History of South Carolina, Volume 5

Yates Snowden, Harry Gardner Cutler

Nabu Public Domain Reprints:

You are holding a reproduction of an original work published before 1923 that is in the public domain in the United States of America, and possibly other countries. You may freely copy and distribute this work as no entity (individual or corporate) has a copyright on the body of the work. This book may contain prior copyright references, and library stamps (as most of these works were scanned from library copies). These have been scanned and retained as part of the historical artifact.

This book may have occasional imperfections such as missing or blurred pages, poor pictures, errant marks, etc. that were either part of the original artifact, or were introduced by the scanning process. We believe this work is culturally important, and despite the imperfections, have elected to bring it back into print as part of our continuing commitment to the preservation of printed works worldwide. We appreciate your understanding of the imperfections in the preservation process, and hope you enjoy this valuable book.

HISTORY OF
SOUTH CAROLINA

EDITED BY
YATES SNOWDEN, LL. D.

In collaboration with
H. G. CUTLER,
General Historian

and an Editorial Advisory Board including Special Contributors

---

Issued in Five Volumes

VOLUME V

ILLUSTRATED

PUBLISHERS
THE LEWIS PUBLISHING COMPANY
CHICAGO AND NEW YORK
1920

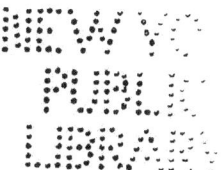

COPYRIGHT, 1920
BY
THE LEWIS PUBLISHING COMPANY

History of South Carolina

CHIEF JUSTICE GARY AND THE SOUTH CAROLINA JUDICIARY. Carlyle tells us that history is the essence of innumerable biographies. With equal truth it may be said that the life-story of one man, well and truly and fully told, is a chapter in the history of his country. Especially so is this the case when the man has spent his life in a high public office, in the service of his country and his state. I purpose to write a brief chapter in the history of our state by giving a sketch of the life of Eugene Blackburn Gary, chief justice of South Carolina. A complete biography it cannot be, for he is still living and in active service; and long may he so continue. This fact also forbids the use of panegyrics and terms of exaggerated praise, nor does it permit the search and exposure of failings, if any there be. It also bids me refrain from invading the privacy and sanctity of his home, no matter how beautiful and attractive the description might be. I can only hope to draw, as it were, an outline sketch, observing the limits that good taste lays down.

There is no higher office, nor one of greater honor and responsibility, than that of judge, whether of the Supreme or the Circuit Court. And there is no state in the Union where judges are held in so high honor as in South Carolina. Yet here, as elsewhere, it is sad to reflect that after death the memory of them is shortened. Read the history of our own or of any state and you will see that while governors, statesmen, generals, are remembered with honor, hardly a reference is made to the judges. It is very true that when they rest from their labors their works do follow them. But those works, in the shape of opinions, decisions and decrees, are pigeon-holed as court records, or bound in calf as law reports, volumes unknown to the historians, and consulted only by succeeding judges and lawyers in search of authorities and precedents. Thus it is that chief justices, chancellors and judges, distinguished in their lifetime for their learning, and honored for their splendid service, are not long remembered after death. They share the common fate to be forgotten ere long, like a dead man out of mind, unless they have done something worthy of note outside of the work of the court. Chancellor Kent is remembered because of his "Commentaries," not because of his chancellorship. Who would ever hear of Judge Longstreet if he had not written the "Georgia Scenes"? A similar fate awaits lawyers; McCrady will be remembered for his "History of South Carolina," when Petigru shall have been forgotten.

It is therefore, to me, a grateful task to contribute to this book on South Carolina a sketch of Chief Justice Gary which may be read by future generations and may show them what manner of man he was.

It has been said that no one is qualified to write the biography of another unless he has known him from his boyhood and all through his life. I may claim to that extent to be qualified; for the boy, Eugene Gary, had me for his schoolmaster for three years; he and I were for nearly twenty years practicing at the same bar, and the same day saw him made associate justice and me a Circuit judge. He was born in Cokesbury, in the old County of Abbeville, on August 22, 1854. Looking back through the three score and six years of his life so far—this is written in 1920—we were bound to say that he has lived through a most eventful period in the history of his state, his country, and the world. He was old enough to remember the terrible times of the Civil war. He saw the sad end of it when President Davis spent the night in his grandfather's house in Cokesbury just the day before he held in Abbeville the last meeting of the Cabinet of the Confederacy.

Then followed, until 1876, the horrible reconstruction period, worse in many respects than the war time, when South Carolina was known throughout the world as the "Prostrate State," ground to the dust under the heels of her emancipated negroes, who were led and controlled by Yankee carpet-baggers and backed by garrisons of soldiers, white and black. The bloodless revolution led by Hampton in '76 put an end to the rule of Yankee and negro. In that revolution no one played a better part than did Gen. Mart Gary, uncle of Eugene.

The year 1886 saw the beginning of the farmers' movement, led by Benjamin R. Tillman, which resulted in 1890 in the election of Tillman as governor, and of Eugene Gary as lieutenant governor. Meanwhile Eugene B. Gary had served one term in the Legislature and had taken an active part in the political strife which waged for several years. For six years he was chairman of the democratic party in Abbeville County. After serving four years as lieutenant governor and president of the Senate, he was electd to the Supreme Court as associate justice in 1893. In 1912 he was elected chief justice, and still occupies that high office.

His has been a successful life. We often hear and read of the secret of success. This is a misleading and inappropriate phrase. There is nothing hidden nor mysterious about it. The cause is plain to anyone who will look for it. Success is a plant of slow growth which requires constant and most careful nursing. The price of success is the proper phrase. A man makes up his mind to reach a certain goal; it may be far off, the road may be a rough and thorny one, and progress may be by painful steps and slow; but he trains himself by education, he devotes all his powers to the attainment of his aim, and in the end succeeds. That was the case with Eugene Gary; he paid the price, he succeeded; and like all truly successful men he deserved success. Let us now look back and trace his course from boyhood and see what was the price he paid.

It was in February, 1869, that I first saw young Eugene Gary. I had opened a classical school in his native town, Cokesbury. He and his two younger brothers came on the opening day. He was in his fifteenth year. I remember well how he looked—a tall lad, slight in build, his pale complexion made to look more pale by the intense blackness of his hair. For three years he was one of my schoolboys. Of the thirty or forty lads who were his schoolfellows, it is pleasant to remember that they all did good work, that they all behaved uncommonly well, that several of them could not be surpassed for diligence and progress in their studies, and none surpassed Eugene Gary. Regular in attendance, he showed each morning that the lessons appointed for study at home had been thoroughly learned. If he had a fault, it was that he was more of a student than a schoolboy; he seemed to have no great liking for the active sports and games of his school fellows.

It is to me a most gratifying reflection that so many of those schoolboys turned out so well in after life. Eugene Gary is not the only one who has attained to high and honorable position. From that group of lads there came a United States senator, a governor of the state, a lieutenant governor, a chief justice, two Circuit judges, a member of Congress, a speaker of the House, a president of the Senate, several members of the Senate and the House, besides lawyers, physicians and business men successful in their various callings. This is a record to be proud of, not unworthy to be placed beside the record of Doctor Waddell's school at Willington, so famous in the history of Abbeville County.

Eugene Gary went straight from the school to the University of South Carolina, from which in due time he was graduated. With his course there I am not familiar, but I am sure he was a most diligent student, that he "lived laborious days" and burned the midnight oil.

After his graduation he read law in the office of his uncle, Gen. Mart Gary, at Edgefield, and was admitted to the bar in his twenty-second year. He immediately opened an office and "hung out his shingle" as an attorney at law at Abbeville Court House, and began the practice of his chosen profession. His determination to join the Abbeville bar showed that the young lawyer had a brave heart. That bar at that time had no superiors in the state, and only one, or perhaps two, that could match it. Armstead Burt, Thomas C. Perrin, General McGowan (afterward judge of the Supreme Court); Edward Noble, William H. Parker, W. A. Lee, James S. Cothran (afterward Circuit judge)—these are the names of the men who then composed the Abbeville bar—all of them lawyers of many years' experience and of large practice. It was a bar that not only controlled the business of Abbeville County, but had a large share in the litigation of all the upper and surrounding counties.

At that time Abbeville County was one of the largest, most populous, and most influential counties in the state. It was a model county in size and shape, and its people were proud of its history. The formation of new counties reduced old Abbeville in influence as well as in size.

But Abbeville was old Abbeville still during the eighteen years in which Eugene Gary practiced law at its bar. The same qualities that had distinguished him as a schoolboy, made him successful as a lawyer; he was diligent in business, faithful to the interests of his clients, always well-prepared and ready for trial of his cases in court. It is not strange, therefore, that he built up an excellent practice.

At this point I may state that Eugene Gary married young, in 1877. Good taste forbid that I should say more than this—that he was most fortunate in his marriage. In the expressive language of Holy Writ, he "obtained favor of the Lord."

We have already seen that in 1893 he was honored with a seat on the Supreme Bench as associate justice; and that in 1912 he was chosen to be chief justice—a well merited promotion and the goal he had aimed at when he began to read law with his uncle. He still holds that high office, the highest and most responsible office in the commonwealth, second only to the chief justiceship of the United States, held in honor not only in South Carolina, but in all her sister states. The Supreme Court of South Carolina has long attracted the attention and gained the respect and confidence of judges and lawyers and text writers in America and in the old country. Its decisions on the principles of the common law, and of commercial law, and upon the ethics of equity jurisprudence, are cited with approval, and many of them as leading cases, in all the courts of the United States and in the high court of Westminster Hall. I well remember how high was the estimation in which our Supreme Court Reports were held by Judge Dillon and Judge Cooley, those learned judges and standard text writers. In conversation with me they both showed they were familiar with our law reports and referred to some of our leading cases in terms of highest praise, naming even the chancellors or the justices who had written the opinions they spoke of.

It is excellent to reflect that our Supreme Court has a traditional reputation for its great learning, judicial ability and the wisdom and soundness of its opinion—a reputation of which the bench and bar and the state at large have good reason to be proud. It would not be proper, nor is it necessary, for me to pass upon the merits of the incumbent chief justice and associate justices. It is enough to say that, judging from the frequency with which their opinions are cited as authority in all the American courts and included with commendation in the volumes of leading cases, they are doing their important work in a manner worthy of the best traditions of our Supreme Court.

And yet it would not be an offense against the canons of good taste to say that Chief Justice Gary is a learned judge. His whole life, since boyhood, has been spent in laying up stores of legal knowledge, of which his numerous opinions afford ample proof. They also show that he is endowed with the judicial cast of mind, and possesses the analytical faculty to discern the real points at issue. They manifest his intimate acquaintance with precedents and aptness in applying them. Whether passing upon statute law or the common law, *lex scripta* or the *lex non scripta*, or upon the fundamental principles of law and equity, his decisions are marked by clearness, conciseness and freedom from technicality; and, greatly to the satisfaction of the members of the bar, those decisions, excepting in rare instances, are brief.

This quality of brevity is much to be commended; all the more so because it is more rarely found in the decisions of courts than formerly. There has been a perceptible lengthening during the last forty or fifty years. Compare a volume of the United States Supreme Court Reports of the year 1800 with a volume of the year 1900, and you will find a great difference in the length of the decisions. In the former they are, with very few exceptions, brief and to the point; in the latter they are nearly all too long and elaborate. This regrettable change may be due to the modern habit of dictating to a stenographer. There is no doubt that when justices wrote their opinions with their own hand, the patience and pen labor encouraged concentration of thought, conciseness and condensation. As little doubt is there that the habit of dictating to a stenographer tends to diffuseness and elaboration and long drawn out argumentation.

As to Chief Justice Gary—I see in the man of 1920 the boy that I knew in 1869—the boy who was without doubt the father of that man. The same qualities are manifest in the chief justice which I remarked in the schoolboy; he is, just as the boy was, a hard worker, painstaking, diligent in business, impatient of delay, eager to finish his task and have "a clean slate." This accounts for the celerity with which he dispatches the business of the court during term time, and the promptness with which he hands down the opinions in the cases assigned to him. No suitor can complain of "the law's delay" when the opinion in his case is to be written by Chief Justice Gary.

Onerous though his labors are as chief justice, he still finds time for respite from those labors in other studies than the strictly legal. Studious by nature and habit, he takes his recreation in much reading of general literature, history seeming to be his favorite branch, if we are to judge by several of his published addresses on historical subjects. In more than one of these addresses he has presented most admirably the case of the Southern Confederacy—a subject which even at this late day receives scant justice at the hands of Northern writers. He has delivered a number of excellent addresses to law students, and even those addresses have a historical tendency, as also have those he has made at the dedication of new court houses. A notable address on legal ethics, which he delivered before the South Caroline Bar Association, was deservedly complimented by Judge Alton B. Parker, of New York, who was in the audience. He rose and congratulated South Carolina on, having at the head of her judiciary one who could produce so admirable a paper.

The chief justice has also been a frequent contributor of articles to law journals. He is said to have written at least 1,800 opinions, before writing which he had to listen with close attention to nearly 4,000 arguments of opposing counsel. Add to this the labor in preparing numerous public addresses and contributions to various journals—is it surprising that his predecessor, the late Chief Justice McIver, himself a hard worker, said that Chief Justice Gary was the hardest working man he ever knew? In 1915 the degree was conferred upon him by the University of South Carolina.

Having given this outline sketch of Eugene Blackburn Gary, let me now look up his pedigree. It is a pedigree to be proud of. He comes of good stock on both the paternal and maternal side of his family. Both the Garys and the Blackburns have a clear claim of descent from early pre-Revolutionary settlers. The Garys are first heard of in Virginia. The first identified Gary ancestor of our chief justice is Charles Gary, who had come with others of the same family name from Virginia and settled in Carolina in what is now called Newberry County. There we find him in 1767.

The Blackburns, his mother's family, are descendants of William Blackburn, who was killed in the battle of King's Mountain, fighting against the British.

But it is through the Porters, the family of his grandmother, Mrs. Thomas Gary, that the chief justice can go farthest back in tracing his descent. That venerable lady—I knew her well—was the lineal descendant of John Witherspoon, a Presbyterian minister, born in Scotland in 1670, who, after having lived in Ulster, the North of Ireland, came to Carolina in 1734 and made his home in the Williamsburg settlement. He was a descendant of John Knox, the great Scottish reformer. He was a brother-in-law of another Witherspoon, the illustrious divine, the president of Princeton College, one of the signers of the Declaration of Independence. He did more than merely sign. There was in the Congress a manifest and natural hesitation to "put their necks in a halter" by signing it, when John Witherspoon came to the front and carried the day. "For myself," said he, "though these gray hairs must soon descend into the sepulchre, I would infinitely rather they should descend thither by the hand of the public executioner than desert at this crisis the sacred cause of my country." On the appeal of that Scotman the declaration was signed.

It thus appears that Chief Justice Gary has reason to be proud of his ancestry. They were all of that excellent stock, usually called Anglo-Saxon, which furnished the Southern colonies with a notable population, from whom have descended the bulk of our present day Southerners, who, being the descendants of those that made America, are the living embodiments of pure and true Americanism. Our

Northern and Western friends have long boasted the marvelous power of the "melting-pot" to assimilate and transform into good Americans all the people of the earth. That was before the Great war. The melting-pot is not so highly thought of now. They would be glad to empty it and get rid of some millions of "undesirables," who decline to be Americanized. Fortunately for the South there has been no such flood of foreign immigration hither as to require the use of that pot. In South Carolina, for example, among the early settlers were three colonies of Huguenots and one of Germans from the Rhenish Palatinate—all of them most desirable as fellow citizens. They have long ago been entirely absorbed and assimilated in our Anglo-Saxon population. Long may the South continue to be the home of true Americanism, the guardian and preserver of liberty and independence; of personal liberty and state independence and self-government.

Proud of his ancestry, Chief Justice Gary has no reason to be ashamed of his immediate kith and kin, but quite to the contrary. His father, Dr. Frank Gary, was a physician eminent in his profession. So was his grandfather, Dr. Thomas R. Gary. His uncle, Thomas P. Gary, was brigade surgeon in the Confederate army, as, indeed, his father, Dr. Frank Gary, had also been. The South Carolina Garys seem to have had a family predilection and aptitude for the medical profession, manifested first by two sons of the ancestor, Charles Gary, already mentioned, and showing in each succeeding generation. In the last and present generation, however, they seem to have taken to law rather than to medicine. Martin Witherspoon Gary—mark his historical name —the uncle already referred to, was a leading lawyer in Edgefield, although he is better known as Maj. Gen. "Mart" Gary, one of the most famous and gallant of the cavalry commanders in the Confederate army. Another uncle, William T. Gary, who had served as major in that army, was afterward a lawyer and a Circuit judge in Augusta, Georgia. Another uncle, S. M. G. Gary, was a lawyer in Ocala, Florida. Then come the two brothers and three first cousins of the chief justice, all lawyers in South Carolina.

The two brothers, Ernest Gary (deceased), and Frank B. Gary, were both Circuit judges at the same time Eugene B. Gary was chief justice. It was the extraordinary, the unparalleled fortune of their mother to see her three sons all honored with seats on the judicial bench. No wonder she was proud of her boys. She lived to a great age, dying in Abbeville in 1918. Before his election to the bench Judge Frank Gary had served an "unexpired term" as United States Senator.

Of the three cousins, the oldest, John Gary Evans, was governor of the state; was a major in the army during the war with Spain, and was placed in charge of the City of Havana after peace was declared. His father, N. G. Evans, who was an officer in the United States Army before the Civil war, became the gallant Gen. "Shanks" Evans of the Confederate Army. South Carolina awarded him a sword and a medal in token of his bravery and success in battle.

The foregoing paragraphs concerning the Gary family abundantly testify that the chief justice comes of a good breed. This is a cause of pleasant reflection not only for himself, but for the people of South Carolina who have honored him so highly, and whom he has served and still serves so well and faithfully. The man who has reason to be proud of his ancestry is also the man who desires to leave an honored name to posterity.

I wish I could finish this without adding a note of sadness. But a sketch of Chief Justice Gary could not be complete without a reference to the great loss and bereavement he suffered during the Great war, in the death of his only son, who bore his own name, Eugene Blackburn Gary.

True to the traditions of his family, when war was declared, young Gary, twenty-seven years of age, at once answered his country's call. Some slight trouble with his eyes twice caused him to be unsuccessful in his eager efforts to join an officers' training corps; but his persistence brought success on his third effort. After the proper training he sailed for France as a lieutenant in a motor-truck company. On the ocean passage he contracted pneumonia and died in the American Hospital at Brest on the very day after landing in France. Dying thus, young Eugene Gary gave his life to his country as fully and patriotically as if he had fallen on the field of battle.

We thus see that Chief Justice Gary has repaid his state and his country for the honors they have abundantly bestowed on him—he has given his son, his only son.—By his old teacher, Former Judge W. C. Benet.

COL. HENRY HARRISON HALL was a dignified, successful and influential business man and citizen of Aiken for over thirty years, and his record is one that commends him to a place among South Carolina's most honored citizens.

He was born in Darien, Georgia, November 22, 1847, a son of Henry Tucker Hall, who was born an English subject on the Isle of Bermuda. The mother of Colonel Hall was Susan Harrison, a native of Georgia and of the distinguished Harrison family of Virginia. She was a granddaughter of President William Henry Harrison and a first cousin of President Benjamin Harrison. The late Colonel Hall was therefore a great-grandson of one of America's most distinguished soldiers and presidents. Colonel Hall has three sisters and two brothers, all now deceased: Mrs. D. O. C. Heery; Phyllis and Marian Hall, of Atlanta, Georgia; T. T. Hall, of Highland, North Carolina, and Horace S. Hall, of Charleston.

At the beginning of the Civil war Henry Harrison Hall was fourteen years of age. His youthful ambition to become a soldier was denied until 1863, when he enlisted as a private, and was in service until the end of the struggle. As a member of Matthews Heavy Artillery he spent most of his time at Battery Wagener and about Charleston, and was with the forces of Gen. Joseph E. Johnston when they surrendered in North Carolina in 1865. At that time he was an acting quartermaster sergeant. He was an ardent defender of his beloved southland, as a soldier was fearless and brave, and while his generous nature prompted him to acknowledge the bravery of his enemies, he regarded the Confederate soldier as his ideal of manly courage

FOUR GENERATIONS
Samuel T. Jenerette, Mrs. Lucinda Cooper, John P. Cooper and Wife,
John P. Cooper, Jr.

and chivalry. He gave to the South the full measure of his devotion, yet after the war he proved his love for a reunited country. He was for many years deeply interested in military affairs, serving for some time as an officer of the local militia, and his title of colonel was bestowed upon him as an officer of the First South Carolina Regiment. His comrades among the Confederate veterans acknowledged his many sterling qualities by making him commander of the local camp, and later he was made colonel on the staff of Gen. B. H. Teague.

At the close of the war he took up the study of pharmacy, completing his studies in Charleston in 1872. At that date his health became impaired and going to Louisville, Kentucky, he engaged in the retail shoe business under the firm name of the Rebel Shoe Company. In 1875 he came to Aiken from Charleston, at the request of some of the physicians of the former town, and formed a partnership with Alfred Holmes to open a drug store. The partnership soon dissolved, and after that Colonel Hall was engaged in business for himself until his death and developed an extensive establishment and a professional reputation well known in Aiken and surrounding territory. He was a real leader in business affairs, and at the time of his death probably the oldest business man in consecutive service at Aiken. His advice was frequently sought, and he never relaxed his efforts in behalf of the general welfare of his community, serving several years as a member of the City Council. He was also at one time a director in the Aiken County Loan and Savings Bank.

He served as a vestryman of the St. Thaddeus Episcopal Church and was closely identified with the affairs of that institution. A devoted husband and father, he did all he could to contribute to the happiness and welfare of his family and showed an interest and sympathy with the lives of others that made his death deeply mourned by the people of the town. The young people were especially fond of him. In November, 1870, he married Miss Emma J. Dawson, of Charleston, who survived him some years. Their children were: Mrs. W. W. Edgerton and Mrs. R. G. Tarrant, both of Aiken; Dr. Huger T. Hall, a prominent physician of Aiken; Charles D. Hall, a pharmacist, who is in business in Washington, D. C., and Henry Harrison Hall, who died at the age of ten years.

JOHN THOMAS LONG, who had three stalwart sons in the World war, has spent a busy life chiefly as an agriculturist in Anderson County, where he owns one of the finest farms in the northern part of that county.

He was born in the county June 25, 1860, a son of Rev. Ezekiel and Anna Matilda (McMurray) Long. His great-grandfather Ezekiel Long was of Irish ancestry, and an early settler in Brushy Creek Township of Anderson County. Ezekiel Long, Sr., the grandfather, was a native of Anderson County and married Bettie Hewey. Rev. Ezekiel Long, father of John T. Long, was born in Anderson County, made a faithful record as a Confederate soldier, and two of his brothers gained special distinction in the Confederate army, James rising to the rank of colonel, while John was a major. Rev. Ezekiel Long died at the age of fifty-two, spent his life chiefly as a farmer and Baptist minister. He married Anna Matilda McMurray, whose father was William McMurray and her mother a Wilson. The McMurrays were also of Irish ancestry. She survived her husband many years, dying at the age of eighty-three. Rev. Ezekiel Long and wife had three sons: James M., John T., both Anderson County farmers, and William M., who is a successful physician at Liberty, South Carolina. The daughters in the family were: Elizabeth, who married N. B. Moore, of Pickens County; Sallie J., who became the wife of W. A. Simpson, of Greenville; and Ella, wife of T. S. Stegall, of Anderson County.

John T. Long grew up on a farm, had a common school education, and from boyhood to the present time has been a practical worker and interested in agriculture. For a few years he was a merchant at Piedmont and in that enterprise and in the oil mill business he was associated with his brother-in-law, W. A. Simpson. When their store burned, entailing a heavy loss, they discontinued business and soon afterward Mr. Long bought and removed to his present farm "Hickory Flat," formerly the Col. D. K. Norris homestead, in the northern part of Anderson County. The handsome brick residence on this plantation was erected by Colonel Norris in 1884. The farm comprises over 700 acres, and under the management of Mr. Long it is one of the chief producers of cotton and livestock in the county. Besides his home place Mr. Long owns 140 acres nearby. He is a member of the Baptist Church.

In 1881 he married Miss Jennie Orr, a daughter of William Orr, of Anderson County. She died leaving seven children: Mamie Jane, George Reese, Weston Homer, John Hovy, Terrell Orr, Cynthia Caroline and Bessie Gertrude. The three sons who wore uniforms of soldiers in the recent war were Weston Homer, John Hovy and Terrell Orr. The only one fortunate enough to be called overseas was John Hovy, who was with a hospital corps in France. Mr. Long married for his present wife Miss Donna S. McCarley. They have children named Anna A., James Thomas, Lewie, Genevieve and Gladys.

JOHN PURLEY COOPER, of Mullins, probably had a distinct genius for commercial affairs, in view of his record. He had hardly attained manhood when he was organizing and taking an active part in the executive direction of several business concerns.

He was born at Mullins, June 30, 1881, son of Noah Bryant and Lucinda (Jenerette) Cooper. His father was also a merchant and farmer educated in the Mullins High School. He began his career as clerk in a general store, and at the age of twenty organized the Palmetto Grocery Company. This business, commanding a capital of $50,000, has felt the impetus and energy of Mr. Cooper from the beginning. He is secretary and treasurer of the corporation. Mr. Cooper is also president and was one of the organizers of the Merchants' and Planters' Bank at Mullins, and is president of the Loris Grocery Company of Loris, South Carolina, and president of the Cooper Smith Company of Conway.

He was only twenty-four years of age when he was elected mayor of Mullins. During the war he was active in behalf of various patriotic causes, being county chairman in the Third Liberty Loan Drive. He is a trustee of the Methodist Episcopal Church and has some active interests in local agriculture, owning and operating a 200-acre farm.

January 21, 1908, he married Miss Ethel Mae Bethea, of Dillon, daughter of Dr. J. Frank Bethea, of Dillon. They have four children: John Purley, Jr., Franklin Bethea, Noah Bryant and Hannah Bethea.

JOHN ORRIN LEA, for many years city treasurer of Charleston, was born in that city July 25, 1845. His father, John Conyers Lea, was born in Smithville, North Carolina, now Southport, March 25, 1815, a son of William Pell Lea, born in Hanover Square, London, England, who came to America in boyhood, going direct to North Carolina and later to Charleston. The mother of John Orrin Lea, Mrs. Caroline Theresa (Stanley) Lea, was also born at Smithville, North Carolina, November 22, 1822. The grandparents on the maternal side were Isaac Davis, who settled in Carteret County, North Carolina, was in the American Revolution, and he was paid for his service on vouchers No. 26 and again on No. 190, and was granted first 300 acres of land, and later 1,735 acres of land, and Stephen Bernard was an officer in the United States Navy during the War of 1812, attached to the naval station at Charleston, South Carolina.

On the paternal side, John Congers was also in the American Revolution, and was paid on voucher No. 2683. John Orrin Lea's father and mother were married at Charleston, July 25, 1844, and became the parents of nine children.

The boyhood days of John Orrin Lea were spent in Charleston, and he attended a private school and the Charleston Academy, and was in the public schools at the time of the outbreak of the war of the sixties. At that time he was a member of the Pickens' Rifles, state troops, which in 1860 did duty at General Ripley's headquarters, Southern Wharf, Charleston, this being regarded as one of the finest companies in the state troops. With the call for troops for the Confederate service this company disbanded, its members volunteering in other companies. During the latter part of the war his mother sought greater safety in Georgia, and in order to be near her he joined the Georgia troops, serving as sergeant major, or acting adjutant of Col. James H. Blount's Battalion of Cavalry, although then only nineteen years of age. The last service performed was while in the Wilderness, winding through Georgia. The battalion was ordered by Gen. F. H. Robinson to burn the bridges between the Chattahooche and Ockmulgee rivers, but when within six or seven miles of Macon, Georgia, they were met by a flag of truce and given the information that General Lee had surrendered and that the war was over. The members of the battalion took the best care they could of themselves and made their way home in different directions. Mr. Lea's father was taken prisoner and confined at Fort Delaware, where he contracted disease and was released, but died on his way home at the South Carolina Hospital, May 10, 1863, at Petersburg, Virginia. His remains now lie in the old Episcopal graveyard at Petersburg.

After the war Mr. Lea returned to Charleston in 1866 and in a few years entered the city treasurer's office. As he had left school at such an early age, he felt the need of further instruction, so attended a night school while working for his uncle, Mr. Stephen Thomas, then city treasurer, as clerk, and when Mr. W. L. Campbell succeeded his uncle he continued in the office as chief clerk. Upon the death of Mr. Campbell in 1893, Mr. Lea was elected city treasurer, continuing as such until the time of his death, June 22, 1919, having been for fifty-two continuous years in service in this department, although five administrations had come and gone since his first election.

Under his administration as city treasurer Charleston was the first city to adopt a uniform system of classification of accounts, of receipts and expenditures of cities over 30,000 population, and he made many other improvements in his department.

Mr. Lea was first married to Susan Bee, born at Charleston, and their children were as follows: Dr. Norman S. Lea, who is a dentist; Campbell Adams, who is deceased, and Mary K. His second marriage was with Harriet Parker, and they had two children, namely: Harriet S. and J. O. Lea, Jr., who served during the great war and is the fourth generation of his family to enter the service of his country. Mr. Lea was a member of Camp Sumter No. 250, Confederate Veterans; of the South Carolina Society of the Sons of the Revolution, and was assistant adjutant general on the staff of the late General Davis and Gen. B. H. Teague, commanding the South Carolina Division of Confederate Veterans. Mr. Lea found in the First Presbyterian Church of Charleston the medium for the expression of his religious faith.

WILLIAM A. G. JAMESON has some unusual distinctions as a successful farmer in the northern part of Anderson County. Reared on a farm, with only a common school education, in 1889 at the time of his marriage he moved to the land he now occupies and with the aid of one small mule put in and gathered his first crop. It was a humble beginning, but he and his wife had the energy, the thrift and the ambition which are the keynotes of success. Into their modest home came by birth seventeen children, fifteen of whom are still living, eleven sons and four daughters. This family of itself constitutes real wealth, and it is a matter of lasting satisfaction to Mr. and Mrs. Jameson that the children have been well reared and given good school advantages.

Mr. Jameson was born in Pickens County January 5, 1862, a son of McElroy and Margaret (Ferguson) Jameson. His ancestry is a derivation of Scotch-Irish, Irish and English stock. His parents were both born in Pickens County. His grandfather William Jameson was a native of Virginia and of Scotch-Irish descent. The maternal grandfather James Ferguson was of Irish lineage and his wife a Miss Dean was English. McElroy Jameson served as a Confederate soldier, and his life occupation was farming.

William A. G. Jameson married in 1880 Miss Lillie Griffin who was born in Pickens County. Mr. Jameson is a deacon in the Baptist Church.

WILLIAM DAVID BARNES. "Through struggle to triumph" seems to be the maxim which holds sway for the majority of our successful citizens, and, though it is undoubtedly true that many fall exhausted in the conflict, a few by their inherent force of character and strong mentality rise above their environment and all which seems to hinder them, until they reach the plane of affluence towards which their face was set through the long years of struggle that must necessarily precede any accomplishment of great magnitude. Such has been the history of William D. Barnes, who through a long, busy and useful life has held the confidence of the people among whom he has labored and with whom he has mingled. In the history of his community his name occupies a conspicuous place, for he has been one of its representative men of affairs, progressive, enterprising and persevering.

William David Barnes was born in Beaufort (now Hampton) County, South Carolina, on August 18, 1859, and is the son of William G. and Eusula (Rivers) Barnes. William G. Barnes, who was a life long resident of Beaufort County, was a soldier in the Confederate army during the Civil war and followed the vocation of farming. His father, William Ransom Barnes, who was descended from old English stock, was also a native of Beaufort, where he became prominent as one of the leading early farmers and planters of that locality. The subject's mother was a daughter of David Rivers, of Hampton County, this state. By her union with William G. Barnes she became the mother of nine children, six sons and three daughters, the subject of this review being the eldest of the children.

William D. Barnes was reared on his father's farm and received a common school education. He remained with his father until he had saved about three hundred dollars, with which he built a small store building, about ten miles north of Brunson and near his birthplace. There he conducted a general store for a few years and met with success in the enterprise. His business experience thus far so encouraged him that he bought a lot at Brunson and built a store, which he operated for about ten years, when the store and entire stock was burned, and, there being no insurance, he lost everything. Nothing daunted, however, he immediately put up a frame building, which still stands and is now used for a warehouse. He again engaged in mercantile operations and again found himself on the road to success. He was keenly alive to his opportunities and, with keen foresight as to the future of this locality, he organized the Moore-Barnes Company in 1012 and erected the present substantial and commodious store building, of brick, 70 by 145 feet in dimensions, two stories high, in which they are now conducting their operations as general merchants. They carry a stock valued at $50,000 and in 1918 did a business of about a quarter million dollars, it being the largest and most successful business enterprise of the kind in this section of the country. In addition to his mercantile interests Mr. Barnes is the owner of several fine tracts of farm land contiguous to Brunson, amounting in all to about 1,800 acres, practically all of which are devoted to general farming. Mr. Barnes also gives considerable attention to the raising and breeding of thoroughbred stock, in which he has been very successful. He is connected with the Brunson Warehouse Company and is identified with a number of enterprises which have had an important bearing on the commercial activity of Brunson. He is a member of the board of trustees of the Brunson High School and was himself mainly instrumental in securing the erection of the new high school building. He has also been actively interested in promoting the development of the artesian wells in this community.

Mr. Barnes has been twice married, first, in 1891, to Angie Brunson, the daughter of F. Brunson, of the town of that name. Mrs. Barnes died and some time afterward Mr. Barnes married Bertha Brunson, a sister of his first wife. This second union has resulted in the birth of two children, William Forrest, who has just returned from France, where he was in the military service of the United States, and Fay Breland, who is now a student at Greenwood, South Carolina.

Fraternally Mr. Barnes is a member of the Ancient Free and Accepted Masons and the Knights of Pythias. His religious affiliation is with the Baptist Church, to which he is a liberal contributor. In the best sense of the term, he is one of the representative men of his community, being public spirited and enterprising to an unwonted degree, while as a friend and neighbor he combines the qualities of head and heart that have won confidence and commanded respect.

LEO WETHERHORN. The gentleman whose life history is herewith outlined is a man who has lived to good purpose and achieved a large degree of success, solely by his individual efforts. By a straightforward and commendable course Mr. Wetherhorn has made his way to a respectable position in the industrial world, winning the hearty admiration of the people of his community and earning a reputation as an enterprising, progressive man of affairs which the public has not been slow to recognize and appreciate. Those who know him best will readily acquiesce in the statement that he is eminently deserving of the material success which has crowned his efforts and of the high esteem in which he is held.

Leo Wetherhorn was born in Charleston on the 25th day of May, 1872. His father, Levy Wetherhorn, who also was a native of Charleston, was a soldier in the Confederate army from 1861 to 1865. He was the son of Marcus Wetherhorn, a native of Poland, who emigrated to the United States and located at Charleston, where he lived the remainder of his life and died. The subject's mother, whose maiden name was Pena Pincus, was a native of Germany, who was brought to Charleston by an uncle, who died here at the age of about seventy-two years. The subject is the third in order of birth of the nine children born to his parents. He was reared here and received his education in the Charleston public schools. At the age of thirteen years he went to work in a planing mill and thus early in life began laying the foundation for the successful and prosperous career which he later was to enjoy. He thoroughly learned every detail of the business, applied himself closely to his work and was wisely economical of his resources, so that in 1894 he was enabled to buy an interest in the business, the firm name becoming Wetherhorn &

Fisher. Subsequently, on the death of Mr. Fisher, the subject became the sole owner of the business. The firm is now known as Wetherhorn & Son and is numbered among the prosperous and enterprising firms of the city. The main business is the manufacture of sash, doors and blinds and the products of this mill are sold at many points outside of Charleston, besides a large and constantly growing trade in the city. About seventy-five persons are constantly employed. Mr. Wetherhorn is also financially interested in other enterprises in Charleston, contributing to the growth and prosperity of the city, particularly in the line of real estate companies. Thus, he is president of the Crown Realty Company, president of the Exchange Realty Company, a director of the Unity Realty Company, and is otherwise giving of his time and finances to enterprises of a laudable order.

In 1896 Mr. Wetherhorn was married to Rosa Kahn and to them have been born eight children, namely: Sophia, Ernest, Raymond, Corrine, Rosalie, Mildred, Leo, Jr., and Lester.

Fraternally, Mr. Wetherhorn is a member of the Masonic order, in which he has taken the thirty-second degree of the Scottish Rite; he is also a member of the Ancient Arabic Order Nobles of the Mystic Shrine and of the Benevolent and Protective Order of Elks. He has taken a keen interest in these fraternal orders and is a past master of his Masonic lodge, a distinct honor in that time-honored order. Religiously he is a member of the Synagogue R. K. B. E., being vice president of that congregation. A lifelong residence in this city has but strengthened his hold on the hearts of the people with whom he has been associated, and today no one enjoys a larger circle of warm friends and acquaintances, who esteem him because of his sterling qualities of character and his business ability.

COL. WILLIAM HANDSFORD DUNCAN. Barnwell County has had the good fortune and distinction of claiming the citizenship of a William Handsford Duncan in each of three successive generations. The first of them was the late Col. William Handsford Duncan, an able soldier, successful business man and public spirited citizen, whose life was a constant influence affecting the advancement and welfare of his community and his state. His death in 1889 removed from South Carolina a substantial and highly esteemed citizen and the many tributes at that time to his high standing in the world of affairs and as a man and citizen attested to the abiding place he had in the hearts and affections of those who knew him and of his work and accomplishment. His career was not a path of roses, but he fought against and conquered adverse conditions that would have utterly discouraged one of less sterling mettle. His military record was marked by courage and ability of a high order, his business record showed that he possessed industry, energy and integrity to a pronounced degree, while his interest in public affairs was of that practical kind that is of real permanent value to the community and state.

He was born in Barnwell County, South Carolina, August 22, 1835, and died December 14, 1889. He was of old Scotch stock and displayed those solid elements of character typical of that race. His father Willis Jennings Duncan was born and reared in Fauquier County, Virginia, and came to South Carolina with his father Joseph Duncan who was a soldier of the War of the Revolution.

William H. Duncan was a resident of Barnwell practically all his life, secured his education in its public schools and began his business career in that community, though his interests later embraced other sections of the state. He applied himself with energy and sound judgment to his varied enterprises, and his progressive attitude made him a factor in various projects for the public good. He constructed and owned the railroad line from Barnwell to Blackville, this being the second railroad chartered in South Carolina. The completion of the road was stopped by the war between the states, much of the material being confiscated and taken to Morris Island where it was used in the construction of breastworks.

At the outbreak of the war Colonel Duncan promptly enlisted as a private but was soon commissioned as captain of Company E of the First South Carolina Regiment, subsequently becoming colonel of that regiment. He proved a valiant and able soldier and served under Gen. Joseph E. Johnston with distinguished gallantry. After the war Colonel Duncan retired to his home farm, called "Duncannon," where he spent most of his time, though he did not by any means shut himself away from the activities about him, maintaining a deep interest in all public affairs and giving his active support to public movements and measures promising permanent value to the welfare of the people and state. He was especially active in the Baptist Sunday School work, to which he gave hearty support with his time and means. In his career no word of suspicion was ever breathed against him. His activities were the result of careful and conscientious thought and when once convinced that he was right no suggestion of policy or personal profit swerved him from the course he had decided upon. His career was complete and rounded in its beautiful simplicity, he did his full duty in all the relations of life, and he died beloved by those near to him and respected and esteemed by his fellow citizens.

Colonel Duncan married Harriet M. Harley, who was born and reared in Barnwell, daughter of Jacob R. Harley, a prominent planter and slave owner of that place. She survived her husband a number of years, her death occurring June 22, 1896. The four children of that union were: Willis J. Duncan, now in business at Edgefield, South Carolina; William Handsford II; Daisy, wife of P. M. Buckingham, whose career is elsewhere sketched in this publication; and Maude, a resident of Barnwell and widow of W. F. Holmes.

In every respect the late William Handsford Duncan, second, was well qualified to adorn the name he bore. He was born at Duncannon, South Carolina, July 14, 1860. For many years he pursued his business as a farmer and planter, and at the same time took an active part in county politics. In 1904 he was elected county auditor of Barnwell County, filling that office until 1910. In 1012 he was elected clerk of the Court of Common Pleas and General Sessions, and gave an earnest and dignified performance of the duties of that office until his death

on January 7, 1920. He lived not quite sixty years, but years alone would hardly offer a proper measure for his influence and achievement. During the World war he was chairman of the local exemption board. From early youth until the end of his career he conducted a farm of several hundred acres, with crops of cotton, corn and garden truck, and also owned landed and other interests at Barnwell. Fraternally he was affiliated with the Knights of Pythias.

June 4, 1888, at Barnwell he married Miss Cornelia Aldrich, a native of Barnwell and daughter of Judge A. P. Aldrich, one of South Carolina's notable figures. Mrs. Duncan died January 4, 1920, just three days before her husband. Her death occurred at Conway, South Carolina, where she was visiting at the home of her daughter Nell, wife of W. A. Freeman. W. H. Duncan II and his wife had six children, two of whom died in infancy, Langdon Chevis and Mary Allen Duncan. The four surviving are: Nell Aldrich, wife of W. A. Freeman; William Handsford Duncan III; Martha Ayer, wife of James C. Patterson, a mechanical engineer now living at Kansas City, Missouri; and Miss Louise Chevis Duncan of Barnwell.

The third William Handsford Duncan has to his credit an interesting military and patriotic record and a place of prominence in the affairs of Barnwell County. He was born October 24, 1890, near Barnwell, was educated in the common and high schools of his native town and began his career in railroad construction work, a line he followed until America entered the war with Germany. He volunteered in Troop A of the South Carolina Cavalry, and was in service altogether twenty-seven months, eighteen months overseas. He went overseas with the Thirtieth Division, and was with that famous organization comprising many South Carolina troops when it broke the Hindenburg line on the Somme River. He was with the Thirtieth in all its terrific engagements, but came through without injury. He went in as a private and wore the stripes of sergeant, first class, when discharged in November, 1919.

Upon the death of his honored father he was appointed by Governor R. A. Cooper to fill the unexpired term as Clerk of Court of Common Pleas and General Sessions of Barnwell County, and has given a splendid administration of the office. At the same time he is the active manager of the extensive planting and farming interests left by his father.

GEORGE G. PALMER. The achievements and leadership of South Carolina in the agricultural affairs of the South are readily demonstrated. Those achievements are due not so much to the unrivaled natural resources of the state, as to the initiative and enterprise of its citizens. In this modern phase of development no individual accomplished more along broader lines than the late George G. Palmer, whose early death was a blow to the business, agricultural and civic interests of his native state. Death always sitting by the highway of life chose a singularly conspicuous victim when it took him away in February, 1920, at the age of thirty-five. Nevertheless he left a record of mature and enduring achievements in the line he had chosen for his life work.

Mr. Palmer possessed a keen intellect, active brain and had the intuition and the breath enabling him to comprehend a great vision, and also the force of character, the grasp of detail to shape and translate a vision into terms of effective reality. For some years he had enjoyed the reputation of a leader as a stock raiser, planter and merchant. While his home and interests were concentrated at his Duroc hog farm at Cartersville, his influence was felt throughout South Carolina. Progressive, broadminded, he was singularly modest and retiring in disposition, and had a personal charm that caused every acquaintance to become a personal frie' His happy, jovial disposition brought him not only the respect and esteem but the admiration and love of all with whom he came in contact.

George G. Palmer was the son of Dr. G. G. Palmer, a well-known physician of Cartersville who died in 1906. The son at once took charge of everything for his mother, including the responsibility of educating his sister and brothers, and forthwith entered upon plans of enlargement and increase in the planting and business interests of the family. He was devoted heart and soul to the raising of the standards of livestock industry in the state, and in bringing in pure bred stock he spared neither money nor effort, and made a wonderful success in that as in everything he undertook. His specialty was pure bred Duroc hogs, and with the establishment of his hog plant known as the Duroc Hog Farms at Cartersville, he gave that town an enviable reputation as the home of some of the best bred hogs in America. He paid what many regarded as fabulous sums for his breeding stock, but for one animal he refused an offer of $10,000, and during the last year of his life his sales of pure bred hogs aggregated over $50,000. Fortunately the business is insured continuance and increased vitality under the efficient management of his wife Mary Keith Palmer.

Mr. Palmer attended school at Thompsons Military Academy in Siler City, North Carolina, spent two years at Guilford College at Greensboro, and one year in Davidson College. He was a concientious and able student, and showed brilliance as an orator and was awarded three medals for his work in that field. He was a member of the college fraternities. On leaving college, while his abilities would have promised him credit and advancement in professions, he immediately began his life work as a planter and stock man. In a comparatively few years he became one of the largest land owners in Florence County, and also a merchant on a large scale. The Duroc hog farms turned out many champions and its products carried off ribbons and prizes wherever exhibited. Mr. Palmer was organizer of the first Duroc Hog Association of the state, and was its secretary until the fall of 1919. He had the satisfaction of knowing that his was the largest hog farm east of the Mississippi. He was in great demand as a speaker on stock raising and agricultural subjects in general, and magazines and newspapers assigned special members of their staff to write up his live stock, his farm, his personal management and ideals.

He was a valued member of the Presbyterian Church, was active in the Masonic Order and Shrine, and was an Elk and Woodman of the World.

In 1907 he married Miss Mary Izler Keith, a daughter of Charles B. and Carrie Keith of Timmonsville and a sister of Maj. James B. Keith of that city. She received her early training in the graded schools of Columbia and Savannah and graduated from the Ursuline Convent at Columbia. Mrs. Palmer as noted above continues the management of the Duroc hog farms and is also carefully superintending the home education and training of her five sons, named: George G. Palmer, Jr., Charles Keith Palmer, Richard Allston Palmer, Joe Bean Palmer and James Bascom Palmer.

The late Mr. Palmer was also survived by his mother, Mrs. Mary Palmer, a sister, Mrs. N. E. Moore of Timmonsville, and his brothers Dr. J. S. Palmer, a prominent physician of Allendale, Capt. O. A. Palmer of the Fourth Cavalry, U. S A, B. M. Palmer of the College of Charleston, B. W. Palmer and Lockwood Palmer of McAllen, Texas.

E. T. H. SHAFFER. Deeds are thoughts crystalized, and according to their brilliancy do we judge the worth of a man to the country which produced him, and in his works we expect to find the true index to his character. The study of the life of the representative American never fails to offer much of pleasing interest and valuable instruction, developing a mastering of expedients which has brought about definite results. The subject of this review is a worthy representative of that type of American character and of that progressive spirit which promotes public good in advancing individual prosperity and conserving popular interests. Members of the Shaffer family have long been identified with affairs in Colleton County, and while their endeavors along material lines have brought them success they have also contributed their share to the general welfare of the whole community.

E. T. H. Shaffer was born at Walterboro, South Carolina, on June 20, 1880, and is the son of A. C. and Amelia (Terry) Shaffer, A. C. Shaffer was a native of Sussex County, New Jersey, whence he came to Walterboro in 1865 and engaged in the mercantile business, to which he devoted himself up to the time of his death. His ancestors originally were from the Rhine Palatinate, Germany. The subject's mother was born in Elmira, New York, the daughter of John K. Terry, a native of Long Island. She died in Walterboro. The subject of this sketch is her only child by her union with A. C. Shaffer.

E. T. H. Shaffer received his elementary education in the public schools of Walterboro, after which he became a student in the Charleston College, where he was graduated in 1902, with the degree of Bachelor of Arts. He at once engaged in the mercantile business and in farming, in which lines he succeeded his father and his maternal grandfather. The general store operated by him was known as one of the leading mercantile establishments of the kind in this locality.

Mr. Shaffer sold all his mercantile interests in 1919. In the fall of 1919 the citizens of Colleton County held a mass meeting to consider what steps should be taken to meet the agricultural changes which would be caused by the boll weevil. Mr. Shaffer, with Mr. Paul Sanders, of Ritter, was sent as a committee of investigation into Southern Georgia and the keynote of their report was that the farmer could continue to prosper only through diversification and that successful diversified farming can only be accomplished by a greater degree of co-operation than ever existed under a one-crop system; that by co-operation alone can the proper handling and the proper marketing of the varied farm products be accomplished.

The Colleton Products' Association, of which Mr. Shaffer is now the president, is a concrete evidence of his idea. It is a $100,000 corporation with head offices at Walterboro and with hundreds of stockholders among the farmers and business men of Colleton County. This company has built a modern grain elevator at Walterboro to handle the increased grain crops, the first in the state and with a capacity of 15,000 bushels. It has also built a chain of sweet potato curing houses over the county to turn the prolific southern sweet potato into the "sugar-spud" for the northern market.

Trained demonstrators are kept at work in the field to instruct the farmer in the new method. Especial attention is also given to seed distribution. As a result of the work of this company Colleton County in 1920 increased its grain acreage sixty per cent and increased Spanish peanuts from zero to 5,000 acres, all with a corresponding loss to "King Cotton."

The people of Colleton County determined that as the county had proven the most effective political unit for reaching the individual in the political sphere, that a county organized as a commercial unit will be found the most effective method of effecting the vast economic change which the boll weevil causes in all parts of the cotton growing South.

Mr. Shaffer owns a business block in the Town of Walterboro and is the owner of about 2,000 acres of excellent farming land in Colleton County, and to which he gives careful attention. He is also a stockholder and a director of the Farmers and Merchants Bank of Walterboro. His entire life has been spent in this locality, and no one enjoys to a greater degree the universal confidence and esteem of the people.

In 1911 Mr. Shaffer was married to Clara Barr, of Greenville, South Carolina, the daughter of George T. Barr, and they are the parents of two children, Jane Terry and E. T. H., Jr.

Fraternally Mr. Shaffer is a member of the Ancient Free and Accepted Masons and the Knights of Pythias. He is also a member of the South Carolina Historical Society, the Carolina Yacht Club, of Charleston, and the Alpha Tau Omega Greek-letter fraternity.

James Aldrich

JUDGE JAMES ALDRICH. Son of a distinguished South Carolina lawyer, patriot and jurist, the late Judge James Aldrich exemplified many of the splendid qualities of his father and also the beautiful side of his mother's nature, and was one of the state's real noblemen. His abilities and character were highly appreciated, and so popular was he that whenever a candidate for public office he never had any opposition.

He represented the eighth generation of an English family that was planted on New England soil at the very beginning of the Massachusetts Bay Colony. His first ancestor was George Aldrich, who married Catherine Seald in 1629, and in November, 1631, they set out from Derbyshire, England, and came to America. George Aldrich became a large land owner in Worcester County, Massachusetts. His son, Jacob Aldrich, born February 28, 1656, lived the life of a Massachusetts farmer. The third generation was represented by Moses Aldrich, born in 1691 and died September 9, 1781. He was an elder of the Friends Society and gave much of his time to the preaching of the Gospel. He married Hannah White in 1711, and their ninth child was Luke Aldrich, born February 22, 1727.

Esek Aldrich, son of Luke and Anna (French) Aldrich, was born September 9, 1753, and married Amy Whipple.

The sixth generation was represented by Robert Aldrich, who was born at Mendon, Massachusetts, February 1, 1780. After completing his education he came to Charleston, South Carolina, about 1800, and went to work in a bookstore, the branch of a Boston establishment. About two years later he and a partner opened a book store of their own, but largely through mismanagement on the partner's score the firm failed. Robert Aldrich then called his creditors together and promised payment in full of all indebtedness, and though it required nearly half of his life to accomplish the task he kept his word and thereby established a character for integrity and intelligence that neither misfortune nor disaster could impair. His work the rest of his life was as manager of the Commercial Wharves of Charleston, and after his death the proprietors of the wharves inscribed upon his monument the following: "Sacred to the memory of Robert Aldrich, who died in this city on the 9th of April, 1851, aged seventy-one years, two months and nine days. He was born at Mendon, Massachusetts, but spent the last fifty years of his life in South Carolina. Forty-two years of which he held the most confidential station on the Commercial Wharves, the duties of which he performed with the most exemplary fidelity. He has left a large family and circle of friends to mourn his death and has gone to his final rest much respected and lamented."

Robert Aldrich married Ann Hawkins Lebby, granddaughter of Nathaniel Lebby, a distinguished South Carolina patriot in the Colonial and Revolutionary period. She died April 22, 1830.

The fourth son of Robert and Ann Hawkins Aldrich was James Thomas Aldrich, whose career as an eminent South Carolinian deserves space in this publication. He was born at Charleston, November 16, 1819. While on account of his father's circumstances he could not acquire a college education, he was a constant reader, devoted to the classics and the best modern literature, and for many years held rank among the state's most cultured gentlemen. He finished his law studies in the office of his brother, Judge A. P. Aldrich, at Barnwell, and was admitted to the bar in 1842. For a time he practiced with his brother and later alone, and through his abilities, his wide learning and his character justly attained distinction and eminence in his profession. After his marriage he enjoyed fourteen years of happiness and success at home, in his friendships and in his profession at Barnwell. Then came the war, and he served as a commissioned officer of the Confederacy, being a captain the last three years of the war. Most of the time he was stationed in Columbia, assigned to department work. In the meantime his home was in the path of the destroying army of Sherman, but was faithfully defended by Mrs. Aldrich, though most of the property and many of the most prized possessions were burnt or despoiled. He resumed the practice of law and though beset by ill health and blindness caused as and by result of his services in the war, and the general misfortunes of the state, he battled bravely until the end, though he did not live to see the final restoration of white rule. He died September 26, 1875.

June 30, 1847, James T. Aldrich married Isabel Coroneus Patterson, who was born at Barnwell May 24, 1829. Her grandparents were Alexander and Elizabeth Patterson, of Scotch ancestry. Her father, Angus Patterson, was born in North Carolina December 5, 1790, and in 1808 came to South Carolina, where he taught school, studied law, and after his admission to the bar located at Barnwell in 1813. He lived at Barnwell until his death in 1854, leaving a distinguished record as a lawyer, citizen and public leader. He represented his county in the General Assembly of the state for thirty-two consecutive years, from 1818 to 1850, the first four years in the House and the remaining twenty-eight years as senator, the last twelve of which he was president of the Senate. Mrs. James T. Aldrich had every educational advantage that cultured parents and wealth could give. She completed her training in Limestone College, graduating with the first honor of her class in her eighteenth year, and was married soon afterward. James T. Aldrich and wife enjoyed a marriage companionship that represented the ideals of a perfect union. Through all the vicissitudes of the darkest and most eventful period of the country's history she did her duty well, proving the faithful helpmate, prudent counselor, frugal housewife and devoted and watchful mother. After the war both she and her husband looked after the education of their children, and both were eminently qualified for those responsibilities. She educated her daughters and prepared, in great part her son for college. She shared with her husband an ardent love of literature, and both had exceptional gifts as writers. She survived her husband more than a quarter of a century.

Judge James Aldrich, who was the only son of James T. and Isabel Aldrich, was born in the village of Barnwell July 25, 1850, and was old enough to appreciate many of the horrors of war and the reconstruction period. He enjoyed a sound physique, and, as noted above, his early education was largely directed by his father and mother. He attended a preparatory school conducted by Rev. B. F. B. Perry until about 1862. During the remainder of the war he lived with his mother on a plantation at Edisto River, and continued his studies under his mother's guidance. In the winter of 1864-65 a company was recruited in Barnwell by Doctor Roper, founder of the Roper Hospital in Charleston. It was known as the "Cradle and Grave" Company, composed of boys and old men. Though only fourteen years of age, when the war ended James Aldrich entered the service, after having twice been rejected before. He took with him for the use of the company his father's carriage, horses and wagon. After the passing of the destroying army he used this equipment to collect some supplies for his destitute family in a region that had not been visited by Sherman's troopers. While on this expedition he used his horses and wagons to haul goods for the merchants from Branchville to Barnwell, a distance of forty miles, and continued that work until the railroad was rebuilt. Then for two years he farmed, performing the common labor of the fields.

In 1869 he entered Washington and Lee University at Lexington, Virginia, and practically completed the course, though he had to leave college in 1872 on account of his means being exhausted. While in college he was a member of the Graham-Lee Literary Society and represented it on several occasions. One of his most prized recollections was that he enjoyed the personal friendship of Gen. Robert E. Lee, and was often a visitor in his home. General Lee was president of Washington and Lee University at the time and died while James Aldrich was in college. He was chosen one of the Guard of Honor to attend the body of the "Matchless Lee" as it lay in state before interment.

Returning to Barnwell in 1872 he took up the diligent study of law under his father and was admitted to the bar January 20, 1873. After his admission he located at Aiken, and early achieved distinction as a lawyer of brilliant powers and enjoyed a large private practice there until 1889. While at Aiken he rendered all the service he could in behalf of peace and order and the restoration of white government. He aided in the organization of the Palmetto Rifles, became first lieutenant and later captain, and commanded the company during its service at the Ellenton and other riots. The company was disbanded by the republican or carpet bag governor, but the men maintained the organization under the guise of a social club, and privately bought Winchester rifles to use in safeguarding society and private property. Later on James Aldrich was one of the attorneys that successfully defended the Ellenton Rioters before the United States Court in Charleston, South Carolina.

Judge Aldrich also became identified with the reconstruction politics of the state. He was an opponent of fusion tickets and advocated a straight-out democratic nomination. On this platform of action he distinguished himself at the democratic convention in May, 1876, but the convention hesitated to adopt his program, though later in the same year Governor Hampton was nominated by the "unterrified democracy," and his election finally redeemed the state from misrule. Judge Aldrich took a prominent part in that memorable campaign. Later he was elected to the House of Representatives from Aiken County, serving from December, 1878, until December, 1884, when he declined re-election. However, he was again elected in December, 1886, and continued in the House until December, 1889.

In December, 1889, he began the service with which his name will be always associated, when he went on the bench as judge of the Second Judicial District, at first including the counties of Aiken, Barnwell, Hampton, Beaufort and Colleton, and later Bamberg. In the first fifteen of the eighteen years he was on the bench he never missed a term of court, and frequently heard cases at night. Many of the trials at which he presided involved important and exciting issues, and he rendered many decisions whose opinions are still quoted as authority.

It was given to Judge James Aldrich to find his calling. He truly loved his work, always finding it a joy. Coming from a long line of lawyers, of which he once counted eighteen judges of the name, the calling was congenial, and as he was possessed of a very impartial mind, and was a student and a scholar, he was eminently fitted for the judgeship. As one paper expressed it when ill health compelled him to resign the work he loved. "His ability was unquestioned as his private life was spotless." A few words but they picture a life of integrity and achievement.

Though his life was distinguished by many achievements and honors, his death at fifty-nine years of age, came when in the fullness of his powers, and was therefore regarded as nothing less than a calamity to his native state. He was always deeply interested in educational affairs, assisting in organizing the Aiken Institute and became its first president. He was a member of the South Carolina Historical Society, was an active Mason, and a prominent layman of the Episcopal Church. He was for years a director of the Bank of Aiken, now the Bank of Western Carolina.

December 15, 1874, Judge Aldrich married Miss Frances Lebby, of Charleston, South Carolina. Of the three children born to their union the only survivor is Anna Lebby, wife of Dr. Huger T. Hall, of Aiken, South Carolina.

FRANCIS WINFIELD TOWLES. It is a compliment worthily bestowed to say that South Carolina is honored by the citizenship of Francis Winfield Towles, of Martins Point, for he has achieved definite success through his own efforts and is thoroughly deserving of the proud American title of self-made man, the term being one that, in its better sense, cannot but appeal to the loyal admiration of all who are appreciative of our national institutions and the privileges afforded for individual accomplishment. Another reason for singling out Mr. Towles for specific mention in this work is the fact that to him is in a large measure due the development of the truck growing industry of the South, for he made the first outside shipments and showed the way to success along new lines, which thousands of others have successfully followed during the subsequent years.

F. W. Towles was born in Savannah, Georgia, on February 29, 1848, and is the son of Daniel Freeman and Ann (English) Towles. His paternal grandparents were James and Mary (Watts) Towles, the former of whom was born at Edgefield, South Carolina, and the latter in the same state. Daniel F. Towles was born in Bryan County, Georgia, as was his wife, who was the daughter of Reuben

English. They were reared and married in Bryan County, Georgia, and reared three sons, Henry A., Francis W. and Daniel H., of whom the eldest and youngest are deceased, the subject being the only member of the family living.

F. W. Towles spent his boyhood days on the parental farmstead in Georgia and reecived such education as was afforded in the log cabin schools of that period. At the early age of fourteen years he began life's battle on his own account. His first employment was as a fireman on the Atlantic & Gulf Railroad, now known as the Coast Line. He performed this work about a year and then went to Alabama and secured a similar job on the Montgomery & West Point Railroad. He was soon promoted to the other side of the cab and ran as passenger engineer on that road until the close of the war between the states. He then returned to Savannah and was employed in a sawmill and at any kind of work which he could find to do. He then came to Martins Point, South Carolina, and worked for his father and William Geraty for a while. Determined to be independent, he then started farming operations on his own account, renting a place on Goose Creek, where he raised a crop of potatoes, but here he lost practically all his money. He then returned to railroad work, serving as engineer on the Savannah & Charleston Railroad for about two years. In 1871 Mr. Towles returned to Martins Point and engaged in farming and merchandising. He also operated a cotton gin and engaged in buying and selling cotton. From the beginning of these last operations he was successful and increased his operations as time went on until he became one of the large land owners of this section, his holdings amounting to about nine hundred acres. He employs on an average about fifty hands and raises a wide variety of products, including besides cotton and corn, vegetables of all kinds. Mr. Towles has been rightfully called the father of the truck growing industry in the South, for it was he who first demonstrated the feasibility and profit in growing and shipping vegetables to outside markets. He proved a successful manager in everything to which he applied himself, and now, in the evening of his life, he is able to rest from his labors and enjoy the fruits of his former efforts.

F. W. Towles has been married three times, first, in 1869, to Annie Allsbrooks, who bore him two daughters, Josephine and Ella. His second marriage was to Mary Geraty, to which union were born three children, Beatrice, deceased; Francis E. and Daniel Q. The third marriage of the subject was to Anna Schaffer, and they have four children living, Frank W., Janice, John O. and Archer Baker.

Fraternally Mr. Towles is a member of the Knights of Pythias. He is a genial and approachable man, who has won and retained a host of loyal friends, for he has shown himself to be the possessor of those qualities which make a true man.

STONEWALL JACKSON RUMPH, one of the leading planters and merchants of Yonges Island, is one of the prominent men of his neighborhood, and one who is held in high esteem because of his uprightness and ability. He was born near Saint George, South Carolina, August 26, 1864, a son of Samuel D. Rumph and grandson of Jacob Rumph. Prior to the American Revolution three brothers by the name of Rumph came to the colonies from Germany, and one settled in Georgia, one in Florida and the third in South Carolina. Samuel D. Rumph was born in what is now Dorchester County, South Carolina, and his wife, who bore the maiden name of Martha F. Bowman, was also born in South Carolina, and was reared near Saint George, her parents being early settlers of the state. The children born to Samuel D. Rumph and his wife were six in number, and of them Stonewall Jackson Rumph was the fourth. Three of these children are still living.

Stonewall Jackson Rumph was reared near Saint George, South Carolina, and attended the Porter Military College at Charleston, following which he learned telegraphy and was operator and agent at different railroad stations, his last position being at Yonges Island. He engaged in general trucking, especially potatoes and cabbage growing and was one of the biggest potato growers until some six years ago. He had invested in rural property, and in 1900 located on his present plantation. He owns three farms and conducts in addition to them two others, so that he has under his active supervision about 1,000 acres of land and has at times employed as many as 300 people. In addition to these responsibilities Mr. Rumph conducts a mercantile establishment and does a business of about $60,000 annually, and has opened another store near Meggett, which will increase the business $35,000 or $40,000 per year. In the past he was extensively engaged in the cotton business, putting out from 1,200 to 2,000 bales annually. In every undertaking Mr. Rumph displays signal business ability and each year's returns proves that he is increasing his production and keeping up his quality.

On January 18, 1893, Mr. Rumph was married to Kate W. Boynton. They have no children. Mrs. Rumph is a very pleasant lady, interested in the development of the state, and a lover of flowers. She delights in caring for the lawn, hedges and directing their care and beautification. During the great World war she was very active in the work of the Red Cross and was chairman of the Red Cross division in her part of the county. She is still an earnest worker in after war needs. Mr. Rumph is a Mason and also belongs to the Knights of Pythias. He is a school trustee and has charge of the roads in his section, to which he gives considerable attention and keeps them good. He has never taken a very active part in politics. He is a director in the South Carolina Produce Association, vice president and director in the Hollywood Manufacturing Co., which manufactures barrels and packages and is doing an extensive business, and is vice president of the South Carolina Cotton Growers' Association. During the great war Mr. Rumph was a member of the County Exemption Board and gave to its duties a faithful and conscientious service. In every relation of life he measures up to the highest standards of American citizenship, and his associates, whether in business or social circles, hold him in high esteem, for they recognize and appreciate his many excellent characteristics.

In 1920 Mr. Rumph has sought to replace the cotton which boll weevil has destroyed, and he has turned his attention and investment to tobacco growing and curing. He has erected two barns and has fourteen acres in tobacco.

He was led to make this experiment in 1920 in

tobacco growing because the boll weevil had destroyed the cotton growing in his vicinity. He feels that success in the venture will result in extensive planting by the farmers while on the other hand a failure will show at his expense just what can be expected. Thus he is serving his community, hoping to succeed, but willing to bear the expense of a demonstration.

His home is one of the handsomest of the community in 1917, and the foundation of which is over one hundred years old, but it is now one of the most modern in the county; beautiful hedges and flowers surround it and are supervised by and under the care of Mrs. Rumph.

JONES HENRY COLUMBUS ALL, a pioneer of Allendale, found his life work in that community as a planter, extensive land owner and business man, and has dispensed his means and influence for many years in a spirit of constructive enterprise that has had much to do with the development of this flourishing little city in the southern part of the state.

Mr. All was born in what was then Barnwell County near the great Saltcahachie Church September 29, 1853. His grandfather All was a native of Holland and settled in South Carolina at the beginning of the nineteenth century. Adam All, the father was also born in the same locality of Barnwell County on August 24, 1812. While most of his years were spent in the operation of his plantation, he was extremely loyal to his home state, and though nearly fifty years of age when the war broke out between the North and South he was not satisfied to fight through the proxy of his four sons, but joined the Home Guards and did what he could to keep the Yankees out of the land when Sherman's invaders came through. After the war he was a member of the "Red Shirt Brigade" and helped reconstruct the state for orderly white government. He died at the age of seventy-two. His wife was Elsie (Williams) All, a native of Barnwell County, of English descent and of an old family of the state. Four of their sons went all through the struggle during the war between the states. George All was in Fort Sumter four years, a sergeant of his company. W. A. All was superintendent of the government repair shop at Charleston. Jack and Jim All were in Captain Smart's Company of Cavalry on the coast.

Jones Henry Columbus All was about eight years old when the war broke out. Consequently the period normally devoted to education was one of confusion and poverty of resources, and he had only the benefit of the interrupted schedule of country schools. At the age of twenty-one in 1874 he began his active career as a merchant at Allendale, and built up and continued a successful business for fifteen years. For the past thirty years his big interest has been farming, now conducted on about 6,000 acres of land he owns in Allendale and Barnwell counties. He has a well organized tenant system, with a large investment in buildings and other equipment, and for years has been one of the leading producers of cotton, corn and peanuts.

Mr. All resides in Allendale, where he owns considerable improved property, and was one of the organizers of the old Allendale Bank. For three or four years he served as a warden of the town and afterwards was intendant or mayor for four years, but whether in office or as a private citizen he has neglected no opportunity to build up and promote the best interests of the town and county. Mr. All is a Mason and a member of the Baptist Church.

July 2, 1873, he married in Barnwell County Theodore Gertrude Bowers, a native of that county. Her father Capt. G. C. Bowers was a prominent planter and of an old South Carolina family of Revolutionary stock and English descent. Eleven children were born to the marriage of Mr. and Mrs. All. One daughter, Edith, died at the age of three, and a son, McIver, at the age of fourteen. There are nine living children, all well established and equipped for life with liberal educations: John E., a preacher in the Seven Day Adventist Church in Columbia; Percy H., whose career is sketched elsewhere; Gertrude, wife of John W. Douglas, of Allendale; Harry W., a cotton buyer and farmer at Allendale; Blanche, wife of H. G. Marsh, a warehouse keeper at Jacksonville, Florida; Bessie, twin sister of Blanche, wife of M. M. Hogan, a real estate dealer at Jacksonville, Florida; Mrs. Gladys Prelliman of Spartanburg; Fred H., a member of the class of 1921 at Harvard University Law School; and Sarah All, who graduated in 1920 from the Boston Conservatory of Music. Mr. Adam All was a large slave owner and after the close of the Civil war kept about seventy-five and took great care of them in every way.

PERCY H. ALL. To the commercial and industrial progress of Allendale, now county seat of the rich and prosperous Allendale County, Percy H. All for a number of years has been one of the chief contributors. He is an electrical engineer by training and early profession, and has done much to promote the cotton and other industries of Allendale.

He was born in 1880, near Allendale, in what was then Barnwell County. His parents, J. H. C. and Theodore Gertrude (Bowers) All, were also natives of the same locality. Percy H. All attended the Allendale schools and graduated as electrical engineer from Clemson College in 1901. The first two years after leaving college he engaged in stock farming on the Savannah River. Then after some associations with a cotton exporting corporation at Savannah he returned to Allendale and engaged in the cotton business for himself. Mr. All in 1914 established the All's Ginnery, one of the largest gins in Allendale County. It has been in successful operation and is one of the leading industries of Allendale. More recently Mr. All extended his initiative and enterprise to a new field. In January, 1920, he established a horse collar and pad factory, one of the few institutions of its kind in the state, and one that will bring increased recognition to Allendale as an industrial center.

Mr. All is a member of the Methodist Episcopal Church. On January 1, 1917, he married Miss Josephine Anthony, daughter of Rev. Bascom Anthony, a prominent minister and member of the South Georgia Conference of the Methodist Episcopal Church, South. Mr. All had the misfortune to lose his wife by death. She was a graduate of Wesleyan College of Macon, Georgia. She was the mother of four children: Percy H., Jr., Raymond Anthony, James Bascom and Frank Ewbank.

Mr. All was an active member of the Georgia

Hussars, of Savannah, Georgia, and an associate member of the Savannah Volunteer Guards.

COL. D'ARCY PAUL DUNCAN. A youthful soldier during the last year of the war between the states, for many years a successful planter, public official of Union County, a former member of the State Railroad Commission, president of the South Carolina State Fair, these and other positions and services have made Col. D'Arcy P. Duncan of Columbia one of the best known citizens of the state.

He comes of a family in which high and scholarly achievement is a tradition. He is a brother of the late Bishop William W. Duncan of the Methodist Episcopal Church. Another brother was James Armstrong Duncan, also a Methodist minister but best known as president of Randolph-Macon College in Virginia. Another brother was the late Maj. D. R. Duncan of Spartanburg, an ex-Confederate officer, prominent as a lawyer and railway president.

These sons were children of David and Alice Amanda (Piedmont) Duncan. David Duncan was born in County Donegal, Ireland, in 1790, of Scotch parents. He was a graduate of the University of Edinburgh. He served four years in the British Navy, and while on a British boat was with the fleet at St. Petersburg when Napoleon and his army read their fate in the flames of Moscow. David Duncan came to America in 1817, and for nearly twenty years was principal of the Norfolk Academy in Virginia, and from 1835 to 1854 was professor of Ancient Languages in Randolph-Macon College. From 1854 to 1881, the year of his death, he was professor of Ancient Languages in Wofford College at Spartanburg, going to that institution the year it was founded. He died at the age of ninety-one. His son William Wallace Duncan had attended the first class of Wofford in 1854, after his graduation filled many pulpits in the Methodist Church and in 1875 was elected to the Chair of Philosophy at Wofford and made financial agent for the college. In 1886, at the General Conference at Richmond, he was elected bishop, a high office he filled with distinction until his death on March 2, 1908. Bishop Duncan is remembered as one of the most gifted, brilliant and scholarly men of the South.

Col. D'Arcy P. Duncan was born in Mecklenburg County, Virginia, in 1846, and was eight years old when his parents moved to Spartanburg. In 1864 he was enrolled in The Citadel, the South Carolina Military Academy at Charleston, and with the Charleston Cadets of State Troops he entered the Confederate Army of defense, serving on James Island and vicinity.

In 1867 Colonel Duncan married Miss Carrie C. Gist, daughter of former Governor W. H. Gist. After his marriage he moved to a plantation in Union County ten miles from the Town of Union on Tyger River, near the Laurens County line. He developed his plantation of 2,100 acres until it became widely known for its successful management and its great productiveness. Colonel Duncan was always a pioneer in the introduction of progressive agricultural methods. It was his prominence as a planter that brought him election in 1881 as president of the State Agricultural and Mechanical Society of South Carolina, the incorporation which has had the management of the State Fair. During his term of office the annual fair at Columbia enjoyed every degree of success and prosperity. Since leaving the office of president he has remained as an ex-officio member of the executive committee of the society.

His first important service in public affairs was rendered when he was elected in 1876 as a member of the Board of County Commissioners of Union County. That was just at the period of restored white rule, and as a result of the carpet bag regime the county was heavily burdened with debt. When he left office in 1880 provision had been made for the payment of every dollar of debt, and Colonel Duncan was complimented by his fellow citizens in bringing about such a desirable result. In 1882 he was appointed by Governor Thomson to fill the unexpired term of Governor Jeter as a member of the Board of Railroad Commissioners, and was connected with that board continuously for twenty-three years. He was a member until 1894, and then for eleven years served as secretary of the board.

Colonel Duncan has been a resident of Columbia since 1904. After severing his connections with the Railroad Commission he represented some of the local railway companies until 1918, and is now enjoying a well earned retirement, though his interests and enthusiasm in all matters touching the welfare of his state and community are as fresh as ever.

Colonel Duncan's first wife died in 1876, and her three living children are Mrs. R. P. Harry, of Union, Mrs. James R. Cogswell, of Darlington, and William Gist Duncan, of Leesville. In 1881 Colonel Duncan married Miss Kate Richardson, daughter of the late Congressman John S. Richardson of Sumter. To this marriage were born four children, Mrs. Harry Nelson Eden, Mrs. Leroy Reeves, Mrs. Ed Brennon, Jr., and James A. Duncan. The son is a graduate with the class of 1917 from the University of South Carolina and is now assistant tutor of physics in Harvard University.

GEORGE BENEDICT CROMER. An unusually busy and fruitful career has been that of George Benedict Cromer, who qualified for practice as a lawyer more than thirty-five years ago, served more than eight years as president of Newberry College, his alma mater, was four times mayor of Newberry, and has long been one of the prominent laymen of the Lutheran Church.

Mr. Cromer was born in Newberry County, October 3, 1857, son of Thomas H. Cromer, a farmer and merchant. Mr. Cromer spent his boyhood days in the country, was farm reared, and had the simple advantages of the country schools, supplemented by the private school of Thomas H. Duckett. He was thus qualified for entrance to Newberry College, where he graduated A. B. in 1877 and A. M. in 1879. From 1877 to 1881 he was an instructor in Newberry College, and while teaching was studying law and was admitted to practice in December, 1881. From that date until January, 1896, he practiced with growing prestige and ability, and three times served as mayor of Newberry, being first elected in 1886 and serving until 1890. Mr. Cromer became president of Newberry College in 1896, and held that office for 8½ years, until 1904. That was a period of great prosperity for his alma mater. Retiring from this office he was elected in 1905 as mayor of Newberry. He is still active in his law practice.

Mr. Cromer was honored in 1901 with the degree LL. D. by Wittenberg College in Ohio and Muhlenberg College in Pennsylvania. He is a member of the American Academy of Political and Social Science and the National Economic League. He is also president of the trustees of Newberry College.

October 11, 1883, he married Miss Carolyn J. Motte, who died in 1888. On November 27, 1890, he married Harriet S. Bittle. He has two children, Carolyn and Beale H.

JOEL SMITH BAILEY, of Greenwood, is a son of Joel S. and Clara (Tarrant) Bailey. His father's rank is well known as a financier and merchant, having been head of one of the largest mercantile firms in Northern South Carolina during the last two decades of the last century.

Joel Smith Bailey for fifteen years has prosecuted many and varied and important interests at Greenwood. He was born in that city August 12, 1883, was educated in public schools, and graduated from Davidson College in North Carolina in 1903. As a newspaper man he is secretary, treasurer and business manager of the Index-Journal. He is a director of the National Loan and Exchange Bank of Greenwood, and is president and treasurer of the Oregon Hotel Company, which built and owns the splendid fireproof five-story hotel at Greenwood. He is also president of the Citizens Trust Company and is one of the three members of the Water and Light Commission of Greenwood.

Mr. Bailey from college days has been deeply interested in athletic sports of all kinds. On May 7, 1914, he married Sarah Caldwell Jamison, of Greenwood. They have one daughter, Margaret Wallace.

CLAUDIUS C. FEATHERSTONE is one of the ablest members of the South Carolina bar, having practiced more than thirty years, and in that time has been called on fifteen different occasions to serve as special judge of the Circuit Court.

Judge Featherstone, whose home is at Greenwood, was born in Laurens County, December 1, 1864, a son of J. C. Calhoun and Addie (Sullivan) Featherstone. His father was likewise a successful lawyer before him. Claudius C. Featherstone was educated in the common schools, attending the high school at Anderson, and had one year of experience in a printing office and also clerked in a store. At the age of twenty he began studying law in the office of his father, and was admitted to the bar in December, 1885. For one year he practiced at Anderson and for twenty years in Laurens, and since 1911 has been a resident of Greenwood, where he became a member of the firm McGhee & Featherstone.

Judge Featherstone has been a prominent leader in the prohibition party in South Carolina for many years. In 1898 he was a candidate on the ticket of that party for governor, and was beaten by only a small majority. In 1910 he was again prohibition candidate for governor against Cole Blease. Judge Featherstone is chairman of the Board of Stewards of the Methodist Episcopal Church, is a Mason and Shriner, and past chancellor of the Knights of Pythias. On October 1, 1893, he married Lura Lucretia Pitts, a daughter of Rev. John D. Pitts, a prominent Baptist minister. To their marriage was born three children: John Douglass, who graduated from the University of South Carolina and was admitted to the bar in 1916, entered the army in 1917 and was a lieutenant and afterwards a captain in the field artillery. Lucia Sullivan, the second child, is a graduate of Winthrop College and a teacher at Greenville. Phoebe Laurens is still a student in Winthrop College.

CAPT. FRANCIS MURRAY MACK is a member of the former Mack family of Fort Mill, distinguished by the scholarship and professional activities of several of its members. Capt. F. M. Mack is a brother of Dr. Edward Mack, long distinguished as a Presbyterian clergyman and theologian, and is also a brother of the brilliant New York lawyer William Mack.

The parents of these sons were Rev. Dr. Joseph Bingham and Harriet Hudson (Banks) Mack. The father was born in New York City of Irish ancestry and came south when a youth. He espoused the cause of the South in the war between the states, and rose to the rank of captain in the Fifty-third Tennessee Infantry. After the war he studied for the Presbyterian ministry, and spent many years in the upbuilding of that church in various states in the South. For several years he served as financial agent for the Presbyterian Theological Seminary at Columbia, South Carolina, and in recognition of that service and his high scholarship the institution awarded him the Doctor of Divinity degree. For twenty years he was engaged in Evangelistic work in Georgia and Alabama. He held a number of prominent pastorates, including Charleston and Fort Mill. He established his permanent home at Fort Mill and died there.

His wife, still living, is a member of the prominent Banks family of this state. Her brother was Prof. Alexander Banks, one of South Carolina's leading educators. He died in March, 1920.

William Mack, mentioned above, was born in Sumter County, South Carolina, October 24, 1865, is a graduate of Davidson College, North Carolina, received his law degree in the University of Missouri, and was admitted to the bar in 1887. Since 1900 he has been secretary of the American Law Book Publishing Company of New York, also editor in chief of its publications, and from 1900 to 1912 was editor in chief of the Encyclopedia of Law and Procedure and since 1914 of "Corpus Juris."

Dr. Edward Mack, D. D., was born at Charleston, July 16, 1868, is a graduate of Columbia Theological Seminary and of Princeton Theological Seminary and has been a minister of the Presbyterian Church since 1889. He held pastorates at St. Louis, Norfolk, Virginia, and other places until 1904. For eleven years he was a professor in the Lane Theological Seminary at Cincinnati, and has held a chair in the Union Theological Seminary at Richmond, Virginia, since 1915. He is author of a number of theological and other books and articles.

F M Mack

Capt. Francis Murray Mack is a junior by twenty years to these distinguished brothers. He was born at Fort Mill in York County in 1887, and was reared in the beautiful Mack home at Fort Mill, where he still lives. He attended public school at Atlanta, spent two years in Davidson College, North Carolina, and two years in Cornell University. Before the World war and since leaving the army he has been engaged in the management of the Mack farm owned by his mother. This is a beautiful and valuable plantation of 800 acres, and adjoins the Town of Fort Mill on the South.

Captain Mack became a private in the Fort Mill Light Infantry and had attained the rank of second lieutenant when he was called to duty with that company on the Mexican border from July to December, 1916. The Fort Mill Company was Company G of the First South Carolina Infantry. This organization was mustered into the National Army April 12, 1917. The first South Carolina with subsequent additions became the One Hundred and Eighteenth Regiment of the Thirtieth, Old Hickory, Division. Concerning the brilliant record of this regiment nothing need be said at this point. Captain Mack joined the colors at Columbia, was at Camp Jackson, and in September, 1917, went to Camp Sevier at Greenville. He went overseas with the One Hundred and Eighteenth in May, 1918. In the meantime he had spent two months of intensive drill in a machine gun course at Fort Sill, Oklahoma, and was made machine gun instructor in his regiment. The One Hundred and Eighteenth Regiment was one of the units called upon for the heaviest service and sustained some of the heaviest losses of any regiment in France beginning with the events of July, 1918, and continuing to the signing of the armistice. While in France Captain Mack was transferred from G Company to the Regimental Intelligence Office of the One Hundred and Eighteenth, and when Captain Pyles was killed he was promoted to regimental operations officer with the rank of captain. After the armistice he was kept on duty in France until the spring of 1919 and was then sent home and received his honorable discharge in July, 1919.

Captain Mack married Miss Elizabeth Nims, of York County. Their two children are Francis Murray, Jr., and Frederick Nims Mack.

JAMES TRAVIS MEDLOCK, deceased, for many years was one of the leading bankers of Greenwood. He was a veteran in banking experience, and filled practically every executive position in a bank. Mr. Medlock was also widely known as one of the most prominent Methodist laymen in the state.

He was born in Laurens County, South Carolina, August 18, 1856, son of James Travis and Cornelia (Jones) Medlock. His father was both a farmer and merchant. The son had a business college education in addition to the advantages of the common schools and for three years was a teacher. With that exception his career has been completely a commercial one. For ten years he was in the mercantile business, four years in Laurens County and six years in Greenwood. He began banking with the Bank of Greenwood, first as assistant cashier for six years and then six years as cashier. Besides his knowledge of banking he had been gaining steadily the confidence of his associates and his reputation for financial management. On leaving the Bank of Greenwood he organized the Loan and Exchange Bank, and served as its cashier and later as its president. This institution was consolidated with the First National Bank, becoming the National Loan and Exchange Bank, and Mr. Medlock was afterward president of the consolidated institution. He was also president of the Citizens Trust Company. He owned the handsome bank and office building, 40x120 feet, a six-story concrete and brick face fire-proof structure that is a substantial evidence of Greenwood's importance as a growing business center. Mr. Medlock was also active vice president of the Durst-Andrews Company, wholesale grocers.

December 15, 1892, he married Miss Kate Bullock, of Greenwood County. They had a family of seven children: Lucile, a teacher; Robert Travis, who during the World war was a sergeant in the Fifty-third Regiment and saw active service with the Expeditionary Forces in France; Bertha Nell, a teacher; James Rogers, a student in Wofford College; Joseph Preston, Melvin Kelly and Mary, all at home.

While Mr. Medlock was daily busy with his affairs in Greenwood he resided on a farm and country estate two miles out of town. He was trustee and secretary and treasurer of the Greenwood City School Board. Mr. Medlock was a steward and treasurer of the First Methodist Episcopal Church of Greenwood, secretary and treasurer of the Sunday school, and for four years was a member of the General Board of Missions of the church and was very prominent in the laymen's missionary movement.

JAMES BENETTE HUNTER is junior member of the law firm of Hunt, Hunt & Hunter, which for years has enjoyed exceptional standing and has represented some of the best abilities in the legal profession in the state. Mr. Hunter has also been active while building up his professional interests in local affairs at Newberry.

He was born in Newberry County, July 18, 1872, son of Robert T. C. and Rebecca J. (Boozer) Hunter. His father was a very progressive factor in the agricultural community of Newberry County. A man of natural mechanical ability, he for many years operated a threshing outfit and a cotton gin and introduced the first steam threshing machine into Newberry County.

James Benette Hunter grew up on his father's farm, had good school advantages, and in 1896 graduated from Newberry College. After reading law privately he was admitted to the bar in 1897. In 1896-97 he taught school. He practiced law for three years at Saluda, and then came to Newberry and has since been a member of the firm Hunt, Hunt & Hunter. While at Saluda he served as intendant of the town for nearly two years, having resigned on moving to Newberry.

He is a prominent layman of the Lutheran Church, is a deacon in his home church and treasurer of its benevolent fund. He is also one of the trustees of Newberry College, and treasurer of one of the endowment funds of the college. Mr. Hunter is a Mason. During the war he served as chief clerk for the local exemption board, and gave practically all his time to those duties to the neglect of his professional duties.

August 27, 1902, he married Minnie McLarnon, of Chester, South Carolina.

THOMAS KENNERLY JOHNSTONE was graduated from Newberry College in 1904, and for the past fifteen years has been actively identified with the commercial affairs of Newberry.

He was born June 13, 1884, a son of Alan and Lilla K. (Kennerly) Johnstone. While his father was a farmer, he was also active in politics and served at one time as a member of the State Senate. Thomas K. Johnstone grew up at his father's home and prepared for Newberry College in the public schools. After leaving college he entered the service of the National Bank of Newberry as collection clerk, and since 1916 has been cashier of that institution. He has served as clerk of the Sinking Fund Commission of South Carolina, and during 1918-19 was an alderman of Newberry. Mr. Johnstone is a member of the Presbyterian Church.

November 24, 1909, he married Miss Jeanne Pelham of Newberry. Their five children are Alan McCrary, Brantly Leavel, Thomas K., Jr., Lilla K. and Ellerbe Pelham.

COL. THOMAS B. SPRATT, of the historic Spratt family of Fort Mill, was lieutenant colonel of the One Hundred and Eighteenth Infantry in the Thirtieth Division and was in active command of his regiment during its glorious participation in the campaign which broke the Hindenburg line during October, 1918. He is one of the distinguished military figures in his native state, and his individual career adds luster to the military annals of the family.

This is one of the oldest families in the northern section of South Carolina, and one inseparably associated with the state's history. The Spratt family have owned and lived continuously upon the Spratt estate at Fort Mill in York County since 1760, a period of 160 years, this land having been given to Kanawha (Thomas Spratt) by the Catawba Indians when he settled among them.

The founder of the name in South Carolina was Thomas Spratt, great-grandfather of Colonel Spratt. He was born in County Down, Ireland, of Scotch parentage, and when a child he came with his parents to America in 1730. His father and two brothers settled at Chester, Pennsylvania. Thomas Spratt about 1758 came southward with his wife and small children and in the southern part of North Carolina crossed the Yadkin River and located on the site of the present City of Charlotte in Mecklenburg County. A son born there is credited with having been the first white child born west of the Yadkin. Historians have also recorded the fact that this was the first white family to cross the Yadkin. The first court of Mecklenburg County was held in the cabin that was erected by Thomas Spratt. He did not long remain there, however, and in 1876 removed to the site of the present Town of Fort Mill in York County, South Carolina, about seventeen miles south of Charlotte. The land was then owned by the Catawba tribe of Indians, and that region was inhabited solely by them. Thomas Spratt was the first permanent white settler among them. The Indians found in him a leader and adviser in their domestic and tribal affairs and also a valuable counselor in their wars. Thomas Spratt led the Catawbas to victory against another tribe on the Kanawha River in what is now West Virginia. After this campaign the Catawbas bestowed upon him the name "Kanawha," by which he is known in history. Largely through the wise and kind leadership of Kanawha Spratt the Catawbas remained faithful and loyal to him and to his descendants, aiding the white people in all their wars beginning with the Revolution and down to the period of the war between the states. Some of the Catawbas were heroes in these wars, a fact permanently testified to by a monument erected to their memory at Fort Mill by John McKee Spratt and Samuel Elliott White. Kanawha Spratt died in 1807. The land given to him by the Catawba Indians at Fort Mill was later granted to him by King George and has never passed out of the family name. Thomas Spratt served as a lieutenant in the Revolutionary war.

Col. Thomas B. Spratt, who was born at Fort Mill in 1878, is a son of John McKee and Susan (Massey) Spratt, the latter still living. John McKee Spratt, who died in 1909, was a son of Thomas D. Spratt and a grandson of James Spratt, who was one of the sons of Kanawha Spratt. During his life of sixty years he was actively and successfully engaged in farming, banking and manufacturing, at Fort Mill, spending his entire life on the old family homestead. Thomas D. Spratt was a man of thorough education. Though he spent three years in the South Carolina College at Columbia and studied medicine in the Medical College of South Carolina at Charleston, he never practiced that profession. He studied law at Yorkville and was admitted to the bar in 1831. His career as a lawyer was also brief. In 1834 he returned to the Spratt place at Fort Mill and busied his years with planting. He died in 1875. His wife was Margaret McKee.

Thomas B. Spratt acquired his education in the South Carolina military school, The Citadel, at Charleston, which has turned out hundreds of men who have achieved fame in war and in civil affairs. After returning home he joined the National Guard of South Carolina. He commanded the Second Battalion, First South Carolina Infantry, during the troubles on the Mexican border. He was on the border during 1916, and when he returned to civil life in 1919 he had been on active duty as a military man for nearly three years. Soon after his return from the South he volunteered in the National Army. He went to France as lieutenant colonel of the One Hundred and Eighteenth Infantry in the Thirtieth Division. The division was largely made up of South Carolina troops and its history is merely a part of the state's military record. He was lieutenant colonel in command of the One Hundred and Eighteenth Infantry, during the great offensive from October 5th to October 20th, and in the absence of the colonel of the regiment he made the plans and gave the command which preceded

the advance and capture of Brancourt, one of the most important objectives attained by the American army in the offensive of the month of October when the Hindenburg line was broken.

Colonel Spratt returned home in December, 1918, having been recommended for promotion, for the purpose of taking command of one of the new regiments being formed. After the armistice he resumed his business duties as president of the First National Bank of Fort Mill, and farming the old homestead.

The vice president and cashier of this bank is his brother, Dr. J. Lee Spratt, who is a graduate in dentistry of the University of Maryland at Baltimore. For several years he has not practiced his profession, having given much of his time to the Spratt Bank and to his farming operations. Doctor Spratt as a civilian rendered valuable service to the Government during the war, serving on Local Exemption Board No. 1 for York County and being chairman of all the Liberty Loan drives for Fort Mill and vicinity. He married Miss Emma Ardrey, daughter of Capt. W. E. Ardrey of Mecklenburg County, North Carolina.

Col. T. B. Spratt married Miss Eleanor Mason Harris. They have three children, named John McKee, Thomas and Eleanor Spratt.

CALHOUN ALLEN MAYS, a lawyer whose talents have brought him wide recognition in South Carolina, has been in practice at Greenwood a number of years, and resumed his work there after his discharge from the army in the winter of 1918-19.

Mr. Mays was born in Edgefield, South Carolina, November 14, 1884, a son of Sampson Butler and Ella (Calhoun) Mays. His father is a farmer and the son made acquaintance with country life and its responsibilities when a youth. He attended the public schools, also the South Carolina Co-educational Institute at Edgefield, where he completed his work in 1902, and then for one year was a teacher. In 1906 he completed a course in Charleston College, and then taught in Georgia, spending some time at Elberton and at Waycross. In 1909 he entered the University of Michigan Law Department, and was admitted to the bar in December, 1910. Mr. Mays has made his home and has had his professional headquarters at Greenwood since September, 1911. He is associated with Henry C. Tillman in the firm of Tillman & Mays. In 1915 he was appointed assistant United States attorney for the Western District of South Carolina. He resigned this office in 1918 to go into the army at the Field Artillery Officers Training School at Camp Taylor, Louisville, Kentucky. He received his honorable discharge November 27, 1918, and then returned to Greenwood to resume the threads of private life and his profession. He is a Mason and is affiliated with the Alpha Tau Omega college fraternity at Charleston.

CHARLES EDWARD SUMMER is president of the Summer Brothers Company, Incorporated, of Newberry, a large and important concern operating on a capital of $100,000. It is an incorporation for general business purposes, doing a large mercantile business, and in addition to this they operate 2,700 acres of plantation. This is one of the notable agricultural undertakings in South Carolina. In the busy seasons sixty-five plows are at work in the fields, and the average annual product from the cotton plantings is 700 bails.

Charles Edward Summer also has during the past thirty years been identified with many other important commercial affairs at Newberry. He was born in Lexington County, November 18, 1858, son of George W. and Martha D. Summers. The Summers family settled in the Dutch Fork of Lexington County nearly a century and a half ago. George W. Summer was a farmer, and while a Confederate soldier died in a Virginia hospital, July 13, 1862. Charles Edward Summer grew up on the home farm and was indebted to his mother for much of his education and the influences which shaped his life. He was trained to farm work and has always had some interests in agriculture. Owing to the limited circumstances of the family he never acquired a college education. He began farming for himself in Lexington County, in 1877, and in 1888 transferred his field of operation to Newberry, where he began merchandising on a small scale. Since then besides the large enterprise noted above he has been identified with the Mollohon Manufacturing Company, the Newberry Warehouse Company, the Standard Warehouse Company, and the Newberry Land and Security Company, serving as an executive officer in these and other local enterprises. He also owns large stocks and leases in oil lands in Kansas, Texas and Oklahoma, is also identified with and owns large stocks in fertilizer plants, of which he is an officer. Mr. Summer is a democrat and is affiliated with the Lutheran Church.

January 1, 1877, he married Leonora Sease, who died in 1884, the mother of three children. On January 2, 1886, he married Mary Jane Sease, sister of his first wife. To this marriage were born six children. Mr. Summer served two terms as an alderman at Newberry and in 1901 began a long service as commissioner of public works, which position he still holds.

WILLIAM KIMBROUGH CHARLES established the first law office in what is now McCormick County, and was associated with Hon. B. E. Nicholson of the Edgefield bar, who was representing the legal interests of many individuals and firms in the Town of McCormick and surrounding country at the time the new county was organized in 1916. Mr. Charles' progress in his profession has been steadily upward since that date.

Mr. Charles was born at Timmonsville in Florence County, April 2, 1892, a son of Kimbrough DuBose and Elizabeth (Keith) Charles. The Charles family was originally from Darlington County.

William K. Charles was educated in the University of South Carolina, graduating from the law department in 1915 and being admitted to the bar the same year. While in Columbia he served as secretary of the committee on agriculture and secretary of the committee on banking and insurance of the State Legislature. For nearly a year after completing his course in the university he was in

Washington, an employe of the Department of Justice and also a student of law at Georgetown University. He then returned home and in 1916 located at McCormick. McCormick, the town as well as the county, has enjoyed a rapid growth and has splendid prospects as the center of a wonderfully rich agricultural and industrial district.

Mr. Charles married Miss Carrie Lou Able, of Leesville, South Carolina. They have a daughter Doris Virginia.

THOMAS B. MADDEN. A happy instance of the rule of special fitness governing political appointments was afforded when Thomas B. Madden received his official commission as postmaster of Columbia on January 21, 1920. If it were not for his comparative youth it might appropriately be said that Mr. Madden has grown old in the service of the postal department of the Government. He is at least a veteran, and his present office is an appropriate reward of a continuously efficient service of more than twenty years.

Mr. Madden was born at Winnsboro, son of Dr. Thomas B. and Margaret S. (Brice) Madden. The Maddens came to South Carolina from the north of Ireland. The grandfather, Dr. Campbell Madden, of Winnsboro, was not only a physician but also a minister of the Associate Reformed Presbyterian Church. Dr. Thomas B. Madden spent his active life as a practicing physician in Fairfield County.

The son was educated in the Mount Zion Academy at Winnsboro, and from there in 1897 he entered the railway mail department of the Government. He also worked in the mail transfer offices in Columbia and Florence and on the Charleston and Augusta division, and in 1904 was assigned to the Augusta postoffice, where during the next six or seven years he had experience in practically every department. Mr. Madden came to Columbia in 1911, was in the general delivery department, was promoted to assistant superintendent of mails in 1913 and in 1915 was appointed assistant postmaster by Postmaster Huggins. He had charge of a large part of the work of the local postoffice during the administration of the late W. H. Coleman, who died in February, 1919. Following the death of his predecessor he served as acting postmaster, and on January 21, 1920, was appointed by President Wilson postmaster of the Columbia office.

Mr. Madden is a member of the Associate Reformed Presbyterian Church and a Mason. He married Miss Willie Brunson, of Dillon, and their three children are Martha, Thomas B. and Addie.

JOHN THOMAS FOOSHE is proprietor of the leading furniture and house furnishing business of the Town of McCormick, county seat of McCormick County. Mr. Fooshe has been in business at McCormick for a number of years, and the esteem accorded him as an enterprising and successful merchant is heightened by the influence he is known to have exercised in behalf of the establishment of the County of McCormick.

Agitation was started to carve a new county from old Abbeville, Edgefield and Greenwood as long ago as 1895, but support of the movement waned, and it was not revived until Mr. Fooshe with others became the active leaders in 1913 and 1914. During the next two years the agitation was carried on with spirit and vigor both in the communities effected and before the State Legislature, resulting in the passage of the act and the establishment of the new county April 12, 1916, with the Town of McCormick as county seat.

John Thomas Fooshe was born at Ninety-Six in Abbeville County, now Greenwood County, South Carolina, October 21, 1873, a son of T. K. and Sallie (Clem) Fooshe. The family is of French origin and the first of the name in South Carolina came from France and located near Ninety-Six about 1700. Mr. Fooshe's grandfather was C. W. Fooshe, born about 1820, and some of his descendants now live in the old home which was built fully 100 years ago by his father. His youngest son, R. L. Fooshe, lives on this place at this writing.

John Thomas Fooshe grew up on the plantation in Abbeville, now Greenwood County. On January 7, 1907, he removed to the Town of McCormick and established a furniture business under the name Fooshe & Strom. After ten months he became sole proprietor and continued the business until the spring of 1910, when the store and most of the business part of the town was destroyed by fire. For about six months he was in business at Lancaster, still retaining his business at McCormick, and aside from that interval has been continuously identified with McCormick for over fourteen years. He is proprietor of the oldest and the first exclusive furniture and house furnishing store in McCormick and in recent years has kept his establishment growing with adequate service to fulfill the new needs and demands of the rapidly developing country around McCormick.

Mr. Fooshe married Miss Hetie Dora Ouzts, of Edgefield County, the daughter of J. Ouzts of Greenwood, South Carolina. They have one adopted daughter, Nellie Norris Fooshe, the daughter of the late J. B. Norris, who died February 29, 1914. Her mother, Emma (Wilson) Norris, died March 3, 1914.

ROBERT S. GALLOWAY was endowed with good business talents and has used those talents during a long and active career largely to promote and handle the several business organizations of the Associate Reformed Presbyterian Church centered at Due West. Mr. Galloway is well known as a publisher and editor of church publications, and was the man chiefly responsible among the local citizens of Due West in giving that historic college community direct connection with the outside world by means of a railroad.

Mr. Galloway was born at Newberry, South Carolina, in 1854, a son of Rev. Jonathan and Martha (Spear) Galloway. His paternal grandparents were natives of Scotland. Rev. Jonathan Galloway was born in York County, South Carolina, and is well remembered as a prominent minister and educator of the Associate Reformed Presbyterian Church. For many years he lived at Newberry but in 1859 moved to Due West, the seat of Erskine College. He was one of the three men who originally conceived the plan of the Due West Female College, and when it was opened in 1860 as an in-

stitution for the higher education of women he became Professor of Latin and Greek. He had been an active minister at Newberry for twenty years. The mother of Robert S. Galloway was born at Lowndesville in Abbeville County.

Robert S. Galloway graduated from Erskine College in 1874. For a time he was a merchant and later organized a company and bought the Associate Reformed Presbyterian, the official organ of the Synod of the church and published at Due West. Mr. Galloway for many years has been business manager of this publication and is assistant editor. Published weekly, the paper circulates to the majority of the homes of the Associate Reformed Presbyterian people in this Synod, and through Mr. Galloway's able management its business administration has been conducted on a most substantial basis. He is also publisher of the Senior Quarterly and Junior Quarterly, the Sunday school publications of the Synod.

Mr. Galloway and his associates among Due West citizens financed and built the Due West Railroad from Donalds to Due West, connecting with the Southern Railway at the former point. The first train was run over the line December 24, 1907. Mr. Galloway is president and treasurer of the railroad and its active manager. He is also a member of the board of trustees of both Erskine College and the Woman's College at Due West.

Mr. Galloway married Mary Eleanor Stone of Louisville, Jefferson County, Georgia, daughter of James Madison and Mary (Lawson) Stone. Mrs. Galloway is active assistant in the management of the "Associate Reformed Presbyterian." Their children, seven in number, were all liberally educated in the Due West colleges and were well trained for lives of usefulness. They are: Jennie, wife of H. D. Kirkpatrick; Mary, wife of J. B. McCutcheon; Helen, wife of E. W. Neal; Lena, who married J. B. Mosely; Robert, Virginia and Kathryn.

N. W. HARDIN is the present mayor, a leading lawyer and for thirty years a source of much of the enterprise which has stimulated the interesting and historic community of Blacksburg.

Blacksburg is the home of the Hardins, one of the notable families of South Carolina. Blacksburg was originally in York County, and upon the creation of Cherokee County in 1897 it was part of the territory used in the creation of that new county division. In and around Blacksburg many prominent families and notable men have lived, not least among them the Hardins. Mr. Hardin's grandfather was Abraham Hardin, who represented Scotch-Irish ancestry. He was a large land and slave owner before the war, for nearly twenty years sat in the General Assembly, was a surveyor, magistrate, deacon in the Baptist Church, and in his generation exercised a great and splendid influence in his community.

N. W. Hardin was born near Blacksburg in 1857, a son of Ira and Elizabeth (Hamilton) Hardin. His father, the late Ira Hardin, was one of the founders of the town of Blacksburg, whose history dates from 1871. The A. & C. Air Line Railroad, now a part of the Southern system, was then being built. Ira Hardin was the means of providing a depot for the company. One of the chief objects of his interest and enthusiasm was education. He caused to be erected the Blacksburg High School Building, the first graded school in that part of the state. He bore over half the expense of establishing the high school. He was also instrumental in founding the Methodist Episcopal Church, South, the first church in Blacksburg. After a life of great usefulness Ira Hardin died in 1917.

While N. W. Hardin has always lived at Blacksburg and has played a role of influence and usefulness in that community, his brothers have elected larger cities in which to make their careers. He has three brothers at Atlanta, Georgia, all men of prominence in the professions. One of them, Dr. S. L. Hardin, is one of the leading surgeons of the South.

Perhaps the most notable of the Hardin brothers is Abraham Tracy Hardin, who is many years younger than the Blacksburg mayor. His career is the record of a remarkable rise of a South Carolina boy to be one of America's foremost railroad officials. Born at Blacksburg in 1880, at the age of fifteen he had learned telegraphy and shorthand, and was an expert railroad telegrapher, his talents attracting the attention of Mr. E. Berkley, superintendent of the Charlotte & Atlanta Air Line, now a part of the Southern Railroad. Mr. Berkley took young Hardin into his office as private clerk. While thus employed he earned money to guarantee his tuition in the University of South Carolina, where he graduated with the first honors of his class in 1903. In university he specialized in higher mathematics and engineering. His record since leaving university has justified all the confidence entertained of his budding abilities. He became private secretary to Mr. R. A. Dodson, general roadmaster of the Southern Railway at Washington. He accepted the many opportunities in that work to acquire the knowledge of an expert in scientific railroading. After two and a half years he went to the New York Central as assistant roadmaster, was promoted to division roadmaster, then division engineer, and from there going into the office of the chief engineer of the system was soon made engineer of maintenance of way. Later he was made assistant to the general manager, became general manager and finally senior vice president of the New York Central System. When the railroads were put under Federal jurisdiction he was appointed Federal manager for all the lines of the New York Central or Vanderbilt system.

N. W. Hardin attended high school at Blacksburg, studied law under the late William C. Black and was admitted to the bar in 1889. For thirty years he has practiced his profession in Blacksburg, and in addition has also looked after a growing and extensive interest as a farmer. By successive elections he has served as mayor of Blacksburg since 1912 and is probably the most popular official that community has ever had. He was elected and served in the Lower House of the General Assembly in 1888 and was again elected in 1914, serving in two regular and two extra sessions of that body.

Mr. Hardin married Miss Mattie A. Black, a daughter of William G. Black. Their six children are Mrs. Willie Davies, S. L. Hardin, James A. Hardin, Kathleen, Louis and Roland Hardin.

MAJ. LINDSAY C. MCFADDEN was one of the "seniors" among South Carolina officers in the great war in France. He was about forty years of age, but in addition to his years he had the advantage of mature business and army experience behind him, all constituting a great advantage as a leader among the men of the One Hundred and Eighteenth Infantry, with which he served as acting commander of the Second Battalion.

Major McFadden has been a prominent merchant at Rock Hill for a number of years. He was born near Rodman in Chester County, son of James C. and Mary R. (Neely) McFadden. His parents still live on their plantation near Rodman. Major McFadden had a good high school education and has been a resident of Rock Hill since 1904. His business career and his residence at Rock Hill have been contemporaneous, though for nearly three years he had to neglect and absent himself from business duties on account of his military service. Major McFadden is vice president of the Diehl-Moore Shoe Company of Rock Hill.

A number of years ago he entered the State National Guard or Militia, and for about twenty years was captain of the Catawba Rifles of Rock Hill. He held that office when the National Guard was called upon for duty on the Mexican border in the summer of 1916. He was called out as captain of the Catawba Rifles in Company H of the First South Carolina Rifles on June 19, 1916, and was on duty during the Mexican imbroglio until December 6th of the same year. April 12, 1917, a few days after the declaration of war against Germany, his company was called into the army and became a part of the One Hundred and Eighteenth Infantry, Thirtieth Division. He retained his rank of captain under the new organization, and was taken into Federal service without further preliminary training. The One Hundred and Eighteenth Infantry trained at Camp Sevier, Greenville, and Company H embarked at New York May 11, 1918, reaching Liverpool May 23d, and soon afterward was on the soil of France. Captain McFadden was practically in command of the Second Battalion throughout the summer and fall of 1918. The regiment and battalion saw its first duty as part of the British sector around Ypres, but had the climax of its duty in the period between September 23d and October 20, 1918, when the battalion took its place in the Hindenburg line just north of Bellicourt. The battalion took its place at this point on September 29th, and during the next day or so the battalion suffered 111 casualties. On the 5th of October the battalion took up its position at Mont Brehain, and in following days it was an important unit in the forward movements of the Thirtieth Division, including the historic points of Brancourt and Brehain. It was in repeated advances until the 14th of October, by which time the battalion had sustained total casualties of over 400, including eight officers, Captain McFadden at that time commanding the battalion. The battalion resumed its place in front line operations the 15th of October, and from October 5th, when the battalion went into position in front of Mont Brehain until relieved on the 20th, the Second Battalion participated in an advance of over twenty kilometers and with the exception of three days was constantly in action. Captain McFadden was one of the five officers of the Second Battalion who continued through the entire action. In the meantime, on October 17th, he had received his commission as major.

The One Hundred and Eighteenth Regiment was cited and commended for unusual performance of duty by Gen. L. D. Tyson, the brigade commander, who in an address said, in addition, referring particularly to the Second Battalion, "that this battalion did more effective fighting than any other battalion in the 30th Division and more actual front line work than any other battalion."

After the signing of the armistice and when the Thirtieth Division was preparing for return to the United States, Major McFadden was transferred to the Third Division and was on duty keeping watch over the bridgeheads of the Rhine. He sailed from Brest August 12, 1919, reaching New York August 20th, and was mustered out and discharged September 12, 1919.

Major McFadden married Miss Maude Grantham, of Florida.

WILLIAM WALKER EDWARDS as merchant, banker and citizen has proved himself a most active spirit in the affairs of the flourishing and rapidly growing Town of Due West, long the seat of Erskine College and in later years developing as a commercial center for a splendid agricultural district.

Mr. Edwards was born near Rock Hill in York County in 1871, but has spent all his life since early infancy in Due West. His parents, Dr. E. H. and Harriett Elizabeth (Roddy) Edwards, natives of York County, moved to Due West in 1873. William Walker Edwards attended Erskine College and as a youth entered a business career. For a number of years he has been the leading merchant of the old college town, and is proprietor of two stores, one is a general dry goods and woman's store, while the other, in a separate building across the street, erected in 1919, handles a complete stock of men's clothing and furnishing goods.

Mr. Edwards was cashier of the Farmers and Merchants Bank of Due West until 1920, when he resigned. He is one of the liberal members of the Associate Reformed Presbyterian Church. He married Miss Isabel Hamilton Miller, daughter of the late Col. McDuffie Miller of Abbeville, now Greenwood, County. Their four children are Margaret Virginia, William Walker, Jr., Harriet Elizabeth and Belle Miller.

THOMAS MOORE ROSS was one of the first attorneys to locate in the new county seat of McCormick County. Highly educated, a young man of influential social connections, he has made rapid progress in achieving secure places in his profession and all around good citizenship.

He was born in Chester County, South Carolina, in 1891, son of Maj. H. M. and Lydia (Moore) Ross. This is an old Scotch family early established in Chester County. His father served with the rank of major in the Confederate army. His mother was a daughter of Dr. Thomas W. Moore of Chester County. Thomas Moore Ross attended school at Bascomville in Chester County and gradu-

ated from the University of South Carolina in 1911. He spent two years in the study of law at Harvard University, and for one year was in the office of Judge Woods of the United States Court. After some months at Columbia he located at McCormick in 1916. McCormick County was organized in that year, and the beginning of his professional career was coincident with the hostory of the new county.

Mr. Ross is a member of the Methodist Church and a Mason. He married Miss Anne McCown, of Florence, South Carolina.

J. JENNINGS DORN. Representative of a family whose enterprise has done much to contribute to the economic resources of the state, J. Jennings Dorn is a business man of the Town of McCormick, is a lumber manufacturer, cotton ginner, planter, banker, and has widespread interests all over that section of the state.

He was born in 1885, at Dornsville, then in Edgefield County. Dornsville, the ancestral home of the Dorns, is four miles east of the present City of McCormick and in the new County of McCormick, situated on Hardlabor Creek. J. Jennings Dorn is a son of J. M. and Visie (Self) Dorn, both natives of Edgefield County. Both his parents died in 1906.

One of the early members of the family and the one to originate an interesting chapter of economic history was Billy Dorn, who about 1835 discovered gold on his property near Dornsville and the present Town of McCormick. He opened and operated a mine, and the records of the United States Treasury show that the Government paid him $900,000 for gold from his mine up to 1858. The mine was again worked after the war, contributing another substantial fortune to the Dorn family. Later a party of New York men leased the property and sunk the New York shaft, and finally the Dorn mining property and many thousands of acres in that section were bought by Cyrus H. McCormick, inventor and manufacturer of harvesting machinery. It was his name that is now commemorated by the present Town and County of McCormick. The county seat stands on land formerly owned by him.

The late J. M. Dorn was one of the leading men of affairs of Dornsville for many years, owning a store, operating a saw and grist mill and cotton gins, all these industries being run by water power.

J. Jennings Dorn has many of the outstanding traits of his family, especially business sagacity and ability. He and his brother M. Gary Dorn comprise the firm of M. G. and J. J. Dorn. They have a large lumber manufacturing plant on the line of the Charleston & Western Carolina Railroad at McCormick, and supply great quantities of lumber, not only for the local demand but for distant shipment. Besides the plant at McCormick they operate from twelve to fifteen additional saw mills at different points in South Carolina. They also own twelve cotton gins at McCormick and four cotton gins at Dornsville, and their aggregate operations make them the largest individual ginners in the state.

Both brothers are also extensively interested in farming. J. J. Dorn has a fine farm at Dornsville, a special feature of which is a fine herd of Hereford cattle. J. J. Dorn is chairman of the McCormick County Commission for Permanent Highways, and through this commission is exerting the full force of his influence for the building of good roads. He is a Knight Templar Mason and Shriner and was one of the organizers and is vice president of the Peoples Bank. He married Miss Nora Cuddy and has one daughter, Mabel Dorn.

WILLIAM C. COBB. While for nearly fifteen years William C. Cobb has been the manager and superintendent of the Ware Shoals Cotton Mills, he achieved that important responsibility and a place among the prominent cotton mill men of the state only as a result of many years of faithful and efficient toil, beginning in the very lowest ranks and coming up step by step on the basis of merit and growing qualities of executive leadership.

Mr. Cobb is a native of South Carolina and was born four miles south of Belton in Anderson County, November 4, 1862, son of G. W. and Laura (West) Cobb. When he was seven years of age the family removed to Banks County, Georgia, where he lived on a farm, did work in the fields and attended country schools in limited sessions. At the age of seventeen he went to work as a track hand on the Northeast Railroad between Athens and Lula, Georgia. In a short time he was made foreman of the section and work train, and continued as such until he met an accidental injury and broke his leg. After being able to walk he attended a school near Pendleton under Mrs. Rebecca Douthit, and he credits her with most of the real education he has acquired, especially in mathematics and spelling.

Since October, 1882, when he engaged as a weaver in the Piedmont mills, Mr. Cobb has been wholly absorbed in the cotton mill industry. On July 4, 1883, he changed his job, going, as he says, "with the generous, big-hearted Captain Smyth as a common weaver." October 14, 1884, he was promoted from weaver to the duties described as "striker," and October 14, 1886, two years later, was promoted to section hand, and after another two years was made second hand in the weave room. June 9, 1890, he was promoted to overseer of weaving in Mills Nos. 1, 2 and 3, comprising over 1,500 looms. This responsibility he held for nearly six years. January 16, 1896, he was transferred to Mill No. 4 to start the operation of the first sheeting looms the Draper Company ever put on the market. March 1, 1900, he became superintendent at Belton and conducted the mill there until September 10, 1905, when he resigned, and on the 18th of September entered upon his duties as manager and superintendent of the Ware Shoals Mills. This is one of the model plants in upper South Carolina, and the mills, the mill village and the entire community comprise one of the "high lights" in the industrial situation of the South. In the upbuilding of the mills and in the creation of the community Mr. Cobb shared with Mr. J. F. MacEnroe and others the credit for this really distinctive achievement.

Mr. Cobb is widely known among cotton mill managers and is an exceedingly popular citizen in his home community. He is a Knight Templar Mason and Shriner. On September 16, 1883, after he had been working in the cotton mills less than a year, he married Miss Hattie Davis. On June 11, 1890, Mr. Cobb married for his present wife Miss Ella P. Walker, of Greenville County. Mr. Cobb is the father of nine children, the oldest, A. C. Cobb, being the son of his first wife, while the others are C. A., Lillian, Lila, Lora, Hazel, W. L., Mary and Frances.

JAMES C. DOZIER. While by no means common, the name Dozier has been conspicuous in a number of communities, especially in the southern states, for many generations. There have been soldiers of the name in various American wars, including the war between the states. Of French origin, there was an interesting appropriateness in the service which James C. Dozier rendered his own country and the country of his remote ancestors during the World war. Both of Lieutenant Dozier's grandfathers were Confederate soldiers and several of his uncles were killed in that war. James C. Dozier was born at Marion, South Carolina, in 1886, son of John H. and Julia (Best) Dozier. His parents have lived for several years at Rock Hill. His mother is a daughter of Capt. James Best of Marion.

James C. Dozier entered Wofford College in the fall of 1915. At that time he was a member of the South Carolina National Guard. In 1916 he went with his company to the Mexican border. He was one of the many gallant sons of Wofford College whose names as soldiers in the World war make a long roll of honor to that institution.

With the declaration of war against Germany young Dozier accompanied his comrades in Company H of the One Hundred and Eighteenth Infantry to training camp at Camp Jackson and later at Camp Sevier, and in the spring of 1918 went overseas to France, where he was transferred to Company G. By service and not through training school he rose from private through the grade of sergeant to second lieutenant and then to first lieutenant, and was ranking first lieutenant of his company when he reached the scene of action in France. The brilliant record of the One Hundred and Eighteenth Infantry, part of the Thirtieth Division, is a matter of common knowledge to South Carolinians. To no one man in that regiment did greater honors fall than to Lieutenant Dozier. The culmination of his brilliant performance of duty came early in October, 1918. At the request of newspaper correspondents Lieutenant Dozier has given some modest account of the action in which his name became memorable, but the service is best told in the formal language of official citation given him by order of General Pershing, as follows:

"Dozier, James C., 1st Lieutenant, Co. G, 118th Infantry.

"For conspicuous gallantry and intrepidity above and beyond the call of duty in action with the enemy near Montbrehain, France, 8 October, 1918.

"In command of two platoons, Lieutenant Dozier was painfully wounded in the shoulder early in the attack, but he continued to lead his men, displaying the highest bravery and skill. When his command was held up by heavy machine-gun fire, he disposed his men in the best cover available and with a soldier continued forward to attack a machine-gun nest. Creeping up to the position in the face of intense fire, he killed the entire crew with hand grenades and his pistol and a little later captured a number of Germans who had taken refuge in a dugout nearby."

Besides this official citation Lieutenant Dozier has been the recipient of the highest military honors. One of these, coveted by every American soldier, is the Congressional medal of honor, which for years has been a badge of distinction. This Congressional medal of honor was bestowed by General Pershing at a review of the Thirtieth Division at Souligne January 21, 1919. Later Lieutenant Dozier was presented with the British military cross in Belgium by Gen. Sir David Henderson of the British Expeditionary Forces. Lieutenant Dozier with his regiment arrived in America March 27, 1919, and he received his honorable discharge on the 20th of April. In the summer of 1919 he was awarded the French Croix de Guerre by Ambassador Jusserand, making a trip to Washington for that purpose. Still later in the same year he received from the President of France the medal of the French Legion of Honor, the highest distinction conferred by the French Government for military valor, and has also been made a Chevalier of the Legion of Honor, an order founded by Napoleon the First. The certificate for this honor reads as follows: "The Grand Chancellor of the National Legion of Honor hereby certifies that on May 5, 1919, the President of the Republic of France conferred upon James C. Dozier, Lieutenant, Company G, 118th Infantry of the American Army, a decoration of the Chevalier of the Order of National Legion of Honor."

Lieutenant Dozier took an active part in the campaign and drive for the Victory Loan in the spring of 1919. The motion picture made under the auspices of the Government and for use in promoting that loan was known as "The Price of Peace" and contained a film illustrating Lieutenant Dozier in the act of charging a nest of machine guns.

Since returning to his home at Rock Hill Lieutenant Dozier has resumed business as an official of the City Wholesale Grocery Company.

While his is one of the most brilliant and outstanding records among South Carolinians in the World war, he had three brothers who yielded nothing to him in patriotic devotion. His brother Sidney W. was sergeant in Company H of the One Hundred and Eighteenth Infantry, having volunteered a few days after war was declared. Leroy Dozier joined the navy and crossed the ocean on duty several times.

The youngest brother, John A. Dozier, was only sixteen years of age when the European war broke out in 1914. Soon afterward in his zeal to become a soldier he went to Canada and joined the famous Princess Patricia Regiment. He was in that regiment at the battle of Vimy Ridge, in which only eighty-three out of something over 900 men comprising the regiment came out unhurt or not killed. He was wounded in that battle, and after leaving the hospital at London received an honorable dis-

charge from the Canadian army. Soon afterward he returned to America and immediately enlisted in the United States Navy and was in service until the summer of 1919.

THOMAS J. PRICE. The lifetime interests of Thomas J. Price have been identified with that section of old Abbeville County now McCormick County and particularly the town and business center and county seat of McCormick. While Mr. Price is best known as a merchant, he has always kept in close touch with agriculture both as a land owner and planter. He was one of the men chiefly responsible for the organization of the present County of McCormick.

He was born in 1867 at the Price homestead four miles from the present Town of McCormick, son of Abraham and Permelia (Beatty) Price. His parents represented two of the older families of Abbeville County. Thomas J. Price grew up on a farm, had a common school education, and on reaching his majority he bought a farm on the edge of the Town of McCormick. Gradually his business affairs became more extensive than his individual farm. He was interested in the oil mill and livestock industry, and about ten years ago engaged in the general merchandise business. His home has been in the Town of McCormick since 1901. He is now head of the T. J. Price Company, a complete organization for an adequate mercantile service, supplying all things required in the home and on the farm, dealing in grain, hay, cotton, farm implements, dry goods, notions and shoes.

The business is a credit to the county seat of one of the richest and most promising counties in the state. Mr. Price for several years labored unselfishly to create sentiment and influence the State Legislature to create the new County of McCormick. After it was established in 1916 he consented at considerable sacrifice of his own interests to accept the office of county superintendent of schools, to which he was elected. His administration has been notable, though he makes little profession of being a practical school man or educator. He has taken sound business judgment and common sense to the administration of the local schools. He started with no school fund for the county, and yet during the past three years the county has paid its teachers, has built new schools, has carried on the system of education without borrowing a dollar, and now has over $7,000 in the treasury. The state superintendent of education calls this the best record made by any county in the state.

Mr. Price married Sallie E. Edmund, of Abbeville County. They have a family of four daughters and two sons: Mrs. Ruth Duncan, Mrs. Ethel Davis, Mrs. Linnie Hurd and Miss Kate Price, Thomas Ansel and Metz Price.

J. CAPERS GAMBRELL. Probably the most complete, thoroughly organized business community in South Carolina is the Village of Ware Shoals, the central features of which are the great cotton mills of the Ware Shoals Manufacturing Company. While operated incidentally and subsidiary to this primary industry, the other departments of the company's enterprise make an imposing aggregate of business in themselves. This group of mercantile, public utility and other industries has as its active manager J. Capers Gambrell, who has occupied his present post of duty and responsibility for the past thirteen years.

Mr. Gambrell was born at Princeton, Laurens County, in 1874, a son of E. B. and Nancy Caroline (Riley) Gambrell. He was educated in the public schools of Princeton, Wofford College at Spartanburg, and had an early business training and experience at Greenwood. June 4, 1906, he came to the Ware Shoals Manufacturing Company. He is the executive manager in charge of the Ware Shoals Bank, various mercantile interests including the ice factory, cotton gin, grist mill, laundry, the dairy farm, and, in general, all the business and industrial interests with the exception of the cotton mills themselves. It is conceded that Ware Shoals is the finest mill town in the United States, where more things are done for the comfort, happiness and prosperity of the citizens than in any similar community anywhere.

Mr. Gambrell takes a particular interest and enthusiasm in the magnificent herd of pure-bred Guernsey dairy cattle, one of the company enterprises and as a result of which the village population has a source of milk supply of unexcelled quality and purity. With good milk, public water supply, ice, free public schools and the many other institutions and improvements that have been instituted and carried out by the company it is easy to understand how the people of Ware Shoals might well be envied for their comfort and prosperity by many larger communities of the country.

Mr. Gambrell is a Knight Templar Mason and Shriner. He married Miss Mary K. McCullough, of Greenville County. She is a niece of the late Col. J. H. McCullough, who was one of the big men of his time in Greenville County, a planter, stock man, merchant and owner of many noted race horses. Mr. and Mrs. Gambrell have five children, James B., Mary, Elizabeth, William and J. Capers McCullough. James B. Gambrell is a graduate of The Citadel at Charleston, and during the war with Germany volunteered in the Marine Corps, served eight months, and rose to the rank of first lieutenant.

JOHN RANDOLPH CHEATHAM. Since early manhood John Randolph Cheatham has given his undivided time and abilities to banking. He helped organized the People's Bank of McCormick, one of the younger and rapidly growing financial institutions in that section of the state.

Mr. Cheatham was born in Edgefield County, member of the South Carolina family of Cheathams which furnish more than one name of prominence and distinction in the South. His grandfather, John T. Cheatham, served in the Confederate army and was especially influential during the carpet bag regime. His wife was an Adams, member of the prominent family of that name in Edgefield. John Randolph Cheatham is a son of John Randolph and Mary (Harvley) Cheatham.

Mr. Cheatham grew up on his father's farm at the Cheatham home place ten miles east of McCormick. He acquired a good common school education and from school went to work to learn the banking business. For seven years he was connected with the Bank of Troy, and in September, 1917, while the People's Bank of McCormick was in process of organization, he assisted through his experience and technical knowledge of banking, and was elected cashier of the new bank. He has been instrumental in building up this strong and successful bank. The People's Bank started with a capital of $25,000 and its present capital is $50,000. The bank owns its own building, a fine three-story modern brick block, with facilities for offices as well as a modern home for the bank. The president of the bank is J. P. Abney of Greenwood.

Mr. Cheatham married Miss Hermine Youngblood, daughter of Dr. D. W. Youngblood and granddaughter of Captain Youngblood of Edgefield. Through her paternal grandmother she is related to the Wigfall family of Edgefield. Mrs. Cheatham's mother was a daughter of Reverend Herman, who was at one time pastor of the Methodist Episcopal Church of Edgefield, South Carolina, and afterward went to North Carolina, where he died. Mr. and Mrs. Cheatham have two children: Herman R. and Mary Wigfall.

STEWART WYLIE PRYOR, M. D. When death stopped his generous heart and stayed his skillful hand on December 27, 1918, at the age of fifty-four, Doctor Pryor had achieved an enviable place among America's most gifted surgeons. While members of his profession in many states marked with a sense of loss his passing, his character appealed to the affection and memory of all classes in his home community of Chester, where he had done his best work and given the best of himself to the highest ideals of service through a period of thirty years. He was one of the most notable South Carolinians who fell victims to the dread plague of influenza in the winter of 1918.

He was born in Spartanburg County January 29, 1864, a son of Stewart Love and Catherine (Haynes) Pryor. His people were pioneers in the states of Virginia and North Carolina, and through his mother he was of Revolutionary stock. His father was a skillful machinist and millwright.

Doctor Pryor spent part of his early life on a homestead in what is now Cherokee County. He had the discipline of regular work, but had only such educational opportunities as were afforded by the home schools. In 1881 he began clerking in a store at Gaffney, left that position to attend a business college at Baltimore, and during 1883-85 was employed as a bookkeeper at Gaffney. At the same time he was trying to realize his boyhood ambition to become a physician, and after saving some money he resigned to enter the Atlanta Medical College, where he was graduated with high honor in 1887. He then practiced for a brief time at Cherokee Spring, then for a few months at Lowryville, and from there came to Chester. Doctor Pryor was a constant student in his profession, specializing in surgery, and took fifteen courses in the New York Polyclinic and also attended the famous clinics of the Mayo Brothers in Minnesota. The skill which he early manifested as a surgeon attracted attention and a large practice from many remote localities, and in response to this patronage and to fill a long felt want he established his first hospital, a part of his own residence at Chester.

This was enlarged from time to time, and in 1904 he built a structure specially designed for hospital purposes and named it, in honor of his wife, the Magdalene Hospital. The facilities of this institution had to be increased from time to time, and it is said that for several years it handled more than 1,000 cases in medicine and surgery during a year. The Magdalene Hospital was destroyed by fire March 20, 1916. After using temporary buildings for a time the splendid Pryor Hospital was completed at a cost of about $100,000. Competent authorities pronounced it one of the best equipped hospitals in the South. Both these hospitals had their charity ward, and while Doctor Pryor seldom mentioned his charity work, it is known that this service alone was maintained at a cost of thousands of dollars.

The work he did through so many years at Chester brought him a well deserved fame and appreciation throughout the state. He had served as president of the County Medical Society, as vice president of the South Carolina Medical Association, as member of the Tri-State Medical Association, the Southern Medical Association, the Southern Gynecological Association, American Medical Association, American Association of Railway Surgeons, and was one of the first surgeons from South Carolina elected to membership and fellowship in the American College of Surgeons. Many papers were prepared by him for medical meetings and medical journals.

Those familiar with the heavy demands upon his time often marveled how he could arrange to give attention to many community, business and civic movements. He served as chairman of the Chester Board of Health, was a trustee of the public schools, and was a director of the Chester Building & Loan Association, National Exchange Bank, Baldwin Cotton Mills, steward of the Bethel Methodist Episcopal Church, chief surgeon of the Carolina and Northwestern Railway, chief surgeon of the Lancaster and Chester Railway, consulting surgeon of the Seaboard Air Line Railway, was a Knight Templar Mason and Shriner, and also owned and supervised the operation of about 2,500 acres of plantation.

Naturally many sincere tributes were paid his life and character after his death. One of the best of them, adopted as the editorial opinion of the South Carolina Medical Journal, was an editorial that appeared in the Columbia State and read as follows: "Not many men in South Carolina have made for themselves in the last quarter a century so high a place in public regard as Dr. Stewart W. Pryor achieved in Chester, where as a physician and surgeon he spent his manhood doing good on an ever enlarging scale. He was one of the pioneers of the extension of modern surgical practice in Upper South Carolina. It was not so long ago that most of the skilled surgeons in this state lived in Charleston—when there was not a hospital even in Columbia. In those days it was necessary for patients requiring hospital accommodation to be taken to Charleston or out of the state. Doctor Pryor built a hospital in Chester at a time when the establishment of an institution of that kind in a small town called for a business courage not far removed from audacity. He saw the need of the people and

resolved to fill it, disregarding the hazard of his means, and he devoted himself to the great work of relieving pain and disease with his whole heart and mind. The people scarcely are aware of the great benefits that have been conferred upon them by the physicians and surgeons whose enterprising spirit has been not less than their fine skill and unselfish zeal. Without hospitals modern surgery would not exist. Now, nearly every town of 4,000 or 5,000 inhabitants has its hospital, and that they have been multiplied so rapidly in recent years is due in a great measure to the vision and toil of men like the late Doctor Pryor, whose death is now mourned by the people of Chester and by thousands of others throughout the state and especially in the Piedmont district."

Almost at the beginning of his profession as a physician and surgeon, on February 14, 1888, Doctor Pryor married Carrie Magdalene Tinsley, daughter of Rufus W. and Sallie (Rogers) Tinsley of Union, South Carolina. It was a happy marriage, and the faithful companionship that followed proved one of the most important sources of the strength and enthusiasm which Doctor Pryor could take to his chosen work. He is survived by Mrs. Pryor and by a family of seven children. The only son is S. W. Pryor, Jr. The daughters are Mrs. Malcolm L. Marion, Mrs. R. H. McFadden, Mrs. E. O. Steinbach, Mrs. Alex L. Oliphant, Miss Ruth and Miss Clara Dale Pryor.

The doctor planned in his will that "Pryor Hospital" should operate under his name by the trustees in charge. It is to go to his son, S. W. Pryor, when he qualifies as a physician.

JOSEPH MURRAY, who began practice at St. George, and is representative of an old and honored family in Dorchester and Berkeley counties, identified himself with the bar of the new county of McCormick in 1917 and is one of the leading lawyers of that section.

He was born at St. George in Dorchester County in 1887, a son of W. T. and Sallie (Judy) Murray and a grandson of Dr. Joseph Murray, who besides being a physician of prominence at one time represented Berkeley County in the House and in the Senate.

Joseph Murray was reared and educated in St. George and graduated in 1911 from the University of South Carolina. He represented Dorchester County in the State Legislature in 1913-14, and began practice at St. George in 1911. He built up a substantial general practice there, and his reputation followed him to McCormick when he came here in 1917.

Mr. Murray married Miss Mary Griffin, of Columbia, member of an old and prominent family of that city, daughter of James and Wilhelmina (Snyder) Griffin. Her grandfather, Ben Griffin, at one time owned much of the land on which the City of Columbia is now built. Her father, James Griffin, was for many years a prominent merchant at Columbia. Mr. and Mrs. Murray have two children, Joseph and James. Mr. Murray is a Methodist and is affiliated with the Masonic Order.

JOSEPH B. WORKMAN, M. D. Graduated with the class of 1907 from the Medical College of the State of South Carolina at Charleston, Doctor Workman located in the environment of Ware Shoals, Greenwood County, and for the past twelve years has practiced medicine and surgery there and rendered valuable professional services in one of the most ideal industrial communities of the state. Ware Shoals when he became a young physician there, was just at the outset of its development as a cotton mill town. Many industries and enterprises have been added as part of the complicated system now comprised under the Ware Shoals Manufacturing Company. Doctor Workman has been adviser and a whole-souled worker in behalf of every movement affecting the welfare and progress of his community and is regarded with peculiar esteem by the residents of the town.

He was born at Woodruff in Spartanburg County in 1882, son of Samuel J. and Hepsy (Barnett) Workman. The Workmans originally came from Dublin, Ireland, to Virginia, thence to South Carolina and the family have been identified with Laurens and Spartanburg counties for more than a century. Doctor Workman attended school at Woodruff, and was graduated A. B. from Furman University at Greenville in 1902. The following year he entered the South Carolina Medical College and remained until graduating. He is a member in good standing of the County, State and American Medical associations, and during the period of the war was chairman for Walnut Grove Township of the Greenwood County Council of Defense.

Doctor Workman married Miss Laura Vivian Murphy, of Charleston. They have a son, Joseph B., Jr.

WILLIAM HUGHES NICHOLSON is a talented lawyer, member of one of the firms doing an immense business in general practice and corporation law, and has been a live factor in the professional and public affairs of Greenwood for a number of years.

He was born in old Edgefield County, December 11, 1879, a son of Benjamin E. and Elizabeth (Hughes) Nicholson. His father spent his active life as a farmer and at the time of his death was clerk of the court for Edgefield County. William H. Nicholson attended private schools, graduated from the University of South Carolina in 1902, and while teaching for two years also read law and was admitted to the bar in May, 1904. In the fall of the same year he moved to Greenwood, and the following winter while building up a practice he also taught school. He was in individual general practice until 1911, when he became junior partner in the firm of Grier, Park & Nicholson, a firm handling an immense corporation practice. Mr. Nicholson was elected to the General Assembly in 1908 and was re-elected in 1910 and 1912. Since 1912 he has been county chairman of the democratic party. His affairs have prospered under his energetic management. Besides his interests as a lawyer he has a farm of 1,000 acres of land. He is a lay leader in the Methodist Episcopal Church and superintendent of the Sunday school.

November 18, 1914, he married Elise Bates of Batesburg, South Carolina. They have had three children, Ellen Bates, deceased, William Hughes, Jr., and Benjamin Edwin Nicholson.

WINTHROP COLLEGE, whose corporate title is the Winthrop Normal and Industrial College of South Carolina, has been a state institution for over a quarter of a century, having previously been maintained largely as an adjunct of the city schools of Columbia for the purpose of training teachers. A brief history of the institution during its earlier years deserves a place here and the record for which can be drawn from the Memorial Address on the origin and early history of Winthrop College written by Dr. Edward S. Joynes on the occurrence of the twenty-fifth anniversary of the opening of the Winthrop Training School. Doctor Joynes, one of the founders of the college, and its able friend and counsellor through all the years, had assisted in organizing the Columbia city schools in 1883, and because of his early acquaintance and observation of David B. Johnson, whom he had known in his school work in Tennessee, recommended that Mr. Johnson be elected the first superintendent of the Columbia schools and, in the words of Doctor Joynes, "among the services it has been my privilege to render to South Carolina, the most valuable of all I consider the fact that I was directly instrumental in bringing David Bancroft Johnson into this state and thus making possible all for which his name now stands."

One of the greatest obstacles Superintendent Johnson had in the Columbia schools was the lack of trained teachers. To supply this deficiency recourse was made to the Peabody Educational Fund, and mainly through the influence of Robert C. Winthrop a promise was secured of $1,500 a year, later increased to $2,000, this sum becoming the sole financial foundation of the Winthrop Training School, and as a recognition of Mr. Winthrop's agency the school has since borne his name. The Columbia School Board accepted this fund from Mr. Winthrop in October, 1886, and proceeded to organize the Winthrop Training School, D. B. Johnson being the first superintendent. The school was first opened in an unused room of the Columbia Theological Seminary and the following year was moved to the "Park Building." The number of pupils continued to increase, the reputation of the school to grow, and in time its original function of supplying teachers for the city schools of Columbia acquired a wider scope. The first attempt to make it a normal school for the state at large was contained in a recommendation by Governor Richardson in 1887. In that year the Legislature granted to the school one scholarship of $150 for each county in the state.

In the meantime the late Benjamin R. Tillman had become an active advocate of a state school for agricultural and industrial education. The principal result of the "Tillman Movement" was of course the establishment of Clemson College, but in his first inaugural address after his election as governor, Mr. Tillman further recommended an industrial school for girls and gave cordial recognition of the work done in that field by the Winthrop Training School. In the meantime the Training School had outgrown its accommodations, and efforts were made to induce the state to take over the institution and insure its continued life and growth as a state normal institution. Doctor Joynes had proposed the matter to Governor Tillman, and subsequently a commission was appointed, with D. B. Johnson as chairman, and in November, 1891, the Columbia School Board tendered the Winthrop Training School to the state with a request that the state provide for its government and maintenance. In his message of 1891 Governor Tillman recommended that an act be passed providing for a State Industrial and Normal College for Women, with the Winthrop Training School as its normal college. This recommendation was carried out in the legislative act of December 23, 1891, and two years later the present title of the Winthrop Normal and Industrial College of South Carolina was adopted. The college was continued at Columbia until September, 1895. In the meantime the board of trustees had secured a location at Rock Hill, and the cornerstone of the new college was laid May 12, 1894.

David Bancroft Johnson, who on February 19, 1895, was unanimously elected president of the new state college, is one of the most distinguished and influential educators in the South. He was born at LaGrange, Tennessee, January 10, 1856, a son of David Bancroft and Margaret E. Johnson. His father was president of a college at LaGrange, and the son grew up in a college atmosphere. He received his A. B. degree from the University of Tennessee in 1877 and his Master of Arts degree from the same university in 1880. South Carolina College bestowed upon him the degree LL. D. in 1905. He was assistant professor of mathematics in the University of Tennessee in 1879-80; principal of the graded schools of Abbeville, South Carolina, in 1880-82. In the words of Doctor Joynes from the Memorial Address above noted, "during my residence at Knoxville I had become acquainted with a young man who had recently been graduated in the University of Tennessee, and had been serving as a teacher in the Knoxville city schools. Later he had been assistant professor in the University in which I was a professor; then he had served in Abbeville as organizer and principal of the schools in that town, and was now superintendent of schools in New Bern, North Carolina. I had watched his career with interest, and was satisfied that he possessed the experience and qualification which we needed in Columbia. So, upon my nomination, he was elected first superintendent of the Columbia Schools." Thus for thirty-five years his name and his work have been written largely in the history of the Columbia City Schools and Winthrop College.

However, Doctor Johnson's great vigor and enthusiasm in behalf of educational ideals have made him a leader in many movements not directly in the routine of his duties at Rock Hill. He established and served as president from 1885 to 1894 of the Columbia Y. M. C. A., and during 1886-95 was chairman of the State Executive Committee of that body. He also organized the South Carolina Association of School Superintendents and the Rural School Improvement Association in 1902. During 1910-11 he was a member of the South Carolina State Commission to revise the school laws. He served as president of the State Teachers' Association from 1884 to 1888 and was vice president of the National Teachers' Association in 1894 and again in 1896-97. In 1909 he was president of the Department of Rural and Agricultural Education of the National Educa-

tion Association, was president of the Normal School Department in 1911 and a member of the National Commission on Normal School Statistics in 1911 of the National Education Association. He was president of the Normal Department in 1908 and the Department of Elementary Education in 1909 and of the Southern Education Association, and was president of the latter association in 1910. One of the highest honors that can be conferred upon a school man is the presidency of the American Education Association, an honor which Doctor Johnson enjoyed in 1915-16.

During the period of the World war Doctor Johnson was unceasing in behalf of many patriotic duties. He was district chairman of the United War Work Campaign in South Carolina, was district chairman of the Jewish Relief Campaign, and helped organize and direct practically all the various patriotic drives in Rock Hill and York County. He is now state chairman for the Young Men's Christian Association in South Carolina and besides founding the Young Men's Christian Association at Columbia founded a similar institution at Rock Hill. Doctor Johnson is a member of the National Civic Association, the National Peace League and the South Carolina Historical Society.

August 6, 1902, he married Mai R. Smith, of Charleston. They have two sons, David Bancroft and Burgh Smith Johnson.

WILLIAM PINCKNEY GREENE, a prominent lawyer and citizen of Abbeville, has been a member of the South Carolina bar for nearly a quarter of a century, and has enjoyed the high honors of his profession and also of business and citizenship.

He was born in Abbeville County, November 24, 1873, a son of James H. and Elvira T. (Bowie) Greene. His father was an Abbeville farmer. The son attended the common schools, also the Preparatory School at Due West, and in 1889 entered Erskine College, where he graduated in 1893, at the head of his class. While teaching for several years he read law in the office of Ernest Moore at Lancaster, and was admitted to practice in December, 1895. The following year he practiced at Greenwood as a partner of the late W. C. McGowan, after whose death in 1897 he removed to Abbeville, where he formed a partnership with William Henry Parker. For over twenty years Mr. Greene has shared in the most important business of the local courts and has tried many important cases in the state courts. He served several times as special judge. He is vice president of the Abbeville Cotton Mills, and owns the Abbeville Press and Banner. He is a member of the Abbeville School Board and a trustee of Erskine College and of the Woman's College at Due West.

March 27, 1907, he married Miss Mary Hemphill. They have two children, Mary Hemphill and William Pinckney, Jr. Mr. Greene is a deacon in the Associate Reformed Presbyterian Church and is a member of the South Carolina Bar Association.

JOHN McKEE NICKLES, the well known Abbeville lawyer and former state senator, has had a prominent part in the public life of his home city and state, and has reason to be especially well satisfied with the part he has played in the modern educational program of South Carolina.

He was born at Due West, South Carolina, August 20, 1876, son of George Newton and Jane (McKee) Nickles. His father was a well to do and successful farmer of Abbeville County and served twelve years as county supervisor of Abbeville County. The son was educated in the public schools and received his A. B. degree from Erskine College. His later interest in education is no doubt derived in part from his own experience as a teacher, an occupation he followed four years. In the meantime he was reading law under James P. Carey, and was admitted to the bar in December, 1904. Since then he has been engaged in a busy general practice at Abbeville, and for seven years served as referee in bankruptcy.

Mr. Nickles was a member of the State Senate during 1915-16-17-18, and then declined to become a candidate for re-election. While in the Senate he devoted much of his time and effort to educational measures. He was one of the authors of the present high school law of South Carolina, and was largely instrumental in the passage and is the author of the Dr. John De La Howe Industrial School Bill. After the passage of that bill he was appointed chairman of the Board of Trustees of the Dr. John De La Howe Industrial School and has interested himself in all its work and development.

About the time the war closed Mr. Nickles, though forty-two years of age, entered the officers training school at Camp Gordon, Atlanta. He is a member of the Knights of Pythias, Woodmen of the World and Junior Order of United American Mechanics and is a deacon in the Presbyterian Church at Abbeville. Besides his law practice he has some farming interests.

JOHN MOORE MARS, whose abilities have commended him favorably to the people of the state at large through his able services in the Legislature, both in the House and Senate, is a successful lawyer at Abbeville, where he has been in practice for the last twelve years.

Mr. Mars was born at Cokesbury, South Carolina, August 17, 1884, a son of Walter and Lucy J. (Moore) Mars. His father was a farmer and merchant. The son was liberally educated, attending the public schools and the conference schools, was a student in Clemson College and afterward attended Erskine College in Abbeville County. In December, 1907, he was admitted to the bar and has since carried the burdens of an increasing general practice at Abbeville. Mr. Mars served as a member of the Lower House of the Legislature in 1909-10 and sat in the Senate during 1911-12-13-14. His most recent public honor came when he was elected mayor of Abbeville in March, 1918. He is a strenuous advocate of every measure that will bring the greatest degree of benefit to the community, county and state.

Mr. Mars is affiliated with the Masonic Order, the Knights of Pythias, Independent Order of Odd Fellows, Junior Order of United American Mechanics and the Woodmen of the World. He is a member of the Methodist Episcopal Church, South.

October 19, 1916, he married Imogen Wilkes, of Laurens, South Carolina.

CHARLES E. COMMANDER, banker and business man of Florence, is possessed and actuated by an essentially constructive spirit and has found the means of influencing and promoting a number of important activities in his home city and district. He prepared for the law and practiced several years, but was not satisfied with the circumscribed range of a professional man and has devoted most of his life to working out problems of practical business.

Mr. Commander was born in Darlington County, South Carolina, in 1882, and was brought as a child by his parents to Florence County. He is a son of R. C. and Sarah (McCurry) Commander. His mother is now deceased. The grandfather, Joseph Commander, was an extensive land owner and planter in Darlington County in ante-bellum days. He gave generously of his means and influence to the promotion of various projects in his home district, providing out of his own funds for the building of the old Mount Hope Church on the Black River. R. C. Commander for a number of years has been a planter in Florence County.

Charles E. Commander grew up at Florence, attended the public schools, and spent five years in the University of South Carolina, three years in the academic course and two years in the law school, where he graduated in 1904. For about a year following his graduation he was field and financial agent for the Alumni Association of the University. For another year he practiced law in Columbia associated with the law firm of Bellinger & Townsend. Returning to Florence in 1906, Mr. Commander entered the real estate and insurance business. Within a few years his business was the largest of its kind in this part of the state. Since 1916 Mr. Commander has been owner of the Florence Motor Sales Company, which he established in Florence and which maintains two departments in that city, one an accessory store and the other a general salesroom and repair plant. The business is both wholesale and retail in automobiles and accessories. Mr. Commander has a great enthusiasm for the present and future of the automobile industry, and is the first vice president of the South Carolina Automotive Trades Association.

Banking circles know him as active president of the City Savings Bank of Florence, which he organized in 1913, and which has a capital and surplus profits of over $35,000 and deposits closely aggregating $500,000, reflecting the wonderful prosperity of the city and adjacent district. Through the ownership and operation of a large body of land Mr. Commander also belongs among the farmer element of Florence County.

He is a charter member of the Florence Rotary Club, which was organized in February, 1920, and is its first vice president. He is affiliated with the Presbyterian Church. He married Miss Adelaide Boyd, of Spartanburg, and their three children are Charles E., Jr., Liela Spands and Adelaide.

JOHN POPE ABNEY is one of the prominent Greenwood bankers, cotton mill officials and to a remarkable degree has been able to utilize and combine the opportunities of a comparatively brief career to achieve prominence in business affairs.

He was born in Saluda County, January 5, 1885, a son of J. R. and Nannie (Clark) Abney. He spent his boyhood days on his father's farm, but acquired a liberal education, supplementing his advantages in the local schools with attendance at Wofford College, where he spent three years, leaving in 1903. His banking experience has been practically continuous since he left college.

For two years he was a messenger boy for the Bank of Greenwood. In 1905 he joined the Farmers and Merchants Bank, and served it successively as bookkeeper, assistant cashier, cashier and president. He resigned the presidency in 1916 to become cashier of the Bank of Greenwood.

Mr. Abney is president of the Grendel and Ninety-Six cotton mills, is president of the People's Bank at McCormick, is vice president of the Greenwood Cotton Mills, and a director in the Farmers and Merchants Bank of Greenwood and the Cambridge Bank at Ninety-Six. His financial interests also extend to various wholesale companies and business organizations of this section of the state.

Mr. Abney married Miss Susie Mathews, of Greenwood County, on June 24, 1913. They have one daughter, Sallie Marian.

JAMES BRADDOCK PARK has practiced law successfully at Greenwood since 1897. He is second member in the well known firm of corporation lawyers, Grier, Park & Nicholson.

He was born in Laurence, South Carolina, November 28, 1873, a son of James F. and Jane (Braddock) Park. His father was a farmer. The son grew up in the country and acquired most of his primary education in a subscription school. He studied law in the University of Virginia and was admitted to the bar in 1894. He practiced one year in his native town of Laurence, but in 1896 came to Greenwood, and soon afterward became associated in practice with Mr. Grier. He served four years as mayor of Greenwood, and was a member of the commission for paving the city streets. He is a deacon of the Presbyterian Church, is a Knight Templar Mason and Shriner, and also a Knight of Pythias and Woodman of the World.

In February, 1906, Mr. Park married Lillias Klugh, of Greenwood County. They have four children: Joe Fowler, Martha Braddock, Julia Glass and Lillias Klugh.

HARRY LEGARE WATSON was trained for the law but inclination, success and other circumstances have combined to keep him steadily in the profession of newspaper man. He is editor of one of the best daily newspapers in South Carolina, The Index-Journal at Greenwood. In the course of time many other interests, both business and civic, have been allotted to him and form the associations by which he is so well known in his section of the state.

Mr. Watson, the only child of Johnson Sale and Charlotte Louise Watson, was born July 11, 1876, at Phoenix, Greenwood County. He attended school in his native locality, and was prepared for college by W. H. Stallworth, Sr., a well known teach-

Chas. E. Commander

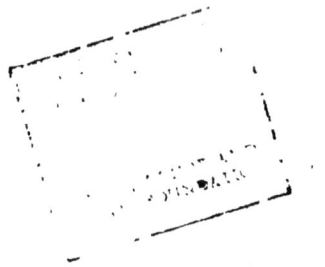

er of that community. For two years he attended Furman University in Greenville and was graduated with the A. B. degree from the University of North Carolina in 1899.

Mr. Watson was admitted to the bar in 1908. He practiced law one year with Maj. H. C. Tillman, and then retired to give his full time to newspaper work. He is president of The Index-Journal Company and editor of The Index-Journal. He is president of the National Loan and Exchange Bank, a director of the Southeastern Life Insurance Company, a director of the Oregon Hotel Company, director of the Chee-Ha Land Company, a director of the Citizens Trust Company, director of Greenwood Chamber of Commerce and a member of Greenwood County Highway Commission. During 1912-13 he was president of the South Carolina Press Association.

Mr. Watson is chairman of the Board of Trustees of the Greenwood city public schools, and a trustee of the Greenwood Carnegie Public Library and a trustee of Furman University and in 1916 was president of the Furman Alumni Association. In 1912 he was a delegate to the Baltimore National Democratic Convention which nominated Woodrow Wilson for President. Mr. Watson is a member and deacon of the South Main Street Baptist Church at Greenwood, is a Knight Templar Mason and member of Omar Temple of the Mystic Shrine, a member of the Greenwood Rotary Club and also belongs to the Kappa Alpha college fraternity.

June 27, 1900, he married Miss Ella Dargan, of Phoenix, daughter of the late Rev. John H. and Elizabeth (Townes) Dargan. To their marriage were born five children: Louise Montague, John Dargan, Elizabeth Sloan, Margaret Josephine and Ella Virginia Watson.

FRANK BARRON GRIER has been a lawyer and an active member of the Greenwood bar since 1897. He is also president and general counsel for the Charleston & Western Carolina Railroad.

Mr. Grier was born at York, South Carolina, December 10, 1869, a son of William Lowndes and Mary (Barron) Grier. His father was a Confederate soldier and captain of his company from Mecklenberg County, North Carolina, and after the war followed the profession of teaching. The son had a public school education and in 1890 graduated from The Citadel at Charleston. For three years he taught in the graded schools at Chester and in the meantime studied law and was admitted to the bar in May, 1893. For three years Mr. Grier practiced at Kingstree, and since 1897 has enjoyed a large general practice with home and offices at Greenwood.

He is a Mason and Shriner. In October, 1898, he married Miss Retta McWillie Withers, of Camden, South Carolina. They have four children, named Mary Barron, Nancy Shannon, Randolph Withers and Frank Barron.

EUGENE SATTERWHITE BLEASE, a former member of the state senate, has been a prominent lawyer at Newberry for the past twenty years, and by continuous and steadfast devotion to the best ideals of his profession has won a high place in the South Carolina bar.

He was born at Newberry, January 20, 1877, a son of Henry H. and Elizabeth (Satterwhite) Blease. His father was both a farmer and merchant. The son was educated in public schools, the Newberry Academy, and graduated from Newberry College in 1895. On leaving college he had made up his mind to become a lawyer. For two years, 1896-97, he taught school, studying law, and in 1899 was admitted to the bar. He has since had a large general practice with offices both at Saluda and Newberry. He was elected and served as a member of the Lower House of the Legislature in 1901-02, and his service in the State Senate was rendered during 1905-06, but he resigned before the close of his term. He also served as city attorney of Newberry four years, resigning that office. He was elected mayor of Newberry in December, 1919, which office he now holds. Mr. Blease married Urbana Neel, of Newberry County.

ZACCHEUS FRANKLIN WRIGHT has been a prominent factor in banking, industry and commercial affairs of Newberry for thirty years.

He was born at Newberry, March 21, 1869, son of Robert H. and Mary Frances (Bowers) Wright. His mother was a daughter of Jacob Bowers of Newberry. His father was a merchant. Zaccheus Wright grew up in the home of well-to-do parents, was given good educational opportunities, and also owes much to the training and influence of his mother. He graduated from Newberry College at the age of nineteen with the class of 1888. The fall of the same year found him established in business as a book and stationery merchant in his native town, and successive years found him burdened with many additional cares and responsibilities in commercial affairs. In 1897 he became cashier of the Commercial Bank of Newberry, an office he filled for many years. He has been a factor in developing the cotton industry in and around Newberry and in 1905 became president of the Newberry Cotton Mill. He was elected president of the Newberry Chamber of Commerce in 1906.

Mr. Wright is a democrat and was reared and for many years has been an active member of the Methodist Church.

THOMAS HUBERT TATUM. Steadily through a period of fifteen years Thomas Hubert Tatum has been rising to distinction as a well grounded, able and hard working lawyer, and in that time has rendered many services to link his name closely with the welfare and progress of his home city of Bishopville.

Mr. Tatum was born in Orangeburg, South Carolina, August 1, 1878, a son of John Samuel Capers and Martha Washington (Smith) Tatum. His father was a planter. The son had the advantages of local schools as a boy, also attended Clemson College, and studied law in private offices and in Georgetown University at Washington. He was graduated with the LL. B. degree in 1902, and the following year began general practice at Bishopville. He was elected and served as a member of the Legislature in 1907-08. He has been county

Vol. V—8

attorney for Lee County, has served Bishopville as city attorney, and is a former trustee of the local schools. Mr. Tatum is a director of the Home Building and Loan Association, is attorney for the People's Bank of Bishopville and the Bank of Bethune, and is local counsel for the Atlantic Coast Line Railway.

He is a steward of the Methodist Church, has been for four years a lay leader for the South Carolina Conference, and is a member of the executive committee of the Layman's Movement for that church. November 22, 1905, he married Bessie McClair Mann, daughter of Rev. Coke D. Mann, for many years a minister of the Methodist Church. They have one daughter, Eliza Milford.

WILLIAM AUGUST HANTSKE, who is manager of the Life Department for the Carolina Life Insurance Company at Columbia, is regarded by his associates as one of the most competent insurance men in the South today. Mr. Hantske knows the insurance business as the result of practically continuous experience and participation from the time he was twenty years of age to the present. The volume of business he wrote in early years as an individual agent has brought him successive promotions, and for over ten years he has been an executive in the life insurance field.

Mr. Hantske was born at Mount Washington, Baltimore County, Maryland, April 28, 1871, son of Morris A. and Emma Augusta Hantske, both now deceased. On both sides he comes of an interesting ancestry. His father was a native of Austria and descended from a family that for generations were noted for their attainments in the science of botany and included some of the most noted botanists of that country. Mr. Hantske's mother was born at Oldenburg, Germany, her father, Hugo Walther, being a noted nurseryman. Through her mother she was descended from the Bosse family, a name long prominent in the annals of the Lutheran Church, many of whose clergymen were of the Bosse family. Mr. Hantske is a grand-nephew of the late Louis Bosse of Spartanburg, South Carolina, who was a Confederate soldier and afterward prominent in the reconstruction period. Morris A. Hantske and wife were married in Germany in 1865 and at once came to America, locating in Maryland, where for many years he was prominent as a florist, nurseryman and botanist at Baltimore.

William A. Hantske acquired his education in the public schools and business colleges of Baltimore, and in 1891, at the age of twenty, made his first effort in the field of life insurance. Later for about one year he was a stock salesman, but with that exception has acknowledged no other dominant interest in business. His work in life insurance has been done in Maryland, Pennsylvania and South Carolina. From 1898 to 1902 he represented the Baltimore Life Insurance Company as manager in Pennsylvania. In 1903 he became an agent with the Metropolitan Life of New York, and in 1906 was promoted to assistant manager of that company and in 1911 to manager. He remained with the Metropolitan until the early part of 1916, when he was called to his present duties by the Carolina Life Insurance Company at Columbia as manager of the Life Department. He is also a member of the South Carolina Life Underwriters' Association.

Like most successful insurance men, his influence has been earnestly directed to the promotion of the best ideals in civic, moral and educational affairs. He has never sought public office though as a democrat he has done what he could to promote clean, progressive politics. He is one of the prominent and well known Lutherans of South Carolina, and during the late war was state chairman for the Lutheran National Commission for the Welfare of Soldiers and Sailors. He is a member of St. Paul's Lutheran Church at Columbia. Mr. Hantske is also affiliated with Richland Lodge No. 39, Ancient Free and Accepted Masons, and is a past grand of the Odd Fellows and chairman of the Finance Committee of the Grand Lodge of South Carolina. He is a member of the Ridgewood Country Club.

In 1894, at Baltimore, he married Mary Cyline George, daughter of John and Catherine E. George. Her father for many years was a farmer in the Dulaney Valley section of Baltimore County. Mr. and Mrs. Hantske have one son, William George, who graduated from Newberry College with the class of 1917.

COLIN BRADLEY RUFFIN, of Bishopville, a talented lawyer, is member of the prominent Ruffin family of North Carolina.

He was born in Edgecombe County of that state, November 7, 1884, a son of Joseph Henry and Zilphi Ann (Lane) Ruffin. His father for many years was identified with the agricultural interests of North Carolina. The son attended local schools, high school, graduated from the literary department of the University of North Carolina at Chapel Hill in 1909 and completed the law course in the same institution. For one year he taught in the high school at Wilmington, North Carolina. Mr. Ruffin was admitted to the bar of his native state in August, 1911, and to that of South Carolina in December, 1912. He came to Bishopville in the latter year and has enjoyed a rapidly growing general practice. He is present county attorney of Lee County, is a director and attorney for the Farmers Loan & Trust Company, during the war was food administrator for Lee County, is a member of the County Board of Education and an alderman of Bishopville. He is also secretary of the Lee County Democratic Club.

November 26, 1913, he married Miss Mabel Fountain, of Tarboro, North Carolina. Their three children are Marion, Mabel and Zilphi A. Lane.

CARROLL JOHNSON RAMAGE, a lawyer who can look back upon the achievements of more than twenty years, has been a prominent factor in the business and civic as well as professional interests of Saluda.

He was born in Edgefield County in what is now the eastern portion of Saluda County, in May, 1874. He attended the local schools and afterward Newberry College, where he distinguished himself as a student. Dr. G. W. Holland was then president of the college and took much interest in him. He graduated and afterward received the Master of Arts degree from Newberry. At his graduation he won medals for English Essay and History.

Mr. Ramage was admitted to the bar in 1897, and since then has practiced at Saluda and has been especially well known as a civil lawyer. He is author of two volumes of Digests of South Carolina Reports, vols. 61 to 100, and served two years as a special judge. He was also a member of the State Board of Education two years and was formerly president and is now vice president of the Planters National Bank of Saluda. In May, 1904, he was happily married to Annie Bell Crouch.

REV. JOHN MCSWEEN, who to distinguish him from his honored father, John McSween, the veteran banker and business man of Timmonsville, writes his name John McSween III, was born at Timmonsville, November 15, 1888. Concerning his father's career a special article is written on other pages.

John McSween had a public school education, graduated Bachelor of Science from Davidson College in 1908, and spent two years in his father's store at Timmonsville. In 1913 he was graduated Bachelor of Divinity from the Presbyterian Theological Seminary at Columbia. For one year he did missionary work for his church in the mountains of North Carolina, and then took a pastorate in the Presbyterian Church at Dillon.

He was commissioned a chaplain with the Second South Carolina Infantry and went to the Mexican border with that organization in 1916. He was mustered out in March, 1917, and on the twenty-fifth of July of the same year again entered the service of the Government as chaplain at Camp Sevier. In May, 1918, he went overseas, and served as chaplain of the One Hundred and Fifth Ammunition Train of the Fifty-fifth Artillery Brigade. He was discharged March 27, 1919.

Mr. McSween married Lina Washington Crews, of Durham, North Carolina, June 11, 1913. To their marriage were born three children: Allen Crews, William Crews, and John IV, who died in 1918.

SAMUEL J. ROYALL. While his able work as a lawyer has made him well known in professional circles at Florence during the past five years, Samuel J. Royall has also achieved fame as one of the officers in the One Hundred and Eighteenth Infantry Regiment, made up of South Carolinians, a unit in the American forces which won lasting fame on the western battlefront of France.

Mr. Royall, who was selected as historian of the regiment by his regimental commander, and whose account of the One Hundred and Eighteenth has been published in book form, was born at Florence in 1889, son of W. N. and Mella (Norris) Royall. The Royalls for many generations have been a prominent family in Virginia and North Carolina. W. N. Royall became a prominent railway official for many years manager of the Atlantic Coast Line Railway with headquarters at Wilmington, North Carolina.

Samuel J. Royall, a native of Florence, was reared and received his early education at Wilmington. He studied law at the University of South Carolina at Columbia, graduating in 1914. He began practice at Florence, but nearly three years of the subsequent time has been taken up in military service for his country. He went to the Mexican border with the old Second South Carolina Regiment of the National Guard in July, 1916. He was on duty there until March, 1917. He then resumed his law practice, but after five months volunteered for the war with Germany and was commissioned lieutenant of Headquarters Company of the One Hundred and Eighteenth Infantry, which as is well known was a part of the Thirtieth Division. He was with this regiment in all its splendid fighting record in France, and returning to America received his honorable discharge April 27, 1919.

Mr. Royall is a member of the Kappa Sigma fraternity, is also a Mason and belongs to the Episcopal Church. He married Miss Elizabeth Willcox, daughter of Dr. James Willcox of Darlington.

HON. JAMES EMMIT BEAMGUARD. Present state senator from York County, James Emmit Beamguard has for many years been one of the solid and substantial citizens of the wealthy and rapidly growing Town of Clover, the leading business center in the upper part of York County.

The Beamguards in South Carolina have always been farmers and planters, though their other qualities have frequently led them into public affairs. Senator Beamguard was born April 9, 1869, in York County, at the family home 2½ miles south of Clover. This old homestead was settled by his grandfather, who was born of Scotch parents and came from the north of Ireland, where the Beamguards had lived for some generations. They are, therefore, of the Scotch-Irish stock. Senator Beamguard is a son of Capt. J. W. and Mona (Stevenson) Beamguard. His father was born in the same locality of York County and served four years as a Confederate soldier, being captain of a company in the Eighteenth South Carolina Regiment.

James E. Beamguard had a common school education, and since early manhood his business affairs have been centered at the ancestral Beamguard place south of Clover. Since 1916 he has also played an important role in the business affairs of Clover, being secretary, treasurer and manager of the Clover Cotton Oil Mill and Ginning Company, manufacturers of cotton seed products and ginners of cotton.

His political experience and participation in public affairs is a record of many years. From 1894 to 1900 he was clerk of the Senate Finance Committee of the General Assembly, then represented his county in the House from 1900 to 1908, and since 1912 has served continuously as senator from York County. He was re-elected in 1916 and was chairman of the committee on privileges and elections and a member of the committee on rules, agriculture and finance. His name has been associated with much of the important legislation enacted in South Carolina during the last twenty years.

Senator Beamguard is a deacon in the Presbyterian Church and teacher of the men's class of the Sunday school, while fraternally he is affiliated with the Masons, Woodmen of the World and Junior Order of United American Mechanics. He married Miss Mittie Dorsett, of York County, on April 2, 1895. Their daughter, Miss Bleeker Beamguard, graduated with the class of 1919 from Chicora College at Columbia.

FREDERICK WILLIAM JAMES GERMANY. In the wholesale district of Columbia stands a large three-story plant, office and cold storage plant, operated under the business title of Germany-Roy-Brown Company. The president of this company is Fred Germany, whose full Christian name has just been given. In a peculiar degree this institution represents the life work and enterprise of Mr. Germany. As it is one of the organizations doing most to establish Columbia as one of the great wholesale centers of the South, there is also the highest degree of personal credit due the president of the company for building up the business and making his individuality and energy count as a powerful commercial stimulus to his native city.

Mr. Germany was born at Columbia February 13, 1872. His parents, William Jackson and Elizabeth E. (Taylor) Germany, are now deceased. Mr. Germany is their only surviving son, and he has three sisters.

To the age of sixteen his life was spent at home and in attending the local schools. At that age he made himself a regular assistant to his father in the grocery business, and after four years of working experience he went north and entered the Eastman Business College at Poughkeepsie, New York, and completed his training for his chosen life-work.

On returning to Columbia Mr. Germany engaged in office work, and for three years was bookkeeper with the wholesale firm of R. B. and D. McKay, one of the well known and old established firms of the South.

The letter-heads of the Germany-Roy-Brown Company bear the words "Established 1894." That date commemorates the independent but exceedingly modest start of Mr. Germany as a retail grocer in Columbia. At that time he had the experience, the training, a sound knowledge of merchandising and business principles, had earned some credit, but had a very limited capital to embark. Moreover he entered business at a time of widespread financial depression. Against those disadvantages were arrayed his energy, ambition, skillful and studious management, and the result was that he was soon handling a capacity trade, and his business grew in volume every year. It is a matter of special interest to note that Mr. Germany still continues the retail grocery business in which he gained his first success and at its original location.

His wholesale business was a direct outgrowth of his retail establishment. In 1914 he entered into partnership with Mr. J. E. Young, making the firm Young & Germany. Mr. Young died in December, 1918, and in January, 1920, the old firm of Young & Germany gave way to the new corporation of Germany-Roy-Brown Company, with Mr. Germany as president, A. F. Brown, vice president, and Mr. T. L. Roy, secretary and treasurer. Their business is groceries, fruit and produce, and in those lines the company has become securely established in the confidence and patronage of a large southern territory. In order to expedite the handling of the growing volume of business the company maintains branch houses at Florence and Spartanburg. They also have a thoroughly equipped and modern cold storage plant at Columbia.

Twenty-five years after his first humble venture as a merchant in Columbia Mr. Germany found himself financially independent, and esteemed as he really is one of the leading business men of the capital city.

He has also found time to cultivate other interests. He is a director in the Carolina National Bank of Columbia and is the owner of two fine farms, one in Richland and the other in Lexington County, both convenient of access to Columbia. Through his ownership of these properties Mr. Germany is deeply interested in agricultural development, and gives his liberal support and encouragement to any movement tending toward improved farming, greater production, good roads, and improved rural conditions. Though taking an interest in clean politics and public questions, he has never been a contender for public office, and has believed that he could render the greatest service to the world by concentrating his attention on his business. He is affiliated with the Independent Order of Odd Fellows and is a member of the Board of Deacons of the First Baptist Church at Columbia.

In the spring of 1899 he married Miss Blanche Smith, of Greenville. She died in 1915. In the spring of 1917 he married Miss Effie Berry, of Wilmington, Delaware. Mrs. Germany is prominent in church, charities and other causes in which the leading women of Columbia participate.

CAPT. C. ALBERT JOHNSON, of Rock Hill, is a prominent business man of that city, member of the wholesale grocery house of Blankenship & Johnson, and was a South Carolina officer in the late war, serving with the rank of captain in the Sixth Division.

He was born at Rock Hill in 1888, a son of J. B. and Ida (Boyd) Johnson. His father for many years was a prominent merchant and capitalist of Rock Hill, and among present connections is president of the York County Cotton Association.

Captain Johnson was liberally educated, attending the Citadel at Charleston two years and graduating from Wofford College at Spartanburg in 1908. On leaving college he entered upon a business career at Rock Hill, and his personal part in the firm of Blankenship & Johnson has been a strong factor in making that one of the leading wholesale grocery houses of the state. In August, 1919, the firm notably expanded its facilities by establishing a branch house at Gastonia, North Carolina.

In August, 1917, Captain Johnson entered the Second Officers Training Camp at Fort Oglethorpe, received a commission as captain, and was assigned to duty with the Sixth Division. He was in camp at Anniston, Alabama, Chickamauga, Tennessee, and Camp Wadsworth, South Carolina, until July, 1918, when he went overseas His division saw its first active duty at the Vosges, and later participated in some of the phases of the great Argonne-Meuse drive. He spent the winter of 1918-19 in France and on the German frontier and returned home and received his honorable discharge May 2, 1919.

Captain Johnson is a member of the Methodist Church, and is affiliated with the Masonic frater-

nity. He married Miss Carrie Anderson, and they have one daughter, Caroline.

FRANK OSCAR BLACK during the ten years since he left college has been devoted to educational work, and his present position in his profession is as county superintendent of schools of Saluda.

He was born in Saluda County, May 10, 1886, a son of John David and Marina (Satcher) Black. He grew up on his father's farm, had some of its duties while attending local schools, and acquired his higher education in the Ridge Spring High School and at Newberry College, where he graduated in June, 1909. He taught school at Prosperity and Little Mountain, also at Bainbridge, Georgia, and was a high school principal four years. In January, 1917, he was elected county superintendent of schools of Saluda County. Mr. Black is a member of the Lutheran Church, is a Royal Arch Mason and a Knight Templar and Shriner, and affiliated with the Woodmen of the World.

June 28, 1911, he married Miss Lillian Hill, of Newberry. They have three children, Francis, Lucy and Susan.

WILLIAM HENRY KEITH. While he inherits the traditions of a family long identified with the business affairs of Timmonsville, William Henry Keith has made his own career a means of increasing the prestige of that city as a commercial center, and has labored faithfully and successfully for a quarter of a century in building up one of the largest concerns of its kind in Florence County.

He was born at Timmonsville, February 7, 1873, a son of Jesse E. and Kate (Sykes) Keith. His father was a merchant at Timmonsville for many years. The son had a public school education, and also attended The Citadel at Charleston. When a young man he went to work in the store of John McSween, his step-father, general merchant at Timmonsville. That business was incorporated in 1899, at which time he became vice president. When Mr. McSween retired he was succeeded by Mr. Keith as president. Mr. Keith is also president of the McSween Mercantile Company at Lamar and is a director of the Bank of Timmonsville and the Merchants and Planters Bank at Lamar. He is also a director of the Timmonsville Oil Mill.

While his time has been well taken up by his varied business interests, he has served acceptably in public responsibilities, being a former alderman and former mayor of Timmonsville. During the war he was chairman of the local exemption board of Florence County. Mr. Keith has been a deacon in the Presbyterian Church since it was organized in Timmonsville. April 14, 1897, he married Miss Cora Byrd, of Timmonsville. They have two children, Dorothy Sykes and Margaret Louise.

MASON DAVIS NESMITH, who is a dental surgeon by profession, has in addition to his professional work performed many interesting public services and been active in business affairs in Lake City, where he has had his home since 1905.

He was born in the old community of South Carolina named for his family, Nesmith, April 15, 1874, son of William Edward and Lydia J. (Joseph) Nesmith, substantial farming people of that vicinity. He was first educated in public schools, atttended Clemson College, and in 1905 graduated from the Atlanta Dental College at Atlanta, Georgia, and finished the pharmacy course in the same year. Since then he has been a resident of Lake City and active in his profession and in business. He is vice president of the Lake City Insurance Company and a director of the Bank of Lake City. Soon after he identified himself with this community he was made chairman of the Committee of Public Works, and helped give Lake City its present splendid water system. He also served as an alderman three years, as trustee of the graded schools, and is now a member of the Board of Assessors for his district. Doctor Nesmith is a deacon of the Baptist Church.

June 14, 1905, he married Virgie Elizabeth Brooks, of Georgia. Their five children are Catherine Lydia, Julia Brooks, Ethel Elizabeth, Daisy Florence and Mason Davis, Jr.

WOODRUFF HOLSTON LOWMAN has been the first and only cashier of the Citizens Bank of Timmonsville. He was identified with the organization of the bank in 1901. At that time its capital was $30,000 but in 1919 this was increased to $75,000. The bank also has surplus of $37,500, while its deposits aggregate $300,000.

Mr. Lowman was born in Edgefield County, South Carolina, June 22, 1861. He acquired his early education in the public schools and his early business experience as clerk and bookkeeper at Batesburg. In 1885 he went to Arkansas and for a time was a bookkeeper at Lonoke. Later he engaged in the general merchandise business at Orangeburg in his native state, and was a general merchant at Timmonsville until he entered the Citizens Bank in 1901. He is also a trustee of the graded schools and has all the best interests of the community at heart. He is a deacon of the Baptist Church.

In March, 1885, he married Miss Sallie Meyer of Batesburg. To their marriage were born four children: Eugene Meyer; Ruby, wife of C. L. Smith; Woodruff H., Jr., who served as a first lieutenant in Company A of the Three Hundred and Tenth Infantry with the Seventy-Eight Division in the Expeditionary Forces; and Norwood, who is still a student.

JOSEPH F. HASELDEN, M. D. For fifteen years Doctor Haselden has practiced his profession at Greeleyville, is the leading physician and surgeon of that community, and both through his profession and through his influence as a citizen has done much to promote the continued growth and improvement of what is one of the most prosperous commercial and home towns in Williamsburg County.

Doctor Haselden was born near the present Town of Johnsonville in Williamsburg County in 1871, son of S. B. and Adele (Johnson) Haselden. The Haseldens are of English ancestry, and the Johnson. family has long been prominent in Williamsburg County, the Town of Johnsonville being named in their honor.

Doctor Haselden prepared for his profession by two years spent in the Medical College of South

Carolina at Charleston, and in 1904 he graduated from the Baltimore Medical College at Baltimore. Immediately after graduation he chose the promising community of Greeleyville as his home, and has found there all the opportunities that an ambitious medical man desires.

Doctor Haselden married Miss Mamie Boyle. She is a niece of Mr. T. W. Boyle, whose noteworthy part in building up the Town of Greeleyville has been described elsewhere. Doctor and Mrs. Haselden have three children: Elizabeth, Boyle and Fleetwood.

HON. JOHN HARDIN MARION. While the family represented by John Hardin Marion, a prominent lawyer and state senator of Chester, has been identified with South Carolina only about a century, it is possible to assert on authentic genealogical evidence that several generations earlier the ancestors of this branch coincided with those of the celebrated Revolutionary leader and South Carolina general, Francis Marion. Francis Marion, the general, was a grandson of Benjamin and Louise (d'Aubrey) Marion. They were French Huguenots, came from the north of Ireland and settled in South Carolina early in the eighteenth century, living near Georgetown.

These French Huguenots had left France after the revocation of the Edict of Nantes and settled in the north of Ireland. Some of them remained there nearly a century after the emigration of the grandparents of General Marion. Between 1815-20 Patrick Marion, who was born at Craigbilly, County Antrim, in 1772, came to America and located in the upper part of Fairfield District. He married Jane McNeely. Their son John Alexander Marion became a planter in Chester County, and through a long life was prominently identified with affairs in that section. He married Margaret Jane Sterling.

Their son James Taylor Marion, long a conspicuous figure in the business life of Chester County, was father of John Hardin Marion.

The late James Taylor Marion was born near Richburg in 1845, and at the age of sixteen enlisted in Company D of the Seventeenth South Carolina Infantry. Later he was transferred to Company B of the Fourth Cavalry, Army of Northern Virginia. At Cold Harbor May 30, 1864, he was captured and spent thirteen months in Elmira prison. Following the war he engaged in merchandising at Lewisville. He is remembered as a man of great energy and public spirit, and became widely known in business, social and church circles. He died in 1911. He, as did also his father before him, served as a ruling elder in the Associate Reformed Presbyterian Church.

James Taylor Marion married Jane A. Hardin, of a prominent Chester County family of English ancestry. The Hardins have lived in Chester County since the Revolution, and among the prominent characters of the name one was the late Peter Lawrence Hardin, who died in 1914 and who for twenty years represented his county in the Lower House and in the State Senate. He was a brother of Jane A. Hardin. She was a daughter of Peter and Rebecca (King) Hardin and was born August 24, 1853, and died June 20, 1916.

John Hardin Marion, who was born in Chester County October 23, 1874, has earned distinctions of his own in addition to those of his ancestry. He acquired his literary and legal education in the University of South Carolina, graduating with the degrees A. B. and LL. B. in 1893. At that time he was only nineteen years old, and it required a special act of the Legislature to admit him to the bar. Returning to Chester, he formed a partnership to practice with Hon. William A. Barber, then attorney general of South Carolina. In later years he has been senior member of the firm Marion & Marion. Since 1902 Mr. Marion has been general counsel for the Carolina and Northwestern Railway. His practice, always large and important, is about evenly divided between corporation and general cases.

One of the eminent members of the Supreme Bench of South Carolina has paid Mr. Marion the following tribute: "He has been a student of the law all of his mature years. He has an ample library of law books. His preparation is tireless and thorough. He is much of an advocate before judge and jury. He has a good voice, pleasing countenance, is apt in anecdote and repartee. He is perhaps at his best before the jury; but before the court he is strong and helpful. His private library of select volumes is full and he diligently studies them. He adds to the accomplishments of a lawyer the attainments of the scholar. He is a man of quiet but determined courage. His word is as good as his bond, and he may be fully trusted in all of the relations of life."

His active career has not been altogether law work. When the Spanish-American war broke out he went in as second lieutenant of Company D, First Regiment, South Carolina Infantry, and afterward served in the National Guard, retiring with the rank of lieutenant colonel in 1907. During the World war he gave a generous part of his time to patriotic causes, having charge of the Speakers' Bureau for the second Red Cross campaign, was county chairman of the United War Work campaign and made many speeches in behalf of all war measures and movements.

Colonel Marion served as a member of the Lower House of the General Assembly from 1898 to 1900, and in 1918 was elected state senator from Chester County, serving in the session of 1919. He has always been greatly interested in education and for several years has been a member of the Board of School Trustees of Chester. He is a member of the Associate Reformed Presbyterian Church, a teacher of its Bible Class at Chester, and is affiliated with the Masonic Order and the Knights of Pythias.

By his marriage he is allied with several historic families. December 31, 1902, Miss Mary Pagan Davidson became his wife. She was born at Chester, daughter of Col. William Lee and Annie Irvine (Pagan) Davidson. Col. William Lee Davidson was a son of Benjamin Wilson and Betsie (Latta) Davidson, of Mecklenburg County, North Carolina. William Lee Davidson served with the rank of colonel in the Seventh North Carolina Infantry in the Confederate army, and gained distinction in that war. His grandfather, Maj. John Davidson, was one of the signers of the Mecklenburg Declaration of Independence, and was a gallant soldier and officer in the Revolutionary war. Annie Irvine

Pagan, mother of Mrs. Marion, was a daughter of Maj. James Pagan of Chester County, who held the rank of major in the Confederate army and for many years was a successful merchant at Chester. James Pagan married Anne Fayssoux, daughter of Peter Fayssoux, who was a son of Dr. Peter Fayssoux of Charleston, the Continental surgeon referred to and quoted by McCready in "South Carolina in the Revolution." Peter Fayssoux, father of Anne, married Rebecca Irvine, whose father, Gen. William Irvine, was a member of Washington's staff and after the Revolution was distinguished by his work in military campaigns and in the civil affairs of Pennsylvania.

WILLIAM TILLMAN MCGOWAN. His associates and clients look upon Mr. McGowan as one of the accomplished younger lawyers, able, hard working, diligent and faithful to all the interests committed to his care. He enjoys a fine position in his profession at Timmonsville.

He was born in Hyde County, North Carolina, October 8, 1882, son of Henry Lawrence and Dell (Stotesbury) McGowan. He spent his boyhood on his father's farm, attended private schools, took his A. B. degree from the University of North Carolina in 1907 and was awarded the degree Master of Science by the same institution in 1908. For four years he was a teacher and superintendent of schools at Lynchburg, South Carolina. Mr. McGowan graduated from the law department of the University of North Carolina in 1911. He was admitted to the South Carolina bar in 1913, and built up his early practice at Bishopville, where he remained until 1915, having now a general practice at Timmonsville.

February 20, 1917, he married Susie Hill, of Abbeville. They have one son, William Tillman, Jr., born November 20, 1917. Mr. McGowan is a member of the Methodist Episcopal Church. He is a thirty-second degree Mason and a member of Omar Temple.

WILLIAM C. DAVIS for many years has been prominent as a lawyer and banker at Manning, and is a member of an old family of Clarendon County. His father, James E. Davis, was for sixteen years clerk of the court at Manning.

William C. Davis was born on his father's farm near Manning February 12, 1870, son of James E. and Anna M. Davis. He was liberally educated and was given a thorough military discipline while a student in The Citadel at Charleston, where he was graduated at the age of nineteen. He began the study of law with Joseph F. Rhame, after which he entered the University of Virginia, and in 1891 was admitted to the Virginia bar. On returning home he formed a partnership with Joseph F. Rhame, his former preceptor. As a young lawyer he also took an active part in local military affairs, and was captain of the Manning Guards, which in May, 1898, was mustered into the United States volunteer service as Company D of the Second South Carolina. He was captain of his company, and served as judge advocate of the Seventh Army Corps while in Cuba. He spent three months in Cuba and was mustered out in April, 1899. During the World war Captain Davis was chairman of the Council of Defense of Clarendon County, and took a permanent part in all war activities.

From 1894 to 1898 he was a member of the Legislature and was on the judiciary committee. He has been interested in various local business affairs, was formerly a director of the Manning Oil Mill, is a director of the Carolina Stock Farms Company and is president of the First National Bank of Manning, which was reorganized in March, 1918, under a national charter.

May 17, 1894, Captain Davis married Clara J. Huggins, daughter of Doctor Huggins of Manning.

RAYMOND CLYDE ROLLINS during the greater part of his active business career since leaving college has been identified with the Bank of Timmonsville. This is one of the strong financial institutions of Florence County and has lent its resources effectively to the upbuilding of that community for many years. The bank is capitalized at $100,000, surplus of $15,000 and its deposits in 1919 aggregated $500,000.

Raymond Clyde Rollins was born at Timmonsville, October 6, 1877, son of William DeLeslie and Addie Eugenia (Morris) Rollins. His father for many years was a railway telegraph operator. The son was educated in public schools and was a member of one of the early classes of Clemson College. On leaving college he entered the Bank of Timmonsville, acquired considerable knowledge of banking at that time, but afterward spent six years as bookkeeper with the John McSween Mercantile Company. In 1901 he returned to the bank as cashier, and has been steadily at his post promoting the interest of the bank and the welfare of its customers for nearly twenty years. In January, 1920, he was made active vice president of the bank. He is also secretary and treasurer and has held those offices since the organization of the Timmonsville Building and Loan Association. Mr. Rollins is a former alderman, is a steward of the Methodist Episcopal Church, superintendent of the Sunday school, is past chancellor of the Knights of Pythias, and past worshipful master of the Masonic Lodge.

July 20, 1899, he married Addie Elizabeth Cokes, of Timmonsville. Their six children are Raymond Clyde, Jr., now a student in Wofford College, Frances Eugenia, who is attending Columbia College, George DeLeslie, Edwin Morris, Ellen Elizabeth and Herbert Cokes.

FREDERICK LESESNE. The name Lesesne is of Huguenot origin, and the family of that name has been numerously represented in South Carolina for many generations. The Lesesnes were among the early settlers on the Santee River in St. Mark's Parish.

Frederick Lesesne, a lawyer of Manning, was born in Clarendon County, April 18, 1875, son of Henry H. and Letitia (Wells) Lesesne. His father was a farmer, and at the beginning of the war between the states entered the Confederate army as first lieutenant of Company I, Twenty-Third South Carolina Regiment. He was later promoted to major of the same regiment and was with Lee at Appomattox. Major Lesesne spent many years as a farmer in Clarendon County and was elected county sheriff in 1878 and had held that office for fourteen years, until his death in 1891. A Camp of Sons of Confederate Veterans was named in his honor.

Frederick Lesesne was educated in the Manning Academy, also took a business college course, and from 1897 to 1915 was employed as a bookkeeper. In the latter year he began the study of law in the University of South Carolina and was admitted to the bar in 1917, since which date he has had a general practice at Manning. Mr. Lesesne is a Royal Arch Mason and Shriner and is a trustee of the Methodist Episcopal Church, South.

JULIAN F. NOHRDEN. The late Julian F. Nohrden, of Charleston, principal of the Mitchell School, was taken from life when in the period of his greatest usefulness, and yet it cannot be truthfully said that his work is ended, for the influence he exerted, the weight of the example of his upright and patriotic actions and the results of his conscientious and intellectual instructions, remain and bear witness to the value of the man and citizen. He was born at Charleston, August 20, 1888, and died in his natal city of typhoid fever August 6, 1918. His parents were F. E. and Florence (Harris) Nohrden.

Julian F. Nohrden was a product of Charleston in every respect, and his death was a distinct loss to his community. Educated at The Citadel, he was orator of his class, and was graduated with honors in 1908, although he had won a scholarship in the Charleston College at the age of sixteen years, resigning it to accept appointment to The Citadel. While he won distinction in educational matters, he was also prominent in athletics, and was a well known figure in both base ball and foot ball. After leaving The Citadel Mr. Nohrden associated himself with the News and Courier as a reporter, with the idea of following newspaper work while he studied law, but changed his mind and accepted the position of assistant principal of one of the public schools of Charleston, and in it found his life work. Later his talents were recognized by his promotion to be principal of the Mitchell School. Subsequently he was further honored by being appointed assistant superintendent of the public schools of Charleston, discharging the onerous duties of both positions at the time of his death. Not only was Mr. Nohrden intellectually fitted to hold the positions to which he was appointed, he had in his heart that inherent love and understanding of children without which no educator can render the best service to his pupils. Inspiring them with a love and winning their confidence and respect, he was able to gain from them a willing and joyous compliance with his regulations which resulted in his school showing remarkable advances in scholarship.

While he left newspaper work for the schoolroom, Mr. Nohrden never entirely lost his liking for literary work, and for several years edited the sporting page of the Charleston American. In addition to all of the multitudinous demands on his time and strength, when this country entered the World war, Mr. Nohrden found opportunity to render efficient service, and led by him the children of all the schools, especially those of the Mitchell School, participated in all of the various war activities taking particular interest in the Red Cross work. As a slight memorial to his memory and in recognition of his efforts in behalf of their children, the members of the Parent-Teachers Association of the Mitchell School awarded a scholarship to the Charleston College.

On June 29, 1911, Mr. Nohrden was married at Charleston to Oriole Walsh, a daughter of James and Mary Walsh, all of Charleston. Mrs. Nohrden was educated at Lucas Academy, from which she was graduated. They had two children, Maynard, who was born June 1, 1912; and Francis Walsh, who was born December 14, 1917.

The funeral services of Mr. Nohrden was held at St. Paul's Episcopal Church, Rev. Harold Thomas officiating. The following acted as pallbearers: Honorary: Messrs. Hames Simons, Julius E. Cogswell, T. W. Passailaigue, Sr., Montague Triest, Andrew J. Riley, Edgar Lieberman and A. Burnet Rhett; active: Messrs. H. F. Barkerdling, H. J. O'Brien, Herbert Schachte, John D. Rooney, P. K. Bremer and Louis Denaro. His remains were laid to rest in St. Laurence Cemetery, Charleston.

Quoting from the tribute paid to Mr. Nohrden by the mayor of Charleston: "Having known him very intimately from earliest childhood, I feel qualified to testify to his very strong personality and high character. He inspired absolute confidence in those with whom he associated, and this quality made him most useful and helpful in our school life. His genuine interest in the individual scholar, and advice cheerfully given to the parents made him the friend of all the homes he touched. He devoted himself most unselfishly to the work as principal. He was most efficient and resourceful in his plans and very faithful in their execution. Our city has lost a devoted, cultured educator and a splendid citizen of the highest type, one who gave his best for the good of our youth and no man can ever render a nobler service."

Mr. Nohrden was a person of poetic instinct and wrote much poetry and short stories under the nom de plume of Martin Maynard. After his decease Mrs. Nohrden collected a number of poems and short stories and published them in a neat little volume. One of the poems—"An Ode"—which he had composed for the memorial exercises at Magnolia Cemetery, May 10, 1915, and which he read there is given herewith:

AN ODE

Winds of the South, blow soft today;
  Whisper, ye branches over head,
A mindful people comes to pay
  Sweet tribute to its hero dead.

O'er their last camp, a sentry stands
  Eternal guard. What spirits rise

Julian F. Nohrden.

To vitalize the nerveless hands?
What visions luminate the eyes?

Northward the guns flash out anew;
Once more the gray forms rush ahead;
Kershaw, he sees, and Pettigrew;
Hampton with knightly Armistead.

Out where the East blends sea with sand
Sumter's dull mutterings begin;
Flouting a navy's wrath, ho! stand
Mitchell—and Elliott—Huguenin.

Far to the West a hill-crest flames;
Up the long slope a thin line crawls;
Hark, how the "rebel yell" proclaims
Marrigault's charge! See, brave Gist falls.

South, as the gun flecked islands lie,
Wagner's frail walls defy the blast.
See, where a barred flag flutters high
Hagood and Ripley standing fast.

North, East they struggled, West and South;
Their strength alone, not their spirit, failed;
Fire and sword, cold, famine, drouth
Threatened. Thru all their faith prevailed.

Here Carolina calls them home;
Here heads are bowed and quick tears start;
While unforgetting daughters come
With blooms to soothe her stricken heart.

Here grateful sons return to give
Thanks for their sacred heritage;
Proud in these glories that ever live,
Humble in this—their pilgrimage.

Winds of the South, blow far today
To the distant realm of Eternity;
Seek out the waiting clans in gray,
Bear them a sign how their children say

That we cherish this shrine as we will alway,
With reverence and love and loyalty.

BENJAMIN FRANKLIN MCKELLAR has for many years been a fixture in the commercial affairs of Greenwood, both as a merchant and banker. His friends claim for him a genius as a financier, and every undertaking with which his name has been associated has had in it some of the elements of real success.

Mr. McKellar was born at Greenwood, June 25, 1872, a son of Benjamin F. and Susan Eliza (Chatham) McKellar. His grandfather was Major Peter McKellar. The grandfather was a man of wealth and great influence in his day, but the grandson, as a result of vicissitudes which frequently overtook southern families in the past century, had to start his own life poor. He received most of his education by night school study. As a boy he worked in a brick yard, also in a furniture store for several years. About that time he was delegated as trustee for an estate, and in its management his business resourcefulness had its first real opportunity. He pulled the estate out of debt, and thereby also earned the confidence of the commercial world. For twenty-two years Mr. McKellar was a successful furniture merchant.

In 1910 he organized the People's Bank of Greenwood, and has been president since the institution was organized. At the beginning $69,900 was subscribed to the capital stock of the bank and the capital is now authorized at $500,000, with from $200,000 to $300,000 paid in and doing over $1,500,000 worth of business. Mr. McKellar is also president of the People's Bank of Hodges, South Carolina, and president of the People's Trust Company.

He married Nora Victoria Summer, of Newberry, South Carolina. Their only son, Benjamin F., Jr., is now deceased. He married Katie Edmonds, of York, and at his death left four children, named Katherine Victoria, Imogene, Alice Frances and Susie Elies.

JAMES WARREN WIDEMAN, a prominent lawyer and present state senator from Clarendon County, bears the same name as his honored father, who was a prominent physician for many years at Due West, South Carolina.

Dr. James Warren Wideman was born in Abbeville County, September 16, 1846, was educated in country schools, in Erskine College, and at the age of seventeen became a member of Company A of the First South Carolina Cavalry. After the war he studied medicine, and was twice honored with the office of president of the Abbeville County Medical Society. On January 23, 1868, he married Emma Lucretia Jordan. Their son, James Warren Wideman, was born at Due West, September 30, 1887, and supplemented his advantages in the local schools with the opportunities of Erskine College, from which he graduated in 1908. He then taught one year in Hickory Grove before entering the Law School of the University of South Carolina. He was admitted to the bar in 1911 and has since had a growing general practice and reputation as a sound and able lawyer at Manning. He was elected a member of the State Senate in 1918 and elected a member of the Democratic State Executive Committee in 1919. Mr. Wideman is a Mason and Woodman of the World.

June 11, 1914, he married Mary Louise Brockinton, of Manning. They have a daughter, Ida Louise, born in May, 1915.

JOHN JACOB SEIBELS was born in Columbia, South Carolina, August 3, 1871. After completing his education at the University of South Carolina, he entered his father's office, then and now known as the insurance agency of E. W. Seibels & Son, one of the oldest agencies in the South. At the age of twenty, Mr. Seibels was appointed Special Agent and Adjuster for the Southern States, for the Manchester Fire Assurance Company. In 1898 the Southern Department was organized with his brother, Edwin G. Seibels, as Manager and John J. Seibels as General Agent, the Glens Falls Insurance Company and the Pacific Fire Insurance Company of New York then comprising the Department. Later the "Rochester-German," "New Hampshire," "American of Newark," "Royal Exchange" of England, "Colonial Fire Underwriters" of Hartford, the Cotton Fire & Marine Underwriters, and others, also entered the office under the same management. Today the office is one of the largest agencies in the South, maintains offices in New York and London, with an annual premium income, both fire and marine, of $2,500,000. The general offices are on the fourteenth and fifteenth floors of the Palmetto Building, and a force of about seventy-five people is maintained. The Palmetto Construction Company, which owned and built the fifteen story Palmetto Building, was organized by Mr. John J. Seibels, president of the company, who especially planned the two upper floors for the Southern Department offices. In 1910 the South Carolina Insurance Company was organized, Mr. Seibels being its secretary.

Among other companies in which Mr. Seibels is a dominant factor may be mentioned the Greenfield Construction Company, the Consolidated Holding Company, the City Investing Company, the Palmetto Trust Company, and he is first vice president of the Palmetto National Bank and Palmetto Trust Company, and a director in numerous other companies, including the Southern Railway, Carolina Division, from 1902 to 1919.

Mr. Seibels is a son of Edwin Whipple and Marie J. Seibels. His great-great-grandfather emigrated from Elberfeldt, Germany, to Charleston, South Carolina in 1760. His great-great-grandmother was Sarah Temple, daughter of William Temple, brother of Sir John Temple of England. Mr. Seibels is a democrat in politics, a Master Mason, member of the Chi Phi Fraternity, Columbia Club, Ridgewood Club and a member of Trinity Church, Columbia. Mr. Seibels was married April 25, 1900, to Miss Bertha Willingham, oldest daughter of Calder Baynard and Lila Ross Willingham, of Macon, Georgia. Her great-great-grandfather, Thomas Henry Willingham, came to Charleston in 1790 from Willingham Hall, Market Rasen, present seat of the Willingham family in England. His son, Thomas, married Phoebe Sarah Lawton. Her great-uncle, Ephraim M. Baynard, is referred to as the chief founder and benefactor of the College of Charleston. The Ross family came from Scotland to Virginia and Mrs. Seibels great-grandfather, Luke Ross, moved to Macon, Georgia, from Williamston, North Carolina, in 1821. Mr. and Mrs. Seibels have two children. Calder Willingham and Mary Ross Seibels, these children being the fourth generation to live in the old Seibels home, which is still occupied by the Seibels family, and which was built in 1790.

JAMES MONROE WALKER. The talents of a good lawyer turned to the business of life insurance have brought James Monroe Walker through successive responsibilities, beginning as solicitor, until he is now assistant general manager and associate counsel of the Carolina Life Insurance Company of Columbia.

Mr. Walker, who was born in Colleton County, June 5, 1879, combines the blood of several old and prominent families of the state. His great-grandfather, George Walker, came from England over a century ago, and was a pioneer of Colleton County. His son George became a Baptist minister, widely known over several southern states. Rev. George Walker was the father of Isham David Walker, who for many years operated and lived on a fine plantation in Colleton County. Isham David Walker married Emma V. Hiers, a daughter of Jacob and Rebecca Hiers. Jacob Hiers was of an old time planting family in Colleton County, and as a comparatively young man entered the Confederate army and was killed in battle, giving his life for the cause of the South.

James Monroe Walker grew up on the plantation of his father, Isham David Walker, and acquired his early education in the public schools of Colleton County. He has to his credit three years of efficient work as a teacher in the public schools of his home county. At the age of twenty he began the study of law in the office of Howell & Gruber. His preceptors were men of distinction and great learning, leaders of the southern bar, the individuals of the firm being Major M. P. Howell and Colonel W. B. Gruber. Mr. Walker was admitted to the South Carolina bar December 9, 1902, and for about ten years was busily engaged in a growing practice, both at Walterboro and St. Matthews.

He acquired his first practical knowledge of the life insurance business as a solicitor and field agent of the Carolina Life Insurance Company. He entered the service of that company on September 1, 1913. In volume and quality of business he quickly showed his class even among older and more experienced men in the business. He was promoted to assistant superintendent of the local agency at Columbia and engaged in that work three years. Then, in 1918, he was made superintendent of the Charleston district and in February, 1919, was returned to the home office at Columbia as assistant general manager and associate counsel.

Aside from his record in helping to build up one of South Carolina's most important business and financial institutions, Mr. Walker had some part in public affairs while he was a lawyer, representing Colleton County in the State Legislature during the sessions of 1905-06. A democrat he is primarily interested in the promotion of clean politics in community and state. Mr. Walker is affiliated with the Independent Order of Odd Fellows and Knights of Pythias and is a member of the Baptist Church.

At Walterboro April 3, 1903, he married Susan Annie Caldwell. She was also born in Colleton County, daughter of Thomas H. and Susan A. (Marsh) Caldwell, the Caldwells and Marshs having been people of honorable distinction in Colleton and other sections of South Carolina through several generations. Mr. and Mrs. Walker have four children: James Monroe, Jr., Leon Waldo, Thelma Gertrude and David Thomas.

DAVID WILLIAM GALLOWAY. Both by intellectual talent and personal character David William Gallo-

way is peculiarly fitted for success as a lawyer, and the early years of his practice have justified every promise entertained of a brilliant future. Mr. Galloway's ambition is in the line with the best traditions of the law. He from the first has regarded the law not as a trade but as a profession, and it has signified for him, in the words of an eminent jurist, "a mental and moral setting apart from the multitude—a priesthood of justice."

He was born in Dillon County, at that time Marion County, South Carolina, in 1889, son of James S. and Mary Lou (Bethea) Galloway. The Galloway ancestors came to this country from the north of Ireland, and represented a fine sturdy stock of people, especially identified with Marlboro County and its improvement into one of the richest sections of the South. James S. Galloway was a Confederate soldier, serving throughout the war in the Twenty-Third South Carolina Infantry. This regiment was a part of Lee's Army of Northern Virginia, and was almost constantly on duty in Virginia except for a period when engaged in the Vicksburg campaign in Mississippi. James S. Galloway enlisted as a private, became a commissioned officer of the Twenty-Third and no braver soldier or more efficient officer served in the Confederate armies, according to the tributes of his old army comrades in arms. A bullet wound received in the head in one battle was the ultimate cause of his death, although he lived many years after the war and was a successful planter in that part of Dillon County originally a part of Marion, and he died at his home there in 1910.

Mary Lou Bethea, also deceased, was a member of the prominent Bethea family of Marion, Marlboro and Dillon counties. This ancestry originated in France and was established in Virginia in early colonial times. The first Bethea to come to South Carolina located in what is now Dillon County about 1746. The Betheas were extensive planters, many of them have been soldiers, and many have appeared as prominent figures in public and political affairs.

David William Galloway has always expressed a great debt to the influence of his mother, who was a woman of great nobility of heart and mind, and exceedingly charitable. Mr. Galloway was educated in Wofford College at Spartanburg and in the University of South Carolina. He finished his law course in the latter school in 1913, and in the same year was admitted to the bar. He began practice at Hartsville in Darlington County, and in 1914 was elected magistrate of Hartsville, filling that office for two years in addition to his general practice. His talents as a lawyer plainly called for a larger field, and he finally abandoned his growing business at Hartsville and established himself at Columbia in November, 1919. Mr. Galloway is a thorough student, and much of his success is due to the conscientious and thorough manner with which he undertakes every important commission assigned to him.

He is a member of the Methodist Church, and fraternally is affiliated with the Masons, Knights of Pythias, Odd Fellows and Woodmen of the World. He married Miss Lois Shores, of Spartanburg. Their three children are David William, Jr., Mary Shores and Roslyn.

JEROME P. CHASE, SR., was one of the leading business men of Florence. He was born in Tennessee, July 28, 1838. He received most of his education at Washington, D. C., and at the age of twenty-one became a telegraph operator in South Carolina. During the war he was part of the time a soldier and afterwards a military telegraph operator for the Confederate Government and finally served for 1½ years in the Quartermaster's Department. After the war he became a Florence merchant but later engaged in the real estate and insurance business and became officially interested in nearly all local business enterprises. He was elected to the Legislature in 1878 and also served as mayor of Florence. He married in 1866 Miss Hattie McLeod.

Jerome P. Chase, Jr., was born in Florence, May 13, 1872. He was educated in the public schools and Wofford College and for several years was associated with the electric light plant at Florence, built by his father. He managed the company through the period of its difficulties and sold out the business in 1904. Since that date he has been engaged in the real estate and insurance business. He is manager and treasurer of the Chase Land & Improvement Company owned by the Chase family, and is a director of the Bank of Florence.

EDWIN EUGENE BRUNSON has spent most of his life in and around Florence, was reared on a farm, and for the past ten years has been one of the leading real estate men of the city.

He was born October 4, 1884, a son of Robert C. and Anna (Phinney) Brunson. His father was a farmer. He received the advantages of private and country schools, attended the University of South Carolina three years, and in 1910 entered the real estate business. He is member of the well known firm Lucas & Brunson of Florence. Mr. Brunson is president of the Pinewood Club and is present city tax assessor of Florence. He is unmarried.

JAMES CALVIN HEMPHILL. The Hemphill family of old Abbeville district has furnished many distinguished names to South Carolina. One of the present generation is James Calvin Hemphill, of Greenwood, formerly a part of old Abbeville County, and he is earning high reputation for himself in the profession of architecture.

He was born at Abbeville in 1889, a son of Robert Reid and Eugenia Cornelia (Taylor) Hemphill. His grandfather was Rev. William Reid Hemphill, for many years pastor of the Associate Reformed Presbyterian Church at Cedar Springs in Abbeville County. An uncle of James C. Hemphill is Major J. C. Hemphill, who was formerly editor of the Charleston News and Courier, the Charlotte Observer and the Richmond Times Dispatch. He is now editor of the Spartanburg Journal.

Robert Reid Hemphill, father of the Greenwood architect, was a Confederate soldier in Orr's Rifles. He played a creditable part in the war and at the end of the reconstruction period was a member of the noted Wallace House of 1876. For some years he was editor of the Abbeville Medium, was member of the State Senate from Abbeville County, and for fourteen years clerk of the South Carolina Senate. He is now deceased.

James Calvin Hemphill acquired a liberal education, attending the College of Charleston two years. He studied architecture in Boston, taking a short course in Harvard University and another course with the Boston Architectural Club. He established himself in practice at Greenwood in 1913, and the past five years have been exceedingly busy and have presented many opportunities for him to prove his skill and develop it. He was fortunate in selecting Greenwood as his home, since it is one of the wealthiest and fastest growing cities in South Carolina. Mr. Hemphill has designed and superintended the construction of several public and private buildings, the most recent being the Abbeville County Memorial Hospital at Abbeville and the addition to the Greenwood Hospital. He is also architect of the fine modern residences of C. C. Wharton, Dr. W. A. Barnett, W. H. Mays, and J. B Walton, in Greenwood

Mr. Hemphill is a member of the South Carolina Chapter of the American Institute of Architects.

In August, 1919, he married Miss Milwee Davis, daughter of Mr. and Mrs. A. J. Davis of Greenwood. Mrs. Hemphill became well known over the state through her work as an organizer for the State Sunday School Association.

WILLIAM JAMES BROWN for over a quarter of a century has been one of the strong and resourceful men in the financial and business affairs of Florence, and has lent his influence and help readily to every movement for the community's advancement and welfare.

He was born in Florence County October 30, 1858, and has lived in the City of Florence since 1869. He had to be satisfied with the meager advantages offered by the private schools of the impoverished period following the war. As a boy he began earning his living as clerk in stores, and from 1887 to 1892 was one of the independent merchants of Florence.

In 1892 Mr. Brown was one of the organizers of the Bank of Florence, served it many years as cashier and is now president. He has also been secretary and treasurer since organization of the Florence Gas Company, and was similarly officially identified with several building and loan associations.

Mr. Brown served as alderman of Florence from 1889 to 1893, and for three years was mayor of the city. He has long been prominent in the Baptist Church, and for twenty-eight years has been treasurer of the church at Florence. October 11, 1881, he married Miss Anna E. Mouzon, of Charleston. Six children were born to their marriage. The two now living are: Gedney M., cashier of the Bank of Florence, and Leroy King, assistant cashier in the bank. Charles Seignious, who was accidentally killed on the railroad in his automobile December 25, 1919, was second assistant cashier of the bank. This youngest son during the war was in the Sanitary Department of the Eighty-First Division with the Expeditionary Forces in France. The three oldest children of Mr. and Mrs. Brown are also deceased. They were: William James, Jr., who died at the age of twenty; Mattie Seignious, who died when five years old; and Furman Evans, who died at the age of fifteen months.

ALLARD HENRY GASQUE, who represents old French Huguenot stock in South Carolina, has devoted his active life to educational affairs and for fifteen years has been busily directing the public school system of Lawrence County in the capacity of county superintendent.

He was born in Florence County March 8, 1873, son of Wesley and Martha (Kirton) Gasque. His father was a merchant and planter. The son was educated in the public schools and as a young man before going to college taught school three years in some of the country districts of Florence County. He was graduated from the University of South Carolina in 1901, and the following year was principal of the Waverly School. He then took a year of post-graduate work and in 1902 was chosen county superintendent of education, beginning his first term in January, 1903. He was elected five times in succession for two year terms, without opposition, and in 1916 was elected for a four year term, receiving a large majority over two rival candidates.

Mr. Gasque is well known among South Carolina educators and is a former president of the South Carolina Teachers' Association. He has been a member of the State Executive Committee of the democratic party for eight years and chairman of the city democratic organization at Florence six years. He is a Mason, Knight of Pythias, and a past state counsellor and national representative of the Junior Order United American Mechanics. His religious connection is with the Baptist Church. He married, March 5, 1908, Bessie Hawley, of Richland County. They have three children, Martha Elizabeth, Doris and John Allard.

JOHN DESAUSSURE GILLAND, a prominent and well known attorney of Florence, has been in practice in that city for the past five years and is at this time acting city recorder.

He was born in Kingstree, South Carolina, November 3, 1883, a son of Thomas McDowell and Louise (Brockington) Gilland. His father was also an attorney, was educated in public schools, and took both his academic and law courses in the University of South Carolina. Mr. Gilland while in school and university became well known in athletic circles, and after leaving university was for three years a professional baseball player. He began the practice of law at Kingstree in 1909 and from that city moved to Florence in 1914. He has been admitted to practice in both the State and Federal courts.

April 22, 1913, he married Jane Allen. Their three children are J. D., Jr., Ruth Allen and Louise.

JOHN WILBUR HICKS, member of the prominent Florence law firm of Arrowsmith, Muldrow, Bridges & Hicks, is a native of South Carolina but finished his legal education in Chicago.

He was born in Florence County, March 24, 1885,

a son of Elijah Myers and Elizabeth C. (Welch) Hicks. His father was a minister of the Baptist Church. Mr. Hicks was educated in public schools, attended the Orangeburg Collegiate Institute until 1899, and from 1900 to 1904 was a student of the Welsh Neck High School. He graduated A. B. from Furman University in 1909, and then entered the law department of the University of Chicago. From this institution he received the degree J. D., Juris Doctor, in December, 1911. On returning to South Carolina Mr. Hicks was employed in the real estate department of the Atlantic Coast Line Railway, on business connected with the Interstate Commerce Commission, until the following May, when he was admitted to the bar and has since been engaged in general practice as a member of the firm above noted.

Mr. Hicks is a member of the Phi Psi college fraternity. He is also affiliated with the Junior Order United American Mechanics and is a thirty-second degree Scottish Rite Mason and Shriner. He belongs to the Baptist Church.

PHILIP H. ARROWSMITH is senior member of one of the prominent law firms in eastern South Carolina, that of Arrowsmith, Muldrow, Bridges & Hicks at Florence.

Mr. Arrowsmith, who was formerly a lawyer at Lake City, was born at Winnsboro, South Carolina, August 8, 1888, a son of Frances H. and Louise (Heller) Arrowsmith. His father was a hotel man. The son attended the public schools of Atlanta, Georgia, took his literary course in Trinity College at Durham, North Carolina, and in 1911 graduated from the law department of the University of South Carolina. Soon after being admitted to the bar he opened his office at Lake City and handled his clientele and business at that point from 1911 to 1919, when he removed to Florence.

July 30, 1912, he married Helen Thames, of Manning, South Carolina. They have two sons, Mitchell Heller and Philip Heller, Jr.

WILLIAM H. MALLOY has been an active business man of Florence for many years, though during the past twenty years his business abilities have been required almost altogether by the city. He has held the office of mayor or city treasurer for an aggregate of seventeen years.

Mr. Malloy was born at Cheraw, South Carolina, July 30, 1859, a son of Dr. A. and Henrietta (Coit) Malloy, of Scotch-Irish ancestry. He received his early education in common schools and the Cheraw Academy, gained his early business experience in Cheraw, and in 1891 removed to Florence. He was bookkeeper for one of the local firms several years, traveled in Texas one year, and then engaged in business as a merchandise broker at Florence. He was elected mayor of the city in 1896 and held that office for six years, until he felt obliged to resign to look after his private affairs. In 1908 he was first elected city treasurer and by repeated re-election annually he has filled that office to the present time. Nearly all the improvements which make a modern city of Florence have been instituted and carried out during his official connection as mayor or treasurer.

Mr. Malloy was for a number of years deacon of the Presbyterian Church at Cheraw. He first married Kate Wilson in 1885. January 28, 1892, he married Hannah Pawley Waring.

HENRY EDWARDS DAVIS was admitted to the bar in 1904, is member of the law firm Willcox & Willcox at Florence, and is division counsel for the Atlantic Coast Line Railroad.

Mr. Davis, who has earned his high place in the South Carolina bar by unremitting industry and hard study, was born at Gourdin, South Carolina, October 4, 1879, a son of James Edwards and Emma W. (Chandler) Davis. He grew up on his father's farm in Williamsburg County, attended local schools, and graduated in June, 1902, from the Presbyterian College of South Carolina. The next fall he entered the law department of the University of South Carolina and continued his studies there until January, 1904. He was then in the office of Associate Justice C. A. Woods at Marion until March, 1906, and since then has been an associate of the law firm of Willcox & Willcox at Florence. Mr. Davis served four years as city attorney of Florence finally resigning that office. He is now and has been for two years a member of the school board, and is a trustee of the Presbyterian College of South Carolina and an elder of the Presbyterian Church.

September 26, 1906, he married Miss Lillian Erskine, of Anderson County. Mrs. Davis was a successful teacher for five years until her marriage. They have two daughters, Maud Elizabeth and Virginia Erskine.

DAVIS C. DURHAM, one of the prominent merchants and citizens of Greenville, where he has had a business career of forty years, is president and treasurer and principal owner of Gilreath-Durham, Inc., jewelers and silversmiths. This is now one of the oldest business firms of that city with a continuous record, and is a landmark of the commercial district. The principal lines carried are jewelry, fine china and fancy goods.

Mr. Durham, who was born at Shelby, Cleveland County, North Carolina, in 1867, is a member of a very historic and prominent family. His parents are David Noah and Esther Ruth (Coleman) Durham, the former now deceased. The original seat of the Durham family was in England. The first to come to America located in Virginia early in the eighteenth century, and some of them later moved to North Carolina. The City of Durham, North Carolina, was named in honor of the family. The name stands for the best there is in American character and some of the Durhams have achieved very high distinction. On the whole, they have been lawyers, merchants, ministers and educators. David Noah Durham and his son Davis C. as merchants are rather exceptions to the general rule. David N. Durham at the age of sixteen was fighting in the uniform of a Confederate soldier, and in 1879, he removed from Shelby, North Carolina, to Greenville, South Carolina, and was a business man in that city for many years.

A brother of Davis C. Durham is Dr. Charles L. Durham of Cornell University. He was born at Shelby in 1872, received his Master of Arts degree from Furman University at Greenville in 1891, was an instructor in that school until 1896, and in 1897 became instructor of Latin at Cornell University and since 1909 has held the chair of Latin in that great institution and is also secretary of the College of Arts and Sciences. He is a man who is held in the highest and most affectionate esteem by every Cornell man (all of whom know "Bull Durham") and for many years has been one of the most popular members of the university's staff. His public spirit is as notable as his classic scholarship. During the war with Germany he devoted much of his time to speaking for the Liberty Loan and other war measures throughout the East and Middle West. Doctor Durham is well known at Greenville, where he spent most of his boyhood and early manhood.

Davis C. Durham, who was born at Shelby in Cleveland County, North Carolina, in 1867, acquired his early education there. Shelby is a town notable for many prominent characters who were born and reared there and attended the same school. Among them are Thomas Dixon, the author and lecturer, and his brothers, Rev. A. C. and Rev. Frank Dixon, and also the Webbs, two prominent jurists of North Carolina. Davis C. Durham is a contemporary of some of these famous people who once lived in Shelby. After coming to Greenville Mr. Durham attended Captain Patrick's Military School.

His father as noted above put on a Confederate uniform at the age of sixteen. At a similar age Davis C. Durham, the country being then at peace and no incentive to fire a boy's military ambition, enlisted in the army of commercial travelers, and was one of the first to travel out of Greenville for a Greenville concern. He became known as the "boy drummer" and for a number of years represented his firm on the road in South Carolina and also portions of North Carolina and Georgia. Mr. Durham was always closely connected with all activities of the traveling men and is a member of the Travelers Protective Association, served as president of his local post and later as state president.

Counting his youthful experience as a clerk and traveling salesman he has been constantly in business at Greenville for forty years, and in the same section of Main Street where his present business is located. This business has been built up on character and through it Mr. Durham has come to realize the ideals of a man's responsibilities and service to the world at large.

Mr. Durham is a member of the First Baptist Church and for fifteen or twenty years was superintendent of the Sunday School of this fine old church. Now and for a number of years he has been giving much attention to work and enlargement of the Greenville Woman's College, being vice president of the Board of Trustees and chairman of the Executive Committee of this institution. He is also a member of the Board of Education of the Baptist State Convention of South Carolina.

For a long number of years he was president of the Merchants Association of Greenville and was one of the founders of the Chamber of Commerce. He was chairman of the Traffic Bureau of the Chamber of Commerce and represented that body in behalf of equitable freight rates for Greenville at various sessions of the State Railroad Commission and the Interstate Commerce Commission, attending many meetings held with the railroad officials of the South. Mr. Durham is credited with having brought about adjustment of freight rates that have played a most important part in making Greenville the commercial center that it is today. Mr. Durham served as a member of the Greenville County Council of Defense during the war and was one of the three or four members of that body who took upon themselves the great bulk of its work and achievement. He was also one of the prime movers in the matter of building the Masonic Temple at Greenville, and is president and treasurer of the Masonic Temple Company and manager of their handsome office building on South Main Street.

Mr. Durham was happily married early in his business career. His wife was formerly Miss Stella Louise Ferris of Spencer, Tioga County, New York. A graduate of the New England Conservatory of Music and a finished musician, she came to Greenville as head of the voice department of the Greenville Woman's College.

Richard Durham, son of Mr. and Mrs. Davis C. Durham, earned distinction as a soldier in France. He is a graduate of Furman University and was a student at Cornell University when in June, 1917, he volunteered in the American Field Service. This was a volunteer organization of American young college men for service under the French government. He paid all his own expenses while with the field service. He was in the first section of the volunteers to be transferred to the American Expeditionary Forces. The unit to which he belonged was decorated three times by the general of the division and once by General Gouraud of the Fourth French Army. Richard Durham participated in some of the most terrific warfare, practically throughout the campaign of 1918. He was in the Aisne retreat from May 27 to June 4, in the third battle of the Somme August 10 to 23, in the second battle of the Marne from September 26 to November 6, and through special gallantry during the Aisne attack at Soissons in June, 1918, he was cited and decorated with the French Croix de Guerre. He was still in France in the spring of 1919.

B. F. BEDINGFIELD who died December 8, 1919, had been a resident of Spartanburg thirty years, and while he began his career without special resources he achieved a place of dignity, influence and real success.

Mr. Bedingfield was born on a plantation in Henderson County, North Carolina, October 3, 1854, oldest of the ten children of George and Nancy (Bayne) Bedingfield of the same county. Five of those children are still living, one daughter being a resident of Greenville, South Carolina.

B. F. Bedingfield left home at the age of fourteen, and during a sojourn in Texas found employment as a farm hand. He largely educated himself and early learned the lessons of self reliance. For several years he was a farmer in Arkansas, and then returned east and locating at Greenville, South Carolina, engaged in the grocery business. From there he removed to Spartanburg, and long before his death had acquired a competency by his good business judgment. He was highly thought of in the

THE NEW YORK
PUBLIC LIBRARY

community, was esteemed for his upright Christian life and character. For many years he was active in the Methodist Church, and distinguished himself by his public spirit in local affairs, and was affiliated with the Woodmen of the World, the Knights of Pythias and the Independent Order of Odd Fellows.

Mr. Bedingfield married for his first wife Miss Dolly Huff of Spartanburg. By that marriage he had one son, Frank, now a resident of Columbia, who married Miss Jeffords of Florence, a graduate of Winthrop College. B. F. Bedingfield married for his second wife Sally Neal of Lawrence.

Mr. Bedingfield is survived by his widow who before her marriage to him was Mrs. Eunice Gilmore Robbs, widow of Dr. James R. Robbs. The only child of this union died in infancy. Mrs. Bedingfield was the youngest of four children and was born in Chester County, April 27, 1864, daughter of Charles and Vermilla (Osborn) Gilmore. Her father's family came originally from Fitchburg, Massachusetts, and for many years he was a planter and died in 1887. Her mother died in 1900. Mrs. Bedingfield's oldest brother, J. E. Gilmore, died in 1918. Her sister, Alvinia, is married and living on the old homestead. Mrs. Bedingfield is a well read and cultured woman, enjoys a comfortable and commodious home in Spartanburg, and is an active member of the Duncan Methodist Church.

RICHARD ASHE MEARES, of the family of that name in Wilmington, North Carolina, has been a resident of South Carolina more than thirty-five years. His permanent home and chief interests have been in Fairfield County.

Mr. Meares, who is a member of the Legislature from Fairfield County and maintains a city home for his family at Columbia, was born in New York City, July 4, 1858. He graduated from St. Stephen's College at Annandale, New York, in 1878, and in the same year came South and studied law in the famous law school of Judges Dick and Dillard at Greensboro, North Carolina. He completed his course in 1879, and for three years practiced at Winston-Salem. In January, 1884, he established his home at Ridgeway in Fairfield County, where after a few years he retired from the practice of his profession in favor of his farming and manufacturing interests.

Mr. Meares first came into public note when he served as a member of the Constitutional Convention in 1895. In 1896 he was elected a member of the House of Representatives, serving during the sessions of 1897-98, and was again chosen to that body in 1910 for the sessions of 1911-12, and in 1918, for the third time, was elected to serve his constituency of Fairfield County. He has been one of the leaders in the legislative program adopted by the sessions of 1919-20. In the last Legislature he was a member of the committee on banking and insurance and other important committees.

Mr. Meares is a prominent layman of the Protestant Episcopal Church. He was a member of the delegation of deputies from the Diocese of South Carolina to the General Convention at Detroit, in October, 1919.

Mr. Meares married Miss Louise Woodward Palmer, of Ridgeway, in 1883. Their son, Gaston Meares, was a corporal in Company M of the Three Hundred and Twenty-first Infantry in the Eighty-First or Wildcat Division, and saw several months of active service in France.

MANCIL JAMES OWINGS. The standing and success achieved by Mr. Owings in business affairs in his native County of Laurens rates him as one of the men of exceptional enterprise, thorough integrity and all around ability. Mr. Owings had little to start with as a young man, and his extensive accumulations of business interests stand as a justified reward of his services and abilities.

He was born on a farm May 5, 1865, a son of Benjamin Lewis and Jane (Smith) Owings, also natives of Laurens County, and a grandson of Mancil James and Susan Owings, the former also a native of Laurens County. His maternal grandparents were Franklin and Frances Smith, of the same county. Benjamin L. Owings spent his active life as a farmer and was also a Confederate soldier. He lived to the age of seventy-four, while his wife died at sixty-four. She was a Methodist and he a Baptist.

Their family of five daughters and two sons all grew up on the old farm, and as a farm boy Mancil James Owings attended the district schools. At the age of eighteen he went to the home of his uncle, John R. Owings, and at the age of twenty-two opened a country store on his uncle's farm. He conducted it for four years, until the death of his uncle. He then came to Laurens and became a competitor with old established merchants. He pushed his business with commendable energy and his affairs have been growing rapidly since then. In 1913 he organized the Farmers National Bank and became its president, and has made that institution one of the solidest in Laurens County. He has also bought stock in other banks and corporations and has been inclined to put most of his profits in farm lands. He is now one of the largest farm land owners, in the county, and has done much to promote the agricultural welfare of his section.

Mr. Owings, who has never married, is an active and public spirited citizen, though he has never sought a public office. He is a trustee of the Baptist Church, a trustee of Greenville Female College, and is affiliated with the Masonic Order and Knights of Pythias.

SAMUEL CRAIG BYRD, D. D., president of the Chicora College for Women at Columbia, has for a quarter of a century been distinguished by his work and leadership in church and educational affairs. With the exception of a few years while he was pastor of Presbyterian churches his career has been spent in his native state of South Carolina.

He was born at Laurens October 24, 1868, a son of Capt. Jonathan Downs and Evelyn (Craig) Byrd. He acquired a liberal education, graduating with the A. B. degree from the Presbyterian College of South Carolina at Clinton in 1889 and receiving his Master of Arts degree from the same institution in 1892. In the latter year he also graduated from the Columbia Theological Seminary. He received his Doctor of Divinity degree from the Presbyterian College in 1906.

During 1892-93 he was tutor of Hebrew in the Columbia Theological Seminary and left that work to become assistant pastor of the First Presbyterian Church of New Orleans. In 1894 he was ordained to the Presbyterian ministry and until 1897 was pastor of Lafayette Church in New Orleans.

He then returned to Columbia and from 1898 to 1902 was adjunct professor in the chair of English Bible, and again tutor of Hebrew in the Theological Seminary. In the meantime he was managing editor of the Presbyterian Quarterly and the Religious Outlook in Columbia in 1898-99 and then gave all his time to his duties as a member of the faculty of the Theological Seminary until 1902. From 1903 to 1906 he was pastor of the Scion Church of Winnsboro, South Carolina, and in 1906 was called to his duties as president of Chicora College at Greenville, South Carolina. July 1, 1915, this institution was consolidated with the College for Women at Columbia, and the educational work of the combined colleges has since been continued at Columbia under the name of Chicora College for Women, with Doctor Byrd as president.

Doctor Byrd was also a trustee of the Presbyterian College of South Carolina, serving for many years as president of the board, during the establishment of the college, and the growth and success attained reflects in no small degree the result of his personal efforts and labor. He is a Royal Arch Mason, a Knight of Pythias, and a member of the Pi Kappa Alpha fraternity.

October 3, 1893, he married Wilhelmina Law Cozby, of Newberry and their only son, James Cozby Byrd, is now a junior student in the University of Pennsylvania.

ISAIAH DAVIS DURHAM, M. D., is son of Edmund Durham and Mary Lee of the distinguished family of Robert E. Lee and a grandson of Richard Durham, who married Jane Davis, a near relative of President Jefferson Davis. The Durhams are of English ancestry and many prominent members of the family have their home in North Carolina, where the City of Durham commemorates them. The Durhams in the different generations have been distinguished as forceful business men and equally prominent in public and professional affairs.

Dr. I. D. Durham was a physician, dentist, minister and journalist and was publishing the Confederate Baptist, a weekly newspaper in Columbia when that city was occupied and burned by General Sherman's army. A brother of I. D. Durham was the late Dr. A. K. Durham, a life-long minister of the Baptist Church, and one of the distinguished men of that denomination in South Carolina. He was one of the founders of the present Baptist Courier, and was also actively identified with educational work for many years.

Dr. I. D. Durham was born in 1832, in Cleveland County, North Carolina. He did not have many advantages of an education in early life but he began preaching at the early age of seventeen and by help from the churches and his own exertions he attended Furman University for several years. He graduated from the Medical College of Pennsylvania at Philadelphia in 1859 with honors.

Returning home he practiced his profession very successfully for years. He was a Baptist minister of note and a very forceful and magnetic orator and many churches and associations were organized by him. He was quite an original and independent character and was possessed of his mountaineer and liberty loving traits.

He was very determined and conscientious, so much so that he left North Carolina before he reached his majority, because he opposed the principle of paying poll tax. When it became law in South Carolina he still opposed the principle and claimed that it was unconstitutional and a badge of slavery. He would not pay the tax himself nor would he allow his friends to do so, consequently he had several trials in court and in one case served one day in Aiken County Jail.

He was married in 1855 to Miss Mary Anne Smith, of Laurens County, South Carolina, who died in 1866. Of this marriage only one son survived, William Davis Durham. In 1869 he was married to Miss Elizabeth M. Knotts of Lexington County, South Carolina.

Doctor Durham took a live, independent and conscientious interest in everything that pertained to the welfare of his country, and in 1882 was greenback candidate for superintendent of education. He was a most devoted man to his family and friends. He died in 1890.

Dr. William Davis Durham, only child of Dr. Isaiah Davis Durham, was born in 1859, at Winnsboro, South Carolina. A physician and dentist, he graduated in medicine at the Augusta Medical College, Augusta, Georgia, in 1881. The same year he married Miss Ida Norris of Batesburg, South Carolina, who lived only a year. In 1885 he was married to Miss Lula McLane of Fairfield County, South Carolina, a daughter of John Hendrix McLane of Columbia, South Carolina. John Hendrix McLane a generation ago was one of the leading public characters of the state. He filled various public offices and was a leader of the reform movement in national politics beginning about 1879. At one time he was greenback candidate for governor.

Dr. W. D. Durham was a very affable man with high and noble ideals and quite a success in his professions. He practiced medicine and dentistry chiefly in Aiken County. He died in 1913, leaving six children, four boys and two girls: Davis McLane Durham, Isaiah Davis Durham, Robert Blakley Durham, Virgil Clayton Durham, Ruby Elizabeth Durham and Mary Lee Durham.

Davis McLane Durham was born in 1886, in Aiken County, South Carolina. A very energetic and applicable business man of good moral stamina.

Dr. Isaiah Davis Durham, who was named for his grandfather, was born in Orangeburg County, South Carolina in 1889. While his professional career has been comparatively brief Dr. Durham has done justice to the noble record of his family and ancestors in the history and affairs of South Carolina. Receiving a good common school education he graduated in medicine in 1913 from the University of Georgia, at Augusta, Georgia. Before moving to his present home in Columbia, South Carolina, several months ago, he practiced his profession in New Brookland and surrounding territory. He has built a large general practice in medicine and surgery and a reputation for skill and efficiency that makes him a valuable asset to his community. He was married to Miss Pauline M. Whitehead of Augusta, Georgia. Their two children are William Vernon and Isaiah Davis, Jr.

Dr. Robert Blakley Durham was born in Orangeburg County, South Carolina, in 1892. Receiving a good common school education he graduated in medicine from the University of Georgia, at Augusta, Georgia, in 1913. He practiced his profession at Perry, South Carolina, until moving to Columbia, in 1917. He volunteered in the medical corps, June 5, 1917, and was given a commission of first lieutenant. He was called to report for duty August 20, 1917. On September 6, 1917, he sailed for France. Doctor Durham served twenty-three months in France with the Twenty-Sixth Division, that saw about ten months in the trenches, being one of the first American divisions to Europe. He took part in all major engagements, namely, St. Mihiel, Meuse- Argonne, Chateau Thierry, etc. During service with the Twenty-Sixth Division he was battalion surgeon of the One Hundred and First Infantry and later was given command of the One Hundred and Second Ambulance Company. Dr. R. B. Durham was promoted to captain in February, 1919. While in France he attended the University of Bordeaux for four months, taking special courses in surgery. He was discharged August 4, 1919. Doctor Durham is now practicing his profession in Columbia, South Carolina.

Virgil Clayton Durham was born in Orangeburg County in 1894. He received a common school education. On July 30, 1917, he volunteered as a private in Major Johnson's Battalion of Engineers of South Carolina, in Company B, which was later a part of the One Hundred and Seventeenth Engineers of the Forty-Second Division. He sailed for France, October, 1917, served about nineteen months overseas. He was in action nine months and was engaged in all important battles which the Americans fought, namely, St. Mihiel, Meuse-Argonne, Chateau Thierry. Virgil Clayton Durham received his discharge April 19, 1919.

These two young men were gallant soldiers and faithfully upheld the traditions of their ancestors.

JOSEPH BROWN FELTON had been continuously a teacher and school administrator in Anderson County for nineteen years, and was serving in his third consecutive term as county superintendent when he was appointed State Agent for Colored Schools in South Carolina, October 1, 1919, with headquarters at Columbia.

Mr. Felton was born in Anderson County, May 14, 1882, son of Joseph Bryant and Cinderella (Brown) Felton. He acquired a good education, graduating June 15, 1900, from the Patrick Military Institute at Anderson. In addition to the literary training he received there he had four years of military instruction and has a practical knowledge of military science and technique.

Mr. Felton began teaching in Anderson County in the fall of 1900, and for eleven years was connected with local schools. In 1912 he was elected county superintendent of education, and was reelected without opposition in 1914, and in 1916 received a third term of four years with four opposing candidates. Incidental to his primary work as an educator Mr. Felton has maintained some farming interests for a number of years.

He has always been a stanch democrat and is a member of the Baptist Church. Fraternally he is affiliated with the Knights of Pythias at Townville, being keeper of records and seal in 1912, is a member of the Improved Order of Red Men at Anderson, serving as sachem for 1918, and is a member of the Independent Order of Odd Fellows.

At Townville December 29, 1901, Mr. Felton married Miss Maggie Elizabeth Speares, daughter of Joseph C. and Janie (Bruce) Speares. Her grandfather, the Rev. Kit Speares, was a noted educator of his day in northwestern South Carolina. He spent practically his entire life in the schoolroom, and many of the best business men of that section received their training either in whole or in part from him. One of his former pupils is Ex-Governor Ansel. Mr. and Mrs. Felton have five children: Herbert Newton, Joseph Bruce, Andy Theodora, Emmie Louese and Margaret Elizabeth.

MARVIN LAMAR PARLER, M. D. While the scene of his professional and other commendable activities during the past twenty years has been Wedgefield in Sumter County, Doctor Parler belongs to that sturdy and successful family of Parlers who since Revolutionary times have lived in the old Orangeburg District. There were three French brothers who came to America either with Rochambeau or LaFayette to assist in the struggle for American freedom. After the war they chose the Colonies as their permanent home, and located in the old Orangeburg District in the vicinity of the present Town of Parler, which was named for the family. The Parlers have lived continuously in that section of Orangeburg County since 1790.

Doctor Parler was born there in 1879 and is a son of Eugene M. Parler, a prominent merchant, planter and land owner and a native of the same vicinity.

Doctor Parler was educated in the public schools of his neighborhood, also at Elloree, and attended Furman University at Greenville. He studied medicine in the Medical College of South Carolina at Charleston, graduating with the class of 1900. In the same year he located at Wedgefield, and has achieved enviable rank as the leading physician and surgeon of that rich and growing section of Sumter County. He has been president of the Sumter County Medical Society and is a member of the State and American Medical Association.

Doctor Parler has been a leader in all local affairs, and is a planter and owner of substantial landed interests at Wedgefield. He is a director of the Commercial Bank & Trust Company of Sumter and during the war was chairman of all the Liberty Loan campaigns for Wedgefield and vicinity and also had charge of the food conservation and was connected with other measures incident to the war. He is a Knight Templar, Mason and member of Omar

Temple of the Mystic Shrine at Charleston, and he and his wife are Baptists.

Doctor Parler married Miss Josie Platt, daughter of Rev. John B. and Celestia (Mims) Platt. Her father was a prominent minister of the South Carolina Conference. Her mother was a daughter of Thomas Mims of Charleston. Doctor and Mrs. Parler have two children: Mary Celestia and Marvin Lamar, Jr.

DAVID DUNCAN WALLACE seems to have been predestined for a teacher and writer. His parents both made enviable reputations as teachers. His father left his professorship in the Columbia Female College after a few years for the freer life of journalism. As founder and for many years the editor of the Newberry Observer, he was one of the most influential members of the South Carolina press.

Dr. Wallace's mother, née Miss Alice Amanda Lomax, spent many years of her life before her marriage on Wofford College campus in the home of her maternal grandfather, Professor David Duncan. Her education at Barhamville was followed by the regular work of the Wofford curriculum under the guidance of her grandfather, and though the rules of the college did not permit her to appear in the classroom, they did not prevent the old Professor of Greek from intimating to his boys that he had a young lady privately studying the same course with whose work their own did not always compare favorably. To this day she can read her Latin and Greek far better than any of her grandchildren after the most earnest preparation of the day's lesson. She is a student whom it is never safe to contradict on a matter of historical fact.

Professor Wallace's father was born in Laurens County, near Mudlick Creek, just across the line from Newberry, near the large brick country house known as Belfast, which was purchased while he was a boy by his father and still remains in the family. His family was Baptist. He joined the Methodist church on account of attending Wofford College, from which he graduated in 1871. The Methodist remains the church connection of all his branch of the family.

David Duncan Wallace was born in Columbia, South Carolina, May 23, 1874, in the old Columbia Female College, now the Colonia Hotel. The only other child was a girl, who died in childhood. When the boy was two years old his parents moved to Newberry, where he lived until he left home for college. He attended the Newberry Male Academy and the preparatory department of Newberry College. Entering the Freshman class of that institution, young Wallace, along with several other overly youthful "town boys", threw away a year by devoting himself more industriously to ringing the college bell at hours not prescribed by the schedule, heaving brickbats against classroom doors, and in other ways plaguing the college authorities, from the white haired old negro janitor to the President. His father effectually corrected these flippant tendencies by putting him at steady work in his printing office for a year. The youth really valued an education, and when the next October rolled round was quaking with dread at the possibility of being denied the privilege of re-entering college. From that moment to the present he has never spent an idle week and rarely an idle day.

Taking up his work again at Newberry College, he came under the influence of that noble Christian gentleman Dr. George W. Holland, and that master of class room instruction, Asbury Sumter Laird, who as Professor of Latin gave an example of thoroughness and inspiration in exact scholarly work that constituted a valuable part of his pupils' equipment for life. It was largely the inspiration of Professor Laird's teaching that stirred him to the efforts that won him the prize for the highest average on all work during the Freshman year.

Wofford College was a family tradition in the Wallace home. At real sacrifice the parents sent their son in 1891 to enter the Sophomore class of the old college, where he graduated in 1894. Among the honors conferred upon him by his college mates were the positions of intercollegiate debater, Founder's Day orator, and editor-in-chief of the Wofford College Journal.

Though the associations with his friends, particularly of the Kappa Alpha fraternity, and the whole life at Wofford were rich in inspiration, the influence of the President, Dr. James H. Carlisle, stands out as one of the most beneficent and potent forces in his life. So profound was the conviction of moral values received from that great teacher, supplementing the same influences from his parents, that he has all his life perhaps underestimated material values. From the influences at Wofford that helped to make the man cannot be omitted the wonderful charm and intellectual stimulus of Dr. Henry Nelson Snyder's teaching of English literature and the stirring spiritual appeal of the preaching of Professor, afterwards Bishop, John C. Kilgo.

After dabbling in law reading for a few weeks the young graduate decided on teaching as his lifework. He studied English, Economics, and History at Vanderbilt University for three years, 1894-6 and 1898-99. Turning more and more to History, he was awarded the degree of Doctor of Philosophy with that as his major in 1899. His published doctoral thesis was on "The Constitutional History of South Carolina from 1725 to 1775."

Dr. Wallace had already taught English and History for the two years, 1896-8, in the Carlisle Fitting School at Bamberg, South Carolina. Immediately after taking his degree he entered upon his duties as adjunct professor of History and Economics in Wofford College, where he has worked ever since, except for the half of the college year of 1917-18, during which he gave advanced courses in American History in the University of Michigan. Though having a strong taste for practical affairs, Dr. Wallace has never felt invitations or opportunities to enter business or administrative positions as serious temptations, as his love for investigation and teaching are so much greater as to prevent his feeling that other things are in comparison really worth while in terms of ultimate values.

Dr. Wallace has contributed largely to the daily, weekly and magazine press on topics connected with history and economics. In 1915 he issued a voluminous Life of Henry Laurens, with the fullest sketch yet published of his distinguished son Lieutenant

Colonel John Laurens.* Henry Laurens was the largest national figure that South Carolina contributed to the American Revolution. He touched the life of the country in so many ways, social, economic and political, during the last half of the eighteenth century as to make his biography a large part of the history of his times. The editor of the American Historical Review so valued the book, as one "of such quite exceptional quality" that he sought to secure a review of it by Sir George Otto Trevelyan, the foremost authority on that period; but the aged scholar had ceased all composition except his correspondence. Perhaps the last book notice ever written by Earl Cromer was a long review of the Laurens in the London Spectator, evincing the great empire builder's profound interest in the story of how British politicians of a former generation had practiced the art of empire destruction.

The following is from a review in the Boston Transcript of September 18, 1915:

"For this biography students of the Revolutionary epoch have waited long. Nor is their expectation disappointed now that, at last, the story of Henry Laurens is adequately told. . . . . An unusually vivid portrait—a remarkable one, considering how little anecdote, biography's "high light", is used. . . . . The background of the picture is also clear. We see the life of the southern American colonies; its curious and picturesque mingling of primitive and luxurious conditions, its conflicting ideals—political and industrial—before and after the Revolution. . . .

"Mr. Wallace throws much light upon several mooted historical subjects, among them: The Conway Cabal, the French Alliance, the Wilkes Fund dispute, the Deane-Lee affair."

Dr. Wallace's two-fold task in the Life of Laurens was the difficult one of writing in one narrative both the scholar's and the general reader's account of the great South Carolina business man, planter, statesman, and diplomat. How well he succeeded is testified by the fact that the most exacting historical critics gave the work cordial approval, while a journal of the popular appeal of the New York *World* devoted an entire page to review and quotations.

Dr. Wallace's interest in political science is only second to his interest in history. In 1906 he prepared a small volume, The Civil Government of South Carolina and the United States, which has been ever since the State adopted school text.* Scholars in several other States have requested permission to combine the national part of the book with State treatments of their own commonwealth governments.

A larger work published in 1916 is The Government of England, Central, Local and Imperial.** This as a straightforward, untechnical account of the British ministerial system free from the historical and legalistic lumber that so commonly repels the general reader from a subject so important to the citizens of any free country, or any country that would be free. The *Presbyterian Advance* described

* G. P. Putnam's Sons, New York and London.
*Southern Publishing Company, Dallas, Texas.
**G. P. Putnam's Sons, New York and London.

it as "a fascinating book on government," while the New York Tribune spoke of it as follows:

"Just as some of the best works on the government of America have been written by Britons and Frenchmen, so some of the best on the British government have proceeded from American pens. . . . As a clear, concise, illuminating and convincing analysis of the British system of government, and an instructive and suggestive comparison of it with the American, it has no superior and leaves little, indeed, to be desired."

Dr. Wallace is at present planning work in some important phases of Reconstruction history in South Carolina. While Dr. Wallace is a Methodist who values highly the special mission of his own church, he entertains a broad tolerance towards all, not excepting those detestables of so many Evangelicals—Catholics and Unitarians. A democrat by principle as well as training, he takes a constant interest in state and national politics, so far as even to derive a certain pleasure in acting as manager at a primary election, attending a ward club meeting, or serving as delegate to a Democratic County Convention. He was an active worker for establishing the South Carolina Industrial School for Boys, for which the chief credit belongs to Mrs. Martha Orr Patterson. He was for the first six years of the existence of that institution a member of its Board of Trustees, acting as Treasurer and later as Vice-president. He was one of the first members of the State Board of Charities and Corrections, and was elected President of the Board upon the resignation of its first President, Dr. George B. Cromer.

Dr. Wallace's family life is blessed with a most charming wife, who was Miss Sophie Willis Adam, to whom he was married January 10, 1900, and four interesting and promising children. Though his chief form of recreation comes from contact with Mother Earth in the vegetable garden, the diversions that he likes best are mountain tramping and swimming.

Dr. Wallace is above all else a teacher, but a teacher who is in constant touch with the great living world. He has been rewarded by the esteem and affection of his students.

CHARLES A. JEFFERIES, M. D. For a number of years Doctor Jefferies had a large and busy practice in his home community of Gaffney, and since surrendering his professional interests for the sake of his health he has had an almost equally strenuous career looking after some extensive business affairs, particularly as a land owner, farmer and druggist.

Doctor Jefferies, who is one of the potent factors in the growth and upbuilding of Gaffney and of the surrounding territory, belongs to one of the oldest families in that section of the state. He was born seven miles southeast of the present city of Gaffney, in what was then Union, now Cherokee, County in 1868, a son of William and Ramath (Hames) Jefferies. The Jefferies family came originally from England. In England one of the most famous of the family, spelling his name somewhat differently, was the great jurist and statesman Jeffreys. The American branch of the family settled in Virginia, and prior to the Revolutionary war established homes in what is now Cherokee County, South Carolina.

Doctor Jefferies is also a descendant of the Curry family, his father's mother having been a Curry. Through this line his great-great-grandfather was Nicholas Curry, a soldier in the battle of King's Mountain. The Currys are of Scotch origin, and, coming from Virginia to South Carolina, settled in the upper part of Union County before the Revolutionary war.

William Jefferies, father of Doctor Jefferies, was a prominent South Carolinian. He was born in the same vicinity as his son, spent his life there, and died in 1906. He owned large parcels of land, was a planter, and had many business interests in Gaffney and other places. He was chosen to represent Union County in the State Legislature as early as 1858, when only twenty-one years of age. He was a Confederate soldier throughout the war, and had an active part in reconstruction. He was a member of the famous Wallace House of 1876. He was the first state senator from the new county of Cherokee after its organization in 1897. Many years prior to that he was one of the first to advocate the creation of a new county. Active in the Methodist Church, he was prominent in Sunday school work. He was one of the builders of the first cotton mill at Gaffney.

Charles A. Jefferies graduated from Wofford College at Spartanburg in 1887 and took his medical work in Tulane University at New Orleans, where he graduated in 1892. He first practiced in his home community and in 1896 located at Gaffney. Several years ago his arduous duties resulted in a threatened breakdown of his health, and he gave up medical practice and has since been entirely devoted to his business and farming interests. These interests alone constitute him one of the most useful men of Cherokee County. He is principal owner of the Cherokee Drug Company in Gaffney, a director of the First National Bank, and is chairman of the Board of Directors of the American State Bank at Gaffney, which was organized in 1919. He is also one of the most extensive cotton planters in the state and the owner of a number of farms in Cherokee County. One of them, the largest and the one in which he takes most pride, lies in the upper part of Union County, and he owns and controls about 3,000 acres.

He has never held or aspired to any public office, being a quiet, easy, plain citizen.

J. ROY FANT. The late John A. Fant established the Monarch Mills at Union in 1900, and was president and treasurer of that important industry for the manufacture of wide print cloths and sheetings until 1907. Thus the name Fant has been associated with the textile industry of Union County through two decades, and the initiative and enterprise of the elder Fant are projected into the present by his capable son J. Roy, who is now managing the Lockhart plant of the Monarch Mills.

John A. Fant was born in Union County and for many years was a prominent merchant at Union, in partnership with his brother under the firm name of Fant Brothers until 1900, after which date he gave all his time and energy to the development of the business of the Monarch Mills and made it one of the largest and most successful textile mills in the South. He was frequently honored with public responsibilities, being mayor of Union, three terms, resigning that office voluntarily. For several years he was chairman of the Board of Trustees of Union, and was a trustee of Furman University at Greenville. He made an endowment to Furman University of $1,000 for the benefit of one student from Union County. Mr. Fant was in every sense a highly useful and gifted citizen. His death in 1907 came when he was in the prime of his activity. The mother was a McJunkin, of a historic family of Union County. John A. Fant married Ora Wilkes, who was born at Wilkesburg in Chester County, daughter of the late Major John W. Wilkes, and she is still living.

J. Roy Fant was born at Union in 1885, and secured a liberal education, at Furman University one year, graduated from the University of South Carolina in 1906, and also attended the Eastman Business College at Poughkeepsie, New York. In January, 1907, he became an associate with his father in the cotton mill business in the Monarch Mill at Union. Later he became an active associate of Mr. Emslie Nicholson, who succeeded his father as president of the Monarch Mills. In 1913 Mr. Fant was made vice president of the Nicholson Bank & Trust Company at Union and held that office two years. In August, 1914, he came to the Lockhart Mills at Lockhart as assistant treasurer, and in the latter part of 1917 this mill was merged with the Monarch Mills at Union, being now known as the Lockhart plant of the Monarch Mills. Mr. Fant has active charge of the Lockhart plant, which has 57,184 spindles and manufactures sheetings and prints. The development of Lockhart as a manufacturing village has taken place largely under the eye and direction of Mr. Fant. His sound judgment and ability had contributed not only to the success of the plant but he has been equally enthusiastic in the making of Lockhart a beautiful and modern village where contentment and prosperity are in evidence on every hand. Mr. Fant is president of the Lockhart Bank and vice president and a director of the Nicholson Bank & Trust Company at Union.

Mr. Fant married Miss Nathalie Hunter, who is a native of Union County but was reared at Columbia in the home of her grand mother, Mrs. Robert W. Gibbes, and is therefore a member of the historic Gibbes family of South Carolina. Mr. and Mrs. Fant have two sons, J. Roy, Jr., and Murray Gibbes.

JAMES FITZ-JAMES CALDWELL. Though one of the most retiring and modest of men, James Fitz-James Caldwell has rendered many conspicuous services to his state, as a soldier, author, lawyer and man of affairs.

He was born September 19, 1837, at Newberry, where he is also passing his declining years. He is a son of James John and Nancy Morgan (McMorries) Caldwell. His great-grandfather, John Caldwell, came from County Antrim, Ireland, in 1770. The grandfather, Dan Caldwell, was born in 1769 and spent his life as a farmer. James J. Caldwell, who was born in Newberry County January 13, 1799, acquired his early education in the Mount

Robert W. Gibbes, M.D.

Bethel Academy, and in December, 1815, entered South Carolina College, graduating three years later. He was admitted to the bar in 1820 and practiced at Newberry until 1843, when he removed to Columbia. He was a man of high principles, and it is said that he was once defeated as a candidate for the State Legislature because he refused to subscribe to the usual practice of furnishing free liquor to voters. Later he was elected and served in the Legislature from 1830 to 1835, and was then chosen solicitor for the Southwestern District, and in 1846 was elected to the Chancery Bench, an office he filled with great ability until his death in 1850. Chancellor Caldwell has been called one of the ablest orators the state ever produced.

James Fitz-James Caldwell, who was one of a family of nine children, attended school at Columbia, Anderson and Pendleton, and the South Carolina College. He received no degree because he refused a position offered at graduation, and thus forfeited his diploma. Afterwards he pursued the study of law for several months in the University of Berlin. He was admitted to the bar in January, 1859, having studied in the office of General James Simons of Charleston.

Mr. Caldwell was in the Confederate army throughout the war, serving in the First Regiment of South Carolina Infantry, Gregg's Regiment. He was promoted from the ranks for "skill and valor on the field of battle," and finally served as aide de camp to Gen. Samuel McGowan in McGowan's South Carolina Brigade. While there he collected in memory and notes the data from which he prepared a "History of a Brigade of South Carolinans," which has been pronounced one of the best contributions from either side to the literature of the Civil war. This book was published in 1866. Three-fourths or more of it was written in camp.

From 1870 to 1890 Mr. Caldwell practiced law in partnership with Major Suber. He is now practically retired from professional work. He has served as director and attorney of the National Bank of Newberry, the Newberry Savings Bank and National Bank of Greenwood, and has represented other important interests. He became chairman of the County Democratic Executive Committee at its organization in 1868, and in that year Newberry was one of the few counties in the state in which democracy was successful. He was again chosen county chairman in 1877. He has been in politics for the sake of good government, and has never been interested in political honors for himself. In fact the only public office he ever held was as trustee of the University of South Carolina. He is a member of the Protestant Episcopal Church.

At Cokesbury, South Carolina, September 29, 1875, he married Rebecca Capers Connor, daughter of Francis A. Connor of Cokesbury.

ROBERT W. GIBBES, M. D. While for a number of years he was a physician of large general practice at Columbia, Doctor Gibbes' work is now limited to the X-Ray, and as a specialist in that field he ranks as the foremost in South Carolina.

While Doctor Gibbes was born at Quincy, Florida, August 20, 1872, he is a member of the South Carolina Gibbes, a family of real renown and widely known prominence of achievement and personal character. His parents were Colonel James Guignard and Rhoda (Waller) Gibbes. Doctor Gibbes' great-great-grandfather was a planter on the Island of Barbadoes, and afterwards removed to Charleston, founding the family in this state. Many of the name have been prominent in the professions, in politics, as soldiers, engineers, and in various fields of practical achievement. Dr. Gibbes is the third Robert W. Gibbes to pursue the profession of medicine and surgery. One of them was his grandfather, and the other an uncle. One very notable member of the family was Major Wade Tampton Gibbes, who served with the rank of Major of Artillery in the Confederate army, and subsequently was a prominent official, merchant and banker at Columbia.

Colonel James Guignard Gibbes was born in Columbia January 6, 1829, was a graduate of South Carolina College in 1847, and pursued special studies in mathematics and engineering in the South Carolina Military Academy at Charleston. In 1852 he became chief engineer of the New Orleans, Opelousas and Great Western Railway, the first railroad built west of the Mississippi, now a part of the Southern Pacific System. In 1854 he began the construction of the Columbia and Augusta Railroad, which was not completed until after the war. Following the war he built several of the Plant lines in Florida and Georgia. Because of his interests as a railroad builder he moved to Florida in 1870, but returned to Columbia in 1890. About 1887 he was made chief engineer of the Pensacola and Mobile Railroad, later a part of the Louisville and Nashville System.

Colonel Gibbes had a prominent part in the fortunes of his State during the Confederacy. He contributed millions to help the Confederacy, and was much impoverished in consequence. While he enlisted as a soldier he was detailed by the Government to take charge of his Saluda factory to make cloth for the Confederacy. He was also successful in negotiating a Confederate cotton loan in Europe, and while abroad attended the marriage of the Prince of Wales. He was chosen mayor of the city of Columbia the day after it was burned by Sherman, holding the office two years. He served as collector of internal revenue during 1865-66. From 1890 he was state land agent, and is credited with having put on the tax books a million acres of land. He was twice married, his marriage to Miss Rhoda Waller, then Mrs. Gilchrist, being celebrated August 8, 1870.

Dr. Robert W. Gibbes was graduated from the South Carolina University in 1892 and finished his work in South Carolina Medical College in 1895. He was an honor graduate of his medical school and during 1895-96 was resident physician of the Charleston City Hospital, locating in Columbia in 1896. In 1905, and again in 1909, he made extensive tours through Europe, visiting the various hospitals and medical colleges, where he pursued intensive clinical research, particularly at the University of Vienna where he enjoyed special opportunities and privileges, under the personal guidance of Professor Holtzneck, head of the Roentgen Department of the

University, and a noted pioneer in Gastro-Intestinal work.

Some years ago Dr. Gibbes became the pioneer X-Ray specialist in Columbia. In fact he began his studies of this marvelous discovery soon after it was announced from Europe, and acquired his first X-Ray equipment soon after the value of the X-Ray was demonstrated as an essential in modern medical and surgical practice. In passing years he has devoted himself exclusively to this line of work. His laboratory is at 1508 Sumter Street, and is one of the most complete in the South. He is the X-Ray scientist for the medical profession in Columbia and his part of the South, and is a member of a number of scientific societies relating to the X-Ray. He is also a member of the Columbia Medical Society and the State and American Medical Associations. November 29, 1900, Dr. Gibbes married Miss Ethel Dole Andrews of Woodworth, Wisconsin.

A cousin of Dr. Gibbes is the eminent Dr. J. Heyward Gibbes of Columbia, who as a specialist in internal diseases is one of the ablest men in the South. He was educated also at the University of South Carolina, receiving his A. B. and B. S. degrees from that institution, while his degree in medicine was awarded by Johns Hopkins University. He was resident physician in the hospital of Johns Hopkins University for two years before beginning practice in Columbia. He has also spent much time abroad in Europe in post-graduate study and investigation.

SAMUEL B. GEORGE, a former clerk of the court of Lexington County, is president of the Home National Bank of Lexington, and has been an active and influential factor in that part of the state for many years. He organized the Home National Bank in 1908 with a capital of $25,000, this capital being increased in 1919 to $50,000. The bank has a surplus of $10,000 and deposits averaging $300,000.

Mr. George also organized and is secretary and treasurer of the Citizens Telephone Company, operating 550 telephones in and around Lexington. Among other interests he owns and operates a 200-acre farm.

Mr. George was born at Laurel Falls Homestead, near Lexington, July 27, 1871, a son of E. J. and Bedia (Taylor) George. He is descended from Ludwig George, who came from Switzerland and joined the American army at Charleston toward the close of the Revolutionary struggle. He afterwards settled in Lexington County, where he died in 1807.

E. J. George was a planter and miller, a very capable and industrious man, and gave his son plenty of work to do to develop habits of industry and judgment. Samuel B. attended the local schools, also the public schools of Lexington, and acquired a good education by study at night and by constant use of the opportunities presented by papers and good magazines and other literature. From the age of nineteen he for several years had charge of his father's flour mills, cotton gins and corn mills. On his twenty-first birthday he was commissioned a notary public and on December 19, 1892, was made official court deputy of the clerk of court. He was elected to that office in 1900, and held it for eight years. He was also commissioner of elections for delegates to the constitutional convention in 1895, and has served as member of the County Board of Education. He has been a prominent official of the Methodist Episcopal Church, South, at Lexington, and is a Knight Templar Mason, a Shriner, member of the Knights of Pythias, Junior Order of United American Mechanics and Sons of Confederate Veterans.

December 29, 1896, he married Miss Olga O. Hendrix, a daughter of J. S. and Martha Hendrix. To their marriage were born five children, Celeste O., now Mrs. Henry Wienges, Samuel A., Juanita O., Francis C. and Sol Irby.

ROBERT THOMAS JENNINGS, M. D. An important use of the opportunities and privileges of the medical profession has been made by Dr. Robert Thomas Jennings, formerly of McCormick and for the past ten years of Columbia. Doctor Jennings in addition to a large private practice in medicine and surgery is resident physician for the South Carolina State Penitentiary and for the Reform Institute for Colored Youth near Columbia.

He was born at Edgefield, South Carolina, in 1876, and comes of a family of physicians. The Jennings family is of English origin and was established several generations ago in Edgefield District of South Carolina. His parents are Dr. W. D. and Mattie Elizabeth (Turner) Jennings, who now reside at Augusta, Georgia, where his father has carried on a large practice for many years. Dr. W. D. Jennings was also born and educated in Edgefield County. He enlisted at the age of sixteen in the Confederate army and performed the duties of a private soldier, while his uncle, Dr. J. H. Jennings, was a surgeon in the Confederacy.

Robert Thomas Jennings received his early education in a private school at Edgefield, and took his medical course in the Medical Department of the University of the South at Sewanee, Tennessee, graduating with the class of 1897. For a time he practiced at Augusta, Georgia, then for twelve years was at McCormick, South Carolina, and since 1909 has found a larger scope for his experience and abilities in the capital city of the state. Doctor Jennings is a member of the Executive Board of the Columbia Hospital, and is affiliated with the Columbia Medical Society and the State and American Medical associations. He is a member of the Masonic Order and belongs to the Main Street Methodist Church, South, in Columbia.

He married Miss Lillie May Talbert of McCormick County, daughter of Dr. R. J. Talbert. They have two children, Permelia and William Robert Jennings.

CHARLES C. STANLEY. For over twenty years Doctor Stanley has enjoyed a substantial professional reputation as a dental surgeon at Columbia. In this time he has also served in the U. S. army in a professional capacity in two wars.

In the fall of 1919 he resumed his private practice after having been continuously on duty sixteen months in the dental department of the United States Army. He offered his services to the Government through Secretary Baker soon after the beginning of the war in April, 1917. He passed the

examination required for military dental service and was commissioned a first lieutenant in November, 1917. He was called to active duty May 26, 1918, with the First Battalion of the Fiftieth Infantry, stationed at Curtis Bay Ordnance Depot, South Baltimore. Later he was transferred to the Third Battalion of the same regiment at Potomac Park, Washington. His most important work, and the experience which counted for the greatest good to him in a professional way and through which he rendered his greatest service in the war, was his work in the dental infirmary of St. Elizabeth's Hospital in Washington. Here he had charge of the dental infirmary and in this institution many thousands of soldiers and sailors were treated. Under Doctor Stanley was a staff of ambitious and capable young dentists. The duties of this staff were both examination and treatment, and many of the soldiers were for the first time in their lives impressed with the importance of the care of the teeth. Beside the practical benefit of this work to the young men in fitting them for military efficiency it will have an untold value in all future years as a means of proper education and understanding of measures necessary for good health. Doctor Stanley received his discharge from the army dental service September 4, 1919, and shortly afterward received his commission as Captain U. S. Reserves, this commission having been held up on account of the signing of the armistice.

Doctor Stanley was born and has spent most of his life in Columbia, where he represents one of the oldest and most substantial families. His great-grandfather was a large property holder in the city. He owned the entire block within which stands the First Presbyterian Church. He donated part of this land to the church and is buried in the church yard.

Doctor Stanley's grandfather was R. H. Stanley, a civil engineer and one of the pioneer settlers of Butler County, Alabama. A brother of R. H. Stanley, Capt. W. B. Stanley, a veteran of the famous Palmetto Regiment, was president of the old Central National Bank of Columbia, president of the Columbia Gas Company, President of the Board of Regents of the State Hospital and one of the wealthiest and most influential citizens of Columbia in his day. He was one of the city's aldermen when Sherman entered Columbia and was the first to occupy the office of intendant or mayor after the redemption of the state from "carpet bag rule."

John Calhoun Stanley, Doctor Stanley's father, entered the Confederate Army at the age of seventeen and was badly wounded at the battle of Malvern Hill. Though crippled in body and fortune by the war, yet with undaunted courage, he came to Columbia at the close of the war and soon became one of the city's most successful business men. He was a member of the Board of School Commissioners which established the present system of graded schools, and as a member of the City Council from Ward three he did much to further the interests of the schools.

Doctor Stanley's mother was Miss Mary Isabel Carrington, whose paternal ancestors were among the early settlers of Concord, Massachusetts.

Charles Carrington Stanley was educated in the public schools of Columbia, in Professor Clarkson's private school, and in Patrick's Military Institute at Anderson. He studied dentistry at the University of Maryland, graduating in 1894, did his post-graduate work in 1895 and for a year was demonstrator in extraction in the Dental School of the University. Then followed several busy years building up a practice in his home city. During the Spanish-American war Doctor Stanley was given the Government contract for the dental work of the First and Second South Carolina regiments. He is a member of the State, National and Army Dental associations. Doctor Stanley represented Ward Three in the City Council.

He married Miss Annie Wilson, of Monongahela, Pennsylvania. Their only son, John Carrington Stanley, was the youngest graduate of the University of South Carolina in the class of '17. He was instructor of chemistry and junior law student at the university at the outbreak of the war, when he volunteered for the Aviation Corps and was stationed at Kelly Field, Texas. Since the close of the war he has been employed as chemist in the Duquesne Steel Works near Pittsburgh, Pennsylvania.

OLIVER P. LOYAL. While he is recognized as one of the younger business men of Columbia, Mr. Loyal has made his initiative and enterprise count as influential factors in several important lines, each contributing towards the advancement of the Capital City as a business and commercial center. He is an official of the Palmetto National Bank, one of the leading financial institutions of the South; secretary of the Carolina Wholesale Hardware Company; treasurer of the Southern Motor Company, and president of the Loyal-Covin Contracting Company.

Mr. Loyal is of Scotch and French ancestry and was born at Garnett in Hampton County, December 7, 1891. His parents were Louis Charles, Jr., and Fannie (Bostick) Loyal, the former a native of Hampton County. The Bosticks are a Scotch family of lower Carolina. The grandfather, Rev. Louis Charles Loyal, was born in France, and on coming to South Carolina in the early forties settled in Hampton County, where for a number of years he was widely known as a Methodist minister.

Oliver P. Loyal attended the Garnett graded schools and also Wofford College at Spartanburg, and has been a resident of Columbia since 1907. After two years of employment with the passenger department of the Southern Railway, he entered the Palmetto National Bank, and on the merit of good service has been promoted to the assistant cashiership, an office he has held since 1917.

Mr. Loyal is one of the organizers and is joint owner with Mr. L. S. Covin of the Southern Motor Company. This well known Columbia concern are distributors for the Marmon, American Six, Scripps-Booth Six automobiles, and the White truck. Since taking up his work as a building contractor Mr. Loyal has done an extensive business in Columbia. He is one of that city's hardest working young business men, and is closely identified with its every movement for advancement and progress.

Mr. Loyal married Miss Lidie Richbourg of Dillon, South Carolina. They have one son, Henry Richbourg Loyal.

SEWALL KEMBLE OLIVER is a graduate engineer and has given his professional services largely to the cotton mill industry of the South and has achieved especial prominence. With headquarters at Columbia, he represents one of the leading cotton mills of the state as their agent.

Mr. Oliver was born at Baltimore, Maryland, June 25, 1884, a son of Charles K. and Catherine C. (Reed) Oliver. He had a private school education, and afterward prepared at Worcester Academy, Worcester, Massachusetts, and finished with a chemical and general engineering course at Yale University in the Sheffield Scientific School. The cotton industry and cotton milling have been familiar to him practically since early youth, since his father was connected with and interested in several mills and organized the Columbia Mills of this city and helped develop the water power at Columbia. Mr. Oliver during 1908-09 was superintendent of the Druid Mills and in 1909 came to Columbia as superintendent of the Columbia Mills Company. He is also a bank director and is one of the busy and successful men of the capital city.

October 23, 1909, he married Miss Lucy Hardy, of Norfolk, Virginia. Her father, Caldwell Hardy, is a former president of the Norfolk National Bank and the Norfolk Savings & Trust Company and agent of the Richmond district, of the Federal Reserve Bank. Mr. and Mrs. Oliver have three children: Sewall Kemble, Jr., Hardy and Lucy. Mr. Oliver is a member and vice president of the Rotary Club and also a member of the Ridgewood and Columbia Clubs.

COLUMBIA MILLS. The first cotton mills in South Carolina and, in fact, in the United States, to be completely electrically driven were the Columbia Mills, which also enjoy another well earned distinction as among the largest heavy duck mills in the world.

These mills were organized by Mr. Charles K. Oliver and building started early in 1892. Operation of the mills was begun in 1893. The motive power were the first induction motors ever manufactured larger than 15 H. P. All the electrical equipment was supplied by the General Electric Company. The powerhouse was located between the canal and river, and electric power was developed from water taken from the Columbia Canal. There was a distinct advantage in this, since through transmission of electric current the necessity was eliminated of locating the mills in the low ground along the canal or river, thus securing a more elevated position than had been therefore possible for any of the cotton mills operated direct by water power.

Up to 1900 the mills were continued under the original management, with Aretas Blood as president and Charles K. Oliver treasurer, secretary and general manager. During those early years the well known Aretas brand achieved its reputation. In 1900 the Mount Vernon-Woodberry Cotton Duck Company of Baltimore acquired a large part of the stock.

The product has probably exceeded that of the combined output of all the other mills in Columbia. In 1916 nearly $700,000 were paid out for labor, figures that graphically indicate the tremendous importance of the mill as a source of prosperity to Columbia. At that time about 1,700 names were on the payroll.

The mill village is situated on high ground on the Lexington side of the river and for years the people of Columbia and the managers of the mill have taken pride in the model character of this village. All the facilities for welfare, recreation, education, and other means of enlightenment have been introduced, and probably no mills in the state are surrounded by a more permaent and contented and prosperous class of working people.

For the past eleven years the agent of the Columbia Mills Company has been Sewall K. Oliver, a son of the founder of the industry, Charles K. Oliver.

FREDERICK HARGROVE HYATT entered the life insurance business thirty-five years ago, and on the basis of accomplished results he has become one of the most widely known insurance men in the South. For many years he was general manager for South Carolina with the Mutual Life Insurance Company of New York.

He was born in Anson County, North Carolina, June 14, 1849, son of Davis and Louisa (Pumbleton) Hyatt. He is of remote German ancestry on his father's side and of English through his mother. His mother was a relative of Bishop R. K. Hargrove of the Methodist Church. His father was a farmer and manufacturer, and Frederick H. grew up on his father's farm and early learned the value of hard labor as a means to success. He acquired his early education in the Field schools, also attended Anson Academy and Rutherford College, each in North Carolina, paying the greater part of his expenses while in school, by clerking at night and Saturdays in one of the local stores. His favorite subjects in school and since have been mathematics and commercial law.

In 1884 Mr. Hyatt became superintendent of the agents of the Valley Mutual Life Insurance Association of Virginia. He soon determined to ally himself with the "old line" branch of insurance, for about two years was a sub-agent with the New York Life Insurance Company, and subsequently became district agent for the Mutual Life Insurance Company. In 1892 he was appointed general manager of the Mutual Life for the states of North and South Carolina.

A number of important enterprises have been promoted and have been benefited by his participation and influence. From 1894 to 1896 he served as president of the Columbia and Eau Claire Railroad Company. He has been a director of the National Loan and Exchange Bank, of the Columbia Loan and Trust Company, vice president of the Public Service Company, treasurer of the Southern Cotton Association of South Carolina, secretary of the Hyatt Brick Company, and president of the South Carolina Marble Works. He has been interested in dairy farming for a number of years and is owner of much valuable real estate, having laid out and developed "Hyatt Park," a suburb of Columbia.

In 1896 Mr. Hyatt became president of the Young Men's Christian Association of Columbia, and has served as a member of the board of trustees and

on the executive committee of Columbia College. He may justly be called the founder of this institution, since in addition to a very liberal cash donation he gave the land upon which the college buildings were erected, besides devoting his time and effort in raising the additional funds necessary for the building and establishment of the college. He is a democrat, and one of the leading laymen of the Methodist Episcopal Church, South. He became superintendent of the Washington Street Methodist Sunday School in 1900 and served as president of the State Sunday School Association during 1894-95. He has also been identified with the good roads movement, and his influence and example both in private and business life have been a source of constant value to his home city and state.

August 12, 1874, Mr. Hyatt married Miss Lena S. Kendall. She was the mother of eleven children. April 13, 1908, Mr. Hyatt married Miss Daisy Bartlett Kistler, of Columbus, Ohio, and to them have been born three daughters.

CLAUDIUS M. LIDE is a prominent building contractor of Columbia and has been one of that city's progressive young business men for nearly twenty years.

Bishop Gregg's well known "History of the Cheraws" contains numerous references to the Lides and their kinsmen the Colters, as among the historic families of the Pee Dee section of South Carolina. The Lide family according to this authority came from Wales, where they had lived for generations, to America about 1740, settling in the old Cheraw district. There were three brothers, John, Thomas and Robert. The name was originally spelled Lloyd. Colonel Thomas Lide, second of the three brothers, settled on the Pee Dee River at Cheraw Hill. He had an active part in the organization of St. David's parish, giving the land for the church buildings and afterwards continuing generous contributions to the maintenance of the church. One of his daughters was the mother of the late Governor John Lide Wilson. The youngest of the three brothers was Major Robert Lide, who served as an officer in the Revolutionary war under General Francis Marion. Hannah, one of his daughters, married Thomas Hart, for whom the town of Hartsville was named. One of Thomas Lide's sons was Charles Motte Lide, to whom history has assigned a high place as a lawyer of genius and a famous orator.

Claudius M. Lide was born at Darlington, South Carolina, in 1878, son of John Miller and Eliza (Edwards) Lide, the latter a native of Georgia. John M. Lide was also a native of Darlington, son of Evans James Lide. He was educated in Furman University and from that school entered the Confederate army, serving four years.

Claudius M. Lide attended the famous St. John's graded school in Darlington, and began his business career as an architectural draftsman in the office of C. C. Wilson and W. A. Edwards, architects, at Columbia. His home has been in Columbia since he was eighteen years of age. Mr. Lide for several years has had an established and independent business as a building contractor. He has specialized somewhat in the building of fine residences in Columbia and over the State, and has also built a number of public buildings and business structures. A complete list of his achievements would be hardly practicable, but some of the more representative include the Darlington High School building, the Girls' Industrial School near Columbia, the Kirkland Apartments in Columbia, the Taylor store building in Columbia, the residence of Dr. Robert W. Gibbes on Calhoun Street in Columbia.

Mr. Lide is a member of the Rotary Club, and is a thirty-second degree Scottish Rite Mason and a member of Omar Temple of the Mystic Shrine at Charleston.

DR. LAURENCE P. GEER came to South Carolina as a member of the Public Health Service of the Government during the war, and after resigning from that work determined to remain in this state and is founder and active head of the pathological laboratory of the Baptist Hospital at Columbia.

Doctor Geer, though he was born and reared and educated in the heart of New England, feels a kinship with South Carolina, since one branch of his English ancestors, who settled in New England in the seventeenth century, came south and founded the widely known Geer family in this state.

Doctor Geer was born at Lynn, Massachusetts, in 1891, a son of Charles W. and Izzette (Patten) Geer. His mother was a native of Lynn, while his father was born at Norwich, Connecticut. Charles W. Geer died at Lynn in 1913.

Laurence P. Geer was graduated with the degree Bachelor of Science from the Massachusetts Institute of Technology in 1915. He specialized in biology and public health work, and that training has been the basis of his vocation and profession. At the beginning of the war with Germany he volunteered in the United States Public Health Service, and his previous training made him a valuable adjunct to that service. He was assigned to duty at Camp Jackson, Columbia, and continued there until the close of the war, when he resigned and in the summer of 1919 established the pathological laboratory of the Baptist Hospital. He has a fully equipped laboratory for all kinds of tests and scientific research as an adjunct to the hospital and to the medical profession in general. Doctor Geer is a man of thorough scientific training and tastes and his presence at Columbia is an important contribution to that city.

JESSE BENJAMIN BALLENTINE after finishing his college education entered upon a career as a teacher, and was identified with the schools of Batesburg prior to his leaving educational work and entering banking, which is the field in which his energies and talents are employed with conspicuous success.

Mr. Ballentine was born in Lexington County August 19, 1888, a son of William Jonas and Helen (Riser) Ballentine. He grew up on his father's farm, attended country schools, the high school at Lexington, received his Master of Arts degree from Newberry College and was also a student in South Carolina College. In 1913 he became principal of the Prosperity High School, remained there two years, was principal of the Brightsville High School one year, and for two years was superintendent of the Batesburg schools. In August, 1918, he was made manager of the Batesburg branch of the Bank of Western Carolina. In addition to the responsibilities of that position he is vice president of the local Board of Trade, and chairman of the local Red Cross. He is a prominent member of the Lutheran Church.

March 19, 1917, he married Mary Sue Griffin of Greenwood. They have a son James Bruce, born June 21, 1918.

LARKIN LeROY CLIPPARD. While one of the younger figures among the cotton manufacturers of South Carolina, Larkin LeRoy Clippard of Enoree has an interesting record as a builder and reviver of industry. He learned cotton milling when a boy, and is still a comparatively young man. In 1915 Mr. Clippard in association with Mr. Allan J. Graham of Greenville bought the Enoree Mills at Enoree in Spartanburg County. They faced a prospect that might have discouraged men of less enterprise and confidence in their own judgment and abilities. Not a wheel had turned in the plant for nearly a year. The mills presented a picture not only of idleness but of settling ruin. The new owners bought the industry from a receiver and started at once to completely make over the facilities at hand. While they have been in charge less than five years, the result is now one of the finest cotton manufacturing plants in the state. The Enoree Mill has 36,000 spindles, 842 looms, and manufactures enormous quantities of sheeting and drills. The mill is capitalized at $600,000. The president and treasurer of the company is Mr. Graham, while Mr. Clippard is vice president and general manager.

The Enoree mill is located on the Enoree River. A dam and water power are the source of electricity for operating the plant and other local industries. The prosperity of the business itself has been reflected in the model mill village which has been developed and is in process of development. Those at the head of the business are guided by high ideals and purposes in line with the most advanced and progressive thought of the new industrial aids. In less than five years the village and its homes have been practically rebuilt, most of the old houses being replaced by new ones. Important public utilities are electric lights, water works, ice plant and laundry. The ground about the individual homes, will be beautified and public playgrounds and recreation spots will be laid out and constructed. The company at its own expense has erected a handsome new school building at a cost of $30,000. Six teachers are employed in this building and practically all the salaries are paid by the company. Many other features of modern community and welfare work have been instituted, such as girls' clubs, mothers' clubs, a canning club which in 1918 put up 2,000 cans of fruit and vegetables furnished by the company. During the summer of 1919 plans were under way for a Young Men's Christian Association and Young Women's Christian Association Building and hardly a phase of community progress has been neglected.

Mr. Clippard in July, 1919, married Miss Katharine Murchison of Camden, South Carolina. She is a member of an old and prominent Scotch family of lower South Carolina.

BENJAMIN FRANKLIN PERRY LEAPHART began his career over thirty years ago as a bank clerk at Columbia, has been a figure of increasing importance and influence in the financial life of the capital city, and among other things to his credit was the founding of the Columbia Clearing House Association.

He was born at Columbia December 27, 1867, a son of John Samuel and Martha Virginia (Janney) Leaphart. His father is remembered for his long service of a quarter of a century as assistant postmaster of Columbia, holding that position under various postmasters. The son was educated in private schools, in the South Carolina College, and his first bank clerkship was with the Commercial Bank of Columbia. Later he became one of the organizers of the Bank of Columbia and was its bookkeeper and assistant cashier fifteen years. He was then elected president of the Columbia Savings Bank and Trust Company, and in 1907 established the Columbia Clearing House Association of which he has since been secretary, treasurer and manager. The Clearing House Association has a membership of ten banks, and these institutions clear $16,000,000 through the association every month.

Mr. Leaphart is a member and former deacon of the First Baptist church and is affiliated with the Knights of Pythias. On April 17, 1900, he married Miss Annie Louise Bruce of Columbia, daughter of Horace E. Bruce. Her father was a native of England and for many years a merchant at Columbia. Mr. and Mrs. Leaphart have two children: Benjamin Franklin Perry, Jr., a student in the University of South Carolina; and Edwin Bruce, attending high school.

THOMAS WALTER BOYLE. Every man has a proper pride in the growth and success of his individual business and affairs. When that pride is enlarged and seasoned with a sincere public spirit, derived from the growth and prosperity of an entire community, it is deserving of special praise and commendation. It is the enthusiasm which he has always shown in the upbuilding of the Greeleyville community in Williamsburg County that distinguished Thomas Walter Boyle beyond the average successful business man. He went to that locality in 1886, nearly thirty-five years ago, when it was known as Greeleyville and a flag stop on the Atlantic Coast Line Railroad. Though at that time he was only a saw mill laborer, Mr. Boyle has furnished much of the enterprise for several of the institutions that give Greeleyville its business significance, and all the various lines of development, benefiting every person living in that section, have been matters of the deepest satisfaction to Mr. Boyle.

He was born near Ridgeway in Fairfield County in 1856, son of William C. and Virginia (Hogan) Boyle. His father was born about thirteen miles north of Columbia in Richland County on the Winnsboro Road, but subsequently lived on a plantation near Ridgeway in Fairfield County some twenty miles north of Columbia. He left his plantation at the beginning of the war between the States, and while serving as a Confederate soldier was killed in the battle of Lookout Mountain in 1863.

Besides the loss of his father Thomas Walter

Boyle had the other handicaps imposed upon every South Carolina youth by the extreme poverty of the state in the reconstruction period. He lived on a plantation, worked in the fields, and was well satisfied with the wage of twenty-five cents a day.

Mr. Boyle was taken into the firm of Boyle & Hogan, and five years later E. G. Mallard acquired an interest. By mutual agreement the name of the company has emphasized the oldest member of the firm. Therefore this business is known as the Mallard Lumber Company, with Mr. Boyle as vice president. While the manufacture of lumber constitutes his oldest interest in the community, Mr. Boyle is also president of the Bank of Greeleyville, is president of the Greeleyville Land & Improvement Company, and through these companies exercises a controlling influence in local lumber manufacture, merchandising, planting and other interests.

When Mr. Boyle came to Greeleyville it had only a saw mill, a store and two dwelling houses, the nearest school was five miles away, and the nearest telegraph office and passenger train station was at Foreston, six miles away. Considering the present resources of Greeleyville it is easy to understand Mr. Boyle's pride and satisfaction in what has been accomplished during the past thirty years. He is an active member of the Methodist Church, is affiliated with the Masons, Knights of Pythias and Woodmen of the World. He married Mrs. Ella Boyle Hogan.

THOMAS KETCHIN ELLIOTT, for over forty years a prominent banker, manufacturer and citizen of Winnsboro, was born in the years before the war and grew up in the straitened atmosphere of the State during the war and reconstruction.

His birth occurred in Fairfield County October 8, 1855, son of a merchant and banker and farmer, Henry Laurens Elliott. Though his mature career has been spent in business affairs, Thomas K. Elliott had some active acquaintance with manual toil as a boy in the fields and on the farm. He attended country schools, and in 1875 graduated from the Virginia Military Institute ranking third in a class of forty-five. He left school to take the position of teller in the Winnsboro National Bank. He has been with that institution for over forty years, and for a number of years has been its president and active executive head. Mr. Elliott was also president of the Fairfield Cotton Mills at Winnsboro and president of the Wylie Mills at Chester for many years. As a successful business man he has had a sense of responsibility to his community and to all the interests entrusted to his charge, and he has given a splendid account of his stewardship.

Mr. Elliott is a democrat, and for many years has been a member and elder in the Associate Reformed Presbyterian Church. November 26, 1879, he married Miss Carrie Aiken. To their union were born seven children.

DAVID B. FRONTIS, M. D. For fully thirty years Doctor Frontis has practiced medicine and surgery at Ridge Spring in Saluda County. The enviable standing he has achieved in his profession is supplemented by an active and influential leadership in every movement affecting that rich and prosperous and enlightened section.

While so long a resident of South Carolina Doctor Frontis is a native of North Carolina and member of an old and prominent family of that State. He was born in Iredell County in 1856, son of Rev. Stephen and Rachel (Beaty) Frontis. In the paternal line he is of French ancestry, though men of that name frequently intermarried with Scotch-Irish people in a section of North Carolina prevailingly Scotch-Irish, Mecklenburg, Iredell and Rowan counties. The Beaty family also has prominent connections in the same counties, one of the earliest settlers having established his home at Beaty's Ford in Mecklenburg County. The ancestors of Doctor Frontis were the founders of Presbyterianism in that section, beginning about 1750. Doctor Frontis' father was one of the founders of Davidson College in North Carolina, an institution which has graduated many well known men including Woodrow Wilson. Rev. Stephen Frontis was financial agent and raised much of the money among Presbyterians for the founding of Davidson College during the forties. For some time he was also a professor of the college, though his life work was that of a minister.

David B. Frontis also was a student for two and a half years in Davidson College, during 1875-76. He studied medicine in the University of Maryland, graduating in 1880. He practiced at Lexington, then for four years at Wadesboro, North Carolina, and in 1889 removed to Ridge Springs. For several years until 1910 Doctor Frontis was a member of the State Board of Health of South Carolina and one of its executive committee. He was member and examining physician for the local draft board of Saluda County and gave much of his time to that patriotic duty for eighteen months. He is a member of the County, State and American Medical associations and of the Presbyterian Church.

He married Miss Annie McKay of Baltimore. They have four children: Grace, Mrs. Ruby Watson, J. B. Frontis and Mrs. Mary Watson.

NEIL ALEXANDER MCMILLAN is a name that should go down in any authentic history of Marion County as one of the founders of what is frequently referred to as the New School of Agriculture in South Carolina.

Mr. McMillan was born in Marion County April 18, 1855, a son of Malcolm S. and Elizabeth (Williamson) McMillan. His father was a planter, and at the time of the war between the states was employed by the Confederate Government in the steamboat service, and died during the war. In helping his mother conduct the farm after the death of his father, he learned early in life to use all his faculties of observation, and, reasoning from effect to cause, he became by the time he began business for himself, convinced that the old, slipshod way of conducting farm operations which had been in vogue since slavery days, must give place to a more efficient system. From then on, he became an apostle of intensified and diversified agriculture. He has always stood for a greater and more intelligent use of commercial fertilizers; for home mixing of ingredients, based on his observation of their effects on his soil and crops; for the best and purest breeds of farm animals; for the growing on his own farm of all the farm supplies that his soil and climate could produce; for the planting of the best seed obtainable and the maintaining of the purity of the seed used, and as he believes that perfection in development is never reached, for the still further development of all seeds, and breeds of animals as well.

N. A. McMillan has always been a public spirited man. Forty-five years ago, when it was difficult to obtain fertilizers except through local agents and the prices asked therefor were almost prohibitive to the farmer, based on a credit system, he advocated the idea of the farmer mixing the ingredients himself, and by combining the needs of the farmers in his community and getting the materials in car-load lots for cash, they have been able to fully supply their demands at a minimum cost to the individual farmer. He has given his time, his thought and his best services unsparingly in thus helping and bringing together the farmers of his community, and the great progress which has been made in recent years in the upbuilding of the community in which he lives, and the community spirit which exists there may be said to be more largely due to his efforts than to any other influence. In order to better carry out his ideas of co-operation and combined energies as the most necessary and the strongest forces in the development of the country, he built and fitted up the "McMillan Hall," free of charge, as a meeting place in the town of Mullins for the farmers or for any other gathering looking to the upbuilding of the town or surrounding country.

As a result partly at least of his efforts, among other things might be mentioned the formation of a company during the fall of 1919 to buy distress cotton, which in ninety days declared a dividend of forty per cent. to stockholders; also, of a recent organization with a capital stock of $100,000 to buy, store and sell all kinds of farm produce.

Mr. McMillan has been twice married. On December 30, 1879, he married Eunice Irene Davis of Florence County. From this marriage, there are the following named children now living: Jeter Davis McMillan, Malcolm Yullee McMillan and Blanche McMillan Austin, all of Winter Garden, Florida, and Neilie McMillan, Sallie McMillan and George Reaves McMillan, all now residing in South Carolina. On June 12, 1907, he married Janet Wilson Northcross of Virginia, and they have one daughter, Lucy Lee McMillan.

JAMES R. WESTMORELAND. Westmoreland is an old English name, and the family has been one of equal distinction and of residence for almost two centuries in America. Three of the Westmorelands left England about 1732 and settled, one in Pennsylvania, one in Virginia and one on the Enoree River in what is now the southwest section of Spartanburg county and in the upper part of Laurens county. Those ancestors had a grant from the King of England to a large tract of land in that section. Some of that land has been owned and lived upon continuously by Westmorelands nearly two centuries. Through the many generations the family has performed a great deal of effective service, has rendered duty in army, in business, industry and other affairs, though few of them have aspired to the conspicuous honors of politics. Probably a majority of the men of the name have been planters, lawyers or doctors.

James R. Westmoreland, who has an interesting place in South Carolina's industrial affairs, is local manager of the Pacolet Manufacturing Company at Pacolet in Spartanburg County. He is a grandson of James R. Westmoreland and a son of John A. and Margaret (Rush) Westmoreland. He was born on the Westmoreland ancestral estate on the Enoree River in the upper part of Laurens County, adjoining the Spartanburg County line, in 1876. He is a graduate of The Citadel with the class of 1900, and is now a member of the Committee of the Alumni Association which has in charge the raising of the "Greater Citadel Fund," to promote the interests of South Carolina's famous military college and is also a member of its Executive Committee. After leaving The Citadel Mr. Westmoreland was connected for a time with the Central National Bank of Spartanburg County, and subsequently organized and for five years was connected with a bank at Woodruff. Since then he has held his present office as local manager for the great cotton mills of the Pacolet Manufacturing Company. The president of the company is Mr. Victor M. Montgomery, and in an article which follows his name is contained something of the history of this splendid industrial institution.

Mr. Westmoreland married Miss Eugenia Childs of Columbia. Her father was the late Colonel W. G. Childs of that city, builder of the Columbia, Newberry & Laurens Railroad, founder of the Bank of Columbia, and otherwise prominently identified with the leading business interests of the state. Mr. and Mrs. Westmoreland have two children, William Childs and Margaret Rush Westmoreland.

ELBERT NEWTON WHITMIRE is a well known banker in Greenville County, has been a resident of Greenville since 1912, and is president and cashier of the Textile Bank of Greenville, South Carolina, having been one of the incorporators of that bank.

Mr. Whitmire was born in Macon County, North Carolina, in 1880, and has six brothers and three sisters. His great-grandfather, John Whitmire, was born in old Pickens District, South Carolina, and lived on the Keowee River not far from old Pickens courthouse. The grandfather, William Whitmire, was born and lived in the same locality for some years, but finally moved to Rabun County, Georgia. John Columbus Whitmire, a farmer, father of the Greenville banker, was born in Rabun County, Georgia, and is still living in that state. He lived for several years in Macon County, North Carolina, where he married Miss Jane Elizabeth Williams. When Elbert Newton Whitmire was four years old, in 1884, the family returned to Georgia and located at Clayton, where Mr. Whitmire was reared on the farm and received a common school education.

He began his business career in early life. For five years, until 1905 he was identified with the management of the Norris Cotton Mills Company Store

at Cateechee, in Pickens County, South Carolina. While there he married Miss Hattie Wilson a school teacher, of Belton, South Carolina. Mrs. Whitmire is a daughter of John A. and Lucy (Horton) Wilson, both representatives of old line families in South Carolina. She is also a granddaughter of John A. Horton, who was a citizen of Anderson County near Pendleton and well and favorably known about "Old Pendleton."

In 1905 Mr. Whitmire moved to Spring Place, Murray County, Georgia, and established the Cohutta Banking Company, remaining in charge for two years. He then returned to Cateechee as manager of the Norris Cotton Mill Company's store and was again identified with that institution for five years until 1912, when he established his permanent home at Greenville.

Mr. Whitmire has had an increasing part in the commercial and financial enterprises of Greenville and vicinity. For some time he was senior member of Whitmire-Cozby Company, wholesale produce merchants. In 1918 he took the office of cashier of the Citizens Bank of Taylor. This bank is located in the prosperous and growing community of Taylor ten miles east of Greenville. In September, 1919, he was one of the incorporators and largest stockholders in The Textile Bank, which has been established at West Greenville in the midst of the many cotton mills of that section, and as stated is president and cashier.

Mr. Whitmire is a member of the Baptist Church and a Mason. He and his wife have two children, Lucy and Elbert Newton, Jr.

WILLIAM L. KIRKPATRICK, M. D. A graduate in medicine twenty-five years ago Doctor Kirpatrick has had a busy and useful career, and for a number of years has been the company physician and surgeon at Trough in Spartanburg County.

This town is distinguished as the home of the great cotton mills of the Pacolet Manufacturing Company, one of the largest textile plants and finest cotton mill villages in the South. As physician and surgeon for the community and its environs Doctor Kirkpatrick is a very active and busy practitioner, and enjoys a high place in the affection of the people he serves.

He was born in Haywood County, North Carolina, in 1870. The Kirkpatricks were originally Scotch-Irish Presbyterians among the pioneer settlers of Mecklenburg County in North Carolina. Many of them are still found there and through all the generations they have furnished prominent and patriotic citizens and leading figures in the annals of that historic section. Doctor Kirkpatrick is a son of M. A. and Annie Laurie (Byers) Kirkpatrick, and is a grandson of Silas F. Kirkpatrick, a native of Mecklenburg County. M. A. Kirkpatrick was a Confederate soldier and was severely wounded at the battle of Seven Pines.

As a boy Doctor Kirkpatrick attended local schools, acquired his academic training in Weaver College at Asheville, and is a graduate with the class of 1894 from Vanderbilt University Medical Department in Nashville, Tennessee. For several years he practiced in Haywood County, his native locality, and then after a year spent in Texas came to Trough in Spartanburg County. His magnificent home built for him by the company is one of the finest in Upper South Carolina. Doctor Kirkpatrick is a member of the County, State and American Medical associations, belongs to the Methodist Episcopal Church South and is affiliated with the Masons, Knights of Pythias and Loyal Order of Moose.

He married Miss Mary J. McCracken of Haywood County, North Carolina. They have three children, Orville Y., John W. and Mary S. Orville has been in the United States Navy since 1914 and is now in the Hospital Corps of the Navy, stationed at Atlanta.

JAMES EDWIN MCDONALD, SR. Professional, business and public distinctions in large number have marked the career of James Edwin McDonald, Sr., as a lawyer and resident of Winnsboro. The esteem in which he is held as a lawyer was indicated by his election as president of the South Carolina Bar Association.

Mr. McDonald was born near Richburg, Chester County, December 15, 1856, son of Rev. Laughlin and Malissa Lucinda (Stinson) McDonald, being of Irish stock on his mother's side and of Scotch through the McDonalds, a family that has been identified with the Southern states since about 1760. His father was for years a minister of the Associate Reformed Presbyterian Church.

James Edwin McDonald was not gifted with physical strength but developed a robust physique by active outdoor work and also developed a fondness for the sports of hunting and fishing that still prevails upon him occasionally. His education in the country schools was supplemented by a full course in Erskine College in Abbeville County, where he graduated A. B. July 4, 1877. At that time there was no law school in South Carolina and having definitely determined to enter the legal profession he studied in the offices of McCants and Douglass from January, 1878, to January, 1880, when he was admitted.

Mr. McDonald has been a resident of Winnsboro nearly forty wears. He soon had a profitable clientage, including his work as attorney for the Winnsboro Granite Company. Later for some years he was attorney for the Southern Power Company, assistant counsel for the Southern Railway, and has represented a number of corporate and business firms.

So far as he could consistently without sacrificing family interests he has responded to calls for public service. From 1884 to November, 1892, he was circuit solicitor. He has frequently been appointed special judge, and in 1894 was elected mayor of Winnsboro. He has served as county chairman of the democratic party in Fairfield County, is a member of the Winnsboro Commercial Club, is a Knight Templar Mason and Shriner and a Knight of Pythias. He has been true to the faith in which he was reared and for many years has been an elder in the Associate Reformed Church.

October 12, 1882, he married Miss Lillie M. Elliott. Six children were born to their marriage.

JAMES EDWIN MCDONALD, JR., has for the past ten years been the partner of his father in practice at Winnsboro.

He was born at Winnsboro, January 8, 1886, son of J. E. and Lillie (Elliott) McDonald. The career of his honored father, a former president of the South Carolina Bar Association, is told in preceding sketch. The son was educated in Mount Zion Academy, graduated in 1906 from The Citadel at Charleston, and took his law course in the University of South Carolina, graduating LL. B. in 1908. Since then he has been in active practice with his father and with increasing experience has added much to the prestige of the firm.

July 6, 1908, he married Miss Lucy Pride Heyward of Columbia. Their three children are Lucy Pride, J. E. III and Elizabeth Heyward.

LOWRY S. COVIN is one of the very active young men in the business affairs of Columbia. Many of the customers of the Palmetto National Bank came to know him and appreciate his good service and courtesy in the office of receiving teller in that institution. Mr. Covin, due to the increase of his private business affairs, left the bank recently and now is active manager of the Southern Motor Company, one of the leading automobile concerns of the capital city.

He was born in 1887 at Mount Carmel in Abbeville county, son of Phillip Augustus and Martha Virginia (Sanders) Covin. His mother was a daughter of Doctor Sanders, at one time a prominent physician of Abbeville county. The Covin family is of French Huguenot ancestry and members of it were among the first settlers at Mount Carmel in Abbeville county. Phillip A. Covin was a Confederate soldier and was still in the Military Hospital at Columbia when Sherman's army occupied the city.

Lowry S. Covin acquired a good common school education at Mount Carmel and McCormick and was sixteen years of age when in 1903 he acquired his first banking experience, with the First National Bank at Batesburg. He remained with that institution three years and in 1908 came to Columbia and entered the Palmetto National Bank. He was receiving teller for seven years, finally resigning in March, 1919, to give his entire time to the automobile business. About two years previously he and a fellow associate in the Palmetto National Bank, O. P. Loyal, had organized the Southern Motor Company, and they are still owners of the business. It has grown and prospered until it was necessary for Mr. Covin to resign his connection with the bank and devote his time and attention to the affairs of the Southern Motor Company, of which he is general manager. This company occupies a first class plant on Sumter street and are distributors for the Scripps-Booth Six, the American Six and the Marmon cars and also the White Truck.

Several years ago Mr. Covin also established the Covin Candy Company, but later sold his interest in that business. He was also a factor in the organization of the Carolina Wholesale Hardware Company, and is now vice president of the same. Mr. Covin is also secretary of the Loyal-Covin Contracting Company, doing a general building and construction business.

He is a member of the Automotive Trades Club of Columbia, is a Mason and a Presbyterian. He married Miss Mary Beckman of Columbia and their one son is Lowry S., Jr.

FREDERICK DOUGLAS MARSHALL was born at Fort Mill, South Carolina, on August 14, 1875. He is the son of John Wilson Marshall and Mary Clawson Marshall; his father, Captain Marshall was born of Scotch and English ancestry, and descended from the Charleston family of that name. He served in the Confederate army with distinction throughout the entire war and was a member of the famous Hampton Legion, participating in all battles of his command in Virginia. In 1865 he moved to York County, where for many years he held a prominent place and had the esteem of that community. His wife, Mary Clawson Marshall, was the daughter of Thomas I. Clawson and Martha Williams Clawson. Her grandfather, Col. Thomas Williams, was a member of the Legislature of South Carolina from 1820 to 1824, and lieutenant-governor during 1828 to 1831; his wife was Martha White Crawford. Colonel Williams moved to Montgomery, Alabama, in 1835, from which state he was sent to Congress in 1841. This family was closely connected with the Witherspoons, Crawfords, Whites, and other prominent families of York County, and it is but natural that Fred Marshall should feel a special pride in his people.

In 1905, December 14th, Mr. Marshall married Miss Mallie Gladden Friday; their children are Mary Elizabeth and Mallie Margaret. Mrs. Marshall is a descendant of some of the earliest settlers of this state, whose names are synonymous with the best traditions of South Carolina. She is a member of the Daughters of the American Revolution and United Daughters of the Confederacy.

Fred Marshall was educated in the local schools of Rock Hill, and also attended Clemson College. At the beginning of the Spanish-American war he volunteered and was First Sergeant, Company G, Catawba Rifles, Rock Hill, First Regiment National Guard. On leaving the army in 1898 he was connected for some months with the Columbia Railway Gas & Electric Company, afterwards with the Southern Bell Telephone Company, Atlanta, Georgia. He had several years experience when he was promoted to district manager for South Carolina, which position he resigned early in 1919 and organized the Marshall-Summers Seed & Grain Company. During his long residence in Columbia he has gained esteem both in business and social circles and has interested himself in good government. He has been elected to the city council. He is a member of the Columbia Club and of the Rotary Club and is a member of St. John's Episcopal Church. In fraternal circles he is a Mason, Odd Fellow, Elk, Knight of Pythias, Woodman of the World and a Moose.

TOLLIVER CLEVELAND CALLISON is a lawyer and in ten years has gained a dignified and successful position as a member of the bar of Lexington.

He was born at the town of Callison in Edgefield County July 17, 1884, a son of Preston Brooks and Mattie Ella (White) Callison. His father was a

farmer and merchant and served two terms as a member of the Legislature, and the Callison family has for generations been prominent in Edgefield County. Tolliver C. Callison was educated in the public schools and Bailey Military Institute at Greenwood and studied law at the University of South Carolina. He was admitted to the bar in the spring of 1909 and at once began practice at Lexington. He is now a member of the prominent firm of Timmerman, Graham & Callison. Mr. Callison did some valuable work in his community during the World war, serving as chief clerk to the local board of the county and as a member of the County Food Administration and did much to carry the county over the top in various war campaigns. He was lieutenant-colonel on the staff of Governor Cooper. Politically he is a democrat.

He is affiliated with the Masons, Knights of Pythias and Woodmen of the World. For three years he was superintendent of the Baptist Sunday School at Lexington. December 17, 1913, he married Miss Margaret Elizabeth Reel of Edgefield. They have three children, Ruby, Tolliver Cleveland, Jr., and Helen.

DANIEL FRANKLIN EFIRD. As a young man Daniel Franklin Efird made a definite choice of agriculture as the work and business of his life. A successful farmer he has been for over thirty years, has been a real leader in the agricultural activities of Lexington County, and from his farm his influence has extended to many unrelated affairs, church, the legislature, and practically all the interests of his community.

He was born in Lexington County January 25, 1861, a son of Rev. Daniel and Henrietta (Dreher) Efird. His people have long been prominent in the Lutheran Church. The maternal grandfather was Rev. Godfrey Dreher, a leader and organizer among the Lutheran chuches of Lexington County. His father, Rev. Daniel Efird, was not only a minister of the Gospel but a farmer and merchant and at one time treasurer of Lexington County.

Daniel Franklin Efird had experience during his youth both as a farmer and in mercantile affairs. He was educated in local schools, in Pine Ridge Academy and completed his junior year at Newberry College. Since the age of twenty-one he has given his business attention primarily to farming. Has served in one official capacity and another in the management of the South Carolina State Fair Association; first as a member of the executive committee, then general superintendent for nine years and since May 13, 1913, he has served as secretary.

He has always been interested in politics and church. He was first elected a member of the South Carolina Legislature in 1896 and was re-elected, serving continuously until 1904, when he was chosen a member of the State Senate. Some of his work while in the Legislature was devoted to putting his home county upon a sound financial basis. Retiring voluntarily from the Senate, he was chosen chairman of the democratic party of his county, which position he held for six years. As a young man Mr. Efird served as lieutenant of a militia company. During the World war he was chairman of the local draft board from the time it was organized. Fraternally he is affiliated with the Independent Order of Odd Fellows, and the Knights of Pythias.

Mr. Efird is one of the prominent Lutheran laymen of the South. In 1914 he became a charter member of the United Lutheran Synod of the South, one of the three general bodies governing the Lutheran Church in America. He was chosen a member of a committee which had charge of the printing and other matters continuously until this synod was merged into the one general body. In January, 1919, an even greater distinction came to him when he was one of the three men of the South selected on the general committee of the United Lutheran Church of America to look after the printing for the united body.

ALBERT CLIFTON HINDS has had a very busy and profitable law practice at Kingstree for the past ten or twelve years, and has also come to be regarded as one of the leading citizens of Williamsburg county, a willing worker in every movement for the welfare of his section and state.

Mr. Hinds was born in Williamsburg county April 4, 1884, a son of Charles Magnus and Ellen (Jaudon) Hinds, substantial farmers of that community. He grew up on his father's farm, attended public schools, and acquired a liberal education in the University of South Carolina, graduating with the A. B. degree in 1905 and receiving his law degree in 1906. He has since practiced at Kingstree, in partnership with John A. Kelley under the name of Kelley & Hinds. Mr. Hinds is president of the Kingstree Building and Loan Association, president of the Kingstree Board of Trade, and is also chairman of the County Democratic Committee. He was a delegate from South Carolina to the St. Louis National Convention of 1916.

December 14, 1911, Mr. Hinds married Miss Nancy Meadors of Kingstree. Her father was Rev. W. P. Meadors, a well known minister of the Methodist Church.

WASHINGTON PRICE TIMMERMAN, M.D. While his own career has been that of a hard working and successful physician and surgeon, since 1902 identified with the Batesburg community, Doctor Timmerman comes of a family whose interests show a natural inclination to politics and public affairs. He is a brother of Hon. George Bell Timmerman of Lexington, present solicitor of the Eleventh Judicial Circuit and who in the campaign of 1919 made a very close race for the democratic nomination for Congress.

Doctor Timmerman was born at the Timmerman community, named in honor of the family in Edgefield County near Phillipi Church in 1869, son of W. H. and Pauline (Asbill) Timmerman.

The late Doctor Washington Hodges Timmerman, his father, who died in 1908, earned a place among South Carolina's most distinguished citizens. He was born in historic Edgefield County, his home and plantation being at Timmerman. His birth occurred in 1832. His father was Ransom Timmerman, who married a member of the prominent Bledsoe family of English ancestry. His grandfather was Jacob Timmerman, who came from Germany and settled in Edgefield County about 1770. Washington H.

Timmerman graduated in medicine at the Charleston Medical College in 1854. In December, 1861, he left his profession to become second lieutenant of Company K, Seventeenth South Carolina Regiment and was soon promoted to first lieutenant, and in April, 1862, was elected Captain of his company. He served until the following July when compelled to resign on account of physical disability. In the meantime he was under General Bragg and had command of a regiment during the retreat from Corinth. In November, 1864, he resumed duty as captain of Company B, Second Regiment, State troops. When Sherman's army entered the state he was detailed by the governor for duty as physician in Edgefield County. Following the war he practiced medicine in Edgefield County until 1892. For several years he lived in Columbia where he had prominent connections with business and financial affairs, and was also a resident of Batesburg, and during that time was president of two of the local banks. For some time he was president of the Farmers Bank at Edgefield and a vice-president of the Farmers and Mechanics Bank of Columbia.

With all the duties and burdens of a large medical practice he became conspicuous in the public life of his county and state. He was elected to the Legislature in 1882, and again in 1890, resigning to enter the State Senate for an unexpired term, being re-elected in 1892. He served as president pro tem. of the Senate and became acting lieutenant-governor when Judge Gary was promoted to the Supreme Bench. He was elected without opposition to the office of lieutenant-governor in 1894 and served until January, 1897, following which he became state treasurer and was twice elected to that office without opposition. He served as a member of the Constitutional Convention of 1895. Captain Timmerman married in 1856 Pauline Asbill, who died in 1873, the mother of six children. Captain Timmerman in 1879 married Henrietta M. Bell.

Dr. W. Price Timmerman attended local and private schools, and graduated in 1891 from the Medical College of the State of South Carolina at Charleston. For the first two years he practiced at Kirksly in what is now Greenwood County. Then for nine years he practiced at Timmerman and in 1902 moved to Batesburg. He is one of the leading physicians and surgeons of Lexington County, enjoys a large general practice and is also local surgeon for the Southern Railway. He is a member of the County, State, Tri-State and American Medical associations and has been district councilor in the State society. He is also a member of the Association of Southern Railway Surgeons. He is a member of the Democratic County Executive Committee, and for a busy doctor exercises considerable influence in local and state politics.

In 1896 Doctor Timmerman married Miss Saidee Moore of Abbeville County, who died leaving no children. For his present wife he married Miss Mary Swygert in 1905. They have four children: W. Price, Jr., William Bledsoe, Mary Elizabeth and John Swygert. Also an adopted daughter, Mrs. Pauline Timmerman Asbell.

IRA CROMLEY CARSON has for a number of years been a prominent figure in financial, business and civic affairs at Batesburg, where he is active vice president of the First National Bank.

He was born in Edgefield (now Saluda) County October 9, 1871, a son of Charles and Carrie (Cromley) Carson. His father was a farmer and the son grew up in the country, attending local schools. He continued his education in the high school at Johnston and in Clemson College.

Mr. Carson has been a factor in the life of Batesburg since 1906, when he was made cashier of the First National Bank. He has been the active vice president of that institution since 1917.

December 6, 1911, Mr. Carson married Grace Ridgell, of Batesburg, daughter of Dr. Edgar C. and Ella (McFall) Ridgell. They have two children, Edgar Charles, born in 1912, and Ella Carrie.

ALEXANDER SCOTT DOUGLAS. Since the close of the war for a period of over half a century the name Douglas has been associated with some of the best achievements of the legal profession and many influential connections with business, civic and social life of Winnsboro.

Alexander Scott Douglas who died January 5, 1914, went to Winnsboro soon after coming out of the Confederate army. He was born in Fairfield County, South Carolina, December 25, 1833, son of Alexander and Jennet (Simonton) Douglas. His grandparents, Alexander and Grace (Brown) Douglas came from County Antrim, Ireland, 1790, and settled in Fairfield, South Carolina. Alexander Douglas was a farmer and planter, and a man who took a very prominent part in local affairs in the Fairfield District.

Alexander Scott Douglas grew up in a rural atmosphere, and was greatly indebted to his mother for his moral and spiritual development. He attended New Hope Academy and in 1853 at the age of twenty graduated A. B. from Erskine College. He studied law from that year until August 17, 1854, under Ex-Governor B. F. Perry at Greenville, and then took the full law course at the University of Virginia. He began practice at Spartanburg in 1856. He wielded a special influence in the affairs of Upper South Carolina from January, 1857, to August, 1861, as editor of the Spartanburg Express. Much of the public opinion in that section of the state was molded by the Express during those critical years. He served as a delegate to the State Democratic Convention at Charleston in 1860.

In August, 1861, Mr. Douglas left his chair as editor and entered the Confederate army as second lieutenant of Company C of the Thirteenth South Carolina Volunteers, McGowan's Brigade, Jackson's Corps, Army of Northern Virginia. For almost four years he was steadily devoted to the fortunes of the South as a soldier and was at the surrender of Appomattox on April 9, 1865. At that time he was a lieutenant in Company C of the Thirteenth Infantry.

It was not many months after the war that Mr. Douglas located at Winnsboro in January, 1866, and began the practice of law. In course of time he had many influential connections and a large general practice. For ten years he was attorney of the Winnsboro National Bank, also attorney for the Winnsboro Bank and for cotton mills and other corporations. He has expressed his political faith

always through the democratic party, and became an elder in the Presbyterian Church at Winnsboro in 1866 and served in that post continuously and also as superintendent of the Presbyterian Sunday School for over forty years.

November 6, 1860, he married Miss Mary E. Byers. On December 17, 1878, he married Miss Sallie McCants, who died September 20, 1901. By his first wife he had three children and by his second marriage four. One son is W. D. Douglas of Winnsboro.

GEORGE JAMES GRAHAM is one of the prominent and historic characters in the life and affairs of Williamsburg county. He was a Confederate soldier during his youth, and while his business interests have always been closely allied with the farm, he has played an interesting part in public affairs.

He was born in Florence county February 23, 1842, son of Miles N. and Hester B. (Myers) Graham. His parents were also natives of this state, and the family were leading planters in antebellum times. George James Graham grew up on his father's farm, attended country schools, and at the age of nineteen in 1861 entered the Confederate army. He became a private in Company K of the Sixth South Carolina Infantry, later being promoted to corporal, and was with that regiment in all its brilliant campaigns and marches and battles in Virginia and elsewhere. The war over he returned to his farm, and so far as his public engagements permitted has remained by preference a tiller of the soil ever since.

Mr. Graham had a prominent part in the redemption of Williamsburg county from the reconstruction regime. He served as a lieutenant but frequently in actual command of a local company of "Red Shirts" and more than once he led these men to scenes of trouble, due to riots caused by negroes and carpet baggers, and was always prompt and resourceful in taking the measures necessary for peace and good order. Mr. Graham was elected a member of the Legislature in 1878, serving one term, and afterwards was a member of the Constitutional Convention. In 1891 he was elected sheriff of Williamsburg county and in only one campaign had opposition for that office. He was sheriff of the county continuously for twenty years, being at this time the oldest sheriff in the State of South Carolina.

GLENN WALKER RAGSDALE is a lawyer of over thirty-five years experience, and a man of the highest standing in his profession and in the community of Winnsboro, where he has had his home for many years.

He was born in Fairfield County June 3, 1857, a son of Elijah and Nancy (Stanton) Ragsdale. He grew up on his father's farm, had a public school education, and after that paid his own way while training for a professional career. He spent two years in Furman University at Greenville, and then taught two years. He read law and was admitted to the bar in 1882, and since that date has been engaged in a general practice at Winnsboro. He has been the recipient of numerous public honors, serving in the Legislature two terms and sat as a delegate in the Constitutional Convention of 1895.

April 16, 1887, Mr. Ragsdale married Miss McMeekin, daughter of John W. McMeekin. Five children were born to their marriage: Ethel, Mrs. John McLaurin, a farmer and druggist of Dillon, South Carolina; Inez, Mrs. G. G. McLaurin, attorney at Dillon; William Glenn, attorney in Winnsboro, who served in the ambulance corps of the American army in France; Robert Walker, a law student in his father's office; and Edith McMeekin, a student in Winthrop College.

CYPRIAN MELANCHTHON EFIRD. This is one of the most widely known lawyers of South Carolina. That reputation is based in part upon the authorship of Efird's "Digest of South Carolina Reports," comprising volumes from 43 to 60. This monumental work was published in 1904 while he was serving as state reporter. He is a lawyer of high standing and of successful practice for over thirty-five years and has been prominent in the bar and public affairs of Lexington County.

He was born in Lexington County December 18, 1856, son of Rev. Daniel and Henrietta M. (Dreher) Efird. His mother was a granddaughter of Godfrey Dreher, a pioneer Lutheran minister in Lexington County. His father also gave his life to the ministry of the Lutheran Church.

Mr. Efird grew up in a country district, worked on a farm, prepared for college in the Pine Ridge Academy in Lexington County, and graduated A. B. from Newberry College in 1877. In the meantime he taught school and studied law and was admitted to the bar in June, 1882. Since then his home and professional interests have been at Lexington. After getting a secure status as a lawyer, he interested himself in politics, was elected state senator in 1892, serving four years, was a member of the Constitutional Convention of 1895, and was appointed state reporter in 1896, an office he held for over twelve years. He has served as a member of the board of trustees of Newberry College, and as a member of the board of directors of the Theological Seminary of the United Synod of the South. December 28, 1882, he married Miss Carrie Boozer, a daughter of Dr. Jacob and Eva C. Boozer of Lexington County.

EZEKIEL BARMORE RASOR, of Cross Hill, Laurens County, was born in Abbeville County January 27, 1868, son of Ezekiel Barmore and Eliza (Latimer) Rasor.

His parents were also natives of Abbeville County, his maternal grandfather being Dr. Harrison Latimer. His paternal grandparents were Ezekiel and Pamelia (Barmore) Rasor, the former a native of Abbeville and a son of Christian Rasor, a native of Virginia and who was of Dutch ancestry. Ezekiel Rasor, Sr., was a farmer and died at the age of seventy-five, while his wife died at the age of forty-nine. Five of their eleven children are living.

Ezekiel Barmore Rasor grew up on a farm and was educated in public schools, including the high school at Honea Path. At the age of twenty-one he began merchandising at Cross Hill, and in 1906

Vol. V—5

became cashier of the bank of that town. He was in that post of responsibility for ten years and since then has been engaged in the general life and fire insurance and also operates a small farm. He is a member of the Baptist Church.

EDWIN CHRISTOPHER EPPS. While banking has been his chief business for a number of years the people of Williamsburg County regard Mr. Epps as broadly representative of the county's leading interests whether of a business, civic or patriotic nature.

He was born near his present home town of Kingstree, April 7, 1873, son of a farmer and merchant, William Epps and wife, Mary R. (Watts) Epps. He was educated in public schools, spending about one year in school at Charleston, when he was about fourteen. He also attended the Patrick Military Institute at Anderson, and his first business experience was when as a boy he clerked in his uncle's store at Kingstree—later serving in like position at Manning. From 1896 to 1900 was engaged in merchandising on his own account. Since 1901 he has been a banker, being selected in that year cashier of the Bank of Kingstree. He remained with that institution five years, resigning in 1906, to become cashier of the Bank of Williamsburg, the largest financial institution of the county.

He was also one of the organizers and served as the first president of the Kingstree Insurance, Real Estate and Loan Company and is an ex-president of the Williamsburg County Fair Association. He served as trustee of the graded schools of Kingstree continuously from 1906 to 1916, and spared no effort on his part to make those schools adequate to the fulfillment of every aim of education. Mr. Epps is largely interested in the establishment of the tobacco market at Kingstree and serves as director in several other of the town's enterprises.

Like many South Carolina bankers he devoted much of his time during the war to the success of the various patriotic campaigns. He was chairman for Williamsburg County in the first, third, fourth and fifth Liberty Loans. He represented the county in State Senate for two terms from 1910 to 1918. In which body he served on the important committees on Education and Finance and was chairman of the Committee on Banking and Insurance. Mr. Epps is a trustee of the Methodist Episcopal Church South.

May 1, 1906, he married Nannie L. Snider of Orangeburg County. They have two children, Mary Catherine and Carlyle.

JOSEPH BENJAMIN JOHNS is superintendent of the South Carolina Industrial School and Farm at Florence. He is an educator of ripe experience, and his personal qualifications make him admirably adapted for the task of superintending the education and training of the boys who are members of this state institution.

Mr. Johns was born in Newberry County May 16, 1875, a son of William Wesley and Elliott (Busby) Johns. He grew up on his father's farm, attended high school at Cherokee Springs, and graduated in 1897 from Furman University. Mr. Johns for sixteen years was engaged in school work in Greenville and Spartanburg counties, and for eight years of that time had charge of the State High School. June 1, 1913, he took up his present duties at the Industrial School at Florence. He has 190 boys under his care and supervision, and operates the farm of 580 acres as an adjunct to the school.

Mr. Johns is affiliated with the Masonic Order and Woodmen of the World, and is a member of the Baptist Church. September 4, 1898, he married Mary Ellie Stroud, of Greenville County. They have two children, William Clayton and Bonnie Kate.

LUECO GUNTER, who for six years served as supervisor of rural schools for South Carolina, has recently accepted the newly established Chair of Education at Furman University. He is one of the best known educators in South Carolina, recognized as a leader in the educational thought of the state.

He was born in Aiken County, South Carolina, near what is now the Town of Wagener, March 26, 1879, son of James A. and Theoria E. Gunter. His early schooling was supplied by the public schools near and at Wagener until the fall of 1895. During the school year 1895-96 he attended the Blackville High School, preparatory for college. He then entered South Carolina College, now the University of South Carolina, in the fall of 1896, and received his A. B. degree in 1900. During 1900-03, while teaching at Columbia, he took a post-graduate course at the university and received his Master of Arts degree in 1903.

Professor Gunter was principal of Waverley Graded School, a suburban school of Columbia, in 1900-01, and during 1901-03 was a teacher in the Presbyterian High School of Columbia. He became superintendent of the Beaufort public schools in the fall of 1903, and remained as superintendent until the summer of 1910. At that date he was appointed assistant state superintendent of education, but resigned the offices in the summer of 1911 to become superintendent of the public schools at Rock Hill. He was there three years, and in July, 1914, accepted the post of state supervisor of rural schools, resigning that position after six years of efficient work to take the Chair of Education at Furman University.

Professor Gunter married, August 10, 1904, Miss Laura K. Perry, of Columbia.

LEROY LEE, who has been a lawyer and public official of Williamsburg County for many years, had just graduated in law when the Spanish-American war broke out, and in July, 1898, he volunteered as a private in Anderson's Heavy Artillery, serving with that organization until honorably discharged on October 16, 1898.

Mr. Lee was born in Florence County, South Carolina, May 21, 1875, son of Henry B. Lee, a prominent planter of that section of the state, and Margaret J. (Lynch) Lee. LeRoy Lee supplemented his public school education by three years in the University of South Carolina in the literary course, and graduated LL. B. from the law department in June, 1898. He began practice at Kingstree, and has always enjoyed a good business, and

since 1900 has filled the official responsibilities of county attorney.

July 12, 1900, he married Eva C. Riser, of Newberry. They have one child, Serena Margaret.

GEORGE WALTER SUMMER. Largely with an equipment that was due to a determined purpose and utilization of meager opportunities during youth, George Walter Summer began an active business career as a merchant at Newberry thirty-five years ago, and since then has become one of the real leaders and executives in the broader commercial affairs of that city.

He was born at Lexington, South Carolina, July 15, 1861. His ancestors came to America from Germany about 1775. He is a son of George W. and Martha D. Summer. His father was a Confederate soldier, and died in a hospital in Virginia on July 13, 1862. George Walter Summer therefore never knew his father, and the influences upon his formative character were derived largely from his mother, a woman of beautiful character. He grew up on a farm, participated in its labors as soon as his strength permitted, and had only a country school education. In November, 1884, he took upon himself the role of merchant in Newberry, and has been a busy factor in that city ever since. Some of the larger institutions with which he has been identified are the Mollohon Manufacturing Company, of which he was president; Newberry Warehouse Company, which he served as president; the Commercial Bank of Newberry; Security Loan & Investment Company of Newberry, in all of which he has been a director. Mr. Summer was the originator of the Summer Brothers opened in November, 1884. For five years he was a trustee of the Newberry graded schools, and is now trustee of Newberry College.

Mr. Summer is a Shriner, Mason, and a Knight of Pythias, is a Lutheran in religion and a democrat in politics.

Outside of business he has found his greatest pleasure in his home circle. On October 13, 1881, he married Miss Polly L. Long. They became the parents of ten children, seven of whom are living.

FRANCIS FISK JOHNSON found his real vocation when a young man, and though he allowed his energies to be diverted by a professional career for a few years, he then returned permanently to the business of planting and agriculture, in which he is one of the leading exponents in Bamberg County.

Mr. Johnson was born in Orangeburg County, not far from the scene of his present activities, on December 28, 1860. He is a member of a family that has been in South Carolina from Revolutionary times. Both his father, Alexander Hamilton Johnson, and his grandfather, Dr. W. S. Johnson, were successful physicians and surgeons and practiced for many years in the old Barnwell District. Dr. Alexander Hamilton Johnson married Addie Powers Hays, who was born in the present Bamberg County section of Barnwell County, her father being a native of Ireland.

Francis Fisk Johnson was the third in a family of seven children, and was educated in the private and public schools of Bamberg. He began farming when a boy, but later studied dentistry and practiced that profession about eight years. Since then he has given his entire attention to farming. He has about 1,000 acres, most of it under cultivation. He is one of the largest cotton growers in Bamberg County. Mr. Johnson is affiliated with the Masonic fraternity and the Knights of Pythias.

LEVI M. CECIL is proprietor of Cecil's Business College at Anderson. This is an institution which in the ten years since it was established has performed an indispensable service in the training of young men and women for business careers, and the value of its work has been greatly enhanced by the fact that Mr. Cecil is himself a business man of wide and generous experience and training.

He was born at Thomasville, North Carolina, March 22, 1880, a son of Jesse W. and Elizabeth (Moffitt) Cecil, both deceased. They were also natives of North Carolina, and his father was a minister of the Reformed Church of the United States.

As a boy in his native state Mr. Cecil attended the Catawba College, and completed the course of the Smithfield Business College in North Carolina and the Philadelphia Business College. For several years he was employed in general office work in Pennsylvania, Virginia and North Carolina, and acquired a practical training which has been invaluable to him since directing the affairs of the business college which he established at Richmond in 1909. Many students from Anderson and adjoining counties have been enrolled and have gone from the college well qualified for business work, and some of them are among the prominent young business leaders of the state today.

Besides the management of the business college Mr. Cecil is secretary and assistant treasurer of the Anderson Mattress and Spring Bed Company and of the Anderson Underwear Company, two of the city's best industrial organizations. He is a deacon in the First Presbyterian Church, and both he and his wife are prominent socially. In 1910 Mr. Cecil married Inez F. Felder, of Summerton, South Carolina.

SIDNEY JACOB DERRICK, who in June, 1918, was called to the responsibilities of Newberry College, was awarded his well earned degree Bachelor of Arts from that institution about a quarter of a century previously, and had long been identified with the preparatory and collegiate departments. Mr. Derrick was one of the broad-minded educators and social and religious leaders in the state.

He was born in Lexington County, South Carolina, November 10, 1867, and as a farm boy had the opportunity to attend only a few brief school terms in his neighborhood. Later he attended Mount Tabor High School in Newberry County, and in the fall of 1888 entered the sophomore class of Newberry College. He was not prepared to carry all the studies in this class, but made up his "conditions," and though he had to discontinue his residence at college for several terms, teaching to pay his way, he kept up his work and remained with his class and when he graduated in 1892 was awarded second honors, and also the medal for the best senior essay.

Then followed a period of teaching, and in 1896 he resigned the principalship of the Lexington High School to accept the principalship of the Preparatory Department of Newberry College. His usefulness in that institution has been a matter of steady growth. In 1903 he was appointed assistant in the Department of History and in 1906 elected professor of history and economics. From the congenial duties of that chair he was called on June 4, 1918, to the presidency, to succeed John Henry Harms, when Doctor Harms left Newberry to occupy a pastorate in Philadelphia.

While busied with many interests outside the strict routine of teaching Mr. Derrick has been constantly a student. He was carrying on studies while teaching which qualified him for the degree of Master of Arts awarded by Newberry College in 1897. He also attended summer schools at Cornell University in 1901 and Columbia University in 1907.

At the time of his election to the presidency a college bulletin contained an article written by E. B. Setzler which may be properly quoted concerning some other interesting facts in the career of Mr. Derrick.

"Professor Derrick has always manifested a broad interest in educational matters. He served two years on the Board of Education of Lexington county, and twelve years on the Newberry County Board; and he is at present a member of the State Board of Education, having been appointed by Governor Manning in April, 1916. The Governor also appointed him chairman of the Newberry County Exemption Board in April, 1917.

"Professor Derrick has likewise shown an active interest in the work of the church. He was confirmed as a member of Holy Trinity Lutheran church, Little Mountain, in May, 1893, during the pastorship of Rev. S. L. Nease. He has been a member of the Board of Deacons of the Church of the Redeemer, Newberry, since 1899, and chairman of that board since 1912; and for the last five years he has been a member of the Lutheran Board of Publication.

"In 1898 Professor Derrick was married to Miss Mary V. Hiller, of Lexington, and to her he attributes—and rightly, we imagine—much of the success which he has achieved.

"President Derrick is—as the above sketch plainly shows—preeminently a self-made man. The church, through the Board of Trustees of the College, has now called him to the biggest task to which he could possibly have inspired. His friends are confident that he will meet its demands with the same unyielding determination which has characterized his efforts in the past. The measure of his success, however, will depend largely upon the way in which the friends of the college rally to his support."

THAD JEROME COTTINGHAM. While his home and principal interests for a number of years have been at Lake City, Mr. Cottingham is widely known all over that section of South Carolina on account of his banking interests. He has made banking a profession, and has exhibited striking ability in financial matters, and was active in the organization and in the subsequent management of several well known banks in his part of the state.

Mr. Cottingham was born in Marion County, September 20, 1883, a son of Daniel Sinclair and Ida (Legette) Cottingham. His father was a substantial farmer and grew up in the country, attending first the public schools of New Holly, and was a student in Wofford College from 1900 to 1903. The following two years he was a teacher, and for another two years kept a set of books for a merchandise company. Since then all his work has been in the banking business. For two years he was cashier of the Bank of Olanta and since 1909 has been identified with the Farmers and Merchants National Bank of Lake City. He was cashier until 1915, then becoming vice president and became president in September, 1919. Mr. Cottingham is also vice president and executive officer of the Farmers and Merchants Bank at Cowards, helping to organize that institution. He reorganized the Farmers & Merchants Bank of Florence, of which he is president. He organized the Farmers and Merchants Bank of Pamplico since September, 1919, also the Farmers and Merchants Bank of Johnsonville, and reorganized the Bank of Cades, South Carolina. He is also president of the Peoples Bank at Moncks Corner, South Carolina.

Mr. Cottingham is a York Rite Mason and Shriner, a member of the Benevolent and Protective Order of Elks and for the past eleven years has been a steward of the Methodist Episcopal Church South. While a very busy man he has found time for recreation in the out of doors, and when business permits he delights in hunting, fishing and tennis.

April 25, 1905, he married Margaret Cox of Rowland, North Carolina. Her father was Chalmers B. Cox, a farmer in that state. The four children of Mr. and Mrs. Cottingham are William Arrowwood, Harriet Cox, Chalmers Daniel and Thad Jerome, Jr.

OLIVER PRESTON RICHARDSON, who served as a captain in the Eighty-first Division in France, was one of the prominent young business men of Gaffney and had resumed his civil pursuits and occupations only a brief time after his honorable discharge when death stayed his hand on August 31, 1919.

He was born near Spartanburg May 25, 1884, a son of W. and Anna (Wingo) Richardson. His parents were natives of South Carolina and were a well known family of the upper part of the state. Captain Richardson attended school at Charlottesville, Virginia, and was a graduate of Wake Forest University, North Carolina. He was in business for several years as a cotton broker at Milledgeville, Georgia, and returning to his home state was with the well known firm of Jennings & Bryant at Spartanburg and Greenville.

Early in the war he joined an Officers Training Camp and was made captain of the Three Hundred and Sixteenth Field Artillery in the Eighty-first Division. He was sent overseas, and spent nine months in France. After his return he engaged in his former business, until his death. He was well known and enjoyed the highest esteem of his business and civic associates at Gaffney.

Captain Richardson married Miss Irene Bayne Wheat, a daughter of H. D. and Anna (Cannon) Wheat, of Gaffney, and member of a well known family of that section. Captain Richardson is survived by one daughter, Anna Wheat Richardson. He was an active member of the First Presbyterian Church of Gaffney.

JAMES STRONG MOFFATT, D. D. President of Erskine College since 1907, Doctor Moffatt has spent over thirty years in the ministry of the Associate Reformed Presbyterian Church. While he is not a native of South Carolina and while much of his work has been in other states, he represents one of the old and distinguished families of earlier generations of South Carolina. In his present office he has the satisfaction of presiding over one of the oldest institutions of Christian education in the South.

Erskine College has recently celebrated the eightieth anniversary of its founding in 1839. At the time of its organization there was not a single institution in South Carolina that afforded the advantages of a college training under Christian influences. It opened its doors under the presidency of Rev. E. E. Pressly. Robert C. Grier was the president from 1847 to 1858 and again from 1865 to 1871. For twenty-eight years its president was Dr. William Moffatt Grier, whose daughter is the wife of Dr. James Strong Moffatt.

Many of the ablest men whose careers are described in these pages acknowledge their debt to Erskine College for some of the most stimulating influences of their early lives. Erskine College, while not aspiring to the rank of a university, has for years done thorough work as a co-educational institution. Under the presidency of Doctor Moffatt it is better equipped than ever. The campus has six modern buildings, and the facilities for a thorough college education are supplied in the midst of a quiet and classic atmosphere and with every safeguard to the spiritual and moral welfare of the students.

Dr. James Strong Moffatt was born in Fulton County, Arkansas, July 17, 1860, a son of Rev. William Samuel and Martha Jane (Wilson) Moffatt. The Moffatts are a Scotch family that came from Scotland and settled in Chester County, South Carolina, in 1772. Doctor Moffatt's great-great-grandfather Moffatt was an American soldier in the Revolution. His grandfather was a merchant in Greenville County, South Carolina, where was born Rev. W. S. Moffatt, who spent the greater part of his life as a minister of the Associate Reformed Presbyterian Church. Martha Jane Wilson was born in Tennessee.

When James Strong Moffatt was a child his parents moved to Uniontown, Belmont County, Ohio, where his father was pastor of a church and where James Strong Moffatt lived until he was nearly grown. For a time he attended school at St. Clairsville in that county, also attended school at Xenia in Western Ohio, spent two years as a student in Erskine college and two years in Muskingum College at New Concord, Ohio, where he graduated A. B. in 1883. He graduated in 1886 from the United Presbyterian Theological Seminary at Allegheny, Pennsylvania. He also did post-graduate work in philosophy in Western University, now the University of Pittsburg, and in recent years Cooper College in Kansas awarded him the degree Doctor of Divinity.

He was ordained to the Associate Reformed Presbyterian ministry in 1886, and his present work was as pastor of the First Church at Charlotte, North Carolina, in 1886-87. He was pastor at Chester, South Carolina, from 1887 to 1907, for a period of twenty years. On January 1, 1907, he was called to the presidency of Erskine College at Due West. He is also a trustee and treasurer of the Associate Reformed Presbyterian Theological Seminary at Due West.

Doctor Moffatt is president of the Farmers and Merchants Bank of Due West. November 22, 1886, he married Jennie Moffatt Grier, daughter of the late Dr. William Moffatt Grier and his wife Nannie (McMorris) Grier of Newberry County. Doctor and Mrs. Moffatt have nine children.

WILLIAM BLACKBURN WILSON. This is the name of a prominent lawyer of Rock Hill. Distinction and eminence as a lawyer and public leader attaches to the name in a previous generation as a result of the services and abilities of William Blackburn Wilson, Sr. Today there are two William Blackburn Wilsons, he of the third generation being also a lawyer.

This branch of the Wilson family is of English origin. They came from England about the close of the Revolutionary war and settled in the lower section of South Carolina, in Colleton County. The grandfather of William Blackburn Wilson of Rock Hill was Rev. William Stanyarne Wilson, a son of John Wilson (who had married Miss Stanyarne of Johns Island). Rev. William S. Wilson was a man of education and the highest scholarly attainments. He married a Miss Blackburn, daughter of Professor George Blackburn. Professor Blackburn, a graduate of the University of Dublin, became a professor of mathematics and astronomy after coming to America, and was connected with the faculties of Asbury College, Baltimore, William and Mary College and the South Carolina College. He was also a technical expert on the boundary commission which fixed the boundary between North and South Carolina.

The late William Blackburn Wilson, father of the present holder of that honored name, was a lawyer whose leadership and abilities gave him a just fame all over the State of South Carolina. For many years he practiced at Yorkville, and his position in the profession made that city a distinctive point in the annals of the South Carolina Bench and Bar. He married Arrah Minerva Lowry, of Yorkville, South Carolina.

Their son William Blackburn Wilson was born at Yorkville, January 12, 1850, and was educated in private schools. He attended schools taught by Dr. Robert Lathan and by Professor William Currell, two teachers of note in Yorkville, and was also a pupil in the Kings Mountain Military School under Col. Asbury Coward. In 1867 he entered the University of South Carolina, where he graduated with the class of 1869. He at once took up the study of law under his father, was admitted to the bar January 9, 1871, just two days before reaching his majority, and beginning his practice at Yorkville moved to Rock Hill in February, 1876, and that city has been his home for over forty years. A man forceful in every way—fine physique, strong mental caliber, remarkable insight, and splendid advocate—always standing squarely in his client's shoes, he has enjoyed a large general practice, and at different times has represented some of the chief business and industrial leaders of York County and elsewhere in the state, and his name has appeared in connection with many important trials. Shortly after his admission to the bar—on account of his alleged connection with the Ku Klux Klan—he concluded that it would be convenient to go to Texas; and he remained there several years—until the excitement was over. He was always proud of the occasion of his going, and often spoke entertainingly of his varied western experiences, as cowboy, etc.

Commencing in 1884, he was elected and served two terms in the Lower House and then one term in the State Senate from York County (without offering a second time), and was one of that county's representatives in the State Constitutional Convention of 1895. He is a communicant of the Episcopal Church, and a Mason, and a friend indeed to all his friends.

Mr. Wilson is owner of valuable farming interests, and on many occasions has shown his public spirit in behalf of the community. He was especially active in procuring for Rock Hill Winthrop College, now one of the state's finest educational institutions. He was also the founder of Rock Hill Land and Town Site Company, which built Oakland, the residential section of Rock Hill.

Mr. Wilson owns and with his family occupies one of the beautiful homes in South Carolina, situated in the Oakland section, where he and his wife are always at home to their many friends.

In 1875 Mr. Wilson was most happily married to Miss Isabella Hinton Miller, daughter of Dr. W. R. Miller of Raleigh, North Carolina, and they have ten children, viz. Arrah Isabella, wife of Rev. J. W. C. Johnson of Gastonia, North Carolina; William Blackburn, Jr., whose early career as a lawyer gives promise that he will add to the distinctions of his honored name; Miss Fannie Britton Wilson, a graduate of the University of Pennsylvania and also a member of her father's law firm; William Miller, lawyer; Margaret, wife of C. J. Walker, of Rock Hill; Minerva Stanyarne, widow of J. M. Wylie; Dr. Oscar Wilson, of Spartanburg; Miss Loulie Meriwether, a professor of Latin in St. Mary's College at Raleigh, North Carolina; York Lowry Wilson; and Mary Blackburn Wilson; and also eighteen grandchildren.

On April 30, 1920, after the above sketch had been prepared, Mr. Wilson patiently yielded to the last call, from a sickness that had come upon him nearly four months previously. The issue of life—so far as he was permitted to take part in it—was most bravely and heroically fought; for time and time again it seemed that the end was at hand, as humanly speaking it would in all reason have been but for his sturdy constitution and his wonderful will power. His taking and the manner of it has left a deep sorrow upon the hearts of his family and his friends, while at the same time there was a sympathetic response throughout and beyond the limits of his native county. He was indeed an all-round man: of commanding stature, virile in body, alert in mind, gentle in spirit, tender in heart; and so he had to be—as he was in very truth—a loving husband and father, a warm friend, a faithful lawyer, an upright citizen, a diligent seeker after truth. "By their fruits ye shall know them." Requiescat in pace.

FRANKLIN WILLIAM FAIREY is distinguished among the business men of Williamsburg County by his evident capacity for successfully handling varied interests. He is a lawyer by profession and training, is also a banker, an extensive farmer, and his advice and assistance have been considered invaluable in a number of important civic movements and public improvements in his home community.

Mr. Fairey was born at Branchville, South Carolina, February 26, 1880, son of Franklin Ernest and Laura E. (Berry) Fairey. As he grew up, spending most of his early years on his father's plantation, he attended public schools, the Carlisle Fitting School and Wofford College. He finished his education in the Smith Business College at Lexington, Kentucky, and for two years was a general merchant. In the meantime he studied law and in 1904 was admitted to the bar, and for three years was the industrious partner in practice with John A. Kelley of Kingstree. He gave up his active professional work to become cashier of the Bank of Kingstree, an office he has held to the present time. He is also a director of the Williamsburg Milling Company, is president of the Williamsburg Motor Company, a firm handling automobiles, and is individual owner of about 4,000 acres of the rich and productive soil around Kingstree. His farming operations are carried on with the aid of many workers and much equipment. He operates twenty-five plows. Mr. Fairey helped give Kingstree its modern improvements of water supply and electric light, and has laid out several additions to the town. He has served as alderman and mayor pro tem, and is deeply interested in every movement affecting his community. He is chairman of the Building Committee of the Methodist Episcopal Church, and he has served as a member of the board of stewards of the same church for ten years.

June 27, 1907, Mr. Fairey married Miss Alma Boyd Kelley, daughter of a former law partner, John A. Kelley. To their marriage were born five children: Elizabeth, Franklin William, Jr., Virginia, Rachel and John Kelley.

WADDY THOMPSON is known all over the South as an author, historian and journalist, and bears a name which would readily be associated even by school children with the most brilliant epochs and personalities of South Carolina.

His great-grandfather also bore the name Waddy Thompson, and as a judge and chancellor was one of South Carolina's most distinguished jurists. One of the most eminent South Carolinians and Americans of the first half of the nineteenth century was

Hon. Waddy Thompson II, a son of Judge Waddy Thompson. He represented South Carolina in Congress, but is best known through being minister to Mexico at the time Texas secured its independence from that country and for the assistance he gave to the Americans whose lives were imperiled in Mexico at the time. His work "Reminiscences of Mexico," published in 1846, contains many thrilling accounts, and is particularly valuable as an authoritative explanation of the history of the relations of the United States with the neighboring republic.

Mr. Waddy Thompson is a son of the late Governor Hugh S. Thompson, who was the fifty-second governor of South Carolina. Governor Thompson was born at Charleston in 1836, son of Henry Tazewell and Agnes (Smith) Thompson. He graduated from The Citadel, the military college of South Carolina at Charleston, in 1856. In 1858 he was made lieutenant professor of French in the Arsenal Military Academy at Columbia, and later was captain and professor of Belles Lettres in The Citadel at Charleston. During the war he served bravely as captain of the Battalion of State Cadets in Charleston and other parts of the state. His command made a glorious record in the war. It fired the first gun, January 9, 1861, upon the Federal warship Star of the West in Charleston Harbor, and subsequently participated in the defense of Charleston, Fort Sumter and the South Carolina coast. This organization was not disbanded until after the surrender of Johnston's army.

After the war he took charge of the Columbia Male Academy, but in 1876 was called to larger and more important duties when he was elected state superintendent of education. He was re-elected in 1878 and 1880. He had in the meantime taken an active part in the redemption of South Carolina from carpet bag rule. The educational system of South Carolina owes a distinctive debt to Hugh Smith Thompson. While the carpet bag regime brought ruin to every department of state life, the effect was particularly disastrous upon schools, and it is almost literally true that the state had no system of education when Mr. Thompson entered upon his duties as state superintendent. His name is intimately associated with reforms which cleared the educational system from debt and restored it to life and vitality. Against strong opposition he established the plan of supporting the schools by local taxes. He instituted summer normal schools for the training of teachers, and generally popularized education when the attitude of most people was one of apathy.

In 1882 Hugh Smith Thompson was elected governor of South Carolina and re-elected in 1884. Before the close of his second term, in July, 1886, he resigned to become assistant Secretary of the United States Treasury under President Cleveland. In the absence of his chief he acted as Secretary of the Treasury. As chief magistrate of South Carolina, Governor Thompson discharged his duties with thorough ability and was elected for a second term without opposition. As acting head of the treasury he handled various responsibilities masterfully. This was particularly true when in the financial panic of 1887 the power of the Government was invoked to prevent a money depreciation from running into disaster. In that Federal post he added greatly to the fame associated with his name in his home state.

In February, 1889, he was made democratic member of the Civil Service Commission by President Cleveland. His appointment was not confirmed by the Senate during the closing days of Cleveland's term, but he was reappointed by President Harrison in May, 1889. His colleague on the commission was Theodore Roosevelt. He continued a member of the commission until May, 1892. At that date he resigned to become comptroller of the New York Life Insurance Company of New York City, and served there with credit for several years. When President Cleveland was making up his cabinet for his second administration, he offered Governor Thompson the choice of the Secretaryship of the Interior or the Postmaster Generalship, showing the esteem and confidence which President Cleveland reposed in him. Governor Thompson died November 15, 1904. In every position, state, national and in private life, Governor Thompson showed the highest qualities. He was conscientious, energetic and capable, a man of marked tact and courtesy, and possessed the rare quality of administrative statesmanship.

In 1856 he married Elizabeth Anderson Clarkson, daughter of Thomas B. Clarkson of Columbia. Their son, Waddy Thompson, was born in Columbia August 13, 1867. He acquired a liberal education in the University of South Carolina, graduating A. B. in 1887, and for the following eight years engaged in newspaper work, and since then has been in the life insurance and publishing business.

Mr. Waddy Thompson has had a busy career as a historian. He is known as author of "A History of the United States," published in 1904; "A Primary History of the United States," published in 1910; and more recently of "History of the People of the United States," and "History of the United States for Beginners."

Mr. Thompson is a member of the Columbia Club, and of the Round Table Club of New Orleans, is a Phi Beta Kappa, and also a member of the Alpha Tau Omega. He is a member of the Louisiana Historical Society, and the United Sons of Confederate Veterans. While Mr. Thompson is a Columbian, his business office is at Atlanta, in the Candler Annex. He married Pauline Spain, of Darlington, South Carolina, October 30, 1895.

JOHN M. SIFLY. In the City of Orangeburg, where he was born and reared, John M. Sifly has been a business man for the past fifteen years, and while he had the struggles and anxieties of a man starting with little capital, his position is now one of substantial credit and his establishment is regarded as an important commercial asset of the city.

Mr. Sifly was born at Orangeburg February 5, 1879, and acquired a liberal education at Wofford College in Spartanburg. In 1905 he engaged in business as local representative and distributor of some standard lines of buggies and wagons. With the growing popularity of the automobile he began the distribution of that vehicle, and has since conducted both lines, handling also the accessories of the trade. Mr. Sifly is the authorized Ford agent at Orangeburg, and conducts a finely equipped service station, and his establishment throughout is one of the most complete and modern in the state.

Mr. Sifly has never established a home of his own through marriage. His father was the late John L. Sifly, a native of Charleston, whose remote ancestors were English and German. The Sifly family has been in South Carolina for many generations, and some members of the earlier generations were Revolutionary soldiers. John L. Sifly earned the love and respect of his fellow men through the many arduous years he devoted to the Methodist ministry. He became a traveling or itinerant minister in 1867, and gave forty years to the duties assigned him by the Methodist Conference. After he was superannuated he lived for seven or eight years in Orangeburg, until his death in 1907. Rev. John L. Sifly married Sue (Townsend) Sifly, who was born at Cokesbury, near Greenwood, South Carolina, and her people were also old South Carolinians of English descent. Her father, Rev. Joel Townsend, was also one of the pioneer Methodist ministers. John M. Sifly has one brother, M. T. Sifly, an Orangeburg merchant, and his sister Lillie is the wife of Dr. J. L. Jeffries of Spartanburg. Mr. Sifly is a Methodist and is affiliated with the Lodge of Elks at Orangeburg.

JOHN FRAMPTON MAYBANK. Representing one of the old and historic families of Charleston, John Frampton Maybank has for many years been identified with its business affairs as a cotton merchant.

He was born in Hampton County January 31, 1870. His original ancestor, David Maybank, came from England and settled in Christ Church Parish of Charleston about 1680. One of the descendants was Joseph Maybank, who served as a lieutenant-colonel of the Berkeley County Militia. David Maybank, father of John F., was born at Mount Pleasant, South Carolina, December 10, 1841. He was educated in Charleston and in King's Mountain Military Academy, and early in the War between the States enlisted in the Rutledge Mounted Rifles. Going to Virginia, he joined the Boykin Rangers, and afterward was temporarily placed with the Jeff Davis Division under Col. W. T. Martin. As a member of that Legion he took part in Stuart's raid around McClellan's army in front of Richmond. Upon the organization of the Second South Carolina Cavalry under Col. M. C. Butler he became a private in Company A. He was in active service all through the war, and at the time of Lee's surrender was in a hospital at Augusta. After recovering he engaged in planting in Beaufort County, South Carolina. He married in Hampton County March 18, 1866, Mary Pope Frampton. Her father was John Frampton, one of the signers of the Ordinance of Secession in 1860. The Framptons were an English family and John Frampton married a Miss Hay of Scotch origin. In 1878 David Maybank returned to Charleston, and was bookkeeper for Thomas P. Smith & Company, and remained with the corporation of Thomas P. Smith McIvor Company until about 1916, when he retired. David Maybank and wife had three sons and three daughters: Dr. Joseph Maybank, John F., Mrs. J. H. Wyman, Mrs. Ed. M. Royall, Theodore, who died January 14, 1919, and Mary, at home with her parents.

John F. Maybank was reared and educated in Charleston, and for many years has been in the cotton business. After leaving school he spent several years in Georgia. He returned here in 1900 and founded the business of Maybank & Company, cotton merchants, also The Maybank Fertilizer Company, and has conducted these with increasing success to the present time.

Mr. Maybank married Eleanor S. Johnson, of Charleston. Their six children are Mary, David, Eleanor, Ann, Theodore and John F., Jr. Mr. Maybank is a member of clubs and social organizations at Charleston, is a Mason and a member of Grace Episcopal Church.

JUDGE R. BURTON HICKS. With the largest population of any county in the state, also one of the wealthiest as the center of the great textile industry, Spartanburg County naturally contributes an immense volume of business and many delicate and important problems of adjustment for the Probate Court. No office in the county touches more vitally the well being and financial interests of a larger number of people than that of the Chancery administration.

The county is fortunate in its present probate judge, R. Burton Hicks. He is a native of the county, is known to most of its citizens as a capable lawyer, has had service in the Legislature, and is giving a most careful and painstaking administration of his present office.

He was born at New Prospect, Campobello Township of Spartanburg County, in 1883, a son of R. L. and Sarah (Burton) Hicks, but moved to Spartanburg with his parents in 1895. He is a graduate of Wofford College with the Class of 1909, and also took post-graduate studies in Columbia University of New York. Before entering the law he was a successful teacher, being at one time superintendent of the schools at Woodruff and later in the same position at Honea Path. He used all his spare time while teaching to give to the study of law, and was admitted to the bar in 1913. He began practice in the same year, with home at Woodruff, and he was elected and served as a member of the Spartanburg County delegation to the Legislature in the session of 1916.

In the campaign of 1918 he received the democratic nomination for judge of the Probate Court, was elected in November, and began his official term January 1, 1919. He was also for some time editor of the Woodruff News, and is a director of the Bank of Commerce, Spartanburg.

Judge Hicks is a member of the Masonic order, of the Elks, of the Knights of Pythias and the Woodmen of the World, and is one of the leading lay members of the Baptist Church in Spartanburg. He married Miss Myrtle Lanford, of Woodruff. They have two children, Burton, Jr., and Myrtle.

HON. ARTHUR R. YOUNG has earned a high place in the South Carolina bar and his own merits and achievements have conferred additional credit upon a family name that is one of the oldest and most honorable in the South.

Mr. Young, who is now representing the County of Charleston in the State Senate, was born in Sewanee, Tennessee, July 3, 1876, a son of Henry E. Young, a grandson of Rev. Thomas John Young, and a great-grandson of William Price Young, who was of English ancestry and came to South Carolina from Pennsylvania. Grandfather Rev. Thomas John Young was at the time of his death assistant rector of St. Michael's Episcopal Church at Charleston. Henry E. Young, who was born in Charleston, was when he retired from practice in 1916 the oldest member of the Charleston bar, in continuous service for sixty years. He had begun practice in 1856, and his legal career was only interrupted by his duties to the Confederate Government at the time of the war. He served as a judge advocate on General Lee's staff. He died April 9, 1918.

Senator Young's mother was Elizabeth Underwood Rutledge, who died February 16, 1918, only a few days before her husband. She was born at Bowling Green, Kentucky, daughter of Arthur Middleton Rutledge, a native of Tennessee, and granddaughter of Henry Rutledge, who went west from South Carolina. The father of Henry Rutledge was a signer of the Declaration of Independence, and a brother of John Rutledge, the first Governor of South Carolina after the British rule. Henry E. Young and wife had a family of six children, three of whom reached mature years. Arthur R. was the second child and oldest son, and has one brother still living, Joseph Rutledge Young, a Charleston cotton merchant.

Senator Young was educated in private schools in Charleston and graduated A. B. in 1896 from the University of the South at Sewanee, Tennessee. He read law in his father's office, was admitted to the bar in December, 1898, and was associated with the elder Young in practice until 1915. Since then he has been a member of the firm Hagood, Rivers & Young, handling a general law clientage.

Mr. Young served as assistant United States attorney from 1911 to 1914. He was a member of the General Assembly in 1917-18, and in the latter year was elected to the State Senate. He is a member of the Carolina Yacht Club and of Charleston Lodge No. 242 of the Benevolent and Protective Order of Elks.

December 19, 1907, he married Nannie C. Conner, a daughter of General James Conner of Charleston. They have three sons, named Arthur Middleton, James Conner and Joseph Rutledge.

FRANK RAVENEL FROST. In the thirty years since he was admitted to the bar Frank Ravenel Frost has always commanded a large clientage and has done a valuable practice as a lawyer. He is one of Charleston's most public spirited citizens, and has found time to attend to the interests of many organizations outside of his immediate profession.

Mr. Frost was born at Society Hill, South Carolina, October 17, 1863, a son of Elias Horry and Frances Ravenel Frost. While the Frosts are an English family the Ravenels were French Huguenots. His father was a native of Charleston, was educated in Yale College, and became a prominent merchant and banker. He lived to be seventy years of age. He was at one time president of the Chamber of Commerce. While a business man, he was also distinguished by his love and knowledge of books and literature. His wife, Frances Ravenel Frost, was born at Charleston and lived to be seventy-three years of age. Frank Ravenel Frost is the second of five children, and the only son still living. His two sisters are Mrs. Ella R. Porcher and Mrs. Harriet H. Parker, both of Charleston.

Mr. Frost attended private school at Charleston, spent one year at Sewanee, Tennessee, and in 1886 received his A. B. degree from Harvard University. He then returned to Charleston and read law in the office of Smythe Lee and was admitted to the bar in 1888. After that he practiced as a member of the firm Smyth, Lee & Frost until 1911, since which date he has been alone in his profession.

During the Spanish-American war in 1898 he served as captain in the Third Regiment of the United States Volunteer Infantry under Colonel P. H. Ray, and saw some service in Cuba. He is a trustee of the Porter Military Academy at Charleston, and gives much of his time to that institution. He is also a chancellor of the Episcopal Church for the diocese of South Carolina. He has served as a member of the Charleston School Board and in 1914 was chairman of the Democratic City Convention and in 1919 chairman of the City Democratic Executive Committee. At different times he has given his services to various political, charitable and other boards, is a member of the Charleston Club, Country Club, the Carolina Yacht Club, and other social organizations.

In 1900 he married Miss Celestine H. Preston, daughter of John and Celestine E. Preston. They have two sons, E. Horry and John Preston.

GEORGE WALTON WILLIAMS, former president of the Carolina Savings Bank of Charleston, was born at Charleston in 1860 and attended the well known schools of Dr. Bruns and Professor Sachtleben in his native city. He prepared for Harvard College at Adams Academy in Quincy, Massachusetts, and spent a year and a half abroad in travel and study. During that time he was a student in the University of Bonn on the Rhine.

Returning from abroad to Charleston he engaged actively in business. For a time he was connected with the management of the Charleston Iron Works, and left that firm to become a partner in the cotton and fertilizer firm of Robertson, Taylor and Williams. After a few years he retired from mercantile pursuits to become identified with the Carolina Savings Bank, and was successively its cashier, vice president and president.

After an active business life of thirty-seven years Mr. Williams resigned the presidency of this bank and has since devoted his time and energies to work among the orphans of South Carolina and elsewhere. This has been a really significant service and the facts speak eloquently. He is chairman of the Board of Commissioners of the Charleston Orphan House, an institution founded in 1790 and with a continuous record of beneficence covering 129 years.

Mr. Williams is also chairman of the Board of Trustees of the Epworth Orphanage at Columbia and has had much to do in shaping the life of that home for dependent children. In the cause of the orphans he has devoted his best thought and service for a number of years, and has visited the best institutions of the kind both in Europe and America. He is directly interested in the welfare of many thousands of children at this time.

For many years Mr. Williams has served as trustee of the William Enston Home, an institution "to make old age comfortable," and was for twelve years an alderman of the City of Charleston. He is a member of the Charleston Club, the Carolina Yacht Club and the Charleston Country Club.

Mr. Williams married Margaret Adger, of Charleston, and their children are: Margaret, wife of Andrew M. Law, of Spartanburg; George W., Jr., Nashville, Tennessee; Ellison A., of Charleston, South Carolina; Susan S., of Charleston; and Martha, wife of Henry J. Blackford, of Englewood, N. J.

Hon. ANDREW JACKSON BETHEA, who recently retired from the office of lieutenant governor, is not only one of the attractive personalities in South Carolina public life, but a man of undoubted ability and true leadership with a proven record in professional and business affairs.

He was born August 17, 1879, at Free State, now in Dillon County, but formerly in the upper portion of Marion County. His early years were spent on a farm and in the invigorating environment of the country. His father, Dr. Andrew J. Bethea, a native of Marion County and a graduate of the South Carolina Medical College of Charleston, was both a physician and planter. During the war between the states he experienced hard and distinguished service as a Confederate soldier and afterwards was equally useful and influential as a citizen and physician. He died in the prime of manhood at the age of forty-three in 1881. His wife was Annie M. Allen, who was born in Marlboro this state October 22, 1843, and died June 19, 1919. Her father, Rev. Joel Allen was a well known Baptist minister. A woman of great refinement and culture, she demonstrated her force of character when as a widow with five children, three sons and two daughters, she reared and educated them and proved a model mother and is remembered for her exceptional gifts and attainments.

Andrew Jackson Bethea attended Centerville Academy and Dalcho School in Dillon County and took his college work in Wake Forest College, North Carolina, where he graduated B. A. in 1902 and Master of Arts in 1904. During 1905 he was a student of the University of Tennessee, and he received the Master of Arts degree from the University of South Carolina in 1910.

Mr. Bethea, who has been a resident of Columbia since 1907, has made for himself a name in several sections of the state. For one term he was principal of the Downer Institute of Beech Island, in Aiken County, for one term was principal of the Hopkins Graded School in Richland County, and for a like time was principal of the Camden graded school. For a brief time he also edited and published the Darlington Press, now The News and Press at Darlington.

Mr. Bethea was appointed private secretary to Governor Martin F. Ansel and served as such from 1907 to 1911. He was admitted to the bar by the Supreme Court of South Carolina in December, 1910, and is also licensed to practice in the Federal Courts. During his legal career he has successfully handled many important cases, and enjoys an unusually select practice. Mr. Bethea was elected code commissioner of South Carolina on the first ballot by the Joint Assembly, and served from 1911 to 1915, during which time he codified the laws of the State of South Carolina which is known as the Code of 1912.

His service as lieutenant governor was from 1915 to 1919. He was twice elected, each time over strong competitors. During his second campaign he received the largest vote ever given a candidate with opposition for a state office in South Carolina. In 1918 Mr. Bethea was a candidate for governor, making the question of loyalty paramount in his campaign. He received a splendid vote and is regarded as a strong and aggressive political leader in his state.

Mr. Bethea is a democrat not only in a partisan sense, but in the literal interpretation of the word, and has always made his influence count in the battle for the rights and rule of the people. In many ways he has been active in movements for the advancement of his party. He attended the democratic convention at Baltimore when Woodrow Wilson was first nominated, and later campaigned for him in doubtful states and also made many speeches to aid in the re-election of President Wilson in 1916.

Mr. Bethea has taken an active part in military affairs having been a member of the South Carolina State Reserve Militia since its organization. In 1917 he volunteered for service in the European war and later at his own request was inducted as a private into the United States Army. In 1918 he entered the Officers Training Camp at Camp Humphreys, Virginia, and was transferred to Camp Kendrick, New Jersey, and completed training in the Training Battalion and U. S. Gas School, taking the full course in gas defensive and offensive warfare. He received a certificate of graduation and was recommended for a commission as major, and later was commissioned with that rank in the army and now holds that rank in the reserves.

In the midst of a busy life, however, Mr. Bethea has found time to serve on several business boards and is interested in a number of financial enterprises. He has made a decided success in business, although he began life without means, educating himself and relying upon his own resources to become established. In this respect he is typical of what is best in modern commercial life and is representative of the highest type of American citizen.

Mr. Bethea is a prominent member of the Baptist denomination and has served in many important positions in his church. He is president of the board of trustees of the South Carolina Baptist Hospital; is a member of the Board of Deacons of the historic First Baptist Church of Columbia, in which the Secession Convention was held, has served as the chairman of the board, and for

several years was superintendent of a flourishing Sunday school in this church. Mr. Bethea is also a member of the Board of Trustees of the Southern Baptist Theological Seminary, Louisville, Kentucky, and acted as chairman of the committee that organized and established the Young Women's Christion Association, of Columbia.

Mr. Bethea is a Mason, an Elk, a Knight of Pythias, and a Woodman of the World, and is affiliated with many other organizations, institutions and movements to advance the material, industrial, social, political and moral life of the state and nation.

ROBERT WILSON, D. D. Trained for the profession of medicine and serving as assistant surgeon in the Confederate army during the war between the states, Dr. Robert Wilson after the war prepared for the ministry of the Episcopal Church and for half a century has been one of the dignified leaders and scholars in that church, not only in South Carolina but in other states.

Reverend Doctor Wilson was born at Charleston October 28, 1838, son of James M. and Ann Isabel (Gibbes) Wilson. He represents several well known colonial families and is of Scotch, English and French ancestry. His father at one time was a leading merchant in Charleston. He is descended from a Dr. Robert Wilson who came from Scotland in 1750 and became one of Charleston's most noted physicians of colonial times. In the maternal line he is also descended from Governor Robert Gibbes, who came from England in 1670 via Barbados and became one of the Proprietary Governors of the Province of Carolina.

Robert Wilson received his early education in private schools, attended the College of Charleston, and afterward the Medical College of the State of South Carolina, where he graduated in 1859. For two years he practiced medicine at Pineville, later at Camden, and at the beginning of the war enlisted his services in behalf of the Confederate Government and was appointed assistant surgeon in the army. He performed all the varied duties required of him until 1864. On leaving the army he entered the Theological Seminary at Camden, graduated, and in 1883 Washington College at Chestertown, Maryland, conferred upon him the degree D. D. He was rector of Claremont Parish at Statesburg, South Carolina, afterward at St. Paul's, Kent, Maryland, and for thirteen years was in charge of St. Peter's Parish at Easton, Maryland. He then returned to his native city and became rector of St. Luke's Parish, which he served for seventeen years, and then had four parishes as missionary until August, 1917. He has also been vice president of the Church Home, president of the Charleston Library Society, president of the Huguenot Society of South Carolina, and of the Elliott Society, has acted as commander of Camp Sumter of the United Confederate Veterans, and twice as colonel of the Charleston Regiment, U. C. Veterans, as chaplain of St. Andrew's Society, is affiliated with the Phi Kappa Psi College Fraternity, the Huguenot Society of America and of London, England. In 1870 he published "Confirmation Lectures" and in 1883 "The Sower," and is author of many briefer articles and papers found in the periodical press, both religious and secular.

November 22, 1859, Doctor Wilson married Mary Susan Gibbes. On April 22, 1862, he married Ann Jane Shand. And now, 1920, they have been married almost fifty-nine years. Of the eight children born to them but two are living, Dr. Robert Wilson, Jr., of Charleston, and Mary, widow of Elias Ball, also of Charleston. Doctor Wilson, Sr., has nine grandchildren. The eldest granddaughter, Miss Mary W. Ball, an artist, is in the service of the United States Government Engineer Department in the map-making drafting department.

EDWARD W. DURANT, JR. A northern lumberman, coming to Charleston about fifteen years ago to look after the mills and other interests of his associates in this state, Mr. Durant has found here opportunities for his ambition as a developer and has become absorbed in a growing list of enterprises that not only aroused his complete enthusiasm but are of direct benefit to the changing agricultural and industrial program of South Carolina.

Mr. Durant was born at Stillwater, Minnesota, in 1864, and was graduated from Yale University with the class of 1887. He is therefore a product of the rugged pioneer circumstances of the great Northwest, and also of one of the finest institutions of learning in America. He returned to Minnesota from university to enter the lumber industry. He worked in lumber camps, and acquired a technical knowledge of every branch of the business. Eventually he became an individual timber owner and lumber manufacturer and was associated with a group of men prominent in that business in the Northwest. Like many other such organizations, with the decrease of the timber supply in the North they began acquiring holdings in the South. It was for the purpose of taking charge of these interests and mills in South Carolina that Mr. Durant located at Charleston in 1904.

It was not long before he was awake to the wonderful natural wealth and the inducements to capital in developing agricultural and other enterprises, and he decided to make Charleston his permanent home. There is no native son more enthusiastic concerning the great future of Charleston and its surrounding rich territory than Mr. Durant. His capital and personal energy have been responsible for a number of enterprises, but two of them, perhaps of greatest significance, are his stock farms, one being the T Farm at Rantowles, fourteen miles south of Charleston in Charleston County, and the other the Pine Grove Farm in Berkeley County, adjoining the Town of Mount Holly. The T Farm comprises over 5,000 acres of very rich land originally a rice plantation, but for several years before it was acquired by Mr. Durant the land had been neglected and impoverished. Mr. Durant spent $50,000 or more developing this land into a modern stock farm. It is a large and profitable enterprise in itself, and has also been frequently pointed out as a practical demonstration of the results that follow judicious combination of livestock husbandry with diversified crop growing. It is the home of a very fine herd of pure bred Hereford cattle headed by registered bulls, and of registered Duroc-Jersey hogs. Mr. Durant has made similar and about equally extensive improvements on the Pine Grove Farm, which is also the breeding ground for Duroc-Jersey and other high grade registered livestock. Part of this farm comprises the Pine Grove Club. By his practical efforts on these farms Mr. Durant anticipated by several years the now general propaganda for diversifying South Carolina agriculture with the raising of livestock as a means of combating the threatened menace of the boll-weevil.

Mr. Durant is president of the Pine Grove Livestock Company, president of the Pine Grove Club, president of the Southern Stock and Farming Company owning the T Farm, is vice president of the E. P. Burton Lumber Company, secretary-treasurer of the Cooper River Corporation, and president of the Filbin Corporation.

He has always enjoyed some of the honors of public life. He is a republican and during the four years of the administration of William H. Taft served as collector of customs for the Port of Charleston. He is a member of the Charleston Chamber of Commerce, the Country Club and a number of other social and business organizations.

Mr. Durant married soon after coming to Charleston a daughter of William Porcher Miles, of one of the old and distinguished families of Charleston.

JULIAN MITCHELL is a prominent Charleston lawyer, and counting his services three generations of the family have been identified with the Charleston community as able professional men and conscientious and public spirited citizens.

Mr. Mitchell was born at the summer home of his parents at Flat Rock, November 21, 1867. His grandfather, Dr. Edward Mitchell, of English ancestry, was for many years a prominent physician and was a native of Edisto Island. Julian Mitchell, Sr., was also born on Edisto Island, and for many years was a prominent leader in educational affairs in his home city and state. He was chairman of the school board of Charleston a number of years and was chairman of the educational committee in the State Constitutional Convention of 1895. One of the school buildings of Charleston is named in his honor. His wife was Caroline Pinckney, daughter of Rev. Charles Cotesworth Pinckney, for several years rector of Grace Episcopal Church of Charleston and of the Revolutionary family of Pinckneys.

Julian Mitchell, Jr., was the only child of his parents. He was educated in the Charleston High School, spent one year in Charleston College, one year in the University School at Petersburg, Virginia, for three years attended Harvard University and finished his law course in the University of Virginia. He was admitted to the bar in 1890, and since that date has enjoyed a large general practice as attorney and counsellor. He is senior partner of Mitchell & Smith. He is also a director of the Bank of Charleston, the Charleston Savings Institute and the Exchange Banking & Trust Company, and for many years has been interested in politics. He was a member of the Legislature from 1896 to 1900.

In 1895 he married Belle W. Witte, a daughter of C. O. Witte. They have two sons, Julian and Cotesworth Pinckney.

ROBERT ALBERTUS DOBSON, a young lawyer of genuine distinction and a prominent member of the Gaffney bar, has twice been a member of the Legislature from Cherokee County, first elected in 1910 and again in 1916. The outstanding feature of his second term was his influence in procuring the bond issue of $225,000 for good roads for Cherokee County. It was this bond issue that put Cherokee County ahead of most of the other counties in South Carolina in matters of good roads, and as attorney for the Cherokee Highway Commission Mr. Dobson has handled most of the legal work in connection with this great improvement.

He was born near Yorkville, South Carolina, September 3, 1877, a son of William and Elizabeth (McCarter) Dobson. The Dobsons are an old time family in York County, while the McCarters are kin of the prominent Wallace family in the old Bethel section. Mr. Dobson's great-grandfather was John Dobson of York County, conspicuous in his time as a teacher and surveyor.

Mr. Dobson grew up on his father's farm, attended the public schools at Yorkville, and in 1900 graduated A. B. from Furman University at Greenville. Like many successful professional men he did his turn at school teaching, and was principal of the schools at York, Kershaw and Laurens. He also studied law, was admitted to the bar in 1904, and in 1908 after resigning his position in the Laurens School he located at Gaffney. There he became associated with Solicitor J. C. Otts under the name Otts & Dobson. In 1913 Mr. Dobson formed his partnership with T. K. Vassy, under the name Dobson & Vassy. They have a large general practice, and also served as attorneys for the City of Gaffney and County of Cherokee. Mr. Dobson is secretary-treasurer of the Farmers & Mechanics Building and Loan Association, and during the war was a member of the local conscription board. During his service in the Legislature he was a member of the judiciary and other important committees. He has served as moderator of the Broad River Baptist Association, and fraternally is affiliated with the Knights of Pythias, Masons, Junior Order United American Mechanics and the Improved Order of Red Men.

Mr. Dobson married Miss Alice E. Williams of Lancaster, daughter of Judge D. A. Williams. They are the parents of four children named Raymond, Nannie Williams, Robert A., Jr., and Sarah Elizabeth.

JAMES BARRE GUESS. As to a proper policy of agricultural management in America many strong and convincing claims have been put forth in favor of extensive rather than intensive cultivation and management. The working of extensive tracts of land under one administrative unit has been a prevailing practice in the old as well as the new South, and possesses all the advantages of efficiency and economy and satisfies the co-operative principle without the obvious faults and weakness of co-

operation as generally applied to industrial undertakings.

Perhaps one of the most successful of these large scale plantations in South Carolina is that owned by the Guess family of Denmark. James Barre Guess, who for over thirty years has sustained the active responsibilities of this business, was born in Leesville, South Carolina, November 7, 1859.

His father, Dr. S. D. M. Guess, was a man of real distinction and achievement. A country dentist as well as a planter, he spent four years in the Confederate army and returned home to find his property destroyed by the invaders and his wife and only child almost starving. With that courage which enabled many southern gentlemen to begin life anew, and with the assistance of his household and some hired help, he reorganized his affairs, and his associates and friends claimed that few men accomplished more in a shorter time by economy, good judgment and hard work. He had a noblewoman for his wife, Sarah Eloise Barre. In war times in the absence of her husband she managed the business, paid the war taxes, and supervised both the household and the fields. She saw the Union soldiers burn her property and carry off the food she needed for daily subsistence. She continued with the same loyal co-operation and shared in the success enjoyed by the family after the war, and lived to the age of eighty-two.

James Barre Guess graduated from the Carolina Military Institute, now The Citadel, June 13, 1879, with the rank of Cadet Captain of Company A. There was no thought of a professional career and he immediately returned home and became a helpful factor in the management of the plantation. Here he found his educational training in engineering mechanics and agricultural science of great advantage to him. In 1885 he was made a full partner in his father's business, under the firm name of S. D. M. Guess & Son. A few years later he became general manager, the business at that time comprising extensive plantations, a store or commissary supplying all the needs of the farm and its workers in a commercial way and a great deal of other expensive equipment required for the operation of a large southern cotton plantation and the production of the food supplies to sustain the home and plantation workers. In 1889 the firm organized the first bank in the Town of Denmark, Doctor Guess assuming its presidency, at which time the full responsibilities of the plantation devolved upon the son. For thirty years that business has continued to grow and prosper and even today is one of the larger agricultural units in the state.

Until the demands of his private business absorbed all his time Mr. Guess was able to take part in various public duties. In 1880, the year after he graduated from the military college, he was made a captain in the South Carolina State Militia, and held a commission until the fall of 1886, when he resigned. In that year he was elected a member of the House of Representatives, and served with a creditable record from 1886 until 1890. He then withdrew altogether from politics in order to give his undivided time to his business. Mr. Guess was a director in the Bank of Denmark until its recent reorganization, when he retired from the management.

The conditions that have prescribed "a solid South" inevitably have brought southern gentlemen into the ranks of the democratic party. Mr. Guess is a democrat without rancor or bitter partisanship. He is a Mason and Knight of Pythias, and his chief interest for many years outside of business and home has been the Methodist Episcopal Church, South, which he has served as trustee, steward and for thirty years as superintendent of its Sunday school.

Mr. Guess has had an ideal and happy family relationship. He was three times married. October 27, 1880, at Denmark, he married Hattie Ramell Wroton, a daughter of W. H. Wroton. August 12, 1884, at Batesburg, Sallie Sophia Mitchell, daughter of J. A. Mitchell, became his wife. She was the mother of all his children. He married for his present wife at Ridge Spring, South Carolina, September 30, 1914, Sudie Catherine Mitchell, daughter of McKendree Mitchell. Mr. Guess has six children: James Barre, Jr., who married Mary Wiggins Connor; Hattie Lee, wife of Hubert W. Matthews; W. Samuel, who married Annie Lou Collins; Sarah Ellen, wife of George Milton Crum; Emmie Ruth, who married Renold Connor Wiggins; and Mary Frances.

MRS. GEORGIANA AUSTIN SAULS. The life history of the estimable and popular lady whose name heads these paragraphs happily illustrates what may be attained by faithful and continued effort along a definite line. Her career has been dignified and womanly, her manner unaffected and her actions have been a blessing to all who have come within range of her influence. She is a representative of one of the sterling old families of this section and enjoys to a notable degree the confidence and regard of the people with whom she has associated for so many years.

Mrs. Georgiana Austin Sauls was born in Lexington, South Carolina, in 1840, and is the daughter of Davis and Mary (Williamson) Austin, both of whom also were natives of Lexington. Davis Austin was the son of Davis and Inabniette Austin and Mary Williamson was a daughter of Thomas Williamson. Davis Austin, Jr., was for many years a prominent merchant in Atlanta, Georgia, but in 1864, during Sherman's historic march to the sea, he lost everything and fled to Savannah. Subsequently he located at Orangeburg, where he followed farming pursuits during the remainder of his active life, his death occurring in 1897, at the age of eighty-six years. His wife had died at the early age of thirty-one years. They were the parents of the following children: Lavinia married a Mr. Livingston, of Orangeburg, and is now eighty-one years old; Morgan was a member of the Thirty-fourth Regiment during the war between the states and was killed in battle; Charles Wesley married a Miss Johnston, of Colleton; Davis Kirkland was married to Jane Croutch, of Edgefield; Jane Kathleen was married to a Mr. Ziegler, of Bamberg.

Mrs. Georgiana Sauls received her educational training in private schools of her home town. In 1859 she became the wife of Caleb Sauls, who was born on a plantation near Walterboro, the son of Isaac and Olive (Savage) Sauls. He received his education in the public schools of Walterboro and then devoted himself to the operation of his plantation. He was also a mail and express carrier, in which positions he rendered efficient and faithful service. During the war between the states Mr. Sauls was a soldier in the Confederate army and was stationed at Sullivan's Island. His death occurred in 1887.

After her husband's death Mrs. Sauls was almost continuously in the hotel business until recently, when she retired, her experience in this line of effort covering a period of practically forty years. She has been a resident of Walterboro for more than fifty years and during these years she faithfully served the public in a manner which was duly appreciated, as her continued patronage by the same persons year after year testified. Though now seventy-nine years old, she still retains to a remarkable degree her physical powers, while mentally she is as keen and alert as ever. In addition to the hotel building which she occupies, Mrs. Sauls is also the owner of a fine business block in Walterboro.

By her union with Caleb Sauls, Mrs. Sauls became the mother of children who are briefly mentioned as follows: Julia became the wife of James DeLetreville, of Charleston; Davis is mentioned elsewhere in this work; Hattie became the wife of a Mr. Peoples, of Moggetts; Morgan is deceased; Minnie became the wife of J. J. Jones, of Augusta; Sallie became the wife of J. Hagood, of Columbia; Charlie, Edward and Norman are deceased. The last named was married to Ida Ackermann, of Cottageville, and they are the parents of seven children; Edgar Pierce; Norma Evelyn; Henry Caleb; Ruth and Naomi, twins, who are deceased; Davis Austin and Elizabeth Ida.

Mrs. Sauls has through the years that have come and gone since she first engaged in the hotel business seen many changes take place and she retains a splendid recollection of the happeings which if put in shape for reading would make an absorbing story. She possesses a charming personality and her circle of friends is as large as her circle of acquaintances.

EDWARD BARNABAS WILLIAMS is one of the best known business men of the southern part of South Carolina, and particularly in Dorchester County, where for many years he has stood for progress and fair dealing, and while he has consistently labored for the advancement of his own interests he has never been neglectful of his duties as a citizen of one of the choicest sections of this great state. Therefore he is held in the highest esteem by all classes in the locality honored by his citizenship, enjoying the confidence and good will of all as a result of his public spirit, fair and straightforward business methods and his exemplary character.

Edward Barnabas Williams was born in Orangeburg, South Carolina, on July 6, 1864, and is the third in order of birth of the ten children born to James Allen and Jane E. (Dukes) Williams. James A. Williams, who also was a native of Orangeburg, was a coachpainter by vocation. He was a soldier in the Confederate army and served throughout the struggle. His father, who was a native of the same place, was of English descent. The subject's mother was a native of Orangeburg County, this state, and the daughter of William A. Dukes, who was a descendant of one of three brothers who came from England and settled in South Carolina. She had one brother, J. W. H. Dukes, who served as a Confederate soldier.

Edward B. Williams was educated in the public schools of his native town, and as soon as old and large enough he began to take up life's battle on his own account. His first work was as an apprentice at the business of carriage manufacturing, but on the conclusion of his apprenticeship period he engaged in the mercantile business at Orangeburg, which occupied his attention for eight years, at the end of which time he sold out, though remaining at Orangeburg. He then returned to his trade of wagonmaker, at which he worked about two years. Then for about one year he was engaged in the cotton business there, but in 1903 he came to St. George, with which locality he has since remained identified. His first enterprise at St. George was as a dealer in wagons and buggies, in which he met with satisfactory success so that the following year he added the cotton business and also acquired some farming interests. He has also bought and sold many horses and mules, in which he has been successful, and in 1918 he opened a brick manufacturing plant at the edge of town, where he is making an excellent quality of brick, which find a ready market. The plant has a daily capacity of 20,000 brick. Because of his indefatigable industry, sound business judgment and accommodating ways, he has met with a well deserved success and is today numbered among the most popular members of the business circles of his community. In 1908 Mr. Williams was elected mayor of St. George, and so satisfactory has been his discharge of his official duties that he has been retained in the office continuously to the present time, his present term expiring in May, 1920.

In 1904 Mr. Williams was married to Minnie Hutto, the daughter of J. S. Hutto of St. George. To this union have been born four children, namely: Mariam, Jane Ellafair, Sue and Edward B., Jr.

Fraternally Mr. Williams is an active member of the Knights of Pythias. Distinctively a man of affairs, he has long filled a conspicuous place in local affairs, and as leader in important enterprises he has attained to an enviable place in the esteem of all who know him.

EDWARD RUFUS CASH has played a role of no secondary importance in the upbuilding of Gaffney as a cotton milling center. While to some degree financially, he has been chiefly identified with local cotton mills as a master of mechanical technique. Probably when a boy he showed a genius for mechanics, and he developed that genius by hard and close application through many years and is regarded as one of the ablest cotton mill superintendents in the state.

Mr. Cash was born in Spartanburg County in 1863, a son of Henry and Lucy (Devine) Cash.

THE NEW YORK
PUBLIC LIBRARY

He was not born to wealth, and the circumstances of his early home life handicapped his taking advantage of even the normal opportunities of the local schools, which were by no means of the highest class. It is said that when he was twelve years of age he was doing all the milking, cooking and hoeing of a "one-horse farm." His mother was then in ill health, and the son and father had to remain on the farm and do all the work both in the fields and in the house. A year or so later he drove an ox wagon, hauling the wood to burn the brick that built the first mill at Clifton, South Carolina. When the job was completed he remained an employe and learned the machinist's trade. At the end of three years he was made master mechanic, and was elevated to a position superior to that of the man who taught him his trade. In 1891, leaving the Clifton mills, he joined the D. A. Tompkins Company at Charlotte, the pioneer mill machinery of the two Carolinas. He was with this firm until 1893, and then identified himself with Gaffney, which at that time contained only two or three stores, two bar rooms and a restaurant. He was therefore a participant in the first movement for the making of Gaffney an industrial center, and during the past quarter of a century his interests and energies have never flagged in behalf of everything that concerns the welfare of this town. He came to Gaffney as master mechanic and superintendent of the Gaffney Manufacturing Company, which in 1893 built the first cotton mill of the town. He remained in that position until 1900, and then took an active part in the organization and building of the Limestone Cotton Mills, having personal supervision of the building, and when it was completed remaining as superintendent. Out of the Limestone grew the Hamrick mill, Dr. W. C. Hamrick being an active official in both organizations, while the venerable merchant, J. A. Carroll, was president of the Limestone mill. Mr. Cash has been superintendent of these mills since they were started. In July, 1919, he organized the Cash Mills of which he is president and treasurer and also the East Side Manufacturing Company at Shelby, North Carolina, of which he is also president and treasurer. He has had a number of other business and investment interests, and for many years has been prominent in the Cherokee Avenue Baptist Church of Gaffney. He is chairman of its Board of Deacons. This church, now housed in a handsome building, grew out of what was first known as the Cherokee Avenue Sunday School, organized in Mr. Cash's home.

In 1885 Mr. Cash married Miss Meda L. Byrd, daughter of David M. Byrd of Darlington. They became the parents of ten children, and the seven living are: Mrs. Marie Estelle Byers, George F., F. Grady, Crowley B., Mrs. Inez Fulmer, Joe Dean Price and Meda Catherine Cash. During the war two of the sons joined the local coast artillery company.

JOHN FRANCIS PRETTYMAN is a veteran lumber manufacturer and merchant. While he has been active head of a large business at Summerville some years, he formerly operated at Marion in this state, also in North Carolina, and acquired his early business experience in the North.

He was born at Philadelphia, Pennsylvania, May 13, 1857. His father bore the same name and was also a native of Philadelphia. The grandfather, David Prettyman, was a native of Lewis, Delaware. Practically all the Prettymans now living in the United States are descended from two brothers, John and William Prettyman, who came from London, England, in 1682 and settled in Virginia. The mother of John F. Prettyman of Summerville was Elizabeth McClure, a native of Philadelphia and of Irish ancestry. He was one of a family of four children, being the oldest.

Mr. Prettyman as a boy in Philadelphia attended the public schools. He engaged in the lumber business in 1877, and has been a manufacturer and producer for over forty years. About 1893 he moved his headquarters to Newbern, North Carolina, and after about seven years there came to Marion, South Carolina, and since 1909 has had his home at Summerville. At this time he formed the firm of J. F. Prettyman and Sons and built the present milling plant, about one mile west of Summerville, under the firm name of J. F. Prettyman & Sons. This lumber plant is of strictly modern construction, and turns out a high grade of material. The timber is supplied by about twenty miles of standard gauge railroad, all of which is owned and operated by the firm, as a means of bringing in their logs and timber, of which they have a sufficient supply to operate the manufacturing plant indefinitely. Mr. F. P. Prettyman, secretary-treasurer of the company, manages the manufacture, sale and shipment of the mills' product, while Mr. C. F. Prettyman manages the land, timber and railroad and logging operations of the company. At the present writing Mr. T. M. Prettyman is not actively connected with the mill operation, he being in Texas engaged in geological survey work in connection with the University of Texas.

January 8, 1885, Mr. Prettyman married Miss Virginia Fleming, a daughter of Dr. T. M. and Virginia (Pemberton) Fleming. Mrs. Prettyman was reared and educated near Richmond, Virginia. They have four children: Frank P., Cannon F., Thomas M. and Virginia Selden. Frank married Isabel Cross, of Marion and has two children, Virginia Fleming and Howard Cross. Cannon married Louise Selden, of Richmond, Virginia. Virginia is the wife of Dr. R. B. Rhett, of Charleston. Thomas M. is unmarried. Mr. and Mrs. Prettyman and their children are members of the Episcopal Church.

LAWRENCE ALLEN WALKER is a banker of long and active experience for a man of his years, and is president of the Bank of Summerville. He was born and received his early banking training in Charleston. His birth occurred February 17, 1879. He is a brother of Mr. Legare Walker of Summerville. He was reared and educated in Charleston and Summerville, attending the Misses Brownfield's school at Summerville, The Citadel, the Charleston High School and Porter Military Academy. As a young man he went to work in the Miners and Merchants Bank of Charleston and remained with that institution for thirteen years, most of the time as teller. On removing from Charleston to Summerville he engaged in the real estate and insurance business, and in September, 1916, when the Bank of Summerville was organized and incorporated he was made its president. Mr. Walker is affiliated with the Knights of Pythias Lodge at Summerville. He was the Red Cross county treasurer and chairman of both War Fund drives for Dorchester County during the World war. He is president of the Summerville Business Men's League, president of the Summerville Tobacco Warehouse Corporation and has given up time to promote agriculture and business of community. He served two complete terms as alderman of the Town of Summerville, and resigned in his third term to serve on the board of public works of the Town of Summerville.

In 1915 he married Margaret W. Buswell, of Hackensack, New Jersey, daughter of Fred C. Buswell, who was vice president of the Home Insurance Company of New York. They have three children, Lawrence A. Jr., Margaret Buswell and Eleanor Buswell.

THOMAS MIDDLETON RAYSOR is one of the oldest lawyers of Orangeburg, and by his work in his profession, in civil and educational affairs, is a man of recognized prominence all over the state.

He was born at Orangeburg, a son of Capt. Peter A. and Anna M. Raysor. His father was a planter and served throughout the war as a captain in the Confederate army. Thomas M. Raysor was educated in the public schools, took his A. B. degree from Wofford College in 1878 and read law under Hon. Samuel Dibble. He was admitted to the bar in December, 1880, and has since commanded a large general practice, much of his work having been in connection with litigation for railroad, telegraph companies and other large corporations. He is also a noted criminal lawyer. He was one of the organizers and the first vice president of the Bank of Orangeburg, and is now its president.

Mr. Raysor served as a member of the Legislature from Orangeburg from 1884 to 1890 and was a member of the State Senate from 1901 to 1910. He is a trustee of Converse College, was trustee of the University of South Carolina, chairman of the board of trustees of the graded schools of Orangeburg and was one of the organizers of the public school system. He and his family have been factors in the educational uplift of South Carolina for several generations. He has served as a member of the State Board of Education, and while in the Legislature he supported the bill to rebuild The Citadel, the state military college at Charleston. His father was a graduate of The Citadel and his grandfather was much interested in that school in his early days. Mr. Raysor was one of the pioneers in promoting a compulsory system of education for the state. In recognition of his many varied services to education Wofford College bestowed upon him the degree LL. D. During the war Mr. Raysor was chairman of the local board of exemption and supported the Government in all its policies and plans. He is a member of the Episcopal Church and in politics has been a delegate to a number of state and national conventions of the democratic party. Mr. Raysor married Mattie Mandeville Rogers, of Darlington, South Carolina.

WYLIE C. HAMRICK. Though a graduate of the Baltimore College of Physicians and Surgeons, and having earned a deservedly high place in his profession, Mr. Hamrick has made his career count for most through the promotion and management of cotton industries and has built up at least four great factories that furnish a large proportion of the industrial assets of Cherokee County.

Mr. Hamrick was born in Cleveland County, North Carolina, in 1860, and though a resident of Gaffney since 1895, his home and work are not far distant from the scenes of his birth and early childhood. His parents were Cameron Street and Almera (Bridges) Hamrick. The Hamricks are an old family of Cleveland County, a county notable for its many distinguished characters. The Hamricks have lived there since before the Revolution. Mr. Hamrick's grandparents were Moses and Sarah (Robinson) Hamrick. His great-grandfather Robinson was a Revolutionary soldier and through him Mr. Hamrick has membership in the Sons of the American Revolution.

He grew up and received his literary training in Cleveland County, and in 1882 took his degree from the Baltimore College of Physicians and Surgeons. He practiced his profession at Grover and Shelby, North Carolina, and for one term of two (1888-90) years represented Cleveland County in the North Carolina Legislature. Upon locating at Gaffney in 1895, Mr. Hamrick continued his professional work for several years. In 1900, associated with J. A. Carroll, A. N. Wood and others he organized the Limestone Mill at Gaffney, and for a number of years has been its secretary and treasurer. This mill was started with 10,000 spindles and 300 looms and in 1904 its facilities were increased by 15,000 spindles and 240 looms, without increasing the capital stock. The business has paid many large dividends, even in adverse years, and the industry is now one valued at $1,000,000, and furnishing employment to 250 or more operatives.

The success of this institution encouraged Mr. Hamrick to further efforts in mill building. In 1907 he organized the Hamrick Mill at Gaffney and since then its capital stock has been increased from $150,000 to $250,000, and its facilities from 10,000 spindles and 300 looms to over 25,000 spindles and over 500 looms. The mill employs approximately 225 people. Mr. Hamrick is president and treasurer of the company. These two industries at Gaffney produce about 4,000,000 pounds of print cloth annually. The third milling enterprise established by Mr. Hamrick was Broad River Mill at Blacksburg, organized January 1, 1913. The company purchased the old Whittaker Mill, a yarn mill, and in 1916 enlarged it until it has about 14,000 spindles and 324 looms. On February 26, 1920, he organized the Musgrove Mills, a million dollar corporation of Gaffney, South Carolina.

The community is indeed fortunate when its industrial affairs are entrusted to a man of such character and ideals as Mr. Hamrick. His abilities measure up to those of the keenest and most successful practical business men, and yet through all

the hand of the administrator is guided by settled convictions and purposes that keep the technical machinery of business always subservient to the welfare of the humanity involved. The Limestone, Hamrick and Broad River mills are the workshops for communities of prospering and enlightened people and nowhere do churches, schools and every factor of a modern social community receive more encouragement.

In civic and public life Mr. Hamrick's most important work at the present time is as chairman of the Cherokee County Highway Commission, an office he accepted in 1917, when the commission was entrusted with the expenditure of the proceeds of a bond issue of $450,000. Under his wise and able administration these and other large sums of money have been expended for good roads, and Cherokee County stands among the first in the state in the matter of improved highways. Mr. Hamrick was elected as a member of the State Senate in 1910. He was prominent in the movement for the formation of the new county of Cherokee in 1897.

Mr. Hamrick married Miss Turner of Grover, North Carolina. They have five children: Volina; Waite C., who is now actively associated with his father in cotton manufacture; Ethel, Alma and Lyman A.

WILLIAM WHETSTONE WANNAMAKER, a lawyer by profession, is head of one of the oldest and most prosperous cotton milling industries in the state at Orangeburg.

He was born at Allendale, South Carolina, August 17, 1872, a son of Rev. Thomas Elliott and Sarah Ann (Boyd) Wannamaker. His father was a minister of the Methodist Episcopal Church, distinguished by long and devoted service. The son was educated in public and private schools, graduated in 1893 from the academic department of the University of South Carolina, and in 1894 completed the law course in the same institution. He was in active practice at Orangeburg until January, 1905. In 1898 he had volunteered for service in the Spanish-American war, becoming captain of Company E of the Second South Carolina Infantry. He saw some active service in Cuba and was on duty until mustered out in April, 1899.

Mr. Wannamaker is sole owner of the Orange Cotton Mills, which is the successor of the Orange Mills established by George H. Cornelson, one of the southern pioneers in cotton manufacture. Since 1909 W. W. Wannamaker has been sole owner. Mr. Wannamaker served two years as an alderman of Orangeburg City. For two years, 1918-19, he was grand master of Masons in South Carolina. He has served as trustee of the city schools for six years and is a director of the People's Bank of Orangeburg. He is a member of the Methodist Church.

June 1, 1899, he married Harriet Lyall Matheson, of Bennettsville, South Carolina. They have four children: William W., Jr., who graduated from The Citadel at Charleston in 1919; Alexander James Matheson, a high school student; Lyall Matheson; and Thomas Elliott, Jr.

THOMAS WHITE COTHRAN. On the basis of his experience and proved achievements Thomas White Cothran of Greenwood is one of the leading civil and construction engineers of his native state. He comes of a prominent family of old Abbeville and Greenwood counties, and was born in a portion of Abbeville that is now Greenwood County in 1874.

His parents were Wade E. and Sarah Elizabeth (Chiles) Cothran. Both the Cothrans and the Chiles families have been long and prominently identified with South Carolina. The Chiles family came to this state from Virginia, and is numerously represented in all the South Atlantic States. Mr. Cothran's great-grandfather was Samuel Cothran, a son of Alexander Cothran, who came to South Carolina about 1815. Originally the Cothrans were north of Ireland people, and on coming to America first settled in Connecticut, and arrived in South Carolina about 1793. Samuel Cothran, the great-grandfather, married Mary Richardson.

John Cothran (1799-1860), grandfather of Thomas White, was the second son of his parents. He was a prominent planter and business man in antebellum days, owning large tracts of land and many slaves. His homestead was at Millway in Abbeville County, now a part of Greenwood County. Wade Elephare Cothran (1837-1899), was the third son of John Cothran and Elephare Rushton. The other sons of the union died without issue.

In the Millway community Wade E. Cothran spent most of his life. He was a graduate of The Citadel at Charleston in the class of 1858. He was a student of medicine in the South Carolina Medical College at Charleston when the Civil war began. He left his medical studies and became a lieutenant in Company C of the Seventh South Carolina Infantry. After a brief service he was promoted to captain of his company and later assigned to the Engineer Corps. Shortly after rejoining his command he was severely wounded at Harper's Ferry and was unable to resume duty either as a soldier or in private business until 1867. Returning to Millway he spent his life as a planter. On the formation of Greenwood County he was elected its probate judge, and was in that office until his death in 1899.

Thomas White Cothran was born and reared on the old plantation at Millway, and was a member of the first class that graduated from Clemson College in 1896. In that splendid institution he received the fundamentals of his training as an engineer. He was retained at Clemson the first year after graduation as instructor in drawing. For two years he was connected with the United States Geological Survey, being on duty in Texas, Indian Territory and Iowa. In 1900 he became an assistant engineer and later chief draftsman in the chief engineer's office of the Seaboard Air Line Railway, and was in that position for several years, though for a brief time he was with a coal mining corporation. Subsequently he was made principal assistant engineer to George A. Kent, chief engineer of the South and Western Railway (C. C. & O.), and in 1905 became resident engineer of the A. B. & A. Railway at Warm Springs, Georgia. July 1, 1906, Mr. Cothran assumed new duties as principal assistant engineer on construction of the Norfolk & Southern Railway, between Raleigh and Newbern in North Carolina.

Since September, 1908, Mr. Cothran has been practicing his profession on his own account and with permanent home at Greenwood. He does a general engineering business and has built up an organization adequate for handling large construction contracts. This organization has put up a number of prominent buildings in Greenwood and adjoining towns and cities, among them being the Clemson College Young Men's Christian Association building.

Mr. Cothran married Miss Maud Boswell, of Portsmouth, Virginia. Their six children are Thomas W., Jr., Virginia, Mary Nelson, William Benjamin, Sarah Elizabeth and Perrin Chiles. Mr. Cothran is a member of the American Society of Civil Engineers, is a member of the American Water Works Association, a Scottish Rite Mason, also a Knight Templar and Shriner, a member of the Rotary Club and served several years as member of the South Carolina Highway Commission.

THOMAS B. BRYANT. Another member of the Bryant family whose interests and activities for so many years have been identified with the old Orangeburg district, Thomas B. Bryant is one of the largest land owners and planters of the state, and for the past thirty years has made his home and business headquarters at Orangeburg.

Mr. Bryant, who is a brother of Uston G. Bryant, under which name many of the interesting particulars in the family's history will be found, was born in Colleton, now Dorchester County, September 5, 1861. He was educated in the common schools of his native county, and at the age of seventeen began a business career. For over thirty years he and his brother Uston were closely associated in their varied business affairs. Their first undertaking was in the lumber business, and in 1883 they moved to Fort Mott, where they conducted a plantation for seven years. In 1889 they removed their business headquarters to Orangeburg, and as Bryant Brothers operated as a livestock firm, buying, selling, raising and breeding stock. In 1911 the brothers separated their interests, and since then Thomas B. Bryant has continued in the stock business under the name of T. B. Bryant.

As a planter Mr. Bryant is one of the largest producers of corn and cotton in South Carolina. One of his plantations has an historic interest apart from its productiveness. It lies in the eastern part of Orangeburg County, in what was at one time known as the Upper St. John's Parish. The old battlefield of Utah Springs, the scene of one of the decisive battles of the Revolution, especially so far as the Carolinas were concerned, is on the plantation. Mr. Bryant has 1,850 acres of land in that tract, and uses between 900 and 1,000 acres for his corn and cotton crops. Another farm of 417 acres is in that portion of Calhoun County formerly Orangeburg County, and practically all of this is used for crop growing. Another highly improved farm contains 150 acres and is close to Orangeburg.

Mr. Bryant for five years was interested in the Peoples National Bank as a director and stockholder, and then retired. He owns the brick building in Orangeburg on Main Street, where he has his business headquarters, and has one of the attractive homes and other property interests in the city.

Mr. Bryant is an active member of the Baptist Church and is affiliated with the Masonic fraternity. He has been twice married. In February, 1893, Miss Lelia Wertz, of Newberry, became his wife, but she died on the 20th of October of the same year. In June, 1895, he married Tulu Ray, a native of Orangeburg, and a daughter of Thomas Ray, who came from Ireland. Her mother, Angeline Jackson, was descended from a South Carolina family of Revolutionary stock and of English descent. Mr. and Mrs. Bryant have a family of one son and eight daughters: Pauline, wife of D. P. Courtney, a business associate of Mr. Bryant, has one child Bryant Courtney; Ruby, wife of H. C. Richards, of Orangeburg; Marie and Maud, students in Coker College; Doris and T. B., Jr., both in high school, Helen and Angie Ray in the grade schools; and Mamie, the youngest.

JAMES ALEXANDER CARROLL. The history of several important towns in South Carolina is largely a repetition of one name woven through all the expanding life and enterprise of the community. This is notably true of Gaffney, today one of the hubs of industry and commerce in upper South Carolina. The name most frequently repeated here during a half century of growth and development is that of James Alexander Carroll, who has been well described as a composite personality of merchant, manufacturer, banker, broker, jobber, farmer, builder and booster, and through it all has ran an eminent public spirit which might well make him deserving of the appellation philanthropist.

He was born May 19, 1852, in York County. His parents were Thomas and Lucinda (Hullender) Carroll. His father was a Confederate soldier and lost his life in the siege of Petersburg. The paternal ancestry is one branch of the distinguished Carroll family of Maryland and Virginia. The famous Charles Carroll, of the "Carrolls of Carrollton" signer of the Declaration of Independence, has probably had no more worthy descendant than the Gaffney business man.

James A. Carroll spent his youth in a period of lamentable ruin and destruction in the South, and he came to manhood with his character strengthened by the shock of circumstance and many vicissitudes. He had a farm training, attended local schools only until he was sixteen, and spent much of his youth with a noted citizen of Whittaker's Mountain, the late Ira Hardin. On leaving home he worked for a while on the building of the first railroad, the old Richmond & Danville, now the Southern, and during his later teens clerked in a number of country stores for Mr. Hardin.

In 1869 at the age of seventeen he first came to Gaffney, then known fitly as Gaffney's Old Field, and clerked in the town's first store owned by I. Hardin. He had little capital, but had showed himself worthy of trust, and not long afterwards he established a little store of his own at Gowdeysville near Gaffney. He conducted that four years, and in 1877 returned to Gaffney, and now for over forty years has been the city's most prominent

business factor. Until 1881 he conducted a business under his individual proprietorship, and then took into partnership the employe whom he held in highest regard, W. C. Carpenter. The firm of Carroll & Carpenter continued for nearly a quarter of a century. In 1900 George C. Byers bought an interest, and the organization was Carroll, Carpenter & Byers until February, 1904, when Mr. Carpenter withdrew. Since then the business has been Carroll & Byers, established in a completely fitted and modern building of its own known as the Carroll & Moore Block. The firm of Carroll & Byers is now a complete merchandise organization, carrying over $100,000 of stock, the main store being devoted to general dry goods and men's and women's clothing, with also a wholesale and jobbing department. The firm has at another location a grocery store, established since 1905. The firm are extensive dealers in fertilizers and through the Carroll Cotton Company buy most of the cotton produced in that territory. The members of the firm are also interested in farming and real estate.

Mr. Carroll established the cotton buying firm of Carroll & Stacy in 1881, and for many years it was the largest plant of its kind in the state employing about 100 men and in some seasons buying over $1,000,000 worth of cotton. Mr. Carroll was one of the original stock holders of the Cherokee Falls Cotton Mill, and served as its president twelve years, from 1888 to 1900. He made the first subscription, $10,000, to the Gaffney Manufacturing Company in 1892 for the purpose of building the first cotton mill in Gaffney. He has been president of the Limestone Mill since its organization, and has been a director from the start in the Gaffney Manufacturing Company, the Hamrick, Globe, Cherokee Falls and Broad River mills, and is a director of the Victor Cotton Oil Company. For twenty years he conducted the great lime works in Gaffney, producing about 100,000 barrels of lime annually.

Mr. Carroll appeared in the role of a banker when in 1891 becoming associated with F. G. Stacy he established Carroll & Stacy, Bankers. In 1896 this bank took out a national charter becoming the National Bank of Gaffney, and later became the First National Bank.

These varied activities of themselves obviously constitute a great public service in the community. Mr. Carroll has been generous of his time and means in helping out many worthy causes. He has been particularly interested in supplying educational facilities for young men and women, partly from a consciousness of a lack of these facilities during his own youth. Several years ago he made a donation of $15,000 to Limestone College, and in April, 1919, there was announced an additional gift from him of $25,000 to this institution.

Mr. Carroll married in 1871 Miss Mary Humphries. Their two daughters are Mrs. G. G. Byers and Mrs. Doctor A. C. Cree.

THOMAS BOONE FRASER, who has been an associate justice of the Supreme Court of South Carolina since 1912, has his home at Sumter, where he was born June 21, 1860, and is a son of Judge Thomas Boone and Sarah Margaret (McIver) Fraser. As a boy he intended to become a lawyer, doubtless through the influence of his father, who for many years was a leader in the South Carolina bar and at one time judge of the Third Circuit Court.

The son graduated A. B. from Davidson College in North Carolina in 1881, and read law under his father, being admitted to the bar in 1883. He steadily practiced law at Sumter for thirty years. From 1901 to 1912 he served as a member of the South Carolina House of Representatives, and was chairman of the judiciary committee five years. In 1912 he was elected to the Supreme Court, and for a time filled an unexpired term as chief justice. He was re-elected in 1916.

Judge Fraser is a member of the Presbyterian Church. December 16, 1886, he married Emma M. Edmunds, of Sumter.

JAMES LAWRENCE QUINBY is one of many successful men who regard it as a privilege to refer gratefully to the community of Graniteville as their birthplace and early home. With Mr. Quinby this pride and interest are increased because Graniteville has been his permanent home and the scene of his busy career for over half a century.

He was born at Graniteville in 1851, son of Lawrence and Martha (Powell) Quinby. His father, a native of Charleston, moved from that city to Graniteville in 1845. He was an associate of the distinguished Charleston citizen William Gregg in the building of the Graniteville cotton mill. This was the first cotton mill in the state, and has remained in continuous operation for over seventy years.

The mill and its surrounding community stand out as a high light in southern industry. As soon as the mill and village were completed and the force of help assembled Mr. Gregg established a free school, and while without power to do so by strict law he practically provided for a system of compulsory education for all children between the ages of seven and twelve. Thus in that little mill village more than seventy years ago was begun, in practice, the required attendance of children at school for stated periods of the year, a principle which was not given full effect over the state in general until 1919. From the first no one under twelve years has ever been allowed to work in the mill at Graniteville, and as a result of that liberal and enlightened provision the mill company has paid larger dividends on its capital than many others that made no effort along educational lines. Furthermore, wholesome sanitary conditions, comfortable housing, beautiful surroundings, features which have been widely advertised by other mill communities in the South, though only of recent establishment, have been the prevailing rule at Graniteville for three quarters of a century.

In November, 1907, the Hickman Memorial Hall was dedicated at Graniteville. As a prominent member of the community who knew most of its history James Lawrence Quinby was called upon for an address at the exercises. He spoke conservatively and yet brought out facts which may be a source of lasting pride to Graniteville for all time to come. He spoke of the unequalled conditions socially, industrially, morally and religiously that have always existed at Graniteville, and as a result of these advantages the large number of strong and successful men and women who in their youth either worked in the mill or were members of mill families. He reviewed the past representation of Edgefield and Aiken counties in the Legislature and found men who had at one time been mill workers at Graniteville, and also referred to by name many county officials not only in Aiken, but in Georgia, Alabama and other states, named physicians, lawyers, judges, soldiers, statesmen and ministers, bank presidents, cotton mill executives, merchants and educators, all of whom were indebted in some way or other to the influences of the Graniteville community. Besides those who began as mill workers and sought other fields of labor, better fitted for their talents, there were many who continued work in the mill and acquired comfortable and substantial homes and farms. In the words of Mr. Quinby, "but the most of the girls have become wives and mothers, which after all is the most perfect and glorious achievement."

It is indeed a pardonable pride and satisfaction on the part of Mr. Quinby that he has so long been associated intimately with the community and its people. He received his early schooling at the Graniteville Academy. At the age of thirteen and a half he began work in the mill, and in that time his own expectations and those of his family looked toward a career as a cotton manufacturer. Instead, in 1871, he engaged in the mercantile business, and has been a merchant at his present location for nearly half a century. His store is one of the largest and most attractive in that section of the state. Mr. Quinby is also president of the Bank of Graniteville, and has much valuable farm land and town property. He has always been a leader in Graniteville affairs, working for good churches, schools and the improvements that mean most in his locality. He has been a member of the Legislature from Aiken County and a member of the state tax board. During the war he had charge of Liberty Loan drives for Aiken County and was an unstinted worker and giver in behalf of war loans, Red Cross and other auxiliary campaigns. Mr. Quinby is a Methodist.

His first wife was Ellen Turner, of Edgefield County. She left him one son, James Lawrence Quinby, Jr., now an associate in his father's business. Mr. Quinby married for his present wife Caroline Wyers, of Brunswick, Missouri.

JOSEPH J. MAJOR. The mature years of his life Mr. Major has spent as a successful farmer in Anderson County, gained a competence in agriculture before the era of tremendous prosperity now enjoyed by the farmer, and is personally well known all over the county and a member of an old and prominent family of the state.

He was born on his father's plantation in that county October 26, 1855. The family was founded in South Carolina by James Major and his two brothers, Elijah and Enoch, who came to this state from Virginia. James Major first lived in Fairfield County, and later settled in Anderson County, east of the City of Anderson. He was of English descent, and the family on coming to America first lived in Pennsylvania and later in Virginia. James Major married at Pendleton, Margaret (Peggy) Breazeale. They had eleven children, Lavina, Pinckney D., Caroline, Hiram B., Hezekiah, James A., Margaret, E. Jenkins, Sallie, Joseph W. and Kennon. The daughter Margaret was accidentally killed at the age of two years, but all the others lived to be more than thirty years of age. All the sons except the first, who was too old, were Confederate soldiers, and Joseph W. and Kennon sacrificed their lives to the cause.

E. Jenkins Major married Elizabeth, the daughter of Ezekiel Long, a pioneer in the northern part of Anderson County. E. Jenkins Major was a farmer, and he and his wife reared their children on the farm. These children were Margaret, Ezekiel Aiken, Joseph J., Willie, who died at the age of three years, John A. and Allie.

Joseph J. Major was reared on a farm, acquired a good education and training for serious responsibilities, and after his marriage located on the old homestead which he still owns. Along with farming he was associated with others in the fertilizer and buggy business at Anderson for several years, but his chief prosperity has been won from the soil. He owns several tracts of farm lands, and with his family lives at 1429 South McDuffie Street in Anderson, where he built a few years ago a beautiful and spacious home. He and his family are all members of the Baptist Church.

January 25, 1887, he married Margaret J. Harris, Mrs. Major is a sister of Dr. J. C. Harris of Anderson. Of their marriage the first child, Joseph Harris, died at the age of fourteen. The second is Elizabeth, usually known as Bessie. The three younger children, sons, are Ezekiel, Roy and Harold. All were soldiers in the great war, though much to their regret their time was spent in training camps on this side of the ocean. Ezekiel became a lieutenant, while the other two sons were privates.

HON. THOMAS BOTHWELL BUTLER. A distinguished lawyer and one of the ablest and most resourceful public men of the state, Thomas Bothwell Butler has been a member of the Cherokee County bar since the organization of that county, which was one of the first public movements in which he took an active and effective part. He has served as mayor of Gaffney and is now a member of the State Senate.

He was born near Santuc, Union County, January 11, 1866, son of Dr. Pierce Picken and Arsinoe (Jeter) Butler, being a member of some of the oldest and most prominent families in the state. Doctor Butler was a brother of the eminent Gen. M. C. Butler, whose career is an indelible part of South Carolina history. Senator Butler is also a nephew of the late Governor Thomas B. Jeter.

When he was twelve years old Thomas B. Butler left the farm home of his parents to live with his uncle, Governor Jeter, at Union, and acquired most of his early training from his scholarly relative and also from the public schools of Union. After the death of Governor Jeter he continued to live with his widow, and from the Jeter home he entered the University of South Carolina, where he

took both the literary and law course. Soon after his admission to the bar he located at Gaffney in 1895 and during the following year was leader in the agitation before the Legislature for the formation of Cherokee County with Gaffney as county seat. As a lawyer he has climbed to the heights of success and has measured his abilities with many of the best of his contemporaries. For twenty years he has been employed on one side or the other in nearly every important case tried in the courts of his county. In a business way he is a director of the People's Building and Loan Association of the American State Bank and Cash Mills.

Again and again positions of honor and trust have been conferred upon him. In 1900 he was almost the unanimous choice of his county for a seat in the House of Representatives, and in 1901 he defeated two strong and popular men for the State Senate. After the close of his term he devoted himself assiduously to the practice of law, and in 1908 formed a partnership with W. S. Hall. He has been county chairman of the democratic party several terms, for a number of years state executive committeeman, has been mayor of Gaffney, United States commissioner, national elector at large, and in 1918 was again returned to a seat in the Senate, where he is a member of the Judiciary Committee. Three times he was candidate for Congress, and made a most creditable race against the veteran congressman, D. E. Finley. Some years ago he was elected lieutenant-colonel of the Third South Carolina Regiment, and served with similar rank on Governor Ansel's staff. Colonel Butler is chairman of the board of trustees of the Buford Street Methodist Church.

He married Miss Annie Wood, daughter of A. N. Wood. They have a son and daughter, Thomas B., Jr., and Ann Jeter.

DAVID ROBERT COKER, of Hartsville, is one of a family long prominent in agricultural leadership, as upbuilders of the great cotton industry in the South, promoters of education, and distinguished both in war and peace.

The family of Coker has been longest identified with the community known as Society Hill. At Society Hill was born James Lide Coker on January 3, 1837, a son of Caleb and Hannah (Lide) Coker. James L. Coker was educated in St. David's Academy at Society Hill, in the South Carolina Military Academy at Charleston, and made a special study of botany and chemistry in the Laurens Scientific School of Harvard University. He is the recipient of the honorary degree LL. D. from the University of South Carolina.

Shortly after beginning his business career he was called to the stern duty of war. In the fall of 1860 he organized the Hartsville Light Infantry, and commanded that company in several great battles, including that of Fredericksburg. He was severely wounded at Lookout Mountain, Tennessee, afterward fell into the hands of the enemy, and did not return to service. He was promoted to major of the Sixth South Carolina Volunteer Infantry about the time he was wounded. He served as a member of the South Carolina House of Representatives in 1864-66.

From 1866 he became a factor of increasing prominence as a merchant and manufacturer at Hartsville. From 1874 to 1881 he was also a member of the firm of Norwood & Coker, cotton factors, at Charleston.

In 1881 he organized and for a number of years served as president of the Darlington National Bank. He was the first president of the Darlington Manufacturing Company in 1884, and in 1889 built a short line of railway from Floyd to Hartsville. He and his oldest son established the Carolina Fiber Company at Hartsville, manufacturing pulp and paper from native wood. He also served as president of the Southern Novelty Company, was a partner in the firm of J. L. Coker & Company, a director of the Hartsville Cotton Mill, Hartsville Oil Mill, and was director and president until 1910 of the Bank of Hartsville. He has served as trustee of Coker College for Women at Hartsville, as president of the Pee Dee Historical Association, has been prominent in the Baptist Church, and was affiliated actively with the Southern Historical Association, the South Carolina Historical Society, the American Historical Association, the American Red Cross, American Institute of Civics and many other societies.

March 28, 1860, James L. Coker married Susan Stout, of Alabama, who died in 1904.

His younger son, William C. Coker, born at Hartsville in 1872, is a Doctor of Philosophy from Johns Hopkins University, is a distinguished botanist, and since 1907 has been Professor of Botany in the University of North Carolina. He has done a great deal of original work, his travels and investigations having taken him to many foreign countries, and he is widely known for his work as a teacher and original contributor in the botanical field.

David Robert Coker, another son of James L. Coker, was born at Hartsville, November 20, 1870, being the fifth of ten children, seven of whom reached mature years. He was educated in the public schools, in St. David's Academy at Society Hill and for four years was a student in South Carolina College, graduating with the degree of A. B. in 1891. In 1892 he entered his father's mercantile business at Hartsville, was promoted to a partnership in 1894, and for many years has been managing partner of a firm that does an imposing aggregate of the mercantile business of the county. He organized and is president of the Pedigreed Seed Company and the Coker Cotton Company. He is also interested in the Hartsville Oil Mill, the Carolina Fiber Company, the Southern Novelty Company, the Hartsville Fertilizer Company, is a director of the Federal Reserve Bank at Richmond, is one of the trustees of the University of South Carolina and was chairman of the State Council of Defense during the World war.

Aside from his business he has given much of his time to the promotion of agricultural interests, and especially to the breeding, introduction and marketing of better and larger varieties of cotton. His work in these respects has resulted in changing the territory around Hartsville from short staple to long, and has added millions of dollars to the profit of the farmers of the South. He was one of the twenty-five men who constituted the National Agricultural Advisory Commission of the United States in 1918. He was also a member of the Agricultural Committee of eight sent to Europe to investigate and report on agricultural conditions in September-October, 1918. He is president of the Plant Breeders Association of South Carolina.

In 1894 he married Jessie Richardson, of Timmonsville. She died in May, 1914, the mother of Catherine, Hannah, Eleanor, Robert and Samuel. In August, 1915, Mr. Coker married May Roper, a daughter of D. C. Roper, Commissioner of Internal Revenue. By this union there is one daughter, Martha.

DeWYAT RAHN RISER, a prominent South Carolina educator, is present superintendent of the Abbeville schools, and has been teaching and engaged in school administration since early manhood.

He was born in Edgefield County, South Carolina, December 20, 1875, son of James Howard and Matilda (Etheredge) Riser. He grew up on his father's plantation, attended the local schools, was also a student of Newberry College, and completed his work at Yale University in 1905. The successive positions and responsibilities he has held in the teaching world were in the Mount Pleasant Collegiate Institute in North Carolina, two years as superintendent of the Ridgeway schools, two years head of the Science Department of the Columbia High School, two years superintendent at Aiken, also as superintendent of the Manning public schools for five years and in 1917 was promoted to his present duties as superintendent of the Abbeville school system. He has now twenty-eight teachers on his staff and the enrollment in the local schools is twelve hundred.

Mr. Riser is a member of the State Teachers Association and the Superintendents Association, and is affiliated with the Knights of Pythias. June 27, 1912, he married Mabel Pearl Johnson, of Ridgeway, South Carolina.

COLIN JASPER McCALL, whose business record in Marion County extends back thirty-five years, still has many important interests in and around Mullins.

Mr. McCall was born in Marlboro County, South Carolina, December 10, 1850, a son of Lauchlin and Susan (McDonald) McCall. He grew up on his father's farm and received a country school education. In 1873 he came to Marion County, locating at Temperance, where he was in the turpentine industry and later conducted a store and a farm. For a number of years he was a lumber manufacturer, also operating cotton gins and other enterprises. In 1893 Mr. McCall removed to Mullins and for thirteen years was agent and chief representative of Alexander Sprunt & Son. Since then he has engaged in the cotton brokerage and fertilizer business, also owns some valuable farming land and is a director of the Bank of Mullins. He has been elder of the Presbyterian Church and superintendent of the Sunday school for seven years.

December 10, 1874, Mr. McCall married Annie Virginia Page, of Marion County. Nine children were born to their marriage: Ida, wife of J. D. Platt, editor and owner of the Mullins Enterprise, Clifford Simpson, a cotton broker in North Carolina; Edna, at home; Walter Vernon, a farmer at Mullins; Bess, wife of Dr. F. A. Smith; McDonald Laughlin, engaged in lumber manufacturing; Irene, wife of Duncan McDuffy, of Marion; Elbert Duncan of Savannah, Georgia; and Jessie Dunlap, wife of M. H. Granger, a farmer in Lee County, South Carolina.

OLIN SAWYER, M. D. While he has enjoyed as busy a practice as any physician in Georgetown County, Doctor Sawyer has yielded to the pressure of duty and the urging of friends to perform many services outside the immediate limits of his profession. He has been a member of the Legislature, held town offices, has been prominent in civic, patriotic and business affairs, and is one of the best known men in his section of the state.

He was born in Edgefield County, January 1, 1875, a son of Ptolemy Searon and Frances De Laura (Crouch) Sawyer. His father was a planter and merchant. Doctor Sawyer attended the public schools of Trenton and Johnston, finished his literary education in the University of South Carolina, and in April, 1901, graduated from the Medical College of the State of South Carolina at Charleston. He largely paid his own way through medical college. As a young man he had worked on a farm and clerked in a drug store and also taught school two summers. He began the practice of medicine at Georgetown and from the first has enjoyed substantial connections. He is chief surgeon of the Atlantic Coast Lumber Corporation, and also the Georgetown & Western Railroad Company, and when that line was taken over by the Seaboard Air Line he remained as local surgeon. Doctor Sawyer has served as a member of the Board of Aldermen in Georgetown and was a member of the Legislature from that county from 1907 to 1913. In 1915 he was elected mayor of Georgetown and served two terms. He was in all the democratic state conventions from 1902 to 1912, was chairman of the County Democratic Organization from 1906 to 1912, and a presidential elector in 1904. During the war Doctor Sawyer was chairman of the county Red Cross campaign, was a Four Minute Man of the committee on public information during the World war and as such spoke and actively worked for the putting through of all the Red Cross campaigns, also Liberty and Victory bond drives, Young Men's Christian Association and United War Work Community drives, and for Jewish relief. He served four years as chairmen of the local Board of Health. He is president of the Georgetown Medical Society and a member of the State, Southern and American Medical associations and the Association of Southern Railway Surgeons. In 1903 Governor Heyward commissioned him regimental surgeon with the rank of major, First Regiment Volunteer Cavalry, and he served in two encampments, until a change was made in the system of the militia organization of the state. Doctor Sawyer for four years was a director of the Georgetown Chamber of Commerce. He is a Presbyterian and is affiliated with the Masonic Order, Knights of Pythias, and the Benevolent and Protective Order of Elks.

November 27, 1901, he married Lulie Boyd of Ridgeway, South Carolina, daughter of Dr. John

D. and Lucy (Bryant) Boyd. They have twin daughters, Olin and Ray.

GEORGE WILLIAM DARGAN was born at "Sleepy Hollow" in Darlington County, South Carolina, on May 11, 1841. He was educated at the academies of his native county and at the South Carolina Military Academy at Charleston. In 1861 he married Miss Ida Louise Hunter, also a native of Darlington County. He was admitted to the bar in 1872; was elected as a democrat to the State Legislature without opposition in 1877; was elected solicitor of the Fourth Judicial Circuit of South Carolina without opposition in 1880, and served with distinction as a member of the Forty-eighth, Forty-ninth, Fiftieth and Fifty-first Congresses of the United States, from the Sixth Congressional District of South Carolina. He died at Darlington, South Carolina, on the 29th day of June, 1898, and was survived by his wife, Ida Louise, and five children, namely, Lawrence, George Edwin, Emile Bacot, Sarah DuBose and Archie Shaw Dargan.

Mr. Dargan was the son of Dr. William Edwin Dargan and Sarah DuBose, and was the grandson of Timothy Dargan, whose father was also named Timothy, all of whom were residents of Darlington County, which has been the home of the Dargan family since a time prior to the Revolutionary war. The family has furnished some conspicuous names to the history of the state. Among them were George Washington Dargan, a distinguished chancellor of South Carolina; Julius A. Dargan, an eminent lawyer and one of the signers of the South Carolina Ordinance of Secession; and Lieut.-Col. Alonza T. Dargan, of the Confederate Army, who was killed in action at Petersburg, Virginia, in 1864, all of whom were uncles of George William Dargan.

He was a modest and retiring gentleman of unimpeachable character, an able and successful lawyer, a ripe scholar and a faithful and fearless public servant.

WILBUR L. RODRIGUES. While his name was added to the Charleston bar only a few years ago, Wilbur L. Rodrigues has won a large following and many successes in his chosen profession.

He has been a resident of South Carolina most of his life, but was born at Jacksonville, Illinois, in 1894, son of L. L. and Minnie (Vieiera) Rodrigues, who now reside at Orangeburg, South Carolina. L. L. Rodrigues, of Portuguese ancestry, was also born at Jacksonville, Illinois. The grandfather, a native of Portugal, was a missionary and on coming to America settled in Illinois. L. L. Rodrigues brought his family to Orangeburg County in 1898.

Wilbur L. Rodrigues attended his first schools in Orangeburg and after completing his public school work began the study of law there. He continued the reading of law in the office of Mr. B. A. Hagood at Charleston and was admitted to the bar in 1917. In three years his abilities have been tested and his qualifications proven in the handling of an increasing general practice.

Mr. Rodrigues is affiliated with Landmark Lodge of Masons. He married Miss Ethel Goddard of Charleston and their two children are Wilbur L., Jr., and Mary Ethel.

RICHARD LEWIS BERRY. Forty years ago Richard Lewis Berry had earned some considerable success as a druggist and dealer in timber lands. Incidental to his main business and to express a youthful enthusiasm which he had cherished for the practical art of printing, he established a small job printing plant at Orangeburg in 1881. Not long afterward some destructive fires swept away the greater part of his timber holdings, involving his other invested capital, and on reorganization his assets he found little left except the printing plant. It was a discouraging situation, but proved in fact a blessing in disguise, since by giving all his energies to printing he discovered his real genius and ability and the work to which his enthusiasm and efforts have been wholly devoted during all subsequent years.

Mr. Berry was born in Orangeburg County, January 23, 1850. While remotely of Irish stock, the Berrys have been in America for many generations and are of Revolutionary stock. Richard E. Berry, his father, was born in the lower part of Orangeburg County, and owing to his age was not called into service by the Confederacy until 1863, and thereafter served chiefly on guard duty with the state troops until the close of the war. He held the rank of lieutenant. Otherwise he devoted his years to farming. His wife was Mary Ott Berry, also a native of Orangeburg County, and one of her brothers was a Confederate soldier. She died in 1850.

Richard Lewis Berry was six months old when his mother died, and an aunt reared him until he was twenty years of age. He had regular duties on the farm in proportion to his years and strength, but also attended local schools and spent one term in Wofford Preparatory School. On leaving home at the age of twenty Mr. Berry moved to Branchville and engaged in the drug business. The license he received at that time from the State Pharmaceutical Board he still preserves. He was a druggist ten years, and also became interested in the timber industry in that vicinity. Then came the critical stage and the turning point in his career above described.

He developed his printing plant to profitable proportions and in time expanded his business by establishing the Enterprise, a weekly newspaper. He continued it for two years, until the financial depression of 1893. Later he employed his printing plant to publish the "Cotton Plant" for Dr. W. J. Stokes. This was a weekly agricultural paper, and Doctor Stokes had bought it to further his political ambition, and was elected to Congress largely through the influence wielded by the paper. The Cotton Plant had a circulation of 8,000, and was published by Mr. Berry for two years.

Later Mr. Berry organized the firm of R. Lewis Berry & Company, the personnel of which consisted of himself, his son W. D. Berry and A. C. Dibble. The company published the Southern Christian Advocate in 1900-01. Later, under the same name, the father and son in 1904 established the Orangeburg Evening News, issued daily except Sunday. The publication of this splendid daily paper was continued until 1917, and proved a great asset to the city. However, Mr. Berry's ideas were somewhat in advance of his time, and the patronage of the News was not all it should have been. One of the contributing causes for the discontinuance was the rapidly mounting high prices of both printing paper and labor, and it was only after the publication was discontinued that the business man and citizen generally of Orangeburg appreciated the usefulness of the organ.

Through all these years the job printing plant has been continued. In May, 1919, Mr. Berry organized the Orangeburg Sun Company, being associated with James I. Sims, Henry R. Sims, Hugo S. Sims, W. D. Berry and C. C. Berry. This company bought the Orangeburg Sun, a semi-weekly, from Mr. Fred Wannamaker, acquiring the publication plant at the same time. Soon afterward the Sun became a weekly and has so been published. The company is incorporated for $10,000, with R. L. Berry as president, C. Clifford Berry, secretary and treasurer. The Sun enjoys a large circulation among the farmers of the county and exemplifies some of the best standards of country journalism in the state.

Mr. Berry has always been a Methodist, and is affiliated with the Masonic order. At Branchville, December 24, 1876, he married Miss Frances M. Howell, a native of that town and daughter of William H. and Mary A. Howell. The two sons of Mr. and Mrs. Berry have already been noted in the business record of the father. Their names are Walter Douglas and Charles Clifford Berry. The former now has charge of the printing department of the Epworth Orphanage at Columbia. In 1911 he married Miss Otes Ransdale, a native of Orangeburg and a daughter of Lendo Ransdale. They have one child, W. D., Jr. Charles C. Berry married June 29, 1909, Annie Mackay, a native of Orangeburg and a daughter of W. E. Mackay. Three children have been born to Mr. and Mrs. C. C. Berry, C. C. Jr., Frances and Richard Bruce.

CORDIE PAGE is a well known lawyer of Horry County, was born in that section of South Carolina, and most of his life has been spent there, though for a time he was engaged in law practice at Florence.

He was born at Galivants Ferry, Horry County, August 19, 1884, a son of William and Mary Jane (Lewis) Page. He grew up on his father's farm, attended Zion School, graduated from the schools of Conway in 1905, and took his Bachelor of Science degree from the University of South Carolina in 1909. For one year he taught school in his native county and in 1912 received his LL. B. degree from the law department of the state university. In January, 1913, he formed a partnership with C. J. Gasque at Florence, but from 1915 to September, 1917, was in practice alone in that city. At the latter date he returned to Horry County and enjoys a splendid practice at Conway. He is secretary of the G. T. Walker Company, a clothing firm of Florence, and was one of the original charter members and organizers of the Pee Dee Fair Association. From April, 1918, until the close of the war he was a member of the local draft board at Conway. Mr. Page is also a leader in the affairs of the Methodist Episcopal Church.

JOHN MARTIN KINARD. A very busy and useful career, based upon self attainment and wisely directed ambition, has been that of John Martin Kinard, the well known banker and industrial leader at Newberry.

He was born at Kinards, Newberry County, May 17, 1862. He acquired his early literary education in Newberry College and afterward took a special course in South Carolina College and while there won the debaters medal given by the Christopher Society. He became interested in public affairs and for ten years served as clerk of court of Newberry County. Mr. Kinard was made president of the Commercial Bank of Newberry at the time of its organization in 1896, and has wisely directed the affairs of that institution for over twenty years. He is also a director of the Newberry Cotton Mill, and is president of the Newberry Knitting Mill. He married Miss Margaret Lee Land, of Augusta, Georgia, June 5, 1895.

ROBERT MILTON SHIRLEY. A large part of the business rendered at Honea Path has been supplied by members of the Shirley family. One of the most prominent of them was the late Robert Milton Shirley, for a quarter of a century a banker and from early boyhood an abundant source of business enterprise to that community.

Mr. Shirley died January 29, 1918, in the house where he was born March 14, 1858. His parents were John Jasper and Frances (Mattison) Shirley. John J. Shirley was born on Little River, five miles south of Honea Path, July 18, 1825, and during his infancy his parents removed to Honea Path, where he grew up and was long one of the most conspicuous figures in the town. He built the home where his son Robert M. was born and where the latter's widow still lives. John J. Shirley died March 9, 1907, when in his eighty-third year. Though well advanced in years at the time, he served as a loyal soldier of the Confederacy in Company E of the Twenty-First Regiment, under Colonel Keith, and as first lieutenant had command of the company part of the time. On account of ill health he was sent home in 1863. He served as the first station agent and performed the duties of that office for twenty-eight years at Honea Path. He was also the first postmaster, was a merchant, and built the Shirley Hotel, which was operated under his management for over fifty years. In 1855 John J. Shirley married Miss Frances Mattison. They had three sons, William A., a furniture dealer and undertaker at Honea Path; Robert Milton; and Dr. John Fletcher Shirley, of Honea Path. John J. Shirley also had farming interests. He was a deacon in the Baptist Church.

Robert Milton Shirley grew up in his home town, attended the public schools, and was not more than ten years of age when his special genius for business prompted him to become a clerk in a local store. Thus he had a thorough training in business at a time when most boys are engaged in their books and school routine. In 1883 he started in business on a small scale as a general merchant. He gave up his mercantile interests in 1893 to organize the Bank of Honea Path. He became its president and served that institution faithfully and well for nearly a quarter of a century. Mr. Shirley had the character and the ability which made him implicitly trusted by all who knew him. In every sense he was

a leader in the community, taking an active part in organizing the Honea Path Cotton Mills and serving as vice president; was for a long time interested in the Honea Path Lumber Company and part of the time president; and owned extensive farming interests. He was active in the establishment of the Carnegie Library, and was a member of the Town Council many years. He was an elder in the Presbyterian Church and was a member of the Knights of Pythias.

November 13, 1890, he married Miss Sallie Hill Erwin, a daughter of Malcolm Erwin of Erwin's Mill in Abbeville County, and his wife, Margaret (McMurtry) Erwin, who were natives of County Antrim, Ireland. The Erwin family came to the United States in 1865, locating at Erwin's Mill in Abbeville County. Malcolm Erwin was a brother of Thomas Erwin, who was the first of the family to come to South Carolina and from Abbeville County moved to Charleston, where he lived for many years. Mrs. Shirley's grandfather, Arthur Erwin, brought his family to the United States and lived near Abbeville Court House. The Erwins are Scotch-Irish. Mrs. Shirley was born in Abbeville County. She is the mother of a son and daughter, Malcolm John Shirley and Frances Eileen Shirley, the latter now Mrs. Clyde Mann. Both children were liberally educated, the son graduating Bachelor of Science from Davidson College, in North Carolina in 1915 and taking his law degree from the University of South Carolina in 1917. The daughter graduated in 1919 from Chicora College. Malcolm John Shirley, who was born December 29, 1893, enlisted in the National army November 26, 1917, and was called to active duty December 15, 1917. For seven months he was in the Quartermaster's Training School at Camp Johnston, Florida, and was sent overseas June 5, 1918. He remained in France nearly a year, until May 18, 1919. During the war he was stationed at an intermediate section in supply work. He received his honorable discharge June 3, 1919.

JOHN ELBERT STEADMAN is a young lawyer of Denmark, a community in which he has spent practically all his life, and in which he is highly esteemed as a citizen.

He was born there August 9, 1891. The Steadmans came to South Carolina during the Revolutionary war. His grandfather was a native of Lexington County, and he took part in the war between the states. His father is John E. Steadman, who was born in Lexington County and was a merchant and died in his seventy-seventh year. He was a second lieutenant in the war between the states, and was wounded. The mother, Sarah Merritt, was born in Lexington County and is still living, a resident of Denmark. Her parents were from Alabama.

John Elbert Steadman was the sixth child and third son in a family of eight children, all living. He has three brothers in Denmark. Boyce, and Elmore were in the World war, Elmore a finance officer at El Paso, Texas, and Boyce was in the quartermaster's department at Bordeaux. Gordon is with the Atlantic Coast Line Railroad. He was well educated, spending one year in Clemson College and taking the law course in the University of South Carolina, where he graduated in 1915. He was admitted to the bar in June of the same year, and at once opened his office at Denmark, specializing in commercial law. In addition to his growing and substantial law practice he represents some of the leading fire insurance companies, and is also owner of a farm in Bamberg County.

In 1919 he married Miss Dessie Hungerpiller, a daughter of J. E. Hungerpiller, of Elloree, South Carolina. They are planters and South Carolinians.

ARNOLD A. RIVERS. The name of Arnold A. Rivers of Brunsson, needs no introduction to the people of his community, where he spent practically his entire life, and where he was successfully engaged in business as the result of rightly applied principles, which never fail in their ultimate effect when coupled with integrity, uprightness and a congenial disposition, as in his case, judging from the high standing he maintained among his fellow citizens, whose undivided esteem he justly won and retained, for his life was one of untiring industry and honorable dealings with his fellow men.

Arnold A. Rivers, who was the popular and efficient cashier of the Merchants and Planters Bank at Brunson, was born in that town on February 23, 1886, and was the fifth in order of birth of the six children born to the union of J. E. and Mildred (Smith) Rivers. J. E. Rivers was born in Hampton County, South Carolina, and has there spent his entire life. He is the son of J. D. Rivers, who was born at what is now known as Rivers Bridge, Barnwell County, South Carolina, and whose father, a native of England, was the first of the family to settle in South Carolina. The subject's mother, who was born in Hampton County, South Carolina, is the daughter of Thomas Smith, who also was a native of that county and of English origin.

Arnold A. Rivers attended the schools of Hampton, where he was graduated from the high school, and he then took a complete course in a business college in Columbia, South Carolina. He was engaged in the fertilizer business for a number of years at Brunson, in which he was successful, and in 1918 he was chosen as cashier of the Merchants and Planters Bank of Brunson, which position he filled until the time of his death in February of 1920. Mr. Rivers was also the owner of a splendid farm, to the operation of which he gave proper attention. He was considered a splendid type of business man, a leader of men in his community and a stanch supporter of every movement calculated to advance the interests of the locality in any way, giving his hearty support to those objects which promised to benefit the public welfare.

In 1906 Mr. Rivers married Lillie Hughes, the daughter of L. F. Hughes, and they were the parents of one son, Louis. Mr. Rivers was a member of the Ancient Free and Accepted Masons and the Knights of Pythias. In the course of an honorable career he was successful in his business efforts and enjoyed the confidence and good will of those with whom he had been associated in either a business or social way.

At the death of Mr. Rivers his brother, John C. Rivers, was elected to succeed him as cashier of the Merchants & Planters Bank. John C. Rivers was born March 23, 1889, near Brunson. He attended the public schools and graduated from the Hampton High School. He was engaged with his brother James T. Rivers in the mercantile business in Brunson for about four years. He then carried the United States mail for three years, until February, 1920, when he was elected cashier of the bank. Mr. Rivers is the owner of and conducts a farm of about 255 acres near Brunson. His crop has been principally in cotton, but he grows corn and grain as well. He is a member of the Knights of Pythias.

John C. Rivers married December 21, 1916, at Brunson, to Ivy Lee Brunson, a native of Brunson and daughter of William R. Brunson. The Brunsons are of an old South Carolina family, the town of Brunson being named in their honor. Mrs. Rivers' grandfather was a soldier in the Confederate army. Mr. and Mrs. Rivers have one child, Miss Mildred Lavonia.

HERBERT KING GILBERT is a veteran in the service of the Atlantic Coast Line Railway, and is now division storekeeper at Florence.

He was born at Charleston, March 21, 1873, a son of Hezekiah Mix and Eveline (King) Gilbert. His father spent his active life as a merchant and in 1858 opened the first general store at Florence. Herbert K. Gilbert was educated in public schools and left school to become a messenger boy in the general offices of the Atlantic Coast Line Railway. He has been promoted steadily during his quarter of a century of service and now holds one of the important posts in the railway service in South Carolina.

He has also been prominent in local affairs. For two terms he was an alderman, resigning that office, served three years as a member of the Board of Health, and from 1907 to 1913 held the office of mayor for three terms. In the fourth campaign he was beaten by thirteen votes, but in 1917 was again elected mayor, and in that year received the largest number of votes ever given to one candidate in a municipal election at Florence. Mr. Gilbert has been a director and treasurer of the Young Men's Christian Association at Florence since it was organized. He is secretary of his Masonic Lodge and a member of the Chapter and Council, and is a steward in the Methodist Episcopal Church South. April 19, 1898, he married Edith May De Berry of Florence County. They have two children, Herbert McTyeire and Clyde Lee.

HON. FRANK BOYD GARY. After his admission to the bar in 1881 Frank Boyd Gary began practice at Abbeville, and has never changed his residence from that old and historic city. In the meantime, however, his abilities have won him state wide and national prominence, and it is doubtful if there is a better known man in the state, or a lawyer or jurist in whom the people in general feel more complete confidence as to his integrity, ability and adequacy.

Judge Gary, a former United States Senator from South Carolina, and present judge of the Eighth Judicial Circuit, was born at Cokesbury in Abbeville County, March 9, 1860, son of Dr. Franklin F. and Mary Caroline (Blackburn) Gary. In different generations members of this family have been people of high position. Judge Gary's paternal grandmother was of the Witherspoon family, which was identified with the very earliest settlement of South Carolina. They first located near Kingstree in Williamsburg County, whence they scattered throughout the state, after having withstood the hostility of Indians and the incursions of wild animals in the frontier days, and after having established a church, which today is one of the oldest in South Carolina. The Witherspoons came to this country to escape persecution, and lineage goes directly to the reformer John Knox.

Judge Gary through his mother is a member of the Blackburn family, which numbers among it many scholars, and two of the Blackburns were killed in the battle of Kings Mountain in the Revolutionary war. Dr. Franklin F. Gary, father of Judge Gary, was a prominent physician, and also took an active part in public affairs, serving as a member of the General Assembly, as president of the State Medical Association, as member of the State Board of Health and representing in every way the highest character and attainments. Dr. Franklin Gary and his wife were honored by three distinguished sons, who were simultaneously Chief Justice of the Supreme Court, Judge of the Fifth Circuit and Judge of the Eighth Circuit. The Chief Justice is Eugene Blackburn Gary, a sketch of whom appears elsewhere in this publication. There is also a daughter, Mrs. M. G. Eason, of Charleston.

Frank Boyd Gary was educated in the Cokesbury Conference School, and then entered Union College at Schenectady, New York. On account of ill health he withdrew from college in his senior year and was admitted to the South Carolina bar in 1881, and at once began practice at Abbeville and continued a leading figure in his profession in that part of the state until 1912. While busied with the law he accepted many opportunities to serve the public. For about nine years he was bill clerk of the House of Representatives, serving under the late James Simons of Charleston, speaker, and during that experience acquired much knowledge of legislative proceedings and especially of parliamentary law. In 1890 he was elected a member of the House, and was re-elected for four consecutive terms, serving until 1900. In 1906 he was again elected a member of the Legislature. He was three times elected speaker of the House, and in 1895 was a member of the Constitutional Convention. On March 6, 1908, Judge Gary was elected by the General Assembly of South Carolina to fill the vacancy in the United States Senate caused by the death of Senator A. C. Latimer. During this service he made several speeches, one of which —his speech on immigration—attracted wide attention and favorable comment, especially in New England. Upon the expiration of his time in the Senate he was elected without opposition judge of the Eighth Judicial Circuit, and has been successively re-elected, having served ten years and is now at the beginning of another four year term.

One of the important incidents in his career, which added to his reputation abroad, was his appointment upon the recommendation of the then Chief Justice Pope of the Supreme Court by Gov-

ernor Hayward to preside at the trial of James H. Tillman in Lexington County. This was a famous trial. Tillman was charged with the murder of Editor Gonzales. The trial lasted twenty-two days, and was followed with intense interest all over the United States, all of the metropolitan papers giving much space to the proceedings. While the result of the trial may have been disappointing to many, but little if any criticism was indulged as to the presiding judge, and many expressed themselves as pleased with his fairness and impartiality in the conduct of the case.

Judge Gary served as delegate at large from South Carolina to the National Democratic Convention in 1908. He is a director of the People's Savings Bank of Abbeville and is active in Masonry, having been Potentate of Oasis Temple of the Mystic Shrine in 1907, Oasis at that time being the Temple for both Carolinas. He is a member and steward of the Methodist Episcopal Church South.

January 6, 1897, at Florence, South Carolina, Judge Gary married Maria Lee Evans, daughter of Dr. James and Maria Antoinette (Powell) Evans. Their only son is Midshipman Frank Boyd Gary, Jr., now a second classman or junior in the United States Naval Academy at Annapolis.

GEORGE WARREN. In a brief sketch of any living citizen it is difficult to do him exact and impartial justice, not so much, however, for lack of space or words to set forth the familiar and passing events of his personal history, as for want of the perfect and rounded conception of his whole life, which grows, develops and ripens, like fruit, to disclose its true and best flavor only when it is mellowed by time. Daily contact with the man so familiarizes us with his many virtues that we ordinarily overlook them and commonly underestimate their possessor. There are, however, a number of elements in the life record of George Warren, one of the representative citizens of Hampton, South Carolina, that even now serve as examples well worthy of emulation, and his fellow townsmen are not unappreciative of these. He is a splendid example of the virile, progressive man who believes in doing well whatever is worth doing at all, a man of keen discernment and sound judgment, and enjoying to a marked degree the confidence of his fellow men.

George Warren, solicitor for Beaufort, Jasper, Hampton and Colleton counties, was born in Hampton County, South Carolina, on November 25, 1887, and is the son of Jefferson and Clara E. (Riley) Warren. The father, who was born and reared in Colleton County, was a prominent and successful lawyer in Hampton, where his death occurred in 1897. He was a soldier in Company C, Fifth South Carolina Cavalry, Butler's Brigade, Confederate States of America, during the Confederate struggle, serving throughout the war, which he entered at the age of fourteen. His father, George Warren, who was a native of Colleton District, was sheriff of that district and was commanding officer of the South Carolina Militia, with the rank of brigadier general. His father, also named George, was a native of England, who came to America prior to the War of the Revolution. The subject's mother, whose maiden name was Clara E. Riley, was a native of Barnwell County, South Carolina, and was the daughter of J. W. Riley, of Barnwell, but who was a native of Ireland. Prior to her marriage to Mr. Warren she had been married to E. J. Webb, to which union three children were born. The subject of this sketch is the only child born to her union with Mr. Warren.

George Warren received his elementary education in the public schools and then entered Clemson College, where he was graduated in 1908, with the degree of Bachelor of Science. Then, having determined to make the practice of law his life work, he entered the office of his uncle, E. F. Warren, at Hampton, under whose direction he read law for a year, being admitted to the bar in 1909. Immediately thereafter he opened an office in Hampton and has since then been devoted to the active practice of his profession. His abilities were quickly recognized and he has been engaged in much of the most important litigation in the courts of this and neighboring counties. Mr. Warren was elected a member of the House of Representatives in 1912, and was twice re-elected, serving in that body until 1916. In the latter year he was elected judge of the Circuit Court, but he declined this position and was then elected solicitor by the people, in which position he is still serving for the counties of Beaufort, Jasper, Hampton and Colleton. He has also held other local offices.

In 1911 occurred the marriage of George Warren to Rita L. Lightsey, who died on October 13, 1918, leaving a son and a daughter, George and Rita Louise. Fraternally Mr. Warren is an appreciative member of the Masonic fraternity, in which he has attained to the thirty-second degree of the Scottish Rite, and also belongs to the Ancient Arabic Order of Nobles of the Mystic Shrine, the Knights of Pythias, the Junior Order of United American Mechanics and the Woodmen of the World. He has earned a reputation as a progressive, enterprising man of affairs and a broad-minded and upright citizen, which the public has not been slow to recognize and appreciate. The honorable distinction which he has already achieved in his profession is but an earnest of the still wider sphere of usefulness which lies before him, for he is a close observer of the trend of the times and an intelligent student of the great questions and issues upon which the thought of the best minds of the world are centered.

BENJAMIN S. WILLIAMS was a gallant and hard-fighting youthful soldier and officer in the Confederate army, serving with a regiment from the State of Georgia. Not long after the war he came to South Carolina, and for many years has been a lawyer, planter and public official in Hampton County.

Mr. Williams was born in Savannah, June 25, 1843, son of Gilbert W. M. and Esther Williams. Although born in Georgia, he passed practically his entire life in South Carolina. This branch of the Williams family is one of the oldest in America, and its authentic records and traditions go far back into the middle ages of Great Britain. The tradition is that the family descended from Marchudel, chief of one of the fifteen tribes of North Wales, in the ninth century. Marchudel was also the progenitor of the royal houses of Tudor. The root meaning of the name is "Guard" or "Sentinel," the word being derived from the old Briton or Cambrian word "gwylio" meaning "to watch." The coat of arms is a sable, a lion rampant, argent armes and languid gules. Crest is a fighting cock, symbol of watchfulness. Motto: Y Fyno Dwy Y Fydd "What God willeth will be." The side motto is: Cognosce Occasionem—"Watch your Opportunity." A traveler in Wales finds this coat of arms at every turn, cut in stone monuments, engraved upon mural tablets in churches and upon brass plates on pew doors.

In America all the colonial as well as later wars had their representatives in the Williams family. Descendants have no trouble in establishing eligibility to the much coveted membership in the Society of Colonial Wars. Colonel Ephraim Williams of Massachusetts fell in the battle near Lake George. He was the founder of a free school at Williamstown, which has since become Williams College. Joseph Warren, who fell at Bunker Hill, was the fifth in descent from Robert Williams, one of the Pilgrims at Plymouth Rock. William Williams, also a lineal descendant of Robert, was member of Congress in 1776 and one of the signers of the Declaration of Independence.

Mr. Williams' great-grandfather was Hon. John Williams, of South Carolina, whose mother was a Miss Caldwell, sister of the mother of Hon. John Caldwell Calhoun, the South's greatest statesman. Mr. Williams' paternal grandmother was Elizabeth Legare Martin, whose mother was Elizabeth Legare of Charleston.

In the cemetery at Savannah, Georgia, there is a modest monument bearing the epitaph "To the memory of Rev. Gilbert W. M. Williams, Colonel of the Forty-Seventh Georgia Infantry, who fighting gallantly for the cause of the Confederacy died September 1, 1863,—a soldier, a patriot and a Christian." Gilbert W. M. Williams' name is in the archives of the State of Georgia as a signer of the ordinance of session, carrying Georgia, his adopted state, out of the Union, following his native State of South Carolina. He then organized and commanded the Forty-seventh Regiment of Georgia Volunteer Infantry in the Army of the West until his death, which occurred in September, 1863. He was a Baptist minister, and was widely known for his forcefulness and eloquence in debate.

Benjamin S. Williams was only eighteen years of age when his father took up arms in behalf of the cause which he believed right. The son followed him, enlisting in 1861 as a private in the Twenty-fifth Georgia Infantry and rising through the grades of corporal, sergeant and first lieutenant. In 1862 he was appointed adjutant of the Forty-seventh Georgia Infantry, his father's regiment. He served throughout the remainder of the war with that famous regiment, known as "the Bloody 47th Georgia."

After the war the young soldier returned to his devastated home and engaged in farming and planting. He also studied law, located in Hampton County, and for many years has been one of the leading cotton planters of that section of the state. He had an active part in politics, particularly in reconstruction times. From 1876 to 1880 he was auditor of Hampton County. He also served as sheriff and has represented the county in the Legislature. He was in the Legislature from 1880 to 1890. Politically Mr. Williams is an ardent democrat, and has always emphasized the "State's Rights" principles in the party.

On November 7, 1867, in Beaufort District, South Carolina, he married Miss Josephine Richardson, daughter of James Cameron Richardson. Mrs. Williams was the beautiful and pious daughter of a wealthy planter, and in her life distinguished herself by faithfulness as a wife, affection as a mother, and the full performance of her duty as a Christian. Mr. Williams has the following children: Gilbert James, Albert Richardson, Kate Cameron, Josephine Caldwell, Esther Ashley and Elizabeth Legare. Only one son is married, Gilbert James.

HARRY ALEXANDER BRUNSON, a prominent member of the Florence bar, formerly a well known educator, is present probate judge of Florence County.

He was born at Florence, November 4, 1868, a son of William Alexander and Antoinette Taylor (Chandler) Brunson. His father before him was a prominent lawyer and for ten years held the office of probate judge. The son was educated in private schools, attended South Carolina College, now the University of South Carolina, being a member of the class of 1889. At intervals of other work principally teaching, he read law under his father and was admitted to the bar in December, 1894. He made little attempt to build up a practice, and gave his time to teaching and educational affairs until 1911, when he succeeded his father as probate judge and has held that office continuously. During his teaching career he taught at Lynchburg, Batesburg, was principal of the Florence High School, principal of schools at Georgetown and for three years connected with the schools of Spartanburg.

Judge Brunson is a director of Palmetto Bank & Trust Company and also director of the Farmers and Mechanics Bank. He is a member of the Masonic Order, Junior Order United American Mechanics and Knights of Pythias January 1, 1908, he married Miss Annie Louise McIntosh of Lynchburg, South Carolina. They have two daughters, Sarah Antoinette and Edith Woods. Judge Brunson is an active member of the Methodist Episcopal Church South.

ELIAS EARLE CHILD was born in Pickens County, South Carolina, May 24, 1880, a son of Rufus Alexander and Essie (Holcombe) Child. His father was an attorney and for twenty-five years was a hard working member of the Methodist Conference.

He married on December 2, 1903, Miss Nola Klugh, daughter of William W. and Ida (Franklin) Klugh. Her father was a planter. To their marriage were born two children named William Klugh and Earl Holcombe.

Mr. Child is president and treasurer of the Glenn-Lawry Manufacturing Company, a $2,000,000 cotton goods mill, and president of the Bank of Whitmire, Whitmire, South Carolina.

JACOB GEORGE WANNAMAKER, M. D. Though a graduate in medicine of forty-five years standing Doctor Wannamaker used his professional talents chiefly as a business man, was a druggist, banker and was prominent in the affairs of his native city up to the time of his death.

He was born in Orangeburg County, April 14, 1852, son of Jacob G. and Matilda (Colclasure) Wannamaker. His father was a large planter and served through the war between the states as captain in the Confederate army. Doctor Wannamaker was a descendant of Lieut. Jacob Wannamaker of Revolutionary fame.

Doctor Wannamaker was educated in private schools, attended the University of South Carolina and was graduated from the Medical College of South Carolina at Charleston in 1874. He began practice at Orangeburg and in 1875 entered the drug business. From 1887 to 1892 he was in the wholesale drug business in Columbia and Charleston, but returned to Orangeburg and enlarged his drug business, the firm being known as the J. G. Wannamaker Manufacturing Company. He was president of this concern up to the time of his death.

Doctor Wannamaker was president and one of the organizers of the Bank of Orangeburg, was chairman of the Board of Commissioners of Public Works of Orangeburg for many years and was vice president of the South Carolina Pharmaceutical Association. He was always active in the affairs of his city and state.

On October 7, 1875, Doctor Wannamaker was married to Carrie E. Connor, daughter of Lewis E. and Mary (Mellerd) Connor. To this union there were born seven children. The oldest boy, Walter M., died in 1900, and the second daughter, Janie Mae, died in 1910. The following children surviving the subject of this sketch are: Goldie C., wife of Robert C. Holman, of Barnwell; Jacob George, Jr., Carrie B., wife of Howard P. Dew; Lewis C., and William J., all of Orangeburg.

Doctor Wannamaker died on May 17, 1919, at the age of sixty-seven years.

HON. HENRY JOHNSON, the first state senator from Allendale County, has been an able lawyer at Allendale since he began practice ten years ago.

Senator Johnson was born at Bowman in Orangeburg County, September 10, 1888, a son of John W. and Lorena (Bowman) Johnson. The town where he was born has been the home of the Bowmans for several generations, and the town was named for his maternal ancestors. Senator Johnson's great-grandfather Johnson came from Massachusetts to Charleston about 1800. The grandfather, Henry L. Johnson, was born at Charleston and in early life settled at Williston in Barnwell County, where the family has since lived. John W. Johnson was born in Barnwell County.

Senator Johnson grew up in Barnwell County, attended school at Williston, and graduated with the class of 1906 from The Citadel at Charleston. He is a graduate of the law department of the University of South Carolina of the class of 1909, and in the same year began practice at Allendale. He is said by all to be an exceptionally capable and skillful lawyer and has more than a local reputation in his profession.

He was elected state senator from Barnwell County in 1916, serving during the sessions of 1917-18. The new county of Allendale, with Allendale as county seat, formed from portions of Barnwell and Hampton counties, was organized in January, 1919, and at that time Mr. Johnson resigned as senator from Barnwell and was chosen for the new county.

During the war Senator Johnson was chairman of the Third Liberty Loan campaign for the Second Congressional District, was a member of the Legal Advisory Board, and earnestly supported all measures for the vigorous prosecution of the war. Senator Johnson married in 1909 Miss Alene All, of Allendale. They have one daughter, Ida Doris Johnson.

EUGENE GIBSON HINSON. Qualified for the practice of law in 1917, Eugene Gibson Hinson spent nearly two years in the army, and in the spring of 1919 he appropriately chose as his home and place of practice the Town of Allendale, recently established as the county seat of the new County of Allendale. This is a rich and promising section of South Carolina, and Mr. Hinson entered practice with every qualification for an able and successful career.

He was born at Marion, South Carolina, in 1894, son of L. L. and Lulu (Gibson) Hinson. The Hinsons for several generations have been planters on James Island. Mr. Hinson grew up at Marion and acquired a liberal education, graduating in both the literary and law courses from the University of South Carolina. He was a member of the class of 1917.

Soon after the outbreak of hostilities with Germany he entered the First Officers Training Camp at Fort Oglethorpe, and was commissioned second lieutenant. He was first assigned to duty with the Eighty-first Division, later was transferred to the Fourteenth Division and stationed at Camp Custer, Michigan. While there he was promoted to first lieutenant. After twenty-two months in the army he received his honorable discharge February 28, 1919.

Mr. Hinson then located at Allendale and has rapidly adapted himself to his new environment, and has a substantial law practice. He is a member of the Presbyterian Church and a Mason in fraternal affiliation.

Mr. Hinson married Miss Agnes Katharine Gibbs, of Atlanta. However, she is a member of the historic Gibbs family of Charleston. Her father was Charles E. Gibbs of Charleston.

LEROY WILSON has been a resident of Allendale nearly all his life, and for over twenty years has been an effective and public spirited factor in the advancement and upbuilding of that city not only as a commercial center but as the seat of justice of the recently organized Allendale County. Mr. Wilson was one of the leaders of the new county movement.

Mr. Wilson, who is president of the Citizens Bank of Allendale, was born in Bamberg County,

South Carolina, in 1876, son of Capt. LeRoy and Mary E. (Brabham) Wilson. Both the Wilson and Brabham families are of Scotch ancestry, and the Brabhams have long held a high place in the history and social affairs of Bamberg County. Capt. LeRoy Wilson was a native of Barnwell, now Allendale County, and lived in Allendale from 1878. He was a planter and merchant, conducted a farm in the neighborhood of Allendale and was a non-commissioned officer in the Confederate army. The Wilsons are of an old South Carolina family, antedating the Revolutionary period and coming from England. Mr. Wilson took part in the Red Shirt brigade during the reconstruction period. He was active in Masonry during his younger days, and died at the age of eighty-four in February, 1911.

The family moved to Allendale in 1878, and here LeRoy Wilson was reared and educated. As a youth he chose commercial pursuits, and the accrued wisdom and experience of passing years has given him a dominating position in the community. The Citizens Bank was organized in 1909. Under the presidency and active management of Mr. Wilson this is a strong financial institution, and has furthered in many ways the expansion of his home community. The bank has a capital stock of $30,000, surplus and undivided profits of about $13,000, and deposits aggregating about $350,000.

In November, 1919, Mr. Wilson organized the Allendale Grocery Company, with capital of $50,000, engaged in the wholesale grocery business. This institution has already served to emphasize Allendale's position as the center of an important and flourishing trade territory. Mr. Wilson is president of the company. The new County of Allendale, in the creation of which Mr. Wilson had a creditable part, comprises territory originally in Bamberg and Barnwell counties. Mr. Wilson was also a leader in the various patriotic movements in his locality during the World war.

He married Miss Ge Delle Brabham, of Bamberg County, daughter of H. J. Brabham, of Bamberg. They have two children, Mary Adele and LeRoy, Jr.

CHARLTON DURANT, former state senator, lawyer, business man and banker of Manning, has been a prominent factor in the life and affairs of that community for over twenty years.

He was born at Bluffton, Georgia, in 1874, son of E. C. and Virginia (Tinsley) DuRant. His ancestors were French, Scotch and Irish. His early advantages were limited to the common schools and he has been the architect of his own fortune and career. By close study he was admitted to the South Carolina bar in 1897, and began practice as member of the firm of Wilson & DuRant at Manning with whom he continued till 1906. In the meantime from 1890 to 1894 he was an express messenger and thus earned his living while preparing for his professional career. Since 1916 he has been a member of the firm of DuRant & Eller Company.

Mr. DuRant organized in 1911 and has since been president of the Home Bank & Trust Company of Manning. This institution has $25,000 capital, surplus of $15,000, while its deposits aggregate over $500,000. He is also member of the firm of DuRant & Floyd, and attorney and manager of the Clarendon Building & Loan Association and president, Clarendon Telephone Company. Mr. DuRant was a member of the State Senate during 1916-17-18.

BENJAMIN HART MOSS has practiced law at Orangeburg since 1883, is still a busy lawyer, and has handled many interests and responsibilities outside the direct limits of his profession.

He was born in Orangeburg County, January 17, 1862, son of William C. and Rebecca C. (Raysor) Moss, and a grandson of Stephen Moss and the great-grandson of Stephen Moss, who established the family in South Carolina from Virginia prior to the Revolutionary war. Benjamin Hart Moss grew up on a farm near Orangeburg, attended local schools, including the Orangeburg High School, and afterward entered Wofford College, where he graduated in 1883. He has preferred the steady practice of law and business to politics, though in 1899 he was elected a member of the Legislature, serving one term and voluntarily retired. He has also been a circuit judge. He has been and is president of the Edisto National Bank of Orangeburg, has served as trustee of Wofford College, and has been especially interested in education, serving repeatedly on the Orangeburg School Board. He is a democrat, a member of the Methodist Episcopal Church, South, is affiliated with the Masonic Order and the Woodmen of the World.

November 16, 1892, he married F. Agnes Dibble, daughter of Hon. Samuel Dibble, one of the most prominent names in the Orangeburg bar. To their marriage were born four children, three of whom reached mature years, Samuel Dibble Moss, May Caroline Moss and Agnes Henley Moss.

ADAM HOLMAN MOSS has been a member of the Orangeburg bar for many years, and while the law has commanded the better part of his time he has also been a factor in public affairs at different times.

He was born at St. Matthews, South Carolina, September 16, 1871, a son of James M. and Margaret (Holman) Moss. He grew up on his father's farm, attended private schools, and graduated from Wofford College in 1892. Mr. Moss studied law in private offices and was admitted to the bar in 1895. For two years he taught school, but for a quarter of a century has been engaged in the practice of law. He served as a captain in the Spanish-American war. He served two terms as a member of the Legislature, having been elected from Orangeburg in 1900 and 1904. He is chairman of the County Democratic Committee and director of the Bank of Orangeburg. Mr. Moss is affiliated with the Order of Elks.

He married Anne Norwood, of Greenville, and their two children are James Alexander and Louisa Norwood.

CHARLES G. DANTZLER. A number of distinguished South Carolinians have borne the family name of Dantzler. The Dantzlers came originally from Germany and established their homes in the Carolinas prior to the Revolution. Charles G. Dantz-

ler was born at Orangeburg, March 19, 1854. His grandfather, Jacob M. Dantzler, was prominent in public life. His father, Olin M. Dantzler, was trained as a lawyer, but followed the business of planter, and during the war between the states commanded the Twenty-second South Carolina Volunteers and was killed in battle in 1864. His wife, Caroline Glover, was a daughter of Dr. Charles Glover, who attained eminence as a physician.

Charles G. Dantzler was educated at Mount Zion Institute, Winnsboro, attended King's Mountain Military School at Yorkville, and from 1871 to 1875 was a student of Wofford College, where he graduated with honors. He then took up the practice of law and for over forty years his name has stood in the front rank of the Orangeburg District. He was elected in 1884 and served for six years as representative of Orangeburg County in the Legislature. In January, 1902, he was elected Circuit Judge of the First Judicial Circuit. Judge Dantzler is a member of the Masonic Order, is affiliated with the Methodist Episcopal Church, South, and has served as a trustee of Wofford College. He married in 1876 Laura A. Moss. He has two daughters, Carrie M. and Annie W.

DAVID K. BRIGGS, M. D. After thirty-six years devoted to his chosen vocation Doctor Briggs is still active as a physician and surgeon, going his daily rounds, and keeping in close touch with the affairs of his home community at Blackville and also with the larger interests of his profession.

A resident of Blackville most of his life, Doctor Briggs was born at Charleston, February 5, 1862. His father was David Briggs, whose life was one of more than ordinary interest and achievement. Born at Sidney, Maine, in 1819, he was a New England farmer, and about 1840 came to South Carolina. He lived in Charleston for several years, and in 1849 with a party of friends sailed around Cape Horn to the California gold fields. After some more or less profitable but very interesting experiences on the Pacific Coast he returned to Charleston and engaged in the paint and oil business. In 1870 he moved to Blackville, and after that lived on a plantation and followed farming until his death in 1888. While a native of the North, he espoused the cause of the South in the time of war, though on account of physical disabilities was not in the Confederate army. However, he did some valuable service as a blockade runner, bringing in supplies to Charleston Harbor. Because of some of his exploits the Federal Government offered a large reward for him dead or alive. Throughout his life he exemplified the character of a good, plain citizen, and gave his best energies to the welfare of his chosen state. He was of English descent, while his wife, Sarah A. Keene, was Scotch. She was born at Augusta, Maine, and died in 1889.

Doctor Briggs received his first advantages in the schools of Charleston, later attended school at Blackville, and in 1884 graduated M. D. from the College of Physicians and Surgeons at Baltimore. He has never allowed any important interests to interfere with a fixed devotion to his profession. He is local surgeon for the Southern Railway Company, has been president of the county and district medical societies, and during the war was examining physician for the Selective Draft Board. He is also a member of the American Medical Association. Doctor Briggs has never found time nor inclination for activity in politics. He is a York Rite Mason and Shriner, a Knight of Pythias and Woodmen of the World.

Doctor Briggs helped organize the Presbyterian Church at Blackville in 1893, was chosen one of its first elders, and has discharged the duties of that office for a quarter of a century. He married in 1887 Ida C. Dodenhoff, a native of Blackville. Her father, Capt. Henry Dodenhoff, was born in Hanover, Germany, while her mother was of an old southern family.

PHILIP ALSTON WILLCOX, senior member of the law firm of Willcox & Willcox, Florence, South Carolina, was born in Marion, South Carolina, on the 4th of December, 1866. He graduated from the University of South Carolina, in 1888, and was admitted to the bar in 1889. He is general solicitor for the Atlantic Coast Line Railroad Company, and represents several large corporate interests, among them being the Standard Oil Company, the Southern Bell Telephone & Telegraph Company, and the Western Union Telegraph Company. He was president of the South Carolina Bar Association 1919-1920; is a member of the general council of the American Bar Association, and a trustee of University of South Carolina. He is an officer and director of several business institutions, banks, etc.

MILES J. WALKER, M. D. For over sixty years the Walker family of York County has been distinguished by the abilities and attainments of its representatives in the profession of medicine and surgery. Dr. Miles J. Walker has practiced steadily for nearly forty years, while his brother, Dr. George Walker, of Baltimore, has earned national and international fame as a surgeon and scientist. The Walkers were of Revolutionary stock. Six of Dr. Miles J. Walker's father's brothers were in the Confederate army during the war between the states.

Dr. Miles J. Walker was born in York County in 1857, son of Dr. William Millard and Mary Ellen (Hudson) Walker. This is a very old family in York County. Dr. W. M. Walker was born there, a son of John Walker, and spent all his active life as a practicing dentist. He was also a Confederate soldier, serving throughout the war.

Dr. Miles J. Walker acquired his literary training in the King's Mountain Military Academy at York while it was under the direction of that venerable educator Colonel Coward. He graduated in medicine from the Louisville Medical College in 1879, and after a brief practice in Union County removed to York. He has taken post-graduate work in the Johns Hopkins University and is widely known for his attainments and services in the medical profession. He was district counsellor for the Fifth District, State Medical Association, has been chairman of the Board of Health of York for twenty years, and is a member of the county, state and American associations. Dr. Miles J. Walker was surgeon for the First Regiment of Militia for ten years, but had to leave the service on account of a broken limb. He retired with the rank of major.

Doctor Walker married Miss Nannie E. Walker, of Union County. Their children are Mrs. R. E. Sharp, Mrs. J. E. Nesbit, Mrs. John Porter Hollis, and Mrs. Henry Grady Hardin.

Though for many years a resident of Baltimore, a brief sketch of Dr. George Walker has an appropriate place in this volume. He was born at Yorkville, now York, July 27, 1869, was educated in South Carolina College and in the medical department of the University of Maryland. From the time of his graduation in 1889 until 1895 he practiced at York, South Carolina, and since 1895 has lived in Baltimore. He was connected with the Johns Hopkins University, and in 1905 was made associate in surgery in that institution. He became chairman of the Maryland Statewide Vice Commission in 1913, and is a director of the Social Service Corporation of Baltimore. He is an honored member of a number of professional and scientific organizations, and is an honorary member of the York Medical Society.

The work which has brought him his greatest fame was during the World war. In 1917 he was commissioned major of the Medical Reserve Corps, and is a member of the Johns Hopkins Unit which went to France in June, 1917. The personnel of that unit included several other physicians of world renown. After a few months, with the approval of General Pershing, Dr. George Walker was put in complete charge of venereal diseases for the entire American Expeditionary Forces and was promoted to the rank of colonel. It was through the original methods adopted at the instance of Colonel Walker that the venereal disease rate in the American army was reduced below that of any other army in Europe. Since returning to America Doctor Walker has given his entire time and talents to a nation-wide campaign against venereal diseases. He has worked for the co-operation of governors, legislators and other organized bodies of public opinion to secure the enactment of suitable legislation to reduce the ravages of such diseases and safeguard the public against them. All this work Doctor Walker has undertaken at his own expense and as a continuation of the social and scientific service in which he has long been engaged.

FRANKLIN JACOB GEIGER, M. D. While his individual record was impressive on account of his service as a Confederate surgeon, and the many years he gave to a large country practice in what is now Calhoun County, Dr. Franklin Jacob Geiger was not the only conspicuous member of his family in the state.

The first of the name was Herman Geiger, who immigrated either from Switzerland or Germany, and settled in Saxe Gotha Township on the Congaree River, about eight miles below the City of Columbia in 1737. The Salley Documentary Sources of State History from 1704 to 1782 make reference to the Geiger family, and another reference is found on page 302 of Logan's History of South Carolina. The fourth son of Herman Geiger was John Geiger, the third son of John was William, and the first son of William was John Conrad Geiger.

John Conrad Geiger, father of Dr. Franklin Jacob Geiger, was born August 24, 1801, and died March 10, 1870. He owned a large plantation, many slaves, was prominent in state politics, was a member of the Legislature and was a member of the Secession Convention and a signer of the Ordinance of Secession. He married Ellen Baker who was born in January, 1809, and died May 28, 1881, being a daughter of William Baker of Lexington County.

Franklin Jacob Geiger was born at Sandy Run in Lexington County, December 20, 1835. He was educated in the Sandy Run Academy and the Shirley Institute at Winnsboro and was graduated from the Medical College of the State of South Carolina with the class of 1858. Soon afterward he removed to Mississippi and practiced in that state until the outbreak of the war between the states, when he returned to South Carolina and joined the Confederate army. He was in the service from the beginning until the end of the war, and as an assistant surgeon was stationed with the defenses around Charleston, Fort Sumter, Battery Wagner and other points. The fortunes of war left him in straightened financial circumstances, and he then settled in the northern section of Orangeburg, now Calhoun County, and for more than forty years diligently practiced his profession and also looked after his farming interests. His character entitled him to the respect and esteem he enjoyed, and a large family of children feel themselves honored to count him as their father. He died November 30, 1910.

He served as trustee of the local schools, was a democrat, was a believer in State's Rights, and during the reconstruction period had an active part in his locality in restoring white rule. He served as worshipful master of Oliver Lodge No. 133, Ancient Free and Accepted Masons, and was a member and elder of the Sandy Run Lutheran Church.

At Charleston, March 8, 1860, he married Anna Elizabeth Geiger, daughter of Godfrey Herman and Elizabeth (Lorick) Geiger. Her father was a Lexington County farmer and her mother was a daughter of Michael Lorick, likewise an extensive planter in Lexington County. Mrs. Doctor Geiger died July 20, 1905. They were the parents of thirteen children, briefly noted as follows: Elizabeth Horlbeck; Ellen Baker, who married P. H. E. Derrick; Dr. Charles Blum, a prominent physician at Manning, a sketch of whom appears elsewhere; William Henry, who was burned to death in a fire at Manning, December 13, 1895; John Franklin, a dentist at Manning; Herbert Lorick, who married Leola Wolfe; Godfrey Herman, who married Susan Whitefield; Stephen Elliott; Mary Louisa; Anna Esther; Rufus Baker, who married Gertrude Smith; Percy Lee and Harold Conrad.

CHARLES BLUM GEIGER, M. D. Oldest son of Dr. Franklin Jacob Geiger, Dr. Charles Blum Geiger's professional career was coincident with that of his father for about twenty years. He has been a physician and surgeon since 1889, and faithfully and well has served the innumerable calls upon his time and energies not only in the strict routine of

his profession but in many other community interests. As his father was a Confederate soldier, so Dr. Charles B. Geiger was for over a year a member of the Medical Reserve Corps of the United States army during the World war.

Charles Blum Geiger was born in Lexington County, South Carolina, June 19, 1867, and grew up in the St. Mathews section of Orangeburg County, where, owing to the reduced circumstances of his father's fortune after the war and during the reconstruction period he had only the limited advantages of country schools and had many duties on the farm. By night study he prepared himself for entrance to the South Carolina Medical College in 1889, and was graduated in 1892. For one year he served as house physician and surgeon in St. Francis Xavier Infirmary at Charleston, and since then has been in active practice at Manning. For a quarter of a century, with the exception of a period spent in the war, he has been on almost day and night duty as a physician and surgeon at Manning. For four years he served as a member of the Manning Board of Health, is a member of the County Pension Board, for two years was a member of the Board of County Commissioners and has been active in the County, State and Medical Association and a director of the Bank of Clarendon.

Doctor Geiger served with the rank of first lieutenant in the Medical Corps from August 16, 1917, to November 30, 1918. He is a Royal Arch Mason and a Woodman of the World. On June 19, 1907, he married Miss Nettie Weinberg of Manning.

His brother, John Franklin Geiger, has been a leading dental practitioner at Manning for over twenty years. He was born in Orangeburg County, August 23, 1871, and is a graduate of the Baltimore College of Dental Surgery with the class of 1895. He is a member of the State and National Dental Societies. John F. Geiger married December 23, 1896, Belle Gallughat. Their five children are Emily, William Erving, Virginia, Rosa Lee and Anna Belle.

DRAYTON MARGARET CROSSON, M. D. More than thirty-five years ago Doctor Crosson began the practice of his profession, and since then many enviable distinctions have crowned his work as a physician and surgeon, as a business man and a public leader.

He is one of a family of many distinguished members and of long and influential residence in Newberry and Lexington counties. He was born at Prosperity in Newberry County, September 29, 1858, a son of John Thomas Pressley and Rosa Catherine (Cook) Crosson. For more than a century his people have been identified with Newberry County. His great-great-grandfather, Alexander Crosson, came from Ireland. His grandfather was James Crosson, a merchant, planter and magistrate of Newberry County, who married a member of the Halfacre family. John Thomas Pressly Crosson graduated at Erskine College, and taught until married, then was also a planter. Rosa Catherine Cook was a daughter of John Cook, a well known and wealthy planter who married a sister of Sen. John C. Hope.

Vol. V—7

Doctor Crosson grew up at a time when the State of South Carolina and its citizens were suffering from the blight of war, but he had good home advantages, and especially from both his mother and father received every encouragement for intellectual development. He developed a good physique on his father's farm, and when only a boy determined to become a physician. He paid part of the expenses of his preparatory course in the Prosperity Academy, was a student for three years at Erskine College and in 1879 entered South Carolina Medical College. Two years later he was graduated and in 1883 completed his medical course in the University of Tennessee at Nashville with first honors in his class and has since from time to time took courses in Baltimore and New York. Since his graduation he has carried the heavy and continuous burdens of a physician and surgeon. He served a number of years as president of the County Medical Society of Lexington County, and has also been active in the State Medical Association.

Doctor Crosson has acquired extensive farm interests and at one time and probably now is the largest planter in Lexington County. He has served on the medical examining board for Lexington County and volunteered for service with the medical reserve corps. Just before the armistice was signed he would have gone to France, if needed. He has found time for participation in public affairs, serving as county chairman of the democratic party, and in 1900 was elected to the State Senate and was re-elected in 1908 and served until 1912. He has recently taken active steps to organize the Farmers and Merchants Bank of Leesville, South Carolina, his home town, and was without opposition unanimously elected its president. He is chairman of the Lexington County Cotton Growers' Association and takes an active interest in all agricultural affairs, both state and national. While in the Senate he introduced the first good roads (highway) bill and advocated a state highway department and engineers, and a license on automobiles for its maintenance. He has lived to see these ideas all put into effect. The National (Highway) or Good Roads Association has made him a life member. He is always an advocate for progressive advancements, professionally, educationally, socially, financially and religiously, and of everything that will upbuild the country. He is a Mason, Knight of Pythias, Odd Fellow and Woodmen of the World, and a Methodist in religious affiliation. Doctor Crosson married Miss S. C. Bodie in 1883, and to their union were born seven children. Two of them are living.

GEORGE WILLIAM BOYLSTON. One of the most interesting men in the old community of Blackville is George William Boylston, who before he was eighteen years of age entered the Confederate army, served all through the war, never surrendered, and for more than half a century has been identified with planting and other interests in his home locality. In Confederate reunions for many years he has been one of the most picturesque figures, and he has a rare memory for the events in which he participated, and the fact that he saw many of the most important phases of warfare in his native state gives his reminiscences unusual value.

Mr. Boylston was born at Blackville, near the Edisto River, February 27, 1843. His parents were Austin and Mary (Reed) Boylston. His great-grandfather was William Boylston, who was born July 24, 1802, of Scotch parentage. His grandfather was born in Virginia. His mother's father, Samuel Reed, was sent to America with an appointment as surveyor by King George III. He received a crown grant of 5,000 acres of land, some of which is in the possession of his descendants to this day. He came to South Carolina from Ireland in 1774. His daughter was born in December, 1801. Two of Mr. Boylston's great-uncles fought in the Revolution. His paternal grandmother was Alice Cloud, wife of George Boylston. His maternal grandmother was Mary Clark, wife of Samuel Reed. His maternal great-grand uncle, Malcolm Clark, was reported missing in the Revolutionary war. He was a justice in Orangeburg District in 1775, and was commissioned by President Rutledge justice of the peace in 1776.

The Boylstons have always been planters. George W. Boylston acquired his early education in what is now Barnwell County. He really had a double enlistment for the war. The first company he joined did not attain its full quota and therefore in September, 1861, he enlisted in heavy artillery under Capt. afterwards Col. Tom Lamar, who appointed him ordnance sergeant of Company B, Second Regiment, Heavy Artillery. He received his baptism of fire on June 16, 1862, an engagement in which forty-three of his comrades were killed or wounded. Mr. Boylston seems to have led a charmed life, since on countless occasions he was exposed to danger and had many narrow escapes. One time a bullet passed through the top of his hat and killed has friend, Captain Reed. His company was the first encamped on James Island in the defenses around Charleston, and for days and months they were exposed to constant fire. Mr. Boylston was present on the occasion when the timely arrival of the Louisiana Tigers compelled the enemy to draw off from what promised to be a successful advance upon the southern fortifications. At Fort Johnson Mr. Boylston had charge of the magazine. Shells from the enemy's ships struck and exploded the magazine, killing all the men inside, Mr. Boylston being fortunately on the outside, and escaped with serious shock and disability from duty for a time. He also recalls the enemy gun which the Confederates named "The Swamp Angel" located on the upper end of Morris Island. Shells from this gun carried six miles into Charleston, passing over Mr. Boylston's battery.

It was the duty of Mr. Boylston to fuse all the shells. He noted a difference in the carrying power, and one day General Beauregard came to him and asked why some of the fuses were so much less effective than others, and his reply was that some were much softer and therefore probably defective. The general promised to send better fuses, and did so the next day.

Mr. Boylston is the only member of the original battery alive today. He has a personal knowledge of the facts in one of the interesting stories told by the old veterans, when Confederate guns were trained on 600 southern soldiers, and Mr. Boylston in recalling the event says that while it was a matter of general congratulation that none of the 600 men was wounded, their escape was not creditable to southern marksmanship. These men afterward became known as the Immortal Six Hundred, and their story has been told and retold at Confederate reunions.

Mr. Boylston also recalls the occasion when a number of Federal barges loaded with troops were stealing up under cover of darkness for a surprise on the southern forts, when they were themselves surprised and the majority of the men on the transport killed. At one time, says Mr. Boylston, the enemy were advancing on the works which had been thrown up after the magazine explosion, and the Federal color bearer planted his flag on the edge. He was shot down, and the Confederates made an effort to capture the colors, but it was rescued before they could do so. As the Federals retired they reached over the works and seized a Confederate and carried him away a prisoner of war.

Mr. Boylston is also one of the surviving Confederates who can give from personal examination an accurate description of the first submarines, which as history shows were originally perfected by the southern government and first put into use during the war. These boats were called "The Davids." He can describe them in detail, and it is his confirmed belief that the American who later gained fame as the inventor of the modern submarine undoubtedly took his ideas from the undersea boats used by the Confederacy. A description of these submarines appeared in the Columbia Record of March 27, 1917, and Mr. Boylston, who has examined that account, says that in the main it is correct, though it is not true that hand pumping was resorted to, since he especially noticed how the pumps were geared in with other machinery, and it was explained how this mechanism was worked.

When Sherman took Atlanta and came north through the Carolinas Mr. Boylston and his comrades left Charleston May 18, 1865, passing up into North Carolina, where they had several fights with Sherman's advance guard. After Lee's surrender Mr. Boylston had several narrow escapes from capture and from death. He was delegated to carry messages to the pickets, the last time all alone, and he always returned safely. After Lee's surrender and in the resulting confusion the commanding officer told Mr. Boylston and his comrades that they could go, and thirteen of them set out for home through a country filled with the enemy. They were practically without food, and they kept their one colored servant constantly scouting for supplies. This negro declared he had asked for food in the name of every northern general he could remember. After an exposure to innumerable hardships and difficulties for eleven days Mr. Boylston reached his home community and participated in a joyful reunion with his loved ones. It has been a matter of lasting satisfaction that he is one of the thirteen men who never surrendered and who never took the oath of allegiance.

The years following the war Mr. Boylston has

devoted to planting, and though now seventy-seven years of age he is still active, goes about his affairs with the energy and spirit of many younger men, and his wife also possesses the spirit of youth. They enjoy life to the full in their attractive home in Blackville. Among the many mementos of his war service Mr. Boylston carefully preserves and cherishes the Cross of Honor bestowed upon him for bravery and courage. He and his wife are earnest members of the Baptist Church.

Mr. Boylston was the first school trustee appointed on the Edisto River after the Civil war, holding that office for many years, finally resigning in favor of a nephew. He is a member of Morrall Camp of Confederate Veterans. Mr. Boylston has been a worker in the Baptist Church for sixty-two years and served eighteen years on the executive committee of the Baptist Association. He and his two brothers were reared in the Baptist faith, married daughters of Methodist ministers, but all became Baptists and reared their children in that faith.

Mr. Boylston was married three times. His first wife was Fanny Crum, daughter of Rev. Lewis Crum. His second wife was Carrie Euphrasia, daughter of Daniel Riley. The present Mrs. Boylston bore the maiden name of Emma Warren, whose father, Frederick Warren, was related to the famous Warren family of Boston, Massachusetts. Her father died on a ship he commanded, a victim of yellow fever, and was buried at sea four months before Mrs. Boylston's birth. Her mother was Jane Mirvin. Mrs. Boylston received a superior education at Charleston, and she heard the first gun fired in the harbor, marking the beginning of the Civil war. She is of Irish-American ancestry and is a member of Davis-Lee Chapter, United Daughters of the Confederacy. Her first husband was Elijah Samuel Reed, by whom she had six children, three of whom died after they were married, leaving descendants. Her grandson Gilmore Mixon is the father of her first great-grandchild, Eva Corrine. Mrs. Boylston was born at Charleston, February 14, 1854.

Mr. Boylston had a son by his first wife, Eugene Boylston, of Blackville. His daughter Leila Estelle married Dr. George Hair of Bamberg, and their daughter, Mrs. J. J. Cudd, of Spartanburg, presented Mr. Boylston with his first great-grandchild, Aileen. He has four grandchildren. By his second marriage there were two sons and two daughters. Mr. Boylston has in his home a speaking likeness of a beautiful young daughter, Ella, who gave promise of achieving great fame in the musical world, but who died in early girlhood.

MAJOR HENRY CUMMING TILLMAN, one of the two sons of the late Senator B. R. Tillman, has for a number of years practiced law at Greenwood, though for a year and a half all his time was given to the government as an army officer in the great war.

Major Tillman is a graduate of Clemson College, which was founded during his father's administration as a governor. He received the Bachelor of Science degree in 1903 and took his law course at Washington and Lee University, graduating in 1905. He began practice at Greenwood in 1906, and is senior of the law firm Tillman, Mays & Harris, with offices in Greenwood and Anderson.

Prior to the war with Germany he was captain of the Fifth Company, Coast Artillery, National Guard, of South Carolina. As commander of that company he was mustered into the National Army in July, 1917, and later was transferred to the command of Headquarters Company, Sixty-First Artillery, Coast Artillery Corps. He went overseas to France in July, 1918, and before the signing of the armistice was promoted to major of the Second Battalion and transferred to the Sixty-Second Artillery. Major Tillman returned home in February, 1919, and upon his release from the army resumed his law practice.

Major Tillman has always been a keen student of politics and public questions, and has given an example of good citizenship in his home community. He is associated with a number of fraternal orders and is a member of the Episcopal Church. He married Miss Mary Fox, of Batesburg. Their three children are: Mary, Adeline and Sarah Stark.

CHARLES VALK BOYKIN is distinguished among the successful business men and executives of Charleston by the power of a creative faculty, which, supplemented with a high degree of business courage and energy, has enabled him in a few short years, from original resources consisting largely of "vision" of the future, to build up a great industry.

Mr. Boykin was born in Charleston in 1878, at the home of his mother, though his parents, Allen J. and Elizabeth C. (Courtney) Boykin, at that time lived in Kershaw County. The Boykins are a very prominent and historic family of Camden and Kershaw counties. Many details of the family history are contained in the work "Historic Camden" published a few years ago. The founder of the family came from England about 1760, and for his services in the Indian wars was given a crown grant of land consisting of about 11,000 acres a few miles below Camden. The Boykins have owned and occupied portions of that land ever since. The ancestral residence, now more than a century old, is still standing. Mr. Boykin's grandfather, Alexander Hamilton Boykin, though strongly opposed to secession, when secession became an actuality organized and fitted up at his own expense, including horses and other equipment, the noted Boykin Rangers. He commanded this body of men two years, most of his service being in Virginia.

Charles Valk Boykin came to Charleston when a boy and learned the trade of machinist in the shops of the old Valk and Murdoch Company on the waterfront. In a few years his qualifications stood as an expert machinist, particularly on boilers and marine machinery and equipment.

The Charleston Dry Dock & Medicine Company is chartered under the laws of the State of Delaware with a capital stock of $2,500,000. The pay roll of the company averages $15,000 per week, many highly paid skilled mechanics being employed. The company is noted for its fine work in the manufacture of marine boilers. The traveling and portable cranes, lathes, drill presses, and particularly the electric welding and compressed air machinery, are of the most modern type. The dry dock can take care of any ships that come into Charleston Harbor. Electric power is used exclusively. Adjoining property in addition to the original plat mentioned above has been purchased, affording ample room on the water front for further expansion. One feature is a yacht basin, built to give private dockage facilities for yachts. As the leading industrial enterprise of Charleston, a large degree of the credit due the present status of the company belongs to the indefatigable energy and enthusiasm of Charles V. Boykin.

Mr. Boykin married Miss Sarah Pearson Allen, of Charleston, daughter of Mr. and Mrs. James P. Allen. Their three children are Mary Allen, Elizabeth Courtney and Charles V., Jr.

RT. REV. MGR. P. L. DUFFY, V. G., LL. D., LITT. D. It is not alone the people of the diocese of Charleston who appreciated the scholarly character and services of Doctor Duffy. His wisdom and learning and the ripe fruits of his experience were assets to the culture of the state as a whole.

Doctor Duffy, who was vicar general of the Catholic diocese of Charleston, spent most of his life in that city, making his preliminary studies in the public and private schools of Charleston. From there he entered Mount St. Mary's College at Emmitsburg, Maryland, graduating with the first honors of his class and the Bachelor of Arts degree in 1875. On completing his course in theology he was accorded the degree A. M. in 1879, received the degree LL. D. in 1894, and the honorary degree Litt. D. was bestowed upon him in 1908 upon the occasion of the delivery of the Centennial Ode at the Centenary of that institution. Cardinal Gibbons, who conferred the degree, pronounced this ode a masterpiece.

In 1908 Doctor Duffy published a volume of poems, "A Wreath of Ilex Leaves," which was accorded generous and deserved praise by the press. He lectured before the College of Charleston on "The Ideal in Literature and Art," and also before the South Carolina Military Academy and elsewhere. He was a contributor to the Catholic Encyclopedia, the Library of Southern Literature, and other publications. At the request of the Daughters of the Confederacy he composed and read the ode on Memorial Day and on several occasions delivered memorial addresses.

Through all the years since his graduation, more than forty in number, Doctor Duffy was a very busy clergyman, devoting himself to the interests of his parish, especially to his schools and general educational work. He was appointed vicar general of the diocese of Charleston in 1911 and was made a prelate of the Papal Court with the title of Monsignor by Pope Benedict in 1917.

The Rt. Rev. Mgr. P. L. Duffy, V. G., was born March 25, 1851, at Waterford, Ireland, and died July 22, 1919, at Charleston, South Carolina.

SAMUEL VINCENT TAYLOR is owner of the S. V. Taylor Department Store at Greeleyville, a business founded by his father, the late Samuel J. Taylor, who deserves the historical credit of being the founder of Greeleyville, and for many years closely associated with every phase of its development and improvement.

Samuel J. Taylor was born at Charleston in 1840. In 1861 at the age of twenty-one he entered the Confederate army, serving as color bearer of the Sixth South Carolina Regiment, Jenkin's Brigade, Longstreet's Corps. He was a soldier from the beginning to the end of the war and saw much of the strenuous fighting in Virginia. In the ten years that followed the war he was stanchly allied with the good citizens of South Carolina in striving to save the state from the ruin of reconstruction and took a prominent part in the campaign of 1876 which restored white man's government and resulted in the election of Governor Wade Hampton. He was appointed a member of the staff of Governor Hampton.

In the meantime Samuel J. Taylor had come to the present site of Greeleyville in 1872. In partnership with S. J. Hudson he bought several hundred acres of timber, and began the manufacture of turpentine and rosin. Later he bought out his partner and took in his brother-in-law, W. S. Varner, and they were associated for a number of years. Samuel J. Taylor was an expert in the naval stores industry, and his enterprise was the source of most of the prosperity of the people then living in this vicinity. His timber holdings became exhausted after about fifteen years. It had been his intention to remove his turpentine equipment to new territory. However, he was very much attached to Greeleyville, had acquired a large body of land there, and had also begun the mercantile business and for both financial and sentimental reasons he elected to remain at Greeleyville.

In promoting a town community here he was actuated by the most liberal motives and wisdom. He practically donated building lots to every industrious and capable man who applied and who would agree to construct and improve a good home. He also gave land freely for street, churches and schools, and long before his death had the satisfaction of seeing his dreams realized in a beautiful town with good streets, good homes and business institutions, and surrounded by a fine civic atmosphere.

Samuel J. Taylor died January 12, 1912, after forty years of residence at Greeleyville. He married Julia Marie DuBose, who is also deceased. Her father was Dr. James M. DuBose of Sumter. Samuel J. Taylor was the father of four children: Lula T., wife of M. D. DeLong, of Charleston; Samuel V.; Dr. E. O., who died October 23, 1918, a practicing physician of Greeleyville, and a graduate of the University of Maryland; and Dr. W. L., a practicing dentist of Kingstree, South Carolina.

Samuel Vincent Taylor was born at Greeleyville November 24, 1878. He attended the local schools and the Furman University at Greenville, and as a young man found employment in his father's store. He mastered the business, assumed many of the responsibilities of its management, and before his father's death he bought the business and has since conducted it as the S. V. Department Store. This business supplies all the varied demands for merchandise in and around Greeleyville, and the stock is carried in a large and well equipped building, 93 by 100 feet.

Mr. Taylor is a Scottish Rite Mason and Shriner,

being a member of Omar Temple of the Shrine at Charleston. He married Miss Martha Elizabeth Murchison of Camden. They have one son, Samuel Vincent, Jr.

Hon. BENJAMIN RYAN TILLMAN. Probably the most impressive tribute to the late Senator Tillman consists in the simple fact that at the end of his long life his old associates and admirers could speak of him not in the exaggerated terms of partisan hero-worship, but could depict in him real greatness as a man and public leader with many of the frailties of human nature. Error is part of struggle and aspiration, or, as another great American expressed it, the successful man decides and executes promptly and makes a few mistakes.

Therefore it was the supreme good fortune of Mr. Tillman that his life story could be told without qualifications or apologies, and doubtless few biographies of South Carolina's eminent men will better stand the test of time and criticism than his. A good, brief outline of his career is that written by his friend and associate Mr. J. Broadus Knight, clerk of the United States District Court at Greenville. With some abbreviation and modifications Mr. Knight's article as it appeared in the "News and Courier" July 4, 1918, the day following Senator Tillman's death, is quoted as follows:

"Benjamin Ryan Tillman, of Trenton, Edgefield county, South Carolina, was born August 11, 1847, on his father's plantation about twelve miles southwest of the present town of Edgefield. He was the son of Benjamin Ryan Tillman and Sophia Hancock and was the youngest of eleven children. There were seven boys, one of whom, Thomas F. Tillman, was killed in the Mexican war. Another, George D. Tillman, served as Congressman from that district for nineteen years.

"Young Tillman's father died when he was two and one-half years old, and he was brought up by his mother on the plantation. He studied at home under private tutors, one of whom was Miss Annie Arthur, a sister of Chester A. Arthur, later president of the United States. When he reached the age of fourteen his mother sent him to a high school at Liberty Hill in Edgefield county, and for three years he studied under the famous teacher, George Galphin. It was here that he secured the foundation for an education which was later to be broadened by extensive reading. He was especially proficient in Latin, and for years spent several hours each day acquainting himself with works of the old masters. In July of 1864 he quit school and volunteered for service in the Confederate army. While on his way to the army he was taken ill, and as a result of this attack lost his left eye by an abscess and was an invalid for two years.

"He returned to his home and spent the next twenty years, from 1866 to 1886, with the exception of a year in Florida, reading and studying and looking after his farming interests. Having a retentive mind he forgot nothing practically that he ever read.

"In 1876, while a member of a local military company, the Sweetwater Saber Club, he took part in the Hamburg riot just across the Savannah River from the city of Augusta, Georgia. In this riot one white man and a score or more of negroes were killed. Some two weeks later as a member of the same club he participated in the Ellenton riot, where many additional blacks were killed. The negroes were in absolute control of the politics in South Carolina, and strong measures were necessary for the whites to maintain supremacy. These riots caused a Congressional investigation by President Grant, but resulted in nothing.

"In 1885 Tillman began his agitation for higher education for the boys and girls of the farming class in South Carolina. It was in this year, when thirty-eight years of age, that he faced his first audience in the state. This speech was known as his Bennettsville speech and created deep interest among the farmers all over the country. During the next three years he continued writing a series of letters to the Charleston papers pleading for the farmers to assert their rights against the politicians around the court houses in the various counties who were then parceling out the political offices.

"He was urged to run for Governor in 1888, but declined. In 1890, as the result of his continued agitation, the farmers' movement had gained such headway and there was such a demand for him to offer himself for Governor that he could not refuse. He entered the race and after one of the most bitter campaigns in history was overwhelmingly elected. In 1898 he was reelected Governor.

"One of the most notable acts of his career as Governor was the establishment of what is known as the primary system. Under this system the people of South Carolina have a right to go to the polls, and a farmer's vote counts for just as much as that of a lawyer's or court house politician. In this way the state was freed from ring-rule, and the people in each county were given a voice in naming the candidates for election to the various offices. Thus was displaced the small coterie of politicians who had heretofore met and slated their candidates behind closed doors.

"True to his promise made on the stump, Tillman set about to establish higher institutions of learning for the boys and girls of the state. His efforts in this behalf resulted in the establishment of Clemson Agricultural and Mechanical College for boys at Fort Mill, Calhoun's old home in Oconee county, and the establishment of Winthrop Normal and Industrial College for girls at Rock Hill. Under a system of scholarships it was made possible for boys and girls of scant means to attend college.

"His next step was the passage of a law to curtail whiskey selling. South Carolina had at that time local option, or the old bar room system. After months of study and thousands of miles spent in travel in making investigations Tillman asked the Legislature to pass what was later known as the dispensary law. Under this act the state undertook to manufacture and dispense alcoholic drinks to its citizens. Many restrictions were thrown around the sale of intoxicants, and in this way considerable curtailment of whiskey drinking resulted. When first established the dispensary was looked on with great disfavor in certain sections of the state and, under authority given him by law, Tillman appointed detectives to hunt down violators. These came to be known as 'Tillman's Spies.' At Darlington, in 1894, feeling ran so high that a riot resulted and several citizens and constables were killed. The

Governor promptly called out the State Militia and the riot was quelled. Thousands of dollars were poured into the treasury of the state in profits derived from the dispensary. But in after years the management of the dispensary fell into the hands of unscrupulous and dishonest men, and the institution was brought into disrepute. Then, too, there was a widespread sentiment favoring prohibition sweeping the country, and the people demanded further curtailment, which was not permissible under the dispensary law. By many the dispensary was regarded as a failure, but as a step toward ultimate prohibition it must be deemed to have been a decided success.

"In 1894, after having served the state as Governor for four years, Tillman entered the race for the United States Senate against Gen. M. C. Butler. He was easily elected and went to Washington in 1895. He was opposed to the policies of President Cleveland, and soon after entering the Senate made what has become known as his 'pitchfork speech.' This speech was a masterpiece and is, perhaps, one of the bitterest arraignments of a president ever made in the history of this country. At the next election the republicans came into power, and as a member of the minority from that time until 1913 he had to content himself with watching the republicans pass what they considered by them 'necessary legislation.' At one time during this period the Senate consisted of ninety members, sixty of whom were republicans. As a result the minority could do little more than 'make them go slow,' as Tillman said.

"Tillman's fame as an orator and stump speaker had preceded him, and from 1896 to 1908 his services were in great demand by managers of lecture bureaus. He traversed the country from ocean to ocean and visited practically every state in the Union. He had many subjects, but probably the most famous speech delivered on such occasions was 'The Race Problem,' which did much toward educating the people of the North as to the true conditions in the South.

"In 1906, with the republicans still in control, and while a member of the committee on interstate and foreign commerce, the republican members of that committee disagreed among themselves as to who should handle an important piece of legislation on the floor of the Senate known as the rate bill. Rather than see one of the republican members get the honor three or four of them joined with the democratic members and placed Tillman in charge. Perhaps this is the first instance in history where a member of the minority party was given the task of handling important majority legislation. Few people know that Senator Tillman prepared and had inserted in this bill what is known as the anti-free pass amendment, but it was through his individual efforts that this legislation was obtained.

"Soon after Senator Tillman entered the Senate he was placed on the great committee on naval affairs, and as a member of that committee he became greatly interested in everything pertaining to the navy and its welfare. One of his greatest efforts in the Senate was to compel the manufacturers of armor plate to sell their product to the government at a reasonable price. His exposure of the Armor Plate Trust in 1897 saved the government hundreds of thousands of dollars.

"In 1902, while a member of this committee, the Senator conceived the idea of a great navy yard on the South Atlantic coast. There was a naval station at Port Royal, South Carolina, but on account of its location, and upon the recommendation of a board of engineers of the navy, it was decided to place the station at Charleston. This he had done, and that was the beginning of the present Charleston Navy Yard. This yard is seven miles from the ocean and has the advantage of being out of reach of shells from an enemy fleet in the open sea.

"After his handling of the 'rate bill' and the notoriety that came to him as a result, Tillman's services as a lecturer were still more in demand and for six months, in 1907, he spoke almost daily. This, coupled with his arduous duties in the Senate in the winter of 1907-1908, brought about a paralytic stroke in February of 1908. This disabled him for several months, and in the summer of that year, with Mrs. Tillman, he took an extended trip through Europe. In the fall he returned in much better physical condition and resumed his work in the Senate. In 1910, while on a visit to his home in Trenton, he suffered a second stroke and for several weeks was compelled to remain at home.

"Senator Tillman possessed all the attributes of a great man. He sprang from the common people and devoted his life to the upbuilding of his people and his state. He was a farmer, and his great life work consisted principally in helping the farmers of South Carolina and trying to give them greater opportunities in life.

"Those with whom Senator Tillman associated soon learned that he had the utmost contempt for idleness. He was never idle a moment himself, and to see anyone around him idle seemed to make him nervous and irritable, and he soon suggested something for the idler to do. He was industrious and diligent, and as a result of those great characteristics he left monuments to his name as he passed along his long political career—monuments which will grow greater and bigger as the years pass by. He was honest and sincere, and has been known for many years throughout the nation as 'Honest Ben.' He was frank and blunt in his expressions, and never spoke a word he did not sincerely believe to be the truth. He was kind and sympathetic and never lost the opportunity to do good to his fellow men; and he loved his own people, the farmers of South Carolina, with a devotion which is rarely equalled. Lastly, Senator Tillman was a brave and courageous man, and being once convinced of the justice of his cause, he went into the battle unafraid. Truth and justice were his only guides."

Another source of interesting information concerning Senator Tillman is Col. August Kohn, of Columbia, who as a newspaper man began his career when Tillman was making his first campaign for governor, and was an intimate of the Senator for nearly thirty years. In describing some of the elements of his political strength and his public achievement Colonel Kohn writes:

"No man in South Carolina has gone through more heated campaigns than Senator Tillman. There never was a more bitter or more intense campaign than those of 1890 and 1892. Senator

Tillman was a keen observer, an apt coiner, a user of trite phrases and expressions, and had a way of reaching his audiences that was peculiar to him. There has never been a public man in South Carolina who could so effectively reach an average audience as Tillman. I remember that in 1892, at one of the campaign meetings, before the speaking began, it was generally agreed that the audience was hostile to him. He appreciated that fact and saw there were very many in the audience who were antagonistic to him, and instead of trying to placate the crowd he proceeded to curse them out for their indifference to him and his work, and finally, when the returns were received he carried the county, and the general impression was that he had won to himself an audience that, at the beginning, was entirely in opposition to him. One of the strongholds that Senator Tillman had on the people of South Carolina, particularly in the days when he made his county to county canvass, was the absolute faith in the honesty of Ben Tillman. There is no question about the fact that the vast majority of people in South Carolina then, as now, believed absolutely in the personal honesty of Senator Tillman. That was his strength in South Carolina, and subsequently in Washington."

Of his work while governor and United States Senator Colonel Kohn writes:

"Of course the dispensary will always be one of the big facts to be credited or charged to Senator Tillman. His real reasons for advocating the dispensary were, first, to abolish the bar rooms, and, second, to save the state from prohibition. At the time that the dispensaries were inaugurated there is no question to the fact that Senator Tillman was opposed to prohibition. He sincerely believed that the dispensary was a great system and if it had been honestly conducted would have been the best solution of the problem. Later on he stated that the dispensary had brought South Carolina nearer to prohibition by showing that the liquor question could be handled.

"But it is going to take a great deal of space to go into all of these matters. Senator Tillman in his final message to the General Assembly recounted his achievements in this summary: 1st: The erection and endowment of Clemson College. 2d: The overthrow of the Coosaw monopoly. 3d: The just and suitable assessment of taxes on railroads and other corporations and the victory of the courts compelling them to pay. 4th: The passage of the dispensary law and the destruction of the bar rooms. 5th: Refunding of the state debt, which saves seventy-eight thousand a year in interest. 6th: The establishment of Winthrop Normal and Industrial College for Women. 7th: Election of the railroad commissioners by the people, and allowing them to fix passenger and freight rates. 8th: The inauguration of the primary system of party nominations for all offices in the gift of the people.

"In his career as United States Senator he laid claim to the constitutional convention held in South Carolina in 1895; to the Charleston Navy Yard, to the enlargement of the navy, to the handling of the armor plate by the Government, to Camp Jackson at Columbia, the placing of South Carolina in its proper light before the country, and other matters."

In 1868, when twenty years of age, Mr. Tillman married Miss Sallie Starke, of Elbert County, Georgia. To this union were born six children, including: Benjamin Ryan Tillman, Jr., Capt. Henry C. Tillman, Melona, who married Charles S. Moore, a lawyer of Atlantic City, New Jersey; Miss Sophia, who married Henry Hughes; Sallie May, who married John Shuler.

Colonel Kohn describes some of his early visits to the Tillman home, when Mr. Tillman was governor. "He always showed the greatest affection for his family, and there has never been a whisper or unkind word about his family life. He and Mrs. Tillman were married in 1868, have always been the most devoted of companions, and she was the one person in the world who had final influence over him. Whatever Mrs. Tillman said was final with him, and it was really beautiful to see the utter devotion of Senator Tillman to his wife and children. One of the sorest afflictions of his married life was the killing of his eldest daughter, Addie, by lightning."

Colonel Kohn also has this interesting paragraph concerning his literary gifts and output: "Some day someone will collect, and perhaps publish, some of the very excellent things that Senator Tillman has left in writing, and they will show what a master of language he was. There are a large number of pamphlets containing addresses and speeches prepared by Tillman, but perhaps the best of these are his speeches made at the constitutional convention on the suffrage question, and why South Carolina, in his opinion, had to restrict the ballot; then his speech on 'Massachusetts and South Carolina in the Revolution,' delivered in the United States Senate on Thursday, January 30, 1902; his address delivered at the Red Shirt reunion in Anderson in August, 1905, describing the struggles of the people of Edgefield county in 1876; his speech in the United States Senate in 1907, on the race problem, brought about by the Brownsville raid; his speech in the United States Senate in 1903, on 'Trusts and Monopolies'; his speech on Bimetallism and Industrial Slavery, in 1896, and his eulogy on Senator Earle. In this connection it is well to note that his messages as Governor of South Carolina are very illuminating as to the conditions that existed at that time. He always wrote forcefully, and up to the day when he was stricken in his last illness, so acute was his mind that he dictated with his well recognized terseness and virility and kept several stenographers on the 'jump' keeping up with his correspondence."

BENJAMIN R. TILLMAN for many years was closely associated with his honored father, the late Senator Tillman, as his principal aide and office manager during the Senator's long political career at Washington. For twenty years he was continuously with his father as chief secretary and in other capacities. His last years in Washington were spent as clerk of the Naval Affairs Committee of the Senate, the committee of which his father was chairman. Since the death of Senator Tillman the son has resumed his residence on the Tillman plantation at Trenton.

Mr. Tillman was born in 1878, at the old Tillman home place, ten miles from the plantation where

Senator Tillman lived for so many years. This is in Edgefield County on the Augusta-Abbeville road. Benjamin R. Tillman now has charge of the Tillman plantation and estate near Trenton. He is a graduate of Clemson College with the class of 1896. He studied law at Georgetown College, but never practiced that profession. While so much of his time was spent with his father in politics and public affairs, Mr. Tillman has a comprehensive knowledge and keen enthusiasm for scientific agriculture, which was one of the hobbies of his honored father. The Tillman plantation, while always emphasizing the cotton crop, has been particularly famous as the first home of the commercial asparagus industry of South Carolina. The growing of asparagus on a commercial scale is one of the achievements properly credited to Senator Tillman, but frequently omitted from the long list of his achievements. Under the management of the son the Tillman plantation supplies a considerable part of the asparagus sent from Trenton to the northern markets.

Mr. Tillman is a Shriner, being a member of Hijiz Temple of Greenville, South Carolina, a member of the Episcopal Church.

HON. DAVID WILLIAM GASTON, JR. The name Gaston has been one of the most prominent in the South since early colonial times. Originally settled in Virginia, the Gastons in a later generation established their home in Aiken County, South Carolina. The great-grandfather of David William Gaston, Jr., had seven brothers, and from them have descended many branches of the family, including prominent citizens not only of South Carolina but of states further west, especially of Alabama and Texas.

In his own generation David William Gaston, Jr., has justified the honorable family traditions in his work as a lawyer and business man. He was born at Aiken, April 29, 1889, and is a son of David W. and Allie (Weathersby) Gaston. His father is one of the wealthy and representative citizens of Aiken, is an extensive planter and is president of the First National Bank of Aiken.

The son graduated from the Aiken Institute in 1906, from The Citadel at Charleston in 1910, and received his law degree from the University of South Carolina in 1912. Since then he has steadily gained increasing reputation as a lawyer at Aiken, and has a large and busy practice. Besides his professional work he is a planter and gives his supervision to the conduct of three excellent farms in Aiken County.

He was elected a member of the Lower House of the General Assembly in 1918 to represent Aiken County. During the following session he was a member of the committees on banking and insurance, accounts, incorporations and privileges and elections.

In 1913 Mr. Gaston married Miss Belle Glover, of Graniteville, South Carolina. They have three children, two daughters, Katharine and Emma, and a son, David William Gaston, third, born May 8, 1920.

CAPT. CHARLES WESLEY MULDROW, member of the law firm of Arrowsmith, Muldrow, Bridges & Hicks of Florence, twice gave up his promising position as a young lawyer to respond to the call of patriotic duty, at first on the Mexican border and then to go overseas and fight in France. He is an able lawyer as well as a splendid soldier.

He was born at Florence, June 17, 1886, son of James F. and Emma Lee (Hudgins) Muldrow. Captain Muldrow has acquired a very liberal education from different sources. He attended the graded schools at Florence, the South Carolina Citadel at Charleston, and the Law School of the University of South Carolina at Columbia and also the Council of Legal Education (Inns of Court) at London, England.

Early in his career as a lawyer he was elected and served as a member of the House of Representatives of South Carolina in 1915-16. Having been educated in a military school, he organized Company K of the Second South Carolina Infantry, and was commissioned its captain June 19, 1916, was inducted into the Federal service July 4th, and shortly after that date until about March 20, 1917, was on duty along the Mexican border at El Paso, Texas.

Then followed a brief interval when he resumed his law practice, but on July 25, 1917, answered the call of the President and was assigned to the One Hundred and Twentieth Infantry at Camp Sevier. He was transferred to the One Hundred and Fifth Ammunition Train as adjutant of a Motor Battalion April 19, 1918, and left Camp Sevier for overseas duty May 21st of that year. He was with the Fifty-fifth Field Artillery Brigade throughout the active service of that organization. March 1, 1919, he was ordered to England on detached service from Le Mans, France, and returned to the United States July 18, 1919, and was discharged at Camp Dix, New Jersey, July 26th.

Since he returned to his home state he was appointed August 5, 1919, a lieutenant colonel on the staff of Governor R. A. Cooper.

Captain Muldrow, whose home is at Florence, is unmarried. He is a Knight Templar and Scottish Rite Mason, is affiliated with Omar Temple of the Mystic Shrine, and is a member of Charleston Lodge No. 242 of the Elks, Gate City Council No. 105, Junior Order United American Mechanics and Walnut Camp No. 52, Woodmen of the World.

ROBERT L. GUNTER recently rounded out ten years of consecutive service as solicitor of the Second Judicial Circuit. As a lawyer his name has been recognized as representing all the ablest qualities of the profession in Aiken County for the past twenty years.

Mr. Gunter also represents an old and prominent family in the state. The Gunters came to South Carolina from Virginia prior to the Revolution. One of the name was killed during the war for independence. In subsequent generations the name has become known also in the states of Georgia, Alabama and Texas, and in those localities is associated with men of wealth and prominence.

Richard Gunter was grandfather of Robert L. The latter was born in 1869, in that part of Lexington County now included in Aiken County and is a son of M. T. and Tabitha (Sawyer) Gunter. His father

was a Confederate soldier and was first lieutenant of Company I, Twentieth Regiment South Carolina Volunteers. He was wounded in the Valley of Virginia near the Berryville Turnpike, while leading his company. He served in the Legislature for two terms. R. L. Gunter's mother's father was George Sawyer, a prominent citizen of Edgefield District, of the section now known as the "Ridge Section." Her mother was a Lovelace of the same section and at one time represented Aiken County in the Legislature.

Robert L. Gunter acquired his high school education at Leesville, attended Newberry College, and graduated in 1892. He studied law one year in the University of Michigan and one year in the University of South Carolina, graduated from the latter institution in 1895. He was admitted to the bar in 1895 and began practice the same year. He also had the special honor and responsibility of being a delegate to the Constitutional Convention in 1895. He was one of the youngest members of that body, but his youth was no bar to effective counsel and much hard work in formulating the new organic law of the state.

Mr. Gunter has had his home at Aiken since 1900, and he developed a large general practice. In 1910 he was elected solicitor of the Second Judicial Circuit, and his tenure of that office has been made continuous by reelection based on the high quality of the service which he has rendered. His circuit embraces Aiken, Barnwell, Bamberg and Allendale counties. Mr. Gunter was also a member of the Legislature in 1901-02. He has been more or less identified with the politics of his county and state since 1895.

During the war he was especially active in behalf of Liberty Loan and Red Cross drives. He is a member of the Masonic order and the Lutheran Church. He married Miss Lula P. Jackson, of Aiken County, in 1898.

HON. JOSEPH ANDREW BERRY, of Orangeburg, lawyer and present speaker pro tempore of the House of Representatives, has among other distinctions the unique one of being the youngest grandson of a Revolutionary soldier in America.

His grandfather and Revolutionary patriot was James Berry, who was born in County Cork, Ireland, about 1736. It is probable that the original spelling of the name in Ireland was Barry. With his young wife and child James Berry came to America about 1758, locating in the Orangeburg district. He was a weaver by trade, and a century or more ago he wove dress goods and other clothes on hand looms, most of his output being used for ladies' apparel. James Berry was about forty years of age when the colonies revolted and began their struggle for independence. He joined with the Carolina patriots in that struggle and fought gallantly as a soldier. James Berry rounded out almost a century of life, dying in the thirties. The wife he brought with him from Ireland died, and in the Orangeburg district he married a second time.

By his second wife he was the father of James Brewton Berry, who was born near Branchville in 1806 and died near there in 1888. James Brewton Berry was a man of prominence in his community and helped in the building of the old Charleston and Hamburg Railroad, one of the first railroads built in America, and now a part of the Southern Railway system. He was also twice married, Sallie Street, of St. George, South Carolina, the mother of Joseph A. Berry, being his second wife.

Joseph Andrew Berry was born at Branchville in Orangeburg County, June 1, 1876, his birth occurring about a hundred and forty years after the birth of his grandfather and just a century after the Declaration of Independence, which the soldier service of his grandfather helped to make valid.

The vicinity of Branchville is the ancestral home of the Berry family, and there Joseph A. Berry spent his early life. His mother died when he was eight years of age, and his aged father died four years later. He was then without anyone to give him parental attention, and the rest of his boyhood days were very hard and entirely without any promise. However, he had attended local schools pretty regularly up to the time of his father's death and thereafter whenever it was possible for him to do so. His education was very limited. He did not have the opportunity to attend even a high school, but in 1897 he entered the law offices of Glaze & Herbert at Orangeburg for the purpose of reading law, and was admitted to the bar by the Supreme Court in May, 1898. This was just at the outbreak of the Spanish-American war. He immediately volunteered for service with the Edisto Rifles of Orangeburg, under command of Capt. D. O. Herbert. With the muster into service of his company as a part of the Independent Battalion he was appointed a corporal, and when the Second South Carolina regiment of infantry was organized under the command of Col. Wilie Jones he was transferred to Company K and appointed first sergeant, with which command he was mustered out of the service in Augusta, Georgia, on April 19, 1899, after almost a year's service, a part of which was spent in Cuba. After the Spanish-American war he re-enlisted in the Edisto Rifles, served as a lieutenant and for several years as captain of this company in the South Carolina National Guard. Subsequently he was major on the staff of Gen. Wilie Jones.

Mr. Berry has resided and practiced his profession in Orangeburg since 1900, with William C. Wolfe, his law partner, under the firm name of Wolfe & Berry, with a splendid degree of success. He is a member of the State Bar Association and has been honored with the position of first vice president. He served as secretary and treasurer of the Orangeburg County Democratic Executive Committee from 1904 to 1918, and has been the member of the State Democratic Executive Committee for Orangeburg County since 1914. He was elected to represent Orangeburg County in the House of Representatives in 1914, and his service has been made continuous by subsequent elections. In 1917 he was chosen speaker pro tempore and was similarly honored by his colleagues in the House in 1919. He is also chairman of the judiciary committee and the chairman of the committee on rules; a member of the state canal commission, and the special committee of the Legislature appointed to revise the tax laws of the state. In the Legislature he has displayed ability of leadership, force as a debater, and delivered some of the best speeches heard in the House of Representatives since he became a member. Conspicuous among his speeches may be mentioned those made by him in behalf of the establishment of a state highway commission, a state budget law, the institution and retention of the state tax commission, the building of a larger Citadel and a bill to repeal the law prohibiting Greek letter fraternities in state institutions. The judiciary committee at the close of the 1920 session presented him with a magnificent gold watch in appreciation of his services.

Mr. Berry missed an education himself, but he is a strong advocate of the subject and has urged it in many a schoolhouse in his county. He has also supported with enthusiasm the establishment and growth of the Dixie Library in Orangeburg and is a life member of the organization. During the World war he was county chairman of the War Savings Stamp campaigns, and was on duty as a speaker with nearly every patriotic drive made in the county. Mr. Berry is a member of the Methodist Church, is a past chancellor of the Knights of Pythias, past exalted ruler of the Elks and also a member of the Masonic order.

October 10, 1900, he married Miss Fannie Pike, of Orangeburg. Their three children are James Brewton, Richard Pike and Joseph Andrew.

CLARENCE J. FICKLING, the active president and manager of the Commercial Bank of Blackville, is a member of an old and honored Barnwell County family, and was a successful farmer in this locality before he became a banker.

Mr. Fickling was born in Barnwell County, December 30, 1881. Four brothers named Fickling came out of England and were settlers in the southern states prior to the Revolutionary war, taking part in that struggle. His great-grandfather was Rev. William Fickling, a Baptist minister, who was active in the organization of the Blackville Baptist Church in 1846, and for many years carried on the work of the ministry in the southwestern portions of South Carolina. The grandfather of the Blackville banker was Henry S. Fickling and the father, F. G. Fickling, both natives of Barnwell County. The latter is still active as a farmer. He married Emma J. Hair, daughter of J. Pinckney and Mary E. (Owens) Hair, both of whom were also natives of South Carolina.

Henry S. Fickling, subject's grandfather, served as a soldier in the Confederate army, and was in active service throughout the entire war.

Clarence J. Fickling was second in a family of three sons. He was reared and educated in Barnwell County, finishing his education in Clemson College. After his college course he returned to the farm and was interested in agricultural matters for several years. He still owns some valuable and extensive planting interests in the county. From 1909 to 1912 he served as cashier of the Bank of Western Carolina, and in February, 1917, was instrumental in organizing the Commercial Bank of Blackville. Since its organization he has served as vice president and manager and is now president and manager.

October 30, 1902, he married Miss Maude G. Hair, a daughter of James Marshall Hair, of Williston, South Carolina. Mrs. Fickling's sister is a member of the Daughters of the American Revolution. Her father served in the Confederate army, was wounded and left for dead on the field. He was hit in the right temple by a Minnie ball, which cut his right optic nerve and took out a molar on the left side of his jaw. Life was discovered in him the next morning, and he was taken and cared for. After the war he married and raised a large family. He moved to Williston, South Carolina, where he followed the business of planting until his death at the age of seventy-one, in 1911. Mr. and Mrs. Fickling have four living children: Sarah, Edina Bell, Sophia and Robert Bruce. Mr. Fickling is affiliated with the Knights of Pythias, and is a prominent member of the Blackville Baptist Church, having served as deacon and treasurer for the past ten years. He has been an active factor in the practical matters of the town, and served two years, 1918-19, as mayor. He is a member of the County Board of Education, 1919-1920.

CHARLES AURELIUS SMITH. While he came Timmonsville a young college graduate with no special recommendation and without capital, the late Charles Aurelius Smith long before his death was one of the foremost men in business, banking and citizenship in that community. He ran for governor of South Carolina, in 1914 and served his state as lieutenant governor for four years.

Mr. Smith who died March 31, 1916, was born in North Carolina January 22, 1861, son of Joseph Smith, and of an old North Carolina family. He lived his early life on his father's farm, attended the rural schools, but for his higher education had to resort to close economy of his resources and even to borrow money to complete his education in Wake Forest College. He prepared for college in the Reynoldson Male Institute in Gates County, North Carolina. On borrowed money he entered Wake Forest College in 1879 and by good use of his time and opportunities earned his A. B. degree in 1882. He at once began teaching school in order to pay off his debt, and it was school work that brought him to Timmonsville, South Carolina. From school work he' soon entered on a business career, and the energy and good judgment with which he prosecuted every enterprise brought him to the head of many of the leading companies in Florence County. He was president of the Citizens Bank of Timmonsville, president of the Timmonsville Oil Company, president of the Charles A. Smith Company, general merchandise, president of the Smith-Williams Company of Lake City, and was also organizer and president of the Bank of Lynchburg, South Carolina. He was a democrat in politics and held the office of mayor of Timmonsville for several years beginning in 1903.

The late Mr. Smith was one of the most prominent Baptist laymen in South Carolina. He was chosen president of the Baptist State Convention in 1903, was made vice president of the Southern Baptist Convention in 1905, and for a number of years was also moderator of the Welsh Neck Baptist Association. He was president of the Board of Trustees of Furman University, trustee of Greenville Female

College, and a trustee of Welsh Neck High School. As a man he was quiet and unobtrusive in spite of the energy with which he directed his affairs, and his career throughout was one of high service.

January 3, 1884, he married Fanny L. Byrd. They were the parents of nine children.

C. Ray Smith, who has succeeded his father as head of the Citizens Bank of Timmonsville, was born in that town July 29, 1889. He was educated in the local public schools and in 1906 took his A. B. degree from his father's alma mater, Wake Forest College in North Carolina. For two years he was assistant cashier of the Citizens Bank, was manager of the Charles A. Smith Company, and upon the death of his father became president of this company, president of the Citizens Bank, vice president of the Smith-Williams Company of Lake City, and a director of the Timmonsville Oil Mill. He is also active in Baptist affairs, is trustee of Coker College and superintendent of a Sunday school. November 25, 1915, he married Miss Hallie Carrison of Camden, South Carolina. They have one daughter, Margaret Carrison.

Another son of Charles A. Smith is Charles Lucien Smith. He attended the Hartsville High School and for two years was a student in Furman University. He began his business career as assistant manager in the Charles A. Smith Company at Timmonsville and is now vice president and manager and a director of the National Bank of Lamar. He married Ruby Lowman of Timmonsville. They have two children, Frances Myers and Jane Lowman.

THOMAS LOWNDES WRAGG, who is manager of the Western Carolina Bank at Blackville, has had an active business career of more than a quarter of a century. Most of his life has been spent in other states, but he belongs to one of the old colonial families of Charleston, where the Wraggs settled about 1700.

They are of English ancestry, and all accounts show that in South Carolina they have been a family of substantial means and exceptional social position and character. During the earlier generations the intermarriages were practically restricted to persons of the same section, and the first arrivals intermarried at once with members of the French Huguenot colony.

The first immigrants to South Carolina of the Wragg family were two brothers, Samuel and Joseph Wragg. While the exact date of their coming has been lost, there is an interesting historical record concerning Samuel Wragg, who on the 6th of March, 1710-11, delivered to the council a letter from the Lords Proprietors. In 1712 he was a member of the Provincial House of Commons and in 1717 was a member of the council.

In 1718, while outward bound from Charleston to England, his vessel was overtaken by the pirate "Blackbeard" just off the Charleston bar, and he was despoiled of a large amount of specie, threatened with death, subjected to many hardships and humiliations before being released and allowed with his young son, William, to return to Charleston.

When the province was transferred to the Crown, Samuel Wragg was a member of the council, as was later his brother Joseph. These brothers were merchants in Charleston, as they had apparently been in London, probably in connection with their uncle, William Wragg, who seems to have been a wealthy merchant of London. Family tradition makes the two brothers sons of a Mr. John Wragg of Chesterfield, Derbyshire. On coming to the province they were well provided with capital, and their means must have been substantially increased, since they ranked among the wealthy citizens of the Carolinas, and when they died both left large fortunes for that period. The brothers married sisters, daughters of Jacques du Bosc, a French Huguenot immigrant who became a merchant at Charleston.

Samuel Wragg purchased and settled the Ashley Barony on Ashley River. William Wragg, who was the son captured by Blackbeard, achieved rank as a man of ability, fortune and the highest character. He declined from delicacy and disinterestedness the position of chief justice of the colony, though he served as a member of the council. In 1777, for his loyalty to the Crown, he suffered expulsion from his native land and on his voyage to England was drowned off the coast of Holland. According to the writer, Henry A. M. Smith, he was the only native born South Carolinian to whom a memorial exists in Westminster Abbey.

On a chart published in the July, 1918, issue of the "South Carolina Historical and Genealogical Magazine," the authority for the Wragg descent prior to the two brothers who came to South Carolina is largely traditional from a manuscript made by the late William Wragg Smith for Henry A. Middleton. The connection between the brothers and their uncle, William Wragg, and the latter's children is from records in this country and other old records and are the data for the later descent. The chart is as accurate as possible.

The oldest example of the Wragg coat of arms is an old piece of silver, the hall mark of which is about 1731. This came down to the descendants of Joseph Wragg, and is described "Or, a fesse azure, a canton azure charged with a fleur de lys." In books apparently owned by Mrs. Milward Poyson, a daughter of Hon. William Wragg, is a book plate showing a coat of arms with crest and motto above the name "William Wragg," but it is not apparent whether it was the Hon. William Wragg who died in 1777 or his son William who died in 1802. One volume in which the book plate is printed was published in 1801 and the other in 1803. The son may have used the book plate of his father. On this plate the canton is argent, likely a mistake, since by heraldic laws one metal argent should not be charged on another metal, so this canton should likely be azure as on the old piece of silver. On this book plate the crest is a demi-eagle with open wings, the motto "Est Ulubris."

Incidentally it should be noted that Mary Ashby, daughter of Shukbrugh Ashby of Quenby, England, married Rev. William Breckwith Wragge, vicar of Frisby, while in this country Samuel Wragg married Mary Ashby I'On, a descendant of John Ashby of Quenby in South Carolina, a collateral branch of Ashby of Quenby, England.

Considering now the immediate ancestry of Thomas Lowndes Wragg, his great-grandfather, Samuel Wragg, and his grandfather, Dr. John Asby

Wragg, were both natives of Charleston. His grandfather practiced medicine for many years at Savannah, Georgia. The father of the Blackville banker, Thomas Wragg, was born at Savannah, and also earned a high position in the medical profession. He married Joseph L. Cooper, a native of Florida, her parents being natives of Georgia.

Thomas Lowndes Wragg, who was the second in a family of three children, was born at Thomasville, Georgia, April 15, 1872, and was reared and educated in Florida. At the age of eighteen he began his active career as a bookkeeper in St. Louis, Missouri. He was in that city nine years, spent three years in Charleston, and for five years was in the general offices of the Southern Railway at Washington. Mr. Wragg came to Blackville, South Carolina, in 1906, as cashier of the Bank of Blackville. Upon the merging of this with the Bank of Western Carolina he accepted the increased responsibilities of manager of the bank.

Mr. Wragg is a member of the Episcopal Church and is affiliated with the Masonic fraternity and Woodmen of the World. In 1905 he married Miss Sevena Andrews, a daughter of John Andrews of Orangeburg. They have two children, Dorothy and Helen.

WILLIAM ELLIOTT SPANN. Those who note the notable figures in Bamberg County agriculture have no hesitation in pronouncing William Elliott Spann one of the most enterprising factors and one of the ablest cotton growers in the state. It is said that Mr. Spann had only seventy-five cents to his name when he came to Bamberg County, and he has used his opportunities and abilities so wisely as to accumulate a large plantation and has been one of the premier cotton growers of the county for a number of years.

He was born near Leesville in Lexington County, South Carolina, November 29, 1859. His grandfather was Henry Spann, a native of South Carolina, and one of the early circuit rider Methodist preachers of the state. His father was Philip C. Spann, who served as a Confederate soldier during the war and otherwise spent his time as a farmer. He married Jane Steadman, of Lexington County.

William Elliott Spann is the oldest of a family of nine children, all of whom are still living. He grew up on a farm and was twenty-two years of age when he came to that portion of old Barnwell County now Bamberg County. He soon distinguished himself by his ability to make a farm produce maximum crops of cotton and grain, and has greatly extended his possessions until he now has about 1,200 acres, mostly all of which is devoted to cotton, corn and tobacco. In several different years he has gathered 350 bales of cotton from 350 acres of land. Mr. Spann is a leader in agriculture, has considerable interests in local banks, and is known to have invested a large sum in Liberty bonds.

He married Miss Minnie Hutto, now deceased, and she was the mother of three children, Elliott Leland, Eva May and Blanche. Mrs. Spann came from one of the old South Carolina families.

The Spanns are an old South Carolina family and besides his father, the subject had three uncles in the Confederate army, one of whom lost his life in one of the engagements. The family is of old Revolutionary stock and of English descent. At an early age William E. Spann had to start in to make his own way, as the war had destroyed the wealth of the Spann family. He is a member of the Knights of Pythias fraternity.

ALBERT PERRY MANVILLE is an honored veteran of the Confederate war, and for nearly half a century, from the close of the war until he retired, was one of the leading merchants of Barnwell.

Mr. Manville is of northern birth and ancestry. He was born in Milford, Connecticut, March 13, 1839. His grandfather, Uri D. Manville, was of French ancestry and was also a native of Milford, Connecticut. His father, Pernett Perry Manville, a native of Milford, was a carpenter by occupation. When Albert Perry was a small child the father came south to follow his trade in Florida and later located at Thomasville, Georgia. While there he was injured during his work and took up merchandising. In 1849 he went west to California, around the Horn, and died in that state. His wife was Harriet Buckingham, a native of Connecticut and of English ancestry.

Albert Perry Manville was the oldest of six children. He spent his boyhood days at Thomasville, Georgia, and at the age of twelve years came to live with his uncle, J. C. Buckingham, in Barnwell, South Carolina. His mother returned north to Connecticut. He worked at the tailor's trade, and was thus employed when the war broke out. He was one of the first to enlist in Captain Brown's company, and he heard the first guns in the war at Fort Sumter and the last fighting just before the surrender at Appomattox. He was in Company C of Kershaw's Second Regiment until after the battle of Fredericksburg, when he became a member of Company E, Colonel Hagood's First Regiment, being made orderly sergeant. He was wounded in the left arm at Savage Station on the York River Railroad, and after a period in hospital was granted a furlough of sixty days. He then rejoined his command and was transferred to Captain Wood's Company E, and continued with that gallant regiment of South Carolina troops until the close of the war. During the reconstruction days he took his part as a good citizen in putting down the radical rule.

He was treasurer of the democratic party during reconstruction days, and it is a known fact that Barnwell County was the best organized county in the state.

The war over he returned to Barnwell and engaged in merchandising, a business he followed until he retired. On March 27, 1867, Mr. Manville married Miss Alice Hart, daughter of Rev. Allen Hart, a Baptist minister, and granddaughter of John Hart. Both her father and grandfather were natives of South Carolina. Mrs. Manville was the second in a family of five children, and was reared and educated at Barnwell. To Mr. and Mrs. Manville were born seven children, and the two now living are Hattie B. and George W. Mr. Manville also has a grandson, Daniel P. Hartley, now fifteen years of age. Their son George is cashier of the Western Carolina Bank of Barnwell. Mr. and Mrs. Manville are active members of the Baptist Church.

The members of this church helped them celebrate their golden or fiftieth wedding anniversary in 1917.

THOMAS GORDON McLEOD. In his home county of Lee Thomas Gordon McLeod long ago established his prestige as an able and learned member of the bar. His services have not been within the strict limits of his profession, however, and again and again he has been called upon to act in positions of trust and responsibility involving large and important issues. For four years he was lieutenant governor of the state, has been a member of both houses of the Legislature, and in all his record there has been nothing to detract justly from his reputation as a lawyer, an upright gentleman and a forward-looking citizen.

He was born at Lynchburg, Sumter County, South Carolina, December 17, 1868, and is descended from James McLeod, a Scotchman, who came to the Carolinas before the Revolutionary war. His father William James McLeod was a merchant and farmer, and served as captain of Company E of the Sixth South Carolina Regiment throughout the war between the states. He married Miss Amanda Rogers, whose father William Rogers was of New England stock and came to the Carolinas from Connecticut in 1835.

Thomas G. McLeod once wrote in regard to his parentage, inheritance and early influences the following words: "My parents were both devoted Christians and the home influences were of the best. My mother died when I was but ten years of age; but her place was taken by my step-mother, and to her training and influence I am as much indebted for whatever success I have attained as I am to any other influence in my life. My early experience in my father's country store brought me in contact with all classes of people; and the knowledge there gained of human nature and the friendly meeting with people of all kinds and classes, appears to have been to me the most useful part of my life training and the foundation certainly of whatever success I have attained in public life."

Besides the incidents and experience thus noted Mr. McLeod also came in contact with the practical work of the South Carolina farm and is strictly speaking country bred, though most of his boyhood was spent in the Village of Lynchburg. He attended private schools and in 1892 finished the classical course and was awarded the A. B. degree by Wofford College. He also took a summer course in law at the University of Virginia. For a year he taught at Bethel Academy and another year at Line Academy and in 1896 was admitted to the bar. He soon returned home to take charge of the family business affairs during the last illness of his father and was thus engaged until 1903, when he removed to Bishopville and began the practice at law about the same time that Lee County was created.

For fully twenty years he has been regarded as a leader in the public life of his community. He was elected to represent Sumter County in the Legislature until 1901. In 1902 he was chosen the first senator from Lee County, and was a delegate to the National Democratic Convention of 1904. He was elected lieutenant governor without opposition in 1906 and 1908.

Mr. McLeod is possessed of a magnetic personality and has many of the qualifications of the true orator. He was one of the most effective platform speakers in every cause and movement related to the prosecution of the World war, speaking in behalf of Liberty Loans, Red Cross and other drives. He was appointed chairman of the local exemption board of Lee County and for nearly two years patriotic work had priority over all his private interests.

Mr. McLeod has extensive farm interests. He is attorney for and director of the Bishopville National Bank, is president of the Bishopville Telephone Company and was formerly president of the W. J. McLeod Company. Recently he was appointed a member of the State Central Committee for the purpose of reducing the cotton acreage. For years he has been a working member of the Methodist Episcopal Church South and as district director he spent much time in the movement for raising funds for the Methodist Church. In 1916 he was appointed a trustee of Winthrop College and is still on the board. Fraternally he is affiliated with the Masons, Knights of Pythias and Woodmen of the World and is a member of the Kappa Alpha College fraternity.

December 31, 1902, he married Miss Elizabeth Alford, daughter of W. McD. and Sarah E. Alford of Marion County. Mr. and Mrs. McLeod have four children: Alford McD.; Thomas G.; Lucy Wood and Yancey Alford.

GEORGE ALEXANDER JENNINGS, the present county treasurer of Bamberg County, is an honored resident of that locality and a man who for his advancement in the world has depended almost entirely upon the virtues of hard work and an honest and straightforward character.

Mr. Jennings was born in Orangeburg County, January 22, 1854. Three months after his birth his father, George Jennings, was accidentally killed. George Jennings was a farmer and a son of John Jennings, a native of Orangeburg County. This branch of the Jennings family was established in South Carolina, coming from England, about 1737. The mother of George Alexander Jennings was Harriet L. Moody, who was born in Orangeburg County, a daughter of John Moody. She was the mother of five children, George Alexander being the youngest.

The latter lived on a farm in Bamberg County from the age of thirteen and had a common school education, supplemented by advanced training in a military academy at Charlotte, North Carolina, and at Porter Military Academy at Charleston. After completing his education he held positions as bookkeeper for such prominent men as Col. John F. Folk, Rice Coplin, H. C. Folk and General Bamberg. He was with General Bamberg at the time of the latter's death. After that for some years Mr. Jennings represented the Simmons Hardware Company until he was elected county treasurer of Bamberg County in 1912. He has had no opposition for that office and has given a faithful and efficient administration of its affairs. Mr. Jennings has been active politically and for several terms was secretary of the County Democratic Club. He was a member of the city council for two terms. He is a member of the Methodist Episcopal Church, South, and fraternally is affiliated with the Knights of Pythias.

November 22, 1876, Mr. Jennings married Miss Julia Slater, a native of Bamberg County, and daughter of John D. Slater. The Slaters are an old South Carolina family of Revolutionary stock and English descent. Mrs. Jennings is a niece of Gen. F. M. Bamberg, whose sketch appears elsewhere in this work. Mrs. Bamberg is the elder sister of Mr. G. A. Jennings. Mrs. Jennings is an aunt of the Slater brothers of Orangeburg. Mr. and Mrs. Jennings have two children: Allie Aleen, wife of A. M. Denbow, of Bamberg, president of the Peoples Bank; and John S., of St. George, South Carolina.

ASBURY LAWTON KIRKLAND. While for the past several years he has been the esteemed and efficient clerk of courts of Bamberg County, Asbury Lawton Kirkland is primarily a farmer and planter, a business to which he has given his best years since leaving college.

He was born in Bamberg County, August 31, 1874. He is a great-grandson of William Kirkland, a soldier of the American Revolution, and who lost an arm in that struggle. He was born in Scotland. The grandfather was Reuben Kirkland, a native of Edgefield County, South Carolina. His father is Dr. N. F. Kirkland, a native of what is now Bamberg County, and still living in his eighty-ninth year. For many years he practiced medicine and became a physician of wide repute and success in what is now Bamberg County. Doctor Kirkland married Jennie M. Lawton, a native of Hampton County, daughter of Joseph M. Lawton, of the same county. The Lawton family was also established in South Carolina prior to the Revolution.

Asbury Lawton Kirkland, the youngest of a family of five sons and one daughter, was reared and educated in his home county, attended common schools and spent one year in Wofford College. He took up planting, and now operates about 500 acres in general and diversified farming. Mr. Kirkland was elected clerk of courts in 1916.

In 1899 he married Miss Carrie Brabham. They have six children: N. Fletcher, Elizabeth, William, Inez, Asbury, Jr., and Frank. Mr. Kirkland is affiliated with the Masonic order, the Knights of Pythias, and is a trustee of the Methodist Episcopal Church, South.

ALBERT MURRAY DENBOW. While he has lived in the state only a comparatively few years, Albert Murray Denbow is widely known as a financier and as an executive officer in half a dozen banks and business corporations in the southern part of the state.

Mr. Denbow, whose home is at Bamberg, where he is president of the Peoples Bank, was born in Canandaigua, New York, April 12, 1884, third among the five children of Alfred and Cora (Howard) Denbow. The parents are both natives of England and immigrated from Devonshire in 1870, first settling at Canandaigua, New York. Alfred Denbow spent his active career as a banker. He was active in New York politics, and was prominent in the financial world. He died in 1890.

Albert Murray Denbow was educated in New York State, and at the close of his schooling located in Richmond, Virginia. He was engaged in the banking business in Richmond with John L. Williams & Sons, bankers. In 1908 he located at Aiken, South Carolina, where he became assistant cashier of the First National Bank. His home has been at Bamberg since 1912. He served successively as cashier, vice president and since 1916 as president of the Peoples Bank at Bamberg. He is also president of the Commercial Bank of Blackville, which he organized in 1917; is organizer of the First National Bank of Barnwell, which was established in 1917, and is organizer and vice president of the Citizens Bank of Aiken. He organized and is active head of the Denbow Tobacco Warehouse of Bamberg, and was one of the organizers and is a director of the Bankers National Life Insurance Company of Orangeburg.

Mr. Denbow is prominent in Masonry, being affiliated with Orangeburg Commandery of the Knights Templar and a member of the Scottish Rite Consistory of Charleston. He is a member of Omar Temple, Order of the Mystic Shrine at Charleston, South Carolina. He is also an Odd Fellow and is district deputy of the Third District, Knights of Pythias of South Carolina. In 1916 Mr. Denbow married Mrs. Allie Jennings O'Hern, daughter of George A. and Julia Jennings, of Bamberg. Mrs. Denbow is a member of one of the oldest South Carolina families, which contributed much to the history of the state in the past. Several members of her family took part in the Confederate struggle. She is also a niece of the late Gen. Francis Marion Bamberg.

ELBERT HERMAN AULL has been editor of the Newberry Herald and News for thirty-five years. While he has been devoted to his profession of journalism, his career on the whole has been a varied one and of many useful services. Several years ago a writer describing his career said: "While at college he intended to be a lawyer, but circumstances were such that he commenced work as an educator instead of as a legal practitioner. When he had almost determined to continue teaching for an indefinite period conditions changed and he was gradually drawn into newspaper work. Finding that he could not carry on both lines at the same time, and believing that the newspaper field offered the most immediate returns, with, perhaps, better opportunities for advancement, he gave up teaching and has since been doing efficient work in the editorial profession."

He was born in Newbury County August 18, 1857, son of Jacob Luther and Julia (Haltiwanger) Aull. His grandfather Rev. Herman Aull was a pioneer Lutheran minister. The father was a miller and farmer. Elbert H. Aull lived in a country district when a boy and though his early opportunities were confined to country schools he did much to develop a many sided and versatile nature. He worked on the farm, as a carpenter, and in flour and saw mills. In 1877 he entered the sophomore class of Newberry College and graduated with the A. M. degree in 1880. For one year he taught at

Abbeville and during the following two years was an instructor in Newberry College and was studying law at the same time. He was admitted to the bar in 1883.

In 1885 he took up his duties as editor of the Newberry Herald and News, and in March, 1887, became financially interested in the paper. In September, 1907, he also became editor of the South Carolina Pythian, the official organ of the Grand Lodge of the Knights of Pythias of the state. He was elected president of the South Carolina Press Association in 1894 and held that office for sixteen years by re-election.

Mr. Aull in 1899 was journal clerk of the State Senate and in June of the same year became private secretary to Governor McSweeney, remaining four years, and also served with the rank of lieutenant-colonel on his staff. During 1903-04 he was a member of the State Legislature and among the measures credited to him was introducing and securing the passage of an act establishing free libraries for public schools in rural communities. During 1905-06 he was chief clerk of the engrossing department of the Legislature and in November, 1906, was again elected a member of the Legislature for two years. Mr. Aull was superintendent of education for Newberry County, and is now superintendent for the fourteenth decennial census of the third district.

He is a member of the Lutheran Church and is affiliated with the Knights of Pythias, the Independent Order of Odd Fellows and the Improved Order of Red Men. On February 14, 1881, he married Miss Alice Kinard who died in July, 1911. They became the parents of six children, four of whom grew up. Mr. Aull married for his present wife Miss Mae Amiek, in June, 1915, and has two sons by this marriage.

Of the three sons of his first marriage who grew to manhood John Kinard Aull is the court stenographer of the Fourth Judicial Circuit of South Carolina and James Luther Aull and Humbert Mayer Aull are associated with their father in the publication of The Herald and News.

PERRY M. BUCKINGHAM. Through an active and interesting career duty has ever been the motive of action of Perry M. Buckingham, manager of the Bank of Western Carolina at Barnwell, and usefulness to his fellowmen has not been by any means a secondary consideration. He has performed well his part in life, and it is a compliment worthily bestowed to say that his locality is honored in his citizenship, for he has achieved definite success through his own efforts and is thoroughly deserving of the proud American title of self-made man, the term being one that, in its better sense, cannot but appeal to the loyal admiration of all who are appreciative of our national institutions and the privileges afforded for individual accomplishment.

Perry M. Buckingham was born in Barnwell, South Carolina, on November 6, 1862, and it is an unusual fact worthy of note that he was born in the same house, in the same room and on the same bed now occupied by him. His father, J. C. Buckingham, was born in Milford, Connecticut, but came to South Carolina about 1840. During the Civil war he served on the side of the Confederacy as a member of the Home Guards. For many years he was engaged in the mercantile trade in Barnwell and lived to the age of eighty-three years. He was the son of Samuel Buckingham, also a native of Connecticut. The subject's mother, whose maiden name was Esther Rebecca Gildersleeve, was born in Connecticut, the daughter of Sylvester Gildersleeve, also a native of Connecticut and of a family of ship builders. He lived to the advanced age of ninety-six years. Esther Rebecca Buckingham bore her husband four children, of whom the subject of this review is the only survivor, and she lived to the age of seventy-eight years.

Perry M. Buckingham attended the common schools, and then became a student in St. Paul's School at Concord, New Hampshire, a preparatory school, where he was graduated in 1881. Soon afterward he entered in a modest way on the career which has led him to his present plane of activity, usefulness and comfort. His first employment was as cashier for a railroad at Richmond, Virginia, whence he was later transferred to Jacksonville, Florida, as train master. After filling that position for three years he returned to Virginia as general freight and passenger agent, with headquarters at Richmond. He filled that position about three years, at the end of which time he came to Barnwell and accepted the position of cashier of the Citizens Savings Bank, holding that position until 1890, when he became cashier of the Bank of Barnwell, filling that position until 1908, when he became president of that institution. In 1909 the Bank of Barnwell was merged, along with several other banks of Aiken and Barnwell counties, into what is known as the Bank of Western Carolina, at which time Mr. Buckingham became vice president of the new institution and manager of its branch bank at Barnwell, which relations he still sustains. Thoroughly qualified by natural aptitude and experience for the banking business, Mr. Buckingham has proven a decided success in this line and much of the splendid success which has attended this bank has been directly due to his sound discretion, mature judgment and personal popularity. He has taken an active part in all movements for the upbuilding and development of this community, and during the recent war activities he was especially prominent, serving as chairman of the Liberty Loan drive and treasurer of the Barnwell Chapter of the Red Cross Society ever since its organization. He has been deeply interested in educational matters, and for the past eighteen years has rendered effective and appreciated service as a member of the board of trustees of the Barnwell school board. In 1918 he was a member of the County Board of Education, and in many other ways has exhibited a commendable attitude towards all movements for the public welfare.

On October 5, 1892, Mr. Buckingham was married to Daisy Duncan, the daughter of the late Col. William H. Duncan, a review of whose life appears elsewhere in this work. All who come within range of his influence are outspoken in their praise of his admirable qualities and the high regard in which he is held, not only in business life, but socially, which indicate the possession of attributes and characteristics that fully entitle him to the respect and good will of his fellow men which is freely accorded him throughout the community where he lives. He is an Episcopalian.

WILLIAM JASPER YOUNG, M. D. For over forty-five years the name of Dr. William J. Young, of Fairfax, has been a household word in his section of the state, where he has built up a large and lucrative practice, being numbered among the representative citizens of this locality, having ever been known to be an able, reliable and progressive physician and patriotic in citizenship. He is esteemed for these commendable traits, together with his cordial disposition and genuine worth, and although he has been more or less active in various relations with his fellow men, his name stands out more prominently in connection with the medical profession, in which he has so long been a prominent figure.

William Jasper Young is the eighth child in order of birth of the ten children born to Frederick and Annie Miley (Blatts) Young, his birth having occurred in Barnwell County, South Carolina, on February 10, 1851. The subject's mother was born at Rivers Bridge, Barnwell County, and remained in that county after her marriage to Frederick Young, they passing the remainder of their lives there.

William J. Young received his elementary education in the common schools of his native locality, and then attended the high school at Charleston. Having determined to devote his life to the practice of medicine, he then matriculated in the medical department of the University of Maryland, where he was graduated in 1872, with the degree of Doctor of Medicine. He spent the following two years in the Roper Hospital at Baltimore, where he gained valuable experience. In 1874 Doctor Young came to Fairfax and entered upon the active practice of his profession, and has remained here ever since. He is a member of the Barnwell County Medical Society, the South Carolina State Medical Society and the American Medical Association. During the years of his professional work in this community Doctor Young has enjoyed to a notable degree the absolute confidence of the people. He has kept closely in touch with all the latest advances in his profession and has been remarkably successful in his treatment of disease. The best part of his life has been given to the service of the people of this community, and his long and faithful service has been rewarded with a competency that would permit him to retire from active labor if he so desired. He has been generous in his attitude towards worthy objects, and among his contributions may be mentioned a gift of $25,000 to the library of the medical department of the University of Georgia.

Doctor Young was married to Virginia Durant, who died in 1906, without issue.

JAMES PRESTON MCNAIR has been one of the prominent business men of Aiken County for over thirty years. He has been a manufacturer, farmer, merchant and banker.

Mr. McNair was born in Robeson County, North Carolina, July 14, 1860, a son of Duncan and Betha Jane (Alford) McNair. His father was a farmer. Mr. McNair was educated in public schools and the Red Springs Academy, and in early life entered the industry of manufacturing turpentine. Later he located at Kitchings Mills in Aiken County, was a merchant there from 1885 to 1905, and also developed extensive farming interests. In 1906 he organized the Farmers and Merchants Bank of Aiken, and has been president of that institution from the beginning. He also owns a large amount of farm land and other real estate both in Aiken County and in Georgia.

Mr. McNair has neglected none of those calls made upon a citizen for public work. He served as a member of the Public Works Commission for Aiken City. He is an elder in the Presbyterian Church. He married for his first wife Cora Kitchings, of Aiken County, and by that union had six children. On September 15, 1909, he married Hattie Roland, of Laurens. They have one child.

CHARLES THOMAS MASON of Sumter though his name is probably not so widely known as some others who have identified themselves with politics and public affairs, has been one of the most useful men of South Carolina, and as an inventor and business manager has an almost international fame in the industrial arts.

He was born at Sumter June 6, 1855, son of Charles Thomas and Judith G. (Britton) Mason. He comes by his talents naturally, his father having been a pioneer in electrical invention. His father during the war made telegraph instruments for the Southern Confederacy and was inventor of a practical electric fan.

Mr. Mason has spent all his life as a mechanical and electrical engineer. When twelve years old he made a working model of an engine which was awarded a silver medal by the State Fair at Columbia. For some time he gave much thought and study to solve the great problem of mechanical picking of cotton, and as early as 1880 invented a cotton picking machine that would discriminate between fibrous and non-fibrous material. His chief business, however, has been the manufacture of telephones. He began making telephones in Sumter in 1893, organizing the Sumter Telephone Manufacturing Company, and was its president and general manager until he sold out his interests a few years ago.

Mr. Mason is the inventor of the ignition system used on many types of aeroplanes in the United States, England, France and Italy. Between the telegraph, which was the first practical application of electricity to modern life, and the aeroplane, rapidly becoming a commonplace marvel of the twentieth century, is represented a profound epoch in industrial art, and at many points the Masons, father and son, have contributed to the advancement recorded.

Mr. Mason is a director of the Bank of South Carolina, and a former director of the Bank of Sumter. He is a member of the Franklin Institute of Philadelphia and the Royal Society of Arts of London.

At Baltimore, Maryland, November 16, 1875, he

married Emma Stewart, a daughter of John H. Stewart. They have four children: Emma S., wife of E. K. Friar; Eleanor, wife of W. I. Crowson, Jr.; C. Stewart Mason, who married Miss Marie Brown; and Carl T. Mason, who married Ollie Delgar.

PERONNEAU FINLEY HENDERSON has been a prominent member of the South Carolina bar for twenty years, and has added much to the prestige in which the name Henderson is held in legal circles at Aiken and that part of the state.

He is a son of Daniel Henderson of Aiken and was born in that city November 29, 1877. He is a graduate of the Aiken Institute and took his college work in Davidson College, North Carolina, where he was an honor man of his graduating class in 1897. He read law with the firm of Henderson Brothers, was admitted to the bar in 1898, and has steadily practiced law ever since. Mr. Henderson is a director of the Real Estate & Fidelity Company, of the Carolina Light & Power Company, of the Highland Park Hotel Company, the Powells Hardware Company and is secretary-treasurer of the Aiken Hospital Association.

He was district chairman of the Second Congressional District and had charge of the Liberty Loan drives in that district during the war, and is a member of the South Carolina Memorial Commission under appointment of Governor Cooper. He is now grand chancellor of the Knights of Pythias of the State of South Carolina.

On June 29, 1904, at Aiken, he married Miss Grace A. Powell, a native of Aiken and daughter of James Powell, of Aiken, retired. He was head of the Powell Hardware Company. They have two children, Adelaide and Eleanor.

J. LEROY DUKES is an Orangeburg lawyer and since March, 1914, has been United States commissioner of his district.

He was born at Orangeburg, October 13, 1889, son of John H. and Sophie (Johnson) Dukes. His father was a planter and also prominent in public affairs in Orangeburg County, serving sixteen years in the office of sheriff and for three terms, six years, representing the county in the Legislature. J. Leroy Dukes after attending public schools entered Wofford College at Spartanburg and was graduated in 1908. He then studied law, was admitted to the bar in 1910, and since that date has been busy in building up a general practice at Orangeburg. He is a York Rite Mason and Shriner and Elk.

October 16, 1918, he married Margaret Keener Summers, of Calhoun County. Mr. Dukes is steward and trustee of St. Paul's Methodist Episcopal Church at Orangeburg.

ROBERT LIDE. Few men in Orangeburg have larger interests both in their home community and over the state than Robert Lide, long prominent as a lawyer, banker and public official.

He was born at Greenville November 25, 1871, a son of Rev. Thomas P. and Martha Caroline (Hawkins) Lide. He is of Welsh ancestry, and his family history goes back to Robert Lide, who was born in Virginia in 1734 and came to South Carolina with a relative and settled in the Darlington district, and was later a major in the Continental army under General Marion. The second of his five sons was Hugh Lide, of Darlington, remarkable, says an old history, "for strength of character and solidity of understanding." A son of Hugh was Evan James Lide, and the latter was the father of the late Thomas P. Lide, who died August 2, 1906, after a life-long devotion to the Baptist Church. He was one of the most prominent ministers of that faith in the Pee Dee Association.

Robert Lide spent his youth in the various communities where his father was pastor. His father was able to send him to college, and he graduated from Wake Forest College in North Carolina in June, 1892. From that time forward he was dependent upon his own energies and exertions, and by work in a lawyer's office and agency work for an insurance company prepared for a professional career. He studied law with B. H. Moss at Orangeburg, and was admitted to practice in 1894. The firm of Moss and Lide has been a prominent one in the South Carolina bar for a quarter of a century.

Mr. Lide was appointed a United States commissioner in 1895, and held that office for a number of years. From 1900 to 1904 he represented his county in the House of Representatives, and was elected and served as a state senator from 1908 to 1916. From 1904 to 1914 he was county chairman of the democratic party and represented Orangeburg County as a member of the State Democratic Executive Committee. He has unusual gifts as a political organizer and has been one of the most influential men in the circles of his party in the state. He was a delegate to the Democratic National Convention at St. Louis in 1916. From 1917 to 1919 he served as mayor of Orangeburg. For twelve years Mr. Lide was also Orangeburg correspondent for the Charleston "News and Courier." He has been a member of the Orangeburg County Board of Education, and is a deacon in the Baptist Church, and long has been prominent in the fraternal orders. He is a past chancellor of the Knights of Pythias lodge, and past consul commander of his camp in the Woodmen of the World. He is a past head consul of South Carolina, and since 1909 has represented the state head camp in the sovereign camp of the United States.

He helped organize the Bank at Elloree in Orangeburg County, where his father was once pastor, in 1904, and has ever since been president of the bank, which is now the First National Bank of Elloree. He is also director and attorney for the First National Bank of Holly Hill.

June 2, 1897, Mr. Lide married Ethel Mildred Lowman, daughter of Dr. J. W. Lowman of Orangeburg. They have three daughters, Mildred, Evelyn and Ethel.

J. STOKES SALLEY, a lawyer and business man of Orangeburg, has been one of the progressive factors of the affairs of his native community since early manhood.

He was born at Orangeburg October 27, 1880, a son of George Lawrence and Mattie (Stokes) Salley. Reference is made to the career of his father on other pages. The son was educated in the local high school, attended Wofford College, and for five years was deputy county clerk. While in that office he was diligently preparing for his profession as a lawyer, and was admitted to the bar in 1904. For one year he served as circuit solicitor and has since applied himself to the private practice of law. He is also a director of the Peoples National Bank, the Orangeburg Packing Company, is president of a bottling company, and is secretary of the A. C. Watson Company, a general insurance agency.

November 15, 1905, he married Lizzie C. Salley, of Orangeburg. They have three children: J. Stokes, Jr., Elizabeth C., and Jane Bruce.

ISAAC CALHOUN STRAUSS, a lawyer by profession and training, has found his activities widely engaged in numerous business relations.

He was born at Florence, South Carolina, May 10, 1873, a son of Alfred A. and Amelia (Weinberg) Strauss. His father was a native of Germany, spent his boyhood in France, and on coming to America settled at Charleston, South Carolina. His wife was a native of South Carolina.

Isaac C. Strauss was educated in public schools, also under private tutors, attended high school at Atlanta, Georgia, one year at the University of South Carolina, and took a course at Eastman's Business College at Poughkeepsie, New York. He was an office boy with the well known law firm of Lee & Moise at Sumter, studied law with them, and upon his admission to the bar in 1896, became associated with his former preceptors and employers. From 1898 to 1918, twenty years, Mr. Strauss served as referee in bankruptcy, finally resigning that office. In that capacity he did a great deal of work, hardly compensated by any of the material rewards paid him for his services, and resulting in many nice adjustments of business interests, and altogether his record was a happy combination of the judicial temperament and thorough business acumen.

Mr. Strauss is president of the Palmetto Insurance Company, president of The Sumter Trust Company, vice president of the City National Bank, is a director and general counsel for the Sumter Telephone Company, a director of Harby Company, director of the Interstate Clay Company, director of the Bank of Haygood and Bank of Pinewood. He is president of the "Congregation Sinai" at Sumter, and throughout his career has extended his personal energies and means in behalf of many charitable causes.

September 4, 1900, he married Hattie Ryttenberg of Sumter, daughter of Harry and Rose (Nussbaum) Ryttenberg.

HON. JAMES BENJAMIN BLACK. While he has had half a century in which to do the work of his life, few men employed their years and talents and opportunities with better distinction than Dr. James Benjamin Black of Bamberg. Until recent years he was engaged in the practice of medicine. He is one of the prominent physicians of South Carolina. Many business affairs have also presented themselves to his attention, and for a quarter of a century he has been a potent figure in the politics of the southern part of the state. The state as a whole knows him through his long service in both the House and Senate, where his influence has been exerted in helpful ways in behalf of an enlightened program of constructive legislation.

Doctor Black was born in Colleton County July 19, 1849. His father, Robert Black, who was of English and Irish descent, served as captain in the State Troops during the war between the states, and while a farmer and planter he also became prominent in county politics, serving as sheriff for twenty years and also as county treasurer. Robert Black married Elizabeth Caldwell, who was born in Colleton County, while her father came from Ireland.

James Benjamin Black though reared in the impoverished period of the war and reconstruction times, acquired a liberal education, attending the common and high schools of his native county, took one course of lectures in the South Carolina Medical College and finished his medical education in the University of Maryland at Baltimore. In 1872 he began practice in Colleton County, and after seven years moved to Bamberg, where he continued to employ his strength in meeting the heavy demands made upon his professional talents until about five years ago, when he retired except for office and consultation work. In the meantime many other interests have developed. For forty years he has conducted a drug store on one spot in Bamberg. Farming on a modest scale has also been one of his interests, and for a quarter of a century he was associated with his brother Thomas Black in the livestock business.

On the death of Thomas Black in October, 1918, Dr. Black's son C. E. Black took the active management of this business. Doctor Black also has stock in the Bamberg Banking Company, in the Enterprise Bank, recently changed to the First National Bank of Bamberg, is a former president of the Bamberg Bank and now a director in the two institutions.

Doctor Black has given an almost continuous service in the Legislature for a quarter of a century. He was in the House eight years and has been in the Senate for sixteen years. Some of the causes with which his work in the Legislature has been especially identified are prohibition, good roads, education and public health. He is chairman of the Senate committee on medical affairs, and for several years has been one of the trustees and vice president of the Medical College of the State of South Carolina. His home locality has long considered him the chosen leader in the democratic party, and he has served as chairman of the Central Committee and chairman of the Bamberg Democratic Club. He is also a former mayor of Bamberg. Fraternally Doctor Black is a past master of Lodge No. 38, Ancient Free and Accepted Masons, is a past district deputy grand master of the Grand Lodge, a York Rite Mason and Shriner. He is also a past chancellor of the Knights of Pythias and a member of the Independent Order of Odd Fellows and Woodmen of the World. Doctor Black is a deacon in his home Baptist Church and for over thirty years has been a teacher in the Sunday school. He served as moderator of the Barnwell Baptist Association for several years and as presi-

dent of the County Sunday School Convention also for a number of years. When he was a young man and doing his first work as a physician in Colleton County he received a commission from Governor Wade Hampton as captain of a local cavalry company.

While his purposes and ideals in life have been expressed in a large degree of individual service and achievement, Doctor Black has every reason to be proud of the family of children who have grown up in his home. He married in Barnwell, now Bamberg County, August 1, 1872, Miss Hattie Ayer, a daughter of Charles F. Ayer. Her father was a grand-nephew of General Ayer, a distinguished character in the military affairs of the early state. Ten children were born to Doctor and Mrs. Black, seven of whom are still living: Mary Elizabeth, now deceased, was the wife of Col. F. N. K. Bailey, who conducts the well known military school at Greenwood, South Carolina; J. Benjamin, who died in infancy; Miles Jackson, a traveling salesman; Minnie Quincy, wife of Fred W. Free, of Bamberg; Doctor Robert, a practicing physician at Bamberg; Doctor Thomas, a dentist at Bamberg; Dr. Charles F., who also qualified as a physician and practiced until his death at Bamberg; Clarence Ervin, an attorney by profession, but, as mentioned above, is now in charge of his father's stock business; Miss Ethel, a teacher at Estill, South Carolina; and Miss Urma, a music teacher at Bamberg.

JONATHAN INGELL HAZARD has been a Georgetown business man thirty years, first as a merchant, but for the greater part of the time as a banker and developer of various projects in and around the city many of which have directly contributed to Georgetown's growth and prosperity.

Mr. Hazard was born at Conway in Horry County, South Carolina, November 8, 1864, a son of Benjamin I. and Sarah Freeborn (Ingell) Hazard. The Hazard family came to South Carolina from Rhode Island in 1849. Jonathan I. Hazard was educated in private schools and in business college and at the age of seventeen went to work in his father's merchandise store as office boy. After a time his father made him assistant bookkeeper and after laying the foundation of a sound business experience he removed to Decatur, Alabama, in April, 1888, and engaged in the house furnishing business under the name Hazard & Wright. Selling out in 1890 he returned to his native state in 1891 and took an active part in organizing the Bank of Georgetown, serving as its first cashier. He is now vice president and cashier. This bank has long been a bulwark in the financial affairs of Georgetown. It has a capital of $100,000, a surplus of $100,000 and undivided profits of $30,000. Mr. Hazard as a factor in the real estate business is president of the Hazard Addition Company, is secretary and treasurer of the Carolina Farm Land Development Company, an organization which has been instrumental in colonizing many tracts of South Carolina with northern people, is secretary-treasurer of the Rhem Dock and Terminal Company, secretary-treasurer of the Washington Park Real Estate Company, and secretary-treasurer of the Georgetown Land Association.

Mr. Hazard is also a director of the Chamber of Commerce, and was one of the citizens of Georgetown who worked hardest and most faithfully for the installation of an adequate water and sewerage system. He served as a member of the City Commissioners. He was also a member of the Volunteer Fire Department as president of the Winyah Hose Reel Company. He served during the World war as chairman of the County Council of National Defense, and as chairman of the Four Minute Men. He served as treasurer of Georgetown Chapter of the American Red Cross, as well as of the successive war fund campaigns. Mr. Hazard is junior warden of Prince George Winyah Episcopal Church.

January 4, 1888, he married Miss Fannie Wright of Bucksville, Horry County, South Carolina. They have three children. The son, J. I., Jr., who graduated from the University of South Carolina in 1911 and is now assistant cashier of the Bank of Georgetown, served as ensign in the navy from February, 1918, until mustered out in February, 1919. The two daughters, Ruth Hattie and Sarah Ingell, are both graduates of Converse College.

J. LAMB PERRY. The legal profession is one that demands much and requires of its devotees implicit and unswerving devotion to its exactions. Long and continued study; natural ability and keen judgment with regard to men and their motives, are all required in the making of a successful lawyer. That so many pass beyond the ordinary in this calling and become figures of note, demonstrates that this profession brings out all that is best and most capable in a man. For ages the most brilliant men of all countries have turned their attention to the study of the law, and especially is this true in the United States, where the form of government gives opportunity to the man of brains to climb even into the very highest position within the gift of the people, and it is a notable fact that from among the lawyers have more of our great men come than from all of the other callings combined. One of the men who is notable as a lawyer and a public-spirited citizen of Charleston, J. Lamb Perry, exemplifies these facts, and was born here in the '60s, a son of Archibald Simpson Johnston Perry, a native of South Carolina, and grandson of Benjamin Perry, at one time Secretary of State, and who was also born in South Carolina. The mother of J. Lamb Perry bore the maiden name of Martha Henrietta Lamb, and was born at Charleston, a daughter of James and Mary (Somers) Lamb, natives of England and South Carolina, respectively. J. Lamb Perry is the only son of his parents, but he had two sisters, namely: Jane Johnston, who married Duke Litta-Visconti-Arese of Italy, died in February, 1920; and Mary Lamb, who married Blackburn Hughes, died about 1911.

J. Lamb Perry attended a private school of Charleston until he matriculated at Union College at Schenectady, New York, from which he was graduated in 1879. He then studied law and was admitted to the bar at Columbia, South Carolina, in 1881, following which he returned to Charleston, where he has since been engaged in an active practice. In addition to his profession Mr. Perry has business interests and is president of the Johnston-Crews Company, wholesale dry goods dealers, the oldest established business of its kind at Charleston, or in fact in the country.

In 1883 Mr. Perry was united in marriage with Miss Caroline Stuart Buist, who died in 1913 leaving three sons, namely: Archibald Simpson, James Lamb, Jr., and Edward Henry Buist, and one daughter, Martha Henrietta. For a number of years Mr. Perry has been a member of the Presbyterian Church, which he is now serving as an elder. His career is interesting, for his success is due to his own ability. He has reaped only where he has sown, and the harvest with its valuable aftermath is now his. He has reached his high professional standing through no favors of influential friends, but because of his knowledge of the law and his fearlessness in interpreting it and bringing to bear upon the conduct of his cases the force of his keen intellect and the benefit of his long and varied experience which made him from the first able to judge correctly of men and their motives. Without this latter qualification few men are able to prosecute their calling as lawyers, for it is necessary to understand the complex workings of a man's mind in order to get at the true facts in a case.

DANIEL HAZEL MARCHANT is a veteran business man of Orangeburg, where he has been a merchant nearly forty years.

He was born in Graniteville, in what is now Aiken, then Edgefield, County, in 1854, a son of Wesley and Charlotte (Hook) Marchant. The Marchant family is of French Huguenot descent. The first of the name on coming to America settled at Tidewater, Virginia, and later in Lower South Carolina, in the vicinity of Charleston. In different generations this family has always produced strong and able men and upright citizens. Wesley Marchant was a native of South Carolina. His wife was a member of the well known Hook family, with prominent connections in Lexington County. Great-grandfather Martin Hook came from Hesse, Germany, during the Revolutionary war, but was not a typical "Hessian," since he joined the American patriot forces against Great Britain. This Revolutionary soldier married Sarah Senn. The maternal grandfather of Daniel H. Marchant was Nicholas Hook.

When Daniel H. Marchant was six years of age his parents left Graniteville and moved to a farm about three miles from Columbia in Lexington County. He was there until about fifteen and subsequently lived for several years at Columbus, Georgia. September 1, 1881, he identified himself with Orangeburg, and that city has since been his permanent home. For ten years he had charge of the piano department of the general mercantile establishment of George H. Cornelson. Thus fortified with a wide experience and acquaintance he became engaged in the merchandise business for himself. His store is one of the principal ones of the kind in this section of South Carolina. He is a dealer in pianos, organs and talking machines, and a varied line of musical goods.

Mr. Marchant is a Knight Templar Mason and Shriner and a member of the Methodist Episcopal Church. At Columbus, Georgia, he married Miss Julia Bond, daughter of Rev. William D. Bond, a Methodist minister. They have five children, Atticus Hagood; Daniel H., Jr.,; Lela Estelle, wife of J. G. Smith, Jr.; Julia Belle, wife of J. W. Culler; and William Wesley Marchant. One child, Albert Andrew Marchant, died in 1916, at the age of thirty-six. D. H. Marchant and all of his family on both sides are one hundred per cent American.

BENJAMIN HUGER RUTLEDGE, member of one of the prominent families of Charleston, has been an active and diligent member of the bar of that city for over thirty-five years. He has given his time to his profession with few outside interests, though frequently appointed to offices of trust.

Mr. Rutledge was born at Charleston September 4, 1861, a son of Benjamin Huger and Eleanor Maria (Middleton) Rutledge. He acquired his early education in Charleston, graduated in 1880 from the Virginia Military Institute at Lexington, and received his A. B. degree from Yale College in 1882. He was admitted to the South Carolina bar in 1884, and practiced for many years as a member of the law firm Mordecai, Gadsden & Rutledge and still later as senior partner of Rutledge, Hyde & Mann.

Mr. Rutledge has served with the rank of major in the South Carolina National Guards. He was elected a member of the South Carolina General Assembly in 1890, and for years was clerk of the judiciary committee of the Legislature. In 1884 he was chosen electoral messenger from South Carolina at the time of Cleveland's first election. Mr. Rutledge was delegate at large to the Universal Congress of Lawyers and Jurists at St. Louis in 1904. He is a member of the St. Cecilia Society, and the Episcopal Church. On October 5, 1882, he married Miss Emma Blake, of Fletcher, North Carolina.

GEORGE H. MOMEIER, former member of the Legislature from Charleston, has been a hard working lawyer in that city for over twenty years.

He was born at Charleston October 8, 1873. He was educated in grammar and high schools in his native city, and was admitted to the bar in 1895. Mr. Momeier's father was a native of Germany, came to Charleston when a boy, received his education in that city, and married Miss Louise C. Hase, a native of Charleston, daughter of John and Dorothea Hase, who had come from Germany at an early date.

Mr. Momeier achieved success in the law after a few years' practice and is one of the most popular and able lawyers of the Charleston bar. He is solicitor for a number of business concerns and served as a member of the Legislature in 1915-16. He is affiliated with the Knights of Pythias, the Woodmen of the World and the Fellowship Society.

April 28, 1898, he married Ernestine Peters, a daughter of C. H. Peters. They have five children: Roland H., Erna W., Arthur George, Frederick L. and Margaret L.

WILLIAM RISH LOWMAN, M. D. For over thirty years Doctor Lowman has been engaged in the heavy work of his profession at Orangeburg. He is a former secretary of the South Carolina Medical Board of Examiners, has given much of his time to educational affairs in medicine and public health, and his services and attainments have made him widely known over the state at large.

He is a son of the late Jacob Walter Lowman, also a physician and distinguished as the first democratic member of the State Legislature after reconstruction days. Dr. Jacob Walter Lowman was born in Lexington County, March 11, 1837. He was a descendant of David Lohman, who came from Germany to Virginia in 1770 and whose son Malachi Lohman settled at Dutch Forks, South Carolina, in 1814. Jacob W. Lowman was a son of Daniel and Nancy (Hiller) Lowman. He began the study of medicine under his brother-in-law, Dr. John K. Kneece, and in 1858 graduated from the Medical Department of the University of Georgia. He taught school and practiced medicine near Batesburg, South Carolina, and during 1863-65 was a lieutenant in the Confederate army. After the war he resumed practice in Lexington County and in 1872 was elected a member of the Legislature from that county. On leaving the Legislature he moved to Orangeburg, where for thirty years he was a leader in his profession and equally prominent in business and civic affairs. He served as vice president of the Edisto Savings Bank, as a director of the Orangeburg Manufacturing Company, was surgeon to the Atlantic Coast Line Railway and also to the C. N. I. A. and M. College of South Carolina. He published a book on hygiene and medical practice in 1879. He was an active Baptist. His death occurred January 14, 1905. He married Lodusky Rish, daughter of Levi and Mary Rish, in 1858.

Dr. William Rish Lowman was born in Lexington County, December 3, 1866, and has lived at Orangeburg since he was eight years of age. He graduated from high school there in 1886 and finished his course in the College of Physicians and Surgeons at Baltimore in 1888. Afterwards he took post-graduate courses in New York. Besides a large private practice he has been surgeon of the Atlantic Coast Line and was a lecturer in the Orangeburg Collegiate Institute, was secretary of the trustees of the C. N. I. A. and M. College of South Carolina, has been president of the trustees of Orangeburg Institute, and has been medical examiner for many insurance companies. He is a member of the National Science Association of America, the State and Tri-State Medical societies and the American Medical Association. He is a Knight Templar Mason and Shriner, and is a past master and past high priest of his lodge and Royal Arch Chapter.

December 27, 1891, he married Elvira Earle Izlar, daughter of Judge B. P. Izlar and niece of General James F. Izlar of Orangeburg.

CARLOS HARTH ABLE, M. D. Doctor Able was the pioneer citizen, business and professional man of the community of Norway in the western part of Orangeburg County. Soon after graduating in medicine he located in that section, and saw the brush burned away to make room for the first houses built. No one is better known and esteemed and has been more conspicuously useful than Doctor Able.

He was born in Lexington County in 1863, a son of Carson and Priscilla (Stedman) Able. Both his father and grandfather were natives of Lexington County, where the Able family settled about the time of the Revolutionary war. The ancestry is English. Doctor Able's grandfather helped build the first Baptist Church in Lexington County. His father, still living at the age of eighty-nine at his old home in Lexington County, was a Confederate soldier in Captain Kaufman's company. He was in active service throughout the struggle, but never received a wound.

Doctor Able attended common schools and studied medicine in the medical department of the University of Georgia at Augusta. He was graduated with the class of 1884, and in the same year settled at the present Town of Norway. All the older families of that community have looked upon him as their first resource as a physician and surgeon. He also conducts a general drug store in Norway and has helped make that town one of the best of its size in the state, situated as it is in the midst of a rich and progressive section. Doctor Able was one of the founders and is president of the First Bank of Norway, a splendid institution, very strong financially and occupying its own building, a modern three-story office structure that would be a credit to a much larger city. Doctor Able is also owner of some valuable planting interests in Orangeburg County, consisting of 195 acres adjoining the town and planted in cotton, corn and general produce.

His first wife was Miss Emma Johnson, of Aiken County, daughter of Edward Johnson, of that county. She was the mother of five children, Annie, Grover, Gerhard, Ruth and Gordon. Doctor Able married for his present wife Mrs. Nannette Brenneke.

Grover is engaged in the merchandise business at Norway. Gerhard is in the insurance business at the same place, and Gordon is attending college at Charleston, now taking the pre-medical course.

JOHN HENRY BURNEY. It is in keeping with the ancient and honorable traditions of South Carolina that some of the most vital and progressive movements in recent times should originate in the state. A movement affecting a numerous class was the recent organization of the Roadmasters and Supervisors Association of America, the founder of which and the secretary-treasurer of the association is John Henry Burney of Orangeburg.

Mr. Burney, whose home has been at Orangeburg since 1909, was for a number of years road supervisor of the Southern Railway. Road supervisors and roadmasters are highly important and responsible men in relation to the welfare and physical maintenance of American railways. Until recently, however, they were not organized or associated with a view to furthering their interests. Realizing the necessity for such organization, especially in view of the federalization of the railroads, Mr. Burney took the preliminary steps toward organization, carrying on the work entirely by correspondence. In order to give his entire time to the business he resigned from the Southern Railway in the fall of 1918, and in October, 1919, he had the satisfaction of seeing the Roadmasters and Supervisors Association of America consummated, embracing officials of that class not only in the United States but in Canada, and therefore an international organization. The offices and official headquarters are at Orangeburg, with Mr. Burney as secretary-treasurer and managing head. Already through negotiations carried on with the railroad administration at Washington many direct benefits have accrued to this class of railroad men, not only in the matter of salaries but other advantages in working conditions.

Mr. Burney was born at Clarkton, Bladen County, North Carolina, in 1883, a son of A. F. and Sarah Ellen (Benson) Burney. He was reared and educated in Clarkton and has been a railroad man since sixteen years of age. He went to work for the Georgia Central Railroad at Savannah, Georgia, in the roadway department. Later he was in the operating department of the same road, first as flagman and later as train conductor. In the fall of 1908 he became section foreman for the Southern Railway at Charleston, and in November, 1909, was promoted to road supervisor, with home and headquarters at Orangeburg. His supervision extended to the lines from Branchville to Columbia and from Kingsville to Kershaw, including the Sumter branch. Upon him in that office devolved the physical maintenance of way, obviously one of the larger responsibilities of railroad work.

Mr. Burney is a Mason and a member of the Presbyterian Church. He married Miss Eugenia Griner of Statesboro, Georgia. Their three children are Eugenia, Edith and John H., Jr.

JOHN HENRY CALDWELL. While his home and interests for a number of years have been in one of the quiet rural communities of Spartanburg County, John Henry Caldwell has performed a service to the entire cause of agriculture not only in the South but everywhere, that should justify his being better known throughout his home state.

Mr. Caldwell has the distinction of being the first to use dynamite in practical farming. In recent years a great propaganda has been launched for the use of blasting materials in many forms of farm work, and the process of disturbing and shattering the original strata, especially where hard, compacted or in the shape of hard pan, is now generally commended and recommended by agricultural authorities. But it was Mr. Caldwell who gave first practical proof of the method and carried it out on a scale admitting of broad tests.

As a result of what he has done in this direction Mr. Caldwell is widely known as "Dynamite Caldwell." Mr. Caldwell was born in Haywood County, North Carolina, April 11, 1854, but has been a resident of Spartanburg County since 1872, when he was eighteen years of age. His father was Alford Caldwell, a native of Spartanburg County, and the grandfather, Hughie Caldwell, was born in the same section of South Carolina. The family were pioneer settlers of the Tyger River in Upper South Carolina. Mr. Caldwell's great-grandfather donated the land where the old Nazareth Church now stands, the second oldest church in that section of the state. The Caldwells were of Scotch origin and came to the Carolinas from Virginia. Alford Caldwell married Sarah Hannah, a native of Haywood County, North Carolina, and a daughter of Evins Hannah of English ancestry and a native of North Carolina.

John Henry Caldwell is the only son of his parents. His one living sister is Mary Ann Caldwell. He spent his boyhood days in Haywood County and was educated there. His first experience in the use of dynamite was as a loader with a firm of contractors on the Asheville Division of the Southern Railroad. For about fifteen years he was employed as an expert in the use of dynamite, in mines, in the blasting of wells, and in general construction work.

In the meantime he bought a farm at Wellford, and continued the practice of agriculture there for twenty-seven years. In 1903 Mr. Caldwell bought his present home at Ardella, four miles west of Spartanburg. He now has 118 acres. The land cost him at purchase only $3,200. It is now conservatively valued at $32,000. Mr. Caldwell states that the land in 1903 produced only ten bushels of corn to the acre or one bale of cotton to three acres. In 1919 some of the same land showed a production of 100 bushels of corn to the acre, while he grew seventy-six bales of cotton on fifty acres. These results seem nothing less than remarkable, and Mr. Caldwell attributes the change almost entirely to the use of dynamite. He has placed heavy charges of that explosive beneath the soil, and the subsequent blast has thoroughly stirred both the top soil and sub-soil and mixed the different elements, and made available latent quantities of plant food which could never have been made available by any known processes of cultivation, even with the deepest plow. The results speak for themselves, and Mr. Caldwell is convinced that while the use of dynamite entails a heavy initial expense, it is cheaper in the long run than commercial fertilizer.

Mr. Caldwell is also interested in a store at Ardella. In that community he is known as a man of public spirit, and one who has the courage to back his convictions and vision by actual demonstrative proof. He has used his influence in behalf of educational and school enterprises, and is also credited with some of the work that brought an electric lighting system to his locality. He has been in politics to some extent, and was a candidate for the Legislature, being defeated by only a few votes. For sixteen years he was a member of the Knights of Honor, for eight years was affiliated with the Woodmen of the World, and as a youth from 1872 to 1875 served as a member of the Ku Klux Klan.

In 1876 he married Isabel Ann Jane Cooper, daughter of W. A. Cooper of Spartanburg County. Nine children were born to their marriage. One son and one daughter are now deceased. The oldest of those living is Martha Elizabeth, wife of Eber Johnson; Susie is the wife of F. L. Bradley; J. M. married Miss Cora Jackson of North Carolina; Jesse Valentine married Eva Steadman;

Austell, Toy Thomas and Roy Max are all at home. The sons Austell and Toy were soldiers in the World war with very creditable records. Both of them enlisted before the draft was issued. Austell served in the First Division and spent twenty-six months in France. He was in eleven distinct battles before he was wounded and he was again wounded, both times by shell fire. He served all through as a private. The son, Toy, was in Company F of the One Hundred and Eighteenth Infantry and saw all the overseas service with the Thirtieth Division.

CHARLES A. MOBLEY, M. D. Doctor Mobley is a Fellow of the American College of Surgeons, and for several years has confined his practice exclusively to surgery, a field in which he has well merited prominence throughout the state. Doctor Mobley recently founded the Orangeburg Hospital, and the direction of that modern institution is now his chief care.

Doctor Mobley was born at Rock Hill, South Carolina, in 1888. He comes of a family of physicians and surgeons, and represents the historic Mobley ancestry which has been in South Carolina since about 1758, founded by Edward Mobley. His grandfather is Dr. James Mobley, a retired physician whose home is in Florida. His maternal grandfather Hope was also a physician. The parents of Doctor Mobley were Frel and Anna (Hope) Mobley, the latter still living.

Doctor Mobley acquired his literary education in the University of Tennessee at Knoxville, and took his medical course in the Medical College of South Carolina at Charleston, where he graduated in 1910. His first home as a physician was at Van Wyck, in Lancaster County, whence he removed to his native city, Rock Hill. For several years at Rock Hill he was associated with Doctor Fennell, a prominent surgeon of that city. In 1919 Doctor Mobley chose the rich and rapidly growing City of Orangeburg as his permanent home, and in September opened the Orangeburg Hospital. This is a modern hospital with every facility and appliance for surgical work and the care of patients. A nurses' training school has been established, and there is a separate building for negro patients.

Doctor Mobley every year has interrupted his work a few weeks or months for further training and association with eminent men of his profession. Several times he has been an observer of the methods and technique of the famous Mayos in Minnesota, and has also attended clinics in Boston, New York, Philadelphia, Baltimore and Chicago. Besides being a Fellow of the American College of Surgeons, he is a member of the American Medical Association.

Doctor Mobley married Miss Susie Bailey, of Edisto Island, a daughter of Edward D. and Louisa (Whaley) Bailey, both natives of Edisto Island and from old South Carolina families of Revolutionary ancestry and English descent. Doctor and Mrs. Mobley have one son, Charles A., Jr.

GEORGE NIXON BUNCH. The community of Spartanburg gained a very high appreciation of the professional talents and the splendid character of the late Doctor Bunch during the eight years he practiced dentistry there.

Doctor Bunch, who was stricken in the early prime of his career and when he had most to live for, was born at North Augusta, Edgefield County, South Carolina, January 24, 1888, and died at his home in Spartanburg, February 3, 1920. His parents were Evan Medling and Ollie (Nixon) Bunch, also natives of South Carolina. Doctor Bunch acquired his early education in country schools, grew up on a farm, also attended private school at Augusta, and a private school at Columbia. He acquired a liberal education, at Clemson College, studying for his profession in the Atlanta Dental College. He was graduated May 12, 1911, and after a brief residence and practice at Gray Court, South Carolina, and at Greenwood, came to Spartanburg in 1912. He was a popular member of the community, belonged to a number of social organizations, and was a thirty-second degree Scottish Rite Mason and Shriner. He had some valuable business interests, including property in Edgefield County inherited from his father's estate. He was a liberal contributor to the Bethel Methodist Episcopal Church and a member of its Sunday school.

April 24, 1910, Doctor Bunch married Jessie E. Wallace, daughter of Watson W. and Martha (Kelly) Wallace. Mrs. Bunch was the youngest of four daughters and one son. Her father was born in Laurens County, South Carolina, and her mother in Spartanburg County. Mrs. Bunch finished her education in Lander College. She became the mother of four children: George Wallace, deceased; Martha Wallace; Evden Hunter, deceased; and George, Jr.

F. M. BRYAN has been a hard working member of the Charleston bar for over twenty years.

He was born at Charleston June 22, 1875, son of Judge George D. and Mary M. Middleton (King) Bryan. His parents were also natives of Charleston, where his father for a number of years was judge of the Probate Court. F. M. Bryan was educated in the Episcopal High School of Virginia, and studied law in South Carolina College. He was admitted to the bar in 1897, and since then has been engaged in a widely diversified general practice. He served six years as an influential member of the State Legislature at Charleston, and has always taken a useful citizen's part in politics. He is now probate judge of Charleston County, having succeeded his father by election in October, 1919. He is a member of several local clubs and societies, including the Masons and the Hibernian Society.

JUDGE JERRY MILES HUGHES. An able lawyer, now serving his second term as probate judge of Orangeburg County, Judge Hughes has accepted many calls and opportunities to devote his talents to the larger objects and aims of his home community.

He was born at Orangeburg in 1884, son of J. M. and Margaret S. (Mack) Hughes, the former a native of James Island, South Carolina, and the latter born near Cordova in Orangeburg County. J. M. Hughes died in 1907.

Jerry Miles Hughes was a studious youth, acquired his local education in the Orangeburg High School, and spent four years in the University of South Carolina. Three years of that time he was in the general academic department and finished his law course in one year, graduating in 1907. The following year he began practice at Orangeburg. He soon left and went west to Oklahoma, which had recently been admitted to the Union, and remained in that state two years. He returned to Orangeburg in 1910 and for several months taught school, resuming his law practice in 1911.

One of the best services he has rendered Orangeburg County has been in connection with the Orangeburg County Fair. This association was established in 1911, with Judge Hughes as secretary, an office he has filled continuously. Orangeburg is justly proud of its fair. The fair has exerted a tremendous influence in developing and improving the agricultural welfare of the community. The management has been such as to make this one of the best fairs in the entire state. During November, 1919, the receipts of the annual fair were $20,000.

Judge Hughes was elected county attorney in 1914, filling that office two years. In 1916 he was chosen judge of probate to fill an unexpired term, and in 1918 was re-elected at the regular election. He is a most competent and faithful official, a very popular citizen, and enjoys every evidence of trust and popular esteem. He is president of the Home Building and Loan Association of Orangeburg.

Judge Hughes is a Methodist and is affiliated with the Knights of Pythias and Masons. He married Miss Oressa Collier, and they have one son, Jerry Miles, Jr.

WILLIAM HENRY COLEMAN. In the death of William Henry Coleman, which occurred January 27, 1919, South Carolina lost one of its oldest, bravest and most efficient public servants. He had been a boy fighter in the Confederate army and from the close of the war until his death had given about a third of a century to public office. He was a former sheriff of Richland County, and at the time of his death was serving as postmaster of Columbia.

He was born in Pickens County, South Carolina, March 9, 1850. For a few years of his boyhood his parents lived in Tennessee. At the age of fifteen Mr. Coleman enlisted in the Confederate army and was with the army during the last six months of the war. He then located at Columbia and for some years was a farmer in that vicinity. During the reconstruction period he was a member of a Red Shirt company commanded by Captain Lykes.

His first important public service was as deputy sheriff under S. W. Rowan. He was deputy sheriff in Richland County for eighteen years, during the administrations of Sheriffs Rowan and Cathcart. He was then elected to that office himself and filled it for twelve years, until he voluntarily retired. It was his work in the sheriff's office which brought him his well deserved reputation throughout Richland County and over a large part of the state. As is often true of really brave men, Mr. Coleman had a modesty which would seldom permit him to speak of the many exciting experiences of his life. But others knew his trustworthiness, his fearlessness in the presence of danger, and his undaunted determination to discharge his duty at all hazards. Throughout the long service he rendered in the sheriff's office no prisoner was ever taken from him.

Mr. Coleman was appointed postmaster of Columbia in February, 1916, and was the courteous head of that office for nearly three years. Fraternally he was a member of the Masonic order, the Independent Order of Odd Fellows, Knights of Pythias and Elks, and was a member of Ebenezer Lutheran Church. He married Miss Annie Taylor Moore of York County and a descendant from an ancestry long and prominently identified with the state. On the paternal side she is a direct descendant of James Moore, the first governor of South Carolina, and on her mother's side, a descendant of Col. Thomas Taylor, the donor of the land upon which the City of Columbia now stands. Mrs. Coleman survives her husband and is the mother of seven children, four daughters and three sons. The daughters are, Mrs. F. F. Hough, of Richmond, Virginia, Mrs. J. A. Krentzlin, of Washington, District of Columbia, Mrs. J. B. Sylvan, of Columbia, and Miss Myrtle Coleman, of Columbia. The sons are, William Augustus Coleman, George Trezevant Coleman, and Samuel Rowan Coleman, all residents of Columbia.

WILLIAM AUGUSTUS COLEMAN. The distinctively modern trend of business and civic development in Columbia has had a tireless and effective ally in William A. Coleman, whose time and energies are devoted to several commercial organizations, and he has shown the same aptitude for public administration as his late father, whose career is included in this publication.

Mr. Coleman was born near Columbia in Richland County, March 27, 1880, son of William H. and Annie Taylor (Moore) Coleman. His early education was limited to five years in the public schools of Columbia, and for the rest he has depended upon his experience and the moulding power of his own ambition and character. His longest and most consistent business association has been as a wholesale druggist, having spent twenty-three years with the Murray Drug Company. He then established himself in business as president of the Covin Candy Company, in association with Mr. W. D. Drew as vice president and secretary.

In April, 1920, the Covin Candy Company was succeeded by the Coleman-Drew Company, which under the same management and with increased capitalization, engaged in the wholesale drug business at Columbia. Mr. Coleman is vice president of the Liberty National Bank, and a director of several building and loan and trust companies. In May, 1918, he was elected commissioner of finance and police of Columbia. As his record proves he is the right sort of man in public office, progressively minded, devoted to the public welfare, and when his convictions are made up he is aggressive and fearless in action.

Mr. Coleman is a member of the Odd Fellows, the Ridgewood, Columbia and Rotary clubs, and is affiliated with the Episcopal Church. June 19, 1903, at Columbia, he married Frances Maner Mixson, daughter of Col. F. M. Mixson. Their family

consists of three children, Nell P., William F. and Lucy M. Coleman.

JAMES ALLAN. Though he has been a member of the bar five years, and nearly two years of that time sacrificed his practice in order to serve his country during the war, James Allan has more than justified the anticipations of his admiring friends who had followed closely his brilliant career through college and university.

Captain Allan was born at Summerville, South Carolina, November 14, 1889. His father, James Allan, was a native of Charleston, was educated in the city schools, also abroad in Switzerland, and was in the wholesale jewelry business. He died when about forty-eight years of age. The grandfather was also named James Allan and was a native of Scotland, coming to South Carolina about 1840. He was also in the jewelry business. James Allan II married Mary Doar Tupper, a native of Charleston, and member of one of the oldest families in the South and New England. Her father was George Tupper and her grandfather Tristram Tupper. Tristram Tupper was president of the South Carolina Railroad when it enjoyed the distinction of being the longest railroad in the world. The Tuppers came from England about 1637 and settled in Massachusetts. The old home at Sandwich, built in 1637, is still owned by the Tupper Family Association.

Capt. James Allan is the younger of two sons. His brother, Samuel, was accidentally killed in 1907. Captain Allan was educated in the Charleston High School and the Porter Military Academy, where he was awarded three medals, for scholarship, classics and declamation. He took his college literary course at Davidson College, North Carolina, and during his career there won three medals for debating. He graduated A. B. and in 1912 was awarded his master's degree by the University of South Carolina. Here again he was awarded two medals for debating and oratory, and for the first time in twenty-five years won the "All Southern Oratorical Contest" for the University of South Carolina. In 1913 he was awarded a law degree by the university and in 1914 did special work in the Harvard Law School. He was admitted to the bar in 1913 and began practice in Charleston the following year.

Captain Allan joined the Charleston Light Dragoons for service on the Mexican border in 1916-17, and served as corporal and sergeant. At the outbreak of the war with Germany he was appointed first lieutenant of a squadron of cavalry being organized by Wyndham Manning. This organization was never perfected. He was then appointed a junior grade lieutenant in the National Naval Volunteers, but the original plans for this organization were never carried out, due to the fact that the Naval Militia was federalized. He then entered the Second Officers Training Camp at Fort Oglethorpe, Georgia, and was commissioned a captain in the field artillery. He was an instructor in the Third Training Camp at Camp Jackson. He then transferred to the Three Hundred and Eighth Cavalry when Pershing called for fifteen regiments of cavalry. He was then stationed at Douglas, Arizona for six months. In August, 1918, all the National Army Cavalry by order of the War Department was transformed into field artillery. Captain Allan was then sent for intensive instruction to the School of Fire at Fort Sill, Oklahoma, and completed his course in reconnoissance and gunnery. He was assigned to the Fifty-sixth Field Artillery, then in training for immediate overseas service, but was kept at Fort Sill until after the armistice was signed. He received his honorable discharge December 6, 1918, and at once returned to Charleston and resumed his law practice.

Captain Allan is a member of St. Andrew's Society and the Carolina Yacht Club. March 31, 1917, he married Marian Aley, of Wichita, Kansas. They have one son, James Allan, Jr., born October 17, 1919.

GEORGE LAWRENCE SALLEY has been a notable figure in the public affairs of Orangeburg County for a number of years, and since December, 1892, has held the post of county clerk. His official record has been as satisfactory and honorable as it has been long. It is interesting to note that his grandfather, Samuel P. Jones, was clerk in Orangeburg District in 1812. A hundred and two years later George L. Salley in the course of his official duties recorded some papers which had been signed by his grandfather. Mr. Salley's maternal ancestors were of English origin and came to America in colonial days. One of the colonial governors of South Carolina, William Bull, appointed by the king of England, was a grandfather of Mrs. Sheldonia (Bull) Salley, the mother of G. Lawrence Salley.

George Lawrence Salley was born in Orangeburg County, February 28, 1847, a son of Nathaniel Moss and Sheldonia (Bull) Salley. He grew up on his father's plantation and had a common school education. He was only fourteen when the war broke out, and later he went into active service as a member of Company D of the Seventh Battery of Artillery. When the war was over he went back to the farm and plantation and was called from that quiet routine to the duties of his present office in December, 1892. For ten years he also served as registrar and supervisor of elections. He is a director of the Peoples National Bank of Orangeburg. Mr. Salley is one of the prominent members of the Methodist Episcopal Church of Orangeburg, serving as trustee and forty years as recording steward.

December 12, 1875, he married Martha Stokes, of Barnwell County. They became the parents of six children. Nathaniel Moss is a member of the faculty of the State College for Women at Tallahasse, Florida. Mary E. is the wife of W. P. Pollock, present United States senator from South Carolina. J. Stokes Salley is a prominent lawyer at Orangeburg. Ada Lockhart is the wife of John C. Evans. James Raworth is a lawyer and deputy clerk under his father, while the youngest, Katherine Moss, is the wife of Dr. N. Bruce Edgerton.

C. DEAN GADSDEN, one of the younger business men of Charleston, has built up an important business and extensive clientage in real estate, stocks, bonds and insurance.

He was born at Charleston, and is a member of an old and prominent family represented in the affairs and history of the city for five generations. His great-grandfather, John Gadsden, was born at Charleston, son of an Englishman and an early settler in the city. His grandfather was Rev. Christopher Philip Gadsden, founder of St. Luke's Episcopal Church. He was a native of Charleston and his chief lifework was in connection with the church which he founded. His father was John Gadsden, a native of Charleston, a graduate of Washington and Lee University at Lexington, Virginia, and a civil engineer by profession. He died at the age of fifty-one. John Gadsden married Mary Joanna Deas, who is still living in Charleston. Her father was Lieut. Charles Deas, a lieutenant in the United States Navy, who died while in foreign service. The Deas family is of Scotch ancestry. John Gadsden and wife had six children, five of whom are still living: Christopher Philip, a traveling salesman; Ann Deas, wife of James Adger, of Charleston; Charles Deas; Mary Porcher, wife of John P. B. Sinkler, of Philadelphia; and Joanna Stuart, wife of Joseph E. Jenkins, of Charleston.

Charles Deas Gadsden was educated in the schools of Charleston and in Porter Military Academy. In 1909 he entered the real estate, stocks, bonds and insurance business. Mr. Gadsden enlisted in the navy in 1918 for a term of four years and served to the time of the armistice, then being transferred to the reserve list, where he is at present.

In 1917 he married Marie N. Bogert, daughter of Rev. Harry Howe Bogert of Birdsboro, Pennsylvania. They have a daughter, Marie Bogert. Mr. Gadsden is a member of the Carolina Yacht Club, Charleston Country Club, the Masonic order, St. Andrews Society, and has taken an active part in public affairs.

COL. JAMES HENRY CLAFFY. Historically South Carolina presents an interesting combination of the conservative and the progressive. The bulk of its people have steered clear equally from the standpat and reactionary and also from dangerous radicalism. Nevertheless some of the most wholesome movements effecting social and economic life have received their earliest recognition in South Carolina, and this state has given to such movements many prominent leaders.

One of the most important units in the proposed great federation of American agriculture is the Farmers' Union, the president of which for South Carolina is Col. James Henry Claffy of Orangeburg. Colonel Claffy is a practical farmer himself, but for many years has been a leader in various movements affecting the best interests of state agriculture. He was born at Columbia, in 1858, a son of James and Eliza (McKenna) Claffy. Both his father and mother were natives of Ireland. They came to America some time before the Civil war, locating at Columbia, and later moving to a farm at Fort Motte in Orangeburg County.

James Henry Claffy was twelve years old when his parents moved to the farm at Fort Motte. He kept his residence in that vicinity until 1893, and since that year Orangeburg has been his home.

He came by his military title justly. It was during the year 1893 that the Darlington riot occurred, when a number of the units of the National Guard of the state refused to obey the orders of the Governor, Tillman. Colonel Claffy, with the aid of several others then organized a company of citizens, numbering seventy-five men, and reported with them to the Governor within twenty-four hours after the call for volunteers was made. A permanent organization of this company was then perfected, Colonel Claffy being commissioned as captain. He held this position for twenty years, although his resignation was repeatedly offered. It was as many times refused, the men refusing to permit him to sever his connections with the company. In 1910 he was elected a major, and after serving in this capacity for two years was elected lieutenant-colonel of the Second South Carolina Infantry. He served in this capacity until 1916, when he retired from the service.

Shortly after moving to Orangeburg Colonel Claffy was elected president of the State Farmers' Union, and while serving in this capacity organized the Farmers Union Bank and Trust Company and served as vice president and cashier for several years. He was also the leader in organizing the Orangeburg County Fair Association, which is conceded to be the most successful effort ever made in this direction. Organized in 1910 and capitalized at $20,000.00, of which $10,000.00 was paid in, this association in 1920 has accumulated real estate valued at $50,000.00 after paying off all indebtedness. In the year 1916 he organized the Orangeburg County Farmers Mutual Fire Insurance Association, which has been remarkably successful. Beginning business without a dollar's capital, at the end of four years has accumulated a surplus of $15,000.00 in cash and business to the amount of $1,500,000.00. In 1919, while president of the Farmers' Union, he was foremost in organizing the Orangeburg County Marketing Association, which gave to the farmers of the county "for the first time" the market price of their products.

Besides being president of the State Farmers' Union, Colonel Claffy is one of the leaders of the American Cotton Association. At the organization of the association at New Orleans in 1919, he was elected one of the directors from South Carolina. In December of the same year he was elected vice president of the South Carolina Division, and also a member of the State Executive Committee. He is also president of the Orangeburg County Cotton Association.

Many conspicuous war activities are to the credit of Colonel Claffy. He was food administrator in charge of speeding up production among the farmers of the state, and his work in that role brought him the especial commendation and a medal from the Food Administration at Washington. Colonel Claffy is a prominent democrat and has frequently been a delegate to state conventions. He is a member of the Catholic Church.

He married Miss Mana E. Rickenbaker, of Orangeburg County. Her mother was a member of the Elliott family of that County. They have two daughters, Mana, wife of Dr. B. M. Montgomery, of Kingstree, and Miss Kathleen Claffy.

James H. Claffy.

SAMUEL DIBBLE, LL. D., was an eminent lawyer, a constructive statesman, an educator and scholar, and none can read the history of South Carolina and his personal record without realizing how deeply his life was impressed upon that of the state at large, and his home community of Orangeburg in particular.

He was born in the City of Charleston, September 16, 1837, and died just seventy-six years later, September 16, 1913, in a sanitarium near Baltimore, whither he had gone in the vain hope of recovering his health. He was a direct descendant in the paternal line from Thomas Dibble who came from England to Dorchester, Massachusetts, in 1630 and in 1635 was one of the founders of Windsor, Connecticut.

Samuel Dibble was the oldest son of Philander Virgil and Frances Ann (Evans) Dibble. Philander and his brother Andrew when young men came from Bethel, Connecticut, to Charleston and engaged in business together as hatters. Ann Evans was descended from the Gabeau family of French Huguenots and the Henley family of England.

Samuel Dibble acquired his early education in his native city at the schools of Misses Caroline and Mary Gray and Mr. John Gray, spent one year in a common school near his grandfather's farm in the Town of Bethel, Connecticut, and in 1849 entered the high school under Henry M. Bruns, the principal, and was admitted to the College of Charleston in 1853. He completed his junior course and in 1855 entered Wofford College, where he graduated A. B. in July, 1856, being the first graduate of that famed institution, which was then under the presidency of Rev. William M. Wightman, afterward Bishop Wightman. While at Wofford he was a member of the Calhoun Literary Society. After forty years of devotion to literary and professional labors he received the degree LL. D. from his alma mater. He considered this the highest honor he ever attained.

On leaving college he taught in Shiloh Academy and Pine Grove Academy in Orangeburg District in 1856-57, and was assistant teacher of the Wofford Preparatory Department in the spring of 1858. Then and during the year 1859 he studied law under Jefferson Choice of Spartanburg, and Lesesne and Wilkins of Charleston, and was admitted as an attorney to the law course in December, 1859, and as a solicitor in equity in 1865, having studied equity under Hon. Charles H. Simonton. In January, 1860, he began the practice of law at Orangeburg.

He was soon called from his office and cases to a sterner field of duty. January 3, 1861, he volunteered as a private in the Edisto Rifles in Col. Johnson Hagood's First Regiment of South Carolina Volunteers. He was with that company throughout the war, attaining the rank of first lieutenant. The company later became a part of the Eutaw Regiment, Twenty-Fifth South Carolina Volunteers, under Col. Charles H. Simonton, a part of Hagood's Brigade, Hokes' Division of the Army of Northern Virginia.

Toward the close of the war he married, with the return of peace began the practice of law at Orangeburg, and in 1867 formed a partnership with Hon. James F. Izlar under the name Izlar & Dibble. During his earlier years as a lawyer he also edited the Orangeburg News. The firm Izlar & Dibble became one of the widest known and strongest legal firms of the state. The Orangeburg Bar in resolutions passed after the death of Mr. Dibble spoke of his record as a lawyer in the following words: "Mr. Dibble studied law as a science and was profoundly versed in its underlying principles. He argued many notable causes, involving new and difficult questions and of the gravest importance to society. When great principles were to be determined his genius was equal to the task, and when authorities were to be invoked to sustain that which already had been settled, he furnished them inexhaustless store and used them with the skill of a master. Mr. Dibble was a learned lawyer and adorned the Bar with the wealth of learning, but as a distinguished public servant he belongs also to the state. His conspicuous and valuable services in public station and in private walk have become part of the rich heritage of the state. He was a leader of men and was ready at all times to do all things and to dare all things for the public good."

Having ventured his life and his fortune for the sake of the South in the war, he was equally ready with all he had to redeem his state from the wretched conditions of reconstruction. He was an able lieutenant of Wade Hampton and did his part in the restoration of white rule. He served as democratic county chairman of Orangeburg County in the Seymour and Blair campaign of 1868. When for the protection of the white people a military company was organized in Orangeburg County, the Edisto Rifles were reorganized in June, 1876, and he was made captain. He was elected to the State Legislature as a member of the House in 1877, and while in that body did good work for the improvement of the educational resources of the state. He was elected one of the trustees of the South Carolina University in 1878, when the vagabond professors and negro students were driven out. He was chairman of the executive committee of the South Carolina Agricultural College and Mechanics Institute for colored students, a branch of the State University. He was appointed one of the Board of School Commissioners of Orangeburg County and formulated the present subdivision of the county into school districts.

In 1880 Mr. Dibble was a delegate to the National Democratic Convention that nominated Hancock and English and was chosen a presidential elector that year. In 1881, on the death of Hon. Michael P. O'Connor, member of Congress, he was elected to the vacancy in the Forty-Seventh Congress and was subsequently reelected as a democrat for four more successive terms, serving until the close of the Fifty-First Congress in 1891, when he declined reelection and retired to occupy his time with other interests. He took high rank among the strong men in Congress and was admittedly among the ablest men this state sent to the nation's councils.

To his reputation as a lawyer and public leader he added that of a wise and able business man. He helped organize the Edisto Savings Bank, now the Edisto National Bank of Orangeburg, was chosen its first president April 3, 1889, and served until April 1, 1902. The Bowman Land and Improvement Company was organized April 11, 1891, and the Branchville and Bowman Railroad Company September 6, 1890, Mr. Dibble serving as president of these institutions.

At this point should be quoted another paragraph from the resolutions above cited: "Mr. Dibble was essentially a constructionist. He possessed great administrative ability and was both a builder and benefactor. He was a man of broad vision, with a clear insight into our industrial conditions and he had the most optimistic faith in the destiny of this section of the state. He appreciated its resources and contributed his capital and talents to develop them. He evinced the deepest interest in improved agricultural methods, in the drainage of our lowlands and in the construction and improvement of the public highways. He developed and brought into a high state of cultivation a large area of practically abandoned territory in the lower portion of this county, stimulating the energy of the people and adding largely to its prosperity. He established and was chiefly instrumental in building the thriving town of Bowman, and with his own means he constructed a railroad from that town to Branchville in order to give the people of that section railroad communications with the outside world. The growing town and the surrounding country with its prosperous farms and intelligent citizenship will ever remain a monument to his genius and energy."

Mr. Dibble joined Shibboleth Lodge No. 28, Ancient Free and Accepted Masons, at Orangeburg May 2, 1867, Eureka Chapter No. 13, August 24, 1867, and was high priest of the Royal Arch for a number of years. He was president of Young American Steam Fire Engine Company and chief of the fire department of Orangeburg. He was township commissioner of Bowman Township during the latter part of his life, and as such assisted largely in widening and improving the highways of the county and state. He was also quite active in securing to Orangeburg its present railroad facilities; was appointed superintendent of the St. Paul Methodist Episcopal Sunday School in 1860, and after the war reorganized it and served until April 18, 1879. On his resignation the Methodist Conference passed resolutions thanking him for his long, intelligent and earnest work as superintendent.

Of other attributes of his mind and character the Bar Resolutions said: "Mr. Dibble was in no sense an ordinary man. He possessed many remarkable characteristics. He was naturally endowed with a strong mind, which he cultivated to a very high degree. He was possibly the best educated and most broadly informed man in the county. Familiar with the classics, a master of several languages and especially gifted in the higher mathematics, he was deeply cultured in the truest sense."

November 10, 1864, Mr. Dibble was happily married to Miss Mary Christiana Louis, of Orangeburg, daughter of Deopold and Ann Agnes Louis. Mrs. Dibble, who survived her husband, has been universally beloved for her admirable character and charming personality. She is the mother of four children: Mrs. B. H. Moss, Mrs. W. W. Watson, Samuel Dibble and Louis V. Dibble.

SAMUEL DIBBLE. The name Dibble has long figured conspicuously in Orangeburg County. The late Samuel Dibble was a prominent lawyer long associated with Judge Izlar and other prominent practitioners of the Orangeburg bar. He is also remembered for his services in Congress during the eighties.

A son of Congressman Dibble and his wife, Mary C. Louis, is Samuel Dibble, Jr., whose work as a civil engineer has brought him in close touch with much of the construction enterprise of the South. He was born at Orangeburg November 25, 1868, and was educated in public schools and the University of South Carolina, where he graduated in the chemistry course in 1890, with the degree B. S. He has employed his technical ability as an engineer in connection with the reclamation and development of large tracts of waste land in Orangeburg County, and through that work has conferred benefits upon the present and all future generations. He owns a large amount of farm property.

At one time he lived at Bowman, South Carolina, and was one of the city fathers there. In 1898 he enlisted for the Spanish-American war in the United States Engineers and served as first lieutenant. He was in service from May, 1898, until discharged on May 20, 1899, and part of that time was on duty in Cuba. Mr. Dibble is unmarried.

LEE A. KLAUBER. Members of the Klauber family have been prominent in mercantile and banking circles in the southern part of the state for over forty years. His life and services well entitled Lee A. Klauber to the rich esteem and veneration in which his name is held and his memory cherished.

He was the founder of the family in South Carolina. Born in Bohemia, he located at St. George in Dorchester County in 1877. His initiative and public spirit proved a valuable addition to the resources of that community. He was a merchant and banker, and found many opportunities to express his generous ideals of service to his community and his fellow men. He was president of the St. George Cotton Seed Oil Manufacturing Company, and personally controlled about 2,000 acres of land at St. George, some of it in timber and the rest in cotton and corn. For a number of years he operated a large sawmill a mile and a half from St. George and cut great quantities of lumber for the South Carolina and Georgia Railroad.

Lee A. Klauber was a member of the Masonic lodge and a member of the Jewish Synagogue at Orange, New Jersey, where he had a brother living. A sister, Mrs. Louisa Plodkin, is now living at Atlanta, Georgia. Lee A. Klauber died September 1, 1919. His character and his generosity made him greatly beloved by all classes of people, both white and black. Many times he was known to have befriended, in a way that amounted to a studious and customary practice, poor women and their families. It is said that on the day of his death probably 500 negroes, stricken with grief at their loss, came to his home.

Lee A. Klauber married Sarah Alice Harbeson, member of an old South Carolina family of English and Scotch-Irish ancestry. She was an active member of the Methodist Church. Her father, William I. Harbeson, of St. George, served four years as a member of the Confederate cavalry during the war, part of the time under Gen. Joseph E. Johnston. He was also prominent in his section during the reconstruction period and served as a member of the "red shirt" brigade.

Two sons of the late Lee A. Klauber are successful South Carolina bankers. One, Robert Lee Klauber, was born at St. George October 19, 1884. He was educated in the local public schools, attended The Citadel two years, and also spent two years, 1901-02, in South Carolina Military Academy. He finished his education in Sullivan, Creighton & Smith's Business College, Georgia, in 1903, and at once returned to St. George and joined his father in the mercantile business. He is now president of the L. A. Klauber Company, a concern whose assets are rated at over $125,000, and is also president of the Bank of St. George, the oldest bank in the community. He is a director in the Farmers Bank & Trust Company of St. Matthews, is connected with the Liberty Bank of Charleston, and operates a thirty horse farm near St. George.

At St. George Robert L. Klauber married Emily A. Howell. Her father, John J. Howell, was for a number of years editor of the Dorchester Democrat and later served as county superintendent of education. Mr. and Mrs. R. L. Klauber have two children, Katherine and Vivian. Mr. Klauber is a Mason, and while never active politically served a term as a member of the Town Council. Fishing and hunting are his favorite recreations and he is a great lover and a judge of dogs and for several years has maintained a fine kennel.

William Adolph Klauber, the other son, who for the past eighteen years has been a banker and merchant at Bamberg, was born at St. George February 17, 1882. He was liberally educated, attending the common schools and the St. George High School, and graduated from South Carolina's famous military school The Citadel with the class of 1902. Soon after completing his education he came to Bamberg and engaged in merchandising, and is still active head of a large business in that line. On January 28, 1920, he bought the interests of the former president of the Enterprise Bank of Bamberg, and at once reorganized, taking in a number of prominent men of Bamberg as his associates and securing a new charter under the name of the First National Bank of Bamberg. The change in name and management became effective May 7, 1920. The officers of the bank are: W. A. Klauber, president; Dr. Robert Black, vice president; W. D. Coleman, cashier; while the directors are Aaron Rice, Dr. George F. Hair, C. J. S. Brooker, Dr. Robert Black, G. A. Ducker, Dr. F. B. McCracken, W. D. Coleman, D. C. Crum, J. D. Copeland, W. E. Free, Dr. J. B. Black and W. A. Klauber—all men of the highest standing in that community.

Mr. Klauber is also a director in the Bank of St. George and is vice president of the Citizens Building and Loan Association and a director in the Bamberg Realty Company.

In recent years he has also taken much part in local and state politics, and was one of the leading supporters of Governor Manning's aspirations for the gubernatorial office. He served four years on the staff of the governor as lieutenant colonel. Fraternally he is affiliated with Ornan Lodge No. 38, Free and Accepted Masons.

February 22, 1903, Mr. Klauber married at St. George Murchy Judy, a native of that community. Her father is Dr. Perry M. Judy, of St. George, of an old colonial family of English and Irish descent. Her grandfather was a surgeon and lieutenant colonel in the Confederate army. Mr. and Mrs. Klauber have three children, Louis A., Perry McSwain and William A., Jr.

S. OLIVER O'BRYAN. How large a place an able and hard working young lawyer may fill in a community's activities is well exemplified in the career of S. Oliver O'Bryan of Manning.

A graduate of the law department of the University of South Carolina in 1905, he began general practice in Manning the same year. He has served as city councilman, county attorney, is present city attorney of Manning, is a trustee of the Manning graded schools, and since 1914 has been chairman of the democratic party of Clarendon County. During the war he was chairman of the County War Savings Stamps Committee, a member of the Council of Defense, chairman of the Legal Advisory Board, chairman of the Home Section of the Red Cross and active in every other war cause. He is superintendent of the Sunday school, president for several years of the Sunday School Association, and an active member of the Presbyterian Church.

Mr. O'Bryan was born in Clarendon County, July 28, 1883, a son of William M. and Mary Gertrude (Oliver) O'Bryan. He was educated in the common schools, in the Presbyterian College at Columbia, in Clemson College preparatory to his law course. In 1906 he became associated as a partner with Judge John S. Wilson under the name Wilson & O'Bryan. In 1907 Mr. Wilson was elected to the bench and since that date Mr. O'Bryan has been associated with Robert O. Purdy, under the firm name of Purdy & O'Bryan. Mr. O'Bryan is a director of the First National Bank of Manning, president of the Bank of Paxville, and president of the Manning Ice & Light Company. He is a Royal Arch Mason and a Past Chancellor Commander of the Knights of Pythias, a member of the Eastern Star and the Woodmen of the World. June 28, 1911, he married Frances Davis of Manning, a daughter of J. Elbert and Sarah Rawlinson Davis. Her father is a former sheriff of Clarendon County. Mr. and Mrs. O'Bryan have four children: William, Leila, Samuel Oliver and Eugenia.

GEORGE FELDER HAIR. The Hairs are an old and prominent family of the old Barnwell district. While farming has always been a dominant interest in the family, the present generation is numerously represented in the professions, several of the sons having been physicians or dentists, including Dr. George Felder Hair, who for twenty years has been a resident of Bamberg and is a former president of the State Dental Society.

The remote ancestry of the Hairs is German, though members of the family have lived in the South since colonial times. The late Judson E. Hair was born in Barnwell County June 30, 1847, and died June 16, 1919. He was a student in the University of Georgia at Athens when the war between the states broke out, and he and the other members of his class volunteered and went to Charleston to enter the Confederate service. He was with Lee's army for eleven months, and was a musician in the band. His mature years were spent as a farmer and merchant in and around Blackville. He was one of the prominent Baptist laymen, being one of the founders and leaders of the church at Blackville and a deacon. Judson E. Hair married Maggie Capres Felder, who was born near Branchville, South Carolina, in 1850, and is still living at Blackville. When she was a small girl her father died as a result of hardship and exposure endured while a Confederate soldier. The family of Judson E. Hair and wife comprised twelve children, seven of whom are living: Lorena Blanch, who was married to Thomas J. Martin, of Anderson, in 1886; Dr. George F.; Arthur B., a hardware merchant and farmer at Blackville; John Pinckney, deceased; Joseph Koger, deceased; Dr. Isaac Murray Hair, a dentist at Spartanburg; Dr. Harry B., also a dentist practicing at Columbia; Mary E., deceased; Mrs. D. D. Walters, of Columbia; Mrs. Maggie E. Still and Mrs. Abigail Sanders, of Blackville; and Dr. Judson E., deceased. Of the younger generation some mention should be made of the two sons of Mrs. Lorena Blanch Martin, of Anderson. These sons, Haskell Hair and Rhett Felder Martin, are both married, but when the war came on and they were called in the draft they claimed no exemption. The older went overseas as a lieutenant, and saw much of the front line service with the Expeditionary Forces. He was at Chateau Thierry and other historic points on the French front. He is now practicing as an architect at Greenville. The other, Rhett Felder Martin, who is in the coal and wood business at Anderson, was on a transport bound for France when the armistice was signed, and the boat was then turned about and landed him in America. Earl Walters, a son of Mrs. D. D. Walters, of Columbia, was a volunteer at the age of eighteen in the World war and was overseas with the first forces sent to France and remained throughout the war. He was a sergeant and participated in all the important engagements of the Expeditionary Forces. Like all the others he had many narrow escapes from death, but he escaped without a mark.

George Felder Hair, who was born at Blackville October 31, 1870, was liberally educated, attending the common and high schools of his native town, graduated in a business course at Newark, New Jersey, in 1888, and during the following year was employed by the S. S. White Dental Manufacturing Company at Staten Island, New York. This experience aroused his interest in the dental profession and he entered the oldest dental college in the world, the Baltimore College of Dental Surgery, where he was graduated with the class of 1892. Doctor Hair practiced at Anderson for ten years, and since 1901 has been busy in his profession at Bamberg. He has filled all the important offices in the State Dental Society, including the office of president, and is now a member of the State Board of Dental Examiners. He is also affiliated with the National Dental Society. Doctor Hair is a Scottish Rite Mason and Shriner, also a member of the Knights of Pythias, Independent Order of Odd Fellows, Woodmen of the World and Improved Order of Red Men. He has never been active in politics, and is a leader in the Baptist Church at Bamberg, being a deacon and a teacher in its Sunday school. On May 5, 1892, he married Miss Leila E. Boylston, of Blackville. Her father is a veteran ex-Confederate soldier, George W. Boylston, for many years a prominent citizen of Blackville. Doctor and Mrs. Hair have two children. Blanche, the daughter, is the wife of J. J. Cudd, a financier and farmer at Spartanburg. The son, P. Belton Hair, received his A. B. degree from Furman University at Greenville, and while there served as a volunteer for three months in the Students Army Corps until the signing of the armistice. He is now in his third year of the Atlanta Dental College of Georgia, preparing for the profession in which his father and some of his uncles have done such distinguished work.

ARTHUR BYRON HAIR. A Blackville business man and planter of long standing and successful and influential connections, Arthur Byron Hair is a member of the old and prominent Hair family in that section of South Carolina, being a son of Judson E. Hair.

He was born near Blackville June 22, 1872, and acquired a liberal education. After common and private school instruction he entered Furman University at Greenville, and in 1893 graduated from Sullivan & Crichton's Business College at Atlanta, Georgia. While there he became proficient in shorthand, and when soon afterward he entered Clemson College, in addition to his regular studies he acted as secretary to the president, E. B. Craighead. Mr. Hair left Clemson in 1895, and for a year was bookkeeper for a mercantile house at Pelzer.

In 1896, nearly a quarter of a century ago, he engaged in the hardware business at Blackville, and has been in that line ever since, his time being divided between his store and his extensive farming interests. Mr. Hair owns and supervises a twenty-horse farm near Blackville. He does farming on a diversified scale, dividing his fields among cotton, peanuts, corn, and small grains, with some asparagus and garden truck.

So far as his business duties would permit, Mr. Hair has accepted those community responsibilities thrust upon him by his fellow citizens. For ten years he was an alderman of Blackville and has been mayor of the town two terms. He has served as school trustee for ten years and for the past four years has been president of the board. He is a deacon in the Baptist church and for twenty

years has been secretary and treasurer of its Sunday school. Fraternally he is affiliated with the Masonic order.

In 1898 Mr. Hair married Cornelia Ada Rush, daughter of C. C. Rush of Blackville. By this union he is the father of six children, Arthur Byron, Jr., and David Harold, both students of Clemson College, James, John Pinckney, Charles and Elizabeth. Mr. Hair married for his second wife Dot Hamel, of Kershaw, on June 24, 1915. They have one son, George Hamel Hair.

RICHARD LEE ROBINSON, D. D., entered upon his duties as president of the Woman's College of Due West July 1, 1910, just after the college had fitly celebrated its semi-centennial anniversary. Doctor Robinson is now in the tenth year of his presidency, and has guided the affairs of the institution with wisdom and energy to a record of results and achievement that justify the institution in the modern life of South Carolina as fully as at any time in the previous history of the college.

This college, one of the oldest for the higher education of women in South Carolina, has an interesting history. Two ministers of the Associate Reformed Presbyterian Church, Rev. John I. Bonner and Rev. Jonathan Galloway, conceived the idea of a school in which young women should have equal educational advantages with young men. In a conference between these two ministers and Rev. R. C. Grier in 1859 the first plans were proposed, and in the same year a board of trustees was elected. This board took over a girl's academy, previously directed by Miss Elizabeth McQuerns, and the college was opened in the academy building January 8, 1860, with Rev. J. I. Bonner as the first president of the school. The cornerstone of the first college building was laid August 7, 1860, and the first class, five in number, graduated in 1861. Doctor Bonner was president of the Due West Female College, which it was originally called, until his death April 29, 1881. "He lived and worked for it with all the energy of his nature. It was the center of all his plans and the unfailing stimulus to his ceaseless toil. He was one of that noble group of educators who rendered such splendid service to the South after the terrible Civil war, a group containing such names as Robert Calvin Grier, James H. Carlisle, John Maurice Webb, John Bunyan Shearer and William Moffatt Grier." Succeeding Doctor Bonner in the presidency came John P. Kennedy, who had been a professor in the college since 1866 and who remained as president until April, 1887, and faithfully carried on the ideals and plans of his predecessor. For eight years Mrs. L. M. Bonner was principal, and in June, 1895, Rev. C. E. Todd was elected president, to be succeeded by Rev. James Boyce in 1899. Doctor Boyce was president for ten years, and during his administration the ownership and control of the college was transferred from a joint stock company to the Associate Reformed Presbyterian Church. Doctor Boyce died January 27, 1910, and was then succeeded by Dr. Richard Lee Robinson.

"During the first half century of its history the college enrolled over 4,000 students and sent out 1,030 graduates. They are to be found in every Southern state and in some of the Western and Northern states. Some have gone to the mission fields of Egypt, Mexico, Japan, China and India. Wherever they have gone their hands and heads and hearts have been freely given for every good work."

Richard Lee Robinson was born at Lancaster, South Carolina, October 31, 1872, a son of Nathaniel Pressly and Agnes Elizabeth (Lathan) Robinson. He is of Scotch ancestry on both sides. His paternal grandmother was a Craig. The Craigs, Robinsons and Lathans are all well known families of South Carolina. Doctor Robinson received his A. B. degree from Erkine College at Due West in 1892, and was awarded the degree Doctor of Divinity in 1912. For four years after leaving college he was teacher and principal of high schools and in 1899 he graduated from Princeton Theological Seminary. In the same year he was ordained a minister of the Associate Reformed Presbyterian Church, and for the next ten years served as pastor of the church at Camden, Alabama. During 1909-10 he was pastor at his home town of Lancaster, and from that post was called to the presidency of the Woman's College.

December 22, 1903, Doctor Robinson married Miss Anna Marshall, of Millersburg, Kentucky. She is a graduate of the Millersburg College and Dean of the Woman's College of Due West.

JOHN CART from the age of fifteen has been identified with the cotton business and for nearly thirty years has been located at Orangeburg.

Mr. Cart was born at Charleston May 5, 1866, a son of Francis G. and Annie M. (Gray) Cart. His father was both a cotton planter and factor. The son, who was educated in the public schools of Charleston and Porter Military Academy, at the age of fifteen entered business and since 1891 has been a resident of Orangeburg, where he established himself in the cotton buying business. He is a member of the Episcopal Church

In 1891 he married Pauline Gervais Prentiss, daughter of Dr. Christopher J. and Pauline Gervais (Miller) Prentiss. Her father was a prominent Charleston physician. Mr. and Mrs. Cart have three children: Pauline Gervais, wife of Charles Matthews Lindsay, a graduate of The Citadel, who' served as a major during the World war; John, Jr., a graduate of The Citadel at Charleston and served in France as first lieutenant of the Three Hundred and Thirty-fifth Infantry; and Gladys, wife of William Clifton Wallace, who is also a graduate of The Citadel and is a lieutenant in the United States Navy.

RUDOLPH SIEGLING. When in 1919 the Siegling Music House of Charleston celebrated the centennial anniversary of its founding, emphasis was very properly placed upon the artistic quality as well as the commercial feature of the achievement. There are a number of strictly commercial establishments that have existed longer than the Siegling Music House, but this business, established in 1819 at Charleston, not only makes good its claim as the oldest music house in America but also as the center from which have radiated many of the choicest influences affecting the musical and artistic life of the South. It would be a serious omission, indeed, not to include the Siegling Music House as one of the most potent factors in the history of South Carolina culture.

The founder of this business was John Siegling, who was born in Erfurt, Germany, in 1789. His father was an eminent mathematician, who included among his scholars the great scientist Humboldt. More remotely the family ancestry goes back to John Siegling, a Saxon knight, who was one of the six knights chosen to protect Luther in his retirement in the Wartburg.

John Siegling decided at the early age of seventeen to leave his home for another land where he could support himself and relieve his parents. His first experience in the business world was in Paris in 1809. With no assistance save his sterling character and abilities he entered the services of Messrs. Erard Brothers, manufacturers of musical instruments, in their large factory where they employed several hundred workmen. Possessing great mechanical skill and proficiency and having a passion for music, he was soon promoted to a prominent position, and equally as soon acquired the trust and confidence of the Erards, his employers. In 1780 the Erards constructed the first piano, the first instrument of the kind manufactured in France. Later they produced their first double movement harp, and in 1823 crowned their work by producing their model grand piano forte.

John Siegling remained with the Erards for ten years, first in Paris and then in London and Dublin to establish and manage branches of this firm. He always felt that he owed much to the Erards for his success in business life.

It was a choice between two alternatives that led John Siegling to America. When he was in readiness to start for foreign lands he found two vessels sailing, one for St. Petersburg, Russia, and the other for Charleston, South Carolina. The latter obtained his decision as being more promising in its destination. He embarked for Charleston in September, 1819. At that time Charleston was one of the largest cities in commercial importance in the United States. On his arrival he decided to locate and quickly took out papers of naturalization and became an American citizen.

In November, 1819, his first place of business was located on the south side of Broad Street, nearly opposite the Court House—a large brick building which was demolished for postoffice grounds and park. It was next moved to the southeast corner of Broad and King streets, where he established a house for the importation of musical instruments. In 1828 his establishment was moved from King and Broad streets to the southwest corner of Meeting and Horlbecks Alley. From there it was moved in 1830 to the southwest corner of King and Beaufain streets, where the present Siegling Music House stands. At the same time a branch house was established in Havana, Cuba. The original store at that location was destroyed by fire April 27, 1838, but a new and the present building was completed in the fall of 1839.

For nearly half a century John Siegling was the business genius who guided this establishment and not only extended its trade but inspired it with the ideals which have been so carefully cherished by his successors. Hundreds of the grand pianos and other musical instruments that contributed to the culture and gaiety of many of the best homes in the Carolinas in ante-bellum days were bought directly from the Siegling Music House at Charleston.

John Siegling died in 1867, at the age of seventy-eight. He married after coming to Charleston Mary Schneli, whose brother was a mayor of Charleston in the early part of the last century.

Many South Carolinians will recall the fame that attended the career of a daughter of John Siegling, Mary Regina Siegling, who was born in Charleston in 1824 and died at London in December, 1919, just a few days before her ninety-fifth anniversary. She became the wife of Edward Schuman-Leclercq. Mrs. Leclercq had a long and distinguished career as a musician. She sang as a soloist in Ole Bull's concerts when that great musican was a young man, and appeared in concert in New York, Havana and most of the European capitals. She was intellectually gifted as well as a wonderful musician and enjoyed delightful associations and friendships with notable personages over a period of three-quarters of a century both in Europe and America. Her reminiscences in the volume "Memoirs of a Dowager," written by her in later years, is a fascinating account of an artistic career, and has had a host of readers both in America and abroad. The volume is naturally greatly prized by members of the Siegling family.

The successor of John Siegling as head of the Siegling Music House was his second son, Henry Siegling, who was born February 13, 1829. While he never served such a long technical apprenticeship as did his father, he was in every other respect as well qualified as his father to conduct the growing business. He was a man of excellent taste and judgment on artistic matters, and was true to the best mercantile ideals, placing all the resources of his house behind its merchandise, and making the name Siegling synonymous with reliability, confidence, sincerity and honesty. Henry Siegling died May 28, 1905, at the age of seventy-six, and it was his good fortune that the great business conducted by him for nearly forty years be left in the capable hands of his sons. When fourteen years later the centennial of the business was celebrated the management of the Siegling Music House was in the hands of the following executives: Rudolph Siegling, president and treasurer; Henry Siegling, vice president; John A. Siegling, secretary; and J. Forrest Greer, who for over forty years had been with the firm as manager.

To describe the wares that have been handled and sold by the Siegling House during a century would be in the nature of an inventory of musical merchandise and tastes with the striking contrast presented by the historic spinets and harpsichords and the modern talking machines. During this period the Siegling House has figured not only as importers but also as manufacturers of musical instruments and music publishers. John Siegling began importing pianofortes from London as early as 1820, and he personally brought over the first harp

THE NEW YORK
PUBLIC LIBRARY

ever imported to America, and he was also the first importer of band instruments to the United States. During the war between the states under stress of patriotic necessity John Siegling diverted his artisans from their regular duties to the manufacture of drums for the Confederate forces.

A happily worded tribute to this firm is found in an editorial in the columns of the News and Courier of November 19, 1919: "The celebration tonight by the Siegling Music House of the one hundredth anniversary of its establishment in Charleston is an event of general interest. In this new country there are not many business establishments which have survived the vicissitudes of so long a time. The Siegling Music House is the oldest music store in America.

"A history of the Siegling Music House would make entertaining reading, we are sure, and would go far toward reflecting the musical atmosphere and musical development of Charleston and of South Carolina throughout the period of its existence. Its founder, John Siegling, had had his training with Sebastien Erard, the celebrated French manufacturer of musical instruments who was distinguished especially for the improvements he made upon the harp and the pianoforte, and whose reputation was world-wide. The importations which John Siegling made of fine musical instruments of all kinds from Europe, as illustrated in the advertisements which he published in the newspapers of that day, are an index to the wealth and culture that existed in Charleston in 1819 and the years following.

"The Siegling Music House has never been content with the selling of musical instruments. From the time of its establishment it has contributed always to the maintenance and development of sound musical ideals in Charleston, and it has always been one of the city's musical centers. The business methods of its founder won for it the confidence of the community and his successors have so conducted its affairs as to retain that confidence in a worthy manner. The News and Courier joins with music lovers and the public generally in extending its congratulations on the celebration which it holds today and in wishing for it a long career of ever widening usefulness and prosperity."

The late Henry Siegling married Miss Kate Patrick, whose father was Doctor Patrick, a prominent dentist of Charleston, and who had several sons also eminent in that profession.

Mr. Rudolph Siegling, now president and treasurer of the Siegling Music House, was born in Charleston in 1878 and was educated at Nazareth Hall, Nazareth, Pennsylvania. He was only sixteen years of age when he became an employe of the music house, and at first was assigned such duties as carrying bundles. His association has now been continuous for a quarter of a century and since the death of his father in 1905 he has been the active executive head.

Rudolph Siegling married Fannie Odell DeMars, of Orangeburg, South Carolina. Their two children are Rudolph Siegling, Jr., and Charles Casimir Siegling.

Mr. Siegling is a member of the Charleston Chamber of Commerce, and is also vice president of the Retail Merchants Association. He is secretary and treasurer of St. John's Lutheran Sunday School and, as a member of the Masonic fraternity, has served as senior warden of Union Kilwinning Lodge No. 4.

FRANK YOUNG PRESSLY, D. D. Quite recently Doctor Pressly, president of the Erskine Theological Seminary, rounded out forty-five years of continuous and efficient work as a minister, educator and leader in the Associate Reformed Presbyterian Church. In educational and religious circles he is one of the distinguished men of the state.

He was born at Due West in Abbeville County January 18, 1853, son of James Patterson and Mary (Young) Pressly. His grandfather was David Pressly. David Pressly was an uncle of Dr. Ebenezer E. Pressly, first president of Erskine College. James Patterson Pressly was also an educator and a clergyman of the Associate Reformed Presbyterian Church, and was connected in an official and teaching capacity with Erskine College and Erskine Theological Seminary from 1842 until his death in 1877.

Frank Young Pressly grew up from childhood in the atmosphere of the old college town of Due West, was graduated from Erskine College in 1871, following which he took the Seminary course and was licensed by the Second Presbytery September 20, 1873. The following winter he spent in the United Presbyterian Theological Seminary at Allegheny, Pennsylvania, following which he did preaching in the Ohio A. R. P. Presbytery, and in October, 1874, was ordained by the Second Presbytery. From October, 1874, to September, 1876, he was stated supply at Mount Zion Church, Auburn, Missouri, for four years did missionary work in Louisville, Kentucky, and from 1880 to 1886 was pastor of Mount Zion Church. He was pastor at Starkville, Mississippi, from 1886 to 1890 and while there taught in the Agricultural and Mechanical College. Returning to his native state he was stated supply of Abbeville from 1890 to 1894. In 1893 the Synod elected him Professor of Greek and German in Erskine College, and he entered upon the duties of that office a year later. In November, 1899, he accepted the presidency of Erskine College, and filled that office until 1907, since which date he has been president of the Erskine Theological Seminary.

He has held many other offices and performed numerous duties for the advancement of his church, college and home community and people. He was moderator of the Synod in 1893 and at Due West has served as member of the Board of Trustees of the local school district, as intendant of the town, and has handled a heavy burden of administrative and civic duties. The Doctor of Divinity degree was conferred upon him by Westminster College in Pennsylvania in 1896, and the degree of Doctor of Laws by the University of South Carolina in 1903.

CAPT. LIONEL K. LEGGE. While Captain Legge was qualified for and began practice as a lawyer at Charleston six years ago, nearly three years of that time were devoted more or less actively to military duties. Captain Legge went overseas with one of the units of South Carolina troops in 1918, and did not return to this country and resume his practice until the middle of 1919.

Captain Legge was born in Charleston in 1889, son of Claude L. and Elizabeth J. (Hutchinson) Legge, the former a native of Spartanburg County and the latter of Summerville, South Carolina. His father, who was an educator, died at Charleston in 1913.

A younger brother of Captain Legge is Lieut.-Col. Barnwell Rhett Legge, a graduate of The Citadel, and received a commission as second lieutenant in the regular army before the beginning of the war with Germany. He was promoted through successive ranks as first lieutenant, captain, major to lieutenant-colonel and with that rank is still in the army. He was with the Expeditionary Forces in France and for his services overseas won both American and French decorations, and was one of the first southern men to be given the French Legion of Honor.

Lionel K. Legge received his education in Charleston, graduating from Charleston College with the class of 1909. The next three years he taught school in Georgetown and Charleston, South Carolina, after which he studied law in the office of Smythe & Visanka, and was admitted to the bar in 1913. He received his preliminary military training as a member of the old National Guard in Troop 6, later Troop A of the South Carolina Cavalry. Soon after America entered the war with Germany he went to the First Officers Training Camp at Fort Oglethorpe, receiving a commission as captain. Following that he was on duty at Camp Jackson and Camp Sevier, and in the summer of 1918 went overseas with the Eighty-first or Wildcat Division. He served as regimental adjutant and operations officer on the staff of the Three Hundred and Twenty-fourth Regiment, and saw active duty during the last phase of the great Meuse-Argonne campaign. For gallantry and bravery under fire he received his citation and after the armistice remained abroad until the spring of 1919.

Prior to his war service Captain Legge was a member of the successful law firm of Legge & Allan at Charleston, and returned home to resume his relations with the same firm and find his prestige as a lawyer undiminished by his absence. Captain Legge is post commander of Charleston Post of the American Legion. He is a member of the Episcopal Church.

MILLEDGE LORENZO BONHAM STURKEY. A great deal of interesting local history might be told incidental to the career of Mr. Sturkey, the pioneer merchant and leading citizen of the town of McCormick. He and his brothers were the first merchants in that town, and for over thirty-five years his influence has been one of the chief factors in molding the commercial, civic and social standards of the community.

Mr. Sturkey, who recently retired from active business as a merchant, was born only a mile from the present town of McCormick, then in Edgefield County, in 1861, son of Jefferson and Lucy (Self) Sturkey. His great-grandfather Sturkey was a native of Alsace Lorraine, France, and with three brothers came to America in 1766. A number of the descendants of these brothers are still found in Lexington and Orangeburg counties. The family was established in Edgefield County by Jefferson Sturkey.

Mr. M. L. B. Sturkey grew up on a farm, and he owns the land today on which he was born. When he was six years of age the family moved to Lincoln County, Georgia, where he attended school and where he lived until 1882.

The town of McCormick was established in 1882. In that year Mr. Sturkey returned to his native community and the following year established his permanent home at McCormick. Associated with his brothers he engaged in business. They were the pioneer merchants, and now after more than a third of a century has passed it is especially interesting to note that they were the dominant influence whereby McCormick was incorporated as a "dry" town, being the first village incorporation to prohibit the sale of liquor in South Carolina. It was through the influence of the same men that Edgefield County was freed from the evils of the old dispensary saloons.

In 1887 M. L. B. Sturkey engaged in business for himself, and until 1918 he had a large trade over an extensive territory in hardware, groceries, farm implements, wagons and buggies and other supplies. Though he has not been a merchant since August, 1918, he is still a planter and cotton buyer.

Mr. Sturkey, as this record faintly indicates, is a man of progressive character, of advanced and modern thought, and wherever possible has lent his influence to securing practical results in behalf of national and local welfare. His prohibition aim and attitude is a matter of record, and he has long been an advocate of woman's suffrage. He reared and educated his children for practical and serious purposes of life.

Mr. Sturkey is one of the few citizens of the present McCormick County who can claim an active share in the first agitation for the creation of that new county. He was allied with the movement nearly a quarter of a century ago. He was one of the two delegates that went to the Constitutional Convention at Columbia in 1895 to present the wisdom of creating a new county from portions of old Edgefield, Abbeville and Greenwood counties. Nothing came of the movement at that time, but Mr. Sturkey did not neglect opportunities to keep the subject alive during the twenty years that followed until the new county was finally created in 1916.

Mr. Sturkey has been four times married. There were no children by his first two wives, who were sisters, Fannie and Mary Willingham, of Lincoln County, Georgia. His third wife was Miss Annie Martin, and she was the mother of four daughters: Mary F., Marian E., Bertha C. and Wessie. By his present wife, Miss Lucy Anderson, daughter of P. H. Anderson, of Waterloo, South Carolina, Mr. Sturkey has three children: Lucy Harriet, M. L. B., Jr., and Annie Laurie. Mr. Sturkey would never consent to accept office, although tendered him many times.

Milledge. L. B. Sturbuy

JULIAN BOOTH SALLEY. A lawyer at Aiken and a citizen whose career has been attended both with material prosperity and dignified service, Julian Booth Salley is a member of the old and prominent Salley family which has been in South Carolina for upwards of two centuries.

He was born in Orangeburg County March 23, 1878, near the Town of Salley in Aiken County. His ancestor Henry Salley settled in South Carolina in 1735. A son of this pioneer was John Salley, who commanded a company in the Revolutionary war. Other members of the family have been prominent in the professions, as planters and public officials.

The father of Julian Booth Salley was Capt. Henry H. Salley, who was born near the Town of Salley, and served all through the war between the states as captain of Company I of the Twenty-second Regiment of Infantry. He was wounded seven times, and for many years suffered from these wounds, but lived until 1893. He also took a prominent part in the campaign for the restoration of white rule in the reconstruction era. His life was spent as a planter. Captain Salley married Margaret Elizabeth Corley, who is still living at the old homestead at Salley, near which place she was born. Her people were of English descent and of Revolutionary stock.

Julian Booth Salley was educated in The Citadel at Charleston, took his law course in the University of South Carolina in 1903, and soon afterward had achieved his first successes as a young lawyer at Aiken. He has built up a large general law practice, which he still carries on. He is also a director of the Bank of Western Carolina and a director of the Real Estate Fidelity Company.

Mr. Salley served as mayor of Aiken from 1904 to 1910, for three successive terms, and has been a delegate to numerous county and state conventions of the democratic party.

His professional and other interests were completely subordinated during the period of the World war to the various services imposed upon him in his community. He was county chairman of the registrars, registering men under the draft and organizing the country districts, was also county chairman of the Exemption Board, was county chairman for the Thrift Stamp campaign and a leader in all the Liberty Loan and Red Cross drives. The governor also appointed him an examiner of county boards of exemption. Just before the armistice Mr. Salley registered for the draft, and waived exemption on any ground.

December 20, 1906, Mr. Salley married Eulalie Chafee, a native of Aiken and a daughter of the late G. K. Chafee. She is of English and French ancestry and of colonial and revolutionary stock. They have two children, Eulalie and Julian, Jr., both attending school at Aiken.

DANIEL ALFRED JACKSON BELL, M. D. Doctor Bell has a record of thirty years of honest, self-denying and skilful professional work, divided between two communities, Parksville, where he had his home for nearly a quarter of a century, and for the past six years at McCormick, county seat of McCormick County.

Doctor Bell has been a valuable man outside of his profession to his present community. He was one of the men who worked earnestly to bring about the establishment of the present county of McCormick. He employed his ability as a writer to promote publicity work through various newspapers of the state in behalf of the organization of the new county. He is author of a number of articles on the history of those sections of Edgefield, Abbeville and Greenwood counties that are now comprised in the new county of McCormick.

Doctor Bell was born at Pleasant Lane in Edgefield County in 1860, a son of J. Milton and Martha (Faulkner) Bell. His great-grandfather, John Bell, a native of Scotland, on coming to America settled in Pennsylvania and died there. The doctor's grandfather, Isaac Bell, subsequently moved to Edgefield County.

Doctor Bell spent his early life on a farm. His youth coincided with the period in which South Carolina and the entire South were suffering from the effects of the war, and the resources of his family did not avail him beyond the meager opportunities of the common country schools. He spent several years teaching in order to earn money for his medical education. He was twenty-nine years of age and had married when he completed his medical course. He graduated from the University of Georgia at Augusta in 1889, and the same year began practice at Parksville, where he lived for twenty-four years. In 1913 he moved to McCormick, and three years later had the satisfaction of seeing that town established as the county seat of McCormick County. While at Parksville he served as intendant or mayor and was a member of the town council for eighteen years. Doctor Bell has also been in the drug business at McCormick. During the war he was county food administrator and member of the Volunteer Medical Reserve Corps.

Doctor Bell is a Baptist, having joined the old Mountain Creek Baptist Church when seventeen years old. He was soon elected superintendent of its Sunday school, since which time he has been continuously in the work either as superintendent or teacher. His family were religiously inclined, his grandfather, Isaac Bell, having only four grandsons by the name of Bell, three of whom were deacons in the Baptist Church and the fourth a distinguished Baptist preacher. Doctor Bell was made a deacon in his twenty-eighth year, and has served in the several communities in which he has lived, always moving his membership to the nearest Baptist Church. He is now a leader in the McCormick Baptist Church, having contributed liberally to the new fifty thousand dollar church building in process of erection.

Doctor Bell married Miss Mamie Middleton, of Edgefield County. They have an interesting family of six children: John Milton; Nettie, wife of T. R. Cartledge; Addie, wife of Lieut. James Parks; Sergt. Dan A. Bell, who was in the Medical Reserve Corps; Eddie Bell, who was also with the Expeditionary Forces for several months; and Miss Martha Bell, who graduated from the Woman's College at Due West in 1920. Doctor Bell has been a strong prohibitionist all his life, and worked for the success of its becoming a law.

WILLIAM MARION STEINMEYER. The County of Beaufort numbers among its citizens many skillful physicians, lawyers of state repute, well-known manufacturers and business men of more than local reputation. While proud of them, she is not lacking in others who have achieved distinction in callings requiring intellectual abilities of a high order. Among the latter William M. Steinmeyer, of Beaufort, the popular and efficient superintendent of education, occupies a deservedly conspicuous place. No one is more entitled to the thoughtful consideration of a free and enlightened people than he who shapes and directs the minds of the young, adds to the value of their intellectual treasures and moulds their characters. This is pre-eminently the mission of the faithful and conscientious teacher, and to such noble work is the life of the subject of this review devoted.

William Marion Steinmeyer was born in Berkeley (now Dorchester) County, South Carolina, on February 16, 1870, and is the fifth in order of birth of the eleven children born to John Henry and Matilda (Evans) Steinmeyer. The father was born in Charleston and spent his life there, being prominently identified with large business interests. He was president of the Steinmeyer Lumber Company of Charleston, and his father, who bore the same name, had also been identified with the lumber trade in Charleston, his native place. His father, George W. Steinmeyer, the great-grandfather of the subject of this sketch, was a native of Wurtemberg, Germany, and who on immigrating to the United States made his first location in Pennsylvania, afterwards locating in Charleston, South Carolina, with which city the family has been identified ever since. The subject's mother was a daughter of J. W. Evans, who moved from Baltimore, Maryland, to Charleston, where the daughter was born, her birth occurring in the Marine Hospital, of which her father was at that time superintendent. John H. Steinmeyer was in the Confederate army during the Civil war, being captain of Company A, Twenty-fourth Regiment, South Carolina Infantry, and his death occurred at the age of sixty-nine years. His wife died when fifty-nine years old. Of their eleven children, seven grew to maturity.

William H. Steinmeyer secured his education in his native city, attending the common schools, the high school and The Citadel. He then went to Baltimore, where he took a thorough course in dentistry, after which he located at Beaufort, where he has ever since been actively engaged in the practice of his profession. He is a most excellent workman, careful and honest, and enjoys a high reputation as a professional man, nearly twenty years of successful practice having established him in the esteem of the people. Mr. Steinmeyer has always evinced the highest interest in educational matters, giving hearty support to everything calculated to benefit the schools in any way. His interest and ability were recognized when, in 1914, he was made superintendent of education, which position he is still filling to the entire satisfaction of the people of his county.

In 1903 Mr. Steinmeyer was married to Alma Devereaux Gantt, the daughter of Richard P. and Ella (Mackay) Gantt, of Barnwell County, and they have become the parents of six children, namely: Ella Rachel, John Henry, Maud Douglas, William Marion, Jr., Alma G. and Marie Therese.

Fraternally Mr. Steinmeyer is a member of the Ancient Free and Accepted Masons, and has been honored by being elected six times as master of the lodge in Beaufort. He is also high priest of the Chapter of Royal Arch Masons. He also holds membership in the Knights of Pythias and the Woodmen of the World. His religious affiliation is with the Presbyterian Church, of which he is an elder. Owing to his probity of character, his genuine worth and genial disposition, he has gained a position in his community as one of the earnest men whose depth of character and strict adherence to principle has called forth the admiration of his contemporaries.

HON. FRANK COOK ROBINSON was the first state senator representing the new County of McCormick, and was a member of the Lower House of the Legislature and had charge of the bill providing for the organization of that county from old Abbeville. Mr. Robinson for many years has been a prominent business man and banker at the town of McCormick.

He was born October 2, 1870, at the old Robinson homestead three miles from McCormick, in what was then Abbeville, now McCormick, County. His parents were Captain R. J. and Frances (Cook) Robinson. His grandfather was John Robinson, and his great-grandfather was of Scotch ancestry and came from the north of Ireland and settled on Long Cane in Abbeville County about 1800. Capt. R. J. Robinson was born and lived practically all his life at the plantation three miles from McCormick. He went from Abbeville County in the army and rose to the rank of captain in the Confederate forces. His wife, Frances Cook, lived on an adjoining plantation.

Frank Cook Robinson grew up on the home farm, graduated from Furman University in 1902, and for two years was principal of the graded schools at McCormick. For ten years he was in the railway mail service, toward the end being on the Charleston & Western Carolina Railway.

Mr. Robinson organized the Farmers Bank at McCormick in 1907. This institution has had a remarkable growth and enjoys great prosperity in keeping with the fortunate district in which it is located. Its progress has been especially rapid since the organization of McCormick County in 1916. The bank has a capital stock of forty thousand dollars, surplus and undivided profits of twenty-five thousand dollars, deposits of three hundred fifty thousand dollars, and aggregate resources of approximately half a million dollars. Its resources are adequate to meet the financial demands and needs of the community, and its officers and directors are men of standing in the business community and have carefully safeguarded and promoted all legitimate enterprises in McCormick County. The

president of the bank is J. B. Harmon, and Mr. Robinson has held the post of cashier for a number of years.

Mr. Robinson was a member of the House of Representatives from Abbeville County in 1913-16, and worked in close co-operation with other citizens from his community in bringing about the organization of McCormick County. He was elected the first senator from the new county in 1916, serving during the sessions of 1917-18. Mr. Robinson was a 1920 delegate to the National Democratic Convention in San Francisco, and in that year was re-elected to the State Senate. He was chairman of the committee on railroads and internal improvements and a member of the finance committee.

During the war Mr. Robinson gave much of his time to war work. He was chairman of the local draft board, county chairman for the War Savings Stamps campaign, and was chairman for the town of McCormick in all of the five Liberty Loan Campaigns.

Mr. Robinson married Miss Annie P. Talbert, member of an old and honored family of Abbeville and McCormick counties. They have a daughter, Margaret, born in September, 1918.

HENRY GRIGGS BURCKMYER. That the plenitude of satiety is seldom attained in the affairs of life is to be considered a most beneficial deprivation, for where ambition is satisfied and every ultimate end realized, if such be possible, apathy must follow. Effort would cease, accomplishment be prostrate and creative talent waste its energies in inactivity. The men who have pushed forward the wheels of progress have been those to whom satisfaction lies ever in the future, who have labored continuously, always finding in each transition stage an incentive for further effort. Henry G. Burckmyer, merchant and farmer of Port Royal and Beaufort, is one whose well directed efforts have gained for him a position of desired prominence in the various circles in which he moves, and his energy and enterprise have been crowned with success, and, having ever had the interests of his county at heart and sought to promote them in every way possible, he has well earned a place along with his enterprising fellow citizens in a permanent history of his locality.

Henry G. Burckmyer was born in Blackville, South Carolina, on February 9, 1870, and is the second in the order of birth of nine children born to John A. and Anna (Hagood) Burckmyer. The family is originally German, but has been established in America for several generations. John A. Burckmyer was a native of Charleston, South Carolina, where he was reared and where he engaged in mercantile business. During the Civil war he was in the custom house and then, after the conclusion of that struggle, he again engaged in business. Eventually he moved to Blackville, this state, where he spent the rest of his days. He was twice married, first to a Miss Davant, to which union seven children were born. His second union, which was with Anna Hagood, was blessed with nine children.

Henry G. Burckmyer was reared in Blackville and secured his education in the common schools. He remained in his native town until 1902, when he came to Port Royal and engaged in the mercantile business, which has occupied his attention continuously since that time. He has a well stocked store and commands a very satisfactory trade from the representative people of his community. In addition to his mercantile interests he also gives considerable attention to truck farming, being the owner of two plantations, with an aggregate acreage of about five hundred acres. In all his enterprises he has been very successful and enjoys an excellent reputation as an enterprising and progressive man. He maintains his home in Beaufort, where he has a comfortable and attractive residence.

In 1902 Mr. Burckmyer was married to Virginia Grimsley, the daughter of Judge D. A. Grimsley, of Culpeper, Virginia. To this union have been born three children, namely: Margaret Sloyd, Virginia Grimsley and Henry Griggs, the latter dying in infancy.

Fraternally Mr. Burckmyer is a member of the Ancient Free Masons. He is a man of splendid personal qualities, and is proud of the fact that his forefathers fought on the side of the colonies in the Revolutionary war, and some of them afterward became early settlers of South Carolina, bearing their full share of the burden of the new community.

JAMES EDWARD BRITT is the recognized dean and veteran in the business life of the town of McCormick, which gained increased distinction as the county seat of the newly organized McCormick County. Mr. Britt has been an influential man there for over a quarter of a century and is active vice president of the oldest bank in the town and the first banking organization in what is now McCormick County.

He also belongs to a prominent and old time family of this section of South Carolina. He was born in 1872, six miles from the present town of McCormick, in what was then Abbeville, but now McCormick County. His parents were Charles and Mary (Foster) Britt. His great-grandfather was Charles Britt, a noted character in the early days of Abbeville district. When a child in 1760 he came with his mother and other members of the family from England and settled in Abbeville district in the Buffalo neighborhood on Long Cane Creek. Charles Britt at the age of sixteen ran away from home and joined the Continental forces in fighting the British in South Carolina. After the Revolution he married a Miss Longelle, who represented a strain of French Huguenot ancestry, her people having settled at Bordeaux in Abbeville County.

James Edward Britt is a grandson of Jacob Britt. His father, Charles Britt, like his ancestor of Revolutionary fame, was also sixteen years of age when he went to war, joining the Confederate army. James E. Britt grew up in the country, attending local schools and Furman University, and in 1892 engaged in merchandising at McCormick. In 1901 he became one of the founders of the Bank of McCormick, served for a number of years as its cashier and is now its active vice president. The oldest bank in the town, it is also one of unsurpassed record as to integrity and ability of management and resources. The bank has a capital stock of sixty-eight thousand dollars, surplus and undivided profits of fifty-seven thousand dollars, and has been the bulwark of nearly every commercial and many of the individual careers in and around McCormick.

Mr. Britt was one of the leading members of the local committee promoting the movement for the organization of the new county of McCormick, and was especially influential in securing the location of the county seat at the town of McCormick. Mr. Britt owns a large amount of land and is busily engaged in planting. He married Janie Belle Kennedy. Their four children are named Edward, Frances, Mary Elizabeth and William Lewis.

JAMES B. HEYWARD entered upon his career as a Charleston lawyer in 1912, and as a member of the firm McMillan & Heyward is busied with the interests of a large clientage and already has secured a position as a skillful and effective counselor.

Mr. Heyward was born in McPhersonville, South Carolina, May 29, 1891, a son of Robert B. and Florida M. (Hutson) Heyward. His father was a native of South Carolina, for many years was a rice planter and died December 16, 1918. The Heyward family is of English descent and has been located in and about Charleston since about 1680. In the maternal line Mr. Heyward is a grandson of Dr. Thomas W. Hutson, and the Hutson family came from England to South Carolina about 1720. Robert B. Heyward was twice married. His first wife was Laura Porcher, who left him one daughter, Caroline H., now the widow of E. E. Douglas and living at Greenville, South Carolina. By his second marriage there were two children, Augusta H., wife of Edward B. Sinkler, of Savannah, Georgia, and James B. Heyward.

James B. Heyward was educated in Porter's Military School at Charleston, graduating in 1907, and received his Bachelor of Science degree from the University of South Carolina in 1911. He read law in the office of Joseph B. Barnwell, was admitted to the bar in December, 1912, and for two years did law work in the office of William Henry Parker. On January 1, 1915, he formed his present partnership with Mr. Thomas S. McMillan.

Mr. Heyward is a member of the Knights of Pythias, being a past chancellor, is also a Mason, belongs to the Kappa Alpha fraternity of the University of South Carolina, and is a member of the St. Cecilia Club.

GIOVANNI SOTTILE came from Italy to Charleston, South Carolina, as a young man of sterling character, excellent scholastic attainments and purposeful ambition. He encountered a full quota of adverse conditions and proved himself a master of the situation which confronted him in the land of his adoption. He achieved eventually the material success and the high personal standing which the United States ever offers to energy, ability and determination, and he became not only a representative business man of Charleston but also served with distinction as Italian consular agent in this city, a position to which he was appointed by the Italian government, May 31, 1899, and of which he continued the incumbent until his death, which occurred June 28, 1913. Of his service in this office the following estimate has been given: "He did much to strengthen the cordial relations between the two governments and to aid those of his countrymen who, like himself, had sought the opportunities afforded in America. In just appreciation and recognition of his services the Italian government conferred upon him an order of knighthood, with the title of chevalier."

Giovanni Sottile was born at Gangi, Italy, June 29, 1866, and was a son of Salvatore and Rosina (Albergamo) Sottile, the family of which he was a scion having been one of special distinction in connection with educational affairs in Italy for many years. Salvatore Sottile was numbered among the patriotic sons of Italy who served with Garibaldi in the historic struggle for liberty in 1870. Giovanni Sottile was a studious youth, and his early educational discipline was largely supervised and directed by one of his aunts, a talented woman who held the position of superintendent of the schools of Gangi. Later he continued his studies in the college at Palermo, where he became specially proficient in mathematics. After leaving school he served four years in the Italian army, in which, by reason of his ability and superior education, he was promoted and assigned to responsible service in the accounting department. After leaving military service Mr. Sottile, moved by worthy ambition, determined to seek the superior advantages which he believed were to be found in the United States. He arrived in New York City in the autumn of 1889, and forthwith sought employment. At that time there was an insistent demand for workmen in the phosphate mines in South Carolina, and groups of men were being sent almost daily from the national metropolis to engage in this work. A stranger in a strange land, with only a superficial knowledge of actual conditions, it is not strange that the young Italian immigrant soon found himself en route to South Carolina, after having accepted a seemingly attractive offer to take the position of accountant in one of the phosphate camps, not far distant from Charleston. Of the deplorable conditions, the brutal treatment of the laborers, most of whom, like Mr. Sottile, had been imposed upon by the crafty "padrones," it is not necessary to enlarge, but it may be stated that the actual experience and the knowledge gained during his period of service in the phosphate camp formed the basis of the great service which he was later enabled to render his countrymen in America.

After a short sojourn, Mr. Sottile left the uncongenial phosphate camp and made his way, on foot, to Charleston. His personality gained him stanch friends in the city, and among those who manifested kindly interest in the young stranger was the wife of Commander Hitchcock, who was in charge of the lighthouse service in this district. Mrs. Hitchcock, recognizing his talent and sterling character, aided him in securing employment as an instructor in the Latin and Italian languages. He soon became established in Charleston, and it was not long before he was joined by his four brothers, of whom more specific mention will be made in a later paragraph and who came to America upon his ad-

vice. It is not necessary in this brief review to enter into details concerning the achievement and rise of Mr. Sottile as one of the valued citizens and representative business men of Charleston, where the Giovanni Sottile & Brothers Company became an important factor in connection with commercial progress.

In 1896 Mr. Sottile returned to Italy, where was solemnized his marriage to Miss Carmela Restivo, a friend of his childhood days in Gangi, where she likewise was born and reared. Mr. and Mrs. Sottile became the parents of four children, Salvatore, Rosina, Giovanni and Carmelina, all of whom were born in Charleston, where they remained with their widowed mother.

Of the four brothers, mentioned above, Nicholas Sottile came to Charleston in 1890. He is president of the company conducting a leading china and glass emporium on King Street, and is actively associated with other business activities, especially in the handling of real estate and the incidental furtherance of the development of Charleston. Santo Sottile, who arrived in Charleston in 1895, is president of the Sottile Cadillac Company of Charleston, where he also has other important interests. Albert Sottile was but fourteen years old when he came to this city in 1891, and he is now president and treasurer of the Pastime Amusement Company. He is one of the prominent theater owners and managers of the south, and he built and now operates the Victory, the Princess and the Garden theaters in Charleston. James Sottile came to Charleston in 1900, and, like his brothers, has here achieved marked success. He is president of the Charleston-Isle of Palms Traction Company; is vice-president and general manager of the Charleston Hotel Company, and is interested in other representative enterprises in his home city.

PAUL M. MACMILLAN had practiced law only four years when he was elevated to the bench as judge of the Civil and Criminal Court of Charleston, and has been doing such effective work in that position that his services have been retained by the urgent voice of opinion, though probably at the sacrifice of his personal and financial interests.

Judge Macmillan, who was born in Charleston, March 5, 1884, a son of Oswald and Emily Mary (Smith) Macmillan. His father was a native of Scotland, coming to South Carolina direct from his native land. For many years he has been an active business man of Charleston. Emily Mary Smith was a native of this city and a daughter of Thomas Henry Smith. The parents had four children, two sons and two daughters, Judge Macmillan being the youngest.

He graduated from high school in 1900 and finished his literary education in the College of Charleston, where he graduated A. B. in 1903 and with the Master of Arts degree in 1904. He studied law in the University of the South, receiving his legal diploma in 1906. He forthwith engaged in practice at Charleston, and in 1910 was elected to his present office.

He is a member of the Knights of Pythias, the First Presbyterian Church and in 1918 was the commodore of the Carolina Yacht Club. In 1917 he married St. Clair Walker, a daughter of B. Wilson Walker.

HON. SAMUEL HODGES McGHEE. A lawyer and banker, Mr. McGhee has been one of the honored and useful residents of Greenwood all of his life and enjoys a well earned and justified leadership in local affairs.

He was born in Cokesbury, Abbeville County, in 1873, son of W. Z. and Sophronia R. (Hodges) McGhee. His paternal ancestor Michael McGhee came from Ireland, and was a North Carolina soldier in the war for American independence, after which he settled in Abbeville County, South Carolina. The Hodges family has also lived in Abbeville County for a number of generations.

Samuel McGhee was the son of a merchant, and reverses which overtook his father a short time before his death made the matter of securing a liberal education one of great difficulty to the son. But in intervals of other employment he received all those advantages that are an index to a man of sound culture. He attended the Cokesbury Conference School, the Greenwood High School, and in 1895 graduated with the A. B. degree from Wofford College and in 1896 received his Master of Arts degree from the same institution. He taught school in Marion County from 1895 until 1899. The following three years he was editor of the Greenwood Index. In the meantime, in 1898, he had been admitted to the bar, and has been in active and regular practice since 1902, though his professional work has been varied with many other business duties. He was elected president of the First National Bank of Greenwood in 1903 upon its organization. He is also president of the Panola Cotton Mills and the Bauna Mills.

His father was a delegate to the National Convention of the democratic party in 1884 when Cleveland was first nominated. The son also served as a delegate to the National Conventions of 1900 and 1904, and Mr. McGhee is a member of the State Senate, having been elected to that office in 1917. He is a Knight Templar Mason and Shriner, a Knight of Pythias, and in former years was affiliated with the gold standard wing of the democratic party. He is a member of the Methodist Episcopal Church, South.

Mr. McGhee married in 1906 Miss Laurie Harrall, of Bennettsville, South Carolina.

SIMEON HYDE is a Charleston lawyer whose name has been identified prominently with various law partnerships and with much of the important litigation in the courts of the city and state for forty years.

He was born at Charleston October 11, 1856. His father, Simeon Hyde, was of an old Connecticut family, but came to South Carolina when a young man. His mother was Ann Eliza Tupper, daughter of Tristram Tupper, for many years a prominent Charleston business man.

Simeon Hyde received his preparatory education in Charleston, and entered Charleston College in 1871, graduating in 1875. He studied law in the office of Pressley, Lord & Inglesby, a law firm of the highest standing, and that early association Mr.

Hyde has always regarded as a chief contributing cause to his success. He was admitted to practice in November, 1877, and was busy building up an individual clientage until 1883, when he became junior partner of the firm of Lord & Hyde. After several years he again resumed individual practice. In 1906 he became a member of the firm Mordecai, Gadsden, Rutledge & Hagood, which after the retirement of Mr. Hagood became Mordecai, Gadsden & Rutledge. He was with this firm until August 1, 1917, when he retired. The firm of Mordecai, Gadsden & Rutledge was dissolved in October, 1918, and at that time Mr. Hyde became associated with Mr. Benjamin H. Rutledge in the firm of Rutledge & Hyde. In January, 1920, Mr. G. N. Mann was admitted to partnership and the firm name changed to Rutledge, Hyde & Mann. They handle a general law practice and are also Division Counsel in Charleston of the Atlantic Coast Line Railroad Company, and represent a number of other corporations and extensive business interests.

Mr. Hyde is also known to the profession as one of the authors of "Chisolm and Hyde Index—Digest of South Carolina Reports," published in 1882. He was a member of the Charleston Delegation in the South Carolina House of Representatives from 1886 to 1888. For many years he was prominent in the State Militia, serving as a commissioned officer, and retiring with the rank of captain in 1888. In 1917, when United States entered the European war, he was commissioned captain of Company B, First Regiment, South Carolina Reserve Militia, established by the Legislature as a military force within the state while the National Guard and other state troops were enrolled in the National Army. Mr. Hyde was for many years in charge of the Mission work of The Citadel Square Baptist Church in Charleston and is a deacon of that church.

THOMAS EMMETTE THROWER was born at Summerville, Georgia, in 1880, and was reared and educated in Atlanta schools, growing up in the magnetic atmosphere of that great and rich southern metropolis. This environment did much to improve his native talents as a commercial salesman. He was on the road selling goods at the age of seventeen. Few young men in the South have a finer record in their profession than Mr. Thrower.

Mr. Thrower, whose parents were O. A. and Fannie (McDaniel) Thrower of Atlanta, enlisted his talents, enthusiasm and service in behalf of the automobile industry about the time motor cars achieved real popularity and recognition in the South. He has been one of the most prominent factors in extending the industry over the southeastern states. Several years ago he located at Columbia, where he owns and manages the Thrower Automotive Company. This company distributes the Premier car in North and South Carolina, Georgia and Florida, with a branch at Atlanta, Georgia and Jacksonville, Florida, and also are southern distributors for the Allen and Skelton cars.

He has been one of the most prominent and active members of the Columbia Automotive Trade Association and one of the leaders in the formation of the South Carolina Automotive Trades Association. As chairman of the Show Committee of this association he has charge of, and was responsible for those special features of the Automobile Show in Columbia in March, 1918, that caused competent critics to pronounce that the best exposition of its kind ever held in the capital city.

Having been so successful in his venture, he was selected in 1920 as general chairman of all committees of the Great Spring Exposition which was held in Columbia in March, the greatest exposition of its kind ever attempted in the United States.

Mr. Thrower has enlisted his enthusiasm and support for many other movements in his home city and state, being the originator of the Minute Men of Columbia, a unique organization having for its members the leaders of all organizations in the city. This movement rejuvenated Columbia and brought about such a spirit of co-operation and civic activity as had never been experienced before resulting in a greater Columbia. He is an advocate of good roads and has exerted a very helpful influence in retaining Columbia's prestige as one of the leading automobile centers in the South.

Mr. Thrower married Miss Luta Beard of Troy, Alabama. They have three children: Frances, Emmett and Nell.

J. WATIES WARING. A lawyer with a large practice, many influential social and civic connections, J. Waties Waring has gained his professional success in the same city where he was born.

A native of Charleston, born July 27, 1880, he is a son of Edward P. and Anna (Waties) Waring, who were also natives of Charleston. His father spent his life at Charleston, and was a railroad man. The grandfather, Thomas R. Waring, was a native of the same city and for a number of years was cashier of the Bank of the State of South Carolina. The Warings came to South Carolina direct from England.

J. Waties Waring was the youngest in a family of three sons and one daughter. The other sons are Thomas R. and E. P., while the daughter is Margaret, wife of Wilson G. Harvey.

Mr. Waring graduated in 1900 from the College of Charleston, and prepared for the bar in the office of Bryan & Bryan. He was admitted to practice in 1901, and since that time his name has been connected with an increasing volume of the legal business of the city. For about five years he was a member of the firm Von Kolnitz & Waring. The firm now is Waring & Brockinton.

Mr. Waring is the present assistant United States district attorney for South Carolina, appointed to that office in 1914. He is a member of the Carolina Yacht Club, South Carolina Society, was for several years a member and captain of the Charleston Light Dragoons, is a member of the Alpha Tau Omega college fraternity, is a past master of the Masonic Lodge, a member of the Knights of Pythias and belongs to various other social organizations. He has been quite active in democratic politics, though never as an aspirant for honors on his own account.

October 30, 1913, Mr. Waring married Anne S.

Gammell, a daughter of William Gammell. They have one daughter, Anne Gammell Waring.

JOHN HODGES DAVID, M. D. In the present day of keen competition in all lines of industry, success calls for the possession of superlative ability. Whether in the professions, in productive lines, in work of a promotive character, or in the great markets of the world, keen strife is invariably found; and when the fight is made with vigor, nerve and discernment, when success is acquired, half the compensation other than financial independence is derived from the satisfaction of having come a victor from a conflict worthy of one's steel. Of the men of Dillon County who have fought a worthy fight and who have been led to but further achievements by the keenness of the fray, is Dr. John Hodges David, formerly a leading and successful medical practitioner, but of more recent years largely engaged in business as a planter in the vicinity of Dillon.

Doctor David was born at Bennettsville; South Carolina, July 23, 1856, a son of Dr. William J. and Rebecca (Spears) David. The original ancestor of the David family in America was one Owen David, who emigrated from Wales to this country about 1776 and settled in South Carolina, where, in Marlboro County, John Hodges David, the grandfather of Doctor David, was born and passed his entire life as a farmer and planter. In that county also was born Dr. William J. David, who was engaged in the practice of medicine at Bennettsville at the time of the outbreak of the war between the states, in which he served four years as a surgeon in the army of the Confederacy. Following the close of that struggle, he established himself to practice at Bennettsville, Marlboro County, and there passed the remaining years of his life. He was a man who was highly respected and esteemed both in his profession and in social circles, and was a man of influence and worth in his community. He married Rebecca Spears, daughter of James Spears of Marlboro County, South Carolina, and of their eight children, Dr. John H. was the first born.

John Hodges David attended the public school at Bennettsville and further prepared himself at Ansonville, North Carolina, following which he enrolled as a student at the Medical College of South Carolina, at Charleston. He was graduated from that institution with the class of 1879 and his cherished medical degree of Doctor of Medicine, and at once embarked in practice at Little Rock, where he remained ten years. Although he had built up a large and lucrative practice and was a successful physician and surgeon, his various business interests had become so heavy and important as to need his undivided attention, and he accordingly gave up his practice and came to Dillon, where he established himself in the midst of business affairs and began to be at once an influencing factor in the enterprises that were rapidly moving this community toward prestige. He was the main actor in the building of a cotton seed oil mill at Dillon and was president of the company which operated it, and subsequently became manager for the company when it was sold to the Southern Cotton Oil Company. After a number of years of successful connection with this and other enterprises, in 1916 he moved from Dillon to a farm two miles south of the city, where he has over 1,000 acres under cultivation, this land being devoted to cotton, tobacco and corn. He is known as one of the successful and thoroughly informed planters of his community, and his business affairs are in a decidedly prosperous condition owing to his excellent management, while his standing in business circles is of the highest, due to the recognition by his associates of his sterling integrity and honesty of purpose.

Doctor David was married in 1879 to Miss Arletta Ione Manning, a sister of Senator J. H. Manning, a sketch of whose career will be found on another page of this work, and to this union there have been born five daughters and one son: Anna, Edna, Mrs. H. E. Dixon, whose husband is in partnership with her father, Helen and Alice, and Lieut. John H., who met a hero's death on a battlefield in Flanders, as the first officer from South Carolina killed in action, and who now lies buried at Theaucourt, St. Mihiel, American Cemetery, in France. Doctor David is a thirty-second degree Scottish Rite Mason and has numerous business, social and civic connections. He was elected from the Sixth Congressional District of South Carolina a delegate to the Democratic National Convention at San Francisco which he attended.

WILLIAM CAPERS MILLER. It is nearly forty years since W. C. Miller was admitted to the bar and began practice at Charleston. During that time his name has been associated with some of the most eminent lawyers of South Carolina and the largest law firms, and the firm of which he is senior member today has a standing and clientage probably not exceeded by any other organization of legal talent in the state.

Mr. Miller was born in Georgetown, South Carolina, February 25, 1858. His great-grandfather, John Miller, was of Pennsylvania Dutch origin and came from Pennsylvania to South Carolina in pioneer days. His grandfather, John C. Miller, was a native of Charleston. Mr. Miller's father, Dr. William C. Miller, was a native of Charleston but practiced medicine in Georgetown, South Carolina, for a number of years and died at the early age of thirty-seven. His mother was Elizabeth M. Cuttino, of a French Huguenot family that came to South Carolina in colonial times. He has one sister, Mary C., unmarried and living in Charleston.

He was reared and educated in Charleston and as a boy attended the Sachtleben School, one of the most noted preparatory schools of the South forty or fifty years ago. After graduating there he entered Furman University at Greenville, later the University of Virginia, and leaving college in 1879 applied himself to the study of law at Charleston until admitted to the bar in the fall of 1881. He was first associated in practice with Mr. Charles Inglesby. Later he was associated with George M. Trenholm and R. G. Rhett, under the name Trenholm, Rhett & Miller. Subsequently he became senior member of the firm Miller & Whaley, which by subsequent changes became Miller, Whaley, Bissell & Miller then Miller & Miller, and the present partnership is Miller, Huger, Wilber & Miller.

Mr. Miller is attorney for many prominent business firms and corporations, including banks, fertilizer companies and general commercial concerns.

Mr. Miller is a past master of Orange Lodge No. 14, Accepted Free Masons, and was at one time district grand master of the Grand Lodge. He is an ex-president of St. Andrews Society, which was organized in 1729, being the oldest St. Andrews organization in America, and among the very first societies of any kind to become established in South Carolina. There is still preserved an unbroken roll of the signatures of the members of this society, from the date of its organization to the present. He is vice president of the Huguenot Society of Charleston, treasurer of the Carolina Art Association, and a trustee of the Charleston Library Society. He was a member of the first Board of Law Examiners of the state, holding office about six years. He has been a working member of the democratic party, though never a candidate for office. He has always attended worship with the Baptist faith.

In 1887 he married Georgia H. Gordon, daughter of James Gordon of Abbeville, South Carolina. They have two children, Gordon and Margaret. The son is junior member of his father's law firm.

Hon. EDGAR CLIFTON RIDGELL whose name is a subject of frequent mention in the press of the state as one of the leading members of the State Senate, has many interests and distinctions to his credit in his home community of Batesburg in Lexington County. He was at one time a practicing dentist and president of the South Carolina Dental Association. He has not been active in his profession for more than twenty years and has given his time to planting and fruit growing. He is one of the leading laymen of the Baptist Church and as a man of large means and great influence has worked untiringly in behalf of many forward movements in his home county and state.

Mr. Ridgell was born in Lexington County where the town of Batesburg is now located, November 6, 1859, a son of Joel and Susannah (Fox) Ridgell. The Ridgell family is of English origin and first settled at Charleston. Joel Ridgell spent all his life in Lexington County. He owned the land on which the Town of Batesburg was built, and was a highly honored character there for many years. The Fox family is likewise one of long residence in the county.

The birthplace of Edgar C. Ridgell was part of the original plantation now in the City of Batesburg. The old home was burned some years ago and Senator Ridgell replaced it with his present residence. He was educated in the public schools at Prosperity in Newberry County and attended the sessions of 1880-81, in the Baltimore College of Dental Surgery. He began practice in 1881 at Prosperity, and in 1885 returned to his old home at Batesburg, where for twelve years until 1897 he gave his chief time to his professional work. Since then he has devoted his attention to his property interests and agriculture.

The farm where he does his planting and fruit growing is a portion of the old plantation and is in Batesburg. Mr. Ridgell is president of the Lexington County Corn Growers Association and was one of the organizers and president and treasurer of the cotton mill at Batesburg, which was built in 1885.

While his own affairs have demanded so much of his time he has apparently made one of the ruling principles of his life an ambition for service in behalf of his civic community, church and every worthy movement. While practicing dentistry he was honored with the office of president of the State Dental Association. He has served as town councilman, was president of the Batesburg Board of Trade, and for seven years was honored with the position of moderator of the Ridge Baptist Association. This is one of the largest and most prosperous associations in the state, having a membership of nearly four thousand. He was also president of the Ridge Baptist Sunday School Convention for many years. Mr. Ridgell at present has charge with others of the campaign in this association's jurisdiction to raise its apportionment of the $5,000,000 fund now being acquired by the Southern Baptist Church for general educational and religious purposes. He was president of the Interdenominational Sunday School Convention of Lexington County for a term. Mr. Ridgell is a deacon in the Batesburg Church, has been superintendent of its Sunday school for twenty years, and was for several years a member of the board of trustees of the Baptist Hospital at Columbia. He served as chairman of trustees of public schools in Batesburg, also president of Tri-County Fair Association.

He was first sent to the Legislature from Lexington County in 1909-10. He served in the House and in 1916 was elected to the Senate for a term of four years. During the 1919 session he was a member of the important Finance Committee and chairman of the Police Regulation Committee. He was author of the bill in the Legislature, appropriating $500,000 to build an office building for the various state departments which passed the Senate at the 1920 session but failed in the House.

For more than twenty years, Doctor Ridgell has taken a leading part in the prohibition movement, both in his county and the state, serving much of the time as county chairman of the party in Lexington County. He was also active in the various drives made in the interest of the Liberty Loans. He was appointed chairman for Lexington County, in the campaign for funds for the American Red Cross, organized the county work and raised more than the apportionment asked for. He has had prominent part in advancing the cause of education, serving as school trustee for a number of years. He is also a director in the First National Bank, of Batesburg.

December 20, 1881, Doctor Ridgell married Miss Ella McFall of Prosperity. Their six children are Daniel Effingham; Lottie, wife of G. F. Norris of Greenville; J. McFall Ridgell; Miss Rosa; Grace, wife of Ira C. Carson; and Miss Louise.

Hon. JOHN FREDERICK WILLIAMS. During a continuous service of over ten years as a member of the Lower House and the State Senate of Aiken County, Mr. Williams has rendered services that have brought him wide recognition as one of the state's most useful leaders in public affairs.

Col Robert C. Emanuel

Amongst the bills he advocated were compulsory school attendance, medical and dental examination of school children and better pay for teachers, all of which were enacted. In his home city he has been a successful lawyer since 1905.

Mr. Williams was born near Salley in Aiken County, February 26, 1884, son of W. S. and Mary (Williamson) Williams, both deceased. His great-grandfather Williams was born in England. W. S. Williams was born in that section of Aiken, formerly a part of Lexington County. Senator Williams' maternal grandfather was Thomas Williamson, and the Williamsons are one of the oldest families of Lexington County.

John Frederick Williams grew up on his father's plantation, attended the Smythe Academy near Salley and took his literary and law courses in South Carolina College. He pursued special academic courses and the law course three years, graduating in law in 1905. He was prominent in student activities at the University and was chiefly responsible for organizing the Criminal Moot Court of the law school. In college he was a leader in oratory, being once monthly orator of the Claraosophic Literary Society, and his talents in that direction have improved with his service as a lawyer and legislator. He has practiced steadily at Aiken, first as a law partner of C. E. Sawyer, under the name Sawyer & Williams, and since then has been in individual practice. He has a large interest in both State and Federal Courts.

Mr. Williams was elected to represent Aiken County in the Lower House of the General Assembly in 1908, serving in the sessions beginning in 1909 and including 1912. In the latter year he was elected to the State Senate and was reelected for a second term of four years in 1916. He is one of the Senate leaders, being chairman of the committee on education, ex-officio trustee of Winthrop College and University of South Carolina, and a member of the judiciary and other committees. In May, 1920, he attended the National Conference on Education at Washington, D. C., under appointment from the governor.

Mr. Williams was one of the organizers and is a director of the Bank of Windsor in Aiken County. He and his wife are members of the Baptist Church. He married Miss Etta Turner, of Graniteville, South Carolina, in 1908. Their two children are Mary and Sargent Pickens Williams.

COL. ROBERT COCHRAN EMANUEL. This name serves to recall not only a very useful and highly dignified figure in the old regime of South Carolina, but also by the manner of his death, at the hands of assassins, the peculiar horrors of the early reconstruction period. Some of his family are still living in old Marlboro County, including his daughter, Mrs. P. L. Breeden, of Bennettsville.

The family trace descent from Michael and Flora Emanuel, a young married couple with children who came from London to Charleston, South Carolina, in the late 1780's. Simeon Emanuel, their youngest child and the father of Col. Robert C. Emanuel, was born in Charleston, South Carolina, in 1800. He came to the Marlboro District, South Carolina, when quite a young man, and was successful in business. He married Miss Maria Cochran, a granddaughter of Thomas Cochran, who was a brother of Dr. John Cochran, Gen. George Washington's surgeon-general, also a brother of Maj. Robert Cochran, who was in command of Fort Edward with 500 men when Burgoyne crossed the St. Lawrence River from Canada into the United States, and immediately retreated. Thomas Cochran came to Marlboro District on the Big Pee Dee River in 1736. This was the Welsh settlement on the Great Pee Dee. He married Miss Lucrecia Council, the daughter of Capt. Henry Council, who served in the Rangers under Gen. Francis Marion, Marion's Brigade. Thomas Cochran's chart from George III for 200 acres of land has been preserved and is now in the possession of Mrs. Breeden. Strange to say, this 200 acres of land lies in a large body and was owned by her husband at his death on October 10, 1919.

Maria Cochran Emanuel was a woman of no ordinary mental ability. Simeon Emanuel was a chaste, peaceful and refined business man. He and his wife were consistent members of the Baptist Church, and both died in full fellowship with the church. Both Simeon Emanuel and his son Robert Cochran Emanuel belonged to the Masonic Lodge.

Col. Robert Cochran Emanuel was born in Marlboro County, August 16, 1825, son of Simeon Emanuel, who was born, as stated above, in Charleston in 1800. Simeon Emanuel became a very prominent and wealthy merchant at Brownsville in Marlboro County, and operated several stores and also conducted a line of steamboats on the Pee Dee River. In managing his extensive plantation and in business affairs he employed the service of a large number of slaves. He was one of the progressive men of his day.

Concerning the life and character of Colonel Emanuel, who lost his life near his residence in Marlboro District, June 16, 1866, the best account is a contemporaneous one, written by a friend a few weeks after he was murdered, showing the esteem in which he was held and some of the emotions his assassination caused in a community then suffering from the waste and devastation of war and anticipating the heavier burdens of reconstruction rule. The chief portions of this "In Memoriam" follows: "In the prime of manhood and in the midst of a career of prosperity and usefulness, he was cut short in a manner revolting to all feelings of humanity. He began life early, having married in his minority, and to the end battled with obstacles with a steadiness and success rarely to be seen. Deprived of the benefits of a finished education, he labored under the disadvantages consequent therefrom. By relying on his own resources and strong native sense, he conquered where others more favored have failed, and won for himself a name for intelligence and successful industry which challenges comparison and is worthy of emulation. By prudent management and untiring effort, he elevated himself from poverty to wealth, and made himself admired by all who have a proper appreciation of the energetic man. Kind in disposition, gentle in deportment, and lavish in hospitality, he had drawn around him a large number of admiring friends, and even those with whom he had unwittingly excited prejudice were glad to have the benefit of his prudent counsel and advice in the hour of trouble and need. Few men in the district, if any, wielded more influence than the deceased, certainly none in his own immediate neighborhood. Though possessed of a large and dependent family, he did not hesitate to leave all in response to his country's call in our recent struggle for liberty. He was among the first to raise and carry into service a company from Marlboro, and with them cheerfully endured the privations of a soldier's life; and doubtless to his training may be ascribed the effective service and noble conduct of these men throughout the war. To the soldier in the field he was stern, but ever just and kind, to the soldier's family at home he was ever benevolent. At any time his loss would have been felt in this community; but especially is it serious at the present juncture, when the example of just such men is needed to teach our oppressed people never to despair, as all losses may be repaired and all difficulties surmounted by determined resolution. As a neighbor he was obliging, as a citizen public spirited and patriotic, as a friend, steadfast, and as a son, husband and parent, gentle, kind and affectionate. It is seldom we see more devotion and attachment to one's family than ruled his breast; it was in the family circle he most closely evinced his striking and lofty traits of character. Here his good qualities were brightly revealed through the intensity of his love and devotion to his own.

"The deceased was not a professed Christian, but admired the beauties of religion, and but a short time preceding his death he expressed to his most intimate friends his resolution to identify himself with the church.

"Our sympathy and condolence for the bereaved wife and family are sincere. To them his loss is irreparable; and while the present generation lasts, many will be the regrets in the community of Brownsville at the untimely death of its most useful member."

Colonel Emanuel received his title colonel while serving with a militia regiment during the '50s. This was State Regiment No. 37.

Colonel Emanuel married Sarah Johnson DuPre, daughter of Thomas Johnson James DuPre and granddaughter of James DuPre, who was one of the original Huguenot settlers coming to South Carolina from France. James DuPre was a noted planter and slave owner in colonial times. A list of the children of Colonel Emanuel is as follows: Margaret Elizabeth; James Simeon and Henry C., both deceased; Alice M., wife of J. G. W. Cobb of Bennettsville; Eleanor, who died in young womanhood; Francis M., deceased; Sarah Della, wife of H. P. Johnson, of Bennettsville; Theodosia, deceased wife of Enos Watson; Bulah, deceased wife of Isham Watson; Sarah, wife of John Watson; and Thomas Johnson James, married and father of a family.

Margaret Elizabeth Emanuel was born in the Brownsville settlement of Marlboro County, August 18, 1843, and was liberally educated in the South Carolina Female College at Columbia. She married Capt. P. L. Breeden and became the mother of six children. Alma Estelle, the oldest, is the widow of John H. Burkhalter, living at Columbia. Julius A. lives in Bennettsville. Alice is the deceased wife of Frank P. Siegnious. Mary Bristow died at the age of four years, and the fifth child died in infancy. Margaret Elizabeth is the wife of J. E. B. Holladay, lawyer of Suffolk, Virginia. Mrs. Breeden is an active member of the Baptist Church.

COL. JAMES SIMONS, of Charleston, a South Carolinian of national distinction who died at the age of nearly fourscore years, was a link connecting the modern present with a period of the state that is becoming more and more a matter of historical record.

James Simons, whose death occurred on July 4, 1919, a day whose associations were always deeply significant to him, was born at Charleston, November 30, 1839, of French Huguenot ancestry with a strong admixture of Scotch and English blood. Just a century before his death another member of the family, Col. Keating Simons, was taken away from the community of Charleston, and at that time an orator said: "The name of Simons is with the people of Charleston clarum et venerabile nomen, great in science, great in medicine, great in the law, great in divinity and amiable in all the duties and charities of life." The same significance has attached to the name during the last century. Colonel Simons was the third to bear the name James. His grandfather was a distinguished officer in the Continental Army, serving under Col. William Washington at Cowpens. His father was a man of very striking appearance and distinguished scholarship and was speaker of the House of Representatives at Columbia at the time of the beginning of the war between the states, holding that post for a longer period than any other man in the history of South Carolina. Colonel Simons was a son of James and Sarah L. (Wragg) Simons.

He grew up and had associations from early boyhood with distinguished men in his state. He served as a page in the Legislature while his father was speaker. He was educated in the South Carolina College when Judge Longstreet was its president. Later he attended the University of Leipzig, Germany, and studied law with his father. Hobart College and the University of South Carolina both bestowed upon him the honorary degree LL. D. He returned from abroad just before the war and was admitted to the bar in 1860. He went with his state when South Carolina voted for secession and became first lieutenant in Bachman's Battery and later was made its captain. Members of this company had all enlisted for five years and the circumstances of the organization were such that Mr. Simons refused any other promotion and was with the battery throughout the war, participating in such battles as Seven Pines, Seven Days' Battle around Richmond, Second Manassas, Sharpsburg, Fredericksburg and Gettysburg and many of the operations between Savannah and Charleston. He never surrendered his company, disbanding it when the news of the capitulation of Johnston's Army reached him. After recovering from the effects of this service he and his father returned to Charleston, where he began the heavy task of rehabilitat-

ing his fortunes and establishing himself in his profession. He and his father were together in practice until the latter's death in 1879, and later he was associated with Gen. Rudolph Siegling and John D. Cappelmann under the name Simons, Siegling & Cappelmann. Though he announced his intention to retire from his profession he was never able to do so completely and his name remains as one of the most distinguished in the annals of the bar of South Carolina during the last half century.

For a quarter of a century also Colonel Simons was prominent in affairs at Charleston as president of the News and Courier Company. For many years he kept his resolution to abstain from politics, but was finally drawn into the struggle for the restoration of the state of white rule, and was a member of the House of Representatives from 1878 to 1891 and speaker of the House from 1882 to 1890. As a member of the rules committee he revised the rules of the House after the radical regime, and those rules today bear the impress of his services. He was a distinguished parliamentarian, and his services in that position were consistent with those rendered by his honored father many years previously.

Much has been said and is a matter of current knowledge concerning his work as chairman of the Board of Public School Commissioners at Charleston during the last twelve years of his life. It was his aim to keep the schools out of debt and at the same time to enlarge and advance their standards to meet the growing needs of the community. The school system of Charleston at the time of his death was unburdened with debt or incumbrances, and a record of constructive work includes the building of the Mitchell School and the Colored Industrial School.

For many years Colonel Simons was devoted to the patriotic organization the Sons of Cincinnati, and it is said he was present at every meeting of that order in Charleston for half a century, attending one of the meetings during the war while in the uniform of a Confederate soldier. Many of his friends felt that his death on the 4th of July was particularly significant. He was president of the State Society of the Order from 1898 and since 1902 had been vice president general of the National Society. He was also president of the Carolina Arts Association.

The following comments on his personal life and character found in a Charleston paper will be of interest: "Mr. Simons was one of the most charming of men in his personality and a man of much scholarship and varied accomplishments. He not only kept up his interest in classical learning but all his life was a student of music. He slept very little, generally working or reading until after midnight, and rising by or before six in the morning, when he usually played the violin until breakfast. On the streets of the city his has been one of the best known and most familiar figures and his passing will be looked upon as removing one who was not only a type of all that was best in the Old South but an example of that sort of citizenship which feels that useful public service comes ahead of everything else.

Colonel Simons married, October 16, 1890, Miss Elizabeth Potter Schott, of Philadelphia, Pennsylvania. She survives him. Colonel Simons was a brother of Dr. Manning Simons, a physician and surgeon of Charleston who died in 1911.

REV. PLEASANT EDGAR MONROE is the president of an increasingly well known institution for the higher education and training of young women, Summerland College at Summerland, founded and maintained under the auspices of the Joint Conference of the South Carolina Conference of the South Carolina Synod of the Lutheran Church.

The first plans for the founding of this institution for the education of young women within South Carolina were made in April, 1909, and in the winter of 1911-12 the Summerland Inn property was secured and in this building the college was opened October 1, 1912. The college has a wonderful location in the Piedmont region of South Carolina, and its facilities are now availed of by an average of 100 students, and there is a corps of nine teachers on the staff, headed by Rev. Mr. Monroe.

Mr. Monroe was born in Salsbury, North Carolina, December 18, 1875, son of Thomas B. and Victoria (Cress) Monroe. He grew up on his father's farm, attended local schools and Episcopal schools and was a student in the North Carolina College, where he was graduated in 1898, A. B., and in the Chicago Theological Seminary, where he was graduated in 1901. Then followed an active career as a pastor, being in charge of the Lutheran Church at Pulaski, Virginia, two years, six years at Ehrhard, South Carolina, five years at Johnston in this state, and in 1913 was called to his duties as president of Summerland College. He is looked upon as one of the leaders in the Lutheran Church in South Carolina. In 1919 he received the degree of D. D. from Newberry College.

April 2, 1902, he married Julia Houseal Hentz of Newberry. They have a daughter Mary Catherine.

COOPER FAMILY. The Cooper family, represented at Denmark and some other localities of South Carolina, is one of the first families of the state in point of lineage, prominence and patriotism. The first Coopers came from England as Quaker followers of Sir William Penn and settled in Pennsylvania. About two generations ago the Coopers began breaking away from their faith as Quakers, and most of them became Baptists.

Jeremiah Cooper, grandfather of the branch of the family in South Carolina, came from Pennsylvania to upper South Carolina in 1774. An Indian trader, he married Miss Charity Clark. They often made the journey back to Philadelphia to visit relatives. Members of this generation all figured prominently in the Revolutionary war. Letters and documents tell of the journey of Jeremiah Clark Cooper to Atlanta, Georgia, in 1824, when Atlanta was simply a small trading post for Indians. These facts and many others are all substantiated in Landrum's History of Upper South Carolina.

The father of those Coopers still found near Graham (now Denmark) was Clark Columbus Cooper. In 1818 he was born in Laurens County, South Carolina, and in 1837, before he was twenty-one, moved to Denmark. He was the youngest of eleven children. From Denmark he soon removed to Augusta, Georgia, but soon returned. February 16, 1847, he married Miss Alice Reed, granddaughter of the well known Malcolm Clark, justice of the peace in Orangeburg District in 1775-76. They were married on the plantation granted by King George to Malcolm Clark, who had served as a crown surveyor under appointment by that king. This plantation remains in the possession of the family today. A brother of Clark Columbus Cooper, Micajah, served in the Mexican war, and another brother, Sam, in the Florida Indian war. Clark Columbus Cooper was the father of: Samuel Powell, deceased; Marion Reed Cooper, a noted figure in South Carolina politics living in Port Royal; Georgie, who married Robert Gibbs Center and both are deceased; Jerome, deceased; William Sumpter, living on the old plantation; Elizabeth, who married William Clark; Perry H., deceased; James Clark, deceased; Julia D., at home; Alice, deceased; and Lillie, still at the old home. William Sumpter Cooper married Augustus Faust and has two sons, Perry and Angus. He lives on Cooper Street, on the old plantation opposite his sisters, Julia and Lillie, who occupy the old home to which their father brought his bride in 1847, and where all the children were born and where the children died. This property is entailed and some of the two hundred acres are within the city limits.

When the war of the states broke out Clark Columbus Cooper was too old for active service and became a member of the Reserves, Barnwell District, Eighth Battalion, as a first lieutenant and afterward as captain. All the members of this organization were either too old or too young for regular army service. One of those too youthful was James H. Bush, who was in Captain Cooper's Company. One precious relic of the war period is a book in which the Northern prisoners in Captain Cooper's care wrote their names and rank. In exquisite pen and ink the first page is embellished with the inscription "Autographs of Federal Officers, Prisoners of War of Charleston, South Carolina, presented to First Lieut. C. C. Cooper." A letter signed by Capt. H. J. McDonald, Eleventh Connecticut Volunteers, and William C. Locke, first lieutenant Connecticut Volunteers, describes how Captain Cooper did everything to alleviate their sufferings compatible with his duty as a Confederate officer, even using his own money. It asked all Northerners to treat him as a gentleman and Mason. Among names in the autograph book are many known to fame. In the book of autographs of southern men are those of G. T. Beauregard, general of the Confederate States Army; R. S. Ripley, brigadier-general; John H. Winder, brigadier-general; M. C. Butler, the famous South Carolinian; Gen. J. B. Hood, Wade Hampton, Lieut.-Gen. W. H. Wallace, Brigadier-General Hagood and many others of fame.

After the war Captain Cooper came back home and heroically gathered up the little left by Sherman's army, and after the war, as during it, lived a hero and a patriot and died at the homestead in 1894.

Mrs. Clark Columbus Cooper died in March, 1920, when nearly ninety years of age. She was an object of love and reverence, and old and young made pilgrimages to her home just to see her even at the last when she could not talk to them. Teachers and pupils alike came to her for first hand information and dates of the Civil war and to listen to thrilling accounts of Sherman's march, when it required four full days for the army, four abreast each side of the Cooper home, to pass it. In her home Wheeler's Scouts ate dinner, a few hours later Brigadier-General Williams occupied the opposite end of the house, eating and sleeping there while tents filled the spacious yard, and one day later General Sherman arrived, riding his famous black horse, and ate his dinner in the lovely parlor today filled with invaluable mementoes of the Cooper family and of the war between the states. In front of the house still stands the black jack oak to which Sherman's horse was tied. In the parlor are the tables and chairs used by the northern officers, and also a child's chair of mahogany and rosewood, looted from some home near and which the soldiers placed on the fire and the Coopers recovered. Their silver spoons in anticipation of the raid had been buried in soft mud, and though the soldiers poked about with their bayonets they were not discovered. A large sum of money and a quantity of handsome silver sent to Orangeburg for safety were all carried away by the enemy. At the beginning of the war Clark Columbus Cooper had in a safe (still standing in the home) a large sum of money to erect a magnificent mansion. The bricks had been hauled, but he gave the money to his beloved South for uniforms and food for its army, and the brick he sold for the same purpose. Thus the wonderful historical old home still stands, a rambling white cottage enclosed with a fence made of the pickets placed there by an English workman and which cost what was then a fabulous sum, twelve dollars per panel to make.

Clark Columbus Cooper was also a member of the Ku Klux Klan. His sword and uniform of gray are cherished possessions of Miss Lillie Cooper. He had feared the worst for his family when Sherman marched through. However, beyond the incidents above noted, they were safe from Sherman and his men, though two stragglers lingered when the enemy marched off, and demanding Mrs. Cooper's gold watch, were just setting the house on fire when an orderly galloped up and scared them off.

This house is now an objective for many visitors from all over the United States. They are always welcomed and Miss Lillie and her sister Julia open the house with its priceless treasures for inspection. Many articles eventually will be given to the various museums, and others distributed among the family.

MISS LILLIE COOPER, youngest child of Clark Columbus Cooper and Alice (Reed) Cooper, was born in the historic Cooper home, whose location many years ago was known as Graham's Turnout, then Graham, and now as Old Denmark, the newer town of Denmark being about a mile away. Old Denmark is a flag station. Miss Cooper recently delivered a talk on this subject to the United Daughters of the Confederacy, telling them that Mr. Graham made the deed with the proviso that the moment the railroad ceased to use it as a station it reverted to his heirs. His son is living and a grandson, Winchester Graham, lives at New Denmark. The flag station thus must always be in use.

Miss Lillie Cooper is a true daughter of the South, a gentlewoman whose influence is felt not only in her home and town but throughout her beloved state. She lives in the old home with her sister Julia. It is a peaceful, beautiful spot, surrounded by stately trees, with about two hundred acres in the estate. The columns of the wide old gates were demolished by Sherman's raiders, a portion of one still standing.

Miss Julia and Miss Lillie Cooper intend to bequeath many of their heirlooms to state institutions. Both were educated near their home, which both love above the ordinary love for a home. Their mother came here as a bride, the children were all born here, the father and mother died here, and it is a hallowed spot. They have heard their parents tell of the thrilling events which took place in this home while it was used successively as headquarters for Wheeler's Scouts of the Confederate army and for General Sherman and Brigadier-General Williams of the Northern army. From memory the sisters have an impressive testimony as to the destructive effect of Sherman's raiding army. No family of South Carolina or the entire South gave more or suffered more than the Cooper family.

In their home is a piece of the iron rail used in building the first railroad in South Carolina. They have counterpanes over a hundred years old, grandmothers caps from one to two hundred years old, and other articles of clothing of similar age. One is a dressing sacque worn by their great-grandmother, Alice Cloud, and one of the grandmother caps was worn by Mary Reed, daughter of Malcolm Clark. In every room are priceless treasures—the huge glass shades placed over candles, a spinning wheel, a mirror that has hung in one place over seventy years, miniatures, silver, china—these and others that might be noted in an inventory are still retained, while many treasures were stolen in the war. General Wheeler was expected, his rooms were supplied with the best of the house, but instead General (Federal) Williams occupied it and when he left the soldiers despoiled all that could be carried away. Many think the Cooper home should be the property of the state, but Captain Cooper strictly entailed it. Miss Lillie Cooper has a fortune for herself and her sister in Confederate bonds which their father bought and in Confederate money, if these could be redeemed. They also have South Carolina money of the issue of 1779.

Miss Lillie Cooper organized the first Daughters of the Confederacy in Denmark, was its first president and has always been its most valued speaker and historian. She is now in great demand as a speaker and writer. Constant study and research have made her an authority on history, but she is also widely versed on other subjects of the day. She was a member of the Arlington committee and a leader in all work for the World war, and is recorder of crosses of the South Carolina Division and a director of World war records. She has now taken the place of her mother, and the pupils and teachers of the schools come out to the old home for information on historical subjects. She and her sister, Miss Julia, are gracious hostesses to the visitors from all over the United States and even from England and other countries.

Their's is a wonderful home, presided over by two Southern ladies, than which there is no higher title in the world.

SAM L. SWEENEY. Farmers and stock men all over the State of South Carolina are familiar with the name and business of Sam L. Sweeney of Columbia. He has handled livestock, especially horses and mules, for over thirty years, and he knows domestic animals and the business of handling them as only a man can with the benefit of thirty years of practical and intimate experience. His success in business has meant more than mere money making, and has stood firmly from the beginning on the bedrock of integrity and character. He has earned a good name and his associates in Columbia and over the state vouch for the fact that his word is as good as his bond and that the latter is gilt edged.

Mr. Sweeney is entirely a self-made man, and educated himself by contact with the world of business and men. He was born in Columbia, August 25, 1874, a son of John C. and Mary (Hill) Sweeney. He has been in the livestock business since he was thirteen years of age, and from that time has depended upon his own efforts to advance him in the world. For several years he was located at the Columbia stock yards, later bought the Rhea livestock business, and since January, 1919, has been located at 1413 Assembly Street. He has been a hard worker, and the disposition of his means indicates a thorough faith in Columbia as a coming commercial metropolis. He owns over thirty houses and lots in Columbia. For four years he was a member of the city council and is now serving on the Civil Service Commission. He is also a director in the National State Bank, and the Homestead Bank, both of Columbia.

Doubtless the greatest inspiration to his business career has been his happy family life. He married Miss Catharine Koneman of Columbia, and his greatest misfortune was her death in 1912. She was a young woman of true nobility of character and in the few years of her association with her children impressed her characteristics upon them so that even in the eight years since she died her influence has been a constant one in their growth and development. Mr. Sweeney now has two grown daughters, both educated in good schools and college, and have shown splendid preparation and equipment for life's serious work. The daughters are Georgia F. and Hilda S. Sweeney. The latter made an especially notable record as a student at St. Genevieve's School in Asheville, North Carolina. The only son is Sam Louis Sweeney, born in 1909. At the age of ten he is already a willing and cheerful assistant to his father in business, and shows every promise of a fine young manhood. While the children have had every advantage at home and at school, they have never shown the slightest inclination to idleness, and voluntarily have chosen means and accepted opportunities to do useful work and assist their father.

OSCAR E. JOHNSON, president of the Southern Home Insurance Company, is one of the most aggressive business men of Charleston, where his operations have made him a well known man. He was born at Charleston, December 25, 1853, a son of Oscar E. Johnson, also a native of Charleston, of English extraction. His mother was prior to her marriage Miss Gabriella A. Strobel, one of the best known instructors in languages in the city, and she came of German ancestry. The Johnson family was founded in South Carolina at a very early day in its history, the descendants of the original settler taking part in the constructive work of developing the country from colonies of England. Daniel Strobel, the maternal great-grandfather of Oscar E. Johnson, came to South Carolina from Germany in 1752, when he was nineteen years of age, and located at Charleston, becoming active in the life of the city, and lieutenant of a company of home guards. His death occurred in 1786 after a residence at Charleston of fifty-four years. Oscar E. Johnson, Sr., and his wife were the parents of six children, of whom Oscar E. Johnson, Jr., is the eldest, and four of the six are still living.

Oscar E. Johnson attended the grammar and high schools of his native city and the College of Charleston, of which he is now a trustee. Upon leaving school Mr. Johnson engaged in the insurance business, with offices on Broad Street, and has been in it for fifty years, during which time he has represented some of the most prominent and trustworthy companies in the world, and selling a vast amount of insurance. He has served as president of the Charleston Board of Underwriters, the oldest board of underwriters continuously in existence in the United States. He was president of the State Association of Fire Insurance Agents, and is therefore one of the best known insurance men in South Carolina. In 1911 Mr. Johnson organized the Southern Home Insurance Company, of which he was elected president, and which he is conducting upon lines which have made it a success, and firmly established it in the confidence of the people. He also represents a number of marine insurance companies and the Department of Insurance for United States shippers, including the fleet corps. Always interested in Charleston, he has been active in civic matters and for two terms of four years each has been a member of the City Council, and has served on many of the important committees of the Council. His offices, which are the finest in the Peoples Building, are occupied by his force of fourteen assistants. A member of the Presbyterian Church, he has always given that organization generous and faithful support.

In 1879 Mr. Johnson was married first to Lila Boozer, who died in 1887, leaving three children, namely: Maud, Lila and Lewis. In 1889 Mr. Johnson was married to Maud Boozer, a sister of his first wife, and they have had one child, Louise, who married Robert S. Small of Charleston. Lila is the wife of A. P. Steele, of Statesville, North Carolina.

Lewis Johnson, the son, was educated at Clemson College, South Carolina, after which he studied the insurance business and now occupies a fine position in the Alabama insurance field. He married Kathleen Dunn, a daughter of Judge Norvell Dunn, of Jasper, Alabama, and they have two children.

ALBERT HORACE NINESTEIN. The community of Blackville in Barnwell County recognizes Mr. Ninestein as one of its ablest lawyers and best citizens. Mr. Ninestein has come up to his present position after many hard struggles and against adversities.

He was born at Palmyra, New York, February 13, 1875, eighth among a family of twelve children born to Edward and Augusta (Naskow) Ninestein. The parents were both born in the old country and were brought to America as children. Albert Horace Ninestein was thirteen years of age when his father died, and the next year he left home to earn his own way in the world. In succeeding years he did a great many things. One time his salary was three dollars and a half a week and he paid three dollars for board. He not only made a living, but also supplied the deficiencies in his early education, and earned the money to equip himself for better and broader things. He studied law in a lawyer's office, and on December 5, 1907, was admitted to the bar at Columbia, South Carolina. The same year he located at Blackville. He reached Blackville with his wife and two children, and his entire capital consisted of $142.00. While he did not know a person in town he had the training and ability to make his talents appreciated, and was soon enjoying a living practice. Since then he has handled some of the most important cases in Barnwell County. He has also been honored with the office of mayor of Blackville, and is now president of its Chamber of Commerce. He is also city attorney. For the past two years he has been chancellor commander of the Knights of Pythias Lodge.

In October, 1900, he married Miss Florence Jarret, a native of Archdale, North Carolina. They have a family of six children, Dorothy, Florence, Edward, Albert, Jr., Theodore and Eleanor.

EDWARD WALTER HUGHES. The steady and faithful devotion he has given to the profession of law for over thirty years has been accompanied with many honors that have made Mr. Hughes prominent in the public life of his home city of Charleston and in the state.

He was born at Summerville, South Carolina, April 21, 1864, son of Edward T. and Anna Gillard (White) Hughes, his ancestors coming from England and France and some of them serving in the Revolutionary army. His father was a banker of Charleston.

Mr. Hughes attended preparatory schools at Charleston, was graduated Bachelor of Science from the University of the South at Sewanee, Tennessee, and in 1885 completed his law course in the University of Virginia. The following year he took up the work of his profession at Charleston and has risen to real distinction as a lawyer. He

was a member of the Legislature from 1888 to 1894. From 1894 to 1898 he was assistant United States attorney, and in 1898 was appointed referee in bankruptcy, which position he still occupies. He was a candidate in 1903 for mayor of Charleston, and was one of two candidates to run in the second primary, 1913, for Congress. His name was prominently considered in connection with the federal judgeship at the time of the appointment of Judge Ham Smith. He is prominent in club life and has been commodore of the Yacht Club, president of the Country Club and president of the Charleston Club.

February 20, 1890, Mr. Hughes married Miss Virginia Randolph Pinckney.

PERRY McQUEEN SMOAK. While he began his business career modestly as a clerk in local stores, Mr. Smoak for twenty years has been one of the most influential figures in the commercial affairs of Orangeburg.

He was born in Orangeburg County August 21, 1869, son of Andrew James and Ann A. (Bair) Smoak. The Smoak family are of old South Carolina Revolutionary stock. His father was a Confederate soldier and a farmer, and he was the son of a soldier, the grandfather having spent four years in the service and was wounded through the thigh by a minie ball at the Battle of Gettysburg. Five of his sons were also soldiers. At one time he held a reunion in Orangeburg County,—at which 108 members of the family were present. Perry McQueen Smoak received a common school education, and in early life, began his business career as clerk in a general store. For four years he managed the shoe department of the store of George H. Cornelson at Orangeburg. He engaged in the wholesale grocery business under the firm name of Jennings & Smoak in November, 1898. He was active in that concern until 1910, when he organized the Orangeburg Fertilizer Works, and thus gave the city one of its important industries. He is still president of the Fertilizer Works. His talents and ability as an organizer have resulted in several other substantial local enterprises. He organized the Orangeburg Coca Cola Bottling Company, the Newberry Coca Cola Company, and the Orangeburg Packing Company. He is a director of the Edisto National Bank, and owns and directs the management of 2,000 acres of farm land.

December 29, 1902, he married Miss Gertrude Boliver, of Orangeburg. They have two children, Dorothy McQueen and Perry McQueen, Jr. Mr. Smoak is a Royal Arch Mason, an Elk, and is a senior deacon in the First Baptist Church of Orangeburg.

W. HUGER FITZ SIMONS began the practice of law in his native state of South Carolina thirty-five years ago, and the success and reputation for ability now associated with his name are in proportion to the length of years spent in close and conscientious devotion to his profession.

Mr. Fitz Simons was born in Charleston January 8, 1861, and most of the years of his lifetime have been spent in his native city. He is a son of Christopher and Susan Milliken (Barker) Fitz Simons, also natives of Charleston, where his father was a well known medical practitioner for many years. The grandfather, Christopher Fitz Simons, was also a native of South Carolina, descended from an Irish ancestor who came to the Carolinas soon after the close of the Revolution. The Charleston lawyer's mother was born at Charleston, a daughter of Samuel Gaillard Barker, a native of the city and for many years a lawyer of prominence.

W. Huger Fitz Simons is the fifth of seven children, all still living. He graduated from Charleston College in 1881 and spent about a year in a law office on Wall Street, New York City. Returning to Charleston in 1882, he continued his studies and was admitted to the bar in 1883, soon after taking up practice for himself and in 1886 forming the partnership of Barker, Gilliland & Fitz Simons. In 1892 he joined George H. Moffett in practice, their association continuing until about 1900. During the following fifteen or sixteen years Mr. Fitz Simons looked after his law business alone and since 1916 has had as an associate his son Samuel G.

In January, 1887, Mr. Fitz Simons married Anne Palmer Cain, a daughter of Maj. William Henry Cain, of Pinopolis, South Carolina. Their five children are James C., W. H., Jr., Samuel G., Margaret and R. C. Three of the sons were soldiers in the World war. James C. was a first lieutenant with the One Hundred and Seventeenth Engineers in the Forty-second or Rainbow Division, and was on active duty in France for fourteen months. Samuel G., now his father's law partner, also served with the rank of first lieutenant, was an aviator, and was on duty in France about twenty months. W. H., Jr., was a first lieutenant of artillery and later transferred to the Aviation Corps and received his "wings" three days after the signing of the armistice. The senior Mr. Fitz Simons is a member of the South Carolina Society and of the Charleston Ancient Artillery Company.

HON. JOSEPH WALKER BARNWELL is one of the oldest members of the Charleston bar, having recently rounded out a half century since his admission to practice. He has enjoyed many honors both in and out of his profession and his life has been one of signal usefulness and service.

He was born at Charleston October 31, 1846, a son of Rev. William H. and Catherine Osborn Barnwell. He attended private school at Charleston, Beaufort College in 1861, also private schools at Columbia and The Citadel at Charleston in 1864. There he was a member of the corps of Cadets and as such rendered active service to the Confederacy and was wounded in the leg in a skirmish along the Charleston and Savannah Railroad December 7, 1864. After the war he entered South Carolina University, and during 1869 studied abroad at the University of Goettingen, Germany.

Mr. Barnwell was admitted to the bar in 1869, and along with a large law practice has many times been called to duty in public offices. He was a member of the House of Representatives from Charleston County from 1874 to 1876, and took an active part in the Hampton campaign. He was chief of staff to Governor Hagood in 1880 and

1882, was senator from Charleston County from 1894 to 1896, and again from 1898 to 1902, declining further election and was candidate for attorney general on the Haskell ticket in 1890. In 1895 he was, together with J. C. Hemphill, William G. McGowan, John T. Sloan and others, a member of the committee which met in conference with Governor Tillman, former Governor Evans, Judge Ira B. Jones, and Hon. C. M. Efird, representing the Tillman faction, the object of the conference being to bring about an agreement between the opposing factions, whereby the Constitutional Convention, which was about to meet, might be conducted upon a non-partisan basis and in the broader interests of the public welfare, and while such an agreement was easily arrived at, it was not carried out by the faction then in power. Mr. Barnwell took a prominent part in the restoration of Charleston after the earthquake of 1886, serving as chairman of the relief committee. He was chairman of the democratic party of his county in 1880, and has been an official of the Charleston Library Society, the South Carolina Historical Society, and the Charleston Club. He has spent many years of earnest and successful effort in promoting and sustaining the Charleston Library Society. While not the author of any history of the state, he has contributed many interesting and valuable articles to the magazine published by the South Carolina Historical Society, and has delivered many notable addresses before literary, patriotic, and educational associations of the state.

January 17, 1900, occurred the death of his wife, whose name was Harriott Kinloch Cheves, daughter of Dr. Charles M. Cheves. The surviving children of Colonel and Mrs. Barnwell are: Capt. Joseph W. Barnwell, Jr., now with the State Highway Department at Columbia; Charles Edmund Barnwell, of New Orleans; and a daughter, Harriott Kinloch, wife of Esmond Phelps, Esq., of the New Orleans bar.

THOMAS HILLER DREHER, A. M., M. D. To speak of him merely in the terms of nearly thirty years of steady medical practice, the greater part of the time at St. Matthews, would be doing an injustice to the broad usefulness and influence of Doctor Dreher in that community. A skillful man in his profession, he has also turned his versatile talents into other avenues presenting means of doing good to his community and the people of his home state.

Many people outside of Calhoun County who know nothing of him as a physician have read and been influenced by his published views and writings. Doctor Dreher has the gift of literary skill and a splendid facility in translating his experiences and well matured judgment into concise and entertaining language. Recently he contributed to a number of the American Lutheran Survey an article entitled "Experiences of an Exemption Board Chairman," in which he describes a number of the incidents that came under his observation and which indicate both the weak and the strong qualities of a community engaged in war. Doctor Dreher as a "rock-bottom democrat" is a man of decided independence of opinion and an original thinker, as is well indicated in the views he expressed in pages of the Manufacturers Record in opposition to the ratification of the League of Nations treaty. Introductory to the article which he contributed to the Record the editor gave a concise description of the author in the following words: "Dr. T. H. Dreher is a prominent physician of South Carolina. He was County Democratic Chairman for many years in his county and chairman of the board of trustees of St. Matthews School for a long time. He was also chairman of the Local Exemption Board during the entire war. Doctor Dreher has always taken a prominent part in public affairs."

He was born near Irmo in Lexington County, South Carolina, November 11th, 1861, a son of Jacob W. and Anne A. (Hiller) Dreher. His Dreher ancestors came out of Germany and settled in Lexington County in the colonial period, some years before the Revolutionary war. Their home was in the vicinity of the present town of Irmo.

Doctor Dreher acquired his early training at home, and on January 1, 1880, matriculated in Newberry College, where he was graduated with first honors in 1885. The following four years he remained as principal of the preparatory department of Newberry College.

He studied medicine in the College of Physicians and Surgeons, now the medical department of the University of Maryland, graduating in 1891. After a brief practice at Lexington he established his home in St. Matthews Parish, then in Orangeburg, now the county seat of Calhoun County. Doctor Dreher took a leading part in the campaign for the organization of the County of Calhoun, was president of the new county association and when the new county was organized was made county chairman of the Democratic Executive Committee, serving as such until 1916. He held for several years the position of chairman of the Board of Trustees of St. Matthews Grade and High schools, and has been vice-president of The Home Bank of St. Matthews since its organization. He is a member of the County, State and American Medical associations and is an ex-president of the District Medical Society. He was reared a Lutheran but for many years past has been active in the Methodist Church.

Doctor Dreher married Miss Frances Wannamaker, daughter of the late Captain Francis Wannamaker of St. Matthews. Articles on other pages give in detail the career of her father and other members of this noted family of Calhoun County.

AUGUSTINE T. SMYTHE is a lawyer and well known business man of Charleston and bears the same name as his honored father, with whom he was associated in practice for a time. Considering their career together the name has been a distinctive one in the legal, civic and business life of Charleston for over half a century.

The late Augustine T. Smythe, who died in 1914, was born at Charleston October 5, 1842, son of Rev. Thomas and Margaret M. (Adger) Smyth. Rev. Thomas Smyth, D. D., came from Belfast, Ireland, in 1830 and for over forty years was pastor of the Second Presbyterian Church of Charleston. He was also a gifted speaker and writer. Margaret M. Adger was a daughter of James Adger, who came from County Antrim, Ire-

Thomas Hiller Dreher

land, in 1790. The names Smythe and Adger have for a century been conspicuous in the business, professional and all the varied interests of the City of Charleston.

Augustine Thomas Smythe always acknowledged a great debt to his parents and next to them to Professor Sachtleben, whose excellent private school he attended as a boy. In 1860 he entered South Carolina College, and remained a student until he entered the army. As a member of the College Cadets he assisted in the defense of Charleston Harbor at the first attack on Fort Sumter. In 1862 he was mustered into the regular Confederate army as a member of the Washington Light Infantry, which became Company A of the Twenty-Fifth South Carolina Volunteers. He was with that organization until the close of the war, doing duty in the Charleston defenses and at the end of the war was a member of a Cavalry Brigade. After the war he accepted his own poverty as the common lot of the South and endured a time of stress and struggle until he could become established in his profession. He studied law in the office of Simonton & Barker at Charleston and was admitted to the bar in 1867. He at once began practice and continued active in the profession for nearly half a century. For a number of years he was senior partner in the well known firm of Smythe, Lee & Frost.

From 1880 to 1894 he was member of the State Senate, and during a large part of that time was chairman of the judiciary committee. In earlier years he was the president of the Pioneer Fire Company, one of the volunteer fire companies of his city, and always kept up an interest in the local militia, serving for a number of years as major of the Washington Light Infantry. He was also prominent in Masonry, being grand master of the Grand Lodge and grand high priest of the Grand Chapter and commander of South Carolina Commandery No. 1. He was also a thirty-second degree Scottish Rite Mason. From 1890 to 1896 he served as a trustee of South Carolina College and was a trustee of Clemson Agricultural College from 1900 to 1906. He was the first commodore and one of the organizers of the Carolina Yacht Club, and at one time was president of the Hibernian Society. For many years and until his death he was an elder in the Presbyterian Church. On June 27, 1865, he married Miss Louisa McCord, of Columbia. She was a daughter of Col. D. J. McCord, prominent as a lawyer, and the granddaughter of Judge Langdon Cheves.

Augustine T. Smythe, Sr., left surviving him three daughters and two sons. The eldest of his surviving sons is the Rev. L. Cheves McC. Smythe, who has been a missionary of the Presbyterian Church for several years in Japan, and who was during the World war with the Red Cross in Russia. Mr. Smythe is a graduate of the University of Virginia, where he received an M. A. degree, and of Princeton Theological Seminary. In 1916 he married Miss Mary Fletcher, daughter of Judge James H. Fletcher, of Accomac, Virginia. The daughters are Louisa C., wife of Samuel G. Stoney, of Charleston; Hannah McC., wife of Anton P. Wright, of Savannah, Georgia; and Susan S., wife of John Bennett, of Charleston.

Augustine T. Smythe, Jr., the younger son, was born at Charleston, January 25, 1885, and was graduated in 1903 from the University School of Charleston. He received his Bachelor of Arts degree from the University of Virginia in 1907 and in 1909 completed his preparation for law in the Harvard Law School. He was admitted to the bar the same year and began practice at Charleston with his father's firm, Smythe, Lee & Frost. He is now a member of the firm Smythe & Visanska. Mr. Smythe is a director of the Southern Home Insurance Company, Charleston Savings Institution, Dime Bank and Trust Company, and has many other business connections. He is a member of the Carolina Yacht Club and is a Mason and Knight of Pythias.

He married Harriott Ravenel Buist, a daughter of the well known Charleston citizen and lawyer, Henry Buist. They have two children, Frances R. and Augustine, Jr.

WILLIAM ELIJAH FREE began the practice of law at Bamberg in 1908, and has a substantial general practice and also a good business in real estate at Bamberg.

He was born in Bamberg County July 31, 1876. His people have lived in that section of the old Barnwell District, now Bamberg County for several generations. His grandfather, Jacob E. Free, was a native of Barnwell County, served as a Confederate soldier, and before the war was a planter and slave holder. His wife, Elizabeth (Dowling) Free, was a daughter of William B. Dowling, who was the son of Elijah Dowling, the grandfather of Ellen E. (Dowling) Cox so that Mr. W. E. Free's great-great-grandfather on both his father's and mother's side was both one and the same man. Both the Free and the Dowling branches of the family are of Revolutionary stock, the former being of Irish descent and the latter of Scotch descent. A brother of Elijah Dowling settled in the pre-Revolutionary period in what is now Darlington County. Elijah Dowling was a lieutenant in the Continental army.

The late Charles Benjamin Free, father of the Bamberg lawyer, was owner of extensive planting interests, employing many people. He was born July 6, 1852, and died December 24, 1914. He was the first clerk of court of Bamberg County, beginning his official duties in 1897 and holding the office uninterruptedly until his death. He never had opposition in election after the first time. His wife was Sallie Dowling, a native of Barnwell County, and a daughter of A. J. and Ellen E. (Dowling) Cox. She was born in 1856 and died in 1896, the mother of four sons and two daughters. Charles B. Free was three times married. His second wife was Amanda R. Stephens, who became the mother of two children, while his third marriage was to Lizzie M. Jenkins. To the third union were born two daughters. Of these ten children in all nine reached mature years and are still living.

William Elijah Free was educated in the high school at Bamberg, attended Furman University at Greenville for three years and studied law in the office of the late John R. Bellinger. He was admitted to the bar in January, 1908, and since then has been busily engaged at Bamberg. For seven years he was a member of the law firm of Mayfield & Free, since which time he has practiced alone. He also operates in real estate and loans and is a stockholder, director and counsel for the First National Bank of Bamberg, and a stockholder in the Bamberg Banking Company.

June 17, 1909, he married Miss Birdie Gill, daughter of W. T. and Senie (Brown) Gill of Bamberg, one of the old and original South Carolina families. He has two sons, William E., Jr., born July 17, 1911, and Joseph D., born July 13, 1915. Mr. Free is a trustee and treasurer of the Baptist Church, and a member of the Executive Board of the Barnwell Baptist Association.

PETER LOWRY LEA. The most elaborate history is perforce a merciless abridgment, the historian being obliged to select his facts and materials from manifold details and to marshal them in concise and logical order. In every life of honor and usefulness there is no dearth of interesting situations and incidents, and yet in summing up such a career as that of Mr. Lea, the writer must needs touch only on the more salient facts, giving the keynote of the character and eliminating all that is superfluous to the continuity of the narrative. The gentleman whose name appears above has led an active and useful life, not entirely void of exciting events, but the more prominent have been so identified with the useful and practical that it is to them almost entirely that the writer refers in the following paragraphs.

Peter Lowry Lea, a well known and successful merchant at Burton, South Carolina, was born in Sumter (now Lee) County, South Carolina, on April 9, 1863, and is the son of William P. and Saphronia (Carter) Lea. William P. Lea was a native of North Carolina, who later became a resident of Charleston, South Carolina, but who followed the sea for many years. His father, William Lea, was a native of Virginia. The subject's mother was a native of Charleston, of which city her father was an early settler. He was a contractor, and among the many early structures erected by him there was the historic Bank of Charleston. The subject of this sketch is the third in order of birth of the five children who were born to his parents.

Peter L. Lea attended the public schools of Charleston, and was a student in the old St. Phillips Street School. At the age of fourteen years he began a seafaring career, and after spending four years before the mast he, at the age of eighteen years, entered an apprenticeship at Port Royal as pilot. During the following twenty years he followed the sea as pilot, and gained a reputation as a man of unusually high qualifications in that line. However, in 1899 Mr. Lea decided to spend the remainder of his life on solid land and engaged in the mercantile business at Burton, Beaufort County, where he is still engaged. He has by strict attention to business and catering to the wants of his patrons built up a large and representative patronage, and has been successful even beyond his anticipations. He carries a general line of goods of well selected grades and his evident desire to please his customers and his uniformly courteous treatment of them has gained for him an enviable reputation. In addition to his mercantile interests Mr. Lea is also the owner of about 150 acres of excellent truck land, on which he raises all the crops of vegetables common to this locality. He is also a stockholder in the Southern Furniture Company of Charleston, of which he is the vice president.

Mr. Lea has been married twice, first in 1887, to Sarah Hay, to which union was born a daughter, Lilla, who is now the wife of R. A. Long, Jr., of Beaufort, South Carolina. Mr. Lea's second marriage was with Eva Fink and they are the parents of two children, Peter L., Jr., and Eva Hampton. Fraternally Mr. Lea is a member of the Ancient Free and Accepted Masons, in which he has attained the degrees of the Royal Arch, and to the Knights of Pythias. He has taken a commendable interest in local public affairs, though without ambition for public office, but he gives his support to every movement having for its object the betterment of the community in any way. Because of his fine personal qualities and business success he enjoys to a marked degree the confidence and esteem of the entire community.

THOMAS FREDERICK BRANTLEY has practiced law in his native city of Orangeburg since 1896. He has also been a member of both branches of the Legislature, and as a political leader and speaker has been an important aid in several democratic national campaigns.

He was born at Orangeburg January 28, 1867, a son of Ellison W. and Angelina (Ulmer) Brantley. His mother's ancestry included men who were soldiers in the Colonial and Revolutionary wars. Ellison W. Brantley was a farmer. The son grew up on his father's farm and early learned the toil of the fields. He was two years old when his mother died, and many of the influences that shaped his early life were supplied by his grandmother. As a boy he looked beyond the farm to a career, and as a preliminary step in his progress he borrowed the money that enabled him to attend the famous Bingham Preparatory School in North Carolina. In 1892 he graduated A. B. from the South Carolina University. He was prominent as a debater in the university, won the debater's medal from his society, and was a member of the Pi Kappa Alpha Fraternity. He next entered the law department of Georgetown University at Washington, and graduated LL. B. in 1905. He was one of the Georgetown Debating Team which carried off the honors in contest with Columbian University. While at Washington he was appointed chief of division of the Treasury Department, winning that appointment after examination. He was dismissed from this office because of his activity in behalf of the election of W. J. Bryan in 1896. On leaving Washington he returned to Orangeburg and has since been busy in a general practice. In 1898 he was elected a member of the Legislature and re-elected the following year, and in 1902 was chosen a member of the State Senate. He resigned that office to become a candidate for Congress. He was

a delegate to the democratic convention at Denver in 1908, where he again warmly supported Bryan as a candidate for the presidency, and was a member of the Notification Committee. Mr. Brantley is a member of the Baptist Church.

Mr. Brantley still owns the original home settlement, which was acquired prior to the Revolutionary war by Mr. Brantley's great-great-grandfather and which has been handed down to successive generations until the present time. It is still one of the old landmarks of this section of the county and is located about seven miles east of the Orangeburg courthouse. It is in the famous "Four Holes" section referred to frequently in Simm's historical novels of South Carolina. Mr. Brantley's father, Ellison W. Brantley, was one of the leaders of the Ku Klux Clan which did so much toward the restoration of South Carolina to white rule. Going back in the geneological tree, Mr. Brantley dates his ancestry to Swiss-German origin, this ancestry settling in this immediate section about 1740.

April 26, 1905, Thomas F. Brantley married Miss Estelle Fairey, daughter of John W. Fairey of Orangeburg. They have four children: Mary Ellison Brantley, Henrietta Estelle Brantley, Thomas F. Brantley and John W. Brantley.

Mr. Brantley is a Mason; a member of Orangeburg Lodge of Elks, of which he is a past exalted ruler; and a member of the Uniform Rank Knights of Pythias, of which he is past chancellor commander.

He is at present engaged in the practice of law in Orangeburg County, and is the head member of the firm of Brantley and Zeigler, which is one of the leading firms in that part of the state.

CAPT. THOMAS S. SINKLER. A capacity for sticking to a purpose and confining one's efforts to a single line of endeavor brings about very desirable results in most instances, and especially is this true in the case of Capt. Thomas S. Sinkler, who, beginning his business career in his present concern, has risen from office boy to be part owner of the wholesale coal company of Johnson, Sinkler & Stone, one of the leading firms of its kind at Charleston. Captain Sinkler was born in Berkeley County, South Carolina, January 7, 1861, a son of William Sinkler, and grandson of James Sinkler, who was born in Scotland, but came to the United States and located in Berkeley County, South Carolina. William Sinkler was born at St. Johns, South Carolina, and he was married to Mary Simons, born at Charleston, a daughter of Dr. Thomas Y. Simons, one of the skilled physicians of a past generation, and a native of Charleston, his family having been founded in this city in the very earliest days of its history. There were ten children in the family born to William Sinkler and his wife, all of whom are living.

When he was a lad Thomas S. Sinkler was brought to Charleston by his parents and was educated in Porter's Military Academy. Entering upon a commercial career, he has been in the employ of but one concern, and his persistence and faithfulness have been rewarded by his steady advancement, and he now owns a half interest in the business. This concern does a very large foreign business, and also handles coal at retail, and the annual sales are enormous.

In 1887 Mr. Sinkler was united in marriage with Caroline Finley, a daughter of W. W. and Carrie (Glover) Finley, members of one of the prominent families of Charleston. Mr. and Mrs. Sinkler have three children, namely: Thomas S., who is a graduate of West Point and a captain in the regular United States Army; Caroline, who is the widow of Watson C. Finger, lives at Charleston; and Allen, who lives at home. Hr. Sinkler is a director of the Security Bank, his connection with it being of long standing. Fraternally he belongs to the Knights of Pythias. His social connections, which are very pleasant, are with the Charleston, the Charleston Country, and the Charleston Yacht clubs. For many years he has been a consistent member of St. Philip's Church of Charleston.

During the great war Mr. Sinkler rendered signal service to his country in the Charleston Reserve Corps, Charleston Light Dragoons, of which he is still captain. Not only did he assist in organizing this company, but through his personal example and enthusiasm brought his men into a high state of efficiency, and won from them and the community generally a respect which will not be forgotten. In days which tried men's souls and brought out their real selves, Mr. Sinkler proved his metal, and earned the right to be accounted one of the true-blue American citizens and patriots, whose deeds are as worthy of perpetuation on the pages of history as are those of the ones who had the privilege of going to the front.

JOSEPH BLAIN CASH, M.D. The community in and around Chesnee, in both Spartanburg and Cherokee counties, has many reminders of the business enterprise and public spirit of the Cash family. Dr. Joseph Blain Cash has recently undertaken to give Chesnee a model private hospital, affording increased facilities for his own extended practice as a physician and surgeon and an institution which would do credit to a large city.

Doctor Cash is a son of Columbus Cash, who has long been one of the leading business men and property owners in the Chesnee community. He was born two miles east of Chesnee, in what is now Cherokee County. He came to manhood in very humble circumstances. He had no regular schooling, and by plowing for small wages and by many severe struggles he finally got started, and the struggling years have given place to prosperity until he is now one of the largest and wealthiest land owners in Spartanburg and Cherokee counties. He operates several fine farms. Columbus Cash is owner of an historic spot in South Carolina, of interest not only to this state but to the nation. This is the Cowpens battle ground, not far from Chesnee, and included in a farm of about four hundred acres owned by Columbus Cash. Every American school child knows of the battle of Cowpens as one of the marks of progress by the American armies in their struggle for independence. Recently Columbus Cash set aside five acres of his land as a gift to the Daughters of the American Revolution, and thus the scene of the battle will become a permanent park, with a suitable monument erected thereon. Columbus Cash owned all of the land on which the village of Chesnee is located, and still has much of the valuable property in that village.

Dr. Joseph Blain Cash, who is a son of Columbus and Susan (King) Cash, was born February 25, 1891, two miles southeast of Chesnee. He took several courses in the Wofford Fitting School at Spartanburg, and afterward continued the regular study of medicine in the Atlanta Medical College, now the Medical Department of Emory University. He was graduated in 1914. For four and a half months he did post-graduate work at Tulane University in New Orleans and also spent five months in the New York Polyclinic and three months in the Grady Hospital at Atlanta. He had begun the practice of his profession in the meantime at Chesnee in 1914. His abilities and experience have led him more and more to the practice of surgery. He has been ambitious not only to succeed but to excel in his profession. Pending the building and completing of his new private hospital, Doctor Cash in July, 1919, entered the New York Lying-in Hospital for a six months' course.

He began the construction work on his new hospital at Chesnee about the first of July, 1919. It is a modern new brick building, two stories and basement, the building and equipment costing about sixty thousand dollars. It exemplifies all the modern ideas of hospital construction and is on an ideal site, comprising nearly two acres on a gently sloping elevation in the east part of the town of Chesnee. It has the pure atmosphere of the upper Carolina region, pure water, and otherwise is an ideal place for treatment and convalescence. The hospital will be open to all classes of patients except those suffering from contagious diseases. Just recently Doctor Cash has incorporated the hospital with a capital stock of $75,000.00, and it will be known as Mountain View Hospital. This will be completed and ready for patients on the 1st of July, 1920.

Doctor Cash, like his father, owns valuable business property in Chesnee and much farming land, and has ample financial resources for carrying out any enterprise in which he embarks.

CHARLES R. VALK, vice president and treasurer of the Charleston Dry Dock and Machine Company, is one of the substantial men of Charleston. He was born at Compo, Connecticut, on October 6, 1848, a son of Charles P. L. Valk, a native of Charleston who moved to Connecticut and there died. His widow returned to Charleston, bringing with her Charles R., then but one year old. He grew up at Charleston and attended the Octavius Porcher School at Abbeville, South Carolina. At the age of fifteen years he entered the Confederate army in the Third South Carolina State Troops, Colonel Goodwin's regiment, but after six months' service peace was declared between the states, and he returned to Charleston.

His military experience made him feel too old for school, so he began an apprenticeship in the foundry of William S. Henerey, and was there from 1866 to 1870, when he became superintendent for the Stono Phosphate Company. In 1871 he formed a partnership with J. Ralph Smith under the style of Smith & Valk, which continued until the name of the Valk & Murdoch Iron Works was adopted, of which Mr. Valk was made president. The plant was moved to the foot of Calhoun Street, and later the business was reorganized as the Valk & Murdoch Company, and again as the Charleston Dry Dock and Machine Company. The company does a general marine business and gives employment to 400 people, its annual volume of product showing a healthy increase.

In 1889 Mr. Valk was united in marriage with Miss E. F. Weyman, of New York City, and they have three children, namely: Elizabeth, who is the wife of G. Lee Holmes; Martha Lawrence and Courtney.

Mr. Valk is chairman of the Hampton Park Association, vice president of the William Austin Home, and is identified with other organizations in the city. A man of wide outlook and unusual capabilities, he has risen to be a strong factor for good in his community. The same enthusiasm which sent him a youth of fifteen years into the army has carried him on in many a conflict with conditions which did not meet with his approval, and in most instances brought him through a victor, for right was always on his side. Deprived of a father's fostering care so early in life, he has had necessarily to make his own way in the world, but early hardships have but developed his character and strengthened his resistance, and he feels that he is all the better for having to earn his living by the "sweat of his brow."

HON. JAMES WILLARD RAGSDALE. A great loss to South Carolina and the nation was experienced in the death of James Willard Ragsdale, which occurred at Washington July 23, 1919, while he was in the midst of his duties as representative from the Sixth South Carolina District in Congress. He was in his fourth consecutive term in Congress, and his work and influence were greatly appreciated both by his fellow members in the House of Representatives and the Senate.

Mr. Ragsdale for many years had been a prominent lawyer and banker at Florence, and in that city and in Eastern Carolina his friends and supporters were most numerous. Mr. Ragsdale was born at Timmonsville, South Carolina, December 14, 1872, son of Littleton Russell and Ellen Adelaide (Byrd) Ragsdale. His mother was a daughter of Doctor Byrd of Timmonsville, a greatly beloved physician and citizen. J. W. Ragsdale acquired his early education in the schools of Timmonsville and at Darlington. For several years he lived at Wilmington, North Carolina, where he was employed in the general offices of the Atlantic Coast Line Railway Company. As a student in the University of South Carolina he studied law under the late Doctor Pope, and began practice at Florence. He was a law partner of Judge Shipp and later of R. E. Whiting and D. G. Baker, under the firm name Ragsdale, Baker & Whiting. Mr. Ragsdale was regarded as one of the ablest criminal lawyers of the state. As a banker he organized the Farmers and Mechanics Bank of Florence, and was its president at the time of his death, and also was a director of the Citizens Bank of Timmonsville, and the People's Bank of Darlington. He owned and con-

ducted several of the finest farms in Florence and Darlington counties.

Mr. Ragsdale early entered politics, and was elected to the Legislature from Florence County for two terms and afterwards served as a member of the State Senate. He resigned from the Senate to make the race for attorney general, but was efeated in that campaign. His first aspirations for a seat in Congress were also defeated by J. E. Ellerbe, whom he finally succeeded in 1913. Among other important committees he served on the Committee on Foreign Affairs. Mr. Ragsdale was a Methodist, was a trustee of the South Carolina Industrial School, and was a member of the Columbia Club of South Carolina and the Army and Navy Club of Washington.

November 15, 1900, he married Marie Louise Joynes, of Columbia, daughter of the late Dr. Edward Southey Joynes, the distinguished South Carolina educator whose career is briefly sketched elsewhere. Mr. Ragsdale was survived by two children: James, aged eighteen, and Marie, aged fourteen.

Besides the many tributes paid the life and work of Mr. Ragsdale by members of Congress and of his home community, the following interesting comments are found in an article by the Washington correspondent of the Columbia State:

"It is probable that from the time Mr. Ragsdale entered Congress as the successor to the late J. E. Ellerbe of Marion until the death of Mrs. Ragsdale's father, the late Dr. E. S. Joynes of Columbia, no one entertained official and social Washington more elegantly and lavishly than he and Mrs. Ragsdale. Their first home in the fashionable section of Washington, on Connecticut Avenue, was often the scene of magnificent functions, and later when they moved to the old William J. Bryan residence, Calumet Place, this entertainment was continued. About a year and a half ago, upon the death of Doctor Joynes, this public entertaining naturally ceased for a time and Mrs. Ragsdale since then has mostly remained at her home at Florence.

"Mr. Ragsdale's influence in certain departments of Washington was frequently commented upon. It was often stated that he could get more appointments for his constituents from the state department than almost any other member of the House. There are now many men from South Carolina in the diplomatic service due to his efforts. There was also a strong link between Mr. Ragsdale and the War Department, and during the momentous days of the war he landed many excellent assignments for men from South Carolina in various departments of the service. He was especially close to General Enoch Crowder, judge advocate general of the army and provost marshal general.

"It has frequently been noted in Washington that Mr. Ragsdale was always willing to do whatever he could for any man from South Carolina if it came to his knowledge that his services were needed, and during the early days of his official career he took the initiative in this matter and stamped himself as being always at the command of any South Carolinian with a worthy cause.

"Mr. Ragsdale was close to the late Senator Tillman, and last summer, just before Senator Tillman's death, Mr. Ragsdale had under consideration for some time the question of entering the race for the United States Senate, but always said that he never would do so while Senator Tillman was a candidate. As events of last year turned out, the situation developed so that after Senator Tillman's death it was too late for Mr. Ragsdale to enter the race. He had many urgent suggestions from friends in different parts of the state offering their support in the event that he should become a candidate. His loyalty to Senator Tillman was unquestioned and remained so throughout his life and that of the Senator."

EDWARD SOUTHEY JOYNES, M. A., LL. D., who died in Columbia, South Carolina, June 18, 1917, was one of America's most distinguished educators. He was born in Accomack County, Virginia, March 2, 1834. He was a son of Thomas R. and Anne Bell (Satchell) Joynes, a grandson of Maj. Levin Joynes of the Continental army, and a descendant of some of the earliest English settlers on the eastern shore of the Old Dominion. After receiving his preparatory training at the celebrated Concord Academy, Virginia, and at Delaware College, he entered the University of Virginia in 1850, and graduated from that institution with the degree of A. B. in 1852 and M. A. the following year. On his graduation in 1853, he was appointed Assistant Professor of Ancient Languages, under the distinguished Dr. Gessner Harrison, and remained at the University of Virginia in this capacity until 1856. To prepare himself more completely for his life-work, he then went to the University of Berlin, 1856-1858, where he studied under the most famous professors then living. While still abroad, he was, in 1858, elected Professor of Greek and German in William and Mary College. Here, in Williamsburg, Virginia, long famed for its brilliant social life, he met, and married, December 14, 1859, Miss Eliza Waller Vest. To this union were born four children: Capt. Walker W. Joynes, of the United States Revenue Cutter Service; Mrs. Alex. G. Fite. of Nashville, Tennessee; Mrs. Robert Macfarlan of Darlington, South Carolina; and Mrs. J. Willard Ragsdale, of Florence, South Carolina.

In 1861 William and Mary College having closed, Professor Joynes was appointed chief clerk in the Confederate States War Department in Richmond, where he served until 1864. From 1864 to 1865 he taught Modern Languages in Hollins Institute, Virginia. In 1866 he became Professor of Modern Languages and English in Washington College (now Washington and Lee University) at Lexington, Virginia, and regarded his service under Gen. Robt. E. Lee, who was president of the college, as the greatest privilege of his life. In 1875 he was elected Professor of Modern Languages and English in Vanderbilt University, and in 1878 to the same chair in the University of Tennessee. The degree of LL. D. was conferred upon him by Delaware College in 1875, and by William and Mary in 1878. In 1882 he entered upon his duties as Professor of Modern Languages and English at the South Carolina College, and continued his work there until he was retired by the Carnegie Board in 1908, after fifty-four years of educational work, for "unusual and distinguished services as Professor of Modern Languages." He was at once made Professor Emeritus of the University of South Carolina.

In addition to his long service as professor, Doctor Joynes was distinguished as a successful author of many well known text-books in German and French, which are now regarded as classics in the world of letters, and are used all over America. Of these, the most important are his well known grammars of German and French; his "Maria Stuart" in German, and his "La Mare au Diable" in French.

Doctor Joynes was always deeply interested in public school work in Virginia, Tennessee, and South Carolina. He assisted in founding and organizing the graded school system in South Carolina, and was one of the founders and trustees of Winthrop College. It was due to his untiring efforts that the University charter was secured for the South Carolina College. This fact is referred to in the dedication of the Year Book for 1907, as follows:

"To Dr. Edward Southey Joynes, Professor of Modern Languages, eminent as teacher and scholar, a distinguished author, patron of the Literary Societies, and 'Father of the University,' this volume is affectionately dedicated."

As a conversationalist Doctor Joynes was brilliant and fascinating, as a writer he was an acknowledged master of English prose; as a teacher he was scholarly and inspiring. His varied attainments and charming personality drew around him an admiring circle of devoted friends. A cultured gentleman of the Old South, he was imbued with the youthful zeal and progressive spirit of the New South. His long experience as an educator, the text-books which came from his pen, and the ripe scholarship which characterized his writings and addresses, made him more than a state figure,—he was known nationally. His is a name mentioned with reverence and affection wherever scholars are gathered together, a name that is a synonym for sound learning, pre-eminent ability, and scholarly production.

The New York Nation says of Doctor Joynes: "Probably few, if any American professors, have personally taught so many students in foreign tongues, and certainly no other American professor has so widely influenced the study of Modern Languages in America."

THOMAS CALVIN STEVENSON has been an engineer for a quarter of a century, and as president of the Charleston Engineering and Contracting Company has been identified with many important constructive enterprises, both private and public works, in Charleston and up and down the coast.

Mr. Stevenson was born in Chester County, South Carolina, September 3, 1873. His father was Daniel R. Stevenson. His mother, Nancy Beaty, was born in Fairfield County, South Carolina, a daughter of James Beaty, a native of Ireland, of Scotch-Irish parentage. Thomas C. Stevenson was the youngest in a family of seven children, five of whom are still living. He completed his education at The Citadel at Charleston, graduating in 1894. He then took up engineering as a Government employe, and spent several years in fortification work. He then entered contract construction, and in 1910 organized the Charleston Engineering and Contracting Company, of which he has been president. Mr. J. A. McCormack is secretary-treasurer.

Mr. Stevenson married in 1904 Miss Nell Williams, of Alabama. They have five sons, Thomas C., Jr., Jere W., Dan R., Fred W. and Norman W. Mr. Stevenson is a Mason and member of the Chamber of Commerce, and is an elder in the Westminster Presbyterian Church.

BENJAMIN MASON ANDERSON was a son of the late Maj. Franklin L. Anderson. His father was distinguished as a Confederate soldier and officer, and one of the finest representatives of the chivalry and ideals of the South. Major Anderson during the greater part of his life lived at the beautiful ancestral estate of the Anderson family, Holly Hill, in Spartanburg County.

At Holly Hill, one of the beautiful landmarks of upper South Carolina, Benjamin Mason Anderson was born September 9, 1874. As noted in the sketch of Major Anderson, he was a child of his father's second marriage, his mother being Ada Eppes.

Though Benjamin Mason Anderson died September 13, 1918, at the age of forty-four, in a comparatively brief career he had emulated the high character of his honored father and left a record of good citizenship and practical achievement that gives his name a lasting affection in the hearts of Spartanburg County people. He was liberally educated, and became inspired with his responsibilities and opportunities for service to the agricultural development of his region. It was the part he played as a farmer that constitutes his best business achievement. He was long regarded as an authority on the subject of agriculture, and his extensive farms were and are today models of progressive culture and management in the Piedmont section. He always believed that farming was one of the highest vocations which can command the services of men, and he took pride in studying it from a scientific standpoint and adopting every progressive device to the handling of his own property and encouraging his neighbors in similar progressive systems. The country home where he lived with his family and where he died was in the Reidville section of Spartanburg County.

His work and influence were by no means confined to his immediate possessions. He regarded the interests of his home community as his own, and was always willing to perform service for the upbuilding of the county and state. He was reared in the old home church of the Anderson family, the Nazareth Church of the Presbyterian denomination. At the time of his death he was an elder in the Reidville Presbyterian Church, this organization having grown out of Nazareth. His funeral services were conducted in the church where he had worshiped in earliest childhood.

Mr. Anderson married Miss Mary Philson of Clinton, South Carolina. She and five children survive, the children being Kathryn, Sadie, Henrietta, Benjamin and Mary Agnes Anderson. Mrs. Ander-

son was well educated for the responsibilities she has carried since her marriage, and has radiated a wonderful influence in her home and has also shown the qualities of good business judgment. She has been a worker in many women's organizations in the county, both church and patriotic.

CAPT. HARRY OGIER WITHINGTON, a prominent young Charleston business man, was commander of the Motor Battalion of the One Hundred and Fifth Ammunition Train practically the entire time this splendid body of Charleston soldiers were on active duty in France, from July, 1918, until after the signing of the armistice.

Captain Withington was born at Charleston in 1882, son of William A. and Julia M. (Thrower) Withington. The Withingtons are of English ancestry and on coming to America established their home in Massachusetts. William A. Withington was also born at Charleston, son of Perez Withington.

Captain Withington was reared in Charleston, had a public school education, and prior to the World war and since returning from abroad has been in active business life as secretary of the Lanneau Art Store and secretary and treasurer of Melcher's Studio.

Many years of training and discipline with the state troops gave Captain Withington preparation for the duties he performed as an officer in the American Expeditionary Forces. As a boy he joined the Washington Light Infantry. He was a member of that organization eighteen years, ten years of the time as captain. The Washington Light Infantry, whose history as a military unit has been continuous since 1807 and whose members have participated in all the wars of the nation since that date, was Company B of the Second South Carolina Infantry prior to the war with Germany.

Captain Withington gave nearly three years to the military service of the nation. He was in command of his company on the Mexican border from June, 1916, to March, 1917. He and the company were called into Federal service in July, 1917, and was on guard duty at Camp Jackson until September of that year and then in training at Camp Sevier until the spring of 1918. While at Sevier the company became the nucleus of the One Hundred and Fifth Ammunition Train of the Thirtieth Division. As such it sailed from Montreal for France May 26, 1918. In France the One Hundred and Fifth Ammunition Train was assigned for active front line duty in various divisions, being changed about according to the exigencies of the service. Captain Withington was on duty during the Somme-St. Mihiel drive, at the Argonne, in the defense of the Toul sector, and also on the Woevre Plains. There was seldom a letup to the service at and near the front lines beginning with the great offensives of July and ending with the armistice.

After reaching France Captain Withington was made battalion commander of the Motor Battalion of the One Hundred and Fifth Ammunition Train. From the time his men received their final inspection at Le Mans until the embarkation for home Captain Withington was in command of the entire One Hundred and Fifth Ammunition Train, comprising seven companies and numerous detachments, a total of 1,300 men. Captain Withington left France March 13, 1919, reaching Charleston toward the end of the same month, and was discharged April 3, 1919.

Captain Withington is a member of Bethel Methodist Church and is affiliated with the Knights of Pythias. He married Miss Jennie Connor, of Branchville, South Carolina, daughter of David and Annie Connor and granddaughter of General Stokes, a distinguished Confederate officer. Mrs. Withington is deceased, and is survived by a daughter, Julia Elizabeth Withington.

J. ARTHUR WIGGINS, active vice president and manager of the Bank of Denmark, first identified himself with that community of Bamberg County in the capacity of an educator. For a number of years he was head of the Denmark schools, finally resigning to take up banking.

He was born at Holly Hill, South Carolina, July 26, 1871. He is of English ancestry, the family coming to America in the 1600's and taking part in the Revolution. His grandfather, James Wiggins, was a farmer, while his father, James B. Wiggins, is a successful physician and surgeon. Dr. J. B. Wiggins was a surgeon in the Confederate army, taking an active part throughout the struggle, and was prominently identified with the famous "red shirt" brigade during the period of reconstruction. He was active in the political world, in which he exercised a wide influence. He was called upon several times to serve in public office and filled the offices of county treasurer and county auditor. In addition to his professional and political duties he owned and operated about 4,000 acres in what is now Orangeburg County, cultivating what is known as a twenty-plow farm. He was prominent in the Methodist Church at Holly Hill, in which he was a steward. He died in 1910. Doctor Wiggins married Mary C. Brownlee, a native of Holly Hill. Both the Brownlee and Wiggins families were early settled in South Carolina.

J. Arthur Wiggins was reared and educated in his home community and received his A. B. degree in 1895 from Wofford College at Spartanburg. He spent ten years as superintendent of the high school at Denmark, and in 1906 accepted the post of cashier in the Bank of Denmark, and since 1915 has been its active vice president and manager. He exercises a wide influence in financial matters of the district. The bank is one of the strong ones of Bamberg County, and has a capital of $50,000, and belongs to the State and National Banking Associations. D. N. Cox is president.

Mr. Wiggins takes an active part in the work of the Methodist Episcopal Church, South, being a steward and trustee. He is affiliated with the Masonic fraternity, the Knights of Pythias and the Woodmen of the World.

In 1896 he married Miss Mattie Connor, a native of Holly Hill and a daughter of Fred Connor, a farmer of Holly Hill. The Connors are an old South Carolina family of Revolutionary stock. Fred Connor was a soldier in the Confederate army and served until the close of the war. He was a man of sterling character and was an ardent supporter of all measures looking toward the general welfare of the community. He became one of the wealthiest and most prominent men of the Holly Hill section. He died in 1910. Mr. and Mrs. Wiggins have four sons and four daughters: Reynold, Vera, Martha, James, Fred, Grace, Frances and Hugh.

Reynold C. Wiggins is auditor of the Edisto National Bank at Orangeburg. He married Ruth, a daughter of Capt. J. B. Guess of Denmark, one of the most prominent farmers in this section of the state. The Guess family is of Revolutionary stock.

EDWARD H. McIVER, who for twenty years has had an active business career at Charleston, where he is now secretary of the Leland Moore Paint & Oil Company, is a grandson of the distinguished Hon. Henry McIver and member of the historic family of that name in the old Cheraw District of South Carolina, frequently referred to in Bishop Gregg's notable work, the History of the Cheraws.

Hon. Henry McIver was born in Darlington County, South Carolina, in 1826, and graduated from South Carolina College in 1846. The following year, after studying law with his father, he was admitted to the bar, and three years later, when his father died, he was solicitor and continued to fill that office until the close of the Civil war. In 1877 he was elected an associate judge of the Supreme Court, and upon the death of Chief Justice Simpson was elected chief justice. He was a member of the Secession Convention of South Carolina and served as an officer in the Fourth South Carolina Cavalry under General Hampton, being successively promoted from second lieutenant to first lieutenant and finally to a captaincy. Judge McIver married Caroline Powe, daughter of Dr. Thomas Powe, of Cheraw.

Edward H. McIver was born at Cheraw, in Chesterfield County, a son of Thomas P. and Susan (Duvall) McIver, the father now deceased. When a boy he came to Charleston and finished his education in the Charleston High School and the College of Charleston. He then began his business career, and for a number of years has been associated with the Leland Moore Paint & Oil Company. In January, 1920, this corporation increased its charter from $40,000 to $150,000, to provide funds for the building of a new plant with greatly enlarged manufacturing facilities for the making of paints and oils. With this new plant it will become one of the larger industrial concerns of Charleston.

Mr. McIver is a member of the St. Cecelia Society, the Charleston Country Club, the Carolina Yacht Club, the Young Men's Christian Association, the Chamber of Commerce, the Masonic order and St. Philip's Church. He married Miss Kate Bull, of Orangeburg.

G. FRANK BAMBERG. The Bambergs are one of the oldest families of South Carolina. They were transplanted from Germany to the Carolina colonies about 1700. For two centuries they have been prominent planters, business men and citizens in the southern part of the state.

G. Frank Bamberg of Bamberg is owner and director of some of the largest plantations in the southern part of the state and is also a leading banker at Bamberg. He was born in that city October 8, 1873. His great-grandfather was John George Bamberg, a native of Lexington County, South Carolina, a minister of the Lutheran Church. He died in 1800. The grandfather, John Frederick Bamberg, was a native of that portion of Barnwell County now Bamberg. The father of the Bamberg banker was Francis Marion Bamberg, who was born in what is now Bamberg County and was a prominent banker, stock farmer and planter. He was a member of Hart's Battery, Hampton's Legion, during the Confederate struggle, and served throughout the war as a lieutenant. During the reconstruction period of 1876 he was a prominent figure among the "Red Shirts," and although a natural leader among men, he never aspired to political honors. The Town of Bamberg was named for his uncle, W. C. Bamberg, while the county was named in his honor. The United Daughters of the Confederacy also named their chapter in Bamberg in his honor. He was a rugged, fearless American whose unwavering kindness endeared him to all. He helped every one he could and would buy any honest man a farm to start him right. At the time of his death, which occurred in his sixty-seventh year, he left $300,000 in mortgages with instructions to his son to never foreclose one of them, an order which the latter, G. Frank Bamberg, has never violated. Mr. F. M. Bamberg was affiliated with the Masons. He married Mary Ann Jennings, who was of English ancestry. The Jennings family was established in South Carolina in 1737. She was a daughter of George P. and Harriet Ann (Moody) Jennings and a granddaughter of John Jennings, a native of Orangeburg County.

G. Frank Bamberg was the third in a family of eight children. He was educated at Wofford College in Spartanburg, and at the age of twenty began business for himself as a livestock dealer and planter. Today he owns 2,500 acres, with about 1,500 acres under cultivation, being one of the largest producers of cotton in the southern counties of the state. Mr. Bamberg is president of the Bamberg Auto Company, and of the Bamberg Banking Company, which operates on a capital of $55,000. He is vice president of the B. E. & W. Railroad. Mr. Bamberg is a member of the Masonic order.

In 1896 he married Nell Elizabeth McGee, a daughter of J. B. and Mollie (Cobb) McGee. They have two sons and one daughter: Francis Marion, Joseph McGee and Nell Jennings.

C. M. BENEDICT has for a number of years been a factor in the public utilities business of South Carolina. He is vice president of the Charleston Consolidated Railway and Light Company.

He had a thorough training in the technical as well as the business departments of public utilities. He was born at Gloversville, New York, June 7, 1872, son of Joseph E. and A. (Morgan) Benedict. He is of English ancestry. He was the only son of his parents and had a high school education and also attended the Fort Edward Institute in his native state. Some of his younger years were spent in the lumber business, and at the age of twenty-one he gained his first experience in the gas industry, with the old Gloversville Gas Company. He

began as a pipe fitter, and went through various grades of promotion until at the end of seven years he was made manager of the company. This plant was owned by a larger corporation having headquarters at Philadelphia, to which city Mr. Benedict was called. In the spring of 1910 he came to Charleston and was made assistant treasurer of the Charleston Consolidated Railway and Light Company. In November, 1917, he was promoted to his present office as vice president.

He is a member of the Chamber of Commerce, the Charleston Club, Country Club, Otranto Club, also of the Manufacturers Club of Philadelphia and of the Presbyterian Church. He married Marvie Rhodes, of Gloversville, New York. They have two sons, Joseph B. and Clarence M., Jr. Joseph B. was an ensign in the United States Navy and was engaged in transport duty during the war. He resigned from the service, effective June 21, 1920.

JESSE FRANCIS CARTER. After working his way through school, paying expenses of his living and of his education and with the aid of his versatile and brilliant talents, Jesse Francis Carter has won an enviable position as a lawyer at Bamberg.

He was born near the little town of Lodge in Colleton County, September 12, 1873. His father, Miles McMillin Carter, was a native of the same county and spent his active life as a farmer. He is of an old South Carolina family of English descent. He married Janie Irene Kinard, a native of Barnwell County, and daughter of Jacob Francis Kinnard, also an old South Carolina family of Scotch-Irish descent. Miles Carter after his marriage moved to a plantation in Colleton County where his six sons were born, all of whom are still living, named: Jesse Francis and Bert Dean Carter, attorneys at law in Bamberg under the firm name of Carter, Carter & Kearse; Joseph Edgar Carter of Wilmington, North Carolina; Alonzo B. Carter of Maxton, North Carolina; Wilbur Lee Carter of Greensboro, North Carolina; and Miles J. Carter of Florence, Alabama, all of whom are engaged in some phase of insurance work, Wilbur Lee and Miles J. owning controlling interests in the business which they conduct.

Jesse Francis Carter as a small boy had opportunities to occasionally attend a log cabin school in Colleton County, a term of only a few weeks each year. He was thirteen when his father died, at which time he took charge of the farm and assisted his mother in rearing his infant brothers. His mother died when he was twenty years of age, after which he attended the graded schools at Bamberg, also a classical institute, and as a means of support taught a number of summer terms. He finally entered Peabody College in Nashville, Tennessee, where he graduated in 1900, and after teaching for a while, he graduated with the degree A. B. from the University of Nashville in 1903. In 1904 Mr. Carter entered the Law School of the University of South Carolina and took two years' work in one, receiving his LL. B. degree in 1905. He then located at Bamberg, and has rapidly made his way to the front as a lawyer. In 1908 he again took special post-graduate work in Chicago. He is engaged in general practice and is a member of the firm Carter, Carter & Kearse of Bamberg, South Carolina. Mr. Carter owns and as a means of recreation conducts some small farming interests in the neighborhood of Bamberg.

In college and university Mr. Carter gave all the time he could to literary and debating societies. He won several debates, including the debater's medal of his society at the University of South Carolina. He was also a winner in the oratorical contest, and was president of his literary society in the University of Nashville and was made permanent secretary of his class at graduation.

He is affiliated with the Masonic order and the Knights of Pythias, and has held many of the offices in both orders. He is a member of the State Bar Association and was attorney for the local board of Bamberg County during the war, also government appeal agent, a member of the State Council of Defense, and a leader in the second Red Cross campaign and in many other war activities. He is a member and deacon of the Missionary Baptist Church and teacher of its Men's Bible Class. Mr. Carter has never been a seeker for political honors, but is one of the most influential men in his party in Bamberg County and is the present chairman of the democratic county committee, serving his second term in that office. Mr. Carter is president of the Home Building & Loan Association, which has an issued capital of $200,000. This is a recently organized company, Mr. Carter being one of the organizers. The company starts off with bright prospects.

In 1911 Mr. Carter married Lydia Jenkins, a daughter of B. M. Jenkins of Kline, South Carolina. They have three daughters: Lydia Frances, Janie Elizabeth and Martha Jaudon Carter.

JAMES HAYES ROBERTS, M. D. The veteran physician and surgeon of Ehrhardt is Dr. James H. Roberts, who began practice there nearly thirty years ago. He has had much to do with the professional, business and civic life of this community.

Doctor Roberts was born at Allendale in old Barnwell County March 2, 1863. His grandfather, Richard Roberts, according to the best information obtainable, was a native of France. The father, Dr. Richard Creech Roberts, was a native of Barnwell County, was reared and educated there, and for fifty years practiced dentistry. He served as a lieutenant of cavalry in the Confederate army and was at one time a member of the Legislature and in other ways prominent in local affairs. He was a major in the State Militia. He died at the age of sixty-nine. His wife was Sarah Emily Durin, of Barnwell County. Her father was born in Ireland and came to Barnwell County when a young man and was a contractor and built many of the early houses in that county.

Dr. James Hayes Roberts was the second in a family of six children, five of whom reached mature years and two are still living, the other being Boyce H.

Doctor Roberts was liberally educated, attending the Porter Military Academy and The Citadel at Charleston, and graduating from the South Carolina Medical College on March 4, 1887. For three years he practiced in his native town of Allendale, and in 1890 located at Ehrhardt. During 1906-07 he was in practice at Great Falls, but then returned to Ehrhardt. He is a member of the Bamberg County Medical Society, the State Medical Association, is vice president of the Farmers and Merchants Bank of Ehrhardt, and is affiliated with the Masonic order, the Knights of Pythias and the Woodmen of the World.

February 25, 1891, Doctor Roberts married Lottie O. Barber. She died July 18, 1895, the mother of two children: Sarah Elizabeth, wife of B. D. Carter, a Bamberg attorney, and Lottie, who died at the age of nine months. October 9, 1901, Doctor Roberts married Laura Dunbar, widow of James Dunbar. They have had seven children: James Heyward, Richard C., Furman, Catherine, Lucile, deceased, Louise and Carlisle.

JUNIUS T. LILES, lieutenant governor of South Carolina in 1919-20, has given a notably constructive service to the legislative and public affairs of South Carolina for eight years. He is a business man of Orangeburg and was born at Lilesville, Anson County, North Carolina, August 25, 1876, son of Col. Edward R. and Frances (Fladger) Liles.

His father, for many years prominent in North Carolina politics, died when the future lieutenant governor of South Carolina was but six years old. Later his mother, a daughter of Rev. Charles B. and Jane (Givee) Fladger of Marion County, South Carolina, became the wife of Capt. John H. Hamer of Little Rock, South Carolina.

Through industrious efforts and thrifty management of his meager opportunities and financial resources Junius T. Lides came to manhood with a good education. After attending private and public schools in Marion County he entered the University of North Carolina at the age of seventeen, but could only attend one year. He then became a bank clerk and salesman in Marion County, and after two and a half years of such work had saved enough to enter Wilmore College of Kentucky. His studies in that institution were interrupted by the outbreak of the Spanish-American war, during which he enlisted in the Second Kentucky Infantry.

In 1901 Mr. Liles engaged in the insurance business, and his success in that line has made him one of the most prominent figures in the insurance world in South Carolina. In 1908 he became general manager for this state for the Jefferson Standard Life Insurance Company. He is associated with his brother in the General Insurance Agency of Liles & Liles of Orangeburg.

All his enthusiasm was given to business until his success was assured, and his career in politics did not begin until 1912, when he was elected to the Legislature from Orangeburg County. He led the ticket in the first primary with fourteen in the race, and was re-elected in 1914 and 1916, winning out by a handsome majority each time in the first primary.

His business experience and other qualifications enabled him to take a leading part in legislative activities and in 1916 was made chairman of the Ways and Means Committee of the House of Representatives. His name was associated with some of the most progressive and creditable legislation during the past eight years.

Among the most notable features of his legislative record, he was connected either as author or sponsor with some measures of far-reaching importance, including the acts creating the tax commission, laws of great benefit to the educational system of the state, the law that made it a chain-gang offense without the alternative of a fine to sell whiskey illegally, and also the act providing the necessary appropriation for eradicating from the state the Texas cattle fever, the enforcement of which has lifted the most serious obstacle to the development of the cattle industry in South Carolina.

Throughout his entire membership in the House of Representatives he was regarded as a leader and was selected by the governor as pilot for some of the most important measures that have been enacted into law in the state for many years. His political career was an open book to the public, and he demonstrated the value of honorable methods in dealing with the affairs of government, a policy which in itself is a permanent contribution to the betterment of state politics.

In 1918 he was elected lieutenant governor of South Carolina, and notwithstanding the fact that he had every assurance of re-election to that position in 1920 declined to run again and withdrew from politics, stating that while he desired no longer to hold office, he would yet hold himself in readiness to respond to the call of the people if at any time his services should be needed for the advancement of the welfare of his state.

In 1899 Mr. Liles married Miss Gertrude Jones, of Meridian, Mississippi. To their marriage have been born four children.

FRANCIS Q. O'NEILL. The name O'Neill has been a distinctive one in the commercial, financial and civic affairs in Charleston for more than half a century.

The father of Francis Q. O'Neill, long prominent as a merchant and banker, was Bernard O'Neill, who was born in Ireland and came to Charleston in 1840. He was a merchant and banker, built up a large wholesale house and at one time was president of the Hibernia Bank, Loan & Trust Company. He was a member of the Legislature of 1876 when white government was restored in the state. His ability as a banker was an important resource in restoring the state's credit. He was at one time acting mayor of the City of Charleston, and lived to be eighty-three years of age. His wife was Elizabeth Quale. They had five sons and three daughters, and two sons and two daughters are still living, all at Charleston.

Francis Q. O'Neill was born in Charleston July 13, 1857. He grew up in a good and comfortable home with every encouragement to develop his talents. He was graduated with the first honors of his class from the College of Charleston in 1878. In the following year he began his business career as a clerk and in 1884 became a member of his father's firm. For several years he was president of the Combahee Fertilizer Company. He was also president of the Hibernia Bank. He is now a director of the First National Bank, a director of the

Bank of Western Carolina, is vice president of the Equitable Insurance Company, president of the Jacksonboro Lumber Company and has long been interested in various business and industrial organizations.

In 1894 he was acting mayor of Charleston, and beginning in 1898 served as alderman for many years. He is a trustee of the College of Charleston, the Charleston Library Society and the Charleston Orphan House, and has been a member of various public boards. He is a member of the Charleston Club, the Charleston Yacht Club, Chamber of Commerce and is a prominent member of St. John's Cathedral of the Catholic Church. In 1905 he married Emma Fourgeaud McGahan. Their two children are Emma T. and Francis Q., Jr.

ROBINSON P. SEARSON has practiced law at Allendale since 1907. His reputation as a lawyer is by no means confined to one community of the state. For several years he represented Barnwell County in the State Legislature. As an Allendale man there was committed to him the responsibility of representing interests of his constituents in agitating for a new county organization. He discharged those responsibilities with his characteristic ability and influence, and it was largely through him that the program was carried to the Legislature for the creation of Allendale County. This is one of the smallest but one of the richest counties in the state, and with Allendale as the county seat the new civil unit, which came into existence in January, 1919, is justifying all the hopes and expectations of its zealous advocates.

Mr. Searson was born at Allendale, February 5, 1881, and most of his life interests have been in that community. His father was R. P. Searson, of South Carolina; his mother was Bonita Arnold, a daughter of William Wynne Arnold, a prominent equity lawyer of Georgia, to whom the Georgia State Legislature erected a monument at Zebulon in 1854; and his great-great-grandfather, John Robinson Searson, who married a niece of Commodore Hull of the "Constitution," was of English ancestry and was an American soldier in the Revolution under General Marion.

The late R. P. Searson, who died in 1916, was one of the first settlers in the town of Allendale and for thirty years was its postmaster and a merchant and druggist of long standing. He was also a Confederate soldier serving in Butler's Cavalry. He personally assisted General Butler to the rear at the battle of Seven Pines, when this gallant Confederate officer had his leg shot off.

Robinson P. Searson was educated in the Johnston Institute, in Clemson College, and took both the literary and law courses in the University of South Carolina. He received his LL. B. degree in 1902. Following that he practiced at Hampton two years, three or four years at Barnesville, Georgia, then locating at Allendale. He enjoys a large general practice, and has exercised much influence both in local and state politics. In 1918 he was candidate for the democratic nomination for attorney general. He represented Barnwell County in the State Legislature for six years.

Mr. Searson was also identified with all the organizations in his home county and state for the better prosecution of the war. He was a member of the Legal Advisory Board for Barnwell County and chairman of the Victory Loan for the Second Congressional District. Mr. Searson is a Baptist and is affiliated with the Elks and Knights of Pythias. He married Miss Mattie Tea Turner, of Macon, Georgia, and they have one son, R. P. Searson III.

EDMUND B. JACKSON. A new chapter is being written in the history of southern banking and one that serves to obliterate the older picture of the banker as an obstacle to the progress of the southern farmer. One of South Carolina's bankers whose activities and influence are a constructive example in this new era is Edmund B. Jackson, of Wagener, Aiken County.

Mr. Jackson, who is president of the First National Bank of Wagener, and himself an extensive planter, was born in Aiken County, ten miles from the Town of Wagener, in 1881, son of W. Q. and Laura (Jeffords) Jackson. His early life was spent on a farm, and from boyhood he has had an experience that gives him a practical knowledge of cotton production. He was thoroughly educated, graduating from The Citadel at Charleston in 1901.

Several years later Mr. Jackson became one of the organizers of the Bank of Wagener, established in August, 1907. He was its cashier until 1912 and since has been president. However, on February 14, 1914, the bank took out a national charter as the First National Bank. Its capital stock is $30,000 and the deposits now aggregate nearly half a million. The service of the bank has been much more than that of a routine banking institution. It has been one of the primary factors in the growth and development of the Town of Wagener and the surrounding rich agricultural territory, which is admittedly the best agricultural part of Aiken County. Within a few years Wagener has become the chief cotton market of the county, and is a town growing and prospering, with a number of important mercantile institutions.

Ever since he became a banker Mr. Jackson has devoted his best talents and energies to the welfare of cotton farmers, not as a philanthropist, but as a far-sighted business man who conceives the welfare of his patrons as inextricably bound up with that of himself and his bank. Having grown up in the community, he knows what the problems of the farmers are and their needs. His greatest satisfaction has been derived from the part his bank has had in the prosperity of his cotton growing customers. Mr. Jackson was the first banker in South Carolina to lend money to cotton farmers at six per cent. His was also the first bank to enlist the Federal Land Bank system for extending financial assistance to farmers. Between ninety and ninety-five per cent of the loans made by the First National Bank are to farmers. Contrary to a deep seated prejudice among some older bankers, the records show that this bank has never lost a cent of money on such loans. This record is due above all to Mr. Jackson's personal judgment. It is said that he knows every farmer in his section, also knows his land, his stock, and his character and reputation, and stands in the relation of a personal adviser to everyone who comes into his bank requesting a loan. Much of his lending is on the "moral risk," but his faith has always been justified by the results.

Mr. Jackson owns several fine plantations, and for years has been one of the most extensive cotton growers in Aiken County. He has also carried on a large real estate business, and during the past two years had carried out a broad plan for the dividing up of large plantations and individual holdings and selling at auction to small owners. The result of this program has been to bring about an era of intensive production. Mr. Jackson as a banker and farmer has used his best efforts to rid his district of the old evils of the credit system, under which cotton farmers were usually bound in virtual slavery to merchants, being always in debt. He has encouraged farmers to borrow money for their necessities at a low rate of interest and then pay cash for all their goods.

Mr. Jackson is a prominent member of the Baptist Church of Wagener, being chairman of its Finance Committee and one of the leaders in the building of the beautiful new church. He is a teacher of the Bible class. In Masonry he is a Scottish Rite and member of Omar Temple of the Mystic Shrine at Charleston.

He married Miss Fannie L. Lybrand, daughter of Mr. and Mrs. J. W. Lybrand, of Wagener. Their two children are Lybrand and Hazel Jackson.

JOHN F. FICKEN, a Confederate veteran, former mayor of Charleston and a lawyer of over half a century's experience, has lived a life of practically uninterrupted service to his own city and state from early youth to old age.

He was born at Charleston June 16, 1843, son of John F. Ficken, Sr., who was a merchant and factor. He was educated in private schools at Charleston and received his A. B. degree from the College of Charleston. He was a youthful soldier in the Confederate army, and at the close of the war began the study of law with Col. John Philips. Subsequently he was a student at the University of Berlin. He was admitted to the bar in 1868, and for several years practiced in partnership with Col. Isaac Hayne, and later with Edward W. Hughes, Esq., and is still practicing in copartnership with his son, Henry H. Ficken, Esq., and H. L. Erckman, Esq. He was elected a member of the Lower House of the State Legislature in 1877, and served seven consecutive terms, representing Charleston County until he resigned in 1891 to become mayor of Charleston. He filled that office four years and declined re-election. In 1876 he was elected as a delegate to the National Democratic Convention which met at St. Louis, Missouri, which body nominated Samuel J. Tilden for President of the United States. In 1902 he was made president of the South Carolina Loan & Trust Company. He is also president of the Board of Trustees of the College of Charleston, is president of Charleston Library, president of the Carolina Art Association, and president of the St. John's Lutheran Church. Among other services rendered to the public he was a member of the Board of Commissioners of the South Carolina Institution for the Education of the Deaf, Dumb and Blind; trustee of Newberry College, and vice-president of the board of trustees of the Medical College of the State of South Carolina. He was one of the directors and general counsel of the South Carolina Inter State and West Indian Exposition. Mr. Ficken is a thirty-third degree Mason. He also served as one of the District Deputy Grand Masters of the Grand Lodge of Masons of South Carolina.

He was twice married, first to Miss Margaret Buckingham Horlbeck, and some years after her death to Miss Emma Julia Blum, both of whom are descendants of John Horlbeck, a soldier of the American Revolution.

JOHN F. RILEY, proprietor of the John F. Riley Foundry and Machine Works of Charleston, is one of the sound business men and public-spirited citizens of this city, and a person whose word is regarded as good as another's bond. He was born at Charleston, July 20, 1859, a son of Patrick and Ann (Collins) Riley. Patrick Riley was born in the north of Ireland and came to the United States in young manhood. Locating at Charleston, he found it more profitable to manufacture gas than to work at his trade of weaving, and was so engaged when Charleston with other southern cities became involved in the war between the states, and he, naturally, gave his support to the Confederacy and enlisted in its army. The authorities, however, decided that he could do the cause more good by continuing the production of gas, so was returned to civilian life. His widow survived him many years, living until she was seventy-nine, but he passed away at the age of sixty-two years. They had five sons and four daughters, seven of whom are living and residents of Charleston.

Growing up at Charleston, John F. Riley attended its schools and then served his apprenticeship at the foundry and machine trades, which he learned with the Charleston Iron Works. In 1884 he began business for himself upon a very small scale, increasing his plant as his trade warranted until he has one of the largest iron works and machine shops in South Carolina, and is now, as he has been from the beginning, sole owner of the establishment. He was a member of the State Democratic Executive Committee from 1902 to 1904. A strong democrat, he succeeded his brother, Andrew J. Riley, in the City Council, and has represented his ward in that body for the past nine years, during that period being connected with some very important constructive work in behalf of the municipality. He is a director of the City Banking & Trust Company and the Hibernia Mutual Fire Insurance Company, and has other interests in the city. A Catholic, Mr. Riley is a member and official of St. Patrick's Catholic Church of Charleston, and he belongs to the Knights of Columbus. A sound, practical and efficient man, Mr. Riley has steadily forged ahead until he is a leader in his line. Having had to practically make his own way in the world, he sympathizes with those less fortunate than he, and his benefactions are many, although the majority of them are never made public. The indigent of his ward have great reason to give him a grateful re-

spect, for he has proven himself their friend upon many occasions. For his native city Mr. Riley has much affection, and it is a source of pride to him that the recent improvements here have been the result of the efforts of him and his associates in the Council, backed by the best men of the community.

GEORGE L. BUIST. There have been five generations of the Buist family represented in the citizenship of Charleston. The first of the family in the city was a very able Presbyterian clergyman. One of his sons, a grandson, great-grandson and great-great-grandson have been lawyers. The name given at the beginning of this paragraph was his grandson.

Rev. George Buist, D. D., was born in Fifeshire, Scotland, in 1770, and was educated at Edinburg University. In 1793 he was called to Charleston as minister of the First Presbyterian church, and served that congregation ably for a number of years. He died at Charleston in 1808. In that city he married Miss Somers, and he left six children.

His son George Buist was born at Charleston in 1805 and died there in 1877. He was educated at South Carolina College, and during the greater part of his active life practiced law. His wife was Mary Edwards Jones, and among their thirteen children one was the late Major George L. Buist.

Major George L. Buist, who filled so conspicuous a place in the affairs of Charleston for upwards of half a century, was born in that city in 1838 and died there in 1907. He also attended Charleston College. The best tribute to his life and character is found in an editorial in the *News and Courier* of June 1, 1907. It reads as follows: "Yesterday the mourners went about the streets and would not be comforted. There was not one who did not have a good word to say about the model citizen who had passed away without a moment's notice, after a busy day spent in the service of his people. The lawyers who had practiced with him at the Bar, the men who had served with him in the affairs of State, those who had been intimate with him in the management of large business concerns, his associates in the educational affairs of the city, his comrades who had stood with him in the shock of battle, his neighbors and friends, white and black, the people of the whole community, indeed, spoke of him and his good deeds, and sorrowed because they should see his face no more.

"It is rare, even in such a community as this, that the emotions of a people are so stirred by the death of any citizen as Charleston was touched to the heart by the news yesterday that the Honorable George Lamb Buist had ceased to exist here. Four months ago Major Julian Mitchell, for many years identified with the educational interests of Charleston, passed out of this life while in the very act of speaking to a brilliant assemblage upon the subject in which his heart was most deeply concerned; Thursday night after returning to his home from the Commencement exercises of an Academy in whose success he felt a deep interest, Mr. Buist, the successor of Mr. Mitchell as chairman of the City Board of School Commissioners, answered the same dread call which had come to his associate, as it must come to all. In the church yard at Melrose Abbey an old time-worn gravestone arrests the attention of every passer-by. On it there is no name, but only this inscription: 'Be thou also ready; great and small are here.' None can stay the hand of the destroyer. The best that can be hoped for is that when our summons comes to join the innumerable caravan that is ever moving on, we shall be able with unfaltering trust to meet our friends who having lived uprightly here, have taught us how to live and how to die.

"Major Buist was nearly seventy years of age. He was born in Charleston and had lived here all his life. He was a splendid citizen. His conduct was never influenced by any but the best and highest motives, and no worthy cause was ever presented to him that did not enlist his support and sympathy. Possessing the thorough confidence of the public, he was trusted by the public in all questions affecting the public welfare. For forty-seven years a member of the Charleston Bar, he was never without clients, and during this long period in the midst of all the changes which have come to the profession he lived up to its best traditions. His advice to his clients was always sound, his appeals to the jury in his more active days were irresistible, and to the last he possessed the unbroken confidence of those who engaged his services.

"As representative and senator from Charleston County in the Legislature, he worked with untiring zeal for the good of his constituents and with never a thought of personal promotion and emolument. He did not seek any benefit for his people which he would not have cheerfully extended to the people in other parts of the State. While his disposition was entirely pacific he did not seek to escape any responsibility when the interests of his constituents required the exercise of the sterner qualities of statesmanship. He intentionally gave offense to none so it came to pass that none gave offense to him.

"Major Buist was the representative for many years of a number of the most important business and financial institutions in Charleston. He had excellent judgment, great business acumen, and was engaged in the settlement of many grave questions affecting large interests. His associates placed the most implicit confidence in his good faith and lofty personal character.

"With the educational concerns of Charleston Major Buist was closely allied for years, as trustee of the College of Charleston, as Commissioner of the City Public Schools, and for the last four months as Chairman of the Board. His heart was wholly enlisted in this work and his death is especially deplored by his associates.

"In the church Major Buist had been deeply interested nearly all his life. He was for years chairman of the Vestry of St. Paul's church, Radcliffboro, and when he withdrew from this important post about a year ago his retirement was made the occasion of very flattering resolutions by those who knew what he had done to keep the light of a pure faith burning in this shrine.

"In his private and personal life Major Buist was above reproach. He was never false to any friend, or disloyal to any obligation as man or citizen.

Everybody liked him and everybody trusted him. Wise in counsel, strong in conviction, loyal in friendship, brave in battle and true in every trust, his death is a serious blow to the community in which he dwelt."

Major Buist married Martha Allston White. He was survived by seven children, one of whom is Henry Buist.

Henry Buist was born at Charleston March 3, 1863, and was graduated from Yale University in 1884. He has practiced law over thirty years, having read law in the office of Buist & Buist, and attended lectures under the celebrated John B. Minor of the University of Virginia. He was admitted to the bar in December, 1885, and is now head of the firm of Buist & Buist, attorneys, at Charleston.

On October 20, 1887, he married Miss Frances Gualdo Ravenel. They have four children: George L. Buist, who was born in 1888 and is now practicing law at Charleston, having graduated from Yale University in 1910; Mrs. Harriott Ravenel Smythe, born in 1890; Henry Buist, Jr., born in 1895, a graduate of the class of 1919 in Yale University; and Frances Gualdo Ravenel Buist, born in 1897.

FRANK BURBIDGE. Fealty to facts in the analyzation of the character of a citizen of the type of Frank Burbidge, president of the Etiwan Fertilizer Company of Charleston, is all that is required to make a biographical sketch interesting to those who have at heart the good name of the community, because it is the honorable reputation of the man of standing and affairs more than any other consideration that gives character and stability to the body politic and makes the true glory of a city or state revered at home and respected in other and distant localities. Mr. Burbidge is regarded as one of the leaders in business circles in his city, and thirty years of identification with the industrial and commercial life of this locality have but confirmed the high position he holds in the hearts of those who know him.

Frank Burbidge is a native of London, England, where he was born on February 4, 1857, and is the son of Enoch and Caroline (Green) Burbidge, also natives of that place. Five children were born to these parents, of which number the subject is the third in order of birth. He was reared in his native city and received a good practical education in the public schools of that locality. In 1873, when seventeen years of age, Mr. Burbidge came to the United States. During the subsequent seventeen years he was located at various places, but in 1890 he came to Charleston, being engaged to build the plant of the Chicora Fertilizer Company. He became thoroughly familiar with the business of manufacturing and preparing fertilizers for the market, and in 1900 he was chiefly instrumental in organizing the Etiwan Fertilizer Company, of which he became president, and which took over the old Etiwan fertilizer plant which had first been started in 1868 and which is located on Cooper River. This concern, under the able management of Mr. Burbidge, has enjoyed a steady and healthy growth and is now numbered among the most important enterprises in its line in this section of the South, its products being shipped to practically every part of the Union. In the promotion of modern methods in the manufacture of fertilizer Mr. Burbidge may be regarded as a pioneer, for it was he who first introduced the burning of pyrites, instead of the former method of using sulphur, an ingredient mostly imported from Italy. This newer process not only resulted in greatly reducing the cost of manufacture, but also increased both the quantity and the value of the output, and is now in universal use in all modern fertilizer plants. Mr. Burbidge takes a live interest in the general commercial advancement of his city and gives his support to every movement looking to the general public betterment. He is a director of the Atlantic Savings Bank of Charleston.

In October, 1875, Frank Burbidge was married to Matilda Mathison, a native of Sweden, the ceremony occurring in New York. To them have been born two sons, Frank A. and Theodore A. Mr. Burbidge is a member of the Masonic order.

Mr. Burbidge is not only a progressive man of affairs, successful in material pursuits, but a man of modest and unassuming demeanor, a fine type of the reliable, self-made man who has ever stood ready to unite with his fellows in any good work.

RT. REV. WILLIAM T. RUSSELL, as Bishop of Charleston has brought to his diocese and the state of South Carolina singular abilities and a brilliant record of achievement in his church. Bishop Russell came to Charleston from one of the greatest churches in America, St. Patrick's Church at Washington, which he served as rector for nine years.

He was born at Baltimore October 20, 1863, a son of William T. and Rose Russell. As a boy he served at the altar of old St. Patrick's Church and attended parochial schools. At the age of fourteen he began his studies at St. Charles' College at Ellicott City, Maryland, where he remained five years, but on account of failing health he went to Loyola College, where he spent a year under the care of a physician. He then re-entered St. Charles' College and spent four years more. From St. Charles' College he went to Rome, Italy, where he finished his studies in philosophy, but his health again failing he returned to the United States and resumed his studies in theology at St. Mary's College in Baltimore, Maryland. He was ordained a priest June 21, 1889. His first appointment was at Hyattsville, Maryland, where he served as pastor of St. Jerome's Church from 1889 to 1894. It was a small church, and he had time to spend several days of each week in study at the Catholic University of America at Washington. At the end of two years he was given the degree of Licentiate of Sacred Theology. He has since been honored with the D. D. degree by St. Mary's Seminary, and that of LL. D. by Mount St. Mary's College.

It was his work in his first parish of Hyattsville which attracted the attention of Cardinal Gibbons, and he was assigned to duty in the Cathedral as secretary to his Eminence, serving from 1894 to 1908.

February 23, 1908, he was installed as pastor of St. Patrick's Church at Washington. His predecessor, the late Rev. D. J. Stafford, had earned a great fame for himself and his church through his

+Wm. T. Russell,
Bishop of Charleston.

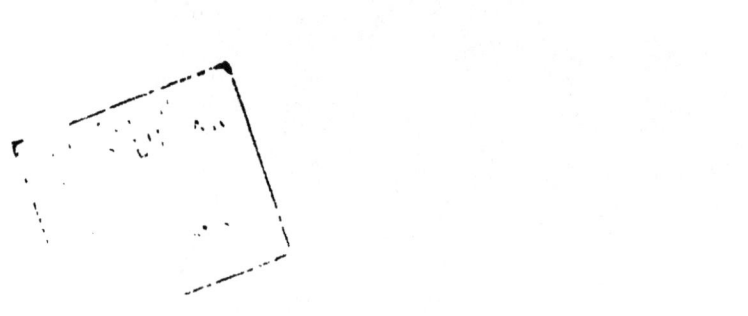

eloquence, and Bishop Russell therefore was confronted with a most difficult task when he assumed the pastorate. What he lacked in eloquence he made up in initiative and constructive progress, and in ten years, it is the opinion of church authorities, he made St. Patrick's in many respects the first parish in the United States.

During this time he realized an important aim in making it a national parish, in keeping with the character of the city and community it serves. One of his notable achievements was founding the League of the Good Shepherd, which held its meetings in St. Patrick's, and was established November 1, 1908. This League has since grown until it is now a feature of many parishes throughout the country. In the year 1909 Bishop Russell inaugurated the Pan-American Thanksgiving Celebration at Washington, a celebration attended by President Taft and the representatives of twenty-one American Republics. Since then the Pan-American Mass has been an annual feature of St. Patrick's. Cardinal Gibbons at the Thanksgiving service of 1916, in referring to Bishop Russell's work in inaugurating the annual festival, said: "He has impressed it with a dignity and solemnity which has won nation-wide, yes, world-wide fame and which commands for him the highest respect and gratitude of the citizens of Washington and even of the nation. This celebration of Thanksgiving day has been going on now for some years and I am satisfied that it would be impossible to duplicate a festival of this kind with all its consequences and with all its surrounding circumstances."

Another achievement of Bishop Russell was "The Field Mass," celebrated at an altar erected on the Monument Grounds only a short distance from the Washington Monument. It was for these services and celebrations, in addition to a growing program of usefulness, dignity and beauty in St. Patrick's regular service that Bishop Russell achieved his great fame among the Catholic clergy of America. A leading Catholic publication said: "The imposing celebration held in St. Patrick's church made him known personally or by reputation to many people throughout the country. There were tasks of importance, however, concerning the general welfare of the church and its people, accomplished without any display, of which only the few knew and for which only the few could offer thanks. He now goes to a difficult field of labor, but those who know him are persuaded that he will go with a heart full of courage and a soul full of zeal and enter into his work with all that God has given him. We do not hesitate to say that when he has finished his task the name of Bishop Russell will be written large in the annals of the Charleston Diocese."

That prediction and hope have been well fulfilled. Bishop Russell was elected December 7, 1916, and consecrated bishop of Charleston, March 15, 1917, and March 19, 1917, was installed at the Cathedral of Charleston. He has handled the difficult task of diocesan administration with rare skill and ability and has assumed many additional burdens, especially those resulting from the great war. He was one of the four bishops of the National Catholic War Council of the Executive Committee directing all Catholic activities in the war.

In September, 1919, at a meeting in Washington of the old Catholic Hierarchy, Cardinal Gibbons presiding, was inaugurated "The National Catholic Welfare Council." An administrative committee was elected by the prelates present. The administrative committee is divided in four parts, viz., Education, Publicity, Social Welfare and Lay Societies. Bishop Russell was placed in charge of Publicity, Press and Literature.

Bishop Russell before coming to Charleston bore the title Monsignor Russell, having been created a Domestic Prelate through Pope Pius X on June 20, 1911. He has served as president of St. Vincent's and St. Joseph's Orphan Asylums at Washington and is a member of the American Historical Association, the Maryland Historical Society and among other results of his scholarship has achieved no small reputation as an historian. He is author of the History of Archdiocese of Baltimore in the Catholic Encyclopedia, and his most widely known work is "Maryland, the Land of Sanctuary," published in 1907.

JOHN L. SHEPPARD. Charleston has been especially honored in the character and career of her active men of industry and commerce—men who have been born to leadership in the various vocations, men who have dominated because of their superior intelligence, natural endowment and force of character. It is always profitable to study such lives, weigh their motives and hold up their achievements as incentives to greater activity and higher excellence on the part of others. These reflections are suggested by the career of one who has forged his way to the front ranks of the favored few and who by a strong inherent force and superior business ability, directed and controlled by intelligence and judgment of a high order, has stood for many years one of the leading men of his city.

John L. Sheppard is a native son of the city now honored by his citizenship, having been born here on January 14, 1842. He is a son of Thomas Coates and Mary (Leefe) Sheppard, both also natives of Charleston. The subject's paternal grandfather was a native of Philadelphia, Pennsylvania, whence he came to Charleston and here spent the latter part of his life. To Thomas C. and Mary Sheppard were born five children, three sons and two daughters, namely: Christianna, Anna W., John L., Benjamin Taylor and Thomas C. The two last named were soldiers in the army of the Confederacy during the Civil war and gave up their lives in that struggle.

John L. Sheppard received his education in the old B. R. Carroll private school of Charleston, which he attended until the age of fourteen years, when he entered the office of a cotton dealer, with whom he remained until the outbreak of the Civil war. He was a member of Company A, Twenty-fifth Regiment, South Carolina Infantry, and held the rank of sergeant. Toward the close of the war, by order of the medical board, he was compelled to accept an appointment in the transportation department. On the conclusion of his military service Mr. Sheppard again entered the cotton business under his former employer, though now he was stationed at Augusta, Georgia. Eventually, however, Mr. Sheppard, ambitious to engage in business on

Vol. V—11

his own account, returned to Charleston and began dealing in rice. From that time to the present he has remained identified with the handling and sale of that product and is distinguished as being one of the oldest rice dealers in the South in point of years of consecutive connection with the business. During these years not only has he enjoyed prosperity but, which is of far more importance, he has held the fullest confidence of the business world, standing among the commercial leaders of Charleston. He has been identified with many phases of the city's development and progress, being always counted on as a supporter of every laudable movement for the public good. He is president of the Charleston Merchants Exchange, whose membership, while not large, embraces the largest wholesale merchants of the city, and is of considerable importance in relation to the commercial life of the community.

Mr. Sheppard is a member and the present commander of Camp Sumter No. 250, United Confederate Veterans. He is also president of the Washington Light Infantry Veterans, the members of which are survivors of three companies, upwards of 440 young men, who in 1862 volunteered "for the war," and less than twenty-five now survive. The organization was instituted many years ago, with the specific object of preserving the roll of old company and keeping in touch with old comrades. At that time there were about 100 members. He is also treasurer of the Washington Light Infantry Annuity Fund, a fund which since the close of the war has distributed nearly $40,000 among widows and orphans.

On April 24, 1873, Mr. Sheppard was married to Margaret Henderson Gilliland, and to them have been born seven children, namely: John L., Jr., William G., Margaret H., Sarah Bryan, wife of Frank Martin; Katie, wife of Robert R. Pregnall; Daniel G., who is now in the service of his country in France, and Thomas C.

Fraternally Mr. Sheppard is a member of the Masonic order and is a member of the Baptist Church. While he has through the years carried on a special line of business in such a manner as to gain a comfortable competence for himself, he has also belonged to that class of representative men of affairs who promote the public welfare while advancing individual success. His sterling traits of character have commanded uniform confidence and regard and he is honored by all who know him.

ROBERT SPANN CATHCART, M. D. This well known surgeon of Charleston has achieved real distinction in his profession, and his name is known for the abilities and attainments associated with it far beyond the borders of his home city and state.

Dr. Cathcart was born at Columbia, South Carolina, September 25, 1871, of Scotch-Irish ancestry and a son of Colonel William R. and Elizabeth (Kelley) Cathcart. The Cathcarts were English but came to America from Ireland. His grandfather, George Cathcart, was born in County Antrim, Ireland. Colonel William Richard Cathcart was a native of Columbia and lived there most of his life. During the war between the states he was in the signal corps and was stationed nearly four years at Fort Sumter. Dr. Cathcart's mother was a daughter of William Aiken Kelley, who came to Charleston from Philadelphia. She was the mother of six children, and Colonel Cathcart after her death married Kate S. Kelley, by whom he had a daughter and son.

Dr. Cathcart acquired his primary education at Columbia, and in 1890 graduated from the School of Pharmacy of the University of South Carolina. Three years later, in 1893, he was graduated from the Medical College of South Carolina at Charleston. He served as interne in the Charleston Hospital one year, and then for fourteen years was engaged in the general practice of medicine. For the past twelve years his work has been limited to surgery. He is a Fellow of the American College of Surgeons, is professor of the Abdominal Surgery Medical College of South Carolina, is surgeon for the Charleston Consolidated Railway and Light Company, surgeon of the Atlantic Coast Line Railway, surgeon to the Seaboard Air Line, surgeon to The Citadel, the Military College of South Carolina, surgeon-in-chief to the Roper Hospital at Charleston, and was medical aid to the governor in selective draft service and was a major in the Medical Reserve Corps. He also served as chief surgeon of the Base Hospital at Camp Woodworth, South Carolina, and chief of the surgical staff of General Hospital No. 24 at Pittsburg.

Dr. Cathcart is president of the Medical Society of South Carolina and is retiring president of the Tri-State Medical Association, comprising North Carolina, South Carolina and Virginia. Dr. Cathcart is a Chapter and Knight Templar Mason and Shriner and an Elk.

January 5, 1898, he married Katherine J. Morrow, of Birmingham, Alabama. They have four children: Mary Frances, Katherine Morrow, Robert S., Jr., and Hugh.

As a boy from 1887 to 1889 Dr. Cathcart served as a page in the House of Representatives at Columbia.

JAMES F. IZLAR was born in Orangeburg County November 25, 1832, of Swiss and Scotch descent. Until his seventeenth year he attended local schools, when he entered Emory College of Georgia, graduating with first honors in 1854. He began the study of law in 1855, and was admitted to the bar and began practice at Orangeburg in 1858.

During the war he served for a year with the First South Carolina Regiment, then as third lieutenant of the Edisto Rifles, and finally was captain of that company, a part of the Twenty-fifth Regiment. He was a participant in some of the hardest fighting in Virginia from 1863 until made a prisoner, and at the close of the war was on Governor's Island in New York. He resumed practice at Orangeburg in 1866. He was elected judge of the First Circuit in 1889, and later was twice elected a member of the State Senate. He was mayor of Orangeburg, a trustee of South Carolina College, and in 1894 was elected to fill a vacancy from the First District in the Fifty-third Congress. Judge Izlar married Frances M. Lovell.

CHARLES W. KOLLOCK, M. D., one of the eminent physicians and surgeons of South Carolina, has specialized for over thirty years in diseases of the eye, ear, nose and throat, and is a recognized authority in ophthalmology.

Doctor Kollock was born at Cheraw in Chesterfield County, April 29, 1857, son of Dr. Cornelius and Mary Henrietta (Shaw) Kollock. His father was a native of Marlboro County and practiced his profession for about fifty years. His grandfather was Oliver Hawes Kollock, a native of Wrentham, Massachusetts, who came south when a young man. A lawyer by profession, he turned his energies to planting in South Carolina. The mother of Dr. C. W. Kollock was born at Boston, Massachusetts, and was educated there and abroad in Europe. Doctor Kollock is a great-nephew of John L. Wilson, who was governor of the State of South Carolina in 1822 and was author of the Duelling Code of the State.

Doctor Kollock was educated in the common schools of Cheraw and the Academy there, and at the age of sixteen entered the Virginia Military Institute at Lexington, graduating in 1877. He took up the study of medicine in his father's office, and in 1878 entered the University of Pennsylvania in the Department of Medicine, graduating in March, 1881. For three years following his graduation he served as interne at the Philadelphia Hospital, Children's Hospital and the Wills Eye Hospital of that city. In 1884 he attended eye and ear clinics in London and Paris. He began private practice at Charleston in 1885 and has always confined his attention to the eye, ear, nose and throat.

With an extensive experience of a third of a century Doctor Kollock has contributed many reports and special papers to medical journals and to the transactions of the South Carolina Medical Association. For many years he made a special study of the "Eye of the Negro," and has contributed much to the original knowledge of that subject. He has served as ophthalmic and aural surgeon in the Charleston City and Roper hospitals and to the Shirras Dispensary, and for a number of years has been professor of diseases of the throat and nose in the Medical College of the State of South Carolina. He is a member of the South Carolina Medical Association, the Medical Society of South Carolina, American Medical Association, American Ophthalmological Society, the Otolaryngological Society, the Tri-State Medical Association of Virginia and Carolinas, and the Association of Air Surgeons, and he also belongs to the St. Cecilia Society, Charles Library Society, and the Alpha Tau Omega college fraternity. He was a lieutenant in the Charleston Light Dragoons from 1886 to 1895, and later became captain, in which capacity he served for four or five years.

Governor McSweeney appointed him special aide with the rank of colonel on the staff of President Roosevelt during Roosevelt's visit to the Exposition of Charleston in 1902. For four years Doctor Kollock was a member of the city council and on the board of health twenty years. During the war with Germany he was commissioned captain in 1917 and was put in charge of examination of men for the aviation section of the Signal Corps. Later he was sent to Mineola, New York, and was in training as a flight surgeon, subsequently being ordered to Kelley Field, Texas, as flight surgeon. He was commissioned a major in the Medical Corps in August, 1918, and received his honorable discharge in December, 1918. His son William G. was a captain in the air service, and has been for a number of years a resident of Los Angeles, California.

November 10, 1885, Doctor Kollock married Miss Gertrude E. Gregg, of Charleston, granddaughter of William Gregg. They were the parents of two children: William Gregg and Henrietta Shaw. Mrs. Kollock died in 1904. In 1906 he married Miss Sarah Elizabeth Irvin, of Washington, Georgia. The three children born to this union are Charles W., Jr., Sarah Irvin, Jr., and Nancy Hicks.

SIDNEY C. SNELGROVE, who for over two years was in actual service with the United States Navy during the World war, and is still a reserve officer, is a graduate of The Citadel at Charleston, and he and his wife have for a number of years been leading merchants in that city.

He was born January 23, 1880, at Mount Willing, now in Saluda County, formerly part of Edgefield County. His father, Eli Snelgrove, is still living, a prosperous farmer and substantial citizen of the Mount Willing community, member of the district school board and a man of standing and influence in that locality. The mother, Mary Miller Snelgrove, who died in 1896, was a daughter of Lydia Sawyer, a member of the well known Sawyer family of Lexington County. The Snelgroves, of English ancestry, have long been identified with the older generations of Edgefield County. The home at Mount Willing is nine miles from Batesburg, and became part of Saluda County when it was formed out of portions of Edgefield, Aiken and Lexington counties.

Sidney C. Snelgrove spent about two years as a student in Leesville College. He had the honor of being selected as the first beneficiary student of The Citadel from the then new county of Saluda, and entered that school in the fall of 1896. He was graduated with the class of 1900, and following that for two years taught school, being principal of Limestone School in Orangeburg County. After his marriage he located at Charleston, and they soon established the millinery business well known as the French Hat Shop at 258 King Street in the heart of the best retail district. Mr. Snelgrove is actively associated with his wife in the management of this shop, which enjoys a high class and exclusive patronage. The success and prestige of their business is due to the tireless energy, ability, and artistic sense of Mrs. Snelgrove, no less than to the assistance of her husband.

Mr. Snelgrove married December 16, 1903, Miss Blanche Caughman, of Columbia, daughter of Mr. and Mrs. Banks L. Caughman, of that city, the Caughmans being an old Edgefield County family. Banks L. Caughman was the first state senator from Saluda County, has served as state railroad commissioner, and has long been prominent in South Carolina public life. Mr. and Mrs. Snelgrove have an adopted son, Sidney C., Jr., now a student in the Porter Military Academy.

Mr. Snelgrove is secretary and treasurer of Grace Episcopal Church Sunday School; a member of St. Andrews Society; the South Carolina Society; Carolina Yacht Club; the Rotary Club; and is a past master of Orange Lodge No. 14, Ancient Free and Accepted Masons, and a member of the Mystic Shrine.

Partly due to his training at The Citadel and partly through natural inclination he has always had an active interest in military and patriotic affairs. He was a member of the South Carolina Naval Militia, a branch of the old National Guard establishment, and was commissioned lieutenant in the Naval Militia on May 10, 1915. At the same date he was appointed disbursing officer, and was with the Reserve Fleet in the summer cruises of 1915-16.

The detailed record of his service during the World war is as follows: Mobilized April 6, 1917, reporting to the commandant of the Sixth Naval District, United States Navy; ordered to duty as assistant to the supply officer of the Charleston Navy Yard April 8, 1917; detached from the Charleston Navy Yard February 19, 1918, and ordered to duty as disbursing officer, U. S. Naval Air Station, Pensacola, Florida, reporting to the commandant at that station February 21, 1918; remained in active service there until relieved and put on the inactive list July 23, 1919; confirmed lieutenant (Pay Corps) U. S. N. R. F., Class 2, for General Service by General Order No. 400 of July 1, 1918. Since relieved from active duty he has been retained as a reserve officer in the United States Navy.

THOMAS GRANGE SIMONS. No other profession during the last half century has accomplished the progress and development that have been made by the medical. This has not been the work of those who became learned by knowledge obtained from books, or the experiences of a past generation, but by those who rose to new occasions, who thought in new lines and did new things, for "New occasions teach new duties; time makes ancient good uncouth." The man of original thought and action, whose text-book forms but the basis for future work, has ever moved forward, taking his profession with him; he becomes a leader, and those that follow reap lasting benefit from his work. Such a man has been Dr. Thomas Grange Simons, for a period of nearly a half century one of the best known medical men of the South and a man who has distinctively honored the city of his residence. In considering the character and career of this eminent member of the medical fraternity, the impartial observer will be disposed to rank him among not only the most distinguished members of this important branch of science of this generation, in which he has few peers and no superiors, but also as one of those men of broad culture and genuine benevolence who have honored mankind in general. Through a long and busy life he has known none but the highest motives, and to the practice of his profession he has brought rare skill and resource, while his quick perception and almost intuitive judgment have rendered him expert in diagnosis. As a citizen he has easily ranked with the most influential of his compeers in affairs looking toward the betterment of his city and state. His course has ever been above suspicion, and those who have been favored with an intimate acquaintance with him have been profuse in their praise of his virtues and upright character, that of the true gentleman.

Thomas Grange Simons was born in Charleston on May 10, 1843, and is a son of Thomas and Mary Ann (Bentham) Simons. He has spent practically his entire life of more than three-quarters of a century in the city of his birth. His general education was received in W. M. Rivers' school and in Charleston College. He left the latter institution in his junior year and entered the Confederate army. He became first sergeant of the Washington Light Infantry, Twenty-fifth Regiment of South Carolina Volunteers, which became a part of Hagood's Brigade. He saw service along the South Carolina coast and was wounded at Secessionville on June 16, 1862, and again at Battery Wagner, Morris Island, on September 6, 1863. He served around Petersburg and Richmond in Virginia, and along the Carolina coast during 1864-5 and was captured by General Sherman's forces at Cheraw, South Carolina, in April, 1865.

Immediately after the close of the war Mr. Simons began the study of medicine under the direction of Dr. William H. Huger, and then attended two courses of lectures at the Medical College of the State of South Carolina, where he was graduated in March, 1867. He was then appointed interne at the Charleston City Hospital, where he remained until 1869, when he entered upon the private practice of his profession, which he has continued to the present time.

Doctor Simons is a member of the Medical Association of the State of South Carolina, of which he was president in 1888-9, and during the two following years he was president of the Medical Society of South Carolina; a member of the Charleston County Medical Society; the Southern Surgical and Gynecological Association; the Medical Society for the Relief of Widows and Orphans of Medical Men; the Howard Medical Association, Memphis, Tennessee, in 1878; the American Public Health Association, and a member of its advisory council; formerly a member of the State Board of Medical Examiners; a member of the State Board of Health and chairman of its committee on quarantine; a member of the board of trustees of the Roper Hospital, Charleston; a member of the Conference of Yellow Fever Experts, Montgomery, Alabama, 1889. Doctor Simons was city dispensary physician during the yellow fever epidemic in Charleston in 1871-73; served at Fernandino, Florida, during the yellow fever epidemic of 1877 and at Memphis, Tennessee, during the epidemic of the following year; was medical director pro tem. of the Howard Medical Corps.

Of Doctor Simons' contributions to medical literature the following are specially noteworthy: "Yellow Fever," transactions of the Medical Association of South Carolina, 1877; "Atresia Vaginae," 1890; "Acute Infective Haemoglobinaemia" idem

1890; "Ante Partum (Accidental) Hemorrhage," idem, 1891; "Laceration of the Cervix Uteri as a Factor in Placenta Previa," transactions of the Southern Surgical and Gynecological Association, 1892. The Doctor has made some original researches in relation to the use of the tendons of rats and squirrel tails as surgical ligatures, and has also been deeply interested in the perfection of quarantine procedures and modern maritime sanitation, as well as land quarantine. He has been assistant demonstrator of anatomy in the Medical College of the State of South Carolina and now professor of materia medica; assistant professor of the practice of medicine and of clinical medicine at the same institution, 1883-6; was physician to the Charleston city dispensary, 1869-72; physician to Shirra's Dispensary, 1873-9, and to the City Hospital, 1873-4.

Along with the multitudinous professional interests which have enlisted his attention, Doctor Simons has found time to give intelligent attention to local public affairs and has always given his support to all worthy public movements. In 1873 he was a member of the city council, as alderman from the sixth ward, and served as chairman of the committee on sewerage.

Doctor Simons is a member of the Charleston Survivors Association, Confederate States Army, Camp Sumter No. 250, North Carolina Veterans, and surgeon of the Washington Light Infantry Veterans Association, Confederate States Army; and he is an appreciate member of Landmark Lodge No. 76, Ancient Free and Accepted Masons.

Dr. Thomas G. Simons was married on November 11, 1879, to Serena D. Aiken, of Charleston, and they have become the parents of five children, namely: Joseph Aiken, Thomas Grange, Jr., Robert Bentham, William Lucas and Albert. All these sons served in the late war, three of them overseas. The wife and mother died in Charleston, January 4, 1917.

Doctor Simons' long and useful life as one of the world's workers has been one of devotion, almost consecration, to his calling, and so he has dignified and honored the profession by his able services in which, through long years of close application, he has attained notable distinction and unqualified success. He has been universally regarded as a splendid citizen, of lofty character, sturdy integrity and unswerving honesty. He has done his full share in all the relations of life and now is secure in the confidence and sincere regard of all who know him and his work.

He is now chairman of the board of sewer commissioners of the City of Charleston. He was an early advocate of the modern system when a member of the council. He has fought for it ever since until the point was won. Doctor Simons feels this to be one of his most important works and that will endure. The city is installing an extensive system and already the improvement in general health is noted. He is still in the general practice of medicine and is the physician of the Charleston Orphan House and lectures at the college. He is active and well preserved mentally and physically.

COL. JULIUS E. COGSWELL has played a notable part in the affairs of Charleston for over thirty years as a lawyer, public official, military man and citizen.

He was born in Columbia, May 13, 1865, a son of Harvey and Mary (Keller) Cogswell. His father was a native of Charleston and was a publisher and manufacturing stationer and during the war between states was Confederate Government printer and manufactured the Government bonds and money. His plant was originally in Charleston, but during the war, as a matter of protection, was moved to Columbia. When Sherman burned Columbia Mr. Cogswell's printing plant was destroyed and his business swept away. He had a foresight of the future and its development and saw that milling was going to have a great development through the South. With Mr. Benjamin F. Evans, his brother-in-law and former partner, he started in the milling business. They built a cotton mill near Augusta, Aitkin County, South Carolina. This mill is still running under the name of the Kalmia mill, one of the oldest cotton mills in the state. Thus Mr. Cogswell was one of the pioneer mill builders of South Carolina.

Having started the mill business under northern capital and with every prospect of a great success, when northern capital was withdrawn the little company was forced into failure, and the foundation that had been so well laid was absorbed by others and developed into a great business. It was then called the Langley Mills.

Before the Civil war broke out the printing firm was known as Walker, Evans & Cogswell, but Mr. Walker withdrew and went into the paper manufacturing business, and the firm became Evans & Cogswell, and this was the firm that did the printing of bonds and money for the Confederate Government. After the war had ruined the business of the old partners a reorganization was effected and the old firm of Walker, Evans & Cogswell was reorganized at Charleston and so still exists, although all the founders have died and the business is now carried on by their descendants. Mr. W. H. Cogswell is its president and in January, 1921, will be celebrated the centennial of its founding. A complete history of the firm for the occasion is being prepared by the present president.

Harvey Cogswell died in Charleston in 1901, at the age of ninety-four years. The widow, at the age of eighty-five (1920), still hale and strong, resides in Charleston with her son Col. J. E. Cogswell. Their home is one which for over fifty years they have occupied. This was the early home of the South Carolina Lee family of which Gen. Stephen D. Lee of Confederate fame was one.

The grandfather of Colonel Cogswell was Harvey Cogswell, a native of Massachusetts, and of an early English family. He came to South Carolina about 1820. His wife was E. Susan Mouzon, connected with one of the early French Huguenot families of Charleston. Mary Keller Cogswell, mother of Colonel Cogswell, was born in Orangeburg County, South Carolina, and represented one branch of the Palatinate Germans of that old district. Colonel Cogswell was one of a family of four sons and one daughter, all still living: The others are William Harvey, of Charleston; Sumter of Alabama; F. J. P., a resident of Greenville, South Carolina; S. Julia, wife of Samuel E. Owen of Mathews, South Carolina.

Julius E. Cogswell was the fourth child and third son. When he was about two years old his parents returned to Charleston and he grew up and received his education in that city. He graduated from South Carolina College in 1886, and then entered the law department of Georgetown University at Washington, District of Columbia, completing his course in 1888. For thirty years he has been a dignified and useful member of the Charleston bar. He gave all his time to a general practice until 1893, when he was elected by the Legislature Register of Mesne Conveyance for Charleston County, and by repeated re-elections has held that office now for over a quarter of a century. He also served as City Hospital commissioner in 1893.

Colonel Cogswell is a York Rite Mason, is a past potentate of Omar Temple of the Mystic Shrine and a past grand patron of the Eastern Star. He is also affiliated with the Knights of Pythias and the Independent Order of Odd Fellows.

He was for eleven years captain of the historic Washington Light Infantry at Charleston. He had severed his connection with this organization several years before the beginning of the World war, and though he made repeated efforts to get into the active service he was unsuccessful. In order to do what he could as a citizen trained to arms he enlisted as a private in the South Carolina Reserve Militia, being soon promoted to captain of the Worthington Light Infantry Reserve and subsequently to lieutenant-colonel of the South Carolina Reserve Militia, and finally became colonel commanding the entire reserve of the state.

ALEXANDER ROBINSON BANKS. South Carolina in this day of unexampled material prosperity can well afford to pause and consider a life of such disinterested and unselfish service as that of the late Alexander Robinson Banks. Human character was the material with which he worked, and there was no dearth of this and his enthusiasm never flagged through good times and ill for more than half a century.

This unique figure in southern education was born at Hazelwood, Chester County, South Carolina, May 27, 1847, son of Rev. William and Mary E. (Harrington) Banks. The first of the family to come to this country was Samuel Mandeville Marjoribanks, who for convenience abbreviated the name to Banks. The Marjoribanks family was descended from Robert Bruce through his daughter Marjorie. Samuel Marjoribanks established a fuller's mill on Fishing Creek, South Carolina, near where the Great Falls electric power development now is.

His father, Rev. William Banks, was a man of great piety and pulpit power. He was the bosom friend of Palmer, Girardeau, Thornwell, Woodrow and other men great in the Southern Presbyterian Church. A graduate of the University of Georgia and the Columbia Theological Seminary, Rev. William Banks served as chaplain in the Fourth South Carolina Cavalry of the Confederate army, was president of the Board of Trustees of Davidson College, chairman of the board of Columbia Theological Seminary, and for a quarter of a century stated clerk of the Synod of South Carolina. His faith was illustrated by an incident. He was called by a country church to pray for rain. Although it was a cloudless day he warned the people to go to their homes in haste. The rain came that afternoon and found him expecting it.

A. R. Banks received his early instruction from the best of the old school masters of those times, including his father, who was at one time very early in life at the head of the Mount Zion Institute at Winnsboro, then a collegiate institution of great reputation. From two other forebears A. R. Banks got his love for teaching, "Jake" Hudson, a maternal great-uncle, who presided over Mount Zion Institute in its best days, and Captain John W. Harrington, a maternal uncle. After serving as a young soldier in the last months of the War of Secession, where he became a drill master of recruits, A. R. Banks attended Davidson College, from which he graduated with distinction in 1869. In 1871 Davidson awarded him the Master of Arts degree.

He at once began teaching and for fifty-one years had spent his life in a work for which he had a genuine passion. Being suspected with having a prominent connection with the activities of the Ku Klux Klan in York County, he along with Doctor Bratton, Doctor Avery and others was forced into exile in 1872. He established at Pleasant Ridge, Alabama, a boys' school, afterwards removed to Tuscaloosa, where for many years it flourished. In 1875 Professor Banks was recalled to South Carolina by the death of his father, and soon afterward established the Fort Mill Academy, from which he sent many young men to colleges, especially to Davidson and Princeton, more than fifty of whom became ministers of the Gospel. His "boys" were admitted to colleges without examination. After teaching and farming at Fort Mill successfully for some years he was invited by the late J. Spratt White and others to remove to Rock Hill, then a town of eight hundred. In 1888 he opened with a hundred fifteen pupils the first public school in South Carolina in a building erected especially for graded school purposes. In his three years in the Rock Hill graded school the attendance grew to more than four hundred.

In 1891 he and his friends established in Rock Hill the Presbyterian High School. The high school property later was absorbed by Winthrop College, whose location in Rock Hill is due in part to the inspiration for education which Professor Banks gave to the community. He taught subsequently in Yorkville, Lancaster and Columbia.

His work was essentially that of a preceptor. Perhaps he was the last of the old fashioned school masters. Among the communities in which handsome new school buildings were erected, due in

great part to his effort, were Rock Hill, Kershaw, Lancaster, Bethune, Hyatt Park and the Presbyterian High School.

At the breaking out of the war with Germany Professor Banks made repeated efforts to get into the service as a Young Men's Christian Association teacher or otherwise. He was eager to go to France in some capacity with the old First South Carolina Regiment. But his age was against him. He gave one son to this cause and one to the Spanish-American army. He assisted in many war drives in 1917-18.

For the last few years he had been teaching public schools and tutoring young boys in entrance examinations for colleges. He declared that he was then doing the best work of his life, and the results showed that he rarely failed to get his "boys" in when they competed for scholarships at West Point and Annapolis. Among his former pupils were seven fighting colonels and lieutenant colonels, George H. McMaster, W. W. Lewis, and T. B. Spratt among them, and a large number of captains and majors. He was particularly proud of this fact. He was one of the charter members of the South Carolina Teachers' Association, an organization which he greatly loved. He was one of the first secretaries and filled other offices.

While Professor Banks was proud of his long and unbroken service in the school room, he was equally proud of his record of half a century as Sunday School superintendent and teacher of the Bible. He was a Master Mason and had been master of the Fort Mill Lodge when it was one of the best in the country.

Though frequently urged to offer for state office, he never entered politics. In 1876 he was prominent in Red Shirt activities in York, Chester and Lancaster counties, and rode at the head of a patrol for law and order. By Governor Hugh S. Thompson he was appointed aide with the rank of lieutenant colonel. By appointment of Governors Evans, Ellerbe, McSweeney, Heyward and Ansel he had served on the State Board of Education until he removed from the Fifth District. There is a record of fifty years continuous service on the executive board of Davidson College shared by him and his father, who was president of the board when he died.

When he heard of Professor Banks' death one of his old "boys" said: "He loved life, he was abounding in it; he loved youth, his heart had never grown old; he loved nature, he loved his God and he loved children. Therefore he got out of life the best that life had to offer." He was greatly loved by every boy whom he ever taught. A man of superb physical manhood, he dominated, led and inspired his pupils. He was "master" of the schoolroom; and his purpose was to teach the young to think, to be manly.

In 1875 Professor Banks married Miss Sallie A. McMullen, of Pleasant Ridge, Alabama, who died in 1911. They are survived by three children: William Banks, Mrs. J. Allen Long and John McMullen Banks.

The death of Professor Banks occurred at Ridgeway, South Carolina, February 25, 1920. Few men go into the Great Beyond leaving such a broad wake of inspiration and influence. Many loving testimonials came to the family. Here was a man who had given his life for others and he was rich in their esteem. While he had prepared for college many men noted in annals of state and nation, he was proudest of those, numbering more than fifty, who had come under his influence and had become ministers of the Gospel, a privilege that perhaps no other man in the state had ever enjoyed.

It was his fortune in life to have the handling of many boys who, in the vernacular, were termed "Black Sheep." He appeared to have a deep affection for that kind of lad, and many of them he succeeded in firing with ambition and pride, and getting them started anew upon successful careers. This was his greatest joy in life. He died in the harness, happy in the consciousness of that fact, and his only unfulfilled wish was to be permitted to retire that he might prepare a few simple text books, arithmetic and English grammar, to aid the groping minds of children sometimes confused by modern publications.

WILLIAM BANKS, chairman of the South Carolina Public Service Commission, is one of the men who graduated from the newspaper profession into the larger responsibilities of business and public affairs.

He is a son of that distinguished South Carolina educator the late A. R. Banks, and was born at Fort Mill, South Carolina, July 12, 1877. He attended his father's old school, Fort Mill Academy, and graduated from his father's alma mater, Davidson College, with the class of 1897. He is a member of the Beta Theta Pi college fraternity. His education was very carefully superintended and as he grew up in a literary atmosphere his literary talents were given every opportunity to develop.

As early as twelve years of age he began writing for newspapers. During his last year in college, 1896-97, he was associate editor of the Rock Hill Herald. He then came to Columbia and was city editor of the Columbia Register, a post he resigned to enlist as a private in the Spanish-American war. He was with the First South Carolina Regiment, and was in the ranks except when detailed as clerk at regimental headquarters. He also acted as camp correspondent for the state, and his "War" letters earned him his first real recognition as a newspaper man. It is told that when at the age of twelve he received his first telegraph order for a story of six hundred words, a report of one of Ben Tillman's speeches, he suffered the stage fright that afflicts young reporters.

After his army experience he was connected with the state for more than twelve years as reporter, city editor and news editor. During that time he reported numerous exciting political campaigns, including the overthrow of the state dispensary, in which undertaking his work was conspicuous. Mr. Banks was for a time editor of the Anderson Daily Mail and Anderson Daily Intelligence, and during 1915-17 was editor of the Columbia Evening Record. He served as vice president eight years and two terms as president of the South Carolina Press Association, and has made numerous addresses on journalism and woman's suffrage, and has been a contributor to Collier's and other publications.

Mr. Banks resigned his newspaper work to become a member of the State Council of Defense early in the war, and also held an appointment from President Wilson in connection with explosives regulation. In order to remain in war work in South Carolina he declined a call to a prominent Canada daily publication. He was a member of the "Committee of Nine" chosen during the war to assist in preserving order and to assist in war activities, and he also acted as state publicity director for a number of successful campaigns for Liberty Bonds and other drives. Governor Manning appointed him a member of the State Council of Defense, and he was chairman of its reclamation committee.

Mr. Banks was appointed by Governor Cooper chairman of the South Carolina Public Service Commission, and has served in that office of great responsibility since 1919. One important feature of the work of this Commission during his time was the reduction of rates on electricity and gas in Columbia, following a tedious inquiry. Mr. Banks served as aide with the rank of lieutenant colonel on the staff of Governor Heyward and afterward on that of Governor Ansel. Governor Manning appointed him a trustee of the State College at Orangeburg. He is a charter member of the Columbia Rotary Club, serving twice as delegate to international conventions; is a York and Scottish Rite Mason, Odd Fellow, and a member of the Columbia, Ridgewood, Rotary and Forum Clubs. He has been a delegate to county and state democratic conventions, and more than once declined state office.

Mr. Banks married Miss Louise Vance, of Laurens, South Carolina. They have two children, Caroline Vance Banks and William Banks, Jr. Mr. Banks is secretary of the diaconate of the First Presbyterian Church.

PRESTON C. JOHNSTON. Only those who come into personal contact with Preston C. Johnston, of St. George, clerk of courts of Dorchester County, scion of one of the worthy old families of South Carolina, and for many years one of the popular and successful teachers of this section of the state, can understand how thoroughly nature and training, habits of thought and action have enabled him to accomplish his life work and made him a creditable representative of the enterprising class of professional people to which he belongs. He is a fine type of the sturdy, conscientious, progressive American of today—a man who unites a high order of ability with courage, patriotism, clean morality and sound common sense, doing thoroughly and well the work that he finds to do and asking praise of no man for the performance of what he conceives to be his simple duty.

Preston C. Johnston was born in Colleton County, South Carolina, on December 24, 1840, and is the son of A. R. and Mary L. (Interbinet) Johnston. The father was born in Colleton County, but moved to Beaufort County in 1842, and there became quite prominent in local public affairs. He represented St. Peters in the House of Representatives and afterward served seven years as a member of the State Senate. He died when about sixty years of age. His father was John Johnston, a native of Beaufort, and he was the son of Capt. Nathan Johnston, who was a captain in the patriot army during the War of the Revolution and who is supposed to have been a native of England. The subject's mother, who was born in Colleton County, South Carolina, was the daughter of John N. Interbinet, a large land owner and slave holder prior to the war. The subject is the younger of two sons born to his parents, his brother, William I., being a graduate of Charleston Medical College and for many years a successful medical practitioner in Eastern Texas.

Preston C. Johnston passed his boyhood days in Beaufort, to which place the family had moved shortly after his birth. After attending the common schools he was a student in Lautenville Academy, Mt. Zion College and, finally, Walford College, where he was graduated in 1861, with the degree of Bachelor of Arts. Subsequently he received from his alma mater the degree of Master of Arts. At the outset of the war between the states Mr. Johnston was among the first to enlist, though he served but a short time. He engaged in teaching school, which with few short intermissions has been his lifelong vocation. He first went to Texas, where he followed his profession for ten years and then returned to South Carolina and was engaged continuously as a teacher until his election to the office of clerk of the courts of Dorchester County. So entirely satisfactory has been the discharge of his official duties in this responsible position that he has twice been elected as his own successor, thus he is now serving his third consecutive term.

In 1861 Preston C. Johnston was united in marriage to Annie C. Smith, of Spartanburg, South Carolina, and to them were born fifteen children, of which number twelve, eight sons and four daughters, were reared to maturity. Of the eight children who are yet living, three of them are physicians, one is a dentist and another is postmaster of St. George. In 1911 Mr. and Mrs. Johnston celebrated the fiftieth anniversary of their marriage, a joyous occasion, participated in by all their surviving children and descendants.

Fraternally Mr. Johnston is a member of the Ancient Free and Accepted Masons and has long been an active and influential member of the Methodist Episcopal Church. In every relation of life he has so ordered his actions as to earn the confidence and esteem of all who know him. As a teacher he was deservedly well liked, for no one is more entitled to the thoughtful consideration of a free and enlightened people than he who shapes and directs the minds of the young, adds to the value of their intellectual treasurers and moulds their characters.

DAVID G. DWIGHT for the past fifteen years has been a figure of growing importance in the fertilizer industry at Charleston, is a graduate of The Citadel, was formerly commandant of the Porter Military Academy at Charleston, and has always been deeply interested in the splendid and historic institution of which he is an alumnus.

FRANKLIN GORHAM BURROUGHS

Mr. Dwight was president of the Association of Graduates of The Citadel from June, 1918, to June, 1920, and for several years has taken an influential part in the alumni organization. As president of the association he deserves much of the credit for the movement now approaching success for the building of the greater Citadel. Work on that ambitious project has already begun, and under the leadership of the association it is possible to predict fulfilment of a plan which every patriotic South Carolinian has long desired, to put this historic and famous school on a sound financial basis and provide for it a home that would be a source of pride to the entire state.

Mr. Dwight was born at Winnsboro in Fairfield County, South Carolina, in 1871, son of William Moultrie and Elizabeth (Gaillard) Dwight. His family on both sides has prominent connections in South Carolina. His father was born at Cedar Grove plantation in Berkeley County, that being the ancestral home of this branch of the Dwight family. More remotely the Dwights came from Wales to Massachusetts and were among the early settlers in the low country of South Carolina. The first to come to South Carolina, one Daniel Dwight, was a missionary of the Church of England. The paternal grandfather of David G. Dwight was Isaac Marion Dwight. On the maternal side he is a grandson of David Gaillard, of French ancestry. The Gaillards appear frequently in the history of prominent families in lower Carolina. David Gaillard in 1836 removed to Fairfield County, taking with him a large number of slaves. As an extensive planter he had two estates in the county, Springfield, located a few miles north of Winnsboro, and Clifton, adjoining the town of Winnsboro.

David G. Dwight was educated in Mount Zion College in Fairfield County and graduated from The Citadel at Charleston in 1890. The next two years he taught in the public schools of Winnsboro, and then became an instructor in Porter's Academy at Charleston. From instructor he was made commandant, and for several years that well known institution was under his executive management. He gave up educational work in 1905, when he resigned from the Porter School, and entered the fertilizer business. For several years Mr. Dwight has been general manager and treasurer of the McCabe Fertilizer Company, one of the largest firms in South Carolina manufacturing commercial fertilizer.

Mr. Dwight is a communicant of St. Michael's Church. He married Miss Susan Chisholm, member of the old and well known Charleston family of that name. Their two children are Susan and David G., Jr.

FRANKLIN GORHAM BURROUGHS. Out of an insufficiency of early opportunity, and acting in an epoch which was one of peculiar hardship to the entire state, the late Frank Gorham Burroughs achieved that success and character that justify an enduring memory, particularly in the City of Conway, where he lived so much of his life.

He was born near Williamston, North Carolina, December 28, 1834, son of Anthony and Ethelinda (Cobb) Burroughs. Altogether his formal school advantages did not amount to more than six months in a country schoolhouse, nevertheless he used his natural gifts and judgment well. In August, 1857, he moved to Horry County, South Carolina, and after a few months of service as deputy sheriff engaged in the turpentine and mercantile business in a small way. That was his work until the opening of the Civil war. Leaving his business in 1861, he volunteered at the organization of the Brooks Guards, and for four years was in the Western Army in Company B of the Tenth South Carolina Regiment in Manigault's Brigade. He was captured at Franklin, Tennessee, in 1864, and until the end of the war was confined at Camp Douglas, Chicago.

After the war he returned to Conway, and resumed the mercantile and turpentine business, with practically no capital. The title of the firm in 1866 was Gurganus & Burroughs, which later became Burroughs, Hart & Company, and subsequently Burroughs & Collins, his partner of longest standing being B. G. Collins. This firm was largely instrumental in the development of transportation in this section. They brought about the establishment of a line of sailing vessels between New York and points on the Waccamaw River. For a number of years this was the only means of transportation in this region. The firm built the first steamboat ever constructed in Conway, and operated it regularly on the Waccamaw River. The firm was also largely instrumental in establishing the first bank in the county, and is probably entitled to the credit of having established the first steam cotton gin in the county. The firm of Burroughs & Collins was incorporated in 1895 as the Burroughs & Collins Company. Though Franklin G. Burroughs died about two years later the business has been continued through his sons, and has been closely identified with all movements for the development of the county up to the present time, including the promotion and building of the Conway Coast and Western Railroad. The late Mr. Burroughs was intensely interested in the cause of education, partly due no doubt to his own early limitations. He co-operated in the establishment of the first regular school in the town, a school that later became and has been known as the Burroughs High School. He was a democrat and Mason, and was strongly in the fight under Hampton in the period of reconstruction for the overthrow of the Carpet Bag Rule in South Carolina.

At Conway, November 15, 1866, Franklin G. Burroughs married Adeline Cooper, daughter of Timothy and Harriet Cooper. A brief record of the children born to their marriage is as follows: Effie T., who married Dr. J. L. Egerton of Hendersonville, North Carolina; George Burroughs; Beulah Burroughs; Claudia Burroughs; Frank A. Burroughs, who married Iola Buck, of Bucksport, South Carolina; Ruth Burroughs; Ella E. Burroughs, who became the wife of Hal L. Buck, of Conway; Arthur M. Burroughs, who married Frances Coles, of Conway; Sarah Best Burroughs, who is the wife of Edwin Sherwood, of Conway, South Carolina; Donald McNeill Burroughs, who married Georgia

Rodgers, of Spartanburg; and Lucille Burroughs, wife of S. G. Godfrey, of Cheraw, South Carolina.

CHARLES R. ALLEN. While his home has been in Charleston only ten years Charles R. Allen has developed a successful business as a merchant and broker, and has identified himself very closely with the various civic and commercial projects which are energetically utilizing every resource and opportunity for the expansion of Charleston as a great commercial and port center.

Mr. Allen was born at Columbus, Georgia, in 1890, son of Charles H. and Mary S. (Robertson) Allen. He was well educated, graduating in 1910 from the Alabama Technical Institute at Auburn, Alabama. In the same year he came to Charleston and was soon making headway as a merchandise broker, and his business under his energetic and skillful management has already become one of the larger concerns of its kind in the state. In 1917 Mr. Allen organized the Southern Fertilizer Company, with headquarters at Charleston. He is president of this company, which carries on an extensive business in fertilizer material from the various army camps of the South. The Southern Fertilizer Company has offices in Fayetteville, Atlanta and Louisville. They are now developing what promises to be their most important business, the making and distributing of portable and permanent steel buildings, known as Prudential Steel Buildings, sanitary, fire proof and rat proof. While only thirty years of age Mr. Allen has also distinguished himself by his good judgment and keen foresight in the handling of various real estate deals and property investments in Charleston. He is a member of the Chamber of Commerce and other local organizations.

He married Miss Gene Montgomery, of Pulaski, Tenn., and they have a daughter, Mary Elizabeth Allen.

VERNON COSBY BADHAM. The success of men in business or any vocation depends upon character as well as upon knowledge. Business demands confidence, and where that is lacking, business ends.

The life history of him whose name heads this sketch is closely identified with the history of the southeastern portion of the state, where for many years he has been a prominent and influential figure in industrial affairs. His life has been one of untiring activity and has been crowned with a degree of success attained by comparatively few men of this section. He is of the highest type of progressive citizenship, and none more than he deserves a fitting recognition among those whose enterprise and ability have achieved results that have awakened the admiration of those who know him and of his work.

Vernon Cosby Badham was born in Edenton, Chowan County, North Carolina, on November 19, 1856, where his ancestors had lived for many generations. His father, Major Henry Alexander Badham, was a graduate of William and Mary, Williamsburg, Virginia; by profession a planter and lawyer, serving in the Army of the Confederacy four years, with the rank of major. He was a great-grandson of William Badham, second son of Charles Badham of the Manors of Badham and Swaffham in Norfolk, England, who emigrated to North Carolina in 1711. He became a leader in the affairs of the province, serving many years in the House of Burgesses, and when North Carolina became a crown colony, was appointed one of the justices of the Supreme Court. He became a man of wealth, was one of the founders of the Episcopal Church in that state and donated the land upon which was erected St. Paul's Church—the oldest church edifice in North Carolina, and still in use for religious worship.

The subject's mother, Cornelia Cosby, was born on Briarfield plantation, Buckingham County, Virginia, a daughter of Dabney Cosby, Eq., a descendant of the Cosbys who settled in Warwick County, Virginia, in 1645.

Vernon C. Badham was reared and educated in North Carolina, studied law, but desiring a more active life embarked upon a business career and moved to Columbia, South Carolina, in 1882, where he was engaged in business until 1902, when he established the Dorchester Lumber Company of Badham, South Carolina, of which he is the sole owner. This company has had a phenomenally prosperous career, and is numbered among the really big concerns of the state. Its operations are on a large scale, and the town of Badham, with electric lights and water, church and school, is born of this enterprise. An adjunct of this business is a railroad thirty-five miles in length, which serves the needs of the farmers of this section. Along with this it owns about 20,000 acres of timber lands.

In 1912 Mr. Badham erected one of the finest residences in South Carolina. This beautiful colonial home is modern in every respect, being exquisitely furnished throughout and in many respects is unexcelled in the state. Its splendid library is filled with rare books, and objects of art, selected with infinite care, make it a home of which the entire community is justly proud. Mr. Badham also owns 15,000 acres of land in Hampton County on the Savannah River, with a large and handsome house, which is the delight of his friends during the hunting season. He is now devoting much of his energies to the development of this place, and it bids fair to become one of the great estates of the South.

Mr. Badham takes a lively interest in all public affairs, and has given his support to every movement having for its object the advancement of the general good of the state. He is progressive in the broadest sense of the term, and enjoys in a marked degree the confidence of all classes. He was a delegate from the first district to the democratic national convention at St. Louis in 1916, and again to the convention held in San Francisco in 1920.

In 1909 Mr. Badham married Leila, the daughter of the late William Young Johnston, of Eufaula, Alabama. Mrs. Badham belongs to the Colonial Dames of Virginia, being a lineal descendant of Col. John Washington, the founder of the Washington family in Virginia. She is also a descendant of William Byrd of Westover. Mrs. Badham belongs to the Daughters of the American Revolution, through the Butlers and the Laniers.

PAUL T. PALMER. Except for nearly two years of military service, with the rank of lieutenant in field artillery, Paul T. Palmer has been a practicing lawyer at Charleston since 1911.

Mr. Palmer, who ancestry goes back to colonial days in South Carolina, was born at Woodruff, Spartanburg County, in October, 1886. He is a son of Peter P. and Eliza H. (Horry) Palmer, now living at Charleston. His mother is a member of the historic Horry family of lower Carolina. The Palmers are descended from Thomas Palmer, an Englishman, who came to South Carolina in 1705. He had a grant of land from the English Crown on the Santee River in St. Stephen's Parish, and there became a large and prosperous planter. Peter P. Palmer was born in St. Stephen's Parish of Berkeley County, and in 1884 removed with his family to Woodruff in Spartanburg County, and from there in 1899 located at Charleston.

Paul T. Palmer was thirteen years of age when he came to Charleston, and finished his education in The Citadel, where he graduated with the class of 1908, and where he gained his first knowledge of military technique. After reading law in the offices of Legare & Holman of Charleston, he was admitted to the bar in 1911, and at once began practice. His knowledge, his personality and his devotion to every interest have brought Mr. Palmer a substantial law clientage. His offices are at 57 Broad Street, and since June, 1919, he has also performed the duties of magistrate for Charleston.

Mr. Palmer, like many other young professional men gave up his business to volunteer early in the war against Germany, He entered the first training camp at Fort Oglethorpe in May, 1917, and was commissioned second lieutenant, later being promoted to first lieutenant. From August, 1917, to May, 1919, he was at Camp Jackson in the Three Hundred and Eighteenth Field Artillery. Then followed other assignments to duty. From Camp Jackson he was sent to the School of Fire at Fort Sill, and had intensive training and instruction there three months. He received his commission as first lieutenant December 31, 1917. During the summer of 1918 Lieutenant Palmer was detailed as artillery aerial observer for the Twenty-Fifth Field Artillery at Camp McClellan, Alabama, and returned to that post of duty from Camp Mills. He received his honorable discharge January 30, 1919, and soon afterward resumed his law practice at Charleston.

COTESWORTH PINCKNEY SANDERS. His professional associates and fellow citizens in general testified in most unmistakable manner to the qualities that distinguished the late Cotesworth Pinckney Sanders as an able lawyer, and as a man whose life and character justified every honor that was bestowed upon it. At the time of his death in February, 1919, he was the recognized dean of the Spartanburg bar, and, very appropriately, president of the Spartanburg Bar Association.

He was past seventy-two years of age when he died, having been born in Colleton County, South Carolina, November 25, 1846, a son of Burrell and Ann Jackson (Ferebe) Sanders. He had four brothers, being the last survivor; John B., Edward, Philemon and Archibald. John B. lost his life in the war between the states.

The late Mr. Sanders spent his boyhood days in the lower part of the state, attended schools in Walterboro, South Carolina, and at an early age entered The Arsenal, a military school at Charleston now known as Porter's Military Academy. He left that school at the age of sixteen with a company of cadets for field service in the Confederate army, and participated in one battle against Sherman's invading army near Beaufort. He also saw service in North Carolina. Returning to his home in Colleton County, he attended the University of South Carolina, but was unable to complete the four years' course because of the financial condition of his father, who before the war was a successful planter and a man of means, but suffered many reverses in the years following the close of the war.

It was the earliest ambition of Mr. Sanders to become a lawyer, but there were many difficulties in attaining that goal. He was not the least discouraged, however, and with a heart full of hope and a determination to succeed he set out to follow the bent of his mind. He earned his own living and read law at night, often times a pine knot blaze and tallow dip furnishing the only light for him to read. Finally he went to Spartanburg, where he had previously met Miss Clara Elizabeth Wilson, daughter of James H. and Altimara Wilson, and on December 8, 1869, they were married. He worked in various stores in Spartanburg as clerk, among them being the late A. G. Floyd and ———— Twitty, and all the while made use of every opportunity by reading his law books.

At one time he engaged in the mercantile business in Bamberg, South Carolina, but this venture did not prove to his liking, nor was it successful, and in the early '70s he returned to Colleton County and located in Hendersonville, where he farmed and in 1874, while living at this place, he was admitted to the bar at Walterboro, South Carolina. He returned to Spartanburg, but did not immediately enter upon the practice of law. He secured a position in the freight depot of the Southern, at that time the old Spartanburg Union & Columbia Railroad, a road in later life he served as division attorney. He also held a position in the office of Fowler & Robinson, manufacturers of wagons and buggies.

In 1877 Mr. Sanders decided to practice law and moved to Gaffney. The first few years were lean and hard ones for the struggling young attorney, for clients were few and fees were small. With a wife and four small children it was a difficult matter to make ends meet. At first he could not afford to rent an office, so he fitted up a room in his dwelling and used that as an office until his practice was such that he could afford more pretentious quarters.

Probably his first work as a lawyer that attracted attention was in securing evidence for the Charlotte & Atlanta Air Line Railroad in a number of cases that had been brought against the company by the owners of a lot of cotton that had been stored on a railway platform and burned, the plaintiffs alleging that the fire was caused by sparks from the engine. The law firm of Duncan & Cleveland, of Spartanburg, composed of David R. Duncan and John B. Cleveland, attorneys for the railroad, employed Mr. Sanders to secure evidence for the company. He displayed much ability for a young lawyer in securing the evidence and he was taken in as a member of the firm. When Mr. Cleveland retired from the law in 1880, Mr. Sanders returned to Spartanburg and became junior partner of Duncan & Sanders. This firm was terminated with the death of Major Duncan in 1902. In 1903 H. E. DePass became associated with Mr. Sanders, and their partnership continued until the death of the senior member.

While at Gaffney Mr. Sanders was local attorney for the Charlotte & Air Line Railroad, now the Southern, his partner, Major Duncan, being at that time division attorney. Mr. Sanders succeeded his senior as division attorney at Spartanburg, and his firm represented the interests of that railroad corporation, and he was also attorney for the Spartanburg Light, Power & Railways Company and enjoyed much large and profitable practice representing many prominent firms and individuals.

For more than forty years Mr. Sanders devoted all his talents to his profession and at all times was a zealous champion for the truth. He acted as his conscience told him to do, and at all times endeavored to discharge every duty faithfully, whether as a lawyer, citizen or churchman. If he was distinguished for any one mental characteristic more than other perhaps it was his sound judgment, which enabled him to act discreetly in difficult cases and rendered him a safe counselor to others.

To the public generally he was known as a hard and aggressive fighter as a lawyer and a citizen—and he was. If he felt that a cause he represented was just and right he never gave up until it had gone through the court of the last resort. As a citizen he never compromised where a moral question was involved. However, there was a soft and gentle side to his nature that was admired by those who knew him best. At all times sympathetic, he was ready to render service to a worthy cause or to his fellow man. He loved the beautiful and the good in everything. He had an especial fondness for out-door life, particularly the mountain country of Western North Carolina, where several years ago he purchased a farm and began the development of an apple orchard. All nature appealed to him.

His character as a lawyer was well set forth by one of his contemporaries and oldest associates, Ralph K. Carson, who said: "Mr. Sanders was an extremely industrious and strenuous lawyer. For years he has been regarded as the leader of the Spartanburg bar and the peer of any man in the state, as far as legal talent is concerned. He possessed a fine judgment and was a prodigious worker. Mr. Sanders was essentially a strong lawyer, not ornate or flowery. His success was due to his industry and his sheer strength of mind."

Mr. Sanders was a life-long member of the Methodist Church, and from the Central Methodist Church of Spartanburg became identified with the Bethel Church upon its organization and at the time of his death was one of the leading lay members.

He represented his county in the legislature two terms.

Mr. Sanders is survived by his widow, Mrs. Clara Elizabeth Wilson Sanders, and by a number of children and grandchildren. His oldest daughter, Nora, died a number of years ago. The surviving children are: C. Eugene, of Saluda, North Carolina; May, wife of J. Frank Fooshe, of Suffolk, Virginia; Miss Tocoa, of Spartanburg; Anna, wife of Donald M. Fraser, of Spartanburg; Marion, wife of L. A. Emerson, of Columbia; Kathleen, wife of Capt. J. Hertz Brown, of Spartanburg; Miss Marcelene; Donald P., who was a lieutenant in the American army; and David D., who was born in Spartanburg in 1890, graduated from the law department of the University of South Carolina with the class of 1916, served in the World war as a member of the Coast Artillery and is now practicing law at Spartanburg.

A well considered tribute to the late Mr. Sanders, with special emphasis upon his work as a lawyer and citizen, is quoted from the editorial columns of the Spartanburg Herald:

"Mr. Sanders was one of the builders of Spartanburg. He came here in the days of the city's villagehood, without means, but with character and resolution to succeed despite obstacles that would have discouraged one of less forceful character. Very soon after being admitted to the bar and taking up his practice here he became identified with the Southern Railway as counsel, this association determining in great measure his career and bringing him into prominence in his chosen field of the law, which carried him into the courts most often as the representative of corporate interests. He was not the 'corporation lawyer' of the type that has brought that term to mean one who placed the dollar above human beings, but he sought justice for the interests he represented and fought for that and nothing more.

"He had the highest conceptions of his duties as a citizen, though at times he took his responsibilities in that direction intemperately and went to extremes. His zeal in those things was due to his hatred for evil and for the appearance of hypocrisy. He believed himself right and when convinced there was no middle ground upon which he could stop. He was to those who knew him best always seeking the truth and anxious to further justice.

"To illustrate his devotion to justice, it was Mr. Sanders who first conceived the idea that a negro man, charged with criminal assault in this country a few years ago, was not guilty. It was a delicate matter to handle, since the negro had been identified by the white woman as her assailant, had been arrested and saved from the fury of a mob after a night of rioting about the county jail, but with the fear in his heart that this poor negro might be convicted of a crime he had not committed, Mr. Sanders set about the difficult and delicate task of saving that man. He did so. The negro was tried by a Spartanburg County jury and acquitted. He was not interested in the negro, but in the cause of justice.

"Mr. Sanders' death marks the passing of one of the forceful, able and good citizens who have con-

tributed to the better ideals of this city, this county and the state."

JACOB N. NATHANS. While during a quarter of a century of active practice his services have brought him distinction as a member of the Charleston bar, Mr. Nathans has in addition performed many voluntary services to his home city and state, and at present is a member of the State Board of Education of South Carolina.

He was born at Charleston in 1874, son of Jacob N. and Alice G. (Cohen) Nathans, the parents both deceased. His father was also born in Charleston, where the family has lived for several generations. His father was also a prominent lawyer and contemporary and of a class with a group of men who lent distinction to the Charleston bar, including such as Samuel Lord, J. E. Burke, Julian Mitchell, Augustine Smythe, George Lamb Buist, A. Markley Lee, Edward McCrady, Theodore G. Barker, Charles H. Simonton, W. H. Brawley, Kennedy Bryan and James Simons.

Jacob N. Nathans, Jr., acquired his education in private schools and the high school of Charleston, the McCabe School at Petersburg, Virginia, and finished his education in the University of Virginia, where he graduated with the class of 1895. At the same time he was diligently studying law, his chief instructor being the late Samuel Lord, mentioned above. He was admitted to the bar in 1895, and has steadily devoted himself to the interests of a large clientage. Mr. Nathans is a member of the Masonic order. He married Miss Annie C. Smith, and their two children are Jacob N., Jr., and R. Macbeth.

BONNEAU HARRIS, the worthy representative of a sturdy line of pioneer ancestry, was elected commissioner of agriculture in 1918, a place of usefulness for which he was well endowed by nature and mental habits of study and philosophy, as well as by a passion to serve the people and to lead the poorer element of the farming classes out of illiteracy and constraint.

On a large plantation in old Pendleton district, Bonneau Harris was born December 31, 1851. His parents were Benjamin Harris, of South Carolina, and Orpha Harris, of Alabama, of the same name but no relation. To them nine children were born, five girls and four boys, two of whom served in the army of the Confederate States. Bonneau Harris was too young to participate in the struggle, but was just old enough to receive some indelible impressions which have shaped the course of his life. He was prevented by the war, and by its more dreadful aftermath, from receiving schooling, for his father, like many others, saw nearly all of his property swept away. B. Harris attended the common schools only ten months after he was ten years of age, but he has educated himself by reading. For many years he has read the Grange and live stock and farm publications, in addition to the daily newspapers, but most particularly has he been a constant reader and close student of the Bible, the one great text book of his life. For many years he has been an elder in the Presbyterian Church, and a member of Pendleton Masonic Lodge No. 34.

At the age of twenty-three he married Miss Nannie Hudgens, of Laurens County, and to them eleven children were born, eight sons and three daughters. Three of the sons were in the service of their country in the World war and four more were ready to go if another call had been made.

The war records in Washington show that his great-great-grandfather, John Harris, was a Revolutionary soldier and served from May, 1778, to 1781. He enlisted with his father and fought under the leadership of Andrew Pickens, one of South Carolina's greatest partisan leaders, and under Sampson Matthews of Virginia at the battle of Cowpens. John Harris was shot through the head at a battle on the Savannah River. John Harris was born on the eastern shore of Maryland, December 6, 1762, and married Mary Pickens, daughter of Gen. Andrew Pickens, February 22, 1784. To them eleven children were born, seven sons and four daughters. After the war he resided in Pendleton district, was a member of the State Convention of 1790, was sheriff for a short time and held the office of ordinary of Pendleton and Anderson district for forty years. He also practiced medicine in connection with managing his extensive farming interests at the confluence of Seneca River and Conneross Creek, about two miles east of Townville. There his children were born and there was born Bonneau Harris.

John Harris, the progenitor of this family of sturdy South Carolinians, was a native of Yorkshire, England, immigrated to Philadelphia, Pennsylvania, with his wife, Esther, before the year 1700. He was licensed to trade with the Indians, and shortly afterward established himself at what is now Harrisburg, Pennsylvania, situated on the east bank of the Susquehanna, 104 miles west of Philadelphia. Here he established a ferry across the mile-wide river, and the place for nearly one hundred years was known as Harris' Ferry. His son John was born there and founded the town which was named Harrisburg, and was incorporated as a town in 1785. In 1812 it was made the capital of the state. John Harris, the settler, died in 1748, and was buried on the river bank in front of his home. The tombstone erected over his grave contains the following inscription:

John Harris, of Yorkshire, England,
the friend of William Penn and
Father of the Founder of Harrisburg,
Died December, 1748,
In the Communion of the Church of England.

At the close of the War of Secession Bonneau Harris, a lad of fourteen, had to go to work as a laborer on his father's plantation. Naturally of a strong mind and of an inquiring nature, he acquired useful information from reading and from association with the well informed people of the community. When twenty-five years of age he moved from Oconee County to old Pendleton, a short distance away, the seat of the Pendleton Farmers Society, now 110 years old, and bearing upon its rolls the names of many illustrious men, including John C. Calhoun and others who practiced diversified agriculture a century ago.

It was here that Mr. Harris began his farming career. After finishing two crop years with cotton he found himself getting deeply into debt. He reasoned that he was doing the wrong kind of farming in buying fertilizers, buying rations for negroes and having nothing to say about the price of his product. Therefore he decided to make an effort in the live stock line.

He made a small start thirty-nine years ago. His farm has prospered. He is the only live stock man in the state today who was engaged in that business then. He says that many fell out of the work because they tried to make too pretentious a beginning. He started in a small way, but with good stock, and has always been able to command his own price for the animals he raised—the secret of success in any business, being able to get the other man to come to your price.

Mr. Harris was a pioneer in breeding in this state Jersey cattle, Berkshire hogs, standard bred horses and Percherons. He is proud of his success with raising grade Percherons which he declares are the only suitable work animals for this section. He has also bred with success a number of horses that have made good records on the track.

He was the first president of the State Farmers Union and in two years had got 6,000 farmers to join it. He is yet devoted to the principles of the Union and declares that this organization could be made to flourish in the South. He was the first man in the state to make a real fight against the low price of cotton. In 1902 he called a meeting of the farmers of Anderson County. In 1903 this had grown into the State Cotton Association, which later became well organized throughout the South. He also made it possible in 1919 to organize the American Cotton Association. He saw that the farmers should not unassisted be required to make the fight for the emancipation of the cottentots and to bring better prices so that the people might have education and home comforts which they had been denied for fifty years. He therefore appealed to the State Bankers Association for co-operation—and got it. Cotton at the moment, in February, 1919, was in danger of going to fifteen cents. When the bankers gave their backing to the farmers to hold the 700,000 bales of cotton then on hand, the price steadied and followed Mr. Harris' prediction by going from twenty-two cents to thirty-five cents in July and thus saving the farmers of the state not less than $65,000,000.

"The right forces must be organized to get behind the agriculture of the state," said Mr. Harris upon taking office. "We must organize and perfect a plan for financing the farmers. Three-fourths of the fight depends upon the financing. I believe that it will not be a difficult matter to organize a bank with a capital of a million dollars to help the farmer of the state in the fight which comes up every time they have a crop to market."

Organization, co-operation, diversification — these have been the three planks in his platform for life. He has been advocating publicly for thirty-five years the diversifying of the crops, and he was the first man in the state to free his farm from the Texas fever tick. He started on this when he first began to raise cattle, for he found that the tick was sickening his cattle and reducing their sale value. He greased his cattle once a week with crude kerosene oil for a year and killed out the tick.

"There are the greatest possibilities in farming today for young men who will go into it intelligently," says Mr. Harris, "provided that they will comply with common sense rules and regulations. Farming is the foundation upon which all other business is based. If agriculture should be neglected in the next few years the South will lose out. Our young men cannot fail to heed the call. The opportunity is too inviting. The farmer is wide awake. He isn't going back to sleep."

The home of Bonneau Harris at Pendleton is an ideal Southern plantation of the old days, with all the comforts and conveniences of the new. Its hospitality is unbounded, and the courtesy and friendliness of its atmosphere are such as to make the visitor feel that there is a lot of good left in the old world, after all.

JAMES O'HEAR. In the course of a busy career at Charleston for thirty years, involving active associations with a number of commercial enterprises, James O'Hear has found his interests and enthusiasm more and more enlisted in those larger and broader projects which are dependent for their fulfillment not on individual resources but the collective energies, wise planning and the processes of long intervals of time. While his work is preeminently practical, and a part of current progress, Mr. O'Hear's eye and vision are looking to the future, when the City of Charleston will realize its proper destiny as one of the big commercial and transportation centers of the Atlantic Coast.

The dominating feature of his life work and planning has been loyalty to his native city. Mr. O'Hear was born in Charleston in 1866, son of Dr. John S. and Anna Berwick (Legare) O'Hear. Legare is one of the most conspicuous names among the French Huguenot colonists of Charleston. His mother was a cousin of Hugh S. Legare and a daughter of John Berwick Legare.

In the paternal line his earliest known ancestors lived in Ireland, and part of them were Protestant and part Catholic. The Protestant branch, from which James O'Hear descends, sojourned in France for several generations, and came from that country to Charleston about the middle of the eighteenth century. The first of the name to settle in Charleston was Hugh O'Hear. Mr. O'Hear's grandfather was also named James. Dr. John S. O'Hear was a graduate of Jefferson Medical College in Philadelphia and for many years bore an honored name in his profession at Charleston. He was an uncle of Governor Johnson Hagood, who served as governor of South Carolina from 1880 to 1882.

James O'Hear was graduated from Wofford College at Spartanburg in the class of 1886. For several years he practiced as a civil engineer and surveyor, and that professional equipment has been an invaluable resource to him in his later business enterprises. His business efforts for a number of years have been devoted especially to the development of North Charleston, both as an industrial and residential section. He deserves a large part of the credit for bringing about this important addition

to Charleston's wealth and resources. Mr. O'Hear is secretary and general manager of the North Charleston Corporation, is president of the North Charleston Development Company, which was organized for the purpose of building homes, making public improvements and otherwise developing that section of North Charleston. He is also president of the North Charleston Water and Light Company and interested in several other corporations for development work in the city and vicinity.

Through his influence and enthusiasm Mr. O'Hear has been able to unite other prominent citizens of Charleston on some noteworthy projects of city planning and development. He is naturally a leader in the new spirit of progress and growth and expansion that have supplemented the big impetus given to Charleston by the Government during the war, making possible the continuous development of the great commercial resources centering in the port, the terminal facilities and the rich and prosperous inland country behind Charleston. As his individual contribution to this larger program, which the present animated spirit of the city community insures fulfillment, Mr. O'Hear originated a project for building a boulevard 200 feet wide on the Meeting Street road leading north from the city. This is one of the most pretentious and valuable features of public improvement ever undertaken in Charleston.

An honor which Mr. O'Hear especially appreciated came in January, 1920, when he was elected secretary of the board of directors of the Charleston Chamber of Commerce, an organization comprising the best business men and other citizens and working collectively for the building of the greater Charleston.

Mr. O'Hear married Miss May Powell Jones, of Charleston. Their three children are James, Roberta Jones and John Legare.

GEORGE WILLIAM DICK. While his home for many years has been in Sumter, and his practice as a dental surgeon has brought him numerous professional honors. Doctor Dick is perhaps most widely known over the state on account of his long and effective service in the Legislature, as a former mayor of the City of Sumter, and through an active and influential connection with civic and business programs.

He was born in that portion of Sumter County now Lee County August 21, 1864. His paternal ancestors were Scotch. For many generations on both sides of the Atlantic there have been numerous physicians in the family. Doctor Dick's parents were Capt. T. Hassell and Margaret (Cooper) Dick. His father was an extensive planter and slave owner before the war.

George William Dick received every advantage that could be bestowed by well to do parents. He attended the Fort Mill Academy, where he had as his teacher a widely known educator, Col. A. R. Banks; also the Boys' High School at Charlottesville, Virginia, under the celebrated legal author, Armstead Gordon of Staunton, Virginia; was also a student at Davidson College, North Carolina, and in the University of South Carolina, and in May, 1885, when not yet twenty-one years of age, he received his degree Doctor of Dental Surgery from the University of Pennsylvania.

Doctor Dick for many years has been regarded as one of the highest qualified men in his profession in the state. His professional brethren frequently honored him and he served as president of the South Carolina State Dental Association as a member of the State Board of Dental Examiners, and as a member of the Southern Dental Association and the National Dental Association. His chief business activities aside from his profession have been planting, and at different times he has owned large plantations on Black River and on the high hills of Upper Sumter County.

Doctor Dick's service as mayor of the City of Sumter was embraced in the two years 1905 to 1907. Continuously from 1907 to January, 1915, when for business reasons he resigned, he sat as a member of the State Legislature from Sumter County. His membership was distinguished by much more than the ordinary routine of legislative activity. When he left the legislature and for several sessions preceding he had been chairman of the Ways and Means Committee and chairman of the State Sinking Fund Commission. He served as a member on the commission to examine into the affairs of the State Hospital for the Insane, and the majority report adopted by him and his confreres was the basis for action taken by Governor Manning with regard to that institution. He was a member of Governor Manning's military staff, rank of lieutenant-colonel. Doctor Dick was also a member of the legislative commission, consisting of two from the House and two from the Senate, sent to Washington to confer with President Woodrow Wilson and others on the proposed twenty-four million dollar cotton bond issue. Both in the Legislature and as a private citizen he threw the full force of his influence to appropriate for military preparation and efficiency. He was appointed postmaster by President Wilson and resigned for professional reasons, after serving four years.

Doctor Dick is a democrat, and is known as a broad-minded thinker, but his positive convictions have never left him "on the fence" on any issue. Doctor Dick is a Knight Templar Mason, a member of Omar Temple of the Shrine at Charleston, the Knights of Pythias, and is past grand chancellor of the state, having served as grand chancellor of the Domain of South Carolina from 1914 to 1915. He also belongs to the Shrine Club and the Elks Club, the Sumter Club and other social bodies at Sumter, and is a deacon in the Southern Presbyterian Church.

May 18, 1887, at Rock Hill, South Carolina, he married Carrie V. Hutchison. Her father, A. E. Hutchison, was an extensive cotton mill owner and operator and was a member of the famous "Wallace House" of 1876. Mrs. Dick was born at Rock Hill, and was educated in the schools of that town and also at Charlotte, North Carolina, and at Columbia, South Carolina. Doctor and Mrs. Dick have a family of five children, Hassell Hutchison, Henry Noble, Susie Dunlop, Caroline Virginia and George W., Jr. The oldest son, Hassell Hutchison, has made a name for himself in United States consular service, having been consul to Japan, Jerusalem and

Switzerland. The daughter Susie Dunlop married Lieut. William Hammond Bowman, of the United States Navy. They have one child, Mary Caroline.

OCTAVUS COHEN. While his name has long been associated with a large and successful law practice at Charleston, Octavus Cohen has also earned and enjoyed the dignity of a high-minded citizen, and one whose influence has been steadily exerted for better things in Charleston and the state at large.

His own career serves to increase the prestige of the family, which has been in Charleston and vicinity for nearly 200 years. He is a descendant of Moses Cohen, a native of London, England, who came to Charleston about 1715 and built the first Jewish place of worship in the South, and the second church for Hebrew worship on the Continent of North America. A son of this distinguished rabbi was Jacob Cohen, great-grandfather of the Charleston lawyer. Octavus Cohen, however, was born at Montgomery, Alabama, September 30, 1860. His father was Joseph Cohen and his grandfather also bore the name Jacob Cohen. The Cohen family has furnished soldiers to every war in which America has been engaged, beginning with the Revolution. His great-grandfather Jacob was an officer from Charleston in the Continental army. His grandfather Jacob was in the War of 1812 and the Mexican war. Joseph Cohen was a civil engineer and an officer in the Confederate army.

While Mr. Octavus Cohen had to be satisfied to express his patriotism through various efforts and influences as a civilian, his only son, Octavus Roy, made sixteen attempts to get into the war with Germany. Mr. Cohen's son-in-law, John K. Gowen, Jr., was a lieutenant of aviation in the war.

Octavus Cohen was the second of seven children, and was reared and educated in Charleston, attending private schools and also being tutored by his father. During the '90s he was editor of the Charleston Daily World and for several years was engaged in newspaper work in New York City. He read law in Saratoga County, New York, and in Charleston, and after his admission to the bar began a busy practice in his home state. He also has offices at Monks Corner, though is legal residence is in Charleston. Mr. Cohen has never been an aspirant for political honors. However, in 1918 he became a candidate in the primaries for the office of lieutenant governor, and though virtually unknown in politics he carried Charleston by a large majority and also Berkeley County, and received a surprisingly large vote throughout the state, although he did not attend the state campaign meetings.

In 1890 Mr. Cohen married Rebecca Ottolengui, a native of Charleston and member of an old and prominent family of that city. Mr. and Mrs. Cohen have a son, Octavus Roy, and a daughter, Dora Moise. The latter is the wife of John K. Gowen, Jr., now a member of the editorial staff of the Boston American.

The son Octavus Roy Cohen is one of the distinguished Americans in literary centers and a resident of Birmingham, Alabama. He was born at Charleston, June 26, 1891, graduated in 1908 from Porter Military Academy, and from Clemson College with the class of 1911. He was employed as a civil engineer by the Tennessee Coal, Iron & Railroad Company during 1909-10 and the following two years was with editorial departments of a number of prominent city papers both south and north. He was admitted to the South Carolina bar in 1913, and for two years practiced law. Since 1915 he has given his time exclusively to writing. He is a co-author of "The Other Woman," published in 1917, is also the author of "Six Seconds of Darkness," published in 1918, "Gray Dusk" and "Polished Ebony," and has written over 300 short stories and a number of other articles.

Successful stage plays written by him include "The Crimson Alibi," "The Scourge," "Every Saturday Night," "Come Seven," "Shadows" and "Twilight Land." He is also the author of a considerable number of motion pictures.

The younger Mr. Cohen is perhaps most famous (as he is unquestionably best known) as the author of the phenomenally popular series of negro stories which have been appearing for the last couple of years in the Saturday Evening Post.

Mr. Cohen is a member of the Author's League of America. He married Inez Lopez, of Bessemer, Alabama, in 1914.

USTON G. BRYANT, an old and prominent business man of Orangeburg, has a distinguished lineage connecting him both with New England and the South, and his own activities and character serve to establish the family name still more securely among the notable ones of South Carolina.

Many studies have been made of the Bryant ancestry, and the lineage goes back to Sir Guy de Briant, who in the reign of Edward III of England had a seat in the castle of Hereford. From him was descended the most notable of the Bryant families of colonial times in New England. Stephen Bryant, a native of England, settled at Plymouth, Massachusetts, as early as 1632, and he and his descendants were citizens of substantial character in the colonial days. A great-great-grandson of Stephen Bryant was the great American poet William Cullen Bryant.

Still another branch of the Stephen Bryant family came at an early date to South Carolina, and in this state the Bryants for the most part have been identified with the industry of agriculture. In that portion of Colleton County that is now Dorchester County was born Thomas R. Bryant, and he spent his active life as a farmer and stock man, though for several years he was in the uniform of Confederate soldier and played a gallant part in behalf of the Lost Cause. He married Drucilla Wimberley, who was born at St. George in Dorchester County, of an old South Carolina family of Revolutionary stock. Four of her brothers were in the Confederate army.

Uston G. Bryant and his brother Thomas B. Bryant, sons of Thomas R. and wife and lineal descendants of Stephen Bryant, the immigrant, have for many years been prominently identified with the development and progress of Orangeburg County. Uston G. Bryant was born in what is now Dorchester County February 19, 1860, and acquired a common school education. He grew up on a farm, and

has always been interested in agriculture, though between the age of seventeen and twenty-four he was in the lumber business in Dorchester County. After that his interests were farming and merchandising in Orangeburg County, and in 1889 he established a home at Orangeburg, though he still continues in the livestock and farming industry.

With Thomas B. Bryant he was associated for over thirty years under the name Bryant Brothers. They were in business together fifteen years before coming to Orangeburg, and at Orangeburg they continued for twenty-two years, from 1889 to 1911. After they dissolved partnership Uston G. Bryant established the firm of U. G. Bryant & Sons, continuing his extensive operations as a livestock farmer and planter.

The largest of his several farms is in Richland County, comprising 1,400 acres, 900 of which are under cultivation, the chief crops being cotton and corn. Another farm of 600 acres is in Calhoun County, and this is also a cotton and corn plantation. Mr. Bryant owns a number of other properties, including the building at Orangeburg where he has his business headquarters, and the adjoining brick garage, both on the main street of the city. Mr. Bryant is vice president and a director of the Bank of Orangeburg, having been associated with that institution for over fifteen years. He is one of the leading Baptist laymen of the state, and has served his home church as deacon for forty years.

At Branchville, South Carolina, December 28, 1882, he married Mary Julia Reeves, a native of Orangeburg County and a daughter of John C. Reeves, who was of English descent and of Revolutionary stock. John Reeves was a Confederate soldier assigned to duty as a railroad man. Mrs. Bryant died June 11, 1884, leaving one son, William Raymond Bryant. He has been associated with his father in business for a number of years. This son married Miss May Reeder, of Charleston, and they became the parents of two children, William Raymond, Jr., and Alton Houston Bryant, the former now deceased.

March 5, 1885, Mr. U. G. Bryant married Miss Margaret Dukes, a native of Orangeburg. Her father, J. W. Dukes, Sr., was sheriff of Orangeburg County prior to the War between the States. To Mr. Bryant's second marriage were born eight children: Frank Cullen Bryant, whose brilliant career in business has been sketched elsewhere; Ada; Tom R., who married Irene Lancaster, of Bamberg County; Lelia; Pearl, wife of George R. Wheeler, of Wellsburg, West Virginia; Belle, deceased; Gladys, a college student; and U. G., Jr.

FRANK CULLEN BRYANT. While the individual destiny ordinarily seems to have little influence on the broad current of life, at rare intervals comes a death that seems to make an entire community pause and when activities are resumed it is with a distinct sense of loss of a personality and character long regarded as indispensable. Such was the experience of Orangeburg and Orangeburg County with the death of Frank Cullen Bryant on February 23, 1920, at the age of thirty-four.

While he lived he lived intensely, carried out many plans that would have fulfilled the ambition of many older men, and he exemplified that faculty remarked as characteristic of men of the finer ability of being able to do many things well and at the same time have leisure for the cultivation of friendship and interests not in the direct line of his business. In fact he was one of the most popular young men of the county, threw himself with singular ardor into community welfare projects, and was liberal of his means and time and had an unfailing cheerfulness and a generosity that endeared him to hundreds outside of his immediate family, upon whom his sudden death fell as a most tragic blow.

He was born January 20, 1886, at Fort Mott, then in Orangeburg County, now in Calhoun County. A liberal education preceded his entry into practical affairs. He attended the common and high schools of Orangeburg, Clemson Agricultural College, and graduated in the banking and bookkeeping and stenography courses of the Georgia-Alabama College at Macon, Georgia, in 1905.

He had thirteen years in which to accomplish his human destiny. His first employment was as clerk in the bank of Orangeburg, and he won rapid promotion to teller, assistant cashier, and at the time of his death was vice president and active president with the full responsibility and burden the office carries.

Other extensive interests grew apace. Besides a 500-acre plantation near Orangeburg, to which he gave much of his time, he was one of the largest growers of oranges at Waresdale, Florida, where he possessed large holdings. It is estimated that the crop of his sixty-five acre grove there will produce 25,000 boxes of oranges in 1920. Only a few months before his death he had bought several other groves in that district. Mr. Bryant was also financially interested in some of the up country cotton mills of South Carolina. The financial power and influence that came to him he wielded always for the welfare of his community and state, and his friends assert that he was absolutely above the unscrupulous use of wealth.

Political honors were frequently urged upon him, including the office of mayor of his home city. He might have been elected to that office by inclination, but refused the honor since his immediate business interests required his full time. However, he did serve as an appointive member of the commission in charge of the street paving of the city.

He held the rank of colonel on the Governor's staff, and served actively in the Red Cross and Liberty Loan drives in his community. One of the last causes to which he devoted himself was the campaign of the Baptist Church of America to raise a fund of $75,000,000, and he spoke in behalf of that cause in many parts of the county. He served one term as president of the Chamber of Commerce, and fraternally was affiliated with the Knights of Pythias, Independent Order of Odd Fellows, Junior Order of United American Mechanics, and the Elks.

A wife and four children survive him and cherish the memory of his character and deeds. He married in April, 1908, Miss Elizabeth Seignious, of Charleston, daughter of James M. Seignious and member of the old and prominent family of that name in Charleston. The four children are Elizabeth, Francis C., Jr., James S. and Margaret.

COL. JAMES ARMSTRONG. It is a service almost unique that Col. James Armstrong has rendered Charleston, not merely in length of years but in orderly and prompt performance. Since 1871 he has been harbor master of that city.

Colonel Armstrong, one of the state's most eloquent orators, and a prominent veteran of the Confederacy, was born at Philadelphia in 1842, son of James and Margaret (O'Rourke) Armstrong. His father was a native of Londonderry, Ireland, and became converted to the Catholic Church, and that religious faith has been the faith of his son, Colonel Armstrong. James Armstrong, Sr., married Margaret O'Rourke, a native of Western Ireland. He came to America in early manhood, living for a time in Philadelphia, and during the middle '40s came to Charleston.

Col. James Armstrong was a child when brought to Charleston and was educated in local schools and for two years had the advantages of education in Europe. He was one of the first volunteers to the military forces of South Carolina when the state seceded. December 27, 1860, as a non-commissioned officer in the First Regiment of South Carolina Rifles, he participated in the capture of Castle Pinckney. He was in the state service until after the fall of Fort Sumter, and then enlisted in one of the companies of Irish volunteers organized in Charleston, being elected junior second lieutenant. This company was the nucleus of Col. Maxy Gregg's regiment of the First South Carolina Volunteers. Colonel Armstrong was second lieutenant in Company K until the latter part of 1861, when he was promoted to first lieutenant and after the battle of Sharpsburg was acting captain until he received his regular commission with that rank in 1864. With his regiment as a part of McGowan's Brigade he fought all through the war in Virginia, Maryland and Pennsylvania, serving until wounded and captured at Sutherland Station a few days before the surrender. He was slightly wounded at Sharpsburg, was wounded at Fredericksburg and again at Gettysburg while carrying the colors of his regiment. He was again wounded at Spottsylvania Court House and at Sutherland Station his right leg was shattered. He was in a hospital at Washington eleven months and therefore did not return to Charleston until early in 1866. His wounds did not heal until 1871, in which year he was appointed harbor master of Charleston. Colonel Armstrong, who served as a member of Governor Hampton's staff, has long been prominent among the Confederate veterans of the state and again and again has been called upon to address them in the annual reunions. For several years Colonel Armstrong has also been the commercial and financial editor of the Charleston News and Courier.

ELIAS BURNETT was one of the strong and resourceful men in the agricultural and civic affairs of Spartanburg County for a long period of years. In his long lifetime he probably experienced all the vicissitudes and obstacles which beset South Carolina agriculture and industry in general, but overcame them all, and worked steadily toward larger attainments, and is remembered as one of the ablest representatives of agriculture in Upper South Carolina.

He was born in Spartanburg County December 28, 1822, son of Woodson and Susan (Burnett) Burnett. His people were early settlers of South Carolina from Virginia. Elias Burnett grew up in his native county, and spent a normal healthy youth, with an education acquired in private schools. He was associated with his father in the work of the home plantation until his marriage.

August 27, 1846, he married Malissa Gilbert. They began housekeeping on a farm, and his first wife died July 18, 1888. Of their nine children only two are now living: Mary Fowler and Farzina McCallister.

October 16, 1890, Mr. Burnett married Elizabeth J. Coggin. Mrs. Burnett, who is still living in Spartanburg County, was born in that locality November 6, 1860, a daughter of Stephen E. and Sarah (Wolf) Coggin, also natives of South Carolina. Her father was a soldier in the Confederate army all through the War between the States. Mrs. Burnett was the fourth in a family of nine children, all of whom but one reached mature years. Mrs. Burnett was well educated in her native county. Life has brought her many responsibilities, all of which she has discharged faithfully. She is the mother of two children: Elma C., wife of B. L. Lancaster; and Malissa F., wife of J. S. McDowell.

The late Elias Burnett many years ago operated a distillery in Spartanburg County. However, his chief business was farming, and he acquired the ownership of 700 acres, all well improved and highly productive. He died March 8, 1920. He was a member of the Baptist Church, and active in its work. Mrs. Burnett enjoys the comforts of a fine home in Spartanburg County, and is capably managing a large agricultural property which she owns.

ISAAC MAYO READ. Charleston as the second city of commercial importance in the South attracts to it some of the best business men of the country, whose efforts are directed toward a maintenance of this prestige through the successful conduct of large industrial plants. One of these men deserving of much more than passing mention, not only on account of his material possessions, but also because he has the best interests of the city at heart and contributes liberally of his time and influence to secure improvements along all lines, is Isaac Mayo Read, vice president of the Read Phosphate Company. He was born in Charlotte County, Virginia, July 1, 1867, a son of William Watkins Read, a graduate of Hampden-Sydney College, and later one of its trustees. He married Paulina Carrington, a daughter of Col. H. A. Carrington. The paternal grandfather, Col. Isaac Read, commanded a regiment in the Mexican war, while another ancestor, Col. Clement Read, gained his title commanding a regiment in the American Revolution. Later he became county clerk and also commanded a troop of Virginia Militia. A daughter of his married

MR. AND MRS. ELIAS BURNETT, ELMER AND MELISSA

Col. Paul Carrington, later a judge and a very prominent man in civic affairs. Col. Clement Read was a very religious man, and was active in church work. The Read family is of English origin.

Isaac Mayo Read was one in the family of nine children born to his parents, three of whom were sons and six daughters, and all survive with the exception of the eldest, William Howard Read, who after becoming one of the leaders in the production of fertilizers died in the prime of life. Abram Carrington Read, the other brother, is president of the Read Phosphate Company.

Growing up in his native state, Isaac M. Read was educated at Hampden-Sydney College. He began his business career in the office of a phosphate company in Syracuse, New York. He came to Charleston in 1893, and has since developed the business of the Read Phosphate Company to large proportions.

Mr. Read was married at Charleston to Margaret C. Darbey, a daughter of Dr. John T. Darbey, of Columbia, South Carolina, an eminent surgeon, a graduate of Jefferson Medical College, Philadelphia, Pennsylvania, who spent some time in France and New York City. Mr. and Mrs. Read have three sons, namely: William Watkins, Isaac Mayo and John Thompson Darbey. The Charleston, the Charleston Country and the Charleston Yacht clubs hold his membership, and furnish him congenial social companionship and recreation. Since coming to Charleston he has belonged to St. Michael's Episcopal Church.

BUDD C. MATTHEWS as a merchant, manufacturer and banker has had a busy career at Newberry, South Carolina, covering thirty years. He came to Newberry a young man of thorough and liberal education and of considerable business training and experience.

He was born in Edgefield County, South Carolina, November 23, 1868, a son of William E. and Sarah (Watkins) Matthews. While he grew up on his father's farm he was given good advantages at home, attended the Pleasant Grove Academy several years, the University of South Carolina in 1886, and Roanoke College at Salem, Virginia, in 1887. He graduated at Smith's Business College, Lexington, Kentucky, March 16, 1888. Prior to coming to Newberry he spent some time as a clerk in a mercantile house at Atlanta, Georgia. In Newberry his first position was as a clerk and bookkeeper with a dry goods house, with which he spent several years. He then organized the B. C. Matthews Brick Manufacturing Company and was its chief executive for ten years. He also established the Mercantile House of Matthews & Cannon, and was associated in that enterprise for several years, selling it out at a good profit.

Since January, 1909, Mr. Matthews has been president of the National Bank of Newberry, Newberry, South Carolina, it being one of the oldest banks in the Upper Carolina, having been established in 1871. When Mr. Matthews took charge of it in 1909 it had deposits of only $90,000. In May, 1920, it had deposits of approximately $1,500,000. He has always extended a helping hand to the agricultural class of people, the people who produce the food and clothing to feed and clothe the world.

The height of his ambition has been and is to help the boys and girls better their condition in life by helping them get a fair price for the food and clothing raised by their own labors, thereby making better citizens out of them and at the same time encouraging them to remain on the farm to raise more food and more clothing than ever before. No honest person could object to this. Do right and stick at it and you can't help but succeed.

He owns considerable farm land and keeps in touch with agricultural conditions around Newberry. Mr. Matthews is a member of the First Baptist Church.

September 29, 1890, he married Miss Clara Belle Crotwell, of Newberry, a most excellent and refined lady who delights in helping her husband. They have four children. The oldest, Alfred C., is the assistant cashier of the First National Bank of Barnwell, South Carolina. The three younger children are Miss Margherita, William E., and Samuel C. Matthews.

ARTHUR MIDDLETON HUGER, United States Commissioner at Charleston, has been engaged in the practice of law in his native city for many years and has a commanding position as a lawyer, citizen and in social life.

He was born at Charleston, a son of Arthur Middleton, Sr., youngest son of Judge Daniel Elliott Huger, and descended from one of the early French Huguenot families of South Carolina. Mr. Huger's mother was Margaret C. King, a native of Charleston, daughter of Hon. Mitchell King, who was of Scotch ancestry.

Arthur M. Huger was educated in Charleston, attended Furman University at Greenville, and since his admission to the bar has given his best talents and energies to law practice. He has been United States Commissioner since 1913. Always a stanch democrat, he has made his influence count for good government and better standards of political life. He is vice president of the Charleston Evening Post.

FRANCIS JULIAN CARROLL, M. D. Doctor Carroll had practiced medicine, had achieved success, the comforts of good living and the prestige and respect of a community for nearly twenty years when America entered the war with Germany. He gave up his practice for the time being, heartily volunteered and enrolled as a medical officer, and spent several vivid and interesting months of arduous work on the battlefields of France.

Doctor Carroll, who resumed his private practice at Summerville in 1919, was born in South Carolina, October 10, 1874, a son of Edward and Fannie (Larligue) Carroll, his father a native of Charleston and his mother of Hampton County. His maternal grandfather was Col. Isidore Larligue, a native of Augusta, Georgia. Doctor Carroll's grandfather and his great-grandfather both bore the name B. R. Carroll. The great-grandfather was a native of Ireland and a son of Maj. Charles Rivers Carroll. Grandfather B. R. Carroll was well known in educational circles and was author of "Carroll's Collections," a text book widely used at one time in colleges and universities.

Doctor Carroll was the youngest of five children. He was educated in Porter Military Academy and the Medical College of the State of South Carolina, graduating with his Doctor of Medicine degree in 1896. For a year he served as house surgeon in St. Francis Hospital at Charleston, and for a short time was on quarantine duty. In 1897 he came to Summerville, and steadily practiced in that community for twenty years. He served one term as mayor, declining re-election. He was also county chairman of the democratic committee and delegate to the National Democratic Convention at Denver in 1908 when Bryan was nominated. Early in the war he volunteered for the Medical Reserve Corps and was called to active duty August 10, 1917, at Camp Greenleaf. Later he was assigned with the Eighty-Second Division at Camp Gordon, and on October 20, 1917, was put in the Three Hundred and Twenty-Seventh Field Hospital of the Three Hundred and Seventh Sanitary Train. With this organization he sailed for France in May, 1918, and was commissioned captain. He was on duty in the Toul sector, but subsequently, beginning with the major operations of the American Expeditionary Forces, had a place in the San Mihiel drive and in the critical battles of the Argonne Forest. Doctor Carroll on his return landed at New York City May 6, 1919, and on the 11th of the same month received his honorable discharge at Camp Dix, New Jersey. On June 9, 1919, he was commissioned major, M. R. C.

In 1897 he married Charlotte A. Doan. Their six children are Lottie F., F. Julian, Jr., Mary L., Edward, E. M. and James D.

Doctor Carroll is a member of the County, State and American Medical associations, and also the Association of Southern Railway Surgeons, being one of the local surgeons employed by the Southern Railway. He is a Mason, Knight of Pythias, Woodman of the World, a member of the Episcopal Church and is post commander of the American Legion for Dorchester County.

HON. WILLIAM JUDGE MOORE, lawyer and planter of Greenwood County, was born December 27, 1859, near Cokesburg in Abbeville County (now a part of Greenwood County), son of William A. and Margaret Louise (Wardlaw) Moore. His parents were also natives of Abbeville County. The Wardlaws were an especially conspicuous family in the state.

William Judge Moore graduated from Furman University in 1878, read law in Governor Ansel's office at Greenville and was admitted to practice in 1881. In 1898 he was elected master in equity for Greenwood County, and filled that office for eighteen years, until he retired in 1916. In 1918 he was elected a member of the House of Representatives from Greenwood County, and is a member of the Judiciary Committee and is author of a bill creating county courts in Greenwood County. Mr. Moore is now president of the Greenwood County Cotton Association.

He is the owner of several plantations in Greenwood County. One of them is the old home place near Cokesburg where he was born and reared. For many years Mr. Moore has produced great quantities of cotton on his land. As a leading cotton planter he has been active in increasing the welfare of cotton planters generally, and has vigorously cooperated with the modern movement for the regulation of cotton production so that adequate compensation may be insured to the farmer who expends his capital and labor in raising the crop. He is also a director of the National Loan and Exchange Bank of Greenwood.

His first wife was Miss Carrie Ellesor, of Newberry. She died August 11, 1899. On June 27, 1905, he married Miss Mamie Clardy, of Laurens. His four children were by his first marriage: Rebecca, wife of John D. Talbert; Miss Margaret Wardlaw; Lieutenant William A.; and Lieutenant Gray E. Moore. Both sons were officers in the World war. William A. is a graduate of The Citadel at Charleston, received a lieutenant's commission at Camp Jackson and served as an instructor in various camps. Gray is a graduate of Wofford College, was also awarded a lieutenant's commission at Plattsburg, and was on duty as military instructor at Syracuse University, New York. Both young men were discharged in 1919. Mr. Moore is a member and officer of the Methodist Church.

JOSEPH KOGER FAIREY. The one big interest of Doctor Fairey's life and the source of many and long continued benefits to his fellow men has been his profession as a physician and surgeon, to which he has devoted himself with practically no interruption and no important diversion for nearly thirty years.

Doctor Fairey, whose home is at St. Matthews, in Calhoun County, belongs to the historic Fairey family of the Orangeburg District, and he was born in the county of that name February 28, 1868. The Faireys are of English and Irish ancestry, were represented in the Revolutionary war, and came to Orangeburg County early in its history. Philip W. Fairey, father of Doctor Fairey, was a native of Orangeburg County, spent his life as a corn and cotton farmer, and served as a first sergeant in the Confederate army until he was wounded in 1864, the day before the battle of Cold Harbor. He died in 1888.

Joseph Koger Fairey acquired a liberal education, attending South Carolina College at Columbia and receiving his M. D. degree at South Carolina Medical College in Charleston. He was graduated in 1891, and for the following seventeen years practiced at Creston, in Orangeburg County, and since 1908 has been a resident of St. Matthews. Particularly in early years he showed no consideration for his strength and endurance in meeting the heavy demands of his practice in town and country, and his ability and professional enthusiasm have brought him a high reputation in medical circles. He is a member of the County and State Medical societies and the American Medical Association. During the World war he was a medical member of the Calhoun County Exemption Board. While never active in politics Doctor Fairey has been keenly interested in education, and ever since he was twenty-three years of age has held the office of school trustee in

his home communities. He is now chairman of the Board of School Trustees at St. Matthews. He also owns a farm near Creston. Doctor Fairey is a Knight Templar Mason, being affiliated with Izlar Lodge No. 170, Ancient Free and Accepted Masons, and with the Commandery at Orangeburg.

April 16, 1891, at Creston, he married Miss Florence Holman Keller, a native of that community, and daughter of Dr. Thomas K. Keller. The Kellers were among the early settlers of South Carolina and some of Mrs. Fairey's ancestors were identified with the colonial cause at the time of the war for independence. Doctor and Mrs. Fairey have three sons: Philip W., in the automobile business at Orangeburg; Dr. Thomas J., who gained his early experience with his father and is now winning a high place for himself as a physician; and Joseph K., Jr., an automobile man at Orangeburg.

WHITFIELD W. WANNAMAKER, SR. The noted Wannamaker family of old Orangeburg have always been distinguished for their close ties with the agricultural industry of South Carolina, and it is to farming and planting that Whitfield W. Wannamaker, Sr., of St. Matthews, has given the best efforts and abilities of his life.

The Wannamakers were colonial settlers in the old Orangeburg district about 1740. Some of the colony that came with the Wannamakers lived in the Dutch Fork region around Lexington. The Wannamaker original stock was Holland Dutch, and they gave the name of the district in honor of Duke Orange of Holland. One of the Wannamakers was a lieutenant in Rumph's Minute Men near St. Matthews. Dr. Whitfield Wesley Wannamaker, father of Whitfield W., Sr., was also born near St. Matthews and became a successful physician, being a graduate of the Charleston College of Medicine. He served as a lieutenant under Captain Edwards in the Confederate Cavalry. While he enjoyed a large medical practice, he was also extensively interested in planting, and prior to the war owned more than 100 slaves.

Whitfield W. Wannamaker, Sr., was a member of the class of 1873 at Wofford College in Spartanburg. While his education and social position would have qualified him for a successful professional career, he chose almost instinctively the vocation of agriculture, and on leaving college took charge of a plantation given him by his father situated two miles from St. Matthews. For nearly half a century farming has been his big interest and he has made a practical business of it. He owned originally 650 acres, which he afterwards increased to about 1200 acres, practically all of which is under cultivation. One piece of land he owns is the ground on which the famous character Rebecca Motte lived, and is near old Fort Motte, named in honor of that South Carolina heroine. Mr. Wannamaker has never been a[ctive in] politics, and his only fraternal affiliation is [the] Knights of Pythias.

[Novem]ber 14, 1877, at St. Matthews, he married [Emm]a Louise Banks, daughter of Rev. Martin [B]anks, who was a Methodist minister and of [Eng.] colonial and revolutionary stock. The children [of] Mr. and Mrs. Wannamaker are Arthur Banks, Adella Keitt, Truetlen Miller, Whitfield William, and Luther Banks Wannamaker. Arthur, who is now engaged in business at Denver, married Selma Shuman, of that city. Truetlen Miller was named in honor of one of the Colonial governors of Georgia, from whom he is a lineal descendant. This governor was murdered by the Tories during the Revolution, and he was buried six miles from St. Matthews. Truetlen married Belle Barton, of Franklin, Kentucky. Whitfield William graduated from Clemson College in 1907 and immediately began the business of raising fine cotton seed, an industry in which his success has been little short of marvelous. His product is authoritatively regarded as the finest seed in the South, and all that he can produce is shipped to supply demands in all the cotton growing states. In recognition of valuable work done in seed breeding a certificate of merit was conferred upon him by Clemson College in 1920. This was especially in reference to the development of the Wannamaker Big Boll cotton, which is conceded to be one of the best varieties for average conditions in the Southern states.

He married Lucile Long, of Darlington, South Carolina. Luther Banks Wannamaker, the youngest son, was in the navy during the war and is now associated with his brothers Truetlen and Whitfield in the seed business.

C. R. I. BROWN left the Charleston High School to go to work in a bank. The routine of banking was his university. Few young men in the state have made more rapid advancement in their chosen vocations. Mr. Brown, without money to start on, on the basis of his personal efficiency and merit, has become president of the Citizens Bank, one of the stronger financial institutions of Charleston.

He is a member of an old and noted family of Charleston, where he was born August 11, 1884, son of B. H. and Sallie (Inness) Brown. Members of six generations of the Brown family have been merchants in china and glass. The family were in that business in England. His great-grandfather was not only a merchant but also a missionary priest of the Episcopal Church, and carried on the work of his church in many parts of South Carolina. The grandfather was Benjamin Henry Brown, a native of Charleston. B. H. Brown, father of the banker, is still a merchant at Charleston.

Sallie Inness, mother of Mr. Brown, is a daughter of Charles Inness. Charles Inness was a brother of George Inness, Jr., an American artist whose work has been in the galleries and salons of Europe and this country for many years, and during the past decade has received a measure of appreciation such as to stamp it with permanent genius. The Inness family originated in Scotland and contains many well known men. B. H. Brown and wife had five sons and three daughters, all living. B. H. Inness Brown, the oldest, is a prominent lawyer of New York City. C. Inness Brown, the second, is vice consul of the American Government in Spain and was one of the four attaches of the American Government left in Germany at the breaking out of the war. E. M. Inness Brown is a planter. H. A. Inness Brown while a student at the University of Virginia won the Woodrow Wilson medal for the best essay, the honor being awarded to him out of

2,000 contestants. He left the University of Virginia to join the American army before the United States entered the war with Germany, was appointed a lieutenant in command of an ambulance unit, was cited twice for bravery and promoted to a captaincy, and has since been designated by his commanding officer to write the history of the American Ambulance Corps during the war. The daughters are: Bessie, wife of Maj. A. H. Silcox of the American Expeditionary Forces; Azile, wife of Lyon Tyler, of New York; Sadie Inness, unmarried and at home.

C. R. I. Brown was the third among the children. He was educated in Charleston, attending the high school three years, and then took one of the humblest positions in a local bank to learn the business. He became teller of the Enterprise Bank, and in 1911 was made cashier of the Citizens Bank and promoted to the presidency in 1913. He is also a member of the Executive Committee of the Charleston Clearing House. He is treasurer of a local fertilizer company and has an interest in many other business concerns.

Hon. ARTHUR M. KENNEDY, whose work as a member of the State Senate from Barnwell County has made him widely known over the state, is a prominent banker of Williston and member of a family that has been active in local affairs there for many years.

Mr. Kennedy was born at Williston August 11, 1868. The Kennedys came to South Carolina prior to the Revolutionary war. His grandfather, John Kennedy, was also a native of Barnwell County. His father, William Hamilton Kennedy, a native of Barnwell County, served as captain in the Confederate army. He was wounded in one of the last battles of the war. After the war he took up merchandising at Williston, and for many years was successfully identified with the business and civic affairs of that community. He died in his eighty-second year. His wife was Elizabeth Merritt, a native of Lexington County, South Carolina, who died when about fifty-eight years of age. Her father, James Merritt, was widely known as a Baptist minister in his native state.

Arthur M. Kennedy was the oldest of five children. He grew up and received his education at Williston and is also a graduate of the famous military school, The Citadel, at Charleston. He completed his work there in 1887, and then returned home and joined his father in merchandising. This business, now a completely stocked department store, is still known as W. H. Kennedy & Son. The Bank of Williston was organized in 1906, and from that time to the present Mr. Kennedy has been its president. The bank has a capital of $25,000 and surplus of over $30,000.

Mr. Kennedy was elected a state senator to fill out the unexpired term of J. Henry Johnson. He was on the finance committee in the Legislature, and is greatly interested in that subject and in tax reforms for South Carolina. He is now a candidate for the Legislature with no opposition. He has always been interested in local affairs, and has been particularly interested in church and education. He is chairman of the local school board, and for a number of years has been a deacon in the Baptist Church. He is also a member of the Masonic Order.

Mr. Kennedy has been twice married, and both wives are now deceased. His first marriage was to Agnes Roberts. She was the daughter of P. Brown, a prominent dentist of Allendale and who was born in Allendale. He served in the war of the states as lieutenant and was also a member of the Legislature from South Carolina, representing Barnwell County. Her mother was a Miss Dunn, also a native of Allendale. Mrs. Kennedy was born in 1868 and died in 1914. She was the mother of his three children: William Roberts, James Arthur and Ruth, wife of John A. Latimer, of Williston. All the children were born in Williston. James Arthur enlisted and was sent to Texas in the World war. He had been attending the University of Virginia (law course), but on his return he entered the George Washington at Washington, D. C., and graduated in 1920 and returned to Williston, where he will open an office and practice his profession. He is the youngest son. James Arthur while in Texas married a Miss Ruckman. William Roberts is in the store with his father. Senator Kennedy's second wife was Emma Harley, of Williston.

ISIDOR ARTHUR MONASH, a prominent young Charleston lawyer, grew up in that city and has been in the active practice of his profession for the past seven years.

He was born in New York City March 17, 1887, a son of I. Morris and Anna (Schaul) Monash. His father was born in Germany and was brought when a boy to this country, being reared and educated in New York City. His mother was born in New York City and her parents came from Germany. Isidor A. Monash was four years old when his parents settled in Charleston, and he received his education in the local schools. He graduated LL. B. from the Law Department of the University of South Carolina in 1912, and in the same year began his career as a lawyer. He was admitted to practice in the United States courts in 1915.

In December, 1918, Mr. Monash married Miss Ray Bluestein, of Savannah, Georgia. He is worshipful master of Friendship Lodge No. 9, Ancient Free Masons, a member of the Scottish Rite and Mystic Shrine, also of the Benevolent Protective Order of Elks, and a member of the Hebrew Benevolent Society of Charleston, of Dan Lodge No. 592, Independent Order B'nai B'rith, the Society of Sons of Joseph of New York, and is an active democrat. He is also class football and class baseball manager and first violinist in the university orchestra.

CAPT. AUGUST J. W. GORSE has been a resident of Charleston over forty years, has achieved a place as leading business man, and his executive ability, his civic prominence and his long record of unselfish service to his community make him one of the most useful members of the present city government as an alderman at large.

Captain Gorse was born at Lehe, Hanover, Germany, in 1865, and was eleven years of age when his

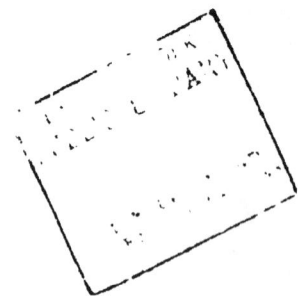

Colonel Olin M. Dantzler

father, Peter N. Gorse, also a native of Hanover, came to Charleston in 1876. His father for a number of years was a retail grocery merchant, but finally returned to his native country and died there.

Captain Gorse had no knowledge of the English language when he came to Charleston, but rapidly mastered the tongue and made good progress in school, finishing his education in the German Academy. As a boy he became self-supporting, and later years have brought him numerous connections with business affairs of the city. His principal interest for a number of years has been ice manufacturing. He is secretary and assistant manager of the Consumers Ice Company, one of the most successful plants of its kind in the state. He is also president and treasurer of the Peoples Life Insurance Company.

Captain Gorse has long been a student of the city's best interests, and his business record and public spirit were accountable for his election in November, 1919, as alderman at large in the City Council. He is therefore one of the men responsible for the carrying out of the large plans now under way to insure Charleston the prestige and power commensurate with its wonderful advantages as a port and commercial center. Captain Gorse and family are members of St. Matthew's Lutheran Church.

He married Miss Mamie Kamp, also a native of Germany. Their four children are August J. W., Jr., Mrs. Anna Elizabeth Martin, Miss Mary E. and Miss Dora W. Gorse.

MORTIMER OWENS DANTZLER is proprietor of Pecanway Place in Orangeburg County. Thousands of people outside of South Carolina recognize the phrase "Pecanway Place" as a result of the judicious and efficient advertising campaign inaugurated by Mr. Dantzler as a means of marketing and distributing the produce of his pecan orchard. Quantities of Pecanway nuts have been shipped to every state in the Union, and to most civilized countries, and everywhere they have served as an ingratiating booster of one of South Carolina's specialized industries.

Pecanway Place is a beautiful plantation containing about a hundred acres, all in the highest state of development. The commercial pecan orchard contains forty-five acres, mostly of the Schley variety. The crop for 1919 amounted to 15,000 pounds. While these nuts are of the popular "paper shell" variety, Mr. Dantzler has developed some individual qualities in his pecans, particularly in the proportion of meat to shell, the proportion of the kernel in weight being from 10 to 20 per cent higher than the average cultivated pecan. Mr. Dantzler inaugurated a systematic sales campaign in 1919, and by well placed advertising in national journals has developed an overwhelming demand for all the crop of his orchard.

Another feature of Pecanway Place is thirty acres of Crimson Clover. This is one of the legumes which is making a wonderful showing in southern agriculture, and Mr. Dantzler's particular field won the first prize carried on by the "Progressive Farmer" in competition with all the southern states, even including such clover growing states as Tennessee and Kentucky.

The Dantzlers are a historic family of Orangeburg. They came out of Germany and settled in Orangeburg district in the early colonial period, and several of the family were conspicuous as American patriots in the winning of independence. In the home of his ancestors in St. Matthews Parish in Orangeburg County Mortimer O. Dantzler was born and has spent his active career. He built up and is president of the No-Filler Fertilizer Company. This is a co-operative concern and a large number of Orangeburg and Calhoun County farmers are interested in the business.

Mr. Dantzler takes great interest in the New Welfare Board, of which he was appointed a member by the United States Government. He was head of the county committee in the second Red Cross drive, which went far above its quota of $18,000, raising $31,000. He married Miss Emma Cornelson, daughter of George H. Cornelson, a pioneer of Orangeburg and builder of the first yarn mill in this country, one of the prominent men of South Carolina. He came here from Germany when a young man, and was at first a merchant. His life is reviewed elsewhere in this history.

Mr. Dantzler is a Shriner through both the York and Scottish Rite, and is an honorary member of the Knights of Pythias.

He received his education at Mt. Zion School at Winsboro, and afterward went to the Carolina Military Institute at Charlotte, North Carolina.

His parents were Colonel Olin M. and Caroline (Glover) Dantzler.

Colonel Dantzler at the outbreak of the war between the states was a member of the South Carolina Senate from Orangeburg County. He resigned and volunteered as a private, becoming lieutenant colonel of the Twentieth Regiment and afterward was promoted to colonel of the Twenty-second South Carolina Volunteers. He was the gallant commander of this regiment at the time of his death. He fell near Petersburg, Virginia, June 2, 1864, while making a charge on the breastworks of the enemy. He was then thirty-nine years of age. A writer said of him "No braver man fought for the independence of the Southern States; no hero ever sacrificed his life upon the altar of his country with sublimer courage." The late Lewis M. Ayer of Anderson, a member of the Confederate Congress, reported to a member of the family that Colonel Dantzler had been promoted to brigadier general, but that the commission had not reached him at the time of his death.

When Colonel Dantzler was killed in Virginia he wore a Masonic pin, which with other belongings was returned with the body. The stars on the collar of his uniform, however, had been cut away by Mr. Griggs of Connecticut, First Artillery. He saw Colonel Dantzler fall and cut the stars off and carried them away. About ten years ago O. G. Dantzler received a letter from the chief of police of Charleston enclosing a letter sent to him from the chief of police of Hartford, Connecticut, a Mr. Bill, wanting to locate the relatives of Colonel Dantzler, killed at Bermuda Hundred, June 2, 1864.

He replied, and the chief of police, Mr. Bill, wrote a letter and sent the stolen stars to him, stating that Mr. Griggs had died and his widow took up the matter with Captain Bill of the First Connecticut Regiment, with the result stated.

Mr. M. O. Dantzler is also a fertilizer manufacturer.

THEO W. PASSAILAIGUE. One of the most important chapters in the history of any city is the development of its transportation system. On the subject of the building and operation of street railways in the City of Charleston there is one acknowledged authority, the general superintendent of railway of the Charleston Consolidated Railway & Lighting Company, Theo W. Passailaigue. His experience and service as a street railway man runs back forty-four years, to a time beyond the memory of the majority of the citizens and when Charleston took more or less pride in the three or four horse cars that ambled up and down the chief thoroughfares.

Mr. Passailaigue was born in Charleston in 1861, son of Louis J. and Esther Ann (Ellis) Passailaigue. The Passailaigue family came originally from Bordeaux, France, and for a generation or so were planters in San Domingo. At the time of the race insurrections of the Napoleonic era the family settled at Charleston. Louis J. Passailaigue was also a transportation official, being connected with the old South Carolina Railroad.

The education of Theo W. Passailaigue was acquired in one of the best boys' schools of the time, the old Holy Communion School at Charleston, whose history is continued in the present Porter's Military Academy. He was fifteen years of age when in 1876 he went to work as office boy in the office of the old Enterprise Railroad Company, which owned and operated the street railway system of Charleston of that date. In a few years he had promoted himself to more important responsibilities, and in the past forty years there has been hardly a phase of the management of the local transportation situation in which he has not been identified. Eventually he became president of the Enterprise Company, and held that office when its property was consolidated with the Charleston City Railway in 1897. In that year the lines were electrified. Mr. Passailaigue became superintendent of the consolidated company, and has been one of the executives in charge during several changes of ownership and management. The street railway system of the city is now conducted by the Charleston Consolidated Railway & Lighting Company, with Mr. Passailaigue as general superintendent of the railway division. This company now operates thirty-eight miles of track and gives Charleston a street railway service of the first rank.

He has also been associated with the group of business men most interested in public and civic improvements. Since 1904 he has served continuously as a member of the Charleston Board of School Commissioners and is chairman of the Committee on new school buildings. He is a director of the Charleston Fidelity Corporation, a member of the Chamber of Commerce, St. Andrew's Society, New England Society, Hibernian Association, and the Order of Elks. He and his family are communicants of Grace Episcopal Church.

Mr. Passailaigue married Miss Kate Ficken Melchers. Her father was the late Capt. Theodore Melchers, one of Charleston's prominent wholesale merchants. To their marriage were born eight children: Theo W., Jr., Edward P., Jack, Beatrice Helen, wife of W. C. De Lorme, and Misses Lillian Agnes, Katherine, Lurline and Frances. Mr. and Mrs. Passailaigue also have an adopted son, Frederick McKeown.

Capt. Edward P. Passailaigue, second of the three sons, is a graduate of the University of South Carolina, where he was a football star and prominent in other athletics, and volunteered his services in the war with Germany. He attended the training camp at Fort Oglethorpe, and was made captain of Company G, Third Ammunition Train, and was with that command in its operations in France. Since the war he has practiced as a lawyer, being a member of the Charleston bar.

GEORGE WASHINGTON FAIREY is one of the most interesting figures in the agricultural, commercial and political life of the St. Matthews community in the southern part of the state. The significant quality of his career seems to have been progressive thought and leadership. While in some respects conservative, he always welcomed better methods even when their application means the overturning of some venerable traditions.

This progressiveness was exemplified early in his connections with agricultural affairs around St. Matthews. He is credited with being the first farmer to plant on a commercial scale corn, oats and pecans in his vicinity. The old time cotton planters among his friends ridiculed his efforts, but he went ahead with a faith that results justified, and it was not many years before his neighbors quietly followed his lead, and for years corn and oats have been field crops ranking only second to cotton. Mr. Fairey raised his first pecan tree from a nut which he planted, and the fruit of that tree he used for further propagation and in time had a considerable acreage of pecan orchard. There are now few places in this district where the pecan tree does not flourish and is not considered a part of the income producing farm management. Thus an important industry has developed from this little experiment that Mr. Fairey made many years ago.

George Washington Fairey was born November 11, 1853, near Branchville, South Carolina. His father, John F. Fairey, was a native of the same community, and soon after the birth of his son, George W., he went west and died in Texas. Members of the Fairey family were associated with the Wannamakers in the very early settlement of Orangeburg County. The name Fairey is of Irish stock, and members of the family were represented in the Revolutionary war.

George Washington Fairey grew up in a period of unprecedented discouragement and lack of advantages resulting from the war and reconstruction. He had to be satisfied with a common school education. He came to manhood about the time the good citizens of South Carolina were working to redeem the state from carpet bag rule, and all his

enthusiasm was enlisted in that movement. He served as a lieutenant in the famous "Red Shirt" brigade of 1876, when negro domination ceased and white government was restored under Governor Hampton.

Mr. Fairey as a young man clerked in a store at Branchville for three years, but then began farming in that vicinity, and in 1879 moved to St. Matthews. Here his farming interests have been continued and with an enlarging scope. Besides his pioneer effort in introducing new crops, he has always demonstrated success with livestock, hogs, sheep and cattle. He owns, leases and conducts farming operations on 425 acres with about 200 acres of permanent pasture. His chief field crops are cotton, corn and oats.

At odd times for about twenty years Mr. Fairey conducted a saw mill, finally selling out in 1919. He is a director of the St. Matthews National Bank, vice president and director of the Farmers Bank and Trust Company of St. Matthews, and is a stockholder in the Anderson Motor Company, the Seminole Fertilizer Company and the Lime-Cola Company.

His name has been actively associated with farmers' movements in South Carolina, and he is a charter member and one of the organizers of the Cotton Association. He has also been active in politics and served as a member of the House from 1896 to 1899, and in 1920 was elected to fill the vacancy caused by the resignation of J. C. Redman. For many years he has been a delegate to state and local conventions, and has served on county and state committees of the democratic party. Mr. Fairey is a Mason and is affiliated with the Methodist Church in which he is a director. He has always taken a deep interest in church work ever since he attained manhood and has always taken an active part, attending all the state conferences of the Methodist Church and was superintendent of Sunday schools for twenty-three years. He was one of the original movers and agitators in establishing Calhoun County, cutting this territory out of Orangeburg and Lexington counties. He was named as one of the twelve commissioners having in charge the establishment of the county. These same commissioners built the present court house. During the war he was active in the drives for the liberty loans.

His first wife was Miss Annie Griffiths, of Branchville, who died in 1881. She was the mother of his only child, Mary Elizabeth, who is the wife of G. F. Crutchfield, of St. Matthews. In 1884 Mr. Fairey married Miss Harriet E. Weeks, of Lone Star, South Carolina.

WHITEMARSH SEABROOKE SMITH. While he was appointed city treasurer of Charleston in December, 1919, Mr. Smith's service in that office is a matter of at least ten years' experience. His appointment as chief of the office was a well merited promotion to one who has always had the city's best interests at heart and has demonstrated exceptional abilities and qualifications in the handling of the city's funds and accounts. His office administration is a model of the kind. It is organized for efficient and expeditious service to the public, each day's record is complete, all books being totaled and balanced at the end of each work day, all of which is in harmony with the most advanced ideas as to business and municipal administration.

Mr. Smith was born at Charleston in 1880, and is related to some of the city's historic families. One of his paternal ancestors was Whitemarsh B. Seabrooke, who served as governor of South Carolina from 1848 to 1850. He is a son of Josiah Edward and Mariah (Huguenin) Smith. His mother's people were of French Huguenot origin.

Whitemarsh Seabrooke Smith was reared in Charleston and received his education in the Porter Military School and The Citadel. For a few years he held clerical positions in the local freight offices of the Atlantic Coast Line Railway and was a subordinate in the office of the city treasurer before he was given his present duties. Mr. Smith is a member of the Carolina Yacht Club, and fraternally is affiliated with the Elks, Masons, and the German Friendly Society.

MICHAEL FRANCIS KENNEDY, veteran real estate dealer, banker and fraternalist of Charleston, has been a resident of that city for three-quarters of a century, and many of his interests have made him widely known over the state and outside the state.

He was born at Charleston September 26, 1844, and acquired his early education in public and private schools. As a youth he worked as a printer in the office of the Charleston Courier. He served four years as a Confederate soldier, beginning as a youth of seventeen and being connected with the South Carolina troops as a member of the Jamison Rifles, under Capt. T. Y. Simonds and later in the Torpedo service, serving with the Eighth Battalion, South Carolina troops.

Mr. Kennedy entered the real estate and insurance business in 1879, organizing the firm of M. F. Kennedy & Brother, and for forty years has had his offices on Broad Street. He was elected in 1882 and served four years in the House of Representatives. Mr. Kennedy has served for thirty years as secretary and treasurer of the Hibernian Mutual Insurance Company and has been a director of the Dime Savings Bank of Charleston since its organization. For twenty-five years he has been state assessor for the city and county of Charleston for the Fourth Ward.

He has served as grand dictator of the Knights of Honor of South Carolina, as grand master of the Ancient Order of United Workmen, a fraternal insurance order, is a former president of St. Patrick's Benevolent Society, and state president of the Ancient Order of Hibernians, a member of the Irish-American Historical Society of New York, and is affiliated with the Barnett Rhett Camp of United Confederate Veterans. In 1882 he attended a Land League Convention at Philadelphia, taking an active part in the organization. He is a member of the Hibernian Society of Charleston, and also a member of the Knights of Columbus, and has freely given of his time and resources to the welfare and advancement of his home city. For many years he has served as a vestryman in St. Mary's Catholic Church.

In 1867 he married Margaret C. Butterly, of New York. She died in 1912, the mother of eight children.

FRANK KERCHNER MYERS, master in equity for Charleston County, has been a resident of Charleston for over twenty years, and has earned many important honors in the legal profession.

He was born at Wilmington, North Carolina, March 7, 1874. His father, Charles D. Myers, was of English ancestry, was a native of New York City, and during the '50s located at Wilmington, North Carolina, where he spent the rest of his life as a merchant. During the war between the states he was on the staff of General French of the Confederacy. He married Lossie de Rosset, of Huguenot ancestry, and a daughter of Dr. A. J. de Rosset. Judge Myers' father died at Wilmington at the age of fifty-eight and his mother at seventy-four. Of their twelve children nine reached mature years and eight are still living, Frank Kerchner being the ninth in age.

As a boy at Wilmington he attended public school, the Cape Fear Academy under Washington Catlett, and began the study of law there but later finished his course in the office of P. A. Wilcox at Florence. He was admitted to the bar in April, 1896, and in the same year located at Charleston. For ten years he was reporter for the First Circuit and afterward for the Ninth Circuit, and in February, 1908, was appointed master in equity for Charleston County, for which office he has been four times renominated without opposition. While the duties of these offices have left him little time to develop a private practice, Judge Myers is regarded as one of the ablest members of his profession in the City of Charleston.

He is president of the Charleston Kiwanis Club, the Musical Art Club, and ex-president of the Charleston Club and Commercial Club, is secretary and treasurer of the Charleston Ancient Artillery Society, and during the recent war was prominent in all patriotic movements, being chairman of the War Camp Community Service. He is a member of the Chamber of Commerce. He is past chancellor of Carolina Lodge No. 9, Knights of Pythias, and was grand chancellor of the state. He is also a past master of Landmark Lodge No. 76, Ancient Free and Accepted Masons.

In 1896 he married Miss Roberta Atkinson Smith, of Raleigh, North Carolina. Mrs. Myers is a great-grandniece of President James Madison. They have two daughters and one son, Josephine Macon, now Mrs. John A. Vincent, of Springfield, Illinois, and Elizabeth de Rosset and Francis Kerchner, at home.

RT. REV. WILLIAM ALEXANDER GUERRY, Bishop of the Protestant Episcopal Church in the Diocese of South Carolina, has enjoyed thirty years of continuous labor and increasing responsibilities since he was ordained a priest.

Bishop Guerry was born at his maternal grandfather's place, known as Pine Grove, in Sumter County, South Carolina, July 7, 1861, son of Rev. LeGrand Felder and Margaret Serena (Brailsford) Guerry. His father, also for many years a minister of the Episcopal Church in South Carolina, was a direct descendant of Pierre Guerri, a Huguenot emigrant to South Carolina from France in 1695. Margaret Serena Brailsford was a direct descendant of Gen. William Moultrie, the historic defender of Fort Moultrie and Charleston Harbor during the Revolution. The family of which Bishop Guerry is a member has furnished many honored names to the life and affairs of South Carolina during past generations.

Bishop Guerry attended the Porter Military Academy at Charleston from 1876 to 1881. He was a student in the University of the South at Sewanee, Tennessee, from 1881 to 1884, receiving his Master of Arts degree in the latter year. He then entered the Theological Seminary at Sewanee in 1885, graduating Bachelor of Divinity in 1888. Upon his ordination as Bishop in 1907 he received the degree D. D. Honoris Causa from Sewanee.

He was made a deacon in 1888 and a priest in 1889. His first active work was at St. John's Church at Florence, and in 1889 he built St. John's Church there. He was rector at Florence, Marion and Darlington until 1893, when he was appointed chaplain and professor of Homiletics and Pastoral Theology at the University of the South. He held those offices until 1907, and during that time came in contact with hundreds of young men preparing for the ministry. In 1907 he was consecrated Bishop Coadjutor and nine months later, upon the death of Bishop Capers in 1908, became Bishop of South Carolina. Since 1917 he has also been president of the Synod of the Fourth Province of the Episcopal Church, and is now chairman of the Social Service Commission of the Fourth Province.

Bishop Guerry was one of a number of bishops of the Episcopal Church to engage in overseas service during the late war. He did that work under the auspices of the Young Men's Christian Association as "Special Preacher and Lecturer" from August, 1918, to March, 1919. He was in England and Scotland and France and also for a time in Germany with the Army of Occupation.

Bishop Guerry is a member of the Sigma Alpha Epsilon college fraternity of Sewanee, was a member of the Red Ribbon Society of the University of the South, a democrat in state politics and independent in national affairs. On November 27, 1889, at St. Luke's Church at Lincolnton, North Carolina, he married Miss Anne McBee, daughter of Vardry Alexander McBee and Mary Sumner McBee of Lincolnton, North Carolina. In the paternal line her prominent family connections are noted on other pages. She is descended from Gen. Jethro Sumner of Revolutionary fame. Bishop and Mrs. Guerry have five children: Alexander, who married Charlotte Patten, of Chattanooga; Sumner, unmarried; Anne, wife of Lieut. James Young Perry, of Greenville, South Carolina; and Moultrie and Edward Brailsford, both pursuing their academic studies at Sewanee, Tennessee.

The Bishop through the kindness of friends in the diocese will attend the sessions of the Lambeth Conference in England, which meets only once in ten years to consider the great problems which are before the world at this time. The Archbishop of Canterbury has written him a personal letter asking him to be present and to submit notes

TRISTRAM T. HYDE, who served as mayor of the City of Charleston in 1915-1919, began his business career in his native city at the age of fifteen and for over thirty years has been one of the chief factors in real estate, insurance and banking.

He was born at Columbia, July 3, 1862, son of Simeon and Anne Eliza (Tupper) Hyde. His father came to South Carolina when a small child, while the mother was a daughter of Tristram Tupper and was born at Charleston.

Mayor Hyde was educated in a private school taught by his sister and in the Charleston High School. At the age of fifteen he became a clerk in a general produce store. Later he was with a real estate firm and on reaching his majority was made a partner, the busines being known as Eben Coffin & Company, real estate and insurance. After five years Mr. Hyde bought out his senior's interests and continued the business under his own name until about 1908, when he took in his two sons. The firm is now Tristram T. Hyde & Sons, real estate and insurance. Mr. Hyde was identified with the organization of the Commercial Savings Bank in 1905, was elected its president, and has continued to fill that office in the reorganized Commercial National Bank. For twenty years or more he has been active in building and loan associations and various real estate developments.

Always interested in local affairs and politics, he was chairman of the City Democratic Committee. He was elected mayor in December, 1915, and was head of the municipal administration of Charleston until 1919. For twenty-seven years he was a member of the Sumter Guards, serving seventeen years as captain, and later was commissioned inspector with the rank of major.

In 1886 he married Miss Minnie D. Black, a daughter of Samuel C. Black, of Charleston. He has six living children: Tristram T., Jr., Samuel Black, Simeon, Jeannie, wife of C. B. Jenkins; Minnie B., wife of Herbert T. Taylor, and Edwin. The mother of these children died in 1905. In 1907 Mr. Hyde married Sue Estelle Thomas, daughter of John P. Thomas, of Union, South Carolina. Mr. Hyde is a prominent member of The Citadel Baptist Church at Charleston, is a deacon, and for twenty-six years has been superintendent of the Sunday school. During his superintendency the Sunday school has grown from a membership of 5 to 1,400, and is one of the largest Sunday schools in the state.

LEMUEL A. GREENE. While his business interests as a farmer, cotton grower and cotton manufacturer have been chiefly confined to Upper South Carolina, around Greenville, Mr. Greene is probably one of the best known men in the South to the cotton growing interests, largely because of his inventions and long continued educational propaganda for promoting a practical knowledge and skill in the grading of cotton, so that this knowledge and skill may be at the service of every cotton planter of ordinary intelligence. Latterly Mr. Greene has contributed another invention, having designed what is probably the lightest weight practical tractor-cultivator ever perfected.

Mr. Greene was born east of Chick Springs in Greenville County, South Carolina, July 16, 1864, son of William B. and Nancy (Taylor) Greene, who were also natives of the same locality. His grandfather, George Greene, and his maternal grandfather, Thomas Taylor, were among a party of twelve that migrated from Culpeper County, Virginia, to Greenville County, South Carolina, in 1786, making this pioneer journey through the wilderness on horseback and carrying with them all their possessions, swimming their horses over rivers and enduring all the hardships of pioneer travel. They settled at what has since become known as Chick Springs. The waters of this spring possessed fine medicinal properties, and made the places famous for more than a century. Mr. L. A. Greene's uncle, Alfred Taylor, developed the possibilities of the spring and for several years conducted a large resort hotel there.

Lemuel A. Greene grew up on a farm and has always been associated with some practical phase of the cotton industry, as a planter, cotton manufacturer and designer of cotton growing implements. In 1882 he became interested in a cotton mill business with his cousins, the Morgan boys, at Crawfordsville in Spartanburg County. He was in the cotton mills there for five years. Then he removed to what was then known as Cedar Hill in Greenville County, northeast of Greenville, and engaged in the general mercantile business with his uncle, I. L. Greene. Later he lived at Greer and in 1907, for the purpose of giving his daughters proper educational facilities, established his home at Greenville. Mr. Greene has a fine farm near the Laurens County line at Tumbling Shoals, and Mrs. Greene also has a farm on the Fork Shoals Road, twelve miles from Greenville.

Early in his experience Mr. Greene as a cotton planter discovered the handicaps and disadvantages at which the grower was placed by reason of the superior knowledge and skill of the buyers representing the cotton exchange. For a long period the grading of cotton was an arbitrary power in the hands of the exchanges, and it was to the advantage of this class of business men to throw as much mystery and confusion over the subject of grading as possible, and probably not one farmer in a dozen was able to determine the grade of his own staple or if he did know the grade insist upon its acceptance. It was to remedy this situation Mr. Greene started upon his educational propaganda and invented and patented a cotton-grader, which, it has been demonstrated, any man of ordinary intelligence can use to assist him in determining sufficient for all commercial purposes the grade of his own cotton. Thousands of these cotton graders are now in use in various Southern states, and for the purpose of promoting its further use and giving cotton growers the benefit of all the knowledge they require from a central agency Mr. Greene has promoted the organization of the Cotton Growers' Educational Union.

In studying the problem of adapting a tractor machine to field cultivation Mr. Greene was first of all impressed by the fact that none of the standard tractors was light enough and mobile enough to make them useful for cultivating growing plants and in soft soil. It is obvious that the average tractor must have great weight in order to have tractive power. Mr. Greene, without entering into details on his invention, solved the problem by producing a frame or chassis driven by gas motor and weighing altogether about 300 pounds. To this is attached the cultivator, consisting of revolving blades, attached to the carriage wheels. The significant feature is that the implement in turning not only cuts and cultivates the soil but furnishes propelling force and thereby overcomes the usual difficulty in which the drive wheels of the average tractor is also adapted to pulling sweep cultivators or other light attachments, efficient for their purpose in cultivating growing crops.

Mr. Greene married Miss Sallie Cureton, daughter of Paschal D. Cureton, who was clerk of the United States District Court. They have three daughters, Elvira, Minnie and Ruth.

While these interests seem to constitute the program of a very busy man, Mr. Greene has been a deep thinker along the other lines. He is probably one of the best informed Bible students in the state, and for a quarter of a century has been working with a view to solving some of the problems of exegesis presented by Ezekiel's Visions, and other difficult passages of old testament scripture. The product of this work is found in twenty-three chapters of manuscript, embracing his revelations of the problems found all the way from Genesis to the Revelations. While Mr. Greene, like other Bible students, recognizes the symbolical character of old testament scripture, he feels that the symbolism is by no means a literary style, but was designed for the express purpose of disguising from Satan the key to the wisdom of God found in all creation. It is through Ezekiel's Visions that Mr. Greene finds, in its symbolic language, the keys to this wisdom of God, designedly uttered for the guidance of humanity. More than that Mr. Greene sees a complete harmony existing between the physical structure of man and the divine structure of the Universe. And in his chapters he has been able to coordinate and give the proper and vital significance to the resemblances involved between the mortal temple of man and the temple of God. As he sees it, the time has come for Christ to give to the world his relation to material power that has been concealed in the tabernacle and the temple for nearly two thousand years. These witnesses will testify to this power being lived into existence by Christ. Satan used false witnesses against Christ, Christ will use only true living witnesses that this power came through Christ.

JOHN F. HUCHTING. One of the interesting and historical landmarks in Charleston is the drug store at the corner of King Street and Broad, conducted under the title of C. F. Schwettman & Son. Investigations at different times have failed to reveal anywhere in the United States an older drug store. The business was founded in 1780, nearly a century and a half ago, and its association and service with the people of Charleston has been continuous ever since.

While the business is still conducted for historical reasons under the old name, the present owner since 1913 has been John F. Huchting. Mr. Huchting, who is one of the prominent pharmacists of the state, was born at Beaufort, South Carolina, in 1887, son of John F. and Angela (Campbell) Huchting. His mother was a native of Charleston, while his father was born in Germany and came to Beaufort in early youth.

Educated in the public schools of Beaufort, John F. Huchting took the full courses in pharmacy in the Medical College of the State of South Carolina, and graduated with the class of 1908 and with the degree Ph. G. However, his practical experience in pharmacy had begun five years earlier, in 1903, as an employe of Elliott's pharmacy in Beaufort. While in college at Charleston he also worked in the local drug store. On graduating in 1908 he went with the Olar Drug Company at Olar, South Carolina, and was in business for himself at Branchville. He returned to Charleston in 1912, and for a year was pharmacist with the Paragon Drug Company. He then bought the C. F. Schwettman & Son business.

Mr. Huchting is a member of the State Pharmaceutical Association, of the National Retail Druggist Association, and when in the fall of 1919 there was organized at Charleston the Ninth District Pharmaceutical Association he was honored by election as its first president. The object of this association is to promote the general welfare not only of the constituent membership of druggists but also the public as well, protecting the public from impure and unsafe preparations offered for sale, and also to co-operate with the federal and local authorities in preventing the sale of narcotics and alcoholic remedies as beverages. He is a member of Solomon Lodge No. 1 of the Masonic order.

Mr. Huchting married Miss Nora Barker, of Olar, South Carolina, and they have two children, John F., Jr., and Amy.

JOHN ALEXANDER KELLEY. In all the years that he has practiced law, now approaching fifty in number, John A. Kelley has diligently sought to make his profession, his personal influence and his example a means of useful service to his community, and the respect in which he is held in Williamsburg County indicates that his ambition has been amply satisfied.

Mr. Kelley was born in Clarendon County, South Carolina, July 20, 1848, son of Joseph J. and Ann J. (Campbell) Kelley. His paternal grandfather, Daniel J. Kelley, came from Ireland to America just after the Revolutionary war. His maternal grandfather was brought from Scotland to this country before the Revolution, and was an ardent patriotic soldier in the War for Independence.

John Alexander Kelley was three years old when his father died, and was reared in a humble home, though throughout his life he has always regarded as the strongest single influence for good the care and direction he received from his mother. She encouraged him in habits of industry and to the extent of her abilities enabled him to attend school.

He was reared at Manning in Clarendon County, and attended the academy there taught by John W. Ervin. When he was sixteen years of age he entered the Confederate army, and fought for the southern cause during the last year of the war. In the meantime he had determined to become a lawyer, and in 1866 he entered South Carolina University. He did not have the means to remain until graduation. He carried on his studies with books and some personal assistance from Johnson & Johnson of Marion, and in 1869 began teaching in Marion County.

Mr. Kelley was admitted to the bar in 1872. For several years thereafter he was associated in the practice of the profession at Marion with the late Hon. Joshua H. Hudson of Bennettsville. At first the firm was Hudson & Kelley, and afterwards Hon. W. W. Sellers came into the firm and it became Sellers, Hudson & Kelley. In the year 1877 Captain Kelley located in Kingstree, where he has since continuously resided. At the time he came to Kingstree, Williamsburg County was dominated by the negroes and carpet-baggers under the leadership of one S. A. Swails, a notorious imported negro politician who was president of the South Carolina Senate during the radical regime. He at once lent himself assiduously to the task of ridding the county of that humiliation. He was made captain of his red shirt company, and his untiring efforts and the inspiration aroused by his uncompromising zeal and courage contributed very largely to the final triumph of white democracy in the county. He was chairman and spokesman of a committee appointed in 1878 to notify S. A. Swails to leave the county in twenty-four hours. Swails received the notice promptly and left in half the allotted time. That was the end of the political trouble with the negroes in Williamsburg.

The subject of this sketch was on Governor Hagood's staff, was member of the South Carolina House of Representatives in 1888 and 1889, served two terms as mayor of Kingstree, and in many ways has rendered much valuable service to his town and county in their progress through the numerous vicissitudes of the last half-century. In all of that long period he was always to be found on that side of all movements and issues which had for its purpose the betterment of the interest of the community. One of his chief distinctions is that, contrary to common experience, even in his advanced age he readily adopts himself to new methods and customs, looks forward and has a keen perception of the beneficial results of progressive enterprises.

It was through his efforts that the Bank of Kingstree, the first bank established in Williamsburg County, was organized. He has served as vice president and attorney of this institution since its organization. He was especially interested in giving his home town adequate school facilities, including the erection of a handsome school building. Mr. Kelley is a democrat, a member of the Methodist Church and is affiliated with the Masons and Knights of Pythias.

For many years he has been recognized as one of the leading lawyers of the Pee Dee section. He was studious and industrious, constantly giving to his clients his best efforts. While he has been notably generous, contributing freely to various worthy causes and repeatedly giving his services, without remuneration, to those in need, he has accumulated a comfortable estate. He has always had the courage to express, and adhere to, his conviction and to his associates has been ever a staunch friend or a worthy foe. To those in trouble he was as sympathetic and tender-hearted as a child, but with the man who attempted to force him to surrender his convictions he would battle with relentless ardour.

October 29, 1872, the same year he was admitted to the bar, he married Elizabeth B. Boyd, daughter of Robert J. and Rachel B. Boyd. Her father, Dr. Robert J. Boyd, was long a prominent member of the South Carolina Methodist Conference. To Mr. and Mrs. Kelley were born three children: Joseph, who died when four years of age, Elizabeth B., wife of W. C. Claiborne, a hardware merchant of Kingstree, South Carolina, and Alma, wife of F. W. Fairey, a banker and prominent man of Kingstree.

LAWRENCE M. PINCKNEY. The business prominence enjoyed by Lawrence M. Pinckney in his native City of Charleston may be judged from his connection with numerous commercial and civic organizations, including the City Bank & Trust Company, of which he is a director; the Charleston Hotel Company, of which he is secretary; the Charleston I. of P. Traction Company, of which he is secretary; the Clyde Realty Corporation, of which he is president; the Exchange Building & Loan Association, of which he is president; the General Realty Investment Company, president; Leiten Realty Corporation and Windsor Real Estate Corporation, president, and the South Carolina Insurance Company, of which he is a director.

Mr. Pinckney, who has been a prominent figure in the realty and insurance business for over fifteen years, was born December 13, 1872, son of Douglas Pinckney, and a grandson of R. Q. Pinckney, who was born in Charleston in 1802, of English ancestry, and died in that city in 1860. Douglas Pinckney spent his active career as a cotton man. He was born in 1837 and died in 1883, at the age of forty-six. His wife was Jane Vander Horst Dawson, who was born at Charleston in 1840 and died in 1885.

Lawrence M. Pinckney was the youngest of seven children. He had a public school education and at the age of thirteen was left an orphan and has found his way to success largely through his individual effort. For a number of years beginning January 1, 1905, he was a member of the City Council, served as chairman of the Committee on Ways and Means, the Board of Exchanges, and is chairman of the Dock Committee. He is a member of the Charleston Club, Charleston Country Club, Carolina Yacht Club and a number of other social organizations. He is a member of Elks Lodge No. 242, belongs to the Bankers Club of New York, the New York Press Club, and has been a lifelong democrat.

His first wife was Claudia Smith, who died in 1911, leaving one son, John Dawson. Mr. Pinckney married for his present wife Elizabeth Allen de Saussure.

GASPER LOREN TOOLE. It would be difficult to exaggerate the values to the community and state radiating from the presence of such a family as the Tooles through many generations. In the country comprised in the old Barnwell District they have been progressive workers in agriculture and planting, have held enviable stations in public affairs, and one of the busiest and most influential members of the family in recent years has been Gasper Loren Toole of Aiken. Mr. Toole has exemplified a rare faculty of doing a number of things well, and most of his activities have had a public bearing. He is a prominent member of the Aiken bar, has been in both Houses of the Legislature a number of terms, and is one of the able leaders among southern cotton planters today.

Mr. Toole was born at Montmorenci, April 13, 1867. His birthplace was in that section of the old Barnwell District now a part of Aiken County, five miles east of the City of Aiken. The Tooles, of Irish ancestry, first settled in Pennsylvania, where one of them married a sister of Benjamin Franklin. Those who founded the southern branch came to South Carolina by way of Virginia and East Tennessee. The first of them in South Carolina came about 1740 and located in Barnwell District, about twenty miles southeast of Aiken, in the locality where the father of the Aiken lawyer was born. The parents of Gasper Loren Toole were Gasper Loren and Susan (Hardin) Toole. His paternal grandmother and his mother were members of the Hardin and Woodward families, both prominent in South Carolina. Susan Hardin's grandfather, William Hardin, was a Revolutionary soldier, while her mother was a Lanier of the illustrious Georgia family of that name. Gasper Loren Toole, Sr., was born in 1817, a son of Isaac and Elizabeth (Woodward) Toole. Mrs. Toole died in 1882 and Mr. Toole remarried, his second wife being Mrs. Fannie Quarles Perrin of Abbeyville County. Since Mr. Toole's death in 1890 she has made her home with the subject of this sketch, having been a great comfort and help to him. She belongs to the old school of southern hospitable and Christian ladies. Beginning in the late '70s Gasper L. Toole, Sr., was a pioneer fruit grower in Barnwell and Aiken counties. He developed an extensive peach orchard, and in some seasons shipped a carload of fruit daily. He was also by profession an educator and taught school at Beach Island. For a number of years he was in the general merchandise business at Montmorenci, holding the office of postmaster there.

Gasper Loren Toole, Jr., was one of ten children, all of whom reached mature years. He attended local schools and the University of South Carolina, and in 1892-94 was superintendent of education of Aiken County. In 1896 he was chosen a member of the Legislature, serving during the sessions of 1897-98. At that time he took his family, consisting of his wife and two children, to Columbia and entered upon the diligent study of law in the university. After completing his course he began practice at Aiken, and has achieved enviable distinction as a lawyer. The large law practice that has accumulated during the past thirty years is now left largely in the hands of his son Frampton W. Toole, who is a graduate of the University of South Carolina.

Mr. Toole was again elected a member of the Legislature in 1902, was re-elected in 1904, and then was chosen a member of the State Senate, serving two years. Again, in 1910 and 1912, he was chosen to the Lower House. He also made the race for Congress in the Second District, standing second among the four aspirants. Mr. Toole is a former director of the First National Bank of Aiken.

His chief productive interests are in his home place "Park in the Pines" at Arbutus Hills in the western edge of Aiken. Here he has a fine farm of 106 acres and also owns 700 acres 1½ miles away on Bridge Creek, at what is known as Kennedy Crossing. His holdings include other valuable property in the country and in Aiken city. As a planter he is specializing in the early Toole wilt-resisting earliness to meet the boll-weevil menace. This cotton has been developed through several generations of use on the part of the Toole family. Planters in other sections have had most satisfactory results with this strain, and a full test of its qualities will shortly be completed in Aiken County where the boll-weevil made its first appearance in the summer of 1919.

Mr. Toole is solidly behind all movements for bettering the condition of and bringing more profit to the cotton farmer. He is at the head of the Aiken County branch of the American Cotton Association. He was appointed a delegate to the first meeting of this association, and in September, 1919, by appointment of Governor Cooper, was a delegate to the World's Cotton Conference at New Orleans. Mr. Toole has always been known as a man of convictions, ready to fight for principles. Many years ago he led the campaign for prohibition in Aiken County when prohibition sentiment was by no means the prevailing popular one.

Besides meeting all the ordinary demands upon his time and means in behalf of patriotic causes, including participation in the speaking campaigns for raising the various war loan and Red Cross funds in Aiken County, Mr. Toole personally volunteered his services to the Young Men's Christian Association and was a Y worker for four months at Camp Jackson, beginning in the summer of 1918. He is a member and clerk of the Aiken Baptist Church, and is affiliated with the Independent Order of Odd Fellows, Woodmen of the World, Junior Order of United American Mechanics and Improved Order of Red Men.

Mr. Toole married Miss May Eunice Perrin, of Abbeville County, member of the well known family of that section. Mrs. Toole comes of one of the old South Carolina families of Revolutionary stock. The family is of French Huguenot descent, coming to America in the early 1700's. Mrs. Toole's father was a non-commissioned officer in the Confederate struggle and was a cousin of Col. Abner Perrin, after whom was named one of the camps of the Southern Confederacy at Edgefield. They have six children: Frampton W., Cleora, Fannie May, Julia Bell, Lorena and Perrin Toole.

Mr. Toole is an indefatigable worker and never drifted with the tide. He has his opinions and sticks to them. He has worked hard in the interest of the cotton industry, and was the author of the first ten land laws for the cotton mill operatives. He worked five years to get the legislation through and being convinced not only of its justice but its importance in establishing an equilibrium between mill owners and workers, kept at it until his efforts were successful. This was the first ten laws of its kind ever put on the statute books of South Carolina. Likewise he worked for the passage of the child labor law to keep children under fourteen years of age out of the cotton mills.

His solution to the high cost of living is greater production, particularly in farm products and that there will have to be an effort to get the people out of the congested centers back to the land. Mr. Toole's farm is adjacent to that of his brother's, Frank P. Toole, who is considered one of the most successful farmers in the county. He is a prominent man in his district, his many charities causing him to be beloved by all those with whom he comes in contact. He was born near Montmorenci, June 21, 1851, and has devoted his life to farming. At his advanced age he is the personal manager of twenty plows.

JAMES REID JOHNSON, a coal merchant of Charleston, has for years been one of the most prominent Masons of the state. He has taken all the various degrees in the York Rite and is a thirty-second degree Scottish Rite Mason. He served as grand master of the Grand Lodge in South Carolina in 1910-11; was grand master of the Royal and Select Masters and eminent commander of South Carolina Commandery No. 1 of the Knights Templar; was potentate of Oasis Temple of the Mystic Shrine about 1907. He has taken a great deal of interest in Memorial Hall for the preservation of Masonic relics.

Mr. Johnson was born at Charleston April 6, 1862. His parents were William and Mary Mellichamp Johnson. The father, also a native of Charleston, established the coal business in 1852 and was active in its management until his death when about seventy-six years of age. The grandfather was James S. Johnson, also a native of Charleston.

James Reid Johnson was the oldest of four children, was educated in the grammar and high schools of Charleston, and early became associated with his father in the firm of Johnson & Company. After his father died he became associated with T. S. Sinkler and A. Marion Stone, and they have one of the leading firms in South Carolina for wholesale and retail coal and the mining of coal. Mr. Johnson is also interested in other business affairs. He has not been active in politics, but served for eight years as chairman of the Board of Public Works under Mayor Rhett. He served all the time the board existed except at the time of its creation, when J. B. Adjer served for a few months.

He married for his first wife Elizabeth Wilson Rouquie, who died June 1, 1914. In 1916 he married Ellen Adams Brooks, a niece of the noted Preston Brooks, of South Carolina.

BERRY WASHINGTON MILEY. In 1919 Judge Miley has the satisfaction of looking back over a quarter of a century since his admission to the bar, and it was an enviable record that he could review. He has not only been a lawyer but a leading public spirited citizen of Bamberg County, former probate judge, and has held many official honors at the hands of his fellow citizens, including the office of representative from the county.

Judge Miley was born at Smoaks Cross Roads in Colleton County, August 14, 1871. His great-grandfather, Robert Miley, came to South Carolina from Pennsylvania about the close of the Revolutionary war. He was twice married and reared a large family. The grandfather of Judge Miley was James Miley, a native of the old Barnwell District. He was a soldier in some of the Indian wars, and otherwise followed the life of a planter. Joseph C. Miley, father of Judge Miley, was born in Colleton County, and at the age of sixteen enlisted as a private in the Confederate army. He served until he was wounded and lost a foot. After the war he followed planting. He married Amanda E. Kinsey, a native of Colleton County and daughter of William Kinsey, who came from North Carolina when a young man.

Berry Washington Miley, the oldest of five children, was reared and educated in Colleton and Bamberg counties, and after the common schools attended Wofford College in Spartanburg one year, spent one year in the University of South Carolina, and graduated from the law school of South Carolina College. He was admitted to the bar in 1894, and during the following five years practiced at Denmark in Bamberg County. In 1899 he was elected and began his duties as probate judge, at that time removing his residence to Bamberg. He gave a careful administration of the office of judge for six years, and then resumed private practice and has handled much of the important litigation in Bamberg County. He began his service in the Legislature in 1907, and served two years, 1913 and 1914. In 1918 he was again elected to represent Bamberg County. Judge Miley has been active in politics and has repeatedly represented his party in both county and state conventions. He has also been a commissioner of elections, county and city attorney, and in every sense a local leader. He has planting interests in the county, which he supervises in addition to his law business.

Judge Miley is a stockholder in the People's Bank of Bamberg and in the B. E. & W. Railway. He owns some farming interests, including land which his great-grandfather owned when he first came to South Carolina. Judge Miley is affiliated with the Knights of Pythias and is a member of the Methodist Church.

WILSON GODFREY HARVEY is one of South Carolina's most prominent bankers, and was one of the founders and for twenty-five years has been actively identified with the management of the Enterprise Bank of Charleston. This institution is one of the largest banks in South Carolina, having aggregate resources of more than $1,500,000.

Mr. Harvey was born at Charleston September

8, 1866, son of Wilson G. and Cornelia Julia (Elbridge) Harvey. His father was also a native of Charleston, as was his grandfather, James E. Harvey. The Harveys came to South Carolina prior to the Revolution from Bermuda, and Mr. Harvey's great-grandfather was a member of the Continental forces fighting for independence. His father, Wilson G. Harvey, was a Confederate soldier. Wilson G. Harvey, the son, was fifth in a family of eleven children, four of whom are still living.

He was educated in the grammar and high schools of Charleston, and at the age of fifteen took up a business career as an employe of the business department of the News-Courier. At the age of twenty-one he was manager of the World and Budget. Leaving newspaper work, he became manager of the Charleston agency of the Bradstreet Company.

He organized the Enterprise Bank in 1894 and was elected its first cashier. Since 1904 he has been president. The Enterprise Bank has a capital of $50,000, surplus of $25,000, and its deposits aggregate more than $1,300,000.

Mr. Harvey has served as president of the South Carolina Bankers Association and as president of the Charleston Clearing House.

While one of the busiest men of Charleston, he always found time to take an active part in various fraternal organizations and civic affairs. He has served as president of the South Carolina Society Sons of the American Revolution and vice president of the national organization of the Sons of the American Revolution. He was adjutant general of the Fourth Brigade of the South Carolina Volunteer Troops for several years and major of the Second Battalion. He has held the office of grand chancellor in the Knights of Pythias of the state, and for twenty-two consecutive years has been elected by unanimous vote grand master of the exchequer of the order. He has also served as grand master of the Independent Order of Odd Fellows, past senior consul of the Woodmen of the World, and is a past master of Solomon's Lodge No. 1, Ancient Free Masons, one of the oldest Masonic lodges in America. For eight years he was an alderman of Charleston and in 1910 mayor pro tem. He has served as president of the Chamber of Commerce and is chairman of the Sanitary Commission of the county. He is a former president of the Charleston Automobile Club, is secretary and one of the board of managers of the Charleston Country Club, a member of the Carolina Yacht Club and other social organizations, and is a deacon in the First Presbyterian Church of Charleston.

April 12, 1894, Mr. Harvey married at Macon, Georgia, Mary Franklin Butler. They have three children: Franklin, wife of D. A. Brockinton; Ruth; and Mary Butler. June 24, 1914, Mr. Harvey married Miss Margaret Waring.

COL. THOMAS J. MOORE. In the life of the late Col. Thomas J. Moore, of the historic family of Moore of Spartanburg County, there was fulfilled every demand of adequacy. His was a long and eventful life, full of experience and achievement, bearing responsibilities and promoting the happiness of others.

The interest in his individual career is supplemented by that of his ancestry. His paternal grandfather was Charles Moore, whose ancestors, tradition says, went from Scotland to the north of Ireland with the Duke of Hamilton, to whom large landed possessions were given by the King of England. It is likely that the Moores were of the same kinship or clan as the Duke of Hamilton. Charles Moore, who was born in the north of Ireland in 1728, was a man of education, and is said to have been a graduate of Trinity College at Dublin or of Oxford. When a young man he came to America with his wife, Mary Moore, first settling in Pennsylvania, and soon afterward coming south to Spartanburg County, South Carolina. He reached that isolated section of the frontier some time between 1760 and 1763, and, as the date indicates, was one of the very first settlers. In 1763 he took up a grant of land on the Tyger River, ten miles south of the present City of Spartanburg, in the locality where his grandson, Colonel Moore, had his home. Thus the Moores have lived in Spartanburg County from practically the close of what is known as the French and Indian war throughout all the intervening period, covering all the history of the United States as a nation. The oldest child of Charles Moore was Margaret, who married Capt. Andrew Barry, also a Scotchman, who had come to Spartanburg County, and in the War of the Revolution was commander of the American forces in that county and region. Margaret Moore Barry is known in history as "Kate Barry" and was a heroine of the Revolution, whose deeds of valor and devotion form an interesting chapter in the annals of Upper Carolina. All of Charles Moore's sons-in-law took a prominent part in the Revolutionary war. His son, Gen. Thomas Moore, although a young man at the time, played a conspicuous part in the winning of independence, and in the War of 1812 served with the rank of Major General. General Moore, who died in 1822, represented his district for several years in Congress.

Dr. Andrew Barry Moore, father of Colonel Moore, was born within two miles of his son's present home in 1771. He died there in 1848. He graduated in 1795 from Dickinson College at Carlisle, Pennsylvania, and then studied the profession of medicine. He was a physician of real distinction and his eminence was such as to give him a permanent name in the medical profession of South Carolina. Practically all his life was devoted to the arduous service of his profession in his home community in Spartanburg County. But his fame went abroad and every year for many years young men were studying medicine at his home, which might be considered one of the earliest medical colleges of South Carolina. At Dickinson College Doctor Moore was a classmate of Roger B. Taney, who afterward became a figure in our national life as Chief Justice of the United States Supreme Court. Dr. Andrew B. Moore married Nancy Miller Montgomery, a member of the well known Spartanburg County family of Montgomery, concerning which record is made on other pages of this publication.

A son of these worthy parents, Col. Thomas J. Moore, was born April 29, 1843, and his birthplace

and the home of all his years has been on the land originally settled by his grandfather, as above noted. Since 1883 this community has been known as Moore, being a station on the C. & W. C. Railway. The Moore possessions here comprise about 4,000 acres.

Thomas J. Moore was pursuing his studies at South Carolina College at Columbia when the cloud of war broke into a storm. When Fort Sumter was fired upon he joined the college cadets, and was sent to Charleston, arriving there April 12, 1861. After a month the cadets returned to college, but subsequently were ordered to the defense of Port Royal. Again resuming college work, Colonel Moore remained until March, 1862, when he joined Company E of the Eighteenth South Carolina Infantry in the regular Confederate service. This regiment was sent to Virginia, where its first important engagement was the second battle of Manassas, where the brigade suffered more than any other, losing 67 per cent of its men. A loss that came especially near to him was the death of his only brother, Andrew C. Moore, a brilliant young man of great promise, a graduate of South Carolina College and a law graduate of the University of Virginia. Some time after this battle Mr. Moore was transferred from the Eighteen Infantry to Company A of the Holcombe Legion, and became color sergeant of that organization. He saw continued dangerous and arduous service in Virginia, Georgia, Florida, South Carolina and North Carolina, and during the last year of war was in the Petersburg campaign. At the battle of Five Forks near the close of the war he was captured and as a prisoner was confined on Johnson's Island in Lake Erie until July, 1865.

Not long after the war Colonel Moore was appointed to organize the Thirty-sixth Regiment of Militia of South Carolina, and was made a colonel. He also served with the rank of colonel on the staff of Gen. Clement Evans, Gen. John B. Gordon and Gen. C. Irvine Walker, Commanders in Chief of the United Confederate Veterans.

Colonel Moore was a member of the South Carolina Legislature in 1872 and 1874, before the reconstruction era was completed. During the '80s he served a four year term in the State Senate. For over forty years before his death he was a member of the Board of Commissioners of the South Carolina School for the Deaf and Blind at Cedar Springs, and during most of this long period he was chairman of the board. In April, 1919, he was unanimously elected a member of the Confederate Pension Board for Spartanburg County. For many years he was an honored ruling elder and Sunday school superintendent of the Presbyterian Church at Moore.

Throughout his life he was a most lovable and popular man, held in the greatest esteem, and to a degree such as is seldom found utilized many opportunities to serve his community and to promote many worthy causes. Hence, though death came to him when he had lived more than three quarters of a century, the event was viewed as a calamity by his host of friends and by all members of his community. Colonel Moore passed away August 19, 1919.

He married Miss Mary Anderson, a daughter of Capt. David Anderson, a granddaughter of James Anderson and great-granddaughter of Maj. David Anderson, one of the early settlers of Spartanburg County and an officer in the Revolutionary war. Colonel and Mrs. Moore have five living children: Dr. Andrew C. Moore, professor of biology of the University of South Carolina; Paul V. Moore, former secretary of the Spartanburg Chamber of Commerce; Miss Harriett Moore; Mrs. Arthur R. Craig; and Miss Nancy Moore.

JOSEPH BELL HYDE has been continuously associated with the business affairs of Charleston for over a quarter of a century. His connections and interests have been those of several of the largest and best known firms in the state.

He was born at Charleston February 3, 1849, second son of Simeon and Ann Eliza (Tupper) Hyde. His father came to South Carolina from New York. His mother was a daughter of Tristram Tupper, one of the leading figures in Charleston's business affairs for many years.

Joseph Bell Hyde attended preparatory schools in Charleston and was a student in high school until the outbreak of the war. His father early in the war moved his family to Columbia and afterward to Greenville and Anderson. Joseph attended school in those cities and toward the end of the war, when the state looked to its boys to fill up the depleted ranks of the Confederacy, he volunteered and was on duty in the closing months of the struggle.

When the war was over he returned to Charleston and engaged in business. From the first year to the present Mr. Hyde has been continuously associated with practically one group of men, except for such changes as have occurred through death and other causes. He was with the firm George W. Williams & Company, at one time foremost among Charleston's merchants, also with its successors, Robertson, Taylor & Williams, and afterward the Ashepoo Fertilizer Company, which was established by Robertson, Taylor & Williams. Mr. Hyde is now local treasurer of the American Agricultural & Chemical Company at its Charleston office. He is a director in the Carolina Savings Bank.

Mr. Hyde for all his active devotion to business has been a lover of good books and has cultivated the amenities of social life. He has accumulated a fine private library and is a trustee and secretary of the Charleston Library Society.

EDGAR PHILMORE EDWARDS. With only forty years allotted him of mortal existence, the late Edgar Philmore Edwards fulfilled all the essentials of a successful business career and eminently public spirited citizenship. While the future held out wonderful promise, the record which had already been written when he died on February 24, 1920, contained every item that a man of worthy ambition and high character could desire.

Mr. Edwards, who for ten years was a resident of Spartanburg, South Carolina, was born at Carthage, North Carolina, September 30, 1879. He comes of a scholarly family. His brother I. N. Edwards, is a member of the faculty of the University of Chicago, and his sister, Alma Edwards, for several years has been the head of the Latin Department of Guilford College. Other surviving members of his family are Mrs. Lucy A. Edwards, his mother, and L. W. Edwards, his brother of Carthage, North Carolina, and Mrs. T. A. Johnson of Liberty, North Carolina.

Mr. Edwards had a normal and wholesome youth, was educated in the public and private schools of North Carolina and began his business career at Columbia, South Carolina. For several years he was connected with Swift & Company, and rapidly rose to the distinction of becoming the youngest district manager of that firm. In 1905 he and his brother, L. W. Edwards, established in Columbia the "Edwards Brothers" retail grocery stores. Here he continued with success until 1910, when he with T. B. Pearce opened the Pearce-Edwards wholesale fruit and produce company of Spartanburg. Later other branch houses were established, including the Pearce-Edwards Company at Union, the Pearce-Woods Company at Greenville and the Pearce-Prince Company at Greenwood. Mr. Edwards was interested in all these.

In addition to his business qualifications Mr. Edwards had a remarkable personality and a genius for friendship, and was one of the best known and best beloved members of the Spartanburg community. He was always ready with his aid in behalf of any progressive movement, and contributed liberally of his time, enthusiasm, energy and funds.. He was a member of the United Commercial Travelers and the Travelers Protective Association, and had served as president of the latter order. He was also a Mason, was a charter member of the Rotary Club of Spartanburg, was vice president of the Chamber of Commerce, district deputy of the Elks, and past exalted ruler of the Spartanburg Lodge. He was a steward in the Bethel Methodist Church.

Mr. Edwards was married on January 5, 1917, to Miss Flora Wilson White, the daughter of Rev. and Mrs. W. A. White of Guilford College, North Carolina. Mrs. Edwards is the niece of Ex-Senator James M. Dixon of Montana, and is descended from a long line of Pennsylvania Quakers.

The three short years of his home life was the crowning virtue of "A man who was clean inside and out; who neither looked up to the rich nor down to the poor; who was too brave to lie, too generous to cheat; who took his share of the world and let other people have theirs."

THOMAS S. MCMILLAN. While a busy lawyer Thomas S. McMillan has been almost equally busy with his varied outside interests in Charleston. He is actively connected with several commercial organizations, is a leader in the democratic party and is well known as an athlete and an athletic coach.

He was born at Ulmers, in Barnwell County, South Carolina, November 27, 1888, a son of James C. and Mary J. (Cave) McMillan. His father was born in Barnwell County in 1844 and he spent his active life as a farmer. He is now living retired. The parents celebrated their golden wedding anniversary December 27, 1917. Of their eleven children six died in infancy, and all the others are still living, namely: Claude, of Albany, Alabama; Alonzo B., of Covington, Kentucky; Thomas S. and John B., twins, the latter being the soldier representative of the family, having been with the American Expeditionary Forces in France; and Willa Low, who is a teacher in the public schools at Gaffney, South Carolina.

Thomas S. McMillan was the eighth among the children. He was educated in public schools near Ulmers, this school being known as the Hickory Hill School, was graduated in 1900 from the Ulmers High School, and in 1907 completed his course in the Orangeburg Collegiate Institute. From there he entered the University of South Carolina at Columbia, taking the A. B. degree in 1912 and his legal diploma in 1913. In the same year he was admitted to the bar, and has since been building up a reputation and practice at Charleston. In 1915 he formed a partnership with J. B. Heyward. The firm of McMillan & Heyward is one of the most successful in Charleston.

Mr. McMillan has been a member of the House of Representatives since 1916, has served as chairman of the Charleston delegation in the Legislature, and is a member of the Ways and Means Committee of the House. He has been a member of the Democratic State Executive Committee, and was a member of the Democratic Convention in 1918.

Mr. McMillan has a rather notable record in athletics. He played professional baseball five years with the South Atlantic League. He was captain of the University of South Carolina baseball team in 1912, and from 1916 to 1919 was coach of The Citadel ball team, and is now president of the Charleston Baseball Club.

He is a member of the Chamber of Commerce, is a Scottish Rite Mason, a member of Dalcho Consistory No. 1, and a Noble of the Mystic Shrine. He is active in The Citadel Square Baptist Church at Charleston and teacher of its Baraca class. Mr. McMillan is interested in the Liberty Transport Company of Charleston, the Campbell Fuel Company and as an attorney represents several other business organizations.

December 14, 1916, he married Miss Clara Gooding, a native of Hampton, South Carolina, and a daughter of W. J. and M. W. Gooding.

EDWARD THERON KELLEY, M. D. In the fifth generation of a South Carolina family that has been noted for its religious convictions, its patriotism, and all the sterling qualities required of home builders and state builders, Doctor Kelley of Kingstree has earned individual distinction as a physician and surgeon, and in all respects has lived up to the best traditions of his family line.

There have been interesting men and women in every generation of the family. His great-grandfather, who was the founder of the family in the United States in the paternal line, was David Kelley, one of the early settlers in Darlington County. Prior to the Revolutionary war and when a mere lad he left his home in Ireland against his parents' will. His mother followed him to the vessel, and when her entreaties failed to dissuade him from his purpose she endeavored to remove him

by main force. Slipping out of his jacket to which she held on, he disengaged himself and, hiding among the cargo of the ship, crossed the ocean in his shirt sleeves. Landing at Charleston, he took the first honest work that offered, clearing new ground, but eventually located in what is now Darlington County, near the Cheraw line, where he reared a large family and acquired considerable wealth. His old home is still standing in a good state of preservation. The name of his wife was Elizabeth Tyna. They seem to have been a godly couple and to have lived an ideal life. They had daily family worship, in which the slaves about the house were permitted to take part. On his tombstone in the old Kelley burying ground it is recorded that he was for fifty years deacon of Gum Branch Baptist Church, and for two years he and his wife were the only attendants upon this church. On her tombstone it is written: "She was a mother in Israel."

The next generation was represented by Capt. Wiley Kelley, a man of wealth and influence. His residence, a mansion in its time, surrounded by beautiful grounds, is still preserved.

George Kelley of the third generation of the family spent his active life as a farmer. He married October 24, 1855, Jane McDowell, a woman of beautiful character and representing a family of great prestige in the South. Her parents were Rev. Archibald and Mary (Drakeford) McDowell, the former a well known Baptist preacher in his day, but, like others who followed that calling, was not dependent upon his ministerial salary, giving attention to farming and milling and achieving considerable wealth which he invested in farming lands and slaves. Jane McDowell had a brother, Archibald McDowell, Jr., who was born in Kershaw County in 1818, graduated from Wake Forest College in 1849, and for many years was a distingushed educator, becoming president of the Chowan Institute in 1862.

Reference to Jane McDowell's maternal ancestry is found in the volume "Historic Camden," in which appears the following: "John Drakeford and his brother Richard came from Fairfax county, Virginia, and settled on Flat Rock Creek in the upper part of Kershaw county about the middle of the eighteenth century. The old land titles show that John was here as early as 1754. The two brothers were gallant patriot soldiers in the Revolution. Richard was desperately wounded by a sword cut on the head, but he recovered and raised a large family. One of his sons was Colonel William Drakeford. Richard died in 1825. John lived to a great age, dying in 1850. The first Drakefords came to this country from England. Many in this state and Alabama trace their lineage to the branch of the family that settled here." Jane McDowell Kelley was a granddaughter of Richard Drakeford mentioned in the quotation.

The father of Doctor Kelley was Alex Kelley, son of George and Jane (McDowell) Kelley. James Alex Kelley, to give his full name, was born October 12, 1858, had a public school education, and also attended Wake Forest College. He became a farmer and mechanic and achieved wealth and civic prominence in Florence County. He was a Methodist. Alex Kelley married Florence Horton, who was born October 11, 1863, daughter of Dr. J. J. and Sarah A. Horton. The old colonial home in which she and her mother were both born and married is still standing on the Camden and Lancaster road.

Dr. J. J. Horton, maternal grandfather of Doctor Kelley, was graduated in medicine at Nashville, Tennessee, in 1860, and soon afterward entered the Confederate army. While home on a furlough he married Miss Sarah A. Ingram. Directly after his marriage he returned to Virginia, where he was in constant service until the close of the war in 1865. Sarah Ingram was the daughter of Capt. James Ingram and Ann M. Young. The grandparents of Ann M. Young were also Irish. On the occasion of her marriage a grandfather's clock was sent over from Ireland as a gift to the bride. The Youngs were all Presbyterians, attending old Pine Tree Church not far from New Bethune. Capt. James Ingram owned extensive tracts of land and slave property before the war. Like all Ingrams he was a Methodist in religious belief. At the age of sixty-five he died, his death being due to exposure from Sherman's raid.

Any man however high his station might be proud of such an ancestry as this and no doubt the knowledge of the kind of people his forbears were has been a constant stimulus to Edward Thereon Kelley. Doctor Kelley was born October 10, 1886, and first attended a rural school, later the Timmonsville graded school, and in 1904 entered South Carolina Medical College, from which he was graduated in 1908. He has been a constant student of his profession and has neglected no opportunity to keep in touch with its advancement. In 1912 he took post-graduate work at the New York Polyclinic Medical School and Hospital, spent part of 1917 in the New York Post-Graduate School, and for several weeks during 1919 and 1920 attended clinics at the Mayo Brothers institution at Rochester, Minnesota.

After graduating in 1908 Doctor Kelley located in Kingstree for the practice of his profession as a physician. By reason of a proficiency he displayed during his student career, constant study and application, and conscientious and untiring efforts, though still a young man, he has succeeded in acquiring an unusually large practice and his attainments are generally recognized in this section of South Carolina. Doctor Kelley loves his profession, has a high conception of its duties and responsibilities, and possesses a wealth of energy and indomitable will. In pursuance of a long cherished purpose and at his own expense he has constructed and for two years has successfully conducted at Kingstree a splendid hospital, a much needed and appreciated institution. He has performed all the major operations at his institution, and those who are in a position to appraise his talents bespeak for him prominence among the surgeons of the state.

Doctor Kelley was honored with the office of first vice president of the State Medical Association in 1919. He is a member of the Williamsburg County Medical Society, the Southern Medical Association and the American Medical Association. At the outbreak of war Doctor Kelley was appointed on the

Exemption Board of Williamsburg County. Religion was a big factor in the lives of his ancestors and for years he has been affiliated with the Methodist Episcopal Church, South, and for the past eleven years has served as a steward in the church at Kingstree.

May 29, 1910, at Kingstree Doctor Kelley married Lorena Jeannette Ross, and he has had the constant inspiration of his wife, his children and his home. Mrs. Kelley after finishing her work in the Kingstree graded schools entered Winthrop Normal and Industrial College, graduating in 1906. Her ancestors on both sides came from Scotland, were stanch Presbyterians, and like so many of the early settlers were honest tillers of the soil. The records also show that they were brave and patriotic, and promoters of education, her grandfather having been a noted teacher in his day. Her father, Marion Alexander Ross, a lumberman and electrician, has done much for the upbuilding of Kingstree, having served on the town council a number of times and also on the school board. As one of the strongest pillars in the Baptist Church he has served as a deacon for years. Mrs. Kelley's mother was Margaret Caroline Harrington. The three children of Doctor and Mrs. Kelley, all born at Kingstree, are Margaret Florence, May 6, 1911; Evelyn Jeanette, December 6, 1916; and James Alex, February 13, 1919.

FRANCIS H. BOLD, M. D. A competent and popular physician and surgeon of Charleston, Doctor Bold spent several months in the Medical Reserve Corps of the United States Army during the recent war.

He was born at Savannah, Georgia, June 16, 1884, son of Charles H. and Helen S. (Van Giessen) Bold, being the second of their seven children. His mother was a native of Macon, Georgia, and his father was born in South Carolina, and when Francis H. was a child returned to his native state. Doctor Bold received his early education in the public and private schools of Charleston and in 1903 graduated from the South Carolina College of Pharmacy. Six years later he completed his work in the South Carolina Medical College, and has been a hard working physician for ten years. He was commissioned a first lieutenant in the Medical Reserve Corps July 5, 1918, and later promoted to captain. He was assigned to duty for thirty days at Fort Oglethorpe, Georgia, was then sent on special duty to the Base Hospital at camp McClelland for sixty days, after which he was assigned to the Ninety-Eighth Division, then being formed and trained for overseas duty. The armistice intervened before the division embarked. Doctor Bold then worked with various organizations, and at his special request was granted an honorable discharge February 7, 1919, and returned to Charleston to resume his private practice. He is a member of the County and State Medical societies, and is affiliated with Charleston Lodge No. 242 of the Elks, is a York Rite Mason and Mystic Shriner. In 1913 he married Bertha G. Lambach, a native of Germany. To them were born two children, Francis H., Jr., now deceased, and Margaret L.

Doctor Bold has taken an active interest in political affairs and is now serving his second term as alderman at large from the Tenth Ward. He is a member of the American Legion and the Charleston Rifle Club.

EDGAR C. GLENN. One of Hampton County's leading business men is Edgar C. Glenn, the well known vice president and general manager of the Big Salkehatchie Cypress Company at Varnville, whose great success has been due in no small measure to his able management and judicious counsel. His methods have ever been progressive and he is quick to adopt new ideas which he believes will prove of practical value in his work. Indolence and idleness are entirely foreign to his nature, and owing to his close application to his business and his honorable methods he has won prosperity that is richly merited, while he enjoys the friendship and esteem of the people of this community. He is a public spirited citizen and withholds his co-operation from no movement which is intended to promote public improvement. What he has achieved in life proves the force of his character and illustrates his steadfastness of purpose. By his own efforts he has advanced to a position of credit and honor in business circles and is numbered among the truly representative men of his section of the state.

Edgar C. Glenn was born at old Fort Kearney, Nebraska, on the first day of February, 1874, and is the son of Thomas Brittain and Ellen Frances (Doom) Glenn. The latter was a native of Virginia and the daughter of Robert Goodlet Doom, also a native of Virginia. He was a democratic member of the Nebraska Legislature and was known as "Silent Bob." His brother, James, was also a member of the Legislature from the republican party and was known as "Crowing Jim." Robert Doom's father, Robert Erskin Doom, was a native of Scotland. Thomas Brittain Glenn was a native of North Carolina. He was a graduate of the John Hopkins University of Baltimore, Maryland, where he graduated with the degree of M. D. He practiced in Nebraska until his death in 1892. He was a Knight Templar Mason. His father, Morgan Robert Glenn, also a native of North Carolina, was one of the first brave and hardy souls from the East to brave the perils and dangers of the long trip across the plains to the West in 1842.

Edgar C. Glenn was reared in Louisiana, but received the bulk of his education in Nebraska, completing his studies in Omaha. Then for eight years he was on a sugar plantation in Louisiana, at the end of which time he became identified with the lumber business at White Castle, Louisiana. In 1901 he became connected wtih the F. B. Williams Cypress Company at Patterson, Louisiana, and sometime later they transferred him as manager to the St. Bernard Cypress Company at New Orleans, where he remained until 1914. In that year Mr. Glenn came to Varnville, South Carolina, and associated himself with R. L. Montague, R. H. Downman and H. B. Hewes, under the corporate name of the Big Salkehatchie Cypress Company, the present evidence of which is the big plant now in operation at Varnville, the largest and best equipped plant of its kind in the state. They employ an

average of about 335 people and turn out an immense volume of lumber, which is shipped to all sections of the eastern part of the United States. Of this plant Mr. Glenn is the active manager and devotes himself indefatigably to its operation.

In 1898 Mr. Glenn was married to Phelia Levy, the daughter of Dorothy Levy, and to them have been born four children, Jonas B., now a member of the junior class of the law school in the Carolina University, Ellen, Bessie and Edgar, Jr. Mr. Glenn is an appreciative member of the Masonic fraternity, in which he has attained the thirty-second degree of Grant Consistory of the Scottish Rite at New Orleans, and the Knight Templar, Indivisible Commandery No. 1 of New Orleans. He is also a member of the Louisiana Historical Society. Mr. Glenn enjoys the respect and esteem of those who know him for his friendly manner, business ability, his interest in public affairs and upright living, and he is regarded by all as one of the substantial and worthy citizens of the community with which he has identified himself.

JOSEPH A. PATLA is a prominent Charleston lawyer and his varied personal abilities have brought him professional success and distinctive leadership and influence in his home city, where he is assistant corporation counsel of the City of Charleston.

He was born at Savannah, Georgia, April 12, 1886, a son of Maurice and Simmie (Jacobs) Patla. His parents were both born in Europe and are now living at Charleston, his father being a dealer in antiques. Maurice Patla moved to Charleston in 1888. The grandfather, Abram I. Patla, for many years was a school teacher and is now retired and living at Charleston. Joseph A. Patla is the oldest of five children. His next younger brother, Nathan, was a first sergeant in the National Army. Sophie is the wife of Benjamin Olasov, a real estate dealer. Dora is unmarried and Jack is still in high school.

Mr. Patla was three years old when brought to Charleston, was educated in that city, attended the Bennett High School and graduated in 1910 with his legal diploma from the University of South Carolina. He was admitted to the bar the same year and has since been earning honors as a lawyer engaged in general practice. On the basis of his scholarship record at the university he was awarded at graduation the Joseph Daniel Pope medal.

He is a leader in democratic politics, being president of the democratic party in the Seventh Ward. He is a member of the Board of Park Commissioners of Charleston. Mr. Patla is a thirty-second degree Scottish Rite Mason, a member of Omar Temple of the Mystic Shrine and adjutant of Omar Patrol. He is also affiliated with the Moose, the Benevolent and Protective Order of Elks, the Fellowship Society, the Travel Club of America, and is a member of the B'nai B'rith and the Jewish Synagogue.

Mr. Patla was married to Rose Lewis, of Hendersonville, North Carolina, on the 6th of January, 1920.

JOSEPH EMILE HARLEY. In the history of South Carolina as applying to the professional interests, the name of Joseph E. Harley, of Barnwell, occupies a conspicuous place, for through a number of years he has been one of the representative men of affairs—progressive, enterprising and public spirited. Such qualities always insure success, and to Mr. Harley they have brought a satisfactory reward for his well directed efforts, and while he has benefited himself and the community in a material way he has also been an influential factor in the educational, political and moral welfare of the community. He is one of the best known lawyers of this locality, enjoying distinctive prestige among the members of his profession because of his success in legal practice and his splendid personal qualities.

Joseph Emile Harley was born in Williston, Barnwell County, South Carolina, on September 14, 1880, and is the son of Lunsford and Mary Elizabeth (Hummell) Harley. The latter was the daughter of Dr. Edwin Hummell, who "refugeed" from Charleston to Williston during the Civil war. He was a native of Germany, who came to the United States in young manhood, locating in Charleston, where he engaged in the drug business until the breaking out of the war between the states. Lunsford Harley was a native of Barnwell, a farmer by vocation, and was the son of Dr. Joseph Harley, who also was a native of Barnwell County and District, and who represented his county in the State Legislature for many years, beginning about the year 1820. His father, and the great-grandfather of the subject of this sketch, who also was born in Barnwell, was of English descent. Thus the Harley family has been resident of Barnwell County for several generations, during which time its various members have borne their share of the burdens of the community and have taken their full part in its various phases of activity, always standing for those things which have tended to the upbuilding and development of the best things in the community life. The subject of this sketch is the fourth in order of birth of the eight children born to Lunsford and Mary Elizabeth Harley, all of whom grew to maturity and are still living, Eva, wife of W. H. Croghan, of Charleston; Marie, who has been postmistress at Williston for twenty years; Ellen, widow of S. A. Wise, at Aiken; J. E. Harley; Michael, at Williston; Marguerite, wife of W. C. Cunningham, of Williston; Pamela, wife of J. C. Thomas, of Aiken; and Louis, deputy clerk of court of Barnwell County.

Joseph E. Harley attended the common schools of his home community, and then attended Bailey Institute at Edgefield. He then became a student in the South Carolina College, where he pursued the course in law, graduating in 1902. He returned to Barnwell and entered upon the active practice of his profession, his career since that time having been one of continued successes as a practitioner, until he came to be acknowledged as one of the leaders of the local bar. He has been employed in much of the most important litigation in the courts of this section of the state and enjoys a high reputation as a trial lawyer. He is at the present time district counsel for the Seaboard Airline Railway Company, having in charge all legal matters for this company in many counties of Southern South Carolina, through which that road runs.

He is also assistant division counsel for the Southern Railway Company, having in charge several counties for this company, is local counsel for the Atlantic Coastline Railway Company and the Charleston and Western Carolina Railroad Company, and represents many other corporations in Bamberg, Barnwell and Allendale counties.

In addition to his professional interests Mr. Harley is interested in local business affairs, being president of the First National Bank of Barnwell. He is the owner of large tracts of fine farming land located in and around the Town of Barnwell, and gives considerable attention to its cultivation, in which he has been splendidly successful. Mr. Harley volunteered in the Spanish American war in 1898 in Company L, First South Carolina Regiment, and was mustered out as sergeant of the company. He was captain for several years of the Barnwell Guards, which was Company E of the Third Regiment, National Guard Infantry of South Carolina. He was also colonel of the only Uniform Rank, Knights of Pythias, in South Carolina.

Mr. Harley has for many years taken a deep interest in public affairs and has been active in political campaigns since attaining his majority. Soon after he had attained his twenty-first year he was elected to the Legislature by the largest vote ever cast in the county, as well as the largest majority, and at the following election he was chosen to succeed himself. In 1908 he was chosen as a delegate from South Carolina to the Democratic National Convention which met at Denver, and at which William Jennings Bryan was nominated for the presidency. In 1912 he was elected mayor of Barnwell and held the office continually until 1918, when he was elected for another term of two years, but was forced to decline the office because of the ruling of Secretary of the Treasury McAdoo, who, as director general of railways ruled that attorneys for railroads could not at the same time hold any political office. In 1920 he was chosen a delegate from South Carolina to the Democratic National Convention meeting at San Francisco, which resulted in the nomination of James Cox for the presidency.

On November 11, 1907, Mr. Harley was married to Sarah Agnes Richardson, daughter of Lawrence G. and Susan A. Richardson, of Barnwell, and they became the parents of two sons, Joseph Emile, Jr., and William Hummell. Fraternally Mr. Harley is a member of the Knights of Pythias, of which he is a past chancellor. He has also other fraternal associations. A man of forceful individuality and marked initiative power, he has been well equipped for the larger duties of life and for leadership in his community, while his probity of character and his genial personality have gained for him universal esteem and friendship in the community where his entire life has been passed.

Lunsford Harley was a soldier in the Confederate army for four years, serving from the beginning and taking an active part in all important engagements, including the battles of Bull Run, Chancellorsville, and Gettysburg. He was wounded several times and was made a life cripple by reason of these wounds. He died December 15, 1911.

Hon. Murdoch McNeill Johnson graduated in law from the University of South Carolina in 1912, and practiced for several years at Jefferson, where he was mayor of that town from 1913 to 1916. In the latter year he moved to Camden, and has achieved a successful position as a lawyer and also as a public spirited citizen in that wealthy and historic community.

Mr. Johnson was born at Bethune, Kershaw County, September 30, 1888. His parents, Henry T. and Flora (Hough) Johnson, still live at Bethune. Henry T. Johnson, whose mother was a member of the historic McNeill family of Moore and Cumberland counties, North Carolina, was born at Drowning Creek in Moore County, and came when a young man to Bethune, in Kershaw County, where his life has been spent as a successful planter.

Murdoch McNeill Johnson was educated in the Welsh Neck High School and Wake Forest College in North Carolina, and had a law course at the University of South Carolina. He had good advantages and training at home and in some of the best schools in preparation for his professional career. Mr. Johnson was elected a member of the House of Representatives from Kershaw County in 1918, and during the session of the following year was a member of the Judiciary Committee. He is a Mason and a Presbyterian. His wife was Miss Amelie Blume, of Blackville, South Carolina. They have one son, Henry Lewis Johnson.

George Henry Cornelson. In the years immediately following the close of the War between the States some fate or destiny directed the steps of George Henry Cornelson, a young German only recently arrived in the country and in search of business opportunity, to Orangeburg, then a small country town. His location was providential both for himself and for the community, and during half a century probably no one individual did more to build up the commercial and industrial life of the city, and none dispensed his accumulating wealth more generously and to better purpose.

Mr. Cornelson was born at Ottersburg, Germany, December 7, 1842, and was in his seventy-fourth year when he died July 22, 1916. He acquired a good education and some commercial training in the old country, and landed in New York at the age of twenty-three. After a brief employment as bookkeeper he came South, and, as already noted, identified himself with Orangeburg. Here he invested his modest means in a stock of general merchandise, and his business grew rapidly and for forty years he was one of the most extensive merchants in this part of the state. The ability to direct business profitably was only one of his many versatile resources. Though foreign born, he acquired complete ease and fluency in speaking the English language. For many years to accommodate his trade he did all the banking business for the city and the surrounding country.

He built and operated the first cotton factory in the lower part of the state. This factory manufactured a high grade of yarn, the quality of which was such as to constitute for it a particular standard in cotton yarn, resulting in an insistent demand for the product that always taxed the ca-

pacity of the machinery to supply. The reputation of this yarn is still part of the common technical knowledge in cotton circles, and it is now, as ever, in demand. Mr. Cornelson personally gave his energies to the direction of the factory until 1904, when on account of advanced age he sold out.

Mr. Cornelson built and operated the first waterworks in Orangeburg in 1897, and for a number of years this plant supplied the city with water, pumped from artesian wells sunk with his capital. These were the first wells of the kind ever developed in the county. He finally sold the plant and it is now municipally owned and operated. He also built and operated the first ice factory in this section of the state, and not only Orangeburg but a wide section of adjacent country was supplied with ice from this plant. He built the first telephone line in Orangeburg between his place of business and his home, and operated it for years. Space would not permit a complete enumeration of all his varied interests. He invested much of his surplus capital in land and its development, and one large farm he owned he so improved that its productiveness made it one of the show places of the state.

Obviously no one could direct so many enterprises with such success without possessing wonderful energy. His energy was combined with common sense, and apparently he made every undertaking prosper. If he had failures, they were unimportant in his own career, since he made them mere stepping stones to larger achievements. Undoubtedly an important factor in his success was his complete integrity. His word was his bond and whatever he said or promised was as good as gold itself. His business affairs went on even through times of depression, held up and maintained by the rugged strength and integrity of his character.

It is said that Mr. Cornelson was nearly a millionaire, yet much the greater part of the fortune which he achieved was dispensed in a way to benefit the community. He was kindly and deeply interested in young men struggling to achieve independence, and more than once he saved older men from bankruptcy. He had a simplicity of character and a lack of ostentation that prevented him from claiming the smallest share of credit or posing as a philanthropist, though as a matter of fact he was a philanthropist in the truest and best sense of the word. He gave liberally to charitable causes, and like Job, 29:16, of old "the cause he knew not of he sought out."

He was a Christian in personal and daily practice, and a very liberal member of the Presbyterian Church of Orangeburg. He was a member of the Home Missionary Committee of the Charleston Presbytery for many years, and through his personal influence he provided large funds for various church causes. He was also deeply interested in the Thornwell Orphanage, and among his bequests was a donation to the Thornwell orphans and also another to the Presbyterian College of South Carolina.

The world knew his business strength, his inflexible honor and to some degree his liberality, but his home circle appreciated these qualities, and also knew him as a kindly, tender and devoted husband and father. January 1, 1869, he married Miss Angie M. Holman. There are four children, all well known and prominent people. The oldest is Rev. George H. Cornelson, Jr., now pastor of the First Presbyterian Church of New Orleans. Emma J. is the wife of M. O. Dantzler, a prominent Orangeburg business man. Annie L. became the wife of Rev. J. L. McLees, who for the past thirty-one years has been pastor of the First Presbyterian Church of Orangeburg, and whose personal record is detailed elsewhere. Charles Arthur Cornelson, the youngest, is an educator, professor of English in the University of Washington state.

REV. J. L. McLEES. Hundreds of families in the old community of Orangeburg have learned instinctively to turn to the beolved pastor of the First Presbyterian Church in times of sorrow and of need. For thirty-one years Mr. McLees has been their pastor, and the practical service he has rendered and the influence he has wielded have made him one of the most valuable citizens of the community.

Rev. Mr. McLees was born at Greenwood, South Carolina, May 24, 1855. He is the grandson of a Revolutionary soldier. This grandfather came from Ireland and first lived in Newberry County and later in Anderson County. The father of Reverend McLees was Rev. John McLees, a native of Anderson County, and also a Presbyterian minister. Rev. John McLees married Sarah Cornelia Anderson, a native of Anderson County. Her grandfather and also her father were physicians. Her grandfather rode from Philadelphia with his saddle bags, and for many years practiced as a pioneer physician in Anderson County, South Carolina.

Rev. J. L. McLees was reared on a farm. His boyhood coincided with that unexampled period of depression and poverty of war and reconstruction time, and his father was unable to give him an education. By thrift and often ingenious use of his resources, he succeeded in paying for his own education, working his way through college. He received the A. B. degree from Adger College at Walhalla in 1879. Thus equipped he went to Brunswick, Georgia, and for two years taught school. By much self denial he was able to complete his course in the Theological Seminary at Columbia, where he graduated in May, 1885. Of thirty-five years in the ministry all but four have been spent at Orangeburg. For 2½ years he was pastor of the church at Providence, North Carolina, and for eighteen months at Charlotte in the same state. He was called to his duties at Orangeburg in 1889, and year in and year out has remained faithful to his post of duty and to a remarkable degree has availed himself of all the many opportunities for service. For ten or more years, without compensation, he rode to St. Matthews (fourteen miles) and preached in a rented hall. Soon he organized a Presbyterian Church with only a handful of members, mostly ladies. It grew slowly at first, but has now become self-sustaining and today is a church of some importance and influence in Calhoun County.

While his pastorate constitutes a heavy duty,

Reverend Mr. McLees is also extensively engaged in agriculture. He has a farm of 1,200 acres just outside the city limits of Orangeburg, and employs this land for diversified crop production. His chief crops are cotton, corn and oats. More recently he has engaged in hog raising, and his farm, the Oakleigh Farm, is now known as the home of some of the finest Duroc Jersey stock in the state. Reverend Mr. McLees is also a director in the People's Bank of Orangeburg, and has various other commercial interests in the city.

February 2, 1893, he married Miss Annie L. Cornelson, daughter of George H. and Angie (Holman) Cornelson. The honored career of her father is sketched elsewhere. Her mother was of an old South Carolina family of English descent and Revolutionary stock. Reverend and Mrs. McLees are the parents of five children: Angie Louise, wife of Jerome B. McMichel, of Orangeburg; Sarah Cornelia, wife of J. E. Elliott, of Columbia; George Cornelson, who was in the navy during the World war is a farmer in Orangeburg County, married Almer Keller, a native of Orangeburg; J. L. McLees, Jr., who during the war was a member of the Students' Army Training Corps of Davidson College, North Carolina; and Arthur G., the youngest, a schoolboy at Orangeburg.

THOMAS JEFFERSON KIRKLAND is a Camden lawyer of more than thirty years active experience in the profession, and is also organizer and president of the Loan & Savings Bank of Camden and has achieved many other interests in his home locality.

He was born at Camden, in Kershaw County, May 9, 1860, son of William Lennox and Mary Miller (Withers) Kirkland. His maternal grandfather was Judge Thomas J. Withers. One of his ancestors was a Huguenot who came to Charleston about 1690, and another line of his ancestry was represented by a colonist from Wales to Virginia in 1685.

Thomas J. Kirkland spent his early life in the vicinity of Camden. From 1870 to 1885 he was a student in the Camden Academy, but during 1875-76 was at the Charlotte Military Academy in North Carolina, and he prepared for the legal profession largely through study and reading at home. He regularly engaged in the practice of law on January 1, 1887. He served in the State House of Representatives from 1890 to 1894, and from 1894 to 1896 was state senator. For a number of years he was chairman of the Board of School Trustees of Camden District, was direct tax agent of his state at Washington in 1891, and has maintained a record of independent thinking in politics. He is a Presbyterian, and has also been interested in outdoor sports and pastimes. He is a co-author of "Historic Camden," an interesting work of local history published in 1905. He has been president of the Camden Historical Society.

September 25, 1889, he married Fredericka Alexander. They are the parents of nine children.

CLARENCE J. OWENS. For many years identified with the educational affairs of South Carolina, Doctor Owens has for several years been one of the distinguished figures in American life. The title conferred upon him by popular consent of "father of the Federal Farm Loan System" is an honor that might well satisfy those most ambitious for achievement and large service. Doctor Owens has had his chief opportunity for influencing national life and promoting the welfare and advancement of the South as Director General of the Southern Commercial Congress.

Clarence Julian Owens was born at Augusta, Georgia, July 4, 1877, a son of Alfred and Fannie Augusta (Easterling) Owens. His mother is still living. Alfred Owens, who died in the City of Washington, December 7, 1918, at the age of seventy-six, was a successful southern business man. He was a merchant at Augusta, Georgia, later at Williston, South Carolina, and during the war he served as a member of Company D of the Third South Carolina Cavalry and was one of Joe Wheeler's scouts. During the last two years of his life he lived at Washington and took the greatest pleasure in the meetings and reunions of the Confederate veterans. He was laid to rest among his comrades in the Confederate section of the national cemetery at Arlington. He was a Baptist, and for many years was identified with the Knights of Pythias. Alfred Owens married Fannie Augusta Easterling on June 22, 1872. They had four children: Mrs. R. A. Weathersbee, of Williston, South Carolina; Dr. Clarence J.; Albert E., who is past commander of the Maryland Division of the Sons of Confederate Veterans; and Mrs. Hugh E. Phillips, of Washington.

Clarence Julian Owens was reared in Barnwell County, South Carolina, was educated in the public schools of Augusta, Georgia, and in 1894 received his A. B. degree from the South Carolina Institute at Williston, now the Bailey Military Institute at Greenwood. At the age of eighteen he took the position of Commandant of Cadets at the Orangeburg Collegiate Institute. Just before he was twenty-one he was elected president of that college, being the youngest college president in America. In the meantime, in 1897, he had pursued courses at Cornell University, and while head of the Orangeburg Institute he made monthly journeys to the Columbian, now George Washington, University at Washington, and as a result of his studies received the degree of Master of Arts in 1900. Later the degrees Doctor of Philosophy and Doctor of Laws were conferred upon him. He was president of Orangeburg College from 1898 to 1901, and from 1901 to 1903 was president of the Sumter Military Academy. He was president of Anniston College in Alabama from 1903 to 1906, and was president of the Southeast Alabama Agricultural College from 1906 to 1910. He has long been prominent in the United Sons of Confederate Veterans, holding every grade of rank in continuous service, and was elected Commander-in-Chief of that organization, serving from 1909 to 1911.

The Southern Commercial Congress owes its direct origin to an annual meeting of the Southern Secretaries' Association held in Chattanooga in 1908. On December 8th of the same year the congress was organized at Washington, and it was incorporated July 21, 1911. Throughout its history the Southern Commercial Congress has existed as a

body of southern men representing not any one department of southern life and affairs but all the vital interests of the South and as an organization to "utilize resources, improve conditions, and fittingly announce the advantages of the South to the world." Its slogan is "For a greater Nation, through a greater South."

On June 3, 1910, Doctor Owens began his duties as Commissioner of Agriculture and Immigration of the Southern Commercial Congress, and on August 1, 1911, was elected secretary and treasurer of the Congress, and since June 6, 1912, has been its managing director. In 1919, by act of the Southern Commercial Congress, the title of his position was changed to director general.

It was on the direct initiative of the Southern Commercial Congress, in its annual convention of 1913, that a thorough investigation of the European systems of agricultural co-operation was proposed. This investigation was pursued by commissions designated by the Congress of the United States, one being the United States Commission on Rural Finance, and the American Commission composed of representatives of the United States and Canadian Provinces. These commissions co-operated in a survey of agricultural organizations in eighteen countries of Europe. President Wilson in 1913 appointed Doctor Owens a member of this commission, and he was chosen director general of the American Commission. Based upon the evidence accumulated by this commission the Federal Farm Loan Act was passed by Congress and approved by the President, July 17, 1916.

The honor of being the "father of the Federal Farm Loan System" is given Doctor Owens on account of the fact that he assembled the American Commission, secured the incorporation of a plank in the platforms of the great political parties, approving the adoption of the system; prepared the initial literature published by the Government on the subject; had the privilege from President Wilson of nominating his six associates on the United States Commission; prepared the joint resolution unanimously adopted by the Congress of the United States invoking diplomatic recognition for the commission; personally directed the survey of investigation in America and Europe; and as a member of the United States Commission aided in the preparation of the law. Under this law there have since been organized twelve great banks, 4,000 farm loan associations, which up to 1919 have loaned more than $200,000,000 to farmers. The system, though still in its infancy, has, even in the opinion of critics not yet satisfied with the system as it is, opened the way for a financial and economical policy with respect to agriculture that will do more than anything else to keep alive that industry and promote a fair distribution of the opportunities and privileges of farm and country life.

Affiliated with his work in the Southern Commercial Congress, Doctor Owens is executive secretary of the House of Southern Governors, executive director of the Shipping Board of the Southern Commercial Congress, which during the period of the war was affiliated with the United States Shipping Board. He organized and is executive director of the National Association of State Commissioners of Agriculture, and in March, 1919, the commissioners of the forty-eight states represented in this organization presented him with a loving cup as a tribute of their appreciation of his work. By appointment of President Wilson he is a member of the United States Commission on Rural Credits. He is a member of the Pan-American Financial Congress, appointed by Secretary McAdoo and reappointed by Secretary Carter Glass. He is a member of the Latin-American Trade Committee by appointment of the Secretary of State and Secretary of Commerce. Doctor Owens organized and directed the mission to the Republic of Panama under Act of Congress of Panama, and by appointment of President Porras conducted an economic survey of that country and organized for it a system of rural credits similar to the United States. He also organized for the Panama government a system of agricultural extension work. He initiated the plan and is the executive director of the Pan American College of Commerce at Panama City, of which John Barrett, director general of the Pan American Union, is president.

Doctor Owens was on the staff of the Governor of South Carolina with the rank of colonel, 1900-02. He was vice-president of the Alabama Educational Association in 1905-08. For a number of years he has been a lecturer on historical and economical subjects. He is a member of the University Club, president of the Southern Society of Washington and a member of other social organizations. He is a Knight Templar Mason and Shriner, is past chancellor commander of the Knights of Pythias and past noble grand of the Odd Fellows.

His home is Riverdale Park, Maryland. He is a member of the Calvary Baptist Church of Washington and teaches the Owens Bible Class of one hundred men at Hyattsville, Maryland. He is also a member of the Washington Board of Trade, The City Club of Washington, and the Washington Chamber of Commerce and is owner of the Southern Drug Company and the Owens Motor Car Company of Washington. At Riverdale Park he belongs to the board of trustees of the local schools, is chairman of the Citizens' Temperance Union of Prince George's County, and led the fight that made Prince George's County dry. He is president of the Chamber of Commerce and Agriculture of Prince George's County, organized, was first president and is chairman of the board of Prince George's Bank at Hyattsville, and was a member of the ratification committee on constitutional prohibition for the State of Maryland. He is the business associate of Dr. James Harris Rogers in the handling of the extensive business affairs based upon Doctor Rogers' epochal discovery of underground and subsea radio.

December 27, 1899, at Williston, South Carolina, Doctor Owens married Marie Louise Kennedy. Her father, Capt. W. H. Kennedy, was a banker and merchant, served with the rank of captain in the Confederate army, and was one of the leading men of business and civic life at Williston for many years. Doctor and Mrs. Owens have seven children: Marie Louise, Clarence Julian, Jr., William Hamilton, Alfred Arthur, Quincy Kennedy, Frances Elizabeth, and Mary Custis Lee Owens. Doctor Owens has a beautiful home, "Oak Villa" at Riverdale

Park, originally a part of the Lord Baltimore estate. The Lord Baltimore mansion adjoining Oak Villa is the suburban home of Senator Hiram Johnson of California.

WILLIAM MCWILLIE SHANNON during an active career of forty years has accumulated a splendid prestige as a lawyer, and has been one of the busiest and most successful practitioners in his section of the state. His home is at Camden, where the name Shannon has been prominent in the making of legal history for at least two generations.

His father, William Shannon, was also a Camden lawyer. William McWillie Shannon was born at Camden, October 11, 1855, son of William and Henrietta (McWillie) Shannon. He finished his education in the University of the South in Sewanee, Tennessee, and was admitted to the bar in January, 1880. For several years he engaged in general practice with his father. He has been attorney for many banks and corporations, including all the banks in Camden, also the Camden cotton mills. He organized the first bank at Camden and the first building and loan association there, also the first cotton mill. He was once nominated by petition as candidate for mayor, but refused to make the race. He is progressive in all local affairs, and for forty years has been a vestryman in Grace Episcopal Church.

In April, 1879, he married Camilla Agnes Nelson, of Sumter County. They have three daughters: Emma S., Mrs. A. McGriffin, of Columbia, South Carolina; Harriet, wife of George W. Brunson, Jr., of Chicago; and Agnes Nelson, a student.

HENRY LAKIN PARR, whose name and energies have been identified with many of the most important constructive commercial affairs in Newberry for many years, was left an orphan early in life, and made his own way to the front by dint of his indomitable energy and determination to succeed.

He was born near Parr Shoals in Fairfield County, South Carolina, February 7, 1872, son of Henry Wilson and Edwina (Smith) Parr. His father in addition to farming was also interested in railroad building. Henry Lakin Parr was three years old when his mother died and six when he lost his father. As opportunity presented he attended the public schools of Jenkinsville, did some farming, and from early manhood was distinguished by a peculiar breadth of outlook and a determination and resolution in every undertaking in which he was engaged. He spent sixteen years in completing the plans and developing the Parr Shoals Water Power Company, now one of the important sources of power for industries. Mr. Parr is president of the Exchange Bank of Newberry, and was head of that bank when in 1918 a handsome brick block 58 by 65 feet was built for its accommodation. He is also president of the Maxwell Farm & Development Company, handling a reclamation project of over twenty thousand acres in Florida.

February 13, 1895, Mr. Parr married Mary Boyd, of Newberry. They have three children: Eddie Mae, wife of Ralph Baker, a wholesale merchant of Newberry; and Azlie and Callie Boyd, the former a student in the Woman's College of Due West, and the latter a student in Newberry College.

LAURENS TENNEY MILLS. Mr. Mills for the past fifteen years has been engaged in a growing general practice as a lawyer at Camden.

He was born in Fairfield County, South Carolina, July 27, 1874, son of Rev. William Wilson and Sarah Edith Ann (Smith) Mills. His father was a minister of the Presbyterian Church. He moved to Camden, South Carolina, in 1884. The son attended the public schools of Camden, and the private school conducted by Leslie McCandless. In 1894 he graduated from Davidson College in North Carolina with the A. B. degree. Then for eight years he taught school in South Carolina. He graduated in law from the South Carolina College in 1904 with the degree of B. L., and at once located at Camden in general practice. Mr. Mills has been for over twenty years connected with the County Board of Education. He represented his county in the State Legislature in 1915-16. He is a Royal Arch Mason, a past master of Kershaw Lodge No. 29, Ancient Free and Accepted Masons, and is district deputy grand master of the order. He is also vice president of the Library Association and is an elder of the Presbyterian Church.

In November, 1904, he married Margaret Law Johnstone, of Newberry, South Carolina. Five children were born to their marriage: John Laurens, Margaret Law, Lillian Kennerly, Job Johnstone and Sarah Smith.

LORENZO T. GREGORY, M. D. On March 18, 1896, Doctor Gregory received his degree as a Doctor of Medicine from South Carolina Medical College, and practically from that date his service and practice have been continuous at Kershaw, where he is honored for his gifts and service as a citizen as well as his unusual abilities in medicine and surgery.

He was born in Lancaster County, South Carolina, July 2, 1870, son of William H. and Queen E. (Gregory) Gregory. His father was both a farmer and merchant. Doctor Gregory attended public schools, also Furman University, and had a good literary education preparatory to his work in the medical department of South Carolina College. For ten years he was a member of the Kershaw Board of Health, was elected mayor of Kershaw in January, 1919, for one year, and re-elected in 1920. He was chairman of the Board of Trustees of the graded schools until the schools were out of debt. For a number of years he has been an active member of the Baptist Church, serving on practically all important committees. Doctor Gregory was past master of Abney Lodge No. 211, Ancient Free Masons, and is past chancellor of Hanging Rock Lodge No. 42, Knights of Pythias.

December 14, 1898, he married Miss Lula Truesdale, of Kershaw. They have three children: Burke Harrison, a student in the University of South Carolina; Evelyn, a student in Winthrop College; and Edith, a student in the graded school of Kershaw.

GEORGE W. CROFT. While of a very distinguished family lineage in South Carolina, the abilities of the late George W. Croft were not obscured by his illustrious connections. He was an eminent lawyer, and measured his powers with credit against many

of the great lawyers of the state during his time. He was also a tried and trusted leader in politics, and death came to him while he was serving his state in Congress.

He was born at Newberry, December 29, 1846, and died March 10, 1904. The Crofts were of English ancestry, and came to America in the late 1600s. His Revolutionary ancestor was George Croft, one of the followers of Francis Marion, and who subsequently formed a partnership with a man named Greenwood and operated a mercantile business at Georgetown, South Carolina. The father of George W. Croft was Theodore Gaillard Croft, a son of Edward and Lydia (Gaillard) Croft, the latter a member of the famous family of that name of Charleston and a sister of Senator John G. Gaillard. Edward Croft was a lawyer and moved from Charleston to Greenville in 1821. Theodore Gaillard Croft married Eliza Webb (D'Oyley).

Their son George W. Croft was educated at The Citadel at Charleston, acquired his legal education in the University of Virginia, and from his admission to the bar in 1869 until his death in 1904 was busily engaged in a law practice at his home town of Aiken. Particularly during the last twenty years of his life he appeared as counsel in nearly every important case tried in his section of the state. One of the most notable of these was his appearance as leading counsel for Lieutenant Governor Tillman in his defense of the killing of Editor Gonzales at Lexington.

Before he was admitted to the bar he had been a youthful soldier of the Confederacy and the spirit of loyalty that always actuated him led him into the reconstruction movement for the restoration of white rule. He was a member of the Red Shirt Brigade in that critical time of the state's history. In other important epochs of the state's politics he was chairman of the Democratic County Convention, and was captain of a militia company during the Ellenton riots. He was elected a member of the State Senate in 1888 and also served several times in the lower house of the Legislature. The Second Congressional District sent him to Congress in 1902, and his death two years later came at a time when he stood high in the affections of his home people. He was owner of some large landed interests in his county and was affiliated with the Masonic order.

In November, 1873, he married Miss Florence McMahan, daughter of an old Alabama planter. She is now living at Aiken.

Of their children the oldest was the late Theodore Gaillard Croft, who was born November 26, 1874, and died March 23, 1920, after a brilliant career as a lawyer and public leader. He attended the Bethlehem Military Academy at Staunton, Virginia, graduating with first honors in 1894, and in 1897 received his law degree from the University of South Carolina. From that time until his death twenty-three years later he practiced law at Aiken, but was always responsive to his duties as a citizen and had many of the honors of politics. He represented his county in both the Senate and House, being elected to the Senate twice, serving from 1907 to 1911, and was a member of the House in 1905-6. He was elected to Congress to fill the unexpired term of his father. During the World war he was chairman of the local board at Aiken and accepted and discharged that duty with such a high sense of responsibility and patriotism as to gain the commendation of the Government and the community. Before the war ended, though past the draft age, he volunteered and was a member of an officers' training camp at Camp Zachary Taylor in Louisville when the armistice was signed. He was a member of the Masonic order. April 3, 1907, he married his cousin, Mary C. Croft, a daughter of Theodore Gaillard Croft, whose career is sketched elsewhere in these volumes.

The younger children of the late George W. Croft were George W., Jr., and Otis Chafee Croft, both of whom died in infancy; W. McM. Croft, a merchant at Augusta, Georgia; Randall De Bohun Croft, a mechanical engineer who died at Providence, Rhode Island, in 1911, at the age of twenty-nine; Laurence E., mentioned below; Edward S., also referred to hereafter; Henry De Bohun Croft, who died in 1897, at the age of seven years; and George Mason Croft.

Laurence E. Croft was educated in Clemson College, in the law department of the University of South Carolina, was admitted to the bar in 1907, and practiced at Greenville from 1908 to 1911 and at Aiken from 1911 to 1919. He then retired from his profession and is now busied with his farming interests. In June, 1915, he married Florence Ella Croft, a daughter of Dr. T. G. Croft.

Edward S. Croft, who was also educated for the law and achieved prominence in the same profession as his father, was born September 8, 1885, in Aiken, where he attended the public schools, took his advance preparatory work in Clemson College, and is a graduate of the University of South Carolina, receiving his A. B. degree in 1905 and the degree LL. B. in 1907, taking these degrees at the same time and in the same class as his brother Laurence. For two and a half years he practiced law at Greenville and for seven years enjoyed a promising practice in Atlanta, Georgia. He returned to his home town of Aiken in 1917, and has since been engaged in the real estate, bond and investment business. Mr. E. S. Croft has never taken an active part in politics, but in June, 1920, was appointed master in equity for Aiken County. He married, October 2, 1914, Miss Mary S. Crosswell, of Wilmington, North Carolina, daughter of William J. and Mary (Gower) Crosswell. Her father for a number of years was district manager for the Southern Express Company. To their marriage have been born two children: Edward S., Jr., and William Crosswell Croft.

George Mason Croft, the youngest of the family, was born in 1897 and graduated with the degree electrical engineer from Clemson College in 1918. He immediately began his service in the navy as an ensign, and since the war has been practicing his profession as an electrical engineer at Birmingham, Alabama. February 15, 1920, he married Miss Thelma Callaway, a daughter of W. R. Callaway, an Aiken merchant.

JOHN M. FARRELL. While he returned home from college to take up a business established by his father at Blackville and has always had his home in that community, John M. Farrell is widely known over a large section of the state as a banker, merchant and cotton mill owner.

He was born at Blackville December 19, 1873. His father, Patrick William Farrell, was born at Clonmel in County Tipperary, Ireland, in 1841. The family, consisting of himself, his two sisters, one brother and their parents, came to America in 1850, and all of them remained in New York state except Patrick, who came to South Carolina, and about the time he reached his majority proved his loyalty to his home state by enlisting in the Confederate army. He wore the gray uniform four years, and at the same time his brother John was in the northern army. For all the dangers and hardships of this four years of service Patrick William Farrell received only a dollar and a quarter and was allotted a snake bitten horse and a mule. He began trading on the mule, and that might be considered as the humble beginning of a large and prosperous business at Blackville today, directed by his son, John M. Farrell. Patrick Farrell was a merchant and planter in the Blackville community until his death in 1906, having survived his wife just ten days. Patrick Farrell married Carolina Columbia Rush. Her maternal ancestors were the Daniels, one of whom was the colonial Governor of South Carolina under the lords proprietor, and others took part in the Revolutionary struggle for independence. In the maternal line she was English, while her paternal ancestors were German.

John M. Farrell finished his education by graduating with the A. B. degree from Mount St. Mary's College at Emmitsburg, Maryland. Soon afterward he returned to Blackville, assisted his father in the mercantile business, and his own energies have made that business grow and expand. While he is practically the sole owner, he has it incorporated as the Mutual Trading Company of Blackville. It is a concern doing an annual business valued at a million dollars, chiefly in cotton, cotton seed and fertilizers.

Mr. Farrell is an able business executive. He also owned and conducted four thousand acres as a cotton, grain and truck plantation near Blackville, though in 1920 he disposed of twenty-five hundred acres. In 1918 he established a hosiery mill, which has a designed capacity for two thousand dozen pair of hose per day, though at this writing it makes only that number weekly, since the complete equipment of machinery has not been installed. The mill is as modern as any in the world, being electrically equipped, and with modern sanitary and lighting arrangements. About sixty people are employed. This mill is entirely the fruit of Mr. Farrell's enterprise and was financed entirely from his individual resources. Mr. Farrell also built a hotel and other buildings in Blackville, and was one of the organizers and is a director of the Bank of Western Carolina. The head bank is at Aiken, with nine branches at Blackville, Barnwell, Johnston, Wagner, Salleys, Batesburg, Lexington, Ellenton and North Augusta.

Mr. Farrell is affiliated with the Knights of Columbus, the Elks and Woodmen of the World.

WALTER B. WILBUR. While his name for several years has been associated with one of the leading law firms of South Carolina, Mr. Wilbur is also an interesting example of a new kind of leadership, involving an unselfish interest and co-operation with the forces devoted to social welfare, not only in his home City of Charleston but in the state at large.

Mr. Wilbur was born at Charleston in 1883, a son of Thomas S. and Mary Ella (Sumner) Wilbur. His parents are still living, his mother being a native of Louisa Court House, Virginia. His father was born in Charleston, and the Wilburs have lived in Charleston since about 1800, when Mr. Wilbur's great-grandfather settled there.

Walter B. Wilbur was educated in the Charleston High School, graduated A. B. from the College of Charleston in 1904, and went north to take his law course in the Harvard University Law School, from which he received his LL. B. degree. After returning to Charleston he was for a short time associated with the law firm of Miller & Whaley, and then formed a partnership with Mr. Alfred Huger under the name Huger & Wilbur. Subsequently the firm became Huger, Wilbur & Guerard, continuing until the death of Mr. Edward P. Guerard, Jr. Since then the firm of Miller, Huger, Wilbur & Miller has been regarded as one of the leading law firms of the state.

Even while in college Mr. Wilbur was prompted by a deep sense of personal obligation on behalf of the welfare of those less fortunate than himself. His continuing interest in that line has led to his being honored with important places of leadership. He was at the time of its merger with other boards into the State Board of Public Welfare a member of the State Board of Correctional Administration. He is president of the Juvenile Protective League of South Carolina, a member of the Juvenile Welfare Commission of Charleston, president of the South Carolina State Conference of Social Work, president of the Social Workers' Club of Charleston, chairman of the State Child Welfare Commission, an unofficial commission appointed by Governor Cooper to make a general survey of the field of child welfare in the state, and to draft a tentative children's code for consideration by the State Legislature. Mr. Wilbur is also president of the Associated Charities Society of Charleston.

He is a member of The Citadel Square Baptist Church, a member of Phi Kappa Sigma, and fraternally is a past master of Union Kilwinning Lodge No. 4, Accepted Free Masons and a Knight of Pythias. He married Miss Ruth Pearson Cooper of Batesburg, South Carolina. They have three children, Lucy Lee, Elizabeth Cuttino and Ruth Pearson.

HON. JOE COPELAND MASSEY. Every year since 1909 when he was admitted to the bar has witnessed an increasing business accumulating in the law offices of Mr. Massey at Kershaw. At the same time he has worked public spiritedly in the affairs of his home community and is regarded as one of the best friends of that rich agricultural section

of which Kershaw is the business center. Kershaw is claimed by two counties, half of the town being in Lancaster and the other half in Kershaw County. For several years Mr. Massey lived on the Lancaster side, and was chosen to the Legislature from that county. He is now a resident of Kershaw County and is a member of the State Senate from that county.

He was born at Taxahaw in Lancaster County May 18, 1881, son of Henry B. and Rosa (Gregory) Massey, who still reside at Taxahaw. His great-great-grandfather came from Virginia and settled in Chesterfield County in early days. Senator Massey's grandfather and great-grandfather were both residents of Lancaster County, so that the family is one of the oldest in that section of the state.

Joe Copeland Massey had a common school education, and spent five years in the University of South Carolina, three years in the literary course and two years as a law student. He graduated from the law school in 1909. While in the university he was honored with the office of president of the Law Association and was junior president of the Clariosophic Society. Mr. Massey has served as intendant or mayor of Kershaw two terms. He was elected from his native county to the House of Representatives in 1912, serving four years. In 1918 he was elected state senator for a term of four years. Senator Massey is a Knight Templar Mason and Shriner and a member of the Elks. He is married and has one daughter, Ethelyne.

CYRIL THOMAS WYCHE, M. D. The record of this well known physician and citizen of Prosperity has been one of distinguished service not only in his profession but to the cause of education. All who believe in the essential soundness and health of American life must be encouraged by the disinterested and unselfish labors of such men as Doctor Wyche.

He was born on the Tar River in Granville County, North Carolina, May 26, 1857, son of William Evans and Sallie (Reavis) Wyche and a grandson of James Wyche and Pamela Evans. The Wyche family ancestry is traced in an unbroken line to the thirteenth century in old England. Some of the names in the earlier generations, notable in the fields of business, patriotism, scholarship and politics, are mentioned briefly elsewhere in this publication.

The first American ancestor of Doctor Wyche was Henry Wyche, whose name first appears in the records of Surry County on the south side of the James River in Virginia in 1679. His will was dated August 1, 1712. His son, George Wyche, lived in Sussex County, Virginia, and his will was dated October 5, 1753. He was the great-great-grandfather of Doctor Wyche. His son Peter was born October 30, 1748, and died December 10, 1843, and Peter's son James, born in 1785, in Brunswick County, Virginia, was the pioneer founder of the family in Granville County, North Carolina, in 1825, living there until his death, March 28, 1845. He was a member of the State Senate at the time of his death, and also was president of the Raleigh and Gaston Railroad. His wife, Pamela Evans, was a daughter of Lieut. William Evans, an officer of the Revolutionary war.

Dr. Cyril Thomas Wyche, in spite of the obvious difficulties and disadvantages of his youth being contemporaneous with the war and reconstruction period, achieved a liberal education, beginning in the common schools of North Carolina, followed by a summer course in the University of North Carolina, and graduated from the College of Physicians and Surgeons at Baltimore. He also took several special courses in New York hospitals. He was a teacher in early life and from that experience acquired the deep and lasting interest he has always retained in education.

Doctor Wyche has had his home in South Carolina since 1882, first practicing in Edgefield County and later at Prosperity. He led the movement for establishing the State Health Department, and at a meeting of the State Medical Association at Anderson was elected delegate to the American Medical Association of Chicago. He served as first vice-president of the South Carolina Medical Association.

It could well be said of him that he has been alien in sympathy to no human interests. His greatest enthusiasm is for the cause of education, and to that he has unselfishly devoted both time and other personal resources. He led the fight for establishing the high school at Prosperity and was chairman of its board of trustees for many years. He finally realized his ambition when the modern high school building was erected. Not content with the popular tribute of "father of the public school system at Prosperity," he is constantly planning and working to improve the common schools of the state and the higher institutions of learning. For many years he was chairman of the committee on education in the House of Representatives. His term of service in the Lower House of the Legislature was for fourteen years, and during his term he was unanimously elected speaker pro tem. He was also member ex-officio of the board of trustees of Winthrop College and the University of South Carolina, and took an active interest in the welfare of both institutions. As a legislator his name is associated with much important legislation. He was author of the pure food law and was appointed by Governor McSweeney to represent South Carolina at the Pure Food Conference at Washington. He also advocated the dispensary as a step toward prohibition and has been one of the warmest friends of the prohibition movement. Only recently he had the satisfaction of seeing enacted the compulsory education law along the lines which he had advocated for many years both in the Legislature and out. He served several terms as mayor of Prosperity, and fraternally is affiliated with the Masonic order.

Doctor Wyche married Miss Carrie Sease, representing a name long distinguished in the legal profession of South Carolina. She was a sister of Judge Thomas S. Sease of Spartanburg and a daughter of the late Leonard Sease, who died in 1918, at the age of ninety-four. Leonard Sease was the father of twelve children, eleven of whom are still living, and one of his daughters was past seventy-five at the time of his death. Doctor and

Mrs. Wyche have two sons, Major C. C. Wyche of Spartanburg and C. G. Wyche of Greenville, both prominent lawyers, and the former a distinguished veteran of the World war; and two daughters, Mrs. James F. Goggans of Columbia, and Miss Caro Wyche of New York City.

C. NORWOOD HASTIE is a member of the firm W. S. Hastie & Sons, general insurance, the oldest established insurance agency operating continuously under one name in South Carolina.

Mr. Hastie was born at Charleston January 9, 1878, a son of W. S. and Julia (Drayton) Hastie. His father was a native of New York and was brought to South Carolina when a child. The grandfather, W. S. Hastie, Sr., was also a native of New York and in 1869 established the insurance business at Charleston which has been operated by his family ever since.

C. Norwood Hastie was educated in the public schools of Charleston and graduated in 1897 from Lawrenceville Preparatory School in New Jersey. Since then he has had an active part in the firm W. S. Hastie & Sons. He is prominent in other business affairs, being a director of the Exchange Bank & Trust Company, a director of the Drake-Inness-Green Shoe Company, a director in the Follin-Wingo Company and in various other local enterprises.

In 1913 he married Miss Sara Calhoun Simons, daughter of E. A. and Sarah (Simonds) Simons. Her grandmother was Sarah Calhoun, a niece of John C. Calhoun. Mr. and Mrs. Hastie have two sons, C. Norwood, Jr., and John Drayton. Mr. Hastie is a member of the Carolina Yacht Club, Charleston Country Club, and has taken the more important degrees in Masonry, but is not active in the order at present. Mr. Hastie's family have always owned the famous Magnolia Gardens near Charleston.

ANTHONY ABRAM SARRATT. The patriotism which is expressed in military service is a crowning achievement in the life of a nation. America could show few families whose record is more faultless in this respect than that of the late Anthony Abram Sarratt, nine of whose family wore the colors in the World war, eight of them being commissioned officers. The state and the nation properly take pride in the records of such distinguished sons.

The qualities that make good soldiers also make good citizens, and the substantial character of the Sarratts has been esteemed in South Carolina for a century and a half. As a family they settled on Sarratt's Creek in upper South Carolina some time between 1765 and 1775.

The late Anthony Abram Sarratt was born December 11, 1843, at Grassy Pond in Spartanburg County, son of Gilbert and Charlotte Lucretia (Irvine) Sarratt. Charlotte Lucretia Irvine was a daughter of Edmund and Sarah (Graham) Irvine and a granddaughter of Col. William Graham of the Revolutionary army, and a member of Provincial Congress in 1775, several of whose descendants are found in Greenville and in North Carolina.

Anthony Abram Sarratt acquired a liberal education before the war in Limestone Springs under Mr. Lisle, and in Furman University at Greenville. At the age of seventeen he volunteered in the Confederate war, and was a lieutenant in Company K of Holcomb Legion, Evans Brigade. After more than two years of strenuous fighting service he was made a prisoner, and endured confinement in northern prison camps thirteen months in 1864-65, at first at Point Lookout and afterward at Fort Delaware. He lost his only brother, Edwin Sarratt, in the war.

After the war he bravely took up his burdens in a state impoverished and with its best men gone or disfranchised, and after his marriage made his home at Schull Shoals in Union County, where he achieved success as a planter and merchant. In early manhood he joined the Methodist Episcopal Church and was devoted to the church and its institutions both as a worker and with his means. He was also elected to the Legislature from Union County, serving as representative six years. For four years he was director of the penitentiary and at home, in his business and in his public relations bore himself in a manner to deserve the trust and confidence of his fellow men. Death came to him on November 14, 1898, and he was laid to rest at Gaffney, South Carolina.

September 15, 1868, at Watola, in Union County, Anthony A. Sarratt married Miss Mary Pacolet Walker. She was born March 25, 1850, being the only child of Dr. Allen Oliver and Sarah Ann (Hoey) Walker. Several of Mrs. Sarratt's uncles were in the Confederate war, including Capt. Sidney S. Walker, Capt. Felix Walker, Capt. Amos Hoey and Capt. Sam Hoey, while her mother was a granddaughter of Capt. Amos Davis of the American Revolution, and a descendant of David Daniel Davis of Colonial history. Mrs. Sarratt by her character and culture had much to do with the training of her noble family. She was educated in schools near her old home and in the Methodist institution, St. John's College at Spartanburg. Her death occurred September 13, 1896.

Of their marriage thirteen children were born, whose individual records more or less briefly are contained in following paragraphs. The names of the children in order of age are: Evelina Sarratt Rice, Col. Edwin Oliver Sarratt, Inez Sarratt Wood, Dr. Sidney Gilbert Sarratt, William Judson Sarratt, Annie Sarratt Hames, Maj. James Anthony Sarratt, Ethel Sarratt Talbott, Clara Sarratt Drain, Melvin Walker Sarratt (who was born February 28, 1889, at Schull Shoals in Union County, and died December 7, 1897), Grady Sarratt (who was born November 8, 1890, and died January 6, 1891), an infant son, born March 7th and died March 9, 1892, Vivian Sarratt Gillespie.

EVELINA SARRATT RICE. The oldest child of the late Anthony Abram Sarratt is Sarah Evelina, who was born at Tulehoma, North Pacolet, in what was then Union, now Cherokee County. Her early training was acquired in the local schools, and continued in the Union Female Academy and later in the Columbia Female College. February 1, 1888, she became the wife of Spencer Morgan Rice.

Mr. Rice was born in Laurens County, June 2, 1859, son of Col. William G. and Sarah E.

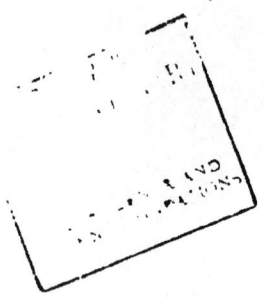

(Sims) Rice, and a descendant of Capt. Charles Sims and his wife, Isabella Sims, of the Revolutionary war. When he was young his father moved to Abbeville County, now Greenwood County, and he acquired his education in the community schools there. Before he was of age he became self-supporting, and was employed for a time by the contracting firm of Rice & Coleman in the building of the Spartanburg and Ashville Railroad. Subsequently he located at Union and engaged in the mercantile business, and at the time of his death had a prosperous establishment dealing in furniture, pianos, organs and other musical instruments. He died May 27, 1912. In early life he joined the Methodist Episcopal Church, South, and his life throughout was one of consecration and piety. He was a pioneer prohibitionist in Union County and lived to see some of the things he had advocated and hoped for practically realized.

Mr. and Mrs. Rice were the parents of five sons and two daughters. The oldest son, Paul Sarratt, died when about eight and a half years of age. The daughter, Sarah Pacolet, after finishing graded and high schools in her home town entered Columbia College, graduating in 1910, and just a year later she became the wife of Beverly Crump Lewis, Jr., of Richmond, Virginia, where they reside. Mr. Lewis is secretary of the Virginia Fire and Marine Insurance Company. They have two children, Beverly Crump Lewis III and Kate Westwood Lewis.

The oldest living son is Robert Coleman Rice, who was born at Union, finished the high school course in his native town, and for two years was a student in Wofford College at Spartanburg. Since then he has been in the office of the Virginia Fire and Marine Insurance Company. As the chief support of his mother and younger brother and sister he was unable to volunteer during the World war, but was actively identified with all branches of home service.

Mrs. Rice had two sons in the war, one in the army and one in the navy. Oliver George, who was born at Union, finished the course of the Union High School with a scholarship to The Citadel, and spent two years in that famous school at Charleston. April 25, 1917, he volunteered, joining the Coast Artillery as sergeant under Capt. F. M. Elerbe. He was with his company at Fort Moultrie in Charleston Harbor, and after a few months joined the Reserve Officers' Training Camp at Fort Oglethorpe, and completed his intensive training in the Saumur Artillery School in France. He was commissioned a second lieutenant, Field Artillery, National Army, and was on duty in France from April 28, 1918, to July 12, 1919. Part of the time he was zone major in the Billeting Department at the towns of Rennes, Messac, Baine and LaRochelle, France. He received his honorable discharge August 8, 1919, at Camp Dix, New Jersey, and still holds a commission in the Reserve Army. On leaving the army he took a course of practical instruction in automobile mechanics at Flint, Michigan, and is now connected with an automobile company at Charlotte, North Carolina.

William Anthony Rice, who was also born at Union, received a scholarship from the high school to Clemson College. He was there only a few months when he won an appointment to the United States Naval Academy at Annapolis, beginning his work there in June, 1916. During the war he was on active duty as a midshipman and completed his course at the academy in June, 1919, receiving his commission as ensign. Since his graduation he has been on the U. S. S. Pennsylvania, the flag ship of the Atlantic fleet.

The youngest son of Mrs. Rice is Sidney Clough Rice, who was born in Union, attended grammar and high school there, but before completing his high school course entered the Massey Business College at Richmond, Virginia, where he remained during 1918-1919. After an active business experience for a few months he resumed his education, and is now a student in Clemson College. The youngest child is Agnes Morgan Rice, a student in the public schools of her native town of Union and now qualified for high school.

COL. EDWIN OLIVER SARRATT, U. S. Army, son of Anthony Abram Sarratt and Mary Pacolet Walker, was born August 8, 1871, at Schull Shoals, Union County, South Carolina. He was married in New York City, July 3, 1902, to Charlotte Jane Norton, daughter of Milford Henry Norton and Martha Green Johnson, of San Antonio, Texas. Their children, with place and date of birth, are: Edwin Oliver Sarratt, Jr., The Presidio, San Francisco, California, July 21, 1903; Henry Norton Sarratt, Fort Hamilton, Brooklyn, New York, December 5, 1906; Charlotte Jane Sarratt, Washington, District of Columbia, September 24, 1910; and Charles Starr Sarratt, San Antonio, Texas, September 24, 1917.

Colonel Sarratt's schools and colleges were: A. B., University of South Carolina, Columbia, South Carolina, 1891. Taught school in South Carolina, 1891 to 1893; cadet U. S. M. A. 1893; graduate, United States Military Academy, West Point, New York, 1897; assigned as second lieutenant to Third Artillery; instructor in mathematics, U. S. M. A., West Point, New York, 1900; graduate School of Submarine Defense, Fort Totten, New York, 1905; graduate Army War College, Washington, District of Columbia, 1910; student officer general staff college, Washington, District of Columbia, 1919. His military record is as follows: Peace: Garrison and staff duty, Atlantic and Pacific coasts of United States, Philippines and Panama. War: Spanish American war, Philippine insurrection, and World war. In the World war commanded the 309th Field Artillery (155 m/m short), 153rd Field Artillery Brigade, 78th Division, September 4, 1917, to May 15, 1919; 309th Field Artillery, composed of New York and New Jersey men (National Army), trained at Camp Dix, New Jersey, and Meucon, Brittany, France; demobilized at Camp Dix, New Jersey, May 15, 1919. In American Expeditionary Force one year. Colonel Sarratt was presented a silver service set by his men after their return from France.

His major operations were: San Mihiel offensive (with 90th Division), Meuse-Argonne offensive (with 78th Division and 42nd Division). His minor operations were: Toul Sector, Pre'ny raid (offensive) and Grand Pre' attack (offensive), November 11, 1918, en route to join second American Army in offensive against Metz.

MAJ. JAMES ANTHONY SARRATT. Maj. James Anthony Sarratt, son of the late Anthony A. Sarratt, of Union County, was born in that county March 10, 1881, and for twelve years has been in the service of his country as an army officer. He acquired his education in the Gaffney Seminary, in the Clemson Agricultural College, and at Washington, District of Columbia.

He received a commission in the United States Regular Forces September 25, 1908. During the next several years he was with the 5th United States Infantry at Plattsburg Barracks, New York, and Governor's Island in New York City, went with the 8th United States Infantry to the Philippine Islands, and was with the 17th Infantry at Eagle Pass, Texas.

Major Sarratt accompanied the Punitive Expedition into Mexico under General Pershing. Soon afterward, at the beginning of the World war, he was appointed an instructor at the Reserve Officers' Training Camp at Fort Oglethorpe, Georgia. While at camp at Fort Oglethorpe he was presented with a gold watch by his men, showing their appreciation. He was later assigned to headquarters of the 76th Division, which was in France from July, 1918, until after the armistice. Returning from France he commanded the First Battalion of the 73rd Infantry of the 12th Division until demobilization, and has since been on duty with the Military Intelligence Division, General Staff, at Washington. His home address is 1617 S. Street, N. W., Washington.

Major Sarratt married August 30, 1915, Constance Kathryn Watkins, of New York City, daughter of Thomas Parke and Mary (Browne) Watkins. Two children were born to their marriage: James A., Jr., who died January 5, 1918, and Anthony Melvin, born at New York City March 6, 1919.

SAMUEL SYLVANUS WOOD, one of the leading farmers and planters in Spartanburg County, is a member of a family that has been identified with this section of the state for more than a century.

He was born in Spartanburg County, April 6, 1862, son of William Lipscomb and Mary (Austell) Wood. His parents were also born in Spartanburg County. The grandfather, William Wood, a native of Virginia, came to South Carolina and settled in the upper part of the state more than a century ago. William L. Wood was born October 5, 1819, and died June 10, 1893. Though past forty years of age, he bore arms as a Confederate soldier during the War between the States. His wife was born February 20, 1834, and died February 18, 1917. Of their six children five reached mature age, and two sons and two daughters are still living.

Samuel S. Wood, the third child, was well educated, and grew up in the Pacolet district of Spartanburg County, where his chief interests have been concentrated. He assisted his father on the plantation and for over thirty years has been engaged in the superintendence of some extensive farming interests. He owns about fifteen hundred acres, most of which are now rented out and operated by tenants.

Mr. Wood married for his first wife Emma Meieg. His second wife was Helen Hamilton. The present Mrs. Wood was Inez Sarratt, member of the prominent Sarratt family sketched on other pages. They had three children, the only one now living being Samuel S., Jr. The family are members of the Methodist Church.

INEZ SARRATT WOOD was born at Tulahoma, Union County, was educated at the Union Female Academy and the Columbia Female College and resides at Pacolet, South Carolina. October 5, 1910, at Union, she became the wife of Samuel S. Wood of Pacolet. They had three children: An infant son that died February 21, 1912; Mary Pacolet Wood, born March 26, 1913, at Union, and died March 25, 1914; and Samuel Sidney Wood, born April 23, 1915, at Spartanburg.

DR. SIDNEY GILBERT SARRATT was born at Schull Shoals in Union County, was educated in the Gaffney High School, graduated in medicine at the University of Maryland in Baltimore in 1897, and subsequently did special work at the Mayo Brothers' clinics and in New York. In the World war he was commissioned a captain, served in the army hospital at Brest, France, for nearly a year, from September 22, 1918, to August 19, 1919, and was honorably discharged at Camp Gordon, Georgia, September 6, 1919.

Doctor Sarratt served as chairman of the Board of Stewards of Grace Methodist Church, and is chairman of the Union County Board of Health; president of the Union County Medical Association, and a member of the Home Service Committee of Union County Chapter, American Reserve Corps. He was offered the rank of major in the Reserve Army, and is practicing medicine at Union, South Carolina.

WILLIAM JUDSON SARRATT was born at Schull Shoals, attended the Gaffney graded schools, and was president of his graduating class at Clemson College in June, 1897. He subsequently took special courses in New York and Baltimore, and at his father's death he and an older brother, Dr. Sidney Sarratt, took charge of the farm. He was elected and for two years represented Cherokee County in the Legislature, 1900-01. For two years, 1908 to 1910, he was a lieutenant in the United States Army in the Philippines, and in the World war was a chemist, making ether at the Government plant at Nitro, West Virginia. He is at this writing a merchant's agent (super cargo) for the International Merchant Marine Company of America and is on the ship St. Anthony on a trip to Greece, Italy, Roumania and Turkey.

ANNIE SARRATT HAMES was born at Schull Shoals, Union County, educated in the Gaffney High School and the Clifford Seminary, and for a number of years has been prominently identified with church and patriotic organizations.

She was secretary and treasurer of the William Wallace Chapter, United Daughters of the Confederacy at Union, and was organizing regent of the Fair Forest Chapters, Daughters of the American Revolution, 1915-1918, and state historian of the South Carolina Daughters of the American Revolution, 1917-1920.

She was awarded a Red Cross service badge for her services during the World war in the Union County Chapter, American Red Cross, and was chairman of supplies and vice-chairman of this Red Cross chapter.

December 26, 1800. Annie Sarratt became the wife of Landy Jones Hames, of Union. Landy Jones Hames is the son of Thaddeus Lemuel and Addie McWhirter Hames, great-grandson of John Jones, for whom the town of Jonesville was named, and descendant of John Floyd, lieutenant, later captain, in the Revolutionary War. His father, T. L. Hames, was commissary sergeant, and a brave Confederate soldier, entering the war at eighteen years of age. The Jonesville Chapter, N. D. C., was named for his uncle, Capt. John Hames. Another uncle, Sergt. Charles Hames, was killed at the second battle of Manasses. Landy Hames lives in the town of Union and is a successful wholesale merchant and planter. He has always been closely identified and interested in the welfare of his town and state.

He is a trustee and steward of Grace Methodist Church; trustee of the Union Carnegie Library, since its organization in 1905; director in the Union Chamber of Commerce, and has served this body as president; director and vice president of the Merchants and Planters National Bank; commissioner of public works 1910 to June, 1920; served as alderman for Ward One for several years.

Landy Hames and his wife have two sons: Sarratt Thaddeus, educated in the Union graded and high schools, two years at The Citadel, Charleston, South Carolina, and is now a cadet at the United States Military Academy, West Point, New York. Landy Jones Hames, Jr., is a student at the Union High School. The youngest brother of Landy Hames, Walter Hames, was commissioned a lieutenant in the 372d Regiment, which was attached to the French army during the World war, and was awarded the Distinguished Service Cross by the American Government, the Croix de Guerre with Palm by the French Government, and made a cavalier in the Legion of Honor of France.

ETHEL SARRATT TALBOTT was born at Schull Shoals, attended the graded schools of Gaffney and Converse College at Spartanburg, and on November 23, 1904, at Gaffney, became the wife of Lieut. Col. Samuel Greaner Talbott. Colonel Talbott, whose record finds an appropriate place in this family history, was born at Richmond, Virginia, February 24, 1877, son of Samuel Greaner and Lucy (Lewis) Talbott. He was educated in the public schools of his native city and graduated with the class of 1899 from the Virginia Military Institute at Lexington. He came of a military family, his father having been with the Otey Battery in the army of Northern Virginia, while his maternal grandfather was a lieutenant in the 59th Virginia Infantry in the war between the states. Colonel Talbott was commissioned a second lieutenant in the regular army in 1902, and in February of that year was sent to the Philippines with the 28th Infantry in the War between the States. Colonel in 1913 went to the Mexican border and subsequently was under General Funsten at Vera Cruz. When America entered the war against the Central Empire he was serving as adjutant of post at Fort Slocum, New York, and was presented with a very handsome watch by the men whom he had in charge. He was soon promoted to lieutenant colonel, and was given the responsibility of organizing a camp at Syracuse, New York. He became commandant at camp at Syracuse in July, 1918, at which time 11,000 men were mobilized there. From Syracuse he was sent to Camp Devens, Massachusetts, later to New York City, and after the armistice was made adjutant general of the United States Army of Occupation at Coblenz, Germany, where at this writing he is still stationed. His wife and daughter being with him. Mrs. Ethel Talbott assumed very unusual and arduous responsibilities during the war as a Red Cross worker, and so highly were her services esteemed at Camp Syracuse that she was called the "mother of the army." Colonel and Mrs. Talbott's daughter is Ethelyn Sarratt Talbott, born at Columbus, Ohio.

CLARA HOEY SARRATT DRAIN, who was born in Schull Shoals, and educated in the grammar schools of Gaffney and the College for Women at Columbia, South Carolina, was married at Union, June 7, 1910, to Maj. Jesse Cyrus Drain of the United States Army.

Maj. Jesse C. Drain was born at Braddock, Pennsylvania, September 25, 1883. His parents, Henry Drain and Caroline Ebert Drain, were of English descent. J. C. Drain was one of nine children, six boys and three girls, and was educated in public schools of Braddock, Pennsylvania. In 1902, J. C. Drain won a competitive examination for West Point, held at Pittsburgh, attended Bethel Academy preparatory school, Virginia, and later the United States Military Academy, West Point, New York, from which institution he was graduated in 1907, and assigned to the 28th Infantry, stationed at Matanzas, Cuba. While stationed in Cuba this officer was mentioned in Army of Cuban Pacification orders for exceptional services performed; later served at Fort Snelling, Minnesota, Fort Sam Houston, Tientsin, China, with China Expeditionary Force, 1912 to 1915; Laredo, Texas, border patrol and professor of military science and tactics, Shattuck School, Faribault, Minnesota. On the outbreak of war, J. C. Drain was appointed examining officer for the State of Minnesota, and also served at the First Officers' Training Camp held at Fort Snelling, Minnesota. In August, 1917, he was detailed to the Infantry School of Arms, Fort Sill, Oklahoma, and remained on duty there until August, 1918, during which time he was director of the small arms department and author of "Grenade Training Manual" and "Hand to Hand Fighting Manual," pamphlets accepted by the Training Committee, General Staff. In August, 1918, he was detailed to staff class, Army War College, graduating with honors and assigned to Training Committee, General Staff, for duty. In January, 1919, he returned to

Infantry School, Camp Benning, Georgia, for duty as director of Close Combat Department. In September, 1919, and March, 1920, he was appointed director of special courses in physical and bayonet training, held pursuant to War Department orders, for which services he received a special letter of commendation from Secretary of War Mr. Newton Baker. He is at present on duty as director of non-commissioned officers' course, Infantry School, Camp Benning, Georgia.

Major Drain and wife have one son, Jesse Cyrus Drain, Jr., who was born at Union, South Carolina, on September 27, 1911.

VIVIAN IRVINE SARRATT GILLESPIE, who was born at Gaffney, attended the Union graded schools and Converse College at Spartanburg, and on June 7, 1917, at Union, was married to Lieut.-Col. James Albert Gillespie, of whom a brief record follows. They have one child, Vivian Gillespie, born at Spartanburg.

LIEUT.-COL. JAMES ALBERT GILLESPIE, who married a daughter of the late Anthony A. Sarratt of Union, is therefore properly included among the distinguished members of this military and fighting family of the South.

Colonel Gillespie was born at Erie, Pennsylvania, December 7, 1886, sixth among the children of Andrew James and Sarah (Shaw) Gillespie. His parents were Scotch-Irish Presbyterians who came to the United States from the North of Ireland in 1881, locating at Erie, where the mother died in 1893, when her son was six years old. The father died in 1916.

James A. Gillespie was educated in the public schools of his native city, graduating from high school in 1905. He accepted an appointment to the United States Military Academy at West Point, entering July 15, 1907. He graduated, No. 30 in his class, June 12, 1912. As a second lieutenant in Field Artillery he was assigned to the Second Field Artillery at Vancouver Barracks, Washington, and in July, 1913, accompanied the Second Artillery to the Philippine Islands, where he was on duty until October, 1915. Returning to the United States, he was with the Fifth Field Artillery at Fort Sill, Oklahoma, and July 1, 1916, was promoted to first lieutenant and assigned recruiting duty at Fort Slocum, New York. He was promoted to captain May 15, 1917. Assigned to the Fifteenth Field Artillery, he joined his command at Syracuse, New York, June 20, 1917, taking command of Battery C. July 22, 1917, he was sent to the School of Fire at Fort Sill as student officer, completing the course and graduating September 15, 1917. Ordered to the Sixteenth Field Artillery at Camp Robinson, Wisconsin, he took command of Battery F, and with that battery went to Fort Snelling, Minnesota, as senior instructor, Field Artillery in the Second Reserve Officers' Training Camp. He trained and commissioned 300 reserve officers out of 375 candidates at that camp. Then with Battery F he was ordered to Camp Greene, North Carolina, where the Fourth Division was being assembled preparatory to going overseas. As commander of Battery F of the Sixteenth Field Artillery, Fourth Regular Division, he sailed for France May 10, 1918, landed at Brest May 23rd, and proceeded to Camp de Souge, an artillery training center near Bordeaux, where he remained training with French guns until July 28th, when he and his battery entrained for the front, detraining at Chateau Thierry and marching to the front lines. He first went into action along the Vesle River near Fismes, and was on duty until August 17, 1918, when the Sixteenth Field Artillery was relieved and sent to a rest area near Chaumont. On the 3rd of July he was promoted to major, and was then assigned and joined the Thirteenth Field Artillery in the same division, taking command of the Second Battalion at Cirey les Mareilles, August 27, 1918. He commanded that battalion through the St. Mihiel and Meuse-Argonne offensives until October 18, 1918, when he was ordered to the Army Line School at Langres, France, as student officer. He graduated, again as No. 30 in the class of 260, on December 28, 1918. In the meantime, October 26, 1918, he had been promoted to lieutenant-colonel, and was ordered after graduating to rejoin the Thirteenth Artillery in the Army of Occupation in Germany. He remained as second in command of this regiment throughout its tour in Germany, and had duties as military commander at various times of the towns of Ulmen, Buchel, Alflen, Alf and Ahrweiler, Germany. July 18, 1919, Colonel Gillespie sailed from Brest, landing at New York July 31st, after an absence of fifteen months, and participation in four of the great offensives of the western front—Aisne-Marne, Vesle Champaign, St. Mihiel and Meuse-Argonne. After a brief leave he reported at Camp Dodge, Iowa, and has since been in command of the Thirteenth Field Artillery. Colonel Gillespie married Miss Vivian Irvine Sarratt at Union, South Carolina, June 7, 1917.

T. GRANGE WARING, who recently was one of the leaders in establishing a large automobile accessory industry and business at Charleston, saw twenty-seven months of active service as a lieutenant in the navy during the World war.

For a number of years he has been an enthusiastic yachtsman, as a member of the Carolina Yacht Club. In pursuit of that pasttime he was not content with the technical achievements of good seamanship in handling a boat under all sorts of conditions, but made a very thorough examination of the coast, its various harbors and inlets, and acquired much of that intuitive sense that distinguished the old time blockade runners of the South. Therefore, when on March 17, 1917, a few weeks before America entered the war with Germany, he volunteered in the navy, he was very appropriately assigned to duty as commander of the coast patrol for the third section of the Sixth Naval District. He was given the rank of lieutenant, junior grade. His section extended from McClellanville to St. Helena Sound and embraced the waters of Charleston Harbor. The fleet under his command was comprised of submarine chasers and patrol boats, and they were used principally in the vicinity of Charleston Harbor. In October, 1918, Mr. Waring was transferred to the staff of Admiral Beatty, in command of the Sixth Naval District, with headquarters at Charleston, and was made district en-

rolling officer. In the meantime he had been promoted to lieutenant, senior grade. Lieutenant Waring remained in active duty until June 28, 1919, when he was released from active service, but is still held on the reserve list.

Mr. Waring was born at Charleston, son of T. M. and Frances Caroline (Simons) Waring. Sketches of historic families of Charleston make frequent mention of both the Warings and the Simonses. T. Grange Waring was educated in public and private schools at Charleston, and after leaving school was in business as a cotton buyer about fifteen years, until he entered his country's service.

In the fall of 1919, when he resumed business relations at Charleston, he became one of the organizers and is president of the Motor Accessory Supply Company. This is a wholesale and distributing business for an extensive line of automobile accessories and supplies, and has proved a welcome addition to the increasing commerce of Charleston. The company occupies a building arranged for its special purpose at 320-322 Meeting Street.

Mr. Waring married Miss Kate Fuller Porter. Her grandfather was the late Rev. Dr. Porter, founder of Porter's Military Academy. Mr. and Mrs. Waring have two children: Frances Caroline and Kate Porter. Mr. Waring is a member of the Carolina Yacht Club and of St. Andrews Society.

JOHN C. WIETERS, M. D. While he is a well qualified physician and surgeon, and served as medical officer in the army and navy during the late war, Doctor Wieters since being released from active duty has for a temporary period at least taken up active business as owner of the Charleston Bill Posting Company, the oldest concern of its kind in South Carolina.

Doctor Wieters was born in Charleston in 1890, son of John C. and Marguerite (Schroeder) Wieters. His father, a native of Germany, came to Charleston when a youth and was a Confederate soldier throughout the war between the states. After the war he became prominent in Charleston commerce. He was associated for a number of years with his older brother, Otto, in the wholesale grocery business, taking the chief responsibility of that concern upon the death of Otto, and the business is still a large and prosperous one, having been continued from the death of John C. Wieters by his younger brother, Mr. E. F. A. Wieters. Mrs. John C. Wieters, who is still living, was born near Bremen, Germany. Prior to the outbreak of the European war she returned to that city to be with her two daughters living there and has since remained.

Dr. John C. Wieters was educated in private and public schools of Charleston, and had the advantage of very extensive travel and instruction in Europe. He attended schools and universities in Germany, Austria and Switzerland, and on returning from abroad began the study of medicine in the Medical College of the State of South Carolina at Charleston, where he graduated in 1912. This was followed by post-graduate work in the University of Berlin, and in 1913 he began the active work of his profession in Charleston.

Doctor Wieters volunteered his services as a medical officer in the United States Army in March, 1917, some weeks before this country entered the war. He was on duty with the rank of lieutenant in the Medical Corps of the army until June, 1917, when he was transferred to the navy. Doctor Wieters was assigned to duty at the Naval Hospital in Charleston in charge of the section of contagious diseases. For nearly two and a half years all his professional talents were given to the Government, and while released from active duty in August, 1919, he is still retained with a reserve commission.

It was his intention to resume private practice, but having in the meantime acquired the ownership of the Charleston Bill Posting Company he found that its greatly expanding business demanded all his attention. The business is growing in proportion to Charleston's remarkable development along all lines, and as a means of putting its service on a plane with the high reputation of the company a new and modern building has been erected for its home on North Meeting street.

Doctor Wieters married Miss Lucile Davis, member of an old and prominent Charleston family. Their two children are John Davis and Charles August.

REDDING CAROLAS HARDWICK is the veteran member of the bar of Denmark, Bamberg County, where he has practiced steadily for twenty-six years.

He was born in Burke County, Georgia, August 12, 1869, son of Andrew and Alice (Chance) Hardwick, both natives of Georgia. He is a descendant of Lord Hardwick of Ireland. Three Hardwick brothers came to America in colonial times, one locating in New York, another in North Carolina, and the third established the branch of the family in Georgia. Subject's uncle was named.

Redding Carolas Harwick was the eighth among nine children, three of whom are still living. He was reared and educated at Waynesboro, Georgia, first attending country schools. As a young man he took up the business of contracting and building, followed that occupation in Georgia, and in 1888 located at the Town of Graham, which subsequently had its name changed to Denmark. He continued as a building contractor here for several years. During his working hours he studied law, beginning in the fall of 1892, and was admitted to the bar December 15, 1893. He had also served a time as chief of police of the town. He has enjoyed a steadily growing general practice as a lawyer, and for fourteen years was actively interested in farming until he sold his farm property in 1917.

In 1890 Mr. Hardwick married Mary Carroll, a native of Blackville, Barnwell County. Mr. Hardwick is affiliated with the Knights of Pythias, and has been identified with that order since 1892. Since he was fifteen years of age he has been a member of the Methodist Episcopal Church South and takes an active part in church work and has also played a leading part in the Sunday school. Thomas W. Hardwick of Atlanta, Georgia, is subject's first cousin. He was in Congress sixteen years, senator ten years. Now running for governor of Georgia. Subject's wife's parents were from Ireland. Her father, E. D. Carroll served in War of States for

Confederacy. He suffered greatly being left on post when his companions left him without relieving him. He stuck to his post without food until their return, three days later. He was on an island near Charleston.

JOHN PULASKI THOMAS. In the quarter of a century since he completed his education at The Citadel and took his place among the young business men of Charleston, John Pulaski Thomas has wielded an increasing influence and power in commercial and industrial affairs of his home city.

He was born at Santuc in Union County, South Carolina, in 1873. His parents, Dr. J. P. and Susan (Rivers) Thomas, are now deceased. The Rivers family was long prominent on James Island, South Carolina. Dr. J. P. Thomas, a native of the Santuc community of Union County, was a graduate of the Medical College of South Carolina at Charleston, spent his active life as a practicing physician, and at one time represented Union County in the Legislature.

A graduate of The Citadel at Charleston with the class of 1893, John P. Thomas during his career as a successful business man has taken a deep interest in the welfare of that historic institution. He is a member of the Board of Visitors of The Citadel, and at the present time is chairman of the Building Committee in charge of the building of the greater Citadel, a work on which plan began early in 1920, and the purpose of which is to provide a fitting home for this school. At the annual meeting of the Board of Visitors December 11, 1917, Mr. Thomas moved that a committee of four members be appointed to take into consideration a new site for the college. His motion was adopted and Mr. Thomas was appointed Chairman of the committee. Thus plans for the greater Citadel were started and have been steadily going forward. Consequently it is shown that Mr. Thomas was really the one to officially suggest and start the project which will result in the greater Citadel. Mr. Thomas has also, partly as a result of his early training at The Citadel, taken much interest in local military affairs, and as a young man was a member of the Carolina Rifles and served as a captain several years. During the World war he was a member of the first War Board at Charleston by appointment of the Governor, and gave much of his time to the different departments of war and patriotic work.

The business efforts of Mr. Thomas have been variously bestowed, but his name is now chiefly identified with the General Asbestos Rubber Company, of which he is treasurer, and the Cameron & Barkley Company, a leading machinery house of the city, of which he is secretary and treasurer. Both of these have been important contributors to the industrial and commercial welfare of Charleston: Mr. Thomas is a member of various social and business organizations, is a past master of Kilwinning Lodge No. 4, Ancient Free and Accepted Masons, and a deacon in The Citadel Square Baptist Church and vice president of the Young Men's Christian Association. He married Miss Lottie Reeves, and their family of six children are Claudia, Sue Rivers, John P., Jr., Matthew Reeves, Charlotte Reeves and Mary Stone.

REV. JESSE ALEXANDER CLIFTON was a greatly beloved minister of the Methodist Episcopal Church in South Carolina for many years. He was born at Chester, a son of Jesse C. and Mary (Walker) Clifton and was of Scotch-Irish descent. Both he and his father were Confederate soldiers. As a boy he attended the Ebenezer High School in York County, and also studied at the University of Virginia. He joined the Confederate Army in Company D of the First South Carolina Volnuteers, Hampton's Brigade, and was a courier and scout in the army of Northern Virginia. After the war he became a minister of the gospel and served actively for over a third of a century. For a number of years he was pastor of the church at Sumter. He was twice a delegate to the general conference of the church. In 1893 the degree Doctor of Divinity was conferred upon him by Rutherford College in North Carolina.

Rev. Mr. Clifton married Mary Hicklin, daughter of Dr. W. J. Hicklin.

WALTER EDWARD RICHARDSON, the well known banker and business man of Beaufort, South Carolina, has been prominently identified with the business interests of this section of the state for many years, and while his varied affairs have brought him success they have also advanced the general welfare by accelerating commercial activity. Mr. Richardson has spent his entire life within the borders of his native state and is the scion of one of its excellent old families.

Walter Edward Richardson was born in Hampton County, South Carolina, on June 19, 1881, and is the third in order of birth of the eight children born to the union of C. G. and Hattie (Bunson) Richardson. C. G. Richardson was also a native of Hampton County, as was his father before him, James Richardson. Mrs. Hattie Richardson was the daughter of Edgar Bunson, of Hampton County. Walter E. Richardson attended the common schools of his native locality until the age of thirteen years, since which time he has been continuously identified with the banking business. His first employment was as office boy in the Bank of Hampton, at Hampton, and he has ever since been connected with that institution. In 1904 he became its cashier, was made its vice president in 1908 and in 1913 became its president, which position he still holds. He early demonstrated to a marked degree those peculiar qualities essential to successful banking and his interests in that line have steadily extended until today he is connected with a number of the best banks in this section of the state. In 1907 he organized a bank at Varnville, of which he is the president and in 1909 organized the Beaufort Bank, of which he was made cashier and of which he is now president. In 1912 he organized the Bank of Yemassee, of which he is the president, and also occupies a like position with the Merchants and Planters Bank at Bunson. These banks are all solid and influential institutions and have been a great incentive to the general business development of this section of the state. In addition to his banking interests, Mr. Richardson is also heavily interested in truck farms, of which he owns about one thousand acres. During the recent World's war he organized the American Ship Building & Dock

Corporation and also became interested in the building of concrete barges, these projects being projected as adjuncts to the war activities of the government. Mr. Richardson is a half owner in the People's Ice and Fuel Company, in addition to which he is financially interested in many other important and successful enterprises, all of which have contributed in a very definite degree to the business prosperity of the community.

In 1909, Mr. Richardson was married to Lucy C. Moore, the daughter of James W. Moore, a prominent lawyer and politician, and former member of the State Senate. To Mr. and Mrs. Richardson have been born two children, Elizabeth and Randall. Fraternally Mr. Richardson is a member of the Ancient Free and Accepted Masons, the Ancient Arabic Order of Nobles of the Mystic Shrine and the Knights of Pythias. In his relations with his fellow men, Mr. Richardson has been thoroughly upright and conscientious, gentlemanly, considerate and courteous in his personal and social contact, and enjoys to a marked degree the confidence of his business associates and the esteem of all who know him. Public spirited and enterprising, he has consistently given his support to every movement tending to advance the public welfare and has at all times advocated the best things for the community.

JOHN McALISTER. What made the life of the late John McAlister distinctive in Charleston was the quality of personal service and personal kindliness which pervaded all his activities. His record is one that can be set down with every mark of honor, and is completely due to the good citizenship he so long exemplified.

He was born at Cushendale, County Antrim, Ireland, June 22, 1864, and died at Charleston January 7, 1920. He was of the best Scotch ancestry. The McAlister clan has a long record of noble deeds in Scotch history, and some of his early ancestors were of kinship with Robert Bruce.

When John McAlister was five years of age his parents came to America and settled near Walhalla in Oconee County, South Carolina. When he was about fifteen, having received only a common school education, he moved to Charleston and joined his brother James in the livery business. Eventually he bought out that business, and in 1886 he qualified himself for the undertaking profession by graduating from the Clarke Embalming School of Brooklyn, New York. It is said that Mr. McAlister was the first licensed embalmer in Charleston. The McAlister undertaking business has been a reliable service in Charleston for over thirty-five years. In connection Mr. McAlister conducted a livery business until about two years before his death, when he sold that department to the Charleston Transfer Company. In June, 1919, Governor Cooper had appointed him a member of the State Board of Embalming Examiners, and he was serving in that capacity when overtaken by death.

He was not only a successful business man but one of the most loyal of Charleston's citizens. He was connected with a number of other business enterprises, and some of them owe much to his influence and abilities. He was a director of the Citizens and the Liberty banks, the Kopp-Isenhour Realty Company, the Commonwealth Building and Loan Association, the Follin-Wingo Company, the Southern Drug Syndicate, and was a member of the Advisory Board of the American Publishing Company. He was also a member of the National Funeral Directors Association and the South Carolina Funeral Directors Association.

Among the fraternal orders of which he was a member are the Elks, Knights of Columbus, Ancient Order of Hibernians, Woodmen of the World, Hibernian Society, Fraternal Aid Society, Loyal Order of Moose and the Fellowship Society.

The place he filled in the community for so many years is well expressed in an editorial tribute taken from the Charleston American: "In the death of John McAlister this community loses a splendid citizen. There is hardly a home to which the sad news did not come as a personal grief. For years he has gone about his quiet way doing untold good, helping the helpless and softening the keen pangs which sorrow brought only too often mixed with the double affliction of poverty. Nobody knows how boundless were his works of charity. Loved, honored and respected, he lived a blameless life and left a noble name. To his family he was devotion itself, to his friends, loyalty, to the community, service, and to the poor and stricken a genuine Samaritan. He knew neither class nor creed, but toward all extended the touch of human sympathy."

Mr. John McAlister married Miss Mary L. McAlister, of Brooklyn, New York. He is survived by Mrs. McAlister and five children: Iona, Catherine and Margaret and James A. and John, Jr. The undertaking business is carried on by the two sons, James A. and John. James Archibald McAlister, the older son, has the distinction of being the youngest licensed embalmer in the state and one of the youngest in the country. He attended the Barnes School of Anatomy, Sanitary Science and Embalming in New York, and received his certificate from that institution on September 30, 1912, just three months after he was fifteen years old.

JOHNSON HEYWARD COPE has for many years been a prominent figure in the planting, manufacturing and financial affairs of Bamberg County. Among other interests he is now active president of the Bamberg Banking Company.

Mr. Cope was born in Barnwell County in that part now included in Bamberg County, June 30, 1861. The Copes came originally from Holland. His father Jacob Martin Cope was a native of the same section of South Carolina, spent his life as a farmer and planter, and was a soldier in the Confederate army. He died when about seventy-four years of age. His wife was Mary Burnett, a native of Barnwell County, who died at the age of forty-five, the mother of four sons and four daughters.

Johnson Heyward Cope was the fifth child and third son and was reared and educated in Orangeburg County. He graduated in 1879 at Moore's Business College at Atlanta, and on the first of September of that year became bookkeeper for H. J. Brabham & Brother at Bamberg. He was there four years, and then engaged in the mercantile business in the same city until 1900. In that year he was made secretary and treasurer of the Bamberg Cotton Mills, having in the meantime sold out his mercantile interests. Later he was elected president and treasurer of the cotton mills, but left the active management of 1919 and for several years was primarily interested in farming and planting at Cope, South Carolina. January 1, 1916, he returned to Bamberg and became active vice president of the Bamberg Banking Company and later became its president which position he now holds. He is also president and treasurer of the Bamberg Cotton Mills, and on July 1, 1919, was elected president of the Santee Cotton Mills at Orangeburg. On January 1, 1920, the Bamberg Mills were taken over by the Santee Mills and are now being operated as the Bamberg branch of the Santee Company. Mr. Cope owns about a thousand acres of farm lands and has fully half of it devoted to cotton, tobacco, peanuts and various food crops.

The Cope family is one of the old South Carolina families of Revolutionary stock of Dutch and English ancestry. The Town of Cope in Orangeburg County was named after subject's father, Jacob Martin Cope.

In 1884 he married Miss Hattie Antley, daughter of D. D. and Emma C. Antley of Orangeburg County. His only son is Glenn Willard, actively associated with his father in farming. Mr. Cope is affiliated with the Knights of Pythias, is a steward in the Methodist Episcopal Church, South, and is a member of the Board of Control of the Carlisle School at Bamberg. He has also served on the town council and as mayor.

JOHN T. RODDY. While his affiliations are with the progressive and younger element in Charleston's business body, Mr. Roddy is by experience a veteran commercial man, and for more than a quarter of a century has been one of the earnest, hard-working personal factors in the business affairs of the city.

He was born at Charleston in 1876, son of Thomas R. and Ann (Robinson) Roddy. His father, who was born in Ireland in 1836, came to Charleston when a boy with his parents, and for a long period of years enjoyed as proprietor of a grocery store a large and extended trade. His name was for a number of years also influentially associated with public affairs. He served several terms as alderman from Ward 3.

The education of John T. Roddy was acquired in parochial and city schools and in Professor Finger's private school at Charleston. He was only a boy when he was given an opportunity to work at a modest salary with the prominent mercantile house of Molony & Carter Company, and with that organization he was actively associated for twenty-five years. He had earned promotion with that concern until for the last twelve years of his service he was secretary of the company and a member of the corporation. July 1, 1919, having severed his connection with Molony & Carter Company, he established himself in business at 35 Broad Street as a dealer in commercial fertilizers, grain, molasses feeds, lumber and other commodities, and serves a large clientage throughout the state territory of Charleston.

Mr. Roddy is also secretary-treasurer of the Commonwealth Building & Loan Association, a director in the Hibernian Mutual Fire Insurance Company, is treasurer of the Hibernian Society, and a member of the Chamber of Commerce, the Carolina Yacht Club and of the Kiwani Club. He is a Catholic in religion. In 1918 he married Miss Catharine A. Buckley, of Washington, D. C.

McPHERSON G. ELLIOTT, M. D. To achieve an eminent standing in as exacting a calling as the medical profession requires something more than mediocre talents—a fidelity to duty and the happy faculty of winning and retaining the confidence and good will of all classes. These qualifications the gentleman whose life record is briefly outlined in the following paragraphs seems to possess, for he has, unaided, gradually overcome all obstacles until he stands in the front rank of the medical profession of Beaufort County.

McPherson Gregorie Elliott is the scion of a long line of sterling ancestors who have honored the locality where he now resides. The Elliott family had its origin in England, but in a very early day representatives of the family came to America and eventually made settlement in South Carolina, where they have lived continuously to the present time. Four generations at least of the family have been born and reared in Beaufort, beginning with the subject's paternal great-grandfather, William Elliott, his grandfather, George Parsons Elliott, and his father, William Waight Elliott. The latter was married to Elizabeth Martha Gregorie, the daughter of James M. and Martha (McPherson) Gregorie. The subject's mother is still living, in the ninetieth year of her age. Of the four children Mary B., William W., George P. and McPherson G. born to her union with William Waight Elliott, the subject of this sketch is the youngest. He was born at Beaufort, South Carolina, on April 6, 1872, and was reared at home, securing his elementary education in the local schools. He was then a student in Porter Academy at Charleston, South Carolina, in addition to which he had a private tutor. Then, having determined to devote his life to the practice of the medical profession, he matriculated in the Medical College of the State of South Carolina, where he was graduated on April 1, 1898, with the degree of Doctor of Medicine. Immediately thereafter he located in Beaufort, and has remained in the practice of his profession here since that time, reaping not only a satisfactory financial return but, what is of more value, the respect and confidence of the people among whom he has worked and associated. Doctor Elliott is a member of the Beaufort County Medical Society, the South Carolina State Medical Society and the American Medical Association. Fraternally he is a member of the Ancient Free and Accepted Masons, in which he has attained the degree of the Royal Arch.

In 1899 Doctor Elliott was married to Janie T. Holmes, the daughter of Rutledge Holmes, of Charleston, South Carolina, and they have become the parents of six children, three sons and three daughters namely: Elizabeth G., Emily H., Janie H., William W., Rutledge H. and McPherson G., Jr. Aside from his professional interests Doctor Elliott has always evinced a commendable interest in the

welfare of the community, being a consistent supporter of everything that is calculated to advance the general welfare in any way.

CHARLES A. SPEISSEGGER, JR., M. D. The problems of health are really the problems of life and must pertain to all questions of human interest, therefore unquestionably the physician and surgeon is the most important man in his community. He must possess a wide range of general culture, be an observant clinician and well-read neurologist, even though he never specializes along any special line. To take his place among the distinguished men of his profession he must bear the stamp of an original mind and be willing to be hard-worked, while at the same time his soul oftentimes faints within him when studying the mysteries of his calling. Acquainted with the simple annals of the poor, and the inner lives of his patients, he acquires a moral power, courage and conscience which permit him to interfere with the mechanism of physical life, alleviating its woes and increasing its resistance to the encroachments of disease. No wonder that a skilled, learned and sympathetic medical man commands such universal admiration and respect, and one of them who measures up to the highest standards of his profession is Dr. Charles A. Speissegger, Jr., of Charleston.

Doctor Speissegger was born at Charleston on August 4, 1880, a son of Charles A. Speissegger, also a native of Charleston, who is connected with railroad affairs. Doctor Speissegger is the eldest son of his parents' six children. After attending the grammar and high schools of Charleston he spent three years at special work in the College of Charleston, and four years at the Medical College of the State University of South Carolina, being graduated from the latter institution in 1905. After one year spent at Roper Hospital, Charleston, and two years in New York City, Doctor Speissegger returned to his native city, where he has since been engaged in a general practice, winning and holding the confidence of his patients and the community generally. He is surgeon for the General Asbestos Company, examining physician for the Western Union Telegraph Company and other corporations, his skill and training being held in such high regard that those concerns who have the welfare of employes truly at heart endeavor to secure his services, knowing if he is in charge of the health of these people favorable health conditions will prevail, as he is one of the practitioners who firmly believes in the necessity of prevention rather than the method of waiting until a disease becomes epidemic before trying to handle it. As a member of the Charleston Medical Society, the South Carolina State Medical Society and the American Medical Association Doctor Spiessegger is highly valued by his associates. He is a member of various fraternal and social organizations, being a past exalted ruler of the Charleston lodge of Elks. For fifteen years he was P. A. surgeon for the South Carolina Naval Militia. Also first lieutenant of the Medical Reserve Corps, U. S. Army.

In October, 1918, Doctor Speissegger was married to Beulah Maebelle Frost, R. N. (registered nurse), a daughter of Charles Edward Frost, of Sumter, South Carolina. They have one son, Charles A. Speissegger, 2nd. Doctor Speissegger is strikingly characterized not only by his scholastic predilection and intellectual eagerness, but also for his facility and promptitude in handling difficult cases, while his sympathetic personality and natural charm of manner win him friends almost without number.

E. B. CHASE. Many thoughtful people who endeavor to discriminate in their judgment and appreciation as to the usefulness of men and their work have long regarded the efficient in the ranks of railroad operation as worthy of all the honors and rewards they can receive. Among such men, a place of real eminence is enjoyed by E. B. Chase, a veteran in the service of the Southern Railway and now in the fortieth year of his profession and vocation.

Mr. Chase is known among a host of friends and travelers on the Southern line between Columbia, South Carolina, and Asheville, North Carolina, as Captain Chase or Capt. Bouey Chase. He was born in Washington, District of Columbia, April 4, 1857, a son of Gen. Jacob and Mary Elizabeth (Bowen) Chase and of Virginia and South Carolina ancestry.

In 1880 at the age of twenty-three he became a baggage man on the old Spartanburg and Columbia Railroad. This position he filled about two years being then promoted to conductor, with a run between Spartanburg and Alston. His service has been continuous on lines forming a part of the railway in South and North Carolina, and for a number of years past he has been passenger conductor of the Carolina special between Columbia and Asheville. Captain Chase is an ideal type of railway man, and despite his long continued, faithful service and allegiance to the discipline of railroading he has preserved his health and strength to a remarkable degree. A few months before entering on his railway career as above noted, Mr. Chase married Isabel Vernon Smith, a daughter of Rev. Angus Smith, a prominent Presbyterian minister, in his time, and Caroline Golding Smith. Mr. Chase's home is at Mountville, South Carolina, in Laurens County, the old ancestral home of Mrs. Chase. Six generations of Mrs. Chase's people have lived on this plantation. Around this old colonial home are many beautiful trees, some of which were planted more than a century ago. The house contains much quaint old furniture, silver and other articles, some dating back to colonial times. The old home has been extensively remodeled and now has all modern improvements. Captain and Mrs. Chase have seven living children and nine grandchildren. Captain Chase is a York Rite and thirty-second degree Scottish Rite Mason and Shriner.

JAMES BENEDICT EHRHARDT. Ehrhardt, one of the thriving commercial centers of Bamberg County, owes its founding to the enterprise and initiative of members of the Ehrhardt family. Conrad Ehrhardt was a native of Germany and came to South Carolina when a very young man. It is said that he and his wife when they married had only twenty-five cents in capital. Their industry and thrift enabled them to accumulate a large amount of property in what is now Bamberg County, and his business initiative as a merchant and miller gave the nucleus to the industrial character of the little City of Ehrhardt. At the time of his death Conrad Ehrhardt owned a large part of the present townsite, and besides other property each of his four children received 1200 acres of land.

One of his sons was Jacob Ehrhardt, who for a number of years was a member of the firm C. Ehrhardt & Sons, general merchants and owners and operators of gins, saw and grist mills, rice mills and other local industries. Jacob Ehrhardt died in 1915 at the age of fifty-seven. He married Catherine F. Cline, a native of South Carolina, daughter of Wallace A. Cline. Five of their children are still living: Frances, wife of F. H. Copeland; Edrie, wife of O. D. Richie, of Albemarle, North Carolina; James Benedict; Mamie, wife of J. P. Griffin, of Ehrhardt; and Jacob L.

James Benedict Ehrhardt, who is cashier of the Ehrhardt Banking Company, was born in the village named for his family August 10, 1891. He was educated in the public schools and graduated with the Bachelor of Science degree from Newberry College in 1912. He then assisted his father in the store and postoffice until January 1, 1915, when he was made postmaster of Ehrhardt. He resigned that office to become cashier of the Ehrhardt Banking Company on August 1, 1918.

October 8, 1913, he married Ruth Groseclose, daughter of Rev. D. B. Groseclose, a Lutheran minister. They have two children: Jacob Bittle and Margaret Frances.

WILLIAM HAMPTON MIXSON. In the commercial and industrial growth and development of Charleston William Hampton Mixson has had a prominent and active part, and for more than thirty years has been numbered among the business men of that city. He is the founder and president of the Southern Fruit Company, president of the W. H. Mixson Seed Company, president of the Atlantic Coast Distributors, vice president of the Leland Moore Paint & Oil Company, and is also a director in the Charleston Guarantee & Insurance Company, the Home Friendly and Life Insurance Corporation, the North Charleston Development Company, and the North Charleston Corporation, all of which have been potent factors in the modern development of the state's metropolis.

Mr. Mixson is a native of the Palmetto state, a descendant from a long line of sturdy ancestry whose names are prominently connected with the history of the state from the time of its formative period. The Mixson family is of English origin, and upon coming to South Carolina settled in the western section, where William Mixson, the grandfather of our present subject, was a well known and extensive planter. His son, Josiah Seth Mixson, born and reared in Barnwell County, became a civil engineer, and ran many of the boundary lines in the then new territory. He married Caroline Brabham, who was also a native of Barnwell County. She, too, came of a line of ancestry who had had part in the early history of the state, as the Brabhams, who were of Scotch-Irish descent, had settled in South Carolina prior to the Revolution.

William Hampton Mixson was born in Barnwell County, South Carolina, October 18, 1860, the eldest of a family of ten children born to Josiah Seth and Caroline (Brabham) Mixson. His boyhood days were spent in his native county, and amidst the surroundings and limited advantages common to the youth of that locality and period. The common schools of the neighborhood afforded the opportunity for a preliminary education, which was supplemented by the careful instruction of his father, a gentleman of exceptional attainments and training. He was an ambitious youth whose boyish fancy led beyond the narrow limitations of the plantation and the country village, and at the early age of seventeen years he went to Augusta, Georgia, and there he entered upon the career in the business world which has since claimed his attention and which has brought substantial recognition and reward.

In 1884 Mr. Mixson located in Charleston, where he continued his business experience, acting in a clerical capacity. In 1889, having decided to engage in business for himself, he organized and established the Southern Fruit Company, which under his continued guidance and management has grown to such magnitude as to merit recognition as one of the largest and best known concerns of its kind on the Atlantic Coast. The volume of the business transacted has shown a steady increase from the beginning, and extends into foreign as well as domestic marts. Incidental to the handling of fruits and produce an extensive seed business was developed, in 1910, and in 1917 was incorporated as a separate business under the name of the W. H. Mixson Seed Company. An experimental and developing farm, which is being made a model of its kind, is conducted by this company not far from Charleston.

In 1915 Mr. Mixson and his brother, J. S. Mixson, organized and established the Atlantic Coast Distributors, a company whose function is the distribution of the food products, more especially those of a perishable kind, and of which great quantities are grown in the territory tributary to Charleston. Mr. Mixson both by careful study of marketing conditions as well as by his early experience in the farming districts knew the difficulties with which the farmer had to contend in finding ready market for his produce at a time and place where it might be disposed of at a reasonable profit. He clearly foresaw the advantage to be had through the establishment of some central organization, or company, whereby the shipment of food supplies might be intelligently directed towards markets where the demand was greatest, and where favorable prices prevailed. Though primarily established to serve the producers of Charleston County, the business of the Atlantic Coast Distributors has assumed such proportions that it now serves a much larger section, and at this time does a business of approximately a million dollars annually, figures which in themselves bespeak the benefit it has brought to the community and to the state at large.

In addition to the many interests of a strictly commercial nature which have demanded his attention Mr. Mixson has not been neglectful of those duties of a semi-public character which go hand in hand with good citizenship, and has given freely of his time and means in the promotion of those movements which make for the public welfare and the

uplift of the community in which he has lived and prospered. He is a member of the Charleston Chamber of Commerce, serving that body as its president in 1916-17. For twenty years he has been a director of the Young Men's Christian Association, and for five years was its president. He is a vestryman and chairman of the finance committee of St. John's English Lutheran Church. In the Masonic fraternity he is a member of South Carolina Commandery No. 1, the oldest commandery of Knights Templars in America. He is also a member of Omar Temple, Nobles of the Mystic Shrine, and a Woodman of the World.

November 16, 1886, he married Hannah M. Quirollo, a native of Charleston, and their four children are: L. Harry Mixson, now vice president and manager of the W. H. Mixson Seed Company; Erma B.; William Hampton, Jr., secretary and general manager of the Southern Fruit Company; and Ashley St. Julian, secretary of the W. H. Mixson Seed Company.

Such, in brief, is the record of a busy life in which industry and unswerving determination of purpose have brought substantial reward. Enough has been said to show that the efforts have ever been directed along constructive and creative lines. With the vision to perceive opportunity, Mr. Mixson has possessed the courage to launch new ventures, and the business ability to bring them to successful fruition. What he has, he has created and developed. His success, therefore, has not been won at the price of another's downfall but has come as the direct result of his individual industry and efforts.

M. S. ELLIOTT. It is proper to judge of a man's life by the estimation in which he is held by his fellow citizens. They see him at his work, in his family circle, in church, hear his views on public questions, observe the operation of his code of morals, witness how he conducts himself in all the relations of society and are therefore competent to judge of his merits and demerits. After a long course of years of daily observations it would be out of the question for his neighbors not to know the truth, for, as has been said "actions speak louder than words." In its connection it is not too much to say that the subject of this sketch has always stood high in the estimation of his neighbors and acquaintances, for his conduct has been honorable in all the relations of life and his duty well performed, whether in public or private life. His family is one of the oldest in this section of the state, and its various members have honored the community by their activities and their adherence to right principles of living, so that the name is one that deserves perpetuation in the record of their community.

M. S. Elliott was born in Beaufort, South Carolina, on the 10th day of May, 1841, and is the son of Rev. Stephen and Ann (Habersham) Elliott. The father, who also was born in Beaufort, was a son of William Elliott, a native of the same place, as was his father, who also was named William. The latter was a brother of Stephen Elliott, who was a son of Stephen Elliott, a well known botanist and who was also high in the ministry of the Protestant Episcopal Church, being Bishop of Georgia.

He had a son R. M. B. Elliott, who also was a bishop of the Episcopal Church in Western Texas. The subject's mother was born in Beaufort, the daughter of John Habersham, a lifelong resident of that place. To Stephen and Ann Elliott were born the following children: Stephen, John H., Ralph E., William, Middleton S. and Ann B. Sometime after the death of his first wife, Rev. Stephen Elliott married again and two children were born to that union, Henry and Louis.

Rev. Stephen Elliott was a chaplain in the Confederate service during the Civil war for about two years, and took pride in the fact that five of his sons fought for Southern rights. Capt. Stephen Elliott, of the Beaufort Volunteer Artillery and promoted to major of artillery, was chosen by General Beauregard to command Fort Sumter, then being bombarded by the Union Fleet and batteries on Morris Island. He performed arduous and heroic service, was promoted to lieutenant colonel and given a regiment then in North Carolina. A short time later he was made brigadier general and put in command of Mathias Brigade, then in Virginia. Ralph E. Elliott joined the Palmetto Guards as a private and participated in every battle in Virginia. After Captain Cuthbert's death, he was elected captain and was killed in the battle of Coal Harbor, Virginia. In one of the battles in Virginia he was shot through the body, but recovered and returned to the front. His body lies in Hollywood Cemetery, Richmond. William Elliott enlisted at the commencement of the war in the Brooks Guard of Charleston as lieutenant. He was in every battle in Virginia. The Guards became an artillery company. Later on William was chosen as chief of staff by Gen. Stephen D. Lee with the rank of lieutenant colonel and was in the siege of Vicksburg and in the battles out West. Henry D. Elliott joined the Beaufort's Artillery when a mere boy, and was one of the youngest volunteers in the service. John Habersham Elliott, the second son, was an Episcopal clergyman, and his standing in the church was very high. His last duty was in Washington, District of Columbia, where he was rector of Ascension Church, which he was instrumental in building.

Middleton S. Elliott was reared under the parental roof and secured his elementary education in the public schools. He then became a student in The Citadel Military School in Charleston, where he was graduated in 1862. While at school he enlisted for service in behalf of the Confederacy and was among the cadets who were posted at Morris Island. Later he volunteered and became a member of the artillery company which his eldest brother commanded, it being in the artillery branch of the service. Though he enlisted as a private he was detailed to perform the duties of a second lieutenant as surveyor and engineer. His service was mainly in the section of country in which he lived, and in the spring of 1864 he received a second lieutenant's commission in the engineers. He then saw active service in Virginia, including the front at Petersburg, and was severely wounded at the crater. As a consequence he was compelled to remain at home for about forty days, after which he returned and served until the close of the struggle. Upon returning home he devoted himself to the re-establishment of his home in Beaufort, and thereafter gave his attention to the buying and selling of cotton, but at the present time is to a great extent retired from active business life. He has always taken a keen interest in public affairs and has occupied a leading position in his community. In 1886 he was appointed by President Grover Cleveland to the position of deputy collector of customs, in which he rendered faithful and effective service. While he has during the years of his active life carried on a special line of business in such a manner as to gain a comfortable competency for himself, he has belonged to that class of representative citizens who promote the public welfare while advancing individual success. Owing to his probity of character, his genuine worth, and his kindly and genial disposition, he has long occupied a position in his native city as one of the earnest men whose depth of character and strict adherence to principle has called forth the admiration of his contemporaries. He is a faithful member of the Episcopal Church.

In 1867 Middleton S. Elliott was married to Ann Stuart Rhett, the daughter of Hon. Edmund Rhett, and to them have been born six children, Phoebe Waight, Edmund, Middleton S., Jr., Stuart, Mary Williamson and John H. Two of the sons took an active part in the World war. Middleton S. served in the Medical Corps of the United States Army, with the rank of captain, and Stuart held the rank of lieutenant colonel in the Twentieth Corps of Engineers, being among the last United States soldiers to leave France.

ARCHIBALD E. BAKER, M. D., F. A. C. S. In the professional, industrial and civic development of every commonwealth certain men stand forth among their fellows as the result of individual effort and unusual achievement. Such men rise into prominence and become objects of high consideration in public estimation only through the development of the best attributes of manhood, for the accidents of birth and fortune, and the adventitious aid of chance and circumstance can do little to give them enduring place in history. Such characters, presenting in combined view the harmonious blending of material success with completeness of moral attribute, stand forth as proof of human progress, and the illustration of human dignity and worth.

In no other field of human endeavor can be found greater opportunity, nor has greater success been achieved, than in the science of surgery and materia medica. The patient physician, the skilled and able surgeon who, fighting against heavy odds, wins back a single human life, or restores again to health and strength a wrecked and shattered body is more justly entitled to the victor's laurel wreath than all whose fame and glory have been won amidst carnage and destruction too often concealed beneath "the pomp and panoply of war."

Archibald E. Baker, an honored member of the medical fraternity of Charleston for thirty years, has won especial distinction as a surgeon, and by election is a Fellow of the American College of Surgeons, a membership which in itself is a tribute to his professional ability and standing.

He is the founder and surgeon in charge of the Baker Sanatorium overlooking Colonial Lake in the City of Charleston. Erected in 1912 at a cost of more than $130,000, which figures indicate its completeness in both capacity and equipment, it stands as a thoroughly modern hospital, affording special facilities for surgical work, and was designed and constructed with the object of supplying the very best and most modern appliances for the successful treatment of surgical and gynecological cases, and it is doubtless true that in completeness of detail and equipment it is unexcelled by any other institution in the country. Although it was primarily designed to care for Doctor Baker's personal practice, its advantages and use have ever been at the disposal of his professional brethren, many of whom have availed themselves of the opportunity thus afforded, and thus the institution has become a powerful factor for the welfare of the public by providing the advanced facilities for the treatment of suffering humanity, otherwise denied them.

Doctor Baker was born at Maxton, North Carolina, August 29, 1862. He is descended on both the paternal and maternal sides from a long line of Scotch ancestry whose rugged and sterling integrity and industry have been typified in his entire career. His father, Angus Baker, was a successful planter in Robinson County, North Carolina, where his grandfather, Archibald Baker, was also born, while his mother, Harriet McEachern, was also born in Robinson County and was a direct descendant from the distinguished family of that name.

Doctor Baker graduated from Davidson College in 1883, and soon thereafter began the study of medicine at the Medical College of South Carolina, graduating in 1889, following this with a post graduate course at the New York Polyclinic in 1892.

In 1889 he had located in Charleston and for eighteen years was engaged in general practice, for fourteen years of which time he was associated with the late eminent surgeon, Dr. R. B. Rhett.

His rapidly increasing practice, together with the signal success he had achieved in surgery, made it necessary for him to resign his general practice in 1907, since which time he has devoted his attention exclusively to the treatment of surgical cases, and the still further increasing demands upon his services made necessary the construction of his sanatorium in 1912.

In addition to his personal practice Doctor Baker has continued to be a close and careful student, keeping fully abreast of the modern strides of progress made in the profession, and has upon many occasions associated himself with many of the eminent surgeons of this country in consultation and otherwise, thus keeping in close touch with the work of the fraternity. He is a former president of the Charleston Medical Society; former president of the Tri-State Medical Association, which includes the states of Virginia and the Carolinas, and is chairman of the board of counsellors of the Medical Association of South Carolina. He is clinical professor of gynecology and abdominal surgery in the Medical College of South Carolina, also a member of the staff of visiting surgeons at Roper Hospital, while in fraternal circles he is a member of the time honored Masonic order.

In 1894 Doctor Baker married Adele Jennings,

daughter of Dr. Julius Jennings, of Bennettsville, South Carolina, and to this union have been born five children. Their only daughter, Beatrice, died at the age of one and one-half years. Of the four sons, Archibald E., Jr., and Barnwell Rhett, are both students at the Medical College of South Carolina; Angus S. and Robert are still at home.

M. T. LAFFITTE is a prosperous young business man at Estill in Hampton County, and enjoys the well deserved honor of two terms as mayor of the city.

Mr. Laffitte was born in Sylvania, Georgia, about thirty-five years ago, a son of Charles A. and Martha (Boston) Laffitte. He comes of an old South Carolina family. His grandfather, Dr. David Montague Laffitte was a native of France, and when a young man came to South Carolina and settled in that portion of old Barnwell District now Hampton County. He practiced medicine for many years and enjoyed those quiet distinctions which are associated with a man of service and character, in a community. Charles A. Laffitte was born in Hampton County, and in later years moved to Georgia.

M. T. Laffitte spent his early life at Sylvania, and finished his education at Mercer University in his native state. He entered business as soon as he came out of college, and in 1904 located at Estill. He has been a factor in the growth and expansion of that rich and growing town and surrounding country. For several years he has had a prosperous automobile and automobile accessory business. He is a Mason, an Elk and a Knight of Pythias.

He was elected mayor of Estill in 1918 and re-elected in 1919. He has given a thoroughly business-like administration, and he is one of the group of citizens who are making for better and larger things for this town. Mr. Laffitte married in November, 1919, Miss Elizabeth Lucius, of Lee County, South Carolina.

COL. OLIVER JAMES BOND. No one institution in South Carolina, not even excepting the State University, has furnished more of the influences and discipline for the training of young men than the famous Citadel, which popularly and no doubt justly has been called the "West Point of the South." To that great body of former students who have enjoyed its advantages during the past third of a century, the name Col. Oliver James Bond has the significance of an old friend, adviser and counsellor.

Colonel Bond, who since 1908 has been president of The Citadel, and has been continuously a member of its teaching force since he graduated in 1886, was born at Marion, South Carolina, May 11, 1865, son of Dr. Oliver J. and Sarah Ann (Wayne) Bond, both of Marion, where his father for many years was a dental practitioner. His grandfather, Henry J. Bond, came when a boy to South Carolina from Maryland, and in 1827 married Mary Denny, locating in Marion, where they reared a family of eight children. Doctor Bond, born in 1831, was the oldest of this family. Through his mother Colonel Bond's ancestry goes back to some of the earliest Huguenots of the Carolinas. while one of his great-grandfathers was a cousin of the celebrated Gen. Anthony Wayne. Sarah A. Wayne was the daughter of Francis Asbury Wayne and Elizabeth Legette, both of Marion. Her grandfather, William Wayne, came from Pennsylvania to Charleston, where he married in 1777 Esther Trezevant, a great-granddaughter of Daniel Trezevant. Daniel Trezevant was one of the Huguenots who immigrated from France to the Carolinas after the revocation of the Edict of Nantes in 1685 and was founder of the extensive family of that name in America. Esther Trezevant, his great-granddaughter, was married May 8, 1777, to Rev. William Wayne, who was born in 1734 and died in 1818. Rev. William Wayne was a son of Gabriel Wayne, and a grandson of Capt. Anthony Wayne, who was born in 1666. Capt. Anthony Wayne was a native of Yorkshire, England, and was the grandfather of Gen. Anthony Wayne, the hero of the Revolution. Colonel Bond's parents were married in 1851, and his father died in 1891 and his mother in 1898.

Colonel Bond, seventh child of his parents, had the advantages of excellent schooling under Prof. William H. Witherow, an educator of great ability, first at Marion and from 1877 to 1881 at Chester. In October, 1882, he matriculated as one of the two beneficiary cadets from Chester County at The Citadel, then just reopened after a period of seventeen years' occupation by United States troops. He was graduated with the class of 1886, and was elected assistant professor of mathematics for the following session. Later he served as professor of mechanical drawing and astronomy, and in 1908 succeeded Col. Asbury Coward as head of the college.

During the years 1891-95, while teaching on the faculty of The Citadel, he pursued a non-resident course in mathematics with the Illinois Wesleyan University, where he went for final examinations in 1895 and was awarded the degree Ph. D. after submitting a mathematical thesis. The honorary degree LL. D. was conferred upon him in 1912 by the University of South Carolina. Doctor Bond has always been interested in mathematics and astronomy, and was teacher of those subjects at several of the summer schools at Winthrop College. He is author of a novelette "Amzi" published in 1904, based on a series of astronomical observations.

While at college he was affiliated with the Sigma Alpha Epsilon fraternity, in later years has become prominent in the Knights of Pythias, being grand chancellor of the state in 1919-20. For many years he has been a vestryman of St. Paul's Episcopal Church at Redcliffeboro; is vice president of the St. Andrew's (Scotch) Society of Charleston; is a member of the Charleston Chamber of Commerce, with which he has served as chairman of the educational committee and of the military and naval committees; and is a member of the Charleston Country Club, of which he was president in 1917-19. Colonel Bond for a number of years has been a devotee of the ancient game of golf. He was one of the organizers of the Carolina Golf Association, composed of the clubs of North and South Carolina, and was honored with the office of president of the association in 1912-14. His studio is adorned with several trophies won in contest on the links. Another diversion that indicates some of the mathematical qualities of his mind is the game of chess. He was one of the organizers of the Charleston Chess Club, now defunct.

Colonel Bond married Mary Fishburne Roach, daughter of Dr. William Fishburne Roach, of Charleston. Their only son, Capt. Oliver J. Bond III, is a young South Carolinian who was in service with the American armies in France nearly two years. He was born July 5, 1890, and spent three years, 1905-08, as a student of the College of Charleston. He was an aide in the United States Coast and Geodetic Survey five years. In 1916 he entered the field artillery branch of the United States Army, and was in service with the First and Second American armies from November, 1917, until June, 1919, in France. January 16, 1912, Captain Bond married Nellie Hall Sinkler, of Charleston, and has a daughter, Mary Ellen, born in 1916.

HARRY DESAUSURE CALHOUN. In all that constitutes true manhood and good citizenship Harry D. Calhoun, president of the Home Bank of Barnwell and one of the best known and most substantial of Barnwell County's citizens, is a notable example and none stands higher than he in the esteem and confidence of the community honored by his citizenship. He is a man of good judgment and pronounced views and, keeping himself well informed upon current events and taking a lively interest in public affairs of his community, he has won to a marked degree the reputation of a man of progressive and up-to-date ideas, standing ever ready to support with his influence and means all measures for the material and moral welfare of his community.

Harry D. Calhoun was born in Barnwell County, South Carolina, on October 31, 1869, and is the fourth in order of birth of the seven children born to his parents, William B. and Annie Walton (Owens) Calhoun. The family is of Irish origin on the paternal side, being descended from the Ezekiel Calhoun branch of the family. The American progenitors of the subject are, first, James Y., a native of Barnwell County, South Carolina, then his son of the same name and nativity, who was the father of William B., father of the subject of this sketch. The subject's mother was a daughter of James and Elizabeth (Overstreet) Owens, natives of Barnwell County, the former being the son of Col. William A. Owens. Elizabeth Overstreet was the daughter of James Overstreet, who represented the Barnwell District in Congress from 1814 to 1822. He drove all the way from his home to Washington, D. C., in a "gig," a typical conveyance of that period, and while on one of these trips his death occurred at China Grove, North Carolina, where he was buried, and where Congress had a monument erected to his memory. The Overstreet family was of English origin, and Elizabeth Overstreet was a direct descendant, through the maternal line, from the Randolph family so prominent in the early life of our nation. Mr. Calhoun's father, William B. was a soldier in the Confederate army, Colcock's regiment and served throughout the war. He was one of the men sent back to direct and look after the home community and to see that they had the means of livelihood and in other words, he was in charge of the settlement and its welfare.

Harry D. Calhoun is indebted to the common schools of his native community for his educational training, which he has liberally supplemented through the subsequent years by close reading and keen observation of men and events, being today considered a man of wide and accurate general information. When practically only a boy he engaged in business, and for fifteen years he was on the road as a traveling salesman. He was successful in his affairs and wisely economical of his resources, so that in 1910 he quit his former vocation and, returning to Barnwell, organized the Home Bank, of which he has been the president since its organization. This has been a prosperous institution, being numbered among the solid and influential banks of this community. It has a capital and surplus of $45,000. Mr. Calhoun is also financially interested in the Home Furniture Company, one of the leading enterprises of the town. He also assisted in the building of the splendid school building at Barnwell, of which he is one of the trustees.

In 1901 Mr. Calhoun was married to Eva Duncan, the daughter of James and Anna (Miller) Duncan, of Charleston, South Carolina, and of Scotch descent. To them have been born two sons, Duncan and James Overstreet, seventeen and eleven years of age. The family are members of the Episcopal Church, while fraternally Mr. Calhoun is a member of the Ancient Free and Accepted Masons, the Benevolent and Protective Order of Elks, the Modern Woodmen of America, the Knights of Pythias, the Farmers Union, the United Commercial Travelers and the Travelers Protective associations. In all the relations of life—family, church, state and society—he has displayed that consistent gentlemanly spirit, that innate refinement and unswerving integrity that have gained for him the sincere respect of all who know him.

W. I. JOHNS. Nowhere in the state has the staple crops, high class livestock and the general business of planting reached a higher degree of perfection than in that peculiarly rich and fertile section lying along the Savannah River and included in the newly organized county of Allendale. That the old time prestige of this agricultural district has not been lost is due to the peculiar genius of a group of men who in the face of many obstacles have been able to adapt their business to changed circumstances and have maintained the efficiency of centralized operation and administration of great holdings.

One of the largest producers of cotton in the entire state, as well as one of the ablest and most influential business men, is W. I. Johns, whose home is at Allendale, but whose interests as a planter are widely extended over the southern counties.

The Johns family is of Scotch-Irish origin and have lived in Bamberg County for several generations. Mr. Johns was born at Ehrhardt in Bamberg County in 1869, a son of Alfred and Martha (Brown) Johns. His great-great-grandfather was a soldier in the Revolutionary struggle. Alfred Johns was all through the War between the States, and gave additional service in the reconstruction

period. He had three brothers in the war: William, a lieutenant who was killed at Gettysburg; Perry, who was killed in the second battle of Manassas; and Jasper, who was wounded at Gettysburg. Martha Brown Johns was the daughter of a Confederate soldier, and her family was of Revolutionary stock and long established in South Carolina.

W. I. Johns grew up on his father's plantation near Bamberg, attended the schools of that town, and in 1893, more than a quarter of a century ago, established his home at Beldoc, near Allendale, in what was then Barnwell County. In 1917 he moved his home to Allendale, though his chief interests are still centered at Beldoc. He owns extensive plantations there and around Allendale, and the claim made for his being one of the largest individual cotton planters in the state is borne out by the ownership and operation of between 6,000 and 7,000 acres under cultivation. He is not only a planter but operates gins, maintains commissary stores, and has various other enterprises so as to make his plantation a business on an independent footing.

In introducing livestock into his planting scheme he was content only with the very best. He has the largest herd of Hereford cattle in the state, and also raises great numbers of Duroc and Poland China hogs. His stock is all registered, and he is able to take pride not only in the registry but in the profitable features of handling stock of this quality.

Mr. Johns is a director of the Citizens Bank of Allendale and one of its organizers. He is a director in the Charleston and Western Carolina Railroad. As one of the new county's largest property owners he naturally took a leading part in the organization of the new county of Allendale in January, 1919. He was named by Governor Cooper as member of the Board of County Commissioners and has been its chairman ever since. He is a member of the executive committee of the South Carolina Agricultural and Mechanical Society.

In 1918 he was appointed by Governor Manning a trustee of the John Del La How Orphanage in what is now McCormick County. This orphanage, with its property comprising 2,000 acres of land, was taken over by the state two years ago, and the trustees are now engaged in the construction of a home that will cost $150,000. When the present plans are wholly completed the cost of the main building will be about $400,000.

During the war he was a member of the South Carolina State Council of Defense, but his most active work was as chairman of the Barnwell County Selective Draft Board. Probably no work required of civilians during the war was of more exacting nature than the duties imposed on the local draft boards. Mr. Johns gave practically all his time for a period of eighteen months to those official duties, and properly shares in the credit and commendations freely bestowed upon the work of the draft board organization.

Mr. Johns was also county chairman of the State Memorial for the World war veterans. Though this was the baby county of the state it was the first to go over the top, its quota for that purpose being exceeded at one meeting in which the speakers were Governor Manning, Mrs. F. S. Munsell and Mr. Johns. The influence of the action taken in the new county helped to make the State Memorial a success. Mr. Johns is a Baptist and was organizer for the Allendale County's quota in the campaign for $75,000,000 for the Southern Baptist Church in November, 1919.

He first married Miss Eveline Wilson, daughter of Oda Wilson, one of the largest farmers in Barnwell County and a former member of the South Carolina Legislature. He has four children by this union, Gladys, wife of Hon. Frank W. Shealy, of Lexington, chairman of the State Board of Railroad Commissioners; Miss Eunice, a graduate of Brenau College in Georgia; Wilson, a graduate of the University of South Carolina; and Jasper, now a student at Furman University. May 22, 1911, Mr. Johns married Miss Montez McKee Bramlett, a daughter of John Bramlett, a member of the Bramlett family of Greenville County of long residence in the state and of Revolutionary stock. Mr. and Mrs. Johns have two children: Martha and Virginia.

Mrs. Johns was county chairman of the Victory Loan drive and various other war drives, each and every one of which produced more than the quota assigned. Mrs. Johns spent a large part of her time in war work. Allendale was the youngest county in the state, and Mrs. Johns received a number of telegrams congratulating her and the county organization for the big things achieved.

JOHN LEWIS COPELAND, M. D. While he has been burdened with the cares and responsibilities of a large private practice ever since locating in Bamberg County, Doctor Copeland has also played a prominent part in the founding and subsequent growth and development of his home community of Ehrhardt.

He was born in what is now Bamberg County March 14, 1871, son of Josiah Isaac Copeland, a native of the same county, and of remote German ancestry. Grandfather Isaac Copeland was born in Barnwell County and became a successful planter and large slave owner. He lived to be about eighty years of age. Josiah Isaac Copeland served four years as a Confederate soldier, but was never wounded. He is still living, in his seventy-fifth year, and enjoys good health. He married Elizabeth Durr, daughter of John Durr, and a native of Colleton County. Doctor Copeland was the second in a family of eight children, four sons and four daughters, seven of whom are still living.

Doctor Copeland was educated in the country schools, in an advanced school in Orangeburg, attended Newberry College, and in 1893 graduated from the Atlanta Medical College. He spent one year in the Savannah Hospital after graduating, and in the fall of 1903 was appointed assistant surgeon in the United States Marine Hospital service. He also took advanced work in the New York Post-Graduate School in 1904 and 1915. Doctor Copeland came to Ehrhardt in 1894 and was one of the men who laid out the town and from the first has taken a deep interest in its civic and business enterprise. In 1905 he organized the Ehrhardt Banking Company, and has been president of that institution from the beginning. He also organized and helped install the local telephone system. He is now a partner in the local drug firm of Copeland and Farrell. Doctor Copeland is a member of the Bamberg County Medical Society, the District Association, including the five counties of Bamberg, Barnwell, Orangeburg, Hampton and Calhoun, the State Medical Association, the Tri-State Association of North and South Carolina and Virginia and the Southern Medical Association. He has served on the town council many years and the school board, and has directed his influence along lines that would mean most to the prosperity and advancement of his community.

June 10, 1896, Doctor Copeland married Mamie Lide, daughter of Rev. T. P. Lide. She died two years after their marriage. For his present wife he married Lottie Farrell, daughter of R. L. and Irene Farrell. Doctor and Mrs. Copeland have two sons and one daughter, Chester F., Claud F. and Mildred F.

COL. WILLIAM R. DARLINGTON. Only his older and more intimate friends are aware of the fact that Colonel Darlington served four years as a Confederate soldier. His vigor in business, his erect and active figure, would never betray the years which the service in that war indicates.

Colonel Darlington has been in many ways one of the most influential citizens in that section of South Carolina included in the present county of Allendale. He was the first chairman of the Board of Commissioners which had charge of the work of bringing about the new county organization, consummated in January, 1919.

Colonel Darlington was born on the Darlington plantation near Dunbarton in Barnwell County in 1842, a son of Thomas and Emily (Boyd) Darlington. His grandfather was Job Darlington and his great-grandfather, John Darlington. The latter was a descendant of the Darlingtons of England, whose American progenitors settled at West Chester, Pennsylvania, in the early part of the eighteenth century. It is presumed that the citizen for whom Darlington County in South Carolina was named, according to Ramsey's History of South Carolina, was a kinsman of this family, although authentic records establishing that connection are not available.

The John Darlington above mentioned was married at Wilmington, Delaware, to Eleanor Armstrong, his second wife. The first official record of his settlement in South Carolina is a transfer of a grant of land to him in Barnwell District in 1795. Presumably he came to the state a year or so previous to that date. The Darlingtons are a strong, vigorous race of people both intellectually and physically.

For a long number of years the title of Colonel has been bestowed as a matter of southern courtesy by his friends upon William R. Darlington on account of his prominent connection with the secession war and the militia organization of the reconstruction and succeeding periods. He acquired his early education at the Barnwell Male Academy, and at the beginning of the war volunteered his services and was mustered into the First South Carolina Infantry at Charleston. He was in Charleston at the time of the attack on Fort Sumter. Later he was with the Army of the West, taking part in the fight at Belmont, Missouri, and Corinth, Mississippi, and other early engagements in the upper Mississippi Valley. In 1862 he was returned to South Carolina, where he became a member of the Second South Carolina Artillery, under Colonel Lamar, and was in the combined artillery and infantry service during the remainder of the war. He was in Battery Reid, which was cited for conspicuous bravery at the battle of Secessionville. As part of General Hardee's corps he was in the engagement at Cheraw, South Carolina, Averysboro and Bentonville, North Carolina, and soon afterward was surrendered with General Johnston's army at Greensboro. For three years, up to the close of hostilities, he was orderly or top sergeant.

Since the war for a period of more than half a century Colonel Darlington has followed the ancestral occupation of planting. He is the owner of valuable city and plantation properties at Allendale, and has been a citizen who could be depended upon for active support of every effort to build up and expand that thriving commercial center.

In the late '60s Colonel Darlington married Miss Lucy Allen, of Barnwell County, member of the well known family for whom Allendale was named. At her death she left four children: T. D.; Miss Laura Stoney Darlington; Miss Lucy O. H. Darlington; and William R., Jr.

T. D. Darlington, who also bears the title of Colonel through his service with that rank on the staff of Governor D. C. Heyward, is manager of the Coe, Mortimer & Ashapoo companies at Charleston, dealers in fertilizers, and also as manager of the A. A. Company at Savannah, Georgia. He married Lyde, daughter of Dr. William Irby, of Laurens, South Carolina, and they have two daughters, Lucy Vance and Claudia.

William R. Darlington, Jr., who is the third member of the family to bear the title of colonel, a title he acquired as member of Governor Richard I. Manning's staff, is a resident of Allendale, engaged in the fertilizer business and as a farmer and stock raiser. He married Miss Mary Hanson Johnston, a daughter of George and Martha E. Johnston, of Greensboro, Alabama. Their two daughters are Martha Elizabeth and Eleanor Allen Darlington.

The death of Miss Laura Stoney Darlington in December, 1917, was not only a grievous blow to her father but terminated influences and activities that had made her a greatly beloved character in more than one sphere. She was cultured in the finest sense and had versatile attainments and gifts. She was an artist in oil painting, china painting and tapestry, and a talented musician. She later took up nursing at the Memorial Hospital at Richmond, Virginia, graduating there, and accepted the position of superintendent of the Johnston-Willis Sanatorium for eight years. Here her gifts had a splendid scope of usefulness and service. She possessed exceptional business ability and manager the hospital and her business affairs with great skill and foresight. She possessed that balance of qualities and

charms which made her a lovable character wherever she was known.

Colonel Darlington married for his present wife Elizabeth Porcher Stoney, daughter of Peter Gaillard Stoney, of Charleston. Through her mother she is a member of the noted Porcher family of Charleston, a name frequently mentioned in this publication. Her father's house where she was born, on the Cooper River at Charleston, was originally the home of Landgrave Thomas Smith, Governor of South Carolina under the Lords Proprietor and was the first brick house built in South Carolina outside of the City of Charleston.

WILES T. RILEY, SR. The interests controlled and managed by Wiles T. Riley, Sr., constitute some of the most productive agricultural operations around Allendale, where he has long been a moving and influential figure.

Mr. Riley, who on both sides is of Irish descent, and descended from families long resident in South Carolina and of Revolutionary stock, was born in Hampton County April 1, 1857. His father, Capt. James W. Riley, was born in Barnwell County and died in 1887. His life was spent on a plantation and for several years he was a magistrate. He formed a company to go in to the Confederate army, but an attack of rheumatism invalided him and kept him out of active warfare. He married Emily Caroline Murray, a native of Barnwell County.

Mr. W. T. Riley, Sr., in spite of the impoverished conditions of South Carolina during and following the war obtained a substantial education, partly in public schools and partly in the North Carolina Military Institute at Charlotte. For a time he was a telegraph operator for the old Port Royal Railroad, but after his marriage he settled down to farming in Hampton and Barnwell counties and has directed his affairs with such good judgment and capability as to steadily prosper in spite of the fluctuations and vicissitudes of agriculture. He owns and controls between 1,800 and 3,000 acres, operated by tenants, the chief crops being cotton, corn and peanuts.

Mr. Riley is an active member and trustee of the Methodist Church. In 1884, in Barnwell County, he married Miss Julia Ellis Williams, a native of Barnwell County, and daughter of J. Angus and C. A. Williams. Reference to this well known old family of South Carolina is made elsewhere. Mrs. Riley died in December, 1902, the mother of four children: Wilmot T. Riley, president of the First National Bank and mayor of Allendale, as noted elsewhere; James McIver Riley, clerk of the Court of Allendale County; Emily Rebecca, wife of W. Robert Kennedy, a merchant of Williston, South Carolina; and Angus Wilson Riley, a cadet in The Citadel with the class of 1920.

THOMAS FRANKLIN HOGG, M. D. In the daily laborious struggle for an honorable competence and a solid career on the part of a business or professional man there is little to attract the casual reader in search of a sensational chapter; but to a mind thoroughly awake to the reality and meaning of human existence there are noble and imperishable lessons in the career of an individual, who without other means that a clear head, strong arm and true heart, directed and controlled by correct principles and unerring judgment, finally wins, not only pecuniary independence but, what is far greater and higher, the deserved respect and confidence of those with whom his active years have been spent.

Thomas Franklin Hogg was born in Barnwell (now Allendale) County, South Carolina, July 27, 1880, the oldest of the six children of John T. and Agnes (Williams) Hogg, and is of Revolutionary stock and Scotch-Irish descent. His parents were both born and reared in Barnwell County. His maternal grandfather was James Wilson Williams, a native of South Carolina and of English descent. The paternal grandfather was Thomas Franklin Hogg, a native of South Carolina. John T. Hogg at the age of fifteen entered the Confederate army in Captain Kirkland's Company, and despite his youth proved his quality and valor as a good soldier, remaining until the end of the war. He had a brother, Richard R. Hogg, a lieutenant, who died from pneumonia resulting from exposure in Virginia before the close of the war. After the war John T. Hogg spent the active years of his life as a farmer, and died when about seventy years of age.

His son, Doctor Hogg, acquired an elementary education in the common schools of his native county, spent two and a half years in Clemson Agricultural College, and by that time having definitely determined his choice among the professions and vocations he entered the medical college of the State of South Carolina at Charleston, where he was graduated in April, 1903, with the degree Doctor of Medicine. At that time he located at his present residence, about six and a half miles north of Allendale, and by nature and training being well equipped success attended his labors from the beginning, and he was soon in command of a large and lucrative practice among the best people of the community. This practice he continued for about ten years, when he relinquished his professional work and has since devoted himself to the operation of his farms. He owns and controls approximately 685 acres of fine farming land, giving employment to about sixty persons, and raises all the crops common to this locality, cotton and corn being his principal crops. He is systematic and methodical in his work and has acheevd more than ordinary success as a farmer, due to the exercise of the same elements that insured his professional success, namely, painstaking care, attention to detail, and concentration on whatever he has in hand to do.

In 1905 Doctor Hogg married Mollie F. Creech, daughter of Henry C. Creech. While in the active medical work he was a member of the Barnwell Medical Association and the South Carolina State Medical Society. In Masonry he is a member of the Lodge, Royal Arch Chapter, Knight Templar Commandery and Shrine. Doctor Hogg has been the architect of his own fortunes, and upon his entire career there rests no blemish, for he has been true to the highest ideals in professional, business, civic and social life. He is a man of great energy and rare judgment, which he has carried into all affairs in which he has been interested. In all of life's relations he has been true and faithful to duty and to his obligations to the community, and he has thereby won the unqualified confidence and respect of his fellow men.

AUGUST KOHN. After having passed the half-century milestone of a life of fruitful achievement in journalism, business and various specialized generosities, August Kohn, of Columbia, South Carolina, is today one of the vigorous, resourceful leaders of the state without asking political preferment for himself, although he has been one of the men of South Carolina whose sage advice has been the directing cause of other men being lifted to high office.

He is of pure Jewish ancestry. His paternal ancestors were from Bavaria, Germany, and his maternal of Austria. From youth he possessed all the virile virtues and commercial characteristics of his race, the harsher tendencies of the mart being softened by a liberal education and the fibre of his manhood transmuted in the assay of the sufferings of others which he so often saw.

The father of Mr. Kohn, Theodore Kohn, came to the United States when a mere lad from Munich, Germany, and the mother, Rosa Wald Kohn, from Zeben, Austria. They settled in Orangeburg, South Carolina, and to them were born three surviving sons, August, Sol and David, who are leading citizens of this state. Theodore Kohn engaged in commercial pursuits in his adopted city, and there was a marked success as a citizen and a business man.

August Kohn, born at Orangeburg, South Carolina, February 25, 1868, was prepared for college under H. G. Sheridan, of his home city, matriculating at the South Carolina College (now University of South Carolina) in September, 1885. On his graduation he received the degree of Bachelor of Arts, cum laude, and sometime afterward entered the service of The News and Courier, of Charleston, South Carolina. His newspaper work was as the representative of the Columbia bureau at the University. At the suggestion of N. G. Gonzales he was offered a place on the local reportorial staff of The News and Courier, and was told that if he "made good" he would get a raise in salary over the $9.00 per week at which he began his newspaper work. He remained for two years as a versatile and accurate member of the local staff. On February 14, 1892, he was promoted to the management of the Columbia Bureau to succeed Matthew F. Tighe, who replaced the late N. G. Gonzales when the latter became the first editor of The State, then just established. Mr. Kohn retained his Columbia newspaper connection until 1906, when he retired from active journalistic work to devote his attention more thoroughly to his accumulating and varying business interests, but for many years thereafter was very active in his reportorial work. In more recent years he had confined his newspaper work to special articles and reporting the sessions of the General Assembly, which task he has undertaken without interruption since 1892—twenty-eight years.

At the Jewish Synagogue, Charleston, South Carolina, March 1, 1894, Mr. Kohn was married to Miss Irene Goldsmith, of that city, who has been described as one of the most lovable, cultured and highly-patriotic women who ever became a citizen of Columbia. Mrs. Kohn before her sudden death at Sullivan's Island, July 16, 1913, was identified with many of the women's organizations of the state and was largely instrumental in making the Daughters of the Confederacy, of which she was state president for several years, a vital force among the women of South Carolina. Those most intimately acquainted with the family say that she was the inspiration of her husband and was one of the moving causes for his pronounced success. To them were born three children, Helen Kohn, who on April 28, 1920, became the bride of Julian H. Hennig, of Columbia, who was overseas in the World war as a commissioned officer; August Kohn, Jr., who graduated with the degree of Bachelor of Arts at the University of South Carolina, class of 1920, and in the fall of the same year, matriculated at Harvard University, taking the law course there; at the time of the armistice in the World war he was at Camp Zachary Taylor in training for a commission, having been selected for a commission by the R. O. T. C., of the University of South Carolina; and Theodore Kohn, his youngest son, who is an undergraduate student and hopes to be a physician.

Since his graduation Mr. Kohn has combined his journalistic skill and penchant for facts with his business acumen—an unusual thing for a newspaper worker—to such effect that he is reputed to be one of the most substantial men of Columbia, South Carolina. Along business lines he is an executive or director in many of the leading enterprises of that city, and has always been an optimist as to the future of South Carolina and Columbia. He is the head of August Kohn & Company, dealing in real estate, bonds and stocks. He is vice-president of the City Development Company, the owners and developers of "Wales Gardens," Columbia's most fashionable residence section; member of the finance committee, National Loan and Exchange Bank; vice president of the Acme Building and Loan Association; vice president of the South Carolina Insurance Company; director of the Columbia Savings Bank and Trust Company; director of the Homestead Building and Loan Association; director of the Standard Warehouse Company; treasurer of Liberty Realty Company and of the Mutual Holding Company; and director of the United Realty Company of Charleston.

Mr. Kohn's chief reputation rests on his newspaper work in South Carolina. He was a painstaking, accurate and accomplished delineator of facts. He did not deal in hypothetical theories, unless his deductions were imbedded in and bedrocked on fact. As manager of the Columbia Bureau of the News and Courier his reputation was secure. He "handled" some of the largest and most gripping "stories" written for a newspaper in a decade; and, in the parlance of the press, he had no "comeback" on his facts; his signature was sufficient guarantee of the accuracy of the "story."

When Mr. Kohn was detailed to take charge of the Columbia Bureau of the News and Courier, South Carolina was in the midst of the tense political feeling incident to Governor Tillman's regime and the Dispensary. The then young reporter gained a reputation for his accurate recording of

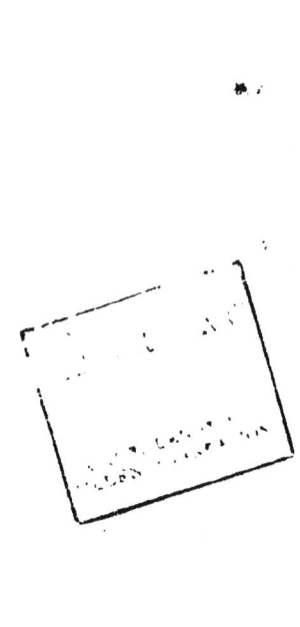

facts, and throughout his more than twenty years of active newspaper work the overshadowing character of his daily record was that whatever was written over his signature "A. K.," was absolutely dependable as to facts. Many wagers are said to have been determined by an agreement to settle the issue on what "Kohn reported." In those days the news service was somewhat different, the Associated Press was not as full and the general news not so competently handled as now, and it was not uncommon for the initials "A. K.," to be subscribed to an entire page of seven columns of news, representing a single day's work.

Mr. Kohn's delight has always been along political and industrial lines, and in these he made a reputation, but Maj. J. C. Hemphill, managing editor of the News and Courier during most of the years of Mr. Kohn's active charge of the bureau, gave him carte blanche as to his work. He was assigned to and reported five state-wide campaigns—notably those of Tillman and Sheppard, Tillman and Butler, and McLaurin and Irby. Whenever an important trial or considerable industrial enterprise was launched, or a lynching was rumored, or a railroad was opened, there August Kohn was sent to get the story. Sometimes he would ask for instructions and invariably Major Hemphill would reply "use your own judgment."

In 1893, before his marriage, Mr. Kohn was visiting his intended wife when the great coastal storm occurred. He went to Beaufort and sent from there the first report of the dreadful disaster. He remained there for a month following the work of Clara Barton and others. So it was that while located in Columbia his newspaper work was really state-wide. His collegiate career demonstrated that Mr. Kohn was destined for service in the press, although his ambition was to become a lawyer; as an undergraduate he was the first managing editor of "The Carolinian," the collegiate publication, and during the year of his graduation he became its editor-in-chief. He was prominent in all collegiate literary activities, and as a member of the Clariosophic Society won the debater's medal.

It was his marked ability to get facts, some call it "a nose for news," that caused the late Mr. N. G. Gonzales, as narrated in the foregoing, to send for Mr. Kohn when he later became ill with typhoid fever to temporarily take charge of the Columbia Bureau of the News and Courier, at that time the most powerful moulder of public opinion in South Carolina. Mr. Kohn was successor to such journalistic figures and scholars as Carlyle McKinley, J. Calvin Hemphill, Matthew F. Tighe and N. G. Gonzales.

He "covered" such stirring South Carolina political campaigns as the famous Tillman-Butler race for the United States Senate in the '90s, and the Tillman-Sheppard campaign, reported the details of the "Darlington Rebellion" in April, 1894, when the State of South Carolina was almost in arms because of the tragic upheaval due to the clash between the constabulary and local citizens in the enforcement of the Tillman Dispensary Law; the trial of James H. Tillman; the Dispensary investigations, and single-handed "handled" the South Carolina Constitutional Convention of 1895, giving detailed reports each day which often covered two solid pages of the News and Courier. For this latter noteworthy achievement he was given the thanks of the convention and a substantial appreciation by his paper.

Since 1892 Mr. Kohn annually has reported one of the Houses of the South Carolina General Assembly, and his close acquaintance with South Carolina public men for over a decade and his knowledge of their political alignments, past and present, make his narratives of particular historic value. His yearly post reviews of the work of the various legislatures have been studied assiduously by the people of the state for years; they are the authority. His "style" may be typified as "newspaper style," which, regardless of the hyperpurists, is fitted to impart thought through unambiguous phrases and unpedantic words. His primary idea always has been to use the Anglo-Saxon derivatives to lend clarity to his language. He writes for instruction—not literature—and to record facts. However, his literary achievements are not limited to the form of the press; he is the author of several treatises which have had a large bearing on the industrial life of South Carolina—"The Cotton Mills of South Carolina" and "The Water Powers in South Carolina." Both, by an amazing statistical analysis of the potential forces of South Carolina, developed and undeveloped, have brought many hundreds of thousands of wealth into the state.

Mr. Kohn is intensely patriotic, although, unlike his father, who served the full four years in the Confederate army with the Twenty-fifth South Carolina Volunteer Regiment, he has not been actively engaged in war, but has contributed largely of himself and his means to his country, in peace and in war. During the Spanish-American war he was sent by the News and Courier as war correspondent with the First South Carolina Regiment, when it departed for Chickamauga for training preparatory to being ordered to Cuba for service. The call to Cuba did not come, but Mr. Kohn was prepared to go. In a tribute written to his services at that time by his friend, the brilliant and lamented Paul M. Brice, was this extract: "Though the opportunity was not given him of thus distinguishing himself, nevertheless he won equally as much glory, in one sense, in reporting fully and accurately the life of the soldier boys in camp; for the dear ones at home cared not so much just then as to what was happening in Cuba as to how their loved ones were faring in camp—how they were enduring the hard life which patriotism called them to undergo; whether if sick they were receiving kind attention, or, if well, whether really they would in the end have to face the bullets of the Spanish army. It was keeping the people at home so well informed as to all these matters, often in the smallest particulars, that won for Mr. Kohn the heartfelt gratitude of hundreds of families in South Carolina."

Mr. Kohn was beyond the age for active service when the United States became a belligerent in the World war, but he entered unreservedly into those auxiliary enterprises at home which had so much to do with the winning of the war. He was the chairman of the conservation and publicity sections of the South Carolina division of the United States

Food Administration, and was in some measure connected with every Liberty Loan campaign and those movements for the raising of funds for humanitarian activities, such as the Red Cross, Young Men's Christian Association, Knights of Columbus, Salvation Army, Jewish Welfare Board and others. In these movements he invariably was chairman of the foreign corporation committee, which through his influence received large sums of money which were credited to South Carolina's quotas; otherwise they probably would have gone to other states. He was chairman of the Welfare Board's work at Camp Jackson, Columbia. He was state chairman for the campaign for Jewish relief, and raised $30,000 over South Carolina's allotment of $100,000, with the very smallest amount of expense—after it was said that it could not be done in such a small state. This was the first time in the history of the state that an Jewish movement for funds was conducted along nonsectarian lines; and Protestant, Catholic, infidel, all, willingly and unstintedly, gave of their means.

The work that has been nearest the heart of Mr. Kohn has been his indefatigable and patriotic service in behalf of his Alma Mater, the University of South Carolina. For years he has been a trustee of the institution and a driving force for the progressive upbuilding and expansion of the University. As chairman of the finance committee he was largely responsible for the policy of the institution in submitting itemized and explicit statements of expenditure each year to the General Assembly, and it is believed that this method of handling the fiscal affairs of the University has been the primary cause for the friendship the South Carolina legislators have extended the institution in later years. When he went on the Board of Trustees the income of the institution was $27,000, while, in 1920 the direct appropriation made by the Legislature aggregated $286,515. As chairman of the building committee he has been the directing head of the past and present construction operations undertaken at the University; and his business acumen has seen to it that the institution has received the maximum benefit from its expenditures. Although an extremely busy man, the University has taken up much of his time and he has given unstintedly of it.

Under a seemingly calculating and commercial exterior, there beats a warm heart in the body of Mr. Kohn; he has been the financial foster-father of many an aspiring boy whom he has helped through college, either by direct financial gift or other means. He has been a trustee of the Alumni Loan Fund of the University of South Carolina since its inception. Although he would not speak of this phase of his character, it is recognized by his friends, particularly among the newspaper men of the state, whose particular mentor he appears to be. For years president of the South Carolina Press Association, many youthful members of the craft have not in vain asked of him assistance. His advice has righted many financially dubious newspaper enterprises.

Religiously, Mr. Kohn is the president of the Tree of Life Congregation of Columbia, South Carolina, and is president of the Hebrew Benevolent Society of Columbia. His versatility is demonstrated by the fact that when a rabbi of his congregation is not available he presides in his place and delivers the service very creditably, it is said. Fraternally he is a member of several organizations, and a thirty-second degree Mason and a Shriner. He has enjoyed the distinction of being an aide-de-camp, with the rank of lieutenant-colonel, on the staffs of two South Carolina governors—the late Miles B. McSweeney and D. C. Heyward, and this accounts for his being called "Colonel" Kohn.

Of course, with his varied interests and the many activities in which he has been engaged during his eventful life, Mr. Kohn has not done all that he wishes to do, but, while he is wholeheartedly responsive to friendships, he does not let the animosities of others worry him. His present address is 1520 Senate Street, Columbia, South Carolina; his business address is 407 National Loan and Exchange Bank Building, Columbia, South Carolina.—By William J. Cormack.

HORACE JOHNSTON CROUCH. The record of Horace Johnston Crouch gives him a high place among South Carolina educators. At times he has engaged in business, not without considerable success, but his main work since early boyhood has been teaching and school administration, and for ten consecutive years he served as county superintendent of education for Barnwell County.

Mr. Crouch was born at Trenton, South Carolina, March 18, 1882, son of George Edward and Sallie (Oregon) Crouch. When he was two years old his father died, and his mother then married Willie A. McCullough. Mr. Crouch was deprived of the care of both his step-father and mother before his twelfth birthday. Among his close relatives is a half-sister, Pearl McCullough. His only sister, Bessie Crouch, died at the age of two years. His brother, George E. Crouch, aged thirty-four, is a rural mail carrier and farmer at Elko, South Carolina.

Though his boyhood home was several times broken up, as the above record indicates, Mr. Crouch received a good education, attending private and public schools at Trenton, and also a public school at Elko. He graduated from the Williston High School in 1900, and spent three years at Furman University at Greenville, graduating A. B. in June, 1903. For the two school sessions, 1903 to 1905, he was principal of the Elko graded school, and for another two years, from 1905 to 1907, was principal of the Lebanon High School at Pendleton, South Carolina. Leaving school work temporarily, he was employed by the Gilreath-Durham Company at Greenville during 1907-08, and the following year was a member of Crouch & Wooley, general merchants at Elko. He was also a partner in Crouch Brothers at Elko in 1910. For the past ten years in addition to his educational responsibilities he has handled some farming interests.

Mr. Crouch was elected county superintendent of education in Barnwell County in 1908 over two opponents on the first ballot. Since then there has been no opposition to his candidacy and in 1918 he was re-elected for a four-year term beginning July 1, 1919. In October, 1918, he was appointed

South Carolina mill school supervisor, but was unable to accept this work on account of the small financial compensation. Mr. Crouch has undoubtedly chosen well in his line of work, and while the financial opportunities are not and probably never will be great, he has that satisfaction which comes from a service performed to society. Under the revised draft law of 1918 he registered on September 12, 1918, and was assigned to Class 3, Division D. In politics Mr. Crouch calls himself an "ultimate democrat." He is a member of Williston Lodge No. 21, Knights of Pythias, and for several years was active in the order, serving in subordinate offices and as chancery commander. He is a member of the Baptist Church.

In the Lebanon Baptist Church near Pendleton, December 26, 1907, he married Miss Inez Breazeale, daughter of R. A. Breazeale of Anderson County. She was next to the youngest of five sisters and also had five brothers. One brother was with the Medical Replacement, Twenty-fifth Unit, in the American Expeditionary Forces in France.

HON. JOHN P. GRACE, of Charleston, a lawyer by profession, former newspaper man, has for a number of years been one of the thoughtful, courageous and forceful leaders in state and city politics.

He was born at Charleston December 30, 1874, son of James I. and Elizabeth (Daly) Grace. His father was born in Charleston in 1845 and his mother in Troy, New York, in 1849, being brought to Charleston by her parents in 1854. All of Mr. Grace's grandparents were natives of Ireland, his grandfathers born in Tipperary, one grandmother in Limerick and the other in County Meath, twenty-one miles from Dublin in Trim, at the foot of Tara's Hill. James I. Grace and wife were married in 1870, and were the parents of six sons and four daughters, John P. being the fourth in age.

Mr. Grace attended the Christian Brothers' School at Charleston until that school was closed by the earthquake in 1886, and thereafter attended high school, but owing to family circumstances left in the second class and at the age of fourteen went to work as office boy for F. W. Wagener & Company. He soon removed to Greenville and was employed by an uncle in the general merchandise and cotton business for about two years, and after returning to Charleston worked as checker at the Commercial Cotton Press and subsequently with Paul S. Felder in the cotton business. For a year and a half he was bookkeeper for Samuel H. Wilson & Company, and then removed to New York, where he lived for about two years and was assistant secretary to the vice president of the Old Dominion Steamship Company. Leaving New York he spent a short time in Rochester and traveled through Ohio, Indiana and Michigan and other localities of the middle west, most of the time selling encyclopedias and also doing some newspaper work.

Mr. Grace returned to Charleston early in 1896. While so much of his life up to that time had been spent in practical business affairs, his early environment had been such as to foster his intellectual development. His father was a graduate of Charleston College and his mother had been educated according to the highest standards of her time. Mr. Grace therefore from earliest childhood received the strictest mental discipline and direction. He had left school not because of disinclination for learning, but for other circumstances. Thereafter while earning his living by hard work he never failed to spend several hours a day in intelligent reading, and pursued this reading thoroughly and with the purpose of mastering some special branch. While in New York he was a member of Cooper Union, and was especially interested in the classes of political economy. He frequently took part in the debates, and he met personally and knew rather intimately such great thinkers of the day as Henry George, Tom Johnson, Daniel De Leon, Doctor McGlynn and others. The great economic question of that time was the money question. His experience in the middle west had brought him in contact with both sides of the controversy over bimetalism or free silver, and before he returned to Charleston he had read everything written on that subject. Though he found employment as bookkeeper for the Tidewater Oil Company, his heart and mind were absorbed in the fiscal revolution then sweeping over the country, under the leadership of Bryan.

After unsuccessful efforts for a few years in the oil business to fight the Standard Oil Company, and after a few months employment as assistant bookkeeper for the Geer Drug Company of Charleston, Mr. Grace when about twenty-five years of age found an opportunity and privilege to become secretary to Congressman William Elliott from the old First South Carolina District. It was a situation pregnant with opportunity and particularly since it offered him the leisure to study law at Washington. He graduated from the Georgetown Law School in 1902, and at once returned to South Carolina to assist from Columbia in the management of Colonel Elliott's campaign for the United States Senate. During the summer a political situation developed in Charleston which demanded that he become a candidate for the State Senate. It was a party issue in which he threw his influence with those who were endeavoring to keep the party standards and records clean and free from the taint imposed upon it during the campaign of 1896, when so many democrats supported McKinley for the gold standard wing of the democratic party. Mr. Grace carried the City of Charleston but lost the outlying districts in the county and was defeated by a narrow margin.

He was also an unsuccessful candidate for the office of sheriff in 1904. Another peculiar situation in state politics developed in 1908 which demanded that he become a candidate for the United States Senate. He entered the race merely as a "sacrifice," but his campaign effected the object in view.

In Charleston Mr. Grace is perhaps most widely known because of his efficient term as mayor of the city. He was elected to that office in 1911. In 1915 he was the leading figure in the campaign still well remembered in that city. He was defeated according to the official count by eighteen votes, but those well informed on the situation are convinced that was not the real verdict of the people. It was a campaign of great excitement and even bloodshed, and at the urging of his friends Mr. Grace refrained from a legal contest of the ballot.

For a number of years he has been engaged in the

practice of law as a member of the firm Logan & Grace. Mr. Grace established the Charleston American in 1916, and continued as its editor until December, 1917, when an arbitrary ruling of the postmaster general compelled him to abandon the editor's chair on the ground that he was not sufficiently loyal to the British Government. Since then the postoffice department has granted him permission to resume his editorial work, but he has not availed himself of the opportunity.

Mr. Grace is a Catholic, a member of the Knights of Columbus, the Hibernian Society of Charleston and the Elks. He married Miss Ella Barkley Sullivan November 27, 1912. She is a daughter of D. A. J. and Ella (Barkley) Sullivan of Charleston.

ROBERT CAPERS HOLMAN. The legal profession of Barnwell County has an able representative in the person of Robert Capers Holman, of Barnwell, one of the leaders of the bar, whose success has given him an enviable standing in the courts of this section of the state. He has spent his life in this community, being the representative of an excellent old family, members of which have ever sought to promote such movements as have for their object the general betterment of their locality. His life has been one of hard study and research since his youth and of laborious professional duty, and the high position which he has attained is evidence that the qualities which he possesses afford the means of distinction under a system of government in which places of honor and usefulness are open to all who may be worthy of them.

Robert C. Holman was born at Barnwell, South Carolina, on March 6, 1867, and is the son of Jacob Wannamaker and V. (Ashley) Holman. The father was a native of Orangeburg County, South Carolina, followed farming during all the active years of his life, and died at the age of about fifty-seven years. He was the father of six children, of which number the subject is the fourth in order of birth.

One of Mr. Holman's brothers was W. A. Holman, of Charleston, South Carolina, now deceased, who was an eminent lawyer and jurist. E. W. Holman is a successful merchant and farmer at Barnwell. One sister is Hattie A., wife of Congressman J. O. Patterson, of Barnwell, South Carolina. The second sister is Maggie I., wife of N. G. Walker, a farmer and banker of Barnwell. The third sister is Flossie, wife of Pickings Butler Hagood, a farmer and son of Ex-Gov. Johnson Hagood, of Barnwell. Mrs. Holman was a native of Barnwell County and the daughter of William Ashley, one of the largest planters in the state. All of her brothers were soldiers in the Confederate army, serving throughout the struggle. Mrs. Holman died at the age of seventy-two years. She was a devout Christian and took a prominent part in all church work. She was a member of the Methodist Episcopal Church. The Ashley family is one of the old American families of Revolutionary stock and English descent.

Robert C. Holman attended the common schools at Barnwell and the high school at Orangeburg, where he was graduated. He then entered the Kings Mountain Military Academy, where he was graduated. Then, having determined to make the practice of law his life work, he applied himself to the study of Blackstone, Kent and other legal authorities, and was admitted to the bar in 1893. He immediately thereafter located at Barnwell and has ever since been engaged in the active practice of his profession here and during the subsequent years he has been connected as counsel with most of the important litigation in the courts of this and adjoining counties. He has been eminently successful as a lawyer and enjoys marked prestige among his professional colleagues. As a practitioner he employs none of the arts and tricks of oratory, but his speeches are eloquent in the clearness of statement, the broad common sense of reasoning, the force of logic, earnestness and power. His career at the bar offers a noble example, while he has never been known to fail in that strict courtesy and regard for professional ethics which should ever characterize the members of the bar. He is a member of the law firm of Holman & Boulware, general practitioners. Mr. Holman was honored by receiving an appointment from Governor Manning as special judge to hold a court of general assizes at Barnwell. He was honored by the electors of Barnwell in his election as mayor of that town. Aside from his professional labors Mr. Holman is deeply interested in agricultural pursuits, owning about 1,500 acres of fine farming land, on which he raises all the crops common to this locality.

On January 17, 1900, Mr. Holman was married to Goldie C. Wannamaker, the daughter of Dr. J. G. Wannamaker, of Orangeburg, South Carolina. To this union have been born two children, Carrie W. and George Robert, the latter being deceased. Fraternally Mr. Holman is a member of the Ancient Free Masons and the Knights of Pythias. He is an enterprising and progressive man, intensely interested in his profession, but not permitting his life to be bounded by its limitations, taking a commendable interest in everything pertaining to the welfare of the community. He is financially interested in the Atlantic Savings Bank and the Exchange Banking and Trust Company of Charleston. He stands consistently for the best things in life and is acknowledged as a leader of men in his locality. Because of his high personal character, his professional ability, his business success and his genial disposition, he enjoys the confidence and good will of all who know him.

NORMAN HORACE BLITCH began his career as an industrious boy on a truck farm, and his life has been one of wide and significant influence to the agriculture of the South. For many years he has retained his interest in truck farming, is president of the Combahee Fertilizer Company, and also one of the prominent officials of the Standard Truck Package Company.

He was born at Elabelle, Georgia, January 15, 1865, son of Henry J. and Lavinia (English) Blitch. His ancestors came from Germany and were members of the original colony of Georgia founded by Oglethorpe. Thomas Blitch was a Revolutionary soldier and was killed at the battle of Brandywine. Henry J. Blitch was a grandson of this Revolutionary patriot, and spent his active life as a farmer

Robert C. Holman

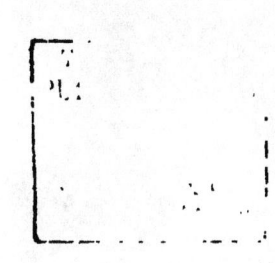

and also served during the '50s as sheriff of his county. He and his wife had fifteen children.

Norman Horace Blitch grew up in a remote country district, nine miles from the nearest railroad. One of a large family, he had to contribute his labor to the support of the household, working on a turpentine farm and at other duties. He could attend school only a few months each year, and had to walk the distance of three miles between his home and the schoolhouse. In 1885, at the age of twenty, he became foreman of the truck farm of his brother on Yonges Island and in a few years was engaged in truck farming on his own account. He was one of the pioneers in developing the great market garden industry of South Carolina. It was almost as an incident to this industry that he became active in the Standard Truck Package Company, a corporation with a factory on Yonges Island and main office at Charleston, manufacturing vast quantities of the package containers used in marketing vegetables. Another logical development of his career as a truck farmer is his position as head of the Combahee Fertilizer Company.

Mr. Blitch for a number of years has lived in Charleston, has been active in the Commercial Club, Country Club and other social organizations, is a democrat and a member of the Catholic Church. November 22, 1887, he married Miss Emily A. Commins, daughter of John Commins of Charleston. They have three living children.

THOMAS TALBIRD. There is no member of the Beaufort County bar who occupies a higher position in the estimation of the people than does he whose name forms the caption to these paragraphs. During his years of practice he has built up a very large clientele and is regarded as an exceedingly safe counsellor in all matters pertaining to legal questions. It speaks well for any man who may have the confidence of the people to such an extent that he is regarded as especially adapted to the settlement of estates and matters of equity. Such a position the subject has occupied, and has discharged his duties to the entire satisfaction of all. His services are likewise in large demand where the drawing of intricate papers is involved—in fact, as a lawyer he is easily the peer of any of his professional brethren in his section of the state. He is a close observer of the trend of the times and an intelligent student of the great questions and issues upon which the thought of the best minds of the world are centered.

Thomas Talbird, eminent lawyer and one of the best known citizens of Beaufort, was born in that city on July 3, 1855, and is of the fourth generation of his family to live in this community. His father, Franklin Talbird, a veteran of the Civil war, was also born here and in the same house, the old home having been built in 1820, 100 years ago, by the subject's grandfather, Thomas Talbird, who also was a native of Beaufort. His father, and the subject's great-grandfather, John Talbird, were born in this county and the latter served as an officer in the patriot army during the war of the Revolution. Thomas Talbird, Sr.'s, wife, Annie Talbird, subject's grandmother, was the daughter of Col. Thomas Talbird, who was also an officer in the Revolutionary war. Henry Talbird, the first of the name to locate in South Carolina, was a native of Ireland. His original family name was "Talbot," but certain legal papers having been made out in England in the name of "Talbird," he adopted that spelling. The subject's mother, whose maiden name was Johana M. O'Grady, was a native of Ireland, but came to the United States under the auspices of Archbishop Hughes of New York. She received her education in the Convent of the Sacred Heart in New York City, and took the first prize in music in that institution. Three of her uncles were officers in the English army.

Thomas Talbird, the immediate subject of this review, is the eldest of the three children born to Franklin and Johana Talbird, and is the only one now living. After completing the public school course he became a student in Manhattan College, New York City, and later entered Washington and Lee University at Lexington, Virginia, of which institution Gen. Robert E. Lee was president at one time. Mr. Talbird took the full law course there and was graduated in 1878. Immediately afterward he was admitted to the bar and at once returned to Beaufort and entered upon active practice, in which he has since been engaged, a period of about thirty years, during which time he has been connected with most of the important litigation in the local courts. During this period he has taken an active interest in local public affairs, and in 1896, and again in 1900, he was elected to the State Senate. He was also elected judge of the Probate Court of Beaufort County, in which he added to his already enviable reputation. He is at present attorney for the City and County of Beaufort, which positions he has occupied for several years. He is also a member of the State Democratic Executive Committee for Beaufort County. He was at one time captain of the Beaufort Volunteer Artillery, one of the oldest military organizations in the state. An earnest democrat in his political views, Mr. Talbird has sat in the councils of his party and served as a delegate to the Democratic National Convention in 1900, which nominated Mr. Bryan for the second time for the presidency.

In 1888 Mr. Talbird was married to Jeanne Canter and they are the parents of two daughters, Therese and Christine, the latter the wife of J. Heyward Jenkins, an attorney, and partner of Mr. Talbird. Personally Mr. Talbird is a man of gracious and kindly personality, and because of his splendid character and honorable career he enjoys to the fullest measure the confidence and esteem of all who know him.

J. L. DAVID. In recent years hardly a business undertaking of any consequence has been noted in the commercial affairs of Charleston with which the name and influence of J. L. David has not been associated in some manner. Mr. David until recently was head of the largest outfitting store for men and women in South Carolina, and is president of the Dime Savings Bank.

He was born at Charleston August 18, 1856, son of R. L. and Pauline (Falk) David. His parents were both natives of Germany and settled in Charleston in 1849. Of a family of thirteen children nine reached mature years, J. L. being the fifth in age.

J. L. David received his education in the public and commercial schools of Charleston. In 1877, at the age of twenty-one, his father dying, he succeeded his father in business. At that time he had the smallest store in the town, but under skillful management it grew until it was the largest of its class in the city for men and women's furnishings, etc. In 1920 Mr. David disposed of his store, selling out his entire stock to give his entire attention to the Dime Bank and Trust Company, which had become one of the prominent fiduciary institutions of Charleston. He was president of the company owning the store and has been president of the Dime Savings Bank since 1909.

In 1896 he married Lizzie Westendorff, of Charleston. They have two children, Winnetta, a student in Wellesley College, and Paul, at home.

AUGUSTUS THEODORE ALLEN, while he has a home at Columbia convenient to the educational centers where his children are being trained, spent practically all his life and has his chief business interests at Allendale, the county seat of the new Allendale County, a name that of itself is a distinct tribute to the long residence and prominence of the Allen family in that community.

Allendale was formerly in Barnwell County, and among the more prominent members of the Allen family there have been Leroy Allen, Wesley Allen and in more recent years the late George Pierce Allen, a banker and influential figure in state politics.

P. H. Allen lived about a mile northwest of the present town of Allendale, and was the first postmaster of that community. When the railroad was completed on July 4, 1872, he was instrumental in having founded the present town of Allendale, named in honor of the Allen family.

A brother of P. H. Allen was John M. Allen, grandfather of Augustus Theodore Allen of Columbia and Allendale, and who was a state senator from the Barnwell district. A. T. Allen, who is a brother of the late George Pierce Allen above noted, was born near Allendale, April 5, 1864, son of Augustus T. and Jane (Roberts) Allen. His father was a Confederate soldier. Augustus Theodore Allen was a very small boy when the Town of Allendale was established. He still has extensive and valuable planting interests in that vicinity. His efforts and enterprise have made him prominent in that section, and he was one of the men chiefly instrumental in the movement which brought about the organization of the new County of Allendale in January, 1919. This is one of the richest small counties in the state. Mr. Allen is president of the National Motor Sales Company of Columbia, which company is a large southern distributor of automobiles and trucks. He is a director in the First National Bank of Allendale, associated with W. T. Riley, Jr., who is president.

Mr. Allen is a member of the staff of Governor Cooper with the rank of lieutenant colonel. In order to give his family educational advantages he established a home in Columbia in 1915. This fine home is at the corner of Gervais and Pickens streets. He and his wife have two children, Augustus T., Jr., and Miss Dorothy Grace Allen.

Augustus T. Allen, Jr., went with the first thirty from the University of South Carolina to Camp Hancock in the machine gun service and had finished about half of the course when the armistice was signed. He returned to the college and graduates with the class of 1921.

WILLIAM H. GRIMBALL comes of a family well known in public and professional affairs in South Carolina, was educated for a technical career, but has followed the example of other members of the family and is today a well known and prosperous Charleston lawyer, member of the firm Whaley, Barnwell & Grimball.

Mr. Grimball was born in Charleston February 2, 1886. The Grimball name is supposed to be of Welsh origin. One prominent representative was Paul Grimball, secretary to the Province of South Carolina in colonial times. His grandfather, John Berkley Grimball, was a native of South Carolina and a rice planter. The father, John Grimball, now living retired, was an officer in the Confederate Navy and during his active career was a rice planter and also a lawyer. The mother of William H. Grimball was Mary G. Barnwell, a native of South Carolina, and of the prominent Barnwell family of this state.

William H. Grimball is the oldest of four sons. He was educated in Charleston College and in 1906 graduated from the Mechanical Engineering Department of Lehigh University. He soon afterward took up the study of law in the office of Joseph W. Barnwell and was admitted to the bar in 1909. In 1913 he formed a partnership with Richard S. Whaley and N. B. Barnwell, and this firm has enjoyed a commanding place in the legal profession. Mr. Grimball is a former solicitor for the Ninth Judicial Circuit and has been a member of the Charleston City Council, and is now corporation counsel for that city.

April 30, 1913, he married Miss Panchita Heyward, daughter of Frank and Frances (Ferguson) Heyward. They have three children, John, William H. and Frances F. Mr. Grimball is a member of the South Carolina Society, St. Andrews Society, Carolina Yacht Club, Charleston Club, has filled all the chairs in the Knights of Pythias, and is a member of St. Michael's Episcopal Church. For a number of years he has been an influential leader of the democratic party.

R. C. SIEGLING is president and treasurer of the News and Courier of Charleston, was educated for the law, and followed that profession, honored and adorned by several of his ancestors, until he gave up his practice in 1915 to become officially identified with the News and Courier.

He was born at Charleston April 13, 1888, a son of Rudolph and Effie (Campbell) Siegling. His father was also born in Charleston, a son of John Siegling, a native of Germany who came to America early in the nineteenth century. Rudolph Siegling was a lieutenant in the Confederate army, and was long prominent as a lawyer and business man at Charleston. At the time of his death he was presi-

dent of the Bank of Charleston and of the News and Courier. He died in 1894. His wife was a daughter of Robert Campbell, an attorney of Walterboro, South Carolina, and a granddaughter of Robert Campbell, also a lawyer and a native of Scotland.

R. C. Siegling, the only son of his parents, was educated in private schools at Charleston, and in 1910 graduated from Princeton University. Returning home, he studied law and was admitted to the bar in 1911, and engaged in a general practice until 1915. He is a member of the Carolina Yacht Club and the Charleston Country Club. April 26, 1916, he married Lucile Bee Lebby, daughter of Robert B. Lebby.

JUDGE RICHARD M. JEFFERIES. In no profession is there a career more open to talent than is that of the law, and in no field of endeavor is there demanded a more careful preparation, a more thorough appreciation of the absolute ethics of life or of the underlying principles which form the basis of all human rights and privileges. Among the members of the legal profession who have not only gained for themselves the respect of their fellow lawyers, but who have also rendered service of a very definite character to their country, none occupies a more enviable position than Richard M. Jefferies, judge of probate of Colleton County.

Richard M. Jefferies was born on what is known as the Star Farm in Union County, South Carolina, on February 27, 1888, and is the son of Capt. John R. and Mary Henrietta (Allen) Jefferies. Captain Jefferies, who was born at the same place, was a soldier, with a commission of captain, in the war between the states. His father, Col. James Jefferies, also a native of Union County, was a soldier in the early Indian wars, where he earned his official title. He was the son of Capt. Nathaniel Jefferies, who fitted out his own company for service in the war of the Revolution and paid all its expenses. The Jefferies family, which is from sterling old English stock, immigrated to this country and first settled in Virginia in 1733. In about 1763 they moved to the headwaters of Thicket Creek. The subject's mother, who was born and reared at Cedar Spring, Spartanburg County, South Carolina, was a daughter of Woodward Allen, who was of English descent and who was a soldier in the Confederate army during the War between the States. The family from which he is descended were numbered among the early settlers of South Carolina.

Of the eleven children born to Capt. John R. and Mary H. Jefferies, the subject of this review is the youngest. He was reared on the paternal farmstead, securing his elementary education in the schools of the neighborhood and at Gaffney graded schools and then became a student in the South Carolina University, where he was graduated in 1910, with the degree of Bachelor of Arts. He then engaged in teaching school at Ridgeland, Jasper County, and incidentally it might be recorded that he took an active part in the creation and organization of the latter county. For a time he was engaged in the publishing business, editing a paper at Ridgeland. In the meantime Mr. Jefferies was giving serious attention to the study of law, with the intention of eventually making the legal profession his life work, and in 1912 he was formally admitted to the bar. In January, 1913, he came to Walterboro, and for about a year was identified with the newspaper business, but was appointed master in equity, succeeding Col. C. G. Henderson, who had resigned from the office. In 1916 the subject was elected to succeed himself in that position, and in 1918 his office was consolidated with that of probate judge, in consequence of which action the judge is now discharging the important duties which formerly pertained to both offices. That he has so handled the multitudinous details of his office in a manner as to win the approval of all who have had dealings with the office is a matter of common comment. Possessing all the requisites of the able lawyer, Judge Jefferies has devoted himself conscientiously to the honest discharge of his duties, with the idea that he is a servant of the people, a viewpoint too often lost sight of in these busy days.

Judge Jefferies keeps closely in touch with local public affairs and gives his unreserved support to every agency which promises to be of benefit to the community at large. He is an earnest advocate of the best educational facilities that can be provided, and while a resident of Jasper County he gave an impetus to educational work during his term as superintendent of education, he being the first incumbent of that office in the newly created county. Politically he is actively identified with the democratic party organization, having served in 1912 as a member of the State Executive Committee, and he has been a member of many of the important councils of that party. Fraternally he is a member of the Ancient Free and Accepted Masons, the Knights of Pythias and the Woodmen of the World, in all of which bodies he has held official positions.

In 1911 Judge Jefferies was married to Annie K. Savage, of Walterboro, the daughter of Capt. C. A. and India D. (Dunwoody) Savage, and the niece of Gov. Johnson Hagood. To this union has been born a daughter, Annie Keith, and a son, R. M. Jefferies, Jr. The splendid success which has come to Judge Jefferies is directly traceable to the salient points in his character, for he started in life practically at the bottom of the ladder, which he has mounted unaided. He is a splendid example of the virile, progressive, self-made men who believe in doing well whatever is worth doing at all, a man of keen discernment and sound judgment, broad minded and at the same time a follower of the principles embodied in the Golden Rule in all his relations with his fellow men, and therefore he enjoys their confidence and good will.

JOSEPH M. WHITSETT is vice president and general manager of The Carolina Company of Charleston. He has been a resident of Charleston since 1908, and while a comparatively young man, is a veteran in his active experience in the shipping industry.

Mr. Whitsett was one of the founders of The Carolina Company. This company is making history for Charleston commerce, and in this connection a brief quotation should be made from the recent report of J. L. Ferguson, president of the Cotton Exchange, who after referring to the gratifying and unprecedented increase of cotton receipts at the Charleston port for the season of 1919, explains the increase as follows:

"This increase in receipts has been due in large measure to the efforts of The Carolina Company, an organization composed entirely of Charleston men, many of whom are members of this exchange. The Carolina Company has been instrumental in bringing to Charleston since August last eighty-one thousand bales of through cotton from a far range of territory, even from Arkansas and Oklahoma. These shipments of through cotton exceed to an enormous extent anything accomplished in that line for the past twenty-five years. It is but right that the members of this exchange know the good work for Charleston which The Carolina Company has brought about. The company was started in June, 1919, with an authorized capital of $500,000, and operates a fleet of ten steamships under its own flag. These ships aggregate 68,000 dead-weight tons and have a carrying capacity of 16,000 to 20,000 bales per ship."

Mr. Whitsett was born at Huntsville, Alabama, in 1881 and is a member of a family long identified in different branches with Virignia, North and South Carolina.

Joseph M. Whitsett was a southern boy who made his own opportunities. At the age of fourteen he left home and while working at Montgomery, Alabama, attended a business college. Hard work has been the chief item in his career ever since, with very few vacations, and he has never hesitated to attack a hard problem and rely on his personal resources to solve it. Thus by unaided effort he has achieved a high place in trade and commerce. Some years he lived in Savannah, Georgia, being associated with the firm of Strachan & Company, extensive ship owners. He was also in the shipping business at Fernandina, Florida.

When he came to Charleston in 1908 it was as representative for Strachan & Company, and he remained with that organization until he became one of the founders of The Carolina Company, of which he is vice president and general manager. As noted in the above quotation, this company is the largest single factor in the present concerted movement for making Charleston one of the leading American ports.

Mr. Whitsett married Miss Ruth Prescott, of Florida, and they have a son, Joseph M., Jr.

HON. HAMPTON P. FULMER, formerly of Norway, but recently of Orangeburg, began his business career when a very young man. Not chance or circumstance, but indefatigable industry and intelligently applied effort have been responsible for his present position as one of the wealthiest and most prominent business men and planters in that section of South Carolina.

Mr. Fulmer, who is also widely known in public life, was born near Springfield in Orangeburg County, June 23, 1875, son of James R. and Marthena (Corley) Fulmer. His mother, who is still living at the age of eighty-five, is a member of the well known Evans family of Aiken and Orangeburg counties. The father, now deceased, was a prominent planter in that section of Orangeburg County originally a part of Lexington County. He served all through the four years of the war of secession, was wounded and captured at Charleston and suffered the untold hardships of war.

Hampton P. Fulmer was educated in the Springfield High School and graduated from Massey's Business College at Columbus, Georgia, in 1897. He is still a comparatively young man, and has accomplished his success in about twenty years. Mr. Fulmer is senior partner of the Fulmer-Jones Company, a large mercantile house of Norway; is president of the Farmers National Bank of Norway; president of the Norway Livestock Company, the Fulmer-Garrick Motor Company, and the Farmers and Merchants Warehouse Company; and is secretary-treasurer of the Norway Ginning Company. One of his most valuable interests is the noted Barnes plantation, comprising 1,000 acres lying six miles southeast of Norway. As owner of this plantation he is one of the principal producers of agricultural crops in Orangeburg County. He recently removed to Orangeburg to engage in banking and real estate, but continues his business in Norway.

Many responsibilities and honors have come to him in public affairs. He is a former mayor of Norway and in 1916 was elected a member of the Lower House of the Legislature to represent Orangeburg County. He has been a leading member of the sessions of 1917, 1918, 1919 and 1920, and is a member of the Ways and Means Committee of the House. In the summer of 1919 he was a popular candidate, though without a campaign organization, for the position in Congress vacated by Congressman Lever. He made a creditable race against the five other aspirants for the office. His name has been announced as a candidate for the campaign of 1920, and his many friends are confident that he will be the next congressman from the Sixth District. He is a Mason and a deacon in the Baptist Church.

During the war Mr. Fulmer was chairman and leader of all the Liberty Loan drives for the Norway section, and also in the War Camp Community Service, Red Cross and other campaigns. He married Miss Willa E. Lybrand, of Wagener, Aiken County, in 1901. Their three children are Margery Louise, Ruby Maxine and Willa Juanita.

LAMB BUIST KERRISON. In referring to Doctor Kerrison, who for the past eight years has been one of the leading dental surgeons of Charleston, it is appropriate to include reference to his family connections, many of whom have played notable and distinguished parts in South Carolina commerce, politics and industry through several generations.

The Kerrison family is of English origin. William Kerrison, grandfather of Lamb Buist Kerrison, was a brother of C. and E. L. Kerrison, founders of the noted Kerrison mercantile establishment in Charleston which had a long and honorable history. They began as dry goods merchants in 1831 at 211 King Street. The business in 1884 passed to Philip D. Kerrison, a son of Charles Kerrison. Doctor Kerrison, in order to free himself from the restrictions of business upon his professional practice, sold out this store. Doctor Kerrison is now a highly

regarded medical authority of New York City, being a specialist in diseases of the eye, ear, nose and throat, and a recognized authority on the mastoid operation.

The father of Lamb Buist Kerrison was Charles Kerrison, a native of Charleston. He was a Confederate soldier with the Palmetto Guards, and with that organization fought under General Lee in the Army of Northern Virginia, participating in all the historic battles, including Gettysburg. One of his brothers, Edwin Kerrison, was killed at the battle of Spottsylvania. Charles Kerrison for thirty years efficiently filled the office of register of mesne conveyance for Charleston County, and died while in office.

Charles Kerrison married Rosa Pinckney Heriot. The Heriots lived in Scotland and from there a branch came to South Carolina prior to the Revolutionary war. Some of the Heriots were patriot Americans in the War of the Revolution, and for several generations the family followed rice planting in the Georgetown district of South Carolina.

Lamb Buist Kerrison was born at Charleston in 1887, a son of Charles and Rosa Pinckney (Heriot) Kerrison. He has four brothers and three sisters living: Dr. Edward Kerrison, Dr. Charles Kerrison, Dr. Harry H. Kerrison, William Kerrison, Mrs. Charles de Saussure Clarkson, Mrs. Alfred Aldridge Patterson and Miss Elizabeth Kerrison.

He acquired his literary education in the public schools of Charleston and Porter's Military Academy and studied dentistry in the Atlanta Southern Dental College at Atlanta, graduating in 1912. His practice has been continuous at Charleston since that date, and has brought him a high rank as a dental surgeon. He is a member of the State and National Dental associations. Doctor Kerrison and family are communicants of St. Paul's Episcopal Church.

He married Miss Hermina Legare, of Charleston, and they have one son, George Legare Kerrison. Mrs. Kerrison is a daughter of George S. and Fannie (Islar) Legare. In this connection the tribute of a brief paragraph should be paid to Mrs. Kerrison's honored father.

Hon. George S. Legare, who was a son of Ned and Kate (Graves) Legare, combined in his character the best and strongest traits of the French Huguenot ancestors, who were among the founders of Charleston. He was educated in Porter's Military School at Charleston, in Washington and Lee University, and as a young man took up the practice of law. He died in 1912 while a member of Congress. He was one of the most talented and brilliant men ever sent to Congress from this state and also one of the youngest. He was only forty-two years of age when he died, and had represented the Charleston district for fourteen years. At the memorial services held in his honor in Congress splendid tributes were paid by the leading members of both houses and by representatives of both parties. Mr. Legare is survived by his widow, a daughter of the late Judge Izlar, of Orangeburg, and three other children besides Mrs. Kerrison, William Legare, Julia and Fernandina Legare.

JAMES REID BOYLSTON is one of those forceful personalities who radiate a tremendous amount of influence for good in every line in which their interest and enthusiasm center. Fortunately Mr. Boylston's interests are not circumscribed. His most valuable influence has no doubt been exerted through his long and wide experience as a cotton seed oil expert. For over fifteen years he has been manager of the Allendale plant of the Southern Cotton Seed Oil Company. By no means all his time has been given to this one plant. He is a traveling man, and has come in contact with the farmers, cotton growers and other business interests of many of the Southern States.

He was born at Winsboro, South Carolina, and represents two very prominent families of that city, being a son of Samuel Cordes and Margaret (DuBose) Boylston. On his mother's side he is descended from some of the earliest French Huguenot settlers of Charleston. The Boylstons were originally in Massachusetts, and the name Boylston has a significant prominence in Boston. The Boylstons have lived in Charleston since the early part of the nineteenth century. Samuel Cordes Boylston was a graduate of The Citadel at Charleston, and from that institution entered the service of the state troops in December, 1860, and went all through the war on the Confederate side.

James Reid Boylston has been in the cotton seed oil business continuously for thirty-five years, and has well earned a high and conspicuous place in that industry. He came to Allendale at the time the present plant of the Southern Cotton Seed Oil Company was established in 1893, and for many years has been its manager. Of all the varied work he has done he finds the greatest satisfaction in his career as a traveling man. His duties in the cotton seed oil business take him "on the road" a great deal of the time. He is a very fine type of the high class traveling man. For two years he was state president of the Travelers Protective Association of Georgia. He is also a member and ex-officer of the United Commercial Travelers, Council 312, Augusta, Georgia.

With the invasion of the boll weevil into South Carolina in 1919, cotton seed oil interests have naturally been looking to other products so as to completely utilize their industrial plants and safeguard them during the period of decreased cotton production. In the falls of 1916-17-18-19, Mr. Boylston made an extensive tour of Alabama, Georgia and other Southern States, gathering much useful data in connection with peanut growing. He has been a propagandist for peanut culture among the farmers of the southern counties in South Carolina. His company recently bought a beautiful tract of eight and a half acres adjoining Allendale. Here in November, 1919, was begun the erection of a modern plant equipped with elaborate peanut separating machinery. This plant will be in complete operation during the season of 1920, in addition to the present cotton seed threshing plant.

Mr. Boylston is also enthusiastic over the modern process of dehydrating food products. There is a dehydrating department in the Allendale plant, equipped for extracting the water from sweet potatoes and sending to the markets of the world the dehydrated product. Government analysis has shown that the dehydrated sweet potatoes make an almost perfect and complete ration.

Obviously Mr. Boylston's interest is deep and sincere in many phases of agriculture. He is a member of and president of the famous Ellenton Agricultural Club of Ellenton, South Carolina.

His first wife was Georgia Ford Baxter, of Sparta, Georgia. She was the mother of three children: Cordes DuBose, Kate Baxter and Bessie Boylston. Cordes DuBose was educated in the Bailey Military Institute and the University of Colorado, and volunteered and served throughout the war in the United States Navy. Mr. Boylston married for his present wife Miss Zilphia Allen, member of the Allen family for whom Allendale was named. They have two children: Sarah Margaret and James Reid Boylston.

THOMAS RICHARD WARING, who has been editor of the Charleston Evening Post since 1895, represents the seventh generation of the Waring family in the Colony and State of South Carolina. The Warings came from England, and for more than 200 years theirs has been a name of honorable associations in Charleston and vicinity.

Mr. Waring was born at Charleston, December 7, 1871, son of Edward P. and Anna T. (Waties) Waring. He attended the Porter Military Academy of Charleston and finished his education in Hobart College at Geneva, New York. After leaving college he had several years' experience in a railroad office but since 1895 has been one of the hard working men on the editorial staff of the Evening Post, and has been the responsible editor of the Post since February, 1897.

Mr. Waring served as a delegate to the National Democratic Convention in 1908 at Denver, and has a number of other services to his credit in politics and public affairs of his home city and state. He is a member of St. Paul's Episcopal Church in Charleston.

At Charleston, November 23, 1898, he married Laura Campbell Witte, daughter of Charles O. and Lottie R. Witte. They have three children: Charles W., born in 1899; Rosamond, born in 1903; and Thomas R., Jr., born in 1907.

DR. DAVID CUNNINGHAM SCOTT, of Kingstree, Williamsburg County, has to his credit not only forty busy years of professional work, but also an energetic participation in business affairs and public matters that have directly enlarged the life of his community and built up his section of the state. He has demonstrated by his own successful example many things that are making Williamsburg one of the most prosperous parts of the country.

Doctor Scott was born at Kingstree, November 23, 1849, third son of John Ervin and Mary McCrea Gordon Scott. His father was a descendant of John Scott and his mother of Archibald McCrea, who in the early part of the eighteenth century were friends and neighbors in Scotland, emigrated from there to Ireland, and in 1734 settled in Williamsburg Township, twenty square miles of territory granted to Scotch-Irish Presbyterians. Thus Doctor Scott's people have been South Carolinians for nearly two centuries.

The war and resultant temporary alien occupation seriously hampered Doctor Scott's father in schooling his children, yet he secured the best possible governesses and tutors for them, paying at least one tutor what was then the large salary of $1,000 a year, and many other men's children in the community profited by the elder Scott's efforts. The intensity of the time had its influence on the future doctor, as well as did the traditions of the heroism of his forefathers in making and saving this land, and he utilized well his time at Mayesville Military Academy and at the Lutheran College at Walhalla. He has always had the reading habit. The best books of the world, some of them browned by more than a century of use, fill the shelves of his library. History, politics, science, things—all knowledge is interesting to him. He knows as much about literature and of life as the best of his generation.

Doctor Scott was too young to participate actively as a soldier in the War between the States, yet old enough to realize that the same foe to individual rights and personal freedom that his ancestors had fought for ages was again undertaking a relentless campaign under changed conditions and another color. And when he saw the alien, the atheist, the cuckoo and the carpet bagger essaying revelry where the sacred fires of his fathers had burned, he became a member of the Invisible Empire that again showed the spirit of the Scotch-Irish invincible. And when the Second '76 satisfied the world that this section belongs to the men who made it, the souls of his kindred who had fallen to make and to maintain it must have looked on him as altogether worthy of the head and the heart he had inherited.

Doctor Scott was graduated from the Medical College of South Carolina in 1876 and soon thereafter began the practice of medicine in Kingstree. He was markedly successful in his profession, soon learning the practical value of the healing touch that emanates from a comprehending mind and a sympathetic soul. He knew and knows the use, as well as the abuse, of drugs, and realizes that much medicine is frequently a weariness to the flesh. Years ago he retired from the active practice of his profession, although yet he remains a source of great strength to younger doctors who come to him in time of trouble, giving them graciously out of his vast fund of information and depth of his discretion.

However many pains he has made to cease and wounds he has helped to heal, Doctor Scott's greatest work has been as a community builder. He saw the possibilities of Williamsburg County years ago when he was led all over its territory to minister to the sick; and by kindly, tactful suggestion and striking personal exemplification has helped his people into the better life of today and stimulated them into anticipating with eagerness what tomorrow must bring.

Twenty years ago Doctor Scott was largely instrumental in establishing the Bank of Kingstree, the first bank in Williamsburg County. He became its first president, which office he yet holds. For a number of years he gave personal attention to every detail of the institution, knowing the moral and financial history and condition of almost every man

Yours respectfully
D. C. Scott

in these parts, and so well has this bank been conducted that it has never lost a dollar.

Doctor Scott was chairman of the board of trustees of schools when the Kingstree school emerged from the best then obtainable into the present modern graded system. He had long labored for a better institution and was greatly gratified when the Kingstree school grew into one of the best of its class in the state.

He was one of the founders and president of the Real Estate Company, established in 1905. He was the moving spirit of the Kingstree Electric Light Company and of the Ice Manufacturing Company. In 1912 he erected the Scott Warehouse, which has since been used for storing and handling a large part of the cotton and tobacco produced in Williamsburg County.

Doctor Scott has been deeply interested in farming and stock raising all his life. He now owns a large and valuable plantation, near Kingstree, which is devoted to agriculture and high grade stock raising.

No more striking illustration of the working of Doctor Scott can be suggested than by the following: For a great many years, he owned and operated a drug store in Kingstree, selling many farm and garden seeds all over this section. He learned the seeds best adapted to the county and sold them only, giving his patrons the benefit of his own experiments and telling them what agricultural journals declared valuable and expedient.

It may be that the material seeds he has been instrumental in sowing have made two ears of corn grow where one had grown. Certainly some of the spiritual seeds he has dropped, even by the wayside, have brought forth an hundred fold.

There are many real things in Kingstree and in Williamsburg County into which Doctor Scott has breathed the breath of life.

Doctor Scott inherited exceptional mental and physical strength and has failed to accept few opportunities to develop and increase his force. So wisely and so well has he adjusted himself to the storm and stress period he has lived that now at more than three score and ten years his arms are yet strong, his eyes undimmed, and his mind still approaches its zenith. One by one he has done things, quietly and unostentatiously, founding institutions and fostering them until they have grown strong, then leaving them in other hands that he has helped to train.

So kindly has he lived and so patient is he with human weakness that some of his younger friends find it difficult to realize that his nature is rooted in the Rock of Ages and that he cannot be moved save towards better things.

Doctor Scott is a member of the democratic party, the Masonic Order, and the Methodist Episcopal Church, South. His heart is in all of them and his hands help sustain them.

December 11, 1884, Doctor Scott married Martha, daughter of Dr. John F. and Elizabeth Scott Brockington, and to them were born four children: Helen, wife of William W. Boddie; John Heyward, who died in the military service, November 16, 1918; David C., Jr., of Kingstree; and Mary Elizabeth, who died in infancy.

MRS. MARTHA SARAH SEABROOK. In a brief sketch of any living citizen it is difficult to do exact and impartial justice, not so much for lack of space or words to set forth the familiar and passing events of the personal history, as for want of the perfect and rounded conception of the whole life, which grows, develops and ripens, like fruit, to disclose its true and best flavor only when it is mellowed by time. These thoughts are prompted by consideration of the life record of one of Charleston's most beloved citizens, whose life still casts its beneficent influence like a benediction over the lives of the thousands who know her and admire and love her.

Mrs. Martha Sarah Seabrook, widow of the late William Seabrook, who after a long and active life largely devoted to public service, is now retired and living quietly in her comfortable home in Charleston, is descended from a long line of sterling ancestry in both the paternal and maternal lines, as was her late husband. The Seabrook family is of English origin, the emigrant ancestor of the South Carolina branch of the family having been Capt. Robert Seabrook, who came to the Carolina province prior to June, 1680. It is thought that he came from Dunstable, in the County of Bedford. In April, 1697, he bought 2,700 acres of land in Colleton County, South Carolina. He became a commissioner under the Church Act of November 4, 1704, was a member of the General Assembly of the province and was elected speaker of the House in 1705. During the French invasion in 1706 he commanded a company from the Carolina islands. In many respects he was one of the leaders of the colonists and was active in many lines of effort in behalf of the young community. His death occurred on December 7, 1710, in the fifty-ninth year of his age. He was the father of three sons, John, Robert and Joseph. Among the latter-day descendants of this worthy ancestor was William Seabrook, whose untimely death at the comparatively early age of forty-one years was deeply regretted by all who knew him. Well educated and soundly versed in law, he also possessed the charm of eloquence, being considered one of the leading orators of his day. At the time of his death he was city attorney of Charleston and a most promising career was cut short by his death. By his marriage to Martha Sarah Baynard there was born a daughter, Sarah Annie, who became the wife of James Swinton Whaley, of Edisto Island. Her death occurred on January 15, 1915.

Joseph Baynard, father of Martha Sarah (Baynard) Seabrook, was the son of Joseph and Sarah Baynard. He was blessed with a brilliant mind, evidences of which were shown at such an early age that when but twelve years of age he was sent by his mother to Princeton to be prepared for college. There he pursued his studies and graduated, but during his educational period he had pursued his investigations and researches into channels unthought of perhaps when he began his college life. The philosophy of life and its problems had attracted him, as had the great questions of statesmanship and politics, which were then uppermost in men's minds. As a result, he became an antisecessionist in his views and opposed his cousin, Governor Seabrook, who was an outspoken nullifier. Eventually he became an Episcopalian minister, in which he gained considerable note, being a man of broad vision and deep spiritual insight. He left Edisto Island and went to Bluffton, where, on his own plantation, he established a school and built a church. There, in the Town of Bluffton, he gave freely of his services to the white population. Later he studied law, and for a time was engaged in the practice of that profession in Charleston, but because of failing health he was compelled to relinquish the practice and moved back to Edisto Island. At his own expense he built a church at Bluffton in 1849 and in 1859 he built another church in St. Paul's Parish. During the War between the States he was pastor of Grace Church, in Charleston, but shortly afterward became pastor of St. Mark's (colored) Church, in Charleston, to which he continued to minister until his death. During the last three years of his life he rendered efficient service as superintendent of the city schools of Charleston. He was a fluent and able writer and a forceful and eloquent speaker. He was one of the most highly esteemed citizens of his section of the state, which was honored by his residence for so many years, during which time he did much for the people with whom he mingled. In all of the relations of life—family, church, state and society—he displayed that consistent, gentlemanly spirit, that innate refinement and unswerving integrity that endeared him alike to man, woman and child.

Joseph Baynard was married three times. His first union was with Sarah Ann Baily, to which union were born the following children: Martha Sarah, who became the wife of William Seabrook, as has been already mentioned; Caroline Cecil, who became the wife of Frank Whaley; Ephraim, who married Harriet Whaley, and who is mentioned more specifically in a later paragraph; Perronnean Finly, who married S. Baily. Joseph Baynard's second union was with Lydia (Baily) Whaley, a daughter of Charles Baily and a sister of his first wife. She became the mother of two children, namely: Lydia, who married her cousin, Franklin Seabrook, and Isabelle, who became the wife of John Lewis Jervais. Mrs. Lydia Baynard died at Rockville on July 27, 1858, at the age of thirty-six years, and subsequently Mr. Baynard was married to Martha Katherine Beckett, who bore him one child, Martha Katherine.

Ephraim Baynard, whose short but active career gave great promise of usefulness, was born on Edisto Island. After completing his elemental studies he went to Princeton College, where he graduated with high standing in his classes. He won the college medal in rhetoric, his subject being Scott's "Ravenwood." He studied law, was admitted to the bar, became solicitor for the State of South Carolina and rose to an enviable standing in his profession. He possessed literary talent of high order and was a contributor to the press on various subjects, his essays attracting more than ordinary attention. An easy speaker and fluent writer, he exerted a distinct influence among his contemporaries. As a friend he was noble, frank and generous. At the time of his death, which occurred when he was but thirty-seven years old, he was serving as city attorney of Charleston.

Mrs. Martha S. Seabrook received a good education and during all her long life she has given of her talents to others in one way or another. In two distinct avenues of usefulness she is widely known and well remembered, that of educator and writer. For the long period of thirty-eight years she was a teacher in the negro schools of Charleston, devoting herself unselfishly and devotedly to this labor, which to her was largely a labor of love, for her heart was in her work. In the field of literature she has contributed many splendid productions, which have entertained thousands, and even now, at the age of eighty-three years, she is still contributing to magazines and is compiling a book of her own poems. She is a spiritualist in her belief, being an ordained minister in that organization. Her mind is a rich storehouse, filled with treasures, and her friends regard it as a rare privilege to spend an evening with this noble woman whose ripened years sit so lightly upon her.

Mrs. Seabrook's life has unfolded like a beautiful flower; full of promise in her girlhood days, in the fulness of time it has burst into bloom, scattering its fragrance into the lives of those around her. Into her life have come many of the experiences common to the lot of mankind. The pathway has led her over many rough places and through trying ordeals, which have only strengthened the beauty of her character and broadened her sympathies. Charitable and kind, she has never lost an opportunity to say a helpful word to all with whom she has come in contact, and she has lived a life of exalted purpose, the value of which cannot be estimated.

ROBERT PICKETT HAMER, JR. Of that spirit of the farms which is the chief source of stability for our national life hardly any South Carolinian was a more conspicuous exemplar than the late Robert Pickett Hamer, Jr. Of his material achievements as a planter there is abundant evidence in the lands he accumulated, improved and managed. However, some of his best work was more intangible, and consisted in his associations with men and organizations and in a influence steadily directed for the elevation and improvement of country life in particular and the welfare of his community and state in general.

The handicaps imposed upon every son of the South as a result of the desolation of war were his, and a boyhood of struggle to surmount these obstacles and adversities seemed to have been the chief source of that resolution and energy which he applied so successfully in his mature years. He was born at the home of his maternal grandmother near Hopewell Church in Darlington County, April 10, 1863, son of Robert Pickett and Sarah (McCall) Hamer. He was English on his father's side and Scotch-Irish on his mother's. The Hamers had settled in Maryland about 1750, while William McCall came from Ireland to the colonies in 1770. The father was a planter and manufacturer, one of the outstanding citizens of his community, and from his mother the late Mr. Hamer drew the qualities of a fine character and a strong personality.

Mr. Hamer was reared on a farm, living in the country twenty-two miles from a railroad or county seat. It is said that when a boy he was given a small piece of land to work for his own profit, being

required to keep a strict account of the outlay on the land and the income, and personally to bear the expense of fertilizers. This was one of the practical experiences in the making of himself a good farmer, one of his first ambitions. His intellectual training was not neglected in the meanwhile. He attended the high school of Little Rock, South Carolina, was graduated from the noted Bingham School at Mebane, North Carolina, a military institution still conducted by Col. Robert Bingham, but now at Asheville. Mr. Hamer graduated from the South Carolina College with the Bachelor of Arts degree in 1885, and was president of his literary society and valedictorian of his class. In college he received distinction both as a thorough student and a social leader.

One of the chief benefits of a liberal education is that it enabled a young man to overcome the limitations of circumstances and environment, and to choose a vocation suited to his inclinations and talents. Mr. Hamer became a planter by conscious choice, and no one could deny that he chose wisely and well. Early in 1886, following his graduation from college, he began his career as a farmer. Thereafter he relied upon his intelligent management of the resources of the soil for all his wealth and prosperity. He had the satisfaction of seeing his business grow, his scope of management expand from year to year, until he was one of the largest planters in the state, operating at one time it is said 160 plows with his lands in four counties of South Carolina and two counties in North Carolina. On his home plantation grew up a small village known as Hamer, one of the chief industries of which is the Hamer Cotton Mills, and he was instrumental in building these and served as president and treasurer of the mill for a number of years. However, these mills and other commercial enterprises were always made incidental to his main business of planting. He served for fifteen years as postmaster at Hamer, was for fourteen years agent for the Atlantic Coast Line Railway Station at that point, and also general manager of the South Atlantic Cotton Oil Mill there. The Town of Hamer was named for him in 1891.

Mr. Hamer early became interested in the project for creating a new county from a portion of Marion County, and when he consented to serve as a member of the House of Representatives in 1909-10 from Marion County he was chosen for the distinctive purpose of furthering the creation of the new county and he introduced the bill creating Dillon County.

Mr. Hamer was one of the most prominent members of the South Carolina Agricultural and Mechanical Society, and served as its president for three consecutive terms. At this point should be quoted a portion of the memorial resolution adopted by the society in February, 1914, as follows: "He was president of the Society when the location was changed from Elmwood avenue to our present location, which entailed a great deal of onerous work and close attention, he having been on the committee which inspected several locations and finally chose our present grounds."

The memorial continues: "He was elected by the two branches of the General Assembly as a trustee of the University of South Carolina (serving from 1904 until his death), and was a member of the Board of Visitors of Clemson College. He was consecutively chosen as executive committeeman of the democratic party of South Carolina and was in attendance upon a meeting of this committee in the City of Columbia, considering the memorable Blease and Jones contest, when taken sick, and left for his summer home in Saluda, North Carolina, where he died soon afterwards on the 9th day of September, 1912. He knew no binding when principle was involved. He was an indefatigable worker in all matters undertaken by him. His integrity in everything was questioned by none. His name was prominently mentioned for governor of South Carolina and no son ever served more faithfully or loved her more."

Mr. Hamer in 1907 served as commissary general with the rank of colonel on the staff of Governor Ansel. In college he was a member of the Alpha Tau Omega fraternity, and was a Mason and Knight of Pythias and an elder in the Presbyterian Church at Hamer.

January 7, 1886, only a few months after graduating from South Carolina College, he married at Mineral Springs Janie B. McCallum, who survived him. Mrs. Hamer was born in Robison County, North Carolina, of which county her parents were also natives. Her father and mother were of Scotch ancestry. Brown McCallum was a very successful business man, was prospered in his life, and as a man of integrity commanded marked respect and confidence from all who knew him. Mrs. Hamer was liberally educated in Floral College of North Carolina and Peace Institute at Raleigh. To Mr. and Mrs. Hamer were born five children: Robert Cochrane, who married Jane Porcher DuBose; Sarah D., who became the wife of Alfred Scarborough; Flora J. and Brown McCallum Hamer, both unmarried, and Katharine Brown, who died January 5, 1907, at the age of eighteen.

A fitting conclusion for this brief outline was found in an editorial in the columns of the State a few days after his death: "The commonwealth of South Carolina could ill afford to lose at this time or any other time so good and true a citizen as Robert Pickett Hamer of Dillon. In the prime of his useful and fruitful manhood he is cut down. Twenty-seven years ago he received his diploma from the South Carolina College, and all of his years have been spent in right and honorable living. He was a great planter, a believer in the soil of his mother state, was a producer of wealth and happiness. He believed moreover that back of all prosperity lay honest and clean government, and he was always ready to respond with hand and heart and purse to help social and political causes that promise improvement for the people of every kind and condition. Without pretense, without expectation of reward, he was to be depended upon when his services were needed, and he was prompt, energetic and fearless in doing his duty. He was a man of genuine worth and ability, deserving of any honor that his state might bestow. As a member of the board of trustees of the University of South Carolina he was especially valuable; indeed, it is not going too far to say that he was one of the three or four most valuable members. He contributed to every good work in his home community and in his county, and he will be sorely, sorely missed by the hundreds of friends throughout the state who knew that they could call upon him whenever there was work to be done for South Carolina. We can not put in words how deeply we sorrow that he is dead nor how severe is the loss of the people of South Carolina that he is gone from them."

THEODORE WILBUR THORNHILL, president of the Charleston Oil Company, and one of the alert and capable young business men of the city, is making a record of which he may well be proud. He was born at Summerville, South Carolina, on September 12, 1892, a son of J. T. E. Thornhill, born in Virginia, who came to South Carolina about 1889, and is still a resident of Summerville. His wife, formerly Lula Wilbur, was born at Charleston. They have three children, namely: Edwin Jesse, Theodore Wilbur and Mary Cuttino.

Theodore Wilbur Thornhill was reared and educated at Summerville and Charleston, and was graduated from the Clemson Agricultural College in 1914 with the degree of Bachelor of Science in electrical and mechanical engineering. During the great war he was commissioned in the reserve corps on May 5, 1917, and called to active service May 8th. On August 3d he was sent to camp at Chickamauga Park, Georgia, and from there sent to Panama, where he remained until May 28, 1918, and was then returned to the United States. During June of that same year he was sent overseas, where he remained until March 20, 1919, when he was returned to the United States to resume his former occupations. During his service he was in the St. Mihiel offensive from September 12 to 16, 1918; Verdun offensive from September 29 to October 10, and the Meuse-Argonne offensive, October 15 to November 11, 1918, after which he was a member of the Army of Occupation from December 14, 1918, to January 12, 1919, with the rank of first lieutenant. Like other veterans of this great conflict, he does not care to dwell upon his experiences, although he displayed the valor belonging to the real American, which resulted in the defeat of the enemy when confronted by it.

Mr. Thornhill was married on November 8, 1916, to Ama Van Noy Smith, a daughter of D. Van and Mamie (Gadsden) Smith, of Summerville, South Carolina. Fraternally Mr. Thornhill is a Mason and Knight of Pythias. His social connections are with the Charleston Country Club. He is also active in the Charleston Chamber of Commerce, and he belongs to the American Society of Mechanical Engineers and to the Rotary Club of Charleston.

JACOB CALVIN KINARD has spent all his life in the community now known as Bamberg County. His years have been spent profitably and pleasantly in the planting industry and for a number of years he has been identified with the Town of Ehrhardt, which he is now serving in his sixth consecutive term as mayor.

Mr. Kinard was born in what was then Barnwell County, June 28, 1853. The Kinards have lived in South Carolina for several generations, and the Holland Dutch contributed at least one strain to the ancestry. His grandfather, George Kinard, was a native of Newberry and a farmer. The father, Adam Kinard, was born in Barnwell County, served for a short time in the Confederate army, and spent his life as an industrious farmer. He married Elizabeth Baggle, a native of Barnwell, now Bamberg, County. They had twelve children, Jacob Calvin being the youngest. Ten reached years of maturity. In 1876 Jacob Calvin Kinard took part in the riots of the period of reconstruction. He had four brothers who were soldiers in the Confederate army. They were Alfred; John, who was killed in the second Manassas battle; George, who was slightly wounded, and Daniel. Alfred and Daniel came home without suffering injury in the struggle.

Jacob Calvin Kinard was reared and educated in the community where he was born and in early manhood followed farming. He has been a resident of Ehrhardt since 1898 and has an interest in the hotel business and other lines of enterprise. His plantation consists of 110 acres, which he now leases on the crop sharing plan.

In 1870 Mr. Kinard married Miss Malinda Chassereau, a native of Barnwell County and daughter of John Chassereau. He has raised two orphan children, who are now happily married and residents of the Ehrhardt district. Willis Chassereau married Mr. Kinard's niece, Dora Kinard. Minerva Chassereau married Mr. Kinard's nephew, Quillie Kinard.

Mr. Kinard was an alderman several terms before entering upon his duties as mayor. He is affiliated with the Masonic order, the Ehrhardt Baptist Church, and is vice president of the Ehrhardt Banking Company.

CAPT. JAMES W. MARTIN is engineer of the Drainage Commission of Charleston. He was born in Edgefield, South Carolina, October 21, 1882, a son of William M. and Sarah (Collins) Martin, his father a native of Georgia and his mother of Edgefield. He was the oldest of three children. His brother, Jesse H., is deceased, and his sister is the wife of Dr. J. G. Moore, of Birmingham, Alabama.

Capt. James W. Martin received his education in the public schools of Graniteville, South Carolina, and is a graduate with the Bachelor of Science and Civil Engineering degrees from the South Carolina Military Academy at Charleston. He completed his course there in 1905. During the late war he was with the Fifth Training Regiment and also with the Tenth Division, U. S. Army. He is a member of Omar Temple, Nobles of the Mystic Shrine, of the American Society of Civil Engineers, of the South Carolina Society and the American Legion.

MAJ. ALFRED HUGER, of the Charleston bar, is one of the leading authorities on the Atlantic Coast on admiralty law. His special abilities in that field were recognized during the period of the war when he was in the service of the Government with the United States Shipping Board, as the board's admiralty counsel and in other capacities.

Born at Charleston, October 10, 1876, he is a representative of one branch of the Huger family that was established in South Carolina in 1685, following the revocation of the Edict of Nantes, when thou-

sands of French Huguenots were expelled from their country; many of them coming to the American colonies. His grandfather was Capt. Thomas Bee Huger, also a native of Charleston, an officer of the United States Navy and later commander of the Confederate fleet at New Orleans, where he was killed in action on the deck of his ship. Captain Huger's wife was a sister of General Meade, who commanded the United States forces at the battle of Gettysburg. Major Huger's father was Thomas Bee Huger, who was also born at Charleston. He was engaged in the steamship and cotton business until his death at the early age of thirty-five. He married Caroline Banks Smith, who was of Scotch ancestry, a granddaughter of Hugh Rose Banks, for many years a prominent citizen of Charleston. Major Huger is the only son of his parents. His sisters are Elizabeth Smith and Caroline Rose Huger, both living in Charleston with his mother.

Alfred Huger received his primary education in the Brownfield and the John Gadsden schools at Summerville, attended the Craft public school at Charleston and graduated from the Porter Military Academy in 1895. During the five years following he was employed in various capacities with the South Carolina Railway Company and the Southern Railway at Charleston, in the freight, claims and passenger departments. Later he entered the Cornell University College of Law, where he was graduated with the LL. B. degree in 1903. Major Huger, following his university career, went abroad as private secretary to Hon. Andrew D. White, former ambassador of the United States to Germany. With Mr. White he traveled in North Africa, Italy and southern France. He assisted Dr. White in writing his biographical memoirs. After his return to this country he passed the New York state bar examinations and became a law clerk for the firm Sackett, McQuaid & Chapman in New York City, general counsel for the New York Tribune and other important interests. After about a year there he became a senior law clerk to Butler, Notman & Mynderse, 54 Wall Street, having special charge of certain large railroad claims arising out of the burning of the Stuyvesant docks at New Orleans, Louisiana. He was made one of the arbitrators for determining the losses arising out of that great fire. While in New York he specialized in the practice of admiralty law there until the fall of 1907, when he returned to Charleston and, being admitted to the South Carolina bar under an order of the State Supreme Court, formed a partnership with Walter B. Wilbur, the firm later being known as Huger, Wilbur & Guerrard. Since Major Huger's return from army service he has been member of the firm Miller, Huger, Wilbur & Miller.

On June 1, 1917, Major Huger was appointed admiralty counsel for the United States Shipping Board at Washington. On April 6, 1918, he was commissioned major in the United States Army and assigned to duty in the Quartermaster's Corps under General Goethals, who ordered him immediately to duty in France as representative of the Shipping Control Committee in France. This committee was given power over the operation of troops and cargo ships in war service as well as the private American merchants ships. In France he was assigned to general headquarters and placed on duty with the First Section of the General Staff, S. O. S. He sailed from Brest in December, 1918, under orders to report for duty in New York City. In January, 1919, upon his application, he received honorable discharge from the U. S. Army and returned to Charleston, where he resumed the practice of his profession.

General Pershing awarded Major Huger a citation for exceptionally meritorious and conspicuous services as representative at general headquarters of the Shipping Control Committee in France. The French Government also awarded him the decoration of Chevalier de l'ordre National de la Légion d'honneur.

While in Cornell University Major Huger was chairman of the senior law class and secretary to the dean. He was named among the twelve memorial speakers, coming out second and receiving honorable mention. In 1903 he was chosen as one of the six contestants for the Woodford gold medal for oratory, and was awarded that prize. The same year he was appointed by his university its representative at the inter-collegiate contest held at Wheeling, West Virginia.

In April, 1906, at New York City, Major Huger married Margaret Mynderse, of Brooklyn, New York, daughter of Wilhelmus Mynderse. They have one son and two daughters, Alfred, Jr., Margaret and Jeanne. Major Huger at one time was commodore of the Carolina Yacht Club of Charleston. He was also a member of the vestry of St. Michael's Church, is a member of the Charleston Club, Chamber of Commerce, St. Andrew's Society, Knights of Pythias, and is a Mason.

In 1920 Major Huger was elected by the State Legislature a member of the Board of Trustees of the Medical College of the State of South Carolina. In 1920 he was elected a member of the Executive Committee of the Maritime Law Association of the United States.

CHARLES F. MIDDLETON. It is not always easy to discover and define the hidden forces that have moved a life of ceaseless activity and large commercial success; little more can be done than to note their manifestation in the career of the individual under consideration. In view of this fact, the life of the distinguished business man and public-spirited man of affairs whose name appears above affords a striking example of well defined purpose with the ability to make that purpose subserve not only his own ends but the good of his fellow men as well.

Charles F. Middleton, well known for many years as one of the largest cotton exporters of Charleston, is a native of the city now honored by his citizenship and was born on August 15, 1859. His father, Charles F. Middleton, who also was a native and lifelong resident of Charleston, was a marine engineer and was chief engineer on the S. S. Lelia during the Civil war. He went down with his ship on her initial trip in 1865, attempting to run the blockade. The subject's paternal grandfather, Philip Francis Middleton, was born and reared in London, England, whence he came direct to Charleston. The subject's mother, whose maiden name was Augusta

Loftus Jordan, was a native of Charleston and the daughter of Edward and Sarah (Shea) Gartside Jordan, her parents having been natives of Ireland. Charles F. Middleton is the elder and the only survivor of the two sons born to his parents. He was reared and educated in Charleston, completing his studies in the Holy Communion Church Institute, now Porter's Military Academy.

His first experience in active business was in the capacity of junior clerk in the cotton factor's office of A. J. Salinas. Later he was employed in the same capacity with the firm of Carrigan & Silcox, cotton factors. Having acquired a thorough knowledge of the details of the business, Mr. Middleton then entered into a partnership with E. A. Seckendorf, under the firm name of Seckendorf & Middleton. This was subsequently absorbed by the firm of Middleton & Ravenel, of which the subject was the senior member. During this period Mr. Middleton was enjoying a prosperous business, the exports of cotton growing with phenomenal strides year after year, until this became one of the best known in Charleston. The last change in the personnel of the firm was when it was reorganized as Middleton & Company, of which the members are Charles F. Middleton, Jr. and Sr., and G. Abbott and Augustus L. Middleton, sons of the subject. The latter have assumed a large part of the detail of management, thus relieving their father of much of the burden entailed by so vast a business. Charles F. Middleton is also interested in other business enterprises of Charleston, being president of the Middleton Compress and Warehouse Company and a stockholder and director in other concerns. A man of great business capacity and of the highest principles of integrity and honor, he has made his influence felt along diverse lines and has long been a leader in the promotion of legitimate industrial and semipublic enterprises which have conserved the welfare of his city.

On August 4, 1881, Charles F. Middleton was married to Lois Hazlehurst, the daughter of George Edward Hazlehurst, and to them have been born five sons and three daughters, namely: Lois Hazlehurst, Charles F. Jr., E. Willoughby, George Abbott, Augustus Loftus, Thomas H., Dorothy and Eunice. Three of these sons demonstrated their loyalty by enlisting in the service of their country in the recent World war: Ed Willoughby, a lieutenant of field artillery, Augustus L. a lieutenant in the aviation corps, and Thomas H., an ensign in the navy. Also a son-in-law, Frederick R. Baker, was in the service, with the rank of captain of field artillery.

Fraternally Mr. Middleton has for many years been a member of the Masonic order, and his religious membership is with the Protestant Episcopal Church, of which he is an earnest and generous supporter. In addition to his long and creditable career in business he has proved an honorable member of the body politic, rising in the confidence and esteem of the public. He has been essentially a man among men, having ever moved as one who commanded respect by innate force as well as by ability.

FRANCIS MARION WHALEY, a well known young Charleston business man, of university training and prominent social connections, was a lieutenant in the navy during the World war and had a most interesting experience and service.

Mr. Whaley, though born in New York City in 1888, is a member of an old and prominent family of Charleston. His father, William Whaley, was born at Charleston and for many years has been one of the city's prominent lawyers. He practiced his profession for fifteen years in New York City. William Whaley married Louisine McCready, a native of New York.

Francis Marion Whaley was educated in the Charleston High School, attended the Browne and Nichols preparatory school at Cambridge, Massachusetts, and finished his education in Princeton University. He was graduated from Princeton University in 1909, and at once returned to Charleston and took up a business career. Prior to the war with Germany his principal associations were in the lumber business, and for the past year he has been connected with the Southern Home Insurance Company of Charleston. He was elected in 1916 and served in 1917-18 as a member of the State Legislature from Charleston.

Mr. Whaley volunteered in the navy in the summer of 1917, and was on duty continuously until March 24, 1919. For some time he was assistant paymaster with the rank of ensign and finally was promoted to lieutenant of the junior grade. For fifteen months he was stationed at Admiral Sims' headquarters in London. While not on active duty, he is still a member of the Naval Reserves.

He married, July 6, 1909, Gabriella M. Grimball, daughter of Harry Morris and Emily (Trenholm) Grimball, of Charleston. They have one child, Francis Marion, Jr.

JAMES JULIAN BUSH. James Julian Bush, though a young man, has gained many of the most substantial honors and successes of his chosen profession, the law. He is junior member of the firm Brown & Bush at Barnwell, whose reputation has become widely extended not only through the bar of South Carolina but to other states as well.

Mr. Bush was born October 2, 1890, at Ellenton, South Carolina. After the usual preparatory course he entered the University of South Carolina, majoring in literature and graduating in 1910. Following that he took the regular course of the law department, graduating in 1914, and at once moved to Barnwell and began practice. In January, 1916, he formed his present partnership with Edgar A. Brown, and in less than four years this has become one of the busiest law offices in the state.

In 1916 Mr. Bush married Miss Gladys Brown, daughter of Charles and Bertha (Vogel) Brown, of Barnwell. Her parents have been residents of Barnwell for many years. The one child born to their union is James Julian Bush, Jr.

The present achievements and the promise of many larger distinctions that have come to Mr. Bush fulfill the anticipations derived from his distinguished ancestry. In the paternal line he had a great-great-uncle, Col. Isaac Bush, who achieved fame as a Revolutionary soldier. The grandfather, David Bush, was a man of prominence in his day and married Clarissa Ashley, whose ancestry on both sides went back prior to Revolutionary war times. Mr. Bush's maternal grandfather was Robert Dunbar, of old Revolutionary stock, whose wife traced her ancestry through Elizabeth Randolph of Virginia to the famous John Randolph of Roanoke.

The father of the Barnwell lawyer was the ardent South Carolina soldier and fighting man, James H. Bush, one of the picturesque figures during the reign of terror in the reconstruction period. He was one of the leaders of the white men in the Ellenton riot. He was greatly feared by the negroes, who knew well his dauntless courage and powers of leadership. He was in the thick of the fighting at Ellenton, and when more than 2,000 blacks were massed at the ginnery dam on Upper Bull's Run, opposed by a mere handful of whites, a negro courier was sent to Colonel Butler demanding James H. Bush, promising if he was given to the negroes they would at once disburse and return to their homes. Colonel Butler replied "Go to Hell," and the fighting was renewed more fiercely and on that spot James H. Bush was badly wounded, the leader of the blacks was killed, and the negroes so demoralized that they began to run in every direction. That was the culminating event in a long series of race riots, and at that time the threat of negro domination of South Carolina passed away forever.

James H. Bush was one of the few men for whom the Federal Government issued warrants who was never arrested. He was a splendid officer in the War between the States, his commission as captain being signed by Wade Hampton. This document is carefully preserved by his son James J. at Barnwell. After the war James H. Bush was honored by his own community in election to the Legislature. James H. Bush married the widow of Clinton E. Buckingham, and to their marriage were born two sons.

James Julian Bush is a member of the Masonic order, the Elks and the Woodmen of the World, is affiliated with the Christian Church, and is the present mayor pro tem of Barnwell. While closely devoted to his profession he has also acquired some valuable interest in land and banks, and is associated with the group of men who are doing most for Barnwell's general adavncement and improvement.

HERMANN D. LUBS. Continuously for more than a quarter of a century Hermann D. Lubs has been one of the employes and for many years one of the active officials of C. D. Franke & Company, of Charleston. As one of the great commercial houses of Charleston and of the entire South his office as secretary and treasurer of the company gives Mr. Lubs a distinctive honor in commercial affairs, and one that he has well deserved on the score of his personal abilities, his hard work and his fidelity.

Mr. Lubs was born at Charleston in 1874, son of C. F. and Magaretha (Wittschenn) Lubs. The parents were both born in Germany. His father, who came to Charleston about 1854 and spent the rest of his life in this city, was a Confederate soldier, being a member of the famous German Artillery of Charleston commanded by Capt. F. W. Wagener. For many years he was a prosperous merchant of Charleston.

Hermann D. Lubs acquired his education in the old German Academy under Prof. C. H. Bergmann, one of the best teachers of his time. However, since he was fifteen years of age his time and energies have been absorbed in practical business. His first employment for a year and a half was with the wholesale grocery house of G. W. Steffens & Sons on Bay Street. He also worked in the livery stable of George B. Lee. Realizing the need of a better commercial training, he left Charleston and entered Eastman's Business College at Poughkeepsie, New York, remaining there until he graduated in 1892. In that year he returned home, and became associated with the firm of C. D. Franke & Company.

C. D. Franke & Company is a Charleston concern of the highest rating in the commercial world. Their business is wholesaling in carriage materials, automobile accessories and heavy hardware. The main business offices are in the modern building at 170-172 Meeting Street, while the wholesale department is in the rear of the office building. The main building is 250x107 feet, three stories high, containing fifteen different floors, and there are other warehouses and buildings, all crowded with the product in which the company deals. A private railroad track connecting with all the railroads of Charleston enables the company to handle both its incoming and outgoing freight without the use of trucks. The business is one requiring the services of sixty people the year around, and its traveling representatives cover all the territory from Virginia to the Gulf of Mexico.

The founder of this business was the late C. D. Franke, who made his success in business a means of general good and philanthropy in his home city. In honor of his deceased adopted son, C. D. Franke left a fund providing for the Jacob Washington Franke Lutheran Hospital and Home at 261 Calhoun Street, and the fund and the institution were placed under the direction of the Evangelical Lutheran Charities Society, which was chartered in 1892, and of which Hermann D. Lubs is treasurer.

At the 153rd anniversary celebration of the German Friendly Society held in January, 1919, Mr. Lubs was honored by being elected president of the society. No other social and benevolent institution of Charleston has a finer record of service than the German Friendly Society. It was founded in January, 1766, by Michael Kalteisen, who had come to Charleston from Germany. The principal objects of the society are charity and congeniality, and for many years after its founding its chief work was giving instruction in the English language to German immigrants to Charleston. The society also developed a system of pensions and benefits for the widows and children of the deceased members. This fund has always been a large one. The society has carried on many good and noble works, and its history and traditions are deeply cherished not only by its members but by all good citizens of Charleston.

Mr. Lubs is a Master Mason, a past chancellor of the Knights of Pythias, and is a member of the Arion Society, the Charleston Rifle Club, and vestryman of St. Matthew's Lutheran Church. He is also a director in the Carolina Mutual Insurance Company.

By his marriage to Miss Ernestine Augusta Habenicht, of Charleston, Mr. Lubs has seven children: Herbert Louis, Victoria Alma, Claire Imogene, Milton Edgar and Erline Margaret, twins, Norma Natalie and Karl Raymond.

JEROME MARQUIS DAVIS, M. D. As a physician and surgeon Doctor Davis has been busied with the cares of a large practice in Orangeburg County for nearly thirty years, and is the pioneer physican and one of the earliest residents of the Town of North in that county.

He was born in Orangeburg County in 1861, a son of John W. and Ann (Johnson) Davis. His father was also born in the same locality, about twelve miles west of the Town of North. Doctor Davis attended the South Carolina College at Columbia through his junior year, and afterward entered the Medical College of the University of Georgia at Augusta, graduating in 1889. He at once began practice and in 1891, at the time of the founding of the Town of North, bought property there and the following year established his residence. He has been one of the most useful members of that community ever since. Doctor Davis also has the honor of being a member of the board of trustees of the Medical College of South Carolina. He belongs to the County, State and American Medical associations.

At the Town of North he has a beautiful and commodious residence built on the generous plan of the old South in colonial style, and equipped with waterworks and all modern conveniences. Doctor Davis has been twice married. His wives were daughters of J. George Salley, deceased, a planter at Seivern in Lexington County. The first Mrs. Davis was Anna Salley, who had two children, Dr. Legare S. Davis, a dentist in North, and a graduate of the Atlanta Dental College, and Mrs. Norma Davis Thatcher, of Greenville, whose husband is in the cotton business. By his second wife, Celeste Salley, he has one son, J. N. Davis, who is in his junior year in the University of South Carolina. Doctor Davis is a Knight of Pythias, a Shriner and a Baptist, and has been a deacon in his church for twenty-five years.

His wives' parents were of famous Revolutionary stock in South Carolina. Doctor Davis traces his ancestry back to John Davis, a soldier in the Revolution, who married a daughter of Colonel Avery, of North Carolina. His son, Dr. Needham Davis, came from Upper South Carolina to Aiken County, then Orangeburg District, in 1805, where he practiced his profession. Sidney Marquis Davis, his son, died in 1832. John W. Davis, always a planter, was a Confederate soldier, serving during the whole four years of the war. The mother of Jerome M. Davis also came of Revolutionary stock. Subject is president of the Bank of North, capitalized at $60,000. He assisted in its organization in 1905, was on its board of directors, then vice president and has been president since 1914. In college he belonged to the E. A. E. Fraternity.

EDWARD FROST PARKER, M. D. For many years a specialist in diseases of the eye, ear, nose and throat, Doctor Parker is a physician and surgeon of general distinction, and has been a hard working member of his profession at Charleston for thirty years.

He was born at Charleston, December 16, 1867, a son of Franois LeJau Parker, M. D., LL. D., and Elizabeth (Frost) Parker. His family is a historic one in South Carolina. His great-grandfather, Thomas Parker, was appointed by President Washington soon after the close of the Revolution as United States district attorney for South Carolina. The great-great-grandfather of Doctor Parker was William Henry Drayton, at one time chief justice of the Colony of South Carolina. Still another ancestor was Rev. Dr. Francis LeJau, rector of Goose Creek Church from 1707 to 1717. Doctor Parker's grandfather was Capt. Thomas Parker, who commanded the Abbeville volunteers in the Seminole Indian war in Florida. Captain Parker married Eleanor Legare.

Doctor Parker was liberally educated, attending private and high schools of Charleston, the South Carolina Military Academy and the University of Virginia. He took his medical degree from the Medical College of the State of South Carolina in 1889, and was awarded the first honors of his class and the college cup. For one year he served as interne in the Charleston City Hospital (Roper). He engaged in the practice of general medicine for several years before specializing in eye, ear, nose and throat diseases. He went abroad to study in London, England, in 1895, and received clinical appointments in the Royal Ophthalmic Hospital and in the Golden Square Nose and Throat Hospital of London. Since his return he has confined his work to his specialties. He is professor of eye and ear diseases in the Medical College of the State of South Carolina, a fellow of the American College of Surgeons and of the American Medical Association and a member of scientific and social organizations. He is ex-dean of the Medical College and an ex-president of the State and County Medical associations. He has contributed many reports and special papers to medical journals and the transactions of medical societies. He is author of a "History of Surgery in South Carolina," published in the Transactions of the South Carolina Medical Association in 1893. This was awarded the prize offered by the South Carolina Medical Association.

November 5, 1907, Doctor Parker married Harriet Horry Frost Prioleau, daughter of E. Horry Frost and Frances Ravenel.

FRANK VICTOR JAMES was for many years in the service of the Atlantic Coast Line Railway, but finally resigned to engage in banking at the Town of Denmark. He is president of the Citizens Exchange Bank of that city.

Mr. James was born in Williamsburg County, South Carolina, October 25, 1872, and is descended from the James family which was established in this state in Revolutionary times. His father, Joseph Allston James, a native of the state, was a physician and surgeon. He entered the Confederate army as a private and at the end was chief surgeon of Kershaw's Brigade. His commission is in the relic room of the Confederacy in Columbia. Doctor James married Sarah McCutchen, a native of South

PAUL H. ALLEN

Carolina, her parents being of pure Scotch blood. Her brothers, T. M. and James McCutchen, were soldiers in the Confederate army.

Frank Victor James was fifth in a family of eight children. He spent his early life in Cheraw, was educated there, and as a young man entered the service of the Atlantic Coast Line Railway. He was with that company about twenty years, in the different capacities of freight agent, ticket agent and telegraph operator. Mr. James was one of the organizers of the Citizens Exchange Bank of Denmark in 1909, and filled the post of cashier until 1913, since which date he has been its president.

In 1898 he married Sarah E. Guess, a daughter of Joseph G. H. and Mattie A. (Prothro) Guess. Mr. James is a deacon in the Presbyterian Church, and his father for many years was a Presbyterian elder. Fraternally he is affiliated with the Knights of Pythias and is a Shriner through the York Rite in Masonry.

HUGH RUTLEDGE TISON, M. D. The work and responsibilities of a competent and high minded physician and surgeon have engaged Doctor Tison at his native Town of Allendale for the past fourteen or fifteen years. Upon the organization of the new County of Allendale in February, 1919, he was honored by being elected first president of the Allendale Medical Society.

Doctor Tison was born at Allendale October 23, 1881, son of Perry H. and Sarah Elizabeth (Allen) Tison. His mother, still living, is a daughter of Paul H. Allen, for whom Allendale was named in the manner recounted in later paragraphs. The Tisons are an old time family of Lower Carolina, their ancestors on coming from England settling at Charleston. Doctor Tison's grandfather and great-grandfather were born and lived in Hampton County and were successful planters.

The late Perry H. Tison spent practically all his life in that section of Barnwell County that is now Allendale County. After having been honorably discharged from the army on account of physical disability he offered himself for any duty he might perform and was put in the conscript bureau, where he served the Confederacy until about a year before the close of the war, when he was compelled to retire on account of ill health.

In writing of Perry Hamilton Tison for the Confederate Veteran, Col. W. R. Darlington, Sr., has to say: "He was born in old Beaufort District, South Carolina, May 2, 1839, and died in Allendale, Barnwell County, November 18, 1918. He entered the Confederate army thoroughly equipped, having been educated at the State Military Academy of Charleston, but on account of physical disability he was forced to take an honorable discharge soon after going into service. He served as major in the 12th Regiment, South Carolina State Troops, under his brother, Colonel John A. Tison, who commanded the regiment.

"In his death is recognized the loss of a devoted and affectionate husband and father, an exemplary citizen of the old type, and a loyal friend. No truer heart ever beat for the cause of the Southern Confederacy, and through the long years of his life he adhered to his allegiance. He was always true to a principle and his name and honesty were synonymous.

"It is comforting to his friends and loved ones to know that he is free from the physical suffering he endured so many years and is now in communion with those that have gone before in an eternal reunion.

"He is survived by his wife, who was Miss Sallie E. Allen, of Allendale, and by three daughters and one son, namely: Mrs. Lucy A. Tison, Mrs. J. Gaillard Stoney, Miss M. Agnes Tison and Dr. Hugh R. Tison, all of Allendale, the county seat of the new County of Allendale."

Hugh Rutledge Tison attended the graded schools of Allendale, graduated with the Bachelor of Science degree in 1901 from Clemson College, and took his medical work in the University of Georgia at Augusta, receiving his M. D. degree in 1904. He was valedictorian of the medical class and was also one of the ten founders of the Chi-Zeta Chi medical fraternity, organized in Augusta in the fall of 1902. He is at the present time state regent for South Carolina for this fraternity. Another honor Doctor Tison greatly appreciated was when he was called upon to deliver the alumni address at the Clemson Agricultural College in 1913.

For a year he was senior interne in the Augusta City Hospital, and after about one year of residence and practice in the Town of Denmark he returned to his native town and has found abundant opportunities to prove his abilities and secure a substantial reputation as a physician. He also owns valuable farming interests in Allendale County. Doctor Tison is a member of the State and American Medical Association, a Methodist, a Royal Arch Mason and a past master of Allendale Lodge No. 109, Ancient Free and Accepted Masons, is past chancellor of Allendale Lodge No. 60, Knights of Pythias, and past consul commander of the Woodmen of the World.

November 23, 1904, at Allendale, Doctor Tison married Miss Edith Stoney, daughter of Dr. J. S. and Mrs. Laura (Allen) Stoney, of the prominent Charleston family of that name. They have three children, Perry H., Agnes and Hugh R., Jr.

PAUL H. ALLEN. The Town of Allendale was named in honor of Paul H. Allen, father of Mrs. Sarah Elizabeth (Allen) Tison. In telling the story of this event Mr. J. W. Ogilvie in the Christian Advocate says:

"About the period stated (1849) the necessity for better postoffice facilities began to move the people to petition Uncle Sam to grant them a postoffice in a line direct from Barnwell Court House. The prayer was answered and a public meeting held at the Swallow Savannah Camp Ground now in forest. Two serious difficulties had to be surmounted at this meeting. First, to find a man who would accept the postmastership of a country postoffice.

"Paul H. Allen, a pillar in the Methodist Church

and a staunch pillar in the support of anything good, as well as a heavy pillar to crush out everything mean and corrupt—a stay-at-home and mind his own business sort of a man—was pitched upon as the individual who possessed all the elements needful to manufacture a first-class country postmaster if—yes, if—if he could be persuaded to allow himself to be put in the department. He was induced to undergo the metamorphosis and then came the second difficulty—the name. Swallow-Savannah that marked and localized the section of country for miles around was a great, big pond and had a long euphonious name. It would not do, though it had named the country and had named the Methodist congregation, the latter for forty years, the former so far back that neither the memory of man or traditions ran to the contrary—still it would not do now for a postoffice.

"Quite a discussion sprang up. Who of us, surely none who were present, dreamed that all this good humored wrangling was but the travailing throes attendant upon the birth of a name. * * * In the midst of the innocent fun someone received an inspiration. The fact is one exclaimed 'call it Allendale.' It acted as oil upon the troubled waters. There was a great calm. The Allen was there individualized, quiet, unassuming and submissive to the popular will."

THEODORE GAILLIARD CROFT, M. D. This was one of the most widely known physicians and surgeons of the state. He graduated as valedictorian of his class from the Medical College of South Carolina at Charleston, March 5, 1875. His professional career was spent in Aiken and many of the best honors of professional and civic life were bestowed upon him. He was president of the South Carolina Medical Association in 1901-02 and in 1904 became a councilor of the association. He was made vice president of the Aiken County Medical Association in 1904. He was a member of the American Medical Association and the Tri-State Medical Association and the Association of Surgeons of the Southern Railway.

Doctor Croft was born at Greenville July 10, 1845, a son of Theodore Gailliard and Eliza Webb (D'oyley) Croft. Edward and John Croft came from the West Indies or direct from England to Charleston about 1700. Doctor Croft was a nephew of John-Gailliard, who represented South Carolina in the United States Senate for twenty-four years, while another member of the same family was Judge Theodore Gailliard. Doctor Croft's father was also a physician as well as a planter.

Doctor Croft had a normal life and routine of the boy born of good ancestry and member of a prominent family until the outbreak of the war between the states. From 1861 to 1862, during his fifteenth year, he served as sergeant of the Sixteenth Regiment of Confederate Volunteers and from 1862 to 1865 was member of a battalion of Citadel Cadets in the South Carolina Military Academy. After the war he chose to make his way by independent exertions and gained his professional education without pecuniary assistance from anyone. His education was acquired in Pierce's School and Furman University at Virginia. Before he studied medicine he was employed as superintendent of a draying and trucking outfit at Rome, Georgia, and from 1872 and 1873 was outdoor superintendent of the Aetna Iron Works in the same state.

Doctor Croft for many years was a surgeon for the Southern Railway, was examiner for many life insurance companies, for eight or ten years was surgeon for the First Regiment of South Carolina State Troops, was made a member of the South Carolina State Board of Medical Examiners in 1902, and has been untiring in his devotion to his profession and the great human service it represents. He was a democrat in politics and had been a vestryman and for twenty years at least was senior warden of St. Thaddeus Episcopal Church at Aiken. He died in March, 1915. A peculiar coincidence is that T. G. Croft and his brother, Congressman G. W. Croft, died on the same day of the month from the effects of the same disease, the former dying March 10, 1915, and the latter on March 10, 1903.

Doctor Croft was the first president of the First National Bank of Aiken, taking part in its organization. This position he only held until the bank was started and on its feet, but he was a director up to the time of his death. About four years before his death the Legislature elected him a trustee of the medical department of the University of South Carolina at Charleston, which office he held until the day of his death.

April 5, 1877, Doctor Croft married Miss Mary Ella Chafee. In July, 1904, he married Miss Estelle Alliston. A remarkable fact connected with the Croft family is that the T. G. Croft of each of the last three generations graduated as first honor men from the medical department of the University of South Carolina. The last Dr. T. G. Croft, a son of the subject and brother of George W. Croft, graduated about 1913. He served two years in the New York Hospital at Blackwell's Island. He was in the Twenty-sixth New England Division, One Hundred and Third Infantry Regiment, serving two years in France, and was one of four of twenty-nine officers who went into the Battle Chateau Thierry. He was commissioned a lieutenant. He is now practicing medicine in Jacksonville, where he is city physician, a position which he resumed upon his return from service.

GEORGE W. CROFT, an Aiken lawyer, is a son of the well known South Carolina physician and surgeon, Dr. Theodore Croft. He was born at Aiken, July 15, 1881, and was liberally educated, attending public schools, The Citadel at Charleston; had two years of academic work and took his law course in the University of the South at Sewanee, Tennessee. He finished his course in 1904 with the degree A. B. and until June, 1919, was engaged in a large general practice at Aiken and also assisted his father in the conduct of his farming properties, comprising about 10,000 acres.

In 1919 George W. Croft gave up his law practice to engage with his cousin, L. E. Croft, a son of the late G. W. Croft, in the development of the farm land belonging to the estates of Dr. T. G. and G. W. Croft, these estates now consisting of about 8,000 acres. At present the land is being handled under the share crop system and is planted largely to cotton and corn.

George W. Croft is the executor of the will of his father. He is a vestryman in the Episcopal Church, having been such for ten years.

February 12, 1907, he married Marie C. Chafee, a native of Lancaster, South Carolina, and a daughter of Nathaniel Chafee, a native of South Carolina and a merchant of Lancaster.

He was a soldier in the Confederate Army and during the third year of the struggle married Rosa Clara Gregg, a daughter of William Gregg, who was the pioneer in the cotton mill business in the South. Mr. and Mrs. Croft have one son, W. Crafee Croft, born November 22, 1907.

HON. EUGENE RANDOLPH BUCKINGHAM. While he was one of the active members of the Legislature during the sessions of 1919-20, Mr. Buckingham does not regard himself as member of the official class, and in fact this is the only political office he ever held or desired to hold. His activities nevertheless have been of an important nature in his home community of Ellenton in Aiken County, where he is a constructive leader in all matters affecting the agricultural interests.

Mr. Buckingham was born at Ellenton, August 22, 1871. This town was named in honor of his mother, Ellen Dunbar Buckingham, who was born there, daughter of Robert Dunbar, the town having been built on the Dunbar plantation. The father of Mr. Buckingham was Clinton E. Buckingham, also deceased. He was born in Barnwell, son of J. C. Buckingham.

Home and family associations are always an important element in any man's career, and it is a matter of interest to examine some of Mr. Buckingham's connections. The Buckingham line runs back to the time of the Mayflower, and when they first crossed the ocean his ancestors settled in New England and eventually came to South Carolina. The name Randolph is due to the lineage from Elizabeth Randolph of Virginia, a direct descendant of the historic John Randolph of Roanoke. Some of the old Randolph family silver is still carefully preserved by the Buckinghams.

His grandfather on his father's side was Esther Gildersleeve, representing one of the oldest families in England, the family lineage tracing from 1200 straight without deviation to the present day. Honors and emoluments were accorded the Gildersleeves in every generation. Richard Gildersleeve carried the line to America in 1630, and the career of this stanch Puritan is a matter of history interwoven with that of America from almost the beginning. A man of wealth and honors, he substantially founded the Gildersleeve family of America.

Mr. Buckingham's great-grandmother danced with General Lafayette and conversed with him. She must have made a great impression on that gallant soldier and gentleman, since he gave her his silver snuff box and the sash he was wearing, both of which are in the possession of the family today. Mr. Buckingham has an uncle, the well known financier and banker of Barnwell, Perry Buckingham. He also has two half brothers: J. J. Bush, an attorney at Barnwell, and Perry Bush of Ellenton, named for his uncle, Perry Buckingham, of Barnwell.

Mr. Buckingham, though a small child at the time, has a vivid memory of the terrible Ellenton riots. He watched the fighting at Upper Bull Run from the windows of his grandfather's plantation home, and the last great fight took place on the plantation itself. As a child he acquired a deep and lasting love of the old plantation and wanted to call it his, but it was not his lot to inherit it, so he went to work to realize his dream. By the most strenuous exertions he gradually bought back the old plantation until he now owns nearly all of it. It is one of the most beautiful in the South, fifteen hundred acres of land as level as a floor, picturesque and beautiful. He may be justly proud of his achievement, and his son and only child loves it as he does and promises to carry on the family traditions. The home in Ellenton is built on a part of the plantation and from it the old place is always in view. The first three cotton gins run by power were sent to this plantation by Governor Rutledge and Mr. Buckingham's maternal great-grandfather, Robert Dunbar, was manager. The plant was erected at Upper Bull Run, and was known as Crohn's Mill. Some of the timbers are visible today in the bottom of the creek.

Through the work and other affiliation with the soil Mr. Buckingham has achieved his best success in life, and is one of the men who confer dignity upon this ancient and honorable vocation. He completed his education in The Citadel at Charleston, where he remained a student three years. Mr. Buckingham now owns two fine plantations, one in the town of Ellenton and the other nearby. Both border the Savannah River. These plantations, under the ownership and management of Mr. Buckingham, have produced many fine crops of the cotton staple, and that crop is still the principle source of revenue. However, Mr. Buckingham has been a keen observer of the signs of the times and has been adapting farm work to new conditions. He raises much corn and small grain and has been carrying out experiments with small acreage devoted to cotton, peanuts, and other crops that seem to provide satisfactory results in a diversified scheme of agriculture.

One of his chief hobbies is the Ellenton Agricultural Club, the first organization of that kind being effected in 1894. It is completely non-political, its purpose being to promote the interests of agriculture and a great deal of value has been realized in that way. In a sense it is an agricultural study class, the meetings being devoted to selected topics and personal experiences, discussion of agricultural matters. Once a month a fine barbecue dinner is given. In December the names of the twelve men who will be hosts next year are drawn. Presidents of the club since the organization have been: A. W. Bailey, James H. Bush, L. A. Bush, Dr. M. A. Turner, Judge T. S. Dunbar and H. M. Cassels, while the present president is James Reid Boylston. This club and about seven similar clubs comprise the Association of Agricultural Clubs in the Savannah Valley.

Mr. Buckingham entered politics by being elected

to the State Legislature by the largest majority ever given a candidate in Aiken County. He was elected in 1918, and though a new member he proved his usefulness in both sessions of the general assembly. He is a member of the Christian Church and is affiliated with the Masonic Order.

June 7, 1893, Mr. Buckingham married Miss Florence Dunbar, of Barnwell County, daughter of Thomas Smith Dunbar and Eugenia (Bush) Dunbar. Thomas Smith Dunbar, whose name Smith comes from the lineage of Governor Thomas Smith, of South Carolina, was appointed a magistrate of Barnwell District by Governor Chamberlain in 1875, but on account of his stanch allegiance as a democrat was deposed. Upon the election of Wade Hampton and the restoration of white rule he was reappointed, and served continuously in that office from 1876 to 1911. Not one of his decisions as a magistrate was ever reversed, a record of distinction in itself. During reconstruction times he was a notable figure, served as chief of the Ku Klux and in other ways preserved peace and good order in the country. When Cole L. Blease was elected governor he forsook precedents and invited Magistrate Dunbar to administer the oath of office, which was impressively performed.

Mrs. Buckingham's mother, Eugenia Bush, was a daughter of the noted Capt. David Bush, who represented Barnwell County in the Legislature. Her great-great-grandfather, Isaac Bush, was a Revolutionary soldier and afterwards prominent in the legislative halls of South Carolina. Of the Bush family James H. Bush was an uncle of Mrs. Buckingham and step-father of Mr. Buckingham. James H. Bush served in the Legislature and was one of the few men for whom Federal warrants were issued who were never placed under arrest. He was a figure in the Ellenton riots, and, in fact, the leader upon whom the vengeance of the black man was chiefly threatened. When Colonel Butler told the negro mob that Mr. Bush would not be delivered to them, the battle was renewed with great intensity, and in the fighting Bush was wounded, but at the same time the leader of the negroes was killed and the backbone of negro domination was finally broken. The negro leader was buried under a tree stump on the banks of the creek near Crohn's Mill, the stump being still in evidence.

All those associated with Mr. Buckingham by ties of kinship, friendship or business are his stanch admirers, and all unite in the statement that he is intensely loyal in all his personal relations. This admiration has been frequently expressed in the sentence, "One thing you can say of Eugene—he always 'totes fair.'"

The only son of Mr. and Mrs. Buckingham is Philip Harold Buckingham, a young business man, now actively in charge of the Buckingham plantation. He volunteered in the United States Navy, serving two years and three months, covering the entire period of the war with Germany. He was a first class fireman on the transport Pocahontas, which gained an enviable record in the American transport fleet, being credited with fifteen round trips to France. He is now mayor of Ellenton.

LEGARÉ WALKER, a lawyer of twenty years' experience, has justly earned a place among the members of the South Carolina bar. His reputation is that of a diligent, painstaking, conscientious and broad minded attorney and citizen, whose skill and judgment have been availed of by a large and important clientage. Mr. Walker is also one of the prominent democrats of the state.

He was born at Charleston, August 4, 1875, a son of Legaré J. and Emma Josephine (Trenholm) Walker. His family history on both sides is linked with many prominent families. The history of the Trenholm family is detailed at length in Volume XVI, Chapter 4, South Carolina Historical and Genealogical Magazine. His paternal grandfather, G. Walker, was descended from an English gentleman who came to America from Edinburg prior to the Revolution and settled in Virginia. G. Walker married Elizabeth Lawrence Adams, directly descended from Henry Adams, who came to America between the years of 1630 and 1635. Henry Adams' son, Hugh, was the ancestor of John Adams and John Q. Adams. Another son of Henry was Matthew, whose son, William, was captured by Black Beard, the pirate, but afterward released; David was a son of William, and his son, David, Jr., was an officer in the Revolutionary army. A son of the latter was David Lawrence Adams, father of Elizabeth Lawrence Adams.

Legaré J. Walker served throughout the war between the states as a captain in the Confederate army and was wounded four times, twice seriously. He was one of the original railroad commissioners of South Carolina, was a deputy collector at the port of Charleston, and afterward a merchant. His second wife was Emma Josephine Trenholm, of Charleston, whose father was George A. Trenholm, of Charleston, one of the most prominent cotton merchants and statesmen of his day and distinguished in Confederate history as secretary of the treasury in President Davis' cabinet.

Legaré Walker attended Miss Caldwell's and Miss Porcher's school at Charleston, graduated from the Charleston High School June 29, 1892, and received his Bachelor of Arts degree from the College of Charleston June 30, 1896. He also pursued a finishing course in law at the University of Virginia during the summer of 1897, after studying law under William C. Miller, a leading member of the Charleston bar. He was admitted to practice May 6, 1898, and since then has spent twenty busy years in the practice of his profession at Charleston and Summerville. He is a director and solicitor of several banks located in the county, for twenty years served as corporation counsel of the Town of Summerville, is counsel for large timber and other corporate interests, and during the war filled the exacting position of chairman of the local board of Dorchester County under the Selective Service Act, and chairman of the Red Cross chapter of that county, both of which were highly commended for their effective management and accomplishments.

He has been in all campaigns, national, state, county and local, and has been an important factor in promoting the success of the democratic party.

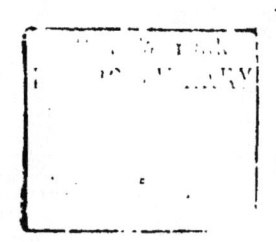

He has for many years represented Dorchester County in the State Executive Committee of his party. Mr. Walker is a member of the American Bar Association, the South Carolina Bar Association, the Alumni Association of the College of Charleston, the Political Science Association, and various other organizations. His religious affiliation is with the Episcopal Church.

At Savannah, Georgia, April 8, 1903, he married Ellen W. Axson, a daughter of Randolph Axson, of Savannah, Georgia. Her grandfather, Rev. I. S. K. Axson, was for more than thirty-five years pastor of the Independent Scotch Presbyterian Church at Savannah. Randolph Axson married Ella Law, daughter of Judge William Law, of Savannah. The first Mrs. Woodrow Wilson, whose maiden name was Ellen Axson, was a niece of Randolph Axson, and, therefore, a first cousin of Mrs. Walker.

Mr. and Mrs. Walker have six children, Ellen Axson, Legaré, Josephine Trenholm, Randolph Axson, William Law and Lawrence Adams.

MAJ. JOHN DIEDRICH ERNEST MEYER is a young man who has already marked his career with distinguished achievement that has reflected honor upon his native State of South Carolina. His record of service in the Thirtieth Division (Old Hickory) in its gallant activities as a part of the American Expeditionary Forces in France during the late World war was such as to reflect lasting honor upon his name; as a representative younger member of the bar of the City of Charleston he has proved himself in his admirable work as a resourceful trial lawyer and well fortified counsel; and in the election of November, 1919, he was "The Young Men's Candidate" for the office of probate judge of his native county. In his career as a soldier in the World war he won promotion to the rank of major.

Major Meyer was born at Charleston, South Carolina, on the 27th of August, 1890, and here he acquired his early education in the public schools, which he continued to attend until his graduation in the high school. Later he was graduated in The Citadel, South Carolina's historic old military college, and finally he entered the University of South Carolina, in which he continued his studies until his graduation in the law department, as a member of the class of 1915, his admission to the bar of his native state having occurred June 8th of that year. While attending the university he pursued the study of law under the preceptorship of James S. Verner and the firm of Cooper & Cooper, at Columbia, and as an undergraduate he served as president of the Law Association of the University. Before completing his professional education Major Meyer had taught school in North Carolina and incidentally served as commandant of cadets in the institution with which he was thus connected.

Immediately after his admission to the bar Major Meyer opened an office in the City of Charleston, and within less than six months thereafter he was retained, together with the law firm of Stoney & Cordes, as counsel in the celebrated bloodhound case of The State versus Brown. In this connection he played a conspicuous part in the achieving of a signal victory and established a high reputation for ability as a trial lawyer—at the very inception of his professional career. The decision in this special case has been reported in annotated legal reports throughout the United States, as in many particulars it constituted a precedent. The alert and vigorous mind of Major Meyer has caused him to take loyal and active interest in political affairs in his native state. His uniform courtesy, broadness of vision, tact and initiative have proven great factors in his success in business.

It is extraneous to the assigned province of this publication to enter into details concerning the splendid military records made by South Carolina men in the World war, but consistency renders it imperative to offer a succinct record concerning the achievement of Major Meyer, who has from his early youth taken deep interest in military affairs. He became affiliated with the Washington Light Infantry, one of the finest military organizations in South Carolina, and was a member of the rifle team which represented the state at the international contests held at Camp Perry, Ohio, in 1913. In 1915 he was appointed captain and adjutant of the Second South Carolina Infantry, which made a noteworthy record in the Mexican border service in 1916-17.

In July, 1917, Captain Meyer was mustered into the Federal military service as captain and adjutant of the Second South Carolina Infantry at Georgetown, this state. Upon the formation of the Thirtieth (Old Hickory) Division, at Greenville, he was assigned to duty as captain and adjutant of the One Hundred and Fifth Train Headquarters and Military Police, of which position he was the incumbent when, with his command, he sailed for France in May, 1918. In the training area in France Captain Meyer spent about one month, during which he gave special attention to studying the British staff system and the technical and practical questions pertaining to ammunition supply. Finally his division was thrown into the line near the City of Ypres, and it was while advancing to take up this position that Captain Meyer was assigned to the moving of the property and supplies of one of the brigades to the front—a task which he achieved in one day and set a record, as the other brigade required two days to accomplish this result. He was probably the first American officer with a combat American division to move into Belgium. His exceptional work in the connection noted above resulted in his being detailed as assistant G-1, in addition to his other duties. Shortly afterward he was relieved as Adjutant of Divisional Trains and appointed Division Ammunition Officer, besides retaining the office of assistant G-1. As division ammunition officer he had entire charge of, and was responsible for, all ammunition of the division. He was charged with the duty of procuring the ammunition and delivering the same to the troops, and upon him devolved the responsible duty of designating the quantity and types of ammunition to be used. Captain Meyer took part in all of the engagements in which his division participated, and was always regarded as a fearless officer who took good care of his men. The record of the gallant Old Hickory Division has become a part of the history of the great war in the annals of time and of that of the American Expeditionary Forces. To review that record is not requisite—nor is it possible—in this sketch, but it may be stated that the division endured the full tension of the great conflict on the blood-stained fields of France and Belgium and played an important role in connection with the splendid achievement of American arms. It is but consistent, however, to offer in this connection the following estimate given of the division by Sir Douglas Haig, the distinguished field marshal: "On the 29th of September you took part with distinction in the great and critical attack which shattered the enemy's resistance in the Hindenburg line, and opened the road to final victory. The deeds of the Twenty-seventh and Thirtieth American Divisions will rank with the highest achievements of this war."

After the signing of the historic armistice Captain Meyer brought his professional talents into requisition and made a splendid record as counsel for comrades appearing for trial at court martial. His service in this capacity was such that the commanding general caused him to be appointed trial judge advocate. In this position he proved that he could prosecute as well as defend. Shortly before leaving France the commanding general of his division assigned him to defend an American soldier who had been accused by some French citizens of committing a heinous offense—one that might have brought about international complications. The prosecution was represented by a judge of the Kentucky bench and also by two other able lawyers of that state. Major Meyer so effectively espoused the cause of his client as to bring about an acquittal for the latter.

It was for his efficient service at the front that Captain Meyer was recommended for promotion to the rank of major. The armistice temporarily delayed this promotion, but on the 21st of February, 1919, the merited recognition came, in consonance with the recommendation of the commanding general and other high officers of the division.

After the close of his service as a soldier Major Meyer returned to his native land, and after receiving his honorable discharge he resumed the practice of his profession at Charleston, where he is meeting with the success that ever attends ability and sterling character. His name is still enrolled on the list of eligible young bachelors in his native city, where his popularity is of unqualified order and where he holds membership in numerous fraternal and social organizations of representative type, including the American Legion, the Masonic fraternity, the Loyal Order of Moose, the Arion Society and the Charleston Rifle Club.

ARTHUR LLOYD AGNEW was born and received his early business training at Columbia, where the Agnews have been prominent in commercial affairs for several generations. Mr. Agnew for ten or twelve years has been a resident of Charleston and is manager of the Terry Fish Company, one of the city's oldest business houses, founded in 1827.

Arthur Lloyd Agnew was born at Columbia in 1881, a son of John and Jennie (Saunders) Agnew, both now deceased. His grandfather was also named John Agnew, and was one of the early merchants of Columbia and one time served as mayor of that city. The Agnew business house on Main Street, at what is now the Mimnaugh corner, comprised in the early days a group of one and two-story buildings, which with the grounds extended back almost to Assembly Street. The business was hardware, groceries, wagons, buggies, and other supplies for city and plantation use, and the patronage was drawn from many of the back counties as well as the country immediately contributary to the state capital.

The younger John Agnew grew up in this business, was associated with his father until the latter's death, and then continued it until death overtook him in his labors in 1897, when he was just in the prime of his years. In the meantime his other affairs, particularly his interests as a farmer, had somewhat dwarfed the mercantile business at Columbia.

The public schools at Columbia gave Arthur Lloyd Agnew his early education, and as was the rule in the family he began to learn business at an early age. For some time he was with the firm of R. O. Jones at Columbia and later in the brokerage business at Gaffney. He has been one of the active men in the Terry Packing Company at Columbia since 1906 and is vice president of that corporation. In 1908 he came to Charleston to take charge and management of the Terry Fish Company, a subsidiary of the Terry Packing Company. The Terry Fish Company has branch houses at Savannah, Augusta and Columbia, and is one of the largest enterprises and organizations of its kind on the South Atlantic Coast.

Mr. Agnew is a member of the Charleston Club and the Charleston Country Club and has had his home in that city since 1908. He married Miss Mary Forster Miller, a member of a prominent Virginia family at Winchester in that state. They have one son, Lloyd Campbell Agnew.

HORATIO WARING MITCHELL, who for eighteen consecutive years (appointed in 1902) has been Master for Charleston County, is a lawyer of wide experience and thorough ability, and has been a member of the bar since 1878.

He was born at Charleston August 28, 1852. The family originated in Scotland, and his great-grandfather, Dr. John Mitchell, was one of the early physicians of South Carolina. The grandfather, James Dean Mitchell, was a native of Charleston and a lawyer by profession and at one time held the office of probate judge. Horatio Waring Mitchell, father of Judge Mitchell, was a native of Charleston, spent his active career as an accountant and died in his eighty-ninth year. His wife was Eliza Maria Gantt, a native of Charleston and a daughter of Thomas J. Gantt, a native of South Carolina, and a granddaughter of Judge Richard Gantt, of Baltimore, Maryland.

Horatio Waring Mitchell was the third in a family of seven children, five of whom reached mature years. Only two are now living, the other being Eliza Hall Mitchell, of Charleston.

Judge Mitchell first attended school under the Misses Lannean, Pitt Street, Charleston. At the age of eight years was a pupil in what is now the Bennettville, South Carolina, and in private schools conducted by Mr. William Glenn and later Dr. William

H. Tarrant, of Charleston. In 1870 he entered and in 1874 was graduated with the first honors of his class from the College of Charleston. He read law under Rutledge and Young, Simons and Simons and J. N. Nathans of the Charleston bar and was admitted to practice in 1878. He enjoyed a profitable share of the general practice of the Charleston bar until 1902, when he was chosen Master for Charleston County, and has held that office continuously since that date. At one time he was in practice with W. Gibbes Whaley under the name Mitchell & Whaley.

Mr. Mitchell is a past master of Solomon Lodge No. 1, Ancient Free Masons, by which the degrees were conferred upon him. He dimitted to Pythgorean Lodge No. 21, of which he is now a member, and is a past chancellor of Pythgorean Lodge No. 6, Knights of Pythias, a member of the South Carolina Society, the Arion Society, and at one time was a member of Company B of the First Regiment of South Carolina Militia. Mr. Mitchell is also an ex-president of the Alumni Association of the College of Charleston.

WILLIAM MILTON STRICKLAND. This well known farmer and merchant at Evergreen in Anderson County has a career of special interest to those who meet adversity and conquer problems along life's road. He is a member of an old and well known family of Anderson County and was born near Craytonville September 15, 1869.

His grandfather John Strickland was a native of Abbeville County, but moved to Anderson County during the war times. William M. Strickland is a son of Stephen Elbridge and Drusilla (Wright) Strickland. His father who was born in Abbeville County in 1845 died in Anderson County in 1894, suffered when a youth the common and familiar disease "white swelling," which made him a cripple and shortened his life. In spite of this handicap he volunteered his service to the Confederate Government and for two years was employed as a wagoner. He had learned the shoemaker's trade, but after the war and his marriage gave his time to farming. His wife Drusilla Wright was a daughter of James and Mahala (Martin) Wright of Hart County, Georgia. Mahala Martin's father, Rev. William P. Martin, was a prominent Baptist minister who lived for many years at Belton, South Carolina, and was pastor of several churches in that vicinity. Mrs. Drusilla Strickland is still living, occupying a farm adjoining that of her son William. She was the mother of thirteen children, five still living. W. M. Strickland is the second child and oldest son.

Up to the age of fourteen Mr. Strickland managed to attend school a few weeks each year, but after that his education was regulated largely by experience and by a habit of constant observation. As the oldest son he had to become the mainstay of the family and at the age of fourteen was practically given free rein in the management of the home farm. He continued on the farm, living with his parents until the age of twenty-one. He then hired out to a farmer for $10 a month and board. This arrangement was terminated because he was stricken with typhoid fever. Not long afterward Mr. Strickland married and returned to his mother's place. He had little to do with, but the future kept encouraging him, until his wife died. After this reverse he had a severe struggle to start anew. After his second marriage he established another home, resumed farming and also opened a store at Evergreen. Through many vicissitudes Mr. Strickland has now achieved a really gratifying success, represented in the ownership of valuable farm lands and a prosperous business as a general merchant.

In 1894 he married Eliza Hewin. She died in 1900 leaving one son, Elbridge D. Strickland now a merchant at Starr, South Carolina. In 1901 Mr. Strickland married Mrs. Minnie E. (Winter) Peek, a daughter of Joseph C. Winter of Holland's Store, South Carolina. Mr. and Mrs. Strickland have three living children, Holcomb, Vera and Charlotte. The family are members of the Baptist Church, Mr. Strickland being a deacon. He and his son Elbridge are Knight Templar Masons and both joined the Mystic Shrine at the same initiation service.

MAJOR WILLIAM S. LANNEAU is president of Lanneau's Art Store of Charleston, a business widely known and patronized not only in Charleston, but over the State of South Carolina.

Major Lanneau was born at Charleston, November 30, 1869, a son of William S. and Isabella (Calder) Lanneau. His parents were also natives of Charleston. The Lanneaus were one of the original families of French Huguenots to establish their homes in Charleston. He established the Art Store in 1899 and has been president since the business was incorporated as a stock company. He has a number of other business interests and is a director of the Commercial National Bank.

In 1906, while captain of the old historic Washington Light Infantry, the company bought their present armory, which they opened on the 22nd of February, 1907, celebrating the centennial of the command. In 1908 he was major of the First Battalion of the Third Infantry of the South Carolina National Guard, and retired with the rank of major in 1909. During the time of the World war, he was again captain of the Washington Light Infantry, Company A of the First South Carolina Reserve Militia.

Major Lanneau was an alderman of the City of Charleston under the Hyde administration, 1915-1919. He was chairman of the committee on water supply of the city council, and it was while chairman that the purchase of the present plant was made. He was then made one of the commissioners on the Board of Public Works, which had charge of the municipal water supply.

Major Lanneau is a member and vestryman of St. Johns Lutheran Church and superintendent of the Sunday school. He is also a member of the Masonic Order.

In 1902 Major Lanneau married Miss Mary Siegling, daughter of Henry and Kate Rutledge (Patrick) Siegling, of Charleston.

HERMAN G. LEIDING, who is founder and active head of the H. G. Leiding Company, brokers, exporters and shipping agents, established in 1896, in Charleston and Havana, Cuba, in 1919, one of the most important commercial houses of Charleston, has more than the position of a successful business man. He has carried his business enterprise and public spirit into direct relation with many of the larger movements for the upbuilding and expansion of southern trade and commerce, particularly as these movements affect the city and port of Charleston.

Born at Charleston in 1878, he is a son of the late Herman Leiding, for many years a prominent Charleston manufacturer, and Catharine Jenkins (Prentiss) Leiding. His mother is a daughter of the late Rev. W. O. Prentiss, well remembered in Charleston and over the state for his long continued work as an Episcopal clergyman.

The late Herman Leiding was born in Germany. For many generations the Leidings inhabited what is now Lorraine. His father, Count Leiding, was a member of the German nobility and served as a general in the German armies during the Napoleonic campaigns. Acquiring a thorough distaste and hostility for the enforced military system of the German State, Herman Leiding left that country in early youth. He acquired an extensive experience as a world traveler and student, and among his Charleston associates was distinguished by his ripe scholarship and his versatile gifts. During the Civil war he was in the Confederate army. He had many exciting experiences in the blockade running operations, and helped get many ships with supplies for the Confederacy in and out of Charleston Harbor.

Herman G. Leiding derived many helpful influences from his father and mother during his youth and was educated in the grammar and high schools of Charleston. Since early youth his career has been one of practical business. The H. G. Leiding Company in twenty years has developed a large business, and in addition to the main offices at Charleston conducts a successful branch house in Havana, Cuba. The company controls and operates a number of canneries and warehouses.

With his long experience in export and import trade, Mr. Leiding has proved an invaluable adviser in the present movement for the expansion of Charleston's ocean commerce. With other public spirited citizens interested in the same matter he has organized a series of activities that already have given substantial impetus in this direction. He is a member of the Midwest-Gulf-South Atlantic Foreign Trade and Transportation Committee, the object of which is the development of southern ports in the handling of export shipments from the Middle West. In this connection Mr. Leiding, accompanied by other prominent members of the Charleston Chamber of Commerce, participated in the hearing before the committee on commerce of the United States Senate at Washington in January, 1920. A vast array of data and proof were submitted at the time, as a result of which the southern business man was practically assured of the maintenance of favorable railroad rates from the Middle West to the southern ports, notwithstanding powerful opposition from the great interests representing northern ports. Mr. Leiding is a member of the Foreign Commerce Committee of the Charleston Chamber of Commerce.

He married Miss Harriet Kershaw, of Charleston, daughter of Rev. Dr. and Mrs. John Kershaw. Her father is rector of St. Michael's Church in Charleston and is also a member of the historic Kershaw family of Kershaw County.

Mr. Leiding is a member of the Charleston Club, the Charleston Country Club, Carolina Yacht Club, and the South Carolina Society.

EDWIN GARLINGTON SIMPSON, M. D. At least one community in South Carolina, Cross Hill, has an abiding and affectionate memory of the life and character of the late Dr. Edwin Garlington Simpson, though his abilities were such as to command for his professional services a much wider appreciation.

He was born at Laurens, South Carolina, November 12, 1815, and died at his old home in Cross Hill March 4, 1901, when in his eighty-sixth year. He was a son of William Wells and Nancy (Garlington) Simpson, and both of these families have long been prominent in South Carolina and America, and have given their country distinguished men in all the professions and walks of life and many of them served with credit and some of them gave their lives during the Colonial, Revolutionary, Civil and more recent wars.

Edwin Garlington Simpson graduated from the "Medical College of Charleston," South Carolina, and soon afterward located at Cross Hill, where for more than half a century he performed the duties and upheld the highest traditions of the medical profession. In his profession as in his citizenship and private life he was ever true and faithful, and was a man of marked generosity and of most exalted patriotism. For many years he served as an elder in the Liberty Springs Presbyterian Church, and his remains now rest in the old churchyard.

On April 29, 1841, Edwin Simpson married Rachel Goulding Campbell, a daughter of Dr. Robert Erskine Campbell and Elizabeth Goulding. Mrs. Simpson possessed a wonderful symmetry of character, and it is said that she recognized no duties higher and more sacred than those to her God and family, and was a living embodiment of charity and good will. Upon her soul was deeply wrought the love of God, "Where beyond these voices there is peace." She descended from a long line of Scotch Presbyterian ancestry, including men of rare scholarship and vigorous mentality. Her mother's brother, Thomas Goulding, was founder and first president of the Presbyterian Theological Seminary at Columbia, South Carolina.

To the marriage of Doctor Simpson and wife were born two children, McNeil Turner Simpson, who married Susan Young Watts; and Nancy Elizabeth.

Nancy Elizabeth Simpson was married May 19, 1865, to Napoleon Bonaparte Davenport. Mr. Davenport, who was born in Newberry County, South Carolina, December 11, 1842, was a son of John Gilliam and Sarah Ann (Williams) Davenport. When he was two years of age his mother died and he was reared by his maternal aunt, Theresa Williams. His father, a man of cultivated mind and of large estate, gave him the best educational advantages, and at the age of sixteen he entered the Confederate army as a volunteer in Company B of the James Battalion. A year later he was transferred to Company E of the Seventh Cavalry, under

Col. A. C. Haskell, and performed all the duties and obligations of the brave and gallant soldier for four years. The cause of the Southern Confederacy was very dear to him, and his deathbed request was that the Confederate flag be his winding sheet. The B. W. Ball Chapter of the United Daughters of the Confederacy placed the old flag on his casket, surrounded by a wealth of floral offerings. His remains also rest in Liberty Springs cemetery. He died at Cross Hill May 5, 1916. Deafness made it impractical for him to realize his brilliant mental qualifications in a public career and he therefore turned his attention to farming at the old homestead in Newberry County, and was one of the leading planters of that region for many years. He was in bearing dignified, a courteous gentleman, a lover of books, who spent much of his time in his library, studying science, and was well versed in ancient and modern history and a student of Latin and Greek. He was a splendid type of those worthy and unostentatious citizens who performed conspicuously their part for their country in those trying times, "when then, as now, Princes and Lords were but the breath of Kings, but an honest man is the noblest work of God."

To the marriage of Napoleon B. Davenport and Nancy Elizabeth Simpson were born eleven children, five of whom are still living: Theresa Rachel, Edwin Garlington, John Gilliam, Sarah Ann, who is the wife of Perrin Ball Watts and has a son, Barrett Simpson Watts; and Robert Campbell Davenport, who married Louise Bailey and has one daughter, Mary Elizabeth Davenport.

DANIEL S. HENDERSON. While the home of the Hendersons has always been at Aiken, there is hardly a better known and more distinguished name in the legal circles of the state, due to the cumulative labors of the Hendersons as lawyers during the past half century. Daniel S. Henderson is the oldest of the lawyers who for many years have practiced under the simple title of "Hendersons." Daniel S. Henderson was admitted to the bar in 1872, began practice at Aiken, and was one of the first lawyers to open an office in that city after the formation of the new county. In 1880 he was joined in practice by his brother Edward P. Henderson and they practiced as Henderson Brothers until January, 1899, when a son of Daniel S. Henderson, P. F. Henderson, was admitted and the firm name became Hendersons.

Daniel S. Henderson was born at Waltersboro in Colleton County April 19, 1849, a son of D. S. and Caroline R. (Webb) Henderson. His parents were both natives of South Carolina and the immigrant ancestor was Daniel Henderson who came from the North of Ireland in 1790 and settled in Charleston. D. S. Henderson, Sr., was also a lawyer by profession.

Daniel S. Henderson was educated in local schools. He entered the Confederate service in Culwaks Cavalry before he was eighteen and served as courier to Gen. Stephen Elliott until the end of the war. Graduated from Charleston College in 1870, with first honors, studied law in that city, was principal of the Male Academy at Chester while pursuing his law studies, and upon admission to the bar in 1872 located at Aiken. He almost at once had a busy practice and every volume of the Supreme Court Reports from 1872 to the present time shows from one to six cases argued before the Court by Mr. Henderson or his partners.

For many years he was likewise prominent in the democratic party, attending most of the democratic conventions, was a delegate to the National Convention of 1884 when Grover Cleveland was first nominated. He served six years in the State Senate, but practically retired from politics in 1880. He was author of the bill to prevent duelling in South Carolina, especially the duelling oath which has to be taken by every officer in the state from governor to coroner and which has stopped the practice of duelling in the state. He first introduced it in the Legislature in 1881 and afterward had it inserted in the Constitution of 1895 he being a prominent member of that convention. Mr. Henderson has been a trustee of South Carolina College, the Presbyterian Theological Seminary, University College—the College of Charleston and Davidson College, and is president of the Aiken Institute, and for many years an elder in the Presbyterian Church.

In 1875 he married Miss Ripley, a daughter of T. R. Ripley of Atlanta, Georgia, her mother was a Conner of South Carolina; and she is a relative of Gen. Roswell Ripley, a commandant of Fort Sumter in the War between the States. The ancestry of Mrs. Henderson is of Revolutionary stock, Mrs. Henderson being a Regent of the Esther Marion Chapter, Daughters of American Revolution.

HENRY ORR BRITTON, who was one of the boy soldiers of the Confederacy in the war between the states, and had three sons in the World war, has been a lifelong resident of Williamsburg County and for the past twelve years has filled the office of clerk of court.

Mr. Britton was born at Indiantown, Williamsburg County, August 15, 1848, son of Thomas Nelson and Rebecca Ervin (Gordon) Britton. He grew up on his father's plantation, had a public school education, and on September 1, 1864, was enrolled in the Confederate army as a private in Company E of the Seventh Infantry. He performed the soldier duties required of him until the close of the great struggle in April, 1865. Following the war he took up civil pursuits as a farmer, and farming and planting has been his occupation for over half a century.

Mr. Britton served eleven years as deputy sheriff of Williamsburg County, and was elected to his present office as clerk of court in 1906. He gave much of his time to various patriotic activities during the war, and has since been deeply interested in a plan for compiling and preserving short biographies of every soldier and sailor representing Williamsburg County in the great war.

Mr. Britton is a deacon of the Presbyterian Church. Mr. Britton's first marriage was to Miss Carrie Ford, and he has one child by that marriage: Ula, who is the wife of W. S. Booth of Manor, Georgia. In February, 1889, he married Mary A. Daniel of Williamsburg County. They are the parents of four children: Mary is Mrs. F. J. Watson of St. Matthews, South Carolina. The three sons are Harry, John Daniel and William Johnson. Harry entered the service in May 1918, and served overseas with the Three Hundred and Twenty-Fourth Regiment in the Eighty-First Division. John Daniel spent the greater part of his enlistment period with a supply company at Camp Sevier. William Johnson went with the Federalized National Guard of South Carolina to the Mexican border in June, 1916, and afterwards entered the World war as a member of the Charleston Light Dragoons, and was with the division headquarters of the Thirtieth Division in France.

DAVID CHARLES SHAW, who has gained exceptional prestige in the automobile business in South Carolina, began handling cars about eleven years ago at Sumter, where he still has his home, though his business organization is now centered at Columbia.

Mr. Shaw was born in Sumter County, June 27, 1871, son of Ervin and Lilles (Whitworth) Shaw. The Shaw and Whitworth families have long been prominent in this section of the state. David Charles Shaw came to manhood largely in the environment of his father's farm and with only the advantages bestowed by the common schools of the neighborhood. When he left home at the age of twenty-one he entered the service of D. W. Alderman & Sons Company. That company then as now was extensively engaged in the manufacturing of lumber, and maintained an industry of very ramified proportions, involving lumber camps, private railroads, stores and commissaries and all the equipment and facilities necessary to such an industry. Mr. Shaw was put in charge of the mercantile interests of the firm, and he not only handled his responsibilities successfully but acquired a business training and knowledge that could have been gained in hardly any other school of experience.

Leaving this firm in 1909 he established the Shaw Motor Company at Sumter. A few years later his organization had the reputation of being the largest dealer in Ford motor cars in the entire South. Since then Mr. Shaw's interests in the automobile industry have extended to various cities and his organization still directs a large share of the distribution of automobiles throughout the state. He is president of the Shaw Motor Company at Columbia and is also owner and proprietor of the Columbia Sales Agency, which handles several of the best makes of cars. Mr. Shaw is owner and proprietor of the Colonial Hotel in Columbia, and is a stockholder in several banks throughout the state.

He is a democratic voter, but has regarded his business and other interests as more important than office holding. He and his family are members of the First Presbyterian Church in their home City of Sumter and he is an elder in this church.

In Sumter County, December 27, 1892, Mr. Shaw married Lula Alderman. She is a daughter of D. W. Alderman, head of the D. W. Alderman & Sons Company. Her father for years has been one of the leading lumbermen of the South, and the family is one of prominence both in business and social circles. Mr. and Mrs. Shaw became the parents of seven children: Ervin David, Gifford W., Paul Whitworth, David Charles, Jr., Martha Priscilla, Bartow Solomon and Lula May. Another page is reserved for the appropriate tribute to the distinguished soldier son, Ervin David Shaw.

ERVIN DAVID SHAW. Patriotic sacrifice will always have a deep significance to South Carolinians who recall the name and service of Ervin David Shaw.

A son of Mr. and Mrs. David Charles Shaw, of Sumter, he was born at Alcolu in Clarendon County, September 13, 1894, but was reared and educated at Sumter, graduating from the Sumter graded school and continuing his education in Davidson College, North Carolina, and in the Georgia School of Technology at Atlanta.

He was the first Sumter man to qualify for the aviation corps, receiving his early training at Columbus, Ohio. He was selected as one of five to be sent to the training school of the Allies at Oxford, England, and at the beginning of 1918 was sent to the front. He was an American aviator serving with the British as a lieutenant of the Forty-eighth Squadron, R. A. F. The major of this squadron, writing July 10, 1918, to Mrs. Shaw said: "On the evening of 9th July in Bristol No. b1113, Lieutenant Shaw with Sergeant Smith as observer went out on a single machine reconnaissance (that means alone). When he failed to return we made all inquiry and were told by observers on the ground near our front line that they had seen one Bristol fighting its way back against three enemy scouts. After a long struggle the Bristol was seen to fall in pieces in the air. We all feel Shaw's loss badly as he was one of our bravest and coolest lads, always cheery and stout-hearted no matter what work was wanted. He shot down two enemy scouts during hard fighting and would have won honors had he been allowed to continue his good work aloft."

The esteem in which he was regarded at home i perhaps best described in the words of his former school superintendent: "Ervin Shaw was a young man of extra fine qualities. He had to a high degree the qualities of loyalty, gentleness and honor. Few young men in Sumter were ever more deservedly popular. Ervin Shaw was noted for his generosity of soul and the fulness of his affections. His friends were devoted to Ervin; because Ervin was devoted to his friends. He has achieved an earthly immortality not only because of his heroic death in behalf of a righteous and glorious cause, but also because 'to live in the hearts of those we love is not to die.'"

But that rare kind of tribute that stands every test and comes the closest to determining the significance of his young character and service is contained in a letter by his comrade Lieutenant Battey, also an American, who explained in his message to Mrs. Shaw that her son was always known among his comrades in camp as "Molly." He wrote: "The story of Molly's success here I could tell you at length, but no doubt you have had from his own pen the account of his actual work as a fighting pilot. He did not tell you though how highly his work was regarded by his fellow pilots. This he could not know and it is this that I purpose to tell In this life of ours out here there is little thought of compliments. If one does well it is but his duty done. But let a man not do his best, he hears of it shortly. Among ourselves, sharing each day the same dangers, we are not apt to think one another brave. One is abnormal only if he is not brave. With Molly it was a bit different. He not only always

did his best but from the day he arrived his best was the equal of the squadron's best. I know that we all regarded Molly as the most daring and skillful pilot among us. A 'stout' chap we say out he.c, this among flying men being the greatest tribute we can pay to our heroes. When Molly was ordered to go back of the line fifteen miles on a dangerous reconnaissance he went back eighteen or twenty to bring in a better and more accurate report. When he met Huns, though the odds were greatly against him, he fought them. Molly Shaw has served his country well.

"The circumstances of his passing are not known to us here in any detail. It is known that as he was coming back to the lines after a long reconnaissance he was attacked by three Hun machines. Their fire must have cut some vital member of the machine's framing, for it broke up in the air, according to a report from one of our advanced battery positions. I at the time must have been quite close. I was flying below a great white cloud. Just a bit of a plane dropped through it and fluttered idly down, down. I did not know then, did not even guess that one of our men was fighting alone above the cloud.

"Molly was my best friend out here, and though I had known him but a little while, I was proud of the knowing. Always at night before he went to bed he knelt down by his cot and prayed. I loved him for that. In this time of sorrow know that you have given the great cause for which your country is fighting a true man."

ANGUS BETHUNE PATTERSON, M. D. For nearly half a century Doctor Patterson has enjoyed the qualifications and has performed the service of a physician and surgeon. While one of the oldest active men in the profession in the state, he is in many respects one of the youngest. His intellectual curiosity, his ardent passion for learning, his patience and disinterested zeal have served to keep him in touch with every phase of advancing thought and knowledge and have also called him more than once from the pleasant and congenial routine of his profession to some of its heavier and less agreeable responsibilities.

Doctor Patterson, whose home the greater part of his life has been at Barnwell, was born in that town March 23, 1851. The Pattersons were Scotch, and came to America following the battle of Culloden Moore. Their early settlement was in North Carolina, and soon after the Revolutionary war they came to South Carolina. Doctor Patterson's grandfather, Angus Patterson, lived at Barnwell, was a lawyer by profession, and for thirty-two years represented the county in the Legislature, during twenty-two of which he was president of the Senate. Edward Lawrence Patterson, father of Doctor Patterson, saw active service as a Confederate soldier in the Trans-Mississippi Department in Louisiana. Edward Lawrence Patterson married Sarah Louise Myers, a native of Fairfield County, South Carolina, and of Revolutionary stock and of German descent.

Angus Bethune Patterson grew up in a home of more than average comfort, received his early training under a private tutor, and took his first course in medicine in the University of South Carolina during 1869-70. In 1871 he received his degree in medicine from Louisville Medical College in Kentucky. In that year he began practice at Barnwell, but from 1889 for ten years enjoyed a large practice and a high position among the medical fraternity of Atlanta, Georgia. With the exception of that decade his home has been at Barnwell practically all his professional career.

Many times he has interrupted his private practice to pursue advanced studies, and has spent literally a fortune in improving his education. He has taken post-graduate work in hospitals of London, Paris and New York, and during June and July of 1919 took his fifth post-graduate course, while in 1920 he attended clinics and lectures at Tulane University at New Orleans. During 1889 he was a student in Paris, and was also assistant in two hospitals in London, the Royal Opthalmic Hospital and the Golden Square Throat Hospital. He has long been a student and research worker in bacteriology, and in many respects is regarded as one of the best educated physicians in the state.

In 1875 Doctor Patterson served one year in the Regular Army as assistant surgeon. He left the army to join the "Red Shirt Brigade" and take part in the Ellenton riots, the culmination of the struggle for supremacy between the whites and the blacks of South Carolina. On account of his previous army record during the Spanish-American war he was appointed by Surgeon General Sternberg as assistant surgeon in Colonel Ray's Seventh Immune Regiment. During the World war he was a member of the Volunteer Medical Service Corps. Doctor Patterson's brother, James O. H. Patterson, was a distinguished South Carolina lawyer, served many years in the Legislature, and for six years represented the state in Congress.

While a very busy professional man, Doctor Patterson has always been deeply interested in farming and owns a splendid plantation on the Edisto River. This plantation includes land that has never been out of the family from the time of King George III. He has 700 acres, devoted to diversified crops and operated by tenants.

Doctor Patterson served in the Legislature eight years. In 1907 he was elected to the House, and served four years, while in 1913 he entered the Senate for a four year term. Doctor Patterson left his private practice to take charge of the State Park Hospital for the Insane at Columbia, and remained at that post of duty for twelve months. He accepted the appointment from a sense of duty and from a desire to find out the defects in hospital administration. He quickly analyzed the situation, and forthwith prepared the bills for the Legislature to correct the abuses there. Altogether it was an exceedingly valuable service to the state. Doctor Patterson has been a member of the South Carolina State Medical Society since 1872, and is also a member of the American Medical Association. He is a member of the Episcopal Church, is a Royal Arch Mason, Knight of Pythias and Independent Order of Odd Fellows.

March 24, 1877, at Gillesonville, South Carolina, he married Miss Sophie M. Tillinghast, a daughter of Hon. Robert Tillinghast, a lawyer and former state senator from Beaufort County. To their marriage were born four children: Edwarda Elizabeth, wife of E. J. DaCosta, a Columbia merchant; Sophia Tillinghast, Robert Bethune and Mary Pierce Patterson. Doctor and Mrs. Patterson also have an adopted son, C. H. Harrison, now in business at Columbia. He is a grandson of Capt. William Henry Harrison of Georgia, known as "Captain Tip," head of the Confederate Veterans of Georgia.

DANIEL W. ELLIS, M. D. Professional success results from merit. Frequently in commercial life one may come into possession of a lucrative business through inheritance or gift, but in what are known as the learned professions advancement is gained only through painstaking and long-continued effort. Prestige in the healing art is the outcome of strong mentality, close application, thorough mastery of its great underlying principles and the ability to apply theory to practice in the treatment of diseases. Good intellectual training, thorough professional knowledge and the possession and utilization of the qualities and attributes essential to success, have made the subject of this review eminent in his chosen calling and he stands today among the scholarly and enterprising physicians in a community noted for the high order of its medical talent.

Daniel W. Ellis was born in what was formerly known as the Allendale district, now Barnwell County, South Carolina, on May 30, 1853, and is the son of Dr. William D. and Susan Emily (Hay) Ellis. William D. Ellis, who died at the comparatively early age of thirty-four years, was a native of the Beaufort district of South Carolina. He graduated from medical college and practiced his profession about twelve years prior to his untimely death. His father, Isaac Ellis, was a native of Virginia and the first of his family to settle in South Carolina. The family is originally of Welsh origin and is possessed of those sturdy qualities which are characteristic of that nationality.

The subject's mother, whose maiden name was Susan Emily Hay, traced her ancestral line back to Scotland, where was born William Hay, the first of the family to cross the Atlantic and establish a home in the new world. Among his sons was Michael Hay, who was the father of Col. Ann Hawks Hay, who was born on the Island of Jamaica and who held the rank of colonel in the patriot army during the war of the Revolution. Among his children was Lewis Scott Hay, a native of New York State and the father of the subject's mother. The latter was born at Boiling Spring, Barnwell County. The subject of this review is the sixth child in order of birth of the seven children born to William D. and Susan E. Ellis.

Daniel W. Ellis is mainly indebted to his brother, Judge W. D. Ellis of Atlanta, for his educational training, and he made the best of his opportunity, gaining a good practical general knowledge. Though without means, he was ambitious for a professional career, and having decided to make the medical science his life work, he matriculated in the Medical College of Charleston in 1886. He graduated at that institution in 1888 and at once located at his present home on James Island and began active practice. During the years which have elapsed since that time Doctor Ellis has stood as one of the most successful, best known and most popular physicians in this section of the state. As a natural sequence his success as a practitioner has brought with it financial gain and he is today in very comfortable circumstances. He owns a fine plantation of six hundred acres, which he has devoted very largely to the raising of sea island cotton, and also has large interests at Atlanta, Georgia, and other places.

Dr. Daniel Ellis was married twice, first to Rena L. McLeod, to which union was born one daughter, Rose M. The doctor's second marriage was with Mary S. Rivers, the daughter of Capt. E. L. Rivers, of James Island, who during his lifetime was one of the principal planters of that locality. Mrs. Ellis is of the tenth generation of her family to live on James Island. She is the mother of two children, namely: Kate, the wife of George L. Dickson, of Greenwood, and Daniel W., Jr., ten years of age. Doctor Ellis takes a deep interest in all those things which look to the advancement of the highest and best interests of the people among which he lives and has membership in the Episcopal Church, of which he has been a vestryman for many years. Not only in his profession has Doctor Ellis been accorded evidences of popular confidence and regard, but also in other directions, while he has ever ordered his course according to the highest principles and ideals, so that he has been found true to himself and to all men.

HON. GEORGE W. SEIGNIOUS, a member of the Legislature from Charleston County and for many years a prominent figure in local politics, has by his business and public record contributed further honors to one of the old and honored families of Charleston. The name is of French origin and Mr. Seignious, his father, as well as his grandfather, were all natives of Charleston.

George W. Seignious was born in 1873, son of John F. and Anne Eugenia (Schroeder) Seignious. His father was a Confederate soldier throughout the war between the states. At the time of his death in 1915 a local paper paid him the following tribute:

LAID TO REST IN MAGNOLIA

Capt. John F. Seignious Served the Confederacy

"Another link in the treasured chain of Confederate comradeship has been broken by the death of Capt. John F. Seignious, whose funeral services were held yesterday afternoon at No. 130 Spring Street, the Rev. D. M. McLeod officiating. Among the sympathizing friends present were the members of Capt. A. Burnet Rhett, United Confederate Veterans, who were there to pay a touching tribute of respect to their dear, dead comrade; to one who acceptably filled the office of adjutant and who had ever been devoted to the interest of the camp, and to the welfare of its members.

"After doing gallant and meritorious service with the Twenty-third regiment of South Carolina Volunteers, Captain Seignious was appointed by Gen. N. G. Evans one of his couriers, and the prompt and efficient manner in which he performed trying and perilous duty elicited not only the admiration, but also the warm regard of that distinguished brigade commander, and at times he was called upon to act as a staff officer. Although separated from his comrades of the rank and file, alongside of whom he had marched and fought, his affection for them re-

James F. Congdon

mained unchanged. It is not alone at the household hearth that Captain Seignious will be missed; there will be deep regret at the meetings and social gatherings of Camp A. Burnet Rhett, occasioned by his absence, for his warm words and faithful work found favor with the good and gallant men, who with bowed heads and tear-bedimmed eyes reverently stood at Magnolia Cemetery yesterday afternoon, the last resting place on earth of so many of the devoted defenders of the South."

Educated in Charleston's public schools, George W. Seignious graduated from the pharmacy department of the Medical College of South Carolina with the degree Ph. G. in 1896. Since that date he has been actively engaged in the retail drug business, and his store at the corner of Spring and Ashley streets is one of the leading pharmacists of the city. He is also vice president of the National Life Insurance Company of Charleston.

From the fact that he has always regarded his business as a means of service to the people of Charleston, and as a result of his public spirit and personal popularity, Mr. Seignious has for years enjoyed the complete trust and confidence of his fellow citizens. For four years he was a member of the Board of School Commissioners. For several years past his public duties have been of a peculiar responsibility to the public in the office of food and milk inspector, and he has exercised the power and instrumentalities of that position with a view solely to the best welfare of the community. Mr. Seignious received the honor of election as one of the representatives from Charleston County to the Legislature in December, 1919, beginning his duties as a legislator on January 13, 1920.

Mr. Seignious is affiliated with the Elks, Odd Fellows, Junior Order of United American Mechanics, and is a member of the Bethel Methodist Episcopal Church, South. He married Miss Josie Bernice Flynn, of Augusta, Georgia. Their son, George W., Jr., is attached to the naval establishment at Charleston Navy Yard in the capacity of assistant to the Labor Board.

JAMES F. CONDON. Some of the business accomplishments of modern men read like romance. To one who has no practical knowledge of the subject it seems almost incredible that a poor lad, starting out at a tender age without any backing of money or influential friends, could rise within little more than a couple of decades to be president of one of the most prosperous merchandising firms of a city of the size of Charleston, and yet in the case of James F. Condon it is true, and he is proud of the fact that he owes his present affluence to his own industry, thrift and acumen. James F. Condon is a native of Charleston, where he was born August 28, 1857, a son of William Condon. The latter was born in Tipperary, Ireland, from whence he came to the United States in boyhood, and after a period spent in New York City, came south to Charleston. A merchant tailor by trade, he was employed as such until the outbreak of hostilities between the North and the South, when he offered himself to the Confederacy, enlisting in a South Carolina regiment, in which he served until the close of the war, dying in 1867, when about forty-nine years of age. Although he left his son James F. and his twin brother, William J., little worldly possessions, they inherited from him the quick intelligence, cheerful optimism and aptitude for hard work so characteristic of the sons of Erin, and because of these qualities were able to forge ahead of their less aggressive associates. Their mother, who bore the maiden name of Fannie Scannell, was born at Cork, Ireland, and came to Charleston to visit her brother, already domiciled here, where she met and was married to William Condon, whom she survived for many years, dying in 1894, when eighty-two years of age.

Until he was eleven years old James F. Condon attended the public schools of Charleston, but then owing to the death of his father he felt the force of necessity compelling him to earn something to aid his mother, and so commenced to learn the trade of ship joiner. Before long he found that this line of work was utterly uncongenial and so became bundle boy in a mercantile establishment, receiving five dollars per week for his services. In time his abilities received recognition and he was made stock boy and afterwards a salesman, his salary gradually increasing. For twenty years he continued as salesman, all of the while carefully conserving his resources, and then, in 1897, began business for himself in a very modest way, his total sales the first year aggregating only $11,000. At present the aggregate of James F. Condon & Sons, Incorporated, run close to the $1,000,000 mark annually. Although his stock at the initial beginning was small, Mr. Condon studied his customers, and rendered such excellent and considerate service that those who bought of him once were almost sure to return again and again. Their patronage brought others, for nothing is more true than that success begets success, and in time he was able to branch out, adding more stock, and including other commodities. The present large store on King Street has a frontage from No. 431 to No. 435, of 90 feet frontage with a depth of 169 feet and occupying two floors. The business grew to such an extent that in 1912 it was incorporated, with James F. Condon as president and treasurer; Matthew A. Condon as secretary; James J. Condon as vice president and manager and William F. Condon as second vice president and assistant manager, the last three being his sons, who had grown up in the business. The store employs about sixty salespersons, and is patronized by all classes desiring dependable merchandise, both throughout Charleston and the adjoining vicinity. In addition to his mercantile interests, Mr. Condon is a director of the Citizens Bank, president of the General Realty and Investment Company, custodian of the Irish Volunteers and director of the American Publishing Company, in the conduct of which he takes an active part. He belongs to the Knights of Columbus, being a past Grand Knight of P. N. Lynch Council 704; Catholic Knights of America, Branch 152, of which he served for sixteen years as treasurer; Woodmen of the World and the Hibernian Society, and is also treasurer of the Society of Friends of Irish Freedom.

James F. Condon was married to Mary A. McLaughlin, who was born in Charleston, the second child of Matthew A. and B. Magrath McLaughlin, both of whom were natives of Ireland. In addition to the three sons mentioned above, Mr. and Mrs. Condon have two daughters, namely: Ella V. and Mary F., both of whom are managers in the millinery department of the store, and are also stockholders in the corporation with their father and brothers.

WILLIAM SMITH STEVENS. It is a well authenticated fact that success comes not as the caprice of chance, but as the legitimate result of well applied energy, unflagging determination and perseverance in a course of action once decided upon by the individual. Only those who diligently seek the goddess Fortuna find her—she was never known to smile upon the idler or dreamer. The subject of this sketch clearly understood this fact early in life, so he did not seek any royal road to success, but sought to direct his feet along the well-beaten paths of those who had won in the battle of life along legitimate lines. In tracing his life history it is plainly seen that his present high standing has been won by commendable qualities, and it is also his personal worth which has gained for him the excellent standing he has long enjoyed in the city which is honored by his citizenship.

William Smith Stevens traces his paternal ancestral line far back in the history of the New World, to the period not long subsequent to the historic days of the Pilgrim Fathers, the American progenitors of the family settling in Massachusetts, and later a number of the New England colonists made early settlement in Charleston, South Carolina. Among their descendants was William Smith Stevens, who was born and spent his entire life in Charleston. He was a physician by profession and during the War of the Revolution he served as a surgeon in the patriot army. He was the father of Joseph L. Stevens, a physician and planter on Johns Island, though a native of Charleston. Among his children was the subject's father, William Smith Stevens, also a doctor and planter, who was born in Charleston, where he was reared, educated and followed his professional career. He married Henrietta Maria Carmichael, who was born in Augusta, Georgia, the daughter of John and Mary (Eve) Carmichael. Mr. Carmichael, though born near Belfast, Ireland, was of Scottish descent.

William Smith Stevens was born January 20, 1864, and was the third of the four children born to his parents, William Smith and Henrietta (Carmichael) Stevens. He was reared and educated in Charleston, receiving a good practical education. At the age of sixteen years he began to work in the cotton fields, and was employed in various capacities until 1898, when he became a clerk in the establishment of which he is now occupying the responsible position of general manager, the Baily, Libby Company, one of the well known and most important concerns in Charleston. Mr. Stevens has not reached this enviable position by outside influence, but his promotion from a mere clerkship to the highest position in the personnel of the administrative force of the concern is the strongest sort of testimonial as to his efficiency, industry and honesty.

In 1892 Mr. Stevens was married to Nina A. Patrick, and they are the parents of three children, namely: William Smith, Jr., Henrietta Elizabeth and John Stangarme. Mr. Smith is extremely popular in the social circles of Charleston and is a member of a number of its leading clubs, including the Charleston Club, the Carolina Yacht Club, the Country Club, the Kiawata Club, and the Cincinnati Society of the State of South Carolina, of which has great-grandfather, William Smith Stevens, was one of the charter members. In many phases of the city's activities Mr. Stevens has taken an active part and has invariably given his earnest support to every movement having for its object the advancement of the city or community in any way. Genial and unassuming in manner, he easily makes friends and always retains them, for he is in the best sense a man among men and an honor to his community.

ANTON RHODY. While Anderson County's citizenship is largely made up of native sons, and many of the families have been here for generations, an important exception is found in the person of Anton Rhody who was born in Germany and came to South Carolina nearly forty years ago. His career is notable because from hard work and the thrifty characteristics of his race he has achieved a definite place among the successful men of his adopted county.

He was born in Germany September 10, 1849, and was left an orphan at an early age. He grew up in the home of his uncle Frederick Rhody, who afterwards came to the United States in 1882 and also became a resident of Anderson County where he lived until his death. Anton Rhody had to serve three years in the German army, and one year of that time Germany was engaged in its war with France known as the Franco-Prussian war. In 1876 he married Gusta Marquet. Their three children were born in Germany, Frank J., Arthur and Gretchen.

In 1881 Mr. Rhody brought his family to the United States, landing in New York and coming direct to Anderson. The following year he worked on the farm of the late W. G. Watson. Then for eight years he was in the employ of the late Sylvester Bleckley at the City of Anderson. He had an ambition to gain independence as a farmer, and out of his modest savings he bought ninety-two acres near Anderson. Year after year has brought him steadily increasing accumulations until today he owns extensive farm lands, equipped with the best improvements, and is one of the wealthy men as well as one of the most capable farmers of Anderson County.

Anton Rhody long ago became thoroughly identified with American life and the spirit of American institutions. During the recent war he was a liberal purchaser of Liberty Bonds and contributor to the various war funds. In church relations he is a Presbyterian.

His first wife and the mother of his children died soon after coming to America. Later he married her sister Rosa. Mr. Rhody's children are all residents of Anderson County. His son Frank married Miss Augusta Dean, while Arthur married Miss Bessie Louise Dean. Both sons are prosperous farmers and business men.

HON. JAMES FRANCIS BYRNES is now rounding out a decade of continuous service as representative of the Second Congressional District of South Carolina, and has been one of the most useful and efficient members of the state's delegation in Congress.

In the Sixty-Second Congress Mr. Byrnes called into conference the representatives who had introduced bills providing for Federal aid in the improvement of public roads, and induced them to discard their bills and agree to support a bill which the conferees proceeded to draft and which was subsequently enacted into law. He also took an active part in the framing of the Federal Reserve Law, especially the section providing for the rediscount of notes secured by agricultural products.

Mr. Byrnes resides at Aiken, South Carolina, but is a native of Charleston, in which city he received a public school education. In 1900 he was appointed official court reporter. While holding this office he also edited a newspaper, the Journal and Review of Aiken, South Carolina. He studied law under Judge James Aldrich of Aiken and was admitted to the bar in 1903. In 1908 he was elected solicitor of the Second Circuit and in 1910 was elected to represent the Second District in the Sixty-second Congress. He was reelected to the Sixty-third, Sixty-fourth, Sixty-fifth and Sixty-sixth congresses. His district comprises nine counties, Aiken, Allendale, Bamberg, Barnwell, Beaufort, Edgefield, Hampton, Jasper and Saluda. He is now a member of the Appropriations Committee, one of the most important committees in the House.

Mr. Byrnes married Miss Maude Busch, of Aiken, on May 2, 1906.

DAVID FARNUM MOORE. With interests touching nearly every line of business activity in the Brunson community, David Farnum Moore is a man of great achievement and enterprise and his associates know him not only as a man who usually carries out what he undertakes but also as a strict exemplar of commercial integrity and honor.

He comes of an old English family of Revolutionary stock and was born in the Beaufort District of what is now Hampton County, February 7, 1860. His grandfather, Humphrey P. Moore, was well educated, possessed abilities above the ordinary, and gave many years to school work and his services were in regular demand to perform the legal writing and land conveyancing for the people in the Beaufort and Barnwell districts.

The father of the Brunson business man was David Farnum Moore, who was born in 1825 in Colleton County and died in June, 1902. He moved to the Beaufort District about 1842 and became a successful farmer. During the war between the states he had charge of the commissary and also performed other responsible duties with the army. He was a Mason. His wife was Mary Elizabeth Gibson, of Scotch-Irish descent and of an old South Carolina family. She was born in Barnwell District and died in January, 1920, at the advanced age of ninety years.

David Farnum Moore of Brunson had to be satisfied with a country school education. To the age of twenty he lived on his father's farm and then took up railroad work as agent and telegraph operator on the Central Georgia Railroad and its auxiliary line the Charleston & West Carolina and also the Atlantic Coast Line. He gave up railroading to go into business for himself at Brunson, contracting for cross ties and lumber and dealing in horses and mules. Those and affiliated branches of business have occupied him ever since. It is said that Mr. Moore has sold more mules than any other individual in the United States. His chief business interest at present is real estate and the handling of timber lands. For the past twenty years he has been associated on terms of partnership with Mr. W. E. Barnes under the firm name of Moore & Barnes, later as Moore, Barnes & Company, and finally as the Moore-Barnes Company. Mr. Moore is president of the company, which operates a department store whose annual business is between $200,000 and $300,000. The firm are extensive buyers of cotton, and have kept in close and beneficial touch with the productive centers of agriculture in their community. They have done much to encourage development and farming, and many times have advanced their credit to families struggling through the early period of farming. While Mr. Moore has been only nominally interested in politics he served a period of thirty-one years from December 24, 1883, to 1914 as postmaster of Brunson. He is affiliated with the Knights of Pythias.

July 6, 1887, he married Miss Annie Yoemans, a native of Hampton County, daughter of Thomas and Emma Yoemans, who were of English descent and Revolutionary stock. Her father was a soldier in the Confederate army. Mrs. Moore, who died January 24, 1892, was the mother of two children. The daughter Annie Lee is the wife of J. J. Gray of Beauford, South Carolina. The son, David Farnum, Jr., is a graduate of The Citadel at Charleston, is in the automobile and hardware business at Brunson, and by his marriage with Miss Marion Lightsey, a daughter of Jacob A. Lightsey, has two children, Mary and Elizabeth.

GEN. THOMAS QUINTON DONALDSON, who held the rank of brigadier-general in the United States Army in the Inspector General's Department at Washington, is an old army man of nearly forty years' experience, and only for a brief time have his services required his presence in his native state, to which, however, he is devoted personally by reason of the distinguished history of his family, which has centered in South Carolina for many generations.

The Donaldsons are an old family of Greenville County. One of the early members of the family there was Nimrod Donaldson, a lifelong citizen of Greenville County and described as a man of unusual stability of character. He had a special mechanical genius, resulting in the invention of one of the first cotton planters in successful use. He patented this machine and for many years it was employed in the cotton fields of the South. Nimrod Donaldson was a cabinet maker by trade, and for many years had a large shop and factory in the lower part of Greenville County. Some recent achievements of his descendants lend a special interest to the fact that early in the nineteenth century he was an ardent believer in the ability of men to navigate the air and contrive some form of self-propelled vehicle such as the modern automobile.

A son of this Greenville pioneer was the late Thomas Quinton Donaldson, father of the general of the same name. Thomas Q. Donaldson was born in Greenville County August 27, 1834, and died only a few years ago. To the age of sixteen he lived on his father's farm, attended country schools, and then for three years was a pupil in a classical school in South Carolina taught by Wesley Leverett, whose work became famous because of the brilliant achievements of some of his students. In that school he acquired a knowledge of English, Greek, Latin and Mathematics, and subsequently was a teacher. In March, 1853, he began the study of law, and was admitted to practice by the Supreme Court at Columbia in the fall of 1855. He was engaged in practice with his preceptor, Charles J. Elford, until 1861. In April of that year he joined the Butler Guards, and saw some active service in Virginia, including the first battle of Bull Run, until failing health compelled him to retire in May, 1862. Soon after returning home he was appointed collector of the war tax for Greenville County, and discharged the duties of that office until the close of hostilities. In succeeding years he devoted himself to the handling of a large law practice. He was elected in 1872 to the State Senate, serving four years and declining a reelection. Besides his work as a lawyer he was distinguished by many public-spirited enterprises. He was chairman of the committee which raised subscriptions for the Air Line Railway, and was the first president of the Huguenot Plaid Mills, and later a director in several of the largest cotton mills in Greenville County. The governor appointed him one of the three commissioners to revise the state tax laws, and for a number of years he was chairman of the board of trustees of the graded schools of Greenville. In religion he was a faithful member of the Baptist Church. In November, 1859, he married Miss Susan B. Hoke. They had four children, two sons and two daughters. Three of his children, Mrs. Albert Barnes, Mrs. Davis Furman and A. H. Donaldson, a practicing attorney, are still living at the old home place in Greenville.

Col. M. L. Donaldson, one of the sons, who for many years represented Greenville County in the State Senate, and at one time was prominently mentioned for the United States Senate.

Gen. Thomas Quinton Donaldson was born in Greenville June 26, 1864. He was appointed a cadet in the West Point Military Academy in 1883, graduating with the class of 1887. Commissioned a second lieutenant of cavalry, he was assigned to the Seventh Cavalry and his first post of duty was Fort Riley, Kansas. He was with the Seventh Cavalry during the Indian troubles of 1890-91 in South Dakota, when the outbreak from the Pine Ridge Agency occurred. These troubles were marked by the battles of Wounded Knee and the Mission. From 1891 to 1895 Lieutenant Donaldson was assigned by the War Department as instructor in tactics, first at the Patrick Military Institute at Anderson, South Carolina, and afterwards at Clemson College, South Carolina, where he had the distinction of organizing the military department. He also taught mathematics in both these institutions.

During his duties at Clemson he was promoted to first lieutenant, assigned to the Eighth Cavalry, and left his native state in October, 1895, to join his regiment at Fort Yates, North Dakota. In October, 1899, his regiment was ordered to Huntsville, Alabama, where after preparation it was ordered to Cuba in November, its first station being at Nuevitas, later at Puerto, Principe. In December, 1899, Lieutenant Donaldson's squadron was returned to the United States and sent to Fort Riley, Kansas, and thence he was sent on detached service in command of a troop at Fort Gibson, Indian Territory, during the disturbances caused by Crazy Snake, the Indian chieftain who objected to the Indian allotments of the Dawes Commission. During that service he was promoted to the rank of captain and assigned again to the Eighth Cavalry. Before leaving the Indian Territory his troop was ordered to Fort Reno, Oklahoma, where it was on duty until 1903, and was then sent to Fort Sill, where were then stationed three other troops belonging to the squadron. From Fort Sill in June, 1905, Captain Donaldson was ordered to the Philippine Islands. During his stay at Fort Sill he made two inspections of the entire National Guard of Oklahoma.

In the Philippines Captain Donaldson, with the remainder of his regiment, was stationed at Fort William McKinley, about six miles from Manila, until May, 1907. The regiment was then returned to the United States and stationed at Fort Robinson, Nebraska. In August, 1908, Captain Donaldson was ordered to the Army School of the Line at Fort Leavenworth as a student, completing his course in June, 1909, as a distinguished graduate. He was then detailed to take the course at the Army Staff School at the same place, beginning September 1, 1909, and completing his work in June, 1910, and during August of that year was in attendance at the army maneuvers at New York. He rejoined his regiment at Fort Robinson, Nebraska, in November, 1910. He went to the Philippines in December of that year and was at Camp McGrath in the Southeastern Luzon, near Batangas, until June, 1913. His regiment was then transferred to Camp Stotsenberg, about sixty miles north of Manila.

In March, 1914, Captain Donaldson was relieved from duty in the Philippines and returned to the United States, making the journey with his family through Asia and Europe. He arrived in the United States June 29, 1914, and when his leave expired in the early part of August he was assigned to duty in the Inspector General's Department at Governor's Island, New York. Soon afterward he was promoted to lieutenant colonel, and after a brief interval to colonel of cavalry.

In October, 1917, some months after America entered the World war, Colonel Donaldson was ordered to duty in the inspector general's office at Washington. On February 18, 1918, he was commissioned brigadier general, National Army, in the Inspector General's Department, and in August of that year was ordered to France and assigned to duty as inspector general of the Services of Supply with station at Tours. He remained in this duty until June, 1919, when he returned to the United States and was assigned to duty in the office of the

James Oscar Williams

inspector general of the army, where he is still on duty with the rank of colonel, his regular army rank. While in France General Donaldson had conferred on him the decoration of the Legion of Honor of France by Marshal Petain. He also received the Distinguished Service Medal of the United States. The citation accompanying the latter medal reads as follows: "Brigadier General T. Q. Donaldson of the United States Army: For exceptionally meritorious and distinguished services. As Inspector General of the Services of Supply, by his energy, sound judgment and able management, he organized and brought to a state of marked efficiency the Inspector General's department in the Services of Supply. He proved a most potent factor in raising the standard of discipline throughout the command, rendering service of conspicuous worth."

In 1892, as a young lieutenant, General Donaldson married Miss Mary Elizabeth Willson. Her father is a distinguished South Carolina educator, Rev. Dr. J. O. Willson, now president of Lander College at Greenwood. General and Mrs. Donaldson are the parents of one daughter and three sons: Miss Mary Sue Donaldson; First Lieut. Thomas Quinton, Jr.; Capt. J. O. Donaldson and Ensign Augustus Hoke Donaldson. The sons apparently all have the military genius of their ancestry, and their individual records are well known to South Carolina people. Augustus Hoke graduated from the Naval Academy at Annapolis in June, 1919, was assigned to duty on the United States transport Imperator, and is now in service at San Diego, California. Thomas Quinton, Jr., graduated from West Point Military Academy in 1918, was with the School of Fire at Fort Sill and later at Camp Benning, Georgia, until June, 1919, when he was sent to France and assigned to the Army of Occupation at Coblenz.

The people of the two Carolinas justly took a great deal of credit to themselves in 1919 from the remarkable performances of two army aviators, one being Lieut. B. W. Maynard, formerly of Wake Forest College, North Carolina, winner of the Transcontinental Aeroplane Derby, while the second place in that remarkable exploit of crossing and recrossing the continent between New York and San Francisco was assigned to Capt. John O. Donaldson, a former student of Furman University at Greenville, South Carolina.

Capt. John Donaldson attended Furman during 1915-16, and while there was awarded the Thomas-Keys Bible Medal as the most proficient Bible student. Later he was a student at Cornell University and by special dispensation at the age of nineteen was permitted to enter the flying service and was in Europe fourteen months on active duty with the British aviation service in France. He distinguished himself by bringing down nine enemy planes, and on September 1, 1918, after bringing down one of three Bodie planes which he was attacking, his own was brought down and he was made prisoner. He escaped twice. On the first occasion he with one companion got through the German lines, but was recaptured just as he was almost within the British lines. After being again confined for eleven days he with four companions escaped a second time, successfully, going north through Belgium and into Holland. The story of his thrilling escape and adventures is interestingly told in Harper's Magazine for July, 1919. Captain Donaldson was cited six times for gallantry, and was awarded the Distinguished Flying Cross by the British government, the presentation being made in New York by the Prince of Wales when the latter was on his visit to the United States in the spring of 1920. It was in October, 1919, that Captain Donaldson participated in the transcontinental air flight, taking second honors in that 5,400-mile journey by air.

HARLEY B. LINDSAY. A native South Carolinian, reared and educated in that state, Doctor Lindsay after practicing as a dentist for two years at Union, sought the larger opportunities of New York City, and for over twenty years has been engaged in a busy practice in that city.

Doctor Lindsay was born at Greenville, South Carolina, in 1874, son of Rev. W. C. and Margaret (Steen) Lindsay. Many communities of South Carolina recall with peculiar affection and esteem the character and service of Rev. W. C. Lindsay. He was born in Virginia of Scotch ancestry but during the many years of his ministry with the Baptist denomination lived in South Carolina. From Greenville he removed to Columbia in 1877 and was a resident of the capital city nearly forty years. Most of that time he was pastor of the old First Baptist Church known historically as the Secession Church. He had every talent and qualification requisite for his calling and he exercised an influence for good among thousands of individuals and in many communities.

Harley B. Lindsay grew up at Columbia from the age of three years, attended the local schools there, and is a graduate of the University of South Carolina with the class of 1893. He has always been deeply interested in his alma mater and has many other interests to attach him to his home state. Doctor Lindsay studied dentistry in the University of Maryland at Baltimore, graduating in 1896. For two years he practiced at Union in his native state and has been a resident of New York since 1898. He is a member of the various dental societies and his address in New York is 40 East Forty-first Street.

Doctor Lindsay married Miss Leize Gimball of Charleston, who shares her husband's interest in South Carolina. Through her mother she is a member of the historic Trenholm family of Charleston. George A. Trenholm of this family was secretary of the treasury during the Confederacy, while Col. William L. Trenholm was comptroller of currency during President Cleveland's administration.

JAMES OSCAR WILLIAMS, whose active business career has been spent at New York City where he is a prominent stock broker and member of the New York Stock Exchange House, is a member of the noted Williams family of Lancaster County, many of whom have gained eminence in public affairs, in law and in business.

James Oscar Williams was born at Lancaster, May 6, 1868, son of Judge David A. and Sarah (Clyburn) Williams. The family came originally from Wales, and after residence in Maryland and Virginia came to South Carolina. Judge D. A. Williams was a Confederate soldier, was admitted to the bar, but never practiced law owing to his long continued duties as county judge and clerk of court of Lancaster County. Two of his sons, Thomas Yancey Williams and David Reece Williams, are prominent lawyers of the state, both of whom served in the Senate.

James Oscar Williams received his early education at the University of South Carolina, at Columbia. In January, 1893, at the age of twenty-five, he elected to seek success in the highly competitive field of New York City, where he later became a member of the firm of Daniel O'Dell & Co., stock brokers and members of the New York Stock Exchange and of the New York Cotton Exchange. During a quarter of a century Mr. Williams received recognition and success in the world's great financial center, and is now one of the partners in the firm of Hicks & Williams, stock brokers and cotton brokers, and members of the New York Stock Exchange and the New York Cotton Exchange, with offices at 74 Broadway.

Though for many years a resident of New York, Mr. Williams retains the liveliest interest in and concern for the people of his native State. Mr. Williams was married in 1908 to Miss Alice Pickett Caskin, who is also of a prominent South Carolina family, on her paternal side being the daughter of the late Theodore Clarke Caskin, a native of Charleston, whose mother was Sara Pinckney of Charleston. Mrs. Williams' mother, Lida Pickett of Virginia, was of close relationship with General Pickett, hero of the famous charge at Gettysburg. Mr. and Mrs. Williams, whose home is at Short Hills, New Jersey, have one daughter, Miss Alice Gwendolyn Williams.

MITCHELL CAMPBELL KING is a dealer in cotton oil and phosphate rock at Atlanta, Georgia, represents a very prominent South Carolina family, with names of recognized prestige in the business and social life of the state since the early colonial period. For many years one of the ablest jurists in the country was Judge Mitchell King, whose home at Charleston was a notable center of culture. A representative of the present generation is Judge Alexander C. King, one of the greatest lawyers of the South, now serving as judge of the United States Circuit Court of Appeals at Atlanta. In the maternal line might be mentioned two prominent lawyers, Judge Josiah Evans and Gen. Robert Blair Campbell, the former a United States senator and judge from South Carolina, while the latter was in the United States diplomatic service as consul at London.

Mitchell Campbell King was born in Dorchester County, South Carolina, August 27, 1878, a son of Alexander Campbell and Mary Lee (Evans) King. His father was a cotton planter. The son was liberally educated, attending South Carolina Military Academy at Charleston, and since then has been engaged in the brokerage business. He moved to Atlanta in 1901 and has been at the cotton oil and phosphate rock business since then, the M. C. King Company being one of the widely known brokerage houses in these lines. He is also interested in some local banks and manufacturing companies, as a director and stockholder, and takes an active part in the social life of his home city. He is a member of the Episcopal Church and on November 27, 1910, married Jeanette Swift.

WILLIAM WALLACE GAINES. One of the modern industrial communities of South Carolina is Ninety-Six in Greenwood County, seat of the Ninety-Six Cotton Mills, a thriving textile industry of which William Wallace Gaines, former mayor of the town, is secretary and manager.

Mr. Gaines is descended from the prominent Gaines family of Virginia. He is a son of J. M. Gaines, who was born in Chester County and when a young man came to what is now Greenwood then Edgefield County. He established himself as a planter and his enterprise gave rise to a community named in his honor Gaines, where a postoffice is still maintained. Gaines is about two miles from Phoenix, and while formerly a part of Edgefield is now in Greenwood County. J. M. Gaines followed planting for a number of years and as a resident of Greenwood is the general agent for the Life Insurance Company of Virginia. He was a member of the State Senate from Edgefield County in 1896-97, and lent all the power of his influence to the movement for the organization of Greenwood County. J. M. Gaines married Mamie Williams.

William Wallace Gaines was born at the Village of Gaines in 1881, was educated in local schools, and spent two years in Richmond College in Virginia. All his time since leaving college has been spent in the textile industry. For three years he was cotton buyer for the Greenwood Cotton Mills. He came to Ninety-Six in 1904 as paymaster and in charge of the shipping department of the Ninety-Six Cotton Mills. Later he was promoted to his present office as secretary and treasurer of the company, and has active management of the entire plant. These mills, manufacturing print cloths, are equipped with 567 looms and 24,192 spindles. The company of which Mr. J. P. Abney of Greenwood is president is capitalized at $400,000.

Mr. Gaines was elected mayor of Ninety-Six in 1915 and filled that office with credit and efficiency for four years until October, 1919. He is present worshipful master of Eureka Lodge No. 47, Ancient Free and Accepted Masons, is a member of Greenwood Chapter Royal Arch Masons and a Knight of Pythias. He married Miss Evelyn Tompkins of Greenwood County. Her father Col. J. H. Tompkins was at one time private secretary to Governor Tillman and later was secretary of state of South Carolina.

COL. JOHN F. HOBBS. While deeply attached to South Carolina as his native state and the home of his ancestors comprising distinguished men and beautiful women, Colonel Hobbs in his own life has been a Ulysses, has traveled far and seen much of men and many places remote from the scenes of his youth, and for a quarter of a century has been a well known resident of New York City, where he still continues his profession as a lawyer and is also a publisher.

Colonel Hobbs was born in 1860 in the famous

John Fletcher Hobbs

"Dutch Fork" section of South Carolina, in a locality then in Lexington County now part of Newberry County. His parents were Dr. Lewellyn Pickens and Mary A. C. (Hope) Hobbs. His grandfather, Edward Hobbs, was, at one time, the wealthiest planter and merchant in the Liberty Hill section, and owned and ably directed many extensive interests. Dr. Lewellyn P. Hobbs gave his active lite to the practice of medicine and served as a surgeon in the Confederate army. He was born at old Liberty Hill in Edgefield County.

Mary (Hope) Hobbs was a great-granddaughter in the maternal line of Col. John Adam Summer, whose father and family was driven from Germany in 1697 for fighting Kaiserism then and whose title and Baronial estates were confiscated by the German Government. They came to America before the Revolutionary war. He was given a grant by King George III to land embracing what later became known as the Hope, Eichelberger and Hobbs plantations. He was founder of the "Dutch Fork" colony. He served as colonel on the Colonists' side in the American Revolutionary war and fought the battle of Granby opposite where Columbia now stands. Colonel Hobbs' maternal grandfather was Hon. John Christian Hope of the "Dutch Fork." He was a member of the South Carolina Senate for thirty years and wielded a wide influence in the public affairs of his community and state.

Colonel Hobbs well recalls his first teacher, Mrs. Cummings Swygert (nee Chapman), at the old St. John's School near Hope Station. She is now living at Pomaria, South Carolina, not far away. Later he attended Bethel Academy, now the Pomaria High School, and received his higher education at Newberry College. He graduated A. B. with the class of 1879 and with the highest honors of his class. Three years later the college conferred upon him the Master of Arts degree, and many years later, June 13, 1913, on his birthday, Newberry College gave him the honorary degree of LL. D., and he was the first and only alumnus so honored by that institution, though she has given it to distinguished men all over the world.

His law studies were directed by the late Chief Justice Pope of South Carolina, and he was admitted to the bar in Columbia in 1880, before reaching his majority, his age having been erroneously chronicled by one year. For a time he practiced at Columbia and Lexington, until failing health caused him to abandon his profession. He sought health, recreation, and also the satisfaction of his spirit of adventure by extensive travels that took him to practically every part of the world. During much of the time he was a newspaper correspondent, and was able to impart real color and vigor to his descriptions, since when in far distant regions he was a soldier and officer as well as a correspondent. During those years he fought with the savage tribes of Australia, was in the Samoan Islands commanding the native troops against the Germans in the battle of Apia, and soon was wounded there in the New Hebrides, in the Orange Free State in Africa, in the Sudan, and came to know many of the savage peoples of the earth. By the natives in Samoa he was made a war chief with the title of prince, and, as such it was that opposed the German oppression of the natives there. In the Orange Free State he was made a brigadier general on the staff of Commanding General Evarts. He is one of the few white men who have crossed entirely the Australian desert. For thirteen years Colonel Hobbs lived this life of adventure, and thoroughly enjoyed every bit of it. The American title of colonel is due to his appointment on the staff of the late Governor W. D. Simpson of South Carolina. He declined a brigadier generalship of the Ninth South Carolina, tendered by the same governor because of failing health and having to go abroad.

Colonel Hobbs has lived in New York permanently since 1895. While he still practices as a lawyer, he is also president of the Caterer Publishing Company, and is one of the influential men in New York City politics. He is a member of the Executive Committee of Tammany and of the Sixteenth Assembly District of this famous democratic organization. A number of honors including that of two proposed nominations for Congress have been offered him, but he has never been a candidate in New York, though he held the appointive position of commissioner of city revenue under the McClellan administration.

Colonel Hobbs is one of the prominent southerners in New York, is a member of the New York Southern Society, is president of the Thirteen Club, and, in Masonry, is a member of Roome Lodge No. 746, Ancient Free and Accepted Masons, Jerusalem Chapter, Royal Arch Masons, Palestine Commandery No. 18, Knights Templar, the Scottish Rite Consistory, thirty-second degree, and Mecca Temple of the Mystic Shrine. Colonel Hobbs married Miss Ella Collin of New York and they have two daughters, Ethel M. and Claire A.

JAMES ELLIOTT HART is a solid business man of Edgefield whose career is significant because of his long and steady adherence to one line and to one institution.

He was born in the Meeting Street section of Edgefield County, March 5, 1868, a son of W. C. Hart, and of English and Scotch ancestry. He was educated in the Edgefield County schools and at the age of thirteen began clerking in his uncle's dry goods store. In 1887 he took a business course in the Eastman Business College at Poughkeepsie, New York. In 1891 Mr. Hart was made a junior partner in the firm of Alvin Hart & Company, where he had been working since he was a boy, and in 1896 after the death of Alvin Hart he bought the business and has expanded and broadened its scope, being its directing head. Until the year 1910 when, owing to ill health he sold the business in Edgefield, South Carolina, which is still his home, and became southern representative for the Phillips Jones Corporation of that city traveling along the southern territory.

November 12, 1891, Mr. Hart married Zillah L. LaGrone.

WILLIS G. TOWNES. Of South Carolinians who have made their careers outside the limits of their native state perhaps none has achieved more extensive and more important connections with the world's business and affairs than Willis G. Townes of New York.

Born in Edgefield County April 2, 1871, Mr. Townes is a son of Henry Howard and Sarah Virginia (Harris) Townes and a grandson of Samuel H. Townes. His father was a native of Greenville and the family has been one of distinction in that section of upper South Carolina since Samuel A. Townes, the son of a wealthy Virginia planter, established his home on the Townes plantation in 1792. Some of the eminent men of this family are mentioned on other pages of this publication. Henry Howard Townes removed from Greenville to Edgefield County, was for many years a successful planter, was a Confederate soldier throughout the war and served in the State Legislature.

Willis G. Townes grew up on his father's plantation and was educated in private schools in South Carolina. His strong and self-reliant character took him into independent action at an early date. His first experiences were in newspaper work on the old Augusta Herald in Georgia. Subsequently he established several county papers in South Carolina. Confident of himself and his powers he next sought a larger arena for his real career, and in 1894 established his home in New York. His dominant activity ever since has been the coal business. In this great and essential industry he has achieved a substantial fortune and a place of high standing in commercial and financial circles both in his home country and abroad. Mr. Townes is active vice president of the Archibald McNeil & Sons Company of New York, miners and exporters of coal. This is one of the largest concerns of its kind in the world, and its trade relations are of international importance. The corporation and its auxiliaries own a fleet of ocean steamships engaged in coal export trade, and has various other transportation systems connected with the coal carrying industry.

A brief summary of the corporations in which Mr. Townes is an active official will give some idea of the nature and extent of his interests: President of the United States Coal and Coke Company; president of the United Coal and Coke Corporation; chairman of the board of directors of the Coalburg Mining Company; chairman of the board Oriole Steamship Lines; president, New River Consolidated Colliery Company; president, Lookout Colliery Company; president Boone Colliery Company, Kemdon Colliery Company, Royal Colliery Co., Wright Colliery Company, which operates lines of steamers between the port of Baltimore and Rotterdam and Liverpool; member of the executive committee of the Tidewater Coal Exchange, which was established under the auspices of the Government and the United States Railway and Fuel Administrations, for the purpose of taking over coal for reshipment.

Mr. Townes has been crossing the Atlantic on business missions for a number of years, and his duties in connection with the exportation of coal to Europe have demanded his presence for several months annually abroad. He is regarded as an authority on the coal industry of Europe as well as of his home country. During the Taft administration he was selected by Secretary of State Knox to go to Europe and develop coal markets for American coal on the Continent. This mission he accomplished entirely at his own expense. During the war he was a member of the National Fuel Administration, and was delegated with special responsibilities by the government requiring frequent trips to Europe.

Mr. Townes is also a prominent man in the democratic party and for a number of years has been associated with the national leaders of that party. He was until the San Francisco Convention chairman of the Financial Committee of the National Democratic Executive Committee. He has membership in the following clubs: International Sporting, New York Athletic, American Yacht, Apawamis Golf, Lawyers, Transportation, New York Press and Algonquin. Mr. Townes married Miss Robina Prothero of Westchester County, New York. Their daughter, Robina Townes, was born in Paris, France, January 3, 1916.

Hon. D. A. Brockinton, who is a representative of Charleston County in the State Legislature, is a young lawyer, and has attracted much attention for his learning and other substantial qualifications in his profession and citizenship.

He was born at Kings Tree in Williamsburg County, South Carolina, July 3, 1890. His father Joseph E. Brockinton represented the fourth generation of the family in Williamsburg County and like his ancestors was a planter. He died at the age of forty-nine. Joseph E. Brockinton married Martha Annie Davis, a native of Smithfield, North Carolina, and of a family of early settlers in that state. David A. Brockinton was the tenth in a family of twelve children, three of whom died in infancy and eight are still living. He spent his early days on his father's farm, and in 1908 graduated from the Kings Tree High School. He entered the University of South Carolina, graduating in the classical course and with the A. B. degree in 1912. The following year he spent managing an insurance business at Gaffney, South Carolina. He re-entered the university in 1913 in the law department and finished his course in 1915. He was admitted to the bar and for about a year was private secretary to Judge Charles A. Woods, judge of the Federal Court of Appeals at Richmond, Virginia. Mr. Brockinton has been engaged in a general practice of law at Charleston since May 1, 1916.

He was elected to the Legislature in 1918, and is serving as a member of the Judiciary Committee. He is a member of a number of social and civic organizations at Charleston. December 12, 1916, he married Annie Franklin Harvey of Charleston, daughter of Wilson G. Harvey of that city. They have one son, David Arthur, Jr.

James Douglas Nisbet, M. D. Of the several eminent physicians and surgeons of New York who claim South Carolina as their native state one is Dr. James Douglas Nisbet, a widely known authority and specialist in diseases of digestion.

Doctor Nisbet was born in the Waxhaw section of Lancaster County, South Carolina, July 30, 1861. He is a son of Dr. John Newton and Jane (Phifer) Nisbet. His paternal grandmother was a Douglas and both the Nisbets and Douglases were among the Scotch Presbyterian colonists who in the Carolinas founded a race of sturdy, God-fearing people.

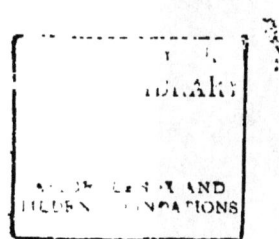

whose first and continued concern in life was the building of character. There is no disparagement of the high personal attainments of Doctor Nisbet to say that he has been greatly profited by the inheritance from his ancestors.

His father Dr. John Newton Nisbet was born in Union County, North Carolina, was a graduate of the South Carolina Medical College, and practiced medicine for over half a century. His life would have presented a generous theme for a eulogy upon the old time country doctor, a man whose good deeds were almost innumerable and whose character is a heritage to be prized by his descendants.

James Douglas Nisbet had the worthy example of his father before him as he grew to manhood. He was liberally educated, graduating A. B. from Davidson College in North Carolina in 1881. During 1882 he was a student in the Charleston Medical College and received his M. D. from Louisville Medical College in 1886. After graduating he practiced in his native county for several years, and during 1889-90 pursued post-graduate study in the New York Polyclinic. He has been a resident of New York for thirty years. He began practice as a specialist in diseases of the digestive system in 1890, but in 1892 went abroad and sought all the advantages of residence and study in Europe, attending the University of Paris in 1892, was at Tuebingen in 1893, and at Berlin in 1894. He resumed his practice as a specialist in 1895.

For many years Doctor Nisbet has enjoyed an undisputed place of leadership in his special field. One of the standard works in medical libraries is "Diseases of the Stomach," of which Doctor Nisbet is the author. This was first published in 1898. Doctor Nisbet was formerly Professor of Diseases of the Digestive System in the New York Polyclinic. He is a member of many professional and social organizations, including the New York Academy of Medicine, American Academy of Medicine, Society of Medical Jurisprudence, New York State Medical Society, American Medical Association, Association for the Advancement of Science, the National Association for the Study and Prevention of Tuberculosis, and the National Sculpture Society. Doctor Nisbet has been a frequent visitor to his home state, and finds some congenial fellowship with other southern men in the New York Southern Society. He is a member of the Kappa Alpha fraternity, the Alumni Association of the University of Kentucky, and the Laurentian Club of Canada. October 22, 1908, Doctor Nisbet married Emma Beulah Hayes of Lewisburg, Pennsylvania.

OLIVER FRANKLIN HART of Columbia is probably known to every Mason in South Carolina. For many years he has devoted his time and study to the ancient craft, and has been an official in nearly all the orders and rites and branches of Freemasonry.

Mr. Hart was born at York in York County, July 14, 1879, a son of George Washington Seabrook and Ellen A. Hart. He was well educated in his native town, attending the public schools and the Banks High School. From 1894, when he was fifteen years of age, until 1914, a period of twenty years, Mr. Hart was actively engaged in the drug business. During 1013-14 he served as president of the South Carolina Pharmaceutical Association.

He joined Richland Lodge No. 39, Ancient Free and Accepted Masons. July 21, 1903, was elected Master for the year 1908, elected a life member in 1911, and was chosen trustee of the lodge in 1919. For the year 1909 he was appointed grand steward of the Grand Lodge, junior grand deacon for 1910, and was elected grand secretary December 14, 1910.

In the Royal Arch he joined Columbia Chapter No. 5, April 1, 1904, served as high priest for the year 1910, and September 21, 1910, was appointed grand secretary of the Grand Royal Arch Chapter to succeed Jacob T. Barron, deceased, and was regularly elected to that office February 14, 1911. He joined the Grand Convention of Anointed High Priests February 8, 1910, and was elected grand recorder February 14, 1911.

Mr. Hart joined Union Council No. 5, Royal and Select Masters, September 26, 1907, was illustrious master for the year 1911, in May, 1910, was appointed grand recorder of the Grand Council, was elected grand recorder February 14, 1911, was elected grand master April 13, 1915, elected general grand steward of the General Grand Council of Royal and Select Masters of the United States of America, August 31, 1915, and elected general grand conductor of the Council, October 1, 1918.

In the Order of Knights Templar he joined Columbia Commandery, April 17, 1906, served as eminent commander in 1918, and was appointed grand captain of the guard for the year 1919. He has been affiliated with Omar Temple of the Mystic Shrine since October 16, 1907, and was elected potentate for the year 1917.

In the Scottish Rite he joined Aleph Lodge of Perfection August 6, 1906, was elected venerable master for 1912 and 1913, joined Buist Chapter No. 1 of the Rose Croix, Bethlehem Council No. 1, Knights of Kadosh and Dalcho Consistory No. 1, Masters Royal Secret, receiving the thirty-second degree October 11, 1911.

Mr. Hart is a democrat in politics, a member of the Columbia Cotillion Club and the Columbia Rotary Club, and is an active member of the Trinity Episcopal Church and superintendent of the Sunday school of St. Timothy Episcopal Mission.

January 1, 1902, at Columbia he married Nancy Childs, daughter of William Gion and Alice (Gibbes) Childs. Seven children were born to their marriage: William Augustus, Oliver Franklin, Jr., deceased; Eleanor, Nancy, deceased; George Childs, Oliver James and Frances Hart.

ROBERT SPANN CATHCART, M. D. This well known surgeon, of Charleston has achieved real distinction in his profession, and his name is known for the abilities and attainments associated with it far beyond the borders of his home city and state.

Dr. Cathcart was born at Columbia, South Carolina, September 25, 1871, of Scotch-Irish ancestry and a son of Colonel William R. and Elizabeth (Kelley) Cathcart. The Cathcarts were Scotch but came to America from Ireland. His grandfather, George Cathcart, was born in County Antrim, Ireland. Colonel William Richard Cathcart was a native of Columbia and lived there most of his life. During the war between the states he was in the signal corps and was stationed nearly four years at Fort Sumter. Dr. Cathcart's mother was a daughter of William Aiken Kelley, who came to Charleston from Philadelphia. She was the mother of six children, and Colonel Cathcart after her death married Kate S. Kelley, by whom he had a daughter and son.

As a boy from 1887 to 1889 Dr. Cathcart served as a page in the House of Representatives at Columbia.

Dr. Cathcart acquired his primary education at Columbia, and in 1890 graduated from the School of Pharmacy of the University of South Carolina. Three years later, in 1893, he was graduated from the Medical College of South Carolina at Charleston. He served as interne in the Charleston Hospital one year, and then for fourteen years was engaged in the general practice of medicine. For the past twelve years his work has been limited to surgery. He is a Fellow of the American College of Surgeons, is professor of the Abdominal Surgery Medical College of South Carolina, is surgeon for the Charleston Consolidated Railway and Light Company, surgeon of the Atlantic Coast Line Railway, surgeon to the Seaboard Air Line Railroad, surgeon to The Citadel, the Military College of South Carolina, surgeon-in-chief to the Roper Hospital at Charleston. Was medical aid to the governor in selective draft service and was a major in the Medical Reserve Corps, U. S. Army during the World war. He also served as chief surgeon of the Base Hospital at Camp Woodworth, South Carolina, and chief of the surgical staff of U. S. A. General Hospital No. 24 at Pittsburgh.

Dr. Cathcart is ex-president of the Medical Society of South Carolina and ex-president of the Tri-State Medical Association, comprising North Carolina, South Carolina and Virginia. Dr. Cathcart is a Chapter and Knight Templar Mason and Shriner and an Elk.

January 5, 1898, he married Katherine J. Morrow, of Birmingham, Alabama. They have four children: Mary Frances, Katherine Morrow, Robert S., Jr., and Hugh.

FRANK E. TOWLES. It is given to some men to rise above their associates and to become towering figures in the industrial, commercial or political world. Having made a success in one line, they are naturally called upon to assume added responsibilities, and these honors but serve to bring out other desirable qualities and enable them to serve all their undertakings efficiently. Frank E. Towles, of Meggetts, is one of these men of many activities, for he is vice president of the Meggetts Produce Company, president and general manager of the Point Farm Company, president and manager of the Yonges Island Plant Company; president, treasurer, director and manager of the Farm Auto Repair Company, manager of the Fenwich Farm Corporation, and was manager of the Ashepoo Corporation, secretary and is treasurer of the Dale Farms Company, director of the Argyle Hotel of Charleston and director of the South Carolina Produce Association. He is also a member of the Agricultural Society of South Carolina, a member of the Sanitary and Drainage Commission and secretary and treasurer of Sea Island Yacht Club.

Frank E. Towles was born at Wadmalaw Island, Charleston County, South Carolina, October 8, 1880, a son of F. W. Towles, a sketch of whom appears elsewhere in this work. He was educated in the country schools of his native county and at a business college, and then entered the business arena in which he has achieved such gratifying results.

On July 25, 1905, Mr. Towles was united in marriage with Martha Sara Wilson, a daughter of J. J. and Annie (Baily) Wilson. Mr. and Mrs. Towles have one son, Frank J., who was born April 7, 1908. Mr. Towles belongs to the Masons and has risen in that order to the Commandery and Shrine and he is also a member of the Knights of Pythias. Each advancement of Mr. Towles' has brought him a broader sense of responsibility and further developed the tact, courtesy and sound judgment for which he is noted, and he is universally recognized as a useful, competent and progressive citizen of the highest type.

JUDGE GEORGE W. NICHOLLS, of Spartanburg, has for many years past been looked upon as one of the leaders of the bar of upper South Carolina, and in the course of more than forty years of active practice has achieved an unusual number of the real successes and honors of the law of citizenship.

His personal career serves to bring to attention one of the oldest and best known families of Spartanburg County. He was born on the old Nicholls home place on the Tyger River south of Spartanburg in 1849, son of George and Catharine M. (Crook) Nicholls. In the maternal line the Crook family has helped make history in Spartanburg County. Judge Nicholls' maternal great-grandfather, Capt. Andrew Barry, was captain of the Spartan Rifles during the Revolutionary war.

The Nicholls family have taken part in every war since and including the Revolution. His great-grandfather, George Nicholls, came to Spartanburg County from Virginia prior to that war and was one of the first white settlers here. The grandfather was Benjamin Nicholls. Judge Nicholls had several other brothers who were in the Cnfederate army. One of these was the late Dr. B. F. Nicholls of Philadelphia, who subsequently removed to that city and for many years was a physician in high standing. Doctor Nicholls' son, Joseph Clapp Nicholls left a large law practice in Philadelphia to become judge advocate general with the rank of major during the recent war.

George W. Nicholls attended the school at Woodruff in Spartanburg County and Furman University at Greenville and read law in the office of Evins & Bomar in Spartanburg. Admitted to the bar in 1876 he was elected in the same year probate judge of Spartanburg County and served as such by successive biennial elections for ten years. Since then he has applied himself to a growing private practice, and in later years has shared his clientage with his son.

Judge Nicholls married Miss Minnie L. Jones, daughter of Rev. Dr. Samuel B. Jones of the Southern Methodist Church. Judge and Mrs. Nicholls had the misfortune to lose two sons in the flower of their youth: George Williams Nicholls, who graduated from the Virginia Military Institute with the highest honors of his class; and William Montague

Nicholls, their third son. The latter had almost finished a four years' course in the Naval Academy at Annapolis, and resigning from that institution took up the study and practice of law with his father at Spartanburg. He had hardly become settled in his professional career when the World war broke out in the summer of 1914. He was one of a number of young Americans whose military enthusiasm was challenged by the issues of that conflict, and he gave his life to the cause long before America entered the lists against Germany. September 1, 1914, he left for Toronto, Canada, where he tried to enlist in the Canadian army. He was rejected as the citizen of a neutral country. Returning to New York he sailed for England and in London made further effort to join the British army, but for a long time without success. Finally a volunteer regiment for service in France was organized by some wealthy Londoners and young Nicholls was permitted to enroll. His previous experience brought him quick recognition by his superior officers, and he was made second lieutenant in the Royal Artillery, Kitchener's Expeditionary Forces. He arrived at the front in France in the latter part of January, 1915, and on March 23d of that year was wounded at the battle of Chappelle. He was returned to England for treatment in hospital, but later rejoined the command, and was killed in action at the battle of Loos, September 26, 1915. He had been a star football player in the Naval Academy at Annapolis and was a splendid specimen of physical manhood and a patriot without fear or reproach.

Judge and Mrs. Nicholls have three living children: Congressman Samuel Jones Nicholls; Kate Montague, wife of Mr. T. S. Perrin of Spartanburg; and Lottie Lee, wife of Robert P. Hazlehurst, assistant paymaster in the United States Navy.

Hon. Samuel Jones Nicholls, who was born in Spartanburg May 7, 1885, is one of the most prominent men of South Carolina in the present generation. He was educated in Wofford College at Spartanburg, in the Bingham Military Institute at Asheville, North Carolina, and in the Virginia Polytechnic Institute, where he spent three years. He studied law with his father and also attended the law school of the University of Chicago. He was admitted to the bar in 1906, and at once began practice with his father under the firm name of Nicholls & Nicholls. In that year, though only twenty-one years of age, he was elected to the Legislature and served one term. While still a very young man he served by special appointment as associate justice of the Supreme Court of South Carolina. He also served as city attorney and county attorney of Spartanburg in Spartanburg County. With all the military spirit of his ancestors he organized in Spartanburg Company I of the First Infantry, National Guard of South Carolina, and for three years was its captain. He is a past exalted ruler of Spartanburg Lodge of Elks and past great sachem of the Improved Order of Red Men.

He was elected to the Sixty-Fourth Congress in 1914 over five opponents by a handsome majority, and in 1916 was re-elected by a majority of 12,000 votes over two opponents in the democratic primaries. In the general election his opponent received only seventy-four votes. In 1918 he was elected to the Sixty-sixth Congress, in which his previous congressional experience and his many substantial abilities gave him an important influence in the reconstruction problems of the nation. Throughout the war with Germany he served as a member of the committee on military affairs. In May, 1919, by mutual agreement, he was transferred to the Naval Affairs Committee. He won his election against some of the strongest and most powerful men in the Fourth District, a district embracing the counties of Spartanburg, Greenville, Laurens and Union, comprising what is perhaps the richest and most important section of South Carolina. Congressman Nicholls is a member of the Central Methodist Church, South. March 7, 1915, he married Miss Eloise M. Clark of Green Bay, Wisconsin.

Hon. Samuel Jones Nicholls who was born in Spartanburg, May 7, 1885, is one of the most prominent men of South Carolina in the present generation. He was educated in Wofford College at Spartanburg, in the Bingham Military Institute at Asheville, North Carolina, and in the Virginia Polytechnic Institute, where he spent three years. He studied law with his father and also attended the law school of the Universtiy of Chicago. He was admitted to the bar in 1906, and at once began practice with his father under the firm name of Nicholls & Nicholls. In that year though only twenty-one years of age, he was elected to the Legislature and served one term. While still a very young man he served by special appointment as associate justice of the Supreme Court of South Carolina. He also served as city attorney and county attorney of Spartanburg in Spartanburg County. With all the military spirit of his ancestors he organized in Spartanburg Company I of the First Infantry, National Guard of South Carolina, and for three years was its captain. He is a past exalted ruler of Spartanburg Lodge of Elks and past sachem of the Improved Order of Red Men.

He was elected to the Sixty-fourth Congress in 1914 over five opponents by a handsome majority, and in 1916 was re-elected by a majority of 12,000 votes over two opponents in the democratic primaries. In 1918 he was elected to the Sixty-sixth Congress, in which his previous congressional experience and his many substantial abilities gave him an important influence in the reconstruction problems of the nation. Throughout the war with Germany he served as a member of the Committee on Military Affairs. In May, 1919, by mutual agreement he was transferred to the Naval Affairs Committee. He won his election against some of the strongest and most powerful men in the Fourth District, a district embracing the counties of Spartanburg, Greenville, Laurens and Union, comprising what is perhaps the richest and most important section of South Carolina.

Congressman Nicholls is a member of the Central Methodist Church, South. March 17, 1915, he married Miss Eloise M. Clark of Green Bay, Wisconsin.

Edward Holbrook Wyman, M. D. Almost immediately after graduating in medicine, Doctor Wyman established his home in a country community of Hampton County, of which the Town of Estill, founded after the building of the railroad about 1891, has since become the center. He has practiced there nearly thirty years, and has seen the town grow from nothing until is is the best little city in Hampton County and one of the best of its size in the state.

Doctor Wyman is a member of a notable family in Hampton County, where he was born July 20, 1870, son of Edward Holbrook and Clara E. (Vincent) Wyman. His birthplace was the old home of his grandfather in what is now the extreme eastern part of Hampton County on the Salkehatchie Swamp, in what was originally Beauford District.

His grandfather was Dr. Joel Wentworth Wyman, a native of Worcester, Massachusetts, and of New England ancestry. He acquired a thorough practical education in the famous Worcester Academy, and in later years was known as a Latin and Greek scholar and man of the highest intellectual attainments. About 1834 he came to South Carolina and settled in Beaufort County, where he married Miss Catherine Clementine Hay. While teaching the old Boiling Springs school in what is now Allendale County, he studied medicine, and for a long period of years served an extensive community around his home in a professional capacity.

This veteran doctor of Hampton County had four sons who became soldiers of the Confederacy, one of them being Edwar Holbrook Wyman. The others were Capt. Benjamin F. Wyman; Hamblin Hay Wyman, who was killed at the battle of Swift Creek, Virginia, in May, 1863, and Harry Hastings Wyman. Capt. Benjamin F. Wyman, who distinguished himself as a Confederate officer, was graduated from the Charleston Medical College in 1868 and for many years pursued a successful career as a physician and surgeon at Columbia.

Edward Holbrook Wyman, father of Doctor Wyman, was a lieutenant of Company F in the Eleventh South Carolina Regiment and served the entire four years of the war. In earlier life he was a planter at the home place in Hampton County and subsequently became a hardware merchant at Aiken.

Doctor Wyman studied medicine at the University of Georgia at Augusta, graduating with the class of 1890. While still a comparatively young man, Doctor Wyman represents the old fashioned ideals of the country doctor. He has been a physician not only for physical ills, but to the soul, and has been a constant friend and adviser to those coming to him with their troubles. The sorrows and tragedies, the family secrets of a country community have been freely entrusted to him, and he has been the means of saving many lives from being wrecked and homes from being dismembered. It is for this intensely human and personal service he has rendered the community that he will be best remembered. Doctor Wyman is a member of the County, State and American Medical associations.

Doctor Wyman has three living brothers and one sister. One brother, John Frampton Wyman, was accidentally killed at the age of thirteen while fishing in a swamp with a friend. One sister, Rosalie Vincent Wyman, died at the age of thirty-two.

His brothers are Joel Wentworth Wyman, a doctor at Denmark, South Carolina; Hugh Vincent Wyman, a hardware merchant at Aiken, South Carolina, and DeLacy Eviline Wyman, a hardware merchant at Estill. His sister is Catherine, wife of Rev. F. D. Jones, a Presbyterian minister of Clinton, South Carolina.

His first wife was Miss Pauline E. Lawton, member of the well known Lawton family of Hampton County. She was the mother of four children: Mrs. Lilla Dale Theus, John Frampton, Edward Holbrook, Jr., and Hugh E. Wyman. Doctor Wyman also has four children by his second wife, whose maiden name was Annie E. Weathersbee. These children are named Chester Graham, Joel Wentworth, Charles Vincent and Kathryn Clementine.

JAMES CASH WARING, M. D. McClellanville and the surrounding country have every reason to know and be grateful to Dr. James Cash Waring, for he has ministered to them in sickness and endeavored through sanitary regulations to keep them in good health once he had cured them. He was born at New Florence, South Carolina, October 31, 1871, a son of Col. A. H. and Hannah Elizabeth (Pawley) Waring, the former of whom was born near Charleston, South Carolina, on a plantation long in the family. On it Morton A. Waring, grandfather of Doctor Waring, was also born. The Waring family was established in South Carolina by English forebears in 1695, the first male of the line in this country being Benjamin Waring. The ancestry is traced down from Benjamin through Josiah Waring and Thomas Waring, to Morton A. Waring. The mother of Doctor Waring bore the maiden name of Pawley, and her father, George Pawley, was born in South Carolina a son of George Pawley. Pawley Island is named for the Pawley family. The elder George Pawley was the one who came to South Carolina from England and from him all of this name in the state, as well as in other states, are descended. Doctor Waring is the fifth in a family of six children born to his parents.

Carefully reared Doctor Waring was sent to private schools until his parents came to Charleston, when he attended the schools of that city. After receiving his classical training at the University of West Virginia, he matriculated in the medical department of the University of South Carolina, and was graduated therefrom in 1894, following which he settled in Beaufort County, North Carolina, and was there engaged in practice until 1906, when he located permanently at McClellanville. He is also a graduate in theology, and while a resident of Beaufort County, was rector of an Episcopal Church. Doctor Waring belongs to the Charleston County Medical Society, the South Carolina State Medical Society and the American Medical Association. He is a Mason and a Knight of Pythias, and also belongs to the Greek Letter College fraternity, Sigma Alpha Epsilon.

In 1912 Doctor Waring was married to Katherine Wyman Vincent, a daughter of Howard Evelyn Vincent of Charleston. Doctor and Mrs. Waring have no children.

WILLIAM HARVEY COGSWELL, born in Charleston, March 19, 1860, son of Harvey Cogswell and Mary (Keller) Cogswell.

Mr. Cogswell first attended the Charleston public

ASTOR, LENOX AND
TILDEN FOUNDATIONS

schools and was later a pupil of Professor Sachleben, who enjoyed fame as a teacher of young men, especially in the Humanities.

When he was prepared for it, young Cogswell matriculated at the Carolina Military Academy at Charlotte, North Carolina, an institution founded by the late Col. John Pierre Thomas to provide educational facilities for the high-born youth of the South, who were suffering by reason of the havoc created by war and its sequelae.

Many men of distinction in this and other states received their education at this institution, for under Colonel Thomas and his assistants the grounding was thorough. The moral code was high, the esprit was clean, evinced by the student body, models for young men anywhere. The standard of honor was that of Southern gentlemen, which meant then the highest in the world. Almost every man which that institution turned out has made his mark, and has been a force in his community.

Shakespeare said: "Let all the ends thou aimest at be thy country's, thy God's and truth's."

And again: "First, above all, to thy own self be true; and it must follow, as the night the day, thou canst not then be false to any man."

Young Cogswell made an obedient and devoted son. He honored his father and mother. He made a consistent and hard student at school and at the higher institutions he attended.

He entered the office of the Walker, Evans & Cogswell Company, a house founded in 1821, of which he is now president and general manager, studied the business, learned it and became a part of it. Then he went on the road, and became acquainted with the important matter of selling the firm's output. This he also studied, digested and mastered. Thus he was first, above all, true to himself.

To the last of Shakespeare's requirements he has been loyal all his life, for he demands truth from others and makes it his pole-star. No employer of labor can long retain the confidence of his employes unless his character is above reproach. He must be rigidly truthful, honorable and fair-minded. Added to which there must be sympathy with the worker's point of view.

Judged by so rigid and inflexible a standard, Mr. Cogswell has stood the test. He has the confidence, good will and affection of the large force under his control.

With such qualities, it is natural to expect that he would be a force in his community and such has been the case. Head of a company that boasts a full century of honorable dealing, descended from men who crossed the seas to have freedom to worship God according to their consciences, he could not be true to himself without measuring up to a high standard of conduct in all the relations of life.

Mr. Cogswell is a life-long member of Bethel Methodist Episcopal Church, South, and has always been foremost in its activities and in the councils of the great religious body which it represents. He has been chairman of Bethel Board of Stewards for the past twenty years. He is a member of the Commission on Finance of the South Carolina Conference, and a trustee of the District Conference. Mr. Cogswell is on the Board of Managers of the Charleston Bible Society, the oldest in the United States, antedating the American Bible Society by several years.

Charleston is headquarters for the Grand Lodge of Masons and Mr. Cogswell is a Mason and a Shriner. He is a member of various social organizations, namely the St. Andrew's Society, founded in 1729, and the oldest social organization in the southern states; the South Carolina Society, founded in 1737; the German Friendly Society, and the New England Society, of which he is likewise a steward. He is also a member of the Charleston Chamber of Commerce and of the Rotary Club; and in all these organizations he has been a force, showing active interest in all that pertains to their welfare.

To every appeal for a worthy object he has made liberal response. He is alive to the needs of his community and to the far-flung call of humanity, and to every call of public duty he has immediately responded, whether the duty asked was at home or elsewhere. He loves his state and her history, is proud of it and of the historic city in which he was born and lives. He has shown unswerving devotion to his country, without asking anything in return.

During the World war he was a worker, throwing into it the whole force of his nature and responding with his means. Three of his sons saw service in France.

William Harvey Cogswell, Jr., his eldest son, answered the call of the President for European war; acted as train adjutant 105th Ammunition Train, September 15, 1917, to March 1, 1918. Promoted captain S. O. No. 57 W. D., March 2, 1918. Served as adjutant throughout the active duties of the Ammunition Train in defensive and offensive operations in the Toul sector, France, August 25 to September 11, 1918; St. Mihiel offensive, September 12-16, 1918; Meuse-Argonne offensive, September 26 to October 8, 1918; Woevre sector, October 11 to November 8, 1918, and the Second Army offensive, November 9-11, 1918. His brigade was commended in orders for service in battle, and on the colors of its three regiments are service ribbons with names that shall live so long as history shall endure.

Julius Chesnee Cogswell graduated at The Citadel April 7, 1917, two months ahead of class, to enter U. S. Marine Corps. Commissioned second lieutenant after graduation. Went into camp at Paris Island, South Carolina, then to Quantico, Virginia. From there he went to France with the Second Battalion of the Sixth Marines, a famous organization, on January 19, 1918. The Sixth Marines belonged to the Second Division. He spent three months in the trenches before going into the battle of Belleau Wood, Chateau-Thierry sector, in which the Marines won glory. Wounded first on June 3d, Lieutenant Cogswell refused to return to the rear, being unwilling to leave his men. However, he was forced to do so on June 8th, when he received the wound which he now bears. He was decorated with the American Distinguished Service Cross in Paris for skill and bravery. He was relieved from active service with the Marine Corps August 26, 1919.

Vernon Cogswell, at the age of eighteen, with the consent of his father, enlisted for the European war as private in Headquarters Troop, First Battalion, Second South Carolina Infantry. While at Camp Sevier he answered a call for volunteers for replacements in General Pershing's headquarters regiment, First Army American Expeditionary Forces, and was immediately transferred to France. He was assigned to Co. B and served with this unit throughout the war.

Mr. Cogswell married on June 11, 1890, Miss Edna Muckenfuss, who died December 30, 1918, leaving the following children: William Harvey, Julius Chesnee, Vernon, Mary Louise, Lucile, Elizabeth, Thomas Keller and Edna Muckenfuss.

On November 4, 1919, he was married to Miss Lucia Fishburne Walker of Charleston.

Here is a well-rounded, successful life, not often seen in any country. Of distinguished ancestry, Mr. Cogswell turned himself at once to showing of what stock he came; for which reason he has right to be proud of his ancestry. He is still holding the banner.

His success in business came from study of his line, devotion to duty, and the putting forth of the uncommon qualities with which nature endowed him.

"'Tis not in mortals to command success," and few attain it who appear to deserve it.

But a wise man has said that life is a game to be won by the best players. Moreover it is a man's game, calling for every ounce of strength, for every faculty, for the bracing of physical, moral and mental sinews. There are rich prizes to be won, and he who fits himself sternly and sets himself squarely to the winning of them may hope to achieve success. So William Harvey Cogswell thought, and on that principle he acted.

With a New Charleston in which opportunities are multiplied a thousand-fold, he is ready for the larger life, for the extended horizon. He is now a commanding figure in his community, and, in the course of nature, is destined to exert influence for many years yet in the community, of which he is so worthy a member.

The Cogswell family, W. H. Cogswell's forbears, was one of distinction in England, but the first man of the house that came to America was John Cogswell, who came over in the "Angel Gabriel," the same ship in which Sir Walter Raleigh sailed to Guiana on his last and fatal voyage.

John Cogswell had eight children, seven of whom came with him. One daughter remained in London and married there. The "Angel Gabriel" was wrecked off Pemaquid, Maine, and went to pieces, probably being worm-eaten, for she had sailed many seas. The cargo was thrown overboard. On a raft, amid this wreckage, John Cogswell and his family safely landed on the rock-bound coast of New England and settled at North Hampton, Massachusetts. Among the passengers on the same ship was Rev. Increase Mather, grandfather of the memorable Rev. Cotton Mather. John Cogswell landed in 1635.

In each generation the Cogswells have been men of distinction. Oliver Wendell Holmes and Ralph Waldo Emerson each belonged to different branches of the family, being descended in the maternal line from John Cogswell, of the "Angel Gabriel." Many members of the family saw service in the Revolution and one, Col. Amos Cogswell, was made head of the New Hampshire branch of the Society of the Cincinnati for distinguished conduct in the war.

The father of Harvey Cogswell married Miss Susan Mouzon, of French Huguenot descent, of Charleston, and it was in this city that Harvey Cogswell was born in 1831. He was a successful business man, a loyal friend and a devout Christian. He died in March, 1902.

Both Harvey Cogswell and his brother-in-law, the knightly B. F. Evans, who crossed the ocean during the war between the states to secure lithographers for the Confederate Government, volunteered for service in the field on the outbreak of war. However, the Confederate Government needed them worse in their printing establishment and called both in. Their names were carried on their company's rolls to the end of the war—a fine tribute from their comrades.

Of the house, at whose head William Harvey Cogswell stands, a volume could be written. It celebrates its centennial of founding January 1, 1921. This is perhaps the longest term of life of any house in the southern states.

Founded by John C. Walker, January 1, 1821, it ran with varying fortunes until the war between the states, when Harvey Cogswell and Benjamin F. Evans, its heads at that time, were taken out of army service and put in charge of the printing and lithographing establishment at Columbia, whence bills and other papers, needed by the Confederacy, were issued. Almost swamped by the collapse of the Confederacy, they began business anew in Charleston and soon were on a firm foundation. Both members of the firm, together with C. Irvine Walker, also a member, entered heartily into the movement for redeeming the state.

The company did what printing was required by the democratic party, taking chances on their success for being paid. Later, when the state was a year behind in taxes and the several counties could not pay cash, Walker, Evans & Cogswell, extended long term credit. A similar policy was pursued in various southern states. This company published The Southern Christian Advocate and The Rural Carolinian for years. They also published Porcher's Resources of Southern Fields and Forests, Johnson's Defense of Fort Sumter and Charleston Harbor, Colonel Thomas' History of the South Carolina Military Academy, and other standard works.

During the War between the States, when lithographers could not be had, B. F. Evans went to England and Scotland, secured the men and brought them back through the Federal blockade, coming via Nassau, in the Bahamas.

The liberal policy of this distinguished company is being steadily pursued by its present president, who completely reorganized the business and brought it up to modern standards and methods.

HON. WILLIAM JUDGE MOORE, lawyer and planter of Greenwood County, was born December 27, 1859, near Cokesbury in Abbeville County (now a part of Greenwood County), son of William A. and Margaret Louise (Wardlaw) Moore. His parents were also natives of Abbeville County. The

Wardlaws were an especially conspicuous family in the state.

William Judge Moore graduated from Furman University in 1878, read law in Governor Ansel's office at Greenville and was admitted to practice in 1881. In 1898 he was elected master in equity for Greenwood County, and filled that office for eighteen years, until he retired in 1916. In 1918 he was elected a member of the House of Representatives from Greenwood County, and is a member of the Judiciary Committee and is author of a bill creating county courts in Greenwood County. Mr. Moore is now president of the Greenwood County Cotton Association.

He is the owner of several plantations in Greenwood County. One of them is the old home place near Cokesburg where he was born and reared. For many years Mr. Moore has produced great quantities of cotton on his land. As a leading cotton planter he has been active in increasing the welfare of cotton planters generally, and has vigorously cooperated with the modern movement for the regulation of cotton production so that adequate compensation may be insured to the farmer who expends his capital and labor in raising the crop. He is also a director of the National Loan and Exchange Bank of Greenwood.

His first wife was Miss Carrie Ellesor, of Newberry. She died August 11, 1899. On June 27, 1905, he married Miss Mamie Clardy, of Laurens. His four children were by his first marriage: Rebecca, wife of John D. Talbert; Miss Margaret Wardlaw; Lieutenant William A.; and Lieutenant GGray E. Moore. Both sons were officers in the World war. William A. is a graduate of The Citadel at Charleston, receiving a lieutenant's commission at Camp Jackson and served as an instructor in various camps. Gray is a graduate of Wofford College, was also awarded a lieutenant's commission at Plattsburg, and was on duty as military instructor at Syracuse University, New York. Both young men were discharged in 1919. Mr. Moore is a member and officer of the Methodist Church.

SAMUEL EDWARD MCFADDEN, of Chester, is a lawyer of secure place, prestige and recognized ability in his profession. While many make the profession of law and through it make a living and render a fair degree of service, Mr. McFadden is one of the exceptional few who are recognized masters in that profession. He has a well-earned fame as a general practitioner, specializing, however, in corporation and criminal law, and is also widely known for his gifts and services as an orator.

Mr. McFadden was born in Chester, December 7, 1869, a son of John C. and Margaret Louise (Waters) McFadden. He is of Scotch-Irish ancestry. The McFaddens and their kinsmen, the McKinneys, were pioneers on Fishing Creek and the Catawba River in the eastern part of Chester County. John C. McFadden and his father, Samuel E. McFadden, were both natives of Chester County, where the family has been represented since prior to the Revolutionary war. John C. McFadden was elected in 1884 and served in the office of clerk of court for twenty-four years.

Samuel E. McFadden was educated in the graded schools at Chester, graduated in 1886 from the Bryant & Stratton Business College at Baltimore and in 1887 entered Furman University at Greenville, where he received his Master of Arts degree in 1890. He then taught for two years in the Chester public schools, read law with J. L. Glenn at Chester, and in 1894 graduated from the law department of the South Carolina College. He has been in active practice since 1894.

Mr. McFadden specializes in corporation law and represents a number of the leading industrial and commercial interests of his section of the state. It is said that only one other law office in South Carolina has a finer library and other equipment for the busy lawyer than that of Mr. McFadden, which occupies the entire second floor of a building at Chester. Mr. McFadden has made a definite choice, partly as a matter of diversion from his routine work as a corporation lawyer, of criminal practice. During his career thus far he has successfully defended about a hundred capital criminal cases. He is widely known for his effective and logical presentation of cases at trial, and is also an orator of justified reputation on other subjects. His friends always refer to him as the "silver-tongued orator." His talents as a speaker were in great demand during the war, and he spent much of his time campaigning in behalf of the various Liberty Loans, Red Cross and other drives. He has never held public office, not has he ever offered for the same.

Mr. McFadden is a director and attorney for the National Exchange Bank, Spratt Building and Loan Association, Chester Machine & Lumber Company, Lancaster & Chester Railway, Springstein Mills, Eureka Mills, Travelers Insurance Company, and other corporations. He was a member of the Kappa Alpha fraternity in college. November 14, 1900, he married Miss Ethel Means, daughter of Capt. J. D. Means of Chester, and a representative of a family that came to this part of South Carolina from Mecklenburg County, North Carolina. Mr. and Mrs. McFadden have five children, Joseph Means, Louise, Jessie, John C. and Samuel E.

MERCER SILAS BAILEY, a veteran business man, banker and manufacturer at Clinton, was born in Laurens County, November 9, 1841.

Though reared on a farm he gained some youthful experience by clerking in a country store, and in 1859 took a clerkship at Clinton and soon after the close of the war became an independent merchant there. He has been in the mercantile business continuously for over half a century. Many other enterprises have responded to his ability as a manager. He spent several years in the saw mill, flour and grist mill business. In 1886 he became head of Bailey's Bank at Clinton, an institution that has had a good record for over thirty years. He established the Clinton Cotton Mill in 1896 and in 1902 the Lydia Cotton Mill, and is still president of both these enterprises.

In 1861 Mr. Bailey married Rosanna Lydia Abrams, daughter of Joseph Abrams. Nine children were born to their marriage, seven of whom are still living. Mr. Bailey is an elder in the Presbyterian Church.

VICTOR E. RECTOR, one of the most useful men in the State Department of Education, has an almost unsurpassed knowledge of educational conditions in the state, and either as a student or a teacher has come in touch with every class of school and every problem of education.

He was born in Spartanburg County February 3, 1882. He had a public school education and worked his way through the University of South Carolina, depending entirely upon his own efforts and enterprise and having not a dollar of aid from any other source. He is one of the alumni of the university who reflects credit upon the institution. He graduated with the degrees L. I., A. B. and M. A.

Mr. Rector has taught in practically every kind of school in the state, including the summer normal for teachers, and for one year taught in the university. For two years he was a teacher in the Philippine Islands and incidental to that experience made a voyage around the world. For one term he served Darlington County in the State Legislature, and has been a candidate for state superintendent of education. Mr. Rector is a Knight of Pythias and Woodman of the World and is a member of the Baptist Church. He married Miss Corrie Henderson, daughter of Rev. Thomas Henderson. They have two daughters, Sara Olivia and Anna Kathrine.

LANG N. ANDERSON is one of the young and capable lieutenants of the great southern cotton manufacturer, Col. Leroy Springs, of Lancaster. Mr. Anderson entered the cotton mill business before he had finished his college course, and with the benefit of sound qualifications and close study of every consecutive responsibility and duty has been promoted until he is now the active manager of the Kershaw Cotton Mills, one of the leading plants in the Leroy Springs group of cotton mills.

Mr. Anderson was born at Williamston in Anderson County, October 23, 1891, son of G. Lang and Ida (Holland) Anderson. His grandfather, George W. Anderson, a native of Laurens County, was a prominent planter both before and after the war between the states. He served in the Confederate army and about the close of the war moved to Williamston.

Lang N. Anderson was educated in the Williamston High School and in Clemson College. His first important post in the cotton mill business was as manager of the Brevard Yarn Mill, the head offices of which were at Greenville. Later he was at the Maplecroft Mills at Liberty, South Carolina, and in 1917 came to his present work as secretary and treasurer and active manager of the Kershaw Cotton Mills at Kershaw. This is one of the best mills of its size in the state, its output being fine lawns.

FRED A. GOSNELL. Among South Carolinians whose work and positions have taken them to the City of Washington during recent years, one is Fred A. Gosnell, now disbursing clerk of the Census Bureau and member of a well known family in Spartanburg County, where he grew up and had his early business training.

Mr. Gosnell was born in what is now Campobello Township in Spartanburg County in 1891. His parents are J. Holland and Corrie (Setzler) Gosnell. His father for many years has been prominent at Inman in that county as a merchant and farmer. A brother of Fred A. Gosnell has attracted much attention by his scholarship honors. This brother is Prof. Cullen B. Gosnell, who graduated from Wofford College in 1916, was a teacher in his native state, and is now associate professor of English in Vanderbilt University at Nashville, where he is pursuing his advanced work leading to the doctor's degree.

Fred A. Gosnell grew up at Inman, attended school there, spent a brief time in Wofford College, and acquired his business training in his father's store.

On March 8, 1915, he entered the government service as a clerk in the Census Bureau at Washington, and has now lived in the capital city for five years. His work was of a quality to win him successive promotions, and in July, 1919, official announcement was made of his fifth promotion when he was advanced to the responsibilities of disbursing clerk. He has performed the responsible duties of that office during the taking of the census and much of the appropriation required in this work passes through his hands.

Mr. Gosnell is a member of the Baptist Church. He married Miss Addie Sue Fite, of a North Carolina family. They maintain their home in Washington and have three children, Susan Katharine, James Robert and Helen Grace.

JAMES ADOLPHUS JONES. Nowhere in the state has agricultural enterprise been better diversified and developed than in Anderson County, and there naturally are found some of the best farmers in the state. One of them is James Adolphus Jones, member of an old and prominent family of that section, whose country home is near Holland.

He was born in that county June 18, 1868, son of James Thomas Crayton and Sarah Josephine (McGee) Jones, grandson of William and Elizabeth (Dean) Jones, and great-grandson of James and Elizabeth (Austin) Jones. The latter were among the first settlers at what was then known as Butlersville, now Starr, in Anderson County. This family has a peculiar distinction in the fact that members of three generations rendered service to the Confederacy in the great war between the states. James Jones, though an aged man, volunteered and was assigned the duty of bringing back the soldier dead from the battlefields and hospitals to their homes. His son William was a captain in the Confederate Army, while James T. C. Jones served as a lieutenant in the ranks. James Jones settled in Anderson County from Greenville County. Josephine McGee also brings a prominent family into this history. She was a daughter of Elias McGee, and her grandfather, Jesse McGee, was one of the early settlers of Anderson County.

James Adolphus Jones spent his early life on the farm, and as the oldest of twelve children, nine sons and three daughters, learned at an early age that great lesson in life of unselfishness and doing for others. While his days in school were limited he acquired a good practical training on the farm and elsewhere.

October 31, 1889, he married Lillah Belle Stucky, daughter of James Thomas and Mary Ann (Long) Stucky. Her great-grandfather was a Revolutionary soldier and was killed while on a furlough at Long Cain by the Tories. Mrs. Jones' paternal grandfather was Robert Stucky, of Abbeville County. On the maternal side the Longs are of Irish lineage, her great-grandfather, James Long, coming from Ireland and settling in Anderson County, where her grandfather, William Long, was born.

Mr. and Mrs. Jones have two sons, James B., who married Florence May Manning, and Joseph Adolphus, who married Nell Elizabeth Martin. About 1905 Mr. and Mrs. Jones bought their present homestead at Holland, and throughout his active career of thirty years farming has been his chief occupation. In 1909 he opened the Holland store with a stock of general merchandise, and conducted that in connection with his farm until recently, when he turned over its management to his son James. Mr. and Mrs. Jones are members of the Baptist Church, and he is affiliated with the Knights of Pythias.

R. EUGENE BURRISS, of Anderson, is a business man of keen mind and ready outlook, who has been identified energetically with several important manufacturing concerns of the state, and is now proprietor of the Burriss Milling Company of Anderson.

He was born in Anderson County, January 25, 1872, spent his early life in the country and attended country schools, was also a student in the Patrick Military Institute at Anderson and went from there to Furman University. He did not finish a university course because in 1892 he accepted the offer to become secretary of the board of directors of the South Carolina State Prison at Columbia. He held that office and performed its duties from January, 1893, until January, 1901. On resigning he returned to Anderson and became secretary of the Anderson Fertilizer Company. After the business was reorganized under the name of the Anderson Phosphate and Oil Company he continued as its chief clerk for two years, and then went on the road as salesman for its products for five years. Following that he performed similar duties for the Union Guano Company of Winston-Salem, North Carolina, but resigned in September, 1915, to devote his entire time to the Burriss Milling Company.

Mr. Burriss had established this business in April, 1915. For some time he had recognized the increasing interest and demand for cereals made from the whole grain, and the business of the Burriss Milling Company has been chiefly to supply and meet that demand. The articles they manufacture comprise whole corn meal and cereals from the whole wheat. The industry has grown in volume and recently the new mill of 100 barrels daily capacity of flour and 200 bushels corn for table meal has been put in operation.

Mr. Burriss is a democrat, is a member of the board of aldermen of Anderson and is a member of the Baptist Church. In 1894 he married Birdie Hawkins, of Columbia, and their only son Robert E., Jr., was in the aviation department of the army during the World war. He was in France eighteen months and remained in service twenty-six months, during which time he received four promotions.

J. REID GARRISON is the chief representative of the varied activities found in the Village of Denver, Anderson County, where he is a farmer, merchant and postmaster.

He was born in Anderson County, December 1, 1869, a son of William Dunkling and Esther (Reid) Garrison, the former a native of Greenville and the latter of Anderson County. The mother was a daughter of Thomas L. Reid. The paternal grandfather, Edmund B. Garrison, was a native of South Carolina, and the father of ten children: William Dunkling Garrison, the oldest of these children, was in the Confederate army four years. He married in Anderson County and settled at Autun. For several years he managed the farm interests of the Pendleton Manufacturing Company under Benjamin Perry and finally bought farm lands at Denver, where he farmed on his own account until his death at the age of sixty-four. His widow is still living and resides on the old homestead. In their family were six sons and four daughters.

J. Reid Garrison grew up on his father's farm and had a common school education. He started out for himself at the age of twenty-one. Buying his stock of general merchandise and the store of Mr. Eskew, a merchant at Denver, he operated that business for several years and sold the general stock. He is now dealing in buggies, fertilizers and cotton, operates a gin, and is also an extensive farmer. The Denver postoffice is in his store.

Mr. Garrison is a member of the Woodmen of the World and the Travelers Protective Association. In 1889 he married Miss Maggie Watkins, of Anderson County. They are the parents of a large family of six daughters and five sons, and the chief ambition of their lives has been to prepare and educate these children for useful and honorable places in life. Four of the daughters have already received superior educational advantages.

JAMES MORTON CARPENTER, one of the comparatively newer residents of Brushy Creek Township, Anderson County, where he is engaged in business as a farmer, had a long and active experience involving much travel and change of environment as a structural iron worker, but is well content to settle down to the quiet and profitable routine of farming.

He was born on a farm near Tryon in Polk County, North Carolina, May 28, 1866, son of James and Nancy (Edwards) Carpenter. His father was born in Rutherford County, North Carolina. The grandfather James Carpenter was a native of North Carolina. Nancy (Edwards) Carpenter was born in that state and the Edwards family originated in France and the first Americans of the name settled in Culpepper County, Virginia. James Carpenter, Jr., was a farmer and also a tanner and died in 1901 at the age of seventy-six. James Morton Carpenter was one of nine children. He has a common school education and up to the age of twenty lived at home and helped on the paternal farm.

With youth's natural desire for travel and change he went to Texas, and learned the structural iron business. For several years he was in the employ of the Southern Pacific Railroad building iron bridges and other iron work, and then entered the service of the American Bridge Company, being employed at many points in the Middle West.

In 1910 Mr. Carpenter married Mrs. Emma Lucretia (Richardson) Wyatt, a daughter of Mathias B. Richardson of Anderson County. Since his marriage Mr. Carpenter has lived in Brushy Creek Township and been engaged in farming. He and his wife are members of the Baptist Church. Mrs. Carpenter's first husband was Joseph William Wyatt, a son of William Franklin Wyatt of Brushy Creek Township. Joseph W. Wyatt was born November 16, 1859, and died July 5, 1907. His children were Vada Emma, Eugene Franklin, Sadie Lucas, deceased, Clarice Edith, deceased, Willa May and Sarah Elizabeth. Of these Eugene Franklin had some overseas service with the American Expeditionary Forces in the Motor Truck Division. Mr. and Mrs. Carpenter have one son, James Morton, Jr.

ROBERT CALVIN BROWNLEE. During colonial history three Brownlee brothers landed at Charleston. One of them subsequently went West, and so far as known all the Brownlees in the state today, constituting a numerous and prominent family, are descendants from one or the other of the two brothers who remained. One of the brothers was the ancestor of the Charleston Brownlees and the other is acknowledged as the forefather of the "up-state" Brownlees. The substance of this brief sketch is mainly concerned with a branch of the family long prominent at Due West and in that vicinity.

George Brownlee, Sr., married a Miss Caldwell, of the Caldwell family of Abbeville and Newberry counties. He reared his children at or near Due West. His son George Brownlee, Jr., married a Miss Richey, lived at Due West, and had a family of six sons and four daughters. One of the sons was Samuel Robinson Brownlee, and he and his wife had three sons: James Lawrence Brownlee, who graduated from Erskine College and became a Presbyterian minister; Samuel D. Brownlee, of Anderson; and Robert Calvin Brownlee.

Robert Calvin Brownlee spent practically all his life at Due West and achieved success as a merchant. He was born there May 31, 1858, and died June 21, 1915, being a son of Samuel Robinson and Mary Louise (Padget) Brownlee. When he was a small boy and while the war was still in progress he lost his father, and the widowed mother had three children of her own and a daughter of her sister to rear. After the war the Brownlees shared in the general poverty of the entire state and its population, and they endured many hardships and privations. Robert Calvin Brownlee in spite of this obvious lack of opportunities finished the course at Erskine College, and went to work to earn his living as clerk in a mercantile establishment. For two years he was in Greenville and in 1880 he and his cousin J. D. Brownlee formed a partnership and opened a general store at Due West. This partnership relation lasted for over twenty years, being terminated by the death of J. D. Brownlee. The business was then continued by Robert Calvin Brownlee until his death, and it is now carried on successfully by his sons O. Y. and W. L. Brownlee, whose place of business is the same store building which their father occupied thirty or forty years ago. Robert Calvin Brownlee achieved success by sheer force of industry, integrity of character and worthy ambition. He always acknowledged a great debt to his mother, whose encouragement was an ever present aid to her children.

In 1880 Mr. Brownlee was happily married to Miss Fannie Foster Bonner. She is a daughter of the late Rev. John I. Bonner, a minister of the Associate Reformed Presbyterian Church and the able president of the Woman's College at Due West. Mrs. Brownlee survives her husband and resides at Due West. Her oldest son, John Irwin Brownlee, married in 1910 Miss Nell Orr, daughter of Dr. W. W. Orr, of Charlotte, North Carolina. They have three children, Robert Orr Brownlee, John Irwin Brownlee, Jr., and Pauline Harvey Brownlee. Mary Louise Brownlee, second child of the late R. C. Brownlee, is the wife of Rev. Samuel W. Boyce. Oliver Young Brownlee married Eva Clinkscales, and William Lawrence Brownlee married Otis Hannah. Robert Calvin Brownlee, Jr., is unmarried and several other children died in infancy.

The late Mr. Brownlee was a life-long member and for many years a deacon in the Associate Reformed Presbyterian Church. His wife is of the same faith and they reared their children in that denomination. A democrat in politics, the late Mr. Brownlee was never a candidate for public office, and the interest he took in politics was in behalf of his friends and the good of his party.

YATES SNOWDEN, college prof.; b. Charleston, S. C., May 8, 1858; s. William S. (M. D.) and Mary A. (Yates) S.; grad. Coll. of Charleston, 1878 (LL. D., 1910); admitted to bar, 1882; post-graduate work Columbia U., 1904-5; m. Annie E. Warley, of St. John's parish, Berkeley Co., S. C., Oct. 25, 1894. On staff Charleston News and Courier, 1886-1904; prof. history, U. of S. C., Sept. 1905—. Mem. Hist. Commn., S. C.; curator S. C. Hist. Socy.; mem. Hist. Assn.; corr. mem. hist. socs. of Va. and Md. Democrat, Mason. Club: Kosmos. Contbr. to hist. bibliog. and other periodicals.

To the foregoing, extracted from "Who's Who in America" (1920-21), the publishers add that Dr. Snowden completed his labors as supervising editor of this history shortly before Thanksgiving of 1920.

WITHDRAWN
WRIGHT STATE UNIVERSITY LIBRARIES

KIDNEY ELECTROLYTE DISORDERS

KIDNEY ELECTROLYTE DISORDERS

Edited by

James C. M. Chan, M.D.

Professor and Vice Chairman
Department of Pediatrics
Virginia Commonwealth University
Medical College of Virginia
Richmond, Virginia

John R. Gill, Jr., M.D.

Scientist Emeritus
Hypertension-Endocrine Branch
National Heart, Lung, Blood Institute
National Institutes of Health
Bethesda, Maryland

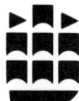

CHURCHILL LIVINGSTONE
New York, Edinburgh, London, Melbourne

Library of Congress Cataloging in Publication Data

Kidney electrolyte disorders / edited by James C.M. Chan, John R. Gill, Jr.
   p.   cm.
   Includes bibliographies and index.
   ISBN 0-443-08639-7
   1. Water-electrolyte imbalances.   2. Kidneys—Diseases—Complications and sequelae.   I. Chan, James C. M.   II. Gill, John R.
   [DNLM: 1. Kidney—physiopathology.   2. Water-Electrolyte Imbalance—physiopathology.   WJ 300 K4522]
   RC630.K53   1990
   616.6′1—dc20
   DNLM/DLC
   for Library of Congress   89-17460
                                                                          CIP

© Churchill Livingstone Inc.   1990

All rights reserved. No part of this publication may be reproduced, stored in a retrieval system, or transmitted in any form or by any means, electronic, mechanical, photocopying, recording, or otherwise, without prior permission of the publisher (Churchill Livingstone Inc., 1560 Broadway, New York, NY 10036).

Distributed in the United Kingdom by Churchill Livingstone, Robert Stevenson House, 1–3 Baxter's Place, Leith Walk, Edinburgh EH1 3AF, and by associated companies, branches, and representatives throughout the world.

Accurate indications, adverse reactions, and dosage schedules for drugs are provided in this book, but it is possible that they may change. The reader is urged to review the package information data of the manufacturers of the medications mentioned.

The views expressed in Chapter 4 are those of the authors and do not necessarily reflect the views of the National Institutes of Health or the Department of Health and Human Services.

The Publishers have made every effort to trace the copyright holders for borrowed material. If they have inadvertently overlooked any, they will be pleased to make the necessary arrangements at the first opportunity.

Acquisitions Editor: *Linda Panzarella*
Copy Editor: *Kimberly Quinlan*
Production Designer: *Jill Little*
Production Supervisor: *Sharon Tuder*

Printed in the United States of America

First published in 1990

Contributors

Uri Alon, MD
Associate Professor, Department of Pediatrics, University of Missouri–Kansas City School of Medicine; Attending Nephrologist, The Children's Mercy Hospital, Kansas City, Missouri

J. Williamson Balfe, MD, FRCP(C)
Associate Professor, Department of Pediatrics, University of Toronto Faculty of Medicine; Acting Director, Department of Pediatric Nephrology, The Hospital for Sick Children, Toronto, Ontario

Frederic C. Bartter, MD†
Professor, Department of Medicine, University of Texas Medical School at San Antonio; Attending Staff, Audie L. Murphy Memorial Veterans Hospital, San Antonio, Texas

Norman H. Bell, MD
Professor, Department of Medicine and Pharmacology and Director, Division of Bone and Mineral Metabolism, Medical University of South Carolina; Staff Physician, Veterans Administration Medical Center, Charleston, South Carolina

Fred Birch, MD
Chief, Division of Nephrology and Assistant Professor, Department of Medicine, University of South Dakota School of Medicine, Rapid City, South Dakota

Murray F. Brennan, MD
Professor, Department of Surgery, Cornell University Medical College; Chairman, Department of Surgery and Alfred P. Sloan Chair in Surgery, Memorial Sloan-Kettering Cancer Center, New York, New York

Ben H. Brouhard, MD
Director of Research, Department of Pediatric and Adolescent Medicine, Cleveland Clinic Foundation, Cleveland, Ohio

James C. M. Chan, MD
Professor and Vice Chairman, Department of Pediatrics, Virginia Commonwealth University Medical College of Virginia, Richmond, Virginia

---

† Deceased.

Robert J. Cunningham III, MD
Director, Section of Pediatric Nephrology and Hypertension, Cleveland Clinic Foundation, Cleveland, Ohio

Catherine S. Delea, AB
Instructor in Research, Department of Medicine, University of Texas Medical School at San Antonio, San Antonio, Texas

Cristobal G. Duarte, MD
Medical Officer, Division of Cardio-Renal Products, The Food and Drug Administration, Rockville, Maryland; Chief, Department of Nephrology, Bay Pines Veterans Administration Hospital, Bay Pines, Florida

Leonard G. Feld, MD, PhD
Assistant Professor, Departments of Pediatrics and Physiology, State University of New York at Buffalo School of Medicine and Biomedical Sciences; Chief, Division of Pediatric Nephrology and Director, Children's Kidney Center, The Children's Hospital of Buffalo, Buffalo, New York

John W. Foreman, MD
Associate Professor, Department of Pediatrics, Virginia Commonwealth University Medical College of Virginia; Attending Nephrologist, University Children's Medical Center, Richmond, Virginia

Donald S. Gann, MD
Professor and Associate Chairman, Department of Surgery, University of Maryland School of Medicine, Baltimore, Maryland

Denis F. Geary, MB, BS, FRCP(C)
Assistant Professor, Department of Pediatrics, University of Toronto Faculty of Medicine; Director, Hemodialysis Service, The Hospital for Sick Children, Toronto, Ontario

John R. Gill, Jr, MD
Scientist Emeritus, Hypertension-Endocrine Branch, National Heart, Lung, Blood Institute, National Institutes of Health, Bethesda, Maryland

Todd S. Ing, MD
Professor, Department of Medicine, Loyola University Stritch School of Medicine, Maywood, Illinois; Program Director, Section of Nephrology and Hypertension, Ed Hines Jr. Veterans Administration Hospital, Hines, Illinois

Joseph L. Izzo, Jr. MD
Associate Professor of Medicine and Pharmacology, Department of Medicine, State University of New York at Buffalo School of Medicine and Biomedical Sciences; Chairman, Department of Medicine, Millard Fillmore Gates Hospital, Buffalo, New York

Mary Jacob, PhD
Professor of Nutrition, Department of Home Economics, California State University, Long Beach, California

Gad Kainer, MB, BS, FRACP
Attending Nephrologist, Prince of Wales Children's Hospital, Randwick, New South Wales, Australia

Pardon R. Kenney, MD, MMSc
Assistant Clinical Professor, Department of Surgery, Harvard Medical School; Chief, Department of Surgery, Faulkner Hospital, Boston, Massachusetts

Saulo Klahr, MD
Joseph Friedman Professor of Renal Disease, Department of Medicine, Renal Division, Washington University School of Medicine; Staff Physician, Barnes Hospital, Saint Louis, Missouri

Robert E. Lynch, MD, PhD
Associate Professor, Department of Pediatrics, Saint Louis University School of Medicine; Attending Nephrologist, Cardinal Glennon Hospital, St. Louis, Missouri

James M. May, MD
Associate Professor, Department of Medicine, Diabetes Research and Training Center, Vanderbilt University School of Medicine, Nashville, Tennessee

Donald E. Oken, MD
Professor, Department of Medicine, Virginia Commonwealth University Medical College of Virginia; Attending Nephrologist, Veterans Administration Medical Center, Richmond, Virginia

H. John Reineck, MD
Clinical Professor, Department of Medicine, University of Texas Medical School at San Antonio, San Antonio, Texas

Anthony G. Salem, MD
Professor, Department of Medicine, University of South Dakota School of Medicine; Chief, Medical Service, Royal C. Johnson Veterans Administration Medical Center, Sioux Falls, South Dakota

Fernando Santos, MD
Professor, Department of Pediatrics, University of Oviedo School of Medicine; Attending Staff, Hospital "N.S. Covadonga", Oviedo, Asturias, Spain

James E. Springate, MD
Assistant Professor, Department of Pediatrics, State University of New York at Buffalo School of Medicine and Biomedical Sciences, Buffalo, New York

Jay H. Stein, MD
Professor and Chairman, Department of Medicine, University of Texas Medical School at San Antonio, San Antonio, Texas

Luther B. Travis, MD
Professor, Department of Nephrology and Diabetes, University of Texas Medical School at Galveston, Galveston, Texas

Noboru Tsuru, MD, MedDSc
Associate Professor and Chairman, Department of Pediatrics, Fukuoka University School of Medicine; Chairman, Department of Pediatrics, Chikushi Hospital, Fukuoka-ken, Japan

Charles O. Watlington, MD
Professor, Department of Medicine, Virginia Commonwealth University Medical College of Virginia, Richmond, Virginia

I. David Weiner, MD
Department of Medicine, Renal Division, Washington University School of Medicine, Saint Louis, Missouri

Edward T. Zawada, Jr, MD
Freeman Professor and Chairman, Department of Medicine, University of South Dakota School of Medicine, Sioux Falls, South Dakota

Preface

There is no short cut to mastering the complexities of renal and electrolyte disorders. On the contrary, the road to understanding begins with a thorough grounding in basic principles, which requires time, effort, and attention to detail. Therefore, this book begins with clear explanations of such basic concepts as acid-base balance and fluid electrolytes, and is directed toward students of medicine in the early stages of their careers.

For the more complex clinical problems, the best approach to their resolution most frequently lies in an understanding of the pathophysiology of the particular disease process. Thus, the later chapters of this book will provide more advanced students of medicine with concise discussions of the pathophysiology and the most current therapies for practical use in the treatment of special problems.

Our efforts in producing this treatise will have had their intended end if the road we have mapped leads to a greater understanding of kidney electrolyte disorders.

James C. M. Chan, MD
John R Gill, Jr, MD

Acknowledgments

We would like to offer our appreciation to Linda Panzarella and Robert Hurley at Churchill Livingstone Inc. for their patience in seeing us through, to Virginia Murrell, for shepherding all the manuscripts through to completion in this last year of dedicated effort. Also, we would like to thank Martha D. Wellons, Faith S. Boyle, and Martha D. Massie for their meticulous proofreading of the page proofs. We are grateful to Harold M. Maurer at the Medical College of Virginia and Harry R. Keiser at the National Institutes of Health for providing the atmosphere for us to complete this task. Finally, we are deeply indebted to the contributors for their excellent chapters. This is their book, which is dedicated to all students of medicine everywhere.

Contents

GENERAL CONSIDERATIONS

1. Disorders of Acid-Base Metabolism 1
   Saulo Klahr and I. David Weiner

2. Disorders of Sodium Metabolism 59
   H. John Reineck and Jay H. Stein

3. Disorders of Water Metabolism 107
   Frederic C. Bartter and Catherine S. Delea

4. Disorders of Potassium Metabolism 137
   John R. Gill, Jr, Fernando Santos, and James C. M. Chan

5. Disorders of Calcium Metabolism 171
   Gad Kainer, James C. M. Chan, and Norman H. Bell

6. Disorders of Phosphate Metabolism 223
   James C. M. Chan and Norman H. Bell

7. Disorders of Magnesium Metabolism 261
   Cristobal G. Duarte

8. Disorders of Trace Mineral Deficiency and Parenteral Nutrition 307
   Uri Alon, Mary Jacob, and Murray F. Brennan

SPECIAL PROBLEMS

9. Special Problems in Fluid and Electrolyte Management in Surgery 343
   Donald S. Gann and Pardon R. Kenney

10. Special Problems of Fluid and Electrolyte Metabolism in Diabetic Patients 363
    James M. May and Charles O. Watlington

11. Special Problems of Electrolyte, Water, and Acid-Base Metabolism in Children 421
    Ben H. Brouhard, Robert J. Cunningham III, Robert E. Lynch, and Luther B. Travis

12.	Pathophysiology and Management of Chronic Renal Failure John W. Foreman, Noboru Tsuru, and James C. M. Chan	457
13.	Special Problems of Chronic Peritoneal Dialysis in Children J. Williamson Balfe and Denis F. Geary	491
14.	Special Problems of Hemodialysis and Peritoneal Dialysis in Adults Edward T. Zawada, Jr, Fred Birch, Todd S. Ing, and Anthony G. Salem	507
15.	Special Problems of Acute Renal Failure: Pathophysiology, Diagnosis, and Treatment Donald E. Oken	527
16.	Special Considerations in Hypertension Leonard G. Feld, James E. Springate, and Joseph L. Izzo, Jr.	565
	Index	601

Disorders of Acid-Base Metabolism

Saulo Klahr
I. David Weiner

Clinical disorders of acid-base balance are seen frequently in medical practice. These disorders relate to an increase or decrease in the number of hydrogen ions entering or leaving the extracellular fluid (ECF), or to an extracorporeal gain or loss of base. Sustained disorders of acid-base balance most often result from altered functioning of one of the two major organs concerned with acid-base regulation—the lung and the kidney. The clinical and, particularly, the laboratory manifestations of acid–base disturbances are determined by the interplay between two opposing forces: (1) the pathophysiologic factors that operate to lower or raise the hydrogen ion activity (or pH) of body fluid, and (2) the defense mechanisms that attempt to restore pH toward normal.

DEFINITIONS: ACIDS, BASES, pH

A rational approach to the diagnosis and management of acid-base abnormalities requires an understanding of the physiologic processes concerned with hydrogen ion regulation. The understanding of acid–base metabolism has been abetted by the widespread use of the Brönsted-Lowry concept of acids and bases.[1] According to the Brönsted-Lowry definition, an acid is a proton donor and a base is a proton acceptor.

$$HA \rightleftarrows H^+ + A^-$$

In this equation, HA is an acid because it is capable of donating a hydrogen ion (proton), and A^- is a base because it accepts a hydrogen ion. Acids and bases vary in "strength" depending on how readily they donate or accept a hydrogen ion. A strong acid donates its H^+ readily; a weak acid does not. For example, HCl dissociates almost completely to $H^+ + Cl^-$; organic acids, typically weak acids, dissociate only partially to H^+ and the conjugate base.

The H^+ concentration of the internal environment of man and higher animals is closely regulated. Precise regulation of body fluid pH is necessary for the optimal functioning of enzyme systems in cells and the maintenance of normal membrane permeability. The central nervous system is particularly prone to functional derangements with large fluctuations in pH.[2]

The normal pH range of arterial blood is narrow, between 7.35 and 7.45, with a mean value of 7.40. Since pH = $-\log[H^+]$, equal numerical changes in pH from 7.40 do not represent equal concentration differences for H^+, for example:

pH	H$^+$ (nM)	ΔH$^+$ (nM)
7.00	100	
		60
7.40	40	
		24
7.80	16	

Because pH measurements are logarithms of actual concentration, it is incorrect to take arithmetic means of pH values or to refer to percentage changes in pH. These operations are appropriate only in the case of a linear scale.

BUFFERS

Buffers are substances that minimize changes in hydrogen ion concentration (and hence, pH) by converting strong (completely ionized) acids and bases into weaker (less completely dissociated) bases and acids, respectively.[3] Buffers consist of mixtures of a weak acid and its conjugate base. Their operation may be illustrated by the reaction occurring when a strong acid is added to a buffered solution:

HX + a$^-$ $\rightleftarrows$ Ha + X$^-$
Strong + Conjugate $\rightleftarrows$ Weak + Anion
acid   base   acid

The weak acid takes most of the added hydrogen out of solution since it dissociates less readily than the strong acid. Hence, the concentration of free hydrogen ions is reduced, and the fall in pH is ameliorated.

Similarly, when a strong base reacts with a weak acid to form the conjugate base and water, the following reaction takes place:

OH$^-$ + Ha $\rightleftarrows$ a$^-$ + H$_2$O
Strong + Weak $\rightleftarrows$ Conjugate + Water
base   acid   base

Hence, buffers protect against large shifts of pH in either the acid or alkaline direction. The pH range in which a buffer is effective is determined by the pK$_a$ of the buffer. Approximately 91 percent of the total buffering capacity of a buffer occurs in the pH range from pK$_a$ − 1 to pK$_a$ + 1.

Table 1-1. Classification of Buffers Present in Plasma and Erythrocytes

Plasma	Red Cell
HCO$_3^-$ − H$_2$CO$_3$	Hb$^-$ − H·HB
P$_r^-$ − H·P$_r$	HbO$_2^-$ − H·HbO$_2$
HPO^{2-} − H$_2$PO$_4^-$	Organic phosphates
	HCO$_3^-$ − H$_2$CO$_3$

Hb = hemoglobin; HbO$_2^-$ = oxyhemoglobin; P$_r^-$ = protein.

Buffers in Body Fluids

There are two general categories of buffers in body fluids: the bicarbonate buffer system and the nonbicarbonate buffer system. This division is logical in view of the very unique properties of the bicarbonate system.

Tables 1-1 and 1-2 summarize the classification of buffers present in plasma and erythrocytes, and the quantitative importance of each buffer component. An important aspect is that through the bicarbonate buffer system, the buffer systems in erythrocytes and in plasma interact rather freely. Roughly half of the buffering of whole blood is due to the bicarbonate buffer

Table 1-2. Quantitative Importance of Each Component of Blood Buffers*

Buffer System	% Buffering in Whole Blood
Nonbicarbonate buffers	
Hemoglobin and oxyhemoglobin	35
Organic phosphates	3
Inorganic phosphates	2
Plasma proteins	7
Total nonbicarbonate buffers	47
Bicarbonate buffers	
Plasma bicarbonate	35
Erythrocyte bicarbonate	18
Total bicarbonate buffers	53

* (From Winters RW and Dell RB Regulation of acid base equilibrium. In Yamamoto WS, Brobeck JR (eds): Physiological Controls and Regulations. WB Saunders, Philadelphia, 1965, with permission.)

system (principally in the plasma), with the other half due to nonbicarbonate buffers (principally hemoglobin in the erythrocytes).

The Bicarbonate-Carbonic Acid Buffer System

In man and other mammals, the bicarbonate–carbonic acid pair is the major physiologically active buffer system of the extracellular fluid (ECF). The interrelations of the various chemical species of the bicarbonate system are as follows:

$$CO_2 + H_2O \rightleftarrows H_2CO_3 \rightleftarrows H^+ + HCO_3^-$$
Hydration Dissociation

CO_2 and water form carbonic acid (H_2CO_3), the weak acid component of the bicarbonate buffer system. HCO_3^- is the conjugate-base component of this buffer pair.

The actual concentration of carbonic acid is not easily measured in clinical circumstances, but the vapor pressure of dissolved CO_2 can be. The Henderson–Hasselbalch equation[4] allows the hydrogen ion activity to be calculated as shown below:

$$pH = pK_a' + \log \frac{[HCO_3^-]}{\alpha \cdot pCO_2}$$

where pK_a' is $-(\log_{10} K_a')$, and α is the solubility coefficient of CO_2 (0.0301 mmol/liter/mmHg). Generally, the pK_a' has been measured as 6.1 in normal plasma. The Henderson-Hasselbalch equation can be rewritten as:

$$pH = pK_a' + \log \frac{[HCO_3^-]}{(0.0301) \cdot pCO_2}$$

where $[HCO_3^-]$ is in mEq/liter and pCO_2 is in mmHg.

The major physiologic importance of the bicarbonate–carbonic acid buffer system is achieved beause it is an "open-ended" buffer system. In most buffer systems ("closed-ended"), buffering results in the conversion of the base (or acid) to its conjugate form, and the total amount of buffer remains constant. As increasing amounts of acid (or base) are buffered, the conjugate base (or acid) is consumed and less remains available for further buffering. With the bicarbonate–carbonic acid buffer system, CO_2 is relatively independently controlled (to be described in more detail below); it can be adjusted back to normal levels by changes in alveolar ventilation. Thus, relatively high amounts of both components of the buffer system remain available. Theoretical considerations suggest that an "open" buffering system has approximately twenty times the buffering capacity of a "closed" system.[5] The ability to excrete or retain CO_2 is a major factor enabling the bicarbonate–carbonic acid buffer system to play the major role that it does in acid-base homeostasis.

ROLE OF THE LUNGS IN REGULATION OF ACID-BASE BALANCE

The lungs play a major role in acid-base regulation by regulating the carbon dioxide tension in the blood. Carbon dioxide is an integral part of the bicarbonate–carbonic acid buffer system because it is in equilibrium with carbonic acid, as discussed previously. Accumulation of carbon dioxide results in an increase in carbonic acid levels and an elevation in hydrogen ion concentration. This could correct alkalosis or cause acidosis, depending on the pre-existing acid–base status of the individual. Similarly, decreases in carbon dioxide result in decreases in carbonic acid levels, and therefore a decrease in hydrogen ion concentration. Alkalosis or correction of acidosis would then ensue. Changes in CO_2 concentration in the plasma can either cause or help correct acid-base disturbances.

Carbon dioxide is produced in large amounts by the metabolism of substrates;

the total daily production of CO_2 is generally assumed to be approximately 13,000 to 15,000 mmole. The lungs are the organs primarily responsible for the removal of appropriate amounts of CO_2 via the equilibration of plasma CO_2 with CO_2 in the gas to be exhaled. The carbon dioxide tension of the plasma is inversely proportional to alveolar ventilation rates. A doubling of alveolar ventilation results in a halving of CO_2 tension, and vice-versa.

Alveolar ventilation appears to be controlled, in large part, by the pH of the interstitial fluid of the central nervous system. Central chemoreceptors in the medulla oblongata appear to sense the cerebral interstitial pH and control alveolar ventilation; peripheral chemoreceptors in the aortic arch appear to be less important to this function under normal circumstances.[6] Acute metabolic acidosis results in a sharp decrease in pH of the extracellular fluid of the brain[7] (a marker of the interstitial fluid pH of the CNS), thereby stimulating the central chemoreceptors to increase alveolar ventilation.[8] Carbon dioxide appears to diffuse rapidly across the blood-brain barrier; changes in peripheral CO_2 concentrations almost simultaneously change the pCO_2 and thus the pH of the CNS interstitial fluid. As a result, changes in peripheral pCO_2 normally result in rapid changes in alveolar ventilation.

The ventilatory response to acid–base disturbances is quite important. In metabolic acidosis, ventilation may increase from the normal of 5.0 liter/min to greater than 30 liter/min as the arterial pH falls from 7.4 toward 7.0. This decreases the dissolved CO_2 concentration and returns the pH toward normal. Conversely, when the plasma bicarbonate concentration is increased in a patient with metabolic alkalosis, hypoventilation with a consequent elevation in pCO_2 reduces the pH toward normal. These respiratory compensations in metabolic acidosis and alkalosis are extremely important, and can turn a life-threatening change in pH into one that is much less dangerous. In contrast to the renal compensation for respiratory disorders in acid-base balance, which takes from three to five days to respond completely, the respiratory adaptation to metabolic disorders of pH is rapid, beginning within minutes and reaching its maximum effect within 12 to 24 hours.

ROLE OF THE KIDNEY IN REGULATION OF ACID–BASE BALANCE

The kidney serves two main functions in the regulation of acid-base balance. First, it regulates the plasma bicarbonate level by controlling bicarbonate reabsorption.[9] Second, it effects net hydrogen ion excretion in the form of titratable acids[10,11] and ammonium.[12]

Under normal physiologic conditions, the kidneys maintain a constant concentration of extracellular bicarbonate of approximately 22 to 26 mEq/liter. The kidney does so by delivering to the ECF compartment (via the renal vein) more bicarbonate than is delivered to the kidneys (via the renal artery), by an amount just sufficient to neutralize the net amount of hydrogen ion added to the ECF by daily metabolism. The typical American diet results in the metabolic production of significant amounts of noncarbonic acids (sulfuric acid, phosphoric acid, and various organic acids). In combination with the excretion of base in the stool, this results in a net "endogenous" production of H^+ of slightly less than 1 mEq/kg body weight/day (approximately 60 mEq/day).[13] These noncarbonic acids, represented by HA, cause an increase in hydrogen ion concentration and titrate body buffers, mainly HCO_3^-, thereby tending to reduce the extracellular bicarbonate concentration and to increase the concentration of A^-, as shown below:

$$HA + HCO_3^- \rightleftarrows A^- + H_2CO_3$$

The resultant H_2CO_3 is excreted as CO_2 by the lungs. By providing a net input of bicarbonate into the ECF that is equal to the net endogenous acid production, and by excreting A^- in the urine at a rate equal to the rate of A^- accession to the ECF, the kidneys prevent a decline in extracellular HCO_3^- concentration and consequent increase in A^- concentration.

The kidneys therefore maintain systemic acid–base equilibrium by: (1) recycling the ECF HCO_3^- delivered to them, and (2) regenerating the HCO_3^- and other body buffers exhausted in the process of neutralizing the approximately 60 mEq/day of H^- that is produced endogenously.

Control of H^+ and HCO_3^- Transport

Transport of H^+ and HCO_3^- occurs by different mechanisms in different portions of the renal tubule. The proximal tubule, made up of both the proximal convoluted and proximal straight segments, provides most (~85 percent) of the total tubular HCO_3^- reabsorption.[14,15] Yet it is unable to generate a significant pH gradient. As a result, it cannot reabsorb all of the filtered bicarbonate. The distal tubule, consisting of the cortical and medullary collecting tubules and the papillary collecting duct, provides the remainder of H^+ and HCO_3^- transport. It provides relatively less total capacity for H^+ and HCO_3^- transport, but is able to generate and maintain H^+ gradients of as much as 1000:1.[16–18] As a result, the distal tubule provides for the remainder of HCO_3^- reabsorption, and can provide for the net excretion of hydrogen ions into the urine.

Proximal Tubule H^+ Secretion

The major mechanism of H^+ secretion in the proximal tubule is via a luminally located Na^+/H^+ exchanger.[19] This exchanger mediates a 1:1 exchange of luminal Na^+ for intracellular H^+. Since the net electrochemical gradient for proton movement is from the lumen into the cell,[20] the exchange of intracellular H^+ for luminal Na^+ respresents a form of active transport.[21] The energy for this active transport is provided by the transcellular gradient of Na^+. Intracellular Na^+ concentrations are maintained at approximately 10 mM by sodium, potassium adenosine triphosphatase (Na^+, K^+, ATPase) located in the basolateral membrane of the luminal cell.[22,23] Luminal Na^+ concentrations remain high throughout the proximal tubule since proximal tubule fluid reabsorption is essentially isosmotic. The 10:1 or greater Na^+ gradient across the luminal membrane of the proximal tubule drives H^+ secretion. The secreted H^+ rapidly combines with HCO_3^- in the luminal fluid to form carbonic acid (H_2CO_3). The breakdown of carbonic acid to H_2O and CO_2 occurs in a reaction catalyzed by luminal-bound carbonic anhydrase.[24] Carbon dioxide rapidly equilibrates across the luminal membrane into the cytoplasm of the cell. There, intracellular carbonic anhydrase catalyzes its hydration with water to form carbonic acid, as shown in Figure 1-1. The dissociation of intracellular carbonic acid to H^+ and HCO_3^- then replaces the H^+ secreted across the luminal membrane. The result is a net movement of HCO_3^- from the lumen into the cell with Na^+. The final step in reabsorption is transport of HCO_3^- from the cell to the peritubular capillaries. This is accomplished primarily by an electrogenic $Na^+(HCO_3^-)_n$ (n > 1) symporter,[25,26] with a small contribution by a sodium-coupled, chloride/bicarbonate exchanger.[27] The electrochemical gradient for HCO_3^- is from the cell into the peritubular space, and thus transport in this direction does not represent active transport. Bicarbonate is then returned to the systemic circulation via the renal vein, resulting in net reabsorption of the filtered bicarbonate.

6 • Kidney Electrolyte Disorders

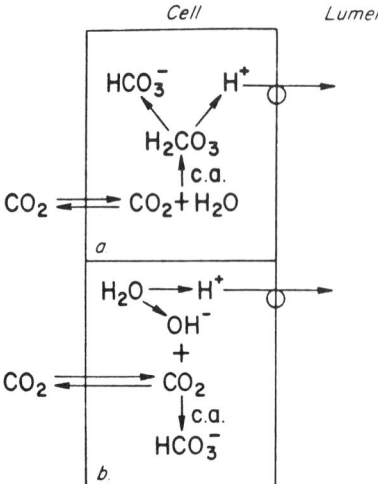

Fig. 1-1. Generation of intracellular hydrogen ions (H$^+$) through hydration of carbon dioxide (CO$_2$) as shown in (A), or through redox mechanisms involving splitting of the water molecule, as shown in (B). The H$^+$ produced in the cells is secreted into the tubular lumen, and the bicarbonate (HCO$_3^-$) left behind is transported across the base of the cell and eventually into the peritubular capillary. The hydration of CO$_2$ is catalyzed by carbonic anhydrase (c.a.)

Some studies have suggested that a small amount of H$^+$ secretion may be sodium independent and occur via a hydrogen-ion-translocating ATPase.[28–30] The secreted hydrogen ion combines with luminal bicarbonate in exactly the same fashion as do hydrogen ions secreted via the Na$^+$/H$^+$ exchanger, and the remainder of the reabsorption process is indistinguishable from the mechanism described above.

For several reasons, bicarbonate transport can occur at relatively high rates in the proximal tubule. First, the large brush-border membrane present in proximal tubule cells greatly increases the surface area available for transport. Second, luminal bicarbonate concentrations are higher in the proximal tubule than elsewhere in the nephron, thus providing greater amounts of bicarbonate for reabsorption. Finally, the Na$^+$/H$^+$ exchanger is able to rapidly exchange the two cations and thus allow for the relatively rapid reabsorption of HCO$_3^-$.

The major limiting factor for HCO$_3^-$ reabsorption in the proximal tubule is the ability of the proximal tubule to maintain a pH gradient from lumen to blood. The maximal acidity of luminal fluid appears to be a pH of approximately 6.7.[31] Several features account for this limitation. First, as the luminal pH falls, the luminal-to-intracellular concentration gradient of H$^+$ increases and can become a limiting factor in hydrogen ion secretion via the Na$^+$/H$^+$ exchanger. Second, the proximal tubule is relatively permeable, perhaps ten times more so than the distal tubule, to the backleakage of HCO$_3^-$ from the peritubular capillaries into the tubule.[32,33] The rate of backleakage depends on the bicarbonate gradient, thus limiting the bicarbonate concentration gradient that can be developed and thereby limiting the pH gradient. Third, the proximal tubule is sufficiently permeable to hydrogen ions that despite hydrogen ion concentrations on the order of 40 to 300 nmol/liter, there is a significant backleakage of hydrogen ions from the lumen to the blood.[34] Estimates of the magnitude of this backleakage suggest that it is approximately one-third of the backleakage of HCO$_3^-$. It is easy to see that several mechanisms prevent the formation of a significant pH gradient across the proximal tubule.

Loop of Henle H$^+$ and HCO$_3^-$ Transport

The loop of Henle participates in bicarbonate transport to a small degree. Transport may occur via passive mechanisms in the upper thin descending limb of the loop of Henle. Water abstraction in this region increases the concentration of bicarbonate in the tubular fluid, thereby causing a gradient to be formed, and passive reabsorption of bicarbonate occurs. In addition, the pCO$_2$ is lower in the medulla than in the cortex, resulting in a gradient for CO_2 exit from the lumen in the medullary portions of the loop of Henle. In the cortical thick ascending limb of the loop of Henle, bicarbonate absorption appears to be sodium-dependent[35] and stimulated by furosemide. The exact relevance of these findings to clinical medicine is uncertain, especially since they have not been confirmed by all investigators.[36,37]

Distal Tubule H^+ and HCO_3^- Transport

The distal tubule is fundamentally different from the proximal tubule in its handling of H^+ and HCO_3^-. The mechanisms of H^+ and HCO_3^- movement, the relative permeability to H^+ and HCO_3^-, and the quantity of HCO_3^- that can be reabsorbed are all very different in the distal tubule than in the proximal tubule.

Bicarbonate reabsorption in the distal tubule is primarily independent of luminal Na^+, in contrast to the case in the proximal tubule.[38] Instead of being linked to luminal Na^+/H^+ exchange, H^+ secretion appears to occur via a luminally located, sodium-independent, electrogenic, H^+-translocating ATPase.[39,40] This ATPase is capable of secreting hydrogen ions against very large gradients, as much as 3 pH units or +180 mV.[41] The luminal secretion of H^+ is balanced by the exit of HCO_3^- across the basolateral membrane via a Cl^-/HCO_3^- exchanger, thereby maintaining a relatively constant intracellular pH.[42] The net effect is proton secretion into the luminal fluid and the return of HCO_3^- into the systemic circulation.

The cortical collecting tubule appears to have cells specialized for H^+ and HCO_3^- transport. The "dark" or intercalated cells appear to have, as their primary function, active H^+ transport.[43] The "light" or principal cells appear to mediate Na^+ and K^+ transport. In addition, there may be two types of intercalated cells. One, the so-called α-intercalated cell, appears to be primarily responsible for H^+ secretion via the mechanism described above. The β-intercalated cell appears to be responsible for HCO_3^- secretion into the luminal fluid (which is apparently necessary for recovery from metabolic alkalosis, as described below). Direct evidence for this latter cell type in humans is currently lacking, but indirect evidence[44] and numerous studies in the rat,[45] rabbit[46] and turtle bladder[47] suggest its presence. The β-intercalated cell appears to have a basolaterally located H^+-ATPase and a luminal Cl^-/HCO_3^- exchanger. Hydrogen ions are secreted from the cell into the peritubular space by the H^+-ATPase, while HCO_3^- is secreted into the luminal fluid down its electrochemical gradient in exchange for Cl^-. Chloride then exits the cell via a basolateral Cl^- channel. Other portions of the distal tubule, the medullary and papillary collecting ducts, appear to have only a single cell type, and there appears to be no β-intercalated cell dedicated to bicarbonate secretion.

The distal tubule is able to generate a considerable pH gradient (as shown in Fig. 1-2), for several reasons. First, the electrogenic proton-translocating ATPase is able to pump protons against a much greater electrochemical gradient than the Na^+/H^+ exchanger in the proximal tubule. It can translocate hydrogen ions against electrochemical gradients of up to 180 mV (equivalent to a H^+ gradient of 1000:1, or 3 pH units). Second, the distal tubule has a much lower permeability to hydrogen ions and bicarbonate than does the proximal tubule. Much higher gradients of hydrogen ions and/or bicarbonate exist in the distal tubule without significant backleakage of either ion. The limiting factor for the pH gradient is therefore the ability of the electrogenic, proton-translocating ATPase to transport hydrogen ions. The distal tubule is therefore able to reduce the urinary pH to approximately 4.4.[48]

8 • Kidney Electrolyte Disorders

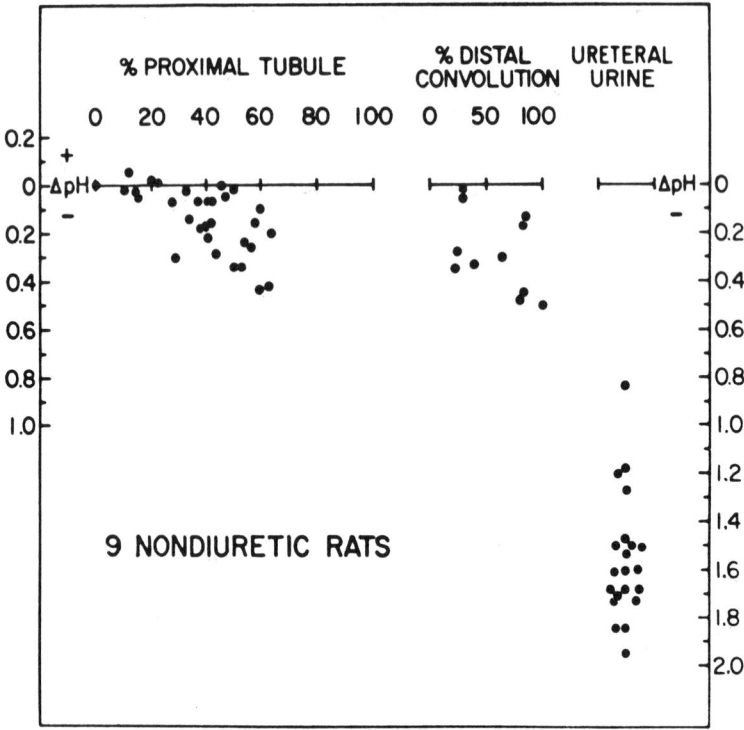

Fig. 1-2. Change in pH (ΔpH) of the tubular fluid along the nephron of the rat. (From Gottschalk C, et al.,[16] with permission.)

The ability to generate large pH gradients allows the distal tubule to participate in net proton excretion. In ordinary circumstances, approximately 85 percent of filtered bicarbonate is reabsorbed by the proximal tubule; this leaves approximately 15 percent for reabsorption in the distal tubule. This amount is easily reabsorbed in the cortical and medullary collecting tubules. However, metabolism of a normal American diet results in the generation of slightly less than 1 mEq/kg (of lean body weight) of acid per day.[13] For the average 70 kg patient, the excretion of ~60 mEq of hydrogen ions in a buffer-free, maximally acid urine (pH 4.4, with a free hydrogen ion concentration of ~40 μM) would require a daily urine output of almost 1400 liters. The presence of buffers allows the excretion of much larger amounts of hydrogen ions with smaller changes in the hydrogen ion concentration. The pK_a of each of these buffers is significantly less than 7.4 (ranging from 6.8 for inorganic phosphate to 4.9 for creatinine). The effective pH range of a buffer is only in the range of 1 pH unit above and below the pK_a of the buffer. It is the ability of the distal tubule to generate and maintain large pH gradients that allows each of these buffer systems to play a significant role in hydrogen ion secretion.

Regulation of Bicarbonate Reabsorption

Proximal Tubule

Several factors have been shown to affect proximal tubular bicarbonate reabsorption. These factors include intracellular pH, ECF volume, potassium levels, and perhaps some hormones. Intracellular pH appears to be an important regulator of such reabsorption. Acute changes in systemic pCO_2 result in changes in bicarbonate reabsorption as the pCO_2 changes.[49,50] This effect appears most likely to be mediated through changes in intracellular pH. Recall that increases in pCO_2 result in an increased intracellular CO_2 content due to the high permeability of CO_2 across cell membranes. The increased CO_2 then reacts with water under catalysis by intracellular carbonic anhydrase to form carbonic acid, which rapidly dissociates to free hydrogen ions and bicarbonate.[51]

A second factor affecting bicarbonate reabsorption in the proximal tubule appears to be the total body potassium store. Chronic hypokalemia appears to cause enhanced proximal tubular bicarbonate reabsorption.[52,53]

Extracellular fluid volume is a third factor affecting bicarbonate reabsorption. Although the exact mechanism is controversial, it is clear that ECF volume regulates proximal tubular bicarbonate reabsorption.[54,55] As shown in Figure 1-3, volume expansion appears to decrease bicarbonate reabsorption and volume contraction appears to stimulate it.

Some hormones, such as parathyroid hormone (PTH), have been shown to affect bicarbonate reabsorption in the proximal tubule.[56,57]

Distal Tubule

The control of hydrogen ion transport in the distal tubule is affected by different factors than in the proximal tubule. An example is that mineralocorticoids have no effect on the proximal tubule, but appear to directly stimulate acidification in the medullary collecting duct.[58]

Intracellular pH appears to be a second modulator of bicarbonate reabsorption in the distal tubule. In the turtle urinary bladder, a model of the cortical collecting tubule, Cohen and Steinmetz, using the ^{14}C-DMO method of estimating intracellular pH, showed that proton secretion was an increasing function of apparent intracellular hydrogen ion concentration.[59]

Third, sodium delivery to the distal tubule may have effects on proton and bicarbonate transport. Increased absorption of sodium in the distal tubule results in the generation of a lumen-negative potential difference. This results in a decrease in the electrochemical gradient against which the proton-translocating ATPase must function, and thereby results in an increase in proton secretion and bicarbonate reabsorption.

Chloride delivery to the distal tubule, especially the cortical collecting tubule, may be important for regulating bicarbonate secretion. Bicarbonate secretion in the cortical collecting tubule appears to occur via a luminally located chloride–bicarbonate exchanger.[60] Therefore, in states of volume depletion, in which chloride delivery to the distal tubule may be decreased due to increased reabsorption in the earlier segments of the nephron, bicarbonate secretion may not occur, resulting in a metabolic alkalosis caused by chloride depletion.

Net Acid Excretion

As discussed previously, simple acidification of an unbuffered urine to pH 4.4 cannot allow for the sufficient excretion of free hydrogen ions. Renal ammoniagenesis and urinary buffer excretion in the form of titratable acid allow the excretion of sufficient amounts of hydrogen ion in normal volumes of urine to maintain acid-base homeostasis, and to correct it if necessary. The difference between the sum of ammonium and titratable acid and the amount of bicarbonate present in the urine is referred to as the net acid excretion. Newly gener-

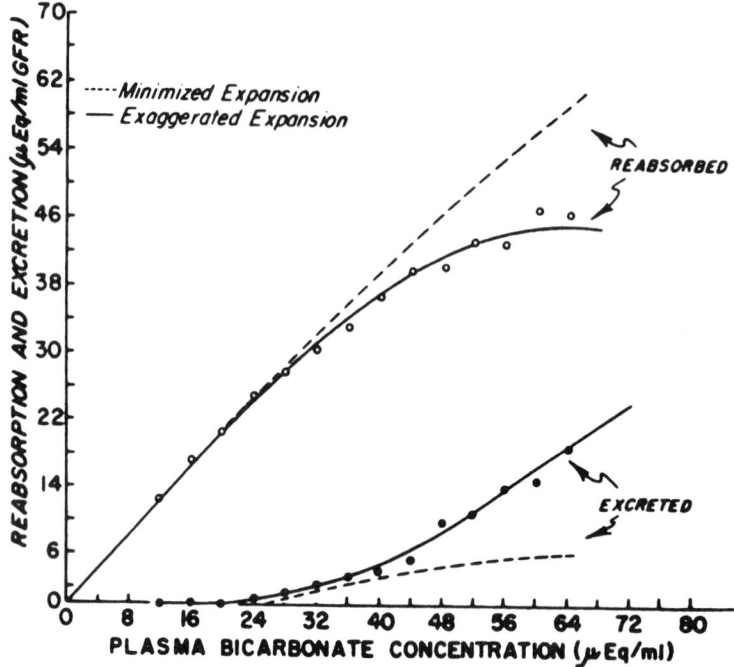

Fig. 1-3. Bicarbonate titration curves, showing both bicarbonate reabsorption and bicarbonate excretion in rats studied under conditions of minimized and exaggerated ECF volume expansion. (From Purkerson ML, Lubowitz H, White RW, Bricker NS: On the influence of extracellular fluid volume expansion on bicarbonate reabsorption in the rat. J Clin Invest 48:1754, 1969, with permission.)

ated bicarbonate is returned to the ECF via the renal vein in an amount equal to net urinary acid excretion.

Ammonia*

Urinary ammonia excretion has long been known to be an important modulator of the renal response to acid–base disturbances. In acute or chronic metabolic acidosis, ammonia excretion can rise significantly. In chronic metabolic acidosis it can rise as much as tenfold over several days in an attempt to maintain acid–base homeostasis. Given such effects, renal ammoniagenesis is one of the major mechanisms of acid-base regulation.

Traditionally, ammonia has been viewed as having the role of a urinary buffer.[61] However, the pK_a of the ammonia buffer system

$$H^+ + NH_3 \rightleftarrows NH_4^+$$

is approximately 9.3. Over 99 percent of total available ammonia is therefore present as ammonium ion (NH_4^+) when the luminal fluid pH is below 7.3. Consequently, urinary ammonia is not a significant buffer of protons secreted into the luminal fluid. Instead, the metabolic production of ammonium by the kidney appears to be responsible for net bicarbonate formation.

Ammonium is produced in the kidney via the metabolism of glutamine. Renal glutamine metabolism can proceed by either of the two pathways shown below[62]:

---

* The term ammonium will be used to refer solely to NH_4^+; ammonia will refer to both NH_3 and NH_4^+.

Glutamine $\rightleftarrows$ 3 CO_2 + 2 NH_4^+
+ 2 HCO_3^-

Glutamine $\rightleftarrows$ ½ Glucose + 2 NH_4^+
+ 2 HCO_3^-

The bicarbonate formed is returned to the systemic circulation via the renal vein, and the ammonium produced can be excreted into the urine. The net effect of the metabolism of one molecule of glutamine can be the production of two molecules of bicarbonate.

Some ammonium resulting from glutamine metabolism is not excreted by the kidney, but is instead returned to the systemic circulation via the renal vien. This ammonium is metabolized by the liver to urea, in a reaction consuming bicarbonate.[62] As a result, when ammonium is not excreted in the urine, the bicarbonate generated by renal ammoniagenesis is consumed by the liver, resulting in no net bicarbonate generation.

Two mechanisms can regulate the renal production of bicarbonate resulting from renal ammoniagenesis. First, ammonium that is not excreted into the urine but finds its way into the systemic circulation via the renal vein results in consumption of the bicarbonate formed in the kidney, and therefore negates the renal generation of bicarbonate. Therefore, factors that affect the distribution of NH_4^+ between the urine and the renal vein will affect the net generation of bicarbonate by the kidney.[63] Second, the rates of renal ammoniagenesis can vary according to the systemic acid–base status, and can contribute to regulating renal bicarbonate generation through ammoniagenesis.

Factors affecting the renal handling of ammonia are currently undergoing active investigation. For several years, the nonionic diffusion of NH_3 was thought to be the main mechanism of ammonia transport. The uncharged NH_3 molecule was believed to be in equilibrium throughout the cortex.

Trapping of the less permeable, positively charged ammonium ion (NH_4^+) in the relatively acid distal tubule was thought to result in the preferential excretion of ammonia into the urine, rather than its return to the systemic circulation via the renal vein. This is now known not to be the only mechanism of ammonia transport.[64] NH_4^+ can be transported via the Na^+/H^+ exchanger in the proximal convoluted tubule.[65] In the thick ascending limb of the tubule, NH_4^+ can substitute for potassium in the Na^+, K^+, $2Cl^-$ transporter.[66] In addition, NH_4^+ has been shown to substitute for potassium in the Na^+, K^+, ATPase in the proximal and collecting tubules.[67,68] In acidosis, an increase in papillary interstitial NH_3 concentration, independent of any decrease in pH of the collecting duct fluid, appears to play a significant role in the increase in ammonia secretion by the collecting duct.[69]

Other factors besides acid–base status can affect ammoniagenesis. In patients with renal insufficiency, NH_4^+ excretion is proportional to the remaining renal mass.[70–72] This decrease in hydrogen excretion may be responsible for much of the metabolic acidosis observed in renal failure.[73] A recent study suggests that the decrease in NH_4^+ excretion following a reduction in renal mass is due at least partly to reduced entrapment of ammonia in the collecting tubule, rather than to decreased ammonia production.[74] In addition, NH_4^+ excretion is affected by changes in the effective circulating volume. Beyond this, potassium depletion increases and hyperkalemia decreases ammoniagenesis,[75] while hypercalcemia decreases and hypocalcemia increases ammonia production.[76] The regulation of ammoniagenesis continues to be under active investigation.

Titratable Acids

Besides generating ammonia, the kidneys are also able to secrete protons and reabsorb bicarbonate via the excretion of titratable acids. This term refers to those buffer systems that can reversibly bind significant numbers of protons and thus allow the net excretion of protons into the urine without significant changes in luminal fluid pH. The major buffers include inorganic phosphate, creatinine, uric acid, and citrate.

Inorganic phosphate is the primary urinary buffer under most circumstances.[70] By rearrangement of the Henderson-Hasselbalch equation to:

$$pH - pK_a = \log \frac{HPO_4^=}{H_2PO_4^-}$$

$$(pK_a = 6.8),$$

one can calculate that approximately 70 percent of inorganic phosphate in glomerular filtrate (pH ~7.25) is present as the conjugate base ($HPO_4^=$), and can therefore bind hydrogen ions. The great majority of the filtered phosphate can therefore buffer hydrogen ion secretion. Because the pK_a for inorganic phosphate is 6.8, it is an excellent buffer as the pH of the urine decreases from 7.25 in the initial ultrafiltrate to 5.8. At a pH of 6.8, 50 percent of the buffer is in the $HPO_4^=$ form, and there still is a large amount of buffer capacity available to bind H^+. At pH 5.8, less than 10 percent of the buffer is in the $HPO_4^=$ form, and the capacity of the buffer has been almost totally exhausted. Other buffers may be utilized to bind hydrogen ions when the urine pH is less than 5.8. Creatinine and uric acid have a pK_a' of 4.9 and 5.6, respectively. They can continue to effectively buffer hydrogen ion secretion until maximum urine acidification, at a pH of approximately 4.4, is achieved.

Several factors affect the rate of formation and excretion of titratable acid. These include the relative tubular transport of the acid and conjugate-base forms of the buffer, and the amount of buffer available for excretion. Chronic, but apparently not acute, metabolic acidosis stimulates phosphaturia via uncertain mechanisms.[77,78] The relative transport of $HPO_4^=$ versus $H_2PO_4^-$ in the proximal tubule appears to be pH sensitive. Alkalosis appears to selectively increase the rate of $HPO_4^=$ reabsorption,[79] reducing the amount of luminal $HPO_4^=$ available to bind hydrogen ions, and this effectively decreases the ability of phosphate to buffer hydrogen ion secretion. Alterations in acid-base status can also affect phosphate reabsorption by altering the affinity of the sodium-phosphate cotransporter for sodium,[80] and by altering the number of phosphate transporters.[64] Indirect factors that may play a role in regulating phosphate reabsorption in disorders of acid-base balance include alterations in Na^+/H^+ exchange, gluconeogenesis, and other metabolic changes present in acid-base disorders.[81]

Citrate has also been postulated to be important in titratable acid excretion and the maintenance of acid-base balance.[82,83] Excretion of citrate increases in alkalosis and decreases in acidosis. Since unexcreted citrate is metabolized by the liver, with the generation of bicarbonate, the urinary excretion of citrate is equivalent to bicarbonate excretion. As a result, changes in the urinary excretion of citrate appear to play a role in maintaining acid-base homeostasis.

An Overview of the Normal Regulation of Acid–Base Balance

A series of overlapping defense mechanisms tends to maintain the pH of ECF within narrow limits. These defense mechanisms consist of at least three well-defined systems. The first consists of extra- and intracellular buffers, which provide an almost instantaneous first line of defense against changes in pH. The second is compensation, a process much slower in its onset of action than buffering, but somewhat more effective in returning the pH toward normal. The respiratory system constitutes the compensatory defense in metabolic disorders, while the kidney assumes this role in respiratory disorders. The third process is the correction of the factors causing the initial acid-base abnormality. This process occurs only when the disease causing the primary disorder is cured or so modified that the lungs can correct the respiratory component of the acid–base equation, and the kidneys can completely correct the metabolic component.

An understanding of the acid–base regulatory system may be facilitated by tracing the course of a hydrogen ion that enters body fluids in the course of normal metabolic processes. The sequence to be described is depicted in Figure 1-4. A hydrogen ion entering body fluids is shown to combine with bicarbonate in the ECF. Bicarbonate is a relatively strong base, and the collision between the hydrogen ion and the bicarbonate ion results in the trapping of the former by the latter, with the formation of carbonic acid. Similarly, the hydrogen ion can combine with the base of any of the other buffer systems listed in Table 1-1. The hydrogen ion thus disappears from solution. Consequently, were the bicarbonate buffering mechanism to be the only defense against the intrusion of hydrogen ions, there would be a decrease in bicarbonate ion concentration in the ECF, an increase in hydrogen ion activity, and an associated acid shift in pH. This sequence, however, does not constitute the complete regulatory system. The second phase of the control system also is depicted in Figure 1-4. As the bicarbonate ion concentration diminishes and the carbonic acid concentration increases, the CO_2 tension (pCO_2)

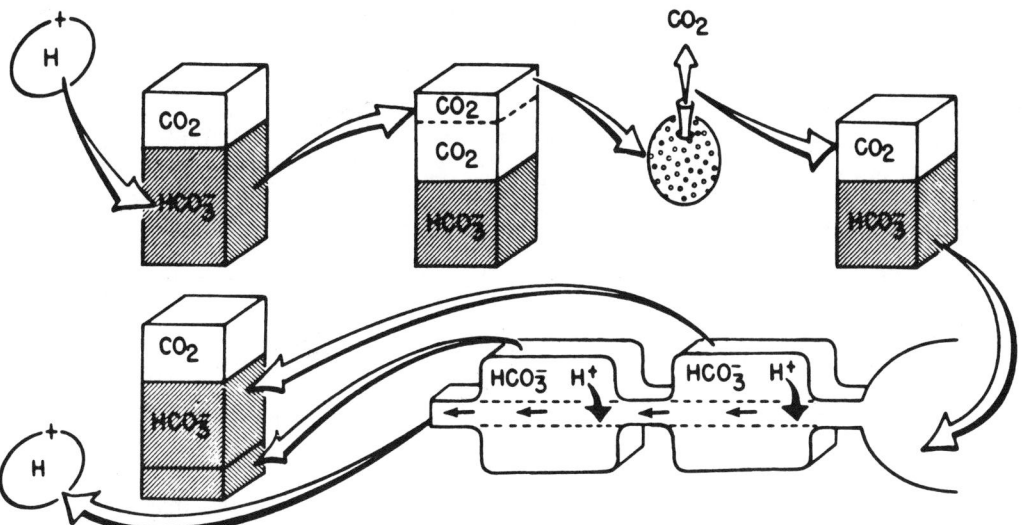

Fig. 1-4. Schematic representation of the system responsible for acid–base regulation. As H^+ ions enter body fluids, they are buffered by HCO_3^-. As a consequence, H_2CO_3 is generated, which in turn increases the pCO_2. The lung excretes the excess CO_2 and prevents the pCO_2 from rising. The bicarbonate consumed (shown by the decrease in the height of the bar marked HCO_3^-) has to be generated in the kidney. Renal mechanisms will reclaim all of the filtered HCO_3^- and generate an amount of HCO_3^- identical to the amount consumed in the buffering of H^+. In the steady state, the de novo synthesis of HCO_3^- is equal to net acid excretion, which in turn is equal to H^+ entering body fluids. (From Bricker NS, and Klahr S: Disorders of acid-base metabolism. Modern Treatment 5:635, 1968, with permission.)

will rise because H_2CO_3 is in equilibrium with CO_2. Either the increase in pCO_2, the increase in hydrogen ion concentration, or both will stimulate the respiratory center, producing an increase in the depth and rate of respiration and an increase in the pulmonary excretion of CO_2.[84] This will help correct the deviation of extracellular pH, because as CO_2 is excreted, the carbonic acid (H_2CO_3) concentration diminishes, and the concentration of hydrogen ions in the ECF diminishes. This respiratory contribution will restore the pH toward its initial value, but it will not completely correct the alteration. The bicarbonate and other buffer-system bases consumed in the initial buffering of the hydrogen ions must still be replenished. This is done by the kidney.

The initial biologic function of the kidney is to reabsorb the bicarbonate present in glomerular filtrate. It must also synthesize new bicarbonate in an amount equal to that utilized in the initial buffering of hydrogen ions. This process is referred to as bicarbonate regeneration. Besides replacing the bicarbonate consumed in the initial buffering reaction, the bicarbonate that is generated also allows the non-bicarbonate buffer systems to release the hydrogen ions they have buffered, thereby returning the entire buffer system back toward its baseline state.

When the integrated regulatory system becomes damaged, or when its regulatory capacity is exceeded, abnormalities develop in the pH of body fluids. This will be the subject of the remainder of this section.

Laboratory Considerations

In evaluating the acid–base status of a patient, it is necessary to determine any two of the three values pH, pCO_2, and HCO_3^- in the Henderson-Hasselbalch equation; the third value may then be easily calculated. The initial screening procedure traditionally employed in evaluating the acid-base status of a patient is the examination of the "carbon dioxide (CO_2) content" of plasma or serum. Because of the relatively small amount of carbonic acid in plasma (~1.2 mM at a pCO_2 of 40 mmHg), the value for the CO_2 content approximates, and is frequently referred to as, the bicarbonate concentration of the ECF. Normal values for the plasma "CO_2 content" are 23 to 25 mmol/liter and can be measured in venous blood. A low CO_2 content is found in metabolic acidosis in which the bicarbonate concentration has been diminished by the buffering of an increased load of hydrogen ions. But the CO_2 concentration is also diminished in respiratory alkalosis when the kidneys have excreted bicarbonate to compensate for a primary reduction in the pCO_2 of body fluids due to hyperventilation. An increased plasma CO_2 content is found in metabolic alkalosis when bicarbonate concentrations are increased proportionately more than the pCO_2. The plasma CO_2 content is also increased, however, in respiratory acidosis in which the kidneys have synthesized more than the normal amount of bicarbonate in response to a primary retention of CO_2. Although the clinical setting will often aid in evaluating a deviation in the CO_2 content from normal, the latter determination alone is rarely sufficient to allow the precise analysis of an acid–base disturbance. Thus, the appropriate interpretation of an acid–base abnormality and the subsequent design of the treatment for it must begin with measurement of the blood pH.

Sampling of blood from an artery is not a difficult procedure, and measurement of the blood pH is available in most clinical laboratories. Only one other analysis need be performed on the same sample of anaerobic arterial blood to obtain all of the data needed to evaluate an acid–base abnormality. The additional parameter measured can be either the pCO_2, using a pCO_2 electrode, or the "CO_2 content," measured manometrically. With any two of the three values for pH, pCO_2, and CO_2 content, the third value can be derived using a standard nomogram or the formula:

$$pH = pK_a + \log \frac{HCO_3^-}{0.03 \cdot pCO_2}$$

$$(pK_a = 6.1)$$

It should be remembered that pH and pCO_2 values should ideally be determined in arterial blood. The pH of venous blood is usually about 0.03 units lower than that of arterial blood, but has sufficient variation to make it unreliable for clinical use.

METABOLIC ACIDOSIS

The hallmark of metabolic acidosis is a decrease in blood pH (an increase in H^+ concentration) characterized by a primary decrease in plasma bicarbonate concentration. The bicarbonate concentration can be decreased in three ways: (1) by the addition to body fluids of a readily dissociated (strong) acid that is buffered by bicarbonate; (2) by the loss of bicarbonate from body fluids via the gastrointestinal tract or the kidneys; and (3) by the rapid dilution of the ECF space.

The sequence of events that transpires with an increased rate of addition of hydrogen ion to body fluids is exactly the same qualitatively as that depicted in Figure 1-4 for normal metabolism. The only difference is that the load is greater and the compensation is incomplete. The added hydrogen ions are buffered by bicarbonate ions, resulting in the conversion of bicarbonate to carbonic acid and a much smaller change in pH. This diminishes the bicarbonate ion concentration. The respiratory center is stimulated, alveolar ventilation is increased, and pCO_2 values are reduced below normal as a result of the augmented rate of pulmonary excretion of carbon dioxide. But the arterial pH nevertheless remains on the acid side of normal because the pulmonary compensation is less than complete. A key factor in controlling the decrease in hydrogen ion activity, and ultimately in restoring the pH to normal, is the rate of reconstitution of bicarbonate ions. The kidney, by regenerating bicarbonate via net acid excretion, will effect a definitive restoration of pH toward normal. Obviously, the administration of bicarbonate or interruption of the events leading to the enhanced rate of delivery of hydrogen ions into the ECF will decrease the time required for the definitive correction of metabolic acidosis.

It must be emphasized that respiratory compensation for chronic metabolic acidosis takes from 12 and 24 hours to maximize, and is never complete. Therefore, the pH never returns to pre-existing normal values, although with a very mild acidosis it may decrease only to the lower limits of normal. By determining the response in many patients, a predictable relationship between the decline in plasma bicarbonate and the decrease in arterial pCO_2 has been established. In general, to estimate the degree of appropriateness of the respiratory compensation for metabolic acidosis, it has been suggested that for every decrement in plasma bicarbonate of 1 mEq/liter, the arterial pCO_2 should fall by 1.0 to 1.3 mmHg (Table 1-3). If lesser or greater changes in arterial pCO_2 are observed, a mixed acid–base disturbance involving a primary respiratory disorder should be suspected.

Clinical Features of Metabolic Acidosis

The clinical manifestations of metabolic acidosis depend in part on the signs and symptoms of the primary disorder responsible for its occurrence. Depending on its severity, however, acidosis per se may directly produce signs and symptoms. With severe metabolic acidosis, left ventricular function is depressed and peripheral vascular resistance falls. This may cause a de-

Table 1-3. Usual Magnitude of Compensatory Changes in Acid–Base Disorders

Metabolic acidosis	pCO_2 should decrease by 1.0–1.3 mmHg for every 1 mEq/liter fall in HCO_3^-
Metabolic alkalosis	pCO_2 should increase by 0.5–1.0 mmHg for every 1 mEq/liter rise in HCO_3^-
Acute respiratory acidosis	HCO_3^- concentration increases, but seldom above 30 mEq/liter
Chronic respiratory acidosis	HCO_3^- concentration should increase by 0.4 mEq/liter for every 1 mmHg rise in pCO_2
Respiratory alkalosis	HCO_3^- concentration should decrease by 0.3 mEq/liter for every 1 mmHg fall in pCO_2. HCO_3^- seldom falls below 16–18 mEq/liter

crease in blood pressure due to decreased myocardial contractility and/or arteriolar vasodilation. Pulmonary edema[85] and arrhythmias, particularly ventricular fibrillation,[86,87] may develop. Decreased oxygen delivery can result from alterations in the oxyhemoglobin dissociation curve (Bohr effect) and 2,3-diphosphoglycerate (2,3-DPG) depletion.[88]

The respiratory compensation for metabolic acidosis is typically manifested by an increase in the depth of respiration with minimal changes in the rate,[89] sometimes referred to as Kussmaul respiration, which is especially prominant when the plasma bicarbonate has decreased to 15 mEq/liter or less. Central nervous system manifestations may occur including changes in mentation, confusion, and sometimes convulsive disorders.[90] Profound metabolic acidosis may produce hypotension unresponsive to the use of pressor agents, and restoration of the normal pressor response may be achieved only after correction of the acid–base abnormality. Chronic acidosis may lead to osteopenia and osteoporosis, owing to the buffering of hydrogen ions by calcium carbonate in bone.[91,92] This may contribute to bone disease, particularly in conditions such as chronic renal failure and renal tubular acidosis. In children, chronic metabolic acidosis may result in stunted growth and development.[93,94]

centration and, as a compensatory mechanism, a decrease in arterial pCO_2. Serum electrolyte measurements will reveal a decrease in the total CO_2 content. The anion gap is very important diagnostically and is discussed in more detail below. Plasma potassium concentrations may be normal or increased (even in the face of some total body potassium deficits), due to the shift of intracellular potassium into the ECF compartment as the intracellular hydrogen ion activity increases. The urine pH, although typically acid, may be alkaline, depending on the nature of the disturbance. In general, the kidney responds to metabolic acidosis by increasing its excretion of acid and regenerating bicarbonate through an increase in net acid excretion. The excretion of ammonium can increase by as much as sixfold over its baseline valve over a period of 4 to 5 days. Titratable acid also increases, by up to two- or threefold,[73,95] but reaches a maximum within two days, and contributes relatively less to net acid excretion. Urinary ammonium excretion can be estimated from the "urine anion gap." If urinary $[Na^+] + [K^+] - [Cl^-]$ is less than -5 to -10 mEq/liter, then significant amounts of ammonium are being excreted in the urine. If the urine anion gap is not negative, then ammonium excretion is not increased, suggesting a primary renal abnormality as the etiology of the acidosis.

Laboratory Findings in Metabolic Acidosis

The laboratory hallmark of metabolic acidosis is a decrease in plasma pH. There is a decrease in the plasma bicarbonate con-

Anion Gap

From a clinical viewpoint, metabolic acidosis is best classified as either a normal anion gap (or hyperchloremic) or as an increased anion gap metabolic acidosis.[96] The anion gap consists of the anions not measured in routine laboratory studies. The magnitude of the gap is estimated by subtracting the sum of the chloride and bicarbonate concentrations from the sodium concentration in the plasma or serum. Normally, a difference of 8 to 16 mEq/liter exists. Unmeasured anions are predominantly anionic plasma proteins, phosphates, sulfates, and organic anions.[97,98]

The differential diagnosis of metabolic acidosis may be approached by dividing the causes of this disorder into the two categories of metabolic acidosis occurring with a normal anion gap (hyperchloremic acidosis) and metabolic acidosis with an increased anion gap (see Figure 1-5). If hydrogen ions have been added to the ECF with an anion other than [Cl], then the bicarbonate concentration will decrease, the chloride and sodium concentrations will remain relatively constant, and a widening of the gap will be observed. The conditions in

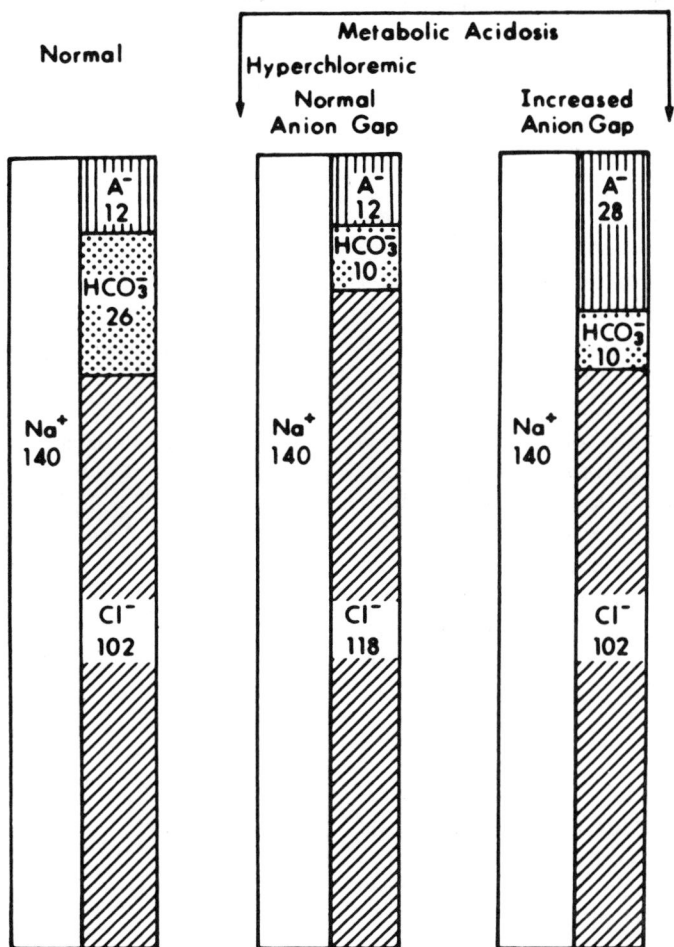

Fig. 1-5. Anion gap under conditions of normal acid–base balance and during metabolic acidosis. Values are given in milliequivalents per liter. (From Klahr S: Differential Diagnosis of Renal and Electrolyte Disorders. Arco, New York, 1978, with permission.)

which metabolic acidosis occurs with a normal anion gap are usually due to external losses of bicarbonate (either via the gastrointestinal tract or the kidneys), or to the systemic addition of HCl (e.g., ammonium chloride- or arginine hydrochloride-containing solutions). The only exception to this relates to dilution of the extracellular space by chloride-containing solutions. Table 1-4 presents a detailed list of the potential causes of metabolic acidosis.

Normal Anion Gap (Hyperchloremic) Acidosis

Renal Loss of Bicarbonate

Renal Tubular Acidosis

Renal tubular acidosis (RTA) is a syndrome of normal anion gap metabolic acidosis in the absence of or out of proportion to any azotemia that may be present.[99] Patients with renal disease may develop metabolic acidosis because of a number of functioning nephrons insufficient to allow adequate net acid excretion; they are not included in this syndrome, but are instead discussed separately later in this chapter. There are three major forms of renal tubular acidosis. They are referred to as distal (also referred to as Type I or classic) RTA, proximal (Type II or bicarbonate wasting RTA), and hyperkalemic RTA (Fig. 1-6). Hyperkalemic RTA is also known as Type IV or hyporeninemic hypoaldosteronism.

Distal Renal Tubular Acidois. Also referred to as classic or Type 1 RTA, distal RTA is characterized by an inability of the distal nephron to maintain the hydrogen ion gradient that a normal nephron can.[100,101] The normal kidney can produce an acid urine of pH 4.4. By contrast, the patient with classic RTA cannot usually excrete a urine with a pH below 6.0, irrespective of

Table 1-4. Differential Diagnosis of Metabolic Acidosis

Metabolic Acidosis with Normal Anion Gap (Hyperchloremic Acidosis)
  Renal loss of bicarbonate
    Use of carbonic anhydrase inhibitors
    Renal tubular acidosis
      1. Distal (Type I)
      2. Proximal (Type II)
      3. Type IV
  Gastrointestinal loss of bicarbonate
    Diarrhea
    Fistulas or drainage of the small bowel or pancreas
    Ureteral sigmoidostomy or ileal loop conduit
    Use of anion exchange resins
  Other causes
    Addition of HCl, NH$_4$Cl, arginine, or lysine hydrochloride
    Hyperalimentation
    Dilutional acidosis

Metabolic Acidosis with Increased Anion Gap
  Increased acid production (non-carbonic acid)
    Increased β-hydroxybutyric and acetoacetic acid production
      Insulin deficiency (diabetic ketoacidosis)
      Starvation or fasting
      Ethanol intoxication
      Hypoglycemia with ketosis and low alanine levels in plasma
    Increased lactic acid production
      Tissue hypoxia (circulatory insufficiency, etc.)
      Muscular exercise
      Administration of phenformin, particularly in diabetic patients
      Ethanol ingestion
      Systemic diseases (leukemia, diabetes mellitus, cirrhosis, pancreatitis)
      Type I glycogen storage disease
      Fructose-1,6 diphosphatase deficiency
    Conditions in which the nature of the organic acid responsible for the acidosis has not been clearly established
      Methanol intoxication
      Ethylene glycol intoxication
      Paraldehyde intoxication
      Salicylate intoxication
      Methylmalonic aciduria
      Propionyl CoA carboxylase deficiency
    Increased sulfuric acid
      Methionine administration
  Decreased acid excretion
    Acute renal failure
    Chronic renal failure

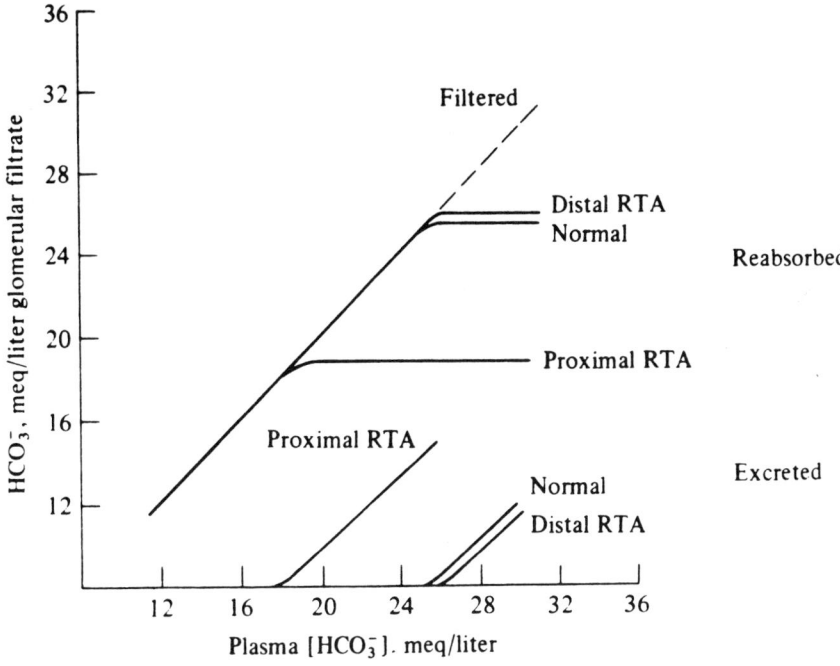

Fig. 1-6. Relation between the plasma concentrations, tubular reabsorption, and urinary excretion of HCO_3^- after a bicarbonate load in patients with proximal and distal RTA and in normal subjects. In normals and patients with distal RTA, all the filtered HCO_3^- is reabsorbed until the plasma HCO_3^- reaches 26 mEq/liter. Above this level, HCO_3^- appears in the urine. By contrast, in patients with proximal RTA, bicarbonaturia may occur when the plasma HCO_3^- concentration approaches 18 mEq/liter, a finding consistent with impaired HCO_3^- reabsorption. (From Rose BP: Clinical Physiology of Acid-Base and Electrolyte Disorders. McGraw-Hill, New York, 1977, with permission.)

the severity of the sytemic acidosis. Filtered bicarbonate is incompletely reabsorbed; a mild bicarbonaturia of 1 to 3 percent of the filtered load ensues and results in a continually worsening acidosis. There is generally a submaximal stimulation of ammonium excretion despite a normal capability for ammoniagenesis, thereby limiting bicarbonate regeneration.[102] As a result, the urinary anion gap will not be negative. The urine pH of 6.0 also limits the excretion of titratable acid. Remember that the pK_a of inorganic phosphate, the main buffer responsible for the excretion of titratable acid, is 6.8. Hence, a significant portion of filtered phosphate is not utilized to buffer hydrogen ions at a urinary pH of 6 or above. The continuing loss of bicarbonate and the failure to regenerate the bicarbonate consumed in buffering daily endogenous acid production results in the development of a progressively worsening metabolic acidosis.

Although the rate of ammonium excretion in patients with distal RTA is high for the relatively alkaline urine, it is insufficient to provide the cation necessary for the excretion of fixed anions, such as bicarbonate, sulfate, or phosphate, in the urine. Hence, these anions obligate the urinary excretion of cations such as sodium, potassium, and calcium.[103,104] This results in depletion of these cations with a reduction of ECF volume, potassium depletion, and rickets or osteomalacia. The increased excretion of calcium and phosphate, along with decreases in citrate excreted into the urine, often causes nephrocalcinosis and/or nephrolithiasis.

Since proximal reabsorption of most of the filtered bicarbonate is intact in distal RTA, the amount of sodium bicarbonate required to correct the hyperchloremic acidosis is relatively modest. In adults the amount of base required is only that necessary to buffer endogenous acid production plus that lost in the urine as bicarbonate. Typical amounts are 1 to 2 mEq/kg/day. In children, increased amounts of bicarbonate may be needed during periods of increased growth. This modest amount of sodium bicarbonate also prevents bone demineralization, nephrocalcinosis, and nephrolithiasis.

Interestingly, the acidifying defect seen in distal RTA may not always lead to metabolic acidosis. Patients with an acidification defect of the distal variety but with a normal plasma bicarbonate are referred to as having incomplete RTA. These patients exhibit a persistently elevated urinary pH but an absence of metabolic acidosis. Apparently, they can increase ammoniagenesis sufficiently to increase their net acid excretion, and thus prevent an acidosis despite an elevated urinary pH. Why these patients can augment their NH_3 production, in contrast to those with a complete form of distal RTA, is not known. It is also of interest that patients with incomplete distal RTA may manifest the complications of hypercalciuria, nephrocalcinosis, nephrolithiasis, and low urinary citrate excretion seen in distal RTA.

Distal or "classic" RTA occurs in: (1) a congenital, primary form[105]; (2) certain hypergammaglobulinemic states[106-109]; (3) nephrocalcinosis[110]; which may result from a number of genetic and metabolic disorders including hyperthyroidism,[111,112] hyperparathyroidism,[113] and hereditary fructose intolerance[114]; (4) nephrotoxicity due to substances that affect the distal nephron, such as amphotericin B,[115-117] vitamin D, toluene,[118] and lithium; (5) medullary sponge kidney[119,120]; (6) renal transplantation[121]; (7) possibly pyelonephritis[122]; (8) collagen vascular diseases[123,124]; and (9) Sjögren's syndrome.[125,126]

Proximal Renal Tubular Acidosis. Dysfunction of proximal tubular HCO_3^- reabsorption results in a distinctive picture of metabolic acidosis. Proximal RTA is characterized by an inability of the proximal tubule to reabsorb normal quantities of filtered bicarbonate. Increased amounts of bicarbonate are delivered to the distal tubule, overloading its bicarbonate reabsorption mechanisms. Significant bicarbonaturia develops, resulting in metabolic acidosis. As the serum bicarbonate level falls, the bicarbonate concentration in the glomerular filtrate also falls. Eventually the filtered bicarbonate concentration decreases to a sufficient degree that proximal tubular bicarbonate reabsorption, although limited, is appropriate for the serum bicarbonate level. Normal amounts of bicarbonate are then delivered to the distal tubule. Since the distal tubule is normal, it can then reabsorb all of the delivered bicarbonate. As a result, the distal tubule can acidify the urine and allow for sufficient net acid excretion to regenerate the bicarbonate consumed in buffering daily endogenous acid production. Acid–base homeostasis ensues and, unless other disease processes occur, there is no further worsening of the metabolic acidosis.

As described earlier in this chapter, proximal tubular bicarbonate reabsorption depends on sodium transport across the luminal membrane of the proximal tubular cell. Proximal renal tubular acidosis is therefore frequently accompanied by disorders of other sodium-linked reabsorptive processes, such as those for glucose, amino acids, and phosphate.[127] Glycosuria, aminoaciduria, and hyperphosphaturia frequently occur in association with proximal renal tubular acidosis in the disorder called Fanconi syndrome.

Attempts to restore the serum bicarbonate to normal levels by administering bicarbonate to patients with proximal RTA can be difficult. The higher the plasma bicarbonate, the larger the quantity of bicarbonate that escapes proximal reabsorption. This bicarbonate, which exceeds the maximal reabsorptive rates of the distal tubule, is eventually lost into the urine. The predominant cation accompanying this urinary bicarbonate is potassium. The resulting kaliuresis may result in significant hypokalemia. Consequently, increases in bicarbonaturia with alkali replacement produce a marked kaliuresis and hypokalemia unless large quantities of potassium are simultaneously given.[128,129] Some of the bicarbonate lost in the urine is balanced by sodium. The loss of sodium in the urine results in contraction of the ECF volume, which in turn enhances aldosterone secretion. In the presence of elevated aldosterone levels and elevated distal tubular sodium delivery, kaliuresis worsens and can magnify the hypokalemia that already exists. Although hyperaldosteronism generally stimulates distal tubular hydrogen ion secretion, this is probably already maximally stimulated by the acidosis, and is not affected by the elevated levels of aldosterone.

Demineralization of the skeleton in proximal RTA results from phosphate loss, buffering of the acidosis by bone matrix, and secondary hyperparathyroidism. The inability to correct the hyperchloremic acidosis completely, except with large amounts of sodium bicarbonate, the worsening of urinary potassium loss with alkali therapy, the ability to reduce urinary pH at low levels of plasma bicarbonate, and the frequent association with other defects in proximal tubular reabsorption all help to distinguish proximal from distal RTA.

Proximal RTA can occur in association with many different diseases. Multiple proximal tubular defects, such as in Fanconi syndrome[130,131] and genetically transmitted systemic diseases (e.g., cystinosis,[132] Wilson's disease,[133,134] hereditary fructose intolerance, and Lowe's syndrome[135,136]) can cause proximal RTA. Intoxications due to heavy metals (lead, cadmium poisoning)[137] or drugs (outdated tetracycline) have also been implicated.[138,139] Proximal RTA may be seen in disorders of increased protein excretion such as the nephrotic syndrome[140-142] and multiple myeloma,[143] as well as during vitamin D deficiency.[144] It may be seen as a primary disorder, either sporadic,[145] or inherited,[147] without any other defects of proximal tubular function. Acute rejection in renal transplantation can result in proximal RTA,[147] as can methylmalonic aciduria.[148]

Type IV Renal Tubular Acidosis. Patients with a non-anion-gap metabolic acidosis, associated with hyperkalemia instead of hypokalemia, are referred to as having Type IV RTA. This may be the most common form of RTA encountered in clinical practice.[128] Most of these patients have mild chronic renal insufficiency, but the hyperkalemia and acidosis are out of proportion to the degree of renal insufficiency.

A relative lack of responsiveness to aldosterone is the underlying abnormality in most patients with Type IV RTA; a few have end-organ resistance to aldosterone. In many patients a hyporeninemic state leads to hypoaldosteronism. Normally, aldosterone increases both potassium and H^+ secretion in the distal nephron.[149] The deficiency of aldosterone results in decreased H^+ and K^+ secretion in the distal nephron, leading to systemic acidosis and hyperkalemia. Furthermore, the hyperkalemia due to impaired K^+ secretion directly inhibits ammoniagenesis and thus worsens the acidosis.[150] In the presence of both chronic renal insufficiency and hypoaldosteronism, most patients exhibit an acid urinary pH of 5.0, indicating the role of the renal failure and hyperkalemia as the major factors in the pathogenesis of the acidosis.[151] Treatment may utilize several approaches. Mineralocorticoid replacement is effective in cases of hypoaldosterone-mediated Type IV RTA, but can lead to significant sodium retention and volume overload. Oral alkali therapy is also effective but has similar side effects. Therapy with the loop diuretic furosemide appears to be very effective in many patients.[152] It stimulates kaliuresis and hydrogen ion secretion. At the same time, it results in a mild natriuresis that may be beneficial if volume overload is present as the result of the underlying renal insufficiency.

Carbonic Anhydrase Inhibitors

Carbonic anhydrase inhibitors inhibit the enzyme responsible for the hydration of carbon dioxide. This enzyme is critical for the secretion of H^+ and consequently the reabsorption and regeneration of bicarbonate by the kidney (described in detail earlier in this chapter). As a result, one of their pharmacologic effects is increased bicarbonate excretion in the urine and the development of metabolic acidosis. Among the carbonic anhydrase inhibitors the drug most commonly implicated is acetazolamide. It is used in glaucoma to decrease intraocular pressure, for the prevention and treatment of acute mountain sickness, and occasionally as a diuretic. An adequate history should reveal whether or not the patient is using such drugs. Methazolamide, another inhibitor of carbonic anhydrase, is frequently used in the treatment of glaucoma and appears to have less effect on acid-base status.

Gastrointestinal Loss of Bicarbonate

The loss of bicarbonate from the gastrointestinal tract decreases the serum bicarbonate concentration without a direct effect on serum pCO_2 levels. The Henderson-Hasselbalch equation shows that metabolic acidosis will then develop. Sodium is lost from the ECF in amounts equal to the amount of bicarbonate lost. As a result, the anion gap remains unchanged. Bicarbonate may be lost from the gastrointestinal tract in many ways, including diarrhea, drainage of gastrointestinal tract secretions, use of the gastrointestinal tract for urine excretion, and through the use of cation exchange resins.

Diarrhea may be characterized by the excretion of fluid containing bicarbonate in excess of the concentration present in plasma. With severe diarrhea, the stool may contain concentrations of bicarbonate between 30 and 50 mEq/liter. Large quantities of potassium may also be lost, and metabolic acidosis with hypokalemia may be seen.[153,154]

Secretions of the small bowel, pancreas, and biliary tract are rich in bicarbonate. Exterior losses of such fluids may lead to marked hyperchloremic acidosis. Bile may contain as much as 60 mEq/liter of bicarbonate.[155]

Patients who have had complete cystectomies (i.e., for malignancy of the bladder) undergo the construction of artificial bladders either in the form of ureteral sigmoidostomies or ileal loop conduits. While the former has been almost completely abandoned, many patients who had this procedure performed two or more decades ago frequently developed hyperchloremic acidosis. The mechanism for this probably involves retention of urine in the sigmoid colon, with reabsorption of water and exchange of chloride for bicarbonate. This leads to a decrease in the bicarbonate concentration of body fluids and an increase in their chloride content. In addition, NH_4^+

may be reabsorbed, thereby decreasing net acid excretion.

Hyperchloremic acidosis is uncommon with ileal loop conduits. However, in certain instances in which the ileal segment is long, when an antiperistaltic loop has been constructed, or when the stoma of the ileal loop is obstructed, a non-anion-gap metabolic acidosis may occur. Under these conditions, prolonged exposure of the urine to the ileal mucosa will occur, with exchange of chloride for bicarbonate and a loss of bicarbonate from body fluids. A non-anion-gap metabolic acidosis may be the first evidence of stenosis of an ileal loop stoma.

Gastrointestinal losses of bicarbonate may also occur during the use of certain anion-exchange resins. Cholestyramine, the nonreabsorbable anion exchange resin used to treat bile acid retention and hyperlipidemia, can exchange chloride for bicarbonate. The use of this resin in patients with renal impairment has occasionally led to a non-anion-gap metabolic acidosis due to increased loss of bicarbonate via the stool and inability of the kidney to generate new bicarbonate to replace those losses.[156]

Miscellaneous Causes

Dilutional acidosis is occasionally seen as a mild, non-anion-gap metabolic acidosis resulting from expansion of the ECF volume with chloride-containing solutions. The serum bicarbonate concentration is decreased by dilution, but CO_2 concentrations are independently and rapidly regulated via central nervous system (CNS) control mechanisms, and are therefore not diluted to the same degree. In addition, volume expansion inhibits proximal tubular bicarbonate reabsorption, resulting in loss of bicarbonate into the urine. A non-anion-gap metabolic acidosis is the result. This is a mild and easily corrected abnormality, and the decreases in plasma bicarbonate are modest.[157]

The administration of hydrochloric acid or other substances, such as ammonium chloride, lysine hydrochloride, or arginine hydrochloride, which may yield hydrochloric acid as their final product, can result in hyperchloremic acidosis.[158] The administration of hydrochloric acid, a substance that dissociates almost completely and is buffered by bicarbonate, leads to an increase in the plasma concentration of chloride and a decrease in the plasma concentration of bicarbonate.

Amino acid infusates such as FreAmine I and Neoaminosol contain organic cations in significant excess of organic anions, and may also cause a non-anion-gap metabolic acidosis. Metabolism of amino acid cations in these infusates by the liver results in the release of hydrogen ions. The accompanying anion in the infusates is usually chloride. The net result is the effective addition of hydrochloric acid and a non-anion-gap metabolic acidosis. When the cationic amino acids are exactly balanced by organic anions, metabolic acidosis is avoided because metabolism of the organic anions consumes the hydrogen ion released by organic cation metabolism.[159]

Metabolic Acidosis Associated with an Increased Anion Gap

Increased Acid Production

Ketoacidosis

Ketoacidosis results from the incomplete oxidation of free fatty acids to CO_2 and water. This leads to increased production of beta-hydroxybutyric and acetoacetic acids. Ketoacid overproduction appears to depend on two factors: (1) enhanced lipolysis, which increases the supply of free fatty acids; and (2) preferential conversion of free fatty acids in the liver to ketoacids rather than triglycerides. This latter process appears to depend on the activity of the enzyme acylcarnitine transferase (ACTase), which facilitates the entry of free fatty acids into the mitochondria of hepatocytes, where the conversion to ketoacids takes place. Normally, insulin is a potent inhibitor of ketone production because of its effect in reducing lipolysis and ACTase activity. In the absence of insulin, or in a prolonged fast, lipolysis and ACTase activity are enhanced, resulting in ketone acid accumulation in the ECF and metabolic acidosis. Glucagon may also directly promote ketone synthesis by enhancing lipolysis and ACTase activity. In conjunction with insulin deficiency, endogenous hypersecretion of glucagon and catecholamines can contribute to the development of hyperglycemia and ketoacidosis in uncontrolled diabetes mellitus.

Diabetes mellitus is the most common cause of ketoacidosis, and may result in a pH below 7.00 and bicarbonate concentration of less than 5.0 mEq/liter.[160-162] Fasting can also cause a mild, self-limited ketosis due to decreased insulin secretion. With continued fasting, ketones replace glucose as the principal metabolic fuel of the body. Occasionally, the combination of alcohol ingestion and poor dietary intake produces ketoacidosis.[163] This clinical state results from a poor carbohydrate intake plus the effects of alcohol in inhibiting gluconeogenesis. In addition, ethanol directly enhances lipolysis.

The diagnosis of ketoacidosis requires a demonstration of ketones in the blood. This is usually done with nitroprusside (Acetest) tablets. In a patient with metabolic acidosis, a 4+ nitroprusside reaction to serum diluted 1:1, and a high anion gap, strongly suggest ketoacidosis. Nitroprusside reacts with acetoacetate and acetone but not with beta-hydroxybutyrate. Since beta-hydroxybutyrate comprises about 75 percent of the circulating ketones in diabetic ketoacidosis and 90 percent of the ketones in concurrent lactic acidosis or alcohol ketoacidosis, the nitroprusside test is insensitive and frequently underestimates the severity of the ketoacidosis.

Lactic Acidosis

An increase in the production of lactic acid can occur in a variety of conditions. By far the most common cause is a decrease in tissue oxygen delivery. This can result from hypotension of any etiology, peripheral arteriovenous shunting, such as in severe sepsis, acute arterial occlusion (e.g., embolization), and severe hypoxemia. Some studies suggest that insulin-dependent diabetic patients appear to be at increased risk of lactic acidosis.[164] Lactic acidosis may also be seen during extreme muscular exercise. Phenformin,[165] an oral hypoglycemic agent, can uncouple oxidative phosphorylation and result in life threatening lactic acidosis. It has been removed from the market for this reason. Acute leukemia and glycogen storage disease Type 1 (van Gerke's disease)[166] have been implicated as other causes of lactic acidosis, as has hereditary fructose-1,6-diphosphatase deficiency.

Lactic acid is produced in muscle by the anaerobic metabolism of pyruvic acid originating from the metabolism of glucose and amino acids (Fig. 1-7). Normally, 45 percent of the glucose metabolized yields lactic acid. This lactic acid is rapidly buffered by the ECF bicarbonate. In the liver, 80 percent of the lactate is converted to CO_2 and water, and 20 percent to glucose. Either of these reactions results in the regeneration of the bicarbonate lost in buffering the lactic acid, thus maintaining acid-base balance. However, if production of lactic acid is enhanced, the capacity of the liver may be overwhelmed, resulting in lactic acidosis.

The normal plasma lactate concentration is 1.0 to 2.0 mEq/liter, and that of pyruvate is 0.1 to 0.2 mEq/liter. Any condition that enhances glycolysis increases pyruvate and lactate formation. In these states, the lac-

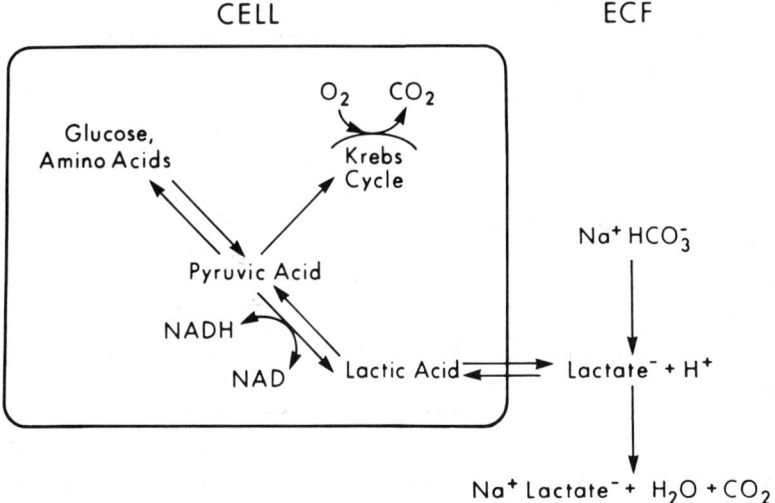

Fig. 1-7. Schematic diagram of lactic acid production. Glycolytic metabolism of glucose and, to a lesser extent, amino acids, results in production of pyruvic acid. This normally is further metabolized by entering the Krebs cycle. The equilibrium between pyruvic and lactic acids is governed by the ratio of NADH:NAD. In anaerobic conditions, the NADH:NAD ratio is increased, favoring production of lactic acid by the enzymatic activity of lactic dehydrogenase. Upon release from cells, lactic acid immediately dissociates and is buffered by ECF bicarbonate. In the liver, lactate uptake and utilization proceeds by reversal of these steps.

tate/pyruvate ratio remains normal (10:1). Acidosis is not a problem, since most of the pyruvate is converted to CO_2 and water. In clinical disorders of lactic acidosis, the overproduction of lactate results in an elevation of the lactate/pyruvate ratio, distinguishing the elevated lactate of acidosis from normal states of enhanced glycolysis.[167]

The concept of excess lactate or an increase in the ratio of lactate to pyruvate has been used to indicate the two ways in which lactate levels can be elevated. If the pyruvate concentration is elevated, the lactate concentration will increase but the ratio will remain unchanged. If anaerobic glycolysis is accelerated (e.g., by hypoxia) and sufficient nicotinamide adenine dinucleotide (NAD) is not available to reconvert lactate to pyruvate, lactate will increase out of proportion to pyruvate, and an increased ratio of lactate to pyruvate will result. In general, it is this latter circumstance that is associated with metabolic acidosis with an increased anion gap.

Toxin-Associated Anion Gap Metabolic Acidosis

Methanol and Ethylene Glycol Ingestion

Severe metabolic acidosis associated with an increased anion gap is occasionally found to be due to the toxic metabolites of methyl alcohol (methanol), often known as wood alcohol, or ethylene glycol, the solvent in radiator antifreeze. Frequently this occurs in alcoholic persons who are attempting to find inexpensive sources of alcohol.

Initially, ingestion of methyl alcohol has CNS effects similar to those of ethanol. Approximately 12 to 18 hours later, after metabolism of the methanol to formic acid by alcohol dehydrogenase, symptoms occur.

The most prominent symptoms are abdominal pain, vomiting, headache, and visual disturbances. Profound metabolic acidosis and retinitis also occur. Methyl alcohol is extremely toxic. Doses of as little as 30 ml may produce toxicity; 200 to 250 ml may prove lethal.

Formic acid appears to be primarily responsible for the acidosis and the anion gap in methanol ingestion,[168] although methanol and its metabolites may interfere with normal oxidative metabolism, leading to elevated lactate levels and associated lactic acidosis.

Therapy includes correction of the acidosis and inhibition of further metabolism of methyl alcohol. Correction of the acidosis with sodium bicarbonate appears to retard the toxic effects, including retinitis, of the metabolites of methanol. The metabolism of methanol can be inhibited by ethanol, since both alcohols are metabolized by the same enzyme, alcohol dehydrogenase. Ethanol should be administered intravenously, and serum ethanol levels should be maintained at 100 to 200 mg/100 ml. The doses typically required are a 0.6 g/kg loading dose followed by ~0.1 g/kg/hr continuous infusion, with an extra 7.2 g/hr (not gm/kg/hr!) given during hemodialysis.[169] Hemodialysis is generally recommended for patients with methyl alcohol levels above 50 mg/100 ml, profound acidosis, or visual impairment.[168]

Ingestion of ethylene glycol can lead to CNS disturbances, cardiovascular collapse, respiratory failure, severe metabolic acidosis, and acute renal failure. The initial metabolic degradation involves alcohol dehydrogenase, with the formation of glyoxylic acid, an intermediate that is further metabolized to oxalic acid and formic acid. The acidosis is due to accumulation of organic acids, particularly lactate, that are formed when formic acid interferes with oxidative metabolism. Oxalate accumulation is felt to be the major factor in the acute renal failure that develops. Oxalate crystals in the urine may be evident, and an accumulation of oxalate crystals may be seen in renal tubules on biopsy.[170]

The major modes of treatment include ethanol administration and hemodialysis. Since ethylene glycol is metabolized by alcohol dehydrogenase, ethanol is an effective inhibitor of ethylene glycol metabolism. Consequently, the administration of ethanol allows for increased renal excretion of ethylene glycol and less systemic toxicity.[169] The doses of ethanol used are the same as for methanol intoxication. Hemodialysis effectively clears ethylene glycol and its toxic metabolites from the system, and is recommended therapy for ethylene glycol intoxication.[170]

Early recognition of intoxication with these two alcohols is necessary, since both agents are extremely toxic and relatively specific therapy is available. Intoxication with either methanol or ethylene glycol should be considered in any alcoholic patient with an anion gap metabolic acidosis. A quick screening test is an increased osmolal gap, the difference between the measured and calculated serum osmolality. One commonly used formula to calculate osmolality is:

$$S_{osm} = 2 \times [Na^+] + [Glucose]/18 + [BUN]/2.8 + [Ethanol]/4.6$$

An osmolal gap greater than 15 to 20 mOsm/kg strongly suggests the possibility of methanol and/or ethylene glycol intoxication in the appropriate clinical situation.

Paraldehyde Poisoning

Chronic ingestion of paraldehyde may cause moderate to severe metabolic acidosis.[171,172] The acids responsible for the increased anion gap in this condition have not been definitively identified. The disturbance is seen with fresh as well as outdated or decomposed paraldehyde. Occasionally, a false positive test for blood ketones may be obtained under these conditions, and may confuse the clinical picture. The history of paraldehyde intake is important in establishing the diagnosis.

Salicylate Poisoning

Accidental, therapeutic, or suicidal ingestion of large amounts of salicylate compounds or derivatives may lead to serious metabolic acidosis.[173,174] Salicylates may produce an initial stimulation of the respiratory center that leads to hyperventilation, a decrease in arterial pCO_2, and marked excretion of bicarbonate in the urine. Shortly thereafter, a metabolic acidosis ensues from the accumulation of lactic acid, pyruvic acid, ketones, and serum amino acids. The bicarbonate further decreases and the anion gap increases.

Salicylate intoxication should be suspected in patients with a history of aspirin ingestion, chronic pain, nausea, vomiting, and the finding of unexplained hyperventilation. Laboratory tests suggesting salicylate intoxication include a prolonged prothrombin time and a positive urine ferric chloride test. The diagnosis can be confirmed by determining the blood levels of salicylate. Initial therapy includes cardiovascular support with parenteral fluid, correction of the acidosis with parenteral sodium bicarbonate, stabilization of the airway, and gastric emptying. Serum salicylate concentrations and the time after ingestion of an acute overdose of salicylate are useful in predicting the severity of the toxicity. In patients with severe CNS impairment, systemic alkalinization to a pH of approximately 7.50 may reduce unbound levels of salicylate, allowing rapid improvement.[173]

Methylmalonic Aciduria

Since 1967, over 100 infants with prominent abnormalities in methylmalonic acid metabolism resulting in severe acidosis have been documented. The clinical presentations of these children can include severe recurrent metabolic acidosis, ketonemia or ketonuria, hyperammonemia, recurrent vomiting, dehydration, muscular abnormalities, and developmental retardation.[175] Life-threatening metabolic ketoacidosis has been the clinical hallmark in about 80 percent of these children. Several children had the onset of their disease within the first month of life. Arterial pH values of 6.9 to 7.1 are not unusual, and have been associated with serum bicarbonate concentrations of 5 mEq/liter or less.

The response of these children to vitamin B_{12} administration has allowed their separation into two distinct categories: those who respond to vitamin B_{12} administration with a reduction in methylmalonic acid excretion, and those whose methylmalonic aciduria is unaffected by vitamin B_{12} supplementation. Treatment of both groups consists of dietary protein restriction and pharmacologic doses of vitamin B_{12}. Patients whose enzymatic abnormality allows the correction of methylmalonic acid concentrations in the blood or urine with vitamin B_{12} appear to have a markedly improved prognosis.[175]

Propionic Acidemia

In 1961, Childs and associates[176] described a male infant with episodic metabolic ketoacidosis, protein intolerance, and a remarkably elevated plasma glycine concentration. More than 100 children with similar clinical and biochemical findings have since been described.[177] Although many of these children were subsequently found to have methylmalonic aciduria, no methylmalonic acid was detected in the urine of many, indicating that methylmalonic aciduria and propionic acidemia are not identical diseases. These children appear to have a primary defect in propionyl CoA carboxylase, the enzyme that catalyzes the conversion of propionyl CoA to

D-methylmalonyl CoA. Their clinical course is characterized by recurrent attacks of ketoacidosis, precipitated by infections or protein ingestion, and by developmental retardation, electroencephalographic abnormalities, and osteoporosis.[177] Therapy consists of protein restriction and a trial of biotin supplementation. Bouts of ketoacidosis are treated with parenteral $NaHCO_3$.

Increased Sulfuric Acid–Methionine Administration

The administration of 13.9 g of D,L-methionine to normal subjects for 5 to 6 days has been shown to produce a small reduction in serum CO_2 content associated with acidification of the urine and increased excretion of ammonium. The changes in acid excretion have been shown to be related to the observed reductions in serum CO_2 content and to the calculated acid retention.[179]

Decreased Acid Excretion

Acute or Chronic Renal Failure

In the acidosis of renal failure, the rate of production of hydrogen ions in the body may not be excessive, but the decreased renal function, especially the marked decrease in glomerular filtration rate, prevents excretion of sufficient NH_4^+ and titratable acids to allow regeneration of the bicarbonate consumed in buffering daily endogenous acid production. With acute renal failure and the almost total cessation of glomerular filtration, the daily acid load resulting from diet and metabolism is handled by the ability of the skeletal system to buffer a significant amount of the daily acid load.[179] A marked fall in plasma bicarbonate may occur, as much as 2 mEq/liter/day. In the presence of fever, infection, trauma, or an increased catabolic state, the accession of hydrogen ions from tissues may markedly increase, and the acidosis may become extremely severe.

In general, acidosis is of three major types. The most common type is a metabolic acidosis characterized by an increased anion gap due to accumulation of phosphate, sulfate, and organic anions. As renal mass decreases, a compensatory increase occurs in the rate of net acid excretion per nephron, especially in the form of ammonium. This allows for maintenance of the acid–base balance for prolonged periods. As the number of nephrons is reduced below a critical level, the acid-base balance can no longer be maintained and metabolic acidosis results. As renal function decreases, the ability to excrete titratable acid remains almost intact, but the total amount of ammonium excreted per day decreases. Under normal conditions, about two-thirds of the acid excreted by the kidney is excreted in the form of ammonium and one-third in the form of titratable acid (approximately 40 mEq/day in the form of ammonium and 20mEq/day in the form of titratable acid). With chronic renal disease, titratable acid excretion is preserved until late in the course of the disease. However, ammonium excretion decreases progressively, and an inversion in the ratio of excretion of ammonium to titratable acid occurs. Net acid excretion falls and metabolic acidosis develops.

In some patients with chronic renal failure caused by diseases that mainly affect the renal interstitium, such as hypercalcemia, medullary cystic diseases, or interstitial nephritis, a loss of NH_3 production causes acidosis at an earlier stage of the disease (a higher GFR) than in other forms of chronic renal failure. This appears to be due preponderantly to the destruction of tubular function while the GFR is maintained. When this occurs, the GFR is sufficient to prevent significant retention of organic acid anions. In this situation, a non-anion-gap metabolic acidosis develops. Potassium excretion is not affected, and serum potassium levels generally remain normal.

In some patients with chronic renal failure who develop a hyperchloremic metabolic acidosis relatively early in the course of their disease, hyperkalemia is also observed. This is known as Type IV RTA and has been discussed above.

In summary, three clinically distinguishable types of metabolic acidosis are associated with chronic renal failure: an increased anion gap acidosis; a non-anion-gap, normokalemic metabolic acidosis; and a non-anion-gap metabolic acidosis with hyperkalemia (Type IV RTA).

METABOLIC ALKALOSIS

The hallmark of metabolic alkalosis is an increased blood pH due to a primary increase in the concentration of plasma bicarbonate. The increase in plasma bicarbonate concentration may occur because of: (1) net loss of hydrogen ions from the ECF, (2) net addition of bicarbonate or its precursors to the ECF, or (3) loss of chloride from the ECF in a concentration greater than bicarbonate. In some instances the kidney cannot excrete sufficient bicarbonate, and metabolic alkalosis develops. It may help to consider the pathogenesis of metabolic alkalosis as occurring in two phases. The generation of metabolic alkalosis requires either the addition to the body of alkali, the removal of acid, or the loss of chloride in excess of the loss of bicarbonate. The gain or loss of alkali or acid may occur through any combination of renal or extrarenal routes. In most circumstances, generation of alkali or acid is either related to renal responses to electrolyte or volume abnormalities, loss of acid through the gastrointestinal tract, or the administration of pharmacologic agents to the patient. These will be discussed in detail below. Under normal circumstances, however, the kidneys have the ability to excrete extremely large quantities of alkali. Normal adults can ingest up to 24 mEq/kg/day of bicarbonate without developing a significant metabolic alkalosis, because of the ability of the kidneys to rapidly excrete bicarbonate.[180,181] Clearly, the pathogenesis of metabolic alkalosis requires not just the generation of metabolic alkalosis, but also a mechanism for its maintenance.

The maintenance of metabolic alkalosis requires a stimulus to the kidney to continue inappropriate proton secretion. The two major etiologies of this are ECF volume contraction and hyperaldosteronism. Extracellular fluid volume contraction may directly stimulate proximal tubular bicarbonate reabsorption, as discussed previously. Secondary hyperaldosteronism directly stimulates distal tubular bicarbonate generation and assists in the maintenance of metabolic alkalosis. Primary hyperaldosteronism can, in and of itself, maintain metabolic alkalosis through direct stimulation of distal tubular proton secretion. Recent evidence suggests that a third mechanism may also exist to maintain metabolic alkalosis.

This third possible mechanism may be chloride depletion. It appears that total body chloride depletion may lead to an inability of the kidney to excrete maximal amounts of bicarbonate. Replacement of chloride, independent of changes in GFR or plasma volume, appears to be able to correct metabolic alkalosis in certain circumstances.[182] The cortical collecting tubule contains a luminal chloride–bicarbonate exchanger. Total body chloride depletion may result in decreased delivery of chloride to the cortical collecting tubule, and therefore inhibition of the ability of this segment to secrete bicarbonate.

Differential Diagnosis of Metabolic Alkalosis

The initial differential diagnosis of metabolic alkalosis regards its generation. Was it due to a net loss of hydrogen ions from the ECF, to a net addition of bicarbonate or its precursors to the ECF, or to the external loss of a fluid containing chloride in a greater concentration and bicarbonate in a lesser concentration than the ECF? Hydrogen ions can be lost from the ECF via the gastrointestinal tract or the kidneys. If the loss of hydrogen ions is greater than the net access of acid from the diet and catabolism, plasma bicarbonate concentrations will rise. Loss of acidic gastric secretions, for example, due to gastric drainage or vomiting, will result in metabolic alkalosis. The kidney also secretes hydrogen, thus generating new bicarbonate which is added to body stores. When the process of hydrogen ion secretion by the kidney is accelerated in such a way that it exceeds the need to reclaim filtered bicarbonate and excrete the daily acid load, the plasma bicarbonate will rise above the normal range. This situation probably occurs in hyperaldosteronism. The excess mineralocorticoid hormone obligates increased reabsorption of sodium in the distal nephron, with continued secretion of hydrogen ions and regeneration of bicarbonate, resulting in the generation of metabolic alkalosis. Metabolic alkalosis can also be generated by potassium loss from the body. Under these conditions, as extracellular potassium decreases, there is increased urinary ammonium excretion and the generation of metabolic alkalosis.[183]

The administration of bicarbonate or organic compounds capable of generating bicarbonate, such as acetate, lactate, and citrate, at a rate greater than that of daily acid production will lead to a rise in the plasma bicarbonate concentration.[184] In the presence of normal renal function, the excess bicarbonate will be eliminated and the metabolic alkalosis will be only modest.

Under certain conditions, fluid may be lost from the extracellular space, in which the concentration of chloride is greater than that of bicarbonate. This may occur, for example, with the use of certain diuretics that induce sodium and chloride losses without bicarbonate losses, and in certain gastrointestinal diseases characterized by diarrhea with a high chloride content.[185]

Clinical Features of Metabolic Alkalosis

There are no specific symptoms or signs that point to the diagnosis of metabolic alkalosis. The disorder should be sought in patients with a history of vomiting, gastric drainage, diuretic therapy, muscle cramps and weakness, or hypertension in association with hypokalemia (i.e., primary hyperaldosteronism). Physical examination may reveal neuromuscular irritability, such as tetany or hyperactive reflexes. These signs will be more pronounced if hypocalcemia is an accompanying feature, since the serum ionized calcium concentration decreases as the pH rises. Hypokalemia usually accompanies the development of metabolic alkalosis, so some of the clinical manifestations of metabolic alkalosis may be related to a decrease in ECF potassium concentration.

Laboratory Findings in Metabolic Alkalosis

Laboratory findings in metabolic alkalosis reveal an elevated serum pH, an increased plasma bicarbonate, and an increased arterial pCO_2. The pCO_2 elevation, however, very seldom exceeds values of 50 mmHg, since an alveolar pCO_2 above 50 mmHg would reduce the arterial oxygen tension. The reduced oxygen tension in arterial blood would stimulate chemoreceptors, thereby tending to restore ventilation and arterial oxygen content toward normal.

Hypokalemia is almost universally present in metabolic alkalosis. Hypovolemia, if present, may lead to elevations of the blood urea nitrogen (BUN) and creatinine concentrations. If volume depletion is present, the hematocrit may also be increased, due to hemoconcentration. The anion gap may be increased by as much as 5 to 6 mM/liter owing in part to elevated lactic acid concentrations[186] and in part to increased concentrations of undefined anions. However, the changes in anion gap do not have diagnostic significance, as they do in metabolic acidosis. Changes in urine pH also do not assist in the differential diagnosis.

The concentration of chloride in the urine is a very important tool in the differential diagnosis of the conditions underlying metabolic alkalosis. It may serve to distinguish between metabolic alkalosis that is accompanied by volume expansion mainly related to mineralocorticoid excess and metabolic alkalosis due to volume depletion. A spot urine chloride concentration greater than 20 mEq/liter in the presence of metabolic alkalosis indicates that neither ECF volume depletion nor chloride availability is a critical factor in maintenance of the metabolic alkalosis, and points to a diagnosis of excess mineralocorticoid activity as the cause of the alkalosis. A spot urine chloride below 20 mEq/liter indicates that volume depletion may be playing a significant role in maintenance of the metabolic alkalosis. The only word of caution in analyzing urine chloride concentrations relates to the possibility of the patient having received diuretics within the preceding 24 to 48 hours. In such patients, the above considerations may not be valid because of the direct increase in urinary chloride caused by the diuretic.

The urinary sodium concentration may be falsely elevated despite volume depletion. Ongoing bicarbonaturia requires the excretion of cations to maintain electroneutrality of the urine. Sodium is one of the major cations excreted in this situation. As a result, urinary sodium concentrations do not necessarily reflect volume status in patients with metabolic alkalosis.

Differential Diagnosis of Metabolic Alkalosis

Most of the conditions responsible for the development of metabolic alkalosis are listed in Table 1–5. From a clinical viewpoint, it is helpful to divide metabolic alkalosis into two major categories: those characterized by ECF volume contraction, usually with secondary hyperaldosteronism, and those characterized by ECF volume expansion, usually the result of primary mineralocorticoid excess (either endogenous or exogenous). The latter group is consistently characterized by the presence of hypertension. This hypertension may be accompanied by high levels of renin and aldosterone. Patients with ECF volume contraction, with the possible exception of Bartter's syndrome, have low chloride concentrations in their urine (usually below 10 mEq/liter). In the volume-expanded, mineralocorticoid excess group, urinary chloride concentrations usually are in excess of 20 mEq/liter.

Table 1-5. Differential Diagnosis of Metabolic Alkalosis

ECF volume contraction (urinary Cl < 10 mEq/liter)
  Gastrointestinal loss of H^+
    Vomiting, gastric drainage
    Villous adenoma of the colon
    Diarrhea with high chloride content
  Renal loss of H^+
    Diuretic therapy; current or remote
    Laxative abuse
  Other
    Bartter's syndrome
    Cystic fibrosis
ECF volume expansion with mineralocorticoid excess (urinary Cl > 20 mEq/liter)
  Primary or secondary aldosteronism
  Cushing's syndrome
  Licorice abuse
  Liddle's syndrome
Excessive bicarbonate loads
  Excessive intake of HCO_3^- or alkalinizing salts.
  The milk-alkali syndrome
  Conversion of accumulated or administered organic acids (lactate, acetate) to bicarbonate
  Glucose induced alkalosis during fasting
  Posthypercapnic state

Metabolic Alkalosis Characterized by Volume Contraction

Loss of Hydrogen Via the Gastrointestinal Tract

Vomiting or Gastric Drainage. Excessive loss of acid gastric juice due to vomiting or gastric drainage will result in the development of metabolic alkalosis[187] (see Fig. 1-8). The parietal cells of the gastric mucosa secrete high concentrations of hydrogen ions into the gastric lumen and return bicarbonate to the systemic circulation. The loss of hydrogen ions via vomiting or continued gastric aspiration therefore results in the net addition of bicarbonate to the ECF, and the generation of metabolic alkalosis. Initially, the increase in plasma bicarbonate results in a marked bicarbonate diuresis. Sodium and potassium accompany the bicarbonate to maintain electroneutrality. Hypokalemia and volume depletion develop. The ECF volume depletion stimulates aldosterone release. The resulting hyperaldosteronism results in further kaliuresis and distal H^+ excretion, worsening the hypokalemia and metabolic alkalosis.

Villous Adenoma of the Colon. A number of patients have been described in whom a villous adenoma was responsible for diarrhea characterized by high concentrations of protein, sodium, potassium and chloride

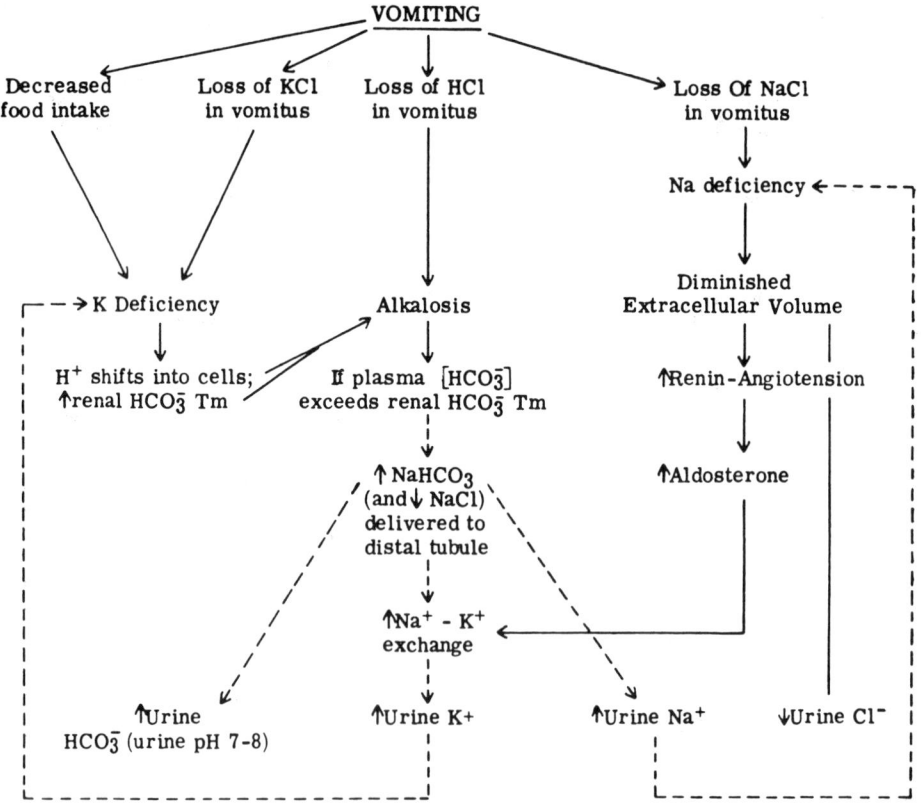

Fig. 1-8. Pathophysiology of metabolic alkalosis secondary to vomiting. (From Seldin DW, Rector FC: Symposium on acid-base homeostasis. The generation and maintenance of metabolic alkalosis. Kidney Int 1:306, 1972, with permission.)

in the stool. In these patients, metabolic alkalosis with hypokalemia results from the loss of chloride in a concentration greater than its plasma concentration, and from the resulting volume depletion with secondary mineralocorticoid excess.[188] In other cases it appears that hypokalemia from K^+ losses in the stool probably caused the alkalosis, since the diarrhea itself was alkaline.[189] However, most cases of colonic villous adenoma result in metabolic acidosis from net bicarbonate loss in the stool.

Congenital Chloridorrhea Darrow and Gamble and associates have described a syndrome consisting of congenital alkalosis and diarrhea.[190,191] The syndrome is characterized by watery diarrhea in which the stool chloride content is higher than the stool sodium plus potassium, and in which an acid stool, metabolic alkalosis, and a chloride-free urine are present. The primary defect in this entity has been postulated to be an inability of the gastrointestinal tract to absorb chloride; the chloride then acts as an osmotic agent and causes diarrhea. The diarrhea also results in loss of potassium in the stool and hypokalemia. Volume contraction, secondary hyperaldosteronism, and possibly total body potassium depletion result in maintenance of the alkalosis.

Renal Loss of Hydrogen

Diuretic Therapy. Apart from losses of hydrogen via the gastrointestinal tract, diuretic administration is a common cause of ECF volume contraction with mineralocorticoid excess.[192,193] If the diuretic is given to a normotensive subject or one whose hypertension has been corrected by treatment, the patient may display high levels of renin and aldosterone. In this instance, the hyperaldosteronism results from diuretic-induced volume contraction. In the absence of diuretic use, this would minimize further urinary excretion of sodium and chloride. However, chronic diuretic administration may successfully inhibit sodium and chloride reabsorption, even during volume contraction. The resulting distal delivery of sodium salts in the presence of hyperaldosteronism (generated by the volume contraction) accelerates potassium and hydrogen losses, predisposing to the development of hypokalemic metabolic alkalosis. If the urine is examined after the cessation of diuretic action, it may contain little potassium or sodium, and may therefore lead to an impression of extrarenal generation of hypokalemic alkalosis. If the urine is examined in the presence of diuretic activity, it may contain large amounts of sodium, potassium, and chloride, a pattern suggesting the renal generation of hypokalemic alkalosis. It is therefore mandatory to define the state of diuretic action, either current or remote, in any evaluation of the renal or extrarenal generation of hypokalemic alkalosis.

Bartter's Syndrome. This is a disorder characterized by juxtaglomerular hyperplasia and a very high plasma renin level, with normal or low blood pressure, secondary hyperaldosteronism, and hypokalemic alkalosis.[194-196] More recent studies indicate that renal prostaglandin synthesis and urinary prostaglandin excretion are markedly increased.[197] Treatment with cyclooxygenase inhibitors, such as aspirin or indomethacin, may result in a reversal of many of the abnormalities seen in Bartter's syndrome.[198] Volume contraction in Bartter's syndrome is probably secondary to salt wasting, and may in some way be mediated by increased renal levels of prostanglandins. The two most likely etiologies of Bartter's syndrome appear to be primary renal Cl^- wasting or primary renal K^+ wasting.[199] Clinically, a high percentage of patients evaluated for possible Bartter's syndrome are found to have surreptitious vomiting and/or diuretic abuse. A spot urine

Cl⁻ will be low in patients with surreptitious vomiting but should be high in those with Bartter's syndrome. Diuretic abuse can be difficult to discern from Bartter's syndrome, and may require analysis of the urine for thiazide or loop diuretics.

Other Causes

Cystic Fibrosis. This is a generalized disorder of exocrine and sweat glands.[200] Malbsorption from a deficiency of pancreatic enzymes is the leading problem in childhood. Chronic pulmonary infection, emphysema, bronchitis, pulmonary fibrosis, and cor pulmonale constitute the major problems seen later in childhood and adolescence. A defect in the control of excretion of electrolytes in sweat—specifically an excess of sodium and chloride—can be an important feature of the disease. Several cases of children with cystic fibrosis have been reported in which metabolic alkalosis occurred, presumably due to a marked loss of chloride in excess of bicarbonate in sweat. Combined with a low salt diet and ECF volume contraction, this results in the generation and appropriate setting for the maintenance of metabolic alkalosis.

Metabolic Alkalosis Characterized by Extracellular Fluid Volume Expansion

In the syndromes of volume expansion with mineralocorticoid excess, as long as dietary salt intake is normal, the delivery of sodium salts to the distal segments of the nephron will be plentiful. This is a particularly characteristic feature of this disorder, and different from the pattern of sodium retention in edematous states, such as cirrhosis with ascites, congestive heart failure, and nephrotic syndrome. In these latter disorders, there is also mineralocorticoid excess that persists in the face of adequate dietary salt intake. Due to a disturbance in Starling's forces in the circulation, the retained salt and water are sequestered in the interstitial spaces or behind the failing left ventricle, so that there is no expansion of effective arterial blood volume. Sodium reabsorption in proximal segments of the nephron may be increased. As long as the patient is untreated, distal delivery of sodium tends to be low. By contrast, in patients with primary mineralocorticoid excess, ECF volume expansion occurs, suppressing proximal reabsorption and allowing a continuous and abundant supply of sodium chloride to the distal tubule. Mineralocorticoid excess plus dietary salt intake result in volume expansion with a gain of two or three liters of body fluid (a gain in body weight of 2 to 3 kg). This increase in weight is not unrelenting, since an "escape" type of phenomenon occurs so that balance is restored, but at the expense of an expanded ECF volume. Edema very seldom if ever occurs under conditions of primary mineralocorticoid excess. There is continued distal delivery of sodium chloride which, in the presence of mineralocorticoid excess, results in losses of potassium with the development of hypokalemia and potassium deficiency, and the generation of metabolic alkalosis. Most of these patients have impaired urinary concentrating ability and polyuria with hypernatremia.

Volume Expansion with Mineralocorticoid Excess (Chloride Resistant)

Primary or Secondary Aldosteronism

Excess aldosterone secretion stimulates distal tubular H⁺ secretion in excess of that needed to maintain acid–base equilibrium, thereby resulting in metabolic acidosis. Different stimuli may be responsible for excessive mineralocorticoid activity, but patients exhibiting such activity can be divided into two groups, depending on the status of the renin-angiotensin-aldosterone system. In some patients, excess secretion of aldosterone is the initiating event. Hypertension and mild volume expansion ensue from the aldosterone-stimulated distal tubular sodium reabsorption. Clinical examples include adrenal adenomas, adrenal carcinoma, and bilateral adrenal hyperplasia. These syndromes are rare, but should be tested for in all patients with newly diagnosed hypertension, by screening for hypokalemia and metabolic alkalosis (prior to the use of diuretics or other medical therapy for hypertension).

Primary stimulation of the renin-angiotensin system may also be the initiating factor in stimulating the aldosterone system. Renal artery stenosis, accelerated or malignant hypertension, and intrarenal vascular diseases are well-recognized causes of hyperreninemia, resulting in nonedematous hyperaldosteronism.[201,202] Autonomous renin production from a renin-secreting tumor occasionally results in hyperreninemic hyperaldosterone-induced metabolic alkalosis.[203]

Excess of Other Adrenal Steroids

Some patients may exhibit evidence of excessive mineralocorticoid activity attributable to compounds other than aldosterone. In cases of adrenocorticotrophic hormone (ACTH)-producing tumors, primary adrenal hyperplasia, and some adrenal tumors, there may be an increased production of glucocorticoids and other related corticosteroids. Deoxycorticosterone seems to be the principal mineralocorticoid in two types of adrenogenital syndrome. In 17-α-hydroxylase deficiency, the obstruction to hydrocortisone synthesis is associated with high levels of corticosterone and deoxycorticosterone, as well as the absence of adrenal androgens and estrogens.[204] In addition to hypokalemic alkalosis and hypertension, these patients display evidence of a failure of secondary sexual development at puberty, with amenorrhea and hypogonadism in girls and ambiguous genitals in boys. In 11-β-hydroxylase deficiency, the obstruction to hydrocortisone synthesis results in excessive secretion of androgens, with virilization and excessive mineralocorticoid activity due to deoxycorticosterone.[205] Deoxycorticosterone has also been shown to be secreted in large amounts by certain adrenal tumors.

Aldosterone-like Compounds in Common Products

A major component of natural licorice, glycyrrhizic acid, resembles aldosterone in its chemical structure, and possesses similar activity. It has been associated in certain patients with a syndrome of mineralocorticoid excess closely simulating hyperaldosteronism.[206] However, most licorice prepared in the United States contains an artificial licorice flavor that lacks glycyrrhizic acid. Other examples of substances that may have an aldosterone-like effect include carbenoxolone,[207] chewing tobacco,[208] and some nasal sprays.[209]

Liddle's Syndrome

Liddle and his associates have reported a syndrome in which there is an intrinsic increase in distal sodium reabsorption resulting in hypokalemic alkalosis and hypertension, but low levels of renin and aldosterone.[210]

Excessive Bicarbonate Loads

Excessive Intake of Bicarbonate or Alkalinizing Salts

It is extremely difficult to produce metabolic alkalosis in individuals with normal renal function by the simple administration of sodium bicarbonate. Quantities as high as 140 g of sodium bicarbonate given daily to normal subjects may result in only slight elevation in the serum concentration of bicarbonate. The striking capacity of the kidney to excrete bicarbonate is due to an apparent limiting Tm, or transport maximum, for bicarbonate reabsorption. The steady-state human serum concentration of bicarbonate of 24 to 26 mEq/liter is close to the threshold for bicarbonate, and the apparent Tm for bicarbonate (28 mEq/liter/100 ml GFR) is also close to these figures, so that small elevations in the serum bicarbonate concentration quickly exceed the threshold and are rapidly excreted into the urine. Second, the administration of sodium bicarbonate tends to expand ECF volume, which in turn decreases bicarbonate reabsorption in the proximal and distal tubules. Even in patients with some degree of renal insufficiency, the ability to excrete bicarbonate is well preserved. Patients with renal failure tend to excrete sodium bicarbonate more rapidly than equivalent amounts of sodium chloride. In addition, in advanced renal failure, the bicarbonate threshold and the Tm for bicarbonate are depressed, which are conditions that favor the excretion of bicarbonate via the kidney. Consequently, the administration of sodium bicarbonate in renal failure usually does not result in the generation of metabolic alkalosis. If, however, concomitant deterioration of the circulation exists in such a way that the administration of sodium salts cannot expand the effective arterial blood volume, alkalosis may result.

The Milk-Alkali Syndrome

The milk-alkali syndrome may occur in patients with peptic ulcer disease or gastric distress who are treated with antacids containing calcium and absorbable alkali such as $CaCO_3$, or antacids and large amounts of milk.[211] The syndrome is characterized by alkalosis, hypercalcemia without hypercalciuria, calcinosis (especially band keratopathy), and severe renal insufficiency with azotemia. The mechanism responsible for metabolic alkalosis probably relates to increased alkali ingestion with impaired renal bicarbonate excretion due to decreased glomerular filtration. Other factors may play a role. Hypercalcemia apparently accelerates bicarbonate reabsorption by a direct effect on the renal tubules. It also may do so by decreasing the levels of circulating parathyroid hormone (PTH). Chronically, nephrocalcinosis may result in chronic renal insufficiency. This decreases the filtered load of HCO_3^- and impairs renal excretion. Hypokalemia, which is a frequent concomitant finding in this syndrome, tends to maintain the metabolic alkalosis.

Metabolism of Organic Acids to Bicarbonate

Metabolic alkalosis may occasionally occur immediately after the treatment of an acute metabolic acidosis.[212-214] The usual setting is that of a metabolic acidosis with a high production of metabolizable acid, such as lactic acid or ketones. These acids have the potential of being reconverted to bicarbonate once the metabolic derangement has subsided. For example, patients in shock with lactic acidosis may, once the circulatory collapse is corrected, metabolize the excess lactate, resulting in bicarbonate and a rebound-type of metabolic alkalosis. Acids such as lactate and ketoacids have been termed "potential bicarbonate" in the sense that unlike the acids that accumulate in uremic acidosis or hyperchloremic acidosis, they may be metabolically converted to bicarbonate without the intervention of the kidney. The reversal of the primary condition responsible for the acidosis, and the accumulation of organic acids with their potential for bicarbonate generation, may result in severe metabolic alkalosis. Some degree of metabolic alkalosis can also be observed in patients undergoing dialysis in whom acetate or lactate are used as organic acid. Prolonged use of solutions containing excess amounts of acetate or lactate, especially during peritoneal dialysis, may result in excessive generation of bicarbonate from these organic acids, and hence in metabolic alkalosis.

Glucose-Induced Alkalosis During Fasting

The mechanisms responsible for the alkalosis and salt retention that develop during starvation or with the resumption of food intake are not completely understood.[215] These effects of refeeding are more pronounced when glucose is the substance administered.[216] In obese patients, the period of starvation is usually characterized by a mild metabolic acidosis, presumably ketonemic in nature, with an increased anion gap accompanied by sodium, potassium, and chloride retention. Despite metabolic acidosis, the bicarbonate Tm, as measured by bicarbonate titration studies, may be increased. During glucose refeeding, a frank metabolic alkalosis associated with a further increase in the apparent bicarbonate Tm occurs, and further sodium retention may result in edema. The factors responsible for an increasing bicarbonate resorptive capacity during fasting, and its further augmentation during glucose refeeding, have not been identified. Neither potassium deficiency nor a reduced effective arterial blood volume can be implicated in the enhanced bicarbonate resorptive capacity. It is possible that metabolism of ketone bodies to bicarbonate when glucose is fed would result in an increase in plasma bicarbonate. Why this phenomenon restores bicarbonate concentrations to higher than normal but not normal levels is not known.

Posthypercapnic State

The posthypercapnic state develops when the hypercapnia (CO_2 retention) of respiratory acidosis is corrected rapidly in a setting in which the kidney is stimulated to reabsorb sodium and hence to reclaim bicarbonate.[217,218] One factor that is important in determining the retention of bicarbonate after hypercapnia has been corrected is salt balance. It has been shown in experimental animals on a salt free diet that the abrupt removal from an atmosphere high in CO_2 does not result in a decrease of serum bicarbonate into the normal range. A respiratory acidosis in patients with chronic pulmonary disease can be acutely converted by mechanical ventilation into a metabolic alkalosis. This problem can be avoided by maneuvers that tend to increase salt and bicarbonate excretion via the kidney. However, in patients with lung disease, congestive heart failure, and a tendency to retain salt, a posthypercapnic state may result in profound metabolic alkalosis. Caution is therefore indicated when the rapid correction of a chronic hypercapnia is undertaken. Obviously, salt restriction or edema-forming states will perpetuate the alkalosis.

RESPIRATORY ACIDOSIS

Respiratory acidosis is a disorder characterized by a primary increase in CO_2 tension (pCO_2) resulting in a decrease in blood pH. This disorder reflects an imbalance between CO_2 production from metabolism and CO_2 excretion by the lungs. The accumulation of carbon dioxide will lead to an increase in the carbonic acid concentration of the ECF (and also of the intracellular fluid), and thereby a decrease in pH. Like any other disturbance of acid–base balance, the first line of defense in respiratory acidosis consists of the reactions by which the increased H_2CO_3 is buffered to mitigate the marked fall in pH. This buffering occurs via nonbicarbonate systems (particularly protein, phosphate, etc.), and occurs mainly in the intracellular compartment.[219] The second line of defense relates to the role of the kidney in respiratory acidosis. As intracellular pH falls, presumably as a consequence of increased carbonic acid accumulation within cells, the renal tubular cells increase their hydrogen ion secretion, which in turn generates new bicarbonate. In the initial phases of respiratory acidosis, the increased pCO_2 is a stimulus for the generation and secretion of hydrogen ions. The exact mechanism is not known, but may involve stimulation of insertion of the proton-translocating ATPase into the luminal membranes of proximal and distal tubule cells.[220] Increased excretion of titratable acid and ammonium occurs and results in the de novo generation of bicarbonate.[221,222] Thus, during the period of adaptation to hypercapnia (respiratory acidosis), there is an increased urinary excretion of ammonium and chloride, which leads to an increase in the plasma bicarbonate and a decrease in the plasma chloride concentration. When a "steady-state" hypercapnia is reached, excretion of ammonium will return to normal and the excess hydrogen secreted will be utilized to reabsorb the greater amount of bicarbonate filtered. This persistently increased hydrogen ion secretion will therefore maintain the plasma bicarbonate concentration at levels greater than normal, a mechanism that would tend to increase the numerator of the Henderson-Hasselbalch equation (HCO_3^- concentration), and hence to restore pH toward normal. The only definitive way of correcting the acid–base disorder is the correction of defective ventilation. In the final analysis, only the restoration of ventilation to normal will result in the disappearance of the acid–base disorder that characterizes respiratory acidosis.

Clinical Features and Systemic Effects of Respiratory Acidosis

The acute onset of hypercapnia is usually accompanied by hypoxemia, which may dominate the clinical manifestations. The patient may present with signs or symptoms of acute respiratory distress, with marked restlessness, tachypnea, and marked dyspnea. As the process progresses to chronic hypercapnia, other manifestations may occur, including fatigue, weakness, confusion, occasional hyperactivity, and even manic periods and headache. With a high pCO_2, semicoma and coma can occur. The physical signs observed include tremor, asterixis like that in hepatic coma, weakness, incoordination, occasional cranial nerve signs, papilledema and retinal hemorrhages, and frequently, abnormal pyramidal tract signs. Tendon reflexes are most often decreased or absent. Other eye signs noted in these patients (chemosis, edema, and cyanosis of the conjunctiva, dilated dark retinal veins, and abnormal arborization of the macular area) are probably due to hypoxia and other factors. Coma begins at various levels of pCO_2 from 70 to 100 mmHg, depending on arterial pH and on the rapidity of elevation of pCO_2. Acute elevations of pCO_2 would probably produce coma at levels of 70 to 80 mmHg. The syndrome of pseudotumor cerebri with increased CSF pressure and papilledema is sometimes produced by respiratory acidosis. The picture may be quite deceptive, since in addition to marked papilledema with increased retinal venous engorgement, a variety of neurologic signs may sometimes be found. The key to diagnosis is recognition of the pulmonary problem and the marked pCO_2 elevation. Control of the pCO_2 usually produces prompt regression of the neurologic signs. Some patients, however, show a slow clearing of neurologic signs when their pCO_2 is brought down rapidly, especially if coma has been prolonged or severe. Although arrhythmias are uncommon in clinical respiratory acidosis, there is some suggestion that they can occur in special clinical circumstances. Although cardiac output usually rises with CO_2 inhalation, cardiac activity may be adversely affected by a high pCO_2. The increase in pCO_2 produces vasoconstriction in the pulmonary circulation, with a marked vasodilation in vessels of most other areas. Cerebral, renal, extremity, and coronary blood flows have been shown to increase. CO_2 apparently also produces vasoconstriction of the splanchnic vascular bed. The rise in pCO_2 may also affect airway resistance (bronchoconstriction). However, the findings in this respect are somewhat conflicting. The metabolic effects of pCO_2 elevation are not well understood. Severe interference with normal metabolism is believed to be present, especially in the central nervous system, particularly due to changes in intracellular pH. Respiratory acidosis may alter autonomic reactions in several ways. A rise in epinephrine and norepinephrine has been noted in human blood during the inhalation of 7 to 14 percent CO_2. During severe acidosis, the responses of pulse and blood pressure to injected catecholamines are altered.

Patients with stable chronic respiratory acidosis may have few if any signs or symptoms related directly to hypercapnia. The signs and symptoms of chronic pulmonary disease, with or without cor pulmonale, usually predominate.[223,224]

Laboratory Findings in Respiratory Acidosis

The arterial blood in respiratory alkalosis is characterized by a marked increase in the partial pressure of pCO_2, and sometimes by a moderately elevated plasma bicarbonate. The plasma bicarbonate in acute respiratory acidosis rarely exceeds 30 mEq/liter, although in chronic compensated respiratory acidosis the bicarbonate level may be as high as 40 mEq/liter. Usually the partial pressure of oxygen is decreased. There is an increased total plasma CO_2 content, although with chronic acidosis there is a marked decrease in plasma chloride. Under most circumstances the urine pH is acid in acute respiratory acidosis,[225] and may be either acid or alkaline in chronic respiratory acidosis.

Differential Diagnosis of Respiratory Acidosis

The causes of respiratory acidosis are summarized in Table 1-6.

Acute Respiratory Acidosis

Airway Obstruction

The most common cause of respiratory acidosis, both acute and chronic, is airway obstruction. The causes of airway obstruction may be grouped as endomural, intramural, and extramural. Endomural causes include bronchial secretions and aspirated foreign bodies; intramural causes include benign and malignant neoplasms, edema, and fibrous strictures; extramural causes are mainly due to enlargement of lymph nodes and other structures, with airway compression. The effects of obstruction vary according to its location and whether it is complete or partial.

Tracheal obstruction is uncommon. Foreign bodies either impact in the larynx or descend beyond the bifurcation. External compression of the trachea may occur from goiter, thymic tumors, or neoplastic lymph nodes. Such pressures initially cause an irritating, nonproductive cough that may progress to severe obstruction with stridor. Localized bronchial obstruction does not

Table 1-6. Differential Diagnosis of Respiratory Acidosis

Acute Respiratory Acidosis
  Airway obstruction
    Aspiration (vomit, food)
    Foreign body
    Severe bronchospasm
    Laryngeal edema
  Suppression of the respiratory center
    Hypnotics, sedatives, other drugs
  Hypoventilation due to muscular or neuromuscular disorders
    Myasthenia gravis
    Brainstem or high spinal cord injury
    Guillain-Barre syndrome
    Botulism
    Hypokalemia
  Disease of the lung or thoracic wall
    Flail chest
    Pneumothorax
    Pneumonia
    Smoke inhalation
    Severe cardiogenic pulmonary edema
    Pulmonary embolization

Chronic respiratory acidosis
  Lung disease
    Progressive lung disease associated with chronic obstructive emphysema and chronic bronchitis
    End-stage interstitial lung disease
  Neuromuscular abnormalities
    Poliomyelitis
    Diaphragmatic paralysis
    Myasthenia gravis
  Chronic depression of the respiratory center
    Chronic use of narcotics
  Obesity with a decrease in alveolar ventilation (Pickwickian syndrome)
  Primary or idiopathic alveolar hypoventilation

interfere with resting air flow unless it is severe; it is more likely to cause infection distally by interfering with mucus flow. When obstruction is nearly complete, overdistention of the distal lung tissue (obstructive emphysema) may occur; complete obstruction eventually results in atelectasis.

Suppression of the Respiratory Center

Barbiturates, opiate derivatives (morphine, etc.), and tranquilizers, as well as other drugs, may depress the respiratory center. Under these conditions, an inadequate response of the respiratory center to increases in pCO_2 retention may occur, with the development of respiratory acidosis. A careful history may reveal the administration or use of some of the drugs mentioned above. Urine and serum drug screens can be helpful in the uncooperative or comatose patient.

Hypoventilation Due to Muscular or Neuromuscular Disorders

Neurologic or muscular disease may cause either peripheral or central respiratory failure. Peripheral respiratory failure results when the skeletal musculature of the diaphragm, chest wall, abdomen, and neck becomes so weakened that it cannot move a sufficient amount of air to ventilate the lungs. Potential causes of peripheral respiratory failure include: (1) diseases of respiratory muscles, such as progressive muscular dystrophy, myotonic muscular dystrophy, and polymyositis; (2) diseases and disorders of the myoneural junction, such as myasthenia gravis, botulism, anticholinesterase poisoning (parathion and DFP), hypersensitivity to curare, and pseudomyasthenia (malignancy); (3) peripheral neuropathies, including Guillain-Barré syndrome, diphtheria, and acute intermittent porphyria; (4) anterior horn cell diseases, such as poliomyelitis and amyotrophic lateral sclerosis; and (5) lesions of the spinal conducting pathways, such as high cervical trauma, acute myelitis, high spinal compression, or malignancy.

The symptoms and manifestations of peripheral respiratory failure depend partly upon which muscles are affected first. Patients suffering from progressive paralysis of the chest wall or abdominal muscles frequently have few symptoms until their diaphragms are involved, at which time no respiratory reserves are left. On the other hand, patients whose diaphragms are paralyzed initially may feel breathless almost immediately. It should be remembered that patients with acute peripheral respiratory failure almost never become hypoxemic or hypocarbic until ready to collapse. Therapy, to be effective, must be started before cyanosis appears or abnormalities appear in blood gas values. Central respiratory failure results when the respiratory integrating neurons in the medulla oblongata become damaged or diseased. Common causes of this include infections (encephalitis, encephalitic poliomyelitis, disseminated encephalomyelitis), trauma, brainstem hemorrhage, neoplasia, and craniovertebral abnormalities. Central respiratory failure produces defects in the respiratory rate and rhythm, and symptoms that usually evolve through progressive stages. Patients may report that they cannot sleep or that they must concentrate on the breathing act. The breathing pattern may be frankly irregular. Respiratory sensitivity to carbon dioxide is reduced, and hypoxia and CO_2 retention develop unless treatment is instituted.

Diseases of the Lung or Thoracic Wall

Respiratory failure with acidosis may occur with diseases of the chest wall in which the muscles of respiration become ineffective, such as flail chest. A history of previous injury to the chest wall may help in the differential diagnosis. Acute development of pneumothorax or severe pneumonia may also impair the exchange of CO_2 and lead to acute respiratory acidosis. Other causes of respiratory acidosis include pulmonary edema and massive pulmonary embolism. Electrocardiographic changes, chest x-rays, physical examination including a careful examination of heart and lungs are essential in the differential diagnosis.

Chronic Respiratory Acidosis

Chronic Obstructive Lung Disease

This term embraces a number of clinical syndromes of varying etiology and pathology, with the common feature of increased hindrance to the flow of air out of the lungs, resulting from an intrapulmonary pathologic condition. In some of these syndromes air flow obstruction is reversible, and the clinical presentation is one of asthma; in others, air flow obstruction is continuous and associated with either chronic bronchitis, emphysema or both, and the clinical presentation varies depending upon the degree to which the pulmonary condition results in disturbance of pulmonary and circulatory function. Typically, the patient with chronic airway obstruction is a cigarette smoker between 50 and 60 years old who may or may not have a long history of chronic bronchitis with recurrent winter bronchitis. Cardinal symptoms are breathlessness on exertion, often with wheezing, worse in the morning, and associated with a sensation of tightness. There is typically intolerance on sudden exposure to cold air or smoky atmospheres, which induce coughing, tightness, and breathlessness. There is often orthopnea along with shortness of breath on stooping.

Neuromuscular Abnormalities and Chronic Depression of the Respiratory Center

These conditions have been considered above.

Cardiorespiratory Failure of Extreme Obesity

Cardiorespiratory failure has been described in association with extreme obesity, the average weight being approximately 325 pounds. The similarity in appearance and behavior of these patients to those of the fat boy, Joe, in *Pickwick Papers*, has led to this association being termed the Pickwickian syndrome. Prominent cyanosis, tachycardia, an increased central venous pressure with cardiac dilatation, functional tricuspid incompetence, hepatomegaly, and peripheral edema may be observed.[226,227]

Primary or Idiopathic Alveolar Hypoventilation

This term denotes a rare clinical syndrome occurring in patients with normal pulmonary and thoracic cage mechanics in whom the primary abnormality is alveolar hypoventilation. The syndrome is characterized by symptoms of headache, drowsiness or somnolence, and exertional dyspnea, and signs of cyanosis and congestive heart failure. The majority of patients are between 30 and 50 years of age, with a preponderance being male. Symptoms have usually been present for many years, but the presentation has sometimes been more acute, usually in response to a respiratory infection. The causes of this syndrome are unknown. Resistance to breathing and the patient's respiratory muscular power are essentially normal, which distinguishes idiopathic alveolar hypoventilation from hypoventilatory abnormalities of the thorax.[228,229]

RESPIRATORY ALKALOSIS

In respiratory alkalosis there is a decrease in pCO_2 (hypocapnia) leading to a decrease in carbonic acid concentration, a decrease in hydrogen ion concentration, and therefore a rise in blood pH. Since the metabolic production of CO_2 is usually constant, a negative CO_2 balance can be achieved only through increased excretion via increased alveolar ventilation. Hyperventilation can have two main origins: (1) increased neurochemical stimulation of ventilation via the respiratory center, and (2) assisted or controlled mechanical ventilation. Just as in any other acid–base disturbance, body buffers constitute the initial line of defense in respiratory alkalosis. Within minutes after an acute change in pCO_2, the pH change is buffered by non-bicarbonate buffer systems.[230,231] The change in the hydrogen ion concentration of the blood is limited to approximately 0.75 nmole/liter/mmHg change in pCO_2. This buffering is complete within 5 to 10 minutes; no further changes are apparent for several hours. In chronic hypocapnia, bicarbonate is excreted by the kidney in an attempt to return the pH toward normal. Although the plasma bicarbonate may be decreased to values as low as 15 mEq/liter at an arterial pCO_2 of 15 mmHg, one should suspect that at a plasma bicarbonate below 18 mEq/liter, the process is more likely related to metabolic acidosis than to acute respiratory alkalosis. The second line of defense in respiratory alkalosis occurs at the level of the kidney.[232] The kidneys respond to the rise in pH by diminishing the rate of hydrogen ion secretion into the tubular fluid, which leads to a bicarbonate diuresis that tends to restore the pH toward normal. The process can also be accomplished by reducing the generation of new bicarbonate which serves to replace that consumed in the daily buffering of the metabolic hydrogen load. The kidney also decreases the excretion of ammonium so as to decrease the generation of new bicarbonate.

As the excretion of NH_4^+ decreases, there must be increased excretion of another cation in order to maintain urine electroneutrality. In experimental animals it has been shown that sodium or potassium excretion increases to electrically balance HCO_3^- excretion.[232,233] After a new steady state is reached, excretion of these electrolytes returns to normal. The process of renal adaptation to respiratory alkalosis occurs slowly, and probably takes 48 to 96 hours to become maximal.

The third or corrective phase of defense against respiratory alkalosis depends on the total reversal of the causes responsible for the hyperventilation that maintains the negative CO_2 balance. This can be accomplished either by removal of the neurochemical stimulus to the respiratory center or modification or cessation of the assisted ventilation causing the abnormality.

CLINICAL FEATURES AND SYSTEMIC EFFECTS OF RESPIRATORY ALKALOSIS

Respiratory alkalosis may be manifested by symptoms and signs attributable to neuromuscular irritability.[234,235] Patients frequently complain of paresthesia in the perioral region and in the extremities.[236,237] Muscle cramps may be present and tinnitus may occur. Tetany and seizures may occur in some patients, and an increase in deep tendon reflexes may be observed.[238,239] Respiratory alkalosis causes vasoconstriction of the cerebral circulation, with a reduction in blood flow to the brain that may result in cerebral hypoxia.[240] Pseudoangina and ischemic electrocardiographic (ECG) changes can result from acute hyperventilation.[241,242] The electrocardiographic changes produced by hyperventilation are clinically important; patients with hypocapnia may present with symptoms suggestive of myocardial ischemia, and the electrocardiographic changes can interfere with the interpretation of exercise stress tests. Inability to concentrate, anxiety, and reduced psychomotor performance with increased irritability are also frequent findings in acute hypocapnia. The occurrence of vertigo and syncope is well known and may be explained by reduced cerebral blood flow. The clinical observation that hypocapnia may precipitate an attack of petit or grand mal epilepsy led to study of the electroencephalographic patterns in hypocapnia. Abnormal electroencephalographic tracings, showing an increase in the number of slow, high voltage waves, have been observed in experimental animals and normal human subjects as well as in epileptic patients. The occurrence of a "typical" epileptic electroencephalographic pattern during hyperventilation in patients known to have epilepsy and whose electroencephalogram (EEG) between the attacks was normal has led to the routine use of the "hyperventilation EEG" in clinical practice.

Laboratory Findings in Respiratory Alkalosis

The hallmark of respiratory alkalosis is a decrease in the carbon dioxide tension of body fluids. As a consequence, there is an elevated arterial pH and a potential decrease in plasma bicarbonate as a compensatory mechanism. The serum electrolytes remain within normal limits in chronic respiratory alkalosis unless another disorder is also present. The urine pH is not usually helpful in the differential diagnosis, and usually remains on the acid side. A rise in the blood concentration of lactic and pyruvic acids in response to an acute reduction in pCO_2 appears to occur[243] but is not present in chronic hypocapnia.[244] The development of a bicarbonate deficit and with a simultaneous rise in the lactic and pyruvic acid concentrations should be kept in mind in this disorder, since it may be confused with the findings seen in metabolic acidosis with an increased anion gap.

Differential Diagnosis of Respiratory Alkalosis

Hyperventilation and respiratory alkalosis have been observed in the clinical states listed in Table 1-7. Many of these entities cause an increase in ventilation by

Table 1-7. Differential Diagnosis of Respiratory Alkalosis

CNS
    Head trauma
    CNS tumor
    Fever
    Anxiety
    Idiopathic hyperventilation syndrome
Decreased O_2 delivery
    Anemia
    Hypoxemia
    Hypotension
Respiratory stimulation
    Pulmonary embolism
    Congestive lung failure
    Interstitial lung disease
    Pneumonia
Unknown
    Hepatic insufficiency
    Gram negative sepsis
Iatrogenic
    Mechanical hyperventilation
Pharmacologic or hormonal
    Salicylates
    Methylxanthines
    Nicotine
    Progesterone (i.e., in pregnancy and the luteal phase of menstrual cycle pregnancy)

central stimulation of the medullary respiratory center, including anxiety, fever, and salicylate intoxication or mechanical irritation of the brain due to trauma or a tumor. Stimulation of the peripheral pathways to the medullary respiratory center occurs in pulmonary-thoracic disorders that cause hypoxemia, and in disorders that decrease lung compliance without necessarily causing hypoxemia. Mechanical ventilation may produce respiratory alkalosis if the rate and tidal volume are set so that the pulmonary excretion of CO_2 exceeds CO_2 production. However, an increased minute ventilation is often needed to deliver adequate quantities of oxygen to patients with severe pulmonary insufficiency. Some of the entities described above and in Table 1-7 will be detailed below.

Hepatic Cirrhosis and Hepatic Coma

Respiratory alkalosis occurs frequently in patients with hepatic insufficiency.[245] However, in addition to respiratory alkalosis, other acid–base disturbances may be encountered in hepatic disease, and mixed acid–base disturbances may be observed. The mechanisms responsible for respiratory alkalosis in hepatic cirrhosis are not known, although increased pulmonary shunting, hyponatremia, and increased blood ammonia levels have been implicated.

Salicylate Intoxication

Hyperventilation is the outstanding clinical sign in salicylate intoxication in adults. The associated disturbance in acid–base balance is characteristically marked by an early respiratory alkalosis followed by a late metabolic acidosis (see the section on metabolic acidosis). The hyperventilation and subsequent respiratory alkalosis probably result from a direct stimulation of the respiratory center by salicylate. The metabolic acidosis occurs late in the course of salicylate intoxication. The decrease in serum bicarbonate produced by the initial phases of respiratory alkalosis contributes markedly to the development of the subsequent metabolic acidosis.

Exercise

Hyperventilation in response to muscular exercise, especially in untrained subjects, is well known and considered to be a reflex effect, the exact mechanism of which is not clear. Investigation of the bicarbonate concentration in severe exercise indicates a progressive bicarbonate deficit concomitant with a reduction in pCO_2. It is difficult to distinguish between respiratory alkalosis and metabolic acidosis as the initial event, since increased lactic acid levels frequently accompany severe muscular exercise.

Fever

A pathologic increase in body temperature or environmental temperature precipitates hyperventilation. The exact mechanism responsible for this is unknown. It is reasonable to assume, however, that it is a homeostatic reflex mechanism mediated through the temperature control center. This assumption is based on the well-known role of the lungs or, more specifically, the respiratory tract mucosa in the regulation of body temperature.

Pulmonary Diseases

Many forms of respiratory disease are associated with respiratory alkalosis. Examples include interstitial lung disease, pneumonia, pulmonary embolism, and pulmonary edema. Vagus nerve stimulation by receptors in the parenchyma of the lung appears to play a role in the pathophysiology of the respiratory alkalosis.[246,247]

The Idiopathic Hyperventilation Syndrome

Clinical recognition of the hyperventilation syndrome is important, since the presenting complaints are multiple and nonspecific, and can quite often mimic an organic illness. The following is probably an incomplete list of some of the various presenting complaints that have been reported in the idiopathic hyperventilation syndrome; the order in which they are listed does not necessarily correspond to the frequency of their occurrence:

1. Severe precordial chest pain, including a sensation of tightness around the chest; precordial palpitations
2. Dyspnea
3. Attacks of weeping and a state of depression
4. Experience of fear and panic; loss of voice
5. Giddiness and lightheadedness, dizziness, syncope
6. Weakness and excessive fatigue
7. Blurred vision
8. Nausea and vomiting
9. Tingling and paresthesia in the upper and lower extremities
10. Sensation of coldness of the extremities
11. Muscle cramps and muscle tightness
12. Emotional excitement and anxiety states
13. Profuse sweating or sweating of the hands
14. Diarrhea or constipation; epigastric or lower abdominal cramps
15. Flushing of the face and dryness of the throat

Clinical management of this syndrome is difficult because its symptoms frequently heighten the anxiety of the patient, resulting in worsening of the hyperventilation. Breathing into a closed system (i.e., a paper bag) may result in CO_2 retention, normalization of blood pH, and interruption of the cycle. Occasionally, anxiolytic agents may be necessary.

MIXED ACID–BASE DISTURBANCES

The entities described above—metabolic acidosis, metabolic alkalosis, respiratory acidosis, and respiratory alkalosis—represent simple acid-base disturbances. They denote the presence of a single primary process and its appropriate physiologic response. A mixed acid–base disturbance refers to the co-existence of two or more simple acid–base disturbances. Since these disturbances may have either additive or nullifying effects on plasma pH, mixed acid–base disturbances may produce dramatically extreme deviations or disarmingly minor or undetectable deviations of hydrogen concentration. The coexistence of two or more simple acid–base disturbances is quite common in hospitalized patients. The presence of a mixed acid–base disturbance is often suspected from a careful analysis of the patient's acid–base values. When the magnitude of the secondary change in pCO_2 or bicarbonate concentration (in metabolic and respiratory disorders, respectively) is inappropriate with respect to the magnitude of the initiating process (see Table 1-3), a mixed disturbance should be considered. Even when a seemingly appropriate relationship exists between an initiating disturbance and an anticipated secondary response, such a relationship may merely be the fortuitous consequence of a dual or even a triple acid–base abnormality. To avoid this diagnostic pitfall, clues to the presence of complicating acid–base disturbances should be sought from a close examination of other laboratory data, and particularly from the patient's history.[248]

The following are frequently encountered examples of mixed acid-base disturbances. Chronic respiratory acidosis may coexist with metabolic alkalosis, particularly in patients with pulmonary insufficiency and cor pulmonale who are treated with diuretics and a low salt diet. The metabolic alkalosis can be unmasked suddenly when a low-grade hypercapnia is partially corrected by mechanical ventilation or by other means.

A combination of chronic and acute respiratory acidosis may be seen in patients with moderately severe CO_2 retention due to chronic obstructive lung disease who experience a sudden worsening of pulmonary function from the use of hypnotics or sedatives capable of depressing the respiratory center, or because of correction of their hypoxia by oxygen therapy, or from acute superimposed infections such as acute pneumonitis.

Metabolic acidosis plus acute respiratory acidosis is common in patients with acute cardiopulmonary arrest, and results from lactic acidosis (triggered by poor tissue perfusion) and CO_2 retention. A similar picture may be seen in severe, acute pulmonary edema. Extreme decreases in plasma pH may be observed under these conditions.

Respiratory alkalosis later converting to metabolic acidosis is typified by salicylate intoxication, and reflects the independent effects of the causative salicylates on ventilation and cellular metabolism. Patients with gram-negative sepsis may also have this combination, since lactic acidosis, renal failure, or both are common complications of such sepsis and may appear in conjunction with primary hyperventilation.

TREATMENT OF ACID-BASE DISORDERS

Metabolic Acidosis

No empiric or uniform approach to the treatment of all forms of metabolic acidosis exists. The therapy must depend on the nature of the underlying defect and the severity of the acidosis. When the rate of hydrogen delivery into the ECF is increased, definite correction of the acidosis requires reversal of the underlying abnormality. In diabetic ketoacidosis, for example, correction of the altered glucose metabolism is essential. Insulin administration will increase glucose entry into the cell, increase the metabolism of beta-hydroxybutyric and acetoacetic acids to CO_2, and decrease the generation rate of hydrogen ions. The underlying abnormality in lactic acidosis must also be reversed if possible. If shock is responsible for the increase in glycolysis, transfusion, the use of volume expanders, pressors, or other techniques must be employed in an effort to reverse shock. The potential beneficial effect of dichloroacetate in patients with lactic acidosis has recently been reported,[249] and a recent study has examined the effect of this compound in dogs with lactic acidosis. In chronic renal disease, restriction of dietary protein and elimination of factors leading to increased catabolism will diminish the rate of accumulation of hydrogen ions. If exogenous proton donors are being administered in the form of medications, discovery of this fact will permit a reduction in the total load of protons entering the ECF. Finally, a normal acid–base balance can be restored by the administration of alkali. In most clinical situations, sodium bicarbonate is the mainstay of therapy in metabolic acidosis. Sodium lactate, sodium citrate, and Tris buffer have been used, but offer no particular advantages over sodium bicarbonate and may be more expensive. Oral citrate solutions tend to be more palatable and may be preferred if oral therapy can be utilized. One milliliter of the solution is metabolized in the liver to provide 1 mEq of bicarbonate. Solutions are available with Na^+, K^+, or both as the cation.

The initial goal of therapy should be to increase systemic pH to a safe level. Once the pH exceeds 7.2, arrhythmias become less likely and cardiac contractility and responsiveness to catecholamines will be restored. The amount of bicarbonate required to correct the acidosis can be calculated from the bicarbonate deficit multiplied by the bicarbonate space. In metabolic acidosis, bicarbonate is distributed through roughly 60 percent of the lean body weight. If the normal plasma bicarbonate concentration is 24 mEq/liter and the observed bicarbonate concentration is 8 mEq/liter, then the amount of bicarbonate needed to correct the deficit would be:

(0.6 × lean body weight in kilograms)
× (24 − 8 mEq/liter).

However, the distribution space increases as the severity of the acidosis worsens. If the serum pH is less than 7.10, the volume of distribution may be 0.80 liter/kg of lean body weight.[250] There is no need to correct the entire bicarbonate deficit acutely, and once plasma bicarbonate levels exceed 16 to 17 mEq/liter, replacement can continue more slowly. In some forms of rapidly developing metabolic acidosis, ECF volume depletion occurs, such as in diabetic ketoacidosis. Restoration of the ECF volume to normal is essential to maintaining cardiovascular integrity and supporting adequate renal function. A decreased cardiac output and/or hypotension complicating any form of metabolic acidosis may not only impair the renal excretion of acid, but may also result in increased formation of lactic acid due to decreased tissue perfusion. Hence, restoration of the ECF volume is important. In diabetic ketoacidosis, for example, the therapeutic goals include: (1) the restoration of normal carbohydrate metabolism by the administration of insulin; (2) replacement of ECF volume losses by the administration of sodium chloride and water; and (3) prevention or correction of potassium depletion during the recovery phase by the administration of carefully regulated quantities of potassium. Other forms of metabolic acidosis, such as in methanol or ethylene glycol intoxication, may require dialysis to treat both the acidosis and the acute renal failure that may develop, and also for removal of the toxins.

Metabolic Alkalosis

If metabolic alkalosis occurs with a loss of ECF volume, the ability of the kidney to correct the alkalosis will be impaired. Accordingly, repair of the the alkalosis will require restoration of the ECF volume to normal. Administration of sodium chloride will in most instances correct part of the metabolic alkalosis. In a patient with hypokalemic alkalosis, potassium chloride should be used to replace potassium deficits, since chloride depletion is an accompanying event. Organic potassium salts, such as potassium triplex or potassium gluconate, are not recommended for the correction of alkalosis associated with potassium depletion, unless sodium chloride is administered concomitantly. In most instances, potassium can be replaced orally. When oral therapy is inadvisable, intravenous solutions containing potassium in a concentration no greater than 60 mEq/liter may be infused, generally at a rate no greater than 10 mEq/hr. In cases of severe hypokalemia and arrhythmia, K^+ can be administered at rates as high as 20 to 60 mEq/hr via a central venous access, with continuous ECG monitoring in an intensive care unit and frequent measurement of serum K^+ levels. Any patient receiving intravenous potassium should be followed carefully so as to avoid the occurrence of hyperkalemia. In a patient with hypochloremic alkalosis who is on a salt-restricted diet and who does not respond to correction of the cause of the alkalosis or to correction of potassium depletion, chloride depletion must be considered. In general, the administration of modest amounts of chloride, either in the form of sodium chloride or potassium chloride, will obviate any contribution of chloride depletion to the perpetuation of metabolic alkalosis.

Inhibition of carbonic anhydrase with acetazolamide can result in increased bicarbonate and K^+ excretion by the kidney. Acetazolamide is available in both oral and intravenous forms, and can be useful in patients with volume overload or other contraindications to volume expansion.

For all practical purposes, the indications for administering acid in the treatment of metabolic alkalosis are restricted to life-threatening situations, of which the best example is the uremia in the patient who is overtreated with alkali and develops refractory convulsions. The hydrogen ions can be administered intravenously as ammonium chloride, arginine hydrochloride, or dilute HCl. If ammonium chloride is used intravenously, it must be given slowly and under close supervision, particularly in patients with suspected hepatic involvement. Both arginine hydrochloride and ammonium chloride are metabolized to urea, and may be relatively contraindicated in azotemic patients. In addition, arginine hydrochloride may cause potassium to exit from cells, resulting in severe hyperkalemia.[251] It should probably not be used. Dilute hydrochloric acid at 100 mmol/liter can be administered via a large central vein,[252,253] and is probably the therapy of choice.

If all other methods fail or are contraindicated, then hemodialysis using a high chloride, low base (whether acetate or bicarbonate) bath can be utilized.[254]

Respiratory Acidosis

In acute respiratory acidosis, immediate attention must be directed to the underlying cause of the impaired gas exchange. If airway obstruction exists, it must be eliminated. If bronchospasm contributes, bronchodilators are indicated. If respiration is impaired because of central nervous system and neuromuscular disorders, mechanically assisted respiration may be necessary.

The treatment of chronic respiratory acidosis also centers on improving alveolar ventilation and gas exchange. The use of bronchodilators and antibiotics to treat infection may be necessary. If viscous secretions contribute to impaired gas exchange, sputum liquefiers, often combined with postural drainage, may be useful. Glucocorticoids may decrease the amount of secretions in patients with chronic bronchitis. Breathing exercises may be necessary. In extreme cases tracheostomy may be indicated. Drugs known to depress the respiratory center should be avoided in patients with chronic respiratory acidosis. Drugs such as barbiturates, narcotics, benzodiazepines, non-barbiturate sedatives such as glutethimide and chloral hydrate, or tranquilizers such as chlorpromazine should be avoided. Care should also be taken when treating acute CO_2 retention in patients with chronic lung disease, since such an event may be followed by a paradoxical shift in pH to the alkaline side of pH 7.4, owing to the patient's inability to excrete the extra bicarbonate retained during the period of hypercapnia.

Respiratory Alkalosis

Treatment of respiratory alkalosis should be directed at reversing the underlying cause of hyperventilation. For example, in patients with salicylate intoxication, removal of the drug by dialysis or by increasing the excretion of urine through the use of osmotic diuresis represents an important part of the therapeutic regimen. In the patient with emotionally induced hyperventilation, sedation may be helpful, but during the period of acute hyperventilation, rebreathing of CO_2 simply by placing a bag over the patient's head will prevent severe alkalosis. In the case of hepatic disease, correction of the responsible abnormality will provide the only mechanism for eliminating the hyperventilation.

REFERENCES

1. Relman AS: What are "acids" and "bases"? Am J Med 17:435, 1954
2. Relman AS: Metabolic consequences of acid base disorders. Kidney Int 1:347, 1972
3. Pitts RF: Buffer mechanisms of tissues and body. In Physiology of the Kidney and Body Fluids. 3rd Ed. Year Book Medical Publishers, Chicago, 1974
4. Hasselbalch KA: Die Berechnung der Wasserstoffzahl des Blutes aus der frein und gebundenen Kohlensaure desselben, und die Sauerstoffbindung des Blutes als Funktion der Wasserstoffzahl. Biochem Z 78:112, 1916
5. Siggard-Andersen O: The Acid–Base Status of the Blood. Williams & Wilkins, Baltimore, 1974
6. Kaehny WD, Jackson JT: Respiratory response to HCL acidosis in dogs after carotid body denervation. J Appl Physiol 46:1138, 1979
7. Javaher S, Clendening A, Papadakis N, Brody JS: Changes in brain surface pH during acute isocapnic metabolic acidosis and alkalosis. J Appl Physiol 51:276, 1981
8. Javaher S, Herrera L, Kazemi H: Ventilatory drive in acute metabolic acidosis. J Appl Physiol 46:913, 1979
9. Pitts RF, Lotspeich WD: Bicarbonate and the renal regulation of acid base balance. Am J Physiol 147:136, 1946
10. Pitts RF, Lotspeich WD, Schiess WA, et al: The renal regulation of acid base balance in man: I. The nature of the mechanism for acidifying the urine. J Clin Invest 27:48, 1948
11. Pitts RF, Alexander RS: The nature of the renal tubular mechanism for acidifying the urine. Am J Physiol 144:239, 1945
12. Pitts RF: The role of ammonia production and excretion in regulation of acid-base balance. N Engl J Med 284:32, 1971
13. Lennon EJ, Lemann J Jr, Litzow Jr: The effects of diet and stool composition on the net external acid balance of normal subjects. J Clin Invest 45:1601, 1966
14. Cogan MG, Maddox DA, Lucci MS, et al: Control of proximal bicarbonate reabsorption in normal and acidotic rats. J Clin Invest 64:1168, 1979
15. Karlmark B, Danielson BG: Titratable acid, pCO_2, bicarbonate and ammonium ions along the rat proximal tubule. Acta Physiol Scand 91:243, 1974
16. Gottschalk CW, Lassiter WE, Mylle M: Localization of urine acidification in the mammalian kidney. Am J Physiol 198:581, 1960
17. Steinmetz PR, Lawson LR: Effect of luminal pH on ion permeability and flows of Na^+ and H^+ in turtle bladder. Am J Physiol 220:1573, 1971
18. Al-Awqati Q: H^+ Transport in urinary epithelia. Am J Physiol 235:F77, 1978
19. Aronson PS: Mechanisms of active H^+ secretion in the proximal tubule. Am J Physiol 245:F647, 1983
20. Roos A, Boron WF: Intracellular pH. Physiol Rev 61:296, 1981
21. Aronson PS: Identifying secondary active solute transport in epithelia. Am J Physiol: 240 (Renal Fluid Electrolyte Physiol 9):F1, 1981
22. Kimura G, Spring KR: Luminal Na^+ entry into *Nectarus* proximal tubule cells. Am J Physiol 236:F295, 1979
23. Wang W, Messner G, Oberleithner H, et al: The effect of ouabain on intracellular

activities of K^+, Na^+, Cl^-, H^+ and Ca^{++} in proximal tubules of frog kidneys. Pflugers Arch 401:6, 1984
24. Lucci MS, Tinker JP, Weiner IM, et al: Function of proximal tubule carbonic anhydrase defined by selective inhibition. Am J Physiol 245:F443, 1983
25. Alpern RJ: Mechanism of basolateral membrane $H^+/OH^-/HCO_3^-$ transport in the rat proximal convoluted tubule: a sodium coupled electrogenic process. J Gen Physiol 86:613, 1985
26. Yoshitomi K, Fromter E: Cell pH of rat proximal tubule in vivo and the conductive nature of HCO_3^- (OH^-) exit. Pflugers Arch 402:300, 1984
27. Sasaki S, Yoshiyama N: Interaction of chloride and bicarbonate transport across the basolateral membrane of rabbit proximal straight tubule. Evidence for sodium coupled chloride/bicarbonate exchange. J Clin Invest 81:1004, 1988
28. Chan YL and Giebisch G: Relationship between sodium and bicarbonate transport in the rat proximal convoluted tubule. Am J Physiol 240:F222, 1981
29. Mello-Aires M, & Malnic G: Sodium in renal tubular acidification kinetics. Am J Physiol 236:F434, 1970
30. Kinne-Saffran E, Beauwens R, Kinne R: An ATP-driven proton pump in brush-border membranes from rat renal cortex. J Membr Biol 64:67, 1982
31. Cassola AC, Giebisch G, Malnic G: Mechanisms and components of renal tubular acidification. J Physiol 267:601, 1977
32. Holmberg C, Kokko JP, Jacobson HR: Determination of chloride and bicarbonate permeabilities in proximal convoluted tubules. Am J Physiol 241:F386, 1981
33. Warnock DG, Yee VJ: Anion permeabilities of the isolated perfused rabbit proximal tubule. Am J Physiol 242:F395, 1982
34. Hamm LL, Pucacco LR, Kokko JP, et al: Hydrogen ion permeability of the rabbit proximal convoluted tubule. Am J Physiol 246:F3, 1984
35. Good DW: Sodium-dependent bicarbonate absorption by cortical thick ascending limb of rat kidney. Am J Physiol 248:F821, 1985
36. Seldin DW, Rosin JM, Rector RC, Jr: Evidence against bicarbonate reabsorption in the ascending limb, particularly as disclosed by free water clearance studies. Yale J Biol Med 48:337, 1975
37. Iino Y, Burg MB: Effect of acid-base status in vivo on bicarbonate transport by rabbit renal tubules in vitro. Jpn J Physiol 31:99, 1981
38. McKinney TD, Burg MB: Bicarbonate absorption by rabbit cortical collecting tubules in vitro. Am J Physiol 234:F141, 1978
39. Gluck S, Kelly S, Al-Awqati Q: The proton translocating ATPase responsible for urinary acidification. J Biol Chem 257:9230, 1982
40. Gluck S, Al-Awqati Q: An electrogenic proton translocating adenosine triphosphatase from bovine kidney medulla. J Clin Invest 73:1704, 1984
41. Al-Awqati Q, Mueller A, Steinmetz PR: Transport of H^+ against electrochemical gradients in turtle bladder. Am J Physiol 233:F502, 1977
42. Fisher JL, Husted RF, Steinmetz PR: Chloride dependence of the HCO_3^- exit step in urinary acidification by the turtle bladder. Am J Physiol 245:F564, 1983
43. Breyer MD, Jacobson HR: Mechanisms and regulation of renal H^+ and HCO_3^- transport. Am J Nephrol 7:150, 1987
44. Rosen RA, Julian BA, Dubovsky EV, et al: On the mechanism by which chloride corrects metabolic alkalosis in man. Am J Med 84:449, 1988
45. Atkins JL, Burg MB: Secretion and absorption of bicarbonate by rat collecting ducts. Clin Res 31:423, 1983
46. Star RA, Burg MB, Knepper MA: Bicarbonate secretion and chloride absorption by rabbit cortical collecting ducts. Role of chloride/bicarbonate exchange. J Clin Invest 76:1123, 1985
47. Cohen L: HCO_3^-/Cl^- exchange transport in the adaptive response to alkalosis by turtle bladder. Am J Physiol 239:F167, 1980
48. Steinmetz PR, Lawson LR: Effect of luminal pH on ion permeability and flows of Na^+ and H^+ in turtle bladder. Am J Physiol 220:1573, 1971.
49. Sasaki S, Berry CA, Rector FC, Jr.: Effect of luminal and peritubular HCO_3^- concentrations and pCO_2 on bicarbonate reabsorption in rabbit proximal convoluted tu-

bules perfused in vitro. J Clin Invest 70:639, 1982
50. Jacobson HR: Effects of CO_2 and acetazolamide on bicarbonate and fluid transport in rabbit proximal tubules. Am J Physiol 240:F54, 1981
51. Maren TH: Carbonic anhydrase: chemistry, physiology, and inhibition. Physiol Rev 47:595, 1967
52. Kunau RT, Frick A, Rector FC, et al: Micropuncture study of the proximal tubular factors responsible for the maintenance of alkalosis during potassium deficiency in the rat. Clin Sci 34:223, 1968
53. Kurtzman NA, White MG, Rogers PW: The effect of potassium and extracellular fluid volume on renal bicarbonate reabsorption. Metabolism 22:41, 1973
54. Bichara M, Paillard M, Corman B, et al: Volume expansion modulates $NaHCO_3$ and NaCl transport in the proximal tubule and Henle's loop. Am J Physiol 247:F140, 1984
55. Cogan MG: Volume expansion predominantly inhibits proximal reabsorption of NaCl rather than $NaHCO_3$. Am J Physiol 245:F272, 1983
56. Iino Y, Burg MB: Effect of parathyroid hormonal bicarbonate reabsorption by proximal tubules in vitro. Am J Physiol 236:F387, 1979
57. McKinney TD, Myers P: PTH inhibition of bicarbonate transport by proximal convoluted tubules. Am J Physiol 239:F127, 1980
58. Stone DK, Seldin DW, Kokko JP, et al: Mineralocorticoid modulation of rabbit medullary collecting duct acidification: a sodium-independent effect. J Clin Invest 72:77, 1983
59. Cohen LH, Steinmetz PR: Control of active proton transport in turtle urinary bladder by cell pH. J Gen Physiol 76:381, 1980
60. Schuster VL, Bonsib SM and Jennings ML: Two types of collecting duct mitochondria-rich (intercalated) cells: lectin and band 3 cytochemistry. Am J Physiol (Cell Physiology 20) 251:C347, 1986
61. Pitts RF: Production and excretion of ammonia in relation to acid-base regulation. p 445. In Orloff J, Berliner RW, Geiger SR (eds): Handbook of Physiology: Urinary Renal Physiology. American Physiological Society, Washington, D.C., 1973
62. Vinay P, Lemieux G, Gougoux A, et al: Regulation of glutamine metabolism in dog kidney in vivo. Kidney Int 29:68, 1986
63. Tizianello A, Deferrari G, Garibotto C, et al: Renal ammoniagenesis during the adaptation to metabolic acidosis in man. Contrib Nephrol 31:40, 1982
64. Hamm LL, Simon EE: Roles and mechanisms of urinary buffer excretion. Am J Physiol 253 (Renal Fluid Electrolyte Physiol. 22):F595, 1987
65. Nagami GT: Luminal ammonium entry in the isolated perfused proximal tubule. Clin Res 34:604, 1986
66. Good DW, Knepper MA, Burg MB: Ammonium and bicarbonate transport by thick ascending limb of rat kidney. Am J Physiol 247 (Renal Fluid Electrolyte Physiol 16):F35, 1984
67. Garvin JL, Burg MB, Knepper MA: Ammonium replaces potassium in supporting sodium transport by the Na-K-ATPase of renal proximal straight tubules. Am J Physiol 249 (Renal Fluid Electrolyte Physiol 18):F785, 1985
68. Knepper MA, Good DW, Burg MB: Mechanism of ammonia secretion by cortical collecting ducts of rabbit. Am J Physiol 247 (Renal Fluid Electrolyte Physiol 16):F729, 1984
69. Good DW, Caflisch CR, DuBose TD Jr: Transepithelial ammonia concentration gradients in inner medulla of the rat. Am J Physiol 252 (Renal Fluid Electrolyte Physiol 21):F491, 1987
70. Wrong O, Davies HEF: The excretion of acid in renal disease. QJ Med 28:259, 1959.
71. Gonick HC, Kleeman CR, Rubini ME, et al: Functional impairment in chronic renal diseases. II. Studies of acid excretion. Nephron 6:28, 1969
72. Dorhout-Mees EJ, Machado M, Slatopolsky E, et al: The functional adaptation of the diseased kidney. III. Ammonium excretion. J Clin Invest 45:289, 1966
73. Simpson DP: Control of hydrogen ion homeostasis and renal acidosis. Medicine 50:503, 1971
74. Buerkert J, Martin D, Trigg D, et al: Effect of reduced renal mass on ammonium handling and net acid formation by the superficial and juxtamedullary nephron of the rat. J Clin Invest 71:1661, 1983

75. Sastrasinh S, Tannen RL: Effect of potassium on renal NH₃ production. Am J Physiol 244 (Renal Fluid Electrolyte Physiol 13):F383, 1983
76. Tannen RL: Ammonia metabolism. Am J Physiol 4:F265, 1978
77. Mahnensmith R, Thier SO, Cooke CR, et al: Effect of acute metabolic acidemia on renal electrolyte transport in man. Metabolism 28:83, 1979
78. Mizgala CL, Quamme GA: Renal handling of phosphate. Physiol Rev 65:431, 1985
79. Brunette MG, Beliveau R, Chan M: Effect of temperature and pH on phosphate transport through brush border membrane vesicles in rats. Can J Physiol Pharmacol 62:229, 1984
80. Amstutz M, Mohrmann M, Gmaj P, et al: Effect of pH on phosphate transport in rat renal brush border membrane vesicles. Am J Physiol 248 (Renal Fluid Electrolyte Physiol 17):F705, 1985
81. Gmaj P, Murer H: Cellular mechanisms of inorganic phosphate transport in kidney. Physiol Rev 66:36, 1986
82. Cohen JJ, Kamm DEA: Renal metabolism: Relation to renal function. p 141. In Brenner BM, Rector FC (eds): 2nd Ed. WB Saunders, Philadelphia, 1981
83. Simpson DP: Citrate excretion: a window on renal metabolism. Am J Physiol 244 (Renal, Fluid and Electrolyte Physiol 13):F223, 1983
84. Irsigler GB, Stafford MJ, Severinghaus JW: Relationship of CSF pH, O_2, and CO_2 responses in metabolic acidosis and alkalosis in humans. J Appl Physiol 48:355, 1980
85. Malck AB: The role of metabolic acidosis in the pulmonary vascular response to hemorrhage and shock. J Trauma 18:108, 1978
86. Gerst P, Fleming W, Malm J: A quantitative evaluation of the effects of acidosis and alkalosis upon the ventricular fibrillation threshold. Surgery 59:1050, 1966
87. Wildenthal K, Mierzwiak DS, Myers RW: Effects of acute lactic acidosis on left ventricular performance. Am J Physiol 214:1352, 1968
88. Bellingham AJ, Detter JC, Lenfant C: Regulatory mechanisms of hemoglobin oxygen affinity in acidosis and alkalosis. J Clin Invest 50:700, 1971
89. Epstein FH: Signs and symptoms of electrolyte disorders. p 499. In Maxwell MH, Kleeman CR (eds): Clinical Disorders in Fluid and Electrolyte Metabolism. McGraw-Hill, New York, 1980
90. Posner J, Plum F: Spinal fluid pH and neurologic symptoms in systemic acidosis. N Engl J Med 27:605, 1967
91. Litzow JR, Lemann J Jr, Lennon EJ: The effect of treatment of acidosis on calcium balance in patients with chronic azotemic renal disease. J Clin Invest 46:280, 1967
92. Burnell JM: Changes in bone sodium and carbonate in metabolic acidosis and alkalosis in the dog. J Clin Invest 50:327, 1971
93. Nash M, Torrado AD, Greifer I, et al: Renal tubular acidosis in infants and children. J Pediatr 80:738, 1972
94. Levy J, New MI: Growth in children with renal failure. Am J Med 58:65, 1975
95. Sartorius OW, Roemmelt JC, Pitts RF: The renal regulation of acid-base balance in man. IV. The nature of the renal compensation—Ammonium chloride acidosis. J Clin Invest 28:423, 1949
96. Narins RG, Emmett M: Simple and mixed acid-base disorders: a practical approach. Medicine 59:161, 1980
97. Oh MS, Carroll JH: The anion gap. N Engl J Med 297:814, 1979
98. Gabows PA, Kaehny WD: The anion gap: Its meaning and clinical utility. Kidney Int 12:5, 1977
99. Soriano JR, Edelmann CM, Jr: Renal tubular acidosis. Annu Rev Med 20:363, 1969
100. Morris RC Jr: Renal tubular acidosis: Mechanisms, classification and implications. N Engl J Med 281:1405, 1969
101. Morris RC, Sebastian A: Renal tubular acidosis. p. 1808–1820. In Stanbury JB, Wyngaarden JB, Fredrickson DS, Goldstein JL, Brown MS (eds): The Metabolic Basis of Inherited Disease. McGraw-Hill, New York, 1983
102. Chan JCM: Renal tubular acidosis. J Pediatr 102:327, 1983.
103. Sabastian A, McSherry E, Morris RC Jr: Impaired renal conservation of sodium and chloride during sustained correction of systemic acidosis in patients with type 1, clas-

sic renal tubular acidosis. J Clin Invest 58:454, 1976
104. Sebastian A, McSherry E, Morris RC, Jr: Renal potassium wasting in renal tubular acidosis (RTA). J Clin Invest 50:667, 1971
105. Buckalew VM Jr, Purvis M, Shulman M, et al: Hereditary renal tubular acidosis. Medicine 53:229, 1974
106. Mason AMS, Golding PL: Hyperglobulinaemic renal tubular acidosis: a report of nine cases. Br Med J 3:143, 1970
107. McCurdy DK, Cornwell GG III, DePratti VJ: Hyperglobulinemic renal tubular acidosis. Report of two cases. Ann Intern Med 67:110, 1967
108. Morris RC Jr, Fudenberg HH: Impaired renal acidification in patients with hypergammaglobulinemia. Medicine 46:57, 1967
109. Cohen A, Way BJ: The association of renal tubular acidosis with hyperglobulinaemic purpura. Australas Ann Med 11:189, 1962
110. Ferris T, Kashgarian M, Levitin H, et al: Renal tubular acidosis and renal potassium wasting acquired as a result of hypercalcemic nephropathy. N Engl J Med 265:924, 1961
111. Huth EJ, Mayock RL, Kerr RM: Hyperthyroidism associated with renal tubular acidosis. Am J Med 26:818, 1959
112. Zisman E, Buccino RA, Gorden P, et al: Hyperthyroidism and renal tubular acidosis. Arch Intern Med 121:118, 1968
113. Reynolds TB, Bethune JE: Renal tubular acidosis secondary to hyperparathyroidism. Clin Res 17:169, 1969
114. Morris RC Jr: An experimental renal acidification defect in patients with hereditary fructose intolerance. II. Its distinction from classic renal tubular acidosis: its resemblance to the renal acidification defect associated with the Fanconi syndrome of children with cystinosis. J Clin Invest 47:1648, 1968
115. Patterson RM, Ackerman GL: Renal tubular acidosis due to amphotericin B nephrotoxicity. Arch Intern Med 127:241, 1971
116. Douglas JB, Healy JK: Nephrotoxic effects of amphotericin B, including renal tubular acidosis. Am J Med 46:154, 1969
117. McCurdy DK, Frederic M, Elkinton JR: Renal tubular acidosis due to amphotericin B. N Engl J Med 278:124, 1968
118. Taher SM, Anderson RJ, McCartney R, et al: Renal tubular acidosis associated with toluene "sniffing." N Engl J Med 290:765, 1974
119. Baehner RL, Gilchrist GS, Anderson EJ: Hereditary elliptocytosis and primary renal tubular acidosis in a single family. Am J Dis Child 115:414, 1968
120. Deck MDF: Medullary sponge kidney with renal tubular acidosis: A report of 3 cases. J Urol 94:330, 1965
121. Batlle DC, Moses MF, Manaligal J, et al: The pathogenesis of hyperchloremic metabolic acidosis associated with renal transplantation. Am J Med 70:786, 1981
122. Cochran M, Peacock M, Smith DA: Renal tubular acidosis of pyelonephritis with renal stone disease. Br Med J 2:721, 1968
123. Tu WH, Stearn MA: Systemic lupus erythematosus and latent renal tubular dysfunction. Ann Intern Med 67:100, 1967
124. Jessop S, Rabkin R, Mumford G, et al: Renal tubular function in systemic lupus erythematosus. S Afr Med J 47:132, 1973
125. Talal N, Zisman E, Shur PH: Renal tubular acidosis, glomerulonephritis and immunologic factors in Sjögren's syndrome. Arthritis Rheum 2:774, 1968
126. Shioji R, Furuyama T, Onodera S, et al: Sjögren's syndrome and renal tubular acidosis. Am J Med 48:456, 1970
127. Chan JCM, Alon U: Tubular disorders of acid-base and phosphate metabolism. Nephron 40:257, 1985
128. Morris RC Jr: Renal tubular acidosis. N Engl J Med 304:418, 1981
129. McSherry E: Renal tubular acidosis in childhood. Kidney Int 20:799, 1981
130. Lee DB, Drinkard N, Rosen JP, et al: The adult Fanconi syndrome. Medicine 51:107, 1972
131. Hunt DD, Stearns G, McKinley JB, et al: Long-term study of family with Fanconi syndrome without cystinosis (DeToni-Debre-Fanconi syndrome). Am J Med 40:492, 1966
132. Worthen HG, Good RA: The deToni-Fanconi syndrome with cystinosis. Am J Dis Child 95:633, 1958
133. Morgan HG, Stewart WK, Lowe KG, et al: Wilson's disease and the Fanconi syndrome. QJ Med 31:361, 1962

134. Wilson DM, Goldstein NP: Bicarbonate excretion in Wilson's disease (hepatolenticular degeneration). Mayo Clin Proc 49:394, 1974
135. Oetliker O, Rossi E: The influence of extracellular fluid volume on the renal bicarbonate threshold: A study of two children with Lowe's syndrome. Pediatr Res 3:140, 1969
136. Matsudy I, Takeda T, Sugai M, et al: Oculocerebrorenal syndrome. Am J Dis Child 117:205, 1969
137. Chisolm JJ, Harrison HC, Eberlein WR, et al: Aminoaciduria, hypophosphatemia, and rickets in lead poisoning. Am J Dis Child 89:159, 1955
138. Fulop M, Drapkin A: Potassium-depleted syndrome secondary to nephropathy apparently caused by "outdated tetracycline." N Engl J Med 272:9865, 1965
139. Wegienka LC, Weller JM: Renal tubular acidosis caused by degraded tetracycline. Arch Intern Med 114:232, 1964
140. Sebastian A, McSherry, Ueka E, et al: Renal amyloidosis, nephrotic syndrome and impaired renal tubular reabsorption of bicarbonate. Ann Intern Med 69:541, 1968
141. Stickler GB, Rosevear JW, Ulrich JA: Renal tubular dysfunction complicating the nephrotic syndrome: The disturbance in calcium and phosphorus metabolism. Mayo Clinic Proc 37:376, 1962
142. Stanbury SW, Macaulay D: Defects of renal tubular function in the nephrotic syndrome. QJ Med 26:7, 1957
143. Maldonado JE, Velosa JH, Kyle RA, et al: Fanconi syndrome in adults. A manifestation of a latent form of myeloma. Am J Med 58:354, 1975
144. Muldowney FP, Freaney R, & McGeeney D: Renal tubular acidosis and amino-aciduria in osteomalacia of dietary or intestinal origin. QJ Med 38:517, 1968
145. Rodriguez-Soriano J, Boichis H, Stark H, et al: Proximal renal tubular acidosis. A defect in bicarbonate reabsorption with normal urinary acidification. Pediatr Res 1:81, 1967
146. Winsnes A, Monn E, Stokke O, et al: Congenital persistent proximal type renal tubular acidosis in two brothers. Acta Paediatr Scand 68:861, 1979
147. Wilson DR, Siddiqui AA: Renal tubular acidosis after kidney transplantation. Ann Int Med 79:352, 1973
148. Wolff JA, Strom C, Griswold W, et al: Proximal renal tubular acidosis in methylmalonic acidemia. J Neurogenet 2:31, 1985
149. Marver D, Kokko JP: Renal target sites and the mechanism of action of aldosterone. Miner Electrolyte Metab 9:1, 1983
150. Schambelan M, Sebastian A, Hutter HA: Adrenal cortical excess and deficiency syndrome. p 232. In Brenner BM & Stein JH (eds): Acid-Base and Potassium Homeostasis. Churchill Livingstone, New York, 1978
151. Sebastian A, Schambelan M, Lindenfeld S, Morris RC Jr: Amelioration of metabolic acidosis with fludrocortisone therapy in hyporeninemic hypoaldosteronism. N Engl J Med 297:576, 1977
152. Sebastian A, Schambelan M, Sutton JM; Amelioration of hyperchloremic acidosis with furosemide therapy in patients with chronic renal insufficiency and type 4 renal tubular acidosis. Am J Nephrol 4:287, 1984
153. Phillips RA: Water and electrolyte losses in cholera. Fed Proc 23:705, 1964
154. Teree TM, Mirabel-Font E, Ortiz A, Wallace WM: Stool losses and acidosis in diarrheal diseases of infancy. Pediatrics 36:704, 1965
155. Phillips SF, Sumerskill WHJ: Water and electrolytes in gastrointestinal disease. p. 897. In Maxwell MH, Kleeman CR (eds): Clinical Disorders of Fluid and Electrolyte Metabolism. 2nd Ed. McGraw-Hill, New York, 1972
156. Kleinman PK: Cholestyramine and metabolic acidosis (Letter). N Engl J Med 290:861, 1974
157. Garella S, Chang BS, Kahn SI: Dilution acidosis and concentration alkalosis: review of a concept. Kidney Int 8:279, 1975
158. Relman AS, Shelburne PF, Talman A: Profound acidosis resulting from excessive ammonium chloride in previously healthy subjects. N Engl J Med 264:848, 1961
159. Heird WC, Bell RB, Driscoll RB Jr: Metabolic acidosis resulting from intravenous alimentation mixtures containing synthetic amino acids. N Engl J Med 287:943, 1972
160. Felig P: Diabetic ketoacidosis. N Engl J Med 290:1360, 1974

161. King AJ, Cooke NJ, McCuish A: Acid-base changes during treatment of diabetic ketoacidosis. Lancet 1:478, 1974
162. Adrogue HJ, Wilson H, Boyd AE, et al: Plasma acid-base patterns in diabetic ketoacidosis. N Engl J Med 307:1603, 1982
163. Fulop M, Hoberman HD: Alcoholic ketosis. Diabetes 24:785, 1975
164. Fulop M, Hoberman HD, Rascoff JH, et al: Lactic acidosis in diabetic patients. Arch Intern Med 136:987, 1976
165. Conlay LA, Loewenstein JE: Phenformin and lactic acidosis. JAMA 235:1575, 1976
166. Field M, Block MB, Levin R, Rall DP: Significance of blood lactate elevations among patients with acute leukemic and other neoplastic proliferative disorders. Am J Med 40:528, 1966
167. Huckabee WE: Abnormal resting blood lactate. I. The significance of hyperlactatemia in hospitalized patients. II. Lactic acidosis. Am J Med 30:833, 1961
168. McMartin KE, Ambre JJ, Tephly TR: Methanol poisoning in human subjects. Role of formic acid accumulation in the metabolic acidosis. Am J Med 68:414, 1980
169. Peterson CD, Collins AJ, Himes JM, et al: Ethylene glycol poisoning: In pharmacokinetics during therapy with ethanol and hemodialysis. N Engl J Med 304:21, 1981
170. Parry MF, Wallach R: Ethylene glycol poisoning. Am J Med 57:143, 1974
171. Gutman RA, Burnell JM: Paraldehyde acidosis. Am J Med 42:435, 1967
172. Hadden JW, Metzner RJ: Pseudoketosis and hyeracetaldehydemia in paraldehyde acidosis. Am J Med 47:642, 1969
173. Temple AR: Acute and chronic effects of aspirin toxicity and their treatment. Arch Intern Med 141:364, 1981
174. Snodgrass WR: Salicylate toxicity. Pediatr Clin North Am 33:381, 1983
175. Matsui SM, Mahoney MJ, Rosenberg LE: The natural history of the inherited methylmalonic acidemias. N Engl J Med 308:854, 1983
176. Childs B, Nyhan WL, Borden M: Idiopathic hyperglycemia and hyperglycinuria: New disorder of amino acid metabolism. I. Pediatrics 27:522, 1961
177. Rosenberg LE: Disorders of propionate, methylmalonate and vitamin B_{12} metabolism. p 474. In Stanbury JB, Wyngaarden JB, Fredrickson DS, et al (eds): The Metabolic Basis of Inherited Disease. McGraw-Hill, New York, 1983
178. Lemann J, Jr, Relman AS: The relation of sulfur metabolism to acid-base balance and electrolyte excretion: The effects of D,L-methionine in normal man. J Clin Invest 38:12, 1959
179. Lemann J Jr, Litzow JR, Lennon EJ: The effects of chronic acid loads in normal man: further evidence for the participation of bone mineral in the defense against chronic metabolic acidosis. J Clin Invest 45:1608, 1966
180. Singer RB, Clark JK, Barker ES, et al: The acute effects in man of intravenous infusion of hypertonic sodium bicarbonate solution. I. Changes in Acid-Base balance and distribution of the excess buffer base. Medicine 34:51, 1955
181. van Goidsenhoven GMT, Gray OV, Price AV, et al: The effect of prolonged administration of large doses of sodium bicarbonate in man. Clin Sci 13:383, 1954
182. Galla JH, Bonduris DN, Luke RG: Effects of chloride and extracellular fluid volume on bicarbonate reabsorption along the nephron in metabolic alkalosis. Reassessment of the classical hypothesis of the pathogenesis of metabolic alkalosis. J Clin Invest 80:41, 1987
183. Jaeger P, Karlmark B, Giebisch G: Ammonium transport in rat cortical tubule. Relationship to potassium metabolism. Am J Physiol 245:F593, 1983
184. Husted FC, Nolph KD, Maher JF: $NaHCO_3$ and NaCl tolerance in chronic renal failure. J Clin Invest 56:414, 1975
185. Bieberdorf FA, Gorden P, Fordtran JS: Pathogenesis of congenital alkalosis with diarrhea. Implications for the physiology of normal ileal electrolyte absorption and secretion. J Clin Invest 51:1958, 1972
186. Swan RC, Axelrod DR, Seip M, et al: Distribution of sodium bicarbonate infused into nephrectomized dogs. J Clin Invest 34:1795, 1955
187. Kassirer JP, Schwartz WB: The response of normal man to selective depletion of hydrochloric acid: Factors in the genesis of persistent gastric alkalosis. Am J Med 40:10, 1966

188. Eisenberg HL, Kolb LH, Yam LT, et al: Villous adenoma of the rectum associated with electrolyte disturbance. Ann Surg 159:604, 1964
189. Babior BM: Villous adenoma of the colon. Am J Med 41:615, 1966
190. Darrow DC: Congenital alkalosis with diarrhea. J Pediatr 26:519, 1945
191. Gamble JL, Fahey KR, Appleton J, et al: Congenital alkalosis with diarrhea. J Pediatr 26:509, 1945
192. Cannon PJ, Heinemann HO, Alber MS, et al: "Contraction" alkalosis after diuresis of edematous patients with ethacrynic acid. Ann Intern Med 62:979, 1965
193. Kassirer JP, London AM, Goldman DM, et al: On the pathogenesis of metabolic alkalosis in hyperaldosteronism. Am J Med 49:306, 1970
194. Bartter FC, Pronove P, Gill JR Jr, et al: Hyperplasia of the juxtaglomerular complex with hyperaldosteronism and hypokalemic alkalosis. A new syndrome. Am J Med 33:306, 1970
195. Cannon PJ, Leeming JM, Sommers SC, et al: Juxtaglomerular cell hyperplasia and secondary hyperaldosteronism (Bartter's syndrome): a re-evaluation of the pathophysiology. Medicine 47:107, 1968
196. White, MG: Bartter's syndrome: a manifestation of renal tubular defects. Arch Intern Med 129:41, 1972
197. Fichman MP, Telfer N, Zia P, et al: Role of prostaglandins in the pathogenesis of Bartter's syndrome. Am J Med 60:785, 1976
198. Gill JR, Jr, Frolich JC, Bowden RE, et al: Bartter's Syndrome: A disorder characterized by high urinary prostaglandins and a dependence of hyperreninemia on prostaglandin synthesis. Am J Med 61:43, 1976
199. Westerfelder C, & Kurtzman NA: Bartter's syndrome: a disorder of active sodium and/or passive chloride transport in the thick ascending limb of Henle's loop. Miner Electrolyte Metab 5:135, 1981
200. Gottlieb RP: Metabolic alkalosis in cystic fibrosis. J Pediatr 79:930, 1971
201. Laidlow JC, Yendt ER, Fornall AG: Hypertension caused by renal artery occlusion simulating primary aldosteronism. Metabolism 9:612, 1960
202. Laragh H, Ulick H, Januszewicz S, et al: Aldosterone secretion and primary malignant hypertension. J Clin Invest 39:1091, 1960
203. Conn JW, Cohen EL, Lucas CP, et al: Primary reninism. Hypertension, hyperreninemia, and secondary aldosteronism due to renin-producing juxtaglomerular cell tumors. Arch Intern Med 130:682, 1972
204. Biglieri ES, Stockigt JR, Schambelan M: Adrenal mineralocorticoids causing hypertension. Am J Med 52:623, 1972
205. Goldsmith O, Solomon DH, Horton R: Hypogonadism and mineralocorticoid excess: The 17-hydroxylase deficiency syndrome. N Engl J Med 277:673, 1967
206. Conn JW, Roune DR, Cohen EL: Licorice-induced pseudoaldosteronism JAMA 205:492, 1968
207. Davies GJ, Rhodes J, & Calcraft BJ: Complications of carbenoxolone therapy. Br Med J 3:400, 1974
208. Blachley JD, Knochel JP: Tobacco chewer's hypokalemia: licorice revisited. N Engl J Med 320:784, 1980
209. Funder JW, Adam WR, Mantero F, et al: The etiology of a syndrome of factitious mineralocorticoid excess: a steroid-containing nasal spray. J Clin Endocrinol Metab 49:842, 1979
210. Liddle GW, Bledsoe T, Coppage WS: A familial renal disorder simulating primary aldosteronism but with negligible aldosterone secretion. Trans Assoc Am Physicians 76:199, 1963
211. Orwell, ES: The milk-alkali syndrome: Current concepts. Ann Intern Med 91:242, 1982
212. Seldin DW, Tarail R: The metabolism of glucose and electrolytes in diabetic acidosis. J Clin Invest 29:552, 1950
213. Litwin M, Smith L, Moore FD: Metabolic alkalosis following massive transfusion. Surgery 45:805, 1959
214. Mattar JA, Weil MH, Shubin H, et al: Cardiac arrest in the critically ill. II. Hyperosmolal states following cardiac arrest. Am J Med 56:162, 1974
215. Veverbrants E, Arky RA: Effects of fasting and refeeding. I. Studies on sodium, potassium and water excretion on a constant electrolyte intake. J Clin Endocrinol 29:55, 1969

216. Stinebaugh BJ, Schloeder FX: Glucose-induced alkalosis in fasting subjects: relationship to renal bicarbonate reabsorption during fasting and refeeding. J Clin Invest 51:1326, 1972
217. Refsum HE: Hypokalemic alkalosis with paradoxical aciduria during artificial ventilation of patients with pulmonary insufficiency and high plasma bicarbonate concentration. Scand J Clin Invest 13:481, 1961
218. Schwartz WB, Hays RM, Polak A, et al: Effects of chronic hypercapnia on electrolyte and acid–base equilibrium. II. Recovery, with special reference to the influence of chloride intake. J Clin Invest 40:1238, 1961
219. Giebisch G, Berger L, Pitts RF: The extrarenal response to acute acid–base disburbances of respiratory origin. J Clin Invest 34:231, 1955
220. Schwartz GJ, Al-Awqati Q: Carbon dioxide causes exocytosis of vesicles containing H^+ pumps in isolated perfused proximal and collecting tubules. J Clin Invest 75:1638, 1985
221. Carter NW, Seldin DW, Teng HC: Tissue and renal response to chronic respiratory acidosis. J Clin Invest 38:949, 1959
222. Schwartz WB, Brackett NC, Jr, Cohen JJ: The response of extracellular hydrogen ion concentration to graded degrees of chronic hypercapnia: The physiologic limits of the defense of pH. J Clin Invest 44:291, 1965
223. Kilburn K: Neurologic manifestations of respiratory failure. Arch Intern Med 116:409, 1965
224. Hodgkin JE, Balchum OJ, Kass I, et al: Chronic obstructive airway diseases. Current concepts in diagnosis and comprehensive care. JAMA 232:1243, 1975
225. Brackett NC, Jr, Cohen JJ, Schwartz WB: Carbon dioxide titration curve of normal man: Effect of increasing degrees of acute hypercapnia on acid-base equilibrium. N Engl J Med 272:6, 1965
226. Zwillich CW, Sutton FD, Pierson DJ, et al: Decreased hypoxic ventilatory drive in the obesity-hypoventilation syndrome. Am J Med 59:343, 1975
227. Sutton FD, Jr, Zwillich CW, Creagh E, et al: Progesterone for outpatient treatment of Pickwickian syndrome. Ann Intern Med 83:476, 1975
228. Fishman AP, Goldring RM, Turino GM: General alveolar hypoventilation: A syndrome of respiratory and cardiac failure in patients with normal lungs. QJ Med 35:261, 1966
229. Fishman A, Turino GM, Bergofsky EH: The syndrome of alveolar hypoventilation associated with obesity. Am J Med 44:881, 1968
230. Arbus GS, Herbert LA, Levesque PR, et al: Characterization and clinical application of the "significance band" for acute respiratory alkalosis. N Engl J Med 280:117, 1969
231. Gledhill N, Beirne GJ, Dempsey JA: Renal response to short-term hypocapnia in man. Kidney Int 8:376, 1975
232. Gennari JF, Goldstein MB, Schwartz WB: The nature of the renal adaptation to chronic hypocapnia. J Clin Invest 51:1722, 1972
233. Gougoux A, Kaehny WD, Cohen JJ: Renal adaptation tc chronic hypocapnia: dietary constraints in achieving H^+ retention. Am J Physiol 229:1330, 1975
234. Trimble C, Smith DF, Rosenthal MH, et al: Pathophysiologic role of hypocarbia in post-traumatic pulmonary insufficiency. Am J Surg 122:633, 1971
235. Weiner MW, Epstein FH: Signs and symptoms of electrolyte disorders. p 629. In Maxwell MH, Kleeman CR (eds): Clinical Disorders of Fluid and Electrolyte Metabolism. 2nd Ed. McGraw-Hill, New York, 1972
236. Rice RL: Symptom patterns of the hyperventilation syndrome. Am J Med 8:691, 1950
237. Saltzman HA, Heyman A, Sicker HO: Correlation of clinical and physiological manifestations of sustained hyperventilation. N Engl J Med 268:1431, 1963
238. Edmondson JW, Brashear RE, Li TK, et al: Quantitative interrelationships between calcium and alkalosis. Am J Physiol 228:1082, 1975
239. Kilburn KH: Shock, seizures, and coma with alkalosis during mechanical ventilation. Ann Intern Med 65:977, 1966
240. Wasserman AJ, Patterson JL Jr: The cer-

ebral vascular response to reduction in arterial carbon dioxide tension. J Clin Invest 40:1297, 1961
241. Evan DW, Lum LC: Hyperventilation: an important cause of pseudoangina. Lancet 1:155, 1977
242. Lary D, Goldschlager N: Electrocardiographic changes during hyperventilation with normal coronary arteriograms. Am Heart J 87:383, 1979
243. Eldridge F, Salzer J: Effect of respiratory alkalosis on blood lactate and pyruvate in humans. J Appl Physiol 22:461, 1967
244. Gennari FJ, Goldstein MB, Schwartz WB: The nature of the renal adaptation to chronic hypocapnia. J Clin Invest 51:1722, 1972
245. Mulhausen R, Eichenholz A, Blumentals A: Acid-base disturbances in patients with cirrhosis of the liver. Medicine (Baltimore) 46:185, 1967
246. Kornbluth RS, Turino GM: Respiratory control in diffuse interstitial lung disease and diseases of the pulmonary vasculature. Clin Chest Med 1:91, 1980
247. Madias NE, Cohen JJ: Determinants of arterial carbon dioxide tension and carbon dioxide balance. p 307. In Cohen JJ, Kassirer JP (eds): Acid-Base. Little, Brown, Boston, 1982
248. Cohen JJ, Kassirer JP: Mixed acid-base disturbances. p 226. In Maxwell MH, Kleeman CR (eds): Clinical Disorders of Fluid and Electrolyte Metabolism. 3rd Ed. McGraw-Hill, New York, 1980
249. Stacpoole PW, Harman EM, Curry SH, et al: Treatment of lactic acidosis with dichloroacetate. N Engl J Med 309:390, 1983
250. Garella S, Dana CL, Chazan JA: Severity of metabolic acidosis as a determinant of bicarbonate requirement. N Engl J Med 289:121, 1973
251. Bushinsky DA, Gennari FJ: Life threatening hyperkalemia induced by arginine: Ann Intern Med 89:632, 1978
252. Knutsen OH: New method for administration of hydrochloric acid in metabolic alkalosis. Lancet 8331:953, 1983
253. Williams DB, Lyons JH Jr: Treatment of severe metabolic alkalosis with intravenous infusion of hydrochloric acid. Surg Gynecol Obstet 150:315, 1980
254. Swartz RO, Rubin JE, Brown RS, et al: Correction of postoperative metabolic alkalosis and renal failure by hemodialysis. Ann Intern Med 86:52, 1977

2

Disorders of Sodium Metabolism

H. John Reineck
Jay H. Stein

The vast majority of osmotically active solutes in the extracellular fluid (ECF) space are sodium salts. Given this consideration and the fact that sodium salts are primarily confined to the ECF, it follows that total body sodium is the most important determinant of ECF volume. In mammals, maintenance of a normal total body sodium depends on the kidneys' ability to excrete or conserve dietary sodium. If renal sodium excretion is impaired, total body sodium increases, and as a result, fluid from the intracellular fluid space is osmotically drawn into the ECF. In addition, thirst mechanisms are activated and antidiuretic hormone (ADH) release is stimulated, resulting respectively in increased water intake and renal water conservation. The net effect of these phenomena is excessive water accumulation within the ECF space, and edema. When renal sodium conservation is impaired, no effect on ECF volume will occur unless the renal losses exceed dietary intake. If this occurs, or if nonrenal losses exceed dietary sodium intake, a diminution in total body sodium results, and the ECF volume is diminished. Thus, disorders of sodium metabolism manifest themselves as disorders in ECF volume homeostasis (i.e., edematous states and volume depletion). It should be stressed that both of these disorders may be accompanied by abnormalities in the serum sodium concentration. Such disorders of tonicity are the result of impaired water metabolism; these states are discussed in Chapter 3 of this volume.

EDEMATOUS STATES

Edema may be defined as the abnormal accumulation of fluid within the interstitial space. Such an accumulation results from alterations of the normal Starling forces across the peripheral capillary walls. Under normal circumstances the mean capillary hydrostatic and oncotic pressure gradients along the length of the capillary are in equilibrium, and therefore no net movement of fluid occurs across the capillary wall. In edematous states this equilibrium is upset, so that the mean intracapillary oncotic pressure is no longer sufficient to prevent the transcapillary movement of fluid due to the hydrostatic pressure gradient between the intravascular and interstitial spaces. Although anatomically limited alterations in Starling forces may occur in localized areas, as occurs in venous or lymphatic obstruction or angioneurotic edema, this chapter deals only with disorders associated with generalized edema—conditions that share a single common pathogenetic mechanism, renal sodium retention.

Before discussing the clinical entities associated with generalized edema, it is first appropriate to discuss briefly a somewhat nebulous but conceptually important term: *effective circulating blood volume*. Assuming that the kidney's regulation of sodium balance is at least teleologically designed to maintain plasma volume (rather than total ECF volume) and thereby assure adequate tissue perfusion, one must view the "effective" plasma volume as the relationship between vascular capacity and absolute volume. Peters suggested considering this relationship as the "fullness" of the circulation.[1] This concept is perhaps best illustrated by several clinical and experimental conditions. Opening an arteriovenous fistula results in avid renal sodium retention despite the fact that absolute plasma volume is entirely normal at the time the fistula is opened.[2] Similarly, standing up, which results in "pooling" of blood but no absolute change in volume, also results in increased renal sodium reabsorption.[3] On the other hand, exposure to cold[4] or immersion in water to the neck[5] increase the effective circulating blood volume and are associated with decreased renal sodium reabsorption. It is thus clear that despite its unmeasurable nature, alterations in the effective circulating blood volume may provide the afferent signal for the salt retention that leads to edema formation.

CIRRHOSIS OF THE LIVER

Edema and ascites constitute major clinical findings in patients with advanced liver disease. By convention, these findings classify such patients as having "decompensated" cirrhosis. Although the literature abounds in the terms "compensated" and "decompensated," this classification is merely descriptive and fails to define the presence or absence of altered renal sodium handling in this disorder. In 1952, Papper and Rosenbaum described excessive renal sodium retention in patients with cirrhosis who were free of edema and ascites and who were given a high sodium diet.[6] Thus, the use of these terms fails to further our understanding of the pathogenesis of edema formation in hepatic cirrhosis.

Afferent Limb

Pathogenesis of Ascites Formation and Its Relationship to Renal Sodium Retention

In discussing the afferent limb (i.e., the manner in which the kidney perceives a decrease in effective circulating blood volume), it is necessary to address the relationship between ascites formation and renal sodium retention. As will be apparent, this relationship is central to our understanding of the pathophysiology of salt retention, and has profound implications for a rational therapeutic approach to the treatment of this disorder.

Most authorities now agree that the most basic pathophysiologic abnormality associated with ascites formation is obstruction to hepatic venous outflow. Beyond this most fundamental understanding and despite several decades of extensive research, controversy continues to surround our knowledge of the mechanism of ascites formation and its relationship to renal sodium retention.[7] Figure 2-1A schematically summarizes the "traditional" theory of ascites accumulation. As hepatic parenchyma is progressively destroyed and replaced by fibrous scar, venous outflow becomes impaired and sinusoidal pressure increases. This process results in the transudation of hepatic lymph into the peritoneal cavity. As portal hypertension develops, large collateral venous complexes form and "sequester" a large portion of the vascular blood volume within the splanchnic circulation. In

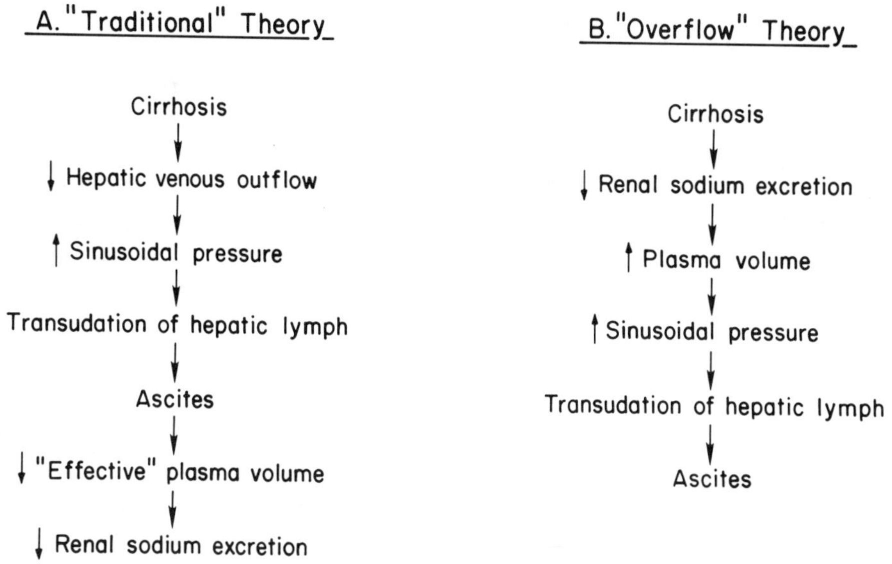

A. "Traditional" Theory

Cirrhosis
↓
↓ Hepatic venous outflow
↓
↑ Sinusoidal pressure
↓
Transudation of hepatic lymph
↓
Ascites
↓
↓ "Effective" plasma volume
↓
↓ Renal sodium excretion

B. "Overflow" Theory

Cirrhosis
↓
↓ Renal sodium excretion
↓
↑ Plasma volume
↓
↑ Sinusoidal pressure
↓
Transudation of hepatic lymph
↓
Ascites

Fig. 2-1. Comparison of the 'traditional' and 'overflow' theories of ascites formation in hepatic cirrhosis. (From Levinsky,[7] by permission.)

addition, this portal hypertension results in fluid transudation from splanchnic capillaries and further accumulation of ascitic fluid. These events then lead to a decrease in the "effective" (nonsplanchnic) plasma volume, with renal salt retention as the consequence. According to the proponents of this theory, the finding of a normal or increased plasma volume in cirrhosis[8] is explicable by the sequestration of a large portion of the plasma volume in the dilated venous plexus of the splanchnic bed.

Several observations tend to support this theory. First, expansion of the intravascular compartment by saline[9] or dextran[10] administration to cirrhotic patients results in a significant increase in urinary sodium excretion. Second, the intravenous infusion of ascitic fluid has been shown to elicit a natriuresis in patients with cirrhosis.[11] These observations, while suggestive of a decrease in effective blood volume, must be interpreted with some caution because of constitutional changes in the plasma (e.g., decreases in hematocrit and oncotic pressure) and possible increases in arterial pressure that result from these "exogenous" infusions. To circumvent these problems, Epstein and colleagues have applied the head-out water immersion technique to the study of sodium handling in cirrhosis.[12] Figure 2-2 illustrates the effect of this maneuver on urinary sodium excretion in 16 patients with "decompensated" cirrhosis. As can be seen, half of these individuals responded with a natriuresis that was quantitatively similar to or greater than that observed in normal controls. Additional circumstantial evidence supporting the traditional view of ascites formation is obtained by observations relating to the renin-angiotensin system in this disorder. Most investigators have reported that plasma renin activity is elevated in patients with "decompensated" cirrhosis.[13-15] If this parameter accurately reflects the status of the effective circulating blood volume, these findings suggest that this factor is indeed decreased. Furthermore, Schroeder and co-workers reported that when the angiotensin II antagonist saralasin is administered to salt-replete, decompensated cirrhotic pa-

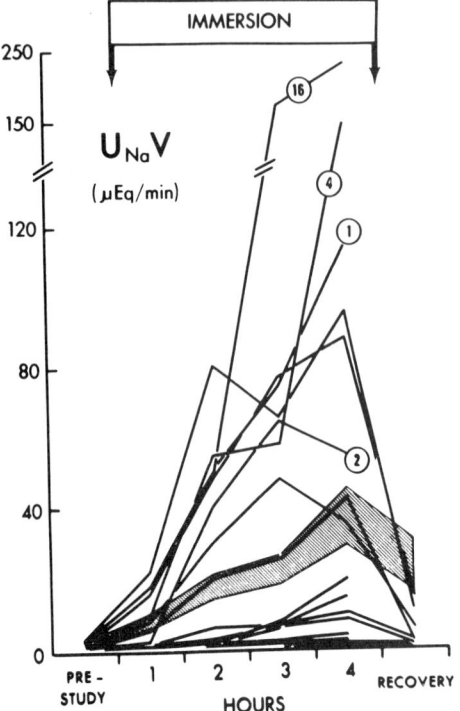

Fig. 2-2 Effect of head-out water immersion on urinary sodium excretion in 16 patients with cirrhosis and ascites. Shaded area represents values observed in normal individuals. (From Epstein,[12] by permission.)

tients, a significant fall occurred in the mean arterial pressure.[16] These results are in sharp contrast to those seen in salt-replete normal individuals, but are similar to those obtained in salt-depleted normal subjects.[17] Finally, the results of the continuous systemic infusion of ascitic fluid via a peritoneovenous (LeVeen) shunt deserves comment. Several groups have reported that this produces a resolution of ascites and at least short term improvement in renal sodium retention.[18,19] On the other hand, a recent study by Greig and colleagues found that six of seven patients in whom this device functioned for 5 to 29 months demonstrated significant salt retention when challenged with a 100 mEq/day sodium diet.[19a] This study therefore raises serious problems for proponents of the traditional theory.

The alternative to this theory of ascites formation, the "overflow" theory, is schematically summarized in Figure 2-1B. According to this view, renal sodium reabsorption is stimulated by some mechanisms that are yet unclear. The result is expansion of the ECF volume which, in the presence of increased hepatic sinusoidal pressure, results in transudation of hepatic lymph and ascites formation. In a setting of portal hypertension, this expansion further engorges the splanchnic vasculature, which also contributes to ascites accumulation.

The initial evidence favoring this theory was reported by Lieberman and Reynolds and co-workers over a decade ago.[8,20,21] As noted earlier, these investigators found that the total plasma volume was increased rather than decreased in cirrhotic patients with ascites and edema. Later, utilizing indirect techniques, they found that the nonsplanchnic vascular volume was also increased in this setting. Among observations by these investigators which supported the overflow theory were that: (1) when "compensated" cirrhotic patients were given a salt retaining mineralocorticoid hormone, they failed to "escape," and ascites and edema formed; (2) when paracentesis was performed, the rate of reaccumulation of ascites was not accelerated and the plasma volume did not contract; (3) during spontaneous resolution of ascites, no change in plasma volume could be detected.

Although these observations are clearly supportive of the overflow theory, the conclusions were, by necessity, indirectly derived. More recently Levy, studying a unique model of cirrhosis in dogs, has marshalled more direct evidence favoring this postulate.[22,23] This model, first described by Manning, is created by the ingestion of dimethylnitrosamine, which results in histologic evidence of portal cirrhosis, portal hypertension, and hepatic insufficiency within two months.[24] Figure 2-3 demon-

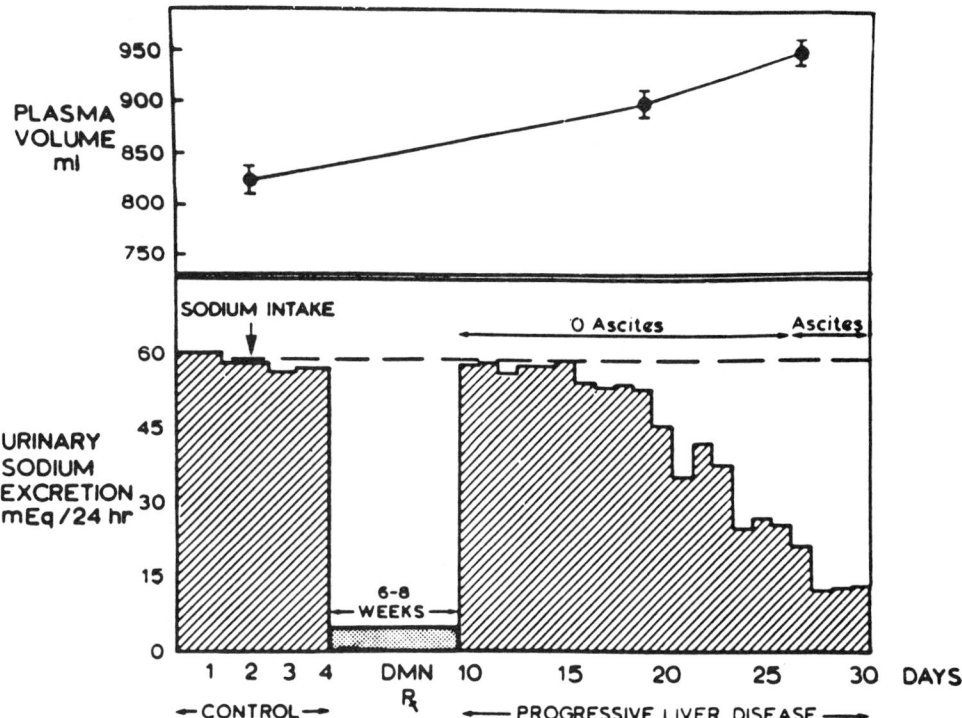

Fig. 2-3. Relationship between ascites formation, plasma volume and sodium balance in dogs with dimethylnitrosamine-induced (DMN) hepatic cirrhosis. (From Levy,[22] by permission.)

strates Levy's finding that renal sodium retention clearly antedated the formation of ascites in these animals.[22] Further, the increase in plasma volume preceded ascites formation and, though not shown in Figure 2-3, nonsplanchnic plasma volume was also increased prior to the formation of ascites. In this same study the author demonstrated that following the partial removal of ascitic fluid, the reaccumulation of ascites was paralleled by renal salt retention, and that when dietary sodium was withheld, the plasma volume remained stable and the reaccumulation of ascites was prevented. Recent studies in the rat, employing another chemical model of cirrhosis, have confirmed these findings.[25] Levy and Wexler directly evaluated the possible role of the splanchnic sequestration of plasma in the formation of ascites.[24] In this study they prevented the development of portal hypertension by end-to-side portacaval shunting prior to the induction of cirrhosis. As in animals without this procedure, renal sodium retention occurred and preceded the formation of ascites.

Obviously a considerable body of evidence has accumulated in favor of both the tradition and overflow theories of ascites formation and its relationship to renal sodium retention. In considering these respective postulates, two additional observations deserve consideration. First, Shear and co-workers, studying patients with cirrhosis, edema, and ascites, observed significant reaccumulation of ascites following paracentesis.[26] Levy has noted that the difference between these patients and his experimental model may lie in the presence of peripheral edema in the former.[22] Indeed, Shear and co-workers observed that in the presence of peripheral edema, ascites accumulated more readily than in its absence.[26] Nonetheless, ascites reaccumulation did occur in the latter setting. A second observation that must be considered is the all-too-frequent occurrence of electrolyte imbalance, hypotension, oliguria, and occasionally, irreversible renal failure after over-aggressive paracentesis.[27–29]

Neither of these observations, however, necessarily rules out the conclusions drawn by Levy. It is possible that early in the course of liver disease, renal sodium retention occurs independent of ascites formation. Once severe liver damage and ascites are present, however, some equilibrium of Starling's forces between the hepatic sinusoids and the peritoneal cavity must be established. Under these circumstances rapid removal of ascitic fluid would result in a sudden disequilibrium, and those forces favoring ascites reaccumulation would be expected to predominate.

Cardiac and Systemic Hemodynamic Considerations

If the overflow theory of ascites formation is indeed correct, what other factors might provide the afferent signal that induces the avid renal retention of sodium? This issue remains an enigma. Numerous investigators have reported that cardiac output is typically elevated in patients with cirrhosis,[30–32] and on this basis some have exonerated the heart as a cause for the renal salt retention. Tristani and Cohn, however, found that an increase in cardiac output is not a universal finding, and that this parameter is, in fact, reduced in some patients.[10] In a series of intriguing experiments, Cohn and colleagues have examined cardiac function and systemic hemodynamics in patients with cirrhosis. They found that when the low systemic peripheral resistance was elevated to normal levels by the intravenous administration of angiotensin, pulmonary wedge pressures rose significantly, indicating a degree of left ventricular dysfunction.[33] Further, Knauer and Lowe have demonstrated that tense ascites may diminish venous return, and thus decrease right atrial pressure and cardiac output.[34] Additionally, Cohn has observed that in patients with liver disease and very high cardiac outputs, portasystemic shunts may function as arteriovenous fistulas. Indicator dilution techniques also suggest that in active liver disease, significant arteriovenous shunting occurs within the hepatic vasculature.[35] Dal Palu and colleagues have shown that significant arteriovenous shunting occurs in the skin and lungs as well.[36]

Although these alterations in cardiac function and systemic hemodynamics provide some insight into the pathophysiology of salt retention in cirrhosis, they still do not fully explain the afferent limb of this abnormality. As will be seen later in this chapter, the mechanisms of salt retention in the presence of heart failure and arteriovenous shunts are also poorly understood. Further, it should be pointed out that these circulatory abnormalities cannot fully explain the avid salt retention in all cases of liver disease. In his animal model of cirrhosis, Levy has clearly demonstrated that increased renal sodium reabsorption precedes any alterations in cardiac output, peripheral resistance, central venous pressure, or renal blood flow.[22,37] Nonetheless, it is possible, and in fact quite likely, that these abnormalities contribute to sodium retention at some later stage in the evolution of cirrhotic liver disease.

Efferent Limb

Regardless of the nature of the afferent limb of sodium retention in cirrhosis of the liver, the efferent component (i.e., the mechanism by which the kidney retains sodium) is also of obvious interest and importance. Theoretically, either a fall in the glomerular filtration rate (GFR) or enhanced tubular reabsorption of sodium could account for the sodium retention. Although many patients with chronic liver disease may manifest a compromise in GFR, the bulk of evidence indicates that the most important abnormality is an increase in tubular reabsorption.[38]

Nephron Site Responsible for Salt Retention

Clearance studies in humans with cirrhosis have suggested an increase in proximal tubular sodium reabsorption.[39,40] Two additional studies in man also implicate enhanced distal reabsorption of sodium.[41,42]

Micropuncture studies in experimental models of liver disease are equivocal. Several groups of investigators have applied this technique in evaluating proximal tubular reabsorption in animals with thoracic inferior vena cava constriction, a model in which hepatic venous congestion occurs and results in ascites and edema formation. Studying chronic thoracic inferior vena cava constriction, Auld, Alexander, and Levinsky found no evidence of enhanced proximal reabsorption.[43] Levy also concluded that the distal nephron was the primary site of salt retention in this model.[44] Cirksena, Dirks, and Berliner, however, reported enhanced proximal reabsorption after an acute saline load in these animals.[45] Investigators performing micropuncture studies in animals with chronic bile duct ligation have also found increased proximal sodium reabsorption.[46,47] Finally, two studies have examined proximal tubular reabsorption in models of chemically induced cirrhosis. Examining his dog model during avid salt retention, Levy reported normal proximal reabsorption of sodium.[48] Lopez-Novoa and colleagues performed micropuncture studies on rats with carbon tetrachloride-induced cirrhosis in the presence of ascites.[49] They reported a marked increase in proximal reabsorption. The reason for the varying results in these studies is not clear. It seems likely, however, that differences in cardiac function and in systemic and renal hemodynamics exist between the various models. Furthermore, differences in these variables may exist on the basis of duration of salt retention, severity of liver congestion, and possibly dietary sodium intake. In any event, a reasonable conclusion might be that enhanced proximal and distal sodium reabsorption probably occurs at some time during the natural history of cirrhosis.

Mechanisms of Renal Salt Retention

A variety of factors have been invoked to explain the avid tubular reabsorption of sodium in cirrhosis. These potential mechanisms are listed in Table 2-1.

Renal Hemodynamics in Cirrhosis

Total renal blood flow (RBF) varies in patients with cirrhosis. In general, patients with compensated cirrhosis are noted to have normal rates of renal perfusion. As liver disease worsens, however, lower rates of RBF tend to be observed, and with the so-called "hepatorenal syndrome," marked reductions in RBF occur.[50] Since RBF is decreased even in the presence of normal systemic arterial pressure, renal vasocon-

Table 2-1. Proposed Mechanisms of Sodium Retention in Cirrhosis

Renal hemodynamic alterations
   Renal vasoconstriction
   Redistribution of renal blood flow
Renal nerve stimulation
Aldosterone
Non-aldosterone humoral factors
   "Natriuretic" factor
   Decreased estrogen synthesis
   Decreased prostaglandin synthesis
   Decreased kallikrein-kinin activity

striction is apparently present. Further, it is of interest that this renal vasoconstriction occurs in the presence of systemic (nonrenal) vasodilation, indicating that the hemodynamic change is unique to the renal vasculature.[10,51]

The mechanism responsible for the renal vasoconstriction in cirrhosis is poorly understood. As was noted earlier in this chapter, most investigators have reported that plasma renin activity is increased in cirrhosis.[13-15] In addition, Saruta and co-workers have documented that circulating angiotensin II levels are also elevated in cirrhosis, despite a decrease in renin substrate.[52] It therefore seems reasonable to suspect that the renin-angiotensin system may be at least partially responsible for the renal vasoconstriction in this setting. Experimental data confirming this suspicion are, however, difficult to obtain. As mentioned earlier, pharmacologic inhibition of angiotensin II with saralasin results in systemic hypotension in cirrhotic patients, and as a result, the nature of any changes in RBF in specific response to this agent cannot be identified.[16] Studies in dogs with thoracic inferior vena cava constriction have had conflicting results. Freeman and colleagues[53] and Taub and co-workers[54] reported that competitive antagonists of angiotensin II increased RBF in this model. Studies by Slick, DiBona, and Kaloyanides failed to observe this effect, however.[55] In a recent review, Hollenberg concluded that these conflicting results derived from methodologic and pharmacologic differences, and that intrarenal angiotensin II does at least partially mediate the renal vasoconstriction in this model.[56]

Enhanced renal adrenergic nerve activity has also been implicated as a cause of the decreased RBF in cirrhosis. Epstein and co-workers reported that the intrarenal administration of the alpha adrenergic blocking agent phentolamine failed to increase RBF in cirrhotic patients.[57] In that study, however, a decrease in systemic blood pressure may have masked the potential for this maneuver to increase renal perfusion. Indeed, Baldus reported that when albumin is administered simultaneously with another α-adrenergic antagonist, phenoxybenzamine, thereby preventing systemic hypotension, a significant increase in RBF is observed.[58] Thus, it seems at least quite possible that the renal vasoconstriction of cirrhosis is partially mediated by increased adrenergic activity.

Finally, it should be considered that renal vascular resistance is the sum of vasoconstrictor and vasodilating stimuli or substances. Although little information is available on renal vasodilating prostaglandins in cirrhotic patients, it is at least conceivable that prostaglandins are inadequately produced by the kidney in this setting. The observation that RBF falls when inhibitors of prostaglandin synthesis are administered to cirrhotic patients indicates that prostaglandins are attempting to maintain RBF.[59,60] Wong has recently summarized the data relating to another naturally occurring vasodilator substance, bradykinin.[61] He has reported low to undetectable levels of circulating kinins in cirrhotic patients, and postulates that this deficiency, when coupled with stimulation of the pressor arc of the system, angiotensin II, may contribute to the decrease in RBF.

The manner in which alterations in RBF might influence renal tubular handling of sodium has been recently reviewed by Skorecki and Brenner.[62] Briefly, net proximal reabsorption of salt and water is influenced by the peritubular oncotic and hydrostatic pressures. An increase in oncotic pressure or a decrease in hydrostatic pressure is associated with an increase in proximal sodium reabsorption. An increase in the former parameter requires an increase in filtration fraction in the absence of a colloid infusion. Since most studies in cirrhotic patients indicate that GFR and RBF are reduced proportionately, the filtration fraction is usually normal and one would not expect the peritubular oncotic pressure to be increased. Ichikawa and Brenner have recently emphasized the profound effect of peritubular hydrostatic pressure on proximal reabsorption.[63] Since the systemic arterial pressure is low to normal in cirrhotic patients, and the increased renal vascular resistance must reside proximal to the peritubular microvasculature, it follows that peritubular hydrostatic pressure must be diminished. The possibility that this low hydrostatic pressure is partially responsible for the salt retention in cirrhosis is supported by early studies done by Laragh and colleagues.[64] These investigators administered angiotensin II to patients with cirrhosis and ascites. When doses sufficient to raise the renal perfusion pressure were given, a marked increase in urinary sodium excretion was observed, even when the filtration fraction increased. Clearance studies performed during these infusions suggested that both proximal and distal sodium reabsorption were effected by the increased perfusion pressure. The distal effect is of considerable interest in view of later micropuncture findings by Stumpe and colleagues and Bank and co-workers that increases in perfusion pressure decrease sodium reabsorption in the loop of Henle in the rat.[65,66]

Others have also presented findings consistent with the view that hemodynamic abnormalities may contribute to the renal sodium retention in cirrhosis. Systemic or renal arterial infusions of renal vasodilating agents have been reported to increase urinary sodium excretion in some[67-70] but not all patients with cirrhosis.[67,69,71,72] The reason for these varying results probably stems from differences in renal perfusion pressure and differing degrees of renal insufficiency and hepatic dysfunction.

Although the data just reviewed suggest that renal hemodynamic abnormalities probably contribute to the sodium retention in cirrhosis, other studies clearly illustrate that this mechanism is not solely responsible. Levy has shown that sodium retention precedes any measurable change in RBF in his dog model of chemically-induced cirrhosis.[22] In addition, he has reported that renal vasodilatation, with or without increases in renal perfusion pressure, failed to increase urinary sodium excretion, even in the presence of ascites and edema.[48] It should be noted, however, that no enhancement of proximal sodium reabsorption was evident in this study. Thus, if renal vasoconstriction exercises its primary influence on proximal tubular sodium handling, as suggested by Skorecki and Brenner,[62] it is perhaps not so surprising that renal vasodilatation failed to elicit a natriuretic response.

A redistribution of renal cortical blood flow has also been implicated in the sodium retention of cirrhosis. Kew and colleagues, using the inert gas washout technique, reported a redistribution of blood flow from the outer to the inner cortex in patients with cirrhosis.[73] The notion that such a redistribution of blood flow might influence urinary sodium excretion was first postulated by Goodyer and Jaeger in 1955, and was based on the anatomic observation that the deeper inner cortical nephrons were longer and therefore possibly capable of quantitatively greater sodium reabsorption than the shorter superficial nephrons of the outer cortex.[74] More recently, micropuncturists have invoked this redistribution as a mechanism of enhanced proximal reabsorption in an animal model of cirrhosis.[49] These investigators found that the single nephron GFR was normal in these animals, and therefore reasoned that even in the face of a normal "whole kidney" filtration fraction, this parameter would be increased in superficial nephrons. The resulting increase in peritubular oncotic pressure would then mediate increased proximal reabsorption. As attractive as these theories may be, experimental data confirming their validity are still lacking. In fact, serious methodologic and interpretative criticism has been leveled at the inert gas washout technique.

Further, a consistent relationship between inward redistribution of renal cortical blood flow and urinary sodium excretion has not been established.[75]

Renal Nerve Stimulation

The observation that acute renal denervation results in a marked increase in urinary sodium excretion was first made over a century ago.[76] Until recently it was assumed that this phenomenon was mediated through either changes in GFR or renal hemodynamics. The reports of Muller and Barajas documenting direct tubular innervation, however, prompted renewed interest in the possible role of the renal nerves in the regulation of urinary sodium excretion.[77,78] Since that time a growing body of physiologic data has accumulated to indicate a direct effect of renal adrenergic nerve activity on tubular sodium transport. DiBona and colleagues found that renal nerve stimulation decreased renal sodium excretion, and that this effect was independent of any changes in GFR or renal hemodynamics,[79] while Bello-Reuss and colleagues[80] observed no changes in these parameters accompanying the natriuresis of renal denervation. More recently, Bello-Reuss reported a direct effect of both L-norepinephrine and isoproterenol on increasing sodium and water reabsorption in the isolated perfused proximal tubule of the rabbit.[81] This observation confirmed the earlier indirect observations, which concluded that the adrenergic effect on tubular sodium transport was independent of hemodynamic changes, angiotensin II, or renal prostaglandins.

In view of these findings, it is not surprising that increased renal nerve stimulation has been suggested as a possible mediator of sodium retention in cirrhosis. Studying dogs with chronic thoracic inferior vena cava constriction, Gill and colleagues[82] and Levy[83] found that ganglionic blockade or beta-adrenergic blockade partially corrected the renal salt retention. In studies in which selective hepatic vein constriction was utilized to induce hepatic congestion, no effect of renal denervation on sodium excretion could be demonstrated.[84] Similarly, Levy was unable to increase urinary sodium excretion by either renal denervation or beta-adrenergic blockade in his canine model of cirrhosis.[48] Again, it should be remembered that proximal reabsorption is normal in that model, and since most data implicate this nephron site as responsive to renal nerve stimulation, this finding is not entirely surprising. Thus, at least a partial role for adrenergic nerve activity in mediating salt retention at some stage in the evolution of hepatic cirrhosis remains a viable possibility.

Aldosterone

Elevated levels of aldosterone have been repeatedly demonstrated in cirrhotic subjects with edema and ascites,[52] and this hormone clearly enhances distal tubular sodium reabsorption.[85-87] Inevitably, therefore, early observers associated the salt retention in cirrhosis with hyperaldosteronism.[88] A large body of evidence in man and experimental animals now indicates that this mineralocorticoid hormone is of relatively minor importance in mediating sodium retention in this setting. The administration to cirrhotic patients of spironolactone, a competitive inhibitor of aldosterone, results in a very mild natriuretic response at best.[7,89] Epstein has shown that the increase in urinary sodium excretion that he observes in some cirrhotic patients in response to head-out water immersion is unaffected by the simultaneous administration of exogenous desoxycorticosterone, a potent mineralocorticoid hormone.[12] As shown in Figure 2-4, Epstein has demonstrated that plasma aldosterone levels decreased in all of his cirrhotic subjects in

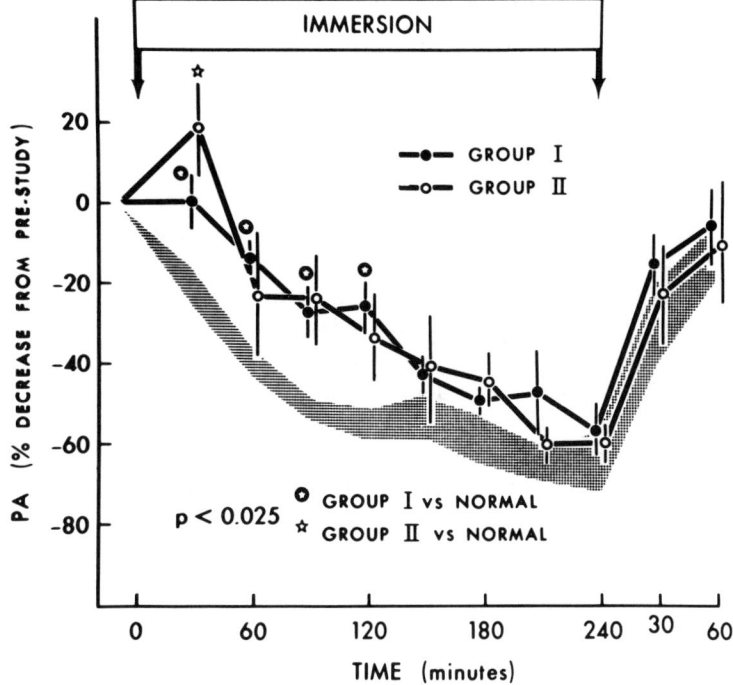

Fig. 2-4. Effect of head-out water immersion on plasma aldosterone levels in cirrhotic subjects with (Group II) and without (Group I) a natriuretic response to immersion. Shaded area represents values obtained in normal subjects. (From Epstein et al.,[90] by permission.)

response to immersion, but that only half of such individuals manifested an increase in sodium excretion.[90]

Chonko and co-workers have reported similar findings in cirrhotic patients ingesting a very high sodium diet. Roughly half of the patients studied responded with a marked fall in plasma aldosterone activity, but all continued to retain sodium.[91] Rosoff and colleagues approached the relationship between salt retention and aldosterone even more directly. They administered aminoglutethiamide to three patients with cirrhosis and ascites. This agent, which is a potent inhibitor of adrenal steroid synthesis, caused a profound fall in plasma aldosterone levels, but avid salt retention persisted.[15] Finally, studies by Levy in dogs with chemically induced cirrhosis clearly demonstrate that salt retention precedes any increase in plasma renin or aldosterone.[48] More recently, Levy reported that prior adrenalectomy failed to prevent ascites formation in these dogs.[92] It therefore seems fair to conclude that aldosterone, while usually elevated in patients with decompensated cirrhosis, is not a major mediator of renal salt retention.

Non-aldosterone Humoral Factors

Since the classic studies in which de-Wardener and colleagues demonstrated in 1961 that factors other than GFR and aldosterone are operative in the excretion of an acutely administered salt load,[93] numerous authors have postulated the existence of a "natriuretic hormone." Further, as recently reviewed by Seely and Levy, a considerable body of circumstantial evidence suggests that such a substance may indeed exist.[94] If this is the case, it is conceivable that this elusive factor is underproduced in cirrhotic patients, either because the liver is the source of its production, or because some nonhepatic volume receptor fails to perceive volume expansion in the milieu of chronic liver disease. To date, only a few studies reflect these possibilities. Kramer has reported that a fraction of plasma derived from volume-expanded normal individuals markedly inhibits the short-circuit current in the frog skin. When this same fraction is prepared from plasma of patients with cirrhosis, ascites, and edema, and applied to the mucosal surface of frog skin, no effect on the short-circuit current is observed.[95] Wilkinson and co-workers fractionated the urine of four cirrhotic patients to whom mineralocorticoid had been chronically administered. The "natriuretic" fraction of the urine from two of the subjects who escaped from the salt retaining effect of the mineralocorticoid caused increased urinary sodium excretion when administered to rats. The same urine fraction obtained from patients who had failed to "escape" from the mineralocorticoid failed to produce a natriuretic response in this bioassay system.[96] These studies clearly tend to support the concept that some circulating substance may be inoperative in the salt retention of cirrhosis. On the other hand, Epstein and colleagues reported that the natriuresis of water immersion in normal subjects is associated with the elaboration of a "natriuretic substance" in the urine during the immersion maneuver.[97] Since Epstein also reported that the urinary sodium excretion of cirrhotic subjects is increased in response to immersion,[12] it is difficult to implicate the absence of such a substance in the salt retention of cirrhosis.

Elevated estrogens or estrogen metabolite concentrations have long been postulated to exist in cirrhotic patients, on the basis of clinical findings such as testicular atrophy, diminished libido, gynecomastia, and spider angiomata. With the advent of the radioimmunoassay, this suspicion was recently confirmed with the finding of elevated plasma levels of estradiol in cirrhotic subjects.[98,99] Studies by Preedy and Aitken demonstrated a salt retaining effect of estradiol in cirrhotic patients.[100] More recently, Cristy and Shaver reviewed the influence of estrogens on renal sodium handling.[101] They concluded that the salt retaining property of these hormones was partially mediated through the stimulation of aldosterone release, and that the nonaldosterone effect was mild and may result from nonrenal systemic effects. Levy serially measured the changes in plasma estradiol levels in his dog with portal cirrhosis.[48] Although levels of this hormone were elevated in the presence of ascites, the salt retention of the pre-ascitic phase of the disease was not associated with increased estradiol concentrations. Thus, while no data are available to refute the concept that estrogens may contribute to the avid salt retention of cirrhosis, other factors must also be operative.

As mentioned earlier in this chapter, prostaglandins and the kallikrein-kinin system may influence sodium reabsorption by influencing renal and/or nonrenal hemodynamics. In addition, a direct tubular effect of these hormonal substances has been postulated. As recently summarized by Lifschitz and Stein, however, a considerable body of conflicting and inconclusive literature addressing this issue has been presented.[102] Currently, there is no good evidence that either of these substances directly influences renal tubular sodium transport in cirrhosis.

Treatment of Salt Retention in Cirrhosis

As was pointed out at the beginning of this section, the mechanism of ascites formation and its relationship to renal sodium retention has profound implications for its treatment. If the overflow theory of ascites is correct, one might expect that early prevention of sodium retention would prevent the development of both ascites and edema. Likewise, reducing ECF volume should reduce the accumulation of ascites, and paracentesis should not result in significant depletion of the intravascular blood volume. On the other hand, if the more traditional theory applies, diuretic therapy and/or paracentesis are potentially dangerous therapeutic interventions, since salt retention is a physiologic and necessary response designed to maintain a "full" circulation and afford adequate tissue perfusion. Thus, until the issue of the mechanism of ascites formation and its relationship to renal salt retention is resolved, our therapeutic principles remain controversial and are based primarily on empirical observations. Despite these considerations, several general principles should be kept in mind. First, ascites and edema in cirrhosis must be viewed as a sign of disease rather than as a disease per se. Therefore, in the absence of respiratory embarassment or dermatologic complications of severe edema, the "knee-jerk" compulsion to diurese or paracentese should often be resisted. Second, the successful employment of diuretics requires the mobilization of edema and ascites. This phenomenon results from renal losses of salt and water and from transient changes in Starling's forces across microvascular beds which favor the movement of interstitial (or ascitic) fluid into the vascular space. As has been illustrated by Shear and colleagues,[26] the rate at which fluid can be mobilized is clearly limited. These investigators found that peripheral edema is mobilized at a much faster rate than ascitic fluid. Further, they found that in patients with ascites but no edema, ascitic fluid was particularly difficult to absorb. On the basis of these observations, Shear and his colleagues recommend that one attempt a daily weight loss of 1 kilogram in patients with ascites and edema, and 0.2 to 0.3 kilograms in patients with ascites and no edema. Applying these guidelines, Gregory and coworkers evaluated the morbidity and mortality of diuretic therapy.[103] They found that the incidence of death, fluid and electrolyte abnormalities, encephalopathy, and renal failure were no greater in diuretic-treated patients than in salt- and water-restricted subjects. Moreover, the cumulative loss of weight and ascites was significantly greater in the former group.

In addition to diuretic therapy, abdominal paracentesis has also been employed as a method of reducing ascites. As noted earlier in this chapter, there is some debate about the reaccumulation of ascites after this procedure. Most authorities would agree, however, that as long as patients continue to ingest dietary sodium, some degree of reaccumulation does occur. As a result, this procedure is probably temporizing at best. Furthermore, overly aggressive paracentesis may precipitate a variety of complications.[27-29] Nonetheless, carefully selected, closely monitored patients with tense ascites may benefit from limited removal of ascitic fluid. As illustrated by Knauer and Lowe (Fig. 2-5), a significant improvement in cardiac output may accompany the aspiration of up to one liter of ascitic fluid.[34] Beyond this amount the beneficial effects are decreased, and the data of Knauer and Lowe suggest that removal of greater than 1500 ml might be counterproductive and result in a fall in cardiac output. The hemodynamic determinations by these authors and others[104] suggest that the limited benefit from paracentesis results from decompression of the inferior vena cava and an increase in venous return and right heart filling pressures. It should be pointed out, however, that no consistent increase in urine output or sodium excretion was shown to accompany the improvement in cardiac output.

All too frequently, patients with cirrhosis and ascites become refractory to conventional diuretic therapy. As shown in Figure

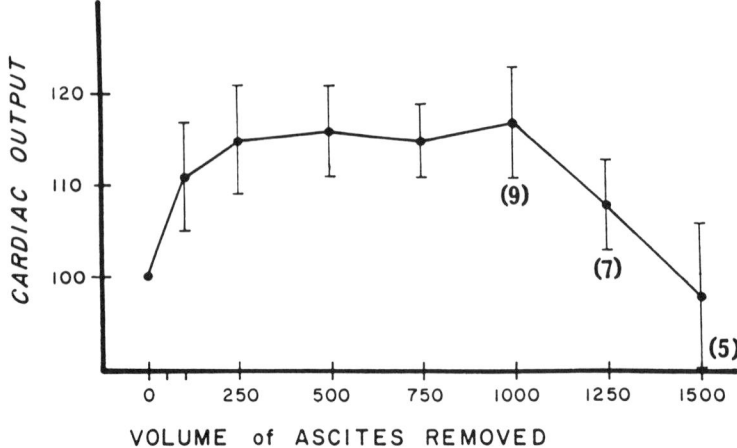

Fig. 2-5. Effect of paracentesis on cardiac output in patients with cirrhosis and ascites. (From Knauer and Lowe,[34] by permission.)

2-6, Eknoyan and co-workers demonstrated that the combination of intravenous ascites infusion and furosemide, a potent loop-acting diuretic, dramatically increased urinary sodium excretion.[105] Although not shown in this figure, these investigators also reported that this combined therapy was much more effective than the administration of furosemide alone. Additionally, it should be pointed out that ascites reinfusion increased RBF in these patients and had no deleterious effect on GFR. Finally, it is important to note that Eknoyan and his group caution that the cumulative volume of ascitic fluid infused should not exceed the urine volume by more than 500 ml because of the risk of overexpansion of the intravascular volume and subsequent precipitation of variceal hemorrhage.

As noted earlier, a number of studies have found a salutory effect of the peritoneovenous (LeVeen) shunt on volume homeostasis in patients with cirrhosis and ascites. Schroeder and colleagues[106] and Blendis and co-workers[107] have shown that the successful use of this device also improved renal hemodynamics and GFR. As recently cautioned by Epstein, however, a wide variety of serious conditions, including disseminated intravascular coagulation, variceal hemorrhage, infection, air embolism and pulmonary edema may complicate the employment of the shunt.[108] It seems reasonable, therefore, to recommend that the use of the LeVeen shunt be limited to carefully selected patients, and that its more routine use awaits the results of carefully designed and performed randomized trials. Finally, the repeated intravenous infusion of hyperoncotic albumin[108] and glucocorticoids[109] has been reported to provide a natriuretic effect in cirrhotic subjects. Unfortunately, these benefits are generally transient at best, and the potential dangers of such repeated therapy preclude its routine or chronic use.

HEART FAILURE

As in the case of hepatic cirrhosis, renal sodium retention often plays a prominent role in the clinical presentation of heart failure. Historically, our understanding of the pathogenesis of edema formation in this condition is quite analogous to the current controversy surrounding ascites formation in cirrhosis. In 1832, Hope first elaborated the "backward failure" theory, stating that

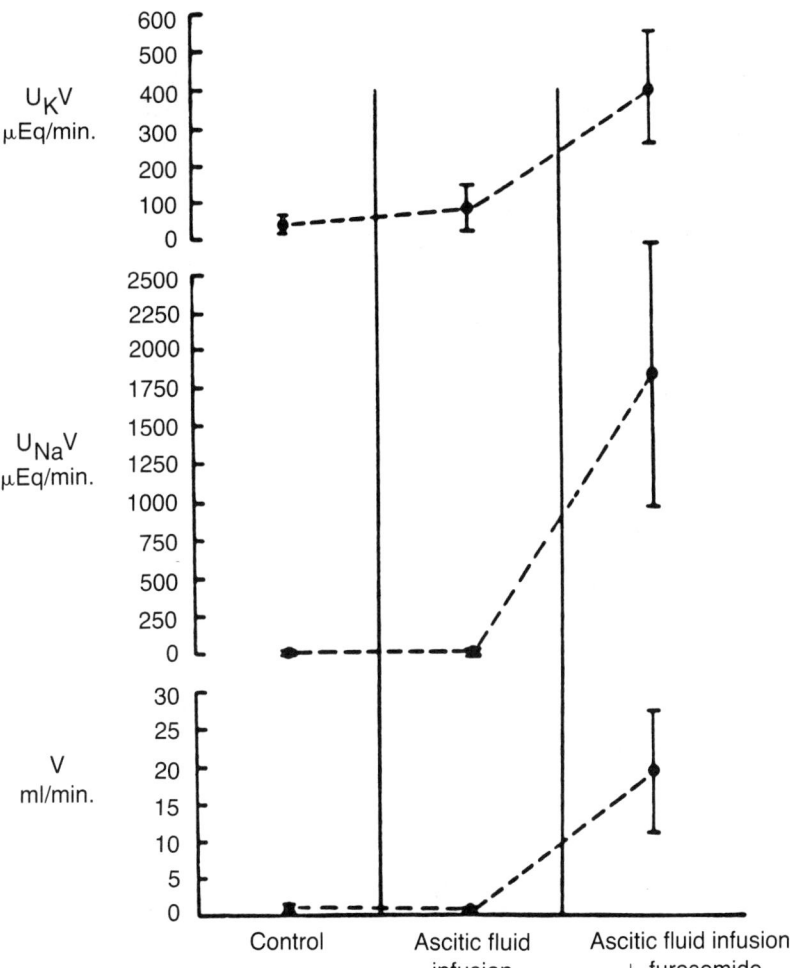

Fig. 2-6. Effect of intravenous ascites reinfusion alone and in combination with furosemide on urinary volume and sodium and potassium excretion. (From Eknoyan et al,[105] by permission.)

as a result of increased right atrial pressure, peripheral venous pressure also rose, and as a consequence, fluid transudation from the intravascular to the interstitial fluid compartment occurred.[110] This loss of intravascular volume triggered renal sodium retention in an attempt to restore vascular volume. This explanation of edema formation was widely held until 1917, when McKenzie presented the "forward failure" theory.[111] According to this postulate, the renal retention of salt and water occurred as a primary event in heart failure, and, in analogy to the "overflow" theory of ascites formation in cirrhosis, this resulted in altered Starling's forces across peripheral capillary beds, and thereby in edema formation. Definitive proof of this series of events was lacking until 1944, when Warren and Stead published their classic study of fluid dynamics in this condition.[112] These investigators studied patients with chronic congestive heart failure, and rendered them asymptomatic and edema free with conventional therapy. They then placed these individuals on a relatively high salt diet and sequentially measured their body weight, plasma volume, and venous pressure. The subsequent salt retention clearly preceded any increase in the last of these parameters. While these findings clearly indicate that the avid renal reabsorption of sodium is a primary event leading to edema formation, it does not exclude the importance of venous pressure in the actual transudation of fluid between the vascular and interstitial spaces. Rather, this study indicates that renal salt retention is at least partially responsible for the elevation in venous pressure.

Before discussing the mechanisms of sodium retention in heart failure, it is appropriate to briefly address our current teleologic concept of this phenomenon. Figure 2-7 depicts the Frank-Starling relationship between cardiac output and left ventricular end diastolic volume (LVEDV). Curve A represents this relationship in the normal heart and curve B, that in the failing myocardium. As can be seen, a direct curvilinear relationship exists between cardiac output and LVEDV in both cases, but at any given LVEDV, cardiac output is less in the failing than in the normal heart. Since venous return and therefore plasma volume are primary determinants of LVEDV, it is evident that one mechanism by which cardiac output can be improved in the diseased heart is by increasing plasma volume and LVEDV. It is therefore apparent that renal sodium retention is much more than an interesting and sometimes troublesome clinical problem. Rather, it represents a physiologic adjustment by which the organism attempts to maintain cardiac output and thereby adequate perfusion of critical tissues.

Afferent Limb

The afferent limb of salt retention, whereby the organism perceives a decrease in effective arterial blood volume and therefore signals the kidney to enhance sodium reabsorption, is poorly understood. Nevertheless, a number of interesting and important observations shed some light on this issue and deserve consideration.

Cardiac Output

Warren and Stead proposed that the low cardiac output that often characterizes heart failure may provide the afferent limb of sodium retention in this condition.[112] Although these investigators suggest that the decrease in cardiac output might be associated with a decrement in RBF, it is also possible that some arterial receptor "senses" inadequate perfusion, and through neuroendocrine mechanisms triggers the avid renal sodium reabsorption. Certainly, baroreceptor mechanisms on the arterial or high pressure side of the circulation have been conclusively implicated in mediating the volume stimulus to antidiuretic hormone (ADH) secretion.[113] By analogy, it is reasonable to suspect that a similar system might serve to perceive a

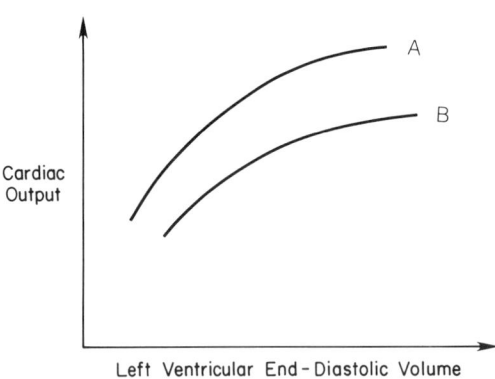

Fig. 2-7. Frank-Starling relationship between cardiac output and left ventricular end-diastolic volume. A direct curvilinear relationship exists in both the normal (curve A) and failing (curve B) myocardium.

need for sodium retention. The elegant studies of Epstein, Post, and McDowell[2] demonstrated that the acute opening of an arteriovenous fistula results in a prompt fall in urinary sodium excretion, a decrease in diastolic blood pressure and peripheral resistance, and no change in RBF and GFR. While consistent with the concept of an arterial volume receptor, however, these acute studies may not be applicable to chronic heart failure. As noted earlier in this chapter, many investigators have applied the model of thoracic inferior vena caval obstruction to the study of salt retention in cirrhosis. Schrier and colleagues have demonstrated that this maneuver is not only associated with hepatic congestion, but also with a decrease in cardiac output.[114] Moreover, the same group found that acute constriction of the thoracic superior vena cava, a model in which hepatic congestion does not occur, is also associated with a fall in cardiac output and antinatriuresis.[115] Lifschitz and Schrier examined systemic hemodynamics in dogs with chronic inferior vena cava constriction and concluded that the body perceived a state of salt retention because of an imbalance between cardiac output and peripheral vascular resistance (i.e., vascular volume and holding capacity).[116]

Some authorities have argued that the concept of an arterial volume receptor that responds to changes in cardiac output is untenable because of the salt retention that accompanies high-output cardiac failure such as that in anemia, thiamine deficiency, or thyrotoxicosis. As pointed out recently by Levy and Seely, however, such an argument is "circuitous" since the high cardiac output may be *due to* antecedent renal salt retention. That this is indeed the case is suggested by the observation that not all high cardiac output states are associated with heart failure. In fact, renal salt retention and expansion of the ECF volume occurs in high cardiac output states even in the absence of heart failure.[2] Thus, the existence of high-output congestive heart failure as a clinical entity does not mitigate against the possibility of a cardiac output-sensitive receptor in the arterial vascular tree that perceives alterations in effective arterial blood volume.

The anatomic localization of such a receptor has to date remained elusive. The only volume-sensitive receptor in the arterial circulation to be identified with certainty is the juxtaglomerular apparatus of the kidney. As will be discussed in more detail below, activation of the renin-angiotensin-aldosterone system through this apparatus may play an important role in the salt retention of congestive heart failure.

Thoracic Venous Pressure

Because of the relatively high compliance of the thoracic venous (low pressure) vasculature, these vessels are excellent candidates to house volume receptors. Indeed, the release of ADH in response to volume stimuli has been shown to result from inhibition of tonic-suppressive stimuli from this system.[117] Further, volume receptors have been documented in the cardiac atria as well.[118,119] The possibility that the salt retention of heart failure may result from an afferent signal in this low pressure system was first postulated in the often-cited study of Hollander and Judson.[120] These investigators studied two groups of patients with severe left ventricular dysfunction. One group of patients was edematous and retained sodium when placed on a relatively high sodium diet. The second group was edema-free and maintained sodium balance when placed on the same dietary sodium intake. Cardiac output, peripheral resistance, pulmonary artery pressure, and oxygen consumption were similar in the two groups. The only parameter that correlated with the salt retention was a significantly higher right ventricular end diastolic pressure in the salt retaining, edematous group of patients. Hollander and Judson, as well as others, have interpreted these observations to implicate elevations in central venous pressure in the afferent limb of sodium retention in heart failure. This interpretation is made somewhat suspect by other findings which indicate that patients and animals with cardiac dysfunction, normal central venous pressure, and no "clinical" evidence of edema have significantly expanded ECF volumes.[121-123] In addition, it will be recalled that Warren and Stead found that urinary salt retention preceded the rise in central venous pressure in their patients.[112] It seems quite likely that the "non-edematous" patients in Hollander and Judson's study had already been through a period of salt retention and had reached a new steady state of sodium balance at an expanded intravascular volume. Further, it is possible that the edematous patients had retained even greater amounts of salt and water, and that their elevated right ventricular end-diastolic pressure was the effect of (rather than the cause of) this greater degree of salt retention. Finally, at first glance it is difficult to reconcile the concept of elevated central venous pressure causing renal sodium retention with the natriuretic response of normal individuals to the supine posture, saline infusion, or to water immersion, since these conditions are associated with increases in central venous pressure. Studies by Zehr and co-workers[124,125] and Greenberg and colleagues[126] offer a possible explanation for this apparent paradox. These investigators describe a blunting of the normal atrial receptor response to changes in transmural pressure under conditions of chronic venous hypertension. Zehr and co-workers found that dogs with chronic mitral stenosis had a diminished ADH response to decreases in venous pressure induced by nonhypotensive hemorrhage.[125] Greenberg and colleagues reported that the frequency of atrial nerve discharge in response to increments in atrial pressure was decreased in dogs with chronic right-sided heart failure.[126] Thus, chronic increases in central venous pressure may not be a direct afferent stimulus to sodium retention, but rather may serve to dampen the normal natriuretic response to increases in intrathoracic vascular volume.

Finally, it should be considered that there may be no extrarenal afferent limb that perceives a diminution in effective arterial blood volume. It is at least conceivable that the salt retention of heart failure is solely due to alterations in intrarenal factors (discussed below), or that the afferent receptor is located within the kidney itself and is thereby tightly linked to the afferent limb of sodium reabsorption.

Efferent Limb

Nephron Sites Responsible for Salt Retention

As was the case for cirrhosis, evidence for enhanced proximal and distal sodium reabsorption has been obtained in humans with congestive heart failure and in animal models of this condition. Free water clearance studies by Bell, Schedl, and Bartter in patients with congestive heart failure suggested that proximal reabsorption is increased in this population.[127] Studies using pharmacologic distal blockade reached a similar conclusion,[128] as did clearance studies in dogs with chronic arteriovenous fistulae.[129] Recent studies of glomerular dynamics in rats with surgically induced myocardial infarcts would also predict increased proximal reabsorption.[130]

Numerous micropuncture studies have marshalled evidence for increased distal sodium reabsorption as well. Studies in dogs[131] and rats[132] with arteriovenous fistulae have shown that the impaired natriuretic response to volume expansion in this model is due to enhanced distal reabsorption. A similar conclusion was derived from micropuncture studies in dogs with pericarditis and salt retention.[133] Stumpe and colleagues placed this enhanced distal reabsorption to the loop of Henle.[132] The exaggerated generation of free water through the administration of mannitol to patients with congestive heart failure is consistent with this localization.[127]

Mechanisms of Salt Retention

Renal Hemodynamics in Heart Failure

As recently reviewed by Humes, Gottlieb, and Brenner, alterations in renal hemodynamics may play an important role in the salt retention of congestive heart failure, especially at the level of the proximal tubule.[134] The manner in which these factors influence sodium reabsorption was briefly summarized in the preceding discussion of salt retention in cirrhosis. Vander and co-workers have documented that the fall in RBF in patients with congestive heart failure usually exceeds any decrement in GFR, and an increase in the filtration fraction is therefore the general rule in this condition.[135] This hemodynamic adjustment, presumably due to efferent arteriolar vasoconstriction, results in an increased peritubular oncotic pressure and, at normal renal perfusion pressure, a fall in peritubular hydrostatic pressure. These alterations in peritubular Starling's forces may well mediate the enhanced proximal reabsorption observed in heart failure.

Hemodynamic changes may also modulate increased sodium reabsorption beyond the proximal tubule. Stumpe and colleagues found an inverse relationship between renal perfusion pressure and sodium reabsorption in the loop of Henle.[65] If this association holds for medullary perfusion pressure, and the renal vascular resistance is increased proximal to the medullary circulation, it is conceivable that this mechanism mediates the avid loop reabsorption found in some models of heart failure.[44,132]

The factors responsible for these intrarenal hemodynamic alterations are not completely understood. By virtue of their ability to effect renal vasoconstriction and increase the filtration fraction, angiotensin and catecholamines are prime candidates for mediating these phenomena.[136] Oliver and colleagues have recently demonstrated that both the renin-angiotensin system and the adrenergic nervous system play a role in mediating the renal hemodynamic response to an acute reduction in cardiac output.[137] They also found that vasodilatory renal prostaglandins tend to modulate these changes. Studies by Hall and co-workers have demonstrated that the salt retention of dietary sodium restriction can be at least partially reversed by the infusion of a competitive antagonist of angiotensin II, and that the increase in sodium excretion correlated with a decrease in filtration fraction.[138] Numerous authors examining animal models of heart failure have described a decrease in renal vascular resistance and an increase in urinary sodium excretion in response to either competitive antagonists of angiotensin II or inhibition of angiotensin converting enzyme.[53,56,139-142] These findings are difficult to interpret, however, because of the profound decrements in systemic arterial pulmonary wedge and right atrial pressures and the increase in cardiac output that accompany their vasodilatory effects.[143] Thus, it is at least possible that the changes in RBF and sodium excretion in congestive heart failure are due to changes in the afferent as well as the efferent limb of the pathophysiology of this condition. In addition, these pharmacologic agents also cause a fall in plasma aldosterone levels, which could theoretically mediate their natriuretic response. In any event, it should be pointed out that while angiotensin II-mediated changes in renal hemodynamics may be one of several components active in renal salt retention, other factors are also clearly involved. Chonko and colleagues emphasized this point by demonstrating that despite suppression of plasma renin activity, salt retention persisted in patients with congestive heart failure ingesting a high salt diet.[91]

Circulating or intrarenal catecholamines released via renal nerve stimulation could also mediate the renal hemodynamic changes of heart failure. The natriuresis of adrenergic blockade in dogs with thoracic inferior vena cava constriction[82] and in normal human subjects[144] is consistent with this possibility. Additionally, abundant evidence indicates an augmented sympathetic tone in congestive heart failure.[137,145-148] Further, Brod and co-workers described a consistent fall in filtration fraction in patients with severe congestive heart failure in response to α-adrenergic blockade.[149] In that study, however, profound systemic hemodynamic alterations often accompanied the renal vasodilatation, and urinary sodium excretion either remained unchanged or was only minimally increased. Finally, it should also be pointed out that in the studies by Gill and colleagues, the natriuresis induced by adrenergic blockade occurred independent of changes in glomerular filtration rate, RBF, and filtration fraction.[82,144] These observations suggest that the influence of the adrenergic nervous system on sodium reabsorption in heart failure may occur by a direct tubular effect rather than through an alteration in intrarenal hemodynamics.

An inward redistribution of RBF and/or GFR has also been proposed as an efferent hemodynamic mechanism for salt retention in congestive heart failure. Barger and Herd, utilizing the inert gas washout technique, described such an inward redistribution of RBF in dogs with pulmonic stenosis, tricuspid regurgitation, and renal salt retention.[150] Studies employing the Hanssen technique to evaluate the distribution of GFR, and radioactive microspheres to determine distributional changes in RBF, have, however, been unable to confirm these findings.[151,152] Furthermore, as pointed out earlier, the association between changes in RBF distribution and urinary sodium excretion has been seriously questioned.[75]

Renal Nerve Stimulation

Evidence favoring a role for the renal nerves in at least partially mediating renal salt retention in congestive heart failure was summarized above, and the potential for this mechanism to modulate renal sodium transport independently of renal hemodynamics is clearly established. Carpenter[152a] and colleagues, in studies with dogs, transplanted one kidney into the neck and removed the contralateral kidney prior to thoracic inferior vena cava constriction.[153] The denervated, transplanted kidney demonstrated the same avid sodium retention as do in-situ, innervated kidneys. Although these authors did not present data reflecting either RBF or GFR in the transplanted kidney, these results certainly suggest that renal nerve stimulation is not an essential component of salt retention in this model. These findings, however, do not exclude the possibility that this mechanism is partially involved in the salt retention of heart failure under "normal" pathophysiologic conditions. The observation of Chidsey and co-workers[148] that sympathetic nerve activity is particularly increased with exercise in heart failure, and the well recognized diuretic effect of bed rest in this condition, are at least consistent with such a partial role.

Aldosterone

In 1950, Deming and Luetcher described a salt-retaining steroid in the urine of patients with congestive heart failure.[153] Subsequent to the identification of this substance as aldosterone, various roles were assigned to this hormone in the salt retention of heart failure. Early studies by Davis and colleagues underlined the importance of aldosterone when they reported that bilateral adrenalectomy resulted in a prompt natriuresis and resolution of ascites and edema in dogs with chronic thoracic vena cava constriction.[154] Since that time, considerable data have indicated that aldosterone is not the sole factor, and possibly not a major factor in the salt retention of congestive heart failure. First, when given chronic, large doses of exogenous mineralocorticoid, normal individuals only transiently retain sodium, and "escape" from the salt retaining effects without developing edema.[155] Individuals with heart failure fail to "escape." Second, spironolactone, a competitive antagonist of aldosterone, causes either no increase or a very small increment in sodium excretion in patients with congestive heart failure.[156] Third, suppression of aldosterone may occur with a high dietary sodium intake, yet avid sodium retention persists.[91] Taken together, these observations seem consistent with the concept that aldosterone plays a "permissive" role in the salt retention of congestive heart failure. In other words, some finite amount of aldosterone must be present in order for other efferent mechanisms to manifest their salt retaining effects. That this may be the case is suggested by the studies of Davis and co-workers, who described salt retention and edema formation in adrenalectomized dogs with thoracic inferior vena cava constriction and in adrenalectomized dogs with pulmonic stenosis when these animals were given only small, fixed replacement doses of mineralocorticoid for maintenance.[154,157]

Non-aldosterone Humoral Factors

The inability of patients with congestive heart failure to elaborate a yet unidentified "natriuretic hormone" is a potential mechanism for the salt retention in this condition. To our knowledge no study has supported this possibility. Mittleman and Levy, on the other hand, attempted to isolate a nonmineralocorticoid, salt-retaining substance from both the urine and plasma of dogs with chronic thoracic inferior vena cava constriction, but were unsuccessful.[158]

As noted earlier in this section, Oliver and co-workers have presented convincing evidence that endogenous renal prostaglandins serve to dampen the efferent arteriolar vasoconstriction mediated by angiotensin II and catecholamines in dogs with acute thoracic inferior vena cava constriction.[137] In their study, no effect of these hemodynamic changes on urinary sodium retention was evident, however. Thus, while it is possible that prostaglandins (or a relative lack of prostaglandins) may in some manner participate in at least the hemodynamically mediated component of salt retention, definitive proof for such a role is still lacking. While similar or even more direct involvement of the renal kinin-kallikrein system is possible, we are unaware of data that bear directly on this possibility.

Treatment of Salt Retention in Heart Failure

Although the exact nature of the afferent and efferent limbs of the salt retaining mechanism in heart failure are poorly understood, considerable success has been achieved in the treatment of this disorder. In considering therapy, it should be remembered that the abnormal renal handling of sodium is not a primary event in heart failure, but rather occurs as the result of inadequate or ineffective cardiac function. A rational approach to the treatment of heart failure should therefore attempt to interrupt the afferent limb of sodium retention by improving cardiac performance. To this end, cardiac glycosides provide the cornerstone of therapy. In addition, surgical intervention may be indicated when valvular or septal abnormalities exist or when a dyskinetic segment of myocardium underlies the low cardiac output. It should also be remembered that left ventricular stroke volume varies inversely with left ventricular afterload (peripheral vascular resistence).[159] As a result, improvement in cardiac output (and diminished sodium retention) may be accomplished by the administration of systemic vasodilators. While this therapy is obviously applicable to patients with concomitant heart failure and hypertension, its efficacy has also been documented in normotensive and even hypotensive subjects. The beneficial effect in the latter circumstances takes advantage of the very basic physiologic fact that blood pressure is the product of cardiac output and peripheral resistance. If left ventricular performance improves sufficiently and cardiac output increases in proportion to the fall in resistance, no change in pressure will occur, but tissue perfusion will be improved. If a sufficient increase in cardiac output does not occur, however, therapy with vasodilator agents may precipitate frank hypotension and shock. Thus, the institution of such therapy in normotensive or hypotensive patients should be undertaken only with careful monitoring of cardiac function.

In many instances, therapy designed to interfere with the afferent limb of the salt retaining mechanism is ineffective or inadequate, and diuretics must be employed to interrupt the efferent limb. In so doing it is necessary to recall the Frank-Starling relationship between right heart filling and cardiac output (Fig. 2-7), and the possibility that "successful" diuretic-induced losses of salt and water may decrease cardiac output and lead to further underperfusion of critical organs. On the other hand, alleviating pulmonary congestion may improve oxygenation and secondarily improve cardiac output.

The choice of diuretics is largely empirical. In general, thiazide diuretics are usually effective, and some potentiation may be obtained from the concomitant use of spironolactone or triamterene. In more severe cases, the more potent loop acting diuretics, furosemide or ethacrynic acid, may be necessary. These agents may be particularly useful in the treatment of acute pulmonary edema. In addition to their diuretic effect, they provide extrarenal hemodynamic benefits. Lesch and co-workers reported that the improvement in pulmonary edema in response to ethacrynic acid preceded an increase in urinary sodium excretion.[160] Dikshit and associates described a similar response to intravenous furosemide.[161] As shown in Figure 2-8, furosemide resulted in a prompt increase in lower leg venous capacitance and a fall in left ventricular filling pressure before any increase in urine output occurred.

Occasionally, patients with congestive heart failure are refractory to even the most potent diuretics.[162-165] Under these circumstances, nephron avidity for sodium reabsorption is presumably so marked in sites unaffected by these agents that there is either very little sodium presented distally or the sodium escaping proximal and loop reabsorption is reabsorbed along the distal tubule or collecting ducts. Several studies have now documented that a combination of afterload reduction (i.e., vasodilator therapy) and potent diuretics may result in an effective diuresis.[162-165] In acute pulmonary edema, sodium nitroprusside is an ideal vasodilator because it affords careful control of arterial blood pressure, and is also a venodilator and therefore reduces preload (venous return). Whether or not vasodilator therapy in conjunction with diuretics will be effective in the treatment of chronic congestive heart failure has not been adequately tested. In a recent study, however, oral, long-acting isosorbide nitrate produced a significant improvement in myocardial performance, and this agent may therefore potentiate the response to diuretics.[166]

Finally, the treatment of edema in pa-

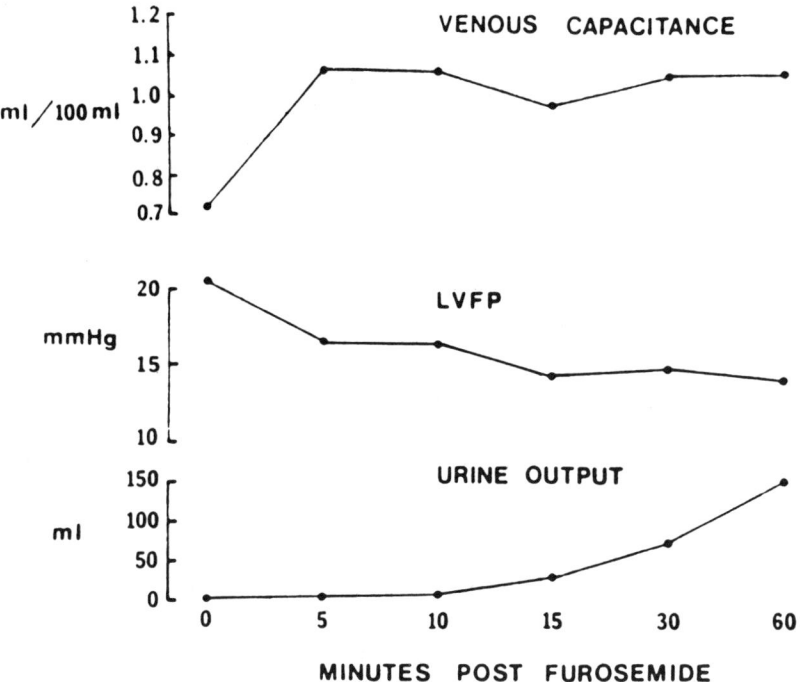

Fig. 2-8. Effect of intravenous furosemide on venous capacitance, left ventricular filling pressure (LVFP) and urine output in patients with pulmonary edema. (From Dikshit et al,[161] by permission.)

tients with primarily right sided heart failure due to chronic lung disease must be addressed. Under these circumstances pulmonary congestion is uncommon, and as a result, aggressive diuretic therapy is rarely indicated. In the setting of cor pulmonale, in which hypoxia and borderline oxygen delivery to peripheral tissues already exists, a further reduction in cardiac output due to diuretic therapy may have disastrous consequences. In addition, the metabolic alkalosis that sometimes occurs as a complication of potent diuretic therapy may further reduce alveolar ventilation and precipitate additional carbon dioxide retention and hypoxia.[167]

NEPHROTIC SYNDROME
Afferent Limb

Generalized edema is a cardinal clinical feature of the nephrotic syndrome, and according to the classic theory, the renal salt retention in this condition ultimately results from urinary losses of albumin and from hypoalbuminemia. The consequent reduction in plasma oncotic pressure gives rise to the transudation of plasma salt and water into the interstitial space, and contraction of the plasma volume. This reduction in volume then activates the afferent and efferent limbs of volume homeostasis, and the kidney avidly reabsorbs sodium. It should be noted that if this scenario is correct, the pathogenesis of salt retention in this condition differs markedly from that seen in decompensated cirrhosis and heart failure. The primary difference centers on the fact that in the previously discussed entities, edema is the result of renal sodium retention. If this classic view is correct, the renal salt retention in nephrotic syndrome results from edema formation.

Although this classic theory seems reasonable and its simplicity makes it most attractive, several observations suggest that it may not be universally applicable. First, several clinical states of hypoalbuminemia, particularly congenital hypoalbuminemia,[168] and some cases of cirrhosis, are not associated with edema. Second, in experiments in which hypoalbuminemia is induced by plasma exchange, a fall in plasma volume is not observed.[169-171] Third, as recently reviewed by Dorhout Mees and associates, plasma volume is normal or increased, rather than decreased, in over 50 percent of nephrotic subjects, even when measured during a period of severe hypoalbuminemia, salt retention, and active edema formation.[172] Studying 10 adult patients with "minimal change" nephrotic syndrome before and after steroid-induced remissions, these authors found that plasma volume fell significantly upon disappearance of the syndrome. Further, plasma renin activity tended to rise with remission, and blood pressure decreased. Meltzer and associates described patients with membranous nephropathy who had normal or expanded blood volumes and low plasma renin activity, and patients with minimal lesions who had low blood volumes and high plasma renin activity.[173] Thus, while the classic theory of edema formation and consequent renal salt retention may be applicable to some patients with the nephrotic syndrome, it clearly does not apply in all instances. It is possible, of course, that some nephrotic patients distribute their vascular volume abnormally. For instance, if the afferent limb of volume recognition resides in the venous circulation, and total blood volume is maldistributed to the arterial and peripheral capillary beds, volume depletion could be sensed, yet renin activity would be suppressed and absolute intravascular volumes would be normal or increased. Evidence for such a redistribution of blood volume in this or any other condition is lacking, however. Finally, it is possible that the holding capacity of the vasculature is increased in nephrotic patients, and that as a result the normal absolute blood volume is inadequate to "fill" that capacity. However, the finding that mean arterial pressures are higher during the edematous phase of the disease than following remission suggests that this is not the case.[172]

Efferent Limb

The reduction in GFR that often accompanies the nephrotic syndrome could in part contribute to renal salt retention. In patients with minimal lesions, however, GFR is often well maintained or may even be abnormally increased (presumably due to a low glomerular capillary oncotic pressure, which opposes filtration), yet edema formation and salt retention still occur. Furthermore, non-nephrotic subjects with an impaired GFR are usually able to maintain perfectly normal sodium homeostasis. Thus, as in heart failure and cirrhosis, enhanced tubular reabsorption of sodium must also be invoked in the nephrotic syndrome.

Nephron Site Responsible for Salt Retention

If a high peritubular capillary oncotic pressure is an important prerequisite for enhanced proximal sodium reabsorption, an astronomically high filtration fraction would be necessary to raise this value above normal in severely hypoalbuminemic nephrotic patients. Indeed, Grausz, Lieberman, and Earley suggested that proximal reabsorption was normal or decreased in nephrotic patients studied during the blockade of distal reabsorption with diuretics.[174] Clearance studies in nephrotic children, on the other hand, were interpreted as indicating that proximal reabsorption is enhanced.[175] More recently, Bernard and colleagues performed micropuncture studies on a nephrotic rat model, and found that following a saline infusion the nephrotic animals displayed even less proximal reabsorption than normal rats.[176] Further, they found that sodium delivery to the late distal tubule of superficial nephrons was virtually identical in the two groups. On the basis of these findings, Bernard and his co-workers implicated the collecting duct or some unidentified segment of deep nephrons in the salt retention.

Mechanisms of Salt Retention

In the cases of cirrhosis or congestive heart failure, circumstantial evidence has been cited for a role of renal hemodynamic alterations in mediating avid sodium reabsorption. Evidence for such a role in the nephrotic syndrome is difficult to obtain, however. As noted above, extremely high filtration fractions would be required to raise peritubular oncotic pressures to levels adequate to enhance proximal reabsorption. Furthermore, studies in man before and after steroid induced remission of minimal-change nephrotic syndrome found a rise rather than a fall in this parameter in response to therapy.[172] In these studies, however, only patients with normal or expanded blood volumes were studied. It is possible that the opposite circumstances exist in nephrotic individuals with depleted blood volumes and stimulation of the renin-angiotensin system or catecholamine release. In this situation it is at least conceivable that postglomerular hydrostatic pressure might be decreased, and thereby mediate increased sodium reabsorption along the proximal tubule and/or the loop of Henle. In this regard it is pertinent to note that Dusing and colleagues were unable to increase urinary sodium excretion in nephrotic subjects with the infusion of saralasin, a competitive antagonist of angiotensin II, despite an increase in mean arterial pressure.[177]

Oliver and co-workers have shown that urinary catecholamine excretion is increased in the nephrotic syndrome.[178] Insofar as this may represent enhanced renal sympathetic nerve stimulation, it is possible that this phenomenon partially mediates the enhanced sodium reabsorption. On the other hand, it must be remembered that most data suggest that distal nephron segments are primarily involved in this condition, and that evidence for a distal effect of catecholamines has not yet been reported.

Both plasma and urinary aldosterone levels are elevated in many, but not all patients with the nephrotic syndrome.[91,179] In view of the distal site of action of this mineralocorticoid, and evidence for enhanced distal reabsorption, it is attractive to attribute at least part of the salt retention to this hormone. That this mechanism is not an essential component of salt retention, however, is emphasized by observations of edema formation in the face of low aldosterone levels.[91,173] To our knowledge, the possibility that some non-aldosterone humoral substances are involved in the salt retention has not been assessed.

Treatment of Salt Retention in the Nephrotic Syndrome

Although the classic theory of salt retention in the nephrotic syndrome may not be applicable to all nephrotic subjects, it remains clear that proteinuria is intimately involved, and that either drug-induced or spontaneous remissions in proteinuria are associated with a diuresis and restoration of normal sodium handling. Thus, the ideal therapy for this condition is correction of the excessive urinary loss of albumin. Unfortunately, such therapy is reliably effective only to those patients with minimal-change disease, which usually responds to relatively short courses of corticosteroids and/or cytotoxic agents. Over the past decade, several investigators have issued reports that nonsteroidal anti-inflammatory agents decrease proteinuria in nephrotic patients with a variety of glomerulopathies.[180-183] These beneficial effects, however, have not been uniformly observed or may be only transient.[184,185] Furthermore, numerous reports have now surfaced indicating that these agents may have profound deleterious effects on renal function.[186-189] In view of these considerations it seems inappropriate to recommend the use of nonsteroidal anti-inflammatory agents in the treatment of the nephrotic syndrome, especially in individuals with compromised renal function.

Prior to the availability of orally effective diuretic agents, dietary management provided the main therapeutic modality for the nephrotic syndrome, and consisted of salt restriction and a high protein intake. The latter is effective in maintaining a positive nitrogen balance, which is particularly important in children, but is not very effective in promoting the mobilization of edema. Strict dietary salt restriction is effective in arresting or slowing the rate of edema formation, but unless coupled with the use of diuretics seldom eliminates edema. Nonetheless, since the magnitude of negative sodium balance depends upon the extent to which urinary sodium exceeds sodium intake, it is obvious that sodium restriction potentiates the benefits of any given natriuretic response to diuretics. Finally, an important word of caution is appropriate about the use of diuretics in the nephrotic syndrome. Overzealous use of these drugs may precipitate frank volume depletion, which can result in deterioration of renal function and hypoperfusion of other organ systems. Indeed, acute renal failure has been reported in nephrotic patients, and may occur as a complication of diuretic therapy.[190-192] Since edema per se is only a sign of the underlying pathology and is not harmful in itself, it does not demand specific therapy. Therefore, when diuretics are employed it is imperative that patients be examined for signs and symptoms of intravascular volume depletion and that renal function be regularly monitored. When these complications occur, diuretic therapy must obviously be discontinued.

ACUTE GLOMERULONEPHRITIS

Acute poststreptococcal glomerulonephritis represents a prototype of so-called "nephritic" edema, a term utilized to distinguish the pathophysiology from that of the "nephrotic" edema just discussed. In that latter entity, as well as cirrhosis and heart failure, an afferent component of salt retention has been either postulated or demonstrated, and in each, a reduction in effective arterial blood volume has been invoked to explain the body's perceived need to retain sodium. Studies of the pathogenesis of nephritic edema seem to clearly deny any real or relative alteration in blood volume that could provide the afferent signal for avid salt retention and edema formation. A large and conclusive body of data recently reviewed by Glassock indicate that effective arterial blood volume is increased in acute glomerulonephritis.[193] These data include: (1) an increase in absolute plasma volume in the disease, (2) an increased mean arterial blood pressure, (3) venous hypertension, (4) an increased cardiac output, (5) suppression of the renin-angiotensin-aldosterone system, (6) low arteriovenous oxygen differences, and (7) depressed sympathetic nervous activity. It therefore appears that the salt retention of acute glomerulonephritis is a relatively unique phenomenon in that it represents a *primary* renal event rather than an adaptive response to some nonrenal systemic abnormality.

Although the renal salt retention appears to occur in the absence of an afferent mechanism, and in this respect differentiates acute glomerulonephritis from the previously discussed entities, the mechanism of edema formation is similar to that described for heart failure, cirrhosis, and the nephrotic syndrome. Specifically, it occurs as a result of an imbalance of the normal Starling forces across the peripheral capillary beds. Further, since edema may form even in the absence of hypoalbuminemia, it is obvious that the transudation of fluid is often a direct consequence of increased capillary hydrostatic pressure.

Efferent Limb

Acute glomerulonephritis is characterized by a sudden decrement in the rate of glomerular filtration, and as a consequence, a fall in the filtered load of sodium. It is not unreasonable to suspect that such a decrease would result in at least transient salt retention and expansion of the ECF volume. On the other hand, some abnormality of tubular function must be operative, since the decrease in tubular sodium reabsorption that normally results from even mild ECF volume expansion fails to occur in this setting, and as a result further expansion follows, ultimately resulting in edema accumulation.

Nephron Site Responsible for Salt Retention in Acute Glomerulonephritis

Clinical studies of patients with acute glomerulonephritis indicate that their filtration fraction is usually decreased.[194] Insofar as this parameter varies directly with proximal reabsorption at any given plasma oncotic pressure, one would predict that proximal reabsorption would be decreased in this disease. Indeed, micropuncture studies in animal models in which the filtration fraction is documented to be decreased have found absolute proximal reabsorption to be diminished.[195–200] As shown in Figure 2-9, Maddox and co-workers found that glomerular tubular balance was demonstrable

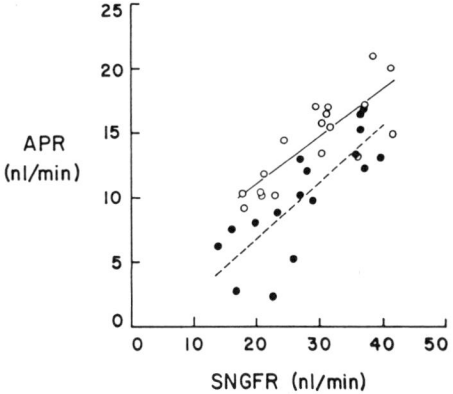

Fig. 2-9. Relationship between single nephron glomerular filtration rate (SNGFR) and absolute proximal reabsorption in normal (O——O) and acutely nephritic (●- - - - -●) rats. At any given SNGFR, APR was decreased in animals with acute nephritis. (From Maddox DA et al[198] with permission.)

in animals with acute glomerulonephritis as well as normal rats.[198] Yet absolute proximal reabsorption tended to be decreased at any given filtration rate in the nephritic rats. In this study, therefore, fractional proximal reabsorption was less in nephritic animals. Maddox and colleagues also measured determinants of proximal reabsorption and concluded that the decrease in proximal reabsorption was explained by a decrease in peritubular oncotic pressure and a slight increase in peritubular hydrostatic pressure.

Wagnild and Wen examined proximal reabsorption in a dog model of glomerulonephritis before and after acute volume expansion.[200] During hydropenia, fractional proximal sodium reabsorption was not different from that in control animals. After an acute saline infusion, this parameter decreased appropriately, but fractional sodium excretion increased only minimally, suggesting enhanced distal reabsorption. Rocha and associates found that fractional reabsorption of sodium was normal throughout the superficial nephron of nephritic rats, yet because of a diminished filtration rate, absolute sodium excretion was decreased.[196] Unfortunately, these investigators did not examine segmental sodium reabsorption after acute volume expansion. In that setting, enhanced fractional reabsorption may have been detected along distal nephron sites.

Despite these data implicating more distal segments in the salt retention of acute glomerulonephritis, other investigators have reported an increase in proximal reabsorption as well. Godon found that proximal reabsorption was markedly enhanced in rats with acute glomerulonephritis,[201] and similar results were reported by Kuroda, Aynedjian, and Bank.[202]

From these considerations it seems fair to conclude that since proximal reabsorption may be decreased, normal, or increased in nephritic kidneys, and since decreased urinary sodium excretion uniformly occurs in glomerulonephritis, avid distal reabsorption must be an essential component of sodium retention in this condition.

Mechanism of Salt Retention

Renal Hemodynamics

As noted above, a decrease in filtration fraction is commonly observed in acute glomerulonephritis. Considering that the plasma protein concentration is normal to decreased and the systemic arterial pressure is normal to increased, it is unlikely that hemodynamically mediated changes in peritubular factors could contribute to the enhanced proximal reabsorption reported by Godon[201] and Kuroda and co-workers.[202] In fact, in a study in which postglomerular protein concentrations were calculated from filtration fraction and plasma protein concentrations, Godon concluded that peritubular oncotic pressure could not account for the avid proximal sodium reabsorption.[203] It is possible that a decrease in postglomerular hydrostatic pressure mediates enhanced loop reabsorption. However, Maddox and colleagues reported normal pertibular hydrostatic pressures in their model of acute glomerulonephritis.[198] Finally, it should be noted that Wen and Wagnild reported no difference in the distribution of renal blood flow or glomerular filtration between normal rats and rats with acute glomerulonephritis.[199]

Aldosterone

As in other edematous states, aldosterone has been implicated by some as mediating the augmented distal sodium reabsorption in acute glomerulonephritis.[203] Although plasma levels of this hormone are normally depressed in nephritic patients, it is possible that even those low levels are inappropriately elevated in view of the expanded ECF volume, and thereby contribute in part to the salt retention.[204] On the other hand, both normal individuals given exogenous mineralocorticoid and patients with primary aldosteronism fail to retain sodium to the point of edema formation. Thus, as in the previously discussed edematous states, aldosterone probably plays a minor or "permissive" role in the salt retention and edema formation in acute glomerulonephritis.

Non-Aldosterone Humoral Factors

Bricker and colleagues have accumulated an impressive body of data suggesting that chronically uremic subjects, including those with chronic glomerulonephritis, elaborate a natriuretic substance that plays an integral role in the ability of these individuals to maintain normal sodium homeostasis.[205] Fine and co-workers using the isolated perfused rabbit cortical collecting tubule, presented evidence that this hormone diminished distal sodium reabsorption.[206] Considering that the bulk of micropuncture studies ascribe the avid salt retention of acute glomerulonephritis to the distal nephron, it is possible that in this condition, patients fail to produce this natriuretic substance, or that the nephron is resistant to its action. In this regard, Godon has suggested that this is indeed the case.[201] He found that rats with acute glomerulonephritis failed to produce a natriuretic substance in response to acute saline loading. It should be pointed out, however, that Godon placed the effect of this substance at the level of the proximal rather than the distal tubule. In addition, a very important study of Wagnild and Gutmann suggests that lack of a circulating natriuretic hormone is not important in the diminished natriuretic response of the nephritic kidney to an acute saline load.[207] These investigators created a unilateral model of acute glomerulonephritis by the intrarenal infusion of nephrotoxic serum. The nephritic kidney not only had a lower basal fractional excretion of sodium but also had a blunted response to saline loading. Since the control kidney responded normally, it is unlikely that these animals failed to produce a natriuretic substance. Alternatively, it is possible that the nephritic kidney was either resistant to the action of the putative hormone or that the hormone is intrarenal in both origin and action.

The possibility that renal prostaglandins or kinins participate in the salt retention of acute glomerulonephritis has not, to our knowledge, been investigated. Similarly, we are unaware of data implicating enhanced renal nerve activity in this condition.

Treatment of Salt Retention in Acute Glomerulonephritis

As was noted earlier, acute glomerulonephritis is a condition characterized by *primary* renal salt retention, which results directly in ECF volume expansion, hypertension, and occasionally, pulmonary vascular congestion.[208] As a result, diuretic therapy not only decreases edema, but is also usually effective in treating the hypertension and diminishing pulmonary vascular congestion when it is present.[209] Although thiazide diuretics are occasionally effective, most nephritic patients require more potent loop-acting agents.[209] Because patients with this condition usually have some degree of renal insufficiency, the potassium-sparing diuretics, spironolactone and triamterene, are contraindicated because of the risk of hyperkalemia. It should also be pointed out that even in the presence of pulmonary congestion and a gallop rhythm, digitalization is not effective, a fact that underscores the lack of a cardiac component in the sodium retention of glomerulonephritis.[210] Finally, occasional patients with more severe disease may be oliguric and refractory to diuretics. Under these circumstances hemodialysis may be necessary for either a reduction in volume (and hypertension and/or pulmonary congestion) or control of hyperkalemia.

IDIOPATHIC EDEMA

Idiopathic edema, which has also been termed "cyclical edema," is a disorder limited to women and characterized by salt retention and generalized edema formation in the absence of hepatic, cardiac, or renal disease. Although the disease may be episodic in some patients, with periods of freedom from edema and maintenance of a normal sodium balance, other individuals may chronically retain sodium and require continuous dietary sodium restriction and/or diuretic therapy. The pathophysiology of idiopathic edema, as its name implies, is unknown. Nevertheless, several interesting observations have been made and will be considered here.

Afferent Limb

Because idiopathic edema occurs most frequently in premenopausal women, elevated estrogen levels or activity have been implicated in the pathogenesis of the salt retention of this condition. It is possible that estrogen, as a vasodilator substance, induces an increase in vascular capacity that precipitates a fall in effective arterial blood volume and thereby signals the kidney to retain sodium. As discussed below, estrogens have also been held to have a direct sodium retaining effect on the renal tubule. Regardless of whether their effect is indirect or direct, it should be stressed that Preedy and Aitken have shown that the sodium retention is transient, and that normal individuals demonstrate an "escape" from chronic estrogen administration.[211] In addition, Ferris and colleagues described a case of idiopathic edema in a postmenopausal woman with undetectable urinary estradiol excretion.[212]

Hypoalbuminemia has been reported to occur in idiopathic edema.[213] Gill, Waldmann, and Bartter found that the cause of the hypoalbuminemia varied in these patients, but that it was accompanied in all cases by a low plasma volume, even when the latter was measured in the presence of edema. Thus, these authors concluded that an absolute decrease in circulating albumin, and consequently plasma volume contraction, provided the afferent limb of sodium retention in this condition. Unfortunately, others have been unable to confirm the presence of hypoalbuminemia.[213,214] Emerson and Armstrong[216] and Clarkson and co-workers[217] reported individuals with an abnormally high capillary permeability to albumin, and attributed the edema to this defect. Because this abnormality has been observed in so few patients, it may not apply to all individuals with idiopathic edema, but instead may represent only a small subset of patients with this problem.

Kuchel and associates[214] and Streeten and co-workers[215] have reported studies suggesting that women with idiopathic edema have an exaggerated antinatriuretic response to assuming an upright position. On the basis of findings of orthostatic hypotension, increased morning-evening weight differences, and increased renin response to the upright position, these authors attributed the salt retention to enhanced orthostatic pooling of blood volume in the lower extremities and a subsequent decrease in effective arterial blood volume.

All of the afferent mechanisms postulated above for salt retention are based on a decrease in absolute or effective arterial blood volume. As pointed out by Ferris and colleagues, these postulates would therefore predict activation of the renin-angiotensin system.[212] Studying eight patients with idiopathic edema, these investigators reported that neither initial plasma renin activity nor the renin response to salt loading differed from values obtained in normal subjects. These observations, therefore, question the existence of an afferent limb in the pathophysiology of idiopathic edema, and raise the possibility that the salt retention is a primary renal abnormality reflecting an inappropriate tubular avidity for sodium. Other investigators, on the other hand, have found elevated plasma renin activity in this entity.[218]

Efferent Limb

Nephron Site Responsible for Salt Retention

Because no animal model of idiopathic edema exists, there are few data reflecting the nephron site (or sites) responsible for avid sodium reabsorption. To our knowledge only one study has addressed this issue. Ferris and associates noted that in response to a very high sodium chloride intake, patients with idiopathic edema, but not control subjects, developed a mild hyperchloremic metabolic acidosis.[212] This observation suggested to these authors that proximal reabsorption (reflected by bicarbonate reabsorption) was appropriately depressed by the patients' volume expansion, but that hyperchloremia developed as a result of enhanced distal reabsorption.

Mechanism of Salt Retention

Hemodynamic Alterations

Hemodynamic alterations are unlikely to mediate the salt retention of idiopathic edema since systemic blood pressure, GFR, and renal blood flow are usually normal in this condition.[92] Renal nerve stimulation could increase sodium reabsorption. Gill and colleagues reported elevated urinary catecholamine excretion in volume-depleted patients with idiopathic edema.[218] Direct evidence of a role for renal nerves in this condition is lacking, however.

Aldosterone

Aldosterone has been implicated as an important effector mechanism in idiopathic edema. Gill and co-workers found increased aldosterone secretory rates in their patients.[217] They also reported that individuals with idiopathic edema showed a greater natriuretic response to spironolactone than did control subjects. Interestingly, when these investigators administered a self-retaining steroid to their patients, the resultant weight gain and positive sodium balance did not differ from that observed in normal women. This finding seemed at odds with the reports that women with idiopathic edema fail to "escape" from long term mineralocorticoid administration.[92] However, Gill's patients were on bed rest during their study, and Marieb and Mulrow reported a patient who "escaped" while remaining supine, but developed edema during forced ambulation.[219] Parenthetically, it should be pointed out that this finding supports the view that orthostatic factors are an important afferent component in this disease. Additionally, failure to escape from mineralocorticoid-induced salt retention (whether in the supine or upright position) indicates that efferent factors other than aldosterone must also be operative in mediating the salt retention. Furthermore, Ferris and co-workers were unable to demonstrate hyperaldosteronism in their patients,[212] and Thorn reported a poor natriuretic response to spironolactone.[220]

As noted above, estrogens can be theoretically implicated in both the afferent and efferent limb of salt retention in idiopathic edema. For reasons previously noted, however, this hormone cannot be of primary importance, at least in most patients with this disease.

MacGregor and associates have recently presented intriguing data relating the pathogenesis of idiopathic edema.[221] They studied 10 women with this disorder and found that all were intermittently taking diuretic agents, and that 8 of these patients had elevated plasma renin activity and urinary aldosterone levels. Upon discontinuation of the diuretics, 9 of the 10 women experienced a weight gain that was associated with edema formation, and the magnitude of the weight gain correlated directly with the initial elevation in plasma renin and urinary aldosterone levels. Within 20 days, however, seven patients were free of edema and two others also subsequently became edema-free. Only one of the subjects continued to experience intermittent edema over a follow-up period of three years. MacGregor and his associates also noted a history of dietary carbohydrate restriction in many patients with idiopathic edema. Studying four normal women, they found that when four days of a low sodium, low carbohydrate diet was followed by a high sodium, high carbohydrate diet, all four subjects gained weight and developed edema. On the basis of these findings, and citing evidence that carbohydrate restriction stimulates catecholamine production, MacGregor and his group concluded that idiopathic edema may result from diuretic-induced stimulation of aldosterone and "starvation"-induced stimulation of circulating catecholamines.[221]

Treatment of Idiopathic Edema

Some authorities recommend dietary sodium restriction and/or diuretic therapy for women with idiopathic edema.[92] The study by MacGregor and his colleagues, however, indicates that these measures may only rarely be necessary. It now seems reasonable to recommend that patients with this condition be thoroughly counseled about the possible role of diuretics and salt and carbohydrate restriction in the development of edema, and the likelihood that such therapy may serve to perpetuate rather than resolve the patients' difficulty. Every effort should then be made to convince the patient to abstain from diuretic use and consume a normal diet for several weeks, and that the long-term benefits will outweigh the transient discomfort of the patient's edematous condition. If the findings of MacGregor and his associates are applicable to the majority of women with idiopathic edema, such an approach should sharply reduce the number of patients requiring indefinite salt restriction and/or diuretic therapy.

SODIUM DEPLETED STATES

Sodium depleted states are the antitheses of edematous states, and just as a sodium surfeit results in ECF volume expansion, a sodium deficit results in contraction of that fluid compartment. The clinical manifestations of volume depletion (e.g., orthostatic hypotension, tachycardia, azotemia and cerebral ischemia) are primarily due to a decrease in plasma volume. Thus, the clinical severity of sodium depleted states depends upon the degree to which the plasma volume participates in the reduction of total ECF volume. As recently summarized by Anderson and Linas, this depends not only on the quantity of the sodium deficit, but also on the rapidity with which the loss occurs.[222] The ability to preferentially replenish plasma volume has been demonstrated by Bauer and Brooks, who measured changes in fluid compartments in human subjects in response to acute and chronic diuretic administration.[223] These investigators found that the acute negative sodium balance induced by diuretics was accompanied by a decrease in both plasma and interstitial volumes. With continued chronic diuretic therapy, however, plasma volume returned to the pre-diuretic level and the interstitial fluid space bore the brunt of the reduction in ECF volume. Although the mechanism of this adjustment is not clear, the decrease in arterial blood pressure in response to the diuretic treatment, as well as a transient increase in plasma oncotic pressure, may have altered Starling's forces across peripheral capillary beds and thus favored the movement of interstitial fluid into the vascular space. Alternatively, changes in pre- and postcapillary sphincter tone could influence Starling's forces even in the absence of changes in mean arterial pressure.

In addition to the aforementioned signs of intravascular volume depletion, the clinical findings in sodium deficient states also include dry mucous membranes, poor skin turgor and, in severe cases, sunken eyes and skin mottling due to intense vasoconstriction. Patients' complaints are often nonspecific and may include enhanced thirst, muscle cramps and weakness, headache, and lassitude. If volume depletion is superimposed on moderate renal insufficiency, a dramatic worsening of renal function may occur and precipitate symptoms of frank uremia. Laboratory findings, while not pathognomonic, often aid in detecting more subtle degrees of sodium depletion. An increase in hemoglobin concentration (hemoconcentration), a disproportionate rise in blood urea nitrogen relative to that of the serum creatinine concentration, and increased plasma renin activity are common findings. It should be stressed that the serum sodium *concentration* bears no direct relationship to ECF volume and may be low, normal, or increased depending on the concomitant water balance. Nonetheless, since volume depletion is a potent nonosmotic stimulus to both ADH release and thirst, hyponatremia is often present if free access to water exists.

Causes of Sodium Depletion

The causes of sodium depletion are extensive, and generally may be divided into those due to extrarenal sodium losses and those due to excessive urinary sodium excretion (Table 2-2 and Table 2-3). These two broad categories can be distinguished by determining the urinary sodium concentration. In conditions associated with extrarenal sodium losses, avid renal sodium retention occurs and the urine sodium concentration is less than 10 mEq/liter. Values greater than 20 mEq/liter are indicative of a renal etiology. One very important exception to this rule should be noted, however. In cases of metabolic alkalosis due to nonrenal causes (e.g., vomiting or nasogastric suction), urinary sodium concentration may be quite high, particularly if this value is determined during the generation of the alkalosis.[224] Under these conditions, determining the urinary chloride concentration will accurately distinguish renal from nonrenal causes of salt depletion.

Nonrenal Causes of Sodium Depletion

The nonrenal causes of sodium depletion are listed in Table 2-2. Gastrointestinal losses are probably the most common clinical cause of volume depletion. Table 2-4 lists the various gastrointestinal fluids and the ranges of volumes and electrolyte concentration that they are likely to have. Vomiting (or nasogastric suction) results in the removal of up to 3 liters of water per day, and concomitant sodium losses may amount to 240 mEq/day. Because of the concomitant hydrogen ion loss and the volume depletion-induced enhancement of renal bicarbonate reabsorption and generation, metabolic alkalosis commonly accompanies the volume depletion. In addition, the volume stimulus to secondary aldosteronism in a setting of increased distal delivery of sodium bicarbonate leads to excessive urinary potassium excretion and hypokalemia.[224]

Diarrhea results from either a decrease in absorption of foodstuffs and gastrointestinal secretions or an increase in the rate of secretion that overwhelms the reabsorptive capability of the gut. In either case, stool volume (and water) is increased. As shown in Figure 2-10, the sodium concentration of stool water is relatively constant, ranging

Table 2-2. Nonrenal Causes of Sodium Depletion

Gastrointestinal losses
  Vomiting or nasogastric suction
  Diarrhea
  Ileostomies
  Pancreatic or biliary fistulas
  Internal sequestration of ECF
Skin losses
  Excessive sweating
  Burns

Table 2-3. Renal Causes of Sodium Depletion

Causes intrinsic to the kidney
  Chronic renal failure
  "Salt-losing" nephropathies
  Nonoliguric acute renal failure
  Diuretic phase of acute renal failure
  Postobstructive diuresis
Causes extrinsic to the kidney
  Solute diuresis
  Diuretics
  Aldosterone deficiency states
    Addison's disease
    Enzyme deficiencies
    Renal resistance to aldosterone

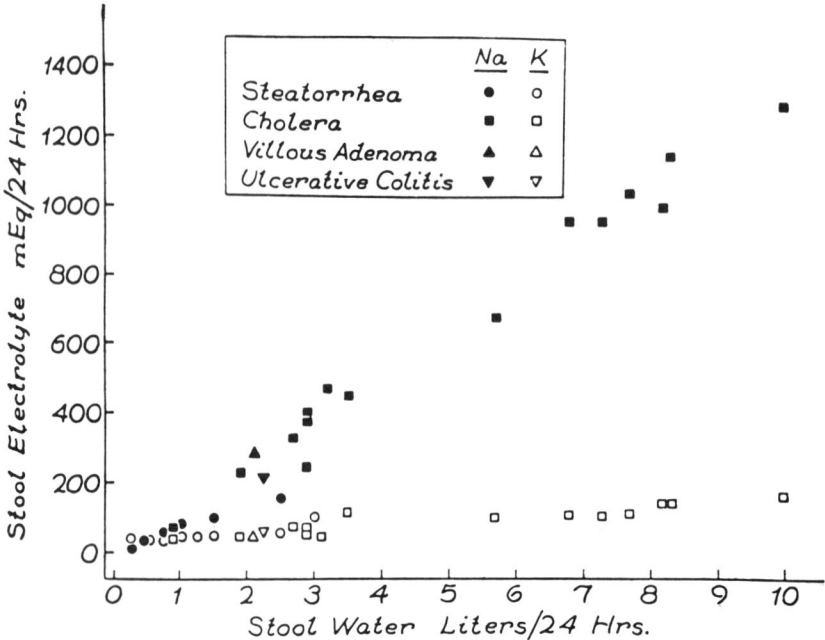

Fig. 2-10. Relationship between stool volume and electrolyte losses in patients with a variety of diarrheal disorders. Note that the sodium concentration is relatively constant and stool losses increase linearly with increasing stool volume. (From Fordtran JS, Dietschy JM: Sodium and potassium losses in diarrhea states. Gastroenterology 50:263, 1966, with permission.)

from 100 to 140 mEq/liter. Thus, the amount of the sodium deficit resulting from diarrhea depends upon the volume of stool water. In some conditions (e.g., cholera) this may amount to as much as 20 liters/day.[225] Most diarrheal conditions result in the loss of potassium and bicarbonate as well as sodium. As a result, hypokalemia and a hyperchloremic metabolic acidosis often accompany the volume depletion of these conditions.

Ileostomies are generally not associated with significant salt and water deficits since the amount of water and electrolytes lost through these fistulas are usually well under the normal dietary intake of these substances (Table 2-4). When dietary intake is restricted, however, this "obligatory" salt and water loss can be of clinical significance. Further, these losses can be markedly increased in diarrheal disease states.

Pancreatic and biliary fistulas may result in varying degrees of volume and electrolyte loss. Neither is likely to lead to significant sodium depletion as long as a normal intake of salt and water is maintained. Pancreatic fistulas, however, may lead to profound metabolic acidosis due to the very bicarbonate-rich nature of pancreatic fluid.[226] In addition to these external losses of fluid and electrolytes, gastrointestinal disorders may also cause significant sodium depletion by the *internal sequestration of ECF*. Examples of such conditions include mechanical bowel obstruction, pancreatitis, and peritonitis.

The skin provides the only other potential extrarenal source of sodium depletion. Sweat, which is usually hypotonic to ECF, contains 40 to 80 mEq of sodium per liter, and the volume of sweat may exceed one liter per hour under conditions of a high metabolic rate and ambient temperature. As recently reviewed by Knochel, these values may be influenced by acclimatization, phys-

Table 2-4. Gastrointestinal Fluids: Volume and Ionic Composition

Fluid	Normal volume (ml/day)	Na+	K+	HCO3−
Gastric	300–3000	40–80	5–15	0
Stool water	<50	100–140	10–30	10–30
Ileostomy	100–1000	120–140	15–20	10–30
Bile	100–1000	140–160	0–10	40
Pancreatic	100–1000	130–150	0–10	100

(Adapted from Anderson and Linas[222] by permission.)

ical conditioning, or volume depletion itself.[227] Nevertheless, it is obvious that failure to replace sweat-related losses of salt and water can result in profound volume depletion and shock. When severe, such a deficit can lead to the devastating clinical syndrome of heat stroke. Finally it should be noted that burn victims may suffer severe sodium depletion. Moncrief has estimated that in the first 24 hours following thermal injury, the sodium needed to restore ECF volume and cardiac output amounts to 0.5 to 0.7 mEq/kg per percent of body surface burned.[228] Thus, a 70 kg individual with a 30 percent burn would experience a 1,000 to 1,500 mEq sodium deficit, representing a 50 to 70 percent reduction in ECF volume.

Renal Causes of Sodium Depletion

Inappropriately high urinary sodium excretion may result from either a primary renal lesion in which tubular sodium transport is limited, or from some nonrenal factor that prevents the normal renal tubule from reabsorbing sodium. The renal causes of sodium depletion are listed according to these two broad categories in Table 2.3

Causes Intrinsic to the Kidney

Many early studies described renal sodium wasting in patients with chronic renal failure of diverse etiologies.[229–232] These studies indicated that most individuals with renal insufficiency could maintain sodium balance when the dietary sodium intake was "normal," but when acutely deprived of sodium were unable to elaborate a sodium-free urine, leading to volume depletion. Although the explanation of this "salt wasting" in chronic renal failure is still unknown, a recent study by Danovitch, Bourgoignie, and Bricker sheds further light on the clinical significance of this phenomenon.[233] These investigators studied five patients with chronic renal failure and found that four of these subjects became volume depleted with abrupt decreases in dietary sodium. When sodium intake was gradually decreased over a 4- to 14-week period, however, all five patients were able to reduce their urinary sodium content to less than 10 mEq/day without evidence of significant volume depletion. This finding indicates that patients with chronic renal failure require a prolonged period to reduce their urinary sodium excretion, but like normal individuals retain their ability to do so. On the other hand, the study by Danovitch, Bourgoignie and Bricker[233] re-emphasizes the potential danger of abrupt reductions in dietary sodium in this patient population.

Occasionally, patients with interstitial renal disease will have a marked defect in renal sodium reabsorption, in which urinary sodium excretion may approach 200 mEq/day even when dietary sodium intake is negligible.[222] Such salt wasting may be particularly prominent in patients with medullary cystic disease,[234,235] and probably explains the prominence of enuresis in these patients. Whether or not these individuals would respond to slow, progressive decrements in dietary sodium intake in the same manner as the subjects studied by Danovitch and his co-workers is not clear.

Patients with nonoliguric acute renal failure may also suffer from inappropriate urine sodium excretion. Anderson and associates found that mean urine volume and urinary sodium concentrations averaged 1280 ml/day and 50 mEq/liter, respectively, in patients with this entity.[236] Assuming that this represents "obligatory" sodium excretion, this would amount to a sodium deficit of 64 mEq/day if sodium intake were nil. Over a prolonged period, the accumulative negative sodium balance could result in significant ECF volume depletion.

The so-called diuretic phase of acute renal failure is also characterized by an inability of the kidney to respond appropriately to alterations in sodium intake. As recently reviewed by Levinsky and colleagues, the excretion of massive amounts of salt and water described in the earlier literature is now only rarely reported.[237] Nonetheless, if sodium intake is severely limited, significant deficits in sodium balance may occur.

Finally, the diuresis that may follow the relief of urinary tract obstruction may rarely result in significant volume depletion.[238] Falls and Stacy have recently emphasized that even the massive diuresis that occasionally occurs transiently in this setting is often explicable on the basis of a marked sodium excess that accumulates during the period of obstruction.[239] Thus, despite unequivocal experimental evidence for a defect in tubular sodium transport during the postobstructive period,[240] clinically significant volume depletion seems to be quite rare.

Causes Extrinsic to the Kidney

Solute diuresis induced by the presence of excessive amounts of either reabsorbable or poorly reabsorbable substances in the renal tubular lumen can result in significant urinary losses of both water and sodium. Endogenous solutes that fall into this category include urea, glucose, and sodium bicarbonate. Urea accumulates in the plasma as a result of impaired glomerular filtration, and in the steady state, the amount present in the ultrafiltrate is, therefore, not excessive. Following the relief of urinary obstruction, however, the increased filtered load of urea probably contributes to the postobstructive diuresis. The glucosuria of diabetic ketoacidosis and hyperosmotic nonketotic coma can result in profound volume depletion. Tyler estimates that deficits of 6 to 8 liters are common in the latter condition,[241] and McCurdy attributed nearly half of the deaths in her series of 84 patients to profound volume depletion.[242] Bicarbonate concentrations may become very high in metabolic alkalosis, and by virtue of the limited ability of the renal tubules to reabsorb this anion, its urinary excretion may obligate the inappropriate excretion of sodium.[224]

Exogenously administered solutes including urea, mannitol, and radiographic contrast media may also induce significant increases in urinary sodium excretion. Gennari and Kassirer found that large doses of mannitol can result in the urinary excretion of as much as 20 to 30 percent of the filtered load of sodium.[243] Because radiographic contrast media are not given over a prolonged period, the osmotic diuresis they induce is generally not the cause of severe dehydration. On the other hand, when patients are prepared for radiologic procedures by methods that also induce volume depletion, the additional volume deficits created by the osmotic diuresis may precipitate clinically significant sodium depletion.

Diuretic agents are obviously capable of producing volume depletion when used in the treatment of either edematous or nonedematous states. The use of loop-acting diuretics in repeated doses, as in the treatment of hypercalcemia, may result in severe volume depletion, since the patients receiving these agents are often dehydrated from hypercalciuria prior to such therapy.[244]

Aldosterone deficiency states are well known to be associated with renal salt wasting. Three general categories of this condition have been identified, and all are associated with hyperkalemia. First, primary adrenal insufficiency (Addison's disease) results in a deficiency of both mineralocorticoid and glucocorticoid hormones. As a result, patients with this condition manifest not only salt depletion but also hyperpigmentation and occasionally hypoglycemia. Second, isolated hypoaldosteronism may occur as a result of adrenocortical enzyme deficiencies that do not interfere with glucocorticoid synthesis. The most common of these so-called "adrenogenital syndromes" is a 21-hydroxylase deficiency.[245] Because this defect causes a shunting of precursor hormones toward the synthetic pathway for androgen production, virilization is commonly observed. Rare enzymatic defects that result in renal salt wasting include deficiencies of 18-hydroxylase, 18-dehydrogenase,[246] or 22,23-cholesterol desmolase.[247] Aldosterone deficiency has also been reported to occur as a complication of chronic heparin therapy.[246] To our knowledge the mechanism of this effect has not been elucidated. The third form of hypoaldosteronism, hyporeninemic hypoaldosteronism, was originally described by Schambelan and co-workers in 1972, and ascribed to a primary deficit in renal renin production.[249] This entity, which is most commonly observed in the setting of diabetes or interstitial nephritis with moderate renal insufficiency, is seldom if ever associated with renal sodium wasting, however, and is usually manifested by hyperkalemia and hyperchloremic metabolic acidosis. In view of the hypoaldosteronism, one might question why the affected individuals are not "salt wasters." There are several possible explanations, the most obvious being that aldosterone is decreased but not absent in this condition. Alternatively, several authors have described patients with this entity who are volume expanded and in whom the hyporeninemia and hypoaldosteronism are the result of this volume expansion.[250–252]

Finally, it should be pointed out that a small number of children with salt-wasting conditions show evidence of a tubular resistance to the sodium retaining effect of aldosterone. Schwartz and Spitzer recently reviewed this entity, which they termed "pseudohypoaldosteronism," and found only 22 cases reported in the literature.[253]

Treatment of Sodium Depleted States

The initial, acute treatment of sodium depletion obviously calls for restoration of the sodium deficit and repletion of the ECF volume. This is best accomplished by sodium chloride administration, since anions other than chloride are less well reabsorbed by the renal tubule and their administration may result in obligatory urinary sodium excretion and/or increases in urinary potassium excretion. The amount of sodium chloride to be administered depends upon the degree of volume depletion, and since there is usually no reliable method to accurately quantitate the sodium deficit, therapy is often empirical and dictated by the clinical response. If the pre-volume depletion weight is known, one liter of normal saline per kilogram of weight loss is a reasonable estimate of the sodium requirement. If hemoconcentration is present and neither hemorrhage nor hemolysis have occurred, the percentage increase in hemoglobin will reflect the percentage decrement in volume. When sodium losses are ongoing, as in diarrhea, these losses must be added to the estimated deficit. It should also be pointed out that once the initial deficit is corrected, such ongoing losses can be estimated by accurate daily weighings. In this regard it is appropriate to note that when effective caloric intake is limited, the consequent catabolic state will result in a loss of 0.2 to 0.3 kg of tissue mass per day. If this weight loss is not taken into account, a patient with diarrhea, for instance, who is given sufficient normal saline to maintain a constant body weight over 10 days, would have a two-liter ECF volume surplus.

The tonicity of the initial sodium chloride replacement solution is dictated by the serum sodium concentration. If severe volume deficits are present, however, isotonic saline is preferable in all cases, even in the presence of hypertonicity, since correction of tonicity is less important than repletion of volume in this setting. Solutions used for the maintenance replacement of ongoing losses should be chosen on the basis of sodium content of the fluids being lost.

REFERENCES

1. Peters JP: Body Water: The Exchange of Fluids in Man. Charles C Thomas, Springfield, IL, 1935
2. Epstein FH, Post RS, McDowell M: The effect of an arterial venous fistula on renal hemodynamics and electrolyte excretion. J Clin Invest 32:233, 1953
3. Epstein FH, Goodyer AVN, Lawrason FD, Relman AS: Studies on the antidiuresis of quite standing: The importance of changes in plasma volume in glomerular filtration rate. J Clin Invest 30:63, 1951
4. Wesson LG: Physiology of the Human Kidney: Sodium Chloride, Monovalent Anions. Grune and Stratton, New York, 1969
5. Arborelius M, Baldwen VI, Lilja B: Hemodynamic changes in man during emersion with the neck above water. Aerospace Med 43:592, 1972
6. Papper S, Rosenbaum JD: Abnormalities in the excretion of water and sodium in "compensated" cirrhosis of the liver. J Lab Clin Med 40:523, 1952
7. Levinsky NG: Refractor ascites in cirrhosis. Kidney Int 14:93, 1978
8. Lieberman FL, Reynolds TB: Plasma volume in cirrhosis of the liver: Its relation to portal hypertension, ascites and renal failure. J Clin Invest 46:1297, 1967
9. Goodyer AVN, Relman AS, Lawrason FD, Epstein FH: Salt retention in cirrhosis of the liver. J Clin Invest 29:973, 1950
10. Tristani FE, Cohn JN: Systemic and renal hemodynamics in oliguric hepatic failure: Effect of volume expansion. J Clin Invest 46:1894, 1967
11. Yamihiro HS, Reynolds TB: Effects of ascitic fluid infusion on sodium excretion, blood volume, and creatinine clearance in cirrhosis. Gastroenterology 40:497, 1961
12. Epstein M: Renal sodium handling in cirrhosis. p. 35. In Epstein M (ed) The Kidney in Liver Disease, Elsevier-North Holland, New York, 1978
13. Ayers CR: Plasma renin activity and renin-substrate concentration in patients with liver disease. Circ Res 20:594, 1967
14. Kondo K, Nakamura R, Saito I, et al: Renin, angiotensin II and juxtaglomerular apparatus in liver cirrhosis. Jap Circ J 38:913, 1974
15. Rosoff L, Zia P, Reynolds T, Horton R: Studies of renin and aldosterone in cirrhotic patients with ascites. Gastroenterology 69:698, 1975
16. Schroeder ET, Anderson GH, Goldman SH, Streeter DHP: Effect of blockade of angiotensin II on blood pressure, renin and aldosterone in cirrhosis. Kidney Int 9:511, 1976
17. Posternak L, Brunner HR, Gavras H, Brunner DB: Angiotensin II blockade in normal man: interaction of renin and sodium in maintaining blood pressure. Kidney Int 11:197, 1977
18. LeVeen HH, Wapnick S, Grosberg S, Kinney MJ: Further experience with peritoneovenous shunt for ascites. Ann Surg 184:574, 1976
19. Wapnick S, Grosberg S, Kinney MJ, LeVenn HH: LeVeen continuous peritoneal-jugular shunt. JAMA 237:131, 1977
19a. Greig PD, Blendis LM, Langer B, et al: Renal and hemodynamic effects of the peritoneovenous shunt. II. Long-term effects. Gastroenterology 80:119, 1981
20. Lieberman FL, Ito S, Reynolds TB: Ef-

fective plasma volume in cirrhosis with ascites. J Clin Invest 48:975, 1969
21. Lieberman FL, Denison EK, Reynolds TB: The relationship of plasma volume, portal hypertension, ascites and renal sodium retention in cirrhosis: The overflow theory of ascites formation. Ann NY Acad Sci 170:202, 1970
22. Levy M: Sodium retention and ascites formation in dogs with experimental portal cirrhosis. Am J Physiol 233:F572, 1977
23. Levy M, Wexler MJ: Renal sodium retention and ascites formation in dogs with experimental portal cirrhosis but without portal hypertension or increased splanchnic vascular capacity. J Lab Clin Med 91:520, 1978
24. Madden JW, Gertman PM, Peacock EE: Dimethylnitrosamine induced hepatic cirrhosis. A new canine model of an ancient human disease. Surgery 68:260, 1970
25. Lopez-Novoa JM, Rengel MA, Hernando L: Dynamics of ascites formation in rats with experimental cirrhosis. Am J Physiol 238:F353, 1980
26. Shear L, Ching S, Gabuzda, GJ: Compartmentalization of ascites and edema in patients with hepatic cirrhosis. N Engl J Med 282:1391, 1970
27. Nelson WP, Rosenbaum JD, Strauss MB: Hyponatremia in hepatic cirrhosis following paracentesis. J Clin Invest 30:738, 1951
28. Papper S: The role of the kidney in Laennec's cirrhosis of the liver. Medicine 37:299, 1958
29. Papper S, Belsky JL, Bleifer KH: Renal failure in Laennec's cirrhosis of the liver. I. Description of clinical and laboratory features. Ann Intern Med 51:759, 1959
30. Murray JF, Dawson AM, Sherlock S: Circulatory changes in chronic liver disease. Ann J Med 24:358, 1958
31. Kowalski HJ, Abelman WH: The cardiac output at rest in Laennec's cirrhosis. J Clin Invest 32:1025, 1953
32. Cohn JN, Khatri IM, Groszman RJ, Kotelanski B: Hepatic blood flow in alcoholic liver disease measured by an indicator dilution technique. Am J Med 53:704, 1972
33. Lemas CJ, Guiha NH, Lekagrel O, Cohn JN: Impaired left ventricular function in alcoholic cirrhosis with ascites: Ineffectiveness of ouabain. Circulation 49:775, 1974
34. Knauer CM, Lowe HM: Hemodynamics in the cirrhotic patient during paracentesis. N Engl J Med 276:491, 1967
35. Cohn JN: Renal hemodynamic alterations in liver disease. p. 225. Suki WN, Eknoyan G (eds): The Kidney in Systemic Disease. Wiley & Sons, New York, 1976
36. Dal Palu C, Donaggro G, Dal Zotto I, Pessina AC: Arteriovenous shunts in cirrhotic patients studied with human serum albumin macroaggregates tagged with ^{131}I. Scand J Gastroenterol 3:425, 1968
37. Levy M, Allotey JBK: Temporal relationships between urinary salt retention and altered systemic hemodynamics in dogs with experimental cirrhosis. J Lab Clin Med 92:560, 1978
38. Klingler EL, Vaamonde CA, Vaamonde LS, et al: Renal function changes in cirrhosis of the liver. Arch Intern Med 125:7070, 1970
39. Schedl HP, Bartter FC: An explanation for experimental correction of the abnormal water diuresis in cirrhosis. J Clin Invest 39:249, 1960
40. Papper S, Saxon L: The diuretic response to administered water in patients with liver disease. Arch Intern Med 103:750, 1959
41. Vaamonde CA, Vaamonde LS, Presser JJ, et al: The role of vasopressin and urea in the renal concentrating defect of patients with cirrhosis of the liver. Clin Sci 41:441, 1971
42. Charmovitz C, Szylman P, Alroy G, Better OS: Mechanism of increased renal tubular sodium reabsorption in cirrhosis. Am J Med 52:198, 1972
43. Auld RB, Alexander EA, Levinsky NG: Proximal tubular function in dogs with thoracic caval constriction. J Clin Invest 50:2150, 1971
44. Levy M: Effects of acute volume expansion and altered hemodynamics on renal tubular function in chronic caval dogs. J Clin Invest 51:922, 1972
45. Cirksena WJ, Dirks JH, Berliner RW: Effect of thoracic cava obstruction on response of proximal tubular sodium reabsorption to saline infusion. J Clin Invest 45:179, 1966
46. Yarger WE: A micropuncture study of salt retention associated with bile duct legation in rats. Clin Res 22:551A, 1974

47. Bank N, Aynedjian HS: A micropuncture study of renal salt retention in chronic bile duct obstruction. J Clin Invest 55:994, 1975
48. Levy M: Sodium retention in dogs with cirrhosis and ascites: Efferent mechanisms. Am J Physiol 233:F586, 1977
49. Lopez-Novoa JM, Rengel MA, Rodicio JL, Hernandez L: A micropuncture study of salt and water retention in chronic experimental cirrhosis. Am J Physiol 232:F315, 1977
50. Conn HO: A rational approach to the hepatorenal syndrome. Gastroenterology 65:321, 1973
51. Epstein M, Schneider N, Befeler B: Relationship of systemic and intrarenal hemodynamics in cirrhosis. J Lab Clin Med 89:1175, 1977
52. Saruta T, Kondo K, Saito I, Nakamura R: Characterization of the components of the renin-angiotensin system in cirrhosis of the liver. p. 207. In Epstein M (ed): The Kidney in Liver Disease. Elsevier-North Holland, New York, 1978
53. Freeman RH, Davis JO, Vitale SJ, Johnston JA: Intrarenal role of angiotensin. Circ Res 32:692, 1973
54. Taub KJ, Caldicott JH, Hollenberg NK: Angiotensin antagonists with increased specificity for the renal vasculature. J Clin Invest 59:528, 1977
55. Slick GL, DiBona GF, Kaloyanides GJ: Renal blockade to angiotensin II in acute and chronic sodium-retaining states. J Pharmacol Exp Ther 195:185, 1975
56. Hollenberg NK: Renin, angiotensin, and the kidney: Assessment with angiotensin antagonists. p. 187. In Epstein M (ed): The Kidney in Liver Disease. Elsevier-North Holland, New York, 1978
57. Epstein M, Berk DP, Hollenberg NK, et al: Renal failure in patients with cirrhosis. The role of active vasoconstriction. Am J Med 49:175, 1970
58. Baldus WP: Etiology and management of renal failure in cirrhosis and portal hypertension. Ann NY Acad Sci 170:267, 1969
59. Boyer TD, Reynolds TB: The effect of indomethacin on renal blood flow and creatinine clearance in patients with cirrhosis. Gastroenterology 70:121, 1976
60. Zipser R, Hoefs J, Speckart P, et al: Prostaglandins: A critical modulator of renin release, blood pressure, and renal function in liver disease. Clin Res 25:151A, 1977
61. Wong PK: The Kallikrein-Kinin and related vasoactive systems in cirrhosis of the liver. p. 299. In Epstein M (ed): The Kidney in Liver Disease. Elsevier-North Holland, New York, 1978
62. Skorecki KL, Brenner BM: Body fluid homeostasis in man: A contemporary overview. Am J Med 70:77, 1981
63. Ichikawa I, Brenner BM: Mechanism of inhibition of proximal tubule fluid reabsorption after exposure of the rat kidney to the physical effects of expansion of the extracellular fluid volume. J Clin Invest 64:1466, 1979
64. Laragh JH, Cannon PJ, Bentzel CJ, et al: Angiotensin II, norepinephrine, and renal transport of electrolytes and water in normal man and in cirrhosis and ascites. J Clin Invest 42:1179, 1963
65. Stumpe K, Lowitz H, Ochwad B: Fluid reabsorption in Henle's loop and urinary excretion of sodium and water in normal rats and rats with chronic hypertension. J Clin Invest 49:1200, 1970
66. Bank N, Aynedjian H, Bansal V, Goldman D: Affect of acute hypertension on sodium transport by the distal nephron. Am J Physiol 219:275, 1970
67. Cohn JN, Tristani FE, Khatri IM: Renal vasodilator therapy in the hepatorenal syndrome. Med Ann DC 39:1, 1970
68. Bennett WM, Keefe E, Melnyk C, et al: Response to dopamine hydrochloride in the hepatorenal syndrome. JAMA 135:964, 1975
69. Arieff AI, Chidsey CA: Renal function in cirrhosis and the effects of prostaglandin A_1. Am J Med 56:695, 1974
70. Espiritu CR, Mendoza JP, Yeh BK: Effects of intravenous infusion of dopamine in cirrhotics. Proc Soc Exp Biol Med 141:331, 1972
71. Bernardo DE, Baldus WP, Maher FT: Effects of dopamine on renal function in cirrhosis. Gastroenterology 58:524, 1970
72. MacGaffey K, Jick H: Studies on the mechanism of sodium diuresis following dopamine. Clin Res 13:311, 1965
73. Kew MD, Varma RR, Williams HS, et al:

Renal and intrarenal blood flow in cirrhosis of the liver. Lancet 2:504, 1971
74. Goodyer AVN, Jaeger CA: Renal response to non-shocking hemorrhage in the dog. Am J Physiol 180:69, 1955
75. Stein JH, Lameire NH, Earley LE: Renal hemodynamic factors and the regulation of sodium excretion. P. 739. In Andreoli TE, Hoffman JF, Fanestil DD (eds): Physiology of Membrane Disorders. Plenum, New York, 1978
76. Bernard C: Leçons sur les Proprietés Physiologiques des Liquides de L'Organisme. Bailliere, Paris, 1859.
77. Muller J, Barajas L: Electron microscopic and histochemical evidence for a tubular innervation in the renal cortex of the monkey. J Ultrastruct Res 41:533, 1972
78. Barajas L, Muller J: The innervation of the juxtaglomerular apparatus and surrounding tubules: A quantitative analysis by serial section electron microscopy. J Ultrastruct Res 43:107, 1973
79. DiBona GF, Zambraskie EJ, Aquilera AJ, Kaloyanides GJ: Neurogenic control of renal tubular sodium reabsorption in the dog. Circ Res 40:SI-127, 1977
80. Bello-Reuss E, Pastoriza-Munoz E, Colindres RE: Acute unilateral renal denervation in rats with extracellular fluid volume expansion. Am J Physiol 232:F26, 1977
81. Bello-Reuss E: The effect of catecholamines on fluid reabsorption by the isolated proximal convoluted tubule. Am J Physiol 238:F347, 1980
82. Gill JR, Carr AA, Fleischman LE, et al: Effects of pentolinium on sodium excretion in dogs with constriction of the vena cava. Am J Physiol 212:191, 1967
83. Levy M: Effects of acute volume expansion and altered hemodynamics on renal tubular function in chronic caval dogs. J Clin Invest. 51:922, 1972
84. Levy M: Renal function in dogs with acute selective hepatic venous outflow block, Am J Physiol 227:1074, 1974
85. Hurholzer K, Wiederholt M: Some aspects of distal tubular solute and water transport. Kidney Int 9:198, 1976
86. Gross JB, Imai M, Kokko JP: A functional comparison of the cortical collecting tubule and the distal convoluted tubule. J Clin Invest 55:1284, 1975
87. Gross JB, Kokko JP: Effects of aldosterone and potassium sparing diuretics on electrical potential difference across the distal nephron. J Clin Invest 59:82, 1977
88. Giuseffi J, Week EE, Larson PV, et al: Effect of bilateral adrenalectomy in a patient with massive ascites and postnecrotic cirrhosis. N Engl J Med 257:796, 1957
89. Epstein M, Pins DS, Schneider N, Levinson R: Determinants of deranged sodium and water homeostasis in decompensated cirrhosis. J Lab Clin Med 87:822, 1976
90. Epstein M, Sancho J, Haber E: Renin-aldosterone responsiveness in decompensated cirrhosis. p. 225. In Epstein M (ed): The Kidney in Liver Disease. Elsevier-North Holland, New York, 1978
91. Chonko AM, Bay WH, Stein JH, Ferris TF: The role of renin and aldosterone in the salt retention of edema. Am J Med 63:881, 1977
92. Levy M, Seely JF: Pathophysiology of edema formation. p. 723. In Brenner BM, Rector FC (eds): The Kidney. WB Saunders, Philadelphia, 1981
93. deWardener HE, Mills IH, Clapham WF, Hayter CJ: Studies on the efferent mechanism of the sodium diuresis which follows the administration of intravenous saline to the dog. Clin Sci 21:249, 1961
94. Seely JF, Levy M: Control of the extracellular fluid volume. p. 371. In Brenner BM, Rector FC (eds): The Kidney. WB Saunders, Philadelphia, 1981
95. Kramer HJ: Natriuretic hormone—Its possible role in fluid and electrolyte disturbances in chronic liver disease. Postgrad Med 51:532, 1975
96. Wilkinson SP, Alam A, Moodie H, Williams R: Renal retention of sodium in cirrhosis and fulminant hepatic failure. Postgrad Med 51:527, 1975
97. Epstein M, Bricker NS, Bourgoinie JJ: Presence of a natriuretic factor in urine of normal men undergoing water immersion. Kidney Int. 13:512, 1978
98. Chorpra IJ, Tulchinsky D, Greenway FL: Estrogen-androgen imbalance in hepatic cirrhosis. Studies in 13 male patients. Ann Intern Med 79:198, 1973
99. Kley HK, Nieschlag E, Wiegelmann W, et al: Steroid hormones and their binding in

plasma of male patients with fatty liver, chronic hepatitis and liver cirrhosis. Acta Endocrinol 78:275, 1975
100. Preedy JRK, Aitken EH: The effect of estrogen on water and electrolyte metabolism. II. Hepatic disease. J Clin Invest 35:430, 1956
101. Cristy NP, Shaver JC: Estrogens and the kidney. Kidney Int 6:366, 1974
102. Lifschitz MD, Stein JH: Renal vasoactive hormones. P. 650. In Brenner BM, Rector FC (eds): The Kidney. WB Saunders, Philadelphia, 1981
103. Gregory PB, Broekelschen PH, Hill MD, et al: Complications of diuresis in the alcoholic patient with ascites: a controlled trial. Gastroenterology 73:534, 1977
104. Guazzi M, Polese A, Magrini F, et al: Negative influences of ascites on the cardiac function of cirrhotic patients. Am J Med 59:165, 1975
105. Eknoyan G, Martinez-Maldonado M, Yium JJ, Suki WN: Combined ascitic fluid and furosemide infusion in the management of ascites. N Engl J Med 282:713, 1970
106. Schroeder ET, Anderson GH, Smulyan H: Effects of portocaval and peritoneal venous shunts in the hepatorenal syndrome. Kidney Int 15:54, 1979
107. Blendis LM, Greig PD, Langer B, et al: The renal and hemodynamic effects of the peritoneo-venous shunt for intractable hepatic ascites. Gastroenterology 77:250, 1979
108. Wilkinson P, Sherlock S: The effect of repeated albumin infusions in patients with cirrhosis. Lancet 2:7266, 1962
109. Redeker AG, Kuzman OT, Reynolds TB: An effective treatment of refractory ascites in cirrhosis of the liver. Arch Intern Med 105:594, 1960
110. Hope J: A Treatise on the Diseases of the Heart and Blood Vessels. William Kidd, London, 1832
111. Mackenzie J: Diseases of the Heart. Oxford Medical Publishers, London, 1917
112. Warren JV, Stead EA: Fluid dynamics in chronic congestive heart failure. An interpretation of the mechanisms producing the edema, increased plasma volume and elevated venous pressure in certain patients with prolonged congestive failure. Arch Intern Med 73:138, 1944
113. Schrier RW, Berl T, Anderson RJ, McDonald KM: Nonosmolar control of renal water excretion. P. 149. In Andreoli TE, Grantham JJ, Rector FC (eds): Disturbances in Body Fluid Osmolality. American Physiological Society, Bethesda, MD 1977
114. Schrier RW, Humphreys MH: Factors involved in the antinatriuretic effects of acute constriction of the thoracic and abdominal inferior vena cava. Circ Res 29:479, 1971
115. Schrier RW, Humphreys MH, Ufferman RC: Role of cardiac output and the autonomic nervous system in the antinatriuretic response to acute constriction of the thoracic superior vena cava. Circ Res 29:490, 1971
116. Lifschitz MD, Schrier RW: Alterations in cardiac output with chronic constriction of thoracic inferior vena cava. Am J Physiol 225:1364, 1973
117. Gauer OH, Henry JP: Circulatory basis of fluid volume control. Physiol Rev 43:423, 1963
118. Johnston JA, Moore WW, Segar WE: Small changes in left atrial pressure and plasma antidiuretic hormone titres in dogs. Am J Physiol 217:210, 1969
119. Gauer OH, Henry JP, Behr C: The regulation of extracellular fluid volume. Annu Rev Physiol 32:547, 1970
120. Hollander WM, Judson WE: The relationship between cardiovascular and renal hemodynamic function to sodium excretion in patients with severe heart disease but without edema. J Clin Invest 35:970, 1956
121. Chobanian AV, Burrows BA, Hollander W: Body fluid and electrolyte composition in cardiac patients with severe heart disease but without peripheral edema. Circulation 24:743, 1961
122. Walser M, Duffy BJ, Griffin HW: Body fluids in hypertension and mild heart failure. JAMA 160:858, 1956
123. Barger AC, Wilson GM, Price HL, et al: Relationship between exchangeable sodium and rate of sodium excretion in dogs with experimental valvular lesions on the heart. Am J Physiol 180:387, 1955
124. Zehr JE, Johnson JA, Moore WW: Left atrial pressure, plasma osmolality, and ADH levels in the unanesthetized ewe. Am J Physiol 217:1672, 1969

125. Zehr JE, Hawe A, Tasarkis AJ: ADH levels following non-hypotensive hemorrhage in dogs with chronic mitral stenosis. Am J Physiol 221:312, 1971
126. Greenberg TT, Richmond WH, Stocking RA, et al: Impaired atrial receptor responses in dogs with heart failure due to tricuspid insufficiency and pulmonary artery stenosis. Circ Res 32:424, 1973
127. Bell NH, Schedl HP, Bartter FC: An explanation for abnormal water retention and hypoosmolality in congestive heart failure. Am J Med 36:351, 1967
128. Bennett WM, Bagley GC, Antonovic JN, Porter GA: Influence of volume expansion on proximal tubular sodium reabsorption in congestive heart failure. Am Heart J 85:55, 1973
129. Johnston CI, Davis JO, Robb CA, MacKenzie JW: Plasma renin in chronic experimental heart failure and during renal sodium "escape" from mineralocorticoids. Circ Res 22:113, 1968
130. Hostetter TH, Pfeffer JM, Pfeffer MA, et al: Glomerular dynamics in rats with myocardial infarcts. Abstr Am Soc Nephrol 13:96A, 1980
131. Schneider EG, Dresser TP, Lynch RE, Knox FG: Sodium reabsorption by the proximal tubule of dogs with experimental heart failure. Am J Physiol 220:952, 1971
132. Stumpe KO, Solle H, Klein H, Kruck F: Mechanism of sodium and water retention in rats with experimental heart failure. Kidney Int 4:309, 1973
133. Mandin H: Cardiac edema in dogs. I. Proximal tubular and renal function. Kidney Int 10:591, 1976
134. Hume HD, Gottlieb MN, Brenner BM: The kidney in congestive heart failure with special emphasis on the role of the renal microvasculature in the pathogenesis of sodium retention. p. 51. In Brenner BM, Stein JH (eds): Sodium and Water Homeostasis. Churchill Livingstone, New York, 1978
135. Vander A, Malvin RL, Wilde WS, Sullivan LP: Re-examination of salt and water retention in congestive heart failure. Am J Med 25:497, 1958
136. Ferris TF, Gordon P: Effect of angiotensin and norepinephrine upon urate clearance in man. Am J Med 44:359, 1968
137. Oliver JA, Sciacca RR, Pinto J, Cannon PJ: Participation of prostaglandins in the control of renal blood flow during acute reduction of cardiac output in the dog. J Clin Invest 67:229, 1981
138. Hall JE, Guyton AC, Trippodo NC, et al: Intrarenal control of electrolyte excretion. Am J Physiol 232:F538, 1977
139. Freeman RH, Davis JO, Spielman WS, Lohmeier TE: High-output heart failure in the dog: Systemic and intrarenal role of angiotensin II. Am J Physiol 229:474, 1975
140. Watkins L, Burton JA, Haber E, et al: The renin-angiotensin-aldosterone system in congestive heart failure in conscious dogs. J Clin Invest 57:1606, 1976
141. Cannon PJ: The kidney in heart failure. N Engl J Med 296:26, 1977
142. Williams GM, Davis JO, Freeman RH, et al: Effects of the oral converting enzyme inhibitor SQ 14225 in experimental high output failure. Am J Physiol 236:F541, 1978
143. Davis R, Ribner HS, Keung E, et al: Effect of captopril in heart failure. N Engl J Med 301:117, 1979
144. Gill JR, Mason DT, Bartter FC: Adrenergic nervous system in sodium metabolism: Effects of guanethidine and sodium retaining steroids in normal man. J Clin Invest 43:177, 1964
145. Chidsey CA, Braunwald E, Morrow AG: Catecholamine excretion and cardiac stores of norepinephrine in congestive heart failure. Am J Med 39:442, 1965
146. Chidsey CA, Braunwald E, Morrow AG, Mason DT: Myocardial norepinephrine concentration in man: Effects of reserpine and congestive heart failure. Science 145:1439, 1964
147. Kramer RS, Mason DT, Braunwald E: Augmented sympathetic neurotransmitter activity in the peripheral vascular bed of patients with congestive heart failure and cardiac norepinephrine depletion. Circulation 38:629, 1968
148. Chidsey CA, Harrison D, Braunwald E: Augmentation of plasma norepinephrine response to exercise in patients with congestive heart failure. N Engl J Med 267:650, 1962
149. Brod J, Fejfar Z, Fejfarova MH: The role of neurohumoral factors in the genesis of

renal hemodynamic changes in heart failure. Acta Med Scand 148:273, 1954
150. Barger AC: Renal hemodynamics in congestive heart failure. Ann NY Acad Sci 139:276, 1966
151. Stumpe KO, Solle H, Klein H, Kruck F: Mechanism of sodium and water retention in rats with experimental heart failure. Kidney Int 4:309, 1973
152. Boudreau R, Mandin H: Cardiac edema in dogs. II. Distribution of glomerular filtrate and renal blood flow. Kidney Int 10:578, 1976
152a. Carpenter CG, Davis JO: Sodium excretion in denervated autotransplanted kidneys in dogs with inferior vena cava obstruction. Am J Physiol 189:241, 1958
153. Demming QB, Luetscher JA: Bioassay of desoxycorticosterone-like material in urine. Proc Soc Exp Biol Med 73:171, 1950
154. Davis JO, Howell DS, Southworth JL: Mechanism of fluid retention in experimental preparation in dogs. III. Effect of adrenalectomy and subsequent desoxycorticosterone acetate administration on ascites formation. Circ Res 1:260, 1953
155. August JT, Nelson DH, Thorn GW: Response of normal subjects to large amounts of aldosterone. J Clin Invest 37:1549, 1958
156. Gill JR: Edema. Annu Rev Med 21:269, 1970
157. Davis JO, Holman JE, Hyatt RE: Sodium excretion in adrenalectomized dogs with cardiac failure produced by pulmonic artery constriction. Am J Physiol 183:263, 1955
158. Mittelman J, Levy M: Failure to demonstrate nonaldosterone salt retaining substances in urine, plasma and liver extract of chronic caval dogs. Can J Physiol Pharmacol 50:1162, 1972
159. Braunwald E, Ross J, Sonnenblick HE: Mechanism of Contraction of the Normal and Failing Heart. Little, Brown, Boston, 1976
160. Lesch M, Caranasos GJ, Mulholland JH: Controlled study comparing ethacrynic acid to mercaptomerin in the treatment of acute pulmonary edema. N Engl J Med 279:115, 1968
161. Dikshit K, Vyder JK, Forrester JS, et al: Renal and extrarenal hemodynamic effects of furosemide in congestive heart failure after acute myocardial infarction. N Engl J Med 288:1087, 1973
162. Cohn JN: Blood pressure and cardiac performance. Am J Med 55:351, 1973
163. Guiha NH, Cohn JN, Mikulic E, et al: Treatment of refractory heart failure with infusion of nitroprusside. N Engl J Med 291:587, 1974
164. Kovick RB, Tillisch JA, Bereus SC, et al: Vasodilator therapy for chronic left ventricular failure. Circulation 53:322, 1976
165. Cohn JN, Matthew KJ, Franciosa JA, Snow JA: Chronic vasodilator therapy in the management of cardiogenic shock and intractable left ventricular failure. Ann Intern Med 81:777, 1974
166. Gomes JAC, Carambar CR, Moran HE, et al: The effect of isosorbide dinitrate on left ventricular size, wall stress and left ventricular function in chronic refractory heart failure. An echocardiographic study. Am J Med 65:794, 1978
167. Heineman HO: Right sided heart failure and the use of diuretics. Am J Med 64:367, 1978
168. Keller H, Morell A, Nosede G: Analbuminemia: Pathophysiologische Unlersuchungen an ienem fall. Schweiz Med Wochenschr 102:71, 1972
169. Matthews CME: Effect of plasmapheresis on albumin pools in rabbits. J Clin Invest 40:603, 1961
170. Andersen SB, Rossing N: Metabolism of albumin and -6-globulin during albumin infusions and plasmapheresis. Scand J Clin Lab Invest 20:183, 1967
171. Wraight EP: Capillary permeability to protein as a factor in the control of plasma volume. J Physiol 237:39, 1974
172. Dorhout Mees EJ, Roos JC, Boer P, et al: Observations on edema formation in the nephrotic syndrome in adults with minimal lesions. Am J Med 67:378, 1979
173. Miltzer JI, Keim HJ, Laragh JH, et al: Nephrotic syndrome: Vasoconstriction and hypervolemic types indicated by renin-sodium profiling. Ann Intern Med 91:688, 1979
174. Grausz H, Lieberman R, Earley LE: Effect of plasma albumin on sodium reabsorption in patients with nephrotic syndrome. Kidney Int 1:47, 1972

175. Gur A, Adefuin PY, Siegel NJ, Hayslett JP: A study of the renal handling of water in lipoid nephrosis. Pediatr Res 20:197, 1976
176. Bernard DB, Alexander EA, Couser WG, Levinsky NG: Renal sodium retention during volume expansion in experimental nephrotic syndrome. Kidney Int 14:478, 1978
177. Dusing R, Vetter H, Kramer HJ: The renin-angiotensin-aldosterone system in patients with nephrotic syndrome: Effects of 1-sar-8-ala-angiotensin II. Nephron 25:187, 1980
178. Oliver WJ, Kelch RC, Chandler JP: Demonstration of increased catecholamine excretion in the nephrotic syndrome. Proc Soc Exp Biol Med 125:1176, 1967
179. Leutcher JA, Johnson BB: Observations on the sodium retaining corticoid (aldosterone) in the urine of children and adults in relation to sodium balance and edema. J Clin Invest 33:1441, 1954
180. Michselsen P, Lambert PP: Effects du traitement par les corticosteroides et l'indomethacine sur la proteinurie. Bull Mem Soc Med Hop Paris 118:217, 1967
181. Conte J, Suc JM, Mignon-Conte M: Effect anti-proteinurique de l'indomethacine dans les glomerulopathies. J Urol Nephrol 73:850, 1967
182. Arisz L, Douker AJM, Breutjeus JRH, van der Hem GK: The effect of indomethacin on proteinuria and kidney function in the nephrotic syndrome. Acta Med Scand 199:121, 1976
183. Tiggeler RGWL, Hulme B, Wydeveld PGAB: Effect of indomethacin on glomerular permeability in the nephrotic syndrome. Kidney Int 16:312, 1979
184. Rose G: Medical research council trials. p. 174. In Vogt RA, Batsford SR (eds): Glomerulonephritis. John Wiley & Sons, New York, 1977
185. German Glomerulonephritis Research Group: A controlled multicenter trial of cyclophosphamide and indomethacin in chronic glomerulonephritis. p. 196. In Kluthe R, Vogt A, Batsford SR (eds): Glomerulonephritis. John Wiley & Sons, New York, 1977
186. Kimberly RP, Plotz PH: Aspirin-induced depression of renal function. N Engl J Med 296:418, 1977
187. Kimberly RP, Bowden RE, Keiser HR, Plotz PH: Reduction of renal function by newer nonsteroidal anti-inflammatory drugs. Am J Med 64:804, 1978
188. Walshe JJ, Venuto RC: Acute oliguric renal failure induced by indomethacin: Possible mechanism. Ann Intern Med 91:47, 1979
189. Tan SY, Shapiro R, Kish MA: Reversible acute renal failure induced by indomethacin. JAMA 241:2732, 1979
190. Yamauchi H, Hoppu J: Hypovolemic shock and hypotension as a complication in the nephrotic syndrome. Ann Intern Med 60:242, 1964
191. Chamberlain MJ, Pringle A, Wrong OM: Oliguric renal failure in the nephrotic syndrome. Q J Med 35:215, 1966
192. Conolly ME, Wrong OM, Jones NF: Reversible renal failure in idiopathic nephrotic syndrome with minimal glomerular changes. Lancet 1:665, 1968
193. Glassock RJ: Sodium homeostasis in acute glomerulonephritis and the nephrotic syndrome. Contrib Nephrol 23:181, 1980
194. Earle DP, Farber SJ, Alexander JD, Pelligrino ED: Renal function and electrolyte metabolism in acute glomerulonephritis. J Clin Invest 30:421, 1951
195. Allison MEM, Wilson CB, Gottschalk CW: Pathophysiology of experimental glomerulonephritis in rats. J Clin Invest 53:1402, 1974
196. Rocha A, Marcondes M, Malnic G: Micropuncture study of rats with experimental glomerulonephritis. Kidney Int 3:14, 1973
197. Van Liew JB, Von Baeyer HR: Proximal tubule volume reabsorption in anti-GBM nephritic rats. Physiologist 17:348, 1974
198. Maddox DA, Bennett CM, Deen WM, et al: Control of proximal tubular fluid reabsorption in experimental glomerulonephritis. J Clin Invest 55:1315, 1975
199. Wen SF, Wagnild JP: Acute effect of nephrotoxic serum on renal sodium transport in the dog. Kidney Int 9:245, 1976
200. Wagnild JP, Wen SF: Micropuncture study of dogs with normal, glomerulonephritic, and remnant kidneys before and after volume expansion. Kidney Int 8:464, 1975
201. Godon JP: Evidence of increased proximal sodium and water reabsorption in experi-

mental glomerulonephritis. Role of a natriuretic factor of renal origin. Nephron 21:145, 1978
202. Kuroda S, Aynedjian HS, Bank N: A micropuncture study of renal sodium retention and nephrotic syndrome in rats: Evidence for increased resistance to tubular fluid flow. Kidney Int 16:561, 1979
203. Godon JP: Sodium and water retention in experimental glomerulonephritis. Kidney Int 2:271, 1972
204. Birhenhager WH, Schalekamp MADH, Schalekamp-Kuyken MRA, et al: Interrelations between arterial pressure fluid volumes and plasma renin concentration in the course of acute glomerulonephritis. Lancet 1:1086, 1970
205. Bricker NS, Fine LG: The renal response to progressive nephron loss. p. 1056. In Brenner BM, Rector FC (eds): The Kidney. WB Saunders, Philadelphia, 1981
206. Fine L, Bourgoignie JJ, Kwang KH, Bricker NS: On the influence of the natriuretic factor from uremic patients on bioelectric properties and sodium transport of the isolated mammalian collecting tubule. J Clin Invest 58:590, 1976
207. Wagnild JP, Gutmann FD: Functional adaptation of nephrons in dogs with acute progressing to chronic experimental glomerulonephritis. J Clin Invest 57:1575, 1976
208. Shahaddin SH, Nor MM, Abdullah AM, Mosdeen F: Plasma renin activity and hypertension in acute glomerulonephritis. Aust NZ J Med 9:250, 1979
209. Repetto HA, Lewy JE, Brando JL, Metcoff J: The renal functional response to furosemide in children with acute glomerulonephritis. J Pediatr 80:660, 1972
210. Binak K, Sirmaci N, Vcak D, Harmanci N: Circulatory changes in acute glomerulonephritis at rest and exercise. Br Heart J 37:883, 1975
211. Preedy JRK, Aitken EH: The effect of estrogen on water and electrolyte metabolism. J Clin Invest 35:423, 1956
212. Ferris TF, Chonko AM, Williams JS, et al: Studies of the mechanism of sodium retention in idiopathic edema. Trans Assoc Am Phys 86:310, 1973
213. Gill JR, Waldmann TA, Bartter FC: Idiopathic edema. I. The occurrence of hypoalbuminemia and abnormal albumin metabolism in women with unexplained edema. Am J Med 52:444, 1972
214. Kuchel O, Horky K, Gregnova I, et al: Inappropriate response to upright posture. A precipitating factor in the pathogenesis of idiopathic edema. Ann Intern Med 73:245, 1970
215. Streeten DHP, Dalakos TG, Souma M, et al: Studies on the pathogenesis of isopathic edema. Clin Sci Molec Med 45:347, 1973
216. Emerson K, Armstrong H: High protein edema due to diffuse abnormality of capillary permeability. Trans Am Clin Chem Assoc 67:59, 1955
217. Clarkson B, Thompson D, Horwith M, Luckey EH: Cyclical edema and shock due to increased capillary permeability. Am J Med 29:193, 1960
218. Gill JR, Cox J, DeLea C, Bartter FC: Idiopathic edema. II. Pathogenesis of edema in patients with hypoalbuminemia. Am J Med 52:452, 1972
219. Marieb NJ, Murlow PJ: Failure to escape. A mechanism in idiopathic edema. J Clin Invest 43:1279, 1964
220. Thorn GW: Approach to the patient with "idiopathic edema" or "periodic swelling." JAMA 206:333, 1968
221. MacGregor GA, Roulston JE, Markandu ND, et al: Is "idiopathic oedema" idiopathic. Lancet 1:397, 1979
222. Anderson RJ, Linas SL: Sodium depletion states. p. 154. In Brenner BM, Stein JH (eds): Sodium and Water Homeostasis. Churchill Livingstone, New York, 1978
223. Bauer JH, Brooks CS: Acute and chronic effects of diuretic therapy on body fluid composition. Kidney Int 19:164, 1981
224. Seldin DW, Rector FC: The generation and maintenance of metabolic alkalosis. Kidney Int 1:306, 1972
225. Phillips RA: Water and electrolyte losses in cholera. Fed Proc 23:705, 1964
226. Phillips SF: Water and electrolytes in gastrointestinal disease. p. 1267. In Maxwell MH, Kleeman CR (eds): Clinical Disorders of Fluid and Electrolyte Metabolism. McGraw-Hill, New York, 1980.
227. Knochel JP: Clinical physiology of heat ex-

228. Moncrief JA: Burns. N Engl J Med 238:444, 1973
229. Platt R: Sodium and potassium excretion in chronic renal failure. Clin Sci 9:367, 1950
230. Nickel JF, Lowrance PB, Leifer E, Bradley SE: Renal function, electrolyte excretion and body fluids in patients with chronic renal insufficiency before and after sodium deprivation. J Clin Invest 32:68, 1953
231. Coleman AJ, Arias M, Carter MW, et al: The mechanism of salt wastage in chronic renal disease. J Clin Invest 45:1116, 1966
232. Gonick HC, Maxwell ME, Rubini ME, Kleeman CR: Functional impairment in chronic renal disease. I. Studies of sodium-conserving ability. Nephron 3:137, 1966
233. Danovitch GM, Bourgoignie J, Bricker NA: Reversibility of the salt-losing tendency in chronic renal failure. N Engl J Med 296:14, 1977
234. Murphy RV, Coffman EW, Pringle BH, Iseri LT: Studies of sodium and potassium metabolism in salt-losing nephritis. Arch Intern Med 90:750, 1952
235. Gardner KD: Evolution of clinical signs in adult-onset cystic disease of the renal medulla. Ann Intern Med 74:47, 1971
236. Anderson RJ, Linas SJ, Berns AS, et al: Non-oliguric acute renal failure. N Engl J Med 296:1134, 1977
237. Levinsky NG, Alexander EA, Venkatachalan MA: Acute renal failure. p. 1181. In Brenner BM, Rector FC (eds): The Kidney. WB Saunders, Philadelphia, 1981
238. Wilson B, Reisman DD, Moyer CA: Fluid balance in the urological patient: Disturbances in the renal regulation of the excretion of water and sodium salts following decompression of the urinary bladder. J Urol 66:805, 1951
239. Falls WF, Stacy WK: Post-obstructive diuresis: Studies in a dialyzed patient with a solitary kidney. Am J Med 54:404, 1973
240. Hanley MJ, Davidson K: Study of isolated nephron segments in a rabbit model of obstructive uropathy. Kidney Int 19:202, 1981
241. Tyler FH: Hyperosmolar coma. Am J Med 45:485, 1968
242. McCurdy DK: Hyperosmolar hyperglycemic non-ketotic diabetic coma. Med Clin North Am 54:683, 1970
243. Gennari JF, Kassirer JP: Osmotic diuresis. N Engl J Med 291:714, 1974
244. Reineck HJ, Stein JH: Mechanism of action and clinical uses of diuretics. p. 1097. In Brenner BM, Rector FC, (eds): The Kidney. WB Saunders, Philadelphia, 1981
245. Iverson T: Congenital adrenocortical hyperplasia with disturbed electrolyte regulations: (dysadrenocorticism). Pediatrics 16:875, 1955
246. Jacobs DR, Posner JB: Isolated analdosteronism: II. The nature of the adrenocortical enzymatic defect and influence of diet and various agents on the electrolyte balance. Metabolism 13:225, 1964
247. Shakleton CHL, Snodgrass GHAI: Steroid excretion by an infant with an unusual salt-losing syndrome: A gas chromatographic-mass spectrophotometric study. Ann Clin Biochem 11:91, 1974
248. Wilson ID, Goetz FC: Selective hypoaldosteronism after prolonged heparin administration. Am J Med Sci 36:635, 1964
249. Schambelan M, Stockigt JR, Biglier EG: Isolated hypoaldosteronism in adults. N Engl J Med 287:573, 1972
250. Oh MS, Carroll HJ, Clemmons JE, et al: A mechanism for hyporeninemic hypoaldosteronism in chronic renal disease. Metabolism 23:1157, 1974
251. Oster JR, Perez GO, Rosen MS: Hyporeninemic hypoaldosteronism after chronic sodium bicarbonate abuse. Arch Intern Med 136:1179, 1976
252. Perez GO, Lespier LE, Oster JR, Vaamonde CA: Effect of alterations of sodium intake in patients with hyporeninemic hypoaldosteronism. Nephron 18:259, 1977
253. Schwartz GJ, Spitzer A: Disorders of renal transport of sodium, potassium and magnesium. p. 1079. In Edelman CM (ed): Pediatric Kidney Disease. Little, Brown, Boston, 1978.

3

Disorders of Water Metabolism

Frederic C. Bartter*
Catherine S. Delea

RELATIVE VERSUS ABSOLUTE DEFICIENCY AND EXCESS OF BODY WATER

Deficiency or excess of body water may be "absolute" or "relative." "Absolute" as usual connotes total body water. The term "relative" applied to a deficiency or excess of body water is here used to describe a body water content that is respectively less than or in excess of that required to maintain the normal osmolality of body fluids. Absolute deficiency or excess of body water is considered in this chapter only when there are also abnormalities of tonicity. Thus, generalized edema in which body fluids retain normal tonicity is considered in Chapter 2, even though it represents an absolute excess of body water. This is appropriate, since sodium is the most important determinant of the osmolarity of extracellular fluid (ECF); when body fluids have normal tonicity, the total ECF volume depends upon the total body sodium content. When the total body sodium is excessive because of abnormal sodium retention, and water has been retained pari passu, there is no relative excess of body water. In contrast, hypernatremia of whatever cause is taken to represent a relative deficiency of water.

The tonicity of body fluids depends ultimately on the balance (intake minus output) of solute and the balance of water. Disorders of body fluid can thus be resolved into those of solute excess or deficit and those of water excess or deficit. It should be noted that by the definition here assumed, an absolute excess of body solute results in a relative deficiency of body water (hypertonicity of body fluids), unless water has been retained with the solute. Unfortunately, such a syndrome was recently produced by the inadvertent salt-loading of infants. The terms *relative excess* and *relative deficiency* of body water are thus used here to describe states of hypotonicity (hypo-osmolality) and hypertonicity (hyperosmolality), respectively, of body fluids. In almost all instances, the serum sodium concentration is below normal when there is relative

---

* We are much saddened by the death on May 5, 1983 of Frederic C. Bartter during the preparation of this chapter. His collaborator of over 30 years, Catherine S. Delea, completed their manuscript based on the outline and notes he left behind. This chapter represents Dr. Bartter's last scientific contribution to the community that he had served so well during his long and distinguished career, which was devoted to studying the relationship between the kidney and hormones.

water excess, and above normal when there is relative water deficiency.

The tonicity of osmolality of a 24-hour urine pool depends on (1) total urinary solute (milliosmoles excreted in the urine per day), and (2) total urine volume (liters of urine excreted per day).* The ratio of (1) to (2) is the osmolality of the 24-hour urine. Normally, this equals the osmolality of the total intake, the total number of milliosmoles ingested or derived from metabolism and destined for urinary excretion, divided by the total fluid intake, as liquid or as water of oxidation minus water lost in the feces and through the lungs and skin as "insensible" loss.

The term "insensible water loss" is generally taken to mean water lost from the lungs and skin which cannot be measured directly. Whereas water of sweat and fecal water can be measured in suitably designed experiments, it is customary to include both of these as "insensible" losses in estimates of water balance. The insensible water loss for a normal adult of average size in a moderate environment may amount to a liter a day; much higher values may be found in a hot environment or in a febrile patient.

For relative dehydration, the available water (intake minus loss) must be less than that required to maintain normal plasma tonicity: hypertonicity of plasma is the hallmark of such simple dehydration. Since the plasma membrane of all but a few body cells acts as a semipermeable membrane, intracellular tonicity must equal extracellular or whole-body tonicity.[1] Thus, the immediate consequence of hypertonicity of the ECF is the loss of water from cells, with a consequent derangement of metabolic processes generally.

ROLE OF ANTIDIURETIC HORMONE

Isotonicity is primarily maintained by antidiuretic hormone (ADH, arginine vasopression in man).* The nonapeptide hormone arginine vasopressin (AVP) is produced in the supraoptic and paraventricular nuclei of the hypothalamus, and is initially bound to a protein, neurophysin II. The bound complex travels down the supraopticohypophyseal and paraventriculohypophyseal tracts of the neurohypophysis, where it is stored in large neurosecretory cells. As the arterial blood supplying the supraopticohypophysis and the thirst centers becomes hypertonic, the AVP is released into the hypophyseal portal blood, with cleavage of the AVP from the neurophysin. The AVP then travels through the bloodstream to reach the collecting ducts of the kidney, where it increases the permeability of the duct cells to water. This increased permeability allows the collecting ducts to reabsorb water from the duct lumen, thus decreasing the volume of tubular fluid destined for urinary excretion and increasing the urine osmolality. Water continues to be recovered from the renal tubules until enough has been recovered to lower the plasma osmolality to normal.

In conjunction with the foregoing mechanism, an increased tonicity of the arterial blood bathing the hypothalamic "thirst centers" will induce drinking, with the ingested

---

* Strictly speaking, osmolarity is the number of osmoles per liter of solution, whereas osmolality is the number of osmoles per kilogram of water. For a mixed solution such as urine, osmolality is determined directly from a colligative property, such as freezing-point depression. For practical purposes, osmolarity, calculated as the sum of the known number of osmoles in a liter of such a solution, is often used. The error introduced by doing this, which includes the variable dissociation of electrolytes and different specific volumes of solutes, is not large.

* Since arginine vasopressin is the antidiuretic hormone in man, the terms AVP and ADH will be used interchangeably. We prefer to use AVP when speaking of the chemical being produced and secreted in the supraoptic nuclei, and ADH when speaking of the effective agent in the nephron.

water also acting to lower the tonicity of the arterial blood. The paraventricular and supraoptic nuclei then decrease or stop their secretion of AVP, and the collecting ducts become unable to reabsorb water, yielding a dilute urine.

The mechanism by which urine osmolality is controlled involves two functions of the kidney: the formation of "free" water and the reabsorption of water without solute. Free water, that is, filtrate freed of chloride and sodium, is formed in the thick ascending limb of the loop of Henle by the active reabsorption of sodium and chloride[2,3]* (see Fig. 3-1). Since this portion of the tubule is impermeable to water, the solutes are reabsorbed without water. Free water is formed under all conditions, during states of dehydration as well as during hydration. If this free water is lost in the urine, the urine is hypotonic with regard to the plasma, and the tonicity of body fluids rises correspondingly.

Concentration of the urine depends on ADH acting to increase the permeability of the collecting ducts to water. Since the normal tonicity of the renal medullary interstitial fluid is considerably higher than that of plasma, this action of ADH can "reclaim" all the free water that has been formed proximally, leaving the urine isotonic. Indeed, it can also reclaim to the body additional water to leave the urine hypertonic to plasma. The principal role of ADH is thus to reclaim to the body filtered water that would otherwise be lost in the urine. As we shall see, the classic examples of relative deficiency and excess of body water represent deficiency and relative excess, respectively, of ADH. It is clear that an understanding of the control of ADH secretion is of paramount importance in the understanding of relative body fluid derangements.

CONTROL OF ADH (AVP) SECRETION

Osmolality of Plasma

Physiologically, the most important stimulus to AVP secretion and release is a function of the tonicity of the blood bathing the supraoptic and paraventricular nuclei: hypertonicity causes release and hypotonicity inhibits release of AVP. This mechanism is extremely sensitive: the release of AVP has been shown to increase in response to a rise of plasma osmolality by one third of one percent[4] (Fig. 3-2). Whereas this effect has been shown for various osmoles, it clearly does not depend on osmolality alone. Thus, urea is a relatively poor regulator of AVP release, and glucose lacks this effect altogether.[5] Specifically, osmoles that cannot readily enter the cells of the supraoptic and paraventricular nuclei (and thus can abstract water from these cells) are effective in AVP control.

Hypovolemia

Hypovolemia constitutes a second, though physiologically much less important, stimulus to AVP release. This was shown by Weinstein and his associates by the demonstration of an increase in jugular venous AVP resulting from controlled hemorrhage in the dog.[6,7] Robertson found that the slope relating AVP release to plasma volume could be increased experimentally in the dog by successive depletions of blood volume, but that such changes in slope were quantitatively relatively inconsequential until decrements in blood volume of some 10 percent or more had been induced.[8,9] Volume related (specifically, hypovo-

---

* Whereas chloride reabsorption was formerly thought to be "primary active," since chloride is reabsorbed against an electrochemical gradient, it is now generally agreed that chloride reabsorption is "secondary active," since the transport of sodium, depending on Na-K-ATPase, is the "primary active" event, with chloride reabsorption following as sodium-plus-chloride cotransport, or possibly sodium-plus-chloride-plus-potassium cotransport.[2,3]

110 • Kidney Electrolyte Disorders

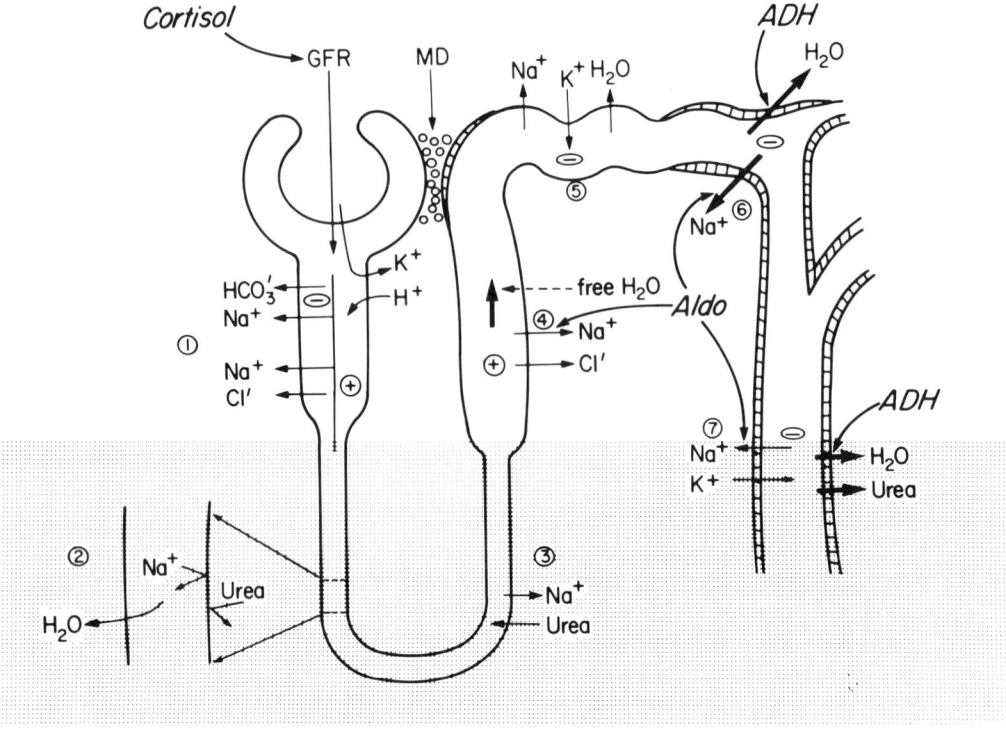

Fig. 3-1. The formation of "free" water and the reabsorption of water in the kidney tubule. Free water is formed in the thick ascending limb of the loop of Henle by the reabsorption of sodium and chloride; the water flowing distally is reabsorbed in the distal tubule and in the collecting duct under the influence of antidiuretic hormone (ADH). MD = macula densa, Aldo = aldosterone.

lemic)* stimuli to AVP release are largely independent of osmotic stimuli, and are mediated in large part through low-pressure afferent impulses arising in the right atrium and central veins via the vagus nerve, and/or through high-pressure efferent impulses through glossopharnygeal nerves and afferent carotid sinus, as well as aortic baroreceptor impulses.[10-12] Despite the insensitivity of the control mechanism, decreases in blood volume or pressure are probably responsible for the inappropriate AVP release that is found in some patients with liver cirrhosis or cardiac failure, and in most cases of undertreated Addison's disease.

Neurogenic Stimuli

In the 1940s, Verney showed that faradic stimuli to the skin of a conscious dog caused a prompt decrease in urine volume and increase in urine conductivity, his only available measure of tonicity.[13] He correctly discerned that this represented secretion of AVP. Minor trauma, such as these stimuli, and major trauma, such as surgical operation, regularly induce inappropriate secretion of ADH. The upright posture, especially quiet standing, may cause ADH release, and regularly does so when it causes hypotension.[14] Fainting and near-fainting because of quiet standing constitute

---

* It is clear that a sudden reduction in blood pressure without a change in volume, such as occurs with vasodilatory drugs, is read by this system as a volume change.

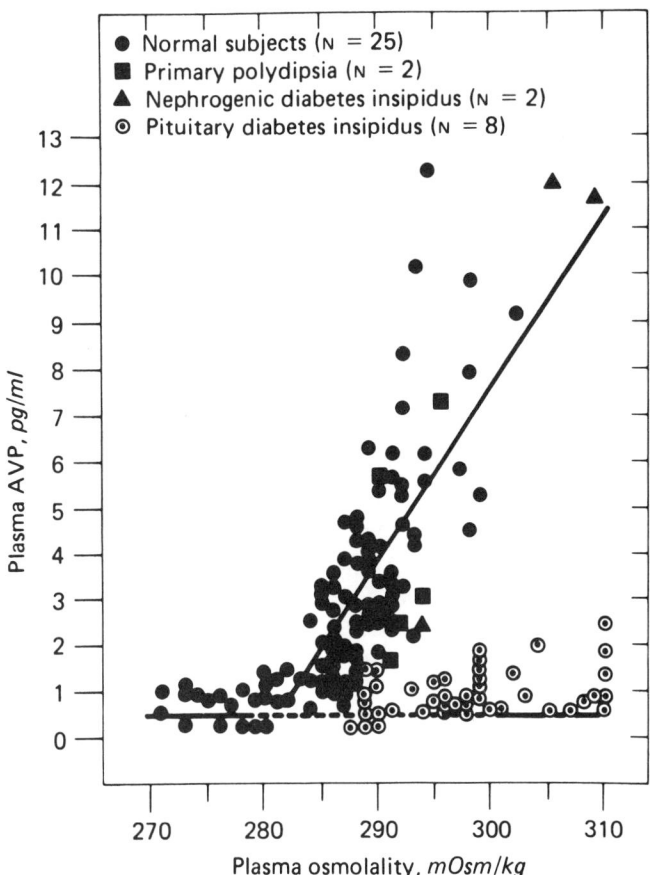

Fig. 3-2. The relationship of plasma vasopressin (AVP) to plasma osmolality in normal subjects and in patients with polyuria. (From Robertson et al,[91] with permission.)

potent stimuli to ADH release. This release results from both the relative central hypovolemia and the hypotension that occur with pooling of blood in the lower parts of the body, and is presumably neurogenic in origin. A special case of neurogenic AVP release is seen with the onset of nausea, even before vomiting appears.[15] The neural pathways involved have not been elucidated.

Drugs

Certain drugs, such as carbamazepine, can cause ADH release and consequent concentration of the urine. If the water intake is high enough, this will produce hypotonicity of body fluids. If the drug is continued, the ADH secretion may continue inappropriately. Other drugs, such as chlorpropamide, potentiate the action of ADH on the kidneys, and this may cause the syndrome of inappropriate secretion of ADH (SIADH) if (1) water intake is high, and (2) some AVP is present.[16] The role of drugs in SIADH is discussed in detail in the section on relative water excess.

Inhibition with Alcohol

Alcohol can block the secretion of AVP by direct action on the supraopticohypophyseal system. It may override such stimuli as hypertonicity of the plasma or hypovolemia. It can be used to distinguish overproduction of AVP caused by tumors from overproduction in response to stimuli to the supraopticohypophyseal system in disorders involving cortisol or thyroid deficiency or intracranial or pulmonary disease.[17,18]

Resetting of the Osmostat

The normal person maintains the tonicity of body fluids within narrow limits: the addition of water to the body promptly results in diminished secretion of AVP, with the excretion of dilute urine until the osmolality of the serum returns to normal. There is a group of patients, however, whose responses to changes in osmotic pressure are regulated about a subnormal tonicity. This has been considered as "a resetting of the osmostat." This possibility has been reported in patients with decompensated cirrhosis,[19] tuberculosis,[20] and psychogenic polydipsia.[21] All of these patients had striking hyponatremia, and responded to a standard water load with a further drop in tonicity, the inhibition of ADH, the excretion of a dilute urine, and the return of the serum sodium and osmolality to their original low concentrations. The administration of a sodium load either acutely or over a period of several days did not correct the hyponatremia to within the normal range, although treatment of the underlying disease regularly restored the serum sodium to values in the normal range. In the case of the patients with psychogenic polydipsia, it was originally thought that the antipsychotic drugs with which they were being treated might have induced the hyponatremia, but treatment with these drugs resulted in improvement of the polydipsia with resulting normal values for serum sodium. Plasma values for AVP were not obtained in any of these patients.

CONTROL OF WATER INGESTION

Thirst and Dehydration

Another important factor controlling water metabolism is thirst. Thirst is the stimulus to water drinking and is activated in response to cellular dehydration. Some of the same factors that activate the production and secretion of AVP also activate thirst, and osmotic or volume sensors may therefore be implicated in this sensation.

Cellular dehydration, which is detected by the osmoreceptors, can be caused by water deprivation, the infusion of hypertonic solutions (especially sodium), or potassium depletion. With cellular dehydration, such as is found with intravenous infusions of hypertonic saline, water leaves the cells to re-establish the tonicity of the extracellular fluid (ECF). The increased tonicity (hyperosmolality) of the fluid coming into contact with the osmoreceptors of the brain induces the organism to initiate drinking. A change in the concentration of osmoles that reflects about a 2 percent deficit in body water is sufficient to trigger the thirst mechanism. The osmoreceptors are believed to be located in the area of the brain where there is no blood-brain barrier, such as the subfornical organ and the organum vasculosum of the lamina terminalis of the third ventricle. Studies by McKinley[22] have shown that ablation of the organum vasculosum and adjacent midline tissue of the optic recess of the third ventricle greatly reduced water drinking in sheep that were receiving intracarotid infusions of hypertonic saline. This led McKinley to suggest that the tissue of that area is usually involved in the osmolar changes that elicit water drinking.

The extracellular dehydration caused by sodium depletion, nausea, profuse vomiting, hemorrhage, or any abrupt removal of ECF can be detected by the volume or stretch receptors in the atrium and the capacitance vessels in the thorax, which elicit afferent nerve activity to stimulate thirst. The kidney, by means of the renin-angiotensin system, has also been implicated in the volume regulation of water intake in some animals.[23,24] Although there is no direct, firm evidence of this in the human being, clinical observations of thirst related to intravenous infusions of angiotensin, and thirst experienced by patients with renal failure[25] and those with renin-secreting Wilms' tumors,[26] suggest that angiotensin may play a role in eliciting thirst in some volume-depleted conditions.

Fitzsimons,[27] one of the foremost researchers in this field, believes that the kidney, with its control of water and solute excretion and its renin-angiotensin system, is a major regulator of thirst. With extracellular dehydration in particular, angiotensin II can be logically implicated in such a mechanism. The dehydration is perceived as hypovolemia, which can stimulate receptors in both the arterial and low-pressure circulation, resulting in sympathetic activation of the juxtaglomerular apparatus to produce renin, and the consequent generation of angiotensin II to stimulate the thirst centers to initiate water drinking, thus restoring the ECF volume. Angiotensin II may either stimulate the thirst centers directly or sensitize them to respond to other stimuli. The structures of the brain most sensitive to the angiotensin II stimulus to water drinking are the subfornical organ and the organum vasculosum of the lamina terminalis in the wall of the anterior third ventricle,[28-30] which are also the structures sensitive to osmolar changes. Other substances in the renin-angiotensin system also induce drinking, and it has been found that all the components of this system are in the brain.[31,32] It has even been suggested that angiotensin II is generated centrally and acts in situ to stimulate drinking.

Other pharmacologic agents are also known to stimulate thirst, but play no role in the normal physiologic mechanisms governing this sensation. Several recent reviews by Fitzsimons[27] and Andersson[33] treat the subject in great detail.

PITUITARY DIABETES INSIPIDUS AS A MODEL FOR RELATIVE WATER DEFICIENCY

In pituitary diabetes insipidus, the patient is unable to secrete or release AVP. As a result, the collecting ducts are unable to reclaim free water, and it is lost in the urine. This leads to a relative deficiency of body water resulting entirely from water loss.

SIADH AS A MODEL FOR RELATIVE WATER EXCESS

It has been shown that normal subjects given long-acting vasopressin preparations and sufficient water to drink retain enough of the water to dilute body fluids.[34] Despite the hyponatremia so induced, aldosterone secretion decreases and there is a paradoxical increase in urinary sodium excretion. In a number of clinical conditions (vide infra), sustained secretion of endogenous ADH is found.[18] In these syndromes of SIADH, the secretion of ADH continues inappropriately* despite the intake of enough water to lower the plasma osmolality to values well below normal. There are also secondary results of the paradoxical loss of sodium that compound the disorder. Initially, it represents a relative excess of body water resulting entirely from water retention.

---

* Inappropriately vis-a-vis plasma tonicity, the usual and physiologically most important factor controlling ADH secretion.

RELATIVE WATER DEFICIENCY

Causes

Table 3-1 lists some of the causes of relative water deficiency. These are conveniently classified as conditions of solute excess, those of water loss (essentially "free" water), and those of combined solute excess and water loss.

Solute Excess: Excessive Solute Load for Available Water

A particularly disastrous syndrome of acute solute excess has been found in infants who received formula to which sodium chloride had been erroneously added in place of sugar.[35] The first such reported episode resulted in the death of 6 of the 14 patients so poisoned, and permanent disability in 2 others. The excessive ingestion of sodium chloride by deranged or psychotic individuals has also led to relative deficiency of water.[36] The use of concentrated sodium injected into the uterus as an abortifacient has led to hypernatremia and plasma hypertonicity in reported cases in which the salt gained access to the circulation.[37,38]

Patients receiving total parenteral nutrition or protein concentrates parenterally or orally are at risk for water deficiency whenever the load constituting the metabolites of the administered solute is greatly in excess of the amount of solute sufficient to bring the available water to isotonicity. In such a situation there is continuing loss of "insensible" water without solute. Whereas this water is not measurable under normal clinical conditions, it must be estimated in the plan for therapeutic restoration of the normal tonicity of body fluids. Excessive solute loading may also result from the excessive addition of solute by the proportioning pump in hemodialysis systems, an eventuality that could result from mechanical defects or user error.[39,40]

Finally, the hyperosmolar states produced by uncontrolled diabetes mellitus, with or without ketoacidosis, depend on

Table 3-1. Relative Water Deficiency: Causes

Excessive solute load for available water
   Hypertonic feeding to infants
   Sodium chloride ingestion
   Use of sodium chloride as an abortifacient
   Parenteral protein administration without adequate water
   Hemodialysis error
   Diabetic ketoacidosis and hyperosmolar coma
Excessive loss of water without solute
   Diabetes insipidus, central
   Diabetes insipidus, renal
      X-linked recessive
      Potassium depletion
      Calcium-induced
      Drugs: Lithium, methoxyflurane, democlocycline
      Medullary washout
      Excessive use of osmotically active agents excreted in urine
      Renal failure with loss of concentrating ability and nitrogen retention
   Gastroenteritis with vomiting and/or diarrhea
   Excessive skin and lung losses
      Fever with hyperpnea
      Desert exposure
Combined solute excess and water loss
   Uremia
   Ocean raft survivors drinking sea water
"Essential" or central hypernatremia

both the retention of excessive solute and the loss of excessive solute in the urine.[41] The urinary solute, by producing an osmotic diuresis wherein the kidney's ability to conserve an adequate amount of filtered water is prevented by the tubular solute load, aggravates the hyperosmolality of the plasma if additional water is not supplied.

Excessive Loss of Water Without Solute

In central diabetes insipidus, the patient is unable to secrete or release ADH from the posterior pituitary. As a result, the collecting ducts are unable to reclaim free water, and it is lost in the urine. This leads to a relative deficiency of body water resulting entirely from water loss. The consequent hypertonicity of body fluids leads to thirst and therefore to drinking. If the amount of fluid drunk is inadequate to match urinary and insensible losses, the dehydration and body fluid hypertonicity increase in severity. Without treatment, death may ensue, caused by "pure" water loss.

The major causes of central diabetes insipidus are head trauma and hypophysectomy.[42,43] The latter is usually performed to remove suprasellar or intrasellar tumors such as chromophobe adenomas, pinealomas, and craniopharyngiomas, and to alleviate carcinoma of the breast and the retinopathy of diabetes mellitus. Other unusual etiologies include granulomatous disorders such as tuberculosis and sarcoidosis, vascular problems including aneurysms and thrombosis, infections and immunologic disorders, histiocytosis and a rare familial form presenting in childhood of diabetes insipidus.[44,45]

Diabetes insipidus following head trauma or hypophysectomy is usually of abrupt onset, with polyuria resulting within a day or two. If the patient is unconscious, care must be taken to monitor the serum osmolality (or sodium) and to provide an adequate fluid input. The diabetes insipidus may be partial or complete,[46,47] which can be determined by the dehydration test, urinary concentrating ability, and plasma vasopressin concentration. Patients with diabetes insipidus respond readily to vasopressin, but the condition may also be controlled with some oral agents that stimulate the production of AVP or potentiate its action on the renal tubule. (Treatment will be discussed in more detail later.)

So-called renal or nephrogenic diabetes insipidus produces a physiologically similar picture to that described above, in which the kidney, unable to respond to ADH, continues to excrete dilute (hypotonic) urine, with the same consequences. Classical hereditary renal diabetes insipidus is an X-linked heritable disorder, found in severe form in males.[48-51] In this condition, the production (indeed, even compensatory overproduction) of vasopressin is not impaired, but the collecting ducts are incapable of responding to vasopressin.

In several metabolic conditions, a similar but reversible state results from acquired renal disease.[52] The tubules lose the ability to concentrate the urine by a vasopressin-induced increase in the permeability of the collecting ducts. The result is a vasopressin-resistant form of renal diabetes insipidus. Depletion of potassium with hypokalemia produces such a situation.[53,54,55] As potassium depletion promotes the secretion of renal prostaglandin E2[56] and vascular prostacyclin,[57] it has been reported that the prostaglandins act to prevent passive transport of water across the collecting ducts.[58] Other studies suggest that potassium depletion also limits the ability of the supraopticohypophyseal system to release vasopressin in response to a rise in plasma tonicity.[59] An additional factor in the lack of vasopressin responsiveness may be the inability of the kidney to generate a sufficiently high interstitial tonicity,[60] possibly due to abnormal solute reabsorption in the ascending limb of the loop of Henle.[61]

Sustained hypercalcemia and hypercalciuria are also associated with an inability to concentrate the urine. Originally, it was thought that parathyroid hormone impaired the release of vasopressin,[62] but Baylis and associates in 1981 showed that there was no defect in the release of the hormone in response to an osmotic stimulus either in patients with hyperparathyroidism or with the hypercalcemia of malignancy.[63] In fact, studies by Weiss and Robertson[64] have demonstrated a role for hypercalcemia in potentiating the sensitivity of the vasopressin response to osmotic stimuli. As in hypokalemia, the defect in concentrating ability can be traced to the nephron, where a decrease in interstitial hypertonicity has been reported with hypercalcemia.[65-67] Other studies have demonstrated that hypercalcemic subjects are vasopressin resistant,[68] indicating a defect in the permeability of the collecting duct to water. There is growing evidence for an important role of calcium in the actions of vasopressin in the renal tubule.[52]

A variety of dissimilar drugs may also produce nephrogenic diabetes insipidus. Among them are lithium carbonate, used in the treatment of affective disorders,[69-71] the anesthetic methoxyflurane,[72] and the antibiotic demeclocycline.[73,74] The polyuria induced by lithium is due to an inhibition of the actions of both adenylate cyclase and cyclic AMP in the renal tubule, and a reduction in the renal medullary osmotic gradient.[75] Weiss and Robertson[64] have also shown that lithium therapy can result in primary polydipsia, which may contribute to the polyuria. The etiology of the tubular defect caused by methoxyflurane is not known. Demeclocycline is believed to inhibit both cyclic AMP production and action.

In addition to these other sources, renal diabetes insipidus may be seen in neurotic or disturbed patients who suffer from compulsive polydipsia. After such subjects have consumed excessive amounts of water over prolonged periods, the renal medulla may, by "washout" of sodium salts and urea, lose its hypertonic state. Under such conditions, a state of pitressin-resistant diabetes insipidus may ensue. This may be misdiagnosed as heritable or metabolic renal diabetes insipidus because of the absence of a response to exogenously-administered vasopressin. It is, however, completely reversible upon the administration of sodium salts in quantities sufficient to restore medullary tonicity.

The excessive use of loop diuretics such as furosemide can produce a renal diabetes insipidus-like syndrome. These agents, by diminishing or preventing the reabsorption of sodium and chloride in the thick ascending limb of the loop of Henle, inhibit or prevent the accumulation of these solutes in the renal medulla. As a result, the ability of the collecting ducts to reabsorb water without solute, and therefore the renal concentrating ability, are impaired.

Renal failure leads to the largest proportion of adult cases of relative water depletion. In early renal failure, the changes in renal function seen with a loss of concentrating ability will lead to relative water loss by renal as well as insensible routes in a subject who was previously well hydrated, unless it is prevented by a corresponding increase in water intake. The situation is aggravated by the retention of solutes such as urea. This not only leads directly to a hyperosmolar state, but also, by producing osmotic diuresis, increases the relative water loss by the kidneys. Excessive water loss may be induced without a pre-existing failure of renal concentrating ability when agents that directly induce an osmotic diuresis are administered as treatment. An example is the use of urea as a diuretic.

The injudicious use of hypertonic fluids in peritoneal dialysis, especially ones containing a solute that is not rapidly metabolized, may lead to hypertonicity of the plasma and a relative water deficiency. As the fluid is removed, it contains relatively more water than the infusate.

Gastrointestinal loss of water can be effected through vomiting or diarrhea. Repeated vomiting can clearly cause the body to lose water and so can contribute to a relative deficiency of body water.[76] Such a deficiency is rarely an important sequel of vomiting, however, except in three situations. First, water deficiency can clearly develop if "selective" vomiting of ingested water and fluids is accompanied by relative retention of food. Second, a relative deficiency of water can result from intestinal obstruction, such as that found with pyloric stenosis, in which secreted digestive juices are lost in vomitus. Third, in conditions such as the Zollinger-Ellison Syndrome, in which hypertrophic gastritis is present and voluminous hypotonic gastric secretions result, the repeated vomiting of such secretions can lead rapidly to relative water loss. Protracted diarrhea may also result in a relative deficiency of body water.[77,78] This is especially likely to accompany so-called osmotic diarrhea, in which a non absorbed solute in the gastrointestinal tract leads to excessive loss of water in the stool. As this solute is generated in the gastrointestinal tract, the water it draws into the tract osmotically is selectively removed from the body fluids. Thus, hyperosmolality and hypernatremia ensue, with the usual consequences.

Relative water deficiency can also be due to excessive loss of water from the skin and lungs, particularly with fever or a high environmental temperature.[79] This loss of water without sodium does not lead to volume contraction unless sustained over several days. The affected patients have a normal ECF volume and normal total body sodium content. Children with fever frequently have hyperpnea, and their deep breathing hastens the water loss from the lungs. The dry air usually found in winter in centrally-heated homes may contribute to the water loss. If such losses are not treated promptly with the ingestion of fluids, hypernatremia will result. Since the osmoreceptors respond normally to the hypertonic stimulus, AVP is released, renal water is retained, and the urine becomes hypertonic.

The most common clinical example of relative water deficiency is found in subjects whose water supply is inadequate, such as those exposed to a desert environment. As relative water deficiency ensues in such a subject, the osmolality of the urine quickly becomes maximal. When dehydration threatens, there are two measures available to the organism to restore and protect body fluid tonicity: ingestion of water and loss of solute. In patients with maximal urine tonicity, the loss of solute by the kidneys is already maximal for the obligatory loss of urinary water. Whereas sweating constitutes an additional potential route for loss of solute, it is of no protective value to the dehydrated organism, since sweat is invariably hypotonic to plasma.[80] Indeed, because sodium depletion, tending to produce hypovolemia, often accompanies such water depletion, the sodium concentration of sweat, and thus its osmolality, generally decreases with dehydration as aldosterone secretion is potentiated.[81] Clearly, such conservation of sodium with continued loss of water in sweat ultimately tends to augment the hypertonicity of the plasma, producing hypernatremia.

Combined Solute Excess and Water Loss

In states of renal failure, there is an increased urea concentration that contributes to the plasma osmole concentration. As the glomerular filtration rate (GFR) drops, the amount of urea and reabsorbable solutes in the plasma rises to alarming osmolar values. An acute renal failure leads to an abrupt increase in osmoles that is frequently associated with neurologic abnormalities. A gradual increase in the urea concentration of the plasma is not associated with neurologic signs or symptoms because the urea penetrates slowly into brain cells and does not produce dehydration as intracellular osmoles enter the ECF. However, the increased tonicity that results exerts its usual effect. In addition, there are idiogenic osmoles produced in the brain cells after a few weeks of a high plasma urea concentration, and these enter the ECF to increase the plasma osmolality even further. Since the GFR can be reduced to minimal levels, the quantity of ions regularly excreted by the kidney (e.g., sodium, potassium, calcium, magnesium, chloride and phosphate) is retained by the body and increases the serum osmolality which, in the absence of the renal response to increased ADH, causes cellular dehydration in the brain. The manifestations of this in the central nervous system include headaches, seizures, twitching, and coma. Even though little water is lost from the kidneys, the body's ordinary insensible water loss contributes to a state of dehydration.

Survivors of a prolonged lack of fresh water in an ocean environment also suffer a relative (albeit clearly not an absolute) deficiency of water. Since the osmolality of ocean water is above that of plasma (e.g., 1000 mOsm/kg of water in the Gulf of Mexico), and indeed, close to the maximal tonicity of human urine (circa 1200 mOsm/kg), it is clear that the human kidney can reclaim no water from ingested sea water. Thus, if the subject drinks sea water, the salts in this water only aggravate the relative water deficiency.

"Essential" or Central Hypernatremia

Another unusual and rare situation in which there is an excess of solutes with no evident deficit in volume has been described by Welt as "essential" hypernatremia.[82] A hypernatremia of strikingly elevated values (159 to 188 mEq/liter reported) has been found in the course of workups for various complaints in patients who appear to be relatively healthy. There was no history of polydipsia or polyuria in any of these patients. In fact, hypodipsia was the rule. The syndrome includes hypernatremia without a volume deficit, normal secretion of ADH in response to nonosmotic stimuli, and the ability of the renal tubules to respond to ADH. The original description by Welt[82] included the hypothesis that there was a resetting of osmoreceptors, with the responses of thirst and ADH secretion functioning around a higher than normal osmolality. Sridhar and colleagues [83] reported that there was impaired secretion of ADH around a wide range of osmolalities, and suggested that the syndrome should be considered one of hypodipsia, hypernatremia, and partial diabetes insipidus. Their premise was strengthened by the reports of three investigators[84-86] that treatment with chlorpropamide, a drug known to increase the secretion of AVP, was effective in restoring thirst, with rehydration and consequent lowering of the serum sodium to normal values.

Metabolic Consequences

Relative water deficiency implies by definition hypertonicity of ECF. Since virtually all cells of the body act as osmometers, separated from the ECF by the semipermeable membrane, the immediate result of ECF hypertonicity is a loss of water from cells, whose intracellular fluid assumes the osmolality of the ECF.[87] Whereas widespread biochemical consequences follow such cellular dehydration, central nervous system changes are clinically the most prominent and most threatening to life.[88,89] These may range from lethargy to stupor to coma, and may be accompanied by convulsions. Despite the progression to coma, the signs may include great irritability and exaggerated deep tendon reflexes.

Measurement of Relative Water Deficiency

In evaluating the degree of relative water deficiency, the relatively simple analyses of sodium with a flame photometer and of osmolality with a freezing-point depression apparatus or a vapor-pressure measuring instrument are used. The more definitive measure of ADH involves a complex radioimmunoassay under conditions of varying degrees of hydration or dehydration. The amount of the patient's water deficit can be calculated with the following assumptions: (1) that the water loss is distributed throughout the total body water (approximately 60 percent of body weight expressed in kilograms for adults), and (2) that 140 mEq/liter is the normal serum concentration of sodium. Accordingly, for a 75 kg adult: 75 kg × 0.60 = 45 liters total body water. If the serum sodium is 154 mEq/liter, 154/140 × 45 liters = 49.5 liters of body water are needed to dilute the serum sodium from 154 to 140 mEq/liter. Consequently, 49.5 liters − 45.0 liters = 4.5 liters deficit.

The Dehydration Test

The diagnosis of central diabetes insipidus consists of demonstrating that vasopressin is not released in response to a rising tonicity of the blood bathing the supraopticohypophyseal region. The optimal stimulus used clinically to establish the tonicity-AVP response is the dehydration test under rigidly controlled conditions.[90] Blood is drawn for plasma sodium, osmolality, and AVP measurement, and body weight is measured in the hospitalized patient in the early evening, at about 1600 hours. This time is selected so that any signs of severe dehydration will occur on the following day when a full nursing staff is available if prompt treatment is needed. After the 1600 hour blood drawing, the patient is fed a dry diet with no dietary liquid or extra water. A complete, if possible, 24-hour urine specimen is collected for volume and osmolality measurements. The urine will serve as a check on the compliance on the patient, since the volume can be equated with the weight loss. At 1600 hours on the second day, which should coincide with the closing of the 24-hour urine collection, blood is again drawn for plasma sodium, osmolality, and AVP measurement, and body weight is again measured. The next available voided urine specimen, however small, is taken for measurement of the "maximal" urine osmolality. If a quick estimate of the specific gravity of this specimen reveals that the urine is hypotonic (below 1.005 s.g.), an intravenous injection of one unit of vasopressin can be given and another urine specimen collected 15 minutes later for an osmolality measurement before the patient is allowed to drink. This permits a test of renal response to AVP.

With this dehydration procedure, normal subjects will usually lose less than 1 percent of their body weight, serum sodium and osmolality will remain in the normal range, and urine osmolality may show a concentration above 1000 mOsm/kg. Those patients with central diabetes insipidus will lose more than 3 percent of their body weight and their serum sodium and osmolality will rise. The first voided specimen will be hypotonic to serum, with an osmolality below 300 mOsm/kg of urine. The renal response to the intravenous dose of vasopressin will be normal, with an osmolality above 300 mOsm/kg (usually 600 to 700 mOsm/kg) being achieved.

Some patients may lose water and body weight very rapidly, and may not be able to undergo the full 24-hour dehydration without symptoms of acute distress. They may be so desperate for water that they drink from any available source, including the toilet bowl. If clinical signs of confusion and inordinate thirst appear, the study should be terminated with the measuring of body weight, the drawing of blood for sodium, osmolality, and AVP measurement, and the collecting of the next voided urine sample. The dehydration test will be achieved even though the test was completed in 12, 18, or 20 hours. The patient will quickly drink enough water to become normally hydrated.

Although the diagnosis of diabetes insipidus has been made for many years without the laboratory assay of ADH, this analysis is now available by sensitive radioimmunoassay in a few laboratories.[91]

Treatment of Relative Water Deficiency

The treatment of hypernatremia is a complicated procedure that can frequently result in cerebral edema and convulsions. Only general principles will be given here. More specific treatment for hypernatremia of various causes should be sought in the literature.[92-94]

Since all patients with water deficiency present with hypernatremia, it is important to assess the cause of this as quickly as possible, in order to start immediate therapy for the hypernatremia and to establish a long-term program to remove the underlying cause. Again, we will consider the therapy in the three distinctive states of water deficiency:

1. Excessive solute load for available water.
2. Excessive loss of water without solute.
3. Excessive loss of water and solute excess.

Excessive Solute Load for Available Water

If there has been an excessive solute load for the available water, oral water replacement should be begun if the subject is conscious. However, a deficit of more than two liters is difficult to replace in one day with water limited to oral intake only, and may require supplementation with an intravenous infusion. If the subject is unconscious, intravenous dextrose (5 percent) and water should be given with diuretics to remove the excessive sodium. In cases of salt poisoning, peritoneal dialysis with hypertonic glucose (8 percent) has been used to reduce the tonicity of the ECF.[95] In the case of diabetic ketoacidosis and hyperosmolar coma, insulin should be given to correct the hyperglycemia.

Excessive Loss of Water Without Solute

The outstanding example of a state of relative water deficiency caused by excessive loss of water without solute is diabetes insipidus. Specific treatment for central diabetes insipidus includes the regular ingestion of water plus vasopressin in the form of pitressin tannate in oil, synthetic lysine vasopressin (Diapid), or desmopressin acetate (DDAVP). Pitressin in oil has a relatively slow onset of action but has persisting effects that allow control of the diabetes with a single daily injection. The usual dose is from 2 to 5 U/day, which controls the renal reabsorption of water for 24 to 72 hours. Overhydration must be avoided. Synthetic lysine vasopressin has a short duration of action and requires two or more doses per day. It is given as a nasal spray containing 50 units (3.7 µg/unit or 0.185 mg/ml). It can cause local nasal irritation. Desmopressin acetate (DDAVP), a synthetic analogue of AVP, has a longer period of action, producing antidiuresis for 6 to 20 hours. It is available in 2.5 ml vials containing 0.1 mg/ml of the drug for intranasal use. The usual daily dose is from 5 to 20 µg. It is supplied with an apparatus that can be calibrated to administer the designated dose.

Some patients with partial diabetes insipidus respond to treatment with oral agents such as chlorpropamide, which potentiates the action of even a small amount of secreted vasopressin on the kidneys. Other drugs, such as carbamazepine and clofibrate, also stimulate release of AVP in patients with partial diabetes insipidus, but because of their adverse side effects are not recommended for routine therapy.[94]

Since patients with nephrogenic diabetes insipidus do not respond to vasopressin, other means of reducing their urinary output include restriction of dietary protein and salt, and the use of thiazide diuretics.

Excessive Loss of Water With Solute Excess

When there has been excessive loss of water together with solute excess, such as in the case of exposure on a raft and drinking seawater, the diagnosis is hypernatremic dehydration. The volume of the ECF must be repleted at the same time as the excess sodium is removed from the body. A combination of 0.45 percent sodium chloride with diuretics will correct the condition. Any infusion to correct the deficit should be given slowly, over 48 hours if possible.

General Principles for Therapy

Among the general principles set forth by Finberg[93] for restoration of the serum sodium to normal are that:

1. The objective is to replace fluid volume, to restore water distribution, and to correct the complicating disturbance.
2. Any fluid that is infused to correct the water deficit should be administered over no less than 48 hours.
3. Water alone (as D5/W) causes cerebral edema. Glucose crosses the blood-central nervous system barrier by active transport. The increased water causes swelling of brain cells with a resulting rise in central nervous system pressure. A number of nervous system functions are affected, and many of the complications can be the result of the "therapy." To avoid cerebral edema in children, and particularly infants, Finberg recommends that the "repair" solution be prepared with consideration of the volume, the content of glucose, sodium, potassium, anion, and calcium, and the rate of administration. The total volume needed, as calculated from the volume deficit, should be infused over a period of 48 hours. Any rate faster than this can lead to complications of the therapy. If the patient is in shock or circulatory distress, 20 ml/kg of 5 percent albumin are recommended to expand the intravascular space.

RELATIVE WATER EXCESS

In 1957, a syndrome was described[16] that resulted entirely from water retention, and represented a relative excess of body water. Two patients with pulmonary tumors (oat-cell type), when drinking water, gained body weight, developed hyponatremia and hypotonicity of the plasma, but continued to lose sodium in the urine. A urine hypertonic to plasma was produced. Despite the plasma hypotonicity, which normally inhibits the production of ADH, the hormone continued to be produced (Fig. 3-3). Accordingly, the syndrome was named "the syndrome of inappropriate secretion of ADH" (SIADH). The term "inappropriate" was used vis-a-vis plasma tonicity, the physiologically most important controlling factor in ADH secretion.

The "model" for this syndrome had been

122 • Kidney Electrolyte Disorders

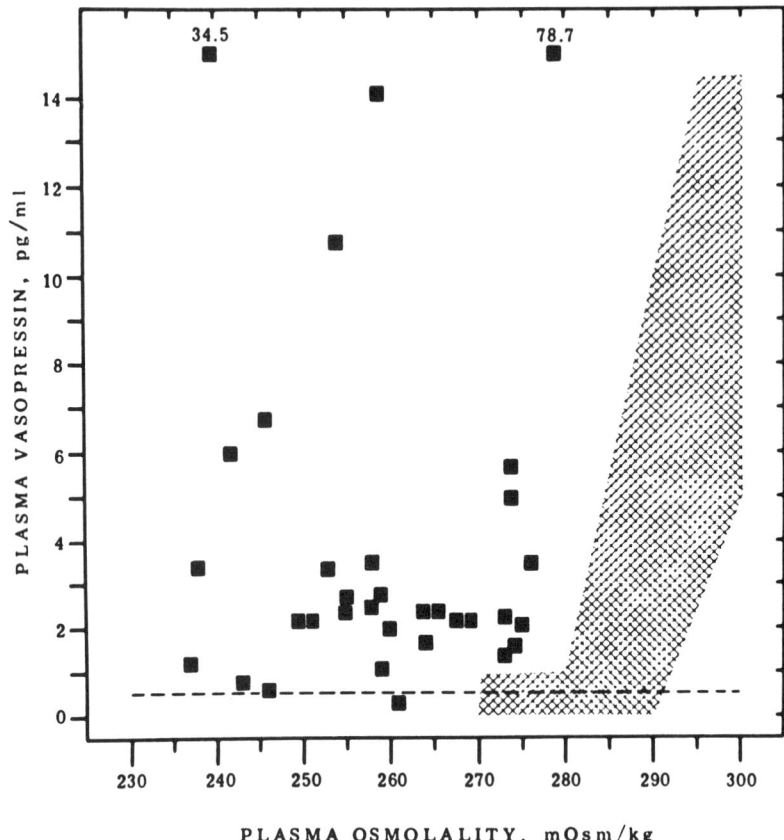

Fig. 3-3. The relationship of plasma vasopressin to plasma osmolality in patients with SIADH. The hatched area represents the data in normal subjects. It is important to note that although all the values for AVP are not high, they are high when considered in relation to the plasma osmolality. (From Robertson GL: Clinical Fluid and Electrolyte Management II. p. 70. Sept 19–21, Veterans Administration, Oklahoma City, Oklahoma 1978, with permission.)

described a few years earlier by Leaf and associates,[34] when they reported the results of treatment with long-acting pitressin (AVP) in normal subjects receiving a constant intake of food and water. The results were clear-cut: the urinary tonicity rose to and remained at a near maximum, water was retained, body weight rose, and serum sodium fell. Although the retained water decreased the serum sodium concentration, the subjects continued paradoxically to excrete more sodium than they were taking in, so that the serum sodium decreased even further. In later studies by Bartter and coworkers,[96] it was shown that this continued urinary sodium loss was accompanied by a decrease in aldosterone secretion (even though the serum sodium was falling) and an increase in the GFR, and thus an increase in the filtered load of sodium (Fig. 3-4). The expansion of total body water produced the hyponatremia, the decreased aldosterone secretion, and a decreased proximal sodium reabsorption, thus leading to a significant natriuresis. With the inability to excrete a free water load, the urinary sodium was excreted in a small volume of urine which was less than maximally dilute.

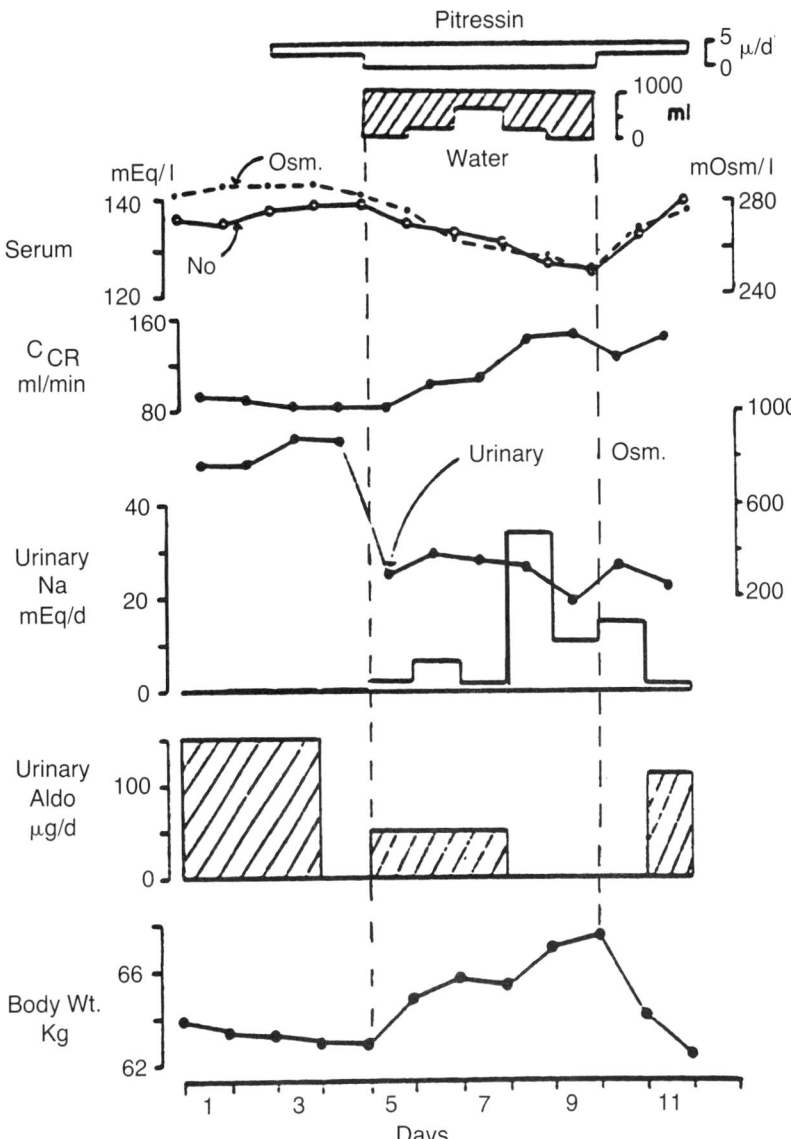

Fig. 3-4. The model for the syndrome of inappropriate secretion of antidiuretic hormone (SIADH). The effect of pitressin and water on serum sodium (Na), and osmolality (Osm), creatinine clearance (C_{cr}), urinary sodium (Na), aldosterone (ALDO), and body weight in a normal subject. (From Bartter JFC: The syndrome of inappropriate secretion of antidiuretic hormone. R Coll Physicians, London 4:264, 1970, with permission.)

Table 3-2. Relative Water Excess: Causes

Syndromes of inappropriate secretion of ADH
  The Model: vasopressin plus water intake
  Tumors secreting ADH
  Intracranial disease
  Pulmonary disease
  Trauma and hemorrhage
  Miscellaneous disorders
  Affective disorders
  Drugs
  Endocrine disorders
  Disorders in which SIADH may play a part: cirrhosis, cardiac failure

One of the cardinal features for the diagnosis of SIADH is that the urine be more concentrated than appropriate for the given solute and water intake: a urine that is less than maximally dilute in the presence of plasma hypotonicity provides clear evidence that there is a defect in water excretion. The syndrome also usually includes normal or low values for blood urea nitrogen, and a normal to high GFR.

Although the syndrome as initially described was first associated with a pulmonary tumor, syndromes of inappropriate secretion of ADH have been seen with other intrathoracic diseases, intracranial disease, severe trauma, and endocrine disease, and with the administration of some drugs.[18,97] Some of the causes of SIADH are listed in Table 3-2 and will be discussed in more detail in the following sections.

Causes

In SIADH, excessive ADH can be produced ectopically by tumor tissue or in response to an unusual sustained stimulus to the supraopticohypophyseal tract. Tumors are the most common cause of SIADH. These include bronchogenic carcinoma of the lungs; carcinoma of the pancreas, duodenum, and ureter; lymphoma; and Ewing's sarcoma.[97-101] Recently, SIADH has been seen in two patients with nasal neuroblastoma[102,103] and in a patient with multiple myeloma.[104] In many of cases it has been demonstrated that the tumor itself produces AVP from amino acid precursors.[97,101,103,105] Its release is independent of normal physiologic controls. These tumors have also been shown to produce neurophysins, a group of peptides that bind ADH.[106] When possible, treatment of the underlying disease by resection, as in the case of olfactory neuroblastoma,[102] or by chemotherapy in patients with small cell carcinomas of the lung,[99] resolves the hyponatremia.

Intracranial and nervous system disorders are frequently associated with SIADH. Since the signs and symptoms seen with severe hyponatremia (a serum sodium concentration below 120 mEq/liter) are usually those of brain edema, the differential diagnosis must be made quickly so that appropriate treatment can be given. The syndrome has been reported for trauma, subarachnoid hemorrhage, meningitis, encephalitis, Guillain-Barré syndrome, stroke, epilepsy, and brain tumor.[97,107] In 1985, Butrus and associates[108] reported a case in which bilateral *Pseudomonas* endophthalmitis and expulsive choroidal hemorrhages were associated with SIADH. Complete remission of the hyponatremia followed bilateral evisceration, suggesting that the infected orbital contents were causing it. In three cases of craniofacial surgery, SIADH developed within 48 hours postoperatively.[109] Several authors suggest that the increase in ADH with cranial disorders, particularly stroke and surgery, is "appropriate," and that the hyponatremia is due to the excessive fluids given in such cases.[110,111] Since this is true of most operations in which pain, trauma, and hemorrhage can appropriately stimulate ADH production, it has become the general practice to limit fluid intake during the first 48 hours postoperatively. If fluid is given, the syndrome (SIADH) will manifest itself.

In 1983, Kirkland and colleagues[112] reported a patient with histologically verified sarcoidosis with polyuria, hyponatremia, severe thirst, and evidence of excessive ADH secretion. Although polyuria has previously been seen with sarcoidosis, this was the first account of SIADH in this disease. At autopsy, extensive granulomatous infiltration of the basal meninges, hypothalamus, and frontal and temporal lobes was found.

Among other disorders reported as being accompanied by SIADH are tetanus,[113] herpes zoster,[114] and systemic lupus erythematosus.[115] All of these disorders probably stimulated the secretion of ADH by way of the nervous system. Rocky mountain spotted fever has been shown to produce SIADH. Although the mechanism is not known, the invasion by Rickettsia of the vascular endothelial cells can result in a decreased intravascular volume, which can stimulate the production of ADH. Water ingestion and consequent hyponatremia then result in SIADH.[116] Patients who have experienced the severe trauma of burns frequently show the symptomatology of SIADH.[117,118] In the report by Shirani and colleagues,[118] 17 patients with hyponatremia had plasma AVP values ranging from 1.6 to 14.3 pg/ml, while the normal values for the authors' laboratory were below 0.5 pg/ml. Nine of these patients, without renal failure or sepsis, demonstrated the full syndrome and four responded to a water loading test with a further reduction in their serum sodium concentration. [A discussor] of this paper proposed that the secretion of ADH was "appropriate," since there was a reduced blood volume and trauma, two factors that are normal stimuli to ADH production and secretion. However, since the hyponatremia persisted for up to 10 days after the burn, at a time when the blood volume had been restored, and the ADH was not suppressed vis-a-vis the plasma osmolality, the patients' condition, by definition, was SIADH.

Patients with pulmonary disease such as pneumonia, tuberculosis, cavitation caused by aspergillosis, and acute respiratory disease have also presented with SIADH.[97] Although it is thought that the hormone is released endogenously from the supraopticohypophyseal tract in these disorders, there has been one report in which ADH was extracted from granulomatous tissue in the lung at autopsy.[119]

Patients with affective disorders, particularly psychoses, mania, and schizophrenia, frequently induce water intoxication by compulsive drinking. In a few such patients with intakes of 20 to 25 liters of fluid a day, the intake exceeds the maximal renal output and some water is retained, with the dilution of body fluids. This is usually not SIADH. However, in three patients reported by Zubenko and associates[120] and six reported by Viewez and colleagues,[121] SIADH was present, with a plasma AVP concentration in the range of 3.4 to 5.6 pg/ml, and hypoosmolality, excessive urine volume, and a urine osmolality in the range of 100 to 154 mosm/kg of water (not maximally dilute despite the excessive urine volume). All of the patients responded to fluid restriction, but the symptoms recurred with renewed drinking until adequate treatment of the affective disorder was given.

Unfortunately, drugs that are used to treat affective disorders have also been implicated in the production of SIADH. Among them are amitriptyline, haloperidol, desipramine, fluphenazine, thioridazine, thiothixene, tranylcypromine, carbamazepine, nortriptyline, amoxapine, and doxepin.[122,123] The data supporting this association are not scientifically strong, since in some instances the hyponatremia has remitted spontaneously, the drug has been stopped and restarted later with no recurrence of the hyponatremia, only a few patients have been tested with water loading, and of the large number of patients who receive these drugs only a few have become symptomatic with SIADH. The mechanism of action for the SIADH is unknown, and no well controlled studies of its development have been done. These patients can usually be managed on the drugs they are receiving as long as their water intake is restricted.

Among other agents implicated in the production of SIADH are drugs used in chemotherapy, particularly vincristine and cyclophosphamide.[97,124] The syndrome has been attributed to the neurotoxic effects of the drugs, which may include the constant nausea and vomiting so frequently accompanying chemotherapy. Since nausea and emesis readily stimulate ADH, any patient in whom the condition is present may induce the syndrome by excessive ingestion of fluid. If this is the responsible mechanism, it is surprising that more patients on chemotherapy do not present with SIADH.

Drugs that are used to treat diabetes insipidus can also cause SIADH. Physician-administered vasopressin, in the form of pitressin or DDAVP, if given regularly without controlled water intake, can produce the syndrome. This is a danger in patients with diabetes insipidus in whom the thirst mechanism is defective.[125] Drugs such as chlorpropamide, which stimulate the production and potentiate the action of ADH, have been implicated as culprits in SIADH.[97,126–128] The chlorothiazide series of drugs, by inducing a limitation in free water clearance, coupled with a high fluid intake, have also been shown to produce the syndrome.[129–131]

Disorders of the endocrine system, particularly hypothyroidism, adrenal cortical insufficiency, and hypopituitarism, have been reported to produce SIADH. Patients with hypothyroidism are frequently found to have hyponatremia.[132–134] The inability to excrete a water load, which causes the hyponatremia, has been ascribed to excessive water retention in the presence of inappropriate secretion of ADH,[132] to decreased renal function, particularly a diminished GFR,[135] or to a possible downward resetting of the osmoreceptors in the hypothalamus.[136] All investigators agree that treatment with thyroxine restores the ability of the kidney to excrete a water load, after which the serum sodium returns to normal. Why the hyponatremia does not occur in all patients with hypothyroidism is a major question. If it is due to an inappropriately high ADH concentration, a low ingestion of water would mask the syndrome. The SIADH has not been reported to be associated with either an overt or occult neoplasm, since it can recur after a period of two years.[134] In 1978, Skowsky and Kikuchi[137] showed that the basal AVP concentration was elevated in 15 of 20 subjects with hypothyroidism, and was not completely suppressed with a standard water load. After the achievement of a euthyroid state by treatment with thyroxine, the concentrations of AVP were normal in both the basal and water-loaded states.

The defect in water excretion in Addison's disease is thought to have three contributing factors: an absence of aldosterone and cortisol and an increased ADH secretion. The lack of aldosterone is associated with decreased sodium reabsorption and decreased free water formation in the renal tubule, and hypovolemia. The lack of cortisol is associated with a decreased GFR and a decreased filtered sodium load, with a resulting decrease in free water formation. An additional decrease in systemic arterial pressure and cardiac output, with a diminution in stroke volume, has also been reported by Schrier and associates.[138] The increase in ADH is thus thought to be the combined effect of the stimuli from the decreased ECF and the decreased arterial pressure and cardiac output. This latter hemodynamic effect depends on intact arterial baroreceptor activity in the carotid sinus.[139]

The hyponatremia seen in hypopituitarism is probably the result of both the thyroxine and cortisol deficiencies, since it can be ameliorated by treatment with these steroids.

Whether the hyponatremia of cardiac failure or cirrhosis of the liver with ascites is due to SIADH is a matter of debate. In both disorders there is a limitation in the formation and excretion of free water. This is believed to be the result of a limited delivery of sodium and water to the thick ascending limb of the loop of Henle, due primarily to abnormally high proximal tubular sodium reabsorption.[140,141] Thus, patients with these disorders may have hyponatremia, inappropriate concentration of the urine, and an inability to excrete a water load. The plasma concentration of AVP has been reported to be elevated in patients with congestive heart failure[142,143] in the basal state. In the study by Goldsmith and associates,[143] there was no correlation between AVP concentration and plasma sodium: AVP was elevated in patients whose plasma sodium was in both the low and normal ranges. They suggested that there is a possible disruption of the normal osmotic regulatory mechanism, since both cardiopulmonary receptors and sinoaortic baroreceptors (which can normally provide nonosmotic stimuli to ADH secretion) may be abnormal in congestive heart failure.[144]

Bichet and colleagues[145] reported in 1982 that patients with cirrhosis who excreted less than 80 percent of a water load (non-excretors) had higher plasma concentrations of AVP than did excretors who did not retain the water. In further studies with head-out water immersion, they demonstrated a diminution in effective blood volume in non-excretors.[146] They concluded that the diminished effective blood volume is associated with a baroreceptor-mediated increase in nonosmotic AVP release. The role of ADH in these two disorders is not fully characterized.

Metabolic Consequences

The inappropriate secretion of ADH promotes water retention, an expansion of ECF volume leading to hypotonicity of the plasma, decreased aldosterone secretion, an increased GFR, and an increased urine sodium concentration. The increase in urine sodium is enhanced by a decrease in the proximal tubular reabsorption of sodium in the volume-expanded state.

The symptoms of SIADH are those of water retention and ultimately water intoxication. The rate of fall of the plasma sodium determines the symptoms. The plasma sodium may fall gradually over a period of days to 120 mEq/liter with only headache, muscle weakness, and apathy contributing to the patient's discomfort. Many patients are asymptomatic at this level of tonicity. When the plasma sodium falls rapidly, the patient experiences anorexia, nausea, and vomiting. With a further fall to below 110 mEq/liter, the neurologic symptoms become more severe. The patient may become confused, lethargic, uncooperative, and hostile, and if the extreme hyponatremia persists, may become convulsive and comatose. Abnormalities in body temperature and respiration may develop, and reflexes may disappear.

The brain chemistry of this disorder is not well-defined. The neurologic symptoms have been attributed to brain swelling due to water entering the cells to maintain osmotic equilibrium. In 1940,[147] however, Yannet reported that the brain cells do not respond to dilution of the ECF in the same manner as other cells of the body. He found, from a direct analysis of brain tissue in hyponatremic animals, that brain cells lost potassium as sodium entered the cells with no net gain of intracellular water. On the other hand, Arieff and Guisado[148] speculate that there may be initial brain edema with a secondary increase in intracranial pressure. With prolonged hyponatremia, the brain becomes depleted of both potassium and sodium, thus imposing a limit on the brain water content. In addition, sodium depletion results in a diminuition in brain energy metabolism, and interferes with the release of amino acid neurotransmitters at the synapses. All of these changes may affect the functioning of the central nervous system.

Measurement

The routine analyses of plasma and urinary sodium and plasma and urinary osmolality are usually sufficient to make the diagnosis of SIADH. The more sophisticated measurement of AVP by radioimmunoassay will confirm it.

If the patient has profound hyponatremia (i.e., below 120 mEq/liter), the foregoing analyses should suffice. If, however, the patient has been fluid restricted and the plasma sodium has risen to the range of 130 to 135 mEq/liter, and yet the syndrome is suspected, a water load may be given to test the kidneys' ability to excrete free water. The water load is given by the oral ingestion of 20 ml of water per kilogram of body weight, taken over a half-hour period. Plasma should be collected for measurement of the sodium concentration, osmolality, and AVP concentration prior to the ingestion of the water load and at the end of a 4-hour period, during which time the urine is collected in hourly aliquots. The urine should be measured for volume and analyzed for osmolality and sodium. A normal subject should excrete 70 percent of the water load during the 4-hour period, with only a minimal decrease (8 to 10 mosm/liter) in the plasma osmolality and a fall in AVP concentration below 0.5 pg/ml.

Difficulties may arise in interpreting the test if the subject has previously been dehydrated or if the underlying disease, such as cardiac failure or cirrhosis, is accompanied by an intrinisic defect in free water excretion. Patients with adrenal insufficiency or hypopituitarism will also have a problem in excreting a water load. If there are signs of dehydration, hypotension, and elevated plasma potassium concentration, and excessive urinary sodium loss, blood should be drawn for assay of the plasma cortisol concentration.

The plasma sodium may be falsely low as an artifact of measurement in patients with hyperlipidemia or the hyperglobulinemia of multiple myeloma. In these instances, the plasma osmolality should be taken as a more accurate measure of the fluid status. As noted earlier in this chapter, sodium is measured by flame photometry, osmolality by freezing point depression or vapor pressure analysis, and AVP by radioimmunoassay.

Treatment

The treatment of SIADH must include treatment of the underlying disorder. Most important is the early recognition of adrenal insufficiency or hypopituitarism where cortisol or another carbohydrate-mobilizing steroid must be given promptly.

The treatment of choice for the hyponatremia of SIADH is water restriction. This treatment is appropriate if the patient is conscious, mentally alert, and has a plasma sodium above 125 mEq/liter.[97] Water restriction may be required for two to three days before the plasma sodium reaches the normal range.

Chronic treatment is directed toward increasing the sodium intake, promoting the excretion of free water, and antagonizing the renal action of ADH. A variety of agents have been suggested that perform one or several of these actions. Among them are lithium,[149] demeclocycline,[150-152] urea,[153] furosemide,[154,155] and hypertonic saline.

Lithium salts can increase free water excretion by producing a form of renal diabetes insipidus, but their toxic effects outweigh their usefulness. Demeclocycline[150-152] operates in the same way but has fewer side-effects, and can be given chronically in cases in which the underlying disorder requires a long period of treatment. It is contraindicated, however, in patients receiving chemotherapy.

Decaux has made an intensive study of the therapy of SIADH, and believes that demeclocycline, urea, and long-loop diuretics are the most effective agents. When rapid resolution of the hyponatremia is required, an osmotic diuresis can be promoted by giving the patient 30 g of urea orally two to three times a day, or by infusing 80 g of urea as a 30 percent solution over a 6-hour period, coupled with water restriction to less than 500 ml/day and sodium supplements of 120 to 360 mmoles/day.[156] Urea is particularly effective in cases in which the GFR is low (i.e., 40 to 60 ml/min).

Long-loop diuretics such as furosemide (40 mg/day) or ethacrynic acid (50 mg/day) have been successfully used, together with water restriction, 3 g of sodium chloride taken orally, and 50 mg of triamterine to reduce the potassium loss usually induced by the diuretics. After the first few days of treatment, the water intake can be liberalized and the sodium intake should be adjusted in relation to the urinary loss.[155]

Rapid correction of hyponatremia has been related to central pontine myelinolysis.[157] "Rapid," however, is a relative term, and there is no definite consensus among neurologists, internists, or pediatricians as to how fast the plasma sodium can be corrected without brain damage. Ayus and associates cite two sets of data in which the mean rate of correction was 2.0 (+ or −1.7) mEq/liter/hr, with 86 percent and 93 percent survival, respectively. He stresses that the change in plasma sodium was from low (107 to 110 mEq/liter) to mildly hyponatremic (120 to 125 mEq/liter), rather than all the way to the normal range.[157]

A new group of drugs called "aquaretics" are being tested experimentally in animals. These agents are antagonistic to vasopressin at the renal epithelial receptors, and may prove to be the treatment of the future for SIADH.[158,159]

REFERENCES

1. Maffly LH, Leaf A: The potential of water in mammalian tissues. J Gen Physiol 42:1257, 1959
2. Eveloff J, Silva P, Kinne R: Evidence for a coupled Na/Cl transport in plasma membrane vesicles from the thick ascending limb of Henle's loop. Fed Proc 39:734, 1980
3. Gregor R: Chloride reabsorption in the rabbit cortical thick ascending limb of the loop of Henle. A sodium dependent process. Pfluegers Arch 390:38, 1981
4. Robertson GL, Shelton RL, Athar S: The osmoregulation of vasopressin. Kidney Int 10:25, 1976
5. Robertson GL, Athar S, Shelton RL: Osmotic control of vasopressin function. p. 125. In Andreoli TE, Grantham JJ, Rector FC Jr (eds): Disturbances in Body Fluid Osmolality. American Physiological Society, Bethesda, MD, 1977
6. Weinstein H, Berne RM, Sachs H: Vasopressin in blood: Effect of hemorrhage. Endocrinology 66:712, 1960
7. Share L: Acute reduction in extracellular fluid volume and concentration of antidiuretic hormone in blood. Endocrinology 69:925, 1961
8. Robertson GL: The regulation of vasopressin function in health and disease. Recent Prog Horm Res 33:333, 1977
9. Share L: Control of plasma ADH titer in hemorrhage: Role of atrial and arterial receptors. Am J Physiol 215:1384, 1968
10. Henry JP, Gauer OH, Reeves JL: Evidence of atrial location of receptors influencing urine flow. Circ Res 4:85, 1956
11. Baisset A, Montastruc J: Polyurie par distension auriculaire chez le Chien: Role de l'hormone antidiuretique. J Physiol (Paris) 49:33, 1957
12. Share L: Effects of carotid occlusion and left atrial distention on plasma vasopressin titer. Am J Physiol 208:219, 1965
13. Verney EB: The antidiuretic hormone and the factors which determine its release. Proc R Soc Lond [Biol] 135B:25, 1947
14. Segar WE, Moore WW: The regulation of antidiuretic hormone release in man. J Clin Invest 47:2143, 1968
15. Andersson R, Larsson S: Inhibitory effect of emesis on water diuresis in the dog. Acta Physiol Scand 32:19, 1954
16. Schwartz WB, Bennet W, Curelop S, Bartter FC: Syndrome of renal sodium loss and hyponatremia probably resulting from in-

appropriate secretion of antidiuretic hormone. Am J Med 23:529, 1957
17. Kleeman CR, Rubini ME, Lamdin E, Epstein FH: Studies on alcohol diuresis. II. The evaluation of ethyl alcohol as an inhibitor of the neurohypophysis. J Clin Invest 34:448, 1955
18. Bartter FC, Schwartz WB: The syndrome of inappropriate secretion of antidiuretic hormone. Am J Med 42:790, 1967
19. Early LE, Sanders CA: Effect of changing serum osmolality on release of antidiuretic hormone in certain patients with decompensated cirrhosis of liver and low serum osmolality. J Clin Invest 38:545, 1959
20. DeFronzo RA, Goldberg M, Agus ZS: Normal diluting capacity in hyponatremic patients. Ann Intern Med 84:538, 1976
21. Hariprasad MK, Eisinger RP, Nadler IM, et al: Hyponatremia in psychogenic polydipsia. Arch Intern Med 140:1639, 1980
22. McKinley MJ, Denton DA, Leksell LG, et al: Osmoregulatory thirst in sheep is disrupted by ablation of the anterior wall of the optic recess. Brain Res 236:210, 1982
23. Fitzsimons J: Thirst. Physiol Rev 52:468, 1972
24. Fitzsimons JT: The physiology of thirst and sodium appetite. Monogr Physiol Soc No. 35, 1979
25. Rogers PW, Kurtzman NA: Renal failure, uncontrollable thirst and hyperreninemia. JAMA 225:1236, 1973
26. Sheth KJ, Tang TT, Blaedel ME, Good TA: Polydipsia, polyuria and hypertension associated with renin-secreting Wilm's tumor. J Pediatr 92:921, 1978
27. Fitzsimons JT: The physiological basis of thirst. Kidney Int 10:3, 1976
28. Simpson JB, Epstein AN, Camardo JS: Localization of receptors for the dipsogenic action of angiotensin II in the subfornical organ of the rat. J Comp Physiol Psychol 92:581, 1978
29. Hoffman WE, Phillips MI: Blockage of blood pressure and drinking responses to angiotensin by anterior third ventricle obstruction. Fed Proc 34:374, 1975
30. Nicolaides S, Fitzsimons JT: La dependence de la prise de'eau induite par l'angiotensine II envers la fonction vasomotrice cerebrale locale chez le rat. C R Acad Sci (D) (Paris) 281D:1417, 1975
31. Fischer-Ferraro C, Nahmod VE, Goldstein DJ, Finkielman S: Angiotensin and renin in rat and dog brain. J Exp Med 133:353, 1971
32. Ganten D, Marquez JA, Granter P, et al: Renin in dog brain. Am J Physiol 221:1733, 1971
33. Andersson B, Leksel LG, Rundgren M: Regulation of water intake. Annu Rev Nutr 2:73, 1982
34. Leaf A, Bartter FC, Santos RF, Wrong O: Evidence in man that urinary electrolyte loss induced by pitressin is a function of water retention. J Clin Invest 32:868, 1953
35. Finberg L, Kiley J, Luttrell CN: Mass accidental salt-poisoning in infancy. A study of a hospital disaster. JAMA 184:187, 1963
36. Johnston JG, Robertson WO: Fatal ingestion of table salt by an adult. West J Med 126:141, 1977
37. Cameron JM, Dayan AD: Association of brain damage with therapeutic abortion induced by amniotic fluid replacement: Report of two cases. Br Med J 1:1010, 1966
38. DeVillota ED, Cavanilles JM, Stein L, et al: Hyperosmolal crisis following infusion of hypertonic sodium chloride for purposes of therapeutic abortion. Am J Med 55:116, 1973
39. Bleumle LW: Current status of chronic hemodialysis. Am J Med 44:749, 1968
40. Smith RJ, Block MR, Arieff AI, et al: Hypernatremic hyperosmolar coma complicating chronic peritoneal dialysis. Proc Clin Dial Transplant Forum 4:96, 1974
41. DeGraeff J, Lips JB: Hypernatremia in diabetes mellitus. Acta Med Scand 157:72, 1957
42. Coggins CH, Leaf A: Diabetes insipidus. Am J Med 42:807, 1967
43. Tan MH: Changing factors in the etiology of diabetes insipidus. Nova Scotia Med Bull 50:153, 1971
44. Forssman H: On hereditary diabetes insipidus with special regard to sex-linked form. Acta Med Scand 159(Suppl):1, 1945
45. Blotner H: The inheritance of diabetes insipidus. Am J Med Sci 204:261, 1942
46. Lipsett MB, Pearson OH: Further studies of diabetes insipidus following hypohysectomy in man. J Lab Cin Med 49:190, 1957
47. Miller M, Dalakos T, Moses AM, et al:

Recognition of partial defects in antidiuretic hormone secretion. Ann Intern Med 73:721, 1970
48. Forssman H: Om arftlighetsgangen vid diabetes insipidus. Nord Med 16:3211, 1942
49. Williams RH, Henry C: Nephrogenic diabetes insipidus: Transmitted by females and appearing in infancy in males. Ann Intern Med 27:84, 1947
50. Carter C, Simpkiss M: The "carrier" state in nephrogenic diabetes insipidus. Lancet 2:1069, 1956
51. Robinson MG, Kaplan SA: Inheritance of vasopressin-resistant ("nephrogenic") diabetes insipidus. Am J Dis Child 99:164, 1960
52. Berl T, Teitelbaum I: Effects of hypokalemia and hypercalcemia on water metabolism. p. 543. In Schrier RW (ed): Vasopressin. Raven Press, New York, 1985
53. Schwartz WB, Relman AS: Metabolic and renal studies in chronic potassium depletion resulting from overuse of laxatives. J Clin Invest 32:258, 1953
54. Rubini ME: Water excretion in potassium deficient man. J Clin Invest 40:2215, 1961
55. Berl T, Linas SL, Aisenbrey GA, Anderson RJ: On the mechanism of polyuria in potassium depletion. The role of polydipsia. J Clin Invest 60:620, 1977
56. Dusing R, Attallah AA, Prezyna AP, Lee JB: Renal biosynthesis of prostaglandins E2 and F2: Dependence on extracellular potassium. J Lab Clin Med 92:669, 1978
57. Dusing R, Scherhag R, Tipplemann R, et al: Arachidonic acid metabolism in isolated rat aorta: Dependence of prostacyclin biosynthesis on extracellular potassium concentration. J Biol Chem 257:1993, 1982
58. Galvez OG, Bay W, Roberts BW, Ferris TF: The hemodynamic effects of potassium deficiency in the dog. Circ Res 40(1):11, 1977
59. Rutecki GW, Cox JW, Robertson GW, et al: Urinary concentrating ability and antidiuretic hormone responsiveness in the potassium-depleted dog. J Lab Clin Med 100:53, 1980
60. Gottschalk CW, Mylle M, Jones NF, et al: Osmolality of renal tubular fluids in potassium-depleted rodents. Clin Sci 29:249, 1965

61. Gutsche HU, Peterson LN, Levine DZ: In vivo evidence of impaired solute transport by the thick ascending limb in potassium-depleted rats. J Clin Invest 73:908, 1984
62. Allen FNA: Hyperparathyroidism: A diabetes-insipidus like syndrome in hyperparathyroidism. Proc Staff Mt Mayo Clinic 6:684, 1931.
63. Baylis PH, Miles JJ, Wilkinson R, Heath DA: Vasopressin function in hypercalcemia. Clin Endocrinol 15:343, 1981
64. Weiss NM, Robinson GL: Effect of hypercalcemia and lithium therapy on the osmoregulation of thirst and vasopressin secretion. p. 281. In Schrier RW (ed): Vasopressin. Raven Press, New York, 1985
65. Manitius A, Levitin H, Beck D, Epstein FH: The mechanism of impairment of renal concentrating ability in hypercalcemia. J Clin Invest 39:693, 1960
66. Bank N, Aynedjian H: On the mechanism of hyposthenuria in hypercalcemia. J Clin Invest 44:681, 1965.
67. Levi M, Peterson L, Berl T: Mechanism of concentrating defect in hypercalcemia. Role of polydipsia and prostaglandins. Kidney Int 23:489, 1983
68. Gill JR Jr, Bartter FC: On the impairment of renal concentrating ability in prolonged hypercalcemia and hypercalciuria in man. J Clin Invest 40:716, 1961
69. Lee RV, Jampol LM, Braun WV: Nephrogenic diabetes insipidus and lithium intoxication-complications of lithium carbonate therapy. N Engl J Med 284:93, 1972
70. Singer I, Rotenberg D, Puschett JB: Lithium-induced nephrogenic diabetes insipidus: In vivo and in vitro studies. J Clin Invest 51:1081, 1972
71. Forrest JN Jr, Cohen AD, Torretti J, et al: On the mechanism of lithium-induced diabetes insipidus in man and rat. J Clin Invest 53:1115, 1974
72. Churchill D, Knaack J, Chirito E, et al: Persisting renal insufficiency after methoxyflurane anesthesia. Report of two cases and review of literature. Am J Med 56:575, 1974
73. Castell DO, Sparks HA: Nephrogenic diabetes insipidus due to demethylchlortetracycline hydrochloride. JAMA 193:237, 1965

74. Singer I, Rotenberg D: Democlocycline-induced nephrogenic diabetes insipidus. In vivo and in vitro studies. Ann Intern Med 79:679, 1973
75. Christensen S, Kusano E, Yusufi ANK, et al: Pathogenesis of nephrogenic diabetes insipidus due to chronic administration of lithium in rats. J Clin Invest 75:1869, 1985
76. Fordtran JS, Dietschy JM: Water and electrolyte movement in the intestine. Gastroenterology 50:263, 1966
77. Bruck E, Abal G, Aceto T Jr: Pathogenesis and pathophysiology of hypertonic dehydration with diarrhea. Am J Dis Child 115:122, 1968
78. Phillips SF: Diarrhea: A current view of the pathophysiology. Gastroenterology 63:495, 1972
79. Finberg L: Hypernatremic dehydration. p. 78. In Finberg L, Kravath RE, Fleischman AR (eds): Water and Electrolytes in Pediatrics. WB Saunders, Philadelphia, 1982
80. Conn JW: Electrolyte composition of sweat. Arch Intern Med 83:416, 1949
81. Bartter FC, Liddle GW, Duncan LE Jr, et al: Regulation of aldosterone secretion in man: Role of fluid volume. J Clin Invest 35:1306, 1956
82. Welt LG: Hypo- and Hypernatremia. Ann Intern Med 56:161, 1962
83. Sridhar CB, Calvert GD, Ibbertson HK: Syndrome of hypernatremia, hypodipsia and partial diabetes insipidus. A new interpretation. J Clin Endocrinol Metab 38:890, 1974
84. DeRubertis FR, Michelis MF, Beck N, et al: "Essential" hypernatremia due to ineffective osmotic and intact volume regulation of vasopressin secretion. J Clin Invest 50:97, 1971
85. Mahoney JH, Goodman AD: Hypernatremia due to hypodipsia and elevated threshold for vasopressin release. N Engl J Med 279:1191, 1968
86. Bode HH, Harley BM, Crawford JD: Restoration of normal drinking behavior by chlorpropamide in patients with hypodipsia and diabetes insipidus. Am J Med 51:304, 1971
87. Leaf A, Chatillon JY, Wrong O, Tuttle EP Jr: Mechanism of osmotic adjustment of body cells as determined in vivo by volume of distribution of large water load. J Clin Invest 33:1261, 1954
88. Arieff AI, Guisado R: Effects on the central nervous system of hypernatremic and hyponatremic states. Kidney Int 10:104, 1976
89. Covey CM, Arieff AI: Disorders of sodium and water metabolism and their effects on the central nervous system. p. 212. In Brenner BM, Stein JH (ed): Sodium and Water Homeostasis. Churchill Livingstone, New York, 1978
90. Bartter FC, Delea CS: Diabetes insipidus: Its nature and diagnosis. Lab Management 20:23, 1982
91. Robertson GL, Mahr EA, Athar S, Sinha T: Development and clinical application of new method for radioimmunoassay of arginine vasopressin in human plasma. J Clin Invest 52:2340, 1973
92. Berl T, Anderson RJ, McDonald KM, Schrier RW: Clinical disorders of water metabolism. Kidney Int 10:117, 1976
93. Finberg L: Therapeutic management of hypernatremic dehydration. p. 129. In Finberg L, Kravath RE, Fleishman AR (eds): Water and Electrolytes in Pediatrics. WB Saunders, Philadelphia, 1982
94. Verbalis JG, Robinson AG: Hypothalamic diabetes insipidus. p. 1. In Krieger D, Bardin W (eds): Current Therapy in Endocrinology 1983–1984. BC Decker, Philadelphia, 1983
95. Miller NL, Finberg L: Peritoneal dialysis for salt poisoning. N Engl J Med 263:1347, 1960
96. Bartter FC: The role of aldosterone in normal homeostasis and in certain disease states. Metabolism 5:369, 1956
97. Bartter FC: The syndrome of inappropriate secretion of antidiuretic hormone (SIADH). p. 1. In Dowling HF (ed): Disease-a-Month. Year Book Medical Publishers, Chicago, November 1973
98. Passamonte PM: Hypouricemia, inappropriate secretion of antidiuretic hormone, and small cell carcinoma of the lung. Arch Intern Med 144:1569, 1984
99. Hainsworth JD, Workman R, Greco FA: Management of the syndrome of inappropriate antidiuretic hormone secretion in small cell lung cancer. Cancer 51:161, 1983
100. Lai CL, Wu PC, Lin HJ, Wong KL: Case

report of symptomatic porphyria cutanea tarda associated with histiocytic lymphoma. Cancer 53:573, 1984
101. Zimbler H, Robertson GL, Bartter FC, et al: Ewing's sarcoma as a cause of the syndrome of inappropriate secretion of antidiuretic hormone. J Clin Endocrinol Metab 41:390, 1975
102. Strigley JR, Dayal VS, Gregor RT, et al: Hyponatremia secondary to olfactory neuroblastoma. Arch Otolaryngol 109:559, 1983
103. Singh W, Ramage C, Best P: Nasal neuroblastoma-secreting vasopressin. Cancer 45:961, 1980
104. Nanji AA: Multiple myeloma and syndrome of inappropriate secretion of antidiuretic hormone. South Med J 76:270, 1983
105. George JM, Copen CC, Phillips AS: Biosynthesis of vasopressin in vitro and ultrastructure of a bronchogenic carcinoma. J Clin Invest 51:141, 1972
106. Hamilton BPM, Upton GV, Amatruda TT Jr: Evidence for the presence of neurophysin in tumors producing the syndrome of inappropriate antidiuresis. J Clin Endocrinol Metab 35:764, 1972
107. Robertson GL, Aycinena P, Zerbe RL: Neurogenic disorders of osmoregulation. Am J Med 72:339, 1982
108. Butrus SI, Sessums SO, Henderson BC, Ganley JP: Syndrome of inappropriate antidiuretic hormone secretion. Arch Ophthalmol 103:759, 1985
109. Brones MF, Kawamoto HK Jr, Renaudin J: Inappropriate antidiuretic hormone syndrome in craniofacial surgery. Plast Reconstr Surg 71:1, 1984
110. Bouzarth WF, Shenkin HA: Is "cerebral" hyponatremia iatrogenic? Lancet 1:1061, 1982
111. Joynt RJ, Feitel JH, Sladek CM: Antidiuretic hormone levels in stroke patients. Ann Neurol 9:182, 1981
112. Kirkland JL, Pearson DJ, Goddard C, Davies I: Polyuria and inappropriate secretion of arginine vasopressin in hypothalamic sarcoidosis. J Clin Endocrinol Metab 56:269,272, 1983
113. Potgieter PD: Inappropriate ADH secretion in tetanus. Crit Care Med 11:417, 1983
114. Ingraham IE Jr, Estes NA, Bern MM, DeGirolami PC: Disseminated varicella-zoster virus infection with the syndrome of inappropriate antidiuretic hormone. Arch Intern Med 143:1270, 1983
115. Agus B, Nayar S, Patel DJ, McGrath M: Inappropriate secretion of ADH in a patient with systemic lupus erythematosus. Arthritis Rheum 26:237, 1983
116. Kaplowitz LG, Robertson GL: Hyponatremia in rocky mountain spotted fever: role of ADH. Ann Intern Med 98:334, 1983
117. Collentine GE, Waisbren BA, Lang GE: Inappropriate secretion of ADH as an accompaniment of burn injury. p. 509. In Matter P, Barclay TL, Kronickova A (eds): Research in Burns, Transaction of 3rd International Congress in Research In Burns. Hans Huber, Bern, 1971
118. Shirani KZ, Vaughan GM, Robertson GL, et al: Inappropriate vasopressin secretion (SIADH) in burned patients. J Trauma 23:217, 1983
119. Vorherr H, Massry SG, Fallet R: Antidiuretic principle in tuberculous lung tissue of a patient with pulmonary tuberculosis and hyponatremia. Ann Intern Med 72:383, 1970
120. Zubenko GS, Altesman RI, Cassidy JW, Barreira PJ: Disturbances of thirst and water homeostasis in patients with affective illness. Am J Psychiatry 141:436, 1984
121. Vieweg WV, Rowe WT, David JJ, et al: Evaluation of patients with self-induced water intoxication and schizophrenic disorders. J Nerv Ment Dis 172:552, 1984
122. Sandifer MG: Hyponatremia due to psychotropic drugs. J Clin Psychiatry 44:301, 1983
123. Abbott R: Hyponatremia due to antidepressant medications. Ann Emerg Med 12:708, 1983
124. Lee MR: Effects of drugs on water metabolism. Br J Clin Pharmacol 12:289, 1981
125. Robertson GL: Abnormalities of thirst regulation. Kidney Intern 25:460, 1984
126. Linshaw MA, Sey M, DiGeorge AM, Gruskin AB: A potential danger of oral chlorpropamide therapy: impaired excretion of a water load. J Clin Endocrinol 34:562, 1972
127. Hayes JS, Kaye M: Inappropriate secre-

tion of antidiuretic hormone induced by chlorpropamide. Am J Med Sci 263:137, 1972
128. Moses AM, Numann P, Miller M: Mechanism of chlorpropamide-induced antidiuresis in man: evidence for release of ADH and enhancement of peripheral action. Metabolism 22:59, 1973
129. Kennedy RM, Earley LE: Profound hyponatremia resulting from a thiazide-induced decrease in urinary diluting capacity in a patient with primary polydipsia. N Engl J Med 282:1185, 1970
130. Beresford HR: Polydipsia, hydrochlorothiazide, and water intoxication. JAMA 214:879, 1970
131. Horowitz J, Keynan A, Ben-Ishay D: A syndrome of inappropriate ADH secretion induced by cyclothiazide. J Clin Pharmacol 12:337, 1972
132. Goldberg M, Reivich M: Studies on the mechanism of hyponatremia and impaired water excretion in myxedema. Ann Intern Med 56:120, 1962
133. Crispell KR, Parson W, Sprinkle P: Cortisone-resistant abnormality in diuretic response to ingested water in primary myxedema. J Clin Endocrinol 14:640, 1954
134. Pettinger WA, Talner L, Ferris TF: Inappropriate secretion of antidiuretic hormone due to myxedema. N Engl J Med 272:362, 1965
135. Papper S, Lancestremere RG: Certain aspects of renal function in myxedema. J Chronic Dis 14:495, 1961
136. Hochberg Z, Benderly A: Normal osmotic threshold for vasopressin release in the hyponatremia of hypothyroidism. Hor Res 17:128, 1983
137. Skowsky WR, Kikuchi TA: The role of vasopressin in the impaired water excretion of myxedema. Am J Med 64:613, 1978
138. Schrier RW, Linas SL: Mechanisms of the defect in water excretion in adrenal insufficiency. Min Electrolyte Metab 4:1, 1980
139. Berl T, Cadnapaphornachai P, Harbottle JA, Schrier RW: Mechanism of stimulation of vasopressin release during beta adrenergic stimulation with isoproterenol. J Clin Invest 53:857, 1974
140. Schedl HP, Bartter FC: An explanation for an experimental correction of the abnormal water diuresis in cirrhosis. J Clin Invest 39:248, 1960
141. Bell NH, Schedl HP, Bartter FC: An explanation for abnormal water retention and hypo-osmolality in congestive heart failure. Am J Med 36:351, 1964
142. Yamane Y: Plasma ADH levels in patients with chronic congestive heart failure. Jpn Circ J 32:745, 1968
143. Goldsmith SR, Francis GS, Crowley AW, et al: Increased plasma arginine vasopressin levels in patients with congestive heart failure. J Am Coll Cardiol 1:1385, 1983
144. Zucker IH: Mechanism of adaptation of left atrial stretch receptors in dogs with chronic congestive heart failure. J Clin Invest 60:323, 1977
145. Bichet D, Szatalowicz V, Chaimovitz C, Schrier RW: Role of vasopressin in abnormal water excretion in cirrhotic humans. Ann Intern Med 96:413, 1982
146. Bichet DG, Groves BM, Schrier RW: Mechanisms of improvement of water and sodium excretion by immersion in decompensated cirrhotic patients. Kidney Int 24:788, 1983
147. Yannet H: Changes in brain resulting from depletion of extracellular electrolytes. Am J Physiol 128:683, 1940
148. Arieff AI, Guisado R: Effects on the central nervous system of hypernatremic and hyponatremic states. Kidney Int 10:104, 1976
149. White MG, Feiner CD: Treatment of the syndrome of inappropriate secretion of antidiuretic hormone with lithium carbonate. N Engl J Med 292:390, 1975
150. DeTroyer A, Demanet JC: Correction of antidiuresis by demeclocycline. N Engl J Med 293:915, 1975
151. Cherrill DA, Stote RM, Birge JR, Singer I: Demeclocycline treatment in the syndrome of inappropriate secretion of antidiuretic hormone. Ann Intern Med 83:654, 1975
152. Forrest JN Jr, Cox M, Hong C, et al: Superiority of demeclocycline over lithium in the treatment of chronic syndrome of inappropriate secretion of antidiuretic hormone. N Engl J Med 298:173, 1978
153. Decaux G, Brimioulle S, Genette F, Mockel J: Treatment of the syndrome of

inappropriate secretion of antidiuretic hormone by urea. Am J Med 69:99, 1980

154. Decaux G, Waterlot Y, Genette F, Mockel J: Treatment of the syndrome of inappropriate secretion of antidiuretic hormone with furosemide. N Engl J Med 304:329, 1981
155. Decaux G: Treatment of the syndrome of inappropriate secretion of antidiuretic hormone by long loop diuretics. Nephron 35:82, 1983
156. Decaux G, Unger J, Brimioulle S, Mockel J: Hyponatremia in the syndrome of inappropriate secretion of antidiuretic hormone: Rapid correction with urea, sodium chloride and water restriction therapy. JAMA 247:471, 1982
157. Ayus JC, Krothapalli RK, Arieff AJ: Changing concepts in treatment of severe symptomatic hyponatremia. Rapid correction and possible relation to central pontine myelinolysis. Am J Med 78:897, 1985
158. Kinter LB, Dubb J, Huffman W, et al: Potential role of vasopressin antagonists in the treatment of water-retaining disorders. p. 553. In Schrier RW (ed): Vasopressin. Raven Press, New York, 1985
159. Hofbauer KG, Mah SC: Vasopressin antagonists: Present and future. Kidney Int 32(Suppl 21):S-76, 1987

4

Disorders of Potassium Metabolism

John R. Gill, Jr
Fernando Santos
James C. M. Chan

GENERAL ASPECTS OF POTASSIUM METABOLISM

The normal extracellular potassium concentration ranges from 3.5 to 5.0 mEq/liter, with serum concentrations exceeding plasma concentrations by 0.4 mEq/liter; this is due to the fact that potassium is released when blood clots.[1] The intracellular potassium content is about 98 percent of the total body potassium, and its concentration ranges from 140 to 150 mEq/liter.[2] The maintenance of this 1:30 gradient between extracellular and intracellular potassium depends on a variety of factors that affect potassium transport, such as sodium-potassium-ATPase (Na^+, K^+-ATPase), insulin, catecholamines, aldosterone, glucocorticoids, glucagon, thyroid hormone, growth hormone, acid-base balance, exercise and osmolality. Normally, Na^+, K^+-ATPase, which is located in the basal membrane, maintains the ratio between extracellular and intracellular potassium by actively transporting potassium into cells as it pumps sodium out,[3,4] thereby counterbalancing the cellular outleak of potassium that occurs because the plasma membrane is permeable to potassium. In the steady state, the uptake and loss of potassium from cells are equal, and potassium concentrations are stable.

Insulin and catecholamines buffer changes in blood potassium that follow a dietary potassium load.[3] These hormones prevent an abrupt rise in the extracellular potassium concentration after a potassium load by augmenting the entry of potassium into cells. The kidneys respond to the increase in intracellular potassium by increasing their excretion of potassium. Although the kidneys readily excrete a sodium load, their response to a potassium load is slower, requiring several days.

The extracellular potassium concentration is usually maintained within a narrow range. Changes in potassium intake or excretion that lead to hyperkalemia (potassium concentration in excess of 5.5 mEq/liter) or hypokalemia (potassium concentration less than 3.0 mEq/liter) are associated with rapid shifts of potassium between cells and extracellular fluid (ECF) that tend to re-establish normokalemia (potassium concentration 3.5 to 5.0 mEq/liter). As a consequence, the extracellular potassium concentration is a useful clinical index of total body potassium stores. In the case of acid-base disturbances, exercise, or changes in osmolality, internal shifts of potassium may occur that change the extracellular potassium without changing total body potassium stores, which are normally 50 to 55 mEq/kg body weight.[3]

CELLULAR ASPECTS OF POTASSIUM METABOLISM

Potassium homeostasis plays a critical role in maintaining the resting cellular membrane potential. Severe potassium imbalance may adversely affect membrane excitability at the neuromuscular junction. Neuronal excitation depends primarily on a change in cellular membrane potential that is partly determined by arterial pH and the serum calcium concentration. Thus, in following the clinical effects of hypokalemia or hyperkalemia, it is as important to monitor neuromuscular electrical potentials by electrocardiography as it is to monitor the absolute serum potassium concentration.

The resting cell *membrane potential*, $-61 \times \log$ [potassium concentration inside (K_i) ÷ potassium concentration outside (K_o)], is -86 millivolts (mV) inside the cell.[4] Upon excitation of the neuromuscular junction, acetylcholine is released, and the sodium permeability of the cell membrane, which is normally low, is increased.[3,4] As a result of increased sodium entry, electronegativity inside the cell decreases. The decrease in membrane potential associated with excitation is called depolarization. Permeability to sodium and, in turn, the rate of sodium entry depend upon the magnitude of depolarization. If depolarization is minimal, sodium entry is proportionately small; in this case, because the permeability of potassium is greater than sodium, the rate of potassium efflux may exceed the rate of sodium entry, returning the membrane potential toward baseline. If sodium permeability is facilitated, so that sodium entry exceeds potassium efflux, then the cell interior may become electropositive, generating a *threshold potential* followed by an action potential.[4] During the repolarization that follows, the cell membrane potential and permeability return to baseline values and electronegativity is re-established by potassium efflux. Sodium that entered the cell during depolarization is pumped out, and potassium that was lost during repolarization is pumped in. This recovery process is complete when the cell constituents have returned to normal. The propagation of these cycles is responsible for neural transmission and muscle contraction.

The difference between the resting potential and threshold potential determines the degree of neuromuscular *membrane excitability*; the greater the difference between these two potentials, the less sensitive the cell is to excitation. Since the resting membrane potential depends principally on the ratio between the intracellular and extracellular potassium concentrations, small changes in extracellular potassium concentration may change the resting potential appreciably. *Hyperkalemia*, which is associated with a decrease in the ratio of intracellular to extracellular potassium concentration, reduces the resting potential and increases membrane excitability. When hyperkalemia is severe, the resting potential may be reduced below the threshold potential. This may prevent repolarization after an action potential, resulting in paralysis.[5] In addition to causing neuromyopathy, hyperkalemia may affect the conducting fibers of the heart and produce characteristic electrocardiographic changes that consist of elevation of the T wave, depression of the P wave, and widening of the PR interval and QRS complex; these changes may progress to ventricular fibrillation.

Hypokalemia increases the ratio between the intracellular and extracellular potassium concentration and thus increases the resting potential. An increase in resting potential without a change in threshold potential decreases membrane excitability. When hypokalemia is severe, excitability may decrease to the point that flaccid paralysis results. The effects of hypokalemia may vary, depending on the ability of cellular stores of potassium to minimize changes in the ratio of intracellular to extracellular potassium. For example, during chronic potassium depletion, potassium may shift from cells to the ECF so as to preserve the normal ratio of potassium. In contrast, in hypokalemic periodic paralysis, there is a rapid shift of potassium from the ECF into cells, increasing the ratio of intracellular to extracellular potassium and leading to flaccid paralysis.[6]

Neuromuscular membrane excitability is also regulated by the *ionized calcium* concentration through its effects on the threshold potential. Calcium regulates the threshold potential through its effects on sodium permeability. Hypocalcemia increases membrane excitability by increasing sodium permeability so that sodium entry exceeds potassium efflux at a membrane potential of -75 mV instead of at -65 mV, as is usually the case.[4] In contrast, hypercalcemia decreases membrane excitability. The effect of calcium on the threshold potential has important clinical implications. For example, the neuromuscular hyperexcitability associated with hyperkalemia may be improved by calcium infusion.

A low arterial pH also decreases membrane excitability, probably in part by increasing the concentration of ionized calcium. Conversely, a high arterial pH increases membrane excitability. Changes in arterial pH also affect the distribution of potassium between cells and the ECF. Acidosis causes potassium to shift from the intracellular to the extracellular space in exchange for hydrogen ions, whereas alkalosis causes extracellular potassium to enter cells.[2] These changes in potassium distribution may lessen the overall effects of changes in arterial pH on membrane excitability.

RENAL HANDLING OF POTASSIUM

Most of the dietary potassium ingested each day, from 60 to 100 mEq, is excreted by the kidneys. Only small amounts of potassium (from 5 to 20 mEq/day) are excreted in the stool.

Almost all of the 600 to 700 mEq of potassium filtered through the glomerulus each day is reabsorbed: 70 to 80 percent by the proximal tubule and 15 to 20 percent by the early distal tubule.[3,4] Although the descending limb of the loop of Henle may secrete potassium, the ascending limb reabsorbs virtually all that is secreted, so that little net secretion occurs.[3] The distal tubule, especially the cortical collecting tubule, is the principal site of potassium secretion.[7] Secretion is increased when potassium intake is increased and is decreased when potassium intake is restricted. During potassium depletion, secretion of potassium by the distal tubule ceases and reabsorption occurs.[8] Secretion of potassium by the distal tubule is passive and is determined by the electrochemical gradient, membrane permeability, and rate of flow of distal tubular fluid.[3] The electrochemical gradient is determined by the potassium concentration in tubule cells and their uptake of sodium from the tubular fluid. The primary factors that regulate potassium secretion are *aldosterone* and the extracellular potassium concentration. An increase in dietary potassium intake raises first the extracellular and then the intracellular potassium concentration, which leads to a stimulation of aldosterone secretion. Aldosterone, in turn, promotes renal potassium secretion by two mechanisms: (1) stimulation of Na^+, K^+-ATPase to transport potassium from the peritubular fluid into tubule cells, and (2) augmentation of permeability of the luminal membrane to sodium.[3,4] Na^+, K^+-ATPase is very sensitive to aldosterone and, in the absence of this hormone, potassium secretion is impaired.[3]

The effect of aldosterone on potassium and sodium excretion may vary, depending on the contribution of other determinants; thus, for example, an increase in dietary potassium intake increases potassium excretion, in part by stimulating aldosterone secretion. An associated effect of the increase in potassium intake is a reduction in sodium and water reabsorption by the proximal tubule and the loop of Henle.[9] The increased delivery of sodium and water to the distal tubule tends to balance the aldosterone-induced sodium reabsorption that occurs there. Thus, aldosterone-induced distal potassium secretion may be associated with little change in net sodium balance. In congestive heart failure, the inability to maintain an effective circulating blood volume stimulates aldosterone secretion and sodium retention, but rarely leads to renal potassium wasting because the tubular flow rate is also diminished, and this limits potassium secretion.[10]

When the ECF volume is expanded, aldosterone secretion is suppressed, so that the increase in tubular flow rate that occurs does not result in potassium wasting.[11] Thus, excess sodium is excreted and potassium balance is preserved. If, however, an increase in distal flow rate is associated with normal or increased aldosterone secretion, as may occur with an aldosterone-producing adenoma, renal potassium wasting and hypokalemia ensue. Potassium wasting may also be stimulated by some diuretics which increase the tubular flow rate in association with an increase in aldosterone secretion.[12]

A *transepithelial potential difference* of -48 mV across cortical distal tubular cells, produced by the reabsorption of positively-charged sodium ions, facilitates the secretion of positively charged potassium ions into the negatively charged tubular lumen.[3,4] If the potential difference were further increased by replacing the chloride ion with a poorly reabsorbable anion such as sulfate, this would further enhance the movement of potassium ions into the tubular lumen.[13] This may explain why potassium wasting and hypokalemia tend to be associated with the antibiotic carbenicillin, which, like sulfate, is also a poorly reabsorbed anion.[14]

Conversely, diuretics such as amiloride or triamterene that reduce the luminal membrane permeability to sodium, inhibit sodium reabsorption and thereby lower the transepithelial potential difference.[12] As the transepithelial potential difference decreases, potassium secretion decreases.[12,15]

EXTRARENAL REGULATION OF POTASSIUM METABOLISM

Potassium homeostasis relies on a remarkably efficient process for distributing potassium between extracellular and intracellular fluids. This first line of defense attenuates increases in extracellular potassium that may result in fatal hyperkalemia. In addition, 50 percent of an oral or intravenous potassium load is excreted in the urine within 6 hours.[16,17] The movement of potassium from ECF into cells normally depends on Na^+, K^+-ATPase, insulin, catecholamines, aldosterone, glucagon, thyroid hormone, growth hormone, and exercise. Changes in arterial pH, osmolality, and rate of cell breakdown, as well as factors associated with certain chronic diseases, may also affect the distribution of potassium.

Sodium-potassium-ATPase is normally responsible for transporting potassium from ECF into cells. The important role of Na^+, K^+-ATPase in maintaining the serum potassium concentration is illustrated by the severe hyperkalemia that may develop when this pump is inhibited by digitalis.[18]

When potassium is ingested, excess potassium enters cells with the help of insulin and catecholamines.[19,20] Insulin promotes the uptake of potassium by stimulating its entry with glucose into liver and skeletal muscle.[21] Catecholamines promote potassium entry into cells by stimulating β-2-adrenergic receptors.[19] Propranolol and other beta-adrenergic blocking agents may cause a sustained increase in potassium concentration after a potassium load by reducing the cellular uptake of potassium.[19] Although a deficiency of insulin or catecholamines may impair the cellular uptake of potassium following a potassium load, it does not prevent it.[22] Also, diabetes mellitus or propranolol administration causes only a slight or transient elevation of the basal serum potassium concentration.

The role of aldosterone as an extrarenal regulator of potassium metabolism remains unsettled. The observation that aldosterone may decrease the plasma potassium concentration without a negative potassium balance has been suggested as support for an extrarenal action of aldosterone.[23,24] A high fecal potassium concentration in patients with primary and secondary hyperaldosteronism is consistent with a stimulation of potassium secretion by aldosterone in the colon, but the difficulties associated with determining accurate potassium balances raise questions about the validity of these observations.[25] In any case, the extrarenal effects of aldosterone are likely to be minimal compared to its actions on renal potassium excretion. A transient increase in plasma potassium concentration may be observed in response to glucocorticoid administration, but this lasts for only 24 hours.[26]

Glucagon administration initially causes hyperkalemia and hyperglycemia, followed by hypokalemia and normoglycemia. The initial hyperkalemia is due to release of potassium from the liver, and may be attenuated by α-adrenergic blockade.[27] The development of hypokalemia as blood glucose returns to normal appears to be caused by secretion of insulin or somatostatin.[28]

Thyroid hormone increases the activity and number of Na^+, K^+-ATPase units, and this is the basis for the increase in ouabain-sensitive potassium influx, sodium efflux, and oxygen consumption, as well as for the increase in ouabain binding in rats treated with thyroid hormone.[29,30] Treatment of hypothyroid children with thyroid hormone increases the potassium concentration in muscle cells.[31] Paradoxically, thyrotoxic patients may show a reduced intracellular potassium concentration that may account for the muscle weakness in this disease.[32]

Growth hormone administration may decrease potassium excretion without affecting the plasma potassium concentration, presumably because it stimulates the uptake of potassium by cells.[33,34] In hypophysectomized rats, growth hormone has been observed to increase the potassium content of muscle.[35] In man, growth hormone, like insulin, has been shown to stimulate the uptake of potassium by forearm muscles.[36] This effect of growth hormone appears to be long-lasting, since patients with acromegaly show a greater than normal uptake of potassium by the forearm.[36]

Exercise is associated with a release of potassium from muscle cells; the resulting increase in blood potassium produces vasodilation and increases blood flow to muscle.[37] The increase in serum potassium is accompanied by an increase in plasma norepinephrine and epinephrine.[38] The increase in these catecholamines attenuates the increase in serum potassium during exercise by beta-adrenergic stimulation, and by α-adrenergic stimulation it limits the decrease in serum potassium following exercise.[38] Although alpha-adrenergic stimulation also occurs during exercise, and tends to accentuate the rise in serum potassium, the attenuating effects of beta-adrenergic stimulation appear to predominate.[38] Treatment with a beta-adrenergic blocking agent may therefore expose a patient to the risk of hyperkalemia during strenuous exercise.[39] It should be noted that the common practice of repeatedly making a fist after the application of a tourniquet for venipuncture may increase the potassium concentration and lead to an overestimation of serum potassium by as much as 2 mEq/liter.[40]

Normally the serum potassium concentration closely reflects total body stores of potassium. In certain pathologic conditions such as chronic renal disease, changes in arterial pH, hyperosmolality, and cell lysis, the normal relationship between intracellular and extracellular potassium may be altered.

Chronic renal disease, because of an inhibition of Na^+, K^+-ATPase activity, is associated with a loss of potassium from and entry of sodium into cells.[19,41,42] This may result in a depletion of total potassium stores by up to 15 percent.[43] Hyperkalemia is not encountered until the end-stage of renal disease because the kidneys excrete the excess extracellular potassium. This compensation is adequate until the glomerular filtration rate (GFR) falls below 25 percent of normal.[43]

Acidosis and alkalosis affect the distribution of potassium between cells and ECF. In metabolic acidosis due to nonmetabolizable net acid accumulation associated with chronic renal failure or diarrhea, 60 percent of the hydrogen ions are buffered intracellularly.[44] As hydrogen ions enter cells, sodium and potassium ions must leave in order to maintain electrical neutrality, since only a small amount of chloride enters cells. Each decrease of 0.1 unit in arterial pH is accompanied by an increase in potassium concentration of 0.2 to 1.7 mEq/liter.[45] In the case of alkalosis, potassium enters cells. Whereas the addition of sodium to ECF may have little physiologic consequence, the change in potassium concentration may produce important effects.

Hyperosmolality increases the extracellular potassium concentration; with each increment of 10 mmol/kg of H_2O in osmolality, the plasma potassium concentration increases by 0.4 to 0.8 mEq/liter.[46] Although in normal subjects hyperglycemia induces the release of insulin and stimulates uptake of potassium, in diabetic subjects hyperglycemia may lead to hyperkalemia.[47]

Breakdown of cells as a result of trauma, thermal injury, rhabdomyolysis, gastrointestinal bleeding, or hemolysis is associated with release of potassium into the extracellular space. Whether or not hyperkalemia develops depends on the rate of uptake of potassium by liver and muscle, and on its rate of excretion by the kidneys. In contrast, rapid cellular proliferation, such as may occur in leukemia, results in potassium deposition in cells, and may lead to hypokalemia. Similarly, patients with megaloblastic anemia may also develop hypokalemia due to increased platelet and red cell production in response to folic acid and/or vitamin B_{12} administration.[48]

HYPERKALEMIA

Hyperkalemia is rarely encountered in healthy subjects because of the effective cellular buffering of acute potassium loads and the renal excretion of the excess potassium that usually occurs within six hours. When potassium is given slowly over a period of time, very large amounts may be tolerated. This process is called *potassium adaptation*, and results from facilitated entry of potassium into liver and muscle cells and excretion of potassium in urine.[3] An increase in aldosterone secretion plays a role in both cellular and renal potassium adaptation.[49] Renal adaptation to an increase in potassium intake is manifested by increased potassium secretion by the cortical and medullary collecting tubules. This occurs because Na^+, K^+-ATPase activity is elevated in the cells of these tubular segments and leads to an enhanced uptake of potassium from the peritubular fluid. As discussed in detail below, this renal adaptation to an increase in body potassium is the major mechanism accounting for potassium homeostasis in chronic renal disease. Another adaptation occurs in the colon, where an increase in Na^+, K^+-ATPase activity may increase potassium secretion to as much as 40 percent of the dietary potassium intake during end-stage renal disease.[50]

Causes of Hyperkalemia

The etiology of hyperkalemia is summarized in Table 4-1. *Spurious hyperkalemia* must be differentiated from true hyperkalemia. Spurious hyperkalemia is due to the release of potassium from cellular elements

Table 4-1. Etiology of Hyperkalemia

Spurious hyperkalemia
    Thrombocytosis, leukocytosis, hemolysis, ischemic venipuncture, familial pseudohyperkalemia, infectious mononucleosis

True Hyperkalemia
    Decreased Renal Excretion
        Prerenal azotemia
        Renal disorders: acute and chronic renal failure, hyporeninemic hypoaldosteronism, sickle cell disease, interstitial nephritis, systemic lupus erythematosus, amyloidosis, lead nephropathy, obstructive uropathy, pseudohypoaldosteronism types I and II, post-renal transplantation
        Adrenal disorders: Addison's disease, 21-hydroxylase deficiency, corticosterone methyloxidase deficiency
        Pharmacologic agents: spironolactone, triamterene, amiloride, converting enzyme inhibitors, nonsteroidal anti-inflammatory agents, heparin

    Increased Release from Cells
        Acidosis: metabolic and respiratory
        Insulin deficiency with hyperglycemia
        Familial hyperkalemic periodic paralysis
        Cell lysis: crush injury, tumor lysis, hemolysis, rhabdomyolysis
        Hyperosmolality
        Exercise
        Pharmacologic agents: Beta-adrenergic blocking drugs, digitalis, arginine, succinylcholine

    Increased Intake
        Potassium penicillin, potassium salts, aged blood, geophagia

after blood has been drawn. This is most apt to occur in blood samples from patients with platelet counts exceeding $10^6/mm^3$ or white cell counts exceeding $5 \times 10^5/mm^3$, especially when the sample remains unseparated for as long as two hours. To avoid spurious hyperkalemia, chemical analyses should be performed on plasma from freshly drawn blood. The most common cause of spurious hyperkalemia is *hemolysis* due to mechanical trauma, associated with prolonged application of a tourniquet (ischemic venipuncture).

The erythrocytes of a family of otherwise healthy individuals leak abnormal amounts of potassium when their drawn blood stands at room temperature. This phenomenon of spurious hyperkalemia has been called *familial pseudohyperkalemia*.[51]

Patients with *infectious mononucleosis* may also exhibit spurious hyperkalemia because their leukocytes and erythrocytes tend to leak potassium abnormally when their blood is drawn.[52]

True Hyperkalemia

True hyperkalemia (Table 4-1) is the result of one or more of the following factors: (1) decreased potassium excretion, (2) increased release of potassium from cells, and (3) increased potassium intake.

Decreased Excretion of Potassium

Urinary excretion of potassium may be very limited in certain pathophysiologic conditions such as renal failure, depletion of ECF volume, or impairment of the renin and aldosterone systems.

Hyperkalemia may be associated with oliguric as well as nonoliguric *acute renal failure*; in the latter case it is usually mild. During oliguric acute renal failure, the concentration of extracellular potassium may increase by 0.4 mEq/liter per day; if renal failure is complicated by trauma, burns, infection, or other catabolic states, it may increase by 0.7 mEq/liter per day or more.[53] Normally the kidneys can excrete a potassium load resulting from catabolism, but in acute renal failure they cannot, because of the reduction in glomerular filtration and in distal tubular flow rate. When acute tubular necrosis or acute interstitial nephritis precipitates acute renal failure, distal tubule cells responsible for potassium secretion may be too severely damaged to respond to the potassium load, and unable to increase their secretory activity.

In contrast, hyperkalemia is not commonly encountered in *chronic renal insufficiency*, despite an impairment in the transport of potassium into cells.[3,54] Despite nephron loss, potassium balance is maintained by increased excretion per nephron and by an adaptation of the colon that increases potassium secretion.[50] These adaptations are partly the consequence of an increase in aldosterone secretion and Na^+, K^+-ATPase activity, and are only effective in maintaining potassium balance until the GFR falls below 25 ml/min/1.73m^2 (Fig. 4-1).[43] Within 24 hours, dogs adapt to ablation of 80 percent of renal mass with a fourfold increase in potassium excretion by the remaining nephrons and with a further increase in potassium excretion over the ensuing week.[55] This adaptation is associated with an increase in Na^+, K^+-ATPase activity of the distal tubule. Increased catabolism, cell breakdown, hypoaldosteronism, or an excessive potassium intake may predispose patients with chronic renal insufficiency to hyperkalemia.[56] Even a mild deficiency in mineralocorticoid secretion limits renal adaptation.

Prerenal azotemia results from a decrease in absolute or effective circulating blood volume or from a sequestration of intravascular fluid in interstitial spaces, and may impair renal function sufficiently to cause hyperkalemia.[57] The decrease in potassium secretion is a consequence of a reduced GFR and distal tubular flow.

Disorders that impair function of the renin and aldosterone systems are characterized by hyperkalemia and hyperchloremic metabolic acidosis, or so-called type 4 renal tubular acidosis.[58] The severity of aldosterone deficiency determines the degree of renal sodium wasting and the predisposition to develop hyperkalemia. Hyperkalemia may in part lead to acidosis by decreasing the production of ammonia,[58] and possibly also by decreasing the reabsorption of bicarbonate.[59] These effects of hyperkalemia may be at least partly mediated by the movement of hydrogen and sodium ions out of cells as potassium enters.[60] Adrenal insufficiency, when it occurs in infancy, is usually due to adrenal hypoplasia or aplasia. In older children or adults, an autoimmune dysplasia or more rarely, tuberculosis, amyloidosis, acute adrenal hemorrhage, or infarction is the cause of adrenal failure. When sodium intake is adequate, normal serum sodium and potassium concentrations and a normal carbon dioxide content are maintained, provided an *acute adrenal crisis* does not occur.[61]

Hereditary enzymatic defects in cortisol or aldosterone biosynthesis may also cause hyperkalemia. The congenital adrenal hyperplasia that results from *21-hydroxylase deficiency* prevents the conversion of 17-hydroxyprogesterone to 11-deoxycortisol and results in increased adrenocorticotrophic hormone (ACTH) secretion and excessive production of adrenal androgens, with virilization. The conversion of corticosterone to aldosterone requires the enzymes corticosterone methyloxidase I and II. A deficiency of either enzyme results in an autosomal recessive, *hereditary isolated defect in aldosterone biogenesis*.[62] Affected infants may present with a hyperkalemic metabolic acidosis that is aggravated by sodium chloride wasting with volume depletion.[62] The disorder may present in the adult as asymptomatic growth failure.

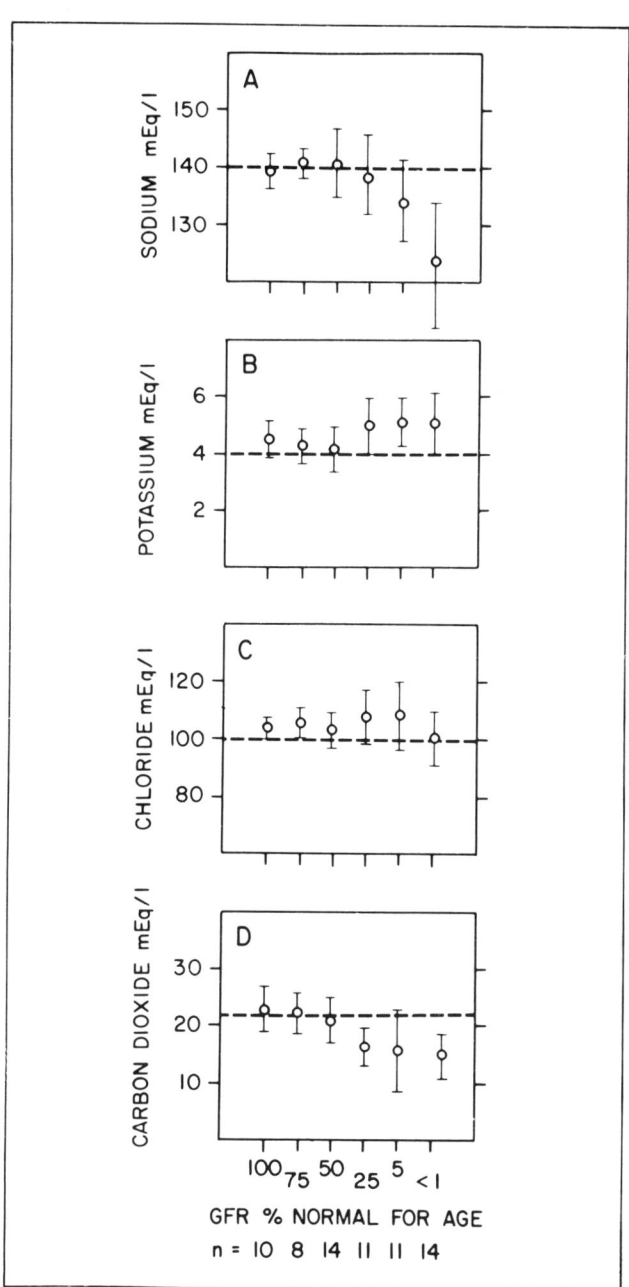

Fig. 4-1. Hyperkalemia is not commonly encountered until the glomerular filtration rate is less than 25 percent of normal. (From Chan JCM, Goplerud JM, Papadopoulou ZL, et al: Kidney failure in childhood. Int J Pediatr Nephrol 2:201, 1981, with permission.)

The syndrome of *hyporeninemic hypoaldosteronism* may be the basis for 50 to 70 percent of cases of unexplained hyperkalemia in patients who do not have renal failure and who are not ingesting an excessive amount of potassium or using potassium-sparing diuretics.[63,64] This syndrome is characterized by low plasma renin activity, a low plasma aldosterone concentration, a GFR between 20 and 75 ml/min/1.73 m², and hyperchloremic metabolic acidosis. Approximately half of these patients have diabetes mellitus.[65] Other diseases associated with hyporeninemic hypoaldosteronism are chronic obstructive uropathy, interstitial nephritis, hypertension, gout, nephrolithiasis, lead nephropathy, sickle cell disease, amyloidosis, renal transplantation, and lupus erythematosus.[65]

Renal tubular hyperkalemia includes a group of isolated, tubular secretory defects with hyperkalemia out of proportion to the mild renal insufficiency that may accompany it. The renal tubule is resistant to circulating aldosterone in physiologic concentrations, as the result of a primary renal tubular disorder such as pseudohypoaldosteronism type I or pseudohypoaldosteronism type II, or impaired distal tubular function caused by sickle cell disease,[65] obstructive uropathy, systemic lupus erythematosus,[66] amyloidosis,[67] lead nephropathy,[68] interstitial nephritis,[69] or renal transplantation.[65]

Pseudohypoaldosteronism type I presents in infancy and is characterized by growth failure, hyperkalemic metabolic acidosis, and hyponatremia caused by renal wasting of sodium and chloride.[70] The hyperreninemia and hyperaldosteronism result from tubular resistance to aldosterone.[66]

Pseudohypoaldosteronism type II presents in adolescence or adulthood with hypertension and hyperkalemic metabolic acidosis, and with an aldosterone concentration that is normal or slightly elevated despite a low plasma renin activity.[71] The primary defect is presumed to be a markedly increased chloride reabsorption in the distal tubule, with increased sodium reabsorption but impaired potassium secretion.[71]

Obstructive uropathy leads to renal resistance to aldosterone and is regarded as the most common etiology of type 4 renal tubular acidosis.[60,72]

Systemic lupus erythematosus is often associated with defective potassium secretion out of proportion to the degree of renal functional impairment. The pathogenesis is unclear, but may be related to interstitial immune-complex injury to the renal tubules.[69]

A large number of *pharmacologic agents*, such as the potassium-sparing diuretics triamterene, spironolactone, and amiloride, block potassium secretion by the distal tubule.[3] These medications should not be used in renal failure.[3]

Captopril and other angiotensin converting enzyme (ACE) inhibitors cause hyperkalemia because they block the formation of angiotensin II from angiotensin I and lead to hypoaldosteronism.[73] Thus, patients treated with these drugs may resemble patients with the syndrome of hyporeninemic hypoaldosteronism, except that in captopril-induced hyperkalemia the plasma renin concentration is high.

Nonsteroidal anti-inflammatory agents such as indomethacin can cause severe hyperkalemia by inhibiting renin release, thereby inducing a reversible form of hyporeninemic hypoaldosteronism. Furthermore, prostaglandin inhibitors may also contribute to the development of hyperkalemia by reducing glomerular filtration and decreasing the rate of distal tubular flow.[74]

Heparin and related compounds may inhibit renin secretion and lead to hypoaldosteronism and hyperkalemia.[75] These effects may be seen as early as one week after the beginning of treatment when these agents are given to patients with renal insufficiency.[76] Cyclosporine, used in patients undergoing renal and heart transplantations, causes hyperkalemia with or without hyporeninemic hypoaldosteronism.[77] Because hyporeninemia is not a consistent finding, it is possible that cyclosporine inhibits renal excretion of potassium.

Release of Potassium from Cells

Redistribution of potassium from the intracellular to the extracellular compartment may be caused by (1) metabolic and respiratory acidosis, (2) rapid lysis of cells, and (3) pharmacologic agents.

Both *metabolic* and *respiratory acidosis* may be accompanied by hyperkalemia. Buffering of hydrogen ions in body cells leads to a movement of potassium to the extracellular space, increasing the plasma potassium concentration. This occurs more in metabolic than in respiratory acidosis.[78] Because of complex factors that relate the degree of acidosis to hyperkalemia, the previous estimation that each 0.1 unit decrease in blood pH is correlated with a 0.5 mEq/liter increment in potassium is imprecise.[3] With an increase in excretion of hydrogen ion, distal tubular potassium secretion is curtailed, predisposing patients to hyperkalemia despite any increase in distal tubular flow rate.[65]

Rapid release of intracellular potassium to the extracellular space (Table 4-1) occurs in exercise, insulin deficiency with hyperglycemia, familial hyperkalemic periodic paralysis, crush injury and cell breakdown from tumor lysis, hemolysis, and rhabdomyolysis.

Diabetic ketoacidosis is frequently associated with hyperkalemia despite depletion of cellular potassium stores.[78] Two mechanisms operate to promote a shift of potassium from cells: (1) the increase in osmolality of ECF associated with hyperglycemia[78] leads to a loss of water and potassium from cells; (2) insulin deficiency limits potassium movement into cells. Ketoacidosis, unlike acidosis caused by nonmetabolizable acids, is not associated with loss of potassium from cells.[78] The tendency of patients with acidosis to develop hyperkalemia may be aggravated by the presence of diabetic nephropathy, diabetic neuropathy, or sympathetic blockade by β-adrenergic blocking agents.[3,65]

Familial hyperkalemic periodic paralysis is an autosomal dominant disorder characterized by recurrent episodes of muscle weakness and paralysis.[79] Attacks are precipitated by exposure to cold, may occur during the resting period after exercise, and usually last less than two hours.[80] During an attack, the serum potassium concentration rises as the muscle potassium concentration falls. This change in the ratio of intracellular to extracellular potassium concentration leads to muscular weakness.

Cell breakdown associated with crush injury,[81] tumor lysis,[82] or hemolysis[83] releases considerable amounts of potassium into the extracellular space and may lead to hyperkalemia, especially if it occurs in patients with renal impairment.

Rhabdomyolysis, when associated with acidosis, dehydration, or shock, may give rise to acute tubular necrosis. Myoglobin released from dead muscle in the process of rhabdomyolysis is not a nephrotoxin; thromboplastin or another tissue constituent is responsible for the renal tubular damage that occurs in this condition.[3] Strenuous exercise, hypernatremia, hyperthermia, or a deficiency of muscle phosphorylase increases the risk of developing rhabdomyolysis with acute renal failure and hyperkalemia.[3,65]

Pharmacologic agents that cause a loss of potassium from cells and predispose patients to hyperkalemia include digitalis,[18] β-adrenergic blocking agents,[3] arginine hydrochloride, and succinylcholine (Table 4-1).

Arginine hydrochloride behaves as a strong acid in the body because it dissociates completely. With entry of hydrogen ions into cells, potassium is extruded, increasing the extracellular potassium concentration.

Succinylcholine, used in general anesthesia as a muscle relaxant, depolarizes cell membranes, causing intracellular potassium to move into the extracellular space.[84] This tendency to produce hyperkalemia is aggravated if succinylcholine is used in patients with burns, crush injuries, or tetanus. Tubocurarine counteracts the risk of hyperkalemia.

Increased Intake of Potassium

Hyperkalemia tends to develop in response to an increase in potassium intake only when renal potassium handling is compromised. This may occur in patients with impaired renal function who are given large doses of penicillin, which contains 1.7 mEq of potassium per million units, or who are taking potassium salts, which contain up to 13 mEq of potassium per gram, as salt substitutes.[85] Multiple transfusions of blood aged in storage have been reported to cause hyperkalemia and cardiac arrest.[86] Geophagia of red clay with a high potassium content may result in hyperkalemia in patients with compromised renal function.[87]

Pathophysiologic Consequences of Hyperkalemia

Profound muscle weakness and paresthesia of the upper and lower extremities, followed by flaccid paralysis ascending symmetrically toward the trunk and involving the respiratory muscles, are due to changes in the resting membrane potential and to the muscle excitability induced by hyperkalemia.[88,89] The resting membrane potential depends on a concentration gradient of 1:30 between the extracellular and intracellular potassium concentrations. As the extracellular potassium rises, the ratio falls, and the resting membrane potential decreases.[90] When the resting electrical potential falls close to or below the threshold, the conduction velocity decreases, the action potential cannot be sustained, and paralysis results.[5] In hyperkalemic periodic paralysis, the attacks may be precipitated by a small increase in serum potassium to 5.5 mEq/liter,[79] although neuromuscular manifestations are typically not encountered until the serum potassium exceeds 8 mEq/liter.[90]

Myocardial conduction fibers are also very susceptible to the effects of hyperkalemia. *Cardiac arrhythmias* and *ventricular fibrillation* may be precipitated by acute elevations of potassium,[90] especially if additional predisposing factors are present, such as hyponatremia,[91] acidosis,[92] or hypocalcemia.[93] On the electrocardiogram, T wave elevations ("tenting"), representing ventricular repolarization, start to appear when the plasma potassium concentration reaches 5.5 to 6.0 mEq/liter.[90] Widening of the PR interval and QRS complex, representing delayed conduction by the His-Purkinje and ventricular fibers, may be seen at potassium concentrations of 6.0 to 7.0 mEq/liter.[93] The P wave becomes flattened due to impaired atrial conduction when the potassium concentration is 7.0 to 7.5 mEq/liter.[93] As the potassium concentration rises above 8 mEq/liter, the changes described above progress to a sine-wave pattern in which the T wave is merged into a markedly widened QRS complex.[93] This pattern may be mistaken for ventricular tachycardia.

If the rise in potassium concentration is gradual, cardiac toxicity from hyperkalemia may be minimal.[89] Cardiac toxicity is potentiated when the rise in potassium concentration is rapid,[93] and may be further aggravated by intercurrent hyponatremia,[91] acidosis,[92] or hypocalcemia.[93]

Diagnostic Evaluation of Hyperkalemia

A careful history is important in the identification of causes of hyperkalemia and associated factors that may aggravate it (Table 4-1). Specifically, one should inquire about current and past renal disease, disorders that may be associated with cell breakdown, adrenal disorders, diabetes mellitus, periodic paralysis and muscle weakness, intercurrent medications, and possible sources of an increase in potassium intake (Table 4-1). Physical examination is necessary to evaluate muscle strength, state of hydration, or signs of diseases that predispose to hyperkalemia (Table 4-1). The initial laboratory workup should include a repeat determination of the serum potassium concentration. If spurious hyperkalemia is suspected, simultaneous analysis of the serum and plasma potassium concentrations should agree within 0.3 mEq/liter. Routine determinations of blood chemical values for glucose, urea nitrogen, creatinine, sodium, carbon dioxide content, and calcium help in the differential diagnosis. An electrocardiogram is important for monitoring the effects of hyperkalemia on myocardial conduction.

A useful diagnostic approach is to evaluate the patient in terms of the three major pathogenic categories of hyperkalemia: (1) decreased excretion, (2) increased release from cells, and (3) increased intake (Table 4-1).

Spurious hyperkalemia may be suspected if the electrocardiogram is normal and there is no apparent cause of the hyperkalemia. Confirmation of hyperkalemia by analysis of a carefully drawn aliquot of blood rules out the possibility of ischemic venipuncture and suggests that thrombocytosis or leukocytosis is the cause of the elevated potassium concentration.

A history of ingestion of potassium penicillin, potassium salt substitutes, or clay, or of having received aged blood suggests that increased potassium intake may be partly responsible for the hyperkalemia. A careful search should be conducted for contributing factors such as medications or impaired renal function. The evaluation of renal function should include urinalysis, measurement of the creatinine clearance, and determination of the ability to conserve sodium. Quantitation of urinary potassium excretion may be helpful if the urinary potassium is low at a time when the serum potassium is rising. This suggests an impairment in the renal excretion of potassium and/or a defect in the renin and aldosterone systems.[65]

If renal impairment is not sufficient to account for the hyperkalemia, or if the patient is not taking a medication that impairs potassium excretion, such as triamterene, spironolactone, amiloride, captopril, a nonsteroidal anti-inflammatory agent, heparin, a β-adrenergic blocking agent, arginine, or succinylcholine, then determination of the plasma renin activity, plasma aldosterone, and cortisol is necessary to test for possible deficiency of, or an abnormal renal tubular response to, an adrenal steroid.

If the initial values for renin and aldosterone are low, then furosemide, 23 mg/m^2, should be given at 6 P.M. the day before and at 6 A.M. on the day that blood is drawn for a repeat determination of plasma renin activity and plasma aldosterone, to ensure their maximal stimulation.

Adrenal insufficiency and hyporeninemic hypoaldosteronism are seen more often in adults than in children, whereas 21-hydroxylase deficiency, corticosterone methyloxidase deficiency, and pseudohypoaldosteronism types I and II are usually present in infancy and childhood. These disorders may present as a hyperkalemic metabolic acidosis, and may also show the specific features presented in Table 4-2.

150 • Kidney Electrolyte Disorders

Table 4-2. Clinical Features of Hormonal Disorders That Predispose to Hyperkalemia

Disorder	Plasma Renin Activity	Plasma Aldosterone	Plasma Cortisol	Diagnostic Features
Hyporeninism	Low	Low	Normal	Renin unresponsive to stimulation
Adrenal insufficiency	High	Low	Low	ACTH high or low
Congenital adrenal hyperplasia, 21-hydroxylase defect	High	Low to high	Low	High progesterone, 17-OH progesterone
Corticosterone methyloxidase defect	High	Low	Normal	High $\frac{\text{18-OH corticosterone}}{\text{aldosterone}}$
Pseudohypoaldosteronism				
Type I	High	High	Normal	Hypotension, sodium wasting
Type II	Low	Low to high	Normal	Hypertension, normal sodium conservation

Treatment of Hyperkalemia

The two aims of therapy for hyperkalemia are first to reverse its acute effects by increasing the transport of potassium from ECF into cells and by eliminating excess potassium from the body, and second, to correct the underlying cause(s) of the hyperkalemia. If the serum potassium concentration exceeds 8 mEq/liter, treatment of neuromuscular irritability may be required. Membrane excitability may be temporarily restored toward normal by the administration of 10 to 30 ml of a 10 percent solution of calcium gluconate given intravenously over 1 to 3 minutes while monitoring the electrocardiogram (Table 4-3).[3,65] Because hypercalcemia predisposes to digitalis toxicity, calcium infusions should not be given to patients taking digitalis unless the hyperkalemia is so severe that the electrocardiogram shows P waves lost in a widened QRS complex.[65] When calcium is given to patients taking digitalis, it should be infused over half an hour in 100 ml of 5 percent dextrose solution with or without insulin (the solution should not contain bicarbonate, in order to avoid precipitation of calcium).[65] If necessary, the calcium infusion may be repeated after half an hour.

In a hyponatremic patient, the effects of hyperkalemia may be minimized by administering 50 to 100 mEq of sodium as a 3 percent solution of hypertonic saline given intravenously over 10 minutes (Table 4-3).[3,94,95] Hypertonic saline may also decrease the extracellular potassium concentration by promoting transport of potassium into cells and by diluting extracellular potassium. These effects are of little benefit in the patient with a normal serum sodium concentration.[96]

Treatment with sodium bicarbonate 50 to 100 mEq, given intravenously over 5 minutes, raises the pH of ECF; this promotes the movement of potassium into cells and increases the ratio of intracellular to extracellular potassium (Table 4-3).[3,65,97] As filtration of the administered sodium bicarbonate exceeds the threshold for bicarbonate reabsorption, the increased delivery of sodium to the distal tubule enhances renal tubular potassium secretion. Occasionally, treatment with sodium bicarbonate may be complicated by pulmonary edema or seizures.[65]

Glucose and insulin increase the entry of

Table 4-3. Therapy for Hyperkalemia

Therapy	Dosage	Onset	Duration of Effect
Antagonism of membrane effects of hyperkalemia			
1. Calcium gluconate (10%)	10–30 ml, IV	A few minutes	60 minutes
2. Hypertonic saline (3%)	50–100 mEq, IV	10 minutes	2 hours
Stimulation of potassium uptake into cells			
1. Sodium bicarbonate	50–100 mEq, IV	30 minutes	2 hours
2. Glucose and insulin	1 unit regular insulin per 5 g glucose, IV over 1 hour	30 minutes	6 hours
3. Hypertonic saline	50–100 mEq IV	10 minutes	2 hours
Removal of potassium from the body			
1. Cation-exchange resin	20–50 g per rectum or per os with sorbitol	60 minutes 120 minutes	6 hours
2. Peritoneal dialysis or hemodialysis	—	A few minutes	variable
3. Diuretics (furosemide)	40 mg IV	Starts with diuresis	variable

potassium into muscle cells.[2,28] Regular insulin, 1 unit per 5 g of glucose, given as 10 units of insulin in 500 ml of 10 percent glucose solution, decreases the serum potassium concentration by 1 mEq/liter; this effect begins within 30 minutes and lasts about six hours (Table 4-3).[3] In patients with poorly controlled diabetes mellitus and hyperglycemia, potassium stores are usually depleted, and hypokalemia may develop when the blood glucose is reduced by insulin.

Removal of potassium from the body may be achieved by cation-exchange resins, diuretics, and peritoneal or hemodialysis (Table 4-3). Sodium polystyrene sulfonate (Kayexalate) is a readily available cation-exchange resin that binds 0.5 to 1.0 mEq of potassium per gram of Kayexalate; it may be given orally or as a retention enema.[3,65] The usual oral dose is 20 g of Kayexalate in 100 ml of 20 percent sorbitol; it may be repeated every four to six hours, as needed.[43] The usual dose for rectal administration is 50 g of Kayexalate in 50 ml of 70 percent sorbitol solution, and it may be repeated in one hour (Table 4-3).[3] The duration of action of the enema is six hours. A retention enema of Kayexalate begins to lower the serum potassium in one hour, whereas oral Kayexalate may require two hours. The major complication of treatment with Kayexalate is pulmonary edema caused by sodium retention in patients with pre-existing congestive heart failure and oliguria. Other complications are nausea, vomiting, and constipation. Occasionally, hypokalemia may follow excessive potassium loss.

Peritoneal dialysis or hemodialysis may be used to remove potassium from the body if the medical interventions outlined above fail to reverse the hyperkalemia or in the case of a massive release of cellular potassium associated with intercurrent hypercatabolism (from trauma or cell lysis). Peritoneal dialysis removes potassium at a slower rate than hemodialysis, reducing serum potassium by 50 percent for every 12 hours of dialysis (Figure 4-2).[43]

Diuretics, such as ethacrynic acid, furosemide, or thiazides, inhibit tubular reab-

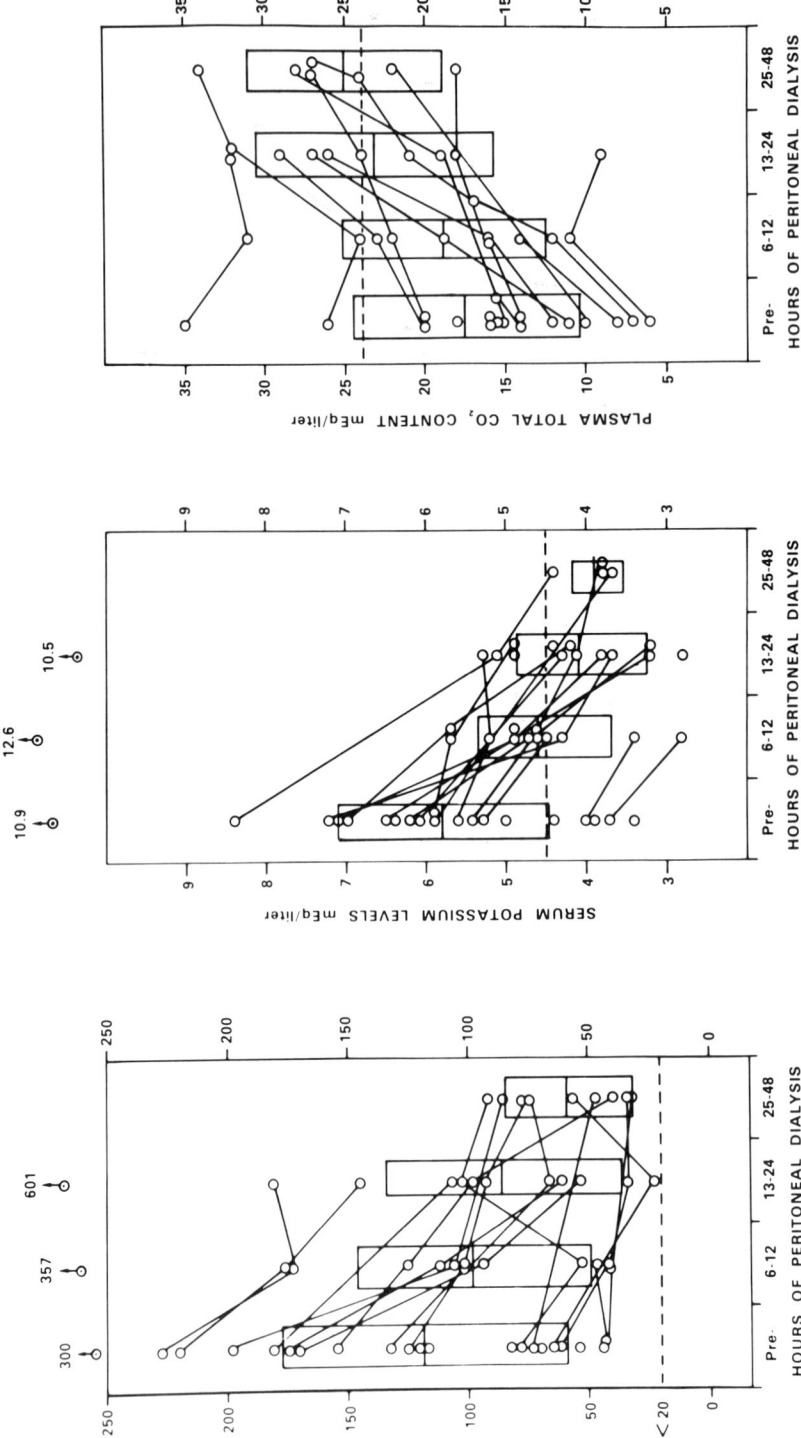

Fig. 4-2. Peritoneal dialysis corrects electrolyte disturbances in acute renal failure. The hyperkalemia is reduced by 50 percent every 12 hours. (From Chan JCM: Peritoneal dialysis of renal failure in childhood: clinical aspects and electrolyte changes as observed in 20 cases. Clin Pediatr 17:349, 1978, with permission.)

sorption of sodium chloride and water and stimulate potassium secretion. Although diuretics are not used specifically as primary agents for treating hyperkalemia, they are very useful for treating hyperkalemia complicated by fluid retention.

Chronic hyperkalemia requires treatment of the underlying disorder. If pharmacologic agents are responsible for the hyperkalemia, such medications should be discontinued (Table 4-1). If chronic renal failure with decreased excretion of potassium is responsible for the hyperkalemia, the dietary intake of potassium should be restricted to less than 60 mEq/day.

Treatment for hyperkalemia associated with abnormalities of the renin and aldosterone systems depends on the nature of the underlying disorder. Fludrocortisone, 0.05 mg/m^2/day, is an effective replacement for aldosterone in patients with corticosterone methyloxidase deficiency.[63] In hyporeninemic hypoaldosteronism, supraphysiologic doses of fludrocortisone (0.5 mg/m^2/day) may be needed because of resistance to aldosterone.[16,64,65] In patients with type II pseudohypoaldosteronism, treatment with a thiazide diuretic corrects the hypertension, hyperkalemia, and acidosis.[71]

In children with congenital adrenal hyperplasia and 21-hydroxylase deficiency, adequate replacement with hydrocortisone and fludrocortisone is essential to correct depletion of extracellular volume and hyperreninemia, virilization, and growth retardation.[98] Fludrocortisone and hydrocortisone may be increased until the plasma renin activity and 17-hydroxyprogesterone concentration are restored to normal.[98]

Fludrocortisone is not effective in type I pseudohypoaldosteronism because of the aldosterone resistance.[70] A high sodium intake improves the depletion of ECF volume, increases distal tubular flow, and facilitates potassium excretion.[4]

Patients with hyperkalemic periodic paralysis may be managed with a high carbohydrate diet, which induces hyperinsulinemia and promotes the cellular uptake of potassium.[79] Diuretics such as acetazolamide and thiazides may be helpful.[80] Treatment with a beta-adrenergic agonist such as albuterol has been reported to be beneficial.[99]

In summary, acute hyperkalemia is preferably treated initially with a cation exchange resin unless cardiotoxic effects of hyperkalemia are present, and then rapid reversal may be achieved with calcium infusion under careful electrocardiographic monitoring. Alternatively, administration of glucose and insulin or bicarbonate may be considered. Finally, if the above therapeutic measures are ineffective, peritoneal dialysis or hemodialysis may be initiated. The management of chronic hyperkalemia also requires treatment of the underlying disease or the removal of any pharmacologic agents that may be contributory.

HYPOKALEMIA

Hypokalemia is defined as a serum potassium concentration below 3.5 mEq/liter.[100] Potassium values between 3.5 and 3.8 mEq/liter may be normal, but should alert the clinician to the possibility that hypokalemia may be developing, with its attendant consequences (Table 4-4).

As sodium is the major extracellular ion, so also is potassium the major intracellular ion. Membrane potentials and cellular excitability are determined to a great extent by the relationship between these two principal ions of the extra- and intracellular compartments of the body. The total body potassium is 50 mEq/kg of body weight, or 3500 mEq for a 70 kg man; 75 percent is in muscle and 23 percent in other cells.[3,4] Extracellular potassium constitutes a mere 2 percent of the total body potassium, and is distributed between plasma (one third) and the interstitial space (two thirds).

The distribution of potassium between cells and ECF is not static, and may be

Table 4-4. Etiology of Hypokalemia

Increased renal excretion:

    Renal tubular disorders: Renal tubular acidosis, Bartter's syndrome, magnesium-losing tubulopathy, calcium-losing tubulopathy, 11-beta hydroxysteroid dehydrogenase deficiency, Liddle's syndrome, diuretic abuse

    Adrenal disorders: Aldosterone-producing adenoma, idiopathic hyperaldosteronism, dexamethasone-suppressible hyperaldosteronism, adrenocortical carcinoma, 11-hydroxylase deficiency, 17-alpha hydroxylase deficiency

Increased gastrointestinal loss: Vomiting, diarrhea, congenital diarrhea, laxative abuse

Increased uptake by cells:

    Increased cell formation: Acute myelogenous leukemia, treated megaloblastic anemia

    Hypothermia

    Familial periodic paralysis

    Pharmacologic agents: Insulin, β-adrenergic agonists, barium, toluene

Decreased intake:

    Chronic alcoholism
    Anorexia nervosa
    Geophagia

---

altered by catecholamines. Insulin, β-adrenergic agonists[101] such as epinephrine, terbutaline,[102] and salbutamol, as well as barium[103] and toluene[104] all stimulate the transport of potassium into cells, producing hypokalemia without a deficit in potassium (Table 4-4). Rapid cell proliferation occurring in the course of acute myelogenous leukemia[105] or during the treatment of megaloblastic anemia[106] may produce hypokalemia by causing the deposition of a large amount of potassium in newly formed cells. Hypothermia, if prolonged, induces significant potassium entry into cells, producing hypokalemia.[107] This intracellular shift of potassium may be readily reversed by restoration of the body temperature to normal.

Familial periodic paralysis is a rare, autosomal dominant disorder that affects males more severely than females.[108,109] A sporadic form of this disorder may be associated with hyperthyroidism, and tends to occur more often in Asians.[110] The attacks of muscle weakness and flaccid paralysis usually tend to occur at night or in the early morning, but may occur at any time.[111] Muscles of respiration and deglutition and ocular muscles are rarely involved. The attacks may be precipitated by exposure to cold or by trauma, vigorous exercise, an increased intake of sodium or glucose, and by glucose and insulin administration. The etiology is obscure, but appears to be related to a movement of extracellular potassium into skeletal muscle.[111]

Hypokalemia associated with a depletion of total body potassium may result from insufficient dietary potassium intake or a loss of potassium from the kidneys or gastrointestinal tract. Rarely, excessive sweat loss, such as that associated with prolonged military exercises in a hot climate, may be associated with hypokalemia.[112] Since sweat contains only 10 mEq/liter of potassium, the volume of loss required to produce a deficit must be considerable, and must therefore be an uncommon cause of hypokalemia.

It should be noted that a deficit of potassium may occur without hypokalemia in uremia, congestive heart failure, and diabetic ketoacidosis, as a result of the movement of potassium from cells to ECF.

Insufficient intake of potassium may occur in chronic alcoholism if food intake is decreased and alcohol provides most of the calories consumed. Since many foods, such as meat, oranges, and bananas, contain substantial amounts of potassium, it is difficult to develop hypokalemia from an insufficient potassium intake, except in extreme circumstances. The refusal of food in anorexia nervosa and the binding of potassium by ingested clay in geophagia are extreme examples of dietary potassium deprivation.

RENAL POTASSIUM LOSS

Renal potassium loss may occur in a setting of normal or high blood pressure, and may be associated with high, normal, or low

Table 4-5. Renal Wasting of Potassium Associated with Normal Blood Pressure

High Renin, High Aldosterone
Renal tubular acidosis
Bartter's syndrome
Magnesium-losing tubulopathy
Calcium-losing tubulopathy
Covert diuretic abuse

---

plasma renin activity. In the case of hypokalemia and normal blood pressure, plasma renin activity and the plasma aldosterone concentration are high; in the case of hypokalemia and hypertension, plasma renin activity may be either high with a high plasma aldosterone, or suppressed with either a high or low plasma aldosterone concentration. The state of the blood pressure and the profile of the renin and aldosterone systems indicate what specific disorders should be considered in a patient with renal potassium loss. Those disorders that cause renal potassium loss and are manifested by a normal blood pressure and high plasma renin activity will be considered first (Table 4-5).

Renal tubular acidosis may result in symptomatic hypokalemia in both primary type I and type II renal tubular acidosis and in the secondary types of acidosis such as that in the Fanconi syndrome.[100,113] In type II renal tubular acidosis and Fanconi syndrome, defective proximal tubular reabsorption of bicarbonate results in the delivery of excess sodium, bicarbonate, and water to distal tubular sites, stimulating potassium loss.

In type I and probably in the other types of renal tubular acidosis as well, sodium conservation may be impaired, leading to a contraction of ECF volume, stimulation of the renin and aldosterone systems, and aggravation of potassium loss.[114] Sodium bicarbonate treatment in the type II disorder may impair proximal bicarbonate reabsorption, and the resulting increased bicarbonaturia may aggravate renal potassium wasting. In contrast, bicarbonate therapy in type I renal tubular acidosis may increase hydrogen ion secretion, which is inhibited by an abnormally low pH gradient, with a resulting decrease in potassium secretion. Other mechanisms controlling potassium excretion may also be defective in type I renal tubular acidosis, since the defect in potassium reabsorption persists despite correction of the systemic acidosis in such patients.

Bartter's syndrome is a disorder of tubular transport that may be familial or acquired as a result of a disease such as cystinosis.[115] Drugs such as diuretics that act to increase potassium excretion, or drugs such as cisplatinum, carbenicillin, aminoglycosides, or gentamicin, which may secondarily impair tubular function so as to increase potassium excretion, may mimic Bartter's syndrome. Hypokalemia in Bartter's syndrome is accompanied by mild to moderate alkalosis, hypochloremia and, in some patients, by hypomagnesemia. Hyperuricemia has also been observed.[116]

Defective chloride transport in the diluting segment of the nephron, presumably the thick ascending limb of the loop of Henle, is thought to be the primary cause of Bartter's syndrome.[117] This proposed abnormality in chloride transport not only accounts for the defects in diluting and concentrating abilities, but could also increase urinary potassium excretion by decreasing potassium reabsorption in the thick ascending limb and by stimulating potassium secretion in the distal nephron through an increase in the rate of distal delivery of tubular fluid. This defect in chloride transport may also account for the increased magnesium excretion in Bartter's syndrome,[118] but does not appear to affect calcium excretion, which is normal or low.[119]

Potassium depletion resulting from renal potassium loss appears to be the basis for prostaglandin overproduction.[120,121] An increase in prostaglandin synthesis in vascular tissue, because it tends to produce vasodilation, is associated with compensatory increases in the activity of the renin, angiotensin, and sympathetic nervous systems to maintain blood pressure. Pressor resistance, initially increased by prostaglandins, is further increased by an increase in circulating angiotensin II that leads to the downregulation of angiotensin II receptors.[122] This pathogenic schema is presented in Figure 4-3. Treatment with a prostaglandin synthetase inhibitor corrects the hyperreninemia and increased sympathoadrenal activity, the pressor resistance to angiotensin II and norepinephrine and the hypotensive response to an inhibitor of angiotensin II, presumably because it corrects the overproduction of prostaglandins.[123-125] Although potassium loss may be improved by the inhibition of prostaglandin synthesis,[126] it is not corrected, because the prostaglandin-independent defect in chloride transport that is a major determinant of potassium loss is unimproved.[117]

A defect in the tubular reabsorption of magnesium, causing renal magnesium loss (magnesium-losing tubulopathy), may be associated with renal potassium loss. Because these patients usually have hyperreninemia and hyperaldosteronism, they tend to resemble patients with Bartter's syndrome with hypomagnesemia. However, the two disorders can be distinguished from each other, since magnesium-losing tubulopathy generally has fewer and milder symptoms and is characterized by a normal urinary diluting ability and a relatively intact concentrating ability despite hypokalemia.

A defect in the tubular reabsorption of calcium, causing renal calcium loss (calcium-losing tubulopathy), may be associated with renal potassium loss. This familial disorder usually presents in childhood as polyuria, polydipsia, and failure to thrive. There is frequently a history of prematurity and polyhydramnios.[127] Although calcium-losing tubulopathy tends to resemble Bartter's syndrome because of hypokalemia, hyperreninemia, and high urinary prostaglandin concentrations, the presence of hypercalciuria and a normal urinary diluting ability readily distinguish it from Bartter's syndrome.[128]

Potassium loss as a result of vomiting, diarrhea, or laxative abuse may produce a deficit sufficient to give rise to many of the features of Bartter's syndrome (prostaglandin overproduction, hyperreninemia, hyperaldosteronism, and pressor resistance).[129] Since the potassium concentration in gastric juice is approximately 10 mEq/liter, potassium loss in vomitus may not be great. An increase in potassium ex-

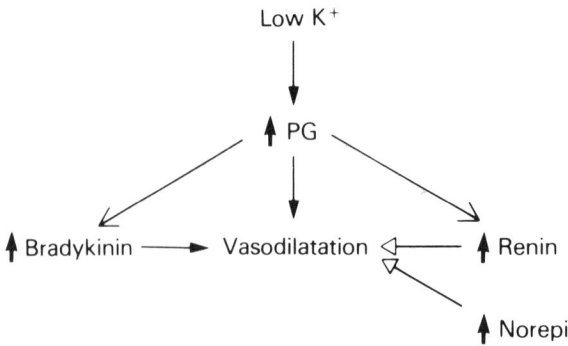

Fig. 4-3. Proposed schema for pathogenesis of Bartter's syndrome. Solid arrows indicate stimulation; open arrows indicate inhibition. The increase of bradykinin is associated with the increase in prostaglandin and may be in response to the increase in plasma renin activity. PG = prostaglandin, Norepi = Norepinephrine.

cretion by the kidney, obligated by hypochloremic alkalosis secondary to the loss of hydrochloric acid in vomitus, may be the more important determinant of overall potassium loss.[130]

The potassium concentration of lower intestinal secretions may be as great as 90 mEq/liter. Normally, intestinal reabsorption results in a potassium output of only 5 to 10 mEq/day in feces. In diarrhea, the decrease in transit time may give rise to considerable losses of potassium and other electrolytes as well as of water. Intermittent, chronic diarrhea with potassium wasting is encountered in villous adenoma,[131] Zollinger-Ellison syndrome,[132] pancreatic islet cell tumors,[133] ganglioneuromas,[133] jejunal bypass,[134] laxative[135] or enema abuse,[136] and congenital diarrhea.[137]

Renal wasting of potassium with hypertension and suppressed plasma renin activity may be associated with a plasma aldosterone concentration that is high or low (Table 4-6). Aldosterone-producing adenoma, idiopathic hyperaldosteronism, dexamethasone-suppressible hyperaldosteronism, and, rarely, adrenocortical carcinoma are adrenal disorders in which aldosterone is overproduced and causes potassium loss.

The sodium retention and ECF volume expansion that result lead to the suppression of plasma renin activity and hypertension. The causes of aldosterone overproduction in idiopathic hyperaldosteronism and in dexamethasone-suppressible hyperaldosteronism are not well understood. In the case of idiopathic hyperaldosteronism, a current hypothesis is that an aldosterone-stimulating factor, possibly of pituitary origin, may either stimulate aldosterone biogenesis or increase the sensitivity of the zona glomerulosa to angiotensin II, or that, both effects may occur.[138]

In dexamethasone-suppressible hyperaldosteronism, ACTH produces a sustained overproduction of aldosterone because of an abnormality of the adrenal glands.[139] A possible explanation for the dependence of aldosterone on ACTH is that corticosterone methyloxidase, an enzyme in zona glomerulosa cells that converts corticosterone to aldosterone, fails to involute normally as the cells migrate to the zona fasiculata, and then acquires 17-hydroxylase activity. Such abnormal fasiculata cells could be the source of aldosterone as well as of the 18-hydroxycortisol and 18-oxocortisol found in the urine of patients with dexamethasone-suppressible hyperaldosteronism.[140]

Renal potassium wasting with hypertension, suppressed plasma renin activity, and a low or suppressed plasma aldosterone concentration results from an overproduction of mineralocorticoids other than aldosterone, or from an increase in the tubular reabsorption of sodium due to an intrinsic tubular abnormality (Table 4-6).

In congenital adrenal hyperplasia, deficiency of the enzymes 11-β-hydroxylase or 17-α-hydroxylase leads to the overproduction of deoxycorticosterone or corticosterone, respectively. An overproduction of either of these mineralocorticoids causes sodium chloride retention, suppression of plasma renin activity and aldosterone production, and potassium wasting.

A deficiency of 11-β-hydroxysteroid de-

Table 4-6. Renal Wasting of Potassium Associated with Hypertension

Low renin, high aldosterone
  Aldosterone-producing adenoma
  Idiopathic hyperaldosteronism
  Dexamethasone-suppressible hyperaldosteronism
  Adrenocortical carcinoma

Low renin, low aldosterone
  17-Alpha-hydroxylase deficiency
  11-Beta-hydroxylase deficiency
  11-Beta hydroxysteroid dehydrogenase deficiency, licorice ingestion
  Liddle's syndrome

High renin, high aldosterone
  Malignant hypertension
  Renal artery stenosis
  Renin-secreting tumor
  Chronic renal disease

hydrogenase, an enzyme responsible for converting cortisol to cortisone in renal tubule cells, results in the accumulation of cortisol and its occupancy of mineralocorticoid receptors in those cells.[141] The sodium retention and potassium wasting that result, and the correction of these abnormalities by spironolactone, a mineralocorticoid antagonist, led to classification of this disorder as an apparent mineralocorticoid excess, because it was thought to be caused by the overproduction of an unidentified mineralocorticoid. Recent studies suggest that the syndrome of apparent mineralocorticoid excess produced by the ingestion of licorice may be caused by the inhibition of 11-β-hydroxysteroid dehydrogenase by glycyrrhizic acid or its metabolite, glycyrrhetinic acid.[142] Licorice compounds do not appear to have a direct action on the renal tubule, because they have no effect in adrenalectomized animals.

Liddle's syndrome, a familial, intrinsic abnormality of the renal distal tubule, is characterized by an increase in sodium reabsorption and potassium secretion. Treatment with spironolactone does not affect the sodium retention or associated potassium loss, thereby excluding mineralocorticoids as pathogenic agents of the syndrome.[143] Although the nature of the increased permeability of the tubular epithelium to sodium is unknown, it can be corrected by potassium-sparing diuretics such as triamterene or amiloride.[143]

Renal potassium wasting with hypertension, high plasma renin activity, and a high plasma aldosterone concentration may be caused by renal artery stenosis, renin-secreting tumors such as hemangiopericytomas, hypernephromas, and Wilms' tumors,[144–147] malignant hypertension, and chronic renal disease (Table 4-6). These disorders may not always produce the pattern of change in the renin and aldosterone systems described above. For example, less than 20 percent of patients with renal artery stenosis show hyperreninemia and hyperaldosteronism.[144]

PATHOPHYSIOLOGIC CONSEQUENCES OF HYPOKALEMIA AND POTASSIUM DEPLETION

Table 4-7 lists the pathophysiologic consequences of hypokalemia. Because the action potential of the cell membrane depends on the ratio between intracellular (K_i) and extracellular (K_o) potassium, and the threshold is directly related to the ratio $K_i:K_o$, hypokalemia brings about important clinical consequences.

Hypokalemia may affect the function of peripheral nerves, especially those of the lower extremities, producing paresthetic sensations of numbness, tingling, prickling, and burning, and even paresis of skeletal

Table 4-7. Pathophysiologic Consequences of Hypokalemia

Neuromuscular
    Peripheral nerves (paresthesias)
    Skeletal muscle (fatigue, weakness, cramps, flaccid paralysis, rhabdomyolysis, myoglobinuria)
    Smooth muscle (paralytic ileus, increased vascular pressor resistance)
    Cardiac muscle (arrhythmia, digitalis toxicity)

Renal
    Concentration defect (polyuria, nocturia)
    Sodium retention
    Increased ammonia production, enhanced bicarbonate reabsorption
    Reduced renal blood flow, decreased GFR
    Predisposition to urinary tract infection
    Interstitial nephritis

Metabolic
    Impaired hepatic glycogen storage
    Carbohydrate intolerance
    Growth retardation

Hormonal
    Impaired growth hormone release
    Impaired insulin secretion
    Decreased aldosterone secretion
    Increased renin release
    Increased synthesis of prostaglandins

muscles.[148] Rhabdomyolysis may be encountered at serum potassium concentrations below 2.0 mEq/liter, and the myoglobinuria associated with the hypokalemia may lead to acute renal failure.[37] Normally, muscular exercise causes a local release of potassium, vasodilation, and increased blood flow to the tissues. In hypokalemia, this shift of potassium from muscle cells is defective, as is synthesis and storage of glycogen by these cells. These defects in skeletal muscle metabolism may result in hypoperfusion, tissue ischemia, rhabdomyolysis, and myoglobinuria.

Hypokalemia of less than 3 mEq/liter may be associated with reduced gastrointestinal motility that may progress to paralytic ileus at a plasma potassium concentration of less than 2.5 mEq/liter.

Potassium deficiency lowers peripheral vascular resistance and diminishes the pressor response to angiotensin II. These effects may be due to increased formation of vasodilator prostaglandins such as prostacyclin by vascular tissue, as well as to a down regulation of angiotensin II receptors.[122,125,149,150]

The increased risk of arrhythmia and propensity to digitalis toxicity are the most dangerous consequences of even mild cases of hypokalemia. Potassium deficiency with a serum potassium concentration of less than 3 mEq/liter causes T wave inversion, ST segment depression, elevated U waves, reduced QRS voltage, and a prolonged atrioventricular conduction time.[90,151] The risk of ventricular arrhythmia in patients with hypokalemia is increased by myocardial infarction, at the induction of anesthesia when associated with pre-existing cardiac disease, or during exercise.[152,153]

Polyuria, polydipsia, and nocturia are well-known features of the lack of urine concentrating ability induced by hypokalemia.[154] The impairment in concentrating ability has been attributed to impaired sodium chloride reabsorption by the thick ascending limb of the loop of Henle, impaired cyclic adenosine monophosphate formation, and increased formation of prostaglandins by renal tissue. The role of prostaglandins is uncertain, because prostaglandin inhibitors do not correct the impaired concentrating ability associated with experimental potassium depletion in the rat. Hypokalemia may predispose to urinary tract infection.[155]

After several months of hypokalemia, there is evidence of swelling and vacuolization of the epithelial cells of the renal proximal tubule, associated with interstitial fibrosis, tubular atrophy, and lymphocyte infiltration. This nephropathy is more likely the result of potassium depletion than a consequence of the recurrent urinary tract infections to which hypokalemic patients are predisposed.[155]

Increased renal ammonia production associated with enhanced bicarbonate reabsorption is also a feature of potassium depletion.[156] The increase in urinary ammonium and net acid excretion in the setting of hypokalemic alkalosis paradoxically perpetuates the metabolic alkalosis.[157] When such an increase in renal ammonia production occurs in patients with hepatic cirrhosis, it may put them at increased risk of developing hepatic coma. Furthermore, severe hypokalemia (serum potassium less than 2 mEq/liter) may impair the tubular reabsorption of chloride and perpetuate the resulting hypochloremia.[157] Other renal functional changes that may be associated with hypokalemia are renal vasoconstriction with reduced renal blood flow and a decreased GFR, and mild renal hypertrophy.

Growth retardation, a feature of children with Bartter's syndrome, also occurs in other conditions of chronic potassium depletion.[158] Impaired growth hormone release, decreased insulin secretion, and reduced synthesis of glycogen and protein in liver and skeletal muscle may be factors contributing to the growth retardation.[159]

Hypokalemia acts directly on the adrenal cortex to inhibit aldosterone secretion through effects on the early and late steps in aldosterone biosynthesis in the zona glomerulosa.[160]

DIAGNOSTIC EVALUATION OF HYPOKALEMIA

A careful history, physical examination, and laboratory analyses, including blood gas and pH determination, are usually sufficient to establish the cause of hypokalemia in most patients. Those patients in whom the etiology of potassium loss remains obscure may be more thoroughly evaluated by putting them on a constant diet with a sodium and chloride intake of approximately 100 mEq/day. A constant, known intake makes it possible to assess daily urinary excretions of sodium chloride, potassium, calcium, and magnesium, and the concentrations of these ions in the serum in a more informative fashion. This "normal" sodium intake provides a convenient reference for interpreting the results of plasma renin activity and plasma aldosterone concentration assays. With this approach, one can usually determine whether potassium is being lost in the urine or from the gastrointestinal tract, and in the case of covert vomiting or laxative abuse, it may be the only way to determine this. Such patients show a low urinary chloride relative to sodium and potassium, or a low urinary sodium relative to sodium intake.[129] In patients with urinary potassium loss, information about urinary calcium and magnesium excretion, plasma renin activity, plasma aldosterone, and blood pressure status allows one to considerably shorten the list of disorders to be considered in the differential diagnosis.

If the blood pressure is high and plasma renin activity is suppressed, an elevated plasma aldosterone suggests that the disorder is a form of hyperaldosteronism (Table 4-6). If, instead, the plasma aldosterone is low or suppressed, this suggests that a mineralocorticoid other than aldosterone is being overproduced, or that there is a deficiency of 11-β hydroxysteroid dehydrogenase, or that a disorder of the renal tubule such as Liddle's syndrome is present (Table 4-6).

If the blood pressure is normal, the plasma renin activity high, and the urinary calcium normal or low, then a tubulopathy such as Bartter's syndrome is the most likely diagnosis, although covert diuretic abuse should always be considered. If hypomagnesemia and hypermagnesiuria are also present, additional studies may be required to distinguish between Bartter's syndrome and a primary magnesium-losing tubulopathy. Determination of the maximal diluting ability, which is impaired in Bartter's syndrome but normal in magnesium-losing tubulopathy, may be very helpful in distinguishing between the two disorders.

TREATMENT STRATEGY FOR HYPOKALEMIA

The treatment of hypokalemia is divided into general and specific measures.

General Treatment of Hypokalemia

In general, potassium depletion should be corrected by the oral administration of potassium supplements. The normal daily intake of dietary potassium is 60 to 100 mEq. Thus, potassium supplementation should be based on the estimated deficit and the normal daily requirement. A decrease in serum potassium concentration from 4 to 3 mEq/liter in a 70 kg adult is associated with a total body potassium deficit of approximately 300 mEq, or 4 mEq/kg body weight.[3] The total body deficit becomes progressively greater as the serum potassium concentration decreases below 3 mEq/liter. For example, a decrease in serum potassium from 3 mEq/liter to 2 mEq/liter in a 70 kg adult is associated with a total deficit of 600 mEq, or 8.5 mEq/kg body weight.[3] When the serum potassium decreases below 2 mEq/liter, it becomes difficult to estimate the total body deficit.[3]

Potassium chloride is used to treat potassium deficiency associated with metabolic alkalosis, because of the frequent association of chloride deficiency with this disorder.[117,130,157] Potassium bicarbonate and potassium citrate are used to treat potassium deficiency associated with metabolic acidosis, such as the hypokalemia of renal tubular acidosis. Commercial preparations of potassium salts are listed in Table 4-8. When oral potassium supplementation raises the serum potassium concentration to 3.5 mEq/liter, supplements may be decreased and the need for supplementation reassessed.

Intravenous potassium administration may be required when hypokalemia is severe; this may be the case when the serum potassium is less than 2 mEq/liter, causing a ventricular arrhythmia or paralysis with or without involvement of the muscles of respiration. Electrocardiographic evidence of severe hypokalemia is an acute emergency requiring intravenous potassium supplementation.[90] Intravenous potassium chloride replacement is also indicated immediately after an operation, when oral potassium administration is not possible. The usual recommendation is that the administered potassium concentration not exceed 40 mEq/liter of intravenous solution, and that it should be given over one hour.[3] In an emergency, a potassium chloride solution containing as much as 100 mEq/liter of potassium may be used, but it should be given slowly over two hours. Ideally, it is better to give no more than 0.75 mEq of potassium per kg of body weight per one to two hours.[2,3] Solutions containing glucose should not be used in the initial treatment of hypokalemia because they stimulate insulin secretion, which may worsen the hypokalemia by increasing the cellular uptake of potassium. Electrocardiographic monitoring should be performed every 15 minutes during intravenous administration of potassium chloride. Because of the complication of phlebitis following the infusion of potassium into a peripheral vein,[2,3] it may be preferable, in an emergency situation, to insert two intravenous lines or to use a large vein such as a femoral vein to deliver the potassium chloride supplementation. The subclavian or jugular veins should probably not be used for the infusion of highly concentrated solutions of potassium because of their proximity to the heart. It is also important to monitor urinary output during the infusion of potassium, since hyperkalemia may be produced if the urine flow decreases.

Specific Treatment of Hypokalemia

Specific treatment of the disorders that produce hypokalemia is summarized in Table 4-9.

Treatment of hypokalemic periodic paralysis with acetazolamide, 250 to 750 mg/day, has been found to decrease the frequency and severity of attacks.[110] Triamterene, 100 to 200 mg/day has also been used successfully.

In renal tubular acidosis, type 1, administration of 50 to 100 mEq/day of bicarbonate may be sufficient to maintain serum carbon dioxide content within the normal

Table 4-8. Potassium Salts

Potassium chloride
   Tablets: K-Dur (Key), 20 mEq/tablet
   Powder: Kato (ICN Pharmaceutical), 20 mEq/4 g packet
   Solution: Kaochlor (Adria), 20 mEq/15 ml
Potassium bicarbonate
   Tablets: Urocit-K (Mission), 5 mEq/tablet
   Effervescent tablets: K-lyte (Bristol), 25 mEq/tablet in solution

Table 4-9. Treatment of Specific Hypokalemic Disorders

Condition	Treatment
Redistribution	Self-limiting
Periodic paralysis	Acetazolamide 25–750 mg/day or triamterene 100–200 mg/day
Insufficient intake or gastrointestinal loss	Supplementation as described
Renal loss	
Renal tubular acidosis	Potassium bicarbonate 50–100 mEq/day
Bartter's syndrome	Potassium chloride 80–160 mEq/day
	Magnesium chloride 30–60 mEq/day
	Triamterene 50–100 mg/day or
	Amiloride 10–20 mg/day
Magnesium-losing tubulopathy	Magnesium chloride 30–60 mEq/day
Calcium-losing tubulopathy	Ibuprofen 800–1200 mg/day
Aldosterone-producing adenoma	Spironolactone or adrenalectomy
Idiopathic hyperaldosteronism	Nifedipine 30 mg/day
	Enalapril 10–20 mg/day
Dexamethasone-suppressible aldosteronism	Amiloride 5–20 mg/day or
	Triamterene 50–200 mg/day
Congenital adrenal hyperplasia	Hydrocortisone
11-Beta-hydroxysteroid dehydrogenase deficiency	Spironolactone
Liddle's syndrome	Amiloride 5–20 mg/day or
	Triamterene 50–200 mg/day

range. This is most readily achieved by treatment with potassium bicarbonate (K-lyte, see Table 4-8). In the case of renal tubular acidosis, type 2, more bicarbonate, 5 to 15 mEq/kg/day, may be required to restore plasma carbon dioxide content to normal. Since children will not grow normally unless the acidosis is corrected, the optimal dose of bicarbonate should be determined. A more detailed discussion of the management of renal tubular acidosis is presented in Chapter 1.

Treatment of Bartter's syndrome requires the administration of sufficient amounts of supplemental potassium and, in those patients with hypomagnesemia, magnesium to control the symptoms of weakness and tiredness and to foster normal growth and development.[161] In some patients this objective may be achieved by giving supplements of potassium, 80 to 160 mEq/day given in three or four divided doses, as the chloride salt (see Table 4-8). Magnesium, 30 to 60 mEq/day given in three or four divided doses, is usually adequate supplementation for those patients with hypomagnesemia. If these dosages of potassium and magnesium are not sufficient to control symptoms, then a potassium-sparing diuretic such as amiloride, 5 to 10 mg, or triamterene, 50 to 100 mg, once or twice a day, may be added. The foregoing regimen is usually adequate for most patients but an occasional patient may require the addition of a prostaglandin synthetase inhibitor such as ibuprofen, 400 to 800 mg, two to three times a day.[161]

The hypomagnesemia and hypokalemia of magnesium-losing tubulopathy are treated by supplements of magnesium and potassium as specified for Bartter's syndrome. Occasionally it may be possible to correct the hypokalemia by magnesium supplements alone. Since magnesium-losing tubulopathy is usually a mild disorder, supplements of magnesium and potassium are all that is required.

Treatment of patients with calcium-losing tubulopathy with a prostaglandin synthetase inhibitor produces marked improvement.[128,161] Ibuprofen, 400 to 600 mg twice daily, decreases the hypercalciuria and improves the polydipsia and polyuria. Hyperreninemia is corrected and leads to a correction of hypokalemia and resumption of normal growth and development. Gastrointestinal side effects may occasionally complicate this very effective therapy.

The optimum treatment for aldosterone-producing adenoma is operative removal of the adrenal gland containing it. This procedure cures the hypertension and hypokalemia in about 80 percent of these patients. Many of those patients who remain hypertensive postoperatively have a family history of hypertension and respond readily to antihypertensive medication. Those patients who are unwilling or unable to undergo an adrenalectomy may be treated with spironolactone, an aldosterone antagonist. Although spironolactone may be very effective therapy, its side effects of mastodynia, gynecomastia, and decreased libido in men, and menometrorrhagia and mastodynia in women may be distressing.

Idiopathic hyperaldosteronism, in most instances, is not cured by adrenalectomy. Nifedipine, 10 mg three times a day, lowers blood pressure and may also decrease aldosterone production.[162] If hypokalemia persists, a potassium-sparing diuretic such as amiloride, 5 mg twice a day, or triamterene, 25 to 100 mg twice a day, may be added. A few patients have been successfully treated with enalapril 10 to 20 mg/day.

The overproduction of mineralocorticoids in dexamethasone-suppressible hyperaldosteronism may be corrected by treatment with dexamethasone. Since the excessive steroid production is an abnormal adrenal response to normal plasma adrenocorticotropin, the effect of dexamethasone is to suppress adrenocorticotropin to subnormal values. Alternatively, administration of triamterene or amiloride (usually 5 to 10 mg per day of the latter drug is sufficient to control blood pressure and prevent hypokalemia) avoids the blunting of the hypothalamic-pituitary axis associated with dexamethasone.

Treatment of congenital adrenal hyperplasia due to deficiency of either 11-β-hydroxylase or of 17-α-hydroxylase is accomplished by providing the hydrocortisone that patients with these enzyme deficiencies cannot secrete. Administration of hydrocortisone restores secretion of adrenocorticotropin to normal, thereby correcting the overproduction of mineralocorticoids. The dose of hydrocortisone is determined by whether the patient is an infant, child, or adult.

Deficiency of 11-β-hydroxysteroid dehydrogenase may be successfully treated by spionolactone, 50 to 200 mg/day. The dose is determined by the amount of antagonist required to correct hypokalemia and to lower blood pressure to normal. Those patients whose deficiency of 11-β-hydroxysteroid dehydrogenase results from ingestion of licorice may be treated by stopping the licorice.

Liddle's syndrome responds readily to amiloride, 5 to 20 mg per day, or triamterene, 50 to 200 mg/day. These medications correct the hypokalemia and usually lower blood pressure to normal.

REFERENCES

1. Lum G, Gambino SR: A comparison of serum versus heparinized plasma for routine chemistry tests. Am J Clin Pathol 61:108, 1974
2. Sterns RH, Cox M, Fieg PV, et al: Internal potassium balance and the control of the plasma potassium concentration. Medicine 60:339, 1981

3. Tannen RL: Potassium disorders. p. 150. In Kokko JP, Tannen RL (eds): Fluids and Electrolytes. WB Saunders, Philadelphia, 1986
4. Guyton AC: Textbook of Medical Physiology. 7th Ed. WB Saunders, Philadelphia, 1973
5. Pollen RH, Williams RH: Hyperkalemic neuromyopathy in Addison's disease. N Engl J Med 263:273, 1960
6. Levitt LP, Rose LI, Dawson DM: Hypokalemic periodic paralysis with arrhythmia. N Engl J Med 286:253, 1972
7. Brenner BM, Berliner RW: The transport of potassium. p. 497. In Orloff J, Berliner RW (eds): Renal Physiology. American Physiological Society, Washington, DC, 1973
8. Stanton BA, Biemesderfer D, Wade JB, et al: Structural and functional study of the rat distal nephron: Effects of potassium adaptation and depletion. Kidney Int 19:36, 1981
9. Stokes JB: Consequences of potassium recycling in the renal medulla. Effects on ion transport by the medullary thick ascending limb of Henle's loop. J Clin Invest 70:219, 1982
10. Seldin D, Welt L, Cort J: The role of sodium salts and adrenal steroids in the production of hypokalemic alkalosis. Yale J Biol Med 29:229, 1956.
11. George JM, Wright L, Bell NH, et al: The syndrome of primary aldosteronism. Am J Med 48:343, 1970
12. Duarte CG, Chomety F, Giebisch G: Effect of amiloride, ouabain, and furosemide on distal tubular function in the rat. Am J Physiol 221:632, 1971
13. Giebisch G, Malnic G, Klose RM, et al: Effect of ionic substitutions on distal tubular potential differences in rat kidney. Am J Physiol 211:560, 1966
14. Lipner HI, Ruzany F, Dasgupta M, et al: The behavior of carbenicillin as a nonreabsorbable anion. J Lab Clin Med 86:183, 1975
15. Garcia-Filho E, Malnic G, Giebisch G: Effects of changes in electrical potential difference on tubular potassium transport. Am J Physiol 238:F235, 1980
16. DeFronzo RA: Hyperkalemia and hyporeninemic hypoaldosteronism. Kidney Int 17:118, 1980
17. Gonick HD, Kleeman HC, Rubini ME, et al: Functional impairment in chronic renal disease. III: Studies of potassium excretion. Am J Med Sci 218:281, 1971
18. Reza MJ, Kovick RB, Shine KI, et al: Massive intravenous digoxin overdosage. N Engl J Med 291:777, 1974
19. DeFronzo RA, Bia M, Birkhead G: Epinephrine and potassium homeostasis. Kidney Int 20:83, 1981
20. Cox M, Sterns RH, Singer I: The defense against hyperkalemia: The roles of insulin and aldosterone. N Engl J Med 299:525, 1978
21. Minaker KL, Rowe JW: Potassium homeostasis during hyperinsulinemia: Effect of insulin level, β-blockade, and age. Am J Physiol 242:E373, 1982
22. DeFronzo RA, Lee R, Jones A, et al: Effect of insulinopenia and adrenal hormone deficiency on acute potassium tolerance. Kidney Int 17:586, 1980
23. Gerstein AR, Kleeman CR, Gold EM, et al: Aldosterone deficiency in chronic renal failure. Nephron 5:90, 1968
24. Alexander EA, Perrone RD: Regulation of extrarenal potassium metabolism. p. 105. In Maxwell MH, Kleeman CR, Narins RG (eds): Clinical Disorders of Fluid and Electrolyte Metabolism. McGraw-Hill, New York, 1987
25. Hayslett JP, Binder HJ: Mechanism of potassium adaptation. Am J Physiol 243:F103, 1982
26. Bartter FC, Fourman P: The different effects of aldosterone-like steroids on urinary excretion of potassium and acid. Metabolism 11:6, 1962
27. Shoemaker WC, Finder AG: Relation of potassium and glucose release from the liver in the unanesthetized dog. Proc Soc Exp Biol Med 108:248, 1961
28. Pettit GW, Vick RL, Kastello MD, et al: The contribution of renal and extra-renal mechanisms to hypokalemia induced by glucagon. Eur J Pharmacol 41:437, 1976
29. Asano Y: Increased cell membrane permeability to Na^+ and K^+ induced by thyroid hormone in rat skeletal muscle. Experientia 32:199, 1978

30. Ismail-Beigin F, Edelman IS: Mechanisms of thyroid calorigenesis: Role of active sodium transport. Proc Natl Acad Aci USA 67:1071, 1970
31. Elliot DA, Cheek DB: Muscle electrolyte patterns during growth. p. 260. In Cheek DB (ed): Human Growth. Lea & Febiger, Philadelphia, 1968
32. Satoyoski E, Murakami K, Kowa H, et al: Myopathy in thyrotoxicosis. Neurology 13:645, 1963
33. Bunner DL, Lewis UJ, Vanderlaan WP, et al: Comparative potency of subtilisin-cleaved and intact human growth hormone measured in growth hormone-deficient human subjects. J Clin Endocrinol Metab 48:293, 1979
34. Henneman PH, Forbes AP, Moldawer M, et al: Effects of human growth hormone in man. J Clin Invest 39:1223, 1960
35. Batts AA, Bennett LL, Garcia J, et al: The effect of growth hormone on muscle potassium and on extracellular fluid. Endocrinology 55:456, 1954
36. Zierler KL, Rabinowitz D: Roles of insulin and growth hormone, based on studies of forearm metabolism in man. Medicine 42:385, 1983
37. Knochel JP, Schlein EM: On the mechanism of rhabdomyolysis in potassium depletion. J Clin Invest 51:1750, 1972
38. Williams ME, Gervino EV, Rosa RM, et al: Catecholamine modulation of rapid potassium shifts during exercise. N Engl J Med 312:823, 1985
39. Lim M, Linton RAF, Wolff CB, et al: Propranolol, exercise and arterial plasma potassium. Lancet 2:591, 1981
40. Brown JJ, Chinn RH, Davies DL, et al: Falsely high plasma potassium values in patients with hyperaldosteronism. Br Med J 2:18, 1970
41. Weffer MI, Mijais SK, Johnson KK, et al: Effect of uremia on Na-K-ATPase in the rat red cell. (Abstr) Kidney Int 33:387, 1988
42. Menkoff L, Gaerther G, Darab M, et al: Inhibition of brain sodium-potassium ATPase in uremic rat. J Lab Clin Med 80:71, 1972
43. Chan JCM, Goplerud JM, Papadopoulou ZL, et al: Kidney failure in childhood. Int J Pediatr Nephrol 2:201, 1981
44. Perez GO, Oster JR, Vaamonde CA: Serum potassium concentration in edematous states. Nephron 27:233, 1981
45. Adrogue HJ, Medias NE: Changes in plasma potassium concentration during acute acid-base disturbances. Am J Med 71:456, 1981
46. Moreno M, Murphy C, Goldsmith C: Increase in serum potassium resulting from the administration of hypertonic mannitol and other solutions. J Lab Clin Med 73:291, 1969
47. Nicolis GL, Kahn T, Sauchez A, et al: Glucose-induced hyperkalemia in diabetic subjects. Arch Intern Med 141:48, 1981
48. Doucet A, Katz AI: Renal potassium adaptation: Na-K-ATPase activity along the nephron after chronic potassium loading. Am J Physiol 238:F380, 1980
49. Silva P, Hayslett JP, Epstein FH: The role of Na-K-activated adenosine triphosphatase in potassium adaptation: stimulation of enzymatic activity by potassium loading. J Clin Invest 52:2665, 1973
50. Hayes CP, Jr., Robinson RR: Fecal potassium excretion in patients on chronic intermittent hemodialysis. Trans Am Soc Artif Intern Organs 11:242, 1965
51. Stewart GW, Corrall RJM, Fyffe JA, et al: Familial pseudohyperkalemia: a new syndrome. Lancet 2:175, 1979
52. Ho-Yen DO, Pennington CR: Pseudohyperkalemia and infectious mononucleosis. Postgrad Med 56:435, 1980
53. Bluemle LW, Webster GD, Elkington JR: Acute tubular necrosis: analysis of one hundred cases with respect to mortality, complications, and treatment with and without dialysis. Arch Intern Med 104:180, 1959
54. Schrier RW, Regal EM: Influence of aldosterone on sodium, water and potassium metabolism in chronic renal disease. Kidney Int 1:156, 1972
55. Schultze RG, Taggart DD, Shapiro H, et al: On the adaptation in potassium secretion associated with nephron reduction in the dog. J Clin Invest 50:1061, 1971
56. Gonick HC, Kleeman CR, Rubin ME, et al: Functional impairment in chronic renal disease: Studies of potassium excretion. Am J Med Sci 261:281, 1971

57. Anderson HM, Laragh JH: Renal excretion of potassium in normal and sodium depleted dogs. J Clin Invest 37:323, 1958
58. Tannen RL: Relationship of renal ammonia production and potassium homeostasis. Kidney Int 11:453, 1977
59. Kurtzman NA, White MG, Rogers PW: The effect of potassium and extracellular volume on renal bicarbonate reabsorption. Metabolism 22:481, 1973
60. Alon U, Kodroff MB, Broecker BH, et al: Renal tubular acidosis type 4 in neonatal unilateral kidney diseases. J Pediatrics 104:855, 1984
61. Nerup J: Addison's disease—Clinical studies. A report of 108 cases. Acta Endocrinol 76:127, 1974
62. Veldhuis JD, Kulin HE, Santen RJ, et al: Inborn error in the terminal step of aldosterone biosynthesis corticosterone methyloxidase type II deficiency in a North American pedigree. N Engl J Med 303:117, 1980
63. Schambelan M, Sebastian A, Biglieri E: Prevalence, pathogenesis, and functional significance of aldosterone deficiency in hyperkalemic patients with chronic renal insufficiency. Kidney Int 17:89, 1980
64. Tan SY, Burton M: Hyporeninemic hypoaldosteronism: an overlooked cause of hyperkalemia. Arch Intern Med 141:30, 1981
65. DeFronzo RA: Hyperkalemic states. p. 547. In Maxwell MH, Kleeman CR, Narins RG (eds): Clinical Disorders of Fluid and Electrolyte Metabolism. McGraw-Hill, New York, 1987
66. Brentjens JR, Sepulveda M, Baliah T, et al: Interstitial immune complex nephritis in patients with systemic lupus erythematosus. Kidney Int 7:342, 1975
67. Timins JE, Hariprasad MK: Isolated hypoaldosteronism with nephrogenic diabetes insipidus and renal amyloidosis. Nephron 30:93, 1982
68. Morgan JM: Hyperkalemia and acidosis in lead nephropathy. South Med J 69:881, 1976
69. Rado JP, Szende L, Szucs L: Hyperkalemia unresponsive to massive doses of aldosterone and renal tubular acidosis in a patient with chronic interstitial nephritis. Clinical and experimental studies. J Med 7:481, 1976
70. Oberfield SE, Levine LS, Carey RM, et al: Pseudohypoaldosteronism: Multiple target organ unresponsiveness to mineralocorticoids. J Clin Endocrinol Metab 48:288, 1979
71. Schambelan M, Sebastian A, Rector FC Jr.: Mineralocorticoid-resistant renal hyperkalemia without salt wasting (type II pseudohypoaldosteronism): Role of increased renal chloride reabsorption. Kidney Int 19:716, 1981
72. Batlle DC, Arruda JAC, Kurtzman NA: Hyperkalemic distal renal tubular acidosis associated with obstructive uropathy. N Engl J Med 304:373, 1981
73. Atlas SA, Case DB, Sealey JE, et al: Interruption of the renin-angiotensin system in hypertensive patients by captopril induces sustained reduction in aldosterone secretion, potassium retention and natriuresis. Hypertension 1:274, 1979
74. Tan SY, Shapiro R, Franco R, et al: Indomethacin-induced prostaglandin inhibition with hyperkalemia. Ann Intern Med 90:783, 1979
75. Schlatmann RJH, Jansen AP, Presner H, et al: A natriuretic and aldosterone-suppressive action of heparin and some related polysulfated polysaccharides. J Clin Endocrinol Metab 24:25, 1960
76. O'Kelly R, Magee F, McKenna TJ: Routine heparin therapy inhibits adrenal aldosterone production. J Clin Endocrinol Metab 56:108, 1983
77. Adu D, Turney J, Michael J, et al: Hyperkalemia in cyclosporine-treated renal allograft recipients. Lancet 2:370, 1983
78. Makoff DL, Da Silva JA, Rosenbaum BJ, et al: Hypertonic expansion: acid base and electrolyte changes. Am J Physiol 218:1201, 1970
79. Gamstrop I, Hauge M, Helweg-Larsen F, et al: Adynamic episodica hereditaria: a disease clinically resembling familial periodic paralysis but characterized by increasing serum potassium during the paralytic attacks. Am J Med 23:385, 1957
80. Pearson CM, Kalyanaraman K: Periodic paralysis. p. 1496. In Stanbury JB, Wyngaarden JB, Frederickson DS (eds): The

Metabolic Basis of Inherited Disease. McGraw-Hill, New York, 1972
81. Lordon RE, Burton JR: Post-traumatic renal failure in military personnel in Southeast Asia. Am J Med 53:137, 1972
82. Arseneau JC, Bagley CM, Anderson T, et al: Hyperkalemia, a sequel to chemotherapy of Burkitt's lymphoma. Lancet 1:10, 1973
83. Fortner RW, Nowakowski A, Carter CB, et al: Death due to overheated dialysate during dialysis. Ann Intern Med 73:443, 1970
84. Birch AA, Jr., Mitchell GD, Playford GA, et al: Changes in serum potassium response to succinylcholine following trauma. JAMA 210:490, 1969
85. Lawson DH: Adverse reactions to potassium chloride. Q J Med 43:433, 1974
86. Le Veen HH, Posternack HS, Lustrin I, et al: Hemorrhage and transfusion as the major cause of cardiac arrest. JAMA 173:770, 1960
87. Gelfand MC, Zarate A, Knepshield JH: Geophagia: A cause of life-threatening hyperkalemia in patients with chronic renal failure. JAMA 234:738, 1975
88. Daughaday WH, Rendleman D: Severe symptomatic hyperkalemia in an adrenalectomized woman due to enhanced mineralocorticoid requirement. Ann Intern Med 66:1197, 1967
89. Fuich CA, Sawyer CG, Flynn JM: Clinical syndrome of potassium intoxication. Am J Med 1:337, 1946
90. Surawicz B: Relationship between electrocardiogram and electrolytes. Am Heart J 73:814, 1967
91. Kumar AM, Gupta RJ, Spitzer A: Intracellular sodium in proximal tubules of diabetic rats. Role of glucose. Kidney Int 33:792, 1988
92. Abrams WB, Lewis DW, Bullet S: The effect of acidosis and alkalosis on the plasma potassium concentration and the electrocardiogram in normal and potassium depleted dogs. Am J Med Sci 222:506, 1951
93. Surawicz B, Chlebus H, Mazzoleni A: Hemodynamic and electrocardiographic effects of hyperpotassemia. Differences in response to slow and rapid increases in concentration of plasma K. Am Heart J 73:647, 1967
94. Levinsky N: Management of emergencies: VI. Hyperkalemia. N Engl J Med 274:1076, 1966
95. Garcia-Palmieri MR: Removal of hyperkalemic cardiotoxicity with hypertonic saline. Am Heart J 64:483, 1962
96. Ballantyne F III, Davis D, Reynolds EW Jr: Cellular basis for reversal of hyperkalemic electrocardiographic changes by sodium. Am J Physiol 229:935, 1975
97. Fraley DS, Adler S: Correction of hyperkalemia by bicarbonate despite constant blood pH. Kidney Int 12:354, 1977
98. Winter JSD: Current approaches to treatment of congenital adrenal hyperplasia. J Pediatr 97:81, 1980
99. Wang P, Clausen T: Treatment of attacks in hyperkalemic familial periodic paralysis by inhalation of salbutanol. Lancet 1:221, 1976
100. Sebastian A, McSherry E, Morris RC: Renal potassium wasting in renal tubular acidosis (RTA): Its occurrence in types 1 and 2 RTA despite sustained correction of systemic acidosis. J Clin Invest 50:667, 1971
101. Bia MJ, Defronzo RA: Extrarenal potassium homeostasis. Am J Physiol 240:F257, 1981
102. Hurlbert BJ, Edelman JD, David K: Serum potassium levels during and after terbutaline. Anesth Analg 60:723, 1981
103. Wetherill SF, Guarino MJ, Cox RW: Acute renal failure associated with barium chloride poisoning. Ann Intern Med 95:187, 1981.
104. Bennett RH, Foreman HR: Hypokalemic periodic paralysis in chronic toluene exposure. Arch Neurol 37:673, 1980
105. Mir MA, Brabin B, Tang OT, et al: Hypokalemia in acute myeloid leukemia. Ann Intern Med 82:54, 1975
106. Hesp R, Chanarin I, Tait CE: Potassium changes in megaloblastic anemia. Clin Sci Mol Med 49:77, 1975
107. Koht A, Cerullo LJ, Land PC, et al: Serum potassium levels during prolonged hypothermia. Anesthesiology 51(suppl):S203, 1979
108. Pudeny RH, McIntosh JF, McEachern D: The role of potassium in familial periodic paralysis. JAMA 111:2253, 1938

109. Talbott JH: Periodic paralysis. A clinical syndrome. Medicine (Baltimore) 20:85, 1941
110. Griggs RC, Engel WK, Resnick JS: Acetazolamide treatment of hypokalemic periodic paralysis. Prevention of attacks and improvement of persistent weakness. Ann Intern Med 73:39, 1970
111. Zierler KL, Andres R: Movement of potassium into skeletal muscle during spontaneous attacks in familial periodic paralysis. J Clin Invest 36:730, 1957
112. Knochel JP, Dotin LN, Hamburger RJ: Pathophysiology of intense physical conditioning in a hot climate. I. Mechanism of potassium depletion. J Clin Invest 51:242, 1972
113. Sebastian A, McSherry E, Morris RC: On the mechanism of renal potassium wasting in renal tubular acidosis associated with Fanconi syndrome (Type II RTA). J Clin Invest 50:231, 1971
114. Gill JR Jr, Bell NH, Bartter FC: Impaired conservation of sodium and potassium in renal tubular acidosis and its correction by buffer anions. Clin Sci 33:577, 1967
115. Godard C, Vallotton MD, Broter M, Roger P: A study of the inhibition of the renin-angiotensin system in renal potassium wasting syndromes, including Bartter's syndrome. Helv Paediatr Acta 27:495, 1972
116. Meyer WJ, III, Gill JR, Jr, Bartter FC: Gout as a complication of Bartter's syndrome. Ann Intern Med 83:56, 1975
117. Gill JR Jr, Bartter FC: Evidence for a prostaglandin-independent defect in chloride reabsorption in the loop of Henle as a proximal cause of Bartter's syndrome. Am J Med 65:766, 1978
118. Shareghi SR, Agus ZS: Magnesium transport in the cortical thick ascending limb of Henle's loop of the rabbit. J Clin Invest 69:759, 1982
119. Rubin A, Sjögren B, Aurell M: Low urinary calcium in Bartter's syndrome. N Engl J Med 310:1190, 1984
120. Galvez OG, Bay WH, Roberts BW, et al: The hemodynamic effects of potassium deficiency in the dog. Circ Res 40 (Suppl I); 1-11, 1977
121. Gullner H-G, Graf AK, Gill JR Jr, et al: Hypokalemia stimulates prostacyclin synthesis in the rat. Clin Sci 65:43, 1983
122. Fujita T, Ando K, Sato Y, et al: Independent roles of prostaglandins and the renin and angiotensin system in abnormal vascular reactivity in Bartter's syndrome. Am J Med 73:71, 1982
123. Sasaki H, Okumura M, Asano T, et al: Responses to angiotensin II antagonist before and after treatment with indomethacin in Bartter's syndrome. Br Med J 2:975, 1977
124. Gullner H-G, Gill JR Jr, Bartter FC, et al: Correction of increased sympathoadrenal activity in Bartter's syndrome by inhibition of prostaglandin synthesis. J Clin Endocrinol Metab 50:857, 1980
125. Bartter FC, Gill JR Jr, Frolich JL, et al: Prostaglandins are overproduced by the kidneys and mediate hyperreninemia in Bartter's syndrome. Trans Assoc Am Phys 89:77, 1976
126. Bowden RE, Gill JR Jr, Radfar N, et al: Prostaglandin synthetase inhibitors in Bartter's syndrome. JAMA 239:117, 1978
127. McCredie DA, Rotenbert E, Williams AC: Hypercalciuria in potassium-losing nephropathy: A variant of Bartter's syndrome. Aust Paediatr J 10:286, 1974
128. Seyberth HW, Rascher W, Schweer H, et al: Congenital hypokalemia with hypercalciuria in preterm infants: A hyperprostaglandinuric tubular syndrome different from Bartter's syndrome. J Pediatr 107:694, 1985
129. Gill JR Jr: Prostaglandins in Bartter's syndrome and in potassium-deficient disorders that mimic it. Miner Electrolyte Metab 6:76, 1981
130. Kassirer JP, Schwartz WB: Correction of metabolic alkalosis in man without repair of potassium deficiency: a re-evaluation of the role of potassium. Am J Med 40:19, 1966
131. Schrock LG, Polk HC Jr: Rectal villous adenomas producing hypokalemia. Am J Surg 40:54, 1974
132. Chisholm JL: Zollinger-Ellison syndrome: intermittent diarrhea, relentless hypokalemia and hypergastrinemia. J Natl Med Assoc 73:1151, 1981

133. Trump DL, Livingstone JN, Baylin SB: Watery diarrhea syndrome in an adult with ganglioneuroma-pheochromocytoma. Cancer 40:1526, 1977
134. Campbell JM, Hunt TK, Karam JH, et al: Jejunoileal bypass as a treatment of morbid obesity. Arch Intern Med 137:602, 1977
135. Basser LS: Purgative and periodic paralysis. Med J Aust 1:47, 1979
136. Foreman JW, Baluarte HJ, Gruskin AB: Hypokalemia after hypertonic phosphate enemas. J Pediatr 94:149, 1979
137. Holmberg C, Perheentura J, Launiala K, et al: Congenital chloride diarrhea. Arch Dis Child 52:255, 1977
138. Carey RW, Sen S: Recent progress in the control of aldosterone secretion. Recent Prog Horm Res 42:251, 1986
139. Gill JR Jr, Bartter FC: Overproduction of sodium-retaining steroids by the zona glomerulosa is adrenocorticotropic-dependent and mediates hypertension in dexamethasone-suppressible aldosteronism. J Clin Endocrinol Metab 53:331, 1981
140. Gomez-Sanchez CE, Gill JR, Jr., Ganguly A, et al: Glucocorticoid-suppressible aldosteronism: A disorder of the adrenal transitional ion. J Clin Endocrinol Metab 67:444, 1988
141. DiMartino-Mardi J, Stoner E, Martin K, et al: New findings in apparent mineralocorticoid excess. J Clin Endocrinol Metab 27:49, 1987
142. Stewart PM, Valentino R, Wallace AM, et al: Mineralocorticoid activity of liquorice: 11-beta-hydroxysteroid dehydrogenase deficiency comes of age. Lancet 2:821, 1987
143. Liddle GW, Bledsoe T, Coppage WS Jr: A familial renal disorder simulating primary aldosteronism but with negligible aldosterone secretion. Trans Assoc Am Phys 76:199, 1963
144. Simon N, Franklin SS, Bleifer KH, et al: Clinical characteristics of renovascular hypertension. JAMA 220:1209, 1972
145. Brown JJ, Lever AF, Robertson JIS, et al: Hypertension and secondary hyperaldosteronism associated with a renin secreting renal juxtaglomerular-cell tumor. Ann Intern Med 79:835, 1973
146. Ganguly A, Gribble J, Tune B, et al: Renin-secreting Wilms' tumor with severe hypertension: report of a case and brief review of renin-secreting tumors. Ann Intern Med 79:835, 1973
147. Dahl T, Eide I, Fryjordet A: Hypernephroma and hypertension: two case reports. Acta Med Scand 209:121, 1981
148. Bilbrey GL, Herbin L, Caster NW, et al: Skeletal muscle resting membrane potential in potassium deficiency. J Clin Invest 52:3011, 1973
149. Tanner RL: Potassium and blood pressure control. Ann Intern Med 98:773–780, 1983
150. Paller MS, Douglas JG, Linas SL: Mechanism of decreased vascular reactivity to angiotensin II in conscious, potassium-deficient rats. J Clin Invest 73:79, 1984
151. Carney P, Stubbs W, Fitchett D, et al: Ventricular arrhythmias and hypokalemia. Lancet 2:231, 1976
152. Boley SJ, Schultz L, Kreiger M, et al: Experimental evaluation of thiazide and potassium as a cause of small bowel ulcer. JAMA 192:763, 1965
153. Hollifield JW, Staton PE: Thiazide diuretics, hypokalemia and cardiac arrhythmias. Acta Med Scand 647:67, 1981
154. Manitus A, Levitin H, Beck D, et al: On the mechanism of impairment of renal concentrating ability in potassium deficiency. J Clin Invest 39:684, 1960
155. Relman AS, Schwartz WB: The kidney in potassium depletion. Am J Med 24:764, 1958
156. Tanner RL: Relationship of renal ammonia production and potassium homeostasis. Kidney Int 11:453, 1977
157. Gariella S, Chazan JA, Cohen JJ: Saline-resistant metabolic alkalosis or chloride-wasting nephropathy. Ann Intern Med 73:31, 1970
158. Podolsky S, Zimmerman HJ, Burrows BA, et al: Potassium depletion in hepatic cirrhosis: a reversible cause of impaired growth hormone and insulin response to stimulation. N Engl J Med 288:644, 1973
159. Manchester KL: Insulin and protein synthesis. p. 267. In Litwack G (ed): Biochemical Actions of Hormones. Vol. 1. Academic Press, New York, 1970
160. McKenna TJ, Island DP, Nicholson WE,

et al: The effects of potassium on early and late steps in aldosterone biosynthesis in cells of the zona glomerulosa. Endocrinology 103:1034, 1978
161. Gill JR Jr: Bartter's syndrome. p. 153. In: Krieger DT, Bardin CW (eds): Current Therapy in Endocrinology and Metabolism 1988–1989. CV Mosby, St. Louis, 1988
162. Nadler JL, Hsueh W, Horton R: Therapeutic effects of calcium channel blockade in primary aldosteronism. J Clin Endocrinol Metab 60:896, 1985

5

Disorders of Calcium Metabolism

Gad Kainer
James C.M. Chan
Norman H. Bell

Calcium is the most abundant mineral in the body. Over 99 percent of total body calcium is in the skeleton and the remainder is in cells and in extracellular fluid (ECF). In a 70 kg man, 1.3 kg of calcium is present in the skeleton as hydroxyapatite [$Ca_{10}(PO_4)_6(OH)_2$], octacalcium phosphate, and amorphous calcium phosphate; 4.3 g is intracellular; and 1.3 g is extracellular.[1,2] Bone mineral is initially deposited as amorphous calcium phosphate that is then converted to hydroxyapatite.

Under normal circumstances, the concentration of serum ionized calcium is maintained within the narrow physiologic limits of 4.4 to 5.2 mg/dl or 1.1 to 1.3 mM. The normal range for serum total calcium is 8.8 to 10.4 mg/dl or 2.2 to 2.6 mM. Variations in the concentration of serum total calcium measured in normal individuals may occur because of differences in serum albumin concentration and state of hydration, and differences in techniques of blood collection and sample handling.[3,4] Elevations in serum calcium of as much as 1.5 mg/dl have been observed after prolonged use of a tourniquet.[5]

Approximately 45 percent of the calcium in serum is bound to plasma proteins and the rest is non-protein-bound or diffusible.[6-11] Of the protein-bound calcium, from 75 to 90 percent is bound to albumin.[7] Globulin binds only a small amount of calcium, from 0.2 to 0.3 mg calcium per gram of globulin (Fig 5-1.). The affinity of albumin for calcium is relatively constant in most diseases,[12,13] but increases with severe hypoalbuminemia, such as sometimes occurs in the nephrotic syndrome.[14] The affinity of plasma proteins for calcium increases with hyponatremia and decreases with hypernatremia.[15] Calcium binding to albumin declines with a reduction in serum pH,[16-18] so that a decrease in pH of 0.1 causes a rise of 0.1 mEq/liter in the concentration of serum ionized calcium.[6] Conversely, a fall in the concentration of serum albumin by 1.0 g/dl produces a decrease in total serum calcium of from 0.8 to 1.0 mg/dl, but the fraction of ionized calcium remains relatively stable.[19]

Approximately 95 percent of diffusible calcium in the ECF is in the form of calcium ions. Most of the remainder is complexed with bicarbonate, phosphate, citrate, and acetate.[20,21] The physiochemical state of calcium in urine is different from that in plasma. Some 28 percent is complexed to

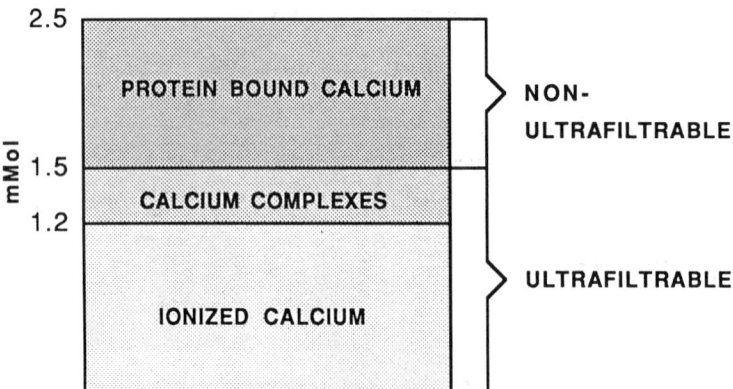

Fig. 5-1. Distribution of calcium in plasma. (Modified from Marx SJ, and Bourdeau JE: Calcium metabolism. Ch 11, p. 208. In Maxwell MH, Kleeman CR, Narins RG (eds): Clinical Disorders of Fluid and Electrolyte Metabolism. 4th Ed. McGraw-Hill, New York, 1987, with permission.)

citrate, 12 percent to sulphates, and 9 percent to phosphate.[22] In the skeleton, most of the calcium does not exchange with calcium in ECF. However, a small "pool" of amorphous calcium phosphate and new and incompletely formed hydroxyapatite crystals participates in the rapid exchange of calcium.[23-25] The concentration of hydrogen ion is an important factor in determining the solubility of hydroxyapatite. Additional characteristics at the crystalline surface exert important limitations on ionic fluxes.[26]

Normally, some 400 mg of calcium are exchanged between the skeleton and ECF compartment each day. The net intestinal absorption of calcium from dietary sources is between 150 and 200 mg/day.[27] In the kidney, although 10 mg/min or 14,400 mg/day of calcium is filtered by the glomerulus, only 1 to 1.5 percent of the filtered calcium is excreted; 60 percent of the remainder is reabsorbed in the proximal tubule, 20 percent in the loop of Henle, and 20 percent in the distal nephron. Reabsorption of calcium in the distal tubule is regulated by parathyroid hormone (PTH)[28,29] (Fig. 5-2).

The skeleton, kidneys, and small intestine are the major organs involved in calcium homeostasis. The concentration of calcium in ECF is closely modulated by calcium-regulating hormones, PTH and 1,25-dihydroxyvitamin D. A physiologic role for calcitonin in this regard is not established in humans. The primary function of PTH is to maintain the serum calcium within the physiologic range. Parathyroid hormone acts in this regard by (1) enhancing the intestinal absorption of calcium, (2) augmenting the tubular reabsorption of calcium, (3) increasing the skeletal release of calcium, and (4) diminishing the tubular reabsorption of phosphate and lowering the serum phosphate concentration.[30] This last effect is important because it reduces the amount of the ion that is complexed to calcium.

INTRACELLULAR CALCIUM

Whereas the total calcium concentration inside cells may be as high as that in extracellular fluids,[31] the concentration of ionized calcium in the cytoplasm is at least three orders of magnitude lower, ranging between 0.13 and 1.3 mM.[32,33] Much of the calcium is sequestered in mitochondria[34,35]

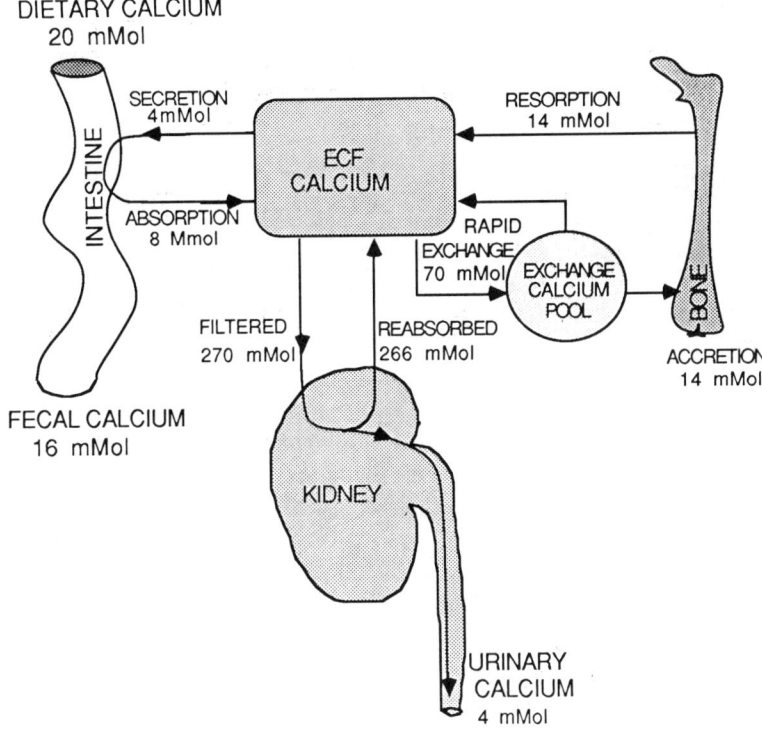

Fig. 5-2. Calcium exchange between body compartments in a 70 kg man, assuming no net gain in total body calcium. (Modified from Marx SJ, Bourdeau JE. Calcium metabolism. Ch 11, p 226. In Maxwell MH, Kleeman CR, Narins RG (eds): Clinical Disorders of Fluid and Electrolyte Metabolism. McGraw Hill, New York, 1987, with permission.)

and smooth endoplasmic reticulum; a smaller fraction is bound to proteins and polyvalent ions such as phosphate and citrate.[36–40] The low concentration of free calcium within cells allows a high concentration of phosphate to exist without precipitation of the two ions.[41] Calcium present at higher concentrations within organelles such as mitochondria and endoplasmic reticulum may take the form of noncrystalline complexes of calcium.[42,43]

A number of methods have been used to measure intracellular calcium. Some are invasive and use calcium-selective microelectrodes, whereas others are noninvasive and use calcium-sensitive photoproteins,[44] metallochromic calcium indicators,[32] and fluorescent calcium indicators such as Quin-2, Indo-2, or Fura-2.[45] The microelectrodes have been used mainly in large invertebrate cells, but have also recently been used in mammalian tissue.[46]

The 1,000- to 10,000-fold concentration gradient of intracellular calcium is maintained by two very active pumps, one that is specific for calcium—the calcium-ATPase system—and one that is coupled to sodium transport and is independent of calcium ATPase.[47–49] Whereas the calcium ATPase-dependent pump system is a high-affinity carrier of calcium, its pumping velocity is some 30 times slower than that of the sodium-calcium countertransport system. The affinity for calcium is reduced by calmodulin, and in heart cells it is regulated by a cyclic adenosine 3′,5′-monophosphate (cAMP)-dependent reaction. In adipose tissue, insulin has been shown to inhibit the system, and may therefore exert a direct effect on calcium homeostasis.[50]

The sodium-calcium countertransport system acts to promote the extrusion of calcium at the basolateral membrane of epithelial cells, and, in contrast to the calcium ATPase-dependent transport mechanism, is not directly dependent upon hydrolysis of ATP but is driven by the electrochemical potential difference for sodium established by Na-K ATPase in the cell membrane.[36,37,51-52] Sodium-calcium countertransport follows a 3 Na to 1 Ca stoichiometry and is linked to Na-K ATPase.[36,53-55] The system is independent of calmodulin but is enhanced at the plasma membrane by elevation of the cytosolic pH.[56]

The electrogenic sodium-calcium countertransport system at the basolateral membranes may control the cytosolic free calcium concentration by varying the electrochemical potential gradient across the cell membrane. The entry of sodium into cells, reduction of the extracellular sodium concentration at the basolateral surface, or depolarization all reduce the electrochemical potential and favor the flux of sodium into the cell, so that sodium-coupled calcium extrusion is inhibited and cytosolic calcium accumulates. In experiments with Ca^{2+}-selective microelectrodes, an increased concentration of ionized calcium in the cytosol was found in proximal tubular cells of *Necturus* when the sodium concentration of the peritubular fluid was reduced.[57] Comparable findings were reported in experiments with isolated perfused tubules from rabbit kidney[58] and in the urinary bladder of the toad.[59]

HORMONAL REGULATION OF MINERAL METABOLISM

Parathyroid Hormone

Parathyroid hormone is a polypeptide made up of 84 amino acids, with a molecular weight of 9,500. The genes for bovine, rat, and human PTH have been cloned.[60-63] In man, a single gene for PTH exists on the short arm of chromosome 11.[64]

Synthesis and Secretion of Parathyroid Hormone

Parathyroid hormone is synthesized on polyribosomes as a precursor pre-pro-PTH that has 115 amino acids.[65] The nascent, hydrophobic N-terminal "pre-PTH" is a leader sequence that directs the precursor hormone across the membrane of the endoplasmic reticulum. Within a period of seconds, the 25-amino acid "pre-PTH" is cleaved by a peptidase, and the 90-amino acid pro-PTH remains in the endoplasmic reticulum. As the molecule is transported to the Golgi apparatus, the N-terminal "pro" sequence containing 6 amino acids is cleaved by enzymes with activities similar to those of trypsin and carboxypeptidase. The remaining 84-amino acid polypeptide or intact PTH is stored in secretory granules. It is either secreted into the extracellular space in response to decreases in ionized calcium or undergoes degradation.

In vitro studies have shown that alterations in the rate of biosynthesis of pro-PTH in response to changes in extracellular calcium take place over a period of hours. It is now established that calcium-mediated changes in hormone synthesis are regulated by alterations in the production of mRNA (or transcription), rather than by biochemical events that occur in response to preexisting mRNA (or translation).[65] Changes in extracellular calcium apparently do not alter the enzymatic conversion of pro-PTH to PTH.

Both in vivo and in vitro studies indicate that neither the "pre" nor "pro" peptide sequences are released by parathyroid tissue into the circulation or into incubation media.[65] However, stores of PTH within the parathyroid glands undergo degradation, and this process varies directly with the concentration of extracellular calcium. Degradation of PTH within the parathyroid glands provides an important means for limiting the amount of biologically active hormone that is secreted. It also contributes to the number of different forms of PTH that are present in the circulation. Conversely, inhibition of the degradation pathway in response to a reduction in extracellular calcium could provide a mechanism for increasing the secretion of readily available PTH before more hormone can be synthesized.

The gene sequence for PTH has been determined, and confirms the reported structure for pre-pro-PTH.[61,62,66-69] Specific defects in the biosynthesis of PTH, such as impaired production of mRNA or defective conversion of pre-pro-PTH to pro-PTH, which could cause hypoparathyroidism, have not been found.

The amino acid sequences of porcine, bovine, and human PTH have been determined, and show a number of differences in amino acid sequence but not in number. All three hormones contain 84 amino acids. These differences in structure may account for some of the variation in cross reactivity among antisera developed against the hormones from different species. Full biologic activity of the native hormone (84 amino acids) resides in the N-terminal, 34-amino acid residue.[70] This portion of the bovine and human hormone has been synthesized and is widely used for investigational purposes. On the other hand, the C-terminal portion of the molecule is biologically inactive.

Secretion of PTH is modulated by the serum ionized calcium concentration, and the serum calcium and serum immunoreactive PTH concentrations are normally negatively correlated with each other.[71] Secretion of the hormone may be regulated in part by cyclic adenosine 3',5'-monophosphate (cAMP). However, it was shown that a decline in calcium stimulated the secretion of both stored and newly synthesized PTH, whereas catecholamines increased the secretion only of the stored hormone.[72] Calcium appears to be the major regulator of PTH secretion. Increases in extracellular calcium increase the concentration of intracellular calcium in parathyroid cells, in contrast to other cells, and this leads to inhibition of secretion of the hormone.[73] In two studies, however, increases in intracellular calcium produced by electroshock and ionophores did not inhibit secretion of the hormone.[74,75] Therefore, increases in intracellular calcium probably do not mediate inhibition of secretion of the hormone. Calcium may act through the G-protein. *Pertussus* toxin, which causes adenosine diphosphate (ADP)-ribosylation of the G protein, prevents the inhibition of secretion of PTH by calcium.[76]

The secretion of PTH is enhanced by phorbol esters, which can stimulate phospholyase C.[77] Supporting this concept is the demonstration that a reduction in the extracellular calcium concentration is associated with an increase in protein kinase C in membranes of dispersed parathyroid cells.[78] Clearly, the whole story about how calcium regulates the synthesis and secretion of PTH is still to be told.

Magnesium acts in a similar fashion to inhibit secretion of PTH, but this effect is not physiologically important. However, magnesium deficiency sometimes causes an impairment in the secretion or action of PTH, and leads to hypocalcemia.[79,80] This could result from diminished production of cAMP, since adenylate cyclase is a magnesium-dependent enzyme.

Serum phosphate is not a direct modulator of the secretion of PTH.[81] Increases in serum immunoreactive parathyroid hormone (iPTH) following ingestion of phosphate are mediated by decreases in the serum ionized calcium. Thus, although PTH enhances renal phosphate excretion, phosphate exerts no direct feedback regulation of secretion of the hormone.[81]

Metabolism of Parathyroid Hormone

As mentioned previously, PTH exists in the circulation in multiple molecular forms. These include the intact native hormone and C-terminal, biologically inactive fragments having a molecular weight of 4,500 to 5,000 daltons.[82] Whereas the half-life of intact PTH and its N-terminal fragments is quite short, perhaps a few minutes, the half life of the C-terminal fragments is longer and approaches one hour. As a consequence, the concentration of C-terminal fragments is higher than that of the other forms, and measurement of the C-terminal fragment or "mid-molecule" portion of the hormone provides a more reliable index of PTH secretion than does measurement of the N-terminal portion of the molecule.[83]

Fragments of circulating PTH are derived from both secretion and peripheral metabolism. The relative contributions of the two processes, however, are not known. The most important organs involved in degradation of PTH are the liver, kidney, and skeleton.[84-88]

The liver is the principal source of the C-terminal fragments of PTH that appear in the circulation. The organ selectively takes up intact PTH and not the N-terminal or C-terminal fragments. The site of cleavage may be the Kupffer cells. The liver is also the site of production of the biologically active N-terminal fragments of PTH, and the rate of production, at least in one species, is regulated by the serum ionized calcium concentration.

The kidney is also a major organ for the metabolism of PTH. The hormone and all of its fragments are filtered by the glomerulus and undergo tubular reabsorption.[87-88] In addition, the biologically active intact hormone and the N-terminal fragment are taken up at peritubular sites, probably by hormone receptors. The C-terminal fragments are excreted by glomerular filtration, the major if not sole means for their removal from the circulation. This accounts for the known high concentrations of immunoreactive C-terminal fragments of PTH in the circulation, and their delayed clearance from the circulation, in patients with chronic renal failure.

The liver accounts for over half of the metabolic clearance of PTH, and the kidney for one-third.[87] Thus, the two organs together remove some 90 percent of the hormone. The skeleton takes up little intact PTH, but does take up a good proportion of the N-terminal, biologically active fragment.

Effects and Mechanism of Action of Parathyroid Hormone

Evidence indicates that the enhanced phosphate clearance effects of PTH on the kidney are mediated by cAMP.[89-91] The hormone binds to highly specific receptors on cell surfaces of the renal tubule and activates adenylate cyclase. This leads to enhanced excretion of "nephrogenous" cAMP or urinary cAMP of renal origin. Nephrogenous cAMP is increased in patients with excess circulating PTH caused by primary or secondary hyperparathyroidism, and is diminished in patients with diminished or absent PTH secretion and hypoparathyroidism. Indeed, the measurement of nephrogenous cAMP is widely used as a diagnostic test for primary hyperparathyroidism.[92]

The effects of PTH on increasing phosphate clearance in patients and laboratory animals with hypoparathyroidism can be reproduced with dibutyryl cAMP.[91,93] Because the dibutyryl moiety is lipid soluble, this synthetic analogue of cAMP readily crosses the cell membrane. It increases the intracellular cAMP concentration by inhibiting phosphodiesterase, an enzyme that degrades the cyclic nucleotide. Parathyroid hormone and cAMP act by inhibiting the tubular reabsorption of phosphate.[94] The effects of PTH on increasing the tubular reabsorption of calcium are also reproduced by dibutyryl cAMP in thyroparathyroidectomized rats.[95] Micropuncture studies indicate that PTH-mediated inhibition of phosphate reabsorption by the kidney occurs in the proximal tubule, whereas enhanced reabsorption of calcium by the kidney takes place from the distal to the proximal renal tubule.[94,96] Parathyroid hormone-responsive adenylate cyclase is found in the renal cortex and along the nephron at several sites, including both the proximal and distal convoluted tubules.[97]

Like cAMP, calcium is also considered a second messenger of PTH.[98] Parathyroid hormone enhances the uptake of calcium by renal tissue, and the impaired excretion of phosphate, which is uniformly present in patients with hypoparathyroidism, is corrected by the administration of calcium and correction of hypocalcemia.[99] It is not known whether calcium administration acts to increase phosphate clearance by increasing the intracellular concentration of cAMP. Parathyroid hormone also activates the phosphatidate polyphosphoinositide cycle.[100,101] Type II pseudohypoparathyroidism, a disease charactered by resistance of target organs to PTH, may be caused by a defective renal tubular response to PTH in which there is a diminished PTH-mediated cellular uptake of calcium. Patients with the disorder exhibit hypocalcemia and hyperphosphatemia, and lack a phosphaturic response to PTH.[102] In untreated patients, the response of urinary cyclic cAMP to PTH is normal. The phosphaturic response to PTH, which is impaired before treatment, is restored by treatment with vitamin D and calcium, and correction of the hypocalcemia.

The extent to which cAMP mediates the effects of PTH on bone resorption is not established. Parathyroid hormone stimulates adenylate cyclase and increases the concentration of cAMP in bone cells.[103] Dibutyryl cAMP increases the serum calcium in thyroparathyroidectomized rats and in patients with hypoparathyroidism, and produces resorption of fetal rat long bones in tissue culture.[91,93,104] Thus, a number of the physiologic effects of PTH on skeletal tissue are mimicked by this synthetic analogue of the cyclic nucleotide. However, in vitro resorption of bone produced by dibutyryl cAMP occurs over a narrow dose range,[105] and the maximum effect is small compared to that produced by PTH.[106] Furthermore, aminophylline, an inhibitor of phosphodiesterase, inhibits rather than potentiates the effects of PTH on bone resorption in vitro.[107]

Whereas osteoblasts synthesize the organic matrix of bone, osteoclasts produce bone resorption. Despite the fact that osteoclasts lack receptors for PTH,[108] the hormone stimulates osteoclastic bone resorption.[109] Available evidence indicates that PTH acts on osteoblasts that have receptors for the hormone to stimulate osteoclastic bone resorption.[109] Indeed, osteoclasts do not stimulate bone resorption in the absence of osteoblasts. The mechanism by which osteoblasts act on osteoclasts is unknown. Presumably, one or more factors produced by osteoblasts in response to PTH mediate the action of the hormone on osteoclasts.

In addition to cAMP, calcium appears to be a second messenger for the skeletal effects of PTH. An initial transient effect of the hormone, which occurs within minutes both in vivo and in vitro, is to lower the calcium in serum and incubation medium, respectively.[110,111] This decline is then followed by an increase in the calcium concentration. In vitro, PTH stimulates the uptake of calcium by skeletal tissue, and the cAMP response to the hormone varies directly with the concentration of calcium in the incubation medium.[112] Moreover, the cAMP enhancing effects of PTH are attenuated by verapamil, an inhibitor of the cellular uptake of calcium, and are exaggerated by the ionophore A 23187, which enhances the cellular uptake of the ion.[113] Dibutyryl cAMP, in contrast to PTH, does not stimulate the uptake of calcium by skeletal tissue.[113] Whereas data show that calcium modulates the response of cAMP to PTH, it is not yet clear that calcium uptake by bone cells exhibits effects that are unrelated to those caused by changes in cAMP concentration.

Calcitonin

Calcitonin is a polypeptide made up of 32 amino acids, with a molecular weight of 3,500 daltons.[114–118] It consists of a straight chain with a disulfide bridge linking two cysteines to form a seven-membered ring of amino acids at the N-terminus of the molecule.

Synthesis and Secretion of Calcitonin

Calcitonin is secreted by the parafollicular cells that are derived embryologically from the last pair of pharyngeal pouches in the primitive foregut.[119,120] In mammals, these cells are distributed throughout the thyroid, where they constitute some 10 to 20 percent of the total number of thyroid cells.[121]

Studies utilizing recombinant DNA techniques and rat mRNA from a transplantable medullary carcinoma of the thyroid that produces calcitonin support the hypothesis that: (1) the hormone is initially synthesized as a larger prohormone with a molecular weight of 15,000 daltons[122]; (2) this is followed by cotranslational glycosylation[123]; (3) a leader sequence is cleaved from the calcitonin precursor; (4) procalcitonin is cleaved by a trypsin-like enzyme; and finally, (5) peptides are removed from both the N-terminus and C-terminus of the molecule, allowing emergence of the native hormone.[124–126]

The calcitonin gene is on the short arm of chromosome 11.[127,128] Three principal peptides are produced, calcitonin, katacalcin, and calcitonin gene-related peptide. Calcitonin and katacalcin, which are present on the C-terminal side of the hormone, represent one precursor, and calcitonin gene-related peptide another.[125,126,128,129] Whether one or the other of the peptides is produced depends on the tissue involved. Both are expressed in the thyroid, but only calcitonin is synthesized in large amounts in the thyroid, while calcitonin gene-related peptide is produced in large amounts in the central and peripheral nervous systems.[129] There is no known biologic role for katacalcin. On the other hand, calcitonin gene-related peptide is a potent vasodilator[129–131] and may serve as a neurotransmitter.[132,133]

The amino acid sequences of calcitonins from a number of species have been determined. There is so much variation in the structure that there is little in the way of immunologic cross-reactivity among them. In contrast, calcitonins from different species all exhibit biologic activity regardless of the animal species tested, and the entire molecule of the hormone is required to elicit this activity. Salmon calcitonin has the greatest biologic activity.[134] This has been shown to occur because of the its high affinity for receptors and its resistance to degradation.[135] Both human and salmon calcitonin have been synthesized and are available for clinical use.

Secretion of calcitonin is modulated by calcium. Serum immunoreactive calcitonin is enhanced by an increase and is diminished by a decrease in the serum calcium concentration.[136] Whereas agents such as glucagon and pentagastrin increase serum immunoreactive calcitonin when given in pharmacologic doses, there is no evidence that glucagon or gastrin plays a physiologic role in secretion of the hormone.[137] In fact, there is strong evidence that in humans, serum ionized calcium is the sole regulator of calcitonin secretion. Orally administered calcium in normal subjects increases the serum calcium, serum immunoreactive calcitonin, and serum gastrin concentrations. However, the increase in serum gastrin occurs earlier than the increases in serum calcium and immunoreactive calcitonin, and there is a significant positive correlation between the serum calcium and serum immunoreactive calcitonin, but not between the serum concentration of the two hormones.

Metabolism of Calcitonin

The half-life of human calcitonin in man is some 10 minutes, and the mean rate of metabolic clearance is about 6 to 9 ml per kilogram of body weight per minute.[138] The major organ for metabolism of calcitonin is the kidney.[139,140] Thus, renal extraction of calcitonin accounts for most of the metabolic clearance of the hormone. It is likely that calcitonin is filtered, reabsorbed, and degraded by the renal tubules, since little of the hormone is normally present in the urine.[140,141]

Calcitonin is present in the circulation in a number of molecular forms.[142-144] Unlike PTH, most of the immunoreactive species are larger than the calcitonin monomer. Some studies suggest that these may be larger derivatives of the prohormone, whereas other investigations indicate that because of the active disulfide bonds of calcitonin, linkages may form between one or more calcitonin molecules or between calcitonin and serum proteins.[144]

Effects and Mechanisms of Action of Calcitonin

Calcitonin lowers the serum calcium concentration by inhibiting osteoclastic bone resorption[145] and tubular reabsorption of the ion.[146] Calcitonin also enhances the renal excretion of phosphorus, magnesium, sodium, and potassium, but these changes are transient and are not sustained.[146]

The effects of calcitonin appear to be mediated by cAMP.[140,147] The hormone binds to specific receptors in both the skeleton and kidney, and activates adenylate cyclase. In bone, the osteoclast is the target cell for calcitonin.[145] As noted already, the "ruffled border" of this cell is thought to be the area of bone-resorbing activity, and calcitonin was shown to decrease the frequency of occurrence of the "ruffled border."[148]

Calcitonin also lowers the serum phosphate concentration.[149,150] Whereas the hormone reduces the serum calcium concentration by inhibiting the release of calcium from the skeleton, it lowers the serum phosphorus by increasing the egress of the phosphate ion from the circulation.

As indicated previously, calcitonin does not appear to have a physiologic role in man. Abnormal calcium homeostasis does not occur either with excess secretion of the hormone, such as occurs in medullary carcinoma of the thyroid, or with its diminished or absent secretion, such as occurs after total thyroidectomy. The hypothesis that calcitonin acts to inhibit postprandial hypercalcemia and to prevent postprandial urinary losses of calcium is an attractive one that will need additional investigation.

The serum immunoreactive calcitonin concentration, both basally and after stimulation with calcium, is lower in women than men and is not altered by age.[140] Secretion rates of monomeric calcitonin are lower in women than in men, and occur because of diminished rates of production rather than enhanced rates of metabolic clearance of the hormone.

Calcitonin is most effective when bone turnover is increased. Thus, it is widely used to treat Paget's disease of bone and hypercalcemia caused by malignancy. It is generally effective in Paget's disease, where the primary event is thought to be increased osteoclastic resorption of bone followed by increased but poorly organized bone formation.

Vitamin D

Vitamin D_2 (derived from irradiated ergocalciferol) is absorbed by way of the intestinal lymphatic system. Bile acids are required, and absorption occurs in the proximal small intestine.[151] Vitamin D_3 (cholecalciferol) is produced by photochemical synthesis from 7-dehydrocholesterol in the skin.[152] When 7-dehydrocholesterol is exposed to ultraviolet light, it absorbs one photon of light energy and is converted to previtamin D_3, which is thermally labile and forms vitamin D_3, which is thermally stable. This temperature-dependent rearrangement of double bonds takes place over a period of several days. As it is produced, vitamin D_3 is removed from the skin by vitamin D-binding protein in the dermal capillaries. Vitamin D-binding protein has a high affinity for vitamin D_3 and a low affinity for previtamin D_3. As a consequence, previtamin D_3 remains in the skin for eventual thermal conversion to the vitamin.

Vitamin D_2 and vitamin D_3 have little biologic activity. Both are hydroxylated in the liver to form 25-hydroxyvitamin D by the enzyme vitamin D-25-hydroxylase.[153] 25-Hydroxyvitamin D, and to a lesser extent vitamin D, are the major storage forms of the vitamin. The serum 25-hydroxyvitamin D concentration varies with the time of year, geographic location, amount of skin pigment, duration of exposure to sunlight or ultraviolet light, and dietary intake. In the northern hemisphere, values are highest in the summer months and lowest in the winter months. Values for serum 25-hydroxyvitamin D are lower in blacks and Mexican Americans, who have more skin pigment than Caucasians.[154,155]

The hepatic 25-hydroxylation of vitamins D_2 and D_3 takes place in both microsomes and mitochondria. In humans, the hydroxylation is apparently regulated by substrate concentration.[156] Thus, in one study it was found that the increment in serum 25-hydroxyvitamin D was higher after a dose of 100 μg/kg body weight than after a dose of 250 μg/kg body weight of vitamin D_3.[156] 1,25-Dihydroxyvitamin D modulates serum 25-hydroxyvitamin D.[157] Studies in laboratory animals indicate that 1,25-dihydroxyvitamin D lowers circulating 25-hydroxyvitamin D, not by decreasing its synthesis, but rather by enhancing the metabolic clearance of this metabolite.[158]

Although previously it was held that 25-hydroxyvitamin D did not influence calcium metabolism, more recent studies suggest that this is not the case. Obese subjects are depleted of vitamin D and have low serum vitamin D,[159] 25-hydroxyvitamin D, and urinary calcium concentrations and elevated serum iPTH and urinary cAMP concentrations.[160] These abnormalities are reversed by 25-hydroxyvitamin D_3.[161] 25-Hydroxyvitamin D is further hydroxylated in the kidney to 1,25-dihydroxyvitamin D by the enzyme 25-hydroxyvitamin D-1α-hydroxylase,[162] a mitochondrial enzyme made up of ferrodoxin reductase, ferrodoxin, and cytochrome P_{450}.[163-165] This hydroxylation is tightly regulated by PTH in adults, but not as closely regulated in children.[166] Values of serum 1,25-dihydroxyvitamin D in infants and children are somewhat higher than in adults.[167] Although production of the metabolite is tightly regulated, seasonal variation of serum 1,25-dihydroxyvitamin D occurs in adults. In human subjects, the metabolites of vitamin D_3 are present in higher amounts in the circulation than are those of vitamin D_2, while the biologic activities of the metabolites of vitamin D_2 and D_3 are thought to be the same.[168]

Parathyroid hormone is a major regulator of the renal production of 1,25-dihydroxyvitamin D.[169] This is emphasized by the fact that serum values of 1,25-dihydroxyvitamin D are elevated in primary hyperparathyroidism and are reduced in hypoparathyroidism.[170] Calcium and phosphate also play a physiologic role in regulating the synthesis of this metabolite. Its production is increased when the intake of either one or the other is reduced, and is decreased by the administration of one or the other.[170-176] Phosphorus is a major regulator of the production of 1,25-dihydroxyvitamin D in man. In normal subjects, serum values for the metabolite vary inversely with phosphate intake.[175]

It is not clear to what extent changes in PTH secretion mediate the alterations in the renal synthesis of 1,25-dihydroxyvitamin D in response to changes in dietary phosphate. Adaptation from a high to a low calcium intake to enhance the intestinal absorption of calcium appears to be mediated by an increased secretion of PTH and the renal synthesis of 1,25-dihydroxyvitamin D.[176] However, calcium also appears to act directly on the renal tubule to modulate the synthesis of 1,25-dihydroxyvitamin D.[173]

Although growth hormone and prolactin have been shown to enhance the renal production of 1,25-dihydroxyvitamin D, their role in the regulation of vitamin D metabolism in man is not established. Serum values for 1,25-dihydroxyvitamin D are normal in patients with prolactin-producing tumors.[176,177] In one study, the short-term administration of growth hormone to growth hormone-deficient children enhanced calcium absorption and lowered serum 1,25-dihydroxyvitamin D.[178] Preliminary evidence in children with growth hormone deficiency suggests that when given chronically, growth hormone may enhance the renal response to endogenous PTH and thereby increase serum 1,25-dihydroxyvitamin D.[179]

The conversion of 25-hydroxyvitamin D to 24,25-dihydroxyvitamin D by the enzyme 25-hydroxyvitamin-D-24-hydroxylase takes place in the kidney as well as other organs.[180] The enzyme is induced by 1,25-dihydroxyvitamin D.[180,181] Whether this metabolite has a physiologic role with regard to bone and mineral metabolism is controversial. It was proposed that 24,25-dihydroxyvitamin D may be important in healing osteomalacia and rickets[182,183] and in regulating the secretion of PTH,[184] and that the 24-hydroxylation of 25-hydroxyvitamin D may be important only as a pathway for degradation of the vitamin. Both 24,25-dihydroxyvitamin D and 1,25-dihydroxyvitamin D may be hydroxylated to 1,24,25-trihydroxyvitamin D. 1,25-Dihydroxyvitamin D may also be converted to calcitroic acid, which has no biologic activity.[185-187] 1,24,25-Trihydroxyvitamin D has biologic activity, but it is much less than that of 1,25-dihydroxyvitamin D.

Vitamin D, 25-hydroxyvitamin D, 24,25-dihydroxyvitamin D, and 1,25-dihydroxyvitamin D are carried in the blood by vitamin D-binding protein, an α_2 globulin that is the group-specific component protein or G_c protein.[188] One molecule of the protein binds one molecule of vitamin D or one of its metabolites. Only 5 percent or less of the binding sites are occupied. Vitamin D deficiency sometimes develops in patients with marked proteinuria as a result of renal loss of vitamin D and its metabolites.

Vitamin D and its metabolites are conjugated in the liver to form glucuronides, which undergo an enterohepatic circulation. Conjugation and biliary excretion appear to be major pathways for excretion of the vitamin and its metabolites. Disruption of the enterohepatic circulation is a potential cause of depletion of vitamin D and its metabolites.

Whereas the half-life of 25-hydroxyvitamin D and of 24,25-dihydroxyvitamin D is on the order of two to three weeks, the half-life of 1,25-dihydroxyvitamin D is much shorter, being less than 24 hours.[189-191] This difference results from differences in the affinity of the metabolites for vitamin D-binding protein.

Both clinical and laboratory studies indicate that hydroxylation of vitamin D at the 25 and 1α positions is required for optimal biologic activity.

Mechanism of Action of Vitamin D

1,25-dihydroxyvitamin D_3 binds to a cytosol receptor in target tissues, and the sterol-receptor complex is transported to the cell nucleus, where it binds to DNA and initiates translation and transcription.[192-195] 1,25-dihydroxyvitamin D_3 also may alter membrane permeability to calcium by a nongenomic mechanism.[196] However, the fact that mutations resulting in substitutions of a single amino acid in the "zinc finger" projections of the DNA-binding moiety of the receptor for 1,25-dihydroxyvitamin D produce defective target-organ responses to the vitamin, provide evidence that nongenomic actions of the vitamin may be of limited physiologic significance.[197b]

The major physiologic actions of 1,25-dihydroxyvitamin D are to enhance the intestinal transport of calcium and phosphate and to stimulate release of calcium and phosphate from the skeleton so that mineralization can occur. 1,25-Dihydroxyvitamin D also stimulates the production of calcium-binding protein in target tissues.[194,197a] Inhibition of the secretion of PTH by 1,25-dihydroxyvitamin D is mediated indirectly through increases in the intestinal absorption of calcium and in the serum calcium concentration, as well as directly.[197,198] With vitamin D intoxication, the serum 25-hydroxyvitamin D concentration is markedly increased, while the serum 1,25-dihydroxyvitamin D is normal or only slightly increased[199] because the renal production of this metabolite is closely regulated by PTH and calcium (see above).[166] At high concentrations, 25-hydroxyvitamin D presumably enters cells of target organs and binds to and activates receptors for 1,25-dihydroxyvitamin D. As already mentioned, this probably also takes place at physiologic concentrations.[161]

1,25-Dihydroxyvitamin D increases the transport of calcium by the small intestine. The movement of calcium from the lumen across the brush border membrane does not require energy or the synthesis of new protein, since it follows a steep concentration gradient.[200] 1,25-Dihydroxyvitamin D_3 promotes the entry of calcium into enterocytes by increasing the permeability of the cell membrane, and appears to alter the structure of the membrane.[201] It increases both the de novo synthesis of phosphatidylcholine and its incorporation into the brush border membrane. The means by which calcium is transported through the cytosol from the luminal to the basolateral membrane is unknown. Mitochondria and a lysosome-like vesicle are suggested as being important.[202] In contrast to the passive entry of calcium at the brush border, the movement of calcium across the basolateral membrane occurs against a steep concentration gradient and requires energy. 1,25-Dihydroxyvitamin D_3 enhances ATP-dependent calcium transport and the activity of Ca^{2+}-ATPase in the basolateral plasma membranes of enterocytes.[203]

Vitamin D–Endocrine System

The regulation of calcium metabolism by PTH and 1,25-dihydroxyvitamin D takes place as follows. Parathyroid hormone enhances the release of calcium from the skeleton and increases the serum ionized calcium which, in turn, inhibits the secretion of the hormone. Parathyroid hormone increases the renal synthesis of 1,25-dihydroxyvitamin D, which enhances the intestinal absorption of calcium and increases the serum calcium concentration. This, in turn, diminishes the secretion of PTH. The parathyroid glands and the skeleton provide a direct negative feedback system for regulation of the serum calcium, and the parathyroid glands, kidney, and intestine provide a second negative feedback system that is indirect. Thus, the regulation of intestinal absorption of calcium by PTH hormone is mediated by changes in the renal synthesis of 1,25-dihydroxyvitamin D.

HYPOCALCEMIA

Pathogenesis of Hypocalcemia

The causes of hypocalcemia are outlined in Table 5-1. In general, hypocalcemia results from abnormal secretion of PTH, abnormal metabolism of vitamin D, or some combination of these two factors. The pathogenesis of hypocalcemia is discussed in detail below.

Table 5-1. Causes of Hypocalcemia

Hypoalbuminemia

Absence or impaired secretion of parathyroid hormone
    Hypoparathyroidism
    Magnesium deficiency

Abnormal metabolism of vitamin D
    Deficiency
        Inadequate intake
        Poor exposure to sunlight
        Malabsorption disease
    Impaired 25-hydroxylation of vitamin D
        Liver disease
    Impaired 1α-hydroxylation of 25-hydroxyvitamin D
        Chronic renal failure
        Hypoparathyroidism
        Hypophosphatemic rickets
        Pseudohypoparathyroidism
        Tumor-induced osteomalacia
        Vitamin D-dependent rickets type I
    Impaired response to 1,25-dihydroxyvitamin D
        Anticonvulsant therapy
        Vitamin D-dependent rickets type II

Miscellaneous
    Acute pancreatitis
    Osteoblastic metastases
    Phosphate therapy
    Chemotherapy

Vitamin D Deficiency

Hypocalcemia and rickets caused by deficiency of vitamin D are not common in children in the United States, and often result from limited exposure to sunlight. An inadequate dietary intake is usually not responsible because milk and dairy products are fortified with the vitamin. Rickets is more prevalent in individuals from other countries, particularly those that are underdeveloped.[204–206] Moreover, exposure to sunlight in northern climates is less than in tropical and subtropical areas. In Great Britain, the disease is found in neonates and infants of immigrants from Asia, and is attributed to pigmentation of the skin, which inhibits the transmission of ultraviolet radiation and dermal synthesis of vitamin D,[207] and to the social customs of avoidance of sunlight and of foods fortified with the vitamin. Maternal deficiency of vitamin D can cause vitamin D deficiency in neonates. Neonatal rickets also occurs in infants of low birth weight.[208]

Similarly, hypocalcemia and osteomalacia caused by deficiency of vitamin D are infrequent in adults in the United States, but occur in individuals from other countries for the same reasons as those mentioned.

Gastrointestinal and Hepatic Diseases

Hypocalcemia of varying degree occurs in patients with gastrointestinal diseases, particularly those that are associated with intestinal malabsorption. These include idiopathic steatorrhea, nontropical sprue, regional enteritis, subtotal gastric resection with gastroenterostomy, and small bowel resection. Because vitamin D is absorbed in the proximal small intestine by a process that requires bile acids, and because the vitamin and its metabolites undergo an enterohepatic circulation, deficiency of the vitamin can result from gastrointestinal diseases that interfere with absorption[209] or the enterohepatic circulation of vitamin D and its metabolites.[210] Malabsorption of vitamin D may occur even in the absence of steatorrhea.

Hypocalcemia sometimes develops in patients with diseases of the liver or pancreas. Parenchymal disease of the liver, or biliary obstruction, may interfere with the synthesis of 25-hydroxyvitamin D or the intestinal absorption and enterohepatic circulation of vitamin D and its metabolites, resulting in deficiency.[211,212] Occasionally the hepatic defect in 25-hydroxylation of vitamin D may be so great that vitamin D may be ineffective, requiring the administration of 25-hydroxyvitamin D$_3$.

Chronic Renal Failure

Hypocalcemia and secondary hyperparathyroidism frequently occur in patients with chronic renal failure. Retention of phosphate[213,214] and loss of renal 25-hydroxyvitamin D-1α-hydroxylase[215,216] are two of the major factors behind this. Even early in the course of the disease, retention of phosphate causes a diminution in the renal production of 1,25-hydroxyvitamin D and absorption of calcium by the intestine, and results in the development of secondary hyperparathyroidism.[216] The defect becomes even more pronounced late in the course of the disease. Lack of inhibition of secretion of PTH by 1,25-dihydroxyvitamin D, owing to low circulating 1,25-dihydroxyvitamin D, also contributes to the development of secondary hyperparathyroidism.[197]

Hypoparathyroidism

In patients with hypoparathyroidism, the serum calcium is reduced, the serum phosphorus is normal or increased, the serum 25-hydroxyvitamin D is normal, and the serum 1,25-dihydroxyvitamin D is low because of lack of PTH.[217,218] As a result, the intestinal absorption of calcium and urinary calcium are also abnormally low.

Hypophosphatemic Rickets

Hypophosphatemic rickets is a familial disease in which hypophosphatemia and renal phosphate wasting characteristically occur. An X-linked dominant inheritance pattern is most common.[219] The primary defect is one in which phosphate transport in the proximal renal tubule is impaired. Screening studies in families of patients with the disorder indicate that fasting hypophosphatemia is the hallmark of the disease.[220] Hypocalcemia is not usually present. The clinical picture varies from asymptomatic individuals who have hypophosphatemia and no clinically evident bone disease, usually females, to subjects with severe osteomalacia or rickets. In infants, skeletal changes of rickets develop in the first year of life and may be associated with delayed dentition. In adults who have received inadequate treatment, bowed legs and short stature are often present without biochemical or radiographic evidence of active skeletal disease. In others, the bone disease is typically advanced osteomalacia. There is no relationship between the extent of bone disease and degree of hypophosphatemia.

The diminished rate of growth in hypophosphatemic rickets probably results from hypophosphatemia. Normal growth rates usually occur in individuals who have a normal or near normal serum phosphate, or in subjects in whom the serum phosphate is restored to normal or near normal by oral phosphate therapy.

Whereas values for serum 1,25-dihydroxyvitamin D are either normal or moderately decreased in patients with hypophosphatemic rickets or osteomalacia, they are inappropriately low for the degree of hypophosphatemia that should increase the renal production of this metabolite.[221,222] Also, the serum 1,25-dihydroxyvitamin D concentrations paradoxically decline in response to treatment with vitamin D or 25-hydroxyvitamin D_3, and responds poorly to exogenously administered PTH.[223] Recent studies indicate that plasma 1,25-dihydroxyvitamin D correlates with the tubular reabsorption of phosphate.[224] These results suggest that the renal defects in phosphorus transport and synthesis of 1,25-dihydroxyvitamin D, both of which take place in the proximal renal tubule, are related. However, it is evident that treatment with 1,25-dihydroxyvitamin D_3 does not correct the renal phosphate wasting, and that correction of hypophosphatemia with orally administered phosphate does not correct the abnormal metabolism of vitamin D.

Pseudohypoparathyroidism

Pseudohypoparathyroidism is a disease in which resistance of the kidneys and skeleton to PTH characteristically occurs. Mental retardation is common. Whereas half of the patients are phenotypically normal, the remainder are phenotypically abnormal and have a short stature, round face, short phalanges, shortening of one or more metacarpals or metatarsals, ectopic calcification, radius curvus, and expressionless facies.[225] Shortening of the phalanges, metacarpals, and metatarsals is caused by early closure of the epiphyses and diminished linear growth of the metaphyseal ends of these bones. Shortening of the fourth and fifth metacarpals is more common and shortening of the first, third, and second metacarpals is less common.[226] As a result of this shortening, a dimple replaces the knuckle when a fist is formed, and is a highly characteristic physical finding. Dental abnormalities occasionally occur and include defects in the enamel and root and unerupted teeth. Calcification of the basal ganglia may be present on skull films.

The classical biochemical features of pseudohypoparathyroidism include a low serum calcium, a normal or elevated serum phosphorus, increases in circulating PTH, and a failure of urinary phosphorus and cAMP to increase in response to PTH.[93,217] The serum alkaline phosphatase is increased in subjects with rickets or osteomalacia. Defective renal conversion of 25-hydroxyvitamin D to 1,25-dihydroxyvitamin D produces a reduction in serum 1,25-dihydroxyvitamin D and in the intestinal absorption of calcium.[227,228] In contrast to the response of patients with hypoparathyroidism, serum 1,25-dihydroxyvitamin D usually does not increase in response to PTH in patients with pseudohypoparathyroidism.[217]

The metabolic defect in pseudohypoparathyroidism that accounts for the lack of response to PTH is caused by an abnormal adenylate cyclase system in target tissues. In some patients with the disorder, there is a 50 percent reduction in the concentration of the guanine nucleotide regulatory protein.[225] Patients deficient in this regulatory protein are almost always phenotypically abnormal (see above). The cause of the defect in the adenylate cyclase system that impairs the response of target organs to PTH in patients with pseudohypoparathyroidism who are phenotypically normal and have normal amounts of guanine nucleotide regulatory protein is unknown.

The guanine nucleotide regulatory protein is present in all eukaryotic cells, and modifies the response of catalytic adenylate cyclase to hormonal stimulation. In patients with a partial deficiency of this nucleotide regulatory protein, an apparently generalized defect in the adenylate cyclase system is evidenced by a number of other endocrinologic abnormalities. These include primary hypothyroidism and primary hypogonadism.[225]

In the kidney, the metabolic defect in

pseudohypoparathyroidism is apparently restricted to the adenylate cyclase system. Evidence for this is that phosphate excretion and serum 1,25-dihydroxyvitamin D are both enhanced by the administration of dibutyryl cAMP.[93,229] The diagnosis of pseudohypoparathyroidism is established by showing an absent or altered response of urinary cAMP and phosphate excretion to PTH[217,225,228] and an increase in serum immunoreactive PTH (iPTH).[228]

Vitamin D-dependent Rickets Type I

Infants with vitamin D-dependent rickets type I appear to be normal at birth and develop characteristic biochemical and clinical features of rickets during the first year of life. Hypocalcemia is a consistent finding and is associated with a normal or low serum phosphorus, elevated serum alkaline phosphatase, increased serum iPTH and urinary cAMP, and diminished intestinal absorption of calcium. The disorder is caused by an absent or inactive form of renal 25-hydroxyvitamin D-1α-hydroxylase, with the result that serum 1,25-dihydroxyvitamin D is markedly reduced.[230,231] Hypocalcemia, rickets, osteomalacia, and the biochemical abnormalities of the disorder are corrected by treatment with 1,25-dihydroxyvitamin D_3.

Tumor-induced Osteomalacia

Tumor-induced osteomalacia is a disease in which rickets or osteomalacia is associated with a benign or malignant tumor and undergoes remission following resection of the tumor.[232] The clinical findings are those of rickets in children and osteomalacia in adults. The serum calcium is normal or low, the serum phosphate is usually low, and the serum alkaline phosphatase is increased. The intestinal absorption of phosphorus is low and renal excretion of phosphate is increased, resulting in a negative phosphorus balance, whereas the intestinal absorption of calcium is low but renal conservation of calcium prevents a negative calcium balance.[233] The serum iPTH is usually normal, even in subjects with an abnormally low serum 1,25-dihydroxyvitamin D and hypocalcemia.

Tumors responsible for the disorder include those of mesenchymal origin, sarcomas, hemangiomas, and giant cell tumors of bone, as well as carcinoma of the breast and of the prostate.[232,234] The pathogenesis of the disease is unknown, but tumors may produce one or more factors that enhance the renal excretion of phosphate and diminish 1α-hydroxylation of 25-hydroxyvitamin D in the kidney.

Treatment is removal of the tumor. Some patients have responded to treatment with 1,25-dihydroxyvitamin D_3 and have shown enhanced intestinal absorption of calcium, correction of hypocalcemia and hypophosphatemia, and healing of the osteomalacia.[233] Other patients have failed to respond to treatment with 1,25-dihydroxyvitamin D_3 alone, but are effectively treated by the addition of oral phosphate. The clinical findings and response to treatment are similar in many respects to those with adult-onset hypophosphatemic rickets.

Anticonvulsant Therapy

Hypocalcemia, rickets, or osteomalacia may occur in patients with epilepsy who are receiving treatment with anticonvulsant drugs.[235,236] The clinical spectrum ranges from asymptomatic subjects with a diminished skeletal mass to patients who have hypocalcemia, clinically apparent bone disease, fractures, and pseudofractures. Patients who receive more than one anticonvulsant drug are more likely to develop bone disease.

Anticonvulsant drugs induce hepatic microsomal mixed oxidase activity. As a consequence, vitamin D and 25-hydroxyvitamin D are converted to more polar, biologically inactive compounds, and the serum 25-hydroxyvitamin D concentration declines.[237] The serum 1,25-dihydroxyvitamin D, however, is normal, so that the bone disease may not be caused by the hepatic alteration of vitamin D metabolism by anticonvulsants. In experimental animals, phenytoin reduces the intestinal absorption of calcium,[238] and both phenytoin and phenobarbital impair mobilization of calcium from bone in vitro.[239] Thus, the anticonvulsant drugs appear to cause hypocalcemia and bone disease by interfering with the peripheral actions of 1,25-dihydroxyvitamin D.

Vitamin D-dependent Rickets Type II

Vitamin D-dependent rickets type II is a rare disease in which the clinical, biochemical, and skeletal findings of rickets or osteomalacia may develop during infancy, childhood, or adolescence.[240,241] Onset is either sporadic or familial, transmission is as an autosomal trait, and patients occasionally are the products of a consanguineous marriage. Alopecia sometimes occurs in patients with the familial disorder. The finding that distinguishes vitamin D-dependent rickets type II from vitamin D-dependent rickets type I is the abnormal elevation of serum 1,25-dihydroxyvitamin D in the former.[240,241] The values of this vitamin D metabolite are generally over 100 pg/ml, and may be much higher in severe cases. Studies with cultured skin fibroblasts show a variety of abnormalities in the uptake and nuclear binding of radiolabeled 1,25-dihydroxyvitamin D_3, and indicate that there is considerable genetic heterogeneity in the disorder.[242] Children with the most profound defects have alopecia, are often difficult to treat, and may die of pneumonia.

As noted earlier, a mutation at two different sites in the "zinc fingers" of the receptor for 1,25-dihydroxyvitamin D in the area of binding to DNA accounted for two separate defects in patients with the disease.[197b]

Signs and Symptoms of Hypocalcemia

The signs and symptoms of hypocalcemia are outlined in Table 5-2.

Neuromuscular

The most characteristic clinical finding in hypocalcemia is tetany. Hypocalcemia lowers the excitability threshold to stimuli, so that the number of spontaneous discharges in nerves supplying the voluntary muscles increases. This is manifested clinically as parasthesias in the hands, feet, and around the mouth, with numbness and cramping of the muscles of the extremities that may progress to a carpopedal spasm characterized by adduction of the thumb and marked flexion of the fingers, which are firmly pressed together at the metacarpophalangeal joint. Plantar flexion of the toes, arching of the feet, and contraction of calf muscles also occur.[243] Despite the association between hypocalcemia and tetany, serum calcium and tetany are poorly correlated in dogs, and tetany is more frequent when alkalosis is present.[244] Hypocalcemia causes respiratory alkalosis by altering the sensitivity of the central mechanism for regulation of respiration in response to changes in CO_2.[245] Thus, hypocalcemia and alkalosis act in concert to cause tetany. The occurrence of tetany is not influenced by the rate of development of hypocalcemia, and is not related to the concentration of ionized calcium in the cerebrospinal fluid (CSF).

Latent tetany can be demonstrated by

Table 5-2. Signs and Symptoms of Hypocalcemia

Cardiovascular
  Electrocardiographic changes

Central nervous system
  Electroencephalographic changes
  Convulsive seizures
    Focal
    Grand mal
    Petit mal
  Calcification of basal ganglia
  Involuntary movements
    Chorea
    Paralysis agitans
    Athetosis
    Dystonia
    Abnormal ocular movements
  Increased intracranial pressure
    Papilledema
  Intellectual impairment
  Organic brain syndrome
    Psychoses
    Neuroses

Dental
  Abnormal tooth development
    Absent or hypoplastic teeth
    Abnormal dentine deposition
    Abnormal enamel
    Delayed tooth eruption
    Caries and infection

Dermal
  Dry scaly skin
  Eczema
  Brittle nails
  Coarse, dry hair

Gastrointestinal
  Diarrhea, loose stools
  Malabsorption and steatorrhea

Neuromuscular
  Tetany
    Paresthesia of hands and feet
    Muscle cramps of extremities
    Cyanosis and spasm of respiratory muscles

Ocular
  Cataracts

tapping over the branches of the facial nerves, which produces twitching of the facial muscles, the so-called Chvostek's sign. The finding is not diagnostic, however, since it may be observed in as many as 25 percent of human subjects.[246] It is therefore of value in following only those patients in whom it is not present when the serum calcium is normal. Latent tetany can be demonstrated by producing ischemia with a blood pressure cuff on one arm inflated to just above the systolic blood pressure (Trousseau's sign).[247] A positive response is indicated by tetany with spasm of the hand muscles and adduction of the thumb and flexion of the fingers at the metacarpophalangeal joints, caused by ischemia of the nerves beneath the cuff.

Central Nervous System

Convulsive seizures of the focal, petit mal, and grand mal types can result from hypocalcemia.[248,249] Electroencephalographic changes include focal or diffuse abnormalities that do not change with correction of the hypocalcemia, and are usually abnormal. Characteristically, the seizures are corrected by treatment of the hypocalcemia. Hypocalcemia itself increases the occurrence of theta waves and paroxysmal discharges in the electroencephalogram.[250] Calcification of the basal ganglia may occur because of hypocalcemia, and may be associated with abnormal involuntary movements, including chorea, paralysis agitans, athetosis, dystonia, and abnormal ocular movements.[248] The abnormalities are caused by calcification and hyaline degeneration of the media and adventitia of the small vessels in the basal ganglia. Calcification observed radiographically on a lateral projection is present from 3 to 5 cm above the sella turcica, and on a frontal projection from 2 to 4 cm lateral to the midline.

Hypocalcemia may cause papilledema and increased intracranial pressure.[248,251] However, the papilledema can be present without an increase in CSF pressure. Some 80 percent of patients with papilledema and hypocalcemia as a result of hypoparathyroidism have a history of convulsions. The papilledema is resolved by treatment of the hypocalcemia.

A spectrum of mental disorders that include intellectual impairment, organic brain syndrome, psychoses, and neuroses may occur in patients with hypocalcemia and hypoparathyroidism.[248] Although a number of symptoms are improved by correction of the hypercalcemia, the response to treatment may be difficult to evaluate.

Dermal

In hypoparathyroidism, the skin is often dry and scaly, and eczema may be present. The nails are brittle and the hair is coarse and dry. Exfoliative dermatitis and eczema sometimes occur after treatment of the hypocalcemia.[252,253] Psoriasis may be worsened by hypocalcemia.[253]

Dental

Hypocalcemia prevents the normal development of teeth but does not alter teeth after they are formed. Tooth development involves four stages: (1) initiation and formation of the tooth bud, (2) matrix formation in dentine and enamel, (3) calcification of dentine and enamel, and (4) eruption. Abnormalities at each stage of tooth development are produced by hypocalcemia: the teeth may be absent or hypoplastic, deposition of dentine may be incomplete, the enamel may be thin and pitted, or tooth eruption may be delayed.[254] Affected teeth are prone to infection and caries.

Ocular

Cataracts are the most frequent complication of chronic hypocalcemia, and the incidence varies with the duration of the disease.[255] Normally, the lens depends upon an active cation transport mechanism in the epithelium of the lens, so that a low sodium concentration is maintained within the lens. A low calcium concentration in the medium surrounding the lens inhibits this transport mechanism and leads to a net increase in the concentration of sodium and water[256] and a net decrease in the concentration of potassium within the lens, causing swelling and disruption of the lens fibers. The calcium concentration of the lens is characteristically elevated in hypocalcemic states, and in advanced cataracts is thought to result from dystrophic calcification. Since cataracts can be prevented and their growth can be inhibited by maintenance of a normal serum calcium, treatment and prevention of hypocalcemia is obviously important. Restoration of serum calcium does not reverse the lenticular changes produced by prolonged hypocalcemia.

Cardiovascular

Hypocalcemia classically produces prolongation of the QT and ST intervals on the electrocardiogram. These abnormalities are frequently present when the serum calcium is less than 7 mg/dl, and are consistently present when the serum calcium is 6 mg/dl or less.[257] The correlation is more consistent when the corrected QT interval is measured in such a way that the QT_c interval and the ST segment vary inversely with the serum calcium. These electrocardiographic changes are corrected when the serum calcium is returned to normal.

Gastrointestinal

Patients with hypocalcemia often have diarrhea or loose stools, and may even develop intestinal malabsorption and steatorrhea.[258] The malabsorption syndrome is entirely corrected by adequate treatment of the hypocalcemia.

Treatment of Hypocalcemia

The goals of treating hypocalcemia are: (1) to bring the serum calcium to within the normal range, alleviate related symptoms, and prevent the occurrence of grand mal and other types of seizures and the development of cataracts; (2) to prevent or diminish the skeletal deformities of rickets or osteomalacia and secondary hyperparathyroidism when they are present; (3) to prevent vitamin D intoxication with hypercalcemia, hypercalciuria, and their sequelae; and (4) to promote normal growth and development of the skeleton in children and infants. Treatment must be individualized and based on the pathogenesis and severity of the hypocalcemia.

Calcium

Hypocalcemia may present with tetany and grand mal seizures, and when it is acute and severe can be a medical emergency. Treatment may be required to prevent laryngeal stridor, which may lead to asphyxia and death. Calcium gluconate can be used to treat hypocalcemia, and should be given slowly by intravenous infusion with 20 to 40 ml of a 10 per cent solution being administered over a period of 1 to 2 hours. Each ml of this solution contains 9 mg of elemental calcium. Calcium can then be given by mouth together with vitamin D, as outlined below.

Administration of elemental calcium is often required. The calcium content of orally administered preparations varies considerably. Calcium carbonate contains 40 percent calcium, calcium chloride 36 percent calcium, calcium lactate 13 percent calcium, and calcium gluconate 9 percent calcium. Therefore, 2.5 g, 2.8 g, 7.7 g, and 11.0 g of these preparations are required, respectively, to provide 1.0 g of elemental calcium daily. Calcium chloride is irritating and should be given only with milk or meals.

Vitamin D

The preparations of vitamin D and its derivatives that are available for use in the United States are vitamin D, 25-hydroxyvitamin D_3, 1,25-dihydroxyvitamin D_3, and dihydrotachysterol. 1α-Hydroxyvitamin D_3 is available in Japan and Europe.

The human daily requirement of vitamin D is 2.5 µg (100 IU) per day. The recommended dietary allowance is 10 µg (400 IU) per day. Using these doses, it takes four to eight weeks for rickets to resolve and for the correction of hypocalcemia. Very large daily doses (750 to 3,000 µg) are needed for the treatment of hypocalcemia in hypoparathyroidism. Dihydrotachysterol is given at dosages of 20 to 100 µg/day for rickets and at 250 to 1000 µg/day for hypoparathyroidism. Calciferol (25-hydroxyvitamin D_3) is given at dosages of 1 to 5 µg/day for rickets and 50 to 200 µg/day for hypoparathyroidism. Calcitriol (1,25-dihydroxyvitamin D) is given at dosages of 0.5 to 2.0 µg/day in two divided doses.

Vitamin D and 25-hydroxyvitamin D_3 have the theoretical advantage of being precursors of 1,25-dihydroxyvitamin D, and will replete stores of 25-hydroxyvitamin D that might otherwise be depleted. 25-Hydroxyvitamin D_3 is indicated for use in patients with liver disease who may have reduced activity of the enzyme vitamin D-25-hydroxylase. The onset of its action is somewhat faster than that of vitamin D.[259] A practical advantage of vitamin D is its low cost and employability in selected patients. In contrast to 25-hydroxyvitamin D_3, however, vitamin D is not chemically stable, and loses its activity during storage. Vitamin D also accumulates in fat and muscle during long-term administration, so that its effects may become cumulative. The serum 25-hydroxyvitamin D concentration can be used to guide treatment with vitamin D and 25-hydroxyvitamin D.[260] For both drugs, the therapeutic dose is near the toxic dose, a long period of time may be required for optimal biologic effects, and activity may persist after cessation of administration, which could be a disadvantage should intoxication occur. Therapeutically, the two sterols are not consistently effective, particularly when the metabolism of vitamin D is abnormal.

The advantage of 1,25-dihydroxyvitamin D_3 is that optimal biologic activity develops after a short period of administration and persists for only a short period of time after the drug is stopped.[261-264] The onset of biologic activity of dihydrotachysterol lies midway between that of 25-hydroxyvitamin D and 1,25-dihydroxyvitamin D.[265] Both drugs may be effective when 1α-hydroxylation of 25-hydroxyvitamin D is impaired. On the other hand, both drugs are relatively expensive, and toxicity can occur spontaneously when they are administered over long periods. Hypercalcemia, however, is readily reversed by stopping the 1,25-dihydroxyvitamin D_3, and can be prevented by lowering the dose.[264,266] 1,25-Dihydroxyvitamin D_3 can be highly effective in stimulating normal or near normal growth and development in children with a deficiency of this metabolite. This may also be true when the other preparations of vitamin D are utilized in adequate doses.

Side Effects and Complications of Treatment

Intoxication is a potential complication when vitamin D or any of its metabolites are administered, and is associated with significant morbidity and mortality. Intoxicated patients are either asymptomatic or may have anorexia, nausea, vomiting, constipation, lethargy, weakness, weight loss, polyuria, polydipsia, a dry mouth, and alterations in mental status. Children and infants are often listless and hypotonic. Hypercalcemia and hypercalciuria are caused by increased intestinal absorption of calcium and mobilization of calcium from the bone; diminution in renal function, nephrocalcinosis, nephrolithiasis, urinary tract infections, renal failure, and death may ensue. Patients who are on long-term treatment with vitamin D and its derivatives are particularly at risk for hypercalcemia and hypercalciuria. Patients being treated with these agents must be carefully followed, since it is not possible to predict when or in whom intoxication will occur.

There is little difference between the toxic and therapeutic doses of vitamin D, 25-hydroxyvitamin D_3, and dihydrotachysterol. On the other hand, toxicity caused by 1,25-dihydroxyvitamin D_3 may result from altered metabolism of the drug.[264] This may also be true for vitamin D, since lower doses are sometimes effective after a hypercalcemic episode. The factors that may play a role in the development of vitamin D intoxication are use of an inappropriately high dose, increments in dose over too-brief intervals, alteration in dietary calcium intake, lack of adequate sequential evaluation of serum 25-hydroxyvitamin D and serum urinary calcium, use of thiazides, and improvement in the underlying disease.

The treatment of vitamin D intoxication involves immediate discontinuation of the drug and any calcium preparations, and forcing of fluids. If hypercalcemia persists or is profound, the administration of glucocorticoids or salmon calcitonin may be required. This usually is necessary only when hypercalcemia is produced by the longer-acting sterols. Reduction of the sterol dose or cessation of calcium after episodes of hypercalcemia is usually sufficient to prevent recurrences. Patients who respond poorly to vitamin D may respond more readily to 1,25-dihydroxyvitamin D_3.

HYPERCALCEMIA

Pathogenesis of Hypercalcemia

In 90 percent of cases, hypercalcemia is caused by either primary hyperparathyroidism or cancer.

The causes of hypercalcemia are outlined in Table 5-3. The pathogenesis of hypercalcemia is discussed in detail below.

Primary Hyperparathyroidism

Primary hyperparathyroidism is a major cause of hypercalcemia. Hypercalcemia results from the PTH-mediated mobilization of calcium from bone and the PTH-enhanced renal tubular reabsorption of calcium. In addition, some patients have elevated circulating 1,25-dihydroxyvitamin D concentrations, and as a result have an increased intestinal absorption of calcium that may lead to hypercalciuria.[267] A major effect of PTH is to diminish the renal tubular reabsorption of phosphate, so that patients with primary hyperparathyroidism often have either a low or low normal serum phosphorus. Patients with primary hyperparathyroidism also have increased nephrogenous cAMP concentrations, and measurements of this cyclic nucleotide have been used as a means for diagnosis of the disease.[268] The renal production of 1,25-dihydroxyvitamin D is stimulated by PTH, a mechanism that is intimately associated with the renal production of cAMP and phosphate transport,[93] and which is inhibited by calcium.[269] Thus, whether or not patients with primary hyperparathyroidism have an elevated serum 1,25-dihydroxyvitamin D with increased intestinal absorption of calcium is related to the net response to these two opposing regulators of PTH secretion. Because PTH increases the renal tubular reabsorption of calcium, the urinary calcium is less than what would be anticipated for the degree of elevation of the serum calcium.[270]

The incidence of primary hyperparathyroidism has risen dramatically since the introduction of automated analysis and frequent measurement of the serum calcium concentration.[271] The incidence increases with age, is higher in men than in women, and peaks in the sixth decade of life. The

Table 5-3. Causes of Hypercalcemia

Primary hyperparathyroidism

Malignancies
  Solid tumors without skeletal metastasis
    Squamous cell carcinoma
      Lung
      Head
      Neck
    Carcinoma
      Ovary
      Pancreas
      Kidney
  Solid tumors with skeletal metastasis
    Carcinoma of the breast
      Estrogen
      Tamoxifen
      Androgens
  Hematologic malignancies
    Multiple myeloma
    T-cell lymphoma
    Hodgkin's disease
    Acute leukemia

Abnormal vitamin D metabolism
  Sarcoidosis
  Tuberculosis
  Other granulomatous diseases

Drugs
  Thiazide diuretics
  Lithium
  Milk-alkali syndrome
  Vitamin A intoxication
  Vitamin D intoxication
  1,25-Dihydroxyvitamin D intoxication

Endocrine diseases
  Hyperthyroidism
  Adrenal insufficiency
  Pheochromocytoma
  VIPoma syndrome

Congenital diseases
  Hypophosphatasia
  Familial hypocalciuric hypercalciuria
  Williams syndrome

Immobilization

incidence is 0.5 to 1 per thousand population.

Primary hyperparathyroidism in 80 to 85 percent of patients is caused by parathyroid adenoma; in another 15 to 20 percent of the patients it results from hyperplasia, and in about 3 percent of cases is caused by carcinoma.[272]

The pathophysiology of primary hyperparathyroidism is not well understood. The normal feedback regulation of PTH secretion by calcium is abnormal. It is likely that a new "set point" of interactive control of calcium is less effective in inhibiting secretion of the hormone in those with the disease than in normal subjects. An increase in the amount of parathyroid tissue mass itself, without a change in the set point for calcium, may be important as well.[273] In parathyroid hyperplasia, an increase in the number of cells per se appears to be of pathophysiologic importance.

The molecular basis for the disease is not known. Most patients do not have a family history of primary hyperparathyroidism or history of irradiation of the neck during childhood. Recent studies indicate that the disease is monoclonal in origin.[274] In two patients with primary hyperparathyroidism, the parathyroid gene was rearranged with DNA at a site known to be a region of two oncogenes.[275]

Malignancies and Hypercalcemia

Patients with hypercalcemia in malignant disease can be divided into three groups: those with solid tumors who do not have skeletal metastasis or so-called humoral hypercalcemia of malignancy (55 percent); patients with solid tumors and skeletal metastasis (25 percent); and patients with hematologic malignancies (15 to 20 percent).[276]

Humoral Hypercalcemia of Malignancy

Humoral hypercalcemia of malignancy is a syndrome in which hypercalcemia occurs in association with a normal or low serum phosphate, a reduction in serum 1,25-dihydroxyvitamin D, normal or low values for serum iPTH, and increases in nephrogenous cAMP.[277] In addition, as compared to patients with primary hyperparathyroidism, a higher urinary calcium is present in patients with humoral hypercalcemia of malignancy,[278] and histomorphometric studies of bone biopsies show an increase in osteoclastic resorption of bone.[279] The syndrome has been shown to result from ectopic production of a peptide made up of 141 amino acids and called parathyroid hormone-related peptide.[279-281] The sequence of the peptide was determined, and 8 of the first 13 amino acids are identical to those of human PTH. However, the remainder of the amino acid sequence is completely different. The gene for the peptide was mapped to the short arm of chromosome 12, whereas the genes for PTH and calcitonin appear on the short arm of chromosome 11.[280] Because the short arms of human chromosomes 11 and 12 are assumed to have been derived from a duplication event, however, the two genes appear to be related.[281]

Northern blot analysis of mRNA from a number of tumors associated with humoral hypercalcemia of malignancy has shown a complex pattern of from three to five hybridizing transcripts.[280] In addition, three hybridizing transcripts were identified in mRNA from normal human keratinocytes, indicating that the parathyroid hormone-like peptide is expressed in these cells and that there are a number of mRNA species that appear in both normal as well as transformed cells.[279-284] The present assumption is that these several species represent alternative mRNA processing.[281] The role of the peptide has not been established, but it may serve an autocrine or paracrine function for skin cells. Evidence in lambs suggests that the peptide may be a regulator of calcium transport by the placenta,[284] and evidence in rats suggests that it may be involved with calcium transport in milk.[285]

Growth factors may also be responsible for the humoral hypercalcemia of malignancy.[276,286] Transforming growth factor α (TGF$_α$), which acts by binding to the receptor for epidermal growth factor (EGF), was found to be responsible for bone resorption in animals with humoral hypercalcemia of malignancy.[286,287] The bone-resorbing activity produced by some tumors was found to be inhibited by anti-EGF receptor antiserum.[287,288] Available evidence indicates that TGF$_α$ is encoded by one gene and that the peptide is synthesized, inserted into cell membranes, and then released by a specific cleavage mechanism.[289,290]

Tumors typically associated with humoral hypercalcemia of malignancy include squamous cell carcinomas of the lung, head, and neck, and carcinomas of the kidney, bladder, ovary, and pancreas.[276,281]

Solid Tumors with Skeletal Metastasis

Hypercalcemia usually occurs in breast cancer as a result of widespread osteolytic bone destruction late in the course of the disease.[290] Some patients, however, appear to develop hypercalcemia by a mechanism similar to that responsible for humoral hypercalcemia of malignancy.[291] On the other hand, some patients develop hypercalcemia following treatment with estrogen or tamoxifen.[292] It is known that human breast cancer cells release prostaglandins in response to estrogens and antiestrogens.[293] However, inhibitors of prostaglandin synthesis have proved not to be effective for the treatment of hypercalcemia in patients with breast cancer. It is also possible that increased renal tubular reabsorption of calcium plays a role in the hypercalcemia of breast cancer.[294] Thus, a number of mechanisms may play a role in the pathogenesis of hypercalcemia related to breast cancer.

Hematologic Malignancies

Hypercalcemia often occurs in multiple myeloma, and is usually associated with a reduction in skeletal density as determined radiographically. Less commonly, lytic lesions are seen. It was shown that the bone-resorbing activity produced by a number of myeloma cell lines was inhibited by antibodies to lymphotoxin,[295] a potent stimulator of osteoclastic bone resorption. Human myeloma cells express mRNA for both lymphotoxin and tumor necrosis factor (TNF). However, the TNF is not secreted by the cells. Thus, lymphotoxin appears to be responsible for the bone resorption in myeloma.

Some patients with lymphoma or Hodgkin's disease and hypercalcemia were found to have elevated circulating 1,25-dihydroxyvitamin D levels.[296] However, other patients with adult T-cell leukemia-lymphoma and hypercalcemia were found to have reduced serum 1,25-dihydroxyvitamin D.[297] In these patients, the pathogenesis of the hypercalcemia is not related to abnormal metabolism of vitamin D.

Sarcoidosis

Hypercalcemia occasionally occurs in patients with sarcoidosis. Hypercalciuria is more common. Abnormal calcium metabolism in this disease results from increased circulating 1,25-dihydroxyvitamin D.[298,299] Hypercalcemia and elevated circulating 1,25-dihydroxyvitamin D usually occur during the summer as a result of increased exposure to sunlight and increased dermal synthesis of vitamin D$_3$.[298,299] Production of 1,25-dihydroxyvitamin D in sarcoidosis is extrarenal, and occurs in alveolar macrophages that are part of the characteristic alveolitis in the disease.[300,301] Increases in circulating 1,25-dihydroxyvitamin D occur because its synthesis by alveolar macrophages is not regulated by the same factors that regulate production in the kidney. Abnormal regulation is evident by an abnormal increase in serum 1,25-dihydroxyvitamin D in response to vitamin D in patients with sarcoidosis but not normal subjects,[302] and by a lack of the suppression of serum 1,25-dihydroxyvitamin D that normally occurs in response to an increased calcium intake.[303] Abnormal calcium metabolism is characterized by hypercalcemia, hypercalciuria, suppressed secretion of PTH and increased intestinal absorption of calcium as a result of the enhancing effect of elevated circulating 1,25-dihydroxyvitamin D on both the intestinal transport of calcium and osteoclastic bone resorption. Patients with sarcoidosis may develop nephrolithiasis and nephrocalcinosis, and are particularly susceptible to renal insufficiency, which can cause death.[298] Since γ-interferon production is increased in alveolar macrophages and pulmonary lymphocytes from patients with sarcoidosis,[304] and γ-interferon was shown to enhance production of 1,25-dihydroxyvitamin D by alveolar macrophages,[305] this interferon may be important in the pathogenesis of abnormal vitamin D metabolism in sarcoidosis.

Tuberculosis

Hypercalcemia and hypercalciuria sometimes occur in patients with pulmonary or miliary tuberculosis, and are associated with suppression of PTH secretion.[306–309] In some patients, the abnormal calcium metabolism results from increased circulating 1,25-dihydroxyvitamin D,[306–308] which is presumably produced in granulomatous tissue. In other patients, values are suppressed, indicating a different pathogenesis.[309] In contrast to its occurrence in sarcoidosis, hypercalcemia in patients with tuberculosis develops spontaneously at any time of year, and is not associated with increased exposure to sunlight. Although one patient had renal failure that apparently resulted from hypercalcemia,[307] the abnormal calcium metabolism appears to be self-limited, renal function is not permanently altered, and treatment is seldom required.

Other Diseases

Hypercalcemia caused by increased values of circulating 1,25-dihydroxyvitamin D was reported to occur in disseminated candidiasis,[310] silicone-induced granulomas,[311] rheumatoid arthritis,[312] and in individuals with no other apparent illness.[313,314] Some degree of impaired renal function occurred in several of these cases. The patient with rheumatoid arthritis had hypercalcemia, hypercalciuria, and nephrolithiasis, and failed to show regulation of serum 1,25-dihydroxyvitamin D when given vitamin D.[312] Lymph node and liver biopsies were unremarkable, and the site of production of 1,25-dihydroxyvitamin D in this case was not known.

Thiazide Diuretics

Thiazides sometimes cause hypercalcemia, and hypercalcemia is more common in individuals with high rates of bone turnover, including those with primary hyperparathyroidism, juvenile osteoporosis, and hypoparathyroidism treated with high doses of vitamin D.[315–317] In acute studies, it was shown that the serum calcium was increased by chlorothiazide in normal subjects and in patients with primary hyperparathyroidism, and that the increases in serum calcium were potentiated by parathyroid extract.[318] Thiazides act directly to increase calcium release from the skeleton and promote tubular reabsorption of calcium. Further, the action of thiazides on the kidney that reduces urinary calcium excretion may be mediated in part by a potentiation of the effects of PTH on the kidney. The evidence for a direct effect on the kidney was the demonstration of decreases in urinary calcium in patients with hypoparathyroidism during treatment with chlorthalidone.[319] The hypocalciuric effect of this drug is also attributed in part to an enhancement of proximal tubular reabsorption of sodium and calcium that results from a depletion of sodium and extracellular fluid volume.[320] The fact that thiazides mobilize calcium from the skeleton is emphasized by the observation that they increase the serum calcium in anephric patients who are on maintenance hemodialysis.[321]

It is evident that hypercalcemia produced by thiazide diuretics is most likely to occur in patients with high bone turnover. Therefore, patients should be evaluated after a thiazide diuretic is stopped, to determine whether hypercalcemia persists and whether other causes of hypercalcemia, particularly primary hyperparathyroidism, may be present.

Lithium

Chronic lithium administration is sometimes associated with mild hypercalcemia, hypermagnesemia, hyperparathyroidism, and relative decreases in urinary calcium,[322-324] and small parathyroid adenomas may be found in patients receiving lithium.[325] The biochemical changes in this disorder resemble those found in familial hypocalciuric hypercalcemia (see below).

Lithium was shown in normal individuals to reduce the fractional renal excretion of calcium and magnesium[324] and to alter the set point of release in vitro of iPTH by bovine parathyroid cells.[326] However, short-term administration of lithium was found not to alter the acute responses of iPTH and urinary cAMP to calcium infusion in normal subjects.[327] Whether long-term administration of lithium will alter the set point of secretion of PTH in human subjects is not established. Until more is known about the possible relationship between lithium and secretion of the hormone, patients in whom primary hyperparathyroidism is a possibility should be evaluated after lithium is stopped, to determine whether hypercalcemia persists.

Milk-alkali Syndrome

The milk-alkali syndrome is caused by excessive intake of calcium and phosphate in the form of milk and absorbable alkali, sodium carbonate, sodium bicarbonate, or calcium carbonate, usually for the treatment of peptic ulcer disease.[328] Because this form of treatment is no longer used, the syndrome is seldom encountered. Hypercalcemia occurs in both acute and chronic manifestations of the syndrome, but hypercalciuria may be present only in the acute syndrome, and may be absent in the chronic syndrome because of impaired renal function. The typical findings include hypercalcemia, alkalosis, hyperphosphatemia, extraskeletal calcification, nephrocalcinosis, and renal failure.[328] Many of the manifestations are reversed when the milk and alkali are discontinued. However, renal function is usually only partially restored, and improvement is related to the duration and extent of renal damage.

Vitamin A Intoxication

Vitamin A toxicity is a rare cause of hypercalcemia and results from the vitamin's enhancement of bone resorption in the skeleton.[329] The diagnosis is made by a history of excessive intake of the vitamin and by measuring the concentration of the vitamin in serum.

Vitamin D Intoxication

Vitamin D toxicity is an uncommon cause of hypercalcemia. Serum values for 25-hydroxyvitamin D are strikingly elevated and values for serum 1,25-dihydroxyvitamin D are either near the upper range of normal or slightly elevated.[199,330] This occurs because whereas the hepatic production of 25-hydroxyvitamin D is poorly regulated, the renal production of 1,25-dihydroxyvitamin D is tightly regulated.[166,302] Hypercalcemia and hypercalciuria occur because of enhanced intestinal absorption of calcium, enhanced osteoclastic bone resorption, suppression of the secretion of PTH, and a consequently diminished PTH-mediated tubular reabsorption of calcium.[330] The diagnosis is made by a history of excessive intake of the vitamin, and is established by showing high values of circulating 25-hydroxyvitamin D.

1,25-Dihydroxyvitamin D Intoxication

Hypercalcemia and hypercalciuria may occur in patients undergoing long-term treatment for hypocalcemia with 1,25-dihydroxyvitamin D_3 regardless of their underlying disease. When it occurs, the abnormal calcium metabolism usually develops spontaneously after stabilization of the serum calcium and months of treatment, and is associated with increases in serum 1,25-dihydroxyvitamin D.[264,266] Since the hormone has a short half-life and is not stored in fat, the hypercalcemia is easily treated by stopping the drug, and can be prevented by decreasing the dose.

Hyperthyroidism

Hypercalcemia occurs in some 8 to 22 percent of patients with thyrotoxicosis.[331] The serum calcium is minimally elevated, and patients are usually asymptomatic. Rarely, the hypercalcemia can be severe and even life-threatening.[331] It results from increased bone resorption caused by a direct effect of thyroxine and triiodothyronine on bone.[332]

Bone turnover is increased in hyperthyroidism,[333] as evidenced by increases in serum alkaline phosphatase and urinary hydroxyproline, and mild changes resembling those of hyperparathyroidism on bone biopsy[334]. Parathyroid function is suppressed,[335] and values for serum 1,25-dihydroxyvitamin D are markedly reduced.[336] These findings account for the characteristically high fecal and urinary calcium that results from decreases in serum 1,25-dihydroxyvitamin D and circulating PTH, respectively, as well as increased bone resorption.

Hyperthyroidism and hyperparathyroidism may occur together in the same patient.[337,338] However, the hyperthyroidism should be treated first. If hypercalcemia persists, patients should be evaluated for other causes of hypercalcemia, especially primary hyperparathyroidism.

Adrenal Insufficiency

Hypercalcemia rarely occurs in patients with untreated adrenocortical insufficiency. Initially, the hypercalcemia was attributed to volume depletion with hemoconcentration, hypercitricemia, and an increased affinity of plasma protein for calcium.[15] Without measurements, it was proposed that the hypercalcemia was not a true hypercalcemia but was due to an increase in binding of calcium to plasma proteins. More recently, however, it was shown that the serum ionized calcium was increased in a patient with hypercalcemia caused by adrenal insufficiency.[339] In this patient, the hypercalcemia was attributed not only to volume depletion but also to diminished renal excretion of calcium and increased bone resorption. The diminished reduction in urinary calcium was attributed to a diminished glomerular filtration and increased tubular reabsorption of calcium.

Interestingly, hypercalcemia occurred in a patient with hypoparathyroidism who developed adrenal insufficiency.[340] It was proposed that the hypercalcemia resulted from increased bone resorption. Since glucocorticoids are known to inhibit prostaglandin synthesis, increased prostaglandin synthesis caused by glucocorticoid deficiency could provide a mechanism for the increased bone resorption in adrenal insufficiency. In support of this is the observation that prednisone in pharmacologic doses produced increases in the cancellous bone of the tibia in both sham-operated and ovariectomized female rats.[341] This presumably occurred because prednisone inhibited prostaglandin synthesis and bone resorption produced by endogenous prostaglandins. Previous studies had shown that adrenalectomy in rats did not alter the uptake of 45-calcium into differentiating bones.[342] It is clear that the hypercalcemia results from volume depletion and glucocorticoid deficiency, since the restoration of extracellular fluid volume by saline and the administration of replacement doses of hydrocortisone corrects the adrenal insufficiency.[339]

Pheochromocytoma

Hypercalcemia sometimes occurs in patients with pheochromocytoma. It is usually successfully treated by removal of the tumor. The hypercalcemia is attributed to a number of mechanisms. These include the occurrence of primary hyperparathyroidism as part of the multiple endocrine neoplasia type II syndrome,[343] ectopic secretion of PTH by the pheochromocytoma,[344] direct catecholamine-stimulated release of PTH by beta adrenergic receptors in the parathyroid glands,[345] catecholamine-stimulated osteoclastic bone resorption,[346] and stimulation of osteoclastic bone resorption by a PTH-related factor produced by the pheochromocytoma.[347]

In view of these considerations, patients with pheochromocytoma and hypercalcemia should first be treated by removal of the pheochromocytoma. If hypercalcemia persists, they should then be evaluated for primary hyperparathyroidism and be treated appropriately.

VIPoma Syndrome

This disorder is characterized by a large-volume secretory diarrhea. The stool water is isotonic to plasma, stool electrolytes account for all of the osmolality, and the diarrhea persists during fasting.[348] Patients have a stool volume of at least 700 ml per day and lose large amounts of potassium and bicarbonate, which results in hypokalemia, acidosis, and volume depletion. Variable features include achlorhydria, hypochlorhydria, hypomagnesemia, an enlarged gallbladder, hypokalemic nephropathy, skin rash, flushing, hyperglycemia, and lacrimal gland hypersecretion and excessive tearing.[348] About half of all affected patients have hypercalcemia. The disease is caused by tumors that produce vasoactive intestinal polypeptide (VIP), which contains 28 amino acids and has a sequence that is similar to the sequences of secretin and glucagon.[349] Since the peptide was demonstrated in neurons of the central and peripheral nervous systems, its major function appears to be that of a neural peptide, neural transmitter, or neural modulator[350,351]. Vasoactive intestinal polypeptide is also a gastrointestinal hormone. The peptide was shown experimentally to increase active intestinal secretion of chloride and bicarbonate.[352]

Patients with hypercalcemia have a negative calcium balance with increased bone resorption.[353] Vasoactive intestinal polypeptide was shown to stimulate bone resorption in cultured mouse bones, and this effect was mediated by cAMP.[354]

The tumors that secrete VIP are present in the pancreas; VIP-containing cells have been identified in tumor tissue and high concentrations of VIP have been identified in the circulation of patients with the VIPoma syndrome. The syndrome is rare, with an incidence rate thought to be 1 per year per 10,000,000 population.[348]

Hypophosphatasia

Hypophosphatasia is a heritable disorder in which diminished skeletal alkaline phosphatase is associated with defective mineralization and increased urinary excretion of pyrophosphate and phosphoethanolamine.[355,356] Infantile or neonatal hypophosphatasia is the most common form, can be diagnosed in utero, is clinically apparent before the age of 6 months, is transmitted as an autosomal recessive trait, and occurs in inbred populations.[355-357] The abnormal calcification is often associated with increased intracranial pressure, hypercalcemia, hypercalciuria, and nephrocalcinosis, which soon ends in death.

Familial Hypocalciuric Hypercalcemia

Familial benign hypercalcemia or familial hypocalciuric hypercalcemia is a heritable disorder characterized by hypercalcemia and hypocalciuria transmitted as an autosomal dominant trait.[358-360] The hypercalcemia is present at birth and persists for life. Patients are usually asymptomatic but may have symptoms often associated with hypercalcemia, including fatigue, weakness, headache, and polyuria.[358] Pancreatitis occasionally occurs and can be life-threatening. The serum iPTH is within the normal range and is not suppressed by the hypercalcemia. The mass of the parathyroid glands is inappropriately large.[358] Despite the hypercalcemia, the urinary calcium concentration is in the range of that observed in normal subjects, and is about half that in patients with primary hyperparathyroidism. This indicates enhanced tubular reabsorption of calcium. However, this "defect" does not result from PTH, since the urinary calcium concentration is not altered by total parathyroidectomy.[358,361] The chronic hypercalcemia does not result in an abnormal renal concentrating ability.[358,362] Interestingly, the response of nephrogenous cAMP to PTH is exaggerated in patients with the syndrome.[363] The pathogenesis of the disease is not known, but insensitivity of the parathyroid glands and renal tubule to calcium was proposed as a mechanism.[358] The disease is usually detected by family screening after a family member is evaluated for hypercalcemia. Often the initial patient is discovered because of persistent hypercalcemia after parathyroidectomy. A modest hyperplasia of the parathyroid glands is typically present.

Williams Syndrome

The Williams syndrome is a congenital disorder of unknown etiology in which mental retardation, supravalvular aortic stenosis, and an elfin facies occur either alone or in association with other cardiac and vascular abnormalities.[364] The disease is usually sporadic but may be familial, and the mode of inheritance is variable, being consistent with X-linked dominant, autosomal dominant, autosomal recessive, and multifactorial transmission.

The so-called hypercalcemia of infancy occurs in some patients, is present during the first few years of life, and may be life-threatening. Patients show increased sensitivity to vitamin D, and balance studies show retention of calcium. The fecal calcium content is low and the urinary calcium is increased.[364] Some patients have elevated values of serum 1,25-dihydroxyvitamin D.[365] Children with the syndrome may show a blunted response of serum immunoreactive calcitonin to a calcium challenge.[366] Hypercalcemia during fetal growth and development has been implicated in the pathogenesis of Williams syndrome, since aortic lesions and somatic changes similar to those described in patients with the syndrome were produced in offspring by the administration of toxic doses of vitamin D to pregnant rabbits.[367,368]

Immobilization

Chronic immobilization consistently leads to loss of bone, with ensuing hypercalciuria and less frequently hypercalcemia.[369,370] Hypercalcemia is more likely to occur in young individuals. Disuse osteoporosis develops in patients who have long-term muscular paralysis as a result of poliomyelitis and those who are paraplegic or quadraplegic because of spinal cord injury.[370] Further, demineralization of the skeleton and hypercalciuria are hazards that may result from weightlessness associated with prolonged spaceflight.[371] In addition to hypercalciuria and loss of bone mass, reduction of serum iPTH, serum 1,25-dihydroxyvitamin D, and nephrogenous cAMP characteristically occur and indicate that these abnormalities result from increased bone resorption.[370]

In experimental animals, immobilization causes an uncoupling of bone remodeling. The bone formation rate declines and the bone resorption rate increases.[372] The increased bone resorption in this animal model appears to be caused by prostaglandins, since it is prevented by indomethacin, an inhibitor of prostaglandin synthesis.[372] The bone formation rate, however, remains suppressed and is not influenced by indomethacin. The mechanism for the decline in the rate of bone formation produced by immobilization is not known.

Signs and Symptoms of Hypercalcemia

The clinical features of hypercalcemia are summarized in Table 5-4. In general, the incidence and severity of the signs and symptoms are related to the degree of hypercalcemia. It is important to be certain that the measured value for total serum calcium is an accurate reflection of the degree of elevation of the ionized calcium. This can best be accomplished by simultaneous determination of the serum ionized calcium with an ion-specific electrode. If this measurement is unavailable, the serum albumin should be measured, since calcium is bound to albumin, and an elevated total serum calcium will represent a more profound degree of hypercalcemia in the presence of hypoalbuminemia. On the other hand, in multiple myeloma, an abnormal elevation of total but not ionized serum calcium can occur because of increased production by myeloma cells of proteins that bind calcium.

Cardiovascular

Cardiovascular findings in hypercalcemia include a reduction in heart rate, elevation of systolic blood pressure, shortening of the QT interval and prolongation of the PR interval on the electrocardiogram, and an increased sensitivity to digitalis.

Neurologic

Neurologic findings produced by hypercalcemia include an overall decline in mentation and state of consciousness with confusion, lethargy, and stupor that can progress to coma.

Dermal

With long-term hypercalcemia, calcium is deposited in the skin, causing pruritis and metastatic calcification, and in the conjunctiva, where it causes band keratopathy and calcification.

Gastrointestinal

Gastrointestinal findings in hypercalcemia include anorexia, nausea, and vomiting which can worsen existing dehydration. These symptoms can be exacerbated by abdominal pain associated with activation of a peptic ulcer or pancreatitis.

Renal

Renal findings in hypercalcemia include a polyuria that is resistant to vasopressin. Patients may present with symptoms that are also found in diabetes mellitus.

Treatment of Hypercalcemia

The management of hypercalcemia is outlined in Table 5-5.

Hypercalcemia can result from increased intestinal absorption of calcium, increased bone resorption, impaired excretion of calcium, or a combination of these factors. For successful treatment in a given patient, it is important to identify the underlying disease and to understand the pathogenesis so that appropriate treatment can be administered. For example, in vitamin D intoxication, hypercalcemia results from increased intestinal absorption of calcium and to a lesser extent from increased osteoclastic bone resorption. Consequently, treatment should be directed at reducing calcium intake and diminishing bone resorption. In patients with multiple myeloma, hypercalcemia results from increased bone resorption; treat-

Table 5-4. Signs and Symptoms of Hypercalcemia

Cardiovascular
  Arrhythmias
    Bradycardia
    Heart block
  Hypertension
  Electrocardiographic changes
  Increased sensitivity to digitalis

Central nervous system
  Impaired concentration
  Increased sleep requirement
  Altered state of unconsciousness
    Confusion
    Lethargy
    Stupor
    Coma
  Mental retardation (infants)

Dermal
  Pruritis
  Metastatic calcification

Gastrointestinal tract
  Polydipsia
  Anorexia
  Nausea
  Vomiting
  Constipation
  Pancreatitis
  Peptic ulcer

General
  Weakness
  Dehydration
  Metastatic calcification

Hematological
  Anemia

Ocular
  Palpebral calcification
  Band keratopathy
  Conjunctival calcification

Renal
  Polyuria
  Diminished concentrating ability
  Nephrolithiasis
  Nephrocalcinosis
  Renal failure

Skeletal
  Joint pains (pseudogout)

Table 5-5. Management of Hypercalcemia

General measures
  Hydration
  Restriction of calcium intake
  Mobilization

Enhancement of urinary calcium
  Intravenous saline
  Diuretics
    Furosemide
    Ethacrynic acid

Inhibition of bone resorption
  Phosphate
  Diphosphonates
  Calcitonin
  Glucocorticoids
  Mithramycin

Treatment of underlying disease

ment should therefore be directed at inhibiting bone resorption.

General Measures

General measures for the treatment of hypercalcemia include hydration. Patients with hypercalcemia may have anorexia, nausea, vomiting, and polyuria caused by a defect in renal concentration. As a result, they are often dehydrated and have reduced glomerular filtration. Restoration of a normal extracellular fluid volume will often diminish the elevated serum calcium, in part by increasing calcium excretion in the urine. If the hypercalcemia is thought to be caused by increased intestinal absorption of calcium, dietary calcium should be restricted to a range of from 200 to 400 mg/day. As noted already, immobilization causes increased bone resorption and can in and of itself result in hypercalcemia. When possible, patients with hypercalcemia should be mobilized with weight-bearing exercise to prevent this.

For more vigorous treatment, diuretics and intravenous saline can be used to promote the urinary excretion of calcium.[373] Saline can be given intravenously in doses of 3 to 6 liters/day, and loop diuretics such as furosemide and ethacrynic acid, which inhibit the tubular reabsorption of calcium, can also be used. The dose of furosemide is 80 to 100 mg every 2 hours, and of ethacrynic acid 20 to 40 mg every 2 hours. These drugs should not be used until patients have been rehydrated. Saline should be administered to prevent dehydration, which if allowed to occur would promote the recurrence of hypercalcemia by preventing calcium excretion.

Phosphate

In the great majority of cases, hypercalcemia results from increased bone resorption. Thus, utilization of drugs that act to inhibit osteoclast-mediated bone resorption provides a specific means of treatment. Phosphate is effective in lowering the serum calcium, but involves raising the serum inorganic phosphate abnormally.

Sodium phosphate does not act by increasing urinary calcium excretion, but causes a redistribution of calcium characterized by a rapid diversion of calcium from the circulation with no effect on calcium entry into the circulation.[374] Phosphate may act by precipitating calcium phosphate salts, since the serum calcium begins to decline within minutes after the start of an infusion of phosphate, and the decline in serum calcium is proportional to the ion product of calcium and phosphate during the infusion.[375] That the precipitation of calcium salts occurs is strengthened by the observation of metastatic calcification in patients receiving phosphate for treatment of hypercalcemia.[376,377] There is no convincing evidence that acute administration of phosphorus for the treatment of hypercalcemia is associated with functional toxicity.[378] Patients receiving phosphate given chronically for the treatment of hypercalcemia need to be followed closely, and the smallest dose possible should be used to prevent soft tissue calcification. The intravenous administration of phosphate is potentially dangerous, since severe and possibly fatal hypocalcemia can be produced.[379] Therefore, patients need to be followed very closely with frequent serial determinations of serum calcium and phosphate.

Phosphate can be given orally, beginning with a daily dose of 1500 mg. Because of toxicity, it is recommended that phosphate not be administered intravenously. Phosphate is effective in lowering the serum calcium, and has been used in such diseases as primary hyperparathyroidism, sarcoidosis, vitamin D intoxication, and multiple myeloma.[375,378,380]

Diphosphonates

Diphosphonates are analogues of pyrophosphate that are potent inhibitors of osteoclastic bone resorption. They are therefore of great value in the treatment of hypercalcemia caused by primary hyperparathyroidism and by cancer. The only diphosphonate available for use in the United States is ethane-1-hydroxy-1,1-diphosphonate (etidronate) or EHDP. Available evidence indicates that when given intravenously, EHDP is effective in the treatment of hypercalcemia caused by malignancy.[381] The drug is given daily at a dose of 7.5 mg/kg body weight until the serum calcium begins to decline. It may then be administered orally, but its intestinal absorption is low so that the drug must be given for a number of weeks before it is effective in correcting the hypercalcemia.[382] There is a narrow range between the therapeutic dose and a toxic dose that may cause impaired mineralization, osteomalacia, and possible fractures. These side effects diminish the potential usefulness of the drug in the long-term management of hypercalcemia.

Other diphosphonates include 3-amino-1-hydroxypropylidene-1,1-diphosphonate (APD) and dichloromethylene-diphosphonate (clodronate). These drugs are also potent inhibitors of bone resorption and were shown to be extremely effective in treating hypercalcemia caused by increased bone resorption.[381-383] They both have the advantage of not impairing mineralization except at very high doses. However, APD is known to produce febrile reactions in high doses, and several patients have developed leukemia while being treated with clodronate.

Calcitonin

Calcitonin acts by blocking bone resorption [384,385] and by inhibiting the renal tubular reabsorption of calcium, which enhances the renal excretion of calcium.[386] Osteoclasts have receptors for calcitonin, and calcitonin was shown to act directly on osteoclasts to inhibit osteoclastic resorption.[387] Salmon calcitonin is quite potent, owing to increased binding of the hormone to receptors in bone and to a diminished rate of degradation.[388] Calcitonin is more effective in diseases in which there is an increased rate of bone resorption. It was shown to be effective in the treatment of hypercalcemia caused by vitamin D intoxication and immobilization, and in the hypercalcemia of infancy, thyrotoxicosis, and malignancy.[389-394] After treatment for a period of hours or days, escape from the hypocalcemic actions of calcitonin occurs.[395] Under these circumstances, treatment should be discontinued for several days before beginning again. Calcitonin was shown to be more effective in the treatment of hypercalcemia related to malignancy when given together with glucocorticoids.[396] The drug is administered either subcutaneously or by intramuscular injection. Salmon calcitonin can be given in doses of 25 to 50 units every 6 to 8 hours.

Glucocorticoids

Glucocorticoids in pharmacologic doses are very effective in the treatment of hypercalcemia in a number of disease states. These include sarcoidosis,[298-299] tuberculosis,[307] rheumatoid arthritis,[312] other granulomatous diseases, and vitamin D intoxication.[330,397] A number of malignancies associated with hypercalcemia are also responsive to treatment with glucocorticoids. These include multiple myeloma, leukemia, Hodgkin's disease, and lymphomas, as well as carcinoma of the breast.[296]

There appear to be a number of mechanisms by which glucocorticoids alter abnormal calcium metabolism. When administered in large doses to normal subjects or patients with normal calcium metabolism, glucocorticoids diminish the intestinal absorption of calcium,[398,399] increase the renal clearance and urinary excretion of calcium,[398,400,401] and enhance the release of calcium from the skeleton.[402] Glucocorticoids appear to act by inhibiting the effects of 1,25-dihydroxyvitamin D on the intestine.[403,404] In addition, glucocorticoids inhibit bone resorption in fetal long bones in organ culture.[405] The mechanism for this is not known, but may be related to inhibition of prostaglandin synthesis, since glucocorticoids have been shown to have this effect in vitro. The administration of prednisone to rats was shown to increase cancellous bone in both sham-operated and ovariectomized animals.[341] This action of the drug is consistent with inhibition of prostaglandin synthesis. As already noted, it is likely that the hypercalcemia associated with adrenal insufficiency results from increased bone resorption caused by lack of suppression of endogenous prostaglandin synthesis. In sarcoidosis, the drug appears to act through its anti-inflammatory effect. Treatment is associated with a reduction of the serum 1,25-dihydroxyvitamin D concentration.[298,299] This also appears to be the case in tuberculosis and lymphomas, where an elevated 1,25-dihydroxyvitamin D is responsible for the abnormal calcium metabolism[296]. Prednisolone in a dosage of 1 mg/kg body weight for two to three days, with reduction of dosage thereafter, is currently recommended.

Mithramycin

Mithramycin is a cytotoxic antibiotic that is derived from *Streptomyces tanashiensis*. Mithramycin inhibits RNA synthesis but does not alter protein or DNA synthesis.[406] It is very potent and is useful in the treatment of hypercalcemia of a variety of causes. The drug was shown to inhibit bone resorption both in vivo[407] and in vitro,[408] an effect attributed to the inhibition of osteoclastic bone resorption. Mithramycin should be given by intravenous injection; the recommended dosage is 25 µg/kg per day for several days. For chronic treatment, it can be administered in one to two doses per week, but should not be given except when hypercalcemia recurs. The toxicity is dependent on the frequency of treatment as well as the total dose.[409,410]

Mithramycin is toxic to the bone marrow, liver, and kidneys. It can produce thrombocytopenia, hepatocellular necrosis, and impaired renal function with proteinuria. In addition, nausea, vomiting, and stomatitis can occur. In general, the toxic effects are reversible, depending on the total dose, but a hemorrhagic diathesis can occur from the impaired synthesis of clotting factors as well as thrombocytopenia. This can proceed to generalized hemorrhagic complications and death.[410,411] Thus, patients being treated with mithramycin need to be closely followed.

REFERENCES

1. Bronner F: Calcium homeostatis. p 43. In Bronner F, Coburn JW (eds): Disorders of Mineral Metabolism. Vol 2 of Calcium

Physiology. Academic Press, New York, 1982
2. Parfitt AM, Kleerekoper M: The divalent ion homeostasis system. Physiology and metabolism of calcium, phosphorus, magnesium and bone. p 269. In Maxwell MH, Kleeman CR (eds): Clinical Disorders of Fluid and Electrolyte Metabolism. McGraw-Hill, New York, 1980
3. Harris EK, DeMets DL: Biological and analytic components of variation in long term studies of serum constituents in normal subjects. V. Estimated biological variations in ionized calcium. Clin Chem 17:983, 1971
4. Pedersen KO: On the cause and degree of intraindividual serum calcium variability. Scand J Clin Lab Invest 30:191, 1972
5. Dent CE: Some problems of hyperparathyroidism. Br Med J 2:1419, 1962
6. Moore EW: Ionized calcium in normal serum, ultrafiltrates, and whole blood determined by ion-exchange electrodes. J Clin Invest 49:318, 1970
7. Pedersen KO: Protein-bound calcium in human serum. Quantitative examination of binding and its variables by a molecular binding model and clinical implications for measurement of ionized calcium. Scand J Clin Lab Invest 30:321, 1972
8. Toribara TY, Terepka R, Dewey PA: The ultrafiltrable calcium of human serum: I. Ultrafiltration methods and normal values. J Clin Invest 36:738, 1957
9. Walser M: Ion association: VI. Interactions between calcium, magnesium, inorganic phosphate, citrate and protein in normal human plasma. J Clin Invest 40:723, 1961
10. Toffaletti J, Savory J, Gitelman HJ: Use of gel filtration to examine the distribution of calcium among serum proteins. Clin Chem 23:2306, 1977
11. Muller-Plathe O, Lindemann K: Ionized calcium versus total calcium. Scand J Clin Lab Invest 43:suppl 165:71, 1983
12. Wills MR, Lewis MR: Plasma calcium fractions and the protein-binding of calcium in normal subjects and in patients with hypercalcemia and hypocalcemia. J Clin Pathol 24:856, 1971
13. Duncan PH, Willis MR, Smith BJ, Savory J: Clinical studies of protein-bound calcium in various diseases. Clin Chem 28:672, 1982
14. Lim P, Jacob E, Chio LF, Pwee HS: Serum ionized calcium in nephrotic syndrome. Q J Med 179:421, 1976
15. Walser M, Robinson BH, Duckett JW: The hypercalcemia of adrenal insufficiency. J Clin Invest 42:456, 1963
16. Katz S, Klotz IM: Interactions of calcium with serum albumin. Arch Biochem Biophys 44:351, 1953
17. Pedersen KO: Binding of calcium to serum albumin: II. Effect of pH via competitive hydrogen and calcium ion binding to the imidazole groups of albumin. Scand J Clin Lab Invest 29:75, 1972
18. Irons LI, Perkins DJ: Studies on the interactions of magnesium, calcium, and strontium ions with native and chemical modification in human serum albumin. Biochem J 84:152, 1962
19. McLean FC, Hastings AB: The state of calcium in the fluids of the body. I. The conditions affecting the ionization of calcium. J Biol Chem 108:285, 1935
20. Coburn JW, Popovtzer MM, Massry SG, Kleeman CR: The physiochemical state and renal handling of divalent ions in chronic renal failure. Arch Intern Med 124:302, 1969
21. Toffaletti J, Gitelman HJ, Savory J: Separation and quantitation of serum constituents associated with calcium by gel filtration. Clin Chem 22:8, 1976
22. Walser M: Divalent cations: Physiochemical state in glomerular filtrate and urine and renal excretion. p 555. In Orloff J, Berliner RW (eds): Handbook of Physiology. Sect 8, Renal Physiology. American Physiological Society, Washington, DC, 1973
23. Clayton B: Table of normal values adjusted for age. p. 146. In Pediatric Chemical Pathology. Vol 1. Blackwell, London, 1980
24. Raisz LG: Bone metabolism and calcium regulation. p 1. In Avioli LV, Krane SM (eds): Metabolic Bone Disease. Vol 1. Academic Press, New York, 1977
25. Harrison HE, Harrison HG. p 53. Disorders of Calcium and Phosphate Metabolism in Childhood and Adolescence. WB Saunders, Philadelphia, 1979
26. Christoffersen J: Dissolution of calcium

hydroxyapatite. Calcif Tissue Int 33:557, 1981
27. Favus MJ: Transport of calcium by intestinal mucosa. Semin Nephrol 1:306, 1981
28. Suki WN: Calcium transport in the nephron. Am J Physiol 237:F1, 1979
29. Suki WN, Rouse D: Hormonal regulation of calcium transport in thick ascending limb renal tubules. Am J Physiol 241:F171, 1981
30. Kleeman CR, Massry SG, Coburn JW: The clinical physiology of calcium homeostasis, parathyroid hormone and calcitonin. Calif Med 114:16, 1971
31. Wacker WEC, Williams RJ: Magnesium/calcium balances and steady states of biological systems. J Theor Biol 20:65, 1968
32. Murphy E, Mandel LJ: Cytosolic free calcium levels in rabbit proximal kidney tubules. Am J Physiol 242:C124, 1982
33. Mandel IJ, Murphy E: Regulation of cytosolic free calcium in rabbit proximal renal tubules. J Biol Chem 259:11188, 1984
34. Bygrave FL: Mitochondria and the control of intracellular calcium. Biol Rev 53:43, 1978
35. Bygrave FL: Calcium transport in mitochondria isolated from normal and injured tissue. p 121. In Anghileri LJ, Tuffet-Anghileri AM (eds): The Role of Calcium in Biological Systems. Vol 1. CRC Press, Boca Raton, 1982
36. Baker PF: Transport and metabolism of calcium in nerve. Prog Biophys Mol Biol 24:177, 1972
37. Blaustein MP: The interrelationship between sodium and calcium fluxes across cell membranes. Rev Physiol Biochem Pharmacol 70:33, 1974
38. Gupta BL, Hall TA: Electron microprobe X-ray analysis of calcium. Ann NY Acad Sci 307:28, 1978
39. Godfraind-DeBecker A, Godfraind T: Calcium transport system: A comparative study in different cells. Int Rev Cytol 67:141, 1980
40. Carafoli E, Cromptom M: The regulation of intracellular calcium in mitochondria. Ann NY Acad Sci 307:369, 1978
41. Carafoli E: The regulation of the cellular functions of Ca^{++}. p. 1. In Bronner F and Coburn JW (eds): Disorders of Mineral Metabolism. Vol 2. Calcium Physiology. Academic Press, New York, 1981
42. Betts F, Blumenthal NC, Posner AS, et al: Atomic structure of intracellular amorphous calcium phosphate deposits. Proc Natl Acad Sci USA 72:2088, 1975
43. Lehninger AL: Mitochondria and the physiology of Ca^{++}. Trans Am Clin Climatol Assoc 83:83, 1973
44. Allen DG, Blinks JR, Prendergast FG: Aequorin luminescence: Relation of light emission to calcium concentration: A calcium-independent component. Science 195:996, 1977
45. Tsien RY, Pozzan T, Rink TJ: Calcium homeostasis in intact lymphocytes: Cytoplasmic free calcium monitored with a new intracellularly trapped fluorescent indicator. J Cell Biol 94:325, 1982
46. Ashley CC, Campbell AK (Eds): Detection and measurement of free Ca^{2+} in cells. Elsevier North Holland, Amsterdam, 1979
47. Moore L, Fitzpatrick DE, Chen TS, Landon EJ: Calcium pump activity of the renal plasma membrane and renal microsomes. Biochim Biophys Acta 345:405, 1974
48. Dipolo R, Beauge L: Mechanisms of calcium transport in the giant axon of the squid and their physiological role. Cell Calcium 1:147, 1980
49. Gmaj P, Murer H, Kinne R: Calcium ion transport across plasma membranes isolated from rat kidney cortex. Biochem J 178:549, 1979
50. Carafoli E: Ca^{2+} pumping systems in the plasma membrane. p. 9. In Bronner F, Peterlik M (eds): Calcium and phosphate transport across biomembranes. Academic Press. New York, 1981
51. Blaustein MP: The interrelationship between sodium and calcium fluxes across cell membanes. Rev Physiol Biochem Pharmacol 70:33, 1974
52. DiPolo R: Characterization of the ATP-dependent calcium efflux in dialyzed squid giant axons. J Gen Physiol 69:795, 1977
53. Chase HS, Al-Awqati Q: Regulation of the sodium permeability of the luminal border of toad bladder by intracellular sodium and calcium. J Gen Physiol 77:693, 1981
54. Ullrich KL, Rumrich G, Kloss S: Active Ca^{2+} reabsorption in the proximal tubule of rat kidney. Pfluegers Arch 364:223, 1976

55. Mullins LJA: A mechanism for Na/Ca transport. J Gen Physiol 70:681, 1977
56. DiPolo R, Beauge L: The effect of pH on Ca^{2+} extrusion mechanisms in dialyzed squid axons. Biochem Biophys Acta 688:237, 1982
57. Lee CO, Taylor A, Windhager EE: Cytosolic calcium ion activity in epithelial cells of *Necturus* kidney. Nature 287:859, 1980
58. Friedman PA, Figureido JF, Maack T, Windhager EE: Sodium-calcium interactions in the renal proximal convoluted tubule of the rabbit. Am J Physiol 240:F558, 1981
59. Taylor A: Role of cytosolic calcium and sodium-calcium exchange in regulation of transepithelial sodium and water absorption. p. 233. In Schultz SG (ed): Ion Transport by Epithelia. Raven Press, New York, 1981
60. Heinrich G, Kronenberg HM, Potts JT Jr, Habener JF: Gene encoding parathyroid hormone: Nucleotide sequence of the rat gene and deduced amino acid sequence of rat preproparathyroid hormone. J Biol Chem 259:3320, 1984
61. Vasicek T, McDevitt BE, Hendy GN, et al: Nucleotide sequence of the human parathyroid hormone gene. Proc Natl Acad Sci USA 80:2127, 1983
62. Hendy GN, Kronenberg HM, Potts JT Jr, Rich A: Nucleotide sequence of cloned cDNAs encoding human preproparathyroid hormone. Proc Natl Acad Sci USA 78:7365, 1981
63. Kronenberg HM, McDevitt BE, Majzoub JA, et al: Cloning and nucleotide sequence of DNA coding for bovine preproparathyroid hormone. Proc Natl Acad Sci USA 76:4981, 1979
64. Naylor SL, Sakaguchi AY, Szoka P, et al: Human parathyroid hormone gene (PTH) is on short arm of chromosome 11. Somatic Cell Genet 9:609, 1983
65. Habener JF, Potts JT Jr: Biosynthesis of parathyroid hormone. N Engl J Med 585:635, 1978
66. Keutmann HT, Sauer MM, Hendy GN, et al: The complete amino acid sequence of human parathyroid hormone. Biochemistry 17:552, 1978
67. Brewer HB Jr, Ronan R: Bovine parathyroid hormone: Amino acid sequence. Proc Natl Acad Sci USA 67:1862, 1970
68. Niall HD, Keutmann HT, Sauer R, et al: The amino acid sequence of bovine parathyroid hormone I. Hoppe Seylers Z Physiol Chem 351:1586, 1970
69. Sauer RT, Niall HD, Hogan ML, et al: The amino acid sequence of porcine parathyroid hormone. Biochemistry 13:1994, 1974
70. Potts JT Jr, Tregear GW, Keutmann HT, et al: Synthesis of a biologically active N-terminal tetratriacontapeptide of parathyroid hormone. Proc Natl Acad Sci USA 68:63, 1971
71. Mayer GP, Hurst JG: Sigmoidal relationship between parathyroid hormone secretion rate and plasma calcium concentration in calves. Endocrinology 102:1036, 1978
72. Morrissey JJ, Cohn DV: Regulation of secretion of parathormone and secretory protein-I from separate intracellular pools by calcium, dibutyryl cyclic AMP, and (1)-isoproterenol. J Cell Biol 82:93, 1979
73. Shoback DM, Thatcher J, Leombruno R, Brown EM: Relationship between parathyroid hormone secretion and cytosolic calcium concentrations in dispersed bovine parathyroid cells. Proc Natl Acad Sci USA 81:3113, 1984
74. Oetting MH, LeBoff MS, Brown EM: Ca^{++} stimulates PTH release in permeabilized parathyroid cells. Clin Res 34:551A, 1986
75. Morrissey J: Cytosolic calcium and parathyroid cell function. Clin Res 34:550A, 1986
76. Fitzpatrick LA, Aurbach GD: Calcium inhibition of parathyroid hormone secretion is mediated via a guanine nucleotide regulatory protein. Program of the Seventh Annual Meeting of the American Society of Bone and Mineral Research. (Abstr 320) Washington, DC, June 15–18, 1985
77. Brown EM, Redgrave J, Thatcher J: Effect of the phorbol ester TPA on PTH secretion: Evidence for a role for protein kinase C in the control of PTH release. FEBS Lett 175:72, 1984
78. Kobayashi N, Russell J, Lettieri D, Sherwood LM: Effects of phorbol ester on subcellular distribution of protein kinase C in bovine parathyroid cells. (Abstr) J Bone Min Res 1 (Suppl):315, 1986

79. Anast CS, Mohs JM, Kaplan SL, Burns TW: Evidence for parathyroid failure in magnesium deficiency. Science 177:606, 1972
80. Anast CS, Winnacker JL, Forte LF, Burns TW: Impaired release of parathyroid hormone in magnesium deficiency. J Clin Endocrinol Metab 42:707, 1976
81. Sherwood LM, Mayer GP, Ramberg CF, et al: Regulation of parathyroid hormone secretion: Proportional control by calcium, lack of effect of phosphate. Endocrinology 83:1043, 1968
82. Canterbury JM, Reiss E: Multiple immunoreactive molecular forms of parathyroid hormone in human serum. Proc Soc Exp Biol Med 140:1393, 1972
83. Mallette LE, Tuma SN, Berger RE, Kirkland JL: Radioimmunoassay for the middle region of human parathyroid hormone using an homologous antiserum with a carboxy-terminal fragment of bovine parathyroid hormone as radioligand. J Clin Endocrinol Metab 54:1017, 1982
84. Hruska KA, Korkor A, Martin K, Slatopolsky E: Peripheral metabolism of intact parathyroid hormone. Role of liver and kidney and the effect of chronic renal failure. J Clin Invest 67:885, 1981
85. Martin KJ, Hruska KA, Lewis J, et al: The renal handling of parathyroid hormone: Role of peritubular uptake and glomerular filtration. J Clin Invest 60:808, 1977
86. Rouleau MF, Warshawsky H. Goltzman D: Parathyroid hormone binding in vivo to renal, hepatic and skeletal tissues of the rat using a radioautographic approach. Endocrinology 118:919, 1986
87. Martin KJ, Hruska KA, Freitag JJ, et al: The peripheral metabolism of parathyroid hormone. N Engl J Med 301:1092, 1979
88. Hruska KA, Kopelman R, Rutherford WE, et al: Metabolism of immunoreactive parathyroid hormone in the dog: The role of the kidney and the effects of chronic renal disease. J Clin Invest 56:39, 1975
89. Kaminsky NH, Broadus AE, Hardman JC, et al: Effects of parathyroid hormone on plasma and urinary adenosine 3',5'-monophosphate in man. J Clin Invest 49:2387, 1970
90. Aurbach GD, Chase LR: Parathyroid gland. Cyclic nucleotides and biochemical actions of parathyroid hormone and calcitonin. p. 117. In Greep R, Astwood EB (eds): Handbook of Physiology. Vol 7. Endocrinology. Baltimore, Williams & Wilkins, 1976
91. Rasmussen H, Pechet M, Fast D: Effect of dibutyryl cyclic adenosine 3',5'-monophosphate, theophylline, and other nucleotides upon calcium and phosphate metabolism. J Clin Invest 47:1843, 1968
92. Broadus AE, Mahaffey JE, Bartter FC, Neer RM: Nephrogenous cyclic AMP as a parathyroid function test. J Clin Invest 60:771, 1977
93. Bell NH, Avery S, Sinha T, et al: Effects of dibutyryl cyclic adenosine 3',5'-monophosphate and parathyroid extract on calcium and phosphorous metabolism in hypoparathyroidism and pseudohypoparathyroidism. J Clin Invest 51:816, 1972
94. Caverzasio J, Rizzoli R, Bonjour J-P: Sodium-dependent phosphate transport inhibited by parathyroid hormone and cyclic AMP stimulation in an opossum kidney cell line. J Biol Chem 261:3233, 1986
95. Agus ZS, Gardner LB, Beck LH, Goldberg M: Effects of parathyroid hormone on renal tubular reabsorption of calcium, sodium and phosphate. Am J Physiol 3:F393, 1978
96. Costanzo LS, Windhager EE: Effects of parathyroid hormone, ADH and cyclic AMP on distal tubular Ca and Na reabsorption. Am J Physiol 246:F937, 1984
97. Charbardes D, Imbert M, Clique A, et al: PTH sensitive adenyl cyclase activity in different segments of the rabbit nephron. Pfluegers Arch 354:229, 1975
98. Borle AB: Calcium and phosphate metabolism. Annu Rev Physiol 36:361, 1974
99. Eisenberg E: Effects of serum calcium level and parathyroid extracts on phosphate and calcium excretion in hypoparathyroid patients. J Clin Invest 44:942, 1965
100. Farese RV, Bidot-Lopez P, Sabir MA, Larson RE: The phosphatidate-polyphosphoinositide cycle: Activation by parathyroid hormone and dibutyryl-cAMP in rabbit kidney cortex. Ann NY Acad Sci 372:539, 1981
101. Hruska KA, Moskowitz D, Esbrit P, et al:

Stimulation of inositol triphosphate and diacylglycerol production in renal tubular cells by parathyroid hormone. J Clin Invest 79:230, 1987
102. Rodriguez HV, Villarreal H, Klahr S, Slatopolsky E: Pseudohypoparathyroidism type II: Restoration of normal renal responsiveness to parathyroid hormone by calcium administration. J Clin Endocrinol Metab 39:693, 1974
103. Rodan SB, Rodan GA: The effect of parathyroid hormone and thyrocalcitonin on the accumulation of cyclic adenosine 3',5'-monophosphate in freshly isolated bone cells. J Biol Chem 249:3068, 1974
104. Vaes G: Parathyroid hormone-like action of N^6-2^1-O-dibutyryl-adenosine-3',5'-(cyclic)-monophosphate on bone explants in tissue culture. Nature 219:939, 1968
105. Klein DC, Raisz LG: Role of adenosine 3',5'-monophosphate in the hormonal regulation of bone resorption: Studies with cultured fetal bone. Endocrinology 89:818, 1971
106. Herrmann-Erlee MPM, van der Meer JM: The effects of dibutyryl cyclic adenosine 3',5'-monophosphate, aminophylline and propranolol on PTE-induced bone resorption in vitro. Endocrinology 94:424, 1974
107. Lerner U: Inhibition of bone resorption and lysosomal enzyme release from calvarial bones cultured for 24 hours: Synergism between cyclic AMP analogues and phosphodiesterase inhibitors. Acta Endocrinol 94:138, 1980
108. Barling PM, Bibby NJ: Study of the localization of [^{3}H] bovine parathyroid hormone in bone by light microscope autoradiography. Calcif Tissue Int 37:441, 1985
109. McSheehy PMJ, Chambers TJ: Osteoblastic cells mediate osteoclastic responsiveness to parathyroid hormone. Endocrinology 118:824, 1986
110. Parsons JA, Neer RM, Potts JT: Initial fall of plasma calcium after intravenous injection of parathyroid hormone. Endocrinology 89:735, 1971
111. Yamaguchi DT, Hahn TJ, Iida-Klein A, et al: Parathyroid hormone-activated calcium channels in an osteoblast-like clonal osteosarcoma cell line. J Biol Chem 262:7711, 1987

112. Peck WA, Kohler G, Barr S: Calcium-mediated enhancement of the cyclic AMP response in cultured bone cells. Calcif Tissue Intl 33:409, 1981
113. Dziak R, Stern PH: Calcium transport in isolated bone cells III. Effects of parathyroid hormone and cyclic 3',5'-AMP. Endocrinology 97:1281, 1975
114. Neher R, Riniker B, Maier R, et al: Human calcitonin. Nature 220:984, 1968
115. Guttman S, Pless J, Huguenin RL, et al: Synthese von salm-calcitonin, einem hochaktiven hypocalcamischen hormon. Helv Chir Acta 52:1789, 1969
116. Niall HD, Keutmann HT, Copp DH, Potts JT Jr: The amino acid sequence of salmon ultimobronchial calcitonin. Proc Natl Acad Sci USA 64:771, 1969
117. Protts JT Jr, Niall HD, Keutman HT, et al: The amino acid sequence of porcine thyrocalcitonin. Proc Natl Acad Sci USA 59:1321, 1968
118. Raulais D, Hagaman J, Ontjes DA, et al: The complete amino acid sequence of rat thyrocalcitonin. Eur J Biochem 64:607, 1976
119. Hamilton WJ, Boyd JD, Mossman HW: Human Embryology. p. 194. Baltimore, Williams & Wilkins, 1952
120. Langman J: Medical Embryology. p. 244. Baltimore, Williams & Wilkins, 1969,
121. Wolfe HJ, Voelkel EF, Tashjian AH Jr: Distribution of calcitonin-containing cells in the normal adult human thyroid gland: A correlation of morphology with peptide content. J Clin Endocrinol Metab 38:688, 1974
122. Jacobs JW, Potts JT, Bell NH, Habener JF: Calcitonin precursor identified by cell-free translation of mRNA. J Biol Chem 254:10600, 1979
123. Jacobs JW, Lund PK, Potts JT Jr, et al: Procalcitonin is a glycoprotein. J Biol Chem 256:2803, 1981
124. Jacobs JW, Chin WW, Dee PC, et al: Calcitonin messenger RNA encodes multiple polypeptides in a single precursor. Science 213:457, 1981
125. Rosenfeld MG, Mermod JJ, Amara SG, et al: Production of a novel neuropeptide encoded by the calcitonin gene via tissue-specific RNA processing. Nature 304:129, 1983

126. Birnbaum RS, O'Neil JA, Muszynski M, et al: A noncalcitonin secretory peptide derived from preprocalcitonin. J Biol Chem 257:241, 1982
127. Hoppener JWM, Steenbergh PH, Zandberg J, et al: Localization of the polymorphic human calcitonin gene on chromosome 11. Hum Genet 66:309, 1984
128. Kittur SD, Hoppener JWM, Antonarakis SE, et al: Linkage map of the short arm of human chromosome 11: Location of the genes for catalase, calcitonin and insulin-like growth factor II. Proc Natl Acad Sci USA 82:5064, 1985
129. Amara SG, Arriza JL, Leff SE, et al: Expression in brain of messenger RNA encoding a novel neuropeptide homologous to calcitonin gene-related peptide. Science 229:1094, 1985
130. Brain SD, Williams TJ, Tippins JR, et al: Calcitonin gene-related peptide is a potent vasodilator. Nature 313:54, 1985
131. McEwan J, Larkin S, Davies G, et al: Calcitonin gene-related peptide: A potent dilator of human epicardial coronary arteries. Circulation 74:1243, 1986
132. New HV, Mudge AW: Calcitonin gene-related peptide regulates muscle acetycholine receptor synthesis. Nature 323:809, 1986
133. Laufer R, Changeux J-P: CGRP elevates cAMP levels in chick skeletal muscle: Possible neurotropic role for a coexisting neuronal messenger. EMBO J 6:901, 1987
134. Keutmann HT, Parsons JA, Potts HT Jr: Isolation and chemical properties of two calcitonins from salmon ultimobronchial glands. J Biol Chem 245:1491, 1970
135. Marx SJ, Woodward C, Aurbach GD: Calcitonin receptors in kidney and bone. Science 178:999, 1972
136. Austin LA, Heath H III, Go VLW: Regulation of calcitonin secretion in normal man by changes of serum calcium within the physiologic range. J Clin Invest 64:1721, 1979
137. Owyang C, Heath H III, Sizemore GW, Go VLW: Comparison of the effects of pentagastrin and meal-stimulated gastrin on plasma calcitonin in normal man. Am J Dig Dis 23:1084, 1978
138. Huwyler R, Born W, Ohnhaus EE, Fischer JA: Plasma kinetics and urinary excretion of exogenous human and salmon calcitonin in man. Am J Physiol 236:E15, 1979
139. Ardaillou R: Kidney and calcitonin. Nephron 15:250, 1975
140. Tiegs RD, Body JJ, Barta JM, Heath H III: Secretion and metabolism of monomeric human calcitonin: Effects of age, sex and thyroid damage. J Bone Min Res 1:339, 1986
141. Snider RH, Moore CF, Silva OL, Becker KL: Radioimmunoassay of calcitonin in normal human urine. Anal Chem 50:449, 1978
142. Singer FR, Habener JF: Multiple immunoreactive forms of calcitonin in human plasma. Biochem Biophys Res Commun 61:710, 1974
143. Sizemore GW, Heath H III: Immunochemical heterogeneity of calcitonin in patients with medullary thyroid carcinoma. J Clin Invest 55:1111, 1975
144. Goltzman D, Tischler AS: Characterization of the immunochemical forms of calcitonin released by a medullary thyroid carcinoma in tissue culture. J Clin Invest 61:449, 1978
145. Chambers TJ, McSheehy PMJ, Thomson BM, Fuller K: The effect of calcium regulating hormones and prostaglandins on bone resorption by osteoclasts disaggregated from neonatal rabbit bones. Endocrinology 116:234, 1985
146. Bijvoet OLM, van der Sluys Veer J, de Vries HR, van Koppen TJ: Natriuretic effect of calcitonin in man. N Engl J Med 284:681, 1971
147. Heersche JNM, Marcus R, Aurbach GD: Calcitonin and the formation of 3′,5′-AMP in bone and kidney. Endocrinology 94:241, 1974
148. Holtrop ME, Raisz LG: Comparison of effects of 1,25-dihydroxycholecalciferol, prostaglandin E_2 and osteoclast activating factor with parathyroid hormone on the ultrastructure of osteoclast cultured long bones of rats. Calcif Tissue Int 29:201, 1979
149. Talmage RV, VanderWeil CJ: The influence of calcitonin on the plasma and urine phosphate changes produced by parathyroid hormone. Calcif Tissue Int 28:113, 1979

150. Talmage RV, Anderson JJB, Cooper CW: The influence of calcitonins on the disappearance of radiocalcium and radiophosphorus from plasma. Endocrinology 90:1185, 1972
151. Schachter D, Finkelstein JD, Kowarski S: Metabolism of vitamin D. I. Preparation of radioactive vitamin D and its intestinal absorption in the rat. J Clin Invest 43:787, 1964
152. Holick MF, MacLaughlin JA, Clark MB, et al: Photosynthesis of previtamin D_3 in human skin and the physiologic consequences. Science 210:203, 1980
153. Ponchon G, DeLuca HF: The role of the liver in the metabolism of vitamin D. J Clin Invest 48:1273, 1969
154. Bell NH, Greene A, Epstein S, et al: Evidence for alteration of the vitamin D-endocrine system in blacks. J Clin Invest 76:470, 1985
155. Dunn JF, Fetchick DA, Liel Y, et al: Alteration of vitamin D metabolism in Mexican Americans. J Bone Min Res 2:(Abstr 434), 1987
156. Whyte MP, Haddad JG Jr, Walters DD, Stamp TCB: Vitamin D bioavailability: Serum 25-hydroxyvitamin D levels in man after oral, subcutaneous, intramuscular, and intravenous vitamin D administration. J Clin Endocrinol Metab 48:906, 1979
157. Bell NH, Shaw S, Turner RT: Evidence that 1,25-dihydroxyvitamin D inhibits the hepatic production of 25-hydroxyvitamin D in man. J Clin Invest 74:1540, 1984
158. Halloran BP, Bikle DD, Levens MJ, et al: Chronic 1,25-dihydroxyvitamin D_3 administration in the rat reduces the serum concentration of 25-hydroxyvitamin D by increasing metabolic clearance rate. J Clin Invest 78:622, 1986
159. Liel Y, Ulmer E, Shary J, et al: Low circulating vitamin D in obesity. Calcif Tissue Intl 43:199, 1988
160. Bell NH, Epstein S, Greene A, et al: Evidence for alteration of the vitamin D-endocrine system in obese subjects. J Clin Invest 76:370, 1985
161. Bell NH, Epstein S, Shary J, et al: Evidence of a probable role for 25-hydroxyvitamin D in the regulation of calcium metabolism in man. J Bone Mineral Res 3:489, 1988
162. Fraser DR, Kodicek E: Unique biosynthesis by kidney of a biologically active vitamin D metabolite. Nature 228:764, 1970
163. Ghazarian JG, Schnoes HK, DeLuca HF: Mechanism of 25-hydroxycholecalciferol 1α-hydroxylation. Incorporation of oxygen-18 into the 12 position of 25-hydroxycholecalciferol. Biochemistry 12:2555, 1973
164. Pedersen JI, Ghazarian JG, Orme-Johnson NR, DeLuca HF: Isolation of chick renal mitochondrial ferredoxin active in the 25-hydroxyvitamin D_3-1α-hydroxylase system. J Biol Chem 251:3933, 1976
165. Yoon PS, DeLuca HF: Purification and properties of chick renal mitochondrial ferredoxin. Biochemistry 19:2165, 1980
166. Stern PH, Taylor AB, Bell NH, Epstein S: Demonstration that circulating 1α,25-dihydroxyvitamin D is loosely regulated in normal children. J Clin Invest 68:1374, 1981
167. Lund B, Clausen N, Lund B, et al: Age-dependent variations in serum 1,25-dihydroxyvitamin D in childhood. Acta Endocrinol 94:426, 1980
168. Hollis BW, Pittard WB III: Evaluation of the total fetomaternal vitamin D relationships at term: Evidence for racial differences. J Clin Endocrinol Metab 59:652, 1984
169. Garabedian M, Holick MF, DeLuca HF, Boyle IT: Control of 25-hydroxycholecalciferol metabolism by the parathyroid glands. Proc Natl Acad Sci USA 69:1673, 1972
170. Haussler MR, Baylink DJ, Hughes MR, et al: The assay of 1α,25-dihydroxyvitamin D_3: Physiologic and pathophysiologic modulation of circulating hormone levels. Clin Endocrinol 5:1515, 1976
171. Boyle IT, Gray RW, DeLuca HF: Regulation by calcium of in vitro synthesis of 1,25-dihydroxycholecalciferol. Proc Natl Acad Sci USA 68:2131, 1971
172. Tanaka Y, DeLuca HF: The control of 25-hydroxyvitamin D metabolism by inorganic phosphorus. Arch Biochem Biophys 154:566, 1973
173. Bikle DD, Rasmussen H: The ionic control of 1,25-dihydroxyvitamin D_3 production in isolated chick renal tubules. J Clin Invest 55:292, 1975

174. Hughes MR, Brumbaugh PF, Haussler MR, et al: Regulation of serum 1α,25-dihydroxyvitamin D₃ by calcium and phosphate in the rat. Science 190:578, 1975
175. Portale AA, Halloran BP, Murphy MM, Morris RC Jr: Oral intake of phosphorus can determine the serum concentration of 1,25-dihydroxyvitamin D by determining its production rate in humans. J Clin Invest 77:7, 1986
176. Adams ND, Garthwaite TL, Gray RW, et al: The interrelationship among prolactin, 1,25-dihydroxyvitamin D and parathyroid hormone in humans. J Clin Endocrinol Metab 49:628, 1979
177. Kumar R, Abboud CF, Riggs BL: The effect of elevated prolactin levels on plasma 1,25-dihydroxyvitamin D and intestinal absorption of calcium. Mayo Clin Proc 55:51, 1980
178. Chipman JJ, Zerwekh J, Nicar M, et al: Effect of growth hormone administration: Reciprocal changes in serum 1α,25-dihydroxyvitamin D and intestinal calcium absorption. J Clin Endocrinol Metab 51:321, 1980
179. Burstein S, Chen I-W, Tsang RC: Effects of growth hormone replacement therapy on 1,25-dihydroxyvitamin D and calcium metabolism. J Clin Endocrinol Metab 56:1246, 1983
180. Holick MF, Schnoes HK, DeLuca HF, et al: Isolation and identification of 24,25-dihydroxycholecalciferol: A metabolite of vitamin D₃ made in the kidney. Biochemistry 11:4251, 1972
181. Tanaka Y, Lorenc RS, DeLuca HF: The role of 1,25-dihydroxyvitamin D₃ and parathyroid hormone in the regulation of chick renal 25-hydroxyvitamin D₃-24-hydroxylase. Arch Biochem Biophys 171:521, 1975
182. Rasmussen H, Bordier P: Vitamin D and bone. Metab Bone Dis Rel Res 1:7, 1978
183. Ornoy A, Goodwin D, Noff D, Edelstein S: 24,25-Dihydroxyvitamin D is a metabolite of vitamin D essential for bone formation. Nature 276:517, 1978
184. Henry HL, Taylor AN, Norman AW: Response of chick parathyroid glands to the vitamin D metabolites 1,25-dihydroxyvitamin D₃ and 24,25-dihydroxyvitamin D₃. J Nutr 107:1918, 1977
185. Boyle IT, Omdahl JL, Gray RW, DeLuca HF: The biological activity and metabolism of 24,25-dihydroxyvitamin D₃. J Biol Chem 251:397, 1973
186. Esvelt RP, Schnoes HK, DeLuca HF: Isolation and characterization of 1α-hydroxytetra-norvitamin D-23-carboxylic acid: A major metabolite of 1,25-dihydroxyvitamin D₃. Biochemistry 18:3977, 1979
187. Esvelt RP, DeLuca HF: Calcitroic acid: Biological activity and tissue distribution studies. Arch Biochem Biophys 206:403, 1981
188. Haddad JG Jr, Walgate J: Radioimmunoassay of the binding protein for vitamin D and its metabolites in human serum: Concentrations in normal subjects and patients with disorders of mineral homeostasis. J Clin Invest 58:1217, 1976
189. Haddad JG, Rojanasathit S: Acute administration of 25-hydroxycholecalciferol to man. J Clin Endocrinol Metab 42:284, 1976
190. Gray RW, Caldas AE, Wilz DR, et al: Metabolism and excretion of ³H-1,25-(OH)₂-vitamin D₃ in healthy adults. J Clin Endocrinol Metab 46:756, 1978
191. Mason RS, Lissner D, Posen S, Norman AW: Blood concentrations of dihydroxylated vitamin D metabolites after an oral dose. Br Med J 280:449, 1980
192. McDonnell DP, Mangelsdorf DJ, Pike JW, et al: Molecular cloning of complementary DNA encoding the avian receptor for vitamin D. Science 235:1214, 1987
193. Burmester JK, Weise RJ, Maeda N, DeLuca HF: Structure and regulation of the rat 1,25-dihydroxyvitamin D₃ receptor. Proc Natl Acad Sci USA 85:9499, 1988
194. Minghetti PP, Norman AW: 1,25(OH)₂-Vitamin D₃ receptors: Gene regulation and genetic circuitry. FASEB J 2:3043, 1988
195. DeLuca HF: The vitamin D story: A collaborative effort of basic science and clinical medicine. FASEB J 2:224, 1988
196. Nemere I, Yoshimoto Y, Norman AW: Calcium transport in perfused duodena from normal chicks: enhancement within fourteen minutes of exposure to 1,25-dihydroxyvitamin D₃. Endocrinology 115:1476, 1984
197. Slatopolsky E, Weerts C, Thielan R, et al: Marked suppression of secondary hyper-

parathyroidism by intravenous administration of 1,25-dihydroxycholecalciferol in uremic patients. J Clin Invest 74:2136, 1984
197a. Wasserman RH, Feher JJ: Vitamin D-dependent calcium-binding proteins. p 292. In Wasserman RH, Corradino RA, Carafoli E, Kretsinger RH, et al (eds): Calcium Binding Proteins and Calcium Function. Elsevier-North Holland, New York, 1977
197b. Hughes MR, Malloy PJ, Kieback DG, et al: Point mutations in the human vitamin D receptor gene associated with hypocalcemic rickets. Science 242:1702, 1988
198. Silver J, Naveh-Many T, Mayer H, et al: Regulation by vitamin D metabolites of parathyroid hormone gene transcription in vivo in the rat. J Clin Invest 78:1296, 1986
199. Hughes MR, Baylink DJ, Jones PG, Haussler MR: Radioligand receptor assay for 25-hydroxyvitamin D_2/D_3 and $1\alpha,25$-dihydroxyvitamin D_2/D_3. J Clin Invest 58:61, 1976
200. Bikle DD, Zolock DT, Morrissey RL: Action of vitamin D on intestinal calcium transport. p 481. In Scott WN, Goodman DBP (eds): Annals of the New York Academy of Sciences. Vol 372. Hormonal Regulation of Epithelial Transport of Ions and Water. The New York Academy of Sciences, New York, 1981
201. Rasmussen H, Fontaine O, Matsumoto T: Liponomic regulation of calcium transport by $1,25(OH)_2D_3$. p. 518. In Scott WN, Goodman DBP (eds): Annals of the New York Academy of Sciences. Vol 372. Hormonal Regulation of Epithelial Transport of Ions and Water. The New York Academy of Sciences, New York, 1981
202. Morrissey RL, Zolock DT, Mellick PW, Bikle DD: Influence of cycloheximide and 1,25-dihydroxyvitamin D_3 on mitochondrial and vesicle mineralization in the intestine. Cell Calcium 1:69, 1980
203. Ghijsen WEJM, van Os CH: $1\alpha,25$-Dihydroxyvitamin D_3 regulates ATP-dependent calcium transport in basolateral plasma membranes of rat enterocytes. Biochim Biophys Acta 689:170, 1982
204. Dunningan MG, Paton JPJ, Haase S, et al: Late rickets and osteomalacia in the Pakistani community in Glasgow. Scott Med J 7:159, 1962
205. Arneil GC, Crosbie JC: Infantile rickets returns to Glasgow. Lancet 2:423, 1963
206. Benson PF, Stroud CE, Mitchell NJ, Nicolaides A: Rickets in immigrant children in London. Br Med J 5337:1054, 1963
207. Loomis WF: Skin-pigment regulation of vitamin D biosynthesis in man. Science 157:501, 1967
208. Roberts WA, Badger VM: Osteomalacia of very-low-birth-weight infants. J Pediatr Orthop 4:593, 1984
209. Thompson GR, Lewis B, Booth CC: Absorption of vitamin D_3-^3H in control subjects and patients with intestinal malabsorption. J Clin Invest 45:94, 1966
210. Arnaud SB, Goldsmith RS, Lambert PW, Go VLW: 25-Hydroxyvitamin D_3: Evidence of an enterohepatic circulation in man. Proc Soc Exp Biol Med 149:570, 1975
211. Imawari M, Akanuma Y, Itakura H, Muto Y, et al: The effects of the liver on serum 25-hydroxyvitamin D and on the serum binding protein for vitamin D and its metabolites. J Lab Clin Med 93:171, 1979
212. Bikle DD, Halloran BP, Gee E, et al: Free 25-hydroxyvitamin D levels are normal in subjects with liver disease and reduced total 25-hydroxyvitamin D levels. J Clin Invest 78:748, 1986
213. Slatopolsky E, Caglar S, Gradowska L, et al: On the prevention of secondary hyperparathyroidism in experimental chronic renal disease using "proportional reduction" of dietary phosphorus intake. Kidney Int 2:147, 1972
214. Portale AA, Booth BE, Halloran BP, Morris RC Jr: Effect of dietary phosphorus on circulating concentrations of 1,25-dihydroxyvitamin D and immunoreactive parathyroid hormone in children with moderate renal insufficiency. J Clin Invest 73:1580, 1984
215. Chesney RW, Hamstra AJ, Mazess RB, et al: Circulating vitamin D metabolite concentration in childhood renal disease. Kidney Int 21:65, 1982
216. Portale AA, Booth BE, Tsai HC, Morris RC Jr: Reduced plasma concentration of 1,25-dihydroxyvitamin D in children with moderate renal insufficiency. Kidney Int 21:267, 1982
217. Lambert PW, Hollis BW, Bell NH, Epstein

S: Demonstration of a lack of change in serum 1α,25-dihydroxyvitamin D in response to parathyroid extract in pseudohypoparathyroidism. J Clin Invest 66:782, 1980
218. Lund BJ, Sorenson OH, Lund Bi, et al: Vitamin D metabolism in hypoparathyroidism. J Clin Endocrinol Metab 51:606, 1980.
219. Graham JB, McFalls VW, Winters RW: Familial hypophosphatemia with vitamin D resistant rickets. III. Three additional kindreds of sex-linked dominant type with a genetic analysis of four such families. Am J Hum Genet 11:311, 1959
220. Greenberg BG, Winters RW, Graham JB: The normal range of serum inorganic phosphorus and its utility as a discriminant in the diagnosis of congenital hypophosphatemia. J Clin Endocrinol 20:364, 1960
221. Lyles KW, Clark AG, Drezner MK: Serum 1,25-dihydroxyvitamin D levels in subjects with X-linked hypophosphatemic rickets and osteomalacia. Calcif Tiss Int 34:125, 1982
222. Insogna KL, Broadus AE, Gertner JM: Impaired phosphorus conservation and 1,25-dihydroxyvitamin D generation during phosphorus deprivation in familial hypophosphatemic rickets. J Clin Invest 71:1562, 1983
223. Lyles KW, Drezner MK: Parathyroid hormone effects on serum 1,25-dihydroxyvitamin D levels in patients with X-linked hypophosphatemic rickets: Evidence for abnormal 25-hydroxyvitamin D-1-hydroxylase activity. J Clin Endocrinol Metab 54:638, 1982
224. Lyles KW, Halsey DL, Friedman NE, Lobaugh B: Correlations of serum concentrations of 1,25-dihydroxyvitamin D, phosphorus, and parathyroid hormone in tumoral calcinosis. J Clin Endocrinol Mctab 67:88, 1988
225. Levine MA, Downs RW, Moses AM, et al: Resistance to multiple hormones in patients with pseudohypoparathyroidism: Association with deficient activity of the guanine nucleotide regulatory protein. Am J Med 74:545, 1983
226. Bronsky D, Kushner DS, Dubin A, Snapper I: Idiopathic hypoparathyroidism and pseudohypoparathyroidism: Case reports and review of the literature. Medicine 37:317, 1958
227. Sinha TK, DeLuca HF, Bell NH: Evidence for a defect in the formation of 1α,25-dihydroxyvitamin D in pseudohypoparathyroidism. Metabolism 26:731, 1977
228. Bell NH, Khairi MRA, Johnston CC Jr, et al: Effects of 1α,25-dihydroxyvitamin D_3 on calcium metabolism and quantitative bone histology in pseudohypoparathyroidism. p. 33. In Copp DH, Talmadge RV (eds): Endocrinology of Calcium Metabolism, No. 421, Excerpta Medica, Amsterdam, 1977
229. Yamaoka K, Seino Y, Ishida M, et al: Effect of dibutyryl adenosine 3',5'-monophosphate administration on plasma concentrations of 1,25-dihydroxyvitamin D in pseudohypoparathyroidism type I. J Clin Endocrinol Metab 53:1096, 1981
230. Fraser D, Kooh SW, Kind HP, et al: Pathogenesis of hereditary vitamin-D-dependent rickets. An inborn error of vitamin-D metabolism involving defective conversion of 25-hydroxyvitamin D to 1α,25-dihydroxyvitamin D. N Engl J Med 289:817, 1973
231. Scriver CR, Reade TM, DeLuca HF, Hamstra AJ: Serum 1,25-dihydroxyvitamin D levels in normal subjects and in patients with hereditary rickets or bone disease. N Engl J Med 299:976, 1978
232. Ryan EA, Reiss E: Oncogenous osteomalacia. Am J Med 77:501, 1984
233. Drezner MK, Feinglos MN: Osteomalacia due to 1α,25-dihydroxycholecalciferol deficiency. J Clin Invest 60:1046, 1977
234. Lyles KW, Berry WR, Haussler M, et al: Hypophosphatemic osteomalacia: association with prostatic carcinoma. Ann Intern Med 93:275, 1980
235. Dent CE, Richens A, Rowe DJF, Stamp TCB: Osteomalacia with long-term anticonvulsant therapy in epilepsy. Br Med J 4:69, 1970
236. Hahn TJ, Halstead LR: Anticonvulsant drug-induced osteomalacia: alterations in mineral metabolism and response to vitamin D_3 administration. Calcif Tissue Int 27:13, 1979
237. Hahn TJ, Birge SJ, Scharp CR, Avioli LV: Phenobarbital-induced alterations in vitamin D metabolism. J Clin Invest 51:741, 1972

238. Koch HV, Kraft D, von Herrath D: Influence of diphenylhydantoin and phenobarbital on intestinal calcium transport in the rat. Epilepsia 13:829, 1972
239. Hahn TJ, Scharp CR, Richardson CA, et al: Interaction of diphenylhydantoin and phenobarbital with hormonal mediation of fetal rat bone resorption in vitro. J Clin Invest 62:406, 1978
240. Brooks MH, Bell NH, Love L, et al: Vitamin-D-dependent rickets type II: resistance of target organs of 1,25-dihydroxyvitamin D. N Engl J Med 298:996, 1978
241. Marx SJ, Spiegel AM, Brown EM, et al: A familial syndrome of decrease in sensitivity to 1,25-dihydroxyvitamin D. J Clin Endocrinol Metab 47:1303, 1978
242. Liberman UA, Eil C, Marx SJ: Resistance to 1,25-dihydroxyvitamin D. Association with heterogeneous defects in cultured skin fibroblasts. J Clin Invest 71:192, 1983
243. Kugelberg E: Neurologic mechanism for certain phenomena in tetany. Arch Neurol Psychiatry 52:507, 1946
244. Wijnbladh H: Postoperative tetany: A study based on 40 treated cases. Acta Endocrinol 10:1, 1952
245. Edmondson JW, Brashear RF, Li TK: Tetany: quantitative interrelationships between calcium and alkalosis. Am J Physiol 228:1082, 1975
246. Hoffman E: The Chvostek sign: A clinical study. Am J Surg 96:33, 1958
247. Lewis T: Trousseau's phenomenon in tetany. Clin Sci 4:361, 1942
248. Frame B: Neuromuscular manifestations of parathyroid disease. p 283. In Vinken PB, Bruyn GW (eds): Handbook of Clinical Neurology. Vol 27. North Holland, Amsterdam, 1976
249. Basser LS, Neale FC, Ireland AW, Posen S: Epilepsy and electroencephalographic abnormalities in chronic surgical hypoparathyroidism. Ann Intern Med 71:507, 1969
250. Swash M, Rowan AJ: Electroencephalographic criteria for hypocalcemia and hypercalcemia. Arch Neurol 26:218, 1972
251. Palmer RF, Searles HH, Boldrey, EB: Papilledema and hypoparathyroidism simulating brain tumor. J Neurosurg 16:378, 1959
252. Dent CE, Garretts M: Skin changes in hypocalcemia. Lancet 1:142, 1960
253. Risum G: Psoriasis exacerbated by hypoparathyroidism with hypocalcemia. Br J Dermatol 89:309, 1973
254. Hinrichs EH: Dental changes in idiopathic juvenile hypoparathyroidism. Oral Surg 9:1102, 1956
255. Ireland AW, Hornbrook JW, Neale FC, Posen S: The crystalline lens in chronic surgical hypoparathyroidism. Arch Intern Med 122:408, 1968
256. Delamere NA, Paterson CA, Holmes DL: Hypocalcemic cataract. I. An animal model and cation distribution study. Metab Pediatr Ophthalmol 5:77, 1981
257. Yu PNG: The electrocardiographic changes associated with hypercalcemia and hypocalcemia. Am J Med Sci 224:413, 1952
258. Clarkson B, Kowlessar OD, Horwith M, Sleisenger M: Clinical and metabolic study of a patient with malabsorption and hypoparathyroidism. Metabolism 9:1093, 1960
259. Parfitt AM: Adult hypoparathyroidism: Treatment with calcifediol. Arch Intern Med 138:874, 1978
260. Mason RS, Posen S: The relevance of 25-hydroxycalciferol measurements in the treatment of hypoparathyroidism. Clin Endocrinol (Oxf) 10:265, 1979
261. Neer RM, Holick MF, DeLuca HF, Potts JT Jr: Effect of 1α,25-dihydroxy vitamin D_3 on calcium and phosphorus metabolism in hypoparathyroidism. Metabolism 24:1403, 1975
262. Davies M, Taylor CM, Hill LF, Stanbury SW: 1,25-Dihydroxycholecalciferol in hypoparathyroidism. Lancet 1:55, 1977
263. Kanis JA, Russell RGG: Rate of reversal of hypercalcaemia and hypercalciuria induced by vitamin D and its 1-hydroxylated derivatives. Br Med J 1:78, 1977
264. Bell NH, Stern PH: Hypercalcemia and increases in serum hormone value during prolonged administration of 1α,25-dihydroxyvitamin D. N Engl J Med 298:1241, 1978
265. Hunt G, Morgan DB: The early effects of dihydrotachysterol on calcium and phosphorus metabolism in patients with hypoparathyroidism. Clin Sci 38:713, 1970
266. Bell NH, Epstein S, Stern PH: Hypercal-

cemia during long-term treatment with 1,25-dihydroxyvitamin D_3 in hypoparathyroidism (letter). N Engl J Med 301:1183, 1979
267. Broadus AE, Horst RL, Lang R, et al: The importance of circulating 1,25-dihydroxyvitamin D in the pathogenesis of hypercalciuria and renal stone formation in primary hyperparathyroidism. N Engl J Med 302:422, 1980
268. Broadus AE, Mahaffey JE, Bartter FC, Neer RM: Nephrogenous cyclic AMP as a parathyroid function test. J Clin Endocrinol Metab 46:477, 1978
269. Hulter HN, Halloran BP, Toto RD, Peterson JC: Long-term control of plasma calcitriol concentration in dogs and humans: Dominant role of plasma calcium concentration in experimental hyperparathyroidism. J Clin Invest 76:695, 1985
270. Peacock M, Robertson WG, Nordin BEC: Relation between serum and urinary calcium with particular reference to parathyroid activity. Lancet 1:384, 1969
271. Heath H, Hodgson SF, Kennedy MA: Primary hyperparathyroidism: Incidence, morbidity, and potential economic impact in a community. N Engl J Med 302:189, 1980
272. Habener JF, Potts JT Jr: Primary hyperparathyroidism: Clinical features. p 954. In DeGroot LJ (ed): Endocrinology. Vol 2. WB Saunders, Philadelphia, 1989
273. Brown EM: Four-parameter model of the sigmoidal relationship between parathyroid hormone release and extracellular calcium concentration in normal and abnormal parathyroid tissue. J Clin Endocrinol Metab 56:572, 1983
274. Arnold A, Staunton CE, Kim HG, et al: Monoclonality and abnormal parathyroid hormone genes in parathyroid adenomas. N Engl J Med 318:658, 1988
275. Arnold A, Kim H, Gaz R, et al: Cloning and characterization of the rearranged PTH gene in a parathyroid adenoma. J Bone Min Res 3(suppl):S210, 1988
276. Mundy GR, Ibbotson KJ, D'Souza SM: Tumor products and the hypercalcemia of malignancy. J Clin Invest 76:391, 1985
277. Stewart AF, Horst R, Deftos LJ, et al: Biochemical evaluation of patients with cancer-associated hypercalcemia: Evidence for humoral and nonhumoral groups. N Engl J Med 303:1377, 1980
278. Stewart AF, Vignery A, Silverglate A, et al: Quantitative bone histomorphometry in humoral hypercalcemia of malignancy: Uncoupling of bone cell activity. J Clin Endocrinol Metab 55:219, 1982
279. Suva LJ, Winslow GA, Wettenhall REH, et al: A parathyroid hormone-related protein implicated in malignant hypercalcemia: Cloning and expression. Science 237:893, 1987
280. Mangin M, Webb AC, Dreyer B, et al: Identification of a cDNA encoding a parathyroid hormone-like peptide from a human tumor associated with humoral hypercalcemia of malignancy. Proc Natl Acad Sci USA 85:597, 1988
281. Broadus AE, Mangin M, Ikeda K, et al: Humoral hypercalcemia of cancer: Identification of a novel parathyroid hormone-like peptide. N Engl J Med 319:556, 1988
282. Stewart AF, Burtis WJ, Wu T, et al: Two forms of parathyroid hormone-like adenylate cyclase-stimulating protein derived from tumors associated with humoral hypercalcemia of malignancy. J Bone Min Res 2:587, 1987
283. Ibbotson KJ, D'Souza SM, Ng KW, et al: Tumor-derived growth factor increases bone resorption in a tumor associated with the humoral hypercalcemia of malignancy. Science 221:1292, 1983
284. Rodda CP, Kubota M, Heath JA, et al: Evidence for a novel parathyroid hormone-related protein in fetal lamb parathyroid glands and sheep placenta: Comparisons with a similar protein implicated in humoral hypercalcaemia of malignancy. J Endocrinol 117:261, 1988
285. Thiede MA, Rodan GA: Expression of a calcium-mobilizing parathyroid hormone-like peptide in lactating mammary tissue. Science 242:278, 1988
286. Sporn MG, Todaro GJ: Autocrine secretion and malignant transformation of cells. N Engl J Med 303:878, 1980
287. Ibbotson KJ, D'Souza SM, Smith DD, et al: EGF receptor antiserum inhibits bone resorbing activity produced by a rat Leydig cell tumor associated with the humoral hy-

percalcemia of malignancy. Endocrinology 116:469, 1985
288. Derynck R, Roberts AB, Winkler ME, et al: Human transforming growth factor-alpha: Precursor structure and expression in E coli. Cell 38:287, 1984
289. Lee DC, Rose TM, Webb NR, Todaro GJ: Cloning and sequence analysis of a cDNA for rat transforming growth factor-alpha. Nature 313:489, 1985
290. Mundy GR, Martin TJ: Hypercalcemia of malignancy: Pathogenesis and treatment. Metab Clin Exp 31:1247, 1982
291. Isales C, Carcangiu ML, Stewart AF: Hypercalcemia in breast cancer. Am J Med 82:1143, 1987
292. Nemoto T, Rosner DH, Patel DJ, et al: Tamoxifen-induced hypercalcemia: In metastatic breast cancer. NY State J Med 80:1980, 1980
293. Valentin-Opran A, Eilon G, Saez S, Mundy GR: Estrogens and antiestrogens stimulate release of bone resorbing activity by cultured human breast cancer cells. J Clin Invest 75:726, 1985
294. Percival RL, Yates AJP, Gray RES, et al: Mechanisms of malignant hypercalcemia in carcinoma of the breast. Br Med J 291:776, 1985
295. Garrett IRB, Durie BGM, Nedwin GE, et al: Production of the bone resorbing cytokine lymphotoxin by cultured human myeloma cells. N Engl J Med 317:526, 1987
296. Breslau NA, McGuire JL, Zerwekh JE, et al: Hypercalcemia associated with increased serum calcitriol levels in three patients with lymphoma. Ann Intern Med 100:1, 1984
297. Grossman B, Schecter GP, Horton JE, et al: Hypercalcemia associated with T–cell lymphoma-leukemia. Am J Clin Pathol 75:149, 1981
298. Bell NH, Stern PH, Pantzer E, et al: Evidence that increased circulating $1\alpha,25$-dihydroxyvitamin D is the probable cause for abnormal calcium metabolism in sarcoidosis. J Clin Invest 64:218, 1979
299. Papapoulos SE, Fraher LJ, Sandler LM, et al: 1,25-Dihydroxycholecalciferol in the pathogenesis of the hypercalcemia of sarcoidosis. Lancet 1:627, 1979
300. Adams JS, Singer FR, Gacad MA, et al: Isolation and structural identification of 1,25-dihydroxyvitamin D_3 produced by cultured alveolar macrophages in sarcoidosis. J Clin Endocrinol Metab 60:960, 1985
301. Adams JS, Gacad MA: Characterization of 1α-hydroxylation of vitamin D_3 sterols by cultured alveolar macrophages from patients with sarcoidosis. J Exp Med 161:755, 1985
302. Stern PH, DeOlazabal J, Bell NH: Evidence for abnormal regulation of circulating $1\alpha,25$-dihydroxyvitamin D in patients with sarcoidosis and normal calcium metabolism. J Clin Invest 66:852, 1980
303. Basile JN, Liel Y, Miller S, et al: Evidence for extrarenal production of 1,25-dihydroxyvitamin D in patients with active sarcoidosis and normal calcium metabolism. J Bone Mineral Res 3:S114, 1988 (Abstr)
304. Robinson BWS, McLemore TL, Crystal RG: Gamma interferon is spontaneously released by alveolar macrophages and lung T lymphocytes in patients with pulmonary sarcoidosis. J Clin Invest 72:1488, 1985
305. Adams JS, Gacad MA: Characterization of 1α-hydroxylation of vitamin D_3 sterols by cultured alveolar macrophages from patients with sarcoidosis. J Exp Med 161:755, 1985
306. Bell NH, Shary J, Shaw S, Turner RT: Hypercalcemia associated with increased circulating 1,25-dihydroxyvitamin D in a patient with pulmonary tuberculosis. Calcif Tissue Int 37:588, 1985
307. Gkonos PJ, London R, Hendler ED: Hypercalcemia and elevated 1,25-dihydroxyvitamin D levels in a patient with end-stage renal disease and active tuberculosis. N Engl J Med 311:1683, 1984
308. Isaacs RD, Nicholson GE, Holdaway IM: Miliary tuberculosis with hypercalcemia and raised vitamin D concentrations. Thorax 42:555, 1987
309. Sullivan JN, Salmon WD Jr: Hypercalcemia in active pulmonary tuberculosis. South Med J 80:572, 1987
310. Kantarjian HM, Saad MF, Estey EH, et al: Hypercalcemia in disseminated candidiasis. Am J Med 74:721, 1983
311. Kozeny GA, Barbato AL, Bansal VK, et al: Hypercalcemia associated with silicone-

induced granulomas. N Engl J Med 311:1103, 1984
312. Gates S, Shary J, Turner RT, et al: Abnormal calcium metabolism caused by increased circulating 1,25-dihydroxyvitamin D in a patient with rheumatoid arthritis. J Bone Min Res 1:221, 1986
313. Schaeffer PC, Fadem SZ, Lifschitz MD, Goldsmith RS: Hypercalcemia due to high serum 1α,25-dihydroxycholecalciferol (1,25-DHCC). (Abstr) Clin Res 26:533A, 1978
314. Frame B, Parfitt M: Corticosteroid-responsive hypercalcemia with elevated serum 1α,25-hydroxyvitamin D. Ann Intern Med 93:449, 1980
315. Duarte DG, Winnacker JL, Becker KL, Pace A: Thiazide-induced hypercalcemia. N Engl J Med 284:828, 1971
316. Parfitt AM: Chlorothiazide-induced hypercalcemia in juvenile osteoporosis and hyperparathyroidism. N Engl J Med 281:55, 1969
317. Parfitt AM: The interactions of thiazide diuretics with parathyroid hormone and vitamin D: Studies in patients with hypoparathyroidism. J Clin Invest 51:1879, 1972
318. Popovtzer MM, Subryan VL, Alfrey AC, et al: The acute effect of chlorothiazide on serum-ionized calcium: Evidence for a parathyroid hormone-dependent mechanism. J Clin Invest 55:1295, 1975
319. Porter RH, Cox BG, Heaney P, et al: Treatment of hypoparathyroid patients with chlorthalidone. N Engl J Med 298:577, 1978
320. Brickman AS, Massry SG, Coburn JW: Changes in serum and urinary calcium during treatment with hydrochlorothiazide: Studies on mechanisms. J Clin Invest 51:945, 1972
321. Koppel MH, Massry SG, Shinaberger JH, et al: Thiazide-induced rise in serum calcium and magnesium in patients on maintenance hemodialysis. Ann Intern Med 72:895, 1970
322. Mallette LE, Eichhorn E: Effects of lithium carbonate on human calcium metabolism. Arch Intern Med 146:770, 1986
323. McIntosh WB, Horns EH, Mathieson LM, Sumner E: The prevalence, mechanism and clinical significance of lithium-induced hypercalcemia. Med Lab Sci 44:115, 1987
324. Miller PD, Dubovsky SL, McDonald KM, et al: Hypocalciuric effect of lithium in man. Miner Electrolyte Metab 1:3, 1978
325. Christiansen TAT: Lithium, hypercalcemia, and hyperparathyroidism. Lancet 2:144, 1976
326. Brown EM: Lithium induces abnormal calcium-regulated PTH release in dispersed bovine parathyroid cells. J Clin Endocrinol Metab 52:1046, 1981
327. Spiegel AM, Rudorfer MV, Marx SJ, Linnoila M: The effect of short term lithium administration on suppressibility of parathyroid hormone secretion by calcium in vivo. J Clin Endocrinol Metab 59:354, 1984
328. Orwoll ES: The milk-alkali syndrome: current concepts. Ann Intern Med 97:242, 1982
329. Frame B, Jackson CE, Reynolds WA, Umphrey JE: Hypercalcemia and skeletal effects in chronic hypervitaminosis A. Ann Intern Med 80:44, 1974
330. Streck WF, Waterhouse C, Haddad JG: Glucocorticoid effects in vitamin D intoxication. Arch Intern Med 139:974, 1979
331. Feely J: Propranolol and the hypercalcemia of thyrotoxicosis. Acta Endocrinol 98:528, 1981
332. Mundy GR, Shapiro JL, Bandelin JG, et al: Direct stimulation of bone resorption by thyroid hormones. J Clin Invest 58:529, 1976
333. Krane SM, Brownell GL, Stanbury JB, Corrigan H: The effect of thyroid disease on calcium metabolism in man. J Clin Invest 35:874, 1956
334. Mosekilde L, Melson F, Bagger JP, et al: Bone changes in hyperthyroidism: interrelationships between bone morphometry, thyroid function and calcium-phosphorus metabolism. Acta Endocrinol (Copenh) 85:515, 1977
335. Mosekilde L, Christensin MS: Decreased parathyroid function in hyperthyroidism: Interrelationships between parathyroid hormone, calcium-phosphorus metabolism and thyroid function. Acta Endocrinol (Copenh) 84:566, 1977
336. Bouillon R, Muls E, DeMoor P: Influence of thyroid function on the serum concentration of 1,25-dihydroxyvitamin D. J Clin Endocrinol Metab 51:793, 1980
337. Breuer RI, McPherson HT: Hypercalcemia in concurrent hyperthyroidism and hyper-

parathyroidism. Arch Intern Med 118:310, 1966
338. Bryant LR, Wolsin JH, Altemeier WA: Hyperparathyroidism and hyperthyroidism. Ann Surg 159:411, 1964
339. Muls E, Bouillon R, Boelaert J, et al: Etiology of hypercalcemia in a patient with Addison's Disease. Calcif Tissue Int 34:523, 1982
340. Walker DA, Davies M: Addison's disease presenting as a hypercalcemic crisis in a patient with idiopathic hypoparathyroidism. Clin Endocrinol 14:419, 1981
341. DeSimone DP, Turner RT, Hannon KS, et al: Prednisone inhibits bone formation and resorption in sham-operated and ovariectomized rats. (abstract G6) Calcif Tissue Int 44:S-38, 1989
342. Rath NC, Reddi AM: Influence of adrenalectomy and dexamethasone on matrix-induced endochondral bone differentiation. Endocrinology 104:1698, 1979
343. Miller SS, Sizemore GW, Sheps SG, Tyce GM: Parathyroid function in patients with pheochromocytoma. Ann Intern Med 82:372, 1975
344. Fairhurst BJ, Shettar SP: Hypercalcemia and pheochromocytoma. Postgrad Med J 57:459, 1981
345. Kalager T, Gluck E, Heimann P, Myking O: Pheochromocytoma with ectopic calcitonin production and parathyroid cyst. Br Med J 2:21, 1977
346. Heath H III, Edis AJ: Pheochromocytoma associated with hypercalcemia and ectopic secretion of calcitonin. Ann Intern Med 91:208, 1979
347. Stewart AF, Hoecker JL, Mallette LE, et al: Hypercalcemia in pheochromocytoma: Evidence for a novel mechanism. Ann Intern Med 102:776, 1985
348. Krejs GJ: VIPoma syndrome. Am J Med 82(suppl 5B):37, 1987
349. Mutt V: Isolation and structure of vasoactive intestinal polypeptide from various species. p. 1. In Said SI (ed): Vasoactive Intestinal Peptide. Raven Press, New York, 1982
350. Fahrenkrug J: Vasoactive intestinal polypeptide: Measurement, distribution and putative neurotransmitter function. Digestion 19:149, 1979
351. Bryant MG, Polak JM, Modlin I, et al: Possible dual role for vasoactive intestinal peptide as gastrointestinal hormone and neurotransmitter substance. Lancet 1:991, 1976
352. Krejs GJ, Barkley RM, Read NW, Fordtran JS: Intestinal secretion induced by vasoactive intestinal polypeptide. A comparison with choleratoxin in the canine jejunum in vivo. J Clin Invest 61:1337, 1978
353. Kofstad J, Froyshov I, Gjone E, Blix S: Pancreatic tumor with intractable watery diarrhea, hypokalemia and hypercalcemia. Electrolyte balance studies. Scand J Gastroenterol 2:246, 1967
354. Hohmann EL, Levine L, Tashijan AH: Vasoactive intestinal peptide stimulates bone resorption via a cyclic adenosine $3',5'$-monophosphate-dependent mechanism. Endocrinology 112:1233, 1983
355. Fraser D: Hypophosphatasia. Am J Med 22:730, 1957
356. Whyte MP, Teitelbaum SL, Murphy WA, et al: Adult hypophosphatasia. Medicine 58:329, 1979
357. Rudd NL, Miskin M, Hoar DI, et al: Prenatal diagnosis of hypophosphatasia. N Engl J Med 295:146, 1976
358. Marx SJ, Brandi M-L: Familial primary hyperparathyroidism. p. 375. In Peck WA (ed): Bone and Mineral Research. Vol 5. Elsevier Science Publishers, Amsterdam, 1987
359. Marx SJ, Attie MF, Levine MA, et al: The hypocalciuric or benign variant of familial hypercalcemia: Clinical and biochemical features in fifteen kindreds. Medicine 60:397, 1981
360. Law WM Jr, Heath H III: Familial benign hypercalcemia (hypocalciuric hypercalcemia): Clinical and pathogenetic studies in 21 families. Ann Intern Med 102:511, 1985
361. Attie MF, Gill JR Jr, Stock JL, et al: Urinary calcium excretion in familial hypocalciuric hypercalcemia: Persistence of relative hypocalciuria after induction of hypoparathyroidism. J Clin Invest 72:667, 1983
362. Marx SJ, Attie MF, Stock JL, et al: Maximal urine-concentrating ability: Familial hypocalciuric hypercalcemia versus typical primary hyperparathyroidism. J Clin Endocrinol Metab 52:736, 1981

363. Marx SJ, Spiegel AM, Sharp MF, et al: Adenosine 3',5'-monophosphate response to parathyroid hormone: Familial hypocalciuric hypercalcemia versus typical primary hyperparathyroidism. J Clin Endocrinol Metab 50:546, 1980
364. Taylor AB, Stern PH, Bell NH: Abnormal regulation of circulating 25-hydroxyvitamin D in the Williams syndrome. N Engl J Med 306:972, 1982
365. Garabedian M, Jacqz E, Guillozo H, et al: Elevated plasma 1,25-dihydroxyvitamin D concentrations in infants with hypercalcemia and an elfin facies. N Engl J Med 312:948, 1985
366. Culler FL, Jones KL, Deftos LJ: Impaired calcitonin secretion in patients with Williams syndrome. J Pediatr 107:720, 1985
367. Friedman WF, Roberts WC: Vitamin D and the supravalvular aortic stenosis syndrome. The transplacental effects of vitamin D on the aorta of the rabbit. Circulation 34:77, 1966
368. Friedman WF, Mills LF: The relationship between vitamin D and the craniofacial and dental anomalies of the supravalvular aortic stenosis syndrome. Pediatrics 43:12, 1969
369. Whedon GD, Schorr E: Metabolic studies in paralytic acute anteriopoliomyelitis. II. Alterations in calcium and phosphorus metabolism. J Clin Invest. 36:966, 1957
370. Stewart AF, Adler M, Byers CM, et al: Calcium homeostasis in immobilization: An example of resorptive hypercalciuria. N Engl J Med 306:1136, 1982
371. Lutwak L, Whedon GD, Lachance PA, et al: Mineral, electrolyte and nitrogen balance studies of the Gemini-VII fourteen-day orbital space flight. J Clin Endocrinol Metab 29:1140, 1969
372. Thompson DD, Rodan GA: Indomethacin inhibition of tenotomy-induced bone resorption in rats. J Bone Min Res 3:409, 1988
373. Suki WN, Yium JJ, Von Minden M, et al: Acute treatment of hypercalcemia with furosemide. N Engl J Med 283:836, 1970
374. Eisenberg E: Effect of intravenous phosphate on serum strontium and calcium. N Engl J Med 282:889, 1970
375. Hebert LA, Lemann J Jr, Petersen JR, Lennon EJ: Studies of the mechanism by which phosphate infusion lowers serum calcium concentration. J Clin Invest 45:1886, 1966
376. Shackney S, Hasson J: Precipitous fall in serum calcium, hypotension, and acute renal failure after intravenous phosphate therapy for hypercalcemia. Report of two cases. Ann Intern Med 66:906, 1967
377. Carey RW, Schmitt GW, Kopald HH, Kantrowitz PA: Massive extraskeletal calcification during phosphate treatment of hypercalcemia. Arch Intern Med 122:150, 1968
378. Goldsmith RS, Ingbar SH: Inorganic phosphate treatment of hypercalcemia of diverse etiologies. N Engl J Med 274:1, 1966
379. Breuer PI, LeBauer J: Caution in the use of phosphates in the treatment of severe hypercalcemia. J Clin Endocrinol Metab 27:695, 1967
380. Goldsmith RS, Bartos H, Hulley SB, et al: Phosphate supplementation as an adjunct in the therapy of multiple myeloma. Arch Intern Med 122:128, 1968
381. Jung A: Comparison of two parenteral diphosphonates in hypercalcemia of malignancy. Am J Med 72:221, 1982
382. Mundy GR, Wilkinson R, Heath DA: Comparative study of available medical therapy for hypercalcemia of malignancy. Am J Med 74:421, 1983
383. Sleeboom HP, Bijovet OL, van Oosterom AT, et al: Comparison of intravenous (3-amino-1-hydroxypropylidene)-1,1-biphosphonate and volume repletion in tumour-induced hypercalcemia. Lancet 2:239, 1983
384. Aer J: Effect of thyrocalcitonin on urinary hydroxyproline and calcium in rats. Endocrinology 83:379, 1968
385. Friedman J, Wu WYW, Raisz LG: Response of fetal rat bone to thyrocalcitonin in tissue culture. Endocrinology 82:149, 1968
386. Ardaillou R, Fillastre JP, Milhaud G, et al: Renal excretion of phosphate, calcium, and sodium during and after a prolonged thyrocalcitonin infusion in man. Proc Soc Exp Biol Med 131:56, 1969
387. Chambers TJ, McSheehy PMJ, Thomson BR, Fuller K: The effect of calcium regulating hormones and prostaglandins on bone resorption by osteoclasts disaggregated from neonatal rabbit bones. Endocrinology 116:234, 1985

388. Marx SJ, Woodward C, Aurbach GD: Calcitonin receptors in kidney and bone. Science 178:999, 1972
389. Milhaud G, Job JC: Thyrocalcitonin: Effect on idiopathic hypercalcemia. Science 154:794, 1966
390. Bijvoet OLM, van der Sluys Veer J, Jansen AP: Effects of calcitonin on patients with Paget's disease, thyrotoxicosis or hypercalcemia. Lancet 1:876, 1968
391. Vaughn CB, Vaitkevicius VK: The effects of calcitonin in hypercalcemia in patients with malignancy. Cancer 34:1268, 1974
392. Sjoberg HE, Hjern B: Acute treatment with calcitonin in primary hyperparathyroidism and severe hypercalcemia of other origin. Acta Chir Scand 141:90, 1975
393. Nilsson O, Almqvist S, Karlberg BE: Salmon calcitonin in the acute treatment of moderate and severe hypercalcemia in man. Acta Med Scand 204:249, 1978
394. Wisneski LA, Croom WP, Silva OL, Becker KL: Salmon calcitonin in hypercalcemia. J Clin Pharmacol 19:219, 1979
395. Raisz LG, Wener JA, Trummel CL, et al: Induction, inhibition and escape as phenomena of bone resorption. p. 446. In Talmage RV, Munson PC (eds): Calcium, Parathyroid Hormone, and the Calcitonins. No 243. Excerpta Medica, Amsterdam, 1972
396. Binstock ML, Mundy GR: Effect of calcitonin and glucocorticoids in combination on the hypercalcemia of malignancy. Ann Intern Med 93:269, 1980
397. Verner JV Jr, Engel FL, McPherson HT et al: Vitamin D intoxication: Report of two cases treated with cortisone. Ann Intern Med 48:765, 1958
398. Pechet MM, Bowers B, Bartter FC: Metabolic studies with a new series of 1,4-diene steroids. II. Effects in normal subjects of prednisone, prednisolone, and 9α-fluoroprednisolone. J Clin Invest 38:691, 1959
399. Hahn TJ, Baran DT, Halstead LR: Effects of short term glucocorticoid administration on intestinal calcium absorption and circulating vitamin D metabolite concentration in man. J Clin Endocrinol Metab 52:111, 1981
400. Zerwekh JE, Pak CYC, Kaplan RA, et al: Pathogenic role of 1α,25-dihydroxyvitamin D in sarcoidosis and absorptive hypercalciuria: Different response to prednisolone therapy. J Clin Endocrinol Metab 51:381, 1980
401. Laake H: The action of corticosteroids in the renal reabsorption of calcium. Acta Endocrinol 34:60, 1960
402. Caniggia A, Nuti R, Lore F, Vattimo A: Pathophysiology of the adverse effects of glucoactive corticosteroids on calcium metabolism in man. J Steroid Biochem 15:153, 1981
403. Kimberg DV, Baerg RD, Gershon E, Graudusius RT: Effect of cortisone treatment on the active transport of calcium by the small intestine. J Clin Invest 50:1309, 1971
404. Favus MJ, Walling MW, Kimberg DV: Effects of 1,25-dihydroxycholecalciferol on intestinal calcium transport in cortisone-treated rats. J Clin Invest 52:1680, 1973
405. Sandberg AL, Raisz LG, Wahl LM, Simmons HA: Enhancement of complement-mediated prostaglandin synthesis and bone resorption by arachidonic acid and inhibition by cortisol. Prostaglandins Leukot Med 8:419, 1982
406. Yarbro JW, Kennedy BJ, Barnum CP: Mithramycin inhibition of ribonucleic acid synthesis. Cancer Res 26:36, 1966
407. Parsons V, Baum M, Self M: Effects of mithramycin on calcium and hydroxyproline metabolism in patients with malignant disease. Br Med J 1:474, 1967
408. Cortes EP, Holland JF, Moskowitz R, Depoli E: Effects of mithramycin on bone resorption in vitro. Cancer Res 32:74, 1972
409. Brown JH, Kennedy BJ: Mithramycin in the treatment of disseminated testicular neoplasia. N Engl J Med 272:111, 1965
410. Ream NW, Perlia CP, Wolter J, Taylor SG III: Mithramycin therapy in disseminated germinal, testicular cancer. JAMA 204:1030, 1968
411. Kofman S, Medrek TJ, Alexander RW: Mithramycin in the treatment of embryonal cancer. Cancer 17:938, 1964

6

Disorders of Phosphate Metabolism

James C. M. Chan
Norman H. Bell

GENERAL ASPECTS OF PHOSPHORUS METABOLISM

Phosphorus is one of the most abundant constituents of all tissues and is a major component of bone. It is a component of many proteins, lipids, and nucleic acids, and is involved in a large number of essential biochemical processes. For example, it is an important constituent of the phospholipids that are components of cell membranes and are essential in the phosphoinositol pathway, which is now known to play a central physiologic role in the regulation of cell metabolism. Virtually all metabolic processes require phosphorus, including the provision of high energy phosphate bonds in the form of adenosine triphosphate (ATP), and the phosphorylation and dephosphorylation of enzymes and the receptors that regulate their biologic activity. ATP is required for a large number of processes including the biosynthesis of proteins, lipids, complex carbohydrates, and nucleic acids; ion transport; the secretion of hormones, neurotransmitters, and enzymes; and contraction of muscles. It is the substrate for the enzyme adenylate cyclase, which synthesizes cyclic adenosine 3′,5′-monophosphate (cAMP).

In biologic systems, phosphorus is present as phosphate. However, in biologic fluids, it is the concentration of elemental phosphorus that is determined and not phosphate, although the terms are used interchangeably.

The total phosphate content in a 70 kg man is approximately 700 g. About 85 percent is present in the skeleton, 14 percent is intracellular, and less than 1 percent is in extracellular fluids. Because the bulk of phosphate is in cells, serum phosphate is not greatly influenced by chronic excess or depletion of phosphate, although acute changes can alter the serum concentration.[1]

In extracellular fluid (ECF), some 10 percent of phosphate is bound to proteins, and one third is complexed to sodium, calcium, and magnesium. Inorganic phosphate is present in the circulation as monohydrogen phosphate, which is divalent, and as dihydrogen phosphate, which is monovalent.[2] At pH 7.4, the composite valency of the two inorganic phosphates is 1.8, and the relative concentrations of monohydrogen and dihydrogen phosphate are 4 and 1, respectively. The composite valency is arrived at by application of the Henderson-Hasselbalch equation:

pH 7.4 = pK 6.8 + log (monohydrogen phosphate/dihydrogen phosphate) where log (monohydrogen phosphate/dihydrogen phosphate) = 0.60, and the antilog is 4. At pH 7.4, 4 mmol (8 mEq) of monohydrogen phosphate exists with 1 mmol (1 mEq) of dihydrogen phosphate, so that there are 9 mEq of phosphate or 5 mmol of phosphate and a valency of 1.8. The concentration of phosphate in plasma or serum is expressed in milligrams per deciliter (mg/dl) or millimoles per liter (mmol/liter). For conversion: mmol/liter = mg/dl × 0.32, and meq/liter = mmol/liter × 1.8.

The concentration of phosphate in serum has a wider physiologic range than that of calcium, and varies with age. It is highest during the neonatal and early childhood periods and declines thereafter (Fig. 6-1). The mechanism for this difference is not established, but may be related to the higher values for circulating growth hormone in growing children as compared to adults, and to the associated increases in the tubular reabsorption of phosphate.[3,4]

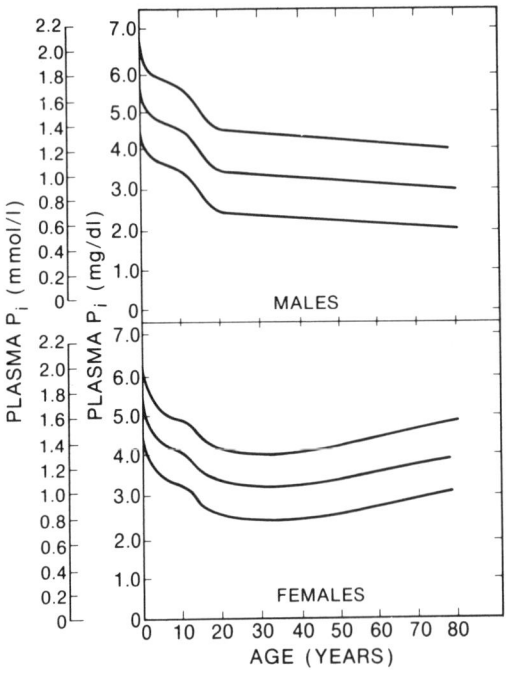

Fig. 6-1. Normal serum phosphate concentration according to age and sex.

The average dietary intake of phosphate is 20 mg/kg/day (Fig. 6-2), which is balanced by fecal and urinary outputs; resulting in a phosphate balance of zero.[5] The internal metabolism of phosphate includes digestive juice secretion and reabsorption, and the formation of bone phosphate. Dietary phosphate is composed of inorganic and organic forms of phosphorus. The latter occur as phosphoproteins, phospholipids, and phosphocarbohydrates.[5]

Intestinal absorption of phosphate occurs maximally at the jejunum, mostly as inorganic phosphate.[6,7] The ratio of organic to inorganic phosphate in the diet varies, depending on the type of food. For example, phosphate in cow's milk is 70 percent inorganic, whereas in animal meat it is mostly organic.[5] Tissue organic phosphate undergoes hydrolysis in the intestinal tract, although certain phospholipids are absorbed in the organic form.[8] If the dietary calcium:phosphate ratio exceeds 4, the excess calcium interferes with intestinal absorption of phosphate because it combines with phosphate to form nonabsorbable complexes.[9] This provides the rationale for the use of calcium carbonate as a phosphate binder to impede the intestinal absorption of phosphate in patients with chronic renal failure.

Data in experimental animals suggest two mechanisms of intestinal absorption of phosphate: (1) Mucosal, sodium-dependent, carrier-mediated transport in the chick jejunum,[10] with phosphate uptake reduced in vitamin D deficiency and normalized by vitamin D supplementation, which operates by enhancing the V_{max} of absorption. This unidirectional, absorptive flux of phosphate has also been demonstrated in the rabbit duodenum, which is sensitive to arsenate, mercuric chloride, and diphosphonate. (2) Serosal, sodium-independent, passive diffusion accounts for phosphate influx and efflux, which are not vitamin D dependent but only concentration dependent.[5]

Under normal conditions, intestinal phos-

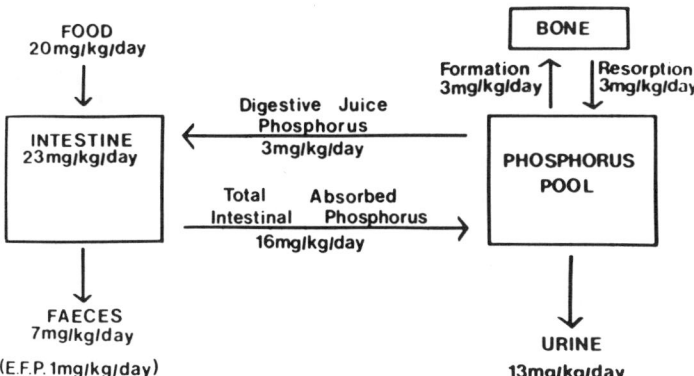

Fig. 6-2. Composite interpretation of phosphate balance: dietary intake, fecal and urinary outputs, and internal homeostasis. (From Nordin BEC, ed. Calcium, Phosphate and Magnesium Metabolism. New York, Churchill Livingstone, 1976, with permission).

phate absorption is principally concentration-dependent. Only under conditions such as dietary deprivation[11] does the active transport process become important. In advanced renal failure, impaired intestinal absorption of phosphate has been demonstrated.[12,13] This is an expected consequence of the lack of 1,25-dihydroxyvitamin D synthesis. However, even in advanced renal failure the bulk of intestinal phosphate absorption is by passive diffusion; thus, unless there is dietary deprivation of phosphate, or phosphate binders are used, the amount of phosphate absorbed usually exceeds what the body needs.

Although absorption of phosphate occurs throughout the intestinal tract, maximal transport of phosphate occurs in the jejunum/duodenum, followed by the ileum.[14] An intestinal phosphate-binding protein has been sought but not found. A calcium-binding protein appears 12 hours after vitamin D administration and more than 4 hours before the start of phosphate absorption, suggesting that the two substances are transported by different mechanisms.

The factors influencing phosphate transport include vitamin D, parathyroid and other hormones, and cations and other dietary components, as well as certain medications. The influence of vitamin D can be gleaned from the observation that the phosphate malabsorption in vitamin D deficiency is reversed with 1,25-dihydroxyvitamin D_3 treatment.[12,13] In studies of isolated rat jejunum, other vitamin D metabolites (e.g., 25-hydroxyvitamin D_3 and 24,25-dihydroxyvitamin D_3) failed to promote phosphate transport.[1,4] Maneuvers designed to stimulate 1,25-dihydroxyvitamin D production (e.g., phosphate or calcium intake restriction) result in increased phosphate absorption. The increased phosphate absorption in primary hyperparathyroidism and the decreased phosphate absorption in hypoparathyroidism suggest that parathyroid hormone (PTH) promotes intestinal phosphate absorption.[15] However, the increased phosphate absorption is probably mediated by increased 1,25-dihydroxyvitamin D production, and is less likely a direct effect of PTH.[16] Contradictory results have been reported concerning calcitonin's effect on phosphate absorption. No disturbances of phosphate transport have been reported in hypothyroid or hyperthyroid subjects.[16] Chronic corticosteroid excess, such as occurs in Cushing's disease, leads to reduced phosphate absorption.[4] Magnesium deficiency promotes phosphate absorption.[17] Increased sodium and potassium concentrations in everted rat gut sacs promote the transport of phosphate against a concentration gradient.[14] Aluminum and magnesium antacids inhibit phosphate absorption.[18] Metabolic inhibitors such as 1-phenylalanine, arsenate, iodoacetate, cyanides, 2,4-dinitrophenol, and ouabain reduce phosphate absorption.[19] Net phosphate absorption decreases with an increased hydrogen ion concentration.[19]

Reducing dietary phosphate intake results in two physiologic responses: (1) the absorption of phosphate increases markedly in rats within three weeks, and increases less so in humans[5,7]; and (2) renal phosphate reabsorption is maximized.[1,4]

Phosphate transport against a concentration gradient requires glucose more as an energy source for cell preservation than specifically for the phosphate transport process per se.[4]

CELLULAR MECHANISM OF RENAL PHOSPHATE TRANSPORT

In contrast to calcium, with its multiple renal tubular sites of reabsorption, phosphate is mainly reabsorbed at the proximal renal tubule in humans.[20,21] Phosphate reabsorption at other sites of the nephron is less well defined.[22] Data on proximal renal tubular transport of phosphate are derived from studies utilizing proximal tubular brush border membrane vesicles; micropuncture techniques; in vitro microperfusion; and the cultured kidney cell line LLC-PK. Evidence obtained to date indicates that phosphate transported at the brush border membrane consists of divalent monohydrogen phosphate coupled electroneutrally with two sodium ions (Fig. 6-3). The favorable electrochemical gradient for sodium entry at the luminal (brush border) membrane comes from the sodium exit at the contraluminal (basolateral) membrane, which is Na^+, K^+-ATPase dependent.[23]

The dependency of phosphate transport on sodium reabsorption is demonstrated by micropuncture studies in which phosphate absorption ceases in the absence of intraluminal sodium.[24] Furthermore, in vitro microperfusion studies have demonstrated that when sodium transport is inhibited by ouabain, phosphate transport also ceases.[21] Finally, brush border membrane vesicle studies have demonstrated that the transport mechanism is cation-specific, because equimolar concentrations of potassium fail to move phosphate into vesicles, even under favorable gradient conditions.[23]

As shown in Figure 6-3, whereas the entry of phosphate into the tubule cell takes place against an electrochemical gradient, requiring saturable, sodium-dependent cotransport across the luminal membrane, the exit of phosphate across the contraluminal membrane into the peritubular fluid is passive, going down a concentration gradient because the intracellular phosphate concentration is higher.[25] This is further augmented by the fact that the intracellular voltage is markedly negative compared with that of the peritubular fluid, setting up an electrochemical gradient to promote exit of the cation. It is unclear whether the cation exists as monovalent or divalent phosphate, although the divalent form is more likely because absorption of phosphate is inhibited when the intraluminal pH is alkaline and not when it is acidic. Robito and colleagues[26] recently demonstrated that phosphate uptake by a cultured kidney cell line (LLC-PK1) is four times greater at the luminal membrane than at the contraluminal membrane. Aside from difficulties in avoiding contamination of the LLC-PK1 cells, this may prove to be a worthwhile method of studying the metabolism of proximal renal tubule cells, because this kidney cell line exhibits the same sodium-dependent, pH-dependent phosphate transport characteristics as proximal renal tubule cells.

In summary, current data on phosphate transport (Fig. 6-3) favor the concept that at the brush border membrane, divalent mo-

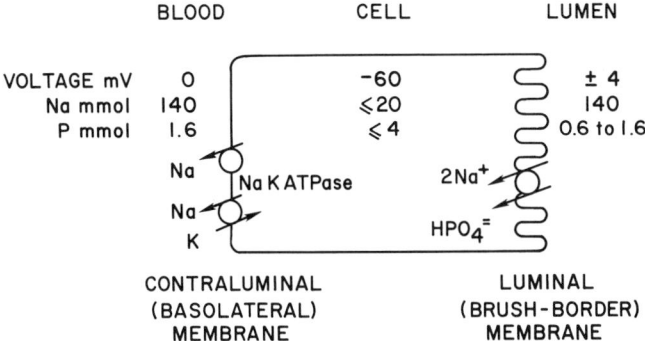

Fig. 6-3. Schematic representation of transcellular phosphate transport. At the luminal (brush border) membrane, divalent phosphate is co-transported with two sodium ions and energized by the continuous exit of sodium ions across the contraluminal (basolateral) membrane.

nohydrogen phosphate is co-transported with sodium ions in an electroneutral fashion, driven by the sharp electrochemical gradient for sodium entry, which in turn is continuously energized by the active extrusion of sodium across the basolateral membrane via Na^+, K^+-ATPase activity. Finally, the exit of phosphate across the basolateral membrane is less well defined but is probably related to passive diffusion of phosphate due to concentration and electrochemical gradients.

RENAL HANDLING OF PHOSPHATE

The kidneys play a pivotal role in the regulation of phosphate homeostatis. Approximately 10 percent of serum phosphate is protein-bound, and the remaining 90 percent consists of monovalent and divalent phosphate anions. By virtue of a number of offsetting factors, the serum phosphate concentration is close to that of the glomerular filtrate.[4] Thus, the filtered load of phosphate can be calculated as the product of the serum phosphate concentration multiplied by the glomerular filtration rate (GFR). The filtered load of phosphate is always larger than the total rate of phosphate excretion, suggesting that there is always a net tubular reabsorption of phosphate.

As mentioned before, the proximal tubular reabsorption of phosphate is saturable. Figure 6-4 illustrates the relationship between plasma phosphate concentration and the renal excretion of phosphate.[27] Because of the initial splaying of the curve in phosphate excretion (Fig. 6-4), the tubular maximum of phosphate excretion per 100 mL of the glomerular filtration rate (TmP/GFR) is extrapolated by extending the phosphate excretion line backwards to cut the abscissa; at this point, the proximal tubular reabsorption of phosphate is saturated. The TmP/GFR respresents the phosphate threshold, beyond which any further increase in serum phosphate concentration will not give rise to any further reabsorption of phosphate; the tubular phosphate excretion parallels the inulin clearance.[28] The maximum rate of phosphate excretion (TmPO$_4$) is the vertical distance between the two slopes (Fig. 6-4). The TmP/GFR is a very useful index of phosphate reabsorption capacity per unit of renal function. Below this "setpoint," all filtered phosphate is reabsorbed; beyond the TmP/GFR, progressively more phosphate is excreted.[27,28] By such means the kidneys maintain a serum phosphate concentration

228 • Kidney Electrolyte Disorders

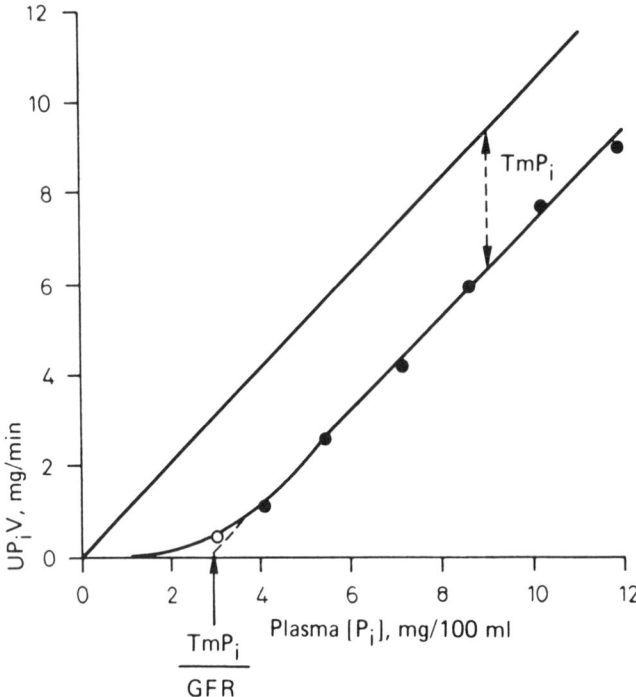

Fig. 6-4. The relationship between plasma phosphate [P] concentration in milligrams per deciliter and the urinary phosphate excretion rate (UP_i V) in milligrams per minute. Fasting data are represented by open circles and data during phosphate infusion are represented by closed circles. The slope of the line for phosphate excretion is identical to the slope of the line for inulin clearance. The $TmPO_4$ (tubular maximum for reabsorption of phosphate) is the vertical distance between the two slopes. The extrapolated tubular maximum of phosphate excretion per 100 ml GFR (i.e. TmP/GFR) represents the saturation or phosphate threshold. (From Bijvoet,[27] with permission).

close to the TmP/GFR. Variations in the serum phosphate concentration are the direct effects of factors influencing the TmP/GFR.

It is not practical in every clinical setting to conduct a phosphate infusion study to determine the TmP/GFR; thus, a useful nomogram has been developed (Fig. 6-5) that takes into account the plasma phosphate (in either milligrams per deciliter or millimoles per liter) and the glomerular filtration rate.[28] By plotting these two known variables, the TmP/GFR in any situation can be determined from a line joining the two points.[29]

As much as 50 percent of the filtered load of phosphate is reabsorbed in the first third of the proximal tubule, as characterized by micropuncture studies and in vivo perfusion of segments of proximal tubule.[30,31] Within this segment, only 10 percent of sodium and water is reabsorbed (Table 6-1). In the last two thirds of the proximal tubule, 20 percent of the filtered load of phosphate is reabsorbed, and in this segment a parallel percentage of water and sodium is also reabsorbed.[21,32] There is no evidence to suggest any transport of phosphate within the loop of Henle. In the distal convoluted tubule, 5 to 10 percent of the filtered load of phosphate is reabsorbed under basal conditions in animals that have undergone parathyroidectomy.[21] This segment of the nephron, however, is responsive to PTH,

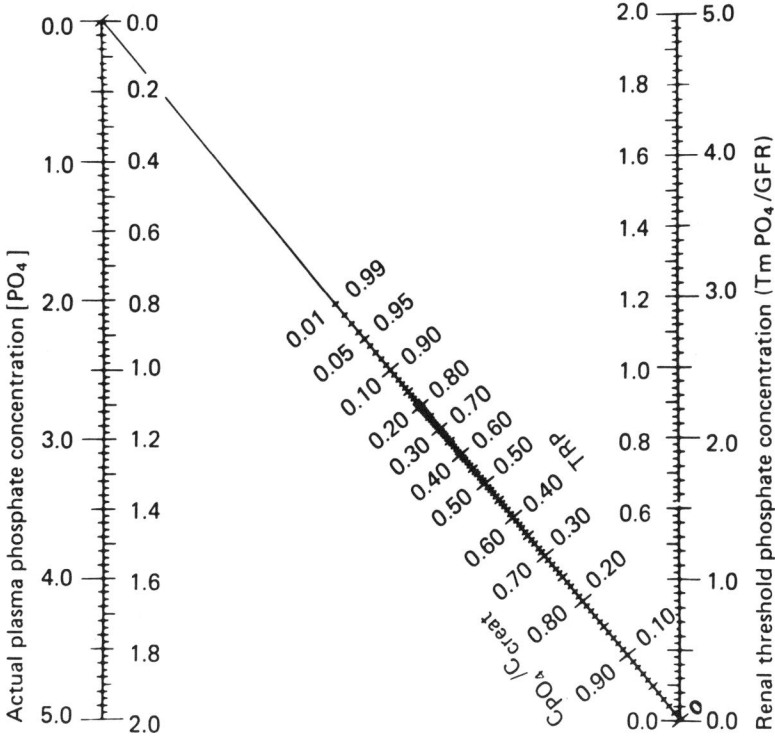

Fig. 6-5. Nomogram to determine TmP/GFR from any two points: the plasma phosphate and the GFR. The lines joining these two points will cross the appropriate TmP/GFR. (From Walton, Bijvoet,[28] with permission).

as are all other segments except the loop of Henle and the collecting duct.[32,33] The administration of PTH results in a lowering of the tubular reabsorption of phosphate by as much as one half, and a lowering of the distal tubular reabsorption from 10 percent to 5 percent.[34] In the collecting duct, up to 3 percent of the filtered load of phosphate is reabsorbed.[4] However, this can be increased to 10 percent in the presence of an increased luminal phosphate concentration or increased flow rates.[1,4]

The superficial and deep nephrons differ in their phosphate handling, with the deep

Table 6-1. Tubular Reabsorption of Filtered Phosphate, Sodium, Water

	Phosphate Reabsorbed	Sodium Reabsorbed	Water Reabsorbed	PTH/PD
Proximal tubule				
First ⅓	50%	10%	10%	↓/↑
Last ⅔	20%	20%	20%	↓/↑
Loop of Henle	0%			—
Distal convoluted tubule	5–10%		60%	↓/↑
Collecting ducts cortical	0–3% (up to 10%)			–/↓

PTH = parathyroid hormone, PD = phosphate deprivation.
↓ = decreased phosphate transport (i.e., increased excretion).
↑ = increased phosphate transport (i.e., decreased excretion).

(juxtamedullary) nephrons reabsorbing a higher percentage of injected phosphate tracers.[21,34] Such differences may account for the variability of past measurements, when microinjections of phosphate were made into superficial cortical nephrons.

In summary, under normal circumstances, the bulk of the filtered load of phosphate is reabsorbed in the proximal tubule, especially in the first one third of the segment of the nephron. The distal convoluted tubule and the collecting duct account for the rest. In all, approximately 80 to 95 percent of the filtered load of phosphate is normally reabsorbed (i.e., the tubular reabsorption of phosphate is 80 to 95 percent under normal conditions).

FACTORS AFFECTING RENAL PHOSPHATE TRANSPORT

In view of the lack of evidence for tubular phosphate secretion, any change in the rate of renal phosphate excretion is modulated by either of two mechanisms: the phosphate load (plasma phosphate concentration × glomerular filtration rate), or the rate of tubular reabsorption of phosphate. The factors that influence proximal tubular phosphate transport (summarized in Table 6-2) will be discussed in this section. Dietary intake of phosphate is an example of a factor that influences the filtered load, and PTH is a factor that in turn influences the tubular reabsorption of phosphate.

Dietary Phosphate Intake

The renal adaptation to dietary phosphate loading is the reduction of phosphate transport and promotion of increased phosphate excretion. This is unrelated to the action of PTH, because within one hour of acute phosphate infusion into rats that have undergone parathyroidectomy, proximal tubular phosphate transport promptly drops.[35]

The renal adaptation to dietary phosphate deprivation is an avid increase in phosphate transport and a reduction of phosphate excretion.[36] In studies with brush border membrane vesicles, phosphate uptake is markedly increased within four hours of phosphate deprivation.[37] In pigs, such an adaptation becomes evident within two days of phosphate deprivation and is similarly independent of PTH or vitamin D activity.[38]

The adaptation is specific to sodium-dependent phosphate transport, because sodium dependent glucose uptake remains unaffected, at least in short-term studies.[39] This renal tubular adaptation to dietary phosphate deprivation occurs in animals that have undergone parathyroidectomy, in vitamin D-deficient animals, and in volume-expanded rats, and is unrelated to serum concentrations of calcium.[39]

Using micropuncture techniques, the adaptation at different nephron sites to different dietary phosphate intakes[35] has been characterized in rats that have undergone parathyroidectomy. With a high phosphate intake, a large fraction of the filtered load of phosphate passes unabsorbed at the superficial proximal tubule. With a low phosphate intake, both proximal and distal tubular reabsorption of phosphate have been demonstrated.

Table 6–2. Factors Influencing Proximal Renal Tubular Phosphate Transport

Increased	Decreased
Phosphate deprivation	Phosphate loading
Growth hormone	Parathyroid hormone
Insulin	Cyclic AMP
Vitamin D	Extracellular fluid expansion
Thyroid hormone	Acute respiratory acidosis
Luminal calcium	Metabolic acidosis or alkalosis
Prostaglandin	Vasopressin
Angiotensin II	Glucocorticoid
	Calcitonin
	Luminal glucose

Using microperfusion techniques,[39] it has been shown that dietary intakes substantially affect the tubular reabsorption of phosphate in both the early and late proximal convoluted tubule.

Using proximal tubule brush border membrane vesicles, a low phosphate diet promotes phosphate intake, even in animals that have undergone parathyroidectomy.[40] Such data[40] suggest that this tubular adaptation is independent of PTH activity. Furthermore, a change in the V_{max} of the sodium dependent gradient for phosphate transport is implicated in this adaptation.[38]

The phosphaturic effects of PTH are blunted in phosphate deprivation. The mechanism(s) involved is unclear. The inhibition probably occurs at a step beyond the tubular site of cAMP production,[41] because PTH administration in the phosphate-deprived state still brings about increased levels of urinary cAMP.

Inhibition of the effects of other phosphaturic hormones (e.g., calcitonin and dibutyryl cAMP) is also encountered in phosphate deprivation.[1,4] Finally, the phosphaturia usually detected after volume expansion as well as after phosphate infusion becomes diminished in phosphate depletion.[4]

Growth Hormone

Large reductions in urinary phosphate excretion, but without substantial changes in serum phosphate concentration, follow the short-term administration of growth hormone to humans and experimental animals.[2,3] In contrast, long-term administration of growth hormone causes not only substantial elevation of the TmP/GFR but also marked elevation of the serum phosphate concentration.[3] Patients with acromegaly, as can be expected, are often hyperphosphatemic, secondary to the elevated TmP/GFR from the chronic oversecretion of the hormone.[42,43] Patients with acromegaly who are treated demonstrate normalization of the serum phosphate level and the TmP/GFR.

The serum phosphate concentrations in infants and young children are higher than normal adult values. Figure 6-1 illustrates that in subjects less than one year old, the mean serum phosphate level is 5 to 7 mg/dl, whereas the corresponding value in adults is 3 to 5 mg/dl. The fact that the serum phosphate concentration decreases to adult values after puberty, when the growth hormone concentration also decreases, implies that the elevation of phosphate concentrations in infancy and early childhood is due to growth hormone effects.[43,44] However, such age-specific changes may not be entirely due to elevated growth hormone concentrations at early ages, because an elevated serum phosphate concentration and TmP/GFR are also seen in pituitary dwarfs.[42] Growth hormone receptors in the renal tubule have been sought but not found, and growth hormone administration seemingly has no effects on gluconeogenesis or cAMP synthesis in isolated proximal tubule fragments.[45] Thus, the mechanisms of action of growth hormone on renal phosphate handling remain unclear. Studies in brush border membrane vesicles confirm that the administration of growth hormone increases sodium-dependent phosphate transport.[46,47] Micropuncture studies suggest an augmentation of proximal renal tubular sodium reabsorption after the administration of growth hormone.[48,49] Systemic sodium retention secondary to growth hormone administration has been demonstrated both in humans[50] and in rats.[51] In view of the sodium and phosphate co-transport in the proximal tubule, the phosphate reabsorptive effect of growth hormone may be mediated by this effect on sodium reabsorption. However, this antinatriuretic action of growth hormone is not a consistent observation.[52]

Evidence has been presented to suggest that growth hormone suppresses PTH secretion.[53] This is based on the observation that growth hormone promotes both 1,25-dihydroxyvitamin D synthesis[54] and intestinal calcium absorption[48]; thus, these two actions may occur in concert and suppress PTH secretion. This accords with the hypercalcemia described in acromegalic subjects.[55]

However, despite these observations that link growth hormone with suppression of PTH secretion, the bulk of scientific evidence[3,48,51] suggests that growth hormone-induced renal tubular reabsorption of phosphate is independent of PTH action. For example, in dogs that have undergone parathyroidectomy,[48] growth hormone increases the TmP/GFR. Furthermore, the phosphatemic effects of PTH have been documented in dogs before and after growth hormone administration.[48]

The hypothesis that growth hormone also exerts its renal tubular effects by way of the somatomedins has received support from the observation that patients with hereditary somatomedin deficiency have reduced serum phosphate concentrations.[56]

In addition, growth hormone increases renal blood flow, GFR,[57] para-amino hippurate (PAH) secretion, and sulfate reabsorption.[58] These hemodynamic changes may increase the filtered load of phosphate, obligating increased reabsorption.

Finally, the possibility that the extrarenal effects of growth hormone may indirectly influence the renal tubular reabsorption of phosphate must be considered. Growth hormone is anabolic, which may prompt a greater need for phosphate, increasing absorption and reducing excretion.[59]

Vitamin D

Controversy exists about the effects of vitamin D on renal phosphate handling. This is due in part to the differences in study conditions and experimental animals employed. Earlier studies[60-62] showed that vitamin D increases the renal tubular reabsorption of phosphate in rachitic animals and humans. This increased TmP/GFR is due to reversal of secondary hyperparathyroidism.[62-64] The phosphate-retaining effect of vitamin D is attributed to inhibition of secretion of PTH and to the vitamin D-induced increase in serum calcium concentration.[62-64] As discussed earlier, the renal tubule adapts to changes in dietary phosphate intake such that phosphate transport varies inversely with dietary phosphate. This response appears to be more efficient in vitamin D-replete than in vitamin D-deficient animals.[64]

There are conflicting data about whether vitamin D and its metabolites directly influence the TmP/GFR. Acute administration of vitamin D increases the TmP/GFR in both parathyroidectomized and vitamin D-depleted rats,[62-64] whereas chronic administration reduces the TmP/GFR.[1,4] Thus, whether vitamin D increases or diminishes the tubular reabsorption of phosphate depends on the duration of its administration. Other studies indicate that phosphate excretion is either unchanged or increased by vitamin D or 1,25-dihydroxyvitamin D_3.[65,66]

It appears that these disparate effects of vitamin D depend on the status of phosphate intake. With hypophosphatemia secondary to phosphate depletion or vitamin D deficiency, vitamin D diminishes renal phosphate excretion. In contrast, with hyperphosphatemia or phosphate repletion, vitamin D and its metabolites enhance phosphate excretion.

The renal handling of phosphate is also indirectly influenced by the effects of vitamin D at nonrenal sites. For example, the healing of rickets in response to vitamin D requires calcium and phosphate to form new bone. Thus, the administration of vitamin D for the treatment of rickets is associated with renal conservation of phosphate. In contrast, vitamin D overdosage results in bone resorption and renal loss of phosphate. These changes in phosphate excretion are clearly not mediated by PTH, because circulating PTH is increased in rickets and suppressed in vitamin D intoxication.

Parathyroid Hormone

Proximal tubular reabsorption of phosphate is inhibited by PTH.[60] This phosphaturic action of PTH is rapid, and occurs within minutes after administration of the hormone.[16] The TmP/GFR is reduced by PTH, and continued infusion of the hormone results in a new steady state with a lower setpoint for the TmP/GFR.

Only a fraction of the cAMP produced by the renal tubules in response to PTH is required for phosphate transport, because further increases in PTH administration produce minimal effects on phosphate clearance while increases in nephrogenic cAMP continue.[20,67]

Parathyroid hormone-sensitive adenylate cyclase is present in both the straight and convoluted segments of the proximal renal tubule, but PTH-sensitive phosphate transport is evident only in the straight segment.[20,67] The reason for this apparent dissociation is unclear.

With parathyroidectomy, proximal tubular reabsorption of phosphate increases within 24 hours as determined by microperfusion studies of isolated segments of nephrons.[67] The tubular fluid (TF) to ultrafiltrate (UF) ratio of phosphate decreases from a range of 0.6 to 0.7 to a range of 0.2 to 0.4.

There is no evidence for the presence of PTH-responsive adenylate cyclase in either the thin or thick ascending limbs of Henle or the cortical collecting ducts.[1] However, responsiveness of adenylate cyclase was demonstrated in the distal tubule.[4]

Figure 6-6 illustrates the process by which PTH inhibits phosphate entry into the cell. At the contraluminal (basolateral) membrane, the hormone activates mem-

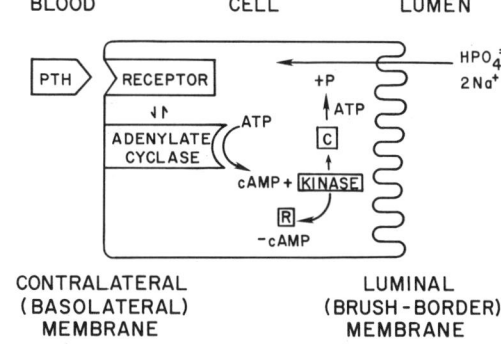

Fig. 6-6. Mechanism of parathyroid hormone action in the proximal renal tubular cell. At the basolateral membrane, the hormone acts upon its receptor, which in turn reacts with the membrane-bound adenylate cyclase system. This leads to conversion of adenosine triphosphate (ATP) to cyclic adenosine monophosphate (cAMP). The binding of cAMP to protein kinase leads to the latter splitting into its regulatory (R) and catalytic (C) subunits. Phosphorylation of brush border membrane proteins inactivates the phosphate transport and inhibits phosphate entry into the cell.

brane-bound adenylate cyclase, which enhances the conversion of adenosine triphosphate to cAMP.[16,20] Protein kinase A, abundantly concentrated in the luminal (brush border) membrane, reacts with cAMP and dissociates into its regulatory and catalytic subunits.[1,4] The phosphorylation of luminal membrane proteins by the catalytic subunit results in an inhibition of sodium-phosphate co-transport, decreasing phosphate entry into the cell. Prompt phosphaturia ensues. The biochemical interactions that lead to this sequence of reactions are unclear.

Parathyroid hormone may also influence phosphate transport by altering the concentration of intracellular calcium.[68] Decreased phosphate transport in brush border membrane vesicles is demonstrated in animals pretreated in vivo with either PTH or cAMP. However, this does not occur if the agents are added in vitro.[69] It is possible that the altered phosphate transport results from changes in the cytosolic ionized calcium concentration brought about by the in vivo administration of PTH or cAMP.[69]

Parathyroid hormone also stimulates phosphoinositol metabolism, which results in activation of the calcium/diacylglycerol, protein kinase C pathway with the probable phosphorylation of proteins. Both this pathway and that produced by the activation of adenylate cyclase can independently mediate the action of PTH on the renal tubular transport of phosphate.[3]

It was suggested that PTH exerts its effect on the proximal tubule by ribosylation of adenosine diphosphate.[70] Nicotinamide adenosine dinucleotide inhibits sodium-dependent phosphate transport but not sodium-dependent glucose transport.[71] Since nicotinamide administered intraperitoneally reverses the renal tubular resistance to PTH as a result of phosphate deprivation, the inhibition appears to be at a site distal to that of cAMP production.[69]

Another hypothesis concerning the mechanism of action of PTH is that it promotes gluconeogenesis by increasing the cytosolic cAMP concentration.[72] Nicotinamide-adenosine dinucleotide, stimulated by the gluconeogenesis, then blocks sodium-dependent phosphate transport.

In summary, PTH inhibits phosphate reabsorption at both proximal and distal sites in the renal tubule. The phosphaturic effects of the hormone are blunted in certain conditions, including phosphate deprivation. In proximal tubular cells, the hormone activates two subunits, one of which, the catalytic subunit, promotes phosphorylation of luminal membrane protein, resulting in inhibition of sodium-phosphate co-transport and phosphate entry. It also stimulates phosphoinositol metabolism and the calcium/diacylglycerol protein kinase C pathway and inhibits the same transport system.

Insulin

Insulin and PTH appear to be physiologic antagonists with regard to the renal tubular transport of phosphorus and gluconeogenesis. Whereas PTH is known to stimulate gluconeogenesis and to inhibit the renal tubular reabsorption of sodium and phosphate (vide supra), insulin was shown to inhibit gluconeogenesis and to enhance the tubular reabsorption of these two ions.[73] Renal receptors for insulin were found in glomeruli and in the luminal brush border membranes and basolateral membranes of proximal tubular cells.[74] Interestingly, stimulation of phosphorylation of the insulin receptor in response to insulin is selective and occurs in the basolateral membranes but not in the brush border membranes. Presumably the insulin receptors in the brush border membranes play a role in modulating phosphate transport, whereas those in the basolateral membranes mediate the biochemical actions of insulin. As occurs in other tissues, the number of insulin receptors in the basolateral membranes is increased in insulin deficiency.

Thyroid Hormone

Elevation of serum phosphate concentrations has been repeatedly observed in hyperthyroid subjects.[75] Conversely, depression of serum phosphate concentrations has been reported in hypothyroid subjects.[75] In well controlled rat experiments, the hormone was shown to promote tubular reabsorption of phosphate. The reports of increased urinary phosphate excretion in hyperthyroid patients may be explained by extrarenal effects of the hormone.[76] Increased appetite and resulting higher dietary phosphate intake, elevated circulating growth hormone concentrations, lowering circulating 1,25-dihydroxyvitamin D concentrations, and higher serum 24,25-dihydroxyvitamin D concentrations seen in hyperthyroid subjects all may influence the renal handling of phosphate.[75,76]

Other Steroid Hormones

In normal and parathyroidectomized rats, cortisone administration leads to phosphaturia.[77] In patients with Cushing's syndrome, serum phosphate concentrations are low. A decrease in the serum phosphate concentration follows the administration of corticotropin or hydrocortisone as a result of increased phosphaturia.[78] It is suggested that glucocorticoids inhibit proximal tubular transport by stimulating gluconeogenesis.

Administration of estrogen to patients with osteoporosis has been reported to inhibit phosphate reabsorption.[79] Increased renal synthesis of 1,25-dihydroxyvitamin D synthesis has been demonstrated in Japanese quail after estrogen injection.[80] But the interaction between 1,25-dihydroxyvitamin D and phosphate handling is not clear. A possible explanation centers on the estrogen inhibition of PTH-induced bone resorption leading to increases in serum immunoreactive PTH (iPTH) and 1,25-dihydroxyvitamin D. The higher iPTH would increase the renal clearance of phosphate.

The diurnal increase in urinary and plasma phosphate concentrations that peak between 6 P.M. and midnight is attributed to the cortisol circadian rhythm and PTH circadian patterns.[81]

Expansion of Extracellular Fluids

The phosphaturia that follows saline solution expansion of extracellular fluid (ECF) volume is probably brought about by PTH acting on the proximal renal tubule.[82] It is postulated that the volume expansion produces a decrease in the serum ionized calcium concentration, which stimulates secretion of PTH. This volume-induced phosphaturia is blunted after parathyroidectomy.[83] Despite these reports of a PTH-dependent mechanism for the phosphaturia that follows volume expansion, several lines of evidence have been presented indicating that the effects are principally due to "passive backflux" and are not PTH dependent. Thus, the serum ionized calcium concentration can be reduced by 25 percent by eidetic acid without major changes in renal phosphate handling.[84] It is also likely that at the proximal tubule, sodium and phosphate transport is parallel but becomes dissociated at the distal tubule. This suggestion is supported by the fact that chronic volume expansion, as encountered in primary aldosteronism and in experimental chronic saline loading, is not associated with phosphaturia because of the dissociation of sodium and phosphate transport at the distal sites.[85]

In obstructive uropathies, the volume-induced phosphaturia is blunted, which may be due to increased sodium and phosphate reabsorption at the proximal tubule.[4]

Calcitonin

Calcitonin administration produces phosphaturia, possibly indirectly as the result of its hypocalcemic effect, which acts to stimulate secretion of PTH or directly on the renal tubule, blocking phosphate transport.[86,87] To avoid the systemic effects of calcitonin, the hormone was directly applied to the surface of exposed proximal tubules and was found to cause phosphaturia.[87] Phosphaturia occurs after calcitonin administration, even when normophosphatemia is maintained by a continuous infusion of phosphate and the hypophosphatemia produced by the hormone is avoided.

The effect of calcitonin on the kidney may be dose dependent. Pharmacologic doses of calcitonin are phosphaturic, whereas lower doses are not.[87] Thus, a physiologic effect of the hormone on renal handling of phosphate is not established. The cAMP concentration is increased after administration of calcitonin, and the sites of tubular concentrations of cAMP do not correspond to the sites of action of PTH. This casts some doubt on the contention that the phosphaturia produced by calcitonin is mediated by PTH. However, this leaves open the possibility that present techniques of measurement may lack the sensitivity required to detect this.

Vasopressin

Antidiuretic hormone (ADH) promotes tubular reabsorption of phosphate through mechanisms that are not yet clearly defined. The antiphosphaturic effects of the hormone are not mediated by its effects on hemodynamic changes in renal blood flow, glomerular filtration rate, or a rise in systolic blood pressure. The action of ADH appears to be independent of PTH.[88] The hyperphosphatemia that follows administration of pharmacologic doses of vasopressin is attributed to its antiphosphaturic effect as well as its extrarenal effect of mobilizing phosphate from tissue into the ECF compartment.[88]

Other Hormonal Factors Influencing Renal Phosphate Handling

"Phosphaturic" factors that are secreted by soft tissue tumors are thought to account for a syndrome characterized by hypophosphatemia, renal phosphate wasting, rickets or osteomalacia, and a depressed serum concentration of 1,25-dihydroxyvitamin D, but without hypocalcemia or an elevated PTH concentration.[89,90] This syndrome is also linked to neurofibromatosis,[91] malignant neurinoma,[91] and fibrous dysplasia of bone.[92,93] Excision of an epidermal nevus from a patient[94] resulted in the reversal of renal phosphate wasting, and the administration of a tumor extract caused phosphaturia in an experimental animal.[93]

Other hormones that affect renal phosphate handling include prostaglandin, which diminishes phosphate excretion in Bartter's syndrome during indomethacin administration,[95] and angiotensin II, which increases the TmP/GFR and reduces phosphate excretion.[96]

As mentioned above, circadian variations in phosphate excretion parallel those of plasma PTH and phosphate concentrations, and are lowest at 8 A.M. and peak at 8 P.M. This pattern is related to the circulating hydrocortisone concentration[97,98] and is apparently independent of feedings,[97] although a contrary observation has described a change in the pattern accompanying 48-hour fasting.[99]

Acid-Base Balance

Contradictory data have been presented concerning the influence of changes in the acid-base balance on renal phosphate handling.[1,4] These contradictions are probably the result of widely different test conditions. In addition, respiratory and dietary changes greatly affect phosphate reabsorption. For example, acute hypercapnia (PCO_2 in excess of 80 mmHg) inhibits proximal tubular phosphate reabsorption and promotes phosphaturia.[4]

In summary, besides respiratory acidosis, acute metabolic acidosis and alkalosis increase phosphate excretion, whereas respiratory alkalosis reduces phosphate excretion. It has been strongly suggested[20,74] that chronic metabolic acidosis is phosphaturic, since it depresses the V_{max} of sodium-dependent phosphate uptake without affecting the K_m. Thus far, the evidence is unclear on how chronic metabolic and respiratory alkalosis affect renal phosphate handling.

Other Factors Influencing Renal Phosphate Handling

Diuretics, (e.g., acetazolamide, thiazides, loop diuretics, osmotic agents, and mercurial diuretics) blunt phosphate reabsorption and increase urinary phosphate excretion. The site of action of most of these diuretics is the proximal tubule and the ascending limb of the loop of Henle, where they inhibit sodium reabsorption and blunt sodium-phosphate co-transport. Potassium-sparing diuretics that act on the distal tubule, (e.g., triamterine, amiloride, and spironolactone) have no effect on phosphate transport because of the dissociation of sodium and potassium transport at that site (vide supra).

Calcium infusion promotes renal tubular reabsorption of phosphate partly by suppressing the secretion of PTH.[100] The antiphosphaturic effect of calcium infusion is prevented by the simultaneous administration of the PTH.[100] In X-linked hypophosphatemic subjects, an additional PTH-independent, calcium-sensitive mechanism that modulates renal phosphate transport can also be demonstrated.[101] In hypoparathyroid patients, calcium acts to decrease phosphate reabsorption.[102] This action is independent of PTH.

Magnesium reduces phosphate excretion by suppressing the secretion of PTH.[103] Conversely, hypomagnesemia produces hypophosphatemia and phosphaturia. The effects of magnesium disorders on renal electrolyte handling are addressed in detail in Chapter 7.

Lithium acts to decrease phosphate excretion by inhibiting the actions of PTH and cAMP on phosphate transport.[1]

Luminal glucose competes with sodium-phosphate co-transport because of the sodium-glucose co-transport discussed earlier in this chapter. It is not clear to what degree the glucosuria found in some patients with X-linked hypophosphatemia adds to the phosphate wasting in this renal tubular transport defect.

The possible role of luminal calcium in directly augmenting proximal tubular phosphate reabsorption is not established.

HYPOPHOSPHATEMIA

Whereas hypophosphatemia (from 1.5 to 3.5 mg/dl, or 0.48 to 1.12 mmol/liter) seldom produces symptoms, severe hypophosphatemia (less than 1.5 mg/dl or 0.48 mmol/liter) often causes symptoms and requires immediate treatment. The causes of hypophosphatemia[104-110] and the consequences of severe hypophosphatemia, as well as its signs and symptoms, diagnostic evaluation, and treatment will be reviewed in subsequent sections of this chapter.

Hypophosphatemia Caused by Decreased Intestinal Absorption and/or Increased Intestinal Loss of Phosphate

In the absence of contributing factors, dietary phosphate deficiency rarely causes clinical hypophosphatemia, owing to the abundance of phosphate naturally present in most foodstuffs (Figure 6-7). Hypophosphatemia can be produced within a single day by selective dietary phosphate deficiency in young, growing rats.[111] The urinary phosphate excretion falls to zero and the fecal output of phosphate declines markedly as well. Thus, phosphate conservation occurs at both the kidney and intestine to prevent deficiency. In older rats, renal adaptation to a reduction in dietary phosphate deprivation is delayed and requires more than one day to develop.[111] In men hypophosphatemia seldom occurs in response to dietary phosphate restriction, whereas mild hypophosphatemia is encountered in women. The mechanism for this difference is still undefined.[112] If fed phosphate-deficient milk, rapidly growing premature infants develop hypophosphatemia and rickets.[113]

Administration of phosphate-binding antacids for the treatment of peptic ulcers,

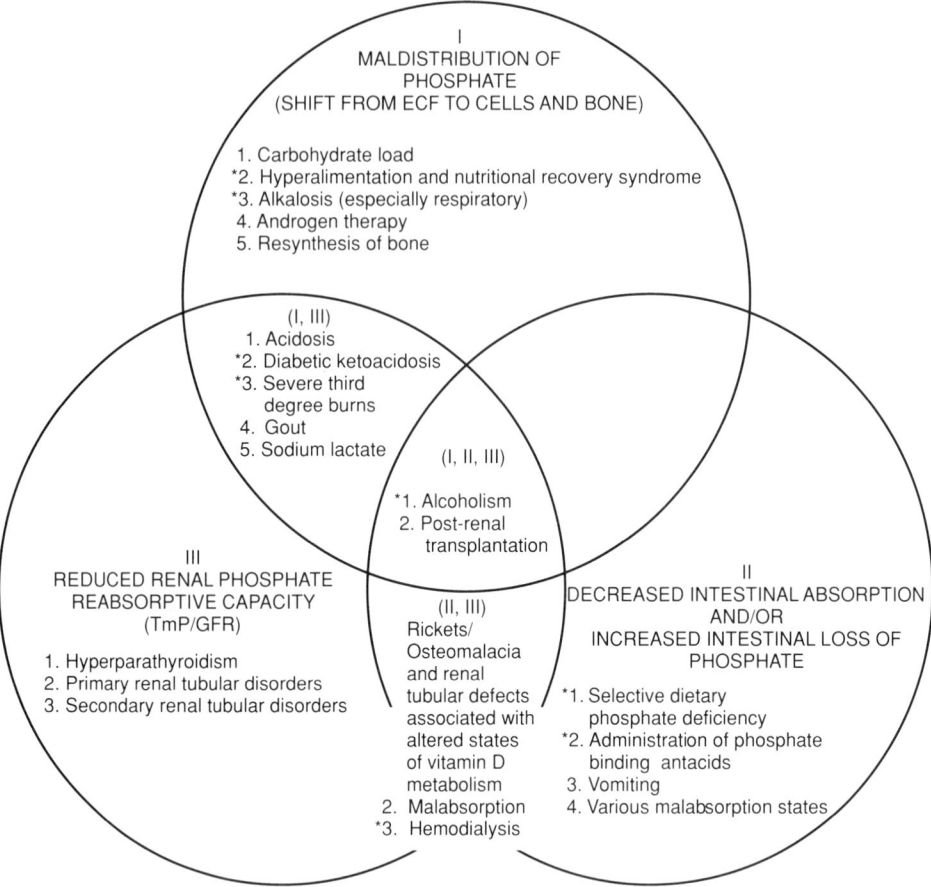

*Conditions which may result in severe hypophosphatemia and other manifestations of the phosphorus depletion syndrome

Fig. 6-7. Classification of hypophosphatemia according to the three principal mechanisms. (From Lee DBN, et al: Disorders of phosphorus metabolism. p 284. In Brenner F, Coburn JW (eds): Disorders of Mineral Metabolism, New York, Academic Press, 1981, with permission.)

chronic renal failure, hypoparathyroidism, and pseudohypoparathyroidism leads to diminished intestinal phosphate absorption.[114] Antacids bind dietary phosphate as well as phosphate secreted into the saliva and intestinal tract.

Hypophosphatemia occurs in response to prolonged vomiting and gastric suction, and is worsened by the associated hypochloremic alkalosis, which aggravates urinary phosphate loss. In addition, the intravenous infusion of dextrose may cause an intracellular shift of phosphate (vide supra) producing further declines in the serum phosphate concentration.

A variety of malabsorption states, including enteropathy, steatorrhea, and intestinal resection or bypass reduce the intestinal absorption of phosphate. Absorption of calcium, vitamin D, and other fat-soluble vitamins is often impaired, contributing to the development of metabolic bone disease.[115]

Reduced Renal Phosphate Reabsorptive Capacity

Hyperparathyroidism causes hypophosphatemia by virtue of the phosphaturic effect of an elevated serum PTH concentration. Hypophosphatemia after renal transplantation is thought to result from the phosphaturic action of elevated concentrations of circulating PTH on the healthy tubules of the allograft.[116] Corticosteroids used for immunosuppression cause phosphaturia, and the intrinsic tubular dysfunction of the allograft contributes to the development of hypophosphatemia.[117]

Primary tubular disorders that are characterized by a reduced renal phosphate reabsorptive capacity include familial hypophosphatemia, Fanconi syndrome, and renal tubular acidosis.

The most predominant type of familial hypophosphatemia is characterized by X-linked dominant transmission. The primary defect is diminished renal tubular transport of phosphate, which results in hypophosphatemic rickets and growth failure in the child and osteomalacia in the adult.[118] Spontaneous dental caries, progressive and marked rachitic deformities, and lateral bowing of the lower extremities are more severe in the male patient. Magnetic resonance spectroscopy done in a few patients showed the presence of normal concentrations of intracellular phosphate.[104] This finding supports the contention that despite marked phosphate wasting and severe extracellular hypophosphatemia, myopathy occurs infrequently because of a normal concentration in intracellular phosphate. However, these findings have not been confirmed in other patients. The pathogenesis of X-linked hypophosphatemia is incompletely understood at this point. Current hypotheses include the following components: (1) an inappropriate tubular response to circulating PTH within the normal concentration range; (2) impaired renal synthesis of 1,25-dihydroxyvitamin D because serum values are inappropriately low for the degree of hypophosphatemia; (3) a defect in the renal primary transport of phosphate. The serum concentration of immunoreactive PTH is usually within the normal range, and even if elevated in some patients is not high enough to cause the degree of hypophosphatemia that is present. In addition, the hypophosphatemia persists following parathyroidectomy in mice with X-linked hypophosphatemic rickets.[119] The concept of an exaggerated phosphatemic response to circulating PTH within the normal concentration range is compatible with a primary defect in proximal tubular phosphate transport,[120] as suggested by studies with isolated renal brush border membrane vesicles.[121] Whether a circulating humoral substance is responsible for the hypophosphatemia remains to be determined.[122]

Fanconi syndrome is characterized by massive proximal tubular defects in the reabsorption of bicarbonate, phosphate, potassium, amino acids, glucose, and uric acid.[123-126] In children, it is associated with cystinosis, Wilson's disease, and heavy metal poisoning.[123,124] In adults, Fanconi syndrome is seen in multiple myeloma, amyloidosis, monoclonal gammopathy, and other disorders. The fact that renal tubular acidosis is also associated with hyperphosphaturia gives rise to the suggestion that one of the mechanisms for phosphate wasting is related to the metabolic acidosis of both conditions. It is also possible that the excess glucose and bicarbonate in the proximal tubule inhibit the reabsorption of filtered phosphate.[4]

Idiopathic hypercalciuria is associated with mild hypophosphatemia and hyperphosphaturia.[127] It is unlikely that increases in circulating PTH play a role in the pathogenesis of impaired phosphate reabsorption, because the hyperphosphaturia persists despite suppression of PTH secretion by calcium infusion. The role of an elevated 1,25-dihydroxyvitamin D concentration in the pathogenesis of the disease is unclear.[128]

Postobstructive diuresis is sometimes associated with hyperphosphaturia and natriuresis.[129] In view of the associated aminoaciduria, uricosuria, and bicarbonaturia, it has been suggested that this may represent a transient Fanconi-like syndrome with alteration in renal tubular transport secondary to urinary tract obstruction.

Hypophosphatemia Secondary to Cellular Shift and Renal Wasting of Phosphate

Metabolic acidosis promotes the intracellular breakdown of organic compounds, releasing inorganic phosphate that is then excreted. Metabolic acidosis suppresses the proximal tubular reabsorption of phosphate,[130] an action that occurs independently of PTH or dietary phosphate intake. Hypophosphatemia is often encountered during treatment of the acidosis, since inorganic phosphate shifts into cells to resynthesize organic compounds.

Severe thermal burns are often associated with profound hypophosphatemia, especially during the recovery phase.[131] The hypophosphatemia initially may develop in response to gram-negative sepsis, respiratory alkalosis, hyperventilation caused by pain, and, later, from increased anabolism during healing.

If untreated, gout may cause hypophosphatemia that is attributed to the hyperphosphaturia from pain-induced hyperventilation, respiratory alkalosis, and uric acid nephropathy.[131]

Sodium lactate infusion gives rise to hyperphosphaturia because of volume expansion.[1] In addition, an intracellular shift of phosphate occurs, since lactate stimulates the hepatic synthesis of glucose.

Hypophosphatemia Secondary to Renal Phosphate Wasting and Decreased Intestinal Phosphate Absorption

Vitamin D-deficient and vitamin D-dependent rickets or osteomalacia are associated with hypophosphatemia that results from a lack of intestinal absorption and impaired renal tubular reabsorption of phosphate because of hypocalcemia and secondary hyperparathyroidism. The diseases result from vitamin D deficiency and from impaired renal production of 1,25-dihydroxyvitamin D (vitamin D-dependent rickets type I), or an abnormal response of target organs to 1,25-dihydroxyvitamin D (vitamin D-dependent rickets type II).

Oncogenic hypophosphatemia is thought to result from a phosphaturic factor produced by mesenchymal tumors that reduces the tubular reabsorption of phosphate. It is unclear why the 1,25-dihydroxyvitamin D concentration is low. Treatment with 1,25-dihydroxyvitamin D does not reverse the defect in tubular reabsorption of phosphate. The tumor is often small and difficult to identify. A high index of suspicion and careful gallium scanning can help locate the tumor. Removal of the tumor corrects the hypophosphatemia.

Removal of phosphate by dialysis and the aggressive concurrent use of phosphate binders have contributed to the hypophosphatemia encountered in patients undergoing dialysis.

Hypophosphatemia Secondary to Transcellular Shifting, Decreased Intestinal Absorption, and Reduced Renal Reabsorption of Phosphate

Diabetic ketoacidosis and alcoholic intoxication are primary examples of hypophosphatemia in which transcellular shifting, decreased intestinal absorption, and reduced renal reabsorption of phosphate are involved simultaneously.

In diabetic ketoacidosis, phosphate intake is reduced because of nausea, anorexia, and vomiting. In addition, the metabolic acidosis promotes intracellular breakdown of organic phosphate, and insulin deficiency prompts a shift of phosphate to the extracellular space so that hyperphosphaturia follows. This renal phosphate wasting is aggravated by the concomitant glycosuria and ketonuria. A deficit of total body phosphate therefore exists before the initiation of insulin therapy to correct the diabetic ketoacidosis. With insulin administration, an abrupt intracellular shift of phosphate occurs to permit oxidative phosphorylation and glycolysis. Additional renal losses of phosphate may occur with re-expansion of the extracellular spaces by what is often aggressive use of intravenous fluid therapy. Thus, it is important to recognize that a number of mechanisms contribute to phosphate depletion, and that severe, life-threatening hypophosphatemia may be encountered within half a day of treatment. The infusion of phosphate with the initiation of insulin therapy will correct a depleted erythrocyte concentration of 2,3-diphosphoglycerate and induce a more rapid reversal of diabetic coma, presumably by improving the cerebral oxygen supply.[132]

Alcoholic patients may become phosphate deficient as the result of a previously decreased dietary phosphate intake and intestinal malabsorption of phosphate from hepatic cirrhosis and recurrent pancreatitis.[133] Absorption of phosphate and calcium may also be impaired as a result of vitamin D deficiency caused by steatorrhea, and by the use of antacids for the treatment of peptic ulcers. Renal wasting of phosphate may result from hypomagnesemia, but also from diabetic ketoacidosis and lactic acidosis as well. An intracellular shift of phosphate may occur in response to the volume re-expansion accomplished with the infusion of glucose, combined with respiratory and metabolic alkalosis caused by delirium tremens, nasogastric suction, hypokalemia produced by diuretics, and intercurrent septicemia. Hypophosphatemia is often mild on admission to the hospital, but profound hypophosphatemia may be encountered within the first few days of hospitalization following treatment with glucose infusions.[133] This is understandable on the basis of the pre-existing intestinal malabsorption as well as the multiple concurrent factors that reduce renal reabsorption of phosphate and present the risk of a cellular phosphate shift. Thus, alcoholics are particularly prone to develop phosphate depletion, and need to be carefully followed during hospitalization.

PATHOPHYSIOLOGIC CONSEQUENCES OF SEVERE HYPOPHOSPHATEMIA

Whereas mild hypophosphatemia (serum phosphate 1.5 to 3.5 mg/dl or 0.48 to 1.12 mmol/liter) causes little disturbance in bodily functions, severe hypophosphatemia (serum phosphate less than 1.5 mg/dl or 0.48 mmol/liter causes major dysfunctions. Phosphate depletion may be life-threatening for two pivotal reasons: (1) severe hypophosphatemia causes a reduction in the synthesis of adenosine triphosphate (ATP) and creatine phosphate, threatening the supply of energy for cellular integrity and functions; (2) severe hypophosphatemia decreases the synthesis of 2,3-diphosphoglycerate in erythrocytes and diminishes their oxygen content. Inorganic phosphate is involved in the Embden-Meyerhof pathway as a substrate in glyceraldehyde-3-phosphate dehydrogenase. Oxidative glycolysis is impaired as a consequence of severe phosphate depletion. Such critical disruptions of basic cellular functions affect virtually all systems (Table 6-3).

Table 6-3. Pathophysiologic Consequences of Severe Hypophosphatemia

Skeletal muscle and cardiovascular dysfunctions
    Clinical: Weakness, proximal myopathy, rhabdomyolysis, cardiomyopathy
    Laboratory: Elevated CPK and aldolase, abnormal EMG, impaired vasopressin sensitivity

Respiratory dysfunctions
    Clinical: Hyperventilation, hypoventilation, respiratory failure
    Laboratory: Decreased vital capacity

Hematologic dyfunctions
    Red cells: Impaired glycolysis, increased rigidity, hemolysis, reduced 2,3-DPG
    White cells: Impaired phagocytosis
    Platelets: Impaired function, thrombocytopenia

Skeletal dysfunction
    Clinical: Arthralgia, bone pain, joint stiffness, pseudofractures, osteomalacia/rickets
    Laboratory: Osteomalacia, osteopenia, decreased bone calcium, phosphate, and magnesium

Gastrointestinal dysfunction
    Clinical: Anorexia, nausea, vomiting, dysphagia, ileus
    Laboratory: Increased absorption of calcium, phosphate, and magnesium due to elevated 1,25-dihydroxyvitamin D

Renal dysfunction
    Clinical: Stones (rare)
    Laboratory: Hypophosphatemia, hypermagnesuria, glucosuria, bicarbonaturia, hypercalciuria

Neurologic dysfunction
    Clinical: Encephalopathy, paresthesia
    Laboratory: EEG anomalies, elevated CSF protein

Hepatic dysfunction
    Abnormal liver function tests

Endocrine/metabolic dysfunctions
    Impaired carbohydrate metabolism, insulin insensitivity, increased 1,25-dihydroxyvitamin D

Skeletal Muscle and Cardiovascular Dysfunction

Both skeletal and smooth muscle are affected by severe hypophosphatemia. The characteristic clinical presentations include weakness or proximal myopathy, elevated serum creatine triphosphokinase and aldolase concentrations, and an abnormal electromyelogram. In malnourished alcoholics, rhabdomyolysis may occur when severe hypophosphatemia is superimposed on a preexisting myopathy.[134] When hypophosphatemia develops after a few days of intravenous glucose infusion, rhabdomyolysis may abruptly follow. It can be prevented by the administration of phosphate.

With hypophosphatemia, myocardial contractility may be impaired, as determined by a decreased left ventricular stroke volume and peak blood flow velocity.[135] These defects are reversed with phosphate repletion.[135]

Vasopressin insensitivity in phosphate-depleted rats has been demonstrated, and is accompanied by a lower mean arterial blood pressure.[105]

Respiratory Dysfunction

Severe hypophosphatemia may produce paresis or weakness of the diaphragm, giving rise to hypoventilation and acute respiratory failure. In severely hypophosphatemic alcoholics, hyperventilation has also been reported to result from hypoxia caused by low 2,3-diphosphoglycerate concentrations in erythrocytes. This may in turn produce respiratory alkalosis and worsen the hypophosphatemia in these patients.

Hematologic Dysfunction

The erythrocyte concentrations of ATP and 2,3-diphosphoglycerate closely parallel extracellular phosphate concentrations.[136] Thus, severe hypophosphatemia adversely affects oxidative glycolysis, resulting in disruption of the intracellular microfilament system, which relies on ATP for energy. Impairment of the microfilament system reduces the flexibility of the erythrocyte membrane, increases the rigidity of the cell, and predisposes the erythrocyte to hemolysis.[137] Chemical hemolysis occurs when the concentration of ATP is half the normal value,[137] which corresponds to a serum phosphate concentration of less than 1 mg/dl (or 0.32 mmol/liter). A reduction in the amount of 2,3-diphosphoglycerate increases the binding of oxygen to hemoglobin and leads to a decreased peripheral release of oxygen into tissues.

Patients with hypophosphatemia are therefore predisposed to diminished phagocytosis and granulocyte chemotaxis because of their reduced ATP concentration. This is especially true in patients who are being treated by parenteral nutrition. Platelet dysfunctions, defective clot retraction, and thrombocytopenia occur in severe hypophosphatemia and are associated with mucosal and subcutaneous hemorrhage and gastrointestinal bleeding.[138]

Skeletal Dysfunction

Arthralgia, bone pain, joint stiffness, pseudofractures, osteomalacia, and rickets have long been associated with phosphate depletion. Bone resorption in hypophosphatemia occurs independently of calcitonin and PTH, because the magnitude of the resorption is not altered by thyroparathyroidectomy in hypophosphatemic rats.[139] Osteomalacia, osteopenia, and decreased bone calcium, phosphate, and magnesium concentrations have been demonstrated in association with hypophosphatemia.[140] In the case of hypophosphatemia, it is unlikely that osteomalacia results from a low circulating 1,25-dihydroxyvitamin D concentration, because hypophosphatemia stimulates the production of the hormone. The rapid bone turnover is not the result of a hypophosphatemia-induced increase in the renal production of 1,25-dihydroxyvitamin D since, although the bone resorption rate can be blunted by vitamin D deprivation, normalization of bone turnover does not occur.[139] The increased bone resorption contributes to the hypercalciuria and hypermagnesuria.

Gastrointestinal Dysfunction

Severe hypophosphatemia leads to anorexia, nausea, vomiting, dysphagia, and ileus, because the intestinal smooth muscle is adversely affected by the reduced ATP concentration and impaired oxidative glycolysis. The absorption of calcium, phosphate, and magnesium is increased as a result of the elevated serum 1,25-dihydroxyvitamin D concentration produced by hypophosphatemia.

Renal Dysfunction

Phosphate depletion is followed by intense renal tubular phosphate reabsorption to conserve this anion. Although increased skeletal release of calcium and magnesium gives rise to hypercalciuria and hypermagnesuria in hypophosphatemia, defective tubular reabsorption of filtered calcium and magnesium also has been suggested as a mechanism for this disorder.[74] Phosphate repletion has been shown to reverse both of these tubular defects. The suppressed secretion of PTH in phosphate depletion may contribute to the development of hypercalciuria, because PTH replacement in phosphate-depleted dogs that have undergone parathyroidectomy decreased the magnitude of their hypercalciuria.[141] Bicarbonate wasting and glucosuria are dependent on the degree and duration of phosphate depletion.[36] Despite the hypercalciuria, renal stones are rarely encountered. The renal adaptations to hypophosphatemia are addressed in detail in earlier sections of this chapter.

Neurologic Dysfunctions

Metabolic encephalopathy associated with severe hypophosphatemia may present as apprehension, irritability, confusion, paresthesia, ataxia, delirium, seizures, and coma. Electroencephalography shows diffuse anomalies compatible with metabolic encephalopathy. The cerebrospinal fluid shows nonspecific elevation of the protein concentration. The nerve conduction velocity is diminished.[142] Neurologic dysfunctions are more likely to be encountered in hypophosphatemic patients who are malnourished.

Hepatic Dysfunction

Tissue hypoxia and impaired glycolysis from the low 2,3-diphosphoglycerate and ATP concentrations in severe hypophosphatemia lead to hepatic dysfunction. Hepatic oxygen extraction is lowered in hypophosphatemic subjects and is restored following correction of their hypophosphatemia.[143]

Endocrine/Metabolic Dysfunctions

Based on the essential role that intracellular inorganic phosphate plays in the cellular uptake of glucose and glycolysis,[104] it can be anticipated that impaired carbohydrate metabolism will occur as a complication of phosphate depletion. This idea is supported by the recently demonstrated relationship between the cellular concentration of inorganic phosphate and the concentration of glucose-6-phosphate,[144] and may help to explain why hyperglycemia, hyperinsulinemia, and insulin resistance occur in phosphate depletion.[145]

Hypoparathyroidism is encountered in hypophosphatemia and results in signs and symptoms of hypocalcemia.[16]

Acetazolamide and other inhibitors of carbonic anhydrase produce a renal loss of phosphate that may lead to hypophosphatemia. Loop diuretics do not cause hypophosphatemia because phosphate is not transported in the loop of Henle. Diuretics that act on the distal tubule rarely cause severe hypophosphatemia, possibly because of the dissociation between the transport of sodium and phosphate at distal tubular sites (vide supra).

DIAGNOSTIC EVALUATION

Severe hypophosphatemia (serum phosphate concentration less than 1.5 mg/dl or 0.48 mmol/liter) most frequently occurs in hospitalized patients as a result of rapid cellular shifts of phosphate (Fig. 6-7).[146,147] Factors that contribute to hypophosphatemia but which by themselves rarely cause severe hypophosphatemia include long-term diuretic treatment for hypertension, chronic respiratory acidosis, postobstructive uropathy, glucocorticoids, idiopathic hypercalciuria, renal transplantation, or losses of phosphate from the upper gastrointestinal tract.[146]

Severe hypophosphatemia often occurs in patients who receive total parenteral nutrition and large amounts of glucose without an adequate supplementation of phosphate.[146,147] Hyperventilation, as a result of salicylate intoxication, pain, sepsis, or anxiety, causes respiratory alkalosis, which can worsen pre-existing hyperphosphaturia and may precipitate an episode of hypophosphatemia. Thus, in patients with severe hypophosphatemia, it is important first to determine whether glucose is being administered inappropriately, and to identify the underlying causes of respiratory alkalosis if this is present.

In patients with severe hypophosphatemia it is important to evaluate the urinary phosphate concentration. In disorders that are associated with hyperphosphaturia (Fig. 6-7), the 24-hour urinary phosphate excretion exceeds 60 mg/m^2 body surface per day in the presence of a serum phosphate below 2 mg/dl or 0.64 mmol/liter.

Whether excess circulating PTH is responsible for increased urinary phosphate excretion can be determined by measurement of the serum iPTH concentration. A clue that this may be the case is the finding of hypercalcemia. Glucosuria, bicarbonaturia, and aminoaciduria are features of the Fanconi syndrome and other diseases of tubular dysfunction.

The diagnostic approach to the different vitamin D-resistant states is summarized in Table 6-4. The Walton/Bijvoet nomogram that relates the TmP/GFR to the serum phosphate concentration (Fig. 6-2) is of practical utility in making the diagnosis. If the urinary phosphate excretion is below these limits, nonrenal causes of hypophosphatemia should be sought. These include the disorders associated with phosphate deprivation, gastrointestinal tract losses of phosphate, excessive use of antacids, and other conditions.

TREATMENT

The goal of treatment in hypophosphatemia is to prevent mild hypophosphatemia (serum phosphate above 2 mg/dl) from progressing to severe, life-threatening hypophosphatemia (serum phosphate less than 1 mg/dl). The presence or absence of alcoholism, diabetes mellitus, hyperalimentation, antacids, dialysis treatment, and other risk factors that may cause severe hypophosphatemia must be determined.

The serum phosphate should be closely followed in hospitalized alcoholic patients because they may be in a state of phosphate depletion at the time of admission. To prevent severe hypophosphatemia, especially

Table 6–4. Differences Between the Main Kinds of Hypophosphatemic Rickets and Osteomalacia

	Vitamin D Deficient	Vitamin D Dependent	Fanconi Syndrome[a]	RTA	XLH or NFH
Plasma Ca (untreated)	N or ↓	↓	N[b]	N	N
PTH (untreated)	↑↑	↑↑	↑	↑	↑
Plasma P$_i$(treated)[c]	N	N	↓	N	↓
Plasma HCO$_3$⁻ (untreated)	↓	↓	↓	↓	N
Plasma HCO$_3$⁻ (treated)[d]	N	N	↓	↓	N
Urinary AA[e] (untreated)	↑	↑	↑	N	N[f]
Urinary AA (treated)	N	N	↑	N	N
Dose of vitamin D (mg/day)	0.25–0.50	1.5–5.0	0.50–1.0–10.0[g]	1.0–2.0	2.0–8.0

[a] Excluding cystinosis, which behaves like vitamin D dependency.
[b] May be low if renal failure is present.
[c] With vitamin D or alkali.
[d] With vitamin D alone.
[e] AA, amino acids.
[f] Except for glycine alone in non-familial hypophosphatemia (NFH)
[g] Varies with degree of renal failure.
N = normal; RTA = renal tubular acidosis; XLH = X-linked hypophosphatemia.
(From Parfitt AM, Kleerekoper M: Clinical disorder of calcium, phosphorus, and magnesium metabolism. Chapter 19 in Clinical Disorders of Fluid and Electrolyte Metabolism. p 947. In: Maxwell MH, Kleeman CS (eds): McGraw-Hill, New York, 1980.)

when intravenous glucose infusion is initiated for rehydration or refeeding, oral phosphate supplementation at a dose of from 15 to 20 mg of phosphate per kilogram of body weight per day should be provided. If oral supplementation is poorly tolerated, and the serum phosphate concentration shows a downward trend, intravenous phosphate supplementation at a dose of 10 mg per kilogram of body weight per day should be given to prevent severe hypophosphatemia. Serial determinations of the serum phosphate and other electrolytes (vide infra) should be used to determine the rate of infusion. Intravenous phosphate should be discontinued when the serum phosphate concentration returns to values above 2 mg/dl (0.64 mmol/liter).

Diabetic ketoacidosis is frequently complicated by severe hypophosphatemia, especially after the administration of insulin and glucose-containing parenteral fluids. Phosphate supplementation in diabetic ketoacidosis promotes rapid normalization of the intracellular concentration of 2,3-diphosphoglycerate,[148] and a more rapid improvement in mental function in patients with hyperosmotic coma.[148] The current recommendation is to provide intravenous phosphate in patients with diabetic ketoacidosis at a dose of 15 to 20 mg of phosphorus per kilogram of body weight per day.[149] Within the first two to three days of treatment, as mental function improves, an oral dosage form of phosphate should be given to replace intravenous administration.[149]

Skim milk is a satisfactory form of phosphate and can be used for this purpose (Table 6-5). It provides both calcium and phosphate. If lactose intolerance precludes the use of milk, commercial phosphate preparations can be used (Table 6-5). The total daily supplement is 2 to 3 g of elemental phosphorus in four divided doses. The dose should be increased slowly because diarrhea will occur with excessive amounts.

Patients who are undergoing dialysis become hypophosphatemic because phosphate is removed by the dialysate or because use of antacids is excessive. The addition of phosphate to achieve a dialysate phosphate concentration of 1.5 to 4 mg/dl, and the temporary discontinuation of antacid administration usually reverses the hypophosphatemia.

Total parenteral nutrition for the treatment of malnutrition or burns often produces hypophosphatemia because phosphate is utilized in the formation of new tissues. Requirements for phosphate supplementation are particularly high in the growing child.[150]

Side effects of intravenous phosphate administration include diarrhea, metabolic acidosis, hyperphosphatemia (especially in renal insufficiency), hypocalcemia, and hypomagnesemia. The diuresis that follows phosphate therapy often gives rise to dehydration, hyponatremia, and hypokalemia. Hypotension caused by volume depletion is a potential complication that requires close monitoring. Finally, potassium-containing phosphate salts (Table 6-5) may cause hyperkalemia in patients with compromised renal function.[151]

In patients with renal failure, intravenous phosphate is absolutely contraindicated because of the inability of the kidney to excrete the phosphate and the likelihood of hyperphosphatemia. Hypocalcemia, hypercalcemia, and hyperkalemia are relative contradictions for parenteral phosphate therapy. If oral phosphate is being administered daily, monitoring of the serum phosphate concentration is required.

As was previously discussed in detail, at a pH of 7.4, the ratio of monovalent phosphate to divalent phosphate is 4:1. The derived valency of phosphate at a pH of 7.4 is 1.8. In computing dosage of phosphate supplementation, it is best to avoid the use of milliequivalents and to use milligrams or millimoles (Table 6-6).

To summarize, the principles of treatment for hypophosphatemia are as follows:

Disorders of Phosphate Metabolism • 247

Table 6-5. Commonly Available Phosphate Preparations

	1000 mg Phosphorus in	Na(mEq)[a]	K(mEq)[a]
For intravenous use			
In-Phos	40 ml	65	8
Hyper-Phos-K	15 ml	0	50
For Oral Use			
Fleet's Phospho Soda	6.2 ml	57	0
Neutra-Phos	300 ml (or 4 capsules)	28.5	28.5
Neutra-Phos-K	300 ml (or 4 capsules)	0	57
Phos-Tabs	6 tab	0	57
K-Phos-MF	8 tab	2.9	1.14
K-Phos No 2	4 tab	5.83	2.25
K-Phos Neutral	4 tab	5.83	2.25
K-Phos-Original	7 tab	13	3.67
K-Phos Alkaline	4 tab	13.9	2.3

[a] In 1 g of phosphorus.
(From Kurokawa K, Levine BS, Lee DBN, Massry SG: Physiology of phosphorus metabolism and pathophysiology of hypophosphatemia and hyperphosphatemia. p 625. In Arieff AI, DeFronzo RA (eds): Fluid, Electrolyte and Acid-Base Disorders. Churchill Livingstone, New York, 1985, with permission.)

Table 6-6. Conversion of Phosphate From mmol to mg

1 mmol of phosphate = 31 mg elemental phosphorus
1 mg of phosphorus = 0.032 mmol of phosphate
1 mmol/L of phosphate = 3.1 mg/dl phosphorus
1 mg/dl of phosphorus = 0.323 mmol/L of phosphate
Conversion instructions
  To convert from mg/dl to mmol/L, multiply by 0.32
  To convert from mmol/L to mg/dl, multiply by 3.1
  To convert from mg phosphorus to mmol phosphate, multiply by 0.032
  To convert from mmol phosphate to mg phosphorus, multiply by 31

(Modified from Puschett JB: Disorders of Fluid and Electrolyte Balance: Diagram and Management. p 76. Churchill Livingstone, New York, 1985 with permission.)

1. Oral phosphate supplementation is preferred.
2. The underlying disorder should be treated.
3. Risk factors, such as total parenteral nutrition, should be identified and measures should be taken that will prevent the development of hypophosphatemia, such as the treatment of symptomatic mild hypophosphatemia, of severe hypophosphatemia (serum phosphate concentration less than 1 mg/dl), and of all moderate hypophosphatemia (serum concentration less than 2 mg/dl).
4. Phosphate therapy is contraindicated in renal failure, and treatment should be discontinued once the concentration of serum phosphate rises above 2 mg/dl, or when hypocalcemia (serum calcium below 8 mg/dl) is encountered.

HYPERPHOSPHATEMIA

By virtue of the unique inverse interrelationship between calcium and phosphate, a rise in the serum phosphate concentration often results in a fall in serum calcium concentration. Precipitation of calcium in soft tissue is not encountered until the calcium-phosphate ion product exceeds 70. A small rise in the serum phosphate concentration is often sufficient to cause a fall in the serum ionized calcium.[4,105]

There are three major mechanisms for the development of hyperphosphatemia (serum phosphate concentration over 5 mg/dl or 1.6 mmol/liter). As summarized in Table 6-7, they are: (1) decreased glomerular filtration, (2) increased tubular absorption of phosphate, and (3) increased phosphate loading. Whereas the input of phosphate to the circulation may be from a host of exogenous or endogenous sources, the major underlying cause of phosphate retention

Table 6-7. Causes of Hyperphosphatemia

Decreased glomerular filtration rate
  Acute and chronic renal failure
Increased tubular reabsorption of phosphate
  Parathyroid dysfunctions:
    Hypoparathyroidism; pseudohypoparathyroidism; transient parathyroid resistance of infancy
  Endocrine dysfunctions:
    Hyperthyroidism, tumoral calcinosis, growth hormone excess; juvenile hypogonadism; postmenopausal state
  High ambient temperature
  Disodium etidronate
Increased phosphate loads
  Exogenous loads:
    Enemas and laxatives; vitamin D intoxication; parenteral phosphate; blood transfusions; white phosphorus burns
  Endogenous loads:
    Cellular shift in diabetic ketoacidosis; lactic acidosis; tissue hypoxia; rhabdomyolysis; cytotoxic therapy of neoplasms; hemolysis; malignant hyperthermia
Miscellaneous
  Familial intermittent hyperphosphatemia

and hyperphosphatemia is impaired renal phosphate excretion.[105] The degree of hyperphosphatemia is a function of the difference between the rate of entry of phosphate into ECF and the renal excretion of phosphate. If renal function is normal, clinically significant hyperphosphatemia seldom develops, unless an event such as massive tissue breakdown (vide infra) occurs and leads to the development of renal failure.

PATHOPHYSIOLOGIC CONSEQUENCES

A serious consequence of hyperphosphatemia is the tendency to the ectopic calcification of amorphous calcium phosphate. The site of this extraosseous deposition of hydroxyapatite crystals depends on a number of local factors. Hypoxic and necrotic tissues are more prone to be the sites of calcium deposition. Ectopic calcification occurs at different sites according to the underlying disease in a particular patient. For example, in chronic renal failure, ectopic calcification tends to occur in the conjunctivae, kidneys, lungs, blood vessel walls,[152] and myocardial conduction system[4] when the calcium-phosphate ion product exceeds 70. In the lungs and conjunctivae, the tissue pH is alkaline because of diffusion of carbon dioxide. The solubility of calcium and phosphate is lowered in a more alkaline medium. No correlation between the severity of calcification and the duration of dialysis or the presumed degree of hyperparathyroidism has been established.[153] The tendency toward periarticular and subintimal calcification[152] is peculiar to end-stage renal disease. On the other hand, a predisposition to calcification at periarticular surfaces of the hips, elbows, shoulders, and other large joints occurs in tumoral calcinosis.

The most serious pathophysiologic consequence of hyperphosphatemia is the increased risk of developing acute renal failure. For example, massive cellular breakdown from chemotherapy for neoplastic diseases results in the release of phosphate. Acute renal failure from the hyperphosphatemia of tissue breakdown is also encountered in rhabdomyolysis, myoglobinuria, autoimmune hemolytic anemia, crush injury, burns, and other catabolic states. The renal failure prolongs phosphate retention and the hyperphosphatemia that occurs with phosphate-containing enemas and phosphate infusions used for the treatment of hypercalcemia. The risk of acute renal failure is compounded by hyperuricemia and hypovolemia.

A third consequence of hyperphosphatemia is hypocalcemia, which may be profound enough to cause seizures, tetany, and hypotension. An impaired response of vascular smooth muscles to vasopressin, impaired myocardial contractility, and arrhythmia are serious consequences of hypocalcemia produced by hyperphosphatemia.

Secondary hyperparathyroidism and

renal osteodystrophy are possible consequences of phosphate retention.[154] The serum phosphate itself does not influence the secretion of PTH, but increases in serum phosphate may indirectly lower the serum ionized calcium concentration, which then stimulates secretion of the hormone.[105]

Although increased concentrations of 2,3-diphosphoglycerate and ATP in erythrocytes correlate with increases in serum phosphate in patients with chronic renal failure,[155] the fact that the increased values persist after renal transplantation and the return of the serum phosphate to normal or low values suggests that hyperphosphatemia is not responsible for the elevated 2,3-diphosphoglycerate concentration in red blood cells. The increases may be a result of corticosteroid treatment.[156] The elevated 2,3-diphosphoglycerate concentration has the potential to provide better oxygenation of peripheral tissues.

In summary, hyperphosphatemia affects multiple systems. When the calcium-phosphate ion product exceeds 70, ectopic calcification becomes an increasing risk, and is characterized by the following features: (1) papular eruptions on the skin and intense pruritus, as well as ischemic necrosis of the extremities that follows calcification of peripheral blood vessels; (2) corneal and conjunctival depositions; (3) cardiac arrhythmia and backward pump failure produced by calcification of the conduction system of the heart; (4) acute renal failure and aggravated deterioration caused by chronic renal failure; (5) dyspnea and pulmonary dysfunction from calcification of the lung and alveolar lining; and (6) melena, anorexia, nausea, vomiting, hematemesis, and paralytic ileus.

DIAGNOSTIC EVALUATION

In early childhood, an elevated serum phosphate concentration is physiologic and is associated with the increased tubular reabsorption of phosphate (TmP/GFR) produced by growth hormone.

On the other hand, acute hyperphosphatemia may follow abrupt and massive cell lysis from a number of causes (Table 6-7).

In chronic renal failure, chronic hyperphosphatemia occurs as a consequence of impaired renal phosphate excretion when the GFR falls below 25 ml/min/1.73 m².[151] Hyperphosphatemia sometimes occurs in patients with normal renal function, from a reduction in phosphate excretion caused by hypoparathyroidism, hyperthyroidism, tumoral calcinosis, and increased circulating growth hormone. Concentrations of phosphate and creatinine in the plasma and urine must be known to permit calculation of the tubular reabsorption of phosphate (TRP) as follows:

$$TRP = \frac{urine\ phosphate}{plasma\ phosphate} \times \frac{plasma\ creatinine}{urine\ creatinine} \%$$

The tubular maximum for phosphate, TmP/GFR, can be obtained from the Walton/Bijvoet nomogram (Fig. 6-3).

The tubular reabsorption of phosphate and the TmP/GFR are low in chronic renal failure and high in hypoparathyroidism, hyperthyroidism, and several other endocrine dysfunctions (Table 6-7).

Laxative abuse, especially with phosphate-containing salts, and the ingestion of large amounts of calcium and vitamin D may cause hyperphosphatemia. Awareness of this sequence of events will lead to a correct diagnosis.

TREATMENT

The treatment for acute hyperphosphaturia is to eliminate the source of phosphate, and if hypocalcemia is present, to administer calcium. For patients undergoing chemotherapy or who have rhabdomyolysis, the administration of fluids in quantities sufficient to produce volume expansion is important for preventing acute renal failure. In patients with hyperthyroidism, hyperphosphatemia is mild and seldom requires treatment. In hypoparathyroidism, correction of hypocalcemia with vitamin D and calcium supplements is usually adequate to correct the hyperphosphatemia. The treatment required for other specific disorders is outlined below.

Decreased Glomerular Filtration Rate

Hyperphosphatemia resulting from renal failure is the most common cause of an elevation of the serum phosphate concentration above 5 mg/dl in adults and 7 mg/dl in infants and children. In patients with chronic renal insufficiency, the serum phosphate concentration usually remains normal until the GFR falls below 25 ml/min/1.73 m².[151]

In patients with acute renal failure, hyperphosphatemia develops when the diminished renal output is exceeded by the dietary phosphate intake or increased endogenous phosphate, which may be especially overwhelming and abrupt following the breakdown of cells in conditions such as rhabdomyolysis or with increased catabolism from a variety of causes (Table 6-7). Hypocalcemia produced by hyperphosphatemia may become symptomatic and require supplementation with calcium. The dosage of calcium required is discussed in detail in Chapter 5 on disorders of calcium metabolism.

In patients with chronic renal insufficiency, the use of dietary phosphate restriction and the administration of phosphate binders such as calcium carbonate immediately before or after meals, to diminish or prevent hyperphosphatemia, is discussed in detail in Chapter 12 on chronic renal failure.

In patients with chronic renal failure, retention of phosphate leads to the development of renal osteodystrophy, ectopic calcification, depression of the renal synthesis of 1,25-dihydroxyvitamin D, and impaired intestinal absorption of calcium. Skeletal resistance to PTH may be aggravated by the hyperphosphatemia. Hyperphosphatemia lowers the serum ionized calcium and stimulates hypertrophy of the parathyroid glands. If judicious use of phosphate binders and dietary phosphate restriction are pursued, calciphylaxis, an extreme form of ectopic calcification, can be prevented. The physician should be familiar with the serious consequences of phosphate retention and indoctrinate patients to restrict their phosphate intake so as to retard the development of such serious complications. If uncontrolled, hyperphosphatemia will lead to additional impairment of renal function and the requirement for kidney dialysis and transplantation.

Increased Tubular Reabsorption of Phosphate

In hypoparathyroidism, hyperphosphatemia is encountered frequently because of reduced excretion of phosphate despite normal glomerular filtration rates. The increased tubular reabsorption of phosphate is caused by lack of PTH. In pseudohypoparathyroidism, the tubular resistance to normally circulating PTH produces hypophosphaturia, hyperphosphatemia, and hypocalcemia. In infancy, hyperparathyroidism is encountered secondary to a transient resistance to PTH.[15] The use of calcium and vitamin D to treat the hypocalcemia is discussed in Chapter 5 on calcium disorders.

The availability of highly potent metabolites of vitamin D, especially 1,25-dihydroxyvitamin D_3, provides a safer means of treating the hypocalcemia in patients with idiopathic and surgical hypoparathyroidism or pseudohypoparathyroidism and reduces the possible risks of prolonged vitamin D therapy and toxicity.[157] It has been suggested that long-term administration of vitamin D reduces the TmP/GFR and reverses hyperphosphatemia in hypocalcemic states. This apparently results from an indirect effect by normalization of the serum calcium concentration.[15,42]

An aim of therapy in patients with hyperphosphatemia is to prevent or reverse abnormally elevated calcium × phosphate product; phosphate binders can be used for this purpose.

Hyperphosphatemia occurs in about one third of patients with hyperthyroidism. It is usually moderate and results in part from increased renal tubular reabsorption of phosphate. Hyperthyroidism also promotes the skeletal resorption of phosphate, which also accounts for the elevation in the serum calcium concentration in this condition.[158]

Treatment of hyperthyroidism restores the serum phosphate to within the normal range. If therapy results in hypothyroidism, hypophosphatemia is sometimes encountered.[4]

Tumoral calcinosis is a rare autosomal recessive disease that is characterized by orange-sized deposits of calcium phosphate over the region of the large joints. Hyperphosphatemia occurs in patients who are less than 20 years of age. The serum phosphorus tends to be normal in older subjects. Values for serum 1,25-dihydroxyvitamin D are increased, and as a result, the intestinal absorption of phosphate and calcium is increased as well.[159,160] The serum iPTH concentration is normal despite a reduction in phosphate excretion, suggesting tubular resistance to the phosphaturic effect of PTH. The serum calcium concentration is also normal, despite the increase in circulating 1,25-dihydroxyvitamin D. The disease appears to be a mirror image of hypophosphatemic rickets. Since the serum 1,25-dihydroxyvitamin D and TmP/GFR may vary directly with each other in both diseases, the abnormal vitamin D metabolism and renal phosphate transport may be coupled. Treatment consists of the dietary restriction of calcium and phosphate, supplemented by phosphate binders. Finally, surgical removal of the calcified tumor may be necessary.

Growth hormone excess, such as that in acromegaly, gives rise to increased renal tubular reabsorption of phosphate. Hypocalcemia does not occur. Irradiation or surgical excision of the growth hormone-secreting pituitary tumor is an effective treatment for acromegaly.

Juvenile hypogonadism is associated with mild hyperphosphatemia secondary to increased tubular reabsorption of phosphate.[105]

Postmenopausal women who are on treatment with stilbestrol have been shown to have phosphate retention as a result of diminished phosphate excretion.[105,106] This is attributed to an effect of the medication.

A high ambient temperature, such as occurs in the summer, has been correlated with an increased tubular reabsorption of phosphate and a rise in the serum phosphate concentration.[161] No treatment is needed for the moderate elevation of serum phosphate concentration, which may rise as high as 6 mg/dl.

Disodium etidronate, which is used for treatment of hypercalcemia, osteoporosis and Paget's disease, enhances the tubular reabsorption of phosphate and causes phosphate retention. However, hyperphosphatemia is seldom encountered if the dosage is kept at or below 5 mg/kg of body weight per day.[162] The highest values for serum phosphate are observed after two weeks of treatment. If severe hyperphosphatemia occurs, the medication should be discontinued.

Increased Phosphate Loads

Hyperphosphatemia from an increased phosphate load arises from two principal mechanisms: (1) exogenous loading by oral or parenteral routes; and (2) endogenous loading from cellular shifts of phosphate, especially with lysis of cells caused by disturbances in acid-base balance or chemotherapy. Treatment is directed at the underlying disorder.

Exogenous loading of phosphate frequently occurs through the administration of phosphate-containing enemas and laxatives (the Fleet enema contains 4.3 g/dl of phosphate). Children are particularly prone to develop this hyperphosphatemia as a consequence of the rapid rate of phosphate absorption in the colon. Children are also susceptible to hypernatremia from the high sodium content of the enema. Hypovolemia may occur and cause impaired renal function. The characteristic laboratory findings are hypovolemia, azotemia, hypernatremia, hyperphosphatemia, and a reduction in the urinary calcium concentration. The anion gap is increased because of the phosphate retention.[4,105] Treatment consists of the discontinuation of enemas, expansion of the body fluid volume, and prevention of acute renal failure caused by hypovolemia.

Phosphate-containing laxatives, taken chronically by laxative abusers, usually do not cause hyperphosphatemia because the kidneys adapt by reducing tubular phosphate reabsorption and eliminate the exogenous load of phosphate. Nephrotoxicity may result from hypercalcemia caused by vitamin D intoxication and/or excess intake of milk and alkali (milk-alkali syndrome) and may compromise the renal capacity to excrete phosphate both by inhibiting the secretion of PTH and by reducing the GFR. When this occurs, hyperphosphatemia sometimes develops. There should be a high index of suspicion in patients who self-medicate; a detailed history of drug utilization is important to establish the diagnosis. Treatment consists of discontinuation of the offending agents.

Parenteral phosphate therapy, formerly used to combat hypercalciuria, is now seldom used for this purpose. Even for the treatment of hypophosphatemia, parenteral phosphate therapy must be used with great caution because of the serious complications of inadvertent hyperphosphatemia and hypocalcemia. This is particularly true in patients with renal insufficiency, who may have an impaired ability to excrete the excess phosphate. In patients with severe hypophosphatemia, the dose of parenteral phosphate should not exceed 8 mg/kg/day.

Blood transfusions, with an increased release of phosphate into the circulation, increase the risk of hyperphosphatemia.[105] Hyperphosphatemia paralleling an increase in lactate concentration has been observed during thoracic and abdominal surgical procedures, and is attributed to tissue breakdown or blood transfusions.[163]

Cutaneous absorption of enough phosphate to give rise to hyperphosphatemia, hypocalcemia, and sudden death was reported as a complication of white phosphorus burns from incendiary bombs.[164]

Endogenous loading of phosphate from cellular shifting of the ion is encountered in diabetic ketoacidosis and lactic acidosis. Acidosis promotes the shifting of phosphate from intracellular to extracellular fluids. Lactic acidosis in particular gives rise to a marked degree of hyperphosphatemia (serum phosphate over 9 mg/dl) compared with that in diabetic ketoacidosis (serum phosphate as high as 6 mg/dl).[165] Metabolic acidosis produced by ammonium chloride does not cause hyperphosphatemia.[165] It seems that whereas organic acids produce cellular shifts in phosphate and hyperphosphatemia, inorganic acids do not. Tissue hypoxia and rapid degradation of ATP probably contribute to the cellular shifting of phosphate.[165] Treatment of the underlying disorder effectively reverses the hyperphosphatemia.

Hyperphosphatemia frequently complicates rhabdomyolysis, a complex muscle breakdown that can be precipitated by a number of metabolic derangements, including prolonged seizures, crush injury, surgical muscle necrosis, heat stroke, hypophosphatemia, hypokalemia produced by volume depletion and secondary aldosteronism, and following influenza and other viral infections. The myoglobinemia and myoglobinuria that follow rhabdomyolysis increase the risk of acute renal failure. Thus, hyperphosphatemia develops both from an increased endogenous phosphate load as well as from compromised renal excretion. The diagnosis is confirmed by elevated serum creatine phosphokinase, uric acid, and lactate dehydrogenase concentrations, and the demonstration of heme-positive urine by dipstick testing in the absence of red blood cells on microscopic examination of the urine. Therapy is directed at the underlying disorder, with maintenance of the ECF volume to avoid volume depletion and alkalinizing of the urine to prevent the development of uric acid accumulation, which predisposes to acute tubular necrosis. Phosphate restriction and dialysis are indicated in the treatment of acute renal failure.

Chemotherapy, such as for Burkitt's lymphoma and lymphoblastic leukemia, can lead to the release of large amounts of phosphate through the breakdown of immature cells. Severe hyperphosphatemia and hypocalcemia may follow within 48 hours of the initiation of chemotherapy.[166] Lymphoblasts are richer in phosphate than are mature lymphocytes. Chronic myelogenous leukemia can give rise to hyperphosphatemia without chemotherapy.[105] In childhood leukemia, chemotherapy may precipitate hyperphosphatemia, hypocalcemia, hyperkalemia, an elevated lactate dehydrogenase level, and severe metabolic acidosis, which is associated with a large anion gap produced by phosphate retention. Treatment consists of expanding the ECF volume, bicarbonate therapy to correct metabolic acidosis and to maintain an alkaline diuresis, administration of allopurinol to reverse hyperuricemia and prevent uric acid nephropathy, and control of hyperkalemia with cation exchange resins. Phosphate restriction and dialysis are indicated for acute renal failure. Details of these therapeutic steps are presented in the chapter on acute renal failure, Chapter 15.

Hemolysis in thalassemia major and paroxysmal nocturnal hemoglobinuria[146] gives rise to phosphate release from intracellular to extracellular fluids, resulting in hyperphosphatemia. The concomitant release of potassium gives rise to hyperkalemia, which if severe may result in cardiac arrhythmia. Hemolysis from mismatched transfusions may precipitate shock, severe hyperkalemia, and hyperphosphatemia. Treatment is directed at combating shock, maintaining the ECF volume, and controlling or preventing hyperkalemia. This may require dialysis.

Malignant hyperthermia is a rare familial syndrome characterized by an abrupt rise in body temperature during the course of anesthesia.[167] It appears to be autosomal dominant in transmission.[167] An elevated serum creatine phosphokinase concentration is found in otherwise normal family members. Hyperphosphatemia results from shifts of phosphate from muscle cells to the extracellular pool. The syndrome has a high mortality rate.

Miscellaneous Disorders

A familial intermittent hyperphosphatemia has been described in three of four children in a family whose members have a history of polyuria and seizures.[168] Serum phosphate concentrations as high as 19.2 mg/dl were reported. The hyperphosphatemia is associated with massive phosphaturia but not with hypercalciuria. Irritability, vomiting, diarrhea, carpopedal spasm, and tetany result from the hypocalcemia caused by the hyperphosphatemia. Treatment during such episodes consists of rehydration and correction of hypocalcemia with parenteral calcium gluconate. Between attacks the children are well, and the results of extensive renal-endocrine-metabolic workups are entirely normal, including measurements of serum iPTH, corticosteroids, amino acids, renal concentration-dilution capabilities, and the erythrocyte 2,3-diphosphoglycerate and ATP concentrations. The pathogenesis of this disorder remains to be elucidated.[168]

In summary, hyperphosphatemia in infants and adolescents, as well as in postmenopausal women, is physiologic and requires no treatment. Acute hyperphosphatemia produced by rhabdomyolysis and rapid cell lysis from chemotherapy, and by laxative abuse or excess phosphate loading needs to be treated by elimination of the phosphate load and careful treatment of symptomatic hypocalcemia. Hyperphosphatemia caused by chronic renal failure, hypoparathyroidism, and hyperthyroidism requires treatment of the underlying disease. Chronic renal failure is now the most common cause of hyperphosphatemia, and requires treatment with dietary phosphate restriction and phosphate binders, as well as dialysis therapy. The hyperphosphatemia caused by hypoparathyroidism is reversed by treatment with vitamin D and the correction of hypocalcemia. Hyperphosphatemia found in patients with hyperthyroidism is mild and requires no specific treatment.

REFERENCES

1. Lee DBN, Kurokawa K: Physiology of phosphorus metabolism. p 245. In Maxwell MH, Kleeman CR, Narins RG (eds): Clinical Disorders of Fluid Electrolyte Metabolism. McGraw-Hill, New York, 1987
2. Henneman PH, Forber AP, Moldawer M, et al: Effects of human growth hormone in man. J Clin Invest 39:1223, 1960
3. Corvilain J, Abramow M: Some effects of human growth hormone on renal hemodynamics and on tubular phosphate transport in man. J Clin Invest 41:1230, 1962
4. Lau K: Phosphate disorders. p 398. In Kokko JP, Tanner RL (eds): Fluids and Electrolytes. WB Saunders, Philadelphia, 1986
5. Wilkinson R: Absorption of calcium, phosphorus and magnesium. p 36. In Nordin BEC (ed): Calcium, Phosphate and Magnesium Metabolism. Clinical Physiology and Diagnostic Procedures. Churchill Livingstone, New York, 1976
6. Walling MW: Intestinal calcium and phosphate transport—Differential responses to vitamin-D_3 metabolites. Am J Physiol 233:E488, 1977
7. Walton EJ, Gray TK: The intestinal absorption of inorganic phosphate in humans. Clin Sci 56:407, 1979
8. Plimmer RHA: The metabolism of inorganic phosphorus compounds; their hydrolysis by the action of enzymes. Biochem J 7:43, 1913
9. Clark I: Importance of dietary Ca:PO_4 ratio on skeletal Ca, Mg and PO_4 metabolism. Am J Physiol 217:865, 1969
10. Matsumoto T, Fontaine O, Rasmussen H: Effects of 1,25$(OH)_2$ D on phosphate uptake into chick intestinal brush border membrane vesicles. Biochem Biophys Acta 59:13, 1980
11. Tanaka Y, DeLuca HF: Intestinal calcium transport: stimulation by low phosphorus diets. Science 181:564, 1973
12. Chan JCM, Kodroff MB, Landwehr DM, et al: Effects of 1,25-dihydroxyvitamin D_3 on renal function, mineral metabolism and growth in children with severe chronic renal failure. Pediatrics 68:559, 1981
13. Brickman AS, Hartenbower DL, Norman AW, et al: Actions of 1α-hydroxyvitamin D_3 and 1,25-dihydroxyvitamin D_3 on mineral metabolism in man: I. Effects of net absorption of phosphorus. Am J Clin Nutr 30:1064, 1977
14. Hildman B, Storelli C, Danisi G, et al: Regulation of Na^+-P^i cotransport by 1,25-dihydroxyvitamin D_3 in rabbit duodenal brush border membrane. Am J Physiol 242:G533, 1982
15. Harrison HE, Harrison HC: Disorders of Calcium and Phosphate Metabolism in Childhood and Adolescence. WB Saunders, Philadelphia, 1979

16. Stewart AF, Broadus AE: Mineral metabolism. p 1317. In Felig P, Baxter JD, Broadus AE, Frohman LA (eds): Endocrinology and Metabolism, 2nd Ed. McGraw-Hill, New York, 1987
17. Clark I, Belanger L: The effects of alterations in dietary magnesium on calcium, phosphate and skeletal metabolism. Calcif Tissue Int 1:204, 1967
18. Lotz M, Zisman E, Bartter FC: Evidence for a phosphorus depletion syndrome in man. N Engl J Med 278:409, 1968
19. Birge SJ, Avioli RC: Intestinal phosphate transport and alkaline phosphatase activity in the chick. Am J Physiol 240:E384, 1981
20. Knox FG, Oswald H, Marchand GR, et al: Editorial review: phosphate transport along the nephron. Am J Physiol 233L:F261, 1977
21. Dennis VW, Stead WW, Myers JC: Renal handling of phosphate and calcium. Annu Rev Physiol 41:257, 1979
22. Knox FG, Haas JA, Berndt T, et al: Phosphate transport in superficial and deep nephrons in phosphate-loaded rats. Am J Physiol 233:F150, 1977
23. Hoffman N, Thees M, Kinne R: Phosphate transport by isolated renal brush border vesicles. Pflugers Arch 362:147, 1976
24. Baumann K, de Rouffignac C, Roinel N, et al: Renal phosphate transport: inhomogeneity of local proximal transport rates and sodium dependency. Pflugers Arch 356:287, 1975
25. Sacktor B, Cheng L: Sodium gradient dependent phosphate transport in renal brush border membrane vesicles. Effect on an intravesicular-extravesicular proton gradient. J Biol Chem 256:8080, 1981
26. Robito CA: Phosphate uptake by a kidney cell line (LLC-PK). Am J Physiol 245:F22, 1983
27. Bijvoet OLM: Relation of plasma phosphorus concentration to renal tubular reabsorption of phosphate. Clin Sci 37:26, 1969
28. Walton RJ, Bijvoet OLM: Nomogram for the derivation of renal threshold phosphate concentration. Lancet 2:309, 1975
29. Bijvoet OLM: Kidney function in calcium and phosphate metabolism. p 49. In Avilo LV, Krane SM (eds): Metabolic Bone Disease, Vol. 1. Academic Press, New York, 1977
30. Kuntzer H, Amiel C, Gaudebout C: Phosphate handling by the rat nephron during saline diuresis. Kidney Int 2:318, 1972
31. Dousa TP, Kempson SA: Editorial: regulation of renal brush border membrane transport of phosphate. Miner Electrolyte Metab 7:113, 1982
32. Agus ZS, Gardner LB, Beck LH, et al: Effects of parathyroid hormone on renal tubular reabsorption of calcium, sodium and phosphate. Am J Physiol 224:1143, 1973
33. Brazy PC, Gullaus SR, Mandel LJ, et al: Metabolic requirement for inorganic phosphate by the rabbit proximal tubule. Evidence for a crabtree effect. J Clin Invest 70:53, 1982
34. Haramati A, Hass JA, Knox FG: Nephron heterogeneity of phosphate reabsorption: Effect of parathyroid hormone. Am J Physiol 250:F150, 1984
35. Trobler U, Bonjour JP, Fleish H: Inorganic phosphate homeostasis: renal adaptation to the dietary intake in intact and thyroparathyroidectomized rats. J Clin Invest 57:265, 1976
36. Steele TH: Renal response to phosphorus deprivation: Effect of the parathyroids and bicarbonate. Kidney Int 11:327, 1977
37. Hammerman MR, Hruska KA: Cyclic AMP-dependent protein phosphorylation in canine renal brush border membrane vesicles is associated with decreased phosphate transport. J Biol Chem 257:992, 1982
38. Barrett PQ, Gertner JM, Rasmussen H: Effect of dietary phosphate on transport properties of pig renal microvillus vesicles. Am J Physiol 239:F352, 1980
39. Brazy PC, McKeown JW, Harris RH, et al: Comparative effects of dietary phosphate, unilateral nephrectomy, and parathyroid hormone on phosphate transport by the rabbit proximal tubule. Kidney Int 17:788, 1980
40. Cheng L, Liang CT, Sacktor B: Phosphate uptake by renal membrane vesicles of rabbits adapted to high and low phosphate diets. Am J Physiol 245:F175, 1983
41. Stoll R, Kinna R, Murer H: Effect of dietary phosphate intake in phosphate transport by isolated rat renal brush border vesicles. Biochem J 180:465, 1978

42. Corvilain J, Abramow M: Growth and renal control of plasma phosphate. J Clin Endocrinol 34:452, 1972
43. Bullock JK: Physiologic variations in inorganic blood phosphorus content at different ages persists: attempt to explain these in growing child. Am J Dis Child 40:725, 1930
44. Thalassinos NC, Leese B, Latham SC, et al: Urinary excretion of phosphate in normal children. Arch Dis Child 45:269, 1970
45. Guder WG: Hormonal regulation of renal gluconeogenesis in isolated tubule fragments. p 202. In Schmidt V, Dubach VC (eds): Current Problems in Clinical Biochemistry, vol. 6. Renal Metabolism in Relation to Renal Function. Haus Huber, Bern, 1976
46. Rabkin R, Epstein S, Swann M, et al: Effect of growth hormone on renal sodium and water excretion. Horm Metab Res 7:139, 1975
47. Batts AA, Bennett LL, Garcia J, et al: The effect of growth hormone on muscle potassium and on extracellular fluid. Endocrinology 55:456, 1954
48. Corvilain J, Abramow M: Effect of growth hormone on tubular transport of phosphate in normal and parathyroidectomized dogs. J Clin Invest 43:1608, 1964
49. Hammerman MR, Karl IE, Hruska KA: Regulation of canine renal vesicle P transport by growth hormone and parathyroid hormone. Biochem Biophys Acta 603:322, 1980
50. Beck JC, McGarry EE, Dyrenfurth L, et al: Metabolic effects of human and monkey growth hormone in man. Science 125:884, 1957
51. Caverzasio J, Bonjour JP, Fleisch H: Tubular handling of P_i in young growing and adult rats. Am J Physiol 242:F705, 1982
52. Ikkos DE, Luft R, Gemzell CA, et al: The effect of human growth hormone in man. Acta Endocrinol 32:341, 1959
53. Altenahr E, Kampt E: Parathyroid function in rats treated with growth hormone. Virchows Arch [Pathol Anat] 371:363, 1976
54. Spanos E, Barrett D, MacIntyre I, et al: Effect of growth hormone on vitamin D metabolism. Nature 273:246, 1978
55. Nadarajah A, Hartog M, Redfern B, et al: Calcium metabolism in acromegaly. Br Med J 4:797, 1968
56. New MI, Schwartz E, Parks GA, et al: Pseudohypopituitary dwarfism with normal plasma growth hormone and low serum sulfation factor. J Pediatr 80:620, 1972
57. Gershberg H: Metabolic and renotropic effects of human growth hormone in disease. J Clin Endocrinol Metab 20:1107, 1960
58. Gershberg H, Gash J: Effect of growth hormone on sulfate Tm, urea clearance and fasting blood glucose. Proc Soc Exp Biol Med 91:46, 1956
59. Rasmussen H, Bordier P: The Physiological Basis of Metabolic Bone Disease. William & Wilkins, Baltimore, 1974
60. Harrison HE, Harrison HC: The renal excretion of inorganic phosphate in relation to the action of vitamin D and parathyroid hormone. J Clin Invest 20:47, 1941
61. Klein R, Gow RC: Interactions of parathyroid hormone and vitamin-D on the renal excretion of phosphate. J Clin Endocrinol Metab 13:271, 1953
62. Oldham SB, Smith R, Hartenbower DL, et al: The acute effect of 1,25-dihydroxycholecalciferol on serum immunoreactive parathyroid hormone (iPTH) in the dog. Endocrinology 104:248, 1979
63. Puschett JB, Moprany J, Kurnick WS: Evidence for a direct action of cholecalciferol and 25-hydroxycholecalciferol on the renal transport of phosphate, sodium and calcium. J Clin Invest 1:373, 1972
64. Costanzo LS, Sheele PR, Weiner IM: Renal actions of vitamin D in D-deficient rats. Am J Physiol 226:1490, 1974
65. Davis M, Hill LF, Taylor CM, et al: 1,25-dihydroxycalciferol in hypoparathyroidism. Lancet 1:55, 1977
66. Rosen JF, Fleischman AR, Finberg L, et al: 1,25-dihydroxycholecalciferol: its use in the long-term management of idiopathic hypoparathyroidism in children. J Clin Endocrinol 45:457, 1977
67. Knox FG, Lechenon C; Distal site of action of parathyroid hormone on phosphate reabsorption. Am J Physiol 229:1556, 1975
68. Borle AB: Effects of purified parathyroid hormone on the calcium metabolism of monkey kidney cells. Endocrinology 83:1316, 1968

69. Marcus R, Aurbach GD: Adenyl cyclase from renal cortex. Biochim Biophys Acta 242:410, 1971
70. Hammerman MR, Hausen VA, Morrissey JJ: ADP ribosylation of canine renal brush border membrane vesicle proteins is associated with decreased phosphate transport. J Biol Chem 257:1238, 1982
71. Berndt TJ, Knox FG, Kempson SA, et al: Nicotinamide adenine dinucleotide and renal response to parathyroid hormone. Endocrinology 108:2005, 1981
72. Kruesser WJ, Descoeudres C, Oda Y, et al: Effect of phosphate depletion on renal gluconeogenesis. Miner Electrolyte Metab 3:312, 1980
73. DeFronzo RA, Cooke CB, Andres R, et al: The effect of insulin on renal handling of sodium, potassium, calcium and phosphate in man. J Clin Invest 55:845, 1975
74. Kurokawa K, Silverblatt FJ, Klein KL, et al: Binding of ^{125}I-Insulin to the isolated glomeruli of rat kidney. J Clin Invest 64:1357, 1979
75. Espinosa RE, Keller MJ, Yusafi ANK, et al: Effect of thyroxine administration on phosphate transport across renal cortical brush border membrane. Am J Physiol 246:F133, 1984
76. McCaffrey C, Ouamme GA: Effects of thyroid status on renal calcium and magnesium handling. Can J Comp Med 48:51, 1984
77. Laron Z, Crawford JD, Klein R: Phosphaturic effect of cortisone in normal and parathyroidectomized rats. Proc Soc Exp Biol Med 96:649, 1957
78. Anderson J, Forster JB: Effect of cortisone on urinary phosphate excretion in man. Clin Sci 18:437, 1959
79. Young MM, Jasani C, Smith DA, et al: Some effects of ethinyl estradiol on calcium and phosphorus metabolism in osteoporosis. Clin Sci 34:411, 1968
80. Kenny AD: Vitamin D metabolism: physiological regulation in egg-laying Japanese quail. Am J Physiol 230:1609, 1976
81. Arnaud CD, Tsao HS, Littledike T, et al: Radioimmunoassay of human parathyroid hormone in serum. J Clin Invest 50:21, 1971
82. Massry SG, Coburn JW, Kleeman CR, et al: The influence of extracellular volume expansion on renal phosphate reabsorption in the dog. J Clin Invest 48:1237, 1969
83. Frick A: Proximal tubule reabsorption of inorganic phosphate during saline infusion in the rat. Am J Physiol 223:1034, 1972
84. Cuche JL, Ott CE, Marchand GR, et al: Lack of effect of hypocalcemia on renal phosphate handling. J Lab Clin Med 88:271, 1976
85. Rastegar A, Agus Z, Connor TB, et al: Renal handling of calcium and phosphate during mineralocorticoid "escape" in man. Kidney Int 2:279, 1972
86. Anast C, Arnaud CD, Rasmussen H, et al: Thyrocalcitonin and the response to parathyroid hormone. J Clin Invest 45:57, 1967
87. Oberleithren H, Lang F, Greger R, et al: Additivity in the phosphaturic action of parathyroid and calcitonin in the rat kidney. Adv Exp Med Biol 128:129, 1980
88. Kurtzman NA, Rogers PW, Boonjarern S, et al: Effect of infusion of pharmacologic amounts of vasopressin on renal electrolyte excretion. Am J Physiol 228:890, 1975
89. Agus ZS: Oncogenic hypophosphatemic osteomalacia. Kidney Int 24:113, 1983
90. Drezner MK, Feinglos MN: Osteomalacia due to 1,25-dihydroxycholecalciferol deficiency. J Clin Invest 60:1046, 1977
91. Saville PD, Nassim JR, Stevenson FH, et al: Osteomalacia in von Recklinghausen's neurofibromatosis. Metabolic study of a case. Br Med J 1:1311, 1955
92. Dent CE, Gertner JM: Hypophosphatemic osteomalacia in fibrosis dysplasia. QJ Med 45:411, 1976
93. Salveson H, Boe J: Osteomalacia—Report of two cases with the Milkman's syndrome. Acta Med Scand 266:863, 1952
94. Aschinberg LC, Soloman LM, Zeis PM, et al: Vitamin D-resistant rickets associated with epidermal nevus syndrome. Demonstration of a phosphaturic substance in the dermal lesions. J Pediatr 91:56, 1977
95. Donker AJM, de Jong PE, Statius van Eps LW, et al: Indomethacin in Bartter's syndrome. Nephron 19:200, 1977
96. Gantt CL, Carter WJ: Acute effects of angiotensin on calcium, phosphorus, magnesium and potassium excretion. Can Med Assoc J 90:287, 1964
97. Heaton FW, Hodgkinson A: External factors affecting diurnal variations in electrolyte excretion with particular reference to

calcium and magnesium. Clin Chem Acta 8:246, 1963
98. Goldsmith RS, Siemsen AW, Mason AD, et al: Primary role of plasma hydrocortisone concentration in the regulation of normal forenoon pattern of urinary phosphate excretion. J Clin Endocrinol Metab 25:1649, 1965
99. Schaat M, Kyle LH: Diurnal variations of calcium and phosphorus in blood and urine. Clin Res 6:139, 1958
100. Hiatt HH, Thompson DD: Some effects of intravenously administered calcium on inorganic phosphate metabolism. J Clin Invest 36:573, 1957
101. Glorieux F, Scriver CR: Loss of a parathyroid hormone-sensitive component of phosphate transport in X-linked hypophosphatemia. Science 175:997, 1972
102. Eisenberg E: Effects of serum calcium level and parathyroid extracts on phosphate and calcium excretion in hypoparathyroid patients. J Clin Invest 44:942, 1965.
103. Slatopolsky E, Mercado A, Morrison A, et al; Inhibitory effects of acute hypermagnesemia on the renal action of parathyroid hormone. J Clin Invest 58:1273, 1976
104. Smith R, Newman RJ, Radda GK, et al: Hypophosphatemic osteomalacia and myopathy: Studies with nuclear magnetic resonance spectroscopy. Clin Sci 67:505, 1984
105. Brautbar N, Kleeman CR: Hypophosphatemia and hyperphosphatemia: clinical and pathophysiologic aspects. p 789. In: Maxwell M, Kleeman CR, Narins RG (eds): Clinical Disorders of Fluid and Electrolyte Metabolism, 4th Ed. McGraw-Hill, New York, 1987
106. Betro MG, Pain RW: Hypophosphatemia in a hospital population. Br Med J 1:273, 1972
107. Silvis SE, Paragas PD Jr: Paresthetic weakness, seizures and hypophosphatemia in patients receiving hyperalimentation. Gastroenterology 62:513, 1972
108. Schmitker MA, Mattman PE, Bliss TL: A clinical study of malnutrition in Japanese prisoners of war. Ann Intern Med 35:69, 1951
109. Okel B, Hurst JW: Prolonged hyperventilation in man. Associated electrolyte changes and subjective symptoms. Arch Intern Med 108:757, 1961
110. Brautbar N, Leibovici H, Massry SG: On the mechanism of hypophosphatemia during acute hypoventilation: Evidence for an increased muscle glycolysis. Miner Electrolyte Metab 9:45, 1983
111. Day HG, McCullom EV: Mineral metabolism, growth, symptomatology of rats on diet extremely deficient in phosphorus. J Biol Chem 130:269, 1939
112. Dominguez JH, Gray RW, Lemann J Jr: Dietary phosphate deprivation in women and men: Effects on mineral and acid balances, parathyroid hormone and the metabolism of 25-OH-vitamin D. J Clin Endocrinol Metab 43:1056, 1976
113. Reade TM, Scriver CR: Hypophosphatemic rickets and breast milk. N Engl J Med 300:1397, 1979
114. Dodge WF, Travis L: Iatrogenic hypophosphatemia in infants with renal insufficiency. Pediatrics 35:792, 1965
115. Wortsman J, Pak CYC, Bartter FC, et al: Pathogenesis of osteomalacia and secondary hyperparathyroidism after gastrectomy. Am J Med 52:556, 1972
116. Henderson L, Nolph KD, Prischett JB, et al: Proximal tubular malfunction as a mechanism for diuresis after renal transplantation. N Eng J Med 278:467, 1971
117. Chan JCM, Grushkin CM, Malekzadeh M, et al: The adaptation of hydrogen ion excretion associated with nephron reduction in post-transplant patients. Pediatr Res 7:712, 1973
118. Chan JCM, Bartter FC: Hypophosphatemic rickets: effect of 1-α-25-dihydroxyvitamin D_3 on growth and mineral metabolism. Pediatrics 64:488, 1979
119. Cowgill L, Goldfarb S, Lau K, et al: Evidence for an intrinsic renal tubular defect in mice with familial hypophosphatemic rickets. J Clin Invest 63:1203, 1979
120. Short EM, Morris RC Jr, Sebastian A, et al; Exaggerated phosphaturic response to circulating parathyroid hormone in patients with familial X-linked hypophosphatemic rickets. J Clin Invest 58:152, 1976
121. Tenenhouse HS, Scriver CR, McInnes RR, et al: Renal handling of phosphate in vivo and in vitro by the X-linked hypophosphatemic male mouse: Evidence for a defect in the brush border membrane. Kidney Int 14:236, 1978

122. Meyer RA Jr, Meyer MH, Gray RW: Humoral origin of X-linked hypophosphatemia in mice suggested by parabiosis. Fed Proc 46:1393, 1987
123. Roth KS, Segal S: Tubular aspects of hereditary and developmental disorders of the kidney. p 945. In Hamburger J, Crosnier J, Grunfeld JP (eds): Nephrology. John Wiley & Sons, New York, 1979
124. Dent CE, Rose GA: Amino acid metabolism in cystinuria. QJ Med 20:205, 1951
125. Thier SD, Segal S, Fox M, et al: Cystinuria: Defective intestinal transport of dibasic amino acids and cystine. J Clin Invest 44:442, 1965
126. Chesney RW, Kaplan BS, Colle E, et al: Abnormalities of carbohydrate metabolism in idiopathic Fanconi syndrome. Pediatr Res 14:209, 1980
127. Broadus AE, Insogna KL, Lauge R, et al: Evidence for disordered control of 1,25-dihydroxyvitamin D production in absorptive hypercalciuria. N Engl J Med 311:73, 1984
128. Lau YK, Wasserstein A, Westby GR, et al: Proximal tubular defects in idiopathic hypercalciuria: Resistance to phosphate administration. Miner Electrolyte Metab 7:237, 1982
129. Falls WF, Stacey WK: Postobstructive diuresis. Am J Med 54:404, 1973
130. Guntupalli J, Eby B, Lau K: Mechanism for the phosphaturia of NH_4Cl dependence on aciduria but not on diet PO_4 or PTH. Am J Physiol 242:F552, 1982
131. Knochell JP: The pathophysiology and clinical characteristics of severe hypophosphatemia. Arch Intern Med 127:203, 1977
132. Ditzel J: Effect of plasma inorganic phosphate on tissue oxygenation during recovery from diabetic ketoacidosis. Adv Exp Med Biol 37A:163, 1971
133. Frank BW, Kern F Jr: Serum inorganic phosphorus during hepatic coma. Arch Intern Med 110:865, 1962
134. Knochel JP, Barcenas C, Cotton JR, et al: Hypophosphatemia and rhabdomyolysis. J Clin Invest 62:1240, 1978
135. Fuller TJ, Nichols WW, Brenner BJ, et al: Reversible depression in myocardial performance in dogs with experimental phosphorus depletion. J Clin Invest 62:1154, 1978
136. Travis SF, Sugarman HJ, Ruberg RL, et al: Alterations of red cell glycolytic intermediates and oxygen transport as a consequence of hypophosphatemia in patients receiving intravenous hyperalimentation. N Engl J Med 285:763, 1971
137. Jacob HS, Ansden T: Acute hemolytic anemia with rigid red cells in hypophosphatemia. N Engl J Med 285:1446, 1971
138. Craddock PR, Yawata Y, Van Santen L, et al: Acquired phagocyte dysfunction: a complication of the hypophosphatemia of parenteral hyperalimentation. N Engl J Med 290:1403, 1974
139. Baylink D, Wergedel J, Stauffer M: Formation, mineralization and resorption of bone in hypophosphatemic rats. J Clin Invest 50:2519, 1971
140. de Vernejoul MC, Marie P, Kuntz D, et al: Non-osteomalacic osteopathy associated with chronic hypophosphatemia. Calcif Tissue Int 34:219, 1982
141. Grabie M, Lau K, Agus ZS, et al: The role of parathyroid hormone in the hypercalciuria of chronic phosphate depletion. Miner Electrolyte Metab 1:279, 1978
142. Boelens PA, Norwood W, Kjellstrand C, et al: Hypophosphatemia with muscle weakness due to antacids and hemodialysis. Am J Dis Child 120:350, 1970
143. Rajan KS, Levinson R, Leevy CM: Hepatic hypoxia secondary to hypophosphatemia. Clin Res 21:521, 1973
144. Brautbar N, Carpenter C, Baczynski R, et al: Impaired energy metabolism in skeletal muscle during phosphate depletion. Kidney Int 24:53, 1983
145. DeFronzo RA, Lang R: Hypophosphatemia and glucose intolerance: Evidence for tissue insensitivity to insulin. N Engl J Med 303:1259, 1980
146. Betro MG, Pain RW: Hypophosphatemia and hyperphosphatemia in a hospital population. Br Med J 1:273, 1972
147. Juan D, Elvazak M: Hypophosphatemia in hospitalized patients. JAMA 242:163, 1979
148. Keller U, Berger W: Prevention of hypophosphatemia by phosphate infusion during treatment of diabetic ketoacidosis and hyperosmolar coma. Diabetes 29:87, 1980

149. Yu GC, Lee DBN: Hypophosphatemia and phosphate depletion. p 26. In Glassock RJ (ed): Current Therapy in Nephrology and Hypertension. BC Decker, Toronto 1987
150. Lentz RD, Brown DM, Kjellstrand CM: Treatment of severe hypophosphatemia. Ann Intern Med 89:941, 1978
151. Chan JCM, Goplerud JM, Papadopoulou ZL, et al: Kidney failure in childhood. Int J Pediatr Nephrol 2:201, 1981
152. Kuzela DC, Huffer WE, Conger JD, et al: Soft tissue calcification in chronic dialysis patients. Am J Pathol 86:403, 1977
153. Contiguglia SR, Alfrey AC, Miller NL, et al: Nature of soft tissue calcification in uremia. Kidney Int 4:229, 1973
154. Santos F, Chan JCM: Idiopathic hypoparathyroidism: a case study on the interactions between exogenous parathyroid hormone infusion and 1,25-dihydroxyvitamin D. Pediatrics 78:1139, 1986
155. Lichtman MA, Miller DR: Erythrocyte glycolysis, 2,3-diphosphoglycerate and adenosine triphosphate concentration in uremic subjects: Relationship to extracellular phosphate concentration. J Lab Clin Med 76:267, 1970
156. Petty C, Bageanat T: In vitro manipulation of 2,3-diphosphoglycerate levels in acid-citrate-dextrose blood with steroids. Life Sci 14:1279, 1974
157. Bell NH, Stern PH: Hypercalcemia and increases in serum hormone value during prolonged administration of 1 alpha, 25-dihydroxyvitamin D. N Engl J Med 298:1241, 1978
158. Krane SM, Brownell GL, Stanbury JB, et al: The effect of thyroid disease or calcium metabolism in man. J Clin Invest 35:874, 1956
159. Mitmick PD, Goldfarb S, Stetopolski E, et al: Calcium and phosphate metabolism in tumoral calcinosis: response to parathyroid hormone and acetazolamide. J Clin Endocrinol Metab 50:648, 1980
160. Nassim JR, Saville PD, Mulligan L, et al: Effect of stilbestrol on urinary phosphate excretion. Clin Sci 15:367, 1956
161. Iwanami M, Osiba S, Yamada T, et al: Seasonal variations in serum inorganic phosphate and calcium with special reference to parathyroid activity. J Physiol 149:23, 1959
162. DeVries HR, Bijvoet OLM: Results of prolonged treatment of Paget's disease of bone with disodium ethane-1-hydroxy-1,1-diphosphonate (EHDP). Neth J Med 17:281, 1974
163. Clowes GH Jr, Simone FA: Acute hypocalcemia in surgical patients. Ann Surg 146:530, 1957
164. Bowen TE, Whelan JR Jr, Nelson TG, et al: Sudden death after phosphorus burns: Experimental observations of hypocalcemia, hyperphosphatemia and electrocardiographic abnormalities following production of a standard white phosphorus burn. Ann Surg 174:779, 1971
165. O'Connor LR, Klein KL, Bethune JE: Hyperphosphatemia in lactic acidosis. N Engl J Med 297:707, 1977
166. Zusman J, Brown DM, Nesbit ME: Hyperparathyroidism, hyperphosphatemia, and hypocalcemia in acute lymphoblastic leukemia. N Engl J Med 289:1335, 1973
167. Denborough MA, Forster JFA, Hudson MC, et al: Biochemical changes in malignant hyperpyrexia. Lancet 1:1137, 1970
168. Miller WL, Meyer WJ, Bartter FC: Intermittent hyperphosphatemia, polyuria, and seizures—a new familial disorder. J Pediatr 86:233, 1975

7

Disorders of Magnesium Metabolism

Cristobal G. Duarte

Magnesium is the fourth most abundant cation in the body, and in intracellular concentration is second only to potassium.[1,2] It is a regulator of important cellular processes that are essential for life.[1,2] It is a component of chlorophyll and is important for the process of photosynthesis.[1,2] It plays a critical role in the function of ribonucleic acid (RNA) and deoxyribonucleic acid (DNA), and in maintaining normal calcium and potassium homeostasis.[1,2] It regulates a series of important enzymatic processes that are involved in the storage, transfer, and production of energy through the activation of pyruvate kinase, creatine kinase, enolase, phosphoglutamase, alkaline phosphatase, adenylate cyclase, adenosine triphosphatase, and other enzymes.[1,2]

The human body contains approximately 2,000 mEq of magnesium. Less than 2 percent of this total body magnesium is in the extracellular space, 60 percent is in bone, and the rest is distributed almost equally between muscle and nonmuscular soft tissue.[1,2] Of soft tissue, striated muscle and liver have the highest magnesium content.[1] The distribution of magnesium in the adult human body is given in Table 7-1.[3] The serum magnesium concentration correlates better with the bone magnesium content than with the muscle or erythrocyte magnesium.[4] Normally there is an exchange between magnesium in the extracellular fluid (ECF) and in bone in response to an excess or deficit of this element.[3] About one-third of the bone magnesium on the surface of apatite crystals may be available for exchange.[3] The exchange of magnesium between the ECF and bone depends on age, decreasing significantly in older individuals.[3]

Studies of the intracellular concentration and metabolism of magnesium have been difficult because of a lack of accurate techniques and instrumentation for its measurement. Techniques that have been used but are not yet routinely available include light-sensitive dyes that bind magnesium, electron microprobe analysis, nuclear magnetic resonance, and magnesium-selective microelectrodes.[3] Intracellular magnesium exists both as a free ion and complexed to proteins and organophosphates.[3] Different reports give different values for intracellular ionized magnesium, ranging from 5 to 50 percent.[3] Intracellular magnesium is considered to be significantly less available for exchange than potassium.[3]

The plasma concentration of magnesium is maintained at a constant level of approximately 1.7 mEq/liter ± 10 percent of the mean.[2,3] Magnesium is present in plasma

Table 7-1. Distribution of Magnesium in the Adult Human Body

Tissue[a]	Concentration, mEq/liter	% of Total Mg
ECF	1.55–2.1	1.3
ICF		
Erythrocyte	4.6–6.2	0.7
Muscle	7.6	20
Other cells	16	10
Bone		
Cortical	214[b]	67
Trabecular	252[b]	
CSF	2.5	
Sweat	0.6	
Total body magnesium	25[b]	100

[a] ECF, extracellular fluid; ICF, intracellular fluid; CSF, cerebrospinal fluid.
[b] mEq/kg
(From Quamme and Dirks,[3] with permission.)

(as in other biologic systems), as free Mg^{2+}, complexed to anions, and bound to proteins.[5] The method most commonly used to determine the state of magnesium in plasma is ultrafiltration, which separates protein-bound magnesium (which does not cross the filter) from the ultrafiltrate containing free and complexed magnesium.[5,6] Only free magnesium is available for biochemical processes.[5,6] Of the total plasma magnesium, 20 to 35 percent is bound to proteins and the rest is ultrafiltrable, of which 55 percent is free and 11 percent is complexed to phosphates, citrate, and unidentified ions.[2,3] The distribution of magnesium in normal plasma is given in Table 7-2.[7]

The binding of magnesium does not seem to be influenced by magnesium deficiency or excess.[8] It has been reported that the

Table 7-2. Physicochemical States of Plasma Magnesium in Man

	mmoles/liter	% of Total
Free ions	0.53	55
Protein bound	0.30	32
$MgHPO_4$	0.03	3
$MgCit^-$	0.04	4
Unidentified complexes	0.06	6
Total	1.15	100

(From Walser M,[7] with permission.)

serum ionized magnesium concentration increases in experimentally induced acute respiratory alkalosis in the dog, and that acute respiratory acidosis has the opposite effect.[9] The technique most commonly used to determine magnesium is atomic absorption spectrophotometry.[5]

Considering that magnesium is predominantly an intracellular cation, its plasma concentration may not always be an accurate indicator of the total body magnesium content. Tissues such as muscle or bone are not easily accessible for magnesium determination in routine clinical practice. Therefore, attempts have been made to develop more practical methods that will allow indirect estimation of the total body magnesium content by more easily accessible measurements in tissues or cells. The concentration of magnesium in erythrocytes is three times higher than in the plasma, with most of the magnesium existing in bound form in the cell and very little in the membrane.[10,11] Reticulocytes have a much higher concentration of magnesium (10 times higher) than do adult erythrocytes, which decreases as the cell ages.[10–12]

The magnesium content of the erythrocyte reflects the plasma concentration of magnesium at the time of erythropoiesis.[10] A normal concentration of magnesium has been detected in the erythrocytes of rats deficient in this element.[12] As red cells age in magnesium-deficient rats, they develop structural defects in the cell membrane and their survival decreases.[13] The concentration of magnesium in erythrocytes is not a good indicator of the total body content of magnesium. It has been reported that the concentration of magnesium in lymphocytes correlates better with the skeletal and cardiac muscle content of this element than does the red cell magnesium.[14] The concentration of magnesium in mononuclear cells has been reported to provide a good indication of the total body magnesium content.[15]

GASTROINTESTINAL METABOLISM OF MAGNESIUM

The content of magnesium in some common foodstuffs is given in Table 7-3. In general, nutrients that have a high caloric content have a low concentration of magnesium.[2] The average daily dietary intake of magnesium in industrialized countries is considered to be below the normal requirement, and amounts of at least 6 mg/kg have been recommended for maintenance in adult women and 7 to 10 mg/kg in adult men.[16] Under physiologic or pathologic conditions, the recommended amounts may have to be increased to twice those noted above.[16] Figure 7-1 illustrates the dynamics of the gastrointestinal handling of magnesium and its metabolism, assuming a "zero balance" of this element, at which magnesium equilibrium is maintained through the amount of magnesium excreted in the urine and feces equaling the oral intake.[17] Magnesium also reaches the lumen of the gut through secretion with the bile and pancreatic and gastrointestinal fluids.[17,18] The concentration of magnesium in gastric aspirates from humans is 0.9 mEq/liter, in bile 1.1 mEq/liter, in pancreatic fluid 0.4 mEq/liter, and in diarrhea and fistula discharge 5.8 mEq/liter.[19] The absorption of magnesium takes place in the small bowel, mainly in the terminal ileum,[17] but as demonstrated by the hypermagnesemia that has occurred after the administration of enemas having a high magnesium content, absorption from the colon is also possible.[20]

The absorption and secretion of magnesium have been studied by perfusion of the duodenum and ileum in the rat.[21] With a normal diet, the secretion of magnesium was higher in the duodenum than in the ileum, but decreased in the duodenum with the feeding of a diet deficient in magnesium.[21] Absorption was approximately the same in the duodenum and ileum when the diet was normal, but was greater in the duodenum on a magnesium deficient diet.[21] Under normal conditions, 44 percent of the content of magnesium in the diet is absorbed, but increases to 76 percent when the content of magnesium in the diet is reduced to 1 mmol/day, and decreases to 24 percent when the dietary content is increased to twice the normal amount.[18] The belief that calcium and magnesium may share the same transport mechanism in the small bowel[22] has not been supported by perfusion studies of gastrointestinal segments.[23]

The transcellular transport of magnesium proceeds down an electrochemical gradient across the brush border membrane, and is active against an electrochemical gradient across the basolateral membrane.[3] The absorption of magnesium across the paracellular pathway is in response to a chemical gradient and as a consequence of water absorption and solvent drag.[3]

Water and sodium are necessary for the absorption of magnesium in the ileum and colon.[24] Increasing the concentration of sodium in these segments of the gastrointestinal tract enhances the absorption of magnesium.[25] Potassium causes a decrease in the apical membrane electrical potential of the rat colon, and thus inhibits magnesium absorption.[26] Phytic acid and phosphate, by binding to magnesium, exert an effect limiting the absorption of this element in the gut.[27] Lactose inhibits, while glucose enhances the absorption of magnesium.[28]

Table 7-3. Content of Magnesium in Some Common Foods

Food	mEq/kg
Nuts	162
Cereals	66
Seafoods	29
Meats	22
Legumes	20
Vegetables	14
Dairy products	13
Fruits	6
Refined sugars	5
Fats	0.6

(From Aikawa,[2] with permission.)

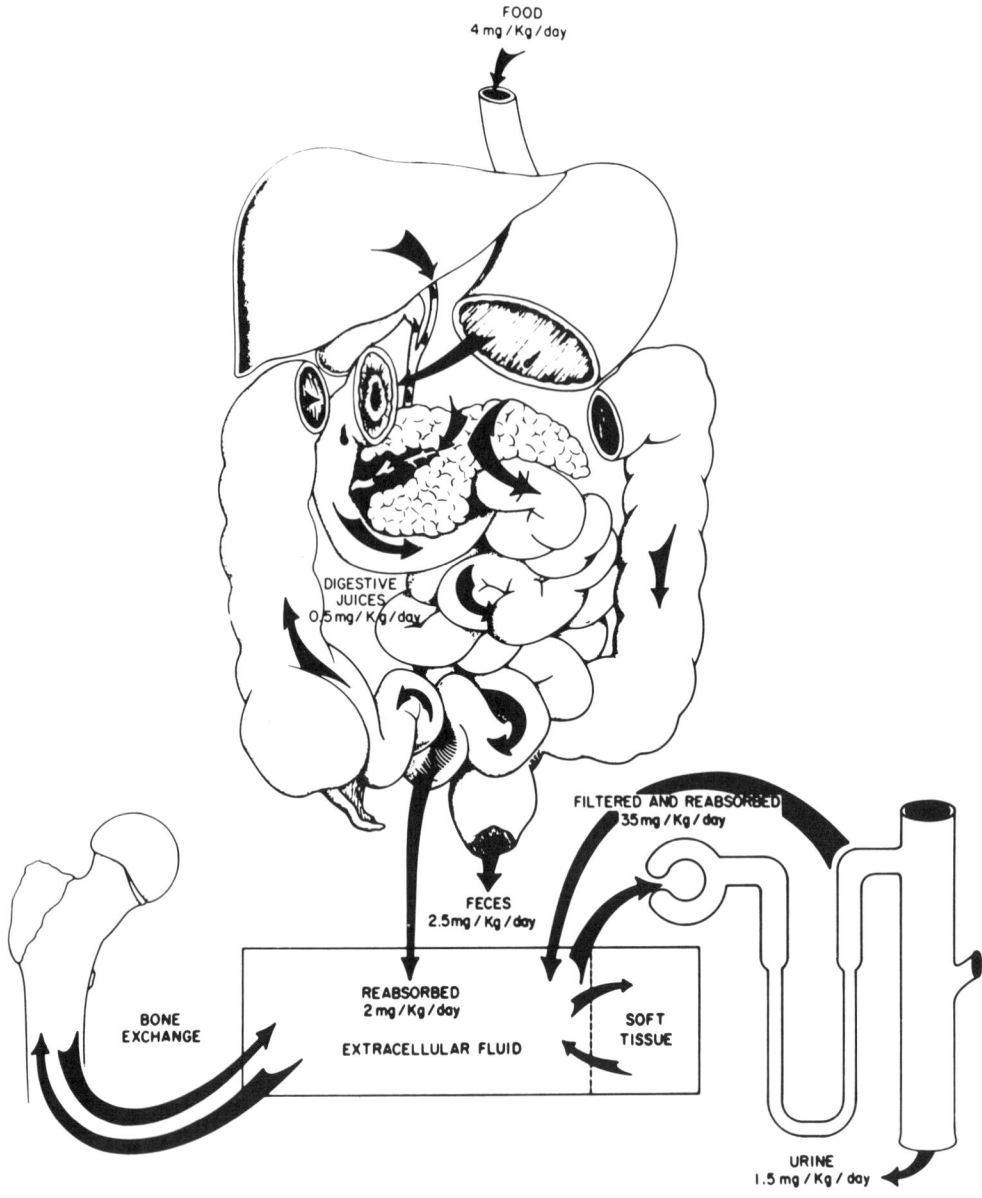

Fig. 7-1. Magnesium metabolism for a normal adult on average magnesium intake and who is in zero magnesium balance. (Adapted from Wilkinson,[17] with permission.)

Increasing the protein intake enhances magnesium absorption.[29] A low-phosphate diet stimulates the absorption of magnesium, but it is not clear whether this is a direct effect or mediated through the increased synthesis of 1,25-(OH)$_2$D.[30]

The absorption of magnesium is enhanced by vitamin D either by a direct effect on magnesium or as a result of calcium and phosphate absorption.[13] Perfusion studies, however, have demonstrated that exogenous 1,25-dihydroxyvitamin D$_3$ (1,25-

(OH)$_2$D$_3$) enhances magnesium absorption in the ileum.[31] The gastrointestinal absorption of magnesium decreases with age[3] and in uremia[23] as a consequence of a deficiency of 1,α,25-(OH)$_2$D$_3$. Parathyroid hormone (PTH) may also enhance magnesium absorption either as a direct effect or by activation of synthesis of 1,α,25-(OH)$_2$D$_3$.[32] The gastrointestinal absorption of magnesium may be stimulated by growth hormone and depressed by aldosterone and calcitonin.[17]

Depletion of magnesium has been induced in healthy human volunteers by limiting the oral intake of this ion. The results have been helpful in elucidating the pathophysiology of clinical magnesium deficiency.[32] As the subjects became depleted of magnesium, hypocalcemia, hypomagnesemia, and hypokalemia developed in spite of an adequate intake of calcium, vitamin D, and potassium.[32] The administration of calcium had only a transitory effect in correcting the hypocalcemia, but with the administration of magnesium there was a prompt return of the plasma magnesium to normal levels, the symptoms of neuromuscular irritability disappeared, and after a delay of days, the plasma calcium normalized.[32]

Attempts at oral loading with magnesium usually result in diarrhea, dehydration, and volume depletion as a consequence of the cathartic effects of this element.

MAGNESIUM AND THE KIDNEYS

Measurements of the magnesium concentration in samples of glomerular fluid obtained by micropuncture of Bowman's space show that 70 to 80 percent of the total plasma magnesium is filtered at the glomerulus.[3,33] The filtered magnesium is in both the ionic form and complexed to different anionic substances such as phosphate, citrate, and oxalate.[3,33] In contrast to sodium, calcium, and potassium, which are reabsorbed isosmotically throughout the length of the proximal tubule and thus maintain a constant intraluminal concentration, the concentration of magnesium increases progressively along the proximal tubule, although to a lesser extent than inulin.[3,33] Therefore, as opposed to sodium, water, and other ions that are reabsorbed extensively in the proximal tubule, this nephron segment has a limited capacity to reabsorb magnesium, and only 20 to 30 percent of the filtered load of magnesium is reabsorbed by the end of the proximal tubule accessible to micropuncture[3,33] (Figs. 7-2A and B). The proximal tubular reabsorption of magnesium is probably an active process.[3,8,33]

The events in the proximal tubule described above and those that take place in the distal convoluted tubules are derived from direct observations obtained by micropuncture of proximal and distal segments of superficial nephrons with short loops of Henle that cannot be micropunctured. Information related to the terminal third of the proximal nephron, the pars recta, and the whole length of Henle's loop has been obtained by exposing the papilla and micropuncturing areas around the bend of Henle's loop. These nephron segments are derived from the deeper juxtamedullary nephrons, with proximal and distal convoluted tubules that are inaccessible to micropuncture. Therefore, when events in these deeper sites are related to the proximal and distal superficial convoluted tubules, it is presumed that there is homogeneity between the short-looped superficial nephrons and the long-looped deeper nephrons. This may not necessarily be the case.

There is no general agreement on the mechanism by which magnesium is transported in the loop of Henle. Studies in the desert jumping mouse *Psammomys* revealed that the fraction of the filtered magnesium remaining at the end of the descending limb was approximately equal to the filtered load of magnesium[34,35] (Fig. 7-2A).

266 • Kidney Electrolyte Disorders

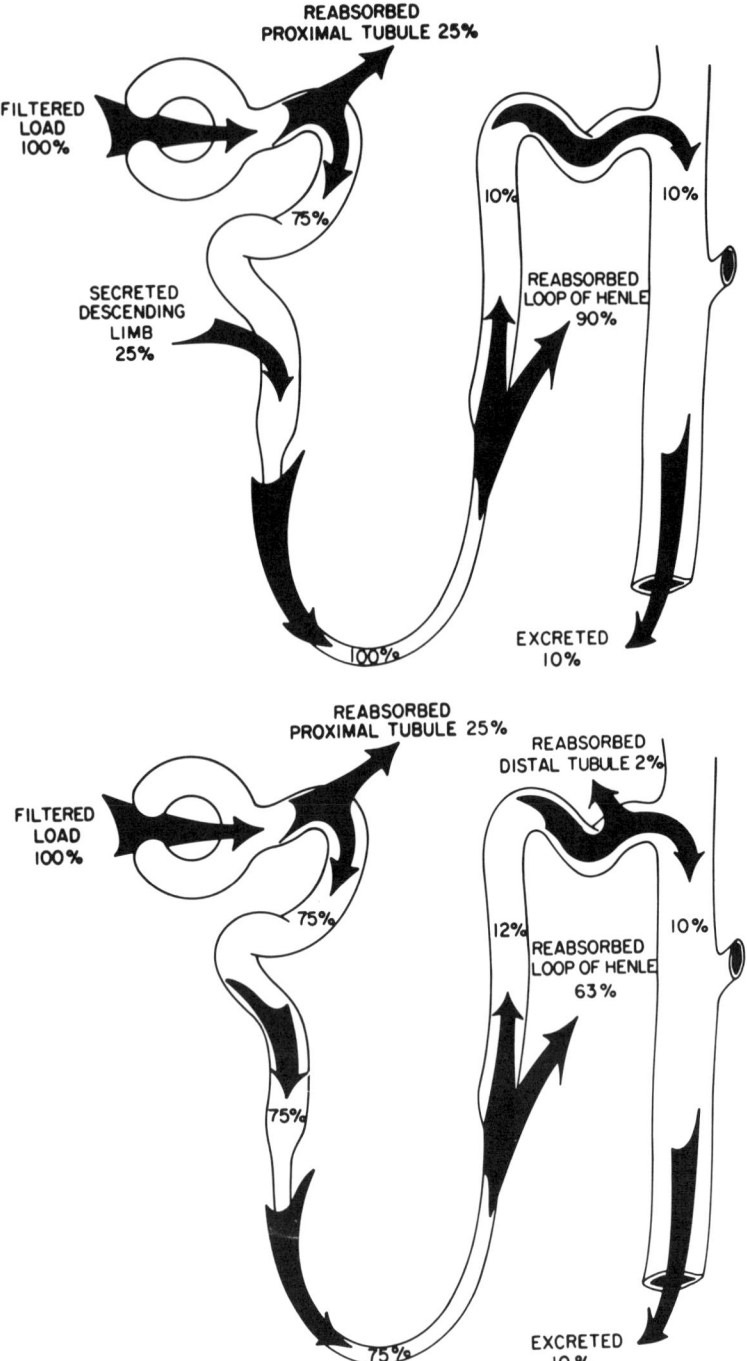

Since there is some reabsorption of magnesium in the proximal tubule, magnesium has to have been added to the lumen of the descending limb of Henle at a point between the end of the proximal tubule and the end of the descending limb.[34,35] This finding was considered to be consistent with the possibility that, as with most other ions, there may be recycling of magnesium in the renal medulla, with the increase in luminal magnesium concentration across the descending limb of Henle's loop being the result of secretion of magnesium in the pars recta of the proximal tubule and/or the descending limb.[34,35] Results reported by others, however, did not support this possibility. In studies in rats, no evidence could be produced to support an input of magnesium to the lumen of the descending limb of the loop of Henle[36,37] (Fig. 7-2B). In microperfusion experiments on superficial loops of Henle with magnesium-free solutions, little magnesium could be detected in the fluid collected from the early distal tubule.[28] In in vitro microperfusion studies of isolated straight segments of superficial and juxtamedullary nephrons, no significant secretion of magnesium could be detected even when the concentration of magnesium in the bath was greatly elevated.[38] Functionally, the isolated segments behaved very much like superficial proximal tubules, demonstrating a limited capacity to reabsorb magnesium.[38] The transport of magnesium in the descending limb of Henle's loop has not been directly investigated.

Studies of magnesium concentration in the earlier portions of the distal tubule showed that the intraluminal concentration of magnesium was significantly lower than the concentration of ultrafiltrable plasma magnesium, and that approximately 60 to 65 percent more of the filtered load of magnesium had been reabsorbed between the end of the proximal convoluted tubule and the beginning of the distal tubule[3,8,33] (Fig. 7-2B). This finding again underlines the differences between the tubular handling of magnesium and that of sodium and calcium, since approximately 30 percent of the filtered load of these two ions is reabsorbed in this segment.[3,8,33] It is presumed that this considerable reabsorptive capacity for magnesium exists in the thick ascending limb.[3,8,33] In vitro studies have provided supportive evidence for this view, and have further demonstrated that this process is voltage dependent.[39] The reabsorption of magnesium on the luminal side of the cells along the ascending limb may be passive, as the consequence of an electrical gradient created by the active reabsorption of chloride[3,8,33] or sodium. On the contraluminal side of the membrane, magnesium may be transported out of the cell in exchange for sodium or by a separate active mechanism[3,8,33] (Fig. 7-3). These proposed mechanisms are hypothetical and need to be explored further[3,8,33] (Fig. 7-3).

The intraluminal concentration of magnesium increases along the more distal portions of the nephron, but to a lesser degree than inulin.[3,8,33] Only 2 to 5 percent of the filtered load of magnesium may be reab-

---

Fig. 7-2. (A) Renal tubular transport of magnesium under normal (control) conditions in *Psammomys*. Only 25 percent of the filtered load of magnesium is reabsorbed proximally. Addition of magnesium into the pars recta and/or the descending limb of Henle's loop increases the content of magnesium at the tip to 100 percent of the filtered load. Most of the load is reabsorbed at the thick ascending portion of Henle's loop, since only 10 percent of the filtered load is delivered to the early portions of the distal convoluted tubules, and most of it is excreted in the urine. (From de Rouffignac et al,[34] with permission.) (B) Renal tubular transport of magnesium under control conditions in the rat. The events along the nephron are similar to those described in (A), except that there is no secretion of magnesium along the descending limb of Henle's loop. (From Brunette et al,[36] with permission.)

268 • Kidney Electrolyte Disorders

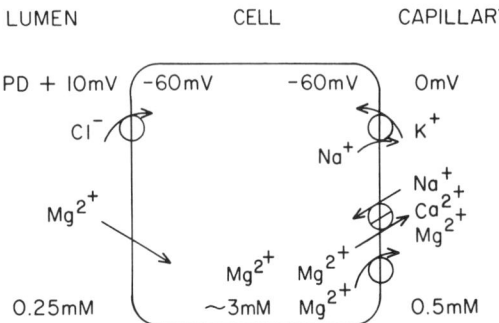

Fig. 7-3. Proposed mechanism of cellular transport of magnesium at the thick ascending portion of Henle's loop. The active transport of chloride at the luminal side creates an electrical gradient, causing magnesium entry into the cell. At the contraluminal side magnesium may be extruded out of the cell in exchange for sodium or by a separate active transport mechanism. The transport of magnesium out of the cell is opposed by a high concentration of calcium or magnesium in the capillary. (From Quamme and Dirks,[8] with permission.)

sorbed in the distal convoluted tubule.[3,8,33] As demonstrated by studies of samples collected by microcatheterization of medullary collecting tubules, there is no reabsorption of magnesium at this site in either intact or thyroparathyroidectomized rats.[40]

Loading and Depletion of Magnesium

During acute intravenous loading with $MgCl_2$ in rats,[37,41] as the filtered load of magnesium increased significantly, the reabsorption of magnesium in the proximal tubule was found either to decrease[37] or remain constant,[41] thus demonstrating again the limited capacity of the proximal tubule to reabsorb magnesium. During loading, there was secretion of magnesium along the pars recta and/or the descending limb, and at the tip of Henle's loop the concentration of magnesium was 130 percent of the filtered load.[34,37] At the earliest portion of the distal convoluted tubule, only 58 percent of the filtered load of magnesium could be recovered, and therefore 72 percent must have been reabsorbed, probably at the thick ascending limb.[37] This portion of the nephron was therefore demonstrated once again to possess a striking ability to reabsorb magnesium. In contrast with some of the results of these studies, secretion of magnesium in the descending portion of Henle's loop during loading with magnesium could not be demonstrated in micropuncture studies of juxtamedullary segments of the terminal descending limb of Henle in the exposed papilla of young rats.[42] These studies demonstrated that the delivery of magnesium to the terminal-descending limb was the same under control conditions in superficial and juxtamedullary nephrons.[42] During loading with magnesium, even when the plasma concentration and urinary excretion of magnesium increased by twofold, the fractional delivery of magnesium to the terminal descending limb did not change.[42] Some studies showed that the amount of magnesium delivered to the early distal tubule was excreted unchanged in the urine,[36] while others elicited a 20 percent secretion in the distal tubule[41] (Fig. 7-4).

A more complete understanding of the mechanism of intratubular transport of magnesium during loading with this element was obtained by microperfusion experiments on Henle's loop.[3,8,33] As the intraluminal concentration of magnesium was increased by microperfusion while the plasma magnesium remained normal, the reabsorptive capacity for magnesium was found to remain constant at 80 percent of the delivered load, with no evidence of saturation of magnesium transport over a wide range of luminal concentrations of magnesium.[3,8,33] When the plasma concentration of magnesium was raised progressively by systemic loading with magnesium, the fractional and absolute reabsorption of magnesium decreased markedly, through an inhibitory effect of hypermagnesemia on magnesium transport at the basolateral membrane.[43]

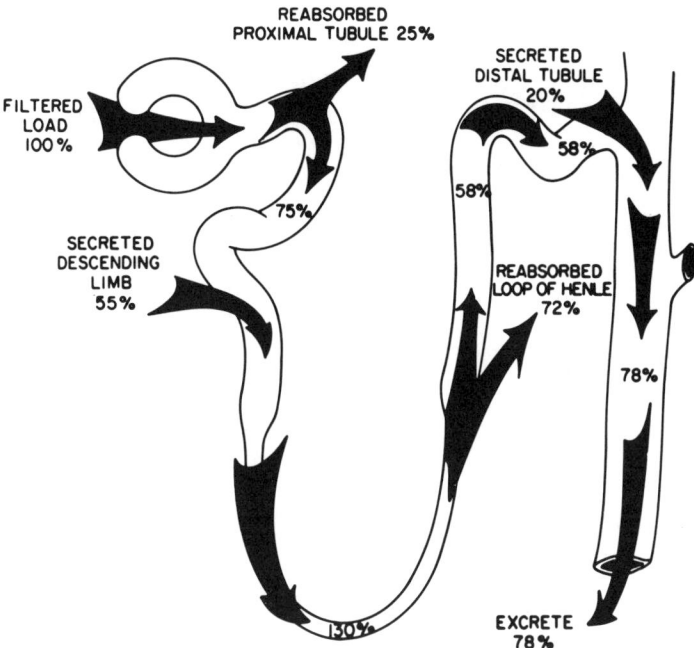

Fig. 7-4. Renal handling of magnesium during magnesium loading in rats. There is little change in the proximal handling of magnesium. Magnesium is secreted along the descending portions of Henle's loop, and the content of magnesium at the bend is 130 percent of the filtered load. Most of this load, however, is reabsorbed at the thick ascending portion of Henle's loop, and only 58 percent of the filtered load is delivered to the distal convoluted tubule. There is secretion of magnesium distally, and 78 percent of the filtered load of magnesium is excreted in the final urine. (From Brunette et al,[37] with permission.)

These results were confirmed by microperfusion studies of isolated segments of the cortical thick ascending limb of the loop of Henle.[39] In these experiments[39] the reabsorption of magnesium was enhanced as the luminal concentration of magnesium was increased, while the bath magnesium was not changed significantly. When the bath magnesium concentration was raised significantly, magnesium reabsorption decreased.[39]

Conflicting results have been reported in studies seeking to demonstrate net secretion of magnesium by maximally stimulating magnesium excretion by loading with this element. Although significant secretion of magnesium was elicited by some investigators under these experimental conditions,[44] these results could not be confirmed by others.[45] In experiments in dogs, a magnesium secretion of small magnitude could be demonstrated during ECF expansion, loading with magnesium, and furosemide administration.[46] Secretion of magnesium has been claimed to contribute to the magnesiuria in phosphate-depleted, magnesium-loaded rats.[47] Magnesium secretion may therefore not be a very important part of the mechanism for the tubular handling of magnesium.

The response of different portions of the nephron to dietary depletion of magnesium has been investigated in adult rats by micropuncture[48] (Fig. 7-5). In magnesium depletion, despite a significant fall in the filtered load, the proximal tubule reabsorbs magnesium at the same fractional levels as in magnesium-replete controls.[48] The loop

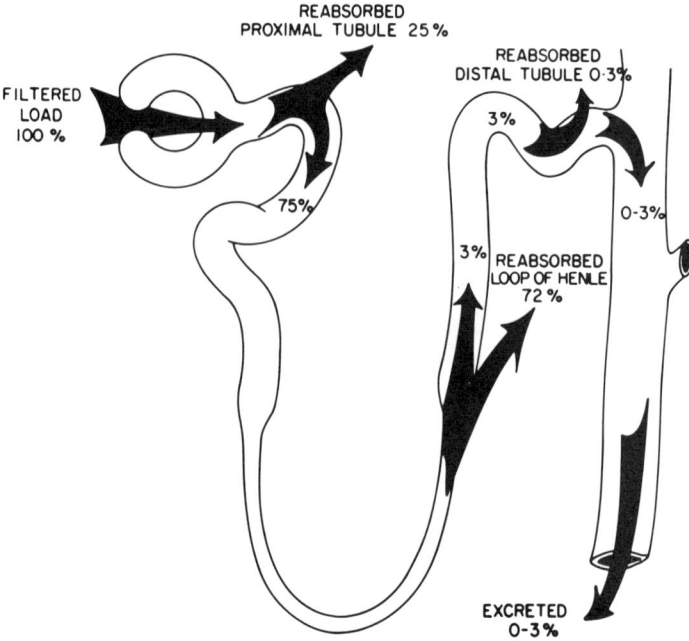

Fig. 7-5. Renal handling of magnesium in magnesium-depleted rats. There are no changes in the transport of magnesium in the proximal tubule. Here again the striking reabsorptive capacity of the thick ascending portion of Henle's loop is demonstrated, since only 3 percent of the filtered load of magnesium is delivered to the distal tubule and excreted in the urine. (From Carney et al,[48] with permission.)

of Henle demonstrated a marked ability to reabsorb magnesium, since only 3 percent of the filtered load was delivered to the early distal convoluted tubule and excreted in the urine.[48] The absolute amount of magnesium reabsorbed in the loop of Henle of magnesium depleted rats, however, was less than in pair-fed controls, and their apparently impaired ability to reabsorb magnesium persisted when the magnesium-depleted rats were loaded with magnesium.[48] It has been proposed that in magnesium-depleted rats there may be a defect or at least a resetting of the magnesium reabsorptive mechanism, and this apparent anomaly exists in the thick ascending limb.[48] The studies in magnesium depleted rats were extended by determining magnesium reabsorption in juxtaglomerular nephrons of young rats with the same degree of magnesium depletion.[49] Under control conditions and during acute loading with magnesium, young magnesium-depleted rats demonstrated that magnesium reabsorption was tightly coupled to the filtered load of magnesium in segments upstream of the juxtaglomerular terminal descending limb and in the whole kidney.[49] A defect in magnesium reabsorption was not evident in the young magnesium-depleted rats.[49] The renal handling of magnesium under different experimental conditions is summarized in Figure 7-6.

Relationship Between the Renal Tubular Transport of Magnesium and Other Ions

The administration of vasodilators causes a significant increase in the urinary excretion of magnesium in spite of a constant

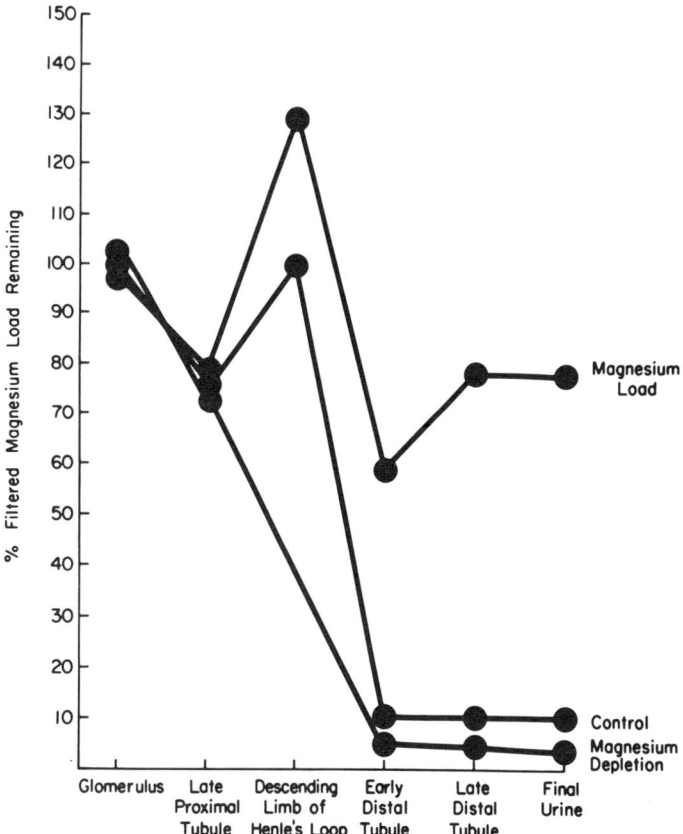

Fig. 7-6. Summary of the renal handling of magnesium under control conditions, acute loading with magnesium, and depletion of magnesium.

filtered load, probably by altering the Starling forces at the peritubular capillary.[50] Expansion of the ECF volume caused a proportional reduction in sodium, calcium, phosphate, and magnesium reabsorption in the proximal tubule.[51,52] There was a relative increase in reabsorption of the load delivered in Henle's loop.[51,52] In these studies there was good correlation between the handling of calcium and sodium in the proximal tubule and that of calcium and magnesium in the thick ascending limb of Henle's loop.[52] Elevations in the intraluminal concentration of magnesium cause a decrease in water permeability and a decrease in sodium reabsorption in the proximal and distal tubules.[53–55]

The urinary excretion of calcium and magnesium increases during loading with either of these two ions,[56] and this effect is still evident even when loading with calcium or magnesium is done during a reduction in the GFR.[57,58] These findings[56–58] suggest that calcium and magnesium compete for a common reabsorptive mechanism in the kidneys. During loading with calcium chloride, calcium reabsorption is depressed proximally, and rises in the loop of Henle but remains unchanged in the distal portions of the nephron as the load delivered from the proximal tubule increases.[59] The handling of magnesium in the proximal tubule is not affected by loading with calcium, but reabsorption is decreased in the loop, thus suggesting a competition for reabsorption between calcium and magnesium at the latter site. Since the load delivered to the distal nephron is not reabsorbed, calcium loading results in a significant magnesiuria.[59] Likewise, systemic loading with magnesium does not affect the proximal handling of calcium but decreases the reabsorption of calcium in Henle's loop.[41] Loading with calcium resulted in a greater increase in the fractional excretion of magnesium than of calcium, while hypermagnesemia caused a more significant magnesiuria than calciuria.[3] These studies were extended by determining the effects of systemic hypercalcemia and hypermagnesemia on the fluid microperfused through Henle's loop.[41] Hypercalcemia reduced the reabsorption of calcium and magnesium in the loop.[60] Hypermagnesemia reduced calcium reabsorption in the loop but had a much less significant effect on sodium reabsorption.[43] Elevations in luminal calcium concentration had little effect on magnesium reabsorption, and a high luminal magnesium concentration did not significantly interfere with calcium reabsorption.[3] These results therefore support the possibility of a competitive reabsorptive mechanism for calcium and magnesium located at the basolateral membrane of the thick ascending portion of Henle's loop.[3]

Rats depleted of phosphate develop a significant calciuria and magnesiuria, and although their gastrointestinal absorption of magnesium increases, their plasma magnesium decreases and the balance of magnesium becomes negative.[61] Soft-tissue concentrations of magnesium were not affected by phosphate depletion, but the bone magnesium content decreased.[61] Thus, phosphate depletion in the rat causes loss of magnesium from bone and a renal leakage of magnesium.[61] In micropuncture studies performed in dogs in order to localize the sites of the tubular defects caused by phosphate depletion, the calciuresis was related to an impairment in calcium reabsorption at a site between the end of the proximal convoluted tubule and the beginning of the distal tubule.[62] The renal handling of magnesium was found to be normal in phosphate-depleted dogs.[62] The administration of phosphate plus parathyroid hormone corrected the defect in calcium reabsorption and enhanced the reabsorption of magnesium in Henle's loop and the distal nephron.[62]

The intratubular effect of sulfate on the transport of electrolytes was studied by microperfusion.[3] Sulfate was reabsorbed almost exclusively in the proximal tubule, and had a modest effect on sodium handling in the nephron[63]; however, it significantly inhibited calcium and magnesium reabsorption in the proximal tubule, Henle's loop, and the distal tubule.[63]

The administration of ethanol, galactose, and glucose causes significant increases in the urinary excretion of calcium and magnesium, without an effect on the GFR.[64] These changes may not be related, as was originally believed, to complexing of these substances to poorly reabsorbable anions or to an increase in the filtered load.[64] Rather, indirect evidence suggests that as a result of an enhancement in sodium reabsorption caused by glucose in the proximal tubule, a delay in the development of a positive potential difference inhibits calcium and magnesium reabsorption.[64]

Similarities in the metabolism of potassium and magnesium have led some investigators to seek the possibility of a relationship between these two ions. Both potassium and magnesium have a high intracellular concentration,[1,65] and both are excreted in the urine of the aglomerular fish.[66] But while the kidneys handle magnesium by a process of filtration and reabsorption, mainly at the thick ascending limb,[8,33] potassium, after filtration, is extensively reabsorbed proximally and secreted in the distal tubules.[67]

Another approach taken to further investigate a possible relationship between potassium and magnesium was that of determining the metabolic response of potassium and magnesium balance to dietary loading or depletion of potassium. In rats fed a high potassium diet for several days (potassium adaptation), the plasma concentration of magnesium declined as the soft-tissue content of potassium and magnesium increased, while the urinary excretion of magnesium did not change.[68] The fecal excretion of magnesium increased in potassium-loaded rats, and the metabolic balance of magnesium showed a net decrease.[68] Thus, the hypomagnesemia in potassium-loaded rats can be related mainly to deposition of magnesium, along with potassium, into tissues, and to increased losses of magnesium in feces.[68]

The renal response to loading with potassium or magnesium was evaluated in control and potassium-adapted rats. In control rats, acute intravenous loading with potassium did not significantly affect the renal excretion of magnesium, and the urinary excretion of potassium did not change after acute intravenous loading with magnesium.[69] When these experiments were repeated in potassium-adapted rats, the urinary excretion of potassium increased in approximately the same proportion upon loading with either potassium or magnesium.[69] Similar results, however, were elicited when potassium-adapted rats were loaded acutely with calcium or hypertonic mannitol.[69] The kaliuresis of magnesium loading may therefore be a nonspecific response of potassium-adapted rats to the enhanced delivery of fluid to the distal sites of potassium secretion, as a consequence of a more proximal rejection of fluid reabsorption due to the volume expansion caused by the loading experiments.[69]

Rats fed a diet deficient in potassium, on the contrary, became hypermagnesemic as a result of transfer of magnesium from tissues into the ECF.[70] As the concentration of magnesium in muscle declined significantly in these potassium-depleted rats, they developed an early magnesiuria, probably as a consequence of an increase in filtered load.[70] Because the secretion of aldosterone is depressed in potassium depletion,[71] and since hypermagnesemia is a finding in adrenal insufficiency,[72] the effects of an exogenously administered mineralocorticoid on the hypermagnesemia of potassium depletion were investigated.[73] When desoxycorticosterone acetate (DOCA) was administered daily to rats during feeding with a diet deficient in potassium there was a partial correction of the elevated plasma magnesium concentration despite a suppression of the magnesiuria. This could be explained by the hemodilutionary effect of plasma expansion, since potassium-depleted DOCA-treated rats retained sodium and water and experienced a significant expansion in plasma volume.[73]

The changes in the metabolism of potassium and magnesium in dietary magnesium depletion have attracted the interest of investigators for many years. The commonly used rat model develops hypomagnesemia and hyperparathyroidism, with hypercalcemia and phosphaturia.[74,75] Despite the maintenance of a normal intake of potassium and a normokalemic state, there is a kaliuresis and depletion of total body potassium. The concentration of potassium and magnesium in muscle is also reduced.[74,75] These events have been explained by proposing that in a state of magnesium deficiency, there is an alteration in cellular permeability that allows a leakage of potassium out of the cell and into the ECF, with the potassium then being excreted in the urine.[74,75] The loss of potassium from the cell may be also related to an abnormality in the cellular transport mechanism caused by a lack of activation of adenosine triphosphatase (ATPase) in the absence of magnesium.[1,74,75] Hyperaldosteronism occurs in magnesium depletion, and may also contribute to the enhanced losses of potassium in the urine.[76] In micropuncture studies, it was found that the renal handling of potassium in magnesium-depleted rats does not differ from that in controls.[77] Loading with magnesium caused a more significant kaliuresis in control than in magnesium-depleted rats.[77] Several other functional and pathologic alterations have been described in experimentally induced magnesium depletion in the rat. The animals become azotemic and develop pathologic changes in the kidneys characterized by microlith formations in the thin limb of Henle's loop, which grow in size by aggregation and fill and distend the lumen of the tubules. Finally, metastatic calcification and calcinosis are observed in the kidneys.[78]

The results of these studies in potassium-adapted rats[69] and in potassium-[70] or magnesium-[74–76] depleted rats seem to indicate that there is a relationship between potassium and magnesium metabolism, primarily at the tissue level, and that the renal response is only secondary to this extrarenal relationship.

Diuretics

Cardiac glycosides, when infused directly into a renal artery, significantly increase the urinary excretion of calcium and magnesium, and to a lesser extent, of sodium.[79] Inhibitors of carbonic anhydrase decrease the reabsorption of magnesium and other ions in the proximal tubule, but do not affect the handling of magnesium in Henle's loop. They therefore cause only a minimal increase in the urinary excretion of magnesium.[33] Mercurial diuretics significantly increase the urinary excretion of magnesium.[80] Mannitol and urea increase the urinary excretion of magnesium by reducing its tubular reabsorption at the loop of Henle.[81] Hyperglycemia also produces a magnesiuria.[3]

The acute and chronic administration of thiazide diuretics has either no effect on urinary excretion of magnesium or produces only a mild magnesiuria.[3,82–84] The effects of thiazide diuretics on the urinary excretion of magnesium may be related to the inhibition of salt and water reabsorption in the more proximal portions of the nephron, and subsequent increased delivery of fluid to the loop of Henle.[3] Micropuncture studies in the distal tubule of the hamster showed that although thiazide diuretics inhibited sodium reabsorption and enhanced calcium reabsorption, there was no effect on magnesium transport.[85] During the chronic administration of thiazide diuretics, a magnesiuria may develop secondary to hypercalcemia and inhibition of parathyroid hormone (PTH) secretion.[86]

The urinary excretion of magnesium has been reported to fall after the administration of spironolactone to normal human subjects,[87] and after the administration of amiloride to subjects with congestive heart failure.[88] The acute administration of amiloride, a potassium-sparing diuretic, to normal human volunteers produced no effect on the urinary excretion of magnesium.[86] In the same studies, hydrochlorothiazide elicited a significant magnesiuria,[86] but when amiloride was added to hydrochlorothiazide there was a blunting of the magnesiuria.[86] In chronic-dosage studies, amiloride reduced the urinary excretion of magnesium, but the change was not significant.[86] The administration of triamterene to sodium-loaded conscious rats produced a significant decrease in the urinary excretion of magnesium.[89] Amiloride also reduced the urinary excretion of magnesium, and blunted the magnesiuria produced by furosemide.[89]

Since the main site of action of the loop diuretics is in the thick ascending limb, which is the main area within the nephron where magnesium is reabsorbed, it is not surprising that ethacrynic acid and furosemide are the most potent magnesiuric agents.[90] When furosemide was microperfused into the loop of Henle in rats, there was a greater inhibition of the reabsorption of magnesium and calcium than of chloride and sodium.[91] The reabsorption of calcium and magnesium was enhanced by PTH even when furosemide was introduced into the lumen of Henle's loop by microperfusion.[91] The same effects were evident in the distal nephron under these experimental conditions.[91] Intraluminal ethacrynic acid had no effect on the transport of electrolytes in the rat.[91]

The prolonged administration of diuretics in clinical medicine has been shown to cause depletion of magnesium.[92]

Magnesium and Acid-Base Metabolism

Changes in the tubular handling of magnesium have been studied by clearance measurements and micropuncture in the dog[93] and in rats.[94] In the dog, acute metabolic alkalosis increased while chronic metabolic acidosis decreased the reabsorption of magnesium.[93] In vitro microperfusion studies in the isolated straight portion of the superficial proximal tubule failed to demonstrate any effect of acid-base changes on magnesium transfer.[95] A correlation between the reabsorption of magnesium in the distal tubule and the intratubular concentration of bicarbonate was demonstrated in these experiments in dogs.[93] It is not clear whether this effect is the result of a direct action of bicarbonate on magnesium transport or is due to alterations in the ionic concentration of magnesium at the antiluminal site.[93] The administration of bicarbonate to thyroparathyroidectomized dogs made acidotic with ammonium chloride caused an enhanced reabsorption of calcium and magnesium in the kidneys.[96]

Acute metabolic or respiratory acidosis had no significant effect on the renal tubular transport of magnesium in rats, but acute metabolic alkalosis enhanced magnesium reabsorption, probably in the pars recta, in studies of juxtamedullary nephrons.[96]

The magnesiuria that occurs at the initiation of fasting is related to metabolic acidosis.[99]

HORMONES AND MAGNESIUM METABOLISM

Parathyroid Hormone

The important role of PTH on calcium homeostasis is well established. Given the close relationship between the tubular transport of calcium and magnesium, it is important to determine some functional aspects of the action of PTH in magnesium metabolism.

The secretion of PTH increased significantly when the parathyroid gland of a goat was perfused directly with solutions having a low concentration of magnesium[98] (Fig. 7-7). This finding is consistent with the enhanced PTH activity that has been noted in magnesium-depleted rats.[74] Hypermagnesemia, on the contrary, has been shown to suppress the synthesis and/or release of the hormone from the parathyroid glands,[99] and to inhibit its biologic activity at the target organs.[100]

In vitro studies of cells cultured from the parathyroid glands have demonstrated a striking relationship between the total concentration of calcium plus magnesium in the medium and the release of PTH.[101] When the concentration of the two ions is altered in such a way that the total concentration remains unchanged, PTH is released at a constant rate except when the concentration of magnesium is very low.[101] At this point, even when the concentration of calcium in the medium is raised proportionately to maintain a constant total concentration of both ions, the secretion of PTH from the cultured cells diminishes significantly[101] (Fig. 7-8). In vivo studies in magnesium depleted subjects indicated that the release, but not the synthesis, of PTH was impaired in magnesium deficiency.[102]

276 • Kidney Electrolyte Disorders

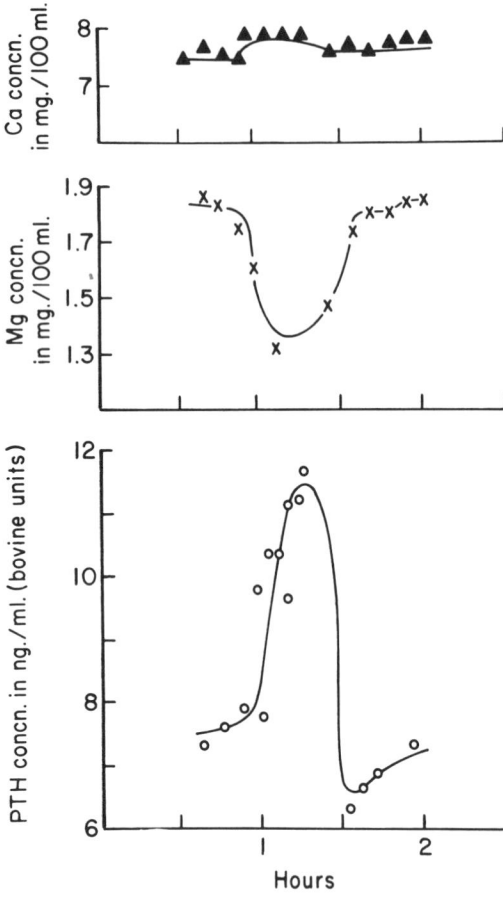

Fig. 7-7. A significant increase in parathyroid hormone secretion is elicited in response to direct perfusion of a parathyroid gland with solutions having a low concentration of magnesium. (From Buckle et al,[98] with permission.)

In vitro studies have also demonstrated that when the concentration of magnesium in a medium containing bone cells is very low, there is an impaired release of calcium from bone in the presence of PTH.[103] These studies indicate that magnesium is necessary for the release of PTH and its action at target organs. Additionally, in vitro studies have indicated that magnesium may promote PTH secretion by enhancing the activation of adenylate cyclase or by competing with calcium for binding at a distinct regulatory system on the enzyme.[104]

It has been difficult to separate the direct effects of PTH on magnesium metabolism from those mediated through the hypercalcemia that results from the release of calcium from target organs.[3] Magnesiuria has been reported as a consequence of the administration of PTH, but this effect may have been secondary to hypercalcemia.[105] In another study, a decrease in the urinary excretion of calcium and magnesium followed PTH administration, while the plasma concentration of calcium remained within normal limits.[3] In yet another study, the magnesiuria and calciuresis provoked by the infusion of magnesium decreased as a result of the concomitant administration of PTH.[106] These studies indicate that an enhancing effect of PTH on magnesium reabsorption can be elicited, but that the results can be obscured by hypercalcemia.

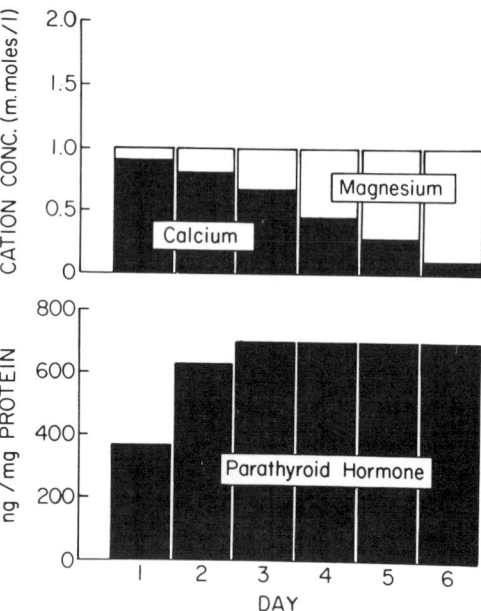

Fig. 7-8 When parathyroid glands were incubated in a medium in which the concentration of calcium plus magnesium was varied in such a way that the total concentration of both ions was kept constant, there was a constant release of parathyroid hormone except at very low concentrations of magnesium (Day 1). (From Targovnik et al,[101] with permission.)

Clearance studies in the golden hamster, an animal species very sensitive to the action of PTH, demonstrated that parathyroidectomy resulted in the urinary excretion of 20 percent of the filtered load of magnesium.[107] Infusions of cyclic adenosine monophosphate (cAMP) or dibutyril produced changes in urinary magnesium handling similar to those elicited by PTH administration.[107] Micropuncture studies in the golden hamster demonstrated an enhancing action of PTH on magnesium reabsorption at a site proximal to the distal tubule.[108] Microperfusion studies of isolated segments of the thick ascending portion of the loop of Henle of rabbits demonstrated that this nephron segment is very sensitive to the enhancing action of PTH on magnesium reabsorption.[109]

It has been reported that PTH stimulates the absorption of magnesium in the gut of thyroparathyroidectomized rats.[40]

Calcitonin

The infusion of magnesium to normal subjects caused a significant increase in plasma levels of immunoreactive calcitonin.[110] The hypermagnesemia was accompanied by a decrease in total and ionized plasma calcium that was related to an increase in the urinary excretion of calcium and suppression of PTH function.[110] In patients with medullary carcinoma of the thyroid, however, the infusion of magnesium produced a striking fall in plasma levels of circulating calcitonin.[111]

The administration of human calcitonin to hormone-deprived rats caused an increase in the GFR and filtered load of magnesium, and a decrease in the urinary excretion of calcium and magnesium.[112] In these studies, calcitonin also caused a fall in the serum calcium concentration,[112] but the sparing effects of calcium and magnesium remained unaltered when hypocalcemia was prevented by the infusion of calcium.[112] Micropuncture experiments in Brattleboro rats were consistent with an enhancing effect of human calcitonin on the reabsorption of magnesium and other ions in the loop of Henle.[113]

Vitamin D and Other Hormones

In man, vitamin D increases the gastrointestinal absorption of calcium and magnesium.[114,115] In studies in rachitic rats, vitamin D was found to enhance the absorption of magnesium from the gut and to cause a magnesiuria, with no changes in the plasma concentration or metabolic balance of magnesium.[116]

Studies in the golden hamster showed that 1,25-(OH)$_2$D$_3$ caused an inhibition of calcium and magnesium reabsorption in the kidneys.[117] Micropuncture studies have demonstrated an enhancing effect of antidiuretic hormone (ADH) on magnesium reabsorption in the loop of Henle of Brattleboro rats.[118] Glucagon has also been shown to enhance the reabsorption of magnesium in the thick ascending portion of Henle's loop in Brattleboro rats.[119] The acute administration of growth hormone causes a magnesiuria,[120] but patients with acromegaly have shown little alteration in their magnesium metabolism.[120] The infusion of atrial natriuretic peptide to normal human volunteers produced an increase in GFR with no change or a decrease in total renal blood flow and an increase in the fractional excretion of magnesium and other ions that could not be explained solely by the increase in filtered load.[12] Other hemodynamic humoral mechanisms or a direct tubular effect may also mediate the magnesiuric action of atrial natriuretic hormone.[121] The acute administration of glucocorticoids to anesthetized dogs caused inconsistent changes in the urinary excretion of magnesium.[122] The magnesiuria observed in Cushing's disease may be related to losses of magnesium from bone.[123] An optimal magnesium concentration is needed for a normal basal and thyroidally stimulated adenyl cyclase activity.[124] Therefore, the synthesis of thyroidal hormones may be impaired in magnesium insufficiency.[124]

Pancreatic and Gastrointestinal Hormones

Insulin administration to nondiabetic subjects stimulates the transfer of magnesium from the extracellular space into tissues, thus conserving magnesium and causing a fall in the plasma concentration of this element.[124,125] Hypomagnesemia enhances[126] while hypermagnesemia decreases[127] the secretion of insulin. The gastrointestinal absorption of calcium, and to a lesser degree of magnesium, is decreased in experimentally induced diabetes mellitus in the rat.[128,129]

The intraduodenal infusion of magnesium significantly stimulates the release of cholecystokinin, pancreatic peptide, and gastrin.[130] The intravenous infusion of magnesium increased the release of cholecystokinin but had no effect on pancreatic peptide or gastrin.[130] Gastrin increased the fecal excretion of calcium, had no effect on fecal magnesium, and caused a small decrease in the urinary excretion of magnesium.[131]

The in vitro release of glucagon from a culture of pancreatic cells is stimulated by the absence of magnesium and suppressed by high concentrations of magnesium.[126] Glucagon and secretin have been shown to induce an increase in the urinary excretion of calcium and magnesium.[132]

Sex Hormones

In vitro studies have shown that the release of gonadotropins from cells of the pituitary gland can be inhibited by a high concentration of magnesium in the medium,[124] and that high and low magnesium levels impair the synthesis of protein by ovarian cells in response to follicle stimulating hormone.[124] The in vitro perfusion of rabbit ovaries with a medium free of calcium and magnesium resulted in rapid rupture of the follicle of an immature ovum.[133]

The changes in magnesium and zinc during the menstrual cycle were evaluated in normally menstruating women.[134] The plasma concentration of magnesium was highest during menses and then declined, reaching its lowest levels during ovulation and then rising during the luteal phase.[134] The content of magnesium in mononuclear cells and red cells did not change significantly as a function of the menstrual cycle.[134]

The concentration of magnesium was found to be low in the semen in infertile subjects.[135] In pregnancy and lactation, magnesium requirements are greatly increased.[16,136] The plasma concentration of magnesium has a tendency to fall during the first half and during the last month of pregnancy.[16,134,135] The hypomagnesemia seen in some stages of pregnancy has been related to hemodilution and transfer of magnesium to the fetus.[124] Others have cited the increase in GFR during pregnancy as the most important factor in the low total and ultrafiltrable plasma magnesium during this time.[137] The plasma concentration of magnesium has been also found to fall in the postpartum period, as a consequence of transfer of magnesium to the child.[124] Magnesium supplementation during pregnancy has been reported to result in fewer hospitalizations, a reduction in preterm delivery, and less frequent referral of the newborn to the neonatal intensive care unit.[138]

The induction of magnesium deficiency has been reported to have embryotoxic effects in pregnant rats.[139]

Women taking contraceptive agents have been shown to have significantly lower plasma magnesium concentrations than normally ovulating women.[124,140–142] Since in these studies the urinary excretion of magnesium was low, it has been proposed that estrogens may decrease plasma magnesium by inhibiting bone resorption or by causing deposition of magnesium into soft tissue.[124,140] A low plasma magnesium concentration might contribute to the increased incidence of thromboembolic disease in women taking contraceptive agents.[143] Other studies, however, have failed to demonstrate any effect of anovulatory agents on plasma magnesium.[124,140] These apparent discrepancies could be explained by the different preparations that were used and the dose administered.[124,140] Progestational agents, on the contrary, have been reported to cause an increase in plasma magnesium.[144]

Because of increased urinary losses, insulin-dependent, diabetic pregnant women are at risk of developing magnesium deficiency.[145] An adverse fetal outcome has been related more frequently to a magnesium deficiency in such women.[145] Hypomagnesemia is a frequent finding in eclampsia, and the intravenous administration of magnesium has been used for many years for the control of eclampsia and pre-eclampsia.[16] The improvement observed after magnesium administration in eclampsia may indicate the correction of a previous magnesium deficiency.[16]

Some studies have indicated that a significant number of women with premenstrual syndrome (PMS) may have subclinical hypothyroidism,[146] and some investigators have also found significantly low levels of red cell magnesium in this syndrome.[147] Many other alterations in hormonal and nonhormonal conditions have been related to PMS,[148] and improvement in symptoms has been detected in women with PMS treated with a preparation having a high content of magnesium, vitamin B$_6$, and other essential nutrients.[149]

Ovariectomy may cause a decrease in plasma magnesium, but testicular castration was shown to have no effect on plasma magnesium.[150]

Renin-Angiotensin-Aldosterone System

The release of renin is stimulated by hypermagnesemia and depressed by a low plasma concentration of magnesium, probably by a direct effect of magnesium on the juxtaglomerular cells.[151] In experimental magnesium depletion there is hypertension and a state of secondary hyperaldosteronism characterized by an increase in granulation of the cells of the juxtaglomerular apparatus and in the width of the zona glomerulosa of the adrenal glands.[152,153] Measurements of hormone levels in samples taken from the adrenal vein have shown an elevated aldosterone concentration in magnesium-depleted rats.[154] When autotransplanted adrenal glands were perfused with solutions having high concentrations of magnesium, the secretion of aldosterone did not change.[155]

The acute administration of mineralocorticoids causes retention of sodium and water, but does not affect the urinary excretion of calcium or magnesium.[156] When mineralocorticoids are administered chronically, however, the urinary excretion of calcium and magnesium rises with the "escape" from the retaining effects of these hormones on sodium.[157] The hypomagnesemia observed experimentally after the chronic administration of mineralocorticoids has been related to the deposition of magnesium into tissue,[158] but most likely is due to external losses.[159]

The effects of aldosterone on magnesium metabolism have also been evaluated by determining the results of endogenous stimulation of aldosterone secretion. Although sodium depletion produced a significant elevation in plasma aldosterone, it yielded no consistent effect on urinary magnesium.[160] A twentyfold increase in plasma aldosterone was elicited in rats fed a diet deficient in sodium, but although the urinary excretion of sodium and magnesium decreased, the plasma magnesium concentration did not change, and the plasma volume was normal.[161] It therefore seems that the magnesiuric effects of aldosterone may be secondary to some primary action of the hormone, such as sodium retention and volume expansion.[157,159–161]

Adrenal Medulla

The secretion of catecholamines is inhibited when the adrenal glands are perfused with solutions having a high concentration of magnesium.[150] Calcium, on the contrary, stimulates the release of catecholamines from the adrenal medulla.[150] The levels of epinephrine in the medullary portion of the adrenal glands have been shown to be low in magnesium deficiency, probably as a result of the release of epinephrine into the circulation.[150] The efflux of noradrenalin increased when peripheral nerves were stimulated in the presence of calcium, but magenesium lacked an effect.[162] The intraperitoneal administration of adrenalin caused hypermagnesemia,[150] whereas the intravenous infusion of adrenalin or the beta-2 agonist salbutamol to human volunteers produced a significant hypomagnesemia.[163] These results were interpreted as supporting the possibility that magnesium fluxes between intracellular and extracellular compartments may be controlled by beta-adrenergic receptors.[163] Thus, the hypomagnesemia that has been observed under conditions of clinical or surgical stress (major surgery, myocardial infarction, insulin-induced hypoglycemia, etc.) may be mediated through increased levels of circulating catecholamines.[163]

NEUROMUSCULAR FUNCTION

The concentration of magnesium in the cerebrospinal fluid (CSF) is higher than in plasma, probably because of secretion of magnesium by the choroidal plexus.[164] There is only a slight increase in the CSF magnesium concentration when the plasma concentration of magnesium increases significantly, and the CSF magnesium concentration decreases in magnesium depletion.[164] In the central nervous system magnesium exerts a stabilizing effect on the synaptic membrane, thus decreasing excitability.[165] At the neuromuscular junction, magnesium competes with calcium and displaces it from its membrane binding sites, decreases the release of acetylcholine, and depresses the excitability of the muscle membrane.[165] In the autonomic nervous system magnesium inhibits acetylcholine release.[165] Intracellular magnesium has an important function, participating in muscular contraction and relaxation.[165]

CARDIOVASCULAR SYSTEM

As an activator of the Na-K-ATPase pump, magnesium plays an important role in regulating the transport of sodium and potassium across cell membranes, including those of cardiac and vascular smooth muscle.[166] The loss of magnesium from tissues may inhibit the activities of Na-K-ATPase and Ca-ATPase, produce alterations in myocardial membrane ion permeability resulting in losses of potassium and magnesium and a gain in calcium and sodium, exacerbate myocardial injury, reduce myocardial contractility, and cause cardiac failure, arrhythmias, and sudden death.[166] The extracellular concentration of ionized magnesium is also important in the control of arterial tone and blood pressure and in the regulation of magnesium-calcium exchange sites.[166] A reduction in the extracellular concentration of magnesium, by allowing excessive entry of calcium and sodium and loss of potassium and magnesium from the arterial wall, can result in sustained vasoconstriction and hypertension. Some type of hypertension may have, as an underlying mechanism, similar alterations in the metabolism of electrolytes.[167,168] Experimentally, an increase in resistance was detected when arteries were perfused with solutions with low magnesium-potassium ratios in relation to calcium.[167,168] Clinically, the replacement of lost gastrointestinal fluids with magnesium-free solutions has resulted in magnesium depletion and hypertension.[168]

Magnesium seems to also play a role in the development of atherosclerosis. It has been noted that there is an inverse relationship between plasma cholesterol and magnesium, with higher plasma magnesium levels corresponding to lower levels of cholesterol.[169] Rabbits fed a low magnesium diet developed hypercholesterolemia and atherosclerosis.[170] The provision of a high intake of magnesium to rabbits fed a high cholesterol diet attenuated the elevation in plasma cholesterol and the atherosclerosis.[170]

HEMATOPOIETIC SYSTEM

Experimental studies indicate that magnesium is necessary for the optimal proliferation and maturation of neutrophils in the bone marrow and for platelet adhesion and aggregation and white cell motion, chemotaxis, and phagocytosis.[171] In experimentally induced magnesium deficiency there is increased myelopoiesis, hyperplasia of lymphopoietic tissues, and leukocytosis with predominant neutrophilia and eosinophilia.[171] The dermatitis seen in severe magnesium deficiency in rats (to a degree incompatible with survival for more than 3 to 6 weeks) may be mediated through degranulation of mast cells and liberation of histamine.[171] Rats with less severe magnesium deficiency develop lymphocytosis, then lymphomas, first in the thymus and then disseminating into retroperitoneal lymph nodes and intravascularly into the spleen, liver, and bone marrow.[171]

The in vitro transformation of lymphocytes depends on the presence of cations,[171] and there is a retardation of the ability to synthesize antibodies in experimental magnesium deficiency.[171] Magnesium participates in the activation of complement through the classical and alternative pathways, as well as in the bactericidal activity of serum.[171]

In experimentally induced magnesium deficiency in animals, there develops a hemolytic anemia characterized by a shortened half-life of erythrocytes and by hemolysis, reticulocytosis, spherocytosis, microcytosis, and by a decreased osmotic fragility of red cells, and erythroid hyperplasia of the bone marrow.[10] Some of these changes may result from a defective activation of ATPase resulting in impaired production of the energy needed for transport functions at the cell membrane.[10] It may also be related to structural alterations in the erythrocyte membrane.[10]

In vitro studies have demonstrated that an increased magnesium concentration inhibits platelet aggregation and release.[10]

The relevance of the observations noted above to clinical magnesium deficiency in humans remains to be established.[10,143]

CLINICAL ASPECTS OF MAGNESIUM METABOLISM

Magnesium Depletion and Hypomagnesemia

The clinical conditions more frequently associated with magnesium deficiency are shown in Table 7-4.

Gastrointestinal Disorders

It has been claimed that the standard American diet,[16] and the dietary intake in European and other American countries[172] provide suboptimal amounts of magnesium. Some factors that have been implicated in

Table 7-4. Causes of Magnesium Deficiency

Nutritional
    Prolonged parenteral fluid administration
    Total parenteral nutrition without magnesium
    Starvation with metabolic acidosis
    Protein-calorie malnutrition
    Kwashiorkor
    Alcoholism

Intestinal
    Chronic diarrhea from any cause (e.g., chronic ulcerative colitis, Crohn's disease, laxative abuse, villous adenoma, adenocarcinoma of the rectum)
    Malabsorption
    Short-bowel syndrome
    Gluten enteropathy
    Pancreatic insufficiency with steatorrhea
    Tropical sprue
    Familial malabsorption of magnesium

Renal
    Disease related
    Renal tubular acidosis
    Acute tubular necrosis (diuretic phase)
    Chronic glomerulonephritis
    Chronic pyelonephritis
    Familial and sporadic renal magnesium loss
    Drug related
    Diuretics (furosemide, ethacrynic acid, thiazides)
    Antibiotics (gentamicin, tobramycin, ticarcillin, carbenicillin, amphotericin B)
    Antineoplastic drugs (cisplatin, combinations of antibiotics and cytotoxic agents)

Endocrine and metabolic
    Primary and secondary aldosteronism
    Hyperthyroidism
    Excessive lactation
    Pregnancy (third trimester)
    Hypercalcemia
    Primary hyperparathyroidism (due to hypercalcemia; immediately postoperatively in patients with osteitis fibrosa cystica)
    Uncontrolled diabetes with marked glucosuria
    Acute intermittent porphyria

Congenital, neonatal
    Maternal diabetes
    Maternal hyperparathyroidism or hypoparathyroidism
    Exchange transfusion (citrate effect)

(From Flink,[261] with permission.)

perpetuating the dietary deficiency of magnesium are loss of magnesium in the process of food refining, the composition of water, and vegetarian diets.[172] In addition, the consumption of some foods that augment the need for magnesium (such as calcium, vitamin D, phosphate, phytase, sodium, potassium, proteins, alcohol, and fat), has increased.[16] A state of chronic, subclinical magnesium deficiency may be more common than usually recognized.[16] But due to the striking ability of the kidneys to conserve magnesium, overt clinical magnesium deficiency is uncommon unless other factors that increase the loss of magnesium in urine or feces, or other metabolic conditions (such as diarrhea, diuretic therapy, pregnancy, stress, cardiac or surgical trauma) are superimposed.[3] An appropriate magnesium intake has been estimated to be between 6 and 10 mg/kg, and this amount may have to be doubled under conditions in which magnesium requirements are increased.[16]

Losses of gastrointestinal fluid containing magnesium, without appropriate electrolyte replacement, constitute a frequent pathologic cause of magnesium depletion. The losses can be in the form of vomiting, nasogastric suction, diarrhea due to infectious enteritis, ulcerative colitis, Crohn's disease, and laxative abuse, among other causes.[173] The magnitude of the decrease in magnesium balance caused by these losses will depend on the volume of fluid lost and its magnesium concentration.[19] Magnesium deficiency has also been observed after total parenteral nutrition without magnesium administration, and in extreme malnutrition.[65,173] Total fasting for obesity produces a catabolic state and an acidosis that causes release of magnesium from bone stores; an increase in the filtered load of magnesium results in the magnesiuria.[173,174] Because of their high protein content, liquid protein diets increase the requirement for magnesium, and if this ion is not administered, magnesium depletion ensues.[16,175]

Since magnesium is extensively absorbed through the small bowel, operations that bypass segments of this portion of the gastrointestinal tract (such as jejunoileal bypass for the treatment of morbid obesity), as well as surgical resection or radiation damage may significantly impair magnesium absorption.[173] In steatorrhea caused by the formation of nonreabsorbable salts, significant amounts of magnesium may be lost in the feces, and depletion of magnesium may develop.[173] In acute pancreatitis, as magnesium precipitates in the necrotic omentum, a significant fall in the plasma concentration of magnesium may be observed.[176]

There is an inborn error characterized by a single defect in the gastrointestinal absorption of magnesium and manifested by hypomagnesemia and hypocalcemia, which is corrected by the administration of magnesium.[165,177] In most cases of this syndrome, serum PTH levels were found to be inappropriately low for the levels of plasma calcium or magnesium, but the calcemic and renal responses to PTH administration were normal.[165,177] Potassium metabolism and adrenal function are normal in this syndrome.[165] Pathologic abnormalities have been found upon renal biopsy.[177] Clinically this condition is manifested by a neuromuscular irritability that responds poorly to calcium or vitamin D administration but is reversed with magnesium therapy.[165,177]

Renal Conditions

Magnesium depletion due to excessive urinary losses secondary to renal tubular damage can occur in postobstructive diuresis, the diuretic phase of renal transplantation,[178] acute tubular necrosis, renal tubular acidosis, and some cases of glomerulonephritis and pyelonephritis.[173] There is an uncommon form of a primary familial defect in the tubular reabsorption of potassium and magnesium that causes hypomagnesemia and hypocalcemia, both of which may respond to magnesium therapy.[179] This may be associated with renal interstitial fibrosis, chondrocalcinosis, osteoarthritis, sensorineural deafness, infertility, nephrocalcinosis, and reduction of the GFR.[179,180]

Several therapeutic agents, such as antibiotic gentamicin and some antineoplastic agents (amphotericin, cisplatinum), can cause tubular damage and result in losses in electrolytes in the urine with hypocalcemia, hypomagnesemia, and inappropriately low levels of PTH.[181–183] Hypercalcemia of any cause (such as in hyperparathyroidism, vitamin D intoxication, malignancy, etc.)[173] and depletion of phosphate[184] can cause increasing losses of magnesium in the urine. Hemodilution and excessive urinary losses account for the hypomagnesemia in patients with inappropriate secretion of antidiuretic hormone (SIADH) and acute intermittent porphyria.[185] Magnesium is an inhibitor of crystallization,[186] and its prophylactic administration has reduced the incidence of calcium stone formation in patients with renal lithiasis.[187]

Diuretics

Although there is general concern about the effects of the administration of diuretics on potassium metabolism, and potassium may be given prophylactically by some physicians to patients receiving diuretics to avoid potassium depletion, a similar awareness of the possibly deleterious effects of diuretics on magnesium metabolism is uncommon. The chronic administration of loop diuretics for the treatment of hypertension or edematous states can result in the renal wasting of potassium, magnesium, and other electrolytes, with hypomagnesemia and hypokalemia.[188,189] Loop diuretics also produce a calciuresis, and the resulting hypocalcemia may stimulate PTH secretion and action.[86] By its action in bone, PTH causes the release of calcium and magnesium, and through the resulting increase in the filtered load of magnesium, the magnesiuria is perpetuated.[86] The mobilization of magnesium from bone retards the clinical manifestations of hypomagnesemia to 8 to 15 days after initiation of therapy with loop diuretics.[86] Once depletion of magnesium is established in the course of the chronic administration of loop diuretics, a decrease in secretion of PTH and resistance to the action of the hormone in the kidneys will perpetuate the negative magnesium balance.[86] The depletion of magnesium may also contribute to the kaliuresis caused by loop diuretics.[123] Later in the course of events, when the secretion of PTH decreases and resistance to its action in bone develops, a compensatory mechanism may become active by which the hypocalcemia may directly enhance the renal tubular reabsorption of magnesium.[86] The negative balance of potassium and magnesium ensuing from the chronic administration of loop diuretics may be further compounded by fluid depletion and secondary hyperaldosteronism, as well as digoxin and insulin therapy.[123]

Most studies have reported that the chronic administration of thiazide diuretics also results in hypokalemia and hypomagnesemia in proportion to the dosage administered and duration of treatment.[189] Although some have noticed a low incidence of hypomagnesemia in patients with uncomplicated hypertension treated with moderate doses of thiazide diuretics,[190] others have detected low concentrations of potassium and magnesium in the muscle tissue of patients after long-term treatment with loop or thiazide diuretics.[188,191] A low concentration of potassium and magnesium was also found in lymphocytes from patients given long-term treatment with furosemide[192-194] or thiazide diuretics.[193] These studies of the tissue content of electrolytes indicate that the incidence of magnesium depletion in patients on long-term diuretic therapy is much higher than the routine plasma determination of magnesium may suggest.

Attempts to prevent or correct diuretic-induced depletion of potassium and magnesium by the administration of potassium have not always been successful,[188,193] but after the administration of magnesium, the content of potassium and magnesium in muscle was found to increase.[195] The administration of amiloride to patients treated with furosemide caused a reduction in the urinary losses of magnesium and potassium and an increase in the plasma and lymphocyte concentration of magnesium.[194]

The administration of amiloride, spironolactone, or triamterene to patients on long-term treatment with thiazide or loop diuretics significantly increases the muscular content of magnesium.[188]

Bartter's Syndrome

Bartter's syndrome is a condition characterized by hyperreninemia, aldosteronism with hypokalemia, alkalosis and normotension, growth retardation, hypertrophy and hyperplasia of the juxtaglomerular apparatus, a decreased pressor response to angiotensin II and norepinephrine, and increased excretion of prostaglandin E_2 in the urine.[196] Some patients with Bartter's syndrome excrete increased amounts of magnesium in the urine and are hypomagnesemic.[196] It has been proposed that in Bartter's syndrome there may be an intrinsic prostaglandin-independent impairment in chloride reabsorption in the loop of Henle.[197]

Acute infusions of magnesium in Bartter's syndrome have been shown to diminish the urinary excretion of potassium.[198] It has been proposed that Bartter's syndrome may be a common expression of three well-defined functional defects of the renal tubules. The first of these (Type I) consists of an isolated defect in potassium transport located in the distal portion of the distal tubule and/or cortical collecting tubules. The second (Type II) consists of a primary defect in sodium chloride reabsorption in the proximal and distal tubules. The third (Type III) consists of a localized defect in sodium chloride reabsorption in the thick ascending portion of Henle's loop.[199] Patients with Bartter's syndrome and magnesium-wasting fall into the last category.[199]

Renal Disease

Although uremic patients may more frequently be hypermagnesemic, the concentration of magnesium in the muscle of such patients, taken as an index of the intracellular content of magnesium, was found to be significantly reduced as compared with that of nonuremic controls.[200] Magnesium depletion has also been shown to occur in uremic patients with malabsorption,[201] and in patients with renal failure, tubular wasting of magnesium, and a hypoparathyroidism that reverted to hyperparathyroidism after correction of the magnesium deficit.[202]

HORMONAL AND METABOLIC ABNORMALITIES

Parathyroid Glands

The plasma concentration of magnesium has been found to be normal or reduced in patients with hyperparathyroidism.[203-206] Some hyperparathyroid patients have a negative magnesium balance due largely to increased losses of magnesium in the urine.[204,206] The magnesiuria in hyperparathyroidism may be partially secondary to the effects of the hypercalcemia blocking magnesium reabsorption.[173] After successful surgical correction of the hyperparathyroidism there may be a further decrease in plasma magnesium, especially in patients with extensive bone disease, and probably caused by the deposition of magnesium into tissue during the process of clinical recovery.[173,204-206] Patients with hypoparathyroidism have increased losses of magnesium in their feces[207] and urine,[173] and are hypomagnesemic.[207]

Thyroid Glands

The plasma magnesium concentration tends to be low in hyperthyroidism and elevated in hypothyroidism.[94,126,208] Hyperthyroid patients excrete greater amounts of magnesium in the urine than hypothyroid patients, and the percentage of magnesium excreted in the feces is greater in hypothyroidism.[126,208] Following treatment of these thyroid diseases, the metabolic balance of magnesium becomes positive in hyperthyroidism and negative in hypothyroidism.[126,208] These results suggest that hyperthyroid patients are depleted of magnesium and that hypothyroid patients have a magnesium excess.[208] There is no definitive information that will allow an explanation for the changes in magnesium balance in thyroid disease. Thyroid hormones may promote the metabolic degradation of vitamin D, causing a decrease in its conversion to 1,25-dihydroxycholecalciferol.[126] The decreased activity of the active form of vitamin D, plus rapid gastrointestinal peristalsis, could explain the decreased gastrointestinal absorption of magnesium in hyperthyroidism.[94] In addition, thyroid hormones may cause an increase in the filtered load of magnesium and a decrease in its renal tubular reabsorption, either directly or through their effects on vitamin D.[126] Since experimental data have also indicated that there is increased secretion of mineralocorticoids in hyperthyroidism, the changes in magnesium metabolism may be mediated through this effect.[126] Additionally, it is possible that thyroid hormones may regulate the influx of magnesium into cells, and that this process is altered in thyroid disease.[126] Most of these possibilities are speculative and await definitive experimental confirmation.

Diabetes

The incidence of hypomagnesemia is high in well controlled, insulin-dependent diabetic patients, but although the muscle magnesium content may remain unchanged,[209] bone magnesium is reduced.[4,210] The hypomagnesemia in insulin-treated diabetic patients has been related to the urinary losses of magnesium and the calciuresis induced by the osmotic diuresis, by a direct effect of insulin and glucose on the renal tubular transport of magnesium,[123] and by the insulin-induced shift of magnesium to erythrocytes[211] and other tissues.[212] The hypomagnesemia in diabetic patients has been considered to be an additional risk factor for diabetic retinopathy[213] and atherosclerotic ischemic heart disease.[214]

In diabetic ketoacidosis, as magnesium exits from cells, there can be a transitory increase in the plasma magnesium concentration; later, however, as a consequence of the renal losses of magnesium and redeposition of magnesium into tissue induced by insulin therapy, the plasma magnesium may fall.[65,174,175]

Hyperaldosteronism

Patients with hyperaldosteronism have increased losses of magnesium in the urine and feces, and may become hypomagnesemic.[215] When patients with hyperaldosteronism are volume expanded, the urinary losses of potassium and magnesium increase further.[216] The kaliuresis and magnesiuria are reduced after the administration of spironolactone,[216] and reversed after surgical removal of the adenoma.[216] The changes in magnesium metabolism in hyperaldosteronism may be secondary to the volume expansion in this condition.[159]

Alcoholism

The urinary excretion of magnesium increases during the acute and chronic ingestion of alcohol.[217,218] The mechanism of the magnesiuria in alcoholism is related to a direct effect of alcohol on the renal tubular transport of magnesium, an increase in tubular flow rate,[218] and decreased tubular transport of magnesium due to the binding of magnesium to lactate as a consequence of the lactic acidosis caused by alcohol.[123,217] Additional factors contributing to the negative magnesium balance in alcoholism are poor dietary intake and starvation, ketoacidosis, vomiting, diarrhea, malabsorption, and hyperhidrosis.[217] The changes in calcium and thiamine metabolism in alcoholism may also alter magnesium metabolism.[174,175,219] There is no evidence of an alteration in parathyroid function or insulin secretion or activity in alcoholism.[123] In alcoholic cirrhosis, the losses of magnesium are compounded by the liver damage and secondary hyperaldosteronism.[174,175] Hypomagnesemia, a low exchangeable magnesium, a low content of magnesium in muscle, and a hypocalcemia that all respond to magnesium administration are all evidence of magnesium depletion in chronic alcoholism.[64,65,174,175,220,221]

During alcohol withdrawal there is a rapid decrease in serum magnesium with respiratory alkalosis and an increased susceptibility to seizures.[217] Chelation of magnesium by fatty acids during alcohol withdrawal decreases the concentration of free magnesium ions, with a consequent increase in susceptibility to neuromuscular excitability and psychiatric symptoms.[222] Some but not all of the symptoms of alcohol withdrawal may be related to the magnesium deficiency.[217]

Cardiovascular Disorders

A number of myocardial ischemic syndromes—arteriosclerosis, coronary spasm, myocardial insufficiency, acute myocardial infarction, arrhythmias and sudden death—have been linked to depletion of magnesium.[223,224] Clinical magnesium depletion rarely occurs as an isolated abnormality, and hypomagnesemia has an effect on the distribution of other ions.[225,226] Therefore, it has been impossible to define an abnormality pathognomonic for magnesium depletion. In a study of critically ill patients admitted to an intensive care unit, 65 percent were found to be hypomagnesemic and one-third were also hypocalcemic.[229] In an evaluation of combined electrolytic abnormalities it was found that hypomagnesemia occurred in 42 percent of patients with hypokalemia, 29 percent of patients with hypophosphatemia, 27 percent of patients with hyponatremia, and 22 percent of hypocalcemic patients.[228]

There is a report of a fatal magnesium-induced cardiomyopathy in a patient who was also hypocalcemic, hypokalemic, and hypophosphatemic.[229] The incidence of ischemic heart disease and sudden death has been reported to be higher in areas with soft water (low in calcium and magnesium) than in areas with hard water (with a higher content of calcium and magnesium).[230] The plasma concentration of magnesium was found to be low in patients admitted with an acute myocardial infarction,[231] and determinations in patients who died of an acute coronary occlusion revealed low levels of magnesium in the myocardium.[232,233] In another study, no differences in the plasma concentration of magnesium were detected in patients admitted with an acute myocardial infarction as compared to normal controls or patients without myocardial disease.[234] However, patients with ischemic heart disease, with or without a myocardial infarction, retained a high proportion of an acute infusion of magnesium.[235] In a study of patients with congestive heart failure treated with diuretics who developed digoxin-induced arrhythmias with normal plasma levels of digoxin, determinations in lymphocytes revealed a low content of potassium and magnesium.[236] With magnesium therapy the arrhythmia subsided.[236] These results indicate that magnesium depletion in patients with ischemic heart disease is more frequent than suggested by routine measurements of the plasma magnesium concentration.

Several mechanisms have been considered as mediating the induction of cardiac arrhythmias in states of potassium and magnesium depletion: there may be a direct arrhythmogenic effect, arrhythmias secondary to digitalis or circulating catecholamines may be potentiated, or there may be an interference with antiarrhythmic drugs and/or an enhancement of the pro-arrhythmic potential of antiarrhythmic therapy.[237] When hypokalemia and hypomagnesemia coexist, potassium therapy alone frequently fails to elevate the serum potassium or to correct the arrhythmia, but the administration of magnesium corrects both the hypokalemia and hypomagnesemia and restores the normal heartbeat rhythm.[237] In a study of patients receiving digitalis, hypomagnesemia was found to be twice as frequent as hypokalemia, suggesting that magnesium depletion may be a more frequent predisposing factor to digitalis intoxication than hypokalemia.[238] Magnesium was found to be effective in the control of intractable ventricular tachycardia, including "torsade de pointes"; massive digitoxin intoxication; and ventricular fibrillation.[239] The administration of magnesium significantly reduced the incidence of arrhythmias in patients admitted with an acute myocardial infarction.[240] In a prospective 6 month follow-up study of patients discharged after an acute myocardial infarction, there was no difference in the plasma concentration of potassium and magnesium, but those patients who did not require diuretic therapy or who were treated with a thiazide diuretic plus amiloride had significantly higher levels of potassium and magnesium in their erythrocytes and lymphocytes than those treated with furosemide and potassium.[241]

Hypertension

The administration of magnesium to hypertensive patients on long-term therapy and receiving diuretics produced a further reduction in blood pressure and better control of their hypertension.[195] Other studies, however, found no beneficial effect of magnesium in hypertensive patients.[242] Currently there is no definite indication for the use of magnesium in the treatment of hypertension.[243]

MISCELLANEOUS CONDITIONS

Cardiac arrhythmias related to a possible hypomagnesemia, which were unresponsive to calcium therapy and which resolved after magnesium administration, were reported during exchange transfusion for erythroblastosis fetalis.[244,245] Complexing to citrate was proposed as the mechanism by which physiologically active ionic magnesium decreased during exchange transfusions.[245] The sometimes symptomatic hypomagnesemia observed in burns may be related to stress and the release of catecholamines, and secondary to hyperaldosteronism and losses of magnesium through burned areas.[246] In severe accidental trauma, the magnesium released from tissue breakdown causes hypermagnesemia and magnesiuria.[18] A negative magnesium balance and hypomagnesemia have been observed for the first three days following a surgical operation, as a result of the surgical trauma and reduction in food intake.[247]

Hypocalcemia and hypomagnesemia have been reported in the toxic shock syndrome.[248] Both total and ionizable plasma calcium are reduced, and the true hypocalcemia in the syndrome has been related to an increase in immunoreactive calcitonin levels in plasma, and to the hypomagnesemia.[248] In cases of tampon-associated toxic-shock syndrome, a low magnesium environment may be induced in the vagina by the binding of magnesium to the fibers of some types of tampons.[249] In vitro studies have confirmed maximum toxin production by strains of *Staphylococcus aureus* in a low-magnesium medium.[250] A symptomatic hypomagnesemic tetany has been reported in a mother with excessive lactation.[251] In a retrospective study, the clinical picture of apnea neonatorum has been reported to be frequently associated with hypomagnesemia and to improve with the administration of magnesium.[252] Depletion of magnesium is difficult to diagnose in the newborn, and because of immature renal function, extreme caution should be used in the administration of magnesium to the neonate.[253]

SYMPTOMS AND SIGNS OF MAGNESIUM DEFICIENCY

Magnesium depletion may remain asymptomatic, show only the manifestations related to the primary disease, or produce florid signs and symptoms of magnesium deficiency[254] (Table 7-5).

Magnesium plays an important role in neuromuscular transmission, and in magnesium depletion there are signs of muscular hyperexcitability.[175,254] Spasm of the facial muscles, tremor, and involuntary movements affecting any of the extremities in an irregular fashion, but more frequently the upper limbs, as well as asterixis, spontaneous or latent tetany with carpopedal spasm, and positive Trousseau and Chvostek signs are manifestations that have been reported in magnesium deficiency.[65,173–175,254] Because of the multifaceted biochemical expressions of magnesium depletion, it is not clear whether the clinical manifestations are related to changes in magnesium, potassium, or calcium metabolism or to the alkalosis in this condition. In many instances, the clinical and chemical abnormalities are corrected after the administration of magnesium alone.[173] The involvement of the autonomic system is sometimes manifested by gastrointestinal dysfunction with dysphagia and intestinal ileus.[259]

The neuromuscular manifestations of magnesium depletion are often accompanied by apathy or agitation, nystagmus, ataxia, vertigo, convulsions, disorientation, and delirium.[65,173–175,255] There are similarities in symptomatology between acute alcoholic withdrawal and magnesium depletion, and on occasion both conditions may coexist in the same patient; however, the response to magnesium therapy is not always consistent in patients with acute alcohol withdrawal.[174,255]

In magnesium depletion there is hypocalcemia with plasma levels of PTH that are depressed or inappropriate for the degree of hypocalcemia.[32,173] Because of a defective activation of magnesium-dependent adenylate cyclase in magnesium deficiency, there is impairment in the release of PTH from the gland and resistance to its action at the kidneys and bone, resulting in the hypocalcemia.[32,173,256,257] In magnesium deficiency there is also an impairment in the function of the Na-K pump, which requires magnesium for its activation by ATPase; this prevents potassium from being effectively reabsorbed by the renal tubules, and there is wasting of potassium in the urine and hypokalemia.[173]

The abnormalities in cardiac function that have been observed as a result of magnesium depletion may result from the malfunction of many enzymatic systems that are activated by magnesium. In moderate magnesium depletion a widening of the QRS complexes and peaked T waves with tachy-

Table 7-5. Symptoms of Magnesium Depletion

Muscular twitching and tremor of any or all muscles including the tongue
Athetoid and choreiform movements (rare)
Vertigo, ataxia and nystagmus (rare)
Muscle wasting muscle weakness
Positive Chvostek sign (fairly common)
Numbness and tingling (fairly common)
Positive Trousseau sign (rare)
Spontaneous carpopedal spasm or tetany (rare)
Convulsions
Sweating and tachycardia
Apathy, depression, and poor memory
Mild to severe delirium (confusion, disorientation, hallucinations, and paranoia)
Premature ventricular beats, ventricular tachycardia, and ventricular fibrillation
Coma
Death

(From Flink,[221] with permission.)

cardia have been described.[225,226] In more severe magnesium depletion there is a prolongation of the PR space, widening of QRS and QT complexes, diminution of the T wave, and occasionally a U wave.[225,226] Hypomagnesemia itself may predispose to cardiac arrhythmias, but the associated hypokalemia may also play an important role in the alterations in rhythm,[226,229] which include supraventricular tachycardia and paroxysmal ventricular fibrillation.[239] Furthermore, the incidence of digitalis intoxication has been reported to be higher and to persist longer in patients with magnesium depletion.[239] In many instances the arrhythmias resulting from digitalis intoxication were refractory to standard treatment, and reversed only after the administration of magnesium.[239]

DIAGNOSIS OF MAGNESIUM DEPLETION

The most practical and commonly used test for the diagnosis of magnesium depletion is assay of the plasma concentration of magnesium. Magnesium deprivation, however, is not always manifested by hypomagnesemia, and normal and even elevated levels of plasma magnesium may be observed at a time when there is tissue depletion of magnesium; furthermore, hypomagnesemia may coexist with normal tissue stores of magnesium.[174] A high degree of awareness is therefore necessary in recognizing those clinical conditions in which there is wasting of magnesium and which may lead to magnesium depletion. Under conditions of normal hydration, a normal plasma albumin concentration, and normal acid-base equilibrium, a low plasma concentration of magnesium is likely, in most instances, to indicate magnesium depletion.[174] Hypomagnesemia has been defined as a plasma or serum concentration of magnesium below 1.7 mg/dl.[123]

When magnesium depletion is induced by extrarenal losses, there will be renal conservation of magnesium, and the urine will be virtually free of magnesium.[123] If the plasma magnesium and urinary excretion of magnesium are normal, magnesium depletion is unlikely.[217] If the plasma magnesium is below 1.0 mEq/liter, the urinary excretion of magnesium is also below 1.0 mEq/liter, and the urinary excretion of magnesium is less than 1.0 mEq/day, magnesium depletion is very likely.[217]

The renal response to intravenous loading with magnesium has been used to estimate the metabolic status of magnesium.[19,258,259] This test, which is being increasingly used, with modifications introduced by different investigators, is contraindicated in patients wih renal failure, when there is a renal tubular leakage of magnesium, and in conditions associated with hypermagnesemia or hypercalcemia.[19,258,259] Medications containing magnesium, such as laxatives, antacids, and diuretics, must be discontinued for 48 hours before the test.[19,258,259] A baseline is first established by determining the plasma concentration of magnesium and the excretion of magnesium in a 24-hour urine collection.[19,258,259] The test is performed by infusing 0.5 mEq/kg magnesium as magnesium chloride or magnesium sulfate in 100 ml of 5 percent dextrose in water (D5W) or normal saline over a 45 minute period. Another 24-hour urine collection is initiated at the end of the infusion, and blood samples for plasma magnesium determination are drawn at the beginning and end of the urine collection. Normally, all the magnesium infused should be eliminated in 24 hours. A retention of 20 to 25 percent or more of the infused magnesium is consistent with magnesium depletion.

A negative magnesium balance that turns positive after treatment with magnesium is also consistent with depletion of magnesium.[165] Hypocalcemia and potassium depletion are frequent manifestations of magnesium deprivation.[165] The metabolic status of magnesium has also been evaluated by measurements of magnesium in red cells,[4] bone,[4] muscle,[4,260] lymphocytes,[14] and mononuclear cells.[15]

TREATMENT OF MAGNESIUM DEPLETION

As a general rule, depletion of magnesium should be prevented by recognizing conditions that may cause excessive losses of magnesium and administering magnesium prophylactically (Table 7-6). Once magnesium deprivation has developed and has been diagnosed, it must be treated immediately. In planning the course of action, it is important to obtain an accurate assessment of renal function, since if the patient is in renal failure, only half the recommended dose should be administered.[261] In all cases, the response to treatment must be monitored by frequent determinations of the plasma magnesium concentration.[261]

Since in most instances it is very difficult to accurately estimate the deficit of magnesium, the replacement is usually based on the best educated guess.[262] It has been estimated that a person with hypomagnesemia has a magnesium deficit of at least 1 mEq/kg. On the first day of treatment it is recommended that 5 g of magnesium sulfate heptahydrate be given intravenously in each of 2 liters of fluid.[261] The same dose can be given intramuscularly by five injections of 2 g at 4 hour intervals.[261] Ampules contain 1 g per 2 ml magnesium sulfate, or a 50 percent solution.[261] One gram equals 8.1 mEq or 4.05 mmoles of magnesium.[261] Treatment should be continued for 3 to 4 days at half the dose given on the first day.[261] The reasons for continuing therapy are that part of the administered dose is excreted daily, the deficit of magnesium may be greater than estimated, and hypomagnesemia may recur if only the first dose is administered.[261] Levels of plasma magnesium must be measured daily.[261]

For emergency treatment in patients with magnesium deficiency who develop convulsions or ventricular arrhythmias, 2 g of magnesium sulfate as a 10 percent solution should be given intravenously over a 2 minute period, followed by the infusion of 12 g (97 mEq) in a liter of fluid over a 12 hour period.[261]

Oral magnesium treatment may be maintained in patients with chronic magnesium losses.[261] Magnesium hydroxide, magnesium gluconate, and magnesium chloride

Table 7-6. Treatment of Magnesium Depletion

The following guidelines are suggested for treatment of magnesium deficiency regardless of etiology:

1. It is important to know that the kidneys are producing urine and that the BUN (blood urea nitrogen) and/or creatinine are normal. Magnesium may be needed and may be administered even in an instance of renal insufficiency, but the treatment must be monitored by frequent serum or plasma level assays.
2. On the first day of therapy at least 1 mEq mg/kg/day should be given parenterally. Subsequently, at least 0.5 mEq mg/kg/day should be given for 3–5 days. If parenteral fluid therapy continues, at least 0.2 mEq/kg/day should be given.
3. Give the above in intravenous infusions if such infusions are being given anyway; otherwise, intramuscular administration is satisfactory.
4. The following schedule for an average adult is safe and effective. (1) Intramuscular route: (ampules with 1 g MgSO$_4$ 7H$_2$O, 50% solution = 8.13 mEq mg) Day 1: 2.0 g (16.3 mEq) every 4 hour for six doses. Day 2–5: 1.0 g (8.1 mEq) every six hours. (2) Intravenous route (same ampules) Day 1: 5 g (41 mEq) in each liter of fluid and at least 2 liters of 83 mEq. Day 2-5: A total of 6 g (49 mEq) distributed equally in total fluids of the day.

If the patient's condition requires continued intravenous infusions, 2 g of MgSO$_4$ should be given daily in the infusion as long as infusions are necessary. When a patient who has a reason to have magnesium deficiency is convulsing, 2.0 g of MgSO$_4$ solution should be administered intravenously in a 10 minute period. For infants and children, the dose should be 0.025 g MgSO$_4$/kg in 10 minutes.

(From Flink,[221] with permission.)

are available in tablets; milk of magnesia and magnesium containing antacids are available in liquid form.[261] A single tablet or a teaspoon of liquid is given twice daily and increased to the point of tolerance.[261] Treatment with oral magnesium salts is limited by diarrhea.[261]

MAGNESIUM EXCESS AND HYPERMAGNESEMIA

The most common condition associated with symptomatic hypermagnesemia is the result of two additive factors: the administration of magnesium to subjects unable to handle efficiently the extra load because of a significant reduction in renal function[263] (Table 7-7).

There is no agreement on the changes that may take place in the gastrointestinal handling of magnesium in uremia. Some studies failed to show any differences in the gastrointestinal absorption of magnesium between uremics and normal controls.[264] Others have shown that the absorption of magnesium is significantly reduced in patients with renal failure.[265] The mechanism by which the excretion of magnesium in feces increases in patients in renal failure has not been established, but on the basis of the finding that magnesium absorption increases after renal transplantation, it has been proposed that the gastrointestinal absorption of magnesium decreases in uremic patients because of defective formation of the active metabolite of vitamin D, 1,25-dihydroxy-D, by the diseased kidneys.[265] Also, because the gastrointestinal absorption of magnesium improves after hemodialysis, it is possible that the elevated magnesium in the ECF of uremic patients retards the gastrointestinal absorption of magnesium.[265]

Micropuncture studies in uremic dogs demonstrated that the filtered load of magnesium was greatly increased in the remnant nephrons secondary to an increase in the single nephron GFR.[286] In these studies the reabsorption of magnesium in the proximal tubules was significantly decreased, and although the delivery of magnesium to the loop of Henle increased, reabsorption in this segment remained constant, thus resulting in an increase in the fractional excretion of magnesium.[266] Factors such as alterations in renal hemodynamics, adaptive increases in the single nephron GFR,[267] and the presence of a natriuretic factor in plasma and urine[268] may exert an enhancing effect on the urinary excretion of magnesium and other ions in uremia.[266] The renal response to PTH was demonstrated to be intact in uremia.[266]

Frank hypermagnesemia is unusual in chronic renal failure unless it is iatrogenically induced,[267] since even under normal conditions, magnesium is already being reabsorbed at a maximal rate, and any increase in the filtered load exceeds this reabsorptive capacity, with the extra load excreted in the urine.[267] In more advanced renal failure, however, when the GFR falls below 10 to 30 ml/min, hypermagnesemia can occur with increasing frequency,[263] and can be easily induced and aggravated by the

Table 7-7. Causes of Hypermagnesemia

Common
    Acute renal failure
    Chronic renal failure with exogenous Mg intake
    Toxemia therapy

Less common
    Chronic renal failure without exogenous intake
    Rectal administration of Mg-containing solutions

Uncommon:
    Parasitosis with exogenous Mg intake producing only small elevations of Mg
    Lithium therapy
    Hypothyroidism
    Certain neoplasms with skeletal involvement
    Viral hepatitis
    Hyperparathyroidism with renal disease
    Pituitary dwarfism
    Milk-alkali syndrome
    Perforated viscus with exogenous Mg intake
    Acute diabetic ketoacidosis
    Addison's disease

(From Nordes and Wacker,[263] with permission.)

administration of magnesium-containing substances such as antacids, enemas, laxatives, and intravenous fluids,[263] as well as after irrigation of the renal pelvis with solutions containing magnesium[269] and after hemodialysis with a dialysate having a high magnesium content.[263]

Hypermagnesemic uremic patients become symptomatic at lower elevations of the plasma magnesium concentration, probably owing to the effects of the high urea concentration causing a transcellular transfer of cations.[221]

The plasma concentration of magnesium may also be significantly elevated in the oliguric phase of acute tubular necrosis.[270] Complicating factors under these circumstances may be continued oral intake or intravenous infusion of magnesium, the catabolic state, and acidosis with the release of magnesium from tissue, such as in rhabdomyolysis.[263]

Depending on the concentration of magnesium in the bath and on the dietary intake of magnesium, the plasma concentration of magnesium may be elevated, normal, or decreased in patients undergoing hemodialysis.[174,262] A post-dialysis induced elevation in plasma magnesium could inhibit the release of PTH, which should have a beneficial effect on the osteodystrophy of chronic renal failure.[262] A 6-month study, however, showed no differences in the plasma concentrations of calcium and PTH in three groups of patients in which the plasma concentration of magnesium was maintained at low, normal, or high levels by changing the concentration in the dialysate.[272] In another study, dialysis with a magnesium-free bath caused a symptomatic depletion of magnesium and depressed PTH function in some patients.[273]

The total body content of magnesium was found to be significantly increased in dialyzed and non-dialyzed uremic patients at autopsy.[274] The increase was more marked in bone, but the content of magnesium was also found to be elevated in red cells and the myocardium, lungs, and skin.[274] No changes were found in muscle and liver.[274] Low concentrations of magnesium in muscle have also been reported in chronic renal failure.[200]

Other conditions found to be associated with elevations in plasma magnesium are lithium therapy,[263,275] pheochromocytoma,[276] hypothyroidism,[124,208] Addison's disease,[72] chronic infections, essential hypertension, oxalate intoxication, untreated acidosis,[174] skeletal involvement with malignancy,[263,277] dwarfism, the milk-alkali syndrome,[263] and viral hepatitis.[263,278] In eclampsia, hypermagnesemia is induced by loading with magnesium as a means of treatment,[279] and children born from eclamptic mothers who have been treated with magnesium may develop symptomatic hypermagnesemia[263] and the meconium-plug syndrome.[280]

Symptoms and Diagnosis of Hypermagnesemia

Excess magnesium induces synthesis of acetylcholine and acetylcholine sterase, suppresses the release of acetylcholine, blocks transmission at the neuromuscular junction, diminishes postsynaptic membrane responsiveness, and antagonizes the effects of calcium.[263] Excess magnesium also diminishes the release of acetylcholine, blocks transmission in sympathetic ganglia, and decreases the output of norepinephrine from adrenergic postganglionic sympathetic fibers and adrenergic nerves.[263] In addition to diminishing the amount of transmitter substance, magnesium may also reduce the sensitivity of the postsynaptic membrane.[263] At levels of magnesium exceeding 4 mEq/L, there is a decrease in deep tendon reflexes, which may disappear when the level of magnesium in plasma reaches 10 mEq/liter, at which point respiratory paralysis may supervene.[221] The P-R interval in the electrocardiogram may become prolonged at plasma levels of magnesium of 5 to 10 mEq/liter, and complete heart block may occur at levels of 15 mEq/liter.[263] Peaked T waves, as well as prolongation of the QT interval and diminution in voltage of the P wave,[263] heart block,[221] and cardiac arrest[263] have been seen in uremia in combination with hyperkalemia and hypermagnesemia. Extreme hypermagnesemia as a cause of hypotension has been reported in a patient with renal failure and in a subject with normal renal function.[271,281] Hypermagnesemia may cause a relaxation of the vascular smooth muscle and a decrease in vascular resistance by displacing calcium from the wall surface.[167]

Increased levels of magnesium interfere with the adhesiveness of platelets and prolong the thrombin-generation time and the clotting time.[263,283] The bleeding disorders in uremia may be explained at least partially by the hypermagnesemia.[263]

It has been observed that the plasma concentration of calcium decreases in patients with hypermagnesemia, and this effect is related to the depressed secretion of PTH and the decreased response of target tissues to the hormone, as well as to increased levels of calcitonin.[263] In hypermagnesemia there is increased deposition of magnesium in bone, causing an alteration in bone calcification and crystallization.[263] Therefore, the abnormalities in bone formation caused by the hypermagnesemia in uremia are among the factors contributing to the osteodystrophy of renal failure.[263]

The possibility of an elevated plasma magnesium concentration should always be considered in patients in the oliguric phase of acute renal failure and in the terminal stages of chronic renal failure, especially if evidence becomes available that the patient was receiving medications containing magnesium.[263] In nonuremic patients the diagnosis is more difficult, and should be suspected in acidotic patients who have a normal or reduced "anion gap."[263,283] Clinically, the patient may complain of nausea and vomiting, have bradycardia and hypotension with cutaneous flushing, and have decreased or absent deep tendon reflexes.[273,263]

Treatment

Hypermagnesemia should be prevented by avoiding the administration of magnesium and medications containing magnesium to patients who, because of a diminution in renal reserve capacity, cannot handle the load.[263] Once the diagnosis of magnesium intoxication has been made clinically and documented by laboratory analysis, all administration of magnesium must be discontinued immediately and calcium must be administered to reverse the effects of magnesium and allow time to prepare the patient for the therapy of choice, which is hemodialysis or peritoneal dialysis with a dialysate having a low concentration of magnesium.[263]

REFERENCES

1. Wacker WEC: Introduction. p. 1. In Wacker WEC (ed): Magnesium and Man. Harvard University Press, Cambridge, MA, 1980
2. Aikawa JK: Biochemistry and physiology of magnesium. p. 47. In Prasad AS, Oberleas D (eds): Trace Elements in Human Health and Disease. Academic Press, New York, 1976
3. Quamme GA, Dirks JH: Magnesium metabolism. p. 297. In Maxwell MH, Kleeman CR, Narins RG (eds): Clinical Disorders of Fluid and Electrolyte Metabolism. 4th Ed. McGraw-Hill, New York, 1987
4. Alfrey AC, Miller NL, Butkus D: Evaluation of body magnesium stores. J Lab Clin Med 84:153, 1974
5. Elin RE: Assessment of magnesium status. Clin Chem 33:1965, 1987
6. Wacker WEC: Measurement. p. 5. In Wacker WEC (ed): Magnesium and Man.

Harvard University Press, Cambridge, MA, 1980
7. Walser M: Ion association. VI. Interaction between calcium, magnesium, inorganic phosphate, citrate and protein in normal human plasma. J Clin Invest 40:723, 1961
8. Quamme GA, Dirks JH: Magnesium transport in the nephron. Am J Physiol 239:F393, 1980
9. Feinroth MV, Feinroth M, Friedman EA, et al: Measurement of serum ionized magnesium (Mg) in acute respiratory alkalosis and acidosis in the dog. Am Soc Nephrol 13:2A, 1980
10. Elin RJ: Role of magnesium in membranes: Erythrocytes and Platelet Functions and Stability. p. 113. In Cantin M, Seelig MS (eds): Magnesium in Health and Disease. SP Medical and Scientific Books, Jamaica, NY, 1980
11. Walser M: Magnesium metabolism. Rev Physiol Biochem Exp Pharmacol 59:185, 1967
12. Elin RJ, Uter A, Tau HK, et al: Effect of magnesium deficiency on erythrocyte aging in rats. Am J Pathol 100:765, 1980
13. Elin RJ, Tau HK: Erythrocyte plaques from rats with magnesium deficiency. Blood 49:653, 1977
14. Ryan MP, Phillips O: Diuretic-induced calcium and magnesium excretion in the rat. Ir J Med Sci 146:303, 1977
15. Elin RJ, Hosseini JM: Magnesium content of mononuclear blood cells. Clin Chem 31:377, 1985
16. Seelig MS: Magnesium requirements in human nutrition. Magnesium Bull 3:26, 1981
17. Wilkinson R: Absorption of calcium, phosphorous and magnesium. p. 36. In Nordin BEC (ed): Calcium, Phosphate and Magnesium Metabolism, Physiology and Diagnostic Procedures. Churchill Livingstone, New York, 1976
18. Wacker WEC: Normal metabolism. p. 52. In Wacker WEC (ed): Magnesium and Man. Harvard University Press, Cambridge, MA, 1980
19. Thoren L: Magnesium deficiency in gastrointestinal fluids. Acta Chir Scand (Suppl) 306:1, 1963
20. Fawcett DW, Gens JP: Magnesium poisoning following an enema of Epsom salt solution. JAMA 123:1028, 1962
21. Petith MM, Schedl HP: Effects of magnesium deficiency on duodenal and ileal absorption and secretion. Dig Dis 23:1, 1978
22. Alcock NW, MacIntyre I: Inter-relation of calcium and magnesium absorption. Clin Sci 22:185, 1962
23. Brannan PG, Vergne-Marini P, Pak CYC, et al: Magnesium absorption in human small intestine. Results in normal subjects, patients with chronic renal disease and subjects with absorptive hypercalciuria. J Clin Invest 57:1412, 1976
24. O'Donnell JM, Smith MW: Uptake of calcium and magnesium by rat duodenal mucosa analysis by means of competing metals. J Physiol (London) 229:733, 1973
25. Ross DB: In vitro studies on the transport of magnesium across the intestinal wall of the rat. J Physiol (London) 160:417, 1962
26. Scharrer E, Schneider B: Inhibitory effect of potassium on magnesium absorption by the rat colon. Nutr Rep Int 37:197, 1988
27. Toothill J: The effects of certain dietary factors in the apparent absorption of magnesium by the rat. Br J Nutr 17:125, 1963
28. Aldor TAM, Moore EW: Magnesium absorption by everted sacs of rat intestine and colon. Gastroenterology 59:745, 1970
29. McCance RZ, Widdowson EM, Lehmann H: Effect of protein intake on absorption of calcium and magnesium. Biochem J 36:686, 1942
30. Branther M, Lee DBN, Coburn JW, et al: Influence of dietary magnesium in experimental phosphate depletion. Bone and soft tissue mineral changes. Am J Physiol 237:E152, 1979
31. Krejs GJ, Nicar M, Zerwekh JE, et al: Effect of 1,25-dihydroxyvitamin D_3 on calcium and magnesium absorption in the healthy human jejunum and ileum. Am J Med 75:973, 1983
32. Shils ME: Magnesium deficiency and calcium and parathyroid hormone interrelations. p. 23. In Prasad AS, Oberleas D (eds): Trace Elements in Human Health and Disease. Academic Press, New York, 1976
33. Sutton RLA, Dirks JH: Renal handling of calcium, phosphate and magnesium. p.

551. In Brenner BM, Rector RC (eds): The Kidney. WB Saunders, Philadelphia, 1981
34. de Rouffignac CF, Morel F, Moss N, et al: Micropuncture study of water and electrolyte movements along the loop of Henle in psammomys with special reference to magnesium, calcium and phosphate. Pflugers Arch 344:309, 1973
35. Jamison RL, Roinel N, deRouffignac CF: Urinary concentration mechanism in the desert rodent *Psammomys obesus*. Am J Physiol 236:F448, 1979
36. Brunette MG, Vigneault N, Carriere S: Micropuncture study of magnesium transport along the nephron in the young rat. Am J Physiol 227:891, 1974
37. Brunette MG, Vigneault N, Carriere S: Micropuncture study of renal magnesium transport in magnesium-loaded rats. Am J Physiol 229:1695, 1975
38. Quamme GA, Smith CM: Magnesium transport in the proximal straight tubule of the rabbit. Am J Physiol 236:F544, 1984
39. Shareghi GR, Agus ZS: Magnesium transport in the cortical thick ascending limb of Henle's loop of the rabbit. J Clin Invest 69:759, 1982
40. Bengele HH, Alexander EA, Lechene C: Calcium and magnesium transport along the inner medullary collecting duct of the rat. Am J Physiol 239:F24, 1980
41. Le Grimellec C, Roinel N, Morel F: Simultaneous Mg, Ca, P, K, Na and Cl analysis in rat tubular fluid. II. During acute Mg plasma loading. Pflugers Arch 340:199, 1973
42. Roy DR: Effect of magnesium loading on magnesium delivery to the juxtamedullary end-descending limb. Am J Physiol 248:F145, 1985
43. Quamme GA, Dirks JH: Intraluminal and contraluminal magnesium on magnesium and calcium transfer in the rat nephron. Am J Physiol 238:F187, 1980
44. Averill CM, Heaton FW: The renal handling of magnesium. Clin Sci 31:353, 1966
45. Alfredson KS, Walser M: Is magnesium secreted by the rat renal tubule? Nephron 7:241, 1970
46. Wen S-F, Wong NL, Dirks JH: Evidence for magnesium secretion during magnesium infusions in the dog. Am J Physiol 220:33, 1971
47. Sachtjen E, Meyer WA, Massry SG: Evidence for magnesium secretion during phosphate depletion in the rat. Proc Soc Exp Biol Med 162:416, 1979
48. Carney S, Wong NLM, Quamme GA, et al: Effect of magnesium deficiency on renal magnesium and calcium transport in the rat. J Clin Invest 65:180, 1980
49. Roy, DR: Magnesium reabsorption in the juxtamedullary loop of Henle. Effects of magnesium deprivation. Can J Physiol Pharmacol 65:1918, 1987
50. Gonda A, Wong N, Seely JF, et al: The role of hemodynamic factors on urinary calcium and magnesium excretion. Can J Physiol Pharmacol 47:619, 1969
51. Wen S-F, Evanson RL, Dirks JH: Micropuncture study of renal magnesium transport in proximal and distal tubule of the dog. Am J Physiol 219:570, 1970
52. Poujeol P, Chahardes D, Roinel N, et al: Influence of extracellular fluid volume expansion on magnesium, calcium and phosphate handling along the rat nephron. Pflugers Arch 365:203, 1976
53. DiBona GF: Effects of magnesium on water permeability of the rat nephron. Am J Physiol 223:1324, 1972
54. Ploth DW, Sawin LL, DiBona GF: Effects of magnesium on rat nephron sodium reabsorption: a segmental analysis. Am J Physiol 226:470, 1974
55. DiBona GF: Effect of magnesium on unidirectional and net sodium fluxes in microperfused rat proximal tubules. Am J Physiol 226:470, 1974
56. Samihy AHE, Brown JL, Globus DL, et al: Interrelation between renal transport systems of magnesium and calcium. Am J Physiol 198:599, 1960
57. Massry SG, Ahumada JJ, Coburn JW, et al: Effect of $MgCl_2$ infusion on urinary Ca and Na during reduction in their filtered loads. Am J Physiol 219:881, 1970
58. Coburn JW, Massry SG, Kleeman CR: The effect of calcium infusions on renal handling of magnesium with normal and reduced glomerular filtration rate. Nephron 7:131, 1970
59. LeGrimellec C, Roinel N, Morel F: Simultaneous Mg, Ca, P, K, Na and Cl analysis in rat tubular fluid. III. During acute

Ca plasma loading. Pflugers Arch 346:171, 1974
60. Quamme GA: Effect of hypercalcemia on renal tubular handling of calcium and magnesium. Can J Physiol Pharmacol 60:1275, 1980
61. Kagussen WJ, Kurokawa K, Aznar E, et al: Effects of phosphate depletion on magnesium homeostasis in rats. J Clin Invest 61:573, 1978
62. Wong NLM, Quamme GA, O'Callaham TJ, et al: Renal tubular transport in phosphate depletion: A micropuncture study. Can J Physiol Pharmacol 58:1063, 1981
63. Quamme GA: Effects of intraluminal sulfate on electrolyte transport along the perfused rat nephron. Can J Physiol Pharmacol 59:122, 1981
64. Lindeman RD: Nutritional influences on magnesium homeostasis with emphasis on renal factors. p. 381. In Cantin M, Seelig MS (eds): Magnesium in Health and Disease. SP Medical and Scientific Books, Jamaica, NY, 1980
65. Wacker WEC, Parisi AF: Magnesium metabolism. N Engl J Med 278:658, 278:712, 278:772, 1968
66. Bieter RN: Further studies concerning the action of diuretics upon the aglomerular fish. J Pharmacol Ther 49:250, 1933
67. Giebisch G, Klose RM, Malnic G: Renal tubular potassium transport. Bull Schweiz Akad Med 23:287, 1967
68. Duarte CG: Magnesium metabolism in potassium-adapted rats. p. 93. In Cantin M, Seelig MS (eds): Magnesium in Health and Disease. SP Medical and Scientific Books, Jamaica, NY, 1980
69. Duarte CG: Magnesium loading in potassium-adapted rats. Am J Physiol 227:482, 1974
70. Duarte CG: Magnesium metabolism in potassium-depleted rats. Am J Physiol 234:F466, 1978
71. Catalona WJ, Palmore WP, Levitin H: Sodium wasting in potassium depletion: the role of aldosterone. Yale J Biol Med 45:33, 1972
72. Wacker WEC, Vallee BL: Magnesium. p. 483. In Comar CL, Bronner F (eds): Mineral Magnesium. Academic Press, New York, 1964
73. Old CW, Siedlecki M, Duarte CG, et al: Effects of DOCA on magnesium metabolism in potassium-depleted rats. Magnesium 3:95, 1984
74. Welt LG, Gitelman H: Disorders of magnesium metabolism. p. 1. Dis A Month 1964
75. Welt LG: Physiological data on magnesium and the kidney. p. 347. In Durlack J (ed): First International Symposium on Magnesium Deficit in Human Pathology. Vittel, France, 1971
76. Francisco LL, DiBona GF: Mechanism of negative potassium balance in the magnesium deficient rat. Kidney Int 16:852, 1979
77. Carney SL, Wong NLM, Dirks JH: Effects of magnesium deficiency and excess on renal tubular potassium transport in the rat. Clin Sci 60:549, 1981
78. Whang R, Oliver J, Welt LG, et al: Renal lesions and disturbance of renal function in rats with magnesium deficiency. An NY Acad Sci 162:766, 1969
79. Kupfer S, Kosovsky JD: Effects of cardiac glycosides on renal tubular transport of calcium, magnesium, inorganic phosphate, and glucose in the dog. J Clin Invest 44:1132, 1965
80. Wesson LG: Organic mercurial effects of renal tubular reabsorption of calcium and magnesium and on phosphate excretion in the dog. J Lab Clin Med 59:630, 1962
81. Wong NLM, Quamme GA, Sutton RAL, et al: Effects of mannitol on water and electrolyte transport in the dog kidney. J Lab Clin Med 94:683, 1979
82. Duarte CG: Effects of chlorothiazide and amipramizide (MK870) on the renal excretion of calcium, phosphate and magnesium. Metabolism 17:420, 1968
83. Eknoyan G, Suki WN, Martinez-Maldonado M: Effects of diuretics on urinary excretion of phosphate, calcium and magnesium in thyroparathyroidectomized dogs. J Lab Clin Med 76:257, 1970
84. Massry SG, Coburn JW: The hormonal and non-hormonal control of renal excretion of calcium and magnesium. Nephron 10:66, 1973
85. Wong NLM, Quamme GA, Dirks JH: Effect of chlorothiazide on renal calcium and magnesium handling in the hamster. Can J Physiol Pharmacol 60:1160, 1982

86. Leary WP, Reyes AJ: Diuretic-induced magnesium losses. Drugs 28(Supp): 182, 1984
87. Mountokalakis T, Merikas G, Skopelitis P, et al: Changes in fractional renal clearance of magnesium after spironolactone administration in normal subjects. Klin Wochenschr 53:633, 1975
88. Coundiham TB, Dunne A, Halley E, et al: The effect of amiloride on urinary, plasma and lymphocyte magnesium in congestive heart failure patients. Ir J Med Sci 147:327, 1978
89. Ryan MP, Devane J, Ryan MF, et al: Effects of diuretics on the renal handling of magnesium. Drugs 28(Supp): 167, 1984
90. Duarte CG: Effects of ethacrynic acid and furosemide on urinary calcium, phosphate and magnesium. Metabolism 17:867, 1968
91. Quamme GA: Effects of intraluminal furosemide on calcium and magnesium transport in the rat nephron. Am J Physiol 241:F340, 1981
92. Smith WO, Kyriakopoulos AA, Hammarsten JF: Magnesium depletion induced by various diuretics. Oklahoma St Med Assoc J 55:248, 1962
93. Wong NLM, Quamme GA, Dirks JH: Effects of acid-base disturbances on renal handling of magnesium in the dog. Clin Sci 70:277, 1986
94. Roy DR, Blouch KL, Jamison RL: Effects of acute acid-base disturbances on renal tubule reabsorption of magnesium in the rat. Am J Physiol 243:F197, 1982
95. Wong NLM, Dirks JH: Differential effects of acid-base changes on proximal straight tubules (PST) transport of calcium and magnesium. Fed Proc 44:1914, 1985
96. Peraino RA, Suki WN, Steibaugh BJ: Renal excretion of calcium and magnesium during correction of metabolic acidosis by bicarbonate infusion in the dog. Min Elect Metab 3:87, 1980
97. Drenik EJ: The effect of acute and prolonged fasting and refeeding on water, electrolyte, and acid-base metabolism. p. 27. In Maxwell MG, Kleeman CR (eds): Clinical Disorders of Fluid and Electrolyte Metabolism. McGraw-Hill Book Company, New York, 1980
98. Buckle RM, Care AD, Cooper CW, et al: The influence of plasma magnesium concentration on parathyroid hormone secretion. J Endocrinol 42:529, 1968
99. Gitelman HJ, Kukilj S, Welt LJ: Inhibition of parathyroid gland activity by hypermagnesemia. Am J Physiol 215:483, 1968
100. Slatopolsky E, Mercado A, Morrison A, et al: Inhibitory effects of hypermagnesemia on the renal action of parathyroid hormone. J Clin Invest 58:1273, 1976
101. Targovnik JH, Rodman JS, Sherwood LM: Regulation of parathyroid hormone synthesis in vitro: quantitative aspects of calcium and magnesium ion control. Endocrinology 898:1377, 1971
102. Allgrove J, Adam S, Fraher L, et al: Hypomagnesemia: studies of parathyroid hormone secretion and function. Clin Endocrinol 21:435, 1984
103. Raisz LG, Niemann I: Effect of phosphate, calcium and magnesium on bone resorption and hormonal response in tissue culture. Endocrinology 85:446, 1969
104. Mahaffee DD, Cooper CW, Ramp WK, et al: Magnesium promotes both parathyroid hormone secretion and adenosine 3′,5′-monophosphate production in rat parathyroid tissues and reverses the inhibitory effects of calcium on adenylate cyclase. Endocrinology 110:487, 1982
105. Heaton DW: The parathyroid glands and magnesium metabolism in the rat. Clin Sci 28:543, 1955
106. Massry SG, Coburn JW, Kleeman CR: Handling of magnesium in the dog. Am J Physiol 216:1460, 1969
107. Burnatowska MA, Harris CA, Sutton RAL, et al: Effects of PTH and cAMP on renal handling of calcium, magnesium and phosphate in the hamster. Am J Physiol 233:F514, 1977
108. Harris CA, Burnatowska MA, Seely JF, et al: Effects of parathyroid hormone on electrolyte transport in the hamster nephron. Am J Physiol 236:F438, 1979
109. Shareghi G, Agus ZS: Magnesium transport in the cortical thick ascending limb of Henle's loop of the rabbit. J Clin Invest 69:759, 1982
110. Suzuki K, Kono N, Onishi T, et al: The effect of hypermagnesemia on serum immunoreactive calcitonin levels in normal

human subjects. Acta Endocrinol 116:282, 1987
111. Anast E, David L, Winnacker J, et al: Serum calcitonin lowering effects of magnesium in patients with medullary carcinoma of the thyroid. J Clin Invest 56:1615, 1975
112. Di Stefano A, Elalouf JM, Garel JM, et al: Modulation by calcitonin of magnesium and calcium urinary excretion in the rat. Kidney Int 27:394, 1985
113. Elalouf JM, Roinel N, deRouffignac C: ADH-like effects of calcitonin on electrolyte transport by Henle's loop of rat kidney. Am J Physiol 246:F213, 1984
114. Hodgkinson A, Marshall DH, Nordin BEC: Vitamin D and magnesium absorption in man. Clin Sci 57:121, 1979
115. Kregs GJ, Nicar MJ, Zerwekh JE, et al: Effect of 1,25-dihydroxyvitamin D_3 on calcium and magnesium absorption in the healthy human jejunum and ileum. Am J Med 75:973, 1983
116. Levine BS, Brautbar N, Walling MW, et al: Effects of vitamin D and diet on magnesium metabolism. Am J Physiol 239:E515, 1980
117. Burnatowska MA, Harris CA, Sutton RAL, et al: Effects of vitamin D on renal handling of calcium, magnesium, and phosphate in the hamster. Kidney Int 27:864, 1985
118. deRouffignac C, Corman B, Roinel N: Stimulation by antidiuretic hormone of electrolyte tubular reabsorption in rat kidney. Am J Physiol 244:F156, 1983
119. Bailly C, Roinel N, Amiel C: PTH-like glucagon stimulation of Ca and Mg reabsorption in Henle's loop of the rat. Am J Physiol 242:F203, 1984
120. Hanna S, Harrison MT, MacIntyre J, et al: Effects of growth hormone on calcium and magnesium metabolism. Bri Med J 2:12, 1961
121. Weidman P, Hasler L, Gandinger MP, et al: Blood levels and renal effects of atrial natriuretic peptide in man. J Clin Invest 77:734, 1986
122. Lemann J, Jr, Piering WF, Lemann EJ: Studies of the acute effects of aldosterone and cortisol in the interrelationship between renal sodium, calcium, and magnesium excretion in normal man. Nephron 7:117, 1970
123. Lau K: Magnesium metabolism, normal and abnormal. p. 575. In Arief AI, De Fronzo RA (eds): Fluid, Electrolyte and Acid-Base Disorders. Churchill Livingstone, New York, 1985
124. Wallach S: Physiologic and critical interrelations of hormones and magnesium, consideration of thyroid, insulin, corticosteroids, sex steroids and catecholamines. p. 241. In Cantin M, Seelig MS (eds): Magnesium in Health and Disease. SP Medical and Scientific Books, Jamaica, NY, 1980
125. Wacker WEC: Biochemistry and physiology. p. 11. In Wacker WEC (ed): Magnesium and Man. Harvard University Press, Cambridge, MA, 1980
126. Leclercq-Meyer V, Marchand J, Malaisse WJ: The effect of calcium and magnesium on glucagon secretion. Endocrinology 93:1369, 1973
127. Bennett LL, Curry DL, Grodsky GM: Calcium-magnesium antagonism in insulin secretion by perfused rat pancreas. Endocrinology 85:594, 1969
128. Miller DL, Schedl HP: Effects of diabetes on intestinal magnesium absorption in the rat. Am J Physiol 231:1039, 1976
129. Schneider LE, Schedl HP: Effects of alloxan diabetes on magnesium metabolism in the rat. Proc Soc Exp Biol Med 147:494, 1974
130. Inoue K, Fried GM, Wiener I, et al: Effect of divalent cations on gastrointestinal hormone release and exocrine pancreatic secretion in dogs. Am J Physiol 248:G28, 1985
131. Barlet JP: The influence of gastrin on the fecal and urinary excretion of water, calcium, magnesium and inorganic phosphorous in sheep. Horm Metab Res 5:124, 1973
132. Pullman TN, Lavender AR, Aho I: Direct effects of glucagon on renal hemodynamics of inorganic ions. Metabolism 16:358, 1967
133. Kobayashi Y, Kitai H, Santulli R, et al: Influence of calcium and magnesium deprivation on ovulation and ovus maturation in the perfused rabbit ovary. Biol Reprod 31:287, 1984
134. Deuster PA, Dolev E, Bernier LL, et al: Magnesium and zinc status during the men-

strual cycle. Am J Ostet Gynecol 157:964, 1987
135. Deger O, Akkus I: Semen magnesium levels in fertile and infertile subjects. Magnesium 7:6, 1988
136. Seelig MS: The role of magnesium in normal and abnormal pregnancy. p. 29. In Seelig MS (ed): Magnesium Deficiency in the Pathogenesis of Disease. Plenum, New York, 1980
137. Rombola G, Benazzi E, De Ferrari MG, et al: Magnesium (Mg) renal handling during pregnancy (P). Kidney Int 28:233, 1985
138. Spatling L, Spatling G: Magnesium supplementation in pregnancy. A double-blind study. Br J Ostet Gynecol 95:120, 1988
139. Gunther T, Ising H, Mohr-Nawroth F, et al: Embryotoxic effects of magnesium deficiency and stress on rats and mice. Teratology 24:225, 1981
140. Smith JC, Brown ED: Effects of oral contraceptive agents on trace element metabolism. A review. p. 315. In Prasad AS, Oberleas D (eds): Trace Elements in Human Health and Disease. Academic Press, New York, 1976
141. Goldsmith NF, Goldsmith JR: Epidemiological aspects of magnesium and calcium metabolism. Arch Environ Health 12:606, 1966
142. Goldsmith NF, Pace N, Baumberger JP, et al: Magnesium and citrate during the menstrual cycle: Effect of an oral contraceptive on serum magnesium. Fertil Steril 21:292, 1970
143. Durlach J: Aspects of chronic magnesium deficiency. p. 883. In Cantin M, Seelig MS (eds): Magnesium in Health and Disease. SP Medical and Scientific Books, Jamaica, NY, 1980
144. Dale E, Simpson G: Serum magnesium levels in women taking an oral or long-acting injectable progestational contraceptive. Obstet Gynecol 39:115, 1972
145. Mimouni F, Miodovnik M, Tsang RC, et al: Decreased maternal serum magnesium concentration and adverse renal outcome in insulin-dependent diabetic women. Obstet Gynecol 70:85, 1987
146. Brayshaw ND, Brayshaw DD: Thyroid hypofunction in premenstrual syndrome. N Engl J Med 315:1486, 1986
147. Sherwood RA, Rocks BF, Stewart A, et al: Magnesium and the premenstrual syndrome. Ann Clin Chem 23:667, 1986
148. Vaitukaitis JL: Premenstrual syndrome. (Editorial). N Engl J Med 311:1371, 1984
149. Chakmakjian ZH, Higgins E, Abraham GE: The effects of nutritional supplement Optivite (R) for women on premenstrual tension syndrome. II. Effect on symptomatology, using a double-blind cross-over design. J Appl Nutr 37:12, 1985
150. Larvor P, Durlach J: Relations entre magnesium et glandes endocrines. p. 251. First International Symposium on Magnesium Deficit in Human Pathology. Vittel, France, 1971
151. Keeton TK, Campbell WB: The pharmacologic alterations of renin release. Pharmacol Rev 32:81, 1980
152. Cantin M: Relationship of juxtaglomerular apparatus and the adrenal cortex to biochemical and extracellular fluid changes in magnesium deficiency. Lab Invest 22:558, 1970
153. Cantin M, Huet M: Histochemistry and ultrastructure of the juxtaglomerular apparatus in magnesium deficient rat. Can J Physiol Pharmacol 51:835, 1973
154. Ginn HE, Cade R, McCallum T, et al: Aldosterone secretion in magnesium-deficient rats. Endocrinology 80:969, 1967
155. Blair-West JR, Cochlan JP, Denton DA, et al: The local action of ammonium, calcium and magnesium on adrenocortical secretion. Aust J Exp Biol Med Sci 6:371, 1968
156. Massry SG, Coburn JW, Chapman LW, et al: The acute effects of adrenal steroids on the interrelationship between the renal excretion of sodium, calcium and magnesium. J Lab Clin Med 70:563, 1967
157. Massry SG, Coburn JW, Chapman LW, et al: The effect of long-term desoxycorticosterone acetate administration on the renal excretion of calcium and magnesium. J Lab Clin Med 71:212, 1968
158. Dawson JK, Watson L: Effects of prolonged administration of aldosterone on potassium and magnesium in the rabbit. Med J Aust 2:304, 1968
159. Hanna S, MacIntyre LT: The influence of aldosterone on magnesium metabolism. Lancet 2:348, 1960

160. Miller TR, Faloon WW, Lloyd CW: Divergence in magnesium, sodium and potassium excretion during stimulation of endogenous aldosterone production. J Clin Endocrinol Metab 18:1178, 1958
161. Duarte CG, Siedlecki M, Phillips R, et al: Effects of sodium depletion on the metabolism of calcium, potassium, sodium and magnesium. To be submitted for publication.
162. Boullin DJ: The action of extracellular cations on the release of the sympathetic transmitter from peripheral nerves. J Physiol (London) 189:85, 1967
163. Whyte KF, Addis GJ, Whitesmith R, et al: Adrenergic control of plasma magnesium in man. Clin Sci 72:135, 1987
164. Fraser CL, Arief AI: Metabolic encephalopathy associated with water, electrolyte, and acid-base disorders. p. 1153. In Maxwell MH, Kleeman CR, Narins RG (eds): Clinical Disorders of Fluid and Electrolyte Metabolism. McGraw-Hill Book Company, New York, 1987
165. Anast CS, Gardner DW: Magnesium metabolism. p. 433. In Brunner F, Coburn JW (eds): Pathophysiology of Calcium, Phosphorus and Magnesium, Vol 3. Academic Press, New York, 1981
166. Altura BM: Ischemic heart disease and magnesium. Magnesium 7:57, 1988
167. Haddy FJ, Seelig MS: Magnesium and the arteries. II. Physiologic effects of electrolyte abnormalities on arterial resistance. p. 639. In Cantin M, Seelig MS (eds): Magnesium in Health and Disease. SP Medical and Scientific Books, Jamaica, NY, 1980
168. Seelig MS, Haddy FJ: Magnesium and the arteries. I. Effects of magnesium deficiency on arteries and on the retention of sodium, potassium and calcium. p. 605. In Cantin M, Seelig MS (eds): Magnesium in Health and Disease. SP Medical and Scientific Books, 1980
169. Rayssiguier Y: Magnesium and lipids interrelationship in the pathogenesis of vascular diseases. Magnesium Bull 3:165, 1981
170. Altura BT, Brust M, Gebrewold A, et al: Oral administration of magnesium lowers serum cholesterol and triglycerides and ameliorates atherogenesis in rabbits. Fed Proc 46:977, 1987
171. Larvor P: Magnesium, humoral immunity and allergy. p. 201. In Cantin M, Seelig MS (eds): Magnesium in Health and Disease. SP Medical and Scientific Books, Jamaica, NY, 1980
172. Maurier JR: Magnesium content of the food supply in the modern-day world. Magnesium 5:1, 1986
173. Rude KK, Singer FR: Magnesium deficiency and excess. Annu Rev Med 32:245, 1981
174. Davilla FP, Tabernero-Romo JM: Fisiopatologia del magnesio. Med Clin 69:206, 1977
175. Geiderman JM, Goodman SL, Cohen DB: Magnesium–the forgotten electrolyte. J Am Assoc Emerg Phys 8:204, 1979
176. Edmonson HA, Berne CJ, Homann RE, et al: Calcium, potassium, magnesium and amylase disturbances in acute pancreatitis. Am J Med 12:34, 1952
177. Paunier L, Radde IC, Kooh SW, et al: Primary hypomagnesemia with secondary hypocalcemia in an infant. Pediatrics 41:385, 1968
178. Davis BB, Preuss HG, Murdaugh HV Jr: Hypomagnesemia following the diuresis of post-renal obstruction and renal transplant. Nephron 14:275, 1975
179. Gitelman HJ, Graham JB, Welt LG: A new familial disorder characterized by hypokalemia and hypomagnesemia. Trans Assoc Am Phys 79:221, 1956
180. Evans RA, Carter JN, George CRP, et al: The congenital "magnesium-losing kidney". Q J Med New Ser 1:39, 1981
181. Bar RS, Wilson HE, Mazzaferri EL: Hypomagnesemic hypocalcemia secondary to renal magnesium wasting. A possible consequence of high dose gentamicin therapy. Ann Int J Med 82:646, 1975
182. Lyman NW, Hemalatha C, Visenso R, et al: Cisplatin-induced hypocalcemia and hypomagnesemia. Arch Intern Med 140:1513, 1980
183. Barton CH, Pahl M, Vaziri ND, et al: Renal magnesium wasting associated with Amphotericin B therapy. Am J Med 77:471, 1984
184. Dominguez JH, Gray RW, Lemann J: Dietary phosphate deprivation in women and men: effects of mineral and acid balances,

parathyroid hormone and the metabolism of 25-OH-Vitamin D. J Clin Endocrinol Metab 43:1056, 1976
185. Nielsen B, Thorn NA: Transient excess in urinary excretion of antidiuretic material in acute intermittent porphyria with hyponatremia and hypomagnesemia. Am J Med 38:345, 1965
186. Rose GA: The medical treatment of renal lithiasis. p. 117. In Wickham JEA (ed): Urinary Calculous Disease. Churchill Livingstone, New York, 1979
187. Johanssen G, Backman U, Danielson BG, et al: Biochemical and clinical effects of the prophylactic treatment of renal calcium stones with magnesium hydroxide. J Urol 124:770, 1980
188. Dyckner T, Wester PO: Intracellular magnesium loss after diuretic administration. Drugs 28:161, 1984
189. Hollifield JW: Magnesium depletion, diuretics and arrhythmias. Am J Med 82:30, 1987
190. Kroenke K, Wood DR, Hanley JF: The value of serum magnesium determination in hypertensive patients receiving diuretics. Arch Intern Med 147:1553, 1987
191. Dorup J, Kajaa K, Clausen T, et al: Reduced concentration of potassium, magnesium, and sodium-potassium pumps in human skeletal muscle during treatment with diuretics. Br Med J 296:455, 1988
192. Ryan MP, Ryan MF, Counihan TB: The effects of diuretics on lymphocyte magnesium and potassium. Acta Med Scand (Suppl) 647:145, 1981
193. Abraham AS, Meshulam Z, Rosenmann D, et al: Influence of chronic diuretic therapy on serum, lymphocyte and erythrocyte potassium, magnesium and calcium concentrations. Cardiology 75:17, 1988
194. Ryan MP, Devane J, Ryan MF, et al: Effects of diuretics on the renal handling of magnesium. Drugs 28(Supp): 167, 1984
195. Dyckner T, Wester PO, Widman L: Effects of peroral magnesium on plasma and skeletal muscle electrolytes in patients on long-term diuretic therapy. Int J Cardiol 19:81, 1988
196. Gill JR: Bartter's syndrome. Annu Rev Med 31:405, 1980
197. Gill JR, Bartter FC: Evidence for a prostaglandin-independent defect in chloride reabsorption in the loop of Henle as a proximal cause of Bartter's syndrome. Am J Med 65:766, 1978
198. Baehler RW, Work J, Kotchen TA, et al: Studies in the pathogenesis of Bartter's syndrome. Am J Med 69:933, 1980
199. Stein JH: The pathogenetic spectrum of Bartter's syndrome. Kidney Int 28:85, 1985
200. Lim P, Chir B, Dong S, et al: Intracellular magnesium depletion in chronic renal failure. N Engl J Med 280:981, 1969
201. Miller PD, Krebs RA, Neal BJ, et al: Hypomagnesemia. Suppression of secondary hyperparathyroidism in chronic renal failure. JAMA 241:722, 1979
202. Mennes P, Rosenbaum R, Martin K, et al: Hypomagnesemia and impaired parathyroid hormone secretion in chronic renal disease. Ann Intern Med 88:206, 1978
203. Agna JW, Goldsmith RE: Primary hyperparathyroidism associated with hypomagnesemia. N Engl J Med 258:222, 1958
204. Tibbetts DM, Aub JC: Magnesium metabolism in health and disease. II. The effects of parathyroid hormone. J Clin Invest 16:503, 1937
205. Mallette LE, Bilezikian JP, Heath DA, et al: Primary hyperparathyroidism: clinical and biochemical features. Medicine 53:127, 1974
206. Sutton RAL: Plasma magnesium concentration in primary hyperparathyroidism. Br Med J 1:529, 1970
207. Jones KH, Fourman P: Effect of infusions of magnesium and calcium in parathyroid insufficiency. Clin Sci 30:139, 1966
208. Jones JE, Desper PC, Shane SR, et al: Magnesium metabolism in hyperthyroidism and hypothyroidism. J Clin Invest 45:891, 1975
209. Levin GE, Maher HM, Milkingston TRE: Tissue magnesium status in diabetes mellitus. Diabetologia 21:131, 1981
210. DeLeew I, Vertommen J, Abs R: The magnesium content of the trabecular bone in diabetic patients. Biomedicine 29:16, 1978
211. Paolisso G, Sgambato S, Passariello N, et al: Insulin induces opposite changes in plasma and erythrocyte magnesium concentration in normal man. Diabetologia 29:644, 1986

212. Ratzman CW: On the insulin effect on magnesium homeostasis. Exp Clin Endocrinol 86:141, 1985
213. McNair P, Christiansen C, Madsbad S, et al: Hypomagnesemia: a risk factor in diabetic retinopathy. Diabetes 27:1075, 1978
214. Mather HM, Nisbet JA, Burton GH, et al: Hypomagnesemia in diabetes. Clin Chim Acta 95:235, 1979
215. Mader TJ, Iseri LT: Spontaneous hypopotassemia, hypomagnesemia, alkalosis and tetany due to hypersection of corticosterone-like mineralocorticoid. Am J Med 19:1187, 1962
216. Horton R, Biglieri EG: Effect of aldosterone on the metabolism of magnesium. J Clin Endocrinol 22:1187, 1962
217. Cronin RE: Magnesium disorders. p. 502. In Kokko JP, Tannen RL (eds): Fluids and Electrolytes. WB Saunders, Philadelphia, 1986
218. Brautbar N, Massry SG: Hypomagnesemia and hypermagnesemia. p. 831. In Maxwell MH, Kleeman CR, Narins RG (eds): Clinical Disorders of Fluid and Electrolyte Metabolism. McGraw-Hill Book Company, New York, 1987
219. Itokawa Y, Tseng L-F, Fujiwara M: Thiamine metabolism in magnesium deficient rats. J Nutr Sci Vitaminol (Tokyo) 20:249, 1974
220. Anderson R, Cohen M, Haller R: Skeletal muscle phosphorus and magnesium deficiency in alcoholic myopathy. Min Elect Metab 4:106, 1980
221. Flink EB: Magnesium deficiency and magnesium toxicity in man. p. 1. In Prasad AS, Oberleas D (eds): Trace Elements in Human Health and Disease. Academic Press, New York, 1976
222. Flink EB, Morano GD, Morabito RA, et al: Plasma free fatty acids and magnesium in the alcohol withdrawal syndrome. p. 73. In Cantin M, Seelig MS (eds): Magnesium in Health and Disease. SP Medical and Scientific Books, Jamaica, NY, 1980
223. Altura BM, Altura BT: Magnesium electrolyte transport and coronary vascular disease. Drugs, 28(Suppl):120, 1984
224. Iseri LT: Magnesium in coronary artery disease. Drugs, 28(Suppl):151, 1984
225. Burch GE, Giles TD: The importance of magnesium deficiency in cardiovascular disease. Am Heart J 94:649, 1977
226. Seelig MS: Magnesium deficiency and cardiac dysrhythmia. p. 219. In Seelig MS (ed): Magnesium Deficiency in Pathogenesis of Disease. Plenum, New York, 1980
227. Ryzen E, Wagers PW, Singer FR, et al: Magnesium deficiency in medical ICU population. Crit Care Med 13:19, 1985
228. Whang R, Oei TO, Aikawa JK, et al: Predictors of clinical hypomagnesemia. Hypokalemia, hypophosphatemia, hyponatremia, and hypocalcemia. Arch Intern Med 144:1794, 1984
229. Kurnik BRC, Marshall J, Katz SM: Hypomagnesemia-induced cardiomyopathy. Magnesium 7:49, 1988
230. Anderson TW, Leriche WH, Hewitt D, et al: Magnesium, water hardness and heart disease. p. 566. In Cantin M, Seelig MS (eds): Magnesium in Health and Disease. SP Medical & Scientific Books, Jamaica, NY, 1980
231. Rector WG Jr., DeWood MA, Williams RV, et al: Serum magnesium and copper levels in myocardial infarction. Am J Med Sci 281:25, 1981
232. Heggveit HA, Tommer P, Hunt B: Magnesium content of normal and ischemic hearts. p. 53. Seventh International Congress of Pathology, Montreal, 1969
233. Seelig MS: Is clinical arteriosclerosis a manifestation of absolute or conditional magnesium deficiency? p. 161. In Seelig MS (ed): Magnesium Deficiency in the Pathogenesis of Disease. Plenum, New York, 1980
234. Ellis VM, Wolmsley RN: A comparison of plasma magnesium values in patients with acute myocardial infarction and patients with chest pain due to other causes. Med J Aust 148:14, 1988
235. Rasmussen HS, McNair P, Goransson L, et al: Magnesium deficiency in patients with ischemic heart disease with and without acute myocardial infarction uncovered by an intravenous loading test. Arch Int Med Assoc 148:329, 1984
236. Cohen L, Kitzes R: Magnesium sulfate and digitalis-toxic arrhythmias. JAMA 249:2808, 1988
237. Packer M, Gottlieb SS, Blum MA: Imme-

diate and long-term pathophysiologic mechanisms underlying the genesis of sudden cardiac death in patients with congestive heart failure. Am J Med (Suppl 3A):4, 1987

238. Whang R, Oei TO, Watanabe A: Frequency of hypomagnesemia in hospitalized patients receiving digitalis. Arch Intern Med 145:655, 1985

239. Iseri LT: Magnesium and cardiac arrhythmias. Magnesium 5:111, 1986

240. Rasmussen HS, Suenson M, McNair P, et al: Magnesium infusions reduces the incidence of arrhythmias in acute myocardial infarction. A double-blind placebo-controlled study. Clin Cardiol 10:351, 1987

241. Abraham AS, Rosenmann D, Meshulan Z, et al: Intracellular cations and diuretic therapy following acute myocardial infarction. Arch Intern Med 146:1301, 1986

242. Cappuccio FP, Markandu ND, Beynon GW, et al: Lack of effect of oral magnesium on high blood pressure: a double blind study. Br Med J 291:235, 1985

243. Maxwell MH, Waks AU: Cations in hypertension. Am J Cardiol 59:108A, 1987

244. Rosevsky JB: Magnesium in exchange transfusion. N Engl J Med 286:843, 1972

245. Bajdpai PC, Sugden D, Stern, et al: Serum ionic magnesium in exchange transfusion. J Pediatrics 70:193, 1967

246. Broughton A, Anderson IRM, Bowden CH: Magnesium-deficiency syndrome in burns. Lancet 2:1156, 1968

247. Heaton FW: Magnesium metabolism in surgical patients. Clin Chim Acta 9:327, 1964

248. Case Records of the Massachusetts General Hospital #4-1986. N Engl J Med 314:302, 1986

249. Rudick JH, Sheehan JP: Hypomagnesemia, hypocalcemia, and toxic-shock syndrome. A case report. Magnesium 6:325, 1987

250. Mills JT, Parsonnet T, Tsai Y-C, et al: Control of production of toxic-shock syndrome toxin-1-(TSS-1) by magnesium ion. J Infect Dis 151:1158, 1985

251. Greenwald JH, Dubin A, Cardon L: Hypomagnesemic tetany due to excessive lactation. Am J Med 35:854, 1963

252. Caddell JL: Magnesium therapy in premature neonates with apnea neonatorum. J Am Coll Nutr 7:5, 1988

253. Tsang RC, Mimouni F: Editorial. J Am Coll Nutr 7:1, 1988

254. Flink EB: Magnesium deficiency. Etiology and clinical spectrum. Acta Med Scand(Suppl 647):125, 1981

255. Vallee BL, Wacker WEC, Ulmer DD: The magnesium-deficiency tetany syndrome in man. N Engl J Med 262:155, 1960

256. Anast CS, Winnacker JL, Forte LR, et al: Impaired release of parathyroid hormone in magnesium deficiency. J Clin Endocrinol Metab 42:707, 1976

257. Suh SM, Tashjian AH Jr, Matsuo N, et al: Pathogenesis of hypocalcemia in primary hypomagnesemia: Normal end-organ responsiveness to parathyroid hormone, impaired parathyroid gland function. J Clin Invest 52:153, 1973

258. Seelig MS: Tests for magnesium deficiency. p. 357. In Seelig MS (ed): Magnesium Deficiency in the Pathogenesis of Disease. Plenum, New York, 1980

259. Flink EB: Therapy of magnesium deficiency. Ann NY Acad Sci 162:901, 1969

260. Dorup I, Skajaa K, Clausen T: A simple and rapid method for the determination of the concentrations of magnesium, sodium, potassium and sodium, potassium pumps in human skeletal muscle. Clin Sci 74:241, 1988

261. Flink EB: Magnesium deficiency. Causes and effects. Hosp Pract 22:117A, 1987

262. Massry SG, Seelig MS: Hypomagnesemia and hypermagnesemia. Clin Nephrol 7:147, 1977

263. Mordes JP, Wacker WEC: Excess magnesium. Pharmacol Rev 29:273, 1978

264. Massry SG, Seelig MS: Hypomagnesemia and hypermagnesemia. Clin Nephrol 7:147, 1977

265. Spencer HA, Lesniak M, Gatza CA, et al: Magnesium absorption and metabolism in patients with chronic renal failure and in patients with normal function. Gastroenterology 79:26, 1980

266. Wong NLM, Quamme GA, Dirks JH, et al: Divalent ion transport in dogs with experimental chronic renal failure. Can J Physiol Pharmacol 60:1296, 1982

267. Kleeman CR, Better O, Massry SG, et al: Divalent ion metabolism and osteodystrophy in chronic renal failure. Yale J Biol Med 40:1, 1967
268. Bourgoignie JJ, Hwang KH, Espinel C, et al: Natriuretic factor in serum of patients with chronic uremia. J Clin Invest 51:1514, 1972
269. Jenny DB, Goris GB, Urwiller RD, et al: Hypermagnesemia following irrigation of renal pelvis. Cause of respiratory depression. JAMA 240:1378, 1978
270. Wacker WEC, Vallee BL: A study of magnesium metabolism in acute renal failure employing a multichannel flame spectrometer. N Engl J Med 257:1254, 1957
271. Mordes JP, Swartz R, Arky RA: Extreme hypermagnesemia as a cause of refractory hypotension. Ann Intern Med 83:657, 1975
272. Gomella M, Bonagluid F, Buzzigoli G, et al: On the effect of magnesium on the PTH secretion in uremic patients on maintenance dialysis. Nephron 27:40, 1981
273. Kenny MA, Casillas E, Ahmad S: Magnesium, calcium and PTH relationships in dialysis patients after magnesium repletion. Nephron 46:199, 1987
274. Contiguglia SR, Alfrey AC, Miller N, et al: Total-body magnesium excess in chronic renal failure. Lancet 1:1300, 1972
275. Mellerup ET, Plence P: Lithium effects on magnesium, calcium and phosphate. Int Pharmacopsychiatry 11:190, 1976
276. Cohen L, Kitzes R: Pheochromocytoma—A rare cause of hypermagnesemia. Magnesium 4:165, 1985
277. Madajewica S, Szymendera J, Zulawski M: Hypermagnesemia in malignant neoplasms. Pol Med J 10:599, 1971
278. Chatterjea NM, Saran A: Serum magnesium in hepatic disease. J Assoc Phys India 24:505, 1976
279. Pritchard JA: Management of preeclampsia and eclampsia. Kidney Int 18:259, 1980
280. Sokal MM, Koenigsberger MR, Rose JS, et al: Neonatal hypermagnesemia and the meconium-plug syndrome. N Engl J Med 286:823, 1972
281. Ferdinandus J, Pederson JA, Whang R: Hypermagnesemia as a cause of refractory hypotension, respiratory depression and coma. Arch Intern Med 141:669, 1981
282. Hughes A, Tonks RS: Platelets, magnesium and myocardial infarction. Lancet 1:1041, 1965
283. Emmett M, Narins RG: (Letter) Ann Intern Med 84:340, 1976

8

Disorders of Trace Mineral Deficiency and Parenteral Nutrition

Uri Alon
Mary Jacob
Murray F. Brennan

The term *trace element* originated from early works, at a time when the precise measurement of many mineral elements occurring in living tissues in very small amounts was not feasible because of lack of adequate analytic methods. The trace elements can be divided into three groups: those that are essential in the diet, those that may be essential in the diet, and those that are not essential in the diet. An element is considered essential if it fulfills the following criteria:[1,2] (1) the element is present in healthy tissues, (2) deficiency of the element consistently produces a functional impairment, (3) the abnormalities induced by deficiency are always accompanied by pertinent, specific biochemical changes, and (4) addition of the element prevents or reverses these abnormalities. The insults associated with profound deficiency may be irreversible, and hence prevention of abnormalities is a better criterion of essentiality than is reversibility. In contrast to nonessential trace elements, the distribution of which reflects environmental concentrations, essential trace elements would be expected to be homeostatically regulated within relatively narrow limits, as well as to be provided in proper quantities to the fetus and in breast milk.

A state of trace element deficiency can result from inadequate intake, decrease availability, impaired reabsorption, excessive excretion, and extracorporeal losses. With the advent of total parenteral nutrition, iatrogenic deficiencies have been noted for several essential trace elements (Table 8-1).

The objective of this chapter is to review the current knowledge on deficiency states for zinc, copper, selenium, chromium, cobalt, manganese, and fluorine, and their implications for the management of total parenteral nutrition (TPN).

ZINC

Zinc was first recognized to be an essential element of human nutrition in 1961, when zinc deficiency was associated with the prevalence of dwarfism and hypogonadism in the Middle East.[3] Spontaneous and experimentally induced zinc deficiency has

Table 8-1. Etiologies of Disordered Trace Element Metabolism

Inadequate intake
   Absolute deficiency—Protein-calorie malnutrition, anorexia, fad diets, low income diets, diets with alcohol providing the bulk of calories, TPN without adequate supplementation.
   Increased requirements—Rapid growth, pregnancy, lactation, tissue anabolism

Decreased availability
   Interactions with other dietary constituents
   GI dysfunction
      Inadequate digestive processes
      Secondary interactions with unabsorbed dietary constituents
   Iatrogenic
      Complexing with drugs
      Drug induced alterations of GI function

Impaired Absorption
   Altered binding factors
      Quantitative or qualitative
      Congenital or acquired
      Competitive uptake of other nutrients
   Inadequate functional surface
      Surgical resection
      GI mucosal disease
      Competitive uptake of other nutrients
   Physiologically appropriate depression of absorption
   Impaired mucosal "packaging"
      Inability to store
      Sequestration

Altered distribution
   Defective transport
      Quantitative or qualitative changes in transport compounds
      Competitive displacement
   Altered tissue receptor sites
   Altered tissue storage compounds
      Inability to store
      Sequestration
   Transient alterations in distribution—Infection, myocardial infarct, stress, etc.

Excessive losses
   Sweat
   Semen
   Menstrual losses, other forms of blood loss
   Urinary—Wastage of nutrient, transport compounds
   Fecal
      A. Pancreatic
      B. Biliary
      C. Gut
   Upper GI losses—Vomiting, nasogastric suction, ostomies
   Other

been observed in several species.[4] Anorexia, skin lesions, loss of taste (hypogeusia) and smell (hyposmia), impairment of reproductive processes, growth retardation, lowered resistance to infections, decreased immune response, and delayed wound healing are some of the most common symptoms observed with zinc deficiency. Most of these effects are reversed by adequate zinc supplements. It would be ideal if specific biochemical defects could be correlated with clinical and pathologic effects of zinc deficiency. Despite considerable effort, however, it has proven difficult to distinguish between the primary and secondary effects of zinc deficiency. Nevertheless, several investigations studying biochemical alterations in zinc-deficient animals have provided important insights into the functional role and mechanisms of action of zinc at the cellular level.[5] The importance of zinc has been primarily related to its key role in over 200 vital enzyme systems, either as an integral structural component of metalloenzymes or as a catalyst in zinc-activated enzyme systems.[6] However, the activity of many of the zinc metalloenzymes does not change when the cellular supply of zinc is inadequate, and zinc is therefore assumed to have additional, nonenzymatic functions. Zinc has been shown to be involved in maintaining the structural and functional integrity of cell membranes by protecting against oxidative damage.[7] Recent evidence derived from the mouse as a model indicates that zinc has a variety of crucial roles in cell-mediated immunity and other, related host defense mechanisms.[8]

The causes of zinc deficiency include low intake, metabolic disturbances resulting in increased need or excessive excretion, and genetic abnormalities. There is evidence that zinc intake is marginal or low in several population groups, such as children of low-income Americans,[9] institutionalized individuals, the elderly, and pregnant teenagers.[10] It is also known that marginal deficiency results from the low bioavailability of zinc in some food sources.[11] Endogenous and exogenous factors known to affect the bioavailability of zinc include components in the diet, zinc binding factors present in the intestinal lumen, constituents of the brush border membrane, intracellular factors, and the availability of plasma carriers of zinc.[12] In adults, approximately 20 to 30 percent of ingested dietary zinc is absorbed. The absorption of zinc from human milk has been reported to be higher (41 percent) than absorption from formulas based on cow's milk (31 percent) or from cow's milk itself (28 percent). This enhanced bioavailability has been attributed to a low-molecular-weight ligand—citrate—isolated from breast milk.[13] Although many aspects of zinc absorption remain unresolved, it is currently visualized as a two-step process. The first step involves carrier-mediated zinc transport at the brush border membrane followed by intracellular interaction of the mineral with low- and high-molecular-weight zinc-binding proteins. In the second step the zinc is transferred by active transport across the basolateral membrane to plasma albumin. There is general consensus that zinc absorption and accumulation in the body are under homeostatic control. It has been shown that the intestinal uptake and re-excretion of zinc are regulated according to the needs of the individual, thus maintaining plasma levels and body stores in the face of variable dietary zinc intakes.[12]

The major pathway of zinc excretion is via the feces. Fecal zinc consists mainly of unabsorbed dietary zinc and a small endogenous fraction. The latter comes from the direct transfer of zinc through the intestinal wall and from pancreatic juice and bile.[4] The urinary excretion of zinc varies from 2 to 6 percent of the normal dietary intake of adults. There is some loss through sweat, in the hair, and by the sloughing of the skin. However, these losses could assume importance in abnormal situations such as those associated with kidney and liver diseases, muscle breakdown, alcoholism, or conditions of excessive sweating.[14] A conditioned deficiency of zinc secondary to metabolic disturbances in various disease states and under conditions of stress has been observed in humans. Abnormal zinc metabolism has been reported in patients with alcoholic cirrhosis, chronic renal disease, pancreatic insufficiency, gastrointestinal disease, burns, and collagen diseases, and in iatrogenically induced situations.[14] A genetic disorder that exhibits clinical and biochemical features of zinc deficiency is acrodermatitis enteropathica. It is a rare, autosomal, recessively inherited disease usually occurring in infants and associated with an impairment in zinc absorption, and is corrected by supplemental zinc.[12] In addition, since zinc deficiency was demonstrated among sickle cell anemia patients, a role for zinc has been proposed in this disease. Zinc protects against sickling by decreasing the binding of hemoglobin to the erythrocyte membrane, resulting in increased oxygen affinity.[6]

Zinc deficiency effects rapidly growing tissues. In rats, maternal deficiency during pregnancy has been shown to cause fetal abnormalities, including a high frequency of defects of the central nervous system.[15-17] Most of this experimental evidence has been derived from animal studies. It has been difficult to establish a causal relationship between zinc deficiency and malformations in the brain in humans.[18-21] However, tentative associations have been drawn from data obtained from anencephalic subjects and zinc deficiency in West Germany,[21] and between inadequate zinc status and various fetal defects in Sweden.[22] Approximately two-thirds of absorbed zinc is transported bound to albumin, and the remainder is complexed with α_2-macroglobulin, transferrin, and some amino acids, such as histidine and cysteine. In the systemic circulation, 80 to 90 percent of the zinc is found in erythrocytes and leukocytes.

The liver plays an important role in the metabolism of zinc, under the control of several hormones, mainly those involved in regulating the body's defense against stress. A relatively large quantity of newly absorbed zinc is taken up by the liver prior to distribution to other tissues. This process has been associated with a low-molecular-weight protein, metallothionein, found in large amounts in the liver as well as in the intestines and kidney. This metalloprotein is induced by zinc and has been suggested to have a protective function in preventing abnormal intracellular concentrations of zinc.[23] Nevertheless, the role of metallothionein remains to be clearly established, since many other factors, including other metals, infections, physiologically active substances such as interleukin-I, and certain drugs increase metallothionein synthesis and thus affect the zinc content of the liver. Chronic administration of prednisone has been shown to depress ^{65}Zn retention in the livers of young rats.[24]

The adult recommended dietary allowance (RDA) of zinc is 15 mg/day, on the basis of human metabolic studies and the turnover of body zinc using ^{65}Zn.[25] The adequacy of this intake is based on the assumption that individuals consume a varied diet containing animal products. Adjustments are made in the adult RDA to meet the needs of growth, pregnancy, and lactation, and also to allow for the availability of zinc from the diet. The requirement for children increases with age (Table 8-2).

The simplest method for assessing zinc status has been the determination of zinc in plasma and urine. However, with the delineation of homeostatic mechanisms that regulate zinc, it has become increasingly clear that plasma zinc is not a reliable indicator of zinc status. Functional tests involving measurements of selected zinc metalloenzymes have been used to detect zinc deficiency.[26] Leukocyte concentrations of zinc show promise in assessing zinc status, but the usefulness and feasibility of this method has not been evaluated in studies among various population groups. The most sensitive test for zinc status would be a well-defined, measurable response to supplemental zinc under controlled conditions.[6] Currently there is no test that definitively indicates a borderline or marginal deficiency of zinc in humans.

COPPER

The importance of copper as a trace element was demonstrated first in 1928 by Hart and associates,[27] who showed that it was required to prevent the development of anemia in rats fed a milk-based diet. Numerous further studies proved copper to be an essential micronutrient in mammals, in whom most of its biologic activities occur through copper metalloenzymes. Yet it was only in 1964 that Cordano and colleagues[28] demonstrated the consequences of copper deficiency in an infant. Eight years later, Danks and co-workers[29-30] reported the connection between Menkes disease and defects in copper metabolism, and Karpel and Peden[31] reported the development of copper deficiency in long-term parenteral nutrition.

The total body copper increases from 10 mg in the newborn to 70 to 150 mg in the adult.[32] The liver and brain are especially rich in copper, and contain about one third of the total body content of this element. Skeletal muscles have a low copper concentration, but because of the large muscular mass they also contain one third of the body copper content.[33] The average

Table 8-2. Recommended Dietary Allowances for Zinc

	Zinc mg/day
Infant, 0–½ yr	3
½–1 yr	5
Children, 1–10 yr	10
Adolescents	15
Adults	15
Pregnancy	20
Lactation	25

daily dietary intake of copper is about 2.0 to 5.0 mg, of which about one third, or 0.6 to 1.6 mg/day, is absorbed.[34,35] The copper is rapidly absorbed from the upper gastrointestinal tract.[36,37] There appear to be two separate mechanisms for copper absorption: passive diffusion and energy-dependent active transport.[38,39] While the simple diffusion mechanism accounts for the absorption of ionic copper,[40] the active mechanism involves the transport of copper-amino complexes to the intestinal mucosa.[41] In man, orally administered ^{64}Cu reaches its peak serum concentration in 1 to 2 hours, mostly bound to albumin but partly to amino acids; this is followed by a sharp drop due to uptake by the liver. As the isotope is incorporated into ceruloplasmin, a secondary rise in the serum concentration of ^{64}Cu is noted for 48 to 72 hours.[42,45] Copper absorption is enhanced in copper-deficient rats and humans.[46] It seems that the active transport mechanism is influenced by the copper status of the body, and that there is no direct relationship between the plasma ceruloplasmin concentration and the rate of copper absorption.[44,47] Most copper excretion occurs through the excretion of bile, with little or no enterohepatic circulation of the element.[48,49] Small amounts of copper leave the body in intestinal excretions, and even smaller amounts through the urine.[34] It seems that excretion through the bile serves as the main homeostatic mechanism for copper[37,50]; however, in cases of interference with bile excretion, a greater amount of copper is excreted in the intestinal fluids and the urine, thus preventing accumulation of copper in the body.[51] Hypercupremia with a normal serum ceruloplasmin concentration was recently described in patients with chronic renal failure.[52] It was hypothesized that this was due to increased intestinal absorption of copper secondary to the zinc deficiency in these patients.

The plasma copper concentration undergoes pronounced developmental changes. It is lowest, approximately 30 μg/dl, at birth, and increases to approach that of adults at the age of 5 months.[53] After 3 years of age, serum copper values decrease markedly until adolescence, when they are approximately 100 to 110 μg/dl. During and after adolescence, the serum copper increases once again, most likely in relation to increased estrogen production.[54] As a result, women have higher serum copper concentrations than men: 130 to 150 μg/dl as compared to 105 to 125 μg/dl, respectively. The blood copper concentration has also been suggested to be an indicator of total body copper status.[55] Hatano and associates[55] found that erythrocyte copper, which constitutes about 50 percent of the whole blood copper, fluctuates with age, and that the activity of Cu,Zn-superoxide dismutase, which contains about 60 percent of the erythrocyte copper, is reduced by copper deficiency and restored by copper supplementation. As a result of the relatively long half-life of erythrocytes, it is possible that erythrocyte copper and/or Cu,Zn-superoxide dismutase activity reflect long-term copper status in the body.

Cuproenzymes are involved in a great number of biochemical processes in mammals, including synthesis of the structural subunits of collagen and elastin (lysyl oxidase) and of the tertiary structure of proteins such as keratin (monoamine oxidase); the adrenal synthesis of catecholamines (dopamine β hydroxylase); the formation of melanin pigment in hair and skin (tyrosinase); mitochondrial energy production through oxidative phosphorylation (cytochrome c oxidase); and the killing of bacteria by white blood cells (Cu,Zn-superoxide dismutase).[56] The mineralization of growing bones seems to be related to copper, either in a cuproenzyme with ascorbate oxidase activity, or in its soluble, ionic form.[32] Copper has a number of functions in iron metabolism, but whether or not serum ceruloplasmin has a physiologically important role in the mobilization of iron is

Table 8-3. Recommended Dietary Allowances for Copper

	mg/day
Infants, 0–½ yr	0.5–0.7
½–1 yr	0.7–1.0
Children, 1–3 yr	1.0–1.5
4–6 yr	1.5–2.0
7–10 yr	2.0–2.5
Adolescents	2.0–3.0
Adults	2.0–3.0

still controversial.[57,58] Copper is also important in the myelination of nerve fibers[59] and the production of neutrophils[60]; however, the mechanisms of its involvement in these functions are not completely understood.

Recommended dietary allowances for copper are shown in Table 8-3. Copper deficiency is an unusual clinical disorder in human beings because almost any diet contains several milligrams of copper. In young children, however, protein-energy malnutrition and diarrhea[60,61] or prematurity,[62–64] especially when associated with a diet based exclusively on cow's milk, can condition the development of copper deficiency. Copper deficiency can impair the growth of children recovering from malnutrition.[65] The most common iatrogenic cause of copper deficiency is prolonged total parenteral nutrition with insufficient supplementation with copper.[66,67,68] In addition to these acquired conditions, Menkes and associates first described in 1962[69] a congenital X-linked recessive disorder with growth retardation, peculiar hair, cerebral degeneration, arterial changes, and death in early childhood. Ten years later, Danks and co-workers[29,30] found that the disorder resulted from an inherited defect in copper metabolism.

Most of the clinical signs observed in states of copper deficiency can be attributed to the reduced activity of one or more of the cuproenzymes.[31,66] In both the congenital metabolic defect and acquired copper deficiency, these signs include low circulating copper and ceruloplasmin concentrations, depigmentation of skin and hair, arterial aneurysms and vascular tortuosity, emphysematous lungs, growth and psychomotor retardation, hypotonia and hypothermia, and skeletal demineralization, which is seen only in infants and young children and may radiologically resemble scurvy or the "battered child syndrome." Patients with Menkes' kinky hair syndrome, besides the characteristic kinky hair, often have seborrheic dermatitis. Those with acquired copper deficiency also develop neutropenia and hypochromic and microcytic anemia as the earliest manifestations of copper deficiency. It is yet unclear why patients with the congenital disorder do not develop anemia and neutropenia.

Whereas all the signs in patients with acquired copper deficiency usually disappear with copper supplementation, this is not the case in Menkes' kinky hair syndrome. In this disorder the basic defect appears to consist of excessive binding of copper to certain tissues, including fibroblasts and the intestinal mucosa.[70–72] The defect in the intestinal mucosa may account for the decreased copper absorption and serum copper concentration, which in turn account for the diminished synthesis of ceruloplasmin. Although parenteral copper administration begun in early infancy raises the serum ceruloplasmin concentration, this does not seem to prevent the progressive cerebral damage in Menkes syndrome. Recently, a milder genetic syndrome, without the usual lethal consequences, has been identified as a partial penetration of the gene responsible for Menkes syndrome.[73]

SELENIUM

During the first half of the twentieth century, interest in selenium was confined to its toxicity in livestock.[74,75] Attention became focused on the physiologic role of selenium in 1957, when Schwarz and Foltz[76] demonstrated that supplementation with selenium prevented the development of liver necrosis in rats, and others[77,78] showed a protective effect of selenium against exudative diathesis in chicks. Shortly afterwards, McLean in New Zealand[79] and Muth and associates[80] in Oregon discovered that muscular dystrophy, occurring naturally in calves and lambs in those areas, was a manifestation of selenium deficiency, and could be prevented by selenium therapy. Subsequently, naturally selenium deficient areas, in which the growth and health of animals were impaired, were demonstrated in many countries, especially New Zealand,[81] Scandinavia,[82,83] and parts of North America.[84] Many of the disorders of animals responsive to selenium were found also to respond to vitamin E, and it was not until 1967 that Thompson and Scott[85] provided conclusive evidence that selenium is a nutritionally essential element with a role beyond that of a substitute for a normal intake of vitamin E.

Selenium is similar to sulfur in many of its chemical properties, and can replace it in disulfide bridges. It can also occur in both organic and inorganic forms. Although many proteins can bind the element, only four selenoenzyme are currently recognized. Very little is known about the incorporation of selenium into these proteins. Recent data suggest the existence of a specific transfer RNA for selenoproteins.[86] Three of the selenoproteins were detected in nonhuman organisms: formate dehydrogenase[87] and glycine dehydrogenase[88] in bacteria, and a selenium containing cytochrome in sheep.[89] The fourth selenoenzyme, found in humans and other mammals is glutathione peroxidase, which contains selenium in its active site in the form of selenocysteine.[90,91] This enzyme catalyzes the degradation of hydrogen peroxide and other peroxides to water while using glutathione as a substrate. In addition, the enzyme is thought to affect cytochrome P450 and prostaglandin metabolism.[92]

Selenium occurs in all cells and tissues of the body in concentrations that vary with the tissue and the selenium content in the diet. Most abundant in selenium are the kidneys, especially the renal cortex, and the liver, pancreas, and pituitary gland.[93] The kidneys and the liver are the most sensitive indicators of selenium status in research animals. Cardiac muscle is consistently higher in selenium than skeletal muscle.[94,95] It should be noted that in some tissues, not all of the glutathione peroxidase contains selenium; in erythrocytes, nevertheless, it is totally a selenoenzyme. The activity of the enzyme depends on the availability of selenium in the diet. A reduction to 15 percent of the normal activity of the enzyme in human tissues was reported by Young and associates following reduction in selenium availability.[96] On the other hand, selenium toxicity, resulting from 10 to 100 times more than the recommended intake, increases selenium content and enzyme activity beyond normal levels, but only to a certain plateau, which in humans occurs at a selenium concentration of 0.14 µg/ml.[97] At this stage, excretion of the trace element equals its absorption.[98] However, it is not only selenium status that affects the activity of the enzyme. Marked differences were observed in different species, age groups, sexes, and clinical conditions. In addition, the activity of glutathione peroxidase is affected by oxidant stress. Therefore, the activity of the enzyme is not a good indicator of selenium status. Thompson and associates[99] stated that each individual might have an optimal level of glutathione peroxidase activity, reflecting the overall effect of several factors.

Selenium is primarily absorbed in the duodenum, and in humans it appears that the absorption is greater than 90 percent of the intake.[97] After absorption it is first carried by the plasma proteins, from which it enters the cells of all tissues. When ^{75}Se is added to human blood, 50 to 70 percent is taken up by cells in 1 to 2 minutes.[101] The intracellular distribution of selenium varies with the tissue, time after administration, and selenium concentration. Most of the element deposited in the tissues is highly labile. Once animals are transferred from a high to a low selenium diet,[102] or following the injection of radiolabelled selenium,[103] the element is removed from the body through excretion into the feces and urine, and in expired air. The biologic half-life of the total body selenium in humans is between 65 and 70 days,[100,104,105] and the main site of excretion is the urine.[106]

The main methods for the assessment of selenium status in humans include measurement of concentrations of the element in whole blood, red blood cells, plasma or serum, urine, and hair. There is a significant correlation between the concentration of selenium in the blood and that in urine and hair.[4] An effective estimation of urine selenium excretion has to be based on a 24-hour collection.[107] The values obtained reflect the absorbable selenium in the diet.[108,109] Blood concentrations of selenium depend on selenium intake, which is affected by geographic area. In the United States, the reference value for adults ranges between 0.10 to 0.34 µg/ml, with a mean of 0.21 µg/ml,[110] whereas in New Zealand it is about one third of these values.[111] As noted earlier, the measurement of glutathione peroxidase activity is also of limited value, since it is poorly correlated with whole blood concentrations above 0.1 µg/ml.[111] In general, since the plasma selenium concentration responds to dietary changes more rapidly than erythrocyte selenium, it is considered a more sensitive index of short-term changes in selenium status, whereas erythrocyte selenium and glutathione peroxidase activity are more indicative of long-term selenium nutrition.[97]

Several animal diseases were recognized as originating from a low-selenium intake. These include liver necrosis in rats[76] and pigs,[94,112] exudative diathesis, encephalomalacia, and pancreatic atrophy in chicks,[78,113,114] muscular dystrophy in lambs, calves, and foals,[79-81,115] periodontal disease in ewes,[116] and heart disease in pigs.[117] In addition, selenium supplementation was shown to promote growth, improve fertility, and reduce postnatal losses among animals in selenium-poor areas.[79,81]

The best known selenium deficiency disease in humans is Keshan disease. The disease is an endemic cardiomyopathy with lethal consequences, occurring in children and young women in Keshan, a province of China.[118-120] The main pathologic feature of the disease, which was first described in 1935, is multiple focal myocardial necrosis scattered throughout the heart muscle, with different degrees of cell infiltration and various stages of fibrosis. Because of some similarities in the pathology of the disease to that of selenium-deficient muscle disease in cattle, the possible involvement of selenium was investigated.[4] The selenium content of the soil and grains in Keshan province was found to be low, and hair and urine selenium and the activity of glutathione peroxidase were reduced in the pediatric population.[118-121] Initial studies, in 1965, about the preventive effect of supplementary sodium selenite gave encouraging results, and in the next decade were further extended, leading to a significant reduction in morbidity and mortality from the disease.[121]

Recently, two other cases of selenium deficiency-induced cardiomyopathy were described. Johnson and associates[122] reported the myopathy in a 43-year-old-man who received parenteral alimentation for two years with hyperalimentation solutions almost devoid of selenium. The patient's erythrocyte selenium concentration and glutathione peroxidase were only 10 percent of normal. Signs of cardiomyopathy included frequent ventricular extrasystoles, bursts of nonsustained ventricular tachycardia, and ventricular fibrillation. A cardiac scan showed great dilatation of the left ventricle and a decreased left ventricular ejection fraction. Postmortem examination of the heart disclosed a histopathologic picture resembling that of Keshan disease, with a reduced content of selenium and depressed activity of glutathione peroxidase. Collipp and Chen[123] described a 2-year-old black American girl who had typical clinical features of Keshan disease including dyspnea, tachycardia, cardiomegaly, and congestive heart failure. The child's blood selenium concentration was much below control values. After 4 weeks of selenium supplementation, her serum concentration returned to normal and the child improved steadily. A dietary history revealed that the child consumed no cereal products, no dairy products, and little meat, thus resulting in a very low intake of selenium.

A selenium-responsive syndrome consisting of myalgia and muscle tenderness has been reported by Van Rig[124] in a patient who received parenteral nutrition for 16 months. Supplementation with selenium enabled the patient to walk again within one week of treatment. In 1983, Kien and Ganther[125] described a child on TPN who developed muscle pain and tenderness and in whom the serum selenium concentration and activity of glutathione peroxidase were very low. Treatment with selenium resolved the clinical and biochemical picture. In 1986, Brown and colleagues[126] reported on a 33-year-old woman on long-term home parenteral nutrition who developed severe muscular weakness and an extremely low activity of glutathione peroxidase in her red and white blood cells. Treatment with selenium given intravenously resolved the clinical and biochemical abnormalities in 6 to 12 weeks. Recently, Vinton and associates[127] reported on low selenium levels in four children receiving long-term parenteral nutrition who developed macrocytosis, loss of pigmentation of hair and skin, and profound muscle weakness. Laboratory data revealed elevated transaminase and creatine kinase activities. All clinical and laboratory findings resolved with selenium supplementation. An endemic muscular syndrome, characterized by muscle aches and tenderness, has been described in inhabitants of the South Island of New Zealand, which is known to be poor in selenium.[97]

Studies in animals, bacteria, and tissue cultures have shown that selenium has a protective effect against the development of experimental carcinogenesis.[128-132] Epidemiologic studies clearly showed the occurrence of several types of cancer to be inversely correlated with both environmental and dietary selenium (Fig. 8-1).[97,130,133] Measurements of body selenium status in patients with malignant diseases gave conflicting data of reduced[134,135] versus normal[136,137] values. Robinson and co-workers[138] have suggested that the low selenium status of some cancer patients was more likely a consequence of their illness than its cause. Further studies to evaluate the place of selenium as a possible cancer-protective agent are indicated.[139] Similarly the role of selenium in cystic fibrosis,[140,141] multiple sclerosis,[142,143] hepatic cirrhosis[144,145] cataracts,[146,147] coronary heart disease,[139] kwashiorkor,[148,149] and cystinosis[150] is unclear as yet. Recently, Hafez and colleagues[151] showed improved erythrocyte survival with combined vitamin E and selenium therapy in children with Mediterranean-type glucose-6-phosphate dehydrogenase deficiency and chronic hemolysis. The recommended dietary allowance (RDS) estimates an adult intake of selenium of about 50 to 200 μg/day. Standards for infants are 20 to 60 μg and for children 30 to 120 μg. Food sources are highly dependent on the soil content of selenium.[152] Usually good sources include seafood, low-fat meats, kidney, liver, and whole grains in areas with selenium rich soil, with additional amounts in vegetables.[97,153,154]

The observation that cord blood and neonatal selenium levels are consistently less than maternal levels suggests that placental transfer of selenium is homeostatically regulated.[97,155-157] The concentration of selen-

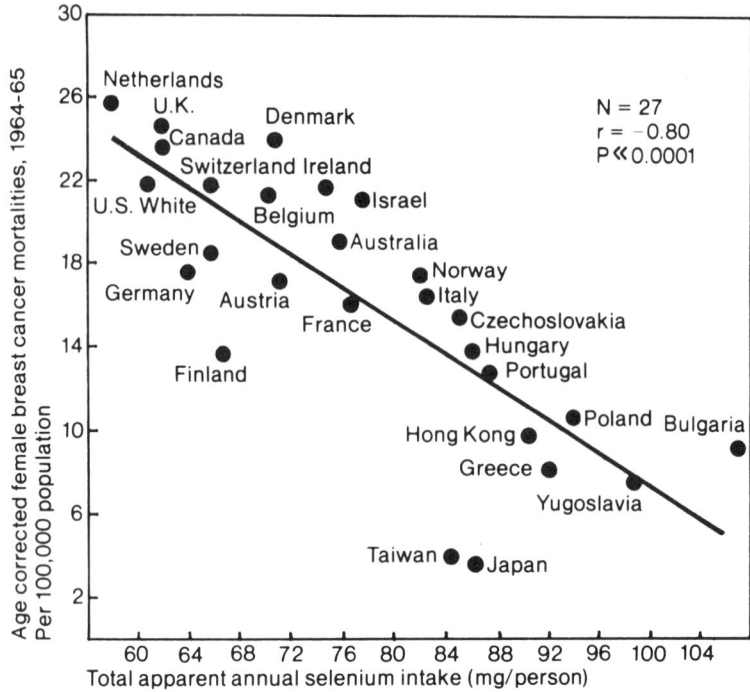

Fig.8-1. Relation of annual selenium intake and breast cancer mortalities. (From Schrauzer et al,[129] with permission.)

ium in breast milk is higher than in bovine milk or formulas.[158,159] The selenium concentration of breast milk varies with geographic area.[158,160] In the United States, the daily selenium intake of breast-fed infants during the first three months of life will be 10 to 12 μg/day as compared to less than 7 μg/day in infants fed formula. During the first month of life, there is a reduction in selenium levels[161,162]; however, breast-fed infants have higher serum concentrations than formula fed infants.[159] Premature infants were found to have lower serum selenium concentrations than term infants and children.[163] The treatment of respiratory distress syndrome further decreased the serum selenium concentration, a situation that was preventable by selenium supplementation but not with vitamin E. It thus seems that some severely sick premature infants may need selenium supplementation.

CHROMIUM

Interest in chromium as an essential trace element was raised in 1959 by Schwarz and Mertz,[164] who showed that trivalent chromium increases the glucose tolerance of rats subsisting on certain diets. Further studies by Schroeder and co-workers[165–167] and Mertz and co-workers[168–170] established the presence of chromium in biologic fluids and tissues and the role of the element as a cofactor with insulin, necessary for normal glucose utilization and for the growth and longevity of rats and mice. The role of chromium as a potentiator of insulin activity in the tissues is so far the only well established physiologic function of the element.[171] Chromium functions biologically as an organic complex with nicotinic acid and amino acids, named glucose tolerance factor (GTF). The detailed structure of the complex has not yet been characterized.

Feeding a diet deficient in chromium leads to impaired glucose tolerance, with a more than 40 percent reduction of glucose removal rates. This can be reversed by chromium supplementation.[172] In chromium-deficient rats, glucose uptake and oxidation, and the incorporation of carbon from glucose into fat were increased in a dose-dependent manner.[172] These effects, however, necessitated the presence of small amounts of insulin.[173] Conversely, it was shown that insulin alone was ineffective in promoting glucose uptake by chromium-depleted tissues, and small amounts of chromium were required for the demonstration of an insulin effect. From these studies and others,[174] it appears that the specific action of GTF is to form a complex between tissue receptors of insulin and the insulin molecule, thus facilitating cellular glucose uptake.

Less clear is the role of chromium in lipid metabolism, particularly as a regulator of the serum cholesterol level.[175] Schroeder[176] reported that feeding rats a diet without chromium resulted in elevation in their serum cholesterol and glucose concentrations. Other studies showed that chromium supplementation to rats on a low-chromium diet caused a decrease in the serum cholesterol concentration,[177] and that administration of chromium led to a reduction in the serum cholesterol concentration of rats fed a hypercholesterolemic diet.[178] Moreover, aortic lipids and the incidence of aortic plaques were found to be increased in chromium-deficient rats, with a 19 percent incidence of aortic plaque in chromium-deficient versus a 2 percent incidence in chromium-fed rats.[179]

Studies in humans of the role of chromium in glucose metabolism examined its effects on the oral glucose tolerance test. Whereas several studies demonstrated no effect of chromium on glucose tolerance in healthy adults,[180–182] a 13 to 17 percent reduction in mean blood glucose concentration was noted in patients with an abnormal glucose tolerance test or overt diabetes mellitus.[181–183] Only the study by Liu and Morris[184] demonstrated a chromium-mediated change in the serum insulin concentration. In 1970, Schroeder and colleagues[166] found that the chromium content in the aorta of people who died from arteriosclerotic heart disease was much lower than that of those who died in road accidents. In another study by this group,[176] chromium supplementation of 2.0 mg daily for six months to a group of institutionalized patients caused a 14 percent reduction from initial values in the serum cholesterol concentration. Recent studies of the effect of chromium supplementation on serum lipid profiles in normal adults, diabetic patients, and hyperlipidemic patients demonstrated no change in total triglycerides and uniform elevation of the high density lipoprotein (HDL) cholesterol by 12 to 36 percent.[180–186] Total serum cholesterol decreased by 5 to 12 percent in some of the studies,[183–186] but remained unchanged in the rest.[180–182] There was no relation between serum cholesterol concentration and the glucose tolerance curve. On the basis of the observation that chromium supplementation improves glucose tolerance in diabetes and can decrease the ratio of total/HDL cholesterol, attempts were made to examine the blood, urine, and hair chromium content of diabetic patients as compared to normal controls. These studies resulted in conflicting data of reduced[187] normal,[184,188,189] and even elevated[190] basal levels of chromium in the diabetic patients. Thus, at the moment, there is not enough evidence for chromium deficiency in diabetic patients.

The main drawback in many of these studies was the lack of standardized, precise, and accurate methods for chromium estimation. Only recently have Kumpulainen and colleagues,[191] using improved technology and standardized methods, found the normal serum chromium concentration to be 0.1 to 0.2 ng/ml, the normal urine concentration to range between 0.06 and 0.20 ng/ml, and daily urine chromium excretion to average 170 mg.

In both animals and humans, the concentration of chromium in tissues of fetuses and newborns is highly elevated.[165-167,176] Because very little chromium was found in the liver of pregnant and postpartum rats, it was reasoned that large quantities of chromium are transported from the mother to the fetus, resulting in large maternal losses. Indeed, whereas Mertz and colleagues[192] showed only little chromium transfer in pregnant rats during the first two trimesters of pregnancy, Wallach and Verch[193] recently found large transfers of chromium during the last trimester of pregnancy. Hambidge and co-workers[194] reported in 1969 that the mean chromium concentration in the hair of multiparous women was significantly lower than that of nulliparous women of comparable age. Further studies evaluating chromium status in pregnant women by measuring hair, plasma, and urine chromium concentrations confirmed that pregnancy depletes chromium stores.[195-200] The relationship of this depletion in chromium stores to results of the oral glucose tolerance test in pregnant women is unclear. In a recent review, Wallach[201] stated that these studies suffer from the same problems of accurate chromium determination as mentioned earlier.

After birth, the chromium concentration in tissues declines rapidly during the first year of life.[176] It is unclear whether this is a normal physiologic event or caused by low chromium intake during this period of life. Breast milk contains chromium at about 390 µg/L,[202] and the total daily intake of breast-fed infants is therefore about 70 µg/kg. Concentrations of chromium in cow's milk and formulas are lower than in breast milk.[171] Chromium deficiency may be a complicating factor in protein-calorie malnutrition in children, since supplementation of chromium to malnourished children in Nigeria and Jordan resulted in significant improvement in their glucose removal rates.[203] Chromium deficiency in states of childhood malnutrition may depend on geographic and dietary factors.[171]

Age has an important influence on the chromium content of human tissues. The chromium content of most tissues among the United States population was found to decrease steadily with advancing age.[165] Similar findings were made in rats.[204] From these observations there arose the question of a possible connection between a depleted chromium state in the elderly and a high incidence of abnormality in the glucose tolerance test and of diabetes mellitus, hyperlipidemic syndromes, and cardiovascular disease in this population. Levine and associates[205] have given 150 µg of chromium daily for periods up to four months to 10 elderly people. In four of these subjects, glucose tolerance returned to normal, but not in the other six. The mean fasting serum chromium concentration in the study group did not differ from that of young controls. Works by Vir and Love[206] and Abraham and colleagues[207] have demonstrated no change in the plasma chromium concentration in the elderly, and recently, Bunker and associates,[208] using modern analytical techniques, have reported a valid chromium balance in this population.

Definite clinical demonstration of the essentiality of chromium in human nutrition has been made in three patients on long-term TPN. Jeejeebhoy and co-workers[209] reported in 1977 that a 40-year-old woman receiving total parenteral nutrition for more than five years developed a 15 percent weight loss, peripheral neuropathy, an abnormal response to the intravenous glucose tolerance test, and a need for treatment with insulin. Her blood and hair chromium concentrations were low. After two weeks of chromium supplementation at 250 µg/day, the insulin therapy could be stopped and the glucose tolerance test returned to normal. With a maintenance addition of chromium to the parenteral nutrition solutions and after another five months, the patient's nerve conduction and well being returned to normal. Two years later, Freund and colleagues[210] reported that after five months of total parenteral nutrition, a 45-year-old woman developed severe glucose intolerance; weight loss; hyperglucosuria; a hyperglycemic, hyperosmolar, nonketotic coma; and encephalopathy. The patient's serum chromium concentration was at the lowest normal level. Supplementation of 150 μg of chromium chloride per day resulted in immediate clinical and metabolic improvement. Recently,[211] another patient on long term total parenteral nutrition was reported to have developed a similar clinical and biochemical picture, which also responded to chromium supplementation.

The mechanism of absorption of chromium has not been fully clarified, but it is known to involve processes other than simple diffusion. Absorption of trivalent chromium in normal human subjects was found to be 0.5 ± 0.3 percent in one study[212] and 0.64 ± 0.08 percent in another.[213] Although hexavalent chromium is slightly better absorbed (2.1 ± 1.5 percent), it is very possible that the hexavalent form is reduced in the stomach by the acid gastric juice to the poorly absorbed trivalent chromium.[212] Thus, it becomes obvious that the average daily intake of approximately 60 μg of chromium will not maintain a positive chromium balance. It therefore seems that the chromium compounds in foodstuffs have a better intestinal absorption rate than do inorganic chromium salts. It is likely that much of the dietary chromium used biologically is ingested as preformed GTF, which is better absorbed than inorganic chromium. The mechanism of chromium absorption is unclear. Hahn and Evans[214] and Huber and Gershoff[215] have suggested that chromium and zinc share a common metabolic pathway in the intestine. Chen and coworkers[216] found that in rats, chromium absorption occurs mainly in the midsection of the small intestine, followed by some absorption in the duodenum and ileum.

Following its absorption, trivalent chromium is carried by transferrin and other serum proteins[217] and hexavalent chromium seems to be bound to the erythrocyte membrane.[218] Circulating chromium is readily taken up by the tissues, the kidneys, and the skeleton, followed by the liver, spleen, lungs, and large intestines.[204,219,220] The metabolic activity of circulating GTF has not been defined, but it is presumably concentrated in tissues that are insulin responsive.[221] The main excretory pathway for chromium is via the urine, with only minor amounts of the element being excreted in the feces through the bile and small intestine, and possibly some excretion also occurring through the skin.[217,222,223]

The Food and Nutrition Board recommends 50 to 200 μg per day of chromium intake for adults and adolescents. Recommended intakes for children are 10 to 40 μg for the first six months of life, 20 to 60 μg for the second half of the first year, 20 to 80 μg from one to three years, and 30 to 120 μg thereafter. Meat, cheese, whole grains, and condiments are good sources of available chromium. Chromium appears to be less available from leafy vegetables, and is very low in polished rice and refined flours and sugars.

MANGANESE

The essential nature of manganese has been recognized since 1931, when Orent and McCollum[224] and Kemmerer and associates[225] observed poor growth in mice and abnormal reproduction in rats fed a diet deficient in the element.

Manganese is a component of two mammalian metalloenzymes: pyruvate carboxylase[226] and mitochondrial superoxide dismutase.[227] Pyruvate carboxylase has not been found to be very sensitive to manganese deficiency.[228] While decreased activity of manganese-dependent superoxide dismutase has been reported for a number of manganese deficient animal species.[229] In rats with manganese deficiency and reduced superoxide dismutase activity there is an increased level of mitochondrial lipid peroxidation, associated with increased susceptibility to ethanol intoxication.[230] In addition, manganese is an activator of several metal-dependent enzymes.[231] Most relevant in this regard are the glycosyltransferases, a group of enzymes involved in the synthesis of glycoproteins and mucopolysaccharides.[232] This role of manganese accounts for many of the symptoms associated with manganese deficiency in animals.

Deficiency of manganese in animals produces skeletal abnormalities, tissue changes in the central nervous system, and ultrastructural changes in the kidney, heart, liver, and pancreas.[232,233] Gestational deficiency of the element produces congenital ataxia in mice, associated with abnormalities of the vestibular apparatus. The skeletal abnormalities and ataxia are thought to result from disruption of mucopolysaccharide synthesis in bone matrix.[234] Manganese may be also involved in brain transmitter metabolism.[235] Feeding a manganese-deficient diet to young chicks resulted in decreased growth and depressed sulfate intake into cartilage uranic acid, with no changes in somatomedin activity.[236] In a recent study, Strause and colleagues[237] found that long-term administration of a manganese-depleted diet to rats resulted in hypercalcemia, hyperphosphatemia, and a reduced bone mineral content, pointing to the possibility of increased bone resorption.

The observation of Rubinstein and associates[238] of a diabetic patient, resistant to insulin, who responded to oral manganese with a lowering of the blood glucose level, coupled with other reports of hypermanganesemia-associated hypoglycemia,[239–241] stimulated research into the role of manganese in carbohydrate metabolism. In manganese deficient rats, glucose tolerance was found to be abnormal and pancreatic insulin release depressed.[242] Guinea pigs born to manganese-deficient dams and fed a manganese-deficient diet had abnormal glucose tolerance curves and histologically demonstrated hypertrophied pancreatic islet tissue with degranulated β-cells and an increased proportion of α-cells.[243] A recent study by Baly and colleagues[244] demonstrated that manganese deficiency in rats results in depressed pancreatic insulin synthesis and enhanced degradation. Korc[245] found that manganese facilitated pancreatic protein synthesis in diabetic rats.

Manganese deficiency has not been reported in humans except for two experimental studies.[246,247] In the first of these,[246] a subject who was taking part in a vitamin K deficiency study was fed a diet inadvertently lacking in manganese. He developed symptoms and signs that included fatigue, weight loss, nausea and vomiting, transient dermatitis, decreased hair growth with a change in pigmentation, hypocholesterolemia, and a prolonged prothrombin time. The disturbance in prothrombin time could be corrected only when both vitamin K and manganese were provided. In a recent balance study,[247] seven young men were fed a low manganese diet. Five of them developed dermatitis which resolved with manganese repletion. In addition, a reduction in serum cholesterol concentration was observed.

Manganese is provided by many items in the human diet. The intake varies from one country to another, being 12.4 mg/day in India, 4.6 mg/day in Britain, and 0.5 mg/day in New Zealand.[248] In a long-term study by Tipton and associates,[249] the mean voluntary manganese intake of one subject was 0.8 mg/day and of another, 2.5 mg/day. The site of manganese absorption is not precisely known, but is believed to be along the extent of the small intestine. Experiments with radioactive manganese estimated the absorption efficiency to be 3 to 4 percent.[251,252] A balance study estimated retention of 12 percent of the dietary intake.[242] Thus it seems that dietary manganese is poorly absorbed. Following absorption, manganese is carried by α_2-macroglobulin in the portal blood to the liver. Once metabolized in the liver, it circulates in the form of Mn^{3+} bound to transferrin. The adult human body has been estimated to contain 10 to 20 mg of manganese, with a large proportion incorporated into the erythrocytes.[253] The major route of manganese excretion is via the bile, and apparently the liver is the key organ in maintaining manganese homeostasis.[254] The magnitude of manganese reabsorption through the enterohepatic circulation is not quantitatively known, but is believed to be low.

The concentration of manganese in the plasma is very low (≤ 1 part per billion), and therefore whole blood manganese has been used as an indicator of body manganese status. Recently, Keen and associates[255] demonstrated that blood manganese reflects tissue manganese concentrations. Normal concentrations of the element in blood are very low, at 10 to 15 parts per billion, requiring highly sensitive and precise analytic methods.

The concentration of manganese in human milk is very low (3.5 to 8 µg/liter), as compared to 20 to 50 µg/liter in bovine milk and 50 to 1300 µg/liter in infant formulas.[256,257] Stastny and associates[257] found that at three months of age, breast-fed infants received 0.42 µg/kg/day of manganese, significantly less than formula-fed infants of the same age, who received 183.22 µg/kg/day. The mean serum manganese concentrations were similar in both groups. However, Collin and co-workers[258] found that at four months of age, formula-fed infants had significantly higher manganese concentrations in their hair than did breast-fed infants, at 0.685 µg/g versus 0.330 µg/g. The values for both blood and hair decline toward adolescence.[258-259] Female adolescents have a significantly higher erythrocyte manganese concentration than males, presumably because of an estrogenic effect.[259] In addition, manganese absorption is increased in iron deficiency, occurring much more frequently in adolescent females than males.[260]

The recommended daily intake of manganese for adults is in the range of 2.5 to 5.0 mg. Recommended daily intakes for infants and children are 0.5 to 0.7 mg during the first six months of life, 0.7 to 1.0 mg for the second half of the first year of life, 1.0 to 1.5 mg for ages 1 to 3 years, 1.5 to 2.0 mg from 4 to 6 years, and 2.0 to 3.0 mg from 7 to 10 years of age. Good sources of manganese include nuts, whole grains, dried legumes, tea, and cloves. Fruits and vegetables are fair sources, depending on the soil content of the element. Meat, fish, and dairy products are low in manganese.

FLUORINE

The association between a high fluorine intake and dental defects was first demonstrated experimentally in rats in 1925.[261] In the 1930s, epidemiologic surveys found that enamel mottling could be related to the presence of excessive amounts of fluorine in the water, and in turn to relatively low caries experience.[262-264] Subsequent studies showed a remarkably close inverse association between the natural fluorine concentrations of domestic water and caries experience.[265,266]

The classification of fluorine as an essential or a nonessential element depends on the criteria employed in determining essentiality. The element assists in the prevention of human dental caries and in the maintenance of a normal skeleton, but fluorine has not been shown to have a vital function in permitting survival. In addition, in contrast to other essential trace elements discussed in this chapter, the biochemical function(s) of fluorine have been elucidated.

Depending upon location, human populations obtain varying quantities of fluorine from the food and water supply and the atmosphere. The latter source is quantitatively important in polluted areas. The occurrence of fluorine in drinking water has been studied in many countries.[267] The amounts in rainwater vary with the distance from urban centers and industrial pollution. The main source of water for humans, surface water, generally contains less than 1 part per million (ppm) fluorine, and in many places only 0.1 ppm or less. Water obtained from deep wells and artesian bores is usually high in fluorine, with concentrations of 4 to 8 ppm. Food is the major source of fluorine for those not exposed to industrial pollution or to naturally or artificially fluorinated water. In fact, the increased usage of fluorinated water in home cooking and in commercial food processing results in increased fluorine concentrations in foodstuff.[268–271] Other sources of fluorine are dentifrices,[272–274] infant formulas and baby foods,[275–278] unintentional ingestion of fluorine from dentifrices,[273–281] and mouthwashes.[281]

Soluble inorganic fluorine is rapidly absorbed, with up to 75 percent being absorbed during the first hour.[282,283] Absorption appears to occur in both the stomach and the small intestine.[283,284] In the body, fluorine circulates in the form of a fluoride ion, and is rapidly deposited as fluorapatite in bone, or excreted by the kidney.[285,286] Throughout life, there is accumulation of fluorine in bone, increasing from 50 to 150 ppm in fetal bone to 7,000 ppm in adult bone. The content of fluorine in teeth and bone varies with respect to the amount, form, duration, and continuity of fluorine consumption. Fluorine is also widely distributed in soft tissues, in non-cumulative, low concentrations of 0.1 to 0.2 ppm. Excretion of fluorine is predominantely through the kidney,[282] and about 10 percent of fluorine is excreted in the feces.

Children continuously exposed to fluorinated water, either natural or artificial, during and after tooth development, benefit by an average reduction of caries experience of 50 to 60 percent and the proportion of caries-free children may increase sixfold.[287] Both deciduous[288] and permanent[289] teeth benefit equally, but because of structural differences, the protection of anterior teeth is better than that of posterior teeth.[289] Apart from reducing the incidence of new caries, fluorine retards the progress of existing lesions.[290,291] Several studies showed that adults can also benefit from an adequate fluorine intake. The protective effect of fluorine is directly related to its concentration in teeth and plaque.[296–299]

The cariostatic mechanisms of fluorine have been extensively studied, but are not completely understood.[299] Fluorine replaces some of the hydroxyl or carbonate ions in hydroxyapatite, decreasing its solubility.[290] The reduced solubility is thought to be the major anticariogenic effect of fluorine. In addition, fluorine inhibits acid dissolution and bacterial enzymes, and may produce minor morphologic changes of the teeth.[290,300] Another hypothesis is that fluorine interferes with bacterial adherence to teeth.[298,301]

The main effect of fluorine in the bone is to stimulate osteoblastic activity.[302,303] It also stimulates a positive calcium balance,[304] and as mentioned earlier, fluoride is incorporated into the crystalline structure of bone as fluorapatite. Since long-term excessive fluorine intake results in fluorosis manifested by osteosclerosis, fluoride was suggested for treating primary osteoporosis. However, in fluorosis, the structure of the bone is abnormal,[305] and supplementation with fluorine might result in strengthened vertebra but weakened cortex-rich tubular bones of the appendicular skeleton.[306–308] Controversy exists about the beneficial effect of fluorine supplementation in osteoporotic patients. Whereas some studies demonstrated no reduction or even an increase in fracture rates,[309,310] others demonstrated improved bone status.[311,312] Improved results might be obtained by combined calcium and fluorine supplementation (at 1.0 to 1.5 µg/day and 20 to 60 mg/day, respectively), providing the required calcium for calcification of the new bone matrix formed with the stimulation of fluorine.[307,313] There might also be a need for vitamin D supplementation.[307,311]

The role of fluorine in the prevention of cardiovascular diseases is even less clear. Early studies demonstrated a reduced frequency of cardiovascular disorder in populations with a high fluorine intake.[314,315] In these studies, however, the populations were also exposed to other, uncontrolled nutritional and environmental factors. In a later study, where the effect of fluorine could be isolated, as 2.5 percent decrease in mortality attributed to heart disease was noted among populations with a high fluorine intake.[316] These findings were not confirmed in two other, similar studies.[317,318]

The recommended daily intake of fluorine for adults is around 1.0 ppm. The most important source is water. Most food sources have a low fluorine content except for seafood and tea. Fluorination of water or supplementation of fluoride to infants and children is recommended in areas with low fluorine concentrations in their water (Table 8-4). However, with increased usage of fluorinated dentifrices and the local application of fluorine, as well as with an increased fluorine content in commercial foodstuffs (vide supra), repeated estimation of the need for optimal supplementation is mandatory.

Table 8-4. Recommended Supplemental Fluoride Doses

Age in Years	Concentration of fluorine in water, ppm		
	<0.3	0.3–0.7	>0.7
Birth–2	0.25 mg	0	0
2–3	0.50 mg	0.25 mg	0
3–13	1.00 mg	0.50 mg	0

COBALT

In 1948, Smith[319] and Rickes and associates[320] discovered that the antipernicious anemia factor in liver, later designated vitamin B_{12}, is a compound containing 4 percent cobalt. Three years later, Smith and co-workers[321] demonstrated that the injection of vitamin B_{12} effected complete remission of all signs of cobalt deficiency in lambs.

In the human body, cobalt occurs in only minute traces in the tissues, and the main storage area is the liver. The normal blood and erythrocyte concentration is about 1 µg/dl. The only known function of cobalt in human physiology is its role as a component of cobalamin, vitamin B_{12}.

Except for one case report by Shuttleworth and colleagues[322] in 1961, there are no other descriptions of cobalt deficiency in humans. The reported patient was a 16-month-old girl who from the age of 4 months was fed only with cows milk from the family's farm. At the time of presentation, the child used to be awakened and "fussy" for hours every night. She became anemic, with a hemoglobin of 6.5 mg/dl, and her hair appeared dry, and was matted and very dull on the occipital area. In addition, the child suffered from severe geophagia. The veterinary surgeon was certain that the child, being fed on milk from cows suffering from cobalt deficiency and behaving similarly, namely eating earth, was also suffering from deficiency of the element. It was therefore suggested that the child be supplemented with cobalt. Within the next two weeks the patient's condition gradually improved, except for her hypochromic microcytic anemia, which necessitated iron therapy. No determinations were made of the cobalt content of the serum or other tissues. Analysis of the farm's soil and hay cobalt content disclosed values well below normal.

Tipton and associates[323] observed the daily adult intake of cobalt to be 160 to 170 μg, and Shroeder and colleagues[324] found it to range between 160 and 580 μg. It seems that daily cobalt intake is greatly influenced by the amounts and proportion of different foods constituting the diet. The quantitative human requirement for cobalt is unknown, but is evidently minute. In patients with pernicious anemia, as little as 0.045 to 0.09 μg daily maintains bone marrow function. Because cobalt is widely distributed in nature and in most foodstuffs, there is practically no problem of insufficient cobalt intake.

TRACE ELEMENT DEFICIENCY AND REPLACEMENT DURING TOTAL PARENTERAL NUTRITION

Prior to the advent of total parenteral nutrition (TPN), trace metal deficiency was rare. However, with the advent of TPN given with solutions that contain only minimal quantities of contaminating trace metals,[325,326] several prospective studies have demonstrated impressive declines in blood and plasma zinc[325-333] and copper[325,328,330,333,334] concentrations during TPN. In addition, deficiency syndromes have been characterized for chromium[209] and selenium.[126,335] Replacement quantities for the various trace elements are much less well documented in patients on TPN,[336-346] and many of these refer to suggested replacement regimens rather than absolutely determined quantities required for replacement.

The most extensive study of trace metal levels in serum and plasma and of attempts at measuring trace metal balance was performed by Jacobson in 1977.[343] This was a short-term study, extending over five days of TPN in four male patients receiving TPN with mixed fat and carbohydrate calories. Supplementation was provided for iron, zinc, manganese, copper, fluorine, and iodine, and 20 trace elements were examined.

Of the four elements that were directly supplemented (cobalt, copper, iron, and zinc) and then subsequently determined, all showed decreased in serum levels despite a positive balance for cobalt and iron over the five-day study. The results of the examinations on the remaining elements are included in Table 8-5. Iodine, fluorine, and manganese were supplemented, but balance studies were not done.

All other studies, while of a longer duration, have tended to address specific trace elements.

Zinc

A syndrome occurring in patients on TPN therapy and related to zinc deficiency in adult humans was described in 1975 and 1976.[327,329,331] This syndrome was characterized by diarrhea, depression, hair loss, and perioral and periorbital dermatitis after prolonged TPN with zinc-free solutions. It was suggested that the diarrhea could occur before marked depression in plasma zinc concentrations. The appearance of the obvious dermatitis is uncommon unless the serum zinc is below 30 μg/100 ml.[330,332] Similar observations were made by others,[347] and progressive decreases in plasma and serum zinc have been described by a number of authors during prolonged parenteral nutrition.[325,328,333,334] Other manifestations of the syndrome of zinc deficiency, such as abnormalities of taste and smell, have been suggested and described.

It has been suggested that certain specific patients are more likely to develop zinc deficiency than others. They include patients with cirrhosis,[348] patients on long-term steroid replacement following bilateral adrenalectomy,[349] and patients with major injuries or diarrheal syndromes.[331,332,336,348-353] Potential zinc depletion can also occur following prolonged starvation or severe protein malnutrition, in which it has been suggested that cumulative losses of 10 to 20 percent of total body zinc stores can occur.[10] The combination of prior body zinc

Table 8-5. Serum Response and Balance Studies of Four Male Patients Undergoing Five Days of TPN

Mean Serum Concentration	Balance	Supplemented
Decreased: Zn, Fe, Co, Mo, Se, Ac, Br, Cs, Hg, Rb, W	Negative: Zn, Mo, Se, As, Rb, Br, Cd, Cs, Hg, La	Yes: Zn, Mn, I, Fe, F, Co
Increased: Cr	Positive: Fe, Cr, Co, Ac, W, Ss	No: Cr, Mo, Se, Ac, As, Au, Br, Cd, Cs, Hg, Rb, W, La, Ss
Not measured: Mn, I, F	Zero: Au	
Unchanged: As, Au, La, Ss, Cd	Not Measured: Mn, I, F	

(From Jacobson and Wester,[343] by permission.)

depletion and increased urinary zinc excretion induced by the infusion of amino acid solutions,[354] coupled with the increased zinc requirements during anabolism,[336] suggests the need for parenteral replacement regimens during TPN. Since the principal form of urinary zinc is that bound to amino acids, the formation of histidyl and cystinyl zinc complexes in blood is associated with increased amounts of these complexes appearing in the urine.[355] However, histidine was not identified as a causative agent of zinc depletion in previous studies of TPN.[354] Other possible mechanisms involve the relationship between the blood albumin concentration and levels of blood amino acids in determining blood zinc and subsequently urinary zinc levels.[356] Any significant decrease in serum albumin concentration, which is common in patients undergoing TPN, further decreases the plasma zinc concentration as zinc is displaced from its carrier protein and readily excreted in the urine.[357] In our own studies, after four weeks of TPN, urinary zinc levels actually decreased to levels not different from normal.[328,330] This followed periods of increased zinc losses early in the course of TPN. Certainly the virtual disappearance of zinc from urine reflects severe total body zinc depletion.[330]

We have tried to prospectively evaluate the response to intravenous zinc in patients undergoing long-term TPN. Maintenance of normal zinc levels or a rapid return of low levels to normal was apparent in these patients when intravenous zinc was administered, as compared to an unsupplemented control group. The urinary zinc balance was consistently positive (500 to 2500 μg/day) in all the supplemented groups. In these studies, any patient with excessive fecal losses or a fistula was excluded from the analysis, suggesting that the urinary balance would reflect a positive zinc balance.[339] On the basis of the weekly response to zinc supplementation in this series, our patients maintained normal serum zinc levels with daily infusions of 70 to 80 μg/kg. Infusion rates below 50 μg/kg were uniformly associated with initially low serum zinc levels. This relationship was even more striking in patients with initially low zinc levels in whom increases in blood levels were noted at rates of 50 to 60 μg/kg/day. Using this dose regimen, no elevated zinc levels greater than 150 μg/dl and no untoward results were noted in any patients, although accidental fatal zinc overdosing with 3000 mg/day has been recorded.[358] This parenteral zinc supplementation rate is supported by other observations,[336] and a minimal replacement level of 2 to 3 mg/day can now be recommended for most parenterally nourished patients. The zinc content of TPN solutions (200 to 500 μg/l) should be considered when such calculations are made.[325,359] A summary of suggested regimens for zinc supplementation is provided in Table 8-6.

Copper

Copper functions as a cofactor for a number of amino acid conversions, most of which are involved in collagen synthesis.

Table 8-6. Recommended Daily Trace Metal Supplementation for Patients Receiving Total Parenteral Nutrition

Author, Reference	Year	Zn (mg)	Cu (mg)	Mn (mg)	I (mg)	Fe (mg)	Cr (mg)	F (mg)
Dudrick[341]	1971	2.8	1.54	2.8	–	1.4	–	–
Shils[337]	1972	2–4	1	1.2	0.07 –0.14	1	0.015	1.2
Wretlind[338]	1972	1.4	0.3	2.3	0.13	3.9	–	0.9
Hull[342]	1974	0.2	0.11	0.2	0.075	–	–	–
Blackburn[340]	1976	10	2	5	0.5	1	0.2	–
Jacobson[343]	1977	3	0.1	–	–	0.5	0.050	–
Wolman[348]	1979	3	1.6	2	0.12	1.8	0.002 –0.02	–
AMA[370]	1979	2.5 –4	0.5 –1.5	0.15 –0.8	–	–	0.001 –0.015	–
Lowry[328,339]	1979	4	2.8	0.4	0.1	–	–	–
Present Authors	1980	5	1.4	0.5	0.06	10[a]	0.02	–

[a] Assumes in-hospital phlebotomy of approximately 100 cc/wk.

Copper deficiency was indeed uncommon until the advent of copper-free TPN.[360] As a consequence of the rarity of copper deficiency, some authors had previously suggested that copper supplementation of TPN solutions was not necessary.[344] However, as experience with TPN has accumulated, cases of severe copper deficiency have been reported in both children[31] and adults.[362,363] In addition, number of longitudinal studies have shown decreases in blood copper over the course of TPN.[325,328,329,333,334] In these copper deficiency situations, variable components of anemia, leukopenia, and hypoproteinemia have been reported.[361,362] The anemia can be rapidly reversed by copper supplementation, as can the leukopenia.[330] An impressive response in the reticulocyte count was seen with copper supplementation for a patient with anemia due to copper deficiency.[330] The low count is thought to be due to an impairment in the formation of ceruloplasmin.[361,362] For this to appear, however, copper levels must usually be less than 25 µg/dl. The exact requirements for copper supplementation in TPN are not known, but in a recent study, we were able to reverse serum copper levels in two of three patients during two weeks of supplementation with a daily infusion rate of between 40 and 70 µg/kg.[339] In a group undergoing prolonged TPN, daily copper supplementation at approximately 60 µg/kg was associated with unchanged or mildly increased copper levels.[339] Previous reports had suggested that lower doses, on the order of 20 µg/kg, would be sufficient.[362] In our present study, despite wide ranges in daily copper intake of between 20 and 100 µg/kg, no evidence of copper deficiency or toxicity was subsequently noted. It would seem reasonable to suggest, under the present regimen, that approximately 1 to 3 mg of copper per day should be a safe and effective maintenance and restorative dosage. Once again, in situations of major trauma and extensive tissue damage, requirements may be greater, although this would seem much more applicable to the requirements for zinc.[351,353]

Manganese

Human manganese deficiency has been described,[246] but has not been seen in studies of patients undergoing TPN. Because manganese appears to be an extremely benign trace element, vigorous efforts to define its limits before supplementing TPN solutions have not been performed. Consequently, the majority of patients have received solutions containing manganese since the commencement of TPN. The adequacy of effectiveness of these quantities is currently unknown, but various quantities are commonly suggested (Table 8-6).

Iron

Since daily losses of iron are extraordinarily small in the adult male and in severely ill females undergoing TPN, menstrual losses are often very low, iron supplementation has not been routinely suggested. This has been compounded by concerns over the use of iron dextran products because of their potential risk of anaphylaxis. Most authors have preferred occasional supplementation with intramuscular injections amounting to about 1 to 2 mg/day (Table 8-6), or the use of blood transfusion.

We have been concerned by the losses of iron in phlebotomy for monitoring severely ill patients on TPN. The iron in hemoglobin constitutes 0.34 percent of this substance, and a 100 cc blood sample can result in a loss of as much as 50 mg of iron. Such losses are not unusual in patients undergoing TPN. We have begun to prospectively elevate the quantity of supplemental iron in TPN mixtures, starting with less than the test dose for an allergic response to iron dextran (0.5 cc of Imferon). We evaluated a dosage of 25 mg/week and subsequently, 87.5 mg/week of iron added to the TPN solution. While some patients showed an improvement in serum iron levels, the high dosage did not universally reverse the deficiency as reflected by serum iron measurements.[363] Unfortunately, serum iron responds, as do other trace metals, to other factors in the severely ill, and may not be a good indicator of iron deficiency. Conversely, because of blood loss and extensive phlebotomy, such a quantity may be insufficient. Further study is required. At the daily intake levels we used, no elevation in serum iron was identified and no allergic response was characterized in over 400 patients' days of administration.

Chromium

Chromium deficiency has recently been recognized in humans. Patients on high carbohydrate loads develop chromium deficiency as a consequence of increased chromium loss.[176] In experimental models, deficiency states have led to growth retardation, decreased glycogen reserves, and impaired amino acid conversion to protein. In situations of chromium deficiency, glucose tolerance can be altered,[205] and this has led to the identification of abnormalities of glucose metabolism occurring in patients on long-term TPN, as a consequence of chromium deficiency.[209,210] Since it has been shown that the administration of a single dose of 200 µg of chromium results in an improved rate of removal of intravenously infused glucose in children with kwashiorkor malnutrition, it would be expected that some glucose intolerance would be identified in patients receiving high glucose loads and long-term TPN.[203,209] Because the typical daily diet is thought to contain approximately 50 to 75 µg of chromium,[176] various suggested quantities of supplemental chromium are currently being used in TPN solutions. It is our practice to supplement daily with approximately 20 µg of chromium (Table 8-7).

Table 8-7. Trace Metal Solution Employed as a Supplement for Total Parenteral Nutrition

Element	Given as	Amount Added to 2 Liters (gm)	Concentration (mg/ml)
Zinc	$ZnCl_2$	2.0	5.00
Copper	$CuSO_4 \cdot 5H_2O$	11.0	1.40
Manganese	$MnSO_4 \cdot SO_4$	3.06	0.50
Iodine	NaI	0.132	0.056
Chromium	$Cr_2(SO_4) \cdot nH_2O$	0.146	0.016

Fluorine

Clear deficiency syndromes of fluoride resulting from TPN solutions have yet to be identified, although some authors suggest that all TPN solutions should be supplemented with fluoride.[337,338] Certainly, fluoride is beneficial in the development of the normal skeleton.

Selenium

Selenium has recently been suggested to cause a previously unidentified deficiency syndrome in patients on long-term parenteral nutrition,[122,124-126,335] on the basis of studies of animal nutrition including primates.[364,365] A selenium-responsive syndrome of muscular pain and weakness has been observed in patients receiving TPN who had known low blood selenium levels before the commencement of TPN[328] or who received prolonged home-based TPN.[126] In their short-term study, Jacobsen and Wester also noted decreased serum levels of selenium and a negative selenium balance in patients receiving TPN solutions containing amino acids, dextrose, and lipid.[343] It would seem reasonable to supplement TPN solutions with selenium in areas of known selenium deficiency.[366] For the general populace this is not currently practiced, but this merely awaits further studies. It is clear that the selenium content of conventional amino acid solutions is low, and no selenium is detectable in synthetic amino acid solutions; in contrast dextrose solutions contain approximately 0.25 to 0.5 μg/ml in 50 percent dextrose. This would mean that from 200 to 400 μg of selenium would usually be provided in the usual amounts of solution administered to an adult patient undergoing TPN within the United States. This compares favorably with the daily intake in the United States of 60 to 150 μg/day.[367] This is in contradiction to the extremely low levels seen in countries such as New Zealand, where the daily selenium intake is between 6 and 70 μg/day.[366] The fact that amino acid solutions used for TPN in New Zealand contain extremely low quantities of selenium may have accounted for the deficiency syndrome reported there.[335] However, since glucose solutions were not analyzed in that study, it may be that the underlying, initially low serum levels were the predominant feature in that deficiency.

Cobalt

The only known human requirement for cobalt is that necessarily contained within the structure of Vitamin B_{12}. Vitamin B_{12} should be routinely supplemented in all TPN solutions as part of the B vitamins. Consequently, it is unlikely that cobalt deficiency could be identified in patients receiving TPN.[368,369]

Other Trace Elements

Deficiencies have not been identified for the remaining trace elements, although the study of Jacobsen[343] (Table 8-5) emphasizes that many trace metals do decrease during TPN even in the short-term, and that this is accompanied by a negative balance. The need for supplementation of these trace metals has not yet been confirmed.

REFERENCES

1. Hemphill DD: Proceedings of the First Annual Conference on Trace Substances in Environmental Health. University of Missouri Press, Columbia, MO, 1967
2. Mertz W: Some aspects of nutritional trace element research. Fed Proc 29:1482, 1970
3. Prasad AS, Halsted JA, Nadimi M: Syndrome of iron deficiency, anemia, hepa-

tosplenomegaly, dwarfism hypogonadism and geophagia. Am J Med 31:532, 1961
4. Underwood EJ: Trace Elements in Human and Animal Nutrition. 4th Ed. Academic Press, New York, 1977
5. Kirchgessner M, Roth HP, Weigand E: Biochemical changes in zinc deficiency. p. 189. In Prasad AS, Oberleas D (eds): Trace Elements in Human Health and Disease, Vol 1. Zinc and Copper. Academic Press, New York, 1976
6. Prasad AS: Zinc. p. 251. In Prasad AS (ed): Trace Elements and Iron in Human Metabolism. Plenum, New York, 1978
7. Bettger WJ, O'Dell BL: A critical physiological role of zinc in the structure and function of biomembranes. Life Sci 28:1425, 1981
8. Fraker PJ, Gershwin ME, Good RA, Prasad A: Interrelationships between zinc and immune function. Fed Proc 45:1474, 1986
9. Hambidge KM, Walravens PA, Breun RM, et al: Zinc nutrition of preschool children in the Denver Head Start Program. Am J Clin Nutr 29:734, 1976
10. Sandstead HH: Zinc nutrition in the United States. Am J Clin Nutr 26:251, 1973
11. Solomons NW: Biological availability of zinc in humans. Am J Clin Nutr 35:1048, 1982
12. Solomons NW, Cousins RJ: Zinc. In Solomans NS, Rosenberg IH (eds): Absorption and Malabsorption of Mineral Nutrients. New York, Alan R. Liss, Inc., 1984, p 125
13. Lonnerdal B, Stanishowski AG, Hurley LS: Isolation of a low molecular weight zinc binding liquid from human milk. J Inorg Biochem 12:71, 1980
14. Sandstead HH: Zinc in Human Nutrition. p. 94. In Bronner F, Coburn JW (eds): Disorders of Mineral Metabolism, Vol 1. Trace Minerals. Academic Press, New York, 1981
15. Hurley LS, Swenerton H: Congenital malformations resulting from zinc deficiency in rats. Proc Soc Exp Biol Med 123:692, 1966
16. Warkany J, Petering HG: Congenital malformations of the central nervous system in rats produced by maternal zinc deficiency. Teratology 5:319, 1972
17. Hurley LS, Mutch PB: Prenatal and postnatal development after transitory gestational deficiency in rats. J Nutr 103:649, 1973
18. Damyanor I, Duty W: Anencephaly in Shiraz, Iran. Lancet 1:82, 1971
19. Gudar AO, Arcasoy A, Baycu T, Himmotoglu O: Zinc deficiency and anencephaly in Turkey. Teratology 22:141, 1980
20. Stewart C, Katchan B, Collipp PJ, et al: Zinc and birth defects. Pediatr Res 15:515, 1981
21. Bergmann KE, Makosch E, Tews KH: Abnormalities of hair zinc concentration in mothers of newborn infants with spina bifida. Am J Clin Nutr 33:2145, 1980
22. Jameson S: Effects of the zinc deficiency in human reproduction. Acta Med Scand (Suppl) 593:5, 1976
23. McCormick CC, Menard MP, Cousins RJ: Induction of hepatic metallothionein by feeding zinc to rats of depleted zinc status. Am J Physiol 240:E414, 1981
24. Jacob M, Chan JCM, Smith Jr JC: Effect of prednisone on growth and zinc metabolism in rats. Nutr Res 4:877, 1984
25. Trace Elements. p. 137. In Recommended Dietary Allowances, 9th Revised Edition, National Research Committee, National Academy of Sciences. Washington, DC, 1980.
26. Solomons NW: On the assessment of zinc and copper nutrition in man. Am J Clin Nutr 32:856, 1979
27. Hart EB, Steenbock H, Waddell J, Elvehjem CA: Iron in nutrition. VII. Copper as a supplement to iron for hemoglobin building in the rat. J Biol Chem 77:797, 1928
28. Cordano A, Baiertl JM, Graham GG: Copper deficiency in infancy. Pediatrics 34:324, 1964
29. Danks DM, Campbell PE, Stevens BJ, et al: Menkes kinky hair syndrome: An inherited defect in copper absorption with wide-spread effects. Pediatrics 50:188, 1972
30. Danks DM, Stevens BJ, Campbell PE, et al: Menkes kinky hair syndrome. Lancet 1:1100, 1972
31. Karpel JT, Peden VH: Copper deficiency in long term parenteral nutrition. J Pediatr 80:32, 1972

32. Hsieh SH, Hsu JM: Biochemistry and metabolism of copper. p. 94. In Karcioglu ZA, Sarper RM (eds): Zinc and Copper in Medicine. Charles C Thomas, Springfield, IL, 1980
33. Mason KE: A conspectus of research on copper metabolism and requirements of man. J Nutr 109:1979, 1979
34. Cartwright GE, Wintrobe MM: Copper metabolism in normal subjects. Am J Clin Nutr 14:224, 1964
35. Klevay LM, Reck SJ, Jacob RA, et al: The human requirement for copper. I. Healthy men fed conventional American diets. Am J Clin Nutr 33:45, 1980
36. Van Campen DR, Mitchell EA: Absorption of ^{64}Cu, ^{65}Zn, ^{99}Mo and ^{59}Fe from ligated segments of the rat gastrointestinal tract. J Nutr 86:120, 1965
37. Owen CA Jr: Absorption and excretion of ^{64}Cu-labeled copper by the rat. Am J Physiol 207:1203, 1964
38. Crampton RF, Matthews EM, Poisner R: Observations on the mechanism of absorption of copper by small intestine. J Physiol 178:111, 1965
39. Marceau N, Aspin N, Sass-Kortsak A: Absorption of copper-64 from gastrointestinal tract of the rat. Am J Physiol 218:377, 1970
40. Mills CF: The dietary availability of copper in the form of naturally occurring organic complexes. Biochem J 63:190, 1956
41. Kirchgessner JR, Markowitz H, Brown CM: The dynamics of copper absorption. p. 277. In Mills CF (ed): Trace Element Metabolism in Animals. Churchill Livingstone, Edinburgh, 1970
42. Bearn AG, Kunkel HG: Metabolic studies in Wilson's disease using ^{64}Cu. J Lab Clin Med 45:623, 1955
43. Bush JA, Mahoney JP, Barkowitz C, et al: Studies on copper metabolism. XVI. Radioactive copper studies in normal subjects and in patients with hepatolenticular degeneration. J Clin Invest 34:1766, 1955
44. Sternleib I: Gastrointestinal copper absorption in man. Gastroenterology 52:1038, 1967
45. Vierling JM, Shrager R, Rumble WF, et al: Incorporation of radiocopper into ceruloplasmin in normal subjects and patients with primary biliary cirrhosis and Wilson's disease. Gastroenterology 74:652, 1978
46. Strickland GT, Beckner WM, Mei-ling L, et al: Turnover studies of copper in homozygotes and heterozygotes for Wilson's disease and controls: Isotope tracer studies with ^{67}Cu. Clin Sci 43:605, 1972
47. Cohen DF, Illowsky B, Linder MC: Altered copper absorption in tumor-bearing and estrogen-treated rats. Am J Physiol 236:E309, 1979
48. Farrer P, Mistilis SP: Absorption of exogenous and endogenous biliary copper in the rat. Nature 213:291, 1967
49. Gollan JL: Studies on the nature of complexes formed by copper with human alimentary secretions and their influence on copper absorption. Clin Sci Mol Med 49:237, 1973
50. Gitlon D, Hughes WL, Janeway CA: Absorption and excretion of copper in mice. Nature 188:150, 1960
51. Mahoney JP, Bush JA, Gubler CJ, et al: Studies on copper metabolism. XV. The excretion of copper by animals. J Lab Clin Med 46:702, 1955
52. Sondheimer JH, Mahajan SK, Rye DL, et al: Elevated plasma copper in chronic renal failure. Am J Clin Nutr 47:846, 1988
53. Tyrala EE, Brodsky NL, Auerbach VH: Urinary copper losses in infants receiving free amino acid solutions. Am J Clin Nutr 35:542, 1982
54. Mason KE: A conspectus of research on copper metabolism and requirements of man. J Nutr 109:1979, 1979
55. Hatano S, Nishi Y, Usui T: Copper levels in plasma and erythrocytes in healthy Japanese children and adults. Am J Clin Nutr 35:120, 1982
56. O'Dell BL: Biochemistry of copper. Med Clin North Am 60:687, 1976
57. Lee GR, Williams DM, Cartwright GE: Role of copper in iron metabolism and bone synthesis. p. 373. In Prasad AS (ed): Trace Elements in Human Health and Disease. I. Zinc and Copper. Academic Press, New York, 1976
58. Osaki S, Johnson DA, Frieden E: The possible significance of ferroxidase activity of ceruloplasmin in normal human serum. J Biol Chem 241:2746, 1966
59. Zimmerman AS, Mattiey J-M, Quareles RH, et al: Hypomyelination in copper de-

ficient rats, pre-natal and post-natal copper replacement. Arch Neurol 33:111, 1976
60. Graham GG, Cordano A: Copper deficiency in human subjects. p. 363. In Prasad AS (ed): Trace Elements in Human Health and Disease. I. Zinc and Copper. Academic Press, New York, 1976
61. Graham GG, Cordano A: Copper depletion and deficiency in the malnourished infant. Johns Hopkins Med J 124:139, 1969
62. Griscom NT, Craig NJ, Neuhauser EBD: Systemic bone disease developing in small premature infants. Pediatrics 48:883, 1971
63. Hillman LS, Martin L, Fiore B: Effect of oral copper supplementation on serum copper and ceruloplasmin concentrations in premature infants. J Pediatr 98:311, 1981
64. Al-Rashid RA, Spangler J: Neonatal copper deficiency. N Engl J Med 285:841, 1971
65. Castillo-Duran C, Uauy R: Copper deficiency impairs growth of infants recovering from malnutrition. Am J Clin Nutr 47:710, 1988
66. Pulimissano DJ: Nutrient deficiencies after intensive parenteral nutrition. N Engl J Med 291:799, 1974
67. Shike M, Roulet M, Kurian R: Copper metabolism and requirements during total parenteral alimentation. Gastroenterology 81:290, 1981
68. Shike M: Copper in parenteral nutrition-deficiency metabolism and requirements. p. 469. In Prasad AS (ed): Essential and Toxic Trace Elements in Human Health and Disease. Alan R Liss, New York, 1988
69. Menkes JH, Alter M, Stegleder GK, et al: A sex-linked recessive disorder with retardation of growth, peculiar hair and focal cerebral and cerebellar degeneration. Pediatrics 29:764, 1962
70. Danks DM, Cartwright E, Stevens BJ, Townley RRW: Menkes' kinky hair disease: Further definition of the defect in copper transport. Science 179:1140, 1973
71. Horn N: Copper incorporation studies on cultured cells for prenatal diagnosis of Menkes' disease. Lancet 1:1156, 1976
72. Onishi T, Inubushi H, Tokugawa S, et al: Abnormal copper metabolism in Menkes cultured fibroblasts. Eur J Pediatr 134:205, 1980
73. Procopis P, Comakaris J, Danks DM: A mild form of Menkes' steely hair syndrome. J Pediatr 98:97, 1981
74. Moxon AL: Alkali disease or selenium poisoning. S Dak Agric Exp Sta Bull 311:1, 1937
75. Rosenfeld I, Beath OA: The influence of protein diets on selenium poisoning. Am J Vet Res 7:52, 1946
76. Schwarz K, Foltz CM: Selenium as an integral part of factor 3 against dietary necrotic liver degeneration. J Am Chem Soc 73:3292, 1957
77. Patterson EL, Milstrey R, Stokstad ELR: Effect of selenium in preventing exudative diathesis in chicks. Proc Soc Exp Biol Med 95:617, 1957
78. Schwarz K, Bieri JG, Briggs GM, et al: Prevention of exudative diathesis in chicks by factor 3 and selenium. Proc Soc Exp Biol Med 95:621, 1957
79. McLean JW, Thompson GG, Claxton JH: Growth response to selenium in lambs. Nature 184:251, 1959
80. Muth OH, Oldfield JE, Remmert LF, et al: Effects of selenium and vitamin E on white muscle disease. Science 128:1090, 1958
81. Hartley WJ, Grant AB: A review of selenium responsive diseases of New Zealand livestock. Fed Proc 20:679, 1961
82. Anderson P: Nutritional muscular dystrophy in cattle. Acta Pathol Microbiol Scand (Suppl) 134:3, 1960
83. Grant CA, Thafvelin B: Selenium and hepatosis diatetica of pigs. Nord Veterinuer Med 10:657, 1958
84. Passwater RA: Selenium as Food and Medicine. p. 3. Keat Publishing, New Canaan, CT, 1980
85. Thompson JN, Scott ML: Selenium deficiency in chicks and quail. p. 130. Proceedings of the Cornell Nutrition Conference for Feed Manufactures, Cornell University Press, Cornell, NY 1967
86. Hawkes WC, Lyons DE, Tappel AL: Identification of a selenocysteine-specific aminoacyl transfer RNA from rat liver. Biochem Biophys Acta 699:183, 1982
87. Pinsent J: The need for selenite and molybdate in the formation of formate dehydrogenases by members of the coliaerogenes group of bacteria. Biochem J 57:10, 1954

88. Turner DC, Stadtman TC: Purification of protein components of the clostridial glycine reductase system and characterization of protein A as a selenoprotein. Arch Biochem Biophys 154:366, 1973
89. Whanger PD, Petersen ND, Weswig PH: Selenium proteins in bovine tissues. II. Spectral properties of a 10,000 molecular weight selenium protein. Biochem Biophys Res Commun 53:1031, 1973
90. Rotruck JT, Pope AL, Ganther ME, et al: Selenium: Biochemical role as a component of glutathione peroxidase. Science 179:588, 1973
91. Flohe L, Gunzler WA, Schoch HH: Glutathione peroxidase: A selenoenzyme. FEBS Lett 32:132, 1973
92. Schwarz K: Essentiality and metabolic functions of selenium. Med Clin North Am 60:745, 1976
93. Dickson RC, Tomlinson RH: Selenium in blood and human tissue. Clin Chem Acta 16:311, 1967
94. Ehlig CG, Hogue DE, Allway WH et al: Fate of selenium from selenite or selenomethionine with or without vitamin E in lambs. J Nutr 92:121, 1967
95. Handreck KA, Godwin KO: Distribution in the sheep of selenium derived from ^{75}Se-labelled reminal pellets. Aust J Agr Res 21:71, 1970
96. Young VR, Nahapetian A, Janghorbani M: Selenium bioavailability with reference to human nutrition. Am J Clin Nutr 35:1076, 1982
97. Thompson CD, Robinson MF: Selenium in human health and disease with emphasis on those aspects peculiar to New Zealand. Am J Clin Nutr 33:303, 1980
98. Cousins FB, Cairney IM: Some aspects of selenium metabolism in sheep. Aust J Agr Res 12:927, 1961
99. Thomson CD, Robinson MF, Campbell DR, et al: Effect of prolonged supplementation with daily supplements of selenomethoionine and sodium selenite on glutathione peroxidase activity in blood of New Zealand residents. Am J Clin Nutr 36:24, 1982
100. Burk RF: Selenium. p. 310. In Hegsted DM (ed): Present Knowledge in Nutrition, 4th Ed. Nutrition Foundation, New York, 1976
101. Lee M, Dong A, Yano J: Metabolism of ^{75}Se-selenite by human whole blood in vitro. Can J Biochem 47:791, 1969
102. Anderson HD, Moxon AL: The excretion of selenium by rats on a seleniferous wheat ration. J Nutr 22:103, 1941
103. Yousef MK, Coffman WJ, Johnson HD: Total rate of body turnover of selenium-75 in rats. Nature 219:1173, 1968
104. Cavalieri RR, Scott KG, Sairengi E: Selenite (^{75}Se) as a tumor-localizing agent in man. J Nucl Med 7:197, 1966
105. Lathrop KA, Johnston RE, Blau M, et al: Radiation dose to humans from ^{75}Se-L-selenomethionine. J Nucl Med 13:7, 1972
106. Greger JL, Marcus RE: Effect of dietary protein, phosphorus and sulfur amino acids on selenium metabolism of adult males. Ann Nutr Metab 25:97, 1981
107. Versieck J, Cornelis R: Normal levels of trace elements in human blood plasma or serum. Anal Chim Acta 116:217, 1980
108. Thomson CD: Urinary excretion of selenium in some New Zealand women. Proc Univ Otago Med Sch 50:31, 1972
109. Burk RF: Selenium in man. p. 105. In Prasad AS (ed): Trace Elements in Human Health and Disease, Vol 2. Academic Press, New York, 1976
110. Allaway WH, Kubota J, Losee F, et al: Selenium, molybdenum, and vanadium in human blood. Arch Environ Health 16:343, 1968
111. Thomson CD, Reas HM, Doesburg VM, et al: Selenium concentration and glutathione peroxidase activities in whole blood of New Zealand residents. Br J Nutr 37:457, 1977
112. Eggert RG, Patterson EL, Akers WT, et al: The role of vitamin E and selenium in the nutrition of the pig. J Anim Sci 16:1032, 1957
113. Century B, Horwitt MK: Effect of dietary selenium on incidence of nutritional encephalomalacia in chicks. Proc Soc Exp Biol Med 117:320, 1964
114. Thompson JN, Scott ML: Impaired lipid and vitamin E absorption related to atrophy of the pancreas in selenium deficient chicks. J Nutr 100:797, 1970
115. Proctor JF, Hogue DE, Warner RG: Selenium, vitamin E and linseed oil meal as preventatives of muscular dystrophy in lambs. J Anim Sci 17:1183, 1958

116. Hart KE, Mackinnon MM: Enzootic parodontal disease in Bulls-Santoft arc. N Z Vet J 6:118, 1958
117. Van Vleeet JF, Carlton W, Orlander HJ: Hepatosis dietetica and mulberry heart disease associated with selenium deficiency in Indiana swine. J Am Vet Med Assoc 157:1208, 1970
118. Keshan Disease Research Group: Epidemiologic studies on the etiologic relationship of selenium and Keshan disease. Chinese Med J 92:477, 1979
119. Keshan Disease Research Group: Observations on effect of sodium selenite in prevention of Keshan disease. Chinese Med J 92:471, 1979
120. Prevention of Keshan cardiomyopathy by sodium selenite: Clinical, nutrition cases. Nutr Rev 38:278, 1980
121. Chen X, Yang G, Chen J, et al: Studies on the relations of selenium and Keshan disease. Biol Trace Elem Res 2:91, 1980
122. Johnson RA, Baker SS, Fallon JT, et al: An accidental case of cardiomyopathy and selenium deficiency. N Engl J Med 304:1210, 1981
123. Collipp PJ, Chen SY: Cardiomyopathy and selenium deficiency in a two-year-old girl. N Engl J Med 304:1304, 1981
124. Van Rij AM, Thomson CD, McKenzie JM, et al: Selenium deficiency in total parenteral nutrition. Am J Clin Nutr 32:2076, 1979
125. Kien CL, Ganther HE: Manifestations of chronic selenium deficiency in a child receiving total parenteral nutrition. Am J Clin Nutr 37:219, 1983
126. Brown MR, Cohen HJ, Lyons JM, et al: Proximal muscle weakness and selenium deficiency associated with long-term parenteral nutrition. Am J Clin Nutr 43:549, 1986
127. Vinton NE, Dahlstrom KA, Strobel CT, Ament ME: Macrocytosis and pseudoalbinism: Manifestations of selenium deficiency. J Pediatr 111:711, 1987
128. Schrauzer GN, Ishmael D: Effects of selenium and of arsenic on the genesis of spontaneous mammary tumors in inbred C_3H mice. Ann Clin Lab Sci 4:441, 1974
129. Schrauzer GN, White DA, Schneider CH: Inhibition of the genesis of spontaneous mammary tumors in C_3 mice: Effects of selenium and of selenium-antagonistic elements and their possible role in human breast cancer. Bioinorg Chem 6:265, 1976
130. Griffin AC: Role of selenium in the chemoprevention of cancer. Adv Cancer Res 29:419, 1979
131. Jacobs MM: Effects of selenium on chemical carcinogens. Prev Med 9:362, 1980
132. Greeder GA, Milner JA: Factors influencing the inhibitory effect of selenium on mice inoculated with Ehrlich ascites tumor cells. Science 209:825, 1980
133. Shamberger RJ, Frost DV: Possible protective effect of selenium against human cancer. Can Med Assoc J 100:682, 1969
134. McConnell KP, Jager RM, Blank KI, et al: The relationship of dietary selenium and breast cancer. J Surg Oncol 15:67, 1980
135. Capel ID, Williams DC: Selenium and glutathione peroxidase in breast cancer. Obstet Gynecol 7:425, 1979
136. Calautti P, Moschini G, Stievano BM, et al: Serum selenium levels in malignant lymphoproliferative diseases. Scand J Haematol 24:63, 1980
137. Broghamer WL, McConnell KP, Grimaldi M, et al: Serum selenium and reticuloendothelial tumors. Cancer 41:1462, 1978
138. Robinson MF, Godfrey PJ, Thomson CD, et al: Blood selenium and glutathione peroxidase activity in normal subjects and in surgical patients with and without cancer in New Zealand. Am J Clin Nutr 32:1477, 1979
139. Virtamo J, Huttunen JK: Selenium in human disease. Ann Clin Res 17:87, 1985
140. Wallach JD, Garmaise B: Cystic fibrosis: A perinatal manifestation of selenium deficiency. p. 469. In Hemphill DD (ed): Trace substances in Environmental Health. University of Missouri Press, Columbia, MO, 1979
141. Lloyd-Still JD, Ganther HE: Selenium and glutathione peroxidase levels in cystic fibrosis. Pediatrics 65:1010, 1980
142. Wikstom J, Westermarck T, Palo J: Selenium, vitamin E and copper in multiple sclerosis. Acta Neurol Scand 54:287, 1976
143. Shukla VKS, Jensen GE, Clausen J: Erythrocyte glutathione deficiency in multiple sclerosis. Acta Neurol Scand 56:542, 1977
144. Shamberger RJ, Rukovena E, Longfield AK, et al: Antioxidants and cancer. I. Se-

lenium in the blood of normals and cancer patients. J Natl Cancer Inst 50:863, 1973
145. Sullivan JF, Blotcky AJ, Jetton MM, et al: Serum levels of selenium, calcium, copper, magnesium, manganese and zinc in various human diseases. J Nutr 109:1432, 1979
146. Whanger, Weswig PH: Effects of selenium, chromium and antioxidants on growth, eye cataracts, plasma cholesterol, and blood glucose in selenium deficient, vitamin A supplemented rats. Nutr Repts Int 12:345, 1975
147. Ostadalova I, Babicky A, Obenberger J: Cataract induced by administration of a single dose of sodium selenite to suckling rats. Experientia 34:222, 1977
148. Burk RF, Pearson WN, Wood RP, et al: Blood selenium levels and in vitro red blood cell uptake of ^{75}Se in kwashiorkor. Am J Clin Nutr 20:723, 1967
149. Schwarz K: Development and status of experimental work of Factor 3-selenium. Fed Proc 20:666, 1961
150. Rhead WJ, Schneider JA: Effect of selenium compounds on selenium content, growth and ^{35}S-cystine metabolism of skin fibroblasts from normal and cystinotic individuals. Bioinorg Chem 6:187, 1976
151. Hafez M, Amar ES, Zedan M, et al: Improved erythrocyte survival with combined vitamin E and selenium therapy in child with glucose-6-phosphate dehydrogenase deficiency and mild chronic hemoglobin. J Pediatr 108:558, 1986
152. Lombeck I, Ebert KH, Kasperek K, et al: Selenium intake of infants and young children, healthy children and dietetically treated patients with phenylketonuria. Eur J Pediatr 142:99, 1984
153. Food and Nutrition Board: Selenium and human health. Nutr Rev 34:347, 1976
154. Anonymous: Studies on selenium. Nutr Rev 33:138, 1975
155. Rudolph N, Wong WL: Selenium and glutathione peroxidase activity in maternal and cord plasma and red cells. Pediatr Res 12:789, 1978
156. Rhead WJ, Cary EE, Allaway WH, et al: The vitamin E and selenium status of infants and the sudden infant death syndrome. Bioinorg Chem 1:289, 1972
157. Haga P, Lunde G: Selenium and vitamin E in cord blood from preterm and full term infants. Acta Paediatr Scand 67:735, 1978
158. Lombeck I, Kasperek K, Bonnermann B, et al: Selenium content of human milk, cow's milk and cow's milk infant formulas. Eur J Pediatr 129:139, 1978
159. Smith AM, Picciano MF, Milner JA: Selenium intakes and status of human milk and formula fed infants. Am J Clin Nutr 35:521, 1982
160. Shearer TR, Hadjimarkos DM: Geographic distribution of selenium in human milk. Arch Environ Health 30:230, 1975
161. Brune D, Samsahl K, Wester P: A comparison between the amount of As, Au, Br, Cu, Fe, Mo, Se and Xn in normal and uraemic human whole blood by means of neutron activation analysis. Clin Chim Acta 13:285, 1966
162. Lombeck I, Kasperek K, Feinendegen LE, et al: The state and supply of selenium in healthy children and dietetically treated patients with inborn errors of metabolism. p. 312. In Kirchgessner M (ed): Trace Element Metabolism in Man and Animals. Vol 3. Freising-Arbeitskreis fur Tierernahrungsforschung Weihenstephan, Weihenstephan, Germany, 1978
163. Amin S, Chen SY, Collipp PJ, et al: Selenium in premature infants. Nutr Metab 24:331, 1980
164. Schwarz K, Mertz W: Chromium III and the glucose tolerance factor. Arch Biochem Biophys 85:292, 1959
165. Schroeder, Balassa JJ, Tipton IH: Abnormal trace metals in man-chromium. J Chron Dis 15:941, 1962
166. Schroeder, Nason AP, Tipton IH: Chromium deficiency as a factor in atherosclerosis. J Chron Dis 23:123, 1970
167. Schroeder HA: The role of trace elements in cardiovascular diseases. Med Clin North Am 58:381, 1974
168. Mertz W, Schwarz K: Relation of glucose tolerance factor to impaired glucose tolerance in rats on stock diets. Am J Physiol 196:614, 1959
169. Mertz W, Anderson RA, Wolf WR, et al: Progress of chromium nutrition research. p. 272. In Kirchgessner M (ed): Trace Elements Metabolism in Man and Animals-3. Technische Universitat Munchen, Ger-

many; Institut fur Ernahrungsphysiologie, Freising-Weihenstephan, 1978
170. Mertz W: Biologic role of chromium. Fed Proc 26:186, 1967
171. Hambidge KM: Chromium. p. 271. In Bonner F, Coburn JW (eds): Disorders of Mineral Metabolism. Academic Press, New York, 1981
172. Mertz W: Chromium occurrence and function in biological systems. Physiol Rev 49:163, 1969
173. Mertz W, Roginski EE, Schwarz K: Effect of trivalent chromium complexes on glucose uptake by epideiymal fat tissue of rats. J Biol Chem 236:318, 1961
174. Saner S: Biochemistry and physiologic role of chromium. p. 7. In: Chromium in Nutrition and Disease. Alan R Liss, New York, 1980
175. Curran GL: Effect of certain transition group elements on hepatic synthesis of cholesterol in the rat. J Biol Chem 210:765, 1954
176. Schroeder HA: The role of chromium in mammalian nutrition. Am J Clin Nutr 21:230, 1968
177. Schroeder HA, Vinton WJ Jr, Balassa JJ: Effect of chromium, cadium and lead on serum cholesterol of rats. Proc Soc Exp Biol Med 109:859, 1962
178. Staub HW, Reussner G, Thiessen R Jr: Serum cholesterol reduction by chromium in hypercholesterolemic rats. Science 166:746, 1969
179. Schroeder HA, Balassa JJ: Influence of chromium, cadmium, and lead on rat aortic lipids and circulating cholesterol. Am J Physiol 209:433, 1965
180. Riales R, Albrink MJ: Effect of chromium chloride supplementation on glucose tolerance and serum lipids including high-density lipoprotein of adult men. Am J Clin Nutr 34:2670, 1981
181. Polansky MM, Anderson RA, Bryden NA, et al: Chromium supplementation of free living subjects—Effect on glucose tolerance and insulin. Fed Proc 40:885, 1981
182. Polansky MM, Anderson RA, Bryden NA, et al: Chromium (Cr) and Brewer's yeast supplementation of human subjects: Effect on glucose tolerance, serum glucose, insulin and lipid parameters. Fed Proc 41:391, 1982
183. Nordstrom JW: Trace mineral nutrition in the elderly. Am J Clin Nutr 36:788, 1982
184. Liu VJK, Morris JS: Relative chromium response to an indicator of chromium status. Am J Clin Nutr 31:972, 1978
185. Elwood JC, Nash DT, Streeten DHP: Effect of high-chromium Brewer's yeast on human serum lipids. J Am Coll Nutr 1:263, 1982
186. Grant AP, McMullen JK: The effect of brewer's yeast containing glucose tolerance factor on the response to treatment type 2 diabetics. A short controlled study. Ulster Med J 51:110, 1982
187. Vecchi C, Tucci PL, Galvan P: Cromo e diabete, Relazione con i livelli sierici di colesterolo, trigliceridi e lipoproteine. Wuad Sclavo Diagn 17:49, 1981
188. Gedik O, Unal S, Koraz Z: Plasma trivalent chromium, glucose tolerance and insulin secretion in juvenile- and adult-onset diabetes mellitus. Isr J Med Sci 16:563, 1980
189. Rabinowitz MB, Levin SR, Gonick HC: Comparisons of chromium status in diabetic and normal men. Metabolism 29:355, 1980
190. Venderlinde RE, Kayne FJ, Komar G, et al: Serum and urine levels of chromium. p. 49. In Shapcott D, Hubert J (eds): Chromium in Nutrition and Metabolism. Elsevier/North Holland, New York, 1979
191. Kumpulainen J, Lehto J, Koivistoinen P, et al: Determination of chromium in human milk, serum and urine by electrothermal atomic absorption spectrometry without preliminary ashing. Sci Total Environ 31:71, 1983
192. Mertz W, Roginski EE, Feldman FJ, et al: Dependence of chromium transfer into the rat embryo on the chemical form. J Nutr 99:363, 1969
193. Wallach S, Verch RL: Placental transport of chromium. J Am Coll Nutr 3:69, 1984
194. Hambidge KM, Chir B, Rodgerson DO: Comparison of hair chromium levels of nulliparous and parous women. Am J Obstet Gynecol 103:320, 1969
195. Saner G: Urinary chromium excretion during prenancy and its relationship with intravenous glucose loading. Am J Clin Nutr 24:1676, 1981
196. Hambidge KM, Droegemueller W:

Changes in plasma and hair concentrations of zinc, copper, chromium, and manganese during pregnancy. Obstet Gynecol 44:666, 1974
197. Imbriani M, Colli, M, Minoia C, et al: Dosaggio del cromo plasmatico nella gravida a termine e nel cordone ombelicale. Quad Sclavo Diagn 15:183, 1979
198. Mahalko JR, Bennion M: The effect of parity and time between pregnancies on maternal hair chromium concentration. Am J Clin Nutr 29:1069, 1976
199. Saner G: The effect of parity on maternal hair chromium concentration and the changes during pregnancy. Am J Clin Nutr 34:583, 1981
200. Davidson IWF, Burt RL: Physiologic changes in plasma chromium of normal and pregnant women: Effect of a glucose load. Am J Obstet Gynecol 116:601, 1973
201. Wallach S: Clinical and biochemical aspects of chromium deficiency. J Am Coll Nutr 4:107, 1985
202. Kumpulainen J, Vuori E: Longitudinal study of chromium in human milk. Am J Clin Nutr 33:2299, 1980
203. Hopkins LL Jr, Ransom-Kuti O, Majaj AS: Improvement of impaired carbohydrate metabolism by chromium (III) in malnourished infants. Am J Clin Nutr 21:203, 1968
204. Wallach S, Verch RL: Radiochromium distribution in aged rats. J Am Coll Nutr 5:291, 1986
205. Levine RA, Streeten DHP, Doisy RJ: Effects of oral chromium supplementation on the glucose tolerance of elderly human subjects. Metabolism 17:114, 1968
206. Vir SC, Love AHG: Chromium status of the aged. Int J Vitam Nutr Res 48:402, 1978
207. Abraham AS, Sonnenblick M, Eini M: Serum chromium and ageing. Gerontology 27:326, 1981
208. Bunker VW, Lawson MS, Delves HT, et al: The uptake and excretion of chromium by the elderly. Am J Clin Nutr 39:797, 1984
209. Jeejeebhoy KN, Chu RC, Marliss EB, et al: Chromium deficiency, glucose intolerance, and neuropathy reversed by chromium supplementation, in a patient receiving long-term total parenteral nutrition. Am J Clin Nutr 30:531, 1977
210. Freund H, Atamian S, Fisher JE: Chromium deficiency during total parenteral nutrition. JAMA 241:496, 1979
211. Anonymous: Is chromium essential for humans? Nutr Rev 46:17, 1988
212. Donaldson RM, Barreras RF: Intestinal absorption of trace quantities of chromium. J Lab Clin Med 68:484, 1966
213. Doisy RJ, Streeten DHP, Levine RA, et al: Proceedings of the Second Annual conference on Trace Substances in Environmental Health. p. 75. University of Missouri Press, Columbia, Missouri, 1968
214. Hahn CJ, Evans GW: Absorption of trace metals in the zinc-deficient rat. Am J Physiol 228:1020, 1975
215. Huber AM, Gershoff SN: Effect of zinc deficiency in rats on insulin release from the pancreas. J Nutr 103:1739, 1973
216. Chen NSC, Tsai A, Dyer IA: Effect of chelating agents on chromium absorption in rats. J Nutr 103:1182, 1973
217. Hopkins LL Jr: Distribution in the rat of physiological amounts of injected ^{51}Cr (III) with time. Am J Physiol 209:731, 1965
218. Polansky MM, Anderson RA: Chromium absorption and retention. Fed Proc 42:925, 1983
219. Jain R, Verch RL, Wallach S, et al: Tissue chromium exchange in the rat. Am J Clin Nutr 34:2199, 1981
220. Lim TH, Sargent T III, Kusubov N; Kinetics of trace element chromium (III) in the human body. Am J Physiol 244:R445, 1983
221. Mertz W: Effects and metabolism of glucose tolerance factor. Nutr Rev 81:129, 1975
222. Anderson RA, Polansky MM, Bryden NA, et al: Urinary chromium excretion of human subjects: Effects of chromium supplementation and glucose loading. Am J Clin Nutr 36:1184, 1982
223. Anderson RA, Polansky MM, Bryden NA, et al: Effects of chromium supplementation on urinary Cr excretion of human subjects and correlation of Cr excretion with selected parameters. J Nutr 113:276, 1983
224. Orent ER, McCollum EV: Effects of deprivation of manganese in the rat. J Biol Chem 92:651, 1931
225. Kemmerer AR, Elvehjem CA, Hart EB: Studies on the relation of manganese to the

nutrition of the mouse. J Biol Chem 92:263, 1931
226. McClure, Landy HA, Kniefel HP: Rat liver pyruvate carboxilase. Preparation, properties and cation specificity. J Biol Chem 246:3569, 1971
227. Weisiger RA, Fridovich I: Superoxide dismutase: Organelle specificity. J Biol Chem 248:3582, 1973
228. Scrutton MC, Griminger P, Wallace JC: Pyruvate carboxylase: Bound metal content of the vertebrate liver enzyme as a function of diet. J Biol Chem 247:3305, 1972
229. DeRosa G, Keen CL, Leach RM, et al: Regulation of superoxide dismutase activity by dietary manganese. J Nutr 110:795, 1980
230. Zidenberg-Cherr S, Hurley LS, Lonnerdal B, et al: Manganese deficiency: Effects on susceptibility to ethanol toxicity in rats. J Nutr 115:460, 1985
231. Keen CL, Lonnerdal B, Hurley LS: Metabolism and biochemistry of manganese. p. 139. In Frieden E (ed): Biochemistry of the Essential Ultratrace Elements. Plenum, New York, 1984
232. Hurley LS: Clinical, Biochemical and Nutritional Aspects of Trace Elements. p. 369. Alan R Liss, New York, 1982
233. Knox D, Cowey CB, Adam JW: The effect of low dietary manganese intake on rainbow trout (Salmo gairdneri). Br J Nutr 46:495, 1981
234. Leach RM Jr, Muenster AM, Wein EM: Studies on the role of manganese in bone formation. II. Effect upon chondroitin sulfate synthesis in chick epiphyseal cartilage. Arch Biochem Biophys 113:22, 1969
235. Lonnerdal B: Trace element nutriton in infancy, childhood, and adolescence. p. 193. In Kretchmer N (ed): Frontiers in Clinical Nutrition. Aspen Publications, Rockville, MD, 1986
236. Bolze MS, Reeves RD, Lindbeck FE, et al: Influence of manganese on growth, somatomedin and glycosaminoglycan metabolism. J Nutr 115:352, 1985
237. Strause LG, Hegenauer J, Saltman P, et al: Effects of long-term dietary manganese and copper deficiency on rat skeleton. J Nutr 116:135, 1986
238. Rubenstein AH, Levin NW, Elliott GA: Manganese-induced hypoglycemial. Lance 2:1348, 1962
239. Hassanein M, Ghaleb HA, Haroun EA, et al: Chronic manganism: preliminary observations on glucose tolerance and serum proteins. Br Ind Med 23:67, 1966
240. Pignatari FJ: Clicimia et lipemia nella intossicaziore de manganese. Fol Med Cracov 18:484, 1932
241. Bellotti RM, Ravera M, Abbona C: Studio in vivo dell' attiveta di alcuna sali de manganese sur metabolism intermedio degli drati di carbonio. Arch Maragliano Patol Clin 12:683, 1956
242. Baly DL, Curry DL, Keen CL, et al: Effect of manganese deficiency on insulin secretion and carbohydrate hemeostatis. J Nutr 114:1438, 1984
243. Everson GJ, Shrader RE: Abnormal glucose tolerance in manganese-deficient guinea pigs. J Nutr 94:89, 1968
244. Baly DL, Curry DL, Keen CL, et al: Dynamics of insulin and glucagan release in rats: Influence of dietary manganese. Endocrinology 116:1734, 1985
245. Korc M: Manganese action on protein synthesis in diabetic rat pancreas: Evidence for a possible physiological role. J Nutr 114:2119, 1984
246. Doisy EA Jr: Micronutrient controls on biosynthesis of clotting proteina and cholesterol. Trace Sub Environ Health 6:193, 1972
247. Friedman BJ, Freeland-Graves JH, Bales CW, et al: Manganese balance and clinical observations in young men fed a manganese-deficient diet. J Nutr 117:113, 1987
248. Wenlock RW, Buss DH, Dixon EJ: Trace nutrients. II. Manganese in British foods. Br J Nutr 41:253, 1979
249. Tipton JW, Steward PL, Dickson J: Patterns of elemental excretion in long term balance studies. Health Phys 16:455, 1969
251. Greenberg DM, Copp DH, Cuthbertson EM: Studies in mineral metabolism with the aid of artificial isotopes. J Biol Chem 147:749, 1943
252. Mena I, Horiuchi K, Burke K, et al: Chronic manganese poisoning: Individual susceptibility and absorption of iron. Neurology 19:100, 1969

253. Schroeder HA, Balassa JJ, Tipton IH: Essential trace metals in man: Manganese. A study of homeostasis. J Chronic Dis 19:545, 1966
254. Bertinchamps AJ, Miller ST, Corzias GC: Interdependence of routes excreting manganese. Am J Physiol 211:217, 1966
255. Keen CL, Clegg MS, Lonnerdal B, et al: Whole blood manganese as an indicator of body manganese status. N Engl J Med 308:1230, 1983
256. Lonnerdal B, Keen CL, Hurley LS: Iron, copper, zinc and manganese in milk. Annu Rev Nutr 1:149, 1981
257. Stastny D, Vogel RS, Picciano MF: Manganese intake and serum manganese concentration of human milk-fed and formula-fed infants. Am J Clin Nutr 39:872, 1984
258. Collipp PJ, Chen SY, Maitinsky S: Manganese in infant formulas and learning disability. Ann Nutr Metab 27:488, 1983
259. Hatano S, Nishi Y, Usui T: Erythrocyte manganese concentration in healthy Japanese children, adults, and the elderly, and in cord blood. Am J Clin Nutr 37:457, 1983
260. Mena I: Manganese. p. 233. In Bronner F, Coburn JW (eds): Disorders of Mineral Metabolism. Academic Press, New York, 1981
261. McCollum EV, Simmonds N, Becker JE, et al: The effect of additions of fluorine to the diet of the rat on the quality of the teeth. J Biol Chem 63:553, 1925
262. McClure FJ: Fluorine Drinking Waters. US Public Health Service, Bethesda, MD, 1962
263. McClure FJ: Water Fluoridation. The Search and the Victory. US Public Health Service, Bethesda, MD, 1970
264. Sognnaes RF: Historical perspectives. p. 321. In Johansen E, Taves DR, Olsen TO (eds): Continuing Evaluation of the Use of Fluorides. Westview, Boulder, CO, 1979
265. Dean HT: Epidemiological studies in the United States. p. 5. In Moulton FR (eds): Dental Caries and Fluorine. American Association for the Advancement of Science, Washington, DC, 1946
266. Hardwick JL: Fluorides and dental health. Forum Medici 13:33, 1971
267. Horowitz HS, Heifetz SB, Driscoll WS: Partial defluoridation of a community water supply and dental fluorosis. Final evaluation in Britton, S Dak. Health Services Rep 87:451, 1972
268. Farkas CS: Total fluoride intake and fluoride content of common foods: A review. Fluoride 8:98, 1975
269. Newbrun E: Water fluoridation and dietary fluoride ingestion—An editorial comment. West J Med 122:437, 1975
270. Toth K, Sugar E: Effect of fluorine content of drinking water on fluorine concentration of foods. Acta Physiol Acad Sci Hung 56:213, 1980
271. Singer L, Ophaug RH, Harland BF: Fluoride intake of young male adults in the United States. Am J Clin Nutr 33:328, 1980
272. Glass RL: The International Conference on the Declining Prevalence of Dental Caries. J Dent Res 61:1301 (Special issue), 1982
273. Glass RL: Secular changes in caries prevalence in two Massachusetts towns. J Dent Res 61:1352 (Special issue), 1982
274. Leverett DH: Fluorides and changing prevalence of dental caries. Science 217:26, 1982
275. Adair SM, Wei SHY: Supplemental fluoride recommendations for infants based on dietary fluoride intake. Caries Res 12:76, 1978
276. Adair SM, Wei SHY: Fluoride content of commercially prepared strained fruit juices. Pediatr Dent 1:174, 1979
277. Ophaug RH, Singer L, Harland BF: Estimated fluoride intake of 6-month-old infants in four dietary regions of the United States. Am J Clin Nutr 33:324, 1980
278. Singer L, Ophaug RH: Dietary sources of fluoride for infants and children. p. 730. In Steward RE, Barber TK, Troutman KC et al (eds): Pediatric Dentistry: Scientific Foundations and Clinical Practice. CV Mosby, St. Louis, MO, 1981
279. Ekstrand J, Ehrnebo M: Absorption of fluoride from fluoride dentifrices. Caries Res 14:96, 1980
280. Ekstrand J, Koch G, Peterson LG: Plasma fluoride concentrations in preschool children after ingestion of fluoride tablets and toothpaste. Caries Res 17:379, 1983
281. Bell RA, Barenie JT, Whitford GM: Fluoride retention in children using self-administered fluoride products. J Dent Res 61:235, 1982

282. Messer HH, Singer L: Fluoride. p. 325. In Hegsted DM (ed): Present Knowledge in Nutrition. 4th Ed. Nutrition Foundation, Washington DC, 1976
283. Carlson CH, Armstrong WD, Singer L: Distribution and excretion of radiofluoride in the human. Proc Soc Exp Biol Med 104:235, 1960
284. Prasad AS: Trace Elements and Iron in Human Metabolism. p. 78. Plenum, New York, 1978
285. Schwarz K: Recent dietary element research, exemplified by tin, fluorine, and silicon. Fed Proc 33:1748, 1974
286. Singer L, Armstrong WD: Regulation of human plasma fluoride concentration. J Appl Physiol 15:508, 1960
287. Adler P: Fluorides in Human Health. World Health Organization Monograph Series No. 59. World Health Organization, Geneva, 1970
288. Rugg-Gunn AJ, Carmichael CL, French AD, et al: Fluoridation in Newcastle and Northumberland. A clinical study of 5-year-old children. Br Dent J 142:395, 1977
289. Backer Dirks O: The benefits of water fluoridation. Caries Res (Suppl 1) 8:2, 1974
290. Schamscula RG, Copper MH, Agus HM, et al: Oral health of Australian children using surface and artesian water supplies. Community Dent Oral Epidemiol 9:34, 1981
291. Sheiham A: The epidemiology of dental caries and periodontal disease. J Clin Periodontol 6:7, 1979
292. Russell AL, Elvove E: Domestic water and dental caries. VII. A study of the fluoride-dental caries relationship in an adult population. Public Health Rep 66:1389, 1951
293. Murray JJ: Water fluoridation and dental caries. Proc Br Paedodont Soc 6:20, 1976
294. Barrett MJ, Williamson JJ: Oral health of Australian Aborigines: Survey methods and prevalence of dental caries. Aust Dent J 17:37, 1972
295. Schamscula RG, Copper MH, Wright MC, et al: Oral health of adolescent and adult Australian Aborigines. Community Dent Oral Epidemiol 8:370, 1980
296. Schamscula RG, Agus H, Charlton G, et al: Associations between fluoride concentration in successive layers of human enamel and individual dental caries experience. Arch Oral Biol 24:847, 1979
297. Schamscula RG, Adkins BL, Barmes DE, et al: WHO Study of Dental Caries Etiology in Papua New Guinea. In: WHO Offset Publication No 40, World Health Organization, Geneva, 1978
298. Agus HM, Schamachula RG, Barnes DE, et al: Associations between the total fluoride content of dental plaque and individual caries experience in Australian children. Community Dent Oral Epidemiol 4:210, 1976
299. Carlos JP: Opening remarks. Mechanisms of action of fluorides in caries prevention. Caries Res (Suppl 1) 11:15, 1977
300. Jenkins GN, Edgar WM: Distribution and forms of F in saliva and plaque. Caries Res (Suppl 1) 11:226, 1977
301. Schamscula RG, Adkins BL, Barnes DE, et al: Caries experience and the mineral content of plaque in a primitive population in New Guinea. J Dent Res (Special Issue) 56:62, 1977
302. Jowsey J, Schenk RK, Reutter RW: Some results of the effect of fluoride on bone tissue in osteoporosis. J Clin Endocrinol 28:869, 1968
303. Jowsey J, Riggs BL, Kelly PJ, et al: Effect of combined therapy with sodium fluorides, vitamin D and calcium in osteoporosis. Am J Med 53:43, 1972
304. Rich G, Ensinck J, Ivanovich P: The effects of sodium fluoride on calcium metabolism of subjects with metabolic bone disease. J Clin Invest 43:545, 1964
305. Posner AS: Relationship between diet and bone mineral ultrastructure. Fed Proc 26:1717, 1967
306. Dambacher MA, Lauffenberger TH, Lammble B et al: Long term effects of sodium fluoride in osteoporosis. p. 238. In: Courvoisier B, Donath A, Baud CA (eds): Fluoride and bones. Hans Huber, Bern, 1978
307. Riggs BL, Hodgson SF, Hoffman DL, et al: Treatment of primary osteoporosis with fluoride and calcium. JAMA 243:446, 1980
308. Editorial: Fluroide and the treatment of osteoporosis. Lance 1:547, 1984
309. Inkovaara J, Heikinheimo R, Jarvineri K, et al: Prophylactic fluoride treatment and aged bones. Br Med J III:73, 1975

310. Harley JB, Schilling A, Glidewell O: Ineffectiveness of fluoride therapy in multiple myeloma. N Engl J Med 286:1283, 1972
311. Budden FH, Bayley TA, Harrison JH, et al: The effect of fluoride on bone histology in postmenopausal osteoporosis depends on adequate fluorine absorption and retention. J Bone Mineral Res 3:127, 1988
312. Riggs BL, Jowsey J: Treatment of osteoporosis with fluoride. Sem Drug Treat 2:27, 1972
313. Riggs BL, Seeman E, Hodgson SF, et al: Effect of the fluoride/calcium regimen on vertebral fracture occurrence in postmenopausal osteoporosis. N Engl J Med 306:446, 1982
314. Bernstein DS, Sadowsky N, Hegsted DM, et al: Prevalence of osteoporosis in high- and low-fluoride areas in North Dakota. JAMA 198:499, 1966
315. Luoma H, Helminen SKJ, Ranta H, et al: Relationships between the fluoride and magnesium concentrations in drinking water and some components in serum related to cardiovascular diseases in mean from four rural districts in Finland. Scand J Clin Lab Invest 32:217, 1973
316. Taves DR: Fluoridation and mortality due to heart disease. Nature 272:361, 1978
317. Schroeder HA, Kraemer LA: Cardiovascular mortality, municipal water, and corrosion. Arch Environ Health 28:303, 1974
318. Newbrun E: Systemic fluorides. An overview. J Can Dent Assoc 46:31, 1980
319. Smith EL: Presence of cobalt in anti-pernicious anemia factor. Nature 162:144, 1948
320. Rickes EL, Brink NG, Koniusky FR, et al: Vitamin B_{12}, a cobalt complex. Science 108:134, 1948
321. Smith SE, Koch BA, Turk KL: The response of cobalt-deficient lambs to liver extract and vitamin B_{12}. J Nutr 44:455, 1951
322. Shuttleworth VS, Cameron BS, Alderman G, et al: A case of cobalt deficiency in a child presenting as "earth eating." Practitioner 186:760, 1961
323. Tipton IH, Stewart PL, Martin PG: Trace elements in diets and excreta. Health Phys 12:1683, 1966
324. Schroeder HA, Nason AP, Tipton IH: Essential trace metals in man: Cobalt, J Chronic Dis 20:869, 1967
325. Fleming CR, Hodges RE, Hurley LS: A prospective study of serum copper and zinc levels in patients receiving total parenteral nutrition. Am J Clin Nutr 29:70, 1976
326. Bozian RC, Shearer C: Copper, zinc and manganese content of four amino acid and protein hydrolysate preparations. Am J Clin Nutr 29:1331, 1976
327. Quarterman J, Mills CF, Humphries WR: The reduced secretion of and sensitivity to insulin in zinc deficient rats. Biochem Biophys Res Commun 25:354, 1966
328. Lowry SF, Goodgame JT Jr, Smith JC Jr, et al: Abnormalities of zinc and copper during total parenteral nutrition. Ann Surgery 189:120, 1979
329. Arakawa T, Tamura T, Igarashi Y, et al: Zinc deficiency in two infants during total parenteral alimentation for diarrhea. Am J Clin Nutr 29:197, 1976
330. McCarthy DM, May RJ, Maher M, Brennan MF: Trace metal and essential fatty acid deficiency during total parenteral nutrition. Am J Dig Dis 23:1009, 1978
331. Kay Rg, Tasman-Jones, Pybus J, et al: A syndrome of acute zinc deficiency during total parenteral nutrition in man. Ann Surg. 183:331, 1976
332. Kay RG, Tasman-Jones C: Acute zinc deficiency in man during intravenous alimentation. Aust NZ J Surg 45:325, 1979
333. Solomans NW, Layden TJ, Rosenberg IH, et al: Plasma trace metals during total parenteral nutrition. Gastroenterology 70:1022, 1976
334. Hankins DA, Riella MC, Scribner BH, Bragg AL: Whole blood trace element concentrations during total parenteral nutrition. Surgery 76:674, 1976
335. Van Rij AM, McKenzie JM, Robinson MF, Thomson CD: Selenium and total parenteral nutrition. JPEN 3:235, 1979
336. Woman SL, Anderson GH, Marliss EB, Jeejeebhoy KN: Zinc in total parenteral nutrition: requirements and metabolic effects. Gastroenterol 76:458, 1979
337. Shils ME: Guidelines for total parenteral nutrition. JAMA 220:1727, 1972
338. Wretlind A: Complete intravenous nutrition: Theoretical and experimental background. Nutr Metab (Suppl) 14:1, 1972
339. Lowry SF, Smith JC, Brennan MF: Zinc and copper replacement during total parenteral nutrition. Am J Clin Nutr 34:1853, 1981

340. Blackburn GL, Bistrian BR: Nutritional care of the injured and/or septic patient. Surg Clin North Am 56:1195, 1976
341. Dudrick SJ, Rhoads JE: New horizons for intravenous feeding. JAMA 215:939, 1971
342. Hull RL: Use of trace elements in intravenous hyperalimentation solutions. Am J Hosp Pharm 31:759, 1974
343. Jacobson S, Wester PO: Balance study of twenty trace elements during total parenteral nutrition in man. Br J Nutr 37:107, 1977
344. James BE, MacMahon RA: Trace metals in intravenous fluids. Med J Aust 2:1161, 1970
345. Jeejeebhoy KN, Langer B, Tsallas G, et al: Total parenteral nutrition at home: Studies in patients surviving 4 months to 5 years. Gastroenterology 71:943, 1976
346. Brennan MF: Total parenteral nutrition in the cancer patient. N Engl J Med 305:375, 1981
347. Okada A, Takagi Y, Itakura T, et al: Skin lesions during intravenous hyperalimentation: Zinc deficiency. Surgery 80:629, 1976
348. Walker BE, Dawson JB, Kelleher J, Lasowsky MS: Plasma and urinary zinc in patients with malabsorption syndromes or hepatic cirrhosis. Gut 14:943, 1973
349. Flynn A, Strain WH, Pories WJ, Hill OA: Zinc deficiency with altered adrenocortical function and its relation to delayed healing. Lancet 1:789, 1973
350. Halsted JA, Smith JC Jr, Irwin MI: A conspectus of research on zinc requirements of man. J Nutr 104:345, 1974
351. Linderman RD, Bottomley RG, Cornelison RL Jr, Jacobs LA: Influence of acute tissue injury on zinc metabolism in man. J Lab Clin Med 79:452, 1972
352. Halbrook T, Helelin H: Zinc metabolism and surgical trauma. Br J Surg 64:271, 1977
353. Fell GS, Cuthbertson DP, Morrison C, et al: Urinary zinc levels an indicator of muscle catabolism. Lance 1:280, 1973
354. Van Rij AM, McKenzie JM, Dunckley JV: Excessive urinary zinc losses and amino aciduria during intravenous alimentation. Proc Univ Otago Med Sch 53:77, 1975
355. Henkin RI, Patten BM, Re PK, Bronzert DA: A syndrome of acute zinc loss. Arch Neurol 32:745, 1975
356. McCance RA, Widdowson EM: The absorption and excretion of zinc. Biochem J 36:692, 1942
357. Hambidge KM, Hambidge C, Jacobs M, Baum JD: Low levels of zinc in hair, anorexia, poor growth and hypogensia in children. Pediatr Res 6:868, 1972
358. Brocks A, Reid H, Glazer G: Acute intravenous zinc poisoning. Br J Med 1:1390, 1977
359. Jetton MS, Sullivan JF, Burch RE: Trace element contamination of intravenous solutions. Arch Intern Med 136:782, 1976
360. Cartwright GE, Gubler CJ, Wintrobe MM: Studies on copper metabolism. XI: Copper and iron metabolism in nephrotic syndrome. J Clin Invest 33:685, 1964
361. Dunlap WM, James GW III, Hume DH: Anemia and neutropenia caused by copper deficiency. Ann Intern Med 80:470, 1974
362. Vilter RW, Bozian RC, Hess EV, et al: Manifestations of copper deficiency in a patient with systemic sclerosis on intravenous hyperalimentation. N Engl J Med 291:188, 1974
363. Norton JA, Peters ML, Wesley R, et al: Iron supplementation of total parenteral nutrition: A prospective study. JPEN 7:457, 1983
364. Andrews ED, Hartley WJ, Grant AB: Selenium responsive diseases of animals in New Zealand. NZ Vet J 16:3, 1968
365. Muth OH, Weswig PH, Phanger PD: Effect of feeding selenium-deficient ration to the subhuman primate (*Saimirj sciureus*). Am J Vet Res 32:1603, 1971
366. Robinson MF: The moonstone—More about selenium. J Hum Nutr 30:79, 1976
367. Schroeder HA, Frost DV, Bolama JJ: Essential trace elements in man: Selenium. J Chronic Dis 23:227, 1970
368. Lowry SF, Goodgame JT, Maher MM, Brennan MF: Parenteral vitamin requirements during intravenous feeding. Am J Clin Nutr 31:2149, 1978
369. Kirkemo AK, Burt ME, Brennan MF: Serum vitamin level maintenance in cancer patients on total parenteral nutrition. Am J Clin Nutr 35:1003, 1982
370. Guidelines for essential trace element preparations for parenteral use. A statement by the Nutrition Advisory Group. JPEN 3:263, 1979

9

Special Problems of Fluid and Electrolyte Management in Surgery

Donald S. Gann
Pardon R. Kenney

The purpose of this chapter is to present some special problems of fluids and electrolyte management in surgery as they relate to the homeostatic response to injury. Trauma (in the operating room or in the field), sepsis, and major burns all set in motion a number of reflexes that attempt to return organ function to normal. In the extreme case, all of these insults may lead to shock—a state of prolonged inadequate tissue perfusion. A common feature of all of these entities is volume loss. Volume loss may occur from hemorrhage, from accumulated wound and tissue fluid (third-space formation), or from the movement of fluid into cells. The classic neural and hormonal response to shock may be potentiated by other factors, including hypoxia, hypercarbia, pain, infection, and anxiety. We will briefly describe some of the responses of the body to injury at both the cellular and the organ-system level, so that we may better delineate therapy to correct them.

EFFECTS OF INJURY

Cellular Level

Initial investigations into the pathophysiology of trauma and shock focused on the response of the whole organism to injurious stimuli. The classic experiments of Walter Cannon[1] are example of this macrophysiologic approach. In recent years the emphasis has shifted to cellular and subcellular responses to injury, in an attempt to understand the response of the organism as a whole.

Regulation of cell volume is disrupted by injury. A membrane-bound, magnesium-dependent, Na-K-ATPase maintains high intracellular potassium and low sodium concentrations. Cell membranes are freely permeable to water, which passively follows sodium. Thus, membrane pump dysfunction leads to diffusion of potassium out of and sodium into the cell, with cell swelling. The classic explanation for this phenomenon is a persistent intracellular energy deficit that occurs in cases of prolonged inadequate tissue perfusion. However, more recent evidence suggests that the production of adenosine triphosphate (ATP) is not impaired in this situation, but that it cannot be utilized.[2] Also, a recent study has shown that cachectin/tumor necrosis factor, a substance released from macrophages exposed to endotoxin, can directly affect cell membrane function.[3] At least in part, this suggests that a variety of host defense factors are responsible for the alterations in cell membrane potential seen in both sepsis and severe shock. The goal of fluid and electrolyte therapy at the cellular level is to improve tissue perfusion. To achieve this, organ system function must be maintained. Let us now review the organ system response to injury.

Organ System Level

The response to injury consists of a triad of interrelated and interdependent actions that are controlled through a variety of mechanisms. Although any one of multiple stimuli may produce this response, the most primal stimulus is loss of blood volume. The three great lines of defense of blood volume are a primary neural response through the baroreceptor reflex, an interrelated hormonal response, and a later response involving restitution of blood volume.

The neural response is the most rapid. Loss of blood volume leads to decreased cardiac output because of decreased venous return. These changes are sensed by stretch receptors in the atria, aortic arch, and carotid arteries, and initiates the classic baroreceptor reflex. This results in increased myocardial contractility and a greater heartbeat rate, attempting to return cardiac output to normal. In addition, systemic vascular resistance increases because of sympathetically mediated peripheral vasoconstriction. Increased peripheral vascular resistance is augmented by the release of vasopressin and angiotensin II, which are powerful vasoconstrictors. Thus, the neural response is interrelated, to a certain extent, with the hormonal response to blood volume loss.

The net effect of the hormonal response to injury is volume conservation. Aldosterone, acting on the distal tubule, and vasopressin, acting on the collecting duct, limit further volume loss. In addition, catecholamines, secreted as part of the neural response to injury, may influence renal water conservation, as shown by Gill.[4] The remaining hormones that participate in the response to loss of blood volume are cortisol and glucagon. These, in addition to the catecholamines and vasopressin, facilitate the restitution of blood volume that is necessary for ultimate stabilization of the cardiovascular system.[5]

The phenomenon of blood volume restitution, also known as transcapillary refilling, has been studied for many years. Restitution of blood volume appears to have two phases. The first, occurring within two hours after injury, is rapid, and is related to decreased capillary pressure. According to the Starling hypothesis, this leads to movement of protein-free water across cell membranes and into the vascular space, as shown by Haddy.[6]

This phase accounts for the restitution of approximately half of the lost volume. The slower second phase is dependent on restoration of plasma protein, as demonstrated by Cope and Litwin.[7] Protein, primarily albumin, moves from the interstitium into the vascular space because of an increase in interstitial pressure that is caused by an increased interstitial fluid volume. Gann and others[8–14] have shown that the origin of this fluid is the intracellular space, and that cortisol plays an essential role in its movement into the interstitium.

In this phase, the primary stimulus for the movement of water out of cells is an increase in extracellular solute, largely glucose with smaller amounts of pyruvate and lactate. The source of this solute is the liver, where glycogenolysis and gluconeogenesis have been stimulated by glucagon, catecholamines, and cortisol. However, along with increased solute production there is also decreased utilization of solute in the periphery. Glucose entry into cells is impeded by epinephrine and also by endorphins,[15] further contributing to the increased extracellular solute content. With this increase, water moves out of the intracellular space down its concentration gradient, and, as noted above, increases interstitial fluid volume and pressure. Lymphatic flow then rises, leading to the return of both water and albumin to the vascular space. This completes the restitution of blood volume. This phenomenon is intimately dependent on the hormonal response to injury, since decreased cortisol, catecholamines, glucagon, and one or more pituitary factors can alter or abolish it.[16-19] Ultimate stabilization of the cardiovascular system depends upon restitution of blood volume.[5]

With smaller hemorrhages (10 to 20 percent), this mechanism is highly effective in restoring blood volume to normal levels. However, with hemorrhage in excess of 25 percent, restitution becomes impaired.[20] The etiology of the impairment is unclear, but may be related to impaired cell membrane function with movement of sodium and water into the cell outweighing the effects of extracellular solute.[21,22]

In addition to the above, there are several other specific renal effects of injury. The first is a decreased ability to excrete potassium. This becomes particularly important in patients with massive crushing injuries or burns, where large quantities of potassium may be released from dead and dying cells. Dangerous levels of hyperkalemia may result. A defect in urinary concentrating ability also exists in this situation, and the patient is unable to excrete a full water load. This will be discussed in detail later. Because the total volume of fluid in the nephron decreases in response to injury, toxic substances may accumulate at concentrations sufficient to damage the nephron. These substances, principally hemoglobin and myoglobin, may also be released in crushing injuries and in burn patients.

The work of breathing increases after surgical operation or trauma, and may require as much as 30 to 50 percent of the cardiac output.[23] Pain and anxiety are powerful stimuli of hyperventilation. In addition, sepsis and/or tissue injury may cause pulmonary membrane damage leading to defective oxygen diffusion and hypoxia, further stimulating ventilation.[24] These factors may be augmented by direct pulmonary injury (pulmonary contusion), and by the harmful effects of postoperative atelectasis.

HYPOVOLEMIA AND ITS THERAPY

Hemorrhage

Hemorrhage becomes hemodynamically significant after the loss of approximately 20 percent of blood volume, as transcapillary refilling and compensatory hemodynamics cannot maintain adequate perfusion. The use of balanced salt solutions is indicated in such situations, as shown by Shires and associates.[25,26] Ringer's lactate is a balanced salt solution and has been the traditional choice of surgeons for rapid replacement of blood loss. It contains 130 mEq/liter sodium, 109 mEq/liter chloride, 4 mEq/liter potassium, 2.7 mEq/liter calcium, and the equivalent in lactate of 28 mEq/liter of bicarbonate. In most situations of emergent volume replacement, Ringer's lactate is the solution of choice until blood is available or indicated. In the occasional exsanguinating patient, type specific, uncrossmatched or O-negative blood may be given, recognizing the risk of transfusion reaction. In this situation the risk of death usually far exceeds this consideration.

The therapy of choice for hemorrhage in excess of 25 to 30 percent is blood. Several caveats must accompany this statement. Blood is stored at 4°C and is usually delivered from the blood bank at or near this temperature. With normal infusion rates, it is usually warmed sufficiently before it reaches the patient. However, with massive and rapid transfusion, significant hypothermia and subsequent ventricular arrhythmias can occur unless the blood is warmed. A variety of devices are currently marketed that can deliver intravenous fluids and blood at extremely rapid rates (in excess of 500 ml/min). Although these devices can rapidly restore blood volume, they can also induce dramatic declines in core body temperature. Hypothermia from these devices is now being recognized as a major source of mortality in otherwise "resuscitated" trauma patients.

As blood ages, the red cells lyse, with release of potassium. Transfusion of old blood can thus cause dangerous hyperkalemia, particularly in the presence of the renal dysfunction that accompanies hypoperfusion.

Old blood also contains particulate matter, the amount of which increases with duration of storage. The particles include aggregates of platelets and white cells, fibrin plugs, and the debris from hemolyzed red cells. These particles are filtered by the lung, and some workers feel that they contribute to the development of the adult respiratory distress syndrome.[27-29] Banked blood is also deficient in clotting factors and platelets, and thus a potentially lethal dilutional coagulopathy can occur with massive transfusion.

Component therapy has been advocated to circumvent many of the problems described above. For moderate blood loss, transfusion of packed red cells will be an adequate replacement for whole blood. Specific defects in clotting parameters can be corrected with fresh frozen plasma or platelet packs, although the risk of hepatitis with the former is appreciable. The advantage of component therapy is the better utilization of blood for appropriate distribution.

Disadvantages of component therapy include the difficulty of rapidly transfusing packed red cells because of their high viscosity. This problem becomes more acute if blood filters are used, since they further slow maximal infusion rates. Viscosity can be decreased by mixing the cells with saline or Ringer's lactate, but this is time consuming in an emergency situation, particularly when several units of blood must be given in 10 to 15 minutes. In general, for life-threatening bleeding, we favor whole blood as therapy. However, if only packed cells are available, an appropriate volume of crystalloid solution (usually 250 ml of saline per unit of packed cells) should be mixed with the cells to decrease their viscosity.

An additional means of treating massive hemorrhage is autotransfusion. Although the principle of salvaging shed blood has been practiced by cardiac surgeons for many years, it has only recently been applied to other surgical procedures. In situations of extensive blood loss without bacterial contamination, such as hepatic vein injuries or elective hepatic surgery, the use of a device to salvage red cells for retransfusion may be lifesaving. A recent additional impetus to the use of autotransfusion has been AIDS. For obvious reasons, retransfusing the patient with his own red cells is far safer than giving him banked blood, and thus this technique should gain substantial popularity in the future.

Dehydration

The onset of dehydration in surgical patients is usually insidious. It is commonly caused by unmeasured abnormal losses without adequate intake of water and electrolytes. The classic example of such a patient is the elderly nursing home resident who develops fever from acute cholecystitis. Oral intake decreases because of general malaise, insensible losses increase because of fever, and dehydration occurs with an increasing urine specific gravity and a progressive rise in blood urea nitrogen (BUN). This is classic *prerenal* dehydration: a defect in extracellular fluid (ECF) volume leading to renal hypoperfusion coupled with intense renal conservation of fluid. It is frequently isotonic, with near normal serum electrolytes and an elevated BUN. Therapy should include ECF volume replacement with saline or Ringer's lactate. These solutions are not equivalent. "Normal" saline has sodium and chloride concentrations of 154 mEq/liter each, and should be used when excessive chloride losses can be demonstrated. This frequently occurs following protracted vomiting, with chloride lost in gastric secretions. If both the sodium and chloride concentrations are normal, then ECF volume expansion with Ringer's lactate is the sensible therapy, particularly since excess chloride may cause hyperchloremic acidosis.

An important source of dehydration in many patients is iatrogenic, either through inadequate fluid replacement or through the use of strong cathartics. The resulting defects in ECF volume may be well-handled by the compensated, awake patient, through sympathetically mediated vasoconstriction and cardiac acceleration. However, the induction of anesthesia for a surgical procedure may block these reflexes, leading to vascular collapse. Correction of ECF volume deficits is mandatory prior to elective or even urgent surgery. In the patient who has been receiving cathartics for several days preoperatively as bowel preparation, this can be easily accomplished by beginning an infusion of Ringer's lactate the night before surgery. Induction of anesthesia is much smoother in such patients, and the intraoperative maintenance of urine output is much easier.

Burns

A complete discussion of burn therapy is beyond the scope of this chapter, but a few observations are pertinent. A major burn is the most severe traumatic insult the body can sustain. Hypovolemia is caused by both increased evaporative water loss and burn wound edema. Under normal circumstances, the skin functions as an effective barrier to water loss, so that no more than 15 ml/m^2/hr of such losses occurs. A burn destroys this protective function, and evaporative losses can approach 200 ml/m^2/hr. This alone can result in severe hypertonic dehydration. It is accompanied by a defect in intravascular volume secondary to massive burn wound edema. Vascular integrity is lost for 24 to 36 hours in the area of the burn, and capillary permeability increases. Fluid rapidly leaks out into the interstitial space, exceeding the removal capacity of the lymphatic system and resulting in diminished intravascular volume. The content of this fluid is similar to that of plasma, although the protein concentration is lower.

Several formulas have been developed to aid the clinician in replacing these fluid losses. All are based on the accurate assessment of percentage of total body surface area (BSA) that is burned. The Brooke formula,[30] developed at the Brooke Army Hospital, estimates the following for the first 24 hours after a burn:

Crystalloid: 2.0 ml/kg/% BSA burned

Water (as D5/W): 2000 ml

The Parkland formula[31] relies solely on crystalloid as Ringer's lactate, estimated on the basis of 4 ml/kg/percent BSA burned. One-half of this is given in the first 8 hours, with the remainder being given over the next 16 hours. It must be emphasized that both of these formulas are only estimates of fluid requirements and should be revised upward or downward depending on the clinical status of the patient and his ability to handle large intravenous infusions. Probably the best guide to adequacy of volume replacement under such circumstances is the urine output. In the face of the concentrating defect that accompanies severe hypovolemia in non-burn patients, adequate solute excretion occurs with production of 30 to 40 ml of urine hourly. However, with severe burns, the renal tubular concentrations of myoglobin and/or free hemoglobin may become toxic. Increased urine flow rates (50 to 70 ml/hr) may prevent the toxic effects of these molecules and the insidious development of renal failure. In the patient with pre-existing renal or cardiac disease, more sophisticated monitoring of volume replacement, such as with the Swan-Ganz catheter, is necessary.

Third Space

A third space is an abnormal compartment of the ECF that develops in response to injury. It can be an important factor in the production of hypovolemia. Originally considered in relation to crushing injuries or burns with massive edema, a third space can also accumulate after other forms of trauma or infection. Functionally, the third space is a slowly equilibrating section of the ECF. As such, it does not participate in ECF changes, and has been termed "parasitic" by Shires.[32] Local injury results in edema and third space formation; the volume of the space is thus directly proportional to the extent and magnitude of injury.

The most common cause of third space formation is operative trauma. Uncomplicated operations with minimal dissection produce only a minimal third space. With more extensive operations, especially those involving substantial retroperitoneal dissection, such as total colectomy or aortic aneurysmectomy, the amount of third space formation will be very large. It is important to take these considerations into account when ordering postoperative fluid. One other common source of third space formation not commonly appreciated occurs with adynamic ileus. In this condition, the secretion of fluid into the intestine may exceed the capacity to absorb it, resulting in fluid sequestration.

Besides direct trauma, the other major source of third space formation is inflammation. Peritonitis, with a minimal increase in the thickness of the peritoneal membrane, produces a massive loss of fluid. The chemical peritonitis of a perforated viscus demands aggressive fluid replacement, since the patient has intravascular volume depletion. It is especially important to replace these losses prior to the necessary urgent surgery, since significant hypotension can occur during induction of anesthesia. Pancreatitis also produces a third space loss, the magnitude of which is directly proportional to the severity of the disease. Fluid requirements during the early stages of the disease may be massive, and such large volume requirements are an ominous prognostic sign.[33,34] The inflammation and edema of pancreatitis have been compared to a third-degree chemical burn of the retroperitoneum, mandating aggressive fluid therapy.

There is no accurate method of quantifying third space losses. The single best guide to adequate fluid therapy is urinary output. During the first postoperative day, many patients will require more fluid than was originally ordered to maintain urine output, because of underestimations of third space accumulation. Patients who remain oliguric after an aggressive fluid challenge need more sophisticated monitoring prior to further volume loading. Occasional patients who have been on long-term diuretic therapy for hypertension may need a small pharmacologic stimulus to initiate urinary output. Here, only after an adequate fluid volume has been infused, very small doses of furosemide can be beneficial (5 to 10 mg IV).

Normally, most patients will begin to diurese third space accumulations within 72 hours after a surgical operation, implying a smooth postoperative recovery. If diuresis does not occur, a septic focus, such as an anastomotic leak, may be causing inflammation and retention of the third space. Another consideration in third space management concerns patients with chronic congestive heart failure (CHF). Resolution of third spaces in these patients can sometimes worsen their CHF and lead to pulmonary edema. This may require the use of diuretics to speed excretion, and sometimes digitalization.

Abnormal Losses

One of the common iatrogenic sources of hypovolemia in surgical patients is inadequate replacement of abnormal gastrointestinal fluid losses. The nature of these losses will vary from site to site in the gastrointestinal tract. Gastric losses are high in chloride, and inadequate replacement can result in hypovolemia and metabolic alkalosis (see below). They are best replaced with isotonic sodium chloride solution. Losses from small bowel fistulas have approximately the serum concentration of electrolytes, with the exception of a lower concentration of chloride. Pancreatic losses are high in bicarbonate, and can lead to metabolic acidosis if not replaced. Uncontrolled diarrhea can also lead to voluminous losses of bicarbonate, sodium, and potassium.

Colloid versus Crystalloid Therapy

Colloid, or more specifically albumin, has long been in the arsenal of fluids for volume replacement. Its indiscriminate use has been questioned recently on two grounds: (1) its cost in comparison to crystalloid; and (2) its potentially deleterious effect on hemodynamic and pulmonary function. Virgilio and associates[35] compared colloid to crystalloid resuscitation with respect to their effects on colloid osmotic pressure, on pulmonary capillary wedge pressure, and on pulmonary shunting. Patients were randomized following aortic aneurysmectomy into a group receiving only crystalloid plus blood, or into a group receiving an albumin-Ringer's lactate mixture and blood. Although the colloid osmotic pressure declined precipitously in the crystalloid group, no incidence of pulmonary edema was noted, and the extent of shunting was unchanged. Thus, no advantage of colloid resuscitation could be shown over crystalloid. Because of its lower cost, crystalloid was recommended as the primary fluid of choice in resuscitation. Similar conclusions have been reached by Moss[36] and Shires.[37]

The second major objection to the use of albumin lies in its effects on the cardiopulmonary system. Plasmanate, which is frequently used in such situations, is a pooled solution of human plasma protein. It contains 16 mmoles of acetate per liter. Acetate, in large doses, is a hypotensive agent and exerts a negative inotropic effect.[38] Also, some batches of plasmanates have been shown to contain a kallikrein activator that leads to the release of bradykinin, another vasodilating agent.[39] The use of albumin alone (salt-poor albumin) does not appear to cause this problem. Large quantities of plasmanate infused into some septic patients may lead to a clinical picture of noncardiogenic pulmonary edema. This seems to be related to alterations in pulmonary capillary permeability, with "trapping" of albumin in the interstitium and a resultant blockage of diffusion.

In the majority of patients, small quantities of albumin are well-tolerated. Massive albumin infusion should probably be avoided, both because crystalloid is cheaper and because the deleterious cardiopulmonary effects of albumin are not yet well-defined.

ACID-BASE CHANGES

An extensive discussion of acid-base balance can be found elsewhere in this volume. Our remarks will be confined to those elements of acid-base metabolism that are relevant to injurious stimuli.

Several patterns of acid-base abnormalities may be seen following injury. Lyons and Moore[23] have shown that alkalosis is more frequently observed than is acidosis in well-compensated patients after mild to moderate trauma. The patient remains well-perfused, without extensive lactate production, and the alkalosis is primarily respiratory in origin. Fear, painful stimuli, head injury, hypoxia, and mechanical ventilation frequently cause hyperventilation and respiratory alkalosis. Two major problems can ensue. First, as potassium moves into cells as a result of the alkalosis, the resultant hypokalemia may produce cardiac arrhythmias and digitalis toxicity. Second, if respiratory alkalosis is prolonged, metabolic compensation develops. When the stimulus to hyperventilation ceases, the patient may rapidly develop metabolic acidosis, hyperkalemia, and ventricular arrhythmias.

Another common cause of respiratory alkalosis is atelectasis. Hypoxemia stimulates chemoreceptors in the aorta and carotid body, leading to hyperventilation. This lowers the arterial CO_2 content, producing alkalosis. These receptors can also be stimulated during hypotension with a low blood flow, even though adequate arterial oxygenation exists. The resulting hyperventilation can be seen in trauma patients who are mildly hypotensive from blood loss but who are still relatively well-perfused.

In the more severely injured patient, metabolic acidosis becomes a prominent finding, frequently coexisting with respiratory alkalosis. As noted earlier, poor tissue perfusion and tissue hypoxia lead to anaerobic metabolism and lactic acid production. Peripheral vasoconstriction contributes to the flow deficit, worsening the acidosis. The requisite respiratory compensation is brought about by hyperventilation, explaining the tachypnea of shock.

The effects of acidosis on the cardiovascular system include decreased myocardial contractility, a decreased response of the myocardium to catecholamines, and cardiac irritability. Acidosis accentuates tissue hypoxia because of its leftward shift of the oxyhemoglobin dissociation curve, and because of vasoconstriction. The work of breathing increases dramatically and may worsen the acidosis. Sustained acidosis at the cellular level leads to rapid cellular degeneration and death.

The correction of metabolic acidosis is brought about by abolishing its origins. The definitive therapy for metabolic acidosis in injured patients is usually replacement of circulating volume. Only after adequate tissue perfusion is restored will lactic acid production cease and the pH rise. As a holding action to protect the myocardium, small amounts of sodium bicarbonate may be given while volume restoration is in progress. Bicarbonate should be used cautiously, since its overzealous administration can lead to hypertonicity and hypokalemia. Bicarbonate administration should be directed by measurements of blood pH.

Vasoconstricting drugs, particularly norepinephrine, can produce severe acidosis if used in high doses. This occurs commonly during resuscitative attempts following ischemic cardiac arrest when a norepinephrine solution is run "wide open" in an attempt to restore blood pressure. This is clearly a manuever designed to buy time, but should be discontinued as soon as possible. There is no place for the use of these drugs in the resuscitation of the hypovolemic patient.

Metabolic alkalosis also occurs in surgical patients. It is seen in response to loss of chloride, potassium, or both. The classic clinical example is the patient with an obstructing duodenal ulcer who is on long-term gastric suction and who loses excessive amounts of chloride and hydrogen ions. Depletion of total body chloride occurs, with concomitant volume depletion. The kidney responds to this by attempting to conserve volume with enhanced sodium reabsorption. This leads to excretion of potassium and hydrogen ions in exchange for sodium, with "paradoxical aciduria" and worsening of the alkalosis. To break the cycle, normal saline must be administered to correct both the volume and the chloride deficit.

A primary loss of potassium, secondary to increased sodium reabsorption and with increased potassium excretion or intense aldosterone stimulation of the kidney, may also lead to alkalosis. Potassium moves out of the intracellular compartment in exchange for sodium ions. This leads to a pH elevation of the ECF that can be corrected by the gradual administration of potassium, but only if volume is normal and chloride is also corrected. In surgical patients, especially those with cardiac disease, an early sign of hypokalemia and hypoxia may be cardiac arrhythmias. Thus, before lidocaine or other antiarrhythmic drugs are given, the potassium and arterial PO_2 should be normalized.

DERANGEMENTS OF ELECTROLYTES AND TONICITY

Since sodium is the principal extracellular cation, the concentration of sodium accurately reflects total body tonicity. Phenomenologically, the concentration of $[Na^+] = [Na_e + K_e]$, where Na_e is total exchangable sodium, K_e is total exchangable potassium, and TWB is total body water.[40] Thus, changes in the total body content of either sodium or potassium (the principal intracellular cation) will be reflected in changes in sodium concentration. As noted above, in the normal individual, pain, anxiety, trauma, and many drugs have been shown to lead to the release of arginine vasopressin (AVP) and adrenocorticotropic hormone (ACTH), which stimulate water and salt retention. This is a normal accompaniment of virtually all surgical operative procedures, and may occur without operation if engendered by one of the other stimuli described above or by anesthesia. Efforts at therapy in the patient with a normal ECF volume should be directed at maintenance of that volume. Despite retention of water and salt, the administration of sodium-containing fluids is required because of abnormal losses and because of sequestration of fluid in injured tissues.

In the face of such changes, injudicious administration of water in excess of salt will lead to hypotonicity and occasionally water intoxication. If the patient is hypovolemic, or if there is a concurrent condition such as CHF that may make it dangerous to further expand the ECF volume, therapy should be aimed at the elimination of excess water. If insensible loss is high, as in the case of fever, simple fluid restriction is the therapy of choice. If there is a tracheostomy, insensible losses may rise to 6 to 10 liters per day if humidified air is not used. Osmotic diuretics may be used on occasion, since they lead to the excretion of water in excess of solute. However, these agents must be used judiciously, since they also lead to transient expansion of the ECF volume. If the patient is hypovolemic, decreased tonicity may be corrected through the use of hypertonic saline.

ECF Deficits and Hypotonicity

Inappropriate or inadequate volume replacement following surgery will lead to a characteristic sequence of events. Losses of ECF are always isotonic. They are primarily caused by losses of blood, of gastrointestinal fluid, and of wound fluid, all of which are in equilibrium with the ECF. in addition, the formation of a third space causes an isotonic decline in ECF volume. This fluid does not exchange easily with the functional ECF, so that it is not useful for the defense of volume status.

The insensible loss of water is an important mechanism contributing to hypertonicity in surgical patients. Normal obligatory insensible losses vary between 500 and 800 ml daily, depending on size and body habitus. In the postoperative patient, these losses may be increased because of increased temperature, sepsis, or poor respiratory care. The loss of water leads to an increase in sodium concentration and to hypertonicity. These losses should be taken into account when planning postoperative fluid therapy.

An inadequate postoperative intake of calories leads to consumption of endogenous fuel stores (fat and carbohydrate), with protection of water and carbon dioxide. Substantial breakdown of body cell mass can thus lead to the production of large quantities of free endogenous water. This offsets, to a degree, the insensible losses mentioned above, but does not effectively expand ECF volume.

The secretion of AVP and aldosterone, and the proximal tubular reabsorption of sodium and water, is increased in response to deficits in ECF volume.[41] As a result, further losses of water and salt are minimized. Urine output in this setting is regulated only by the amount of solute delivered to the kidney for excretion. The amount of such solute is directly proportional to the rate of endogenous protein breakdown, which is very much decreased in starvation. In resting humans, the total amount of solute can be excreted in as little as 400 to 600 ml of urine daily. However, the proximal reabsorption of sodium and water is increased in hypovolemia or trauma. As a result, there is a loss of concentrating ability to the extent that 800 to 1200 ml of urine may be required to excrete the endogenous solute load. Because of high concentrations of AVP, tests of hydration, based on standard water loads, cannot be used in the postoperative patient, since the determinant of excretion is not water but solute. The exception to this rule is the too rapid administration of glucose solutions, which will cause a glycosuria and a spurious increase in urine output, giving the erroneous impression of normovolemia.

Hyponatremia can be observed in surgical patients under several circumstances. First, there may be acute renal failure with insufficient glomerular filtration. Such patients will develop azotemia and will not respond to expansion of the ECF volume. Second, the patient may have functional hypovolemia with prerenal azotemia. In this case, expansion of the ECF volume with a rapid load of saline will increase water excretion.[42] The underlying mechanism in this case involves secretion of vasopressin in response to the hypovolemic stimulus.[43] Finally, the patient may have the syndrome of inappropriate antidiuretic hormone release (SIADH). This condition has been described in burn patients. The water retention in this situation results from excess vasopressin, but there is no obvious stimulus to the release of AVP.[44]

The therapy of ECF volume losses is straightforward. Extrarenal losses are replaced with water and electrolyte solutions, usually at near normal serum concentrations. The solution used may be either normal saline or Ringer's lactate. In the former case, the physician must be aware that an increased chloride load is being administered, whereas in the latter case the physician must be equally aware that a significant fraction of the solution is free water. If an acute volume deficit (e.g., hemorrhage) is being treated, the use of isotonic saline, which is distributed only across the ECF volume, may be preferable to the use of Ringer's lactate, since the significant distribution of the latter across the total body water may impair cardiovascular stabilization. More severe deficits in ECF volume, particularly those associated with shock or anuria, generally imply inadequate intravascular volume from blood loss. In this situation, blood should be given emergently until adequate perfusion pressure is obtained.

Extracellular Fluid Excess

An expanded ECF volume is uncommon, and occurs only when excess fluid is administered or when salt and water are being retained. Clinically significant hypervolemia is manifested either by pulmonary edema or peripheral edema. If the patient is being monitored, pulmonary edema may be preceded by a rise in the arterial pressure, pulmonary arterial pressure, or pulmonary capillary wedge pressure. If the condition is detected early, the treatment of choice is fluid restriction. If significant edema has developed, diuretic therapy may be indicated. However, postoperative patients have a diminished ability to concentrate or dilute the urine, so that attention must be directed to the serum sodium concentration if diuretics are used.[45]

Hypernatremia: Special Considerations

Hypernatremia is uncommon but can be caused by excess salt administration (certain tube-feeding formulas), by excess extrarenal water losses (insensible losses), or by excess renal loss of water (solute diuresis). The administration of excess salt can be prevented by calculating the tonicity of fluids being administered, and by adding sufficient free water to provide adequately for insensible loss. Increased insensible loss occurs most commonly in the presence of fever. However, increased pulmonary insensible loss may be a concomitant of diminished dead space, as in tracheostomy. The most common cause of osmotic diuresis in the postoperative patient is the rapid administration of glucose-containing solutions, usually ordered because of a belief that the physician is providing nutrition and/or free water. However, surgery and injury are accompanied by a transient "diabetic state,"[46] and when glucose is not being metabolized, it is as effective an osmotic diuretic as mannitol.[47] Osmotic diuresis is also produced when the rate of administration of solutions containing amino acids is too rapid.

Finally, an occasional patient will develop hypernatremia because of excess water loss resulting from inadequate secretion of vasopressin. This condition of true diabetes insipidus is commonly seen only after head injury.

OTHER ELECTROLYTE ABNORMALITIES

Hypokalemia

The potassium ion plays a critical role in many important body functions. It is the primary intracellular cation, so that total body potassium measurements can be used to approximate the body cell mass. Although its concentration in ECF is low, deficiencies can produce critical changes in neuromuscular, cardiac, and gastrointestinal function. Hypokalemia is common in the postoperative patient, with many potential causes. Alkalosis causes hypokalemia by promoting movement of potassium into cells in exchange for sodium ions, and by enhancing sodium-potassium exchange in preference to sodium-hydrogen exchange in the distal nephron.[48] The most common cause of sustained alkalosis is long-term nasogastric suction. Other gastrointestinal losses can also lead to hypokalemia. This is especially true in patients with massive diarrhea or small, high-output intestinal fistulas. In starving patients, decreased total exchangeable potassium accompanies decreased body cell mass. Thus, malnourished patients who are treated with total parenteral nutrition (TPN) will require increased amounts of potassium as anabolism occurs.

The diagnosis of potassium deficiency is based on a high index of suspicion, particularly in postoperative patients. Early evidence of cardiac, gastrointestinal, or neuromuscular dysfunction may be a clue to hypokalemia. The first line of treatment should be correction of alkalosis if it is present. Metabolic alkalosis should be treated by administering of chloride ion, whereas respiratory alkalosis may be treated by diminishing the minute volume or by increasing dead space. If hypokalemia persists, and if there is a plausible explanation for excess loss of potassium, the concurrent existence of a deficiency of total body potassium should be considered. If the serum potassium continues to be less than 3.5 mEq/liter, potassium should be infused. A serum concentration of potassium below 3 mEq/liter should be regarded as an emergency because of the potential for development of cardiac arrhythmia.

Hyperkalemia

Hyperkalemia is less frequent than hypokalemia in postsurgical patients. It is seen after shock, massive crushing injuries, occasionally after massive burns, and in renal failure. Severe acidosis causes sodium-potassium exchange across the cell membrane, probably as a result of a change in the efficiency of sodium-potassium ATPase.[49] It should be noted that the commonly hypothesized potassium-hydrogen exchange cannot account for the hyperkalemia of acidosis, since hydrogen ion is present in plasma at a concentration of approximately 10^{-7} molar, whereas potassium ion is present at a concentration of 10^{-3} molar. Hyperkalemia may be accompanied by intestinal complaints including vomiting, nausea, diarrhea, and crampy abdominal pain.

Hyperkalemia caused by acidosis most commonly results from hypoperfusion, particularly of the splanchnic bed. Correction of the acidosis generally requires correction of a volume deficit. If hyperkalemia persists, it should be treated either by the use of glucose and insulin, or by the use of a bicarbonate-containing solution. Glucose and insulin may be ineffective because of the insulin resistance associated with hypovolemia. Chronic hyperkalemia should be treated by dialysis or by the use of cation exchange resins, as discussed elsewhere.

Calcium

Hypocalcemia

The active component of serum calcium is the ionized fraction, which represents between 45 and 50 percent of the total. Since most laboratories measure total calcium, and not the ionized fraction, knowledge of the plasma protein is vital for accurate assessment of the biologically active calcium concentration.

Ionized calcium decreases after all injuries, although this decrease is rarely clinically significant. Decreases in calcium ion to concentrations that will produce tetany are commonly seen only in severe shock[50] and in pancreatitis.[34] Although it is commonly thought that in the latter condition calcium is deposited in the pancreas and retroperitoneum because of saponification of fat, this mechanism cannot entirely account for the observed deficit. Moreover, the proportion of ionized calcium should actually increase because of the acidosis associated with the shock of severe pancreatitis.

Hypocalcemia should be treated in the presence of carpopedal spasm, retrosternal pain, or stridor. Other indications for treatment include electrocardiographic abnormality (a prolonged QT interval), insomnia, and severe occipital headache. The emergent treatment of hypocalcemia should begin with the production of respiratory acidosis by rebreathing. This will permit the slow administration of calcium intravenously, obviating the possibility of an overcompensation that can produce a transient excess of ionized calcium and cessation of myocardial function in systole. Other, less common causes of hypocalcemia include major infections of soft tissue, gastrointestinal fistulas, and alkalosis.

Hypocalcemia is also commonly seen following the removal of parathyroid adenomas, since the function of the remaining glands is suppressed.

Hypercalcemia

In surgical patients, hypercalcemia is usually caused by hyperparathyroidism or disseminated metastatic cancer. Initial warning signs may include polyuria and polydipsia with dehydration. Weakness, loss of appetite, nausea, and vomiting may lead to more severe central nervous system (CNS) symptoms with headache, stupor, and coma progressing to death if not properly treated. Emergent therapy is based primarily on repletion of ECF volume. In addition, some clinicians have used furosemide along with volume infusion to increase renal calcium excretion. Calcitonin can also be used to reduce serum calcium, and less acute correction of hypercalcemia can be accomplished by administering mithramycin.[51] This drug inhibits bone osteoclastic activity, decreasing calcium release into the ECF. Its undesirable side effects include significant reductions in the platelet and white cell counts secondary to bone marrow suppression. Definitive therapy for hypercalcemia caused by metastatic disease may also include radiation and/or chemotherapy if indicated.

Magnesium

In current surgical practice, the most common etiology for magnesium deficiency is inadequate replacement in patients on sustained TPN. Other causes include prolonged losses from intestinal fistulas, malabsorption, and chronic alcoholism.

The physiology of magnesium is still under investigation, but its primary role is that of a cofactor in many enzyme systems. Neuromuscular irritability and hyperactivity of the CNS are the most common symptoms of deficiency. A normal serum magnesium may accompany severe total body depletion, and thus the diagnosis may be based largely on suspicion. Appropriate therapy consists of infusing magnesium.

Hypermagnesemia is distinctly uncommon in surgical patients, and is almost always seen in cases of severe renal failure. Therapy is directed at slowly increasing the ECF volume, and acute symptoms can be treated with a slow infusion of calcium chloride or gluconate.

PARENTERAL AND ENTERAL NUTRITION

Total Parenteral Nutrition

The advent of TPN permitted the salvage of critically ill patients who previously would have died from malnutrition. Nutritional assessment has now become a relatively routine portion of the evaluation of surgical patients. Malnourished patients are at increased risk of disruption of anastomoses and other wounds.

Indications

If TPN is used, its effects should be monitored and its administration should be continued until there is some evidence that it is working. Useful nutritional parameters to measure during TPN include retinol binding protein, transferrin, and albumin.[52]

There are many indications for TPN. Its preoperative use is justified in patients whose primary disease has resulted in weight loss and tissue breakdown. A classic example is the cachectic patient with esophageal carcinoma. Preoperative use of TPN in such a patient can greatly improve the chances of complication-free recovery, since the gastroesophageal anastomosis will heal more quickly and the patient will be better able to defend himself against any septic complications. Similar results can be achieved in patients with inflammatory bowel disease, in which preoperative catabolism may result in a massively negative nitrogen balance. These patients tolerate surgery much better with adequate nutritional stores. Additionally, TPN may be useful where prolonged rest of the gastrointestinal tract is essential, such as in severe pancreatitis or small bowel fistulae. Many small bowel fistulae will heal with complete gastrointestinal rest, but parenteral nutrition must be supplied for this to occur. The hypermetabolic patient who has had a major burn or severe multiple trauma may require more than 5000 calories daily, and this requirement can be met with supplemental TPN.

Solution Composition

A variety of TPN solutions are commercially available. Most feature high glucose concentrations, varying amounts of electrolytes, and amino acids. Casein hydrolysates are no longer used. The optimal ratio of nonprotein calories to grams of nitrogen in TPN solutions is about 150:1, although this varies from one patient to another. In septic patients, where peripheral insulin resistance and hypermetabolism may coexist, the optimal ratio may be higher, in the range of 200:1. In starved, nonstressed patients, the ratio may be as low as 120:1. The ratio must be considered when choosing the proper solution for a given patient. If adequate nonprotein calories cannot be administered, as in glucose-intolerant patients, they may be provided supplementally by using peripheral fat emulsions (see below).

The daily electrolyte requirements of most patients can usually be met with standard TPN solutions. With abnormal losses, additional electrolytes may be added to the TPN solution. Trace elements are now routinely added, as are folate and selenium. (see Ch. 7)

Complications

Technical

The primary technical complications of TPN relate to the catheter. During cannulation, these include pneumothorax or hemothorac, subclavian artery cannulation, thoracic duct injury, and air embolism. The catheter may also be placed in the thorax but outside the vein, with the development of hydrothorax and mediastinal displacement when fluid is administered. Other problems involve catheter dislodgement and occlusion of the catheter. The first can be avoided by meticulous attention to the catheter during dressing changes. The latter can be prevented by using a pump on the intravenous tubing to maintain a constant rate of infusion.

Metabolic

Metabolic complications of TPN therapy are surprisingly infrequent. The most common complication is mild hyperglycemia, which can be managed by the use of small, subcutaneous doses of regular insulin. This is more likely to occur in diabetic patients and during glucose intolerance following severe trauma or sepsis. If neutral protamine Hagedorn (NPH) insulin is required for glucose control, it should be given in divided doses 12 hours apart, since with TPN there is no diurnal variation in glucose input. Insulin can be added to the infusion itself, although the amount of insulin delivered will vary because of its absorption to the plastic containers and tubing used to deliver the solution. Extremely brittle diabetics may require reductions in glucose concentration to 20 or even 15 percent. These non-protein calories can be replaced by using fat emulsions.

A more serious complication of TPN therapy is hyperosmolar, hyperglycemic nonketotic coma. This is characterized by extremely high blood glucose levels, hyponatremia, polydipsia, polyuria with glycosuria, and severe dehydration. Its symptoms include weakness, stupor, and eventual coma. The etiology is usually either the overly rapid administration of TPN or diabetes. The condition is treated by the administration of insulin and free water. Electrolytes and blood glucose must be closely monitored, since rebound hypoglycemia can occur.

Other infrequent complications of TPN include metabolic hyperchloremic acidosis from excess chloride in the synthetic amino acid mixtures used in TPN. Also, hypophosphatemia may occasionally occur with the chronic administration of crystalline amino acids, and may be treated by adding calcium and phosphate to the solution. Essential fatty acid deficiency is seen in patients on long-term TPN. Its insidious onset is heralded by hair loss, scaling dermatitis, and thrombocytopenia. An increase occurs in the triene to tetraene ratio (to greater than 0.3) of serum fatty acids. This problem can be eliminated by the once or twice weekly administration of fat emulsions via a peripheral vein. Trace element deficiencies are another complication of TPN therapy, and numerous syndromes of trace element deficiency have been defined. These are not seen when trace elements are administered routinely.

A final metabolic complication is iatrogenic, and related to the cessation of TPN. Because the rate of glucose infusion is constant, insulin levels reach an elevated steady state. If the infusion of glucose is suddenly stopped, a high circulating insulin concentration can produce dangerous hypoglycemia, which can be fatal in the elderly. If TPN is to be discontinued, the rate of infusion should be gradually decreased, in decrements of 25 ml/hr every two hours, allowing a gradual decline in insulin levels. If the infusion is terminated suddenly because of intentional catheter removal for sepsis or delivery system malfunction, a peripheral infusion of 10 percent dextrose in water (D10/W) should be started to prevent hypoglycemia.

Septic

The most serious complication of TPN is sepsis. Septic complications occur in two peaks. The first occurs 24 to 48 hours after beginning TPN, and is related to a break in sterile technique during catheter insertion. The second occurs from seven days to weeks after initiating TPN, and is caused by contamination of the administration system in the pharmacy or on the ward. One of the earliest clinical signs of sepsis is glycosuria secondary to peripheral insulin resistance. Thus, if a patient who had previously been tolerating TPN suddenly develops glycosuria, sepsis must be considered. Any unexplained fever in a patient who is receiving central TPN should be a cause for concern, and may be an indication for catheter change over a wire, unless another source of fever can be found. Appropriate cultures should be obtained, including peripheral blood cultures, cultures of the catheter tip, and cultures of the TPN solution itself. If the old catheter is subsequently proven to be the source of the sepsis, the new catheter should be removed. Life-threatening sepsis may require catheter removal without replacement.

ENTERAL NUTRITION

Indications and Techniques

The indications for enteral nutrition are similar to those for TPN. In recent years, the admonition "if the gut works, use it" has been applied to many patients with a variety of techniques. Most patients require tube feeding of enteral diets since, with a few exceptions, these diets are unpalatable. Tube feeding can be accomplished through a nasogastric tube, through a gastrostomy, or through a jejunostomy created at the time of surgery. Nasogastric feedings have the disadvantage of tube-related discomfort and failure to tolerate the tube for long periods. This problem has been overcome somewhat by using a soft, small silicone tube introduced with the aid of a mercury weight at its end. These are generally well tolerated by most patients.

One time-honored method of enteral feeding involved gastrostomy. Most patients tolerate gastrostomies well, but a major disadvantage of this technique is the risk of aspiration, especially in elderly or obtunded patients. This risk can be reduced somewhat by elevating the head of the bed at least 30 degrees, and by aspirating the stomach frequently to prevent gastric distension by the diet. Large gastric residuals are not usually a problem if the diet is administered using a pump, since the maximal volume in the stomach at any one time is small. Aspiration more frequently occurs when the diet is fed intermittently in large volumes, as is the case in most chronic care facilities.

The jejunostomy obviates many of these problems but presents a few of its own. Since it is distal to the pylorus, there is effective protection against aspiration. However, because the jejunum cannot function as a reservoir or dilute the diet, the diet cannot be administered by gavage, but must instead be given by using a continuous infusion system. Pumps for this purpose are expensive and require substantial attention from nursing personnel, and many long-term nursing facilities do not have them. Thus, for patients who are destined to reside in extended care facilities, jejunostomies may be less desirable. One real advantage of jejunostomies lies in the ability to begin feeding soon after surgery.[53] Jejunostomies can be created distal to biliary or pancreatic fistulae and beyond areas of anastomosis or resection. These areas can then be given the time and the nutrition to heal in the postoperative period.

Also, a recent study has suggested that the use of enteral feeding early after surgery may help to prevent sepsis.[54] A key substance involved in this process is enterally administered glutamine. This amino acid appears to help maintain the integrity of the gut mucosa during stress. Breakdown of the gut mucosal barrier has been implicated as a potential etiologic agent in the development of major sepsis following injury,[55] explaining the beneficial effects following early use of glutamine-containing enteral diets.

Recently, several feeding tubes have been developed that obviate some of the problems inherent in the use of both gastrostomy and jejunostomy tubes. These double-lumen devices, introduced into the stomach via a standard gastrostomy opening, consist of a long tube that can be threaded into the proximal jejunum through the pylorus, and a shorter, larger bore tube that drains the stomach. Since they require only one enterotomy to insert, the associated infectious risks are reduced, an issue of particular importance in debilitated patients. Also, since the stomach is continuously drained and the feeding occurs directly into the jejunum, the risk of aspiration is negligible.

The accurate identification of patients who need nutritional supplementation is crucial. Most patients who are otherwise healthy and whose gastrointestinal function may normally be expected to return within seven days are not candidates for additional nutritional support. Debilitated patients undergoing emergency surgery, patients with proximal pancreatic and biliary fistulae, and those undergoing major gastric resections are candidates. Distal small- or large-bowel fistulae may undergo spontaneous healing if a defined-formula diet is used for enteral feeding.[56] This may be necessary for many weeks, but it avoids further surgery and the additional risk and expense of central TPN. Defined-formula or elemental diets may also be useful as nutritional supplements in patients with the short-bowel syndrome, necrotizing enterocolitis, advanced inflammatory bowel disease, and end-stage radiation enteritis.

A profusion of dietary supplements are available. Elemental diets minimize the residue presented to the colon, and can therefore be used in patients with ileus, since their major problem is colonic.[57] The major disadvantage of these synthetic diets is poor taste, and they must usually be provided through a tube. Elemental diets are indicated when only a small absorptive surface is available or when rest of a substantial segment of the bowel is desired. Other diets are more palatable but produce substantially more residue. These may be of value in supplementing postoperative oral intake, or can be used preoperatively to improve nutritional status.

Complications

One refreshing aspect of enteral feeding is the paucity of major complications. As with TPN, the diets available should be used carefully in diabetic patients. Because they are hyperosmolar, these diets should also be used with caution in elderly or volume-depleted patients, in whom significant hypernatremia and dehydration can occur from the loss of free water into the lumen of the intestine.

The hyperosmolarity of diets for enteral feeding also leads to their most common complication—diarrhea. Normally, a period of adaptation to these diets is necessary in most patients. The initiation of a full-strength diet at a high speed will produce painful and occasionally dangerous gastrointestinal symptoms in most patients because of the osmolar load. These symptoms include nausea, bloating, distension, vomiting, and diarrhea. For this reason, most patients are started at a low infusion rate (20 ml/hr). Subsequently, the rate is increased on a daily basis until the desired daily volume is reached. Even with these precautions, some diarrhea still occurs, especially with the high osmolarity solutions. This can frequently be controlled by adding small amounts of paregoric or deodorized tincture of opium (DTO) to the solution itself, and by temporarily decreasing the concentration or infusion rate.

REFERENCES

1. Cannon WB: Traumatic Shock. D Appleton, New York, 1923
2. Shires GT III, Peitzman AB, Illner H, et al: Changes in red blood cell transmembrane potential, electrolytes, and energy content in septic shock. J Trauma 23:769, 1983
3. Tracey KJ, Lowry SF, Shires GT, et al: Cachectin/Tumor Necrosis Factor mediates changes of skeletal muscle plasma membrane potential. J Exp Med 164:1368, 1986
4. Gill JR, Casper AJT: Role of sympathetic nervous system in the renal response to hemorrhage. J Clin Invest 48:915, 1969
5. Byrnes GJ, Pirkle JC, Gann DS: Cardiovascular stabilization after hemorrhage depends upon restitution of blood volume. J Trauma 18:623, 1978
6. Haddy FJ, Scott JB, Molnez JJ: Mechanism of volume replacement and vascular constriction following hemorrhage. Am J Physiol 208:169, 1965
7. Cope O, Litwin SB: Contribution of the lymphatic system to the replenishment of the plasma volume following a hemorrhage. Ann Surg 156:655, 1962
8. Drucker WR, Chadwick CDJ, Gann DS: Transcapillary refill in hemorrhage and shock. Arch Surg 116:1344, 1981
9. Gann DS: Endocrine control of plasma protein and volume. Surg Clin North Am 56:1135, 1976
10. Gann DS: Endocrine and metabolic re-

sponse to injury. p. 1. In Schwartz SI (ed): Principles of Surgery, 4th Ed. McGraw-Hill, New York, 1984
11. Gann DS, Carlson DE, Byrnes GJ, et al: Role of solute in the early restitution of blood volume after hemorrhage. Surgery 94:439, 1983
12. Pirkle JC, Gann DS: Expansion of interstitial fluid is required for full restitution of blood volume after hemorrhage. J Trauma 16:937, 1976
13. Pirkle JC, Gann DS: Restitution of blood volume after hemorrhage: role of the adrenal cortex. Am J Physiol 230:1683, 1976
14. Gann DS, Pirkle JC: Role of cortisol in the restitution of blood volume after hemorrhage. Am J Surg 130:565, 1975
15. Amaral JS, Caldwell MD, Gann DS: The effect of naloxone on glucose metabolism in the skeletal muscle. J Trauma 25:119, 1985
16. Byrnes GJ, Engeland WC, Gann DS: Restitution of blood volume after hemorrhage: Inhibition by somatostatin. Endocrinology 110:1945, 1982
17. McLeod MK, Carlson DE, Gann DS: Secretory response of glucagon to hemorrhage. J Trauma 22:629, 1982
18. Pirkle JC, Gann DS, Allen-Rowlands CF: Role of the pituitary in restitution of blood volume after hemorrhage. Endocrinology 110:7, 1982
19. Lilly MP: Cited in Gann DS, Amaral JS. Pathophysiology of Shock and Trauma. In Rutherford RB, Zuidema GD, Ballinger WF (eds): The Management of Trauma, 4th Ed. WB Saunders, Philadelphia, 1984
20. Gann DS, Carlson DE, Byrnes GJ, et al: Impaired restitution of blood volume after large hemorrhage. J Trauma 21:598, 1981
21. Shires GT, Cunningham JN, Baker CRF, et al: Alterations in cellular membrane function during hemorrhagic shock in primates. Ann Surg 176:288, 1972
22. Illner H, Cunningham J, Shires GT: Red blood cell sodium content and permeability changes in hemorrhagic shock. Am J Surg 143:349, 1982
23. Lyons JH, Moore FD: Post-traumatic alkalosis: incidence and pathophysiology of alkalosis in surgery. Surgery 60:93, 1966
24. Moore FD, Lyons JH, Pierce EC, et al: Post-traumatic Pulmonary Insufficiency. WB Saunders, Philadelphia, 1969
25. Canizaro PC, Prager MD, Shires GT: The infusion of Ringer's lactate solution during shock. Am J Surg 122:494, 1971
26. Shires GT, Culn D, Carrico J, et al: Fluid therapy in hemorrhagic shock. Arch Surg 88:688, 1964
27. Blaisdell FW, Schlobolm RM: The respiratory distress syndrome: A review. Surgery 74:251, 1973
28. Carrico CJ: Pulmonary response to injury. Bull NY Acad Med 55:174, 1979
29. Byrne JP, Dickson JA: Pulmonary edema following blood transfussion reaction. Arch Surg 102:91, 1971
30. Pruit BA, Goodwin CW: Burns. p. 291. In Saviston DC (ed): Textbook of Surgery. WB Saunders, Philadelphia, 1981
31. Baxter CR, Marvin JA, Curreri PW: Fluid and electrolyte therapy of burn shock. Heart Lung 2:707, 1973
32. Shires GT, Canizaro PC, Lowrey SF: Fluid, electrolyte and nutritional management of the surgical patient. p. 61. In Schwartz SI (ed): Principles of Surgery, 4th Ed. McGraw-Hill, New York, 1984
33. Ranson JHC, Pasternak BS: Statistical methods for quantifying the severity of clinical acute pancreatitis. J Surge Res 22:79, 1977
34. Ranson JHC, Rifkind KM, Roses DF, et al: Prognostic signs and the role of operative management in acute pancreatitis. Surg Gynecol Obstet 139:69, 1974
35. Virgilio RW, Rice CL, Smith DE, et al: Crystalloid vs. colloid resuscitation: is one better? Surgery 85:129, 1979
36. Moss GS, Lowe RJ, Gilick J, et al: Colloid or crystalloid in the resuscitation of hemorrhagic shock: a controlled clinical trial. Surgery 89:434, 1981
37. Shires GT, Peitzman AB, Albert SA, et al: Response of extravascular lung water to intraoperative fluids. Ann Surg 197:515, 1983
38. Olinger GN, Warner PH, Bonchek LI, et al: Vasodilator effects of the sodium acetate in pooled protein fraction. Ann Surg 190:305, 1979
39. Alving BM, Hojima Y, Pisano JJ, et al: Hypotension associated with prekallikrein activator (Hageman factor fragments) in plasma protein fraction. N Engl J Med 299:66, 1978

40. Adelman IS, Leibman J, O'Meara MP, et al: Interrelations between serum sodium concentration, serum osmolarity, and total exchangable sodium, total exchangable potassium and total body water. J Clin Invest 37:1236, 1958
41. Gann DS, Wright HK, Newsome HH: Prevention of sodium depletion during osmotic diuresis. Surg Gynecol Obstet 119:265, 1964
42. Wright HK, Gann DS: Correction of the free water deficit in postoperative patients by extracellular fluid volume expansion. Ann Surg 158:70, 1963
43. Leaf A, Bartter FC, Sautos RF, et al: Evidence in man that urinary electrolyte loss induced by pitressin is a function of water retention. J Clin Invest 32:868, 1953
44. Shirani KZ, Vaughan GM, Robertson GL, et al: Inappropriate vasopressin secretion (SIADH) in burned patients. J Trauma 23:217, 1983
45. Wright HK, Gann DS: A defect in urinary concentrating ability during postoperative antidiuresis. Surg Gynecol Obstet 121:47, 1965
46. Drucker WR, Kaye M, Kendrick R, et al: Metabolic aspects of hemorrhagic shock: Changes in intermediary metabolism during hemorrhage and repletion of blood. Surg Forum 9:49, 1958
47. Wright HK, Gann DS, Albertson K: Effect of glucose on sodium excretion and renal concentrating ability after starvation in man. Metabolism 12:804, 1963
48. Berliner RW, Kennedy TJ Jr, Orloff J: Relationship between acidification of the urine and potassium metabolism. Am J Med 11:274, 1951
49. Stewart PA: How To Understand Acid Base. p. 155. Elsevier, New York, 1981
50. Trunkey D, Carpenter MA, Holcroft J, et al: Ionized calcium and magnesium: The effect of septic shock in the baboon. J Trauma 18:166, 1978
51. Auerbach GD, Marks SJ, Spiegel AM: Parathyroid hormone, calcitonin, and the calciferols. p. 983. In Williams RH (ed): Textbook of Endocrinology. WB Saunders, Philadelphia, 1981
52. Grant JP, Custer PB, Thurlow J: Current techniques of nutritional assessment. Surg Clin North Am 61:437, 1981
53. Hoover HC, Ryan JA, Anderson EJ, et al: Nutritional benefits of immediate postoperative jejunal feeding of an elemental diet. Am J Surg 139:153, 1980
54. Border JR, Hassett J, LaDuca J, et al: The Gut Origin Septic States in Blunt Multiple Trauma (ISS-40) in the ICU. Ann Surg 206(4):427, 1987
55. Deitch EA, Winerton J, Burg R: Thermal injury promotes bacterial translocation from the gastrointestinal tract in mice with impaired T-Cell mediated immunity. Arch Surg 121:97, 1986:427, 1987
56. Rocchio MA, Cha CJ, Randall HT, et al: Use of chemically defined diets in the management of patients with high-output gastrointestinal cutaneous fistulas. Am J Surg 127:48, 1974
57. Woods JH, Erickson LW, Condon RE, et al: Postoperative ileus: A colonic problem? Surgery 84:527, 1978

10

Special Problems of Fluid and Electrolyte Metabolism in Diabetic Patients

James M. May
Charles O. Watlington

The fluid and electrolyte disorders found in diabetes mellitus encompass a broad spectrum of abnormalities which are often, but not always, related to insulin deficiency. The most obvious result of insulin deficiency or resistance is an osmotic diuresis due to hyperglycemia. It must be emphasized, however, that changes in water and electrolyte homeostasis result not only from the effects of a pure osmotic diuresis, but also depend on the response of the kidneys to metabolic acidosis, changes in intravascular volume, changes in oxygen delivery, and variations in hormonal stimulation (e.g., by aldosterone). Hyperglycemia and its effects on salt and water metabolism in the diabetic may be related to other hormones (such as glucagon, epinephrine, cortisol, and growth hormone) that play deleterious roles by virtue of their antagonism to insulin at the tissue level, even when measurable insulin concentrations are not low. Direct effects of insulin on renal water and electrolyte metabolism may also be important, and by their absence may contribute substantially to the abnormalities observed.

Even in the absence of uncontrolled hyperglycemia, diabetics may experience a variety of acid-base, water, and electrolyte abnormalities. Chronic abnormalities of renal function associated with diabetes appear to be causative or at least contributory. Abnormal renal function is common in patients with diabetes of over 15 years duration. It is due not only to diabetic glomerulosclerosis but also to other causes of renal failure, such as hypertension or chronic pyelonephritis.[1]

This chapter will review the various clinical abnormalities of fluid and electrolyte metabolism seen in diabetes mellitus. It will emphasize the pathogenesis of these abnormalities, particularly as they are related to multiple interacting causes such as insulin deficiency, excess of antagonistic hormones, and renal or adrenal dysfunction.

ROLE OF GLUCOREGULATORY HORMONES IN FLUID AND ELECTROLYTE BALANCE

Effects of Insulin on Ion Homeostasis

Although there has been considerable debate about whether the effects of insulin on ion transport are due to elevated local glu-

Table 10-1. Summary of Insulin Effects on Fluid and Electrolyte Balance

Sodium
  Stimulates sodium efflux in various tissues
  Causes renal sodium retention
Potassium
  Transfers potassium into cells
  Little effect on renal potassium handling
Calcium
  Enhances urinary calcium excretion (probably at the distal tubule)
Phosphorus
  Counteracts glucose-induced phosphaturia
  Enhances distal tubular phosphate reabsorption
  Increases phosphate transfer into cells
Magnesium
  Increases renal magnesium excretion

cose concentrations or to the direct effects of the hormone, recent studies, described below, have clearly established a role for insulin that is independent of glucose transport and metabolism. The major actions of insulin on ion homeostasis are summarized in Table 10-1.

Sodium

Insulin stimulates the efflux of sodium from various tissues, including the brain,[2] uterus,[3] and skeletal muscle of the rat,[4] human lymphocytes,[5] and skeletal muscle of the frog.[6] In rat[7] or frog[8] skeletal muscle, the stimulation of sodium efflux by insulin has been found to be independent of glucose transport, but does appear to require energy, since adenosine triphosphate (ATP) is consumed in the process.[2] Cellular metabolism and oxygen consumption are stimulated by insulin in muscle preparations.[9,10] Insulin-stimulated cellular metabolism may in fact be linked to ion transport, as suggested by studies in frog sarcolemmal membranes, in which it appears that the specific effect of insulin on sodium transport results from activation of a membrane-bound, magnesium-dependent, sodium-potassium-adenosine triphosphatase (Na^+,K^+ ATPase).[2] Stimulation of sodium efflux has also been attributed to a similar enzyme in lymphocytes.[5]

Although insulin may contribute to the maintenance of sodium balance in many tissues, its major effects on extracellular fluid (ECF) volume and sodium homeostasis are probably exerted in the kidney. Insulin has long been known to stimulate transcellular sodium transport in amphibian skin[11–14] and bladder,[15] which, as in muscle, is independent of glucose transport. Insulin also favors sodium retention in the isolated perfused dog kidney.[16] Early studies in humans demonstrated that withdrawal of insulin caused a marked natriuresis in excess of that which could be attributed to hyperglycemic osmotic diuresis, while insulin treatment caused a marked fall in urinary sodium excretion.[17,18] In addition, in better controlled studies a reduction in urinary sodium excretion following insulin administration was observed in normal subjects undergoing either a water or glucose diuresis,[19] and in insulin-deprived diabetics following reinstitution of therapy.[20] Correction of the osmotic diuresis with insulin certainly causes a major decline in urinary sodium loss, but there is evidence to suggest a direct insulin effect. Using the hyperglycemic and euglycemic clamp techniques in dogs, DeFronzo and colleagues[21] found that the decrease in sodium excretion associated with insulin treatment was due to insulin itself rather than to an attendant decrease in urinary glucose. The glucose clamp technique involves infusion of a specified amount of insulin, with concomitant glucose infusion at rates sufficient to maintain the plasma glucose at a constant level.

The antinatriuretic effect of insulin has also been demonstrated in human studies by DeFronzo and associates[22] with the use of the euglycemic clamp technique. In six subjects undergoing water diuresis, urinary sodium excretion decreased by 50 percent during an insulin infusion sufficient to produce insulin concentrations between 98 and

193 μU/ml (normal insulin concentrations are 5 to 20 μU/ml), while glucose concentrations were maintained in the normal range by simultaneous glucose infusion. Under these conditions free water clearance increased significantly. There was a slight fall in plasma glucagon, but there were no changes in the subjects' low plasma aldosterone concentrations, glomerular filtration rate (GFR), or renal plasma flow. Since infusion of insulin directly into the renal artery also caused a fall in sodium excretion,[16,21] it is likely that the effect was induced primarily by insulin rather than by glucagon. Micropuncture studies in dog kidneys further indicated that the decrease in sodium excretion occurred distal to the proximal tubular puncture site, either in the loop of Henle or in the distal tubule.[21] DeFronzo has recently reviewed these studies.[22,23]

To summarize, the role that insulin plays in sodium homeostasis under normal circumstances is uncertain. However, in developing diabetic ketoacidosis, insulin deficiency very likely increases the sodium loss that occurs during the osmotic diuresis. Conversely, the treatment of poorly controlled diabetes mellitus with insulin probably contributes substantially to the observed sodium retention. Because of the complicating effects of glycosuria on renal sodium handling, quantitation of the direct effects of insulin absence during poor diabetic control is difficult.

Potassium

Since potassium excretion in sweat or in gastrointestinal secretions is minimal under normal conditions, the kidney plays a dominant role in potassium balance. Control of renal potassium excretion depends on the concentration of potassium in the pericapillary space of the distal convoluted and collecting tubules,[23,24] as well as on the concentration of aldosterone, which acts on the distal tubule to enhance potassium secretion and sodium retention.[25] Whether or not potassium secretion is directly coupled to sodium reabsorption is controversial, as reviewed by Knochel.[26] The secretion of aldosterone is largely dependent on the renin-angiotensin system,[27] although hyperkalemia can also exert a direct stimulatory effect on aldosterone secretion that is independent of the concentration of angiotensin II, intravascular volume, and sodium balance.[28-30] Aldosterone has also been shown to play a major role in the development of tolerance to the acute administration of potassium to animals.[31] This latter phenomenon has been more difficult to demonstrate in humans.[32] It has long been known that there exist acute extrarenal adaptations to potassium loading that involve extracellular to intracellular transfers,[33,34] but potassium tolerance mediated by aldosterone requires several days to develop.[31] Thus, other factors than aldosterone also appear to play a role in both the acute response to potassium and in the maintenance of normal potassium concentrations.[35] One of the major factors appears to be insulin.

The effects of insulin on potassium homeostasis do not involve modification of renal handling of the cation,[23] but rather its transfer from the extracellular space into cells.[36,37] Perfusion of human forearm musculature with increasing doses of insulin resulted in an increased potassium uptake that was independent of glucose uptake.[36] Similarly, it was shown over 50 years ago that stimulation by insulin of glycogen deposition in the liver was associated with potassium uptake.[37] Subsequent studies in isolated perfused rat liver have demonstrated that the addition of insulin causes a prompt uptake of potassium before any effects on glucose transfer.[38,39] Even human erythrocytes have been shown to take up potassium in response to insulin, although this may have been an indirect effect, since it occurred only after in vivo insulin administration, but not following in vitro treatment of erythrocytes with insulin.[40] It may well be that the membrane-bound Na^+, K^+ ATPase that insulin activates to stimulate sodium efflux also results in the observed potassium uptake.[2] As noted previously with regard to insulin's effects on sodium transport, this enzyme activity does not directly require glucose uptake.

The effectiveness of insulin in modulating potassium redistribution is exemplified by studies involving the administration of quantities of potassium that are too large to be handled quickly by the kidneys. Experimental animals have been shown to remove much of a near lethal dose of potassium chloride from ECF, and this tolerance required either the presence of the pancreas or insulin infusion in pancreatectomized animals.[41-43] Similarly, cellular uptake of an acute potassium load was markedly impaired in a diabetic hemodialysis patient,[44] and in diabetic patients with only slightly reduced renal function.[45] Insulin and glucose (to prevent hypoglycemia) are frequently given to reverse acute hyperkalemia in humans, regardless of the presence or absence of diabetes mellitus.[46]

Some question remains about whether insulin plays a role in the maintenance of normal potassium concentrations,[47] since high physiologic concentrations of insulin were required to induce forearm muscle potassium uptake.[36] On the other hand, the liver is probably very important in potassium removal, and it is exposed to much higher insulin concentrations in the portal vein than are peripheral tissues.[48] Studies suggesting that insulin does maintain basal potassium concentrations were performed by DeFronzo and colleagues in normal volunteers.[49] They found that suppression of insulin secretion by the infusion of somatostatin resulted in an increase in serum potassium. This occurred before the rise in plasma glucose, and was not explained by altered renal excretion of the ion. Similar somatostatin infusions caused no rise in serum potassium in insulinopenic diabetics (in spite of a similar fall in plasma glucagon). Moreover, the hyperkalemic effect of somatostatin in normal dogs was abolished by insulin replacement. It was concluded that somatostatin-induced hyperkalemia was due solely to insulin deficiency. Further, it appears that extremes (particularly low extremes) of potassium concentration are linked to insulin secretion,[49] suggesting that a feedback mechanism may exist.

There is considerable evidence, both in vitro and in vivo, that increases in serum potassium can stimulate insulin secretion. Studies in the isolated perfused pancreas, in pancreatic slices, and in islet-cell preparations have shown that increases in medium potassium concentrations evoke a prompt release of insulin.[50-53] Acute hyperkalemia in dogs has also been associated with a rise in circulating insulin concentrations,[41,43,54] although small changes in serum potassium may be ineffective.[49] In normal human volunteers who had previously been on a low potassium diet (40 mEq/day), an acute increase of serum potassium to 6 mEq/liter caused prompt elevations in serum insulin concentrations.[55] On the other hand, acute potassium loading following a daily intake of potassium of 100 mEq caused no changes in plasma insulin.[55] Although elevated potassium levels in blood can clearly increase the insulin concentration (which in turn causes potassium transfer into cells), it remains to be demonstrated that physiologic changes in serum potassium lead to increases in serum insulin concentrations in humans.[47]

Studies in humans by Saglid and coworkers[56] on the other hand, have shown that total body potassium depletion (range: 200 to 500 mEq) following ingestion of a potassium binding resin impaired intravenous glucose tolerance and insulin responses, even though serum potassium and fasting glucose concentrations did not change. Furthermore, potassium infusion normalized the responses to intravenous glucose. There is additional evidence that diuretic-induced hypokalemia also impairs insulin secretion,[57] as will be discussed later.

In addition to insulin and aldosterone, epinephrine has also been shown to enhance extrarenal potassium uptake, particularly in muscle and liver.[35,58] In fact, counterregulatory secretion of epinephrine during insulin-induced hypoglycemia has been shown to intensify the hypokalemia caused by insulin.[58]

From the foregoing it appears likely that aldosterone and insulin are important in the maintenance of potassium homeostasis, and that insulin secretion and potassium homeostasis are linked by feedback controls. The coordination of insulin and aldosterone will become even more apparent as specific electrolyte problems in diabetic patients are discussed, such as ketoacidosis and hyporeninemic hypoaldosteronism.

Calcium

Urinary calcium excretion is enhanced following either oral glucose[23,55-57] or insulin administration.[57] In the studies by DeFronzo and colleagues in humans,[23] glucose was infused to maintain normal blood glucose concentrations, while insulin infusion produced plasma insulin concentrations between 98 and 193 µU/ml. Under these conditions urinary calcium excretion increased by 75 percent, suggesting that insulin mediated the effect in the absence of glycosuria. Subsequent micropuncture studies in dogs indicated that the increased urinary excretion of calcium caused by insulin might be due in part to decreased fractional calcium reabsorption in the proximal tubule, although no significant increase in the final urinary calcium excretion was noted in that particular study.[21] Since sodium and calcium reabsorption are coupled in the proximal tubule,[60-62] the decreased sodium excretion and increased calcium excretion with hyperinsulinemia are not readily explained by a single proximal tubular effect. Thus the site of opposite, insulin-mediated effects on sodium and calcium excretion may be the distal tubule. Certain diuretics,[63,64] as well as mineralocorticoids[64,65] with sites of action in the distal tubule, are also known to cause sodium and calcium countertransport.

On the other hand, kidneys from rats made diabetic with streptozotocin showed diminished calcium reabsorption, and not because of the effects of an osmotic diuresis, since calcium reabsorption was measured in isolated perfused kidneys.[66] Early treatment of the rats with insulin enhanced the ability of subsequently perfused kidneys to reabsorb calcium. Similarly, Raskin and associates[67] found that the renal calcium "leak" associated with poorly controlled diabetes was reversed by optimal insulin treatment. While the osmotic diuresis probably contributed substantially to the renal calcium loss in the clinical studies, it is clear that the observed effects of insulin on renal calcium handling depend upon the clinical situation.

Extensive in vitro studies have established that adequate calcium is required for pancreatic insulin secretion[51,68-70] and for the action of insulin on target tissues such as muscle.[71] Although adipose tissue does not require calcium in the tissue culture medium to demonstrate an insulin response,[72] calcium has been implicated in the mechanism of insulin action in the adipocyte.[73] In humans with hypercalcemia caused by hyperparathyroidism, glucose-induced plasma insulin responses were increased.[73] On the other hand, in subjects with hypocalcemia due to idiopathic hypoparathyroidism or pseudohypoparathyroidism, glucose-induced insulin responses were decreased compared to those in normal subjects, a finding felt to be related to serum calcium rather than serum parathyroid hormone (PTH) concentrations.[74] In experiments with dogs in which secondary hyperparathyroidism was induced by dietary manipulation, PTH was found to have no effect on tolbutamide- or glucose-stimulated insulin release,[75] further implicating calcium rather than PTH in the abnormal insulin secretory pattern. The observation that normal glucose tolerance is preserved regardless of the variation in insulin response has been taken to indicate a compensatory change in peripheral sensitivity to insulin.[76,77] It is not known whether the small variations in serum calcium in normal individuals affect insulin secretion; very likely it is the free or ionized calcium that is important.

Phosphorus

Interrelations of phosphate excretion, plasma glucose concentration, and glucoregulatory hormones are quite complex. Hyperglycemia in man[78,79] and dogs[80] increases urinary phosphate excretion, probably as the result of a glucose-induced osmotic diuresis. On the other hand, DeFronzo and associates[21] demonstrated in dogs that sustained subthreshold hyperglycemia and hyperinsulinemia (to 40 μU/ml) caused a significant fall in phosphate excretion. The decrease in excretion was probably the result of enhanced distal tubular reabsorption, since micropuncture studies in dogs showed an 8 to 14 percent decrease in proximal tubular phosphate reabsorption, an effect that could have been counteracted only in the distal tubules. Glucose and phosphate are thought to share a common transport pathway in the proximal tubule.[81] Thus, increased unreabsorbed glucose may cause competitive inhibition of phosphate reabsorption at that site.[21] The decrease in fractional excretion of phosphate associated with hyperglycemia may depend more on elevated insulin concentrations than on hyperglycemia.

Insulin administration is known to cause a fall in urinary phosphate clearance,[23,79,82] but this could result from a concomitant fall in plasma phosphate concentration induced by insulin, thus decreasing the filtered load of phosphate. More recently, hyperinsulinemia (to 80 μU/ml) during euglycemic clamp studies in dogs was found to cause a decrease in fractional phosphate excretion in the absence of a change in the filtered phosphate load.[21] Micropuncture studies indicated that an increase in proximal tubular phosphate reabsorption contributed greatly to the decreased phosphate clearance.[21] This contrasts with the findings noted above during hyperglycemia, in which proximal tubular phosphate reabsorption was inhibited by glucose and distal reabsorption enhanced (possibly by insulin). Although the mechanism of this insulin effect is unknown, it is probably direct, since intrarenal insulin infusion produced similar changes in phosphate clearance.[21]

Insulin administration in the absence of hyperglycemia also is likely to increase phosphate transport into cells, since in some studies,[23,79,82] but not all,[21] insulin lowered plasma phosphate concentrations, as noted above. This phosphate lowering effect is probably related to cellular phosphate uptake associated with increased glucose transport, and to phosphorylation induced by insulin, since insulin potentiates the depression of plasma phosphate following glucose administration.[83] The effect is most apparent clinically as hypophosphatemia developing after glucose infusion.[84,85] Insulin secretion in response to glucose in dogs has also been shown to increase during hypophosphatemia induced by dietary deprivation, although glucose tolerance is actually mildly impaired.[75]

In poorly controlled diabetic patients, the institution of optimal insulin therapy caused a decrease in urinary phosphate excretion and an increase in plasma phosphate concentrations.[86] Raskin and Pak felt that the renal effects of insulin on retaining phosphate outweighed the effects of the hormone on driving phosphate into cells under such conditions.[86] It was also thought that insulin, by diminishing the renal calcium leakage present in poorly controlled diabetes, would raise the serum calcium and prevent excessive PTH secretion, thus secondarily increasing phosphate reabsorption.[86]

Magnesium

In general, renal magnesium excretion responds to either glucose or insulin in a manner similar to that for calcium. For example, in humans undergoing symptomatic insulin-induced hypoglycemia (but not developing a hypoglycemia-related antidiuresis), renal magnesium excretion almost doubled, as was the case following 100 g of oral glucose.[61] Although magnesium is required under certain conditions for in vitro insulin release, both calcium and potassium appear to play a more crucial role.[51]

Effects of Insulin on Blood Volume and Vascular Permeability

Rapid intravenous injection of insulin decreases peripheral blood flow and plasma volume in diabetic patients with intact autonomic nervous systems.[87] This effect is associated with increased urinary albumin excretion and a decreased intravascular albumin concentration that may reflect a generalized increase in vascular permeability.[88] Since the effects of insulin on intravascular volume occurred even though the blood glucose did not fall to hypoglycemic concentrations, they were considered to be direct effects of insulin.[87] However, a more recent study in diabetic patients,[89] of rapid insulin-induced decreases of blood glucose to nonhypoglycemic concentrations, demonstrated counter-regulatory increases in epinephrine and cortisol. Insulin injection also elicits what appear to be compensatory increases in plasma norepinephrine and heart rate.[87] In the diabetic patient with hyperglycemia, therefore, changes in blood volume as a result of insulin injection may be due to the combined effects of several hormones. Calculations indicate that insulin-induced glucose translocation out of the vascular space, along with water, can account for only about one-fifth of the observed decrease in plasma volume.[90] The exact mechanism of insulin-induced hypovolemia remains unknown, as does its relevance in nondiabetic individuals or in diabetic patients given subcutaneous insulin.

Diabetes is also associated with glomerular hyperfiltration and increased renal size.[91,92] At least one study has suggested that improved blood sugar control can improve glomerular hyperfiltration, although it cannot reduce the enlarged renal mass.[93]

Other Glucoregulatory Hormones and Ion Balance

Several hormones in addition to insulin are known to affect ion homeostasis as well as glucoregulation. These hormones generally have antagonistic effects to those of insulin, and their concentrations vary inversely with that of insulin in different metabolic states. The interactions of insulin, glucagon, and epinephrine in the control of hepatic glucose synthesis and disposal have been the subject of intensive research; hormonal effects on ion metabolism have received much less attention.

Glucagon

Glucagon has long been known to alter renal electrolyte excretion when administered in pharmacologic doses,[94,95] an effect that is independent of glucagon-induced hyperglycemia.[96] Glucagon infusion into perfused dog kidneys (probably to supraphysiologic concentrations) was also shown to increase the excretion of free water, calcium, magnesium, sodium, chloride, and potassium.[97] Since neither GFR, para-aminohippurate clearance, nor filtration fraction differed between the kidney perfused with glucagon and the opposite, control kidney, the observed effects were thought to be caused by decreased tubular reabsorption.[97] Other studies have demonstrated transient elevations in the GFR following glucagon administration,[98] but not to the extent that increased filtered load could produce the observed changes in water and electrolyte clearance.[99] Saudek and colleagues[100] infused glucagon into fed obese subjects at rates that produced physiologic (fourfold) increments in plasma glucagon, and found that urinary sodium excretion increased significantly, although urinary potassium, calcium, and phosphate excretions were unchanged.

The effect of physiologic concentrations of glucagon on sodium excretion is perhaps best understood from studies of the natriuresis of fasting. Fasting in humans causes a marked increase in sodium excretion that persists for several days and then declines. An antinatriuretic phase follows when refeeding occurs.[101] The natriuresis of fasting is accompanied by marked increases in plasma glucagon[100,102] and aldosterone,[101] both of which decline with carbohydrate refeeding.[101,102] In fasting obese volunteers, the infusion of glucagon in doses sufficient to increase plasma levels only twofold caused a significant natriuresis, thus implicating glucagon in the natriuresis of fasting.[100] Furthermore, similar rates of glucagon infusion also caused refractoriness to exogenous mineralocorticoid in either the fed or fasted state, suggesting that glucagon may produce natriuresis by inhibiting the effects of aldosterone on the distal tubule.[103] It is also possible, of course, that decreases in insulin during fasting, and increases with refeeding, contribute to the changes in sodium excretion described above.

As noted above, glucagon in pharmacologic doses causes an increase in urinary potassium excretion, which may be associated with mild hypokalemia.[96] An initial acute increase in serum potassium following glucagon has also been observed, the cause of which is uncertain.[99] It has further been shown in dogs that potassium infusion elevates plasma glucagon.[41] Additionally studies by DeFronzo and colleagues[49] have shown that somatostatin-induced decreases in plasma glucagon do not affect serum potassium. Furthermore, tolerance to potassium in dogs has been shown to depend on the ability to secrete insulin, not glucagon. It is therefore unlikely that physiologic increases in plasma glucagon normally affect plasma or urinary potassium.

Supraphysiologic doses of glucagon cause hypophosphatemia, possibly related to direct renal effects of this hormone,[96] to decreased bone reabsorption,[104] or to the phosphate uptake required for glucagon-induced glycogenolysis.[105] However, as noted above, insulin also may lower serum phosphate, and it is difficult to dissociate the effects of the two hormones under physiologic conditions. Even though the hypophosphatemic effect of glucagon persists when hyperglycemia is prevented,[105] glucagon directly stimulates insulin secretion from the β-cell.[106,107]

Glucagon infused in supraphysiologic amounts has been shown to slightly lower serum calcium in animals[108] and normal human subjects.[109] It is possible that this effect is related to glucagon-induced stimulation of calcitonin secretion[110] or to an effect of glucagon on inhibition of bone resorption. This could occur either directly[104] or via inhibition of the action of PTH.[111,112] Furthermore, glucagon has been causally implicated in the hypocalcemia of acute pancreatitis.[113] More recent studies have also shown glucagon elevations during acute pancreatitis,[113,114] with[114] or without[113] concomitant increases in calcitonin. However, since infusion of glucagon in the amounts required to produce high physiologic plasma concentrations of the

Catecholamines

Excessive catecholamine stimulation is known to inhibit both the secretion[117] and action[118] of insulin. Under conditions of stress, catecholamines may play a major role in producing and maintaining a state of apparent insulin lack or insulin resistance. Elevated catecholamine concentrations may also increase plasma renin activity,[119] leading to an increase in plasma aldosterone, which in turn may produce sodium retention and potassium loss. Finally, catecholamines also modulate extrarenal potassium homeostasis independently of insulin and aldosterone. Epinephrine, probably from alpha-adrenergic stimulation, causes hepatic potassium release and hyperkalemia when infused acutely.[119,120] On the other hand, β-adrenergic receptors appear to mediate the opposite and probably clinically more important effect of epinephrine, which is to increase extrarenal potassium disposal and cause hypokalemia.[35,121,122] Beta-blocking agents or sympathetic blockade have in fact been shown to cause hyperkalemia.[123]

Other Hormones

When secreted in excess, both cortisol and growth hormone may impair tissue responsiveness to the effects of insulin.[124,125] These hormones may also contribute to salt and water retention independently of insulin in both Cushing's syndrome and acromegaly. At physiologic concentrations, however, a direct role of these hormones in fluid and electrolyte homeostasis has not been demonstrated.

CLINICAL ABNORMALITIES OF FLUID AND ELECTROLYTE BALANCE IN DIABETES MELLITUS

Diabetic Ketoacidosis

The factors that lead to ketoacidosis in the insulin-dependent diabetic patient are multiple and may include discontinuation of insulin, hyperglucagonemia,[126] infection, or stress, such as from an emotional disturbance or myocardial infarction. These conditions cause a diminished effect of insulin with the consequences summarized in Figures 10-1 and 10-2 and Table 10-2, and detailed below.

Consequences of Hyperglycemia and Osmotic Diuresis

The derangements in fluid and electrolytes encountered in poorly controlled diabetes or in ketoacidosis are probably caused to some extent by the lack of direct insulin effects on renal electrolyte excretion and transport of certain ions across cell membranes, as discussed above, but most of the changes are the consequence of a glucose-induced osmotic diuresis. Early studies, including those of Atchley and associates[17] and Nabarro and colleagues,[18]

Table 10-2. Losses of Water and Electrolytes During the Development of Diabetic Coma

Substance Lost	Ketoacidosis	Hyperosmolar Coma
Water	0.08–0.11 L	0.12 L
Sodium	5–10 mEq	5.3 mEq
Chloride	5–6 mEq	—
Potassium	5–6 mEq	1.8 mEq
Magnesium	0.5–0.8 mEq	—
Phosphorus	0.5–1.3 mM	—

Amounts Lost per Kilogram of Body Weight

372 • Kidney Electrolyte Disorders

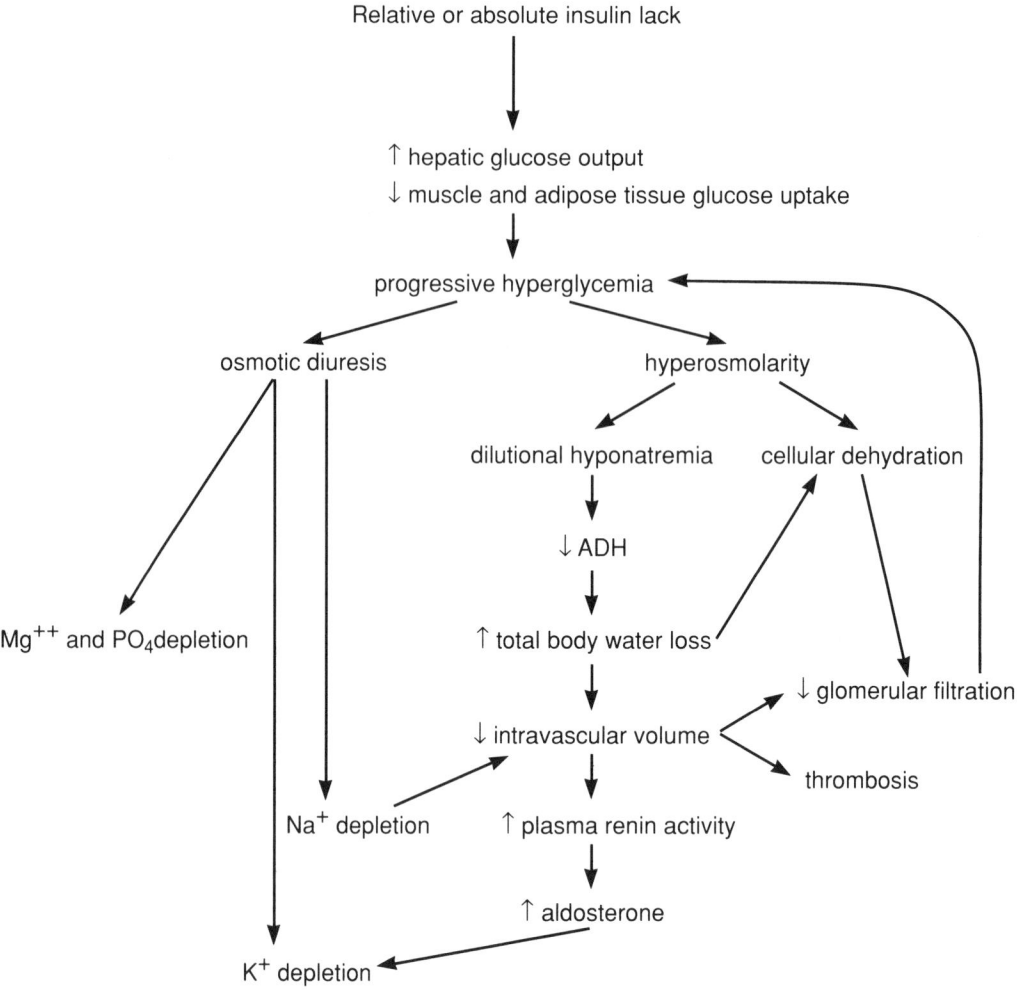

Fig. 10-1 Development of salt and water losses.

documented in detail the progressive deterioration in metabolic status as a result of insulin deficiency. Excessive hepatic glucose output and diminished peripheral glucose uptake due to both a lack of insulin and an excess of counter-regulatory hormones cause progressive increases in blood glucose. Until glucose begins to appear in significant amounts in the urine at a blood glucose above 180 mg/dl, the increase in extracellular osmolality induced by hyperglycemia produces water flow out of cells and into the vascular and extracellular spaces. Electrolytes are not included to any significant extent in this cellular water loss, resulting in a mild dilutional hyponatremia.[127] This hyponatremia may transiently decrease antidiuretic hormone (ADH) secretion (which is insensitive to hyperglycemia), contributing to the loss of free water.[127] As the renal reabsorptive capacity for glucose is overwhelmed by progressive hyperglycemia, an osmotic diuresis ensues and increased water and electrolyte excretion occurs with the glycosuria. During this phase, both water and ions are lost from cells in order to replenish intravascular volume, at the expense of further cellular de-

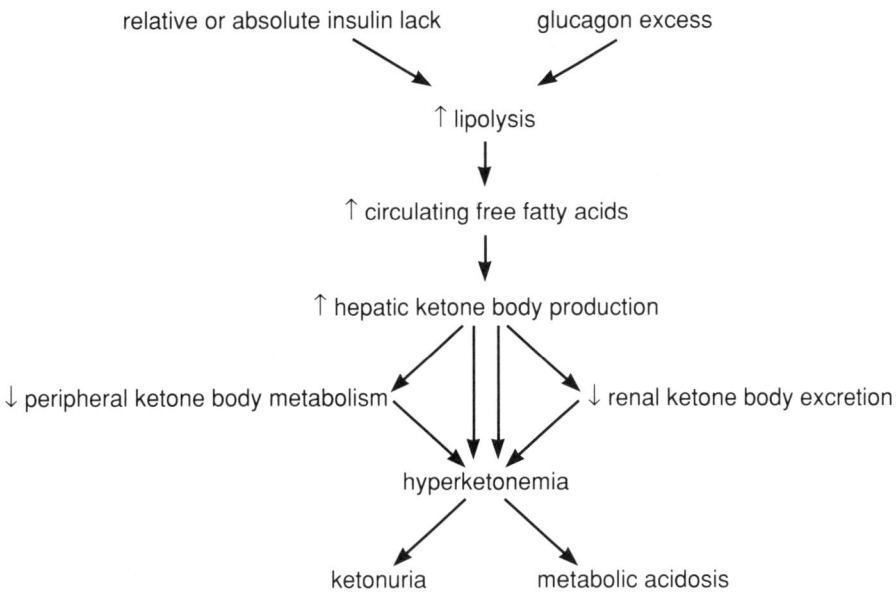

Fig. 10-2 Development of ketosis.

pletion.[128] The fluid and salt losses during an osmotic diuresis correlate well with the severity of the glycosuria,[18,129] while in most cases vomiting and ketonuria make smaller contributions.[130] The osmotic diuresis generally results in water losses greater than those of salt, so that the urine remains hypotonic to the plasma.[17,130] Although this impaired renal concentrating ability may be due primarily to the osmotic diuresis, hypokalemia,[131] decreased glomerular filtration, and other factors may contribute. Whereas ADH secretion may be transiently suppressed during the initial phases of hyperglycemia, as noted previously, the plasma concentration of this hormone become quite elevated, helping to retain free water, in cases of severe volume depletion due to hyperglycemic osmotic diuresis.[132,133] Intense thirst is usually present at this stage, but water losses usually are not replaced, due to concomitant nausea and vomiting, and possibly to the fact that glucose is not as good a stimulant of thirst as other solutes.[134] As volume depletion and cellular dehydration proceed, there occurs a fall in glomerular filtration,[135,136] allowing the blood glucose to rise even higher. The fall in GFR may be as much as 66 percent[136] and is associated with prerenal azotemia.[135,137] Azotemia in diabetic ketoacidosis is said to be due not only to prerenal causes, but also to an excess of nitrogen produced from amino acids during gluconeogenesis.[138] In most instances the azotemia resolves with therapy,[135,136] although acute renal failure leading to death may occur.[135,137] The causes of the decreased renal function are not well understood, but probably include acidosis, dehydration, hypokalemia, and increased blood viscosity.[135,138] A major consequence of decreased glomerular filtration is retention of glucose and worsening of hyperglycemia and hyperosmolarity. The normal person can excrete up to 32 g/hr of glucose,[139] but in ketoacidosis the rate falls to 19 g/hr.[130]

In diabetic ketoacidosis, marked increases in plasma renin activity and aldosterone are noted, probably as a result of the severe volume depletion. Ketoacidosis is thus a state of secondary aldosteronism.[140] Plasma renin activity in ketoacidosis was shown to fall dramatically within 4 hours of beginning treatment, and by 48 hours was no different than values found in controls.[140] In patients with moderate hyperglycemia (a mean blood glucose of 318 mg/dl) but no ketosis, plasma renin activity was normal and unaffected by tight control of blood glucose.[140] During the volume-depleted stage, however, aldosterone may help to maintain intravascular volume by causing sodium and water retention, albeit at the expense of depletion of body stores of potassium.

Hyperglycemic hyperosmolarity is usually but not always present in ketoacidosis at the time of admission to the hospital.[141-145] The hyperosmolarity generally requires several days to develop before admission. Serum osmolality may be measured directly or calculated from the following formula[146]:

$$\text{Serum osmolality} = 2([Na^+] + [K^+]) + \frac{[Glucose]}{18} + \frac{BUN}{2.8}$$

Since blood urea nitrogen (BUN) distributes equally across membranes, some authorities do not include it in the calculated serum osmolality (although osmolarity and osmolality are not the same, clinical usage is not strict in this distinction).

It appears that the depth of stupor in diabetic coma may be best related to the degree of hyperosmolarity and to the rapidity with which it develops,[147,148] although other factors such as ketonemia, azotemia, or acidosis may contribute.[138] In fact, patients with diabetic ketoacidosis but minimal hyperglycemia generally show few mental changes.[141] It has further been noted that the degree of hyperosmolarity correlates with the fatality rate.[144] Coma without significant hyperosmolarity suggests that the altered consciousness is due to causes other than uncontrolled diabetes, such as stroke.[147]

The loss of body water in established diabetic ketoacidosis may be as much as 0.08 to 0.11 liters/kg (Table 10-2), as measured either by retention studies during insulin treatment[18,142,143] or by studies of losses during insulin withdrawal.[17] This loss amounts to a 6- to 7-liter water deficit in a 70 kg patient, or 10 to 15 percent of the total body water. Cellular dehydration is difficult to assess clinically, but is probably reflected by the degree of hyperglycemia and concentration of blood proteins and formed blood elements. For reasons discussed in the next section, the plasma sodium concentration may not be a good index of cellular dehydration. Dehydration contributes substantially to the increased mortality found in severely hyperosmolar patients.[144] Early studies of glucose infusion in dogs demonstrated that extreme hyperglycemia leading to an osmotic diuresis produced intracellular dehydration, hemoconcentration, acidosis, and eventually coma and death,[149] usually associated with liver failure.[150] It is noteworthy in this regard that vascular thrombosis and shock are now leading causes of mortality in diabetic ketoacidosis.[151]

Electrolyte Derangements in Diabetic Ketoacidosis

Sodium

The extent of the loss of sodium during the osmotic diuresis of uncontrolled diabetes may be quite large, as shown in Table 10-2, ranging from 5 to 10 mEq/kg in several studies.[17,18,143,152,153] Even after insulin administration, hyperglycemia and attendant osmotic diuresis may persist for some time, with further loss of sodium chloride in the urine;[17] any direct effect of insulin on sodium retention in the renal tubule[21-23] is apparently overcome by the osmotic effects of glycosuria. However, it has been shown in rabbits made diabetic by streptozotocin that insulin treatment decreased urinary sodium excretion disproportionately to the decrease in glycosuria.[154] This phenomenon has also been described in some poorly controlled diabetic patients treated with insulin.[20] Not only was urinary sodium excretion during insulin treatment lower than expected from the glycosuric diuresis, but some patients actually developed edema. This "insulin edema" will be discussed more fully in a later section.

Although water is lost in excess of solute during the development of diabetic hyperglycemia, the serum sodium is usually normal or low at the time of admission.[143,144] As discussed above, this hyponatremia is primarily due to the hypertonic effect of hyperglycemia, which causes water in excess of sodium to flow out of cells and thus "dilutes" the plasma sodium.[155] Plasma sodium concentrations may also be artifactually lowered by severe hypertriglyceridemia, which may accompany diabetic ketoacidosis.

Chloride is lost in significant amounts during diabetic ketoacidosis, but as noted in Table 10-2, it is spared somewhat as compared to sodium and potassium because β-hydroxybutyrate and acetoacetate constitute the major anions lost in the urine.[18,143]

Potassium

Most balance studies demonstrate a profound loss of potassium during the development of ketoacidosis. Losses estimated from studies of retention of administered potassium average between 5 and 6 mEq/kg of body weight,[17,18,142,152,153] and as with sodium, replacements are generally much greater than the deficits present on admission, due to ongoing urinary losses during the early phases of treatment. Much of the loss in body potassium occurs in the urine, but vomiting may also contribute substantially. The loss of potassium during diuresis induced by a nonreabsorbable solute is generally not as great as that observed during ketoacidosis.[156] This may be due in part to increased loss of potassium from cells in ketoacidosis. Several explanations may be advanced for the translocation of potassium out of cells, into the vascular space, and thence into the urine. The glucose-induced diuresis in diabetes causes volume contraction of the ECF and hypertonicity, producing water and electrolyte movement out of cells in an attempt to maintain vascular volume.[128] The rapid flux of water out of cells may be thought of as creating a "solvent drag," removing ions (primarily potassium) as well. It is also likely that potassium is released from cells as a result of cellular damage related to dehydration,[130,156] excessive glycogenolysis,[37] or lack of a tonic effect of insulin on potassium transport into cells.[49] Metabolic acidosis per se is known to elevate serum potassium by causing it to shift out of cells as hydrogen ion is buffered intracellularly.[157,158] This, however, has recently been questioned on the basis of clinical studies by Fulop,[159] who found in reanalysis of his previous data that as a group, diabetic patients with acidosis tended to have elevated serum potassium levels on admission, but that there was no correlation between serum potassium and blood pH. In addition to increased potassium loss from the intracellular space, renal wastage of the ion is heightened in ketoacidosis. Metabolic acidosis with obligatory excretion of organic ions requires concomitant excretion of sodium, potassium, and hydrogen. Further, in the presence of secondary aldosteronism,[140] sodium is retained at the expense of potassium.

Large total body deficits in potassium, as with sodium, are not reflected in the plasma potassium on admission to the hospital.

Most patients with severe diabetic ketoacidosis have normal or elevated serum potassium concentrations.[18,143] In addition to the mechanisms discussed above for potassium transport from cells into the vascular space, it is possible that decreased glomerular filtration contributes to elevated or relatively elevated serum potassium concentrations, although neither the hematocrit nor the serum urea concentration has been found to correlate with the serum potassium concentrations.[143] A low serum potassium on admission (4 percent in one large series[144]) usually indicates severe potassium deficiency[159] with large requirements for potassium replacement.[160] Although aberrations in serum potassium could not directly account for fatalities in Beigelman's large series,[144] there seems little doubt that the incidence of cardiac arrythmias would be greater in patients with severe extremes of serum potassium.

Calcium and Magnesium

The serum calcium concentration is normal after correction for protein binding in most patients admitted with diabetic ketoacidosis,[144] but administered calcium is usually avidly retained.[17] Even nonketotic patients with poorly controlled diabetes may have significant hypercalciuria.[67] The major portion of calcium lost in the urine is probably a result of the osmotic diuresis.

Serum magnesium concentrations in diabetic ketoacidosis follow a pattern similar to that of serum potassium, with most being normal or elevated before treatment.[143,161] Since the patient with ketoacidosis is severely dehydrated, a low or normal magnesium concentration indicates a deficit of body magnesium.[162] There is about a threefold increase in urinary magnesium loss with glycosuria, so that a prolonged osmotic diuresis may result in large losses of magnesium.[162] Balance studies have shown that the magnesium deficit is between 0.5 and 0.8 mEq/kg in diabetic ketoacidosis (Table 10-2).[18,153]

Phosphorus

There is extensive urinary loss of phosphorus in diabetic ketoacidosis, with deficits between 0.5 and 1.3 mM/kg reported in early studies.[17,18,130,143,153] The urinary loss of cellular phosphorus in the form of phosphate probably has several causes in diabetic ketoacidosis, as reviewed by Kreisberg.[163] These include tissue catabolism, impaired cellular phosphate uptake because of diminished glucose utilization, and increased renal losses resulting directly from the metabolic acidosis[130] and from proximal renal tubular countertransport of glucose and phosphate.[21,80] In spite of severe deficiencies in total body stores, serum phosphorus concentrations are often elevated (71 percent) or normal (18 percent) before therapy,[144] as has been noted for other ions.

One of the major abnormalities related to cellular phosphate depletion in ketoacidosis is the fall in erythrocyte 2,3-diphosphoglycerate (2,3-DPG) concentrations to values about half those of controls.[164,165] In addition to the phosphorus deficiency, metabolic acidosis[166] and even hyperglycemia[167] have been causally implicated in decreasing 2,3-DPG synthesis. Low 2,3-DPG concentrations have in turn been associated with diminished oxygen release from hemoglobin,[168,169] raising the possibility that tissue hypoxia may thereby be produced. On the other hand, this effect is apparently counteracted during established ketoacidosis by the diminished affinity of hemoglobin for oxygen that occurs at subphysiologic pH (Bohr effect). Several groups have shown that the hemoglobin–oxygen dissociation curve in diabetic ketoacidosis is normal because of this balance.[165,170,171] The therapy of diabetic ketoacidosis may disrupt this tenuous balance, however, as discussed below.

Development of Acidosis

Diabetic acidosis results primarily from relative or absolute insulin deficiency, possibly exaggerated by hyperglucagonemia.[172] Not only are β-hydroxybutyric and acetoacetic acids overproduced by the liver, but there is also evidence in diabetic ketoacidosis of decreased peripheral ketone metabolism.[173,174] The abnormalities related to the development of ketoacidosis are diagrammed in Fig. 10-2.

Insulin deficiency, coupled with increased circulating lipolytic hormones such as glucagon and the catecholamines, augments the lipolysis of triglyceride in adipose tissue, resulting in increased circulating free fatty acid concentrations.[170] Free fatty acids provide the necessary substrate for fatty acid oxidation and ketone production by the liver. Once taken up by the liver, the fatty acids are activated to long chain fatty acyl-CoA and then either esterified to triglycerides or oxidized to acetyl-CoA in the β-oxidative pathway of mitochondria. Flux through both pathways is increased in ketoacidosis because of increased substrate concentrations. Triglyceride is deposited in the liver in excessive amounts, causing a "fatty liver," as well as secreted back into the circulation as a component of very low density lipoprotein (VLDL), which may cause diabetic "lipemia." Much of the fatty acyl-CoA, however, is shunted to the mitochondrion for oxidation. Recent work has indiated that the rate-limiting step in this process and of ketogenesis per se is transport of fatty acids across the mitochondrial membranes, which is in turn determined by the activity of the enzyme carnitine acyltransferase.[175,176] The activity of this enzyme is increased in ketoacidosis, due in part to increased carnitine concentrations,[176] but probably also because of a deficiency of malonyl-CoA, a potent and specific inhibitor of the enzyme.[177] Malonyl-CoA is the first committed intermediate in fatty acid synthesis; it is markedly diminished in ketoacidosis, probably due to the prevailing low insulin-to-glucagon ratios.[178] Thus, increased fatty-acyl transport into mitochondria results in increased β-oxidation, the product of which is acetyl-CoA. Acetyl-CoA in turn may enter three major pathways: (1) fatty acid synthesis (which is completely turned off), (2) the Krebs cycle, with oxidation to CO_2 (also probably inhibited in ketosis),[175] or (3) ketone body synthesis. In ketoacidosis the latter pathway predominates, and acetoacetic acid and its reduction product β-hydroxybutyric acid are released into the circulation, usually with a predominance of β-hydroxybutyric acid.[179] In addition to hepatic ketone overproduction, decreased peripheral utilization of ketone bodies by muscle and nervous tissue occurs. Both diabetic dogs[173] and humans[174] clear ketones less rapidly than controls, a defect reversed by insulin administration. Decreased glomerular filtration, as discussed above, may also contribute substantially to the decreased clearance rate of ketone bodies in ketoacidosis.[138] Acetoacetic and β-hydroxybutyric are strong organic acids (pKa 4.8), and over 99 percent dissociated at physiologic pH, so that with continued ketoacid production, bicarbonate buffering capacity is rapidly exhausted and the blood pH falls. Also, because acetoacetate and β-hydroxybutyrate are organic ions, a negative anion gap is produced. The anion gap is normally 12 mEq/liter or less when calculated from the following formula:[180]

$$\text{Anion gap} = ([Na^+] + [K^+]) - ([Cl^-] + [HCO_3^-])$$

The gap is usually over 20 in significant diabetic ketoacidosis. Excess hydrogen ions contribute to the mortality from ketoacidosis in many ways, not the least of which are increasing potassium movement from cells into the extracellular space, inducing a decreased oxygen carrying capacity of hemoglobin (Bohr effect), and, possibly, inhibiting pH-sensitive enzymes.

In rare instances, uncontrolled diabetes with ketosis may result in an alkalosis rather than acidosis. This paradox is thought to be due to the development of a "volume-contraction alkalosis" from incessant vomiting[181,182] or diuretic therapy.[183] Hyperchloremic metabolic acidosis with no increase in anion gap has also been reported in poorly controlled ketotic diabetes. This may be related to concomitant diarrhea or to various renal tubular defects, including renal tubular acidosis,[184,185] a renal tubular defect in the reabsorption of ketone-body anions,[186] and bicarbonate wasting caused by hypophosphatemia.[187]

Treatment of Diabetic Ketoacidosis

Insulin Therapy

Therapy in diabetic ketoacidosis requires prompt attention whenever possible to inciting events such as infection, stroke, or psychologic stress, as well as to providing adequate insulin and replacing fluid and electrolyte deficits. Numerous studies[188-191] have indicated the effectiveness of "low-dose" insulin therapy by various routes in correcting the metabolic abnormalities of even severe ketoacidosis in adults or children. The insulin concentrations provided by such low-dose regimens[189] are still more than adequate to decrease gluconeogenesis and inhibit lipolysis, as pointed out by Clements and Vourganti.[151] They also note that the recent studies of low-dose insulin therapy illustrate the importance of adequate fluid and electrolyte replacement, both in correcting deficits and in actually lowering the blood glucose.

Water and Sodium Chloride Replacement

Two studies highlight the importance of early fluid replacement in diabetic ketoacidosis. In a series of patients eventually treated with a low-dose insulin regimen, Page and colleagues[188] found that in 12 of 18 patients so treated, the blood glucose fell with saline infusion alone over the first 3 hours, and that in most of the 38 patients addition of insulin did not appear to increase the rate of decline in blood glucose. In a more recent evaluation,[192] seven ketoacidotic diabetic patients were treated safely with hypo-osmolal solutions (220 mOsm/kg). All demonstrated significant electrolyte retention as well as decreases in serum osmolality and blood glucose. One patient treated with saline failed to respond. In addition, it was found that volume repletion alone caused reductions in several glucoregulatory hormones (glucagon, epinephrine, norepinephrine, cortisol), as well as in plasma renin activity and aldosterone concentrations. These reports should not be used to suggest the exclusion of insulin from such a regimen, but to emphasize the importance of adequate early volume repletion.

During a severe osmotic diuresis, water is lost in excess of salt, as discussed above. Thus, current recommendations for fluid therapy include hypotonic solutions, generally 0.45 percent saline,[193] although for children or for hyponatremic adults initial therapy should be with isotonic saline.[151,189,190] In the event of hypotension or shock, initial replacement with isotonic saline is required. Recommendations regarding rates of administration in adults vary from 300 to 1000 ml/hr until an adequate urine output is established, which should then be followed by lower rates. Children require proportionately smaller amounts, on the order of 10 to 20 ml/kg/hr.[151] When the blood glucose falls to 250 mg/dl or less, glucose is usually added to the infusate to prevent hypoglycemia[151,188,191,193] and to lessen the risk of cerebral edema[193] (see below).

Most ketoacidotic patients have an increased plasma osmolality on admission, and treatment with hypotonic fluids generally results in a fall in osmolality over the first 13 hours, whereas this may not occur with isotonic fluid replacement.[143] The tonicity of the fluid administered has no effect on the volume retained.[143] As noted in early balance studies,[17,18] expansion of the extracellular space is generally complete within 48 hours after starting therapy, whereas intracellular rehydration may require 6 to 10 days.

At the beginning of treatment, the acidosis is normochloremic with an increased anion gap consisting of ketone anions replacing bicarbonate. Although metabolism of ketone anions should lower the anion gap and lead to the regeneration of previously titrated bicarbonate, even with adequate therapy the serum bicarbonate may in fact not rise.[194] This effect is probably related to ECF volume expansion,[195,196] resulting in an increased distribution space for bicarbonate.[194] Another important cause of the anion gap appears to be a temporary deficit of base equivalents lost as ketone bodies in the urine.[197] Continued treatment usually corrects the lag in serum bicarbonate and acidosis.

Most patients with ketoacidosis have a low or normal serum sodium on admission, but often develop transient hypernatremia during treatment.[143] Uncontrolled diabetes with or without ketosis is one of the more common causes of severe hypernatremia in adults.[198] It is probably not the administered salt per se that produces the hypernatremia. Fluid losses during ketoacidosis are hypotonic and would cause hypernatremia, but this is masked by the osmotic effects of the high glucose concentrations (see above). As the glucose falls, the pre-existing hypernatremia (and hyperchloremia) become manifest.[151] Supportive evidence for this mechanism is that there is an excellent inverse correlation between sodium and glucose concentrations during fluid replacement.[198] The risk of producing initial hypernatremia is probably outweighed by the need to maintain the intravascular volume with isotonic saline. On the other hand, hyponatremia before or during the early stages of treatment should alert one to the possibility of cerebral edema.

Potassium Replacement

Diabetic ketoacidosis is associated with large total body potassium deficits, but the serum potassium is usually normal or elevated on admission.[143,144] After several hours of therapy, however, severe and symptomatic or potentially fatal hypokalemia may occur.[143,144,199,200] Three factors contribute to the fall in serum potassium: fluid therapy tends to dilute the serum potassium, there is continued urinary loss of potassium,[143,201] and there is re-entry of potassium into cells with insulin therapy. The latter results from direct insulin effects on potassium transport, as well as from the correction of acidosis. Although administration of bicarbonate corrects the acidosis more rapidly than does saline, it has also been associated with lethal hypokalemia.[202] Increased potassium requirements have been observed with the administration of large amounts of bicarbonate (>250 mEq).[201] The issue of bicarbonate therapy in diabetic ketoacidosis remains controversial for several reasons, which will be discussed subsequently.

In order to avoid hypokalemia, large amounts of potassium may have to be administered during initial therapy. Generous quantities of potassium are particularly important if the serum potassium is low on admission. Potassium in concentrations of 20 to 40 mEq/liter of intravenous fluids has been recommended from the outset of therapy in recent reviews.[151,193] Such loads might, however, prove fatal if renal failure is also present, and potassium administration is therefore probably safer if delayed until after a good urine output has been established and an electrocardiogram has been taken to help identify the rare case of initial hyperkalemia.[201] Because the usual patient with ketoacidosis is young and without underlying renal insufficiency, current practice usually dictates potassium inclusion in the first fluid administered,[189,191,193] even before a serum potassium result is available. Close observation of the patient's clinical status and frequent serum potassium measurements are essential to avoid hypo- or hyperkalemia.[202] Since the total body potassium deficit may require some time to fully correct, oral potassium supplements should be provided after the acute episode has resolved.

Phosphorus Replacement

Diabetic patients in ketoacidosis have severe deficiencies of phosphorus despite normal or elevated serum phosphate concentrations on admisson.[18,143,203,204,205] Within hours of initiation of treatment with insulin the serum phosphate concentration falls precipitously in almost every patient, sometimes to concentrations below 1.0 mg/dl.[18,143,204] Certainly volume expansion and continued urinary losses contribute to the development of hypophosphatemia,[77,206,207] but undoubtedly the major factor is increased transport into cells for the phosphorylation of glucose in response to the effect of insulin.[36] The incidence of hypophosphatemia has been shown to correlate with the dose of insulin administered,[208,209] but even at low-dose infusion rates of insulin (0.1 U/kg/hr), significant declines in phosphate concentration have been observed.[209]

The complications of profound hypophosphatemia are multiple, and include rhabdomyolysis and acute renal failure,[210] diminished myocardial performance[211,212] with heart failure in rare instances,[213] and acute respiratory failure.[214] It is likely that hypophosphatemia causes decreased phosphorylation of glucose and that the resulting decline in intracellular ATP stores accounts for these consequences of hypophosphatemia.[211] Indeed, it has been shown in hypophosphatemic diabetic patients that treatment with phosphate without insulin improves glucose utilization.[215] There is no doubt that severe hypophosphatemia requires treatment. The current differences of opinion involve whether or not to treat all patients with diabetic acidosis with phosphate-containing fluids in order to prevent even mild hypophosphatemia and rapidly restore diminished red cell 2,3-DPG concentrations.

Several causes, including phosphorus deficiency, contribute to a reduced red cell 2,3-DPG concentration in ketoacidosis. The decrease in 2,3-DPG impairs peripheral oxygen release by hemoglobin (or a decrease in P_{50}), but this is initially counteracted by the effect of acidosis. As the acidosis is treated, however, the effects of decreased 2,3-DPG may become manifest, with impaired tissue oxygen delivery due to a leftward shift in the hemoglobin-oxygen dissociation curve.[170,171] As discussed by Kreisberg,[163] decreased peripheral oxygenation would theoretically require a severalfold increment in cardiac output in order to compensate for the potential decrease in tissue oxygen delivery. Without phosphate supplements it requires 3 to 4 days for red cell 2,3-DPG concentrations to become normal,[165] whereas with phosphate supplementation normality often (but not always[203]) occurs in 12 to 24 hours and presumably prevents the decrease in P_{50} that otherwise occurs.[216,217] In children, 2,3-DPG concentrations in erythrocytes may rise to normal within 24 hours without phosphate therapy.[218] Scant recent data exist to show a clinical benefit from phosphate therapy in ketoacidosis. The study by Franks and associates,[204] done during a time of higher mortality in diabetic ketoacidosis, did suggest that early phosphate replacement allowed more rapid correction of the acidosis, and hastened the resolution of coma and lowered mortality, although other workers[142,203] have not confirmed such an effect. Thus, in a recent study by Keller and Berger,[203] phosphate infusion prevented hypophosphatemia in diabetic ketoacidosis and hyperosmolar coma, but no improvement was observed in mental status or survival in 14 patients. The authors hypothesized that the short duration of hypophosphatemia in their patients, as opposed to the longer duration in the earlier study,[204] may have accounted for the apparent clinical ineffectiveness of phosphate therapy. Since phosphate is required for glucose metabolism, its deficiency could also contribute to a state of insulin resistance. This, in fact, has been demonstrated in dogs[75] and more recently in man.[219]

Phosphate therapy in diabetic ketoacidosis is most simply accomplished by giving phosphate intravenously or orally as a balanced phosphate salt, usually of potassium (about 1.0 mmol/kg). Early balance studies showed that phosphorus was avidly retained, often in amounts exceeding 50 percent of the administered dose.[143,204] However, a recent study showed urinary loss of nearly all administered phosphate, although the serum phosphorus remained normal.[203] Reviews in both the pediatric[220,221] and the adult literature suggest using potassium phosphate salts as the sole source of potassium for replacement. This may not be without hazard, especially in children. One recent study[222] described nine children treated with potassium phosphate solution (with phosphate at 20 to 40 mEq/liter) at rates designed to maintain normal serum phosphorus and potassium concentrations. Six developed transient hypocalcemia, five transient hypomagnesemia. One child with severe hypokalemia, treated with large amounts of potassium phosphate, developed carpopedal spasm responsive to magnesium but not to calcium supplements. In three patients, PTH concentrations were low during hypocalcemia, suggesting hypoparathyroidism, possibly related to magnesium deficiency.[223] These latter findings have recently been confirmed in another study.[224] Although the actual incidence of hypocalcemia and hypomagnesemia in patients treated in this manner is not known and certainly appears to be lower in adults, it may not be advisable to provide all potassium replacements as the phosphate salt.[203] Also, as pointed out by Lavis,[225] administration of phosphate early in the course of treatment to highly volume-contracted individuals with significant renal failure may be catastrophic. However, with proper attention to urinary output before large amounts of phosphate are given, such complications should be avoidable.

Calcium and Magnesium Replacement

In spite of a negative calcium balance in ketoacidosis, and the fact that serum calcium often falls below normal during therapy,[143] symptomatic hypocalcemia is rarely observed, with the possible exception, as noted above, of its occurrence during concomitant phosphate therapy.[222] Calcium supplements are therefore not usually indicated during the acute phase of therapy.

Magnesium concentrations tend to parallel those of potassium, generally falling to levels below normal within the first few hours of therapy.[143,153,161] These changes are related both to continued urinary loss and intracellular transport.[143] Tetany has been observed when acidosis was corrected without magnesium replacement.[153,222] Recommendations have been made for magnesium supplements of 5 mEq/liter of intravenous fluid[226] or a total provision of 0.2 mEq/kg.[143] Replacement of magnesium may also prevent impaired PTH secretion, noted above to be particularly important when phosphate supplements are administered.

Treatment of Acidosis

Concern has been expressed about whether the hazards of bicarbonate therapy outweigh the need for rapid correction of acidosis.[151,227] The effect of acidosis on mortality in the present era may not be as great as previously supposed, since mortality correlates better with the degree of hyperglycemia, uremia, and associated illnesses than with the severity of acidosis.[144,202] It is clear, however, that metabolic acidosis impairs myocardial contractility,[228,229] increases the frequency of cardiac arrhythmias,[230] compromises ventilatory function,[231] interferes with cellular metabolism, and may cause decreased insulin binding to cellular receptors, although increased β-hydroxybutyrate concentrations appear to compensate for this latter effect.[232]

Studies of recovery from ketoacidosis have suggested that there may be no differences in the rates of resolution of acidosis with or without bicarbonate therapy.[227,233,234] Some recent investigations of low-dose versus high-dose insulin therapy have minimized the use of bicarbonate with excellent recovery rates and survival.[189,233,235] Since β-hydroxybutyrate and acetoacetate are metabolized, volume expansion and insulin therapy should theoretically correct the acidosis without supplemental bicarbonate.

There are also several dangers inherent in the treatment of diabetic acidosis with bicarbonate. The distribution space of bicarbonate in severe metabolic acidosis may be over 200 percent of body weight,[236] but studies of acid production[237] have indicated that actual alkali requirements for the correction of acidosis are much smaller than predicted.[238] Excessive or too rapid administration of bicarbonate may accentuate the development of hypokalemia by enhancing potassium transport into cells,[158] result in impaired tissue oxygenation by mechanisms outlined above, and be associated with deepening of the comatose state.[239] The mechanism responsible for worsening of a coma in the face of an improving blood pH may be related to the paradoxical decrease in cerebrospinal fluid (CSF) pH that occurs.[239,240] However, this decrease is no greater with bicarbonate treatment than without,[240] and clinical improvement is usually progressive.[240,241] Current recommendations therefore suggest the use of little[193,242] or no[151] bicarbonate, particularly if the blood pH is above 7.0.

Cerebral Edema

Cerebral edema is a rare but frequently fatal complication occurring during treatment of diabetic ketoacidosis.[243] In the large series reported by Beigelman,[144] there were no identified episodes of cerebral edema. Cerebral edema is also seldom observed in nonketotic hyperosmolar coma, although it has been reported.[244] Typically, the patient is an adolescent diabetic with no underlying illness, often not initially comatose, who several hours after the beginning of therapy lapses into coma, becomes hyperpyrexic, and develops an elevated CSF pressure with papilledema. This episode occurs at a time when blood glucose is falling and blood pH is returning toward normal.[193] Associated factors have included overly rapid insulin and fluid therapy and initial hyponatremia,[193,245] although these have not yet been demonstrated to be causative. Treatment generally consists of large doses of glucocorticoids and mannitol, but the effectiveness of such therapy is not known.

The possible mechanisms of cerebral edema have recently been reviewed by Kreisberg,[163] and include paradoxical central nervous system acidosis, altered central nervous system oxygenation, and unfavorable osmotic gradients. As discussed previously, it is unlikely that paradoxical CSF acidosis deepens coma,[241] and there is no evidence or obvious mechanism to relate CSF acidosis to cerebral edema.

On the basis of the altered affinity of hemoglobin for oxygen during the treatment of acidosis (see above), it has been calculated that cardiac output would have to increase severalfold to maintain adequate oxygen delivery.[163] If such a deficit in oxygen delivery occurs, damage to brain cells would result and produce a breakdown in the blood-brain barrier, thus hastening water transfer down established osmotic gradients.

The major abnormality underlying the development of cerebral edema appears to be a rapid osmotic shift of water into nervous tissue that has remained hypertonic while the plasma osmolality has fallen with treatment.[246,247] A delay of several hours has been noted in the equilibration between CSF and plasma glucose levels following sudden changes in glucose concentrations in dogs.[246] Because CSF concentrations of sorbitol and fructose were elevated, it was suggested that the sorbitol or polyol pathway of conversion of glucose to sugar alcohols had contributed to the generation and maintenance of intracellular hyperosmolarity,[220] since fructose and sorbitol are not transported well across membranes.[248] However, subsequent measurements of sorbitol and other sugars have shown that the amounts present in brain tissue do not account for the degree of intracellular hyperosmolarity that develops.[249] It has been found in rabbits that during sustained hyperglycemia (4 hours), the brain retains intracellular volume by generating osmotically active particles, termed ''idiogenic osmoles'' because they have not yet been identified.[247] These may take some time to dissipate even though the glucose concentration declines in the interstitial space, thus creating an unfavorable osmotic gradient.

The development of an osmotic gradient of greater than 45 mOsm/kg has been shown to cause cerebral edema, a situation that might occur when the blood glucose is lowered rapidly to less than 300 mg/dl.[250] An elevated CSF pressure was found in five patients over the first 10 hours of therapy when the blood glucose was lowered rapidly, but was apparently well tolerated.[251] Although the factors that cause the rare patient to develop cerebral edema have yet to be fully elucidated, it seems clear from accumulated evidence that marked falls in glucose and overly vigorous fluid replacement (greater than 4 liters/m^2/24 hr) should be avoided.[245]

Hyperglycemic Hyperosmolar Nonketotic Coma

Clinical Characteristics

Patients with hyperglycemic, hyperosmolar, nonketotic coma or hyperosmolar coma are distinguished from those with diabetic ketoacidosis primarily on the basis of a serum glucose above 600 mg/dl, a serum osmolality above 350 mOsm/kg, and absent or minimal ketosis and acidosis.[138] There are several clinical differences as well. The syndrome is usually seen in females[252] and in the elderly or infirm, although occurrences have been described in young children.[253] Most patients either have mild diabetes or no previous history of the disease.[252,254-256] It may be brought on by burns,[257,258] by the infusion[259] or ingestion[256] of glucose containing fluids, by dialysis with hypertonic glucose solutions,[259-261] and by hypothermia.[262] In those patients who do manifest glucose intolerance there are usually precipitating illnesses, such as are found in diabetic ketoacidosis, including infection,[252,255,256] stroke,[255,256,263] acute pancreatitis,[264,265] and endocrinopathies such as acromegaly[266] or thyrotoxicosis.[267] Hyperosmolar coma is also uniquely associated with various drugs that are known to inhibit insulin secretion or action, including diphenylhydantoin[268,269] corticosteroids,[270] diazoxide,[271] diuretics,[272] and propranolol.[273]

On presentation, the patient with hyperosmolar coma appears profoundly dehydrated, with obtundation of varying severity but without Kussmaul respirations. Focal neurologic defects or seizures are commonly observed, in contrast to ketoacidosis.[244,256,274] Two additional features that distinguish hyperosmolar coma from diabetic ketoacidosis and probably contribute significantly to the development and maintenance of the hyperosmolarity are a prolonged osmotic diuresis and underlying renal disease. The duration of the prodromal symptoms related to an osmotic diuresis is usually days to weeks rather than hours to days,[254–256,263] allowing greater loss of fluid and electrolytes, and possibly playing a role in inducing hyperglycemia without ketosis.[275] Arieff[138] suggests that this is because patients with impending hyperosmolar coma only become more unresponsive as their illness progresses, while those going into ketoacidosis may manifest symptoms such as hyperventilation, nausea and vomiting, and vascular collapse which bring them to medical attention sooner. On admission, volume depletion in hyperosmolar coma is often so severe that oliguria is present. In most[255,275] but not all[256] instances, renal function improves with therapy; however, there is usually a degree of renal insufficiency present that does not resolve and which may contribute to hyperglycemia.

Effects of Hyperglycemia and Hyperosmolarity

Hyperglycemia in the hyperosmolar syndrome initially develops from a relative rather than absolute lack of insulin, even though peripheral insulin concentrations in the two diseases are often similar.[276] Drugs or stressful illnesses causing tissue resistance to the available insulin, rather than the lack of insulin that occurs in ketoacidosis, are major factors contributing to the hyperglycemia of hyperosmolar coma (see Fig. 10-1).

The development of hyperglycemia produces water flow from cells, and at least temporarily expands intravascular volume. The "threshold" for glucose loss in the urine may be elevated, possibly related to coexisting renal disease, and may prevent significant glycosuria until the blood glucose is 250 to 300 mg/dl. Once begun, the glycosuric diuresis interferes with renal reabsorption of water even in the presence of antidiuretic hormone (ADH), the concentration of which is probably rising at this stage. Perhaps because many patients who develop hyperosmolar coma are not initially acutely ill, they are able to take in enough water to maintain a delicate balance. Even a mild insult at this stage, however, may prevent intake from keeping up with output, and lead to a more rapid progression of the hyperosmolarity. The thirst drive is not appropriate to the state of dehydration.[134] Some patients appear to tolerate very high blood glucose concentrations (and associated serum osmolalities) very well. This tolerance may be related to the chronicity of the hyperglycemia. Progressive unreplaced water losses in the urine are replaced in the ECF by water from cells; greater intracellular dehydration probably occurs in this syndrome than in ketoacidosis, and contributes to the more frequent metabolic-neurologic abnormalities discussed below. The plasma volume eventually falls with the loss of salt and water, leading to marked hemoconcentration and hypotension. Renal blood flow and glomerular filtration decline, serving to further accentuate the hyperglycemia.[135] Hypertonicity and ECF volume depletion also diminish insulin secretion,[255] further compromising the subject's ability to metabolize glucose. The blood glucose may rise above 2000 mg/dl in some instances.

Serum osmolarity, either calculated from

the formula given previously or measured directly, is almost always elevated at the time of admission. The presence of high glucose concentrations creates a dilutional hyponatremia that may obscure the truly hyperosmolar state. On the other hand, significant azotemia, which does not contribute to effective osmotic pressure across the semipermeable cell membrane, will be measured with an osmometer and gives a false impression of the degree of dehydration.[254] The urine osmolality in hyperosmolar coma is low relative to the marked elevations in plasma osmolality;[247] this discrepancy is probably due to the effects of the osmotic diuresis causing greater water than solute loss.[129] The osmotic diuresis, as suggested by Arieff and Carroll,[256] probably protects the kidney from acute tubular necrosis related to markedly decreased renal perfusion.[277] This situation may be reversed when treatment lowers the blood glucose rapidly and the protective effect of the osmotic diuresis is lost.[256]

The renal loss of water in excess of solute in conjunction with severe hyperglycemia produces a hypertonic state,[254] which accounts for most but probably not all of the central nervous system alterations found in hyperosmolar coma.[254,278] Although only short-lived neurologic deficits are produced by agents such as hypertonic urea, which induce only transient water shifts,[279] solutes such as sodium or glucose, which do not leave the extracellular space, produce deficits that last as long as the hypertonicity persists.[130,279] A rapid increase in blood glucose in animals has been shown to cause cerebral dehydration and death within 90 minutes.[280] Dural and intracerebral hemorrhages have also been found following hypertonic saline treatment, but not after hypertonic urea infusions.[279] Such hemorrhages could result from brain shrinkage in the cranial vault.[254]

Extracellular hyperosmolarity has been shown to correlate with changes in the sensorium in hyperosmolar coma;[147,256,281-284] coma seldom develops unless the osmolarity exceeds 350 mOsm/kg.[255] However, this does not always indicate intracellular dehydration, since patients who die with hyperosmolar coma usually do not have evidence of cerebral dehydration at autopsy.[282,285] Because hyperosmolarity develops at a relatively slow rate in hyperosmolar coma, intracellular dehydration may well be compensated. Recent evidence[247] confirms earlier suggestions[279] that protection may arise from the generation of "idiogenic osmoles" within the cells of the brain. Elevation of plasma glucose in rabbits to about 60 mM over a 1-to-2-hour period produces an initial loss in brain water content. This deficit is repaired within 4 hours in the brain but not in skeletal muscle.[247] The increase in brain water is accompanied by an increase in brain solute. Part of this solute (about 50 percent) is explained by increased concentrations of intracellular ions (sodium, potassium, chloride), glucose, polyols, and intermediary metabolites, but much of it cannot be explained.[247] Other studies have also failed to find markedly increased intracellular amounts of glucose,[249] sorbitol,[249] or myoinositol[249] in brain tissue. Although generation of known and unknown solutes may protect the brain from dehydration, it may also have profound effects on cellular processes and cause cerebral dysfunction. Other factors that may contribute to cerebral dysfunction in hyperosmolar coma are the age of the patient, concurrent illness, and cerebral atherosclerosis,[278] with the final effect being decreased oxygen consumption by the brain.[285]

The total body water deficit in hyperosmolar coma (an average of 9 to 10 liters) is about twice that found in ketoacidosis.[138,255,258]

Electrolyte Derangements

Electrolyte deficits in hyperosmolar coma are usually less than those observed in diabetic ketoacidosis (Table 10-2), despite the prolonged osmotic diuresis.

The initial serum sodium concentration is quite variable (120 to 160 mEq/liter),[255,256,275] probably owing to the degree of hyperglycemia and water loss. Retention of sodium over 36 hours of therapy averages 307 mEq, or about 80 percent of the administered amount.[256]

Serum potassium concentrations are often normal on admission,[255,256,263,274] but belie the underlying total body potassium depletion. During 36 hours of therapy, patients with hyperosmolar coma retained an average of 137 mEq of administered potassium.[256] As with diabetic ketoacidosis, potassium loss is primarily through the kidney, and is related to both the osmotic diuresis and the effects of elevated aldosterone concentrations on the distal tubule.[255]

Little attention has been given to losses of other ions in the development of hyperosmolar coma, although phosphorus, calcium, and magnesium deficits probably parallel those in diabetic ketoacidosis.

Change in Acid-Base Status

A mild metabolic acidosis is often observed in adults with hyperosmolar coma,[255,256,263] with the arterial pH seldom below 7.20.[256] In children the pH may be lower, however.[286] The degree of ketosis is by definition mild, but since the nitroprusside reagent commonly used to detect ketones does not give a positive result with β-hydroxybutyric acid, some cases of significant ketoacidosis may be misdiagnosed. Lactic acidosis has been considered a cause of the acidosis in nonketotic coma,[253,287] but recent lactate measurements[256] suggest that lactate excess is not frequent. Acidosis of renal origin may also be a contributing factor, since these patients often have a significant degree of underlying chronic renal failure.[255,256,275] Hypertonic infusions have also been shown to cause severe acidosis in animals,[288,289] possibly owing to the release of hydrogen ions, phosphate, chloride, and other anions from cells. Even patients without acidosis often have an excess of unmeasured anion.[256] In most patients with hyperosmolar coma, therefore, acidosis probably has several causes.

The causes for the lack of ketosis in hyperosmolar coma have not been established, and remain an area of controversy. Peripheral insulin concentrations in the syndrome have been found adequate to inhibit lipolysis as (assessed by circulating free fatty acids) in some[255,256] but not all studies.[290,291] A more likely hypothesis centers on the fact that the liver may be adequately insulinized (receiving blood directly from the pancreas via the portal vein) to suppress fatty acid oxidation to ketones and shunt substrate toward triglyceride and very low density lipoprotein (VLDL) synthesis, but not adequately insulinized to prevent excessive hepatic glucose output.[292] Direct experimental evidence on this point is not yet available.

Treatment of Hyperosmolar Nonketotic Coma

In patients with hyperosmolar coma, as in the case of diabetic ketoacidosis, insulin therapy and replacement of fluid and electrolyte deficits are the major factors in treatment. Precipitating events or concurrent illnesses require close attention, since they contribute substantially to the observed mortality.[255,256]

Therapy of the metabolic disorder involves lowering the extremely high blood glucose concentrations and correcting fluid and electrolyte deficits. Insulin therapy may be effectively accomplished with low-[128,242] or high-dose[255,256] regimens, although the latter may be associated with a higher incidence of hypoglycemia in this disease.[256] It is widely recommended that glucose-containing fluids (5 percent glucose) be included as the blood glucose approaches 250 mg/dl.[128,242,255,273] Insulin should also be given intravenously when hypotension or shock is present.

Initial fluid and electrolyte therapy remains an area of controversy. McCurdy[254] has divided the major aspects of treatment into three stages: repair of marked sodium deficits, rapid but incomplete replacement of water losses, and finally a cautious return of body composition and fluid volume to normal. The use of hypotonic saline (0.45 percent) is recommended by some[255,283,293] in order to restore water losses that have exceeded salt losses during the development of the syndrome, as well as to avoid severe hypernatremia. Relative water and monovalent cation losses (about 60 mEq/liter[256] in fact approximate the NaCl concentration in half-normal saline (77 mEq/liter), and further indicate the use of the latter.[138] Other sources stress the use of normal saline at least initially, to stablize the blood pressure and establish a good urine flow.[254–256,294] Elderly patients, particularly those with known atherosclerotic disease, require placement of a central venous pressure line.[242,255] In a patient who is hypertonic, normal saline is relatively hypotonic. Furthermore, isotonic saline quickly provides the salt necessary to prevent hypovolemic shock and attendant thrombotic complications, while hypotonic saline may not provide salt quickly enough.[254,294] The use of saline should be avoided when the blood pressure is elevated or when congestive heart failure or peripheral edema is present.[254] Significant hypernatremia represents another situation in which isotonic saline may not be indicated.[275]

Once the blood pressure and urine output are stable, McCurdy[254] suggests repair of water deficits. It is estimated that the patient with hyperosmolar coma has lost about 24 percent of total body water,[256,281] one-half of which should be replaced over the first 12 hours and the remainder over the next 12 hours. Also, ongoing losses due to continuing osmotic diuresis should be corrected.[254,256] The treatment must be tailored to the individual patient. During this stage of water replacement, half-normal saline is probably the best fluid to use, supplemented by oral fluid intake where possible. Hypotonic saline repairs residual sodium deficits and provides for losses in the urine, which may continue to be as high as 30 to 50 mEq/liter.[254] Serum sodium is variable during treatment, but usually remains in the normal range,[255] despite the fall in blood glucose and influx of water back into cells.

Total body potassium, as described previously, is depleted, and the serum potassium invariably falls after several hours of treatment.[255] Potassium supplements of 10 to 20 mEq/liter of intravenous fluid are usually given at this point rather than in the initial stage of therapy because of the possibility of oliguria.[242] It has been suggested that initial hypokalemia merits early treatment with larger amounts of potassium.[255]

The replacement of phosphorus and magnesium has generally been given little attention, but as with ketoacidosis, these minerals should be replaced as needed following measurement of their serum concentrations during treatment. In contrast to diabetic ketoacidosis, erythrocyte 2,3-DPG concentrations have not been found to be depressed in hyperosmolar coma.[203]

The second phase of fluid and electrolyte replacement generally ends when the calculated or measured serum osmolality falls to 325 mOsm/kg or below.[254] At this point many patients can take fluids orally, and glycosuria is under control. Renal mechanisms can regulate volume and ECF composition, although as in ketoacidosis, it may take a week or longer to fully correct deficits.

Complications of Therapy

Insulin therapy may rapidly lower the blood glucose in patients with hyperosmolar coma, and this in turn may result in an osmotic gradient down which water flows back into cells. Severe hypovolemia, hypotension, and oliguria may result. This latter sequence of events was presumably the cause of the shock that developed several hours after insulin was given to 6 of 32 patients reported by Arieff and Carroll.[256] Five other patients in the same series developed oliguria without hypotension, effects related by Arieff and Carroll[256] to a decrease in glycosuria and loss of the protective effect against acute tubular necrosis by an osmotic diuresis.[277] The fact that initial treatment with insulin and half-normal rather than isotonic saline may further accentuate such phenomena has recently been confirmed.[295] McCurdy[254] noted a correlation between the dose of insulin and ECF volume contraction, but this has not been confirmed. Even patients who do not present with hypotension or oliguria may therefore be subject to an insulin-induced decrease in ECF volume. The treatment of therapy-induced hypotension involves giving volume expanders such as saline, albumin, or low molecular weight dextran at a rapid rate.[138]

Patients with heart failure and fluid overload, on the other hand, may show symptomatic improvement when insulin treatment lowers a severely elevated blood glucose.[295] Hyperglycemia has also been noted to exacerbate congestive heart failure.[296] This is particularly true when severe renal failure is present and renal loss of glucose cannot occur.[297]

Cerebral edema has been reported in hyperosmolar coma[244] but its occurrence is much less frequent than in ketoacidosis.[255,256] Studies with animal models indicate that an elevated CSF pressure may occur with severe hyperglycemia,[288] but this apparently does not occur in man.[256] Cerebrospinal fluid glucose falls more slowly than plasma glucose during the treatment of hyperosmolar coma.[256] The osmotic balance, however, is maintained by the generation of other solutes in brain tissue, as discussed previously. If the blood glucose is lowered rapidly and hypotonic fluid is administered, the CSF osmolality may lag so far behind the plasma osmolality that convulsions ensue.[298] Irsigler and associates have advocated the use of hypertonic solutions (about 310 to 365 mOsm/kg) in the treatment of hyperosmolar coma in order to maintain a slow, controlled decrease in osmolarity of the ECF (2 to 4 mOsm/hr) and CSF.[299,300]

In light of these studies, it is probably safest to lower the blood glucose slowly. If hypotonic fluids are administered, blood pressure and renal function should be monitored quite frequently.

Lactic Acidosis

Development

Lactic acidosis may sometimes be found in diabetic patients with ketoacidosis,[301–303] although patients whose diabetes is under control generally do not have lactate concentrations greatly different from normal.[304–308] Furthermore, since the removal of phenformin from general use, Kreisberg, in a recent review,[307] noted little association between lactic acidosis and diabetes mellitus. On the other hand, there are several features of diabetes mellitus and particularly ketoacidosis that might predispose to lactate overproduction. These features include poor circulation caused by micro- or macrovascular disease; altered hemoglobin affinity for oxygen related to a decreased erythrocyte 2,3-DPG concentration (in ketoacidosis only) or an increased glycosylated hemoglobin in erythrocytes; increased blood viscosity; and abnormal platelet function.[307]

The sole means of removing accumulated lactate in mammals is to convert it to pyruvate via lactate dehydrogenase (LDH); the equilibrium of LDH lies far to the left:

Pyruvic acid + NADH$_2$

$$\xleftrightarrow{\text{LDH}} \text{lactic acid} + \text{NAD}$$

Circulating lactate concentrations in diabetic patients were found to be slightly elevated.[308] The serum lactate elevation was probably due to increased muscle lactate production (twofold greater than in nondiabetic individuals), which could not be completely corrected by increased hepatic extraction.[308] After 30 minutes of exercise, the excessive lactate production was even more pronounced.[308] The increased muscle lactate production is probably caused by impaired pyruvate oxidation in diabetes. In perfused skeletal muscle, the rate of lactate oxidation in diabetic animals was only one-fourth that of controls.[309] The impairment appears to lie in an inhibition of pyruvate dehydrogenase activity,[310] which decreases pyruvate (and lactate) oxidation and shunts more lactate toward gluconeogenesis.[311] Elevated ketone and fatty acid concentrations may contribute substantially to the inhibition of pyruvate dehydrogenase in uncontrolled diabetes.[312] An experimental rabbit model has been developed in which an irreversible lactic acidosis occurs in one-half the animals.[313] The rabbits were first made diabetic with alloxan, then infused with β-hydroxbutyrate to deplete nicotinamide-adenine dinucleotide (NAD), and finally alkalinized with bicarbonate. The need to produce the diabetic state in these animals in order to cause lactic acidosis may indicate a similar predisposition in human patients with diabetes.

Despite the biochemical tendency to develop increased lactate concentrations and acidosis in diabetes, as noted above, clinical lactic acidosis is not common in diabetes or diabetic ketoacidosis. It is likely that lactic acidosis develops in diabetes because of shock, hypotension, or regional tissue hypoperfusion related to events or illnesses other than uncompensated diabetes per se.

Clinical Diagnosis

The diagnosis of nonketotic diabetic acidosis due to lactate accumulation should be suspected in the diabetic patient with a metabolic acidosis and increased anion gap (25 mEq/liter or greater), but with minimal or absent ketosis.[303] The measurement of lactate in the blood is required to confirm the diagnosis. Blood or plasma lactate concentrations are normally between 0.5 and 1.5 mM.[307] Lactate concentrations of 7 mM or greater are observed if the acidosis is severe,[305] but 4- to 5-mM concentrations in the presence of significant acidosis are considered diagnostic of lactic acidosis.[303,314]

There is a factor that may complicate the diagnosis of lactic acidosis in the diabetic patient with metabolic acidosis when lactate measurements are unavailable. If the patient has ketoacidosis due to increased β-hydroxybutyrate concentrations, the nitroprusside test for serum or urine ketones may be falsely negative, since the reagent detects acetoacetate but not β-hydroxybutyrate.[315,316] Fulop and associates[302] have stressed the possibility of underestimating the degree of ketosis in diabetic patients with acidosis. Diabetic ketoacidosis related to excess β-hydroxybutyrate may not be uncommon,[302,316] and it has been suggested that lactic acidosis may contribute to such a state.[317] On thermodynamic grounds it is more likely that β-hydroxybutyrate acidosis predisposes to lactic acidosis.

Kussmaul-type respirations are usually present on admission in both diabetic ketoacidosis and lactic acidosis. However, the sudden development of such a pattern of hyperventilation strongly suggests lactic acidosis, since ketoacidosis is usually slower to develop.[305] In pure diabetic ketoacidosis, the increase in anion gap usually accounts exactly for the fall in bicarbonate, while in lactic acidosis the anion gap may be greater than the decrease in bicarbonate concentration.[305] The reasons for this discrepancy are unclear, since lactic acid is a strong organic acid (pK_a = 3.8), and is completely dissociated at physiologic pH.

Several conditions may predispose to the development of secondary lactic acidosis in a diabetic patient. Such conditions include shock,[305] ethylene glycol ingestion, salicylate overdose, and acute alcohol intoxication.[307] Alcoholic ketoacidosis may coexist with lactic acidosis,[318,319] but can be distinguished from diabetic ketosis by the lack of a significant elevation in blood glucose. Diabetes, and particularly ketoacidosis in diabetes, may theoretically contribute to the development of lactic acidosis, as discussed above, but most authors of clinical studies suggest that the two occur together because of concomitant underlying tissue hypoperfusion, and not because of ketoacidosis per se.[199,305,307]

The persistence of metabolic acidosis during apparently successful treatment of diabetic ketoacidosis (i.e., in the presence of a falling blood glucose and ketonemia) should also suggest lactic acidosis.[307] During the treatment of ketoacidosis, diabetic patients may have increases in lactate concentrations unrelated to lactate infusion.[301,320,321] In experimental ketoacidosis, blood lactate concentrations have also been noted to increase with insulin therapy.[322,323] This effect was related to the inhibition of gluconeogenesis by insulin, and secondarily to reduced hepatic lactate extraction.[322] Although several cases of fatal lactic acidosis have been reported during therapy for diabetic ketoacidosis,[301,324] these were probably due to severe shock from fulminating gastroenteritis. In the absence of tissue hypoperfusion, increased lactate concentrations occurring during the treatment of ketoacidosis usually resolve spontaneously.[301,321]

Phenformin-Induced Lactic Acidosis

Diabetic patients taking phenformin have shown an increased incidence of lactic acidosis.[303] Although the drug has several effects, excessive lactate production is probably related to impairment of aerobic metabolism in the liver,[325,326] which is essential for the oxidation of NADH. In the presence of renal insufficiency (allowing phenformin to accumulate) or hepatic dysfunction (impairing lactate metabolism even further), the incidence of lactic acidosis in patients treated with phenformin was especially high.[327] The results of the University Group Diabetes Program study also showed that phenformin therapy was associated with a death rate from cardiovascular events about twice that found in insulin- or diet-treated subjects.[328] Primarily because of the "unacceptably high risk" of lactic acidosis (between 0.25 and 4.0 cases per 1,000 users per year), the United States Food and Drug Administration removed phenformin from the general market in 1977.[329]

Therapy of Lactic Acidosis in the Diabetic Patient

The most important factor in the treatment of lactic acidosis, whether diabetes is present or not, is to remove the precipitating causes and improve tissue perfusion. Lactic acidosis may be a preterminal event, but in many instances aggressive volume repletion, assisted ventilation, and more specific treatment may reverse the course of events. As tissue perfusion and oxygenation are improved, lactic acid will be converted to pyruvate with subsequent oxidative metabolism. Despite the fact that insulin treatment may transiently increase blood lactate concentrations, as noted above, the diabetic patient with uncontrolled blood glucose and lactic acidosis must be treated with insulin. This is especially true if a component of ketoacidosis is present that will respond readily to insulin with an increase in pH.

The role of bicarbonate therapy in the treatment of diabetic patients with severe lactic acidosis is uncertain. Alkalinization may enhance lactic acid production by increasing peripheral tissue glycolysis,[313,330] and as noted above, is an essential component in an animal model of lactic acidosis.[313] On the other hand, liver extraction of lactate should also improve as pH increases.[307] Bicarbonate therapy, however, continues to be important in the treatment of lactic acidosis, and bicarbonate requirements in this condition may be quite high.[303]

Recent reports indicate that dichloroacetate may be effective in lowering blood lactate concentrations in many situations of excess lactate production. This phenomenon may be particularly true for lactic acidosis occurring in diabetic patients, since blood glucose may also be lowered with dichloroacetate therapy.[305,306,323,331,332] Dichloroacetate activates pyruvate dehydrogenase in several tissues, and promotes the oxidation of glucose, lactate, and pyruvate.[323,333] This finding may be particularly relevant for the reversal of pyruvate dehydrogenase inhibition in diabetes (see above). Four diabetic patients treated with oral dichloroacetate had dramatic decreases in plasma lactate concentrations, although in only three of them was the lactate elevated (between 1.5 and 3 mM) prior to therapy.[331] Diabetic rats with ketoacidosis have also been shown to respond to dichloroacetate with a lowering of blood lactate concentrations.[323] The response in severe lactic acidosis is not yet known. Neurologic complications associated with the use of dichloroacetate may limit the usefulness of this particular agent.[334]

Other therapies advocated for severe lactic acidosis include the use of vasodilators,[335] oxidation-reduction agents,[303] and dialysis.[336] Only the last appears to be of consistent help in reversing lactic acidosis.

Hypoglycemic Coma in the Diabetic Patient

Several changes related to fluid and volume homeostasis may occur during symptomatic hypoglycemia. As discussed in the section on the effects of insulin on blood volume and vascular permeability, rapid insulinization causes decreased vascular volume and increased vascular permeability.[87] These effects are due to insulin and not hypoglycemia, since they occur even though the blood glucose does not fall to hypoglycemic concentrations.[87]

The falling blood glucose in the intravascular space also induces osmotic fluid shifts toward the intracellular spaces. This fluid movement may be relevant in the causation of the multiple central nervous system abnormalities of hypoglycemic coma, since many patients show evidence of cerebral edema at autopsy.[138] Indeed, the seizures associated with insulin administration have been shown to occur at a time when brain glucose concentrations are normal.[337] An early increase in brain sodium, potassium, and osmolality may also be a direct effect of insulin, predisposing to later water influx and edema formation.[307] While such evidence suggests a role for insulin-induced electrolyte abnormalities in the genesis of hypoglycemic coma, the osmotic effects of a falling plasma glucose concentration or intracellular hypoglycemia may also be operative.

Insulin "Edema"

Edema formation during insulin therapy was described several years after insulin became available,[338] but the mechanism of edema formation is still not completely understood. Diabetic patients in poor control who are treated with insulin and sodium-containing fluids are known to retain sizable quantities of administered sodium.[17,18,143] As discussed in the section on physiologic effects of insulin, it is most likely that the rapid onset of sodium retention relates to a direct renal tubular effect of insulin that increases Na^+ transport.[21,23] In some patients the sodium retention may actually result in clinical edema formation.[338–341] This fluid retention may be particularly evident if one attempts to restore salt and water losses within 12 to 24 hours.[151,339] The phenomenon is not restricted to diabetic ketoacidosis, but may be seen with hyperglycemia in varying severity.[20] Studies in both man[20] and rats[154] have shown that enhanced sodium retention may last for several days. The fall in sodium excretion did not correlate with the decrease in glycosuria or ketonuria, or with the degree of pre-existing sodium depletion.[20,154] Although only two of the humans studied developed overt edema, the average weight gain was 1.45 kg (range: 0.35 to 2.5 kg).[20] Besides a direct insulin effect, other possible factors contributing to the formation of insulin "edema" include elevated aldosterone concentrations, antinatriuresis related to normalization of the serum pH,[151] increased vascular permeability related to insulin therapy,[340,341] and a fall in the glucagon concentration.[154] The latter hypothesis suggests a parallel between insulin "edema" and resolution of the natriuresis of fasting.[154] As pointed out earlier, sustained aldosterone elevations are possible, but plasma renin activity falls rapidly with insulin therapy.

The edema is seldom clinically significant, usually resolves spontaneously over 24 to 48 hours without specific therapy, and is said to respond rapidly to furosemide.[151]

Divalent Cation Homeostasis in Chronic Diabetes Mellitus

Diabetic patients presumably under adequate control (at least not in overt ketoacidosis) have been shown to have abnormalities of divalent cation balance.

Calcium

Uncontrolled glycosuria causes excessive renal loss of calcium in the urine, as discussed in the section on ketoacidosis. Raskin and colleagues[67] studied 20 diabetic patients with poor control of their disease but not ketoacidosis, and found 10 who exhibited significant hypercalciuria (greater than 200 mg/24 hr on a 400 mg/day calcium intake).[342] After vigorous insulin therapy, urinary calcium excretion fell in all but 2 subjects, and 5 of the 10 initially hypercalciuric subjects were no longer hypercalciuric.[67] The fall in urinary calcium excretion correlated well with the fall in glycosuria induced by insulin treatment. The authors suggested that uncontrolled glycosuria causes renal hypercalciuria, which could result in secondary hyperparathyroidism and bone loss. In support of this, urinary cyclic adenosine monophosphate (cAMP) activity was found to be in the high normal range, and decreased significantly following treatment. Parathyroid hormone measurements were not done.

It is possible that hypercalciuria could contribute to the osteopenia that has been observed in both adults[343,344] and children[345] with diabetes mellitus. Such an association, if causal, provides further impetus for closer blood sugar control in diabetes.

Magnesium

In an analysis of 5,100 subjects[346] diabetes mellitus was the disease most commonly associated with hypomagnesemia. Previous studies had also shown a high prevalence of hypomagnesemia in patients with both maturity and juvenile onset diabetes.[347] Of several chronic illnesses, diabetes was associated with the lowest serum magnesium concentrations.[346] Furthermore, the degree of hypomagnesemia was found to correlate with the severity of diabetes as assessed by fasting blood glucose concentrations[346] or by the amount of insulin required for "control."[347] Ketonuria was not present in the diabetic patients with the lowest serum magnesium concentrations.[346] The results have been confirmed in more recent studies[348,349] of both insulin-requiring and non-insulin-requiring diabetic patients. It has been suggested that the glycosuric diuresis in poorly controlled diabetic patients accounts for the low magnesium concentrations observed,[348] as well as for the reportedly decreased soft tissue stores of magnesium.[350] It has also been reported that diabetic patients with more serious retinopathy also had significantly lower concentrations of magnesium than other diabetic patients,[348] thus linking magnesium deficiency with diabetic complications. However, if magnesium loss is related to poor control and associated glycosuria, the retinopathy may well relate to complications of poor control other than hypomagnesmia.

Hyporeninemic Hypoaldosteronism and Diabetes Mellitus

Definition and Association with Diabetes Mellitus

Isolated or selective hypoaldosteronism appears to be a heterogenous disorder with two major forms. The first or primary form is quite rare and is found in subjects (usually infants) with a deficiency or blockage of the activity of the enzymes catalyzing the final steps in aldosterone biosynthesis, 18-hydroxlase[351] and 17-hydroxydehydrogenase.[352] An acquired blockage of 18-hydroxylase activity has also been noted in patients on chronic heparin therapy.[353] In these conditions plasma renin activity is usually normal or elevated. A second disorder of aldosterone deficiency is hyporeninemic hypoaldosteronism, which, as its name implies, is associated with low plasma renin activity and thus may be secondary (at least in part) to a deficit in the renin-angiotensin system.

The syndrome of hyporeninemic hypoaldosteronism was first described in 1957,[354] but was not well characterized for over a decade.[355,356] A major finding in this disorder is hyperkalemia, which is often associated with a mild or moderate degree of renal insufficiency.[355-358] Affected persons are often of advanced age. Plasma renin activity and plasma aldosterone are inappropriately low and respond minimally or not at all to short-term sodium depletion, adrenocorticotropin, upright posture, exogenous catecholamines, and angiotensin II.[355,357,358] Glucocorticoid secretion is normal.[355,358] Important in the current context is that as many as 46 percent of the reported patients have diabetes mellitus.[359] Several features of the diabetic state have been suggested to contribute to the genesis of hyporeninemic hypoaldosteronism, and particularly to its most clinically significant feature—hyperkalemia.

Possible Causes of Hyporeninemic Hypoaldosteronism and Nonuremic Hyperkalemia in Diabetes Mellitus

The renin-angiotensin system in uncomplicated diabetes has been shown to function normally.[360] However, in diabetes complicated by hypertension with nephropathy,[360] or in diabetes with neuropathy and orthostatic hypotension,[361] diminished plasma renin activity and responsiveness to standard stimuli have been found. Rats with alloxan diabetes also showed suppression of plasma renin activity proportional to the degree of hyperglycemia (not necessarily glycosuria) produced in these animals.[362] These observations suggest several factors that might contribute to diminished plasma renin activity in diabetes (see Table 10-3): (1) decreased catecholamine stimulation of renin secretion secondary to autonomic neuropathy,[361] (2) structural renal damage with impairment of function of the juxtaglomerular apparatus,[363] (3) defective renin

Table 10-3. Possible Causes of the Features of Hyporeninemic Hypoaldosteronism in Diabetes Mellitus

Decreased plasma renin activity
 Decreased catecholamine stimulation (autonomic neuropathy)
 Structural damage to the juxtaglomerular apparatus
 Defective renin synthesis
 Suppression from chronic volume expansion
 Hyperkalemia
 Defective renal prostaglandin synthesis (?)

Diminished plasma aldosterone
 Decreased plasma renin activity
 Block(s) in the zona glomerulosa biosynthesis of aldosterone

Hyperkalemia
 Diminished aldosterone effect
 Acidosis
 Specific tubular defect in potassium secretion
 Defective tolerance to chronic potassium overload

synthesis,[364,365] and (4) expanded blood volume related to poor diabetic control.[363,366]

Defective synthesis of renin has been observed in diabetics with neuropathy.[364,365] In these patients most of the renin was in the form of prorenin, which is relatively inactive. The prevalence of defective renin biosynthesis in diabetes is not known, although it could contribute to the low plasma aldosterone concentrations observed. The presence of prorenin may also be related to a damaged juxtaglomerular apparatus caused by diabetic renal disease.[365]

The possibility that either defective or absent renin biosynthesis in diabetes relates to damage to the juxtaglomerular apparatus is quite plausible. Most diabetic patients with decreased plasma renin activity have some degree of nephropathy.[363] Diabetic nephropathy in turn is known to cause either sclerosis of the juxtaglomerular cells or encasement of them in fibrosclerotic material associated with afferent arteriolar hyalinization.[367-369] The sclerosis was observed to separate the macula densa and juxtaglomerular cells.[368,369] Not only were arterioles in the vicinity also observed to be sclerotic, but renin-containing cells were found in decreased numbers.[368] These changes could impair signal transmission to the juxtaglomerular apparatus and result in decreased renin secretion. Not only may low catecholamines in diabetes with autonomic neuropathy lead to decreased renin secretion, but it is also possible that sympathetic innervation of the juxtaglomerular apparatus[370] is disrupted by the sclerotic changes and that this further contributes to decreased renin responsiveness. Sclerosis around and within the juxtaglomerular apparatus appears to be unique to diabetes. Among 602 diseased kidneys demonstrating such changes, there was a previous history of diabetes in all but one case.[368]

The role of renal disease in the pathogenesis of low plasma renin activity in diabetes appears to be important. Taken as a group, diabetic patients with normal or elevated creatinine clearances, irrespective of hypertension, have supine plasma renin activities similar to those of controls.[360,371] Patients with decreased plasma renin activity and orthostatic hypotension also had mean creatinine clearances below 50 ml/min in one study.[371] Another study in which decreased plasma renin activity with neuropathy was found does not give measurements of renal function, except to say that minimal proteinuria was present.[372] Since plasma renin activity in uncomplicated diabetes is normal,[360] and since neuropathy and nephropathy progress together, renal disease may be the most significant factor in causing low plasma renin activity.

The presence of low plasma renin activity in diabetic patients with neuropathy and often orthostatic hypotension[361,372] could also indicate that they may have depressed sympathetic activity or low catecholamine concentrations—both potent stimuli to renin release.[373] Diabetic patients with uncomplicated disease have normal basal and stimulated catecholamines.[374,375] However, some diabetic patients with neuropathy and postural hypotension demonstrate low stimulated catecholamine responses.[372,374,375]

Not all diabetic patients with peripheral neuropathy and orthostatic hypotension have blunted catecholamine responses, however. Cryer and associates[376] found that only 7 of 18 diabetic patients with orthostatic hypotension had diminished norepinephrine responses to standing, and that basal norepinephrine and epinephrine concentrations were often normal in these patients. Diminished catecholamine concentrations have been found in the hearts and blood vessels of diabetic patients with neuropathy dying from causes other than uremia or congestive heart failure.[377] Although diabetic patients are said to have an exaggerated pressor response to infused catecholamine,[378,379] suggesting autonomic denervation, other workers have found blunted pressor responses.[375]

Decreased basal and posture-stimulated plasma renin activity and blunted plasma norepinephrine responsiveness to standing have been found in diabetic patients with neuropathy and hyporeninemic hypoaldosteronism, although basal supine norepinephrine concentrations were similar to those of controls.[375] If autonomic denervation (indicated by decreased catecholamines) accounts for the decreased plasma renin activity in neuropathic diabetic patients, one would expect hyperresponsiveness of the renin system to infused catecholamines. Several studies, however, have shown that diabetic patients with neuropathy and hyporeninemic hypoaldosteronism have decreased or absent plasma renin responsiveness to infused catecholamines.[357,361,375] These latter findings led Tuck and colleagues[375] to suggest an additional defect at the juxtaglomerular apparatus regarding the suppressed renin release. Another possible cause of hyporeninemia, in addition to a damaged juxtaglomerular apparatus, is chronic suppression of renin synthesis and secretion. This might produce neuropathy in the diabetic patient. Chronic suppression of the renin system might occur as a result of decreased catecholamines and thus decreased tonic stimulation of renin synthesis.[375] Another factor that may contribute to chronic suppression of renin synthesis is excessive salt and water retention.

Two patients with diabetes and mild renal failure were found to have an increased ECF volume and total exchangeable sodium with decreased plasma renin activity.[366] Prolonged volume depletion from sodium restriction and diuretic therapy resulted in increases in both plasma renin activity and aldosterone.[366] However, the increases were still inappropriately low for the degree of stimulation provided. Similar results were found in a subsequent study.[380] The incidence of chronic volume expansion in diabetic patients with renal disease is unknown, but hyperglycemia and glycosuria in alloxan-diabetic rats is associated with increased blood volume and decreased plasma renin activity.[362] Poorly controlled diabetic patients, especially with decreased free water clearance related to renal disease, could have an increased ECF volume due to the osmotic effects of hyperglycemia causing water flow from cells. In fact, diabetic patients with hyperglycemia have been shown to have higher blood volumes than when the blood glucose was normal.[140]

If chronic volume expansion causes plasma renin suppression in hyporeninemic hypoaldosteronism, one would expect to find a high incidence of hypertension. In a recent review, Phelps and associates[381] noted that over 50 percent of reported patients with the syndrome did in fact demonstrate hypertension.

Two other possible causes of depressed plasma renin activity have been considered in patients with hyporeninemic hypoaldosteronism either with or without diabetes.[381] A primary elevation in potassium could cause suppression of plasma renin activity.[382,383] However, treatment of the hyperkalemia alone does not restore plasma renin activity to normal.[355,357] Furthermore, in neither Addison's disease[384] nor congenital selective aldosterone deficiency[385] is hyperkalemia associated with decreased plasma renin activity. Defective renal prostaglandin synthesis can cause suppressed plasma renin activity.[386] The role of prostaglandins in the hyporeninemia and hyperkalemia of this syndrome has not been evaluated.[381]

Although decreased catecholamines, volume expansion, or secretion of an inactive renin may contribute to the low plasma renin activity found in some diabetic patients, the common denominator in most patients appears to be renal disease, which as noted above is often associated with sclerosis in or around the juxtaglomerular apparatus.

Diminished Plasma Aldosterone

Two major causes have been suggested for decreased aldosterone secretion and a decreased aldosterone secretory response to stimuli in diabetic patients with hyporeninemic hypoaldosteronism.[363] First, the decreased plasma renin activity and decreased angiotensin II in these patients result in inadequate stimulation of aldosterone secretion. Second, there is evidence for a blockage in aldosterone biosynthesis. Since many patients with hyporeninemic aldosteronism are described as hyperkalemic, and since all have normal glucocorticoid secretion, it does not appear that either hypokalemia or diminished ACTH are involved.

Diabetic patients with or without nephropathy have been shown to have plasma renin activity and aldosterone concentrations that respond in unison to sodium depletion[375,387] and upright posture,[371,375,387] although in the latter group both responses were lower than in controls. In long-term volume depletion, plasma renin activity and aldosterone again tend to rise together to supranormal concentrations.[366] These studies suggest that the renin-angiotensin-aldosterone system is at least partly intact in such patients, and that decreased renin activity may be the primary defect.

Several reports of possible aldosterone biosynthetic defects in diabetic patients have appeared.[356,358,365,388] Low excretion of aldosterone and its metabolites, or of 18-hydroxycorticosterone and aldosterone (and their metabolites) in the presence of normal or elevated precursors (desoxycorticosterone, corticosterone), was taken as presumptive evidence of 18-hydroxysteroid dehydrogenase and 18-hydroxylase deficiencies, respectively, in the zona glomerulosa. Diminished 18-hydroxylated components have also been observed following ACTH stimulation.[355,365] However, as pointed out by Rösler and Ulick,[389] such patterns of secretion may reflect only the steroid secretion pattern of a suppressed zona glomerulosa. Corticosterone is produced primarily in the human zona fasciculata,[390] and both it and its metabolites would therefore be normal in the absence of activity of the zona glomerulosa.[389]

As noted by Phelps and associates[381] the definitive approach to this problem will require simultaneous stimulation of the zona glomerulosa with angiotensin II and suppression of the zona fasciculata with dexamethasone. If altered aldosterone biosynthesis is a primary defect in hyporeninemic hypoaldosteronism, one would further expect plasma renin activity to be elevated.[389] Two separate defects would be required to produce both hyporeninemia and low aldosterone concentrations. The existing data as clarified by Rösler and Ulick[389] seem much more compatible with a primary defect in renin secretion causing secondary atrophy of the zona glomerulosa cells and hyposecretion of aldosterone, rather with than a primary blockage of aldosterone biosynthesis. Furthermore, not all studies confirm adrenal enzyme abnormalities in patients with hyporeninemic hypoaldosteronism.[355] One further piece of contradictory evidence stressed by Williams[391] is that anephric humans do not have blunted aldosterone responses to adrenocorticotropin and potassium, as one might expect from chronic suppression of the zona glomerulosa due to the absence of renin.[392,393]

Diabetes has also been associated with a syndrome of acquired hyperreninemic hypoaldosteronism. In the one well-studied patient reported, there appeared to be defective aldosterone biosynthesis in response to angiotensin II stimulation, although the remainder of adrenal function was normal.[393]

Hyperkalemia

Many diabetic patients with hyporeninemic hypoaldosteronism have hyperkalemia as their major clinical complication. Hyperkalemia is not present in all patients with the syndrome.[355,366,394] As discussed above, most patients have some degree of renal failure, but the degree of renal failure and acidosis is considered inadequate to account for the hyperkalemia observed.[394-396]

The most obvious cause of hyperkalemia is a decreased action of aldosterone on distal tubule potassium excretion. The hyperkalemia in hyporeninemic hypoaldosteronism may be resistant to correction with exogeneous mineralocorticoid, however.[397] As suggested by Knochel,[396] tolerance to chronic potassium elevation, such as that found in an end-stage renal disease,[31] may also be defective. This may or may not depend on aldosterone.[26] Acidosis could also increase serum potassium, although correction of acidosis does not always improve hyperkalemia.[380]

Alterations in renal function, in addition to decreased glomerular filtration, may also contribute to the hyperkalemia in hyporeninemic hypoaldosteronism.[381] As suggested by De Fronzo and associates,[359] a specific tubular defect in potassium excretion in diabetes could cause hyperkalemia and in turn suppress the renin-angiotensin-aldosterone system. On the other hand, the reported cases having such a tubular defect did not have diabetes as a primary illness.[359,398,399] Furthermore, low renin activity and aldosterone concentrations may occur in the absence of elevated potassium,[371] making a primary tubular defect unlikely.

Finally, there is substantial evidence that insulin deficiency contributes to the hyperkalemia found in diabetic patients, particularly those with hypoaldosteronism. As discussed previously, insulin modulates serum potassium primarily by shifting potassium intracellularly. Diabetic animals[3,41] and humans[44,394] demonstrate decreased tolerance to potassium loading. In diabetic patients with hyperkalemia, glucose tolerance was also found to be more severely compromised than in patients without hyperkalemia.[394] Although even low insulin concentrations may prevent the tendency towards hyperkalemia, as suggested by Cox and co-workers,[47] it is possible that insulin resistance (e.g., infection-related) may also involve potassium transfer and cause an elevated potassium in patients with ordinarily adequate insulin concentrations. Thus, diabetic patients with both insulin and aldosterone deficiency are at particular risk for developing hyperkalemia, especially if they are given hypertonic glucose infusions or potassium-sparing diuretics (see below).

Infusions of hypertonic glucose cause intravascular hyperosmolarity, which tends to cause potassium to flow from cells into the extracellular space.[156] In normal subjects, this effect is counteracted by insulin[36] secreted in response to hyperglycemia. Diabetic patients with a limited ability to secrete insulin, have been shown to develop increased serum potassium concentrations[371,400] rather than the usual decrease observed in nondiabetic individuals. This phenomenon usually becomes clinically significant only when there is combined insulin and aldosterone deficiency, such as with diabetics who have selective aldosteronism. Goldfarb and associates[401] found that hyperkalemia correlated well with blood glucose concentrations in diabetic patients. They also were able to suppress the hyperkalemic response by mineralocorticoid pretreatment, and to abolish it with insulin pretreatment.[401,402] The life-threatening nature of combined insulin–aldosterone deficiency is illustrated by one patient reported by Goldfarb and colleagues,[401] who developed ventricular tachycardia while hyperkalemic. There is also a case report of a diabetic patient with normal urinary and plasma aldosterone concentrations and mild renal failure but no acidosis who developed hyperkalemia in response to glucose infusions.[403] The hyperkalemia resolved with insulin therapy and pharmacologic doses of deoxycortisone acetate. The risk of inducing hyperkalemia in diabetic patients with both insulin and aldosterone deficiencies may be substantial. The infusion of high concentrations of glucose in comatose diabetic patients as a "therapeutic test" is to be avoided.[400] This is particularly true since glucose oxidase test strips can be used to detect hypoglycemia within minutes of obtaining blood.

Potassium-retaining diuretics have been shown to increase the serum potassium concentration in diabetic patients even in the absence of renal disease.[404,405] The hyperkalemia in these patients depended on the degree of glucose control; patients with fasting blood glucose levels below 200 mg/dl did not exhibit hyperkalemia.[405] Intravenous glucose (25 g) elicited hyperkalemia in all subjects receiving triamterene who had fasting blood glucoses over 300 mg/dl, although a 100 g oral glucose load elicited hyperkalemia in only one of 11 patients.[405] Other diuretics implicated in hyperkalemia are spironolactone and amiloride.[404] Because of this complication, care must be taken when treating poorly controlled diabetic patients with these agents; oral or intravenous glucose should not be given. Another action that may worsen the tendency to hyperkalemia in susceptible diabetic patients is the treatment of hypertension with angiotensin converting enzyme inhibitors. Although this does not appear to be a major problem,[406–409] loss of the kaliuretic effect of aldosterone could be especially important in diabetic patients with moderate degrees of renal insufficiency.

Therapy of Diabetes and Hyporeninemic Hypoaldosteronism

The diabetic patient with poor glucose control and hyperkalemia may respond rapidly to insulin therapy with a decrease in serum potassium and correction of mild hyperchloremic acidosis.[401,402] However, adjunctive therapy may also be required during the acute episode, if the blood glucose is difficult to regulate, or if the defect in aldosterone synthesis is severe. Treatment with base (sodium bicarbonate or Shohl's solution) may improve the hyperkalemia and acidosis, but rarely corrects them.[396]

A potassium binding resin (polystyrene sulfonate) taken orally was shown to correct the hyperkalemia and mild acidosis in a nondiabetic patient with hyporeninemic hypoaldosteronism.[398] Apparently, hyperkalemia was the primary defect, causing impairment of urinary ammonia (and thus acid) excretion, since urinary ammonium excretion was increased by tenfold when the serum potassium was normalized and the pH was restored to normal.[398]

Mineralocorticoid therapy, usually with fludrocortisone, has been helpful in treating both the hyperkalemia and acidosis in hyporeninemic hypoaldosteronism.[296,410] Larger doses (greater than 0.2 mg fludrocortisone per day) are usually required than in the treatment of simple adrenal insufficiency[296,397,410] possibly because of mineralocorticoid resistance caused by the renal disease.[410]

Each of the above therapies may increase

plasma volume and worsen pre-existing hypertension, edema, or congestive heart failure.[396,410,411] Such volume expansion usually responds well to furosemide and a liberal fluid intake.[396] As mentioned previously, prolonged salt depletion and diuretic therapy may correct the hyperkalemia and acidosis, as well as increase renin and aldosterone secretion.[366] Thus, furosemide may be the preferable initial therapy in patients with hypertension or edema. Fludrocortisone could then be added if hyperkalemia is still a problem. Another therapeutic dilemma may occur in patients who also have neuropathic hypotension. Treatment with fludrocortisone (0.3 to 0.5 mg/day) may correct orthostatic symptoms but produce supine hypertension, which in turn may be associated with cardiovascular complications.[411]

Thiazides and Glucose Intolerance

Thiazides and similar diuretic agents have long been known to impair carbohydrate tolerance in nondiabetic persons.[412,413] In elderly persons or those with a family history of diabetes, clinical diabetes was sometimes precipitated.[412] A causal role for hypokalemia in this condition also received support from the work of Conn, in 1965,[57] in which a high incidence of carbohydrate intolerance was observed in patients with aldosteronism of which a primary feature was hypokalemia. Experimental potassium depletion in rats is well known to induce glucose intolerance.[414] Similarly, induction of potassium depletion (200 to 500 mEq) in humans over a period of several days through the use of an oral ion exchange resin caused a marked decline in tolerance to intravenous glucose, even when serum potassium concentrations had not changed significantly.[56] Treatment with insulin prevented the decline in carbohydrate tolerance, implying that decreased insulin secretion, possibly induced by potassium depletion, was the cause of the glucose intolerance. Hypokalemia in patients with primary aldosteronism was later found to be associated with low insulin secretion and carbohydrate intolerance, both of which resolved with removal of the adenoma producing the aldosteronism and return of the serum potassium to normal.[57]

The prevalence of thiazide-induced glucose intolerance has been found to vary from negligible in one study[415] to 30 percent in others.[416,417] In a group of elderly patients treated with thiazides, glucose tolerance as a whole was abnormal within two years of starting treatment.[417] The decline in glucose tolerance was also found to be related to the degree of decrease in serum potassium.[417]

As discussed previously, provision of adequate potassium is required for in vitro insulin secretion from either the perfused pancreas or isolated islets. Clinical hypokalemia has further been shown to induce an insulinopenic state in which the fraction of biologically active insulin is below that in normal subjects, and in which there is an increase in proinsulin-like components, which have only about 10 percent of the biologic activity of insulin.[418]

These findings probably have little importance for insulin-requiring diabetic patients, who usually have little endogenous insulin secretion. In the nonketotic diabetic, who is often obese, elderly, and hypertensive, thiazides may be an important cause of deterioration in glucose tolerance, perhaps leading to symptomatic diabetes. As noted earlier, glucose concentrations may rise when the serum potassium has fallen only slightly, because body potassium stores are significantly depleted.[56] In the absence of renal failure (causing potassium retention), it is wise to maintain serum potassium concentrations well within the range of normal with oral potassium supplements. In this manner it may be possible to prevent deterioration in glucose tolerance or assuage clinical, adult-onset diabetes treated with thiazides.

Hypertension and Diabetes Mellitus—Role of Sodium–Volume Excess

Diabetes mellitus is often associated with hypertension, even prior to the onset of significant renal failure. Such patients have been shown to have normal concentrations of cortisol and epinephrine,[419] and normal or low concentrations of renin, aldosterone, and norepinephrine.[360,376,378,419] There is evidence that total body sodium and fluid volume may be excessive in some hypertensive diabetic patients. Alloxan-diabetic rats were found to have increased blood volume,[420] and a more recent study demonstrated increased total exchangeable sodium and a clinical response to salt restriction or diuretic therapy in humans.[421]

Renal Failure and Diabetes Mellitus

Fluid or Electrolyte Problems in Diabetic Uremia

Renal failure accounts for almost half of all deaths in patients with diabetes diagnosed before the age of 20.[1] This death rate represents an increased incidence of renal failure, and may reflect an increasing appearance of chronic complications as diabetic patients live longer. However, diabetic patients with renal failure present the clinician with a variety of difficult management problems that are absent in the non-diabetic patient with uremia (Table 10-4). The interval from the onset of significant proteinuria (over 500 mg/day) to early renal failure (creatinine 2.8 mg/dl, BUN >40 mg/dl) averages two years. The interval from the onset of proteinuria to late renal failure (creatinine 8.5 mg/dl, BUN >100 mg/dl) is about four years, with death shortly thereafter unless intervention occurs.[1] This four to five year period is also a critical one for the progression of other complications, especially neuropathy and retinopathy. Metabolic and electrolyte control is probably also important in halting or at least slowing the progression of small-vessel disease. Recently, evidence has accumulated indicating that a low protein diet may not only decrease the glomerular hyperfiltration common to diabetes, but also diabetic proteinuria.[422–424] Whether renal function is prolonged has yet to be determined.

The insulin dosage becomes more difficult to regulate as renal function declines. Urine tests for glucose become unreliable indices of the blood glucose concentration because the number of nephrons capable of excreting glucose falls and the apparent renal threshold for glucose rises. Urine testing is also invalidated by urinary retention due to a neurogenic bladder. A decrease in the amount of functioning renal tissue, as well as a decreased caloric intake, probably accounts for a reduction in the requirement for insulin by an average of 50 percent.[425] Also, the patient may experience an increase in the frequency of hypoglycemic reactions (although this is usually a late event).[425,426] This latter effect is caused both by a decline in renal insulin excretion and a decreased renal capacity to bind and degrade insulin.[427] Patients receiving sul-

Table 10-4. Special Fluid and Electrolyte Balance Problems in Diabetics with Renal Failure

Mid–late renal failure
  Deterioration of renal function after intravenous contrast material
  Rapid blood glucose fluctuations: Hyperosmolar coma
  Hyporeninemic hypoaldosteronism
  Fluctuating serum potassium related to glucose-induced fluid shifts

End-stage renal failure-dialysis
  Hyper- and hypokalemia
  Hyperosmolarity
  Hypercalcemia

Post-renal transplant
  Hyperglycemia-induced hyperkalemia
  "Hyperglycemic pseudorejection"

fonylurea drugs, particularly chlorpropamide, may experience hypoglycemia due to impaired renal excretion of the drug (chlorpropamide) or the effects of its active metabolites (acetohexamide, tolazamide and tolbutamide).[426,428] Patients on insulin may also have rapid swings in blood glucose, in part due to uremic anorexia, nausea, and vomiting, and in part due to an inability to excrete a glucose load.[426]

Approximately 6 percent of diabetic patients develop the nephrotic syndrome,[429] and 12 percent of diabetic patients in end-stage renal failure may experience progressive hypoalbuminemia and weight loss, evidence of severe malnutrition.[425]

Two major problems related to fluid and electrolyte balance in mid- and late-stage renal failure may be identified. Diabetic patients with even mild renal failure (serum creatinine 1.54 to 4.5 mg/dl) may experience renal functional deterioration following intravenous urography[430-436] or other contrast studies. As the creatinine nears 5.0 mg/dl, the risk becomes prohibitive.[431] In most cases the onset of renal failure is prompt, often with oliguria, and is usually reversible in 7 to 10 days.[430-432] Patients with more severe renal failure may not exhibit a return of serum creatinine to baseline concentrations. Certain factors in addition to renal disease per se have been associated with exacerbation of renal failure following excretory urography. These include juvenile-onset diabetes of any duration,[431] older age,[432] the presence of hypertensive renal disease,[432] large or repeated doses of contrast medium[433] and pre-existing dehydration.[434,435] The role of volume depletion and dose of contrast medium has been found to be unimportant by other workers.[431] The causes for renal shutdown are not yet established, but may include a direct vascular toxic effect of the contrast agent[432] or may be the consequences of poor hydration. The latter may be induced either by a pre-existing osmotic diuresis or from a contrast-induced osmotic diuresis,[432] and result in red blood cell sludging and decreased glomerular capillary flow.[431,436] Treatment is usually not effective, although high dose "loop" diuretic therapy and volume expansion have been tried.[431]

Although ketoacidosis occurs in diabetic renal failure, particularly in children,[437] there appears to be an increased incidence of hyperosmolar coma in diabetic patients with renal failure.[426] This increase is certainly related to decreased renal excretion of glucose, despite an osmotic diuresis with attendant fluid and electrolyte loss, as discussed previously. The course and treatment of hyperosmolar coma mirrors that seen with lesser degrees of renal failure, with certain exceptions. Blood glucose may rise rapidly to very high concentrations, especially when vomiting is present, causing cellular dehydration and worsening of the mental status. Since cardiac function for various reasons is often impaired in diabetic patients with significant renal disease, rapid fluid shifts into the vascular space from the cellular space may precipitate acute heart failure.

Hyperglycemia (even to nonhyperosmolar concentrations) may cause a flow of potassium from cells, a process exacerbated by renal acidosis. The patient may present with a blood glucose of 800 to 1000 mg/dl and a serum potassium of 6 to 7 mEq/liter. Insulin treatment alone may rapidly lower not only the blood glucose concentration but also the potassium concentration, frequently to hypokalemic levels.[438] Careful insulin treatment and frequent electrolyte determinations are required in the management of these difficult problems.

Diabetic Renal Failure and Chronic Dialysis

Hemodialysis

Diabetic patients begun on hemodialysis have done less well than nondiabetic patients on chronic hemodialysis, with two year survival rates between 40 and 75 percent.[429] Although progression of large and small vessel disease accounts for much of this increased mortality,[426] metabolic, fluid, and electrolyte problems may also contribute significantly.

Comty and associates[425] have stated that "diabetic control in the dialyzed insulin-dependent diabetic patient resembled that in the labile teenage diabetic patient." Even minor alterations in insulin regimens or meals may cause rises of the blood glucose into the hyperosmolar range with attendant volume overload (but with surprisingly little hypertension), and often with hyperkalemia. Volume-overload hypertension may also be frequent in diabetic patients, particularly with renal failure. Patients usually experience an increase in insulin dosage requirements on hemodialysis, in many instances to greater levels than before the onset of uremia.[425,426] The first few months of hemodialysis are frequently complicated by hyperglycemia, sometimes with ketosis.[425] A split-dose insulin regimen is frequently necessary.[425] The increase in insulin requirement has been attributed to increased appetite and carbohydrate intake, but there may also be loss of insulin during dialysis. Since fluid volume is under control and the kidneys have very little function, the complications of an osmotic diuresis do not occur. However, with the loss of the renal "safety valve" for glucose spillover, hyperglycemia and hyperosmolarity may be recurrent and severe unless controlled by insulin therapy and dialysis against the proper dialysate. In lieu of frequent blood glucose measurements, patients may learn to recognize thirst as a symptom of hyperglycemia.[375] A dialysis glucose concentration of 200 mg/dl has been recommended.[375] Hemodialysis is an effective way to treat severe hyperglycemic hyperosmolarity, although care must be taken to avoid rapid falls in blood glucose and osmotic disequilibrium between the CSF and plasma. A rapid fall in blood glucose may also induce life-threatening hypokalemia,[438] discussed previously. Acidosis and ketosis related to poor diabetic control will also respond to hemodialysis, with buffer capacity added by the dialysate and removal of ketones across the membranes.[425] Surprisingly, development of hyperglycemia to hyperosmolar levels (with or without ketosis) necessitated only 7 percent of admissions of diabetic patients on hemodialysis in one series,[425] and is not frequently reported as a major problem in the more recent literature.

Hypercalcemia has been observed in about 10 percent of diabetic admissions.[425] The serum phosphorus is usually low. The hypercalcemia may be symptomatic, contributing to nausea, anorexia, and vomiting. Causes for hypercalcemia cannot be directly attributed to the diabetic state, although ketosis-induced anorexia may decrease food intake, potentiate upper gastrointestinal bleeding, and result in increased antacid therapy. These in turn bind more phosphate and cause a rise in serum calcium.[425] Secondary hyperparathyroidism due to renal failure may also exist and contribute to the hypercalcemia. Many patients are treated with vitamin D and calcium during some part of their illness. However, two patients of Comty and associates[425] had normal serum PTH concentrations and no hyperplasia at surgery, in spite of hypercalcemia and hypophosphatemia. However, either withholding antacids or giving oral phosphate supplements rectified the problem. In addition, uremic patients with diabetes on hemodialysis have been shown to develop early deposition of aluminum in bone,[439] which could lead to low-turnover osteomalacia and contribute to increased bone pain and fractures.

Fluid retention, weight gain between dialyses, and other electrolyte problems do not appear to be encountered any more frequently in the diabetic than in the nondiabetic patient on hemodialysis.[440]

Peritoneal Dialysis

Long-term peritoneal dialysis in the diabetic patient has been successful for as long as 2 years,[441] with results at least as good as in hemodialyzed diabetic patients.[429] Peritoneal dialysis has been associated with hyperosmolar coma,[261] pleural effusions, and risk of infection.[426] Insulin-requiring diabetic patients generally have fewer episodes of severe hyperglycemia than those with "latent" diabetes, probably because of closer monitoring of blood glucose concentrations and the avoidance of dialysate glucose concentrations greater than 200 mg/dl.[442] Again, an increase in insulin dosage may be required.[438] Sorbitol probably should not be substituted for glucose in the dialysate because sorbitol may also cause hyperosmolar coma [443] and may predispose to the development of acidosis.[438]

Renal Transplantation

Transplantation appears to be the treatment of choice for diabetic patients with end-stage renal disease, particularly early in the course of such disease, in order to minimize the worsening of neuropathy and retinopathy that occurs with symptomatic uremia, and to simplify management.[444,445] Complications causing death are usually related to progressive cardiovascular and peripheral vascular disease.[444] Metabolic, fluid, and electrolyte complications have not been reported with excessive frequency in large series,[444-446] but several features of the diabetic patient with a renal transplant have been emphasized.

Blood glucose control may be difficult because of a decreased apparent renal threshold for glucose, lessening the value of urine testing.[447] High doses of corticosteroids induce insulin resistance, usually increase insulin requirements, and may also predispose to hyperosmolar coma.[270]

Hyperglycemia in the diabetic patient with a renal transplant has been associated with hyperkalemia. This has been observed in the post-transplant period in a patient with normal renal and adrenal zona glomerulosa function.[448] The hyperkalemia occurred only in the presence of severe hyperglycemia, and was attributed to insulinopenia and diminished translocation of potassium from the extracellular space. Rebound hypokalemia after insulin treatment was not recorded.

Hyperglycemia in the transplant patient may also be associated with a rising creatinine concentration in the absence of other evidence of transplant rejection.[449] This phenomenon has been termed "hyperglycemic pseudorejection." It appears to be common and to reflect poor diabetic control, since the reported blood glucose concentrations correlated quite well with serum creatinine concentrations.[449] Lowering the blood glucose with insulin caused the creatinine concentrations to return to baseline. The cause of "hyperglycemic pseudorejection" is not known, but is probably not due to a laboratory artifact or to hyperketonemia.[449] Rather Matas and colleagues[449] suggest that it is related to the dehydration and hyperosmolarity caused by an osmotic diuresis, which in turn reversibly decrease renal function, as described previously with regard to the development of ketoacidotic and hyperosmolar comas.

REFERENCES

1. Knowles HC: Magnitude of the renal failure problem in diabetic patients. Kidney Int 6 (Suppl 1):2, 1974
2. Gavryck WA, Moore RD, Thompson RC: Effect of insulin membrane-bound (Na^+-K^+)-ATPase extracted from frog skeletal muscle. J Physiol (Lond) 252:43, 1975
3. Lostroh AJ, Krahl ME: Insulin action. Accumulation in vivo of Mg^{2+} and K^+ in rat uterus; ion pump activity. Biochim Biophys Acta 291:260, 1973

4. Brodal BP, Jebens E, Öy V, Iversen O-J: Effect of insulin on (Na^+-K^+)-activated adenosine triphosphatase activity in rat muscle sarcolemma. Nature 249:41, 1974
5. Hadden JW, Hadden EM, Wilson EE, Good RA: Direct action of insulin on plasma membrane ATPase activity in human lymphocytes. Nature (New Biol) 235:174, 1972
6. Moore RD: Effect of insulin upon the sodium pump in frog skeletal muscle. J Physiol (Lond) 232:23, 1973
7. Creese R: Sodium fluxes in diaphragm muscle and the effects of insulin and serum proteins. J Physiol (Lond) 197:255, 1968
8. Moore RD: The ionic effects of insulin. Abs. Biophys. Soc. USA FA 12, 1965
9. Manery JF, Gourley DRH, Fisher KC: The potassium uptake and rate of oxygen consumption of isolated frog skeletal muscle in the presence of insulin and lactate. Can J Biochem Physiol 34:893, 1956
10. Smillie LB, Manery JF: Effect of external potassium concentration, insulin and lactate on frog muscle potassium and respiratory rate. Am J Physiol 198:67, 1960
11. Herrera FC, Whittembury G, Planchart A: Effect of insulin on short-circuit current across isolated frog skin in the presence of calcium and magnesium. Biochim Biophys Acta 66:170, 1963
12. André R, Crabbé J: Stimulation by insulin of active sodium transport by toadskin: influence of aldosterone and vasopressin. Arch Int Physiol Biochim 74:538, 1966
13. Crabbé J, Francois B: Stimulation par l'insuline du transport actif de sodium a travers les membranes epitheliales du crapaud, *Bufo marinus*. Ann Endocrinol 28:713, 1967
14. Francois B, de Gasparo M, Crabbé J: Interaction between isolated amphibian skin and insulin. Arch Int Physiol Biochim 77:527, 1969
15. Benjamin WB, Singer I: Aldosterone and insulin induced proteins. (Abstract) Clin Res 22:516A, 1974
16. Nizet A, Lefebvre P, Crabbé J: Control by insulin of sodium, potassium, and water excretion by the isolated dog kidney. Pflugers Arch Eur J Physiol 323:11, 1971
17. Atchley DW, Loeb RF, Richards DW Jr, et al: On diabetic acidosis. A detailed study of electrolyte balances following the withdrawal and reestablishment of insulin therapy. J Clin Invest 12:297, 1933
18. Nabarro JDN, Spencer AG, Stowers JM: Metabolic studies in severe diabetic ketoacidosis. Q J Med 21:225, 1952
19. Miller JH, Bogdonoff MD: Antidiuresis associated with administration of insulin. J Appl Physiol 6:509, 1954
20. Saudek CD, Boulter PR, Knopp RH, Arky RA: Sodium retention accompanying insulin treatment of diabetes mellitus. Diabetes 23:240, 1974
21. DeFronzo RA, Goldberg M, Agus ZS: The effects of glucose and insulin on renal electrolyte transport. J Clin Invest 58:83, 1976
22. DeFronzo RA: The effect of insulin on renal sodium metabolism. A review with clinical implications. Diabetologia 21:165, 1981
23. DeFronzo RA, Cooke CR, Andres R, et al: The effect of insulin on renal handling of sodium, potassium, calcium, and phosphate in man. J Clin Invest 55:845, 1975
24. Giebisch G: Some reflections on the mechanism of renal tubular potassium transport. Yale J Biol Med 48:315, 1975
25. Hierholzer K, Wiederholt M, Holzgreve H, et al: Micropuncture study of renal tubular transtubular concentration gradients of sodium and potassium in adrenalectomized rats. Pflugers Arch 285:193, 1965
26. Knochel JP: Role of glucoregulatory hormones in potassium homeostasis. Kidney Int 11:443, 1977
27. Laragh JH, Angers M, Kelly WG, Lieberman S: Hypotensive agents and pressor substances: The effect of epinephrine, norepinephrine, angiotensin II and others on the secretory rate of aldosterone in man. JAMA 174:234, 1960
28. Laragh JH, Stoerk HC: A study of the mechanisms of secretion of the sodium-retaining hormone (aldosterone) J Clin Invest 36:383, 1957
29. Gann DS, Delea CS, Gill JR Jr, et al: Control of aldosterone secretion by change of body potassium in normal man. Am J Physiol 207:104, 1964
30. Hollenberg HR, Williams G, Burger B, Hooshmand I: The influence of potassium

30. on the renal vasculature and adrenal gland and their responsiveness to angiotensin II in normal man. Clin Sci Mol Med 49:527, 1975
31. Alexander EA, Levinsky NG: An extrarenal mechanism of potassium adaptation. J Clin Invest 47:740, 1968
32. Silva P, Brown RS, Epstein FH: Adaptation to potassium. Kidney Int 11:466, 1977
33. Bourdillon J: Distribution in body fluids and excretion of ingested ammonium chloride, potassium chloride and sodium chloride. Am J Physiol 120:411, 1937
34. Winkler JA, Smith PK: The apparent volume of distribution of potassium injected intravenously. J Biol Chem 124:589, 1938
35. Bia MJ, DeFronzo RA: Extrarenal potassium homeostasis. Am J Physiol 240:F257, 1981
36. Andres R, Baltzan MA, Cader G, Zierler KL: Effect of insulin on carbohydrate metabolism and on potassium in the forearm of man. J Clin Invest 41:108, 1962
37. Fenn WO: Deposition of potassium and phosphorus with glycogen in rat livers. J Biol Chem 128:297, 1939
38. Burton SD, Ishida T: Effect of insulin on potassium and glucose movement in perfused rat liver. Am J Physiol 209:1145, 1965
39. Kestens PJ, Haxhe JJ, Lambotte L, Lambotte C: The effect of insulin on the uptake of potassium and phosphate by the isolated perfused canine liver. Metabolism 12:941, 1963
40. Kalsheker NA, Hales CN: Insulin in vivo increases the in vitro fall of plasma potassium concentration in human venous blood. Eur J Clin Invest 15:113, 1985
41. Santeusanio F, Faloona GR, Knochel JP, Unger RH: Evidence for a role of endogenous insulin and glucagon in the regulation of potassium homeostasis. J Lab Clin Med 81:809, 1973
42. Hiatt N, Morgenstern L, Davidson MB, et al: Role of insulin in the transfer of infused potassium to tissue. Horm Metab Res 5:84, 1973
43. Pettit GW, Vick RL, Swander AM: Plasma K^+ and insulin: Changes during KCl infusion in normal and nephrectomized dogs. Am J Physiol 228:107, 1975
44. Sterns R, Guzzo J, Feig P: Role of insulin in human K^+ homeostasis. (Abstract) Kidney Int 12:475, 1977
45. Smoller S, Rashid K, Perez GO, et al: Kaliuresis after an acute oral potassium load in diabetes mellitus. Am J Med Sci 295:114, 1988
46. Rosenfeld MG (ed): Manual of Medical Therapeutics, Ch. 2. p. 49. Little, Brown, Boston, 1971
47. Cox M, Sterns RH, Singer I: The defense against hyperkalemia: The roles of insulin and aldosterone. N Engl J Med 299:525, 1978
48. Blackard WG, Nelson NC: Portal and peripheral vein immunoreactive insulin concentrations before and after glucose infusion. Diabetes 19:302, 1970
49. DeFronzo RA, Sherwin RS, Dillingham M, et al: Influence of basal insulin and glucagon secretion on potassium and sodium metabolism. Studies with somatostatin in normal dogs and in normal and diabetic human beings. J Clin Invest 61:472, 1978
50. Milner RDG, Hales CN: Cations and the secretion of insulin. Biochim Biophys Acta 150:165, 1968
51. Grodsky GM, Bennett LL: Cation requirements for insulin secretion in the isolated perfused pancreas. Diabetes 15:910, 1966
52. Gomez M, Curry DL: Potassium stimulation of insulin release by the perfused rat pancreas. Endocrinology 92:1126, 1973
53. Henquin JC, Lambert AE: Cationic environment and dynamics of insulin secretion. II: Effects of a high concentration of potassium. Diabetes 23:933, 1974
54. Hiatt N, Davidson MB, Bonorris G: The effect of potassium chloride infusion on insulin secretion in vivo. Horm Metab Res 4:64, 1972
55. Dluhy RG, Axelrod L, Williams GH: Serum immunoreactive insulin and growth hormone response to potassium infusion in normal man. J Appl Physiol 33:22, 1972
56. Saglid U, Anderson V, Andreasen PB: Glucose tolerance and insulin responsiveness in experimental potassium depletion. Acta Med Scand 169:243, 1961
57. Conn JW: Hypertension, the potassium ion and impaired glucose tolerance. N Engl J Med 273:1135, 1965
58. Petersen KG, Schlüter KJ, Kemp L: Reg-

ulation of serum potassium during insulin-induced hypoglycemia. Diabetes 31:615, 1982
59. Lennon EJ, Piering WF: A comparison of the effects of glucose ingestion and NH₄Cl acidosis on urinary calcium and magnesium excretion in man. J Clin Invest 49:1458, 1970
60. Lennon EJ, Lemann J Jr, Piering NF, Larson LS: The effect of glucose on urinary cation excretion during chronic extracellular volume expansion in normal man. J Clin Invest 53:1424, 1974
61. Lindemann RD, Adler S, Yiengst MJ, Beard ES: Influence of various nutrients on urinary cation excretion. J Lab Clin Med 70:236, 1967
62. Walser M: Calcium-sodium interdependence in renal transport. p 21. In Fisher JW, Cafrumy EJ (eds): Renal Pharmacology. Appleton-Century-Crofts, New York, 1971
63. Parfitt AM: The acute effects of mersalyl, chlorothiazide and mannitol on the renal excretion of calcium and other ions in man. Clin Sci 36:267, 1969
64. Beck LH, Goldberg M: Effects of acetazolamide and parathyroidectomy on renal transport of sodium, calcium, and phosphate. Am J Physiol 224:1136, 1973
65. Massry SG, Coburn JW, Chapman LW, Kleeman CR: The acute effect of adrenal steroids on the interrelationship between the renal excretion of sodium, calcium, and magnesium. J Lab Clin Med 70:563, 1967
66. Hoskins B, Scott JM: Evidence for a direct action of insulin to increase renal reabsorption of calcium and for an irreversible defect in renal ability to conserve calcium due to prolonged absence of insulin. Dibetes 33:991, 1984
67. Raskin P, Stevenson RM, Barilla DE, Pak CY: The hypercalcemia of diabetes mellitus: Its amelioration with insulin. Clin Endocrinol 9:329, 1978
68. Milner RDG, Hales CN: The role of calcium and magnesium in insulin secretion from rabbit pancreas studied in vitro. Diabetologia 3:47, 1967
69. Curry DL, Bennett LL, Grodsky GM: Requirement for calcium ion in insulin secretion by the perfused rat pancreas. Am J Physiol 214:174, 1968
70. Malaisse WJ, Brisson G, Malaisse-Lagae F: The stimulus-secretion coupling of glucose-induced insulin release. I. Interaction of epinephrine and alkaline earth cations. J Lab Clin Med 76:895, 1970
71. Gould MK, Chaudry IH: The action of insulin on glucose uptake by isolated rat soleus muscle. 1. Effects of cations. Biochim Biophys Acta 215:249, 1970
72. Letarte J, Renold AE: Ionic effects on glucose transport and metabolism by isolated mouse fat cells incubated with or without insulin. I. Lack of effect of medium Ca^{2+}, Mg^{2+} or PO_4^{3-}. Biochim Biophys Acta 183:350, 1969
73. Kissebah AH, Tulloch BR, Hope-Gill H, et al: Mode of insulin action. Lancet 1:144, 1975
74. Yasuda K, Hurukawa Y, Okuyama M, et al: Glucose tolerance and insulin secretion in patients with parathyroid disorders. Effect of serum calcium on insulin release. N Engl J Med 292:501, 1975
75. Harter HR, Santiago JV, Rutherford WE, et al: The relative roles of calcium, phosphorus, and parathyroid hormone in glucose and tolbutamide-mediated insulin release. J Clin Invest 58:359, 1976
76. Kim H, Kalkhoff RK, Costrini NV, et al: Plasma insulin disturbances in primary hyperparathyroidism. J Clin Invest 50:2596, 1971
77. Lindall A, Carmena R, Cohen S, Comty C: Insulin hypersecretion in patients on chronic hemodialysis: role of parathyroids. J Clin Endocrinol Metab 32:653, 1971
78. Levitan BA: Effect in normal man of hyperglycemia and glycosuria on excretion and reabsorption of phosphate. J Appl Physiol 4:224, 1951
79. Huffman ER, Hlad CJ Jr, Whipple NE, Elrick H: The influence of blood glucose on the renal clearance of phosphate. J Clin Invest 37:369, 1958
80. Ginsburg JM: Effect of glucose and free fatty acid on phosphate transport in dog kidney. Am J Physiol 222:1153, 1972
81. Harter HR, Mercado A, Rutherford WE, et al: Effects of phosphate depletion and parathyroid hormone on renal glucose reabsorption. Am J Physiol 227:1422, 1974
82. Eggleton MG, Shuster S: Glucose and

phosphate excretion in the cat. J Physiol (Lond) 124, 613, 1954
83. Briggs AP, Koechig I, Doisy EA, Weber CJ: Some changes in the composition of blood due to the injection of insulin. J Biol Chem 58:721, 1924
84. Betro MG, Pain RW: Hypophosphatemia and hyperphosphatemia in a hospital population. Br Med J 1:273, 1972
85. Juan D, Elrazak MA: Hypophosphatemia in hospitalized patients. JAMA 242:163, 1979
86. Raskin P, Pak CYC: The effect of chronic insulin therapy on phosphate metabolism in diabetes mellitus. Diabetologia 21:50, 1981
87. Gundersen HJG, Christensen NJ: Intravenous insulin causing loss of intravascular water and albumin and increased adrenergic nervous activity in diabetics. Diabetes 26:551, 1977
88. Morgensen CE, Christensen NJ, Gundersen HJG: The acute effect of insulin on renal hemodynamics and protein excretion in diabetes. Diabetologia 15:153, 1978
89. DeFronzo RA, Hendler R, Christensen N: Stimulation of counterregulatory hormonal responses in diabetic man by a fall in glucose concentration. Diabetes 29:125, 1980
90. Christensen NJ: Catecholamines and diabetes mellitus. Diabetologia 16:211, 1979
91. Wiseman MJ, Viberti GC, Keen H: Threshold effect of plasma glucose in glomerular hyperfiltration of diabetes. Nephron 38:257, 1984
92. Morgensen CE, Steffes MW, Deckert T, Christiansen JS: Functional and morphological renal manifestations in diabetes mellitus. Diabetologia 21:89, 1981
93. Wiseman MJ, Saunders AJ, Keen H, Viberti GC: Effect of blood glucose control on increased glomerular filtration rate and kidney size in insulin-dependent diabetes. N Engl J Med 312:617, 1985
94. Dalle X, Tanghe J, Gryjspeerdt W: Influence du glucagon sur l'excrétion rénale des électrolytes. Arch Int Pharmacodyn Ther 120:505, 1959
95. Charbon GA, Hoekstra MH, Kool DS: The influence of glucagon on the urinary excretion of water, sodium, potassium, calcium, magnesium, chloride and inorganic phosphate. Acta Physiol Pharmacol Neerl 12:48, 1963
96. Elrick H, Huffman ER, Hlad CJ, Jr, et al: Effects of glucagon on renal function in man. J Clin Endocrinol Metab 18:813, 1958
97. Pullman TN, Lavender AR, Aho O: Direct effects of glucagon on renal hemodynamics and excretion of inorganic ions. Metabolism 16:358, 1967
98. Serratto M, Earle DP: Effect of glucagon on renal functions in the dog. Proc Soc Exp Biol Med 102:701, 1959
99. Avioli LV: The effect of glucagon on mineral and electrolyte metabolism. p 181. In Lefebvre PJ, Unger RH (eds): Glucagon, Molecular Physiology, Clinical and Therapeutic Implications. Pergamon Press, Oxford, 1972
100. Saudek CD, Boulter PR, Arky RA: The natriuretic effect of glucagon and its role in starvation. J Clin Endocrinol Metab 36:761, 1973
101. Boulter PR, Spark RF, Arky RA: Dissociation of the renin-aldosterone system and refractoriness to the sodium-retaining action of mineralocorticoid during starvation in man. J Clin Endocrinol Metab 38:248, 1974
102. Muller WA, Faloona GR, Unger RH: Influence of the antecedent diet upon glucagon and insulin secretion. N Engl J Med 285:1450, 1971
103. O'Brian JT, Saudek CD, Spark RF, Arky RA: Glucagon induced refractoriness to exogenous mineralocorticoid. J Clin Endocrinol Metab 38:1147, 1974
104. Tanzer FS, Kennedy JW III, Talmage RV: A comparison of the effects of thyrocalcitonin and glucagon on plasma calcium and phosphate. Proc Soc Exp Biol Med 133:500, 1969
105. De Venanzi F: Comparison between changes in serum organic phosphorus induced by glucose and glucagon in diabetics. Proc Soc Exp Biol Med 90:112, 1955
106. Crockford PM, Porte D Jr, Wood FC Jr, Williams RH: Effect of glucagon on serum insulin, plasma glucose and free fatty acids in man. Metabolism 15:114, 1966
107. Samols E, Marri G, Marks V: Interrelationship of glucagon, insulin and glucose. The insulinogenic effect of glucagon. Diabetes 15:855, 1966

108. Paloyan E, Paloyan D, Harper PV: The role of glucagon hypersecretion in the relationship of pancreatitis and hyperparathyroidism. Surgery 62:167, 1967
109. Birge SJ, Avioli LV: Glucagon-induced hypocalcemia in man. J Clin Endocrinol 29:213, 1969
110. Care AD, Bates RSL, Gitelman NJ: A possible role for the adenyl cyclase system in calcium release. J Endocrinol 48:1, 1970
111. Stern PH, Bell NH: Effects of glucagon on serum calcium in the rat and on bone resorption in tissue culture. Endocrinology 87:111, 1970
112. Lawrence AM: Radioimmunoassayable glucagon levels in man. Effects of starvation, hypoglycemia and glucose administration. Proc Natl Acad Sci USA 55:315, 1966
113. Weir GC, Lesser PB, Drop LJ, et al: The hypocalcemia of acute pancreatitis. Ann Intern Med 83:185, 1975
114. Drew SI, Joffe B, Vinik A, et al: The first 24 hours of acute pancreatitis. Changes in biochemical and endocrine homeostasis in patients with pancreatitis compared with those in control subjects undergoing stress for reasons other than pancreatitis. Am J Med 64:795, 1978
115. Robertson GM, Moor EW, Switz DM, et al: Inadequate parathyroid response in acute pancreatitis. N Engl J Med 294:512, 1976
116. Kuzuya T, Kajinuma H, Ide T: Effect of intrapancreatic injection of potassium and calcium on insulin and glucagon secretion in dogs. Diabetes 23:55, 1974
117. Robertson RP, Porte D Jr: Adrenergic modulation of basal insulin secretion in man. Diabetes 22:1, 1973
118. Sacca L, Eigler N, Cryer PE, Sherwin RS: Insulin antagonistic effects of glucagon and epinephrine in the dog. Am J Physiol 237:E487, 1979
119. Peart WS: Renin-angiotensin system. N Engl J Med 292:302, 1975
120. Craig AB Jr, Mendel PL: Blockade of hyperkalemia and hyperglycemia induced by epinephrine in frog liver and in cats. Am J Physiol 197:52, 1954
121. Vick RL, Todd EP, Luedke DW: Epinephrine-induced hypokalemia: Relation to liver and skeletal muscle. J Pharmacol Exp Ther 181:139, 1972
122. Lockwood RH, Lum BKB: Effects of adrenergic agonists and antagonists on potassium metabolism. J Pharmacol Exp Ther 189:119, 1974
123. Rosa RM, Silva P, Young JB, et al: Adrenergic modulation of extrarenal potassium disposal. N Engl J Med 302:431, 1980
124. Conn JW, Fajans SS: Influence of adrenal corticol steroids on carbohydrate metabolism in man. Metabolism 5:114, 1956
125. Ikkos D, Luft R: Aspects of the metabolic action of human growth hormone. p 117. In Wolstenholme GEW, O'Conner CM (eds): CIBA Foundation Colloquia on Endocrinology, Vol 13. Little, Brown, Boston, 1959
126. Müller WA, Faloona GR, Unger RH: Hyperglucagonemia in diabetic ketoacidosis: Its prevalence and significance. Am J Med 54:52, 1973
127. Loeb JN: The hyperosmolar state. N Engl J Med 290:1184, 1974
128. Feig PU, McCurdy DK: The hypertonic state. N Engl J Med 297:1444, 1977
129. Brodsky WA, Rapoport S, West CD: The mechanism of glycosuric diuresis in diabetic man. J Clin Invest 29:1021, 1950
130. Seldin DW, Tarail R: The metabolism of glucose and electrolytes in diabetic acidosis. J Clin Invest 29:552, 1950
131. Linton AL, Kennedy AC: Diabetic ketoacidosis complicated by acute renal failure. Postgrad Med J 39:364, 1963
132. Zerbe RL, Vinicor F, Robertson GL: Plasma vasopressin in uncontrolled diabetes mellitus. Diabetes 28:503, 1979
133. Walsh CH, Baylis PH, Malins JM: Plasma arginine vasopressin in diabetic ketoacidosis. Diabetologia 16:93, 1979
134. Fitzsimons JT: The physiological basis of thirst. Kidney Int 10:3, 1976
135. Reubi FC: Glomerular filtration rate, renal blood flow and blood viscosity during and after diabetic coma. Circ Res 1:410, 1953
136. Bernstein LM, Foley EF, Hoffman WS: Renal function during and after diabetic coma. J Clin Invest 31:711, 1952
137. Trever RW, Cluff LE: The problem of increasing azotemia during the management of diabetic acidosis. Am J Med 24:368, 1958

138. Arief AI: Kidney, water and electrolyte metabolism in diabetes mellitus. p. 1257. In Brenner BM, Rector FC (eds): The Kidney. WB Saunders, Philadelphia, 1976
139. Seldin DW, Tarail R: Effect of hypertonic solutions on metabolism and excretion of electrolytes. Am J Physiol 159:160, 1944
140. Christlieb AR, Assal JP, Katsilambros N, et al: Plasma renin activity and blood volume in uncontrolled diabetes. Ketoacidosis, a state of secondary aldosteronism. Diabetes 24:190, 1975
141. Munro JF, Campbell IW, McCuish AC, Duncan LJP: Euglycemic ketoacidosis. Br Med J 2:578, 1973
142. Darrow DG, Pratt EL: Retention of water and electrolyte during recovery in a patient with diabetic acidosis. J Pediat 4:688, 1942
143. Martin HE, Smith K, Wilson ML: The fluid and electrolyte therapy of severe diabetic acidosis and ketosis. A study of twenty-nine episodes (twenty-six patients). Am J Med 20:376, 1958
144. Beigelman PM: Severe diabetic ketoacidosis (diabetic "coma"). 482 episodes in 257 patients, experience of three years. Diabetes 20:490, 1971
145. Adrogue AJ, Lederer ED, Suku WN, Eknoyan G: Determinants of plasma potassium levels in diabetic ketoacidosis. Medicine 65:163, 1986
146. Tyler FH: Hyperosmolar coma. Am J Med 45:485, 1968
147. Fulop M, Rosenblatt A, Kreitzer SM, Gerstenhaber B: Hyperosmolar nature of diabetic coma. Diabetes 24:594, 1975
148. Fulop M, Tannenbaum H, Dreyer N: Ketotic hyperosmolar coma. Lancet 2:635, 1973
149. Wierzuchowski M: Overflow diabetes and toxic phenomena due to the infusion of glucose in normal dogs. J Physiol 87:85P, 1936
150. Astwood EB, Flynn JM, Krayer O: Effects of continuous intravenous infusion of glucose in normal dogs. J Clin Invest 21:621, 1942
151. Clements RS Jr, Vourganti B: Fatal diabetic ketoacidosis: Major cause and approaches to their prevention. Diabetes Care 1:314, 1978
152. Danowski TS, Peters JH, Rathbun JC, et al: Studies in diabetic acidosis and coma with particular emphasis on retention of administered potassium. J Clin Invest 28:1, 1949
153. Butler AM, Talbot NB, Burnett CH, et al: Metabolic studies in diabetic coma. Trans Am Assoc Physicians 60:102, 1947
154. Blumenthal SA: Observations on sodium retention related to insulin treatment of experimental diabetes. Diabetes 24:645, 1975
155. Katz MA: Hyperglycemia-induced hyponatremia-calculation of the expected serum sodium depression. N Engl J Med 289:843, 1973
156. Makoff DL, Da Silva JA, Rosenbaum BJ: On the mechanism of hyperkalemia due to hyperosmotic expansion with saline or mannitol. Clin Sci 41:383, 1971
157. Swan RC, Pitts RF: Neutralization of infused acid by nephrectomized dogs. J Clin Invest 34:205, 1955
158. Burnell JH, Villamil MF, Uyeno BT, Scribner BH: The effect in humans of extracellular pH changes on the relationship between serum potassium concentration and intracellular potassium. J Clin Invest 35:935, 1956
159. Fulop M: Serum potassium in lactic acidosis and ketoacidosis. N Engl J Med 300:1087, 1979
160. Beigelman PM: Potassium in severe diabetic ketoacidosis. Am J Med 54:419, 1973
161. Wacker WEC, Parisi AF: Magnesium metabolism. N Engl J Med 278:712, 1968
162. Martin HE: Clinical magnesium deficiency. Ann NY Acad Sci 162:891, 1969
163. Kreisberg RA: Diabetic ketoacidosis: New concepts and trends in pathogenesis and treatment. Ann Intern Med 88:681, 1978
164. Guest GM, Rapoport S: Role of acid-soluble phosphorus compounds in red blood cells. Am J Dis Child 58:1072, 1939
165. Alberti KGMM, Darley JH, Emerson PM, Hockaday TDR: 2,3-Diphosphoglycerate and tissue oxygenation in uncontrolled diabetes mellitus. Lancet 2:391, 1972
166. Guest GM: Relationship of potassium and inorganic phosphorus to organic acid soluble phosphates in erythrocytes. Lancet 73:188, 1953
167. Travis SF, Morrison AD, Clements RS Jr, et al: Metabolic alterations in the human erythrocyte produced by increases in glu-

cose concentration. The role of the polyol pathway. J Clin Invest 50:2104, 1971
168. Benesch R, Benesch RE: The effect of organic phosphates from human erythrocytes on the allosteric properties of hemoglobin. Biochem Biophys Res Commun 26:162, 1967
169. Chanutin A, Curnish RR: Effect of organic and inorganic phosphates on the oxygen equilibrium of human erythrocytes. Arch Biochem Biophys 121:96, 1967
170. Bellingham AJ, Detter JC, Lenfant C: The role of hemoglobin affinity for oxygen and red cell 2,3-diphosphoglycerate in the management of diabetic ketoacidosis. Trans Am Assoc Physicians 83:113, 1970
171. Ditzel J, Standl E: The oxygen transport system of red blood cells during diabetic ketoacidosis and recovery. Diabetologia 11:255, 1975
172. Ungar RH, Orci L: The essential role of glucagon in the pathogenesis of diabetes mellitus. Lancet 1:14, 1975
173. Balasse EO, Havel RJ: Evidence for an effect of insulin on the peripheral utilization of ketone bodies in dogs. J Clin Invest 50:801, 1971
174. Sherwin RS, Hendler RG, Felig P: Effect of diabetes mellitus and insulin on the turnover and metabolic response to ketones in man. Diabetes 25:776, 1976
175. Wieland O: Ketogenesis and its regulation. Adv Metab Disord 3:1–47, 1968
176. McGarry JD, Robles-Valdes G, Foster DW: The role of carnitine in hepatic ketogenesis. Proc Natl Acad Sci USA 72:4385, 1975
177. McGarry JD, Leatherman GF, Foster DF: Carnitine palmitoyl-transferase I—the site of inhibition of hepatic fatty acid oxidation by malonyl-CoA. J Biol Chem 253:4128, 1978
178. McGarry JD: New perspectives in the regulation of ketogenesis. Diabetes 28:517, 1979
179. Stephens JM, Sulway MJ, Watkins PJ: Relationship of blood acetoacetate and 3-hydroxybutyrate in diabetes. Diabetes 20:485, 1971
180. Oh MS, Carroll HJ: The anion gap. N Engl J Med 297:814, 1977
181. Lim KC, Walsh CH: Diabetic ketoalkalosis. A readily misdiagnosed entity. Br Med J 2:19, 1976
182. Roggin GM, Moses D, Kautcher M, et al: Ketosis and metabolic alkalosis in a patient with diabetes. JAMA 211:296, 1970
183. Koett J, Howell J, Steinberg S, Wolf P: Diabetic ketoalkalosis. Clin Chem 25:1329, 1979
184. Giammarco R, Goldstein MB, Halperin ML, Stinebaugh BJ: Renal tubular acidosis during therapy for diabetic ketoacidosis. Can Med Assoc J 112:463, 1975
185. Bailey CC Jr, Steiner RW: Renal acidification defect in diabetes mellitus. (Letter) Ann Intern Med 92:263, 1980
186. Hammeke M, Bear R, Lee R, et al: Hyperchloremic metabolic acidosis in diabetes mellitus. A case report and discussion of the pathophysiologic mechanism. Diabetes 27:16, 1978
187. Fisher AH: Hyperchloremic acidosis and diabetic ketoacidosis. (Letter) Ann Intern Med 90:722, 1978
188. Page MM, Alberti KGMM, Greenwood R, et al: Treatment of diabetic coma with continuous low-dose infusion of insulin. Br Med J 2:687, 1974
189. Alberti KGMM, Hockaday TDR, Turner RC: Small doses of intramuscular insulin in the treatment of diabetic "coma." Lancet 2:515, 1973
190. Edwards GA, Kohaut EC, Wehring B, Hill IL: Effectiveness of low-dose continuous intravenous insulin infusion in diabetic ketoacidosis. J Pediatr 91:701, 1977
191. Fisher JN, Shahshahani M, Kitabchi AE: Diabetic ketoacidosis: Low-dose insulin therapy by various routes. N Engl J Med 297:238, 1977
192. Waldhäusl W, Kleinberger G, Korn A, et al: Severe hyperglycemia: Effects of rehydration on endocrine derangements and blood glucose concentration. Diabetes 28:577, 1979
193. Felig P: Diabetic ketoacidosis. N Engl J Med 290:1360, 1974
194. Oh MS, Carroll HJ, Goldstein DA, Fein IA: Hyperchloremic acidosis during the recovery phase of diabetic ketosis. Ann Intern Med 89:925, 1978
195. Kydd D: Salt and water in the treatment of diabetic acidosis. J Clin Invest 12:1169, 1933

196. Sprague RG, Power MH: Electrolyte metabolism in diabetic acidosis. JAMA 151:970, 1953
197. Oh MS, Banerji MA, Carroll HJ: The mechanism of hypercholoremic acidosis during the recovery phase of diabetic ketoacidosis. Diabetes 30:310, 1981
198. Daggett P, Deanfield J, Moss F, Reynolds D: Severe hypernatremia in adults. Br Med J 1:1177, 1979
199. Holler JW: Potassium deficiency occurring during the treatment of diabetic acidosis. JAMA 131:1186, 1946
200. Abramson E, Arky R: Diabetic acidosis with initial hypokalemia. Therapeutic implications. JAMA 196:401, 1966
201. Soler NG, Bennett MA, Dixon K, et al: Potassium balance during treatment of diabetic ketoacidosis with special reference to the use of bicarbonate. Lancet 2:665, 1972
202. Soler NG, Bennett MA, FitzGerald MG, Malins JM: Intensive care in the management of diabetic ketoacidosis. Lancet 1:951, 1973
203. Keller U, Berger W: Prevention of hypophosphatemia by phosphate infusion during treatment of diabetic ketoacidosis and hyperosmolar coma. Diabetes 29:87, 1980
204. Franks M, Berris RF, Kaplan NO, Myers GB: Metabolic studies in diabetic acidosis. II. The effect of the administration of sodium phosphate. Arch Intern Med 81:42, 1948
205. Kebler R, McDonald FD, Cadnapaphornchai P: Dynamic changes in serum phosphorus levels in diabetic ketoacidosis. Am J Med 79:571, 1985
206. Steele TH: Increased urinary phosphate excretion following volume expansion in normal man. Metabolism 19:129, 1970
207. Forsham PH, Thorn GW: Changes of organic serum phosphorus during the intravenous glucose tolerance test as an adjunct to the diagnosis of early diabetes mellitus. Proc Am Diabetes Assoc 9:101, 1950
208. Piters KM, Kumar D, Pei E, Bessman AN: Comparison of continuous and intermittant intravenous insulin therapies for diabetic ketoacidosis. Diabetologia 13:317, 1977
209. Riley MS, Schade DS, Eaton RP: Effects of insulin infusion on plasma phosphate in diabetic patients. Metabolism 28:191, 1979
210. Knochel JP: The pathophysiology and clinical characteristics of severe hypophosphatemia. Arch Intern Med 137:203, 1977
211. O'Connor LR, Wheeler WS, Bethune JE: Effect of hypophosphatemia on myocardial performance in man. N Engl J Med 297:901, 1977
212. Davis SV, Olichweir KR, Chakko SC: Reversible depression of myocardial performance in hypophosphatemia. Am J Med Sci 295:183, 1988
213. Darsee JR, Nutter DO: Reversible severe congestive cardiomyopathy in three cases of hypophosphatemia. Ann Intern Med 89:867, 1978
214. Newman JH, Neff TA, Ziporin P: Acute respiratory failure associated with hypophosphatemia. N Engl J Med 296:1101, 1977
215. Friedlander K, Rosenthal WH: Uber der Einfluss des Phosphosaureions auf den Blut und Harnzuckle des normalgen und des diabetischen Organismus. Arch Exp Path Pharmakol 112:66, 1926
216. Guest GM, Rapoport S: Electrolytes of blood plasma and cells in diabetic acidosis and during recovery. Diabetes 7:97, 1948
217. Bonnici F: Traitement de la céto-acidose diabétique: intérêt d'un supplément de phosphate de potassium: L'effet sur le 2,3-diphosphoglycerate at l'oxygénation tissulaire. Nouv Press Med 7:3743, 1978
218. Munk P, Freedman MH, Levison H, Ehrlich RM: Effect of bicarbonate on oxygen transport in juvenile diabetic ketoacidosis. J Pediatr 84:510, 1974
219. DeFronzo RA, Lang R: Hypophosphatemia and glucose intolerance: evidence for tissue insensitivity to insulin. N Engl J Med 303:1259, 1980
220. Drash AL: The treatment of diabetic ketoacidosis. (Editorial) J Pediatr 91:858, 1977
221. Bacon GE, Spencer ML, Kelch RP: Diabetes mellitus. p 6. In Bacon, GE (ed): A Practical Approach to Pediatric Endocrinology. Year Book Medical Publishers, Chicago, 1975
222. Zipf WB, Bacon GE, Spencer ML, et al: Hypocalcemia, hypomagnesemia, and transient hypoparathyroidism during therapy with potassium phosphate in diabetic ketoacidosis. Diabetes Care 2:265, 1979

223. Anast CS, Winnacker JL, Forte LR, Burns TW: Impaired release of parathyroid hormone in magnesium deficiency. J Clin Endocrinol Metab 42:707, 1976
224. Winter RJ, Harris CJ, Phillips LS, Green OC: Diabetic ketoacidosis. Induction of hypocalcemia and hypomagnesemia by phosphate therapy. Am J Med 67:897, 1979
225. Lavis VR: Treatment of diabetic ketoacidosis. Diabetes Care 2:385, 1979 (Letter)
226. Butler AM: Diabetic coma. N Engl J Med 243:648, 1950
227. King AJ, Cooke NJ, McCuish A, et al: Acid-base changes during treatment of diabetic ketoacidosis. Lancet 1:478, 1974
228. Thrower WB, Darby TD, Aldinger EE: Acid-base derangements and myocardial contractility. Effects as a complication of shock. Arch Surg 82:56, 1961
229. Cingolani HE, Mattiazzi AR, Blesa ES, Gongalez NC: Contractility in isolated mammalian heart muscle after acid-base changes. Circ Res 26:269, 1970
230. Gerst PH, Fleming WH, Malm JR: A quantitative evaluation of the effects of acidosis and alkalosis upon the ventricular fibrillation threshold. Surgery 59:1050, 1966
231. Nahas GG, Ligou JC, Mehlman B: Effects of pH changes on O_2 uptake and plasma catecholamine levels in the dog. Am J Physiol 198:60, 1960
232. Misbin RI, Pulkkinen AJ, Lofton SA, Merimee TJ: Ketoacids and the insulin receptor. Diabetes 27:539, 1978
233. Kitabchi AE, Ayyagari V, Guerra SMO: The efficacy of low-dose versus conventional therapy of insulin for treatment of diabetic ketoacidosis. Ann Intern Med 84:663, 1976
234. Mcrris LR, Murphy MB, Kitabchi AE: Bicarbonate therapy in severe diabetic ketoacidosis. Ann Intern Med 105:836, 1986
235. Gonzalez-Villalpando C, Blachley JD, Vaughan GM, Smith JD: Low- and high-dose intravenous insulin therapy for diabetic ketoacidosis. JAMA 241:925, 1979
236. Garella S, Dana CL, Chazan JA: Severity of metabolic acidosis as a determinant of bicarbonate requirements. N Engl J Med 289:121, 1973
237. Zimmet PZ, Taft P, Ennis GC, Sheath J: Acid production in diabetic acidosis: A more rational approach to alkali replacement. Br Med J 3:610, 1970
238. Mellemgaard K, Astrup P: The quantitative determination of surplus amounts of acid or base in the human body. Scand J Clin Lab Invest 12:187, 1960
239. Posner JB, Plum F: Spinal-fluid pH and neurologic symptoms in systemic acidosis. N Engl J Med 277:605, 1967
240. Assal J-P, Aoki TT, Manzano FM, Kozak GP: Metabolic effects of sodium bicarbonate in management of diabetic ketoacidosis. Diabetes 23:405, 1974
241. Ohman JL, Marliss EB, Aoki TT, et al: The cerebrospinal fluid in diabetic ketoacidosis. N Engl J Med 284:283, 1971
242. Chisholm DJ: Insulin therapy, recent advances in ketoacidosis, hyperosmolar coma and insulin to test. Med J Aust 2:494, 1976
243. Young E, Bradley RF: Cerebral edema with irreversible coma in severe diabetic ketoacidosis. N Engl J Med 276:665, 1967
244. Maccario M, Messis CP: Cerebral edema complicating treated nonketotic hyperglycemia. Lancet 2:352, 1969
245. Duck SC, Weldon VV, Pagliara AS, Haymond MW: Cerebral edema complicating therapy for diabetic ketoacidosis. Diabetes 25:111, 1976
246. Clements RS Jr, Prockop LD, Windegrad AI: Acute cerebral edema during treatment of hyperglycemia. An experimental model. Lancet 2:384, 1968
247. Arieff AI, Kleeman CR: Studies on mechanisms of cerebral edema in diabetic comas. Effects of hyperglycemia and rapid lowering of plasma glucose in normal rabbits. J Clin Invest 52:571, 1973
248. Kinoshita JH, Futterman S, Satoh K, Merola LO: Factors affecting the formation of sugar alcohols in ocular lens. Biochim Biophys Acta 74:340, 1963
249. Prockop LD: Hyperglycemia, polyol accumulation, and increased intracranial pressure. Arch Neurol 25:126, 1971
250. Stern WE, Coxon RV: Osmolality of brain tissue and its relation to brain bulk. Am J Physiol 206:1, 1964
251. Clements RS Jr, Blumental SA, Morrison AD, Winegrad AI: Increased cerebrospinal fluid pressure during treatment of diabetic ketoacidosis. Lancet 2:671, 1971

252. Wachtel TJ, Silliman RA, Lamberton A: Predisposing factors for the diabetic hyperosmolar state. Arch Intern Med 147:499, 1987
253. Rubin HM, Kramer R, Drash A: Hyperosmolarity complicating diabetes mellitus in childhood. J Pediatr 74:177, 1969
254. McCurdy DK: Hyperosmolar hyperglycemic nonketotic diabetic coma. Med Clin North Am 54:683, 1970
255. Gerich JE, Martin MM, Recant L: Clinical and metabolic characteristics of hyperosmolar nonketotic coma. Diabetes 20:228, 1971
256. Arieff AI, Carroll HJ: Nonketotic hyperosmolar coma with hyperglycemia: Clinical features, pathophysiology, renal function, acid-base balance, plasma-cerebrospinal fluid equilibria and the effects of therapy in 37 cases. Medicine 51:73, 1972
257. Evans EI, Butterfield WJH: The stress response in the severely burned. Ann Surg 134:588, 1951
258. Rosenberg SA, Brief DK, Kinney JM, et al: The syndrome of dehydration, coma and severe hyperglycemia in patients convalescing from burns. N Engl J Med 272:931, 1965
259. Brenner WI, Lansky Z, Engelman RM, Stahl WM: Hyperosmolar coma in surgical patients—An iatrogenic disease of increasing incidence. Ann Surg 178:651, 1973
260. Potter DJ: Death as a result of hyperglycemia without ketosis-a complication of hemodialysis. Ann Intern Med 64:399, 1966
261. Boyer J, Gill GN, Epstein FH: Hyperglycemia and hyperosmolarity complicating peritoneal dialysis. Ann Intern Med 67:568, 1967
262. Wynn V: Electrolyte disturbances associated with failure to metabolize glucose during hypothermia. Lancet 2:575, 1954
263. Vinik A, Seftel H, Joffe BI: Metabolic findings in hyperosmolar, nonketotic diabetic stupor. Lancet 2:797, 1970
264. Davidson AIG: Diabetic coma without ketoacidosis in a patient with acute pancreatitis. Br Med J 1:356, 1964
265. Nielson OS, Simonsen, E: A case of transient diabetes mellitus in connection with acute pancreatitis. Acta Med Scand 185:459, 1969
266. Milloy P: Hyperosmolar nonketotic coma in acromegaly. JAMA 222:814, 1972
267. Jacobson R, Horenstein M, Kassel L: Hyperglycemia and hyperosmolarity in a brittle diabetic with thyrotoxicosis. Diabetes 19:70, 1970
268. Sanbar SS, Conway FJ, Zweifler AJ, Smet G: Diabetogenic effect of Dilantin (diphenylhydantoin). Diabetes 16:533, 1967
269. Goldberg EM, Sanbar SS: Hyperglycemia, nonketotic coma following administration of Dilantin (diphenylhydantoin). Diabetes 18:101, 1969
270. Boyer MH: Hyperosmolar anacidotic coma in association with glucocorticoid therapy. JAMA 202:1007, 1967
271. Charles MA, Danforth E Jr: Nonketoacidotic hyperglycemia and coma during intravenous diazoxide therapy in uremia. Diabetes 20:501, 1971
272. Shapiro AP, Benedek TG, Small JL: Effect of thiazides on carbohydrate metabolism in patients with hypertension. N Engl J Med 265:1028, 1961
273. Podolsky S, Pattavina CG: Hyperosmolar non-ketotic coma: a complication of propranolol therapy. Metabolism 22:685, 1973
274. Maccario M, Messis CP, Vastola EF: Focal seizures as a manifestation of hyperglycemia without ketoacidosis. A report of seven cases with review of the literature. Neurology 15:195, 1965
275. Gordon EE, Kabadi UM: The hyperglycemic hyperosmolar syndrome. Am J Med Sci 271:252, 1976
276. Chupin M, Charbonnel B, Dubin B, et al: Profil hormonale et métabolique du coma hyperosmolaire diabétique. Diab Metab 4:243, 1978
277. Stahl WM: Effect of mannitol on the kidney. N Engl J Med 272:381, 1965
278. Guisado R, Arieff AI: Neurologic manifestations of diabetic comas: Correlation with biochemical alterations in the brain. Metabolism 24:665, 1975
279. Fineberg L, Luttrell C, Redd H: Pathogenesis of lesions in the nervous system in hypernatremic states: Experimental studies of gross anatomic changes and alterations of chemical composition of the tissue. Pediatrics 23:46, 1959
280. Harreveld AV, Hooper NK, Guisick JT:

Brain electrolytes and cortical impedance. Am J Physiol 201:139, 1961
281. Arieff AI, Carroll HJ: Cerebral edema and depression of sensorium in nonketotic hyperosmolar coma. Diabetes 23:525, 1974
282. DiBenedetto RJ, Crocco JA, Soscia JL: Hyperglycemic nonketotic coma. Arch Intern Med 116:74, 1965
283. Jackson WPU, Forman R: Hyperosmolar nonketotic diabetic coma. Diabetes 15:714, 1966
284. Stewart MA, Sherman WR, Kurien MM, et al: Polyol accumulations in nervous tissue of rats with experimental diabetes and galactosemia. J Neurochem 14:1057, 1967
285. Lassen NA: Cerebral blood flow and oxygen consumption in man. Physiol Rev 39:183, 1959
286. Kogut MD, Landing BH: Coma and hyperglycemia in the absence of ketonemia present in a 12-year-old boy. Am J Dis Child 114:676, 1967
287. Daughaday WH, Lipicky RJ, Rasinski DC: Lactic acidosis as a cause of nonketotic acidosis in diabetic patients. N Engl J Med 267:1010, 1967
288. Sotos JF, Dodge PR, Talbot NB: Studies in experimental hypertonicity. II. Hypertonicity of body fluids as a cause of acidosis. Pediatrics 30:180, 1962
289. Makoff DL, Da Silva JA, Rosenbaum BJ, et al: Hypertonic expansion: Acid-base and electrolyte changes. Am J Physiol 218:1201, 1970
290. Bewsher PD, Petrie JC, Worth HGJ: Serum lipid levels in hyperosmolar nonketotic diabetic coma. Br Med J 3:82, 1970
291. Foster DW: Insulin deficiency and hyperosmolar coma. Adv Intern Med 19:159, 1974
292. Joffe BI, Goldberg RB, Krut LH, Seftel HC: Pathogenesis of nonketotic hyperosmolar diabetic coma. Lancet 1:1069, 1975
293. Nelson JK: Hyperosmolar coma in diabetes. (Letter) Lancet 1:1376, 1966
294. Haapenen E: Hyperosmolar coma in diabetes. (Letter) Lancet 1:1154, 1966
295. Brown RH, Rossini AA, Callaway CW, Cahill GF Jr: Caveat on fluid replacement in hyperglycemic, hyperosmolar, nonketotic coma. Diabetes Care 1:305, 1978
296. Axelrod L: Response of congestive heart failure to correction of hyperglycemia in the presence of diabetic nephropathy. N Engl J Med 293:1243, 1975
297. Kaldany A, Curt GA, Estes M, et al: Reversible acute pulmonary edema due to uncontrolled hyperglycemia in diabetic individuals with renal failure. Diabetes Care 5:506, 1982
298. Irsigler K, Kaspan L: Hyperglycemic, hyperosmolar, nonketotic coma: Hypotonic or hypertonic treatment? (Letter) Diabetes Care 2:532, 1979
299. Irsigler K, Kaspar L, Bruneder H, Lageder H: Kein freies Wasser bei der Therapie des "Coma diabeticum hyperosmolare"! Dtsch Med Wochenschr 102:1655, 1977
300. Irsigler K, Kaspar L: Coma diabeticum. Med Klin 74:257, 1979
301. Watkins PJ, Smith JS, Fitzgerald MG, Malins JM: Lactic acidosis in diabetes. Br Med J 1:744, 1969
302. Fulop M, Hoberman HD, Rascoff JH, et al: Lactic acidosis in diabetic patients. Arch Intern Med 136:987, 1976
303. Oliva PB: Lactic acidosis. Am J Med 48:209, 1970
304. Huckabee WE: Abnormal resting blood lactate 1. The significance of hyperlactatemia in hospitalized patients. Am J Med 30:833, 1961
305. Tranquada RE, Grant WJ, Peterson CR: Lactic acidosis. Arch Intern Med 117:192, 1966
306. Anderson J, Mazza R: Pyruvate and lactate excretion in patients with diabetes mellitus and benign glycosuria. Lancet 2:270, 1963
307. Kreisberg RA: Lactate homeostasis and lactic acidosis. Ann Intern Med 92:227, 1980
308. Wahren J, Hagenfeldt L, Felig P: Splanchnic and leg exchange of glucose, amino acids, and free fatty acids during exercise in diabetes mellitus. J Clin Invest 55:1303, 1975
309. Berger M, Hagg SA, Goodman MN, Ruderman NB: Glucose metabolism in perfused skeletal muscle. Biochem J 158:191, 1976
310. Hagg SA, Taylor SI, Ruderman NB: Glucose metabolism in perfused skeletal muscle pyruvate dehydrogenase activity in starvation, diabetes and exercise. Biochem J 158:203, 1976

311. DeMeutter RC, Shreeve WW: Conversion of DL-lactate-2-C^{14} or -3-C^{14} or pyruvate-2-C^{14} to blood glucose in humans: Effects of diabetes, insulin, tolbutamide, and glucose load. J Clin Invest 42:525, 1963
312. Garland PB, Newsholme EA, Randle PJ: Regulation of glucose uptake by muscle. 9. Effects of fatty acids and ketone bodies, and of alloxan diabetes and starvation, on pyruvate metabolism and on lactate/pyruvate and L-glycerol 3-phosphate/dihydroxyacetone phosphate concentration ratios in rat heart and rat diaphragm muscles. Biochem J 93:665, 1964
313. Arieff AI, Kerian A: Lactic acidosis: an experimental model. Metabolism 25:307, 1976
314. Relman AS: Lactic acidosis and a new possible treatment. (Editorial) N Engl J Med 298:564, 1978
315. Lee CT, Duncan GG: Diabetic coma: The value of a simple test for acetone in the plasma—An aid to diagnosis and treatment. Metabolism 5:144, 1956
316. Alberti KGMM, Hockaday TDR: Rapid ketone body estimation in the diagnosis of diabetic ketoacidosis. Br Med J 2:565, 1972
317. Marliss EB, Ohman JL Jr, Aoki TT, Kozak GP: Altered redox state obscuring ketoacidosis in diabetic patients with lactic acidosis. N Engl J Med 283:978, 1970
318. Fulop M, Hoberman HD: Alcoholic ketosis. Diabetes 24:785, 1975
319. Miller PD, Heinig RE, Waterhouse C: Treatment of alcoholic acidosis. The role of dextrose and phosphorus. Arch Intern Med 138:67, 1978
320. Sussman KE: p. 559. In Leibel BS, Wrenshall GA (eds): On the Nature and Treatment of Diabetes. International Congress Series, No 84. Excerpta Medica, Amsterdam
321. Alberti KGMM, Hockaday TDR: Blood lactic and pyruvic acids in diabetic coma. (Abstract) Diabetes 21:350, 1972
322. Blackshear PJ, Alberti KGMM: Experimental diabetic ketoacidosis. Sequential changes of metabolic intermediates in blood, liver, cerebrospinal fluid and brain after acute insulin deprivation in the streptozotocin-diabetic rat. Biochem J 138:107, 1974
323. Blackshear PJ, Holloway PAH, Alberti KGMM: Metabolic interactions of dichloroacetate and insulin in experimental diabetic ketoacidosis. Biochem J 146:447, 1975
324. Waters WC III, Hall JD, Schwarz WB: Spontaneous lactic acidosis. The nature of the acid-base disturbance and considerations in diagnosis and management. Am J Med 35:781, 1963
325. Ungar G, Psychoyos S, Hall A: Action of phenethylbiguanide, a hypoglycemic agent, on tricarboxylic acid cycle. Metabolism 9:36, 1960
326. Searle GL, Siperstein MD: Lactic acidosis associated with phenformin therapy. Evidence that inhibited lactate oxidation is the causative factor. Diabetes 24:741, 1975
327. Assan R, Heuclin C, Girard JR, et al: Phenformin induced lactic acidosis in diabetic patients. Diabetes 24:791, 1975
328. University Group Diabetes Program: A Study of the effects of hypoglycemic agents on vascular complications in patients with adult-onset diabetes. V: Evaluation of phenformin therapy. Diabetes 24: (Suppl 1):65, 1975
329. Phenformin: removal from general market. FDA Drug Bull 7(3):14, 1977
330. Misbin RI: Phenformin-associated lactic acidosis: Pathogenesis and treatment. Ann Intern Med 87:591, 1977
331. Stacpoole PW, Moore GW, Kornhauser DM: Metabolic effects of dichloroacetate in patients with diabetes mellitus and hyperlipoproteinemia. N Engl J Med 298:526, 1978
332. Ribes G, Valette G, Loubatiéres-Mariani M-M: Metabolic effects of sodium dichloroacetate in normal and diabetic dogs. Diabetes 28:852, 1979
333. Whitehouse S, Cooper RH, Randle PJ: Mechanisms of activation of pyruvate dehydrogenase by dichloroacetate and other halogenated carboxylic acids. Biochem J 141:761, 1974
334. Stacpoole PW, Moore GW, Kornhauser DM: Toxicity of chronic dichloroacetate. (Letter) N Engl J Med 300:372, 1979
335. Taradish MR, Jacobson LB: Vasodilator therapy of idiopathic lactic acidosis. N Engl J Med 293:468, 1975

336. Vaziri ND, Ness R, Wellikson L, et al: Bicarbonate-buffered peritoneal dialysis: An effective adjunct in the treatment of lactic acidosis. Am J Med 67:392, 1979
337. Arieff AI, Doerner T, Zelig H, Massry SG: Mechanisms of seizures and coma in hypoglycemia: Evidence for a direct effect of insulin on electrolyte transport in brain. J Clin Invest 54:654, 1974
338. Leifer A: A case of insulin edema. JAMA 90:610, 1928
339. Bradley RF: Diabetic ketoacidosis and coma. p. 361. In Marble A, White P, Bradley RF, Krall LP (eds): Joslin's Diabetes Mellitus, 11th Ed. Lea ane Febiger, Philadelphia, 1971
340. Garcia-Lemo J, Böhm GM, Migliorini RH, DeSouza MZA: Possible participation of insulin in the control of vascular permeability. Eur J Pharmacol 29:298, 1974
341. Bleach NR, Dunn PJ, Khalafalla ME, McConkey B: Insulin oedema. Br Med J 2:177, 1979
342. Pak CYC, Ohata M, Lawrence EC, Snyder W: The hypercalciurias: Causes, parathyroid functions, and diagnostic criteria. J Clin Invest 54:387, 1974
343. Levin ME, Boisseau VC, Avioli LV: Effects of diabetes mellitus on bone mass in juvenile and adult-onset diabetes. N Engl J Med 294:241, 1976
344. DeLeeuw I, Abs R: Bone mass and bone density in maturity type diabetes measured by the ^{125}I photon-absorption technique. Diabetes 26:1130, 1977
345. Rosenblood AL, Lezotte DC, Weber T, et al: Diminution of bone mass in childhood diabetes. Diabetes 26:1052, 1977
346. Jackson CE, Meier DW: Routine serum magnesium analysis. Correlation with clinical state in 5100 patients. Ann Intern Med 69:743, 1968
347. Stutzman FL, Amatuzio DS: Blood serum magnesium in portal cirrhosis and diabetes mellitus. J Lab Clin Med 41:215, 1953
348. McNair P, Christiansen C, Madsbad S, et al: Hypomagnesemia, a risk factor for diabetic retinopathy. Diabetes 27:1075, 1978
349. Mather HM, Nisbet J, Burton GH, et al: Plasma magnesium levels in diabetes. (Abstract) Diabetologia 15:254, 1978
350. Mather HM, Levin GE: Magnesium status in diabetes. (Letter) Lancet 1:924, 1979
351. Visser HKA, Cost WS: A new hereditary defect in the biosynthesis of aldosterone: Urinary C_{21}-corticosteroid pattern in three related patients with a salt-losing syndrome, suggesting an 18-oxidation defect. Acta Endocrinol (Köbenhavn) 47:489, 1964
352. Ulick S, Gautier E, Vetter KK, et al: An aldosterone biosynthetic defect in a salt-losing disorder. J Clin Endocrinol Metab 25:669, 1964
353. Wilson ID, Goetz FC: Selective hypoaldosteronism after prolonged heparin administration. Am J Med 36:635, 1964
354. Hudson JB, Chobanian AV, Relman AS: Hypoaldosteronism: A clinical study of a patient with an isolated adrenal mineralocorticoid deficiency resulting in hyperkalemia and Stokes-Adams attacks. N Engl J Med 257:529, 1957
355. Schambelan M, Stockigt JR, Biglieri EG: Isolated hypoaldosteronism in adults. A renin-deficiency syndrome. N Engl J Med 287:573, 1972
356. Perez G, Siegel L, Schreiner GE: Selective hypoaldosteronism with hyperkalemia. Ann Intern Med 76:757, 1972
357. Weidmann P, Reinhart R, Maxwell MH, et al: Syndrome of hyporeninemic hypoaldosteronism and hyperkalemia in renal disease. J Clin Endocrinol Metab 36:965, 1973
358. Tuck ML, Mayes DM: Mineralocorticoid biosynthesis in patients with hyporeninemic hypoaldosteronism. J Clin Endocrinol Metab 50:341, 1980
359. DeFronzo RA, Sherwin RS, Felig P, Bia M: Nonuremic diabetic hyperkalemia. Possible role of insulin deficiency (Editorial) Arch Intern Med 137:842, 1977
360. Christlieb AR, Kaldany A, D'Elia JA: Plasma renin activity and hypertension in diabetes mellitus. Diabetes 25:970, 1976
361. Christlieb AR, Munichoodappa C, Braaten JT: Decreased response of plasma renin activity to orthostasis in diabetic patients with orthostatic hypotension. Diabetes 23:835, 1974
362. Christlieb AR: Renin, angiotensin and norepinephrine in alloxan diabetes. Diabetes 23:962, 1974
363. Christlieb AR: Renin-angiotensin-aldosterone system in diabetes mellitus. Diabetes 25 (Suppl 2):820, 1976

364. Day RP, Luetscher JA, Gonzales CM: Occurrence of big renin in human plasma, amniotic fluid and kidney extracts. J Clin Endocrinol Metab 40:1078, 1975
365. deLeiva A, Christlieb AR, Melby JC, et al: Big renin and biosynthetic defect of aldosterone in diabetes mellitus. N Engl J Med 295:639, 1976
366. Oh MS, Carroll HJ, Clemmons JE, et al: A mechanism for hyporeninemic hypoaldosteronism in chronic renal disease. Metabolism 23:1157, 1974
367. Bell ET: Renal vascular disease in diabetes mellitus. Diabetes 2:376, 1953
368. Schindler AM, Sommers SC: Diabetic sclerosis of the renal juxtaglomerular apparatus. Lab Invest 15:877, 1966
369. Sparagana M: Hyporeninemic hypoaldosteronism with diabetic glomerulosclerosis. Biochem Med 14:93, 1975
370. Müller J, Barajas L: Electron microscopic and histochemical evidence for a tubular innervation in the renal cortex of the monkey. J Ultrastruct Res 41:533, 1972
371. Perez GO, Lespier L, Jacobi J, et al: Hyporeninemia and hypoaldosteronism in diabetes mellitus. Arch Intern Med 137:852, 1977
372. Fernandez-Cruz A, Lassman MN, Noth RH, et al: Low plasma renin activity in normotensive patients with diabetes and neuropathy. (Abstract) Diabetes 24 (Suppl 2):414, 1975
373. Davis JO, Freeman RH: Mechanisms regulating renin release. Physiol Rev 56:1, 1976
374. Christensen NJ: Plasma catecholamines in long-term diabetics with and without neuropathy and in hypophysectomized subjects. J Clin Invest 51:779, 1972
375. Tuck ML, Sambhi MP, Levin L: Hyporeninemic hypoaldosteronism in diabetes mellitus. Studies of the autonomic nervous system's control of renin release. Diabetes 28:237, 1979
376. Cryer PE, Silverberg AB, Santiago JV, Shah SD: Plasma catecholamines in diabetes. The syndromes of hypoadrenergic and hyperadrenergic postural hypotension. Am J Med 64:407, 1978
377. Neubauer B, Christensen NJ: Norepinephrine, epinephrine, and dopamine contents of the cardiovascular system in long-term diabetics. Diabetes 25:6, 1976
378. Christlieb AR, Janka HU, Kraus B, et al: Vascular reactivity to angiotensin II and to norepinephrine in diabetic subjects. Diabetes 25:268, 1974
379. Barani FR: Abnormal vascular reactions in diabetes mellitus. Acta Med Scand (Suppl 304) 52:3, 1955
380. Perez GO, Lespier LE, Oster JR, Vaamonde CA: Effect of alterations of sodium intake in patients with hyporeninemic hypoaldosteronism. Nephron 18:259, 1977
381. Phelps KR, Lieberman RL, Oh MS, Carroll HJ: Pathophysiology of the syndrome of hyporeninemic hypoaldosteronism. Metabolism 29:186, 1980
382. Maebashi M, Miura Y, Yoshinaga K: Suppressive effect of potassium on renin. Jpn Circ J 32:1265, 1968
383. Vander AJ: Direct effects of potassium on renin secretion and renal function. Am J Physiol 219:455, 1970
384. Brown JJ, Fraser R, Lever AF, et al: Renin, angiotensin, corticosteroids, and electrolyte balance in Addison's disease. QJ Med 37:97, 1968
385. Rösler A, Rabinowitz D, Theodor R, et al: The nature of the defect in a salt-wasting disorder in Jews of Iran. J Clin Endocrinol Metab 44:279, 1977
386. Frölich JC, Hollifield JW, Dormois JC, et al: Suppression of plasma renin activity by indomethacin in man. Circ Res 39:447, 1976
387. Christlieb AR, Kaldany A, D'Elia JA, Williams GH: Aldosterone responsiveness in patients with diabetes mellitus. Diabetes 27:732, 1978
388. Vagnucci AH: Selective aldosterone deficiency. J Clin Endocrinol Metab 29:279, 1964
389. Rösler A, Ulick A: Criteria for diagnosis of aldosterone biosynthetic defects. (Letter) N Engl J Med 295:1383, 1976
390. Ulick S, Vetter KK: Simultaneous measurement of secretory rates of aldosterone and 18-hydroxycorticosterone. J Clin Endocrinol Metab 25:1015, 1965
391. Williams GH: Aldosterone potassium and acidosis. (Editorial) N Engl J Med 294:392, 1976

392. Bayard F, Cooke CR, Tiller DJ, et al: The regulation of aldosterone secretion in anephric man. J Clin Invest 50:1585, 1971
393. Morimoto S, Kim KS, Yamamoto I, et al: Selective hypoaldosteronism with hyperreninemia in a diabetic patient. J Clin Endocrinol 49:742, 1979
394. Perez GO, Lespier L, Knowles R, et al: Potassium homeostasis in chronic diabetes mellitus. Arch Intern Med 137:1018, 1977
395. Michelis MF, Murdoch HV: Selective hypoaldosteronism. An editorial revisited after 15 years. (Editorial) Am J Med 59:1, 1975
396. Knochel JP: The syndrome of hyporeninemic hypoaldosteronism. Annu Rev Med 30:145, 1979
397. Szylman P, Better OS, Chaimowitz C, Rösler A: Role of hyperkalemia in the metabolic acidosis of isolated hypoaldosteronism. N Engl J Med 294:361, 1976
398. Arnold JE, Healy JK: Hyperkalemia, hypertension and systemic acidosis without renal failure associated with a tubular defect in potassium excretion. Am J Med 47:461, 1969
399. De Fronzo R, Cooke CR, Goldberg M, et al: Impaired renal tubular potassium secretion in systemic lupus erythematosus. Ann Intern Med 86:268, 1977
400. Viberti GC: Glucose-induced hyperkalemia: A hazard for diabetics? Lancet 1:690, 1978
401. Goldfarb S, Strunk B, Singer I, Goldberg M: Paradoxical glucose-induced hyperkalemia. Combined aldosterone-insulin deficiency. Am J Med 59:744, 1975
402. Goldfarb S, Cox M, Singer I, Goldberg M: Acute hyperkalemia induced by hyperglycemia: hormonal mechanisms. Ann Intern Med 84:462, 1976
403. Ammon RA, May WS, Nightingale SD: Glucose-induced hyperkalemia with normal aldosterone levels. Studies in a patient with diabetes mellitus. Ann Intern Med 89:349, 1978
404. McNay JL, Oran E: Possible predisposition of diabetic patients to hyperkalemia following administration of potassium-retaining diuretic, amiloride (MK 870). Metabolism 19:58, 1969
405. Walker BR, Capuzzi DM, Alexander F, et al: Hyperkalemia after triamterene in diabetic patients. Clin Pharmacol Ther 13:643, 1972
406. Taguma Y, Kitamoto Y, Futaki G, et al: Effect of captopril on heavy proteinuria in azotemic diabetics. N Engl J Med 313:1617, 1985
407. Hommel E, Parving HH, Mathiesen E, et al: Effect of captopril on kidney function in insulin-dependent diabetic patients with nephropathy. Br Med J 293:467, 1986
408. Moore MP, Elliott TW, Nicholls MG: Hormonal and metabolic effects of enalapril treatment in hypertensive subjects with NIDDM. Diabetes Care 11:397, 1988
409. American Diabetes Association Statement on hypertension in diabetes. Diabetes Care 10:764, 1987
410. Sebastian A, Schambelan M, Lindenfield S, Morris RC Jr: Amelioration of metabolic acidosis with fludrocortisone therapy in hyporeninemic hypoaldosteronism. N Engl J Med 297:576, 1977
411. Chobanian AV, Volicer L, Tifft CP, et al: Mineralocorticoid-induced hypertension in patients with orthostatic hypotension. N Engl J Med 301:68, 1979
412. Shapiro AP, Benedek TG, Small JL: Effect of thiazides on carbohydrate metabolism in patients with hypertension. N Engl J Med 265:1028, 1961
413. Wolff FW, Parmley WW, White K, Okun R: Drug-induced diabetes: Diabetogenic activity of long-term administration of benzothiadiazines. JAMA 185:568, 1963
414. Fuhrman FA: Glycogen, glucose tolerance, and tissue metabolism in potassium-deficient rats. Am J Physiol 167:314, 1965
415. Kohner EM, Dollery CT, Lowry C, Schumer B: Effect of diuretic therapy on glucose tolerance in hypertensive patients. Lancet 1:986, 1971
416. Breckenridge A, Welborn TA, Dollery CT, Fraser R: Glucose tolerance in hypertensive patients on long-term diuretic therapy. Lancet 1:61, 1967
417. Amery A, Berthaux P, Bulpitt C, et al: Glucose intolerance during diuretic therapy. Results of trial by the European Working Party on hypertension in the elderly. Lancet 1:681, 1978
418. Gordon P, Sherman BM, Simopoulos AP:

Glucose intolerance with hyperkalemia: An increased proportion of circulating proinsulin-like component. J Clin Endocrinol Metab 34:235, 1972
419. De Châtel R, Weidmann P, Flammer J, et al: Sodium, renin, aldosterone, catecholamines and blood pressure in diabetes mellitus. Kidney Int 12:413, 1977
420. Christlieb AR: Diabetes and hypertensive vascular disease. Am J Cardiol 32:592, 1973
421. Weidmann P, Beretta-Piccoli C, Keusch G, et al: Sodium-volume factor, cardiovascular reactivity and hypotensive mechanism of diuretic therapy in mild hypertension associated with diabetes mellitus. Am J Med 67:779, 1979
422. Cohen E, Dodds R, Viberti G: Effect of protein restriction in insulin dependent diabetics at risk of nephropathy. Br Med J 294:795, 1987
423. Kupin WL, Cortes P, Dumler F, et al: Effect on renal function of change from high to moderate protein intake in Type I diabetic patients. Diabetes 36:73, 1987
424. Evanoff GV, Thompson CS, Brown J, Weinman EJ: The effect of dietary protein restriction on the progression of diabetic nephropathy. A 12-month follow-up. Arch Intern Med 147:492, 1987
425. Comty CM, Leonard A, Shapiro FL: Nutritional and metabolic problems in the dialyzed patient with diabetes mellitus. Kidney Int 6 (Suppl 1):S-51, 1974
426. Watkins PJ, Parsons V, Bewick M: The prognosis and management of diabetic nephropathy. Clin Nephrol 7:243, 1977
427. Reaven G, Weisinger JR, Swenson RS: Insulin and glucose metabolism in renal insufficiency. Kidney Int 6: (Suppl 1):S-63, 1974
428. Bauer HG: Severe and prolonged hypoglycemic shock during sulfonylurea treatment. Metabolism 14:220, 1965
429. Stone WJ: Renal disease in the diabetic. South Med J 72:203, 1979
430. Diaz-Buxo JA, Wagoner RD, Hattery RR, Palumbo PJ: Acute renal failure after excretory urography in diabetic patients. Ann Intern Med 83:155, 1975
431. Harkonen S, Kjellstrand CM: Exacerbation of diabetic renal failure following intravenous pyelography. Am J Med 63:939, 1977
432. VanZee BE, Hoy WE, Talley TE, Jaenike JR: Renal injury associated with intravenous pyelography in nondiabetic and diabetic patients. Ann Intern Med 89:51, 1978
433. Pillay VKG, Robbins PC, Schwartz FD, Kark RM: Acute renal failure following intravenous urography in patients with long-standing diabetes mellitus and azotemia. Radiology 95:633, 1970
434. MacLachlin MSF, Chick S, Roberts EE, Asscher AW: Intravenous urography in experimental acute renal failure in the rat. Invest Radiol 7:466, 1972
435. Talner LB: Urographic contrast media in uremia. Radiol Clin North Am 10:421, 1972
436. Sobin SE, Fisher WG, Jacobson GJ, Van Eeckhoven EJ: Nature of adverse reactions to radioopaque agents: A preliminary report. JAMA 170:1546, 1959
437. Baladimos MC, Legg MA, Bradley RF: Diabetic glomerulosclerosis in children. Diabetes 20:622, 1971
438. White N, Snowden SA, Parsons V, et al: The management of terminal renal failure in diabetic patients by regular dialysis therapy. Nephron 11:261, 1973
439. Andress DL, Kopp JB, Maloney NA, et al: Early deposition of aluminum in bone in diabetic patients on hemodialysis. N Engl J Med 316:292, 1987
440. Ellenberg M: Metabolic complications (of the dialyzed patient with diabetes mellitus). Kidney Int 6: (Suppl 1):S-73, 1974
441. Blumenkrantz MJ, Shapiro DJ, Minura N, et al: Maintenance peritoneal dialysis as an alternative in the patient with diabetes mellitus and end-stage uremia. Kidney Int 6: (Suppl 1):S108, 1974
442. Chazan BI, Rees SB, Balodinos MC, et al: Dialysis in diabetics. A review of 44 patients. JAMA 209:2026, 1969
443. Raja RM, Moros JB, Kramer MS, Rosenbaum JL: Peritoneal dialysis in the sorbitol dialysate sorbitol complicating. Ann Intern Med 73:993, 1970
444. Najarian JS, Sutherland DER, Simmons RL, et al: Kidney transplantation for the uremic diabetic patient. Surg Gynecol Obstet 144:682, 1977
445. Mitchell JC: End-stage renal failure in juvenile diabetes mellitus. A 5-year follow-up of treatment. Mayo Clin Proc 52:281, 1977

446. Zincke H, Woods JE, Palumbo PJ, et al: Renal transplantation in patients with insulin-dependent diabetes mellitus, JAMA 237:1101, 1977
447. Palumbo PJ, Woods JE, Johnson WJ, Service FJ: Metabolic problems in patients undergoing renal transplantation. Kidney Int 6: (Suppl 1):S58, 1974
448. Rosenbaum R, Hoffsten PE, Cryer P, Klahr S: Hyperkalemia after renal transplantation. Occurrence in a patient with insulin-dependent diabetes mellitus. Arch Intern Med 138:1270, 1978
449. Matas AJ, Simmons RL, Goetz FC, et al: Hyperglycemic pseudorejection in the diabetic transplant patient. Surgery 79:132, 1976

11

Special Problems of Electrolyte, Water, and Acid-Base Metabolism in Children

Ben H. Brouhard
Robert J. Cunningham III
Robert E. Lynch
Luther B. Travis

The problem of fatal dehydration in infants and small children gave added impetus to the development of the science of parenteral fluid therapy. This same problem led to the establishment of pediatrics as a separate discipline and explains the interest of pediatricians in this area of physiology and therapeutics. Though much has been learned about the management of disturbances in water and salt physiology, severe dehydration remains a major cause of infant mortality worldwide. The volume and composition of body water that must be maintained for cellular function is influenced by a variety of inputs. The major responsibility for maintaining the volume and composition of our internal environment rests with the kidney. Patients with normal renal function, access to salt and water, and normal absorptive mechanisms can maintain body water and electrolyte concentrations. When conditions make internal mechanisms incapable of correcting disturbances, intervention is necessary and usually takes the form of parenteral fluid therapy. Although simplicity in the planning of parenteral fluid therapy is not only convenient but also highly desirable, the use of routine treatments is to be discouraged. Experience has demonstrated that an individualized approach based on knowledge of body fluid physiology yields better results. Furthermore, the patient's condition and response to therapy are the final determinants of the accuracy of the calculations. Individualization of fluid therapy must consider two things: the pathogenesis of the fluid and electrolyte abnormality and the age (and thus renal functional capabilities) of the child. In this chapter an attempt is therefore made to review the maturation of the physiology of fluid homeostasis. Common fluid and electrolyte problems of children will also be reviewed. An approach to the child with azotemia and oliguria will be presented, as well as the specialized problems of the malnourished child.

NORMAL PHYSIOLOGY

The body fluids are composed of water and solute. The volume of total body water (TBW) is variously reported as being from

55 to 70 percent of total body weight, greater in lean individuals and less in obese. The newborn has a relatively large TBW, 80 percent at birth and decreasing to about 70 percent at one year. Total body water can be broken down into two large compartments: extracellular fluid (ECF) and intracellular fluid (ICF). Extracellular fluid has been estimated to be about 25 percent of body weight and about 45 percent of TBW; it is usually compartmentalized further into plasma water (5 to 6 percent of body weight), interstitial water (10 to 12 percent), connective tissue and bone water (6 to 7 percent) and transcellular water (1 to 2 percent). The ICF accounts for about 35 percent of body weight or 55 percent of TBW. The electrolyte composition of plasma, plasma water, interstitial fluid, and intracellular fluid (muscle) is listed in Table 11-1. The reason for considering plasma and plasma water separately is that the usual solid content (lipids and proteins) of plasma is about 7 percent. Thus, plasma water is about 93 percent of total plasma volume. In situations where plasma solids increase markedly (e.g., hyperlipidemia), the percentage of the plasma that is water will decrease. Usual chemical analysis would show a reduction in the concentrations of electrolytes; in fact, the actual concentrations in plasma water are unchanged. The electrolyte composition of the muscle cell is fairly representative of intracellular fluids but may not depict the actual intracellular constituents for all cells. As can be noted from this comparison, the composition of the body fluid compartments varies markedly. The major cation of the ICF is potassium, while that of the ECF is sodium. Control of ECF volume depends on the regulation of sodium balance, which is determined by the relationship of sodium intake to extrarenal loss and renal sodium excretion. Since the kidneys can greatly vary sodium excretion, they play a pivotal role in regulating sodium balance and therefore ECF volume.

Water tends to move freely between ECF and ICF; the major forces responsible for this movement are osmotic and hydrostatic pressures. Osmotic pressure is principally determined by the serum sodium, and can be estimated by doubling the serum sodium concentration and adding 10. However, this estimate may not always be a true reflection of the plasma osmolality, as noted above for the case of hyperlipidemia. Two other substances that exert osmotic force are glucose and urea. As the glucose concentration increases, the increased osmotic force pulls water out of the cells to decrease sodium concentration. The sodium concentration will decrease 1.6 mEq/liter for each 100 mg/dl increase in glucose.[1] This fact is important, because with

Table 11-1. Electrolyte Composition of Body Compartments

Electrolytes (mEq/liter)	Plasma (mEq/liter)	Plasma Water (mEq/liter)	Interstitial Water (mEq/liter)	Intracellular Water (Muscle) (mEq/liter)
Cations				
Sodium	142	152.7	145	10
Potassium	4	4.3	4	156
Calcium	5	5.4	—	3
Magnesium	2	2.2	—	26
Anions				
Chloride	102	109.7	114	2
Bicarbonate	26	28.0	31	8
Phosphate	2	2.2	—	95
Sulfate	1	1.1	—	20
Organic acids	6	6.5	—	15
Protein	16	17.2	—	55

hyperglycemia and a normal serum sodium concentration, the serum is hyperosmolar. This effect is not as prominent with urea, since urea can easily penetrate cells to raise the intracellular as well as extracellular osmolality.

The ECF is of immediate interest to the clinician because this fluid compartment is the intermediary between the cell and the external environment. The ECF is in a state of dynamic flux as water and solute are lost via the lungs, skin, gastrointestinal tract, and kidneys, and gained by ingestion. Various mechanisms protect ECF stability and keep the volume and composition of this fluid compartment within relatively close confines (i.e., homeostasis). Under normal conditions water is continuously lost from the body, initially and primarily from the ECF compartment. If these losses are not replaced, the ECF volume contracts, concentrating its solute content. Since water flows down concentration gradients, water from the ICF moves into the ECF so that the water loss is ultimately shared by both compartments. Normal water losses occur by insensible routes and renal excretion.

Insensible losses consist of water lost through evaporation from the lungs and skin. The loss from skin (which is not sweat because insensibly lost water contains no electrolytes) is obligatory and accounts for 70 percent of the total loss. Since the amount lost relates to caloric expenditure, elevated body temperature (e.g., a temperature greater than 38°C will increase water requirements by 12.5 percent per degree of fever), physical activity, and/or an increased metabolic rate increase this loss. Lung losses account for the remaining 30 percent and occur as cool, dry ambient air is humidified. This obligatory loss, also related to caloric expenditure, is exaggerated by hyperpnea, tachypnea, and hyperthermia. Since insensible losses are related to caloric expenditure, they are most appropriately calculated from the metabolic rate. From curves derived by studying the metabolic rates of hospitalized infants and children,[2] an approximation can be made that 45 ml of insensible water are lost per 100 calories metabolized, or approximately 750 to 1000 ml per square meter per 24 hours.

Urine volume, though variable, is also an obligatory loss since water is the vehicle by which the kidney transports solid wastes from the diet and products of catabolism. The volume of urine excreted depends on three major factors: (1) the glomerular filtration rate (GFR), (2) the magnitude of the solute load, and (3) the ability of the kidney to concentrate the urine. As will be noted in a later section, GFR normally varies with the age of the child, with the neonate's GFR being about one-third of the adult's when corrected for body surface area. The GFR attains a normal level on a square meter basis at about the age of two years.[3] The solute load is derived from two sources: metabolism of food intake and waste from normal tissue catabolism. The combination results in an average osmolar load of about 600 mOsm/m^2/day. Thus the kidney must excrete a volume of urine necessary to transport this amount of solute. This load may be increased if the amount of potential nitrogenous waste is increased, such as when the individual is placed on a high-protein diet, or a hypercatabolic state exists. Fasting lowers the load somewhat but exaggerates protein and fat catabolism, so that the load is reduced only to 400 mOsm/m^2/day. If the diet were to supply as much as 60 to 75 g/m^2/day of glucose, protein and fat catabolism would be minimized and the osmolar load would drop to approximately 200 mOsm/m^2/day. Under basal conditions, the final urine concentration, the third factor determining final urine volume, is between 300 and 500 mOsm/m^2/day, or for each osmole, the kidney loses 2 to 3 milliliters of water. Since the usual osmolar load is 600 mOsm/m^2/day, renal water loss would be about 1000 to 1800 ml/m^2/day. Since the normal adult kidney can concentrate up to 1200 mOsm/liter, the same amount of solute could be transported in as little as 500 ml/m^2/day. Since normal concentrating ability is not attained until about two years of age, when solute is increased in infants, additional water will be needed for excretion of the increased load.

The amount of sodium in a standard diet is approximately 60 to 70 mEq/m^2/day. Unless other factors are operational, the mature kidney will excrete this amount and achieve balance. In the presence of severe sodium restriction, the kidney can reduce its excretion to less than 100 mEq/m^2/day. Alternatively, the mature kidney can increase sodium excretion to an amount in excess of 150 mEq/m^2/day in the face of sodium loading. Chloride and potassium losses are, in general, highly dependent on sodium excretion. Chloride losses are generally in the range of 40 to 60 mEq/m^2/day, while potassium excretion ranges from 30 to 40 mEq/m^2/day. Both may increase significantly in the face of increased intake. Bicarbonate excretion is normally less than 1.0 mmol/m^2/day, and in most instances is absent.

Various systems or standards of reference have been proposed for estimating the normal replacement of maintenance fluids (insensible plus renal water loss). The three commonly used systems of kilograms body weight, surface area, or caloric expenditure are compared in Table 11-2. Holliday and Segar[2] provided normal values for energy expenditures by hospitalized infants and children. It is usually assumed that 120 ml of water are required for every 100 kilocalories metabolized. However, endogenous water is provided from the oxidation of carbohydrate, fat, and protein, as well as from intracellular water released during cellular degeneration. If one takes into account these two endogenous sources of water—water of oxidation (17 ml/100 kcal) and preformed water (3 ml/100 kcal)—it becomes apparent that 100 ml of exogenous water must be supplied for each 100 kilocalories metabolized. Thus, caloric expenditures can be calculated as follows:

For the first 10 kilograms of body weight:	100 calories per kilogram
For the next 10 kilograms:	50 calories per kilogram
For each additional kilogram:	20 calories per kilogram

For the sake of simplicity, calories equal milliliters when figuring maintenance fluid requirements; surface area is also convenient and physiologically appropriate, since it emphasizes that water loss is related to heat loss through the skin. As noted in Table 11-2, any of these methods will give approximately the same fluid allotment.

However, some reference measure is necessary for children, since requirements for children of different ages vary markedly. The infant has a large body surface area and a high rate of heat exchange relative to size and weight when compared to the older child or adult. For example, the average newborn weighs only 3 kilograms, yet has a surface area of 0.2 square meter as compared to an average 70 kilogram adult with a surface area of only 1.73 square meters. Thus, the infant's weight is only about 4 percent of the adult's, but its surface area is about 14 percent of the adult's. Consequently the infant loses approximately 100 milliliters of water per kilogram per day. In contrast, the adult has a daily water output of about 40 milliliters per kilogram per day. Thus the infant's normal daily loss of water totals nearly one-tenth of its TBW, but this would amount to only one-twenty-fifth of the TBW in an adult. Since intake must equal output, the consequences of curtailed intake are obvious. If fluids were stopped for individuals of different ages for a 24-hour period, an adult would lose sufficient weight to become 3 to 5 percent dehydrated, with few if any symptoms. An eight-year-old child would lose about 2 kilograms as water and would be clinically dehydrated (6.5 percent water loss). An infant would lose sufficient water to be 10 percent dehydrated; clinical signs and symptoms

Table 11-2. Reference Standards for Replacement Fluids

	Patient Data		Weight		Calories			Surface Area	
Age	Avg. Wt. (kg)	Surface Area (m^2)	Recommended (ml/kg/age)	Actual (ml/day)	Recommended (Cal/kg/age)	Recommended (ml/100 cal)	Actual (ml/day)	Recommended (ml/m^2)	Actual (ml/day)
Birth	3.0	0.2	130	390	100	100	300	1500	300
6 Mos.	7.5	0.35	90	675	90	100	675	1500	525
1 Year	10	0.5	80	800	80	100	800	1500	750
5 Years	20	0.75	60	1200	75	80	1200	1500	1125
8 Years	30	1.0	50	1500	60	80	1440	1500	1500
Adult	70	1.7	35	2450	35	70	1715	1500	2550

would be obvious, and intervention would be necessary. Thus, relatively short periods of uncompensated normal water losses can be serious for young infants and children; with additional stresses from vomiting or other gastrointestinal losses, the outcome can be devastating.

DEHYDRATION

Normal or abnormal water losses with the absence of intake or in excess of intake lead to dehydration. Abnormal losses may take several forms. Fever exaggerates the rate of insensible water loss, primarily from the skin, with each degree rise in centigrade temperature above 38°C increasing losses by about 12.5 percent. An increased metabolic rate not only occurs with fever, but also in hyperthyroidism and salicylism. Hyperpnea can increase pulmonary losses markedly (the pulmonary losses of a diabetic patient with Kussmaul respirations may increase 200 to 300 percent). Sweating, such as during excessive exercise or exposure to high environmental temperatures, increases the loss of both water and electrolytes. Children with cystic fibrosis are particularly prone to such losses. Diarrheal losses may be moderate or extreme, and initially tend to be isotonic with the ECF. Vomiting may result in a particularly serious loss, since it is almost always associated with curtailed fluid intake. In some cases, abnormal urinary losses can lead to dehydration and electrolyte imbalance: diabetes insipidus is an example of almost pure water loss with volumes ranging between 3000 and 8000 ml/m²/day. Other conditions with concentrating defects include nephronophthisis, cystinosis, and distal renal tubular acidosis; furthermore, patients with sickle cell disease, pyelonephritis, or hypokalemia may have mild concentrating defects. Sodium-losing states (adrenal insufficiency, Bartter's syndrome) produce abnormal urinary losses and contracture of the ECF volume.

Without appropriate fluid replacement, such losses lead to dehydration. Although dehydration classically implies a simple deficit in body water, it usually also indicates a decrease in electrolytes. Such abnormalities may result from decreased intake or excessive loss of both water and electrolytes. The body's losses are such that the absolute amount of water lost always exceeds that of solute. Thus, virtually all dehydration has the tendency to be hypertonic; however, the kidneys' ability to regulate excretion and concentration of solute and water prevents hypertonicity in most cases. Another important determinant of final plasma osmolality is tonicity of intake. The various types of dehydration have been classified according to plasma osmolality or sodium concentration. Isotonic dehydration, the most common type, implies that serum osmolality is within the normal range (285 to 295 mOsm/liter or a serum sodium of 130 to 150 mEq/liter). Hypertonic dehydration describes a situation in which the serum sodium is equal to or greater than 150 mEq/liter. This may occur when the degree of water deficit becomes so great that renal circulation is impaired, leading to an inability of the kidneys to compensate fully by excess solute excretion. It may also occur during the development of dehydration if the oral intake is high in salt content. Hypotonic dehydration (a serum sodium concentration less than 130 mEq/liter) tends to occur in two clinical situations: (1) when the child's intake has been virtually electrolyte-free during the course of several days of diarrhea; or (2) in the chronically malnourished child with recurrent bouts of mild to moderate diarrhea and poor intake.

The type of dehydration is determined principally by biochemical parameters; however, the magnitude of the deficit is best estimated by clinical judgment based primarily on physical examination. This aspect is particularly important, since the ability to accurately estimate the degree of deficit will lead to the institution of appropriate therapy. The parameters used to judge degree of dehydration are noted in Table 11-3.

The plan for treating dehydration must have four facets: (1) route of administration, (2) total volume of fluid necessary, (3) rate of fluid administration, and (4) composition of the proposed infusate. Each needs to be considered in light of the clinical evaluation of the child and what is known about the current status of the body's handling of fluids and electrolytes.[3] The route of administration depends on the severity of the dehydration. If it is mild and the child is not vomiting, oral replacement may be attempted.[4-8] Oral electrolyte solutions are particularly suited for patients with diarrhea and 5 to 7 percent dehydration. Numerous studies have noted the effectiveness of such oral rehydration in undernourished and well-nourished children and in infants with hypertonic or isotonic dehydration.[4-7] The solutions used contain 40 to 90 mEq/liter of sodium, glucose, and potassium. Finberg[8] has pointed out that the higher sodium concentration should be used early in the course of the rehydration, with lesser amounts (40 to 50 mEq/liter) used for maintenance hydration. Glucose in these solutions not only provides calories but also facilitates sodium movement across the gut epithelium. Four or 5 percent glucose solutions may produce an osmotic diarrhea; thus, 2 to 2.5 percent solutions are more appropriate. If the circumstances indicate that oral rehydration is not possible, intravenous administration is necessary. The total volume of fluid must be estimated from maintenance requirements, deficits, and ongoing losses. The rate of administration varies with the severity and type of dehydration. If the degree of dehydration is such that intravascular volume is compromised, a push of fluid is needed to ensure expansion of this space. The amount of this push can be an arbitrary 10 ml/kg (this volume may be repeated if an adequate clinical response is not obtained after the initial bolus), or can be estimated from: body weight (in kilograms) × percent plasma volume (6 percent) × percent dehydration. This volume of fluid must not be added into the total volume to be infused. Deficit fluids are calculated by multiplying the percent dehydration times the body weight in kilograms, with the result being the amount of volume deficit in liters. Ongoing fluid losses are usually gastrointestinal (e.g., diarrhea), but may be renal (e.g., diabetes mellitus). For most accurate replacement they should be measured and replaced milliliter for milliliter. However if this is not possible, estimation is used, with 25 percent of the maintainence volume as a reasonable guess. Again the improvement in the hydration status of the patient will provide the best measure of adequacy of therapy.

In the usual case of isotonic dehydration, half of the total replacement fluids can be given in the first eight hours (and half of this in the first two hours) with the remainder given in the next 16 hours. Ensuring adequate intravascular volume early in therapy is important; thus, a more isotonic solution (e.g., normal saline, Ringer's solution) should be used. As hydration continues, replacing water and potassium becomes more important. As stated earlier, all dehydration is initially hypertonic, since water is lost. Water replacement should be completed in the 48 to 72 hours after the start of therapy.

Hypotonic dehydration is uncommon, but its management differs little from that of isotonic dehydration. However, serum sodium levels below 125 mEq/liter are associated with seizures, so a rapid increase in serum sodium may be desirable.[9] Recent data have suggested that correction of hyponatremia may be associated with central pontine myelinolysis. Ayus and colleagues[10] delineate four classes of patients for whom the decision must be made to treat hyponatremia rapidly or slowly. These include symptomatic patients with the syndrome of inappropriate antidiuretic hormone secretion (SIADH), patients with self-induced or iatrogenic water intoxica-

Table 11-3. Findings in Dehydration

Degree of Dehydration	% Acute Weight Loss	Sensorium Status	Mucous Membranes	Skin Turgor	Fontanelle, Eyes	Vital Signs	Urine Output
Mild	3–5%	Clear	N to dry	N to D	N	N	N to D
Moderate	6–10%	Lethargy Restlessness Irritability	Dry	D	D	HR–I Resp–N or I BP–N T–I	D
Severe	11–15%	Stupor Semicoma	Dry to parched	Markedly decreased	Markedly depressed	HR–Markedly I Resp–Markedly I BP–N to D	Markedly decreased
Extreme	>15%	Coma	Dry to parched	Markedly decreased	Markedly depressed	HR–I or D Resp–I or D BP–D T–D	Markedly decreased

N = normal; I = increased; D = decreased; HR = heart rate; BP = blood pressure; T = temperature; Resp = respiration

tion, patients who have undergone surgery, and patients with an idiosyncratic reaction to thiazide diuretics. Patients who are symptomatic should have a rapid correction (2 mEq/L/hr) of serum sodium after assessment of their cardiac status. The serum sodium should be raised to 120 mEq/liter, and should not be brought to normal or hypernatremic values. The formula for calculating milliequivalents of sodium to be given is as follows:[11]

1. 135 ml/liter − observed sodium = cation deficit per TBW (liters)
2. (0.65 − % dehydration) × body weight (kg) = TBW (liters)
3. Cation deficit (mEq/liter) × TBW (liters) = cation to be added

A somewhat rapid correction of volume status can be accomplished over the first few hours of fluid therapy, particularly if the dehydration is severe. However, the degree of dehydration tends to be overestimated in patients with hypotonic dehydration, because water from the ECF moves into the ICF, augmenting intravascular loss. After any necessary acute correction of hyponatremia, fluid replacement can proceed much as in isotonic dehydration.

Hypertonic dehydration requires special attention. Hypernatremic (or hypertonic) dehydration, usually a winter phenomenon, occurs in infants with vomiting and diarrhea, especially if the infant continues to be fed a high-solute formula,[12] thus increasing renal water loss. Overall mortality has ranged from 7 to 29 percent in several series[13−15]; this mortality was markedly increased if the sodium concentration was greater than 158 mEq/liter at presentation. Increases in serum sodium, either acutely or for prolonged intervals, have been shown to increase the brain sodium concentration. In more prolonged studies, an increase in measured brain osmolality occurs with an actual decrease in brain sodium.[16,17] The unknown osmoles (idiogenic osmoles) responsible for this may account for as much as half the increase in intracellular brain osmolality. Rapid lowering of the serum osmolality causes a shift of water into the brain, resulting in cerebral edema. The likelihood of neurologic complications will be increased: (1) for infants and young children with prolonged dehydration of more than four days; (2) when associated with severe hypertonicity; and (3) with rapid correction of the ECF osmolality. To minimize the latter, fluid therapy should consist of an isotonic fluid given at a slow, even rate. Deficit, ongoing, and maintenance fluids are planned for a 48-hour period and infused at a constant rate over that period. The deficit in hypertonic dehydration has a tendency to be underestimated, since the ECF volume is maintained at the expense of ICF volume due to the hyperosmolality of the serum. As therapy progresses, two points should be kept in mind: (1) the infusate solution should have a progressively lower salt content since water is the main deficit; and (2) hypocalcemia, a peculiar aspect of hypernatremic dehydration and dehydration of an unexplained etiology, should be watched for. Potassium also should be added early; theoretically this ion protects against a decrease in intracellular osmolality as water moves into the cell.[12]

The other fluid replacement volume that must be estimated is the amount needed for ongoing losses. If possible, such losses should be collected, their volumes noted, and their sodium and potassium content measured. These losses are most commonly from nasogastric drainage, fistulas, diarrhea, and large urine volumes. Nasogastric drainage contains large amounts of chloride, sodium, and some potassium. Pancreatic, biliary, and small intestinal secretions contain bicarbonate. The latter can be estimated from the sum of the sodium and potassium concentrations minus the chloride concentration. Inappropriately large urine losses, which must also be replaced, can result from inability to reabsorb water (e.g., diabetes insipidus) or inability to reabsorb solute (e.g., resolving acute renal failure). If the former is suspected (e.g., after intracranial surgery), desmopressin acetate (DDAVP) may be used. In the oliguric phase of acute renal failure, all urine output may be replaced; as the polyuric phase is entered, increasing volumes of urine may be produced with larger volumes of fluid replaced. This cycle may become positive, since an increase in ECF may decrease sodium reabsorption from the proximal nephron, so that more urine is produced, requiring more replacement fluid. If this process is suspected, infused fluids should be decreased. If the patient loses weight or becomes dehydrated, the polyuric phase is still present and a large fluid intake is still necessary. If, however, urine output decreases, further decreases in input can be tried.

A total body deficit of potassium is an almost uniform finding in patients with acidosis and/or dehydration. Potassium is lost from cellular stores during acidosis as hydrogen ion is buffered within the cell. This increased level of plasma potassium augments the secretion of aldosterone, as does the ECF contraction caused by dehydration. Increased aldosterone secretion accelerates sodium-potassium exchange in the distal nephron and increases potassium excretion. Additional potassium may be lost in gastrointestinal secretions. Replacement of cellular potassium stores cannot be accomplished rapidly but must be done as early and safely as possible. Potassium is not added to intravenous fluids until renal excretory function is established. To prevent a dangerous rate of administration, the concentration of potassium in intravenous fluids should not exceed 40 to 60 mEq/liter.

Dehydration is also usually accompanied by some degree of acidosis. The kidney is responsible for excreting nonvolatile organic acids derived from tissue catabolism. These organic acids are usually kept to a concentration of 5 to 10 mEq/liter. Their unmeasured anions represent the R fraction, or anion gap,[18] [i.e., (sodium + potassium) − (Cl + HCO$_3$)], which increases markedly as catabolism increases and renal function decreases. The bicarbonate concentration is depressed due to ECF buffering, as is the PCO$_2$ due to hyperventilation, as a compensating mechanism. Both serve to minimize the decrease in plasma pH of the ECF. Since the increase in organic acids is secondary to a decrease in peripheral perfusion and renal function, the acidosis may correct as the dehydration is corrected. However, the acidosis may occasionally be so extreme that survival is threatened (plasma pH less than 7.10). In these instances, judicious use of bicarbonate may be indicated.[19] In general, bicarbonate should not be pushed as a bolus unless there has been a cardiac arrest. Such a bolus can: (1) worsen intracellular and, in particular, CSF acidosis,[20] (2) create hypernatremia, (3) produce tetany by acutely lowering the ionized calcium, and (4) produce hypokalemia.[21] Bicarbonate can be given as part of the rehydration fluid; the dose can be calculated as 2 to 4 mEq/kg, or (measured HCO$_3^-$ − actual HCO$_3^-$) × [0.6 (bicarbonate space)] × body weight (in kilograms)/2 = amount of bicarbonate to be given to correct half of the total deficit. After this dose has been infused, re-evaluation of the laboratory data and the patient's clinical status should be made before more bicarbonate is given. If no bicarbonate is given, one should remember that the serum bicarbonate concentration may be diluted by the rehydration fluids. This condition is known as dilutional acidosis[22]; however, whether it is clinically relevant has been questioned.[23]

If bicarbonate is to be administered, blood gas readings should be obtained. "Correcting" a low total carbon dioxide content obtained with other serum electrolytes may not always be appropriate. Respiratory alkalosis with decreased plasma bicarbonate may be due to central respiratory stimulation. Thus, the bicarbonate is lowered in order to compensate for a decreased PCO_2, and attempts to "correct" the low bicarbonate only exacerbate the alkalemia. Likewise, the metabolic acidosis of acute renal failure should not be treated with intravenous bicarbonate; it usually is not severe, and this treatment will only add excess sodium and may aggravate ECF volume expansion. However, correcting the acidosis of chronic renal failure is appropriate and should be done with orally administered base solutions.

The most important part of fluid resuscitation therapy is monitoring the patient frequently. Those parameters that dictated the patient's degree of dehydration should be monitored to assess improvement. Improved clinical appearance is the most important indication that fluid therapy is adequate. Vital signs should stabilize and normalize early. The sensorium should improve gradually over 16 to 24 hours. Weight gain is another excellent method of following the adequacy of therapy. Urine flow and specific gravity (without proteinuria or glycosuria) may be monitored; an indwelling Foley catheter should not be placed. If the patient does not progress toward normalization, the patient's clinical condition and pertinent laboratory data (e.g., hemoglobin, serum sodium, bicarbonate, potassium and BUN[24]), should be reassessed and fluid therapy recalculated.

METABOLIC ALKALOSIS

Other common causes of dehydration in the pediatric patient are conditions producing metabolic alkalosis. These conditions are most commonly observed in patients with high intestinal obstruction or those being maintained on gastric suction. The primary losses under such conditions are hydrogen, chloride, sodium, and small amounts of potassium. In the child with persistent losses of these ions due to vomiting or suction, the ECF acquires a progressively alkaline character. As hydrochloric acid is secreted into the stomach, bicarbonate is secreted into the ECF and excreted into the urine, causing an alkaline urine. The respiratory center responds to systemic alkalosis by decreasing the rate and depth of respirations in an attempt to conserve hydrogen ion. This response is limited by the requirement for oxygen, but the P_ACO_2 can reach 55 to 60 mmHg. Initially the kidney responds by decreasing the reabsorption of sodium and bicarbonate, producing an alkaline urine. However, as the PCO_2 increases, the kidney responds with more complete bicarbonate reabsorption. Because of the increased losses of sodium and water (gastric and urinary), the ECF volume decreases and aldosterone is secreted. As a result, sodium is conserved and potassium is lost in the urine. Increased bicarbonate reabsorption also occurs with progressive ECF volume contraction and hypokalemia. As urinary potassium losses continue, less potassium is available at the distal exchange site. In its place, hydrogen ion is secreted and the urine becomes acid.

In patients with obstructive lesions in whom surgery is contemplated, the therapy for extracellular alkalosis must be started promptly. Since total body stores of potassium and chloride are depleted, these ions must be supplied during the correction. However, the sodium deficit is mild to moderate. In addition, large amounts of sodium tend to enhance the distal loss of potassium. In the alkalotic child who is not significantly dehydrated, an appropriate fluid would be one that: (1) would supply adequate calories, (2) is sufficiently low in sodium to minimize distal tubular potassium loss, and (3) supplies a safe but effective concentration of potassium and chloride. In the child who is also sodium depleted, the initial fluid must be designed to correct dehydration and sodium deficiency. Until these are corrected, the body will still sense a reduction in plasma volume and continue to secrete large amounts of aldosterone, thus causing increased potassium loss in the urine. Potassium should be given as potassium chloride and not potassium phosphate, since both chloride and potassium are necessary for the total correction of extracellular alkalosis. Unlike patients with acidosis, patients with alkalosis often do not have clinical symptoms or signs; obtaining an arterial pH may be worthwhile since more aggressive therapy may be indicated by a very alkaline plasma pH. Theoretically, the pH maxima compatible with recovery are 6.80 to 7.80. A pH of 6.80 represents a hydrogen ion concentration of 160 mmol/liter of hydrogen (normal is about 40 mmol/liter), or an increase of 300 percent. A pH of 7.80 represents a decrease of only 40 percent hydrogen (16 mmol/liter). Thus the body tolerates and better defends against acidosis than alkalosis. Indeed, it has been noted in adults that a 40 percent mortality exists with an arterial pH in the range of 7.54 to 7.56.[25] If an alkalotic child is not improving clinically and biochemically with fluids, other therapies are available, but blood gases should be followed. A weak acid such as ammonium chloride or hydrochloric acid can be given.[26,27] The dose is calculated much like that of bicarbonate: milliequivalents of ammonium chloride to be given = (measured bicarbonate − desired bicarbonate) × (0.6) × body weight (in kilograms)/2. Although precautions need to be remembered with acid therapy, it can be a useful adjunct to volume, chloride, and potassium replacement.

Although pyloric stenosis or gastic suction are the most common conditions under which marked metabolic alkalosis can occur, there are others of which one should be aware. Cystic fibrosis with marked chloride loss in sweat has presented as metabolic alkalosis.[28] Bartter's syndrome,[29] chloride diarrhea,[30] chloride-deficient formulae,[31,32] and primary hyperaldosteronism[33] have all been associated with metabolic alkalosis. Although diuretic and laxative abuse and surreptitious vomiting[34] have been described in adults presenting with metabolic alkalosis, these abuses are rare in children. Common to all mechanisms is usually some initial decrease in ECF volume with an increase in chloride loss or a decrease in chloride intake.

FLUID AND ELECTROLYTE BALANCE IN THE NEONATE

A small infant presents special problems in fluid and electrolyte therapy. To appropriately plan this therapy for the neonate, one must understand the body composition of preterm and full-term neonates, and the renal functional capabilities of these infants and how they change with age. The magnitudes of stresses imposed on neonates are also much different from those imposed on older children and adults. In planning the fluid and electrolyte therapy of the neonate, the same general considerations of maintenance, ongoing and deficit fluid requirements must be taken into account as in older children; however, limitations of neonatal renal function and the relative degree of stresses imposed must also be considered.

Perinatal Water Flux

The change from the intrauterine to the extrauterine environment is associated with many changes within the fetus, not the least of which is the total dependence of excretory function on the neonate's kidneys. Prior to birth the placenta serves as the organ of excretion, and is extremely active in water exchange. Studies by Hutchinson and associates[35] estimated that at term, 3,500 milliliters are exchanged hourly between the fetus and mother, with the net flux being in the direction of the fetus. In utero, the fetal urine flow rate increases progressively from 12.2 ml/hr at 32 weeks gestation to 28.2 ml/hr at 40 weeks. Conservation of water is not a concern for the fetus since it is bathed in amniotic fluid, and water is provided by the mother. This net transfer of water to the fetus results in a relative increase in total body water. The percentage of total body composition that is water depends on gestational age. The younger the neonate the higher the body water content (Fig. 11-1). As will be discussed later, the initial weight loss seen in all infants is loss of part of this water. At birth, the urine flow rate decreases dramatically at the same time as the source of hydration is cut off. Furthermore, sources of water loss (i.e., evaporation from skin and lungs) are now imposed on the newborn. Thus, without a constant source of fluids and increased losses, the capabilities and limitations of neonatal renal function assume a critical role in water and electrolyte balance. An understanding of neonatal renal physiology is therefore important, especially when parenteral fluid therapy is required.

Neonatal Renal Physiology

As gestational age increases, not only does body water content change but renal function also changes. In studies of 49 newborns, Arant[36] demonstrated that creatinine clearance was directly related to gestational age. He found no significant increase in GFR (as estimated by C_{cr}) before 34 weeks' gestational age; however, after this time there was a progressive increase in C_{cr} from 0.46 to 2.24 ml/min. The finding of 34 weeks as a critical time for an increased GFR is of interest, since anatomic studies suggest that glomerulogenesis stops by 34 weeks' gestation. It has also been proposed that at the same time there is an increase and redistribution of renal blood flow and glomerular filtration to more superficial nephrons. This process is accompanied by a decrease in vascular resistance. Vasoactive hormones and intrarenal hormones such as angiotensin and prostaglandins are likely candidates for mediators of such changes.[37]

Not only is the GFR lower in neonates, but tubular function also has been reported to be less mature than in the adult kidney.

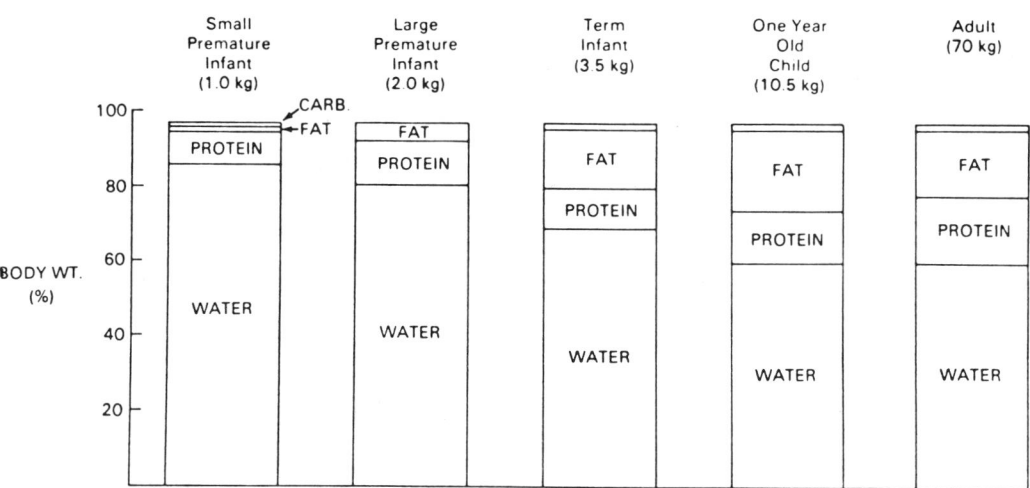

Fig. 11-1. Percentage of water contributing to total body weight in children of various ages. (From Heird WC, Driscoll JM, Schullinger JN, et al: Intravenous alimentation in pediatric patients. J Pediatr 80:351, 1972, with permission.)

The renal bicarbonate threshold is lower in neonates than adults, and serum bicarbonate values are therefore decreased. It has been proposed that this lower threshold may account for the late metabolic acidosis noted in premature infants. However, Schwartz and associates,[38] studying 14 low-birth-weight infants, showed that CO_{2TOT} rose between birth and three weeks of life from a mean of 18.6 to 20.3 mEq/liters. The frequency distribution of CO_{2TOT} values in these neonates showed no significant deviations from normal. Furthermore, Schwartz and his group demonstrated that the ability of their low birth infants to excrete an ammonium chloride load was not related to their acid-base status and indeed was comparable to that of term infants. Other tubular functions that have been studied include the reabsorption of glucose and phosphate. In infants from 25 to 41 weeks' gestational age, Arant[36] found glucosuria in 13.3 percent of infants less than 34 weeks' gestational age and in none of those of more than 36 weeks' gestational age. In these same infants, tubular reabsorption of phosphate was 85 percent or greater in every age group. As feedings were instituted and serum phosphate rose, the tubular reabsorption of phosphate decreased. Taken together, these studies indicate that although absolute values of glomerular and tubular function are low at birth, glomerulotubular balance does exist for most if not all substances handled by the neonatal kidney.

The ability of the neonate's kidneys to handle sodium has been another area of extensive investigation. It has been noted that term infants are unable to excrete a saline load as well as older children or adults. It was hypothesized that the low GFR, in concert with the high aldosterone levels present at this age, promoted sodium retention. However, it has also been noted that preterm infants have a tendency for salt wasting and subsequent hyponatremia. In these infants, proximal tubular sodium reabsorption is less and distal reabsorption is greater than for the adult kidney. In studying 11 preterm infants (with a mean gestational age of 31.7 weeks) weighing an average of 1,670 g, Sulyok and associates[39] found a progressive decrease in distal tubular sodium delivery (or conversely an increase in proximal tubular sodium reabsorption) from 4.96 ± 0.07 ml/min/100 ml GFR during the first week to 3.3 ± 0.41 ml/min/100 ml GFR in the sixth week. They also found a progressive rise in distal tubular sodium reabsorption from 69.5 ± 2.4 percent in the first week to 83.7 ± 1.8 percent in the second week. Arant,[36] investigating fractional sodium reabsorption (T_{Na}/C_{cr}) in preterm infants, found a tendency for sodium loss in neonates of less than 34 weeks' gestational age. Fractional sodium reabsorption for this group was 96.7 ± 3.4 percent, which was significantly less than the 99.6 ± 0.03 percent in the greater than 34 weeks' gestational age group. Arant[40] has proposed that instead of functional immaturity for sodium handling, the neonatal kidney is responding appropriately to the circumstances with which it is presented. Thus, in the term infant without a great deal of excess extracellular water on board (Fig. 11-1), no glycosuria, phosphaturia, or sodium loss is noted; whereas in the preterm neonate with a large excess of ECF volume, proximal sodium reabsorption is diminished. This situation is analogous to the situation in the adult when ECF volume is increased (e.g., SIADH), in which there is increased renal sodium excretion. Not only is sodium reabsorption depressed in states of ECF volume expansion, but bicarbonate, phosphate, and glucose reabsorption also may be affected. Thus, sodium excretion may not depend on the relative maturity of the kidney, but instead on the circumstances to which it is subjected.

Neonates, after the first few days of life, can excrete a maximally dilute urine, with osmolalities of 25 to 35 mOsm/liter. However, concentrating ability is not maximal until about the age of two years. The neonate can generally achieve a level of 600 to 700 mOsm/liter. This inability to concentrate maximally is due in large part to the lack of a suitable osmotic gradient in the medullary interstitium. Due to the anabolic state of the infant, urea excretion is low; consequently, approximately half the osmotically active particles necessary for urinary concentration are missing, and thus the ability to concentrate the urine is lower in the neonate than in the older child. If, however, protein intake is increased, concentrating ability can also be increased. Indeed, following a high protein feeding, infants can achieve maximal urinary osmolalities of 930 mOsm/liter.[41] The renal response to circulating antidiuretic hormone (ADH) appears to approach adult levels. From animal studies it has been postulated that ADH levels in infants are lower than adult levels; given the above data, however, it appears that this is not the only limiting factor to the concentrating mechanism in the neonate.

Fluid Balance

As with older children and adults, fluid balance in the neonate can be thought of in terms of insensible loss, renal loss, and ongoing loss (e.g., gastrointestinal). As previously mentioned, both preterm and full-term infants are born with an increased body water content. This extra water is lost in the first few days of life, accounting for the weight loss seen during this period, and in large part because of the high rate of insensible water loss secondary to infants' relatively large surface area. Studies by Wu and Hodgman[42] and Fanaroff and associates[43] have shown that from 64 to 17 ml/kg/day can be lost as insensible water loss, the highest values being in low birthweight infants (1,000 g). Other environmental factors may also influence the degree of insensible water loss, including radiant warmers, phototherapy, the ambient temperature, the metabolic rate, humidity, heat shields, and postnatal age. Radiant warmers can increase insensible water loss from 101 to 191 percent depending on the size of the infant. Phototherapy, often used to decrease serum bilirubin, can increase insensible water loss greatly; in full-term infants it has been shown to increase insensible water loss from 1.7 to 2.4 ml/kg/hr, while in preterm infants[42] with weights less than 1,500 g, insensible water loss increased from 31.2 to 44.2 ml/kg/hr, and in infants with weights greater than 1,500 g it increased from 19.7 to 42.0 ml/kg/hr. The mechanism of increased insensible water loss under radiant energy heaters or phototherapy is not completely understood. Increased sweating may account for part of the extra fluid loss; however, although full-term infants can sweat, infants of less than 36 weeks' gestation show a limited sweating response, and the neonate of less than 30 weeks' gestation has no ability to sweat. Thus, increased weight loss with phototherapy cannot be explained by sweating alone. However, phototherapy has been shown to significantly increase calf blood flow from 30 to 80 percent above control values; this increase in blood flow may lead to increased evaporative losses,[44] possibly to as much as 8.3 ml/kg/hr.[45]

Increased humidity can greatly decrease insensible water loss. Hey and Katz[46] showed a 30 percent lowering of evaporative water loss at high humidity versus low humidity. Just as humidity is one protection against increased water loss, a heat shield is another. Fanaroff and associates[43] have shown a 25 percent reduction in insensible water loss with the use of such a shield.

Postnatal age also influences water loss. Very low birthweight infants can have very large losses of insensible water due to their relatively larger surface area and larger body water content (Fig. 11-1).

Another source of water loss for the neonate, as for anyone, is renal water loss. Although this is always a loss, its magnitude in the neonate, as with other water losses, is relatively greater because of the inability to concentrate maximally. Thus, more water is required to excrete a solute load. The amount of water required to excrete solutes depends in part on the ingested load and is a function of the protein and electrolyte content of the diet. The larger the osmolar load taken in, the more water will be required to excrete it. A precise figure for this renal water requirement is not possible, since the premature infant may have large losses from the skin and lungs. It has been suggested that a urine osmolality between 75 and 300 mOsm/liter will not unduly stress the concentrating or diluting mechanisms of the neonate.[47] Within this range, a urine volume of 50 to 100 ml/kg/day is required.

Another source of potential water loss is gastrointestinal loss. Obviously, gastroenteritis with diarrhea or vomiting can increase the need for water and electrolytes. However, it must be remembered that phototherapy also increases stool water by increasing the number of stools passed. Stool water loss can amount to 7 ml/kg/day in the jaundiced full-term infant without phototherapy versus 19 ml/kg/day in similar infants under phototherapy.[48] The increase in water content of the stools may be related to the shortened transit time secondary to the photodecomposition products of bilirubin.[49]

Two further factors relating to fluid balance in the neonate are increased fluid requirements due to growth and a decrease in fluids due to water of oxidation. If the goal for neonates is to parallel intrauterine growth after birth, especially for preterm infants, about an extra 15 ml/kg/day must be included for body weights up to 2,000 g, decreasing to about 6 ml/kg/day for a 3,000 g infant.

From the total water requirements, water of oxidation can be subtracted. This water is a function of metabolic rate, and usually amounts to about 12 milliliters per 100 calories expended. Therefore, water of oxidation derived from caloric expenditures of 45 to 130 cal/kg/day equals 5 to 15 ml/kg/day. Consequently, water of oxidation is in the same range as the water required for growth, so that the two cancel each other out.

Assessment of Hydration

From the foregoing discussion it is clear that the neonate has more possible sources of water loss and less reserve than older children. However, the parameters used to monitor the hydration status of the neonate do not differ greatly from those measures used in the infant and adult. Weights are extremely important and should be done at least daily, and in unstable conditions every 12 hours. In this regard it is expected that weight loss will occur in the first few days. However, just because extra water is present is not sufficient reason to withhold fluids during this time. Furthermore, although a weight loss is expected, the infant should not be allowed to become dehydrated; nor should large volumes of fluids be given to prevent weight loss. No hard and fast criteria exist for acceptable weight loss in the first few days of life; however, since very-low-birth-weight infants have a greater proportion of water, they can be expected to lose a greater proportion of their body weight. A reasonable estimate of weight loss is not more than 10 percent of birthweight for infants greater than 1,500 g, and not more than 15 percent for infants less than 1,500 g. Lorenz and associates[50] have presented data that fluid intake in very-low-birth-weight infants (750 to 1,500 g) can be lowered to allow up to a gradual loss of 5 to 15 percent of birthweight during the first week of life without an increase in intracranial hemorrhage, bronchopulmonary dysplasia, dehydration, acute renal failure, or metabolic disturbance.

As in older infants, skin turgor (including that at the fontanelle), blood pressure, and heart rate can also be used to assess dehydration. Other parameters include hemoglobin, hematocrit, serum sodium, plasma osmolality, and blood urea nitrogen (BUN). It must be realized that many factors can influence these biochemical measurements. Hemoglobin/hematocrit can be influenced by hemolysis, occult blood loss, or blood drawing. Serum sodium can be greatly influenced by the renal handling of sodium and the sodium intake. Plasma osmolality can vary normally in the newborn. Davis and associates[51] found no fixed relationship between plasma sodium and osmolality in the first week of life. Furthermore, they showed a normal rise in plasma osmolality from 285 to 300 mOsm/liter in the first 48 hours. Additionally, solute load can influence osmolality.

Urine parameters can also be used as an assessment of hydration. As has been mentioned, keeping the urine osmolality between 75 and 300 mOsm/liter poses no undue stress on the concentrating or diluting mechanisms. Increasing the ingested solute load can cause an obligatory osmolar loss with concomitant water loss and the potential for dehydration. An isolated urine sodium has limited value in estimating hydration or renal handling of sodium. This estimate can only be based on timed aliquots. Urine volume also has been used to help assess hydration. Roy and Sinclair[47] feel that normal urine output should be in the range of 50 to 100 ml/kg/day, with a urine osmolality of 75 to 300 mOsm/liter, or roughly 1 ml/kg/hr as a minimum value. Lower values may suggest dehydration, obstruction, or renal disease. Arant[52] has pointed out the fallability of this approach. Certainly urine volume per se says little about renal function; the urine volume may be quite high with a markedly diminished GFR (e.g., in an infant with a postobstructive diuresis); conversely, a neonate with SIADH may have a low urine output but a normal GFR. As noted, urine volume should be evaluated in the context of urinary solute load and concentration capacity. The higher the solute load and the less able the kidneys are to concentrate, the higher should be the urine volume.

Administered Fluids and Electrolytes

When an infant is being evaluated, some basic decisions need to be made concerning hydration and nutrition. Hydration can be obtained through the gastrointestinal tract or through a central or peripheral vessel. Hydration and nutrition via the gastrointestinal route can be further broken down into oral feedings, intermittent gavage, or continuous duodenal drip feedings. These are beyond the scope of this chapter. Alternatively, hydration can be given through a vessel; this can be a peripheral vein, central vein (usually reserved for total parenteral nutrition), or umbilical artery or vein. The umbilical artery is used particularly when blood gases need to be monitored frequently. When it is clear that intravenous hydration will be necessary, it is best to start fluid therapy immediately.

Again, several decisions need to be made concerning the amount of fluid, electrolytes, and glucose concentration to be used. When deciding on the amount of fluid, such factors as gestational age and use of a radiant warmer or phototherapy need to be taken into account. Fluids are usually limited for the first 24 to 48 hours, due to a decreased GFR and reduced renal blood flow; as renal vascular resistance decreases and these parameters increase, fluid therapy also must be increased. Suggested fluid rates are listed in Table 11-4.[53] Electrolytes are not usually added to intravenous fluids for the first 24 hours, which is a period of sodium retention due to the low GFR; however, after this time 2 to 3 mEq/kg/day of sodium is the usual maintenance sodium requirement. The more immature the infant the greater the sodium loss may be and the

Table 11-4. Suggested Fluid Administration Rates and Electrolyte Content of Fluid for Different Gestational Ages in the First Three Days of Life

Birth weight: 1000 g	
1st day	100–120 ml/kg/24 hr
2nd day	140–160 ml/kg/24 hr
3rd day	180–200+ ml/kg/24 hr
Birth weight: 1000–1500 g	
1st day	80–120 ml/kg/24 hr
2nd day	110–130 ml/kg/24 hr
3rd day	140–180 ml/kg/24 hr
Birth weight: 1500–2500 g	
1st day	65–85 ml/kg/24 hr
2nd day	90–110 ml/kg/24 hr
3rd day	120–160 ml/kg/24 hr
Birth weight: 2500 g	
1st day	65–85 ml/kg/24 hr
2nd day	90–100 ml/kg/24 hr
3rd day on	100–120 ml/kg/24 hr

(From Richardson CJ,[53] with permission.)

more the quantity of sodium that may have to be supplied. Potassium is not added again until after a 24-hour period, and only then when the infant has voided. Dextrose is usually also given in the intravenous solutions. However, hyperglycemia must be watched for and blood glucose levels monitored, especially in low-birth-weight infants. The usual hepatic output of the term infant is 4 to 6 mg/kg/min;[54] thus, infusion rates of glucose should approximate these levels.

Rarely are ions other than sodium and potassium added to intravenous fluids. Calcium should not be added to peripheral intravenous infusions because of the hazard of tissue destruction with extravasation. Bicarbonate is also rarely used in large doses. As has been pointed out, the low serum bicarbonate in neonates is due to decreased reabsorption, which may be secondary ECF volume expansion. Furthermore, since most of the acid-base problems of the neonate are respiratory, bicarbonate is not useful. In fact, such therapy may be contraindicated if adequate ventilation cannot be assured.

The neonate requires special attention to fluid and electrolyte therapy. Total body composition is markedly different not only for neonates as a group but also for different gestational ages. Although glomerular filtration and renal blood flow are decreased, the tubular functions appear to be much as those in the adult kidney. Insensible water loss is large in the neonate, and factors affecting it need to be taken into account when planning fluid therapy. Particularly close attention needs to be paid to fluids and electrolytes in the first few days of life, since changes need to be made on a daily basis. Fluid and electrolyte therapy for the neonate can be approached in much the same manner as for the older child or adult if consideration is given to the functional capabilities and limitations of the newborn.

ACUTE OLIGURIA IN CHILDREN

The management of the child with an acute decrease in urine output requires careful attention to fluid, electrolyte, and mineral metabolism; if the process continues longer than a few days, thought needs to be given to nutrition. Regardless of etiology, four factors have been implicated in the pathogenesis of acute renal failure (ARF)[55]: (1) reduction in renal blood flow, (2) reduction in the K_f of the glomerulus, (3) intratubular obstruction, and (4) back-leakage of filtration markers. No single factor can explain all renal malfunctions of acute renal failure, and all may potentially contribute to the final outcome. From current evidence it seems that the degree to which each of these factors contributes to hypofiltration depends on the degree of injury and the time at which each factor is evaluated. Renal vasoconstriction occurs in both the initiation and maintenance phases of most models of acute renal failure.[47] This factor is most prominent in the early phases of myohemoglobinuric and ischemic forms of renal damage. The K_f is reduced in the gentamycin and uranyl nitrate models of ARF. Intratubular obstruction occurs to a variable extent in all experimental models of ARF. The contribution of backleakage of glomerular filtration marker has been related directly to the severity of tubular cell injury.

Whatever the etiologic mechanisms involved, evaluation of the patient with ARF should include a determination of whether the problem is prerenal, postrenal, or an intrinsic renal process. This distinction can be arrived at by history, physical examination, and appropriate laboratory studies. Management must be aimed at correcting potentially life-threatening conditions, preventing such situations, and reversing conditions contributing to the renal failure.[56]

Etiology

Acute renal failure may be defined as any disease process causing sudden suppression of renal function with a urine output of less than 300 ml/m^2/day. As mentioned, ARF may be conveniently thought of in terms of prerenal, postrenal, and intrinsic renal failure. Prerenal failure is manifest when decreased blood flow to intact kidneys reduces function. This hypoperfusion is sensed by the kidneys as volume depletion, and water and sodium excretion are therefore minimized. This is advantageous during true volume depletion (e.g., diarrhea with dehydration), but may act adversely during times of relative fluid repletion (e.g., congestive heart failure). Due to the maintenance of a relatively normal GFR with enhanced sodium reabsorption, the urinary sodium concentration (<20 mEq/liter), urine:plasma creatinine ratio (>40), renal failure index [(U_{Na}/urinary:plasma creatinine)<1], fractional excretion of sodium [FE_{Na}(<1)], and urine osmolality (>500 mOsm/liter) have been used to identify the patient with prerenal failure.[57] Even before this initial laboratory work is obtained, the history and physical examination may point to dehydration as a cause of oliguria. If the patient's cardiovascular status will permit, a fluid challenge of isotonic saline or another appropriate potassium-free crystalloid at 10 to 20 ml/kg may be diagnostic.[52] Lesser amounts of colloid may be used to achieve the desired increase in intravascular volume.[58]

Postrenal failure may be caused by a variety of anatomic abnormalities that give rise to a partial acute obstruction which rapidly elevates intratubular pressure and reduces the net glomerular filtration pressure. The degree and duration of obstruction determine the urine output in tubular dysfunction and the functional capabilities of the tubules and glomeruli, and thus the urinary indices. Therefore, these values by themselves cannot invariably distinguish prerenal from postrenal failure.[57–59]

Intrinsic renal disease can act by any one of several mechanisms to produce acute azotemia. Specific disorders that may lead to ARF are multiple. Once prerenal (i.e., ischemia) and postrenal (i.e., obstruction) causes of renal failure are eliminated, a search for causes of intrinsic renal damage (glomerular and/or tubular) must be undertaken. As when investigating most diseases, an appropriate history and physical examination are mandatory. In evaluating the history of older children, one must look for antecedent illnesses such as pharyngitis or pyoderma that might precede rapidly progressive glomerular nephritis.[60] A viral upper respiratory illness or diarrheal disease commonly precedes hemolytic-uremic syndrome.[61] Acute interstitial nephritis is often drug-induced.[62] Any member of the penicillin group of drugs may produce such a reaction, although methicillin is most frequently mentioned; sulfonamides, diuretics (including furosemide), phenytoin, phenylbutazone, and allopurinol have also been implicated. Several factors have been postulated to predispose to the well known aminoglycoside nephrotoxicity, including advanced age, pre-existing renal dysfunction, hypovolemia, and other nephrotoxic drugs (e.g., cephalosporins).[63] Because of its volume-depleting effect, furosemide may also potentiate aminoglycoside nephrotoxicity.

Systemic diseases that may be associated with ARF included sepsis, bacterial endocarditis, leukemia, lymphoma,[64] and vasculitis. A history of urinary tract symptoms may point to previous renal diseases. Dysuria, frequency, enuresis, and flank pain are clues that infection may be the cause of ARF. Rhabdomyolysis usually occurs in crush injuries, extensive burns, and muscle inflammation, but may also be found when muscle blood flow and metabolism are disturbed.[65] Thus, nontraumatic rhabdomyolysis may be an important cause of renal failure.

Surgery is a frequent antecedent to oliguria or anuria. In evaluating such patients one needs to know if significant hypotension occurred, what drugs were given, what anesthetic was used (e.g., methoxyflurane), if renal vascular flow was interrupted, if a transfusion reaction occurred, if stitches were placed near the urethral course, or if the ureters were reimplanted or instrumented in such a way that edema could occur. One must also evaluate the adequacy of replacement fluids. From the entire spectrum of surgical patients, an important subgroup of cardiac patients has emerged. Renal dysfunction of some variety has been reported in from 1 to 30 percent of adults and 8 percent of pediatric cases in one series.[66] Important risk factors for the development of ARF are hypoglycemia, duration of surgery, type of operation, and low cardiac output.[67]

Newborns with oliguria or anuria are a special problem.[68] Ninety percent of infants void in the first 24 hours and 98 percent in the first 48; thus, if no urine has been noted by this time, investigation is warranted. Prerenal azotemia secondary to perinatal stress with hypotension, hypoxia, and acidosis can be corrected with a fluid challenge. Anatomic lesions, including posterior urethral valves or severe dysplasia, may present as oliguria. Renal artery embolism from a patent ductus arteriosus or umbilical artery catheter is usually associated with hypertension and gross hematuria. Bilateral renal vein thrombosis may occur in neonates with nephrotic syndrome or in infants of diabetic mothers. Oliguria secondary to excessive secretion of ADH occurs in some infants with pulmonary disease.[69] The recent and widespread use of indomethacin has been associated with elevations in serum creatinine and oliguria or anuria.[70,71] Chevalier and co-workers[72] followed 16 infants with acute renal failure. They identified the lack of oliguria and the presence of identifiable renal perfusion by scintigraphy as favorable factors for ultimate survival.

The physical examination may also give clues about the etiology of ARF. Edema associated with hypoproteinemia and proteinuria represents the nephrotic syndrome and is almost always a sign of intrinsic glomerular disease. Ascites without hepatomegaly also may be present. Ascites with hepatomegaly and oliguria suggests hepatorenal syndrome, particularly if peripheral edema is minimal and liver disease is confirmed chemically.[73] Skin rashes may be important, particularly the malar flush of systemic lupus erythematosus, erythema marginatum, the petichial purpura of polyarteritis, or anaphylactoid purpura. Splenomegaly may suggest malignancy or bacterial endocarditis. Arthralgia and arthritis have been found with systemic lupus erythematosus, polyarteritis, and anaphylactoid purpura. Severe myositis with oliguria is suggestive of viral dissemination, systemic lupus erythematosus, and polyarteritis. With an abdominal mass one must consider hydronephrosis with obstruction; urethral valves with bladder distention; tumors such as Wilm's tumor, neuroblastoma, rhabdomyosarcoma, or lymphoma; or abscess. Finally, one should be alert for bony changes suggestive of rickets and/or short stature. These findings may suggest chronic disease with acute deterioration.

Laboratory Data

The most pertinent laboratory evaluations in neonatal oliguria, at least initially, are urine volume, serum creatinine, BUN, and urinalysis. As previously mentioned, ARF is usually suspected because of oliguria or anuria. However, in the last decade the number of patients with nonoliguric renal failure has increased.[74] In a prospective study of acute tubular necrosis, in which 92 patients were studied, 41 percent were oliguric throughout the azotemic phase.[75] Fifty-four percent were nonoliguric, with a mean daily urine volume of 1280 ± 75 ml. The increased frequency of nonoliguric renal failure may be due to better recognition, an increasing incidence of nephrotoxic antibiotic-induced ARF, and the increased use of potent loop diuretics and mannitol, which may convert oliguric to nonoliguric renal failure.[76,77]

Specific tests of tubular function have proven useful in separating out prerenal from acute intrinsic renal oliguria. As noted, in otherwise normal hypoperfused kidneys, there is intense reabsorption of salt and water, with a resultant increase in urine osmolality. Since proteinuria and glycosuria affect specific gravity, urine osmolality is a more reliable index of concentrating ability. In intrinsic renal azotemia, damaged tubules cannot conserve salt and water, and oliguria is therefore present with relatively lower urine osmolalities. However, considerable overlap has been found between prerenal and intrinsic renal disease.[57] Thus, some investigators have suggested using urine-to-plasma osmolar ratios rather than relying solely on urine osmolalities. Ratios of 1.04 in acute tubular necrosis (ATN) and 1.35 and 1.29 in prerenal azotemia have been reported. Using this index, Eliahou and Bate[78] found no overlap. Some groups have recommended the free-water clearance as an early indicator of tubular damage, especially after cardiac surgery.[79]

Fractional sodium reabsorption also may discriminate between prerenal and renal failure, being very high in the former and lower in the latter. Although the majority of patients with hypoperfused kidneys excrete less than 20 mEq/liter and most with intrinsic renal disease excrete 40 mEq/liter or more, there is again overlap.[80] Patients with nonoliguric ATN may excrete low sodium concentrations (<10 mEq/L).[81] The use of FE_{Na} ($FE_{Na} = U_{Na}/P_{Na} \div U_{Cr}/P_{Cr}$ (where P is plasma) and renal failure index (RFI = $U_{Na} \div U_{Cr}/P_{Cr}$) are attempts to separate out the overlapping groups. Using these two methods the overlap lessens but is still present.[82] One study found the FE_{Na} to be 0.64 percent in prerenal azotemia and 3.77 percent in acute renal azotemia.[83] It is important that a fractional sodium excretion of greater than one is consistent not only with the acutely azotemic patient, but also with volume depletion in patients receiving diuretics.[84] As for the renal failure index, values of 1 percent for prerenal and 4 to 10 percent for intrinsic renal azotemia have been reported.[59] These criteria may need to be modified for the preterm neonate. The FE_{Na} in the preterm fetus has been reported to be 12.8 ± 2.3 percent,[85] while after delivery, low-birth-weight preterm infants can show values as high as 7 percent.[86]

Serum creatinine also may be used as a reliable estimate of renal function. Since creatinine is an end product of creatine phosphate metabolism in muscle, the serum creatinine in infants and children must be measured according to age-appropriate standards.[87] Although the BUN is also inversely proportional to the GFR, its values are affected by more variables than is creatinine. Urea is produced almost exclusively by the liver, and its production can be increased by protein intake, tetracyclines, and hypercatabolic states such as infection, trauma, or burns. As mentioned, both urea and creatinine are freely filtered at the glomerulus; urea is partially reabsorbed, while filtered creatinine is totally excreted (and secreted). Progressive reabsorption of filtrate will markedly increase the concentration of both substances as they traverse the tubules. The normal U/P ratio for urea is usually greater than 14, and in hypoperfused kidneys may reach above 100. In acute oliguric renal failure, values have varied from 2 to 3.4; in nonoliguric renal failure, slightly higher values have been noted.[88] However a large overlap exists; indeed, 40 percent of patients with prerenal azotemia have had ratios commonly considered indicative of ATN. Urine:plasma creatinine ratios show the same problems as U/P urea ratios. For prerenal azotemia their mean values are 43 to 45; in acute oliguric and nonoliguric ATN the values tend to be less than 20.[59] However, many patients with both conditions have ratios between 20 and 40.[89]

Urinalysis with careful attention to the microscopic examination is also useful in trying to separate prerenal from intrinsic renal azotemia. The pH ranges from 5.5 to 7 in ATN, while a strongly acid urine is more suggestive of prerenal azotemia. A positive dipstick reaction to blood is more common with intrinsic renal disease, but the lack of red blood cells on microscopic examination suggests hemoglobinuria or myoglobinuria. The finding of 1+ to 2+ proteinuria is compatible with ATN. Red blood cells suggest intrinsic renal disease, and red blood cell casts localize the hematuria to the kidney. White cells may suggest infection or interstitial nephritis. Hyaline and finely granular casts may suggest prerenal azotemia, while tubular cells and casts suggest ATN. Crystallurias of uric acid, calcium oxalate, and phosphate suggest the etiology of acute renal failure. More recently, Mandal and co-workers[90] used transmission electron microscopy to evaluate the urine sediment of patients with renal disease. Renal tubule cells were a consistent findings and could be divided into three types: type I comprised homogeneous cell populations with a severely altered ultrastructure; type II comprised a similar cell group, but only mildly; type III comprised a heterogeneous population, variably affected. The importance of identifying such cell types became apparent when the clinical outcome for the patient was compared to the various cell types. Of 11 patients with a type I sediment, only two survived. Seven of eight patients with Type II sediment survived; patients with Type III urinary cell populations had an intermediary course. Thus, electron microscopic examination of the urine sediment may be a useful adjunct to routine urinalysis.

Radiologic techniques can often be of use, especially to evaluate postrenal azotemia. The plain film will help delineate the size of the kidneys and the presence or absence of stones. The intravenous pyelogram uses salts of substituted triiodinated benzoic acid for visualization of the parenchyma and collecting structures. However, the increasing number of radiocontrast-induced cases of renal failure makes it necessary for physicians to weigh thoughtfully the need for a contrast study.[91,92] Ultrasonography, to estimate renal size and enlargement of the renal pelvis, may aid in the diagnosis of obstruction without the need for contrast material.

Determination of kidney size may provide important differential information. Kidneys below two standard deviations from the normal in length are a frequent result of chronic sclerosing disease, interstitial nephritis, glomerulonephritis, pyelonephritis, congenital hypoplasia, or dysplasia. Large kidneys result from the nephrotic syndrome, acute glomerulonephritis, ATN, interstitial nephritis, renal vein thrombosis, and pyelonephritis, especially with obstruction. A discrepancy of more than 1.5 cm in renal size suggests dysplasia or renal artery stenosis, a condition that can compromise renal function due to hypertensive nephropathy contralaterally and minimal blood flow ipsilaterally. Measurement of renal size generally depends on plain radiography, tomographic renal shadowing, or sonography. Voiding cystourethrography has been very useful when urethral valves or a grossly anatomically abnormal urinary tract was suspected. Retrograde pyelography remains important in probable intraluminal obstruction, particularly if the kidney is infected and in need of drainage. Computerized axial tomography has been useful in defining renal anatomy in unusual cases.

Renal biopsy may be necessary in some cases of acute renal failure. Indications may include the following: (1) when no obvious cause is found; (2) when oliguria or anuria lasts for two to three weeks; (3) when physical or laboratory findings are suggestive of a primary renal disease, vasculitis, or systemic disease; or (4) when there is exposure to drugs known to be associated with tubulointerstitial disease. Thus, biopsy may be a useful tool in a small number (10 to 15 percent) of patients with ARF.[93,94]

Management

The child with oliguria or anuria may need correction of many abnormalities. These include: (1) fluid and electrolyte imbalances, (2) acid-base imbalances, and (3) endocrinologic and metabolic malfunctions. In terms of ongoing fluid management of the oliguric or anuric child, the basic goal is to maintain normal hydration and electrolyte concentrations without the aid of functioning kidneys. Fluid intake and output should be monitored and corroborated with daily weights and clinical examination. Due to the catabolic state with loss of endogenous fat and protein, a child with ARF should lose about 0.05 percent of body weight per day.[56] If this loss is not occurring, excess fluid may be accumulating. Water allotment should be set at 400 to 600 ml/m²/day to replace insensible water losses. Any other fluid loss may be replaced milliliter for milliliter. Since insensible losses consist of pure water, electrolyte intake should replace losses in urine or gastrointestinal fluid. Intravenous medications that require diluting fluids must also be calculated into the total fluid intake. Additionally, significant amounts of sodium or potassium that may accompany medications such as carbenicillin, cephalosporins, and penicillin should be taken into account. Hyponatremia has the same significance in the oliguric patient as in the patient with normal renal function (i.e., water in excess of sodium). Fluid restriction, diuretics, and ultrafiltration may be used to remove excess fluid; the use of these methods depends on the degree of renal functional impairment. If the serum sodium is less than 120 mEq/liter or if the patient is symptomatic, hypertonic saline (3 to 5 percent) administration may be necessary. The use of a concentrated salt solution is necessary to reduce the fluid volume required to deliver the amount of sodium needed to correct the sodium deficit.

The dangers of hyperkalemia are now well recognized, and death from this complication is rare. Hyperkalemia tends to be more severe in post-traumatic renal failure; certainly other biochemical alterations (such as acidosis) may increase the serum potassium concentration. Although abnormalities on the electrocardiogram (ECG) correlate poorly with serum potassium levels, the ECG is a more accurate reflection of the electrophysiologic condition of the heart.[95] At potassium levels between 5.5 and 6.0 mEq/liter, peaking of T waves and shortening of the QT_c interval are usually evident. As hyperkalemia increases, the electrocardiogram continues to become more abnormal until levels of 8.0 to 9.0 mEq/liter are reached, atrial conduction ceases, the P wave disappears, and conduction to the ventricles produces a widened pattern that merges into the T wave, the so-called sine wave pattern. Hyperkalemia may be deceptively silent until life-threatening sequelae occur. A well-developed normal child with renal failure of sudden onset may show a 2 mEq/liter rise in potassium per day in the absence of major acidosis. This rate of rise depends on several factors, including the patient's muscle mass and adrenal status, the presence of infection or other catabolic phenomena, and the presence of hemolysis.

Life-threatening hyperkalemia may be treated by shifting potassium into cells, antagonizing its cardiac effects, or removing it from the body. Intracellular shifts of potassium are accomplished by correcting acidosis or by infusing glucose and insulin. Many regimens are available; one approach is to add 75 mEq of sodium bicarbonate and 50 units of regular insulin to 450 ml of 25 percent glucose. This solution is administered at a rate of 75 ml/m² for the first hour and 25 ml/m²/hr thereafter, while monitoring serum potassium and glucose. Calcium ions antagonize the cardiotoxic effects of potassium. Intravenous calcium administration is the most immediate method for averting impending cardiac arrest as indicated by severe QRS widening or heart block. One may begin with 10 percent calcium gluconate at a dose of 15 ml/m² per 2 to 4 minutes; however when severe ECG changes are present, calcium should be given by slow intravenous push until effective cardiac contraction and a near normal ECG are obtained. Calcium must be infused slowly to avoid bradycardia; also, the beneficial effects are transient, and additional measures must therefore be undertaken simultaneously. Removal of potassium also may be initiated with sodium polystyrene sulfonate at a dose of 1 to 2 g/kg in sorbitol, repeated every 2 to 4 hours as needed. When using these measures certain precautions must be noted: (1) each 50 ml ampule of 8.4 percent NaHCO$_3$ contains 50 milliequivalents of sodium, (2) alkalosis may provoke hypocalcemia and tetany, (3) calcium gluconate may provoke arrhythmias and should be given only with ECG monitoring, (4) calcium is contraindicated in the digitalized patient, and (5) each ampule of 10 percent calcium chloride contains more than threefold the amount of calcium in one ampule of 10 percent calcium gluconate. For each gram of sodium polystyrene sulfonate (Kayexalate), 1 milliequivalent of potassium is bound in exchange for 1 milliequivalent of sodium. The definitive therapy for hyperkalemia is emergency dialysis, which should be arranged for while temporizing with the above measures.

Hypocalcemia may develop early in the course of ARF. In cases of trauma or rhabdomyolysis, the hypocalcemia may be related to a high calcium:phosphorus ratio and the deposition of calcium phosphate in soft tissue.[96] The etiology in other conditions is unknown, but may be related to the lack of a parathyroid hormone (PTH) response secondary to altered vitamin D metabolism.[97] Hypercalcemia has been rarely reported, but appears not to be related to PTH excess.[98] Hypocalcemia is treated with calcium gluconate if the patient is symptomatic or if the calcium is very low (less than 8.0 mg%) in the absence of hypoproteinemia.

The serum phosphate is generally elevated and is reduced with oral aluminum hydroxide gels. Magnesium levels are usually normal to slightly elevated. Hypermagnesemia may be inadvertently caused by the administration of aluminum-containing antacids, but signs of toxicity are unusual unless levels over 5 mEq/liters are reached.

Metabolic acidosis is a frequent accompaniment of ARF and results from retention of acid end products from the catabolism of dietary proteins. The endogenous acid production is roughly 1 mEq/kg/day. Thus the serum bicarbonate may decrease 1 to 2 mEq/day in ARF. Acidosis may be corrected with oral sodium bicarbonate or sodium citrate (Shohl's solution). The correction should be done over a 12 to 24 hour period, since acute correction may lead to sodium overload and alkalinization, with hypocalcemia and hypokalemia. Maintenance doses of base are about 1 mEq/kg/day.

Hypertension may also be present in ARF, usually due to fluid overload. Defining the levels of hypertension to treat and lower acutely is difficult and somewhat arbitrary. Certainly if the patient is symptomatic, the blood pressure should be lowered quickly. In the asymptomatic patient, our general approach is to acutely treat an infant with parenteral therapy for a pressure above 130/90 mmHg, a small child at 140/100 mmHg, and patients older than 6 to 7 years at 150/110 mmHg. Strokes and other manifestations of hypertensive encephalopathy do occur at these levels and may be preventable. Two potent emergency antihypertensive drugs are diazoxide and sodium nitroprusside. Diazoxide, a powerful peripheral vasodilator with a chemical structure similar to the thiazide diuretics, is given as a 5 mg/kg rapid push, and results in an almost immediate fall in blood pressure that may be followed by further declines. The initial dose may be repeated after 30 minutes, with the total dose not to exceed 20 mg/kg/day.[99] It may also be given in smaller incremental doses to produce a more gradual effect.[100] As with any vasodilator, sodium retention may occur[101]; in addition, hyperglycemia may result.

Sodium nitroprusside is given as a constant infusion of 0.5 µg/kg/min and titrated according to the response. The hypotensive vasodilatory response is rapidly reversed upon stopping the infusion,[102] usually after oral antihypertensives have been started. The patient must be closely monitored for metabolic acidosis reflecting cyanide and thiocyanate accumulation, since poisonings have complicated nitroprusside use.[103] Such accumulation may be particularly rapid in patients with renal compromise unless they are frequently dialyzed.

If fluid overload is the cause of the hypertension, any antihypertensive therapy will be much less effective; dialysis may be indicated. Absolute indications for dialysis include: (1) severe or persistent hyperkalemia; (2) intractable hypertension, congestive heart failure, or pulmonary edema from volume overload; (3) severe and persistent acidosis; and (4) neurologic complications of uremia.[104] The effect of early dialysis remains controversial. Most series are retrospective, but indicate that early dialysis may reduce mortality.[105–108] One small prospective controlled study also supports the concept of early dialysis.[105] Prognosis has been correlated with the maximal height of the BUN,[109] but it is unclear whether lowering the BUN affects outcome.[110] Acute uremia in children is seldom severe enough in itself to be a major threat at presentation. Exceptions do occur, however: BUN levels that are acutely increased above 100 mg/dl in infants, 150 mg/dl in children, and 175 mg/dl in adolescents justify emergency dialysis, even if electrolytes and fluid balance are acceptable. The BUN should be reduced slowly with peritoneal dialysis or short-duration hemodialysis. If untreated, uremia of the degree indicated by such high BUN levels may progress, with a high risk of severe central nervous system depression, seizures, nausea and vomiting, hemorrhage, and pericarditis. It may also be that early dialysis allows other interventions (e.g., total parenteral nutrition) that influence the volume of fluid required for an effective outcome.

As experience with patients in ARF accumulates, it is clear that simply maintaining fluid and electrolyte balance and controlling hypertension are inadequate. Acute renal failure is a catabolic state in which the loss of body mass can be extreme.[111] In order to overcome this catabolic state in the face of anorexia, nausea, and reduced ability to excrete fluid and nitrogenous waste, dialysis plus intravenous nutrition may be required. The composition of the optimal solution is not yet determined, but it should contain sufficient glucose to at least spare protein breakdown (75 kcal/kg/day), electrolytes, minerals, vitamins, and L-amino acids (1.0 to 2.0 grams of protein per kilogram per day). It appears that in addition to the eight essential amino acids, histidine and tyrosine may also be useful. Additionally, nonessential amino acids may be beneficial. These amino acids added to essential amino acids have been shown to increase body weight and plasma albumin in uremic rats.[112] Nonessential amino acids can be given safely to patients with ARF without exacerbating azotemia. The value of amino acids has been demonstrated by Abitbol and Holliday,[113] who showed that when the provision of glucose calories was raised from 20 to 70 kcal/kg/day, nitrogen balance became less negative. However, with the addition of essential amino acids, the nitrogen balance became positive. Other benefits of amino acid and hypertonic glucose therapy include improved survival, improved nitrogen balance, a low incidence of hyperkalemia and hyperphosphatemia, and more rapid recovery of renal function. This therapy is not without complications, including catheter placement injuries, catheter sepsis, and hyperglycemia. The incidence of these complications can be minimized when total parenteral nutrition is administered by a team whose members have knowledge and interest in this area.[114,115] The team should be composed of a physician familiar with the principles of nutrition, a surgeon experienced in catheter placement, a nurse to supervise aseptic technique during catheter manipulation, and a pharmacist to prepare the solutions.

The outcome of ARF is influenced by a number of factors, of which age, underlying disease, and nutrition are only a few. In a large review, infection was found to account for approximately 30 percent of all deaths resulting from ARF.[116] Pulmonary infections may account for 40 to 77 percent; peritonitis in postsurgical and post-traumatic cases may account for 33 to 87 percent. Urinary tract infection is related to catheterization; furthermore, prophylactic antibiotics increase the frequency of infection.[117] The management of infection should begin with avoidance, especially of urinary catheters. The diagnosis of infection requires a high degree of suspicion. Leukocytosis may be present at the onset of ARF. Hypotension, tachycardia, and a marked increase in BUN may be signs of sepsis. Appropriate cultures should be taken. If a central catheter is in place, its removal may be necessary. Antibiotics should be aimed at *Staphylococcus aureus* and gram-negative organisms. Loading doses are necessary initially, and are then adjusted for the degree of renal insufficiency present.[118,119]

In summary, oliguric patients should be evaluated for emergency conditions, including severe volume deficiency leading to shock, volume overload with hypertension or heart failure, dangerous electrolyte abnormalities such as hyperkalemia or hypocalcemia, and severe uremia or other life-threatening complications. When the patient is stable, usual fluid, electrolyte, and drug therapies must be adjusted to allow for the retention of products normally excreted via the urine. Specific therapy when possible, and supportive therapy in general, should be aggressively pursued.

FLUID AND ELECTROLYTE HOMEOSTASIS IN THE MALNOURISHED CHILD

The child who suffers from protein-calorie deprivation presents a conundrum for the physician interested in fluid and electrolyte metabolism. Despite the fact that malnourished infants and children have the clinical stigmata of dehydration, they are in fact relatively overhydrated. During the process of starvation, protein and mineral losses exceed that of water, so that the percentage of body weight represented by water actually increases. Alterations in body electrolyte content also need to be recognized if therapy is to be effective. Numerous investigators have described changes in renal function during starvation;

whether these are in response to or the cause of the aberrations in water and electrolyte metabolism has not been determined. This section will outline the changes that occur in both body composition and renal function in the severely malnourished infant, and then attempt to define the implications for fluid and electrolyte therapy for these patients. Throughout this discussion, changes that occur in pure protein malnutrition (kwashiorkor) will not be distinguished from those due strictly to calorie deprivation (marasmus); all will be treated as the same spectrum of disease. There is a paucity of recent work on this subject, but the extensive monograph by Garrow and associates[120] summarizes much of what is known about this subject.

Fluid and Electrolyte Balance

Total body water is increased in the malnourished infant. Under normal circumstances, water as a percentage of total body weight decreases with increasing fetal age until the infant is one year of age[121] (Fig. 11-1). Thus, as the child becomes progressively more malnourished, total body water increases. Studies supporting this view are of three types: first, whole body (cadaver) analyses of the water and mineral content of malnourished children; second, analyses of the water content in muscle and skin biopsy material taken from malnourished subjects; and third, the use of isotope dilution techniques to estimate whole body water in malnourished patients.

Garrow and associates[122] were able to perform postmortem analyses on five children who died of malnutrition and four children who were relatively normally nourished. They found that, whereas the total solids were markedly reduced (41 to 70 percent of expected), total body water was increased (80 to 125 percent of that expected for a child of equal height). In the early 1900s, German investigators[117] also found a relative increase in TBW.

Biopsies of skin and muscle tissue were performed by Frenk and associates[123] in malnourished Mexican children. He found that the water content in muscle cells was increased and fell as the children recovered. In skin, the range was variable, but some samples had a 100 percent increase in tissue water as compared to samples from controls.[124]

Isotope dilution techniques have utilized either titrated water[124] or deuterium oxide[125] to determine TBW. These studies also revealed that TBW was increased in malnourished subjects. Total body water as a percentage of body weight fell as the children recovered.[126]

Where is this excess proportion of body water located? Unfortunately, the answer to this question is not known at present. Most studies that have used either chloride or thiocyanate as an extracellular marker indicate the increase in water to be in the extracellular space. However, the critical assumption in these studies is that the marker is confined to the extracellular space in malnourished subjects as it is in normal individuals. Since this assumption has not been adequately tested, the conclusions are tentative. In any case, all of the methods used so far have shown that victims of severe malnutrition are water "overloaded." This finding contrasts sharply with the physical appearance of these patients, which is that of "dehydration" because of poor skin turgor and a sunken appearance of the eyes from loss of supporting tissue structure, not from water loss.

Since infants with protein-calorie malnutrition have an excess of body water, they also have a higher than normal total body sodium content (on a per-unit-of-body-weight basis).[127] However, their plasma sodium concentrations are often either lower than normal or in the low end of the normal range,[123,128] so that plasma osmolality is often decreased. It is important to remember that hyponatremia does not necessarily result from sodium deficiency, but can also result from an excess of water. If sodium is given to patients with severe malnutrition, dire consequences may follow. Gordillo and co-workers[129] reported that when hypotonic sodium chloride infusions were given to malnourished, hyponatremic infants, sodium was retained with no change in plasma osmolality. Thus, water shifted from the intracellular to the extracellular space and the patients remained hypotonic.

Tissue analysis also indicates that sodium, which under ordinary circumstances is almost entirely confined to the ECF space, accumulates within cells.[130] Postmortem tissue chemical analyses confirm that sodium is in excess relative to other minerals.[131] The critical point is that even though malnourished children appear dehydrated and have a low serum sodium concentration, they have a high total body content of sodium and an even higher excess of TBW.

There is a large body of evidence indicating that the most profound change in malnutrition may be total body potassium depletion. The evidence includes postmortem chemical analysis, tissue biopsy studies, measurements of the isotope ^{40}K by means of a whole body counter,[119] and potassium balance studies. Hansen[132] performed careful potassium balance studies in South African children suffering from kwashiorkor, and demonstrated a positive potassium balance; this was particularly marked during the first two to three days of treatment, during which children retained 3 to 5 mEq of potassium per kilogram of body weight. He also demonstrated a simultaneous negative sodium balance in these infants. Over the course of treatment, there was a notable shift of plasma potassium from the low and low-normal range to the mid-normal range. Tissue studies by Frenk and co-workers[123] demonstrated that muscle cells have a 10 to 20 percent reduction in potassium concentration. This has been confirmed by Metcoff and associates.[130] Whole body analysis done on cadavers of children who died as a result of malnutrition also have revealed a markedly diminished potassium content.[131]

Garrow[133] performed sophisticated studies on severely malnourished infants before, during, and after recovery. Using a whole body liquid scintillation counter, he determined whole body ^{40}K (the naturally occurring isotope of potassium). Since the ratio of ^{40}K to ^{39}K is constant, by measuring ^{40}K it is possible to calculate total body potassium.[134] Garrow showed that malnourished edematous children had significant potassium depletion, in the range of 20 to 50 percent.

Renal Function

Renal function in the malnourished child is altered; there is a decrease in both renal plasma flow and GFR, a decrease in the ability to concentrate a dilute glomerular filtrate, and a diminished ability to excrete an acid load.[129] The reasons for these changes and whether they are adaptive or maladaptive adjustments to caloric deprivation have not yet been determined.[135]

Decreases in renal plasma flow and GFR have been found consistently.[136] The filtration rate varies from 20 to 50 percent of normal depending on the degree of starvation. Renal plasma flow is also decreased, and this has been attributed to a low cardiac output (40 percent of normal) by some workers. Recent work in Munich wistar rats implicates protein deprivation as the primary determinant of a decreased renal plasma flow and GFR.[137] In this work, two groups of rats were fed isocaloric diets, one low in protein, one high in protein; a third group was given the high protein diet ad libitum. Despite the fact that rats in group 1 (low protein) had essentially the same caloric intake as those in group 2 (high protein, low calorie) for four months, the rats in group 2 weighed significantly more than did those in group 1. In addition, both renal plasma flow and glomerular filtration were decreased by 30 percent in group 1 as compared to groups 2 and 3. These differences were the result of a lower glomerular permeability constant, which is a function of both glomerular surface and of the permeability characteristics of the glomerular basement membrane. Morphologic studies were then carried out and revealed that the cross-sectional area of glomeruli from group 1 rats was significantly reduced as compared to that in groups 2 and 3. Group 2 rats (low calories, high protein) had significantly smaller glomeruli than did group 3 rats (high protein, ad libitum feeding).

The reasons for the contraction of glomerular surface area are unknown; possible contributing factors include an increased level of angiotensin II, an increased level of PTH, other humoral substances, or structural alterations in membrane composition as a result of protein deficiency.

Other consistent observations in protein-calorie malnourished infants are that they put out large volumes of dilute urine and have very hypotonic plasma that is in equilibrium with cells, implying a hypotonic intracellular environment as well.[138] This raises the question of whether or not these patients are capable of secreting and responding to vasopressin. Though vasopressin levels have not been measured, there is evidence that these patients do respond to exogenous vasopressin. Alleyne[138] gave intramuscular pitressin both before and after recovery from malnutrition, and found that in both instances there was a significant increase in urine osmolality. After recovery, however, the children were better able to concentrate their urine than previously; in view of what we now know about the role of urea and medullary hypertonicity in the elaboration of concentrated urine, it is hardly surprising that protein-malnourished children cannot concentrate their urine as well as their normal counterparts.[139] This represents a "washout" or loss of medullary hypertonicity, not an inability to respond to vasopressin.

It has also been found that malnourished children have a diminished capacity to excrete an acid load. However, malnourished infants are able to appropriately increase ammonia production in response to an acid load; the defect that impairs their ability to excrete an acid load lies in their inability to increase titratable acid excretion. Again, this is probably not a result of renal dysfunction but of a decreased availability of buffer; indeed, in adult malnourished patients, titratable acid excretion increases if intravenous phosphate is given.[140] Phosphate deficiency has been demonstrated in children, further adding to the evidence for buffer deficiency.[141]

Of the renal changes described in protein-calorie malnutrition, the decrease in renal plasma flow and GFR are real. The reason for these functional alterations is unknown, and whether this represents an adaptive response to preserve volume or a deterioration secondary to the underlying condition remains to be determined. The concentrating defect and inability to excrete an acid load are the result of an altered milieu, not of changes in kidney structure.

Fluid Therapy

Knowing the changes that occur in body composition, along with an understanding of the renal functional alterations, should make therapy for infants with malnutrition relatively simple. Unfortunately, this is not the case. There are a number of factors involved, among which are that malnourished children appear clinically dehydrated and are therefore often vigorously "resuscitated" with intravenous sodium chloride solutions despite the fact that they are, in reality, both sodium and water overloaded. Skin turgor and general lethargy are not valid indicators of the state of hydration, since these may be due to malnutrition. Probably the best indicators of dehydration in these infants are the pulse rate and the presence of a sunken fontanelle. A child who otherwise appears dehydrated but has a normal or slow pulse rate and a normal fontanelle should be hydrated slowly and not given isotonic sodium chloride solutions. In situations in which hypertonic sodium chloride infusions have been given, two things have resulted: patients retain nearly all of the sodium infused, and the plasma osmolality and plasma sodium concentrations do not change. These effects are due to large shifts of water from the intracellular to the extracellular space, which may result in intracellular dehydration, and have been implicated in the death of one carefully studied patient.[130]

A second reason that children with protein-calorie malnutrition fail to do well is that they are very susceptible to infections, particularly diarrhea. A diarrheal episode superimposed on long term malnutrition will demand the quick replenishment of water and electrolytes. The problem lies in determining an end point for fluid therapy and in choosing an appropriate intravenous solution. Again, armed with the knowledge that plasma and cellular osmolality prior to the diarrhea was probably low (260 to 270 mOsm/liter), it seems that the intravenous fluid should also be somewhat hypotonic. Therefore, solutions such as one-fifth or one-third normal saline are recommended. Clinical guides to the adequacy of therapy should again be the pulse rate and the status of the fontanelle. When these are normal, the child has had adequate fluid resuscitation. Improvement in neurologic status, skin turgor, and general appearance will be slowly forthcoming as the nutritional status improves.

Even in those patients who have protein-calorie malnutrition compounded with chronic diarrhea, oral replenishment of calories and fluids is the method of choice.[142]

Oral rehydration can be accomplished in children with mild dehydration with a standard solution of glucose and electrolytes (sodium 30 mEq/liter, potassium 20 mEq/liter, chloride 30 mEq/liter, bicarbonate 31 mEq/liter, calcium 4 mEq/liter, and glucose 50 g/L). If dehydration is severe, intravenous therapy with isotonic solutions may be required; hypertonic solutions of sodium chloride are contraindicated.[143]

Feeding to establish adequate calories must be advanced slowly, at least in terms of volume. Seventy-five kilocalories per kilogram of body weight are necessary to prevent further weight loss, and this intake should be established within five to seven days of hospitalization. Some authors recommend that milk be used,[143] others avoid lactose and use mixtures of soybean-cathauseedarl, sucrose, and casein. These formulas are commercially available (Osmolite, Portagen).

Most authors recommend that potassium supplements be given for the first five to seven days so that intake is 5 to 8 milliequivalents of potassium per kilogram per day. Magnesium supplements are also recommended (2 to 4 mEq/kg/day).[142] Most authors also advocate vitamin and iron supplementation. The goal of therapy is to reestablish weight gain, which will require an intake of 125 to 150 kcal/kg/day. Early in the course of treatment, a weight loss may be noted secondary to diuresis and loss of excess body sodium.

Magnesium deficiency also appears to be a part of the protein-calorie deficiency syndrome, although the evidence for this relies heavily on balance studies. Montgomery[144] did short term balance studies and demonstrated that there was a positive magnesium balance during therapy. Longer term balance studies were performed by Linder and associates[145] in 13 children with kwashiorkor, and in all but 1 the net magnesium balance was strongly positive. Caddell also[146] performed a double blind study in malnourished Nigerian children who had symptoms of magnesium deficiency. The children given magnesium supplements along with the standard regimen for protein-calorie malnutrition did much better than those who received only standard treatment. The applicability of this study is open to question because of the patient selection. However, most centers do give magnesium supplements as part of the therapy for severe malnutrition.

Of the trace elements, zinc has been the best studied, and it appears that children with either marasmus or kwashiorkor have decreased plasma zinc concentrations if they have evidence of skin lesions.[147] These skin lesions, which are seen in protein-calorie malnutrition, do respond to zinc therapy.[148] Other trace minerals have not been adequately studied, and so their role in the pathogenesis and treatment of protein-calorie malnutrition remains unknown.

REFERENCES

1. Katz MA: Hyperglycemic-induced hyponatremia—Calculation of expected serum sodium depression. N Engl J Med 289:843, 1973
2. Holliday MA, Segar WF: The maintenance need for water in parenteral fluid therapy. Pediatrics 19:823, 1957
3. McCrory WW: Quantitative measurement of renal function during growth in infancy and childhood. p.79. In McCrory WW (ed): Developmental Nephrology. Harvard University Press, Cambridge, MA 1972
4. Pizarro D, Posada G, Levine MM: Hypernatremic diarrheal dehydration treated with "slow" (12-hour) oral rehydration therapy: A preliminary report. J Pediatr 104:316, 1984
5. Aperia A, Marin L, Zetterstrom R, et al: Salt and water homeostasis during oral rehydration therapy. J Pediatr 103:364, 1983
6. Pizarro D, Posada G, Mata L: Treatment of 242 neonates with dehydrating diarrhea with an oral glucose-electrolyte solution. J Pediatr 102:153, 1983
7. Santhosham M, Daum RS, Dillman L, et al: Oral rehydration therapy of infantile diarrhea. N Engl J Med 306:1070, 1982
8. Finberg L: Oral electrolyte/glucose solutions. J Pediatr 105:939, 1984
9. Arieff AI, Guirada R: Effects on the CNS of hypernatremic and hyponatremic states. Kidney Int 10:104, 1976
10. Ayus JC, Krothapalli RK, Arieff A: Changing concepts in treatment of severe symptomatic hyponatremia. Am J Med 78:897, 1985
11. Nash M: Water and solute homeostasis. p 290. In Edelmann CM Jr (ed): Pediatric Kidney Disease, Vol 1. Little, Brown, Boston, 1979
12. Finberg L: Hypernatremic (hypertonic) dehydration in infants. N Engl J Med 289:196, 1973
13. Pullan CR, Dellagrammatikas H, Steiner H: Survey of gastroenteritis in children admitted to hospital in Newcastle upon Tyne in 1971–1975. Br Med J 1:619, 1977
14. Bruck E, Abal G, Aceto T: Pathogenesis and pathophysiology of hypotonic dehydration with diarrhea. Am J Dis Child 115:122, 1968
15. Finberg L, Harrison HE: Hypernatremia in infants. Pediatrics 16:1, 1955
16. Arieff AI, Guisado R, Rozarowitz VC: The pathophysiology of hyperosmolar states. p. 227. In Andreoli TE, Grantham JJ, Rector FC (eds): Disturbances in Body Fluid Osmolality. The American Physiological Society, Bethesda, MD, 1977
17. Colle E, Ayoub E, Raile R: Hypertonic dehydration (hypernatremia): The role of feedings high in solute. Pediatrics 22:5, 1958
18. Emmett M, Narins RG: Clinical use of the anion gap. Medicine 56:38, 1977
19. Kaye R: Diabetic ketoacidosis: The bicarbonate controversy. J Pediatr 87:156, 1975
20. Posner JB, Plum F: Spinal-fluid pH and neurologic symptoms in systemic acidosis. N Engl J Med 277:605, 1967
21. Winters RW: Physiology of acid-base disorders. p. 46. In Winters RW (ed): The Body Fluids in Pediatrics. Little, Brown, Boston, 1973.
22. Shires GT, Tolman J: Dilution acidosis. Ann Intern Med 28:557, 1948
23. Garilla S, Chang BS, Kahn SI: Dilution aci-

dosis and contraction alkalosis: Review of a concept. Kidney Int 8:279, 1975
24. Brill CB, Urelsky S, Gribetz D: Indication of intrinsic renal disease in azotemic infants with diarrhea and dehydration. Pediatrics 52:197, 1973
25. Wilson RF, Gibson D, Percenel AK, et al: Severe alkalosis in critically ill surgical patients. Arch Surg 105:197, 1972
26. Lock JE, Lynch RE, Mauer SM: Metabolic alkalosis in children with congestive heart failure. J Pediatr 87:938, 1975
27. Abouna GM, Voazey PR, Terry DB: Intravenous infusion of hydrochloric acid for the treatment of severe metabolic alkalosis. Surgery 75:194, 1974
28. Beckerman RC, Taussig LM: Hypoelectrolytemia and metabolic alkalosis in infants with cystic fibrosis. Pediatrics 63:580, 1979
29. Gill JR Jr., Bartter FC: Evidence for a prostaglandin-independent defect in chloride reabsorption in the loop of Henle as a proximal cause of Bartter's syndrome. Am J Med 65:766, 1978
30. Beikerdoz FA, Gorden P, Fordtran JS: Pathogenesis of congenital alkalosis with diarrhea. J Clin Invest 51:1958, 1972
31. Linshaw AM, Harrison HL, Gruskin AB, et al: Hypochloremic alkalosis in infants associated with soy protein formula. J Pediatr 96:635, 1980
32. Grassman H, Duggan E, McCammon S, et al: The dietary chloride deficiency syndrome. Pediatrics 66:366, 1980
33. Schambelan M, Slaton PE Jr, Biglieri EG: Mineralocorticoid production in hyperadrenocorticism. Role in pathogenesis of metabolic alkalosis. Am J Med 51:299, 1971
34. Veldhuis JD, Bardin CW, Demers LM: Metabolic mimicry of Bartter's syndrome by covert vomiting. Am J Med 66:361, 1979
35. Hutchinson DL, Gary MJ. Plentl AA, et al: The role of the fetus in the water exchange of the amniotic fluid of normal and hydramniotic patients. J Clin Invest 38:971, 1959
36. Arant BS: Developmental patterns of renal functional maturation compared in the human neonate. J Pediatr 92:705, 1978
37. Brouhard BH, Aplin CE, Cunningham RJ, LaGrone L: Immunoreactive urinary prostaglandins A and E in neonates, children and adults. Prostaglandins 15:881, 1978
38. Schwartz GJ, Haycock GB, Edelmann CM, Spetizer A: Late metabolic acidosis: a reassessment of the definition. J Pediatr 95:102, 1979
39. Sulyok E, Varga F, Gyory E, et al: Postnatal development of renal sodium handling in premature infants. J Pediatr 95:787, 1979
40. Arant BS: The kidney in the newborn. In Rudolph A (ed): Pediatrics 17th Ed. p. 1154. Appleton-Century-Crofts, Norwalk CT, 1982
41. Edelmann CM Jr, Barnett HL, Stark H: Effect of urea on concentrations of urinary nonurea solute in premature infants. J Appl Physiol 21:1021, 1966
42. Wu PYK, Hodgman JE: Insensible water loss in preterm infants: Changes with postnatal development and nonionizing radiant energy. Pediatrics 54:704, 1974
43. Fanaroff AA, Wald M, Gruber HS, Klaus MH: Insensible water loss in low birth weight infants. Pediatrics 50:236, 1972
44. Oh W, Yao AC, Hanson JS, Lind J: Peripheral circulatory response to phototherapy in newborn infants. Acta Paediatr Scand 62:49, 1973
45. Engle WD, Baumgart S, Schwartz JG, et al: Insensible water loss in the critically ill neonate. Am J Dis Child 135:516, 1981
46. Hey E, Katz G: Evaporative water loss in the newborn baby. J Pediatr 75:200, 1969
47. Roy RN, Sinclair JC: Hydration of the low birth-weight infant. Clin Perinatol 2:393, 1975
48. Oh W, Karecki H: Phototherapy and insensible water loss in the newborn infant. Am J Dis Child 124:230, 1972
49. Rubaltelli FF, Largajolli G: Effect of light exposure on gut transit time in jaundiced newborns. Acta Paediatr Scand 62:146, 1973
50. Lorenz JM, Kleinmon LI, Kotagal UR, Reller MD: Water balance in very low-birth-weight infants: Relationship to water and sodium intake and effect on outcome. J Pediatr 101:423, 1982
51. Davis JA, Harvey DR, Stevens JF: Osmolality as a measure of dehydration in the neonatal period. Arch Dis Child 41:448, 1966
52. Arant BS Jr: Renal disorders of the new-

born infant. p. 111. In Tune BM, Mendoza SA (eds): Contemporary Issues in Nephrology, Vol 12. Churchill Livingstone, New York, 1984
53. Richardson CJ: Parenteral fluid therapy. p. 20. Perinatal Pediatrics Housestaff Manual. Galveston TX, 1978
54. Adam PAJ: Control of glucose metabolism in the human fetus and newborn infants. Adv Metab Dis 5:183, 1971
55. Hostetter TH, Wilker BM, Brenner BM: Mechanisms of impaired glomerular filtration in acute renal failure. p. 52. In Brenner BM, Stein JH (eds): Acute Renal Failure. Churchill Livingstone, New York, 1980
56. Lieberman E: Management of acute renal failure in infants and children. Nephron 11:193, 1973
57. Bastl CP, Rudnick MR, Narins RG: Diagnostic approaches to acute renal failure. p. 17. In Brenner BM, Stein JH (eds): Acute Renal Failure. Churchill Livingstone, New York, 1980
58. Perkin RM, Levin DL: Shock in the pediatric patient. J Pediatr 101:163, 319, 1982
59. Miller TR, Anderson RJ, Linas SL, et al: Urinary diagnostic indices in acute renal failure. A prospective study. Ann Intern Med 89:47, 1978
60. Cunningham RJ, Gilfoil M, Cavallo T, et al: Rapidly progressive glomerulonephritis: A report of 13 cases and a review of the literature. Pediatr Res 14:128, 1980
61. Goldstein MH, Churg J, Strauss L, Gribetz D: Hemolytic-uremic syndrome. Nephron 23:263, 1979
62. Richet G, Mayaud C: The cause of acute renal failure in pyelonephritis and other types of interstitial nephritis. Nephon 22:124, 1978
63. Cronin RE: Aminoglycoside nephrotoxicity pathogenesis and prevention. Clin Nephrol 11:251, 1978
64. Lynch RE, Kjellstrand CM, Coecia PF: Renal and metabolic complications of childhood non-Hodgkins lymphoma. Semin Oncol 4:325, 1977
65. Humphreys MH: Rhabdomyolysis. Medical Staff Conference, University of California, San Francisco. West J Med 125:298, 1976
66. Chesney RW, Kaplan BS, Freedom RM, et al: Acute renal failure: An important complication of cardiac surgery in infants. J Pediatr 87:381, 1975
67. Bhat JG, Gluck MC, Lowenstein J, Baldwin DS: Renal failure after open heart surgery. Ann Intern Med 84:677, 1976
68. Norman ME, Asadi FK: A prospective study of acute renal failure in the newborn infant. Pediatrics 63:475, 1979
69. Paxson CL, Stoerner JW, Denson SE, et al: Syndrome of inappropriate antidiuretic hormone secretion in neonates with pneumothorax or atelectasis. J Pediatr 91:459, 1977
70. Freedmon WF, Herschklau MJ, Printz MP, et al: Pharmacologic closure of patent ductus arteriosus in the premature infant. N Engl J Med 295:526, 1976
71. Walshe JJ, Venuto RC: Acute oliguric renal failure induced by indomethacin: Possible mechanism. Ann Intern Med 91:47, 1979
72. Chevalier RL, Campbell F, Brenbridge ANAG: Prognostic factors in neonatal acute renal failure. Pediatrics 74:265, 1984
73. Reynolds TB: Water electrolyte and acid-base disorders in liver disease. p. 1251. In Maxwell MH, Kleemon CR (eds): Clinical Disorders of Fluid and Electrolyte Metabolism. New York McGraw-Hill, New York, 1980
74. McMurray SD, Luft FC, Maxwell DR, et al: Prevailing patterns and predictor variables in patients with acute tubular necrosis. Arch Intern Med 138:950, 1978
75. Anderson RJ, Linar SL, Buns AS, et al: Non-oliguric acute renal failure. N Engl J Med 294:1134, 1977
76. Barry KG: Post-traumatic renal shutdown in humans: Its prevention and treatment by the intravenous infusion of mannitol. Milit Med 128:224, 1963
77. Levensky NG, Bernard DB, Johnston PA: Enhancement of recovery of acute renal failure: Effects of mannitol and diuretics. p. 163. In Brenner BM, Stein JH (eds): Acute Renal Failure. Churchill Livingstone, New York, 1980
78. Eliahou HE, Bate A: The diagnosis of acute renal failure. Nephron 2:287, 1965
79. Balk SM, Brown RS, Shoemaker WC: Early prediction of acute renal failure and

recovery. I: Sequential measurements of free water clearance. Ann Surg 77:253, 1973
80. Handa SP, Morrin PAF: Diagnostic indices in acute renal failure. Can Med Assoc J 96:78, 1967
81. Vertel RM, Knochel JP: Nonoliguric acute renal failure. JAMA 200:598, 1967
82. Ellis EN, Arnold WC: Use of urinary indices in renal failure in the newborn. Am J Dis Child 136:615, 1982
83. Espinel CH: The FE_{Na} test: Use in the differential diagnosis of acute renal failure. JAMA 236:579, 1976
84. Steiner RW: Interpreting the fractional excretion of sodium. Am J Med 77:699, 1984
85. Houston IB: Prenatal renal function. In Spitzer A (ed): The Kidney During Development. Morphology and Function. Ch 43. p. 313. Masson, New York, 1980
86. Siegel SR, Oh W: Renal function as a marker of human fetal maturation. Acta Paediatr Scand 65:481, 1976
87. Schwartz GJ, Haycock GB, Spitzer A: Plasma creatinine and urea concentration in children: Normal values for age and sex. J Pediatr 88:828, 1976
88. Luke RG, Briggs JD, Allison MEM, Kennedy AC: Factors determining response to mannitol in acute renal failure. Am J Med Sci 259:168, 1970
89. Bull GM, Joekes AM, Lowe KG: Renal function studies in acute tubular necrosis. Clin Sci 9:379, 1950
90. Mandal AK, Sklar AH, Hudson JB: Transmission electron microscopy of urinary sediment in human acute renal failure. Kidney Int 28:58, 1985
91. Alexander RD, Berkes SL, Abuelo SG: Contrast media-induced oliguric renal failure. Arch Intern Med 138:318, 1978
92. VanZee DC, Hay WE, Falley TE, Jaenike JR: Renal injury associated with intravenous pyelography in non-diabetic and diabetic patients. Ann Intern Med 89:51, 1978
93. Sraer JD: Renal biopsy in acute renal failure. Kidney Int 8:60, 1975
94. Wilson DM, Turner DR, Cameron JS, et al: Value of renal biopsy in acute intrinsic renal failure. Br Med J 2:459, 1976
95. Kleeman K, Singl BN: Serum electrolytes and the heart. p. 145. In Maxwell MH, Kleemon CR (eds): Clinical Disorders of Fluid and Electrolyte Metabolism. New York, McGraw-Hill, New York, 1980
96. Grossmon HH, Lange H: Hypercalcemia in acute renal failure. Ann Intern Med 69:1332, 1969
97. Ng RCK, Suki WN: Treatment of acute renal failure. p. 229. In Brenner BM, Stein JH (eds): Acute Renal Failure. Churchill Livingstone, New York, 1980
98. Fuss N, Bagon J, Dupont E, et al: Parathyroid hormone and calcium blood levels in acute renal failure. Nephron 20:196, 1978
99. McCrory WW, Kohaut EC, Lewy JE, et al: Safety of intravenous diazoxide in children with severe hypertension. Clin Pediatr 18:661, 1979
100. Boerth RC, Long WR: Dose-response relation of diazoxide in children with hypertension. Circulation 56:1062, 1977
101. Brouhard BH, Lagrone L, Allen WR, Cunningham RJ: Role of sympathetic nerve activity in antinatriuresis after diazoxide and sodium nitroprusside infusion. J Pharmacol Exp Ther 218:148, 1981
102. Shearn DJ, Grim CE: Treatment of malignant hypertension with sodium nitroprusside. Arch Intern Med 133:187, 1974
103. Cole E: The safe use of sodium nitroprusside. Anesthesiology 33:473, 1978
104. Siegel NJ: Acute renal failure. p. 297. In Tune BM, Mendoza SA (eds): Contemporary Issues in Nephrology, Vol 12. Churchill Livingstone, New York, 1984
105. Conger JD: Controlled evaluation of prophylactic dialysis in post-traumatic acute renal failure. J Trauma 15:1056, 1975
106. Terchon PE, Baxter CR, O'Brian TF, et al: Prophylactic hemodialysis in the treatment of acute renal failure. Ann Intern Med 53:992, 1960
107. Parsons FM, Hobson SM, Blogg CR, McCracken BH: Optimum time for dialysis in acute reversible renal failure. Lancet 1:129, 1961
108. Fischer RP, Griffen WO, Reiser M, Clark DS: Early dialysis in the treatment of acute renal failure. Surg Gynecol Obstet 123:1019, 1966
109. Fine LG, Eliahou HE: Acute oliguric intrinsic renal failure. Diagnostic criteria and

clinical features in 61 patients. Isr J Med Sci 5:1024, 1969
110. Kennedy AC, Burton JA, Luke RG, et al: Factors affecting the prognosis in acute renal failure. Q J Med 42:73, 1973
111. Merrill JP: The treatment of renal failure. In Merrill JP (ed): Therapeutic Principles in the Management of Acute and Chronic Uremia, 2nd Ed. Grune & Stratton, New York, 1965
112. Pennisi AJ, Wang M, Kopple JD: Effects of protein and amino acid diets in chronically uremic and control rats. Kidney Int 13:472, 1978
113. Abitbol CL, Holliday MA: Total parenteral nutrition in anuric children. Clin Nephrol 5:153, 1976
114. Dudrick SJ, MacFadyen BV Jr, VanBuren CT, et al: Parenteral hyperalimentation, metabolic problems and solutions. Ann Surg 176:259, 1972
115. Fleming CR, McGill DB, Hoffmon HN II, Nelson RA: Total parenteral nutrition. Mayo Clin Proc 51:187, 1976
116. Montgomerie VZ, Kalmonson GM, Guze LB: Renal failure and infection. Medicine 47:1, 1968
117. Zech P, Bouletreau R, Moskoutchenko JF, et al: Infection in acute renal failure. In Hamburger J, Crosnier J, Maxwell MH (eds): Advances in Nephrology, Vol 1. Chicago, Year Book Medical Publishers, 1971
118. Bennett WN, Muther RS, Parker RA, et al: Drug therapy in renal failure. Ann Intern Med 93:62:286, 1980
119. Appel GB, Neu HC: The nephrotoxicity of antimicrobial agents. N Engl J Med 296:663, 722, 784, 1977
120. Garrow JS, Smith R, Ward EE: Electrolyte Metabolism in Severe Infantile Malnutrition. Pergamon Press, Oxford, London, 1968
121. Friis-Hanson B: Hydronatry of growth and aging in Human Body Composition. Brozeh J. Pergamon Press, Oxford, New York, 1968
122. Garrow JS, Fletcher K, Holliday D: Body composition in severe infantile malnutrition. J Clin Invest 44:417, 1956
123. Frenk S, Metcoff J, Gomez F, et al: Intracellular composition and homeostatic mechanisms in severe chronic infantile malnutrition. II: Composition of tissues. Pediatrics 20:105, 1957
124. Schneider H, Hendrickse RG, Haigh CP: Studies in water metabolism in clinical and experimental malnutrition. Trans R Soc Trop Med Hyg 52:169, 1958
125. Smith R: Total body water in malnourished infants. Clin Sci 19:275–285, 1960
126. Brock JF, Hansen JDL: Body composition and appraisal of nutrition. p. 261. In Brozek J. (ed): Human Body Composition. Pergamon Press, London, 1965
127. Alleyne GAO: Mineral metabolism in protein calorie malnutrition. p. 208. In Olson RE (ed): Protein-Calorie Malnutrition. Academic Press, New York, San Francisco, London, 1975
128. Smith R: Hyponatremia in infantile malnutrition. Lancet 1:771, 1963
129. Gordillo G, Soto RA, Metcoff J, et al: Intracellular composition and homeostatic mechanisms in severe chronic infantile malnutrition. III: Renal adjustments. Pediatrics 20:303, 1957
130. Metcoff J, Frenk S, Yoshida T, et al: Cell composition and metabolism in kwaskiorkor (severe protein-calorie malnutrition in children). Medicine 45:365, 1966
131. Garrow JS, Fletcher K, Holliday D: Body composition in severe infantile malnutrition. J Clin Invest 44:417, 1965
132. Hansen JDL: Electrolyte and nitrogen metabolism in kwashiorkor. S Afr J Lab Clin Med 2:206, 1956
133. Garrow JS: Total body potassium in kwashiorkor and marasmus. Lancet 2:455, 1965
134. Garrow JS: The use and calibration of a small whole body counter in the measurement of total body potassium in malnourished infants. West Indian Med J 14:73, 1965
135. Klahr S, Alleyne GAO: Effects of chronic protein calorie malnutrition on the kidney. Kidney Int 3:129, 1973
136. Alleyne GAO: Cardiac function in severely malnourished Jamaican children. Clin Sci 30:553, 1966
137. Ichikawa I, Purkerson ML, Klahr S, et al: Mechanism of reduced glomerular filtration rate in chronic malnutrition. J Clin Invest 65:982, 1980
138. Alleyne GAO: The effect of severe protein-

calorie malnutrition on the renal function of Jamaican children. Pediatrics 39:400, 1967

139. Jamison RL: Urinary concentration and dilution: The role of antidiuretic hormone and the role of urea. p. 391. In Brenner BM, Rector FC Jr (eds): The Kidney. WB Saunders, Philadelphia, 1976

140. Klahr S, Tripathy K, Lotero H: Renal regulation of acid-base balance in malnourished man. Am J Med 48:325, 1970

141. Waterlow JC, Willis VS: Balance studies in malnourished infants. I. Absorption and retention of nitrogen and phosphorus. Br J Nutr 14:183, 1966

142. Maclean WC, Lopez de Romaua G, Mossa E, Graham GG: Nutritional management of chronic diarrhea and malnutrition: Primary reliance on oral feeding. J Pediatr 97:316, 1980

143. Ashworth A: Progress in the treatment of protein-energy malnutrition. Proc Nutr Soc 38:89, 1979

144. Montgomery RD: Magnesium deficiency and tetany in kwashiorkor. Lancet 2:74, 264, 1960

145. Linder GC, Hansen JDL, Karabus CD: The metabolism of magnesium and other inorganic cations and of nitrogen in acute kwashiorkor. Pediatrics 31:552, 1963

146. Caddell JL: Studies in protein-calories malnutrition: N.A. double blind clinical trial to assess magnesium therapy. N Engl J Med 276:535, 1967

147. Golden BE, Golden HNG: Plasma zinc and the clinical features of malnutrition. Am J Clin Nutr 32:2490, 1979

148. Golden MH, Golden BE, Jackson AA: Skin breakdown in kwashiorkor responds to zinc. Lancet 1:1256, 1980

12

Pathophysiology and Management of Chronic Renal Failure

John W. Foreman
Noboru Tsuru
James C. M. Chan

Nearly 100,000 patients (430 patients per million population) received dialysis for end-stage renal failure in the United States in 1987, at a cost of 2.5 billion dollars.[1] The availability and cost of dialysis for the growing number of end-stage renal disease patients has made tax supported funding for such treatment an important issue over the past 20 years. Despite continuing controversy about the extent of this commitment, the industrialized countries have affirmed government support of treatment programs for end-stage renal disease. During the next two decades, the focus of attention will be optimal medical management to prolong and enhance the quality of life, minimize complications, and maximize growth and development in patients with renal disease before dialysis and transplantation become necessary. In addition, efforts will be made to find alternative forms of treatment and to meet the special needs of infants and children with chronic renal insufficiency. This chapter addresses some of these questions, reviews advances over the past two decades, appraises current concepts, and assesses recent progress in the care of patients with end-stage renal failure.

The progression of chronic renal disease can be divided into four stages.[2,3] Although each has distinguishing features, there is considerable overlap, particularly between the third and fourth stages.

The first stage of chronic renal disease is associated with a glomerular filtration rate (GFR) of 50 to 75 percent of normal, and is characterized by decreased renal reserve with a delicate preservation of the remaining renal excretory and regulatory functions.[2,4] When the GFR falls below 50 percent of normal, elevation of blood urea nitrogen (BUN) and creatinine ensues, and the renal response to fluid-electrolyte changes becomes progressively limited.[5]

The second stage, renal insufficiency, is characterized by mild anemia, hyposthenuria, and nocturia.[6] It is associated with a GFR of 25 to 50 percent of normal. Dehydration and/or intercurrent infections, which cause no difficulties in the first stage, can easily precipitate severe azotemia and acidosis in the second stage because the renal regulation of water-electrolyte balance is vulnerable.[7]

The third stage of chronic renal disease[3] is associated with a GFR of 10 to 25 percent of normal. Increasingly, the signs and symptoms of renal failure become detectable: progressive anemia, severe acidosis, inadequate renal excretion of phosphate and consequent hyperphosphatemia.[8] Intestinal malabsorption of calcium, renal osteodystrophy, and secondary hyperparathyroidism may result either directly from inadequate renal activation of vitamin D and consequent hypocalcemia, or indirectly from hyperphosphatemia.[9]

The fourth and final stage[3] coincides with a GFR of less than 10 percent of normal. Neurologic, intestinal, hematologic, skeletal, and other features of uremia become progressively evident.[10] Preparation for renal replacement therapy—dialysis or transplantation—must be initiated when the patient enters this stage.[11]

ETIOLOGY AND PATHOPHYSIOLOGY OF CHRONIC RENAL FAILURE

An estimated 30 to 80 persons per million general population per year require dialysis or transplantation to maintain life[12]; of these, slightly less than 10 percent are in the pediatric age group (<16 years old). The major causes of end-stage renal insufficiency in adults and children are shown in Table 12-1 and 12-2.

Attempts have been made to arrest or reverse the progression of chronic renal diseases. Immunosuppressive therapy has

Table 12-1. Major Causes of End-Stage Renal Failure

Diagnosis	WM	WF	BM	BF	W	B	M	F	Total	B:W	M:F
Hypertension[a]	12	8	69	48	11.6	40.9	33.5	26.3	**30.2**	5.9:1	1.5:1
Glomerulonephritis[a]	32	16	31	15	28.1	16.5	26.1	14.6	**20.8**	1.0:1	2.1:1
Diabetic nephropathy	13	13	29	34	15.2	22.0	17.1	22.1	**19.5**	2.4:1	0.9:1
Polycystic kidney disease (PKD)	11	7	0	5	10.5	1.7	4.5	5.2	**5.0**	0.3:1	0.9:1
Collagen vascular disease	4	1	1	6	2.9	2.4	2.0	3.3	**2.6**	0.7:1	0.7:1
Hereditary nephritis	1	2	2	0	1.8	0.7	1.2	0.9		1.5:1	1.5:1
Analgesic abuse nephropathy	2	3	2	1	2.9	1.0	1.6	1.9	**1.8**	0.6:1	1.0:1
Other interstitial nephritis	5	16	6	14	12.3	7.0	4.5	14.1	**9.0**	1.0:1	0.4:1
Obstructive uropathies[b]	4	2	2	1	3.5	1.0	2.4	1.4	**2.0**	2.0:1	2.0:1
Amyloidosis	0	1	0	1	0.6	0.3	0.0	0.9	**0.4**	1.0:1	
Multiple myeloma	3	0	0	0	1.8	0.0	1.2	0.0	**0.7**		
Unknown	3	7	8	9	5.8	5.9	4.5	7.5	**5.2**	1.7:1	0.7:1
Other	2	3	1	1	2.9	0.7	1.2	1.9	1.5	0.4:1	0.8:1
Total	92	79	151	135						1.7:1	1.2:1

[a] There was one oriental male in each of these two diagnostic categories.
[b] Both congenital and acquired uropathies.
W = white; M = male; B = black; F = female.
(From Loveluck RJ: Genetic Epidemiological Studies of an End-stage Renal Disease Population. Ph.D. thesis. Virginia Commonwealth University, Richmond, Virginia, by permission.)

Table 12-2. Percent Distribution of Primary Renal Disease in Children with Chronic Renal Failure

	FRG	EDTA	MIAMI	TORONTO	COMBINED
Total Cases	623	3342	81	90	4136
Glomerulonephritis	20	35	27	43	33
Pyelonephritis/OU	36	23	42	24	25
Hypoplasia/dysplasia	9	12	15	—	11
Hereditary nephropathies	19	16	2	11	16
Vascular disorders	4	5	6	—	5
Other	12	9	8	22	10
	100%	100%	100%	100%	100%

Glomerulonephritis category includes children with focal segmental sclerosis and membranous glomerulopathy. Pyelonephritis/OU includes children with reflux nephropathy, urinary tract malformations, and obstructive uropathy (OU). Vascular disorders include renal vein thrombosis and hemolytic-uremic syndrome. Other = other causes including unknown. FRG = Federal Republic of Germany data in Clin Nephr 23:278, 1985; EDTA = European Dialysis Transplant Association data in Proc EDTA 19:16, 1982; Miami data from Int J Ped Nephr 1:30, 1980; Toronto data from Can Med J 122:655, 1980. (From Foreman JW and Chan JCM,[12] with permission.)

been tried in a number of types of glomerulonephritis. Recognizing the various causes of interstitial nephritis (Table 12-3) is important because eliminating the causative agents can save the kidney from further injury. Control of reversible causes of azotemia, such as infection, hypertension, acidosis, and extracellular volume contraction, should also be achieved. In addition to early treatment to prevent complications, good medical management requires genetic counseling in cases of hereditary renal disease.

Although recent data[13] imply that early surgical treatment for obstructive uropathies in childhood does not affect the rate of progression to renal failure, early recognition and suppression of urinary tract infections reduces morbidity. Adequate alkali therapy in type 1 renal tubular acidosis reverses hypocitraturia, reduces hypercalciuria, and diminishes the risk of nephrocalcinosis and renal scarring.[14] Encouraging data have been presented on the use of low protein diets,[15] α-keto analogs of amino acids,[16] and dietary phosphate reduction[17] to prolong life before dialysis and/or transplantation.[17] However, in most renal diseases, deterioration of renal function progresses relentlessly despite medical intervention.

Over the past 20 years, much attention has been focused on the pathophysiology of renal adaptation in maintaining water and solute balance in spite of the limitations imposed by the failing kidney.[17] The surviving nephrons compensate for the reduced GFR by reducing tubular reabsorption of sodium and water and by increasing potassium and

Table 12-3. Causes of Interstitial Nephritis

Infection
Ureteral Reflux
Obstruction
Drugs
  Acute (hypersensitivity)
  Chronic
    Analgesics
    Lithium
Immune
  Lupus
  Sjögrens
  Transplant rejection
Heavy Metals
Metabolic
  Oxalate
  Nephrocalcinosis
  Urate
  Hypokalemia
Radiation
Hereditary
  Medullary cystic
  Cystinosis
Neoplastic
  Myeloma
  Leukemia, lymphoma
Miscellaneous
  Sarcoid
  Balkan

hydrogen ion secretion.[18] This allows a successful but precarious balance to be maintained until the final stages of chronic renal failure.[18]

In the absence of renal failure, compensation after sudden loss of renal tissue, as imposed by unilateral nephrectomy or occlusion of one renal artery, occurs by hyperplasia and/or hypertrophy of the remaining kidney. In early infancy, compensatory growth is achieved by forming new cells (hyperplasia), whereas in adulthood, it is accomplished primarily by the hypertrophy of remaining cells. Within three years after unilateral nephrectomy, the size of the remaining kidney increases by half. Renal function increases within one week to 40 percent of the combined total for the kidneys, and within two months to 90 percent of the GFR before the unilateral nephrectomy.[19]

The diseased kidney also compensates by various adaptive mechanisms. The observation that patients with chronic renal failure can maintain normal water and saline balance led to the "intact nephron" hypothesis: namely, that despite great histologic heterogeneity, the diseased kidney can adapt in a well-organized fashion, so that the delicate balance of body chemistry is maintained until severe reductions in GFR occur.[20-22] Although the "intact nephron" hypothesis has been widely accepted as explaining the adaptation of the diseased kidney, the wide disparity in histologic findings has precluded its universal acceptance. In recent years, the concept of "trade-off" in chronic renal failure, with preservation of certain functions at the expense of others, has gained wider acceptance.

Adaptation of Hydrogen Ion and Potassium Metabolism

The maximum level of hydrogen ion excretion by the diseased kidney is reached early in the course of chronic renal insufficiency.[18] With a further reduction in renal function, severe metabolic acidosis is prevented by the buffering of hydrogen ions with bone salts at the expense of the skeletal system.[21] Thus, a "trade-off" is made between severe acidosis and skeletal demineralization.

Another trade-off occurs between sodium balance and acid-base balance. In order to maintain sodium balance, each functioning nephron decreases its proximal sodium reabsorption, resulting in a decrease in proximal bicarbonate reabsorption. This is the cause of metabolic acidosis observed early in renal insufficiency[18] (Fig. 12-1). Bicarbonaturia may also occur because of elevated parathyroid hormone (PTH) secretion in patients with chronic renal failure.[19] However, increased PTH secretion probably plays only a peripheral role in the development and perpetuation of metabolic acidosis in renal insufficiency.[19]

In a healthy adult, 70 mEq of hydrogen ion is produced per day through the oxidation of sulfur-containing amino acids such as cysteine and methionine, the incomplete oxidation of organic acids, and the hydrogen ion produced secondary to metabolism of phosphoesters.[21] Thus, acid production in normal adults is about 1 mEq/kg body weight per day.[21] In the infant and growing child,[23] an additional component of acid production must be considered because approximately 20 mEq of hydrogen is produced for each gram of calcium deposited as hydroxyapatite for new bone formation. The total acid production in an infant is approximately 2 to 3 mEq/kg body weight per day.[24]

Normally, the amount of acid produced is balanced by an equal amount of renal acid excretion. The net acid excretion is the sum of urinary titratable acid plus ammonium minus bicarbonate.[25] Because urinary titratable acidity is primarily phosphate-buffered hydrogen ion, the availability of filtered phosphate plays an important role in renal acid excretion.[26] With the progression

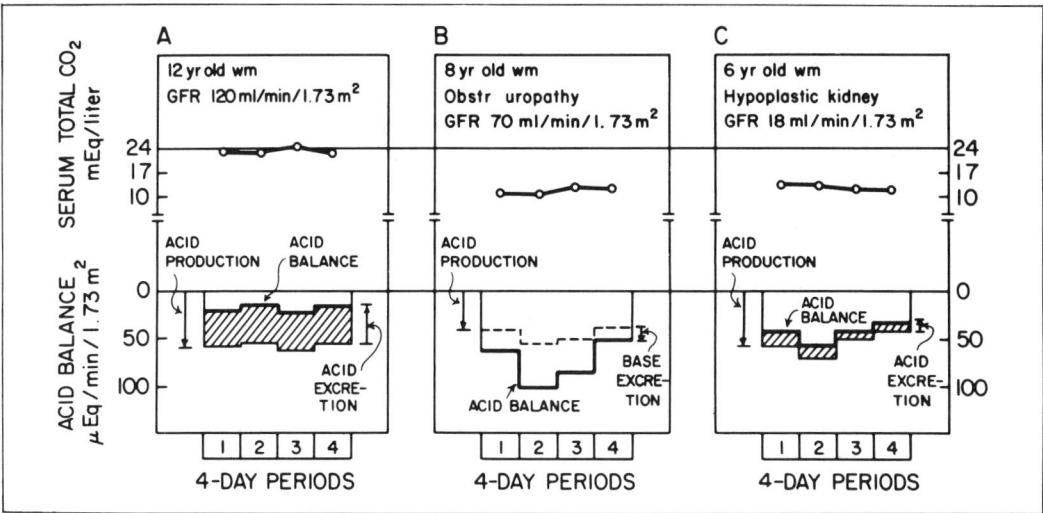

Fig. 12-1. Net acid balance in children with normal renal function and various degress of renal insufficiency. (A) Endogenous acid production and excretion in a child with normal kidney function. (B and C) Acid balance with increasing severity of renal insufficiency. With moderate renal insufficiency (B), a GFR of 70 ml/min/1.73 m², the bicarbonaturia accounts for a significant portion of acid accumulation. The reduced acid excretion in severe renal insufficiency (C) accounts for the acid retention and development of acidosis. The acid production was calculated by the sum of sulfate and organic anion determination and net acid (or base) excretion. (From Chan JCM, et al.,[18] with permission.)

of renal insufficiency, tubular reabsorption of phosphate decreases from normal values of 90 percent to less than 10 percent, so that urinary phosphate availability is not limited in chronic renal failure. However, with a marked reduction in functioning nephrons, the overall amount of titratable acid excreted is inadequate. Overzealous phosphate restriction and the use of phosphate binding agents reduce urinary phosphate excretion, further limiting titratable acid excretion. Another important factor in the acidosis of chronic renal insufficiency is the reduced ammonium excretion. This results from decreased ammoniogenesis due to a reduction in the number of nephrons.[27] Inhibitory factors encountered in uremia also depress ammoniogenesis.

In children with chronic renal failure, acid-base balance is usually maintained until the GFR is less than 25 percent of normal. As shown in Figure 12-1, the production of net acid from endogenous metabolism in a normal child amounts to 50 to 60 µEq/min per 1.73 m², which is matched by an almost equal net acid excretion.[18] A small retention of hydrogen ion can be demonstrated (Figure 12-1), but this is not reflected in any change in blood acid-base status.[18]

The metabolism of each gram of protein produces 0.7 mEq of hydrogen ion, which in turn requires renal excretion.[28] Restricting protein intake in advanced renal failure would reduce the acid production and the need for renal hydrogen ion excretion. In normal subjects, the skeleton stores approximately 35,000 mEq of alkali, which provides a convenient system for buffering extra hydrogen ion.[21] Indeed, calcium balance studies in chronic uremic acidosis show either a negative or suboptimal balance.[29] It is possible that the poor calcium absorption in chronic renal failure is due to inhibition of absorption caused by the metabolic acidosis, as well as to the impaired production of 1,25-dihydroxyvitamin D_3.[30]

The hallmark of uremic acidosis is an increased anion gap due to a reduction in serum bicarbonate without a concomitant rise in serum chloride. This increased anion gap is caused by the retention of phosphate and sulfate. However, non-anion-gap or hyperchloremic metabolic acidosis can be observed in chronic pyelonephritis, obstructive uropathy, or diabetic nephropathy. This metabolic acidosis is associated with hyperkalemia from hypoaldosteronism, and has been labeled type 4 renal tubular acidosis.[31] In ureteral sigmoidostomy, bicarbonate exchange for chloride by the colon in response to an acidic urine leads to the retention of hydrogen ions and hyperchloremia.[32]

Until renal failure is very advanced, the diseased kidneys can maintain external potassium balance by markedly increasing potassium excretion per nephron.[33] Several lines of evidence point to the distal and collecting tubules as the main sites of this compensation.[33] The increased urinary sodium delivery to the distal tubule in chronic renal failure facilitates potassium secretion because a more negative potential is developed in the distal tubule by the avid reabsorption of the excess sodium.[34] Another source of potassium elimination in chronic renal failure is secretion by the colon. This route is negligible in health, but increases in chronic renal failure by an aldosterone-dependent mechanism.[35] Reduced sodium delivery to distal exchange sites, secondary to injudicious salt restriction, can decrease potassium secretion and lead to hyperkalemia. Hyperkalemia can also occur because of selective hypoaldosteronism, which is sometimes associated with chronic renal insufficiency. The Giovannetti diet, which is low in protein, may cause metabolic acidosis and therefore hyperkalemia.[36]

Contradictory data have been presented about the ability of the failing kidney to respond to an acute potassium load.[37] Most of the evidence does not support restricting potassium intake in the average patient with chronic renal insufficiency until the final stages of renal failure. Dietary restriction of potassium is advisable with the occurrence of hemolysis, acidosis, or intercurrent illness because these situations will accelerate catabolism with its concomitant load of potassium.

Other influences on serum potassium are β-adrenergic antagonists, which inhibit cellular potassium entry, and angiotensin antagonists and converting enzyme inhibitors, which may cause hyperkalemia by blunting the stimuli for aldosterone secretion.[37] Indirectly, prostaglandin synthetase inhibitors promote hyperkalemia through the same mechanism. By promoting potassium release from cells, depolarizing muscle relaxants, such as succinylcholine, may precipitate hyperkalemia and should be used with caution in chronic renal failure. Phosphate binders, which induce constipation, may give rise to hyperkalemia by reducing potassium excretion in the colon.

Hyperkalemia may also be precipitated by the excess ingestion of high-potassium foods, such as avocados, almonds, bananas, peanuts, potassium-containing salt substitutes, chocolate, and dried fruits. The injudicious use of the potassium-sparing diuretics triamterene and spironolactone may also produce hyperkalemia in the compromised patient.

Hyperkalemia, especially in diabetic nephropathy, may be secondary to selective hypoaldosteronism associated with abnormalities of adrenocorticoid synthesis and renin conversion.[38] Administration of 9-α-fludrocortisone reverses the hyperkalemia but leaves the acidosis only partially corrected, suggesting that an abnormal sensitivity to mineralocorticoids is intrinsic to the syndrome of selective hypoaldosteronism.[38]

Adaptation of Water and Sodium Metabolism

Moderate polyuria and polydipsia are encountered early in the course of chronic renal failure. There is a loss of normal circadian rhythm, and nocturia is therefore a common early symptom of chronic renal insufficiency. Hyposthenuria, the obligatory excretion of hyposmolar urine, is common in cystinosis, renal dysplasia, and nephronophthisis. Pyelonephritis and obstructive uropathy may also be present with hyposthenuria.

The pathophysiology of isosthenuria in renal failure[3,4] is poorly understood, but is probably related to one or a combination of the following factors: (1) increased solute load to the residual nephron, as suggested by the increase in single nephron glomerular filtration rate (SNGFR); (2) anatomic changes modifying medullary architecture; (3) resistance at the collecting tubule secondary to unresponsiveness of the adenylate cyclase system in the uremic state; (4) increased medullary blood flow leading to washout of the concentration gradient in the interstitium of the medullary collecting tubule; (5) defective sodium chloride transport in the ascending limb of the loop of Henle; and (6) deficient medullary recycling of urea, leading to a low medullary interstitial solute concentration.

The diluting ability is well preserved in chronic renal failure.[2,3] With progressive reduction of renal function, the total free water excretion is diminished, although the fractional free water excretion (free water clearance per milliliter of glomerular filtration) remains normal. Because of the water loss obligated by solute excretion, together with the reduction in concentrating ability, urine volume is unlikely to diminish appreciably in response to dehydration. Thus, water intake should be sufficient and frequent enough to compensate for the polyuria. Prolonged periods of water deprivation should be avoided in uremic patients.

On the other hand, excessive fluid intake, in the face of reduced free water excretion, will give rise to dilutional hyponatremia.

Dietary sodium restriction should not be routine policy in all patients with chronic renal insufficiency.[18] Unlike normal subjects, whose renal sodium excretion adjusts in response to restriction, these patients continue an "obligatory" excretion of sodium that leads to a negative sodium balance, although this salt-losing tendency has recently been found to be reversed if salt intake is reduced gradually over several months rather than stopped abruptly. This salt wasting is even more pronounced in small infants with chronic renal failure, and can have serious consequences. In patients with hypertension, congestive heart failure, or edema, sodium restriction is advisable.[18]

The factors controlling sodium balance in chronic renal insufficiency are sodium intake, aldosterone, GFR, and atrial natriuretic hormone. Atrial natriuretic hormone may be released in excess and catabolized more slowly in uremia.[39] Glomerular/tubular adjustments regulating sodium balance become progressively limited as renal failure advances, so that any undue sodium loading causes edema and hypertension, and any undue salt restriction causes hypotension and circulatory failure, as in Addison's disease.

The increased sodium excretion of functioning nephrons may be related to decreased fractional reabsorption of sodium in the proximal tubule, or other factors, such as reduction in filtration rates, hypoalbuminemia, anemia, and elevation of blood pressure. In chronic renal insufficiency there also appears to be a circulating hormone that inhibits sodium transport, as suggested by the fact that infusion of a factor from the urine of uremic patients causes diuresis in normal dogs.[39]

Sodium intake should be regulated to maintain ECF volume within a normal range. A significant weight gain or edema suggests sodium restriction, while orthostasis indicates liberalization. The serum sodium concentration is not an indicator of the body's need for sodium, since it remains in the normal range until renal function is reduced to 5 percent of normal.[40] Exceptions are salt-wasting diseases of the kidney and interstitial nephritis, in which severe hyponatremia may occur early in the disease.

Abrupt sodium or potassium loads are poorly tolerated by patients with renal insufficiency, and should be avoided. Thus, the physician and others involved in the care of such patients should be cognizant of the electrolyte composition of common foods.

The inability to handle excess water loads results in hyponatremia. Indeed, in chronic renal insufficiency, "dilutional" hyponatremia is a more common type of hyponatremia than that due to salt-wasting. Hyponatremia in chronic renal insufficiency may also be caused by vomiting, diarrhea, sodium depletion, or excessive use of diuretics. Infrequently it is secondary to selective hypoaldosteronism.[41]

Adaptation of Calcium, Phosphate, Magnesium and Other Mineral Metabolisms

In uremic patients, a negative calcium balance is typical and is due to reduced intake from anorexia, a low-protein (and thus a low-calcium) diet, and reduced calcium absorption. The principal sites of calcium absorption are the duodenum and jejunum.[42] This decreased intestinal calcium absorption is caused by impaired activation of vitamin D to 1,25-dihydroxyvitamin D. Activated vitamin D stimulates the synthesis of an intracellular calcium-binding protein[43] and other proteins involved in calcium transport.[44] Vitamin D may also change the lipid composition of the brush border membrane to enhance calcium uptake.[44] The decreased calcium absorption in uremia eventually gives rise to hypocalcemia. Hyperparathyroidism can compensate for this tendency to develop hypocalcemia until the development of advanced renal failure. At this point, skeletal resistance to parathyroid hormone (PTH) may supervene.[42] Hyperphosphatemia, common in chronic renal failure, is another factor in the development of hypocalcemia.

Patients with chronic renal insufficiency are vulnerable to hyperphosphatemia and hypermagnesemia[18] because the kidney is the principal site for disposal of these ions, although an increase in phosphate excretion per nephron permits phosphate balance to be maintained until the GFR decreases to 20 to 25 ml/min/1.73 m^2. With further deterioration of renal function, hyperphosphatemia ensues.

The important role of phosphate retention in the pathogenesis of hyperparathyroidism is emphasized in the reversal of hyperparathyroidism with a phosphate-restricted diet or by the use of phosphate binding agents. Hyperparathyroidism maintains a normal serum phosphate concentration until the later stages of renal failure. However, this is achieved at the expense of progressive bone disease. Thus, it is recommended that phosphate restriction or the use of binders, such as calcium carbonate, be initiated early in the course of chronic renal failure to minimize hyperparathyroidism.[45,46] This was demonstrated in experimental animals fed a diet in which phosphate was decreased in proportion to the reduction in GFR.[47] With this dietary restriction, the elevation of plasma phosphate and parathyroid hormone was prevented.

The plasma magnesium concentration is normal in most uremic patients,[48] especially in the earlier states of renal insufficiency. Injudicious consumption of magnesium-containing laxatives or antacids can cause acute hypermagnesemia. This is a worrisome complication, since hypermagnesemia has been implicated in uremic neuropathy.[49] Hypermagnesemia can impede cellular ion transport, which may account for this neuropathy. Hypermagnesemia in chronic renal failure arises from the decreased ability of the failing kidney to excrete this ion, although its excretion by individual, functioning nephrons is increased. The increased sodium excretion per functioning nephron appears to cause the increased magnesium excretion.

Intestinal absorption of dietary magnesium is low in chronic renal failure. In uremic adults it varies from 16 to 23 percent of intake, without an apparent explanation.[50] Recent data in uremic children indicate that 23 percent of dietary magnesium is absorbed.[48]

Aluminum in patients with renal failure, especially those with end-stage disease, has been a subject of attention in the past decade. Aluminum is linked to an unusual form of encephalopathy occurring in dialysis patients.[51] The intoxication arises from aluminum-containing phosphate binders and from aluminum in the water used in the dialysate. The incidence of this condition has fallen dramatically with better water purification and limitation of aluminum-containing phosphate binders.[52]

More common effects of aluminum intoxication are microcytic anemia and vitamin D-resistant osteodystrophy.[53,54] Infants with renal failure may be at greater risk for aluminum intoxication because of their higher dietary phosphate intake per unit of body weight, and therefore their greater need for phosphate binders.[55] One of the clinical clues to aluminum intoxication is marked sensitivity to vitamin D, as manifested by hypercalcemia.[54] The measurement of serum aluminum is now relatively accessible and reliable, allowing patients at risk to be easily monitored. A high correlation of aluminum-induced bone disease occurs only with serum aluminum concentrations of about 200 mcg/liter[56]; lower serum levels may or may not be associated with bone disease.[56] A more reliable method is to stain bone biopsy specimens for aluminum, but the invasiveness of this procedure limits its applicability.[57] A deferoxamine infusion test may be of some benefit when aluminum-associated bone disease is suspected, especially in excluding it.[58] Aluminum intoxication can be treated with deferoxamine given either intravenously during hemodialysis[30] or intraperitoneally.[59] Obviously the best measure is to prevent this condition by the use of calcium carbonate as a phosphate binder, and by water purification in dialysis.

Zinc deficiency may occur in patients undergoing chronic hemodialysis.[60] The clinical signs of this condition include hypozincemia, impotence, a low serum testosterone, changes in taste, and anorexia.[60] Zinc supplementation has reversed these disorders in most patients, although some may require the administration of 1,25-dihydroxyvitamin D.[60]

Positive zinc balances of 607 ± 270 g/m²/day have recently been documented in uremic children.[48] Zinc absorption rose from 17 percent before to 33 percent after 1,25-dihydroxyvitamin D therapy. However, the serum zinc concentration remained normal after therapy.[48] The effect of long-term treatment with 1,25-dihydroxyvitamin D on the ongoing accumulation of zinc warrants careful follow-up. In addition, the impact of suboptimal zinc absorption resulting from renal failure on growth and development in childhood demands further investigation.

To prevent dental caries, fluoride has been added to drinking water. The possibility that fluoridation may lead to renal impairment, especially in patients with chronic renal insufficiency, has been emphasized by detractors of fluoridation. Reports[61] of an increased incidence of osteomalacia and of exacerbation of renal osteodystrophy associated with the use of fluoridated water raise concern, but the data are inconclusive. Deionization of the water used in the dialysate probably circumvents the problem.

With the advent of long-term dialysis, interest in trace mineral metabolism has increased. Prolonged dialysis with ionized and nonionized water and the concomitant depletion of certain trace minerals (or in the reverse situation, excess of trace minerals), have created concern about potential health hazards for patients. This concern is perhaps magnified in the child, in whom the relationship between trace minerals and normal growth is just beginning to be approached.

During the course of dialysis, toxic amounts of trace elements can be transferred into the blood from the dialysate or the delivery system and tubing. Acute hypercupremia, which presents as hemolysis, nausea, vomiting, leukocytosis, and metabolic acidosis, has been described in hemodialysis patients.[62] The problem occurs when deionizers are unable to remove hydrogen ions from the water used in making the dialysate, allowing the leaching of copper from copper tubing. Because of this, copper is seldom used now in the dialysis delivery system.

RENAL OSTEODYSTROPHY

Renal osteodystrophy is an important complication of chronic renal failure. Infants and children are particularly susceptible to renal osteodystrophy because of their rapid turnover rate of bone.[63] A brief review of osteogenesis is presented to provide a basis for understanding the development of renal osteodystrophy. More extensive treatment of this subject can be found elsewhere.[64,65]

Osteoblasts are basophilic, bone-forming cells derived from mesenchyme. They are particularly rich in alkaline phosphatase and ribonucleic acid. Osteoid tissue is formed from the collagenous fiber and ground substances produced by osteoblasts. With the progressive increase of osteoid tissue and increasing formation of spicules, osteoblasts are imbedded in the bone marrow and become bone cells or osteocytes. The spaces in which these cells are located are called lacunae. Osteocytes send out cytoplasmic processes to communicate with other osteocytes and cortical cells via the canaliculi. The elongation and branching of calcified areas form a network of spongy bone until after birth, when the fetal nonlamellar bone is replaced by lamellar, spongy, and compact bone.

Osteoclasts actively resorb bone under the influence of PTH and vitamin D. Calcitonin has the opposite effect on osteoclasts.

The zone of provisional calcification is the growth-plate region of long bones undergoing active mineralization of the cartilaginous matrix. After chondroblastic resorption, the mineralized cartilaginous spicules remain as the framework for the placement of bone matrix.

The growth of flat bones, unlike that of long bones, occurs by intramembranous deposition, with mesenchymal cells differentiating directly into osteoblasts and forming spicules of immature woven bone. This bone is progressively replaced by mature bone beginning in the third trimester, and the process is completed during the first year of life. Bone growth involves the generation of osteoid mass as well as modeling of the growing bone to its adult stage. Remodeling is an ongoing process throughout life, but in uremia the rate of resorption exceeds that of osteogenesis.

Pathogenesis of Renal Osteodystrophy

Factors leading to the development of renal osteodystrophy include retention of phosphate and hydrogen ion; hypocalcemia from hyperphosphatemia and intestinal malabsorption of calcium; defective vitamin D metabolism; and most importantly, secondary hyperparathyroidism.

Current understanding of renal osteodystrophy involves the skeletal effects of an elevated serum PTH concentration coupled with a depressed serum calcitriol level. Calcitriol, the active form of vitamin D, is formed in the renal tubule from 25-hydroxyvitamin D.[63] The loss of renal mass, especially in those disorders principally affecting the renal tubule, such as congenital dysplasia and obstructive uropathy, leads to decreased calcitriol concentrations and decreased intestinal calcium absorption.[66]

Early in renal insufficiency the normal dietary intake of phosphate suppresses calcitriol production and leads to an increased PTH level in spite of mild fasting hypophosphatemia.[67] Restriction of phosphate intake causes both the serum PTH and calcitriol levels to return to normal. With further reductions in GFR, the serum phosphate level becomes elevated in spite of secondary hyperparathyroidism and increased fractional urine phosphate excretion, leading to further reductions in serum calcitriol and calcium values. In addition, the set point for the inhibition of PTH secretion by extracellular calcium is raised in chronic renal failure, making it more difficult to turn off the secondary hyperparathyroidism.[68] Also, calcitriol may directly inhibit PTH secretion to some extent, and this would be blunted in renal failure due to the low calcitriol levels.[69]

Role of Metabolic Acidosis

The negative calcium balance induced by chronic metabolic acidosis contributes to bone disease.[70] However, healing of the bone lesion can be brought about by administering large doses of vitamin D,[48] even in the presence of persistent metabolic acidosis.[63] Reversal of metabolic acidosis with alkali therapy reduces calcium losses in the urine and stool,[29,70] but an optimal calcium balance is still not achieved. The skeletal buffering of acid releases calcium carbonate, dissolves hydroxyapatite, and resorbs bone.[38,70] The skeletal effects of PTH are enhanced by acidosis.[71] Finally, metabolic acidosis per se has been shown[72,73] to interfere with the renal hydroxylation of 25-hydroxyvitamin D to 1,25-dihydroxyvitamin D, although contrary evidence has also been reported.[74]

Bone Histology in Renal Osteodystrophy

Renal osteodystrophy is histologically a mixture of osteitis fibrosa and osteomalacia. Osteitis fibrosa, caused by hyperparathyroidism, is characterized by osteoclastic activity, the accumulation of woven osteoid, and Howship's lacunae. The woven osteoid of uremic bone is characterized by disorganized collagen fibers, demineralization, a tendency to osteosclerosis, and blurring of any distinction between trabecular and cortical bone. Indeed, in long-standing uremia, trabecular bone tends to replace the thinned-out cortical bone.

Osteomalacia is characterized by defective mineralization associated with wide osteoid seams, and is less common than osteitis fibrosa.[64,65] This can be easily determined by labeling newly formed bone with two doses of tetracycline given several weeks apart. This provides a means of estimating the width of osteoid seams and an approximation of the rate of new bone formation.

In patients with early chronic renal insufficiency associated with a GFR that exceeds 50 percent of normal, Malluche and associates,[75] using bone biopsies, showed an accumulation of woven osteoid indicative of accelerated bone turnover and osteoclastic resorption stimulated by secondary hyperparathyroidism. With further advances of renal failure, renal osteodystrophy becomes overt, with a preponderance of osteitis fibrosa in the United States, Germany, and the Netherlands, and a preponderance of osteomalacia in England, Italy, and Israel. A high calcium × phosphate product is associated with osteitis fibrosa.[64,65] The geographic differences in the incidence of the two conditions may be related to the intake of vitamin D, phosphate, and protein. A low intake predisposes to osteomalacia and a high intake to osteitis fibrosa.

Maintenance dialysis exposes patients to additional risk factors: depletion of trace minerals, amino acid losses, fluctuations in fluoride, acetate, bicarbonate, magnesium, and calcium concentrations, and periodic heparin administration. These variables may modulate the frequency and severity of renal osteodystrophy in patients on dialysis.

Clinical Features of Renal Osteodystrophy

The clinical symptoms and signs of renal osteodystrophy center on two major areas: (1) musculoskeletal—bone fracture, bone pain, arthritis, periarthritis, myopathy, skeletal deformities, growth retardation, and spontaneous tendon rupture, and (2) dermatological—pruritus and calciphylaxis.

Low back pain is a common complaint in renal osteodystrophy and varies in intensity from subtle to debilitating. It may be associated with collapse of a vertebral body from osteomalacia, osteofibrosis, or a combination of the two processes. Other sites of pain include the hips, knees, legs, and ankles, and pain at these sites may suggest arthritis. Chest pain and tenderness may signify nontraumatic rib fracture.

Arthritis and periarthritis from renal osteodystrophy present with localized swelling, pain, and discoloration and are associated with periosteal erosion and hydroxyapatite deposition. Reversal of arthritis and periarthritis symptoms may occur within weeks after parathyroidectomy.

Myopathy in uremia appears insidiously and primarily involves the proximal muscles[76]; thus, the patient cannot lift his arms above his head or easily walk up stairs. Muscle enzymes are not elevated. The pathogenesis of the myopathy is complex. Vitamin D deficiency may play a major role, since treatment with 1,25-dihydroxyvitamin D and 25-hydroxyvitamin D brings prompt reversal. Prompt, marked improvement has also been reported with successful renal transplantation. Other contributing factors in the development of myopathy include uremic neuropathy, protein-calorie malnutrition, and depletion of specific proteins in uremia.

Lateral bowing of the legs from rickets is a common problem in childhood renal osteodystrophy. Limping, with or without localized pain and swelling, may signify slipped femoral epiphyses (Fig. 12-2). Slipped epiphyses may also occur in the lower humerus, radius, ulna, lower femur, and tibia. The characteristic histologic feature of rickets in renal osteodystrophy is osteitis fibrosa, with undermineralized woven bone between the epiphyses and metaphyses.[64] Severe genu valgum is seen in preadolescents.

The growth retardation is a common feature of renal osteodystrophy in children. Growth acceleration typically occurs following treatment with either 1-α-hydroxyvitamin D_3^{30} or 1,25-dihydroxyvitamin D_3^{48}.

Nontraumatic tendon rupture is a well described feature of both primary and secondary hyperparathyroidism. This commonly occurs in the tendons of the quadriceps, triceps, and extensors of the fingers.

Pruritus associated with subperiosteal erosion and other features of secondary hyperparathyroidism is another common complaint. It may be dispelled within days after parathyroidectomy.[77] An elevated calcium

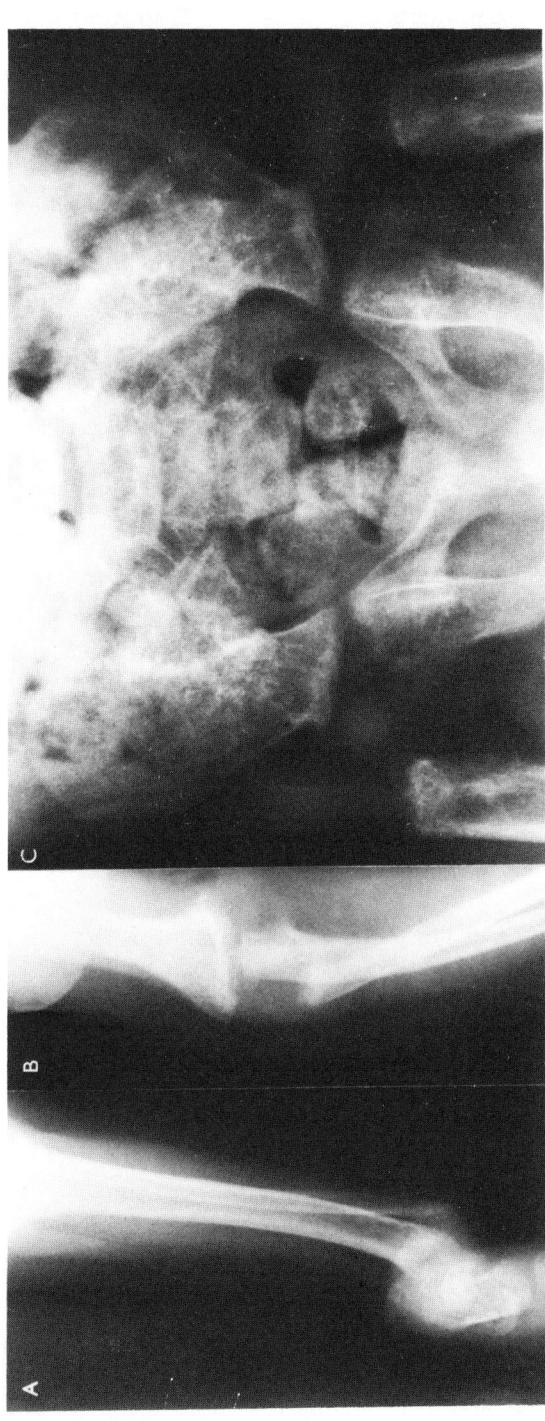

Fig. 12-2. Severe renal osteodystrophy in an 18-month-old boy with congenital hypoplastic kidneys and moderate renal insufficiency. The PTH concentration was significantly elevated at 812 ± 100 μl equivalents/ml. (**A**) Severe erosion of metaphysis and fracture of the tibia and fibula with dislocations of the ankle joints. (**B**) Severe ricket changes, flaring of epiphysis of the elbow joint. (**C**) Severe generalized demineralization of the hips. (From Chan JCM, and Hsu AC,[63] with permission.)

concentration in the skin has been proposed as the cause of pruritus, but the rapid disappearance of pruritus after parathyroidectomy, without a significant decrease in cutaneous calcium content, casts doubt on such an association.[78]

Calciphylaxis of the small and medium-sized arteries of the toes and fingers, presenting with localized ischemic necrosis[77] and cutaneous ulceration,[79,80] may also be associated with secondary hyperparathyroidism.[80] Parathyroidectomy may reverse the symptoms. Calciphylaxis is aggravated by steroids, which put the post-transplant patient at greater risk.

Laboratory Features of Renal Osteodystrophy

In contrast to the insidious and inconsistent signs and symptoms of renal osteodystrophy, blood biochemical values often provide early diagnostic clues to this condition. The serum PTH concentration is usually elevated, with a 50 percent reduction in GFR.[18,81,82] The elevation of PTH in chronic renal failure is theoretically best detected with an antibody to the amino terminus of the hormone, which detects both the intact molecule and the active 1-34 fragment, but not the inactive fragments that accumulate in renal failure. Long-term studies, using an antibody that recognizes the C-terminus of the PTH molecule, have shown a good correlation between levels measured with this assay and bone disease. The elevation in serum creatinine, as an index of GFR, is correlated linearly with the rise in serum PTH concentration (Fig. 12-3). Several laboratories have shown good correlations between serum PTH concentrations and the bone histologic changes of renal osteodystrophy.

Fasting hyperphosphatemia is usually found after renal function has been reduced to less than 30 percent of normal.[18] This occurs in spite of decreased intestinal absorption of phosphate.[48] Hyperphosphatemia inhibits 1,25-dihydroxyvitamin D synthesis.[48] Production of activated vitamin D is also diminished by the reduction in the number of proximal tubule cells in renal failure. Low levels of 1,25-dihydroxyvitamin D give rise to the calcium malabsorption of renal failure.[48] Elevated PTH levels stimulate phosphate excretion, but in advanced chronic renal failure the overall excretion is inadequate to maintain normal plasma levels with the typical dietary intake.[18]

The risk of metastatic calcification increases[17] as the calcium × phosphate product rises above 60. Maintaining this product below 60 requires some dietary restriction and often the use of phosphate binders.[45,63] With advanced renal failure, dialysis is helpful,[79,80] but controlling the phosphate concentration may require subtotal parathyroidectomy[77] to reverse or prevent metastatic calcification.

Hypocalcemia may occur transiently and usually in association with hyperphosphatemia. A persistent total and ionized hypocalcemia that is unrelated to hypoalbuminemia occurs infrequently, even in patients with renal clearances of only 20 to 50 ml/min/1.73 m².

Hypermagnesemia has been found in 30 to 50 percent of patients with renal failure.[83] Severe symptomatic hypermagnesemia with somnolence, hypotension, and a decreased patellar reflex is rare, and usually occurs after the inadvertent ingestion of magnesium-containing antacids or laxatives. This can be reversed with calcium administration.[84] The interaction between magnesium and PTH secretion is not clearly understood. Hypomagnesemia blunts PTH secretion, causing hypocalcemia.[84] Parathyroid hormone administration does not completely normalize hypomagnesemia.

Alkaline phosphatase derived from bone is usually elevated in renal osteodystrophy. Ordinarily, this reflects increased osteoblastic activity, but it cannot be used to discriminate between osteitis fibrosa and

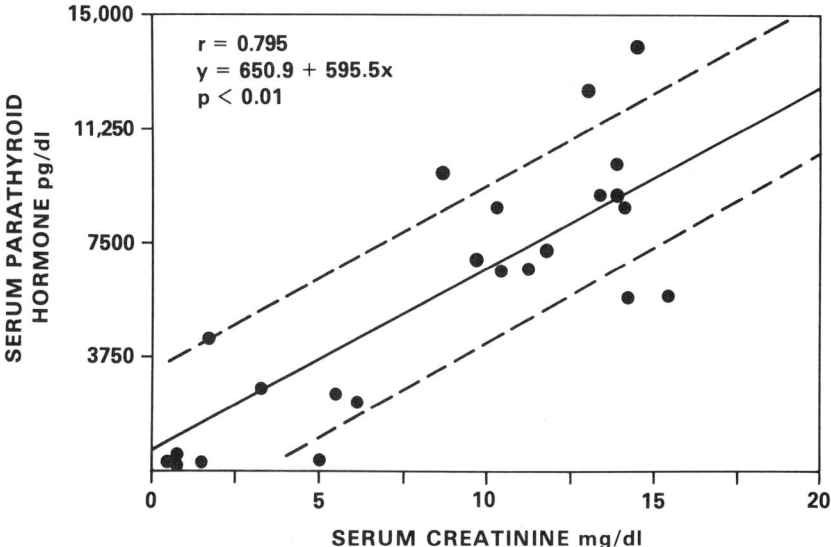

Fig. 12-3. Correlation between serum PTH concentration and serum creatinine. (From Chan JCM and DeLuca HF,[81] with permission.)

osteomalacia. Further, the proper interpretation of alkaline phosphatase levels requires that the age of the patient be considered, since normal infants and children have much higher levels than adults.

Hydroxyproline excretion reflects collagen catabolism, especially if the measurement is made after a 12-hour fast to exclude the effect of dietary intake of this amino acid.[85] The ratio of fasting urinary hydroxyproline to creatinine is normally less than 0.20. An elevation is associated with hyperparathyroidism or osteomalacia. The determination of 24-hour urinary hydroxyproline excretion requires that the patient follow a collagen-free diet for several days prior to collection of the urine. Normally, less than 25 mg/m² of hydroxyproline is excreted per day.

Radiologic Features of Renal Osteodystrophy

Routine radiography detects bone mineral loss only after it is in excess of 30 percent.[65] Bone densitometry, photon absorptiometry, scintiscanning, and computerized axial tomography (CAT) provide earlier detection of bone mineral loss. In 20 to 30 percent of patients with chronic renal failure, osteosclerosis can be demonstrated by routine radiography.[65]

The earliest radiographic feature of renal osteodystrophy in children is widening of the zone of provisional calcification between the epiphysis and metaphysis of the rapidly growing bone plates.[48] Secondary hyperparathyroidism can be suspected from a coarse trabecular pattern of the ulnar and distal femoral metaphyses. Other signs of hyperparathyroidism are subperiosteal cortical resorption of the radial aspect of the middle phalanges of the digits, and erosion of the ungual tuft of the terminal phalanges. Such subperiosteal resorption can also occur at the lateral tip of the clavicle, acromioclavicular joint, symphysis pubis, and sacroiliac joint. Loss of the lamina dura, particularly of the molars, is another feature of hyperparathyroidism.[63] Pseudofractures of the long bones are more common in adult uremic patients, and are characterized by lucent defects surrounded by sclerosis, usually on the medial aspects of long bones such as the femur. Biopsy of such lesions shows severe osteomalacia.[75] Sclerosis of the spine and bending or true fractures of the long bones and rib cage give rise to skeletal deformities. Osteosclerosis of the vertebral body, with a middle zone of lesser density, has been labeled the "rugger jersey" spine. Secondary hyperparathyroidism gives a "salt-and-pepper" appearance to the skull, consisting of mottled areas of density (sclerosis) and lightness (resorption). Generalized osteopenia secondary to the combined effects of hyperparathyroidism, osteoporosis, and osteomalacia occurs in severe chronic renal failure, particularly in adult patients.[65]

A slipped femoral epiphysis is another radiographic feature of renal osteodystrophy in children, especially those with long-standing chronic renal failure. Aggressive treatment of the underlying renal osteodystrophy and pinning of the femoral head may be necessary. Other sites of slipped epiphyses are the radius, ulna, humerus, and tibia.

Brown tumors are cystic lesions, usually found in the metacarpals, distal femur, proximal tibia, and distal radius. They are induced by hyperparathyroidism and are characterized by erosion, with clear-cut margins and areas of new bone formation. Intraosseous bleeding gives rise to the brown discoloration. With treatment of hyperparathyroidism, sclerosis fills in the cystic area.

NITROGEN, CARBOHYDRATE, AND LIPID DISORDERS

Nitrogen Metabolism

Elasmobranch fishes use urea to maintain osmolality.[3] For example, in deep sea sharks, the blood urea concentration may exceed 600 mg/dl. In man, urea is produced by the deamidation of arginine. The regulation of its production is not well delineated,[86] but is correlated with dietary protein intake. Furthermore, the question of increased synthesis and catabolism of urea in chronic renal insufficiency is not settled. In health, one-fifth of the body's urea is catabolized to ammonia in the gastrointestinal tract, and resynthesized into urea by the liver.[87] This rate of recycling remains the same during the course of renal failure. It was hoped that this recycled ammonia could be used in amino acid synthesis in renal failure, but this appears not to be possible. Urea excretion via extrarenal routes is unaffected by elevations in the plasma urea concentration, and remains constant.

Although urea does not appear to be the cause of the uremic syndrome, it is a useful marker of this condition. Symptoms usually appear when the plasma urea nitrogen exceeds 100 mg/dl, and consist of nausea, vomiting, weakness, headache, and poor mentation. However, such symptoms are sometimes absent even when the BUN exceeds 500 mg/dl. Symptomatic improvement after dialysis with dialysate baths containing urea concentrations of 300 to 600 mg/dl, so that the BUN remained extremely elevated, indicated that urea was probably not the uremic toxin.

Creatinine also does not appear to be the toxin in uremic syndrome.[3] It can be converted by intestinal bacteria into creatine, sarcosine, methylamine, and methylhydantoin. These also appear not to be toxic. Of importance is the catabolism of creatinine into methylguanidine.[88] When injected into animals, methylguanidine can cause a uremic-like syndrome, although only at plasma levels that are much higher than those found in uremic patients.[89] Guanidinosuccinic acid is another compound that has been proposed as a uremic toxin, but little experimental evidence supports this postulate. Phenolic acid and hydroxyphenolic acids and their conjugates also accumulate in chronic renal failure.[90] There is

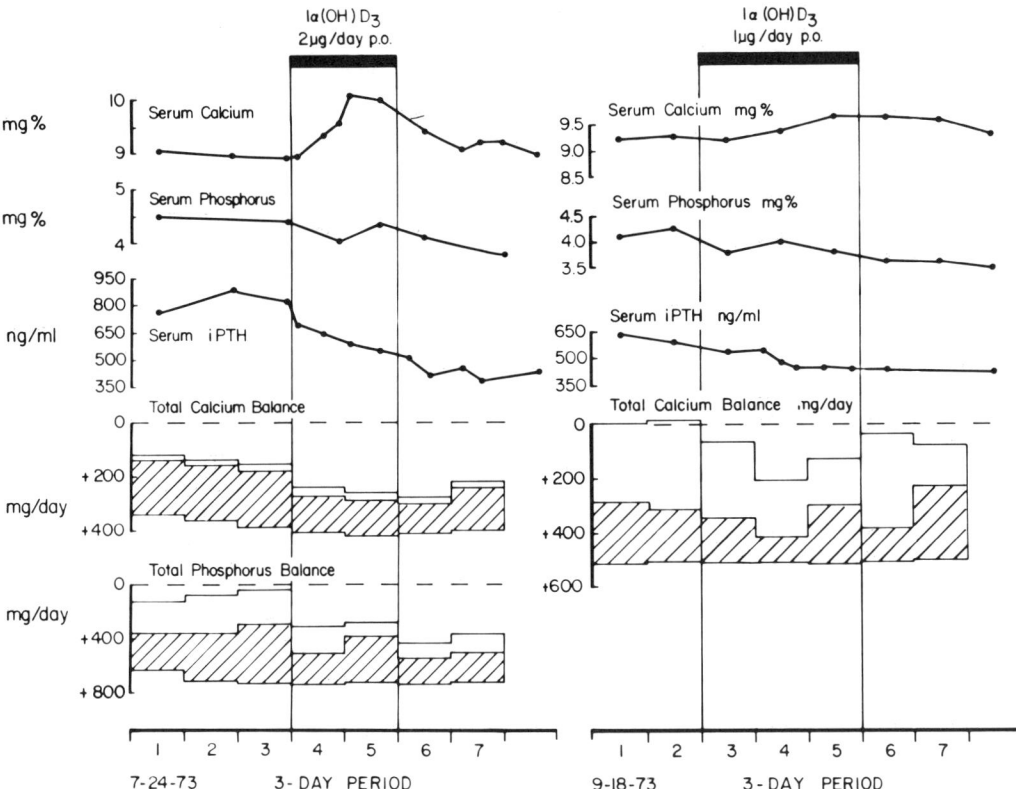

Fig. 12-4. Calcium and phosphorus balance studies in a 16-year-old female with chronic renal insufficiency treated with 1-α-hydroxyvitamin D. Dietary intake plotted from zero line downward and stool mineral data upward and urinary output further upward, so that the distance between the uppermost line and zero line represents the mineral balance. Treatment with 1-α-hydroxyvitamin D_3 resulted in a sharp rise in serum calcium concentrations, a gradual fall in serum phosphorous concentration, and a steady decline in the serum iPTH values. Calcium balance became more positive (increased retention of dietary calcium) after treatment with either dose of 1-α-vitamin D principally by a reduction in fecal calcium. (From Chan JCM, et al.,[30] with permission.)

some evidence that at the concentrations found in uremia they may exert toxic effects, especially on membrane transport.

"Middle molecules" (500 to 2,000 daltons) have also been suggested as the uremic toxin.[91] These compounds were proposed on the basis of the questionable clinical observation that patients on peritoneal dialysis had less uremic neuropathy than those on hemodialysis. Highly sophisticated identification techniques for these compounds have not yielded consistent results. Most of the compounds isolated are peptides and fragments of known proteins. Reducing the concentrations of these compounds with intensive dialysis has not consistently improved uremic complications, casing doubt on their importance in uremia.

Carbohydrate Metabolism

Carbohydrate metabolism in chronic renal insufficiency is characterized by an abnormal glucose tolerance, with normal or elevated fasting plasma insulin concentrations.[92] In response to a glucose load, the plasma insulin concentration rises normally but remains elevated for an abnormal period.[92] Peripheral insulin resistance is present in chronic renal failure, but is reversed with dialysis. This resistance appears to be distal to the insulin receptor. In addition, the rise in plasma glucagon is exaggerated and remains so after a glucose load. Renal degradation of these hormones is also impaired in chronic renal failure. The role of PTH in insulin hypersecretion in uremic patients with secondary hyperparathyroidism is not certain, but it may play a role in these patients' insulin resistance. After subtotal parathyroidectomy, the response to a glucose load is similar to that observed in dialyzed patients without secondary hyperparathyroidism.[93]

Growth hormone is typically elevated in chronic renal failure as a result of decreased renal excretion of the hormone. The release of growth hormone in response to arginine infusion, sleep, or insulin-induced hypoglycemia is normal. The elevated levels of growth hormone may contribute to the insulin resistance of uremia; the normal response to glucose loading is a decreased growth hormone concentration,[94] but in uremia the reverse is seen.[95] Hemodialysis fails to correct this paradoxical response.[94,96]

Lipid Metabolism

Lipid metabolic disorders in chronic renal disease probably result from abnormalities of carbohydrate metabolism,[97] and include elevation of serum triglyceride, very low density lipoprotein (VLDL), and cholesterol concentrations. This is characteristic of carbohydrate-induced, type 4 hyperlipidemia of the Frederickson classification.[98] The etiology of the hyperlipidemia is thought to be related to increased hepatic lipid synthesis and reduced triglyceride removal.[97] The insulin insensitivity in uremia may cause impaired lipoprotein lipase activity. As a result, carbohydrate is diverted to fat synthesis and subsequently to VLDL. The hyperlipidemia is not reversed with dialysis, and may indeed be increased. The risk of cardiovascular disease from hyperlipidemia in such patients is not clearly defined.

Considerable interest has been generated by recent data[99] showing that only 10 weeks of well-controlled exercise training significantly decreased the plasma concentration of triglyceride in hemodialyzed patients. These beneficial effects are thought to be mediated by increased lipoprotein lipase activity induced by exercise. When the exercise regimen was discontinued, the endocrine-metabolic abnormalities returned.[100] Exercise also reduces insulin resistance and improves glucose metabolism in dialysis patients.[100]

IMMUNOLOGIC DISORDERS

The widespread general impression that uremic patients have impaired immunologic defenses reinforces the perception that they have higher morbidity and mortality rates from infections.[101] However, the latter is difficult to document. Twenty years ago, one-third of deaths in nondialyzed azotemic patients resulted from infection, usually from urinary tract infection, pulmonary infection, and/or septicemia, but in recent years, infections have accounted for only 10 percent of such deaths.[101,102] This improvement is attributed to better prophylaxis and treatment of infection.

Delayed wound healing in uremic patients gives rise to a higher incidence of infection during the postoperative and posttraumatic periods.[102] The impaired cellular and humoral immunologic defenses are further compromised by additional factors associated with chronic uremia.[101] Delayed appearance of lymphocytes and macrophages in response to inflammation has been noted using the skin-window technique. In addition, the prolonged survival of skin grafts in uremia suggests that uremic patients have other defects in the immune system. A poor delayed hypersensitivity response to a variety of intracutaneously injected antigens has also been demonstrated. Taken together, these observations suggest changes in cellular as well as humoral immunity in uremia.

Cellular Immunity

Although the total neutrophil count is normal, peripheral lymphopenia and thymic hypoplasia are frequently encountered in patients with end-stage renal failure.[103] The survival of lymphocytes in uremic serum is impaired,[103] but not in serum taken from control patients with other chronic diseases. T-lymphocyte function measured in vitro is inhibited by uremic serum, but this can be improved with dialysis.[104] Vitamin B_6 supplementation has also improved the lymphocyte response. This appears to be related to pyridoxal kinase inhibition in uremia rather than to vitamin B_6 deficiency,[103] although the latter is known to cause impaired cell-mediated immunity in normal animals. Urea and creatinine do not suppress the lymphocyte response, but guanidine and phenols can.[104] Interferon production by lymphocytes is decreased in uremia.[103,105] This defect is not alleviated by hemodialysis or incubating lymphocytes in normal, non-uremic plasma. Phagocytosis, intracellular bacterial killing, and opsonic factors are normal.[106]

Humoral Immunity

In general, humoral immunity is normal or only slightly impaired in uremia.[105] The amnestic response to diphtheria toxoid is normal. The humoral response to influenza A or B vaccine is normal or slightly decreased, and appears to be improved by hemodialysis.

NEUROLOGIC DISORDERS

The principal neurologic abnormalities in adults and adolescents with chronic renal failure are uremic encephalopathy, peripheral neuropathy, and vascular accidents from hypertension or anticoagulation. A progressive encephalopathy consisting of developmental delay and microcephaly has been noted in infants with chronic renal failure. The recognition of and therapeutic approach to these consequences will be increasingly important as more patients' lives are prolonged by conservative medical therapy before dialysis and/or transplantation. The aluminum encephalopathy associated with dialysis and phosphate binding agents will be discussed in the section on complications of hemodialysis.

Encephalopathy

A retrospective study of 23 infants with chronic renal insufficiency noted a progressive encephalopathy that was not related to dialysis dementia or aluminum intoxication.[107] Developmental delay, seizures, myoclonus, hypotonia, chorea, and ataxia were common. In addition, ventricular enlargement or cortical atrophy occurred in 7 of the 12 children who underwent computerized axial tomography. The progressive encephalopathy is thought to be secondary to inadequate nutrition during a crucial period of rapid brain growth, and to be aggravated by a combination of other factors including the accumulation of hydrogen ions and metabolic waste-products of nitrogen metabolism, and hyperparathyroidism.

The early signs of uremic encephalopathy in a child or adult are usually nonspecific, consisting of fatigue, listlessness, a poor attention span, and depression alternating with alertness.[108] Late signs include muscle weakness, cramps, asterixis, slurred speech, mental confusion, frank psychosis, seizures, and myoclonus. Uremic amaurosis may be transient. Decorticate posture and coma occur in terminal cases.

The pathophysiology of uremic encephalopathy has been studied extensively. Because dialysis reverses symptoms of uremic encephalopathy,[109] current opinion favors dialyzable uremic toxins as the causative factors. These include guanidine, aromatic amines, phenolic acids, and possible uremic "middle molecules."

Parathyroid hormone has also been implicated in the pathogenesis of uremic encephalopathy.[110] In animals with experimental renal failure, electroencephalographic (EEG) abnormalities were shown to be related to an effect of PTH on the brain, causing an elevated brain calcium content. Studies in patients with chronic renal failure suggest a similar effect of PTH.[111] Patients with primary hyperparathyroidism often have neuropsychiatric symptoms and EEG abnormalities similar to those in renal failure patients, again suggesting a link between PTH and uremic encephalopathy.[112]

The uremic brains of experimental animals utilized less adenosine triphosphate (ATP), took up less glucose, and consumed less oxygen than those of controls.[113] The decreased cerebral oxygen and glucose consumptions is not due to a decrease in cerebral circulation. Indeed, cerebral blood flow is increased, probably in compensation for the anemia. Rather, the decreased brain metabolism is a reflection of reduced neuronal activity brought about by the accumulation of some or all of the uremic toxins.

Peripheral Neuropathy

Peripheral neuropathy in uremia is usually distal and symmetrical. The early symptoms arise from a sensory disorder of the lower extremities, with complaints of a tingling, prickling sensation—the "restless leg syndrome"—especially in adult uremic patients. Loss of deep tendon reflexes, foot drop, paraplegia, and other motor disorders have also been described. Dialysis rarely improves motor paralysis. However, nerve conduction velocity, which is slowed by chronic renal failure, may improve with hemodialysis and after transplantation.[109,114] Because of such improvement, circulating toxins are presumed to be the underlying cause of uremic neuropathy. With time, an irreversible axonal degeneration occurs.

Hypertensive Encephalopathy

The signs and symptoms of uremic hypertensive encephalopathy are nonspecific. They consist of headaches, nausea and vomiting, reduced mental acuity, and confusion, with progression to focal neurologic deficits (muscular weakness, visual disturbances, nystagmus, asymmetric reflex disturbances, and Babinski signs) or to generalized seizures, coma, and death.[115,116] Cerebral arterial vasoconstriction with reduced blood flow is the constant finding. The cerebrospinal fluid pressure and protein concentration may be normal or high. Diffuse swelling of the brain and necrosis of arterial walls may be found in later stages of uremia.

Treatment is directed at reversing the hypertension and edema and controlling seizures.[116] To these ends, antihypertensive therapy is instituted and, if necessary, cerebral edema is controlled by administering 20 percent mannitol. In addition, corticosteroids (dexamethasone) have been advocated to stabilize the cerebrovascular wall.[117,118]

Uremic Myopathy

Weakness and wasting of proximal muscles, such as the pelvic muscles and the quadriceps, can occur in uremia as a myopathy without neuropathy, as mixed myopathy and neuropathy, or as a neuropathy without myopathy. The secondary hyperparathyroidism of chronic renal failure appears to play an important role in the generation of this myopathy.[117] It is characterized by progressive weakness and pain of the proximal muscles, which can be reversed after subtotal parathyroidectomy. Persistent hypophosphatemia inadvertently produced by excessive use of oral phosphate binding agents can result in severe myopathy associated with osteomalacia, hemolytic anemia, and arthralgia.[119]

GASTROINTESTINAL DISORDERS

Uremia impairs the renewal of the epithelium of the gastrointestinal tract, and in conjunction with gastric basal cell hypersecretion may account for the increased incidence of peptic ulcers in adults with renal failure.[120,121] The duodenum is the most common site of ulceration, followed by the stomach. The increased susceptibility of uremic patients to intestinal tract ulcers has been attributed to at least two factors: (1) the inadequate removal of gastrin by the diseased kidneys, with consequent elevation of the serum gastrin concentration, and (2) the increased incidence of duodenogastric reflux, possibly related to an incompetent pyloric sphincter induced by the elevation of the serum gastrin concentration in uremic patients.[121] However, the exact role of these elevated gastrin levels and peptic ulcer disease is far from clear.

The poor intestinal absorption of calcium, phosphate, magnesium, and zinc is well documented in chronic renal insufficiency. Such malabsorption is reversed by vitamin D, its metabolites, and especially 1,25-dihydroxyvitamin D. Iron is also poorly absorbed in chronic uremia.

Uremia is at times associated with a protein-losing enteropathy.[121] This is further aggravated by changes in bile acid metabolism, with the formation of keto-bile acids and a lack of deoxycholic acid. The protein-losing enteropathy is further compounded by decreased hepatic synthesis of albumin.

ENDOCRINE DISORDERS

The anomalies of nitrogen, carbohydrate, fat, and mineral metabolism in chronic renal failure were discussed previously. This section will deal with thyroid hormones, cortisol, growth hormone, somatomedin, epinephrine, and norepinephrine in uremic patients.

Thyroid Function

Although both hypothyroidism and hyperthyroidism have been described, careful scrutiny of available evidence indicates that uremia, per se, does not cause frank thyroid dysfunction.[122] The basal plasma concentration of thyrotropin in renal failure is normal, even though the healthy kidney catabolizes a significant fraction of thyrotropin. The rise of thyrotropin to a standard challenge of thyrotropin-releasing hormone in renal failure patients is slower than in normal subjects, and its disappearance is slower. This implies alternative sites of catabolism or a reduced rate of production of thyrotropin-releasing hormone.

The plasma concentration of total thyroxine (T_4) is either normal or low,[123] but that of triiodothyronine (T_3) is in the hypothyroid range in 80 percent of uremic patients before dialysis.[123,124] The administration of T_4 to such patients does not bring about the expected rise in T_3, suggesting a defect in the extrathyroidal conversion of T_4 to T_3 in uremic patients. Experimental animal data suggest that this impaired conversion of T_4 to T_3 is reflected in signs of hypothyroidism at the cellular level.

Other Hormones

Plasma cortisol levels are generally normal in patients with chronic renal failure, although they are occasionally found to be elevated. The plasma disappearance of injected cortisol is delayed.[125] Cortisol production in response to injected adrenocorticotropic hormone (ACTH) is normal, as is the suppression of cortisol in response to dexamethasone administration.[126] Plasma ACTH levels are also normal.[127] Adrenal insufficiency may occur in end-stage renal failure patients who have undergone bilateral nephrectomy with inadvertent removal of their adrenal glands.

Growth hormone is elevated in chronic renal failure.[94] This may be secondary to the decreased functioning renal mass, which normally would degrade growth hormone. The functional significance of this elevation is not clear. Somatomedin, which is produced peripherally in response to growth hormone, has been reported to be low.[128] These values depend on whether a biologic or immunoreactive assay is used. Circulating inhibitors of somatomedin activity have been proposed to explain the low biologic activity of this hormone while its immunoreactive levels appear to be elevated.[129] The role these inhibitors play in growth failure in children with uremia is uncertain.

In patients undergoing chronic hemodialysis, the plasma epinephrine concentration was low and that of norepinephrine was elevated.[130] The measurements were made in patients who were supine for an hour. Norepinephrine levels rose in response to a head-up position.

CARDIOVASCULAR DISORDERS

Pericardial and Myocardial Complications

Pericardial effusion can be documented by echocardiography in two-thirds of uremic patients, although only a small number manifest clinical symptoms.[131] Echocardiographic abnormalities documented before dialysis are pericardial effusions, pericardial thickening, left ventricular hypertrophy, and left ventricular dilation. Uremic pericarditis is not common until the BUN consistently exceeds 80 mg/dl.[3]

Uremic pericarditis presents as in pericarditis from other causes. Chest pain, fever, and a friction rub are the most common signs. Hypotension during dialysis and cardiac arrhythmias may occur. Tamponade and constrictive pericarditis are serious complications.

Hypertension

Hypertension secondary to sodium and water retention is common in advanced renal failure and can be reversed by sodium restriction and diuretics. Furosemide is the diuretic of choice, since hydrochlorothiazide is not effective after the GFR has fallen below 50 percent of normal.[132] Dialysis may be necessary to treat volume-dependent hypertension in advanced renal failure. Hyperreninemic hypertension affects less than 15 percent of hypertensive patients with advanced renal insufficiency.[132,133] In the latter form of hypertension, vasodilators such as hydralazine, specific beta blockers such as propranolol or atenolol, and angiotensin-converting enzyme inhibitors such as captopril are effective either singly or in combination.

Minoxidil is a potent vasodilator that is quite useful in patients with resistant, severe hypertension. In many patients, it has obviated the need for bilateral nephrectomy with its attendant risk of exacerbation of anemia, renal osteodystrophy, and mortality. Sodium retention and hirsutism have, however, limited patient acceptance of minoxidil.

PULMONARY DISORDERS

Fluid overload or left heart failure from malignant hypertension may lead to pulmonary edema in advanced chronic renal insufficiency. Increased pulmonary capillary permeability and hyponatremia have also been implicated in the pathogenesis of uremic pulmonary edema by (1) markedly reducing the gradient between the serum colloid osmotic pressure and pulmonary arterial pressure, and (2) increasing the passage of protein-rich exudate into the alveolar fluid via a permeable pulmonary capillary membrane.[134]

Uremic pneumonitis is an extreme form of pulmonary edema.[134] In addition to fluid, fibrin-rich hyaline membranes form in the alveoli. Hemorrhage into the alveoli is also common. Interstitial fibrosis often results as the pneumonic process resolves.

HEMATOLOGIC DISORDERS

One of the most common findings in chronic renal failure is normochromic, normocytic anemia[135] correlated inversely, although poorly, with creatinine clearance and BUN. The etiology is related to impaired erythropoietin production,[135] defective homeostasis, and hemolysis.

Erythropoiesis

The kidneys normally respond to hypoxia by secreting erythropoietin,[136] which in turn stimulates bone marrow erythropoiesis. With progressive destruction of the renal parenchyma, this erythropoietic response becomes impaired by the lack of renal production of erythropoietin and inhibitors of erythropoietin. Parathyroid hormone has been implicated as an inhibitor of erythropoiesis, but evidence for this is not conclusive.

Recently, recombinant human erythropoietin has become available on a research basis. The response to the intravenous administration of this hormone in adult patients with end-stage renal disease was dramatic.[135] The reticulocyte count promptly rose and the hematocrit soon became normal in all subjects. Seizures, possibly related to increased blood pressure, and elevations in serum creatinine and potassium concentrations have been noted as complications in some of the subjects.[135]

In addition, iron utilization is poor in renal failure.[135] Both plasma turnover and erythrocyte incorporation of iron are impaired in uremia. Iron deficiency may result from chronic loss of blood from the intestinal tract, frequent venipuncture, or repeated blood loss associated with hemodialysis.

Deficiencies in folic acid,[137] pyridoxine, histidine, and other nutritional factors due to the uremic state or depletion via dialysis may contribute to the reduced erythropoiesis.

Homeostasis

Platelet function is often abnormal in chronic renal failure, leading to an increased tendency to bleed and to microangiopathy.[138] Reduced platelet production results in thrombocytopenia, although rarely below 60,000/mm^3. The platelet lifespan is normal, but platelet aggregation, adhesiveness, phospholipid content, adenylcyclase, and factor 3 activation are impaired,[139] with consequent poor clot retraction and prolongation of the bleeding time as manifestations of this dysfunction. Guanidinosuccinic acid, phenolic acids,[139] and prostacyclins are implicated in these dysfunctions. Adequate dialysis, with urea nitrogen levels below 80 mg/dl, reverses these platelet abnormalities. Platelet transfusions are not effective. Infusion of desmopressin acetate (DDAVP), the synthetic analogue of vasopressin, is useful for rapid improvement in the bleeding time.[140] Conjugated estrogens are also helpful in correcting the bleeding time.[141] The onset of action is slower, but more prolonged.

Hemolysis

Reduced red cell survival is present in a majority of uremic patients, but there is little correlation between red cell survival and the degree of renal failure. Coomb's test is usually negative in uncomplicated cases of anemia. Red cell 2,3-diphosphoglyceric acid and adenosine triphosphate are increased secondary to the increased serum phosphate concentration. The elevated erythrocyte 2,3-diphosphoglyceric acid content shifts the oxygen dissociation curve to the right, resulting in a reduced hemoglobin-oxygen affinity.[3] This permits the patient with chronic renal failure to tolerate the invariable anemia better than patients with non-uremic anemia.

GONADAL AND SEXUAL DISORDERS

Delayed or absent adolescent growth spurts,[142] amenorrhea, and hypermenorrhea[143] are common in uremic females, and hypospermatogenesis, low testosterone, high prolactin, and elevated luteinizing hormone have been reported repeatedly in uremic males.[144] These abnormalities lead to infertility and decreased libido in both sexes, and impotence in males.

Dialysis has reversed the loss of libido[144] and fertility.[143] Although pregnancy has been described in uremic patients, it has rarely progressed to term in patients whose BUN exceeded 30 mg/dl. Successful pregnancies have been reported in renal transplant recipients. Increased testosterone production and a purportedly increased libido after subtotal parathyroidectomy or 1,25-dihydroxyvitamin D treatment have led to the suggestion that an elevated PTH concentration is responsible for some aspects of sexual dysfunction in advanced renal failure. Another possible mechanism for these complex dysfunctions is suggested by the finding that sexual potency returns after the reversal of hypozincemia by zinc supplementation or during 1,25-dihydroxyvitamin D administration,[60] presumably because of increased zinc absorption.

OTHER SYSTEMIC DISORDERS

Pruritus in uremic patients may be due to many factors, including inadequate dialysis,[77] disorders of calcium and parathyroid metabolism,[78] and peripheral neuropathy. Relief of the pruritus after parathyroidectomy is thought to be related to elimination of the continued microscopic calcium deposition in the epidermis that is associated with severe hyperparathyroidism.[80]

Hyperuricemia is common in chronic renal failure,[3,93] but attacks of gout are uncommon. Metastatic calcification of the periarticular tissues or the bone pain of renal osteodystrophy may mimic clinical gout.[77] Easing of these symptoms follows the correction of hyperphosphatemia and return to a normal calcium × phosphate product.[76,80]

CONSERVATIVE MANAGEMENT

The first principle in the management of chronic renal failure is to treat the underlying cause, such as immunosuppression for glomerulonephritis, surgery for obstructive uropathy, ureteral implantation for gross reflux, and proscription of the offending toxin in interstitial nephritis. However, once chronic renal failure is established, it continues to progress despite effective therapy for the underlying disorder. A number of factors have been identified as causing this progression. Therapies designed to slow or halt the progression have been labeled conservative therapies.

One factor in the progression of renal failure is hypertension.[145] Hypertension is clearly injurious to the kidney, and has been implicated as a cause of renal failure, especially in blacks. The mechanism of the injury is not clearly understood, but may involve vascular hypertrophy leading to ischemic glomerulosclerosis. Systemic hypertension may be mirrored in the intraglomerular blood pressure, causing increased renal blood flow and filtration in individual nephrons. This could lead to endothelial damage and subsequent sclerosis. Effective control of blood pressure appears to slow the progression of renal damage, and in some cases to improve renal function.

Another factor in the progression of renal failure is the protein content of the diet. Glomerular filtration can be modulated in normal animals[146] and man[147] by protein intake. High protein intakes raise the renal blood flow and GFR through vasodilation of renal arterioles, especially in the superficial glomeruli.[148] The increased blood flow leads to increased glomerular capillary pressure.

These increases are not related to the urea, sulfate, sodium, or acid content of food, because feeding these substances will not raise the GFR.[148] On the other hand, infusion of amino acids will increase renal blood flow and glomerular filtration, but not in isolated, perfused kidneys. This implies that circulating factors are responsible for the increased blood flow, and glucagon and prostaglandins appear to be these factors.[149]

Over a lifetime, the higher intraglomerular pressure from a protein-rich diet appears to be detrimental. This is especially so in renal failure. In rats with four-fifths nephrectomy, protein loading led to an increased rate of glomerulosclerosis and progression of renal failure.[148] Proteinuria was also more marked in rats given a high protein diet, and this also may have increased the amount of sclerosis.[148]

Through these experimental data, there has been a rediscovery of the efficacy of low protein diet in patients with renal insufficiency. Restriction of protein to approximately 0.6 g/kg/day can yield a neutral nitrogen balance in many patients whose uremia is not severe, provided that the total caloric and vitamin intakes are adequate.[15,36,150] Giovannetti and Maggiore first pointed out that substantially reduced daily intake of protein (20 to 25 g) could yield nitrogen balance if the proportion of essential amino acids in the proteins supplied was high.[36] This led to the development of a diet for uremic individuals consisting of 0.6 g/kg of predominantly high quality protein plus carbohydrate sources that are low in electrolytes and nitrogen.

Reducing the protein intake to below 0.6 g/kg was not always successful and often led to a negative nitrogen balance.[150,151] This could be overcome by the use of a very low protein diet containing 20 to 25 g of mixed quality protein supplemented with a mixture of essential amino acids.[15,36,152] Histidine has been included in this mixture because it is known to be essential in humans. Initially, it was thought that essential amino acids would allow the recycling of urea nitrogen, but this appears not to be the case. Essential amino acid mixtures are useful because they are efficiently utilized as a source of nitrogen and lead to the lower rates of urea nitrogen appearance.

A number of studies have shown that low protein diets can slow the rate of progression of chronic renal failure.[15,153–159] Restriction of the dietary intake of protein to 0.6 g/kg/day, and of the phosphorus intake to 750 mg/day, led to a slower rise in serum creatinine than did a standard diet in a control population.[153] Similar results were obtained by Johnson and associates.[154] Gior-

Table 12-4. Recommended Protein and Energy Intake for Patients With Chronic Renal Insufficiency

Glomerular Filtration Rate (ml/min/1.73 m²)	Protein (g/kg/day)	Energy (Kcal/kg/day)[a]	Carbohydrate[b] (% total calories)	Fat (% total calories)	P/S Ratio
≥70 without apparent progression	Approximately 1.0–1.2	Sufficient to maintain desirable body weight	As recommended for health enhancement for normal people		
≥70 with apparent progression	0.55–0.60[c]; ≥0.35 g/kg/day of high value protein	≥35	50% primarily complex carbohydrates	The remaining non-protein calories	1.0
25–70	0.55–0.60; ≥0.35 g/kg/day of high value protein or 0.28 g protein/kg/day with 10–20 g/day of essential amino acids or keto acids	≥35	50% primarily complex carbohydrates	The remaining non-protein calories	1.0
5–25	0.55–0.60; ≥0.35 g/kg/day of high value protein or 0.28 g protein/kg/day with 10–20 g/day of essential amino acids or keto acids	≥35	50% primarily complex carbohydrates	The remaining non-protein calories	1.0

P/S = polysaturated/saturated fatty acid ratio.[1]
[a] Energy intake may be reduced in patients with body weight greater than 120% of desirable body weight or who are gaining undesired fat with the recommended energy intake, or who refuse to ingest these levels of energy.
[b] Patients should be encouraged to ingest complex rather than purified carbohydrates.
[c] In patients who are unable to adhere well to this protein intake, the prescription may be changed to 0.60–0.70 g protein/kg/day of which ≥35 g/kg/day is of high biologic value.
(From Hirschberg R and Kopple JD: Requirements for protein, calories, and fat in the predialysis patient. p. 142. In Mitch WE, Klahr S (eds): Nutrition and the Kidney. Little, Brown, Boston, 1988 with permission.)

dano noted that patients with a serum creatinine of 3 mg/dl on a low protein, low phosphorus diet did not progress to dialysis or transplantation for an average of 7.6 years, while those who ate a standard diet progressed to end-stage renal failure after only 1.3 years.[155] The importance of phosphorus restriction in slowing the progression of renal failure was shown in patients in whom phosphorus was restricted to 6.5 mg/kg/day. Renal failure progressed more slowly in these patients than in those in whom only a modest restriction of phosphate to 12 mg/kg/day was made.[156] Several authors have shown the advantage of a low protein diet, containing 20 to 30 g protein per day, plus essential amino acids in slowing the progression of renal failure, as compared to simply restricting the dietary protein to 0.6 g/kg.[157-159] Even further slowing of the progression of renal failure can be accomplished by giving a diet containing protein at 0.28 g/kg/day plus a mixture of essential amino acids and keto acid analogues at 0.28 g/kg/day.[15] However, maintenance of this restricted diet over long periods has been difficult.

From this information, restriction of the dietary protein intake to 0.6 g/kg/day when renal function is mildly to moderately impaired will eliminate uremic symptoms and may slow the loss of residual renal function (Table 12-4). Restricting dietary protein intake to 0.3 g/kg/day, with 0.22 to 0.28 g/kg/day of essential amino acids or a mixture of amino acids and ketoacids when the GFR is below 70 ml/min/1.73 m^2, will further slow the rate of progression of renal failure. However, when renal function falls to less than 5 percent of normal, it is unlikely that conservative management will forestall the need for dialytic therapy. With restriction of protein intake, attention must clearly be given to insuring that the patient remains in neutral nitrogen balance and is receiving adequate caloric, vitamin, and trace mineral intakes.

ACKNOWLEDGMENTS

The authors thank Virginia Murrell for secretarial assistance, and Mrs. Martha D. Massie and Mrs. Faith S. Boyle for research assistance. This work was supported by NIH grants RO1 DK 31370 and RO1 DK 39336-01.

REFERENCES

1. ESRD Facility Survey Tables, Bureau of Data Management, Health Care Financing Administration, Washington, DC, 1989
2. Chantler C, Holliday M: Progressive loss of renal function. p. 773. In Holliday MA, Barratt TM, Vernier RL (eds): Pediatric Nephrology, 2nd Ed. Williams & Wilkins, Baltimore, 1987
3. Schreiner GE, Maher JF: Uremia: Biochemistry, Pathogenesis and Treatment. Charles C Thomas, Springfield, IL, 1983
4. Harris RC, Meyer TW, Brenner BM: Nephron adaptation to renal injury. p. 1553. In Brenner BM, Rector FC Jr (eds): The Kidney, 3rd Ed, Vol 2. WB Saunders, Philadelphia, 1986
5. Gonick HC, Maxwell MH, Rubini ME, et al: Functional impairment in chronic renal disease. I. Studies of sodium-conserving ability. Nephron 3:137, 1966
6. Chan JCM: Urinary tract diseases. p. 467. In Maurer HM (ed): Pediatrics. Churchill Livingstone, New York, 1982
7. Chan JCM: Acid-base and mineral disorders in children: A review. Int J Ped Nephrol 1:54, 1980
8. Slatopolsky E, Rutherford WE, Rosenbaum R, et al: Hyperphosphatemia. Clin Nephrol 7:138, 1977
9. Feinfeld DA, Sherwood LM: Parathyroid hormone and 1,25-(OH)$_2$D$_3$ in chronic renal failure. Kidney Int 33:1049, 1988
10. Hellerstein S, Holliday MA, Grupe WE, et al: Nutritional management of children with chronic renal failure. Pediatr Nephr 1:195, 1987
11. Fine RN: Treatment of end-stage renal disease in children. Pediatr Ann 10:65, 1981
12. Foreman JW, Chan JCM: Chronic renal

failure in infants and children. J Pediatr 113:793, 1988
13. Warshaw BL, Edelbrock HH, Ettenger RB, et al: Progression to end-stage renal disease in children with obstructive uropathy. J Pediatr 100:183, 1982
14. Chan JCM: Renal tubular acidosis. J Pediatr 102:327, 1983
15. Mitch WE: The influence of the diet on the progression of renal insufficiency. Annu Rev Med 35:249, 1984
16. Mitch WE, Walser M, Stein TI, et al: The effects of ketoacid-amino acid supplement to a restricted diet on the progression of chronic renal failure. N Engl J Med 311:623, 1984
17. Mitch WE, Wilcox CS: Disorders of body fluids, sodium and potassium in chronic renal failure. Am J Med 72:536, 1982
18. Chan JCM, Goplerud JM, Papadopoulou ZL, et al: Kidney failure in childhood. Int J Pediatr Nephrol 2:201, 1981
19. Chan JCM, Grushkin CM, Malekzadeh M, et al: The adaptation of hydrogen ion excretion associated with nephron reduction in post-transplant patients. Pediatr Res 7:712, 1973
20. Bricker NS: On the meaning of the intact nephron hypothesis. Am J Med 46:1, 1969
21. Chan JCM: Nutrition and acid-base metabolism. Fed Proc 40:2423, 1981
22. Schultze RG, Weisser F, Bricker NS: The influence of uremia on fractional sodium reabsorption by the proximal tubule of rats. Kidney Int 2:59, 1972
23. Chan JCM: The effect of milk formulae on acid balance. Nutr Metab 16:140, 1974
24. Chan JCM: The influence of dietary intake on endogenous acid production: Theoretical and experimental background. Nutr Metab 16:1, 1974
25. Chan JCM: The rapid determination of urinary titratable acid and ammonium and evaluation of freezing as a method of preservation. Clin Biochem 5:94, 1972
26. Chan JCM, Ma RSW, Malekzadeh MH, et al: Renal response to acute ammonium chloride acidosis in subjects with single kidney. J Urol 111:315, 1974
27. Laski ME, Kurtzman NA: Acid-base physiology and pathophysiology. p. 195. Contemporary Nephrology, Vol 4. Plenum, New York, 1987
28. Broyer M: Acute renal failure. p. 353. In Royer R, Habib R, Mathieu H, et al (eds): Pediatric Nephrology. WB Saunders, Philadelphia, 1974
29. Lemann J Jr, Lennon EJ: Role of diet, gastrointestinal tract and bone in acid-base homeostasis. Kidney Int 1:275, 1972
30. Chan JCM, Oldham SB, Holick NF, et al: 1-alpha-hydroxyvitamin D_3 in chronic renal failure. A potent analog of the kidney hormone, 1,25-dihydroxycholecalciferol. JAMA 234:47, 1975
31. Alon U, Kodroff MB, Broecker BH, et al: Renal tubular acidosis type 4 in neonatal unilateral kidney diseases. J Pediatr 104:855, 1984
32. McConnell JB, Murison J, Stewart WK: The role of the colon in the pathogenesis of hyperchloremic acidosis in ureterosigmoid anastomosis. Clin Sci 57:305, 1979
33. Schultze RG, Taggart DD, Shapiro HS, et al: On the adaptation in potassium excretion associated with nephron reduction in the dog. J Clin Invest 50:1061, 1971
34. Bank N, Aynedjian HS: A micropuncture study of potassium excretion by the remnant kidney. J Clin Invest 52:1480, 1973
35. Hayes CP Jr, McLead ME, Robinson RR: An extrarenal mechanism for the maintenance of potassium balance in severe chronic renal failure. Trans Assoc Am Physicians 80:207, 1967
36. Giovannetti S, Maggiore Q: A low nitrogen diet with protein of high biological value for severe chronic uremia. Lancet 1:1000, 1964
37. Van Ypersele de Strihou C: Potassium homeostasis in renal failure. Kidney Int 11:491, 1977
38. Chan JCM: Acid-base, calcium, potassium and aldosterone metabolism in renal tubular acidosis. Nephron 23:153, 1979
39. Bourgoignie JJ, Hwang KH, Ipakchi E, et al: The presence of a natriuretic factor in urine of patients with chronic uremia. J Clin Invest 53:1559, 1974
40. Danovitch CM, Bourgoignie J, Bricker NS: Reversibility of the "salt-losing" tendency of chronic renal failure. N Engl J Med 296:14, 1977
41. Chan JCM: Control of aldosterone secretion. Nephron 23:79, 1979

42. Chan JCM: Clinical disorders of calcium metabolism in chronic renal failure in children. p. 498. In Grushkin AB, Norman ME (eds): Fifth International Pediatric Nephrology Symposium. Martinus Nijhoff, The Hague, 1981
43. Jacob M, Chan JCM: Effect of variations in dietary calcium on renal and intestinal calcium-binding proteins. Pediatr Res 22:518, 1987
44. Nemere I, Norman AW: Vitamin D and intestinal cell membranes. Biochim Biophys Acta 684:307, 1982
45. Mak RHK, Turner C, Thompson T, et al: Suppression of secondary hyperparathyroidism in children with chronic renal failure by high dose phosphate binders: $CaCO_3$ vs $Al(OH)_3$. Br Med J 291:623, 1985
46. Slatopolsky E, Bricker NS: The role of phosphorus restriction in the prevention of secondary hyperparathyroidism in chronic renal failure. Kidney Int 4:141, 1973
47. Slatopolsky E, Cagler S, Pennell JP, et al: On the pathogenesis of hyperparathyroidism in chronic experimental renal insufficiency in dogs. J Clin Invest 50:492, 1971
48. Chan JCM, Kodroff MB, Landwehr DM: Effects of 1,25-dihydroxyvitamin-D_3 on renal function, mineral metabolism and growth in children with severe chronic renal failure. Pediatrics 68:559, 1981
49. Sorenson E, Tougaard L, Brochner-Mortensen J: Iatrogenic magnesium intoxication during 1-alpha-hydroxycholecalciferol treatment. Br Med J 2:215, 1976
50. Kopple JD, Coburn JW: Metabolic studies of low protein diets in uremia II. Calcium, phosphorus and magnesium. Medicine 52:597, 1973
51. Alfrey AC, LeGendre GR, Kaehny WD: The dialysis encephalopathy syndrome: Possible aluminum intoxication. N Engl J Med 294:184, 1976
52. Santos F, Massie MD, Chan JCM: Risk factors in aluminum toxicity in children with chronic renal failure. Nephron 42:189, 1986
53. O'Hare JA, Murnaghan DJ: Reversal of aluminum-induced hemodialysis anemia by a low-aluminum dialysate. N Engl J Med 307:654, 1982
54. Alfrey AC: Aluminum. Adv Clin Chem 23:69, 1983
55. Andreoli SP, Bergstein JM, Sherrard DJ: Aluminum intoxication from aluminum-containing phosphate binders in children with azotemia but not undergoing dialysis. N Engl J Med 310:1079, 1984
56. Milliner DS, Nebeker HG, Ott SM, et al: Use of deferoxamine infusion test in the diagnosis of aluminum-related osteodystrophy. Ann Intern Med 101:775, 1984
57. Ott SM, Maloney NA, Coburn JW, et al: The prevalence of bone aluminum deposition in renal osteodystrophy and its relation to the response to calcitriol therapy. N Engl J Med 307:709, 1982
58. Malluche HH, Smith AJ, Abreo K, Faugere M-C: The use of deferoxamine in the management of aluminum accumulation in bone in patients with renal failure. N Engl J Med 311:140, 1984
59. Andreoli SP, Dunn D, DeMeyer W, et al: Intraperitoneal deferoxamine therapy for aluminum intoxication in a child undergoing continuous ambulatory peritoneal dialysis. J Pediatr 107:760, 1985
60. Antonio LD, Shalhoub RJ, Sudhaker T, et al: Reversal of uraemic impotence of zinc. Lancet 2:895, 1977
61. Lough J, Noonan R, Gagnon R, Kaye M: Effect of fluoride on bone in chronic renal failure. Arch Pathol 99:484, 1975
62. Manzler AD, Schreiner AW: Copper-induced acute hemolytic anemia. A new complication of hemodialysis. Ann Intern Med 73:409, 1970
63. Chan JCM, Hsu AC: Vitamin D and renal diseases. Adv Pediatr 27:117, 1980
64. Rasmussen H, Bordier P: The Physiological Cellular Basis of Metabolic Bone Disease. Williams & Wilkins, Baltimore, 1974
65. Jowsey J: Metabolic Disease of Bone. WB Saunders, Philadelphia, 1977
66. Chesney RW, Hamstra AJ, Mazess RB, et al: Circulating vitamin D concentrations in childhood renal disease. Kidney Int 21:65, 1981
67. Portale AA, Booth BE, Halloran BP, Morris RC Jr: Effect of dietary phosphorus on circulating concentrations of 1,25-dihydroxyvitamin D and immunoreactive parathyroid hormone in children with moderate renal insufficiency. J Clin Invest 73:1580, 1984

68. Brown EM, Wilson RE, Eastman C, et al: Abnormal regulation of parathyroid release by calcium in secondary hyperparathyroidism due to chronic renal failure. J Clin Endocrinol Metab 54:172, 1982
69. Slatopolsky E, Weers C, Theilan J, et al: Marked suppression of secondary hyperparathyroidism by intravenous administration of 1,25-dihydroxyvitamin D in uremic patients. J Clin Invest 74:2136, 1984
70. Lemann J Jr, Litzow JR, Lennon EJ, et al: Study of the mechanisms by which chronic metabolic acidosis augments calcium excretion in man. J Clin Invest 46:1318, 1967
71. Hruska KA, Kopelman R, Rutherford WE, et al: Metabolism of immunoreactive parathyroid hormone in the dog: The role of the kidney and the effects of chronic renal insufficiency. J Clin Invest 56:39, 1975
72. Langman CB, Bushinsky DA, Favus MJ, et al: Ca and P regulation of 1,25(OH)$_2$D$_3$ synthesis by D-replete rat tubules during acidosis. Am J Physiol 251:F911, 1986
73. Lee SW, Russell J, Avioli LV, et al: 25-hydroxycholecalciferol to 1,25-dihydroxycholecalciferol: conversion impaired by systemic metabolic acidosis. Science 195:994, 1977
74. Kraut JA, Gordon EM, Ransom JC, et al: Effect of chronic metabolic acidosis on vitamin D metabolism in humans. Kidney Int 24:644, 1983
75. Malluche HH, Ritz E, Lang HP, et al: Bone histology in incipient and advanced renal failure. Kidney Int 9:355, 1976
76. Wright RS, Mehl O, Ritz E, et al: Musculoskeletal manifestation of chronic renal failure. p. 342. In Bacon A, Hadler MN (eds): The Kidney and Rheumatic Disease. Butterworth, London, 1982
77. Massry SG, Popovtzer MM, Coburn JW, et al: Intractable pruritus as a manifestation of secondary hyperparathyroidism in uremia. N Engl J Med 279:697, 1968
78. Hampers CL, Katz AI, Wilson RE, et al: Disappearance of "uremic" itching after subtotal parathyroidectomy. N Engl J Med 279:695, 1968
79. Parfitt AM: Soft-tissue calcification in uremia. Arch Intern Med 124:544, 1969
80. Contriguglia SR, Alfrey AC, Miller NL, et al: Nature of soft tissue calcification in uremia. Kidney Int 4:229, 1973
81. Chan JCM, DeLuca HF: Calcium and parathyroid disorders in children: chronic renal failure and treatment with calcitriol. JAMA 241:1242, 1979
82. Norman ME, Mazur AT, Borden S, et al: Early diagnosis of juvenile renal osteodystrophy. J Pediatr 97:226, 1980
83. Walser M: Ion association: VI. Interactions between calcium, magnesium, inorganic phosphate, citrate, and protein in normal human plasma. J Clin Invest 40:723, 1961
84. Coburn JW, Popovtzer MM, Massry SG, et al: The physicochemical state and renal handling of divalent ions in chronic renal failure. Arch Intern Med 124:302, 1969
85. Nordin BEC: Calcium, Phosphate and Magnesium Metabolism: Clinical Physiology and Diagnostic Procedures. Churchill Livingstone, New York, 1976, p. 683.
86. Wassner SJ, Bergstrom J, Bruselow SW, et al: Protein metabolism in renal failure: abnormalities and possible mechanisms. Am J Kidney Dis 7:285, 1986
87. Jones EA, Smallwood RA, Craigie A, Rosenoer VM: The enterohepatic circulation of urea nitrogen. Clin Sci 37:285, 1969
88. Orita Y, Tsubakihara Y, Ando A: The effect of arginine or creatinine administration on the urinary excretion of methylguanidine. Nephron 22:328, 1978
89. Giovannetti S, Balestri TL, Barsotti G: Methylguanidine in uremia. Arch Intern Med 131:709, 1973
90. Wardle EN, Wilkinson K: Free phenols in chronic renal failure. Clin Nephrol 6:361, 1976
91. Bergstrom J, Furst P: Uremic middle molecules. Clin Nephrol 5:143, 1976
92. DeFronzo RA, Andres R, Edgan P, et al: Carbohydrate metabolism in uremia: a review. Medicine 52:469, 1973
93. Massry SG, Sellers AL: Clinical Aspects of Uremia and Dialysis. Charles C Thomas, Springfield, IL, 1976
94. Samaan N, Freeman RM: Growth hormone levels in severe renal failure. Metabolism 19:102, 1970
95. Orskov H, Christensen NJ: Growth hormone in uremia: I. Plasma growth hormone, insulin and glucagon after oral and intravenous glucose in uremic subjects. Scand J Clin Lab Invest 27:51, 1971

96. Wright AD, Lowry C, Fraser TR, et al: Serum growth hormone and glucose tolerance in renal failure. Lancet 2:798, 1968
97. Chan MK, Varghese Z, Moorehead JF: Lipid abnormalities in uremia, dialysis and transplantation. Kidney Int 19:625, 1981
98. Frederickson DS, Levy RI, Lees RS: Fat transport in lipoproteins: An integrated approach to mechanisms and disorders. N Engl J Med 276:34, 1967
99. Zabetakis PH, Gleim GW, Pasternack FL, et al: Long-duration submaximal exercise conditioning in hemodialysis patients. Clin Nephrol 18:17, 1982
100. Goldberg AP, Hagberg JM, Delmez JA, et al: Metabolic effects of exercise training in hemodialysis patients. Kidney Int 18:754, 1980
101. Jacobs C, Brunner SP, Chantler C, et al: Combined report on regular dialysis and transplantation in Europe. Proc Eur Dial Transplant Assoc 14:3, 1977
102. Boulton-Jones JM, Vick R, Cameron JS, et al: Immune response in uremia. Clin Nephrol 1:351, 1973
103. Wilson WEC, Kirkpatrick CH, Talmage DW: Suppression of immunologic responsiveness in uremia. Ann Intern Med 62:1, 1965
104. Touraine JL, Touraine L, Revillard JP, et al: T-lymphocyte and serum inhibitors of cell-mediated immunity in renal insufficiency. Nephron 14:195, 1975
105. Casciani CV, DeSimone C, Bonini S, et al: Immunological aspects of chronic uremia. Kidney Int 8:S49, 1978
106. Bruscarini L, Bassi F: Some aspects of leucocyte behavior in haemodialysis. Acta Hematol 50:223, 1973
107. Rotundo A, Nevins TE, Lipton M, et al: Progressive encephalopathy in children with chronic renal insufficiency in infancy. Kidney Int 21:486, 1982
108. Ginn HE: Neurobehavioral dysfunction in uremia. Kidney Int 7 (Suppl):217, 1975
109. Tyler HR: Neurological disorders in renal failure. Am J Med 44:734, 1968
110. Arieff AI, Guisado R, Massry SG: Uremic encephalopathy. Kidney Int 7:S194, 1975
111. Akmal M, Goldstein DA, Multani S, Massry SG: Role of uremia, brain calcium, and parathyroid hormone on changes in chronic renal failure. Am J Physiol 246:F575, 1984
112. Cogan M, Covey C, Arieff AI, et al: Central nervous system manifestations of hyperparathyroidism. Am J Med 65:963, 1978
113. Van den Noort S, Eckel RE, Brine KL, Hrdlicka JT: Brain metabolism in experimental uremia. Arch Intern Med 126:831, 1970
114. Chan JCM, Eng G: Hemodialysis and nerve conduction studies in children. Pediatr Res 13:591, 1979
115. Jellinek EH, Painter M, Princas J, et al: Hypertensive encephalopathy with cortical disturbance of vision. Q J Med 33:239, 1964
116. Ingelfinger JR: Pediatric Hypertension. WB Saunders, Philadelphia, 1982
117. Letteri JM, Mellk H, Louis S, et al: Diphenylhydantoin metabolism in uremia. N Engl J Med 285:648, 1971
118. Raskin NH, Fishman RA: Neurological disorders in renal failure. N Engl J Med 294:143, 1976
119. Patten BM: Neuromuscular complications. p. 281. In Eknoyan G, Knochel JP (eds): The Systemic Consequence of Renal Failure. Grune & Stratton, Orlando, FL, 1984
120. Shepherd AMM, Stewart WK, Wormsley KG: Peptic ulceration in chronic renal failure. Lancet 1:1357, 1973
121. De Meritt Bischel M: Hepatitis and gastrointestinal abnormalities. p. 185. In Massry SG, Sellers AL (eds): Clinical Aspects of Uremia and Dialysis. Charles C Thomas, Springfield, IL 1976
122. Chan JCM, Hung W: Hemodialysis and thyroid functions in children. J Dialysis 2:387, 1978
123. Spector DA, Davis PJ, Helderman JH, et al: Thyroid function and metabolic state in chronic renal failure. Ann Intern Med 85:724, 1976
124. Ramirez G, O'Neill W Jr, Jubiz W, et al: Thyroid dysfunction in uremia: evidence for thyroid and hypophyseal abnormalities. Ann Intern Med 84:672, 1976
125. Mishkin MS, Hsu JH, Walker WG, Bledsoe T: Studies on the episodic secretion of cortisol in uremic patients on hemodialysis. Johns Hopkins Med J 131:160, 1972
126. Barbour GL, Sevier BR: Adrenal respon-

siveness in chronic hemodialysis. N Engl J Med 290:1258, 1974
127. Gilkes JJH, Eady RAJ, Rees LH, et al: Plasma immunoreactive melanotrophic hormones in patients on maintenance hemodialysis. Br Med J 1:656, 1975
128. Saenger P, Wiedeman E, Schwartz E, et al: Somatomedin and growth after renal transplantation. Pediatr Res 8:163, 1974
129. Lewy JE, Van Wyk JJ: Somatomedin and growth retardation in children with chronic renal insufficiency. Kidney Int 14:361, 1978
130. McGrath BP, Ledingham JGG, Benedict CR: Catecholamines in peripheral venous plasma in patients on chronic hemodialysis. Clin Sci Mol Med 55:89, 1978
131. Winney RJ, Wright N, Summerling MD, et al: Echocardiography in uremic pericarditis with effusion. Nephron 18:201, 1977
132. Chan JCM: Renal and endocrine hypertension. Int J Pediatr Nephrol 4:187, 1983
133. Feld LG, Springate JE: Hypertension in infants and children. Curr Probl Pediatr 18:319, 1988
134. Brigham KL, Bernard G: Pulmonary complications of chronic renal failure. Semin Nephrol 1:188, 1981
135. Eschbach JW, Egrie JC, Downing MR, et al: Correction of the anemia of end-stage renal disease with recombinant human erythropoietin. Results of a combined Phase I and II clinical trial. N Engl J Med 316:73, 1987
136. Spivak JL: The mechanisms of action of erythropoietin. Int J Cell Cloning 4:139, 1986
137. Hampers CL, Streiff R, Nathan DG, et al: Megaloblastic hematopoiesis in uremia and in patients on long-term hemodialysis. N Engl J Med 267:351, 1967
138. Hardisty RM, Hutton RA: Bleeding tendency associated with "new" abnormality of platelet behavior. Lancet 1:983, 1967
139. Rabiner SF, Molinas F: The role of phenol and phenolic acids in the thrombocytopathy and defective platelet aggregation of patients with renal failure. Am J Med 49:346, 1970
140. Mannucci PM, Remuzzi G, Pusineri F, et al: Deamino 8-D-arginine vasopressin shortens the bleeding time in uremia. N Engl J Med 308:8, 1983
141. Liu YK, Kosfeld RE, Marcum SG: Treatment of uraemic bleeding with conjugated estrogens. Lancet 2:887, 1984
142. Chan JCM, Oldham SB, DeLuca HF: Effectiveness of 1-alpha-hydroxyvitamin D_3 in children with renal osteodystrophy associated with hemodialysis. J Pediatr 90:820, 1977
143. Olgaard K, Hagen C, McNeilly AS: Pituitary hormones in women with chronic renal failure: the effect of chronic intermittent haemo- and peritoneal dialysis. Acta Endocrinol 80:237, 1975
144. Lim VS, Fang VS: Gonadal dysfunction in uremic men. A study of the hypothalamopituitary testicular axis before and after renal transplantation. Am J Med 58:655, 1975
145. Baldwin DS, Neugarten J: Blood pressure control and progression of renal insufficiency. p. 81. In Mitch WE, Brenner BM, Stein JH (eds): The Progressive Nature of Renal Disease. Churchill Livingstone, New York, 1986
146. Schoolwerth AC, Sandler RS, Hoffman PM, Klahr S: Effects of nephron reduction and dietary protein content on renal ammoniagenesis in the rat. Kidney Int 7:397, 1975
147. Pullman TN, Alving AS, Dern RJ, Landowne M: The influence of dietary protein intake on specific renal functions in normal man. J Lab Clin Med 44:320, 1954
148. Brenner BM, Meyer TW, Hostetter TH: Dietary protein intake and progressive nature of kidney disease: The role of hemodynamically mediated glomerular injury in the pathogenesis of progressive glomerular sclerosis in aging, renal ablation, and intrinsic renal disease. N Engl J Med 307:652, 1982
149. Hirschberg RR, Zipser RD, Slomowitz LA, Kopple JD: Glucagon and prostaglandins are mediators of aminoacid-induced rise in renal hemodynamics. Kidney Int 33:1147, 1988
150. Lippman RW, Persike EC: Ambulatory management of azotemia and uremia. Arch Intern Med 80:579, 1947
151. Kopple JD, Sorenson MK, Coburn JW, et al: Controlled comparison of 20-g and 40-

g protein diets in the treatment of chronic uremia. Am J Clin Nutr 21:553, 1968
152. Kopple JD, Swenseid ME: Nitrogen balance and plasma amino acid levels in uremic patients fed an essential amino acid diet. Am J Clin Nutr 27:806, 1974
153. Maschio G, Oldrizzi L, Tessitore N, et al: Effects of dietary protein and phosphorus restriction on the progression of early renal failure. Kidney Int 22:371, 1982
154. Johnson WJ, Goldsmith RS, Jowsey J: The influence of maintaining normal serum phosphate and calcium on renal osteodystrophy. p. 56. In Norman AW (ed): Vitamin D and Problems Related to Uremic Bone Disease. Walter de Gruyter, Berlin, 1975
155. Giordano C: Early diet to slow the course of chronic renal failure. p. 71. In Zurukzoglu W, Papadimitriou M, Pyrpaspopoulos M, et al (eds): Eighth International Congress on Nephrology: Advances in Basic and Clinical Nephrology. S Karger, Basel, 1981
156. Barsotti G, Giannoni A, Morelli E, et al: The decline of renal function slowed by very low phosphorus intake in chronic renal patients following a low nitrogen diet. Clin Nephrol 21:54, 1984
157. Alverstrand A, Ahlberg M, Furst P, Bergstrom J: Clinical results of long-term treatment with a low protein diet and a new amino acid preparation in patients with chronic uremia. Clin Nephrol 19:67, 1983
158. Ando A, Orita Y, Abe H, et al: The effect of essential amino acid supplementation therapy on prognosis of patients with chronic renal failure estimated on the basis of the Markov process. Med J Osaka U 32:31, 1981
159. Altman PO, Bucht H, Larson O, Uddebom G: Protein reduced diet in chronic renal failure. Clin Nephrol 19:217, 1983

13

Special Problems of Chronic Peritoneal Dialysis in Children

J. Williamson Balfe
Denis F. Geary

Peritoneal dialysis was first performed on uremic rabbits and later, in 1923, on a uremic patient.[1] Since then, many investigators have demonstrated its life-saving role in adults with renal failure.[2] Peritoneal dialysis has also been used successfully in children with acute[3] and chronic[4] renal failure.

Even though peritoneal dialysis was discovered before hemodialysis, most physicians were reluctant to use it for long-term management of renal failure because it was associated with increased morbidity. The introduction of a permanent catheter, designed by Palmer[5] in 1964 and modified by Tenckhoff[6] in 1968, brought renewed interest in the procedure. The acceptability of peritoneal dialysis was enhanced in 1971 when Lasker[7] introduced the automatic peritoneal cycler, which made home management of the procedure feasible. In 1972, Tenckhoff[8] described a reverse osmosis peritoneal dialysis system that greatly reduced the cost of peritoneal dialysis, making it competitive with hemodialysis. Because no hemodialysis equipment suitable for young patients was available,[9] chronic intermittent peritoneal dialysis was applied to children and proved successful. Home intermittent peritoneal dialysis has also been used in children.[10,11]

The most important recent breakthrough in peritoneal dialysis was the introduction of continuous ambulatory peritoneal dialysis (CAPD) in 1976 by Popovich and Moncrief.[12,13] By exchanging 2 liters of dialysis fluid four times a day, seven days a week, they succeeded in maintaining biochemical control of small (urea, creatinine) and medium-sized molecules. Modifications by Oreopoulos[14] made the technique less cumbersome (by using plastic bags rather than bottles), and reduced the high incidence of peritonitis by improving the technique for dialysis exchanges. Continuous ambulatory peritoneal dialysis has been used successfully to manage children and infants with severe renal insufficiency.[15,16]

INSERTION OF THE CHRONIC PERITONEAL CATHETER

The Tenckhoff catheter is made of silicone rubber, and is available commercially in neonatal, pediatric, and adult sizes. The designs in common use are the Tenckhoff straight catheter, Tenckhoff curled catheter, double-disc Toronto-Western Hospital (TWH) catheter (Oreopoulos-Zellerman catheter), and column-disc or Ash catheter (Lifecath). These catheters are available with one or two Dacron cuffs for fixation. The adult size is used for children over 30 kg body weight, and the pediatric size for those between 10 and 30 kg. On occasion, the neonatal catheter has been used for infants of less than 10 kg. In all three sizes the Dacron felt cuff is fixed 5 cm proximal to the first drainage holes. Proper insertion of the catheter requires special attention in children weighing less than 20 kg. The catheter is implanted surgically; in children this is usually done under a general anesthetic. The patient receives prophylactic antibiotics [tobramycin 1.5 mg and cefazolin (or any first generation cephalosporin) 20 mg/kg body weight intravenously] one hour before the operation.

A 2 to 3 cm midline incision is made below the umbilicus. The peritoneum is opened and the catheter tip directed toward the pelvis. The position of the catheter is checked immediately by radiography; the fenestrated end of the catheter and especially the tip should lie in the pelvis. Often it is necessary to reposition the catheter. It should be mentioned, however, that a normally functioning catheter will sometimes be seen radiographically as curled out of the pelvis. Once the correct position is confirmed, a purse-string suture secures the peritoneum around the catheter, and the Dacron felt cuff is buried between the peritoneum and the rectus abdominis muscle. A 5 cm tunnel created just lateral to the umbilicus leads the catheter from the peri-

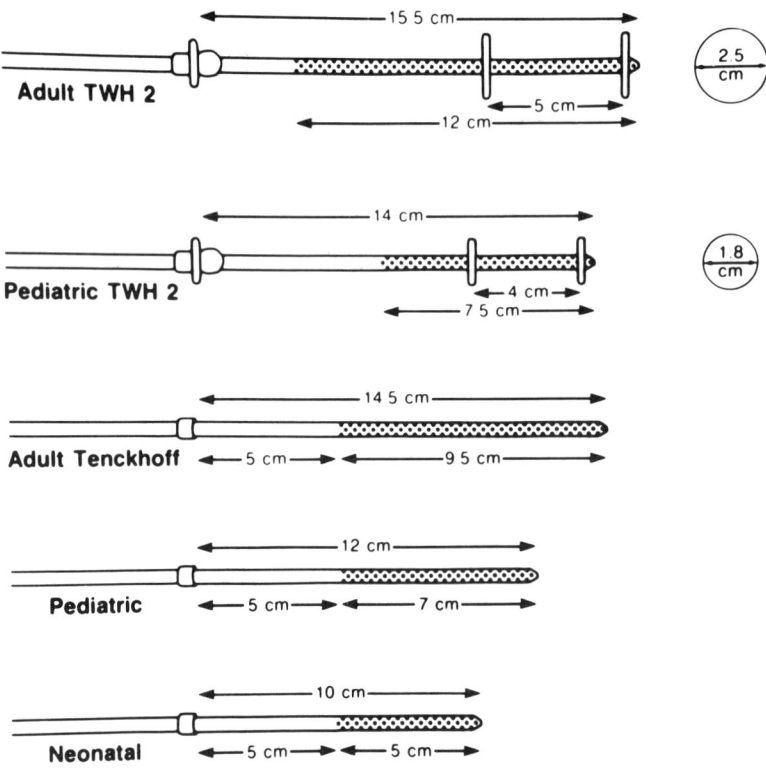

Fig. 13-1. Types of chronic peritoneal catheters.

toneum to the skin exit site. In an attempt to reduce the likelihood of catheter leakage, Helfrich and Winchester[17] suggested the catheter be inserted more laterally, that is, splitting the rectus muscle, being careful to avoid the inferior epigastric artery, in order to have more tissue in which to bury the cuff. We have been impressed with this technique in our patients.

Some centers prefer to have a second Dacron felt cuff near the site where the catheter exits from the subcutaneous tunnel. This second cuff must be at least 2 cm from the exit site to prevent erosion through the skin. Other centers prefer only one cuff. The types of catheters currently used are shown in Figure 13-1.

Hogg and associates[18] reported their pediatric experience using the TWH catheter; our own experience with chronic peritoneal catheters was reviewed by Watson and colleagues.[19] Although initially we preferred the straight single-cuffed Tenckhoff catheter,[20] our current approach is to use a paramedian incision and the TWH catheter. This has markedly reduced one-way failure, which is believed to be due to omental obstruction.

COMPLICATIONS RELATED TO THE CHRONIC PERITONEAL CATHETER

The dialysate is often bloody immediately after catheter insertion, but clears soon after dialysis is started. Abdominal pain is common during the first few weeks after catheter insertion, and can be aggravated by excessive use of concentrated dialysate. Occasionally, the pain is referred to the shoulder. A subcutaneous leak may occur during the first few days or 7 to 10 days after insertion. The leak will seal itself if the dialysis is stopped for a few days, then restarted using a smaller volume. It has been suggested that stopping dialysis electively for a period after the initial break-in process is complete will allow the tunnel to heal, thereby preventing leakage and reducing subsequent infections. Nonetheless, infection at the skin exit site can be a problem, especially if hygiene is poor. Infections are treated with an appropriate oral or intraperitoneal antibiotic, plus daily dressing changes. A tunnel infection or abscess is usually managed by catheter removal and antibiotics.

One-way obstruction (i.e., good inflow but no outflow) may occur as a result of catheter dislodgement and/or blockage by the omentum. One-way obstruction occurring a few days after insertion frequently resists attempts to establish good flow, and thus a new catheter must be inserted. In such cases, an omentectomy at the time of reinsertion should be considered. Since constipation may play a role in catheter dislodgement, a strong laxative may free the obstruction. Complete catheter obstruction can be caused by kinking of the tube or by fibrin in the catheter. The fibrin is treated by adding 500 to 1,000 units of heparin per liter of dialysate for a few days. If dialysis is discontinued for a few days, 3 ml of heparin (1,000 units/ml) is instilled into the catheter to ensure catheter patency. For resistant cases of catheter obstruction by fibrin, an infusion of streptokinase or urokinase into the catheter may be useful. This technique has also been used for suspected catheter colonization with bacteria.[21]

AUTOMATIC PERITONEAL DIALYSIS EQUIPMENT

In North America, the Lasker Cycler (American Medical Products Corporation) is the most frequently used machine for dialysis. It is a simple gravity-type machine consisting of a central pole with eight hooks, each holding a 2 L bag of dialysate, a heater box, a cycler, an outflow or drainage container, two timers (one for the "fill cycle" and one for the time required to drain fluid from the peritoneal cavity), and a counterbalance scale that monitors the volume of fluid draining out. Although the machine is inexpensive, its operating costs are high because commercially purchased bags of dialysate are used.

The reverse-osmosis type of machine (e.g., that made by the Physio-Control Company, Seattle) produces its own sterilized deionized water from tap water. A proportioning pump mixes 19 parts of warmed sterile water with 1 part concentrated solution of electrolyte and dextrose. The machine requires sterilization once every week with formaldehyde solution. Such machines are expensive, but the operating costs are relatively low, and they are associated with a reduced incidence of peritonitis.

Long-dwell pediatric cyclers are the AMP 80/2, Microstar (Medionics), PAC-X (Baxter Healthcare), and Inpersol 1000 (Abbott Labs). The PAC-X, Inpersol 1000, and Microstar, which can all be adjusted for use with small children, are most appropriate for pediatric use; the pediatric model of the AMP 80/2 is limited to settings of 250, 500, 750, and 1000 ml volumes, and is therefore less suited to smaller patients. The Microstar can be set to volumes as small as 10 ml, but the degree of recirculation at these volumes is excessive.

TYPES OF DIALYSIS FLUID AND PERITONEAL CLEARANCE

During peritoneal dialysis, most renal failure patients receive a potassium-free dialysate, although patients receiving digoxin may require potassium added to the dialysate. The usual dextrose concentration of the dialysate is 1.5, 2.5 (especially for anephric CAPD patients), or 4.25 g/dl. However, in some patients a concentration of even 1.5 g/dl dialysate may remove too much fluid; in this case a dextrose concentration of 0.5 g/dl dialysate is used. Recently, more efficient solute clearance and ultrafiltration have been reported using a dialysate containing glucose polymers, although these solutions have yet to gain widespread acceptance.[22]

Many factors can affect peritoneal clearance. One is the surface area of the peritoneum. Esperanca[23] stated that the surface area of the peritoneum was 177 cm^2/kg body weight in an adult, and 383 cm^2/kg body weight in an infant. In contrast, Henderson[24] reported that the peritoneal surface area for an average adult is 1.0 m^2. Peritoneal creatinine clearance in a six-day-old[25] was reported to be 27 ml/min/1.73 m^2, whereas that in adults[26] was 15 ml/min/1.73 m^2. In a study of adults, Robson[27] correlated clearance with body weight.

The peritoneal membrane clears urea and creatinine about 25 percent as effectively as hemodialysis; however, because the peritoneal membrane has a larger pore size, it is more effective in clearing "middle molecules" (molecular weight 300 to 1,500 daltons). This latter property has led workers to speculate that peritoneal dialysis removes the "uremic toxin" more effectively, with a consequent improvement in health.[28]

Hypertonic dialysis fluid (4.25 g/dl) has a greater clearance because it removes more fluid, thereby increasing solvent drag, which enhances the peritoneal permeability.[29] The length of time fluid is left to dwell in the peritoneal cavity affects the removal of water, since most of the ultrafiltrate is removed in the first 10 to 15 minutes.

Characteristics of peritoneal dialysis in older children are similar to those in adults. However, a preliminary report by Kohaut and Alexander[30] suggests that the ability of peritoneal dialysis to ultrafilter water is reduced in newborns. Our studies[31] on children were similar to those of Kohaut. Children less than six years old tend to absorb dextrose from the dialysate more readily than older children. It would appear that the loss of the dextrose osmotic concentration gradient is the major reason for the reduced ultrafiltration characteristics.

Factors that enhance peritoneal clearance are increased temperature,[32] an increased flow or exchange rate of dialysate, an increased dextrose concentration in the dialysate, vasodilators (e.g., nitroprusside in the dialysate),[33] and albumin added to the dialysate. Some factors that decrease peritoneal clearance are the use of dialysate at room temperature, vasoconstrictive agents, collagen-vascular disease,[34] ileus, and a relatively small abdominal cavity.

INTERMITTENT PERITONEAL DIALYSIS REQUIREMENTS

The amount of peritoneal dialysis clearance required is affected by the amount of residual renal function. Most patients require two 20-hour periods of dialysis a week. Each cycle has a 20-minute dwell time. There can be many variations in the dialysis scheduling. Patients with some renal function are able to maintain acceptable biochemistries with less dialysis. Because of protein loss in the dialysate, extra dietary protein is required, on the order of 60 to 80 g/day for adults or 3 to 4 g/kg body weight for children.

CONTINUOUS AMBULATORY PERITONEAL DIALYSIS

Continuous ambulatory peritoneal dialysis has been operational since it was introduced by Popovich and co-workers[13] in 1976, but has provoked controversy and often has been regarded with skepticism. In Canada, CAPD quickly became popular; approximately 30 percent of patients on chronic dialysis are managed by this method. Its usage varies from country to country, and the reasons for its acceptance are numerous. Its usage rates in Australia and the United Kingdom are similar to that in Canada, whereas in the United States, the country of its discovery, the usage rate is only 12 percent. It is less well accepted in some countries, such as France and Germany, and has only recently been introduced in Japan. Although it is premature to predict its impact on the management of end-stage renal disease, CAPD appears to be the dialysis mode of choice for infants and young children.

CONTINUOUS CYCLIC PERITONEAL DIALYSIS

Continuous cyclic peritoneal dialysis (CCPD) was made possible by the availability of long-dwell automated peritoneal dialysis cyclers. The adult experience with this technique was reported by Diaz-Buxo.[35] The patient receives five or six nocturnal exchanges, then disconnects from the cycler to have one long (10 to 12 hour) diurnal exchange. The diurnal dwell volume is often less than that used with the nightly cycles. This technique has been well accepted in numerous pediatric centers.[36,37] Our own recent experience is reflected by von Lilien and associates, who reported that 30 of 70 children on CAPD converted to CCPD.[38] The main reasons are that CCPD is much less labor-intensive than CAPD and does not require a bag change in the middle of the day. The incidence of peritonitis and the metabolic control achieved are similar with CAPD and CCPD. Table 13-1 compares CAPD and CCPD according to several criteria. Because of concern that CCPD provides insufficient dialysis over the long term, CAPD remains the most popular method of dialysis in adults. To overcome this concern, tidal volume peritoneal dialysis has been attempted in adults. This technique requires the instillation of a large dwell volume (approximately 3 liters), which is then partially exchanged several times during an 8 to 10 hour

Table 13-1. Comparison of Chronic Ambulatory and Continuous Cyclic Peritoneal Dialysis

Criterion	Optimal Dialysis	Reason for Preference
Clearance of "middle" molecules	CAPD	Theoretically better with prolonged dwell
Convenience	CCPD	Less need to connect/disconnect
School/work attendance	CCPD	No mid-day exchange
Cost	CAPD	Cycler not required
Freedom to Travel	CAPD	Most cyclers bulky
Risk of Peritonitis	No difference	CCPD theoretically better
Appetite	CCPD	Reduced or no dwell volume during day

period. This method of dialysis is reported to be 20 percent more efficient than intermittent peritoneal dialysis for similar dialysate volumes.

CAPD TECHNIQUE

The current technique for CAPD relies on soft plastic bags. Modifications introduced by Oreopoulos[14] have markedly reduced the incidence of peritonitis. Improvements in technique continue to be made; nevertheless, the peritonitis rate—generally and at our hospital—remains at one episode per 11.8 patient months of dialysis, which is higher than the rate in adults.[38] The chronic peritoneal catheter is fitted with a special titanium adaptor that has a Luer-lok connector to a plastic tube (CAPD solution transfer set) with a locking connection. The catheter ends in a special spike and is easily inserted into the dialysis bag. Strict sterile technique is essential when changing a bag. The tube should be changed only by a person who has been specially trained, or by a nurse who is experienced in CAPD. After the dialysis fluid has entered the peritoneal cavity, the empty bag is clamped off, folded, and carried under the patient's clothing or in a small purse. After six to eight hours, the patient drains the dialysate into the previously folded bag, removes the spike from the used bag, and reconnects it into a fresh new dialysate bag. A variety of methods whereby patients are disconnected from their bag between exchanges [e.g., Ultraset (Baxter Healthcare Corp), Biocap (Abbott Labs)] are undergoing study. These will probably prove more convenient for patients, and may over the long term reduce peritonitis rates.

Most adults require four bag exchanges per day, seven days a week, using a volume of 1 to 2 liters, depending on the patient's size. If the plasma creatinine is less than 12 to 13 mg/dl, it may be possible to perform only three bag exchanges per day. Some adults are maintained on three 3-liter exchanges per day.[39] When five exchanges are required, CAPD is generally considered too laborious and time-consuming for the patient, and another type of dialysis, such as intermittent peritoneal dialysis (IPD) or continuous cyclic peritoneal dialysis (CCPD), should be considered. Chronic peritoneal dialysis is the treatment of choice for children with end-stage renal disease unless contraindicated by the conditions listed in Table 13-2. The problem of patient selection among adults is more difficult.[40] Better means are needed for deciding which patients will do well on CAPD. Twardowski and colleagues have proposed the use of a standardized peritoneal equilibration test to determine which patients are most suited to CAPD as opposed to dialysis modalities

Table 13-2. Contraindications to Chronic Peritoneal Dialysis in Children

Inadequate social circumstances
Severe bowel adhesions
Imminent need for abdominal surgery
Likelihood of early transplant
Colostomy, ileostomy
Diaphragmatic leak, hydrothorax (absolute contraindication)

with short dwell exchanges.[41] Using measurements of creatinine, sodium, and glucose transfer, they have suggested that patients with high average peritoneal solute transfer rates can be differentiated from patients with low solute transfer rates, and the optimal dialysis method prescribed accordingly.

There are basic requirements in setting up a CAPD program.[42] To start hastily without proper organization can be counterproductive. In addition to having the proper facilities and equipment, the doctors, nurses, and patients should be motivated and have a positive attitude. Correct insertion of the catheter is of the utmost importance for effective catheter function; without it the physician is ineffective in caring for the patient. Too often catheter insertion is considered a minor surgical procedure and left to the junior surgical resident. This is inappropriate. The surgeon should be aware that this catheter represents the patient's lifeline, and that its incorrect placement may result in leakage, peritonitis, and potential loss of ultrafiltration ability. Table 13-3 lists the techniques for breaking in a new chronic catheter. Dialysis is started immediately after surgery. The initial volume is small to prevent undue stretching of the wound with consequent fluid leakage. The actual CAPD training takes about two weeks. Patients are taught how to change the dialysis bag, do a dressing change, change the connecting tube, and measure blood pressure. They are also taught the importance of diet, the physiology of dialysis, and the signs and early treatment of peritonitis. Thereafter, they are discharged from the hospital. Blood work should be done initially every two weeks and then monthly. The patient must see the physician every month, and keep in close contact (at least weekly) with the CAPD nurse. Home visits are desirable.

Table 13-3. Chronic Peritoneal Catheter "Break In" Routine

Each case must be individualized to take account of the patient's size and the integrity of the peritoneal membrane. Discuss with the surgeon any concerns, including the initial dialysate volume.

- Initially run 10 ml/kg body weight 1.5% dialysate with no dwell time for four hours. If dialysate is clear and draining well, start a 10-minute dwell time for six hours. Add prophylactic heparin (500 U/L), cefazolin (250 mg/liter), and tobramycin (8 mg/liter) for the first 48 hours.
- After the 10-hour "break in" period, patients who do not need urgent dialysis or entrance to CAPD can be capped off; inject 3 ml (1000 U/ml) heparin into catheter. For patients in need of dialysis and/or entrance in CAPD, start one-hour dwell for 24 hours, then two-hour dwell for 24 hours, and then four-hour dwell for 24 hours.
- The exchange volume is gradually increased, as in the following examples:

	Start (ml)	Finish (ml)
10 kg patient	100	300
20 kg patient	250	500
30 kg patient	300	750
40 kg patient	400	1000

CAPD may commence after the 24 hours of four- to six-hour dwell time. Prophylactic antibiotic and heparin may then be discontinued.

PERITONITIS

Many reports attest to the improved sense of well-being experienced by patients maintained on CAPD. Nevertheless, the major problem of peritonitis must be overcome before CAPD can be truly considered an alternative life-support system for end-stage renal disease. Many episodes of peritonitis can be traced to a break in sterile technique. Cloudy fluid accompanied by fever and abdominal pain are indicative of peritonitis. Infants with peritonitis tend to draw up their legs.

Once almost entirely the preserve of surgeons, peritonitis related to CAPD is now managed by physicians. Although it varies in severity, it can be mild enough to be managed on an outpatient basis when treatment is started early. The suspected patient should be seen as soon as possible by a doctor to establish a diagnosis.

Care must be taken in handling the cloudy peritoneal fluid so that the causal organisms

Table 13-4. Antibiotic Dosing Guidelines for the Treatment of Peritonitis in Chronic Ambulatory Peritoneal Dialysis

	Half-Life (hours)			Dose[a]			
				Initial		Maintenance	
	Normal	ESRD	CAPD	mg/kg	mg/2L bag	mg/L	mg/2L bag
Aminoglycosides							
Amikacin	1.6	39	ND	5.0–7.5	350–500	6–7.5	12–15
Gentamicin	2.2	53	32	1.5–1.7	120	4–6	8–12
Netilmicin	2.1	42	ND	1.5–2.0	140	4–6	8–12
Tobramycin	2.5	58	36	1.5–1.7	120	4–6	9–12
Cephalosporins							
Cefamandole	1.0	10	8.0	—	1000	ND	ND
Cefazolin	2.2	28	27	—	500–1000	125–250	250–500
Cefoperazone	1.8	2.3	2.2	—	2000	500	1000
Cefotaxime	0.9	2.5	2.4	—	2000	250	500
Cefoxitin	0.8	20	15	—	1000	100	200
Ceftazidime	1.8	26	16	—	1000	125	250
Ceftizoxime	1.6	28	11	—	1000	125	250
Ceftriaxone	8.0	15	13	—	1000	ND	ND
Cefuroxime	1.3	18	15	—	1500	250	500
Cephalothin	0.2	3.7	ND	—	2000	250	500
Moxalactam	2.2	20	16	—	1000	ND	ND
Cephradine	0.9	12	ND	—	500	125–250	250–500
					1000 PO	NA	NA
Cephalexin	0.8	19	9	—	1000 PO	NA	NA
Penicillins							
Ampicillin	1.3	15	ND	—	500	50	100
Azthocillin	0.9	5.1	ND	—	500	250	500
Mezlocillin	1.0	4.3	ND	—	3000 IV	3000/12 h IV	ND
Piperacillin	1.2	3.9	ND	—	4000 IV	4000/12 h IV	ND
Ticarcillin	1.2	15	ND	—	2000 IV	2000/12 h IV	ND
Vancomycin and others							
Vancomycin	6.9	161	83	—	1000	15	30
Aztreonam	2.0	7.0	7.1	—	1000	250	500
Ciprofloxacin	4.0	8.0	13	—	750 PO	ND	ND
Clindamycin	2.8	2.8	ND	—	300	150	300
Erythromycin	2.1	4.0	ND	—	300	75	150
Metronidazole	7.9	7.7	11	—	500 PO/IV	ND	ND
Rifampin	4	8	ND	—	600 PO	NA	NA
Sulfamethoxazole	10	13	14	—	1600 PO	100–200	200–400
Trimethoprim	14	33	34	—	320 PO	20–40	40–80
Antifungals							
Amphotericin	360	360	ND	—	0.5	0.5	1
Flucytosine	4.2	115	ND	—	3000 PO	NA	NA
					200	50–100	100–200
Ketoconazole	2	1.8	2.4	—	400 PO	NA	NA
Miconazole	24	25	ND	—	100	50	100

[a] All doses are calculated for a 70 kg person who is using standard 2L bags. The route of administration is intraperitoneal unless otherwise specified. These data should only be utilized as initial "guidelines." Individualized dosing is recommended when possible.

The pharmacokinetic data and dosing recommendations presented here are based on published literature reviewed through January 1987 and personal experience. Those dosage recommendations that differ from product labelling are based on more recent experience.

There is no evidence that mixing different antibiotics in dialysis fluid (except for aminoglycosides and penicillins) is deleterious for the drugs or patients. Do not use the same syringe to mix antibiotics.

ESRD = creatinine clearance at 10 mg/min, patient not on dialysis; NA = not applicable; ND = no data; IV = intravenous; PO = oral.

(From Keane et al,[43a] with permission.)

can be successfully isolated.[43] The choice of antibiotic may be influenced by the gram stain of the fluid. In most centers, a first-generation cephalosporin (e.g., cefazolin) is used routinely for gram-positive organisms and tobramycin for gram-negative organisms. Both antibiotics are used if the gram stain is negative but bacterial peritonitis is suspected. Usually these two antibiotics are adequate; however, depending on the culture, it may be necessary to change the antibiotic. Table 13-4 lists a number of antibiotics that can be used in the dialysate.[43a]

Current management of peritonitis involves lavage of the peritoneal cavity three times with no dwell time, and then with the addition of the appropriate antibiotic plus heparin (500 U/liter of dialysate). The precise treatment of peritonitis is shown in Table 13-5. The initial exchange after lavage contains a loading dose of cefazolin and/or tobramycin. Intraperitoneal antibiotics are continued for 7 to 14 days. In some patients, oral antibiotic is administered for an additional two weeks.

The general trend is toward reducing the rate of peritonitis in centers with established CAPD programs. This reduction is accomplished in part through improved aseptic technique for handling the tubing and quick action whenever a spike has been contaminated. Some centers advocate a tube change, whereas others will soak the spike in povidone-iodine. Peritonitis results are usually calculated by dividing the cumulative total patient dialysis months by the number of episodes of peritonitis, and are expressed as one episode of peritonitis per number of patient-months of CAPD. The average incidence is one episode of peritonitis for every 6 to 12 patient-months on CAPD.

The causal organisms most frequently implicated in peritonitis are from the skin, such as *Staphylococcus epidermidis* and *Staphylococcus aureus*. Eosinophilic peritonitis[44] has also been described, but the etiology is unknown. *Candida* peritonitis has been reported,[45] especially in diabetic patients, and it is usually necessary to remove the chronic peritoneal catheter to eradicate this infection. Singlas[46] described his success with intraperitoneal co-trimoxazole in adults on CAPD. Slingeneyer[47] used an in-line bacteriologic filter (Twen millipore) to prevent peritonitis, with encouraging results; this procedure prolongs the time needed for a bag change, but does offer a back-up system in case of contamination. Ash has reported the effect of using a Peridex filter on peritonitis rates.[48]

The incidence of culture-negative or sterile peritonitis is variable (0 to 30 percent), and is lower in established centers where the cloudy dialysate is thoroughly and meticulously cultured. One must do a careful bacteriologic assessment of a suspected peritoneal fluid, because the organism may be present in small numbers and therefore difficult to culture. Usually the blood culture is sterile. If a gram-negative or particularly a mixed growth is encountered, a bowel perforation should be suspected. Routinely culturing peritoneal fluid to diagnose peritonitis at an early point has been proposed. Zaruba and Oliveri[49] have been able to make an early diagnosis of peritonitis by home culturing.

Table 13-5. Treatment of Peritonitis for Patients on Chronic Ambulatory Peritoneal Dialysis

When peritonitis is suspected:
  Obtain specimen for gram stain, cell count, culture, and sensitivity.
  Three exchanges of dialysate without antibiotic; no dwell time.
  Resume CAPD schedule. If gram-positive organism is found on gram stain, add cefazolin[a] to dialysate (500 mg/liter to the first exchange and 250 mg/liter to subsequent exchanges).
  If gram-negative organism is found, add tobramycin to dialysate (1.7 mg/kg body weight to the first and 8 mg/liter to subsequent exchanges).
  If no organism is found or if gram stain is not obtained, add 500 mg of cefazolin per liter of dialysate plus 1.7 mg/kg body weight of tobramycin for first exchange after lavage, and then 250 mg cefazolin and 8 mg tobramycin per liter of dialysate.

[a] Any first-generation cephalosporin may be substituted.

HEMATOLOGIC RESPONSE

There are many metabolic aspects of CAPD that require further investigation. Many centers have reported an increase in blood hemoglobin concentration, but this has not been adequately explained. Patients on CAPD have less blood loss than those on hemodialysis. Since CAPD is reported to be more efficient in removing middle molecules from uremic patients, it may improve erythrocyte production by the bone marrow. Improved control of hydration, enabling the attainment of a true dry weight and a rise in red blood cell mass unrelated to changes in erythropoietin, has been reported.[50] Early experience using human recombinant erythropoietin is encouraging, and suggests that the frequent transfusions required by many dialysis patients may soon be unnecessary, and that anemia will no longer be a major problem for this population.

NUTRITION

Obesity can be a complication of CAPD for some patients, although it is unusual in children. Patients on CAPD are maintained on a relatively free diet, and in addition receive extra dextrose from the dialysis fluid (approximately 200 g of dextrose per day). The extra dextrose intake may play an etiologic role in causing an abnormal lipoprotein profile. The reduction in low density lipoprotein (LDL) cholesterol[51] associated with the increase in plasma cholesterol and triglyceride is of concern. Thus, CAPD patients may be at increased risk of developing atherosclerosis. Carnitine deficiency in dialysis patients has also been suspected as a cause of lipid disturbance.[52]

GROWTH

Children with severe renal insufficiency do not grow well. This lack of growth is also observed when they are managed by dialysis, and is explained in part by a poor caloric intake.[53] We reported our experience in 17 children aged 0.4 to 18.5 years who were managed by CAPD for longer than five months at The Hospital for Sick Children, Toronto.[54] Growth was considered normal in 10, fair in 6 others and poor in only 1. Growth velocity indices in the CAPD patients were significantly better than in 18 children receiving hemodialysis, and did not differ significantly from 20 who had undergone transplantation. Further details of growth patterns in children on CAPD were provided by Watson and colleagues, who reported poor growth in prepubertal patients beyond infancy, while infants and pubertal children generally grew normally.[55]

While many reasons have been proposed to explain the growth delay seen in children with chronic renal failure, poor nutrition is undoubtedly the major cause. Younger children (less than six years of age) on CAPD absorb more glucose and lose more protein via the peritoneal route than older children.[56] The very young child on CAPD eats very poorly, but the reason is not known. The dialysis compounds this nutritional problem by causing a continuous loss of protein, albumin, and amino acids in the dialysate.[57,58] Although the amount of amino acids lost in the dialysate of adults (about 2 g/day) is not considered significant, this may not be true for small children. Nutritional hypoproteinemia is observed in young patients on CAPD, and edema related to hypoalbuminemia is seen. Amino acids (1 percent Travasol without electrolytes) have been added to 1.5 percent dialysate to prevent amino acid loss.[59] This technique was also used by Jackson and colleagues.[60] We have studied the short-term effects of amino acid dialysis,[61] and long-term trials are currently being conducted to assess the safety and efficacy of this technique. Nasogastric and gastrostomy tubes may also be used to supplement the patient's diet; the presence of gastrostomy tubes is seldom associated with the development of peritonitis.[62]

RENAL OSTEODYSTROPHY

It has been known for a century that renal failure could cause rickets. Renal osteodystrophy is a spectrum of skeletal abnormalities seen in patients with chronic kidney failure. Children seem to be especially sensitive to the metabolic and hormonal disturbances seen in uremia. Hewitt and associates[63] described the experience of 15 children managed by CAPD over a period of 1.3 to 2.4 years. Since CAPD provides a more steady-state control of biochemical values than hemodialysis, it was anticipated there would be a reduced incidence of osteodystrophy. Although most patients experienced improved or unchanged skeletal status, deterioration was noted in some. Paunier and associates[64] reported a similar experience, and demonstrated that higher doses of vitamin D metabolites were successful in normalizing elevated plasma parathyroid hormone (PTH) levels. More recently, Delmez and co-workers[65] have shown that an increased dialysate calcium level causes a slight reduction in circulating PTH levels, and that $1,25\ (OH)_2D_3$ administered intraperitoneally raises ionized calcium and serum $1,25\ (OH)_2D_3$ levels and successfully suppresses PTH. However, further controlled studies are necessary to characterize the pharmacokinetics of vitamin D administered intraperitoneally, as well as the long-term effects of this mode of treatment.

RENAL TRANSPLANTATION

It is possible to perform renal transplantation successfully in patients managed by peritoneal dialysis. In a study of 203 cadaveric renal transplants, Cardella[66] and Stefanidis and associates[67] found that the survival of patients and grafts was the same whether the pretransplant treatment was hemodialysis or peritoneal dialysis. The peritoneal catheter is removed at the time of transplantation or prior to discharge from the hospital after surgery. In patients with unstable renal function following transplantation, the peritoneal catheter is occasionally left in place longer. These catheters are capped off and flushed weekly with heparin to maintain patency. Two of our patients developed *Pseudomonas* peritonitis in this situation. This underlies the need for strict catheter care in such patients, and for catheter removal at the earliest opportunity. Our usual policy is to place the transplanted kidney into the body in a retroperitoneal position. We are concerned about an intraperitoneal transplant in a CAPD patient in view of the serious consequences that could ensue at the vascular anastomosis if peritonitis occurred. In small children, intraperitoneal placement of the transplant may be infeasible because of the size of the donor kidney. In this circumstance, if the donor is a cadaver, the peritoneal catheter is always removed at the time of surgery and a central venous line suitable for hemodialysis is inserted. However, because of improved results, we now recommend the use of living, related donors when transplantation is necessary in children less than three or four years of age. In preparation for transplantation in such children, the peritoneal catheter can be removed electively two to four weeks prior to transplantation, and hemodialysis can be instituted. Alternatively, provided satisfactory growth and development can be attained in infants with chronic renal failure, transplantation may often be postponed until the child is bigger and the likelihood of a successful transplant greater.

CONSIDERATIONS IN SELECTING CAPD AND/OR PERITONEAL DIALYSIS

Neither CAPD nor peritoneal dialysis is any longer a second-choice mode of dialysis. However, a degree of caution is still necessary, since further refinements of both techniques are required. The incidence of peritonitis must be reduced to a rate of not more than one episode per 24 months of CAPD treatment at most. In addition, the contents of the solution must be improved to contain the proper concentrations of calcium, magnesium, and the particular bicarbonate precursor that is used. The efficacy and safety of adding amino acids to the dialysate need to be investigated.

ADVANTAGES OF CAPD

Chronic ambulatory peritoneal dialysis offers many advantages (Table 13-6). Training the patient or parent requires only one to two weeks and is relatively easy. Because CAPD is continuous, it will not cause the "disequilibrium syndrome." It provides certain "freedoms," such as an almost unrestricted diet, freedom to travel (even to go camping), freedom to work or attend school on a regular basis, and more freedom in controlling individual dialysis needs. Furthermore, CAPD implies home dialysis, an important benefit for children who in the past usually required in-center hemodialysis. Since children experience more difficulty undergoing hemodialysis than do adults, those requiring this treatment must live near a specialized pediatric center until a renal transplant can be found. This requirement can present a hardship and major psychological upset for any family whose home is a long distance from the medical center. With CAPD, children can return home and come back to the medical center only when the transplant is available.

DISADVANTAGES OF CAPD

Unfortunately, there are problems with CAPD, the most serious being the risk of peritonitis. Catheter care can be tedious (a daily shower and catheter care versus a weekly dressing change). Abdominal hernias are common in all age groups and usually require surgical repair. Moreover, although CAPD involves less severe cardiovascular stress than hemodialysis, hypotension can be a problem, and may be related to removing components of the renin-angiotensin system.[68] Eventually, patients and/or parents often become weary of the constant routine of CAPD and may require periods of relief (either admission to the hospital or home care assistance).

CONTRAINDICATIONS TO CAPD

There are a number of contraindications to CAPD (Table 13-2). With more experience, it should become possible to predict which patients will not be able to cope with CAPD. Obviously, good hygiene is important. Another problem is the inability of some patients to handle the new freedom and independence that accompany discontinuance of the thrice weekly contacts with the hemodialysis unit. Abdominal stomas may be an additional risk for peritonitis, although we have not found this to be the case in children with urine drainage to the skin. The diabetic patient with end-stage renal disease who is blind or has a severe

Table 13-6. Advantages and Disadvantages of Chronic Peritoneal Dialysis in Children

Advantages	Disadvantages
No abrupt changes in body composition	Peritonitis risk
	Catheter care
Free to travel (even to camp, since no electricity is needed)	Abdominal/inguinal hernia
	Protein loss
Home dialysis, including children	Urea clearance 60% of that with hemodialysis
Nearly free diet	Hypotension
Require less supervision/contact	Fatigue/monotony for patient or parent
No blood loss	
Higher hemoglobin concentration	
Improved school attendance	

reduction in visual acuity can easily contaminate the "spike" while trying to insert it into the dialysis bag. However, CAPD may be the dialysis of choice for diabetic patients, and techniques and equipment have been developed to enable people with poor vision to perform bag changes. Finally, we have seen one child who developed large pleural effusions when CAPD was started, presumably as a result of a pleuroperitoneal connection. This necessitated discontinuance of CAPD.

THE FUTURE

The future for peritoneal dialysis holds great promise. Control of peritonitis and establishment of the ideal dialysate composition are goals that can be attained in the near future. A portable pump peritoneal dialysis system permitting recirculation of the dialysate offers an interesting prospect, since fewer dialysate exchanges (one or two per day) would not only provide more free time but would also reduce the incidence of peritonitis. For the very young and the very old patient, CAPD may be especially beneficial. It can easily be applied to infants, and hopefully will allow them time to attain sufficient growth so that the prognosis for a successful renal transplant will be good. For the very old patient, CAPD may be a realistic alternative to renal transplantation. Continuous cyclic peritoneal dialysis (CCPD) is now being assessed by a number of CAPD programs. With the availability of long-dwell automated pediatric cyclers, pediatric centers are now using CCPD on specific patients, such as infants in whom adequate ultrafiltration is difficult to achieve by the usual CAPD techniques. Dialysis can be done automatically at night, followed by a prolonged daytime dwell. This procedure may prevent parent/patient "burnout." The respective roles of CAPD and CCPD in providing home peritoneal dialysis remain to be seen.

REFERENCES

1. Ganter G: Ueger die Beseitigung giftiger stroffe aus dem Blute durch Dialyse. Munch Med Wochschr 11:1478, 1923
2. Boen ST: Peritoneal Dialysis in Clinical Medicine. p. 128. Charles C Thomas, Springfield, IL, 1964
3. Meadow SR, Cameron JS, Ogg CS, Saxton HM: Children referred for acute dialysis. Arch Dis Child 46:221, 1971
4. Brewer TE, Caldwell FT, Patterson RM, Flanigan WJ: Indwelling peritoneal (Tenckhoff) dialysis catheter: experience with 24 patients. JAMA 219:1011, 1972
5. Palmer RA, Quinton WE, Gray JE: Prolonged peritoneal dialysis for chronic renal failure. Lancet 1:700, 1964
6. Tenckhoff H, Schechter H: A bacteriologically safe peritoneal access device. Trans Am Soc Artif Intern Organs 14:181, 1968
7. Lasker N: Chronic peritoneal dialysis. Pa Med 74:67, 1971
8. Tenckhoff H, Meston B, Shilipetar G: A simplified automatic dialysis system. Trans Am Soc Artif Intern Organs 18:436, 1972
9. Feldman W, Baliah T, Drummond KN: Intermittent peritoneal dialysis in the management of chronic renal failure in children. Am J Dis Child 116:30, 1968
10. Diaz-Buxo JA, Chandler JT, Farmer CD, Smith DL: Chronic peritoneal dialysis at home—A comparison with hemodialysis. Trans Am Soc Artif Intern Organs 23:191, 1977
11. Brouhard BH, Berger M, Cunningham RJ, et al: Home peritoneal dialysis in children. Trans Am Soc Artif Intern Organs 25:90, 1979
12. Popovich RP, Moncrief JW, Dechard JB, et al: The definition of a novel portable/wearable equilibrium peritoneal dialysis technique. (Abstract) Am Soc Artif Intern Organs 5:64, 1976
13. Popovich RP, Moncrief JW, Nolph KD, et al: Continuous ambulatory peritoneal dialysis. Ann Intern Med 88:449, 1978
14. Oreopoulos DG, Robson M, Izatt S, et al: A simple and safe technique for continuous ambulatory peritoneal dialysis (CAPD). Trans Am Soc Artif Intern Organs 24:484, 1978

15. Balfe JW, Irwin MA: Continuous ambulatory peritoneal dialysis in pediatrics. p. 131. In LeGrain M (ed): Continuous Ambulatory Peritoneal Dialysis. Exerpta Medica, Amsterdam, 1980
16. Baum M, Powell D, Calvin S, et al: Continuous ambulatory peritoneal dialysis in children: Comparison with hemodialysis. N Engl J Med 307:1537, 1982
17. Helfrich GB, Winchester JF: What is the best technique for implantation of a peritoneal catheter? Perit Dial Bull 2:132, 1982
18. Hogg RJ, Coln D, Chang J, et al: The Toronto Western Hospital Catheter in a Pediatric Dialysis Program. Am J Kid Dis 3:219, 1983
19. Watson AR, Vigneux A, Hardy BE, Balfe JW: Six-year experience with CAPD catheters in children. Perit Dial Bull 5:119, 1985
20. Vigneux A, Hardy BE, Balfe JW: Chronic peritoneal catheter in children—One or two dacron cuffs? Perit Dial Bull 1:151, 1981
21. Block RA, Taylor B, Frederick G: Intraperitoneal infusion of streptokinase in the treatment of recurrent peritonitis. Perit Dial Bull 3:162, 1983
22. Mistry CD, Mallick NP, Gokal R: Ultrafiltration with an isosmotic solution during long peritoneal dialysis exchanges. Lancet 2:178, 1987
23. Esperanca MJ, Collins DL: Peritoneal dialysis efficiency in relation to body weight. J Pediatr Surg 1:162, 1966
24. Henderson LW: The problem of peritoneal membrane area and permeability. Kidney Int 3:409, 1973
25. Siegel NJ, Brown RS: Peritoneal clearance of ammonia and creatinine in a neonate. J Pediatr 82:1044, 1973
26. Nolph KD, Whitcomb ME, Schrier RW: Mechanisms for inefficient peritoneal dialysis in acute renal failure associated with heat stress and exercise. Ann Intern Med 71:317, 1969
27. Robson M, Oreopoulos DG, Izatt S, et al: Influence of exchange volume and dialysate flow rate on solute clearance in peritoneal dialysis. Kidney Int 14:486, 1978
28. Babb AL, Farrell PC, Uvelli DA, Scribner BH: Hemodialyzer evaluation by examination of solute molecular spectra. Trans Am Soc Artif Intern Organs 18:98, 1972
29. Henderson LW: Peritoneal ultrafiltration dialysis enhanced urea transfer using hypertonic peritoneal dialysis fluid. J Clin Invest 45:950, 1966
30. Kohaut EC, Alexander SR: Ultrafiltration in the young patient on CAPD. p. 221. In Moncrief JW, Popovich RP (eds): CAPD Update: Continuous Ambulatory Peritoneal Dialysis. Masson, Paris, 1981
31. Balfe JW, Hanning RM, Vigneux A, Watson AR: A comparison of water and solute movement in young and older children on CAPD. p. 14. In Fine RN, Schärer K, Mehls O (eds): CAPD in Children. Springer-Verlag, Berlin, 1984
32. Miller RB, Tassistro CR: Peritoneal dialysis. N Engl J Med 281:945, 1969
33. Maher JF: Peritoneal mass transport. Pharmacologic and hormonal influences. Dial Transplant 7:825, 1978
34. Nolph KD, Stoltz ML, Maher JF: Altered peritoneal permeability in patients with systemic vasculitis. Ann Intern Med 75:753, 1971
35. Diaz-Buxo JA, Walker PJ, Farmer CD, et al: Continuous cyclic peritoneal dialysis (CCPD). Kidney Int 19:145, 1981
36. Brem AS, Toscano AM: Continuous-cycling peritoneal dialysis for children: an alternative to hemodialysis treatment. Pediatrics 74:254, 1984
37. Alliapoulos JC, Salusky IB, Hall T, et al: Comparison of continuous cycling peritoneal dialysis with continuous ambulatory peritoneal dialysis in children. J Pediatr 105:721, 1984
38. von Lilien T, Salusky IB, Boechat I, et al: Five years' experience with continuous ambulatory or continuous cycling peritoneal dialysis in children. J Pediatr 111:513, 1987
39. Twardowski ZJ, Prowant BF, Nolph KD, et al: High volume, low frequency continuous ambulatory peritoneal dialysis. Kidney Int 23:64, 1983
40. Fenton SSA, McCready W, Cattran DC, et al: Selected clinical aspects of continuous ambulatory peritoneal dialysis. p. 107. In LeGrain M (ed): Continuous Ambulatory Peritoneal Dialysis. Exerpta Medica, Amsterdam, 1980
41. Twardowski ZJ, Nolph KD, Khanna R, et al: Peritoneal equilibration test. Perit Dial Bull 7:138, 1987

42. Oreopoulos DG: Requirements for the organization of a continuous ambulatory peritoneal dialysis program. Nephron 24:261, 1979
43. Vas SI: Microbiologic aspects of chronic ambulatory peritoneal dialysis. Kidney Int 23:83, 1983
43a. Keane WF, Everett ED, Fine RN, et al: CAPD related peritonitis management and antibiotic therapy recommendations. Perit Dial Bull 7(2)55, 1987
44. Humayun HM, Ing TS, Daugirdas JT, et al: Peritoneal fluid eosinophilia in patients undergoing maintenance peritoneal dialysis. Arch Intern Med 141:1172, 1981
45. Bayer AS, Blumenkrantz MJ, Montgomerie JZ, et al: Candida peritonitis: report of 22 cases and review of the English literature. Am J Med 61:832, 1976
46. Singlas E, Rottembourg J, de Martin A, et al: Pharmacokinetics of Co-Trimoxazole using the peritoneal route: consequence for the treatment of peritonitis in patients maintained on peritoneal dialysis. p. 63. In Moncrief JW, Popovich RP (ed): CAPD Update: Continuous Ambulatory Peritoneal Dialysis. Masson, Paris, 1981
47. Slingeneyer A, Liendo-Liendo C, Mion C: Continuous ambulatory peritoneal dialysis with a bacteriological filter on the dialysate infusion line. p. 59. In LeGrain M (eds): Continuous Ambulatory Peritoneal Dialysis. Exerpta Medica, Amsterdam, 1980
48. Ash SR, Horswell R Jr, Heeter EM, Bloch R: Effect of the Peridex filter on peritonitis rates in a CAPD population. Perit Dial Bull 3:89, 1983
49. Zaruba K, Oliveri M: Early diagnosis of peritoneal infection during continuous ambulatory peritoneal dialysis by the dialysate-digest medium-tube method. Lancet 2:1226, 1980
50. Saltissi D, Coles GA, Napier JAF, Bentley P: The hematological response to continuous ambulatory peritoneal dialysis. Clin Nephrol 22:21, 1984
51. Norbeck HE: Lipid abnormalities in continuous ambulatory peritoneal dialysis patients. p. 298. In LeGrain M (ed): Continuous Ambulatory Peritoneal Dialysis. Exerpta Medica, Amsterdam, 1980
52. Bohmer T, Bergrem H, Eiklid K: Carnitine deficiency induced during intermittent haemodialysis for renal failure. Lancet 1:126, 1978
53. Simmons JM, Wilson CJ, Potter DE, Holliday MA: Relation of calorie deficiency to growth failure in children on haemodialysis and the growth response to calorie supplementation. N Engl J Med 285:653, 1971
54. Stefanidis CJ, Hewitt IK, Balfe JW: Growth in children receiving continuous ambulatory peritoneal dialysis. J Pediatr 102:681, 1983
55. Watson AR, Taylor J, Balfe JW: Growth in children on CAPD: a reappraisal. p. 171. In Khanna R, Nolph KD, Prowant B, et al (eds): Advances in Continuous Ambulatory Peritoneal Dialysis/1985. University of Toronto Press, Toronto, 1985
56. Balfe JW, Vigneux A, Willumsen J, Hardy BE: The use of CAPD in the treatment of children with end-stage renal disease. Perit Dial Bull 1:35, 1981
57. Berlyne GM, Lee HA, Giordano C, et al: Amino acid loss in peritoneal dialysis. Lancet 1:1339, 1967
58. Giordano C, De Danto NG, Capodicasa G, et al: Amino acid losses during CAPD. Clin Nephrol 14:230, 1980
59. Oreopoulos DG, Balfe JW, Khanna R, et al: Further experience with the use of amino acid containing dialysate in peritoneal dialysis. p. 109. In Moncrief JW, Popovich RP (ed): CAPD Update: Continuous Ambulatory Peritoneal Dialysis. Masson, Paris, 1981
60. Jackson MA, Talbot S, Thomas DW, Lee HA: Prevention of amino acid losses during peritoneal dialysis. Postgrad Med J 55:533, 1979
61. Balfe JW, Hanning RM, Zlotkin SH: Amino acid dialysis in children on CAPD. p. 84. In RN Fine, K Scharer, O Mehls (eds): CAPD in Children. Springer-Verlag, Berlin, 1984
62. Levin L, Balfe JW, Geary D, et al: Gastrostomy tube feeding in children on CAPD. Perit Dial Bull 7:223, 1987
63. Hewitt IK, Stefanidis C, Reilly BJ, et al: Renal osteodystrophy in children undergoing continuous ambulatory peritoneal dialysis. J Pediatr 103:729, 1983
64. Paunier L, Salusky IB, Slatopolsky E, et al:

Renal osteodystrophy in children undergoing continuous ambulatory peritoneal dialysis. Pediatr Res 18:742, 1984
65. Delmez JA, Dougan CS, Gearing BK, et al: The effects of intraperitoneal calcitriol on calcium and parathyroid hormone. Kidney Int 31:795, 1987
66. Cardella CJ: Renal transplantation in patients on peritoneal dialysis. Perit Dial Bull 1:12, 1980
67. Stefanidis CJ, Balfe JW, Arbus GS, et al: Renal transplantation in children treated with continuous ambulatory peritoneal dialysis. Perit Dial Bull 3:5, 1983
68. Osmond DH, Loh AY, Abrams J, et al: "Prosubstrate" in plasma and erythropoietic activity in dialysates of humans on chronic peritoneal dialysis (CAPD). Physiologist 23:65(a), 1980

14

Special Problems of Hemodialysis and Peritoneal Dialysis in Adults

Edward T. Zawada, Jr
Fred Birch
Todd S. Ing
Anthony G. Salem

"In brief, all things *are* artificial; for nature is the art of God."
—Sir Thomas Browne, M.D.*

The era of long-term life support by artificial organs began with the successful implementation of chronic hemodialysis therapy over a quarter of a century ago. Chronic dialysis therapy is now commonplace, and is in fact almost mandated as an inalienable patient right. Its ready availability has given rise to a series of ethical problems, among them the appropriateness of offering life support to the most elderly patients (such as octogenarians) with end-stage renal disease. Today's ethical considerations pertaining to dialysis therapy will undoubtedly influence decisions in the future about the extension of other artificial organ support to geriatric patients. In this chapter we will begin with a short history of hemodialysis and peritoneal dialysis. We will then review the technology of the most common forms of dialysis equipment in use, followed by an outline of several special clinical problems faced by patients receiving chronic dialysis. We will conclude with a discussion of the need for research pertaining to yet unsolved problems in long-term human life extension by chronic dialysis therapy.

BRIEF HISTORY OF DIALYSIS

During World War II, Willem Kolff[1] attempted to treat patients with acute renal failure by routing their blood through a prototypic dialyzer: a series of semipermeable membranes soaking in a tank containing Ringer's solution. The blood traveled into this "dialyzer" by gravity; a rotating wooden drum milked the membranes to bring the blood back to the patient. Arterial access was required to deliver a quantity of blood sufficient to allow reasonable removal of waste products. Although successful in prolonging the life of the patient

---

* Favorite author of Sir William Osler, M.D.

and improving uremic symptoms, each dialysis required that a surgical procedure be performed to connect the patient's blood vessels to the dialysis equipment. In the 1960s, Quinton and Scribner[2] described their arteriovenous shunt, which was sewn into the patient's blood vessels. This shunt was made of tubing that was more pliable, caused less inflammation when left in place for a prolonged period, and was less likely to initiate clotting than previous materials used for this purpose. By connecting the arterial end of the tubing with the venous end, a continuous flow through the shunt was established, thus maintaining patency between dialysis treatments and obviating the need for anticoagulation. The Quinton-Scribner shunt allowed multiple use of the same blood vessel access site for dialysis, permitting more frequent dialysis with better control of uremia. In the mid-1960s a blood pump of the roller type was substituted for the rotating wooden drum of the dialyzer, and the semipermeable membrane was configured as a coiled tube designed to be immersed in a reservoir of dialysis solution. Access for hemodialysis was further improved by use of the arteriovenous fistula[3]—a completely subcutaneous connection between a peripheral artery and a peripheral vein, which could be accessed repeatedly by the percutaneous insertion of a needle. The arteriovenous fistula remains the most desirable form of hemodialysis access because it incorporates no foreign materials and because its subcutaneous position affords an effective barrier against bacterial infection. At times, however, the creation of an arteriovenous fistula was technically impossible; for such circumstances, the arteriovenous graft was developed: a vascular bridge made of saphenous vein, bovine carotid artery, Dacron, or Gore-Tex.[4] Most recently, double-lumen catheters were designed to be placed into a large vein by percutaneous insertion, in order to provide hemodialysis access for weeks or months without an unduly high incidence of clotting or infection.[5,6]

The efficiency of diffusive removal of nitrogenous wastes by dialysis was improved in the 1970s when machines were developed that pumped fresh, newly mixed dialysis solution through the dialysate reservoir to provide dialysis solution delivery in a single pass, maintaining at all times a maximum gradient for diffusion between the blood and the dialysate compartments.[7] In addition, ultrafiltration controllers were developed that allow one to remove predetermined amounts of ultrafiltrate during dialysis accurately and at an even pace.[8] Such accurate and even-paced removal of excess fluid minimizes the development of hypotension due to inadvertently abrupt and excessive ultrafiltration. In the mid-1970s, use of a small volume of dialysis solution was made possible through the employment of a sorbent cartridge to regenerate used dialysate on-line.[9] Finally, the geometry of the semipermeable membrane in the dialyzer was changed. The membrane was configured as a series of parallel plates or hollow fibers surrounded by dialysate, rather than in the form of a coil, and a number of membranes made of new, more biocompatible materials were developed.[10]

Peritoneal dialysis was also used to treat acute renal failure. The peritoneal membrane allows the diffusion of nitrogenous wastes from the patient's blood into a dialysate, which is subsequently drained by gravity. Initially, disposable catheters were placed percutaneously into the peritoneal cavity. The dialysate was contained in glass bottles, and a T-tubing arrangement was used to allow its infusion and drainage under sterile conditions. Because the inflexible peritoneal catheter could remain in the abdomen for only about 72 hours due to the risk of peritonitis, peritoneal dialysis was not at first as feasible as hemodialysis for chronic life support of uremic patients. In the late 1960s, Tenckhoff and others developed a pliable peritoneal catheter equipped with two thick cuffs of synthetic material in its middle.[11] The outer (or proximal) cuff allowed the ingrowth of subcutaneous connective tissue, while the inner (or distal) cuff allowed the ingrowth of peritoneal mesothelial cells. Reinforced by such cellular growths, these cuffs sealed off the catheter tract and prevented bacteria from tracking from the skin surface along the catheter into the peritoneal cavity. As a result of this innovation the risk of infection was markedly reduced, making it feasible to perform chronic peritoneal dialysis via a single catheter. Continuous high-flow, and then cyclic, lower-flow delivery systems for peritoneal dialysis solution were produced[12]; these systems allowed patients to perform peritoneal dialysis at night and to be free for normal daily activities in the daytime. In the late 1970s, the concept of continuous ambulatory peritoneal dialysis (CAPD) was developed.[13,14] In this technique a patient would fill, by gravity, his or her peritoneal cavity with dialysis solution contained in a plastic bag, and would then be free to perform routine daily activities while diffusion took place. With CAPD, no machines are used, and its benefits include only a short period of training and a high degree of patient self-sufficiency. Better techniques of connecting the required tubings, utilizing lever-driven systems, ultraviolet light exposure to reduce bacterial contamination,[15] and other novel means, are being developed and refined.

INDICATIONS AND EXCLUSIONS FOR HEMODIALYSIS AND PERITONEAL DIALYSIS

The most common indications for performing dialysis on an acute basis are hyperkalemia, fluid overload, severe metabolic acidosis, and symptoms of uremia.[16] The latter include nausea, decreasing appetite, vomiting, and altered mental status (ranging from somnolence to frank coma). Appearance of a pericardial friction rub due to uremic pericarditis is also an indication for acute dialysis. Often, dialysis is initiated before any of these problems develops if there is a steady rise in the serum urea nitrogen level to greater than 100 mg/dl, or where the serum creatinine value is greater than 10 mg/dl. Dialysis is initiated also when the glomerular filtration rate (GFR), as assessed by renal creatinine clearance, falls below 0.1 to 0.15 ml/min/kg body weight. Dialysis is often begun earlier in diabetic patients, in whom uremic symptoms may occur earlier.[17]

Exclusions for dialysis primarily comprise refusal by the patient or by the appropriate patient advocate; advanced disease in multiple systems of the body (e.g., advanced liver, pulmonary, or heart disease in addition to renal failure); advanced disease of the central nervous system (e.g., dementia due to Alzheimer's disease or multiple cerebrovascular accidents); or advanced malignancy. Two groups of patients previously excluded from dialysis were the very elderly and diabetic patients. In some countries (e.g., the United Kingdom), the very elderly are often not considered for dialysis treatments. In the United States, however, such patients are now commonly offered dialysis therapy without question, to the extent that patients in the 70 to 90-year-old group now represent the fastest growing segment of the dialysis population. In many medical centers, diabetic patients now represent the most numerous group of patients receiving dialysis. Even patients with advanced multisystem disease are occasionally offered dialysis on a trial basis while quality of life, burden on the family, and cost factors (e.g., cost of transportation and of repeated hospitalizations for acute illness) are being assessed. In the past, the presence of an advanced malignancy commonly led to automatic exclusion from consideration for dialysis. Most recently, however, improvement in the survival of patients with prostate cancer, breast cancer, hypernephroma, and multiple myeloma has favored the concept of offering support via dialysis, at least on a trial basis, to patients with various malignancies, even when the latter are far advanced.

The choice of peritoneal dialysis versus hemodialysis is more difficult in the case of chronic than in that of acute dialysis. For acute dialysis, peritoneal dialysis is frequently chosen when treating infants or very young children, or when hemodialysis machines or staff capable of performing hemodialysis are unavailable. Patients commonly excluded from peritoneal dialysis (for acute or chronic renal failure) are those with an unsuitable peritoneal membrane due to the presence of extensive adhesions, fibrosis, or malignancy. However, successful placement of a peritoneal catheter under direct vision, with the aid of a peritoneoscope, can sometimes be achieved in patients with only mild to moderate peritoneal disease.[18] In the chronic situation, peritoneal dialysis is usually chosen over hemodialysis for infants and small children, and for patients with severe cardiovascular disease, those with difficult-to-establish vascular access (e.g., diabetic patients), those who desire greater freedom to travel, and those who wish to perform home dialysis but do not have suitable partners to assist them.

TECHNICAL ASPECTS OF HEMODIALYSIS AND PERITONEAL DIALYSIS

Two main types of delivery system for dialysis solution are in common use today: the single-pass delivery system[19] and the sorbent system.[9] In a single-pass delivery machine, water is first passed through a water treatment unit, which removes ions and organic contaminants. This treated water is then routed into the single-pass machine, which also draws, from one or two separate sources, a concentrated solution of electrolytes (containing acetate or bicarbonate as a base). Apart from some minor differences, the product dialysis solution basically resembles Ringer's solution in composition. The machine also heats this solution to body temperature. A separate pump then draws the prepared dialysis solution into the dialysate compartment, so that the solution will be in contact with the non-blood side of the dialyzer membrane. The used dialysate is then routed to a drain. The dialysis solution flow rate is usually set at 500 to 800 ml/min.

The sorbent dialysis solution delivery system is quite portable and does not need a continuous supply of water, water pretreatment, or drainage. With this equipment, about 6 liters of tap water are poured into a dialysis solution reservoir along with a packet of electrolytes. The dialysis solution is circulated from the reservoir through the dialyzer and back again in a closed loop. A sorbent cartridge inserted distal to the dialyzer purifies the spent dialysate by removing nitrogenous and other wastes that enter the dialysate from the blood. A small infusion pump adds calcium and magnesium to the purified dialysate, since these ions are removed from the dialysate by the cartridge.

Both the single pass and the sorbent dialysis solution delivery systems incorporate a number of alarms or safety devices to assure that a physiologic dialysis solution is being delivered. The machine constantly tests the temperature and conductivity of the product dialysis solution. After returning from the dialyzer the dialysate is monitored for blood leakage by an optical-density measurement method. The blood pump is often incorporated into the dialysis solution delivery machine, so that alarms will turn off the pump if limits for maximal and minimal pressures are exceeded.

Because the diffusion of low molecular weight solutes proceeds quite rapidly during dialysis, their removal rises markedly as blood flow through the dialyzer is increased. The rate of diffusion depends not only on the surface area of the membrane but also on membrane permeability, dialyzer geometry, and dialyzer design. By way of diffusion the concentrations of toxic waste products in the blood are reduced, and abnormal blood electrolyte and acid-base values are corrected.

With regard to ultrafiltration, which also occurs during a hemodialysis treatment, the driving force for this type of transfer is the hydrostatic pressure gradient between the blood and the dialysate sides of the dialyzer membrane. The hydrostatic pressure gradient is the result of (1) the resistance to blood flow in the extracorporeal circuit (positive pressure on the blood side of the semipermeable membrane), and (2) an adjustable negative pressure intentionally created on the dialysate side of the membrane by the dialysis machine. The hydrostatic pressure gradient is called the transmembrane pressure (TMP). Fluid transfer across the membrane will depend not only on the TMP but also on the permeability of the membrane to water, the K_{UF}, which is expressed as the volume in milliliters of fluid that will pass through the membrane per millimeter of mercury of transmembrane pressure per hour.[20] Apart from high molecular weight substances such as proteins or protein-bound solutes, the composition of the ultrafiltrate is similar to that of plasma.

Ultrafiltration during dialysis is used to reduce body sodium and water contents accumulated during the interdialytic period. For most hemodialysis treatments, both diffusion and ultrafiltration occur simultaneously. It is, however, possible to separate the two processes: blood can be coursed through the dialyzer in the usual fashion, while the dialysis solution flow is routed so as to bypass the dialyzer entirely. Diffusion will then not occur, but diverting the dialysis solution away from the dialyzer will create a negative hydrostatic pressure in the enclosed dialysate compartment, allowing ultrafiltration to take place. This procedure is called isolated ultrafiltration,[21] and can be used to treat patients who need removal of excess fluid, but in whom no reductions in plasma solute concentrations are desired.

Peritoneal dialysis is accomplished with a catheter placed transabdominally into the space between the visceral and parietal layers of the peritoneal membrane. In this case the semipermeable membrane separating blood and dialysate consists of the walls of capillaries supplying the abdominal structures, the connective tissue between the capillaries and the peritoneal membrane, and the cells of the peritoneal membrane.[22] For acute peritoneal dialysis an inflexible catheter can be inserted percutaneously over a trocar or guidewire after the peritoneal cavity is filled with a dialysis solution via a smaller, plastic catheter. For chronic peritoneal dialysis a flexible catheter with one or two cuffs is placed into the peritoneal cavity either surgically or percutaneously. The most commonly used catheter for chronic peritoneal dialysis is a simple silastic tube with side ports for drainage and two cuffs for tissue ingrowth. Other catheter styles include those with proximal spirals or even surgically implantable proximal disks. Peritoneal dialysis solution can be introduced through the catheter into the peritoneal cavity from individual plastic bags either by gravity or with the aid of a cycler machine. The latter periodically allows metered volumes of dialysis solution to go into and to come out of the peritoneal cavity.

Diffusive transfer in peritoneal dialysis is similar to that in hemodialysis. The dialysis solution resembles that used in hemodialysis except that large quantities of dextrose are added to allow for osmotic removal of excess fluid. When the dialysis solution comes into contact with the peritoneal membrane, low molecular weight waste products such as urea and creatinine diffuse from the blood into the dialysate. The length of time (dwell time) that a dialysis solution is allowed to remain in the abdomen before it is drained determines the extent of diffusion. In acute dialysis the dwell time is usually about 20 minutes, after which time sufficient diffusion has occurred to result in a substantial transfer of waste products to the dialysate. As diffusion progresses, its efficiency falls due to a lessening of the concentration gradient between blood and dialysate. For this reason, short dwell times, which allow cycling of a larger total volume of dialysate through the abdomen and foster creation of higher concentration gradients, enhance waste product removal. For urea, near-total equilibration between blood and dialysate takes place after approximately 4 hours.[13] In treating patients with chronic renal failure, a popular mode of peritoneal dialysis is CAPD.[22-24] In CAPD, for patient convenience, the drainage of spent dialysate and reinfusion of new dialysis solution (an exchange) is performed every 4 to 5 hours during the day and once in the early morning after a 6- or 8-hour overnight dwell. Another mode of chronic peritoneal dialysis, known as cycler-assisted peritoneal dialysis (CCPD),[24,25] utilizes a cycler to infuse approximately 2 liters of dialysis solution every 2 hours or so during the night while the patient sleeps. During the day, the abdomen may or may not be left filled with a morning instillation of a fresh dialysis solution for a long-dwell daytime exchange. The advantage of CCPD over CAPD is that connection of the catheter to the dialysis solution source is performed only once daily, as opposed to five or six times in CAPD, thereby possibly reducing the risk of infection.

PROBLEMS WITH ACCESS IN PATIENTS UNDERGOING HEMODIALYSIS AND PERITONEAL DIALYSIS

The preferred hemodialysis access is an arteriovenous fistula in the non-dominant upper limb, between the radial artery and the cephalic vein.[26] Placement in the non-dominant upper limb allows the patient use of the dominant upper limb during dialysis for various purposes (e.g., to perform self-care dialysis if required). An arteriovenous fistula has a smaller chance of infection than an arteriovenous graft because it contains no foreign material (other than sutures or staples). Such arteriovenous fistulae can frequently be created in less than an hour of operating time, often under only regional anesthesia. One minor disadvantage of the arteriovenous fistula is that one has to wait a number of weeks before the fistula is mature enough to be used. Maturation is evidenced by dilatation of the veins downstream to the fistula in response to the increase in flow and pressure in these vessels. Such arterialization also results in thickening of the vein walls due to hypertrophy of the muscular layer. Maturation thus adds strength to the access and minimizes the likelihood of vessel tearing during needle insertion. The length of time for maturation of an arteriovenous fistula is variable, ranging from several weeks to several months. For this reason, the need for dialysis should be anticipated and planned in advance. When an arteriovenous fistula cannot be created surgically (usually because of previous vascular access surgery), a synthetic graft can be inserted between an artery and a vein. Placement of a graft is technically more difficult and requires more operating time, as well as, commonly, general anesthesia. In addition, the risks of thrombosis and infection are increased. Arteriovenous fistulae employing a synthetic graft, although not requiring a maturation period, ideally need a minimum period of 2 weeks before they can be used. This amount of time is needed for edema to resolve so as to allow for better palpation of the fistula, and for less traumatic needle insertion. Also, some time is required for fibroblasts to grow into the outer layers of the graft material and for endothelial cells to grow into the corresponding inner layers to strengthen the wall and limit the spread of any extravasated blood.

Access thrombosis and infection are among the most common reasons for hospitalization of hemodialysis patients. Thrombosis most often is presaged by stenosis of the access vein or of the anastomotic site. Often such stenosis is amenable to repair by revision of the anastomosis or by dilatation of a stenotic venous segment using balloon angioplasty. After repair, an access can sometimes continue to be used for ongoing hemodialysis treatments. When thrombosis is due to poor arterial inflow, then a new access must be created at a new site. In such situations a double-lumen catheter in the subclavian vein can often be used to provide temporary access for a period of weeks.[6]

Infection of a hemodialysis access site is also a serious problem, sometimes leading to early access failure and the need for creation of another site. The best treatment is anticipatory, with early treatment at the slightest indication of purulence, or even when hyperemia around the graft suggests only early inflammation. Over 90 percent of hemodialysis access infections are due to *Staphylococcus aureua* or a *Streptococcus species*. Although semisynthetic penicillins, erythromycin, or even first-generation cephalosporins are often effective agents and are occasionally used, the most common therapy given at our center is vancomycin. Vancomycin has the unique properties of being very effective against these bacteria, of not being dialyzed, and of maintaining sustained therapeutic levels for a very prolonged period of time because of renal dysfunction. Therefore, one dose is usually sufficient therapy for simple, early access infections. Complicated access infections can be life-threatening because of the rapid hematogenous spread of infecting organisms, and may demand surgical drainage, prolonged antibiotic therapy, extensive surgical revision of the access, or even removal of the access. In the case of access site infection by *Staphylococcus aureus*, antibiotic therapy is usually continued for at least four weeks to minimize the risk of secondary endocarditis.

Double-lumen subclavian access catheters may occasionally be occluded by fibrin in the absence of infection. In such cases infusion of streptokinase or urokinase into the catheter will occasionally dissolve the clot and restore function.[27] Apart from infection, stenosis and/or thrombosis of the vein may occur when a double-lumen subclavian catheter is left in place beyond several weeks. If an arteriovenous fistula or shunt is subsequently placed in the same upper limb, the impaired venous return may then cause swelling of the entire extremity.

Problems with peritoneal access are also not uncommon. A common problem is erosion of the outer catheter cuff from its subcutaneous site.[24] Cuff erosion facilitates the tracking of bacteria into the catheter tunnel, with consequent tunnel infection and peritonitis. Occasionally, early antibiotic therapy and local irrigation with antiseptic agents can eradicate tunnel infections, but most often, tunnel infection is quite difficult to cure completely; persistent infections lead to recurrent peritonitis, which eventually requires catheter removal and sometimes even a change of therapy from peritoneal dialysis to hemodialysis. Another problem in peritoneal access is plugging of the catheter by fibrin or ingrowth of mesentery into the catheter. Catheter obstruction usually occurs during an episode of peritonitis. Sometimes, infusion of streptokinase or urokinase into the peritoneal catheter can restore adequate drainage.[28] A more serious, and fortunately rare, set of problems related to the peritoneal dialysis catheter is bowel perforation, intra-abdominal hemorrhage, bowel obstruction, or volvulus.

HYPOTENSION

Hypotension during hemodialysis is a rather common complication and must be dealt with in certain susceptible patients during most of their dialysis treatments. Prevention and treatment of intradialytic hypotension is an important task of the dialysis staff and the nephrologist. Hypotension can be due to removal of an excessive amount of fluid by ultrafiltration or to an excessive rate of ultrafiltration. When hypotension occurs, ultrafiltration should be stopped and the patient placed in a Trendelenburg position to enhance venous return (unless contraindicated). An isotonic sodium chloride solution can then be infused or, alternatively, an oncotic agent such as 25 percent albumin can be given. Because dialysis solution containing bicarbonate is relatively difficult to prepare and store, a number of dialysis machines continue to provide a solution containing acetate as a bicarbonate-generating base. Acetate has vasodilatatory effects that may contribute to the occurrence of hypotension.[29] Newer dialysis machines, capable of delivering a bicarbonate-containing dialysis solution, have allowed the elimination of acetate-induced hypotension.[30]

Another cause of hypotension is the intracellular shifting of fluid when the sodium level of the dialysis solution is below that of the plasma. Such fluid shifts have been believed to contribute to the disequilibrium syndrome. Intracellular shifting of fluid can be averted by keeping the sodium concentration of the dialysis solution at or above the plasma sodium value.

The volume of the extracorporeal circuit can contribute to hypotension during dialysis of infants. In adults, the extracorporeal circuit volume is rarely a factor in intradialytic hypotension except in patients with severe cardiac disease who are extremely sensitive to minor reductions in cardiac filling.

Whether or not autonomic neuropathy contributes to intradialytic hypotension is controversial. Although uremia itself can cause peripheral and autonomic neuropathy, impairment in baroreceptor function is found primarily in diabetic patients, the elderly, patients with alcoholic neuropathy, and patients with renal failure due to multiple myeloma. Administration of adrenergic agonists (e.g., intravenous neosynephrine) has been reported to improve blood pressure during dialysis in such patients. Another less common but nevertheless very important cause of intradialytic hypotension is hemodynamically significant pericardial effusion. Because of compression of the right atrium by the raised pressure within the pericardial sac, a high venous filling pressure is ordinarily required to overcome this sac pressure and return blood to the right heart. Should an inordinately large amount of fluid be inadvertently removed from the blood during dialysis, the venous pressure will fall, venous return and hence cardiac output will suffer, and a picture of cardiac tamponade will emerge.[31] The treatment usually recommended for dialysis-related pericardial effusion is vigorous daily dialysis for a period of two weeks or so; if improvement is not obtained with this approach, some form of surgical treatment, such as pericardiostomy, creation of a pericardial window, partial pericardiectomy, or total percardiectomy is recommended.[32] When sonography suggests that the quantity of pericardial fluid exceeds 250 ml, we prefer to promptly perform subxiphoid pericardiostomy followed by a short period of tube drainage,[33] since large effusions have been found to respond poorly to conservative treatments.[34]

Antihypertensive therapy may contribute to hypotension during hemodialysis. In hemodialysis patients, antihypertensive therapy may need to be restricted to non-dialysis days, or to be delayed until after the dialysis session.

Hypotension during peritoneal dialysis is much less common than during hemodialysis, and maintenance peritoneal dialysis is the treatment of choice for patients who are prone to severe hypotension during hemodialysis.

DISEQUILIBRIUM SYNDROME

The disequilibrium syndrome is a constellation of signs and symptoms often seen in severely uremic patients who are dialyzed too vigorously.[35-37] Its clinical manifestations include restlessness, headache, muscle twitching, nausea, vomiting, confusion, coma, and seizures. The exact pathogenesis of the syndrome is unknown, although it is generally believed that cerebral edema is responsible for the development of its clinical manifestations. Explanations for the syndrome include: (1) a decline of urea and osmolality levels in the cerebrospinal fluid (CSF) that is less rapid than their decline in the plasma during dialysis, with the result that water moves into the CSF and increases the CSF pressure; (2) the development of CSF acidosis during dialysis, which can alter the intracellular binding of cations and result in a rise of brain cell osmolality; and (3) a dialysis-related increase in the concentration of idiogenic osmoles within brain cells, leading to the development of cerebral edema. The risk of occurrence of the disequilibrium syndrome can be minimized by using a dialysis solution with a sodium concentration equal to or greater than that of the plasma, and by avoiding, in the acute renal failure setting, the excessive use of dialysis. A small, less-efficient dialyzer should be used, the blood flow rate should be curtailed, and the length of treatment should be limited. It is important to emphasize that the risk of disequilibrium syndrome is initially greatest during the first few dialyses of a patient (or during a dialysis following an abnormally long interdialytic interval). Once regular dialysis has been initiated, more intense dialysis, using larger dialyzers and higher blood flow rates, can commonly be performed safely. In some centers, anticonvulsants are administered prophylactically whenever the risk of disequilibrium syndrome is believed to be high. In patients with a pre-existing seizure disorder, an additional dose of anticonvulsant may need to be given, depending on plasma drug levels and the pharmacokinetics of the agent being used. Administration of mannitol as a bolus or as a constant infusion during a high-risk dialysis is another approach to reducing the occurrence of the disequilibrium syndrome.

Muscle cramps during dialysis tend to occur when the sodium level of the dialysis solution is low, when the patient becomes hypotensive, or when excessive ultrafiltration has been done.[38] The treatment is to administer saline (isotonic or hypertonic) or hypertonic glucose solution intravenously, or to use a dialysis solution with a high sodium level. Quinine sulfate or oxazepam given prior to dialysis may sometimes afford relief.

PERITONITIS

Peritonitis is the main cause of termination of chronic peritoneal dialysis.[22,24,39] Peritonitis usually occurs as the result of an error in the technique of connecting the catheter tubing to the source of peritoneal dialysis solution. A second common route of infection is extension along the catheter tract in the abdominal wall during the course of infection of an exit site or a subcutaneous tunnel. The causative organisms vary according to anatomic site. The majority are gram-positive cocci. However, peritonitis with gram-negative bacilli or even with fungi is not uncommon. Mortality from peritonitis is low but not negligible.

The usual treatment of peritonitis involves the intraperitoneal instillation of antibiotics by way of dialysis solutions. An intravenous loading dose is sometimes given for severe infections. Table 14-1 displays some dose regimens for the intraperitoneal administration of antibiotics.[40] Therapy is usually begun empirically, without waiting for a culture result, as soon as symptoms appear and the peritoneal effluent turns cloudy. A peritoneal fluid cell

Table 14-1. Loading and Maintenance Doses of Antimicrobials for Peritonitis

Drug	Loading Dose[a]	Maintenance Dose
Aminoglyosides		
Amikacin	500 mg	6–7.5 mg/liter
Gentamicin	70–140 mg	4–8 mg/liter
Tobramycin	70–140 mg	4–8 mg/liter
Cephalosporins		
Cefamandole	1000 mg	250 mg/liter
Cefazolin	500–1000 mg	125–250 mg/liter
Cefoperazone	2000 mg	200–500 mg/liter
Cefotaxime	2000 mg	250 mg/liter
Cefoxitin	1000 mg	100 mg/liter
Ceftazidime	1000 mg	50–125 mg/liter
Ceftizoxime	1000 mg	125 mg/liter
Ceftriaxone	1000 mg	125–250 mg/liter
Cefuroxime	1000 mg	75–200 mg/liter
Cephalothin	1000 mg	100 mg/liter
Moxalactam	1000 mg	175 mg/liter
Penicillins		
Ampicillin	500 mg	50 mg/liter
Azlocillin	500 mg	250 mg/liter
Mezlocillin	3000 mg IV	250 mg/liter
Piperacillin	4000 mg IV	250 mg/liter
Ticarcillin	1000–2000 mg	125 mg/liter
Vancomycin and others		
Vancomycin	1000–2000 mg	15–25 mg/liter
Aztreonam	1000 mg	250 mg/liter
Ciprofloxacin	750 mg PO	25 mg/liter
Clindamycin	300 mg	150 mg/liter
Erythromycin	No data	75 mg/liter
Metronidazole	500 mg PO/IV	500 mg PO/IV TID
Rifampin	600 mg PO	600 mg PO q 24 H
Sulfamethoxazole	1600 mg PO	100–200 mg/liter
Trimethoprim	320 mg PO	20–40 mg/liter
Antifungals		
Amphotericin B[b]	1.0 mg IV test dose	30 mg/day IV
Flucytosine	200 mg	50–100 mg/liter
Miconazole	200 mg	50–100 mg/liter

[a] All loading doses, unless otherwise specified, are expressed as milligrams per bag dialysis solution (the volume of dialysis solution is not very important in calculating an IP loading dose).

[b] Causes pain and possibly sclerosis on IP instillation; give IV.

(From Keane WF et al: CAPD peritonitis treatment recommendations: 1989 update by the ad hoc advisory committee on peritonitis management. Perit Dial Int, in press, with permission; and Leehey DJ et al: Peritonitis. p. 252. In Daugirdas JT, Ing TS (eds): Handbook of Dialysis. Little, Brown, Boston 1988, with permission.)

count can be helpful. Infection is usually present when there are more than 100 neutrophils per cubic millimeter.[39] One common form of empiric therapy for peritonitis suspected of being caused by gram-positive bacteria is the use of a first-generation cephalosporin. Some nephrologists also use an antibiotic effective against gram-negative bacteria initially, discontinuing it once culture results show that these bacteria are not responsible for the infection. The choice of antibiotic will be based on the results of culture and sensitivity testing in a given anatomic area.

An acute increase in peritoneal membrane permeability commonly occurs during peritonitis.[24] The result is that patients often have difficulty in ultrafiltering excess fluid, and commonly require dialysis solutions containing higher concentrations of dextrose. Heparin should be added to peritoneal dialysis solutions during an episode of peritonitis because peritoneal inflammation can lead to local activation of the coagulation system and the formation of fibrin, with resulting catheter obstruction.

Recurrent peritonitis may reduce the efficiency of diffusion by impairing the permeability of the peritoneal membrane. Alteration of dialysis schedules may be needed to adjust for these effects. Ultimately, extensive fibrous adhesions or peritoneal sclerosis may render the peritoneal membrane unusable for dialysis, necessitating the abandonment of peritoneal dialysis therapy altogether.[41]

Whereas it was once thought that patients undergoing peritoneal dialysis had a poorer outcome after renal transplantation, this is no longer felt to be the case. Pediatric patients, in whom peritoneal dialysis is the preferred therapy, have recently done quite well after transplantation.

PROBLEMS WITH DIALYSIS IN THE PATIENT WITH HEART DISEASE

The patient with heart disease is more likely to develop angina, arrhythmias, and hypotension during dialysis. Such patients will often tolerate peritoneal dialysis better than hemodialysis. Simply having an arteriovenous fistula in such patients may increase their cardiac output and worsen angina. These patients are frequently balanced on a fine line between developing pulmonary edema from overhydration and suffering from hypotension due to inadequate cardiac filling. Excessively rapid ultrafiltration may induce hypotension in such patients despite evidence of sodium and water excess. Use of a bicarbonate-containing dialysis solution rather than an acetate-based solution is highly recommended. Isolated ultrafiltration is often useful for treating fluid overload in such patients. In some difficult cases, the patient may need to be hospitalized briefly for the removal of excess fluid, using one of the slow, continuous ultrafiltration procedures described below.

The risk of arrhythmias occurring during or after dialysis is increased by the development of hypokalemia, alkalosis, and/or hypophosphatemia[42] if adjustments in dialysate composition are not made to prevent the occurrence of these electrolytic complications. In patients with heart disease, the potassium concentration of the dialysis solution may need to be kept high, even if other potassium-lowering therapeutic measures may have to be taken. In addition, increasing the potassium concentration of the dialysate to 3 mmol/liter or higher may be necessary in patients receiving cardiac glycosides. This step ensures that hypokalemia will not occur during dialysis, in order to avoid the risk of cardiac glycoside intoxication (with its accompanying arrhythmias).

Angina during hemodialysis can be due to hypotension caused by excessive ultrafiltration, the use of acetate in the dialysis solution, or cardiac arrhythmias. In addition, a common cause of angina is a decrease in the patient's hematocrit to below a critical level. The first management strategy for unstable angina in the dialysis patient is to prevent excessive ultrafiltration, avoid the use of acetate-containing dialysis solutions, ensure that blood electrolyte levels are in order, and increase the hematocrit level using androgens, erythropoietin, or blood transfusion. If these measures fail to improve the angina, prophylactic sublingual nitroglycerin, given at the start of a hemodialysis treatment, can prove successful. If chest pain becomes continuous, the patient must be admitted to the hospital and managed in a manner similar to that for any other patient with unstable angina. Careful use of beta-blocking agents, salicylates, calcium-channel blocking agents, and long-acting nitrates may be needed. Cardiology consultation and cardiac catheterization may be required. Patients undergoing dialysis tolerate cardiac catheterization surprisingly well, and have even successfully undergone coronary artery bypass surgery.

In these patients, intraoperative hemodialysis by connection of their dialysis tubing to the cardiopulmonary bypass machine may delay the need for postoperative hemodialysis for 72 hours or longer, thus allowing wounds to heal and minimizing the complications of early postoperative dialysis (such as bleeding problems related to the use of heparin).[43]

A substantial degree of hypoxemia, the causes of which are probably multifactorial, can occur during dialysis.[44] Hypoxemia during acetate-based dialysis may be due to alteration in the respiratory quotient when acetate is metabolized, and also to hypoventilation due to CO_2 loss to the dialysate. With bicarbonate-containing dialysis solutions, alkalemia may depress the respiratory drive, causing hypoxemia. A small component of the hypoxemia may be membrane-dependent, due to complement-mediated pulmonary sequestration of leukocytes. Complement-mediated leukocyte activation should be reduced when employing a reused cellulosic dialyzer (in which the membrane has become coated with plasma protein, reducing its complement-activating ability), or when employing one of the substituted cellulose or synthetic membranes. Some of these latter membranes may adsorb released complement fragments or activate complement to a lesser extent.

Fewer acute problems occur in patients with heart disease if they are managed with CAPD. However, glucose absorption via the peritoneum can contribute to obesity and hypertriglyceridemia. Theoretically, at least, elevated serum triglyceride levels can lower the high density lipoprotein (HDL) cholesterol level, putting the patient at higher risk for atherosclerosis.

PROBLEMS WITH DIALYSIS IN THE DIABETIC PATIENT

In some parts of the United States, diabetes represents the most common cause of chronic renal failure requiring end-stage renal disease management. Since diabetic patients tend to tolerate azotemia poorly,[17,45] they are often begun on dialysis before their creatinine clearance falls below the traditional guideline for initiating dialysis in nondiabetic patients, which is 0.1 to 0.15 ml/min/kg body weight. Diabetic patients are difficult to maintain by hemodialysis. Vascular access is difficult to achieve owing to the frequency of atherosclerosis and calcification of blood vessels. Ischemia of the hands and fingers distal to an arteriovenous fistula may result from a steal syndrome due to poor arterial inflow. This syndrome, which can improve with time, can present as hand muscle weakness, coolness of the hand or fingers, or, rarely, as dry or wet gangrene of the fingers. Surgical correction of the fistula may be necessary for relief. Access infections are also common in diabetic patients, further complicating their maintenance on hemodialysis.

Hypotension during hemodialysis occurs frequently in diabetic patients; the primary cause is believed to be impaired baroreceptor function resulting from diabetic neuropathy. Predialysis hypertension alternates with intradialytic hypotension. Such patients may need to have antihypertensive drugs administered on non-dialysis days, and alpha-agonists during dialysis.

It has been feared that anticoagulation during hemodialysis might worsen retinal hemorrhages in diabetic patients. This is the reason usually given for the preference of peritoneal dialysis for the diabetic patient with end-stage renal disease. However, prospective studies of visual acuity in diabetic patients treated with hemodialysis for as long as three years suggest that the use of heparin during dialysis does not cause worsening of diabetic retinopathy.[46]

Peritoneal dialysis has the advantage of producing less hypotension than hemodialysis in the diabetic patient.[23] The problem of vascular access is also avoided. Insulin can be given intraperitoneally via the dialysis solution, obviating the need for subcutaneous insulin therapy in many patients. Chronic peritoneal dialysis allows ingestion of a more liberal diet and fluid intake. However, peritoneal dialysis also has some disadvantages in diabetic patients. The insulin requirement is increased because of the intraperitoneal glucose load. The glucose load may also elevate serum triglyceride levels. Additionally, diabetic patients may be more prone to peritonitis than nondiabetics. Finally, peritonitis may be more severe and life-threatening in diabetic patients than in their nondiabetic counterparts.

PROBLEMS WITH DIALYSIS IN THE GERIATRIC PATIENT

Although elderly persons were previously often excluded from end-stage renal disease therapy, as noted above, today they represent both the largest and still increasing group of patients being treated with dialysis.[47] The elderly frequently have both diabetes and heart disease, and the problems associated with these illnesses have been outlined above. On the other hand, in many very elderly dialysis patients, nephrosclerosis is the cause of renal failure. These patients have only a limited degree of heart disease, and are surprisingly easy to manage with maintenance dialysis. They are also often very compliant, reducing the difficulty of their management. Because of impaired baroreceptor function, the very elderly are prone to develop hypotension during hemodialysis. All long-term dialysis patients are at greater risk for acute respiratory infections, especially during epidemics of influenza. The geriatric dialysis patient has an even greater risk, since age may be an independent risk factor for respiratory infection. Vaccinations against pneumococcal and influenzal infections should be done. Nutritional insufficiency is common in the elderly, and the poor appetite typical of patients with chronic renal failure only exacerbates the danger of protein-calorie malnutrition as well as mineral and vitamin deficiencies. Poor economic status, an altered sense of taste or smell, and uremia can all lead to such nutritional deficits.

Bone disease is likely to be a serious problem in geriatric dialysis patients. Senile osteoporosis, especially in women, superimposed on renal osteodystrophy, increases the risk of pathologic fractures of vertebrae or long bones. Dairy product intake is lower in the elderly, and they also spend less time in the sun. Renal failure further impairs their vitamin D synthesis, compounding vitamin D deficiency and leading to accelerated metabolic bone disease. Paget's disease is more common in the elderly and may coexist with osteoporosis and renal osteodystrophy. Falls are more common in the elderly due to changes in the proprioception pathways of the central nervous system. Even a minor fall in a geriatric dialysis patient with bone diseases such as that described above can result in a hip fracture. The latter often leads to a steady overall decline in the health of a geriatric patient, and ultimately to death by pulmonary infection. Since some elderly patients do not have partners for home hemodialysis and may not be able to handle CAPD or CCPD themselves, in-center hemodialysis and peritoneal dialysis may be the only workable alternatives. Recent work in our program has shown that elderly nondiabetic patients often tolerate hemodialysis as well as their younger counterparts. Counterregulatory cardiovascular hormone control systems in the elderly respond to the hemodynamic stress of hemodialysis in a manner not unlike that observed in younger patients.

The ethics of extending chronic dialysis therapy to the very elderly are still being explored. The increasing number of individuals in the geriatric age group and their mounting political influence tend to favor the expansion of dialysis services to this population despite the costs involved. On the other hand, people in younger age groups are facing an escalating financial burden for services rendered to older age groups. The question of offering dialysis to the elderly is linked to the increasing use of other invasive therapies in this age group, such as advanced heart surgery, the use of newer and more powerful chemotherapeutic agents, and even transplantation. The use of these therapies increases the risk of renal failure from ischemic or toxic insults in the elderly because of their reduced renal reserve. The management of complicating renal failure adds to the time and expense of such other invasive therapies.

SPECIAL FORMS OF DIALYSIS THERAPY

Three special forms of dialysis therapy are continuous arteriovenous ultrafiltration (CAVU),[48] continuous arteriovenous hemofiltration (CAVH),[49] and continuous arteriovenous hemodialysis (CAVHD).[50,51] Figures 14-1 through 14-3 illustrate each of these modalities, respectively. In the first two procedures a highly permeable membrane is used. Catheters are ordinarily introduced percutaneously into the femoral artery and the femoral vein. No blood pump is used. Arterial pressure is the force that drives blood through the ultrafiltration device. A heparin drip is infused into the arterial tubing. A pump can be used to create a negative pressure to enhance ultrafiltration and deliver the ultrafiltrate into a collection bag. Once set up, CAVU treatment often runs continuously for days. This form of isolated ultrafiltration is not commonly accompanied by any significant changes in the blood pressure. The procedure can slowly and effectively reduce plasma volume while excess fluid can enter the blood from the interstitial space to replenish the circulatory volume. Consequently, CAVU is used to remove excess fluid from patients with inordinately unstable cardiovascular systems, such as patients with oliguria after coronary artery bypass surgery, or those who have had a recent acute myocardial infarction. It can also be used to re-establish the dry weight in a dialysis patient with heart disease in whom conventional hemodialysis has not been successful in removing excess fluid.

Continuous arteriovenous hemofiltration is similar to CAVU, except that a larger volume of ultrafiltrate is removed and a replacement solution is returned to the patient. As a result, changes in the solute composition of the blood can be effected with CAVH. The electrolyte composition of the replacement solution is similar to that of a hemodialysis solution. When required, replacement fluid containing amino acids and/or glucose can also be provided, for the purpose of parenteral nutrition. With CAVH, the difference between the rate of infusion of all replacement solutions and the rate of ultrafiltration in the hemofilter device will be the net rate of excess fluid removal.

With CAVHD, a dialyzer with a conventional membrane or one with a highly permeable membrane can be used. The setup of the extracorporeal circuit for CAVHD is similar to that for CAVU, except that sterile peritoneal dialysis solution is routed through the dialysate compartment of the dialyzer, and ultrafiltration is usually achieved through the osmotic effect of the dextrose contained in the dialysis solution.

In common with CAVU, CAVH and CAVHD are ideally suited for patients with cardiovascular instability. Since changes in body solute composition and body fluid volume occur very slowly, patient tolerance to these renal substitution modalities is markedly improved.

Another special therapy is hemoperfusion.[52] In this procedure, a double-lumen catheter is usually placed into a femoral vein to deliver blood to and from a charcoal hemoperfusion cartridge. Heparinization is

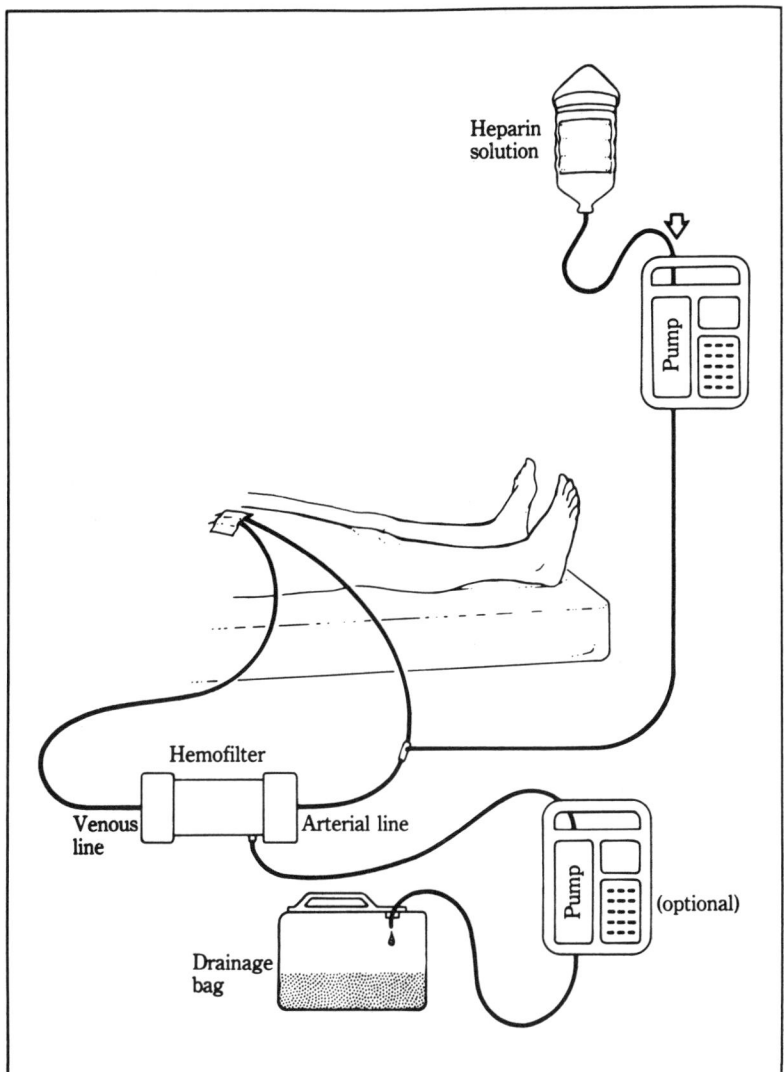

Fig. 14-1. The circuit for continuous arteriovenous ultrafiltration (CAVU). In the diagram, an intravenous infusion pump (optional) is shown interposed in the line draining the hemofilter to control the rate of ultrafiltration. The other pump controls the rate of heparin infusion. (From Daugirdas JT et al: Special procedures. p. 122. In Daugirdas JT, Ing TS (eds): Handbook of Dialysis. Little, Brown, Boston, 1988, with permission.)

required. Hemoperfusion is used to remove toxic substances, usually drugs, from the circulation, often in a situation in which a patient has taken a drug overdose in an attempt to commit suicide. During hemoperfusion, serum drug values should be monitored. A rebound in serum drug level may occur with certain drugs after the therapy has been completed, owing to drug release from tissue stores. Levels of white blood cells and platelets, the hematocrit, and the serum calcium and serum magnesium concentrations should also be monitored during hemoperfusion.

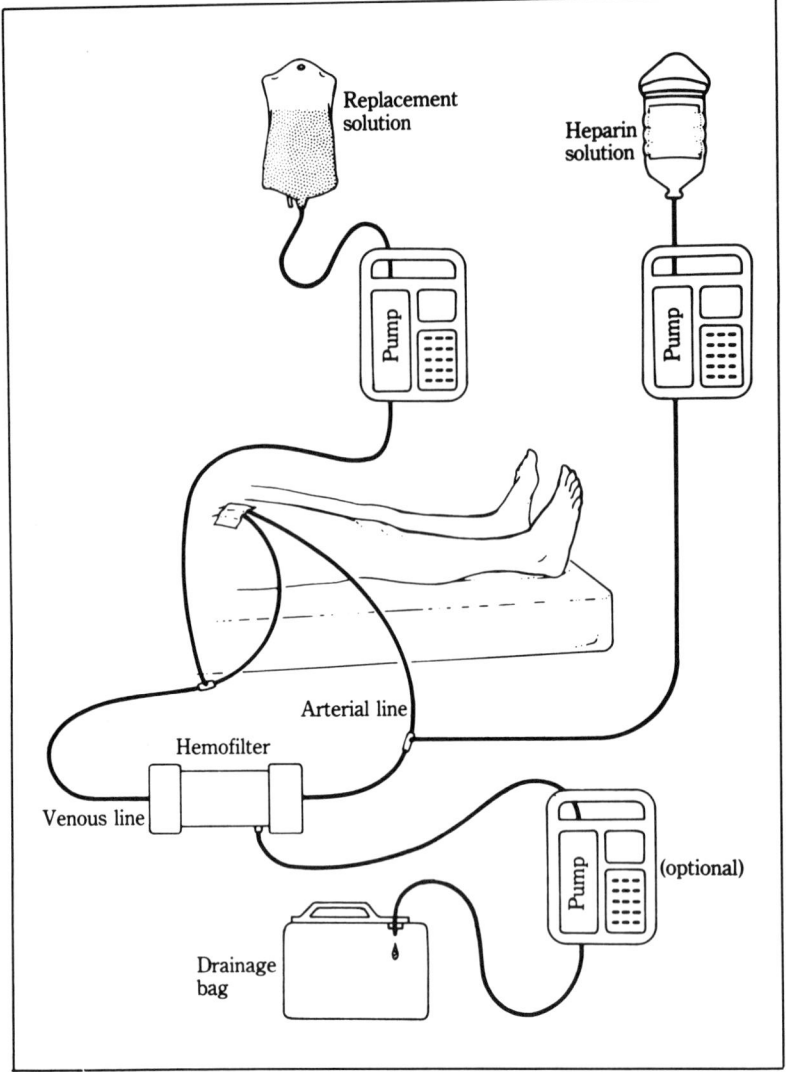

Fig. 14-2. The circuit for continuous arteriovenous hemofiltration (CAVH). The two-pump method is illustrated, with intravenous infusion pumps used to control both the rate of replacement solution infusion and the rate of ultrafiltration. Replacement solution is shown infused into the venous line (postdilution mode). The third pump is used for heparin infusion. (From Daugirdas JT et al: Special procedures. p. 136. In Daugirdas JT, Ing TS (eds): Handbook of Dialysis. Little, Brown, Boston, 1988, with permission.)

FUTURE RESEARCH AND CONCLUSIONS

There are several active areas in which dialysis therapy can be improved. Membranes that are more efficient, more biocompatible, and more adsorptive (with the goal of adsorbing various undesirable substances) than those currently available can be developed. For example, we still do not have an ideal means to remove phosphate from the body; better dialyzer membranes and phosphate-binders for phosphate removal are required. Also, many dialyzer

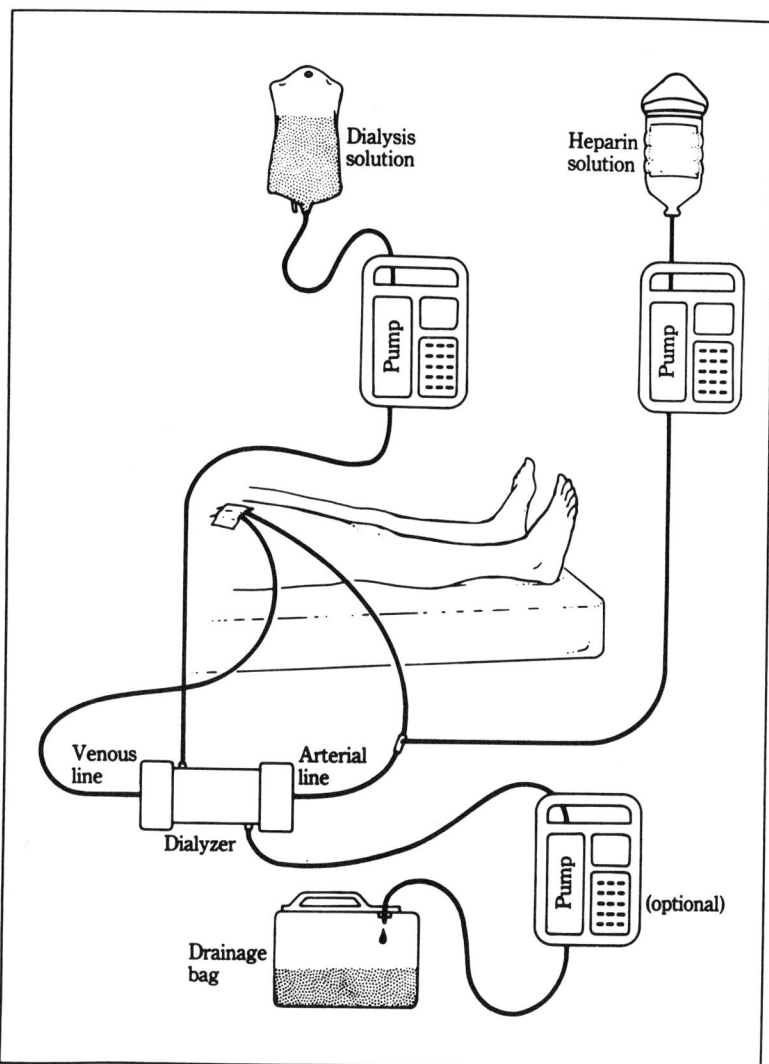

Fig. 14.3. The circuit for continuous arteriovenous hemodialysis (CAVHD). The only change from the circuit shown in Figure 14-2 is that the in-flow fluid is infused into the dialysis solution inflow port of the dialyzer instead of into the blood line. In this diagram, two pumps are used to control the rate of dialysis solution flow. Other methods using only one dialysis solution pump are also available, or the dialysis solution can even be infused by gravity drip. (From Daugirdas JT et al: Special procedures. p. 138. In Daugirdas JT, Ing TS (eds): Handbook of Dialysis. Little, Brown, Boston, 1988, with permission.)

membranes can induce macrophages to produce interleukin 1[53] and tumor necrosis factor.[54] Better membranes, which do not promote the formation of these monokines, should be developed. Nowadays, short-duration dialysis sessions lasting 2 to 2½ hours each can be achieved by using highly efficient dialyzers in combination with high blood and dialysate flow rates, bicarbonate-containing dialysis solutions, and ultrafiltration controllers.[55] Despite the fact that we are approaching the upper limit of dialysis efficiency with the short-duration dialysis method, it is conceivable that still more efficient dialysis procedures will be discovered in the future. Although ultra-compact, implantable dialysis equipment is a long-sought holy grail of dialysis researchers, the use of robots to perform dialysis functions should be possible in the future. Alternative means of anticoagulation are also being explored, such as with prostacyclin and its analogs, which prevent clotting by interfering with platelet activation. Such agents have an extremely short duration of action, and their effects are quickly reversed when a dialysis session is ended. The feasibility of incorporating an anticoagulant into dialyzer membranes, dialysis tubing, and dialysis catheters is under active investigation. The advent of erythropoietin will revolutionize the treatment of anemia in end-stage renal failure patients.[56] Apparently, one has to administer this drug judiciously, so as to avoid the occurrence of such complications as hypertension and clotting problems.

The peritoneoscope is an important new development in peritoneal dialysis; its use has renewed interest in peritoneal dialysis because of the ease with which it permits catheter insertion.[18] The method also has a high success rate. The advent of the peritoneoscope is encouraging more nephrologists to insert chronic catheters in a special procedure room under sterile conditions, rather than requesting a surgical colleague to insert such catheters in a formal surgical operating room setting.

A promising approach to improving the efficacy of peritoneal dialysis is known as tidal peritoneal dialysis.[57] In this method, 3 liters (for example) of a dialysis solution are introduced into an empty peritoneal cavity to constitute an initial filling volume. After an appropriate dwell period, a volume of effluent is removed so that approximately 2 liters of fluid are left behind in the peritoneal cavity. The quantity of effluent removed often amounts to a little in excess of 1 liter (the difference being due to a contribution by ultrafiltrate). A liter of fresh dialysis solution is then introduced and the exchange cycle is repeated. This approach is more efficient than conventional varieties of peritoneal dialysis because contact between the peritoneal membrane and the dialysis solution is much improved.

It will come as no surprise that new and novel means of connecting one tubing to another for the purpose of peritoneal dialysis will come to fruition in the future. One awaits the day when the occurrence of peritonitis will be markedly curtailed by innovations like these.

Finally, the physiologic changes, survival rates, quality of life, and expense of extending management in end-stage renal disease to special groups who have previously been denied such treatment (e.g., the elderly, the patient with other organ system failure, and the patient with a variety of malignancies at different stages of progression) will need to be addressed.

REFERENCES

1. Friedman EA: Introduction. p 1. In Friedman EA (ed): Strategy in Renal Failure. John Wiley & Sons, New York, 1978
2. Quinton WE, Dillard DH, Cole JJ, Scribner BH: Eight months' experience with silastic-teflon bypass cannulas. Trans Am Soc Artif Intern Organs 8:236, 1962
3. Brescia MJ, Cimino JE, Appel K, Hurwich BJ: Chronic hemodialysis using venipuncture and a surgically created arteriovenous fistula. N Engl J Med 275:1089, 1966
4. Dunn I, Frumkin E, Forte R, et al: Dacron velour vascular prosthesis for hemodialysis. Proc Dial Transplant Forum 2:85, 1972
5. Sheldon S, Silva H, Pomeroy J, et al: Percutaneous femoral venous catheterization and reusable dialyzers in the treatment of acute renal failure. Trans Am Soc Artif Intern Organs 10:133, 1964
6. Udall RR, Joy C, Merchant N: Further experience with a double-lumen subclavian cannula for hemodialysis. Trans Am Soc Artif Intern Organs 28:71, 1982

7. Friedman EA, Lundin AP III: Dialysate delivery: Historical, theoretical, and practical aspects. Kidney Int 10, suppl:S33–S43, 1980
8. Flendrig JG, Carpay WM, Dekkers WT: The accurate control of ultrafiltration. Artif Organs 2:144, 1978
9. Roberts M, Daugirdas JT: REDY sorbent hemodialysis. p 146. In Daugirdas JT, Ing TS (eds): Handbook of Dialysis. Little, Brown, Boston, 1988
10. Mujais SK, Ivanovich P: Membranes for extracorporeal therapy. p 181. In Maher JF (ed): Replacement of Renal Function by Diralysis. Kluwer Academic Publishers, Dordrecht, The Netherlands, 1989
11. Tenckhoff H, Schechter H: A bacteriologically safe peritoneal access device. Trans Am Soc Artif Intern Organs 14:181, 1968
12. Boen ST, Mulinari AS, Dillard DH, Scribner BH: Periodic peritoneal dialysis in the management of chronic uremia. Trans Am Soc Artif Intern Organs 8:256, 1962
13. Popovich RP, Moncrief JW, Nolph KD, et al: Continuous ambulatory peritoneal dialysis. Ann Intern Med 88:449, 1978
14. Oreopoulos DG, Clayton S, Dombros N, et al: Nineteen months' experience with continuous ambulatory peritoneal dialysis (CAPD). Proc Eur Dial Transpl Assoc 16:178, 1979
15. Popovich RP, Moncrief JW, Sorrels-Akar PAJ, et al: The ultraviolet germicidal system: The elimination of distal contamination in CAPD. p 169. In Maher JF, Winchester JF (eds): Frontiers in Peritoneal Dialysis. Field, Rich & Associates, New York, 1986
16. Zawada ET Jr: Indications for dialysis. p 3. In Daugirdas JT, Ing TS (eds): Handbook of Dialysis. Little, Brown, Boston, 1988
17. Tzamaloukas AH: p 321. In Daugirdas JT, Ing TS (eds): Handbook of Dialysis. Little, Brown, Boston, 1988
18. Ash SR, Handt AE, Bloch R: Peritoneoscopic placement of the Tenckhoff catheter: Further clinical experience. Perit Dial Bull 3:8, 1983.
19. Van Stone JC: Hemodialysis apparatus. p 21. In Daugirdas JT, Ing TS (eds): Handbook of Dialysis. Little, Brown, Boston, 1988
20. Gotch FA: Solute transport and ultrafiltration in hemodialysis. p 639. In Massry SG, Sellers AL (eds): Clinical Aspects of Uremia and Dialysis. Charles C Thomas, Springfield IL 1976
21. Ing TS, Ashbach DL, Kanter A, et al: Fluid removal with negative-pressure hydrostatic ultrafiltration using a partial vacuum. Nephron 14:451, 1975
22. Nolph KD, Sorkin MI: Continuous ambulatory peritoneal dialysis. p 193. In Brenner BM, Stein JH (eds): Chronic Renal Failure. Churchill Livingstone, New York, 1981
23. Khanna R, Oreopoulos DG: CAPD in patients with diabetes mellitus. p 291. In Gokal R (ed): Continuous Ambulatory Peritoneal Dialysis. Churchill Livingstone, Edinburgh, 1986
24. Mion CM: Continuous ambulatory peritoneal dialysis and continuous cyclic peritoneal dialysis. p 3235. In Schrier RW, Gottschalk CW (eds): Diseases of the Kidney. 4th Ed. Little, Brown, Boston, 1988
25. Diaz-Buxo JA. Continuous cyclic peritoneal dialysis. p 169. In Nolph KD (ed): Peritoneal Dialysis. Kluwer Academic Publishers, Dordrecht, The Netherlands, 1989
26. Tawa NE Jr, Tilney NL: Angioaccess in the renal failure patient. p 218. In Maher JF (ed): Replacement of Renal Function by Dialysis. Kluwer Academic Publishers, Dordrecht, The Netherlands, 1989
27. McNamar TO, Fischer JR: Thrombolysis of peripheral arterial and graft occlusions: Improved results using high-dose urokinase. AJR 144:769, 1985
28. Benevent D, Peyronnet P, Brignon P, Leroux-Robert C: Urokinase infusion for obstructed catheters and peritonitis. Perit Dial Bull 5:77, 1985
29. Bauer W, Richards DW Jr: A vasodilator action of acetates. J Physiol (Lond) 66:371, 1928
30. Graefe U, Milutinovich J, Follette WC, et al: Less dialysis-induced morbidity and vascular instability with bicarbonate in dialysate. Ann Intern Med 88:332, 1978
31. Spodick DH: Acute cardiac tamponade: Pathologic physiology, diagnosis and treatment. Progr Cardiovasc Dis 10:64, 1967
32. Renfrew R, Buselmeier TJ, Kjellstrand CM: Pericarditis and renal failure. Annu Rev Med 31:345, 1980
33. Leehey DJ, Daugirdas JT, Ing TS: Early

drainage of pericardial effusion in patients with dialysis pericarditis. Arch Intern Med 143:1673, 1984
34. Peraino RA: Pericardial effusion in patients treated with maintenance dialysis. Am J Nephrol 3:319, 1983
35. Hakim RM, Lazarus JM: Hemodialysis in acute renal failure. p 767. In Brenner BM, Lazarus JM (eds): Acute Renal Failure. Churchill Livingstone, New York, 1988
36. Blagg CR: Acute complications associated with hemodialysis. p 750. In Maher JF (ed): Replacement of Renal Function by Dialysis. Kluwer Academic Publishers, Dordrecht, The Netherlands, 1989
37. Arieff AI, Lazarowitz VC, Guisado R: Experimental dialysis disequilibrium syndrome: Prevention with glycerol. Kidney Int 14:270, 1978
38. Sherman RA, Goodling KA, Eisinger RP: Acute therapy of hemodialysis-related muscle cramps. Am J Kidney Dis 2:287, 1982
39. Vas SI: Peritonitis. p 261. In Nolph KD (ed): Peritoneal Dialysis. Kluwer Academic Publishers, Dordrecht, The Netherlands 1989
40. Keane WF, Everett ED, Fine RN, et al: CAPD related peritonitis management and antibiotic therapy recommendations. Perit Dial Bull 7:55, 1987
41. Gandhi VC, Ing TS, Daugirdas JT, et al: Failure of peritoneal dialysis due to peritoneal sclerosis. Int J Artif Organs 6:97, 1983
42. Venditti FJ, Marotta C, Panezai FR: Hypophosphatemia and cardiac arrhythmias. Miner Electrolyte Metab 13:19, 1987
43. Zawada ET Jr, Stinson JB, Done G: New perspectives on coronary artery disease in hemodialysis patients. South Med J 75:694, 1982
44. Burns CB, Scheinhorn DJ: Hypoxemia during hemodialysis. Arch Intern Med 142:1350, 1982
45. Kjellstrand CM: Dialysis in diabetics. p 345. In Friedman EA (ed): Strategy in Renal Failure. John Wiley & Sons, New York, 1978
46. Ramsay RC, Cantrill HL, Knobloch WH, et al: Visual parameters in diabetic patients on chronic dialysis. Diabetic Nephropathy 2:30, 1983
47. Stacy W, Sica D: Dialysis of the elderly patient. p 229. In Zawada ET Jr, Sica DA (eds): Geriatric Nephrology and Urology. PSG Publishing Company, Littleton, MA, 1985
48. Paganini EP, Nakamoto S: Continuous slow ultrafiltration in oliguric acute renal failure. Trans Am Soc Artif Intern Organs 26:201, 1980
49. Lauer A, Saccaggi A, Ronco C, et al: Continuous arteriovenous hemofiltration in the critically ill patient. Ann Intern Med 99:455, 1983
50. Ing TS, Purandare VV, Daugirdas JT, et al: Slow continuous hemodialysis. Int J Artif Organs 7:53, 1984
51. Geronemus R, Schneider N: Continuous arteriovenous hemodialysis: A new modality for treatment of acute renal failure. Trans Am Soc Artif Intern Organs 30:610, 1984
52. Winchester JF: Use of dialysis and hemoperfusion in treatment of poisoning. p 437. In Daugirdas JT, Ing TS (eds): Handbook of Dialysis. Little, Brown, Boston, 1988
53. Henderson LW, Koch KM, Dinarello CA, et al: Hemodialysis hypotension: The interleukin hypothesis. Blood Purif 1:3, 1983
54. Lonnemann G, van der Meer JWM, Cannon JG, et al: Induction of tumor necrosis factor during extracorporeal blood purification. N Engl J Med 317:963, 1987
55. Collins A, Ilstrup K, Hanson G, et al: Rapid high-efficiency hemodialysis. Artif Organs 10:185, 1986
56. Eschbach JW, Egrie JC, Downing MR, et al: Correction of the anemia of end-stage renal disease with recombinant human erythropoietin. Results of a combined phase I and II clinical trials. N Eng J Med 316:73, 1987
57. Twardowski ZJ: New approaches to intermittent peritoneal dialysis therapies. p 133. In Nolph KD (ed): Peritoneal Dialysis. Kluwer Academic Publishers, Dordrecht, The Netherlands, 1989

15

Special Problems of Acute Renal Failure: Pathophysiology, Diagnosis and Treatment

Donald E. Oken

The abrupt cessation of renal function presents a dramatic, life-threatening illness that sometimes sorely tries the diagnostic and therapeutic skills of the physician. The more common of the several etiologies are shown in Table 15-1, but here we are primarily concerned with the peculiar syndrome most commonly termed *acute tubular necrosis* (ATN), *acute renal failure* (ARF), or *vasomotor nephropathy* (VMN). Other forms of renal failure will be considered only as they relate to the sometimes vexing problem of differential diagnosis.

The title "acute tubular necrosis" may be misleading, since many patients with this syndrome do not exhibit tubular necrosis at all.[1,2] Some nephrologists thus prefer the name "acute renal failure," but several other renal diseases of widely different etiologies also cause acute renal failure. A more meaningful term thus would be preferable. Grossly reduced renal blood flow is a hallmark of virtually all patients with this syndrome,[3–8] and this abnormality seems to be the principal cause of failed filtration (see below). Hence, the term "vasomotor nephropathy," proposed by Borst[9] and Hackradt[10] over 60 years ago, appears to be an accurate, specific and etiologically meaningful name for the syndrome in man. The oliguria and azotemia of *prerenal failure* also reflect a vasomotor phenomenon, but since there is no intrinsic renal abnormality in this disorder, it is not a true nephropathy. We shall refer to that entity as *functional renal failure* to underscore the fact that it is a purely functional abnormality that is predictably reversed by removing the underlying hemodynamic problem.

THE SYNDROME OF VASOMOTOR NEPHROPATHY

Etiology

The close relationship between vasomotor nephropathy and hemorrhage, volume depletion, sepsis, or hypotension is universally recognized, as is its association with brisk hemolysis, rhabdomyolysis, and the surgical interruption of renal blood flow by arterial clamping. Obstetric complications produce *vasomotor nephropathy* (VMN) in a small but significant number of patients. Septic abortion, especially when followed

Table 15-1. Causes of Acute Renal Failure

Glomerulopathies	Sepsis
Post-streptococcal and other bacterial	Trauma
Viral	Heart failure
Lupus erythematosus	Vasomotor nephropathy (acute tubular necrosis, acute renal failure)
Wegener's granulomatosis	
Heroin nephropathy	All causes of functional renal failure if not adequately treated
Eclampsia	
Hemolytic-uremic syndrome	Blunt trauma
Acquired immunodeficiency syndrome	Burns
Vascular and thrombotic diseases	Surgery
Malignant hypertension	Fractures
Wegener's granulomatosis	Intravascular hemolysis
Hypersensitivity angiitis	Heat stroke
Periarteritis nodosa	Malaria
Thrombotic thrombocytopenic purpura	Snake bite
Hemolytic-uremic syndrome	Electric shock
Schwartzmann reaction (cortical necrosis)	Dissecting aneurysm (e.g., Marfan's homocystinuria)
Scleroderma	
Acute allograft rejection	Septicemia
Fat or cholesterol embolism	Rhabdomyolysis
Renal venous-vena caval thrombosis	Poisons (especially antibiotics, mercury, bismuth, phosphorus, lead, carbon tetrachloride, ethylene glycol, methanol, mushrooms, Lysol). Others[42]
Post-traumatic arterial thrombosis or avulsion	
Aortic coarctation with arterial thrombosis	
Renal artery dysplasia	Hepatorenal syndrome
Interstitial disease	Urinary obstruction (ureter, bladder, or urethra)
Allergic, postinfectious, and idiosyncratic interstitial nephritis	Inflammation
	Stones
Fulminating pyelonephritis	Blood clot
Papillary necrosis	Urate crystallization
Functional renal failure ("prerenal" renal failure)	Tumor
Severe volume depletion	Retroperitoneal mass
Shock	Fibrosis
	Bladder rupture

by clostridial endometritis, still causes renal failure with alarming frequency in some areas of the world.[11] Intra- and postpartum hemorrhage, abruptio placentae, and placenta previa remain as uncommon but important etiologies related to pregnancy.[12] Causes of renal failure other than VMN in this same population include the hemolytic-uremic syndrome (postpartum acute renal failure),[13] disseminated intravascular coagulation,[14] and acute fatty liver of pregnancy,[15] as well as lupus and various glomerular and microvascular diseases that are not unique to the gravid state.

Vasomotor nephropathy is often seen in association with intravascular hemolysis or rhabdomyolysis. The latter is a common result of traumatic crush injury or of prolonged muscle compression in individuals rendered comatose by alcohol, sedatives, narcotics, or carbon monoxide poisoning.[16] Other cases appear after sustained strenuous exercise,[17] heat prostration,[18] convulsions,[19] or, without evident trauma, in the glycogen storage diseases.[20,21] Ethanol intoxication is a frequent forerunner of myoglobinuric VMN, even in the absence of evident muscle trauma or excessive exertion.[22,23] Influenza,[24] polymyositis,[25] amphetamine overdosage,[26] gross hypernatremia,[27] hypothyroidism,[28] and a variety of other disorders are rare causes of this form of VMN.

The association between renal failure and hemolysis has been known for over 100 years.[29] Renal failure due to incompatible blood transfusion, once relatively common, is now quite rare thanks to improved blood banking techniques. Delayed transfusion reactions due to Kidd, Duffy, Lewis, and other minor blood group incompatibilities do still occur, but these tend to produce delayed transfusion reactions[30] that are typically mild and rarely lead to renal failure.[30] Hemolytic "crises" due to glucose-6-phosphate dehydrogenase (G-6-PD) deficiency,[31] paroxysmal nocturnal hemoglobinuria,[32] paroxysmal cold hemoglobinuria,[33] and march hemoglobinuria[34] are rare potential causes of the syndrome. Other uncommon causes of posthemolytic VMN include (among others) intra-amniotic infusions of hypertonic saline,[35] intracervical instillation of cleaning solutions for self-induced abortion,[36] intravenous glycerol therapy of cerebral edema,[37] snake bite,[38] malaria,[39] and arsine poisoning.[40]

A large number of household and industrial chemicals produce VMN by direct nephrotoxicity. The list includes the heavy metals: mercury, uranium, chromate, bismuth, cadmium, and arsenic. Arsine may produce acute renal failure, although chronic renal failure appears to result more commonly.[41] Carbon tetrachloride, methanol, ethylene glycol, and chlorinated hydrocarbon (paraquat, chlordane) poisoning was common in the past, but we see relatively few such cases today. A long list of other toxins that cause ARF of various types may be found in the old but extensive review by Schreiner and Maher.[42] Some of these exert a direct nephrotoxic effect. Others, such as *Amanita phalloides*[43] or *A. verna*,[44] cause severe volume depletion and cardiovascular collapse as the prime contributing factor, and still others lead to myoglobinuria[45] or hemolysis[46] as the essential cause of renal failure.

The aminoglycoside antibiotics, used so commonly in today's medical armamentarium, are without doubt the most common chemical cause of renal failure in this era. Unlike most other antibiotics (e.g., cephaloridine), which produce renal injury in only a small minority of patients, all the aminoglycoside antibiotics except streptomycin are universal nephrotoxins. Neomycin is so nephrotoxic and neurotoxic as to be reserved for oral or topical administration. The aminoglycoside antibiotics as a group are excreted almost exclusively by the kidney, and largely by glomerular filtration.[47] Pharmacokinetic studies by Schentag and co-workers have shown that the half-life of gentamicin in the serum of healthy human subjects is approximately two hours, while that in renal tissue is some four days.[48] The concentration in renal tissue thus increases with each dose given. If excessively high serum concentrations of gentamicin (or amikacin or tobramycin) are avoided by adjusting the dosage of antibiotic to the patient's renal function, the concentration in the kidney usually does not reach frankly toxic levels in a typical 5- to 7-day treatment period. However, nephrotoxic tissue concentrations may be expected when the dosage exceeds that which is appropriate or if treatment is prolonged. Amikacin appears to be comparable to gentamicin in its nephrotoxicity, while tobramycin exhibits somewhat lower tissue accumulation and, by some accounts, less nephrotoxicity.[49,50] Netilmicin, sisomicin, and kanamycin seem no less nephrotoxic.

Amphotericin B is yet another universal nephrotoxin[51] whose detrimental effect on the kidney is universal and clearly dose related. The patient is at risk of progressive and sometimes irreversible renal failure after an accumulated dose in excess of 2 g, whether the drug is taken over a matter of weeks, months, or even years. Cisplatin,[52] used so commonly today in cancer chemotherapy, produces acute, reversible renal failure comparable to that seen with the aminoglycoside antibiotics. Methotrexate appears to cause acute renal failure by the quite different mechanism of intrarenal tubular obstruction.

Iodinated contrast agents employed for intravenous pyelography, arteriography, or computed tomography are reputed to cause "acute renal failure" with startling frequency in some reports.[53-55] Frank renal failure has especially been found in diabetics with pre-existing renal disease,[56] hypoalbuminemia, marked proteinuria, or hyperuricemia.[57] However, close perusal shows that many individuals with essentially normal baseline renal function in some reports had experienced nothing more than a transient and minor (as little as 0.5 mg/dl) rise in the serum creatinine concentration that clearly was not VMN. Such instances may reflect nothing more than an osmotic diuresis and the volume depletion that results from infusions of hyperosmolal contrast medium. Additionally, severe and irreversible renal failure occurring after aortography may, in some cases, reflect unrecognized atheroembolization or other complications of aortic catheterization.

Pathology

Initially normal in size, the kidneys of subjects with vasomotor nephropathy enlarge one to two days after the onset of renal failure and remain large well into the recovery period. On cut section, the renal parenchyma is pale while the medulla is often deep burgundy in color due to engorgement of medullary vessels and/or heme pigment in tubule structures. The glomeruli are entirely normal both on light and electron microscopy,[58,59] although distinct abnormalities have been reported in an occasional experimental model.[60] There is no necessary glomerular endothelial, epithelial, or mesangial cellular proliferation, and both the mesangium and the glomerular basement membranes appear entirely normal. Fibrin-like material in glomerular capillaries,[61] glomerular epithelial reflux,[62] and leukocyte margination in vasa rectae[63] have been reported as potentially important pathogenetic features, but both the frequency and significance of these findings are open to question.[64] Despite the marked attenuation of the preglomerular vasculature seen at angiography, the intrarenal vessels in biopsy and postmortem material appear entirely normal.[1] Presumably, then, the renal hemodynamic aberrations observed (see below) have no fixed anatomic basis. Interstitial edema is a prominent feature of established vasomotor nephropathy, although lacking on the initial day or so. As a result of this edema, tubules no longer lie in intimate contact, as is normal, but are separated by a distinct interstitial space. Small islands of lymphocytes with occasional plasma cells, eosinophils, and polymorphonuclear leukocytes may be found in the interstitium.[65] Profuse infiltration with mononuclear cells, particularly when accompanied by eosinophils and plasma cells, suggests a diagnosis of interstitial nephritis.[66] Bohle[64] has called attention to the fact that tubule lumens typically are not collapsed as in other autopsy and biopsy material, a feature he considers to be of diagnostic importance. The degree of tubule epithelial injury varies from subject to subject (see Pathophysiology), is patchy in distribution within a given kidney, and is frequently most notable at the corticomedullary junction.[67] Little or no change in the cellular architecture may be evident on light microscopy,[1,2] while at the other extreme, a rare patient will exhibit frank tubular necrosis, nuclear pyknosis, cellular disruption, and masses of epithelial debris within tubular lumens. There is, however, no correlation between the severity of the histologic lesions found and the clinical status of the individual patient.[1,2] Electron microscopic examination routinely reveals nuclear and mitochondrial alterations of tubular epithelial cells[64] even when light microscopic changes are minimal, a finding that appears to account for the greatly reduced tubular transport capacity in this syndrome.

It is usually difficult to diagnose vasomotor nephropathy solely from light microscopic examination of the tubular epithelium. Various authors have commented on the smudging and vacuolization of proximal tubule cells and the resemblance of such changes to those resulting from proteinuria, mannitol diuresis, and transient ischemia in kidneys with well maintained renal function.[1] When present, however, widespread nuclear pyknosis and mitoses are clear-cut evidence for frank tubular necrosis and strongly support a diagnosis of VMN in the absence of obvious and severe interstitial inflammatory disease.

THE CLINICAL SYNDROME OF VASOMOTOR NEPHROPATHY

Except for covert poisonings, VMN rarely occurs without an obvious antecedent cause. While a phase of "incipient renal failure" may exist for many hours or even days,[68] frank renal insufficiency usually develops rapidly and in close proximity to the causative insult. Renal failure may be delayed by several days after minor blood-group transfusion accidents[30] and some poisonings,[69] however. Oliguric renal failure is heralded by an abrupt reduction in urine volume to less than 400 ml/24 hr. Nonoliguric renal failure, once considered uncommon, appears in more recent series with an incidence of 20 to 50 percent,[70-72] a change perhaps largely attributable to the widespread usage of nephrotoxic antibiotics and more frequent laboratory screening of postoperative patients. Anderson and co-workers[72] incriminated antibiotics as the cause of 30 percent of their cases of nonoliguric renal failure. Patients with major and extensive burns also seem particularly prone to maintain a relatively high urine volume despite severe, hypercatabolic renal failure.[73] Total anuria may be found initially, but persistent anuria for a period greater than 24 to 48 hours is sufficiently uncommon as to suggest causes other than VMN. Urinary tract obstruction, large vessel or microvascular disease, renal cortical necrosis, allergic interstitial nephritis, glomerulonephritis, and ruptured bladder should be considered as alternative etiologies for prolonged, total anuria.

Whether the patient is oliguric or not, the urine output in our experience increases little if at all in response to either diuretic therapy[74] or the infusion of fluids. Indeed, responsiveness to diuretic agents is employed by some authorities as a test to rule out the diagnosis of vasomotor nephropathy,[75] although others would dispute the validity of that contention.[76] The volume of urine produced is remarkably constant from day to day, wide swings in urinary output being highly atypical. A urine pH of 5.5 to 6.5 typifies both the established and recovery phases of the syndrome of VMN. The urinary sodium concentration almost predictably ranges between 30 and 90 mEq/liter (most commonly 40 to 70 mEq/liter), and the fractional excretion of sodium (FE_{Na}) characteristically far exceeds 3 percent (see below). The osmolality of the urine differs from that of plasma by no more than 50 mOsm/kg H_2O,[77] and the urine creatinine concentration is some 5 to 15 (generally less than 10) times higher than that of plasma.[78] In a given patient, these urinary characteristics change little throughout the period of sustained renal failure.

Whether in oliguric or nonoliguric renal failure, the urine is often cloudy and off-brown in color. It is replete with tubular and bladder epithelial cells, coarsely granular casts, tubule cell casts, "broad" casts, and modest amounts of protein. While the casts may be pigment stained and red blood cells are often seen in the sediment, erythrocyte casts are so decidedly uncommon that their presence, particularly if associated with marked proteinuria and hypertension, should raise the possibility of glomerulopathy or vasculitis as alternate causes of renal failure. Modest leukocyturia may be found, but marked pyuria and leukocyte casts should prompt consideration of acute papillary necrosis (which is rare), infection/obstruction, or acute interstitial nephritis as the cause of renal failure.

Because of the markedly depressed glomerular filtration rate (GFR) in this syndrome, the BUN and serum creatinine concentrations are expected to rise progressively throughout the phase of established renal failure. Muscular individuals with hypercatabolic renal failure or rhabdomyolysis may display a daily rise in creatinine concentration of 4 mg/100 ml or more, while the usual increase is 1 to 2 mg/100 ml or so per day. The rate of blood urea nitrogen (BUN) elevation depends more on the catabolic state of the patient and the intake of protein nitrogen than on the degree of renal involvement. Minimally ill subjects with VMN caused by a mismatched transfusion, for example, may experience a BUN rise of only 10 mg/100 ml/day,[79] while that of hypercatabolic patients and those fed large nitrogen loads may increase by 40 to 60 mg/100 ml each day.[80] Coexistent therapy with corticosteroids or tetracyclines aggravates the rate of BUN increase. As a result of fluctuations in the catabolic rate, the daily BUN rise may be far less constant than that of serum creatinine.

As the patient enters the recovery phase of renal failure, urine volume is seen to increase stepwise on successive days. The BUN and serum creatinine concentrations characteristically continue to rise for a day or so after the urine volume picks up, and then levels off for a period of one or two days before entering a phase of progressive decline.[81] Coarsely granular and tubular epithelial casts may appear in profusion as oliguria is reversed. For much of the recovery phase, the urine sodium concentration, urine:plasma (U/P) creatinine ratio, urine osmolality, and FE_{Na} remain as they were during the oliguric period. Some flexibility in the control of urinary electrolyte excretion and osmolality first becomes apparent as the falling serum creatinine concentration approaches 3 mg/100 ml. Ultimately, the various aspects of renal function are expected to return to a level 80 percent or more of the norm.[82]

Table 15-2. Characteristic Clinical Presentation of Vasomotor Nephropathy

Phase of fixed renal failure
  Sudden onset in close temporal proximity to cause
  Oliguric (urine volume <400 ml/day) or nonoliguric
  Urine volume remarkably constant from day to day if the patient is hemodynamically stable
  Progressive and reasonably constant daily rise in serum creatinine concentration of at least 0.6 mg/day (usually >1 mg/day)
  Virtually no response of urine volume to fluid expansion or diuretics
  Urinary characteristics as in Table 15-3 with little daily variation
  Mean duration of oliguric VMN 11.6 days, nonoliguric 5.2 days before recovery phase starts. Renal failure lasting more than 3 weeks raises suspicion of an alternate diagnosis

Recovery phase
  Serum creatinine concentration continues to rise for 2 to 3 days after urine output starts to increase, plateaus for 1 to 3 days before falling
  Progressive rise in urine output
  Urinary chemistry as in the phase of full renal failure until the serum creatinine approaches baseline
  Recovery period one-half to two-thirds the duration of renal failure phase
  Full recovery, although subtle diminution in maximal concentrating ability and acid excretion may persist

The typical manifestations of VMN are summarized in Table 15-2.

THE CLINICAL CONSEQUENCES OF VASOMOTOR NEPHROPATHY

The clinical consequences of "renal shutdown" are the same no matter what the cause. Substances that depend on glomerular filtration for excretion are almost totally retained, and impaired tubular transport capacity markedly inhibits the excretion of a number of drugs and other organic compounds normally secreted by the proximal tubule.

Except for illness caused by the original cause of renal failure, or that due to severe fluid and electrolyte disorders (see the section on treatment of vasomotor nephropathy), the patient with vasomotor nephropathy is usually totally asymptomatic until the serum creatinine concentration reaches 6 to 8 mg/100 ml. Anorexia and nausea sometimes appear with this degree of azotemia, and are to be expected when the serum creatinine concentration rises much further. Hypertension, when present, is usually attributable to a marked overexpansion of the vascular compartment, and of itself, rarely produces symptomatology. Very severe elevations of blood pressure are more suggestive of malignant hypertension, scleroderma, or glomerular or renovascular disease as the true cause of renal failure. Some degree of anemia, variably attributable to iatrogenic and spontaneous blood loss,[83] resistance to erythropoietin,[84] and a shortened erythrocyte survival time[85] are expected within the first week of renal failure.[86] Acute illness, hypercatabolism, abnormal bleeding, and hemolysis may be further contributors. In the absence of major bleeding or brisk hemolysis, however, the anemia is rarely severe and does not appear to be prevented by frequent and intensive dialysis. Modest leukocytosis is commonly seen even in the absence of devitalized tissue or evident infection.[87]

Late Consequences of Vasomotor Nephropathy

Even when conservative treatment succeeds in preventing major fluid and electrolyte disorders, prolonged renal failure ultimately produces life-threatening uremic complications unless dialysis is introduced. The manifestations of frank uremia usually do not appear until the BUN concentration exceeds 180 mg/100 ml and the serum creatinine concentration is above 12 mg/100 ml. By this time the patient usually feels decidedly unwell, anorexia and nausea are more pronounced, and vomiting may supervene. Anemia may be marked, and platelet dysfunction[88] may be manifested by bleeding of the gums, bruising, metrorrhagia, or even gastrointestinal hemorrhage. Unless dialysis is undertaken, generalized pruritus soon develops, and bothersome muscle cramps, which are not necessarily related to electrolyte imbalance,[89] are common. The patient frequently complains of a metallic taste caused by the hydrolysis of salivary urea to ammonia by bacterial urease. This, together with decreased salivary flow, may produce frank stomatitis. Monilial superinfection of the oropharynx is common, and slowed parotid flow predisposes to the development of acute parotitis.

Undialyzed, the patient is at increasing risk of serious neurologic, infectious, and other life-threatening complications,[90] which will be briefly described below. It is now customary to dialyze patients with any form of renal failure "prophylactically" before such symptoms supervene (i.e., at a BUN concentration of 100 to 120 mg/100 ml or a serum creatinine concentration of 8 to 10 mg/100 ml; see the section on treatment of vasomotor nephropathy).

Altered mentation is usually the first indication of a uremic neurologic disorder in undialyzed or inadequately dialyzed patients. The signs are at first subtle, intermittent, and elusive. Personality changes are common, and depression, irritability, or excitement follow and may be seen in sequence. Asterixis, myoclonus, coarse fasciculation, and tremors usually appear later and appear to be unrelated to electrolyte disorders. Deep tendon reflexes may be hypo- or hyperactive at this time, sometimes asymmetrically and inconstantly. Even vision may be impaired,[91] and a pathologic Babinski reflex may be found. Meningismus may develop, and the spinal fluid protein concentration and pressure may be elevated, although pleocytosis is decidedly uncommon.[91] Confusion, lethargy, disorientation, and convulsions may progress to coma unless the uremic process is reversed. Fortunately, such advanced neurologic manifestations are now rarely seen thanks to early and vigorous dialysis.

Pericarditis, once a frequent concomitant of late uremia[92] and a harbinger of uremic death, is seen far less frequently since the advent of "early" dialysis. Occasionally, however, pericarditis becomes manifest at a relatively low serum creatinine concentration of 5 or 6 mg/100 ml, and in patients who by most other criteria would be considered "well dialyzed." The patient with uremic pericarditis usually will experience precordial discomfort, but may be entirely asymptomatic. Electrocardiographic changes[93] are variably present. The associated pericardial friction rub is classically rough, coarse, and constant, but is so soft, murmur-like, and even evanescent in some patients as to be heard by one skilled examiner and not another listening to the patient's chest an hour later. Fibrinous pleurisy, manifested by a pleuropericardial friction rub, is found only occasionally.[94] Pericarditis may be associated with significant effusion of fluid into the pericardium which, when forming rapidly, can be life-threatening if not treated promptly.[95] Tamponade due to hemopericardium occurs uncommonly.[96]

Gastrointestinal hemorrhage due to diffuse gastritis or peptic ulceration[97] has been noted in up to 40 percent of patients with post-traumatic VMN and, together with sepsis and cardiac abnormalities,[90] is a leading cause of death.[98] Bleeding may occur at any time in the patient's course when due to gastritis or peptic ulcers, but bleeding due to uremic enterocolitis[99] is a complication of advanced uremia and so has become quite uncommon since early dialysis has become routine.

Formerly, it was customary to remove all sources of dietary protein to reduce the risk of life-threatening hyperkalemia and minimize the rate of urea and hydrogen ion formation. The availability of dialysis now obviates the need for such stringent dietary restriction. Major nutritional problems are thus unlikely to appear in subjects who feel well enough to take a reasonable diet. Unhappily, the underlying cause of renal failure itself often leaves the patient severely ill, hypercatabolic, and unwilling or unable to eat. The situation may be further complicated by uncontrolled vomiting or essential gastrointestinal tube drainage. Then, since renal failure may persist for as long as three to four weeks, marked protein malnutrition may present yet another challenge to survival unless parenteral feeding is begun.

Recovery from Vasomotor Nephropathy

With rare exceptions, the kidney returns to its premorbid state if the patient survives the period of renal failure. All biochemical parameters slowly improve as an adequate GFR is restored. Massive diuresis may occur for several days after the serum creatinine concentration begins to fall, particularly if excessively large volumes of fluid have been retained during the oliguric phase. The neurologic status of the patient may actually deteriorate transiently as the BUN falls, especially when the improvement in GFR is rapid and the patient has been excessively azotemic. Full neurologic recovery is the rule. The anemia and platelet abnormalities repair slowly and may persist for some time after renal function is restored. Pruritus is soon lost. However, sepsis remains a threat well into the recovery phase, with up to one-half of septic deaths related to renal failure occurring in this period.[100] In our experience, the recovery phase lasts approximately one-half to two-thirds as long as the period of full renal failure. Thus, with oliguric VMN lasting an average of 11 to 12 days, recovery to a serum creatinine concentration of 2 or 3 mg/dl usually takes about a week after the urine volume first picks up. A shorter recovery period can be expected with renal failure of lesser duration, while recovery may require two weeks or more in the unusual case in which VMN lasts for as long as three to four weeks. A prolonged convalescence is not unexpected in patients whose renal failure was associated with severe illness.

ON THE DIFFERENTIAL DIAGNOSIS OF ACUTE RENAL FAILURE

Renal function may be severely depressed by a host of renal and extrarenal disturbances other than VMN. A broad subclassification of causes has been published elsewhere,[101] and a list of the more common etiologies is given in Table 15-1. More than one potential cause of renal failure may be present in the same patient. Renal failure attributed to VMN in a trauma victim may actually be due to fat or atheromatous embolization suffered either at the time of injury or as the result of subsequent aortography or surgical manipulation of the aorta.[102] Allergic interstitial nephritis or hypersensitivity angiitis may complicate treatment with any of a number of drugs to which such a patient is apt to be exposed.[103] Partial urinary outflow obstruction due to pelvic hematoma, ureteral blood clots, or retroperitoneal hemorrhage may seriously impair renal function and go unrecognized unless specifically excluded by appropriate studies. Traumatic thrombosis of major renal vessels or aneurysmal aortic dissection may be hidden by the severity and extensiveness of abdominal trauma. Sepsis, heart failure, unrecognized severe volume depletion, or hypotension may seriously impair glomerular filtration on a purely functional basis, and rupture of the bladder will produce seemingly total (but false) renal failure.

Other causes for renal failure may at times also be misdiagnosed as VMN. A child with Henoch-Schönlein purpura sent for diagnostic laparotomy may develop postoperative renal failure, not as a result of VMN, but due to the disease process that prompted the surgery in the first place. Addison's disease, uncovered by stress, may cause severe functional renal failure with none of the urinary characteristics expected in volume-depleted patients. Myocardial infarction, cardiac surgery, or sepsis may produce hypotension amenable only to large doses of dopamine or catecholamine. At such doses, these agents worsen rather than ameliorate renal ischemia[104] despite a seemingly encouraging rise in blood pressure, and often are the major contributors to protracted functional renal insufficiency. Covert sepsis may significantly depress renal function before it declares itself. Hyperuricemia in patients undergoing cytolytic therapy for malignancies can result in either acute gouty "infarction" of the kidney or urinary outflow obstruction.[105] Jaundiced patients may experience renal failure due to such diverse causes as VMN, the hepatorenal syndrome,[106] functional abnormalities, or systemic diseases affecting both the kidney and the liver (e.g., leptospirosis, vasculitis, malignancy, vena caval thrombosis). Sustained osmotic diuresis in diabetes may conceal severe volume depletion from those who equate an "adequate" urine volume with euvolemia, and may prompt a diagnosis of nonoliguric VMN as the renal function falls; solute diuresis mounted by burned patients[107] and incomplete urinary outflow obstruction can do likewise. Acute elevations of serum creatinine may follow the introduction of radiographic contrast medium in certain patients.[108] Indomethacin treatment has been reported to cause a moderate depression of renal function in a significant number of cases,[109] as has combined therapy with trimethoprim and sulfamethoxazole (Bactrim).[110]

In short, the number of diseases and other circumstances that cause an acute deterioration of renal function is legion. While it is routine to consider VMN, functional renal failure, and urinary outflow obstruction in the differential diagnosis, other causes must always be borne in mind.

VASOMOTOR NEPHROPATHY VERSUS FUNCTIONAL RENAL FAILURE

It is usually not difficult to distinguish between VMN and functional renal failure on the basis of history, physical examination, clinical course, and the very different urine characteristics with which they present. When the cardiac output of young, otherwise healthy individuals falls to a degree that greatly reduces the GFR, there is a concomitant outpouring of aldosterone and antidiuretic hormone (ADH). With an intact concentrating capacity and distal tubule system, the normal but hypoperfused kidney avidly absorbs sodium (urine sodium concentration 0 to 5 mEq/liter) and concentrates urinary solutes to a far higher concentration than in plasma (U/P creatinine ratio >60, U/P osmolality ratio 2 to 3). Despite the avidity of salt and water absorption, the urine output will generally increase after a large dose of a loop diuretic or mannitol. By contrast, tubular injury is a hallmark of VMN. While on histologic section the renal epithelium usually does not show frank necrosis, the tubules cannot conserve sodium or concentrate their urine no matter how appropriate such responses might be to the patient's hemodynamic status. Thus, as noted earlier, the urine sodium concentration is generally between 30 and 90 mEq/liter, the urine:plasma (U/P) creatinine and urea concentration ratios are low, and concentrating and diluting capacity are essentially lost. Such findings contrast sharply with the "classical" urinary characteristics of functional renal failure.

Unfortunately, the features separating functional renal failure from VMN often become blurred in patients with even very modest antecedent renal disease. Despite severe volume depletion, such individuals often cannot concentrate their urine,[111] their U/P creatinine ratio is apt to be much lower than is usual for functional renal failure, and the urine sodium concentration may far exceed that considered typical of functional renal failure. The urinary findings thus may resemble or be quite typical of those in VMN even when the acute reduction in GFR is entirely functional. In my experience, moreover, this same population seems to respond to severe volume depletion, heart failure, or sepsis with unusually severe functional renal failure, their serum creatinine concentration at times rising many fold. As a further complication, elderly patients who have been seriously volume depleted for some time do not necessarily respond promptly to fluid administration. Rather, they may remain oliguric for up to 24 to 36 hours after the full restoration of the volume deficit is assured by a normal or high pulmonary capillary wedge pressure.[112] Such fluid unresponsiveness may be misinterpreted as an indication of established VMN, and sometimes prompts the unwary to restrict fluids rather than continuing to replace lost volume. However, such patients usually respond promptly to a large dose of a loop diuretic or mannitol after their plasma volume has been restored, a clear signal of the functional origin of their sustained renal insufficiency.

In short, while the urinary characteristics most often will distinguish patients with volume depletion from those with VMN, that happy circumstance does not always prevail.

VASOMOTOR NEPHROPATHY VERSUS URINARY OUTFLOW OBSTRUCTION

Urinary tract obstruction can be complete or incomplete. When outflow obstruction is incomplete, the patient may be oliguric, have a well preserved urine output, or even exhibit polyuria. To produce renal failure, of course, obstruction must either be bilateral or occur in a solitary functioning kidney. (It must be remembered that 1 in 500 members of the population has but a single kidney or exhibits unilateral renal atrophy at autopsy[113].) Lesions involving both ureters simultaneously, or the bladder outlet, are thus the most common cause of obstructive renal failure. In the male, hypertrophy or carcinoma of the prostate, urethral stricture, carcinoma of the bladder and invasive colonic tumors are the most frequent offenders. In females, vaginal and cervical carcinomas replace prostatic causes. Retroperitoneal fibrosis or infiltrative tumors of the retroperitoneum (especially seminoma, lymphoma, or reticulum cell sarcoma) frequently entrap both ureters. Repeated renal stone formation not uncommonly obliterates the function of one kidney at some point in time, subsequent obstruction of the contralateral kidney then causing complete renal failure.

The urine sodium concentration as well as the U/P creatinine concentration and osmolality ratios of subjects with urinary outflow obstruction typically are indistinguishable from their counterparts in VMN. Thus, when the obstruction is silent and incomplete, the two entities can be separated only by employing ancillary diagnostic criteria. Certain clues should point away from a diagnosis of VMN and toward a possible obstructive cause of renal failure. These are: a clear responsiveness of urine output to diuretics; a urine volume that changes by 50 percent or more upward and downward on different days or shows marked variation from hour to hour; a serum creatinine concentration that fluctuates in its upward or downward trend; periods of renal insufficiency alternating with more normal renal function (in the absence of cardiovascular instability); and a history of abnormalities likely to cause urinary tract obstruction.[81] Bladder outflow obstruction may be detectable by abdominal palpation, but in adults the bladder does not become palpable until it is massively enlarged. Straight catheterization is of both diagnostic and therapeutic value if lower tract obstruction exists. Ultrasonography of the abdomen usually will detect urinary stones; establish the presence, location, and size of the kidneys; and reveal obstructive enlargement of the ureters and/or renal pelvis (see below). Increasing numbers of reports of false negative studies have appeared, however, most commonly when ureteral enlargement is limited by the corseting effect of retroperitoneal fibrosis or tumor. If, therefore, upper tract obstruction is suspected and ultrasonography fails to confirm its presence, retrograde pyelography is required for a definitive diagnosis.

VASOMOTOR NEPHROPATHY VERSUS GLOMERULAR/ MICROVASCULAR DISEASES

Diseases that primarily affect the glomeruli or microvasculature but cause little injury usually leave the sodium transport and concentration mechanisms intact. When renal failure supervenes, therefore, the urinary chemical characteristics are quite comparable to those of functional renal failure. In some instances, however, the tubules are notably involved. In such cases the urinary characteristics may be either quite typical of VMN and the tubulointerstitial disorders, or fall into a "gray zone" intermediate between those disorders and functional renal failure. This causes little difficulty if the urine sediment contains the characteristic erythrocytes and red blood cell (RBC) casts, and if there is marked proteinuria. However, microhematuria is commonly found in both VMN and allergic interstitial nephritis, and RBC casts are not always demonstrable in the glomerular and (especially) the microvascular diseases. Indeed, atheromatous microembolization to the kidney classically yields a remarkably benign urinary sediment,[114] and unless other stigmata of these disorders are sought and recognized, they can easily be confused with VMN.

FRACTIONAL EXCRETION OF SODIUM IN DIFFERENTIAL DIAGNOSIS

Because some individual cases believed to represent VMN on clinical grounds have shown urinary characteristics at the cusp of, or outside, the values expected with that diagnosis, more definitive diagnostic tests have been sought. Most notable among these have been the renal failure index (RFI)[115] and the fractional excretion of sodium, FE_{Na}. In the former, the urinary sodium concentration (U_{Na}) is divided by the simultaneous urine:plasma creatinine concentration ratio $(U/P)_{cr}$ so that $RFI = U_{Na}/(U/P)_{cr}$. The FE_{Na} is a very similar test in which the U/P sodium concentration ratio $(U/P)_{Na}$ is substituted for the urinary sodium concentration value. Thus, $FE_{Na} = (U/P)_{Na}/(U/P)_{cr}$; it is customary to convert the FE_{Na} to a percentage by multiplying the result by 100. With the degree of variation in serum sodium concentration generally encountered, the two indices give results that are little different in their diagnostic sensitivity. A fractional excretion of sodium below 1 percent appears to effectively rule out the possibility of vasomotor nephropathy.[116,117] Values between 1 and 3 percent have been considered indeterminate by Miller and associates,[117] and indicative of VMN by Espinel and Gregory.[116]

Both groups of authors have declared the FE_{Na} to be superior to the classically employed indices (U_{Na}, $(U/P)_{cr}$, $(U/P)_{osm}$) as a diagnostic marker. In one of the reports,[116] 11 of the 40 patients stated to have "ATN" (VMN) had a urine sodium concentration below 20 mEq/liter, 16 had U/P creatinine concentration ratios greater than 15, and 13 had urinary osmolalities higher than 350 mOsm/kg H_2O. All 40 of these subjects had an FE_{Na} greater than 1 percent, but 22 values were below 3 percent. Of 55 cases of acute oliguric and nonoliguric renal failure attributed to "ATN" in the other series,[117] 11 reportedly had urine osmolality values between 350 and 500 mOsm/kg H_2O; no oliguric subjects and only 2 of 31 nonoliguric patients had a urinary sodium concentration below 20 mEq/liter, a finding that contrasts sharply with the report of Espinel and Gregory.[116] Seventeen individuals bearing the diagnosis of "ATN"' had U/P creatinine ratios greater than 20, however, and 5 of these were above 40. One oliguric subject and 10 percent of the nonoliguric patients reportedly displayed an FE_{Na} under 1 percent. In both studies, therefore, an extraordinary number of patients considered to have "ATN" had a urinary sodium concentration, and/or a U/P osmolality or U/P creatinine concentration ratio far outside the range generally considered typical of that diagnosis. If, therefore, the FE_{Na} is to be considered an almost perfect diagnostic indicator of VMN, as suggested by these reports, one would have to accept that a urinary sodium concentration below 20 mEq/liter, urine osmolality between 350 and 500 mOsm/kg H_2O, and a U/P creatinine concentration ratio between 15 and 40 occur commonly in this syndrome. However, such findings are so foreign to the prevailing literature and our own experience as to raise serious questions about the accuracy of diagnosis in at least the most exceptional cases.

The GFR of subjects with oliguric VMN is usually less than 5 ml/min, and commonly 1 ml/min.[71,78,100,118,119] The GFR is approximated by the creatinine clearance, which is in turn calculated as the $(U/P)_{cr}$ ratio multiplied by the urine excretion rate (V) [i.e., $GFR = (U/P)_{cr} \times V$]. On rearranging, $(U/P)_{cr} = GFR/V$. Thus, when the GFR and urine flow rate are known, one can easily calculate the corresponding unique value for $(U/P)_{cr}$. Figure 15-1 illustrates the $(U/P)_{cr}$ that must accompany given values for the GFR and daily urine output. It can be seen, for example, that the U/P creatinine concentration ratio must be only 3.6 when the GFR is 1 ml/min and the urine volume is 400 ml/day. With this urine output, in-

Special Problems of Acute Renal Failure • 539

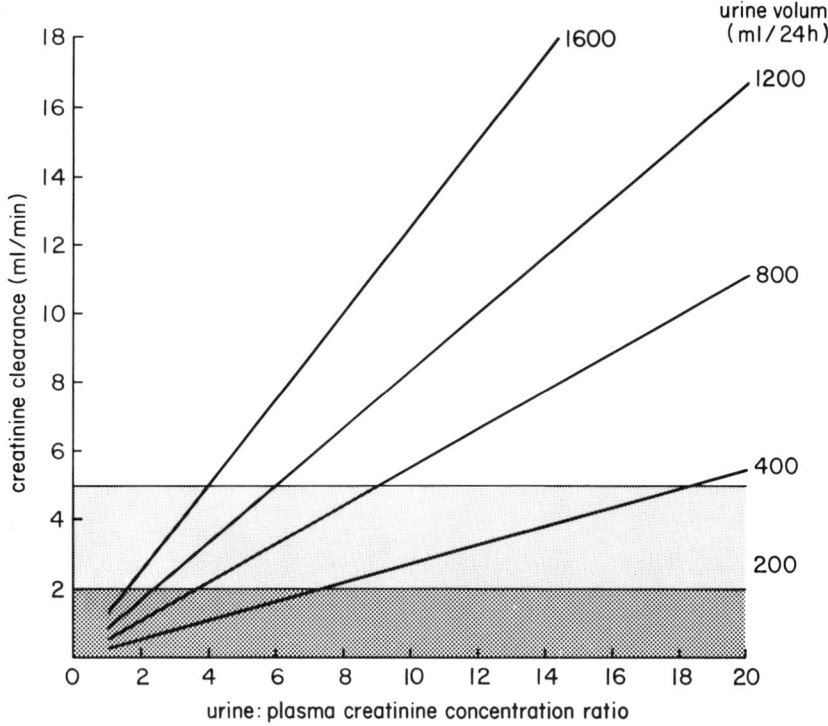

Fig. 15-1. The relationship between the urine:plasma creatinine concentration ratio $(U/P)_{cr}$ and creatinine clearance (GFR,C_{cr}) at different daily urine volumes. The expected range of C_{cr} in oliguric (stippled) and nonoliguric (lighter stippling) renal failure is shown. With $(U/P)_{cr}$ = GFR/V, this figure illustrates the relationship between the C_{cr} and $(U/P)_{cr}$ at various assumed urine volumes. The crosshatched zone at the base of the figure delimits a GFR of 0 to 2 ml/min, while the stippled area reflects a GFR of 2 to 5 ml/min. Note that at these low GFR values and the urine volumes shown, the $(U/P)_{cr}$ ratio is always less than 18. Far higher ratios can be attained only if the GFR is much greater than that expected in VMN. (From Oken DE,[81] with permission.)

deed, the $(U/P)_{cr}$ does not exceed 18 even when the GFR is as high as 5 ml/min; with a nonoliguric urine volume of 1,000 ml/day, the calculated $(U/P)_{cr}$ is 7.2, and a GFR of even 10 ml/min yields a $(U/P)_{cr}$ of only 14.2. It thus is easy to see why, with the GFR usually well below 5 ml/min, the measured $(U/P)_{cr}$ of most individuals with VMN is so low.

Conversely, one can determine the GFR that corresponds to any given $(U/P)_{cr}$ and daily urine volume from the clearance equation. A $(U/P)_{cr}$ ratio of 40 (as found in the studies just cited) with a urine volume of 400 ml/day presupposes a GFR of 11 ml/min; the GFR of a nonoliguric patient with a urine volume of 1,000 ml/24hr and the same $(U/P)_{cr}$ is 28 ml/min. In my experience, a GFR of even 11 ml/min is rather unusual in VMN, and a GFR as high as 28 ml/min is sufficiently atypical as to raise questions about the accuracy of diagnosis when such a high $(U/P)_{cr}$ is found. Since the urinary osmolality relates closely to the U/P creatinine ratio, urine osmolalities of 400 to 500 mOsm/kg H_2O, such as were reported in the studies just cited, imply not only an unusually well maintained GFR, but also a remarkably intact urinary concentrating mechanism.

In our practice, most patients with a *clinical* presentation entirely typical of VMN (see Table 15-3) have had an FE_{Na} of 6 percent and above.[81] Many have exhibited a value between 3 and 6 percent, and a small minority have had an FE_{Na} below 3 percent. However, these lower figures often have been obtained in cases in which, on the basis of the overall clinical presentation, the diagnosis of VMN has been less than certain. It will be recalled that Espinel and Gregory have claimed that an FE_{Na} above 1 percent signifies a diagnosis of VMN, while Miller and associates consider a value of 3 percent as the demarcation point. It thus seems worthwhile to carefully examine the relationship between the urinary sodium concentration, U/P creatinine concentration ratio, and FE_{Na} shown in Figure 15-2.

With an FE_{Na} of 6 percent, we see that the $(U/P)_{cr}$ ratio cannot exceed 15 unless the urine sodium concentration is over 100 mEq/liter. Since a U_{Na} higher than this is unusual in VMN, so too should be a $(U/P)_{cr}$ above 15 at this same FE_{Na}. With an FE_{Na} of 6, moreover, the urine sodium concentration does not fall below 30 mEq/liter unless the U/P creatinine value is less than 3.6 (Fig. 15-2); $(U/P)_{cr}$ ratios lower than this are rarely encountered. Thus, at any FE_{Na} value of 6 percent or higher, both the urine Na concentration and the U/P creatinine (and by extension U/P osmolality) ratios virtually always fall within the "classical" limits.

If we take an FE_{Na} of 3 percent to be the lower limit diagnostic of VMN, the $(U/P)_{cr}$ always falls within the expected value (i.e., <15) at any urine sodium concentration between 30 and 65 mEq/liter; a sodium concentration of 75 mEq/liter is associated with a U/P creatinine ratio of 17.9, only slightly above the usually cited upper limit in VMN. Thus, since a U_{Na} much above 75 mEq/liter is somewhat unusual in VMN, a FE_{Na} of 3 will usually be accompanied by "classical" values for both the U_{Na} and $(U/P)_{cr}$. However, Figure 15-2 also shows that there is a sizeable triangular area in which both the U/P creatinine ratio and urine sodium concentration are entirely typical of VMN, yet the FE_{Na} lies between 1.8 and 3 percent. If, therefore, an FE_{Na} below 3 percent is considered to rule out VMN as the cause of renal failure,[117] at least some patients with $(U/P)_{cr}$ and U_{Na} values within that triangle would be (wrongly?) excluded from that diagnosis. On the other hand, the suggestion that an FE_{Na} as low as 1 percent is diagnostic of VMN fails to consider that values

Table 15-3. Typical Urinary Characteristics of Various Forms of Acute Renal Failure

Condition	U_{Na} (mEq/liter)	$(U/P)_{cr}$	$(U/P)_{osm}$	FE_{Na} (%)	Sediment
Functional[a]	<20	>20	>2	<1	Benign
VMN	30–90	<15	0.95–1.05	>3	"Broad" granular and cellular casts, RBC; no RBC casts
Obstructive uropathy	As in VMN	As in VMN	As in VMN	As in VMN	RBC may be present; WBC if infected
Interstitial nephritis	As in VMN	As in VMN	As in VMN	As in VMN	WBC, WBC casts predominate. RBC may be present; no RBC casts. Eosinophils if allergic etiology
Glomerulovascular[b]	<20	Usually >20	>1	Usually <1	RBC, RBC casts

[a] May resemble VMN if superimposed on chronic renal disease, after loop diuretic therapy, or under the influence of chemical or osmotic diuretics.

[b] May resemble VMN or be intermediate between VMN and functional renal failure if there is prominent tubular injury.

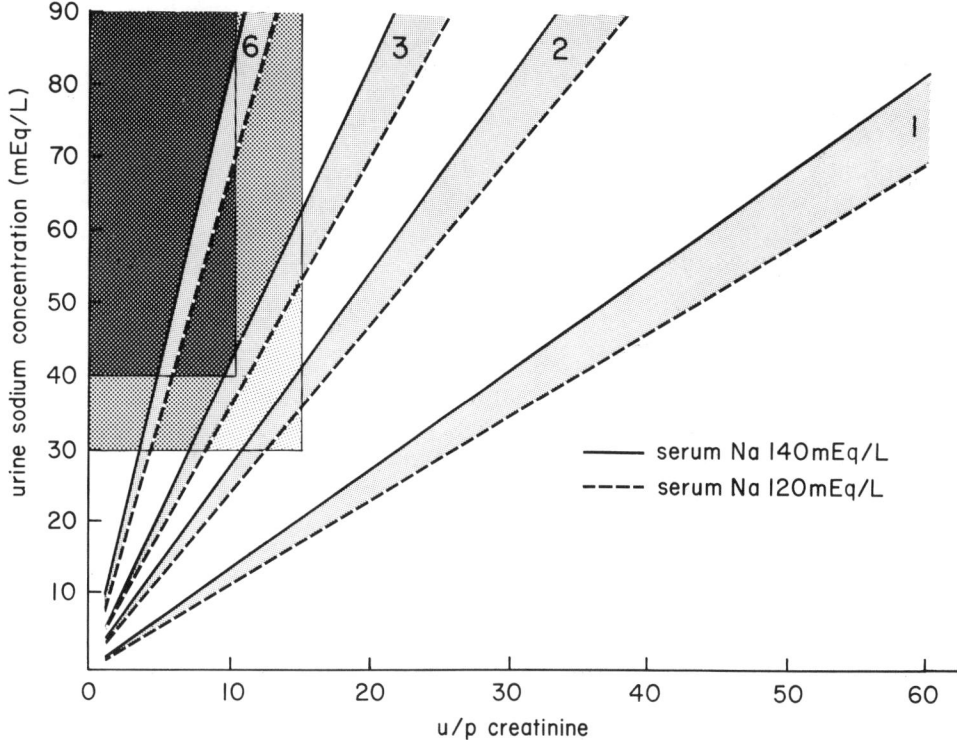

Fig. 15-2 Fractional excretion of sodium (FE$_{Na}$) corresponding to various urinary sodium concentrations (U$_{Na}$) and (U/P)$_{cr}$ ratios, with assumed plasma sodium concentrations of 120 to 140 mEq/liter. Values for U$_{Na}$ and (U/P)$_{cr}$ considered typical of VMN (see text) are shown with shading at the left of the figure, the more usual range of values being shown in the darker zone. Note that a FE$_{Na}$ of 1 percent, which is typical of functional renal failure, never intersects this zone and thus has precisely the same diagnostic implications as the corresponding U$_{Na}$ and (U/P)$_{cr}$ values. It also should be noted that the "classical" U$_{Na}$ and (U/P)$_{cr}$ values usually correspond to an FE$_{Na}$ above 3 percent, but that entirely typical values can coexist with FE$_{Na}$ values below this, as shown in the finely stippled triangle of the figure. A FE$_{Na}$ between 1 and 3 percent is thus considered of uncertain value in the differential diagnosis of acute renal failure. (From Oken DE,[81] with permission.)

even higher than this can be found concomitantly with a (U/P)$_{cr}$ ratio above 60 (Fig. 15-2). In my view, such a creatinine ratio is incompatible with a diagnosis of VMN.[81]

The validity of any study of the presenting characteristics in VMN rests entirely upon proper diagnosis of the patients included. In my experience, most cases of assumed VMN in which the U$_{Na}$, U/P creatinine ratio, and U/P osmolality have departed greatly from the classical values discussed above have also exhibited a clinical course that is not entirely typical of that diagnosis. As noted earlier, acute interstitial nephritis, renal atheroembolism, instances of glomerulonephritis without the characteristic RBC casts, hypersensitivity angiitis, functional renal failure superimposed on pre-existing renal disease, and other renal disorders all may masquerade as VMN. Thus, even when both the "classical" urinary findings and the FE$_{Na}$ are entirely consistent with that diagnosis, one still should examine the history, physical examination, and very importantly, the total clinical presentation (Table 15-3) to minimize the likelihood of a misdiagnosis. Conversely, alternative causes of renal failure should be actively considered whenever *any* aspect of the clinical or laboratory presentation is atypical. To do otherwise may conceal the correct diagnosis and significantly distort one's concept of the true presentation of this disorder.

Limits for urine sodium, osmolality, FE_{Na}, and $(U/P)_{cr}$ in VMN should not be considered inviolable. Urine sodium concentration, U/P osmolality, and creatinine concentration ratios only slightly out of the expected range may be seen with otherwise typical VMN. Nonetheless, the further any value strays from the norm the less likely is this diagnosis to be correct. A calculated creatinine clearance above 5 ml/min in oliguric patients is decidedly suspect. Accordingly, a serum creatinine concentration that rises by much less than 1 mg/dl daily again bespeaks a degree of maintained filtration that deserves note. In hemodynamically stable individuals, a urine volume that fluctuates by 50 percent a day, either spontaneously or as a result of fluid administration and diuretics, is so atypical of VMN as to prompt a search for alternate causes even when all the other urinary characteristics are entirely compatible with that diagnosis. Up-and-down fluctuation or prolonged stabilization of the serum creatinine concentration without the onset of recovery is even more suggestive of diagnoses other than VMN, as is a rapid fall in serum creatinine concentration without the typical plateau heralding the onset of recovery (see above). The finding of red cell and/or white cell casts and marked proteinuria, severe hypertension, peripheral manifestations of systemic diseases likely to produce renal failure, major microangiopathic changes in a blood smear, persistent hypotension, livedo reticularis (suggestive of atheroembolism or vasculitis), and concomitant liver failure all warrant consideration of alternate causes for renal failure.

OTHER DIAGNOSTIC PARAMETERS IN ACUTE RENAL FAILURE

In recent years, the urinary excretion of proximal tubular enzymes and low-molecular-weight proteins (e.g., β_2 microglobulin) has been applied in the differential diagnosis of acute renal failure. Increased excretion of β_2 microglobulin and various tubular enzymes—most prominently alanine aminopeptidase,[120] lactic dehydrogenase,[121] and N-acetyl-glucosaminidase[122]—is a reliable marker of quite low levels of tubular injury. Indeed, significant enzymuria is found routinely in patients given aminonucleoside antibiotics and who have no demonstrable change in renal function.[123] Although on average, enzymuria tends to be greater in VMN than in most other conditions affecting the kidney,[124] the degree of overlap between the various disorders is such as to limit its diagnostic value.

Intravenous pyelography has been suggested as a valuable tool in the differential diagnosis of acute renal failure.[125] With total urinary outflow obstruction, one generally sees normal opacification of the renal cortex, but calyceal filling is lacking; in the presence of incomplete obstruction, sequential films often display increasing calyceal opacification, with faint ultimate delineation of the renal pelvis or enlarged ureters above the point of obstruction. The appearance of a persistent nephrogram immediately after injection of contrast medium has been suggested to be pathognomonic of VMN or acute pyelonephritis with oliguric renal failure. However, we have seen the same phenomenon in other forms of renal failure as well as many instances of VMN in which cortical opacification occurred slowly and increased with time. Thus, while early, dense opacification of the kidneys may be commonly found in vasomotor nephropathy, one perhaps should not put too much reliance on the diagnostic aspects of the nephrographic appearance in the individual patient. In recent years, moreover, it has become recognized that the renal function of patients with diagnoses other than VMN may suffer as the result of injected hyperosmolal contrast medium. Ultrasonography has thus largely displaced the intravenous pyelogram (IVP) in the workup of subjects with acute renal failure.

Sonography is an excellent means of identifying urinary outflow obstruction, and often can indicate the cause of such obstruction when it is due to extrinsic masses[126] or nephrolithiasis. The technique accurately delineates renal size, a feature that may be very useful in differentiating vasomotor nephropathy from acute arterial occlusion, and in separating acute problems from chronic ones. The kidney with VMN is enlarged and exhibits decreased cortical echogenicity.[126] Renal artery occlusion is characterized by a small kidney size with high cortical echogenicity.[126] Uncomplicated functional renal failure should present with normal sized kidneys (unless the patient is in shock at the time of study) with normal echo characteristics. Additional information valuable in the differential diagnosis may be derived by combining sonography with computed radionuclide studies.[127] In the latter, effective renal plasma flow, CFR, and the filtration fraction can be approximated by determining the uptake of ^{131}I-hippuran or ^{99m}Tc–iron ascorbate by the kidneys after intravenous injection. The renal uptake and loss of isotope is followed with a gamma scintillation camera coupled to a suitable computer. The iron ascorbate is excreted exlusively by glomerular filtration, while ^{131}I-hippuran, which is handled by both filtration and tubular secretion, serves as a measure of renal cortical blood flow.[127] Vasomotor nephropathy is typified by markedly depressed cortical blood flow, impaired tubule function, and a negligible GFR, as manifested by delayed radionuclide uptake, slow attainment of peak activity, and (factitiously) an increasing calculated filtration fraction.[127] Again, however, although distinct patterns are said to be characteristic of one diagnosis or another, the technique is most useful in cases of renal artery occlusion, cortical necrosis, or hyperacute rejection, which it easily separates from urinary outflow obstruction. The ability of this tool to reliably differentiate between VMN, atheromatous embolization, interstitial nephritis, hypersensitivity angiitis, and other entities presenting with oliguric renal failure has not yet been established. Indeed, this approach has not found wide acceptance at all in the past several years.

Selective renal arteriography has been employed as a definitive means of separating vasomotor nephropathy from renal cortical necrosis and renal arterial occlusion.[5,6] Traumatic avulsion of the kidney from its renal artery, a frequently fatal accident, can be identified by arteriography, as can involvement of the renal arterial ostia by a dissecting aortic aneurysm, embolus, or atheromatous occlusive disease of the aorta or renal arteries. Except when specifically indicated in looking for these disorders, however, the invasive nature of the procedure precludes its application as a routine diagnostic measure in patients with acute renal failure.

PATHOPHYSIOLOGY OF VASOMOTOR NEPHROPATHY

Experimental techniques that might reveal the mechanisms responsible for the vanishingly low inulin clearance of VMN in man are very limited. They were even more so when this syndrome first became widely recognized, and early physiologic studies of the underlying mechanisms failed to provide definitive answers.[118,119] Pathogenetic theories were therefore based largely on three major abnormalities of renal histology: tubular injury, proteinaceous material or cell debris in tubule lumens, and interstitial edema. Since the glomeruli and the renal vasculature appear entirely normal in this syndrome,[58,59] it was assumed that glomerular filtration should occur at a normal or only modestly reduced rate. If so, it was reasoned, the very low inulin clearance could only be explained by tubular outflow obstruction, the quantitative and nonselective leakage of filtrate across a damaged tubular epithelial barrier, or both. With "passive backflow" of filtrate then assumed, the inulin and para-aminohippurate (PAH) clearance techniques were considered unreliable indicators of the true GFR and renal blood flow. However, the early assumption that normal glomerular and vascular histology necessarily denoted adequate filtration and renocortical blood flow rates had little basis in fact. Indeed, although histologically normal, the intrarenal arteries at angiography are greatly reduced in caliber.[6] The arcuate vessels are notably attenuated, and the fourth- and fifth-order vessels virtually disappear, leaving only scattered wisps of vessels in the outer cortex.[5,6] Such findings signify a major increase in preglomerular renovascular resistance and, by extrapolation, a substantial reduction in renocortical blood flow.

Unlike the PAH clearance technique, the indirect Fick method of blood flow measurement is uninfluenced by any uncertainty about the tubules' integrity, and is thus entirely suitable for use in subjects with VMN. Measured in this way, renocortical blood flow generally averages some 20 to 30 percent of normal,[3-8] a finding consonant with the marked vascular attenuation seen at angiography. Outer cortical blood flow is particularly decreased.[5,6]

Tubular Factors in Human Vasomotor Nephropathy

Although pioneering microdissection studies by Oliver and co-workers[128] suggested that tubular necrosis is the keystone of the syndrome of VMN in man, that view has changed over the years. Indeed, several pathologists (e.g., references 16–19) have emphasized the *paucity* of tubular degenerative changes in most patients dying in "acute tubular necrosis." Those lesions that are seen have been considered to be neither consistent nor diagnostically specific.[16,17] Recently, Solez and Finckh[129] utilized modern statistical methodology to re-review the pathologic material that served as the basis for one of these reports.[1] Twenty of the 28 patients with ARF showed no histologic evidence of proximal tubular injury at all. A like number displayed either no or only slight distal tubular change even though the mean score for these abnormalities was statistically higher in the patients with ARF than in controls. To be considered a key pathogenetic factor in VMN, however, tubular alterations should be present in *all* instances and lacking in controls. That a given abnormality is *on average* found more commonly or is somewhat more severe in a series of patients with VMN, but is often absent or not worse than in some controls, does not satisfy the usual criteria of causality. Thus, this re-examination of old pathologic material demonstrated that anatomic changes may be more common in subjects with renal failure than in controls after all,[129] but the results are still entirely consistent with the original conclusions of Finckh and co-workers[1] and others, to the effect that tubular changes in this syndrome are inconsistent, generally of modest severity, and of unclear pathogenetic importance.

The paucity and inconsistency of overt tubular alterations do not suggest abnormal tubular permeability as an important pathogenetic feature in human VMN, but tubular permeability cannot necessarily be judged from the histology. In considering the role of tubular leakage in human renal failure, the crucial question is not whether some degree of tubular leakage can or does occur, but rather whether tubular damage is an essential contributor without which renal function would be reasonably well maintained. Myers and co-workers[130,131] have examined the possibility of tubular leakage in human VMN by comparing the simultaneously derived clearances of inulin and polydisperse dextrans ranging in size from some 18Å to 42Å [the dextran:inulin (D:I) clearance ratio]. In some patients, the clearance ratio for one or more of the lowest molecular weight dextran moieties was somewhat higher than 1, and the clearance ratio for the larger dextrans was routinely higher than in controls. These results were interpreted to reflect the leakage of 20 to 42 percent of filtered inulin in individual patients.[130] However, the authors acknowledged that the high D:I ratio for the high molecular weight dextrans might be explained as well or instead by changes in glomerular hemodynamics.[130] Indeed, in a separate study of patients with simple heart failure and presumably no intrinsic renal disease at all,[132] the authors had found the 40Å D:I clearance ratio to be some 60 percent higher than the control.

The contribution of tubular leakage to any form of renal failure can be assessed by comparing the measured GFR obtained at any assumed degree of inulin absorption with that expected if leakage had not been present. If inulin, the customary marker of filtration, is passively absorbed, the degree to which the measured whole-kidney filtration rate underestimates the true GFR can be estimated from the equation[133]:

$$C_{in} = C_{in}^{True} (1 - Absn_{in}) \quad (1)$$

where C_{in} is the measured inulin clearance, C_{in}^{True} is the true filtration rate, and $Absn_{in}$ is the fraction of filtered inulin lost by leakage, if any. Based on this equation, Figure 15-3 shows the degree of change in the "true" GFR required to yield any given measured GFR when the latter is reduced by the tubular leakage of inulin (or creati-

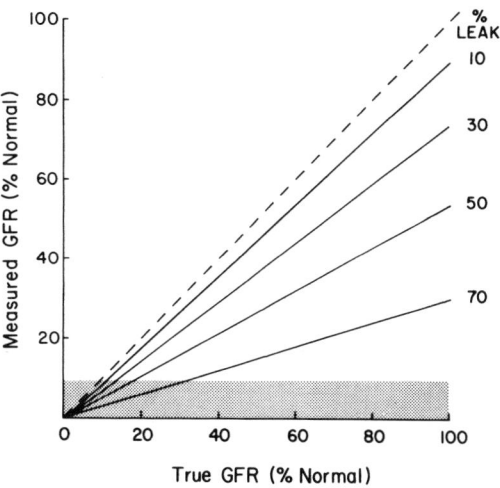

Fig. 15-3. The effect of indiscriminate inulin leakage on the measured GFR at different assumed true GFR values. The stippled area depicts a measured GFR of 10 ml/min, although the GFR in VMN is expected to be 5 ml/min or less. See text below. (From Oken DE,[133] with permission.)

nine). If we assume that the true filtration rate is maintained at its normal value of 125 ml/min, the leakage of as much as 50 percent of all the inulin filtered lowers the measured C_{in} only by one-half (i.e., to some 60 ml/min). It is clear, therefore, that even such a massive permeability change could not by itself yield the customary value of 5 ml/min or less expected in fully established oliguric renal failure (see above). Assuming even this large a degree of tubular leakage, Figure 15-3 shows that a C_{in} typical of VMN could be obtained only if the *true* filtration rate falls concomitantly by at least 92 percent. Leakage then accounts for a mere 3 to 4 percent of the total filtration deficit, and the 20 to 42 percent absorption of inulin reported[130] would contribute even less. Severe renal failure thus would exist whether leakage of such a degree is present or not, and "passive backflow" could at most be a minor contributor to the development of VMN in man.

Tubular Obstruction in Human Vasomotor Nephropathy

The early assumption that tubular obstruction plays a pathogenetic role in human VMN was based on the finding of interstitial edema, luminal debris, and/or protein casts in tubule lumens. Since interstitial edema typically does not appear until 24 to 48 hours after the onset of renal failure, other factors would have to be incriminated in this phase. Later, when edema is maximal, the tubules are dilated[64] and not collapsed as would be expected if interstitial edema were the cause of tubular obstruction. This does not rule out intrinsic tubular obstruction as a contributor to failed filtration. However, luminal debris and casts are not found in abundance in human material,[1,2] and the persistence of those casts that are seen may reflect nothing more than the absence of tubule fluid flow to wash them out of the kidney. If tubular obstruction does cause filtration failure, it should do so by raising luminal pressure. It has not been possible to measure renal tubular pressures directly in man. However, the renal venous wedge pressure appears to be an accurate mirror of proximal tubule pressure,[134] and this parameter is reportedly normal in established VMN.[134,135] This, coupled with the infrequency with which intraluminal casts are found in human pathologic material, in no way supports the concept that tubular obstruction is the key essential factor of renal failure in man.

Glomerular Hemodynamics in Human Vasomotor Nephropathy

Glomerular filtration is a purely passive phenomenon driven by the net hydrostatic pressure gradient across the glomerular capillary wall, and modulated by the ultrafiltration coefficient (K_f) of the filtering surface. Thus:

$$SNGFR = K_f[P_g - (P_{BS} + COP)] \quad (2)$$

where SNGFR is the single nephron glomerular filtration rate, P_g represents glomerular capillary hydrostatic pressure, P_{BS} is the hydrostatic pressure in Bowman's space, and COP is the mean colloid osmotic pressure of plasma proteins within the glomerular tuft.

It is evident from Equation 2 that filtration will be vanishingly low if the K_f becomes sufficiently small, if P_g falls toward a value equal to ($P_{BS} + COP$), or if a large increase in P_{BS} raises this last term to a pressure that approaches P_g. In theory, at least, any one or more of these changes might be the cause of failed filtration in VMN. At a reasonably maintained blood pressure, P_g is almost entirely a function of the relative settings of the preglomerular (R_A) and postglomerular (R_E) vascular resistances. Thus, a fall in glomerular capillary pressure large enough to cause filtration failure presupposes an increase in R_A, a decrease in R_E, or both changes occurring in tandem. Conversely, if the R_A/R_E ratio is documented to be substantially increased, a fall in GFR is inevitable.

Values for the individual determinants of glomerular filtration have been well established for the normal rat and dog, but not for man. However, knowing the whole-kidney GFR and blood flow rate, and with 1 million nephrons per kidney, we can estimate that the mean SNGFR is 60 to 65 nl/min, glomerular blood flow (GBF) approximates 575 nl/min, and the total vascular resistance per nephron is some 1.2×10^{10} dyne sec cm^{-5}.[136] As extrapolated from renal venous wedge pressures, normal Bowman's space pressure is taken to be between 15 mmHg[134] and 25 mmHg,[135] the higher pressure having been reported more recently. Assuming the latter P_{BS}, we have applied network thermodynamic modelling[137] to determine limiting values for the K_f, R_A, and R_E of individual nephrons that would yield the total resistance, filtration rate, and blood flow for normal man shown above. These values were then employed to estimate the degree of change in any of these parameters needed to reduce filtration and blood flow to the degree expected in human VMN.[137]

Such analysis has shown that filtration in man is so very resistant to reduced glomerular permeability that even an 80 percent fall in K_f leaves the filtration rate significantly above one-third of normal.[137] In fact, the filtering surface must become virtually impermeable before a change in K_f alone could yield the extremely low SNGFR expected in VMN.[137] Moreover, it appears that even a massive fall in K_f can reduce the filtration rate very little more when superimposed on the degree of preglomerular vasoconstriction that typifies this syndrome in man.[3-8] Consequently, there is little reason to believe that decreased glomerular permeability contributes meaningfully to the development of VMN in man, the less so since scanning electron microscopy studies show no abnormality of the endothelial fenestrae and capillary wall that would suggest any major permeability change.[138] With tubular obstruction and indiscriminate leakage of filtrate likely to play only a secondary, if any, role in this syndrome (see above), the marked cortical ischemia and preglomerular vasoconstriction evident at angiography become of paramount importance.

With blood pressure essentially normal, as in uncomplicated VMN, the typical 70 to 80 percent reduction in renocortical blood flow denotes at least a threefold increase in total vascular resistance. We do not have any means of precisely quantitating the relative contributions of the pre- and postglomerular vascular beds to this overall change in resistance. However, according to the Poiseuille equation, vascular resistance changes as the fourth power of a vessel's radius. Thus, a threefold rise in resistance corresponds to a mere 25 percent decrease in mean vessel diameter. The very marked attenuation of the preglomerular vessels found at angiography[5,6] bespeaks far more than a 25 percent reduction in vascular caliber, and it thus seems probable that this segment of the vasculature contributes much more to the overall resistance changes than does the postglomerular tree.

Network modelling has shown that a solitary rise in preglomerular resistance large enough to reduce cortical blood flow by only one-half would by itself virtually abolish filtration in man.[137] No change in K_f or P_{BS} need be superimposed.[137] Obviously, then, the more usual 70 to 80 percent reduction in renocortical blood flow would suffice.

Although filtration failure would not be attained if the overall increase in resistance is shared exactly equally by the pre- and postglomerular vascular beds,[137] that eventuality seems improbable in light of the extreme attenuation of the fourth- and fifth-order preglomerular vessels seen (or actually not seen) at angiography. Moreover, modelling has shown that failed filtration still obtains in the presence of a substantial rise in postglomerular resistance, so long as the preglomerular resistance rises only slightly more.[137] In short, all indications point to a vasomotor phenomenon as the primary cause of VMN in man.[137] The cause of this major and persistent change in renal hemodynamics is yet to be determined.

One explanation is found in the "no reflow" hypothesis, which presupposes that a period of reduced blood flow in the initiation phase of VMN leads to endothelial and tubule cell swelling; this then results in both tubular occlusion and patchy renal ischemia.[139] Endothelial swelling, a potential cause of increased glomerular capillary resistance, has been observed on electron microscopy in a single experimental model,[140] but most authors find neither endothelial nor mesangial abnormalities in human pathologic material.[58,59,138] That concept thus finds little experimental support despite its attractive neatness. Moreover, the marked increase in renal blood flow that follows intra-arterial infusions of vasodilator drugs (see below) argues strongly against a fixed, anatomic cause for the cortical ischemia found in this syndrome.

Various authors have suggested that intravascular coagulation plays a key role in the pathogenesis of VMN. Wardle,[141] Clarkson and colleagues,[61] and others have attributed human acute renal failure to the deposition of fibrin(ogen) products in the glomerular capillaries. They theorized that such materials contribute to renal failure both by mechanically obstructing blood flow and by releasing vasoactive agents. Abnormal concentrations of fibrin degradation products have been demonstrated in the serum of both human subjects and experimental animals with this syndrome.[141,142] Fibrinogen utilization has been demonstrated experimentally,[142] and fibrin-like material has been found in glomerular and peritubular capillaries by some authors.[141] It is unclear, however, whether such abnormalities are causally important or are merely associated phenomena, since the usual circumstances in which VMN develops initiate intravascular coagulation whether renal failure develops or not.[143] Moreover, since a detailed search by Baylis could not confirm the presence of fibrin-like material in the renal vasculature,[144] it is not certain that intravascular fibrin deposition is an essential feature of VMN in man.

A *vasomotor* etiology, independent of mechanical obstruction to blood flow, was first envisioned as a cause of renal failure over 70 years ago,[9,10] and has found wide support in the more recent literature.[3-8] Very similar renal hemodynamic abnormalities are met whether renal failure is due to shock, sepsis, chemical poisoning, trauma, hemolysis, obstetric accidents, or the injudicious use of aminoglycoside antibiotics.[6] However, the tenet that renocortical ischemia is the primary cause of failed filtration has been questioned by the finding that vasodilators such as dihydralazine, acetylcholine, and prostaglandin E_2 injected into the renal artery markedly increase renal blood flow but leave glomerular filtration at unmeasurably low levels.[7,8] It thus was reasoned that failed filtration could not be attributed to blood flow reduction. However, these vasodilators increase blood flow primarily through efferent arteriolar relaxation,[144] an effect that would be expected to produce a further *fall* in glomerular capillary pressure and in no way ameliorate the filtration deficit despite the marked improvement in blood flow.

Goormaghtigh proposed 40 years ago that the strategic position of the macula densa between the afferent and efferent arterioles made this structure (and thus the renin-angiotensin system) a likely determinant of vasomotor changes in VMN. An extremely potent vasoconstrictor, angiotensin is formed in situ within the kidney as well as in the lung.[145] Plasma renin titers of patients with VMN are markedly increased, but similar elevations are seen under circumstances in which renal function is not markedly disturbed.[146] Plasma volume expansion suppresses renal renin activity in normal subjects, and appears to protect patients put at risk of renal failure, while volume depletion stimulates renin production and is considered a major risk factor in the development of renal failure. Long-term saline loading, a maneuver that almost totally blocks renal renin formation, offers almost complete protection of renal function in rats challenged with mercury,[147] glycerol,[148] or dichromate.[149] Although such findings tend to incriminate the renin-angiotensin system in the pathogenesis of the syndrome of VMN (if only in the rat), the evidence is purely circumstantial. Immunization against renin or angiotensin[150,151] and the administration of hyperpharmacologic doses of angiotensin antagonists[152] confer dubious protection in the same models in which the syndrome is prevented by saline loading. Angiotensin injected into the renal artery in large doses does not cause acute renal failure in dogs,[153] and indeed, after a period of intense renal vasoconstriction the renal vasculature soon exhibits tachyphylaxis, with recovery of blood flow even when the infusion is continued.[153]

Catecholamine release and neural influences are important concomitants of shock and trauma, and have therefore been incriminated as likely pathogenetic factors in VMN.[154] Since, however, this syndrome occurs with some frequency in totally denervated transplanted kidneys, and phenoxybenzamine treatment has failed to ameliorate established VMN in nontransplanted patients,[155] a neural contribution to sustained renal insufficiency cannot be considered essential.

The close interaction between the prostaglandins, prostacyclines, angiotensin, catecholes, and kinins raises the possibility that prostaglandin deficiency might leave the effects of the constrictor stimuli unopposed in VMN.[156] Intra-arterial infusion of prostaglandin E_2 greatly reduces the degree of cortical ischemia in patients with VMN,[8] but this fact by no means establishes the existence of a prostaglandin deficiency state. Exogenous prostaglandins also abrogate the vasoconstriction produced by angiotensin, catecholamines, and renal nerve stimulation in the absence of prostaglandin depletion. Moreover, it seems unlikely that comparable vasodilation caused by dopamine, dihydralazine, and acetylcholine in human VMN can be attributed to depletion of these particular substances. Thus, a role of the prostaglandins in this syndrome remains entirely speculative.

Despite the vanishingly low GFR and the delivery of scant volumes of filtrate for absorption, reduced tubular transport capacity causes a major increase in the fractional excretion of salt and water in VMN. Since a normal GFR would put the subject at risk of life-threatening volume losses, there may be considerable (though temporary) survival value for filtration to "shut down" in the event of serious tubular injury.[157] One might thus envision some means of "conversation" between the injured tubule and the glomerulus to achieve that end. Adenosine might play precisely this role.

Unlike the other vasoactive agents considered above, adenosine has been reported to produce preglomerular vasoconstriction and a reciprocal fall in postglomerular resistance in the normal rat kidney.[158] Prolonged adenosine infusions do not cause tachyphylaxis,[159] and long-term salt loading inhibits the cortical ischemia otherwise induced by adenosine.[160] Noting an abrupt rise in the adenosine content of rat renal cortex after even brief periods of total renal ischemia, Osswald and associates[161] proposed that this agent would be a rational and attractive mediator of postischemic renal failure. Bidani and Churchill, and Bowmer and colleagues have reported amelioration of renal function in rats with glycerol-induced ARF treated with the adenosine-receptor blockers aminophylline[162,163] or 8-phenyltheophylline.[164,165] The protection obtained was incomplete and inconsistent, however, and these adenosine antagonists have been no more successful in our hands (unpublished data). However, recent preliminary studies have shown essentially total and entirely consistent protection from glycerol-induced myohemoglobinuric ARF in rats treated with the new and highly potent adenosine receptor blocker, BW A1433U.[166] To date, the efficacy of this agent has not yet been assessed with other experimental ARF models, and until it is tried in man, it is entirely unclear whether comparable results will apply in human renal failure. Nonetheless, until evidence appears to the contrary, the possibility that adenosine released by injured tubules plays a key role in human VMN deserves serious consideration.

TREATMENT OF VASOMOTOR NEPHROPATHY

At present, there is no known means of reversing established VMN. The goal of therapy, therefore, must be to maintain the patient's acid-base and fluid and electrolyte status within reasonable bounds, to prevent the development of uremic complications by timely dialysis, to avoid septic complications wherever possible, and to treat infections with some sense of urgency as they become manifest. Close attention should be paid to problems that may be associated with protein-calorie malnutrition and the retention of potentially toxic medications.

The Management of Fluid and Electrolyte Disorders

With a very limited excretory capacity, the fluid volume and serum electrolyte concentration of subjects with VMN are determined largely by their intake. Nowadays, patients seldom receive frankly inappropriate loads of sodium, water, and potassium. Where dialytic treatment is either unavailable or to be avoided, water intake is routinely limited to a volume calculated to approximate the volume of urine and the extrarenal water losses through the lungs and the skin. The latter (so-called insensible loss) varies considerably with the ambient temperature and relative humidity as well as the patient's temperature. Insensible water loss in normal adults averages some 12 ml/kg body weight per day, but febrile patients in a hot, dry environment may lose in excess of 2 liters of fluid a day by this route. By contrast, patients breathing water-saturated air from closed respirator systems have markedly reduced or no insensible fluid losses. Fluid output is partly offset by the water of oxidation of foods or body tissue, and may be overshadowed by the often substantial losses of fluid and electrolytes through burned skin or from the gastrointestinal tract. It has therefore become routine in most centers to rely on body weight as the main indicator of appropriate fluid balance, rather than depending upon assumed values for water of oxidation, insensible water loss, and the frequently inaccurate notations of intake and external losses. Body weight should not be kept constant, however, because the frugal acute renal failure diet causes an expected 0.2 to 0.5 kg (in adults) daily decrease in body tissue mass.

While in the past, stringent guidelines for fluid therapy were applied to forestall the development of congesive heart failure and hyponatremia, routine dialysis permits a somewhat more liberal fluid intake. A water ration of 1 liter per day (or even more when indicated) is probably preferable to the very restricted fluid regimens of old.

Oliguric patients typically excrete only some 10 to 30 mEq of sodium per day in urine, and virtually always excrete a urine far hyponatremic to plasma. In the absence of major extrarenal sodium loss, therefore, the development of hyponatremia reflects excessive water intake. The extent of water overloading may be calculated rapidly by assuming that every 10 mEq/liter decrease in the serum sodium concentration represents 7 percent expansion of the total body water. Thus, a patient weighing 70 kg whose serum sodium concentration has fallen to 130 mEq/liter without excessive extrarenal sodium loss has experienced a 3 liter expansion of body water, and so on. This degree of hyponatremia is best treated by a modest reduction of water intake that will permit the volume surfeit to slowly correct itself in the succeeding days. Sodium salts should not be administered for this purpose unless burns, vomiting, diarrhea, or gastric suction have caused large sodium losses. Inadvisably replacing large volumes of fluid lost via these routes with water alone will cause sodium depletion, and may cause frank water intoxication. Even then, however, dialysis is often the treatment of choice, although the dialysate should be modified to prevent the serum sodium concentration of markedly hyponatremic subjects from rising by more than some 10 mEq/liter/day. Peritoneal dialysis is particularly useful in correcting most fluid and electrolyte disorders, but again, the dialysate may have to be tailored to the patient's needs.

Acidosis is an almost inevitable consequence of renal failure unless hydrogen ion accumulation is equalled or exceeded by gastric acid loss. The serum bicarbonate concentration of most patients with VMN falls by 1 to 3 mEq/liter daily. The rate of acid production and the daily fall in bicarbonate concentration are, however, considerably higher in hypercatabolic patients suffering from severe tissue trauma, sepsis, or extensive abdominal surgery. The correction of acidosis presupposes the administration of base or the removal of gastric acid. Some 30 mEq of bicarbonate, with an attendant cation, are required to raise the serum bicarbonate concentration of a 70 kg adult by 1 mEq/liter. Clearly, potassium bicarbonate should not be given to correct acidosis in most patients, and large amounts of sodium bicarbonate cause unwanted and possibly dangerous extracellular volume expansion. Removing one liter of gastric juice by nasogastric suction increases the serum bicarbonate concentration by some 3 to 4 mEq/liter, and this modality can be a useful way of treating severe acidosis when alkalization is deemed unsafe and dialysis is not possible. For the most part, however, it is not necessary to treat systemic acidosis until the serum bicarbonate concentration falls below 15 mEq/liter. Dialysis is generally the preferable mode of therapy in most instances of serious metabolic acidosis, especially in patients with cardiac or chronic lung disease and when the acidosis is complicated by other major fluid and electrolyte disorders.

Hyperkalemia is among the most serious of the early complications of VMN. Not all patients develop marked hyperkalemia; some do so slowly, while patients with acidosis, sepsis, tissue necrosis, or extravascular blood sequestration may develop potentially lethal levels of hyperkalemia within a matter of two to three days. Potassium released from muscle tissue as the result of starvation further complicates the issue. Each of these abnormalities should be addressed actively, both for its own sake and to reduce the rate at which the serum potassium concentration rises. It is my practice to examine the electrocardiogram daily when the serum potassium concentration reaches 5.5 mEq/liter, and to introduce a therapeutic regimen to limit the rise in serum potassium concentration at this point.

Except in overly catabolic patients, the rate of rise of the serum potassium concentration can be greatly reduced by an ion exchange resin such as sodium polystyrene sulfonate (Kayexalate),[167] and by sorbitol, an osmotic cathartic, given by mouth.[167] Allowed to equilibrate, each gram of resin exchanges about 1 mEq of sodium for an equal amount of potassium (and some hydrogen ion) in the intestinal tract. Thus, the standard dose of 15 g of Kayexalate removes approximately 15 mEq of potassium, and this dose can be repeated two, three, or four times daily, according to need. Sorbitol itself obligates additional potassium loss in the stool,[167] and prevents intestinal concretion of the resin. The resin-sorbitol mixture is unpalatable, however, and is found objectionable by many patients. If the patient's refusal, intestinal ileus, or other problems preclude oral therapy, 30 g of Kayexalate in sorbitol may be given as a retention enema. Ion exchange is a slow process, however, and the slurry requires a residence time of 2 hours for optimal potassium removal. A radiologic barium enema catheter proves highly effective for permitting an adequate residence time for the resin.

Symmetrical peaking of the T waves is

the first electrocardiographic sign of serious potassium intoxication, although comparable peaking may be seen with increased intracranial pressure or acidosis in the absence of hyperkalemia. This change is followed in sequence by loss of the amplitude of the R wave, deepening of the S wave, prolongation of the P-R interval, suppression of the P wave, and an increasing widening of the QRS complex as the serum potassium concentration rises further. With this last EKG change, emergency therapy is mandated to prevent the development of ventricular arrhythmias, ventricular fibrillation, and death. Marked widening of the QRS complex or arrhythmia demands an immediate bolus injection of 50 mEq of sodium bicarbonate and continuous EKG monitoring. The injection is repeated if there is an inadequate response, a beneficial effect usually being observed within minutes. The sodium ion provides partial protection from the cardiac effects of potassium intoxication, and the bicarbonate serves to lower the serum potassium concentration by promoting potassium entry into the intracellular compartment. Calcium gluconate given at a rate of 5 to 10 ml/min as a 10 percent solution gives added protection, and may be given simultaneously with sodium bicarbonate in emergency situations. The two solutions must not be mixed in the same container, however, because of the inevitable precipitation of the calcium as its carbonate salt. Dextrose and insulin, given at a ratio of 1 unit of insulin to 3 to 5 g of dextrose, may be given as a continuous infusion of 50 percent dextrose intravenously. Unlike treatment with bicarbonate and calcium solutions, however, this therapy does not become effective for at least 20 minutes. It is somewhat longer acting in its effect than either bicarbonate or calcium gluconate, but that is often not of paramount importance, since patients with a degree of hyperkalemia that warrants the use of such treatment generally will be dialyzed promptly.

Hemodialysis reverses hyperkalemia very rapidly, by removing the excess potassium from the body rather than merely redistributing it or modulating its cardiogenic effects, as do the chemical therapies. Nonetheless, the other therapeutic modalities may be lifesaving while the necessary machinery for dialytic therapy is mustered. A double-lumen catheter inserted through a femoral vein is an exceedingly useful portal for dialysis in emergency situations in which speed is all important.

Peritoneal dialysis is not a substitute for hemodialysis in the emergency treatment of hyperkalemia. Failure to obtain adequate drainage may waste precious time, and this can have serious consequences for the patient. Furthermore, one can anticipate no more than 60 percent equilibration of potassium between the extracellular fluid (ECF) and the peritoneal solution in a one hour period.[168] Thus, when instilling 2 liters of dialysate into the abdomen of a patient whose serum potassium concentration is 8 mEq/liter, a total of no more than 9.6 mEq of potassium will be removed per exchange. Where hemodialysis is not available, however, even this amount of potassium removal can be of distinct benefit, particularly when sodium polystyrene sulfonate and sorbitol are given throughout the procedure and chemical maneuvers designed to forestall an imminent hyperkalemic death are applied as indicated. Hypocalcemia and hypermagnesemia, expected complications in VMN, rarely require treatment.

Nutritional Problems in Vasomotor Nephropathy

Protein-calorie malnutrition is not a particular problem in patients with VMN uncomplicated by extensive tissue trauma, recent major surgery, or septicemia. On average, oliguric VMN lasts only about 11 days, and nonoliguric renal failure usually runs an even shorter course. Over this time period, excessive utilization of body protein can be prevented in reasonably well patients by administering 100 to 200 g of carbohydrates in divided doses, preferably by mouth. Twenty grams of high-biologic-value protein, typically given as egg and milk, may be offered to provide a source of essential amino acids, but at the cost of raising the BUN concentration by an additional 6.5 mg/dl or so, and adding about 20 mEq of potassium to the body pool per day. Intravenous infusions employing a slow drip of 50 percent dextrose in water can substitute for the oral intake in patients who cannot be fed by mouth. Since the hypertonicity of this solution is likely to produce venous thrombosis if it is infused into peripheral veins, a central line is used routinely. Central infusion lines are not without the risk of septic complications even in the most skilled hands,[169] however, and the procedure is complicated by pneumothorax, venous thrombosis, or hemothorax in a small percentage of patients. It is not at all certain, therefore, that such treatment warrants the potential hazards in patients who are not overtly hypercatabolic. One liter of 10 percent dextrose solution provides 400 kcal which, though inadequate, can greatly lessen the degree of nutritional stress when oral feeding is precluded. This can be given by a peripheral vein.

Nutritional considerations are quite different in severely traumatized, hypercatabolic patients, whose caloric expenditures may be immense.[170] Severe protein-calorie malnutrition is expected to develop quickly in such individuals, and this may contribute to poor wound healing[171] while possibly increasing susceptibility to a septicemic death. The BUN concentration of these patients may rise by as much as 60 mg/dl a day, a change that reflects the net daily production of some 25 g of urea nitrogen and the destruction of 180 g of body protein.

Giordano and subsequent workers[172,173] have amply demonstrated the ability of nonhypercatabolic patients to minimize urea nitrogen formation when adequate calories and basic amounts of essential amino acids are provided. Various authors have shown that the negative nitrogen balance in *uncomplicated* postoperative cases can be lessened by providing amino acid nitrogen in addition to an adequate caloric intake.[174] Such therapy was first extended to the treatment of acute renal failue by Dudrick and co-workers,[174] and the concept was supported in studies by Abel and associates.[175] In a much discussed prospective double-blind study of the efficacy of such treatment, the latter authors[175] randomly assigned 53 patients with VMN to treatment with intravenous essential L-amino acids and hypertonic glucose (renal failure fluid), or to the glucose solution alone. Twenty-one of 28 patients given the renal failure fluid survived, while only 11 of the 25 glucose-treated subjects were equally fortunate. Intriguingly, the creatinine concentration of the group treated with amino acids declined within three days of the beginning of therapy; the control group's creatinine concentration continued to rise for a week after the beginning of the study. Recovery from VMN is typically heralded by a plateau of the serum creatinine concentration for two to three days. Thus, with the serum creatinine concentration beginning to fall on an average of three days after hyperalimentation was started, it might be suggested that the treatment caused an immediate reversal of renal failure. Alternatively, patients on the verge of recovery might have been segregated by chance into the treatment group even though a random selection process was employed in establishing the treatment and control series. Indeed, the number of variables that impinge on survival and the course of this syndrome is so large that a truly "controlled" series is very difficult to achieve.[176] Moreover, the frequency with which septic and other complications occur in VMN increases with the duration of renal insufficiency. Thus, one might question whether the improved survival of the treatment group was the result of their (fortuitously?) prompt recovery of renal function, rather than a true reflection of increased resistance to infectious and other complications leading to death. Baek and co-workers[177] have also reported on an improved survival rate in patients provided hypertonic glucose solution and amino acids, all of whom had been admitted to an intensive care unit because of critical illness. Additionally, this regimen can induce a very beneficial fall in serum potassium concentration despite continued renal failure, and many patients require potassium, phosphate, and magnesium supplementation to maintain an adequate concentration of these ions in the plasma.[176,177]

Improved survival has not universally followed the use of parenteral nutrition with amino-acid-rich mixtures, however. In an uncontrolled study of 139 patients with acute renal failure treated in this way, Abel and co-workers[178] found a mortality rate of 57 percent, which was quite comparable to that of the "control" patients in their earlier series. Leonard and associates[179] obtained no better results in their subjects, and subjecting all the available literature to careful statistical scrutiny, Naylor and colleagues[180] have concluded that evidence for a beneficial effect of hyperalimentation in VMN is at best weak.

Strong support for the concept that hyperalimentation with amino-acid-rich solutions might improve the survival rate and shorten the duration of renal insufficiency in man appeared in a study of mercury-induced acute renal failure in the rat.[181] Massive amounts of essential amino acids in 50 percent dextrose solution were infused beginning 30 hours after rats were injected with mercuric chloride. Measured 18 hours later, the serum creatinine concentration of these animals was only twice that of normal control rats, while animals given glucose solution alone exhibited a 12-fold rise.[180] Since renal failure is typically well established within 24 hours of mercury injection in the rat, it might be assumed that the amino acid infusion begun 30 hours after mercury injection had promptly reversed previously established renal failure. Closely following the protocol of that study, as well as using a variety of amino acid regimens, we have been unable to confirm any significant benefit of amino acid therapy in either mercury poisoned rats or animals with myohemoglobin-induced acute renal failure.[182] The mortality rate of amino acid treated animals was inordinately high, the severity of renal failure was not reduced, and treatment had no discernible effect on the rate of recovery from renal failure.[182]

Clearly, prolonged protein-calorie malnutrition is harmful to any organism, whether renal failure is present or not. On the other hand, evidence that any hyperalimentation regimen shortens the course of renal failure or improves the survival rate in the general population of patients with VMN is weak at best (see above). Thus, the decision to employ such treatment rests on one's conception of the relative risks inherent in protein-calorie malnutrition versus those of the treatment itself in each individual patient. In my view, hyperalimentation probably plays no role in the management of noncatabolic patients who can accept the standard renal failure feedings mentioned above.

Prevention and Treatment of Infection

As noted earlier, infection is a prime cause of death in both the oliguric and recovery phases of VMN. Many patients, particularly those with penetrating wounds of the abdomen, crush injuries of the chest, and surgical disorders of the intestinal tract, may be septic from the outset. Certain infections, however, are either preventable or readily controlled using the principles of good medical and nursing care. Infected wounds should be carefully debrided whenever possible, and cultured and observed for signs of recurring infection. The risk of hypostatic pneumonia in acutely ill or obtunded patients can be minimized by applying standard nursing techniques. Bedridden patients who cannot be moved should be turned frequently if possible, and pulmonary toilet procedures should be followed. Bronchial secretions should not be allowed to accumulate, but should be aspirated using aseptic technique if the patient is unable to cough adequately. Strict asepsis should be observed in caring for tracheostomies and endotracheal tubes. Patients who can be moved from bed to chair rest should be out of bed according to their tolerance, and ambulation (if only with assistance) can be of both psychological as well as physical value. Parotitis and the risks of oral fungal infections can be significantly reduced by providing small volumes of fluid at frequent intervals, stimulating salivary flow by providing thin slices of lemon (the potassium content is negligible), and in comatose patients, by having trained nursing personnel apply glycerine swabs. Mycostatin mouth washes are generally effective in treating superficial oral monilial infections.

While a single straight bladder catheterization may be important in the initial evaluation of the oliguric patient, indwelling catheters are for the most part contraindicated. The indwelling bladder catheter is a prime source of potentially fatal septicemia. Once the presence of oliguria has been established and the diagnosis of VMN made, monitoring the urine volume hour by hour or shift by shift serves little purpose. Catheterization should be employed only if it is suspected that the bladder is overly full, and even here it seems preferable to employ repeated straight catheterization under aseptic conditions rather than to leave an indwelling catheter in place for several days. Bladder catheters should not be inserted into nonoliguric renal failure patients who are capable of voiding spontaneously, an external drainage system sufficing in the presence of urinary incontinence. Whether the patient has been catheterized or not, it is our practice to culture the urine twice weekly and obtain antibiotic sensitivities of any bacteria grown, regardless of the count. If generalized sepsis then becomes manifest, the possibility that it derives from the urinary tract can be evaluated, and a reasonable choice of antibiotic can be made while awaiting the results of blood cultures.

Whenever possible, food and fluids should be given by mouth. Central venous lines or Swan-Ganz catheters should be used only when indicated, and removed promptly when the information requiring their use has been obtained. The extraordinary susceptibility to infection of patients with VMN dictates that venipuncture sites be scrupulously sterilized and, when intravenous infusions are indicated, that both the puncture site and the fluid containers be handled as aseptically as possible.

While in former years it was customary to place patients with vasomotor nephropathy in a single room, isolated from other patients and attended by personnel wearing masks, gowns, and gloves, this "reverse precautionary" technique has distinct drawbacks. First, the cumbersome procedure of preparing to visit the patient is likely to inhibit the frequency with which appropriate visits are made by the nursing staff and physicians alike. With reasonably alert patients, such care often produces considerable anxiety and (appropriately) a feeling of isolation. The efficacy of the procedure as a means of preventing infection has never been adequately established, and its advantages may be outweighed by many potential disadvantages. Nevertheless, it does not seem appropriate to put patients with VMN in close proximity to infected patients in open wards. The need for skilled and intensive nursing care for many patients with postoperative or post-traumatic acute renal failure is readily evident. There is currently no adequate evidence that prophylactic antibiotics are at all valuable in managing patients with renal failure. Until a universal antibiotic becomes available, prophylactic treatment can only modify infections with bacteria susceptible to the particular antibiotic used. Using a broad spectrum antibiotic, one may put the patient at risk of an infection that is not readily responsive to therapy, mask ongoing infections with organisms that are partially suppressed but not eradicated, and put the patient at a small but unnecessary risk of a toxic, allergic, or idiosyncratic reaction. When antibiotics are called for by the presence of established infection, one must be aware of their potential toxicity and the fact that many of them depend upon adequate renal function for their excretion. Dosage schedules may need to be adjusted accordingly (see below).

Drug Retention in Vasomotor Nephropathy

The severity of associated illness in many patients with VMN prompts therapy with a bewildering array of pharmaceuticals, many of which depend largely or exclusively on the kidney for their excretion. Certain of these are nephrotoxic (e.g., the aminoglycosides), while others display extrarenal toxicity. To minimize the risk of untoward reactions, therefore, it is incumbent on the physician to determine the appropriate dosage modification needed for any medicine given in the presence of VMN. This task has been made immeasurably easier by the therapeutic guidelines compiled for most commonly used agents by Bennett and co-workers.[183,184]

It is difficult to memorize the details of the dosage changes needed for such a large variety of drugs. However, many agents are metabolized or excreted largely through extrarenal routes, and so require no adjustment in dose if hepatic function is adequate. Table 15-4 contains a list of such agents. It

Table 15-4. A Listing of Drugs That Do *Not* Require Dosage Adjustment in Patients with Renal Failure and Adequate Hepatic Function

Anticoagulants and antiplatelet agents: Heparin, coumadin, dipyridamole, streptokinase, urokinase
Corticosteroids: All
Antihistamines: Chlorpheniramine, terfenadine
Antihypertensives: As in any patient, dosing with antihypertensive medications is always determined by the blood pressure response.
    Adrenergic agents: All except methyldopa, clonidine, and guanethidine, for which some adjustment may be needed.
    Beta blockers: Metoprolol, nadolol, pindolol, propranolol, timolol
    Calcium blockers: Diltiazem, nifedipine
Antiarrhythmics: Quinidine, lorcainide, lidocaine, mexiletine, amiodarone
Nitrates: Nitroglycerin, isosorbide
Narcotics: Naloxone
Antibiotics: Chloramphenicol, ceftriaxone, clindamycin, timidazole, metronidazole, cefoperazone, isoniazid, rifampin, cloxacillin, dicloxacillin, nafcillin, minocycline, oxacillin, amphotericin B, ketoconazole
Neuromuscular agents: Pyridostigmine, succinylcholine, tubocurarine, vecuronium
Phenothiazines: Chlorpromazine, terfenadine
Tricyclic antidepressants: All
Benzodiazapines: All except chlordiazepoxide, midazolam
Antiparkinsonian agents: Bromocriptine, levodopa, carbidopa-levodopa, trihexyphenidyl
Anticonvulsive: Phenytoin, valproate
Antineoplastic agents: Vinblastine, vincristine, cyclosporin, cytarabine, 5-fluorouracil, busulfan
Oral hypoglycemics: Glipizide, glyburide
Nonsteroidal antiinflammatory agents: All except diflunisal, phenylbutazone, sulfinpyrazone

is often helpful to memorize or carry this list and refresh one's memory as necessary on dosage adjustments for other agents from the drug compendium cited earlier.[184]

According to Bennett and associates[183] certain drugs should not be given to patients with minimal renal function; these include methenamine mandelate; nalidixic acid; nitrofurantoin; phenazopyridine; glutethimide; lithium carbonate; bretylium; gallamine; pancuronium; acetazolamide (except for glaucoma); ethacrynic acid; acetohexamide; furosemide; mercurials; spironolactone; thiazides; chlorpropamide; terbutaline; gold salts; phenylbutazone; probenecid; cisplatin; nitrosourea; and triamterene. Some are totally ineffectual in VMN (e.g., the diuretics, methenamine, and uricosurics) and potentially harmful, while others (e.g., acetohexamide and phenylbutazone), though effective, can have distinctly adverse effects when retained.

Many of the medications apt to be problematic in renal failure are dialyzable. These include[183] flucytosine; penicillins and related drugs; cephalosporins (except cefaclor); colistimethate; quinine; sulfisoxazole; aspirin; aminoglycosides; phenobarbital; lithium; meprobamate; procainamide; methyldopa; primidone; azathioprine; gallium; and cimetidine. When given in large excess and causing problems for the patient (e.g., aminoglycosides, aspirin; phenobarbital), such agents can largely be removed by hemodialysis. By the same token, however, removal of these agents by dialysis may reduce their therapeutic effectiveness unless dosages are readjusted after each dialysis treatment.

DIALYSIS IN THE TREATMENT OF VASOMOTOR NEPHROPATHY

Dialysis has become standard treatment for patients with VMN. Clearly, dialysis is immediately life-saving in certain patients, particularly those with malignant levels of hyperkalemia, severe acidosis, or pulmonary edema unresponsive to conservative therapy. It will forestall the development of most symptoms attributable to uremia, and allows for the removal of certain drugs given in excess and destined to be retained because of renal failure (see above). Markedly hypercatabolic patients whose BUN and serum creatinine concentrations are rising at perhaps 60 mg/dl and 4 mg/dl per day respectively can often be maintained only with the adjunctive use of dialysis. The availability of this form of treatment allows for a reasonable nitrogen intake and makes stringent fluid restriction a thing of the past.

The choice between hemodialysis and peritoneal dialysis is best individualized according to the dialysis center's expertise and facilities, as well as the patient's clinical status. Peritoneal dialysis is rarely feasible in patients whose retroperitoneum has been violated, such as for the repair of an aortic aneurysm, since large volumes of dialysis fluid will be absorbed into the surgical site. Open abdominal wounds and surgical drains also make peritoneal dialysis impractical. On the other hand, marked cardiovascular instability, gastrointestinal or cerebral hemorrhage, and clotting disorders often militate against the use of hemodialysis, while peritoneal dialysis may have particular value in the treatment of peritonitis and pancreatitis.

Both forms of dialysis potentially have an adverse effect on nutrition—hemodialysis by the removal of amino acids[185] and peritoneal dialysis through the loss of albumin into the peritoneal space.[186] Such nitrogen losses carry little consequence for noncatabolic patients requiring infrequent dialysis, but may be of great concern in subjects whose need for daily or twice daily dialysis stems largely from their gross hypercatabolism. These latter patients can ill afford any further amino acid losses, and it is reasonable to give an infusion of 1.4 g of balanced essential amino acids in 25 percent dextrose solution via the venous return tubing of the dialysis system in the terminal hour of each dialysis. Only a small fraction of these amino acids will be lost to the dialysis bath,[185] and the patient's total caloric intake can be further supplemented throughout the dialysis by including glucose in the bath fluid at a concentration of 500 mg/dl; blood sugar concentrations should then be monitored at intervals and insulin given as required.

Early and frequent (so called "prophylactic" dialysis) has been proposed as a means of decreasing the exorbitant death rate of patients with VMN.[187] While such treatment permits more liberal dietary and fluid intake, helps to maintain a normal electrolyte balance, and clearly prevents the complications of frank uremia, it is hard to prove that it also offers a significantly better chance for survival than less frequent dialysis. Prophylactic dialysis has become standard in most nephrology centers, but improved survival, such as was reported by Kleinknecht and colleagues,[187] has not been found universally. Factors that might influence survival in VMN include (among others) age; extent of trauma; cardiovascular status; severe pulmonary disease; sepsis, its source of origin, and its susceptibility to treatment; associated hepatic failure; serious head trauma; coexisting intravascular coagulation; burns; major gastrointestinal hemorrhage; pulmonary embolus; intestinal infarction; coexisting diabetes with its complications; prolonged shock; and fat- or atheroembolization. While patients may be randomly assigned to a treatment or control group for studies of the efficacy of a given treatment, this arrangement will not match for the multiple variables just mentioned. Only with massive numbers of patients can one expect the various risk factors to be equally distributed between groups; without such matching, there is a very real possibility that differences in survival may be obtained purely by chance from one experimental group to another.[176]

REFERENCES

1. Finckh ES, Jeremy D, Whyte HM: Structural renal damage and its relation to clinical features in acute oliguric renal failure. Q J Med 31:429, 1962
2. Sevitt S: Pathogenesis of traumatic uremia—A revised concept. Lancet 2:135, 1959
3. Brun C, Crone C, Davidsen HG, et al: Renal blood flow in anuric human subject determined by use of radioactive krypton 85. Proc Soc Exp Biol Med 89:687, 1955
4. Walker JG, Silva H, Lawson TR, et al: Renal blood flow in acute renal failure measured by renal arterial infusion of indocyanine green. Proc Soc Exp Biol Med 112:932, 1963
5. Hollenberg NK, Epstein M, Rosen SM, et al: Acute oliguric renal failure in man. Evidence for preferential renal cortical ischemia. Medicine 47:455, 1968
6. Hollenberg NK, Adams DF, Oken DE, et al: Acute renal failure due to nephrotoxins. N Engl J Med 282:1329, 1970
7. Ladefoged J, Winkler K: Hemodynamics in acute renal failure: The effect of hypotension induced by dihydralazine on renal blood flow, mean circulation time for plasma, and renal vascular volume in patients with acute oliguric renal failure. Scand J Clin Lab Invest 26:83, 1970
8. Reubi FC, Vorburger C: Renal hemodynamics in acute renal failure after shock in man. Kidney Int 10:S-137, 1976
9. Borst M: Pathologische-anatomische Erfahrunger uber Kriegsverletzungen. Samml Klin Vortrage 735:297, 1917
10. Hackradt A: Uber akute, todliche vasomotorische Nephrosen nach Verschuttung. Inaugural-Dissertation, Munchen, 1917
11. Smith R, McClure-Browne JC, Shackman R, et al: Acute renal failure of obstetric origin. Lancet 2:351, 1965
12. Ober WE, Reid DE, Romney SL, et al: Renal lesions and acute renal failure in pregnancy. Am J Med 21:781, 1956
13. Sheer RL, Jones DB: Malignant nephrosclerosis in women postpartum. JAMA 201:600, 1967
14. Chugh KS, Singhal PC, Sharma BK, et al: Acute renal failure of obstetric origin. Obstet Gynecol 48:642, 1976
15. Morrin PAF, Handa SP, Valberg LS, et al: Acute renal failure in association with fatty liver of pregnancy. Am J Med 42:844, 1967
16. Bywaters EGL, Beall D: Crush injuries with impairment of renal function. Br Med J 1:427, 1941
17. Olerud JE, Homer LD, Carroll HW: Incidence of acute exertional rhabdomyolysis. Arch Intern Med 136:692, 1976
18. Kew MC, Abrahams C, Levin NW, et al: The effects of heatstroke on the function and structure of the kidney. Q J Med 36:277, 1967
19. Diamond I, Aguino, TI: Myoglobinuria fol-

lowing unilateral status epilepticus and ipsilateral rhabdomyolysis. N Engl J Med 272:834, 1965
20. Nixon JC, Hobbs WK, Greenblatt J: Myoglobinuria and skeletal muscle phosphorylase deficiency: Report of a case of McArdle's disease. Can Med Assoc J 94:977, 1966
21. Reza MJ, Kar NC, Pearson CM, et al: Recurrent myoglobinuria due to muscle carnitine palmityl transferase deficiency. Ann Intern Med 88:610, 1978
22. Rubin E, Kantz AM, Lieber CS, et al: Muscle damage produced by chronic alcohol consumption. Am J Pathol 83:499, 1976
23. Nadel SM, Jackson JW, Ploth, DW: Hypokalemic rhabdomyolysis and acute renal failure. JAMA 241:2294, 1979
24. Shenouda A, Hatch FE: Influenza A viral infection associated with acute renal failure. Am J Med 61:697, 1976
25. Sloan MF, Franks AJ, Exley KA, et al: Acute renal failure due to polymyositis. Br Med J 193:1457, 1978
26. Kendrick WC, Hull AR, Knochel JP: Rhabdomyolysis and shock after intravenous amphetamine administration. Ann Intern Med 86:381, 1977
27. Ulvila JM, Nessan VJ: Hypernatremia with myoglobinuria. Am J Med 265:79, 1973
28. Halverson PB, Kozin F, Ryan LM, et al: Rhabdomyolysis and renal failure in hypothyroidism. Ann Intern Med 91:57, 1970
29. Ponfik V: Experimentelle beitrage zur lehre von der transfusion. Virchows Arch [Pathol Anat] 62:273, 1875
30. Solanki D, McCurdy PR: Delayed hemolytic transfusion reactions. An often-missed entity. JAMA 239:729, 1978
31. Owusu SK, Addy JH, Foli AK, et al: Acute reversible renal failure associated with glucose-6-phosphate-dehydrogenase deficiency. Lancet 1:1255, 1972
32. Hartman RC, Auditore JV: Paroxysmal nocturnal hemoglobinuria. 2. Erythrocyte cholinesterase defect. Am J Med 27:389, 1959
33. Gulati PD, Rizvi SNA: Acute reversible renal failure in G-6PD-deficient siblings. Postgrad Med J 52:83, 1976
34. Fleischer R: Ueber eine neue form von hemoglobinurie beim menschen. Berl Klin Worchenschr 18:691, 1881
35. Eisner GM, Piver JS: Acute renal failure after therapeutic abortion by intra-amniotic saline administration. N Engl J Med 279:360, 1968
36. Thomas TA, Galizia EJ, Wensley RT: Termination of pregnancy with utus paste: report of a fatal case. Br Med J 1:375, 1975
37. Hagvenik K, Gordon E, Lins LE, et al: Glycerol-induced haemolysis with haemoglobinuria and acute renal failure. Report of three cases. Lancet 1:75, 1974
38. Sitprija V, Benyajati C, Boonpucknavig V: Further observations of renal insufficiency in snakebite. Nephron 13:396, 1974
39. Rosen S, Hano JE, Inman MM, et al: The kidney in blackwater fever. Am J Clin Pathol 49:358, 1968
40. Fowler BA, Weissberg JB: Arsine poisoning. N Engl J Med 291:1171, 1974
41. Muehrcke RC, Pirani CL: Arsine-induced anuria: A correlative clinico-pathological study with electron microscopic observations. Ann Intern Med 68:853, 1968
42. Schreiner GE, Maher JF: Toxic nephropathy. Am J Med 38:409, 1965
43. Grossman CM, Malbin B: Mushroom poisoning. Ann Intern Med 40:249, 1954
44. Harrison DC, Coggins CH, Welland FH, et al: Mushroom poisoning in five patients. Am J Med 38:787, 1965
45. Carlton BE, Tufts E, Girard DE: Water hemlock poisoning complicated by rhabdomyolysis and renal failure. Clin Toxicol 14:87, 1979
46. Warrell DA, Ormerod LD, Davidson NM: Bites by puff-adder (*Bitis arietas*) in Nigeria, and value of antivenom. Br Med J 4:697, 1975
47. Glselynck AM, Forrey A, Cutler R: Pharmacokinetics of gentamicin: distribution and plasma and renal clearance. J Infect Dis 124:70, 1971
48. Schentag JJ, Plaut ME, Cerra FB, et al: Aminoglycoside nephrotoxicity in critically ill surgical patients. J Surg Res 26:270, 1979
49. de Rosa F, Buoncristiani U, Capitanucci P, et al: Tobramycin: Toxicological and pharmacological studies in animals and pharmacokinetic research in patients with varying degrees of renal impairment. J Int Med Res 2:100, 1974

50. Plaut ME, Schentag JJ, Jusko WJ: Aminoglycoside nephrotoxicity: Comparative assessment in critically ill patients. Am J Med 10:257, 1979
51. Butler WT, Bennett JE, Alling DW, et al: Nephrotoxicity of amphotericin B: Early and late effects in 81 patients. Ann Intern Med 61:175, 1964
52. Abelson HT, Garnick MB: Renal failure induced by cancer chemotherapy. p. 769. In Rieselbach RE, Garnick MB (eds): Cancer and the Kidney. Lea and Febiger, Philadelphia, 1982
53. Older RA, Korobkin M, Cleeve DM, et al: Contrast-induced acute renal failure: Persistent nephrogram as clue to early detection. Am J Radiol 134:339, 1980
54. Harkonen S, Kjellstrand CM: Intravenous pyelography in non-uremic diabetic patients. Nephron 24:268, 1979
55. Jerwell JL, Marden R, Onaindia JM: Renal functional impairment caused by intravenous urography: A prospective study. Arch Intern Med 141:1268, 1981
56. Van Zee BE, Hoy WE, Talley TE, et al: Renal injury associated with intravenous pyelography in non-diabetic and diabetic patients. Ann Intern Med 89:51, 1978
57. Kamdar A, Weidmann P, Makoff DL, et al: Acute renal failure following intravenous use of radiographic contrast dyes in patients with diabetes mellitus. Diabetes 26:643, 1977
58. Olsen TS, Skjoldborg H: The fine structure of the renal glomerulus in acute anuria. Acta Pathol Microbiol Scand 70:205, 1967
59. Dalgaard OZ: An electron microscopic study on glomeruli in renal biopsies taken from human shock kidney. Lab Invest 9:364, 1960
60. Cox JW, Baehler RW, Sharma H, et al: Studies on the mechanism of oliguria in a model of unilateral acute renal failure. J Clin Invest 53:1546, 1974
61. Clarkson AR, MacDonald MK, Fuster V, et al: Glomerular coagulation in acute ischaemic renal failure. Q J Med 39:585, 1970
62. Handa SP: Glomerular lesions in acute tubular necrosis. Postgrad Med J 46:79, 1970
63. Solez K, Kramer EC, Heptinstall RH: The pathology of acute renal failure: Leukocyte accumulation in the vasa recta. Am J Pathol 74:31a, 1974
64. Bohle A, Mackensen-Haen S, Grund KE, et al: Shock kidney. Pathol Res Pract 165:212, 1979
65. Olsen S, Asklund M: Interstitial nephritis with acute renal failure following cardiac surgery and treatment with methicillin. Acta Med Scand 199:305, 1976
66. Solez K, Morel-Maroger L, Sraer JD: The morphology of "acute tubular necrosis" in man: analysis of 57 renal biopsies and a comparison with the glycerol model. Medicine 58:362, 1979
67. Dunnill MA: A review of the pathology and pathogenesis of acute renal failure due to acute tubular necrosis. J Clin Pathol 27:2, 1974
68. Eliahou HE: Mannitol therapy in oliguria of acute onset. Br Med J 1:807, 1964
69. Guild WR, Young JV, Merrill JP: Anuria due to carbon tetrachloride intoxication. Ann Intern Med 48:1221, 1958
70. Cameron JS, Miller-Jones CMH: Renal function and renal failure in badly burned children. Br J Surg 54:132, 1967
71. Meyers C, Roxe DM, Hano J: The clinical course of nonoliguric acute tubular necrosis. (Abstract). Proc Am Soc Nephrol 7:62, 1974
72. Anderson RJ, Linas SL, Berns AS, et al: Nonoliguric acute renal failure. N Engl J Med 296:1134, 1977
73. Eklund J, Granberg PO, Liljedahl SO: Studies on renal function in burns. Acta Chir Scand 136:627, 1970
74. Oken DE: Mannitol and the prevention of vasomotor nephropathy. p. 578. Proceedings of the Sixth International Congress on Nephrology, Karger, Basel, 1976
75. Epstein M, Schneider NS, Befeler B: Effect of intrarenal furosemide on renal function and intrarenal hemodynamics in acute renal failure. Am J Med 58:510, 1975
76. Kjellstrand CM: Ethacrynic acid in acute tubular necrosis. Indications and effect on the natural course. Nephron 9:337, 1972
77. Teschan PE, Post RS, Smith LH, et al: Post-traumatic renal insufficiency in military casualties: 1. Clinical characteristics. 2. Management, use of artificial kidney, prognosis. Am J Med 18:172, 1955
78. Fine LG, Eliahou HE: Acute oliguric intrinsic renal failure. Diagnostic criteria and

clinical features in 61 patients. Isr J Med Sci 51:1024, 1969
79. Maher JF, Schreiner GE: Causes of death in acute renal failure. Arch Intern Med 110:139, 1962
80. Kennedy AC, Burton JA, Luke RG, et al: Factors affecting the prognosis in acute renal failure. Q J Med 165:73, 1973
81. Oken DE: On the differential diagnosis of acute renal failure. Am J Med 71:916, 1981
82. Amerio A, Vercellone A, De Benedictis A, et al: Long-term prognosis in acute renal failure of primarily tubular origin. Minerva Nefrol 19:7, 1972
83. Mason EE: Gastrointestinal lesions occurring in uremia. Ann Intern Med 37:96, 1952
84. Kendall AG, Lowenstein L, Morgen RO: The hemorrhagic diathesis in renal disease (with special reference to acute uremia). Can Med Assoc J 85:405, 1961
85. Stewart JH: Haemolytic anaemia in acute and chronic renal failure. Q J Med 36:85, 1967
86. Naets JP, Brauman H, Kraytman M: Etude de l'erythropoiese au cours de l'insuffisance rénale aigue et chronique. Acta Haematol 24:169, 1960
87. Bluemle LW, Webster GD, Elkinton JR: Acute tubular necrosis. Arch Intern Med 104:180, 1959
88. Eknoyan G, Wacksman SJ, Glueck HL, et al: Platelet function in renal failure. N Engl J Med 280:677, 1969
89. Oken DE: Clinical aspects of acute renal failure (vasomotor nephropathy). p. 1108. In Edelmann CM (ed): Pediatric Kidney Disease. Little, Brown, Boston, 1978
90. Corwin HL, Teplick RS, Schreiber MJ, et al: Prediction of outcome in acute renal failure. Am J Nephrol 7:8, 1987
91. Tyler HR: Neurological complications of acute and chronic renal failure. p. 315. In Merrill JP (ed): The Treatment of Renal Failure. Grune and Stratton, New York, London, 1965
92. Wacker W, Merrill JP: Uremic pericarditis in acute and chronic renal failure. JAMA 156:764, 1954
93. Spodick DH: Differential characteristics of the electrocardiogram in early repolarization and acute pericarditis. N Engl J Med 295:523, 1976
94. Nidus BD, Matalon R, Cantacuzino D, et al: Uremic pleuritis—A clinicopathological entity. N Engl J Med 281:255, 1969
95. Buselmeier TJ, Simmons RL, Najarian JS, et al: Uremic pericardial effusion: Treatment by catheter drainage and local nonabsorbable steroid administration. Nephron 16:371, 1976
96. Guild WR, Bray G, Merrill JP: Hemopericardium with cardiac tamponade in chronic uremia. N Engl J Med 257:230, 1957
97. Stone WJ, Knepshield JH: Post-traumatic acute renal insufficiency in Vietnam. Clin Nephrol 2:185, 1974
98. Montgomerie JZ, Kalmanson GM, Guze LB: Renal failure and infection. Medicine 47:1, 1968
99. Merrill JP: The Treatment of Renal Failure. p. 174. 2nd ed. Grune and Stratton, New York, London, 1965
100. Swan RC, Merrill JP: The clinical course of acute renal failure. Medicine 32:215, 1953.
101. Oken DE: Clinical aspects of acute renal failure (vasomotor nephropathy). p. 1110. In Edelmann CM (ed): Pediatric Kidney Disease. Little, Brown, Boston, 1978
102. McNamara JJ, Molot M, Dunn R, et al: Clinical fat embolism in combat casualities. Am Surg 176:54, 1972
103. Appel GB: A decade of penicillin related acute interstitial nephritis—More questions than answers. Clin Nephrol 13:151, 1980
104. Goldberg LI: Dopamine—Clinical uses of an endogenous catecholamine. N Engl J Med 291:707, 1974
105. Morley CJ, Houston IB, Morris-Jones P: Acute renal failure and gout as presenting features of acute lymphoblastic leukaemia. Arch Dis Child 51:723, 1976
106. Papper S: The role of the kidney in Laennec's cirrhosis of the liver. Medicine 37:299, 1958
107. Eklund J: Studies on renal function in burns. Acta Chir Scand 136:741, 1970
108. Carvallo A, Rakowski TA, Argy WP, et al: Acute renal failure following drip infusion pyelography. Am J Med 65:38, 1978
109. Gary NE, Dodelson R, Eisinger RP: Indomethacin-associated acute renal failure. Am J Med 69:135, 1980

110. Bailey RR, Little PJ: Deterioration in renal function in association with co-trimethoxazole therapy. Med J Aust 1:914, 1976
111. Sporn IN, Langestremere RG, Papper S: Differential diagnosis of oliguria in aged patients. N Engl J Med 267:130, 1962
112. Oken DE: Diagnosis and treatment of acute renal failure. Mod Treat 6:927, 1969
113. Bernstein J, Kissane JM: Hereditary disorders of the kidney. p. 117. In Rosenberg HS, Bolande RP (eds): Perspectives in Pediatric Pathology. Year Book, Medical Publishers, Chicago, 1973
114. Kassirer JP: Atheroembolic renal disease. N Engl J Med 280:812, 1969
115. Handa SP, Morrin PAF: Diagnostic indices in acute renal failure. Can Med Assoc J 96:78, 1967
116. Espinel CH, Gregory AW: Differential diagnosis of acute renal failure. Clin Nephrol 13:73, 1980
117. Miller TR, Anderson RJ, Linas SL, et al: Urinary diagnostic indices in acute renal failure. Ann Intern Med 89:47, 1978
118. Munck O: Renal Circulation in Acute Renal Failure. Blackwell, Oxford, 1958
119. Bull GM, Joekes AM, Lowe KG: Renal function studies in acute tubular necrosis. Clin Sci 9:379, 1950
120. Mondorf AW, Breier J, Hendus J, et al: Effect of aminoglycosides on proximal tubular membranes of the human kidney. Eur J Clin Pharmacol 13:133, 1978
121. Rosalki SB, Wilkinson JH: Urinary lactic dehydrogenase in renal disease. Lancet 2:327, 1959
122. Butterworth PJ, Moss DW, Pitkanen E, et al: Patterns of urinary excretion of alkaline phosphatase in acute renal failure. Clin Chim Acta 11:212, 1965
123. Beck PR, Thompson RB, Chaudhuri AKR: Aminoglycoside antibiotics and renal function: Changes in urinary γ-glutamyltransferase excretion. J Clin Pathol 30:432, 1977
124. Raab WP: Diagnostic value of urinary enzyme determinations. Clin Chem 18:5, 1972
125. Cattell WR, McIntosh CS, Moseley IF, et al: Excretion urography in acute renal failure. Br Med J 9:575, 1973
126. Sanders RC: Renal ultrasound. Radiol Clin North Am 3:417, 1975
127. Schlegel JU, Land EK: Computed radionuclide urogram for assessing acute renal failure. AJR 134:1029, 1980
128. Oliver J, MacDowell M, Tracy A: The pathogenesis of acute renal failure associated with traumatic and toxic injury. Renal ischemia, nephrotoxic damage and the ischemuric episode. J Clin Invest 30:1305, 1951
129. Solez K, Finckh ES: Is there a correlation between the morphologic and functional changes in human acute renal failure? Data of Finckh, Jeremy and Whyte reexamined 20 years later. p. 3. In Solez K, Whelton A (eds): Acute Renal Failure: Correlations Between Morphology and Function. Marcel Dekker, New York, 1984
130. Myers BD, Carie BJ, Yee RR, et al: Pathophysiology of hemodynamically mediated acute renal failure. Kidney Int 18:495, 1980
131. Myers BD, Hilberman M, Spenser RJ, Jamison RL: Glomerular and tubular function in non-oliguric acute renal failure. Am J Med 72:643, 1982
132. Carrie BJ, Hilberman M, Schroeder JS, et al: Albuminuria and the permselective properties of the glomerulus in cardiac failure. Kidney Int 17:807, 1980
133. Oken DE: The pathogenetic significance of tubular leakage in acute renal failure (vasomotor nephropathy). Renal Failure 10:125, 1988
134. Brun C, Crone C, Davidsen HG, et al: Renal interstitial pressure in normal and in anuric man: Based on wedged renal vein pressure. Proc Soc Exp Biol Med 91:199, 1956
135. Lowenstein J, Beranbaum R, Chasis H, et al: Intrarenal pressure and exaggerated natriuresis in essential hypertension. Clin Sci 38:359, 1970
136. Oken DE: An analysis of glomerular dynamics in rat, dog and man. Kidney Int 22:136, 1982
137. Oken DE: Hemodynamic basis for human acute renal failure. Am J Med 76:702, 1984
138. Bohle A, von Giese H, Schubert B, et al: Transmission and scanning electron microscopy investigations on the structure of the ultrafilter of glomeruli in human acute renal failure. Am J Nephrol 8:112, 1988
139. Flores J, DiBona DR, Beck CH, et al: Role of cell swelling in ischemic renal damage

and the protective effect of hypertonic solute. J Clin Invest 51:118, 1972
140. Stein JH, Gottschall J, Osgood RW, et al: Pathophysiology of a nephrotoxic model of acute renal failure. Kidney Int 8:27, 1975
141. Wardle EM: Fibrin in renal disease: Functional considerations. Clin Nephrol 2:85, 1974
142. Carvalho JS, Carvalho ACA, Vaillancourt RA, et al: The pathogenetic significance of intravascular coagulation in experimental acute renal failure. Nephron 22:484, 1978
143. Watanabe T, Imamura T, Nakagaki K, et al: Disseminated intravascular coagulation in autopsy cases. Its incidence and clinicopathologic significance. Pathol Res Pract 165:311, 1979
144. Baylis C, Deen WM, Myers BD, et al: Effects of some vasodilator drugs on transcapillary fluid exchange in the renal cortex. Am J Physiol 230:1148, 1976
145. Brown JJ, Chinn RH, Gavras H, et al: Renin and Renal Function. p. 81. Hypertension. Vol. 172. Springer-Verlag, Berlin, 1972
146. Tu WH: Plasma renin activity in acute tubular necrosis and other renal disease associated with hypertension. Circulation 31:686, 1965
147. DiBona GF, McDonald FD, Flamenbaum W, et al: Maintenance of renal function in salt loaded rats despite severe tubular necrosis induced by $HgCl_2$. Nephron 8:205, 1971
148. McDonald FD, Thiel G, Wilson DR, et al: The prevention of acute renal failure in the rat by long-term saline loading. A possible role of the renin-angiotensin axis. Proc Soc Exp Biol Med 131:610, 1969
149. Henry LN, Lane CE, Kashgarian M: Micropuncture studies of the pathophysiology of acute renal failure in the rat. Lab Invest 19:309, 1968
150. Oken DE, Cotes SC, Flamenbaum W, et al: Active and passive immunization to angiotensin in experimental acute renal failure. Kidney Int 7:12, 1975
151. Flamenbaum W, Kotchen TA, Oken DE: Effect of renin immunization on mercuric chloride and glycerol-induced acute renal failure. Kidney Int 1:406, 1972
152. Hollenberg NK, Wilkes BM, Schulman G: The renin-angiotensin system in acute renal failure. p. 133. In Brenner BM, Lazarus JM (eds): Acute Renal Failure. 2nd Ed. Churchill Livingstone, New York, 1988
153. Fung HYM: Renal Hemodynamic Studies in Acute Renal Failure. Thesis. University of Manitoba, Canada, 1972
154. Knapp R, Hollenberg NK, Busch GJ, et al: Prolonged unilateral acute renal failure induced by intra-arterial norepinephrine infusion in the dog. Invest Radiol 7:164, 1972
155. Thomson AE, Fung HYM: Adrenergic and cholinergic mechanisms in acute renal failure in the dog and in man. p. 74. In Friedman EA, Eliahou HE (eds): Proceedings of the Conference on Acute Renal Failure. DHEW Publication No. (NIH) Washington, DC, 1973
156. Oken DE: Role of prostaglandins in the pathogenesis of acute renal failure. Lancet 1:1319, 1975
157. Oken DE, DiBona GF, McDonald FD: The pathophysiologic correlates of recovery from myohemoglobinuric acute renal failure. p. 122. In Gessler U, Schroeder K, Weidinger H (eds): Pathogenesis and Clinical Findings with Acute Renal Failure. Georg Thieme Verlag, Stuttgart, 1971
158. Tagawa H, Vander AJ: Effects of adenosine compounds on renal function and renin secretion in dogs. Circ Res 26:327, 1970
159. Osswald H: Renal effects of adenosine and their inhibition by theophylline. Naunyn-Schmiedebergs Arch Pharmacol 288:79, 1975
160. Osswald H, Schmitz HJ, Heidenreich O: Adenosine response of the rat kidney after saline loading, sodium restriction and hemorrhage. Pfluegers Arch 357:323, 1975
161. Osswald H, Schmitz HJ, Kemper R: Tissue content of adenosine, inosine and hypoxanthine in the rat kidney after ischemia and postischemic recirculation. Pfluegers Arch 371:45, 1977
162. Bidani AK, Churchill PC: Aminophylline ameliorates glycerol-induced acute renal failure in rats. Can J Physiol Pharmacol 61:567, 1983
163. Bidani AK, Churchill PC, Packer W: Theophylline-induced protection in myoglobinuric acute renal failure:Further charac-

terization. Can J Physiol Pharmacol 65:42, 1987
164. Bowmer CJ, Collis MG, Yates MS: Effect of the adenosine antagonist 8-phenyltheophylline on glycerol-induced acute renal failure in the rat. Br J Pharmacol 88:205, 1986
165. Yates MS, Bowmer CJ, Kellett R, et al: Effect of 8-phenyltheophylline, enprophylline and hydrochlorothiazide on glycerol-induced acute renal failure in the rat. J Pharm Pharmacol 39:803, 1987
166. Oken DE, Reilly KM: Total protection of glycerol-induced acute renal failure (ARF) with an adenosine-receptor blocker. (Abstract) Kidney Int 35:415, 1989
167. Flinn RB, Merrill JP, Welzant WR: The use of a new sodium exchange resin in the treatment of the anuric patient. N Engl J Med 264:111, 1961
168. Boen ST: Kinetics of peritoneal dialysis— a comparison with the artificial kidney. Medicine 40:243, 1961
169. Ryan JA, Abel RM, Abbott WM, et al: Catheter complications in total parenteral nutrition. N Engl J Med 290:757, 1974
170. Hinton P, Allison SP, Littlejohn S, et al: Insulin and glucose to reduce catabolic response to injury in burned patients. Lancet 1:767, 1971
171. McDermott FT, Nayman J, DeBoer WGRM: The effect of acute renal failure upon wound healing: histological and autoradiographic studies in the mouse. Ann Surg 168:142, 1968
172. Giordano C: Use of exogenous and endogenous urea for protein synthesis in normal and uremic subjects. J Lab Clin Med 62:231, 1963
173. Giovanetti S, Maggiore Q: A low nitrogen diet with proteins of high biological value for severe chronic uraemia. Lancet 1:1000, 1964
174. Dudrick SJ, Steiger E, Long JM: Renal failure in surgical patients: Treatment with intravenous essential amino acids and hypertonic glucose. Surgery 68:180, 1968
175. Abel RM, Beck CH, Abbott WM, et al: Improved survival from acute renal failure after treatment with intravenous essential L-amino acids and glucose. N Engl J Med 288:695, 1973
176. Oken DE: Mannitol and the prevention of vasomotor nephropathy. p. 578. Proceedings of the Sixth International Congress on Nephrology, Florence, 1975
177. Baek SM, Makabali GG, Bryan-Brown CW, et al: The influence of parenteral nutrition on the course of acute renal failure. Surg Gynecol Obstet 141:405, 1975
178. Abel RM, Abbott WM, Beck CH, et al: Essential L-amino acids in patients with disordered nitrogen metabolism. Am J Surg 128:317, 1974
179. Leonard CD, Luke RG, Siegel RR: Parenteral essential amino acids in acute renal failure. Urology 6:154, 1975
180. Naylor CD, Detsky AS, O'Rourke K, et al: Does treatment with essential amino acids and glucose improve survival in acute renal failure: A meta-analysis. Renal Failure 10:141, 1987–88
181. Toback FG: Amino acid enhancement of renal regeneration after acute tubular necrosis. Kidney Int 12:193, 1977
182. Oken DE, Sprinkel FM, Kirschbaum BB, et al: Amino acid therapy in the treatment of experimental acute renal failure in the rat. Kidney Int 17:14, 1980
183. Bennett WM, Muther RS, Parker RA, et al: Drug therapy in renal failure: dosing guidelines for adults. Ann Intern Med 93:62, 1980
184. Bennet WA, Aronoff GR, Golper TA, et al: Drug Prescribing in Renal Failure: Dosing Guidelines for Adults. American College of Physicians, Philadelphia, 1987
185. Noree LO, Bergstrom J, Furst P, et al: The effect of essential amino acid administration on nitrogen metabolism during dialysis. Proc Eur Dial Transplant Assoc 7:182, 1971
186. Berlyne GM, Jones JH, Hewitt V, et al: Protein loss in peritoneal dialysis. Lancet 1:738, 1964
187. Kleinknecht D, Jungers P, Chanard J, et al: Uremic and non-uremic complications in acute renal failure. Evaluation of early and frequent dialysis on prognosis. Kidney Int 4:390, 1973

16

Special Considerations in Hypertension

Leonard G. Feld
James E. Springate
Joseph L. Izzo, Jr

Arterial hypertension is a condition that has been recognized in varying forms for centuries. Records from the dynasty of the Yellow Emperor of China in the Third Century B.C. refer to problems associated with "the hardening of the pulse" associated with excessive salt intake. Within the last two centuries, Claude Bernard and other physiologists rediscovered the association between hypertension and cardiovascular pathology. After Korotkoff described our present auscultatory method for blood pressure estimation in 1905, a simple tool for the detection and follow-up of arterial hypertension became readily available.

Yet effective treatment of arterial hypertension is a phenomenon of the last 30 years. Hallmark epidemiologic studies begun in Framingham, Massachusetts after World War II drew attention to the risks associated with hypertension.[1] Other, less publicized epidemiologic studies also underscored the association of hypertension with stroke and cardiac and renal disease.[2,3] As the result of these early studies, a multidisciplinary advisory council was formed to aid in public policy formation. This Joint National Committee on the Detection and Treatment of High Blood Pressure issued its first report in 1977.[4] It established a cutoff point of 140/90 mmHg for defining hypertension, and recommended "stepped care" therapy, which began with diuretic agents and then added sympatholytic and vasodilator drugs if necessary. Many members of this group were instrumental in initiating the Hypertension Detection and Follow-up Project, which yielded positive but somewhat disappointing results for stepped care in the treatment of mild hypertension.[5] The subsequent Multiple Risk Factor Intervention Trial[6] was also disappointing in that it failed to show any benefit of stepped care therapy on ischemic heart disease. Thus, although the first Veteran's Administration cooperative trial[7] demonstrated in 1971 that the treatment of severe arterial hypertension improved morbidity and mortality, debate has increased about whether or not the treatment of mild hypertension is uniformly indicated. On the one hand, because of the large number of subjects with mild hypertension, most of the benefit of reduced morbidity and mortality results from treatment of this group.[8] On the other hand, the absolute risk rate is very low in mild hypertension.[9] Thus, the potential benefit of therapy in a given individual is small. Recently, the Medical Research Council of Great Britain evaluated the treatment of mild hypertension and concluded that 857 individuals must be treated to prevent one stroke annually.[9]

Perhaps the most important aspect of mild hypertension is its interaction with other health problems. The Framingham Study clearly demonstrated that a variety of risk factors contribute in multiplicative fashion to overall cardiovascular risk.[1] An elevated serum cholesterol concentration, cigarette smoking, diabetes mellitus, and the presence of left ventricular hypertrophy amplify the risk of hypertension by 10- to 20-fold. Thus, it is prudent to consider factors other than the blood pressure in determining the level of aggressiveness and type of therapy most appropriate in a given patient. The fact remains that treatment is a statistical exercise with no guarantee of long-term benefit in a given case. If future developments provide better means of identifying individuals specifically at risk for morbid events, it may be possible to aggressively treat certain patients while withholding drug therapy in those with the lowest risk profiles.[10,11]

In summary, although the treatment of hypertension is often considered to be a triumph of public health policy, important questions remain to be answered. Uniform (non-individualized) treatment of patients with mild hypertension and children remains exceptionally problematic, given new data on the heterogeneity of hypertensive individuals. The intent of this chapter is to highlight special problems related to the pathophysiologic understanding of the diagnosis and treatment of hypertension.

DEFINITION AND DETECTION OF HYPERTENSION

The definition of high blood pressure is arbitrary. Its detection therefore requires universal acceptance and application of blood pressure standards and a reliable, consistent method for blood pressure measurement.

Adults

The blood pressure continuum in adults is a skewed normal distribution with no distinct cutoff point.[1-4,8] It has been arbitrarily decided in the United States that hypertension is defined as a diastolic pressure greater than 90 mmHg or a systolic pressure greater than 160 mmHg (if the diastolic pressure is less than 90 mmHg).[4,8,12] Different definitions exist in different countries. For example, in England, it is common practice to define essential hypertension on the basis of repeated office diastolic blood pressure readings in excess of 100 mmHg. As discussed at the beginning of the chapter, the treatment of mild hypertension is an area that may require further evaluation.

The Joint National Committee on Detection and Evaluation of High Blood Pressure has made a series of definitions that are summarized in Table 16-1.[4,12] Of particular note is the attention paid by this ad-

Table 16-1. Classification of Blood Pressure in Adults

Range (mmHg)	Category
Diastolic	
<85	Normal blood pressure
85–89	High normal blood pressure
90–104	Mild hypertension
105–114	Moderate hypertension
≥115	Severe hypertension
Systolic, when diastolic blood pressure is <90	
<140	Normal blood pressure
140–159	Borderline isolated systolic hypertension
≥160	Isolated systolic hypertension

(From The 1988 Report of the Joint National Committee on Detection, Evaluation and Treatment of High Blood Pressure,[12] with permission.)

visory committee to the group listed as having "high normal" blood pressures. At present, two schools of thought exist. The more aggressive school suggests that blood pressures be kept below 130/85 mmHg. The less aggressive school feels that blood pressures in excess of 150/100 mmHg require treatment.

It must be emphasized that standard epidemiologic data are based on blood pressures determined in the physician's office. Office blood pressures are poorly reflective of the cumulative effects of blood pressure elevation because of the marked hetergeneity of stress responses among individuals. At present, "white coat" hypertension is widely recognized.[13] Because of this confounding effect, a growing number of investigators feel that additional information, such as blood pressures taken at the work site or at home, may provide more important information with regard to the prognosis for a given individual.[13-17]

Another technique that has gained acceptance as a research tool is ambulatory blood pressure monitoring.[15,16] Whether or not ambulatory monitoring has a role in the clinical management of hypertensive patients is being debated. There seems to be little doubt that average waking ambulatory blood pressures have importance as prognostic tools in epidemiologic research. In an excellent study performed by Perloff and colleagues,[17] a group of about 550 hypertensive subjects with equivalent pressures in the physician's office were divided into two groups. The first group had blood pressures in excess of the predicted office/ambulatory difference (approximately 10 mmHg). The second group demonstrated the predicted lower blood pressure values expected during ambulatory (compared to office) readings. In essence, the first group experienced similar blood pressures in the physician's office and during ambulatory monitoring, while the second group exhibited at least a 6 mmHg decrease in the mean ambulatory blood pressure compared to the physician's office reading. After 10 years of follow-up, the morbidity and mortality of the group with both office and ambulatory hypertension was twice that of the group whose blood pressures decreased when outside the clinic setting. These impressive results were obtained using a much smaller number of subjects than those required to show altered morbidity and mortality based on physician's office readings. This argues indirectly that the precision and value of non-office blood pressure readings are superior to those of pressures measured in the physician's office.

Other investigators have attempted to quantitate continuous indices of target organ damage with the average (mean) ambulatory blood pressure. The left ventricular wall thickness[15] or left ventricular mass index[16] can be shown to be directly proportional to mean ambulatory blood pressure values. It is interesting to note that in one of these studies, Devereux and co-workers[15] found no relationship between left ventricular wall thickness and blood pressures obtained in the physician's office.

These data provided by ambulatory techniques suggest that an entirely different definition of hypertension may be required. This area is highly controversial at present. However, it is our opinion that the syndrome of essential hypertension may be better defined by the degree of target organ damage that exists than by office blood pressure values.

Children

The 1987 Task Force Report on Blood Pressure Control in Children has provided an excellent discussion of the definition and detection of high blood pressure in pediatrics.[18] Among the points that deserve emphasis are that: (1) Regardless of the clinical setting, several blood pressure measurements are needed to detect hypertension, and (2) accurate equipment, appropriate cuff size, correct measuring technique, and proper patient preparation are important. Even in the best circumstances, blood pressure measurements in children are subject to considerable interobserver variation. The accuracy of indirect diastolic measurements is especially questionable, leading some experts to recommend using systolic blood pressure measurements to detect hypertension in children.[19] Standardized automated blood pressure measuring devices may help eliminate interobserver variability. The data used to construct blood pressure standards in the Task Force Study were generally obtained by experienced health care workers using mercury sphygmomanometers in children and Doppler instruments in infants, under standardized conditions. In theory, only results obtained using these same methods can be interpreted. Although intra-arterial, oscillometric, or home measurement may more accurately reflect "true" blood pressure, their significance is unclear. Ambulatory blood pressure monitoring in children appears to be unreliable.[20]

Some physicians may be confused by the pediatric Task Force's use of different criteria for the definition and classification of hypertension (Tables 16-2 and 16-3).[18] For example, a six-year-old girl with consistent blood pressure readings of 120/75 mmHg would be labeled hypertensive according to the Task Force's definition of high blood pressure based on age- and sex-specific percentiles, but would not have significant hypertension according to the Task Force's classification of hypertension. Because the clinical significance of the Task Force's blood pressure standards is unknown, the diagnosis of childhood hypertension is probably best made using the Task Force's classification criteria (Table 16-3).

We need a standardized approach to the definition and classification of hypertension in children and adults. For example, an older adolescent labeled hypertensive by a pediatrician can be reclassified as having high normal or even normal blood pressure by an internist. Similarly, an adolescent with severe hypertension in the pediatrician's office can have only mild hypertension or even borderline isolated systolic hypertension in another physician's office. Interdisciplinary communication, patient care, and research would benefit greatly from an arbitrary but uniform definition and classification of hypertension.

The pediatric Task Force's algorithm for detecting children with hypertension is presented in Figure 16-1. The value of distinguishing between children with high normal blood pressure and normal blood pressure is unclear. Although some children with high normal blood pressures will continue to have elevated blood pressures years later, and will possibly be at higher risk for hypertension as adults, many will not.[21] The Task Force also recognizes that variables other than chronologic age and sex affect

Table 16-2. 1987 Pediatric Task Force Definition of Hypertension

Term	Definition
Normal blood pressure	Systolic and diastolic blood pressures <90th percentile for age and sex
High normal blood pressure[a]	Average systolic and/or average diastolic blood pressure between 90th and 95th percentiles for age and sex
High blood pressure (hypertension)	Average systolic and/or average diastolic blood pressures ≥95th percentile for age and sex with measurements obtained on at least three occasions

[a] If the blood pressure reading is high normal for age, but can be accounted for by excess height for age or excess lean body mass for age, the patient is considered to have a normal blood pressure.
(From Report of the Second Task Force on Blood Pressure Control in Children,[18] with permission.)

Table 16-3. 1987 Pediatric Task Force Classification of Hypertension

Age Group	Significant Hypertension (Blood Pressure in mmHg)
Newborn	
7 days	Systolic ≥96
8–30 days	Systolic ≥104
Infant (<2 yr)	Systolic ≥112
	Diastolic ≥74
Children (3–5 yr)	Systolic ≥116
	Diastolic ≥76
Children (6–9 yr)	Systolic ≥122
	Diastolic ≥78
Children (10–12 yr)	Systolic ≥126
	Diastolic ≥82
Children (13–15 yr)	Systolic ≥136
	Diastolic ≥86
Adolescents (16–18 yr)	Systolic ≥142
	Diastolic ≥92

(From Report of the Second Task Force on Blood Pressure Control in Children,[18] with permission.)

normal blood pressure in childhood. These variables include maturational age and body size. To account for these additional variables, the Task Force recommends that the weight and height percentiles be determined for children with blood pressure readings between the 90th and 95th percentile for age. If the patient has a high normal blood pressure and a weight and height that are below the 90th percentile, "there is a greater possibility that the blood pressure elevation is the result of some pathologic process and that the child needs special consideration."[18] This recommendation will identify a substantial number of "at risk" children for closer follow-up. At least 3 percent of all children have blood pressures above and heights and weights below the 90th percentile for their age.[22] The Task Force's algorithm for identifying children with high blood pressure will therefore target more than 8 percent of the population for "special consideration" (5 percent with hypertension, more than 3 percent with high normal blood pressure). The significance and appropriateness of this labeling are unknown.

The Task Force Report recognizes that "the choice of the 90th percentile of blood pressure is arbitrary because, if children and adolescents respond to blood pressure elevation as adults do, risk can be expected to increase as blood pressure increases with no absolute cutoff point separating normotension from hypertension."[18] However, it is equally possible that some children with blood pressures in or above the 95th percentile for their age are normal, and that some children with blood pressures below the 90th percentile are abnormal. Their blood pressures may also reflect differences in growth or maturation.[23] No generally accepted method exists for identifying these children. An interesting new approach is the use of vertex-corrected blood pressure measurements.[24] This technique involves measurement of the distance from the mid-upper arm (heart level) to the top of the head (brain level), with use of this measurement as a correction factor for blood pressure measurements obtained in a seated patient (Fig. 16-2). Vertex-corrected readings appear to eliminate variability due to age and height, and also estimate the brain perfusion pressure (a possible index of stroke risk). An extreme example is the erect giraffe, which requires a very high blood pressure at heart level (260/158 – 340/303 mmHg) to maintain a normal arterial pressure in its brain.

In summary, current standards for defining hypertension in children are arbitrary. They are based on the hypothesis that values greater than the 95th percentile for age are abnormal. The significance of this definition in terms of future morbidity is unclear. Nevertheless, serial blood pressure measurements should become a routine part of pediatric health care. Proper interpretation of these measurements requires analysis of the clinical setting and consideration of the severity and chronicity of abnormal values. A persistently high blood pressure in childhood may be the only sign of a potentially serious underlying disease, even though its value in predicting the risk of hypertension in adulthood is unsettled.

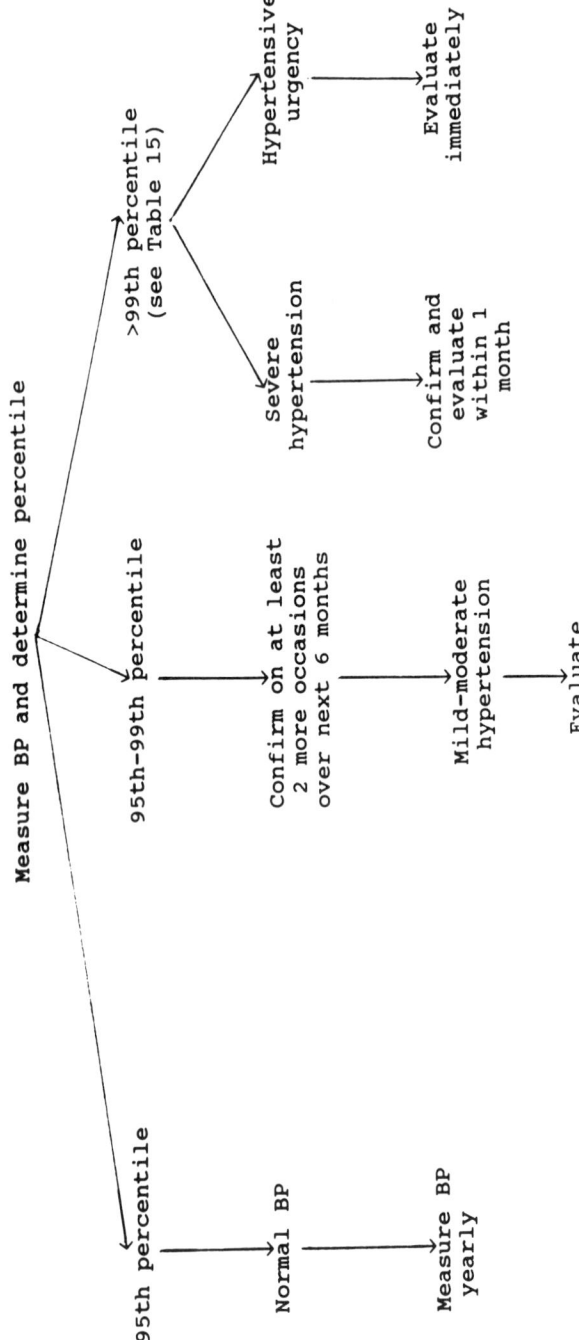

FIG. 16-1. A method for diagnosing hypertension in children. (From Feld LG, et al.[19] with permission.)

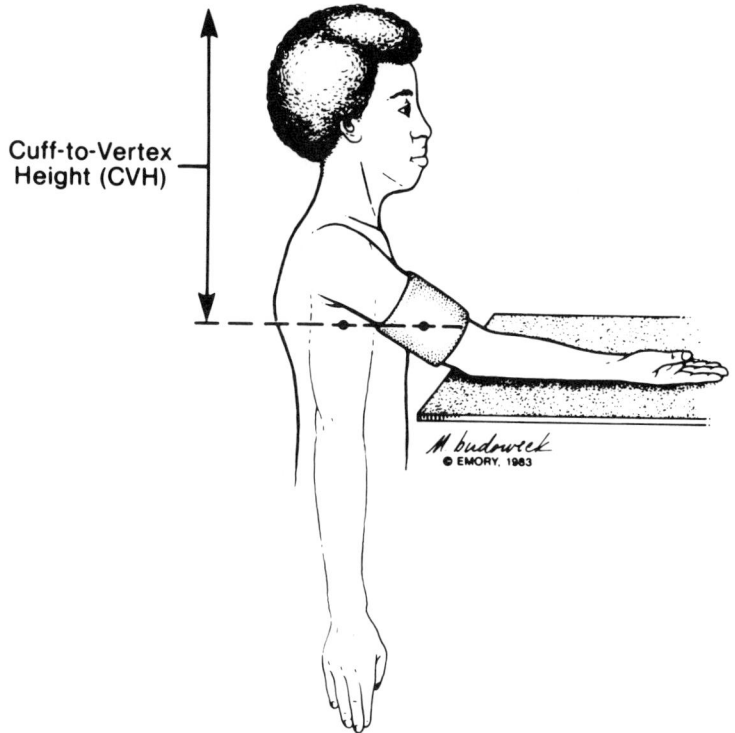

FIG. 16-2. Vertex-corrected blood pressure measurements use the distance in centimeters from the midpoint of the upper arm to the top of the head (CVH) to dampen blood pressure variability due to age and height. Vertex-corrected blood pressure = measured blood pressure − 0.779 (CVH). (From Kahn HS, Bain RP: Vertex-corrected blood pressure in black girls. Hypertension 9: 390, 1987, with permission.)

ETIOLOGY

Essential Hypertension

The etiology, or more probably etiologies, of essential hypertension remain to be fully elucidated. Given the diverse nature of the hypertensive population and the multiplicity of redundant mechanisms contributing to the regulation of arterial pressure, a single cause of hypertension is highly unlikely. Most experts agree that this disorder is a multifactorial phenomenon, an idea put forward most clearly by Irvine Page.[25] Page suggested that subtle abnormalities of several mutually interdependent factors are responsible for the "mosaic" that is essential hypertension. It is generally believed that in each case, systemic vascular resistance is inappropriately high for the level of cardiac output that exists in the affected individual. Thus, hypertension is often considered to be a disorder of the peripheral vasculature. However, it is conceivable that a final common pathway exists to mediate the input of several diverse stimuli, resulting in hypertension. A strong argument can be made that this final common pathway is mediated through rapid changes in cytosolic calcium concentration.

Calcium and Hypertension

Extracellular calcium is absolutely necessary for any type of muscle to undergo contraction. This calcium must enter the cell to effect a series of changes that lead to the phosphorylations directly responsible for muscle contraction. Thus, if one more clearly understood the factors regulating calcium influx, essential hypertension might be more easily understood. At least four major factors directly influence the rate of calcium influx. These are: (1) factors associated with membrane electronegativity, in turn caused by the adenosine triphosphatase (ATPase)-dependent flux of sodium, potassium, and other ions across the membrane; (2) the "potential-dependent" or "slow" calcium channels in the cell membrane; (3) angiotensin II receptor-inositide interactions; and (4) adrenergic receptor-dependent calcium influx.

If each of these diverse mechanisms controlling calcium influx were heterogeneously responsible for a certain percentage of calcium influx, and if these determinants exhibited genetic variation in the population, then both the mosaic theory and the final common pathway theory could be reconciled. In clinical practice, the physician would simply determine (by methods not currently available) which pathway was responsible for the greatest percentage of calcium influx. Because so many antihypertensive drugs are quite specific for one of the four major mechanisms controlling calcium flux, specific pharmacotherapy could then be recommended. This attractive theory remains to be fully tested, but provides an interesting and useful framework for the use of currently available antihypertensive drugs.

Sodium and Hypertension

Recent reviews by Dustan[26] and Weinberger[27] summarize the controversy surrounding the role of salt in hypertension. Tobian and others had previously suggested that increased salt intake caused heightened vascular reactivity, perhaps by directly increasing vascular sensitivity and also by increasing the salt and water content of the cells in the walls of resistance arterioles. This cell "water-logging" then narrowed the lumen of the blood vessels. A flurry of recent investigation has suggested that some individuals are in fact sensitive to sodium chloride while others are not.[28,29] Some investigators have suggested that "salt-sensitive" hypertensive individuals have abnormalities of angiotensin II receptor regulation ("modulation").[28] Another theory proposes that circulating substances in the salt-sensitive hypertensive individual affect membrane pump activities.[28,29] None of these abnormalities appears to apply to all people with hypertension, however.

In order to understand the effects (or lack thereof) of sodium loading on blood pressure, direct cellular effects must be compared to counterbalancing physiologic compensations in the whole animal. For example, slow salt loading causes a volume expansion phenomenon which in turn tends to suppress the activity of the major vasoconstrictor systems: the sympathetic nervous system and the renin-angiotensin system.[30] Conversely, salt restriction activates these systems. In fact, clinical experience suggests that only part of the hypertensive population will respond to sodium restriction or diuretic therapy. In the case of diuretics, the nonresponders appear to have the ability to compensate for sodium restriction by vigorous activation of the vasoconstrictor systems. Only in the case of near total sodium restriction, comparable to levels achieved in the Kempner Rice Diet (less than 10 mEq/day), is a major therapeutic benefit consistently demonstrated. In common clinical situations, where sodium restriction of approximately 20 percent can be achieved, only a small blood pressure decrease was seen.[31]

The most convincing evidence correlating salt intake with high blood pressure in childhood comes from a study by Hofman and associates on the effects of salt restriction on blood pressure in infants.[32] Newborns were randomly assigned to receive a "normal" diet or a diet with 50 percent less sodium. At six months of age, systolic blood pressures in the low-sodium-diet infants were significantly lower than those of the normal-sodium group, without any difference in growth. Follow-up of these infants is eagerly awaited. Studies of various forms of salt-dependent hypertension in animals have revealed a striking age-related susceptibility to increased salt intake.[33] The idea that there exists a critical developmental period of exposure to hypertensive stimuli such as salt may provide new insights into the pathogenesis and prevention of primary hypertension.

Potassium in Hypertension

Significant controversy surrounds the role of potassium supplementation in hypertension. Data exist to indicate that patients with blood potassium levels below 3.0 mEq/liter have an increased likelihood of ventricular arrhythmias.[34] However, contrary opinion suggests that these particular arrhythmias are benign in nature. The general recommendation that potassium supplementation be given to patients taking thiazide diuretics has undergone revisions on two occasions. Recent trends toward a reduction in thiazide dose may improve relative degrees of hypokalemia.[35] At doses of hydrochlorothiazide of 25 mg/day there appears to be less potassium wasting than at previously used doses of 50 or 100 mg.[35] Because the efficacy of low-dose thiazide is almost as great that of higher doses, the former is usually recommended.

Data also exist to indicate that hypertensive subjects tend to have lower potassium diets.[36] Kaplan and others have demonstrated that massive potassium supplementation itself may lower blood pressure by mechanisms that remain to be elucidated.[37] Provocative animal data from Tobian's laboratory suggest that cerebral vascular accidents in stroke-prone rats can be dramatically reduced by a high potassium diet despite minimal lowering of the blood pressure.[38] Further developments in this area should prove interesting.

Age-related Hemodynamic Changes

A major hemodynamic shift occurs in the natural history and evolution of hypertension. In the early years of life, borderline (sometimes called "labile") hypertension is often associated with relative degrees of tachycardia and systolic hypertension.[39] These signs denote the increased cardiac output of younger subjects with hypertension, who are predominantly males. However, in later years, hypertension is not associated with an increase in cardiac output, but rather with increased systemic vascular resistance.[40] This hemodynamic evolution from high-flow to high-resistance hypertension prompted Guyton to propose the theory of "whole-body autoregulation." In Guyton's concept, an abnormality of some physiologic regulatory mechanism, perhaps involving the baroreceptors and mechanisms controlling renal sodium excretion, caused this long-term hemodynamic shift to occur. The precise mechanisms controlling this evolutionary change were never elucidated, however.

It is intriguing to consider the long-range change from flow to resistance in light of several clinical observations implicating the sympathetic nervous system in the pathogenesis of hypertension. First, older hypertensive individuals do not necessarily develop a high-flow state prior to the onset of fixed high-resistance hypertension. Second, it has been observed that in early hypertension, the affected subjects have evidence of sympathetic nervous system hyperactivity.[40] Third, Izzo and co-workers have shown that the sympathetic nervous system contributes to the high vascular resistance of hypertension, independent of age.[41] Thus, it can be argued that the sympathetic nervous system plays an important contributory role in all stages of hypertension.

Several other pieces of information also point to a role for the sympathetic nervous system in a "vascular aging model" of hemodynamic evolution in hypertension.[42] Younger subjects have higher densities of β-adrenergic receptors than older subjects. With age, the activity of the renin-angiotensin system and blood volume also decline. In older age, subjects are thus "high-resistance" hypertensives who actually have low normal blood volumes. It must be mentioned in this context that the "volume-vasoconstrictor" hypothesis forwarded by Laragh and other workers usually equates "low renin" hypertension with "volume excess." In truth, most low renin hypertensives are older individuals[43] with low blood volumes and high levels of vasoconstriction. Thus, aging effects are probably more important than volume effects in interpreting the level of renin and angiotensin activity in a given subject.[43] It is interesting to note that sympatholytic drugs are among the only drugs that are uniformly effective in all forms of hypertension. This observation lends functional significance to a role for the sympathetic nervous system in all levels of hypertension.

Specific Pediatric Issues

Attempts to identify physiologic markers for primary hypertension in childhood have served only to emphasize its diversity. Several studies have indicated that differences in cellular sodium transport can distinguish children with primary hypertension from those with secondary hypertension or normal blood pressures, and can identify individuals at risk for future high blood pressure.[44] Other studies have either failed to confirm these results or have demonstrated a significant degree of overlapping values.[44] Children with primary hypertension, like their adult counterparts, can have low, normal, or high levels of renin secretion, normal or elevated sympathetic nervous system activity, low or normal rates of urinary kallikrein excretion, and normal or impaired erythrocyte deformability.[45-48] The role of differences in cardiovascular reactivity, cardiac output, and systemic vascular resistance in childhood hypertension is also being actively investigated.[49,50] The results of these studies suggest that primary hypertension in childhood is produced by a variety of separate processes rather than by a single, as yet unidentified, abnormality.

Secondary Hypertension

If a secondary cause of hypertension is suspected, this possibility should be pursued. The causes of secondary hypertension are in Table 16-4.

EVALUATION

General Comments

The goals of evaluation are to (1) correctly label individuals with hypertension, (2) detect potentially curable secondary causes of hypertension, (3) establish the presence of other risk factors for cardiovascular disease, and (4) identify the chronicity of hypertension and hypertensive target organ damage. The scope and pace of this evaluation must be regulated by an awareness that the natural history of hypertension is unknown, and that morbidity from the disease relates both to its severity and duration and to the presence of other underlying illnesses and cardiovascular disease risk factors.

These goals can be achieved by a thorough personal and family medical history, physical examination, selected laboratory

Table 16-4. Causes of Secondary Hypertension

Obesity
Renal Parenchymal Diseases[45]
    Acute or chronic glomerulopathies
    Acute and chronic renal failure
    Obstructive uropathy
    Reflux nephropathy
    Cystic renal diseases
    Trauma

Vascular Disease
    Coarctation of the aorta
    Renal artery disorders
    Renal infarction

Endocrine Disease[45,51]
    Adrenocortical disorders
        Cushing's syndrome
        Idiopathic primary hyperaldosteronism
        "Hypertensive" congenital adrenal hyperplasia (11-hydroxylase deficiency, 17-hydroxylase deficiency)
        Dexamethasone suppressible hyperaldosteronism
        Apparent mineralocorticoid excess
    Hyperthyroidism
    Hyperparathyroidism/Hypercalcemia
    Hypothyroidism

Tumor[45,52-54]
    Wilm's tumor
    Pheochromocytoma (isolated or associated with multiple endocrinopathy syndrome, neurofibromatosis or Von Hippel-Lindau disease)
    Neuroblastoma and related neurogenic tumors
    Conn's syndrome (aldosterone-secreting tumor)
    Renin-secreting juxtaglomerular cell tumor

Drug/Toxin[45,55,56]
    Oral contraceptives
    Corticosteroids
    Sympathomimetics (nose or eye drops, "cold" medications)
    Amphetamines
    Methylphenidate
    Imipramine
    Cyclosporine
    Clonidine or guanabenz withdrawal
    Metoclopramide or other intravenous antiemetics
    Methotrexate
    Lead

Neurologic[45,57-59]
    Increased intracranial pressure
    Head injury or cerebrovascular accident
    Guillain-Barré syndrome
    Autonomic dysreflexia (spinal cord injury)
    Posterior fossa lesions

Other[45,60-62]
    Chronic upper airway obstruction/sleep apnea
    Traction-induced
    Severe burns
    Pregnancy
    Intravascular volume overload
    Pain or anxiety

(From Feld LG, et al.,[19] with permission.)

tests, and consistent follow-up. Once hypertension has been detected, evaluation is initiated by formulating a clinical impression about the severity and duration of the patient's high blood pressure, factors influencing patient risk and management, and the possibility of secondary hypertension (see Table 16-4).

Severe Hypertension

Because the likelihood of secondary hypertension is great, patients who may have this condition require further investigation. Serum electrolyte measurements provide inexpensive screening for hyperaldosteronism and for acidosis associated with renal parenchymal disease. Hypokalemia and alkalemia suggest excess mineralocorticoid secretion due to adrenal cortical disorders, renovascular disease, or a renin-secreting juxtaglomerular cell tumor. Although primary hyperaldosteronism without hypokalemia has been described in children, studies in adults indicate that the presence of hypokalemia in the absence of salt depletion or diuretic use is an excellent screening test for this rare but easily overlooked disorder.[18,63] In patients receiving diuretics, serum potassium values of 2.9 mEq/liter or greater are most likely caused by diuretic-induced secondary hyperaldosteronism. However, a serum potassium value below 2.6 mEq/liter is rarely diuretic-induced, and generally represents primary hyperaldosteronism that has been exacerbated by diuretic therapy.

Renal failure as a cause of hypertension cannot be overlooked. The serum creatinine concentration remains the most practical indicator of the glomerular filtration rate (GFR). Results must be interpreted using age-appropriate normal values. An abnormally high result suggests that renal function is no more than 50 percent of normal. Complete blood counts, urine cultures, and serum uric acid levels are often included in evaluations for suspected secondary hypertension,[18] but no form of secondary hypertension is associated with isolated abnormalities of these parameters. Elevated uric acid levels appear to reflect decreases in renal blood flow produced by essential hypertension,[64] and the uric acid concentration is therefore a potential measure of hypertensive end-organ damage rather than a sign of hypertension secondary to impaired renal function. Blood urea nitrogen levels should not be used alone to estimate renal function.

In addition to serum electrolyte and creatinine measurements, renal imaging studies should be obtained in all patients with severe, unexplained hypertension. It is important to remember that at least one-third of affected adults with accelerated hypertension have underlying renovascular disease.[65] Renal disease is also a leading cause of secondary hypertension in childhood, in which many hypertensive renal disorders are not associated with a significant reduction in GFR. Current evidence supports the combination of sonography and radionuclide scanning for imaging the kidney as a possible source of hypertension; intravenous pyelography remains an appropriate alternative.[66,67] This topic is treated in depth elsewhere.[67a] These studies must be done by a radiologist who understands the purpose of their use and is skilled in their interpretation.

Inability to detect a secondary cause for severe hypertension following the above evaluation puts the primary care provider in a troublesome position. Does the patient have primary hypertension or should the search for secondary causes continue? Diagnostic possibilities at this point may still include renovascular disease, pheochromocytoma, and primary hyperaldosteronism. Asymptomatic pheochromocytomas and normokalemic primary hyperaldosteronism are unusual, and their diagnosis and management require specialized care. Renovascular disease is not uncommon in this setting, and its detection and treatment are problematic. Referral to a specialist in hypertension may be appropriate at this point.

Chronic Hypertension with Target Organ Damage

Considerable clinical judgment is needed to identify the group of patients with hypertension in whom there is target organ damage. Previous blood pressure measurements are often unavailable, and organ damage may be difficult to detect. A careful funduscopic examination should be performed, and the urine should be examined for proteinuria, cells, and casts. Peripheral arteries should be palpated and auscultated for bruits. In hypertensive adults, left ventricular hypertrophy is best identified by echocardiography.[15] Early renal involvement can be detected by elevated serum uric acid levels and creatinine clearance measurements.[64,68]

Although definitive pediatric studies on this topic have not been reported, echocardiography and uric acid levels may be of value in determining the chronicity and significance of childhood hypertension. When chronic mild to moderate hypertension or hypertensive end-organ damage is suspected, evaluation of the patient should include serum electrolyte, uric acid, and creatinine measurements as well as echocardiography and renal imaging.[19] If no secondary cause for hypertension is found after this evaluation, the primary care provider can safely choose either to refer the patient or to institute therapy for primary hypertension and associated cardiovascular disease risk factors.

MANAGEMENT

An understanding of the natural history and consequences of hypertension together with a thorough evaluation of the hypertensive patient form the foundation for appropriate management of the disease. Some patients with secondary hypertension can be offered a definitive cure. Others with secondary hypertension and all children and adults with primary hypertension have a potentially chronic problem. These individuals and their physicians must commit themselves to a long-term care plan designed to control blood pressure, eliminate other risk factors for cardiovascular disease, and preserve an acceptable quality of life.

Management strategies can be divided into nonpharmacologic treatment and pharmacologic treatment. Selection of an appropriate care plan depends on clinical judgment based on the severity and duration of high blood pressure, on the presence of other risk factors, and on the presence of other diseases effected by hypertension. A healthy patient with newly diagnosed mild to moderate hypertension may benefit from general information about nonpharmacologic treatment and continued observation. On the other hand, a child or adult with severe hypertension, end-organ damage, hyperlipidemia, or underlying renal disease may require more aggressive nonpharmacologic treatment and antihypertensive medication.

Current recommendations suggest that blood pressure be reduced to "normal" levels of less than 140/90 mmHg in adults and below the 90th percentile in children.[12,18] These recommendations are based on the assumption that the dangers of high blood pressure increase (or decrease) continuously as blood pressure rises (or is reduced). Recent research in hypertensive adults indicates that these treatment goals need to be re-evaluated.[69,70] Blood pressure reduction to less than 130/85 mmHg may actually increase the risk of myocardial infarction and death in certain patients. The significance of these findings for hypertensive children is unknown.

Nonpharmacologic Antihypertensive Therapy

The nonpharmacologic approach to antihypertensive therapy concentrates on the use of lifestyle changes associated with a lower blood pressure and reduced cardiovascular disease risk. All hypertensive patients can benefit from this approach even if antihypertensive medications are used. Family participation should be encouraged.

The evaluation for nonpharmacologic therapy is begun by reviewing information about the patient's current lifestyle and cardiovascular disease risk factors. A dietary record provides a useful semiquantitative method for evaluating salt, fat, and caloric intake. This record is analyzed using a computerized program that constructs an individualized treatment program emphasizing the following points.

Weight Control

Proper control of weight can cure hypertension, eliminate an independent risk factor for adult heart disease, and reduce medication needs for those requiring pharmacologic treatment.[71,72] Achieving and maintaining an ideal body weight is an important part of nonpharmacologic antihypertensive therapy.

Dietary Sodium Restriction

Restriction of dietary sodium intake is a popular but, as discussed above, controversial method of blood pressure therapy. Recently, 13 studies involving 584 people were analyzed for the effect of salt restriction on blood pressure.[31] The participants ranged in age from 16 to 60 years. A small but significant decline in blood pressure was achieved in only 3 of the 13 trials, and only older, more severely hypertensive patients appeared to benefit. Yet it is clear that most people ingest excessive amounts of sodium, that salt-sensitive forms of hypertension exist, and that dietary sodium restriction can reduce blood pressure or antihypertensive medication requirements in certain individuals.[18,71]

In its recent report on nonpharmacologic approaches to blood pressure control, the Joint National Committee on the Detection, Evaluation and Treatment of High Blood Pressure stated that "a prudent restriction of dietary sodium to less than 2 g/day (5 g salt/day) is recommended as a treatment for hypertension.[12] Although long-term studies are sorely lacking, it has been demonstrated that sodium restriction is manageable and safe. Evidence indicates that an adult's average daily intake is about 10 g, more than twice the amount recommended for blood pressure control. Traditional methods for calculating dietary sources of sodium have estimated that as much as 50 percent of sodium intake derives from discretionary sources.[73] These estimates form the basis for the popular recommendation that table and cooking salt be eliminated. More recent and more accurate information using lithium labeling techniques revealed that only 15 percent of sodium intake derives from discretionary use, and that 80 percent of salt intake comes from processed foods.[73] Periodic analyses of dietary records, consultation with a dietician, and the use of newly developed urine dipsticks to estimate sodium intake are useful motivational tools.[74]

Aerobic Exercise, Supplementation of Dietary Potassium, Calcium, Magnesium, and Fiber, and Stress Reduction

These are among other nonpharmacologic methods for blood pressure control. Additional information about these forms of treatment can be found in the 1987 Task Force Report and in the Joint National Committee Report on nonpharmacologic approaches to blood pressure control.[18,71]

Pharmacologic Antihypertensive Therapy

The major issues in managing hypertension with medication include defining which groups of individuals require drugs, and selecting the appropriate antihypertensive medications for patients within them. The 1987 Task Force report states that "the issue of risk versus benefit must be carefully considered before antihypertensive drug therapy is initiated. A definite need must be established before therapy with any of these agents is introduced during the first or second decade of life with the possibility of 50 or 60 years (or more) of continuous hypertensive therapy."[18]

In children, current evidence indicates that pharmacologic treatment is beneficial in severe hypertension, in mild to moderate hypertension unresponsive to nonpharmacologic treatment and associated with end-organ damage, and in secondary hypertension caused by irreversible renal disorders or inoperable tumors. There is no convincing evidence to support the use of drugs in the management of any other child with hypertension. Until clinical research definitively establishes that childhood hypertension as currently defined is unhealthy, and that the benefits of drug therapy of childhood hypertension outweigh its risks, the decision to institute medication is arbitrary. It is probably reasonable to consider the use of drugs only in older children with documented chronic hypertension or with other significant cardiovascular disease risk factors. The decision not to institute drug therapy should not be perceived by the patient or physician as an indication of casual indifference. The importance of nonpharmacologic treatment and close follow-up must be emphasized.

An outline of the traditional "stepped care" approach to drug treatment and a list of usual dosages for antihypertensive medications commonly used in children are presented in the 1987 Task Force report.[18] Table 16-5 summarizes our recommendations for oral antihypertensive medications. Traditional approaches to the pharmacologic treatment of hypertension typically involve initial therapy with diuretics or β-adrenergic blocking agents, and the subsequent combination of these agents in unresponsive patients. It is now apparent that the chronic use of diuretic or β-adrenergic blocking agents can produce a variety of undesirable physiologic, metabolic, and psychological side effects. Initial treatment with α-adrenergic blocking agents, angiotensin-converting enzyme inhibitors, or calcium channel blocking agents is now recommended and can avoid some of these problems.[12] Recent studies have shown that some antihypertensive agents may decrease hypertension-associated left ventricular hypertrophy while others do not.[75] The clinical significance of these findings is unclear but certainly important: left ventricular hypertrophy is not only a sign of hypertensive end-organ damage but also an independent risk factor for premature cardiovascular death.

The final issue in the pharmacologic management of hypertension is designing an appropriate follow-up method. Periodic monitoring for side effects and medication-induced abnormalities in potassium, uric acid, or lipid metabolism is necessary. In addition, many antihypertensive drugs have adverse effects on emotional well-being and athletic, sexual, and cognitive performance.[76]

The 1987 Task Force and 1988 Joint National Committee Report note that a frequently neglected phase of management is step-down therapy or drug therapy withdrawal. "Once an extended course of effective blood pressure control has been accomplished, a gradual reduction in, or withdrawal of, medication may be attempted."[18] These recommendations are based on relatively limited studies of hypertensive adults.[77] More recent and extensive longitudinal data demonstrate that nearly all patients will experience a relapse and require medication again.[77,78] Close observation is needed not only during the period of drug withdrawal but also throughout life, given that permanent remission of high blood pressure appears to be a rare event. Stamler and colleagues have recently reported the results of a four-year trial assessing whether adults with mild to moderate hypertension could discontinue drug therapy through nutritional means (weight loss, and sodium and alcohol restriction).[79] After four years, 39 percent of the patients in the nutritionally treated group remained normotensive without drugs, while only 5 percent of those in whom drug therapy was stopped without nutritional treatment were normotensive.

SPECIAL CONSIDERATIONS

Obesity

Several studies have demonstrated that adults, adolescents, and children with unexplained high blood pressure are often overweight, and that obesity is a risk factor for future hypertension.[18,72] Weight reduction is the preferred treatment for many obese hypertensive patients. The pathophysiology of obesity-associated hypertension has not been clearly defined, but the antihypertensive effect of weight loss appears to be independent of natriuresis or sodium intake. Current research indicates that insulin resistance and hyperinsulinemia are associated with enhanced renal sodium reabsorption and increased sympathetic nervous system activity, although the cause and effect process in this phenomenon remains to be established.[80] Either insulin-induced sympathetic nervous system stim-

Table 16-5. Oral Antihypertensive Medications

	Pediatric Dose	Adult Dose	Frequency	Comments
Diuretics				
Hydrochlorothiazide (Hydro-Diuril, etc.)	0.5–2 mg/kg	12.5–100 mg	qd	Thiazides can cause hypokalemia, hypomagnesemia, hyponatremia, hyperuricemia, and hyperlipidemia, and can interfere with glycemic control
Chlorothiazide (Diuril, etc)	5–10 mg/kg	0.25–1.0 g	qd	More natriuretic than thiazides
Metolazone (Zaroxolyn, Diulo)	0.2–0.4 mg/kg/day	2.5–5.0 mg	qd or bid	Similar to thiazides
Indapamide (Lozol)	Not established	2.5–5.0 mg	qd	
Furosemide (Lasix)	0.5–2 mg/kg	20–80 mg	bid or qd	Potent diuretic useful for hypertension associated with edema or renal failure; in addition to fluid and electrolyte depletion, it can cause hypercalciuria, nephrocalcinosis, and bone demineralization
Bumetanide (Bumex)	Not established	0.5–10 mg	bid or qd	
Central sympatholytics				
Alpha methyldopa (Aldomet)	5–20 mg/kg	0.25–1.0 g	bid	These agents have minimal metabolic side effects; sedation, dry mouth, and other alterations in mental function are common; causes positive Coombs' test, hemolysis, and hepatic injury. Rebound hypertension can occur with abrupt discontinuation of chronic therapy
Clonidine (Catapres)	0.05–0.4 mg	0.1–0.6 mg	bid or tid	As above
Guanabenz (Wytensin)	Not established	4–16 mg	bid	Same as clonidine
β-adrenergic antagonists				
Nonselective agents				
Propranolol (Inderal)	0.5–3.0 mg/kg	0.5–3 mg/kg	bid or tid	Has had widespread use as an initial agent; avoid if there is heart failure or bronchospasm; may complicate diabetic management; impair mental and physical performance, and adversely affect blood lipids
Nadolol (Corgard)	Not established	40–160 mg	qd	Same as propranolol
Timolol (Blocadren)	Not established	5–20 mg	bid	Same as propranolol
Pindolol (Visken)	Not established	5–20 mg	bid	Partial agonist beta-blocker with less bronchospasm, peripheral vasoconstrictor, or cholesterol effect
Selective agents				
Atenolol (Tenormin)	Not established	50–100 mg	qd or bid	Has theoretical(?) clinical advantage of less β-receptor blockage and side effects

Drug	Pediatric dose	Adult dose	Frequency	Notes
Metoprolol (Lopressor)	Not established	100–200 mg	bid or qd	Same as atenolol
Acebutolol (Sectral)	Not established	200–800 mg	qd	Similar to pindolol with longer half-life
α-1-adrenergic blockers				
Prazosin (Minipress)	1–5 mg	1–5 mg	bid or tid	Is acceptable initial agent; watch for syncope when starting or increasing dose
Terazosin (Hytrin)	Not established	1–20 mg	bid or qd	Similar to prazosin with longer half-life
Complex adrenergic antagonists				
Labetalol (Normodyne, Trandate)	Not established	100–400 mg	bid	Is a unique agent with both α- and β-adrenergic blocking actions; less effect on blood lipids
Direct vasodilators				
Hydralazine (Apresoline)	0.5–2 mg/kg	10–50 mg	tid or qid	Usually requires concomitant diuretic, beta-blocker, or both; avoid in coronary artery disease; causes lupus-like syndrome
Nifedipine (Procardia, Adalat)	0.25–0.5 mg/kg	10–30 mg	tid or qid	Duration of action is brief; headaches, flushing, and dizziness may limit compliance
Diltiazem (sustained release) (Cardizem SR)	Not established	60–120 mg	bid	May increase propranolol levels
Verapamil (sustained-release) (Calan SR, Isoptin SR)	Not established	120–240 mg	bid or qd	Is acceptable initial agent; pediatric experience is limited
Minoxidil (Loniten)	0.1–0.5 mg/kg	2.5–20 mg	bid or qd	Advice from specialist recommended
Angiotensin-converting enzyme inhibitors				
Captopril (Capoten)	0.05–0.5 mg/kg (in infants); 0.5–2 mg/kg (in children)	12.5–50 mg	bid to qid	Acceptable initial agent particularly useful in high renin hypertension, watch for first dose hypotension and angioedema; can cause decreased GFR (reversible) in patients with renal artery stenosis, scleroderma or other vasculopathies. In renal failure may cause hyperkalemia
Enalapril (Vasotec)	Not established	2.5–20 mg	bid or qd	Similar to captopril except longer half-life due to requirement for hydrolysis to active form (enalaprat)
Lisinopril (Prinivil, Zestril)	Not established	2.5–20 mg	bid or qd	Similar to enalapril but does not require hydrolytic activation

bid = twice daily; tid = three times daily; qid = four times daily; qd = once a day.
DO NOT EXCEED MAXIMUM ADULT DOSE.
(From Feld LG, et al.[19] with permission.)

ulation is responsible for obesity-associated high blood pressure, or increased sympathetic nervous hyperactivity in obesity causes hypertension and hyperinsulinemia. Starvation or weight loss is known to decrease sympathetic nervous system activity and blood pressure in parallel.[80a]

The diagnosis of obesity-associated hypertension is beset by at least two major problems. First, obesity must be defined.[81] No specific rules for this exist in adults, but a reasonable cutoff point is a body weight in excess of 20 percent of that recommended in standard insurance industry profiles. In children, comparison to an "ideal" or average weight for children of the same sex, height, and age is a reasonable alternative. A weight/height measurement above the 95th percentile or a weight greater than 120 percent of normal is consistent with the diagnosis of obesity if inspection of the patient confirms that the excessive body weight is the result of fat and not lean body mass. The 1987 Task Force Report suggests that obesity-associated hypertension be considered in all children who appear obese and have blood pressures and weights above the 90th percentile for age and sex.[18] This concept can be better quantitated using the method of Lauer and associates, which accounts for the effects of age, sex, height, and weight on blood pressure.[22]

Second, the diagnosis of obesity-associated hypertension must be confirmed. This is best accomplished by examining the affected individual clinically and documenting a reduction of blood pressure with weight loss. Unfortunately, treatment of obesity is often unsuccessful.[81] The diagnosis of obesity-associated hypertension then becomes a matter of clinical judgment. Other causes of secondary hypertension associated with obesity should be excluded, including sleep apnea/chronic upper airway obstruction, Cushing's syndrome, Laurence-Moon-Biedl syndrome, and Turner's syndrome.[60,82,83] As the 1987 Task Force notes, "obese children are unlikely to have a cause for their high blood pressure other than their excessive ponderosity."[18] Nevertheless, obese hypertensive children with severe high blood pressure or with any degree of hypertension refractory to weight reduction should receive the same evaluation and management as their non-obese counterparts. These individuals and their families should also be aware that the persistence of these two disorders in adulthood dramatically increases the risk of heart disease.[72]

Neonatal Hypertension

With the increasing use of neonatal intensive care and growing interest in the natural history of high blood pressure, neonatal hypertension has become an important concern for pediatricians. Hypertension is uncommon in normal newborns, and blood pressure measurements obtained in infancy correlate poorly with measurements obtained later in life.[45,84] This information indicates that routine blood pressure measurement is unnecessary in newborns. Certain factors increase the risk of neonatal hypertension and identify groups of infants which require blood pressure screening. These factors include umbilical artery catheterization, prematurity requiring intensive care, and bronchopulmonary dysplasia.[18,85] The causes of neonatal hypertension have also been fairly well defined (Table 16-6). Renal and vascular diseases predominate, although essential hypertension can be present. Evaluation should include renal imaging using sonography and/or radionuclide studies.

Several issues remain unresolved. The most important of these is the definition of normal and abnormal blood pressure in newborn infants. The 1987 Task Force has established reasonable guidelines for the diagnosis of hypertension in term newborns. Their data and additional information on blood pressure at birth were used to con-

Table 16-6. Causes of Neonatal Hypertension

Vascular[45,86–89]
  Renal artery thrombosis or stenosis
  Coarctation of the aorta
  Renal vein thrombosis

Renal[45,90,91]
  Renal failure from any cause
  Cystic renal diseases
  Obstructive uropathy
  Renal hypoplasia/dysplasia
  Renal tumors

Medications[45,89,92,93]
  Corticosteroids
  Ocular phenylephrine
  Doxapram
  Narcotic-addicted mother

Other[45,89,96]
  Fluid overload
  Increased intracranial pressure or cerebrovascular accident
  Neural crest tumors
  Cushing's disease
  Congenital adrenal hyperplasia
  Hyperaldosteronism
  Thyrotoxicosis
  Genitourinary tract surgery or omphalocele repair
  Hypercalcemia
  Pneumothorax
  Primary hypertension

(From Feld LG, et al,[19] with permission.)

struct Table 16-7.[18,94,95] Because blood pressure is lower in sleeping than awake infants, 7 mmHg should be added to the systolic blood pressure and 5 mmHg to the diastolic blood pressure in measurements obtained on sleeping infants.[18] Clinicians should also be aware that the systolic blood pressure of an awake and sucking newborn averages 6 mmHg higher than that of an awake but quiet infant.[96] Crying can also increase blood pressure values by as much as 25 mmHg.[96] We use a 30 percent increase above age-related upper limits of normal to define severe hypertension requiring immediate attention.

The appropriate management of hypertensive newborns also remains unsettled. Heart failure, encephalopathy, cerebrovascular accidents, and retinopathy have all been described as a consequence of uncontrolled neonatal hypertension.[89,97] Some seriously ill premature infants manifest considerable fluctuations in blood pressure, including occasional hypertensive peaks associated with active and passive movement.[98] This lability in blood pressure can impair cerebral oxygenation and result in intraventricular hemorrhage.

All newborns with severe or symptomatic hypertension require treatment. Diuretics usually control mild high blood pressure. Hydralazine, α-methyldopa, and/or propranolol can be added in more severe cases or if diuretics are not effective.[89] Diazoxide and nitroprusside have been successfully and safely used to treat hypertensive crises in newborns.[89,99] Angiotensin converting enzyme inhibitors can reduce blood pressure in newborns with renovascular hypertension refractory to conventional therapy, but their use risks renal functional deterioration.[89] Sublingual nifedipine is also an effective antihypertensive agent in infants.[100] Chronic diuretic administration can produce electrolyte imbalance, and furosemide may cause nephrocalcinosis and bone demineralization. β-adrenergic blocking agents can exacerbate heart failure and reactive airway disease.

A final unresolved issue in neonatal hypertension is its prognosis. Infants with high blood pressure associated with bronchopulmonary dysplasia or prematurity seem to do quite well.[85,101] Their hypertension is readily controlled and is transient, allowing discontinuation of medications within the first year of life. In general, the outcome for newborns with hypertension secondary to renal artery thrombosis from umbilical artery catheters also appears favorable, if they survive. In a recent study of 12 infants after a mean follow-up period of six years, Adelman found that that their hypertension resolved and that medications could be stopped; however, persistent abnormalities in renal size and function were common, indicating that continued observation is necessary.[102]

Table 16-7. Definition of Hypertension

Age Group	95th Percentile Value (Blood Pressure in mmHg)			
	Birth Wt < 1 kg		Others	
Preterm Infants				
Birth	Systolic	60	Systolic	80
	Diastolic	40	Diastolic	50
	Mean	40–48	Mean	60
7 days	Systolic	?	Systolic	?
	Diastolic	?	Diastolic	?
	Mean	57	Mean	65–70
1 month	Systolic	?	Systolic	?
	Diastolic	?	Diastolic	?
	Mean	63	Mean	71–76
Term Infants				
Birth			Systolic	90
			Diastolic	60
			Mean	70
7 days			Systolic	92
			Diastolic	69
			Mean	77
8 days–1 month			Systolic	106
			Diastolic	74
			Mean	85

(Modified from Feld LG, et al.,[19] with permission.)

Alcohol

Alcohol consumption is strongly associated with high blood pressure in adults.[103] It is recommended that hypertensive adults should reduce their ethanol intake to two ounces per day or less. Two ounces of ethanol is contained in 4 ounces of 100 proof whiskey, 16 ounces of wine, or 48 ounces of beer. Patients who enjoy drinking can still take heart in the knowledge that the consumption of one to two ounces of ethanol per day may be associated with a slightly lower mortality and morbidity from coronary artery disease. A study of school children who drank regularly (about 50 percent of the surveyed population) did not show any association between alcohol consumption and blood pressure.[104] However, the average ethanol consumption in these children was about two ounces per week.

The Hypertensive Athlete

Consistent aerobic exercise usually lowers blood pressure, and even in modest amounts reduces the risk of coronary heart disease and premature death.[18,105] Unfortunately, specific recommendations about athletic activities and hypertensive children are unavailable because no carefully controlled long-term studies have been done on the effect of exercise on blood pressure.[71]

Blood pressure responds differently to isometric and dynamic physical activity.[71] During vigorous aerobic or dynamic exercise (e.g., running, swimming, cycling), the systolic blood pressure rises dramatically while the diastolic blood pressure may rise slightly or even fall. These normal changes reflect an increase in cardiac output and a decrease in peripheral vascular resistance. During static or isometric exercise, both the systolic and diastolic blood pressures rise, reflecting an increase in both cardiac output and peripheral vascular resistance. Levels in excess of 300/160 mmHg have been recorded during heavy weightlifting. The body adapts well to these massive changes in blood pressure which, in different circumstances, would be associated with a hypertensive crisis.

The blood pressure of hypertensive children does not differ from that of normotensive children during exercise.[18] Results of dynamic stress testing cannot be used to identify children destined to have chronic high blood pressure. A recent study has shown that more than 50 percent of adolescents with resting blood pressures greater than the 95th percentile for their age and systolic blood pressures greater than 220 mmHg during bicycle ergometry did not have hypertension 24 months later.[106] The marked increase in diastolic blood pressure during static exercise underlies the recommendation that adults and children with hypertension avoid isometric exercise and participate in dynamic sports activities.[18,71] Fixler and colleagues compared the blood pressure responses to isometric (handgrip) exercise in 107 hypertensive and 74 control children, and found no significant differences in these responses in the two groups.[107] We believe that exercise programs for hypertensive children should center on dynamic activities, although there is no clear evidence that blood pressure changes occurring during static exercise are any more dangerous to hypertensive than to normotensive patients. Weightlifters should also include dynamic exercise in their routines. It has been shown that weight training in hypertensive adolescents maintains blood pressure reductions achieved by running, and may even further reduce their blood pressure.[108]

Before recommending exercise or permitting vigorous athletic competition, hypertensive patients should be thoroughly evaluated. This includes an assessment for cardiovascular abnormalities associated with sports-related sudden death, such as hypertrophic cardiomyopathy, congenital or acquired causes of coronary artery disease, aortic stenosis, mitral valve prolapse, carditis, arrhythmias, and Marfan's syndrome.[109,110] Questioning about exercise-associated syncope, lightheadedness, or chest pain and a family history of sudden syncope or death, hypertrophic cardiomyopathy, or premature atherosclerotic heart disease may provide the only clue that a potentially lethal disorder exists. If electrocardiograms or echocardiograms are obtained, their interpretation must take into account the normal physiologic changes in cardiac structure and function that occur in well-conditioned athletes.[111] Failure to recognize these changes may lead to unnecessary evaluation or unwarranted proscription of athletic activities.

The role of exercise stress-testing in the evaluation of hypertensive patients for sports participation is unclear. Although the 1987 Task Force downplays the value of stress-testing in hypertensive patients, several experts suggest its use prior to permitting athletic activities.[18,112,113] We recommend stress-testing in all patients with sustained mild to moderate hypertension before allowing their participation in strenuous sports, and in all patients being treated for hypertension before endorsing any type of exercise program for them. These patients should probably be re-evaluated periodically in order to exclude evolving cardiac dysfunction. In the patient who develops serious arrhythmias, ischemia, or hypotension during exercise testing, strenuous sports should be avoided. Although the full significance of excessive blood pressure elevations during testing is unknown, systolic levels in excess of 230 to 250 mmHg have been associated with myocardial ischemia.[112] These recommendations are controversial and may not be widely accepted. Nevertheless, exercise stress-testing can be valuable for counseling and reassuring hypertensive patients and their families that participation in strenuous physical activity and competitive athletics is safe.

A final consideration in the management of the hypertensive athlete is the selection of appropriate medications for those who require pharmacologic treatment. Some patients may experience problems with various antihypertensive drugs; hypokalemia from diuretics may alter muscle function and beta-adrenergic blocking agents may reduce dynamic exercise tolerance.[71] Physicians who care for children requiring such medication are urged to watch for medication-induced deterioration in their physical performance. It is possible to control high blood pressure and preserve exercise tolerance through careful medication selection and patient follow-up. Angiotensin converting enzyme inhibitors, calcium channel blocking agents, and alpha-adrenergic blocking agents appear to be the most effective drugs for lowering blood pressure without impairing hemodynamic responses to vigorous exercise.[114-117]

Race

Current data indicate that significant differences exist between blacks and whites with respect to the hemodynamics and neurohumoral makeup of individuals with hypertension.[118] Blacks tend to have higher systemic vascular resistance, lower blood volumes, and lower plasma renin activity than age-matched whites. White subjects tend to have higher plasma renin activity and to demonstrate preferential responses to angiotensin converting enzyme inhibitor therapy.[119] Black subjects, on the other hand, have been said by some investigators to respond better to diuretic therapy and therapy with calcium channel blocking agents.

It has been widely assumed that the consequences of hypertension are more severe in the black population than the white population. In addition, average blood pressures of black subjects tend to be higher than those of comparably age-, sex-, and weight-matched whites. New investigation suggests there may be basic differences in membrane pump activity between black and white subjects,[120] but these data are preliminary and will require corroboration.

Sleep Disturbances

A growing body of information now links the sleep apnea syndrome to hypertension.[121] In this condition, it is postulated that hypoxia stimulates abnormal sympathoadrenal discharge, resulting in hypertension. This form of hypertension is not recognized by many physicians, and its true incidence has not yet been determined. Treatment for this form of hypertension may require primary attention to the reason for sleep-apnea.

Geriatric Considerations

Patients in the older age group are the ones who experience the greatest prevalence of morbidity and mortality attributable to hypertension. It would therefore seem logical to assume that these patients would benefit from intensive therapy. However, it is extremely difficult to calculate risk/benefit ratios for older individuals. In addition, different therapeutic endpoints may be required.

It should be remembered that the aging process contributes to arteriosclerosis, large-vessel stiffness, and a tendency toward systolic hypertension as a manifestation of increased systemic vascular resistance. Elderly individuals also commonly have a reduced blood volume along with increased vasoconstriction, as already discussed in the section on age-related hemodynamic changes. Thus, it might be expected that older patients would respond to vasodilator drugs. This observation has been confirmed in clinical studies, but it must be remembered that pure arterial dilator drugs such as hydralazine may also increase the chance of myocardial ischemia.

The phenomenon of isolated systolic hypertension in the elderly has been addressed in a large, ongoing, multicenter trial. Of interest is the fact that the pilot study for this

Systolic Hypertension in the Elderly Project (SHEP) was difficult to complete because so many of the patients whose systolic blood pressures exceeded 160 mmHg on entry (with diastolic pressures below 90 mmHg) had pressures that fell to within the normal range after extended observation. Of the subjects who qualified for further therapy, approximately 85 percent responded to low-dose thiazide therapy (25 mg hydrochlorothiazide daily).[122] The large trial will not be concluded for several years.

The benefits of treatment in the geriatric population are currently unclear. The only study demonstrating a clear-cut benefit of antihypertensive drug therapy on morbidity and mortality in elderly patients is the European Working Party Hypertension In The Elderly (EWPHE) Study. The patient group in this study had significant elevations of diastolic as well as systolic blood pressure.[122a] Also controversial is the treatment of hypertension in the very old patient. It may be that no benefit of therapy is demonstrable in patients over the age of 80 years.[123] It is our opinion, however, that it is unwise to adopt an age cutoff for the treatment of hypertension. Given the difference between "biologic" and "chronologic" age across the population, it would seem prudent to treat healthy elderly individuals with drugs that do not cause untoward side effects.

Pregnancy

Knowledge of the pathophysiology of hypertension in human pregnancy has been somewhat difficult to accumulate. As a result, unclear classification systems have arisen. At present, there is no uniform classification of blood pressure disorders in pregnancy. It would seem, however, that at least three forms of the disorder exist. Chronic hypertension can be defined as that which antedates the pregnancy. Pregnancy-associated hypertension can develop in any of the three trimesters. Toxemia-eclampsia is that form of malignant hypertension that develops later in pregnancy with potentially dire consequences to both mother and fetus. It seems likely that these different forms of hypertension may have different pathogenic features. An understanding of the possibilities requires a brief review of the physiologic changes that accompany normal pregnancy.[124]

Under usual circumstances, pregnancy is associated with marked peripheral vasodilation that is accompanied by dramatic increases in blood volume and cardiac output (often approximately 50 percent). In the pregnant patient with hypertension, as compared to the nonhypertensive pregnant control, it is a general rule that increased vasoconstriction is accompanied by reduced blood volume. As a result, it is usually recommended that diuretic therapy be withheld except in cases of heart failure or severe edema. In general, it has been feared that excessive diuretic therapy will compromise the placental circulation.

The most extreme group of pregnant subjects are those who present with symptoms of pre-eclampsia or toxemia. These individuals may be different in that they exhibit exaggerated sensitivity to circulating angiotensin II. In normal pregnancies, there is reduced sensitivity to circulating angiotensin II, so that the relative hyperreninemia of pregnancy is of little consequence. In toxemia, the mechanism of abnormal angiotensin II sensitivity is unknown. However, it has been postulated that abnormal prostaglandin synthesis or calcium flux may contribute. An interesting observation by Taufield and co-workers suggests that there is a marked reduction in urinary calcium excretion and increased cellular calcium uptake in toxemic hypertensive patients.[125] The implications of this observation are not completely known, but it is of interest that the time-honored therapy of magnesium sulfate infusion would intuitively be expected to counteract increased cellular calcium uptake.

Chronic therapy can be accomplished in pregnant hypertensive patients by one of several strategies. The more traditional approach employs α-methyldopa and hydralazine therapy. Significant literature also exists to support the use of β-adrenergic blocking drugs in this group of patients. There is a smaller experience with α-adrenergic blocking drugs, which also appear promising. The role of calcium channel blocking agents or angiotensin converting enzyme inhibitors remains to be determined.

Diabetes

It is well known that diabetes mellitus is associated with an increased prevalence of hypertension and renal failure. Diabetic subjects exhibit abnormal sympathetic nervous control[126] and probably have abnormal fluid volume regulation. Many diabetic subjects with severe hypertension actually have low peripheral venous plasma renin activity. Given this, it might be expected that therapy with angiotensin converting enzyme inhibitors would be ineffective in diabetic patients. However, new information about the possible roles of intrarenal angiotensin II and glomerular capillary hypertension in the pathogenesis of renal failure may be the basis for reconsidering the use of angiotensin converting enzyme inhibitors in this population.

It is generally recognized that angiotensin II contributes to an increase in intraglomerular pressure. Brenner and co-workers have suggested that this relative glomerular capillary hypertension is a major driving force for the focal glomerulosclerosis that occurs in diabetes,[127] which in turn reduces the glomerular surface area and single-nephron glomerular filtration rate. With a reduction in nephron mass, a vicious cycle is created in which further increases in pressure and flow rates in remaining glomeruli accelerate the ongoing renal damage. Important work by Mogensen and other Scandinavian investigators indicates that urinary microalbumin excretion rates may be early markers of diabetic nephropathy.[128] Parving and co-workers have demonstrated that adequate control of blood pressure helps reduce the rate of decline of renal function in diabetic patients.[129] Aurell and co-workers have further suggested that angiotensin converting enzyme inhibition may produce additional specific protective effects against further nephron loss.[130] Other studies are ongoing to determine whether urinary microalbumin can be used as a marker of renal damage, and whether the rate of progression of renal disease in diabetic patients can be reduced by specific forms of pharmacotherapy. These questions are currently controversial.

Renal Failure

Hypertension associated with renal failure is generally considered to reflect reduced salt and water excretion and increased blood volume. However, other evidence indicates that abnormal vasoconstriction also exists in this population. Izzo and co-workers have demonstrated increased sympathetic nervous activity in patients with renal failure regardless of its etiology.[131,132] Renal failure patients also experience good therapeutic responses to central sympatholytic drugs, suggesting a major component of sympathetic hyperactivity in the pathogenesis of their hypertension.[132] The role of the renin–angiotensin system in the hypertension of renal failure is complicated; a few individuals respond well to angiotensin converting enzyme inhibition. Individuals with renal failure usually exhibit marked changes in the pressure-natriuresis phenomenon, requiring a higher arterial pressure to adequately excrete a salt load. In this setting, diuretic therapy may be required as an adjunct to other antihypertensive drug therapy to ensure adequate natriuresis at lower levels of arterial pressure.

Hypertensive Crises

Occasionally, hypertension can pose an immediate risk of devastating organ damage or death. In these circumstances, prompt and effective treatment is required, often before a specific cause for the elevated blood pressure has been determined.

The Report by the Joint National Committee on Detection, Evaluation, and Treatment of High Blood Pressure suggested operational definitions for hypertensive crises.[12] It was proposed that emergencies be defined as situations in which elevated blood pressure must be lowered within one hour to stop life-threatening organ damage, while urgencies were situations in which elevated blood pressure should be reduced within 24 hours to eliminate potential patient risk. These definitions have considerable clinical value not only because they provide solid management guidelines, but also because they de-emphasize the role of a specific level of blood pressure in creating these emergent situations.

Both clinical and experimental evidence indicates that the rate of change of blood pressure can be just as important as its absolute level in the pathogenesis of hypertensive emergencies.[45,133] Examples of this concept range from the association between transient hypertensive episodes and intraventricular hemorrhage in preterm infants to the development of eclampsia in pregnant women with relatively mild blood pressure elevations. Gruskin and associates have illustrated this point quite well by describing a six-year-old child with poststreptococcal glomerulonephritis, cortical blindness, and generalized seizures whose admission blood pressure was 110/80 mmHg.[134] Full recovery occurred with treatment, and the patient's blood pressure at discharge, without antihypertensive medication, was 75/50 mmHg. Although this child's admission blood pressure would not have been classified as severe in absolute terms, the marked increase from premorbid levels was presumably sufficient to produce a hypertensive emergency. These authors emphasize that the evaluation of hypertensive crises should include consideration of absolute and relative hypertension. In this regard, knowledge of previous blood pressure measurements obtained during routine office visits can be extremely useful.

On the other hand, some persons can appear perfectly healthy despite a longstanding, severely elevated blood pressure. Although these patients are at high risk for cardiovascular complications in the future, they are probably not in any immediate danger, and their hypertension should not be considered an emergency. Thus, as Ferguson and Vlasses point out, "the level of blood pressure itself may be a poor determinant of the seriousness of the clinical situation and the need for hospitalization or parenteral antihypertensive drugs."[133] Unfortunately, an isolated blood pressure measurement is often all that is available in potentially emergent situations, and an immediate judgment about its significance must be made. For this purpose, guidelines correlating the severity of hypertension with absolute blood pressure level are needed. The 1987 Task Force on Blood Pressure Control in Children has recommended defining severe hypertension as consisting of blood pressure levels exceeding the 99th percentile for age.[18] These levels often exceed the upper limits of normal blood pressure established by the 1977 Task Force by only a few millimeters of mercury. Because the clinical significance of the 1987 Task Force definition of severe hypertension is unclear, we prefer the approach of Gruskin and colleagues in evaluating children for potential hypertensive crises.[134] Their approach is based on evidence in adults that risk related to hypertension increases continuously as blood pressure rises, and that it is the percent increase in blood pressure above normal that constitutes the major risk for hypertensive complications. Until further guidelines become available, a reasonable definition of severe hypertension in children would include blood pressure levels that exceed age-related normal limits (or previous blood pressure measurements) by 30 percent. These recommendations are arbitrary, and their clinical significance, particularly regarding systolic blood pressure levels, is unknown.

In adults, severe hypertension is defined by a diastolic blood pressure greater than 115 mmHg or a systolic blood pressure exceeding 200 mmHg; these values represent at least a 29 percent and 26 percent increase from normal diastolic and systolic levels, respectively.[12] Adults with diastolic blood pressures of 130 mmHg or more may require more urgent treatment.[12] However, hospitalization generally should be reserved for those individuals who demonstrate evidence of acute target organ damage (encephalopathy, renal parenchymal damage, myocardial compromise, etc.).

Hypertensive emergencies are listed in Table 16-8. Each of these situations is life threatening and requires immediate management. The term "hypertensive encephalopathy" was introduced in 1928 to describe the association between marked hypertension and the development of headaches, seizures, and confusion in an adolescent with acute nephritis.[135] It is a clinical syndrome occurring in all age groups, and is defined by the presence of an acute, generalized cerebral dysfunction (severe headache, irritability, diminished alertness, impaired intellectual function, blindness, generalized seizures, or coma) that cannot be explained by other diseases and for which the exclusion of the causes of encephalopathy such as cerebrovascular accident, uremia, infection, and poisoning, as well as improvement in clinical condition following antihypertensive therapy, are crucial parts of the diagnosis.[136] Its etiology seems to relate to exceeding the upper limit of cerebral blood pressure autoregulation, with subsequent cerebral hyperperfusion, damage to arterioles and capillaries, and cerebral edema and ischemia.[137] In the neonatal age group, this syndrome may occur at relatively low blood pressures, as previously described, and is more closely related to the speed of pressure increase than to absolute blood pressure levels.[138]

A closely related form of accelerated hypertension is "malignant hypertension," which is also a medical emergency. This condition is defined by marked hypertension and papilledema, retinal hemorrhages, and soft exudates. It is usually accompanied by evidence of other organ system damage including central nervous system dysfunction, cardiac decompensation, renal failure, and microangiopathic hemolytic anemia. Malignant hypertension occurs in less than

Table 16-8. Hypertensive Emergencies

Condition	Management (Blood Pressure Must Be Reduced Within One Hour)
Hypertensive encephalopathy	Admit to hospital and obtain consultation
Acute heart failure with pulmonary edema	Monitor vital signs and clinical condition frequently
Acute myocardial infarction or unstable angina pectoris	Administer appropriate antihypertensive medications (see Table 16-9); improves when blood pressure is lowered
Cerebrovascular accident or head trauma	Attempt to determine cause of hypertension and extent of organ damage
Dissecting aortic aneurysm	If central nervous system dysfunction, consider structural, metabolic, or infectious process
Eclampsia	

(Modified from Feld LG, et al.,[19] with permission.)

1 percent of patients during the course of either essential or secondary hypertension. It is rarely the first manifestation of hypertensive disease and is unusual in children, the average age of diagnosis being 40 years. Other examples of hypertensive emergencies include severe hypertension or a rapidly rising blood pressure associated with acute heart failure and pulmonary edema, progressive renal insufficiency, cerebral vascular accident, or other conditions described in Table 16-8.

A management plan for hypertensive emergencies is detailed in Table 16-8. These situations are life threatening, uncommon, and often complex. Their management should therefore be closely supervised in the hospital, with the help of experienced personnel. Although their treatment must be expeditious, evaluation of the patient cannot be neglected. This should include an attempt to determine the cause of the hypertension and the extent of organ system damage, as has been noted in other sections. A brief medical history should emphasize underlying diseases, unusual symptoms or events in the immediate past, and use of medications or other drugs. Physical examination should also be brief but comprehensive. It must include an assessment of neurologic function and the ocular fundi. Evidence of heart failure and pulmonary or peripheral edema should be sought. The abdomen should be auscultated for bruits and palpated for enlarged kidneys. The blood pressure in a lower extremity should be measured. Laboratory investigation should include a complete blood count, routine blood chemistries, and urinalysis. In some cases a chest x-ray and cranial computed tomography or magnetic resonance imaging can be useful, but these and other tests must not delay appropriate treatment.

Several antihypertensive medications are available for the treatment of hypertensive emergencies (Table 16-9).[133,134] There is no ideal agent. Intravenous medications are usually required. Oral agents can be quickly substituted or added in most situations. Furosemide is only needed in cases of heart failure or pulmonary edema. In all other situations, appropriate vasodilator therapy is the first choice. It is important to understand that patients with accelerated hypertension have dramatic reductions in blood volume, often in the range of 30 to 40 percent.[139] In some cases, vigorous diuretic therapy has been found to worsen the hypertensive crisis, presumably by stimulating reflex vasoconstriction. The reason for the "volume contracted" state of patients with accelerated hypertension is unknown, but is likely to be related to pressure diuresis.

The exact level to which the blood pressure should be reduced in hypertensive crises is unclear and controversial.[133,137] A common therapeutic goal within one hour is a blood pressure of 160 to 170/100 to 110 mmHg (mean arterial pressure 120 to 130 mmHg) in adults and older adolescents, and about a 25 percent reduction in blood pressure in younger patients. Hypotension will further compromise organ function and must be avoided; if it occurs, antihypertensive medications must be discontinued immediately and saline infusion instituted if necessary. In addition, some patients (including premature infants, elderly or chronically hypertensive patients, and stroke or brain trauma victims) may have impaired or altered blood flow regulation. Too rapid or excessive reduction of blood pressure can produce cerebral, myocardial, or renal ischemia. All patients should be closely monitored for these potential iatrogenic complications.

In less extreme cases of severe hypertension, treatment can begin either inside or outside the hospital, depending on the circumstances. Rapidly acting oral agents or intravenous hydralazine are the preferred medications. Unlike hypertensive emergencies, in which the risk of rapid blood pressure reduction is probably less than that of continued hypertensive organ damage,

Table 16-9. Medications for Treatment of Hypertensive Emergencies

Drug Name (Brand Name)	Route of Administration	Pediatric Dose	Adult Dose	Comments
Sodium nitroprusside (Nipride)	Continuous IV infusion	0.5–0.8 µg/kg/min titrated based on BP response	Same as pediatric dosage	Effect within seconds, dose-dependent and terminates immediately when discontinued. Use only in ICU setting. Problems include photodegradation and metabolite toxicity. Avoid in pregnancy
Diazoxide (Hyperstat)	Rapid IV bolus	1–2 mg/kg (max 100 mg) every 10 min up to 10 mg/kg or 600 mg	150 mg bolus, repeated at 20–40 min intervals to max of 600 mg	Precise, controlled BP reduction not insured. Duration of action variable. Acute hypotension, hyperglycemia, angina, nausea, fluid retention can occur
Labetalol (Normodyne)	Slow IV push or continuous infusion	0.2 mg/kg (max 20 mg) initially then 0.4 mg/kg (max. 40–60 mg) every 10 min up to 3–4 mg/kg or 300 mg total dose	Bolus dosage: 20–200 mg repeated at 0.5–6 hr intervals. Continuous infusion, 0.5–2 mg/min	Limited pediatric experience. Avoid if heart failure, asthma or bradycardia
Hydralazine (Apresoline)	IM or IV bolus	0.2–0.6 mg/kg (max 20 mg) every 1 hr until effect then every 4–6 hr	Same as pediatric dosage	Onset of effect often too slow for emergency. Causes tachycardia, headache, nausea, fluid retention and can exacerbate myocardial ischemia
α-methyldopa (Aldomet)	Slow IV infusion	5–10 mg/kg over 30–60 min (max 500–1000 mg)	250–500 mg q6h	Effect too slow and unpredictable for emergency. Somnolence major side effect

Drug	Route	Dose	Comments
Nifedipine (Procardia, Adalat)	Oral	0.25–0.5 mg/kg (max 20 mg). Repeat in 30–60 min if needed	10–20 mg po; repeat at 20–30 min, then at q6h intervals	Effective within 30 min but relatively short duration of action. Side effects include tachycardia, flushing, fluid retention
Minoxidil (Loniten)	Oral	0.1–0.2 mg/kg/dose (max 0.5 mg/kg or 40 mg/day)	2.5–5.0 initial dose with repeat at 6 hrs.	Maximum effect in 2–4 hrs with duration of 12–24 hrs. Causes tachycardia and fluid retention. Has undesirable side effects with chronic use
Captopril (Capoten)	Oral	0.1 mg/kg (max 6.25 mg) initially then increase to max of 2 mg/kg or 50 mg/dose	25–50 mg initial dose repeated in 30–60 min, if necessary	Usually effective within 30–60 min. Gradually increase dose every 90 min until response. Closely monitor for side effects especially if renal failure, renal artery stenosis or collagen-vascular disease
Enalapril (Vasotec)	Slow IV infusion	Not established	1.25 mg over 5 min	Response in 15 min. Peak effect may not occur for up to 4 hrs
Clonidine (Catapres)	Oral	0.05–0.1 mg/dose (max 1.2 mg/day)	0.2 mg initially, followed by 0.1 mg at 20–40 min intervals to a max of 0.5 mg	Administer dose every 1–2 hr until desired effect. Onset of action 30–60 min with duration of 8–12 hrs. Problems include sedation, nightmares, and "clonidine withdrawal syndrome"
Phentolamine (Regitine)	IV bolus or continuous infusion	0.1 mg/kg (max 5 mg) initially or 1–7 mg/kg/min titrated based on response	5 mg bolus; titrate infusion rate to BP	Brief duration of action. Consider if pheochromocytoma, clonidine or guanabenz withdrawal

(From Feld LG, et al.,[19] with permission.)

blood pressure reduction in hypertensive urgencies should be gradual, in order to avoid unnecessary side effects.

ACKNOWLEDGEMENTS

We greatly appreciate the excellent secretarial assistance of Ms. Paula Hamburg and Ms. Kimberly Pilarski.

REFERENCES

1. Kannel WB, Gordon T, Schwartz MJ: Systolic vs. diastolic blood pressure and risk of coronary disease. The Framingham study. Am J Cardiol 27:335, 1971
2. Pickering G: Hypertension, definition, natural histories and consequences. Am J Med 52:570, 1972
3. Society of Actuaries. 1979 Build and blood pressure study. Ipasca, Illinois 1980
4. Detection, Evaluation, and Treatment of High Blood Pressure. Report of Joint National Committee. National Heart, Lung and Blood Institute, NIH, Bethesda, Maryland, 1977
5. Hypertension Detection and Follow-up Program Cooperative Group: Five-year findings of the hypertension detection and follow-up program. I. Reduction in mortality of persons with high blood pressure, including mild hypertension. JAMA 242:2562, 1979
6. Multiple Risk Factor Intervention Trial Research Group: Multiple Risk Factor Intervention Trial: Risk Factor Changes and Mortality Results. JAMA 248:1465, 1982
7. Veteran's Administration Cooperative Study Group on Antihypertensive Agents. JAMA 213:1143, 1971
8. Hypertension Detection and Follow-up Program Cooperative Group: A Follow-up Report. JAMA 242:2562, 1979
9. Medical Research Council Working Party: MRC trial of treatment of mild hypertension: principal results. Br Med J 291:97, 1985
10. Black HR: A new approach to hypertension. Diagnosis 10:20, 1988
11. Kaplan NM: Hypertension in the population at large. p 1. In Kaplan NM (ed): Clinical Hypertension. 4th Ed. Williams & Wilkins, Baltimore, 1986
12. The 1988 Report of the Joint National Committee on Detection, Evaluation and Treatment of High Blood Pressure. Arch Intern Med 148:1023, 1988
13. Pickering TG, James GD, Boddie C, et al: How common is white coat hypertension? JAMA 259:225, 1988
14. Harshfield GA, Pickering TG, Kleinert HD, et al: Situational variations of blood pressure in ambulatory hypertensive patients. Psychosom Med 44:237, 1982
15. Devereux RB, Pickering TG, Harshfield GA, et al: Left ventricular hypertrophy in patients with hypertension: importance of blood pressure response to regularly recurring stress. Circulation 68:470, 1983
16. Drayer JI, Weber MA, DeYoung JL: BP as a determinant of cardiac left ventricular muscle mass. Arch Intern Med 143:90, 1983
17. Perloff D, Sokolow M, Cowan R: The prognostic value of ambulatory blood pressures. JAMA 249:2792, 1985
18. Report of the Second Task Force on Blood Pressure Control in Children. Pediatrics 79:1, 1987
19. Feld LG, Springate JE: Hypertension in children. Curr Probl Pediatr 6:317, 1988
20. Daniels SR, Loggie JMH, Burton T, et al: Difficulties with ambulatory blood pressure monitoring in children. J Pediatr 111:397, 1987
21. Shear CL, Burke GL, Freedman DS: Value of childhood blood pressure measurements and family history in predicting future blood pressure status. Pediatrics 77:862, 1986
22. Lauer RM, Burns TL, Clarke WR: Assessing children's blood pressure–considerations of age and body size. Pediatrics 75:1081, 1985
23. Katz SH, Hediger ML, Schall JI, et al: Blood pressure, growth and maturation from childhood through adolescence. Hypertension 2, suppl I, 55, 1980
24. Kahn HS, Bain RP, Pullen-Smith B: The interpretation of children's blood pressure using a physiologic height correction. J Chronic Dis 39:521, 1986

involvement in Laurence-Moon-Biedl syndrome. Acta Paediatr Scand 75:240, 1986
83. Virdis R, Contie M, Ghizzoni L, et al: Blood pressure behaviour and control in Turner syndrome. Clin Exp Hypertens A8:787, 1986
84. Zinner SH, Kass EH: Epidemiology of blood pressure in infants and children. p. 93. In Loggie JMH (ed): NHLBI Workshop on Juvenile Hypertension. Biomedical Information Corporation, New York, 1984
85. Friedman AL, Hustead VA: Hypertension in babies following discharge from a neonatal intensive care unit. Pediatr Nephrol 1:30, 1987
86. Blackburn WR: Vascular pathology in hypertensive children. p. 335. In Loggie JMH (ed): NHLBI Workshop on Juvenile Hypertension. Biomedical Information Corporation, New York, 1984
87. Vailas GN, Brouillette RT, Scott JP, et al: Neonatal aortic thrombosis: recent experience. J Pediatr 109:101, 1986
88. Milner LS, Heitner R, Thomson PD, et al: Hypertension as the major problem of idiopathic arterial calcification of infancy. J Pediatr 105:934, 1984
89. Guignard JP: Hypertension in the neonate. Clin Exp Hypertension A8:723, 1986
90. Cole BR, Conley SB, Stapleton FB: Polycystic kidney disease in the first year of life. J Pediatr 111:693, 1987
91. Chan HSL, Cheng MY, Mancer K, et al: Congenital mesoblastic nephroma. J Pediatr 111:64, 1987
92. Isenberg S, Everett S: Cardiovascular effects of mydriatics in low-birth-weight infants. J Pediatr 101:111, 1984
93. Barrington KJ, Finer NN, Torok-Buth G, et al: Dose-response relationship of doxapram in the therapy for refractory idiopathic apnea of prematurity. Pediatrics 80:22, 1987
94. Versmold HT, Kitterman JA, Phibbs RH, et al: Aortic blood pressure during the first 12 hours of life in infants with birth weight 610 to 4220 grams. Pediatrics 67:607, 1981
95. Tan KL: Blood pressure in full term healthy neonates. Clin Pediatr 26:21, 1987
96. Adelman RD: Neonatal hypertension. In Loggie JMH (ed): NHLBI Workshop on Juvenile hypertension. p. 267. Biomedical Information Corporation, New York, 1984
97. Skalina MEL, Annable WL, Kliegman RM: Hypertensive retinopathy in the newborn infant. J Pediatr 103:781, 1983
98. Brazy JE, Lewis DV: Changes in cerebral blood volume and cytochrome aa3 during hypertensive peaks in preterm infants. J Pediatr 108:983, 1986
99. Benitz WE, Malachowski N, Cohen RS, et al: Use of sodium nitroprusside in neonates. J Pediatr 106:102, 1985
100. Rascher W, Bonzel KE, Ruder H, et al: Blood pressure and hormonal responses to sublingual nifedipine in acute childhood hypertension. Clin Exp Hypertens A8:859, 1986
101. Abman SH, Warady BA, Lum GM: Systemic hypertension in infants with bronchopulmonary dysplasia. J Pediatr 104:928, 1984
102. Adelman RD: Long-term follow-up of neonatal renovascular hypertension. Pediatr Nephrol 1:35, 1987
103. MacMahon SE, Norton RN: Alcohol and hypertension: implications for prevention and treatment. Ann Intern Med 105:124, 1986
104. Trevisan M: Alcohol consumption and blood pressure in school children. Int J Pediatr Nephrol 8:25, 1987
105. Leon AS, Connett J, Jacobs DR, et al: Leisure-time physical activity levels and risk of coronary heart disease and death. JAMA 258:2388, 1987
106. Fixler DE, Laird WP, Dana K: Usefulness of exercise stress testing for prediction of blood pressure trends. Pediatrics 75:1071, 1985
107. Fixler DE, Laird WP, Browne R, et al: Response of hypertensive adolescents to dynamic and isometric exercise stress. Pediatrics 64:579, 1979
108. Hagberg JM, Ehsoni AA, Goldring D, et al: Effect of weight training on blood pressure and hemodynamics in hypertensive adolescents. J Pediatr 104:147, 1984
109. Driscoll DJ: Cardiovascular evaluation of the child and adolescent before participation in sports. Mayo Clin Proc 60:867, 1985
110. Neuspiel DR: Sudden death from myocarditis in young athletes. Mayo Clin Proc 61:226, 1986
111. Huston TP, Puffer JC, Rodney WM: The

athletic heart syndrome. N Engl J Med 313:24, 1985
112. Freed MD: Recreational and sports recommendations for the child with heart disease. Pediatr Clin North Am 31:1307, 1984
113. Portman RJ, Robson AM: Controversies in pediatric hypertension, In Tune BM, Mendoza SA (eds): Pediatric Nephrology. Contemporary Issues in Nephrology. p. 265. Vol 12. Churchill Livingstone, New York, 1984
114. Zusman RM: Alternatives to traditional antihypertensive therapy. Hypertension 8:837, 1986
115. de Bono G, Kaye CM, Roland E: Acebutolol: Ten years experience. Am Heart J 109:1211, 1985
116. Feit A, Holtzman R, Cohen M: Effect of labetalol on exercise tolerance and double product in mild to moderate essential hypertension. Am J Med 78:937, 1985
117. Cody RJ, Kubo SH, Cavit AB, et al: Exercise hemodynamics and oxygen delivery in human hypertension: Response to verapamil. Hypertension 8:3, 1986
118. Frohlich ED, Messerli FH, Dunn FG, et al: Greater renal vascular involvement in the black patient with essential hypertension. A comparison of systemic and renal hemodynamics in black and white patients. Miner Electrolyte Metab 10:173, 1984
119. Vlasses PH, Conner DP, Rotmensch HH, et al: Double-blind comparison of captopril and enalapril in mild to moderate hypertension. J Am Col Cardiol 7:651, 1986
120. Smith JB, Wade MB, Fineberg NS, et al: Influence of race, sex, and blood pressure on erythrocyte sodium transport in humans. Hypertension 12:251, 1988
121. Kales A, Bixler EO, Cadieux RJ: Sleep apnea in a hypertensive population. Lancet 2:1005, 1984
122. Perry HMJr, McDonald RH, Hulley SB, et al: Systolic Hypertension in the Elderly Program, Pilot Study (SHEP-PS): morbidity and mortality experience. J Hypertension, suppl 4:S21, 1986
122a. Amery A, Birkenhager W, Brixko P, et al: Influence of antihypertensive drug treatment or morbidity and mortality in patients over the age of 60 years: European Working Party on High Blood Pressure in the Elderly (EWPHE) results: Subgroup analysis on entry stratification. J Hypertension 4:S642, 1986
123. Tuck ML, Griffiths RF, Johnson LE, et al: UCLA geriatric grand rounds. Hypertension in the elderly (clinical conference). J Am Geriatr Soc 36:630, 1989
124. Maikranz P, Lindheimer MD: Hypertension in pregnancy. Med Clin North Am 71:1031, 1987
125. Taufield PA, Ales KL, Resnick LM, et al: Hypocalciuria in preeclampsia. N Engl J Med 316:715, 1987
126. Cryer PE, Silverberg AB, Santiago JV, et al: Plasma catecholamines in diabetes. The syndromes of hypoadrenergic and hyperadrenergic postural hypotension. Am J Med 64:407, 1978
127. Zatz R, Dunn BR, Meyer TW, et al: Prevention of diabetic glomerulopathy by pharmacological amelioration of glomerular capillary hypertension. J Clin Invest 77:1925, 1986
128. Mogensen CE: Microalbuminuria predicts clinical proteinuria and early mortality in maturity-onset diabetes. N Engl J Med 310:356, 1984
129. Hommel E, Mathiesen E, Edsberg B, et al: Acute reduction of arterial blood pressure reduces urinary albumin excretion in type 1 (insulin-dependent) diabetic patients with incipient nephropathy. Diabetologia 29:211, 1986
130. Bjorck S, Nyberg G, Mulec TNN, et al: Beneficial effects of angiotensin converting enzyme inhibition on renal function in patients with diabetic nephropathy. Br Med J 293:471, 1986
131. Izzo JL Jr, Sterns RH: Abnormal norepinephrine release in uremia. Kidney Int 24: suppl 16, S221–S223, 1983
132. Izzo JL Jr, Santarosa RP, Larrabee PS, et al: Increased plasma norepinephrine and sympathetic nervous activity in essential hypertensive and uremic humans: effects of clonidine. J Cardiovasc Pharmacol 10: suppl 12, S225, 1987
133. Ferguson RK, Vlasses PH: Hypertensive emergencies and urgencies. JAMA 255:1607, 1986
134. Gruskin AB, Baluarte HJ, Polinsky MS, et al: Treatment of severe hypertension in

children with renal disease. p. 143. In Strauss J (ed): Acute renal disorders and renal emergencies. Martinus Nijhoff, Boston, 1984
135. Oppenheimer BS, Fishberg AM: Hypertensive encephalopathy. Arch Intern Med 41:264, 1928
136. Healton EB, Brust JC, Feinfield DA: Hypertensive encephalopathy and the neurologic manifestations of malignant hypertension. Neurology 32:127, 1982
137. Hurtig HI, Franklin SS: Hypertensive emergencies. p. 211. In Narins RG (ed): Controversies in Nephrology and Hypertension. Churchill Livingstone, New York, 1984
138. Mace S, Hirschfeld S: Hypertensive encephalopathy: A cause of neonatal seizures. Am J Dis Child 137:32, 1983
139. Dustan HP, Tarazi RC, Bravo EL, et al: Plasma and extracellular fluid volumes in hypertension. Circ Res 32: suppl 1:73, 1973

Index

Page numbers followed by t *represent tables; those followed by* f *represent figures.*

Abortion, septic, 527
Acebutolol, 581t
Acetazolamide
   bicarbonate excretion and, 22
   in hypokalemia, 161, 162t
   in metabolic alkalosis, 48
Acetoacetic acid, ketoacidosis and, 23
Acetylcholine, hypermagnesemia and, 293
Acid
   Bronsted-Lowry definition of, 1
   dietary generation of, 8
   net excretion of, 9–10
   organic, metabolism of
     metabolic alkalosis and, 36–37
   titratable, 11–12
     in metabolic acidosis, 16
     in respiratory acidosis, 38
Acid-base balance. *See also* pH.
   ammonia excretion and, 10–11
   bicarbonate reabsorption and, 8–9, 10f
   buffers and, 2
   carbonic anhydrase inhibitors and, 22
   disorders of. *See also* Acidosis; Alkalosis.
     mixed, 45–46
     treatment of, 46–49
     ventilatory response to, 4
   distal tubule in, 9
   in hepatic disease, 44
   in hyperosmolar coma, 386
   kidney role in, 4–15
     ammonia excretion and, 10–11
     distal tubule in, 7–8, 8f, 9
     loop of Henle in, 6–7
     net acid excretion in, 9–10
     proximal tubule in, 5–6, 6f, 8–9, 10f
     titratable acids and, 11–12
   laboratory evaluation of, 14–15
   lung role in, 3–4
   magnesium and, 275
   proximal tubule in
     bicarbonate reabsorption in, 8–9, 10f
     hydrogen ion secretion in, 5–6, 6f
   in renal failure, 28–29
     chronic, 461
   renal phosphate transport and, 236
   surgery and, 349–351
   titratable acids and, 11–12

Acidosis, 3
   dehydration and, in children, 430
   diabetic, 377–378
     treatment of, 382
   dilutional, 23
   hyperchloremic, 18–23, 19f
     treatment of, 20
   lactic. *See* Lactic acidosis.
   metabolic. *See* Metabolic acidosis.
   nonchloremic, 379
   of renal failure, 28–29
   respiratory. *See* Respiratory acidosis.
   vasomotor nephropathy and, 551
Acromegaly, hyperphosphatemia and, 251
Acylcarnitine transferase, ketoacidosis and, 24
Addison's disease
   sodium depletion and, 95
   water excretion defect in, 126
Adenosine triphosphate synthesis,
     hypophosphatemia and, 241
Adolescent. *See also* Children.
   delayed growth spurts in, 480
   hypertension in, 569t
   obesity in, 579
Adrenal adenoma, aldosterone-producing, 163
Adrenal crisis, acute, 144
Adrenal failure, hyperkalemia and, 144
Adrenal hyperplasia, congenital
   hyperkalemia and, 149, 150t
   potassium wasting and, 157
   treatment of, 163
Adrenal insufficiency
   hypercalcemia and, 197–198
   hyperkalemia and, 149, 150t
Adrenal medulla, magnesium metabolism and, 280
Adrenaline, magnesium metabolism and, 280
Adrenocorticotrophic hormone-producing tumor,
     metabolic alkalosis and, 35
Adrenogenital syndrome
   metabolic alkalosis and, 35
   sodium depletion and, 95
Aerobic exercise, hypertension and, 584
Affective disorder, SIADH and, 125
Aging, hypertension and, 573–574
Airway obstruction, respiratory acidosis and, 39–40, 48

601

Albumin
  calcium affinity of, 171
  hyperoncotic, in cirrhosis, 72
  in idiopathic edema, 88
Alcohol
  antidiuretic hormone secretion and, 111–112
  hypertension and, 584
  hypophosphatemia and, 240–241
Alcoholic ketoacidosis, 390
Alcoholism
  chronic, hypokalemia and, 154
  magnesium depletion and, 286–287
Aldosterone
  in acute glomerulonephritis, 86
  in cirrhosis, 68–69, 69f
  in congestive heart failure, 78–79
  deficiency of. See Hypoaldosteronism.
  effect of head-out water immersion on, 68–69, 69f
  hereditary isolated biogenesis defect of, 144
  hyperkalemia and, 144
  -like compounds in common products, 35
  magnesium metabolism and, 279–280
  in nephrotic syndrome, 83
  plasma
    in diabetes, 396–397
    in nephrotic syndrome, 83
  potassium secretion and, 139–140
  potassium tolerance and, 365
  sodium excretion and, 140
Aldosteronism, metabolic alkalosis and, 34–35
Alkali, in metabolic acidosis, 47
Alkaline phosphatase, in renal osteodystrophy, 470–471
Alkalinizing salt, excessive intake of, 35–36
Alkalosis, 3
  diabetic, 378
  metabolic. See Metabolic alkalosis.
  respiratory. See Respiratory alkalosis.
  surgery and, 349–350
Alpha-adrenergic blocker, 581t
  in cirrhosis, 66
17-alpha-hydroxylase deficiency, potassium wasting and, 157
Alpha-methyldopa, 580t
  in hypertensive emergency, 592t
  in pregnant hypertensives, 588
Aluminum intoxication, in chronic renal failure, 465
Alveolar ventilation
  interstitial fluid pH and, 4
  respiratory acidosis and, 42
Amiloride
  magnesium depletion and, 284–285
  potassium secretion and, 140
Amino acid infusate, hyperchloremic acidosis and, 23
Ammonia
  hyperkalemia and, 144
  hypokalemia and, 159
  in malnutrition, 449
  renal handling of, 11
  urinary excretion of, 10
Ammoniagenesis
  acid-base balance and, 11
  renal, 9

Ammonium
  in distal tubule, 11
  excretion of, in distal tubular acidosis, 19–20
  renal production of, 10–11
  in respiratory acidosis, 38
Ammonium chloride, in metabolic alkalosis, 48
Amphotericin B, nephrotoxicity of, 529
Anemia
  in chronic renal failure, 479
  cobalt and, 323
  copper deficiency and, 310
Angina, dialysis and, 517–518
Angiotensin, thirst and, 113
Angiotensin converting enzyme, hyperkalemia and, 146
Angiotensin converting enzyme inhibitor, 581t
Angiotensin II
  in heart failure, 79
  thirst and, 113
Angiotension II antagonist, in cirrhosis, 61–62
Anion gap
  in diabetic acidosis, 377
  in distal tubular acidosis, 19
  fasting and, 37
  increased, in metabolic acidosis, 23–29, 25f
  in metabolic acidosis, 16
  metabolic alkalosis and, 31
  normal, in metabolic acidosis, 18–23, 19f
  in paraldehyde poisoning, 26
Antacid
  milk-alkali syndrome and, 36
  phosphate reabsorption and, 238
Antibiotic
  -induced vasomotor nephropathy, 529
  in peritonitis, 498t, 516t
Anticonvulsant therapy, -induced hypocalcemia, 186–187
Antidiuretic hormone, 59
  affective disorder and, 125
  alcohol inhibition of, 111–112
  diabetes insipidus and, 113
  diabetic ketoacidosis and, 372
  drugs and, 111
  essential hypernatremia and, 118
  in heart failure, 74
  hyperosmolar coma and, 384
  hypovolemia and, 109–110
  magnesium metabolism and, 277
  neurogenic stimuli and, 110–111
  osmostat resetting and, 112
  plasma osmolality and, 109, 110f
  renal phosphate transport and, 236
  role of, 108–109
  secretion of, 109–112
  thoracic venous pressure and, 75
Antihypertensive agents, 578–579, 580–581t
  emergency, 592–593t
Aquaretic agents, in SIADH, 129
Arginine hydrochloride, hyperkalemia and, 148
Arginine vasopressin, 108
Arrhythmia
  dialysis and, 517
  hyperkalemia and, 148
  hypokalemia and, 159, 573

Index • 603

magnesium depletion and, 288
Arterial carbon dioxide partial pressure, in respiratory acidosis, 39
Arteriovenous fistula
  renal sodium retention and, 60
  urinary sodium excretion and, 75
Arteriovenous shunt, in cirrhosis, 64
Arthritis, renal osteodystrophy and, 468
Ascites, 60
  without edema, 71
  overflow theory of, 61f, 62
  renal sodium retention and, 60–64, 61–63f
  splanchnic plasma sequestration in, 63
  traditional vs. overflow theory of, 60, 61f
  treatment of, 70–72, 72–73f
Asthma, respiratory acidosis and, 41
Atelectasis, postoperative, 345
Atenolol, 581t
Athlete, hypertension in, 584–586
ATPase, -calcium system, 173
Autonomic neuropathy, in dialysis, 514
Azotemia, prerenal
  hyperkalemia and, 144

Baroreceptor, in heart failure, 74
Bartter's syndrome
  diagnosis of, 160
  etiology of, 33–34
  hypokalemia and, 155, 159, 160
  magnesium depletion and, 285
  metabolic alkalosis and, 33–34, 432
  renal potassium wasting and, 155
  treatment of, 162
Base
  Bronsted-Lowry definition of, 1
  extracorporeal balance of, 1
Beta-adrenergic agonist
  in hyperkalemia, 153
  potassium transport and, 154
Beta-adrenergic blocker, 580t
  in hypertension, 579
  potassium metabolism and, 141
Beta-hydroxybutyric acid, ketoacidosis and, 23
11-beta-hydroxylase deficiency, potassium wasting and, 157
11-beta-hydroxysteroid dehydrogenase deficiency
  potassium wasting and, 157–158
  treatment of, 163
Bicarbonate
  in acid-base balance, 13f
  in dehydration, 430–431
  electrochemical gradient for, 5
  excessive intake of, 35–36
  excretion of, 29
    diarrhea and, 22
  extracellular, renal concentration of, 4–5
  glutamine metabolism and, 11
  in lactic acidosis, 390–391
  in neonate, 434
  plasma
    arterial carbon dioxide and, 15
    in metabolic alkalosis, 29
    in respiratory acidosis, 39
  reabsorption of
    hypokalemia and, 155, 159
    kidney in, 4
    limiting factors in, 6
    in proximal tubular acidosis, 20
    in proximal tubule, 6, 8–9, 10f
  renal production of, 11
  transport of
    in distal tubule, 7–8, 8f
    in loop of Henle, 6–7
    in proximal tubule, 6
Bicarbonate buffer system, 2t
Bicarbonate-carbonic acid buffer system, 3
Bicarbonaturia, in distal renal tubular acidosis, 19
Biliary fistula, sodium depletion in, 92
Biliary obstruction, hypocalcemia and, 184
Blood. *See also* Plasma.
  buffers in, 2t
  pH of, 1
  volume of
    in acute glomerulonephritis, 84
    effective circulating, 60
    in idiopathic edema, 88
    insulin and, 369
    restitution of, 344
Blood pressure
  age-related changes in, 573–574
  antidiuretic hormone secretion and, 110
  classification of
    in adults, 566t
    in children, 568t
  diastolic, 566, 566t
  high normal, 567
    in children, 568t, 569
  measurement of, vertex-corrected, 569, 571f
  metabolic acidosis and, 15–16
  monitoring of, 567
  physical activity and, 584
  renal potassium wasting and, 154–155, 155t
  systolic, 566, 566t
    in neonates, 583
Blood urea nitrogen
  in acute renal failure, in children, 445
  in chronic renal disease, 457
  diabetic ketoacidosis and, 374
  hypovolemia and, 30
  prerenal dehydration and, 346–357
Body fluids, tonicity of, 107
Bohr effect, 376
Bone
  fluorine and, 322–323
  immobilization and, 200
  metastatic calcification of, 470
  resorption of
    calcitonin and, 179–180
    cyclic AMP and, 177
    humoral hypercalcemia and, 193
    osteoclasts and, 177
Bone disorder, metabolic acidosis and, 16
Breast cancer, hypercalcemia and, 194
Breast milk
  manganese in, 321
  selenium in, 326
Bronchial obstruction, respiratory acidosis and, 39–40

Bronchitis, chronic
  respiratory acidosis and, 41
Bronchodilator, in respiratory acidosis, 48
Bronchospasm, treatment of, 48
Bronsted-Lowry concept, of acids and bases, 1
Brooke formula, 347
Buffer, 2t
Buffer system
  ammonia, 10–11
  closed-ended, 3
  open-ended, 3
  in respiratory acidosis, 37–38
Bumetanide, 580t
Burkitt's lymphoma, hyperphosphatemia and, 253
Burn injury
  hypophosphatemia and, 240
  hypovolemia and, 347–348
  SIADH and, 135

Calciphylaxis, in renal osteodystrophy, 470
Calcitonin, 178–180
  amino acid sequences of, 178
  circulatory, molecular forms of, 179
  effects and mechanism of action of, 179–180
  in hypercalcemia, 203
  magnesium metabolism and, 277
  metabolism of, 179
  physiologic role of, 172
  renal phosphate transport and, 235–236
  synthesis and secretion of, 178–179
Calcium
  -ATPase system, 173
  body compartment exchanges of, 172, 173f
  in diabetes, 392
  diabetic ketoacidosis and, 376
  dietary, 172
    in hypertension, 578
  glucagon and, 370
  homeostasis of, 172
  hypertension and, 571–572
  intracellular, 172–174
    measurement of, 173
  ionized concentration of, 139
  metabolism of
    in chronic renal failure, 464
    surgery and, 354–355
  plasma, 171, 172f
  reabsorption of
    parathyroid hormone and, 176–177
    renal potassium wasting and, 155t, 156
    treatment of, 163
  renal phosphate reabsorption and, 237
  skeletal-extracellular fluid exchange of, 172
  -sodium countertransport system, 174
  supplementation of
    in diabetic ketoacidosis, 381
    in hypokalemia, 163
  total body, 171
  transport of, 1,25-dihydroxyvitamin D and, 182
  urinary, 171–172
    insulin and, 367
Calcium carbonate, in hypocalcemia, 190
Calcium channel blocker, in hypertension in pregnancy, 588

Calcium gluconate, in hyperkalemia, 150, 151t
Capillary oncotic pressure, in nephrotic syndrome, 82
Capillary wall, in edema, 59
Captopril, 581t
  hyperkalemia and, 146
  in hypertensive emergency, 593t
Carbamazepine, antidiuretic hormone secretion and, 111
Carbohydrate
  in chronic renal failure, 473–474
  restriction of, idiopathic edema and, 89–90
Carbon dioxide
  plasma content of, 14
  production of, 3–4
  rebreathing of, in respiratory alkalosis, 49
Carbon dioxide tension
  lung role in, 3
  in respiratory alkalosis, 43
Carbonic acid
  concentration of, 3
  intracellular dissociation of, 5
Carbonic anhydrase, carbon dioxide hydration and, 6f
Carbonic anhydrase inhibitor
  bicarbonate excretion and, 22
  metabolic acidosis and, 22
  in metabolic alkalosis, 48
Cardiac glycosides, in heart failure, 79
Cardiac output
  cirrhosis and, 64
  in heart failure, 74–75
  left ventricular end-diastolic pressure and, 74, 74f
  paracentesis and, 71, 72f
  renal salt retention and, 75
Cardiomyopathy
  magnesium-induced, 287
  selenium deficiency-induced, 314–315
Cardiorespiratory failure, of extreme obesity, 41–42
Cardiovascular disease
  in chronic renal failure, 478
  dialysis and, 517–518
  magnesium depletion and, 287–288
  prevention of, fluorine in, 323
Cardiovascular system
  in hepatic cirrhosis, 64
  in hypercalcemia, 200
  in hyperkalemia, 148–149
  in hypocalcemia, 189
  in hypokalemia, 159
  in hypophosphatemia, 242, 242t
  in magnesium deficiency, 289–290
  magnesium metabolism and, 280–281
  in metabolic acidosis, 16, 350
  in respiratory acidosis, 39
Carnitine deficiency, in peritoneal dialysis, 500
Carpopedal spasm, hypocalcemia and, 354
Cataract, hypocalcemia and, 189
Catecholamines
  in heart failure, 78, 79
  ion balance and, 371
  magnesium metabolism and, 280
  in nephrotic syndrome, 83
  potassium metabolism and, 137, 141

Catheter, peritoneal. *See* Peritoneal dialysis.
Cation-exchange resin, in hyperkalemia, 151, 151t
Cell membrane
   excitability of, 138
      ionized calcium concentration and, 139
   resting potential of, 138
      in hyperkalemia, 148
   threshold potential of, 138
Cellular immunity, in chronic renal failure, 475
Central nervous system
   in dilutional acidosis, 23
   ethylene glycol ingestion and, 26
   fluid movement and, 391
   in hypercalcemia, 200, 201t
   in hypocalcemia, 188–189
   in magnesium deficiency, 355
   in metabolic acidosis, 16
   methyl alcohol ingestion and, 25–26
   in respiratory acidosis, 38
   in respiratory alkalosis, 43, 44t
   in respiratory failure, 41
   in SIADH, 127
   in water deficiency, 118
Cerebral blood flow, respiratory alkalosis and, 43
Cerebral edema
   diabetic ketoacidosis and, 382–383
   in hyperosmolar coma, 388
Cerebrospinal fluid
   diabetic coma and, 382
   dialysis and, 515
   magnesium in, 280
Chemotherapy
   hyperphosphatemia and, 253
   SIADH and, 126
Chest wall disease, respiratory acidosis and, 41
Children, 421–451. *See also* Adolescent; Infant; Neonate.
   acute oliguria in, 438–446
      etiology of, 439–440
      laboratory data in, 441–443
      management of, 443–446
   body fluids in, normal physiology of, 421–426, 422t, 425t
   dehydration in, 426–431, 428t
   fluorinated water and, 322
   growth delay in, 500–501
   hypertension in
      classification of, 569t
      definition of, 567–569, 568t
      detection of, 568, 570f
      diagnosis of, 568–569, 570f
      etiology of, 574
      treatment of, 578
   malnourished
      fluid and electrolyte homeostasis in, 446–451
      fluid therapy in, 449–451
      renal function in, 448–449
   metabolic alkalosis in, 431–432
   obesity in, 582
   percentage of water contributing to total body weight by age, 433f
   peritoneal dialysis in. *See* Peritoneal dialysis.
   pseudohypoaldosteronism in, 146
   total body water in, 421–422

Chloride
   in cystic fibrosis, 34
   in distal tubule bicarbonate reabsorption, 9
   loss of
      in diabetic ketoacidosis, 375
      metabolic alkalosis and, 29
   in metabolic acidosis, 17f
   transport of, defective
      hypokalemia and, 155
   urinary
      in Bartter's syndrome, 33–34
      in metabolic alkalosis, 31
      in respiratory acidosis, 38
Chloridorrhea, congenital
   metabolic alkalosis and, 33
Chlorothiazide, 580t
Chlorpropamide, in diabetes insipidus, 121
Cholecalciferol, 180
Cholecystokinin, magnesium metabolism and, 278
Chromium
   deficiency of, 316–319
   in TPN, 318–319, 327
   dietary, 317
Chromosome 11, calcitonin gene on, 178
Chronic obstructive lung disease, respiratory acidosis and, 41
Chvostek's sign, in hypocalcemia, 188
Cirrhosis, 60–72
   aldosterone in, 68–69, 69f
   cardiac function in, 64
   compensated, 62
   decompensated, 60
      sodium excretion in, 61
   hemodynamic considerations in, 64
   humoral factors in, non-aldosterone, 69–70
   hypokalemia and, 159
   renal nerve stimulation in, 68
   renal vasoconstriction in, 66
   respiratory alkalosis and, 44
   salt retention in
      afferent limb of, 60–64, 61–63f
      efferent limb of, 64–70, 65t, 69f
      proposed mechanisms of, 65t
      treatment of, 70–72, 72–73f
   SIADH and, 127
Citrate
   in metabolic acidosis, 47
   metabolism of, 12
Clonidine, 580t
   in hypertensive emergency, 593t
Cobalt deficiency, 323–324
   in TPN, 328
Collagen synthesis, copper in, 325
Collecting tubule, cortical
   bicarbonate transport and, 7
   chloride delivery to, 9
   hydrogen ion concentration in, 7, 9
Colloid therapy, 349
Colon, villous adenoma of
   metabolic alkalosis and, 32–33
Coma
   diabetic, water and electrolyte loss in, 371t
   hepatic, respiratory alkalosis and, 44

Coma (*Continued*)
  hyperglycemic hyperosmolar nonketotic, 383–388
    acid-base status in, 386
    clinical characteristics of, 383–384
    electrolyte derangements in, 385–386
    hyperglycemia effects in, 372f, 384
    hyperosmolarity in, 384–385
    treatment of, 386–387
      complications of, 387–388
  hypoglycemic, in diabetes, 391
  respiratory acidosis and, 38
  water deficiency and, 118
Computed tomography, in renal osteodystrophy, 471
Congestive heart failure. *See also* Heart failure.
  cardiac output in, 75
  chronic, salt retention in, 73–74
  salt retention site in, 76–77
  third space and, 348–349
Contraceptives, magnesium metabolism and, 278–279
Contrast agents, nephrotoxicity of, 529–530
Copper
  deficiency of, 310–312
    in TPN, 325–326
  dietary, 311
  plasma, 311
  recommended dietary allowances for, 312t
  total body, 310
Cor pulmonale, heart failure and, 81
Corticosterone, diabetes and, 396
Corticosterone methyloxidase defect, hyperkalemia and, 150t
Corticosterone methyloxidase I, 144
Corticosterone methyloxidase defect
  hyperkalemia and, 150t
    treatment of, 153
Cortisol
  in chronic renal failure, 478
  conversion to cortisone, 158
  ion balance and, 371
Cortisone, renal phosphate transport and, 234–235
Creatinine
  in acute oliguria, in children, 441
  in chronic renal failure, 472–473
Crush injury, hyperkalemia and, 147
Crystalloid therapy, 349
Cuproenzyme, in copper deficiency, 311, 312
Cushing's syndrome, phosphate in, 234–235
Cyclic AMP
  bone resorption and, 177
  calcium and, 173
  parathyroid hormone and, 176
  phosphorus metabolism and, 223
Cyclooxygenase inhibitor, in Bartter's syndrome, 33
Cyclophosphamide, SIADH and, 126
Cyclosporine, hyperkalemia and, 147
Cystectomy, metabolic acidosis and, 22–23
Cystic fibrosis, metabolic alkalosis and, 34

Dehydration
  cellular, 112
  in children, 426–431, 428t
    treatment of, 427–430
  environmental factors in, 117
  extracellular, 112–113
  hyperosmolar coma and, 384
  hypertonic, 426
    treatment of, 429
  hypotonic, 426
    treatment of, 427–429
  prerenal, 346
  surgery and, 346–347
  water loss in, 108
Dehydration test
  in head trauma, 115
  in water deficiency, 119–120
Deoxycorticosterone, 35
Desmopressin acetate, in diabetes insipidus, 120
Desoxycorticosterone, cirrhosis and, 68
Dextrose solution, in water deficiency, 1220
Diabetes
  dialysis and, 518–519
  hypertension and, 588
  lactic acidosis and, 389
  magnesium depletion and, 279, 286
  manganese deficiency and, 320
  nephrogenic, 115
  pregnancy and, 279
  TPN and, 356–357
Diabetes insipidus
  central, 115
  diagnosis of, 119–120
  excessive water loss without solute in, 115
  hereditary renal, 115
  nephrogenic, 115–116
  treatment of, 120–121
  vasopressin-resistant, 115
Diabetes mellitus
  aldosterone in, diminished plasma, 396–397
  calcium balance in, 392
  chronic
    calcium balance in, 392
    magnesium balance in, 392–393
  dialysis and, 401–403
  divalent cation homeostasis in, 392–393
  fluid or electrolyte problems in, 400–401
  hemodialysis and, 401–402
  hyperkalemia and, 397–398
  hyperosmolality and, 114–115
  hypertension and, sodium in, 400
  hypoglycemic coma and, 391
  hyporeninemic hypoaldosteronism and, 393–399
    therapy of, 398–399
  ketoacidosis and. *See* Diabetic ketoacidosis.
  lactic acidosis and, 388–391
  magnesium balance in, 392–393
  nonuremic hyperkalemia and, 393–396
  peritoneal dialysis and, 403
  renal failure and, 400–403
  renal transplantation and, 403
  therapy, 398–399
Diabetic ketoacidosis, 371–383
  acidosis treatment in, 382
  antidiuretic hormone and, 372
  calcium balance and, 376
  calcium replacement in, 381
  cerebral edema and, 382–383
  consequences of hyperglycemia and osmotic

diuresis in, 371t, 372–373f
  development of acidosis in, 377–378
  electrolyte disorders in, 374–378
  hyperkalemia and, 147
  hyponatremia and, 374–375
  hypophosphatemia and, 240–241
    treatment of, 246
  magnesium balance and, 376
  magnesium replacement in, 381
  osmotic diuresis in, 371–374
  phosphorus balance and, 376
  phosphorus replacement in, 380–381
  potassium balance and, 375–376
  potassium replacement in, 379–380
  salt and water losses in, 372f
  sodium balance and, 365
  sodium chloride replacement in, 378–379
  sodium imbalance in, 374–375
  treatment of, 378–383
  water replacement in, 378–379
Diabetic neuropathy, renin synthesis and, 394
Dialysate, in peritoneal dialysis, 494–495
Dialysis
  chronic, diabetes and, 401–403
  continuous arteriovenous hemofiltration, 520, 522f
  continuous arteriovenous ultrafiltration, 520, 521f
  disequilibrium syndrome and, 515
  hemo-. *See* Hemodialysis.
  hemoperfusion, 520–522
  history of, 507–509
  hypermagnesemia and, 293
  hypophosphatemia and, 246
  indications and contraindications for, 509–510
  peritoneal. *See* Peritoneal dialysis.
  phosphate removal by, 240
  renal osteodystrophy and, 468
  in respiratory alkalosis, 49
  trace mineral metabolism and, 465–466
  ultrafiltration in, 511
  in vasomotor nephropathy, 557–558
  water depletion and, 116
Diarrhea
  colon villous adenoma and, 32–33
  congenital alkalosis and, 33
  hypokalemia and, 156, 157
  malnutrition and, 450
  metabolic acidosis and, 22
  metabolic alkalosis and, 30
  sodium depletion and, 91–92, 92f
  water deficiency and, 117
Diastolic blood pressure, 566, 566t
Diazoxide, in hypertensive emergency, 592t
Dichloroacetate, in lactic acidosis, 391
Diet therapy
  in chronic renal failure, 481
  enteral, 357–359
  in hyperkalemia, 153
  in nephrotic syndrome, 84
  total parenteral. *See* Total parenteral nutrition.
Digitalis intoxication, hypokalemia and, 159
1,25-dihydroxyvitamin D
  calcium transport and, 182
  chronic renal failure, and, 184
  intoxication, hypercalcemia and, 197
  mechanism of action of, 182
  parathyroid hormone and, 180–181
  phosphorus and, 181
  physiologic actions of, 182
  in vitamin D-dependent rickets, type II, 187
24,25-dihydroxyvitamin D, 181
1,25-dihydroxyvitamin D3
Diltiazem, 581t
Dimethylnitrosamine, cirrhosis and, 62–63, 63f
Diphosphonates, in hypercalcemia, 203
Disequilibrium syndrome, 515
Disodium etidronate, hyperphosphatemia and, 251
Distal renal tubule
  acidosis, 18–20
  alpha-intercalated cell of, 7
  ammonium ion in, 11
  beta-intercalated cell of, 7
  bicarbonate transport in, 7–8, 8f
  hydrogen ion transport in, 7–8, 8f
  Liddle's syndrome and, 158
  magnesium concentration in, 267
  pH gradient in, 7
  phosphate reabsorption in, 228
  potassium secretion by, 139, 140
  sodium reabsorption in
    in acute glomerulonephritis, 86
    in nephrotic syndrome, 83
  transepithelial potential of, 140
Diuretic, 580t
  in acute glomerulonephritis, 87
  in ascites, 71–72, 73f
  in heart failure, 80
  in hyperkalemia, 151t
  in hypertension, 579, 580t
  in neonates, 583
  in idiopathic edema, 89, 90
  loop
    in acute glomerulonephritis, 87
    excessive use of, 116
    magnesium depletion and, 284
    in SIADH, 129
    sodium depletion and, 94–95
  magnesium depletion and, 284–285
  magnesium metabolism and, 274–275
  metabolic alkalosis and, 33
  in nephrotic syndrome, 84
  potassium secretion and, 140
  potassium-sparing
    in acute glomerulonephritis, 87
    in diabetes, 398
    hyperkalemia and, 146
    renal phosphate transport and, 236–237
    in SIADH, 128–129
    sodium depletion and, 94–95
  thiazide
    glucose intolerance and, 399–400
    hypercalcemia and, 195–196
    magnesium depletion and, 284
Drug therapy
  antidiuretic hormone secretion and, 111
  -induced hyperkalemia, 146, 147–148
  -induced hypertension, 575t
  -induced nephrogenic diabetes insipidus, 116
  -induced renal potassium wasting, 155

Drug therapy (*Continued*)
-induced SIADH, 125–126
retention, in vasomotor nephropathy, 556t
thirst and, 113
Duodenal ulcer, chronic renal failure and, 477
Duodenum, selenium absorption in, 313–314

Echocardiography, in hypertension, 576
Eclampsia, 587, 590t
Edema, 59–60
in acute glomerulonephritis, 84–85
afferent limb in, 88
aldosterone in, 89–90
efferent limb in, 88–89
generalized, 107
hemodynamic alterations in, 89
idiopathic, 87–90
insulin, 391–392
nephritic, 84
nephrotic, 84
salt retention in
mechanism of, 89–90
nephron site responsible for, 88–89
treatment of, 90
Elderly
dialysis in, 519–520
hypertension in, 586–587
Electrocardiography
in acute oliguria, in children, 443–444
in hyperkalemia, 138, 148
in hypermagnesemia, 293–294
in hypocalcemia, 354
in hypokalemia, 159
in vasomotor nephropathy, 551–552
Electroencephalography
in hypophosphatemia, 244
in respiratory alkalosis, 43
Electrolyte balance
in hyperosmolar coma, 385–386
insulin effects on, 364t
in malnutrition, in children, 447–448
surgery and, 353–355
Electrolyte therapy
in neonates, 437–438, 438t
in TPN, 356
Emphysema, respiratory acidosis and, 41
Enalapril, 581t
in hypertensive emergency, 593t
Encephalopathy
in chronic renal failure, 475–476
hypertensive, 476
Endocrine disorder
in chronic renal failure, 477–478
hypertension and, 575t
SIADH and, 126
Endocrine system
in hypokalemia, 158t
in hypophosphatemia, 244
vitamin D and, 182–183
Endophthalmitis, *Pseudomonas*
SIADH and, 124
Enema, retention
in hyperkalemia, 151

Enteral nutrition, 357–359
Enzyme system
acid-base balance and, 1
hyperkalemia and, 144
Epidermal growth factor, hypercalcemia and, 194
Epilepsy
hypocalcemia and, 186
respiratory alkalosis and, 43
Epinephrine, potassium and, 367
Erythrocyte, buffers in, 2t
Erythropoiesis, in chronic renal failure, 479
Erythropoietin, recombinant, 500
Estradiol, in cirrhosis, 70
Estrogen
cirrhosis and, 70
idiopathic edema and, 88
Ethylene glycol, metabolic acidosis and, 26
Exercise
hypertension and, 578
hypokalemia and, 585–586
lactic acidosis and, 24
potassium and, 141
respiratory alkalosis and, 44
Exercise stress testing, 585
Extracellular fluid
acid-base balance and, 1
bicarbonate-carbonic acid buffer system in, 3
calcium in, 171
carbon dioxide in, respiratory acidosis and, 37
cellular dehydration and, 112
in children, 422–423
deficit of, surgery and, 351–352
excess of, surgery and, 352–353
extracellular dehydration and, 112–113
hypertonicity of, 108
internal sequestration of, 92
magnesium in, 261
metabolic alkalosis and, 29–30
osmotically active solutes in, 59
pH of, 12–13
phosphate in, 223
potassium in, 137–138
in proximal tubular bicarbonate reabsorption, 9
third space, 348–349
tonicity of, 107
volume of
in acute glomerulonephritis, 85
in metabolic acidosis, 47
metabolic alkalosis and, 34–35
renal phosphate transport and, 235
sodium and, 59
water deficiency and, 118
Eye, in hypocalcemia, 189

Fainting, antidiuretic hormone secretion and, 110–111
Familial pseudohyperkalemia, 143
Fanconi syndrome
hypokalemia and, 155
hypophosphatemia and, 239
Fasting, glucose-induced alkalosis during, 37
Fatty acid, free
ketoacidosis and, 23

Fever
  respiratory alkalosis and, 44–45
  water deficiency and, 117
Fiber, in hypertension, 578
Fluid balance
  insulin effects on, 364t
  in malnutrition, in children, 447–448
  in neonate, 435–436
Fluid retention, hemodialysis and, 402
Fluid therapy
  Brooke formula, 347
  in burn injury, 347–348
  in children, 417–432, 425t
    for malnutrition, 449–451
  colloid vs. crystalloid, 349
  in dehydration, 346–347
  fat emulsions, 357
  in hemorrhage, 345
  in hyperosmolar nonketotic coma, 386–387
  in malnutrition, 449–451
  in neonates, 437–438, 438t
  Parkland formula, 347
  in vasomotor nephropathy, 550–552
Fluoride, in chronic renal failure, 465
Fluorine
  deficiency of, 321–323
    in TPN, 328
  recommended supplemental doses of, 323f
Foreign body aspiration, respiratory acidosis and, 39
Formic acid, metabolic acidosis and, 26
Fundoscopic examination, in hypertension, 576
Furosemide, 580t
  in ascites, 72, 73f
  in pulmonary edema, 80, 81f

Gastric acid secretion, metabolic alkalosis and, 30
Gastric distress, milk-alkali syndrome and, 36
Gastric drainage, metabolic alkalosis and, 32
Gastrointestinal disorder
  in chronic renal failure, 477
  hypocalcemia and, 183–184
  magnesium depletion in, 281–283, 282t
  in vasomotor nephropathy, 534
Gastrointestinal tract
  bicarbonate loss via, 15, 22–23
  hormones of, magnesium metabolism and, 278
  in hypocalcemia, 189
  in hypokalemia, 159
  in hypophosphatemia, 242t, 243
  magnesium metabolism in, 263–265, 264f
  metabolic acidosis and, 22–23
  potassium loss via, 157
  sodium depletion via, 91t
  water loss via, 117
Geophagia
  cobalt deficiency and, 323
  hypokalemia and, 154
  renal function and, 148
Geriatrics
  dialysis in, 519–520
  hypertension in, 586–587
Glomerular disease, vs. vasomotor nephropathy, 537
Glomerular filtration rate
  in acute glomerulonephritis, 85
  chronic renal disease and, 142, 457–458
  in cirrhosis, 64–65
  in congestive heart failure, 77
  diabetic ketoacidosis and, 373
  diuretics and, 72
  hyperkalemia and, 145f
  hyperphosphatemia and, 250
  hypertension and, 575
  insulin and, 365
  in malnutrition, 448–449
  in neonate, 433–434
  in nephrotic syndrome, 82
  phosphate transport and, 228
  renal failure and, 28
    urea concentration in, 117–118
  renal nerve stimulation and, 68
  in vasomotor nephropathy, 532, 546–549
Glomerulonephritis
  acute
    salt retention in, 84–87
    efferent limb in, 85f
    mechanism of, 86–87
    treatment of, 87
  chronic, humoral factors in, 86–87
  sodium retention in, 85
Glomerulosclerosis, diabetes and, 588
Glucagon
  ion balance and, 369–371
  magnesium metabolism and, 278
  potassium excretion and, 370
  potassium metabolism and, 141
  sodium excretion and, 370
Glucocorticoids
  in cirrhosis, 72
  in hypercalcemia, 204
  magnesium metabolism and, 277
  in respiratory acidosis, 48
Gluconeogenesis, renal phosphate transport and, 234
Glucose
  in hyperkalemia, 150–151, 151t
  -induced alkalosis, during fasting, 37
Glucose tolerance
  chromium and, 316
  in chronic renal failure, 473–474
  thiazides and, 399–400
Glucose tolerance factor, 316
Glutamine, renal metabolism of, 10–11
Glycogen storage disease, lactic acidosis and, 24
Glycolysis, anaerobic, 25
Glycoside, magnesium metabolism and, 274
Glycosuria, diabetes and, 392
Glycyrrhizic acid, 35
Gonadal disorder, in chronic renal failure, 480
Gonadotropin, magnesium metabolism and, 278
Gout, hypophosphatemia and, 240
Granulomatous disorder, diabetes insipidus and, 115
Growth factor, hypercalcemia and, 194
Growth hormone
  in chronic renal failure, 474, 478
  excess of, 251
  insulin and, 371
  phosphate reabsorption and, 249
  potassium and, 141
  renal phosphate transport and, 231–232

Growth retardation
 copper deficiency and, 312
 hypokalemia and, 159
 in hypophosphatemic rickets, 184
 renal osteodystrophy and, 468
Guanabenz, 580t

Heart failure, 72–81. See also Congestive heart failure.
 aldosterone in, 78–79
 "backward" theory of, 72–73
 cardiac output in, 74–75
 edema formation in, 72–74
 "forward" theory of, 73–74
 humoral factors in, non-aldosterone, 79
 hyponatremia in, 126–127
 renal hemodynamics in, 77–78
 renal nerve stimulation in, 78
 salt retention in
  afferent limb of, 74–76
  efferent limb of, 76–77
  mechanisms of, 77–79
  nephron sites for, 76–88
 treatment of, 79–81, 81f
 thoracic venous pressure in, 75–76
Hematocrit, metabolic alkalosis and, 31
Hematologic disorder, in chronic renal failure, 479–480
Hematologic malignancy, hypercalcemia and, 194
Hematopoietic system
 in hypermagnesemia, 294
 hypophosphatemia and, 243
 magnesium metabolism and, 281
 in selenium deficiency, 315
Hemoconcentration, in idiopathic edema, 91
Hemodialysis. See also Dialysis.
 access for, 508, 512–513
 in cardiovascular disease, 517–518
 continuous arteriovenous, 520
 in diabetes, 401–402, 518–519
 disequilibrium syndrome and, 515
 epinephrine and, 478
 exclusions for, 509–510
 future of, 522–524
 in geriatrics, 519–520
 in hyperkalemia, 151, 151t
 hypotension and, 513–514
 indications for, 509–510
 vs. peritoneal dialysis, 510
 peritonitis in, 515–517
  antimicrobial agents in, 516t
 technical aspects of, 510–512
 in vasomotor nephropathy, 552, 557
Hemodilution
 dialysis and, 518
 magnesium depletion and, 284
Hemolysis
 renal failure and
  acute, 528–529
  chronic, 480
 spurious hyperkalemia and, 143
Hemorrhage, hypovolemia and, 345–346
Henderson-Hasselbalch equation, 3, 12

in acid-base status determination, 14
 in respiratory acidosis, 38
Henle's loop. See Loop of Henle.
Heparin, hyperkalemia and, 146–147
Hepatic. See also Liver.
Hepatic disease
 hypocalcemia and, 184
 respiratory alkalosis and, 44
Hepatic function, in hypophosphatemia, 244
Hepatic insufficiency, respiratory alkalosis and, 44
Hepatorenal syndrome, renal blood flow in, 65
Histiocytosis, diabetes insipidus and, 115
Hodgkin's disease, hypercalcemia and, 194
Hormone
 glucoregulatory, effect on fluid and electrolyte balance, 363–371
 hyperkalemia and, 149, 150t
 in hypokalemia, 158t
 magnesium metabolism and, 275–280
 response to injury, 344
Humoral immunity, in chronic renal failure, 475
Hydralazine, 581t
 in hypertensive emergency, 591, 592t
Hydration, assessment of, in neonate, 436–437
Hydrochloric acid
 hyperchloremic acidosis and, 23
 in metabolic alkalosis, 48
Hydrochlorothiazide, 580t
Hydrogen ion
 in acid-base balance, 13f
 buffer and, 2
 donation of, 1
 intracellular, generation of, 5, 6f
 in metabolic acidosis, 15
 proximal tubule secretion of, 5–6, 6f
 regulation of, 1
 in renal failure, chronic, 460–462, 461f
 secretion of
  aldosterone and, 21, 34
  sodium independent, 6
 transport of
  in distal tubule, 7–8, 8f, 9
  in loop of Henle, 6–7
17-alpha hydroxylase deficiency, metabolic alkalosis and, 35
21-hydroxylase deficiency, hyperkalemia and, 144
1,25-hydroxyvitamin D
 chronic renal failure and, 184
25-hydroxyvitamin D, calcium metabolism and, 180
 mechanism of action of, 182
Hyperaldosteronism
 dexamethasone-suppressible, 163
 diuretic therapy and, 33
 idiopathic, 163
 magnesium depletion and, 286
 metabolic alkalosis and, 29
Hypercalcemia, 192–204
 adrenal insufficiency and, 197–198
 ammoniagenesis and, 11
 calcitonin therapy in, 203
 cardiovascular signs and symptoms of, 200
 causes of, 192t
 dermal signs and symptoms of, 201
 1,25-dihydroxyvitamin D intoxication and, 197

diphosphate therapy in, 203
diuretic and, 195–196
familial hypocalciuric, 199
gastrointestinal signs and symptoms of, 201
glucocorticoids in, 204
hematologic malignancy and, 194
hemodialysis and, 402
humoral, of malignancy, 193–194
hyperparathyroidism and, 192–193
hyperthyroidism and, 197
hypophosphatasia and, 199
immobilization and, 200
lithium and, 196
magnesium depletion and, 285
malignancy and, 193
   hematologic, 194
   humoral, 193–194
   solid tumor with skeletal metastasis, 194
milk-alkali syndrome and, 36, 196
mithramycin in, 204
neurologic signs and symptoms of, 200–201
pathogenesis of, 192–200
pheochromocytoma and, 198
phosphate therapy in, 202–203
sarcoidosis and, 194–195
signs and symptoms of, 200–201, 201t
solid tumor with skeletal metastasis and, 194
surgery and, 355
thiazide diuretic and, 195–196
treatment of, 201–204, 202t
tuberculosis and, 195
urine concentration and, 116
VIPoma syndrome and, 198–199
vitamin A intoxication and, 196
vitamin D intoxication and, 197
Williams syndrome and, 199–200
Hypercalciuria
  diabetes and, 392
  diabetic ketoacidosis and, 376
  hypophosphatemia and, 239–240
  sarcoidosis and, 194
  urine concentration and, 116
Hypercapnia, respiratory acidosis and, 37
Hypercatabolism, vasomotor nephropathy and, 533
Hyperchloremia, diabetic ketoacidosis and, 379
Hyperglycemia
  effects on salt and water metabolism, 363
  hyperosmolality and, 384–385
  phosphorus and, 368
  renal failure and, 401
  renal transplantation and, 403
Hyperglycemic hyperosmolality, 374
Hyperglycemic hyperosmolar nonketotic coma, 383–388
  acid-base status in, 386
  clinical characteristics of, 383–384
  electrolyte derangements in, 385–386
  hyperglycemia effects in, 372f, 384
  hyperosmolarity in, 384–385
  treatment of, 386–387
    complications of, 387–388
Hyperinsulinemia
  hyperkalemia and, 153
  hypertension and, 579

Hyperkalemia, 142–153
  ammoniagenesis and, 11, 21
  cause of, 143, 143t
  cellular potassium release and, 143
  of decreased potassium excretion, 143–147, 145f
  diabetes and, 397–398
  diabetic nephropathy and, 462
  diagnostic evaluation of, 149, 150t
  etiology of, 143t
  familial periodic paralysis of, 147
  hormone disorders predisposing to, 149, 150t
  of increased potassium intake, 148
  membrane excitability and, 138
  pathophysiologic consequences of, 148–149
  of potassium release from cells, 147–148
  renal failure and
    acute, 143–144
    chronic, 144, 462
  renal tubular, 146
  renin and, 395–395
  spurious, 143, 143t
    diagnosis of, 149
  surgery and, 354
  trauma and, 142
  treatment of, 150–153, 151t, 152f
  true, 143, 143t
  vasomotor nephropathy and, 551
Hypermagnesemia, 292–294
  causes of, 292t
  chronic renal failure and, 464–465
  enema and, 263
  surgery and, 355
  symptoms and diagnosis of, 293–294
  treatment of, 294
Hypernatremia
  diabetic ketoacidosis and, 379
  essential, 118
  surgery and, 353
  treatment of, 120–121
  water deficiency and, 107
Hyperosmolality, potassium and, 142
Hyperparathyroidism
  in chronic renal failure, 184, 464
  hypercalcemia and, 192–193
  hyperphosphatemia and, 248–249
  hyperthyroidism and, 197
  hypophosphatemia and, 239
  primary, 192–193
Hyperphosphatemia, 247–254
  acute, treatment of, 249–250
  causes of, 247–248, 248t
  decreased glomerular filtration rate in, 250
  diagnostic evaluation of, 249
  familial intermittent, 253–254
  increased phosphate load in, 251–253
  increased phosphate tubular reabsorption in, 250–251
  pathophysiologic consequences of, 248–249
  renal osteodystrophy and, 470
  treatment of, 249–254
Hypertension, 565–594
  adrenergic antagonists in, complex, 581t
  age and, 573–574
  alcohol and, 584

Hypertension (*Continued*)
  aldosteronism and, 34
  alpha-adrenergic blockers in, 581t
  angiotensin-converting enzyme inhibitors in, 581t
  arterial, 565
  in athletes, 584–586
  beta-adrenergic antagonists in, 580–581t
  calcium and, 571–572
  in children. *See* Children, hypertension in.
  chronic, with target organ damage, 576
  crises in, 589–594, 590t
    drug therapy for, 592–593t
  definition of, 565
    in adults, 566–567
    in children, 567–569, 568t, 569t
    in neonates, 584t
  diabetes and, 400, 566, 588
  dietary sodium restriction in, 577–578
  dietary supplements in, 578
  diuretics in, 580t
  in elderly, 586–587
  etiology of
    essential, 571–574
    secondary, 574–575, 575t
    severe, 575–576
  evaluation of, 574–576
  exercise and, 578
  fluid overload in, 445
  geriatric considerations of, 586–587
  glomerular capillary, 588
  high-resistance, 573
  history of, 565
  hypokalemia and, 157, 157t
  labile, 573
  left ventricular hypertrophy and, 566
  low renin, 574
  magnesium depletion and, 288
  malignant, 590–591
  management of, 576–579
    nonpharmacologic, 577–578
    pharmacologic, 578–579, 580–581t
    stepped-care, 565, 579
  mild, 566
  mosaic theory of, 571
  in neonates, 444–445, 582–583, 583t
  obesity and, 579–582
  portal, 60
    ascites and, 62
  potassium and, 573
  in pregnancy, 587–588
  race factors in, 586
  renal failure and, 588
    chronic, 478
  salt restriction in, 572–573
  salt-sensitive, 572
  secondary causes of, 574, 575t
  serum cholesterol and, 566
  severe, evaluation of, 575–576
  sleep disturbances and, 586
  sodium and, 572–573
  "step-care" therapy for, 565, 579
  systolic, in geriatrics, 586–587
  vasodilators in, 581t
  weight control in, 577

Hypertensive crises, 589–594
  drug therapy in, 592–593t
Hypertensive encephalopathy, in chronic renal failure, 476
Hyperthermia, malignant
  hyperphosphatemia and, 253
Hyperthyroidism
  hypercalcemia and, 197
  hyperphosphatemia and, 251
  magnesium depletion and, 285–286
Hyperuricemia, chronic renal failure and, 480
Hyperventilation
  exercise and, 44
  fever and, 44–45
  idiopathic, 45
  pulmonary disease and, 45
  respiratory alkalosis and, 14, 42–44, 44t
  salicylate intoxication and, 44
Hypoalbuminemia
  in idiopathic edema, 88
  nephrotic syndrome and, 81–82
Hypoaldosteronism
  hyperkalemia and, 144
  hyporeninemic. *See* Hyporeninic hypoaldosteronism.
  sodium depletion and, 95
Hypocalcemia, 183–191
  anticonvulsant therapy-induced, 186–187
  cardiovascular signs and symptoms of, 189
  causes of, 183t
  cell membrane excitability and, 139
  central nervous system signs and symptoms of, 188–189
  dental signs and symptoms of, 189
  dermal signs and symptoms of, 189
  gastrointestinal disease and, 183–184, 189
  hepatic disease and, 183–184
  hyperphosphatemia and, 248
  hypoparathyroidism and, 184
  hypophosphatemic rickets and, 184–185
  magnesium depletion and, 288
  neuromuscular signs and symptoms of, 187–188
  ocular signs and symptoms of, 189
  osteomalacia and, 186
  pathogenesis of, 183–187
  pseudohypoparathyroidism and, 185–186
  renal failure and
    acute, 444
    chronic, 184
  rickets and
    hypophosphatemic, 184–185
    vitamin D-dependent, type I, 186
    vitamin D-dependent, type II, 187
  signs and symptoms of, 187–189, 188t
  surgery and, 354–355
  treatment of, 190–191
  tumor-induced osteomalacia and, 186
  vitamin D deficiency and, 183
  vitamin D therapy in, 190–191
  vitamin D-dependent rickets type I and, 186
  vitamin D-dependent rickets type II and, 187
Hypodipsia, essential hypernatremia and, 118
Hypoglycemia, magnesium and, 369
Hypokalemia, 153–154

blood pressure and, 154–155, 155t
in children, 430
diabetic ketoacidosis and, 375–376, 379
diagnostic evaluation of, 160
etiology of, 154t
hypertension and, 157, 157t, 573
in malnutrition, 448
membrane excitability and, 138–139
metabolic alkalosis and, 30, 33
pathophysiologic consequences of, 158t
proximal tubular bicarbonate reabsorption and, 9
renal potassium loss and, 154–158, 155t, 156f, 157t
resting potential and, 138
surgery and, 353–354
treatment of, 160–163, 161–162t
Hypomagnesemia. *See also* Magnesium, deficiency of.
in diabetes, 392–393
diabetic ketoacidosis and, 376
hypokalemia and, 162
treatment of, 162
Hyponatremia
in children, 431–432
in diabetic ketoacidosis, 374–375
osmostat resetting and, 112
Hypo-osmolality, 107
Hypoparathyroidism
hypercalcemia and, 198
hypocalcemia and, 184
hypophosphatemia and, 244
magnesium depletion and, 285
Hypophosphatasia, hypercalcemia and, 199
Hypophosphatemia, 237–247
cardiovascular dysfunction in, 242
classification of, 338f
decreased intestinal absorption and/or increased loss of phosphate in, 237–239, 238f
diabetic ketoacidosis and, 380
diagnostic evaluation of, 244–245, 245t
endocrine dysfunction in, 244
familial, 239
gastrointestinal dysfunction in, 243
glucagon and, 370
hematologic dysfunction in, 243
hepatic dysfunction in, 244
intracellular shifting and renal wasting of phosphate in, 240
metabolic dysfunction in, 244
neurologic dysfunction in, 244
oncogenic, 240
pathophysiologic consequences of, severe, 241–244, 242t
reduced renal phosphate reabsorptive capacity and, 239–240
renal dysfunction in, 243–244
renal phosphate wasting and decreased intestinal phosphate absorption and, 2
respiratory dysfunction in, 242–243
severe, pathophysiologic consequences of, 241–244, 242t
skeletal dysfunction in, 243
skeletal muscle in, 242
transcellular shifting, decreased intestinal absorption, and reduced renal reabsorption of phosphate in, 240–241

treatment of, 245–247, 247t
uremic myopathy and, 477
X-linked, 239
Hypopituitarism, hyponatremia of, 126
Hyporeninemic hypoaldosteronism, 18, 19f, 21–22
diabetes mellitus and, 393–399
hyperkalemia and, 146, 149
treatment of, 153
sodium depletion and, 95
Hyporeninism, hyperkalemia, 149, 150t
Hypotension
in hemodialysis, 513–514, 518
lactic acidosis and, 24
in peritoneal dialysis, 518–519
Hypothyroidism
magnesium depletion and, 285–286
SIADH and, 126
Hypotonicity, 107
Hypoventilation
alveolar, 42
muscular disorder and, 40–41, 40t
neurologic disorder and, 40–41, 40t
Hypovolemia
antidiuretic hormone secretion and, 109–110
iatrogenic, 349
metabolic alkalosis and, 30–31
Hypoxemia, dialysis and, 518
Hypoxia, hypertension and, 586

Ibuprofen, in hypokalemia, 163
Idiopathic hyperventilation syndrome, respiratory alkalosis and, 45
Ileal loop conduit, hyperchloremic acidosis and, 23
Ileostomy, sodium depletion and, 91t, 92
Ileum, magnesium absorption in, 263
Immobilization, hypercalcemia and, 200
Immune complex injury, hyperkalemia and, 146
Immunologic disorder, in chronic renal failure, 474–475
Indapamide, 580t
Indomethacin, hyperkalemia and, 146
Infancy, pseudohypoaldosteronism type I of, 146
Infant. *See also* Children; Neonate.
hypercalcemia in, 199–200
hypertension in, 569t
protein-calorie deprivation in, 447
vitamin D-dependent rickets in, 186
Infection
in hemodialysis, 513
TPN and, 357
in vasomotor nephropathy, 554–556, 556t
Infectious mononucleosis, spurious hyperkalemia and, 143
Insulin
antinatriuretic effect of, 364
blood volume and, 369
calcium balance and, 364t, 367–368
catecholamines and, 371
cerebral edema and, 382
deficiency of
hyperkalemia and, 397
potassium metabolism and, 147
in diabetes, 398

Insulin (*Continued*)
  in diabetic ketoacidosis, 378
  in diabetic uremia, 400
  "edema," 391–392
  hemodialysis and, 401–402
  in hyperkalemia, 150–151, 151t
  ion homeostasis and, 363–369, 364t
  ketoacidosis and, 24
  magnesium metabolism and, 278, 364t, 369
  in metabolic acidosis, 46
  neutral protamine Hagedorn, 356
  peritoneal dialysis and, 402
  phosphorus balance and, 364t, 368–369
  potassium metabolism and, 137, 140–141, 364t, 365–367
  potassium transport and, 154
  renal phosphate transport and, 234
  resistance to, in chronic renal failure, 474
  sodium balance and, 364t
  vascular permeability and, 369
Interstitial nephritis
  causes of, 459, 459t
  in children, 439
  sodium depletion in, 93–94
Intestine, small
  vitamin D absorption in, 183–184
Intracellular fluid, in children, 422–423
Intracranial pressure
  hypocalcemia and, 188
  in SIADH, 127
Intravenous pyelography, in vasomotor nephropathy, 542–543
Ion homeostasis, insulin effects on, 363–369
Iron deficiency, in TPN, 327
Ischemic heart disease, magnesium depletion and, 287
Isosorbide dinitrate, in heart failure, 80
Isotonicity, antidiuretic hormone and, 108

Jejunostomy, enteral feeding and, 358
Juxtaglomerular hyperplasia, metabolic alkalosis and, 33

Kaliuresis, of magnesium loading, 273
Kallikrein-kinin system, sodium reabsorption and, 70
Keshan disease, selenium deficiency and, 314, 315
Ketoacidosis
  alcoholic, 390
  diabetic. *See* Diabetic ketoacidosis.
  diagnosis of, 24
  hyperkalemia and, 147
  metabolic
    methylmalonic aciduria and, 27
    propionic aciduria and, 27–28
  metabolic acidosis and, 23–24
Ketonuria, diabetes and, 392
Ketosis, development of, 373f
Kidney. *See also* Renal.
  acid-base balance regulation in. *See* Acid-base balance, kidney in.
  biopsy of, in children, 443
  in congestive heart failure, 73–74
  hemodynamics of
    in cirrhosis, 65t
    in heart failure, 77–78
  in hypercalcemia, 201, 201t
  in hypokalemia, 158t
  magnesium and, 265–268
  membranous nephropathy of, 82
  parathyroid hormone metabolism in, 176
  physiology of, in neonate, 433–435
  potassium handling in, 139–140
  in respiratory alkalosis, 42
  salt retention and, in cirrhosis, 65–70
  size of, in children, 442–443
  titratable acids and, 11–12
  tubules. *See* Renal tubule.
Kinin-kallikrein system, in heart failure, 79
Kussmaul respiration
  in children, 426
  metabolic acidosis and, 16
Kwashiorkor malnutrition, 327

Labetalol, in hypertensive emergency, 592t
Lactate, plasma concentration of, 24–25
Lactate dehydrogenase, 388–389
Lactic acid, production of, 24, 25f
Lactic acidosis, 24–25, 388–391
  clinical diagnosis of, 389–390
  development of, 388–389
  ketones and, 24
  phenformin-induced, 390
  therapy, in diabetes, 390–391
Lasker Cycler, 493–494
Laurence-Moon-Biedl syndrome, 582
Left ventricular end-diastolic pressure, cardiac output and, 74, 74f
Left ventricular hypertrophy
  antihypertensive agents and, 579
  hypertension and, 566
Left ventricular stroke volume, in heart failure, 80
Leukemia, chronic myelogenous
  hyperphosphatemia and, 253
LeVeen shunt, in cirrhosis, 72
Libido, chronic renal failure and, 480
Licorice, glycyrrhizic acid in, 35
Liddle's syndrome
  metabolic alkalosis and, 35
  potassium wasting in, 158
  treatment of, 163
Lipids
  chromium and, 217
  in chronic renal failure, 474
Lisinopril, 581t
Lithium
  hypercalcemia and, 196
  renal phosphate reabsorption and, 237
  in SIADH, 128
Liver. *See also* Hepatic.
  cirrhosis of. *See* Cirrhosis.
  citrate metabolism in, 12
  parathyroid hormone metabolism in, 176
  in selenium deficiency, 313
  zinc metabolism and, 309–310
Loop of Henle

Index • 615

ascending limb of, bicarbonate absorption in, 7
bicarbonate transport in, 6–7
hydrogen ion transport in, 6–7
magnesium reabsorption in, 265
magnesium transport in, 267–268, 268f
potassium secretion in, 139
sodium reabsorption in, 140
   in heart failure, 77
   in nephrotic syndrome, 83
water reabsorption in, 140
Low density lipoprotein, peritoneal dialysis and, 500
Lung, in acid-base balance regulation, 3–4
Lymphoma, hypercalcemia and, 194
Lysine vasopressin, in diabetes insipidus, 120

Magnesium
  acid-base balance and, 275
  alcoholism and, 286–287
  Bartter's syndrome and, 285
  body distribution of, 262t
  cardiovascular disorders and, 287–288
  cardiovascular system and, 280–281
  deficiency of
    causes of, 282t
    diagnosis of, 290–291
    diuretics and, 284–285
    gastrointestinal disorders and, 281–283
    iron and, 265
    renal disorders and, 283–284
    signs and symptoms of, 289t
    surgery and, 355
    treatment of, 291t
  depletion of, 269–270
  diabetes and, 286, 392–393
  diabetic ketoacidosis and, 376
  dietary, 263t
    in hypertension, 578
  diuretics and, 274–275, 284–285
  in erythrocytes, 262
  excess of, 292–294
  extracellular, 261
  gastrointestinal metabolism of, 263–265
  hematopoietic system and, 281
  hormonal abnormalities and, 285–286
  hyperaldosteronism and, 286
  hypertension and, 288
  insulin and, 369
  intracellular, 261
  kidney and, 265–275
  loading of, 268–269, 269f
  metabolic abnormalities and, 285–288
  metabolism of, 263–265, 264f
    adrenal medulla and, 280
    calcitonin and, 277
    clinical aspects of, 281–285
    gastrointestinal disorders and, 281–283
    gastrointestinal hormones and, 278
    hormones and, 275–280
    pancreatic hormones and, 278
    parathyroid hormone and, 275–277, 276f
    renin-angiotensin-aldosterone system and, 279–280
    sex hormones and, 278–279
    thyroid hormone and, 277–278
    vitamin D and, 277
  neuromuscular function and, 280
  parathyroid gland and, 285
  parathyroid hormone secretion and, 175
  plasma, 261–262, 262t
    in chronic renal failure, 464–465
  renal disease and, 285
  renal potassium wasting and, 155t, 156
    treatment of, 162–163
  renal tubular transport of, 266f
    other ions and, 270–274
  supplementation of, 291t
    in diabetic ketoacidosis, 381
    in hypokalemia, 162–163
  thyroid gland and, 285–286
  toxic shock syndrome and, 288
  urinary, 274–275
Magnesium sulfate, in magnesium depletion, 291
Magnesiuria, phosphate depletion and, 272
Malabsorption
  chronic renal failure and, 477
  hypocalcemia and, 183, 189
  hypophosphatemia and, 238–239
Malignancy. *See also* Tumor.
  hypercalcemia and, 193
    humoral, 193–194
Malignant hyperthermia, hyperphosphatemia and, 253
Malnutrition
  in children, 446–451
    fluid and electrolyte balance in, 447–448
    fluid therapy in, 449–451
    renal function in, 448–449
  kwashiorkor, 327
  magnesium deficiency in, 283
  protein-calorie, in vasomotor nephropathy, 552–554
Manganese
  deficiency of, 319–321
    in TPN, 326–327
  dietary, 320–321
  recommended dietary allowance for, 321
Medulla oblongata, respiratory failure and, 41
Menkes' kinky hair syndrome, 312
Mental status
  in hypercalcemia, 200
  vasomotor nephropathy and, 533
Metabolic acidosis, 15–29
  anion gap in, 16–18, 17f, 18t
    increased, 23–29, 25f
    normal (hyperchloremic acidosis), 18–23, 19f
    renal tubular acidosis and, type IV, 21
    toxin-associated, 25–28
  cellular potassium release in, 147
  chronic
    phosphaturia and, 12
    respiratory compensation in, 15
  clinical features of, 15–16
  compensatory changes in, 16t
  differential diagnosis of, 17–18, 18t
  ethylene glycol and, 26
  hyperchloremic, 16
    chronic renal failure and, 29

Metabolic acidosis (*Continued*)
    cystectomy and, 22–23
    idiopathic edema and, 88–89
    hyperkalemia and, 144
        in pseudohypoaldosteronism type II, 146
    hypophosphatemia and, 240
    increased anion gap, 23–29, 25f
        renal failure and, 28
    laboratory findings in, 16
    methanol and, 25–26
    methylmalonic aciduria and, 27
    non-anion gap
        carbonic anhydrase inhibitors and, 22
        cystectomy and, 22–23
        dilutional acidosis and, 23
        gastrointestinal bleeding and, 22–23
    paraldehyde poisoning and, 26–27
    potassium and, 142
    propionic acidemia and, 27–28
    renal failure and, 28
        in children, 444
    respiratory acidosis and, 46
    respiratory compensation for, 16
    salicylate poisoning and, 27
    surgery and, 350
    treatment of, 46–47
        metabolic alkalosis and, 36–37
Metabolic alkalosis, 29–37
    adrenal steroids in, 35
    aldosteronism and, 34–35
    alkalinizing salt intake and, 35–36
    Bartter's syndrome and, 33–34
    beta-intercalated cells in, 7
    bicarbonate loads in, excessive, 35–37
    in children, 431–432
    chloride depletion in, 9
    clinical features of, 30
    colon villous adenoma and, 32–33
    compensatory changes in, 16t
    congenital chloridorrhea and, 33
    cystic fibrosis and, 34
    differential diagnosis of, 29–30, 31t
    diuretics and, 33
    excessive bicarbonate intake and, 35–36
    gastric drainage and, 32
    glucose induced-, during fasting, 37
    hydrogen loss in
        via gastrointestinal tract, 32–33
        via kidney, 33–34
    hypokalemia and, 30, 159
    hypokalemic, 33
    hypovolemia and, 30–31
    laboratory findings in, 30–31
    Liddle's syndrome and, 35
    milk-alkali syndrome and, 36
    organic acid metabolism and, 36–37
    pathophysiology of, 32f
    potassium and, 142
    respiratory acidosis and, 46
    surgery and, 350–351
    treatment of, 47–48
    volume contraction in, 32f
    volume expansion in, 34–35
    vomiting and, 32, 32f

Metabolic encephalopathy, hypophosphatemia and, 244
Metabolic ketoacidosis, in methylmalonic aciduria, 27
Metabolism
    in hypokalemia, 158t
    in hypophosphatemia, 244
Methanol, metabolic acidosis and, 25–26
Methazolamide, acid-base balance and, 22
Methylmalonic aciduria, metabolic acidosis and, 27
Metolazone, 580t
Metoprolol, 581t
Microvascular disease, vs. vasomotor nephropathy, 537
Milk-alkali syndrome
    hypercalcemia and, 196
    metabolic alkalosis and, 36
Mineral metabolism
    calcitonin regulation of, 178–180
    hormonal regulation of, 174–183
    parathyroid hormone regulation of, 174–178
    vitamin D regulation of, 180–183
Mineralocorticoid hormone, metabolic alkalosis and, 30
Mineralocorticoids
    in diabetes, 398
    excess, metabolic alkalosis and, 34–35
    in heart failure, 79
    magnesium metabolism and, 279
Minoxidil, 581t
    in hypertensive emergency, 593t
    in uremic hypertension, 478
Mithramycin, in hypercalcemia, 204
Mitochondria, calcium in, 172
Mononucleosis, infectious
    spurious hyperkalemia and, 143
Multiple myeloma, hypercalcemia and, 194
Muscular weakness, in hyperkalemia, 148
Myelinolysis, central pontine
    hyponatremia therapy and, 129
Myopathy
    in renal osteodystrophy, 468
    uremic, 476–477

Nadolol, 580t
Nasogastric feeding, 358
Natriuretic hormone
    cirrhosis and, 69–70
    in glomerulonephritis, 86–87
    in heart failure, 79
Nausea, antidiuretic hormone secretion and, 111
Neonate. *See also* Infant.
    electrolyte therapy in, 437–438
    fluid balance in, 432–433, 435–436
    fluid therapy in, 437–438, 438t
    hydration assessment in, 436–437
    hypertension in, 582–583, 583t
        classification of, 569t
    oligo-anuria in, 440
    renal physiology in, 433–435
    rickets in, 183
    water flux in, 432–433
Nephritic edema, pathogenesis of, 84

Nephrocalcinosis
  milk-alkali syndrome and, 36
  renal tubular acidosis and, 20
Nephrotic syndrome
  classic theory of, 81–82
  salt retention in
    afferent limb in, 81–82
    classic theory of, 83
    efferent limb in, 82–83
    mechanisms of, 83
    nephron site of, 82–83
    treatment of, 83–84
Neuroblastoma, SIADH and, 124
Neurologic disorder
  in chronic renal failure, 475–477
  hypertension and, 575t
Neuromuscular irritability, respiratory alkalosis and, 43
Neuromuscular junction
  magnesium at, 280
    potassium metabolism and, 138
Neuromuscular system
  in hypocalcemia, 187–188
  in hypokalemia, 158–159
  in magnesium deficiency, 289
  magnesium metabolism and, 280
Neuromyopathy, hyperkalemia and, 138
Neurophysin, SIADH and, 124
Neutrophil, magnesium and, 281
Nifedipine, 581t
  in hypertensive emergency, 593t
Nitrogen, in chronic renal failure, 472–473
Nitroprusside, in ketoacidosis diagnosis, 24
Nonsteroidal anti-inflammatory agent
  hyperkalemia and, 146
  in nephrotic syndrome, 83–84
Noradrenalin, magnesium metabolism and, 280
Nutrition
  enteral, 357–359
  magnesium depletion and, 281
  total parenteral. *See* Total parenteral nutrition.

Obesity
  cardiorespiratory failure of, 41–42
  definition of, 582
  hypertension and, 575t, 579–582
  peritoneal dialysis and, 500
Obstructive uropathy
  hyperkalemia and, 146
  surgery for, 459
Oliguria
  acute, in children, 438–446
    etiology of, 439–440
    laboratory data in, 441–443
    management of, 443–446
  hypermagnesemia and, 294
Oncotic pressure, peritubular
  in acute glomerulonephritis, 86
  in nephrotic syndrome, 83
Opium, tincture of, 359
Oral glucose tolerance test, chromium and, 317
Oreopoulos-Zellerman catheter, 492
Orthostatic hypotension, diabetes and, 394–395

Osmolal gap, calculation of, 26
Osmolality, tonicity of, 107–108
Osmoreceptor, cellular dehydration and, 112
Osmostat, resetting of, 112
Osmotic gradient, in cerebral edema, 383
Osmotic pressure, osmostat resetting and, 112
Osteitis fibrosa, 467
Osteoblast, 177, 466
Osteoclast, 177, 466
Osteodystrophy, renal. *See* Renal osteodystrophy.
Osteomalacia, 467
  hypophosphatemia and, 243
  vs. hypophosphatemic rickets, 245t
  tumor-induced, 186
  vitamin D deficiency and, 183
Osteoporosis, fluorine and, 322–323
Ovariectomy, magnesium metabolism and, 279
Oxidative glycolysis, hypophosphatemia and, 243
Oxidative phosphorylation, phenformin and, 24
Oxyhemoglobin dissociation curve, metabolic acidosis and, 16

Paget's disease, calcitonin in, 179–180
Pancreas, hormones of, magnesium metabolism and, 278
Pancreatic disease, hypocalcemia and, 184
Pancreatic fistula, sodium depletion in, 92
Pancreatitis
  familial hypocalciuric hypercalcemia and, 199
  glucagon and, 370–371
Para-aminohippurate clearance, in vasomotor nephropathy, 544
Paracentesis, in cirrhosis, 71, 72f
Parafollicular cell, calcitonin secretion by, 178
Paraldehyde poisoning, metabolic acidosis and, 26–27
Paralysis
  familial periodic
    hyperkalemic, 147
    hyperthyroidism and, 154
  hypokalemia and, 139
Parathyroid gland, magnesium depletion and, 285
Parathyroid hormone, 174–178
  amino acid sequences for, 175
  1,25-dihydroxyvitamin D synthesis and, 182–183
  effects and mechanism of action of, 176–178
  function of, 172
  gene sequence for, 175
  insulin and, 367–368
  magnesium metabolism and, 175, 265, 275–277, 276f
  magnesium supplementation and, 381
  metabolism of, 176
  peritoneal dialysis and, 501
  proximal tubular bicarbonate reabsorption and, 9
  in pseudohypoparathyroidism, 185
  in renal osteodystrophy, 467
  renal phosphate handling and, 231–232, 233f
  synthesis and secretion of, 174–175
Parenteral nutrition, total. *See* Total parenteral nutrition.
Parkland formula, 347
Penicillin, hyperkalemia and, 148

Peptic ulcer disease, milk-alkali syndrome and, 36
Periarthritis, renal osteodystrophy and, 468
Pericardial effusion, chronic renal failure and, 478
Pericarditis
    uremic, 478
    vasomotor nephropathy and, 534
Peripheral neuropathy
    in chronic renal failure, 476
    diabetes and, 394-395
    hypokalemia and, 158-159
Peripheral vascular resistance
    cardiac output and, 75
    in heart failure, 80
    hypokalemia and, 159
    metabolic acidosis and, 15-16
Peritoneal dialysis. *See also* Dialysis.
    access problems in, 512-513
    amino acid, 500
    in cardiovascular disease, 517-518
    vs. chronic ambulatory peritoneal dialysis, 501-502
    chronic, in children, 491-503
        automatic equipment for, 493-494
        catheter "break in" routine for, 497t
        catheter complications in, 493
        catheter insertion for, 491-493, 492f
        continuous ambulatory, 495
            advantages and disadvantages of, 502, 502t
            vs. continuous cyclic, 496t
            contraindications to, 502-503
            growth and, 500-501
            hematologic response to, 500
            nutrition and, 500
            vs. peritoneal dialysis, 501-502
            renal osteodystrophy and, 501
            renal transplantation and, 501
        continuous cyclic, 495-496
            vs. chronic ambulatory, 496t
            technique, 496-497
            contraindications to, 496t
        fluid types and peritoneal clearance in, 494-495
        intermittent, 495
        peritonitis and, 497-499, 498-499t
    cycler-assisted, 512
    in diabetes, 403, 518-519
    diffusive transfer in, 511-512
    disequilibrium syndrome and, 515
    exclusions for, 509-510
    future for, 503, 522-524
    in geriatrics, 519-520
    vs. hemodialysis, 510
    history of, 491
    home intermittent, 491
    in hyperkalemia, 151, 151t
    in hypermagnesemia, 294
    hypotension and, 513-514
    indications for, 509-510
    peritonitis in, 515-517
        antimicrobial agents in, 516t
    reverse-osmosis, 491, 494
    technical aspects of, 510-512
    total volume, 495-496
    in vasomotor nephropathy, 552, 557
    water depletion and, 116

Peritoneovenous shunt, in cirrhosis, 72
Peritonitis
    in peritoneal dialysis, 497-499, 515-517
        antibiotic guidelines for, 498t, 516t
        treatment of, 499t
    renal transplantation and, 501
pH. *See also* Acid-base balance.
    blood
        cell membrane excitability and, 139
        measurement of, 14-15
        in metabolic acidosis, 15
    buffers and, 2
    intracellular
        in distal tubular bicarbonate reabsorption, 9
        in proximal tubular bicarbonate reabsorption, 8-9
        in respiratory acidosis, 38
    regulation of, 1
    urinary, in metabolic acidosis, 16
Phenformin, -induced lactic acidosis, 390
Phentolamine
    in cirrhosis, 66
    in hypertensive emergency, 593t
Pheochromocytoma
    asymptomatic, 576
    hypercalcemia and, 198
Phosphate. *See also* Phosphorus.
    calcitonin and, 179
    in chronic renal failure, 464
    conversion from mmol to mg, 247t
    cutaneous absorption of, 252
    in diabetic ketoacidosis, 381
    dietary, 224
        renal adaptation to, 230-231
    homeostasis, 225f
    in hydrogen ion buffering, 12
    in hypercalcemia, 202-203
    intestinal absorption of, 224-225
    parathyroid hormone and, 176-177
    parenteral, 252
    preparations, 247t
    reabsorption of, 229t
        acid-base balance and, 12
        hyperphosphatemia and, 250-251
        in neonate, 434
        parathyroid hormone and, 172
    renal transport of, 227-230, 228-229f, 229t
        acid-base balance and, 236
        calcitonin and, 235-236
        cellular mechanism of, 226-227, 227f
        dietary phosphate intake and, 230-231
        drug therapy and, 236-237
        extracellular fluid expansion and, 235
        factors affecting, 230-237
        growth hormone and, 231-232
        insulin and, 234
        parathyroid hormone and, 233-234
        steroid hormones and, 234-235
        thyroid hormone and, 234
        vasopressin and, 236
        vitamin D and, 232-233
    retention of, 464
    in rickets, 184
    serum

Index • 619

intravenous therapy and, 245–246
  normal, by age and sex, 224f
  parathyroid hormone secretion and, 175
transport of, 225–226
  transcellular, 227f
urinary, insulin and, 368
Phosphaturia
  calcitonin and, 235
  chronic metabolic acidosis and, 12
  extracellular fluid volume and, 235
Phosphoinositol, parathyroid hormone and, 234
Phosphorus. *See also* Phosphate.
  balance of, insulin and, 368–369
  diabetic ketoacidosis and, 376, 380–381
  1,25- in dihydroxyvitamin D production, 181
  metabolism of, 223–226, 224–225f
Pickwickian syndrome, respiratory acidosis and, 42
Pindolol, 580t
Pitressin tannate, in diabetes insipidus, 120
Plasma. *See also* Blood.
  buffers in, 2t
  carbon dioxide content of, 14
  osmolality of, 109, 111f
Platelet function, in chronic renal failure, 479–480
Pneumonitis, uremic, 479
Pneumothorax, respiratory acidosis and, 41
Poisoning
  paraldehyde, 26–27
  salicylate, 27,44
Polydipsia
  chronic renal failure and, 463–464
  compulsive, 116
Polyuria, chronic renal failure and, 463–464
Portasystemic shunt, in cirrhosis, 64
Posthypercapnic state, metabolic alkalosis and, 37
Poststreptococcal glomerulonephritis, acute, 84
Potassium
  adaptation, 142
  aldosterone and, 21
  body store of, 9
  cellular
    diabetic ketoacidosis and, 147
    in hyperkalemia, 147–148
  deficiency of. *See* Hypokalemia.
  in diabetic ketoacidosis, 379–380
  dietary
    in hypertension, 578
    hypokalemia and, 154
    renal adaptation to, 142
    restriction of, 153
  excess of. *See* Hyperkalemia.
  excretion of, 365
    glucagon and, 370
    in hyperkalemia, 143–147, 145f
  extracellular, 137
    distribution of, 153
    potassium secretion and, 139
    trauma and, 142
  homeostasis of, 138, 140
    insulin and, 365–367
  in hyperosmolar coma, 386
  hypertension and, 573
  increased intake of, 148
  ingestion of, 140–141

  intracellular, 137
  intravenous, 161
  in metabolic acidosis, 16
  metabolism of, 137–138
    cellular aspects of, 138–139
    in chronic renal failure, 461–462
    extrarenal regulation of, 140–142
    magnesium depletion and, 273–274, 283
  oral supplementation of, 161t
  reabsorption of, 139
    in intestines, 157
  renal handling of, 139–140
  renal loss of, 154–158, 155t, 156f, 157t
  renal wasting of, 157, 157t
  secretion of
    aldosterone and, 139
  serum
    exercise and, 141
    measurement of, 149
  supplementation of, 160, 161t
    in hyperosmolar nonketotic coma, 387
    in hypertension, 573
    in malnutrition, 450
  in sweat, 154
  total body, 153
    deficit treatment, 160–161
Potassium bicarbonate
  in hypokalemia, 161, 161
  in renal tubular acidosis type I, 162
Potassium chloride
  in hypokalemia, 161, 161t
  in metabolic alkalosis, 47–48
Prazosin, 581t
Pre-eclampsia, 587
Pregnancy
  hypertension in, 587–588
  magnesium supplementation in, 278
Premenstrual syndrome, magnesium metabolism in, 279
Prerenal failure, 537
Propionic acidemia, metabolic acidosis and, 27–28
Propionyl Coenzyme A carboxylase, propionic acidemia and, 27–28
Propranolol, 580t
  potassium metabolism and, 141
Prostaglandin
  breast cancer and, 194
  hypokalemia and, 155–156, 156f, 159
  in salt retention, 79
  sodium reabsorption and, 70
Protein
  -calorie deprivation, 446–447
  dietary, in chronic renal failure, 481–483
  magnesium absorption and, 264
Protein-losing enteropathy, chronic renal failure and, 477
Proteinuria, nonsteroidal anti-inflammatory agents and, 83–84
Proximal renal tubule
  acidosis. *See* Renal tubular acidosis, proximal.
  bicarbonate reabsorption in, 6, 8–9, 10f
  bicarbonate transport in, 6
  in hepatic cirrhosis, 65
  hydrogen ion secretion in, 5–6, 6f

Proximal renal tubule (*Continued*)
  magnesium reabsorption in, 265, 267
  phosphate reabsorption in, 227–229, 228–229f
  phosphate transport in, 231t
  sodium reabsorption in, 140
    in glomerulonephritis, 85
    in heart failure, 76
    in nephrotic syndrome, 83
    single nephron glomerular filtration rate and, 85, 85f
  vacuolization of, hypokalemia and, 159
  water reabsorption in, 140
Pruritus
  in chronic renal failure, 480
  renal osteodystrophy and, 468–470
Pseudohyperkalemia, familial, 143
Pseudohypoaldosteronism, 95
  type I, 146
    hyperkalemia and, 149, 150t
  type II, 146
    hyperkalemia and, 149, 150t
Pseudohypoparathyroidism, hypocalcemia and, 185–186
Pseudotumor cerebri, respiratory acidosis and, 38
Pulmonary disease
  chronic renal failure and, 479
  respiratory alkalosis and, 45
  SIADH and, 125
Pulmonary edema
  furosemide in, 80, 81f
  respiratory acidosis and, 41
Pulmonary embolism, respiratory acidosis and, 41
Pulmonary wedge pressure, cirrhosis and, 64
Pyloric stenosis
  in children, 432
  water depletion and, 117
Pyruvate carboxylase, manganese metabolism and, 319–320
Pyruvic acid, anaerobic metabolism of, 24

Race, hypertension and, 586
Radiography, in renal osteodystrophy, 471–472
Radionuclide scanning, in hypertension, 576
Renal arteriography, in vasomotor nephropathy, 543
Renal artery stenosis, metabolic alkalosis and, 35
Renal blood flow
  in cirrhosis, 65, 67
  in congestive heart failure, 77
  diuretics and, 72
Renal disease
  in children, 439
  chronic
    potassium stores in, 142
    progression of, 457
  diabetes and, 394
  hypertension and, 575t
  magnesium depletion and, 285
Renal failure
  acute
    causes of, 528t
    in children, 438–446
      etiology of, 439–440
      laboratory data in, 441–443
      management of, 443–446
    clinical consequences of, 532–535
    clinical manifestations of, 531–532, 532t
    diagnosis of, 542–543
    dialysis in, 557–558
    differential diagnosis of, 535
      fractional sodium excretion in, 538–542, 539f, 540t, 541f
    diuretic phase of, 94
    drug retention in, 556–557
    etiology of, 527–530, 528t
    fluid and electrolyte management in, 550–552
    vs. functional renal failure, 536
    glomerular hemodynamics in, 546–549
    vs. glomerular microvascular disease, 537
    hyperkalemia and, 143–144
      peritoneal dialysis in, 152f
    hyperphosphatemia and, 248
      treatment of, 250
    hypokalemia and, 159
    infection prevention and treatment in, 554–556
    metabolic acidosis and, 28
    nutritional problems in, 552–554
    pathology of, 530–531
    pathophysiology of, 543–549
    peritoneal dialysis for, 508–509
    recovery from, 534–535
      sodium depletion in, 94
    treatment of, 550–557
    tubular factors in, 544–546, 545f
    vs. urinary outflow obstruction, 536–537
  bicarbonate excretion in, 36
  chronic, 457–483
    aluminum metabolism in, 465
    bone disease in, 16
    calcium metabolism in, 464, 473f
    carbohydrate metabolism in, 473–474
    cardiovascular disorders in, 478
    cellular immunity in, 475
    in children, 459t
    cortisol in, 478
    diet therapy in, 481–483
    economics of, 457
    encephalopathy in, 475–476
    endocrine disorders in, 477–478
    erythropoiesis in, 479
    etiology of, 458–460
    fluoride deficiency in, 465
    gastrointestinal disorders in, 477
    gonadal and sexual disorders in, 480
    growth delay in, 500
    growth hormone and, 478
    hematologic disorders in, 479–480
    hemolysis in, 480
    homeostasis in, 479–480
    humoral immunity in, 475
    hydrogen ion adaptation in, 460–462, 461f
    hyperkalemia and, 462
      dietary restriction in, 153
    hypermagnesemia and, 292–293
    hyperparathyroidism and, 184
    hypertension in, 478
    hypertensive encephalopathy in, 476
    hyperuricemia in, 480

hypocalemia and, 184
immunologic disorders in, 474–475
lipid metabolism in, 474
magnesium metabolism in, 464–465
major causes of, 458t
management of, 480–483, 482t
metabolic acidosis and, 28–29
mineral metabolism in, 463–466
myocardial complications of, 478
neurologic disorders in, 475–477
nitrogen metabolism in, 472–473
pathophysiology of, 460–466
pericardial complications of, 478
peripheral neuropathy in, 476
phosphate metabolism in, 464, 473f
potassium metabolism in, 461–462
protein in, 481
pruritis in, 480
pulmonary disorders in, 479
renal failure and, 144
renal osteodystrophy in. *See* Renal osteodystrophy.
sexual disorders in, 480
sodium depletion in, 93
sodium metabolism in, 463–464
thyroid function in, 477
trace mineral metabolism in, 466
uremic myopathy in, 476–477
water adaptation in, 463–464
zinc deficiency in, 465
diabetes and, 400–403
end-stage, major causes of, 458t
ethylene glycol ingestion and, 26
functional, 527
 vs. vasomotor nephropathy, 536
hypertension and, 575, 588–589
magnesium depletion and, 285
obstetric complications of, 527
peritoneal dialysis in, 152f, 494
water depletion and, 116
Renal function
hyperkalemia and, 149
hypokalemia and, 159
in hypophosphatemia, 242t, 243–244
in malnutrition, in children, 448–449
Renal imaging, in hypertension, 576
Renal insufficiency
chronic
hyperkalemia and, 144, 145f
major causes of, 458t
nephrocalcinosis and, 36
growth delay in, 500
idiopathic edema and, 90
renal tubular acidosis and, 21–22
sodium depletion in, 93
Renal nerve stimulation
in cirrhosis, 68
in heart failure, 78
in idiopathic edema, 89
Renal osteodystrophy, 466–472
bone histology in, 467–468
clinical features of, 468–470, 469f
hyperphosphatemia and, 249
laboratory features of, 470–471, 471f

metabolic acidosis and, 467
pathogenesis of, 466–467
peritoneal dialysis and, 501
radiologic features of, 471–472
Renal transplantation
diabetes and, 403
magnesium depletion and, 283
peritoneal dialysis and, 501
Renal tubular acidosis
bicarbonate loss in, 18–22
bone disease in, 16
distal, bicarbonate loss in, 18–20
hypokalemia and, 155
proximal
 bicarbonate loss in, 20–21
 hypokalemia and, 155
type I, hypokalemia and, 155
 treatment of, 161–162, 162t
type II, 18
 hypokalemia and, 155
type IV (hyperkalemic), 18, 19f
 bicarbonate loss in, 21–22
 hyperkalemia and, 144
Renal tubular necrosis, acute, 527
in children, 441
Renal tubule
acidosis. *See* Renal tubular acidosis.
calcium-losing defect and, 155t, 156
collecting. *See* Collecting tubule.
glomerular filtration rate and, 28
hyperkalemia and, 146
magnesium depletion and, 283–284
magnesium losing defect and, 155t, 156
magnesium transport in, 265–267, 266f
obstruction of, 546
sodium depletion and, 94
titratable acid and, 12
Renin
catecholamines and, 371
in diabetic ketoacidosis, 374
hyperkalemia and, 144
hypertension and, 574
magnesium metabolism and, 279
Renin-angiotensin system
diabetes mellitus and, 393
in hypertension of renal failure, 588
metabolic alkalosis and, 35
thirst and, 113
Renin-angiotensin-aldosterone system
in congestive heart failure, 75
magnesium metabolism and, 279–280
Respiration, surgery and, 345
Respiratory acidosis, 37–42
acute, 39–41
 compensatory changes in, 16t
airway obstruction and, 39–40, 40t
alveolar hypoventilation and, 42
cardiorespiratory failure of obesity in, 41–42
cellular potassium release in, 147
chronic, 41–42
 compensatory changes in, 16t
chronic obstructive lung disease and, 41
clinical features of, 38–39
differential diagnosis of, 39–42, 40t

Respiratory acidosis (*Continued*)
  hypoventilation in, 40–41
  laboratory findings in, 39
  lung diseases and, 41
  metabolic acidosis and, 46
  metabolic alkalosis and, 46
  neuromuscular disorders and, 40–41
  obesity and, 41–42
  respiratory center suppression in, 40, 40t
    chronic, 41
  systemic effects of, 38–39
  thoracic wall disease and, 41
  treatment of, 48
Respiratory alkalosis, 42–45
  atelectasis and, 350
  clinical features of, 43
  compensatory changes in, 16t
  conversion to metabolic acidosis, 46
  differential diagnosis of, 43–45, 44t
  hypocalcemia and, 187
  in children, 431
  laboratory findings in, 43
  salicylate intoxication and, 44
  surgery and, 350
  systemic effects of, 43
  treatment of, 49
Respiratory center, suppression of
  respiratory acidosis and, 40, 40t
Respiratory distress
  acute, 38
  selenium deficiency and, 316
Respiratory failure, 40–41
Respiratory function, hypophosphatemia and, 242–243
Rhabdomyolysis
  hyperkalemia and, 147
  hyperphosphatemia and, 252–253
  hypokalemia and, 159
  vasomotor nephropathy and, 528
Rickets
  hypophosphatemic
    hypocalcemia and, 184–185
    vs. osteomalacia, 245t
  renal osteodystrophy and, 468
  tumor-induced osteomalacia and, 186
  vitamin D deficiency and, 183
  vitamin D-dependent, type I
    hypocalcemia and, 186
  vitamin D-dependent, type II
    hypocalcemia and, 187
Ringer's solution, in hemorrhage, 345
Rocky mountain spotted fever, SIADH and, 125

Salicylate poisoning
  metabolic acidosis and, 27
  respiratory alkalosis and, 44
Saline, hypertonic
  in hyperkalemia, 150t
Salt
  alkalinizing, excessive intake of, 35–36
  hypertension and, 572–573
  lithium, in SIADH, 128
  retention of
    mechanism of
      in acute glomerulonephritis, 86–87
      in cirrhosis, 65t, 69f
      in heart failure, 77–79
      in idiopathic edema, 89–90
      in nephrotic syndrome, 83
    pathophysiology of, 60–64, 61–63f
    treatment of
      in acute glomerulonephritis, 87
      in cirrhosis, 70–72, 72–73f
      in heart failure, 79–81, 81f
      in idiopathic edema, 90
      in nephrotic syndrome, 83–84
Salt wasting
  enzymatic defects in, 95
  in interstitial renal disease, 93–94
Saralasin, in cirrhosis, 61–62
Sarcoidosis
  hypercalcemia and, 194–195
  SIADH and, 124–125
Seizure, insulin and, 391
Selenium
  breast cancer mortality and, 316f
  deficiency of, 312–316
    in TPN, 328
  plasma, 314
  recommended dietary allowance for, 315
Semen, magnesium in, 278
Sensory perception, zinc deficiency and, 324
Sex hormone, magnesium metabolism and, 278–279
Sexual disorder, in chronic renal failure, 480
SIADH. *See* Syndrome of inappropriate antidiuretic hormone secretion.
Skeleton
  in hypophosphatemia, 242, 242t, 243
  in manganese deficiency, 320
  parathyroid hormone effects on, 177–178
  peritoneal dialysis and, 501
Skin
  in acute oliguria, 440
  in hypercalcemia, 201, 201t
  in hypocalcemia, 188
  in hypoparathyroidism, 188
  sodium depletion via, 91t, 92–93
  turgor of, in neonates, 436–437
  water loss via, 117
Sleep, blood pressure and, 583
Sleep apnea syndrome, hypertension and, 586
Sodium
  in bicarbonate reabsorption, 7
  -calcium countertransport system, 174
  in cystic fibrosis, 34
  depletion of, 90–96
    causes of, 91–95
      extrinsic to kidney, 94–95
      intrinsic to kidney, 93–94
    non-renal causes of, 91t
    renal causes of, 91t, 93
    treatment of, 95–96
  in diabetic ketoacidosis, 374–375
  dietary
    in children, 424
    restriction of, 577–578
  edematous states. *See* Salt, retention of.

excretion of
  aldosterone and, 140
  glucagon and, 370
  in vasomotor nephropathy, 538–542, 539f, 540t, 541f
extracellular, insulin and, 364
in hyperosmolar coma, 386
hypertension and, 572–573
metabolism of
  in chronic renal failure, 463–464
  insulin and, 364–365
plasma, in SIADH, 128
reabsorption of
  in cirrhosis, 64–65
  hydrostatic pressure and, 67
  in Liddle's syndrome, 35
renal handling of, in neonate, 434
replacement therapy, 121
restriction of
  in hypertension, 577–578
  in idiopathic edema, 90
retention of
  in acute glomerulonephritis, 85
  aldosterone and, 69
  arteriovenous fistula and, 60
  in cirrhosis, 65t
  estrogen and, 70
  in heart failure. *See* Heart failure, sodium retention in.
  in idiopathic edema, 88
urinary
  excretion of, 61
    effect of head-out water immersion on, 61, 62f
  in metabolic alkalosis, 31
  in SIADH, 128
Sodium bicarbonate
  in hyperkalemia, 150, 151t
  in metabolic acidosis, 47
  in renal tubular acidosis, 155
Sodium chloride
  in diabetic ketoacidosis, 378–379
  in metabolic alkalosis, 47
  in sodium depleted states, 95–96
Sodium citrate, in metabolic acidosis, 47
Sodium lactate
  hypophosphatemia and, 240
  in metabolic acidosis, 47
Sodium nitroprusside
  in children, 445
  in hypertensive emergency, 592t
Sodium phosphate, in hypercalcemia, 202–203
Sodium polystyrene sulfonate, in hyperkalemia, 151
Solute diuresis, sodium depletion and, 94
Solute excess for available water, 114–115
  treatment of, 120
Somatostatin, potassium balance and, 366
Sonography
  in hypertension, 576
  in vasomotor nephropathy, 543
Spironolactone
  in acute glomerulonephritis, 87
  in congestive heart failure, 79
  in heart failure, 80
Starling forces
  in edema, 59–60

in heart failure, 73
Starling hypothesis, blood volume restitution and, 344
Starvation, alkalosis and, 37
Stilbestrol, hyperphosphatemia and, 251
Streptokinase, in catheter obstruction, 493
Stress reduction, in hypertension, 578
Stress testing, exercise, 585
Succinylcholine, hyperkalemia and, 148
Sulfate, intratubular effect of, 272
Sulfonylureas, diabetes and, 401
Sulfuric acid-methionine therapy, metabolic acidosis and, 28
Superoxide dismutase, manganese metabolism and, 319–320
Supraopticohypophyseal system
  alcohol effect on, 111–112
  thirst and, 108
Surgery
  abnormal fluid loss in, 349
  acid-base changes in, 349–351
  burn injury and, 347–348
  calcium disorders and, 354–355
  in children, 440
  colloid vs. crystalloid therapy in, 349
  dehydration and, 346–347
  effects of injury, 343–345
    on cellular level, 343–344
    on organ system level, 344–345
  electrolyte imbalance in, 351–353
  extracellular fluid deficit and, 351–352
  extracellular fluid excess and, 352–353
  hemorrhage and, 345–346
  hypercalcemia and, 355
  hyperkalemia and, 354
  hypernatremia and, 353
  hypocalcemia and, 354–355
  hypokalemia and, 353–354
  hypovolemia and, 345–349
  magnesium deficiency and, 355
  in obstructive uropathy, 459
  preoperative TPN and, 355
  SIADH and, 352
  third space and, 348–349
  tonicity and, 351–353
Sweat
  sodium depletion via, 92
  water loss in, 108
Sympathetic nervous system
  in hypertension, 573–574
  insulin stimulation of, 579–582
Sympatholytic agents, 580t
Syndrome of inappropriate antidiuretic hormone secretion (SIADH), 111
  causes of, 124–127
  in children, 427
  diagnosis of, 128
  history of, 121–122, 122f
  metabolic consequences of, 127–128
  model for, 122, 123f
  as model for relative water excess, 113
  in neonate, 434
  plasma vasopressin-plasma osmolality relationship in, 122f
  surgery and, 352
  treatment of, 128–129

Systemic lupus erythematosus, hyperkalemia and, 146
Systolic blood pressure, 566, 566t
  in elderly, 586–587
  in neonates, 583

Teeth
  fluorine and, 321–322
  in hypocalcemia, 189
Tenckhoff catheter, 491–492, 492f, 493
Tendon reflex
  in respiratory acidosis, 38
  water deficiency and, 118
Terazosin, 581t
Tetany, in hypocalcemia, 187–188
Thalassemia major, hyperphosphatemia and, 253
Third space, 348–349
Thirst, 112
Thoracic venous pressure, in heart failure, 75–76
Thyroid gland
  in chronic renal failure, 477–478
  magnesium depletion and, 285–286
Thyroid hormone
  in chronic renal failure, 477–478
  magnesium metabolism and, 278
  potassium and, 141
  renal phosphate transport and, 234
Thyrotoxicosis, hypercalcemia and, 197
Timolol, 580t
Tonicity, surgery and, 349–353
Toronto-Western Hospital catheter, 492, 493
Total parenteral nutrition (TPN), 355–357
  chromium deficiency and, 318–319, 327
  cobalt deficiency in, 328
  complications of, 356–357
  copper deficiency in, 325–326
  fluorine deficiency in, 328
  hypophosphatemia and, 244
  indications for, 355–356
  iron deficiency in, 327
  magnesium depletion in, 283
  manganese deficiency in, 326–327
  metabolic complications of, 356–357
  recommended daily trace element supplementation for, 326t
  selenium deficiency in, 328
  septic complications of, 357
  serum response and balance study in, 325t
  solution composition for, 356
  technical complications of, 356
  trace element deficiency in, 324–328
  trace metal solution as supplement for, 327t
  water deficiency and, 114
  zinc deficiency in, 324–325
Toxemia, 587
Toxic shock syndrome, magnesium depletion and, 288–289
Toxin
  hypertension and, 575t
  -induced vasomotor nephropathy, 529
  uremic, 494
TPN. *See* Total parenteral nutrition.
Trace element, 307
  deficiency of, 307
  etiologies of, 308t
  in TPN, 324–328
  supplementation of, 451
Trachea, obstruction of
  respiratory acidosis and, 39
Transfusion
  component therapy, 346
  hyperkalemia and, 148
  hypothermia and, 345
Transplantation, of kidney. *See* Renal transplantation.
Trauma
  alkalosis and, 349–350
  antidiuretic hormone secretion and, 110
  cellular effects of, 343–344
  diabetes insipidus and, 115
  extracellular potassium and, 142
  hyperkalemia and, 147
  organ system effects of, 344–345
  SIADH and, 124
  third space and, 348–349
Triamterene
  in acute glomerulonephritis, 87
  in heart failure, 80
  in hypokalemia, 161, 162t
Triglyceride, serum
  in chronic renal failure, 474
Tris buffer, in metabolic acidosis, 47
Trousseau's sign, in hypocalcemia, 188
Tuberculosis, hypercalcemia and, 194
Tumor. *See also* Malignancy.
  hypercalcemia and, 193
  hypertension and, 575t
  -induced osteomalacia, 186
  phosphaturia factors secreted by, 236
  renin-secreting, 158
  SIADH and, 124
  solid, with skeletal metastasis, 194
Tumoral calcinosis, hyperphosphatemia and, 251
Turner's syndrome, 582

Ultrasound. *See* Sonography.
Ultraviolet radiation, rickets and, 183
Umbilical artery catheterization, 582
Urea
  in chronic renal failure, 472
  glomerular filtration rate and, 117–118
  glutamine metabolism and, 11
  in SIADH, 128–129
Uremia, diabetic, 400–401
Uremic encephalopathy, 475–476
Uremic myopathy, in chronic renal failure, 476–477
Urinary outflow obstruction, vs. vasomotor nephropathy, 536–537
Urine
  acid-base balance in, 9–10
  ammonia in, 10–11
  anion gap, in metabolic acidosis, 16
  concentration of, 109
    hypercalcemia and, 116
    hypokalemia and, 159
    SIADH and, 124

in distal renal tubular acidosis, 18–19
osmolality of
  in neonate, 434–435
  mechanism of control of, 109, 110f
tonicity of osmolality of, 107–108
unbuffered, acidification of, 9
volume of, in children, 423

Van Gerke's disease, lactic acidosis and, 24
Vascular disease, hypertension and, 575t
Vascular permeability, insulin and, 369
Vascular resistance
  peripheral. See Peripheral vascular resistance.
  renal, in cirrhosis, 66
  systemic
    cirrhosis and, 64
    hypertension and, 571
    race factors and, 586
Vasoactive intestinal polypeptide. See VIP.
Vasodilator, 581t
  in cirrhosis, 67
Vasomotor nephropathy
  clinical consequences of, 532–535
  clinical manifestations of, 531–532, 532t
  diagnosis of, 542–543
  dialysis in, 557–558
  differential diagnosis of, 535
    fractional sodium excretion in, 538–542, 539f, 540t, 541f
  drug retention in, 556–557
  etiology of, 527–530, 528t
  fluid and electrolyte management in, 550–552
  vs. functional renal failure, 536
  glomerular hemodynamics in, 546–549
  vs. glomerular microvascular disease, 537
  infection prevention and treatment in, 554–556
  nutritional problems in, 552–554
  pathology of, 530–531
  pathophysiology of, 543–549
  recovery from, 534–535
  treatment of, 550–557
  tubular factors in, 544–545, 545f
  tubular obstruction in, 546
  vs. urinary outflow obstruction, 536–537
Vasopressin, renal phosphate transport and, 236
Vena cava
  thoracic inferior, constriction of
    heart failure and, 78
  thoracic superior, acute constriction of, 75, 78
Ventilation
  acid-base disorder and, 4
  mechanical
    respiratory acidosis and, 37
    respiratory alkalosis and, 44
  minute, respiratory alkalosis and, 44
Ventricular end-diastolic pressure, left
  cardiac output and, 74, 74f
Ventricular fibrillation, hyperkalemia and, 148
Ventricular tachycardia, magnesium depletion and, 288
Verapamil, 581t
Very low density lipoprotein, in chronic renal failure, 474

Vincristine, SIADH and, 126
VIPoma syndrome, hypercalcemia and, 198–199
Viral infection, acute oliguria and, 439
Virilization, hyperkalemia and, 144
Vitamin A intoxication, hypercalcemia and, 196
Vitamin B12, in methylmalonic aciduria, 27
Vitamin D, 180–183
  deficiency of
    hypocalcemia and, 183
    hypophosphatemia and, 240
  endocrine system and, 182–183
  human daily requirement of, 190
  in hypocalcemia, 190–191
  intestinal absorption of, 183–184
  intoxication, 191
    hypercalcemia and, 197
  magnesium absorption and, 264–265
  magnesium metabolism and, 277
  mechanism of action of, 182
  peritoneal dialysis and, 501
  renal phosphate transport and, 232–233
Vitamin D2, 180
Vitamin D3, 180
Vitamin K deficiency, manganese deficiency and, 320
Volume expansion syndrome, metabolic alkalosis and, 34
Vomiting
  Bartter's syndrome and, 33
  dehydration and, in children, 426
  hypokalemia and, 156–157
  hypophosphatemia and, 238
  magnesium depletion and, 283
  metabolic alkalosis and, 32, 32f
  water deficiency and, 117

Water
  deficiency of
    causes of, 114–118
    combined solute excess and, 114t, 117–118
    dehydration test for, 119–120
    diabetes insipidus and, 113
    essential hypernatremia and, 114t, 118
    excessive solute loss without water in, 120–121
    excessive, without solute excess, 121
    measurement of, 119–120
    metabolic consequences of, 118
    relative vs. absolute, 107–108
    solute excess for available water and, 114t
      treatment of, 120
    without solute loss, 114t, 115–117
      treatment of, 121
    total parenteral nutrition and, 114
    treatment of, 120–121
  diabetes mellitus and, 114–115
  in diabetic ketoacidosis, 374, 378–379
  excess of, 121–129
    causes of, 124–127
    measurement of, 128
    metabolic consequences of, 127
    relative vs. absolute, 107
    SIADH as model of, 113
    treatment of, 128–129

Water (*Continued*)
  fluorine in, 322
  free, formation of, 110f
  in hyperosmolar coma, 385
  ingestion of, control of, 112–113
  insensible loss of, 108
    in children, 423
    in neonate, 435
  perinatal flux of, 432–433
  reabsorption of, in renal tubule, 110f
  restriction of, in SIADH, 128
  total body
    in children, 421–422
    in malnutrition, 447
Weight control, in hypertension, 577

Williams syndrome, hypercalcemia and, 199–200
Wilms' tumor, thirst and, 113

X chromosome, -linked hypophosphatemia, 239

Zinc
  deficiency of, 307–310
    in chronic renal failure, 465
    in TPN, 324–325
  dietary, 309
  excretion of, 309
  recommended dietary allowance for, 310, 310t
"Zinc fingers," 187
Zollinger-Ellison syndrome, water depletion in, 117